AF781806

Crime and Punishment around the World

Crime and Punishment around the World

AFRICA AND THE MIDDLE EAST

Volume 1

MAHESH K. NALLA, VOLUME EDITOR
GRAEME R. NEWMAN, GENERAL EDITOR

ABC-CLIO

Santa Barbara, California • Denver, Colorado • Oxford, England

Copyright 2010 by Mahesh K. Nalla, Volume Editor

Graeme R. Newman, General Editor

All rights reserved. No part of this publication may be reproduced, stored in a retrieval system, or transmitted, in any form or by any means, electronic, mechanical, photocopying, recording, or otherwise, except for the inclusion of brief quotations in a review, without prior permission in writing from the publisher.

Library of Congress Cataloging-in-Publication Data

Crime and punishment around the world.
p. cm.
Includes bibliographical references and index.
ISBN 978-0-313-35133-4 (set : alk. paper) — ISBN 978-0-313-35134-1 (set ebook) — ISBN 978-0-313-35135-8 (vol. 1 : alk. paper) — ISBN 978-0-313-35136-5 (vol. 1 ebook) — ISBN 978-0-313-35137-2 (vol. 2 : alk. paper) — ISBN 978-0-313-35138-9 (vol. 2 ebook) — ISBN 978-0-313-35139-6 (vol. 3 : alk. paper) — ISBN 978-0-313-35140-2 (vol. 3 ebook) — ISBN 978-0-313-35141-9 (vol. 4 : alk. paper) — ISBN 978-0-313-35142-6 (vol. 4 ebook)
1. Crime. 2. Punishment. 3. Criminal justice, Administration of.
HV6025.C7115 2010
364—dc22 2010021159

ISBN (set): 978-0-313-35133-4
EISBN (set): 978-0-313-35134-1

14 13 12 11 10 1 2 3 4 5

This book is also available on the World Wide Web as an eBook.
Visit www.abc-clio.com for details.

ABC-CLIO, LLC
130 Cremona Drive, P.O. Box 1911
Santa Barbara, California 93116-1911

This book is printed on acid-free paper ∞

Manufactured in the United States of America

This volume set is dedicated to the memory of
Ali Sabeeh of Omara, Iraq, who, while preparing the entry on Iraq,
was kidnapped, tortured, and killed in October 2007

To Amma and Nannagaru

Editorial Advisory Board

Adam Bouloukos, Director of Outreach and Partnerships, UNOPS, Copenhagen, Denmark

Ronald V. Clarke, University Professor, Rutgers University

Adam Graycar, Professor, Australian National University

Martin Killias, Professor, University of Zurich

Jeremy Travis, President, John Jay College of Criminal Justice

Contents

Acknowledgments

The contribution made by the volume editors to this project has been inestimable. A project of this magnitude could not have been achieved without their unceasing efforts to find contributors for large and small countries alike, to manage their contributors' contributions, and to edit them into the style and format required by a publication of this type. They helped overcome a number of crises we met along the way. For this and for their always being on the receiving end of my constant e-mails, I express my sincere appreciation. I thank especially Janet Stamatel for producing the world and regional maps from my sometimes less than adequate databases.

Many authors have contributed to these volumes. Without them, of course, this project would not have been possible. The volume editors and I express our great admiration to our contributors and appreciation for their tolerance of our editorial demands, which oftentimes must have seemed unreasonable. We apologize if your chapter ended up a little shorter than you had wanted. We bear full responsibility for any misconceptions that may have occurred as a result of our at-times heavy editorial hand.

Finally, we thank the Editorial Advisory Board members for being there when we needed them.

—Graeme R. Newman
Albany, NY
December 31, 2009

General Introduction

We humans are fascinated by the diversity of cultures, climates, landscapes, and peoples. It is part of our deep human heritage that we have never been able to stay at home. Since the beginning of human time, our haplogroups have migrated far and wide, stumbling on new fauna and evolving with them, adapting to cold, hot, wet, and dry seasons and climates. Along the way, we have constructed societies and civilizations that have come and gone, none reaching perfection; each having tried its own solutions to the problem of order; each constructing rules, laws, customs, and ways of dealing with those who, for whatever reason, have broken with the sacred commandments of order. Somewhere along the way, no matter what the civilization or society, the idea of justice emerged, perhaps independently of the need for order and, indeed, every now and again in opposition to order. But whatever order's relationship to justice, one thing is certain: order is necessary for societies to survive. And embedded in this necessity is the inevitability that individuals will break laws, rules, and customs and will, as a matter of logic (and justice), be punished for it.

So law (so-called if it is written) and custom (embodying law and rules that may not be written but that are "practiced" and conveyed orally) is universal in all known societies. They are part of the "civilizing" process, which seeks to hold in check the tendency of humans to devour each other. It is true that great thinkers, philosophers, and even scientists have insisted—in the face of the overwhelming evidence of history that stands against them—that humans, if only given a chance, can or could work together for their common good without being coerced to do so. But we know of no society anywhere in which this utopian (if it is utopian) conception of human nature has produced a society without laws or customs and their concomitant punishments. And surely humans have had plenty of chances to construct such utopian societies. Yet each time they try, order takes over, because we know that individuals only grudgingly curb their own desires. They do not like the imposition of order, but they know that they cannot survive without it and its accoutrements. Or at least, we may say that life is much more comfortable if one gives into almost any kind of order. This observation probably applies even to the worst of tyrannical orders, for it is easier to remain in submission than it is to rise up and overthrow a very powerful authority. The 18th-century enlightenment thinkers upon whose ideas much of the world's criminal justice systems are based (whether civil or common) were clearly of the opinion that punishment was a necessary evil, a price paid for the

comfort of living in an ordered society. Its universality certainly attests to the truth of this assertion.

It should come as no surprise, therefore, that getting reliable information about such a touchy subject—essentially how a society, nation, or culture maintains order in the face of a populace that may secretly or even openly resent its imposition—is very difficult. Nations can be very secretive about their crime rates and their punishments, not to mention their procedures for finding guilt and their manner of interrogating suspects. Various organizations have set themselves up to monitor the most egregious violations of individuals in the name of order, such as Human Rights Watch and Amnesty International, but there is a far larger part of the maintenance of order and the processing of lawbreakers by nations and regional governments that also needs constant scrutiny. Violations of human rights in the name of order may easily be hidden inside the bureaucratic inertia and practices of even the most "enlightened" societies. To admit to having a very high rate of murder or incarceration—perhaps one of the highest—of its citizens is not something of which a nation can be especially proud. Such statistics say something about that nation, though what that something is, unfortunately, can be easily misinterpreted. For example, some countries may be criticized for having very high imprisonment rates, but their retort may be that this is because they have very high crime rates, to which it may be asked, but why do you have such high crime rates? The reply may be, "Because we have strict laws that are strictly enforced, which is for the good of our citizens, who are kept safer than those in other countries whose administration of criminal justice is too lax." Provided here is just a taste of the controversies and disagreements concerning the differing levels of crime and punishment in diverse countries, as well as the puzzling relationship or lack thereof between prison rates and crime rates. The riddle can be stated thus: more punishment should reduce crime, but more crime requires more punishment.

One would think that the costs in public relations to a nation would be far too high to allow for the publication of crime and punishment statistics. So it is an amazing achievement that the United Nations World Crime Surveys, whose mission is to collect the official statistics on crime and justice from member nations, have shown steady and significant increases in the number of countries submitting their statistics since they were first collected in the 1970s. From a handful of countries in the beginning, the number providing crime and punishment statistics had grown to about 50 as of 2005. That is the positive spin. In fact, this is only 50 out of 190 member UN nations, and there are signs of decreasing reporting by countries in recent years, according to Jan Van Dijk, author of *The World of Crime* and former UN expert on international crime and justice.

Although it is true that nations are reticent to make public their crime and punishment statistics for reasons of public image, there are many technical difficulties in making comparisons of officially collected crime and justice statistics across countries. Many of these difficulties are serious, and *the reader is warned to use considerable caution in making such comparisons across countries*. These technical difficulties include the following:

- Different legal definitions of offenses make it difficult to compare specific offenses across nations.
- Different reporting and recording practices of the police who generally have first official contact with a crime make comparing statistics from one country to another unreliable without knowledge of these practices.
- Different legal systems may affect the finding of guilt, recording and classification of offenses, and recording of arrests and convictions.
- Inconsistent classifications of crime records and frequent changes over time make it difficult to compare trends in crime or punishment.
- Different bureaucracies and government departments within each nation that collate and publish crime and punishment statistics may produce different statistics. For example, city- or state-level collection of crime rates or prison rates may differ from collection at the federal level, as in the United States.
- Inadequate infrastructure for collecting and processing crime and justice reports, including information technology, may hinder the amount or accuracy of criminal justice data.
- Lack of professionally trained crime analysts and statisticians may limit the reliability and depth of statistical data available.
- Local events or conditions may inflate crime and punishment statistics, such as genocidal events that may or may not be recorded as murders.
- Changing government policies about making crime and justice statistics public may affect trends and the amount and type of data made available. There have been instances where countries have revealed crime and justice statistics to the United Nations, but not to their own citizens. The reverse is also true. There was a time, for example, when the Soviet Union routinely collected crime statistics for its internal use but officially denied to the United Nations that there was any crime at all in the Soviet Union, because there could be no crime in a true communist society.
- In large populous countries, there may be vast differences within those countries. For example, the levels of crime and punishment vary enormously throughout the United States; some states still retain the death penalty, and many do not. There may also be huge differences in amounts and kinds of crime between urban and rural regions. There may even be different legal systems operating within the same country, such as, for example, Quebec in Canada or the several customary, Islamic, and civil law systems operating in Timor-Leste.

If one must make comparisons—and most people are unable to resist it—the best way to overcome these pitfalls is to make sure that one knows as much as possible about the historical and social context within which the statistics are collected. *Crime and Punishment around the World* provides just that context. This encyclopedia describes in detail the crime and punishment practices of each country and, in some instances, specific regions. The four volumes offer a glimpse of the ways in which all the nations around the world try to solve the basic problem

they all face: what to do with those who break the law? They have all enacted either customary or written criminal laws. They have all inherited their criminal laws from their ancestors near and far, not infrequently from other nations that either usurped them or overtook them through migration. They have all developed procedures for the finding of guilt of the accused, and all, of course, follow up the finding of guilt with legislated or customary punishments. These are all essentially the product of their legal systems.

World Legal Systems

For more than 1,000 years, the Roman Empire encompassed just about all the region around the Mediterranean and stretched as far north as Great Britain. Law was probably its major weapon against the peoples it subdued, bringing with it order and a stable means of commerce. Its concepts would form much of the basis of canon law and eventually much of the civil law of Europe. Furthermore, much of the Islamic and customary law of the countries surrounding the south and east of the Mediterranean was deeply affected by Roman law because those peoples were also subjects of the Roman Empire at various times for over 1,000 years. Those countries of Europe that retained more of the Roman law and its procedures would later come to be known as "civil law" countries. Those European countries that managed to put aside Roman law came to be known as "common law" countries. And those of North Africa and the Far East retained Islamic and customary law systems.

Civil law systems account for over 50 percent of the world's legal systems, although many such systems are mixed with other legal systems because of local and historical circumstance. In fact, as a result of constant reforms, it is likely that there are no purely civil law systems left in the world. Most countries have incorporated various aspects of the adversarial system. The main characteristics of civil law systems are the following:

1. Systematically written legal codes are the prime source of authority in legal decisions and procedures.
2. Their procedures are often (though not entirely) based on what is sometimes called the "inquisitorial system"—reaching back to the days of the Roman Catholic Inquisition—in which the process of finding of guilt is conducted by a judge or magistrate who both investigates and conducts the final trial. These trials are usually, though not always, conducted before a magistrate or panel of magistrates.

Probably the prime examples of European civil law systems are those of France and Germany and, to some extent, Italy, which has recently incorporated aspects of the adversarial system.

Common law systems account for another 20 percent of the world's legal systems. These are commonly referred to as "adversarial systems" because the finding of guilt is not conducted by the magistrate who decides and investigates the case as in civil law; rather, a prosecutor (or sometimes an investigating police officer) investigates the case and prepares the case for a trial by judge and jury

(although juries are not always required). The two significant features of common law systems are the following:

1. Cases are decided based on precedent, which views previous cases and decisions as a cumulative wisdom and authority.
2. Cases are a courtroom drama in which the prosecutor is pitted against the defense.

It should be noted, however, that in modern legal systems of common law, there are legal codes that systematize the law, and these may or may not be based on the codification of past legal practice. In the United States, for example, every state, in addition to the federal system, has its own written code. Cases are decided, however, based not only on how well the offender's acts match the written code but also on the cases that came before it—that is, precedent. One sees this tradition played out in the U.S. Supreme Court, which arduously scrutinizes past decisions to conclude whether a particular case was decided correctly or not, in accordance with the supreme law of the land, the U.S. Constitution. The popular view that contrasts these two legal traditions is that civil law is focused more on finding a probably guilty person guilty, whereas common law is focused more on defending a possibly innocent person from a guilty verdict. Both systems do, however, adhere to the presumption of innocence of the accused until proven guilty. The most typical examples of common law systems are those of the United Kingdom, the United States, and Australia.

Islamic legal systems account for about 10 percent of the world's legal systems, although there are probably no purely Islamic systems anywhere in the world. This is because of the early Roman influence on all countries surrounding the Mediterranean and because of the imperialism of the West during the 16th through 20th centuries. In its pure form, the Islamic system of law follows the exact law of God, as interpreted by experts (Mullahs), deriving from the Koran, the Bible, and other sacred texts. Islamic law is often called sharia—the path to follow. Perhaps the most contrasting feature of Islamic law is that it is more a way to live one's life than a set of prohibitions laid down by a state authority as in Roman law and its progenitors. Thus, not only does it include prohibitions, some of which are set out in the Ten Commandments, but it also includes exhortations to lead a good life (e.g., love thy neighbor). No such positive exhortations are found in other Western legal traditions, whose defining principle is prohibition. The procedural rules of Islamic law are those of human reasoning and consensus. One of the problems that faces legal theorists in Islamic law is that there are many offenses that are not specifically covered in any of the sacred texts. For example, sodomy is not mentioned in the Koran or Sunna (another sacred text), but adultery is. So the judge may reason that the two offenses are similar and the punishments prescribed for one may apply to the other. In practice, however, many cases are decided also on custom and precedent, given that in many Islamic countries, tribal customs concerning redress of wrongs (e.g., feuding and vengeance) have developed alongside Islamic and other kinds of law. The majority of countries with Islamic legal systems therefore also have customary law as a major component, especially in dealing with day-to-day infractions. Finally, most Islamic law

countries also have a considerable dose of civil law, especially in the field of commerce, though it has been necessary even there for such countries to develop ways to get around the Islamic prohibition of usury, defined rather broadly.

Customary law is the law that has arisen through oral tradition among tribes and cultures where law is not written down but rather communicated across generations by tribal elders. Village or regional chieftains are usually, though not always, the main repositories of such legal wisdom, and the finding of guilt usually occurs within an informal meeting of interested parties. In many countries of Africa and southern Asia, these kinds of local meetings occur and settlements are reached based on the hearing of all sides of the complaints. Depending on the culture, shamans or others thought to hold special powers may be brought in as expert witnesses and sometimes as judges. However, the most important attribute of customary law is its specificity to the local region or village. These traditions can be very deep and resistant to change or imposition from outside influences. Perhaps a prime example in the 21st century is that of the tribal villages in the mountains of Pakistan and parts of Afghanistan that have defied state authority for hundreds of years. Instead, these tribal areas have their own chiefs and their own informal ways of settling infractions and disputes.

Socialist legal systems are those that have arisen on top of civil law systems, for the most part. Certainly this was the case in the Soviet Union and continues to be the case in Cuba and other communist countries, although China is perhaps an exception. Yet even there, the customary legal system was usurped by Western powers in the 19th century and abolished by the revolution of 1949. However, the emergence in the 1980s of China as an industrial and trading nation required that it develop a legal system that would make commerce possible and more efficient. The result has been that its legal system is based essentially on civil law, with criminal law that codifies edicts of the State and procedures that are largely reflective of the inquisitorial system.

Finally, although there are probably no countries that are purely of one or the other legal system, there are quite a number of countries whose legal systems are mixtures of some or all of the preceding. Many African and some South Asian countries are mixtures of customary, civil, common, and Islamic law. Such countries would include, for example, India, Afghanistan, and maybe Egypt.

How Does Your Country Measure Up?

Although for the reasons recounted earlier, comparing the crime and punishment of countries to each other is a very difficult procedure, it is nevertheless important to get a rough idea of how one country compares to the rest of the world. It is probably one of the main reasons people refer to world encyclopedias of any kind, to get a sense of how one fits in the universe.

To provide a very rough glimpse of how a country's crime and punishment compare to the rest of the world, we have provided a snapshot of some major indicators of crime and punishment for each country at the start of each country essay. We have chosen these indicators because they are readily available and offer a reasonably approximate way of ranking countries along a continuum. Of

the crime indicators, murder is chosen as probably the most reliable for making comparisons because its definition is roughly similar across nations, and in most cases, the statistics have been adjusted to fit the UN standard definition of murder for countries reporting their murder rates. Nevertheless, many countries do not report their murder rates. Prison rates are also reasonably reliable for making comparisons, although they too involve great technical difficulties in measurement, considering that the counting of inmates may occur on different days of the year, and a simple accounting on a particular day does not give any indication of the flow of prisoners in and out of the prison over a given period of time. The snapshot indicators provided for each country or region when available are as follow:

- *Type of Legal System*
- *Murder*—murders per 100,000 people
- *Burglary*—those victimized by burglaries per thousand people
- *Corruption*—levels of perceived corruption
- *Human Trafficking*—how much the country is doing to control human trafficking
- *Prison*—number of prisoners per 100,000 population
- *Death Penalty*—whether the country has the death penalty
- *Corporal Punishment*—whether corporal punishment is available to the criminal justice system

Legal System

The types of legal system were compiled from the United Nations *Global Report on Crime and Justice,* supplemented by information from individual country Web sites and from the University of Ottawa Civil Law Section Web site on World Legal Systems at http://www.droitcivil.uottawa.ca/world-legal-systems/eng-tableau.php.

Murder

These are officially reported statistics on murder supplied by countries to the United Nations World Crime Surveys, supplemented where necessary by individual country information plus homicide statistics from the World Health Organization. Most of the statistics were taken from the revised listing supplied by Jan Van Dijk in his book *The World of Crime,* in which he reported the average murder rates for 1998–2002, supplemented by more recent United Nations surveys. Additional data from INTERPOL and individual country sources, where available, sometimes for a slightly different period of years, were also included. However, such small differences should not matter because we know that murder rates are fairly stable over time. The countries are ranked from highest to lowest murder rate (murders per 100,000 people) and then divided into quartiles, with the middle two quartiles classified as "Medium" and the two outer quartiles labeled "High" and "Low." The world distribution of murder rates can be seen in Map 1, Murder around the World.

Burglary

Obtaining reliable rates of property crime, the most common of which is usually referred to as theft, is especially difficult when relying on officially recorded statistics because definitions and enforcement practices vary enormously across nations. We have therefore included measures of victimization of individuals by burglary. These measures are derived from the International Crime Victim Surveys (ICVS), which are interviews or questionnaires asking samples of a population whether they have been victims of particular offenses over a particular number of years (usually the past year). In this case, the samples were households, and the survey was conducted in many countries, although *limited only to urban populations*. Therefore, they do not, of course, represent the country or region as a whole, though they do, perhaps in the case of burglary, represent most of the population of a given country that there are, generally, many more households in urban settings than in rural settings. These data are taken from Van Dijk's *World of Crime.* Countries were ranked according to their burglary rates (number of victimizations reported per 1,000 people) using quartiles, divided into High, Medium, and Low, with Medium defined by the two middle quartiles.

Corruption

The ways in which crime and punishment are eventually perceived by the public and administered by the State are affected by the level of corruption in a particular country. We have therefore included a measure of corruption, a kind of crime that is neither a violent crime nor, strictly speaking, a property crime. Rather, it is a crime against justice itself. There is also the advantage that data on perceived corruption in countries are much more available, thanks to the source of our data, Transparency International at http://www.transparency.org/policy_research/surveys_indices/cpi. This Corruption Perception Index (CPI) is based on the ranking of "180 countries by their perceived levels of corruption, as determined by expert assessments and opinion surveys" according to Transparency International. We have taken these rankings, added some additional countries in some cases where they were not included in the survey, and then divided them into Low, Medium, and High, using quartiles once again.

Human Trafficking

This measure is taken from the U.S. Department of State three-tier listing of countries it classifies as making a strong effort to control human trafficking, making some effort, or making very little effort. The classifications are taken from the U.S. Department of State *Trafficking in Persons Report 2008*, found at http://www.state.gov/g/tip/rls/tiprpt/2008/index.htm. The classification scheme is derived from the U.S. Trafficking Victims Protection Act of 2000 (TVPA), which defines the minimum standards for the elimination of trafficking. It should be noted, however, that our ratings of "High" "Medium," and "Low" in the rates of human trafficking are only very rough because they assume that countries that comply with the U.S. anti-trafficking standards of enforcement will therefore have low levels of human trafficking. This is not always true. The United States,

for example, is rated as low for human trafficking because it complies with the TVPA anti-trafficking act; however, we know that it is a major destination country for trafficked humans. The classifications are as follows:

- *Low Amount of Trafficking* (Tier 1): Countries that fully comply with the U.S. Department of State standards for anti-trafficking enforcement.
- *Medium Amount of Trafficking* (Tier 2): Countries that do not fully comply with the minimum standards but are making significant efforts to bring themselves into compliance.
- *Medium Amount of Trafficking* (Watch List): Countries on Tier 2 requiring special scrutiny because of a high or significantly increasing number of victims, failure to provide evidence of increasing efforts to combat trafficking in persons, or an assessment as Medium based on commitments to take action over the next year.
- *High Amount of Trafficking* (Tier 3): Countries that neither satisfy the minimum standards nor demonstrate a significant effort to come into compliance. Countries in this tier are subject to potential non-humanitarian and non-trade sanctions.

Prison

The prison rate assessments are derived from the International Center for Prison Studies, King's College, London, and found at http://www.kcl.ac.uk/schools/law/research/icps. The rates are of prisoners per 100,000 population, and countries are ranked from high to low and divided into High, Medium, and Low using the quartile method described previously. These were the most up-to-date and thorough statistics available as of 2008. The world distribution of prison rates is depicted in Map 2: Imprisonment around the World.

Death Penalty

About 65 percent of countries have abolished the death penalty either by legislation or in practice. A few have essentially abolished it while retaining it for especially heinous crimes, although it may not have been used for many years. These countries are classified as "maybe" in our assessment of whether the death penalty is available to countries. Thus, the classifications for whether countries have the death penalty as an available punishment are "Yes," "Maybe," and "No." The information has been taken from the Web site *Info Please* at http://www.infoplease.com/ipa/A0777460.html, which in turn has taken its statistics from Amnesty International. The world death penalty distribution may be seen in Map 3: Death Penalty around the World.

Corporal Punishment

The assessments as to whether countries have available to them the use of corporal punishment, either as a sentence for a crime or for use within the prison system for disciplinary purposes, is based on information provided by the Web site http://www.endcorporalpunishment.org/pages/frame.html, which assesses

mainly the legislative steps that countries have taken to prohibit the use of corporal punishment. The Web site covers the use of corporal punishment in homes and schools as well as in the criminal justice system. Its assessments of countries are based almost entirely on whether legislation has been passed prohibiting corporal punishment either as a sentence in criminal justice or as a means of discipline in prisons. The legal situation is often ambiguous because, as with the death penalty, many countries retain the possibility of corporal punishment's use either as a sentence or in prisons but rarely or never resort to it. Thus, there is a category of "maybe" for those countries. Perhaps surprisingly, less than 20 percent of the world's countries have prohibited by legislation the use of corporal punishment either as a sentence for a crime or for use in prison discipline. Like the death penalty, our classification of the availability of corporal punishment is "Yes," "No," or "Maybe." The world use of corporal punishment is presented in Map 4: Corporal Punishment around the World.

Regions of the Four Volumes

The four volumes are broken up into the following regions:

- Volume 1: Africa and the Middle East
- Volume 2: The Americas
- Volume 3: Asia and Pacific
- Volume 4: Europe

There are any number of ways to classify countries into regions of the world. We have mostly relied on a geographical classification based on the United Nations Statistics Division classification system (http://unstats.un.org/unsd/geoinfo/default.htm). But this method is far from satisfactory. Although geography (relatively speaking) remains the same, the borders of countries do not, mostly as a result of political conflict and other factors such as migration. Furthermore, the definition of what makes a country a country is also very difficult because there are many instances where "principalities" (e.g., San Marino) and "independent nations" (e.g., the Navajo Nation in the United States) exist inside larger nations or countries. The complex histories of colonialism and migration have resulted in particular countries containing a vast variety of peoples, cultures, and social arrangements, such that calling them a "country" or even "nation" gives a misleading impression of a cohesive national system governed by one set of laws. Bosnia and Herzogovina are perhaps a prime recent example of this difficulty.

Given the shifting boundaries and definitions of countries and the social, cultural, and political diversity contained in them, allocating such countries to broad regions of the world is obviously even less precise. The final allocation of countries that were hard to classify—Turkey, for example—was admittedly somewhat arbitrary. We finally placed Turkey, along with Georgia, in Asia, not Europe. And we located countries of the Middle East (itself a very difficult region to define in both geographical and political terms) along with Africa in Volume 1. A number of the countries classified in the Middle Eastern region could just

as easily be placed in Asia, and others are geographically located in North Africa. And the variety of countries found in the Asia and Pacific volume is also vast in terms of both geography and culture; New Zealand and Australia, for example, have much more in common with Europe, from a historical and cultural point of view, than they do with their near and distant neighbors in Asia (although this is probably changing). Thus, comparing regions on any number of crime and punishment factors is fraught with even greater difficulties than comparing individual countries. Some commonalities and patterns, however, do emerge when one peruses the world maps that are provided. It is likely, as editors to the respective volumes point out, that these patterns reflect the colonial past of these regions, although there are no doubt other explanations related to local culture, migration patterns, and political history.

About the Contributors

We have drawn on a variety of authors to contribute to these four volumes. In some cases, these authors are professionals who work for their governments, but in other cases (the majority), these authors are independent scholars. The objectivity of reports written by those who work for governments may perhaps be questioned, but on the other hand, government officials have much greater access to information and statistics than do outsiders. With a couple of important exceptions, all governments, by and large, have a monopoly on crime and punishment information. The exceptions are the international crime-victim surveys described earlier that are conducted mostly apart from governments, because they do not necessarily depend on officially recorded statistics by criminal justice officials. However, more government departments are conducting their own victimization surveys because some governments in the past have been embarrassed by the findings. Various nongovernmental watch groups, such as Amnesty International and Transparency International, also collect crime and punishment information and it is part of their mission to apply value judgments and criticism to governments and their administrators. As editors, we have tried in these chapters, as far as possible, to avoid either advocacy on behalf of the government's interest or criticism of governments, although in some cases the criminality and punitive practices of governments cannot be ignored.

—Graeme R. Newman
University at Albany

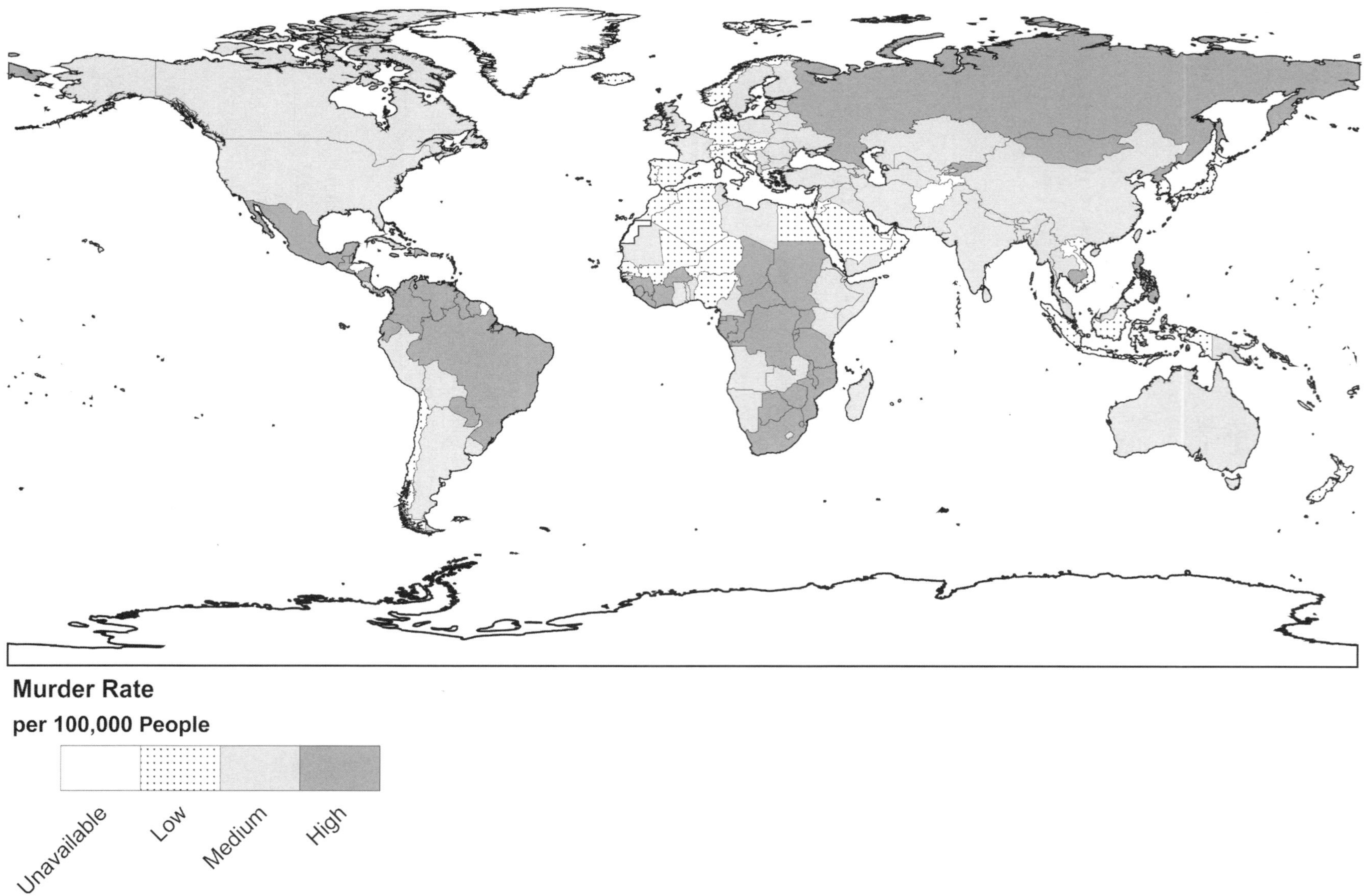

Murder around the World

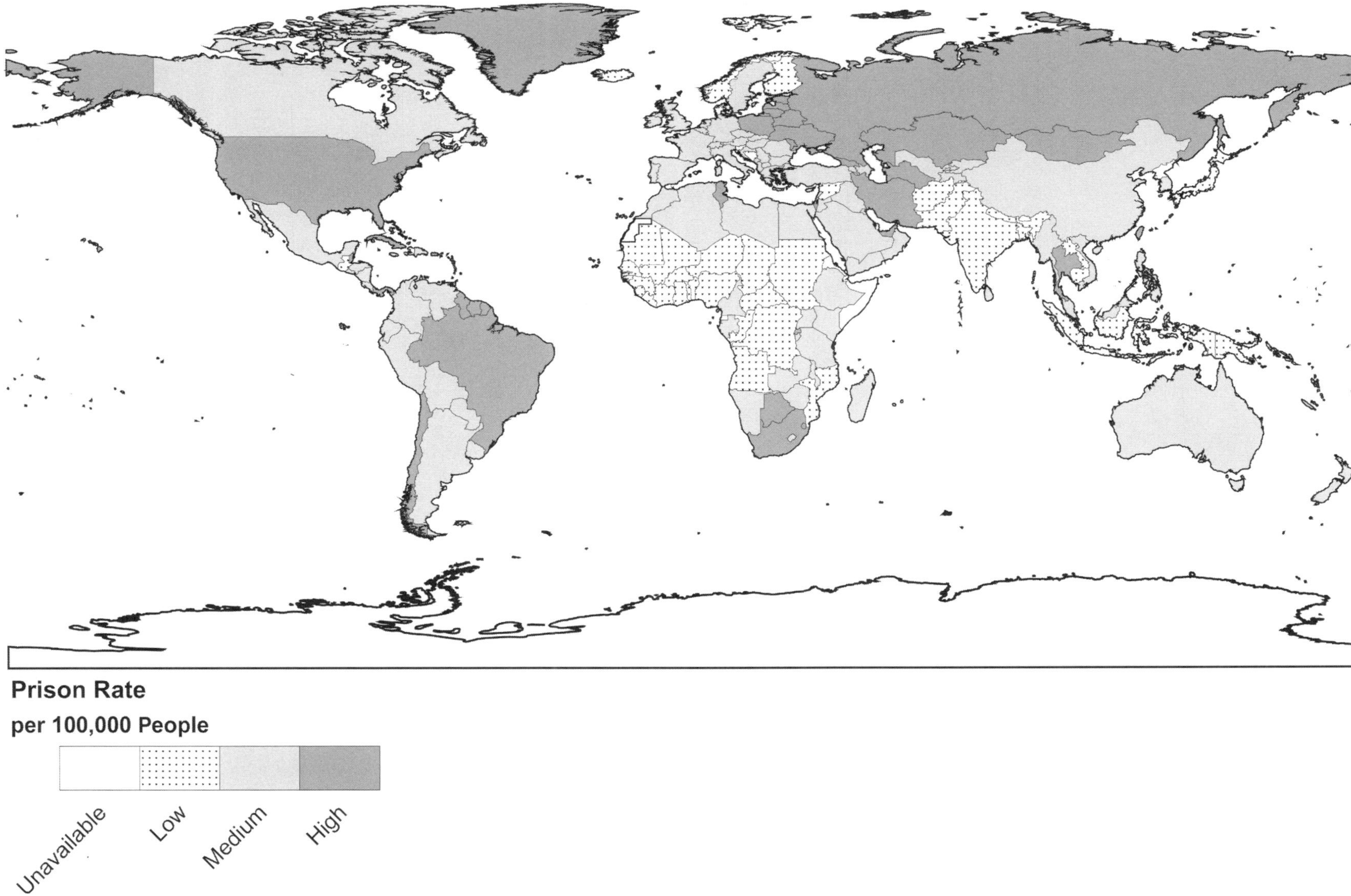

Imprisonment around the World

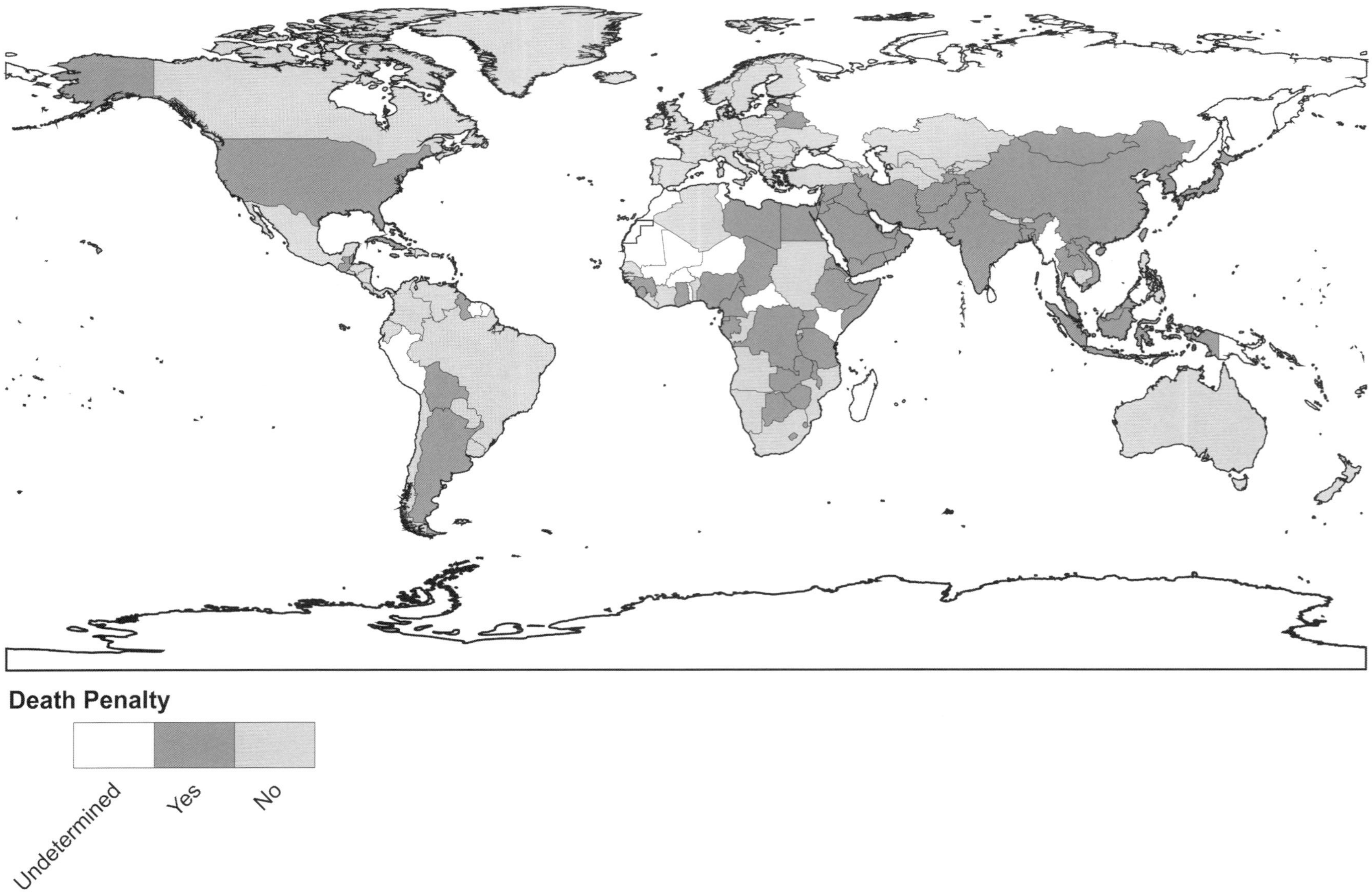

Death Penalty around the World

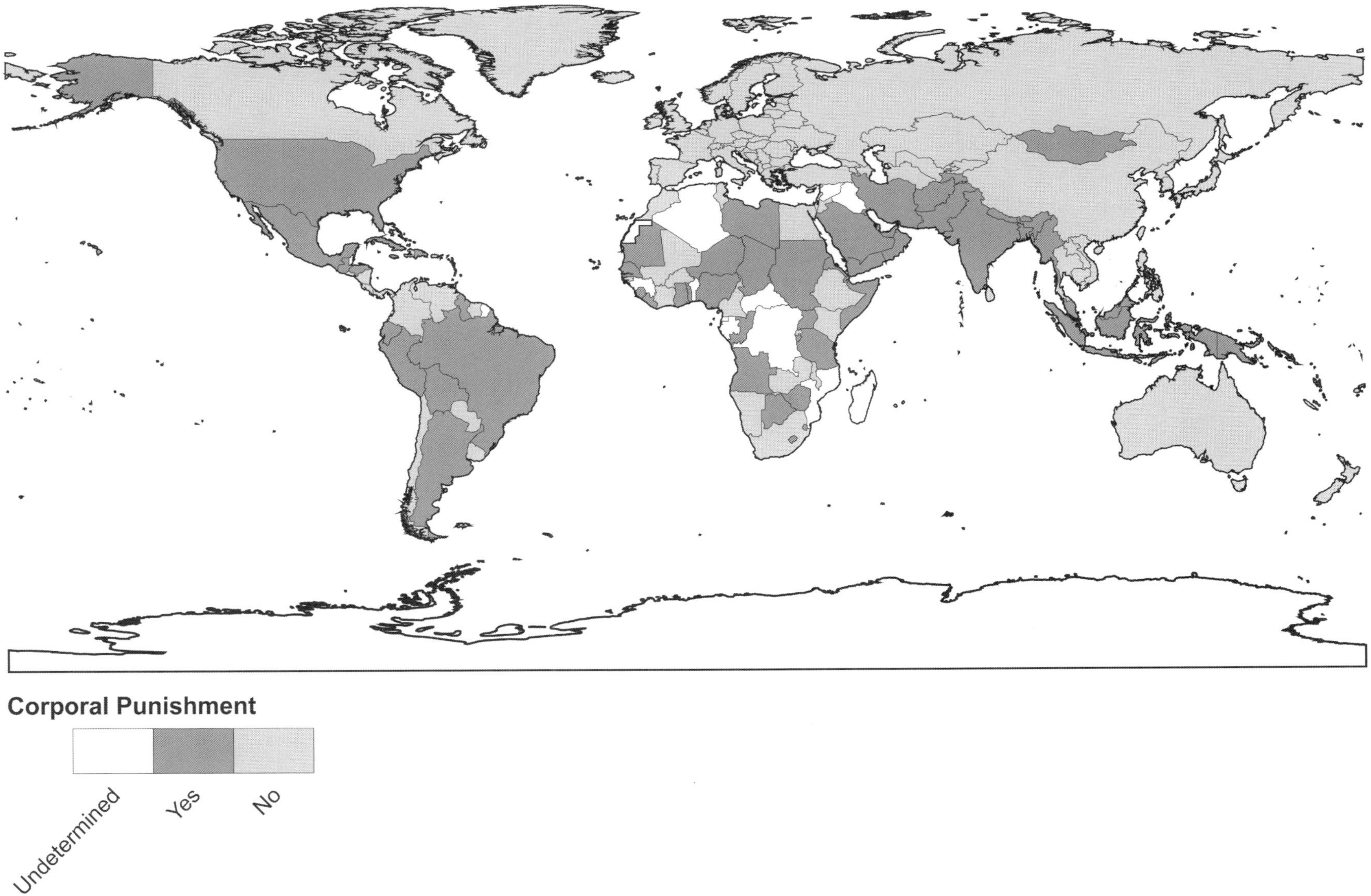

Corporal Punishment around the World

Introduction

Africa has a long and rich history of powerful kingdoms and is home to a variety of civilizations. Around 3000 BCE, the powerful kingdom of Egypt, which then controlled much of North and Central Africa, contributed substantially to the development of Africa through its advances in science, medicine, and technology. Other powerful African kingdoms followed, the most notable being Mali, Dahomey, Ashanti, and the empire of ancient Ghana (present-day southeast Mauritania). Islam entered North Africa around 700 CE and spread across and outside the continent. Among the first Europeans to land in Africa were the Portuguese, who arrived in 1439 seeking gold and slaves. Others soon followed, opening trade routes and setting up forts and bases along Africa's 4,000-mile Atlantic coast.

By 1890, much of Africa was ruled by the British, French, and Germans, who divided the land in straight lines with scant attention paid to ethnic and cultural traditions. Before the 1960s, when most African countries became independent, the colonies of various European superpowers made up most of the continent, with the United Kingdom (31 colonies) and France (23 colonies) in the lead, followed by Portugal (6), Italy (4), Belgium (3), Germany (2), and Spain (2). Today, Africa is the world's second-largest continent, with nearly 12 million square miles, and contains 53 independent countries and 880 million people, who belong to more than 3,000 native groups speaking more than 1,000 languages. Africa has rich natural resources and produces nearly half of the world's gold and diamonds, yet over half of its total population lives on less than US$1 a day. According to a United Nations development program, Sub-Saharan Africa, consisting of 45 countries, has performed well economically over the past eight years, recording a 5 percent growth rate and demonstrating significant strides in democratic governance.

The Middle East, a term much criticized for being Eurocentric, generally refers to the land mass that lies west of Eurasia and east of Africa, with the Mediterranean Sea to the west and the Indian Ocean to the south. Its location and historical development—especially its role as the birthplace of such major religions as Christianity, Islam, Judaism, and Zoroastrianism, among others—make this region a strategic location. The discovery of oil in the area gave even greater strategic, political, and economic importance to this region. The top 7 of the 15 largest oil-producing countries in the world are located in the Middle East, making them some of the richest countries per capita in the world. Like Africa, the Middle East, with the exceptions of Iran and Saudi Arabia, was either colonized or indirectly governed by the English and French until the early 20th century.

Long histories of colonial rule in Africa and the Middle East profoundly influenced not only political and economic development but also the evolution of criminal justice systems. Many of the countries in these regions became independent in the early or mid-20th century. However, civil war, ethnic violence, highly unstable political systems, and military coup d'états have tremendously influenced indigenous mechanisms of social regulation and have shaped the law, the role of police, and the justice system.

Modern forms of justice administration are believed to have been introduced by European colonists, despite strong evidence of the existence of formal and informal mechanisms of social regulation prior to colonization. Notions of crime, law, and justice were introduced by the colonists and were primarily used as a mechanism of social control of the local populations in areas of European investment. The local customary laws in many of these countries were either underused or not recognized until the countries became independent states, when most nations harmonized customary laws and formal justice systems. Few countries in the region can claim little to no influence from colonists in shaping their criminal justice systems. These exceptions include Saudi Arabia, Iran, and Sudan, whose criminal justice systems were arguably built on Islamic laws.

Today, Africa and the Middle East are vibrant and growing regions with the potential to become powerful global players. Globalization has touched and influenced Africa and the Middle East in many positive ways. Yet the regions are plagued by social problems that include violence in the name of custom, tradition, religion, war, and ethnic cleansing. The development of institutions of police and justice are generally considered a measure of political and social progress. Sadly, the subject matter of crime and punishment in Africa and the Middle East has received scant attention from scholars, making it difficult to offer a bird's-eye view of crime and justice in the region. This void is filled in this volume, which offers a current look at the nature and state of crime and punishment in Africa and the Middle East.

Volume 1 of *Crime and Punishment around the World* contains 55 individual entries for the countries making up Africa and 15 individual entries for each of the countries in the Middle East. The purpose of this volume is not to compare and contrast issues of crime and punishment in Africa and the Middle East, but simply to offer insights into developments in this area in individual countries of the two regions. Yet this mosaic of criminal justice systems will provide readers with similarities and differences in the evolution of the regions' criminal justice systems and the extent to which colonial influences shaped the existing forms of social regulation, crime control mechanisms, and social governance. Readers will note that data are sparse and dated on many matters of crime and justice. Though limited, the data also offer clues to the reasons these are the least documented regions in terms of information on crime and punishment; coupe d'états, civil wars, terrorism, and ethnic and other forms of violence related to drugs and illegal trafficking in arms and humans have all had an impact in this regard. The conflict and confusion emerging from multiple legal systems, including colonial legal systems, customary laws, and religious laws, pose additional challenges to the administration of justice. Readers will note that some of these problems in many of the countries included in this volume are direct outcomes of the colonial legacy, which left behind a criminal justice system that was developed to preserve a regime in power, not that evolved as a consequence of the needs of citizens. Also, the new independent rulers often continued with the previous excesses to maintain political and social control.

Each of the entries in this volume begins with a background section that offers a brief history and context to introduce crime and punishment in the specific country. It provides an outline of the legal system; role and functions of police; classification of crimes and crime data, where available; court processes that include investigation, trial, and sentencing; and finally, a section on punishment that includes descriptions of prisons and inmates.

Legal Systems

The legal systems of Africa and the Middle East are categorized as following one or more of the following traditions:

1. Civil
2. Islamic
3. Common law
4. Customary

Only one country has a common-law tradition, and five countries in Africa have a civil legal framework. The remaining countries have some combination of civil, common, Islamic, and customary legal systems. Of the 55 African countries included in this volume, 22 have a combination of civil and customary legal frameworks. The other combinations include civil/Islamic (7), common/customary (6), common/civil (5), civil/customary/Islamic (3), and Islamic/customary/common (3). One country has an Islamic and common law combination, and one other has common law, customary, and civil legal traditions.

Among the Middle East countries, four have Islamic/civil legal traditions, and four others have Islamic/common-law legal systems. Three countries have a combination of civil, Islamic, and common law traditions, and only one does not have any form of Islamic legal tradition, with a combination of common law and customary laws.

Similar to legal systems, policing is rooted in colonial traditions, which were inherently paramilitary in nature and whose styles were adopted by the leadership in the new and fragile independent states, and therefore the consolidation of power continued. For the most part, police organizations in many African countries are underfunded, poorly equipped, and allegedly corrupt. In countries that have long histories of civil war and ethnic conflict, the lines between the military and the civil police are often blurred. Many instances of police brutality and gross violations of civil rights are noted in Amnesty International reports. Policing in the Middle East, on the other hand, is well funded, with well-trained professionals, but seems more paramilitary in nature, with state security as the primary mission.

Crime

The crime data presented in this volume primarily come from police sources. Many of the countries in the African continent do not have recent data, and the Interpol data for some countries are very outdated. A classification of specific crimes, such as murder, into the categories of low, medium, and high (see Map 5: Murder in Africa and Middle East), indicates the seriousness of the problem across the two regions. Parts of western, middle, and southern African countries have high murder rates compared to the northeastern, southwestern, and northwestern regions. None of the countries in the Middle East have a high murder rate. Only four countries—Iran, Iraq, Syria, and Yemen—have medium rates, with the remaining countries having low level murder rates.

Apart from murder, the other forms of violent crime that are frequently reported in Africa include violence against women in the forms of rape, female genital mutilation, and slavery. Drug-related violence; trafficking in women, children, and firearms; and terrorism were among the other crimes commonly noted in country reports. Most countries in the Middle East and Africa have harsh penalties for drug-related crimes, especially when compared to penalties for offenses against women. Some countries also report crimes such as poaching, cattle theft, and piracy. Among the violations noted in some of the Middle Eastern countries were crimes against domestic workers and trafficking in women and children.

Punishment

Nearly half of all African countries and nearly all countries in the Middle East have corporal punishment (see Map 7: Corporal Punishment in Africa and Middle East). A similar number of countries in Africa and all the countries in the Middle East have the death penalty (see Map 8: Death Penalty in Africa and Middle East). A check of these two maps suggests a high concordance rate between corporal punishment and the death penalty. The chapters also record the number of prisons and prisoners in each country (territory). Although far from reliable or current, the data offer an opportunity to determine countries and regions that have high imprisonment rates (see Map 6: Imprisonment in Africa and Middle East). In Africa, 5 countries are rated as high imprisonment countries, 20 countries have medium imprisonment rates, and the remaining have low rates. In the Middle East, Iraq and the United Arab Emirates have high prison rates, and Syria has low rates, with the remaining countries holding medium rates. A majority of African country reports indicate poor prison conditions for inmates and high incidences of human rights violations. It is not uncommon to note the absence or non-practice of due process for suspects in custody; they are often locked up with convicted prisoners and subject to similar harsh and unsanitary prison conditions.

An overview of these two regions and Africa in particular suggests many challenges encountered by governments. These problems are inherent in most all countries with colonial legacies. However, these countries also face additional challenges, such as political instability, weak economies, ethnic tensions, and environmental disasters, which result in a focus more on law and order and less on reforms in criminal justice. As seen in this volume, the legal framework in most of the countries adopts multiple legal systems, making harmonization of the legal system more complex. Countries with police systems that are direct descendants of colonial rulers are more paramilitary than civilian in orientation. The primary mission of police organizations in these states is to protect the state, rather than to protect the citizens by following the principles of democratic policing, rule of law, and the upholding of human rights. Many of the reports from these regions note efforts at judicial reforms and the democratization of civil police, professionalization of police, and efforts in developing community policing. Some countries have reported resources being made available for streamlining court processes and improving correctional services. This is a positive sign. Reform efforts need more than money, but above all, they require political will.

—Mahesh K. Nalla
Michigan State University

Country Key to Africa and the Middle East Maps

Algeria	DZ	Malawi	MW
Angola	AO	Mali	ML
Bahrain	BH	Mauritania	MR
Benin	BJ	Mauritius	MU
Botswana	BW	Mayotte	YT
Burkina Faso	BF	Morocco	MA
Burundi	BI	Mozambique	MZ
Cameroon	CM	Namibia	NA
Cape Verde	CV	Niger	NE
Central African Republic	CF	Nigeria	NG
Chad	TD	Oman	OM
Comoros	KM	Palestinian Occupied Territory	PS
Congo	CG	Qatar	QA
Djibouti	DJ	Reunion	RE
Egypt	EG	Rwanda	RW
Equatorial Guinea	GQ	St. Helena	SH
Eritrea	ER	Sao Tome and Principe	ST
Ethiopia	ET	Saudi Arabia	SA
Gabon	GA	Senegal	SN
Gambia	GM	Seychelles	SC
Ghana	GH	Sierra Leone	SL
Guinea	GN	Somalia	SO
Guinea-Bissau	GW	South Africa	ZA
Iran	IR	Sudan	SD
Iraq	IQ	Swaziland	SZ
Israel	IL	Syria	SY
Ivory Coast	CI	Tanzania, United Republic of	TZ
Jordan	JO	Togo	TG
Kenya	KE	Tunisia	TN
Kuwait	KW	Uganda	UG
Lebanon	LB	United Arab Emirates	AE
Lesotho	LS	Yemen	YE
Liberia	LR	Zaire	CD
Libya	LY	Zambia	ZM
Madagascar	MG	Zimbabwe	ZW

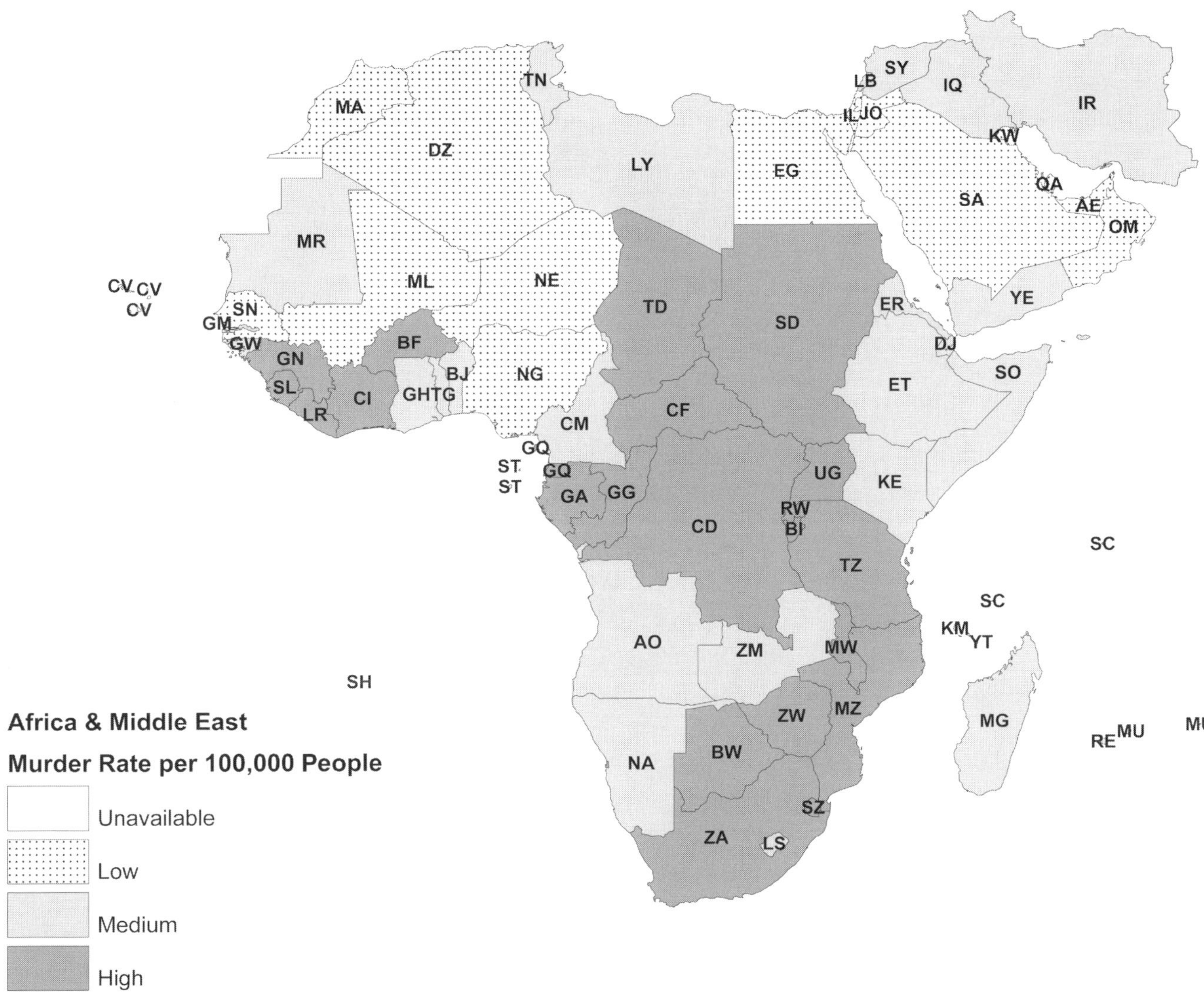

Murder in Africa and the Middle East

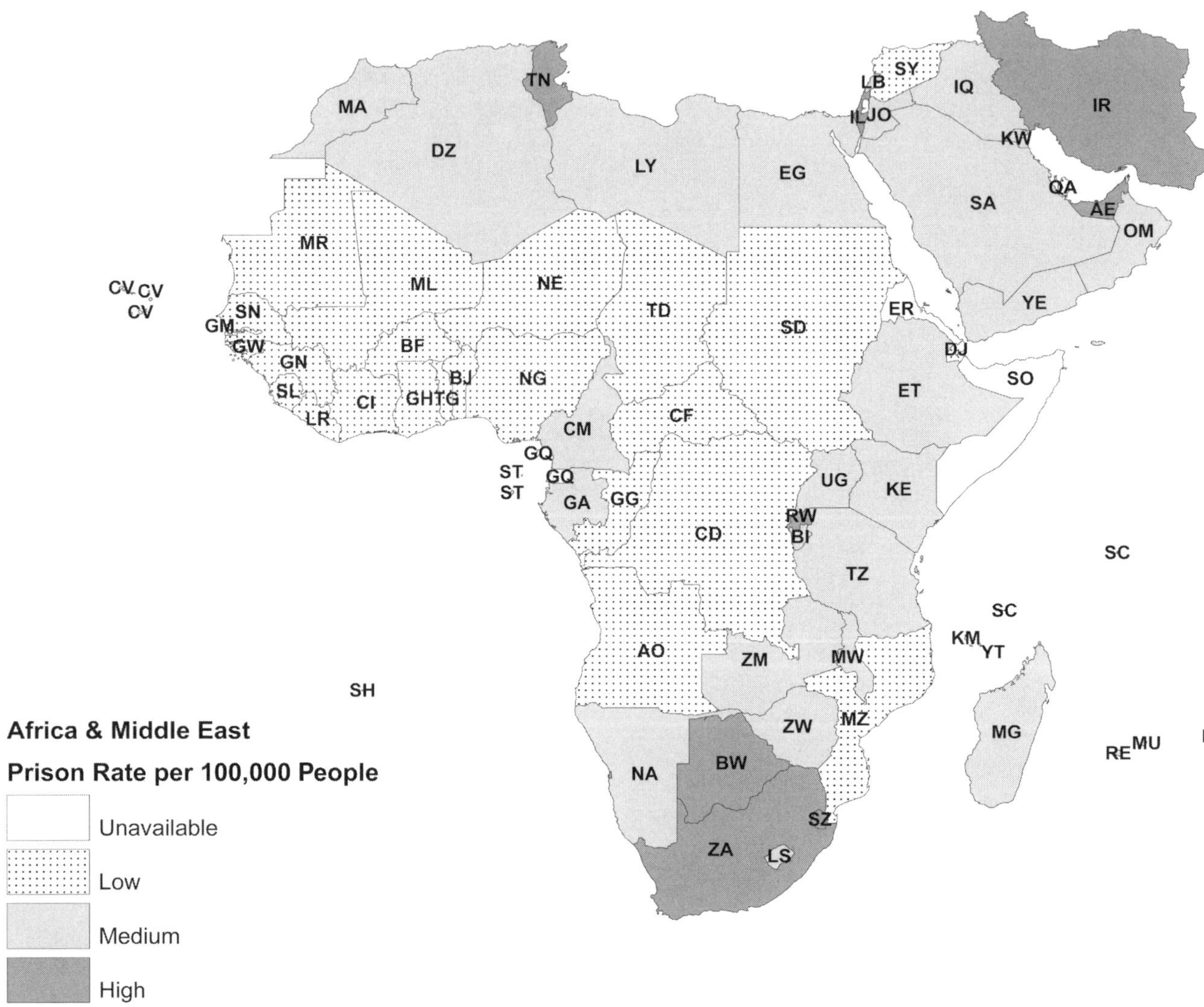

Imprisonment in Africa and the Middle East

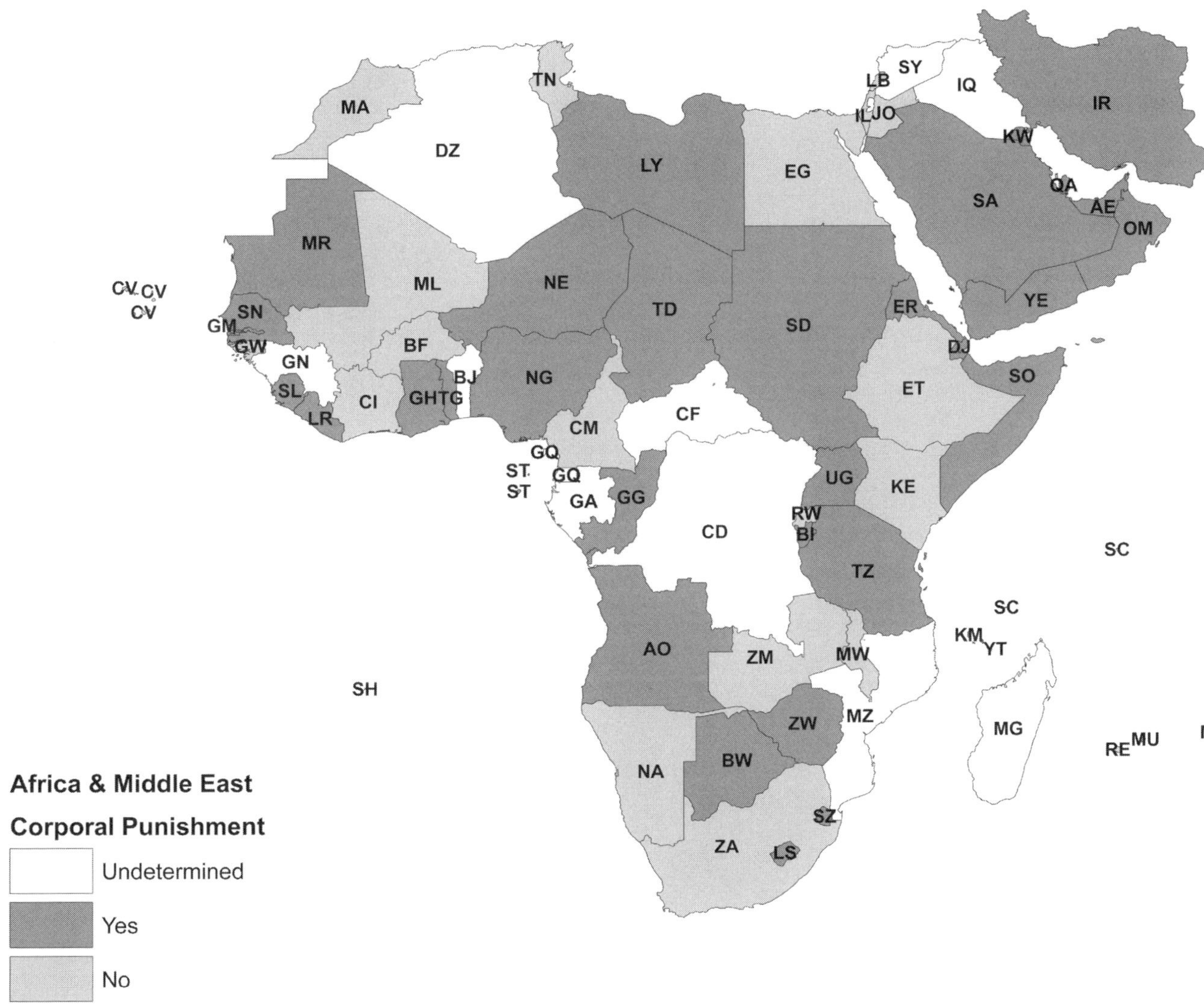

Corporal Punishment in Africa and the Middle East

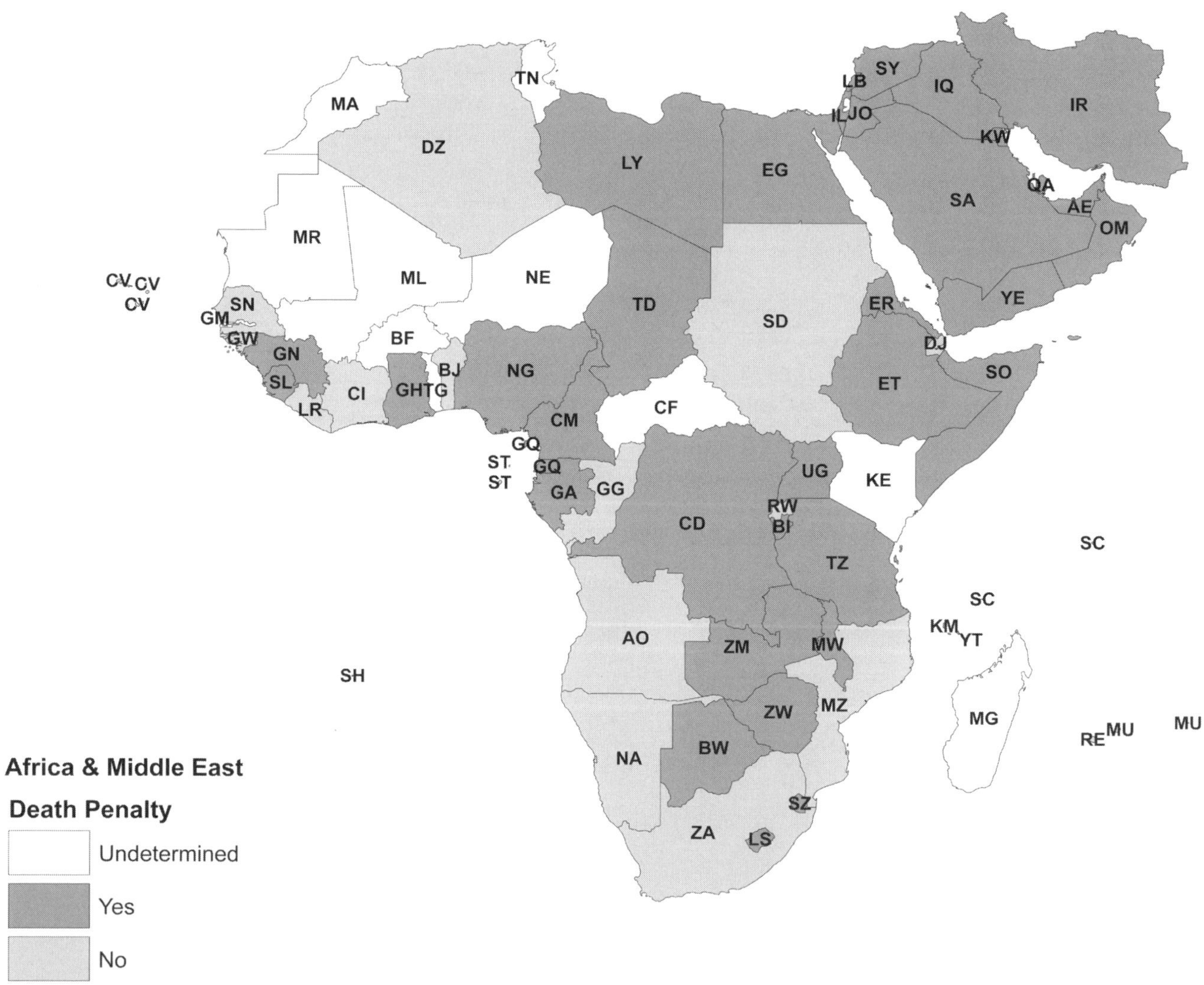

Death Penalty in Africa and the Middle East

Africa

Angola

Legal System: Civil
Murder: Medium
Corruption: High
Human Trafficking: Medium
Prison Rate: Low
Death Penalty: No
Corporal Punishment: Yes

Background

Angola (Republica de Angola) is situated on the southwest African coast with the Democratic Republic of Congo, Zambia, and Namibia as its neighbors. The capital city is Luanda, and Portuguese is the official and widely spoken language. A former Portuguese colony, Angola became mired in a 27-year civil war soon upon attaining independence in 1975. The civil war between the ruling party, the Popular Movement for the Liberation of Angola (MPLA), and the National Union for the Total Independence of Angola (UNITA) left hundreds of thousands displaced internally (IDPs) or killed. The conflict ended in 2002, but the country's development was severely restricted. Post-conflict, Angola's economy began to develop with newfound mineral wealth in oil and precious stones.

Angola, which had its last election in 2008, operates under a multiparty political system with a president who is both the head of state and the head of government. The 1975 Constitution was revised multiple times, with the last revision in 1992 yet to be ratified. In principle, the judiciary and legislature are both autonomous and independent of the executive branch, and members of parliament are elected into office for a term of four years. The legal system is based on the Portuguese civil law system and customary law with the Supreme Court, or Tribunal da Relacao, as its apex court, whose judges are appointed by the president.

Judicial System

Soon after independence, in 1976, Angola established a civilian court system, known as the People's Revolutionary Tribunal (Tribunal Popular Révolucionario), to deal with capital offenses against national security. These courts, composed of three to five judges, had jurisdiction over crimes against the security of the state, mercenary activities, war crimes, and so-called crimes against humanity, and they could unilaterally assume jurisdiction over any criminal case that had a significant impact on national security. Each provincial capital had one of these courts, which were administered by a national directorate in Luanda.

The Supreme Court of post–civil war Angola currently works as a constitutional court and as a first-level court in a number of matters, as a court of appeals for all provincial court decisions, and as a court of appeals for the municipal court decisions in criminal matters. Although the Supreme Court has 16 seats, a 2003 International Bar Association (IBA) report noted that only 9 were filled. There are 19 provincial courts each for criminal and civil matters such as family, labor, children, and minors. Appeals of the provincial courts go directly to the

Supreme Court. Municipal courts have limited jurisdiction in civil and criminal matters in the municipal areas and appeals from these courts go directly to provincial courts and to the Supreme Court in criminal matters. Local courts rule on civil matters and petty crime in some areas. Municipal and provincial courts operate under the authority of the Supreme Court.

The Accounting Court or "Anti-Corruption Court" (Tribunal de Contas) was established in 1996 but did not begin operating until 2001, and it was headed by a judge who was also a deputy in the National Assembly. Community-based courts and judges practice traditional law, outside the jurisdiction of the Constitution and the official legal system. Community-based courts and judges are not a substitute for those that the Constitution provides.

Police

It is widely believed that during the civil war days, very little role was played by the national police. Post-independence Angola's internal security functions were assumed by the Ministry of Defense, State Security, the Ministry of Interior, and the People's Vigilance Brigades (Brigadas Populares de Vigilância—BPV). The Ministry of Defense's Directorate of People's Defense and Territorial Troops (ODP) had over half a million members fighting alongside the army against various insurgent groups, defending bridges and other key infrastructure.

The police organization that existed before independence, Direcao de Informacao e Seguranca de Angola (DISA), which was formally abolished in 1979, was known to be repressive and was widely feared. Very little information is available about the organization, and its functions were subsumed by a new body under the Ministry of Interior, still referred to as DISA. DISA had wide-ranging powers and discretion to conduct investigations, make arrests, detain individuals, and determine how they would be treated. The national police, called the National Angolan People's Police, which evolved from the Portuguese colonial police and the People's Police Corps of Angola, was set

On January 9, 2010, Angolan police escort the bus carrying Ghana's soccer team as it leaves the compound in Cabinda, Angola, where the teams are based. (AP Photo/Darko Bandic)

up in 1976 under the Ministry of Defense. With headquarters in Luanda, the police numbered about 8,000 men and women and was supported by a paramilitary force of 10,000 that resembled a national guard.

DISA was officially abolished in 1979 and recreated in 1980 under the Ministry of State Security, which was carved out of the Ministry of Interior as part of the government reorganization. This new ministry consolidated the DISA's internal security functions with those relating to counterintelligence, control of foreigners, anti-UNITA operations, and frontier security. The Ministry of State Security also had under its jurisdiction the Angolan Border Guard (Tropa Guarda Fronteira Angolana—TGFA). With an estimated strength of about 7,000 in 1988, TGFA's primary goal was to secure Angola's borders with Congo, Zaire, Zambia, and Namibia.

In 1983, the BPV was established to maintain public order, law enforcement, and public service for urban centers. Some of the BPV units were armed but mostly performed public security functions such as intelligence gathering, surveillance, patrols, civil defense, and crime prevention activities. Each unit contained about 100 members and was organized along provincial levels and below, but they were easily mobilized in case of reported insurgencies. In 1987, it was reported that there were nearly 1 million members, a third of them women.

In 1994, as part of the Lusaka Protocol, the Angolan National Police were formally charged with managing public order, a function generally associated with civilian police. Simultaneously, an elite unit called the Rapid Reaction Police (or Policia da Intervencas Rápida—PIR) was created and stationed in strategic locations in a supportive role for maintenance and restoration of order, control of situations of concerted violence, protection against violence and organized crime, protection of strategic installations, and security for important personalities.

The Angolan National Police (NPA) is housed in the Ministry of the Interior. Various legal instruments including the National Police Statute, Angola Decree 20/93 of June 11, 1993, are in place requiring that the police act impartially and subject to the rule of law regarding the civil rights of citizens. However, there have been numerous reports of political bias among police rank-and-file in favor of the ruling party. Despite numerous reports of misconduct, there are checks and balances in place to regulate the police behavior as outlined in the 1975 Constitution, later revised in 1992. Some of the provisions include Angola's commitment to the United Nations (UN) and Organization of African Unity (OAU) charters, equality before law of all its citizens, respect for human dignity, and the provision that no person shall be subjected to torture or inhumane and degrading treatment and punishment, among others.

The organization of the NPA consists of a national command, with provincial, municipal, and communal structures under its overall control. The NPA's departments include public order, criminal investigation, traffic and transport, investigation and inspection of economic activities, and the Rapid Reaction Police. The functions of the NPA are the defense of democratic legality; preservation of public order; respect for fundamental rights and liberties of citizens; defense and protection of state as collective, personal, and private property; prevention of delinquency and reduction of criminality; and collaboration in the implementation of national defense policies, in terms established by the law.

Though many proposals have been made to upgrade and improve the NPA, lack of basic resources severely hampers any development. There are no facilities to train in areas such as criminal investigation and forensics. In 2006, a Higher Institute of Police Sciences was established to minimize the need for sending officers abroad for training.

Police brutality and corruption are areas of concern, according to Amnesty International (AI). AI reports that despite the inclusion of human rights training in the police training curriculum, officers continue to violate human rights, and few perpetrators are ever brought to justice. In almost all the cases of human rights violations, the officers were not held accountable for their actions. There were no investigations carried out, no disciplinary proceedings followed, and no suspected perpetrators were brought to justice. The AI report also notes the NPA culture of total obedience to supervisors that results in officers executing orders without questioning the legality of their actions.

Private security played an important role in Angola's history of military involvement and in its civil war, particularly between 1993 and 1996. In the early 2000s, estimates placed the number of private security companies operating in Angola at around 80. Angola's diamond and oil industries in particular have contributed to the growth of the industry, given that the government was unable to provide security to foreign investors. Although there have been instances of excesses of private security personnel, the government of Angola seems committed to the application of a combination of international, regional, and national legislation to regulate private armies.

Crime

The penal code (1886) and the criminal procedure code are the two main legal documents that guide the criminal justice system in Angola. Both documents are dated. In addition other laws and decrees called sundry laws have passed recently, but this does not necessarily mean that the laws are current and keep up with the social reality of Angola.

Rape: Among felony crimes, rape, including spousal rape, is illegal and punishable by up to eight years' imprisonment. Most cases never reach prosecution stage because of limited investigative resources, low level forensic capabilities, and an ineffective judicial system. Sexual relations with a child under 12 is considered rape. Sex with children between the ages of 12 and 15 may be considered sexual abuse, and offenders can receive up to 8 years in prison. NGOs offer shelter and special services to rape victims and have pressed the Ministry of Interior to increase women police as well as train police officers to improve response to rape allegations.

Trafficking in persons: There are no specific laws for trafficking in persons. Though data are not available for trafficking, there have been unconfirmed reports of trafficking of orphaned children, who are often most vulnerable. Laws criminalizing forced or bonded labor, prostitution, pornography, rape, kidnapping, and illegal entry are used to prosecute trafficking cases. The sentence for some of these related offenses carries a maximum of life imprisonment. There is no single ministry with direct responsibility for combating trafficking.

Prostitution is illegal, but the prohibition is not consistently enforced, once again because of lack of resources. Sexual harassment is common but is not specifically illegal. However, sometimes such cases are prosecuted under assault and battery and defamation statutes.

Terrorism: There is no legislation specifically targeting terrorism. However, other forms of conduct listed in Crimes against the State, Law 7/78 of 26 May, and Law against Mercenary Actions, Law 4/77 of 25 February, could be classified as terrorism. Crimes against the State, Law 7/78, specifically mentions the crime of piracy (article 15), rebel activities (article 19), sabotage (article 21), and explosives (article 22), among others.

Current crime data for Angola are not available. The most recent data available on the INTERPOL Web site are for 1999. The number of crimes reported to INTERPOL in 1999 were as follows:

Homicide/murder	1,047
Rape	248
Serious assault	1,841
Robbery and violent theft	569
Aggravated theft	4,226
Breaking and entering	3,657
Motor vehicle theft	441
Drug offenses	522

Finding of Guilt

Angolan law authorizes the Ministry of State Security to detain persons suspected of having committed serious crimes against the security of the state without charge for up to three months and then if necessary for an additional three months. Unlike common criminals, such detainees do not have any constitutional safeguards such as the right to be brought before a judge within 48 hours of arrest and cannot challenge the basis of detention. Political prisoners must be informed of the accusations against them after six months in detention and then must be referred to a public prosecutor or released. If charges are pressed, there is no stated time period within which a trial must be held, and delays of several years are common.

Lack of training and infrastructure inhibits judicial proceedings, according to the U.S. State Department (USSD) 2004 report. The report notes that as a result of severe disruptions inflicted due to the civil war, inadequate judicial infrastructure in many provinces and municipalities began relying on traditional leaders called *sobas* to decide local cases. Unfortunately, these local traditional or informal courts do not offer the same constitutional safeguards accorded in formal municipal and provincial courts. The International Bar Association (IBA) report noted that few Angolans have access to justice because the number of lawyers is limited. Some provinces such as Moxico, Kuando Kubango, Luanda Norte, and Bié had no lawyers and a further five provinces had only one lawyer. The USSD report noted that the government is making efforts to rebuild courts and train new magistrates and prosecutors to fill all vacancies.

According to the Angolan constitution, a person caught in the act of committing a crime may be arrested and detained immediately. Otherwise, the law requires that a judge or a provincial magistrate issue an arrest warrant or that it be issued by members of the judicial police and confirmed within five days by a magistrate. Typically, arrest warrants (*mandatos de captura*) are issued by police commanders (*comandantes da policia*). Normal police procedures include detaining an individual at a police station for up to 72 hours, but the individual must then be charged or released. Warrants have to be served personally but can be left with relatives or neighbors if the named person is not present. In the past, warrants were sometimes broadcast on the radio or published in the newspaper.

The length of time a suspect can be detained is outlined in the Angolan penal codes. The 2003 IBA report notes that "Angolan law allows people suspected of crimes punishable for up to two years in prison to be detained for a maximum of 120 days; people suspected of crimes punishable for over two years in prison to be detained for a maximum of 135 days; and people suspected of crimes against state security to be detained for a maximum of 215 days." However, the report notes that the prolonged detention was primarily due to lack of resources in the justice system, including lack of personnel.

The Constitution accords protections to citizens from arbitrary arrest. Article 36 states that "no citizen may be arrested or put on trial except in accordance with the law, and all accused shall be guaranteed the right to defense and the right to legal aid and counsel." Additional safeguards are offered by the Constitution. Articles 37 and 38, respectively, stipulate that "preventive detention shall be permitted only in cases provided for by the law, which shall establish the limits and periods thereof" and "any citizen subject to preventive detention shall be taken before a competent judge to legalize the detention and be tried within the period provided for by law or released." Given the large number of indigent suspects who turn up in courts, legal representation becomes an issue. The 2003 IBA report notes that the Angolan Bar Association is able to provide criminal defense lawyers to some of the suspects. The Constitution also provides defendants with the presumption of innocence until a judicial decision is made by a court, with right to counsel, and with public trials.

The age of criminal responsibility in Angola is 16 years. However, the civil responsibility could be vested with parents or the guardians. For youth between 17 and 21 years, the Angolan law considers these persons not completely criminally responsible for their actions. The Juvenile Court, which started functioning in 2003 in Luanda, decrees socio-educational measures for persons within this age group, and oversees compliance.

Punishment

Amnesty International (AI) reported in March 2004 that Angola had abolished the death penalty for all crimes in 1992. Further, Amnesty also notes that article 22 of the Constitution stipulates that "the State shall respect and protect the life of the human person." It also states that the death penalty is prohibited. However, in its 2004 report, AI cited instances of extrajudicial executions by the security forces.

Prison System

Portuguese Angola used prisons as far back as the 1570s, with the first prison built in Sao Migeul in 1576. In post-independence Angola, the Ministry of State Security was responsible for administering the national prison system, with certain prison camps run by the Ministry of Interior. The principal prisons are located in Luanda. The Estrada de Catete prison in the capital and the Bentiaba detention camp in Namibe Province are the principal detention centers for political prisoners. The detention center in Cuanza Sul Province is primarily used as one of the main rural detention centers. This facility, being a former sisal plantation, is utilized as a labor farm for prisoners who perform forced labor and reside in barracks-like dwellings.

Most of these facilities are overcrowded with substandard conditions. Though prison conditions vary widely, some of these conditions include poor diet, sanitation, and medical facilities; prolonged interrogation, beatings, torture, and inhumane treatment; curtailment of visits by family and friends arbitrarily; and holding inmates incommunicado or moving them from one prison to another without notifying the family.

A 2004 U.S. State Department (USSD) report noted that prison conditions were harsh and life threatening and continued to hold as many as five times their built-in capacity. Overcrowding in Luanda prisons was said to be diminished after the completion in November 2004 of the rehabilitation and expansion of the Viana prison, the report noted. A 2004 Freedom House report also noted that prisoners are often kept in detention for long periods awaiting trial in life-threatening, overcrowded, and unsanitary conditions. Outside the capital in the Bengo, Malange, and Lunda Norte provinces, sometimes warehouses were used as prison facilities. Lack of financial resources is directly related to inadequate hygiene, food, and health care for prisoners. Some prisoners relied on their relatives to bring in food, which the underpaid prison staff would sometimes steal.

Police detention cells are also reported to be inhumane. The 2004 USSD report noted that between 8 and 16 prisoners died from asphyxiation in an overcrowded police station detention cell. Police reportedly killed two individuals as the local population protested. The report noted that the national police commander publicly acknowledged wrongdoing and ordered appropriate disciplinary action on the officers involved.

The Constitution and the penal code prohibit all forms of mistreatment of suspects, detainees, and prisoners by security forces and prison officials. However, local and international human rights organizations have noted gross neglect and exploitation of prisoners. The USSD report also noted that sometimes prison officials operated an informal bail system for detainees, allowing their release until their trial date for a price. Female prisoners were kept apart from males, but the prison guards sexually abused female inmates. Some improvements were noted when a new prison opened in Viana with a female-only wing staffed by female guards. Juveniles are often warehoused with adult prisoners and subject to harassment and abuses from both older inmates and prison guards.

The King's College of London World Prison Brief reported that in 2002 there were 4,975 prison inmates, representing a rate of 37 per 100,000 population. In October 2005, the report noted that including pretrial detainees and remand prisoners, there were about 8,300 inmates.

Mahesh K. Nalla and Joseph D. Johnson

Further Reading

Berg, J. (2005). *Overview of Plural Policing Oversight in Select Southern African Development Community (SADC) Countries*. Cape Town: Institute of Criminology.

Cleary, S. (1999). "Angola—A Case Study of Private Military Involvement." In *Peace, Profit or Plunder? The Privatisation of Security in War-torn African Societies,* edited by J. Cilliers and

P. Mason, pp. 141–174. Pretoria: Institute for Security Studies.

Culolo, A. J. P. (2001). "Combating Organized Crime in Angola (Cpt.9)." Monograph No. 56: http://www.iss.co.za/Pubs/Monographs/No56/chap9.html.

Home Office. (2005). *Angola: Country Report.* Country Information & Policy Unit, Immigration and Nationality Directorate, Home Office, United Kingdom: http://www.unhcr.org/refworld/pdfid/429ed3594.pdf.

U.S. Department of State. (2005). *Country Reports on Human Rights Practices—2004:* http://www.state.gov/g/drl/rls/hrrpt/2004/41587.htm.

Basutholand. See Lesotho

Benin

Legal System: Civil
Murder: Medium
Corruption: Medium
Human Trafficking: Medium
Prison Rate: Low
Death Penalty: No
Corporal Punishment: Maybe

Background

Benin is located in Central Africa with Nigeria, Togo, Burkina Faso, and Niger as its neighbors. Until 1975, Benin was known as Dahomey, a name given to it by its colonial master, France. Benin obtained its independence from France on August 1, 1960. The capital city is Porto Novo, with Cotonou being the largest and most commercial city. In 2005, Benin's population was estimated to be 8,439,000, and it occupies an area of 112,622 square kilometers (43,483 square miles).

Today, Benin operates as a multiparty representative democratic political system. The president is both the head of state and the head of government. According to the 1990 Constitution of Benin, the judiciary and legislature are both autonomous and independent of the executive branch. The president is elected into office for two terms of five years each. Members of parliament are elected into office for a term of four years. There are 83 members of Benin's National Assembly, which meets twice yearly. There are currently 12 political parties in the country. For administrative purposes, the country is divided into 12 departments and 77 communes.

Benin's military and policing systems are modeled after the French systems. Its security operatives consist of the armed forces, which are headed by the State Ministry of Defense. The gendarmerie is the security outfit that performs police functions in the rural areas of the country, and it is supervised by the Ministry of Defense. The police have jurisdiction in the larger, more urban centers of the country. This police establishment is under the supervision of the Ministry of the Interior, Security, and Decentralization. It is important to note that all of the security forces, the armed forces, and the police are under the control of civilians through the ministries.

Legal System

With the nation being a constitutional democracy, the Benin Constitution guarantees the independence of the judiciary. The Constitution further guarantees the citizens civil and human rights, and the government generally upholds these rights. Its security forces are under the control of the civilian administration. The armed forces are under the supervision of the minister in charge of defense matters. The police force is under the Ministry of Interior, Security, and Decentralization. The gendarmerie, which polices the rural areas, is under the supervision of the Ministry of Defense. The other police establishment, which operates in urban and bigger cities, is under the supervision of the Ministry of the Interior. However, the delivery of justice in the country is hampered by poverty, illiteracy, and endemic corruption within the judiciary. Furthermore, the citizens find the principles and processes of the state-based legal system incompatible with the African concept of justice. Again, the police use of excessive force and arbitrary detention of suspects undermines the people's confidence in the legal system. As a result, the people seek to resolve their conflicts through the African indigenous justice institutions and may out of frustration resort to lynching and vigilante justice.

The legal system of Benin is based on both the French civil law system and African customary law. Consistent with the constitutional provision, there is a clear division of power among the branches of government. Thus, the judiciary acts independently of the executive branch. The Benin court system operates at both the national and provincial levels. There is one Court of Appeals and one Supreme Court. The Supreme Court has the final jurisdiction on all administrative and judicial matters. The Constitution also provides for a Constitutional Court, which has the original jurisdiction in determining constitutional laws, as well as settling conflicts between the National Assembly and the president. The Constitutional Court also handles disputes resulting from both presidential and legislative elections. Judges of the civil courts are career magistrates appointed by the president. However, the Constitution empowers the Ministry of Justice with supervisory authority over the judges of the civil courts. The ministry assigns judges and can transfer them to any area of the country where their services are needed.

In the event that the president or a minister of the state is the defendant in a criminal proceeding against the state, a High Court of Justice will convene according to the Constitution. Members of the High Court include members of the Constitutional Court, excluding the president of the court, and six deputies elected by the National Assembly

Women walk past the Justice Ministry building in Cotonou, Benin. Benin has seen three peaceful transfers of power in 15 years, making the former Marxist dictatorship—once nicknamed "Africa's Cuba"—an unlikely leader of Africa's checkered democratic rebirth. (AP Photo/George Osodi)

and the Supreme Court. The chairman of the Supreme Court presides over the proceedings of the High Court.

The criminal code distinguishes between juveniles and adults, as well as between first-time offenders and repeat offenders. For example, judges may grant suspended sentences to first-time offenders. The age of criminal responsibility is 18 years. The revised 1994 penal code of Benin replaced the Code of Criminal Instruction of 1958. The code recognizes three levels of offense, namely crimes, misdemeanors, and other violations. Crimes are punishable with between 5- and 20-year prison sentences; misdemeanors are punishable with prison sentences of up to 3 years; and violations are punishable by up to a year in prison. According to Borricand in the *World Factbook of Criminal Justice Systems,* crimes are classified into attacks against persons, property, and public security:

> Attacks against persons include intentional homicide (murder, assassination, infanticide), intentional violence (non-intentional death, harm resulting in a permanent injury), and rape (including rape with more than one offender, aggravating circumstances, simple rape, and rape of a minor under 15 years of age). Attacks against property include theft, robbery, fraud, breach of trust, aggravated robberies and vandalism, public security and counterfeiting.

The penal code also distinguishes between completed and attempted criminal acts. Criminal trials must be public and fair. However, when public order is threatened, the court president may restrict public access to the court to preserve order and protect the individuals involved in the judicial process. Defendants may be granted bail upon the recommendation of the attorney general. An accused is innocent until proven guilty and is entitled to legal representation financed by the state if he or she cannot afford the services of a lawyer. It is the right of the accused to be present in court during trial and to confront any witnesses. The accused must also be granted full access to any evidence in the government's possession.

A lack of qualified judges in Benin is currently hampering the delivery of justice in the country. The salaries of judges are also grossly inadequate, and many contribute to the endemic corruption in the judiciary. Serious attempts were made in 2004 by the government of Benin to curb corruption within the judiciary; several judges and other senior officers of the judiciary who were found guilty of corruption were sentenced to prison. In addition, the salaries of judges have been increased, and ethics training for judges and other senior officers of the judiciary has been instituted.

The language of the courts is French, which the average Beninoise does not understand, and this further limits the people's access to justice. Furthermore, the courts have introduced illegal court fees that judicial authorities claim is necessary to meet court costs for which the government does not provide. This practice of charging fees is another limitation to the average person's access to justice because only the very rich can afford the court fees. Once again, the principles and processes of the government courts are incompatible with the principles and processes of traditional African justice, to which the people have become accustomed. Whereas the goal of the government's courts is the punishment of the offender to deter the offender and others from committing crime, the goal of African indigenous justice is the restoration of the victim, the community, and even the offender. Many Africans therefore are reluctant to patronize the government courts because the "winner take all" approach undermines community bonds and can create community bitterness, which may endure for several years and even generations.

Unfortunately, citizens sometimes resort to lynching crime suspects, out of frustration resulting from their lack of trust in the agents of the criminal justice system. Lynching occurs mostly in the urban areas where the African indigenous justice system is not available. Another major crime problem in Benin is human trafficking, which the security agents are ill equipped to handle. Benin is a major source and transit point for human trafficking. The U.S. Department of State reported, from research conducted by the World Bank and the National Institute of Statistics and Economics, that an estimated 49,000 children from rural areas between the ages of 6 and 16 are trafficked to Côte d'Ivoire and Gabon as agricultural and domestic workers. Some villages are more affected than others. Some villages lose up to 51 percent of their youths to child human trafficking. Although important legislative steps and local NGO efforts have been introduced to stamp out child trafficking, the country remains in Tier 2 of the U.S. 2008 State Department trafficking report. Benin is also a major source and transit point for drug trafficking. Although a small amount of illegal narcotics is produced locally, the drug of choice is marijuana in Benin.

Crime

Benin's crime rate is relatively low, although the country has experienced a slight increase in crime in recent years. According to the available 1998 crime data, INTERPOL reports that the crime rates per 100,000 population for Benin were as follows: murder, 5.12; rape, 2.55; robbery, 4.27; aggravated assault, 102.03; burglary, 4.57; larceny, 59.90; motor vehicle theft, .63; and total crime rate, 179.07. According to the Ministry of Interior, an estimated 17 percent of crimes and misdemeanors were drug-related.

Punishment

Prisons

The prison conditions are very harsh. The eight prisons in the country are overcrowded, holding many more detainees than the maximum capacity. The prisons also lack adequate sanitation and medical facilities. The quality of the food served to inmates is inadequate for nutritional needs. Malnutrition and diseases are common, and family members of detainees are expected to provide food for their loved ones in government custody.

Angela R. Morris and O. Oko Elechi

Further Reading

Borricand, J. Benin. "France." In *World Factbook of Criminal Justice Systems*, edited by Graeme Newman. Washington, DC: U.S. Department of Justice, Bureau of Justice Statistics. 1993, 2002: http://bjs.ojp.usdoj.gov/index.cfm?ty=pbdetail&iid=1435.

Lefort, R. (1999). *Benin: Justice on the Horizon:* http://www.unesco.org/courier/1999_11/uk/dossier/txt22.htm.

Minister of the Interior. (1993). "Aspects of the Observed Criminality in France in 1992" (Ministere de l'Interieur, "Aspects de la criminalité et de la delinquance constatées en France 1992"): http://www.police.online.fr/lawfr.htm.

U.S. Department of State. (2007). *Human Rights Country Report:* http://www.state.gov/g/drl/rls/hrrpt/2007/100466.htm.

Botswana

Legal System: Civil/Common
Murder: High
Burglary: High
Corruption: Low
Prison Rate: High
Death Penalty: Yes
Corporal Punishment: Yes

Background

Botswana is a land-locked nation located north of South Africa, bordering Namibia, Zambia, and Zimbabwe. In 1966, it became independent from the United Kingdom. Botswana has a bicameral parliamentary democracy. It has a House of Chiefs, whose members are leaders of the local communities and appointed by the president. The House of Chiefs serves an advisory role in making decisions regarding customary law and tradition. Members must not have been actively involved in politics for five years prior to appointment and must not be a member of a political party. The nation also has a national assembly elected by direct vote of the population. The national assembly is the law-making branch of the government. These combined represent the national assembly. Although there is some evidence of media manipulation by the government, the most recent presidential election in 2004 was described as free and fair. The government also has firm control over the military and the police.

The Botswana Defense Forces (BDF) is responsible for external security and operates domestically to protect wildlife areas from poachers. The Botswana Police Service (BPS) is the primary agency responsible for maintaining internal security. There are approximately 6,500 police personnel for 1.8 million residents, which represents approximately 1 policeman for every 276 people in the population. The BPS operates under the Ministry of Presidential Affairs and Public Administration. Until March 2008, there were also local and customary police that operated separately from the BPS. These organizations have since been merged into the BPS.

The BPS has low levels of corruption and police brutality. Police command staff indicate some corruption among lower-level police personnel. There is also some evidence of use of excessive force during interrogations. BPS personnel are held accountable by the people and the government. The State Department indicates numerous incidents of police being arrested and fired or imprisoned for committing crimes. In 2006, two police officers were arrested for collaborating with civilian burglars and subsequently dismissed. Between January and September 2008, 31 police officers were arrested for criminal offenses, and 19 of these were brought to trial. It must be noted, these incidents do not indicate high levels of corruption among the BPS, and rather these incidents indicate that police personnel are held accountable for their actions.

More generally, the government has also taken steps to deal with official corruption. Official corruption generally refers to the use of public power for private gain. Prior to 1990, the Botswana civil service was reputed to be efficient and incorruptible. But a number of high-profile corruption cases, including illegal land sales and large unpaid loans to public officials, resulted in the resignation of some high-level members of governments. This resulted in the development of an ombudsman to deal with complaints of corruption by the general public and in the creation of the Directorate of Corruption and Economic Crime (the Directorate or DEC) to deal with high-profile economic crime and corruption.

Some critics indicate the Directorate is merely a tool of the current government in power, but the agency has had a number of successes. Since its creation, the Directorate has heard thousands of complaints. In 1996, the DEC successfully prosecuted 60 of the 95 cases it brought to court. It also successfully lobbied the government to require members of parliament to declare their financial assets and make them available to the public. The Directorate is facing serious man-power shortages and problems in its working relationship with other government agencies. The existence of the ombudsman, the Directorate, and the prosecution of police personnel by the courts indicates a high level of accountability and a drive to reduce corruption.

The peculiarities of its colonial history have influenced the development of Botswana's legal system. Because of the assumption that the country would be annexed by South Africa, the legal system of Botswana was originally based in Roman-Dutch rather than English common law. Roman-Dutch law was the legal system of the British colony of the Cape of Good Hope. At independence, Botswana adopted British common law in criminal codes and contracts. It continues to rely on Roman-Dutch law for rules of evidence and procedural law. South Africa continues to have a significant legal influence on Botswana. Since 1995, the South African Constitutional Law Reports have published decisions of Botswana. South African criminal procedure textbooks are also recognized in Botswana.

Botswana's legal system is heavily influenced by traditional practices. The country has a dual legal system, which includes a Westernized legal system and the customary courts that are based in the traditional practices of the Botswana people. Throughout this entry reference will be made to customary courts and the legal system. The legal system is here defined as the contemporary Western system of common and civil law courts, judges, and attorneys that operate in Botswana. Customary courts are the traditional dispute resolution mechanisms separate from the legal system.

The system of customary courts is incorporated into the formal legal structure of the country. The Botswana Supreme Court has determined that the customary courts are subordinate to the legal system and that traditional leaders are subordinate to the national government. However, the legal protections enshrined in the Botswana Constitution are not applicable in the customary courts. These traditional courts play a major role in dispute resolution and try approximately 85 percent of all criminal cases.

Crime

The crime problem in Botswana is of both domestic and international importance. Evidence regarding levels of crime in Botswana is available, although more recent data are limited.

Classification of Crime

Crimes are classified according to whether they are an offense against the law of Botswana. Crimes are further classified according to the extent they are "serious," from crimes in which the maximum penalty is death to crimes for which the penalty is imprisonment for not less than two years. Information on crime classifications outside of those described is as follows:

1. *Rape:* Section 2 of the Penal Code (Amendment Act) No. 5 of 1998 reads: "Any person who has unlawful carnal knowledge of another person, or who causes the penetration of a sexual organ or instrument, of whatever nature, into the person of another for the purpose of his own sexual gratification, or who causes the penetration of another person's sexual organ into his or her person, without the consent of such person, or with such person's consent if the consent is obtained by force . . . or by means of false pretences."
2. *Defilement:* Rape of a person under the age of 16.
3. *Economic crime:* Bribery, conflict of interest, diversion of public revenue, and possession of unexplained income.
4. *Money laundering:* A person is deemed to have been engaged in money laundering if he engages, directly or indirectly, in a transaction that involves money, or other property, that is the proceeds of a serious offense, whether committed in Botswana or elsewhere.
5. *Crimes involving drugs:* No person shall deal in any habit-forming drug or any plant from which any habit-forming drug can be manufactured; or shall possess or use any such drug or plant.

There exists some tension between the legal system and the customary courts because many traditional rules are not codified within the criminal code. A customary court can find guilty an individual who violates a community rule and punish them accordingly. However, the customary courts must obey the penal law and cannot technically punish a person unless the "crime" he or she committed was established in the penal code.

Crime Statistics

There are a number of different sources of crime data, including INTERPOL data, Afrobarometer data, and other government and nongovernment sources of data. Each is described independently. The most recent crime data available from INTERPOL are for 1996. It is unknown the extent to which those cases handled by the customary courts are incorporated into this INTERPOL data, though it is likely that they reflect crimes reported to the police. These data are as follows:

Homicide	207
Sexual offenses	1,254
Rape	1,101
Serious assault	5,939
Theft (all)	28,549
Aggravated theft	13,642
Robbery and violent theft	1,172
Breaking and entering	123
Theft of motor vehicles	1,799
Other thefts	11,185
Fraud	657
Currency offenses	17
Drug offenses	762
Total	**66,407**

It is unknown whether the preceding data represent current levels of crime. The United Nations Office on Drugs and Crime indicates that all persons treated for drug abuse in Botswana were treated for abuse of cannabis. However, there is some available information on rape and motor vehicle theft. According to police records, in 2002, there were 303 cases of rape of a person under the age of 16 (defilement) and 1,473 cases of rape a person over the age of 16. In 2003, there were 303 cases of defilement and 1,506 incidents of rape. This represents a 28 percent increase in defilement and a 2 percent increase in rape. The level of human trafficking is unknown, and information was not available on prosecutions or convictions for this crime. Motor vehicles are stolen in Botswana to be sold in Zambia, Zimbabwe, Zaire, and Tanzania.

There are additional data available on both victimization and fear of crime among persons who live in Botswana. The Afrobarometer survey interviewed a representative sample of individuals in 22 countries throughout sub-Saharan Africa on a wide range of topics. This survey asked questions on a range of topics, including perceptions of crime, trust in the police, perceived levels of corruption, and difficulties in obtaining police services. Data from this study in 2005 reveal that 64 percent of Botswana citizens have never feared crime in their homes, less fear than South Africans, Zambians, and Lesothans, the nation's neighbors. These data also indicate that 69 percent of Botswana residents have never had something stolen from their house. A large majority (86%) of Botswanans have never been physically attacked.

Information on the perceptions of crime by Botswana police personnel is available. Police personnel indicate they are largely responsible for maintaining order. Lethal violence in Botswana is perceived as rare and generally relates to drunken disputes. There are some indicators of increasing levels of crimes based on these interviews with BPS personnel and a review of available police records. There has also been an increase in serious assaults because of large numbers of squatters. There were very low levels of forcible theft after independence, but levels have increased since the 1990s. Coinciding with this increase in robberies was a movement of police stations to more commercial areas and a growth in private security. Forcible thefts are largely committed by the poor and involve small sums of money. The police have also become more involved in dealing with both thefts and burglaries. The BPS tends to be less concerned with public order crimes and more concerned with maintaining order in urban areas and dealing with rural migrants.

Botswana is dealing with two internal crime and human rights problems of international significance. These include discrimination against women, including domestic violence, and the mistreatment of its ethnic San minority.

Although women have the same civil rights as men, there is still significant discrimination. Traditional laws enforced through the customary courts restrict the property rights and economic opportunities of women in rural areas. Customary law allows husbands to treat their wives as if they were minor children.

Domestic violence is a significant problem in Botswana. Although the law prohibits rape, it does not recognize spousal rape. The law also does not prohibit violence against women. Because domestic violence is not considered a crime in Botswana law, the police do not collect statistics on domestic violence.

The Basarwa ethnic group, also known as the San, represents approximately 3 percent of the country's population. The San are culturally and linguistically distinct from the Tswana majority. Although legally protected from discrimination, the San are marginalized economically and politically, have limited access to education, and are not fully aware of their civil rights.

Finding of Guilt

The Botswana Constitution provides for an independent judiciary. Judicial independence is generally respected by the government. These include the legal system and the customary courts. The customary courts handle minor criminal offenses and civil matters between tribesmen. The legal system has jurisdiction over both civil and criminal matters.

To make an arrest, the police must have an arrest warrant signed by a magistrate that has been substantiated with compelling evidence. Persons arrested have the right to remain silent and must be charged by a magistrate within 48 hours after arrest. A magistrate who charges a person with a crime may hold the accused for 14 days through a writ of detention, and the writ must be renewed every 14 days. In 2008, the government established a new domestic intelligence agency called the DISS. This agency has the authority to enter premises and make arrests without a warrant if the agency believes a person has committed a crime.

Persons accused of a crime in Botswana are innocent until proven guilty. Defendants have the right to a fair and independent court and a public trial. Accused individuals have the right to a trial in a language they can understand. They also have the right to call defense witnesses and cross-examine the accused. The accused also has the right to address the court before judgment.

Although the Botswana people have the right to legal representation, the state provides it only in capital cases. This leaves many defendants without legal representation because they do not have the funds to retain an attorney. A lack of legal representation means that many defendants are not informed of their rights in pretrial or trial proceedings. Legal representation is perceived as a right only at trial, not at the time of arrest or during interrogation by the police. This system of legal representation also does little to protect defendants who cannot afford the services of a lawyer.

Criminal defendants have the right to bail. Bail is not allowed for individuals accused of murder, rape, or treason. Detention without bail is uncommon. When deciding on the right to bail, the court considers the seriousness of the offense, the impact on the victim, the nature of the evidence, and the possibility of the defendant interfering with the victim.

Victims in Botswana have some rights in criminal proceedings. They have the right to request that a case be withdrawn. Victims must be made aware of ongoing developments in their case. Investigating officers also have the duty to update the victim on the progress of an investigation. At the end of trial, the prosecutor is allowed to address the court on behalf of the victim.

Botswana does have a separate juvenile justice system, and juveniles are treated differently under the law. Juvenile courts are located at the same place as the other courts, but they follow different procedures and have different sitting magistrates. Court proceedings with juveniles are closed to the public, and their confidentiality is guaranteed. However, there is some confusion regarding the exact definition of a juvenile. In some laws, a juvenile is defined as any person under the age of 21. In other laws, those under the age of 18 are considered juveniles.

A person who is dissatisfied with the legal process has the right to appeal in both the legal system and the customary system. Appeals may be made within 30 days against both a conviction and a sentence. Dispositions in the customary courts can also be made to the legal system.

The legal system does not have sufficient number of personnel to try cases in a timely manner, resulting often in delays in both criminal and civil matters. It takes an average of 10 months for a person in pretrial detention to be brought to trial. In part because of these delays and staff shortages, the customary court system plays a significant role in the resolution of disputes.

Customary Courts

The system of traditional dispute resolution, also known as the *kgotla,* has been used in Botswana for hundreds of years. The *kgotla,* or customary court, is not an adversarial process. The customary court typically involves the complainant and the defendant discussing their dispute before a judge. It allows every man present to speak for or against the person accused.

The government codified the place of customary law and the customary courts in the Customary Law Act. This act has three provisions. First, customary law in Botswana typically operates at the local level. Only members of a particular community are bound to the laws of that community. Second, the customary law must be "compatible with morality, humanity, or natural justice," but the law does not define exactly what that means. Third, customary laws that conflict with written law are not enforceable. Each customary court operates under a different jurisdiction and has powers mandated by the state. The state mandates the types of offenses each court may handle and the type and severity of punishments they can impose.

There are indications of numerous issues with the administration of justice through the customary court system. These include a lack of legal representation, problems with the competencies of customary court judges, and the frequency of the use of the customary court system.

Customary courts do not provide constitutional due-process protections. Customary courts do not allow for legal representation. There are no standardized rules of evidence. Any party to a dispute in customary court does have the right to have that dispute transferred to a local magistrate's court. It is unknown whether this automatic transfer can occur after a course has been adjudicated by the court or prior to when a decision is made. Lack of knowledge regarding remedies in the legal system and a lack of money to pay for an attorney can keep many disputes in the customary system.

There are indications that only limited numbers of presiding officers (judges) in customary courts have a high school education and that large numbers are not literate. Court officers are expected to apply the penal codes, but these statutes are not written in the vernacular language, only in English and Setswana. The 2008 State Department Human Rights Report indicates that the decisions reached in the customary courts vary considerably, and often defendants lack the presumption of innocence.

Customary courts handle a large number of cases in Botswana. In 1998, there were 27,057 cases registered in customary courts. Of these cases, 9.9 percent of defendants were acquitted, 12.35 percent were pending trial, and 76 percent resulted in a conviction. Of those 20,577 convictions in 1998, only 1.2 percent resulted in an appeal. These court officers can sentence convicted offenders to prison for up to five years. More than two-thirds of prison inmates in the prison system were placed there by customary courts.

The customary court system creates a conundrum for the administration of justice in Botswana. The legal system provides all the procedural and due process protections that any citizen of a Western nation could expect, but it handles a minority of cases. The customary courts, which are bound by rules of tradition rather than constitutional legal protections, handle a large majority of cases. Botswana needs the system of customary courts, but this could also be creating problems with the administration of criminal justice.

Punishment

The legal system and the government developed a system of punishment with the premise of deterring criminals from committing crime. Botswana seeks to deter crime by punishing its offenders severely. Punishments appear to generally involve fines, corporal punishment, or incarceration. The extent that community corrections, such as community service and probation, are utilized is unknown. There is no available information on punishment in the juvenile justice system.

In the early 1990s, the government adopted a number of mandatory minimum sentences to deal with increases in specific crimes. Mandatory minimum sentences have been passed for treason, murder with no extenuating circumstances, unlawful possession of arms and ammunition for war, possession of and dealing habit-forming drugs, motor vehicle theft, road traffic offenses, stock theft, causing grievous harm, aggravated robbery, rape and attempted rape, and defilement and attempted defilement. The government is under the belief that these mandatory minimum sentences will not only deter crime but also ease the workload and expedite the trial process of the courts. They believe it will do this by reducing the amount of information about the convicted person's background that has to be gathered to sentence someone. Prescribed punishments are as follows:

1. *Rape:* 10 years imprisonment; with violence, suspect has HIV: 15 years; if suspect knew he was HIV-positive: minimum of 20 years and corporal punishment.

2. *Attempted rape:* 5 years imprisonment and corporal punishment.
3. *Money laundering:* Maximum of 3 years' imprisonment or fine of 10,000 pula.* If a manager/director of a group, fine not to exceed 25,000 pula.
4. *Possession/use of 40 grams of habit-forming drug other than cannabis:* Imprisonment of not less than 10 years or more than 15 years, fine of 15,000 pula.
5. *Possession/use/sale of less than 60 grams of cannabis:* Imprisonment for up to 3 years, fine of 1,000 pula.
6. *Murder:* Death penalty.
7. *Murder with extenuating circumstances:* 15 to 25 years imprisonment.
8. *Treason:* Death penalty.
9. *Instigating a foreigner to invade Botswana:* Death penalty.
10. *Committing an assault with intent to kill in the course of piracy:* Death penalty.

* In March 2009, 1 pula was equal to approximately .13 U.S. dollars.

Botswana utilizes corporal punishment. The customary courts issue sentences that include corporal punishment such as lashings on the buttocks. Corporal punishment is not to exceed 12 lashings, or 6 lashings for persons under the age of 18. Corporal punishment of females, males sentenced to death, and males believed to be over 40 years old is prohibited. Corporal punishment is also combined with imprisonment for serious offenders.

Botswana retains the right to use the death penalty for normal crimes. The death penalty can be used for persons convicted of murder, treason, instigating a foreigner to invade Botswana, or committing an assault with intent to kill in the course of piracy. Use of the death penalty is prohibited for persons under the age of 18, women who are pregnant, and persons suffering from a disease affecting their mind that makes them incapable of understanding the act. There is no provision for persons with an intellectual or mental deficiency. The president and members of parliament support the use of the death penalty. Members of government have indicated that the population supports the continued use of the death penalty, although there is no evidence available to support this assertion.

Human rights groups indicate significant problems with the implementation of the death penalty by the Botswana government. Under the law, condemned prisoners are not given notice of their execution date until 24 hours before hanging. The International Federation for Human Rights (FIDH) and Ditshwanelo indicate that often there is no public knowledge of an execution until after it occurs. The family and the condemned prisoner's lawyer are not allowed to see the condemned prior to execution, and executions have been carried out while petitions before the African Commission on Human and People's Rights were pending.

Botswana executed 32 prisoners between 1966 and 1998. Since 2001, it has executed a further 6 prisoners. The most recent execution in April 2006 was of a black South African man accused of murdering a police sergeant. Outside of the use of the death penalty, the use of mandatory minimum sentences is increasing the severity of punishments handed down to persons convicted of a crime. The average adult prisoner spends five years in jail after conviction.

Prison

Botswana has approximately 6,300 prisoners, an incarceration rate of 314 prisoners per 100,000. The incarceration rate is lower than what was reported to the United Nations between 1998 and 2000. The Botswana prison system has a capacity of 4,900 prisoners and a total of 23 prisons, including the Center for Illegal Immigrants. Based on available figures, the system is operating at 129 percent of capacity.

In 2004, 25.1 percent of all prisoners were pretrial detainees, and 5 percent of the prison population was female. Approximately 13 percent of the prison population are residents of foreign countries. The prison service does provide voluntary and free HIV testing, peer counseling, and treatment to Botswana citizens in detention. The government will house refugees in local jails.

Overcrowding, combined with high levels of HIV/AIDS and tuberculosis among the general population, is creating a serious health threat within the prison system. The conditions inside the Botswana prison system are described as poor, with conditions worse in male than female prisons. Nongovernmental organizations indicate difficulties in attaining access to prisons to assess conditions.

The State Department indicates that some children under the age of six are being held with their mothers in prison. Juveniles were held with adults, and pretrial detainees and convicted prisoners are held together. In 2000, there were 290 juveniles incarcerated.

There are some opportunities for early release from prison. A prison commissioner has the authority to release a terminally ill prisoner in the last 12 months of his or her sentence. Prisoners who are citizens in Botswana also have the opportunity for work release. This system allows the prisoners to complete "extramural" work at government facilities. These prisoners must have short-term sentences and must have served at least half of their sentence. Prisoners with serious and violent felonies are not eligible for this program.

Mistreatment of prisoners is illegal, but the number of complaints by prisoners was not available. Any allegations of mistreatment or suspicions of mishandling of prisoners are forwarded to the police for investigation. There is some evidence of accountability for abuse, given that three prison officials appeared before a magistrate in 2000 for allegations of prisoner abuse. One of these individuals was fired from his position.

Nathan Meehan

Further Reading

Boko, D. G. (2000). "Fair Trial and the Customary Courts in Botswana: Questions on Legal Representation." *Criminal Law Forum* 11(4): 445–460.

International Federation for Human Rights and Ditshwanelo (The Botswana Center for Human Rights). (2007). *The Death Penalty in Botswana: Hasty and Secret Hangings.* Gabarone: FIDH: http://www.fidh.org/Secretive-and-hasty-hangings-in-Botswana.

Mathumo, Dimpho Margaret. (2006). "Country Report: Botswana." In *Work Product of the 131st International Training Course.* United Nations Asia and Far East Institute for the Prevention of Crime and the Treatment of Offender, pp. 137–144.

Nesereko, Daniel D. (1999). "Minimum Sentences and Their Effect on Judicial Discretion." *Crime, Law, and Social Change* 31: 363–384.

Otlhogile, Bojosi. (1993). "Criminal Justice and the Problems of a Dual Legal System in Botswana." *Criminal Law Forum* 4(3): 521–533.

Roth, F. P. (2007). "Traditional Society and Urban Democratic Policing in Botswana." *Police Practice and Research* 8(1): 63–78.

Burkina Faso

Legal System: Civil/Customary
Murder: High
Corruption: Medium
Human Trafficking: Medium
Prison Rate: Low
Death Penalty: Maybe
Corporal Punishment: No

Background

Burkina Faso (short form Burkina and formerly called the Republic of Upper Volta) is situated in West Africa with Mali, Niger, Benin, Togo, Ghana, and Côte d'Ivoire as its neighbors. Burkina is an ethnically diverse society with a 2006 census of 13.7 million population. In a country where most aspects of state administration are relatively new and underdeveloped, the police, courts, and prisons have historically been few in number and ill-suited to the needs of a society struggling with economic change, demographic growth, social dislocation, and the domestic repercussions of civil war and strife elsewhere in West Africa. Only since 2002, with the start of a comprehensive judicial reform program, has the infrastructure of Burkina's justice system begun to extend more systematically outside the largest cities.

Legal System

Based on the new constitution adopted in 1995, the legislature approved a new organizational structure for the country's court system. At the top, the old Supreme Court was divided into four new entities: a constitutional court to monitor the constitutionality of legislation and certify election results, a council of state responsible for resolving disputes among state institutions, a court of accounts to oversee the management of public finances and resources, and a court of cassation to review and possibly overturn rulings by lower-level criminal and civil courts. There was also provision for a high court of justice, with the authority to hear allegations against the president should parliament vote to lay such charges. The courts that hear and judge major cases are the *tribunaux de grande instance* (TGIs), with separate chambers to take up criminal infractions, commercial disputes, and civil actions involving inheritance, divorce, and other matters or material claims exceeding CFA1 million (about US$2,000). These courts may try cases with panels of up to three judges and several nonprofessional jurors. Trials are generally public, except for certain specified cases—for example, to protect the privacy of a rape victim. Below these tribunals are lower courts at the level of departments and arrondissements, with jurisdiction to hear minor infractions and the authority to impose only small fines or sentences of community service; they may also include nonprofessionals and follow looser, more streamlined rules for hearing cases. In addition, there are a variety of administrative and labor tribunals, a separate system of military courts, and provisions for establishing courts for children and juveniles.

Police

A number of the larger municipalities employ their own police services, with limited powers of detention and enforcement. There is also a well-equipped and highly trained elite police force of about 250 men known as the Compagnie Républicaine de Sécurité (CRS), which is often used to contain riots and other civil unrest and which sometimes takes part in operations against gangs of armed bandits. But the main bodies for carrying out routine policing are the national police and gendarmes. Their duties overlap, although the national police fall under the Ministry of Security and the gendarmes under the Ministry of Defense. The national police generally have been more lightly armed than the gendarmes, and the gendarmes have greater capacity to investigate serious criminal infractions.

In 2002, there was just 1 police officer or gendarme for every 3,686 inhabitants, that is, a total of about 3,400. By the end of 2005, the ratio had improved to 1 police or gendarme for every 2,700 inhabitants (a total combined force of nearly 4,900). The interior ministry reports suggest that there are 112 territorial gendarme brigades and 171 police posts, including one central station for each of the 45 provinces and 126 district stations. The following year, the national police academy graduated another 1,500 new recruits for the national police, gendarmes, judicial services, and municipal police. In August 2007, the minister of security reported that there were only 183 police and gendarmes in that region, or 1 security agent for every 6,185 inhabitants. Moreover, they had just 30 vehicles to cover an area of approximately 14,000 square kilometers.

In response to increasing public complaints about violent crime, many are being reorganized into more visible and active units (*police de proximité*) that regularly patrol neighborhoods and high-crime areas. And to encourage greater public cooperation with the police, "local security committees" were authorized in 2005. Thousands of such committees were subsequently established, each composed of dignitaries, officials, traditional chiefs, and other influential figures, to encourage local populations to remain alert to possible criminal behavior and to provide the police with information.

Although the regular army has resisted occasional calls by politicians and other public figures to become engaged in the fight against armed banditry, the military has taken some modest steps toward helping the national police and gendarmes. In some areas, especially where gangs of armed bandits operate out of heavily forested reserves that are impassable to police vehicles, mobile army units have carried out maneuvers and exercises to make it harder for organized criminal groups to use them as sanctuaries.

In their fight against armed criminals, it also appeared that the police and gendarmes committed serious violations of the law. In early 2002, the country's foremost human rights association charged that the security forces had summarily executed 106 suspected criminals in just the three-month period from October 15, 2001, to January 15, 2002. The group presented to the press photographs of 30 bodies with bullet holes and charged that most of those killed were livestock thieves, not major armed bandits. Amnesty International called on the authorities to open an inquiry into the allegations.

Police extortion or misconduct is just one facet of a wider problem in Burkina: the country's public institutions, though in the past considered only moderately corrupt, are perceived to have become increasingly marked by various forms of corruption. Since 2000, an association of nongovernmental organizations concerned about corruption, known as Ren-Lac (Réseau national de lutte anti-corruption), the local affiliate of Transparency International, has systematically published annual reports on the state of corruption in Burkina, based in part on national public-opinion surveys. The network's first report in 2000 revealed that the police were considered the single most corrupt institution in the country: 82 percent of respondents who said they had personally experienced corruption cited the police as the source, mostly the extortion of small bribes when they wished to pass at roadside checks, to obtain identity documents, or to secure release following arrest.

Crime

Burkina's legal system recognizes the same type and range of crimes as those specified in France, the former colonial power, at the time of independence in 1960. Its penal code is a virtual copy of the French code, with only a few modifications over the years.

Historically, Burkina was considered a country with very low crime rates. According to data supplied to INTERPOL, the murder rate in Burkina in 1998 was 0.38 per 100,000 population. Ethnographic studies of rural communities in particular often indicated that even serious offenses such as murder or theft were handled without any police or other state involvement, sometimes through customary procedures of redress managed by village and lineage elders and sometimes through direct retaliation by the aggrieved individuals or their families. Nevertheless, there appeared to be wide agreement among both Burkinabè citizens and travelers in the region that serious crime was far less prevalent in Burkina than in some of its immediate neighbors, especially in more urbanized coastal countries such as Ghana or Côte d'Ivoire. It is likely that violent crime, particularly homicide, for which the WHO reported a rate of 18.2 per 100,000 population in 2004, are much higher today.

Beyond the more spectacular crimes of murder, armed robbery, drug smuggling, or corruption, which receive some coverage in the national media, many other legal infractions also occur on a daily basis, and some of them are dealt with by the police and courts routinely. Few official statistics are available on such instances. One type of crime that has received some public attention and stirred a degree of debate relates to contraventions of family law or violence against women and girls, which have been highlighted because of recent policy interventions by the legislature and government.

For example, female genital cutting, also known as female excision, was made a penal offense in 1996, punishable by sentences of between six months and three years. With the criminalization of the practice, the power of the police and judicial system was also brought to bear. The police started compiling files on known excisors, and some excisors and parents have been prosecuted under the statute.

Other harmful social behaviors have also been difficult to counter solely through police or judicial enforcement. Among the Gurmantché ethnic group, for example, the practice of kidnapping women and young girls for marriage is widespread. It often involves not just the individuals directly concerned but also their extended families and lineages. The main criminal court in Bogandé, for example, is frequently confronted with such kidnapping cases, although the penal code provides serious sanctions only if the female is under 13 years of age. Sometimes the police resolve cases directly by detaining a member of the family of the kidnapper until the girl is returned. Further complicating the issue, some charges of "kidnapping" are brought by family elders who disapprove of a daughter's decision to elope with a male suitor of her own choosing. Violence against women is also frequent, and a number of civil society organizations actively campaign against the phenomenon. But beatings, sexual assaults, and other forms of violence against women are rarely reported to the police, especially if such acts take place within the conjugal home.

Finding of Guilt

From initial detention to trial, defendants are in theory guaranteed a range of rights protecting them from arbitrary imprisonment or mistreatment. In practice, such rights are not always observed and are sometimes violated flagrantly. A suspect, for example, legally may be detained without charge or access to a lawyer for only 72 hours, renewable for another 48 hours upon approval by the prosecutor's office. Yet it is not uncommon for suspects to be held for weeks before they are charged or released. There also have been numerous reports of beatings and other forms of abuse of people awaiting charge or trial, in some cases as police seek to elicit confessions or obtain information about possible accomplices. Once charged, an accused person may have to wait for many months, sometimes several years or more, before the case comes to trial. Even if the charges are serious, the accused may petition for provisional release pending trial. Given the costs of holding someone for long periods and the overcrowded conditions in Burkina's detention facilities, release may well be granted, especially for defendants facing less serious charges. All accused may retain legal representation, although the costs of hiring a qualified attorney are prohibitive for many. In serious cases, the government can cover the cost of legal representation for poor defendants, and some lawyers willingly take on such cases for nominal fees (if a defendant is found guilty, restitution of court costs may be included in the sentence). Lawyers and other legal professionals have set up a variety of organizations, programs, and services to provide legal advice at low or no cost to citizens facing charges or otherwise engaged in court proceedings.

Because legal reporting is not well developed or systematized, there are almost no consistent official data publicly available summarizing trial verdicts and sentences. Yet because most court proceedings are public, some anecdotal information can be gleaned from news coverage. Overwhelmingly, media reports focus on cases involving high-profile crimes such as murder, armed robbery, assault, and major instances of corruption or fraud, especially those heard in Ouagadougou's larger courts. During 2007, however, a correspondent based in the provincial town of Kaya regularly filed reports on scores of local cases with the national news agency, providing a rare glimpse at some of the more routine and less spectacular trials that take place beyond the national spotlight. Because Kaya, the capital of Sanmetenga Province and of the Center-North region, is a modest-sized town of just 36,000 people, the cases heard and verdicts delivered there may be more typical of the country as a whole than those taken up by big-city courts. According to *Sidwaya Magazine,* the numbers of persons charged for various offenses in 2007 were as follows:

Theft	70
Excision	20
Assault	14
Fraud	10
Property damage	8
Bodily threat	7
Kidnapping	4
Drug use/sale	4
Receiving stolen goods	4
Negligence	1
Child abandonment	1

The overwhelming majority of these defendants were convicted. Fines and prison terms of various lengths were the most common sentences.

Punishment

Death Penalty

The penal code permits the death sentence for murder, treason, and attempted murder of a father or other close relative, with execution by firing squad. Several such trials have been held in the criminal chamber of Ouagadougou's court of appeals.

Public attitudes are divided on the death penalty: A public opinion survey in 1997 found 54 percent opposed to the death penalty. Custodial penalties are the most typical for major cases. Monetary penalties are also sometimes imposed, including in cases of bodily harm. However, such monetary penalties have been most common in cases of theft, embezzlement, or fraud.

Prisons

Burkina has few prisoners. According to the International Centre for Prison Studies at King's College, University of London, the country had a total of approximately 2,800 prisoners in September 2002, the latest year for which the center had data provided by the Burkinabè authorities. Based on the estimated population at the time, this gave a ratio of 23 prisoners for every 100,000 people.

Paradoxically, although the overall prison population is low, the existing prison system is severely overcrowded. In September 2002, the country's 11 prisons had an official capacity of just 1,650, yielding an occupancy rate of 169.7 percent. Of these, 58.3 percent of the prison occupants were pretrial or remand prisoners.

Among the prisons, Ouagadougou's central prison, MACO, is often in the spotlight. Originally built in the early 1960s for a population of about 600 detainees, it housed 1,128 prisoners as of July 2007, that is, more than 40 percent of the country's total prison population. Such crowding inevitably has had a negative effect on other conditions in the prisons, further worsening nutrition, sanitation, health care, and the overall quality of life.

Prison regulations stipulate that different categories of prisoners should be housed separately, for their own security: serious offenders from pretrial detainees or those convicted of minor infractions, women and children from the general prison population. The excessive occupancy rate has made such separations difficult to implement, although as of 2001, only 1 percent of the entire prison population was female, and 2.4 percent were minors. Separate women's blocks exist only in the prisons in Ouagadougou and Bobo-Dioulasso. Nursing mothers are permitted to keep their infants with them until they are old enough to be placed with other family members. As of 2004, only seven of the country's prisons had separate quarters for minors, but there were plans to build such quarters in three more prisons.

As part of the judicial reform program to expand the number of major case courts nationally, each new court was to be accompanied by a new prison as well. That aspect has lagged, but over time, the construction of new prisons and rehabilitation and expansion of the existing ones should in theory ease conditions somewhat—unless the size of the prison population itself also increases significantly.

Within the limits imposed by inadequate financing, MACO and other prisons operate various training, educational, sports, and work programs for inmates to aid in their longer-term rehabilitation and reintegration back into society. Minors attend basic literacy classes, as do some adults. Men and women inmates have access to facilities where they can learn skills in carpentry, welding, soap-making, fabric dying, market gardening, and other trades. All prisoners are required to assist in cleaning their cells and the prison grounds. Participation in craft activities is permitted as a reward for those regarded as well-behaved. Good conduct can also earn prisoners who have served at least a quarter of their sentence special leave to keep medical or legal appointments; to attend funerals, weddings, and other major family functions; or to take up part-time jobs outside the prison. Inmates who have records of good conduct, who have participated actively in prison work programs, or who are in ill-health periodically receive presidential pardons, often on national holidays. They also may be released on parole once they have completed a specified portion of their sentence. Such early releases are one option the authorities employ to keep down the overall size of the prison population.

Ernest Harsch

Further Reading

Englebert, Pierre. (1996). *Burkina Faso: Unsteady Statehood in West Africa.* Boulder, CO: Westview Press.

Harsch, Ernest. (1999). "Trop, c'est trop!: Civil Insurgence in Burkina Faso, 1998–99." *Review of African Political Economy* 81: 395–406.

Harsch, Ernest. (2002). "Cleaning House: Anticorruption Struggles in Ghana and Burkina Faso." PhD dissertation, New School for Social Research, New York.

Lompo, Myemba Benoît. (1995). *Les Tribunaux départementaux et les Tribunaux d'arrondissements au Burkina Faso.* Ouagadougou: Sankofa Editions.

Somé, Kounkinè Augustin. (2007). "Burkina Faso Legal Information and Research." Hauser Global Law School Program Web site: http://www.nyulawglobal.org/globalex/Burkina_Faso.htm.

Burundi

Legal System: Civil/Customary
Murder: High
Corruption: High
Human Trafficking: Medium
Prison Rate: Medium
Death Penalty: Yes
Corporal Punishment: Yes

Background

Burundi is a landlocked country of Central Africa with Rwanda, the Democratic Republic of Congo, and the United Republic of Tanzania as its borders. Its surface area is 27,834 square kilometers, and it has a population over 8 million. The capital city is Bujumbura, and the country is divided into 17 provinces. The executive branch consists of a bicameral parliament with 60 percent Hutu and 40 percent Tutsi seats, with women constituting an overall 30 percent of members. Burundi's legal system is based on German and Belgian civil codes and customary law.

Crime

The Burundian penal code is composed of 444 articles divided into two volumes:

1. Book 1 deals with offenses and punishment in general.
2. Book 2, the most voluminous, is dedicated to a detailed examination of these offenses and in particular to their punishment.

Offenses punishable by prison sentences of more than two months are called infractions. Offenses punishable by more than five years of prison time are crimes. Other offenses are misdemeanors.

Homicide (Voluntary and Involuntary)

A homicide is defined as a murder committed against a known individual, or against someone who is found or encountered, though intent may be dependent on particular circumstances or particular conditions, even if the perpetrator was mistaken as to the identity of the victim of the attack (based on article 141, Burundian penal code).

The Burundian penal code also contains a series of provisions punishing all attempts on human life with heavy penalties. Articles 141 to 155 in particular make homicide and voluntary bodily harm a crime. The right to life is protected from conception, not birth, with the penal code outlawing abortion in articles 353 to 356.

Despite all of these texts ratified by Burundi, and even though the Burundian penal code is clear on matters related to criminality as just described, the data on human rights gathered over the years by the Iteka League (the most renowned Burundian human rights organization) show that the current situation remains nevertheless bleak, especially in the province of Bujumbura-Rural as depicted in the following table.

Crimes against the Person, by Province

PROVINCE	TORTURES		MURDERS		RAPES	
	2004	2006	2004	2006	2004	2006
Bubanza	10	5	47	24	30	38
Bujumbura Capitale	—	—	—	—	—	—
Bujumbura-Rural	199	52	107	77	12	7
Bururi	13	8	27	14	17	15
Cankuzo	11	4	35	32	15	44
Cibitoki	7	13	23	29	15	32
Karusi	—	—	—	—	—	—
Kayanza	20	15	40	42	37	27
Kirundo	14	14	36	22	23	16
Gitega	3	—	29	37	23	16
Makamba	25	8	15	25	35	39
Muramvya	4	1	23	12	32	17
Muyinga	3	—	25	19	7	8
Mwaro	7	4	13	4	5	12
Ngozi	11	16	39	23	36	37
Rutana	1	—	18	4	3	1
Ruyigi	5	—	22	—	13	—
Total	333	140	499	364	303	309
Average	23	13	34	26	21	22

*Totals and averages are calculated only for provinces with data for the two years (2004, 2006) by crime.
Source: Annual Reports, Iteka League

The same source (Iteka League) tells us that these murders were committed by soldiers with the National Army; by members of the current and former rebel movements, CNDD-FDD and Palipehutu-FNL; and by armed bandits and third parties. Forms of social violence such as witch hunts, vigilante justice, and infanticide have likewise claimed many victims.

Torture

Burundi ratified the Convention against Torture and Other Cruel, Inhuman or Degrading Treatment or Punishment on December 31, 1992. The term "torture" signifies any act by which severe pain or suffering, whether physical or mental, is intentionally inflicted on a person for such purposes as obtaining from him or a third person information or a confession, punishing him for an act he or a third person has committed or is suspected of having committed, or intimidating or coercing him or a third person, or for any reason based on discrimination of any kind, when such pain or suffering is inflicted by, at the instigation of, or with the consent or acquiescence of a public official or other person acting in an official capacity. It does not include pain or suffering inherent in or incidental to lawful "sanctions."

No such definition of torture exists in Burundian law. In practice, those who inflict torture are prosecuted and punished based on definitions of offenses in penal law such as "voluntary bodily harm" provided for in articles 145 to 150 of the Burundian penal code. Nevertheless, because it has ratified the previously noted convention, Burundi recognizes the definition contained in the convention and has made it its own. Normally, "all of the States' parties to the Convention see to it that the competent authorities proceed immediately with an impartial investigation whenever they have reason to believe that an act of torture has been committed within any territory under their jurisdiction." Article 25 of the Constitution of Burundi also stipulates, "All women and men have the right to the liberty of their person, in particular, to physical integrity and to liberty of movement."

Indeed, in addition to the fact that torture is not even defined, neither has it yet been established as a punishable offense in the eyes of Burundian penal law. It constitutes only an aggravating circumstance in the offenses of homicide and voluntary bodily harm (articles 145 and 147). To this end, a national law defining the offense of torture as such is needed to implement the convention ratified by Burundi.

Rape

Burundian law defines violence as acts of physical force exercised against people (article 196, penal code). Several cases of violence and discrimination against Burundian women, particularly within their households, were recorded during 2004. Burundian women, especially rural women, are confronted with various forms of physical as well as psychological violence, in particular domestic violence. Yet in the majority of cases, they do not dare to come forward, the tendency in Burundian society being to trivialize these incidents and to reduce women to silence about this dangerous and oppressive scourge. However, according to Doctors Without Borders, the number of rapes reported to women's health centers has reached worrisome proportions.

According to the Iteka League, rape involving children has reached alarming proportions. They note that among the reported cases, 43 percent involve minors, of which 17 percent are children under the age of 10. These rapes take many forms, most notably gang rape and rape involving violence. These types of cases have been reported chiefly in the provinces of Bujumbura-Rural, Bubanza, and Cibitoke. Cases of incest are also found in many provinces. For example, during the night of August 13, 2004, in the city of Gihanga, Bubanza Province, a 55-year-old man was accused of raping his 15 year-old daughter. The victim suffered wounds to her neck and uterus and was treated at the women's health center of Doctors Without Borders–Belgium.

In addition to women and children, rape also affects men. However, many of these cases are not reported, especially when they involve adults who prefer to hide their misfortune, doubtless for reasons of pride. For example, on April 27, 2004, on Nyagatovu hill, in Tangara commune, Ngozi Province, a 17-year-old male servant was raped by his boss, a shopkeeper from the same hill. On March 7, 2004, in the Muzinda sector, Rugazi commune, Bubanza Province, an 18-year-old man raped a 7-year-old boy. The rape was committed in an old house in the Muzinda market.

It should also be noted that rape is used for criminal purposes by known carriers of HIV/AIDS, as these examples show: A man infected with HIV from Muramvyz hill, Mbizi zone, Bujumbura-Rural Province, raped a number of women whom he met in his travels. The police searched for him, but he remained at large. On May 23, 2004, at 7:00 P.M. on the Kwibaru River, Mitakataka zone, Gatura sector, Mpanda commune, Bubanza Province, a 41-year-old widow was raped by more than four men. She was able to recognize three of them, who were, according to locals, HIV carriers. The rapists took 25,000 Burundi Francs (F/Bu) and her clothes, so that she had to return home totally naked. Unfortunately, the victim did not seek medical treatment in time; she arrived at the hospital at Bubanza three days later.

The Burundian penal code contains, however, several provisions punishing indecent assault and rape, in articles 382–387. In addition to the previously cited cases, domestic violence, sometimes fatal, has been reported. These tragedies affect women in particular. This situation is rooted in the practices of concubinage and polygamy, especially in outlying provinces of the country and in the Imbo plains. Polygamy was nevertheless outlawed in Burundi under the Second Republic. However, public authorities seem to turn a blind eye to this widespread trend, which contributes to the spread of HIV/AIDS, as well as to the destabilization of families and its many unfortunate consequences, in particular the violation of women's and children's rights, as the following examples illustrate.

On May 14, 2004, on Matana hill, under Kavuza hill, Bururi Province, a man killed his wife over a lost hoe. The murderer found his son in the fields and accused him of losing the hoe. When the father began to beat the son, the mother jumped in and tried to save her child. Her husband pounced upon her, saying, "It was you I was looking for." He began to beat her severely until she fell unconscious. The victim was taken to the hospital at Matana and was transferred to Bujumbura, where she passed away two days later. After her death, her husband sold her cow and goat. It seems that the victim had previously refused to allow her husband to sell them. On January 8, 2004, in Gacokwe sector and hill, Gisuru commune, Ruyigi Province, a woman went missing. The perpetrator was likely her husband, who strangled her because of constant turmoil in their marriage.

War Crimes and Crimes against Humanity

Burundi has witnessed several periods of serious violence and massacres. The years 1965, 1972, 1988, and 1993 were the bloodiest, resulting from political-ethnic conflicts between the ruling Tutsi party and Hutu rebel movements. These episodes of violence resulted in hundreds of thousands of deaths, in particular during 1972 and 1993.

The current conflict began with the murder of President Ndadaye in 1993 by Tutsi National Army officers. This was followed by massacres of Tutsi civilians throughout the country, leaving several tens of thousands dead. The army reacted with horrific violence, killing several thousand Hutu civilians. The result of these massacres was an ongoing civil war that has not yet ended. To distinguish the civilian population from soldiers, at the end of the 1990s, the national army rounded up thousands of civilians into relocation and refugee camps where serious human rights abuses were the norm.

In August 2004, rebels from the FNL movement, in collaboration with the Mai Mai of Congo and the Interahamwe of Rwanda, massacred Banyamulenge refugees at Gatumba. More than 150 people died, and 106 were wounded. In April 2003 in Kabezi in Bujumbura-Rural Province, Burundian army soldiers and the FNL opened fire on civilians who were fleeing the combat. In September 2003, in Rubiza and Muyire, also in Bujumbura-Rural Province, Burundian soldiers massacred civilians, apparently in reprisal for the assassination of several of their ranks by FNL members in surrounding areas. Administration representatives and other civilians were deliberately killed by FDD soldiers during the same period. They also forcibly recruited civilians to serve in their ranks. In Ruyigi, Bubanza, Kayanza, Bujumbura-Rural, and other parts of the country, women were raped by FDD and FNL combatants as well as by Burundian army soldiers. Civilians were also subjected to forced unpaid labor as porters or guides by members of rebel and militant movements, sometimes in unsafe areas where they were exposed to danger.

There has been no adequate judicial response to these serious crimes against humanity since 2007, perpetuating impunity in Burundi. In a 2003 report, Human Rights Watch writes that the National Transition Assembly adopted the law ratifying the Rome Statute that created the International Criminal Court, but the president still has neither enacted the law nor revealed his intentions as to its fate. In May 2003, a law against genocide, war crimes, and crimes against humanity, long demanded by the Tutsi, was adopted and enacted, but in August, the National Transition Assembly voted provisional immunity into law, exempting a certain number of Hutu leaders returning from exile from all judicial prosecution. These mutual agreements pursuing political ends seem to seek to satisfy claims exclusive to each of the Tutsi and Hutu communities more than to facilitate the administration of justice. The November 2, 2003, protocol extended the notion of immunity to all members of the national armed forces and to all FDD soldiers, without adding any time limit to this protection. Judicial authorities took steps to arrest several persons of interest in the case of the assassination of a World Health Organization representative in Burundi. Military courts failed to pursue or to bring the soldiers implicated in these serious crimes to justice.

In 2005, the Commission of Truth and Reconciliation (CVR) was put into place, composed of six members: two from the government, two from nongovernmental organizations, and two from the United Nations. This commission has the ambitious task of investigating all crimes against humanity and war crimes perpetrated in Burundi since its independence. As the United Nations sees it, the creation of the CVR will also lead to a special tribunal. The commission did not begin its work until April 2008.

Criminal Justice System

The National Police

The national police force was officially created in 2004. It is made up of elements of the former Public Security Police (PSP) and the Judicial Police, the former governmental army and local police, and former armed opposition movements. This latter group constitutes more than one-third of the total members of the new police forces. The Burundian national police force is a civil force operating under the authority of the newly created Ministry of Public Security, formerly an arm of the Ministry of the Interior. It is made up of four commissariats: the Internal Security Police (PSI), the Judicial Police (PJ), the Penitentiary Police, and the Police for Air, Borders and Foreigners (PAFE). The Rapid Mobile Intervention Groups (GMIR), a specialized reserve force created in 2006, was part of the PSI until December 2007, when it became an autonomous force reporting directly to the director of the national police under a police restructuring program.

Judicial police and internal security police officers share responsibilities for prevention and punishment of everyday crimes and have the most regular and direct contact with the population. The judicial police conduct pre-jurisdictional investigations, interrogate suspects, and provide evidence to the prosecutor (Law No. 1/020 of 12/31/04). The internal security police keep watch over public areas, apprehend offenders, and execute search and arrest warrants issued by the prosecutor. Internal security police, including GMIR agents, are not authorized to conduct interrogations or detain suspects.

The integration of former combatants into the ranks of the national police has caused the latter's numbers to swell from 2,300 in 2000 to 15,000–20,000 in 2007. The actual number of police officers is unknown to even police administration because not all have been registered, and some do not have administrative files. It is widely recognized, however, that the police force is far larger than the country needs. In accordance with the conditions established by the International Monetary Fund for future aid, the police force intends to select and demobilize officers to reach a target of 15,000 officers.

Merging these diverse components into a single impartial force to serve citizens of all ethnic groups and political affiliations and ensuring that all police personnel are trained in accordance with necessary standards have proven to be major challenges. Officers from the former police force had been trained for police work, whereas soldiers transferred from the army had military, not police, training. Moreover, some soldiers transferred from the army had not performed well in the military and had been sent to the police because the army did not wish to retain them. More than a third of new police officers were former rebel soldiers without formal military or police training. Some of these new officers are illiterate.

Judicial Procedure

According to Burundian law, judicial procedure consists of two phases. In the inquest phase, the code of criminal procedure accords a certain number of powers to judicial police officers, including the power to deprive a person suspected of breaking criminal law of his or her freedom. They exercise this prerogative, however, under the authority and supervision of the public prosecutor. A pre-jurisdictional arrest cannot last more than 15 days according to the law. Despite judicial police officers' prerogative to restrict citizens' freedom, the fact remains that in principle, the code of criminal procedure has only one concern: to protect all individuals from unlawful detention. The code of criminal procedure was written as much with police and prosecutors in mind as judges. For the police, the code of criminal procedure envisages situations that give rise to the deprivation of freedom, but they are well defined. This deprivation of freedom can take the form of police custody and preventive detention.

The examination phase is an even more important step in that the detainee will see the charges against him or her even more clearly outlined, at least more than they had been by the police. It is during this phase that the case is actually built. The examining judge must, in principle, investigate the case for the prosecution as well as for the defense. The pertinent provisions are found in chapter 2 of the code of criminal procedure, most notably in articles 22–26. The public prosecutor is in fact the guarantor of public order, which means that he has the mission to assure the just and equitable application of the law. His role is to assemble the evidence of guilt. The prosecutor's work is in reality similar to that of the police. However, differences in method can be noted in that the public prosecutor employs manifestly less coercion to persuade detainees to confess.

Nevertheless, Burundian judicial procedure has experienced a fair number of problems, such as the failure to respect preventive detention terms, where months can pass without a judge hearing a person's case. This is the case notably for detainees suspected of participation in the 1993 massacres. There is also the problem of slowness of judgments and of their execution once they are entered.

Prison

As for prisons, Burundi has 11 old buildings at its disposition with an overall capacity for 3,650 detainees. These 11 detention centers are as follows:

1. Central Prison of Mpimba (Bujumbura)
2. Ngozi Men's Detention Center
3. Gitega Detention Center
4. Ruyigi Prison
5. Rutana Prison
6. Muyinga Prison
7. Rumonge Prison
8. Ngozi Specialized Center for Women and Children
9. Bururi Prison
10. Muramvya Prison
11. Bubanza Prison

Today, these prisons house around 7,350 people when all sectors are taken together (convicts, defendants, women, and minors), despite a current capacity of only 3,650. The causes of prison overpopulation are likely the slow handling of cases, irregularities related principally to poor recordkeeping, prison conditions that are lacking, and also the persistent failure to separate groups of detainees (adults and minors) according to the Human Rights League Iteka (2006 annual report) and the October 2007 monthly report of the Division of Human Rights and Justice of BINUB.

Gilberte Nkeshimana and Philip Verwimp

Further Reading

Human Rights Watch. (2000, April). *Neglecting Justice and Making Peace.* New York: Human Rights Watch.

Human Rights Watch. (2003). *Les Civils dans la guerre au Burundi.* New York: Human Rights Watch.

Lemarchand, R. (1994). *Burundi: Ethnocide as Discourse and Practice.* Cambridge: Cambridge University Press.

United Nations. (1996). Report of the Secretary-General on the Situation in Burundi. *Security Council, S/1996/660.* New York: United Nations.

United Nations (BINUB et OHCDHB). *Rapports sur la situation des droits de l'homme et de la justice au Burundi. Rapports mensuels.* Bujumbura: United Nations.

Cameroon

Legal System: Civil/Customary/Common
Murder: Medium
Burglary: Low
Corruption: High
Human Trafficking: Medium
Prison Rate: Medium
Death Penalty: Yes
Corporal Punishment: No

Background

Cameroon is a developing country located in Central Africa with the Atlantic Ocean, Equatorial

Guinea, and Gabon as its borders. Yaoundé is Cameroon's capital city, and Douala, its largest city. The 2006 population estimates indicate that there are over 17 million people in Cameroon spread over 250 tribes. Though English and French are both constitutionally recognized as official languages, French is the common spoken language. Pidgin English is also a commonly used lingua franca in the English-speaking countries of West Africa. Christianity (40%), Islam (20%), and indigenous African beliefs (40%) are the predominant religions in Cameroon. In 1961, southern Cameroon wanted to gain its independence by reuniting with French Cameroun, which had already become independent in 1960, and northern Cameroon wanted to remain a part of Nigeria. In 1961, southern Cameroon and the independent French Cameroun were known as the "Federal Republic of Cameroon."

There are three branches of government. The executive branch is headed by the president. The president is entitled to a seven-year term in office that is renewable once. The president appoints and dismisses the prime minister, cabinet members, judges, generals, provincial governors, prefects, and heads of para-statal firms. The president disburses expenditures and approves or vetoes regulations to implement new laws. The president declares states of emergencies. The prime minister is responsible for implementing polices established by the former head of state.

The legislative branch of government has a unicameral national assembly made up of 180 members with five-year terms. This assembly meets twice yearly, in June/July and November/December. Laws are adopted by the majority vote of the national assembly or by the president himself. Since 1990, when political opposition was legalized, parliament has been represented by more than 168 oppositional parties. The Cameroon People's Democratic Movement (CPDM) has dominated parliament.

The judicial branch of government is part of the executive ministry of justice. The Supreme Court reviews the constitutionality of laws only at the president's request. The traditional courts have a role in domestic, property, and probate law. Tribal and customary laws are honored within the judicial system, when they are not in conflict with national law. Cameroon has made attempts to develop a modern legal system that embraces its heritage and current socioeconomic/political climate. The history of Cameroon's legal system reflects its difficulties in trying to embrace national legislation that has been derived from customary and international laws. As a result of complications stemming from Cameroon's colonial past, there are two foreign legal systems struggling for power in determining the nature and content of its non-uniform laws.

Legal System

This legal system is based on the dual English-French colonial legal heritage. The predominant sources of law in Cameroon are the Constitution, the legislation, judicial precedents, and customary law. Since Cameroon's independence and reunification of the former British Southern Cameroons and the French Cameroun, this country has had three different constitutions with varying amendments. The first constitution was under the French Cameroun, when it became independent in 1960. The second constitution was a 1961 amendment of the 1960 Constitution of French Cameroun. In 1972, after a referendum, a new constitution was developed, and the country's name changed to the United Republic of Cameroon. In 1984, "United Republic" was changed to "Republic."

Judicial precedence as a source of Cameroonian law varies depending on whether a province is an English-speaking Anglophone or French-speaking Francophone Province. The English law uses *stare decisis* under which judicial precedence is major law, which is subject to the complexities of judicial organization of the court system. The Cameroonian courts operate within a unified and decentralized fashion, with a Supreme Court for the entire country. This Supreme Court operates in a manner similar to the French Cour de Cassation rather than as an English court of appeal. The appeals court is the highest in both provinces. Within the Anglophone provinces, precedents are binding within that locale. Within English provinces, precedents have limits to which they are binding because of the "provincialized" system. Controversial cases may be presented in the appeals court and in the Supreme Court;

these cases are not generally handled as appeals in the strict sense of the meaning of the word. The Supreme Court provides persuasive authority. Judicial precedents are important in Anglophone provinces because of the structure and operation of the court system. In Francophone provinces, judicial precedents are not the primary sources of law. However, judicial precedents in superior courts are highly persuasive in Francophone provinces.

Traditional law is important in Cameroon. Traditional laws are based on the customs of the dominant ethnic groups in a province. Traditional law depends on the region and ethnic group trying the case. The British and French enforced this type of law; however, not every type is recognized and utilized. For example, traditional courts have tried the criminally accused for practicing witchcraft, subjecting them to drinking poison. In another example, an Anglophone province, as established by a southern high court, supported and recognized traditional laws that are not repugnant to natural justice or equitable treatment and are in good conscience. Further, traditional law must not be incompatible with any previously established law. Traditional laws are applied if there is consent from both the plaintiff and the defendant. That said, many persons in rural provinces do not know their rights under civil law and have been taught only that traditional law must be enforced. Traditional courts often hear cases that involve property, domestic, and probate matters. Traditional laws most often apply to and are used by persons living in rural areas.

Police

The national police and intelligence service, the gendarmerie, the ministry of territorial administration, military intelligence, the armed forces, and the presidential guard are all responsible for reinforcing Cameroon's security. The president and the civilian minister of defense and head of police are responsible for the security forces. There are 25,000 military personnel, including a 13,000 member security force and 3,000 presidential guards. The presidential guard's main responsibility is maintaining internal security. The national police force has 15,000 personnel and a domestic intelligence network.

Cameroon's security forces have been accused of committing serious human rights violations. Unjustified arrests, detentions, stripping, confinement in overcrowded jails, torture, beatings, denial of access to the toilet and other sanitation facilities, denial of access to health care, disappearances, executions, and murder at times are all instances that have occurred and are said to have been politically motivated. These crimes are often committed with impunity. The Cameroonian government rarely investigates and charges security personnel. These methods are often used to extract confessions.

When unjustifiable detentions occur, these suspects are subject to two kinds of physical beatings. The first is known as the *bastinade*. This form of abuse involves the detainee being beaten on the soles of the feet. The second is known as the *balancoire*. This form of abuse involves the detainee's genitals being beaten.

The police and gendarmes harass citizens by conducting unlawful stops and searches without warrants and by forcefully entering homes. In Douala and Yaoundé, law enforcement sweeps occur regularly. These sweeps are known as "kali-kali" or "rafles." When sweeps occur, law enforcement may close off an entire neighborhood while conducting unlawful stops and searches without warrants, forcefully entering homes, arbitrarily arresting individuals, and seizing contraband and/or suspicious items. At times, law enforcement loot homes during sweeps.

The Cameroonian Constitution prohibits such human rights violations. The law requires arrest and search warrants, except when the criminal is caught in the act of breaking the law. Individuals arrested must be brought before a magistrate, and it is unlawful to detain accused individuals for prolonged periods of time without granting them this privilege. However, detainees are kept for months and even years before seeing a magistrate. The accused may be detained for up to 24 hours for committing a crime, a time frame that is renewable three times, before formal charges are implemented. In Anglophone provinces, the law supports judicial review and release on bail. In instances where British common law is taken into consideration, bail is not likely. In Francophone provinces, the law precludes the judiciary from acting on a case until the administrative authority turns the case over to the prosecution. After a magistrate has issued a warrant to bring a case to trial, the detainee can be held indefinitely until trial. Eighty percent of prisoners within Cameroon's judicial system have not been tried.

Crime

Predatory crimes in Cameroon are the result of famine, mismanagement of financial resources, political conflicts, disease, and persistent economic stagnation. Refugees from neighboring countries, such as Chad and Congo, further contribute to this already fragile political economy. Predatory crimes impact rural and urban Cameroon.

Domestic violence is an example of a predatory crime. Women are quite often victims of domestic violence. Female genital mutilation still occurs in rural areas of Cameroon and causes physical and psychological damage. There aren't any effective gender-specific laws that prosecute men and protect women from domestic violence.

Trafficking of people is an example of a predatory crime. Trafficking of persons is punishable by 10 to 20 years of incarceration. Cameroon is a transit and international destination point for trafficking. Juveniles are trafficked to and from Nigeria, Benin, Niger, Chad, Togo, Congo Kinshasa, and the Central African Republic. Children are trafficked for indentured or domestic servitude and for sexual exploitation. In 2000, the International Labor Organization reported that in Yaoundé, Douala, and Bamenda, trafficking accounted for 84 percent (530,000) of an estimated 610,000 child laborers.

The 1998 INTERPOL data for crime rates in Cameroon for various offenses per 100,000 population were as follows: murder, 0.38; sex offenses, 1.37; rape, 0.45; serious assault, 1.17; theft, 31.73; and total offenses, 78.17. Although the crime rates were reportedly low in 1998, since 1995 crimes have increased fivefold. Between 1995 and 1998, murder increased from 0.23 to 0.38 per 100,000 population; sex offenses from 0.05 to 1.17; theft from 4.69 to 31.73; and total offenses from 13.45 to 78.17. The robbery rate of 0.39 and breaking and entering rate of 1.50 were recorded in 1995, but not in 1998.

Punishment

In 1998, Cameroon's penal institution housed 15,903 inmates, representing a rate of 115 inmates per 100,000 population. Cameroon's prisons are characterized by conditions such as lack of food, overcrowding (four to five times the original capacity), lack of access to health and medical care, and unsanitary conditions. At times, women, men, and juveniles are housed together. Women can be incarcerated with their children, even if their children are babies. Detainees are tortured and beaten. Prisoners are entitled to one meal per day. Inmates are also entitled to 4.4 ounces of soap every six months.

In Douala's New Bell Prison, there were only 7 water faucets for approximately 3,500 detainees, in a space built for 600 detainees. Two thousand of these inmates were pretrial detainees, whose presence exacerbates overcrowding. Maroua's prison is also overcrowded. This prison's capacity is 300 detainees, but it holds 900 prisoners. The Bertoua Prison's capacity is 50 detainees, whereas this institution has 700 prisoners. Yaoundé's Kondengui Central Prison has the capacity for 1,500 detainees but has 3,600 prisoners; the facility has only 16 bathrooms and 400 beds. The Bamenda Central Prison's capacity is 300 detainees, but it has 750 prisoners.

Angela R. Morris

Further Reading

Anyangwe, C. (1987). *The Cameroonian Judicial System.* Yaoundé, Cameroon: CEPER.

Borricand, J. (2009). "France." In *World Factbook of Criminal Justice Systems*, edited by Graeme Newman. Washington, DC: U.S. Department of Justice, Bureau of Justice Statistics. 1993, 2002: http://bjs.ojp.usdoj.gov/index.cfm?ty=pbdetail&iid=1435.

Enonchong, H. N. A. (1967). *Cameroon Constitutional Law: Federalism in a Mixed Common-Law and Civil Law System.* Yaoundé, Cameroon: Centre d'edition et de production de manuels at auxiliaries de l'enseignement.

Fombad, C. M. (1991). "The Scope for Uniform National Laws in Cameroon." *Journal of Modern African Studies* 29: 443–456.

Johnson, W. (1970). *The Cameroon Federation: Political Integration in a Fragmentary Society.* Princeton, NJ: Princeton University Press.

Kofele-Kale, N. (1980). *An Experiment in Nation Building: The Bilingual Cameroon Republic since Reunification.* Boulder, CO: Westview Press.

Ngoh, J. N. (1990). *Constitutional Developments in Southern Cameroons, 1946–1961: From Trusteeship to Independence.* Yaoundé, Cameroon: CEPER.

Cape Verde

Legal System: Civil
Corruption: Medium
Prison Rate: Medium
Death Penalty: No
Corporal Punishment: No

Background

The Republic of Cape Verde is an archipelago consisting of 10 islands located in the eastern Atlantic Ocean roughly 300 miles off the coast of Senegal in western Africa. The former Portuguese colony and province gained its independence on July 5, 1975. This island nation is inhabited by approximately 500,000 residents of mixed ethnic backgrounds. Seventy percent of the population is of Creole descent (a mixture of African and Portuguese), 28 percent of the population is African, and approximately 1 percent of the population is European. Because of a lack of natural resources and domestic production, a majority of the Cape Verdean population is emigrant. Population estimates indicate that approximately 700,000 Cape Verdeans live outside the country's borders (predominately in the United States and Portugal).

After gaining independence from Portugal in 1975, Cape Verde was governed by a one-party system until 1990. The first multiparty elections in Cape Verde were held in January 1991. Since that time, political power has fluctuated between the country's two main political parties, the African Party for the Independence of Cape Verde (PAICV), which split from the PAIGC after a coup in Guinea-Bissau, and the oppositional Movement for Democracy (MPD). Overall, Cape Verde exhibits one of Africa's most stable democratic governments.

The Cape Verdean government is guided by the country's Constitution, which was adopted in 1980 and revised most recently in 1999. The head of state is the president, who is elected to a five-year term by popular vote. The head of the government is the prime minister, who is nominated by the National Assembly and appointed by the president. The National Assembly is the legislative branch of the Cape Verdean government, and it consists of 72 members from four political parties. Like the president, the National Assembly is elected to a five-year term by popular vote.

The judicial branch of the Cape Verdean government consists of a Supreme Tribunal of Justice and numerous regional courts. Members of the supreme court are appointed by the president and the National Assembly. Civil, criminal, and constitutional cases are heard by separate courts and appeals are heard by the Supreme Tribunal.

The primary law enforcement agency in Cape Verde is the Public Order Police, which is made up of the national police, responsible for law enforcement, and the judicial police, responsible for investigations. The police force is organized nationally under the Ministry of Internal Administration and the Ministry of Justice. Also included under the jurisdiction of the Public Order Police are the economic and fiscal police, who are responsible for combating smuggling and related offenses. The police in Cape Verde were controlled by the military until 1994 but are now a separate agency answerable to civilian authority.

Statistics from 2006 list Cape Verde's total police personnel at 3,981 officers. This figure indicates a population per police officer of approximately 110. According to a 2007 UN study on crime and corruption in Cape Verde, there was an overall consensus among respondents that police in Cape Verde do a reasonably good job of preventing and controlling crime. Over 50 percent of the general population and over 70 percent of private sector respondents indicated that the police do at least a "good" job of maintaining law and order.

The law enforcement agencies of Cape Verde face a number of challenges that may limit their ability to effectively operate. According to the 2008 Human Rights Report, logistical constraints, including lack of vehicles, limited communications equipment, and poor forensic capacity, have limited police effectiveness. The Human Rights Report also listed police corruption as a growing problem in Cape Verde. Approximately 12 percent of the citizens surveyed by the United Nations Office on Drugs and Crime said that they considered corruption among police officers a problem.

Crime

The legal system in Cape Verde is similar to that of Portugal because of the heavy Portuguese influence on Cape Verdean government structure and politics. The Portuguese legal code can be classified as a civil law or continental legal system. It is similar to legal systems of other European nations such as France, Spain, Italy, and Germany. A variant of the Portuguese civil law system is recognized in Cape Verde. The Cape Verdean legal system distinguishes more serious crimes as felonies.

Because of its geography, Cape Verde faces some unique challenges when it comes to crime control.

A group of 40 illegal immigrants are escorted by Cape Verde police after they were rescued as their boat drifted off the coast of Cape Verde on June 7, 2007. (Ulisses Moreira/AFP/Getty Images)

The combination of a highly accessible coastline and lack of regulation in the country's maritime ports has caused smuggling to become a growing concern in Cape Verde. Government officials have raised concerns about the smuggling of drugs, small arms, and other contraband into Cape Verde in recent years and have cited this as a contributing factor in observed increases in organized and street crime in some areas. The Cape Verdean government is working to increase security in maritime ports to combat this growing smuggling problem.

Most of the crime that occurs in Cape Verde is classified as property crime, not typically involving violence. Although burglary does not occur at a very high rate in Cape Verde compared to other African nations, it is particularly prevalent in urban areas, especially in the city of Santiago. Recent victimization surveys revealed that more than 10 percent of the residents of Santiago experienced at least one home break-in in the previous five years. According to the U.S. State Department, petty thievery and burglary are common in Cape Verde, especially in crowds, such as marketplaces, festivals, and celebrations. Despite an overall low rate of car ownership, rates of auto theft are relatively high in urban centers when compared to other African cities.

As noted previously, drug trafficking is a growing concern in Cape Verde. A 2007 UN victimization survey revealed that 20 percent of respondents had been exposed to drug problems in the previous year and that approximately 25 percent of respondents felt that drug trafficking was the most dangerous type of crime in Cape Verde. Respondents also rank drug consumption as a leading cause of crime in the country. Police respondents echoed this concern, citing drug use and trafficking as the primary cause of crime in Cape Verde. In response to the growing concern about drug use and trafficking, penalties for drug crimes in Cape Verde are severe. If convicted, offenders can expect long jail sentences and heavy fines.

Violent crime in Cape Verde is relatively rare overall. However, although official statistics are unavailable, rates of violent crime appear to have increased dramatically in recent years. Citing the country's investigative police, the UN Integrated Regional Information Networks (IRIN) reported that violent crimes occurred five times more often in 2007 than in the previous 10 years combined. According to this data source, there were as many as 56 attempted or completed murders in 2007 compared to just two completed murders between 1996 and 2006. Victimization surveys also revealed that robbery and theft with force were growing problems in urban areas. Although the overall rate of violent crime in Cape Verde is relatively low, there has been growing concern about escalating rates of violence in the island nation, especially in urban areas.

Crime in Cape Verde is substantially more prevalent in urban areas than it is in the predominately rural regions of the country. The UNODC victimization survey revealed that citizens in urban areas experienced crime three times more frequently than citizens in rural areas. The nature of this crime appears to be more violent than that occurring in more rural areas as well: victim reports revealed that 34 percent of the crime in urban areas involved violence, whereas only 27 percent of victims in rural areas reported the use of violence. Victimization data also reveal that crime is underreported in Cape Verde, especially in urban areas.

Finding of Guilt

The Constitution and law of Cape Verde provide a justice system that follows a due process model. Arbitrary arrest and detention is prohibited by law, and the government generally observes these prohibitions. Arrest without a warrant by an authorized official is prohibited unless a person is caught in the act of committing a felony. The law requires that an accused suspect be notified of charges within 24 hours and appear in front of a judge within 48 hours of being arrested. According to the 2008 Human Rights Report for Cape Verde, the right to a prompt judicial determination of the legality of detention was generally observed by authorities.

Accused suspects in Cape Verde have the right to a public nonjury trial before an independent judiciary. They are presumed innocent and have the right to legal counsel; free counsel is provided for the indigent. Defendants and their counsel have the right to confront witnesses and evidence against them and also have the right to present witnesses and evidence on their own behalf. Additionally, defendants and their counsel have the right to access any government-held evidence relevant to their case prior to trial. Criminal investigations are conducted by the judicial police branch of the national Public Order Police. Appeals of regional court decisions can be made to the Supreme Tribunal of Justice. The rights of due process are provided to all citizens.

Although the aforementioned due process rights are provided by the Constitution of Cape Verde, numerous barriers exist that may jeopardize the rights of the accused. The judicial system in Cape Verde is overburdened and understaffed, and cases are often dropped without court judgment as a means of clearing cases from the booked docket. This logistical situation has caused lengthy pretrial detention and trial delays to become a serious problem in Cape Verde. Reports suggest that detainees often remain in jail for more than a year while awaiting charge. Another cause for concern is the rights of juvenile offenders. Cape Verde does not have a separate judicial system for juveniles, and they are detained alongside adult offenders.

Punishment

Punishment for serious offenses in Cape Verde typically takes the form of fines and imprisonment. The maximum prison sentence allowed under Cape Verdean law is 25 years. Capital punishment is prohibited, and the last official execution in Cape Verde occurred in 1835, when the country was still under Portuguese rule. The penalty for rape is 8 to 16 years in prison and can be higher if the victim is under the age of 16. Domestic violence, which is considered a major problem in Cape Verde, is punishable by 2 to 13 years in prison but is rarely reported to the police. Government corruption, which also has been identified as a problem in Cape Verde, is punishable by a sentence of up to 15 years in prison. Because of the major concern over drug use and trafficking in Cape Verde, punishments for possession and distribution of drugs are severe. Individuals convicted of drug offenses may face lengthy prison sentences and heavy fines.

Prison conditions in Cape Verde are considered substandard and a major human rights concern. Cape Verdean prisons are characterized by frequent overcrowding, poor sanitation and medical care, and some accusations of prisoner abuse. Although women and men are housed separately, juvenile offenders are housed with adults, and pretrial detainees are housed with convicted offenders. There are 11 total prisons in the Cape Verdean nation, and the official capacity of the prison system is 1,997. Official prison statistics from the national prison administration list a total prison population of 755 inmates, including pretrial detainees. The prison population rate per 100,000 citizens was approximately 178 as of 2007. Approximately 5 percent of the prison population are female, 3 percent are juvenile prisoners, and 37 percent are pretrial detainees. Because of the poor condition of Cape Verdean prisons, medical and psychological health problems are frequently reported. The state of prisons in Cape Verde is one of the country's most significant human rights issues according to the U.S. State Department. Before the country's independence, Cape Verde was home to one of the world's most cruel and infamous prisons, the Tarrafal prison on the island of Santiago. Between 1936 and 1974, the Tarrafal prison, "the swamp of death," was run by the PIDE (Portuguese secret police). Tarrafal was not actually a prison, but rather a concentration camp where political prisoners and opponents of Portuguese colonial rule and fascism were sent to die. Prisoners sent to Tarrafal were often held long after their sentences had been completed or without ever being formally charged or tried. The conditions at the camp were abysmal, and survivors tell stories of isolation and torture on a regular basis. Poor conditions and a lack of medical care caused many prisoners to die from malaria and tuberculosis, among other ailments. Survivor reports describe cement punishment cells where prisoners were intentionally exposed to the sun and mosquitoes for days at a time. The temperatures in these torture chambers often exceeded 150 degrees. The camp was closed in 1954.

Michael S. Caudy and James V. Ray

Further Reading

Kurian, G. T. (2006). "Cape Verde." In *World Encyclopedia of Police Forces and Correctional Systems,* 2nd ed., edited by G. T. Kurian, p. 278. Detroit, MI: Gale.

Shaw, C. S. (1991). *Cape Verde.* World Bibliographical Series (Vol. 123). Oxford, UK: Clio Press.

UN Office on Drugs and Crime. (2007). *Study on Crime and Corruption in Cape Verde.* 2007. http://www.unodc.org.

UN Integrated Regional Information Networks. (2008). *Cape Verde: Urban Crime, Violence Multiplies.* All Africa Global Media: http://allafrica.com/stories/200812011243.html.

U.S. Department of State. (2008). *2008 Human Rights Report: Cape Verde:* http://www.state.gov/g/drl/rls/hrrpt/2008/af/118991.htm.

Central African Republic

Legal System: Civil
Murder: High
Corruption: High
Human Trafficking: Medium
Prison Rate: Low
Death Penalty: Maybe

Background

The Central African Republic (CAR) is a constitutional republic. Its population is estimated to be around 4.4 million. It is located in Central Africa with an area of 240,535 square miles surrounded by Chad to the north, Sudan in the east, Republic of Congo (Brazzaville) and Democratic Republic of Congo to the south, and Cameroon to the east. CAR has a strong executive branch and weak legislative and judicial branches of government

CAR remains a country in which suspected witches and sorcerers are dealt with harshly, despite the existence of a highly bureaucratic civil legal system in which codified law and due process are supposed to take precedence. Unfortunately, this system is circumvented by the government as well as the citizens at every turn. Written codes and Constitution aside, the CAR is very much a country in which mob justice and brutal government repression remain the supreme methods of handling the problem of crime. The country has agricultural, water, and mineral resources, but unfortunately, international bodies such as the United Nations and International Monetary Fund see problems with the way the government runs the country.

Formerly the French colony of Ubangi-Shari, the CAR was formed upon gaining independence in 1960. In subsequent decades, the country has experienced many coups resulting in civil war–like situations, displacing hundreds of thousands of citizens. Many civilians have been killed, kidnapped, or subjected to violence during these times. The failure of the civilian government to control security forces has resulted in a sharp deterioration of the security and humanitarian situation. Further, arms proliferation in the country has complicated the law and order situation, resulting in the deployment of peacekeeping soldiers from neighboring countries.

At the time of independence, the penal code, the code of criminal procedure, and the Constitution were codified such that the criminal justice system resembled the French civil law tradition. As a civil law system, the judicial processes within the CAR are inquisitorial in nature, and the legal profession is highly bureaucratic. The system of policing and the rest of the criminal justice system are also still based very closely on the French structures that were imported during the colonial period. Although there are some remote rural regions in the CAR in which traditional methods of arbitration and conflict resolution are used predominantly, such a situation simply does not exist within the capital, Bangui, and the most populous areas. Moreover, since independence, few changes have been made to either of the two pertinent codes mentioned previously, despite some urgent and very specific crime problems, some of which are seemingly created by the dysfunction of all layers of the criminal justice process.

Unfortunately, the place that the criminal justice system occupies within the greater social and political contexts within the Central African Republic is extremely discouraging. From the perspective of the Central African citizens, the police and the formal judicial process are perceived to hold little legitimacy because of their inability to effectively battle the crime problems of the country. Furthermore, the rule of law is seemingly undermined by discrepancy between popular customary law and the inherited structure and codified law—another problem common to postcolonial African states. As a result of this lack of confidence and support for law enforcement and the judiciary, citizens commonly apprehend and execute suspected bandits or witches through their own brutal methods. Also born out of the feeble crime control system, the government forces and police engage in human rights violations such as summary executions, illegal searches, arbitrary arrests, and torture in attempts to brutally suppress rampant crime problems.

Politically speaking, units of the national police and the gendarmerie are often utilized by the government to quell political dissenters, rebels loyal to the Patassé government—ousted in a 2003 coup—as well as those suspected or accused of supporting such groups. These individuals are often arrested arbitrarily and held for long periods of time without being brought before a judge, and without the benefit of communication with a lawyer or family members. These practices are in violation of international standards, but also of the Constitution, the penal code, and the code of criminal procedure of the Central African Republic.

There are two major police forces operating within the CAR, listed earlier, as well as several notable specialized divisions. Beginning with the two overarching structures, the national police in the CAR are organized under the director-general of the police and the Ministry of the Interior and Public Security, whereas the national gendarmerie is organized under the Ministry of Defense. Literature regarding the Central African Republic has placed little emphasis on the officers of these two forces in general, but rather has most typically discussed the actions of specialized units found under their auspices. The government's inability to pay wages makes both the national police and the gendarmerie vulnerable to corruption. What are considered routine matters for police, such as calls for police assistance, involve victims paying gas money for police.

The police unit receiving the majority of the attention in the CAR, because of the interest of international human rights advocates, has been the Central Office for the Repression of Banditry (OCRB). Formed by the government to combat the high incidence of banditry throughout the Central African Republic, this particular unit is responsible for a great deal of the human rights violations noted previously. It is common for the OCRB to conduct illegal searches, arrest individuals, and then take them to a location where they are tortured and then killed. Most often, the bodies of suspected bandits, or those who are accused of assisting them, are then driven through the villages in open-air government jeeps as a deterrent to crime, before their bodies are dropped off at the local hospital to be picked up by their families.

Although provisions in the penal code referring to the abuse of power by government representatives are strong, by all accounts agents of the OCRB operate with near total impunity; none have recently been prosecuted for their part in the atrocities committed against the Central African people. It is without question that the vast majority of serious crime problems in the CAR are handled in this extrajudicial fashion, with only rare use of the formal judicial process. Also implicated in the aforementioned activities—as well as rape and other atrocities—has been the Section of Research and Investigation (SRI), which originally operated as a unit of the presidential guard. In fact, the predecessor to the SRI was disbanded in 2003, before being reformed and renamed, following the conviction of five members in the rape of a woman. One final force worth noting in this regard is a mixed brigade of armed forces personnel and members of the national police and national gendarmerie formed in 2004 and tasked with matters of security throughout the country. Citizen complaints against military and police personnel have indicated instances of rape, beatings, and torture.

Crime

General infractions contrary to the law within the Central African Republic are broken up into three categories by the country's penal code. Using the best literal translation, and in descending order of seriousness, the three categories are delineated as crimes, offenses, and infringements. As in French law, these types of infraction are distinguished in the code by the punishments that may be incurred on the individual found guilty of committing them. The types of punishment within the CAR are then also broken up into the three corresponding categories. Again using the best literal translation, and in corresponding order, the categories of punishment within the CAR will be referred to as those that are imposed in criminal matters, those that are correctional matters, and last, matters of simple police. For the purpose of organization, the actual punishments that fall within these three categories are discussed in greater detail later in this entry under a separate section regarding punishment.

In the area of juvenile justice, the 1994 publication of the Central African Republic's penal code does not specifically denote an age of criminal responsibility under which an offender holds no culpability whatsoever. What is does specify, however, is that a youth offender is someone 16 years of age or younger, who must go to trial before a youth judge (offenders over the age of 16 then are considered adults by the criminal justice system). The youth magistrate must then decide whether the individual shall be held accountable for his or her crime consistent with the present code, or whether the youth offender is deserving of some lesser punishment. A lesser punishment typically holds a minimum punishment equivalent of "simple police matters," although any judgment that the magistrate finds suitable for the rehabilitation of the offender is acceptable. For those accused who are under the age of 14, the judge may only impose a judgment that contributes to the "reeducation" of the offender. Toward this end, an entirely separate juvenile court system was established in the late 1990s in Bangui, and it was reported in 2006 to have tried cases throughout the year. The U.S. Department of State (2007) also reported that this court had provided counseling services for families and young offenders throughout the year. These findings should be viewed as somewhat of an encouraging step, considering that the juvenile court had gone as long as a year without any operation in the past because of lack of funding and personnel.

Crime Statistics

The Central African Republic has yet to report any official crime or arrest statistics to either the UN or the INTERPOL international crime surveys. In fact, there does not seem to be any available data regarding crime rates published within the CAR or otherwise. Given the situation and current context within the CAR, there are several apparent reasons that this might be the case. First, we should consider the fact that the government simply does not have the resources, personnel, or technological capabilities to produce such a statistical product. Amnesty International (2006) reported that the Ministry of Justice had only one computer and one printer for the entire country. Further contributing to the problem, analysts have estimated that as little as 2 percent of the country's geographic territory is actually under the authority of the federal government.

The second factor that has likely as much, if not more, to do with the lack of official crime statistics within the CAR is the government's aversion to transparency. For many reasons, it would be unfavorable from the government's perspective to provide an accurate and official statement regarding crime and punishment to the international community—again, assuming the government was in fact able to do so. For instance, it would be unlikely that the government would publish statistics for arrest made by law enforcement, when in fact in many cases the suspects were simply tortured and killed extrajudicially by the OCRB or the SRI before being dumped at the local hospital.

Several international sources have indicated that one of the most troubling crime problems within the Central African Republic at present is the trafficking of human beings. The CAR is noted as both a source and a destination for trafficked persons—usually children—who are often sold into bondage or prostitution. The CAR currently has no law on the books prohibiting human trafficking, despite having ratified the Convention for the Suppression of the Traffic in Persons and of the Exploitation of the Prostitution of Others prior to 1992. It should be noted, however, that it is possible under the CAR's current penal code to prosecute human traffickers under articles that are relevant to the trade, such as laws against slavery, sexual assault and exploitation, labor violations, and prostitution and laws governing the mandatory school age for children.

A third prominent crime problem within the Central African Republic is that of rampant banditry. Because very little of the country's actual territory is developed and controllable by the government, bandits are able to operate extensively in the unstable northwestern regions. These groups are thought to be made up of a mixture of common criminals as well as the remnants of organized rebel groups. According to a report published by the United Nations High Commissioner for Refugees in 2005, the bandits are responsible for kidnapping, hostage taking, ambushes, and general pillaging in addition to armed robbery, and they are typically armed with AK-47 assault rifles and grenade launchers. The government of the CAR has taken some steps toward combating banditry in both the remote regions and the capital of Bangui with the deployment of the Central Office for the Repression of Banditry.

Despite the lack of crime data published by the Central African Republic, outside sources provide some information about the existence and nature of more common crime problems within Bangui as well as the rural areas. Although it is noted by Safer Access (2006) that banditry is a growing problem in the city and on the main roads, this problem is typically confined to the remote villages and routes of travel. Right within Bangui, on the other hand, simple muggings are more commonplace. It is also worth noting that the majority of women arrested in Bangui are facing charges of sorcery or witchcraft. Bangui prison officials in 2006 reported that 50–60 percent of women arrested in the capital were accused of witchcraft or sorcery, an offense that carries the death penalty in the CAR.

Finding of Guilt

The judicial system in the Central African Republic is based very closely on French law, so many of the protections enjoyed by the accused are written into the formal codes. From arrest through the entire court process, the penal code and the code of criminal procedure dictate that the accused are treated in a reasonably just and humane manner. Unfortunately, it is these very tenets of justice that are so commonly violated by the government.

The court process in civil law systems such as France and the CAR can be broken up into three phases. First, there is the investigative phase in which the public prosecutor—who is presented the charge by the police—collects evidence and decides whether such evidence is substantial enough to warrant a formal action. From this point, those cases found to be worthwhile by the prosecutor are forwarded to the examining magistrate, or *juge d'instruction,* who again collects evidence and questions witnesses to in preparation for trial and also determines whether the case should proceed. Finally, during the trial process, both the defense and the prosecution are provided with a record of the investigation and are allowed to make their oral arguments to the judge and jury.

According to formal codes, there are a number of rights that can and should be invoked by the accused in the Central African Republic immediately upon arrest. First, and perhaps most importantly, the offender is by law allowed to meet with defense counsel; it should also be noted here that this right is to be provided at the expense of the government in the case of an indigent suspect. Second, there are several rights delineated in formal code that are intended both to ensure the speedy processing of a case and to limit any unnecessary or prolonged pretrial detention. The pretrial process found in the inquisitorial civil law systems is by nature longer than those of common law counterparts; however, provisions regarding a speedy trial process in the CAR are typical when compared to other civil law systems in that regard. Except in cases of national security, those arrested on criminal charges in the CAR are to be taken before a magistrate within 96 hours of arrest, and any request for bail is to be answered by the *juge d'instruction* within five days. At any point during the investigation or examining phase, if the evidence does not support further detention, the suspect is to be released, and if the investigation is longer than one month, the *juge d'instruction* must come forward to formally make known the reason.

It becomes clear when examining what is known that the pretrial process in the CAR is a serious weak link, one that is institutionally flawed to the point where it would literally be impossible for the court system to satisfy the requirements of the country's own Constitution, penal code, and code of criminal procedure. It should be understood that the civil law judicial system imposed on the CAR and adopted at the end of colonial rule is one that relies on a great degree of bureaucracy. The type of bureaucracy employed in other civil law countries, however, is simply not sustainable in the Central African Republic. For instance, as a result of lack of funds and trained personnel, several courts within the CAR have remained out of operation for entire calendar years in recent times. Even when operating to government expectations, the criminal court in Bangui does not operate continuously. The Constitution dictates that the court is to have its sessions set up according to needs by the minister of justice, with a typical expectation being once a year for a period of two months. The effects of the institutional and bureaucratic problems such as these would seemingly preclude the possibility of compliance with the speedy trial provisions written into formal code.

The effectiveness of the judicial bureaucracy is severely hampered by the inadequate number of personnel: 150 judges and only 40 practicing barristers in the entire country, and even these are almost exclusively found in Bangui. Judges and lawyers within the Central African Republic enjoy civil servant status and a flexible merit-based system for promotion and salary increase. However, despite the fact that there are very few judges and prosecutors in the CAR, this status has been greatly diminished because of the government's inability to pay its staff.

Regarding the rights provided to the accused when their case reaches the trial phase and beyond, the failure of ineffective bureaucracy has stripped the meaning from any provisions of law pertaining to due process. Technically, the presumption of innocence exists at every stage of the process until conviction, and as mentioned earlier, the ability to put up an effective defense is in theory guaranteed. Defendants in the CAR are tried before a jury in criminal cases and have the right to be present during their trials, and the defense also has the right to question or call witnesses on defendants' behalf. Unfortunately, judges, underpaid or sometimes unpaid, are particularly susceptible to bribes and are often paid off in some way or another by the lawyers in exchange for an outcome favorable to their cause. Once again, it cannot be overemphasized that the trial process is often moot given that the vast majority of criminal problems are dealt with extrajudicially.

Following a ruling by one of the courts of first authority, an individual convicted of a crime in the Central African Republic is afforded the right to an appeals process. In the French tradition, formal code dictates that an appeal may work its way through the appeals courts of jurisdiction and, if necessary, come before the supreme court of appeals, which is the Court of Cassation.

Punishment

The penal code of the Central African Republic divides punishments applicable under the law into three different categories, which correspond to the three different classifications delineated as general infractions. Beginning with the punishments found in the class of "crimes" under article 1, several harsh options are available at the sentencing phase. Listed primarily in article 6 of the penal code are the punishments of death, perpetual forced labor, and a period of forced labor of between 10 and 20 years. Given the typical process we have discussed already, this is the classification of punishments least likely to be imposed through formal court proceedings in the Central African Republic. A second subheading under article 6 lists some additional punishments that are to be applied by the courts in criminal matters of a political nature. Punishments available in specifically political criminal matters include life imprisonment, a prison term of an unspecified length, banishment, and civic degradation.

Three of the most seriously treated crimes—murder, robbery, and rape—fall into this category of infractions, though they are treated somewhat differently at times by the code. For the crimes of voluntary homicide and armed robbery within the Central African Republic, there exists only one possible sentence: death. Robberies that do not include the use of a weapon but that still utilize violence, on the other hand, can earn an individual a life sentence of forced labor. In contrast with homicide and robbery, rape is treated with a little more ambiguity throughout the code and is liable for a greater amount of judicial discretion. For the simple rape of an individual over the age of 15, a Central African offender can be sentenced to any length of forced labor. Ambiguity again comes in when the penal code states that it reserves the ability to impose stronger punishments on those found to be habitual sexual offenders, as well as those who commit the act of rape on a person under the age of 15. Offenders who are found guilty of lesser sex-related crimes in the CAR, which are separated similarly in Western countries, face a punishment of 5 to 10 years of incarceration.

After listing the death penalty as an option in the category of "criminal matters," the penal code goes on to specify the methods and manner in which the death penalty is to be employed by the state. Somewhat similar to the common practices for summary executions, all those condemned to death in the Central African Republic are to be executed in public, and the only available option for carrying out the death penalty is by firing squad. Once the offender has been executed, the government then turns over the body to the person's family for burial. By law, men and women in the CAR are to be executed in the same manner and by the same means. However, if a woman who is sentenced to death is pregnant, the execution will occur only after she has given birth. Finally, the penal code also prohibits the state from executing convicts on Sundays, or any other religious or national holidays. The Central African government notes that no official death sentence has been imposed in the country since 1981, but again this manifests the lack of formality in executing offenders rather than a progressive stance on the use of the death penalty.

Article 7 of the penal code specifies the punishments for "offenses," which are applicable under our second category of punishments known as "correctional matters." This particular category manifests the punitive philosophy of incarceration and fines. Correctional matters within the CAR are those offenses that are punishable by law through imprisonment for a period of between 1 month and a day and 10 years—except in the case of recidivists or other special cases for which the law has determined different limits. Correctional matters may also carry a punishment of up to 100,000 Central African francs, either in lieu of or in addition to imprisonment.

Burglary and theft in the Central African Republic are both offenses that, under the penal code, merit punishments in the correctional-matters category. Most general forms of theft are said to carry a punishment of one to five years of imprisonment, and a fine of 100,000 to 1,000,000 Central African francs. Burglary, on the other hand, carries the stiffer punishment of 10 to 20 years of forced labor and can result in an even harsher penalty should certain aggravating circumstances be present.

At least through the formal code, the government of the Central African Republic has taken a particularly tough stance against the sale, possession, cultivation, or supply of drugs—also all offenses that are considered correctional matters. In fact, in addition to the development of a special antidrug police force under the OCRB, the law provides for some pretty tough penalties for any form of drug offense. Article 285 of the penal code, found under "special offenses," notes that the aforementioned crime will be punished by 2 to 10 years' imprisonment and a fine of between 100,000 and 5,000,000 Central African francs. It is important to note that this article makes no distinction between growing, selling, possessing, or providing drugs, thus giving the magistrate a great deal of discretion in the sentencing options for any of these listed offenses. Equally peculiar is the fact that there is no difference in seriousness based on classification of drugs; the article tacitly states that hallucinogens will be treated the same way by the law as hashish and other cannabis products.

The final category of punishment listed in the penal code refers to "matters of simple police" and corresponds to the least serious forms of infractions, termed earlier as "infringements." Matters of simple police within the Central African Republic are punishable by imprisonment for a term between one day and one month and by a principle or complementary punishment of a fine between 100 and 50,000 Central African francs. It is also worth noting at this time that the state may confiscate any products or tools of the offense in an infraction that falls into any of the aforementioned categories. In criminal and correctional matters, these items are subject to confiscation as either principle or complementary punishments, whereas for matters of simple police, said items can be confiscated as a complementary punishment.

Prisons

The prison administration is within the Ministry of Home Affairs. The latest official statistics provided by the CAR's National Prison Administration were published by Home Office (2001) and indicated a total prison population of 4,168 individuals with an incarceration rate of 110 per 100,000. At the time, these figures were among the highest from those central African countries that supplied official statistics. Unofficial estimates provided by the International Centre for Prison Studies (ICPS) later estimated the total prison population within the CAR to be 1,000 however, with a much smaller rate of incarceration, totaling 24 per 100,000 in 2006. In 2002, there were 56 prisons with a capacity of 6,000 inmates. Because the larger number of cases is handled informally, prisons appear somewhat underused in proportion to the amount of serious crime. Another contributing factor is the heavy use of extrajudicial killings and other sanctions in recent years. However a number of prisons were destroyed in 2003 during internal conflict following the revolutionary coup, according to the U.S. Department of State Human Rights Report (2007), so that many of the 56 prisons counted in 2002 were out of service in 2005.

Incarceration practices common within the CAR are often in violation of not only international standards but also the nation's own Constitution and code of criminal procedure. For instance, a large percentage of the general prison population is made up of pretrial detainees—approximately half of all inmates in the nation's two largest prisons in 2006. Contrary to international standards and the relevant legislation, these individuals are often held at length without trial or charge and at times are refused the ability to consult counsel or speak with their families. In addition to these issues, children are housed with adult inmates, where they are often subjected to physical or sexual abuse. In fact, aside from the Ngaragba and Bimbo prisons in Bangui—the nation's sole gender-specific prisons—male and female prisoners within the Central African Republic are housed together as well.

In addition to the systematic institutional practices, prisoners within the CAR are also subjected to a number of abuses by the guards and the administration at each individual prison. Evidence of torture by the guards was observed during a 2000 prison inspection conducted by the African Commission on Human and Peoples' Rights. Corruption is rooted in the system and manifests itself in several common practices. For instance, in recent years inmates have been forced to perform unpaid labor at the houses of political elites, as well as magistrates and other government legal professionals. Visitation from family members is allowed in most cases; however, at times the guards must first be bribed. Despite sometimes having to bribe the guards, the families play an important role throughout prisoners' incarceration. It is typically necessary for the families to supply medical amenities to the inmates and sometimes even food—especially in police or gendarmerie cells. In 2000, it was reported that no food was supplied by prison authorities at Berberati prison in Mambere Kadei prefecture for a period of more than seven months. Even inmates who require serious medical attention are typically without the benefit of an onsite physician, are often refused medical attention at local hospitals, and receive it only at their own expense.

Poor health within the institutions of the CAR can further be aggravated by the conditions under which the prisoners are housed. Communal cells are often overcrowded, with inmates sleeping on dirt floors covered only by straw mats. The 2006 U.S. Department of State Report on Human Rights (2007) noted that a five-square-meter cell at the national gendarmerie's Research and Investigation Division was housing 12 inmates, with only a single bucket to serve as a latrine. The same report noted that the cell frequently flooded during the rainy season, further exposing inmates to disease. In fact, it is not uncommon for there to be so many prisoners in a single cell that they do not have enough room to lie down at the same time. The spread of the HIV virus is also an immense concern among prisoners within the CAR, given that prisoners with infectious diseases are not segregated from those who are generally healthy, and the majority of the facilities are coed.

As mentioned previously, the two main prisons within the Central African Republic are found in the capital of Bangui and are the only gender-specific prisons in the country. Aside from a few notable exceptions, the Ngaragba prison houses the country's male inmates in conditions much the same as those noted already. Among the general prison population, there are large communal cells shared by both convicts and those on remand—in which the prisoners are required to sleep on straw mats. A second wing of the prison referred to as the "White House" contains former dignitaries of the Patassé regime who are serving time there as a result of the 2003 coup. Finally, a third wing is maintained in which there are isolation cells to be utilized as a disciplinary measure against the inmates.

For information regarding Bimbo prison in Bangui, the second major prison in the CAR, a report completed following a 2000 inspection provides the best description. Again, Bimbo houses female convicts in the same communal cells as those who are on remand. It is notable that some of the latter had been held without trial for as long as five years and that a large number of both types of prisoners at Bimbo were either accused or convicted of witchcraft. The overall conditions at Bimbo prison during the inspection were in large part similar to those found elsewhere around the country. The four cells there housed 36 prisoners, who were subjected to a damp atmosphere courtesy of a leaky roof and the subsequent mosquito infestation. Similar to Ngaragba, civil servants were kept in a cell separate from the rest of the inmates and were provided more favorable amenities including mosquito nets. Aside from the mere exposure to the conditions described here, there were no complaints of abuse from the prisoners during the visit.

Dale Marsden

Further Reading

Amnesty International. (2006). *Central African Republic: The Government Tramples on the Basic Rights of Detainees:* http://www.amnestyzusa.org/document.php?id=ENGAFR190072006&lang=e.

Central African Republic. (2004). Constitution de la République Centrafricaine 2004.

Code Pénal. (1994). Bangui, Central African Republic: Journal Officiel de la Republique Centrafricaine.

Dankwa, E. V. O. (2001). *Prisons in the Central African Republic: Report of the Special Rapporteur on Prisons and Conditions of Detention in Africa.* Banjul: African Commission on Human & Peoples' Rights.

Human Rights Committee. (2006). "Report of States: Central African Republic": http://www2.ohchr.org/english/bodies/hrc/hrcs87.htm.

United Nations High Commissioner for Refugees. (2005). *Fiche Pays Republique Centrafricaine:* http://www.sangonet.com/ActuDo/santeah/fich-RCA-unhcr2005.pdf.

Woodfork, J. (2006). *Culture and Customs of the Central African Republic.* Westport, CT: Greenwood Press.

Chad

Legal System: Civil/Customary
Murder: High
Corruption: High
Human Trafficking: Medium
Prison Rate: Low
Death Penalty: Yes
Corporal Punishment: Yes

Background

Chad is located in Central Africa with Libya to the north, Sudan to the east, the Central African Republic to the south, and Niger to the west. Chad is home to approximately 10 million individuals. Arabic and French are the official language groups. Islam is the most widely practiced religion.

Chad is a constitutional regime. According to its 1996 Constitution, Chad is a republic founded on the principles of democracy, the rule of law, and justice. Separation of powers is recognized in the Constitution, which established an executive made up of a president elected by the people for a renewable five-year term and a government led by a prime minister appointed by the president. The government is responsible before a single-house parliament (the National Assembly). The National Assembly has the power to remove the other branches of government. The president has the power to remove the National Assembly in the case of excessive conflicts between the executive and legislative branches. The judiciary is established independently, consisting of a supreme court, a court of appeal, tribunals, and a justice of the peace.

Chad's political culture can be grouped as a Romano-Germanic approach of law (sometimes referred to as a "code" law). The legal system is characteristic of a code law system in that it is based on comprehensive legislative statues often bound together as codes. Chad also has maintained traditional and customary laws. Citizen control over the various branches of government is weak. There appears to be general agreement that police and army officials are relatively unconstrained by the paper guarantees of civil liberties, enshrined in various constitutions adopted after 1990.

The rule of law in the Republic of Chad in the past has been and continues to be in a state of flux. Originally the rule of law was based on the framework of French law inherited from the previous colonial rule. Later an austere form of Arab socialism (1969) was incorporated that forbids alcohol, prostitution, nightclubs, and Christian churches. Islamic interpretations were also incorporated into the legal code. All the while, traditional and customary laws were maintained, which often superseded Napoleonic law in practice. Thus, sorting out any definitive set of laws is complicated. These frequent revisions have impacted the Chadian legal system specifically and the Chadian political culture in general.

In 1960, Chad obtained independence and officially received the blessings and diplomatic and economic assistance of France and the Western world. In reality, France encouraged little constitutionalism or free markets in its occupied land. The Constitution adopted in 1990 laid the foundation for political transition but did not provide any explicit blueprint for reform of the security establishment. Ever since Chad's "independence," Chad has been plagued by political violence and recurrent attempted coup d'état. The executive appears to dominate the legislative and judicial branches of government. Members of the judiciary receive death threats, demotion, or removal when they do not cooperate with government officials in terms of granting them immunity for their crimes. Further, evidence suggest that the gendarmerie and the Rapid Intervention Force were formally part of the National Army of Chad (ANT) and received favorable treatment from the executive branch. In fact, it has been suggested that this unit is the real seat of coercive power at the disposal of the ruling elite.

The criminal justice system in Chad has been impacted in numerous ways. Chadians distrust police because they often target unfavorable ethnic groups with verbal abuse, excessive questioning, discriminatory patterns of arrest, and excessive use of force. Because of the breakdown of stability after the 1990 coup, there is considerable pressure for the police to be watchful of certain minorities who might be a threat to the state. What further feeds this officer mentality is that the sheer composition of decision-makers has been based on the preferences or objectives of whoever is in power. That is, positions in the criminal justice system, as in the political system, are often handpicked. This method of selection has resulted in biased policing and ill-experienced officials in general. The inadequacy of the police force has had a ripple effect on the criminal justice system (for example, their inability to protect refugees or control long stretches in the desert). In short, as both the perpetrators of injustice and the protectors of justice, the Chadian criminal justice system's ability to address crime and punishment continues to be problematic.

Moreover, the police act as one of the instruments of the elite in power. Numerous incidents of political harassment as well as coercive action against the press and political parties have occurred. In addition, accusations of extortion and sexual assaults by serving police are common. Officers are paid low wages and have few benefits. In addition, they are held in low esteem by the citizens. Post-independence politics in Chad, as in numerous other African countries, has been to replace or alter the civic public realm inherited from the colonial powers. In the case of Chad, often it has been replaced with rivaling communal or primordial realms.

Chad inherited its structure of policing from French colonial rule, and the police still bear some features traceable to the colonial factor today. As in France, policing is undertaken by a plurality of organizations whose classifications and nature have changed over the years since independence. Specifically, law enforcement in Chad is the responsibility of multiple agencies including the local police, the state police (gendarmerie), the National and Nomadic Guard (NNG), the Police Rapid Action Company (CARP), and the national army and various executively sanctioned investigative organizations.

At independence, various policing agencies existed, some with a remit extending over several French colonies, such as the National Security Police, or Suret. The Territorial Police (renamed the Nomad and National Guard in 1968 and reconstituted in 1996) were entrusted with security for government officials, premises, and regional posts. A national gendarmerie, formally a military unit, was responsible for rural security, and a national police force of uncertain nature also existed. The onset of rebellion led to the restructuring of existing units and the creation of new ones. Under President Habre, a political police known as the Direction de la Documentation et de la Securite (DDS) came into being and is alleged to have been largely responsible for the extrajudicial killings of up to 40,000 people that occurred under this president (Habre is now standing trial). By the Deby era, policing had come to be parceled out among a number of units whose activities were largely under the control of individuals serving the president. These units included the state police force or gendarmerie, a national police force, the Nomad and National Guard, the Rapid Intervention Force, the Republican Guard, and the Presidential Security Force.

Chad's police force is approximately 30,000 strong (Economic Intelligence Unit Limited). The inadequate size and lack of training and regional violence have come to the attention of the United Nations (UN), who are in the process of compromising with Chadian officials to send in troops to protect citizens (particularly in those areas flooded with refugees from neighboring state chaos).

The Ministry of Public Security and Immigration is responsible for the national police. The ANT, gendarmerie, and GNNT report to the Ministry of Defense (which is under the discretion of the president). The national police fall under the Ministry of Public Immigration. The Republican Guard and ANS report to the president.

Crime

The Republic of Chad has chosen to maintain colonial pieces of legislation, until such time that they are replaced by national laws. The most important colonial piece of legislation is the civil code. Chad is still using the 1958 edition of the French Civil Code. In 1999, the government drafted the "Code des personnes et de la famille" to replace the civil code; however, this has yet to be passed into law by parliament. The penal code and the penal procedure code were adopted on June 9, 1967, and the Anti-Corruption Act on February 16, 2000.

Under both the penal law and penal procedure, there is a tripartite distinction of offenses based on their respective seriousness: crimes, misdemeanors, and violations. Under the penal code, crimes and misdemeanors can incur a 20-year sentence and a 5-year sentence, respectively. Crimes are also classified into attacks against persons, attacks against property, and attacks against public security. Attacks against persons include intentional homicide (murder and assassination), intentional violence (nonintentional death, harm resulting in a permanent injury), and rape (including rape with more than one offender, aggravating circumstances, simple rape, and rape of a minor under 15 years of age). Attacks against property include theft, robbery, fraud, breach of trust, aggravated

An alleged looter is detained at the Chadian prime minister's residence in N'Djamena, Chad, on February 11, 2008. Government buildings were looted in the aftermath of a rebel attack on the Chadian capital. (AP Photo/Jerome Delay)

robberies, and vandalism. Illegal drug use, possession, and sale are also taken very seriously by the courts, and convictions carry stiff sentences and fines.

Challenging Crimes

The following information has been compiled from many sources, including reports to and by the United Nations' human rights treaty bodies. Chad has many crimes that are a particular challenge, including (this list is not exhaustive) state-perpetrated crimes, human trafficking, kidnapping, and child labor.

State perpetrated crime is a major issue for Chad and as such has been brought to the attention of the United Nations and other organizations who are trying to address it. According to the United Nations, security forces have committed and continue to commit politically motivated disappearances, and they have officially sanctioned extrajudicial killings of suspected criminals. Indeed, political instability is a contributor to some of the more horrendous crimes in Chad. In eastern Chad, for example, attacks on villages often result in attacks on women who suffer grave human rights abuses, including rape. In one instance, seven women were abducted and brutally attacked in Djimeze Djarma and held by their attackers for 20 days.

Human trafficking is a growing problem in Chad. It is difficult to measure the extent of the problem of commercial sexual exploitation of children in Chad because of the lack of reliable data and the taboo surrounding the subject. It is known that prostitution, including child prostitution, trafficking for sexual purposes, and forced labor exist in Chad. In fact, children in Chad are some of the most at-risk children in the world. The number of street children and children struggling to survive is growing. More than 11,000 children live in the streets and become victims of violence, exploitation, and disease. According to a UNAIDS/WHO report, in 2002, the population of orphans living with HIV/AIDS was 72,000.

Recent media reports of the inability of EUFOR (European Union Force) and MINURCAT (UN Mission in the Central African Republic and Chad) to protect civilians and curb bourgeoning criminality in Chad raise some serious concerns. In 2008, humanitarian agencies reported various human rights violations in eastern Chad including beatings, livestock theft, and the rape of women and children.

Forced military service is another form of internal child trafficking. The Chadian armed forces are known to have recruited children between 12 and 15 years of age. In 2000, the World Organization against Torture reported that many of the children recruited into the military forces and sent to the front line to detect landmines were under 13 years of age. Chad has no effective restriction on the military recruitment of volunteers who obtain the consent of a guardian. The report noted that 30 percent of abducted children in these areas were recruited as soldiers, 13 percent were raped, and 2 percent used as forced labor. It has been estimated that between 7,000 and 10,000 child soldiers operate in Chad national army and rebel and militia groups.

The practice of female genital mutilation, traditional within some of Chad's larger religious groups, is legally prohibited but widely practiced, affecting nearly half of the country's female population. The traditional sale of child wives is common in Chad's more rural areas. The age of consent in Chad is 14 regardless of marital status, but this is also not enforced, nor are most of the laws prohibiting prostitution and the operation of prostitution houses, which have become commonplace in the south.

Crime Statistics

Gauging the incidence of crime in Chad is more of an art than a science given that Chad has not participated in UN surveys or contributed to the INTERPOL. What further complicates gauging the incidence of crime is that many of the perpetrators of these offenses are members of the military and police forces and are rarely prosecuted. Finally, Chadian civilians are at times reluctant to report crimes to the police out of fear of re-victimization. In terms of reliable information regarding crime in Chad, the U.S. Sate Department Counselor Information Sheet provides some qualitative statements. Other information provided hereafter is based on multiple sources such as newspaper articles, various organizations, and basically whatever information the author gauged to have some validity.

Although politically motivated abuses are common, the incidence of violent crime in Chad is on the rise. Petty theft, burglary, and auto theft occur frequently. The Economist Intelligence Unit's analysts have estimated that Chad experiences over 20 homicides per 100,000 people a year. Expatriate U.S. and European tourists are often targeted for armed robbery (and in the process have been assaulted) and are advised against overt displays of wealth. Sexual harassment and sexual discrimination against women is legally permissible and widespread.

Rural areas are extremely dangerous. Armed bandits operate on many roads, assaulting, robbing, and killing travelers. In some cases the motive appears to be robbery. Suspected perpetrators of these crimes were identified as active duty soldiers or deserters. Employees of foreign assistance organizations or nongovernmental organizations (NGOs) have also been targeted. Interethnic violence is increasing in rural areas as well. Particularly, violence resulting from land disputes has been increasing.

Finding of Guilt

The following section discusses the rights of the accused according to the Constitution of the Republic of Chad, which was adopted in March 1996 and promulgated on April 14, 1996. Accordingly, all citizens are equal before the law. Articles 21 through 26 of the Chadian Constitution form the foundation for fundamental rights under the law. Illegal and arbitrary arrests are forbidden. The accused has the right to a self-obtained lawyer or to a lawyer chosen by the state. The accused is presumed innocent until proven guilty, and no individual can be held responsible for a crime he or she did not directly commit. The Constitution does make mention of the state's right to conduct searches in private domiciles as provided by law. Other rights granted by the state include the following: no individual may be detained in a penitentiary institution unless by virtue of a penal law in source. Incarceration before or while awaiting trial is allowed. The accused also has the right to appeal the judge's decision on the grounds of it being unconstitutional.

The gap between practice and policy in terms of these rights is palpable. More specifically, much of Chad's police force is corrupt and functions primarily to secure political objectives at the expense of socially desirable ones. State and local police regularly ignore certain crimes such as prostitution. Politically motivated arrest, detention, rape, and torture are common. Extrajudicial kidnappings and murder are known to be practiced by the gendarmerie against rebels, suspected criminals, and even election observers. In some cases, these extrajudicial actions have been officially sanctioned. Although members of the police force are occasionally prosecuted for criminal violations such as drug crimes, they are rarely if ever brought up on charges of human rights abuses. Though constitutionally prohibited from doing so, Chad's police agencies regularly arrest and detain suspected criminals and enemies of the state without the required warrants. As with many of the freedoms guaranteed by Chad's Constitution, the rights of the citizenry and press are secondary to the political objectives of the ruling party. The press in Chad is routinely controlled through intimidation tactics, police harassment, and detention.

At the national level, the Constitution provides for a Supreme Court, Constitutional Court, and Court of Appeals. At the provincial or local level, there are appeals courts in N'Djamena, Moundou, and Abeche. Chad's legal process begins with the submission that a crime occurred. After crimes are submitted to the criminal courts under the provisions of the criminal procedure code, the judicial process ensues. A hearing takes place, led by the chairman, in which a prosecutor or deputy prosecutor is present. The next phase would involve the courts of divisions, which are separate jurisdictions to which judges are assigned. Civil and commercial cases go to the chairman, and criminal cases go to the state prosecutor. Trials are public; guilt is often assumed, particularly in the case of theft and rape; and in theory, defendants and their attorneys have the right to question their accusers.

Criminal courts are nonpermanent jurisdictions and are made up of a chairman of the Court of Appeals or a counselor, two counselors, and four magistrates' assistants. For civil cases, commercial cases, minor offenses, and police court matters, the criminal courts (also referred to as courts of first instance) are the common law authority. The judicial system consists of 4 criminal courts, 4 magistrates' courts, 4 labor tribunals, 14 district courts (in major cities), 36 justices of the peace (in larger townships), and a court of appeal (the Appellate Court of N'Djamena). Criminal courts convened in N'Djamena, Sarh, Moundou, and Abéché, and criminal judges traveled to other towns when necessary. In addition, each of the 14 prefectures has a magistrates' court, in which civil cases and minor criminal cases are tried. In 1988, 43 justices of the peace served as courts of first resort in some areas.

Chad also has an unofficial but widely accepted system of Islamic sharia courts in the north and east, which have operated for a century or more. Most cases involve family obligations and religious teachings. In most rural areas where there is no access to these formal judicial institutions, sultans and chiefs preside over customary courts. Their decisions may be appealed to ordinary courts.

In other areas, traditional custom requires family elders to mediate disputes involving members of their descent group—that is, men and women related to them through sons and brothers. Civil courts often consider traditional law and community sentiment in decisions, and the courts sometimes seek the advice of local leaders in considering evidence and rendering verdicts.

Originally, a supreme court was inaugurated in 1963 and abolished in 1975. The Court of State Security was established in 1976. Courts-martial, instituted early in the Déby regime to try security personnel, no longer operate, and the remaining military magistrates sit as civilian judges on the N'Djamena Court of Appeals. Following the 1990 coup, the structure and functioning of the judicial system was seriously disrupted. Because of the breakdown of law and order, the judiciary was unable to handle criminal cases. Interference by the government and by the military contributed to the breakdown. Many magistrates went out on strike in 1993 to protest difficult working conditions and nonpayment of salaries.

The new constitution, adopted in March 1996 by referendum, mandates an independent judiciary from the executive and the legislature. Judges remain in office on a permanent basis, and they are only subject to judicial review. The judiciary comprises the Supreme Court, courts of appeal, tribunals, and the justices of the peace.

The administration of the judiciary (including the appointment, promotion, discipline, and responsibility of judges, etc.) is the responsibility of the High Council of the Judiciary (HCJ). The HCJ proposes judges to the president for appointment and promotion. The council is chaired by the president of the republic, with the minister of justice and the chairperson of the Supreme Court, respectively, as first and second vice-chairs. The other members of the HCJ are judges elected by their peers. When sitting on disciplinary matters, the HCJ is presided over by its second vice-chair.

Though steps have been taken to follow these provisions, it is clear that there continues to be significant interference in the independence of the judiciary, including from the executive arm of the government. In 2000, the chief justice of the Supreme Court demoted two Supreme Court justices, reportedly because they made a decision that adversely affected the interests of the chief justice. The president names the chief justice, and 15 councilors are chosen by the president and the National Assembly. Appointments to the bench are for life. A Constitutional Council reviews legislation, treaties, and international agreements before adoption. Nine judges are elected to the Constitutional Council for terms of nine years. The Superior Council of Magistrates oversees and guarantees the independence of the judiciary. In 2001, several justices were sanctioned for malfeasance.

The government of Chad has not put in place appropriate legal provisions to protect children against abuse and exploitation. Chad has ratified most of the relevant child rights treaties. Chad does not have a policy for free primary education or a juvenile justice system. However, the establishment of separate juvenile quarters is on the policy agenda according to a recent meeting between Chad and the international community; the UN committee encouraged and applauded the establishment of juvenile chambers to deal with offenders ages 13 to 18 in courts of first instance; and additional legislation on the treatment of juveniles has been recently adopted. Accordingly, Chad has plans to build facilities to separate juveniles from adults and continue training judges.

Punishment

Punishments typically used in Chad are fines, prison, and various forms of corporal punishments. What follows is a sample of crimes and punishments allegedly associated with those acts. Because of the Chadian blend of various legal frameworks (e.g., French civil law and the inclusion of traditional and Islamic interpretations), types of punishments vary depending on a number of factors, such as geographical region, religion, citizen status (refugee), ethnicity, and police corruption. The latter factor has further complicated any real attempts at gauging crime because authorities contribute heavy-handedly to the prevalence of various crimes, which in turn helps to mask actual crime rates because of underreporting by citizens and officials alike. In addition, police agency incompetence in general has stunted Chad's capability and prevented any sense of progress from entering the professional era of policing.

In part owing to Africa's legacy of using corporal punishment, Chad frequently resorts to this sanction for certain offenses, although not overtly. A recent report posited that in Chad corporal punishment in the penal system as a sentence for a crime is prohibited. It can be used, however, as a disciplinary means whether on a suspect or a convict. In a recent incident, security forces in N'Djamena arrested, detained, and reportedly tortured two individuals who were accused of theft (Bureau of Democracy, Human Rights, and Labor 2007). In a separate case (June 2007), security forces arrested without charge, beat, and detained for one week a lieutenant (Bureau of Democracy, Human Rights, and Labor, 2007).

Legally speaking, the law does not explicitly forbid corporal punishment against individuals, but it mentions in general torture and maltreatment or assault and battery (see article 252 of penal code). The law provides for higher sentences where children are involved. In Chad, corporal punishment in schools was prohibited by decree in 1970. Both lethal and nonlethal and legal and nonlegal forms of corporal punishment are employed by police authorities. In all, acts of democide and genocide—perhaps the most extreme form of punishment possible—over the last half century are responsible for the deaths of 20,000 individuals in Chad.

Economic sanctions are used often as penalties for breaking the law. For example, assault is handled primarily through economic sanction, but there is the option of a prison term ranging from six days to one and a half years (article 252 of the penal code). Where a child below 13 years is the victim of assault and injuries, the sentence may be double. In most cases we see economic sanctions in combination with imprisonment. For example, "pimping," or living off the prostitution of others, is punishable by a fine and imprisonment for six months to two years. If the offense is committed against a minor, the imprisonment increases to two to five years. Operating an establishment for prostitution in a brothel or on other premises is also prohibited. Punishment for the offense is a fine and two to five years' imprisonment.

Those found guilty of engaging in forced marriages face anywhere from six months to two years in prison and a fine of 100 to 500 dollars. Trafficking violations are accompanied by penalties of between 10 months and life imprisonment. If trafficking involves children, the penalty jumps to 10 to 20 years of hard labor in prisons. Rape is punishable by prison. However, it is rarely prosecuted or reported. Homicides are punishable by death or long prison terms accompanied by hard labor. Drug offenses carry fairly long prison sentences; however, ascertaining the length of those sentences was difficult.

With the integration of multiple sources of law, in the northern Muslim areas, the concept of dia, which is payment to the family of a crime victim, is practiced widely. These payments are decided by local leaders and are challenged by non-Muslim populations who support the civil code and claim the practice of dia violates the Constitution.

The death penalty is allowed in Chad. Crimes punishable by death include homicide. However, it appears the people of Chad can be put to death for a variety of reasons, such as protesting, suspicion of belonging to an unfavored group, and so forth. Executions are carried out either judicially or extrajudicially. Extrajudicial killings usually occur outside the capital. The judicial method of execution is execution by firing squad. It is suspected that extrajudicial killings are carried out by a single official. Other methods have included death while in custody as a result of torture and stoning. The 19 death sentences imposed on July 30, 2004, were the first since the November 2003 executions of 9 individuals. Based on available data, Chad has fairly low rates of legal executions. One reason may be because extrajudicial killings help mask those figures.

The Chadian legal system does not respect the right to a full appeal against either conviction or sentence in capital cases, in contravention of international law. The only recourse open to those sentenced to death is to submit a cassation plea on grounds of gross errors of fact or law to the cassation chamber of the Supreme Court. If successful, the case is sent back for retrial. If unsuccessful, the convicted prisoner may appeal for presidential clemency. The 19 men's lawyers have submitted a cassation plea to the Supreme Court. In at least one known case, a man was convicted and put to death while his appeal was being put together by his lawyers.

Prison

According to the International Centre for Prison Studies, Chad's total prison population as of 2007 was roughly 2,800 prisoners, approximately 35 per 100,000 national population. Females make up roughly 2.4 percent of the total prison population. Foreign prisoners constitute 1.3 percent of the total Chadian prison population.

Chad has a total of 46 prisons throughout the country. The central prison is located in the capital city of N'Djamenas and houses over 700 prisoners. All of Chad's prisons are characterized as having harsh and life-threatening conditions. For example, N'Djamena's Central Prison was built to hold 350 prisoners, yet it holds nearly double its capacity. Overcrowding also translates into the mixing of prisoners across categories of those incarcerated (pretrial detainees, convicts, juveniles, men, and women). Available data show very high numbers of pretrial detainees in prisons as well as those awaiting sentencing or the outcome of appeals. These individuals account for anywhere between 50 and 70 percent of the prison population.

Not only are prison conditions in general poor; so too is management of those prisons. The Department of State described Chadian prisons as primitive. Food rations are inadequate, and prisoners usually need an outside connection to food. Prison personnel lack professional training and as a consequence often abuse prisoners. It is not uncommon for individuals to serve their term but not be released because of inadequate record keeping. Juvenile males are not always kept out of sight and sound of adult prisoners. Pretrial detainees are commonly held with convicted prisoners. Although the law authorizes forced labor, reports from human rights organizations suggest that forced labor generally does not occur.

Access to Chadian prisoners is possible under certain circumstances. The primary determinant is whether the prison is civilian or military. For the most part, with the confirmed existence of illegal prisons run by the gendarmerie, national security agency, and the police, Chad officials have granted certain nongovernmental organizations a permanent authorization notice to visit civilian prisons at any time. Other NGOs must obtain authorization from a court or director of a prison. In short, selected prisons are accessible to selected individuals.

Kristan Fox and Michael Fox

Further Reading

Azevedo, Mario, and Emmanuel Nnadozie. (1997). *Chad: A Nation in Search of Its Future.* (Nations of the Modern World.) Boulder, CO: Westview Press.

Bureau of Democracy, Human Rights, and Labor. (2009). http://www.state.gov/g/drl.

Coalition for International Courts. (2009). "Chad": http://www.iccnow.org/?mod=coalition.

Foltz, William J. *Chad's Third Republic: Strengths, Problems, and Prospects.* CSIS Africa Notes, No. 77. Washington, DC: Center for Strategic and International Studies, 1987.

Nolutshungu, S. C. (1996). *Limits of Anarchy: Intervention and State Formation in Chad.* Carter G. Woodson Institute Series in Black Studies. Charlottesville: University Press of Virginia.

Comoros

Legal System: Islamic/Civil
Murder: Medium
Corruption: Medium
Prison Rate: Low
Death Penalty: Yes
Corporal Punishment: Yes

Background

The Union of Comoros consists of three islands named Grande Comore, Anjouan, and Moheli. The island of Mayotte is claimed by Comoros as a fourth island; however, Mayotte is still very much under French control. Comoros is located in the Indian Ocean off the southeastern coast of Africa between Madagascar to the north and Mozambique on the northeast. Comoros, with an area of 863 square miles, is a poor country, with very few natural resources. The population is over 700,000, and transportation among the three islands is insufficient. Ninety-eight percent of the country is Sunni Muslim, and children attend Quranic school for two or three years, beginning around age five. School for older students has more French influence.

Comoros is a federal presidential republic, and the president is the head of the government and head of a pluriform multiparty system. The Constitution of the Union of Comoros was ratified on 2001. Comoros has had a history of political unrest, in part because its Constitution allows for each island to have governmental autonomy in addition to the union government.

Although many disputes are resolved by village elders or small courts, there is a clear criminal process and a criminal code that is a blend of Islamic law and French law. Although the judiciary is independent of the executive and legislative bodies, corruption of government is also an issue of great importance, and there are concerns that judges face pressure to make decisions in favor of government officials or risk removal from office.

Police forces are varied among the islands, with each island supporting its own local police force. Grand Comore and Moheli have a union military and a union gendarmerie that handle both defense and local policing. The union police handle immigration issues and local policing on Grande Comore. Anjouan police authorities may be difficult to distinguish, given that several military groups are armed on the island. Corruption among police forces is rampant, and officers have been known both to take bribes from citizens and to bribe citizens into making false reports. Police officials are attempting to develop their professional skills and raise the integrity of police work in the nation. Attendance at international law enforcement trainings held by the United States allowed Comoros to take part in training on dealing with terrorism, anticorruption, financial crimes, border security, drug enforcement, and firearms. The training also focuses on adhering to the rule of law while supporting democracy.

Crime

There is evidence that transnational crime issues are plaguing officials because assistance has been sought in dealing with these problems from police training agencies, and human rights offenses are reported to be of most concern to the international community. Technology does not appear to pose a problem for collecting criminal data because there appear to be at least 22,000 Internet users on the islands, a sign that the Internet is a reliable communication device and citizens are not without technology skills. The hope is that as Comoros reaches out for assistance from developed nations in addressing these human rights and transnational crimes issues, pressure will be applied on Comorian officials from those providing the assistance to collect data on criminal activity and other activities in the criminal justice system.

The legal system incorporates French and Islamic law, and although violent crime does appear to be uncommon, there is evidence of crimes against human rights, including violence against women, child abuse and child labor, and issues surrounding the trafficking and use of drugs, and there is concern that terrorists seek refuge in the islands. Reports indicate that government leaders are not in denial about these transnational crime issues and are seeking to address them, either through unifying with other African nations to ratify protocols that would establish laws and systems to handle certain crimes or through training provided by U.S. law enforcement and other aspects of criminal justice.

Comoros relies on the French criminal code to prosecute criminal activity; therefore, it would appear that offenses are categorized according to their seriousness as felonies, misdemeanors, and petty offenses. However, it is difficult to pinpoint which crimes fall into these categories. In France, crimes considered felonious include murder, trafficking of drugs, treason, rape, money laundering, certain offenses related to destruction of property, and terrorism, and those considered misdemeanor crimes include some forms of counterfeiting, threatening an individual, certain forms of negligence that cause physical harm to others, and degrading behavior toward another person, including assault. The law does consider unmarried children under the age of 18 as minors, and the U.S. State Department Report on Human Rights Practices suggests that minors are not incarcerated but sent home to parents. There does not appear to be a separate criminal code dealing with juvenile offenders. Because Islamic law also governs, it is important to point out that Islam does prescribe a punishment for criminal offenses as well, which may be employed by courts in Comoros. In Islam, crime is a serious moral problem and has a broad perspective, meaning Islam defines crime as any act forbidden in sharia against a person or his property.

Crimes that represent a particular challenge to Comoros are mostly in the areas of human rights. Reported to officials frequently, crimes such as violence against women, child labor, and child abuse are rarely investigated or prosecuted. Comoros did ratify the Protocol on the Rights of Women in Africa, which establishes the African Court on Human and People's Rights, but critics of the countries that have stepped forward indicate that little has been done in these nations to inform women of their rights and of access to this new forum for resolving these abuses against them. Reports indicate that 28 percent of children ages 5 to 14 are engaged in child labor, some in homes as domestic servants.

Penalties for possession, use, or trafficking of illegal drugs are very stiff, including long terms in prison and very high fines. Information on which drugs in Comoros are declared illegal could not be located; however, reports on other nations in Africa do indicate opiates, cocaine, and heroin among the drugs that are being tracked throughout the continent. Reports indicate that there is a possibility that terrorists have sought safe haven in Comoros. Officials in the nation have taken measures to increase counterterrorism training for military and police officials, relying on the United States to provide much of this training.

Several U.S. and international travel advisories' Web sites warn against mugging and pickpocketing but advise that violent crime is not likely in Comoros. Comoros does not report any crime data to INTERPOL or to the United Nations.

Finding of Guilt

Religious courts, those that make decisions based on Muslim teachings, conduct hearings on family or personal relationships and are scattered throughout the islands. Lower courts, or courts of first instance, are located in towns on the islands and handle small disputes. The High Council reviews the decisions of the lower courts and consists of two members appointed by the president, two members elected by the Federal Assembly, and one elected by the council of each island. This High Council, similar to the U.S. Supreme Court, hears cases involving the constitutionality of laws. Magistrates are appointed by decree.

In Comoros, the law does require that a warrant be issued for a person who is detained; however, in practice, persons may be detained for long periods of time without being charged. Persons detained are advised of their right to an attorney, but with scarce legal resources, this service is rarely available to defendants. Persons are admitted to bail if conditions are met. The law does provide for the right to a fair, public trial, and defendants are presumed innocent until proven guilty. Juries deliberate on criminal cases, and defendants do have the right to appeal their case to a higher court. Many of these rights are also supported by statements in the Constitution of the Union of Comoros, which states that all persons are equal under the law and have the right to defend themselves. Although these provisions are acknowledged as proper and legal practices in Moheli and Grande Comore, citizens on Anjouan are not as lucky. It is reported that journalists, politicians, and teachers have been detained without due process on numerous occasions and held for months. These radical actions likely have resulted from their protests against Bacar, the self-appointed leader of Anjouan. References to prosecution of trials in Comoros indicate that magistrates or judges themselves prosecute cases. Statistical data on the number of lower-court judges in Comoros could not be located. There is no juvenile court system or welfare system to attend to juveniles.

Punishment

The categories of punishment in Comoros are known as *hudud, qisas,* and *ta'azir.* According to these three systems, for certain offenses, such as adultery or fornication, death by stoning is the punishment. For stealing or robbery, the punishment might be cutting off the defendants' hands. In Islam, no man or court has the right to alter the punishment. The most serious form of punishment is capital punishment.

In the French code, prison terms, fines, and reparations to the state or victim are common punishments. Examples of punishments per the French code include 20–30 years' imprisonment for abduction, and 20 years' imprisonment for rape, with all terms carrying very hefty fines to the state. Depending on the severity of the drug offense, life imprisonment might be ordered; in any event, a conviction of possession alone will likely carry at least a five-year prison sentence. There are no statistics available as to the number of state executions of prisoners.

Prison conditions are poor; many of them are overcrowded, are lacking in medical care, and have little or no running water. Women and men are kept separate from each other. The government does allow prisoners to have visitors. Information regarding the number of prisons was not obtainable, however, on the Island of Anjouan; authorities use makeshift prison containers, such as crates or boxes.

Rhonda Gardner

Further Reading

International Regional Information Networks (IRIN) (2008). *Comoros: Too Late to Mediate:* http://www.unhcr.org/refworld/docid/47b46147c.html.

Mufune, Jennifer. (2007, June 20). "African Human Rights Court: Will It Make a Difference for

Women?" *One World Africa:* http://humanrightshouse.org/noop/page.php?p=Articles/6599.html&d=hjuwhxpalalwrud.

Representing Children Worldwide. (2005). *Comoros.* Yale Law School: http://www.law.yale.edu/rcw/rcw/jurisdictions/afe/comoros/frontpage.htm.

U.S. Department of State. (2006). "Africa Review." *Country Reports on Terrorism.* Released by the Office of the Coordinator for Counterterrorism: http://www.state.gov/s/ct/rls/crt/2005/64335.htm.

White, B. (1995). *Socially Conscious or Self-Actualizing?: Micro-Enterprise and Social Change in the Comoros Islands.* Montreal: McGill University.

Congo, Democratic Republic of the (Congo-Kinshasa)

Legal System: Civil/Customary
Murder: High
Corruption: High
Human Trafficking: Medium
Prison Rate: Low
Death Penalty: Yes
Corporal Punishment: Maybe

Background

The Democratic Republic of the Congo (DRC) or the *Republic democratique du Congo* is a Francophone country located in Central Africa. To distinguish it from its neighbor with the same name, it is called Congo-Kinshasa, after its capital. It is also known variously as DR Congo, DRC, or RDC. The DRC has been plagued by social and political turmoil since gaining its political independence from Belgium on June 30, 1960. The name Congo is derived from a major river in the area called Congo or Zaire found in the Bakongo ethnic group enclave. Kinshasa is the largest and capital city of the Democratic Republic of the Congo. The DRC's neighbors include the Central African Republic and Sudan to the north; Uganda, Rwanda, and Burundi to the east; Zambia and Angola to the south; and the Republic of the Congo to the west. It is separated from its neighbor to the east, Tanzania, by Lake Tanganyika. The DRC has a small coastline of 40 kilometers to the west of the Atlantic Ocean and a nine-kilometer access to the Gulf of Guinea through the Congo River. A recent estimate puts the population of the Democratic Republic of the Congo at 66,514,506.

The DRC became an independent country in 1960. The new constitution that came into force on February 2009 allows for the establishment of a bicameral legislature, comprising the Senate and the National Assembly. The executive branch of government consists of a 60-member cabinet, the president, and four vice presidents. The four vice-presidential positions in the DRC government are unique and have earned the president and vice presidents the popular nickname "the 1 + 4." The president is the head of state and commander-in-chief of the armed forces. The party with the majority in parliament is authorized by the Constitution to appoint prime minister and the cabinet. The Constitution allows for the establishment of an independent judiciary headed by the supreme court of the land. The Supreme Court has powers to adjudicate or interpret matters of constitutional significance. However, under the new constitution, the powers of the Supreme Court are to be scaled down with its division into three new institutions, including a constitutional court to perform the functions of the Supreme Court in interpreting constitutional matters.

Crime

The DRC has an independent and relatively autonomous judiciary. The judicial branch is composed of the constitutional court, the appeals court or *cour de cassation,* the council of state, and the high military court, in addition to civil and military courts and tribunals. The DRC's new constitution was adopted on December 18, 2005, following a national referendum. The DRC has accepted International Court of Justice (ICJ) jurisdiction, although with reservations.

Prosecutor Benjamin Bansenga, left, and Judge Midagu Amani conduct a court case in Bunia, Democratic Republic of Congo, on April 23, 2004. The two are part of a small team of judges and prosecutors dispatched here from Congo's capital to help restore the rule of law and central government authority to a region still tense and violent after a five-year war. (AP Photo/Schalk van Zuydam)

Numerous civil wars, economic and political instability, and governmental corruption all have contributed to the destruction of the DRC's infrastructure, making it difficult to maintain law and order in the country. Armed robbery, theft of vehicles, and carjackings are common in the DRC. Despite the presence of the largest UN peacekeeping operations in the area, the Democratic Republic of the Congo is considered a dangerous, high-crime area. Kinshasa has been rated one of the most dangerous crime cities in Africa. The maintenance of law and order in the country has been a challenge because of the social and political upheaval that has plagued the country for several years. Further compounding the security problem in the country are the civil wars in neighboring countries. Kinshasa's homicide rate is about 12.3 homicides per 100,000. Muggings, robberies, rape, kidnapping, and gang violence occur throughout the country. A recent UN report notes that some of the murders, robberies, rapes, lootings, and arsons are committed by a Rwandan rebel group, the Democratic Forces for the Liberation of Rwanda (FDLR). Many view the FDLR crimes against the civilian population as retribution against the people of the DRC for to the DRC's support of the Rwandan government against the rebel group. The frequent attacks on the civilian population by the rebel groups have left many children orphans, homeless, and street beggars. The Congolese army is also involved in the looting and mass rape of the women.

The DRC is also a major source and destination for women, children, and men trafficked for forced labor, sexual exploitation and child armies. Many of the child victims of human trafficking are orphans and street children whose parents were killed or abandoned them while fleeing the war. Reports by UNICEF indicate that there are approximately 15,000 to 40,000 children, from as young as 3 years to 13 years, in the streets of the Democratic Republic of the Congo. Some of the children are abandoned in the streets because their parents or their church pastors have declared them witches. It is also reported that some of the children are driven away from their homes by their parents to reduce the number of mouths they must feed. The children sometimes join criminal gangs for survival.

The Democratic Republic of the Congo is considered one of the biggest producers of cannabis. However, the cannabis produced in the country is for local consumption only. Money laundering is said not to be a problem because the banking and financial systems are underdeveloped. The maintenance of law and order in the DRC is ineffective because the law enforcement agencies lack the financial, technical, and human resources to carry out their duties. Corruption within the government and law enforcement agencies is also a major limitation against effectiveness. However, the MONUC, the UN peacekeeping force, is mobilizing joint civilian groups to help protect civilians against both rebel and military attacks in war-torn areas. The personnel for the joint civilian protection are drawn from the agencies of civil affairs, child protection, human rights, and political affairs.

Police and Punishment

Political corruption, social and economic injustice, exclusion, poverty, and more than 40 years of conflict and wars in the DRC have greatly affected the well-being of the people and their relationship with the government, especially the police. The police force has been politicized, underfunded, ill-equipped, and ineffective. During the regime of Mobutu Sese Seko, one of the branches of the police charged with investigating crimes was converted by the president and used to witch-hunt his political enemies, for example. The Center Nationale de Documentation (CND), formerly known as the Surete Nationale, had authorization from the president to arrest individuals perceived as enemies of the state without regard to constitutional safeguards. The primary function of the CND changed from that of national police to an outfit for the protection of the president. Political opponents and perceived enemies of the state were implicated by the CND for planning or attempting overthrow of President Mobutu Sese Seko and other treasonable felonies.

One of the agreements reached during the recent inter-Congolese dialogue was the creation and reunification of the republican army and police force. This new force is to be well equipped, trained in new technologies, provided better wages, and devoted to the protection of the people and the nation. To enhance the security of persons and property, the new police force will be well equipped to perform security and intelligence services throughout the nation. They also will be involved in the training of specialized units of the armed forces, police, and security services. Other countries such as Nigeria, Israel, the United States, the United Nations, South Africa, Tanzania, and Uganda have provided training, logistics, and resources to the DRC police force.

The DRC enacted a new constitution in February 2006 that included many provisions to protect human rights. It has, however, failed to amend most of its acts of parliament, which give power to the authorities under the military penal code, allowing for military trials of civilians for several offenses. According to the Constitution, the military tribunal has jurisdiction over army and police personnel and not civilians, and the right to freedom from discrimination on several grounds, including sex, is guaranteed. Yet the failure to amend jurisdiction and control of the military tribunals results in many human rights violations. For instance, the Constitution does not make any reference to the death penalty for a number of offenses, including some against the state, yet scores of people are given death sentences by military courts every year, although no executions have been reported since 2003.

Prison

No information is available on corrections in the DRC. Kinshasa, the capital of the DRC, has several prisons. Some of them function within the authority of the courts and tribunals. The places of detention include prison cells under the authority of courts and tribunals; lockups of the Armed Congelese Forces (FAC) and Congolese National Police (PNC); private prisons of certain authorities that include both civil and military offenders; and prisons of the civil and military police forces. Data from 1997 indicate that in Kinshasa, the Kinshasa Penitentiary and Re-education Centre (CPRK, the Central Prison of Makala) is the only official detention center under the authority of the courts and tribunals. This facility houses both military and civilian prisoners, a procedure adopted with the closure of the military prison at Ndolo.

The administration of this facility comes under the Ministry of Justice as well as the Ministry for National Defense. There are about 10 wings, including include one for adolescents and one for women. Though the facility is intended for less than 1,000 inmates, in December 2001, there were an estimated 2,285 civilian and military prisoners. Families can visit detainees every Wednesday, Friday, and Sunday between 10 A.M. and 4 P.M. in all wings with the exception of Wing 1. For Wing 1, visitation is allowed only on Sundays between 12 noon and 3 P.M. Visitation is limited to 10 minutes, but families are allowed to leave food for inmates. Inmates' diet is a serious concern. There are widespread reports of severe malnutrition among the inmate community and, reportedly, a high number suffering from tuberculosis.

The prison of DEMIAP/Central District called "Ouagadougou" is considered one of the most dreaded prisons in the Kinshasa area. It consists of an unfinished multi-storied building with a long corridor containing three narrow cells each measuring 4.5 square meters. Inmates in these cells are subjected to inhumane, cruel, and degrading conditions. The inmates sleep on the ground, in a narrow overpopulated cell with no toilets or other amenities. Rainwater seeps in, and with the heat and stench from stagnant water and no toilets, the conditions are considered inhumane. In addition, prison guards extract money from inmates in exchange for meager food rations. Torture is a common practice, and often, many inmates are kept isolated from any contact with their lawyers or families for months at a time.

O. Oko Elechi and Angela R. Morris

Further Reading

Bedi, S. R. S. (2007). *The Development of Human Rights Law by the Judges of the International Court of Justice.* Hartford, CT: Oxford.

Nelson, Ryan, trans. and ed. (2002). *Prisons in the Democratic Republic of Congo.* Ireland: Refugee Documentation Centre: http://www.unhcr.org/refworld/docid/402d0d764.html.

Onwudiwe, D. I. (2006). "Congo, the Democratic Republic of." In *The World Police Encyclopedia,* edited by Dilip K. Das and Michael J. Palmiotto, pp. 190–195. New York: Routledge.

Congo, Republic of (Congo-Brazzaville)

Legal System: Civil/Customary
Murder: High
Burglary: Low
Corruption: High
Human Trafficking: Medium
Prison Rate: Low
Death Penalty: Yes
Corporal Punishment: Yes

Background

The Republic of Congo, also referred to as Congo-Brazzaville or Congo, is located in Central Africa, bordering Cameroon, Central African Republic, Gabon, the province of Cabinda, the Democratic Republic of Congo, and the Gulf of Guinea. In 1960, after gaining independence from France, the nation's government experimented with the ideas of Marxism. In 1992, after Marxist theories were deserted, a democratic government took office. The democratic government lasted until 1997, when a civil war broke out in Congo. This ultimately led to a period of ethnic and political unrest.

The legal system is based on French civil law and African customary law. In general, the French legal system has developed through several stages, resulting in a blend of both an accusatorial system and an inquisitorial system. Two codes were adopted in France at this time: the Code of Criminal Instruction of 1808 and the Penal Code of 1810. The penal code resulted in a list of definable offense and reforms, including stiffening of punishment for recidivists, parole, and probation, which were used to accommodate the new penal code. Since this time, new reforms have taken the place of the Code of Criminal Instruction, which was replaced by the Code of Penal Procedure. In 1992, a new penal code was established, taking effect in 1994. The new penal code kept the three-part distinction of crime that France had established—crimes, misdemeanors, and violations—and also addressed new issues within the legal system, including new types of crimes.

The security forces in the Republic of Congo include the police, the gendarmerie, and the armed forces. However, the distinction between the three is ambiguous. The police are tasked with maintaining internal control mainly in cities, whereas the gendarmerie focuses its efforts outside cities. A primary and important task for police is to provide election security, whereas the military is responsible for external security. In theory, the police should be the first to respond to incidents, with gendarmes and army units intervening later on, if necessary. How the police forces are divided also remains unclear. The Congo government is unclear not only about how the police are organized, but also about its strength in numbers.

A police officer from the village of Loukolela, Republic of Congo, northeast of Brazzaville, confiscates a knife from a Hutu refugee, who arrived after crossing the Congo River by canoe. Loukolela hosts 6,250 Rwandan Hutus who fled across Congo fearing attacks from Laurent Kabila's Tutsi-led army. (AP Photo/Jean-Marc Bouju)

Estimates suggest that there are currently about 70,000 to 100,000. What is known is that police forces and the military often have operations that overlap and are generally not effective. Since the civil war in 1997, new recruits have mainly come from nongovernmental militias. One of the most infamous groups of security forces are the "Cobra" militiamen under control of President Sassou-Nguesso. The Cobras have been responsible for numerous killings of unarmed civilians believed to be supporters of the Ninjas, former prime minister Bernard Kolela's militia. In 1998, forces considered loyal to President Sassou-Nguesso reportedly killed more than 100 unarmed civilians and raped numerous women.

Moreover, Congo's military is made up of the Congolese Armed Forces (Forces Armees Congolaises, FAC), which includes the army, navy, Congolese Air Force (Armee de l'Air Congolaise), gendarmerie, and Special Presidential Security Guard (GSSP) (2008). Manpower available for military operations is approximately 842,771 for males ages 16 through 49 (2008). As of 2007, women were not allowed to serve. The army remains weak and could again collapse quickly if faced with a serious threat. Although most former belligerents now form the transitional government and formally support the new army, they and their ex-soldiers sometimes ignore orders from the military hierarchy that they consider to be in conflict with the interests of their respective factions. Indeed, the reluctance to move forward with reform in many security structures is a deliberate strategy on the part of the leaders who fought the 1998–2002 war to preserve their ability to respond with force if the elections do not turn out to their satisfaction.

Beating civilians and detainees and raping women is a norm for security forces in the Republic of Congo. In practice, security forces sometimes use beatings as punishment and to gain a confession. Female detainees are often raped. Other acts by the security forces in Congo include beating citizens and stealing from their homes and extorting travelers for money at checkpoints. Often times, no action is taken against the security forces. In 2001, a survey was conducted of 2,000 persons. Of the 81 percent that had contact with the police, more than 65 percent were dissatisfied with the treatment.

Crime

The classification of crime in the Republic of Congo follows the French classification. Under the French Penal Law and Penal Procedure, there are three classifications of offenses: crime, misdemeanors, and violations. These offenses are classified according to their seriousness. For crimes and misdemeanors, a distinction is made between completed and attempted acts. Under the classification of crime, there are three different distinctions: attacks against persons, attacks against property, and attacks against public security. Attacks against persons include crimes such as murder, assassination, infanticide, intentional violence (nonintentional death), and rape. Attacks against property include robbery, theft, and breach of trust, and attacks against public security include counterfeiting. Under the penal code, crimes can draw a 20-year sentence, misdemeanors receive 5 years, and violations receive 2 years. Typically, though, sentence length is 10 years for crimes, 3 years for misdemeanors, and 1 year for violations. The age of criminal responsibility is 18 years of age.

Between the civil war, the problems surrounding the Lissouba-Sassou-Nguesso rivalry, and the security forces, the Republic of Congo has its share of crimes. After attempts to contact numerous officials on the crime status in Congo, one anthropologist, Bruce Whitehouse, stated that the only significant crimes perpetrated in the Republic of Congo since their independence have been those perpetrated by the state, or at least by individuals and networks operating within the apparatus of the state. Whitehouse further goes on to state that according to a Web site (http://www.mwinda.org) run by the political opposition in exile, the newest problem in the Republic of Congo is "operateurs economiques vereux." This means that people in power receive high government contracts but never do any actual work. "Shadow businesses" are being designated on paper, but no actual enterprise is receiving the contracts. In 2005, Transparency International in its survey of Corruption Perceptions Index ranked Congo 130 out of 159 countries surveyed (the higher the rating, the worse the corruption). There were media reports of government bribery and corruption, particularly regarding oil revenues and mismanagement in the government-run diamond industry.

Amnesty International (1999) and the U.S. Department of State (2007) both have released reports about the human rights abuses in the Republic of Congo. In 2006, the Bureau of Democracy, Human Rights, and Labor released its Country Report on Human Rights Practices in the Congo. According to the report, although there have been some improvements in Congo's human rights record, it still remains poor because of the numerous crimes begin committed, mainly by the state. Killing of suspected criminals, mob violence, security force beatings, trafficking in persons, lengthy pretrial detentions, and physical abuse of detainees are just 6 of 24 named problems within the Congo.

Besides human rights violations, other crimes that are of a particular challenge to this country include (but are not limited to) rape, burglary, muggings, and drug trafficking and production. According to the United Nations, crimes against women, particularly rape, constitute a disturbing phenomenon. Although widespread, rape is rarely reported. For example, in 1999, more than 1,000 women were raped during the conflict by soldiers and militiaman. This number may be underestimated because it was based on those who came to the Brazzaville hospital for medical attention. Indeed, the International Rescue Committee (IRC) reports that 3,000 rapes were recorded in the capital of Brazzaville following the beginning of the second conflict between the government and militiaman. When rapes are reported, the government does not effectively enforce the law, which prescribes 5 to 10 years for this conduct. In addition, spousal beating is a major problem. Unfortunately, no specific provisions outlaw spousal battery. Domestic violence is typically handled within the extended family.

According to the U.S. State Department's Consular Information Sheet, the Republic of Congo is best known for its nighttime muggings and petty street crime. In addition, carjacking, rape, murder, armed robbery, gang conflicts, taxi wars, vigilantism, and police shootings frequently dominate newspaper headlines. Travel advice for this country warns against walking the streets after dark and urges tourists to use air travel as opposed to road travel. For the latter, road conditions are cited as being generally poor and deteriorating, leaving the road and railway between Brazzaville and Pointe Noire pass a magnet for criminal gangs who continually rob vehicles and trains. For the most part, males disproportionately commit crimes and are disproportionably at risk. For example, 70 percent of all firearm injuries involve males between the ages of 11 and 30. The Public Health Study finds that at least 15 percent of firearm injuries involve youth under the age of 11.

Because of the strategic geographic position and its highly urbanized characteristics, Congo-Brazzaville is an ideal candidate for drug trafficking and production, muggings, and burglaries, as well as gun trafficking. In 2004, the Republic of Congo adopted laws aimed at reducing illicit drug trade. Prior to the adoption of these two new laws, Congo had only two statutes on its books concerning drugs, laws that dated back to colonial times. Specifically, the two previous laws were the 1929 decree prohibiting the cultivation of hemp and its use as a narcotic and the 1932 decree regulating the possession of poisonous substances. Despite the adoption of drug laws, statistical information regarding drug offenses is minimal.

Finding of Guilt

Because the Republic of Congo's legal system is based on French civil law system and customary law, their court proceedings are generally held in the same manner. The Fundamental Act provides for an independent judiciary, but as the Republic of Congo has shown, this judiciary is generally corrupt. The court system within the Republic of Congo is mainly influenced by politics and is also extremely underfinanced and overburdened. Following the civil wars, much of the records and statistics held within the courts were taken, so nothing remains of law books, case decisions, and judicial records. The courts are also suffering from a severe lack of resources. With all of these problems combined, the court systems within the Republic of Congo are extremely poor. Despite this, the Ministry of Justice began to rebuild the court system beginning in 2001. This rebuilding involved a new

"Law Library and Information Center" that was opened to the public.

In general, there are four courts within the Republic: local courts, courts of appeal, traditional courts, and the Supreme Court. Traditional courts are generally designed to handle local disputes, at least within rural areas. Local disputes include property and probate cases and domestic conflicts that cannot be solved by the family. Defendants have some rights that include access to prosecutorial evidence and testimony. They also have the right to counter this evidence and have a lawyer present during questioning. The accused are tried in a public court of law with a state-appointed magistrate presiding over the case. Besides the right to access evidence and testimony, within the formal courts, defendants also have the right to appeal. One of the many issues with the Republic's courts is the legal caseloads, which affect the defendants' rights. The courts are so overburdened with their caseloads that the judiciary cannot provide defendants with the right to a fair and speedy trial. Other rights of the defendant include the right to a self-obtained lawyer or one appointed by the state and the right to compensation if placed in abusive custody.

The process for bringing a suspect to trial can be elaborate, but it depends on the seriousness of the crime. Generally, there are two procedural stages prior to trial, the police stage and the judiciary stage. The police stage involves an investigation being conducted by the police under the supervision of the prosecutor. During this stage, the suspect is held for supervision for 24 hours. This can be lengthened by the authorization of the prosecutor. The accused is allowed to appeal this decision and request release. The proceedings begin when they are initiated by either the public minister (a government official) or the victim. The public minister decides whether the case should be brought before a judge or handled alternatively, whereas the victim can only force the prosecution to take action by filing a civil suit against the accused. Alternatives to trial are not known. If there is doubt in the case, it is handed over to an examining magistrate who has the power to examine the suspect. At this time, the magistrate can interrogate, confront, bring warrants against the suspect, and arrest the suspect and bring him or her before another judicial authority. If the examining magistrate deems necessary, the case is handed over to the public minister for prosecution. Under the French civil law system and customary law, suspects are not allowed to plead guilty; therefore, every accused shall be presumed innocent until proven guilty, which can be established only at the end of the criminal procedure.

It is unclear how the majority of cases within the Republic of Congo are resolved. It is also unclear how many courts and judges operate in the country. With the rampant corruption in the government and the lax legal system, defendants are not likely to receive a fair trial. With the amount of extrajudicial killings and beatings of detainees taking place in the Congo, it seems as though a majority of criminal cases are "resolved" through nonlegal ways.

One special alternative to going to trial or further in the criminal justice system in the Republic of Congo is through the use of bribes. Specifically, the U.S. Department of State reports that bribes generally determine the length of detention. Because arbitrary arrest is a problem in this country, sometimes detainees awaiting trial are released after a bribe is paid and/or after pressure from external sources to release the individual occurs.

The Republic of Congo does not have a separate system for juveniles. It does, however, have special procedures that differ from adult procedures when handling youth. Most of the officials who work in the child justice sector in the Congo-Brazzaville do not know the various requirements that govern children's rights. Consequently, youth rights are often violated. Furthermore, magistrates in the country have been accused of abusing the rights of children. One report found that when being arrested and held in custody, children suffer violence. Also, some of them are held in custody past the legal time-frame of 73 hours and are detained in the same cells as adults.

One of the biggest cases of maltreatment of detainees in the legal system became well known when Amnesty International (2006) released a report about political prisoners being held in the Republic of Congo. In 2005, at least 25 members of the Congolese security forces were stopped in Brazzaville. According to reports, the group was thought to be plotting the overthrow of current President Denis Sassou-Nguesso. Thirteen of those members were put into jail, and the rest were thrown into a prison in Brazzaville. Members were held for seven months without charges or a lawsuit. In March 2006, Amnesty International talked to the prosecutor, who stated that the examining magistrate in the case had concluded that no charges were being retained. But by November 2006, authorities had not released the prisoners.

During their imprisonment, many of the members were subject to acts of torture and other inhumane, degrading treatment. For four months, the members were retained and held in secrecy, without the ability to contact members of their family or lawyers. Some of the members were in bad health and did not receive proper health care, nor adequate amounts of food. Amnesty International has shown interest and worry in the case because as of the time the report was released (December 2006), some of the members still in detention were being denied the right to dispute the charges and their right to speedy and fair trial.

The case of the political prisoners is a typical example of how the legal system in the Republic of Congo works. Wrongful arrests, illegal detentions, and denial of rights are a frequent occurrence, as is the mistreatment of detainees. As the next section details, there are very few options for those who are detained.

Punishment

Detainees are not given all of their rights, and unlawful detention and arbitrary killing are common. Security forces typically disobey the Fundamental Act and do as they please not only with detainees but even with those not accused of any crimes. Security forces frequently use beatings to coerce confessions or to punish detainees. These practices are used both in institutional settings (jails and prison systems) and on the streets (e.g., security forces beat citizens). For females, there have been reports of rape committed on female detainees by security forces. Other typical punishments include fines (either legitimate or through bribery), corporal punishment, public punishments, and banishment from cities.

The Republic of Congo does have the death penalty. Capital offenses punishable by death include burglary, espionage, murder, treason, robbery, arson during riots of national emergencies, and causing disorder. The method of execution is shooting. Executions are generally closed to the public, and there are no available data for the number of executions that have been carried out.

Often times, Sassou-Nguesso will detain persons thought to be friendly to the opposition. Once they are detained, these persons are subjected to long periods of detention, beatings, and in the case of women, rape. Sassou's militia, Cobras, is responsible for numerous killings. People who are thought to be with the opposition and fail to identify themselves with a Cobra unit are blindfolded, ordered to run, and then shot by the Cobras.

Prisons

Prison conditions in the Republic of Congo are extremely poor and obsolete because of a lack of funding and conformity to the international standard for human rights protection. Facilities are extremely overcrowded, and with a lack of resources, the prisons fail to provide food or health care to those inside. According to the most recent data available from the International Centre for Prison Studies, the total prison population averages around 900 inmates (including pretrial detainees and remand prisoners), a mere .22 percent of the overall population. The prison system consists of one central prison located in the capital, Brazzaville, and six smaller prisons located in Djambala, Dolisie, Impfondo, Ouesso, Owando, and Pointe-Noire. The central prison, built in 1938, has an official capacity of 100–200 prisoners but held as many as 502 prisoners in January of 2007, and all seven institutions were reported to be overcrowded in 2006.

Decay, disease, and violence are commonplace within the prison system. Reports from the United Nations Integrated Regional Information

Networks (UNIRIN) attest to the appalling conditions within the prisons. In the central prison, cells designed for four inmates are shared by up to 12 inmates, with men, women, and juveniles confined together. Prison cells are not ventilated, and most do not have windows. Many inmates suffer from malnutrition because inmates receive only one meal a day, usually bread and fish, and have virtually no access to public health care, but some prisons allow inmates to leave prison facilities during the day for medical treatment when paid for by family and relatives. The cells lack running water or toilets, so prisoners often have to relieve themselves on the same floor on which they sleep.

Overcrowding and poor hygiene combine to create prime conditions for disease and violence. Although no hard data are available, reports from the UNIRIN state that the prevalence rates for rape and sexually transmitted diseases, including AIDS, among inmates are high and increasing. Prison officials have little or no means to prevent incidents of violence or to treat inmates who are ill or injured. As part of its effort to stem the spread of AIDS, the government launched an HIV-prevention program in 2006, but there are no data available to evaluate the success of the program.

The Ministry of Justice began attempting to repair the prisons in 2001, but progress has been slow because of a lack of funds. Detainees who do make it into a prison are subject to overcrowding, beatings, extortion, and other cruel treatments. In 2000, a group of prisoners filed a suit against the prison they stayed in for 16 months. The prisoners claimed they were subjected to cruel and inhumane treatment, including torture. Angered by the slow pace of the suit in Pointe Noire, the prisoners took their suit to a Belgian national court.

The state of prisons in the Republic of Congo is extremely poor with little effort being made to fix them. The policies within the prisons are also poor, with women being imprisoned with men and juveniles being held with adults. Those being held as pretrial detainees are also being held in the same place as convicted prisoners. As is the case with much of the other information on the Republic of Congo, little exists on prisons, except regarding the atrocities being committed there.

Kristan Fox and Nicole Reinsch

Further Reading

Amnesty International. (2006). *Congo. Des detenus politiques dans un vide juridique:* http://www.amnesty.org/en/library/asset/AFR22/003/2006/fr/dom-AFR220032006fr.html. Translated by Babel Fish at http://babelfish.altavista.com/babelfish/tr.

Borricand, J. (1996). *World Factbook of Criminal Justice Systems: France:* http://www.ojp.usdoj.gov/bjs/pub/ascii/wfbcjfra.txt.

Frank, J. C. (2008). *The Failure of Democracy in the Republic of Congo.* Boulder, CO: Lynne Rienner Publishers.

French Ministry of Foreign Affairs. (2007). *The French Legal System*: http://www.ambafrance-au.org/france_australie/spip.php?article459.

Pierre, Englebert, and James Ron. (2004). "Primary Commodities and War: Congo: Brazzaville's Ambivalent Resource Curse." *Comparative Politics* 37(1): 61–81.

Côte d'Ivoire. See Ivory Coast

Djibouti

Legal System: Civil/Common/Customary
Murder: Medium
Corruption: Medium
Human Trafficking: Medium
Prison Rate: Low
Death Penalty: No
Corporal Punishment: Yes

Background

Djibouti is located in northeast Africa, across from the Arabian Peninsula and the coast of Yemen on the Horn of Africa. Off of the Red Sea coast, it is bordered by Eritrea, Ethiopia, and Somalia. Djibouti is slightly smaller than the American state of Massachusetts. The capital of Djibouti is also Djibouti, and more than two-thirds of the country's estimated 650,000 inhabitants live there. Djibouti's population is quite youthful, with more than 43 percent below 15 years and about 53 percent of the population between the ages of 15 and 64. Only about 4 percent of Djibouti's population is over 64 years old.

Legal System

Djibouti is largely a multiparty democracy with at least nine major political parties. There are also three branches of government: executive, legislative, and judicial. Its legal system is based primarily on French civil law. However, since breaking with the French in 1977, Djibouti has coupled French civil law with Islamic Law (sharia) and other more localized traditional practices.

The French-inspired legal system in Djibouti is based on both legislative and executive decrees. That is, in terms of French law and judicial practices, crime is dealt with in a court system. Civil actions are similarly brought into the French-adopted style of courts of law and judicial practice.

Islamic law, or sharia, is more restrictive and takes into concern only civil and family matters, like marriages, for example. Based on the Koran and administered by the Qadi (the country's senior Islamic law judge), Islamic law is then concerned primarily with the Muslim peoples. The exception to this rule is that a non-Muslim man may marry a Muslim woman, though only after converting over to Islam.

Finally, traditional law, or Xeer, is believed to predate Islam, although Islam is thought to have influenced this system. Under this system, elders serve as mediators in disputes to help settle matters. Elders use conflict mediation practices and seek compensation for the victims. In the case of murder and rape, elders use their own, more traditional set of stipulations. For example, a traditional stipulation for crimes of murder and/or rape is a blood price for the crime.

Police

Djibouti has multiple policing agencies. These agencies have been largely French-inspired. More recently however, and specifically since 9/11, various U.S. agencies have extended a hand to help with the training of Djibouti's policing agencies. Officers in Djibouti are being trained in such services as motorcade operations, VIP protection, motorcade route analysis, and improvised explosive devices (IED), as well as in illegal immigration, drug interdiction, and antiterrorism.

In terms of actual policing agencies, Djibouti has an estimated 8,000-member National Police Force (FNP). The FNP's responsibilities largely include internal security and border control. They are responsible to and serve directly under the Ministry of Interior. The Gendarmerie Nationale is a separate police force in Djibouti. Serving under the Ministry of Defense, it is primarily responsible for the president's security. Djibouti also has a national army, coast guard, and a navy, all of which serve under the Ministry of Defense. The country has also retained the elite Republican Guard, an independent unit of the Genadarmerie Nationale. The Republican Guard is a small intelligence firm that reports directly to the president of Djibouti.

Although in recent years Djibouti's law enforcement has benefited from the United States and generally from the war on terror, there are still many issues with funding, materials, and not to mention officer training, development, and accountability. The FNP in Djibouti, for example, is underfunded and lacks such amenities as transportation, fuel, and communications technology and equipment. These issues in turn have affected police responsiveness. Another issue has to do with human rights abuses. Some of Djibouti's policing agencies have been known for their brute-force tactics on civilians. Such acts go beyond and are independent of Djibouti's government rules and standards.

Courts

Djibouti's judicial system is based largely on French Napoleonic code. Under this system, laws can be applied only if they are duly promulgated and published officially. Judges or magistrates are encouraged to interpret the law.

Djibouti's legal system is composed of a lower court, court of appeals, and Supreme Court. Only the Supreme Court can overrule the decisions of the two lower courts. Magistrates serving in Djibouti's courts are appointed for lifelong terms. The country is also developing a Constitutional Council, which rules on the constitutionality of laws, including those of human rights and civil liberties.

Crime

Classification of Crime

Crime in Djibouti is classified as follows:

- Crimes against the individual: homicide, rape, robbery, domestic violence, female genital mutilation, and so on.
- Property crimes: theft, burglary, motor vehicle theft, and so on.
- Crimes against the state: terrorism and espionage, and so on.
- Organized crime: drug trafficking, and so on.

Crime Statistics

Although Djibouti lacks accurate crime statistics, it appears that crime is on the rise. INTERPOL data from 1996 and 1998, the most recent available, for Djibouti indicate some results for index crimes such as murder, forcible rape, robbery, aggravated assault, burglary, larceny, and motor vehicle theft. For that period, the total index crimes increased from 138 in 1996 to 219.35 in 1998, an increase of 58.9 percent within two years. More specifically, murder and other individual and property offenses seem to have increased. It must be noted here, however, that such increases in the basic statistics may be a direct result of new recording practices or data-collection techniques in Djibouti over this two-year time frame.

Nevertheless, the incidence of crime in Djibouti compared to the more industrialized countries is generally low. Most crimes in Djibouti range from petty thefts and pick-pocketing to home invasions. Narcotics smuggling and prostitution are also rife. But importantly, more serious crimes such as murder are rare; however, they are increasing in frequency.

Other crimes include drug offenses. Khat is a local drug and popular, but legal in Djibouti, though it is recognized as a source of social problems by UNICEF and other nongovernmental organizations. However one may receive harsh punishments for the trafficking of other drugs, such as heroin, cocaine and alcohol. Although sharia law prohibits and thus punishes for the use and sale of these various substances, there is little known about Djibouti's drug-abuse prevention and treatment activities.

Domestic violence and child trafficking also exist in Djibouti but are rarely reported to the police. Such issues are dealt with within the more traditional clan structure, in the family, or not at all. Specifically in terms of girls and women, it is estimated that many young women from ages 7 to 10 have undergone FGM, or female genital mutilation. An educational campaign on this issue began in 1988 with the Union of Djiboutian Women (UNFD). And after the 1995 UN conference in Cairo Egypt, the UNFD declared that all forms of FGM should be illegal. There is currently a penalty for FGM of up to five years in prison and a fine of US$5,650; however, under this statute there has not been a single documented conviction.

Some crimes in Djibouti do involve third-country nationals (TCNS). That is to say that Djibouti's international borders are fairly open, and thus there are gaps for terrorists and insurgents to use Djibouti either as a haven or as a sort of gateway to Westerners. In particular, Somalia, a country that borders Djibouti to its south, is known for its increasing terrorist and insurgent presence. On October 29, 2008, a coordinated attack on Djibouti took place in the regions of Somaliland and Puntland. Multiple car bombs against local and international targets were set off almost simultaneously.

Finding of Guilt

Preventive Detention

When one is accused of a crime in Djibouti, the law stipulates that he or she cannot be held more than 48 hours without formal charge from a magistrate.

The exception to this rule is when a prosecutor provides prior approval. The accused then may be held for another 24 hours before having to be released.

Rights of the Accused

Upon being accused of a crime, whether it is petty theft or a kind of political or national security offense, the defendant has the right to be informed of his or her crimes and is allowed to contact family members. Once detained, the defendant has the right to also obtain access to an attorney of his or her choice. Djiboutian law also allows arrangements for bail and guarantees an expeditious trial.

Assistance Provided to the Accused

In Djibouti, the accused has the right to legal assistance when he or she cannot afford an attorney and is without any form of optional legal representation. However, there must be proof that the accused cannot afford an attorney.

Investigation

Following French law, the judge is provided with the powers to investigate and obtain evidence that pertains to the accused crime to determine innocence or guilt. Within these powers, the judge has the right to authorize search and arrest warrants. The judge also has the ability to delegate judicial powers to police officials, allowing them to identify suspects and gather information. Based on the evidence gathered and provided by the judge and/or police officials, the prosecutor then decides whether the case is strong enough for criminal prosecution.

The Criminal Court

A total of three judges hear a single court case. One is the presiding judge, and the other two are considered accompanying judges. Judges are formally considered to be magistrates and are appointed to lifelong terms. Defendants, on the other hand, have the presumption of innocence. While being prosecuted, they have the right to access and view the state's or government's evidence. They also have the right to be present during their trial, question witnesses, and appeal if necessary.

According to Djiboutian law, juveniles are to be provided with separate courts, judges, and all accompanying measures, including a social worker who is legally assigned to his or her case.

Under Djiboutian law, crimes are resolved by trial. That is, there are no guilty pleas or plea bargaining on behalf of the defendant. These latter actions are not allowed in Djibouti.

Punishment

Types of Punishment

Guided primarily by French penal code, in Djibouti there are a variety of punishments that may be handed down by the residing court magistrate. These punishments include fines, community service, probation, suspended sentences, suspended sentences coupled with probation or community service, reparations, incarceration, and expulsion. Importantly, various types of crimes also carry different weights of punishment.

- *Homicide:* In Djibouti, the punishment for murder is 30 years of imprisonment. If the murder is premeditated and/or against a public service official, the accused could receive a prison term of life.
- *Rape:* Any form of penetration or blatant rape receives 15 years of imprisonment. If the victim is under the age of 15, is pregnant, or becomes in some form disabled, or a weapon is used during the incident, the punishment is 20 years of imprisonment. If the rape results in the death of the victim, or torture is involved, the punishment is 30 years to life imprisonment.
- *Theft:* Theft is punishable by anywhere from 3 to 30 years' imprisonment, and the accused is required to pay a fine.
- *Drug offenses:* Drug offenses range from 5 years of imprisonment and a fine for sale and consumption to life imprisonment for organizing the production, manufacturing, or transport of illegal drugs.

Prison

Djibouti's prison system is relatively small. Gabode is currently the only known functional prison in Djibouti, and it houses up to as many as 350 inmates at a time. In Gabode, men, women, and juveniles are incarcerated, but they are separated from one another. Women who have children under a certain age (five years) are allowed to have them in prison with them. Once one is found guilty of a crime and sentenced to imprisonment in Djibouti, the prisoner is allowed visitations. However, because of funding issues, there are no known rehabilitation or educational services or courses provided to inmates in Gabode.

Based on a national population of about 650,000, the prison population rate for Djibouti is estimated to be about 61 per 10,000 people. More specifically, Djibouti has an estimated total of four prison-type institutions. But again, only one facility is known to actually contain national prisoners, Gabode. Located in the city of Djibouti, Gabode is designed to house 350 prison inmates at one time in two-by-two-meter cells. In 1999, Gabode had maxed out its prison facility with more than 384 detainees.

The Death Penalty

Djibouti's last execution was in 1977. In fact, there have been no executions since the country's independence. In 1995, Djibouti went as far as abolishing its death penalty when the penal code and code of penal procedure were enacted and enforced. And in 2005 Djibouti became a cosponsor during the 61st UN Commission on Human Rights to abolish the death penalty worldwide.

Joseph D. Johnson

Further Reading

Constitution of Djibouti (1992, September 4). http://www.chr.up.ac.za/hr_docs/constitutions/docs/DjiboutiC%20(english%20summary) (rev).doc.

Reporters without Borders Annual Review 2004: http://www.unhcr.org/cgi-bin/texis/vtx/refworld/rwmain?docid=46e6910816.

UNICEF Funding Proposal: Protection for Children in Especially Difficult Circumstances: http://www.unicef.org/djibouti/french/FUNDING_PROPOSAL_UNICEF_DJIBOUTI.pdf.

United Nations Development Programme (UNDP), Judiciary Country Profiles—Djibouti: http://www.undp-pogar.org/countries/judiciary.asp?cid=4.

Equatorial Guinea

Legal System: Civil/Customary
Murder: High
Corruption: High
Human Trafficking: Medium
Death Penalty: Yes
Corporal Punishment: Maybe

Background

Equatorial Guinea is located on the west coast of Central Africa, bordering Cameroon and Gabon. With an area of 28,050 square kilometers, Equatorial Guinea has an estimated population of 600,000, mostly of Bantu origin. Equatorial Guinea was first discovered by Portuguese explorer Fernando Po and later was ceded by Portugal to Spain in 1778, remaining under Spanish Rule until October 1968. The new constitution mandated that the republic join the United Nations and coordinate assistance with Spain until the nation had become fully "Africanized." The Constitution was later suspended when President Macias assumed power, making law by decree. Even after the second constitution was approved, Macias retained much of this power.

The government is composed of three branches, the executive, legislative, and judicial; however, the president significantly influences the workings of all three branches. The president is the head of state and is elected for a seven-year term by direct universal suffrage and governs through the Council of Ministers. The executive branch is headed by a prime minister, who is the president's appointee and who is the leader of the majority party in the

House. The body responsible for implementing national policy, which is determined by the president, is the Council of Ministers. The president is also responsible for appointing the governors of the seven provinces. The duty of the Council of Ministries is to propose and implement socioeconomic development plans and draft and execute a budget approved by the president and national assembly.

The legislative branch consists of a unicameral parliament. The House of Representatives of the People consists of 80 members who are directly elected by universal suffrage for a five-year tenure.

The judicial branch of government in the republic is organized around the constitutional law that dictates the necessary organization and powers of courts. Article 83 of the Constitution provides for a judicial system independent of the legislative and executive branches, and article 86 declares the Head of the State as first magistrate of the nation who must guarantee the independence of the judiciary. The president appoints the Supreme Court members for five-year terms. The appointments and dismissals of the justice professionals such as judges and the officials of the justice system are outlined in article 91 of the Constitution. The highest court of the judiciary is the Supreme Court of Justice, which hears all matters. The constitutional court is charged with determining whether challenged laws are unconstitutional and hearing appeals against regulations and acts that violate civil liberties provided for in the Constitution. Lastly, the judiciary is tasked with adjudicating matters independent of the executive and legislative branches. The Constitution also provides for many individual rights, including the right to a fair trial, freedom from double jeopardy, and the presumption of innocence. Despite numerous provisions in the Constitution, the judiciary is seriously undermined by flawed practices in the appointment of senior magistrates and a serious lack of resources for the judicial system.

Police

Policing in Equatorial Guinea is split between the police, who are primarily responsible for the urban areas, and the gendarmes, who are charged with patrolling rural areas and special events. A small paramilitary police force called the Civil Guard (Guardia Civil) consists of about 2,000 personnel and is located at Malabo. These personnel are trained in Guardia Civil schools in Spain. The police are both poorly funded and poorly trained. Law enforcement officials continue to extort money from citizens, and impunity remains a problem. Efforts by the government to investigate these allegations of abuse of power are poorly developed.

Arbitrary arrests are significantly increasing in frequency because vigilante groups belonging to the same tribe, Fang, to which the president belongs assist security forces in illegal arrests, detention, and gross violation of human rights. The 2007 Country Report on Human Rights Practices notes that arrest warrants are not a legal requirement in the Equatorial Guinean criminal justice system, and therefore, individuals may be taken into custody based solely on the verbal instructions of police officials. The abuse of prisoners during or immediately after arrest is of particular issue in some police precincts in Equatorial Guinea. There also have been complaints by foreigners of excessive force and harassment by law enforcement during their detention according to the Country Reports on Human Rights Practices of 2008. However, the 2007 Amnesty International report suggests that the number of arrests in 2007 decreased in frequency from the previous year.

Crime

Violent crime is rare; however, the Global Peace Index of 2008 indicates a homicide rate of 2 and a violent crime rate of 2.5 per 100,000 population, respectively. There has been a significant rise in nonviolent street crimes and burglaries in residential areas. The rise in street crime as opposed to violent crime may be partially explained by the large percentage of the population that is minor children.

The unequal rights of males and females in Equatorial Guinea are reflected in the laws that govern it. Rape is illegal in the republic, and yet the criminalization of spousal rape is not provided for in the law. Rape is considered shameful to the families involved, and as such, the number of actual rapes is unknown. This low social status of women puts them at greater risk of domestic violence and wife beatings, occurrences that are not generally prosecuted. The 2007 Country Report on Human Rights states that domestic violence and spousal abuse is illegal but that the government does not effectively enforce such laws, and thus, violence in the home remains a substantial problem.

Human Trafficking

The 2006 Trafficking in Persons Report notes that Equatorial Guinea is primarily a destination country for children trafficked for the purposes of labor and possibly sexual exploitation. The cause of human trafficking relates to the supply of victims generated by a lack of employment opportunities: poverty, discrimination and violence against women, violence against children, government corruption, armed conflict, and political instability. The booming oil economy has generated a large demand in the agricultural and commercial sectors that encourages the trafficking of children from surrounding nations to work in these sectors. The penalties for trafficking in persons for either sexual or other forms of exploitation are 10 to 15 years in prison and a fine of at least $100,000. However, enforcement officials have done little to investigate let alone prosecute cases of trafficking.

There are minimal efforts in Equatorial Guinea to prosecute human trafficking. The government does not train law enforcement in trafficking, and subsequently law enforcement does not investigate trafficking cases. Not only does the Republic of Equatorial Guinea do little to investigate trafficking cases, but it also fails to adequately protect its citizens from trafficking. There are no shelters for women or children where victims can seek assistance. The Republic of Equatorial Guinea does not comply with the current minimum standards for the elimination of trafficking, but the nation is making an effort to do so. An anti-trafficking action plan is aimed at developing shelters, and campaigns are being made to raise awareness for the new legislation concerning trafficking.

Organized Crime

Other enterprises that have either emerged or gained momentum recently include pirate fishing, unsustainable logging, forced labor, and drug trafficking. There is considerable evidence that officials of Equatorial Guinea participate in the trafficking of drugs, and as such, the republic has been labeled a "narco-state," or a nation whose economy is greatly supported by the production or trafficking of drugs. In general, the nations in western Africa fail to personify good governance because of their inability to control corruption or hold the elite accountable. Such governance will not likely reduce organized crime anytime soon.

Finding of Guilt

The court system of the Republic of Equatorial Guinea is based on the Spanish civil law tradition and tribal custom. This court system consists of the Supreme Court of Justice, two appellate courts, lower provincial or first instance courts, military courts, and customary or traditional courts. The administrative levels of the judicial system begin with the president and his judicial advisors and the Supreme Court, and then in descending rank are the appellate courts, chief judges for the different divisions, and local magistrates. The court system generally operates under customary law, but because of a lack of established practice and ill-experienced personnel, the judiciary is a combination of traditional, civil, and military justice, operating in an informal manner. These customary courts are composed of tribal elders who hear mainly civil and minor criminal offenses. Appeals from first instance courts are rare, and tribal law is honored in the formal system only when it is not in conflict with the provisions of national law.

As noted earlier, the Constitution provides for basic individual rights, but although the Constitution may prohibit arbitrary interference in the privacy of an individual, according to the Country Reports on Human Rights Practices 2007, security forces often arrest suspected criminals, foreign nationals, and other individuals without judicial order. The Constitution also calls for the right to an independent judiciary, and the state fails to meet this provision in practice. The judges represent the will of the president, and cases are sometimes decided on political grounds. It is unclear what procedures are in place to hire judges below the Supreme Court, who are appointed by the president. Judges are not well trained, and rampant corruption makes the judicial system ineffective. The opportunity for criminal offenders to have a fair trial that is heard by an impartial and competent adjudicator is not very likely in practice.

There is a serious issue of pretrial detention. As already noted, the police and gendarme are very corrupt, and the law does not require an arrest warrant to detain an individual. Once an individual has been detained, within 72 hours, they have the right to be aware of the reason for their detainment; however, in practice, this requirement is not often met. The stint of incarceration is sometimes much longer before individuals are informed of the charges pending against them. Insufficient judicial process, staff shortages, corruption, and a lack of monitoring result in an estimated 80 percent of incarcerated individuals being pretrial detainees.

Most trials are indeed public, but juries are not often utilized. Defendants have a right to be present in the courtroom, but they do not usually have the opportunity to confer with an attorney prior to trial. Offenders have the opportunity to question witnesses and present their own evidence or witnesses, but again, this seldom happens. Public defenders may be supplied on request for the accused who cannot afford their own representation, but this right is not typically discussed with the defendant. Appeals are not very common, and defense lawyers do not necessarily represent the wishes of their client. The right of due process is often undermined by the highly centralized and corrupt judiciary.

Tribal elders adjudicate minor criminal and civil offenses in the traditional courts in the countryside. Civil judicial matters may be handled outside of a formal court setting. However, there are no known informal means of mediation besides adjudication by tribal elders. Civil cases do not often go to formal adjudication for fear of an impartial trial and a general misunderstanding of the actual process by the populous.

Punishment

The most common form of punishment appears to be imprisonment. The law prohibits torture and any other forms of cruel and degrading punishment of criminal offenders, but the abuse and torture of detained individuals remains a problem in the prison systems. In addition to the elongated pretrial detainment of suspected criminals and their immediate abuse or neglect, substandard conditions in correctional facilities are also common. Equatorial Guinea has the death penalty, and three prisoners were executed in 2007.

Harsh conditions in the correctional facilities are life-threatening, leaving prisoners without food, medical care, water to drink, or a healthy living space. Medical attention is frequently denied to inmates, and family members of prisoners report that the time allotted for visitation with inmates is merely minutes, and prison guards refuse to distribute food care packages. The Country Reports on Human Rights Practices 2007 found that male and female prisoners were not housed in separate facilities. Females are believed to be sexually assaulted by prison authorities and fellow male inmates. Prisoners are also used as laborers in construction for judges and other officials without pay or other means of compensation. The government has made significant improvements in the nation's three main prisons, including the notorious Black Beach prison, as the result of some major renovation projects. Reports of poor sanitary conditions and insufficient provision of food and water decreased sharply in 2007. According to the Country Reports on Human Rights Practices 2007, a law banning torture can partially account for the improvement in the major prisons, including Black Beach.

Juvenile offenders are prohibited by law from being placed in facilities with adult prisoners, although most often juveniles are not imprisoned. Juvenile offenders tend to be detained in local precinct facilities for a short period of time and later released to their homes with a warning.

Jessica Raber

Further Reading

Heilbrunn, J. R. (2007). "Equatorial Guinea and Togo: What Price Repression?" In *Worst of the Worst: Dealing with Repressive and Rogue Nations,* edited by Robert I. Rotberg, pp. 223–249. Cambridge, MA: World Peace Foundation.

Immigration and Refugee Board of Canada. (2001). *Guinea-Bissau: Judiciary Police, including Function, Jurisdiction, Relations with Other Police Forces and Whether Its Members Have Been Implicated in Human Rights Abuses (1993–February 2001):* http://www.unhcr.org/refworld/docid/3df4be374.html.

International Bar Association. (2003). *Equatorial Guinea at the Crossroads.* London: Human Rights Institute, International Bar Association: http://www.ibanet.org/Search/Default.aspx?q=equatorial%20guinea%20at%20the%20cross roads.

UN Human Rights Council. (2008, February 18). *Report of the Working Group on Arbitrary Detention, Addendum: Mission to Equatorial Guinea (8–13 July 2007):* http://www.unhcr.org/refworld/docid/47fddcc92.html.

Wannenberg, G. (2005). "Organised Crime in West Africa." *African Security Review* 14(4): 5–16.

Eritrea

Legal System: Civil/Customary/Islamic
Murder: Medium
Corruption: Medium
Human Trafficking: Medium
Death Penalty: Yes
Corporal Punishment: Yes

Background

Eritrea is a country in East Africa, between Sudan and Djibouti, bordering the Red Sea. It has a population of nearly 5 million people, in nine ethnic groups, with Asmara as its capital. Eritrea achieved full independence in 1993 from Ethiopia, and its Constitution was ratified in 1997. The Constitution provides for an independent judiciary and democratic freedom. However, in reality, the judiciary is very weak and regularly subjected to executive interference. Free elections have yet to occur. They were originally postponed as a result of the devastating two-year war with Ethiopia from 1998 to 2000 but have not occurred since the signing of the peace treaty in 2000.

Eritrea has a transitional government made up of legislative, executive, and judicial branches. The legislative body (described as the supreme representative of the Eritrean people by the Constitution) is the unicameral Transitional National Assembly. It is composed of 150 members, half elected members of the PFDJ and the rest appointed members of the same party. This assembly has not sat since 2002, and elections have been postponed indefinitely.

The executive body is made up of the president and his 19-member cabinet. It has the highest authority between sittings of the national assembly and is accountable to the assembly when it is sitting.

Police

Given the history and the colonial legacy, police organization resembles the military in many aspects, including the titles and ranks. The policing function after independence was primarily performed by the Eritrean Peoples Liberation Front (ELPF). In 1994, as part of the demobilization, many military personnel who became civilians entered the police force, which was primarily responsible for internal security. Eritrea continues to depend on the military, its reserves, and decommissioned personnel to respond to emergencies within the country.

People's Protection Brigades

People's Protection Brigades were a creation of the Derg, the communist military junta that came to power from the mid-1970s to mid-1980s. They performed several key functions, including law enforcement duties such as protection of public property and enforcement of land reforms. They had police powers, which they exercised following a few months of training. They were deployed not only inside Ethiopia but also in the provinces, including Eritrea.

The current Eritrean police force is not only bureaucratized but also militaristic in many aspects. Although the police force carries out the traditional functions of maintaining law and order, investigation of crimes, patrol, and conducting arrest, it is dependent on the military forces in dealing with emergency situations. Members of armed forces committed human rights abuses during the conflict with Ethiopia, and their record has not substantially improved. Under the law, warrants are required for searches, but in practice, the authorities do not obtain warrants.

Capacity-Building for the Police Department

With the support and cooperation of the Netherlands Ministry of Foreign Affairs, bilateral arrangements were made for capacity building for the Police Department during the late 1990s. The forms of this capacity-building included creation of a police training center and various other units found in police organizations around the world. The overall aim was to gear the capacity-building within the framework of the evolution of a multiparty democracy to help Eritrea build a civilian and professional police force to function in a democratic society.

Crime

Reliable statistics are almost impossible to obtain. The country did not even fully participate in the international survey known as the Global Peace Index 2008. Limited information from 1999–2000 INTERPOL data suggests that crime rates per 100,000 population in Eritrea are as follows: murder, 2.77; rape, 1.69; aggravated assault, 10.26; burglary, 5.8; and larceny, 26.37.

Classification of Crimes

All violations of criminal law, together with those of juvenile law, are divided into major categories, examples of which include felonies and misdemeanors. The most familiar distinction in describing crimes in Eritrea is between felonies (or serious crimes) and less serious crimes. The distinction exists to determine not only which courts have jurisdiction over which category but also the nature of punishment or sanctions appropriate for each category. The serious crimes include the following:

1. *Political crimes.* Perhaps the most discernible category of crimes in Eritrea is political crimes. They are both externally and internally induced. The former is associated with the border conflict between Ethiopia and Eritrea, whereas the latter involves warring internal factions, that is, the conflicts between members of the ruling party and the dissidents. The political crimes are serious, deep-rooted, and spread throughout the social fabric.
2. *Rape and other forms of sexual abuse.* It has been estimated that in 2001, 65 percent of women in the capital Asmara were victims of domestic violence, and 95 percent of women had been subjected to genital mutilation. There is no law against genital mutilation, but when the United Nations still operated in Eritrea, it worked with the government to discourage the practice. Prostitution is illegal, but it is a serious problem in the country.
3. *Human trafficking.* Eritrea is among the countries in the Horn of Africa from which human trafficking originates. However, there is little documentation of the extent and forms of this social problem in Eritrea.
4. *Drug trafficking.* The introduction of drug trafficking in the country has been attributed to the new influx of the children of the Eritrean nationals living in North America.

Juvenile Delinquency

There are relatively small numbers of young offenders in Eritrea in its transitional period. Juvenile offenses including gang involvement, sex offending, substance abuse, property theft, and truancy are the social problems that have yet to appear in Eritrea.

Finding of Guilt

After Eritrea achieved independence, the administration of justice commenced provisionally on the basis of the Ethiopian penal code and the criminal procedure code. These codes were amended to reflect Eritrea independence, but the revisions have not yet been fully completed. Some of the difficulties with the Eritrean legal system can be traced back to the rule of Ethiopia. The transitional Eritrean government inherited a weak and under-resourced judicial system with few qualified judges, prosecutors, and lawyers. It has faced a difficult challenge in building a system to effectively administer justice. When the Ethiopians ruled Eritrea, they systematically used detention and torture as well as military trials and executions. This meant that no traditions of judicial independence or legal defense activism were allowed to be established. A judiciary was formed by decree at independence in 1993. It has never disagreed with the government, and constitutional guarantees are ignored in cases related to state security.

The Eritrean Constitution provides for an independent judiciary and democratic freedom and prohibits arbitrary actions on the part of government officials, including those in policing and those in the judiciary and the penal systems. It contrast, it stipulates protections for the citizens. In theory, the judiciary is deemed independent from the executive branch of the government, but in reality, the judiciary is weak and regularly subjected to executive interference. Article 48 of the Constitution stipulates that "in exercising their judicial power, courts shall be free from direction, control and supervision of any person or authority." However, selected elements of this separation of power have been eroded by arbitrary arrests and detention pursuant to suppression of political crimes according to Amnesty International. In addition, influential administrative authorities' practice of reversing or rescinding court decisions for well-connected individuals has been noted.

The country's original (1993) Constitution was also written to endorse basic universal elements found in multiparty democratic countries. Examples of such elements include presumption of innocence until proven guilty in a court of law; formality, or step-by-step official actions starting from arrest until guilt or innocence is proven; right to an attorney or legal counsel; and appeal process upon conviction followed by sentencing; and protection from double jeopardy.

The current Eritrean system is a combination of traditional laws and laws inherited from its colonizers, particularly Ethiopia. It generally follows a civil law system, with some influence from common law. Sharia law also has an influence. The transitional laws of Eritrea incorporate some pre-independence statutes of the EPLF, revised Ethiopian laws, customary laws, and post-independence enacted laws.

There are three sources of law. The Constitution is the most important source of Eritrean law. It has not yet been fully implemented, and full implementation will see authority move from the executive to the legislature. Customary law is not an official source of law but is very important in practice and can be applied by community courts. Sharia law has de facto status as a source of law and is enforced through separate civil courts.

The Eritrean judicial system has three parts: civilian, military, and special courts. All parts of the system suffer from a lack of trained personnel, inadequate funding, and poor infrastructure. This makes it difficult for the state to grant a fair or a quick trial. However, the low recorded crime rate has allowed the judicial system to function with relatively few delays.

The Supreme Court is the apex court, with high courts serving as the appellate courts and subordinate courts, which have responsibility for initial trials as well as summary jurisdiction over the less serious crimes. The normal court of first instance is known as the Zoba court, or the community court. Community courts have a one-magistrate bench system, filled by elected magistrates. Magistrates have no legal training and base their decisions on local custom. The court operates at both a regional and a subregional level. Decisions of the Zoba court can be appealed to the high court. The high court also functions as a court of first instance in some of the most serious cases, such as murder, rape, and serious felonies. It consists of a panel of three judges and includes a bench that functions as a Supreme Court. Military courts have jurisdiction over penal cases brought against members of the armed forces. They assume jurisdiction over crimes committed by and against members of the armed forces.

Because the Eritrean population is largely rural, most citizens have contact with the legal system only through traditional village courts. Village judges hear civil cases and minor infractions, and trained magistrates hear criminal cases. These community courts have potential to introduce restorative justice, a concept that is becoming popular worldwide, including parts of Africa such as South Africa. Maintaining law and order or simply social order through these courts provides opportunities and challenges in serving social justice in the rural areas. These courts also continue to make justice accessible at minimum financial costs. Further, they continue to provide an opportunity for resolution not only of the legal issues but also of the social issues subsumed under antisocial (or deviant) behavior (e.g., violation of ethnic traditions, customs, and norms). There is a consensus among observers that most petty offenses continue to be adjudicated by the local elders in their traditional village courts. Examples of such offenses include land and property disputes and marriage disputes, including abduction of girls to induce grounds for marriage. The Ministry of Justice also holds training in informal dispute resolution to handle some petty criminal cases.

Defendants in the civilian court system have access to legal counsel, usually at their own expense. Although there is no formal public defender's office, the government has requested that attorneys work without fees to represent defendants without money who are charged with very serious offenses. In 1996, however, the government established special courts. The stated rationale for these was that there was a significant backlog in the civilian court system, caused primarily by the drafting of many civilians into the army. The government also considered that existing courts were too lenient in corruption cases.

Special courts prohibit legal defense counsel and the right of appeal. The hearings are held in private and decisions are not reported. They allow the executive to mete out punishment without due process. Judges in special courts are military officers without formal legal training; they are expected to base their decisions on "conscience." Judges are appointed directly by the head of state, and there are no requirements regarding competence or judicial training. There is no limitation on the punishment that special courts can impose. The special courts have jurisdiction over such offenses as capital offenses, felonies, and large-scale tax evasion and also have the right to reopen cases already processed through the regular criminal justice system. Trials are summary. As well as the lack of opportunity to present a full defense, there is a lack of judicial independence and impartiality.

Special courts were set up as a temporary measure, but there is no sign that they will cease to operate. They operate in a separate jurisdiction not under the control of the chief justice and fail to meet international fair-trial standards. Special courts have been responsible for violations of human rights, in particular failing to protect the rights not to be tortured or unlawfully detained. They hand down prison sentences in summary trials without legal representation or the right to appeal.

This continued use of an executive-directed special court system allows ongoing executive interference with the judicial process. Amnesty International has called for the abolition of the special court.

There are problems in the infrastructure of the courts, both civilian and special. For example, the key court personnel such as prosecutors and judges lack formal legal education and training; funding is limited; and there are court delays. Other related court problems include the crumbling physical infrastructure, facilities, and equipment; lack of housing for court judges; and use of temporary buildings commonly called containers.

Eritrea has embarked on judicial reform as one of the national agendas. Several specific aspects of this reform include crash training programs for members of the judiciary to replace their Ethiopian counterparts, promoting education of a new cadre of judges, replacing archaic infrastructure and facilities, performing procedural assessments, and building judicial associations or work groups.

Punishment

The categorization of the prisons in Eritrea is less discernible than in Ethiopia. That is, prisons are not identified as maximum-security prisons, medium-security prisons, and minimum-security prisons. However, references are made to regular prisons, military prisons, and underground prison cells.

The punishment of offenders is affected by the legacy of Eritrea's rule by Ethiopia, and the subsequent war between the two countries. In 2000, Eritrea detained between 10,000 and 20,000 Ethiopians as prisoners of war, scheduled for deportation and repatriation.

Amnesty International visited a prison in 1999 and reported that conditions appeared to meet international standards. There have, however, been no reports of international NGOs visiting Eritrean prisons subsequent to that date. The International Red Cross has been refused access to the prisons. In addition, prisoners are warned not to discuss prison conditions after release, so accurate information is hard to obtain. All the indications are that prison conditions are difficult. The government permits three visits a week by family members. Women and men are held separately, but there are no juvenile facilities, so children are held with adults. Pretrial detainees are held alongside convicted prisoners.

It is known that religious and political prisoners are held in harsh conditions amounting to cruel, inhumane, and degrading treatment. Many are held in metal shipping containers that are overcrowded, lacking in sanitary facilities, and subject to extreme temperatures. Medical treatment is virtually nonexistent, and prisoners are taken to hospital only when they are near death.

The transitional penal code prohibits torture, but many observers believe that police have resorted to torture and physical beatings of prisoners during interrogation. This torture is not applied solely to those suspected or convicted of criminal involvement; draft evaders and deserters have been arrested and sometimes tortured as well. Government opponents, supporters of opposition groups, and religious prisoners have been tortured.

Arbitrary arrest, often for political reasons, and punishment are also relatively common. Although the penal code specifies a limit of 30 days for those held without charge, in practice, the authorities do sometimes hold people (including Ethiopians, Sudanese nationals, members of opposition groups, and Jehovah's Witnesses) for much longer.

Juvenile justice in Eritrea is in its formative years. These formative forms of juvenile justice are exemplified by the official recognition of the need to take action against juvenile offenders even though no separate juvenile law and juvenile institutions exist. Amnesty International has made investigation into their treatment in adult institutions. Being housed in adult prisons means that juvenile offenders are subjected to the same poor prison conditions whose descriptions appear in the reports of Amnesty International. The death penalty has been effectively suspended since independence in 1993, although it remains as an optional penalty for homicide and treason.

Brian Stout and Ejakait (J. S. E.) Opolot

Further Reading

Kebbede, G. (1992). *The State and Development in Ethiopia.* London: Humanities Press.

Keller, E. (1995). "Remaking the Ethiopian State" In *Collapsed States: The Disintegration and Restoration of Legitimate Authority,* edited by I. W. Zartman, pp. 125–142. Boulder, CO: Lynne Rienner, 1995.

Ethiopia

Legal System: Civil/Customary
Murder: Medium
Corruption: Medium
Prison Rate: Medium
Death Penalty: Yes
Corporal Punishment: No

Background

Ethiopia is a diverse country with an approximate population of 75.1 million, located in eastern Africa. Ethiopia's first legal code, the Fetha Nagast (Law of Kings), is attributed to a 13th-century Egyptian Coptic scholar and was translated into the language of ancient Ethiopia around the 15th century.

The Fetha Nagast combined elements of the Old and New Testaments, Roman emperor Justinian's civil law, early Christian canons, and the Koran. It addressed ecclesiastical and secular law, family law, property law, and public law. The Fetha Nagast was an important first step in the development of the Ethiopian legal system. However, the Fetha Nagast applied only to Christian Ethiopians; Muslims who came under Ethiopian rule were subject to Islamic sharia law.

The Fetha Nagast remained the basis for criminal procedure in Ethiopia well into the 20th century. It was not until 1930 that Emperor Haile Selassie established the first penal code, which defined offenses and prescribed punishments. Increasing interaction between Ethiopia and the rest of the world, however, made it clear that Ethiopia still appeared backward by comparison. The creation of a constitution in 1931 was one attempt at proving that Ethiopia was taking its place among modern nations. Prior to 1931, there had existed a sophisticated unwritten traditional constitution, and tribal judges had possessed complete discretion to render decisions based on their own concept of justice. There had been no conformity from one tribal court to the next. A written constitution served to bring Ethiopia into an era of continuity across the legal system.

By the 1950s, the social and political climate of Ethiopia had changed so dramatically that the 1931 Constitution and penal code were outdated. In 1945, Ethiopia became a founding member of the United Nations. This new alliance brought more opportunities for the introduction of Western ideas. As a result of the changing social situation in Ethiopia, and perhaps because of international pressure, Emperor Haile Selassie revised the Constitution in 1955 and the penal code in 1957.

The revised Constitution expanded on concepts introduced in the 1931 Constitution and introduced entirely new concepts. It outlined the rights of the accused, delineated the functions of parliament, and established the independence of the judiciary. Separation of power between the legislative, executive, and judicial branches was also strengthened.

Emperor Haile Selassie directed the revision under the stated purpose of bringing it up to date with Ethiopia's social progress; however, some speculated that his motives were not so magnanimous. The first 36 articles of the revised Constitution concerned the imperial throne and the rights thereof. The emperor was declared sovereign and his election divine, based on a bloodline tracing back to King Solomon of Israel. The throne would remain attached to the bloodline of Haile Selassie, and only direct male descendents could succeed him. Despite a thin veil of new rights for the people, the powers vested in the emperor by the 1955 Constitution were so extensive that they made Haile Selassie, and those who succeeded him, absolute monarchs.

In 1961, a criminal procedures code drafted by a British scholar introduced English common law into the Ethiopian legal system. The code detailed minimum and maximum punishments for each offense and emphasized the concepts of culpability, willingness to accept responsibility for one's actions, and mitigating or aggravating circumstances.

In 1974, a socialist military regime known as the Derg deposed Haile Selassie and assumed control of the government. Under the Derg and Chairman Lt. Col. Mengistu Haile Mariam, the penal code was amended to reflect socialist philosophy. The code was revised to include the death penalty for antirevolutionary activities, and new laws were applied ex post facto to previous officials. In 1981, the code was revised again to include a new category: economic crimes. Economic crimes were actions in conflict with the socialist state: food hoarding, overcharging, damaging public property, or interfering with the production or distribution of goods.

In 1987, a decade into its rule, the Derg ratified a constitution that ended military rule and provided for a civilian government. Although the layout of the government changed on paper, little changed in practice. The old Derg officials were still in charge, with new titles. Critics claimed that the new Constitution did little to address the needs of Ethiopians as a people or as individuals. It was instead a manifesto affirming the socialist principles of the Derg, much of which was taken almost verbatim from the 1977 Soviet Constitution.

In the late 1980s, insurrections, droughts, and famine eventually brought about the Derg's collapse. In

1991, the Ethiopian People's Revolutionary Democratic Front (EPRDF) advanced on the capital city, Addis Ababa. Members of the Derg, including Mengistu, fled the country. The EPRDF established a transitional government and instituted a charter that functioned as a transitional constitution. Meles Zenawi assumed the role of interim president during the transitional period. Under his leadership, the Constitution of 1994 was ratified, and in August 1995, Ethiopia became the Federal Democratic Republic of Ethiopia. The same year, Ethiopia held its first-ever multiparty election.

Ethiopia's legal codes have been rewritten numerous times, with each version reflecting the current ruler's ideals and purposes. As a result, the current Constitution is still in its infancy. In the decade since the Constitution was drafted, Ethiopia has worked to decentralize government power and give more authority to individual states. In addition to returning the government to the hands of the people, decentralization serves as a guard against the resurgence of the monarchical and despotic rule Ethiopia has experienced in the past.

Police and Courts

Ethiopia has a federal police force, established by the 1994 Constitution. However, because bribery and corruption are widespread in the Ethiopian police force, it has faced serious challenges in establishing legitimacy. Further, decades of bloody political coups have blurred the lines between national security, public order, and general criminal activity. The lack of distinction between political crimes and other criminal acts means the police have become embroiled in volatile political situations. This has resulted in accusations of human rights violations, including the use of torture, massacres of protesters, and political disappearances. The government is working to increase the level of human rights and constitutional law training among members of the police force, but it has a long way to go before the police force reaches a level of professionalism befitting a modern, industrialized country.

The 1994 Constitution provides for two formal court systems: a three-tiered federal court and regional courts, which are arranged in the same three-tiered design as the federal courts. The Constitution also legitimizes customary and religious courts. Ethiopians may consult customary or religious courts in personal or family matters, if both parties agree to this arrangement. Muslim citizens may consult sharia courts, as well. Customary and religious courts handle minor personal disputes that would otherwise bog down the formal court system and are therefore an important part of the criminal justice system.

Crime

The criminal code defines a range of criminal offenses, including offenses against the person, property offenses, moral offenses, technological crimes, and political offenses. The code also contains a number of progressive inclusions, such as penalties for human trafficking and female circumcision. Crimes are classified based on the nature of the offense and whether the offender poses a future danger to society. The less serious offenses are generally punished with reprimand, probation, fines, fines converted to labor, or simple imprisonment, whereas grave offenses are punished by imprisonment, up to life imprisonment, or death. If an individual is found criminally responsible, the court will calculate the penalty taking into account the individual's guilt, disposition, education level, and personal circumstances, as well as the seriousness of the crime.

Those who commit criminal offenses are also categorized by age. Children who have not reached 9 years of age cannot be held criminally responsible for their actions. Youth between the ages of 9 and 15 may be held criminally liable for their actions but do not face adult penalties. Offenders who are older than age 15 but younger than age 18 are tried as adults under the provisions of the criminal code. However, in these cases the court can take into consideration the nature of the crime and the offender's age and, based on these considerations, may sentence the offender to a penalty applicable to young persons. Penalties applicable to young persons include reprimand,

The Federal Supreme Court building in Addis Ababa, Ethiopia. (AP Photo/Anthony Michell)

fines, probation, school or home arrest, admission to a curative or corrective institution, or incarceration in an adult facility where they will be segregated from adult offenders. Youth offenders who are mentally ill or addicted to alcohol or narcotics may be sent to a curative institution, which provides medical care as well as education or training when possible.

Crime Rates and Trends

The International Criminal Police Organization (INTERPOL) crime data for the year 2000 revealed the following rates of crime reported to police per 100,000 persons: homicide, 5.48; rape, 1.12; robbery, 5.01; aggravated assault, 71.61; burglary, 1.79; larceny, 28.92; and motor vehicle theft, 2.06. The combined rate for all offenses was 115.99 per 100,000 persons.

Examination of crime trends shows that there have been increases and decreases depending on the crime in question. INTERPOL data for the years 1995 to 2000 reveal that crime rates have increased for rape, aggravated assault, and motor vehicle theft. However, crime rates have decreased for homicide, robbery, burglary, and larceny. Overall, the crime rate in Ethiopia decreased 6.0 percent between the years 1995 and 2000.

Ethiopia faces crimes of an international nature such as human trafficking, drug trafficking, terrorism, and violations of human rights. It has been found that underage girls have been sent abroad as well as used in urban areas of Ethiopia as child prostitutes. Women have been trafficked for sexual purposes and forced labor. Economic crisis is thought to be a driving force for the trafficking of women and children, given that poor and uneducated children and women may be enticed or forced into labor or prostitution within the country or abroad.

Although Ethiopia is not a major player in the international drug trade, it is situated along major transit routes for narcotics. The United Nations Office on Drugs and Crime Prevention (UNDCP) conducted a study in 1998 that revealed that although Ethiopians were not consuming hard drugs such as heroin and cocaine, there was an increase in the use of khat, cannabis, and inhalants such as glues and solvents. These increases have been most prominent among women and youth. To respond to the problem, Ethiopia has a Counter-Narcotics Unit that works to interdict drugs and traffickers specifically at the Bole International Airport. Although this unit does what it can to suppress trafficking within Ethiopia, financial restraints cause Ethiopia to rely on other countries such as the United States and Germany as well as the United Nations to combat drug trafficking.

As for its role in combating terrorism, Ethiopia's National Intelligence and Security Service (NISS) is responsible for managing counterterrorism efforts. Federal and local law enforcement focus on responding to terrorist events when and if they occur. The 2005 criminal code criminalized financial crimes such as money laundering so as to prevent terrorists from using Ethiopian financial networks to finance their operations. Further, Ethiopia is in the process of drafting its own counterterrorism legislation and also actively participates in the African Union and its efforts to combat terrorism.

Finding of Guilt

The 1994 Constitution of Ethiopia details the protections provided for persons accused of crimes. It guarantees that arrestees will be promptly informed of the charges against them and receive an explanation of those charges before a court, if desired. Arrestees must be informed that they have a right to remain silent and that self-incriminating statements may be used against them. Appearance before the court must be prompt, within 48 hours of arrest. A special exclusion is provided for the reasonable time it takes to transport the accused to the court because in remote areas of Ethiopia, one is likely to encounter mountains, marshlands, or deserts that would greatly impede travel. Bail is also a constitutionally guaranteed right, except when the court determines that no amount of bail will protect society or ensure appearance in court.

The 1994 Constitution also contains trial rights. The accused is presumed innocent until the court determines guilt. The accused has the right to discovery of the evidence against him or her and must be given adequate time to review the evidence and prepare a defense. The Constitution guarantees the right to defense counsel, and in the case of indigents, the court must provide defense at its own expense. Public trials are also a guarantee, except in cases where the safety of those involved is at risk. However, as a general rule, the right to a public trial is of great constitutional importance, and only the gravest circumstances warrant an exception.

There is no jury system in Ethiopia. Instead, prosecution and defense argue their case before a panel of judges. A finding of guilt is determined by a majority vote, and the criminal code is consulted to determine appropriate punishment. Finally, the accused has the right to appeal his or her verdict to a higher court.

Punishment

Conditions in Ethiopia's prisons are said to be less than favorable. Human rights organizations have criticized the country for what they believe is inhumane treatment of prisoners. In the past, prisoners were said to be subjected to beatings, unsanitary conditions, exhausting work, overcrowding, and political propaganda. Further, there were few recreational or rehabilitative opportunities.

Although capital punishment is an option in Ethiopia, the death penalty may be used only for grave offenses such as homicide, genocide, and attacks on the political or territorial integrity of the state. Generally, the method of execution is firing squad. Although the death penalty is an option for some crimes, there have only been two executions carried out since 1998, the most recent occurring in 2007.

Finally, international human rights organizations such as Amnesty International and Human Rights Watch point out that although Ethiopia is moving forward in recognizing human rights, there are still problems to confront, such as police brutality, illegal detention, inhumane prison conditions, and the use of torture and the death penalty. For these reasons, Ethiopia remains under scrutiny by human rights organizations and international governmental groups such as the European Union.

Ashley G. Blackburn and Meredith Matthews

Further Reading

Criminal Code of the Federal Democratic Republic of Ethiopia. (2004). International Labour Organization—NATLX Web site: http://www.ilo.org/dyn/natlex/docs/ELECTRONIC/70993/75092/F1429731028/ETH70993.pdf.

Library of Congress. (2005). "Country Profile: Ethiopia": http://memory.loc.gov/frd/cs/profiles/Ethiopia.pdf.

Nahum, Fasil. (1997). *Constitution for a Nation of Nations: The Ethiopian Prospect.* Lawrenceville, NJ: Red Sea Press.

Tiba, Firew Kebede. (2007). "The Mengistu Genocide Trial in Ethiopia." *Journal of International Criminal Justice* 5: 513–528.

Gabon

Legal System: Civil
Murder: High
Corruption: Medium
Human Trafficking: Medium
Prison Rate: Medium
Death Penalty: Yes

Background

Gabon is a country near the equator in western Africa bordered by Equatorial Guinea to the north, Cameroon Republic to the south, the People's Republic of Congo to the east, and the Gulf of Guinea to the west. The CIA country profile lists Gabon's current population at 1,454,867. Gabon officially became an independent republic on August 17, 1960, but the French influence has continued to modern-day Gabon.

That influence is evident in Gabon's legal system, in that the contemporary civil law and customary law are highly influenced by the French civil law system. Gabon's civil court system has three tiers: the trial courts, the appellate courts, and the Supreme Court. Additionally, there are three courts (judicial, administrative, and accounts) in the Supreme Court, each serving different functions. A constitutional court was also established in 1991, to deal with constitutional issues. National legislation on civil, criminal, and social matters, is maintained by the laws that either were in place and inherited by French colonization or that have been modified to take care of customary laws.

The police in Gabon consist of two groups: the national police, who fall under the control of the Interior Ministry, and the gendarmerie, who work under the Defense Ministry. Exact numbers of police officers are not available, but the national police and gendarmerie, along with the army, navy, and air force, make up a military of approximately 5,000 personnel. The Overseas Security Advisory Council (OSAC) reported in 2007 that Gabon's police infrastructure is inadequate to deal with the country's crime problem, and police assistance for visitors can be expected to be "minimal at best." Police corruption is also alleged, and it is possible that a criminal can be released and never charged—for the right price. Military and police checkpoints are also used randomly throughout the country. The officers at these checkpoints often wind up extorting bribes from individuals who cannot provide requested documentation. In addition to the gendarmerie and national police, there is also an elite, heavily armed unit called the Republican Guard. This unit is tasked with the job of protecting the president.

Crime

In Gabon, the minimum age for criminal responsibility is 13. Although Gabon's justice system is based on the French civil law system, and there can be an assumption that Gabon's crime classification is also influenced by France's crime classifications, one of the shortcomings to researching limited data sources is that there is no direct mention of exactly how the distinction is made between serious and minor crimes.

A wide array of crimes are committed in Gabon. The OSAC notes that petty theft is widely reported. Gabonese criminals commit crimes when the opportunity is right, often preying on those with visible valuables or going after victims who are weak, drunk, or unfamiliar with their surroundings. Violent crimes also occur in Gabon, more often around bigger cities such as Libreville, the capital. Possibly the greatest threat to the public's safety are motor vehicles. OSAC warns travelers of the poor driving skills of average Gabonese drivers who have little regard for traffic laws and drive at high speeds.

Current crime statistics for Gabon are unavailable. The 1996 INTERPOL report provided crime data for some categories. The rate was 105 per 100,000 population for rape; 125 for robbery; and 114 for motor vehicle theft. For murder, the rate in 1996 was not reported, but recent data collected by the WHO indicate that the level is high.

One crime that is of particular challenge to the country is that of human trafficking, especially with children. Children from Benin, Nigeria, Togo, Guinea, Sierra Leone, Burkina Faso, and Cameroon are trafficked to Gabon, usually by boat, for the purpose of forced labor. Young boys are trafficked for forced street hawking and forced labor in workshops, and girls are trafficked for market vending, forced restaurant labor, and domestic servitude. Despite the problem of child trafficking, the Gabonese government does not appear to be making efforts to battle it. Although Gabon does not fully comply with the minimum standards to eliminate human trafficking, efforts toward progress were initiated in 2004. A law passed in 2004 prohibits child trafficking and calls for a punishment of 5 to 15 years' imprisonment with a \$20,000–\$40,000 fine. Gabon has also prohibited child trafficking for the purpose of sexual exploitation. No trafficking convictions were reported within the last year, and there are only 12 to 20 trafficking cases currently in the judicial system. Data from the U.S. Department of State report show that from February 2007 to January 2008, there were 16 female suspected traffickers awaiting trial; three escaped, eight went to trial, and the remaining were released because they needed to care for their children. The report also noted that the government had assigned two judges for two-year terms to work exclusively on trafficking cases.

Another crime challenging Gabon is poaching. About 85 percent of the land is forest, with a tropical climate that makes it one of the most hospitable territories for wildlife. Poaching of elephants, lowland gorillas, and mandrils continues to be a problem. In 2002, Gabon set aside 10 percent of its land for the purpose of establishing national parks with no poaching allowed. Unfortunately, there is no way to keep the animals safe once they wander outside of the park boundaries. According to one report, there were an estimated 4,000 forest elephants in the national parks in 2005. One year later, that number had already dwindled to 3,000. Despite government efforts to stop the illegal poaching of animals, it is still a profitable crime and continues today.

Finding of Guilt

Although the Constitution prohibits torture or cruel punishment, Gabonese security forces still occasionally engage in human right violations. Suspects and prisoners are often beaten and subjected to mistreatment to obtain confessions. The Constitution also prohibits arbitrary arrest and detention; however, the government does not observe such prohibitions. The law states that the police have 48 hours of initial preventive detention, and during that time, police must charge a detainee before a judge. Police do not often respect this law.

If there is to be an ongoing investigation, bail can be set for the prisoner. Pretrial detainees have a right to free access to their attorneys and a speedy trial, a right that is practiced and respected. Pretrial detention cannot exceed more than six months for a misdemeanor and a year for felony charges.

Although some minor disputes may wind up going before a local area chief, the state does not officially recognize such decisions. Procedural safeguards during the trial phase are still lacking, and there have been reported instances where the presiding judge has delivered an immediate verdict of guilt at the initial hearing, if the state presents sufficient evidence.

Gabon has been consistently working to strengthen its national system of human rights promotion and protection. The Ministry of the Advancement of Women and Child Protection, the National Human Rights Commission, the National Observatory on the Rights of the Child, and the National Observatory for Women's Rights and Equality, among others, have all been established to ensure that the rights of Gabonese citizens, including children, women, and the handicapped, are respected.

Punishment

On September 13, 2007, the Gabonese government decided to abolish the death penalty. This was a request by President Omar bongo Ondimba, who was seeking to stop the death penalty because nobody had been executed in over 20 years. Gabon currently has around 2,750 inmates in the country's prison population. Out of the total number of prisoners, approximately 40 percent are considered pretrial detainees or remand prisoners awaiting trial. Statistics were unavailable for the percentage of female prisoners or for the rates of foreign prisoners in Gabon's prison system.

Data are unavailable on the number of prisons and their locations. Some details about the inside of the prisons have been released. Conditions are considered to be life-threatening or harsh, with poor ventilation and sanitation. Food is inadequate for inmates, and medical care is almost nonexistent. With the exception of some rural prisons, detainees are segregated. Accused persons are kept separate from convicted persons, and juveniles are kept apart from adults. Finally, although the government does not impede such visits, there were no known visits by human rights monitors to observe prison conditions during 2001.

Steve Grubbs

Further Reading

Barnes, J. F. (1992). *Gabon: Beyond the Colonial Legacy.* Boulder, CO: Westview Press.

Folefack, E. (2007, October). "The Gabonese Legal System and Legal Research." *GlobaLex:* http://www.nyulawglobal.com/globalex/gabon.htm.

Patt, M. (2008). *Human Trafficking and Modern-Day Slavery: Gabon:* http://www.gvnet.com/humantrafficking/Gabon-2.htm.

Gambia

Legal System: Islamic/Common/Customary
Murder: Medium
Corruption: High
Human Trafficking: High
Prison Rate: Low
Death Penalty: Maybe
Corporal Punishment: Yes

Background

Gambia is located on the west coast of Africa. It is a multiparty democratic republic, having gained independence from Britain in 1965. After independence, it continued to be a member of the commonwealth with a prime minister as its head of government, while being governed under the constitutional monarchy of the British throne. It became a republic in 1970, adopting its own constitution as a sovereign state with an executive president. A new Constitution of the Second Republic came into effect on January 16, 1997. The head of state is an executive president elected by universal adult suffrage. Legislative authority is vested in the national assembly, the members of which serve a five-year term. The assembly is composed of 53 members: 48 are elected, and the remaining 5 are appointed by the president. The president appoints all government cabinet ministers and senior security chiefs.

Legal System

The Gambian judicial system is based on the English common law system, combined with a mixture of customary and Muslim sharia law. The court process is adversarial. Trials are generally public, and defendants generally have the right to a lawyer at their own expense. They also have the right to confront witnesses and challenge evidence presented in their cases. Finally, the accused remains innocent until proven guilty.

The Gambian court structure operates on a two-tier system composed of the superior courts and the lower courts. The superior courts consist of the Supreme Court, which is the highest and final court of appeal in Gambia, with jurisdiction to hear all appeals from the high courts and court of appeal. The court of appeal is the second level of the superior court system. This court hears all appeals arising from cases decided by the high court and the special criminal court. This is followed by the high court, which is the first level of appeal from the lower courts. The court recently created special internal divisions, which are commercial, civil and land, miscellaneous, and family court. And finally, the special criminal court has jurisdiction over all criminal matters.

The subordinate lower courts consist of eight magistrates' courts, the Cadi courts (of the Islamic sharia law), and district tribunals. Most of the magistrates in the magistrates' courts are lawyers by profession. Cases presented before the magistrates' court usually involve a bench trial, in which the magistrate exercises summary jurisdiction. A magistrate can sentence offenders to custodial sentences with hard labor or impose fines on the finding of guilt.

The Cadi courts adjudicate cases relating to the Muslim religion and cover such matters as civil status, marriage, succession, donations, testaments, and guardianship as prescribed by Islamic laws. Before the 1997 Constitution, there were only two Cadi courts, located in the capital region. The 1997 Constitution empowered the chief justice and allowed him to establish a Cadi court anywhere in the country. An ordinary first hearing of the Cadi court is presided over by three members, including a senior Cadi and two qualified Muslim scholars with knowledge of the Sharia law. For review hearings, a Cadi and four other panel members preside.

The district tribunals have jurisdiction to hear less serious criminal and civil matters. They are customary courts headed by a local district chief (*seyfo*), who acts as president, with six or seven other panel members appointed by the Secretary of State for Local Government and Lands. The district tribunal's panel members are usually senior male members of the district who are familiar with local laws and customs. The tribunal's jurisdiction is limited to areas under its geographical command. District tribunals are generally considered the first formal level of adjudication for most rural people.

Police

The Gambian Police Force (GPF) was created by The Police Act of 1949 as amended by Act 5/1988 and comes under the Secretary of State for the Interior. The chief of police is known as the inspector general of police (IGP), a presidential nominee. All other senior ranks are appointed by the IGP through the office of the Secretary of States for the Interior, following the consent of the president.

The recruiting age range for the Gambian police is 18 to 25 years. A recruit is required to have a minimum of a secondary school certificate. There are provisions to appoint people with higher academic qualifications as cadet officer or other senior positions. All such appointments must be approved by the president. Police recruits go through a six-month training at the police training school, located at Yundum, a few kilometers from the capital, Banjul. The training includes physicals, firearms training, and lectures on legal subjects related to the profession.

The Gambian police are made up of about 2,000 sworn officers. The Gambian Police Force rank structure consists of the inspector general of police (IGP), a deputy inspector general (DIG), and 10–20 commissioners of police. Of the remaining senior- and middle-management team, there are at least 15 chief superintendents, 50 superintendents and assistant superintendents of police (ASP) combined, 100 inspectors (including chief inspectors and sub-inspectors), and between 150 and 200 sergeants; the remainder of the force includes corporals, first class constables, constables, and recruits (in training or on probation).

The country is divided into nine police boroughs. The borough commanders are directly answerable to the IGP. A borough commander must have the minimum rank of an assistant superintendent of police (ASP). However, all boroughs are now headed by a police commissioner, who has several police stations under his command. A commissioner of operations based at police headquarters in Banjul, who acts as an operations liaison officer between the borough commanders/commissioners and the IGP, also assists the inspector. All borough commanders are, therefore, expected to coordinate activities with headquarters through the commissioner of operations, which limits their level of discretion in police operational matters.

A police station commander usually bears the rank of an inspector, but a sergeant or corporal may man a smaller station. A station may have fewer than five officers or more than one hundred. Most rural police stations have fewer than 10 officers, whereas the Serekunda police station, Serekunda being the biggest city in Gambia, has up to 200 officers or more.

Crime

Crimes in Gambia are classified into felonies and misdemeanors. Misdemeanor offenses are nonserious offenses and include all minor crimes against a person and property. Felonies include all serious offenses that carry a penalty of up to three years or more. Felonious offenses include homicide, robbery, aggravated assault, aggravated theft, rape, and arson.

Offenses involving actual bodily harm, sexual assault, theft, and serious driving offenses are seriously prosecuted and may involve a custodial sentence. Homosexuality is a felony crime under chapter 5 of the Gambian Criminal Code 1965. Offenses against morality may be punishable by imprisonment for a term of up to 14 years, but no such case has been tried to guilt yet.

The age of criminal responsibility is 18 years. Depending on the nature and seriousness of an offense, crimes can be prosecuted by either the police prosecution unit or the director of public prosecution (DPP). Generally, most cases are prosecuted by the police prosecution unit at the magistrates' court level.

Property theft, minor drug offenses, and petty street crimes, such as pickpocketing, are the most prevalent crimes and account for the most demand on police services. Cannabis or marijuana (*yamba* or *tie* as it is locally known) is the most common drug in Gambia. Most offenses involve the use and trafficking of cannabis. It is illegal to sell or use all common dangerous drugs such as heroin, marijuana, cocaine, and other classes of designer drugs. Penalties for drug offenses can be severe and may include lengthy custodial sentences.

Generally, crime statistics are not readily available. In 1995, the INTERPOL crime data provided the crime rates per 100,000 population as follows: 8 murders; 6 rapes and serious sex offenses; 1,236 larceny thefts; 385 robberies and violent/aggravated thefts; 227 breaking and entering thefts; 331 serious assaults; 55 fraud cases; 300 drug-related offenses; and 4 auto thefts.

The most prevalent crime in the rural areas is cattle rustling, which is constantly reported in the local press. House burglaries are also common. There are also the occasional land-related disputes, most of which are settled at the village *alkalo* or district chief/*seyfo* level.

Petty theft is most prevalent in the urban areas. Gambia is a popular tourist destination for Europeans. The government has demarcated a Tourism Development Area (TDA) that is considered to be one of the safest areas, as it is visibly patrolled by the Army National Guard, with its manned station near a cluster of hotels. Regardless, the TDA attracts petty criminals and tricksters who are involved in the occasional pickpocketing and bag stealing/snatching. Petty drug peddling and the sex industry are also of concern in the TDA, and tourists are known to get in trouble for trying to buy cannabis.

Finding of Guilt

Trials are public, and defendants generally have the right to a lawyer at their own expense. There is no free legal aid system in Gambia. The law requires that there be probable cause to initiate an arrest. Most arrests are post-incident, and a suspect can be arrested and held in custody for up to 72 hours based on a complaint or a report of wrongdoing made to the police.

The Constitution prohibits arbitrary arrest and detention, but the police and other law enforcement units appear to operate with unchecked powers to stop, question, and apprehend a suspect with or without a warrant. The police, army, and National Intelligence Agency (NIA) are known to arbitrarily arrest and detain people. The Constitution requires that arrested subjects be charged and brought to court within 72 hours, but this is not generally observed, especially with political and security-related detainees. Arbitrary arrest and detentions are frequently reported in the local and international press. Such claims can also be verified from former detainees, especially political detainees. Generally, in most ordinary cases, detainees are granted access to family members and a lawyer or are allowed bail.

The Constitution provides for an independent judiciary, but in reality, most cases are subject to several forms of executive pressure. The Constitution provides for a fair trial, but the courts are known to be overloaded with work and lack the capacity to handle the demand.

The police prosecution unit would normally lead on and prosecute all minor offenses at the magistrates' court level. The police are required to charge and bring an accused before the court within 72 hours. There is the presumption of innocence until proven guilty. The police are required to send copies of all prosecutable offenses to the DPP for legal advice. The DPP has the discretion to remand cases back to the police, with legal advice and instructions for the police to prosecute. The police prosecutor, just like the office of the DPP, has some discretion in either bringing formal charges against a suspect or dropping all charges.

An alternate dispute resolution (ADR) facility has recently been set up as an annexed court to provide an alternative form of dispute resolution, which is recognized within the court system. However, in Gambia, dispute resolution exists in both the formal judicial structure and the traditional system. At the village and family level, for instance, such methods as negotiation, mediation, and dispute resolution are used as an alternate to avoid government involvement in what many consider family matters. Customary law and the Muslim sharia law are still considered by many as alternatives, though they are now incorporated as part of the formal legal system. Customary law is designed for non-Muslims to cover marriage and divorce, inheritance, land tenure, tribal and clan leadership, and other traditional and social relations, whereas the sharia law deals with Muslim marriage and divorce matters.

Several petty crimes are also settled informally, post-incident and arrest, but before any formal charges are made. Even within the urban and capital regions, most petty crimes do not go to trial. Only serious criminals are fingerprinted. Arrest bookings usually entail nothing more than a subject's name, his or her address (usually the name of a neighborhood or compound owner), and a brief detail of the offense for which the person was arrested. For instance, in a typical case of home burglary or simple assault, the victim may be satisfied with recovering lost property and have no interest in pressing charges after the suspect has spent a few days in a local police cell. In some cases, especially where the suspect is locally known (perhaps a delinquent juvenile or a known repeat petty criminal offender), family members could mediate by appealing to the victim, who would in turn go to the police or the village head (*alkalo* or chief) to pardon the offender. Police generally tend to drop charges in cases where the victim has recovered his or her property, and there is no further interest to pursue the case by either the police or the victim.

The Children's Act of 2005 was passed to protect the welfare of children, and a children's court has now been set up in Kanifing, which is completely devoted to juvenile cases. The act covers the issues of adoption, custody, maintenance, parentage, and special and criminal cases affecting children, except for the offense of treason where the child is jointly charged with adults. During 2007 several criminal cases were heard regarding rape and abuse of children. However, there were no reported convictions.

Punishment

The death penalty was abolished in 1993 by the previous government but was reinstated in the 1997 Constitution with a provision for the national assembly to review its desirability within 10 years of the introduction of the new Constitution. There have been no known executions; all murder and treason convictions are generally commuted to life imprisonment, which the Constitution clearly made provisions for in section 18(2) (the protection of right to life).

Rape is a crime under the law, and a person who has carnal relations with a girl younger than 16 years is guilty of a statutory felony, which is punishable by a custodial sentence. Gambia is a predominantly Muslim country, which allows the practice of polygamy; however, incest is a crime. The police tend to treat crimes such as domestic violence as incidents outside of their ordinary jurisdiction, and thus rape within the confines of a marriage is rarely heard of. Rape is punishable with a custodial sentence. Punishment for such offenses as theft, burglary, and robbery usually involve a custodial sentence depending on the nature and value of the property involved.

Prisons

Gambia does not keep up-to-date and accurate statistics of its prison population. Gambia prisons have a total capacity of about 780 inmates. Mile 2 Central Prison has capacity for 500, Jeshwang for 200, and Janjanburay for 80. There are about 250 prison wardens altogether. In 2002, the Gambian Prisons Department reported 450 people in prison, including pretrial detainees. Prison statistics are treated with some level of secrecy; therefore, the current figures can only be estimated in relation to the total capacity.

The Prisons Act required the separation of prisoners based on sex and conviction status. Section 36 of the act specifically required separating prisoners by age and separating first-time offenders from recidivists, as well as those on remand from those already convicted. However, the prisons are generally separated into sections for male, female, remand, and security detainees. The Security Wing is known to house a mix of all classes of prisoners, including political prisoners and convicted murderers.

There are three prisons in Gambia, all of which were built during the colonial period or just after independence. The three prisons, as listed previously, are Mile 2 Central Prison, located on the island of the capital city of Banjul, with a capacity for 500 inmates and housing mainly felony convicts and political and remand prisoners; Jeshwang Prison, located in the suburb of Serekunda (the biggest town in Gambia) and with capacity for 200 inmates, who are generally deemed to be of less security importance; and Janjanburay Prison located in the Central River Division, with a capacity of 80 inmates and which typically holds convicts from the rural areas who are considered to be of no or minimal security threat, as well as temporarily remanded security prisoners awaiting transfer to Mile 2 Central Prison.

The central prison at Mile 2 has an official capacity for 500 inmates. It is located exactly two miles from the center of the capital city of Banjul. The only ways off of the main island of Banjul are by ferry or small boat or through the guarded Denton Bridge. All regular ferry and motor crossing points are guarded by armed officer.

Prisoners serving time with hard labor sentences work anywhere within or outside the precincts of their place of confinement. Non–hard labor prisoners, as well as female prisoners, engage in productive activities within their prison of confinement only. Prisoners are supposed to be involved in learning vocational skills, such as carpentry, but there is little to no evidence to suggest that this is in practice because of the lack of resources. Jeshwang prisoners are known to be involved in some poultry farming, and Janjanburay prisoners are known to work on rice and millet fields. The produce from these fields is used to feed the prisoners.

Section 21 of the Prisons Act recognizes the rights of prisoners to have visitors. Prisoners are generally allowed family or private visits according to their conviction status. Most prisoners are allowed one visit a month; however, some get only one visit for every three months. Prisoners can be allowed emergency visits, but this has to be approved by the head of the prison. Visits can last from 15 minutes to an hour. Appointed members of the Prisons Committee are known to occasionally visit prisoners. The Red Cross and other international human rights groups are also occasionally allowed to visit prisoners.

Pa Musa Jobarteh

Further Reading

Constitution of the Republic of the Gambia. (1997). http://www.ncce.gm/files/constitution.pdf.

The Gambia Police Force Five Year Strategy Development Plan 2002–2007. (2002). Draft. Banjul, Gambia: Police Headquarters.

The Point. (n.d.). Online newspaper with a column on the courts that reports cases and decisions: http://www.thepoint.gm/index.html.

Ghana

Legal System: Common/Customary
Murder: Medium
Corruption: Medium
Human Trafficking: Medium
Prison Rate: Low
Death Penalty: Yes
Corporal Punishment: Yes

Background

Ghana is a West African multiethnic nation of more than 24 million people covering 92,000 square miles. Divided into 10 administrative regions, Ghana became a multiparty democracy in January 1993, after years of political instability, especially 12 years of military rule. Ghana's current criminal justice system was first introduced by the British in 1844 when they signed an agreement with eight coastal chiefs of the present-day Central Region of Ghana under which the chiefs relinquished their powers to the British, especially their ancient political and judicial powers to try cases and deal with offenders. The sources of law in Ghana are the 1992 Constitution, legislation, existing law, common law, and native law. Ghanaian law distinguishes between adults and juveniles. A juvenile in Ghana is a person under 17 years of age. The law forbids detention without due process, deprivation of property without due process, and enslavement of any kind.

Criminal Justice System

Ghana's current criminal justice system consists of the Ghana Judicial Service, the Ghana Police Service, and the Ghana Prisons Service. Through these institutions, the Ghanaian society investigates, identifies, accuses, tries, convicts, punishes, and "rehabilitates" those who break the law. The department of the attorney general (AG) and police prosecutors prosecute all criminal cases in Ghana except for homicide and very high-profile cases. The police arrest, investigate, charge, and prosecute most of the criminal cases/offenses in Ghana. Each criminal justice institution has its own personnel selection criteria, training schemes, and career prospects. All the justices of the courts are trained lawyers. Legal education in Ghana is strenuous and expensive. Following the English tradition, lawyers are not permitted to advertise their services, and the media cannot comment on any substantive case before a court of law.

Crime

Crime in Ghana is usually grouped into three broad categories. These are offenses against the person, offenses against property, and offenses against public order, health, and morality. Offenses against the person include murder, manslaughter, threatening, causing harm, assault, abortion, infanticide, rape, defilement, child stealing, slavery and slave dealing, criminal libel, insulting behavior, and attempted suicide. Offenses against property include arson, criminal damage, larceny theft, burglary, and pickpocketing and trust offenses such as fraud, dishonestly receiving, extortion, embezzlement, and swindling. Offenses against public order, health, and morality relate to state or national security, public health and morality, and treason.

Police reports from the Ghana Police Service suggest that among the three broad offense categories, offenses against the person account for 48 percent, followed by offenses against property at 44 percent, and offenses against public order, health, and morality at 8 percent. Most criminal offenses recorded by the police are nonserious or misdemeanors.

Specific crime rates per 100,000 population in 2000 were 448.42 assaults, 2.48 murders, 6.85 rapes, 2.15 robberies, 1.3 burglaries, and 0.08 larceny thefts. In 2002, there were 459 homicide cases, and between January and June 2003, there were 211 homicide cases recorded. During the same period, there were 11,121 cases of threatening; 44,422 assault; 87 rape; 4,920 causing damage; 490 defilement; and 5,508 fraud. In 2006, all the major offenses declined except defilement (sexual assault of a minor), which rose 29 percent, from 428 to 552 cases, and rape, which rose 15.2 percent, from 145 to 167 cases. One growing crime in Ghana is narcotic offenses. Both locals and foreigners arrested for narcotic offenses, including cocaine, methamphetamine, hashish, LSD, and marijuana, as well as organized crime and fraud involving locals and foreigners from the West African subregion have increased recently.

Most offenders in Ghana, 99.7 percent, are young adult males, between 18 and 37 years. Fifty-six percent of the offenders are single and unemployed. Most offenders either do not possess any educational qualification or possess only an elementary school certificate.

Ghana's police headquarters in Accra, where two 16-year-old British girls were being held on suspicion of drug trafficking, July 12, 2007. The two girls from London were allegedly carrying $600,000 worth of cocaine when they were stopped by Ghanian drug officials at the Accra airport. (AP Photo/Kouame Adou)

Finding of Guilt

In Ghana, a distinction is often made between the formal court system introduced by England after 1844 and the informal court system that existed before English colonization. The judiciary has expanded profoundly over the years. There are more than 300 courts of all levels and jurisdictions and more than 430 judges to dispense fair and impartial justice. Ghanaian courts adhere strictly to precedence and follow the common law accusatorial tradition. Ghana's current court system is made up of the Superior Court of Judicature and the lower courts. The Superior Court includes the Supreme Court, Court of Appeal, High Court, and regional tribunals. The Supreme Court consists of the chief justice and no fewer than nine justices, all appointed by the president of Ghana on the advice of Ghana's Council of State and, in the case of the chief justice, approved by Ghana's parliament. The Supreme Court is the highest and final court of appeal in Ghana. The Court of Appeal hears appeals from the High Court and the lower courts. The High Court hears civil and criminal cases. All the Supreme Court justices do not sit at once on a case. The chief justice, the chief executive officer of the Ghana Judicial Service, either presides or empanels a number of the justices, usually five, to decide on a case. Any dissatisfied party or parties may then appeal to the entire justices for a full hearing.

Subordinate to the Superior Court of Judicature are the lower courts whose judges are appointed by the chief justice. Most criminal offenses and civil cases are handled by these lower courts. Plea bargains and grand juries are not utilized in Ghana, but jury trial is guaranteed, especially in murder trials. Murder trials begin at the lower courts before committal to the High Court. Punishment for murder is death, but Ghana has been a de facto abolitionist nation since 1993. By law, suspects and those appearing before the courts have a right to an attorney. Most of the courts are in the urban areas, although over 70 percent of Ghanaians live in the countryside. Consequently, most of the rural residents resort to the native courts for justice or resolution of disputes.

The Native/Customary Court

The native court, also variously called the customary, traditional, chiefs', or informal court, operates under the local (village/town/traditional) chief or ruler and deals primarily with chieftaincy and land disputes, as well as summary offenses such as petty thefts and assault, especially in areas without court and police coverage. Every Ghanaian city, town, and village has a native court. The highest customary court is the Judicial and Arbitration Division of the National House of Chiefs (comprising all the paramount chiefs, heads of the ethnic groups of Ghana) in Kumasi. Each region has its own regional judicial and arbitration court. The native court is nonaccusatorial. Attorney representation is not necessary. Except at the national and regional levels, proceedings of the native courts are not recorded, and statistics of cases pending or adjudicated are not kept. Moreover, the native court cannot order arrest or incarcerate anyone who appears or refuses to appear before it. Rather, the court seeks to maintain communal solidarity through mediation and conciliation. The formal courts have often referred and deferred cases to the native courts. As well, the formal courts have sought the expertise of the native courts on specific matters and issues.

Police

The Ghana Police Service (GPS), with headquarters in Accra, is the sole law and order enforcement agency in Ghana. The head of the GPS is the inspector general of police (IGP). The GPS has several specialized departments, including the Criminal Investigations Department (CID) formed in 1921, the Intelligence and Professional Standards Bureau, the Strategic Direction and Monitoring Department, the Armored Division, and departments of special services, operations, motor traffic, services, welfare, finance, human resources, and legal services. In 2006, a new unit, the Domestic Violence and Victim Support Unit (DOVVSU), was created to assist women and children victims of domestic violence.

Between 1966 and 1969, 1972 and 1979, and 1981 and 1992, the police forged a political alliance with the Ghana Armed Forces to overthrow the lawfully elected civilian governments of Ghana and established police-cum-military administrations to rule the country. Even so, the relation between the police and the military has been one of love and hate. In 1974, the GPS became a self-accounting institution (Police Force Decree, NRCD, 303). Consequently, new and improved service conditions and new units, regions, divisions, and districts were implemented or created. The GPS is a member of several international associations and organizations, including INTERPOL, and has conducted numerous peacekeeping duties and operations; it has also offered technical and training assistance programs to Afghanistan, Bosnia, Cambodia, Kosovo, Liberia, and Sierra Leone.

For law enforcement purposes, the GPS divides Ghana into 12 regional commands, 51 divisions, 179 districts, and over 651 police stations and posts across Ghana. The GPS has undergone tremendous changes since its inception. From the first 120-member Gold Coast Militia and Police (GCMP) to guard the English castles, investigate crimes, and serve summons, the GPS currently has over 18,000 personnel. The police-to-civilian ratio is 1:1,200. The functions of the GPS include crime detection and prevention, apprehension and prosecution of offenders, maintenance of law and order, and the due enforcement of the law (1970, Police Service Act, Act 350).

The highest policy-making body of the GPS is the Police Council, chaired by the vice president of the Republic of Ghana and made up of representatives of some identifiable professional groups and bodies, such as the Ghana Bar Association, as well as individuals appointed by the president of Ghana. The Police Council regulates in the areas of recruitment; promotions; personnel ranks; uniforms; conditions of service, including salaries, pension, gratuities, allowances, authority, and powers of commanders; and code of ethics and discipline and other areas that will ensure the smooth and effective administration of the police. The council also advises the president of Ghana on internal security, budgeting and finance, administration, and promotion above the rank of assistant commissioner of police. Each region has its own regional police council, chaired by the regional minister. As well, each district of Ghana has its own council chaired by the district chief executive.

Among the challenges facing the police in the 21st century are increased violent armed robberies, home invasions, larceny theft, and domestic violence; proliferation of transnational crimes; local and international criminal gangs; "contract" killings; local and international illegal narcotic/drug smuggling and use; laws on intellectual property and piracy; poaching; money laundering; and crowd control. Some of the difficulties facing the police include inadequate and obsolete equipments and accoutrement, poor data and poor criminal record keeping, slow and sloppy investigations, and insufficient and oftentimes unqualified personnel. Widespread cases of bribery and corruption are but two negative activities that continue to tarnish the image of the GPS in the eyes of the Ghanaian public. Real and perceived cases of bribery and corruption have often led to violent confrontations between members of the GPS and sections of the public, which sometimes have resulted in the killing of police personnel. Mistrust of police among Ghanaians is rather profound. The mistrust has oftentimes led to lynching of suspects when police were perceived as not doing their job. As well, increased incidents of police misconduct, such as assaults, both physical and sexual, and sometimes killing of innocent people, are among the concerns expressed by the citizenry and human rights groups and activists. The GPS is currently underfunded and ill-equipped to deal with the crime problem and other challenges facing contemporary Ghana. Several towns and villages do not have a police station or law enforcement presence. Despite these shortcomings, the GPS vigorously maintains law and order by apprehending and prosecuting criminals.

Prison

The Ghana Prisons Service, with headquarters in Accra, receives into lawful custody all adult offenders committed to prison, as well as all the juvenile offenders committed to the Ghana Borstal Institution

(GBI). The current prison system was first introduced by the British after the 1844 agreement. The Prisons Service used to be part of the Ghana Police Service before it was separated in the 1920s. The head of the service is the director-general of prisons, appointed by the president of Ghana on the advice of the Council of State (1992 Constitution, articles 206 and 207). The highest policy-making body of the Prisons Service is the Prisons Council chaired by the vice president of the Republic of Ghana and made up of nominees from various identifiable professional bodies and organizations and individuals appointed by the president of Ghana. The Ghana Prisons Service currently employs over 4,600 people. Most officers perform guard and escort duties. Prison personnel have participated in international assignments and training programs in Liberia, Sierra Leone, and Afghanistan.

There are 47 prisons or correctional facilities, seven of which are female prisons. Almost every prison has a remand block within it. Thirty-four prisons, including all the female prisons, are walled, 2 are camp-prisons, 10 are farmstead prisons, and 1 is a contagious diseases camp. All the female prisons are attached to male prisons, except the largest female prison in Ghana, the Nsawam Female Prison. Of the male prisons, 6 are maximum-security; 1, Nsawam, is medium-security; and 25 are minimum-security. Most of the prisons, including the Kumasi Central Prison (1904) and the Sekondi Central Prison (1905), were built between 1904 and 1930. Few new prisons have been constructed since the 1960s. The Ghana Prisons Service also operates the only correctional facility in Ghana for juveniles between 17 and 21, the Ghana Borstal Institution (GBI).

The Ghana Prisons Service places little emphasis on offender classification because of the nature and conditions of the prison buildings and chronic overcrowding. Only death row inmates and remands are separated from the general population. Offenders sentenced to "Imprisonment Hard Labor" (IHL) are required to work unless declared unfit by a medical officer. Work detail includes farming and poultry, construction, mechanics, laundry, and other menial work. Only a few adult prisoners and the Borstal inmates attend classes to receive formal education or vocational training. By law, every prison inmate has the right to receive visitation from relatives, social workers, friends, philanthropists, and religious leaders. Churches and faith-based groups play a vital role in prisoner welfare in Ghana. Thus, groups and individuals visit, counsel, feed, clothe, and provide medication to several needy prisoners in Ghana daily. Prison Visiting Committees, assigned medical officers, public officials, and human rights groups also visit the prisons frequently to ensure that safe and humane conditions prevail.

The average daily prison population of Ghanaian prisons is in excess of 13,800, of which 98.2 percent are males; 4,218 are remands awaiting trials, and 700 are foreign nationals from over 25 African, European, and the Far Eastern countries. Ghana and Nigeria have frequently exchanged convicted prisoners. Prisoner transfer/exchange negotiations under which the exchanged prisoners complete their sentences in their native countries are ongoing with other West African countries. Most female prisoners were convicted of assault, larceny theft, fraud, or drug/narcotic offenses. Sentences of the female offenders range from six months to life. Ghana has never executed any female offender; female death sentences are always commuted to life. Female prisons are neater, and the conditions are generally better than in the male prisons. Sentences of the male prisoners range from one month of imprisonment to death. More than 70 percent of the convicted male offenders are in prison for less than four years. More than 64 percent of all the offenders are recidivists, having been convicted at least once previously. The Ghanaian prison population is young; more than 98 percent of the offenders are younger than 50 years of age. Ghanaian prisons are notoriously overcrowded. To reduce overcrowding and the negative effects of incarceration, the government has frequently granted amnesty to certain categories of offenders, mostly first and second offenders, as well as nonviolent offenders who have served over half of their sentences. The level of HIV/AIDS among inmates is unknown because of the absence of thorough and periodic medical examinations of the inmates. However, 31 of the 118 deaths reported by the service in 2006 were classified as HIV/AIDS-related. The Ghana Prisons Service is at a crossroads. Many accomplishments have been achieved over the years in the areas of personnel recruitment and improved conditions of service, but there remains a lot to be done.

Outside of the criminal justice system, the Ministry of Employment and Social Welfare operates industrial homes for boys in Accra in Greater Accra, in Swedru in the Central region, and in Jakobu in the Ashanti region for boys and for girls in Kumasi in the Ashanti region, as well as detention centers for juveniles under 17 of both sexes in Accra, Sekondi, Cape Coast, and Kumasi.

Joseph Appiahene-Gyamfi

Further Reading

The Constitution of the Republic of Ghana. (1992). Tema: Ghana Publishing Corporation.

Harvey, William Burnet. (1966). *Law and Social Change in Ghana.* Princeton, NJ: Princeton University Press.

Kimble, David. (1963). *A Political History of Ghana. The Rise of Gold Coast Nationalism 1850–1928.* Oxford, UK: Oxford University Press/Clarendon Press.

Twumasi, Paul Kofi. (1985). *Criminal Law in Ghana.* Tema: Ghana Publishing Corporation.

Guinea

Legal System: Civil/Customary
Murder: High
Corruption: High
Human Trafficking: Medium
Prison Rate: Low
Death Penalty: Yes

Background

Guinea is a country in western Africa with Guinea-Bissau, Senegal, Mali, Côte d'Ivoire, and Liberia as its neighbors. In 2002, its population was 8,444,559, which included refugees and foreign-born residents. The capital city is Conakry, which has a population of 2,000,000. Guinea was a colony of France until 1958, when it gained independence. In 1990, Guinea adopted a new constitution that limited the number of political parties to two and also made it law that the ruling party had a total of five years to establish order in the country prior to the first election.

The Guinean Constitution is known as the Fundamental Law, and it has 96 articles grouped into 12 titles, including Sovereignty, Rights, Fundamental Freedoms and Duties, President of the Republic, National Assembly, Relationship Between the president of the Republic and the National Assembly, Treaties and International Accords, Judicial Power, High Court of Justice, Economic and Social Council, Local Governments, Constitutional Review, and Transitional Provisions.

The Constitution has some very interesting points, including that Guinea will follow the principles of the African Union, the United Nations, and the Universal Declaration of Human Rights. Other interesting inclusions are a separation of governmental powers and 18 specific articles that speak to the duties and rights of all Guinean citizens.

The legislative power in Guinea is held by the National Assembly. Of the 114 members of the assembly, 76 of them are elected from the party's national list and are chosen by a proportional poll. Thirty-eight of the members are elected by a majority system and are drawn from the 33 prefectures and 5 separate communes of Conakry. Each elected member must be at least 25 years old, must be represented by a constituted political party, must be a Guinea citizen by birth or be a naturalized citizen for 10 years, and must have been living in Guinea since being naturalized. Guinea mainly uses an inquisitorial type of legal system. The inquisitorial legal system is characterized by having extensive pretrial interrogations and investigations, with the goal being that no innocent person be tried in a court of law.

Police

The Ministry of Justice and Human Rights has the task of creating rules for the organization, jurisdiction, and operation of correctional services that guarantee human freedoms and ensure the rule of law. The Ministry of Interior and Security has the task of maintaining order, managing internal and external security of the state, protecting the security of people and their property, maintaining public order, preventing terrorism, preventing economic and financial crime, fighting drugs, and fighting organized crime.

Internal security is conducted by the gendarmerie, a part of the Ministry of Defense, and by the national police, which is a part of the Ministry of Security. Although the army is used for external security in most cases, it also may intervene in internal security issues. The Anticrime Brigade, a quasi-police unit used to fight criminal gangs, is used in the capitol of Conakry and in most of the prefectures and regions of Guinea. An interesting fact is that the code of penal procedure states that only the gendarmerie is allowed to arrest people. However, it is well known that the state police, the army, and the Red Berets or Presidential Guard make arrests also.

The 2007 Country Report on Human Rights Practices claimed that the police forces lacked training, were not staffed adequately, had poor administrative controls, and rarely followed the law that they were paid to enforce. The police have also been seen extorting money from citizens at roadblocks and ignoring basic legal procedures. The report also suggested that many citizens viewed the police and security forces as dangerous and ineffective.

In a 2006 study conducted by Human Rights Watch, 35 people, many of them children, were interviewed in Conakry and provided insight into police operations. Many of the individuals complained of torture suffered during the interrogation phase. They told of being severely beaten, abused, burned, bound in painful positions, and hung from a tree. The author of this study has concluded that police torture is commonplace.

Crime

Rape is considered a criminal offense in Guinea, but it is rarely prosecuted because women fear being ostracized and because of social beliefs. Spousal rape is not considered a crime at all, and overall, there are few, if any, prosecutions against rapists. A 2003 study reported that victims of sexual assaults accounted for 20 percent of all female visits to a local hospital. One-half of the victims were young girls, the majority of them knew their attacker, and the crimes took place mainly at schools.

Domestic violence against women is a common issue in Guinea; however, there are no actual statistics to confirm this observation. It is suggested that women fear retribution and stigmatization and rarely report domestic abuse unless it is at a divorce hearing. Beating one's spouse is not specifically prohibited by the law, but assault charges could be filed.

Prostitution is illegal but the law is not enforced. Pimping minors for prostitution is illegal, but the government does nothing when this charge is brought to their attention. Sexual harassment is not against the law; however, the government often speaks negatively about it in the media. Equal treatment from the law is provided for in the Constitution, but women and especially rural women still face discrimination. Typically, men have better divorce settlements than women, and their statements carry more weight in a court of law.

Female genital mutilation (FGM) is illegal. However, it is widely practiced in all regions of Guinea. Underage marriage is illegal, and the legal marriage age is 21 for men and 17 for women. Regardless of the law, underage marriage is allegedly a problem.

Human trafficking is illegal. The U.S. Human Trafficking Report of 2008 concludes that Guinea is a transit point, source, and destination point for human trafficking. It is reported that children, men, and women are trafficked internationally and within the country for illegal labor and for sex. The most common trafficking is taking people from the poorest rural areas in Upper Guinea and then moving them to the urban centers. Children are typically used as labor in diamond mining camps, in agriculture, for prostitution, for domestic work, and for begging.

Another source suggests that many adult and juvenile females are trafficked to Spain, Greece, Nigeria, Côte d'Ivoire, Benin, and Senegal for sexual exploitation and domestic servitude. This report also suggests that women from China are trafficked into

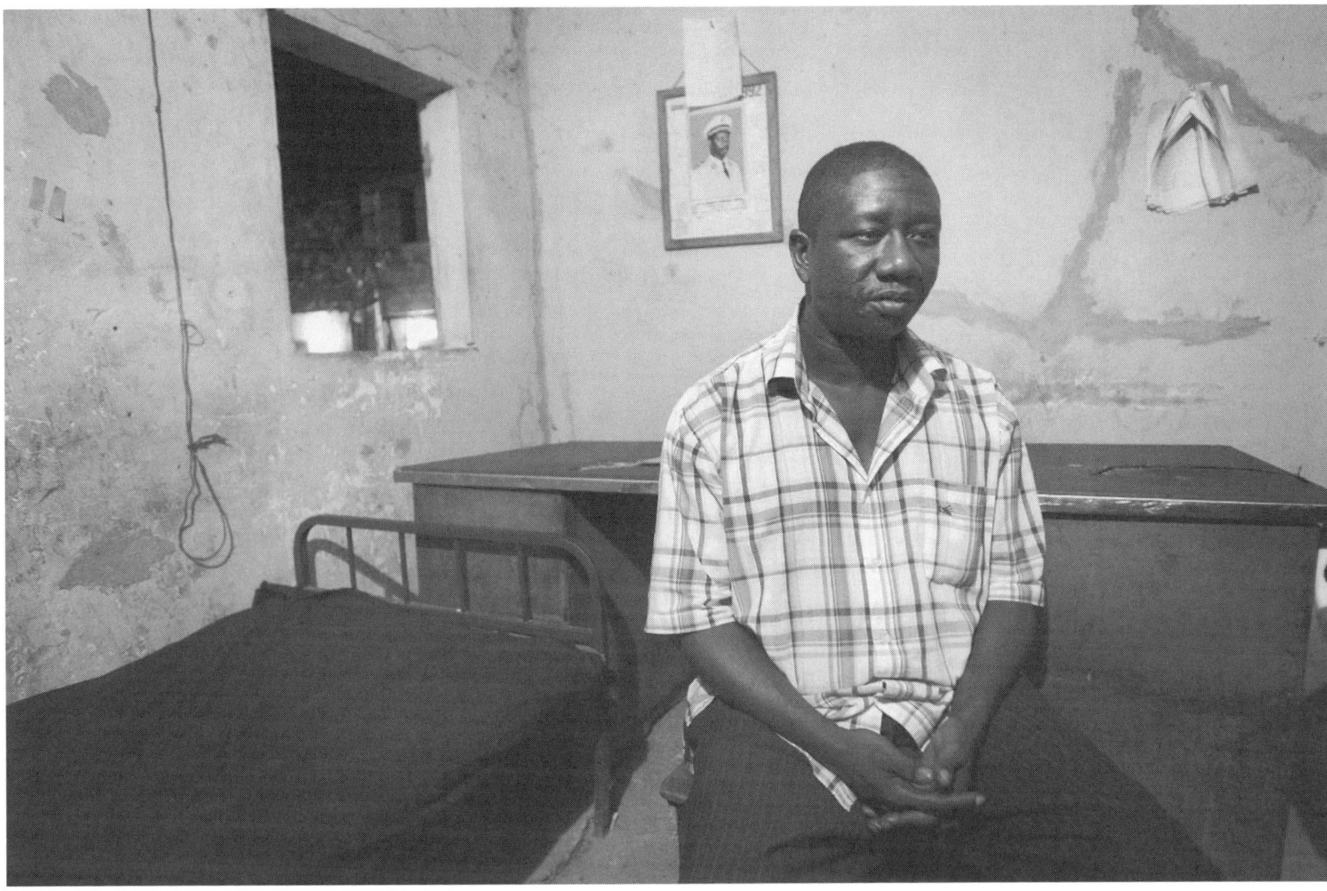

Ousmane Conte, son of Guinea's late President, Lasante Conte, sits in detention in Conakry, Guinea, on March 11, 2008. He admitted in a taped confession that he was in the drug business. (AP Photo/Jerome Delay)

Guinea to be used for sexual exploitation. Lastly, this report concludes that Guinea does not fully comply with minimum expectations for the prevention of trafficking. The country is doing much better than in the past but should pass legislation that would prohibit all forms on trafficking.

Petty street crime is common in Guinea's cities, and the government has imposed a midnight to 6 A.M. curfew as a means to combat it. Along the borders on Sierra Leone and Liberia, banditry has been reported. Criminals have also been reported to target foreign travelers near airports, hotels, traditional markets, and restaurants, often using children to commit the actual crimes. Visitors may receive unsolicited offers of help at hotels and airports from people who are often trying to steal wallets and luggage. The cities of Taouyah, Niger, and Madina are cited as being particular hot spots.

The U.S. State Department suggests that the majority of nonviolent crimes include purse snatching and pickpocketing, and the violent crimes include muggings, assaults, and armed robberies. It is further suggested that the police have not been able to prevent this type of crime and sometimes ask directly or indirectly for bribes when being asked for help. Drugs are an issue in Guinea, which has become a transit point for transnational drug networks.

Business fraud is very prevalent, and the victims are usually foreigners. The common scam is to send unsolicited e-mails to people and companies and promise quick monetary gains. A similar scam is present in legitimate business deals that require payments in advance on large contracts. The business deal might be legitimate, but people who give credit and bank card information sometimes find out that their accounts have been drained of all resources.

Violent crime is increasing in Conakry, the capitol of Guinea, and the nation's economic output has decreased during the past 40 years. Four districts in Conakry have been ruled off-limits to United Nations staff, and life for Guineans who live there is very dangerous because of the large number of firearms held by the residents. With constant power cuts, even walking the streets of Conakry after dark is dangerous.

Refugee camps in Guinea have been used as bases for armed groups and are threats to national security because of the large quantity of small firearms in refugee-populated areas. In 2000, President Conte had more than 450,000 refugees rounded up because he felt that they had caused a wave of violence throughout the country. During this same time, Conte recruited an estimated 7,000–30,000 young Guineans, called Young Volunteers, to push back the refugees. At the same time, Liberia was sponsoring attacks against Guinea, and these attacks usually took place at the refugee camps. As a result, Guinea based numerous militarized groups around the camps to protect the refugees.

Because of the refugee status in Guinea, camp security is probably the largest criminal-justice issue facing Guinea at this time. Inside the camps, the Brigade Mixt (BMS), a mix of gendarmerie and police officers, is charged with camp security. Over 78,000 refugees are distributed over seven camps, Laine, Kouankan, Kola, Nonah, Kuntaya, Telikoro, and Boreah, with an average of 1 BMS guard to every 1,000 refugees, resulting in very little effective security, so that theft, rape, and fistfights are common.

The exchange of sex for food and gifts is widespread in refugee camps. Currently, there are thousands of refugees living in Guinea who are there because they are trying to distance themselves from the war. Furthermore, there have been reports that some UN peacekeepers are to blame for some of the sexual exploitation.

Armed conflicts around Guinea starting in the 1990s have created a heavy financial toll on Guinea. There is a huge cost associated with having several hundred thousand refugees in the country because the military must protect the border and the people, and the government must house and feed the refugees. In turn Guinea's economic growth rate dropped to 2 percent in 2000, which was down from an average of 3.7 percent in 1989–1999.

A result of the Liberian Civil War ending was the 3,800 Young Volunteers who were armed and had not been reintegrated into society, causing huge security concerns in the Forest region of Guinea and concerns that they might be recruited by other armed political organizations.

Crime statistics are hard to find for Guinea. However, NationMaster (2008) has provided some key indicators on how crime and the courts affect business people:

- 1.67 percent of the managers surveyed agreed that crime is a constraint on their business.
- 2.68 percent of the managers surveyed agreed that corruption is a major business constraint.
- 59.01 percent of the managers surveyed agreed that they lack confidence in the courts to uphold property rights.
- 42 percent of the managers surveyed agreed that the courts were a major business constraint.

Finding of Guilt

Human Rights and Legal System

All citizens of Guinea have the following rights guaranteed to them: protection from arbitrary or unlawful deprivation of life; protection from disappearance; protection from torture and other inhumane, cruel, or degrading punishment; protection from arbitrary detention and arrest; the right from to a fair public trial; and freedom from arbitrary interference with home, family, and private correspondence.

Civil and penal proceedings are the two categories of trials in Guinea. Penal cases are designed to protect society from those who threaten it, and civil matters protect public order by applying punishments and seeking a balance between private parties. Penal cases consist of identifying the offender and the application of law. Each court has a unique magistrate charged with gathering all of the facts in the case; this happens during the investigation stage. In some misdemeanor cases, this stage is not even used, and the suspect goes directly to the application of law stage. During the application-of-law stage, every court decision has to be deliberated, and then the sentence can be delivered. The following sentences are then given: a provisional order is given; the suspect is acquitted or released; the suspect is exempt from punishment, such as what happens when the suspect is under 13 years old; a decision of punishment is made, or there is a decision of inadmissibility, in which a case is dropped because the court feels that the case is weak.

Court System

Guinea's court system consists of the Supreme Court, courts of first instance, justices of the peace, the Tribunal of the First Instance, the Second Instance Court, courts for minors, the High Court of Justice, the Court of State Security, the Military Tribunal, tribunals of labor, and the Chamber of Arbitration. Factors such as the crime, a person's age, whether the person has been tried before, and numerous other legalities determine what court a person's case will be assigned to.

The Supreme Court has a first president who is appointed by the president of Guinea. The other members of the Supreme Court are appointed by the president also, and they must retire after they become 65 years old. During their time in the Supreme Court, they cannot be fired at will, but they can be prosecuted for committing a crime.

Ordinary courts, such as the court of first instance, deal with cases for the first time, and the monetary value of the case decides the jurisdiction. Typically, misdemeanors that carry a punishment of up to five years in jail are tried in a court of first instance. Within the courts of first instance, the public prosecutor is in charge of supervising the police officers of the Criminal Investigation Department who investigate cases. The public prosecutor also has to visit police stations as a check and balance against extra long preventive custody and detention. Lastly, the public prosecutor inspects Justices of the peace and makes sure that they are following the correct policies and procedures.

The Second Instance Court is the court of appeal, and there is one in Conakry and one in Kankan. The court in Conakry covers Middle and Lower Guinea and has 7 courts of first instance and 14 justices of the peace under its jurisdiction. The court in Kankan covers Upper Guinea and the Forest Region, where it has 3 courts of first instance and 12 justices of the peace under its jurisdiction.

There is a justice of the peace in every prefecture, and there are a total of 26 justices of the peace and prefectures in Guinea. Justices of the peace must deal with all civil and commercial matters when the value of the case is not more than 50,000 Guinean francs and the ultimate punishment is not more than 15 days in jail.

Courts for minors have the responsibility of dealing with all cases involving a minor. A minor is defined as somebody under the age of 18 the day the offense happened. These courts are presided over by the magistrate for children, who often investigates the offense the minor has committed. Minors are treated differently from adults in the court system, and legislation that impacts minor court cases has to be strictly interpreted.

The High Court of Justice deals with cases against the president and cabinet ministers, which are usually high-treason cases. High Court cases are not eligible for any type of appeal in the Court of Appeal or in the Supreme Court. The High Court of Justice has three full-time judges and three substitutes, and each is chosen on a yearly basis from the pool of Court of Appeal judges.

The Court of State Security is run by one Supreme Court judge and also has two professional judges and two high-ranking military officers on the panel. This court has jurisdiction over the entire country, and it mainly deals with crimes that are political in nature. This court's jurisdiction is optional, and the president can choose to send cases to the courts of first instance.

The Military Tribunal court also has jurisdiction over the entire country and deals with all offenses that are military-based in nature. Some of the types of offenses dealt with in the Military Tribunal court are abuse of authority, damage to the security of the state, treason, destruction of property, embezzlement, and abuse of authority.

Arrest and Pretrial Civil Rights

The Human Rights Practices Report of 2007 suggested that incarceration before trial is allowed with the following rules: suspects cannot be arrested inside of their home between 4:30 P.M. and 6:00 A.M., the government must issue a warrant before somebody is arrested, detainees must be charged within 72 hours of their arrest, the accused can be held until the case is over, attorneys must have access to their clients, and bail is given purely at the discretion of the magistrate. The report also claims that on numerous occasions, these listed rules have not been followed by Guinean security forces.

The Human Rights Watch report of 2008 notes that people charged with a crime are often transferred from the police department to prisons where they are left for years awaiting trial. It is suggested that hundreds of petty criminals and others charged with assault and murder are mainly held in Maison Centrale based on confessions that were obtained by the police using torture as a method to get incriminating evidence. Of the 1,000 people being held in Maison Central, it is estimated that 700 to 800 of them have not yet been tried in a court of law. Human Rights Watch interviewed 20 inmates who stated that they had been incarcerated for more than six years without a hearing.

Punishment

Types of Punishment

Beating of a spouse would not bring a charge of domestic violence in Guinea, but could result in a charge of assault. The penalties for assault include the potential for two to five years in jail and fines ranging from US$13 to $79. Female genital mutilation (FGM) is illegal and holds a three-month prison sentence along with a $26 fine; however, it is still widely practiced in all regions of Guinea. Human trafficking is illegal and carries a punishment of 5–10 years in prison and the forfeiture of all property and money obtained while trafficking humans.

The death penalty was last used in Guinea in 2001. Currently, there are 11 criminals sitting on death row waiting for their punishment. The death penalty was reintroduced in 1984 by Minister of Justice Abou Camara because he wanted to put an end to the general feeling of insecurity among the citizens of Guinea as a result of fighting in Western Africa and an influx of war weapons into the country. Prior to 1984, criminals were often hanged in public so that they would be made an example of. Typically, the public hangings would be politically motivated. Long jail sentences can also be expected for the trafficking, possession, and use of illegal drugs; for sexual contact with a minor; and for using or giving away child pornography.

Prison

As of 2002, there were a total of 3,070 people incarcerated in Guinea, which had a total population of 8.4 million people. This would give it a prison population rate of 37 per 100,000 inhabitants. The largest prison in Guinea is the Maison Centrale, which is located in Conakry. Maison Centrale was designed to hold between 240 and 300 prisoners, but it currently holds around 1,000 inmates on average and had a high around 1,500 in 2006. It has been acknowledged by prison officials that overcrowding is the biggest issue facing this prison. With an average of 1,000 inmates, there are basically 3.3 to 5 inmates for the designed space of 1 inmate. Human Rights Watch reports that many of the inmates spend their entire day in very small and dimly lit cells.

The United Nations has produced the Standard Minimum Rules for the Treatment of Prisoners, which mandates that all inmates receive enough food to remain healthy and strong. Human Rights Watch reported that inmates at Maison Centrale typically get a few handfuls of rice covered with palm oil on a daily basis. Because of this lack of nutrition, seven inmates died of malnutrition and disease in 2004. The authors suggest that this number is actually lower than the true number of inmates who die because the director of Maison Centrale has a policy of releasing inmates who are about to die so that they do not die in custody.

Human Rights Watch reports that the majority of prisons in Guinea are staffed by untrained and unpaid volunteer guards. These guards usually receive their compensation by selling food, clothing, marijuana, cigarettes, and anything of value to the inmates; they also use extortion as a means of making money. One method of extortion the guards use is to house boys with the men. This is against prison policy but is done so that the boys will pay the guards to house them with other boys, so that they will not be victimized by the men.

Mike Mudry

Further Reading

Chonghaile, C. (2002). "Sex-for-Food Scandal in West African Refugee Camps." *The Lancet* 359(9309): 860–861.

Milner, J. (2005). *The Militarization and Demilitarization of Refugee Camps in Guinea:* http://www.smallarmssurvey.org/files/sas/publications/b_series_pdf/AA/Part%20I%2005%20Guinea.pdf.

Sidibe, I. (2008). *Guinean Legal System and Research:* http://www.nyulawglobal.org/globalex/Guinea.htm.

U.S. Department of State. (2008). *Guinea Country Reports on Human Rights Practices* (2007). Bureau of Democracy, Human Rights, and Labor: http://www.state.gov/g/drl/rls/hrrpt/2007/100485.htm.

Guinea-Bissau

Legal System: Civil/Customary
Murder: Medium
Corruption: High
Human Trafficking: Medium
Death Penalty: No
Corporal Punishment: No

Background

Guinea-Bissau is a small nation located in northwestern Africa. Bordered by Senegal to the north, Guinea to the south and east, and the Atlantic Ocean to the east, tiny Guinea-Bissau is slightly less than three times the size of Connecticut. With an area of only 13,948 square miles, Guinea-Bissau has a relatively low population of 1.745 million. Its capital city, Bissau, located in the country's southwest region, is also one of the country's four ports.

Guinea-Bissau has been a republic since its independence in 1974. It has three branches of government: executive, legislative, and judicial. The executive branch is headed by a president, the chief of state, who is elected to a five-year term with no term limits. The president is also head of state, supreme commander of the armed forces, symbol of national unity, and guarantor of national independence and the Constitution. The executive branch also contains a prime minister, the head of government, who is appointed by the president in line with party representation in parliament. In addition to these two figures, there are also 21 ministers of various departments.

Next to the executive, the legislative branch is relatively simple in its composition. Here there is only one main body: the Unicameral National People's Assembly. The assembly is composed of 100 members elected by popular vote for four-year terms. During its term, the assembly is tasked with passing laws and revising the Constitution, if needed. Its power as a body, however, is seemingly less than that of the executive. In times of crisis, the president has the right to dissolve the assembly.

The final branch is the judicial and is based on French civil law. This branch is composed of three levels of courts. The Supreme Court is the apex court. This court consists of nine justices who are appointed by the president and who serve as the final court of appeals in criminal and civil cases. Below this court is a system of regional courts, one in each of the country's nine regions. In addition to serving as the first court of appeals for the courts below it, regional courts also hear all felony cases and civil cases valued at more than $1,000. And at the bottom of the judiciary is a network of 24 sectoral courts. Here civil cases valued at less than $1,000 and misdemeanor criminal cases are heard. But it is worth noting that judges in any of these courts are not necessarily trained lawyers.

A number of parties compete within this political system for power. Though they number in the dozens, only two political parties are of serious consequence. The first is the current ruling party, the African Party for the Independence of Guinea-Bissau and Cape Verde (PAIGC). Also the oldest party in Guinea-Bissau, the PAIGC was begun during the nation's years as a Portuguese colony and led the war for independence. As a result, much of the party's support comes from military veterans and elder citizens. The PAIGC's largest opposition is the Social Renewal Party (PRS). In sharp contrast to the PAIGC, the PRS finds support primarily among urban youth.

Crime

Despite a majority Muslim population, homosexuality is generally tolerated in Guinea-Bissau so long as couples are discreet. As a result, there are no known laws against homosexuality. Additionally, there are no established laws against domestic violence, including wife beating, which is an accepted means of settling domestic disputes. Related to that, there is no law prohibiting sexual harassment either, an oddity considering that the law claims to view the genders equally and prohibits discrimination. Other prohibitions in the law are fairly common. For example, rape (including spousal rape) is prohibited, though government enforcement is weak. Much the same story can be found in prostitution, which is prohibited by law, but allowed to flourish as a result of lack of enforcement.

A seeming contradiction in Guinea-Bissau criminal law also exists in the area of forced labor. The law prohibits forced or compulsory labor, including by children, but reports indicate that such practices occur. The contradiction arises when it is learned that the law, though outlawing forced labor, does not prohibit trafficking in persons. Children are commonly the victims of this contradiction, being trafficked from and within the country to work as domestic servants, to shine shoes in urban areas, and to sell food such as bananas and peanuts on the streets.

The one area of law that does seem of great consequence is drug crime. In light of the nation's recent troubles with the international drug trade, penalties for possession, use, or trafficking in illegal drugs in Guinea-Bissau are severe. Additionally, convicted offenders can expect long jail sentences and heavy fines.

Crime Statistics

Data on crime are not available in Guinea-Bissau, partially because of the great degree of political instability. Instead, international observers are left with only general impressions. And in general, crime rates in Guinea-Bissau are not high. In the case of normal, daytime street crime, the occurrence is fairly low; however, far greater rates are seen in pickpocketing in marketplaces and bandits accosting rural travelers. Conversely, the threat and occurrence of terrorism are exceedingly low.

Drug Trafficking

Also low is the apprehension and conviction of drug traffickers. In spite of the law prescribing severe sentences for drug crimes, the application of the law is rare; traffickers operate with almost complete impunity. In recent years, Guinea-Bissau has become a major transshipment point for Latin American cocaine heading to market in Europe. Conservative estimates say 50 tons of cocaine a year are now being transshipped through West Africa, and Guinea-Bissau is at the center of this problem. The reasons for this are many.

The first is the abject poverty shared by most citizens in Guinea-Bissau, which makes them vulnerable to enticement of the money drug traffickers may offer. Reports indicate this is true from children on up to top government officials. And the enticement is easy to appreciate. The UN Drug and Crime Office has estimated that the national budget of Guinea-Bissau is roughly equal to the wholesale value in Europe of 2½ tons of cocaine.

That value touches on another reason for Guinea-Bissau's selection by drug traffickers. Although demand and prices for cocaine have peaked in the United States, the drug's popularity is exploding in Europe, specifically in England, Spain, and Italy. And because of the value of the Euro, cocaine profits are twice as great in Europe as well. These conditions have led, in part, to a shift in world drug distribution.

Geography also plays a role in Guinea-Bissau's selection. Located on the Atlantic coast of northwestern Africa, the nation is only 400 miles directly south of Spain, one of Europe's growing cocaine markets. Besides location, Guinea-Bissau also features an archipelago of more than 70 islands just off its coast, most uninhabited, each of which provides landing strips for small aircraft and staging areas for the distribution of cocaine. Exacerbating this is the fact that Guinea-Bissau's maritime area is larger than its mainland, making effective patrols difficult, that is, assuming there is a patrol at all. As a small nation, its navy is formed of only two boats, one of which is out of service. Further, the air force has no functioning aircraft of any kind. Even were there regular patrol, there is no guarantee that drug law would be enforced because there are strong suspicions and confirmations of corruption within the military as well.

Although the cocaine trade has taken on national importance, most residents remain ignorant of the narcotics trade. Reports indicate that villagers have even found cocaine bundles floating in the ocean. Not recognizing what they have found, the villagers have used the cocaine to fertilize their crops. Some have even seasoned their food with it.

So now Guinea-Bissau is in danger of becoming a narco-state—a nation run primarily for the benefit of drug gangs. Other countries have acknowledged this fact. To help this struggling country, Portugal, and a handful of other countries, the European Union and the United Nations have pledged more than $6 million to help overhaul the justice system there. But there is much still to be done in this tiny nation. Corruption still reigns in a nation where 674 kilograms of cocaine can disappear from the treasury's vaults. And with more than 33 percent of cocaine arriving in Europe being funneled through West Africa, Guinea-Bissau's battle with drug traffickers is unlikely to be over soon.

Police

The nation of Guinea-Bissau is divided into 37 police districts. These 37 districts are serviced by an estimated 3,500 officers nationally in nine different police forces reporting to seven different ministries. Of these 3,500, 1,300 members of the public order police are under the Ministry of Interior. These officers are responsible for preventive patrols, crowd control, and conventional maintenance of law and order. Although the public order police wield the greatest numbers, the greatest prestige and international attention are awarded to the less than 100 members of the judiciary police under the Ministry of Justice. This group's popularity stems mostly from its responsibility for investigating transnational crime, including Guinea-Bissau's growing drug trade. Other policing groups include the state information service, the border service, the rapid intervention force, and the maritime police. Whichever policing agency is examined, though, all share a dramatic absence of training and other resources. In a nation with 3,500 officers and only two patrol vehicles, this is not surprising. More surprising are reports of traffickers eluding capture because police vehicles ran out of gasoline while in pursuit. This resource poverty is not endemic to the rural police either. Even the elite federal officers of the judiciary police lack handcuffs, only half of them have firearms, and they share one laptop computer. The use of this computer itself is in question too because of the nation's unreliable energy generation. Also unreliable is the payroll. Inspectors in the judiciary police are supposed to make less than $65 a month, but they cannot even rely on that; officers commonly go for several months without pay. Because of this, corruption is not only a temptation but also a widespread reality. This combination of corruption and resource-scarcity has rendered the police ineffective.

Finding of Guilt

Warrants are required for arrests. It is similarly required by law that detainees be brought before a magistrate within 48 hours after arrest and that prisoners be released if no timely indictment is filed. Detainees also have the right against arbitrary arrest and detention and cruel and unusual punishment and the rights to counsel at state expense, to question witnesses, to have access to evidence held by the government, and to appeal. However, many of these rights are normally ignored in practice. At the same time, trials are commonly delayed, and there is no right to a jury trial.

However, Guinea-Bissau's justice system is different in practice than in theory. Like the police, the judiciary is paid poorly, poorly trained, and susceptible to corruption. Accusations of bias and passivity are also common, particularly in respect to court-appointed attorneys and with the judges, where there is no requirement that they have a legal education. Court-appointed attorneys also receive no compensation from the state for representing indigent clients, are not punished for failing to do so, and generally ignore such responsibilities. On a positive note, though, those who go to trial do have their rights respected in practice. There is also a functioning bail system in place.

Punishment

The corrections system is virtually nonexistent in Guinea-Bissau. With its only prison largely destroyed during the civil war of the late 1990s, the nation has no real prison to speak of. In place of a purpose-built prison, Guinea-Bissau now houses its prisoners in a former office building in Bissau, a facility generally without running water and adequate sanitation. The prison's guards consist of two uniformed men standing outside the building's door, only one of whom has a pistol. Inside, approximately 40 prisoners are housed. Pretrial detainees, who constitute the majority of the inmates and convicts, are housed openly together, as are adults and children. With the exception of the serious offenders (who are kept in a padlocked room), nothing stands between the prisoners and freedom but an open door and the two guards. This lack of capacity and security has led to predictable outcomes. Many detainees who are remanded to their homes as a result of space constraints fail to return to face charges. And the poor nutritional quality of food provided has led to the release of thieves and murderers to find something to eat if they promise to return.

Michael Galezewski

Further Reading

Baldauf, S. (2009, March 3). "Guinea-Bissau Assassinations: Is Colombia's Drug Trade Behind Them?" *Christian Science Monitor:* http://www.csmonitor.com/World/Africa/2009/0303/p07s02-woaf.html.

Bureau of African Affairs. (2009, March). *Background Note: Guinea-Bissau:* http://www.state.gov/r/pa/ei/bgn/5454.htm.

Foreign & Commonwealth Office. (2009, February 25). *Country Profile: The Republic of Guinea-Bissau:* http://www.fco.gov.uk/en/about-the-fco/country-profiles/sub-saharan-africa/guinea-bissau?profile=politics&pg=7.

Horta, L. (2007, October). *Guinea-Bissau: Africa's First Narcostate:* http://www.africa.upenn.edu/Articles_Gen/guinbisauhorta.html.

Ivory Coast (Côte d'Ivoire)

Legal System: Civil/Customary
Murder: High
Corruption: High
Human Trafficking: Medium
Prison Rate: Low
Death Penalty: No
Corporal Punishment: No

Background

The Republic of the Ivory Coast (formal name: *République de Côte d'Ivoire*) is situated in western Africa. The Ivory Coast became a French colony on

March 10, 1893, and part of French West-Africa in 1902. It remained a colony until the French Constitution of October 27, 1946, changed it into an overseas territory. As allowed by the French Constitution of October 4, 1958, the Ivory Coast was a Member-State of the French Community. The Ivory Coast became a sovereign republic on August 7, 1960.

The Preamble of the Ivorian Constitution proclaims its dedication to liberal democratic principles and inalienable human rights as expressed in the 1789 Declaration of Rights of Man and the Citizen and the 1948 Universal Declaration of Human Rights. The Ivorian judicial organization, criminal code, and code of criminal procedure have been considerably influenced by the French legal and judicial tradition. Whereas the criminal code defines offenses and determines penalties, the code of criminal procedure dictates rules on the form of the proceedings. Specific offenses, procedures, measures, and/or punishments exist for minors (persons under 18) and members of the armed forces.

Crime

The criminal code is composed of two books. The first book includes general provisions, common to all criminal offenses. The second book, called special criminal law, defines specific felonies and misdemeanors and determines their penalties. Petty offenses and their penalties are determined by decree, and some specific types of criminality, such as drugs, are dealt with in separate criminal laws. The code of criminal procedure contains a preliminary title concerning public prosecution and civil action, followed by five books. The first book concerns the exercise of public prosecution and judicial investigation. The second book concerns the trial courts and tribunals, namely the Assize Court, the Correctional Tribunal, the Police Tribunal and the Appeal Court. The third book lists special remedies such as cassation applications before the Supreme Court. The fourth book describes some specific proceedings, including for criminal offenses committed outside the territory of the republic. Finally, the fifth book concerns procedures for the execution of penalties.

Classification of Crimes

Criminal offenses are categorized according to their seriousness, as felonies, misdemeanors, or petty offenses. Felonies are in principle judged by Assize Courts, misdemeanors by Correctional Tribunals, and petty offenses by police tribunals.

A criminal offense is categorized as felony when it is punished by death, imprisonment for life, or imprisonment exceeding 10 years. It is a petty offense when it is punished by imprisonment of maximum two months and/or a fine of maximum CFA360,000. Misdemeanors are all criminal offenses that are punished neither as a felony nor as a petty crime.

Crime Statistics

The dark figure of crime (a term to describe the amount of crime that is unreported or does not come to the attention of police agencies) is important because many criminal offenses are still resolved according to indigenous laws and customs, by indigenous chiefs or elders, and through negotiations, mediations, and arbitrations.

Officially known criminality has been linked to socioeconomic change related to urbanization; industrialization; labor migration, especially toward Abidjan; proliferation of urban slums; unemployment; and so on.

According to the United Nations Operations in Côte d'Ivoire (UNOCI) report, there were 9,586 inmates on May 30, 2007, of whom 71 percent were convicted inmates and 29 percent were pretrial detainees. Women constituted 2.5 percent of the inmates.

Finding of Guilt

The proceedings in criminal cases are very complex and can be divided into two major parts. First, there are the public prosecution and judicial investigation (book 1) that are primarily secret and written. Next, there are the proceedings before the trial courts and tribunals (book 2) that are generally public and oral.

Ivorian soldiers listen to a judge in a courtroom in Abidjan on November 12, 2008, before their trial on charges of harming public order. Over a hundred soldiers were charged after taking part in violent protests in September in the cities of Daoukro and Yamoussoukro. The soldiers were demanding payment of their war benefits. (Issouf Sanogo/AFP/Getty Images)

In the first title of the first book of the code of criminal procedure, the authorities in charge of public prosecution and judicial investigation are described. They are the Judicial Police, the Public Prosecution, and the Investigating Judge. The second title regards the inquiries divided into the preliminary inquiry and the inquiry in case of flagrant felonies and misdemeanors.

A flagrant felony or misdemeanor is one when, almost immediately after the act, the suspect is chased by hue and cry, or is found in the possession of articles, or has on or about him traces or clues that give grounds to believe that he has taken part in the felony or misdemeanor. Along with a flagrant felony or misdemeanor are felonies and misdemeanors committed inside a house and for which the head of the house calls on a judicial police officer or the Prosecutor of the Republic to ratify them. The Judicial Police officer, who is told of a flagrant felony or misdemeanor punishable by imprisonment, immediately informs the Prosecutor of the Republic, who initiates the investigation. The preliminary inquiry is carried out by Judicial Police officers either on the instructions of the Prosecutor of the Republic or on their own initiative.

The third title concerns the investigating jurisdictions, divided into the Investigating Judge and the Investigating Chamber. A judicial investigation by the Investigating Judge is mandatory when a felony has been committed. It is generally optional for misdemeanors. The Investigating Judge undertakes or procures an inquiry into the personality of the suspects, as well as into his or her material, family and social situation and may order a medical or psychological examination. He has large powers when it comes to home searches and seizures, which are made in all the places where items may be found that could be useful for the discovery of the truth. The summons is designed to give the suspect a notice to appear before the judge at the date and time specified by this warrant. An arrest warrant is an order given to the law enforcement agencies to find the suspect and take him to the prison mentioned in the warrant, where he will be received and detained. Any suspect detained due to those warrants must be heard by the investigating judge within 48 hours. Pretrial detention is supposed to be an exceptional measure in which the modalities depend on the seriousness of the criminal offense. Bail is possible. If the judge concludes that the facts amount to a petty offense, he makes an order referring the case to the Police Tribunal, and if he concludes they amount to a misdemeanor, he refers them to the Correctional Tribunal. If the investigating judge concludes that the charges accepted against the suspect constitute an offense qualified as a felony by the law, he orders the indictment before the Assize Court. Appeals can be filed against orders of the investigating judge before the Investigating Chamber.

Each appeal court includes an investigating chamber, composed of a president and two appeal judges. The duties of public prosecution are performed by the prosecutor general or his deputies. At the investigating chamber, the hearings are held, and the judgments are given in chambers. In pretrial detention matters, the investigating chamber must decide whether to uphold the investigating judge's decision or to quash and modify it. On appeal against closing orders of the investigating judge, if the charges brought against the suspect constitute an offense classed as a felony by law, the investigating chamber does not always order indictment before the Assize Court. If it considers that, because of circumstances, only a penalty for misdemeanors need be pronounced, it may refer the suspect, by motivated order and with due submissions of the public prosecution, to the Correctional Tribunal instead of the Assize Court.

The proceedings before the trial courts and tribunals constitute the second book of the code of criminal procedure. The general principle is that felonies are judged by Assize Courts, misdemeanors by correctional tribunals, and petty offenses by police tribunals.

The Assize Court has full jurisdiction to judge individuals committed for trial before it by the indictment judgment. This means that the Assize Court, which is not a permanent trial court, judges only serious felonies. Assizes are held within the tribunal of first instance. The Assize Court comprises the court proper, which consists of a president and two assessors, and six jurors. The Public Prosecution is represented by the prosecutor general or the prosecutor of the Republic or their deputies. Once the jury is composed, the public hearing can start. The president orders the retirement of the witnesses, and the referring judgment is read. Then the accused is interrogated by the president. Next, the witnesses, who take an oath, make their statements. After each statement, the president may ask questions to the witness. The other parties may also ask questions through his intermediary. When the investigation made in the course of the hearing is ended, the public prosecutor makes his submissions. The accused present their defense arguments. The public prosecutor may reply, but the accused will always have the final word. The president declares the hearing closed. Before the judges of the court and the jurors retire to the deliberation chamber, the president reads out an instruction stipulating that their innermost conviction prevails. The judges of the court and the jurors deliberate and vote on the guilt and the penalty. The president reads out the verdict in the courtroom and informs the accused of the faculty of a cassation application. Because of the complexity and costs of the assizes, they are not often organized. This leads to long-term pretrial detentions in matters of serious felonies.

The Correctional Tribunal judges misdemeanors and felonies referred to it by the Investigation

Chamber. It is composed of a president and two other judges. The public prosecution is exercised by the prosecutor of the republic or his deputies. Suspects arrested in flagrant cases who are under committal warrant of the prosecutor of the republic are forthwith brought before the Correctional Tribunal. Hearings are public. Offenses may be proven by any mode of evidence, and the judges decide according to their innermost conviction. However, they may base their decision only on evidence that was submitted in the course of the hearing and adversarially discussed before them. Confessions, like any other type of evidence, are left to the free appreciation of the judges. The suspect and witnesses, who take an oath, are interrogated and heard by the president. When the investigation at the hearing is over, the prosecutor of the republic makes his submissions, and finally, the suspect presents his defense. The public prosecutor may respond, but the suspect will always have the last word. Judgment is pronounced at the same session as the hearing or at a later date. Every judgment must be motivated. A suspect who is regularly cited but does not appear on the day and at the time fixed by the summons is tried by default. The judgment by default is deemed nonexistent if the defendant files an application to set aside its enforcement. The case will then be tried again by the Correctional Tribunal. Judgments in misdemeanor matters may be challenged by appeal. The appeal is brought before the Appeal Court. The Chamber for Appeals is composed of a president and two appeal judges. The duties of public prosecution are performed by the prosecutor general or one of his attorneys general or his deputies. The rules applicable before the Appeal Court are similar to those set out for the Correctional Tribunal.

The Police Tribunal tries petty offenses. The functions of the Police Tribunal are exercised by the Correctional Tribunal. For most petty offenses, criminal proceedings may be extinguished by the payment of a fine. When it comes to a hearing, the proceedings are similar to those mentioned for the Correctional Tribunal. An application to set aside may be filed, and an appeal can be brought before the Appeal Court.

There are nine Correctional Tribunals in the Republic of the Ivory Coast. To reduce the geographic distance between the citizens and the tribunals, there are 25 delegated sections of the correctional tribunals. Until the reform of 1999, they were usually presided over by one, sometimes, two judges, cumulating the functions of trial judge, investigating judge, and public prosecution. From the judicial year of 2004–2005 on, each delegated section has been composed of a president, an investigating judge, and a deputy prosecutor of the republic. There are three Appeal Courts. Three additional Correctional Tribunals and Appeal Courts are foreseen.

The cassation application is an important special remedy, elaborated in book 3 of the code of criminal procedure. Judgments made by the Investigating Chamber and judgments rendered by courts of final instance in felony, misdemeanor, or petty offense matters may be quashed in the event of a violation of the law. The cassation application is brought before the Supreme Court located in Abidjan.

Punishment

The types of punishments are dealt with in the first book of the criminal code, which is subdivided into five titles. In the first title, the constitutional principle of the equality of all before the criminal law is repeated. The only distinctions that are permitted are those foreseen by law, such as the seriousness of the criminal offense and the social danger the offender presents.

The second title concerns the penalties in more detail. They must be imposed according to the circumstances of the criminal offense, the danger it presents for public order, the personality of the offender, and his possibilities of rehabilitation. The principal penalties are death, different types of imprisonment, and fines. Although the criminal code foresees capital punishment by shooting, the Ivorian government has not employed such executions since its independence.

Title III regards criminal liability and stipulates the grounds for absence or attenuation of criminal liability. For instance, a person is not criminally liable in a state of legitimate defense. The judge may, taking into account the seriousness of the facts and the culpability of the offender, allow consideration of mitigating circumstances. The judge need not justify this decision. The mitigating circumstances may lead to a substantial reduction of the penalties. For instance, the penalty for felonies punished by death may be reduced to an imprisonment for life.

Recidivism, which is defined and elaborated in Title IV, leads to severe penalties; the maximum of the prison sentences may be doubled for repeat offenders.

The execution of penalties may, in conformity with Title V, be partly or totally exempt, through suspension, pardon, prescription, and death of the convicted person. Suspension may be granted, taking into account the seriousness of the offense and the fact that the offender, at the time of the offense, had not yet been convicted and imprisoned for a felony or a misdemeanor. Pardon by the president of the republic may commute a penalty to a lesser penalty. Death, for instance, can be commuted to an imprisonment for life. Prescription of penalties occurs after 25 for felonies, 5 years for misdemeanors, and 2 years for petty crimes. Death of the convicted person obviously ends imprisonment but does not prevent the execution of fines and confiscations.

Prisons

The proceedings for the execution of penalties are described in the fifth book of the code of criminal procedure. The Public Prosecution is responsible for the execution of the criminal penalties. When it comes to imprisonment, the constitutional principle of the prohibition of arbitrary detention is repeated. Parole may be granted to convicts who have given sufficient proof of good behavior and serious efforts toward social rehabilitation. They must also have served part of their prison sentence, with duration depending on the seriousness of the criminal offense and the social danger the offender presents. The parole decision specifies the conditions under which it is granted. In the event of a new conviction, of notorious misconduct, of violation of the conditions, or of a non-observance of the measures determined by the parole decision, it may be revoked.

There is a prison next to each Correctional Tribunal and delegated section. The largest prison is the MACA in Abidjan. The Rule of Law of ONUCI evaluated the prisons of the Ivory Coast in 2005 and 2006 and pointed out that the budget of the prison administration is very limited. Permanent overcrowding is a major problem, and the material conditions of the prisons are generally poor. Men and women are separated, but there is no separation between pretrial detainees and convicted inmates. The dietary conditions are often insufficient, and the medical and sanitation facilities are minimal, leading to a high mortality rate. The inmates have the right to regular visits, and family members often bring them additional food. Prison staffs and guard forces are small relative to the number of inmates. The prisons serve primarily as punitive and custodial institutions, in which little attention is paid to rehabilitation.

Veerle Van Gijsegem

Further Reading

Handloff, R. E. (1988). *Côte d'Ivoire: A Country Study.* Washington, DC: Federal Research Division, Library of Congress: http://www.country-data.com/frd/cs/citoc.html.

Official Web Site of the Ivorian Government: http://www.gouv.ci.

United Nations Operation in Côte d'Ivoire (UNOCI), Unité de l'état de droit. (2007, June). *L'organisation et le fonctionnement du système judiciaire en Côte d'Ivoire:* http://www.onuci.org/.

United Nations Operation in Côte d'Ivoire (UNOCI), Unité de l'état de droit. (2006, August). *Sommaire: Situation des établissements pénitentiaires en Côte d'Ivoire:* http://www.onuci.org/.

United Nations Operation in Côte d'Ivoire (UNOCI), Unité de l'état de droit. *Rapport sur la situation des établissements pénitentiaires en Côte d'Ivoire:* http://www.onuci.org/.

Kenya

Legal System: Civil/Islamic/Customary
Murder: Medium
Corruption: High
Human Trafficking: Medium
Prison Rate: Medium
Death Penalty: Maybe
Corporal Punishment: No

Background

Kenya is an east-central African country sharing borders with Sudan and Ethiopia to the north; Somalia to the east; Tanzania to the south; and Uganda to the west. Kenya's population stood at over 34 million in 2007. A former British colony, Kenya attained political independence in 1963, following a drawn-out indigenous insurrection, which came to be widely known as the Mau Mau, under the leadership of Jomo Kenya, who became the first head of state. It became ostensibly politically stable until the election of Mwai Kibaki in 2002. The two previous regimes had been known to be predatory, scandal-prone, or corrupt and to employ the tactics of divide-and-rule to keep political opponents at bay. In the late 1990s, the Kenya government itself admitted the widespread practice of torture by its security forces.

Crime

In Kenya, as in the other former British colonies, police gather crime data on both adult and juvenile offenses. Data are published on conventional crimes such as armed robbery, assault, homicide, embezzlement, theft, disturbance of public order, and rape. Secondary sources now include the media and special reports by NGOs.

A sample of crime data (2007), available from the Kenyan police Web site (http://www.kenyapolice.go.ke), is as follows:

Homicide	1,912
Offenses against morality	3,673
Other offenses against persons	17,831
Robbery	3,492
Breaking and entering	6,337
Theft of stock	1,568
Stealing	10,749
Theft by servant	2,169
Vehicle and other thefts	1,221
Dangerous drugs	5,401
Traffic offenses	46
Criminal damage	2,770
Economic crimes	1,908
Corruption	177
Offenses involving police officers	32
Offenses involving tourist	10
Other penal code offenses	3,732

The statistics on homicide should be viewed with caution. Taking the average of three years, from 2005 through 2007, the rate per 100,000 population comes to 6.1; however, the WHO estimate for 2004 was 20.8, a much higher rate that most likely includes many homicides that are technically either not recorded or not dealt with by Kenya police because they may fall under the heading of "terrorism" or other such categories. Such crimes as offenses against persons, stealing, breaking and entering, and drugs account for the majority of recorded crime. Additional data suggest that over 2005–2007, the total crime fell by about 16 percent. The Kenya police also report recorded crime by province, showing that Nairobi, Rift Valley, Central, Eastern, Nyanza, Coast, and Western account for the most amount of crime.

Data on rapes, defilement, and other forms of sexual violence against women and children have been relatively sparse or notoriously underreported. Kenya is one of several African countries in which rape and other forms of sexual violence against women and children were on the increase before the elections of 2007. The trend worsened during post-election violence from late December 2007 through March 2008, upon the formation of the joint government. The increased incidents caused fear of HIV infection, especially in the cases of gang rapes.

Kenya has witnessed an increase in environmental crimes in recent years. One of the major dilemmas

Kenyan Wildlife wardens display confiscated elephant tusks at the Kenyan Wildlife offices in Nairobi, Kenya, on November 30, 2009. African wildlife authorities have seized nearly 3,800 pounds of illegal elephant ivory, and the Kenya Wildlife Service has arrested 65 people during the six-nation operation. (AP Photo/Khalil Senosi)

for the Kenya police in general and the wildlife police in particular involves the hidden nature of wildlife crimes. Perhaps the foremost concerns relate to the remote locations where these crimes tend to be committed: for example, deep in isolated forests in the cases of poaching. A second concern relates to the limited budgets and sparse resources, which impose restraints on hiring more personnel to regulate these crimes.

A consequence of these problems has been an increase in environmental crimes such as poaching, smuggling of ivory, and illicit trade in ivory. These crimes are also difficult to detect, investigate, and prosecute for a variety of reasons. For one thing, the offenders are often part of organized criminal gangs, are sophisticated, and use modern technology for communication and committing crime. In its fight against poaching and trafficking in ivory, Kenya has emerged as a pioneer in the use of DNA experiments followed by tracking the origin of poached elephants. The downside of the tourist attraction is that the same precious game parks have also been targets for not only farming but also human settlement, coupled with illegal hunting activities.

Terrorism has been an emerging crime since the 1990s. Illegal firearms are also a rising problem for Kenyan police. The Institute for Security Studies report on a 2001 public survey on attitudes toward arms in Nairobi, the capital of Kenya, indicates that 47 percent of the respondents point out the inability of police in handling the problem. The findings call for greater improvement by the government in a number of key areas, including crime control and policing.

According to a survey conducted by the South Africa-based Institute for Security Studies, in response to the incidents of crime victimization, individual Kenyans have been arming themselves but also forming vigilante groups. The weapons in common use include knives, guns, sticks, and clubs.

Kenya border-crime problems have been around since even before colonial rule. Given its porous borders, cross-border crimes include arms smuggling, cattle rustling, and smuggling of ivory, among others.

Kenya has become a key transit route for heroin and hashish destined for North American streets, according to a new U.S. State Department report on narcotics control. The report also notes police corruption and a network of commercial and family ties linking some Kenyans to southwest Asia, the route for much of the narcotics. The United Nations Office on Drugs and Crime has noted that organized criminal groups have established international networks to carry out both legal and illegal drug trafficking with Kenya as a hub and a route.

Vigilantism

Also called mob justice or market justice, vigilantism is alive and well in Kenya's urban areas and occurs in increasing numbers and with increasing ferocity. Also, police inaction punctuated by corruption has become a notorious contributing factor.

Juvenile Delinquency and Juvenile Offenders

Juvenile delinquency is now a broad, complex concept incorporating a mix of the elements of antisocial or deviant behaviors that encompass street children, and common crimes such as truancy, theft, carjacking, shoplifting, and prostitution. Increasingly, the number of special-needs youth offenders has caught the attention of the media, scholars, and practitioners. A classic example is the youthful offenders with HIV/AIDS whose treatment defies the use of traditional juvenile institutions.

Police

The Imperial British East Africa Company introduced as well as operated private security before 1887. This was similar to the other standard initiatives in East Africa as well as other British possessions, territories, and colonies in the world. The evolution of the colonial police forces did not mean the end of the existence of the private security. Far from it, the two forms of policing coexisted, to a greater or lesser extent. The private security units were present in the private-sector enterprises such as large-scale farming, mining, transportation, and tourism.

The concept of strong centralized police administration became a reality with the central government police forces. The colonial authorities established their police force to undertake tasks dealing with the enforcement of criminal law in the urban areas and to be realigned with those in rural areas under the jurisdiction of the various ethnic customary laws and Islamic law. The central police force was the primary enforcer of criminal law, whereas the tribal police were focused on the customary laws.

The number of police functions increased during the 1940s, thanks to urbanization and the unintended consequence of urban crime. This development was met with expanded recruitment and training activities. By the early 1950s, the Kenya Police Force had the strength of 5,935 personnel.

The Kenya Police Service is under the jurisdiction of the Ministry of Home Affairs; its commissioner reports to the Police Service Commission as the policy-making as well as monitoring authority. Nairobi, the capital, has been the police service's headquarters since the colonial period. By the mid-1980s, Kenya's police force had 19,000 uniformed personnel, including female officers.

There are many special units within the police bureaucracy. These include the paramilitary general services unit, the railways and harbors police, the inspection department, the criminal investigation directorate, the police air wing, and the dog section. Although there has been a great diversity in the form and size of each of these units, their administration somewhat mirrored the central administrative ethos in terms of the rules, procedures, regulations, policies, and budgets and expenditures. In addition, the tribal police force was established to serve as the conduit between the central police and the ethnic authorities. The latter administered exclusively customary laws and Islamic law.

The police service in Kenya has since the dawn of the 21st century been in the midst of responding to the needs and problems of the masses who have been at the receiving end of injustice since the colonial period. There is no doubt that postcolonial police reform in Kenya was made more difficult by the dictatorial regimes of the 20th century. Unlike South Africa, the Kenya political leadership embraced the concept of the ombudsman as a matter of a constitutional move to address, among other things, the past and current human rights violations and, in general, complaints against the police.

Public–Private Partnership for Police Reform

An emerging phenomenon in the Kenya Police Service is the notion of public–private partnership for police reform. It involves sharing resources in funds and technical expertise with the private sector in an effort to improve the performance of the police in selected projects. This development promotes the enhancement of the mutual interests as well as benefits for the participating parties. Public–private partnerships for police reform are exemplified by the Nairobi Central Business District Association, with its express purpose of evolving what is called "community policing." The understanding is that the practice of this concept will lessen the tension between the police and the public segments such as the street children and street commercial vendors and hawkers.

Courts and Judiciary

Prosecution of Crimes

The Kenyan legal system is a mixture of statutory law, common law, and customary law, and thus the responsibility for prosecution has, since the colonial era, been split between the police and the Director of Public Prosecutions. The former has been primarily relegated to the lesser serious crimes under the jurisdiction of the magistrates' courts. The Director of Public Prosecutions' Office has had the staff to handle the trials and appeals in the High Court and Court of Appeal, with jurisdiction over the serious crimes.

Colonial Courts

The colonial courts were structured to constitute a dual court system, meaning that there were central government courts and customary-law grassroots courts. The former had jurisdiction over the criminal law and related laws. They were increasingly bureaucratized. They were subdivided into the high courts and magistrates' courts. The high courts tried the major criminal and civil cases to begin with and were appellate courts, with highest court of appeal being the Privy Council in the United Kingdom, as was the arrangement for all the colonies, possessions, and trusteeships. The customary courts had jurisdiction over disputes in the various ethnic communities.

The African employees in these courts played major roles on behalf of both the government and the masses. The prominent positions they held included those of interpreters, clerks, and intermediaries. Only the clerical personnel weathered the storm of Africanization, and their numbers even increased, with additional courts, during the postcolonial era.

The Postcolonial Courts

Court reform was driven by the commonly shared theme of legal integration in the former British colonies. In Kenya this meant doing away with the customary courts and thereby further expanding the jurisdiction of the high courts and magistrates' courts at the expense of the needs and problems of the masses. The Kenyan courts became elitist. The other development involved the elimination of the Privy Council of the House of Lords as the highest court of appeal; the country has its own called the Supreme Court.

The Court of Appeal is the highest court. Appeals to it come from High Court. The High Court has jurisdiction over civil, criminal, and constitutional matters. Eleven judges sit in it, with one of them being the president.

Subordinate courts are in two categories: resident magistrates' courts and the district magistrates' courts, with the latter being of a lower rank than its counterpart. Other courts include the kadhi's (Muslim) courts, the children's courts, the tribunals or quasi-judicial bodies, the industrial courts, and rent tribunals.

The resilient features of the customary law are limited to civil cases, and they vary from one ethnic group to another, particularly in rural areas. The major restriction imposed in these cases is that they not be in conflict with national or statutory law. Matters dealing with the settlement of personal litigation are within the jurisdiction of Islamic law and indigenous customary law.

Critics of the Kenya Courts

Independence of the judiciary is a universally held as well as practiced norm in the democratic societies in the world. In Kenya the Constitution does provide for it. On occasion it has been practiced during the postcolonial period. Without a doubt, the number of defense attorneys with long track records in challenging the Kenya authorities in the administration of justice has been increasing. Some of them are women lawyers.

The postcolonial courts in Kenya have tended to serve the interests of the government in power and the segments of the general public. Examples of the latter include the media, victims of crime, the defendants, and significant others such as court personnel. Corruption is associated with the latter.

Juvenile Courts

The juvenile courts in Kenya are one of the colonial legacies. They continue to be the equivalent of the adult magistrates' courts and to have jurisdiction over criminal cases, status offenses, and related social problems calling for "protection or discipline" of minors. Status offenses include being "incorrigible," vagrancy, truancy, and running away from home. Related social problems are exemplified by street children.

Presiding over the juvenile courts are the magistrates. They have legal authority to order juvenile offenders to be placed in remand institutions and approved schools in the Prisons Department, as an alternative to institutionalization in the Children's Department. Police lockup of children is under the jurisdiction of the police officials.

Some juvenile offenders under 18 years of age get housed in the adult prisons, thereby literally violating the law, which prohibits such action. Even more disturbing is the discovery that two of the existing reformatories have been underutilized.

The government departments with some jurisdiction over juvenile offenders include the Prisons Service, the Children's Department, and the Probation and After Care Services Department.

Punishment

Stipulated in the Kenya penal code are the following forms of punishment that are available for the courts to impose:

1. Death
2. Imprisonment
3. Detention under the Detention Camps Act
4. Corporal punishment
5. Fine
6. Forfeiture
7. Payment of compensation

Kenya inherited the colonial penal system with the Prisons Service as the core component. The alternatives to incarceration included probation, fines, and juvenile institutions; approved schools, borstals, and reformatories were also side components of the penal system.

Imprisonment brought with it physical punishments reminiscent of those in the early European civilization, including the use of corporal punishment for violation of prison rules and dietary restrictions. As in the case of the police and the courts, the penal system in Kenya was essentially a duplication of the British concepts and practices in penology. This occurred particularly at the central level of government.

The existing penological studies have raised issues pertaining to a variety of problems as follows:

- *Harsh prison conditions.* Harsh prison conditions abound in Kenya, as do reports about them. These conditions range from lack of basic dietary provisions to the death of the inmates.
- *HIV/AIDS in the prisons.* HIV/AIDS continues to be a major concern through Kenya and shows no signs of slowing down, especially in prisons. Homosexuality in the Kenyan prisons is perhaps the newest prison issue in the 21st century. The steps that the prison authorities have taken to address certain aspects at least suggest acknowledgement of its existence, but not necessarily of its causes and impact.

The Death Penalty

The death penalty continues to be one of the contested colonial penal legacies in the 21st century. The penal code stipulates its application for convicted offenders of murder, treason, and armed robbery. Relief from it often occurs upon presidential pardon or amnesty or successful appeal.

At the dawn of the 21st century, there were about 1,000 condemned prisoners locked up in Kenya's notoriously overcrowded maximum-security prisons The government in power entertained the notion of abolishing the death penalty, thereby seeking to join the bandwagon of the worldwide trade.

Probation and Aftercare Services

The Probation and Aftercare Department is a colonial creation dating back to 1943. It has grown and expanded since to become a large bureaucracy. The Office of the Vice President and the Ministry of Home Affairs have joint jurisdiction over it. Its subdivisions are as follows:

Probationers (offenders on probation orders)
Community service orders supervisees/supervisors
Justice agencies
Learning institutions
Civil organizations
The community

Ejakait (J. S. E.) Opolot

Further Reading

Anderson, D. M. (1991). "Policing, Prosecuting and the Law in Colonial Kenya, 1970, pp. 5–39." In *Policing the Empire,* edited by D. M. Anderson and D. Killingway, pp. 183–201. New York: St. Martin's Press.

Deflem, M. (1994). "Law Enforcement in British Colonial Africa: A Comparative Analysis of Imperial Policing in Nyasaland, the Gold Coast, and Kenya." *Police Studies* 17(1): 45–68.

Hill, B. E., and N. Targ. (2001). "The Link Between Protecting Natural Resources and the Issues of Environmental Justice." *Environmental Affairs* 8(1): 33–42.

Lesotho

Legal System: Common/Civil/Customary
Murder: Medium
Burglary: High
Corruption: Medium
Prison Rate: Medium
Death Penalty: Yes
Corporal Punishment: Yes

Background

Lesotho (formerly known as Basutholand) is a landlocked country entirely encompassed by the country of South Africa. In the 1500 and 1600s, the inhabitants of the land were called San Bushmen (a name given by the whites). The Bushmen were hunters and gatherers and lived that way until 1818. At that time, a king named Moshoeshoe (pronounced Moo-shway-shway) brought together nearby communities of different tribes who had survived raids by other African tribes, mainly the Zulu and the Matabele. Between 1818 and 1966, the land was governed mostly by the chiefs. The country gained independence in 1966 from the United Kingdom, and after 23 years of military rule, Lesotho is currently a constitutional monarchy. The Constitution was implemented in 1993.

Criminal law in Lesotho has retained, in part, the customary law that was once the ruling law in the country long before European colonization. In the late 19th century, the paramount chief (at that time, King Moshoeshoe) made a deal with the British colonists that in return for protection from the Afrikaner colonists, the Basothos (black Africans) would allow the land to become a British colony. The British government followed an amalgamation type of law that included both the Roman Dutch law and English law, with the Roman Dutch law consisting of influences by both the Roman law and Dutch customs.

The Sesotho customary law, as it is referred to in Lesotho, is run by what are deemed local and central courts. Most of the criminal law statutory offenses can be found in the Laws of Lerotholi. The Laws of Lerotholi are written in the form of a constitution to be followed by all native citizens of Basutholand (Lesotho). It states that the paramount chief—otherwise known as the king—is in charge of all natives of the land and that anyone who disobeys the laws of the land is liable to be punished.

Three major organizations provide policing and security in modern-day Lesotho. They are the Lesotho Defense Force (LDF), the Lesotho Mounted Police Service (LMPS), and the National Security Service (NSS). The prime minister in Lesotho has authority over both the LDF and the NSS, whereas the typical law enforcement responsibilities fall under the jurisdiction of the LMPS; however, because of the severe lack of resources, equipment, training, and raw number of officers, the police services are severely limited. It is even said that it is common for victims of crimes to be responsible for providing transportation for the LMPS to get to the scene of the crime. The LMPS is divided into three regions, which are further divided into districts in the country. Each region is led by an assistant commissioner of police, and senior superintendents head the districts.

The armed services in Lesotho have, in the past, been greatly influenced by politics and government. Despite efforts to bring the services under civilian control, the South African Development Community was forced to intervene in an army rebellion, for which they arrested LDF soldiers and disarmed the rest of the soldiers. This occurred in 1998, after Parliament (which consisted of 120 members in January 2004) had passed both the Lesotho Defense Act in 1996 and the Regulations for Military Justice in 1997. Both were designed to provide civilian control over the law enforcement agencies. The rebellion was a reaction to Parliament's attempt to take control away from the politicized armed services. Fifty army personnel were then charged with the capital offense of mutiny and high treason in 1998, providing the first instance in which a court-martial prosecuted LDF soldiers for disobeying the Defense Act. All three services are still currently undergoing restructuring, especially since recent allegations of human rights abuses by the security forces.

There are many reports of corruption in the police forces and the government; however, in recent years, action has been taken against it. It had been confirmed that some police officers were accepting bribes to overlook some traffic and other minor offenses. In addition, the police and army were suspected of being involved in a string of robberies, for which one police officer was sentenced to eight years' imprisonment. Human rights abuses allegedly perpetrated by the security forces include torture, excessive force with detainees, and long delays in trials. There are also no laws prohibiting the monitoring of telephone conversations, and there is no requirement for a search warrant to search persons, vehicles, and homes, through the 1984 Internal Security Act.

Crime

The age of criminal responsibility is 18. Juveniles are afforded rights such as special treatment, including the prohibition on children being sentenced to death and the rules that children must be separated from adult offenders, that the state must monitor the treatment of the children, and that the imprisonment of a juvenile should be avoided at all possible instances, with alternative sanctions provided.

Crimes that are a particular challenge to the area include theft, home invasions, armed robbery, physical and sexual assault, and homicide. It is interesting to note that homosexual acts and photography of government buildings are also both considered illegal in Lesotho. In the 1940s and 1950s, a unique practice called medicine murder was becoming a large problem for the country. These murders involved the removal of a person's flesh, before death, and using the flesh (called *diretlo*) to make protective medicines for the native people. These killings were always said to be premeditated, and a group of people worked together to obtain the flesh. Upon completion of the murder, the body was hidden and the death made to seem like an accident or suspicious death. With so much political conflict occurring, the native Sothos felt as though this *diretlo* would provide the medicine they needed to retain their power in the land.

Traditional crimes, or customary rulings that result in the punishment of natives if disobeyed, that are interesting and specific to Lesotho are written in the Laws of Lerotholi. One is that the chief may take away land that has not been cultivated properly because of absence or insufficient reason, and another is that fines can be imposed on individuals who fail to properly cultivate their land.

There is a large deficit of information regarding drug offenses in Lesotho. The International Narcotics Control Strategy Report of 1995 reported that there was little production or consumption of illegal drugs in Lesotho. It also stated that the two major problems are with cannabis (marijuana), which is cultivated as a cash crop, and the transport of Mandrax through the country (although it is not produced or largely consumed there). Lesotho's Drugs and Diamond Smuggling Unit cooperates with South Africa's police force to intervene in the smuggling of Mandrax, but it is ill-equipped to work on its own.

In 2001, Lesotho drafted the Drugs of Abuse Bill, which outline crimes and punishments that pertain to drug trafficking. Specifically, the bill intends to provide punishment for those who disobey drug laws and to deter potential perpetrators from committing such crimes. Another goal of the Drugs of Abuse Bill is to bring Lesotho into line with the recommendations drawn from international drug conferences, including the 1961 Single Convention on Narcotic Drugs and its 1962 protocol, the 1971 Convention against Psychotropic Substances, and the 1988 United Nations Convention against Illicit Traffic in Narcotic Drugs and Psychotropic Substances. One of the suggestions of the bill is that a narcotics commission or unit should be created in Lesotho's government. This unit would have responsibilities such as conducting research on the prevalence and rate of drug use, growth, and trafficking in the country, which would provide information for policy makers to combat the problem. The bill also provides suggestions concerning the funding of the unit. One includes the creation of a Lesotho Fund for Prevention and Control of Drug Abuse. This fund would raise money to provide institutions for those with substance abuse problems, to provide law enforcement agencies with proper resources to carry out the investigative and adjudication processes of the bill, and to create "controlled delivery" practices. This is somewhat comparable to informants in other countries, and it involves an illegal trafficker participating in an assignment of trafficking drugs under the supervision of law enforcement to catch other perpetrators. The bill was passed in 2007.

Specific crimes are defined in Kasozi's *Introduction of the Law of Lesotho: A Basic Text on Law and Judicial Conduct and Practice, Volume 1.* Murder in Lesotho was defined in 1980 during the judgment of the court case of *Rex v. Mota Phaloane* as the purposeful and illegal killing of another human being. The specifics regarding murder are that the deceased must be a human who has taken at least one breath (therefore ruling that abortion is not murder). Lesser charges include negligent homicide and involuntary manslaughter.

The Roman Dutch and English law applied in Lesotho concerning rape consists of three elements: evidence that shows that the woman was violated in a sexual manner, that the accused was the perpetrator, and that the victim did not give the accused her consent. To be classified as theft, a crime must include the intent to steal something that actually can be stolen. When this act of thievery is combined with force, it then becomes robbery. There is a crime titled assault with intent to do grievous bodily harm.

Crime Statistics

The most recent statistics available regarding serious crimes in Lesotho come from 1999 INTERPOL data. The murder rate was 50.41 murders per 100,000 people; 55.54 people per 100,000 were raped; robbery rates came to 64.82 per 100,000 people; aggravated assault came to 156.88 per 100,000; the burglary rate was 250.35 per 100,000; and the motor vehicle theft rate was 30.76 per 100,000 people. There was reportedly an average of 15.5 serious drug offenses per 100,000 people in the years 1990–2000.

In rural areas, most literature focuses on the extreme lack of adequate roads and highways, leading to carjackings. Travel sites give advice on how to avoid such dangerous criminal activity while driving in rural Lesotho, and such tactics include driving in the middle lanes, keeping windows rolled up, keeping a watchful eye on all mirrors, not returning to the hotel if being followed, locking the car doors, and not stopping at roadblocks.

In urban areas, such as the capital, crime mainly consists of "petty street crime," but these are often accompanied by AK-47 rifles. It is said that it is common for this petty street crime to include criminals attempting to steal money, cell phones, or other valuables and utilizing knives or handguns to do so.

Finding of Guilt

According to the Constitution, the accused have the right to a speedy trial; however, the lack of resources in the criminal court system in Lesotho often results in a backlog of cases. For instance, the Royal Lesotho Mounted Police (RLMP) members who were charged with treason (for the previously described army rebellion that occurred in 1998) remained in the maximum-security prison for 18 months without any real progress with regard to finishing their trials.

Lesotho does not follow simply one code of law but rather follows several, including the Constitution, legislation, common law, judicial precedent, customary law, and authoritative texts. Legislation includes laws that have been passed by both houses of Parliament and acknowledged by the king. Precedent, many times, comes from South African courts, but magistrates' court decisions are not considered precedent because they are lower courts.

The prosecution of cases in Lesotho criminal courts is run by the director of public prosecutions (DPP). He or she can personally exercise this authority or can delegate these powers to subordinate legal officers. In any instance in which a charge has been brought forth upon a person, the Constitution provides the DPP with the power to prosecute that person. In addition, if a trial is already taking place, the DPP has the authority to overtake the proceedings at any time. The DPP has the burden of proving beyond reasonable doubt, using evidence and witnesses, that the accused committed the crime. The trials and criminal courts in Lesotho do not utilize juries, and the trials are public.

The courts in Lesotho are split up into (ranking from highest to lowest) the Court of Appeal, the High Court (and a Labor Court), subordinate courts and courts martial, and "tribunals" designated by Parliament to act with judicial functions. The Court of Appeal has the authority to supervise and review all other courts. The High Court generally hears cases that pertain to constitutional issues, and it has no limit on the jurisdiction of its cases in criminal or civil matters. The Labor Court is equal in power to the High Court but hears only cases with issues of industrial and labor matters. Magistrates' courts (which are included under the subordinate courts) follow the High Courts, and local courts deal with customary law.

The Court of Appeal in Lesotho contains a president, justices of appeal (as many as Parliament prescribes), and the chief justice and *puisne* judges of the High Court (see later description). The president is appointed by the king with aide from the prime minister, and the justices of appeal are also appointed by the king, but with assistance from the Judicial Service Commission and the president. The Judicial Service Commission is constituted by the chief justice, as chairman; the attorney general; the chairman of the Public Service Commission (or someone whom the chairman appoints); and an appointed member (appointed by the king with advice from the chief justice) who has held a high judicial office.

The High Court consists of a chief justice and several other judges (referred to as *puisne* judges). The chief justice is appointed by the king, and all subordinate judges are appointed by the chief justice, as he sees fit. The same qualifications as exist for justices of appeal apply to the *puisne* judges, except that the *puisne* judges are only required to have five years' experience in specified qualifications.

The Constitution of Lesotho clearly states that each defendant has the right to be provided legal aide; however, many times, defendants are not read their rights and are not aware that this is a basic right. In addition, lack of resources makes it difficult for any organizations to provide such aide. There are nongovernmental organizations whose goal is to provide aid to indigent defendants, but they are very few, and they rarely have the necessary resources to achieve their goals. Defendants are detained before trials, but bail is often granted (on a reportedly fair basis). The largest problem with pretrial detainment is the huge backlog of cases, resulting in long waits for the detainees who are not offered bail.

Obviously, the advantage of having legal representation is the aid received in deciphering complicated criminal statutes and precedents and forming a defense around them. The defenses that defense attorneys can use include youth (described previously), insanity, intoxication, provocation, mistake of fact, mistake of law, necessity, defense of property, self-defense, compulsion, superior orders, and consent. Kasozi's *Introduction to the Law of Lesotho* outlines these. Insanity includes the inability of the perpetrator to reason. Intoxication can also be said to diminish the capacity of the defendant to reason and therefore can be used as a defense. In addition, provocation can be used to convert a charge of murder to a finding of culpable homicide, if it can be proved that the defendant was provoked in "the heat of passion." Necessity is used in self-defense defenses, and defense of property is just that. Compulsion includes acts that the defendant is coerced or pushed into committing; superior orders refer to those instances in which the defendant was ordered by someone with authority over him or her to commit an act, but the act must not be known to be illegal to the defendant. Lastly, consent is a defense that involves civil law, in situations where the complainant provided consent to the defendant for the act in question.

Punishment

From the time that the Constitution was drafted in 1993, crimes were punishable by prison sentences, fines, or death. However, to address the growing problem of overcrowding in prisons, new attempts to implement sanctions such as probation, judiciary supervision, and community service have been implemented in the sentencing of criminals in Lesotho. Two other new punishments are verbal sanctions and reprimand. The director of probation service in Lesotho, Ntsi'keng Qhubu, is considered the initiator of restorative justice in Lesotho. She has worked in the probation department in Lesotho since 1989. "Restorative justice" was originally coined with regard to juvenile justice; however, it has recently been implemented in adult criminal justice as well. Two villages in Lesotho have taken on restorative justice programs as trial runs, and they deal with such offenses as domestic violence, faulting on rent payments, child abuse, minor conflicts among neighbors, petty theft, and paternity issues involving young girls who became pregnant out of wedlock. Restorative justice advocates and probation advocates came across some difficulties, however. The first was that many traditional leaders, and their followers, did not trust Western law; therefore, they continue to handle criminal activity within their communities, restorative or not. In addition, both prosecutors and magistrates were reluctant to implement restorative justice policies. More recently, prosecutors and magistrates have recognized the importance of probation and restorative justice, partially through conferences and sensitivity training.

When discussing typical punishments for certain crimes, it is important to take into consideration the difference between customary law and the more recent English and Roman Dutch law. In customary law, most often and for most crimes, a verbal apology is the sentence for the defendant. The perpetrator is expected to show remorse, and there is no guilty plea—if a crime is committed, it is expected and assumed that the perpetrator admits guilt and attempts to "fix" his or her wrongdoing. Historically, even passersby were allowed to participate in the deliberation of the punishment for the offender. For murder, a common punishment in traditional villages was the payment of 10 cattle from the family of the perpetrator to the family of the victim. Other serious offenses resulted in the payment of goat or sheep. A punishment that was said to be harsh was community service in the community. The basic understanding in traditional law, however, was that everyone parted ways peacefully once the punishment was handed down.

The punishment in customary law for seducing a girl under the "apparent" age of 16 or any mentally challenged girl is a fine no more than 50 pounds (approximately $70) or imprisonment no longer than 12 months (or both). And any native who refuses or fails to pay his fine may be fined 1 extra pound and a month of imprisonment. The perpetrator has 6 months from the time he is sentenced to a fine to pay it. In the instance that stock is stolen or killed, if the number of stock stolen or killed was between 1 and 10, the debt owed to the victim is 1 stock. If there were 11 to 20 stock stolen or killed, 2 stock are owed to the victim. Lastly, if there were over 30 stock killed or stolen, 3 are owed to the victim.

In terms of drugs, the laws of Lerotholi prohibit the possession, growth, or use of dagga (marijuana). Any person who disobeys this law is required to pay a fine of no more than 25 pounds or is subject to imprisonment for no more than six months, or both.

The death penalty still exists in Lesotho and is used as a sentence for crimes such as murder, treason, and rape. The kind of rape that warrants the death penalty, however, is specific: the death penalty is given only when the perpetrator is aware that he or she is infected with HIV/AIDS. Not all murder, treason, and rape cases result in the death penalty, and this is because they are used only when there are no extenuating circumstances in the case. Hanging by neck is the method of execution used, and for the last execution (which was in 1996), a professional hangman had to be brought in from another country to execute the perpetrator. The death penalty has not been utilized since 1996. Some suggest that this is because all of the Court of Appeals judges but one are from South Africa, where the death penalty is no longer a legal punishment. Therefore, they are likely to find extenuating circumstances in the cases. There is no death penalty sentence for juveniles or pregnant women. Previous statistics show that between the years of 1992 and 1998, six death sentences were handed down to criminals. Three of these, however, were commuted to prison sentences, ranging from seven years to life. There is a unique process for appealing for clemency or pardon for the death penalty, and that involves the perpetrator appealing to a Pardons Committee established through the Constitution. This committee views presentations made by the defense counsel, the accused, the director of public prosecution, judges from the High Court and Court of Appeal, and the district secretary. The main function of the Pardons Committee is to provide the king with advice on giving out clemency to appellants, after the presentations have been made. The reason that the death penalty remains a legal sanction for heinous crimes is because it is considered a deterrent.

Outside of the death penalty, the typical punishment for murder is a lengthy prison sentence. Depending on the severity of the crime, and the extenuating circumstances, these sentences can range from approximately five years to life. Although there is the possibility of parole in Lesotho's correctional policy, little is available in existing literature. In July 2008, however, nine prisoners were released on parole from Teyateyaneng Prison. They were convicted of crimes such as robbery, theft, malicious damage of property, assault, and other offenses. The nine parolees had served at least half of their sentence and were released on positive behavior in prison.

Prison

There are currently 12 prisons located throughout Lesotho, which accommodated 2,924 inmates in January 2007. There is debate over whether to privatize these 12 prisons into one, large institution. The proposal's argument is that this would alleviate the overcrowding and poor conditions that are plaguing the country's existing prisons. Other reported conditions have included lack of sanitation and bedding and poor nutrition, and although it is stated that pretrial detainees and convicted inmates should be housed separately, this is often not the case. In addition, reports abound that corrections officials are abusive toward the prisoners. For example, in Mohale's Hoek Prison, there were reportedly two deaths of inmates in 2004, following a long period of solitary confinement in which they were stripped, soaked in cold water, and beaten. One of these prisoners suffocated himself with his own handcuffs while the cause of death for the other prisoner proved to be the swallowing of nails.

The ombudsman, an official given the authority to conduct inspections on the prison conditions, reported that between 2002 and 2003, the prisons were overcrowded and unsanitary and provided the inmates with no facilities with which to wash themselves and no activities. Three years later, during the follow-up inspection, the ombudsman reported that some improvements were made in the areas of bedding, blankets, and feeding, but there was very little, if any, improvement in overcrowding, accommodations, transportation for officers, washing stations, and the length it took a detainee to be brought to trial.

The largest prison in Lesotho is Maseru Central Prison, located in Maseru, the capital city of Lesotho. Recently, this prison has come under attack for the poor living conditions and especially the high rate of sodomy, causing HIV/AIDS rates to increase among the inmates. Because of the high rate of sodomy, the International Committee of the Red Cross traveled to Maseru to observe the problems and advise authorities on how to alleviate them. Suggestions included HIV/AIDS education, better access to treatment, and the release of the terminally ill; upon conclusion of the briefing, officials in Maseru Central Prison began distributing condoms and working toward simplifying the process of releasing terminally ill inmates. Another major problem in Maseru Central Prison is overcrowding, and in 2005, the prison (which has a capacity to hold 700 inmates) was housing 1,000.

Inmates who are detained prior to a trial are afforded basic human rights, as well as the right to obtain their own food through family, friends, or other outside sources; the opportunity to work (with payment); the opportunity to communicate with their families; the right to be "tried within reasonable time"; and the right to have legal aid free of charge. During the Lesotho Justice Sector Conference, it was stated that females were to be afforded the same rights as male prisoners. The law of Lesotho provides prisoners with the right to receive visitation from families, but many times, the police do not abide by this law.

Chelsea Diem

Further Reading

Dube, B. (2008). *The Law and Legal Research in Lesotho:* http://www.nyulawglobal.org/globalex/Lesotho.htm#_Sources_of_Law.

Duncan, P. (2006). *Sotho Laws and Customs.* Morija, Lesotho: Morija Printing Works.

Government of Lesotho—Government Constitution. (1993). http://www.lesotho.gov.ls/documents/Lesotho_Constitution.pdf.

Kasozi, G. W., ed. (1999). *Introduction to the Law of Lesotho: A Basic Text on Law and Aspects of Judicial Conduct and Practice, Volume 1.* Maseru, Lesotho: Ministry of Justice, Human Rights, and Rehabilitation.

Qhubu, N. (n.d.). *The Development of Restorative Justice in Lesotho:* http://www.doj.gov.za/alraesa/conferences/papers/s4B_qhubu.pdf.

Liberia

Legal System: Common/Customary
Murder: High
Corruption: High
Human Trafficking: Medium
Prison Rate: Low
Death Penalty: No
Corporal Punishment: Yes

Background

Liberia is a relatively small nation located in western Africa. Bordered by the Atlantic Ocean to the west, Liberia is bounded by the nations of Côte d'Ivoire and Sierra Leone, covering an area of approximately 43,000 square miles. The nation's population was nearly 3.5 million in 2008. Liberia is a republic built around three branches of government: the executive, the legislative, and the judicial. The executive branch of the Liberian government is commanded by the president/chief of state elected to a maximum of two terms of six years by popular vote. Liberia has a bicameral legislature with a Senate and House of Representatives. Each of these senators is elected by popular vote to serve nine-year terms. The judicial branch's primary body is the Supreme Court. The high court consists of one chief justice and four associate justices, each nominated by the president and confirmed by the Senate. They commonly serve until retirement or death, though there is a mechanism for removal through impeachment. The Supreme Court of Liberia holds original jurisdiction over cases of constitutional consequence. It is also the adjudicator of those cases involving ambassadors, ministers, or countries as a party.

Crime Statistics

Precise crime statistics are difficult to obtain. Instead, the records of international observers and foreign embassies in Liberia are relied on to generalize crime occurrence. And in general, crime in Liberia is high, likely exacerbated by extremely high unemployment rates. This is true in both the rural and the urban areas of Liberia. Theft, assault, burglary, child abuse, rape, domestic violence, and murder are existing problems of concern in both rural and urban areas.

Rape is especially rampant, even among children. This is, in part, a remnant of Liberia's recent and dark past. So prevalent was rape during the country's 14-year civil war that it is now thought of as commonplace, ranking only as a petty offense to many citizens. So minor is attention to rape now that only five convicted rapists are serving time in the country's largest prison.

The circumstances surrounding the country's murder problem are of special interest too. Aside from the common motivations, Liberia has also experienced murders as a result of land disputes, mob violence, and ritualistic killings. This last occurrence is especially troubling. Occurring with some regularity, these murders happen when body parts are severed as part of a traditional indigenous ritual. The exact number of these ritual killings is, like other Liberian crime statistics, difficult to determine because the police regularly miscategorize these killings as suicides or accidents. This has been true even when body parts were missing. As a consequence, there were no prosecutions of ritual murders in 2008.

The drama of rape and murder aside, most crime in Liberia is opportunistic theft. Weapons used in the commission of theft commonly include knives and machetes, but some thieves have also acquired firearms. Other Liberians are the most common targets and victims of theft; however, relatively wealthy foreign visitors present an enticing target to these thieves as well.

Police

Following years of civil war and political instability, much of Liberia is being rebuilt. That statement extends to its police force as well. As it stands today, the Liberian police do not even have primary security responsibility. Since the 2003 peace agreement, those duties have been mostly assigned to the 15,000 United Nations Mission in Liberia (UNMIL) peacekeepers and United Nations international police

Three men convicted of the rape of four young girls are photographed at the prison in Monrovia, Liberia, on June 2, 2007. According to the girls, the three men, members of the "Never Die" Church, kept them captive and abused them for years until they were able to escape. The men are among the first rapists convicted under the country's revised penal code, a turning point in what people here call a "war on rape." (AP Photo/Rebecca Blackwell)

(UNPOL). This is likely just as well because Liberian police and security personnel carry no weapons because of a 2003 disarmament program.

As part of their mission in Liberia, UN forces are also providing reform, restructuring, and training to the "new" Liberian National Police, a measure prescribed in the now highly influential 2003 Accra peace accord. Established in 1956, the "old" Liberian National Police were found to have lagged in their commitment to and effectiveness in achieving their mission of protecting life and property; maintaining law and order; preventing, detecting and investigating crime; and preserving and enhancing internal security. As part of this restructuring, several thousand "old" LNP officers were dismissed, having not met the new, more stringent standards established by UN forces. This restructuring began in earnest in May 2004 with the recruitment of new officers, with an eventual target of 3,500. Training commenced in July of that year with the reopening of the National Police Academy. By November, the first class of 132 new officers was being deployed to their respective counties. Since then, according to a United Nations report, more than 2,000 more trained officers have followed.

As a result of the new LNP and the UN presence, the security situation in Liberia has improved since 2003 but still remains volatile. International observers still find that the LNP have limited capabilities to prevent crime or provide emergency response. This does vary slightly depending on location according to some reports. Within the capital, Monrovia, services are slightly better but still below acceptable levels. Outside the capital, though, security forces are in near total absence. As a result, many foreign consulates recommend that visitors not even venture outside the capital because of the security situation.

The continued ineffectiveness of the police likely stems from two pressing issues. The first is that, like many other West African nations, Liberian police are resource-poor. The police there have extremely limited logistical, communication, and forensic capabilities, among other things. This severely impacts their ability to successfully investigate crimes of any nature, including murder. Were the LNP even able to investigate adequately, there remains some question about whether they would. As in other areas of the Liberian government, corruption runs rampant through the police too. The situation has improved over recent years, but there are still accounts of bribe solicitation and abuse of citizens by the police. Low and irregular LNP pay has likely contributed to this persistent corruption.

Courts

The judicial branch's primary body is the Supreme Court. The high court consists of one chief justice and four associate justices, each nominated by the president and confirmed by the Senate. They commonly serve until retirement or death, though there is a mechanism for removal via impeachment. Below the Supreme Court there is a system of 15 circuit courts, one in each of the country's 15 counties. These courts are presided over by rotating circuit judges who sit in quarterly sessions. The rotation itself is set by the Supreme Court's chief justice. At the lowest level of courts are a variety of specialized courts. Specialized courts include labor, debt, tax, probate, and juvenile courts as well as others. This is also the level on which courts of first instance such as magisterial and justice of the peace courts exercise their limited jurisdictional authority.

The Liberian Constitution prohibits arbitrary arrest and detention. This is not always observed in practice though. Neither is the constitutional requirement of arrest warrants and prompt appearance before a magistrate. Instead, warrants often have been based on insufficient evidence, and those without the means of hiring an attorney were often held for more than 48 hours before arraignment. At arraignment, Liberian law does provide for bail with the exception of cases involving rape, murder, armed robbery, and treason. If denied bail, detainees must also have prompt access to counsel, familial visits, and a court-appointed attorney in the case of the indigent. Again, these rights are not always observed in practice. This is especially true of court-appointed attorneys. There is no public defender's office established in Liberia, and the indigent rely on the altruism of local attorneys. These attorneys are not required to serve and are not punished for failing to. Consequently, many pretrial detainees languish in jail for long stretches of time. Were the detainees' case to finally proceed to trial (convictions are rare in Liberia), they would find several more constitutional rights. Beyond a presumption of innocence, defendants also have the right to confront or question witnesses against them, to access state-held evidence relevant to their case, to present evidence and witnesses on their own behalf, and to appeal adverse decisions. But because of the corruption present, even in the judiciary, these rights are often denied if a defendant is unable to pay a bribe to the judge.

These wavering rights contribute to a court system that remains barely functional. In addition to endangering the liberty of citizens, the corruption present in the court system has led to inconsistent and unpredictable application of the law. Like the police, the court system suffers from low pay and shortages of all kinds. In personnel shortage terms, the law requires that all magistrates be lawyers. But the relative paucity of the legally trained in Liberia has meant this is not always the case. There are only 22 judges in Liberia. Even when a qualified person is found, the judge often cannot hold court because of a lack of security, supplies, equipment, or even a courthouse. This inability to hold court, whatever its cause, has led to a severe backlog of cases. This backlog now means it might be years before a case is heard. To make matters worse, Liberia's penal code has been out of print since the 1950s. Judges must now rely on blurred photocopies of the statutes during sentencing.

Alongside the Anglo-American system described here is another parallel system of mostly unwritten customary laws practiced within Liberia's indigenous population. Of particular interest is this system's continued use of trial by ordeal in spite of its prohibition by the Supreme Court. This process of physical examination, brutal by Western standards, commonly involves either the ingestion of a substance meant to cause illness or the application of a fire-warmed machete to the legs of the accused. The belief is, essentially, that the innocent will be unharmed by these trials, whereas the guilty will obviously suffer from them. This suffering can and has varied from slight discomfort on up to and including death.

Punishment

Conditions within Liberia's correctional facilities have been generously described as harsh by various sources. In many ways the conditions can also be life-threatening. In spite of having been established over 30 years ago, the correctional system is still in its early stages of development. As it currently exists, the system is overcrowded, underfunded, and plagued by deplorable conditions.

The most prominent issue facing Liberia's correctional system is overcrowding. To illustrate this, the official capacity of Liberia's 15 prison facilities is only 750. But at the end of 2008, they held 1,624 according to the Bureau of Rehabilitation and Corrections. On an individual facility level, the problem is just as grave. Liberia's largest facility, Monrovia Central Prison, has a stated maximum capacity of 150 but regularly houses more than 500, causing single cells to hold 12–15 individuals each. This overcrowding has led to other unfortunate consequences, besides the personal discomfort of inmates. The first is the mixing of different inmate categories. This intermingling exists between genders, ages (juvenile and adult), and status (pretrial and convicted). And because of the vast numbers of inmates and a limited budget, there exists a serious shortage of guards and correctional staff to adequately oversee the prison population. This imbalance was partially to blame for the December 2008 escape of 200 inmates from Monrovia Central Prison. And because of the ineffectiveness of the police, 165 of those inmates have evaded capture. Thankfully, there are renovation and expansion efforts underway at select facilities. Monrovia Central itself is in the process of constructing a new 100- to 150-inmate cell block funded by the U.S. government.

A large part of the overcrowding issue comes from a ripple effect that begins in the courts. Because of the backlog in the courts, cases are not heard in a timely fashion. This has created a large population of pretrial detainees, a population so large it accounts for 97.3 percent of those held in Liberia's correctional facilities. There is also the chance that nearly 4 percent of the prison population should not be there at all according to the law—4.3 percent of Liberia's prison population is under the age of 18, and many magistrates are unaware that many juvenile offenders should not be in prison. Both of these court system factors have contributed strongly to the present overcrowding.

The corrections system, like the police and courts, suffers from lack of funding. This underfunding has led to an insufficient staff and heavy reliance on foreign aid for operating expenses. If not for this foreign aid, many inmates would likely go without medical care. Of even more concern is that if it were not for the World Food program and various nongovernmental organizations, some inmates might not even receive sufficient nourishment.

Similar to the police and courts, the corrections system is showing signs of progress. Juvenile justice, for example, is beginning to receive attention. There still remains no formalized juvenile justice system in Liberia, stop-gap measures do exist. Monrovia's Don Bosco Children's Centre, a pseudo-rehabilitation home, is one such attempt, at least in cases of less serious juvenile crimes such as theft. And in the case of formal detention, there are efforts being made to ensure that children have cells separate from their adult counterparts, though interaction with adults in common areas is still unaddressed.

The adult convict is also finding new, progressive options. Rather than simply prison, the Liberian Bureau of Rehabilitation and Corrections has recently instituted some rehabilitation programs in a number of its facilities. At their core, these new programs look to recruit and train convicts in fields including rice farming, cloth weaving, brick making, soap making, and rabbit farming. Officials hope that if these convicts are trained in a needed skill, their post-release reintegration into society will be more successful. Because the program only began in 2008, no results have been obtained at current date.

Michael Galezewski

Further Reading

Bureau of Democracy, Human Rights, and Labor. (2007). *Liberia International Religious Freedom Report 2007:* http://www.state.gov/g/drl/rls/irf/2007/90105.htm.

Bureau of Rehabilitation and Corrections. (2008, December 31). *Annual Activities Report:* http://www.moj.gov.lr/press.php.

Callimachi, R. (2007, August 7). "Liberian Rape Victims Fighting Back." *The Seattle Times:* http://seattletimes.nwsource.com/html/nationworld/2003824753_liberia07.html.

The Ministry of Justice. (n.d.). *Overview of the Liberia National Police:* http://www.moj.gov.lr/lnp.html.

United Nations Mission in Liberia. (n.d.). *Corrections:* http://unmil.org/1content.asp?ccat=corrections&zdoc=1.

Madagascar

Legal System: Civil/Customary
Murder: Medium
Corruption: Medium
Human Trafficking: Low
Prison Rate: Medium
Death Penalty: Maybe

Background

Madagascar, also known as the Republic of Madagascar, is a southern African country located in the Indian Ocean. It is the world's fourth-largest island, and according to the Central Intelligence Agency's World Factbook, Madagascar had a population of approximately 19,448,815 million people as of July 2007. The people of Madagascar are mostly of Malagasy nationality with cultural ties to Africa and Asia; however, the country was once under the control of France and eventually gained independence in 1960.

The legal system of Madagascar is a mix of civil and customary law. It is based on both the French civil law system and traditional Malagasy law. Therefore, it focuses more on codified law than case law and precedent, as is typical of the common law system. It also uses a traditional *dina* system, which was in use in the country prior to colonization to control resource use, community behavior, and property rights in isolated areas of the country.

Police

The police force in Madagascar has a rich history with roots in the military. While under the control of France, Madagascar fought in many wars for its colonial masters. As such, the armed forces and some state security services still reflect French practices today.

Besides the FAP, or the Forces Armees Populaires, there are five state security services: the National Gendarmerie, the Republican Security Force (FRS), the Civil Police, the Civil Service, and the Antigang Brigade. All of these groups are outside the FAP command with the exception of the National Gendarmerie. The National Gendarmerie has 7,500 members and operates within the Ministry of Defense. There are units of the National Gendarmerie stationed throughout the island, to maintain public order, maintain security in the villages, pursue criminals, protect government buildings, and even prevent cattle thievery. These units are also assisted in some areas by regular army units in operations against bandit gangs and cattle thieves. The gendarmerie has automatic weapons, armored cars, and even aircraft at its disposal. In addition, it operates a maritime police force.

Madagascar police and army patrol the streets before the start of an antigovernment rally in Antananarivo, Madagascar, on January 31, 2009. About 4,500 people joined the rally, called by the capital's mayor after a week of violence in Madagascar left at least 43 people dead. (AP Photo/Jerome Delay)

The Civil Police are also enforcers of the law in Madagascar. Their 3,000 members' presence can be felt mostly in island cities. The Civil Police fall under the jurisdiction of the Ministry of Interior. However, just like the National Gendarmerie and other security forces, the police force tends to overreact during times of civil strife, which has provoked many opponents and protestors. In addition, the Civil Service is a paramilitary force, which is a type of reserve force. Its operations are nonmilitary and involve work in rural and social development programs.

Finally, the Antigang Brigade was established with the help of the French in 1989. This unit also reports to the Ministry of Interior and is used for combating hijackers, terrorism, and dangerous criminals. Moreover, the brigade is trained by French security, as are many other security forces in the country.

The state secretary of the Ministry of Interior for Public Security and the national police are accountable for law and order in the capital city, Antananarivo, and other large cities in the country. In addition, there are traffic police and village-level law enforcement groups that enforce local traditional laws called *dina.* These enforcers are especially prevalent in areas where the government's presence is weak. However, the resources available to these local police services are limited because the majority of the population live in poverty. Therefore, police responsiveness to citizens' calls is, at times, inadequate and ineffective. Crime responses are slow or nonexistent for the average citizen, even in the larger cities. For example, in the capital of

Antananarivo, a district police office will have only one to two police cars available to respond to citizens' calls and crimes. In general, even though the police are mostly capable and professional, a lack of training and equipment, low salaries, and corruption are still apparent within the nation's law enforcement.

Overall, there have been and continue to be reports that police, gendarmes, and *dina* authorities are corrupt and have committed human rights abuses. However, the country and its administration have acknowledged this and have been making strides to try to reduce these acts of misconduct.

Crime

Despite its impoverished economy, the capital city, Antananarivo, has seen a decline in violent crime. The vast majority of crime in the capital is petty street crime, such as pickpocketing and "grab and runs." These crimes of opportunity are the most prevalent; however, other serious offenses do occur.

Classification of Crimes

Crimes in Madagascar are classified as misdemeanors and felonies. Felony crimes include murder, assault, rape, and those of rebellion against the state. Other offenses, such as cattle theft, pickpocketing, and other petty street theft, are considered misdemeanors. However, to be charged with any of these crimes, an offender must be 13 years old, which is the minimum age of criminal responsibility in Madagascar.

The country has recently turned its attention toward the crime of human trafficking. There have been reports of trafficking in women and girls for prostitution between Madagascar and the neighboring islands of Mauritius and Reunion. Children also have been trafficked from rural areas to work as prostitutes in urban areas. Although human trafficking and prostitution are not specifically prohibited, in 2000 the law prohibited pedophilia and sexual tourism. Therefore, traffickers may be prosecuted under the provision that outlaws pedophilia or under laws that prohibit child labor. The trafficking problem is a serious one for the country. In 2005, the government also passed a new adoption law, in part so that children could not be trafficked under the excuse of adoption. However, the lack of resources makes it difficult to combat human trafficking effectively. There are also reports that trafficking is initiated individually and does not involve coercion, force, or fraud. There were reportedly 700–800 child prostitutes in the city of Nosy Be and 2,000-plus in the city of Toamasina in 2005.

In addition, Madagascar law prohibits domestic violence. However, it has been reported by the State Department of the United States that 50 percent of women have experienced domestic abuse. Even so, when women do report domestic violence, the police generally intervene.

Another pervasive problem within the country is theft. Incidents of cattle theft are common. There are special courts to deal with those charged with cattle theft. Agriculture is also a huge component of the country and its economy, so theft of certain crops is an issue. Pickpocketing is also common, especially targeting Westerners who visit. Thieves will steal from unlocked cars as well. Some more serious types of stealing deal with criminal gangs made up of foreign felons, ex-military personnel, and police from former regimes who are known to commit home invasions and kidnapping. These organized gangs patrol areas where they think the wealthy, foreign visitors congregate. Burglary does happen outside the capital as well, but the threat of confrontational crimes is less prevalent in those rural areas.

In Madagascar the prevalence of illicit drugs has been growing in recent years according to the government. Cannabis is a ubiquitous drug in Madagascar. The country is a producer of cannabis, but most of it is used for domestic consumption, and thus, there has been an increase in cannabis use in remote areas. In addition, the country has experienced increasing numbers of people using cocaine, heroin, and Ecstasy, especially among high school–aged youth. Madagascar is also used as a transshipment point for heroin.

Crime Statistics

The only available data relating to the incidence of Madagascar crime were from 1995 INTERPOL data for Madagascar. According to the INTERPOL data, for murder, the rate in 1995 was 1.75 per 100,000 population; rape in 1995 was 1.19; robbery was 3.24; aggravated assault was 21.45; burglary was 16.52; and larceny was 1.24.

Finding of Guilt

The Malagasy penal code affords those accused of crimes with most of the rights and protections granted under French and Western law. The Constitution provides for due process of those people accused. There is a presumption of innocence until proven guilty under the country's penal code. Trials are public, and the accused has a right to attend the trial. The accused also has a general right to an attorney and to be informed of the charges against him or her. However, the government is required to provide counsel only in cases where an indigent defendant is being charged with a crime that carries a punishment of a prison sentence greater than five years. In addition, the rights to confront witnesses and to present evidence are also present in the country.

The law also requires that state agents use warrants unless they are in hot pursuit. However, many citizens are detained and jailed solely on accusations made by others. Therefore, despite legal safeguards, infringement of a person's rights and arbitrary arrest and detention do occur.

Bail exists in the country's criminal justice system; however, in practice, it is not available to many defendants. Because bail is often rejected, it is rarely requested. Instead, the country uses a retaining writ (*mandat de depot*), and the defendant is held in detention during the entire pretrial period. This long pretrial detention is a serious problem. In addition, a crime suspect is to be charged or released within 48 hours. However, this is not always the case in Madagascar In practice, investigative detention often exceeds one year, and many detainees spend longer periods in investigative detention than they would have spent in incarceration for the maximum sentence for what they were charged. Therefore, this lengthy investigative detention is a problem within the country and results in the denial of a person's due process. Poor recordkeeping and a lack of resources are also part of the cause of this. The Ministry of Justice has tried in recent years to reduce this excessive pretrial detention through case reviews and expedited judgments. However, the backlog of cases still remains a problem.

Jurisdiction under the Ministry of Justice has three levels. There are lower courts called the courts of first instance that hear civil cases and criminal cases carrying limited fines and sentences. There is a Court of Appeals, which is also the criminal court of first instance for cases with sentences greater than five years. The Supreme Court hears appeals from the Court of Appeals. A fourth separate and autonomous court, the High Constitutional Court or *Haute Cour Constitutionelle,* reviews the constitutionality of laws, decrees, ordinances, and electoral disputes.

There are also specialized courts that handle matters such as cattle theft and cases that deal with civil disputes within and between villages. These courts deal with traditional *dina* laws, such as property issues. However, in practice, they also address criminal cases, given the isolation of many rural areas and the ineffective police and judiciary outside of the cities. The decisions based on *dina* are not subject to codified safeguards for the accused; however, there are instances where they can be challenged at an appeal court level.

Additionally, there are special military courts that handle all cases involving national security. The defendants in military courts have an appeals process as well. Also, it should be noted that Madagascar accepts compulsory International Court of Justice (ICJ) jurisdiction only with reservations. The ICJ is a court of 15 judges elected for nine-year terms by the United Nations General Assembly and Security Council. Its purpose is to settle legal disputes submitted to it by the member states, such as Madagascar, and to give advisory opinions on legal questions submitted to it.

There is a special Tribunal for Children, which is situated at the first instance courts. If a person accused of committing a crime is 13 to 18 years old, the juvenile judge may decide whether or not to charge the youth. These juvenile judges for the courts are chosen from the courts of first instance depending on their interests and aptitudes in the area. There is also a magistrate designated by the attorney general whose job is to follow children's cases and offer measures to improve their safety. In addition, in Madagascar, a juvenile's name cannot be revealed to the public. However, in practice, the juvenile justice system, like other entities in the criminal justice system, is lacking in resources, judges (there are approximately 50 in the country), specialized training among judges, and social workers to assist the judges. Instead, many juveniles are sent to residential centers without a judge being involved.

The judiciary officials are appointed and elected along with other public officials. For example, the first president is elected by the Superior Council of Prosecutors and General Assembly of the Supreme Court, holds a three-year term, and can be reelected once. The general prosecutor is appointed by the president of the republic acting in the Council of Ministers from a list nominated by the Supreme Council of Prosecutors. This position also holds a three-year term, and the official can be reelected once. The High Constitutional Court has nine members who each hold one six-year term. Three of the members are appointed by the president of the republic, two by the National Assembly, one by the Senate, and three by the Superior Council of the Magistrates.

However, the country's judiciary has lost much trust from its citizens because of the pernicious corruption within the system, and even though the law provides for an independent judiciary, it is susceptible to executive influence. According to the 2007 Transparency International Corruption Perception Index, the country ranked 94th out of 180 countries in amount of corruption.

To combat the corruption, the Malagasy government established an Anti-Corruption National Council in September 2002. In May 2004, an Anti-Corruption Judiciary Unit (CPAC) was established in Antananarivo, which consists of magistrates, public prosecutors, and judges trained in corruption matters. They have offices separate from other judiciary offices to help ensure their impartiality and trustworthiness. The judiciary is one sector affected by corruption because of low salaries, lack of training, and complex judicial proceedings that require a long series of steps before a resolution can be reached. Therefore, bribery can offer an expeditious resolution to a case. Along with the Anti-Corruption Independent Bureau (BIANCO), the CPAC has uncovered and prosecuted many corruption cases. Most tend to be petty corruption within the police and judiciary. These include abuse of power, solicitation of bribes, and extortion. In 2003, 12 magistrates were suspended for corrupt practices, and in September 2005, a judge was suspended for one year for having taken an eight-dollar bribe from the family of a detained prisoner. BIANCO is continuing to battle this low-level corruption by using ethics forums.

Punishment

In Madagascar, punishments for crimes can vary from fines and hard labor to imprisonment and death. Imprisonment is one of the areas in most dire need of improvement.

Types of Punishment

The types of punishment used in Madagascar vary. The country uses fines, probation, prisons, and hard labor. The most severe punishment is death by firing squad, although it is rarely administered. Forced exile is also available as a type of punishment, but there are no cases where it has been used.

Punishments for murder normally range from forced labor to imprisonment. The punishment for rape is usually 5 to 10 years in prison. Rape of a child or a pregnant woman is punishable by hard labor. Punishment for cattle theft tends to be monetary fines when coming before the local-level judiciary, which is limited to monetary damages.

Juvenile punishments vary from adult punishments for the most part. Because the minimum age of criminal responsibility in Madagascar is 13, if juveniles under 13 commit a misdemeanor, they receive a police warning (*admonestation*), and if they commit a serious act, educative measures are taken, such as being returned to their parents. If 13- to 18-year-olds are found guilty of misdemeanors, they are given fines or probation. If the juvenile is 13 to 16 years old, the excuse of being a minor can have the sentence reduced to half that of an adult. For a serious crime, the excuse of being a minor is still retained and can reduce the sentence. If the crime comes with a sentence of death, forced labor for life, or deportation, the juvenile will get 10 to 12 years' imprisonment. If the crime comes with a sentence of forced labor or detention, it is cut in half. If a 13- to 16-year-old is found not responsible for the crime, educative measures are used, and they can be sent to re-educative centers up until they 21 years old. There are two of these centers run under the Ministry of Justice and three that are private. However, judges can reject the juvenile defense of 16- to 18-year-olds and sentence them as adults, with the exception of the death penalty, which is restricted to only adults.

Additionally, in 2001, it was decided that persons accused of rebellious acts could be detained incommunicado and could be subject to indefinite detention if deemed necessary by the government.

Prison

Madagascar has 97 prisons, holding approximately 17,495 prisoners as of December 2006 according to its National Prison Administration. The country has a nationwide prison system, with each of the six provinces in Madagascar having a central prison for inmates serving sentences of less than five years. There are also at least 25 lesser prisons for individuals serving less than two year terms and those awaiting trial. Courts at the local level (subprefecture) maintain jails for lesser offenders serving time for less than six months.

Nevertheless, with all the facilities, the country's prisons still suffer from overcrowding, and according to nongovernmental organizations (NGOs), some prisoners have to be held in storage warehouses. One prison in Ambositra had a capacity of only 80 inmates but actually held 400. Another, Tsiafahy Detention Center, usually reserved for the serious criminals, held up to 620 inmates even though its capacity was supposed to be 200. The reasons cited for the overcrowding include all of the arrests following the political crisis in the country and all of those inmates being held for lengthy pretrial detention. These pretrial detainees make up 64.7 percent of all prisoners. However, the country's overcrowding also stems from the fact that many of those who are tried before a court are expected to pay a court fee before they can receive their judgment. If they cannot pay the fee, they are then returned to jail. Overall, the official capacity of the Madagascar prison system is 13,462; however, the occupancy level was at 130 percent as of December 2006. This was even after the government granted 7,279 pardons to reduce overcrowding.

According to the International Centre for Prison Studies, 3.3 percent of the total prisoners are female. Women prisoners who are sent to serve long prison sentences are usually sent to the Central Prison (*Maisono Centrale*) in Antannarivo. Rape is not an uncommon occurrence for females in prison. In addition, female prisoners are found to engage in prostitution in collusion with prison guards. Gender segregation is not absolute. There have been some reports of rapes committed by other prisoners. Sometimes preschool-aged children are put with their mothers in cells and end up abused as well.

In addition, juveniles are not always held separate from the adult prison population. Those under 18 years of age make up 2.4 percent of the prison population. The pretrial detention inmates are also not always held separate from the general prison population either; 0.1 percent of the total prisoners are foreign.

Besides the overcrowding and mixing of various prison populations, the harsh prison conditions are also life-threatening. Prison cells allow for less than one square yard of space per inmate. Cells built for one inmate can at times hold up to eight, and inmates have to take turns to sleep. A prisoner's diet is usually 100 grams of cassava or rice per day. Usually families or NGOs such as Catholic Prisoners

Chaplain will supplement the food for some of the inmates. Therefore, those inmates lacking relatives can go several days without food. Those prisoners who are brought to the capital to be tried, especially during the times of political turmoil, can go days without food because their families may not be able to afford to travel to see them. The prison cells can also contain several people with only one toilet, no running water, and no electricity.

The medical care is also inadequate. From January 1, 2005, to September 30, 2005, 144 prisoners died from malnutrition, diseases such as malaria and tuberculosis, and neglect. These deaths occurred even though the International Committee of the Red Cross (ICRS) and the Ministry for Health and Family Planning provided disinfection services to help prevent outbreaks and epidemics of disease. A study published in the *Journal of Research in Microbiology* found that the incidence of tuberculosis was 16 times higher in the Antananarivo prison than in the general population.

Rape is commonplace in Madagascar prisons as well. It is used by guards and other inmates to humiliate prisoners. Inmates also can be used as forced labor. The lack of resources makes it difficult to have any type of prison program. However, there have been organizations dedicated to restorative justice in the country's prisons. The Prison Fellowship International has an entity called Fraternite des Prisons au Madagascar. Its aim is to work with prisoners to help heal broken relationships, repair the damage done by the crime, and restore the offender to a productive role in society. This initiative has 50 volunteers in the country who have been involved in restorative justice with 11 Madagascar prisons, working with 7,500 prisoners.

Raquel Hutts

Further Reading

Rasolofo-Razanamparany, V., D. Menard, M Ratsitorahina, G. Auregan, B. Gicquel, and S. Chanteau (2000). "Transmission of Tuberculosis in the Prison of Antananarivo (Madagascar)." *Journal of Research in Microbiology* 151: 785–795.

U.S. Department of State. (2006). *Country Reports on Human Rights Practices:* http://www.state.gov.

Malawi

Legal System: Common/Customary
Murder: High
Corruption: Medium
Human Trafficking: Medium
Prison Rate: Medium
Death Penalty: Yes
Corporal Punishment: No

Background

Formerly known as Nyazal, Malawi is a landlocked country bordered by Tanzania to the north and west and Mozambique to the south. With an estimated population of over 12 million (2003), it is one of the most populated sub-Saharan countries. Colonization introduced new frontiers in the sociopolitical context to the extent that all the indigenous people had to relate to the British rule—politics, law, crime, policing order, judicial process, and punishments or penal system. Prior to colonial rule, there existed forms and practices of crime and punishment in Malawi that the British authorities called Nyasaland. Response to crime was handled in communal ways under the supervision and coordination of the heads of the clans and villages. These were the practices that had to be abrogated or realigned so that the resilient elements coexisted along those of the colonial authorities. Since becoming independent in 1964, the primary goals of the multiparty system have been democracy, rule of law, and human rights.

Crime

Crime Statistics

Crimes and other social problems appear to have been a major concern to the people of Malawi since the mid-1990s. Additionally, a variety of social problems plague Malawian society, including poverty, environmental crime caused by rising human encroachment on the wetlands, and the high rate of HIV/AIDS infection.

Though crime data are not easily available in Malawi, data from the International Crime Victim Surveys (ICVS) suggest fairly high victimization rates among the respondents. In a United Nations survey of 2,984 respondents, 44 percent reported that they were victims of crime between May 2002 and May 2003. The most reported victimization related to theft of crops, livestock, burglary, personal property, and bicycles, suggesting the agrarian background of the victims. Violent crimes such as assault, robbery, murder, and sexual assault were less common; however, for the period August 2000 to July 2002, the police recorded 789 cases of crimes involving small arms.

Illegal Firearms

Malawi has a serious social problem of illegal firearms. According to the Malawi police, a total of 318 illegal firearms were seized between 1996 and 2001 and 105 illegal firearms in the first quarter of 2002. These firearms, which were seized mostly from organized crime syndicates, included AK-47 assault rifles and pistols.

Border Crimes

Malawi's porous borders with Mozambique, Tanzania, and Zambia have been a source of major concerns over border crimes. These concerns have led to at least joint public displays of bilateral and even multilateral courses of action. Perhaps the most ambitious of these courses of action involves completion of the extradition treaty between Malawi and Zambia. The work on this treaty started in 2004.

Trafficking of Women and Children

Although there has been public discourse on trafficking of women, a numerical account of the extent of the problem is unavailable. The discourse circulates around government circles and NGOs. Police actions or those of the military have been ad hoc at best.

Malawi is considered by many observers to be a country of origin as well as transit for trafficking of women and children, both for child labor and for sexual purposes. South Africa is one of the destination countries in this business. Until recent years, there was hardly any documentation of trafficking of women and children. Activities for enhanced documentation are now being carried out by the Center for Social Concern and Center for the Protection of Trafficked Persons. There are several provisions in the penal code with respect to prostitution and indecency. One of the provisions involves imprisonment on conviction.

Juvenile Delinquency

This is an umbrella concept that incorporates a variety of antisocial (or deviant) behavior, on one hand, and legal violations on the other. Youth legal violations include those behaviors for which adults often get prosecuted and those violations for which only persons under 18 years of age get taken to court. An example of the latter is truancy or running from school as well as home. A number of both international and national NGOs have stepped up their efforts to deal with the needs and problems of the street children in Malawi. The national NGOs include the Scouts Association of Malawi; the Street Children's Ministry based in Blantgre, Malawi; and the Chisomo Children's Club.

Corruption

Corruption is probably the most talked about social problem in the circles of the African stakeholders. Data from the International Crime Victims survey (ICVS) suggest that public experience with officials is fraught with problems and concerns. Of a total sample of 2,984, nearly 6 percent (N = 384) noted that they had been asked for money to perform a service that was legally required of officials to conduct.

Despite the crime problems, the number of victims reporting crime to police is relatively low. The ICVS data suggest that the two most common crimes that victims report to police are theft of crops and livestock, though the highest degree of victimization was for housebreaking (32.6%) and theft of personal property (37.5%). Some of the reasons for this include a general perception that the crime was not serious enough to warrant reporting to the police; the victims' sense that they do not have enough evidence to report the matter to police; and the knowledge that stolen property rarely if ever gets returned back to the owner.

Police

The Malawi Police Force (MPS) was first established in 1921 under the Ministry of Justice. It had its headquarters in Zomba along with the regional headquarters to which two dozen or so district commandants reported. As in the other British colonies, the top policy makers and administrators were British, and the Africans occupied the lowest echelons. In terms of organizational structure, there were several divisions aside from the central administration. Examples include Criminal Investigation, the Special Branch for Intelligence, the Immigration Service, the Police Mobile Service, the Police Mobile Force, and Training School. In 2003, there were 7,915 staff with the Malawi police service; a majority of them (61%) are young, between the ages of 18 and 35, with men outnumbering women by a ratio of 5:1. Some estimates indicate that the current strength of the police force is not adequate to carry out the tasks and that an additional 4,625 personnel are needed to reach its strategic goal of 1 police officer for every 1,000 Malawians.

Organizational Structure of the Police Service

The police service is currently one of the major components of the Ministry of Home Affairs. The inspector general of police heads the police service and reports to the minister of home affairs, a concept that also is reflected in the other southern African countries other than South Africa.

Citizens' Complaints

Citizens' complaints against the police, as well as other legal or criminal justice authorities, have a place in a democratic society. Malawi now claims such a society. The previous regime, of Hastings Banda (1961–1994) had notorious young pioneers as a youth branch of its political party. They were involved in conducting dirty tricks against Banda's real as well as imagined political opponents. To bolster citizens' confidence in the police, the Malawi Community Safety and Firearms Control Project (MCSFCP) was implemented through community policing programs that were originally established to deal with crime problems.

Police Reform

By African standards, Malawi joined the ranks of progressive countries in police reform at the dawn of the 21st century. The categories of its police reform include the mission, organizational structure, administrative management, and organizational culture.

For purposes of improving the professional standards of the police, the starting point is the collection and publication of comprehensive crime and policing data. Data should be made available not only for new and emerging crimes but also for those crimes that are traditional in any country, such as homicide, assault, and theft.

Finding of Guilt

Courts

The court system consists of the superior (Supreme Court and the High Court) and subordinate courts (magistrates' courts). Criminal cases are grouped by the seriousness of the offense, in which case serious offenses include murder, armed robbery, and treason. Only the superior courts have jurisdiction in these offenses. The courts are also categorized by their time frames for resolving cases. For example, subordinate courts are essentially the courts of origin for minor or less serious crimes. The higher courts for appeal are structured to start with the High Court, with the Court of Appeal as the equivalent of what in some countries is called the Supreme Court. This appellate court has been considered the most important institution per recent judicial rulings because its judicial interpretations have been palatable to the international community, including Amnesty International and Human Rights Watch. It is also distinguished from the High Court in two respects; it has multiple judges and does not use a jury.

The magistrates' courts and other subordinate courts handle the bulk of the cases at the trial level. After all, they are spread all of over the country and are most accessible to the average citizens at minimum litigation costs. In contrast, the High Court is aloof from the citizens. The Constitution provides for the independence of the judiciary, which was not the case during the Banda regime and to some extent of the immediate post-Banda regime. There have been two major revisions of Malawi's Constitution in recent years. The first one was carried out in 1994 and the second in 1998.

Trial by Jury

As is the case in most former British colonies, in Africa, trial by jury is a special provision of the penal code, but it is reserved for trials of murder cases only. In this case, the High Court makes use of 12 persons. As of mid-1996, there were 1,000 murder suspects awaiting trial. On August 28, 1996, the Inter Press Service English News reported a call by legal reformers to abolish the country's jury system. They suggested replacing it with singular acts of the judge. The difficulty of engaging juries in the criminal justice process has been marred by political interference.

Delays and Other Problems of the Courts

Court delays in democratic societies are publicly condemned. The Malawi courts did not escape the traumas of the economic downturn at the dawn of the 21st century. To make matters worse, the judicial staff went on strike in August 2002. Their leadership accused the members of Parliament of double standards: they gave themselves pay raises while the average workers' demands were rejected.

Legal Reform

The achievements of the post-Banda government regimes in Malawi include legal reform in general, police reform, and penal reform, all of which have helped develop the rule of law and a culture of shared values through participatory discourse.

One of the desired goals of legal reform has been attainment of judicial accountability. This achievement does not come out of the blue; it requires the court policy makers and top administrators to assume primary responsibilities, for which they should be assessed for their performance. The Malawi Law Commission, Parliament, and the police service; the British Home Office and Department of International Development; and nongovernmental organizations such as London-based Amnesty International, the Kenya-based International Resources Group, and the South Africa–based Institute of Security Studies have all contributed to this evolving process. One significant reform in establishing governmental accountability has been the establishment of the Office of the Ombudsman. The aim has been to prevent inconsistent and arbitrary actions reminiscent of the situations in Hastings Banda's regime.

Provisions of the Penal Code

The penal code not only defines crimes but also stipulates their corresponding punishments. The punishment for murder was death by hanging until April 27, 2007, when the judges of the High Court ruled against the imposition of the sentence. By the same token, the death penalty applied to conviction for rape and armed robbery. Malawi has an established Law Commission, which has a major responsibility of periodically reviewing the penal code. It was originally set up to recommend that unprotected sex that spreads HIV should be a criminal offense.

Punishment

The penal system is composed of the prisons, probation, fines, and related penalties. The colonial authorities introduced three major categories of prisons, namely maximum-security prisons, medium-security prisons, and minimum-security prisons. The one maximum-security prison was located at the headquarters in Zomba, whereas there were three medium-security prisons. The open prison farm constituted the minimum-security prison.

The Malawi Prisons Acts

The basic documents that guide the administration of the prisons are the result of three legislative acts: the Prisons Act, the Prisons Regulations, and the Prisons Standing Orders. The prisons in Malawi perform multiple roles, ranging from inflicting pain to so-called rehabilitation. The prison conditions are described by United Nations Commission on Human Rights and other observers as horrible, punctuated by overcrowding, sexual abuse, and physical abuse including torture. On December 3, 2007, there were 10,830 prisoners in Malawi, including pretrial detainees, representing a 173 percent occupancy rate. These conditions continue notwithstanding the provisions of the penal code that call for damages upon successful litigation against prison authorities. In regard to HIV/AIDS in prisons, the proposal by some lawmakers in the National Assembly to provide condoms to inmates has received mixed response.

The Death Penalty

On April 27, 2007, the Malawi judges of the High Court unanimously agreed that the mandatory death sentence for murder was unconstitutional, thereby rendering invalid article 210 of the penal code. This ruling was greeted with cheers by the opponents of the death penalty. On the other hand, there continue to be segments of Malawi society that want to retain the death penalty. Furthermore, this ruling does not as yet mean that the death penalty is abolished, which will require legislation.

Penal Reform

Building more prisons to ease overcrowding has been in the works since the dawn of the 21st century according to the reports from prison policy makers and administrators. Apart from seeking to ease overcrowding, a related goal is to de-emphasize punitiveness, on one hand, and emphasize rehabilitation on the other, according to the *People's Daily Online* (2007). At stake are the issues of not only inadequate but also sporadic budget allocation and other related infrastructure to meet the needs and problems associated with teenagers and young men, whether they are in detention or not. Lack of quality education is the centerpiece of the criticism. In this regard, transfer of the Approved School (institutions of detention for juveniles) to the Ministry of Education has been proposed. Several African countries including Malawi have, through legislation, prioritized making community service an alternative to imprisonment.

One of the service areas in which Prison Reform International been working is the provision of paralegal assistance. It is a borrowed concept from the West geared toward the broad theme of social justice via the provision of inmate legal services, including the availability of law books in the prisons and even the larger jails. Prison Reform International has introduced paralegal assistance as a pilot project in Malawi's four prisons, thanks to funding by the British government's Department for International Development. The project entails, among other things, the coordination and monitoring of selected areas of application of law in real life within the legal or criminal justice system. Paid paralegal assistants are utilized. Already selected prisoners' receipt of bail or bond has been considered a positive outcome of this program.

Reform of Juvenile Justice

Reform of juvenile justice has been underway thanks to the cooperative efforts between UNICEF and the Malawi government. One example of the reform involves establishment of child-friendly courts designed to divert juvenile offenders from adult prisons, a result of the assistance of the British Department for International Development.

A review of the functions and purposes of reformatory schools in Malawi was commissioned by UNICEF and completed in August 2001. The report mentions several major problems dating back to the establishment of the reformatory schools and continuing through their plight in the

21st century. It has been recommended that the government (a) build additional reformatory institutions, (b) institute separation of adult offenders from juvenile ones, (c) provide adequate funding for the reformatory institutions, and (d) provide adequate staffing.

The Office of the Ombudsman

The country's new Constitution provides for the creation of the Office of the Ombudsman. It is to be an independent office with powers of authority to conduct investigations as well as subpoena targeted persons and to render appropriate remedies following findings. The remedies may be administrative and/or legal. There are constitutional grounds upon which the ombudsman may be subject to removal from office.

Aside from the Office of the Ombudsman, the National Juvenile Justice Forum, the Law Commission, and the Human Rights Commission, there are other long-standing constitutional instruments to ensure checks and balances in government. They include the Judicial Service Commission, the Police Service Commission, the Prisons Service Commission, and the Inspectorate of Prisons.

Ejakait (J. S. E.) Opolot

Further Reading

Alvazzi del Frate. (1998). *Victims of Crime in a Developing World.* Rome: UNICRI. Publication no. 57.

DeGabriele, D. (2001). *Review of the Functions and Purposes of Reformatory Schools in Malawi.* http://www.unicef.org/evaldatabase/files/2001_Malawi_Reform_Schools.pdf.

Gould, C., and G. Lamb. (2004). *Hide and Seek: Taking Account of Small Arms in South Africa*: http://www.iss.co.za/pubs/Books/Hide+Seek/Contents.htm.

Malawi Prison Service. (2000). "Correction of Law-Offenders": http://www.sdnp.org.mw/.

Pelser, E., E. P. Burton, and L. Gondwe. (n.d.). *Crimes of Need: Results of the Malawi National Crime Victimization Survey:* http://www.iss.co.za/pubs/Books/CrimesOfNeed/Contents.htm.

Mali

Legal System: Civil/Customary
Murder: Low
Corruption: Medium
Human Trafficking: Medium
Prison Rate: Low
Death Penalty: Maybe
Corporal Punishment: No

Background

The Republic of Mali (henceforth Mali) is a country in West Africa with an estimated (2006) population of 12.5 million. Mali is the largest country in West Africa, occupying an area of 1,240,278 square kilometers, and shares borders with seven other countries: Algeria to the north; Ivory Coast and Guinea to the south; Burkina Faso to the southeast; Mauritania and Senegal to the west; and Niger and Senegal to the east. The capital of Mali is Bamako, with a population of about 1 million.

Mali is a multiparty democracy and has operated under a presidential system of government since becoming independent from France in 1960. The head of state and commander in chief of the armed forces of the country is the executive president. The prime minister is the head of the government. It has a national assembly that has the sole responsibility of making laws in the country.

Police and Crime Data

Mali has about 1,000 police officers. The Ministry of Internal Security and Civil Protection oversees police functions. The gendarmerie is supervised by the Ministry of the Armed Forces. The maintenance of law and order in the urban areas is the responsibility of the police. However, the police and the gendarmerie are responsible for the internal security of the land. The police authority and administration is decentralized, with the commissioners being responsible for the districts. The police commissioners who are in charge of the districts are answerable to the national headquarters. The local police forces are under the Ministry of Security and Civil Protection. The gendarmerie is under the Ministry of the Armed Forces. The police and gendarmes share responsibility for internal security, and the police are responsible for the urban areas only. The police force is decentralized to the district level, with each district having a commissioner who reports to the national headquarters. Available records show that the Malian police are relatively effective despite concerns the corruption in the police force and the criminal justice system. There have been reports of the police collecting bribes at road checkpoints. Other problems plaguing the police include inadequate training and equipment. Despite all these challenges, Mali's crime rate remains relatively low.

Complementing the efforts of the state police are those of the traditional police known as *jeliw* (griots or bards). The *jeliw* employ African principles of justice and conflict resolution to resolve conflicts that arise in the community. This traditional police system is quite effective in maintaining law and order because of its strong ties to the community. They assist victims in restoring their losses and work to reintegrate offenders into the community. Their goal is the restoration of peace and harmony in the community. Just as *jeliw* use shaming as a mechanism to administer justice, they themselves are subject to shaming when they are exposed to abuse and forced to "humble themselves" to keep the respect from the disputing factions.

Crime data are limited and sparse. The incidence of violent crime is low, and the most frequently reported crimes are pickpocketing and theft. According to INTERPOL, data from 1998 (most recent available) reveal the crime rates per 100,000 population as follows: murder, 0.71; rape, 0.46; robbery, 0.05; aggravated assault, 1.45; burglary, 0.77; larceny, 0.94; motor vehicle theft, 0.34. One of the explanations of low crime rates according to researcher A. B. Chikwanha in 2008 is the country's reliance on traditional policing and justice mechanisms, as well as extensive reliance on restorative justice. However, corruption in government remains a big issue. There are many cases of financial mismanagement, corruption, and fraud. Many wealthy individuals and corporations have also been found to evade taxes. The auditor general of the country reported that in 2006, more than US$218 million was lost to corruption and fraud by government officials. Again, about US$15.5 million was lost in the same year to tax evasion.

Domestic violence is widespread in the society despite the fact that assault in marriage is a crime. The police are reluctant to prosecute rape and domestic violence cases because of the prevailing cultural attitudes that condone rape and domestic violence. However, a lot is being done to address the issue, including raising society's awareness of the dangers of domestic violence and rape. Collective efforts by both government and nongovernmental organizations to sensitize the people to the prevalence of rape and domestic violence and also educate women on their rights are currently underway in the country. Women are also receiving education on how to access the justice system and defend their rights.

The problem is further compounded by the definitions of crime. For instance, female genital mutilation is defined as a crime, but women do not report this crime. Additionally, higher illiteracy among women further aggravates their problems. In this patriarchal society, women are poorer than men, and efforts to encourage education for women are frowned upon.

In Mali, the age of legal responsibility varies depending on whether it is a criminal, civil, or social matter. The Constitution stipulates that the age of criminal responsibility is 18 years. However, depending on the crime, minors between the ages of 13 and 18 can be held criminally liable if the court can establish that they knew what they were doing. In civil matters, the Constitution stipulates 21 years as the age of legal responsibility. However, girls 18 years and over can make decisions to marry without parental approval. There have been many documented cases of child trafficking in Mali to other African countries, especially Côte d'Ivoire.

Courts

Mali's legal system is based on the French civil law system and the African customary laws. The Constitution provides for an independent judiciary. In addition to legal responsibilities, the Malian courts also exercise judicial review over legislative acts. The Malian Constitution protects its citizens against arbitrary arrests and detentions. It also guarantees the right to legal counsel for indigent suspects. Citizens' rights to free speech, press, assembly, and association and to practice any religion of their choice are protected by the Constitution. All trials except those involving minors must be held publicly. And defendants are considered innocent until proven guilty. Mali's Supreme Court, which was established in 1969, is the apex court of the land. The Supreme Court has 19 members, including its president and vice president, and they are appointed for five years by the prime minister and the Superior Council of the Magistry. The court performs both judicial and administrative oversight over the three civil chambers and one criminal chamber over which it has jurisdiction. The Supreme Court's primary function is the hearing of appeals from the lower courts.

The Malian Constitution also makes provision for the establishment of the appeals courts. There are three appeals courts located in Bamako, Kayeds, and Mopti. Appeals courts have many jurisdictions, including civil, commercial, labor, criminal, and prosecution functions. The appeals courts hear cases from the lower courts. The Constitution also provides for a High Court of Justice, which hears cases of corruption and abuse of office against the president, ministers, and other members of the National Assembly. Other cases of treasonable felony, national security matters, and constitutional violations are also heard in the High Court of Justice.

There is also the Constitutional Council (or Court), which hears cases pertaining to the Constitution. It reviews the constitutionality of laws before they are enacted. It also reviews the decisions of the National Assembly to make sure they do not violate the Constitution. It also provides opinions and advice on the constitutional implications of conflicts between the various arms of government and also the constitutionality of electoral votes. It consists of nine members. The prime minister, the president of the National Assembly, and the Superior Council of the Magistracy each appoint three members to the Constitutional Court. The president of the Constitutional Court is elected by the members of the court. There are also established customary courts that deal with matters relating to African customs and Islamic traditions. However, these courts are in the process of being abolished.

There is a strong emphasis in Malian culture on relying on informal justice, with an active role for the *jeliw,* who strongly discourage the community from reporting to formal procedures of justice. Chikwanha noted that the *jeliw* often mediate over disputes over such issues as trading spaces, money, and other business-related matters. There is another informal justice mechanism called the jokers, who intervene in cases that mostly relate to assault. They use joking relationships (*anankun*) and cause embarrassment to parties involved in conflict to encourage them to resolve the matter informally.

Punishment

The prison population rate is about 35 per 100,000, and there is a history of degrading and dehumanizing prison conditions. Prisons are overcrowded with minors and adults put in the same prison although in separate cells. Conditions in some of the prisons are quite deplorable. The female prison population is just about 2 percent of the total prison population in Mali. Partly accounting for the low incarceration rate is the stigma that prison attracts in the society. Again, judges are aware that family members also suffer when their breadwinner is locked up. Efforts have been made to address overcrowding in prisons. As a result, two prisons were built in 1991, one for youth and the other for women. Clearly, it has not done much to the overcrowding problem. A 2003 report noted that there were 4,000 prisoners in Malian prisons.

Mali has been applauded by Amnesty International for being one of the few countries in the world without a political prisoner. However, there are many cases of suspects remaining in detention for up to 10 years without trial, an estimated 5,000 in 2003. The

Constitution provides for access to justice for prisoners, but this does not occur. Furthermore, some pretrial detainees are sometimes housed with convicted offenders, and there is no probation or parole.

In addition to formal punishment and restorative justice by the *jeliw*, there is collective punishment where the entire clan can be fined because of one community member's crime. Juveniles are often treated as adults at the time of trial and punishment. They do have their own tribunals and special courts, but the way they are treated is more traumatizing than helpful.

Angela R. Morris and O. Oko Elechi

Further Reading

Chikwanha, A. B. (2008). "Mali's Criminal Justice System: November 2008": http://www.africanreview.org/docs/mali/maliissuenov08.pdf.

Chickwanha, A. B. (2008, December 13). "Mali Crime and Criminal Justice System Dissemination Report." Hotel Azalai Salaam, Bamako: http://www.africanreview.org/docs/mali/dissemrepdec08.pdf.

Pringle, R. (2006). *Democratization in Mali: Putting history to Work, Peace Works.* Washington, DC: United States Institute of Peace.

Touchent, D. (2005). *Guide to Legal Research in Mali:* http://www.nyulawglobal.org/globalex/mali.htm.

Mauritania

Legal System: Civil/Islamic
Murder: Medium
Corruption: Medium
Human Trafficking: Medium
Prison Rate: Low
Death Penalty: Maybe
Corporal Punishment: Yes

Background

The Islamic Republic of Mauritania (Al Jumhuriyah al Islamiyah al Muritaniyah) is located in northern Africa on the North Atlantic, between Senegal to the south, Western Sahara to the northwest, and Algeria and Mali to the west. The estimated population in 2009 was a little over 3 million. The country is divided into 12 regions and 1 capital district and capital city, Nouakchott. Arabic is the official language, and more than half the population relies on agriculture and livestock.

The executive branch consists of the head of state, the president who is elected for five-year terms. The head of the government is the prime minister, who has a council of ministers as his cabinet. The legislative branch consists of 56 seats of senate, or Majlis al-Shuyukh, out of which 53 are elected by municipal leaders to serve six-year terms. The national assembly, or Majlis al-Watani, consists of 95 seats, with members elected for five-year terms by popular vote. Finally, the judicial branch consists of a three-tier system with the Supreme Court as the apex court, plus appeals courts and lower courts.

In the early 1960s through the 1970s, Mauritania's legal system was influenced by the French legal and judicial system, and as the amount of legal cadres rose, so too did attempts to reconcile secular and Islamic laws. Islamic courts coexisted with secular courts that were based off French models with no appellate courts and no constitutional jurisdiction. The Constitution dictated that French laws were to hold fast until they were amended or repealed, as was also the case with French civil, commercial, and penal codes. Until 1965 there was no Supreme Court, and it was not until the early 1970s that new nationality and labor codes were adopted alongside new penal, civil, commercial, and administrative procedures after so many years under French laws and jurisdiction. Moktar Ould Daddah was the country's first president and served from the nation's independence until he was ousted in what was termed a bloodless coup on July 10, 1978; immediately following, the country came under military rule, which lasted until 1992, when the first multiparty elections were held following a referendum of a constitution.

Sharia Islamic code was instituted in 1980 and served as the law of the land in civil matters, with

Mauritanian troops pursue a man during a demonstration protesting an army coup in the city of Nouakchott, on August 8, 2008. (AP Photo/Candace Feit)

an exception being "modern areas" such as nationality law and litigation that involved corporations, automobiles, and aircraft. The code also covered areas of public law such as theft and murder. As with French law, no one was presumed innocent, and therefore, an inability to convince the sitting magistrate that the charges were erroneous in itself constituted proof of guilt; firsthand testimony from a witness or codefendant was viewed in the same light. Defendants were granted the right to counsel and could also appeal a verdict to the Supreme Court so long as it was completed within 15 days. As was the case in the secular courts, circumstantial evidence was not admissible as proof of guilt, and plea bargaining was common.

Today, Mauritanian laws guarantee an expeditious arraignment and trial; however, the judicial system's inadequate funding results in slow and long pretrial detentions. Furthermore, legislation was approved by then-President Daddah just prior to the 1978 coup declaring the authority to detain without trial or appeal anyone who was judged to be a threat to national security.

Currently, the police in Mauritania, known as the national police, are under the direction of the Ministry of the Interior and are responsible for law enforcement and maintaining order in urban areas. The National Guard, also under the Ministry of the Interior, performs security functions in the areas of the country where city police are not present. The gendarmerie, a specialized paramilitary group under the Ministry of Defense, is responsible for maintaining civil order in and outside metropolitan areas. The police have been viewed as unprofessional and unwilling to handle and investigate minor complaints if those making the report or claim are not politically well connected. The police have also been found lacking in equipment and proper training and to act in a manner that is corrupt. Examples of these behaviors have occurred in various regions where former criminals were rearrested and then bribed for their release, and others were just released prior to their trial, with no explanation. The government has often not held security officials accountable, nor have they been prosecuted for abuses.

Crime

The country of Mauritania has no public reports of criminal statistics since 1996. INTERPOL held a conference in 2007 where the need for allocation among African countries was discussed, especially pertaining to drug crimes in Mauritania. Other than this information, it appears that there are no credible recent sources available for Mauritania. The most recent INTERPOL data of crimes recorded by police are for the year 1996, which are as follows:

Homicide/murder	27
Rape	36
Serious assault	989
Robbery and violent theft	347
Aggravated theft	542
Breaking and entering	195
Motor vehicle theft	177
Other thefts	138
Fraud	33
Counterfeit currency	1.0
Drug offenses	81

The U.S. Department of State details potential threats to tourists to be pickpocketing, theft of valuables left in plain sight, and kidnapping. Some information presented on the U.S. Department of State Web site indicated that some trafficking of children for purposes of labor occurs; however, there were no substantial statistics, nor was any follow-up information available.

A problem in reporting crime statistics could stem from the overly large nomadic population. With citizens of Mauritania constantly moving throughout the country and into other neighboring countries, the possibility of crimes occurring and going unnoticed for a period of time because the perpetrators have fled the scene does exist. There is a great amount of land in Mauritania that is underdeveloped, and thus, "bandits" or nomads are able to operate more extensively than in the more controlled parts of the country.

Finding of Guilt

For those accused of a crime in Mauritania, the Constitution and law currently provide for judicial independence, and the judiciary exercises greater independence than in previous years, particularly in acquitting persons of terrorist charges in light of the many alleged police abuses in the process of collection of evidence according to the U.S. Department of State's human rights report of 2008. The executive branch continues to have a significant influence over the judiciary via the ability to appoint as well as pressure judges, many of whom have been found to be poorly educated and trained and thus made susceptible to social, tribal, and financial pressures. The government has continued to work on judicial reform, to incorporate more thorough training of judges, prosecutors, and police/law enforcement entities on correct procedures for application of laws, particularly those that concern human rights, antislavery, money laundering, and trafficking in persons. There has also been an effort to add a layer of professionalism to judges by calling for the hiring of judges from academic circles and by having more advanced training for prosecutors and judges to increase efficiency.

According to the U.S. Department of State, there is a single system of courts consistent with modified principles of sharia law. Departmental, regional, and labor tribunals are the courts of first instance at the lower level, with 53 departmental tribunals, composed of a president and magistrates with traditional Islamic legal training, who hear civil cases that involve sums less than $37 (10,000 ouguiya) and family issues, which include domestic issues, divorce, and inheritance cases. A total of 13 regional tribunals accept appeals in commercial and civil matters from the departmental tribunals and hear misdemeanor cases. Next is the middle level, consisting of three courts of appeal, each having seven chambers (civil, commercial, administrative, and penal chambers, as well as criminal, minors, and labor courts) that hear appeals from the regional courts and have original jurisdiction for felonies.

The Supreme Court is appointed by the president and is subject to annual review; it is nominally independent and reviews decisions and rulings that were made by the courts of appeal to determine their compliance with the law and procedure. The Supreme Court conducts an annual review to determine whether the lower courts have applied the laws correctly and followed protocol. These types of review also serve as a baseline for evaluating the reform process and in reassigning judges based on their individual qualifications.

The current Mauritanian law provides for due process; that is, defendants have a right to a public trial, but juries are not used for all defendants. Regardless of which court and of their ability to pay, defendants have the legal right to representation by counsel during the proceedings. Much like a good portion of the Western world, if the defendant lacks the ability to pay, a court-appointed attorney from a list prepared by the National Order of Lawyers will provide a defense free of charge. There is a presumption of innocence and the right to appeal. Based on the legal principles of sharia, which provides the law and legal procedures. the courts traditionally have not treated women as equals of men.

There is a special court that hears cases for children who are under the age of 18; typically those appearing receive a more lenient sentence than adults, and greater consideration is given to extenuating circumstances in juvenile cases. The minimum age for children to be tried is 12; those between the ages of 12 and 18 are tried, and if convicted, they are sentenced to time in the juvenile detention center. Rape, including spousal rape, is illegal in Mauritania, as is domestic violence; however, several NGOs have reported that the incidence of unreported rape is high. Despite several rape cases being reported, it is also known that wealthy rape suspects have avoided prosecution or, if prosecuted, prison time.

Punishment

There is a paucity of information available regarding the types of punishment that are dealt to offenders who are convicted in Mauritania. There have been reports that the death penalty does exist in Mauritania, but this information could not be supported by credible sources.

Prisons

In June 2008, a new central prison was built in Nouakchott with the design to hold 800 prisoners and to replace the former Nouakchott prison that housed only 250. At the end of 2008, there were 650 prisoners incarcerated in this new prison. It is not known how many other less centrally located prisons there are in Mauritania. The U.S. Department of State reports that there have been serious overcrowding and inadequate sanitation facilities in some of the other prisons, and there have been reports that this has contributed to the spread of diseases such as tuberculosis, diarrhea, and dermatological ailments. Medical supplies, mainly provided by an international nongovernmental organization (NGO), remained insufficient in all prisons. The country's budget allocations to improve prison conditions have remained insufficient in all prisons; those prisoners with high-level connections or status and with families to bring them food, medicines, and reading material as a result have typically fared better than their less privileged counterparts and citizens of other countries. The prison security, known as guard force management, generally enforces the regulations against beatings and torture inside and outside prison cell walls; however, there continue to be credible reports of beatings and abuse in police detention centers and several prisons throughout the country. The children of female prisoners remain with their mothers, or the Ministry of Justice gives temporary custody to other family members. The Noura Foundation, an NGO, works in the women's prison and provides education and vocational training to female prisoners. The Noura Foundation also works with the Catholic charity Caritas to provide education, sports, and vocational services to juvenile offenders. Pretrial detainees in all detention facilities are frequently held with convicted prisoners as a result of overcrowding.

Jennifer Janowski

Further Reading

Amnesty International. (2008). *Mauritania's Security Forces Guilty of Routine Torture:* http://www.amnesty.org/en/news-and-updates/report/mauritanias-security-forces-guilty-routine-torture-20081203.

Handloff, Robert E., ed. (1988). *Mauritania: A Country Study*. Washington, DC: GPO for the Library of Congress.

U.S. Department of State. (2008). *Country Reports on Human Rights Practices: Bureau of Democracy, Human Rights, and Labor: Africa:* http://www.state.gov/g/drl/rls/hrrpt/2007/100493.htm.

Mauritius

Legal System: Civil/Common
Murder: Medium
Corruption: Low
Human Trafficking: Medium
Prison Rate: Medium
Death Penalty: No
Corporal Punishment: Yes

Background

Mauritius, along with the other islands of Rodrigues, Agalega, and Cargados Carajos Shoals, is situated in the Indian Ocean, about 559 miles east of Madagascar and 1,250 miles off the nearest point of the African coast. Mauritius became independent in 1968 from the United Kingdom and has since been a stable democracy with a current population of about 1.1 million inhabitants who mainly speak English in addition to French, Creole, Chinese, and a host of other Indian languages. Mauritius is a republic with a presidential democracy, and the president is head of state and commander-in-chief. The prime minister is the head of government and has full executive powers. Legislative power rests with a unicameral 62-seat national assembly, which is elected by universal suffrage for a five-year term. The country has nine districts and three dependencies.

Legal System

After taking over Mauritius from the French in 1810, the British set in motion the reform of the judicial system. In 1845, it was ordered that French be abolished as the ordinary language used in court. In 1851, a bill was passed that abolished the *la Cour de Premiere Instance* and established a Supreme Court. The right to appeal to the Judicial Committee of the Privy Council was maintained. This left Mauritius once again with a one-tier jurisdiction. Over time, Mauritius returned to a two-tier jurisdiction when the Bail Court, presided over by one judge of the Supreme Court, was established. Also, district courts were presided over by a magistrate with a right to appeal to the Bail Court. Later on, the Intermediate Court and the Industrial Court were established.

As a parliamentary democracy, Mauritius exercises separation of powers between the three branches of the government, namely, the legislative, the executive, and the judiciary. Consistent with the British legal system, it practices the accusatorial system of law by guaranteeing the principle of presumption of innocence and the reasonable legal protection of the accused. The independent republic of Mauritius has a hybrid legal system. The criminal and civil litigation is drawn from the English legal system, and the substantive law is mainly drawn from the French Napoleonic code.

The legal system is composed of the Supreme Court and the subordinate courts. The Supreme Court is the "principal court of original criminal jurisdiction" with criminal trials for serious offenses (e.g., murder and manslaughter) held before a presiding judge and a nine-person jury. Provision is also made for the prosecution of certain offenses such as drug trafficking under the Dangerous Drugs Act, before a judge of the Supreme Court without a jury.

The death penalty was abolished in 1995, but the Supreme Court may inflict sentences of penal servitude for life or sentences for terms not exceeding 60 years.

The Supreme Court has various divisions, with jurisdiction over the Bankruptcy Court, the courts of first instance in civil and criminal matters, the Court of Appeal, the Court of Civil Appeal, Court of Criminal Appeal, and 10 district courts. The final appeals from decisions from the Court of Appeal of Mauritius go to the Judicial Committee of the Privy Council in London. Mauritius has 12 judges and 40 subordinate court judges called magistrates. The subordinate courts are made up of the Court of Rodrigues, the district courts, the Intermediate Court, and the Industrial Court. The legal system has provisions for fair public trials with criminal defendants having the right to counsel and indigents having court-appointed counsel. The president, in consultation with the prime minister, nominates the chief justice and then, with the advice of the chief justice, also appoints the associate judges. The president nominates other judges on the advice of the Judicial and Legal Service Commissions.

Role of Police

The Mauritius Police Force (MFP) has a long history that reaches back to the early French colonial period. The French Royal Government of Louis XVI introduced the first formal police institution after a contingent of the French National Troupe arrived on the island. Its modern state has evolved since then, and it is now a highly structured and well-organized organization. The department is headed by the commissioner of police, who oversees all activities and divisions within the organization. Underneath the commissioner are 10 branches. They include the Anti-Drug and Smuggling Unit, the Central Investigation Division, the Helicopter Squadron, the National Coast Guard, the Passport and Immigration Unit, the Rodrigues Police, the Special Mobile Force, the Special Supporting Unit, the Traffic Branch, and the Western Division. In 2002, the Mauritian police force comprised 10,576 members, with 531 of them being women police officers and with an overall ethnic distribution representing the total population, with 1 officer for 19 citizens. Of these police personnel, 2,876 were nonuniformed, with an additional 780 civilian personnel to take care of administrative duties. The 2004 data suggest a slight increase in the employment, with the police force consisting of 11,137 individuals (10,595 men and 542 women). The country then had a total of 93 police stations and posts.

The Criminal Investigation Division (CID) handles sensitive cases and cases involving the larger public interest. It handles all cases of bribery, fraud, and homicide. The CID has various units: the Fraud Squad looks into cases of fraud concerning immovable property; the Major Crime Investigation Team inquires into all cases of homicide, suspected homicide, and sexual assault; and the Technical Support Unit is made up of draughtsman, photographers, and crime scene officers. The latter are the first to visit the scene of a crime and are responsible for preserving evidence.

The National Coast Guard was earlier known as the marine wing of the police force. In the past, their main role was limited to search, rescue, and coastal patrol. In 1987, the cabinet approved the new structure of the department, and the National Coast Guard came into being as a specialized unit of the Mauritius Police Force. Similarly, the Special Mobile Forces is a paramilitary force that follows training based on conventional military tactics, with an emphasis on internal security operations. Their main function is to ensure the internal and external security of the island. They are organized as a motorized infantry battalion with five companies, an engineer squadron, and a mobile wing that contains two squadrons equipped with armored vehicles. With Mauritius having no regular military force, the Special Mobile Forces plays a critical role for the nation.

The Special Supporting Unit has the primary goal of assisting the regular police in controlling civil unrest when the situation escalates beyond control. They support the regular police in a variety of ways, including providing security at sensitive and vulnerable points, managing crowd control, conducting searches for missing people, tracking criminals, and escorting dangerous prisoners. They are essentially a backup to the regular police to effectively deal with problems associated with maintaining order on the island.

The Western Division and the Rodrigues Police are branches also under the commissioner of police. These two large branches have their own internal subdivisions to control crime in their territories. The last branch under the commissioner of police is the Traffic Branch. This agency is responsible for issuing and controlling driving licenses, both domestic and international. They also maintain a record of convictions of drivers for offenses under the Road Traffic Act.

Technology

The Mauritius Police Force has taken major steps to update and modernize its systems, equipment, and computers to bring themselves to the same level as other modern societies. In 1999, the force launched the Automated Fingerprint Identification System (AFIS) to use as part of the crime records. The AFIS system also stores personal and family information on all convicted criminals, which helps police to generate a suspect list in a matter of minutes when investigating a crime.

In 2000, an information technology unit was created in the Mauritius Police Force to coordinate all information technology activities, identify new projects, and expedite ongoing projects. They also organized and coordinated the training for all members of the force, with the goal of having most policemen computer literate by the year 2005. Another part of this upgrade involved networking AFIS to all the police stations and units. This networking was completed in 2001. The networking of AFIS allowed for the sharing of information regarding wanted criminals, lost and found motor vehicles and other valuable properties, and lost and found persons and firearms. This overhaul of the system allowed the Mauritius Police Force to end the use of paperwork and a large amount of manual entries of information.

Crime

Classification of Crime

Mauritius's Criminal Code Act classifies offenses as crimes, misdemeanors, or contraventions. Crimes are offenses punishable by (a) penal servitude and (b) a fine exceeding 5,000 rupees (approx. US$155). Examples of crimes include crimes against a person such as murder, manslaughter, and abortion; crimes against property such as larceny, extortion and arson; fraud and dishonesty such as forgery, counterfeiting, and embezzlement; offenses against morality such as rape, sodomy, and sexual intercourse with a female under 16; and crimes against the Dangerous Drugs Act.

Misdemeanors are offenses that are punishable by (a) imprisonment for a term exceeding 10 days and (b) a fine exceeding 5,000 rupees. When imprisonment is imposed, the court has the option to mandate punishment with or without hard labor. Examples of misdemeanor offenses are offenses against a person such as wounds and blows not classified as a crime, involuntary homicide, and involuntary wounds and blows; offenses against property such as bicycles and automobiles and other simple larcenies against property; offenses such as disorderly conduct, riots, breach of the peace, poaching, public mischief, and escape from lawful custody; and offenses against the Firearms Act.

Contraventions are, generally speaking, very minor offenses. They are punishable by (a) imprisonment for a term not exceeding 10 days and (b) a fine not exceeding 5,000 rupees. Examples of contraventions are traffic offenses, distilleries/liquor offenses, gambling and public lotteries, drunkenness, and disturbance.

Traffic Offenses

Traffic-related offenses were the most common offense, accounting for 72.8 percent of the offenses, during 2003. Of all offenses, 7.5 percent were property-related, 6.8 percent were offenses against persons, 1.8 percent were license law–related offenses, 1.8 percent were drug-related offenses, 0.2 percent were morality-related offenses, and 8.3 percent other smaller categories. Larceny, breaking and entering, larceny of cellular phones, larceny from motor vehicles, and auto motor larceny are among the most common occurrences.

Drug-Related Offenses

Perhaps the most pressing issue in crime facing Mauritius today is the increase in drug-related offenses. Contraventions under the Dangerous Drugs Act (CDDA) have shown a sustained increase over recent years. As more drugs are captured and offenders arrested, more continue to flow in. The police are in a constant battle to keep drug trafficking and use under control in Mauritius.

The CDDA takes a hard stance on drug use and drug consumers. The act has clear guidelines about possession and dealing of drugs as well. The most common drug is gandia, or cannabis, followed by heroin. Gandia is often illegally cultivated in the mountains, the forest, and cane fields. Heroin is a derivative of opium, and the type available in the open market of Mauritius is known as "brown sugar." It is smuggled mainly by human courier, concealed in suitcases and other carrying devices. It is most in demand in the urban areas. The next most prevalent drugs are psychotropic substances that are legal pharmaceutical products but that are acquired illegally and taken in an abusive manner.

Crime Statistics

The UN Crime Survey noted that from 1990 to 1997, the crime rate per 100,000 population increased from 2,761 to 3,392, representing a nearly 60 percent increase. However, a more comprehensive crime survey was conducted in 2004 by the Mauritius Police Force and Safer Africa, an independent NGO. Though there have been some increases since 2002, the rate of increase in crime was not as dramatic as noted by the UN data in the 1990s. Overall, the rate of violent crime in Mauritius is low. In 2001, there were 27 murders on the island, followed by 24 in 2002 and 26 in 2003. This is a relatively low figure with a rate of only 2 murders per 100,000 people.

Mauritius saw an overall increase in crimes against morality between 2001 and 2003. The number of rapes increased 18 percent during this time span. There were 41 reported rapes in 2001, 37 in 2002, and 50 in 2003. Rape is a crime that has always been difficult to obtain an accurate measurement of because of the underreporting of the offense. One cause for the increased level of reporting could be the domestic violence legislation and elevated awareness created around the need to report crime. The Ombudsperson of Children and the Police Family Protection Unit have also taken a strong stance and have seen positive results in encouraging victims to report crimes of this type. The majority of crimes such as rape take place in private, making proactive policing difficult.

Property offenses constitute the second-largest type of offense in Mauritius. There are 24 types of property offenses, which are divided into crimes and misdemeanors. Crime categories include 13 offenses, about half of which decreased and half of which increased over the 2001–2003 period. A similar pattern of decrease and increase was evident for the 11 misdemeanor offenses. The most frequent type of property offense was larceny from motor vehicles. There were 583 offenses reported in 2001; 1,020 reported in 2002; and 1,172 reported in 2003. This is clearly a major problem that the Mauritian Police Force is working to get under control. The force has implemented more aggressive and frequent patrolling. This includes increased after-hour patrolling by traffic police, roadblocks carried out by the special support unit, stop and search operations, and stronger partnerships between the police and public.

Contraventions against the Dangerous Drugs Act had steady increases from 2001 to 2003. There were 2,966 offenses in 2001; 3,022 in 2002; and 3,361 in 2003, suggesting a sharp increase in those years. Based on the numbers for 2003, Mauritius has a rate of 275 drug offenses per 100,000 people. Fighting the drug problem is a top priority of the police force as well as the government.

Crime in Mauritius occurs throughout the entire country. However, the rural areas are known for the production and growth of illegal drugs. They use the farmlands and forest to cultivate these products for sale. The urban areas tend to have higher instances of property thefts. Larceny is a major problem, and concentrated numbers of people in urban areas create more opportunities for thieves.

Finding of Guilt

Mauritius's Constitution has explicit provisions that offer legal protections and access to legal support. The Constitution prohibits arbitrary arrest and detention of citizens. The Constitution also stipulates that warrants must be obtained for arrests. When this is done, the accused must be read his or her rights. These include the right to remain silent and the right to an attorney. The accused must then be brought before the local district magistrate within 48 hours. The U.S. Bureau of Democracy, Human Rights, and Labor looked into the practices of the Mauritian government and found that the government generally respects these rights. However, in some cases, police delayed suspects' access to defense counsel. They also found that minors who did not know their rights were less likely to be provided with immediate access to an attorney. Those who are not able to afford an attorney are provided one at the expense of the state.

A suspect can be detained for up to a week before bail becomes an issue before the magistrate. However, on police consent, the accused person can be released on bail the same day as the arrest. Those charged with drug trafficking can be detained for up to 36 hours without access to legal counsel or bail. The court system in Mauritius is clogged because of the slow judicial process. The Bureau of Democracy, Human Rights and Labor found that occasionally prisoners were held in waiting for up to four years before they were tried. Time served in waiting did not apply to the later sentences. In 2006, approximately 22 percent of the prison population consisted of pretrial detainees.

Mauritius does not have a separate system for juveniles, but under the Juvenile Offenders Act (JOA), a juvenile is generally considered to be a person below the age of 17. The JOA, which was enacted in 1935, is old and has not been revised in almost 60 years. Save the Children, an NGO, in a report in 1999 called attention to the fact that the government missed an opportunity to bring the JOA in line with the Convention on the Rights of the Child (CRC) when it enacted the Child Protection Act through the national assembly.

The minimum and maximum ages of criminal responsibility for youth in Mauritius are 11 and 18 years, respectively. There are no special judicial arrangements regarding offenses committed by children under the age of 14. According to the national law, minor detainees below 14 appear before a magistrate in chambers, and the proceedings are held in camera and in the presence of a responsible party. Juveniles adjudicated as offenders are sent to a reform institution, rehabilitation center, or probation hostel as decided by the magistrate. No child, however, is deprived of his or her liberty unlawfully or arbitrarily, nor is he or she sentenced to capital punishment or life imprisonment.

There are no juvenile courts, and the magistrates do not have any special training in cases involving young offenders. Convicted minors placed on probation are sent to a rehabilitation youth center or correctional youth center. So-called probation hostels for boys and probation hostels for girls also exist. Convicted juveniles ages 11 and above are sent to correctional youth centers, and those with minor offenses are sent to the rehabilitation youth centers.

Punishment

Types of Punishment

The typical form of punishment is a fine, imprisonment, or a combination of both. The offenses of murder, rape, serious theft/burglary/robbery, and serious drug offenses are all considered crimes under the Mauritian criminal code. Under the sentencing guidelines of a crime, those who commit these acts are subject to a prison sentence and a fine exceeding 5,000 rupees.

The Mauritius government used to practice capital punishment, but in 1995, the country abolished the use of capital punishment. Serious crimes such as murder that carry the possibility of life imprisonment are sent to the Supreme Court for hearing. Medium-level severity offenses are sent to intermediate courts, and lesser crimes are heard in the district courts.

Prison

Mauritius has nine prisons. For adults, there are five prisons for adult males (two maximum-security prisons; a high-security prison; a medium-security prison; and an open prison); one prison for females; and three for juveniles (one correctional youth center, two male/female rehabilitation youth centers, and one prison for Rodrigues Island). The prison system is administered by a commissioner and a deputy commissioner of prisons. As part of the community-based corrections, a Probation and Aftercare Service was formed in 1947 for probation and other related community care services for sentenced and post-release offenders.

The prison population in Mauritius is large and continues to grow. According to the Mauritius Prison Service, as of April 10, 2008, Mauritius prisons had 2,233 inmates. Of these inmates, 1,566 had already been convicted of crimes, but 667 of the inmates were in remand and waiting for their trial. This large number of inmates has caused overcrowding in the Mauritius prisons. The Central Prison, which has a capacity of 677, held more than 1,000 prisoners in 2006. However, despite the overcrowding, inmates remain relatively safe. Prisoners are separated based on danger level, with the most dangerous inmates going to high-security prisons. Behavior of the prisoner rather than the conviction or sentence determines the placement of the prisoner.

The Richelieu Open Prison is unique because it lacks physical barriers. It is bounded only by a thin metallic fence. The low-security prison is designed with a focus on rehabilitation based on self-discipline and the development of the detainees' sense of responsibility. At Richelieu, detainees have the opportunity to learn and work different jobs. There is also a farm where they can learn basic knowledge of cattle and pig breeding.

The Grand River North West Prison was built in 1995. It is a maximum-security prison that can accommodate 325 inmates. In 2006, there were about 171 detainees there awaiting trial and only about 40 convicted inmates. They perform minor work duties. The Phoenix Prison is also a high-security prison; it opened in 1980 and can accommodate a maximum of 25 inmates. This is a special prison for those inmates who commit aggravated prison offenses and for those who either are considered unable to be reformed or are having a bad influence on the other inmates. The New Wing Prison is another high-security prison and was built in 2003. It can accommodate 248 inmates. Another specialized prison is the women's prison. This prison opened in 1951 and can accommodate a maximum of 146 female inmates. Before this women's prison was created, they formally had only a small yard reserved for them at another male prison.

The Petit Verger Prison is a medium-security prison that can hold 416 inmates. This prison gives inmates daily routine work, but they also have the possibility to be trained in cattle, sheep, and goat rearing as well as in agriculture. Many of the inmates also work in the on-site brick factory.

The Correctional Youth Center is a special prison for young male offenders from 16 to 21 years of age. The youths, because of their criminal tendencies and association with antisocial elements, are put under constant supervision and given instruction and discipline to reform their behavior. The system of training used aims at strengthening character and is based on progressive trust toward the development of self-discipline and self-responsibility.

The Rehabilitation Youth Center is divided into two sections, one for boys and the other for girls. These centers accommodate boys and girls below 16 and 18 years old who are found guilty of criminal tendencies and association with antisocial elements or of being involved in deviant behaviors. Also, children who no longer submit to parental authority are sent there on the advice of the probation service. Once the child is released, the probation service provides supervision over the juvenile delinquent to facilitate his or her integration into society. They participate in vocational activities as well as activities that help them acquire a sense of responsibility and self-discipline.

Those incarcerated are allowed to have visitors see them while in prison. Convicts are allowed to have visitors once every 28 days. They are allowed a maximum of three persons. They can be visited on Monday, Wednesday, Friday, or Saturday during the hours of 9 A.M. to 3 P.M. Those in prison on remand are allowed visitors once weekly. The maximum number of visitors is three persons. They are allowed to visit on Tuesdays or Thursdays from 9 A.M. to 3 P.M.

Jason Harris and Mahesh K. Nalla

Further Reading

Agnihotri, A. K. (2003). "Juvenile Delinquency-Scenario in Mauritius." *Anil Aggrawal's Internet Journal of Forensic Medicine and Toxicology* 4(1): http://www.geradts.com/anil/ij/vol_004_no_001/papers/paper003.html.

Crime Statistics Office. (2006). *Crime Statistics 1994–2004 (Police Department)*. Port Louis, Mauritius: Ministry of Finance and Economic Development.

Force, M. P. (2007, March 29). *The Mauritius Police Force:* http://www.gov.mu/portal/site/police/menuitem.2c06d25d9d65fff3d0db7010e2b521ca/.

Koondial, K. (2002). "Republic of Mauritius." In *Kids Behind Bars,* edited by Stan Meuwese, pp. 74–76. Amsterdam, The Netherlands: Stenco: http://www.kidsbehindbars.org/english/docs/RapportKBBtotaal.pdf.

Ramsaran, A. R. (2006). "Mauritius." In *World Police Encyclopedia,* edited by Dilip K. Das and Michael J. Palmiotto. New York: Routledge.

SaferAfrica and Mauritius Police Force. (2004). *Mauritius Crime Survey 2004.* Port Louis, Mauritius: Mauritius Police Force and SaferAfrica.

Mayotte

Legal System: Civil/Islamic
Prison Rate: Medium
Death Penalty: No
Corporal Punishment: No

Background

Since 1974, when Mayotte voted against independence from France, unlike the other three islands of the Comoros, there has been a social and political rift dividing the small island from the island chain known as the Comoros Islands. The small 374 square kilometer country of Mayotte has a population of approximately 209,000 people, 97 percent of which are Muslim and follow, in their own way, the Islamic codes of justice, though the extent to which such codes override French codes is unclear.

Political and Social Context of the Justice System

When the Comoros Islands were split during 1974, a cultural and political rift began to form between the three Comoros Islands and Mayotte. This rift has grown into a general divorcing of all things Comorian by Mayotte, to include languages, dress, national identity, and general cultural characteristics. This shedding of Comorian ways is still ongoing in the justice system of Mayotte, as the Mahorias attempt to rid the country of all customary and Islamic legal practices and use solely the civil legal system of France. Following its independence, there were 19 coups d'états or attempted coups, out of which four were successful, with the last abortive coup taking place on March 21, 2000. Unfortunately, it is not currently known how much of these customary and Islamic legal traditions are used in Mayotte, and therefore, it is difficult to know just how extensive the departmentalization of the country's legal system has become.

Role of the Police

Many of the details surrounding the justice system in Mayotte remain a mystery from tourists and comparative criminologists alike. As a departmental collectivity, Mayotte has cultural independence while still under the ultimate authority of France. These aspects combined with the fact that Mayotte is largely populated by Islamic people and with its unusual loose association with Comoros make understanding exactly what system of justice is practiced in Mayotte extremely challenging to pin down. The CIA World Factbook (2008) states that Mayotte uses French law where applicable, but the highly unpublicized functions of the Mahorian police remain only at the level of speculation. If Mayotte used the law enforcement strategy implemented in France, there would be a centralized system of police, including a national police force responsible for large cities and a national gendarmerie operating in small towns. Because Mayotte has only one major city, Mamoudzou, it is difficult to know whether the French divisions of police forces are used or whether only the Gendarmerie Nationale enforces laws within the borders of Mayotte. It is also possible that Mayotte uses a law enforcement assembly similar to the Comorian Defense Force (CDF) used on the Comoros Islands, which is responsible, along with the gendarmerie, for internal security.

Crime

The breakdown of crimes in Mayotte in terms of lesser and more serious offenses is largely unknown. The assumption is that Mayotte largely follows the legal codes of France with possible additions or changes resulting from its adherence to Islamic law. In Mayotte, the age of universal suffrage for citizens is 18, and in France, 18 is considered the age of majority, even though at 16 and 17, juveniles can be tried as adults. Within France, the seriousness of the crime is an important factor because it determines which court the trial will be held in, as well as distinguishes between serious felonies, less serious felonies, misdemeanors (delit), and violations (contraventions) and determines what punishments will be used in each given situation. In addition, the French penal code is based on five books that give extensive details in terms of sentence lengths, types of punishments, characteristics of certain criminal activity, and attempted versus completed crimes.

Finding of Guilt

The French legal system applies to Mayotte as part of its coverage of all overseas territory in the application of the civil law system, the finding of guilt, and all other aspects of criminal justice. The initial stages of guilt begin with an arrest, which is immediately followed by a period of time spent in jail while the arrestee is questioned by officials called the *guard a vou.* Questioning of suspects can last up to 96 hours without their being formally charged and could vary in duration and intensity in Mayotte.

Where representation is concerned in French law, immediate assignment of an attorney is granted for all defendants except those who are being held on suspicion of terrorism; however, because there are no overt terrorist dealings within Mayotte, this may or may not be the case there. Within French civil law, those accused of crimes are afforded certain rights, including the right to remain silent, the right to retract pretrial confessions, and the right to a fair trial and the ability to make statements while in trial proceedings without being under oath. It is assumed that these procedures are adhered to by Mayotte.

After the investigation is completed by the police in misdemeanor cases or by the felony pretrial process, and the preliminary court proceedings are finished, the findings of the investigation are sent from the *juge d'instruction* to the indicting chamber, where it is determined whether a trial is necessary. The lengthy and detailed pretrial process, though in place to ensure the accused are not falsely accused, can create long stays in jail awaiting the trial. In more serious and felony cases, the judge (or president) presides over the courts of assize and interacts with the jury throughout the proceedings. Along with the president, there are also two other judges (assessors) who can question witnesses and can have investigations increased for more factual evidence.

Alternatives to trials are rare in civil law nations such as Mayotte and its mother country of France because civil law operates under the presumption of

Would-be immigrants trying to reach Mayotte are intercepted at sea by the Gendarmerie Nationale on May 6, 2009. (AFP/Getty Images)

innocence, there is little to no desire to entice prosecutors or court officials to settle cases without trials. A practice called the *ordonnance penale* is used in France as a tool similar to plea bargaining that primarily functions to expedite portions of the investigation and trial process. However, the traditional process of arrest, investigation, indicting chamber, trial, verdict, and sentence is the most common form of the finding of guilt in France and quite possibly Mayotte. Juvenile processes are different in that one judge is responsible for the case from beginning to end, and the parents of the young offender are also required to attend hearings. Restorative and rehabilitative measures are attempted in French juvenile courts through the use of diversion programs as well as special police units aimed at policing juveniles.

Punishment

Types of Punishment

In Islamic countries, there is a tendency by authorities to restrict the number of convicts who are sentenced to prison sentences. Instead, Islamic law leans more toward sentences of corporal punishment, and given that Mayotte is so highly concentrated in followers of Islam, this is highly possible. Typical punishments in Islamic-led nations are determined by the reading and interpretation of the sharia, which relies on the interpretation of the law to administer the punishment that fits the crime. Three main levels of crimes can be committed under sharia, and the breakdown is similar to that of crimes in Western systems: *hadd* crimes are the most serious offenses, *ta'azir* crimes are less serious, and *qesas* crimes are crimes of revenge or restitution. Crimes that fall under the *hadd* category include the most reprehensible offenses according to Islamic law and include murder, theft, robbery, adultery, and partaking of illegal substances. For these crimes to be fully prosecuted and for the defendant to be sentenced, there must be several eyewitnesses who can attest to the fact that the crime was committed, among other things, and although the punishment for these crimes is harsh, there is usually not enough evidence, and the judge refrains from sentencing to the full extent possible. For the offense of theft and robbery, the punishment according to the sharia is for the offender's hand to be cut off at the wrist, and for the offense of drinking or drug use, striking the user with a whip or lash is the prescribed punishment. Capital punishment is also used liberally in Islamic nations. Mayotte, however, has moderated its Islamic punishments under French influence.

Unlike Islamic law and the sharia, French law is based on the civil law system, which uses a very different basis for determining the punishments necessary for certain crimes. The most common and widely used punishments in the French legal system include probation, community orders, fines, day fines, imprisonment, and other alternative punishments. For minor contravention crimes such as assaults and noise violations, the penalty is usually fines, as opposed to delit crimes such as theft, fraud, and manslaughter, which carry a punishment of 6 months to 10 years in the prison system. The most serious crime category includes murder, rape, robbery, and abduction, and these crimes are usually punished with 10 years to a life sentence in prison. Another contrast between the Islamic legal system and the French system is that there is no death penalty in France; this practiced was abolished in 1981 by the French government. These common provisions apply to all French overseas territories.

Mayotte officially became a French overseas department on March 29, 2009, and thus the penal system and laws are in transition. As noted previously, some of the laws have been inspired by Islamic law, which is allowed under article 75 of the French Constitution. The July 11, 2001, law guarantees a local law that differs from the French civil and common law. Customs such as polygamy and inequality of the sexes concerning inheritances are still in effect; however, now that Mayotte's status as a department makes it a part of the French government, all French laws will be in effect in the immediate future. The penal law in Mayotte will therefore become similar to the French. Therefore, such punishments as the death penalty and corporal punishment, which have been in principle allowed in Mayotte, will no longer be legal.

Elisabeth Anne Filemyr

Further Reading

French Ministry of Foreign Affairs. (2007). *The French Justice System:* http://ambafrance-us.org/IMG/pdf/Justice_ag.pdf.

Joireman, S. F. (2001). "Inherited Legal Systems and Effective Rule of Law: Africa and the Colonial Legacy." *Journal of Modern African Studies* 39(4): 571–596.

Walker, I. (2007). "What Came First, the Nation or the State? Political Process in the Comoro Islands." *Africa* 77(4): 582–605.

Wiechman, D. J., J. D. Kendall, and M. K. Azarian. (n.d.). *Islamic Law: Myths and Realities:* http://muslim-canada.org/Islam_myths.htm.

Mozambique

Legal System: Civil/Customary
Murder: High
Burglary: High
Corruption: Medium
Human Trafficking: Medium
Prison Rate: Low
Death Penalty: No
Corporal Punishment: Maybe

Background

The Republic of Mozambique, or Mozambique, is located on the southeastern coast of Africa and has a tropical to subtropical climate. It is bordered by

Tanzania, Malawi, Zambia, Zimbabwe, Swaziland, and South Africa. Mozambique has an estimated population of 21 million, and the official language of the country is Portuguese. Maputo is the capital city of Mozambique.

From 1505 to 1975, Mozambique fell under colonial rule by the Portuguese. During the 1960s, anticolonial sentiment emerged in response to the lack of fundamental opportunities, such as education, which led to the establishment of the Front for the Liberation of Mozambique (FRELIMO), a socialist movement. Following a decade of armed conflict, Mozambique achieved independence on June 25, 1975, and a one-party government was instituted. Political and religious freedoms were subsequently abolished under Marxism. Civil war (1977–1992) ensued between the Mozambican National Resistance (RENAMO), the opposition, and FRELIMO, which resulted in social and economic unrest, population displacement, and mass casualties. In November 1990, a new constitution was ratified with a multiparty, democratic form of government.

With its origin in the Portuguese civil law system, the new constitution provided greater freedoms and liberties for citizens, including the rights to life, property, education, and health care; the right to counsel; freedom of expression; and equal rights protection. In addition, the death penalty was rescinded. Civil rights were later expanded in the 2004 Constitution regarding habeas corpus, legal assistance, preventive detention, and punishment. Separation of powers between the executive, legislative, and judicial branches was established, although the realization of legislation has been hindered by financial difficulties.

There are three departments responsible for law enforcement and security in Mozambique, which are under the jurisdiction of the Ministry of the Interior. They include the Mozambican Police Force (PRM), the Criminal Investigative Police (PIC), and the Rapid Reaction Force (PIR). The PRM has about 18,000 officers, and the PRI has several thousand officers. Additional units have been designated to address organized crime, border protection, and drug trafficking.

Proper training of police (as well as judges and prosecutors) could enhance effectiveness and public perception. In recent years, ethics and professionalism have been incorporated into law enforcement agencies with some success. However, corruption is widespread, and citizen confidence and satisfaction with police is low. In response, a series of public lynchings of known criminals occurred. Allegations of abuse of power, complacency in crime, and torture and summary executions by police have prompted investigations by international human rights organizations. The ratio between police officers and civilians is low, and, according to Deputy Minister of the Interior Jose Mandra, about 1,000 officers are dying each year as a result of AIDS. Police community councils were implemented in 2001 to improve community relations and public safety; however, ordinary citizens with inadequate training possess the authority to address crime and disorder.

Crime

The Mozambican Civil War had a tremendous impact on the criminal justice system. As may occur in newly created democracies, crime rates increased before eventually leveling off. More recent statistics suggest that crime is rising, although it is difficult to ascertain the reliability of crime data or distinguish between the various types of offenses committed. Nevertheless, between 2006 and 2007, crime increased by 16 percent, according to Attorney-General Augusto Paulino. According to Afrik.com, in 2007 there were 26,350 property crimes, 10,161 crimes against persons, and 5,391 public disorder incidents. Other regions have experienced notably larger increases. The majority of offenses are property crimes, followed by crimes against individuals and public disorder.

Organized crime has swelled in Mozambique. Although the extent of transnational crime is unknown, criminal networks have been linked to South Africa, Portugal, Pakistan, Russia, Dubai, and other countries. Crime syndicates may be engaged in drug and arms trafficking as well as motor vehicle theft, human trafficking, and money laundering.

The most common forms of illicit substances smuggled from Mozambique to other destination countries (e.g., Europe and the United States) include cocaine, hashish, and heroin. Moreover, organized crime groups have become more sophisticated and increasingly violent compared to traditional street gangs. Members of law enforcement have systematically been targeted by organized crime groups. One report estimates that between 2006 and 2008, more than 25 police officers were killed or assassinated.

Mozambique is predominantly a source country for trafficking in persons. Poverty, high unemployment rates, and other sociocultural factors contribute to the propensity for human trafficking. Individuals are trafficked to neighboring African nations, Europe, and the Middle East for sexual exploitation, organ removal, compulsory labor, slavery, or indentured servitude. They are also trafficked within Mozambique. Furthermore, border police have been accused of bribery by traffickers. In 2007 and 2008, Mozambique was placed on the Tier 2 Watch List for noncompliance with international standards regarding human trafficking. However, police training and increased efforts have led to the apprehension of human smugglers. In one case, police intervention resulted in the liberation of more than 200 children in transit from Mozambique to South Africa, according to the U.S. Department of State. In 2009, Mozambique was removed from the watch list because it had adopted additional security measures to cope with the problem.

Women and children are particularly susceptible to victimization. Gender discrimination is rooted in traditional social and cultural views toward women in society. Little information exists regarding the extent of interpersonal or intimate partner violence. This may be due to an absence of legislation regarding domestic violence and sex crimes. Although safeguards for the protection of women and children have been implemented by police, domestic violence provisions and education are needed.

Finding of Guilt

Several courts make up the judiciary in Mozambique. The judicial courts consist of the Supreme Court as well as 93 district and 11 provincial courts. The Supreme Court serves as an appellate court and hears cases pertaining to crimes involving high officials or members of public office. Judicial courts handle both civil and criminal cases. Crimes involving punishment up to eight years in prison and civil cases of 30,000 MZM (around US$1130.00) or less fall under the scope of district courts (first or second class, depending on value and length of sentence). District courts may also hear juvenile cases, and recently, a juvenile court was established in Maputo. The age of criminal responsibility in Mozambique is 16. In 2008, Parliament passed a bill regarding court jurisdiction and crime prevention for minors under the age of 16.

In contrast, provincial courts assert jurisdiction for all other criminal and civil cases that exceed 30,000 MZM or carry a sentence of more than eight years in prison. The Constitutional Council is responsible for electoral and constitutional questions. The administrative court, housed in the capital city, has authority over regulatory and financial issues. Community courts located throughout the country are most commonly used by individuals seeking redress for minor offenses or civil infractions, such as housing disputes. Although the Constitution outlines additional court structures for specialized matters (e.g., appellate, administrative, maritime, and labor), budget constraints have impeded their development. Finally, although not recognized by the Constitution, local chiefs may administer traditional forms of justice for dispute resolution.

As previously discussed, the constitutional revisions of 1990 and 2004 broadened the rights of the accused. Despite this, many citizens are unaware of their legal rights. The Public Prosecution Service oversees the PIC, which investigates crimes. Individuals are afforded the right to counsel throughout the legal process, and those who cannot afford an attorney are entitled to free legal assistance provided by the government. However, costs associated with judicial proceedings may be prohibitive for many citizens, and courts are not easily accessible for those residing in rural areas. Suspects may be confined in jail for a maximum of six months prior to formal charges; bail is not typically ordered. The judicial system suffers from inefficiency and is overwhelmed with thousands of cases awaiting trial.

Punishment

Both the criminal procedure code and the criminal code delineate punishment for crimes. However, the availability of public information regarding penalties for specific crimes, such as murder, rape, or robbery, is limited. Fines are often associated with regulatory infractions and minor criminal offenses. Mozambique classifies crimes into three categories: those that may be punishable (1) for up to 1 year of imprisonment, (2) for between 1 and 2 years' imprisonment, and (3) for 2 to 30 years' imprisonment. Community service is not recognized as a form of sentencing. Drug traffickers and individuals convicted of drug crimes face severe penalties, including up to 30 years' confinement. Convicted criminals may also serve consecutive sentences.

Despite high crime rates, incarceration rates are low. In 2006, the National Prisons Services (SNAPRI) was established to maintain custodial oversight, which replaced a previous, bifurcated system that was deemed ineffectual. There are various types of correctional facilities, including central, district, and provincial prisons, penitentiaries, and open prisons. Security levels vary depending on type of offense. Although a women's prison exists, human rights groups have reported that females and minors are often housed with adult male offenders as well as those awaiting trial, a violation of the UN Standard Minimum Rules on the Treatment of Prisoners.

The conditions in Mozambican jails and prisons are extremely poor. Severe overcrowding, food and water shortages, and lack of basic necessities are common problems, according to the Open Society Foundation. During a visit to the Maputo Central Prison, the largest in the country, the Mozambican Human Rights League found that capacity was exceeded by over 200 percent. In addition, penal institutions suffer from lack of repair and routine maintenance. Infirmaries are often ill-equipped to provide adequate medical care for widespread diseases that afflict the prison population. There is some evidence suggesting that HIV transmission is escalating among inmates, which has prompted the introduction of preventive measures, such as condom distribution. Furthermore, there have been allegations of torture and abuse among prison officials. Suspicious deaths of prisoners have also been reported. A notorious case which made international headlines involved the deaths of 93 inmates from asphyxiation, who were held in a jail cell in Montepuez for their activities during a political rally. Although the current situation appears grim, efforts are underway to improve the status of prisons in Mozambique.

Susan Gade

Further Reading

Afrik.com. (2008, May 1). *Crime on the Rise in Mozambique:* http://en.afrik.com/article13436.html.

Horta, L. (2008, September 8). "The Bite of Mamba: Mozambique's Bloody War against Crime." *Africa Policy Forum:* http://forums.csis.org/africa/?p=180.

Open Society Foundation. (2006). "Mozambique: Justice Sector and the Rule of Law." Johannesburg: Open Society Initiative for Southern Africa, pp. 1–146: http://www.afrimap.org/english/images/report/Mozambique%20Justice%20report%20(Eng).pdf.

UNICEF Mozambique. (n.d.). *HIV/AIDS—The Picture:* http://www.unicef.org/mozambique/hiv_aids_2045.html.

Namibia

Legal System: Civil/Common
Murder: Medium
Burglary: High
Corruption: Medium
Prison Rate: Medium
Death Penalty: No
Corporal Punishment: No

Background

Located in southwestern Africa, Namibia's land mass consists of 823,145 square kilometers (320,827 square miles) and shares borders with Angola,

Botswana, and South Africa. Windhoek, its political capital, is also Namibia's principal city and most populous. Namibia's population is estimated around 2 million. A former colony of Germany, Namibia in 1990 became an independent nation.

A unitary democracy, Namibia's government is composed of three branches: the executive, the legislative, and the judicial. The executive is headed by the current president, who shares executive power with his cabinet of prime ministers who can serve only two five-year terms. The legislative branch is embodied by Parliament, which consists of a 72-member National Assembly and a 26-member National Council. Members of the Assembly are elected by registered voters using direct, secret ballots and serve five-year terms. The Namibian judiciary is headed by a Supreme Court that hears appeals from the lower High Court. The Supreme Court itself is made up of justices appointed by the president on the recommendation of a Judicial Services Commission. Beneath the Supreme Court is a High Court that acts as the first appeals court. At the bottom of the judicial system are 30 magistrate courts that act as routine trial courts. Military courts also exist, but they try only military members.

Crime

Namibia's climate and location on Africa's west coast makes it a target for illicit drug growth and transshipment. Correspondingly, criminal penalties for possession, use, or trafficking of illegal drugs in Namibia are severe, and convicted offenders can expect long jail sentences and heavy fines. The same can be said for those dealing in diamonds illegally; those convicted may be fined as much as US$20,000 and may be incarcerated for as long as five years.

Domestic violence is illegal under Namibian law, including beating and spousal rape. Penalties for rape convictions can range from 5 to 45 years' incarceration. The abuse of children, in many forms, is also illegal. Child rape and incest are both of particular prosecutorial interest. Criminal laws are also in place to deter clients and pimps from exploiting children under age 18 through child pornography or prostitution. Trafficking of persons, including children, is illegal. Kidnapping, forced labor, and slavery are all fiercely prohibited. This applies to trafficking both inside Namibia and between Namibia and other nations. If convicted, traffickers may face a sentence as high as US$98,907, 50 years' imprisonment, or both.

Among those activities that are not outlawed are some common sexual activities. Prostitution is legal in Namibia, as is homosexuality, though the latter is frowned upon by mainstream society, and the act of sodomy between males is still illegal. Evidence of this legality but intolerance can be seen in the regular police shutdowns of Windhoek's only gay bar (the Ceibas Café).

Crime Statistics

Detailed crime data are not available for Namibia. The most common crimes in Namibia are nonviolent crimes that include pickpocketing, purse-snatching, vehicle theft, and vehicle break-in (particularly at service stations), all crimes of opportunity. Violent crimes by comparison are far less frequent, but the number of violent incidents has risen in recent years. This prevalence is seen in the widespread occurrence of domestic violence and rape. Though normally underreported, there were 1,100 cases of rape reported in 2008.

Police

The internal security of Namibia falls mostly to two bodies: the Namibian Police Force (NAMPOL) and the Namibian Defense Force (NDF). Despite their shared missions and comparable sizes (12,000 NAMPOL, 16,000 NDF), these two bodies are answerable to different ministries. The NAMPOL is under the Ministry of Safety and Security, and the NDF is under the Ministry of Defense. Most of what is considered police work, though, falls to the NAMPOL. Within the highly centralized structure of the NAMPOL is also a paramilitary unit called the Special Field Force. Approximately half of the NAMPOL's overall 12,000 personnel belong to this unit, which itself is composed mostly of former People's Liberation Army of Namibia soldiers. These former soldiers are normally responsible for guard duties, checkpoints, and general order maintenance. The NAMPOL can be further subdivided into a number of specialized units. These include a crime investigation unit, a drug law enforcement unit, a motor vehicle theft unit, a commercial crime investigation unit, a protected resources unit, a serious crime unit, a special branch, a women and child protection unit, a scene of crime unit, a criminal record center/fingerprint unit, a dog unit, an INTERPOL (Criminal Intelligence Bulletin) unit, a stock theft unit, and an explosive unit.

NAMPOL faces a number of issues. Among these are a string of human and civil rights abuses. In recent years, there have been reports and charges of excessive force, prostitute extortion, and arbitrary arrest, though these tend to be the exception rather than the rule. In general, Namibian authorities respect the rights guaranteed in their Constitution, and Namibia has been lauded as one of the best-performing countries on human rights in Africa. However, this achievement in human rights does not fully translate to other areas of policing. Due to a shortage of personnel, training, and resources, the NAMPOL is routinely ineffective in deterring or investigating street crime. These shortages have not led to as much official corruption as has been seen in some other parts of Africa. Part of this is due to the "zero tolerance" policies of the Namibian government. This policy has been official law since May 2003, when Namibia's Parliament passed the Anti-Corruption Act. Beyond making a new law, the act also created an Anti-Corruption Commission, the body today tasked with enforcing Namibia's zero-tolerance corruption policy.

Finding of Guilt

The Namibian Constitution provides for a number of civil rights that begin at arrest. These include charges being read to the arrestee, appearance before a magistrate within 48 hours, and arraignment. Bail exists as an option though many remain in detention following arraignment. Lengthy pretrial detentions are a concern in Namibia because though trials are required to begin in a "reasonable amount of time," they often do not. The reasons for this include lack of qualified magistrates, the high cost of legal aid, and the glacial pace at which police investigations regularly move. As a result, it can often be years between arrest and trial. This issue is now to such a point that a full 8 percent of the prison population are those awaiting trial. In addition, 50,000 cases languish on court dockets unresolved. Those who do progress to court enjoy a number of rights. The first is a public trial, though that trial is not decided by jurors. The second is legal counsel. If the defendants cannot afford their own counsel, they are provided counsel at public expense. But because of a shortage of public defenders, this right is not always absolute. Something that is absolute is a presumption of innocence. The defendant also has the right to be present at trial, to consult with an attorney in a timely manner, to access government-held evidence, to confront witnesses, and to appeal the court's decision.

Punishment

Modern-day Namibia's correctional system traces back to 1990 and the passage of the Namibian Constitution. That document provides for the correctional system's head, the commissioner of prisons. Appointed by the president, the commissioner acts as the chief administrator of Namibia's 13 prisons and their 4,400 inmates, according to the Namibian Prison Service. Those 13 facilities, found in 9 of Namibia's 13 regions, cover a large range of ages and needs. The ages of these different facilities vary widely, with Swakomund Prison, built in 1909, as the oldest and Oluno Prison, built in 1996, as the newest.

Maximum-security prisons are located in Windhoek, Hardap, Walvis Bay, and Oluno. These prisons offer programs to develop trade skills. Proximity to population centers helps placement in jobs after release as well as greater contact with family.

Namibia's open prison farm is located at Divundu in the Kavango region and houses inmates who are serving sentences of fewer than three years and who are generally first-time offenders.

Luderitz, Keetmanshoop, Gobabis, Omaruru, Grootfontein, and Swakopmund are somewhat transitional facilities designated as district prisons. Capable of serving as maximum-security prisons, these locations instead serve mostly as reception centers for the larger corrections system. Those commonly housed here are pretrial detainees, those in transit to other prisons, and inmates serving sentences of less than two years. However, the use of district prisons for pretrial detainees is expected to decrease as Namibia moves forward with the development of specialized "remand" prisons. Also available for temporary incarceration are prison camps. Small facilities, these prison camps are built to stand only briefly for a specific purpose determined by the commissioner of prisons. Those housed in these temporary prisons are of a specific type and serve inmates who have no more than one year to serve before their release.

This stratification of prisons belies Namibia's progressive attitude toward corrections. So too does the country's juvenile rehabilitation center. Acknowledging the necessity of separating juveniles from adults in prisons, corrections officials have made efforts to ensure that cohabitation does not occur. Currently operating is the Elizabeth Nepemba Juvenile Centre near Rundu. Officials hope to expand these efforts as well.

Namibia abolished capital punishment upon independence and today offers many rehabilitative skill-development programs. Among these are in-house literacy programs, construction education, and self-sustaining agricultural programs. Vocational programs are also offered by domestic nongovernmental organizations such as Criminals Return to Society. Many of these have come about as a result of Namibia's close international partnerships, first with South Africa and increasingly today with the Canadian Prison Service. On the diversionary front, Namibia has shown a degree of innovation by implementing a community service pilot project for those convicted of petty crimes. Latest reports indicate this project is active in 4 of Namibia's 13 regions. For youth offenders, there also exists a pilot prison diversion program utilizing shelters and foster homes.

Although Namibia has made laudable strides in the area of corrections, it is plagued by resource scarcity. For instance, only one medical officer serves the entire prison population. This medical understaffing has led to a number of medical maladies among prisoners. Hypertension today prevails as the most common ailment, and HIV/AIDS is the leading cause of prisoner mortality. Overcrowding is a major problem and can be attributed to two factors. The first is the generally antiquated designs of Namibia's prisons characterized by large walls, tall fences, barred windows, and looming watchtowers. Second, Namibia's incarceration rate is high. In 2004, that rate stood at 264 per 100,000 inhabitants, reflecting a general increase in the corrections population. In 1992, the population stood at only 2,711. By 2001, it had risen to 4,727 before leveling off. All of these factors have led to systemwide issues, with prisons running at anywhere from 130 to 210 percent capacity. Windhoek Central Prison alone generally runs at 155 percent of capacity. In response to these conditions, Namibia is now attempting to divert petty criminals away from incarceration.

The existence of prison gangs presents another issue facing corrections officials. This is especially true at the Windhoek Central Prison, where multiple gangs operate. Notable gangs include Group 26, a gang affiliated with a South African prison gang of the same name, and Group 28, a group known for its facilitation of homosexual sex. Oddly enough, the existence of these gangs does not coincide with the existence of illicit drugs, a common means of finance and trade inside prisons elsewhere. Indeed, the consumption and smuggling of drugs is not noted as a large problem in Namibia's prisons. Most likely displacing such drugs are a variety of fermented fruit drinks that enjoy far greater popularity inside prison walls.

The inmates themselves are mostly males and between the ages of 18 and 35. Only about 2 percent of Namibian inmates are female. In light of this, there are no women-only prisons, but men and women are housed in separate units within the prisons.

Michael Galezewski

Further Reading

High Court of Namibia. (2007). *About the Namibian High Court:* http://www.superiorcourts.org.na/.

Namibian Police. (n.d.). *The Structure of the Namibian Police Force:* http://www.nampol.gov.na/default.aspx.

Schulz, S., and J. Winterdyk. (2004). "Namibian Adult Corrections from the Past into the Present: A Difficult Transition." In *From Adult Corrections: International Systems and Perspectives,* edited by J. Winterdyk, pp. 269–304. Monsey, NY: Criminal Justice Press.

Supreme Court of Namibia. (2007). *History of the Supreme Court of Namibia:* http://www.superiorcourts.org.na/supreme/history.html.

Niger

Legal System: Civil/Customary
Murder: Low
Corruption: Medium
Human Trafficking: Medium
Prison Rate: Low
Death Penalty: Maybe
Corporal Punishment: Yes

Background

Niger is located in western sub-Saharan Africa. Prior to French occupation in the 19th century, Niger was an economic crossroads and the home of numerous empires. Niger was not subject to the same levels of exploitation and intervention as other colonies as long as it paid its taxes and enacted French policies. It gained its full independence from France in 1960 and since then has struggled to sustain a stable democracy. The 1991 democratically elected government established a new constitution and ruled for four years. A new government was established in its current form in 1999.

A cultural divide exists between rural and urban Niger. The French-influenced legal system, bureaucracy, and language are primarily an urban phenomenon. This divide is represented in criminal justice. Traditional dispute resolution typically holds sway in rural areas, whereas urban areas are subject to the Westernized criminal justice system, but the lines between the two are blurred. Tradition affects proceedings in urban areas, and rural citizens utilize the police and prison systems if traditional mechanisms are not able to settle a dispute. Niger is a parliamentary democracy with shared power between a president and a prime minister.

The primary agencies responsible for the internal security of the country are the national police and the gendarmerie. The national police operate under the direction of the Interior Ministry and conduct law enforcement in urban areas. According to a report from the International Institute for Strategic Studies on Sub-Saharan Africa, there are approximately 1,500 national police officers. The gendarmerie is responsible for rural policing and operates under the Ministry of Defense. There are approximately 1,400 members. There are also 2,500 members of the paramilitary known as the Republican Guard. The Republican Guard anecdotally has been involved in law enforcement and dispute resolution in rural Niger. In total, there are 5,400 officers in the gendarmerie, national police, and Republican Guard, a rate of 1 member of law enforcement for every 2,314 persons in the population.

The U.S. State Department and Amnesty International indicate significant corruption and use of excessive force by law enforcement personnel. In 2006, the police were reportedly responsible for excessive force resulting in death and forcibly dispersing demonstrators resulting in injuries. The police are generally considered ineffective because of (1) limited supplies such as vehicle fuel, radios, uniforms, handcuffs, batons, and badges; (2) slow response time; (3) lack of weapons and other police training; and (4) lack of accountability. The gendarmerie is responsible for investigating complaints against the police, but these mechanisms are ineffective.

Law and the legal system in Niger are heavily influenced by the French. This influence includes the creation and application of customary law, placement of control of the bureaucracy in the hands of urban educated elite, and contemporary legal system and criminal procedure. There are three different forms of law in Niger. Throughout this chapter, references will be made to traditional law, customary law, and the legal system. Traditional law is here defined as the ethnic and religious practices carried out in both rural and urban Niger. Customary law is the French codification of elements of traditional law and the creation of dispute resolution systems based on this law. The legal system is the contemporary Western criminal justice system that operates in urban Niger.

Customary law is the French interpretation and codification of some Nigerien traditions. It was created because the French did not want to allocate resources to fully develop a legal system. During this process, the French found that traditional cultural practices did not incorporate a centralized authority or fixed rules, and thus, they created the system of customary law and dispute mechanisms based on their perceptions of traditional society. They gave the traditional chiefs power to make decisions and handle disputes, power that they did not previously have. Customary law was put in place while Niger was a French colony, but its use continued after independence and is currently enshrined in the legal code. Contemporary Nigerien customary law relates to matters including divorce, succession, gifts, testaments, and some commercial contracts. It is similar to Western "civil" law, even though civil remedies through the legal system are also available. Customary law can be used by judges to resolve disputes, but it cannot be applied in criminal matters. The arbitrariness in the creation of customary law and its power structure created wariness among rural people about the use of a centralized legal system and political authority.

The French created a caste of elites known as Evolues, who were put in charge of government bureaucracy. They typically speak French and wear Western clothing. They lack an understanding of traditional practices, viewing those living in rural areas with contempt. The rural–urban divide is especially present in the legal system because those individuals were trained in French legal customs and often educated in France. The rural population relies on languages other than French.

Niger's legal system is a mix of customary and French civil code. The French civil code was fully adopted at independence, and any element of the code that conflicted with the Constitution of Niger was considered null. Systematic assessment to identify the statutory contradictions between the French civil code and the Niger's Constitution was not undertaken, creating significant confusion regarding the status and applicability of specific laws.

The government rewrote its penal code in 2001. The goal behind this revised penal code was to make the code comparable to current Western notions of crime and criminal justice. The code created penalties for sexual harassment, female genital mutilation, intentional HIV transmission, and crimes that damage economic progress. This revised code focused on the right of the individual and limited the traditional Niger custom of punishing a family for the crimes of its members. These revisions sought to make criminal procedures and sentencing more consistent and predictable and to limit the utility of traditional dispute-resolution mechanisms and findings of guilt. Although Niger is primarily a Muslim nation, it has not adopted any elements of Islamic law.

Niger's current Constitution and criminal code are similar to Western notions of human rights and criminal justice. But there still exists a significant schism between the legal code of Niger and the law and dispute resolution in practice. There is a distrust of the urban Francophone government and a divide between rural and urban Niger.

Crime

The crime problem in Niger is of both domestic and international importance. The lack of resources combined with the schism between traditional dispute resolution and the criminal justice system contributes to the crime problem in a number of ways. First, it makes it difficult to determine the extent of the crime problem. Second, it contributes to problems of international importance, such as slavery

Former slave Adidjatou Mani Koraou, center, is flanked by unidentified officials of the Slavery International NGO during her appearance at a court in Niamey, Niger, on April 11, 2008. In a landmark ruling with implications across the region, West African judges on October 27, 2008, fined Niger the equivalent of $20,000 for failing to protect the woman, who was sold into slavery at age 12. (Boureima HAMA/AFP/Getty Images)

and human trafficking. Third, it limits the ability of the police and the government to respond to crime.

Classification of Crime

Crimes are classified according to the extent they cause injury to the body. These include murder; rape; various forms of assault and violence, including castration and female genital mutilation; and threats of violence. Availability of classifications of crime, in terms of seriousness of offense and punishment, is limited.

Crime Statistics

Criminal statistics on Niger are limited. As a result of lack of resources, the rural and urban divide, and police corruption and inefficiency, crimes are often unreported to the police, and data are generally unavailable on investigations and arrests. The most recent crime data available are from 1998 and available through INTERPOL. The number of crimes reported to the police were as follows:

Homicide	83
Sexual offenses	82
Serious assault	1,492
Theft (all)	4,731
Aggravated theft	547
Theft of motor vehicles	65
Other thefts	4,119
Fraud	473
Currency offenses	223
Drug offenses	325

The U.S. State Department indicates crime was at a high level because of thefts, robberies, and residential break-ins in Niamey (the capital) and in some rural areas in 2007. Thefts and petty crimes were common in both daytime and nighttime hours. Armed attacks were occurring at night and usually were committed by groups of two to four people. Instances of banditry have occurred in rural areas of Niger.

The exact extent of rural crime is unknown. The INTERPOL crime statistics described here not only are dated but also represent only crimes reported to the police. The reliance of many people on traditional dispute-resolution mechanisms limits the utility of these statistics. It is unlikely that crime in rural areas is reported to the police. The most common types of crime in rural areas relate to theft of property as well as land disputes, but these crimes are infrequent.

Niger has a number of crime problems of international significance. These include drug trafficking, domestic violence, female genital mutilation, slavery, and human trafficking. These problems are driven by porous and unpoliced borders, culture and tradition, the subservient status of women, an ineffective civil service, and a lack of resources. There have not been any reports of terrorist activity. The most well-known incident in the country related to terrorism relates to the supposed sale of Niger's uranium to Iraq.

Some research indicates that Niger may have a significant drug trafficking problem. According to Country Watch 2008 reports, in 2007, Niger's drug squad made 558 arrests for drug trafficking or use, and the majority of these individuals were residents of Niger. During the 1990s, approximately 4,300 mostly foreign drug dealers were arrested. Also seized during this same time period were significant quantities of marijuana, hallucinogens, and other narcotics. The government has indicated it is a transit point for drugs going to Europe and North Africa. But recent seizures in Niger have been minimal.

The U.S. State Department indicates domestic violence is widespread, but statistics are unavailable. Wife beating is considered common, and the law does not explicitly prohibit domestic violence. Though a wife has the ability to lodge criminal charges for battery, government attempts to enforce these laws are met with unknown success. Domestic violence is often dealt with informally and goes unreported.

Female genital mutilation (FGM) is also practiced by some tribal groups in Niger. FGM is the practice of removing or sewing up parts of the female genitalia. Approximately 5 percent of women had been victims of FGM in 1998 according to a report by the Inter-Parliamentary Union. This practice was more common in the Peul and Zarma ethnic groups. A recent report released by the government of Niger indicates that as of a 2006 survey, 2.2 percent of women were victims of FGM. If this finding is accurate, it would indicate a significant reduction in the prevalence of FGM. Reports indicate that the reduction is due to the severity of punishment for FGM.

Although outlawed in 2003, slavery still is a significant problem in Niger. Slaves are typically used for agriculture, animal rearing, and housework. Slavery is perpetuated in Niger for a number of reasons. It is more common in the rural areas of Niger, where the central government and the criminal justice system have less of a presence. Children born of slaves become the property of their master. A slave master has the right to decide on the education of a slave's children as well as decide whom a slave can marry. This limits the ability to stop slavery and the ability of slaves to gain their freedom.

A 2002 survey interviewed 11,000 slaves regarding their rights and conditions. This research revealed numerous human rights abuses including rape and torture. It is difficult to ascertain the total number of persons currently enslaved. Although the 2002 study indicates there were 870,363 slaves during that year, the same study also indicates this number is inflated. The U.S. State Department indicates a much lower figure: 43,000.

Slavery is outlawed and punishable, but Niger's desire to address the problem is inconsistent. The government acknowledged the problem of slavery and rewrote its legal code in 2003, but it has not implemented or enforced the law outlawing slavery. The trafficking of women and girls for sexual exploitation also occurs within Niger and to North Africa, the Middle East, and Europe. Niger serves as a transit point for the trafficking of persons to Benin, Nigeria, Togo, Ghana, Burkina Faso, and Mali. A 2005 survey found that 5.8 percent of households in Niger claimed at least one member of the household had been a victim of trafficking. Trafficking also occurs for use in forced labor. Boys have been indentured to Koranic teachers who would support their teachers by doing manual labor or begging.

Finding of Guilt

Niger has three systems of dispute resolution, which embody the divide between traditional and urban Niger. They consist of the urban system of police, courts, and corrections typically envisioned by Westerners, the customary dispute-resolution mechanisms created by the French, and the more rural and traditional dispute-resolution and guilt-finding procedures used in rural areas.

Legal System

Nigeriens have access to both civil and criminal remedies. The 1999 Constitution of Niger provides protections similar to those available in Western democratic nations. Niger's Constitution prohibits arbitrary arrest and detention. Detention without charge for more than 48 hours is prohibited. A defendant has the right to a lawyer upon being detained by the police. Bail is available for crimes that carry a sentence of less than 10 years. Detainees have the right to a prompt trial where they are informed of the charges against them. There are also limitations on the time and scope of the criminal trial. Those wrongly detained have the opportunity for financial reimbursement.

Trials in Niger are public, and individuals are tried by juries. The Nigerien legal system is based on the inquisitorial model of the French. In the inquisitorial model, the judge is actively involved in investigating the circumstances surrounding a case; the judge is not neutral as in the English and U.S. legal systems. The defendant has the presumption of innocence. Defendants have the right to be present at their trial and to confront and have witnesses to support them. Defendants have the right to all evidence against them. Those found guilty have the right to appeal, first to the Court of Appeals and then to the Supreme Court. Defendants do have the right to counsel, and the government provides a lawyer to those who are indigent and facing punishments greater than 10 years. Minors are also provided council at public expense.

There persist significant problems in accessing these legal protections. Most law is written in French, and many citizens do not read or even speak the language. Bail is generally not used because of ignorance of the law or lack of money. Although lawyers provide counsel to indigents and minors when requested by the government, they are often not provided compensation for their services. Lawyers are not generally available outside the capital city of Niamey. There is 1 judge for every 80,000 people, and there are 77 practicing lawyers in the country. There are also indications of political interference in the legal system.

Customary Law

Customary law and courts were systems developed by the French through interpretation of traditional law. Little is known about this system. Traditional chiefs are given the authority to act as mediators and counselors and have the authority to try cases. Customary courts can try noncriminal cases, relating to such things as divorce and inheritance. Women have a lesser status in customary courts than men. Disputes tried by chiefs and customary courts are not regulated by law, and defendants adjudicate their case in the legal system if they are unhappy with their verdict.

Traditional Law

Traditional Nigerien law is a mixture of spirit worship and Islam. Spirit worship is based on the belief that humans exist within a world where individual spirits control people's lives and where communication and interaction with these spirits is possible. Nigeriens generally follow the tenants of Sufi Islam; the rules of the Koran are seen as guidelines, and spirit worship is acceptable as long as prayers are only made to Allah.

Traditional law includes a collection of behavioral norms and moral obligations that exert social control over rural Nigeriens, relating to law rights, social ethics, and standards of appropriate behavior. It does not distinguish between private and public or criminal and civil law. There is both tension and redundancy between traditional dispute resolution and the legal system. This is a result of the early French colonial as well as the current government's efforts to implement a uniform legal code and limit traditional power. Criminal procedure laws are contrary to many elements of traditional Nigerien Law. They forbid collective responsibility and do not permit families and communities to resolve their own disputes, punishment involves removal from the community rather than reintegration, and they do not allow for the traditional spiritual methods of ascertaining guilt or innocence. Rural and urban people can access traditional dispute-resolution mechanisms and customary courts for noncriminal matters such as divorce in both rural and urban areas. Rural Nigeriens can access the criminal and civil remedies if they are unhappy with the results of traditional methods or have an uncooperative suspect who is not content to admit his or her guilt. Nigeriens tend to utilize the lowest level of dispute resolution. But there are indications that Nigeriens also choose dispute resolution mechanisms based on which one is likely to provide them with the best outcome.

Traditional law and the legal system are in contradiction. This contradiction is caused by a rural mistrust of the legal system and the imposition of these ideals on traditional practices. The legal system represents Western ideals of equality and due process, but it is difficult to access and is mistrusted by the population.

Punishment

Both the rationale and use of punishment in Niger continues to reflect the rural–urban divide. Little is known about the rationale or use of punishment in the customary legal system, though dispute resolution is probably used in rural areas. The criminal justice system utilizes both fines and incarceration. Rape is punished with 10–30 years' imprisonment; sexual harassment with 3–6 months' imprisonment and fines of \$20 to \$200; female genital mutilation with 6 months' to 3 years' imprisonment, or 10 to 20 years if death occurs; and castration with life imprisonment and death penalty if the victim dies.

The U.S. State Department indicates that crimes involving drugs are severely punished with heavy fines and long jail sentences; however, the actual extent of punishments for drug crimes is unknown. Niger does not currently utilize the death penalty. It retains the death penalty as a legal punishment but has not utilized the death penalty since 1976 and has generally established the practice of not carrying out executions.

Prison

According to the International Centre for Prison Studies, Niger has approximately 5,709 prisoners, an incarceration rate of 46 per 100,000. The prison population largely consists of remand prisoners. Remand prisoners are those who are awaiting trial and sentencing; they have not been officially found guilty or sentenced for their crimes. Remand prisoners are held with sentenced prisoners. The country has only a small percentage (3.2%) of female prisoners. There are 37 prisons in Niger. The official capacity of the prison system is 8,850, and it is operating at 65 percent of capacity.

Despite operating under official capacity, conditions in Nigerien prisons are poor. The U.S. State Department describes the prison systems as underfunded, understaffed, and overcrowded. In Niamey (the capital of Niger) in 2008 there were 718 prisoners in a prison with a capacity of 350, of whom 550 were on remand. A 2008 U.S. Human Rights report noted that though sanitation was poor, and prisoners died of AIDS, tuberculosis, and malaria, prisoners were allowed to receive food and medicines from their visiting families. Prison staff is corrupt, and prisoners could bribe staff to leave for the day and serve their sentences in the evening or serve their entire sentences in the national hospital.

Beyond human rights reports from the State Department, little is known about prison conditions within Niger. The use of incarceration appears low by international standards, but considering the country's economic status, lack of resources, and corruption, the prison conditions are likely to be poor.

Nathan Meehan

Further Reading

Abdelkader, G. K. (2004). *Slavery in Niger: Historical, Legal, and Contemporary Perspectives.* Niamery, Niger: Anti-Slavery International & Association Timidria.

Inter-Parliamentary Union. (2008). *Female Genital Mutilation Legislation and Other National Provisions: Namibia, Netherlands, New Zealand, Niger, Nigeria, Norway:* http://www.ipu.org/wmn-e/fgm-prov-n.htm.

Kelley, T. A. (2006). "Exporting Western Law to the Developing World: The Troubling Case of Niger." *Bepress Legal Series* 1057:1–52.

Kelley, T. A. (2002). "Squeezing Parakeets into Pigeon Holes: The Effects of Globalization and State Legal Reform in Niger on Indigenous Zarma Law." *New York University Journal of International Law and Politics* 34:635–709.

United Nations Office on Drugs and Crime. (2008). *Biannaual Seizure Report:* http://www.unodc.org/unodc/en/organized-crime/bi-annual-seizure-reports.html.

Nigeria

Legal System: Common/Islamic/Customary
Murder: Low
Burglary: Medium
Corruption: Medium
Human Trafficking: Medium
Prison Rate: Low
Death Penalty: Yes
Corporal Punishment: Yes

Background

Nigeria is a country in West Africa. It is bordered on the north by the Niger Republic, on the east by the Chad Republic and the Republic of Cameroon, on the west by the Benin Republic, and on the south by the Gulf of Guinea. It has a total land and water mass of 923,768 square kilometers (356,700 square miles). Nigeria is Africa's most populous country, and in 2007, its population was estimated to be 135,031,164. Nigeria operates a federal government structure of 36 states and Abuja, the federal capital territory. The Constitution that came into effect on May 29, 1999, stipulates a presidential form of government and a bicameral National Assembly consisting of the Senate and House of Representatives. The Senate has 109 seats, three from each state of the federation, and one seat from Abuja, the federal capital territory, and the House of Representatives is composed of 360 seats.

The Legal System

As a former British colony, Nigeria's legal system is founded on the English legal system, especially the concept of the rule of law and the doctrines of equity. In addition, laws made by the English legislature and extended to Nigeria before October 1960, when Nigeria obtained its independence from

Britain, remain valid in Nigeria, unless the appropriate authorities in Nigeria have followed established procedures to repeal such laws. Other major sources of Nigerian laws include the English common law, the 1999 Constitution, sharia (Islamic law), and African customary laws. Sharia is applicable only in the 12 northern states of the country, which are predominantly Muslim. The customary laws are based on African indigenous customs and belief systems and are mostly applicable in the southern states of the country. Customary laws are operational within the ethnic group where such customs are relevant and binding. Because customary laws are mostly unwritten, they must be shown in court to be admissible unless the facts are so commonplace that their applicability is self-evident.

Police

The Nigerian Police Force came into being in 1861 after the British Consul charged with the administration of the Colony of Lagos obtained permission from London to establish a Consular Guard comprising 30 men. This force had a military character and was recruited mostly from the Hausa ethnic group; hence, it was called the "Hausa Guard." The Lagos Police Force was created in 1896. In 1888, the British Colonial Authorities established the Royal Niger Constabulary with headquarters at Lokoja, geared toward the protection of its installations along the River Niger banks. In 1906, the police force and part of the Niger Coast Constabulary were reorganized to form the Nigeria Police Force. The Niger Coast Constabulary became the Southern Nigerian Regiments. These two police authorities continued to operate independent of each other until April 1, 1930, when they were consolidated to form the present Nigerian Police Force, under the authority of the Inspector-General of Police, with headquarters in Lagos.

Section 214 of the 1999 Nigerian Constitution renewed the police mandate to operate, with its headquarters located at the Federal Capital Territory, Abuja. There are 371,800 police officers in the country, and the police force is divided into 12 zonal commands. To enhance its crime control capability, the Nigerian police have further created other specialized units, such as an Anti-Terrorism Squad and Anti-Robbery Squad.

In addition, the National Drug Law Enforcement Agency (NDLEA) was established to deal with the challenges confronting local enforcement agencies in combating transnational crime. Arrest records both within and outside the country show that a significant number of Nigerians are involved in the various stages of drug trade, including the growing, processing, manufacturing, selling, exporting, and trafficking of hard drugs. Nigeria is considered a key transit point between the manufacture of cocaine in South America and its destinations in Europe and North America. Nigerians, according to the NDLEA report, dominate the drug market of sub-Saharan Africa. Nigerian drug traffickers are also involved in the export of marijuana to Europe and other West African countries. Marijuana is the only narcotic that is produced in Nigeria.

Another agency established to tackle a special crime problem is the National Agency for the Prohibition of Traffic in Persons (NAPTIP). This agency came into effect through Act No. 24 of 2003, known as the Trafficking in Persons (Prohibition) Law Enforcement and Administration Act. This act makes it a crime and imposes punishment for any individual or groups of individuals involved in the trafficking of persons, particularly women and children, and other related offenses. The NAPTIP has the authority and responsibility for the investigation and prosecution of offenders as well as for the counseling and rehabilitation of victims of trafficking. Other responsibilities include providing protection for trafficked persons and informants and gathering other information as may be necessary during the course of any investigation related to the trafficking of persons. The agency is administered by a board whose chairman and 12 other members are appointed by the president and commander-in-chief of the armed forces of the Federal Republic of Nigeria for an initial term of four years. The chairman and members of the board are eligible for a second term of four years. The agency operates a secretariat headed by a secretary appointed by the president of Nigeria on the recommendation of the attorney general of the federation. The secretary, who is the chief executive, and the accounting officer of the agency are responsible for the day-to-day operations of the secretariat.

In line with the government's determination to root out international corruption and other financial crimes in the country and also improve its international image, the Economic and Financial Crimes Commission (EFCC) was established. This law enforcement agency is one of the best-known and most popular law enforcement agencies in Nigeria. Its popularity derives mostly from its involvement and success in the investigation, arrest, and prosecution of top government officials who use their offices in money laundering practices and in enriching themselves. The EFCC was established in 2003 and is empowered to investigate financial crimes, including advance fee fraud, popularly known as 419 fraud; money laundering; illegal bunkering; terrorism; capital market; cyber crime; banking fraud; and economic governance. Section 46 of the EFCC Establishment Act of 2004 empowers the agency to investigate, prevent, and prosecute offenders involved in various crimes that include money laundering, embezzlement, bribery, looting, and other forms of corrupt practices such as illegal arms deals, smuggling, human trafficking and child labor, illegal oil bunkering, illegal mining, tax evasion, foreign exchange malpractices including counterfeiting of currency, theft of intellectual property and piracy, open market abuse, dumping of toxic wastes, and prohibited goods.

Crime

The data on crime in Nigeria suggest that over the period of 1994 to 2005, the reported crime slightly increased for some categories such as murder and armed robbery, while some other crimes such as assault, stealing, burglary, and store breaking decreased. Other crimes such as attempted murder, suicide, grievous harm, and wounding remained stable over time. Levels of crime for the most recent year available (2005) are as follows:

Murder	2,074
Attempted murder	11
Suicide	128
Grievous harm and wounding	22,858
Assault	33,991
Rape	798
Armed robbery	2,074
Burglary	4,907
Housebreaking	6,371
Store breaking	4,837

Courts

The judiciary is a separate and independent branch of the government. The country operates a dual court system with both the federal and state governments authorized by the 1999 Constitution to establish and administer their courts.

Federal Courts

The following are the federal courts in order of superiority:

- *The Supreme Court of Nigeria.* The Supreme Court is the highest and final appellate court in the country. The Supreme Court has original jurisdiction in conflicts between the federal government and the state government(s). It also has original jurisdiction in cases between state governments; otherwise, the court's primary function is the hearing of appeals from the Federal Court of Appeal. The head of the Supreme Court is the chief justice of the federation. The number of justices of the Supreme Court is prescribed by an act of the National Assembly but must not exceed 21. Currently, the number of Supreme Court justices seated on constitutional matters is seven; and five are seated on regular cases.
- *The Federal Court of Appeal.* The Court of Appeal consists of the president and 49 justices. At least three of the Court of Appeal justices must be learned in Islamic law, and at least three must be versed in customary law. The Court of Appeal has exclusive jurisdic-

tion to hear appeals from other lower courts as prescribed by law, including the State High Courts, the Federal Revenue Court, the Sharia Court of Appeal, and the Customary Court of Appeal.

- *The Federal High Court.* The Federal High Court consists of the chief judge and other justices, whose number is determined by an act of the National Assembly. The court has original jurisdiction in civil and criminal cases relating to taxation, currency, banking and foreign exchange, customs and excise duties, and so on.
- *The High Court of the Federal Capital Territory, Abuja.* The High Court of the Federal Capital Territory, Abuja, consists of a chief judge and such number of judges as may be prescribed by an act of the National Assembly. The court has original jurisdiction over procedural civil and criminal cases and others referred to it as a result of its appellate and supervisory jurisdiction. The court is duly constituted when there is at least one judge of the court presiding over a case.
- *The Sharia Court of Appeal of the Federal Capital Territory.* The Sharia Court of Appeal has appellate and supervisory jurisdiction over civil matters pertaining to Islamic personal law. The court consists of the grand kadi and such number of kadis (judges of Sharia courts) as prescribed by an act of the National Assembly.
- *The Customary Court of Appeal of the Federal Capital Territory, Abuja.* The Customary Court of Appeal of the Federal Capital Territory consists of the president and such number of judges as may be determined by an act of the National Assembly. The Customary Court of Appeal, in addition to carrying out other legal responsibilities delegated to it by an act of the National Assembly, has jurisdiction in civil matters relating to customary law.
- *Election tribunals.* The Constitution provides for the establishment of one or more election tribunals to be known as the National Assembly Election Tribunals. The tribunal hears petitions concerning the conduct of elections to the National Assembly. In addition, the Constitution stipulates the establishment in each state of the federation one or more election tribunals to be called the Governorship and Legislative Houses Election Tribunals. These tribunals review petitions concerning the conduct of governorship and State Assembly elections.

State Courts

The 1999 Constitution empowers the states to operate their own courts. The following are the courts administered by the states in order of superiority:

- *High Court of a state.* The High Court of a state consists of a chief judge and such number of judges as may be prescribed by a law of the House of Assembly of the state. The court hears appeals and also exercises a supervisory role over other lower courts in the state.
- *Sharia Court of Appeal of a state.* The head of the Sharia Court of Appeal of a state is the grand kadi. The court is also made up of kadis, with the number determined by the state House of Assembly. The court exercises an appellate and supervisory role on matters of Islamic personal law over other lower courts of the state.
- *Customary Court of Appeal of a state.* Similar to the Sharia Court of Appeal of a state, the Customary Court of Appeal of a state has no original jurisdiction on any matter. It has appellate and supervisory jurisdiction over the customary courts. The court is headed by a president and such number of judges as may be determined by the House of Assembly of the state.

Other courts that the states administer include the magistrate courts, the district courts, the customary courts, and the area courts. The magistrate courts are found in every state of the federation and have jurisdiction over civil and criminal matters. There are different classes of magistrate courts, related to the type of cases they handle. The district courts, on the other hand, exist mostly in the 12 northern states of the federation that have adopted the sharia law. The customary and area courts deal with limited civil and criminal matters emanating from customary law. They operate mostly in the southern states of the federation.

Punishment

Crimes are classified in Nigeria according to their seriousness, namely felony, misdemeanor, and simple offense. The length of jail and/or bail amount is reflective of the seriousness of the crime. Accordingly, persons found guilty of misdemeanor offenses may receive fine and/or warnings. They can also be granted probation or ordered to undertake community service. On the other hand, persons convicted of felony offenses are sent to prison, which may be either a maximum-security or a medium-security prison. Those convicted of less serious felony offenses may be sent to either a minimum-security prison or a labor camp. Political dissidents may be sentenced to house arrest. Although there is no parole system in Nigeria, prisoners are frequently granted pardon by the president, governors, or even chief justices of the federation or states. Offenders convicted of treason, murder, or armed robbery may be given the death penalty. Public executions for those convicted of capital offenses are common. There are also reports of many people convicted of capital offenses being executed secretly. The two main forms of execution are public firing squad and hanging in the gallows within the prison institution.

In all cases, it is the judge or magistrate who determines the sentence to be imposed. Because there is no special sentencing hearing in Nigeria, the

A man walks past an information board containing "details of prisoners committed" at the prison in Bauchi, Nigeria, on December 3, 2006. (AP Photo/George Osodi)

judge or magistrate typically sentences the offender to prison immediately after the trial is completed. Generally, government-appointed psychiatrists and social workers play advisory roles in both the pretrial investigations and the administration of penalty.

Prison System

The first prison in Nigeria was established in today's Broad Street, Lagos, by the colonial authorities in 1872. Prisons were built in several regional administrative headquarters of the country by 1910, including Ibadan, Onitsha, Lagos, Degema, and Calabar, under the administration of the colonial authorities. In line with the indirect rule policy of the British colonial authorities, some prisons were operated by native authorities in the northern and western part of the country. This accounts for why Nigeria operated a dual prison system for more than half a century until 1968, when the federal and local prisons were consolidated. Following the amalgamation of the northern and southern protectorates in 1914 by Lord Lugard, the Prison Ordinance of 1916 and Prison Regulations of 1917 were promulgated. The governor acquired the power and authority from this ordinance to establish and regulate the prison administration throughout the country.

The Nigerian Prisons Service is part of the Federal Civil Service. The head of the Prisons Service is the comptroller general of prisons (CGP), who reports to the president of Nigeria through the office of the Minister of Internal Affairs. The NPS has six administrative units known as directorates, and each is headed by a deputy comptroller-general of prisons (DCG).

Prisons are located in the 36 states and Abuja, the federal capital territory. By 1999, there were 148 prisons and 83 satellite prisons or lockups in Nigeria. There were also 10 prison farms and 9 cottage industries scattered all over the country for the training and rehabilitation of prisoners. More than 80 percent of the prisons were built before 1950. By October 1999, the prison population was 44,797, although the prisons had a total capacity for 25,000 inmates. According to available records released in November 2000, the total Nigerian prison population was 42,298, with 24,953 (59%) of this figure awaiting trial. A total of 956 (2.3%) of the Nigerian prison population were females. According to a recent Associated Press report, in 2008, the Nigerian prison population was estimated to be 40,000, with about 65 percent of this figure constituting those awaiting trial.

O. Oko Elechi and Charles B. A. Ubah

Further Reading

Agomoh, Uju, Adedokun Adeyemi, and Victor Ogbebor. (2001). *The Prison Service and Penal Reform in Nigeria: A Synthesis Study.* Lagos: Prisoners Rehabilitation and Welfare Action (PRAWA).

Elechi, O. Oko. (2006). *Doing Justice without the State: The Afikpo (Ehugbo) Nigeria Model.* New York: Routledge.

Oli, Sampson Ike. (2007). *Crime and Social Control: Lessons from Africa.* Ann Arbor, MI: Copley.

Réunion

Legal System: Civil
Murder: Medium
Prison Rate: Medium
Death Penalty: No
Corporal Punishment: No

Background

Réunion is an island located in the Indian Ocean off the coast of southern Africa, east of Madagascar. It has an estimated population of approximately 721,000. It is a quasi-independent department of France. The legal system in Réunion is inquisitorial. This trial system was introduced by the Ordonnance of Colbert in 1791, based on the Code of Penal Procedure written under Napoleon in 1791. It was officially implemented in Réunion after its attachment to France.

Police

Two distinct agencies are in charge of law enforcement in France. The Police Nationale fills five main roles, including the protection of the safety of individuals, material goods, and institutions. The police also must control immigration movements and fight against illegal workers, organized crime, and drug trafficking. This agency is also in charge of the protection of the country against outside threats and terrorism and must maintain public order. There are 145,820 officers in the French national police. The national police branch in Réunion is called the Direction Departementale de la Securite Publique (DDSP) and is composed of 872 officers including 61 medium-ranked officers and 7 high-level managers. The national police force is composed of more than 12 different groups, including the *l'unite de coordination de la lutte anti-terroriste* (anti-terrorist team) and an antidrugs division (MILAD). All these groups can be represented in Réunion when certain events occur such as terrorist attacks or drug trafficking.

The other agency responsible for law enforcement in France is the Gendarmerie Nationale. This agency is under the Ministry of Defense authority and is composed of military personnel as well as civilians. This law enforcement agency is responsible for maintaining law and order in rural areas. The Gendarmerie d'Outre-Mer (the name in non-metropolitan areas) is composed of 3,673 individuals, which includes 735 officers in Réunion. The Gendarmerie d'Outre-Mer has multiple specialized units, including naval, aerial, traffic safety, motorized, and search units. All officers belonging to this agency are military trained, except the civilian staff who are experts in administrative, scientific, and technical services. The gendarmerie groups in Réunion are also specialized in high-mountain rescue search and juvenile delinquency. In case of a military conflict, the military officers of the gendarmerie can be enrolled in the national army. Both the Police Nationale and the gendarmerie work often in cooperation so as to assure the safety of French citizens.

Crime

Classification of Crime

Crimes are classified into five types of infractions: against individuals, against material goods, against the state, organized crime, and victimless crime. Infractions against individuals include rape, torture, and homicide. Infractions against material goods include theft and robbery. Infractions against the state include terrorism and treason.

Each infraction is also divided into three levels of seriousness. Crimes are the most serious infractions, which include murder, rape, armed robbery, and drug trafficking. Under article 131–1 of the penal code, crimes incur a minimum sentence of 10 years of imprisonment. *Delits* are the second type of serious infractions, which include theft and drug dealing. Under article 131–3 of the penal code, delits incur imprisonment of less than 10 years, fines, day fines, community service, and restrictions on the offenders' driver's license or hunting license, for example. Delits are the equivalent of misdemeanors. Finally, the least serious infractions are petty infractions, which include traffic violations. Under article 131–13 of the penal code, petty infractions incur only fines according to the seriousness of the infractions.

The age of penal responsibility is 18 years old. Juveniles under 13 years old are not considered responsible. Juveniles between the ages of 13 and 18 can be handled by the juvenile justice system. Juvenile delinquents who commit extremely serious crimes can be prosecuted by adult courts. However, most juvenile delinquents are sentenced to educational and vocational programs. Incarceration is used only as a last resort for individuals under 18.

Drug Offenses

Drug use and drug trafficking appear as particular challenges to the Réunion authorities. The use of psychoactive legal (alcohol) and illegal substances (Zamal/cannabis) is widespread in Réunion. Zamal (local name for cannabis), which was previously extremely popular in Réunion, is now being replaced by Ecstasy and cocaine, which are now viewed as more attractive by the local youths. The production and distribution of stupefying substances are prohibited under article L 3421–1 of the Code of Public Health. Provocation to traffic incurs a maximum sentence of five years of imprisonment and fines up to 75,000 euros under article L3421–4 of the Code of Public Health. The use of stupefying substances incurs up to a year of imprisonment and a fine of up to 3,750 euros under article L3421–1 of the Code of Public Health. Possession of stupefying substances with intent to sell incurs a maximum sentence of 10 years and up to 500,000 euros in fines. Drug dealing incurs a maximum of five years of imprisonment and up to 75,000 euros in fines under article 222–38 of the penal code. "Guetteurs," those who work with drug dealers as a lookout for police, may face the same punishment as dealers. The length of imprisonment doubles if drugs are sold to minors or in educational areas. The organization of drug trafficking results in prison sentences from 10 to 30 years and up to 7,500,000 euros in fines under article 222–34 of the penal code.

Crime Statistics

The total crime rate in the capital of Réunion, Saint Denis, was 56.16 per 1,000 inhabitants in 2006. The most typical crimes in the most rural area, the arrondissement of Saint Benoit with 101,804 inhabitants, were assaults. There were 284 assaults in 2005. The most typical crimes in the most urban area, the arrondissement of Saint-Denis with 236,599 inhabitants, were theft of two-wheel motor vehicles. There were 421 thefts of this kind reported in 2006.

In 2006, 44 murders were reported to the police and gendarmerie in Réunion, whereas in metropolitan France, 900 murders were reported. The murder rate in Réunion was four times higher, 5.6 per 100,000 inhabitants, than in France, 1.4 per 100,000 inhabitants. Such statistics may imply that Réunion is facing a challenge to reduce its high murder rate. There were 49 robberies and 3,405 burglaries. Out of 184 rapes reported, 124 were rapes of minors. The numbers of drug trafficking or selling reported were 25. The total number of infractions was 31,518, including 5,427 offenses against individuals. Finally, there were 18,452 thefts reported to law enforcement agencies.

Finding of Guilt

Preventive Detention

The office of judicial police can detain a person for up to 24 hours: this is the *garde a vue.* If authorized by the prosecutor, 24 hours can be added to the original detention period (article 63–62 of the code of criminal procedure). After the initial 24 to 48 hours, the prosecutor must release the individual, or further court proceedings must be initiated.

Rights of the Accused

Under article 63–1 of the code of criminal procedure, the accused must immediately be informed of the crimes or infractions for which the investigation is necessary. If the accused is unable to read or write or has a certain disability, an interpreter or a certain method must be found to communicate with him or her.

The individual detained is allowed to make contact with family members, the individual(s) he or she lives with, or his or her employer by phone during the first three hours of detention. (article 63-2 of the code of criminal procedure).

Article 63–3 of the code of criminal procedure guarantees the right of the accused to be examined by a physician. If the detention lasts longer than 24 hours, a second examination can be given at any time. The judicial police officer or prosecutor can also call a physician if deemed necessary. Article 63–5 of the code of criminal procedure also guarantees that body searches will be conducted only by physicians.

Upon detention, the accused has the right to have a self-obtained lawyer or a state-appointed lawyer (*avocat commis d'office*), under article 63–4 of the code of criminal procedure. The meeting is confidential and cannot last longer than 30 minutes. If the detention exceeds 36 hours, the accused has the right to ask for a second meeting with a lawyer.

Assistance Provided to the Accused

Legal aid, or *aide juridique,* is available through the public defender system to those who cannot afford legal advice or litigation under article 63–4 of the code of criminal procedure. The accused must present a lack of means based on monetary resources to the Bureau d'Aide Jurisdictionelle, composed of magistrates and counselors. This aid may cover the amount of legal representation partially or entirely. However, the aid does not cover additional expenses related to the trial or fines assigned to the defendant.

Alternatives to Trial

Individuals who were not considered mentally capable during the completion of their crime(s) may be referred to psychiatric services instead of a formal punishment. Article 122–1 of the criminal code declares the accused free from criminal liability if the court-appointed psychiatric experts declares that the accused suffered from mental illness during the commission of the crime. There are alternatives to trial for juveniles and drug offenders as well. However, the majority of crimes are resolved by trial. Plea bargaining, dispute resolution, and guilty pleas are not allowed.

Pretrial Incarceration

The accused may be kept under supervision if suspected of an offense related to a term of imprisonment longer than three years. In January 2007, 30.6 percent of the accused, 18,483 individuals, were incarcerated before trial. The average length of preventive detention in 2006 was four months.

Investigation

At first, the police lead an investigation to identify potential suspects and obtain a minimum of information. Prosecutors—or in serious cases (delits or crimes), *juges d' instruction*—seek to establish whether the prosecution of the accused is justified. All investigations are under judicial supervision.

The judges have tremendous powers and are required to investigate and obtain evidence and elements of the accuser's guilt. Those judges are *a charge et a decharge,* which means that they are responsible for finding any kind of evidence. These judges can seek evidence proving the innocence of the accused. Indeed, the defense is not allowed to conduct its own investigation in the name of the offender. The judge can transfer some of his or her judiciary powers to police officials using a *commission rogatoire,* which will allow law enforcement officers to investigate. The judge has the right to emit search and seizure warrants as well as arrest warrants, can meet suspects at any time, and can order preventive detention.

The Criminal Court: The Assize Court

The Cour d'Assises, also called the Assize Court, is composed of three professional judges: a president and two assessors. The judges are magistrates who received a law school education and passed three national exams. There is one Assize Court for each department in France, including Réunion (100 courts in total). The Assize Court in Réunion meets in the administrative capital of the department, Saint-Denis. The president of the court is the chief of the chamber or advisor at the appellate court. Assessors are magistrates working in department courts or are advisers at the appellate court. The court is held once every three months for a maximum of 15 days.

Juveniles

The French juvenile justice system was created under the law of February 2, 1945. Its primary aims are reinsertion and rehabilitation of young delinquents between the ages of 13 and 18. Juveniles are treated by special criminal courts with specialized judges. Also, there are specific incarceration and rehabilitation facilities for juvenile delinquents. The Cour d'Assises (Assize Court) also exists for individuals under 18 when they commit serious crimes. Juveniles can also be judged by adult criminal courts when their crimes are extremely serious and can be incarcerated in adult correctional facilities. Each department is responsible for the creation of a support system for juvenile delinquents and their families. There is a juvenile court in Réunion.

Punishment

Types of Punishment

The types of punishments vary greatly, ranging from fines, electronic monitoring, suspended sentences, suspended sentences with probation or community services, probation, reparations, community service, postponement of sentence, incarceration, and half-imprisonment (day in the community, nights and weekends in the correctional facility) to expulsion from the French territory if citizenship cannot be proven.

The typical punishment for murder (article 222–1 of the penal code) is up to 30 years of imprisonment. If the murder follows or is committed during another crime, to facilitate another crime, to escape from controlled facilities, or to guarantee the anonymity of the offender or his or her accomplice, the sentence can be increased, up to life without parole. Premeditated murder is punished with life imprisonment (article 221–3 of CCP). If the murder is committed against a minor under 15 years old or is accompanied with rape, torture, or any barbarous acts, the offender must serve a minimum of 30 years in prison without the possibility of time reduction. Murder also results in life in prison if the individual killed his or her natural or adopted parents or attacked vulnerable individuals who are sick, disabled, or pregnant. The offender also receives up to life imprisonment if he or she murdered any public service official such as a lawyer, judge, or police officer during the exercise of his or her function. Finally, the murder of a witness in a criminal case is also punished by up to life in prison (221–4 of CP).

Rape is punished by up to 15 years of prison. According to article 222–24 of the penal code, offenders are punished with up to 20 years if the rape caused mutilation or permanent disability, was committed on a minor under 15, was committed on a vulnerable individual (disability, age, pregnancy) or known to the offender, was committed on a natural ascendant or individual over which the offender had authority, or was committed with the use of a weapon. Rape is punished by up to 30 years of incarceration if the offender's actions led to the death of the victim. If torture or barbarous acts preceded or followed the rape, the offender receives up to life in prison (article 222–25 of CP).

Theft is punished by up to three years of imprisonment and a fine up to approximately 46,000 euros (article 311–3 of penal code). It can be punished by up to five years of prison and 100,000 euros of fines if it is preceded or followed by violence on the victim (minor injury that does not have an impact on the victim's ability to work). Theft can be punished by up to seven years in jail and 100,000 euros in fines if two aggravating circumstances are present, such as violence on the victim(s) and degradation of personal or commercial property during the commission of the crime. If three aggravating circumstances are present, the offender can receive up to 10 years in prison and a fine of 150,000 euros. The offender can receive up to 15 years of imprisonment if the violence attached to the theft led to a permanent disability of the victim (article 311–77 of the penal code). If prohibited weapons are used or carried during the theft, the offender will receive a term up to 20 years and may receive a fine of 150,000 euros. Finally, robberies committed in group involving weapons lead to up to 30 years' imprisonment for all offenders involved.

The most serious drug offense is the direction or organization of a group that produces, fabricates, exports, transports, detains, offers, and/or sells illegal drugs. This offense leads to possible life imprisonment and up to 8,000,000 euros in fines (article 222–34 of penal code). According to articles 222–35 and 222–36 of the penal code, the production and fabrication of drugs results in 20 years of imprisonment if committed alone and up to 30 years in prison if committed by an organized group.

Suspended Sentence: Le "Sursis"

According to article 132–29 of the penal code, a suspension of punishment can be announced by a court after the conviction of the offender. This is called a *sursis*. This suspension may be ordered when a defendant has not been previously condemned for a criminal act (article 132–30 of PC) and is applicable in particular circumstances (e.g., vehicular manslaughter). The suspension becomes void after five years of its application (article 132–35 of penal code). In case of re-offending, the offender will have to accept the suspended sentence as well as his or her new penalty, which cannot be merged (article 132–38). The convict will be placed under the control of a judge of application of punishments (article 730 of code of penal procedure). There were 146,000 individuals in January 2007 whose sentences were suspended. Most of them had suspended sentences coupled with penal measures such as probation, electronic monitoring, or community service.

The Death Penalty

The death penalty was abolished with law #81908, voted into law on October 9, 1981. Corporal punishment is not authorized either.

Prison

The total number of inmates in France was 58,402 on the January 1, 2007, including 2,152 women and 727 minors housed in 194 facilities. In Réunion, on November 26, 2007, there were a total of 1,293 inmates in three correctional facilities, including 296 men and 32 women housed at the jail of Saint-Denis, 211 men jailed at Saint-Pierre, and 754 housed at the Port. A new correctional facility was scheduled to open in June 2008, which would house 574 inmates, including 40 women and 40 minors.

The largest facility is located at Le Port and houses the most dangerous inmates. It was previously called the Centre Penitentiaire de la Plaine des Galets.

Education Programs and Rehabilitation

All of the Réunion prisons offer educational programs to their inmates, including auto-mechanic training (8 months), mechanic garden equipment formation (7 months), gardener formation (7 months), construction (8 months), and preservation of national monuments formation (2 months). Inmates are remunerated during their professional training up to 2.26 euros/day. In the correctional facility of Saint-Pierre, inmates can participate in workshops on writing and reading, which last for three months and have a capacity of 30 inmates. They can also participate in food production/hygiene and quality of food monitoring, which lasts three months and has a capacity of 16 inmates. At the facility of Le Port, inmates can be trained in construction, maintenance, and auto-mechanism. In general, 29.4 percent of inmates obtain a CAP-BEP (certificate program), 10.6 percent prepare for the French high school final exam ("le Baccalaureat") or university diplomas, and 60 percent of inmates prepare for the equivalent of the GED every year. Twenty-four percent of the inmate population participates in some school formation, and 10 percent of inmates obtain a diploma. Almost all of minors receive some type of educational training. Neither work nor educational programs are mandatory for inmates.

Incarceration Policies

Visiting days and schedules differ for each establishment. However, certain guidelines are applied by all facilities. Individuals placed on preventive detention are allowed a minimum number of three visitations per week. Inmates detained are allowed a minimum of one visit per week. To visit an inmate placed in preventive detention, visitors must obtain a visiting license obtained from the judge. Visitors of inmates detained must bring identification documents. French inmates have numerous privileges, including receipt of mail (except newspapers and packages), the keeping of personal items such as clothes and certain jewelry items such as ring and watch, smoking, participation in sport classes, watching television, and access to a library and to educational programs. Inmates can also work, and they and their families will receive social security benefits up to four years after incarceration. Finally, French inmates can vote during and after being imprisoned.

Anne-Laure Del Cerro and Seigo Nishijima

Further Reading

Bell, John, Sophie Boyron, Simon Whittaker, Andrew Bell, Mark Freedland, and Sylvia Hargreaves. (1998). *Principles of French Law.* New York: Oxford University Press.

French Government, Ministere de l'Interieur. (2007). *Police Nationale:* http://www.interieur.gouv.fr/sections/a_l_interieur/la_police_nationale.

French Government, Ministere de la Justice. (2007). *Organisation de la Justice:* http://www.justice.gouv.fr/index.php?rubrique=10031.

French Government, Ministere de la Defense. (2007). *Gendarmerie:* http://www.defense.gouv.fr/gendarmerie.

French Government, Secretariat General du Gouvernement. (2007). *Service Public d' Acces au Droit:* http://www.legifrance.gouv.fr/.

Kock, Gerald, and Richard S. Frase. (1988). *The French Code of Criminal Procedure.* American Series of Foreign Penal Codes 29. Littleton, CO: Fred B. Rothman & Co.

Scherer, Andre. (1980). *La Réunion.* 4th ed. Paris: Presses Universitaires de France.

Rwanda

Legal System: Civil/Customary
Murder: Medium
Corruption: Medium
Human Trafficking: Medium
Prison Rate: High
Death Penalty: No
Corporal Punishment: No

Background

The Republic of Rwanda is located in central Africa. It is surrounded by Burundi to the south, Tanzania to the east, Uganda to the north, and the Democratic Republic of Congo to the west. It has a total land mass of over 26,000 square kilometers and an estimated 2009 population of about 10.5 million. The majority of the population is Hutu (84%), and Tutsi constitute 15 percent.

Rwanda is a republic that became independent in 1962 from Belgium-administered UN trusteeship. It has a multiparty presidential system. The head of state is the president elected by popular vote for seven-year terms. The head of government is the prime minister, and the president appoints a council of ministers. The legislative branch consists of a bicameral Parliament of 26 seats, out of which 12 members are elected by local councils for eight-year terms. There are 80 seats for the Chamber of Deputies, out of which 53 are elected by popular vote to serve five-year terms. Another 24 seats are reserved for women candidates who get elected by local bodies, and the remaining 3 are selected by youth and disability organizations. The judicial branch consists of the Supreme Court as its apex court, high courts of the republic, provincial courts, district courts, and mediation committees.

Rwanda is dominated by a strong presidency. The predominately Tutsi Rwandan Patriotic Front (RPF) took power in 1994 and formed a Government of National Unity that functioned during the transitional period following the civil war. In May 2003, according to the U.S. Department of State, a country-wide referendum resulted in the approval of a new constitution, which provides for a multiparty system and nullifies the suspension of political activity, although it provides few protections for parties and their candidates. In August 2003, the country held its first multicandidate national elections since independence. President Paul Kagame was elected to a seven-year term in largely peaceful but seriously marred elections. It was in September 2003 that President Kagame's party, the RPF, won the majority of the seats during legislative elections and therefore remained the principal political force that controlled the government. The judiciary, which was not operational for most of the year as the country implemented judicial reforms, was subject to executive influence and suffered from a lack of resources, inefficiency, and some corruption.

The minister of defense holds the responsibility for external security and national defense, and the minister of internal security is responsible for civilian security matters as well as supervision of the prisons and the Rwandan national police. The Rwanda Defense Forces (RDF) is responsible for maintaining external security, and the police maintain the internal security. After the formal withdrawal of all its troops from the Democratic Republic of the Congo (DRC) during 2002, the Rwandan government began to reorganize its military to provide a smaller, more suitable force for territorial defense, rather than for expeditionary actions abroad. It also has been noted that some members of the security forces acting independently committed serious human rights violations as the government authorities failed to exercise adequate control over security personnel.

In 2006, the government of Rwanda instituted a significant reorganization administratively, replacing the previous 12 prefectures with 5 larger multiethnic provinces intended to promote power-sharing and reduce ethnic conflict. The country's economy, adversely affected by the conflict of the early 1990s, continued to recover gradually. Recovery efforts were aided in 2006, when significant debt relief was granted by the World Bank and the International Monetary Fund, and in 2007, when Rwanda joined the East African Community, a regional trade and development bloc.

Crime

According to the United Nations, in September 1994, only 16 months after the establishment of the International Criminal Tribunal for the former Yugoslavia (ICTY), the new government of Rwanda requested that the United Nations establish an International Criminal Tribunal for Rwanda (ICTR) to adjudicate the crimes of genocide, war crimes, and crimes against humanity that had been committed in the country. However, as negotiations over the terms for establishing an ICTR began, Rwanda objected to a number of provisions. Some of these original points of tension remain as issues that may tend to limit or at least to call into question the efficacy of the ICTR.

Police

Prior to 2000, there were three police organizations in Rwanda: The national gendarmerie, a paramilitary force established in 1973 under the Ministry of Defense; the communal police, which was established in 1963 under the auspices of the Ministry of Interior/Home Affairs; and the Judicial Police Inspectors, established to help with the large number of genocide cases and which reported to the minister of justice. In 2000, legislation was enacted to merge all three into one entity that reported to the minister of interior.

The national police is headed by a commissioner-general in charge of many directorates and divisions. One of these divisions is for community policing. In addition, there are a number of services, territorial and support units such as the medical services, the air wing, and an intervention force, as well as five specialized units such as traffic, air, and border police.

Many reforms have been initiated since the genocide. Included among them are greater inclusion of all diverse ethnic groups in the police force, demilitarization and civilianization of police force, and oversight and police accountability systems.

Crime Rate

There is limited information from the United Nations that directly relates to the rate of crime in Rwanda. The Overseas Advisory Security Council (OSAC) has stated that most crimes include automobile break-ins, pickpocketing, purse snatchings, and increasingly, muggings. Political violence in Rwanda has gone down since 2004 because the Democratic Forces for the Liberation of Rwanda (FDLR), which has been the primary source of past political violence, has diminished as a direct military threat and has not conducted any attacks or acts of violence within Rwanda since 2004. Other crimes reported during the genocide attacks in the early 1990s include rape and genital mutilation of local women during the severe and violent attacks.

Finding of Guilt

Rwanda is investigating the possibility of moving toward a common law system from the current Romano-Germanic system. Though similarities between the two systems exist in the areas such as presumed innocence until proven guilty, rights to legal representation, and fair trial, there are fundamental differences. The most important of them is the absence of the jury system.

The Rwandan judicial system is bureaucratic, and cases can be delayed significantly. The Gacaca (pronounced "gachacha") court is part of a system of community justice inspired in Rwanda by tradition and was established in 2001, in the wake of the 1994 attacks, where between 400,000 and 1,000,000 Rwandans, mostly Tutsi, were slaughtered at the hands of the Hutu. It was after the genocide that the new Rwandan Patriotic Front's government was struggling with developing just means for the humane detention and prosecution of the more than 100,000 people accused of genocide, war crimes, and related crimes against humanity. The court system needed a more prompt and efficient means of delivering justice, and thus Rwanda implemented the Gacaca court system, which has roots in the

Rwandan police guard Father Guy Theunis, right, who appears before a Gacaca court in Kigali, Rwanda, on September 11, 2005. The Belgian priest is accused of reproducing articles encouraging the killings of Tutsis by Hutu extremists. Gacaca courts are a new form of community justice that have been used in Rwanda since the Rwandan genocide. The system involves both victims and witnesses in an interactive court proceeding against alleged criminals. (AP Photo/Riccardo Gangale)

traditional, cultural, communal law enforcement procedures. The primary mission of this system is to achieve reconciliation, and it aims to promote community healing by making the punishment of perpetrators faster and less expensive to the state.

The Rwandan Supreme Court has a sixth court called the Gacaca Courts Department to coordinate and supervise the activities of the various courts as well as keep the national and international community informed about the Gacaca courts' activities. In 2002, the Gacaca Courts Department was replaced by the National Service of Gacaca Courts, so as to coordinate the Gacaca Courts activities and speed up this process.

The International Criminal Tribunal for Rwanda (ICTR) is an international court established in November 1994 by the United Nations Security Council to judge those people responsible for the Rwandan genocide and other serious violations of international law performed in the territory of Rwanda, or by Rwandan citizens in nearby states, between January 1 and December 31, 1994 (United Nations Resolution 955, 1994). The tribunal consists of 16 judges in four "chambers"—three to hear trials and one to hear appeals. In addition, there are 9 "ad litem judges," bringing the total to 25. At present, all 9 ad litem judges are assigned to chambers 2 and 3. There is an additional pool of 9 further ad litem judges who may be called on in the case of a judge being absent. The Office of the Prosecutor has an investigation section as well as a prosecution section.

The Registry, headed by the registrar and representative of the Secretary General of the United Nations, is responsible for the overall administration and management of the tribunal and provides judicial and legal support services for the work of the trial chambers and the prosecution. It also serves as the tribunal's channel of communication. The Registry has the Judicial and Legal Services Division and the Division of Administration. Additionally, there is a Witnesses and Victims Support Section consisting of two units: one for prosecution witnesses and one for defense witnesses.

The Gacaca system is representative of a model of restorative justice in that it focuses on the healing of victims and perpetrators, confessions, plea bargains, and reintegration to society. With these characteristics, it is a radically different approach from the retributive and punitive nature of justice of the ICTR and national courts. There has been great hope placed in the ability of restorative justice to contribute to reconciliation at the individual and community level. Overall, it would appear that Rwanda is in fact making a positive move toward having a court system that is effective in deciding the guilt of those brought before it. However, it is evident that the sheer volume of crimes committed has weighed down these courts considerably and that there is still a great deal of work to be done. It seems that moving toward a more Western way of trial by jury would be more effective in time, but now it would not be efficient with the large numbers of cases that have still not been heard.

Punishment

Punishing crimes in Rwanda is a difficult task given the vast number of crimes that occurred in a relatively short period of time, in a country whose laws and statutes are lacking. Those who have committed identical crimes are not necessarily dealt the same punishment, depending on the evidence presented. As discussed previously, there are four categories of convicts, categories in which punishments differ. The first category includes leaders and organizers of the genocide and offenders who committed ghastly murders or sexual torture. Other convicted of homicides are included in category 2. Category 3 includes those who are convicted of grave assaults, and finally, category 4 includes those engaged in property crimes connected with genocide. Category 1 offenses are punishable by death. All categories with the exception of category 1 received reduced sentences as part of guilty pleas. A greater reduction in punishment is available for those who plead guilty before the trial.

The distribution of defendants between the national and international fora has been an area of concern in the implementation of concurrent jurisdiction. Questions have has been raised about the appropriate distribution of defendants, which has caused uncertainty and, at times, tension between national governments and the ICTR. The distribution of offenders has caused tensions between the Rwandan government and the ICTR partly because of miscommunication and more importantly because of a difference in agendas of each of the two groups. The biggest bone of contention came from the manner in which plea bargaining was administered.

The performance levels of the national justice system and of the ICTR remain to be seen, given that that the best form of justice that the ICTR or the national courts will be able to render will be justice delayed, for the reasons previously discussed regarding the large numbers of suspects on trial for crimes that were committed a great many years ago. It is not clear whether Rwanda would benefit more from utilizing international assistance or strictly adhering to the system currently in place.

Prisons

The U.S. Department of State Human Rights Report noted that conditions in prison and detention centers were harsh as a result of overcrowding from large convictions following the Gacaca hearings. The prison population in the 16 central prisons rose sharply from 87,000 at the end of 2006 to 98,000 in July 2007. However, the numbers went down to 58,598 toward the year's end because of a change in Gacaca sentencing structure. Consequently, 2 of the 16 decrepit prisons were closed down. With an increase in the government's interest in human rights in prisons, torture and inmate abuse declined sharply. Prison officials who were found violating inmates' human rights were relieved of their jobs. Conditions in prisons and detention centers remained poor with strong increases in inmate population. The government made strong efforts to improve health care as well as increase food budgets following the release of large numbers of inmates in the middle of 2007. Prison conditions for women prisoners were better relative to conditions in male prisons and detention centers.

Minimal food and water is given to those in prison, limited to a porridge for breakfast and a type of maize meal and beans for lunch. All incoming mail is read by prison officials prior to being handed out, and many inmates are expected to perform community service as part of their sentence. There are showers available for daily use, though they rarely have hot water available. The prisons have a high rate of HIV/AIDS and have few doctors able to treat this ailment. In comparison to the Western world, these conditions are substandard; however, without more substantial help from human rights groups, it seems as though the current conditions will remain.

Jennifer Janowski

Further Reading

Harhoff, Frederik. (1997). "The Rwanda Tribunal: A Presentation of Some Legal Aspects." *International Review of the Red Cross:* http://www.icrc.org/web/eng/siteeng0.nsf/html/57JNZ4.

Human Rights Watch. (2004). *Case Law of the International Criminal Tribunal for Rwanda:* http://www.hrw.org/reports/2004/ij/ictr/index.htm.

Le Mon, Christopher. (2006). *Rwanda's Troubled Gacaca Courts:* http://www.wcl.american.edu/hrbrief/14/2lemon.pdf?rd=1.

Mamdani, M. (2001). *When Victims Become Killers: Colonialism, Nativism, and the Genocide in Rwanda.* Princeton, NJ: Princeton University Press.

Tiemessen, A. (2004). "After Arusha: Gacaca Justice in Post-Genocide Rwanda." *African Studies Quarterly* 8(1): http://web.africa.ufl.edu/asq/v8/v8i1a4.htm.

Saint Helena

Legal System: Common
Death Penalty: No
Corporal Punishment: No

Background

Saint Helena is a British overseas territory located in the South Atlantic Ocean, midway between Africa and South America. The territory of St. Helena includes both the Ascension Islands and the group of islands of Tristan da Cunha. St. Helena is located about 700 miles southeast of Ascension Island and is over 1,000 miles to the nearest West African state. The Tristan da Cunha group of islands, considered the remotest archipelago in the world, lies over 1,500 miles to the south. St. Helena is a small island, about 10 miles by 7 miles, and the major city is Jamestown. There is no air link to the island, and all journeys are by sea, via Cape Town in South Africa, Ascension Island, or Walvis Bay in Namibia. Residents of St. Helena are fondly referred to as "Saints." St. Helena's population consists of a little over 4,000 residents, mostly European descendants. The Ascension Islands have about 3,000 in transient population, mostly American and British military personnel, and the Tristan da Cunha islands have about 300 inhabitants, mostly British. St. Helena's economy is mostly tourism, which has declined in recent years.

Queen Elizabeth II is the head of state and appoints a governor on the advice of the British government. Although responsibility for defense and foreign affairs remain with the United Kingdom, the unicameral legislative council consists of 15 members, 12 of whom are elected for four-year terms. The other three members are the governor and two ex officio members. The governor of St. Helena appoints administrators for both the Ascension Islands and Tristan da Cunha.

Legal System

According to the St. Helena Police Service, St. Helena's legal system consists of common law and statutes, supplemented by local statutes. The executive branch of government is composed of the chief of state, Queen Elizabeth II, and the head of government in St. Helena, the governor and commander in chief (Andrew Gurr as of 2007). The island's executive cabinet consists of the governor, three ex-officio officers, and five elected members of the legislative council. There are no elections because the monarch is hereditary, so the governor is appointed by the monarch. The legislative branch is a unicameral legislative council that holds 16 seats, including the speaker, three ex-officio and 12 elected members who serve a four-year term. Additionally, St. Helena's judicial branch consists of the Magistrate's Court, Supreme Court, and Court of Appeal.

According to the St. Helena Police Service, there is one local police department, which deals with all types of offenses (i.e., criminal, traffic, etc.). St. Helena uses a common law system, which means law and procedure are governed by laws and precedents. Their laws reflect the experience of practitioners, on a case-by-case basis, and the Supreme Court develops law. Truth-finding is limited by pleas and rules of evidence, which limits the fact-finding process as well. Grand and petit juries play a strong role, and there is an overall presumption of innocence until proven guilty.

Crime

Classification of Crimes

The role of the police in St. Helena is to deal with all types of crime, and the military defense of the country is left up to the United Kingdom. According to the St. Helena Police Service, the main legal classification of crime is indictable serious crime. The last criminal-related deaths in St. Helena were manslaughter in 2004 and murder in 1984. Drug offenses in St. Helena usually involve cannabis, which is the main drug there, and there has been one known case of Ecstasy. The most typical crimes in the rural areas of St. Helena are burglaries. The most typical of crimes in urban areas are alcohol-related offenses.

Offense categories for the overall crime rate in St. Helena are based on the following ordinances: assaults, burglaries/thefts, sexual offenses, drug offenses, firearm offenses, criminal damages, arson, and public order offenses. Violent crimes include assaults and disturbance of public order.

Crime Statistics

The St. Helena Police Service implements performance targets based on the criminal reports that they receive. Respectively, each crime category is labeled as recorded, detected, and detection. "Recorded" represents the total number of crime reports received in a year. "Detected" is the number of crimes solved, and "detection" is the percentage of crimes solved. The following data were provided by the St. Helena Police Service for the last three years. These data include the number of crimes recorded (reported), the number detected (solved), and the percentage of detection (detected) from April 1 to March 31 of 2006, 2007, and 2008. These data show that, for the fiscal year of 2005–2006, St. Helena had 213 total crimes reported. Of those crimes, 8 were burglaries, 61 were violent crimes (assaults or public order), and 39 were committed by juvenile offenders. Of the 213 total crimes reported, 141 were solved; 2 of the 8 burglaries were solved; and 60 of the 61 violent crimes were solved. Data for the year 2006–2007 indicate that there was a reduction in overall crimes (184). However, the number of burglaries doubled from 8 to 16 from the previous year. Data for the year 2007–2008 show that the overall crime rate continued to decline, with the exception of a slight increase in the number of violent offenses.

Finding of Guilt

The judicial system consists of four courts: the Supreme Court, the Magistrate's Court, the Small Debts Court, and the Juvenile Court. The chief justice presides over the Supreme Court, which has jurisdiction over criminal and civil cases. Criminal cases are dealt with according to English procedure, as far as local circumstances permit, and the trial of the prisoner is by a jury of eight. The Supreme Court is located in the capital of Jamestown. The court also contains probate, admiralty, and divorce sections. However, the Court of Appeals is located in London. The governor has acted as chief justice in his absence. In the Magistrate's Court, the sheriff doubles as the magistrate and a justice of the peace. The Small Debts Court reviews civil cases not exceeding the amount of 50 dollars. The Juvenile Court is composed of three justices, and the only people allowed in the court are the justices, the police prosecutor, and the child's parents.

In 1990, St. Helena Police performed a search of a ship docked on the island and found five tons of cannabis. As a result, the captain and his crew (four Dutchman and three Ghanaians) were detained, and the ship was impounded. The biggest challenge was providing adequate legal counsel for the accused. Aside from the governor, the island had only one qualified lawyer, who was also the attorney general. A trial was conducted on July 8, 1991, and lasted nine days. After four and a half hours, the jury found the captain guilty of importing cannabis and four of the crew members of simple possession. The captain received nine years' imprisonment, one crew member received three years, and the remaining three received two years in prison.

Punishment

The superintendent of the police was also the superintendent of the prisons in 1973. The prison, located in Jamestown, has a total staff of three, the sergeant/warden, an assistant warden, and a matron. Male and female prisoners are housed in separate wings. In 1970, there were a total of 11 male prisoners. In 1971, this number increased to 20 male prisoners and 1 female prisoner. In 1972, the number decreased to a total of 5 male prisoners and 3 juveniles on remand. By 1973, there were a total of 8 male prisoners and 1 female prisoner. All of the prisoners were employed during their stay by way of carpentry and the use of certain power tools to perform tasks for the community. Corporal punishment is prohibited as a sentence for crime in St. Helena. It is also prohibited as a disciplinary measure in penal institutions.

According to the St. Helena government Web site, some of the key objectives for the prison services in St. Helena are to maintain prison staff without reliance on the police services and to develop rehabilitation programs that will aid inmates in their release back into the community.

Mark Bridge

Further Reading

St. Helena Development Agency. (2009). *About St. Helena:* http://www.shda.co.sh/pages/about_st_helena.html.

St. Helena Government Web site: http://www.sainthelena.gov.sh/.

St. Helena Police Service. (2008). Correspondence and Statistical Data of April 2008, from the CID Clerk at the St. Helena Police Department.

Willms, J. (2008). *Napoleon & St. Helena: On the Island of Exile*. Translated by J. Brownjohn. London: Armchair Traveller/Haus Pub.

Sao Tome and Principe

Legal System: Civil/Customary
Murder: Medium
Corruption: Medium
Prison Rate: Medium
Death Penalty: No
Corporal Punishment: Yes

Background

The Democratic Republic of Sao Tome and Principe (STP) consists of two volcanic islands located in the Gulf of Guinea to the west of Gabon and to the south of Nigeria. Originally a colony of Portugal, STP is one of the smallest independent nations and continues to operate under a democratic multiparty system. There are approximately 160,000 people living in STP with 38 percent of the population geographically situated in urban areas and 62 percent located in rural areas. When STP gained independence in 1975, voters put into action a new constitution, which was subsequently ratified in 1990 following a national referendum and again in 2003.

STP's legal system is based on the Portuguese rule of law along with some customary laws. The Portuguese legal system in turn is based on Roman law and is considered to be in the civil or continental family of legal systems. The court system has three levels including a circuit court at the first level, a Supreme Court, and the Constitutional Court. The Supreme Court is the appellate court of last resort. The Constitutional Court is the court with the highest judicial authority and was only recently created, in 2006. In addition, the Constitution declares that all individuals are given the right to a fair public trial, the right to appeal, and the right to legal representation.

Despite the rights given to those accused and convicted of crimes, the current economic situation in STP has hindered the extent to which individuals are able to access legal resources. The poor economic conditions and limited availability of well-trained lawyers have impeded the right to a speedy trial because of an inability to train and hire judges. This has also led to judges being susceptible to bribery and corruption, decreasing the likelihood that one will receive a fair trial.

The judiciary in STP is designated as an independent entity not to be influenced by the executive branch of government. Based on this design, the judiciary is the only entity to make decisions regarding matters that are related to the constitutional rights of the nation's constituents. However, given that the executive branch controls the salaries of judges and police officers, the executive branch has the ability to influence decisions of judiciary and has reportedly done so in several cases. In response to corruption, amendments were made to the Constitution in 2003 to maintain an equal balance of power between the legislative and executive branches of the government. This entailed several mechanisms to be developed to prevent further manipulation by the executive branch. For example, the Constitution now requires that the executive branch undergo a reform following every election as well as the implementation of a tribunal whose duty it is to oversee the constitutionality of elections, political parties, and legislation.

Political and economic reforms have brought tension to the nation, which in turn has resulted in several challenges to STP law enforcement. Specifically, a recent shift from socialist to democratic rule along with insufficient resources and the recent discovery of oil-rich offshore areas in STP has sparked several liberal rights movements and increasing civil unrest. Several of these movements have come in the form of coups. Police and military authorities have become more adept at dealing with such movements and have settled coup attempts with very little violence. However, three coups against the STP government were initiated by members of its own security forces as a result of discontent with poor working conditions and corruption.

The internal and external security of STP is provided by a 600-person force. Three hundred of these individuals make up the military force, and the other 300 are paramilitary, consisting mainly of part-time fishermen and farmers. In addition to the police and military, STP has both a coast guard and a presidential guard. The police and military force is supervised by the Ministry of National Defense and Internal Affairs and is spread out over eight districts.

The police force has been said to be ineffective in maintaining order, which may be a result of the excessive amount of corruption and impunity among police officers in STP. The police force has also been accused of abusing prisoners and using violent means to deal with peaceful demonstrators. There have been two incidents reported in which arbitrary and unnecessary lethal use of force by officers occurred. However, the STP police have recently combined training with Angolan police, enhancing their capabilities, especially in dealing with nonviolent crowd control. In addition, the lack of resources in STP has had a negative impact on police morale. In response, the government in STP recently increased police salaries and implemented better training strategies, which have both helped to curtail the extent of corruption and low morale among officers.

Crime

For the most part, STP is considered a peaceful nation with very little crime, which is apparent in the results from the seventh annual survey on crime reported by the United Nations (UN). This survey reports on those crimes for STP similar to index crimes recorded by the Federal Bureau of Investigations (FBI). However, the most recent year available that reports crimes for STP is 1994 (statistics on STP in recent reports is not available). According to the UN report, total crime in STP was 344.32 per every 100,000 inhabitants. Their equivalent to murder is intentional homicide, which was reported to be 6.22 per 100,000. Major assaults were 321.78, burglaries were 4.66, and theft was 11.66 per every 100,000 population. Prostitution is deemed illegal by law, but the police reported no incidences of such crimes. The rate for robberies, rape, and auto theft was not reported. Trend statistics from 1990 to 1994 show a consistent decrease in all types of crime with an overall decrease of 10 percent (382.62–344.32).

Both assault and rape against women are restricted by law, and these laws are highly enforced. The penalties for assault depend on the severity of the injury that the victim sustains. Severity is based mainly on the number of days that the victim loses work. Specifically, the law states that for every 10 days of lost work, the offender receives an additional 6 months in prison. Though not common, rape does occur in STP and is also highly punishable. Prosecutions in rape cases are usually successful when there is strong evidence of physical violence. Those convicted can receive anywhere from 2 to 12 years in prison depending on the extent of harm and the age of victim. Although the rate of rape was not noted in the UN report, violence committed against women was common in STP and sometimes included rape. The law specifically protects women from spousal abuse and assault in general; however, most women are reluctant to bring charges against their assaulter either because of ignorance of their rights or because of customs that restrict women from taking disputes outside the family. Laws also have been designed to protect children, specifically regarding child labor. The law states that employers cannot work children more than 35 hours a week or 7 hours a day. However, child labor is a reported problem in STP, yet no cases have been officially prosecuted.

Finding of Guilt

Criminal investigations are conducted by the police, and the law requires that for a suspect to be apprehended, a warrant must be issued by an official who is authorized to do so. However, if an individual is caught by police while carrying out an illegal act, no warrant is necessary to detain the individual. Otherwise, authorities are given 48 hours to determine whether an illegal act has been committed and to charge the accused with the offense. Those accused of a crime are detained until the time of the trial unless able to make bail. The Constitution of STP requires that all defendants be provided with a fair and independent trial before a judge, by whom they are presumed innocent until proven guilty. A jury system is not used in STP. In addition, the Constitution gives those arrested for a crime the right to legal representation, and the state will provide counsel if the accused cannot afford one. Defendants are also provided with the right to confront accusers and witnesses and to view and access evidence against them, and they may also present to the judge witnesses and evidence favorable to their position.

The lack of resources in STP has resulted several legal rights not being honored. For example, there are few well-trained lawyers available to defendants. Although the exact number of judges in STP is not reported, long pretrial detention and docket backlogs are common because of a shortage of competent judges. STP also has a separate juvenile justice system, and this system has performed well compared to other African nations in making the nation child-friendly, according to the African Report on Child Well Being (2008). However, juveniles who have been convicted or are awaiting trial are detained and held with adult offenders.

Punishment

STP has recently taken steps to increase the level of humanity of the treatment that individuals convicted of crimes receive. STP is a signatory on both the International Convention on the Prevention and Punishment for the Crime of Genocide and the Convention against Torture and Other Cruel, Inhuman or Degrading Treatment or Punishment. Although there has not been a recorded execution in the history of the nation, STP abolished the use of the death penalty in 1990 as a potential punishment. Despite these steps to make the legal system more humane, the prison conditions in STP are considered to be extremely harsh because of the lack of resources. Conditions in the prison facilities are described as poor, overcrowded, and unsanitary. Prisoners are also exposed to poor medical facilities and inadequate nutrition.

There is only one prison in STP along with an agricultural holding facility. The prison system is under the guidance of the Ministry of Justice, State Reform, and Public Administration. In 2002, there were a reported 160 prisoners, and between the two facilities, they had the capacity to hold approximately 300 prisoners. The prison rate for STP is 83 per 100,000 of the population, with 2.3 percent of the prisoners being females; 34 percent are pretrial prisoners, 6.9 percent are under age 18, and less than 1 percent is foreign prisoners. The prison rate in STP has steadily increased from 70 in 1992 to 82 in 2005.

James V. Ray and Michael S. Caudy

Further Reading

Hodges, T., and M. N. Newitt. (1988). *Sao Tome and Principe: From Plantation Colony to Microstate.* Boulder, CO: Westview Press.

International Monetary Fund. (2009, April). *Democratic Republic of Sao Tome and Principe and the IMF:* http://www.imf.org/external/country/STP/index.htm.

U.S. Department of Labor: Bureau of International Affairs. (2009, May). São Tomé and Principe: http://www.dol.gov/ILAB/media/reports/iclp/tda2004/sao-tome-principe.htm#_ftnref3534.

U.S. Department of State. (2002). *Country Reports on Human Rights Practices: Bureau of Democracy, Human Rights, and Labor:* http://www.state.gov/g/drl/rls/hrrpt/2001/af/8399.htm.

Senegal

Legal System: Civil/Customary
Murder: Low–medium
Corruption: Medium
Human Trafficking: Medium
Prison Rate: Low
Death Penalty: No
Corporal Punishment: Yes

Background

The nation of Senegal in located in western Africa bordering the nations of Guinea-Bissau and Guinea to the south; Mauritania to the north; Mali to the east; and the Atlantic Ocean to the west. Also along that coast is Senegal's largest city and political capital, Dakar. Senegal's population in 2009 was estimated at a little over 13 million. The vast majority of those who can read and write do so in French, Senegal's official language. A former French colony, Senegal gained independence in 1960 and adopted its own Constitution in 1963. Though it is primarily a single-party state, in 1974, a multiparty democracy was institutionalized.

A relatively small nation, Senegal is divided into only 11 administrative regions, each headed by a governor who is appointed by and responsible to the president. These regions are Dakar, Diourbel, Fatick, Kaolack, Kolda, Louga, Matam, Saint-Louis, Tambacounda, Thies, and Ziguinchor. The executive consists of three principal parts. The executive branch consists of the president with two five-year terms who appoints the prime minister, who in turn appoints a council of ministers in consultation with the president. The legislative branch consists of a bicameral parliament with two houses of government. In both houses, the legislators serve five-year terms.

The judicial branch is a collection of different appeal and trial courts with defined subject jurisdictions. The highest courts include the Constitutional Court; the Council of State; the Court of Final Appeals, or Cour de Cassation; and the High Court of Justice. Each of these courts, with the exception of the High Court of Justice, is made up of justices appointed by the president. These justices are typically senior magistrates or prominent attorneys or academics. In the case of the Constitutional Court, there are five justices, each assigned for a nonrenewable six-year term. This membership is refreshed as a rate of two new justices every two years, resulting in a completely new court every six years while assuring that the court never lacks senior leadership.

According to the Constitution of Senegal, the Constitutional Court rules on eight matters: the constitutionality of the rules of procedure of the assemblies; the constitutionality of the laws; the lawful character of the provisions of legislative form; the constitutionality of the organic laws; the admissibility of the private bills and amendments of parliamentary origin; the constitutionality of international engagements; the exceptions of unconstitutionality raised before the Council of State or the Supreme Court of Appeal and more generally; all the conflicts of competence between the Council of State and the Supreme Court of Appeal and between the executive power and the legislative power.

Juxtaposed against this relatively long list of jurisdictional areas is the Council of State, which rules on administrative matters. The Court of Final Appeal has jurisdiction over criminal and civil matters. Exceptional to these three courts, though, is the High Court of Justice. Composed of eight National Assembly deputies and one professional judge, this court rarely convenes. It only does so when a case arises against a senior government official (e.g., the head of state or a minister) for an act committed in his or her capacity as an official. When such a case does emerge, it must first gain three-fifths of the National Assembly vote for prosecution. If such a majority vote exists, the High Court may then meet. At the same time, a separate military court system exists for the prosecution of armed forces and gendarmerie members.

Crime

Criminal Law

Senegal's criminal code offenses are organized into three groups. Similar to Anglo-Saxon law with its infractions, misdemeanors, and felonies, Senegal has contraventions, delits, and crimes. The first is the least severe. Contraventions carry only a 1-month maximum incarceration penalty. Far broader, and encompassing the most offenses, are delits. These are punishable with a sentence ranging from 1 month to 10 years. Topping this scale are crimes, those offenses punishable by terms of incarceration greater than 10 years.

As a former French colony, much of Senegal's jurisprudence is based on French law. Like many of its neighboring nations, Senegal is facing an increasing problem with illicit drug transshipment along its coasts. Of special attention is the growth in Colombian cocaine shipments routed through Senegal. As a result, Senegal's criminal law provides severe penalties for possession, use, or trafficking in illegal drugs in Senegal, and convicted offenders can expect long jail sentences and heavy fines. The abuse of legal drugs in the form of driving while intoxicated is also severely punished with sentences including imprisonment.

The law also seriously addresses assault. Such acts can result in one to five years of imprisonment and a fine. Further, acknowledging the nation's problem with violence toward women, the law provides increased penalties (in both prison term and fine)

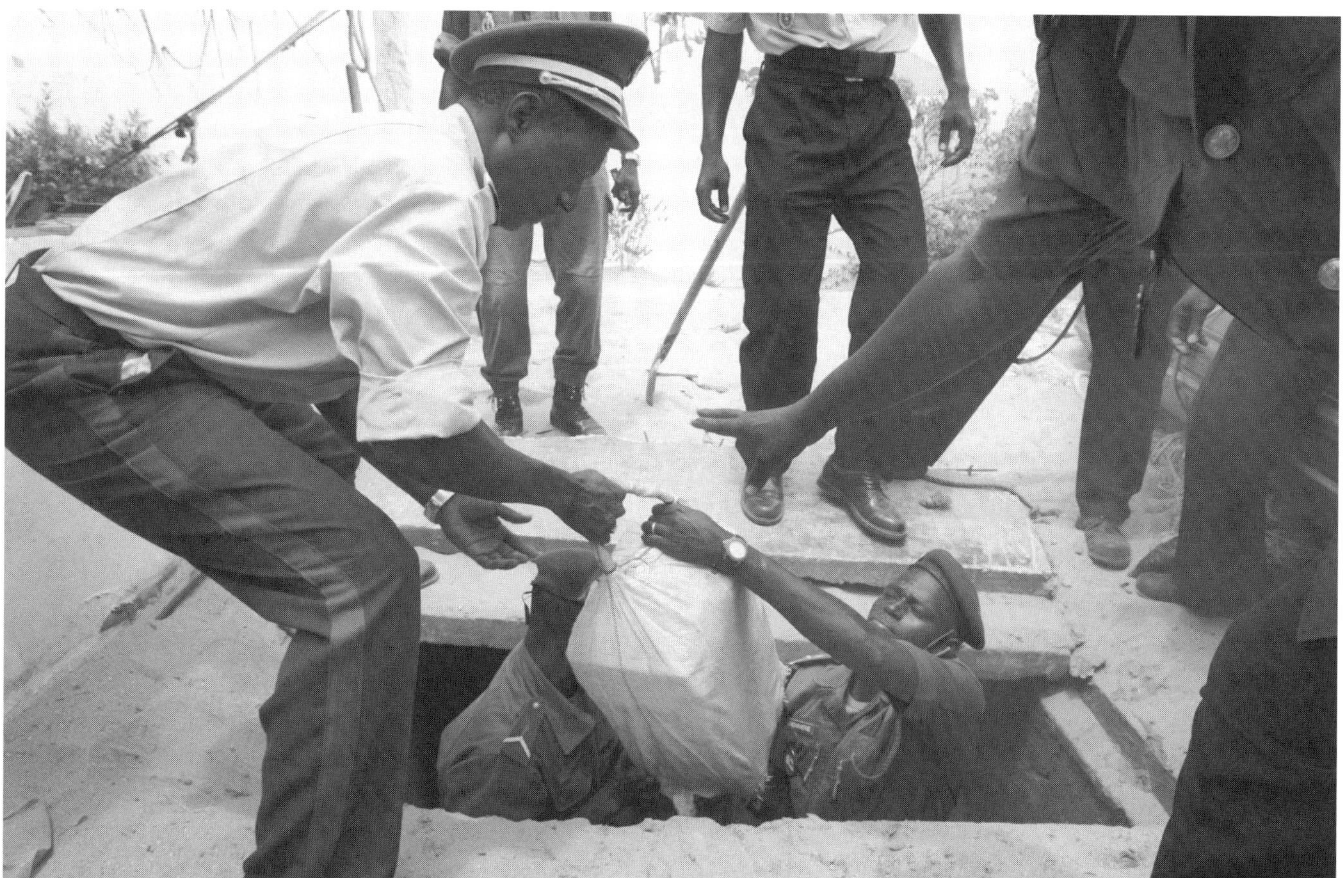

Police officers remove bags of drugs found in an underground cache in a villa south of Dakar, Senegal, on July 2, 2007. West Africa has become a hub for a drug-trafficking industry that threatens regional security. (Georges Gobeta/AFP/Getty Images)

for assault when the violence is directed toward a woman. This stern treatment of assault convicts extends to domestic violence as well. In the event an act of domestic violence results in lasting injuries, that act is punishable with a prison sentence of 10 to 20 years. If it results in death, the law prescribes life imprisonment.

This structuring is reflected in rape statutes. Under Senegalese law, rape is illegal, though spousal rape is not. As with assault, rape is punishable by imprisonment. In general, rape can result in 5 to 10 years in prison. If rape escalates to the point of death, the penalty also escalates to life imprisonment. These penalties are not limited to rape. Several other sexual crimes have severe legal penalties too. The first is sexual harassment. A moderate problem, those convicted of sexual harassment can expect prison terms of five months to three years and fines of $100 to $1,000. Female genital mutilation (FGM), an issue throughout Africa, is similarly punished. If convicted, those directly practicing or ordering the practice of FGM can be sentenced to a term of imprisonment ranging from six months to five years. Even more resolute sentences are doled out for the sexual abuse of children. For that crime, sentences can range from 5 to 10 years' imprisonment. This crime is aggravated by the involvement of family members. If the perpetrator is a family member, the sentence begins on the higher end of the normal scale, near 10 years. In light of these penalties, unexpected sexual freedom is seen in the legality of prostitution. According to Senegalese law, the prostitute must be at least 21 years of age, must register with the police, must carry a valid sanitary card, and must test negative for sexually transmitted infections. In addition, pimping and soliciting customers are illegal practices. Paradoxically, although prostitution is legal (a liberal policy), homosexuality is legally forbidden (a puritanical policy). Much of this can be attributed to Senegal's strong Islamic roots and beliefs, which themselves speak of homosexuality in decidedly harsh tones. As a result, article 319 of Senegal's penal code prescribes a prison sentence of one to five years and a fine of $3,000 for those convicted of homosexuality or, as it is often coined, acts against nature.

Human trafficking remains a significant problem, and the legal code and Constitution outlaw it. The crime itself is more closely defined as the recruitment, transport, transfer, or harboring of persons, whether by means of violence, fraud, abuse of authority, or otherwise for the purposes of sexual exploitation, labor, forced servitude, or slavery. The seriousness of this offense can be seen in its penalties: 5 to 10 years in prison and a fine of $10,000 to $40,000. These punishments can quickly rise if the trafficking offense involves torture, barbarism, the removal of human organs, or the exposure of the victim to a risk of death or injury. In such a case, the prison term can reach 30 years.

Crime Statistics

Reliable crime statistics are difficult to come by in Senegal. More verifiable are the general trends and patterns of crime found there. And in general, street crime is the most prevalent, particularly in Senegal's cities. In larger cities, crimes such as pickpocketing and purse-snatching are exceedingly common and routinely committed by groups of criminals working in concert with each other. A routine scenario is the use of aggressive panhandlers, beggars, or street children to distract the attention of tourists in congested areas (e.g., Leopold Senghor International Airport and the restaurant areas of Dakar and St. Louis) while their accomplice commits the theft itself. Related to these low-level crimes is the regular occurrence of banditry. Contrary to the pickpockets and purse-snatchers, though, these bandits prefer to operate in the rural areas of Senegal, further from the threat of law enforcement. This motivation is further verified by the environment is which the bandits choose to operate, preferring to accost highway travelers under the cloak of darkness in the nation's central and eastern areas, both of which are far removed from the relative safety offered by police in Senegal's major cities, located along the western coast. Further inflaming this problem is the continuing low-level resistance fighting present in the Casamance region of southern Senegal despite a 2004 ceasefire agreement. Noticing these two crime trends, the Senegalese government has acted. Recently a police unit was created with the expressed goal of addressing and ameliorating such tourist-centric crimes. But to date, no reliable information exists on the effectiveness of this tourist police unit.

Perhaps Senegal's best-known crime is fraud. With the explosion of the Internet's popularity over the past decade has also come an explosion of fraud, much of it originating in Senegal. These fraudulent schemes have a variety of forms. One of the most common begins with an unsolicited communication (i.e., e-mail) ostensibly from a conflict refugee or political leader's relative. Many such schemes have seized on the conflict in Sierra Leone to lend realism to their plot. In these communications, the writer promises quick financial gain to the receiver in return for his or her help in transferring large sums of wealth out of West Africa. At that point, one of two options is usually presented: advanced fees or bank account information. Under "advanced fees," the writer requests a sum of money from the receiver to pay either associated taxes or account fees, under the auspices of completing the transfer of the previously mentioned wealth. In essence, the e-mail recipient is led to believe that to collect his or her payoff, he or she must first advance the sender a set amount of money to complete the transaction. In reality, the payoff never existed, and the entire scam was constructed just for the sender to collect the advanced fee. However, if the e-mail's sender instead requests bank account information, the consequences can be worse. Such information is collected under the promise that the previously discussed wealth will be deposited into the receiver's account. Instead, all funds are withdrawn from the receiver's account.

Other crimes also remain problems for local law enforcement, some significant. These include burglary, pimping, underage prostitution, rape, spousal rape, domestic violence, child abuse, human trafficking, and FGM. On the last crime though, FGM, the Senegalese government has made important strides. Prosecution of FGM practitioners continues while the government also partners with nongovernmental organizations to educate the populace about the dangers and consequences of FGM. These efforts have shown progress as well. By one estimate, 1,679 of Senegal's 5,000 communities have abandoned the practice. Still, FGM remains widespread and is still often practiced openly with impunity. It is also of note that FGM and the other crimes discussed traditionally increase in occurrence immediately before religious holidays.

Police

Law enforcement in Senegal falls mostly into two broad groups: the police and the gendarmerie. The first group consists of 10 departments spread throughout Senegal and commanded centrally by the Directorate General of National Safety, which is housed within the Senegalese Department of Interior. These 10 departments are distributed such that each of Senegal's 11 administrative regions has at least one police station and one mobile safety brigade. A greater concentration of these police services is found in the capital and largest city, Dakar. Dakar has 15 stations. Within these stations, the personnel structure roughly mirrors that of American police with a chain of command and span of control. Similarly, ranks include officer, lieutenant, sergeant, and captain.

The second group of police is the gendarmerie, a military body tasked with many of the same responsibilities as the police discussed earlier. Under the authority of the Ministry of Defense, the history of the gendarmerie in Senegal can be traced back over 100 years. However, the modern-day gendarmerie mission came into definition more recently, on June 13, 1974, with decree 74–571. Since then, the gendarmerie has taken on a large, bureaucratic structure composed of numerous compartmentalized divisions, including criminal investigation, marine, and riot police. As a military group, the gendarmerie's ranks are fairly well known, including lieutenants, second lieutenants, warrant officers, and a large number of auxiliary gendarmeries who serve two-year terms of military service. The men and women (women becoming integrated beginning in 2006) who staff these ranks are relatively well-qualified given the recruit requirements laid out by the gendarmerie. Chief among these requirements are Senegalese citizenship, an age of under 30 years at the time of candidacy filing, good physical health, acceptable vision, a certificate of education, and finally, proof of good reputation. Fulfilling these requirements, the gendarmerie candidate then attends the gendarmerie's training academy, the School of Formation of the National Gendarmerie. This process of recruitment and training, though beneficial in its selectivity, does pose an issue to the gendarmerie's stated objective of increased recruitment. As stated by the group itself, the gendarmerie would like to reach a level of 1 gendarme for every 1,000 inhabitants in rural zones and 1 gendarme for 10,000 inhabitants in urban zones. Currently there is 1 gendarme for every 12,000 inhabitants in rural zones and 1 gendarme for every 15,000 inhabitants in urban zones. In addition to this personnel objective, the gendarmerie is also in the process of technological modernization. Of special emphasis are the computerization of units and the modernization of the communication network.

Although the two groups responsible for policing Senegal have different histories and ranks, they share in common a number of powers, as well as vexing issues. Many of these vexing issues can be traced back to inadequate training and supervision, hopefully vestiges of a bygone era in Senegal policing. Today, new members of the police receive training in human rights protection, a step that is hoped to lessen abuse. However, this training has not taken effect just yet. According to the latest reports, abuse, rights violations, and corruption continue. Some of these problems are flamed by the vast power vested in the Senegalese police. An example of this power is visible in the simple order to provide identification. In Senegal, an officer may request identification from a citizen without cause. Failure to provide this identification may result in detainment. Further, police may detain a suspect without filing formal charges for up to 48 hours following arrest and up to 96 hours if so authorized by a public prosecutor. Further, police may detain someone for up to 192 hours in the case of a threat to state security. Power such as this is susceptible to and often responsible for police corruption, an ongoing problem, with officials often attempting to solicit bribes from tourists and others. This corruption extends to questionable investigations and inappropriately long pretrial detentions. These detentions also included abuses ranging from forcing detainees to sleep on floors without bedding to directing bright lights at detainees' pupils, beating detainees with batons, and housing detainees in cells with minimal access to air.

Contrary to this brutal treatment, journalists in Senegal have operated largely free of police harassment. This is expected because Senegal's Constitution provides for freedom of the press. In contrast to that, though, are a number of existing laws that allow the police to curtail that freedom. Such pliable laws prohibit offending the head of state, publishing false news, and threatening public order. In addition, libel is a criminal offense rather than a civil one. All of these have been used by police in the past to limit journalistic freedoms in Senegal. In most cases, the limitation comes in the form of self-censorship. Other times, it is more overt. One recent incident occurred in March 2008 when a Dakar reporter covering a violent antigovernment protest was assaulted by police. Later, police raided the reporter's office and demanded the reporter's materials.

Finding of Guilt

The Constitution of Senegal provides for an independent judiciary. But as with many other aspects of Senegal's criminal justice system, the ideal codified letter of the law does not always come through in the actions of the government. Here corruption and inadequate resources remain a persistent problem. The scarcity of resources has reached such a point that judges have begun to publicly voice their frustration with mounting caseloads, insufficient facilities and transportation, and understaffed offices.

Those issues aside, the legal system itself is complex and difficult to maneuver through without an attorney. These maneuvers, for the typical Senegalian, begin with the first 48 hours of detention following arrest. During these two days, the detainee does not have access to an attorney. Instead, the detainee is allowed a medical examination and, in some cases, access to family members. Finally, after 48 hours of detainment, the detainee may access an attorney, but only at his or her own expense. It is not until the prosecutor has presented its case that the indigent is appointed publicly funded legal counsel. At arraignment, bail also becomes a possibility, though it is rarely used.

If the case is carried through to court, the defendant is typically tried before a panel of judges, not a jury, in civil and criminal cases. Only if the offense is serious, such as murder, does a defendant have a right to a jury trial. Though a jury trial is not assured, a public trial is. Along with this comes a presumption of innocence and the right to be present in court, to confront witnesses, and to present evidence. Also, if the verdict does not go in favor of the defendant, there exists a right to appeal. This right applies to all courts with the exception of the Cour d'Assises and the High Court of Justice.

Punishment

Many NGOs describe Senegalese prison conditions as poor, characterized by overcrowding, lack of medical care, and decaying infrastructure. Given that spending is $0.66 per prisoner per day, these conditions are unsurprising. The overcrowding issue is due in part to a lack of capacity, given that Senegal has not constructed a new prison since 1960. Instead, many of Senegal's current facilities are repurposed office buildings, modified to hold inmates. Dakar's Central Prison was designed to house 500 prisoners. It now holds 1,500. Another facility in Dakar, a penal camp, is currently operating at double its designed capacity of 400. This overcrowding has reached such a point that detainees are not even guaranteed a mattress (there is one for every five inmates), no less indoor housing. Indeed, in Diourbel, detainees were being housed outside in a horse stable, some for as long as two days. The overcrowding has also led to understaffing, with a handful of guards being responsible for the monitoring of hundreds of prisoners. Such was the case in September 2006 when 52 prisoners escaped from the Thies Prison. At the time of the escape, 3 guards were responsible for the prison's 668 inmates. The understaffing problem extends beyond the guards to the medical personnel. At this writing, there is only 1 doctor per 5,000 inmates. As a result, many prisons lack doctors at all. And when doctors are on-site, they often do not have adequate medicinal supplies, forcing those prisoners in need of medical treatment to be evacuated from prison.

Many of Senegal's purpose-built prisons suffer drainage problems during the rainy season and oppressive heat the rest of the year. Weather aside, human conditions inside are poor year-round. As a result of insufficient training and supervision, prisoners have been subject to cruel and degrading treatment by officials. The lack of supervision has also caused a partial failure of Senegal's separation regulations. Under those regulations, pretrial detainees are to be held separately from convicts, and juveniles are to be segregated from adults. But because of overcrowding and little supervision, these regulations are often broken. However, women detainees are regularly held apart from men under the supervision of female guards, as mandated by correctional regulations.

Senegal is not an altogether punitive society, though. In fact, a relatively well-established rehabilitation scheme is in place. This scheme is based on transcendental meditation (TM). Began in January 1987, TM was first introduced by Maharishi Consultants International to a population of 11,000 prisoners in 31 prisons. Since then, the program has reported astonishing improvements. Before the introduction of TM, Senegal prisoners had a 90 percent recidivism rate, in the convicts' first month of release. A study conducted after TM's introduction found that the rate had dropped significantly: Of the 2,400 prisoners released in a June 1988 amnesty, only 200 recidivated during the six-month follow-up. Of those who did recidivate, 80 percent had not practiced TM (though there is no comment on what percentage of the initial 2,400 practiced TM to begin with). As a result of the drop in recidivism following TM, Senegal closed three prisons and idled eight others dramatically below their capacity—

decisions that, given today's overcrowding issues, may not have been advisable.

Michael Galezewski

Further Reading

Busia, N. K., Jr. (n.d.). *The Status of Human Rights Organizations in Sub-Saharan Africa: Senegal:* http://www1.umn.edu/humanrts/africa/senegal.htm.

Gendarmerie Nationale. (2006). *Gendarmerie Nationale:* http://www.gendarmerie.sn/.

Murray, D. M. (1991). "A Powerful Cure? Transcendental Meditation Can Offer Peaceful Road to Rehabilitation." *Corrections Today* 53(7): http://archive.tm.org/news/corrections.html.

République du Sénégal. (n.d.). *Conseil Constitutionnel:* http://www.gouv.sn/institutions/conseil_consthtml.

Seychelles

Legal System: Common/Civil
Murder: Medium
Corruption: Medium
Prison Rate: High
Death Penalty: No
Corporal Punishment: Maybe

Background

The Seychelles legal system is based on English common law, Napoleonic civil law, and customary law. The English common law deals with criminal matters. The Napoleonic civil law, inherited from Seychelles' colonial past, deals with tort, contract, and civil matters.

The first police force was created in 1775 when 15 soldiers were sent to perform security duties in Seychelles, which was then a dependency of Mauritius and France. In 1802, a small police force was established, which was composed of policemen and soldiers sent from the United Kingdom. Police presence increased exponentially until 1903, to reach the number of 79 officers based in 12 different stations in the territory. The force did not sustain dramatic changes until 1964, when a Special Force Unit was created to assist police officers with civil unrest fueled by political changes. The police force continued to endure changes until 1971, with the establishment of an airport police force and a training center. The independence of the colony, obtained on June 28, 1976, did not lead to substantial changes in the administration. However, real changes occurred after Rene's supporters' coup on June 5, 1977, during which police weapons were used by opponents of the ruling party. The corruption of police officers and their possible role during the coup highlighted the need for a complete separation between law enforcement and political movements. The police have since then continued to evolve toward a more innovative and modern approach to policing.

Current Police

The national police practices are based on British practices, and police forces are commanded by a commissioner appointed by the president. The president is at the head of the security apparatus composed of the Seychelles People Defense Forces (SPDF), the National Guard, the Presidential Protection Unit, the Coast Guard, and the police.

The current police force is made up of 500 officers assisted by a 60-member Paramilitary Mobile Unit. Also, a Presidential Guard composed of 300 highly trained members, including European mercenaries, is responsible for the presidents' safety.

The Seychelles police force has been dramatically restructured and reorganized since 2004 to face increasing criminal activities. The commissioner in charge of police forces has created the position of "performance audit officer," who is responsible for counteracting negative events that could impact the public's trust in the force. Also, this officer is in charge of monitoring officers' performance and may make recommendations to improve the quality of policing. The Seychelles police force is now divided into seven divisions: the

Operation Division; the Criminal Investigation Division, which includes the Scientific Support and the Criminal Record Bureau; the Seychelles Police Academy Division; the Special Support Division; the Special Branch Division; the Administration and Finance Division; and the Transport Security Division. The creation of such units now highlights a step toward the modernization of the police force.

The previous decentralized regional policing model was replaced by a Centralized Command Operation System based in the police headquarters in Victoria. The centralization of the police force is a major element of the reform affecting the department, which now holds as key principles of the policing the implementation of higher standards of performance, improved training at every level, better use of the civilian support staff, a more flexible reward system for officers, more effective use of technological advances, and a stronger partnership between the police force and other governmental agencies.

The Seychelles police force is a member of the Eastern Africa Police Chief Association formed in 2000. The Seychelles police have also been cooperating with the U.S. government to prevent possible terrorist attacks.

Crime

Classification of Crime

Crimes are generally classified into three types of offenses: against the person, against morality, and against property and the economy. Offenses against the person include murder, manslaughter, infanticide, abortion, and assaults. Offenses against morality include rape, indecent assaults, and prostitution. Finally, offenses against property and the economy include theft, burglary, robbery, and traffic offenses.

Crime Statistics

In 2006, 9 murders, including 2 manslaughters, were reported to the police. There were 119 robberies and 765 burglaries, which included 138 burglaries, 384 cases of housebreaking and stealing, and 243 cases of breaking into buildings and stealing. Out of 105 sexual assaults reported, 25 were cases of sexual interferences with child. The number of reported cases of drug trafficking or selling was 19. There were 5,669 crimes against individuals reported. Finally, there were 1,321 thefts reported to law enforcement agencies, including 44 thefts from dwelling houses, 3 thefts from hotels, 135 thefts from beaches, 65 thefts from persons, 35 thefts committed by servants, 151 thefts from motor vehicles, and 894 other type of thefts.

Drug Crime

The possession of controlled drugs has become a widespread challenge in recent years. In 2002, 222 cases of illegal possession were reported to the police, and in 2006, the number increased to 492. Drug trafficking has also increased, from 7 cases to 19 cases in 2006. Cannabis seems to be the most common illicit drug. Indeed, of all the individuals treated for drug addiction in 2005, 36 were treated for addiction to cannabis, 28 were treated for addiction to opiates, and 1 individual was treated for the use of amphetamine-type stimulants. The efforts to combat drug problems have led to the replacement of the Anti-Drug and Marine Squad by the National Drug Enforcement Agency. This agency comprises police, immigration, customs, and revenue officers. The legislators have also enacted the Anti-Money Laundering and Proceeds of Crime (Civil Confiscation) Law to support the fight against drug-related incidents. This law enables the state to confiscate property obtained from the profits of drug trafficking. The U.S. government has also joined the nation's efforts in the war against drugs, sending two experts to from CARE—the Campaign for Awareness, Resilience, and Education against Substance Abuse—to train social workers and police officers. CARE focuses on prevention of illicit drug use and provides educational programs to youths. The members of this program also collaborate with the police in the community to support citizens who wish to report cases of drug trafficking.

Finding of Guilt

Preventive Detention

If authorized by a court order, the accused may be held in detention without being charged for up to seven days. A magistrate or judge sets bail for the accused to secure his or her appearance in court. The office of the attorney general of provides relevant information on the accused to determine whether bail should be granted to the offender. Individuals who are unable to pay their bail must remain in custody during pretrial detention. Courts provide bail in most cases.

Rights of the Accused

The rights of the accused cannot be infringed based on a fundamental principle of innocence until proven guilty. The accused must be brought before a magistrate within 24 hours of the arrest, allowing for boat travels from distant islands. Accused individuals are also allowed to make phone calls during the detention. Although the Constitution guarantees the release of prisoners after six months of pretrial detention without any hearing, the inefficiency of the judicial system often prolongs pretrial detention, which causes serious ethical problems. It is not uncommon for prisoners to wait up to three years for trial or sentencing.

Assistance Provided to Accused

The accused can easily obtain defense lawyers in Seychelles because of the high ratio of lawyers in the population. Although free counsel is not a guaranteed right, legal aid is often provided to the accused, including those who are involved in civil cases based on the Legal Aid Act (cap. 110).

Arrest

Police officers in Seychelles are able to make an arrest with or without an arrest warrant, which is issued by the court. To seek an arrest without warrant, the police officer must reasonably suspect that a cognizable offense has been committed. A cognizable offense is defined as when an individual commits a breach of peace in the presence of an officer, obstructs an officer while he or she is on duty, loiters, or possesses housebreaking tools. A civilian can also make an arrest if a suspect commits an offense against an individual or his or her property.

Judicial System

The judicial system in the Seychelles is led by the chief justice of Seychelles. The judiciary is a three-tiered system composed of the Court of Appeal, the Supreme Court, and the other subordinate courts and tribunals. Juries hear cases of murder and treason. The Seychelles Court of Appeal, which is made up of five justices including the president, hears both civil and criminal appeals from the Supreme Court. The right to appeal to the Court of Appeal may be obtained from a judgment, direction, decision, declaration, decree, writ, or order of the Supreme Court. Upon the recommendation of the Constitutional Appointments Authority, the president appoints judges and justices of appeal for terms of seven years.

The Constitution deems the Supreme Court as having an original jurisdiction in issues relating to the application, contravention, enforcement, or interpretation of the Constitution. This court also has supervisory jurisdiction over subordinate courts, tribunals, and adjudicating authority. The Supreme Court is composed of the chief justice, the deputy judges, and the master of the Supreme Court.

The magistrates' courts, comprising one senior magistrate and two magistrates, have jurisdiction in suits for goods seized in execution of judgment or traffic offenses. These courts also treat civil cases, if the amount claimed or valued by the subject does not exceed 25,000 rupees. The Rent Board handles cases that fall under the Control of Rent and Tenancy Agreement Ordinance (cap. 166 of the laws of Seychelles).

Alternatives to Trial

Plea bargaining is a common practice in Seychelles. The accused may enter a plea of guilty after an agreement has been reached between the prosecutor and the defense lawyer. In many less serious cases, plea bargaining occurs at the arraignment stage. The plea bargaining process is an essential tool to assure the swift disposition of cases. The offenders who are deemed incapable of standing trial because of insanity can be sent to a psychiatric facility instead of being incarcerated with the general inmate population.

Juveniles

The minimum age of criminal responsibility is 12 years old. However, criminal prosecution of children between 8 and 12 years of age is still possible under certain conditions. A juvenile under the age of 7 years old cannot be considered criminally responsible. The penal code (section 15) states that a juvenile under the age of 12 years old cannot be convicted of the offense of rape. The juvenile justice system suffers from a lack of community-based rehabilitation programs for juvenile offenders. Also, the Youth Residential Treatment Center offers only a few educational and rehabilitation programs.

Investigation

The criminal procedure code in Seychelles, enacted in 1955, originated from the English procedural law. Police investigations are sent to the office of the Attorney General of Seychelles, where a decision to charge a suspect is made. The British High Commission donated basic equipment for drug testing in 2007, enabling Seychellois police to conduct its own forensic test for drug related offenses.

Punishment

Types of Punishment

There are multiple methods of punishment used in Seychelles, such as fines, compensation, and forfeiture of certain assets. The offenders may also be liable to police supervision and can sign a "security for keeping the peace," making a promise to be law-abiding. Imprisonment is also used as a punishment for offenders. According to the Seychelles penal code, an individual convicted of murder faces mandatory life imprisonment. An offender convicted of rape is also liable to life imprisonment. The typical punishment for robbery ranges from 14 years to life imprisonment depending on the usage of weapon(s) during the commission of the offense. An offender committing a burglary can face up to 10 years in prison, and an individual convicted of theft can be imprisoned for up to 5 years. Prison sentences are considered mandatory or discretionary depending on the offense. Finally, the death penalty was abolished in 1993 by article 15(2) of the 1993 Constitution of the Republic of the Seychelles.

Prison

According to reports made by the U.S. Department of State, there were 305 inmates in Seychelles in 2008, including 185 men in pretrial detention and 7 women. Currently, there is only one correctional facility on the island. In 2003, neighbors of the Long Island Prison complained that inmates sometimes fled from the prison to attend parties and to commit more crimes. Long Island and its neighboring islands boast scenic beaches and are integral parts of the Seychelles tourism industry. Hence, fearing negative effects on tourism, the government began transferring inmates to the prison located on the main island of Mahe. In October 2006, all prisoners of the Long Island Prison were transferred to the newly opened Montagne Posee Prison located on the main island of Mahe. In June 2007, inmates incarcerated at the Grand Police High Security Police Prison were also transferred to the Montagne Posee Prison. A month later, the Grand Police High Security Police Prison was closed, leaving the Montagne Posee Prison as the only correctional facility in the Seychelles. The Montagne Posse Prison has a maximum capacity of 400 inmates; men and women are held in separate locations.

Inmates are not required to work, but training in professional trades is offered in prison. Available classes in prison include carpentry, gardening, mechanics classes, and library. Also, a minor part of the budget is allocated to the rehabilitation of offenders. Counseling, self-esteem workshops, and anger and stress management classes are offered to willing offenders. Finally, programs are being developed to facilitate the reintegration of offenders and to help inmates cope with stigmatization upon release from the prison.

Inmates can receive visits in the facility and receive limited access to radio and television. Such privileges are hindered, however, by the major economic difficulties faced by the facility. Indeed, staff shortages have significantly reduced the time that inmates can spend outside of their prison cells. Also, inmates have been complaining of inadequate sanitation and a lack of water. Such deplorable living conditions ultimately led to a hunger strike in December 2007. Inmates protested for improvement of hygienic and sanitary conditions and for the end of food shortages.

Seigo Nishijima and Anne-Laure Del Cerro

Further Reading

Bwana, Steven J. (1995). *Crime and the Law in Seychelles.* Seychelles: [publisher not available].

Jolicoeur, Shelton M. (2003). *The Law and You.* Mahe, Seychelles: Printec Press Holdings.

Scarr, Deryck. (1999). *Seychelles since 1770: History of a Slave and Post-Slavery Society.* Trenton, NJ: Africa World Press.

Sierra Leone

Legal System: Common/Customary
Murder: Medium
Corruption: High
Human Trafficking: Medium
Prison Rate: Low
Death Penalty: Yes
Corporal Punishment: Yes

Background

Sierra Leone lies on the west coast of Africa with Guinea to the north and northeast, Liberia to the south and southeast, and the Atlantic Ocean on the west and southwest. It covers a total land area of 73,326 square kilometers. The country in 2004 had an estimated population of nearly 5 million.

A former British colony, Sierra Leone was declared a republic on April 19, 1971. The type of legal system in Sierra Leone can be best described as a mixture of accusatorial and customary. The political and social context of the criminal justice system is still evolving in Sierra Leone. The 1991 Constitution established a seemingly complete separation of powers. However, there are still overlaps in the three organs of government—the executive, the judiciary, and the legislature—which sometimes makes it difficult for the criminal justice system to operate effectively.

The criminal justice system in Sierra Leone comprises the police, the judiciary, the law officers department, and the prisons department as major stakeholders. The law officers department contains the office of the director of public prosecution, which supports the police in the prosecution of cases in court. The president appoints the chief justice, the attorney general, and the minister of justice. The latter is the vote controller and accountable officer for the judiciary in the cabinet. By this arrangement, there is every likelihood of interference by the executive in the prosecution and adjudication of matters by the courts.

Police

The Sierra Leone Police (SLP) began as a 600-officer organization during the latter half of the 19th century. The SLP operated as two forces: the Frontier Police and the Civilian Police—with the Frontier Police in charge of the protectorate, the hinterland, while the Civilian Police took control of the colony, the area surrounding Freetown, the present capital of Sierra Leone. Section 174 of the Sierra Leone Constitution of 1978 changed the traditional role of the SLP with the appointment of the chief of police as a member of parliament. The organization consequently became corrupt, ill trained, and poorly equipped, thus losing much of the public trust. This situation was salvaged, however, by the 1991 Constitution of Sierra Leone, which precludes any police officer from getting actively involved in politics. Nevertheless, section 156(10) of the same Constitution formulated the Police Council, which acts as an oversight body to the SLP, with the vice president of the republic serving as chairman and with the minister of internal affairs as a member. This arrangement also has the tendency to cause political interference with the operational independence of the force.

In 1999, the SLP organization was restructured, and officers were retrained to become capable of performing effective police duties in a democratic environment. The strength of the SLP in 2008 stood at 9,642. This number is spread among 29 local command units (LCUs) into which the entire country has been divided for policing purposes. Each command unit is headed by a local unit commander (LUC). Additionally, each of the country's four regions has a regional commander to whom all the LUCs in that region report.

The regional commander of any region is the local police chief for that region. They are at liberty to develop their own strategic plans in line with the mission of the organization, work out their operational plans, and implement as they deem fit. They are accountable only to the Executive Management Board (EMB), which is composed of the inspector general of police (IGP), the deputy inspector general of police, and 12 assistant inspector generals of police. It is chaired by the IGP, and is responsible for strategic decision making for the entire organization.

Crime

Classification of Crimes

Crimes in Sierra Leone are classified into the following four basic levels:

1. *Treason.* Treason is a statutory offense under Sierra Leone law created by the Treason and State Offences Act, 1963, and carries the death penalty.
2. *Felony.* Felonies include capital or noncapital offenses. Capital felonies are punishable by death, and these include such crimes as murder, armed robbery, and robbery with aggravation. Noncapital felonies are punishable only by custodial sentence for a term between one year and life imprisonment. Crimes of this nature include rape, wounding with intent, manslaughter, larceny, receiving stolen goods, burglary, arson, obtaining goods by false pretenses, conspiracy to defraud, forgery, falsification of accounts, uttering counterfeit coin, and sedition.
3. *Misdemeanor.* Misdemeanors are minor offenses regarded as less serious than felonies. They are punishable with imprisonment for not more than five years or with a fine or both. This category of prohibitions includes common assault, indecent assault, driving without due care and attention, and fraudulent conversion.
4. *Customary law violations.* Customary law violations are infractions of the customary law that are punishable by imprisonment of not more than a year or a fine or both. Examples of customary law crimes include adultery, seducing another man's wife, harboring another man's wife, and incest.

Age of Criminal Responsibility

The law presumes that children under 10 are incapable of committing a crime. Between the ages of 10 and 14, a child is liable for any crime he or she commits if the prosecution is able to prove that the child knew what he or she was doing was wrong. Young persons at the age of 14 are liable for criminal acts, but if under the age of 17, they are tried in juvenile courts.

Crime Statistics

The Sierra Leone Police Crime Statistics Report revealed that for the period 2006–2007, a total of 72,802 offenses were recorded in various police stations countrywide. The Western Area recorded the highest with a total of 52,403 (72%); the Eastern Province was second, recording 8,871 (12%), and the Northern and Southern provinces were third and fourth with 7,889 (11%) and 3,639 (5%), respectively.

On April 23, 2009, at a dumping ground at Freetown, Sierra Leone, police officials burn 1,500 pounds of cocaine seized last year at Lungi Airport. A judge handed five-year prison terms to eight foreigners convicted of attempting to illegally import the cocaine in a Cessna plane with Red Cross markings. (AP Photo/Nazia Parvez)

Finding of Guilt

The Constitution of Sierra Leone 1991 and the Criminal Procedure Act of 1965 provide certain rights to accused persons from suspect stage to trial stage. These include the rights to be defended by an attorney or lawyer of their choice, to have a speedy trial, and to plead guilty to a lesser offense or to elect to be tried summarily.

The 1991 Constitution of Sierra Leone also stipulates that all criminal suits be brought in the name of the attorney general and minister of justice on behalf of the government. The real situation is that as a result of the lack of capacity by the law officers department, the director of public prosecution (DPP) grants a fiat to police officers to prosecute matters on his behalf at the magistrates' courts only.

The Sierra Leone legal system has not made provision for alternative dispute resolution. However, with the increase in population and crime rate, the SLP has adopted what is known as an informal resolution (IR) policy where minor cases are settled by police officers out of court. The majority of criminal cases in Sierra Leone are resolved by summary judgment, and a custodial sentence or fine is imposed.

One of the legacies left by British colonial rule in Sierra Leone is the dual court system—the British-oriented general law courts and the local courts. These are organized in a five-tier system:

1. *Local courts.* These courts have limited jurisdiction, adjudicating minor criminal cases involving customary laws. They are presided over by persons who are elders of the local

communities and have a wealth of knowledge in matters pertaining customary law. The country has a total of 287 local courts.

2. *Magistrates' courts.* These courts too have limited jurisdiction and have both original and appellate jurisdiction. They play three main roles. The first is the hearing and disposal of lesser criminal matters punishable by a maximum term of three years' imprisonment or a small fine or both. Their second role is to serve as appellate courts for customary law matters dealt with at the local courts. In such circumstances, the magistrate sits in what is referred to as the district appeal court, with two assessors who are experts in customary law. The third key role of these courts is to hold preliminary investigations or hearings into felony charges and, where there is sufficient evidence against the person charged with the commission of the offense, commit the matter to the High Court. Where there is insufficient evidence, the court will dismiss the case and discharge the defendant. Lawyers have a right of audience before these courts. There are 15 such courts throughout the country, located mostly in towns. To give wider access to the citizens, roving courts, or circuit courts, were introduced in 2006.
3. *High Court.* The High Court comes next in the hierarchy of criminal courts in Sierra Leone. It has original, appellate, and supervisory powers with jurisdiction over felonious cases and those involving treason. The cases are usually tried by judge and jury or, on exceptional cases, by judge alone. The High Court is continuously in session in the Western Area, where much of its work is concentrated. In the provinces, the sessions vary from two to three a year. All superior court judges are appointed by the president on the advice of the Judicial and Legal Service Commission.
4. *Court of Appeal.* Next in the hierarchy of the Sierra Leone court system is the Court of Appeal. This court hears and determines appeals made from decisions and orders of the High Court. The court is constituted by three justices, with the most senior presiding, for the normal business of hearing an appeal. Justices of appeal are usually appointed from the pool of judges on the High Court bench.
5. *Supreme Court.* The highest judicial organ in Sierra Leone is the Supreme Court. The main business of this court is limited to the hearing and determination of criminal appeals from the Court of Appeal. The Supreme Court also has original jurisdiction on issues that have "substantial questions of law" or "of public interest." The court also exercises supervisory jurisdiction over all other courts in the country. It is constituted for regular judicial business by five justices, including the chief justice as president or, in his absence, the most senior justice. Justices of the Supreme Court are usually appointed from justices of the Court of Appeal.

There is a separate system for juveniles. While being investigated at the police stations, juveniles are not supposed to be incarcerated in the same cells as the adults. The juvenile court is usually impaneled with one stipendiary magistrate sitting with two lay justices of the peace. Juveniles are remanded in separate remand homes during trials. When given a custodial sentence, they are sent to a separate prison for children known as an "approved school" for corrective training. Such a facility is available only in Freetown at the moment.

Punishment

Types of Punishment

The types of punishment typically used are fines, compensation, imprisonment, and the death penalty. In civil matters, compensation or reparations and fines are mostly used. In exceptional cases, imprisonment is used as punishment. For criminal matters, fines and/or imprisonment are mostly the case. Compensation is sparsely used in criminal matters, except where the complainant is allowed such compensation to offset medical, transport, and other bills.

The typical punishment for murder is life imprisonment, although the mandatory sentence according to law is death by hanging. Rape, according to law, should be punished by life imprisonment, but the punishment usually dished out is 15 years' imprisonment. The typical punishment for robbery with aggravation is life imprisonment, although there is a mandatory punishment of the death sentence by hanging, in accordance with the 1971 amendment to the Larceny Act of 1916.

The death sentence is also mandatory according to law for cases of treason, and the prescribed method of death should be death by hanging. However, no execution has been carried out since October 1998 in Sierra Leone. According to the Pharmacy and Drugs Acts of 2001, serious drugs offenses should now get a minimum of 10 years' imprisonment.

Prison

The inception of the Sierra Leone Prisons Service dates as far back as the colonial era, when, in August 1792, a jailer was sentenced by Governor Clarkson, then-governor of the Colony, for being found guilty of slave dealing. In the absence of a prison facility, he was confined on board a vessel in iron bars until he was taken to England to serve his sentence. In May 1793, the colonial powers resolved to build a kind of jail on shore. In 1801, a temporary jail was constructed at Fort Thornton in Freetown. After several efforts by successive governors at providing better prison facilities, a modern prison, known as the Freetown Central Prison, was eventually built at Pademba Road in 1914.

The Prisons Service has since grown over the years, with the construction of prison facilities throughout the country. There are currently 15 prisons in all, with a total 2007 population of 2,047 and an overall capacity of 2,235. However, the Freetown Central Prison, with a capacity of 324, had a 2007 population of 1,094, so it is obviously overcrowded, as are other smaller prisons, such as Bo Prison (capacity 80, population 113), Kenema Prison (150 versus 190), and Makeni Prison (75 versus 116). However, the remaining prisons are generally underutilized or nonfunctional.

Freetown Central Prison is located at the central part of Freetown, the capital of Sierra Leone. This location is not ideal because vehicular and human traffic create a lot of inconveniences. Within the prison, there are dormitories named Clarkson House, Blyden House, Howard House, Wilberforce House, Remand Block, Condemn Block, and Separate Cell that accommodate male inmates. The Female Wing is separated from the male blocks by a concrete wall.

In the middle of the prison, there is a long wooden building with different workshops for carpentry, shoemaking, blacksmithery, upholstery, masonry, and welding, among other skills. There are two wooden buildings for tailoring located by the side of the football field. There is also another building for weaving and artistry work. The prisoners are engaged in the these trades. Some of the machines in these workshops are dysfunctional. As a result, the inmates rely on hand tools to do their work. There is a church and a mosque for religious practices for the inmates and the officers.

The administrative structure is as follows: The regional commander is responsible for the supervision of all officers at the Freetown Central Prison and other prison institutions in the Western Area and assists in the general administration. The Officer-in-Charge of Technical Supervision supervises all technical or trades work. The Officer-in-Charge Female supervises all the female prisoners. There are units within the prison such as the record unit and reception unit, with officers who are responsible for the routine activities of the prisoners and the officers. There is a hospital, with one medical doctor and a number of nurses, where the prisoners are treated. Cases that are beyond their management are referred to the specialist doctors outside the prison.

All the administrative staff are answerable to the director of prisons whose office is at the prisons headquarters at New England Ville in Freetown. Inmates are required to work. Short-sentenced prisoners do outdoor labor at government institutions. There is a literacy class at the Freetown Central Prison and a literacy pilot project at the Moyamba Prison, both of which are sponsored by the Justice Sector Development Programme.

Visits are allowed on Tuesdays and Fridays, normally in the morning hours. Relatives, friends, and families do come on those days to see their loved ones. Representatives of humanitarian organizations, nongovernmental organizations, and parliamentary committees also come into the prisons on assessment visits. Lawyers are allowed to visit the prisons to see their clients. All visits are conducted within the prisons' regulations.

Al Shek Kamara

Further Reading

Constitution of Sierra Leone (Act No. 6). (1991). http://www.statehouse-sl.org/constitution/.

Laws of Sierra Leone. (1960). Vol. 1: http://www.britishcouncil.org/jsdp-resources-consolidated-laws-of-sl-volume-one.doc.

Malan, M., P. Rakate, and A. McIntyre. (2002). *Peacekeeping in Sierra Leone.* Pretoria, South Africa: Institute for Security Studies.

Thompson, B. (1999). *The Criminal Law of Sierra Leone.* Lanham, MD.: University Press of America.

The Truth and Reconciliation Commission for Sierra Leone. (n.d.). http://www.trcsierraleone.org.

Somalia

Legal System: Islamic/Common/Civil
Murder: Medium
Corruption: High
Death Penalty: Yes
Corporal Punishment: Yes

Background

Somalia is located in eastern Africa, close to the Middle East. It has approximately 3,025 kilometers of coastline and a population of about 10 million. It borders Ethiopia, Djibouti, and Kenya. Somalia includes the semiautonomous Somaliland in northern Somalia, which declared autonomy in 1991; Puntland, around the horn of Africa, which declared autonomy in 1998; and Somalia, which is primarily southern Somalia. Any reference to Somalia in this entry refers to the southern portion of the country. There appears to be some level of stability in Somaliland and Puntland, but Somalia has not had a functioning government since 1992. It is a failed state, but since 2000 it has begun to develop a central government.

Soon after independence, the government considered the police left over from past colonial administrations as part of the armed forces. There was a police commandant and officers in each administrative district. They received training and aid from Italy, the United States, and West Germany. This Western influence was meant to counterbalance the Soviet support of the rest of the army.

The army and the police were used by the rival clans to gain resources and were used in inter-clan conflict. In October 1969, President Shermaarke was killed by one of his bodyguards, and the military, which prior to this was not involved in politics, rapidly took control of the country under the auspices of the Supreme Revolutionary Council, which appointed Major General Mahammad Siad Barre (Barre) to be president and the de facto dictator of Somalia. Initially, Barre's tenure seemed to be positive. He built new institutions and tried to write down the Somali language.

During the Barre regime, the police were advised by units from the German Democratic Republic, a Soviet client state. In 1972, the police were reorganized into three commands, which included Mogadishu, southern Somalia, and northern Somalia, and they were used by Barre to suppress dissidents and opposition.

Barre began the Ogaden War with Ethiopia in 1977, during which a number of internal Somali groups formed in opposition to Barre. He responded harshly to the actions of these groups and killed thousands of innocent people. After the war, the conflict continued and gradually alienated more of the clans. These dissident groups were armed by Ethiopia, which gave them military hardware and training and allowed these groups to operate out of their country. Barre was ousted from power on January 27, 1991.

The civil war destroyed the infrastructure of Somalia. In May 1991, Somaliland declared itself independent of Somalia. Sharia law was to be its legal basis. The country has worked toward becoming a parliamentary democracy. Somaliland appears to have a functioning police force and is relatively stable. Little is known about the police and security in Somaliland.

In Mogadishu, the capital of Somalia along the southern coast of the country, the civil war continued. This round of civil war destroyed almost everything that was left after Barre was ousted from power. This conflict, the destruction of Somalia's infrastructure, and a drought drove hundreds of thousands of people from the country.

In 1993, the United Nations sent international troops to Somalia to ensure the protection of food. This included personnel from the U.S. military. These UN forces were unsuccessful in their efforts. The United States withdrew from Somalia after the killing of U.S. soldiers during fighting in Mogadishu. The UN withdrew fully from Somalia in 1995. The country continued its descent into lawlessness.

Puntland declared itself an autonomous entity in 1998. Since then, it has worked to develop a government bureaucracy and administration after years of civil war and state collapse. It created a 5,000-strong security force in 1998 that was composed of urban police and paramilitary forces, according to a Puntland Development Research Center Web site Police perform services such as arresting criminals and holding them until they can be tried by the courts. The average police wage is $60 per month, and when the police do not get paid, they stop working. The efforts of the police are made difficult by a well-armed populace, strong clan ties, and limited resources.

While both Puntland and Somaliland were attempting to transform into stable states, fighting in the rest of Somalia continued. In October 2004, the Kenyan government helped to broker a deal that developed the Transitional Federal Government (TFG). The peace deal resulted in the election of Abdullah Yusuf Ahmed as president of the TFG (Yusuf). Yusuf was the former leader of Puntland.

The creation of the TFG did little to immediately improve the security situation. Because of security concerns and instability, the government was not relocated to Mogadishu, which was considered too dangerous. Despite pleas for assistance, Yusuf was not able to gain any assistance from the United States, the African Union, or other regional international organizations that would allow him to retake Mogadishu and begin to set up the TFG.

The main opposition to the TFG in Mogadishu was the Union of Islamic Courts (UIC). The Union of Islamic courts was a system of clan-based sharia courts that fought to gain control of Mogadishu through their militias. The UIC were supported by both Eritrea and the Middle East. By May 2006, the Islamic militias had defeated the warlords of Mogadishu and returned some stability to the city. The UIC defeated the U.S.-backed Alliance for the Restoration of Peace and Counter Terrorism during the fighting. The U.S. government was concerned that the UIC was affiliated with Al Qaeda or other Muslim fundamentalist terrorist organizations.

In December 2006, the Ethiopian military entered Somalia to support the TFG and to deal with the Islamic courts and their militias. Ethiopia had support from the U.S. government. The Ethiopian military was rapidly able to defeat the Union of Islamic Courts. Although the UIC forces were defeated, Ethiopian and TFG forces in Mogadishu and the rest of the country continued to be attacked by dissident groups and rival militias. The security situation in Mogadishu has been tenuous ever since, with suicide bombings, mortar attacks, hit and run attacks, and the use of improvised explosive devices. In 2008, a new president, Sheick Sharif Sheik Ahmed (Sharif) was elected, and Omar Abdirasid ali Sharmarke (Sharmarke) was appointed as prime Minster. The TFG continues to work to build Somali capacity and build governance in Somalia.

The TFG's Transitional Federal Charter outlines a framework for the government of Somalia. The charter describes a five-year plan that should lead to the establishment of a representative government after national elections. The charter outlines the need to have an army and a police force. But this has yet to be put in place. Police stations in Somalia continue to be attacked by antigovernment groups and police personnel executed. This same phenomenon was identified in Somaliland where security makes up approximately 60 percent of the budget. The Somaliland police also operate with impunity and do not maintain order or limit violence.

Crime

In general, Somalia incorporates four distinct legal traditions into one legal mechanism. These include English common law, sharia (Islamic religious law), Somali customary law, and Italian law. The 1964 Uniform Penal Code worked to incorporate these various traditions into one system. The Somali criminal procedure code, which mandates matters of arrest and trial, was based in English common law. The crime problem in Somalia is of both domestic and international importance. Violence in Somalia is common. Weapons are easily available. Somalia's instability has driven it to be an area with a wide variety of international crime and security problems.

Classification of Crime

The Somali penal code was written in 1962 and became effective in 1964. The extent to which the Somali penal code is in use in Somalia or Puntland is unknown. The code noted that written law determined offenses and punishments. Crimes were classified into crimes and contraventions. Crimes are more serious offenses such as murder, rape, and robbery. Violent offenses include rape and various levels of assault such as very grievous hurt, grievous hurt, hurt, assault, robbery, aggravated assault, and assault. Property crimes include robbery and theft.

Contraventions are minor offenses, such as begging, failure to control animals, or other public order and public safety offenses. Contraventions are criminal offenses without criminal intent. These include begging, acts contrary to public decency, and cruelty to animals.

In Puntland, many of the laws and crimes appear to fall under customary law. This customary law is primarily governed by the sharia. For example, there is no insurance or traffic system to deal with car accidents. The rules that are followed are based in customary law, which makes it difficult to classify accidents appropriately. This also means that rules for compensation and responsibility vary from region to region.

Crime Statistics

Criminal statistics in Somalia and Puntland are not available. The U.S. State Department paints a grim picture of crime inside Somalia, including murders, thefts, and kidnappings. But due to instability and limited government capacity, it is not possible to identify levels of crime in Somalia.

The Somaliland Police Force recently released crime statistics in 2008, presumably the numbers of crimes reported to the police. However, it is difficult to understand these statistics because of the obvious lack of specificity of the types of offenses listed. They are as follows:

Deaths	73
Rape cases	126
Theft and robbery	2,467
Trafficking illegal materials and drugs	60
Injuries inflicted upon individuals	2,750

Human Rights Violations

In Somalia, human rights violations are rampant. Violations of human rights do occur in Somaliland and Puntland, but not to the same extent. The U.S. State Department indicates significant violation of human rights in 2008. The Transitional Federal Government, or its agents, and dissident groups were responsible for unlawful and politically motivated killings, kidnappings, torture, rapes, and beatings. Fighting between the TFG and opposition groups killed at least 3,000 civilians in 2008.

Discrimination and Violence against Women

Somali women face a significant amount of discrimination and violation of their human rights. There are laws against rape, but they are not enforced. There are no laws against spousal rape. Sexual assault in the home is reported to be a significant problem. Rape is commonly used by police and military members and during inter-clan conflict. There are no laws against domestic violence, and no statistics are available on its pervasiveness.

The use of female genital mutilation (FGM) is pervasive in Somalia. In Somaliland and Puntland, the practice is illegal, but the law is not enforced, and the practice continues. FGM is the practice of removing or sewing up parts of the female genitalia. UNICEF reports indicate that 95 percent of women in Somalia have undergone FGM. The procedure is primarily performed on young girls between the ages of 4 and 11.

Trafficking in Illicit Firearms

There is an international arms embargo against Somalia, but despite these efforts, firearms are easily available. This causes significant problems for Somalia, Somaliland, Puntland, and their neighbors. Somalia allied itself with both the Soviet Union and the United States at one time or another. The Institute for Security Studies noted that the Soviets reportedly gave $260 million worth of arms to Somalia, and the United States contributed an additional $154 million after that. This built up significant stockpiles of weapons in Somalia. After the fall of the Barre regime, roughly 500,000 weapons went into the hands of militias and other armed groups. These stockpiles, combined with general lawlessness and open borders, have made weapons a problem for this country as well as its neighbors. Small arms and light weapons are easily available. Small arms include such weapons as assault rifles and handguns. Light weapons include machine guns and rocket launchers. Somalia has become a conduit and a shipment point for weapons throughout the region.

Gun possession is an important part of Somali culture. Because Somalians have a herding and nomadic culture, they have come to rely on weapons to protect their resources. Weapons are also considered a symbol of power and wealth. Dowries are often made in the form of weapons. Atta-Asamoah in his research indicates that "a man who is able to offer a gun is believed to make a better husband." Weapons are also used as a source of wealth. Gun owners will reportedly sell their weapons when they are in need of money and then repurchase them after they regained their financial footing.

States bordering Somalia have evaded international efforts to reduce the supply of weapons flowing into the country. There are indications that Djibouti, Ethiopia, Yemen, Eritrea, Iran, Libya, Saudi Arabia, and Syria have broken the arms embargo on Somalia in one form or another. Their actions have included direct delivery of military material to factions, provision of military services, use of their territories for transshipment points, and entering into Somalia with weapons for use by troops.

The Use of Child Soldiers

The use of child soldiers is a longtime practice in Somalia. There are no records of children in the military forces of Somaliland. It is unknown whether child soldiers are fighting in Puntland. In the 2006 conflicts around Mogadishu, children were recruited by all sides including TFG forces, the Union of Islamic Courts, and the Alliance for the Restoration of Peace and Counter-Terrorism. In some cases these organizations forcibly recruited child soldiers. In some instances, it was reported that children as young as eight years old were recruited to fight. The Union of Islamic Courts forcibly recruited many children during its late 2006 fight to gain control of Mogadishu. According to Child Soldiers Web site, headmasters in Mogadishu schools were required to provide between 300 and 600 children to be made into solders. The Alliance for the Restoration for Peace and Counter-terrorism also recruited child soldiers into its ranks. Forced recruitment by this organization is disquieting because the organization was receiving backing from the U.S. government. The TFG openly admits that it has child soldiers in its ranks.

Human Trafficking

Reports indicate that human trafficking is a significant problem in Somalia. Somalia appears to be a transit, source, and destination point for human trafficking. Puntland appears to be the primary point of entry for trafficking activities. The overall response of the Transitional Federal Government, Puntland, and Somaliland to human trafficking has been minimal. Trafficking in children is exacerbated by the poor living situation of many Somali families. Some will surrender the custody of their children to relatives or others in their clan if they can no longer provide proper care. These children are then put at risk of trafficking.

There are reports of persons trafficked for labor to the Gulf states. Somali and Ethiopian women have been trafficked to the Middle East, Lebanon, Syria, and South Africa for domestic labor and prostitution. Somali men have been trafficked to the Gulf states to herd animals and do menial labor. Children have been trafficked for labor and commercial prostitution to Djibouti, Malawi, South Africa, and Tanzania. Cambodian men have been trafficked to work in fishing boats off the Somali coast. Armed militias are also reported to have trafficked women and children for sexual exploitation to both the Middle East and Europe.

International Piracy

Somalia has well over a thousand miles of unmonitored coastline. It is also very close to the shipping lanes of the Suez Canal through the Gulf of Aden. Middleton in his research on piracy in Somalia noted that it is estimated that 16,000 ships pass through the Gulf every year. These factors, combined with rampant poverty, high unemployment, available weaponry, and lawlessness make the coast of Somalia a haven for pirates who capture and hold ships for ransom. A Reuters Web site noted that between 2005 and 2008, the number of reported piracy attacks increased significantly, and between January and March 2009, the number of pirate incidents doubled from 2008. There were 18 attacks in March 2009 alone. These pirates typically operate out of coastal towns in Puntland.

Pirates generally take the captured ships to smaller ports on the Somali coast and hold them until a ransom has been paid. Ransoms for ships generally range from $500,000 to $2 million. Governments, shipping companies, and insurance companies are generally willing to pay the ransoms because of the high value of the ships themselves and the crewmembers on board. The international community is making efforts to deal with the ongoing and increasing threat of international piracy off the coast of Somalia. There has recently been increased activity of naval ships in the area to protect merchant ships and deal with pirates. Dealing with this problem is difficult because of the sheer size of the areas in which these acts are occurring and the continued instability in Somalia and Puntland.

Finding of Guilt

There are a number of different dispute resolution mechanisms utilized in Somalia, Puntland, and Somaliland. These systems are generally a blend of Somalian customary laws, sharia, British common law, and Italian legal codes. In all, available information on the legal systems of the Transitional Federal Government, Somaliland, and Puntland is limited.

Somalia

In 1962, Somalia developed a four-tiered court system. This court system includes a Supreme Court, a Court of Appeals, regional courts, and district courts. There are 84 district courts. The civil district courts handle applications of sharia law, customary law, or lawsuits up to 3,000 Somali shillings. The criminal district courts handle offenses punishable by fines or prison sentences less than three years. There are eight regional courts with three divisions. The ordinary division handles criminal and civil cases more serious than those handled in the district courts. The assize division handles those cases with crimes punishable by more than 10 years in prison. There is also a division that handles labor cases. There are two appeals courts, one in Mogadishu and another in Hargeysa in northern Somalia. There are two divisions in each appeals court, one that deals with ordinary cases and the other that deals with assize cases. The Supreme Court holds ultimate authority to interpret the law and hear appeals of cases of lower courts.

Under the Somali penal code, to be criminally liable, a person must have committed an act or failed to commit an act that caused harm or danger to the person or property of another or the state. In post-independence Somalia, persons are innocent until proven guilty beyond a reasonable doubt. The burden of proof also rests on the state. A person can be only arrested if he or she is seen committing an offense or through a warrant authorized by a magistrate. A person has the right to appear before a judge within 24 hours of arrest. It is unknown the extent that these rights are upheld in practice.

Somaliland

When Somaliland declared itself an independent state, it rapidly worked to develop a legal system. The Somaliland Constitution provides for an independent judiciary. It largely adopted the court structure of Somalia mandated in the Somali Penal Code of 1964. In theory, it should incorporate many of the legal protections enumerated in the penal code. It has a system of district courts, regional courts, appeals courts, and a Supreme Court similar in organization to that utilized in post-independence Somalia.

There are functional courts, but there do not appear to be enough judges, and there is a lack of legal documentation. An Amnesty International report noted that the Somaliland legal system is understaffed and lacks qualified people. In 1999, there were believed to be 10 lawyers in the entire country. The Globalex Web site notes that in 2006, there were 33 functioning courts and 87 judges. These two problems combine to limit the system's ability to build judicial precedence. The judiciary in Somaliland is not independent, officials are reported to have interfered with the courts, and sometimes laws are used to detain people without trial. Corruption appears to be rampant.

Puntland

Puntland operates under a charter that provides for an independent judiciary. But like Somaliland, the judiciary is not independent. There are provisions for a Supreme Court, Court of Appeals, and lower-level courts. The legal system in Puntland appears to be operating through a concurrent system of sharia courts, customary law, and Western legal courts. There are few formally trained lawyers, and those who do exist work in private practice. The judges in the sharia courts lack the formal education or experience to implement court procedure property. It is estimated that 70 percent of the judges in the legal system are informally trained customary (traditional) law judges, according to the Puntland Development Research Center. Most people who are arrested and remanded to prison pending their trial are not represented by attorneys. This occurs because they are unaware of their rights to have an attorney, because they do not have enough money to hire an attorney, or because the government does not have the resources to provide an attorney for them.

The Transitional Federal Government

The Transitional Federal Charter outlines the structure of the Somali court system. But it does not exist in practice. The charter is supposed to ensure an independent judiciary and also establishes the rights of Somali citizens. It establishes equal protection before the law; establishes freedom from detention unless pursuant to an act of a judicial authority or when apprehended committing a crime; calls for judicial proceedings to be open to the public; provides that persons charged with a criminal offense are innocent until proven guilty and have the right to communicate with their relatives and their lawyers; and calls for the provision of free legal services to anyone who cannot afford them and other basic human rights. The Transitional Federal Charter also describes the formation of the judiciary and court system, but outside of traditional dispute resolution and potentially through sharia, courts the legal system is nonexistent.

Punishment

Traditional Somali dispute resolution emphasizes the importance of collective punishments. Not only is the individual punished, but so are the clans or groups to which the perpetrator belongs. This punishment would typically come in the form of a blood price or *diya*. The *diya* is used for all types of crimes, including for homicides. This system of paying the *diya* continued after Somali independence and is still used to this day.

There has been some effort to standardize compensation for *diya*. In Puntland, compensation payment is determined by applying the sharia. The cost of compensation should be borne by the person who committed the crime, but he can ask his family for aid. According to the Puntland Development Research Center, some examples include 100 camels for the murder of a man and 50 camels for the murder of a woman.

The extent to which the *diya* is common throughout Somalia and Somaliland is unknown. *Diya* is paid not only for serious crimes but also for minor crimes. However, it is clear that the *diya* is an important tradition throughout Somalia.

Associated with collective punishment is the customary practice in Somalia of revenge killings. Revenge killings are the killings of innocent relatives of the perpetrator of a crime. Revenge killings can occur for a number of reasons. They can occur because the perpetrator enjoys clan protection and is not brought to justice. They can also occur when compensation for a prior case is not paid or when property taken or looted during a conflict is not returned to original owners.

There has been some movement, at least in Puntland, to eliminate the practice of revenge killings. Traditional leaders in Puntland indicate that a person who commits a revenge killing should lose the protection of his or her clan and be considered to be a criminal. The perpetrator must pay blood compensation (*diya*) on time. All conflict resulting from an incident should be resolved by clan elders, and any property or loot taken during a conflict must be returned. Judicial judgments must be passed swiftly, and legal action must be taken against those who facilitate revenge killings or protect those who commit them.

The Somali Penal Code

The principal punishments for crimes described by the Somali penal code include death, imprisonment for life, imprisonment, and fines. The Somali penal code provides for the death penalty for murder but for imprisonment and fines for other violent and property crimes. The penal code emphasizes that punishment is not to overshadow the need for the moral reeducation of convicted prisoners, suggesting support for the use of rehabilitation. The code requires that all prisoners work during their confinement. In return for their labor, prisoners are to be paid a modest salary. The code also outlaws the imprisonment of juveniles with adults. For contraventions, the typical punishments include imprisonment and fines.

The penal code prohibits collective punishments, which are a part of customary law. But the practice of paying *diya* for the commission of a crime was retained. Sharia was also made applicable in civil matters where disputes arise under the law. The extent that these punishments are in use at present is unknown.

Prison

Available information on the contemporary prison system is limited. In the past in Somalia, prisons held juveniles with adults. Juveniles were often incarcerated at the request of their families as punishment. Females were separated from males, but remand prisoners were not separated from sentenced prisoners. Information about prisons operated by the Transitional Federal Government other than that just provided is limited. There is some information available about the imprisonment in Somaliland and Puntland.

Somaliland

There are eight prisons in Somaliland. According to Amnesty International, in 1996, there were a total of 2,000 male inmates and 20 female inmates. People with mental illness are reportedly also held in these prisons due to a lack of treatment facilities.

In 1999, 70 percent of those prisoners were awaiting trial. In 2008, the main Somaliland Prison of Hargeisa, with a capacity of 150 inmates, had 700 prisoners housed there, according to a U.S. State Department report. That facility is operating at 466 percent capacity. Sanitation is poor, health care is limited, and there is inadequate food and water. The report found that the families of those imprisoned were expected to pay for the costs of detention as well as provide food. The United Nations Development Program and the European Commission recently helped build a new prison in Hargeisa, Somaliland. The prison began operations in December 2008. These prisons were built with the goal of improving prison conditions.

Puntland

The exact number of prisoners in Puntland is unknown. According to the Puntland Development Research Center report, cells in both prisons and lockup are described as having "no adequate space and are not suitable for imprisonment of human beings." There are not separate facilities for juveniles and women. There are no facilities for treating prisoners who are sick or who have a mental illness. Prisoners are not adequately fed or clothed or provided adequate bedding. Because prisons are located in urban areas, prisoners do not have the opportunity to exercise or even go outside. Prisoners are also not separated based on illness, adults and juveniles are housed together, drug offenders are not provided rehabilitation, and convicted and remand prisoners are housed together. The United Nations Development Program and the European Commission have recently helped build a prison in Gardo, Puntland. The prison began operations in December 2008. These prisons were also built with the goal of improving prison conditions.

Nathan Meehan

Further Reading

Cornwell, R. (2006). "Somalia: Distorting Reality." *African Security Review* 15(2): 77–78.

Elmi, A., and A. Barise. (2006). "The Somali Conflict: Root Causes, Obstacles, and Peace Building Strategies." *African Security Review* 15(1): 32–54.

Ganzglass, M. (1971). *The Penal Code of the Somali Democratic Republic.* Rutgers, NJ: Rutgers University Press.

Middleton, R. (2009). *Piracy in Somalia: Threatening Global Trade, Feeding Local Wars.* Chatham House: http://www.chathamhouse.org.uk/files/12203_1008piracysomalia.pdf.

South Africa

Legal System: Civil/Common/Customary
Murder: High
Burglary: Medium
Corruption: Medium
Human Trafficking: Medium
Prison Rate: High
Death Penalty: No
Corporal Punishment: No

Background

In 1652, the Dutch East India Company began building a fort at the Cape of Good Hope, modern-day Cape Town. By the turn of the 18th century, the Cape colony had come under control of Britain. In 1824, the British also established a settlement at the Bay of Natal on South Africa's eastern coast (modern-day Durban). During this same period, newly arrived immigrants, primarily from the Netherlands, Germany, and France, as well as descendents of the early Dutch settlers, established the independent Afrikaner republics of the Orange Free State and the South African (Transvaal) Republic. A result of this history is a hybrid legal system influenced by Roman-Dutch civil law tradition, the British common law tradition, indigenous African law that existed before colonization, and more recently, the international human rights movement. The primary sources of modern South African law include the Constitution, legislation, case authority, and international treaties and conventions.

Crime

South Africa experiences the broad range of crimes found in all contemporary societies, as well as some crimes that are more unique, or restricted, to the African context. The current level of crime is considered by both the general population and government officials to be among the most important domestic issues facing South Africa as it seeks to stabilize the new democracy. Violent crime rates are high. Rape and domestic violence are especially high and are priority concerns of government. The numbers of crimes reported to the South African Police Service for the period April 2007 through March 2008 were as follows:

Murder	18,4871
Attempted murder	18,795
Serious assault	210,104
Rape	36,190
Aggravated robbery	118,312
Resident burglary	237,853

These numbers reflect a general 20 percent decrease over the prior year.

Drug Crime

According to the United Nations Office on Drugs and Crime (UNODC) report of 2007, South Africa is the largest market for drugs entering southern Africa. For the period 2001 through 2005 the South African Police Service reported an increase of 80.9 percent in drug-related crime. Cannabis, is the most prevalent illicit drug used in South Africa, followed by Mandrax (methaqualone). Heroin, cocaine, and Ecstasy use is also reported but at much lower rates, although use of these drugs also appears to be on the rise.

Police

The South African Police Service (SAPS) is a national police service within the Ministry of Safety and Security, with some decentralization taking place at the provincial level. The broad structure and mandate of the SAPS is set out in the Constitution, chapter 11, with more specific direction provided by the South African Police Service Act 68 of 1995. The service is headed by a national commissioner and five deputy national commissioners, each overseeing one of the major divisions of the organization, with the national commissioner reporting directly to the minister of safety and security. Each province is in turn headed by a provincial commissioner, with a structure replicating that of the national head office. As of June 2009, the service had approximately 145,000 police officials (excluding civilians) for a national population of approximately 48,000,000 citizens, resulting in a police population ratio of 1:330. Approximately 22 percent of police officials in the South African Police Service are female.

Municipal police services (MPS) have also been created under the authority of the South African Police Service Amendment Act, No. 83. of 1998. At present there are six MPS agencies, primarily in the largest cities and metro areas in South Africa. The establishment of additional MPS agencies is expected in the near future. Metropolitan police services are intended to supplement the SAPS and ensure that local governments are more able to directly address their own crime control priorities, given that national and local priorities do not always overlap. The mandate of metro police services is to enforce traffic regulations and the policing of municipal by-laws and regulations. The Police Service Amendment Act also added the authority to engage in crime prevention, which in the South African context includes preventive patrol, rapid response to serious crimes, and the investigation of crime. However, the investigation of crime is explicitly denied to municipal police services and thus falls within the exclusive jurisdiction of the SAPS. In addition, the MPS agencies are also limited in their authority to hold evidence and detain arrested persons.

Ministry of Justice

The Independent Complaints Directorate (ICD) is mandated to investigate complaints of brutality, criminality, and misconduct against SAPS and municipal police service (MPS) members and operates

South African police shoot rubber bullets at advancing protesters during a clash with demonstrators from the predominantly Muslim PAGAD (People against Gangs and Drugs) group at the Waterfront Shopping Center in Cape Town, South Africa, on November 3, 1996. Around 5,000 PAGAD protesters demonstrated against local drug barons. (AP Photo/Sasa Kralj)

independently of both the SAPS and municipal police services.

The Directorate of Special Operations (DSO), popularly known as the Scorpions, has had the mandate to investigate organized crime, organized corruption, serious and complex financial crime, and racketeering and money laundering. As a branch within the Ministry of Justice, the DSO's mandate remains outside of the general police functions of the Ministry of Safety and Security. As of 2009, the DSO was to be replaced by the Directorate of Priority Crimes Investigation (DPCI), with a focus on organized crime, commercial crime, and corruption.

The National Prosecuting Authority consists of a national director of public prosecutions, directors of public prosecutions, and prosecutors and has the primary function of the prosecution of criminal cases. The Authority has the power to institute criminal proceedings on behalf of the state and carry out any other functions necessary for instituting criminal proceedings. The national director of public prosecutions determines prosecution policy and the issuance of policy directives but is required to report and answer to the minister of justice, who exercises final authority. The Authority also has responsibility for the Witness-Protection Program, the Asset Forfeiture Unit, and units such as the Sexual Offense and Community Affairs Unit, the Specialized Commercial Crimes Unit, and the Priority Crimes Litigation Unit.

Finding of Guilt

Courts

South Africa's criminal court structure is multilayered consisting of the following courts:

- *Magistrates' courts.* The criminal magistrates' courts, the most numerous of the courts with jurisdiction over criminal matters, are subdivided into regional magistrates' courts and district magistrates' courts. Regional magistrates' courts have jurisdiction over more serious criminal cases in that they are authorized to hear all criminal cases, except treason and murder. A person convicted in the regional magistrates' courts can be sentenced to a maximum of 10 years' imprisonment, whereas district magistrates' courts, upon conviction of an accused, may issue sentences of only up to 3 years. More serious criminal matters are heard in the high courts.
- *High courts.* Currently, the High Court of South Africa is divided into 10 divisions with 3 additional local divisions. The high courts have jurisdiction over all matters in their geographical area, but normally exercise jurisdiction only over civil matters involving more than 100,000 Rand and serious criminal cases. Except where maximum and minimum sentences are prescribed by law, the sentencing discretion of high court judges is unlimited. The maximum criminal penalty in South Africa is a life sentence. The high courts are also the appellate courts for magistrates' courts lying within the jurisdiction of the specific high court.
- *The Supreme Court of Appeal.* The Supreme Court of Appeal is the court of last resort on general jurisdiction. It hears and decides appeals against decisions of the high courts not raising constitutional questions, and its decisions are binding on all lower courts.
- *The Constitutional Court.* Constitutional questions—matters including any issue involving the interpretation, protection, or enforcement of the Constitution—are decided by the Constitutional Court. The court is composed of a president, a deputy president, and nine other judges and decides only constitutional matters and issues connected with decisions on constitutional matters. The court makes the sole and final decision as to whether a question arising is a matter of the Constitution or is connected with a decision on a constitutional matter. Matters before the court must be heard by at least 8 judges, but in practice all 11 judges hear every case.
- *Specialty courts.* Several specialty courts have also been established to address certain crimes, to divert cases from the principal courts, or to uphold traditional law within South Africa's historical tribal structure.
- *Community courts.* The community courts were established to address lower-level offenses principally affecting citizens within a narrowly defined geographic area. Thefts involving low value of loss or those of a frequent nature such as thefts of cell phones and handbags, offenses related to drug and alcohol abuse, and other petty offenses may come within the jurisdiction of community courts.
- *Chief's courts.* Primarily established to handle civil issues, these courts are designed to deal with customary disputes in terms of customary law and are informal hearings. Although decisions of chief's courts have the force of the decisions of magistrates' courts, their jurisdiction is limited to disputes of one African against another African within the jurisdiction of an authorized headman or his deputy. Appeals from the decision of a chief's court are made to the municipal courts having legal jurisdiction in the territory in which a chief's court may sit.
- *Sexual offense courts.* The courts function as specialist courts for sexual offense cases. They are established with the intention to increase sensitivity toward victims and to reduce the incidence of secondary victimization.

Judicial Appointments and Qualifications

The procedures for judicial appointments in South Africa are essentially characterized by the differing roles played by political and judicial officials, depending on the court to which a nominee is to be appointed. All of the procedures, however, are established in chapter 8, section 174, of the Constitution. The majority of judicial appointments are made by the national president on the advice of the Judicial Services Commission (JSC), a constitutionally established body consisting of 23 members. The exact makeup of the commission itself is also specified by the Constitution (chapter 8, section 178). When an appointment is to be made to the Constitutional Court, or the appointment is that of the president or deputy president of the Supreme Court of Appeal, the national president is more directly involved.

Qualifications of Judges

The only criteria specified by the Constitution of South Africa for appointment as a judicial officer are as follows: "Any appropriately qualified woman or man who is a fit and proper person may be appointed as a judicial officer. Any person to be appointed to the Constitutional Court must also be a South African citizen" (chapter 8, section 174[1]). As a matter of practice, "appropriately qualified" has come to mean being qualified by legal education.

Attorney Qualifications

The first requirement for becoming an attorney is completion of the LLB, a four-year program of legal study. After attaining the LLB, a prospective attorney must then serve as a candidate attorney at a law firm or legal aid clinic, complete a practical legal training course that is recognized by a statutory law society, and pass the attorneys admission examination. There are two levels of legal practice in South Africa, attorneys and advocates, with the authority of an attorney being more limited than that of an advocate. Advocates have the greater expertise and are authorized to present cases in court in contrast to attorneys. Advocates are also empowered to give legal opinions and to assist in the drafting of legal documents.

Rights of Arrested, Detained, and Accused Persons

Rights of arrested, detained, and accused persons are quite extensive and are detailed in section 35 of chapter 2 of the Constitution. Specific rights are associated with specific stages of the adjudication process.

Arrested Persons

Every person who is arrested for allegedly committing an offense has the right to remain silent and to be informed promptly of the right and the consequences of not doing so. An arrested person also cannot be compelled to make any confession or admission. He or she has a constitutional right to be brought before a court as soon as reasonably possible and not later than 48 hours unless the courts are not operating within the prescribed 48-hour period. At this appearance, the arrested party has a constitutional right to be charged, informed of the justification for continued detention, or released. If detained, an arrested person has the right to be released if the interest of justice permits.

Detained Persons

Everyone who is detained, including every sentenced prisoner, has the right to be informed promptly of the reason for being detained. Detained persons also have the right to choose, and to consult with, a legal practitioner and to be informed of this right promptly, as well as the right to have a legal practitioner assigned by the state at state expense if substantial injustice would otherwise result. Detained persons have right to habeas corpus petition and the right to be released from unlawful detention. The Constitution also makes broad provision for the conditions of detention, including at a minimum adequate housing, nutrition, reading materials, and medical treatment. Finally, the Constitution requires that a detained person be provided with the opportunity to communicate with and be visited by that person's spouse or partner and next of kin, his or her chosen religious counselor, and his or her chosen medical practitioner.

Accused Persons

Once charged with a crime, every accused person has a right to a fair trial. Fairness means that every accused has the right to a speedy trial, a prohibition against trials in absentia, and the right to a public trial before an ordinary court All accused persons are presumed to be innocent and have the right to remain silent, have the right to not testify during proceedings, and cannot be compelled to give incriminating evidence. The Constitution also prohibits the enforcement of ex post facto laws and provides protection against double jeopardy. If convicted, there is a right of appeal or review by a higher court. Finally, the Constitution makes direct provision for the exclusion of evidence obtained in a manner that violates any right in the Bill of Rights if the admission of that evidence would render the trial unfair or otherwise be detrimental to the administration of justice.

Sentencing

The discretion of judges at sentencing has been broad. However, Parliament passed the Criminal Law Amendment Act, 105 of 1997, mandating minimum sentences for a broad range of offenses. At the high end is life imprisonment. Although historically available, the death penalty was removed by statute in 1997. Judges may vary from the statutory minimums, but only with justification that must be documented. Data from the South Africa Department of Correctional Services on sentenced prisoners in March of 2006 indicate 6,800 inmates were serving life sentences, and another 9,500 were serving sentences of more than 20 years, out of a total inmate population of about 112,000 sentenced prisoners. The modal category was a sentence of 10–15 years (24,000 inmates). Slightly less than one-half of sentenced prisoners were serving sentences of 10 or more years on March 31, 2006.

Punishment

The corrections component in South Africa has been the focus of sweeping reforms since the enactment of the Correctional Services Act (Act 111 of 1998) and the Correctional Services Amendment Act of 2001. They are intended to establish a correctional service whose goals and performance are consistent with modern international standards as well as falling within the framework of the South African Constitution. Although major indicators of progress are readily visible, continuous development of the service can be anticipated for the foreseeable future.

Department of Correctional Services

The Department of Correctional Services (DCS) today operates over 230 correctional centers, of which 8 are exclusively for women and 13 are youth development centers; another 86 centers accommodate women in a special section of a center. The remaining centers are male only. The vast majority of both sentenced male (67%) and female (86%) prisoners are incarcerated in medium-security centers. Both males and females are about as likely to be serving minimum-security sentences (+/− 3%). However, male inmates (31%) are about three times as likely to be serving maximum-security sentences as women (11%). The median sentence for all inmates is 7–10 years with a modal sentence of 10–15 years. Almost three-fourths of sentenced inmates are incarcerated for what are termed aggressive (56%) or sexual (16%) crimes, according to the South African Department OF Correctional Services.

In January 2006, the number of DCS authorized personnel was just over 39,000. Of the total number of positions authorized, slightly over 11 percent were unfilled at the time. The vacancy level presents a significant challenge to the DCS in its efforts to meet new legislative and policy mandates to reform correctional practices and services.

The major challenge for the DCS in the development of rehabilitative programming is the large inmate population. Recent statistics available from the DCS, at the close of the 2007 fiscal year, indicated a capacity of 114,644 beds. However, the total population, of both sentenced prisoners and awaiting-trial detainees (ATDs), was slightly over 161,000. In addition is the challenge of reducing the incarceration of youthful offenders. A youth under South African definition is a person 25 years of age and younger. Within this group are child offenders, those under the age of 18. There were 36,000 sentenced youthful offenders in 2007, of whom less than 1,000 were child offenders. In contrast, out of 25,000 ATD youths, about 1,300 were children. Overall, the challenge to the DCS is that, as of yet, true alternatives have not been put in place to effect change to the correctional system. Reform of the system is ongoing.

Michael E. Meyer

Further Reading

Centre for the Study of Violence and Reconciliation (CSVR): http://www.csvr.org.za/.

Centre of Criminology, University of Cape Town: http://www.criminology.uct.ac.za/.

Correctional Services South Africa: http://www-dcs.pwv.gov.za/.

Institute for Security Studies (ISS): http://www.iss.co.za/.

South African Police Service: http://www.saps.gov.za/.

Swaziland

Legal System: Civil/Customary
Murder: High
Burglary: High
Corruption: Medium
Prison Rate: High
Death Penalty: Yes
Corporal Punishment: Yes

Background

Swaziland gained its independence from Great Britain in 1968 and was established as a constitutional monarchy with a clear separation of governmental powers. In 1973, King Sobhuza II repealed the Constitution and declared himself to be an absolute monarch. Since then, the country has generally been ruled under some kind of state of emergency, and the 1978 Constitution never came into force.

The country is neither a parliamentary democracy nor a constitutional monarchy. Rather, it remains a feudal system based on the absolute monarchy of King Mswati III, who assumed power in 1986 and currently presides over Africa's last remaining absolute monarchy. The king and his traditional advisors monopolize political power.

There is no separation of powers across governmental branches. The king is the ultimate authority over his cabinet, parliament, and the judiciary. He is commander-in-chief of the military as well as the commissioner-in-chief of the police forces. He also appoints any government officials of consequence, including senior civil servants, members of commissions, the cabinet, the prime minister, and superior court justices. Most of these officials are from his royal Dlamini family.

The people do not have the right to change the government, and the king is above the law, conferring on himself the prerogative of approving any proposed legislation. Parliament has no power, and the monarch bans all political parties. When the country finally held its first parliamentary elections in 2008, international observers had to report that the elections fell far short of international standards for fair elections because of substantial governmental interference.

In a tightly controlled process, in which all dissenting opinions were ignored, the king's delegates developed a new constitution. This new constitution went into force in 2005. Ironically, the Constitution actually includes a section titled "Protection and Promotion of Fundamental Rights and Freedoms," which essentially contains a sort of Bill of Rights that provides for various civil and political rights. But the Constitution has little substantive authority.

The National Constituency Assembly (NCA), a group of civic associations, petitioned the High Court to reject the Constitution and declare it null and void. The court rejected the petition. The Constitution formally removed the king's privilege to rule by decree. Yet he has continued to do so. He can also waive any constitutional rights at his whim. He holds absolute authority over the cabinet, parliament, and judiciary while upholding the ban on all political parties, as well as the country's feudal *tinkhundla* system of governance.

The *tinkhundla,* or local council, system involves 55 geographical areas ruled by traditional chiefs. These chiefs are directly beholden to the king. Although these chiefs are supposed to be hereditary positions, the king can, and occasionally does, appoint anyone to be chief over any area. These local chiefs also control elections in the House of Assembly and play prominent judicial roles locally.

Amid this feudal system's absence of any separation of powers, freedoms of press, speech, assembly, association, and movement are all severely restricted. Police frequently and arbitrarily detain and harass journalists, opposition group members, trade union leaders and strikers, and any demonstrators. The lavishly spending, polygamous king presides over a severely impoverished populace, and corruption remains a serious problem.

Societal discrimination against mixed-race and white citizens is problematic in the country in which 97 percent of the people are racially African and 3 percent are of European descent. There are no minorities in the government. Forty percent of the population adheres to a Zionist religion, which is a synthesis of Christian elements and indigenous ancestor worship. A fifth of the population is Muslim, and a tenth is Roman Catholic. Women, children, and homosexuals suffer significant discrimination, and the country maintains the world's highest rates of both HIV infection and tuberculosis. The American-based Freedom House (FH) reports that in recent years, Swaziland has experienced its worst upheavals as a result of labor strife, antigovernment violence, and governmental crackdowns in decades.

Legal System

Swazi jurisprudence is notable for its two distinct legal systems. One is based on South Africa's Roman-Dutch legal tradition as applied in an English-organized courts system. The second system is based on unwritten Swazi customary law and tradition.

The Roman-Dutch Swazi national court system includes the Supreme Court, the High Court, the Court of Appeals, the magistrates' courts, and the judicial commissioner. Civilians are not tried in the military courts. The High Court has unlimited civil and criminal jurisdiction to hear and decide matters brought before it.

The Supreme Court possesses and exercises all the jurisdiction, power, and authority vested in South Africa's Supreme Court. All of the judges presiding over Swaziland's Supreme Court have been foreign-born, primarily retired South African judges. However, it has no jurisdiction over any cases bearing on the institution of the king and other Swazi law and customs. Nor do the courts have jurisdiction over the office of the Queen Mother, the regency, chiefs, the Swazi National Council, or the traditional "regiments" systems.

The High Court interprets the Constitution. It has otherwise unlimited civil and criminal jurisdiction to hear and decide matters brought before it. The Court of Appeals and magistrates' courts operate below the High Court. The 1938 Magistrates' Courts Act governs the magistrates' courts. The criminal jurisdiction of the top-level magistrates' courts encompasses all criminal offenses except treason, murder, sedition, offenses relating to coinage and currency, rape, and any conspiracy or attempt to commit any of these offenses. Civil jurisdiction is limited to cases involving a monetary value not exceeding 1,000 Emolangeni (US$125) and to matters not involving dissolution of a marriage, estates, and determinations as to mental capacity.

The king has judicial powers himself and has the authority to appoint, discipline, and remove judges, including the chief justice and the High Court and appellate court judges as well as all three categories of magistrates: principal magistrates, senior magistrates, and magistrates. The Judicial Service Commission (JSC), appointed by the king, advises him on such matters. When even this level of control displeased the king, he turned to the King's Special Committee on Justice, known as the "Thursday Committee," which has essentially usurped the JSC's role in dealing with judges whose rulings displease the king. The king ignores rulings that displease him, and the Thursday Committee attempts to harass and intimidate errant judges into compliance. When conflicts between superior court judges and the monarch have arisen, judges have been known to resign in unison, sometimes striking for years. For example, in 2002, when they ruled that the king does not legally possess unlimited power or the right to simply rule by royal decree, the king aggressively rejected the ruling, and prompting all of the Court of Appeals judges to resign in protest, precipitating a judicial crisis. Not surprisingly, international legal observers have concluded that the country's Roman-Dutch judicial system is "crumbling" or nearing the "breaking point" and have called for "urgently needed" reforms.

Most of the Swazi population tends to use the 13 traditional Swazi courts in the *tinkhundla* system. Under the 1950 Swazi Courts Act, these courts serve the local chiefs and are responsible for administering unwritten Swazi law and custom. These emphasize a kind of restorative justice, typically meting out fines, and their criminal jurisdiction is limited to petty offenses such as theft, assault, and violations of Swazi law and custom such as the practice of witchcraft. They have limited civil authority and are authorized to administer customary law only "insofar as it is not repugnant to natural justice or morality or inconsistent with the provisions of any civil law in force."

But some traditional laws do conflict with the international treaties to which Swaziland is a party, particularly with respect to the status of women and children. Females have a subordinate status in the traditional courts. Children are deemed to belong to their fathers, and the practice of arranged marriages involving young females continues. So too does polygamy, despite the fact that the Roman-Dutch law prohibits the practice. Court presidents without legal credentials fulfill judicial roles and are usually elders appointed by the monarch.

Police

The country's police force was first established by the British imperial authority as the Swaziland Police Force, and officers were mandated to carry firearms and apprehend suspected lawbreakers. Upon independence, the king changed the name to the Royal Swaziland Police Service (RSPS) and appointed himself commissioner-in-chief. The RSPS is organized into four regional divisions, with different numbers of police posts in the country and with headquarters in the capital city Mbabane.

Police ranks are similar to those in British services, with a commissioner of police, a deputy commissioner, and an assistant commissioner. Below them are directors, senior superintendents, superintendents, and assistant superintendents. Beneath them, in 2002, were about 100 inspectors, 400 sub-inspectors/sergeants, and 2,000 constables. The sub-inspector rank has recently been abolished, though active sub-inspectors benefit from a grandfather clause until they retire.

The RSPS also includes an Operational Support Service Unit, which is assigned to respond to public disorder, bomb disposal, VIP protection, and vehicle or aircraft rescue operations. The RSPS also has a forensic chemistry lab for blood-alcohol content analyses. There is an officer training college, and some officers also train abroad. The U.S. State Department considers the RSPS to be generally professional, but it acknowledges that bureaucratic inefficiency is problematic and that the service is susceptible to political pressure and corruption.

The police commonly spy on labor unions, political groups, religious organizations, and others. They have also forcibly dispersed political demonstrators and strikers, inflicting numerous injuries in the process. Arbitrary arrests, the excessive use of force, assaults on citizens, and the use of sometimes lethal torture during interrogation are serious problems. For example, rangers at the Mkhaya Private Game Reserve are legally permitted to kill poachers whom they catch in the act of violating the Game Act. But in one recent episode, the reserve's general manager and several plainclothes RSPS officers broke into an unarmed man's home and shot him to death despite the absence of any evidence of a crime. More commonly, the Umbutfo Swaziland Defense Force (USDF) soldiers, ostensibly responsible for external security, patrol inside the country, setting up roadblocks, conducting random searches, and killing civilians. Indeed, security forces generally operate with impunity.

There is no independent investigative body to counteract police misconduct. However, the Constitution does provide for a Commission on Human Rights and Public Administration, mandated to investigate complaints related to violations of human rights, corruption and abuse of police power, poor public service, and the misappropriation of funds. It can publish findings and make recommendations. It can also refer matters to the director of public prosecutors or the attorney general, who is the king's principal legal advisor. The king appoints all of these officials, and if they decide not to prosecute police misconduct, and they typically do not, the commission cannot do so itself. The RSPS has its own internal complaints and discipline unit. This is secretive and does not prosecute or discipline its own.

The Service Charter of the Swaziland police calls for commitment to community policing and the formation of partnership with the community, ostensibly to make the police more accountable. In practice, this has meant the use of so-called community police, volunteer officers operating under the direct supervision of traditional chiefs in rural areas. The officers have the authority to arrest suspects and bring them before an inner council within the chiefdom for a customary trial. In cases involving more serious crimes, they turn suspects over to the RSPS.

Crime

According to the United Nations Surveys of Crime Trends and Criminal Justice Systems, the most recent available crime statistics were for the year 2000. The rates per 100,000 population for crimes reported were as follows:

Homicide	88.61
Major assaults	754.35
Assaults	1,356.84
Rapes	121.24
Robberies	259.14
Major thefts	1,093.78
Thefts	1,251.87
Burglaries	810.00

The law criminalizes rape, including spousal rape. According to the 2007 RSPS Annual Report, there were 663 reported rape cases. But the crime is clearly more common than this. Many Swazi men regard it as a minor offense, and many victims feel inhibited from reporting. Acquittal rates are high, and the laws are not effectively enforced.

Despite traditional restrictions against it, domestic violence, particularly wife beating, is common. According to a Central Statistics Office survey, 60 percent of men believed that it is okay to beat their wives. Victims can complain to both the Roman-Dutch and traditional Swazi legal systems. Women in urban areas often do. But in rural areas, women have little recourse because traditional courts are not responsive to the complaints of "unruly" and "disobedient" women. More likely is that women will be fined for wearing pants rather than traditional female clothing in public.

The law protects children under 16 from sexual exploitation, sets the age of consent at 16, and prohibits prostitution and child pornography. But child abuse, including incest and child sexual abuse, is serious. According to the UN Children's fund (UNICEF), one in three females have suffered sexual abuse as children, and one in four have experienced physical abuse. Most sexual abuse occurs within the home, and fewer than half of these crimes are reported.

The U.S. State Department has added Swaziland to its list of countries with the worst human trafficking problems because the authorities are not taking significant steps to comply with the U.S. Trafficking Victims Protection Act. Swaziland law does not specifically prohibit human trafficking, though the statutes prohibit kidnapping, forced and compulsory labor, aiding and abetting "prohibited immigrants" to enter the country, keeping a brothel, and procurement for prostitution.

Children are trafficked internally or from Mozambique for domestic servitude in the homes of wealthy Swazis and through the country to South Africa for domestic servitude and commercial sex exploitation. The International Organization for Migration (IOM) reports that Chinese women are trafficked through the country and sold in neighboring countries. Although the RSPS is generally responsible for enforcing immigration laws and suppressing cross-border crimes, there is no specific agency responsible for dealing with human trafficking or even maintaining records on its prevalence. There have been no known investigations or prosecutions of human traffickers.

Corruption is another serious crime problem. Although corruption is against Swazi law, authorities do not take it seriously. This is not surprising given that business contracts are frequently awarded based on business owners' relationships with government officials. The government has recently set up an Anticorruption Commission with a commissioner and two deputies. But the commission has not taken action yet, and corruption is never investigated or punished. Indeed, journalists who criticize the government, particularly the royals, or report on official corruption risk becoming the subject of libel suits or even arrest and prosecution for supporting terrorists.

Like other authoritarian governments, King Mswati's regime has enthusiastically embraced antiterrorism. A bomb explosion shortly before the parliamentary elections provided the pretext for the passage of the 2008 Suppression of Terrorism Act. Formally, this criminalizes all persons who aid, sympathize with, shelter, or provide logistical support to undesirable organizations, and those who violate the law are subject to arrest and imprisonment for 25 years to life.

The act also lists "specified entities," thus outlawing the Swaziland Solidarity Network (SSN), the Swaziland Youth Congress (SWAYOCO), the Swaziland People's Liberation Army (UMBANE), and the People's United Democratic Movement (PUDEMO). It defines terrorism very broadly so that it effectively criminalizes all progressive political organizations and its members. As Amnesty International and the Human Rights Institute of the International Bar Association concluded, the law is "inherently repressive," violating a range of basic democratic rights and the country's obligations under international and regional human rights treaties.

Finding of Guilt

The Constitution prohibits practices that constitute torture or cruel, inhumane, or degrading treatment or punishment. But the provisions pertaining to law enforcement are located in the "policy" section of the Constitution and are not enforceable in any court or tribunal. Moreover, the law does not specifically prohibit these practices, and they are not punished.

Suspected criminals have been subjected to such abuse even before any authority had decided to initiate any formal arrest and prosecution against them. Punitive mobs frequently beat, whip, and even kill individuals whom they have suspected of committing crimes such as burglary, rape, and assistance with abortions, despite there often being little or no evidence of guilt. Community police working for local chiefs typically participate in these mob attacks, and in one recent incident, a community police officer severely beat several homeless children for having slept in his patrol car overnight. These mobs are never investigated or punished.

The law requires that police officers get arrest warrants except when they observe a crime being committed or believe that a person is about to commit a crime. They are also required to get search warrants from magistrates. But police with the old rank of sub-inspector or higher have the authority to search without one if they believe that evidence might be lost.

Detainees must be charged with violation of a statute within a reasonable time, usually 48 hours, or in remote areas, as soon as the judicial officer appears. However, arresting authorities do not always present detainees within this period. Still, it appears that, in general, authorities promptly inform detainees of the charges against them and allow family members to visit them.

The Constitution includes the right for a detainee's next of kin, personal doctor, and lawyer to be allowed reasonable and confidential access to the detainee. Detainees may consult with lawyers of their choice. Defendants in the magistrate or superior courts are allowed to hire lawyers at their own expense. Unfortunately, widespread poverty is a barrier to general access to justice and fair hearings given that a large percentage of the population cannot afford to pay the legal fees.

There is no legal aid system, and the government pays for lawyers only when defendants potentially face either life imprisonment or execution. Further, defendants in the traditional courts are not even allowed the assistance of legal counsel. They must speak for themselves or be assisted by informal advisors. The Law Society of Swaziland serves as the bar association, including all practitioners. The national legal profession numbers just about 100 advocate lawyers and attorneys.

The absolute monarchy does not respect any right to habeas corpus. It provides only that persons be informed of the reasons for their arrests "as soon as reasonably practicable." During detention, police commonly prefer an interrogation technique known as "tubing." This involves temporarily suffocating detainees by putting rubber tubes around their face and mouth until they "confess."

There is a functioning bail system. If detainees can get a court appearance, they can request bail, except in murder and rape cases. In 2002, the Court of Appeals ruled that decisions to deny bail to detainees simply because they are accused of crimes such as rape are actually illegal. Prison officials have refused to abide by this ruling, prompting the courts to rule the officials in contempt.

Prolonged periods of pretrial detention are common. Ostensibly, authorities hold suspects so long to prevent them from influencing witnesses. Judicial inefficiency and staff shortages also contribute to the problem of prolonged pretrial detention. Some detainees have been exonerated after years of detention.

The director of public prosecutors, who is answerable to the JSC, has the authority to initiate and undertake criminal proceedings. As well, the public prosecutor has the legal authority to determine which court should hear a case. Usually, the police actually make this decision. If the king does not want the public prosecutor to actually prosecute someone, the king will have the prosecutor charged with "malicious prosecution" until the case is dropped.

The Constitution provides defendants with the right to "a fair and speedy public hearing within a reasonable time by an independent and impartial court or adjudicating authority established by law." Trials are to be closed to the public only when necessary in the "interests of defense, public safety, public order, justice, public morality, the welfare of persons under the age of 18 years, or the protection of the private lives of the persons concerned in the proceedings." The judiciary generally abides by the right to public hearings.

Providing speedy trials has proven to be more difficult, and there is a backlog of cases before the courts. There is no independent court budget, and there is a shortage in basic equipment, trained staff, and efficient case management techniques. All contribute to delayed proceedings, as do the inadequate salaries and lack of judges. Only 13 legally qualified magistrates serve on the magistrates' courts.

These financial and efficiency problems are greater in the Roman-Dutch legal systems than they are in the traditional Swazi courts. In the former, defendants not only are entitled to the presumption of innocence and the support of legal counsel, but also are entitled to the adherence of proper formal procedural rules and the keeping of case records. These due process protections do not apply in the traditional courts. Neither system uses juries.

Defendants in the Roman-Dutch system not only can present and question witnesses but also are entitled to access government-held evidence. It appears that they are generally able to get this access even before trials begin. Both defendants and prosecutors have the right to appeal all the way up to the Supreme Court in both civil and criminal cases.

Defendants in traditional Swazi courts may speak on their own behalf and call witnesses. The courts may impose on them fines up to 100 Emolangeni (US$11) and prison sentences up to 12 months. These sentences are subject to review by traditional authorities and can be appealed to the High Court.

Because the Suppression of Terrorism Act is aimed toward groups and individuals deemed threatening to the monarchy, it is not surprising that it generally abrogates the legal protections allowed to those accused of common crimes. For example, the act shifts the burden of proof to the accused, lacks any procedural safeguards during trial, and limits judicial review.

Punishment

The Internal Security Act of 2002 provides for severe penalties for anyone participating in or organizing political demonstrations, and it outlaws "support" for any political parties already banned by the king's proclamation of 1973. Swaziland's most prominent political prisoner is Mario Masuku. He is the leader of PUDEMO, one of the "specified entities" criminalized by the 2008 Suppression of Terrorism Act. Officials have not allowed religious leaders, labor union leaders, or foreign embassy officials to visit Masuku during his prolonged incarceration.

In many interpersonal crimes, however, offenders are unlikely to face significant punishment. Roman-Dutch courts have discretion regarding the punishment for assaults, other than rape, against women. They typically mete out light sentences. Even aggravated rape cases typically incur lenient sentences, despite the fact that they are punishable by up to 15 years' imprisonment.

The law prohibits forced exile, and the monarchy does not use it. Corporal punishment is not a lawful punishment for convicted criminals. However, it is legally and routinely inflicted on school children under age 16 who have committed no crime. Children may be beaten on the buttocks with up to four strokes. The death penalty is permitted by the Constitution. Though two persons have received death sentences, none have been executed since 1983.

The 1964 Prisons Act provides for the organization of the prison system. It also regulates the authority and duties of prison officers such as mandating that they carry firearms. The prison system is administered under the auspices of the Ministry of Justice. According to the World Prison Brief, the system incarcerated 2,546 people in its 12 prisons in 2008. This gave the country an official imprisonment rate of 231 prisoners per 100,000.

Because of the problem of prolonged pretrial detention, 25.1 percent of the prisoners are pretrial detainees. Convicts and pretrial detainees are held together. Foreigners represent 6.0 percent of the prison population, and juveniles represent just 0.5 percent.

Only one facility, Mawelawela, is designated for females. Although they sleep in different quarters within the prison, adults and juveniles are otherwise held together. Further, several children have lived there with their imprisoned mothers.

The government reports that its prison system is at just 89.7 percent of its official 2,838 capacity. This claim lacks credibility. The U.S. State Department concludes that Swazi prisons are quite overcrowded and that conditions are poor. Freedom House agrees and has noted that the prisons lack proper sanitation. As on the outside, HIV/AIDS is a severe problem inside the prisons, and rapes contribute to the epidemic. However, some prevention programs have been introduced inside prisons along with free HIV/AIDS testing, counseling, and antiretroviral treatment.

The torture ban inside the prisons is not enforceable in court. As well, beatings are quite common. The Swaziland Coalition of Concerned Civic Organizations reports that physical punishment of prisoners remains an accepted part of the culture, and authorities do not regard the corporal punishment of prisoners as a human rights violation. Life in Swazi prisons is indeed punitive.

Paul Schupp

Further Reading

Milner, A., ed. (1969). *African Penal Systems.* New York: Praeger.

Reza, A., M. J. Breding, J. Gulaid, J. A. Mercy, C. Blanton, Z. Mthethwa, S. Bamrah, L. L. Dahlberg, and M. Anderson. (2009). "Sexual Violence and Its Health Consequences for Female Children in Swaziland: A Cluster Survey Study." *Lancet* 373: 1966–1972.

UNICEF. (2007). *A National Study on Violence against Children and Young Women in Swaziland.* Swaziland: UNICEF.

U.S. Department of State. (2009, June 16). *Trafficking in Persons Report 2009—Swaziland:*

http://www.unhcr.org/refworld/docid/4a42148e28.html.

Women and Law in Southern Africa Research and Education Trust. (2001). *Multiple Jeopardy, Domestic Violence and Women's Search for Justice in Swaziland.* Mbabane: WLSA Swaziland, Women and Law in Southern Africa Trust.

Tanzania

Legal System: Common/Customary
Murder: High
Corruption: Medium
Human Trafficking: Medium
Prison Rate: Medium
Death Penalty: Yes
Corporal Punishment: Yes

Background

The United Republic of Tanzania consists of Tanganyika and the Zanzibar Islands. The union between the two territories occurred in 1964. Tanzania is located in the eastern part of Africa, sharing borders with Kenya, Uganda, Rwanda, Burundi, Mozambique, Zambia, Malawi, and the Democratic Republic of Congo, with the Indian Ocean on the east. With an area of 945,087 square kilometers, Tanzania's population stands at over 34 million according to the National Census of 2002. The United Republic of Tanzania is divided into 26 regions, with 21 in Tanganyika and 2 in Zanzibar, and with Dar es Salaam as its capital city.

Police

The Tanzanian mainland did not see European-style "civilian" police until 1916 when the German East African Company imported 31 South African Mounted Rifles for civilian police functions, who were in turn replaced by the English-style police in 1919 when Britain look over Tanganyika and established the Tanganyika Police Force and Prisons Service. The command structure was similar to other colonial forces established by the British in other commonwealth countries, with the top hierarchy consisting of white officers and the middle and lower ranks staffed with a mix of Asian and African personnel. In 1961, when Tanzania celebrated independence from Britain, the police force consisted of about 6,000. Changes in policing occurred in the 1960s, with a clear shift in colonial to postcolonial politics and with major expansion in security forces from nearly 3,000 to 40,000–50,000 strong, blurring distinctions between the police and the military. These shifts have been seen as the consequence of redefining national security with emphasis by regimes to safeguard their continued rule.

The Tanzania Police Force (TPF) is a national police force guided by the Police Force and Auxiliary Services Act 2002 (the Police Act), the Police Force Service Regulations 1995 (the Police Regulations), and the Police General Orders. Other legislation such as the penal code (which codifies criminal offenses), the Criminal Procedure Act 1985 (procedural guidelines), the Evidence Act (guidelines for gathering evidence), and the Prevention of Terrorism Act of 2002 all guide police mission and conduct.

The TPF is hierarchically structured. At the headquarters, the department is headed by the inspector general, who is supported by five commissioners: the Zanzibar police commissioner, the director of criminal investigation, the operations and training commissioner, the administration and finance commissioner, and the Dar es Salaam zonal commissioner. Outside the headquarters, the field establishments are spread over 23 regions on the mainland and 5 in Zanzibar consisting of 97 districts. These include the regional and district establishments, specialized units, and training institutions. Each district is headed by an assistant commissioner or a superintendent of police. Each district has many police stations headed by an inspector or a senior non-commissioned officer. The TPF has a number of different units, including the Airports Division, the Air Wing Unit, the Anti-Drug Unit, the Anti-Robbery Unit, the Central Railway Unit, the Anti-Terrorism Unit, and the Traffic Unit, among others. In addition, the TPF has provisions for auxiliary police organizations, 15 of them, most notably in Dar es Salaam, to enforce local government laws, bylaws, and ordinances.

In 1999, Tanzania had about 27,200 police officers (officer-to-population ratio of 1:1,298), and despite a marginal increase in the police officers, the ratio of officers to population got worse (1:1,400), which was insufficient compared to the UN recommended standard of 1:450, making the TPF force ineffective and inadequate to conduct its operations. A report by the Commonwealth Human Rights Initiative identified police pay and living conditions as poor. As an example, they cite that a constable who joined the police in 2003 would have earned Tsh 1,087,440 annually (about US$820) and accommodations with poor living conditions and no access to toilets or water. There is no insurance for police personnel, and the compensation for personnel killed in action is too small to assist families. Conditions at work are poor, and basic equipment is not reliable, nor are the officers adequately trained to use the equipment well. In Dar es Salaam, there is one identification bureau to deal with ballistics and fingerprinting. However, there is no forensic laboratory at the present time.

Community Policing

This program draws its legitimacy from Constitution article 146(2)(b) to deliver the service the public deserves by enlisting the cooperation and participation of the communities it serves and other stakeholders. However, there are other programs that the TPF either has created or supports that involve citizen participation in social regulation.

Auxiliary police: To assist the TPF, under the Police Act, the inspector general police (IGP) has powers to design and supervise auxiliary police to maintain order and protect property in designated areas. The IGP has jurisdiction over training, salary, equipment, and administrative control of the auxiliary police. The auxiliary police have the power to search and arrest and are entitled to the same immunities as police officers; however, they have to surrender an arrestee at the nearest police station. The Dar es Salaam Auxiliary Police Force was established in 2001 to enforce city ordinances, guard city property, and assist local police in investigating crime and making arrests. A number of these units are deployed in Dar es Salaam, which includes the University of Dar es Salaam, Muhimbili National Hospital, Tanzania Harbours Authority, and Tanzanian companies such as the Tanzania National Petroleum and Tanganyika Wattle Company.

Sungusungu

In addition to the auxiliary police force, all across the country there are civilian police that engage in self-policing, the people's militia or the Sungusungu. The Sungusungu began in cattle-breeding regions of Tanzania Nyamwesi and Sukuma areas as a grassroots law and organization, a citizen patrol, to prevent cattle and stock theft resulting from inadequate police presence in these areas. The organization is widely spread across the country and primarily consists of young persons in the age group of 14 to 30 years.

Though they do not have any legal authority, the government amended legislation to formalize their role. They are now governed by a wide range of enactments that include the People's Militia Law 1973, People's Militia (Compensation for Death or Injuries) Act 1973, and the Militia (Powers of Arrest) Act 1975. The Sungusungu do have some police powers such as the right to arrest, but they do not carry weapons, nor do they have investigative authority. The Sungusungu organization differs from place to place, but its power and authority structure in relation to the TPF remains the same. A 1996 household survey in Tanzania suggested that citizens were more satisfied with the Sungusungu than with the TPF.

Crime

Classification of Crimes

Chapter 16 of the penal code (revised edition 2002, issued under cap. 1, s 18) outlines the definitions of crimes for each crime. Chapter 7 of the penal code outlines definitions for treason and murder, which are punishable by death. Chapter 7 also identifies other felonies related to treason, such as treasonable felony (section 40), promotion of warlike undertaking (section 43), aiding prisoners of war to escape (section 46), seditious intention (section 55), and unlawful drilling (section 62).

Sections 195 and 196 of chapter 19a define manslaughter and murder. Other sections in this chapter define "malice aforethought" (section 200), provocation (section 202), "causing death" (section 203), and "when a child deemed to be a person" (section 204). Other offenses related to murder, such as accessory after the fact of murder (section 213), written threat to murder (section 214), conspiracy to murder (section 215), and suicide (aiding suicide, section 216), and attempting suicide (section 217), are provided for in chapter 21. Chapter 24 defines assaults (section 24) and assaults occasioning actual bodily harm (section 241).

Crimes against Morality

Chapter 15 classifies crimes against morality, which also include some forms of violent crime. Sections 130 and 132 define rape and attempted rape, respectively. The punishment for rape is life imprisonment with or without corporal punishment (section 131).

A member of the Tanzanian police ignites a bonfire of over 2,000 confiscated weapons at a stadium near Kigoma on January 23, 2007. The guns were surrendered under a program to rid Tanzania of illegal arms. (AP Photo/Khalfan Said)

There are many provisions in this chapter relating to sexual violence against young women and girls. These include abduction of girls under 16 (section 134), householder permitting defilement of girls under 16 (section 142), defilement of girls under 12 (section 136), and defilement by husband of wife under 12 (section 138). This chapter also penalizes abortion (section 150), abortion by women with child (section 151), indecent practices between males (section 157), incest by females (section 160), and unnatural offenses (i.e., against the order of nature, or animal, etc. [section 154]).

Property Crimes

Chapter 27 covers robbery and extortion. Robbery (section 285) is punishable with imprisonment for 20 years, and if it involves the use of weapon and causes injury, the imprisonment can be life imprisonment with or without corporal punishment (section 286). Other offenses in this category include attempted robbery (section 287), assault with intent to steal (section 288), and various forms of extortion (e.g., demanding property by written threat [section 289] and procuring execution of deed by threats [section 291]). Burglary, housebreaking, and related offenses are covered in chapter 29. These include breaking and entering dwelling house (section 294), entering dwelling house (section 296), and criminal trespass (section 299).

Human Trafficking

According to the U.S. Department of State Trafficking in Persons Report 2008, Tanzania is a source, transit, and destination country for men, women, and children trafficked for forced labor and sexual exploitation. Tanzania's penal code outlines various offenses related to human trafficking in chapter 25—offenses against liberty. These offenses are punishable by imprisonment of up to 10 years and a fine.

Terrorism

Terrorism as a problem in Tanzania has been highlighted since the terrorist bombing of the U.S. Embassy in Dar es Salaam on August 7, 1998. The Criminal Procedure Act of 1985, the Extradition Act, and the Evidence Act of 1965 have provisions to deal with terrorist acts. However, in response to increasing terrorist threats, the United Republic of Tanzania enacted the Prevention of Terrorism Act 2002, applying to both the mainland of Tanzania and Zanzibar.

Other Offenses

Piracy

A common problem in the Gulf of Aden and the Indian Ocean in recent years has been piracy, with increasing attacks on merchant ships occurring on the high seas off the coast of Somalia. According to the IMB Piracy Reporting Center, as of 2008, the pirates had attacked almost 100 vessels and had successfully hijacked nearly 40. Section 66 of the penal code defines piracy, and offenders can be punished with life imprisonment.

Poaching

Tanzania is rich with natural game reserves (84) and national parks (16), with hundreds of animal species. Though hunting is permitted, and the government issues gaming licenses, poachers target a range of wildlife, including zebras, wildebeest, antelopes, gazelles, hippos, and exotic birds. More than 1,300 people were arrested in the 2006–2007 season for illegal hunting, a number lower than that recorded in 2005–2006, when there were 2,303 cases.

Drugs

Illicit trafficking in drugs and psychotropic substances is a problem in Tanzania. The drugs include cannabis, khat (*Cath edulis*), hashish, heroin, cocaine, and Mandrax among others. Although some drugs such as cannabis are grown in the rural areas of the country and transported to the urban area, other drugs such as heroin come from Pakistan and India. Some of these contents are consumed in the country, but most of the drugs move to Europe and North America. The number of cases registered, amount seized, and persons arrested relating to cannabis and khat trafficking during the period 2001 to 2004 showed a fairly consistent increase according to Tanzanian Police records.

Illicit Trafficking in Firearms

Illicit trafficking in firearms is a major concern for Tanzania. Most of these arms are trafficked into Tanzania from neighboring states of Burundi, Rwanda, and Congo because of political instability combined with porous border. Most of these weapons are small arms left over from years of civil wars. The number of firearms seized between the period of January 2001 and December 2005 totals 3,098. Seized illicit firearms are routinely destroyed.

Cattle Rustling

Cattle rustling is a serious crime problem in Tanzania, particularly in the northern regions of Mara, Arusha, Manyara, Tanga, and Kiimanjaro; in the central regions of Dodoma, Shinyanga, and Singida; and on the borders with Rwanda and Burundi. Although people within the country steal cattle to smuggle them outside the country, it is also not uncommon for aliens to cross into Tanzania for the purpose of stealing animals. Sungusungu, originally the rural defense groups formed by volunteers, were among the first to organize to prevent and fight cattle theft in the rural areas of the Shinyanga, Mwanza, Mara, and Singida regions. Police records indicate that from 2001 to 2005, the following numbers of heads of cattle were reported stolen: 31,126 in 2001; 25,120 in 2002; 27,089 in 2003; 28,524 in 2004; and, 25,704 in 2005.

Crime Statistics

Crime data for the year 2000, the most recent year available, were published by INTERPOL, a sample of which follows, showing numbers of offenses reported by police:

Homicide/murder	1,846
Rape	1,758
Serious assault	5,408
Robbery and violent theft	786
Aggravated theft	30,556
Breaking and entering	23,415
Motor vehicle theft	230
Other thefts	29,269
Fraud	223
Counterfeit currency	398
Drug offenses	4,069

A. S. Mapunda reported in 2006 that during an 18-month period, from January 2004 to June 2005, police recorded 140 incidents of armed robbery committed by foreign nationals. However, in general, the number of armed robberies remained fairly similar for the years 2001–2005: 1,047; 1,237; 1,111; 1,175; and 1,080. Mapunda noted a slight increase in motor vehicle thefts during 2002–2005 compared to the years 1998–2000.

Since 1992, police have been seizing counterfeit 1,000 legal tender (bank notes), representing an increase in white collar crime. Since 1995, Tanzanian 5,000- and 10,000-shilling notes were the most popular tender for counterfeiting. Police data on the numbers of cases registered for the years between 2001 and 2005 were 494, 707, 722, 742, and 653, respectively.

Crime in Zanzibar

Mapunda also reported police data on crime in Zanzibar for the years 2000 through 2005. The number of murder cases increased from 18 in 2000 to 43 in 2003 and 25 in 2005. However, the number decreased to 9 in 2001 and 17 in 2002 and 2004. There were no reported cases of armed robbery for most of the years, with the exception of 2002 (5) and 2003 (1). Though drug trafficking cases increased slightly overall during the reported period, the sharpest increase was noted from 2003 to 2004. The sharpest increase in crime was noted for rape.

Finding of Guilt

Courts

Tanzania has a five-level judiciary and combines tribal, Islamic, and British common law. Christians are governed by customary or statutory law in both civil and criminal matters. Muslims may apply either customary law or Islamic law in civil matters. Judges are appointed by the chief justice, except for those for the Court of Appeals and the High Court, who are appointed by the president. Advocates defend clients in all courts, except in primary courts. There is no trial by jury. The law also provides for commercial courts, land tribunals, housing tribunals, and military tribunals.

The Magistrate's Court Act of 1963 introduced a three-tier court system in Tanganyika, including (1) subordinate courts, (2) the High Court, and (3) the Court of Appeals. The subordinate courts consist of primary courts (limited jurisdiction and appeals can be made to the higher courts), districts courts, and resident magistrate's courts. Under the Magistrate's Courts Act of 1984, the primary courts are the lowest court in the country, established in every district. These courts cover all civil suits related to customary and Islamic law and all civil and Christian matrimonial suits. Appeals from primary courts are allowed to the district court. Currently, there are 206 district courts in Tanzania.

The next highest court in the hierarchy is the High Court established by article 108(1) of the Constitution. There are two divisions of the High Court, one in Tanganyika and one in Zanzibar. The High Court is headed by *jaji kiongozi,* the principal judge, and not less than 15 *puisne* judges. The court consists of 37 judges ruling in 11 zones. They are appointed by the president.

The highest court in the land is the Court of Appeals. It consists of the chief justice and four judges who are appointed by the president. The court hears appeals from both Tanganyika and Zanzibar. There are two attorney generals for the United Republic of Tanzania—one serving the mainland and the other serving Zanzibar.

Zanzibar's court system generally parallels that of the mainland but retains Islamic courts to adjudicate Muslim family cases such as divorce, child custody, and inheritance. Islamic courts only adjudicate cases involving Muslims. Cases concerning Zanzibar's constitutional issues are heard only in Zanzibar's courts. All other cases may be appealed to the national Court of Appeals.

The Constitution of Zanzibar came into effect in 1963 upon being granted internal self-government. With independence the Courts Decree 1966 made provision for a High Court, district courts, kadhis' courts, primary courts, and juvenile courts. The most significant development in Zanzibar was the introduction of people's courts in 1970 (People's Courts Decree 1969), which slightly altered the court system. These include, from lower to higher level, (a) the people's area courts, (b) the people's district courts, (c) the kadhis' Courts, (d) the High Court, and (e) the Supreme Council. Further reorganization occurred with the enactment of the High Court Act 1985, which provides for three levels of courts: the High Court of Zanzibar, the kadhis' courts, and the magistrates' courts. The magistrates' courts, like those on the mainland, consist of primary courts, district courts, and the resident magistrates' courts. The kadhis' courts are established in every district deal with the Muslim law relating to marriage, divorce, inheritance, and so on.

Tanzania's criminal trials are governed by the criminal procedure code that governs trials before the primary courts. The Magistrates' Courts Act 1963 governs trials before the subordinate courts and the High Court. An assessor presents a case in the primary or district court, and the director of public prosecutions presents a case in court for the Government.

The Constitution, in article 13(6)(e), ensures equality before the law and requires the state to guarantee that no person is subjected to torture or to inhumane or degrading treatment. The accused have a right to legal representation under section 310 of the Criminal Procedure Act, 1985. This includes the right to be informed of that right to legal representation by the trial court. There is no trial by jury in Tanzania, and criminal trials are open to the press and the public. Criminal defendants do, however, have the right to appeal. All defendants have a right to bail because it is considered a right for any person whose liberty is at stake pending the due process of law. There are three types of bail: the police bail, bail pending trial, and bail pending appeal. Though Tanzania has made great strides in achieving gender equality in the legal system, women are seriously disadvantaged in the application of customary and Islamic law, particularly in the areas of property ownership, inheritance, and custody of children.

Juvenile Justice

Juvenile justice in Tanzania is governed by the Children and Young Persons Ordinance (cap. 13) enacted by the British in 1937 to deal with problem street children, both delinquent and non-delinquent. Today, in addition to cap. 13, the Probation of Offenders Ordinance, the Corporal Punishment Ordinance, the penal code, the Criminal Procedure Act, and the Magistrates' Court Act govern juvenile justice in Tanzania

According to cap. 13, a "child" is a person under the age of 12 years, and a "young person" is 12 years and over but below 16 years. Section 17 specifies a young person above 16 "not to be a child or young person," which highlights concerns for those older than 16 but younger or at the age of 18. The common types of offenses committed by juveniles in Tanzania include pickpocketing, stealing, robbery, sexual offenses, burglary, housebreaking, and aggravated assault. Data on juvenile crimes were not available. In a study that covered the years 2000–2002, data from Lindi, Mbeya, Mwanza, Tabora, Ngara, and Moshi indicate that of the 800 juvenile delinquency cases registered, as many as 443 were brought in primary courts, 353 in district/resident magistrates' courts, and only 4 in the High Court.

The 1985 Criminal Procedure Act, section 56, requires a police officer in charge of investigating an offense that involves a juvenile delinquent to notify parents or guardians. Only in rare instances do police officers notify probation officers. Similarly, like apprehension, in most instances, police officers interrogate young offenders in the presence of parents, guardians, or probation officers.

Section 4 of cap. 13 empowers the officer in charge of a police station to grant bail to an apprehended juvenile offender on the officer's own recognition (bond) unless the offense is punishable by a sentence exceeding seven years or it is in the interest of the offender to be removed from association with undesirable elements. The Criminal Procedure Act, section 64(3), also provides for the offender to be released to parents or guardians if the apprehended juvenile is younger than 15 years.

Section 3 of cap. 13 requires that the criminal hearing against juveniles be held in a different courtroom, and no members other than the members of the court, the relatives of the accused, and parties to the case can be present (section 3[5]). The 1985 Criminal Procedure Act, under section 148, provides for granting of bail during trial with some conditions, such as explaining to the juvenile in simple language the "substance of the alleged offense" or requiring the court to order a hearing if the juvenile pleads not guilty and so on.

Juvenile punishments are outlined under part 3 of cap. 13. The trial magistrate must be guided by the provisions outlined in section 22(2) of cap. 13, which states that "no young person shall be sentenced to imprisonment, unless the court considers that, none of the other methods in which the case may be legally dealt with by the provisions of this or any other Ordinance is suitable."

Punishment

Types of Punishment

The Tanzania penal code (cap. 16) outlines various punishments. These include death, imprisonment, corporal punishment, fine, forfeiture, payment of compensation, and any other punishment provided by the penal code or by any other law or ordinance.

The Death Penalty

The penal code's cap. 16 outlines the two offenses that draw death penalty. They are murder (section 197) and treason (section 40). Death penalty exemption is made if the convicted offender is a female and pregnant, in which instance she will be sentenced to life (section 198). However, recently, the Law Reform Commission has begun to review its position on abolishing the death penalty in response to human rights watchdogs. The last time a person was hanged in Tanzania was in 1994, and the number of inmates on death row was 286 as October 31, 2008.

Corporal Punishment

Corporal punishment is one of the punishments permissible under section 28 of the 1945 penal code and is administered in accordance with the Corporal Punishment Ordinance, 1930; the Corporal Punishment Order, 1930; and Government Notice No. 76 of 1941. Juveniles and females are exempt from corporal punishment under the Minimum Sentences Act (articles 2 and 3). Mandatory corporal punishment was abolished by the Minimum Sentences Act in 1972 but was reintroduced in 1989 by the Written Law (Miscellaneous Amendments) Act. In Zanzibar, special procedures for offenders under the age of 16 years are outlined in the Children and Young Persons Act. Corporal punishment is lawful in prisons. Prison officials can administer punishment (caning) under article 33 of the Prisons Act of 1967 for inmates guilty of offenses within the prison.

Imprisonment and Fines

Imprisonment is the most common form of punishment in Tanzania. Numerous offenses listed in the penal code (cap. 16) are punishable with some term in prison.

Prisons

The Tanzania Prisons Service (TPS) was officially established in 1931 and took over from the police force that was primarily responsible for administering punishments. The Prisons Act of 1967 embodied the guidelines relating to treatment of prisoners listed in the international basic human rights documents. Some of these include humane treatment of the offender as the core value with the overriding philosophy of rehabilitation and community safety. Alternatives to incarceration were introduced, including open farm houses and establishment of educational and vocational training centers in prisons. Further, training programs for correctional personnel were also introduced.

The prison service comes under the jurisdiction of the home ministry. The principal commissioner is the chief administrator who in turn is assisted by three commissioners: those for rehabilitation services, legal and prison affairs, and finance and administration. The prison system consists of 122 institutions, 21 regional offices, 2 staff training centers, 4 vocational training facilities, and a head office, with an overall total employment of nearly 12,000. The regional offices provide administrative oversight, and the head office effect management and administration of all prison stations countrywide. The TPS is responsible for the custody and care of more than 45,000 inmates, but its accommodation capacity is 22,669. This implies that the prisons facilities are overcrowded by more than 100 percent. In 2008, there were 40,613 inmates in Tanzania's prisons, of which a little more than 18,000 were on remand or on trial. Of these inmates, 1,261 were females.

Upon admission to the prison, inmates are segregated by gender, age, and type of sentence. Male and female prisoners are housed separately. The two age categories are those inmates between 16 and 20 and those 21 and above. Based on the nature of offense and repeat offender status, inmates are classified as star class (inmates with good behavior), ordinary class (those unsuitable for star class), and incorrigibles (troublesome offenders). To the extent possible, prisoners awaiting trial, young prisoners, juveniles, and civil offense prisoners are separated from the regular inmates. Even among inmates, to the extent possible, star-class inmates are housed separately.

Prison diet is determined by dietary scales by taking into account the inmates' cultural background and medical conditions. There are a minimum of three inmates to a cell but never less. Inmates charged with rule violations have the right to be heard, the right to appeal, the right to apply for review, and the right to make defense. Those found guilty receive additional punishment, which may be awarded by a subordinate officer or senior officer and may require approval of a qualified medical officer. In some instances, a punishment may require approval by the principal commissioner of prisons before implementation.

Inmates have opportunities for recreation with provisions for outdoor and indoor games. Educational classes are offered for those interested, and reading materials such as magazines, newspapers, and books are available for inmates. In addition, an inmate grievance process is available through meetings called *barazas* about once every month.

Mahesh K. Nalla and Ernest Mallya

Further Reading

Bierwagen, R. M., and C. M. Peter. (1989, April). "Administration of Justice in Tanzania and Zanzibar: A Comparison of Two Judicial Systems." *International and Comparative Law Quarterly* 38: 395–412.

Kijo-Bisimba, Helen, and Chris Maina Peter. (2005). *Justice and Rule of Law in Tanzania: Selected Judgments and Writings of Justice James L. Mwalusanya and Commentaries.* Dar es salaam, Tanzania: Legal and Human Rights Center (LHRC).

Kimaro, L. R., D. M.S. Rutahindurwa, and C.J. Mashamba. (2003). *The State of Juvenile Justice in Tanzania: Report on the Findings of the Research on Administration of Juvenile Justice in Tanzania.* Dar es Salaam, Tanzania: Legal and Human Rights Center.

Mapunda, A. S. (2006). "Crime Trends in Tanzania." Paper presented at a Senior Police Officers' Seminar held on February 13–14, Bwawani Hotel, Zanzibar.

Robertshaw, R., A. Louw, and A. Mtani. (2001). *Crime in Dar es Salaam.* Pretoria, South Africa: Institute for Security Studies.

Togo

Legal System: Civil
Murder: Medium
Corruption: Medium
Human Trafficking: Medium
Prison Rate: Low
Death Penalty: Maybe
Corporal Punishment: Yes

Background

The republic of Togo is a small country situated in West Africa between Ghana to the west, Benin to the east, and Burkina Faso to the north. The capital and largest city of the country is Lome. Roughly 6,300,000 people live in this area of 56,785 square kilometers.

The legal system of Togo combines French Napoleonic code with African traditional law, therefore making it an inquisitorial system. The Napoleonic code went into effect in 1804 and consists of 2,281 rules, or articles, covering a variety of subjects: persons, property, torts, and contracts. The classification as an inquisitorial system means that extensive pretrial investigations and interrogations take place. People are provided with an independent judiciary and are protected from arbitrary interference of privacy.

According to the 1992 Constitution, executive power is vested in the president. The president and the unicameral National Assembly are both elected for five-year terms by the universal adult suffrage committee. The president elects a prime minister, who in turn, with consultation of the president, appoints a cabinet of ministers.

The Constitutional Court of Togo has nine members and is the highest court of jurisdiction for constitutional matters and for preserving the basic freedoms and rights of the people. The Supreme Court, established in 1961, sits in Lome and consists of Court of Sessions, Appeals Courts, and Tribunals. Tribunals are divided into civil, commercial, and correctional chambers. These include a labor tribunal, a tribunal for children's' rights, a military tribunal, and a special state security court. These tribunals are divided into civil, commercial, and correctional chambers. The Court of State Security, established in 1970, judges crimes against the internal and external security of the state. There is also a tribunal for recovery of public funds that handles cases involving misuse of public funds.

The Superior Council of Magistrates was set up in 1964 and is responsible for maintaining the independence of the judiciary system. This makeup of the controlling men of the Superior Council allows for politics to play a large role in the criminal law proceedings. The corruption of the president and his appointed officials has led to many attempted coups to overthrow the government and force the president out. The majority of these have failed, and those that did not were soon reversed by the military controlled by the president.

Policing in Togo is based on the French system. There is a national gendarmerie, which is part of the armed forces and is directed by the minister of defense; a national police force under the authority of the minister of the interior, Security, and Decentralization; and the city police of Lome, responsible for policing the metropolitan area of the capital.

The gendarmerie is a paramilitary police force responsible for maintaining order throughout the country, updating the Central Criminal Archives, performing domestic intelligence duties, and training the Presidential Guard, whose sole responsibility is protecting the president. This force consists of five brigades: air, harbor, traffic, territorial policing, and criminal investigation.

The national police force, commanded by an inspector general, is responsible for the regulatory and administrative aspects of policing. It is also responsible for Togolese security and monitoring potential subversion against the state. This police unit has a number of different divisions, including intelligence (special service), railway, harbor, fire service, and the judicial police. The president has no control over this police force, as he does with the gendarmerie, so he has little trust in its activities. Therefore, he has established duplications of some of the tasks performed by the national police through the development of brigades attached directly to the president.

The judicial police are under the authority of the minister of interior, security, and decentralization and are responsible for criminal investigation. However, although organizationally they are under that control, when they conduct investigations, they come under the jurisdiction of the courts and are supervised by the chief prosecutor. During an investigation, they establish that an offense has occurred, gather evidence, and search for offenders. Once a charge has been developed, they have delegated judicial powers to hold preliminary inquiries, to receive complaints and charges, to search, to detain, and to process a suspect's testimony.

Work conditions are being improved to raise the effectiveness of the judicial police. Police buildings are being renovated and temporary detention facilities properly outfitted, computerization is being introduced, and office materials and stationery is being supplied. Officer ranks are being trained in school for judicial police, modern scientific methods are being introduced, and a minimum graduation certificate is set for judicial police agents.

Crime

Crimes that are a particular challenge to the country are pickpocketing, mugging, assault, theft, residential burglary, carjacking, violent attacks, vigilante/mob justice, domestic violence, human trafficking, drug-related crimes, organized crime, and business fraud. These are the main problems that the Togolese police force must face. They seem common to most countries and big cities in Africa. However, these crimes have a distinction because certain crimes are more focused on foreign visitors than natives of Togo, whereas others are problems of only the Togolese people themselves. Pickpocketing, mugging, theft, and business fraud are aimed at foreign visitors or targeted at businesses in foreign countries, and domestic violence, human trafficking, residential burglary, and drug-related crimes are mainly Togolese-only problems. Crimes such as assault, carjacking, violent attacks, vigilante/mob justice, and organized crime can be problems of foreigners and Togolese alike.

Over the past year, Togo has seen an increase in violent crimes throughout the country, including several machete attacks in poorly lit areas of Lome. Particular areas for foreigners to avoid within Lome, especially during the hours of darkness, include the Grand Marche (Lome's largest market area), the beach road, and the Ghana-Togo border areas. Foreign travelers are advised also to avoid driving late at night on the eastern section of the beach road, where criminals often target cars for theft.

In the first decade of the 21st century, business fraud had increased in Togo. The perpetrators of business fraud often target foreigners, using the facilities of the Internet. These fraud schemes are accredited with starting in Nigeria, but they are now present in western Africa, especially in Togo. These schemes pose a threat of financial loss and physical harm. Typically, these scams begin with an unsolicited e-mail from an unknown individual that promises quick financial gain if the recipient assists in the transfer of a large sum of money or valuables out of the country. The scenario is as follows: An American must pretend to be the next of kin to a deceased Togolese who left a fortune unclaimed in a Togolese bank. The requests are usually for the payment of advanced fees, attorney's fees, or down payments on contracts. The final payoff does not exist, and the purpose of the scam is to get any money possible and to gain information about the victim's bank account.

Human trafficking is a major problem in Togo. Togo has been a transit point for human trafficking from Burkina Faso, Ghana, Côte d'Ivoire, and Nigeria. Although the law does not prohibit trafficking specifically, other statutes such as kidnapping, procuring, and other crimes linked to trafficking allow the prosecution of these people.

Children are the primary victims of trafficking. They are trafficked for indenture and servitude, which amounts at times to slavery. Women are the next most likely victims of trafficking. They are used for the purpose of prostitution or nonconsensual labor as domestic servants. Adult males are the least likely to be involved as victims in trafficking. This could be a result of the fact that they may be harder to control; the majority of the time, they are the people responsible for procuring the victims for trafficking.

Organized crime and drug smuggling are also large problems in Togo, as with all of western Africa. Togo is not a major drug-producing country, but it is an alternate trafficking route for shipments headed for the United States and England. Togo is such a popular trafficking route because of its loosely patrolled borders. These borders allow smugglers to pass through without much resistance from the Togolese police force.

Finding of Guilt

The legal system of Togo is based on the French Napoleonic code combined with African traditional law. The Togolese Constitution prohibits arbitrary interference with privacy and provides for an independent judiciary. Trials are public, and defendants have a right to counsel and to appeal cases from a lower court. The bar association provides attorneys for indigent defenders. Defendants may confront witnesses, present evidence, and enjoy a presumption of innocence. The court systems in Togo are overburdened and understaffed.

The Constitutional Court is the apex court. It is made up of nine members and is responsible for constitutional matters and for preserving the basic rights and freedoms of the people. The civil judiciary system is made up of the Supreme Court, the Court of Sessions (Court of Assizes), and appeals courts. There is a labor tribunal and a tribunal for children's rights. There is also a military tribunal and a special state security court; both hold hearings that are closed to the public, dealing with crimes against the internal and external security of the state. In the countryside, village chiefs or councils of elders try minor civil and criminal cases. Those who reject the rulings of these courts may take their case to the regular courts, which is the starting point for cases that originated in the urban areas of Togo.

There is no evidence of plea bargaining or other alternatives to going to trial. The majority of cases involve a short trial that usually ends in conviction with a sentence of at least a year in prison, plus fines, or one year of probation. The majority of cases end in imprisonment.

Arbitrary arrest and detention are major problems in the legal system of Togo. The law allows authorities to hold arrested persons without charge for 48 hours, with an additional 48 hours for cases that are deemed serious or complex. Detainees can be held without bail for extended periods of time with or without approval of the judge. After the detention period of 48–96 hours, a detainee has the right to access to family members or an attorney, but authorities often delay or deny this privilege. Detainees have a right to be informed of the charges against them; however, police often times ignore this right as well. The law in Togo stipulates that a special judge conduct a pretrial investigation to examine the adequacy of evidence and decide on bail. However, a shortage of judges and qualified personnel results in lengthy pretrial detention, in some cases several years, which would be longer than the actual sentence if the person were tried and convicted.

The courts in Togo are understaffed and overworked. This leads to many backups in trial proceedings. Even with the stipulations and regulations in the Constitution, many rights and procedures are ignored by actors of the legal system.

Punishment

Most information gathered on the types of punishments is based on political crimes. These cases involved some of the members of the political party opposing the president. Charges were brought against these men for expressing their political opinions. These cases ended in varying sentences, ranging from 3–18 months in jail to 6–12 months probation, or $150–$500 fines. However, these were only political crimes based on expressing political opinion. Crimes such as drug smuggling and human trafficking result in long harsh sentences.

Prison

Prison conditions in Togo are very harsh, and overcrowding is a problem. Poor sanitation, unhealthy food, poor medical facilities, and drug use are common in the majority of the prisons. The central prison in Lome, Togo's largest, is built to hold 350 prisoners but is reportedly housing more than 1,500 inmates. Prison guards in the overcrowded civil prison in Lome charge prisoners fees to shower, use the toilet, or have a place to sleep. It is also reported that sick prisoners have to pay guards $2 to gain access to the infirmary.

In April 2007, a UN special rapporteur was invited by the government of Togo to visit prisons, gendarmerie, police, and military detention facilities without prior notice and to conduct interviews of the detainees. Two of the three prisons that the special rapporteur visited were severely overcrowded. Detainees sleep in overcrowded cells, often times in shifts. Food is restricted, and inmates rely mainly on supplies from family members. All prisons in Togo have nurses who provide daily treatment, but that service is provided only to those inmates who can afford the fee. This results in many serious cases going untreated.

Conditions are even worse in gendarmerie and police detention facilities. Detainees sleep on concrete floors in dark cells with little or no ventilation and minimal food and water. Inmates are permitted to use the toilet one time per day, and access to water for washing is restricted. Inmates are even required to be naked day and night to prevent suicide or attempted suicide.

There have been major improvements in the treatment of prisoners since 2005. There are few allegations of ill treatment or torture, but there are many allegations of beatings by guards or other inmates as a means of punishment. Inmates are beaten by wooden sticks, primarily to help in extracting a confession, but also for punishment or intimidation purposes. Verbal threats are also used to intimidate detainees.

Women and minors are housed separately from male inmates. Conditions in these prisons are generally better than in the men's prisons because of the lack of overcrowding. However, women and minors are more likely to be victims of ill treatment or torture. There is a lack of female guards in the women's prisons, which is a violation of international standards. This fact leads to the likelihood that they will be mistreated.

Minors face the greatest risk of torture and ill treatment. At the juvenile detention centers, all the children are held together, regardless of age. Ten-year-old children are held in the same prison as young adults. This is a clear violation of the basic principles of the Convention on the Rights of the Child.

Eric Smith

Further Reading

Das, D. K., and M. J. Palmiotto. (2006). *World Police Encyclopedia.* New York: Rutledge.

Economist Intelligence Unit. (2006). *Politics: Security Risk in Togo:* http://find.galegroup.com.proxy2.cl.msu.edu:2047/itx/infomark.do?&contentSet=IAC-Documents&type=retrieve&

tabID=T001&prodId=AONE&docId=A155839604&source=gale&srcprod=AONE&userGroupName=msu_main&version=1.0.

"Togo—Judicial System." (2007). *Encyclopedia of the Nations:* http://www.nationsencyclopedia.com/Africa/Togo-JUDICIAL-SYSTEM.html.

Uganda

Legal System: Common/Customary
Murder: High
Burglary: Medium
Corruption: Medium
Human Trafficking: Medium
Prison Rate: Medium
Death Penalty: Yes
Corporal Punishment: Yes

Background

Uganda is a landlocked country in East Africa whose modern legal system is based on the common law tradition. The territories now identified with Uganda were placed under the control of the British East Africa Company in 1888. The country was then confirmed a British protectorate in 1894, and the British introduced the English common law system. Prior to this, most parts of Uganda applied customary law, which was unwritten law developed according to the customs and lives of the local communities. Customary law, however, was not abolished and continued to apply in the native courts, using the chieftaincy structures to administer the process. When Uganda gained independence from the United Kingdom in 1962, the government moved to unify the native courts and protectorate courts by enacting the Magistrates' Courts Act (MCA) in 1964.

The System of Criminal Justice

The British introduced a model criminal code in Uganda in 1930. Although the Uganda Penal Code Act (PCA) in its present form is still principally a reflection of criminal law as it existed in Britain in 1930, the 1995 Constitution established the current system of courts of judicature, which include the Supreme Court, Court of Appeal, High Court, magistrates' courts, and other subordinate courts.

The Supreme Court is at the top of the judicial hierarchy and is the final court of appeal. Below the Supreme Court is the Court of Appeal, an intermediate court that was established by the 1995 Constitution. The High Court is the next court of record in the judicial hierarchy, and it is the most important court of judicature in the Ugandan system. It has unlimited jurisdiction over both civil and criminal cases of any value and magnitude. In addition, it also handles appeals from the lower courts, which include magistrates' courts and local council courts.

The magistrates' courts were established by the Magistrates' Courts Act and are responsible for administration of criminal justice as well as civil proceedings in Uganda. At present, there are 26 chief magisterial areas in Uganda; each area is presided over by a chief magistrate with the power to supervise all magisterial courts in that area. Local council courts handle minor offenses and have limited territorial jurisdiction. Judges in Uganda are appointed by the president upon recommendation of the Judicial Service Commission and approval of Parliament.

Role of the Police

The Ugandan police system is hierarchically structured. There are three main departments, the Criminal Investigation Department (CID), the Directorate of Special Branch, and the Mobile Police Patrol Unit, plus other minor departments. Other departments include the traffic police, the Marine Unit, the Department of Private Security and Firearm Control, and the Child and Family Protection Unit. The Constitution mandates the police to cooperate with other security organs. This provision has been applied extensively by the government, which in several instances has deployed the military and other security agencies on law and order duties. The many joint operations between the military and the police have greatly blurred the mandate imposed by the Constitution on these two government forces and contributed to an increasing militarization of the police.

Crime

Classification of Crimes

In Uganda, a felony is an offense that is declared by law to be a felony or that, if not declared to be a misdemeanor, is punishable, without proof of previous conviction, with death or with imprisonment for three years or more. A misdemeanor, on the other hand, is defined as any offense that is not a felony. The PCA further provides that when no punishment is especially provided for any misdemeanor, it shall be punishable with imprisonment for a period not exceeding two years. An offense is referred to as an act, attempt, or omission punishable by law.

Examples of felony offenses punished under the Ugandan penal code are murder, rape, treason, robbery, terrorism, habitual dealing in slaves, theft, and arson. Examples of misdemeanor offenses are unlawful assembly, public riot, insult to religion, common nuisance, keeping gaming houses, fouling water, and criminal trespass.

Specific Criminal Offenses

Rape

The law on rape has been criticized for its narrow definition and failure to recognize that various types of forced sexual acts might have serious impacts on the victim, including psychological trauma. The Uganda Law Reform Commission recommended that the definition be expanded to any act of a sexual nature between two persons without consent. This definition would include homosexual rape and forced oral sex, as well as the use of other parts of the body to penetrate. The burden of proof in rape cases is on the prosecution, which must always prove the offender's culpability beyond reasonable doubt; the onus never shifts.

Cyber-Crime

Uganda enacted the Computer Misuse Act in 2004. The act criminalizes various behaviors, such as distributed denial of service, cyber terrorism, cyber stalking, phishing, identity theft, hacking, and spoofing. The major cyber-crime cases detected so far involved inter-country situations, including within Nigeria, Congo, Kenya, and Canada.

Terrorism

The Anti-Terrorism Act was adopted in 2002 in the aftermath of the 9/11 attacks. Section 7 of the statute defines terrorism as any act that involves "the use of violence or threat of violence with intent to promote or achieve religious, economic and cultural or social ends in an unlawful manner, and includes the use, or threat to use, violence to put the public in fear or alarm." The act has been condemned by human rights organizations, such as the local NGO Foundation for Human Rights Initiative (FHRI) as well as Human Rights Watch and Amnesty International, for its lack of specificity and the vagueness of the offenses' definitions.

War Crimes and Crimes against Humanity

Upon referral from the Ugandan government, the International Criminal Court launched an investigation in 2004 that led to the issuance of five arrest warrants against the top commanders of the Lord's Resistance Army (LRA). The accused have been charged with war crimes and crimes against humanity as provided under articles 7 and 8 of the Rome Statute, namely, murder, cruel treatment of civilians, intentionally directing an attack against a civilian population, pillaging, inducing rape, forced enlisting of children, enslavement, sexual enslavement, rape, and torture.

The charges raised by the ICC concern crimes that are not covered under Ugandan criminal law. The PCA does not provide for crimes of utmost gravity such as the mentioned international crimes. In addition, it is believed that because of the magnitude and gravity of the crimes and atrocities committed by the LRA, the Ugandan judiciary would be in an unlikely position to handle these crimes appropriately. Therefore, there is a belief that local prosecutions would offer a magnitude of challenges, both financially and structurally, that would result in a diversion of resources that could be better put to rebuilding the lives that have been affected by the LRA war in the last 20 years.

Crime Statistics

The crime statistics provided in this section are found in the 2006 and 2007 Annual Crime Reports compiled by the Uganda Police Department (UPD). In 2007, the Ugandan police registered a total of 153,924 crimes that were reported and investigated by the Criminal Investigations Directorate. Of these, only 46,422 cases reached the trial phase by the end of the year, leaving a backlog of 107,502 cases. Out of those brought to court, 12,346 cases secured actual convictions. The distribution of reported crime varies by region, the locality with the highest incidence being Kampala. However, for the country as a whole, there was a decrease in the number of reported crimes in 2007.

Opposition Forum for Democratic Change (FDC) leader Dr. Kizza Besigye, center, listens to his legal team at the High Court in Kampala before resumption of his trial for rape, January 23, 2006. Besigye, who was later an unsuccessful candidate in Uganda's 2006 presidential election, was acquitted of the rape charge on March 7, 2006. (Stuart Price/AFP/Getty Images)

Finding of Guilt

Criminal Prosecutions

There are three ways to initiate criminal proceedings against any person in Uganda. The first mode involves the immediate arrest and detention of a suspect at the police station. This usually occurs in the case of the most serious offenses, when the police decide to promptly arrest a person with or without warrant because there is sufficient evidence for criminal prosecution. The police next lay the charges against the suspect, who will then either be released on bond or, more frequently, be put in detention until the first court hearing within the next 48 hours.

The second way involves the director of public prosecutions, who is Uganda's central prosecuting authority and is appointed by the president upon recommendation of the Public Service Commission. The director of public prosecutions institutes criminal proceedings against a suspect either personally or through authorized officers, who serve as public prosecutors before magistrates' courts in any local area.

The third mode involves the initiation of criminal proceedings by any private citizen who has reason to believe that a crime has been committed. A private prosecutor does not have to be directly involved (e.g., as a victim) in the reported offense; any citizen with knowledge of a crime is entitled to exercise this right. However, the power to initiate criminal action may be exercised only for minor offenses that fall under the jurisdiction of Uganda's lower courts.

Rights of the Accused

The 1995 Constitution details the rights of the accused, including fair and speedy trial and public hearing before impartial court or tribunal. Despite this important provision, there are still enormous flaws in the Ugandan criminal justice system. At the magistrates' courts level, an average trial may take up to three months from the beginning of the trial to the sentencing stage. Proceedings at the High Court may also take from two weeks to several months, especially for capital cases. The lack of basic resources, such as facilities, equipment, stationery, and funds, and the low number of available trial attorneys are major problems that hinder the effectiveness and efficiency of the criminal justice system in Uganda.

According to the Ugandan Constitution, every person charged with a criminal offense is entitled to be represented by a lawyer of his own choice. However, there is no general obligation on the state to provide free legal services to indigent defendants. The availability of public legal assistance at the expenses of the state is limited to cases brought before the High Court, Court of Appeal, and Supreme Court. The Constitution, however, provides that free assistance of a translator be guaranteed to those defendants who do not understand or speak English, Uganda's official language. This provision is important, considering that there are more than 20 languages and many more dialects in the country.

Defendants are presumed innocent until proved guilty by a court of law or until the person has pleaded guilty. There is no jury system. In capital cases tried by the High Court, however, the presence of at least two "assessors" is required. These are Ugandan citizens selected by chief magistrates, whose function is to assess the evidence against the defendant and decide whether he is guilty or not in the light of the special customs, language, and habits of the particular community the defendant comes from. Judges are not bound by the assessors' opinion but must justify any departure from it.

The law provides for pretrial custody of defendants awaiting trial for reasons of public interest, namely, (1) to ensure that the defendant is present at court hearings, (2) to safeguard police investigations against possible attempts to intimidate witnesses or influence prosecuting authorities, (3) to protect material evidence, (4) to protect the accused against retaliations or attacks from victims or their relatives, and (5) to protect the community from potentially dangerous individuals. Recent legislative reforms have substantially reduced the legal period allowed for pretrial custody and have established an automatic release on bail after 16 months for capital cases and after 8 months for all others.

Juvenile Justice

Uganda has introduced aspects of restorative justice in the treatment of youths involved in crime. A separate system for juvenile defendants—under the age of 18 years—has been created in every district, which is dealt with by special Family and Children Courts and which emphasizes children's welfare. Special procedures have been developed to protect the juvenile during the criminal justice process. For example, hearings are held as often as necessary, with closed doors and in camera; parents or guardians are required to be present whenever possible; probation and social welfare officers are also informed and may participate in the parents' absence; and proceedings are generally informal and do not require typical adversarial procedures. Special facilities to hold children on remand awaiting trial are established and kept separate from adult detention centers. In addition, there is a time limit of six months for a child's pretrial custody.

Punishment

Types of Punishment

Death Penalty

The Ugandan penal code (PCA) imposes the death penalty for eight offenses that are considered most serious. The death penalty is mandatory when offenders are convicted of murder, treason, smuggling involving the use of a deadly weapon, or aggravated robbery. The court may choose the death penalty for rape, unlawful sexual intercourse with an underage person, detention with sexual intent, and kidnapping with intent to murder. After the adoption of the Anti-Terrorism Act in 2002, additional offenses carry a possible death sentence.

There are certain limitations with respect to the use of capital punishment. Ugandan law establishes that individuals who, at the time of the offense, were under the age of 18 years cannot be executed. Similarly, a death sentence cannot be pronounced against a pregnant woman; instead, she must be given a sentence of life imprisonment.

The legal method for executions as provided by Ugandan law is by hanging. Statistics on the number of people sentenced to death or executed in Uganda are unfortunately hard to retrieve and may not be entirely reliable. According to a 2005 report by Amnesty International, in December 2004 there were at least 525 inmates on death row in Ugandan prisons. No executions of civilians have been conducted since May 1999, when 28 inmates on death row at Luzira Prison were hanged. Executions are, however, still imposed and carried out by military courts. In February 2006, the chief of Ugandan defense forces stated that 26 UPDF (Uganda People's Defense Force) soldiers had been sentenced to death and executed between 2003 and 2005 for killing civilians while on duty in northern Uganda.

Corporal Punishment

Although considered a controversial means of punishment and conflicting with several human rights provisions, corporal punishment is still practiced in Uganda with respect to a limited number of offenses. It is mandatory if a person commits robbery and attempted robbery, and it is administered in addition to any imprisonment sentence. The judge can also require it at his own discretion in cases of attempted rape, incident assault, and attempted defilement. The law prohibits using corporal punishment for any other offenses.

In fact, there are exceptions to this rule; corporal punishment can be used with offenders younger than 16 years as an alternative or in addition to imprisonment. Corporal punishment is believed to be more appropriate for young offenders and to have a stronger deterrent impact compared to other forms of punishment.

The law specifies 24 strokes as the maximum that can be imposed as a sentence. Women of any age, men over 45 years old, and convicts sentenced to death cannot be subjected to this practice. In addition, a doctor must examine individuals who are to be corporally punished to establish whether they are physically fit to receive it. If this is not the case, another form of punishment is to be preferred. Because corporal punishment is believed to have a major deterrent impact when administered swiftly, the law provides that the sentence must be executed soon after the end of the proceedings, and in any case not after six weeks.

Imprisonment and Fines

Imprisonment is the most common type of punishment for criminal offenses in Uganda. Time in prison must be served at one of the facilities administered by the central government or by a district administration. Illegal detention in secret prisons is forbidden; however, there are allegations that this practice is still used in present-day Uganda.

The practice of imposing fines as a punishment was already in use in precolonial Uganda. Indigenous justice provided that individuals who violated the law pay back with livestock to the local authorities. With the introduction of cash, the system has changed, and now fines are paid in money form. Fines can be imposed as an alternative to imprisonment or in addition to time in prison, especially for serious offenses such as the illegal smuggling of goods.

Other Measures

When the crime consists of assault or any other offense of a personal or private nature not amounting to felony, the judge may propose to settle the dispute peacefully, promoting reconciliation between the offender and the victim. The court may request that the offender financially compensate the victim for the harm suffered, repair a damaged property, or simply offer an expression of remorse and apology.

Compensation may be awarded anytime during normal criminal proceedings. Individuals entitled to receive it include any person who has suffered material loss or personal injury as a result of the offense,—that is, not only the victim but also the prosecuting private party or a witness. Complainants are also allowed to file a civil suit against the defendant to obtain full compensation. In case of property-related offenses, the court may also order the convict to return any property or proceeds that were subtracted from the victim, if—obviously—this is still available.

Probation is an alternative disposition available at sentencing time. Offenders granted probation are allowed to return to their homes under two conditions: (1) that they follow law-abiding behavior and (2) that they remain under supervision by a probation officer. Not all offenses allow for probation, only those for which there is no minimum sentence prescribed by the law.

A different mode of punishment involves police supervision and applies, after their release, to persons who have been sentenced to imprisonment terms other than life imprisonment. It is mandatory for offenders convicted of robbery for up to five years following their discharge from prison; as of 2008 this is the only type of crime for which it has been used. Ex-convicts must comply with a series of obligations, such as reporting personally to the police at certain time intervals and notifying the police supervisors of any changes in residence.

Prisons

The prison system is administered at a central level by the Ugandan Ministry of Internal Affairs. The commissioner of prisons, who is accountable to the minister, is in charge of supervising the 46 central government prisons as well as local detention centers. There are two main types of prisons in Uganda: (1) reception centers—or district prisons—for defendants on pretrial remand and awaiting trial and (2) prisons for convicted offenders. Reception centers of the first type are usually located in urban areas, where defendants can be held close to the court. Convicted offenders serving short-term sentences may also be detained in these facilities. Prisons for convicts are classified in six categories, depending on the offender's characteristics and the type of sentence: "preventive detention" prisons for habitual offenders, "prison farms" for convicts serving medium- to long-term sentences, maximum-security prisons for dangerous offenders and hard-core recidivists, "reformatory schools" for juvenile offenders, special prisons for young offenders, and women's prisons.

Prison conditions in Uganda—especially in the non-central areas—have been condemned by local NGOs and human rights organizations. Recent reports reveal that the majority of inmates lack bedding (mattresses and blankets) and proper uniforms. Overcrowding, lack of transport, extremely poor sanitation, and scarce food also constitute a chronic reality in today's prison system.

The prison population in Uganda has been growing steadily in part because of the inefficiency of the judicial system, which suffers from an enormous backlog. A major problem is the excessive length of the temporary stay of prisoners in custody on remand. In 2005, there were a total of 19,600 prisoners in Uganda, 63 percent of whom were being held on remand. Facilities are, therefore, congested by prisoners on remand, whose costs of maintenance weigh on the government's finances. Most inmates in Uganda are between the ages of 15 and 50 years.

Lack of funding is the most compelling reason behind the appalling state of prisons in Uganda. Most facilities were built in the 1950s and have not been renovated since. The 2001 Human Rights Report by FHRI reveals that, although inmates in central government prisons do not work, in local administration prisons, they are sometimes forced to work in exchange for food and other necessities such as soap, salt, or medication. In some instances, local prison administrators have resorted to the sale of prisoner labor. Prisoners in local facilities are oftentimes overworked and forced to take long shifts without being sufficiently fed.

Other allegations of human rights abuses involve torture and inhumane treatment, such as in the case of prisoners at the Kanungu Local Administration Prison, who have been employed to exhume cadavers at a mass murder site without protective gear. Incidents of violence and other cruel treatment by prison officers and wardens are also common. Despite recent efforts to improve prisoners' conditions, the number of complaints to the Uganda Human Rights Commission remains steady. Between 2003 and 2004, the commission received almost 4,000 complaints.

Under pressure from the United Nations to honor the obligations undertaken in the Brussels Declaration and the Programme of Action for the Least Developed Countries for the Decade 2001–2010, the Ugandan government has initiated a number of reforms in the area of criminal justice. In November 2001, the Community Service Act was implemented. This statute provides that an offender may be sentenced to spend a number of hours working pro bono at a public institution as part of the court's ordered punishment. This measure has contributed to a partial decongestion of prisons and has saved the Ugandan government more than 1.35 billion shillings in anticipated costs of maintaining prisoners in custody. Other initiatives to improve the state of the prison system involve a renovation project of dilapidated infrastructures and the construction of new offices; enhanced machinery and equipment—for example, in prison farms to build self-sustainability in food production for inmates; the purchase of vehicles to ease transportation of prisoners attending trials in courts; and the recruitment of prison officers and wardens to increase the staff-to-prisoner ratio from 1:9 to 1:6 toward the targeted international standard ratio of 1:3.

Roberta Belli and Sheila Atim-Scheijgrond

Further Reading

Allen, Tim. (2006). *Trial Justice: The International Criminal Court and the Lord's Resistance Army.* African Arguments. London and New York: Zed Books.

Nasaba, Alfred P. W. (1998). "Right to a Fair Trial: The Uganda Perspective." In *The Right to a Fair Trial,* edited by David S. Weissbrodt and Rüdiger Wolfrum, pp. 241–285. Beiträge Zum Ausländischen Öffentlichen Recht Und Völkerrecht. Vol. Bd. 129. Berlin and New York: Springer.

Nsereko, David D. N. (1995). "Criminal Law and Procedure in Uganda." In *International Encyclopaedia of Laws,* edited by Lieven Dupont and Cyrille Fijnaut, pp. 1–326. Deventer, The Netherlands, and Boston: Kluwer Law International Publishers.

Tibatemwa-Ekirikubinza, Lillian. (2005). *Criminal Law in Uganda: Sexual Assaults and Offences against Morality.* Fountain Series in Law and Business Studies. Kampala: Fountain Publishers.

Zambia

Legal System: Common/Customary
Murder: Medium
Burglary: High
Corruption: Medium
Human Trafficking: Medium
Prison Rate: Medium
Death Penalty: Yes
Corporal Punishment: No

Background

Zambia is bordered by eight countries: Mozambique, Zimbabwe, Botswana, Namibia, Angola, the Democratic Republic of the Congo, Tanzania, and Malawi. It is also multiethnic with the Banta-speaking ethnic groups forming the majority. The changing sociopolitical contexts from the 1960s through the dawn of the 21st century in Zambia have been extensively chronicled from the constitutional and economic perspectives. They have had and continue to have both positive and negative consequences on crime and punishment in the country. Zambia was an English colony until 1964 when it became independent. English is the official language, and Bemba, Lozi, Nyanja, and Tonga are among the major languages. It has over 70 ethnic groups spread over 9 provinces and is the home to the spectacular Victoria Falls along the Zambezi river. Zambia was the third-largest copper producer in the world after the United States and the Soviet Union in the 1960s and was considered one of the continent's richest countries but became one of the poorest when copper prices crashed in the mid-1960s.

Mr. Kenneth Kaunda, referred to as the father of the nation, ruled Zambia for more than two decades until a multiparty system was established in 1991. This change occurred with the enactment of a new constitution that increased the size of the National Assembly from 136 members to a maximum of 158 members, established an electoral commission, and allowed for more than one party. The executive branch is headed by the president who is elected by popular vote for a five-year term and who appoints the cabinet from among the elected members of the national assembly. The Constitution was amended again in 1996 to set term limits for the president and a requirement that both parents of a presidential candidate be Zambian-born.

Legal System

The unicameral National Assembly consists of 158 seats, of which 150 members are elected by popular vote and the remaining nominated by the president. The judicial system is based on English common law and customary law. The president appoints the chief justice and eight justices to the Supreme Court, the apex court. The president, along with the prime minister, appoints the director of public prosecution and the attorney general. The attorney general serves as the principal legal adviser to the government. Common law is administered by several high courts, which have authority to hear criminal and civil cases and appeals from lower courts. Resident magistrates' courts are also established at various centers. Local courts mainly administer customary law, especially cases relating to marriage, property, and inheritance. The government respects the independence of the judiciary, and trials in magistrate courts are public.

Police

The Zambian police service is located in the Ministry of Home Affairs and has approximately 14,000 officers. The inspector general of police (IG) is the head of the department and appointed by the president. The IG of police is supported by the commissioner of police (COMPOL), who is also appointed by the president of Zambia. Various deputy commissioners of police (DCP) support various divisions.

The criteria for police recruitment, selection, and basic training are not as rigorous as for the gazetted (or senior) police officers who were exclusively European. They could be characterized to be based on hunches and ingenuity or as the senior officers saw fit. On the other hand, the criteria for recruitment, selection, and training of the senior officers were the generally applicable ones throughout the British Empire, with room for modification to suit the territorial sociopolitical contexts. Structural problems in the police department hinder effective policing. The heavily centralized structure leads to delays in decision making and implementation. All the police posts in the country report to one of the nine provincial stations, and these in turn report to the central station.

The organized structure of the police force breaks into two categories: mainstream and the special units. The police headquarters are located in the capital, Lusaka, and regional headquarters are located in each of the provinces. District headquarters are located in each province, as are police stations. The special police units include the Mobile Unit or the Paramilitary Battalion, the Mounted Section, the Marine Service, the Prosecutorial Branch, and the Police Training School.

According to article 104 of the Zambia Constitution, the police functions in the postcolonial era include protection of life and property; preserving law and order; detection and prevention of crime; and cooperation with civilian authorities and security organs, in particular the director of public prosecutions in the Ministry of Legal Affairs.

The Zambian police force is enlisted as a component of INTERPOL's Sub-Regional Bureau for Southern Africa, which includes Angola, Botswana, Lesotho, Madagascar, Malawi, Mauritius, Mozambique, Namibia, South Africa, Swaziland, Zambia, and Zimbabwe. As such, it tends to share some of the attributes of the police services in other countries. The Bureau of Democracy, Human Rights, and Labor in 2004 criticized Zambian police for numerous human rights abuses, including reported extrajudicial killings by the police during the year.

Contributing factors to these abuses were identified as follows:

1. Inadequate training in investigation skills, leading to improper handling of suspects.
2. Insufficient knowledge of human rights law.
3. The absence of a national forensic laboratory, resulting in the application of underhanded methods by overzealous officers.
4. Lack of adequate financial resources and logistical support.
5. Supervising officers' reluctance to expose perpetrators of torture to disciplinary action.

As part of police reforms, the Zambia Police Act was amended (Zambia Police [Amendment] Act number 14 of 1999) to create victim support units in all police stations; to establish the Police Public Complaints Authority, whose members have since been appointed and which is now operational; and to designate custody officers. Despite the spirit of the law, observers such as Human Rights Watch and the Consultative Group characterize Zambian police reform to be very slow.

The Police Public Complaints Authority was created upon the amendment of the Zambia Police Act (cap. 107). Its is required to receive and investigate complaints against police actions and submit its findings and recommendations to the director of public prosecutions and inspector general for disciplinary action or to the Anti-Corruption Commission or any other relevant body or authority.

A review of the police training curriculum was completed during the late 1990s. Among others, the minimum educational requirement was elevated to completion of secondary education. Also now included in the curriculum is sensitivity to human rights with a view to cutting down the number of human rights violations.

A victim support unit was established in 1994. Its inclusion is comprehensive throughout the country. Its offices are located not only at the headquarters and regional offices but also at both the district and local station levels. The jurisdiction of this unit includes both criminal and civil cases involving particularly vulnerable women and children. It has had foreign support, including transportation donations in the form of bicycles and funds for capacity building.

A Police Professional Standard Unit was added in July 2003. Among other things, it conducts investigations pertaining to corruption, abuse of power, and other related extrajudicial activities. It is headed by a senior police prosecutions officer.

HIV/AIDS is a serious problem in the Zambian police department. Estimates suggest about 21 out of the roughly 14,000 officers may be dying of AIDS each month, which translates to about 254 personnel each year. Further, it is estimated that more than 3,000 personnel died of AIDS between January 1991 and April 2003.

Crime

Crime Statistics

There has been a scarcity of official crime statistics. Old crime statistics published in the *World Encyclopedia of Police Forces and Penal Systems* cite the number of crimes reported to police in 1984 as follows:

Murder	569
Sex offenses including rape	456
Rape	341
Serious assault	23,056
All theft	58,864
Robbery and violent theft	3,567
Breaking and entering	25,226
Auto theft	1,173
Fraud	651
Counterfeiting	96
Drug offenses	356
Total offenses	**150,311**

Though recent systematic crime data are not available, Chikwanha in a report in 2007 noted that armed carjacking, mugging, residential burglaries, and petty theft are common occurrences in Lusaka, the Zambian capital. She also noted that burglary victimization was reported by an estimated 10.9 percent of respondents in 2003 in the same region, and the crime of child rape in Zambia had increased by up to 60 percent. According to the NationMaster

Web site, there were a total 59,426 recorded crimes in that year. Of these, 797 were murders; 300 rapes; 2,699 robberies; and 792 car thefts.

Classification of Crime

The conventional crimes include petty theft, assaults, larceny, murder, mugging, burglaries, and armed carjacking, especially in urban areas. Crime and corruption in Zambia have been widely reported by the media. It is public knowledge that members of organized crime—the mafias—have been outwitting the police service in southern Africa of which Zambia is a part.

Zambia was among the more than 40 African countries that became signatories to the United Nations Convention on Organized Crime at the dawn of the 21st century. Its deputy secretary of home affairs spoke loud and clear about the importance of joint efforts to stamp out the menace of organized crime as a transnational crime.

Prostitution

Prostitution, especially child prostitution, has become a pervasive social problem in Zambia, particularly in urban areas. A national survey of the magnitude of this social problem has yet to be documented. On the other hand, many observers seem to have opinions as to its causes as well as impact. In the former case, the causal factors include poverty, Western values, urban migration, school dropout, and unemployment and underemployment. The commonly cited forms of impact are infection with HIV, orphanage, divorce, and criminal activities related to prostitution. Unfortunately, the victims of these social ills are more often than not considered to be the "forgotten" and "voiceless" people.

Street Children

Physical abuse and exploitation of children are known to occur along with missing children, including those who have succumbed to death resulting from HIV/AIDS. Responses to street children vary from the public sector to the private sector. Segments of the former, including the police and the Ministry of Labor, have been ad hoc in the absence of comprehensive national legislation as well as policies. Some semblance of a dent in the problem of the street children has come from the stakeholders in the private sector. These stakeholders include the local and foreign NGOs. Their efforts include the establishment of shelters, fund-raising, and special projects geared toward prevention and control of HIV/AIDS. The U.S. Agency for International Development (USAID) and UNICEF joined the efforts to launch a network of local NGOs and community-based organizations early in the 21st century.

Wildlife Crimes

There are prisoners serving time for conviction for wildlife crimes. This penalty derives from the Zambia Wildlife Act No. 12 of 1998. The nature and form of other penalties vary from one wildlife crime to another. In its efforts to prevent and control wildlife crimes, Zambia joined forces with five other African countries, namely, the Democratic Republic of the Congo, Kenya, Lesotho, Tanzania, and Uganda, to set up an international task force that is now called the Lusaka Agreement on Cooperative Enforcement Operations.

Border Crimes

Border crimes abound in southern Africa in general and Zambia in particular. The responsibility for their prevention and control has belonged to both the Southern African Regional Police Chiefs Cooperative Organization and the Zambian police service.

The southern African region comprises Angola, Botswana, Lesotho, Malawi, Mauritius, Mozambique, Namibia, South Africa, Swaziland, Tanzania, Zambia, and Zimbabwe. These crimes have been committed by perpetrators at large, by bad apples in the ranks of the national police forces, and by some of the retired soldiers, and the Southern African Regional Police Chiefs Cooperation Organization was formed to, among other things, police border crimes, but they suffer poor resources. Its members are primarily the senior police executives from each country. These members meet once a year.

Human Trafficking

An estimated 563,000 children between the ages of 5 and 17 were found in 2000 to be involved in some form of domestic labor or prostitution according to a Zambian government report. Child trafficking for labor is primarily related to work in quarries, stone breaking, household work, cooking in markets, and labor such as construction and carpentry. Minors are at greater risk of being pushed into prostitution in border towns and along trucking routes, particularly along the border between Zambia and Zimbabwe, where truck drivers wait for days to cross the border. Trafficking in female children is also related to sex tourism. The most common place is Livingston, located above Victoria Falls, which has the highest incidence of HIV/AIDS in Zambia, at around 30 percent. Though Zambia has legislation on the protection of children's rights in judicial proceedings, it does not fully comply with the goals of the Convention on the Rights of the Child.

Finding of Guilt

The Zambian Constitution stipulates not only the structure but also the management and operations of the country's courts. In the former case, the court structure includes the following components: The upper-level courts are known as the Supreme Court and the high courts; their counterparts are the local courts and the magistrates' courts. The Supreme Court is strictly limited to appeals; the high courts conduct both trials in major cases and appeals from the magistrates' courts. The local courts have jurisdiction in cases involving customary law, whereas the magistrates' courts are the courts of first instance and summary jurisdiction.

The majority of the rural population relies on customary law administered by local leaders who are not generally considered part of the judicial system in the Zambian Constitution. In spite of this weakness, many citizens use customary justice because of the inaccessibility of the state system. Customary law is also applied by local courts, which occupy the lowest position in the constitutional hierarchy of the Zambian courts. Though the local court structures are part of the formal legal system, they appear to be in trouble because there is no overview or administrative control of the cases that move through the court system. Often, local chiefs are asked to recommend potential candidates for court administration who are knowledgeable of the local customs and who are then given access to considerable power and influence over the institution of justice. Women use the customary courts often for such family-related issues as domestic violence, adultery, and divorce.

Courts are generally congested, and there are significant delays in trials, with a large number held in detention while awaiting trial. In many instances, it may take six months before a magistrate sends a defendant through to the high court. It usually takes the magistrate months to prepare the court record, and once the high-court proceedings begin, they can last over six months. One of the reasons cited for the delay is a high turnover in judicial and court personnel, which is often a result of poor pay and poor working conditions. The increased use of alternatives to imprisonment for minor crimes—community service, probation, and fines—has also been attributed to these courts.

Prosecution of Offenders

The prosecution of offenders is under the jurisdiction of the directors of the department of public prosecution and the police service. The latter does its business primarily in the magistrates' courts, whereas its counterpart works in the Supreme Court and high courts and other courts subject to the provisions of the Constitution.

Punishment

The Zambian penal concepts and practices are aligned with those of the United Kingdom. The definitions of crimes both serious and less serious accrue from the penal code, as is the case with the provisions for their corresponding punishments. Capital punishment is a sentence for murder except in military circumstances, treason, and aggravated robbery. Conviction for trafficking of women and children carries the sentence of between 20 years and life in prison.

Prisons

The administration of the Zambian prisons is conducted within the framework of the Prisons Act and related legislation including the Constitution. The commissioner of prisons is a presidential appointee. The day-to-day administration is strictly defined by the Prisons Act. Zambia is the only African country whose minister of home affairs was an ordained reverend in the 1990s through the dawn of the 21st century. His preaching to prisoners in the industrial region—the Copperbelt—has been extensively reported by the media.

Conditions are harsh and life-threatening in Zambia prisons. Some of the reasons cited are severe overcrowding, inadequate food supplies, lack of potable water, and unhygienic unsanitary conditions. A similar situation applies to inmates in remand awaiting trial. Outbreaks of tuberculosis and dysentery are common medical concerns. The report submitted by the commissioner of prisons submitted to Parliament in 1996 indicated that 975 prisoners had died in prison between January 1991 and December 1995 as a result of illness and harsh conditions. Overcrowding was also a major concern in Zambian prisons, and the Kamwala Remand Prison in Lusaka at one time was operating at three times its capacity. In March 2000, the commissioner of prisons cited slow disposition of cases in courts (resulting in higher numbers of those detained awaiting trial) as a reason for overcrowding, which led to the Magistrates and Judges Association of Zambia decision to make efforts to release all eligible detainees on bail to reduce prison congestion.

The Zambian Prisons Act provides for visits and inspections by officials in their capacity as "visiting justices"; judges, magistrates, the minister of home affairs, and provincial ministers are examples of these officials. Part 19 of the Prisons Act stipulates that during their visits, they must inspect all management and discipline records, visit every part of the prison and see every prisoner, assess the quality and quantity of the food, inquire into complaints by prisoners, and ensure compliance with all standing orders.

HIV/AIDS in the Prisons

It has not been uncommon for the prison staff to make negative commentaries about the prison victims of HIV/AIDS. There have been reports that some of the prison staff have preyed on inmates, especially the young female offenders. There are hardly any accounts of successful strategies on the part of prison authorities to solve the problem of recalcitrant prisoners with respect to repeat sexual activities resulting in the spread of HIV/AIDS. Prison authorities have resorted to segregation or isolation, maximum security, behavior readjustment, and placement in special units dealing with especially violent inmates as stipulated by the Prisons Act and Standing Orders since the colonial era.

Juvenile Justice and Institutions

Since the colonial era, the penal authorities have on occasion had to make three choices in cases of juveniles: detain juvenile offenders in the adult prisons; segregate them into their own institutions, such as the approved schools and the reformatories; or establish alternatives to detention in the public institutions.

Zambia not only is one of the signatories to the United Nations Standard Minimum Rules for the Administration of Juvenile Justice, but also practices some of these rules. The Juveniles Act (chapter 53 of the Laws of Zambia) makes provision for the custody and protection of juveniles in need of care and for the correction of juvenile delinquents. Among other things, these rules emphasize procedural safeguards, including presumption of innocence, use of discretion given the varying needs of juvenile offenders, provisions of alternatives to detention (e.g., community-based diversion), specialization within the police, special police units, and competent authority to adjudicate.

Resurrection of the Crime Prevention Foundation of Zambia

The Crime Prevention Foundation of Zambia, a nonprofit organization, was resurrected in 2006. Its mandate include promoting awareness and education; coordinating units and their operation; and providing technical assistance to organizations that deal with victims of crime, ex-prisoners, and offenders in the country's criminal justice system.

Ejakait (J. S. E.) Opolot

Further Reading

Chikwanha, A. B. (2007). "Zambia—Crime and Criminal Justice." In *Human Security Initiative:* http://www.africanreview.org/docs/zambia/zambiaissue07.pdf.

International Labor Organization–International Program on the Elimination of Child Labor. (2003). *HIV/AIDS and Child Labor in Zambia: A Rapid Assessment.* Geneva: International Labor Organization.

University of Minnesota Human Rights Library. (2001). "Committee against Torture, Consideration of Reports Submitted by States Parties under Article 19 of the Convention." Zambia, U.N. Doc. CAT/C/47/Add.2.

USAID Congressional Presentation (1997). "Zambia": http://www.usaid.gov/pubs/cp97/countries/zm.htm.

Zimbabwe

Legal System: Civil/Common/Customary
Murder: High
Burglary: High
Corruption: High
Human Trafficking: Medium
Prison Rate: Medium
Death Penalty: Yes
Corporal Punishment: Yes

Background

Geographically located in southern Africa, Zimbabwe, also known as the Republic of Zimbabwe, has a population of approximately 11.6 million. This landlocked country borders South Africa, Botswana, Zambia, and Mozambique. It is divided into 10 provinces, with two metropolitan cities having provincial status.

The official language of Zimbabwe is English; however, the majority of the natives speak Shona. Zimbabwe was known as Southern Rhodesia when it was a self-governing colony claimed by the United Kingdom. By the 1970s, many Zimbabwe natives sought violent means to gain independence. A formal agreement proclaiming Zimbabwe's independence was reached in 1979 between the key players, the British government, the African National Union, and the African People's Union. Since its independence in 1980, the African National Union led by President Robert Mugabe has dominated all aspects of the criminal justice system. Currently, deteriorating economic stability and a HIV/AID epidemic plague Zimbabwe.

Zimbabwe operates under a parliamentary democracy. Foreign nations debated this after questioning the past three elections. Although Zimbabwe's Constitution allows for multiple parties to run in an election, the ruling party has consistently used intimidation and manipulation to control the national security forces and committed abuses against those parties running in opposition.

The legal system is a mixture of Roman-Dutch and English common law. At the head of the executive branch lies a majority-elected president who is both chief of state and head of government. The president is elected for a term of five years with no term limit. The president is responsible for appointing two vice presidents and many upper-level administrators in the public service sector, along with both the legislative and the judicial branch. Zimbabwe employs a bicameral legislature. The upper house, the Senate, contains 93 seats, 15 of which are nominated or appointed to the chamber by the president; the House of Assembly, the lower chamber, contains 210 seats all elected by popular vote.

Zimbabwe's Constitution is the supreme law of the nation and calls for an independent judiciary. There are five sources of Zimbabwean law: legislation; case law, or court decisions and precedent; customary law; common law; and authoritative texts. Besides criminal law, the majority of Zimbabwean laws are uncodified. The president appoints judges, typically, to serve until the age of 65. Terms may be extended if the judge remains in good physical and mental health. The Zimbabwe Constitution provides that judges may be removed from the bench only for gross misconduct, and they cannot be discharged or transferred for political reasons. Recent concerns regarding judiciary independence rose in 2001 when the judiciary came under intense pressure to conform to the current government policies.

The responsibility of enforcing the law falls between the Zimbabwe Republic Police and two divisions of the Zimbabwe armed forces: army (ZNA) and air force (AFZ). Zimbabwe has no navy because it is landlocked between other countries. After proclaiming independence in 1980, Zimbabwe set up two national armed forces. Currently, the Zimbabwe National Army has approximately 30,000 active duty members, and the air force approximates that it has around 5,000 active members. Zimbabwe Republic Police (ZRP) law enforcement capabilities have seen dramatic deterioration in recent years, largely as a result of Zimbabwe's economic decline. Because of a lack of sufficient funding, the police are unable to maintain and operate equipment or train new personnel. They have nearly no ability to respond to emergencies; in the case of criminal activity, the police typically need to be provided with a means of transportation to perform any investigative function. Due to the police's limited mobility, criminal incidents must be reported in person to the nearest police station. Given these issues, the ZRP tend to be apathetic toward investigating crime, and as previously stated, they prefer to focus their resources and energies on political acts, especially demonstrations. The ZRP estimate their membership to be approximately 25,000. The police are divided into a variety of units including a uniformed national police, the Criminal Investigation Department, and traffic police. To support each provincial department, the ZRP also includes a paramilitary Police Support Unit, a riot unit, and a Police Internal Security and Intelligence unit. Under the command of the police commissioner-general, who like other upper administrators is appointed by the president, the ZRP is organized by province. The majority of the ZRP patrols the highly urbanized capital, Harare.

Crime

According to the U.S. Department of State, the reported crime in Zimbabwe is a very serious problem and has been shown to be driven by the country's recently deteriorating economy. One of the most prevalent and serious crimes in Zimbabwe is street crime; Americans and other foreign visitors are typically perceived as being wealthy and have found themselves the targets of criminals operating in the close vicinity of hotels, restaurants, and shopping areas in major cities and tourist locales. Purse-snatching is another form of street crime in which teams of two work together, with one of the teammates acting as a diversion. Muggings typically involve younger males who surround and overwhelm their victims in a populated area. The U.S. Department of State lists the majority of crimes in Zimbabwe as being nonviolent, though most of the perpetrators are armed with weapons that usually include firearms. Cellular phones are of great interest to local thieves. Another typical crime is "smash and grab" where thieves break windows of cars at intersections and remove items from inside. Kidnapping is also a crime that has been frequently connected to the political arena; several members of opposing groups have found themselves tied up and left in remote areas or taken into custody of the ZRP and treated poorly under harsh conditions. In 2003, there were 35 reports of politically motivated "disappearances," mostly committed by ZANU-PF supporters, especially in the rural areas where most organized groups were loyal to the government and where there were few opposition organizations. Domestic human rights organizations believe that there were disappearances in rural areas that were not reported because of fear of retribution by pro-government factions. Many abductees were beaten or tortured; others later were found killed.

The country of Zimbabwe has a Ministry of Home Affairs Web site that contains the only statistical data available. This "Crime Statistics Report" details only white-collar crime for the years 2000–2001, providing minimal and vague information, though indicating that white-collar crime (possibly comprising corruption, tax evasion, other crime related to gold trading and precious stones, and currency exchange) increased by some 54 percent from 200 to 2001. The Overseas Security Advisory Council notes an increase in crime rates during 2007, though most of these crimes are nonviolent and less serious. However, the downtown sector remains a concern, especially at night when thieves act with little fear of police.

There are no laws that specifically address trafficking in persons, and there continue to be anecdotal reports that the country is both a point of origin and a transit path for trafficking. Common law prohibits abduction and forced labor, and it is a crime under the Sexual Offenses Act (SOA) to transport persons across the border for sex. Traffickers also can be prosecuted under other legislation such as immigration and abduction laws. The SOA provides for a maximum fine of $0.41 (Z$35 thousand) or imprisonment of up to 7 years for those convicted of prostituting children under 12 years of age. It also provides for a maximum fine of $0.58 (Z$50 thousand) and a maximum prison sentence of 10 years for procuring another person for prostitution or to have sex inside or outside the country. Little information exists on the trafficking of humans beyond known instances for sexual encounters in exchange for money.

Finding of Guilt

Those accused of a crime in Zimbabwe are protected under the Constitution, which provides the right to a fair trial; the judiciary rigorously enforces this right. However, under Mugabe, the judiciary's reputation for independence from the executive branch has been compromised, with the executive refashioning the courts to conform to personal opinions. The law requires that the ZRP inform an arrested individual of the charges against him or her before being taken the person into custody; warrants of arrest issued by the courts are required except in cases of serious crimes or where there is the risk of evidence disappearing. There is a growing problem, especially in rural areas, in which victims or witnesses of crimes who inform the police are charged themselves with the crimes of the perpetrators. According to law, a preliminary hearing before a magistrate must be held within 48 hours of arrest, 96 hours over a weekend. The law typically is disregarded if the accused does not have legal representation. To delay the bail release hearing, the police typically conduct arrests of individuals accused of political crimes.

In general, detainees are not afforded prompt or regular access to their lawyers, with the authorities often informing lawyers who attempt to visit their clients that detainees were "not available." It is also not uncommon for family members to be denied access unless accompanied by an attorney. Detainees, especially those from rural areas without legal representation, routinely are held without communication, leaving family members and attorneys unable to verify that the individual has been detained until he or she is scheduled to appear in court.

Zimbabwean law provides for a unitary court system, consisting of headmen's courts, chiefs' courts, magistrates' courts, the High Court, and the Supreme Court. Civil and customary law cases may be heard at all levels of the judiciary, including the Supreme Court. Military courts deal with disciplinary proceedings; police courts, which can sentence a police officer to confinement in a camp or demotion, handle disciplinary and misconduct cases involving police. Trials in both these courts generally meet internationally accepted standards for fair trials. All accused have the right to appeal to the Supreme Court.

In criminal cases, an impoverished defendant may apply to have the government provide an attorney, but this is granted rarely. In capital cases, the government provides an attorney for all defendants unable to afford one. Those litigants in civil cases can request legal assistance from the NGO Legal Resources Foundation, and all litigants are represented in the High Court. According to the U.S. Department of State, the Zimbabwe Supreme Court instructs its magistrates to ensure that unrepresented defendants fully understand their rights and to weigh any mitigating circumstances in criminal cases, whether or not the accused presents them as part of his or her defense. According to the Zimbabwe Constitution, the right to appeal exists in all cases and is automatically granted in cases in which the death penalty is imposed. Trials remain open to the public except in circumstance involving national security issues. The Zimbabwe Constitution outlines several rights for defendants. Those accused of crimes are presumed innocent until proven guilty. Defendants also enjoy the right to present witnesses and the right to question witnesses against them. Defense attorneys and their clients generally have access to the government-held evidence relevant to their cases.

Punishment

As with the lack of current and reliable crime statistics, relevant information regarding the types of punishment is also not disclosed by the Zimbabwean government. What is understood from the little published information is that the court compiles reports and recommendations regarding appropriate punishments for individual offenders. Besides imprisonment, the Ministry of Justice, Legal, and Parliamentary Affairs mentions the utilization of community service as a proper punishment. Capital punishment exists within the country, but it is unclear what type of conviction must be made for this to occur, though it appears that the rate of usage is low.

Prisons

Zimbabwe's prison system contains 42 prisons divided among four regional headquarters, with the largest and most central prison in the national capital, Harare. Zimbabwe's current prison conditions remain harsh and life-threatening, as prisons nationwide suffer from overcrowding. According to the Ministry of Justice, Legal, and Parliamentary Affairs, the combined holding capacity for the 42 prisons is approximately 17,000 prisoners; however, the ministry estimated the inmate population in 2007 to be fluctuating around 18,000. This estimate seems to represent a low approximation because in that same year, the U.S. Department of State estimated the inmate population to be around 25,000. Of the total prison population, approximately 70 percent are convicted prisoners, and the other 30 percent are awaiting trial. The majority of the Zimbabwe inmate population is between the ages of 18 and 40 years. Female prisoners represent only 3 percent of the total inmate population. An inspection done in December 2004 by the Law Society of Zimbabwe (LSZ) at Khami Maximum Prison in Bulawayo revealed that the prison, which had been built to accommodate 650 prisoners, actually housed 1,167 inmates.

In 2006, convicted juveniles represented 1.8 percent of the total inmate population; however, presently, they are not held separately from adults. The Prison Fellowship of Zimbabwe, a local Christian organization working with former inmates, has estimated that there are more than 200 children living in the country's prison system with their detained mothers. Prison cells are divided into groups to separate pretrial detainees from convicted offenders. Large group cells typically hold pretrial detainees until their bail hearing, and once charged, the detainees are moved to separate remand prisons.

According to the Ministry of Justice, Legal, and Parliamentary Affairs, unconvicted detainees are permitted one visitor per week. For convicted prisoners, the number of visits depends on the inmate's classification. Prisoners in class A, the lowest security risk, are granted up to three visitors once every two weeks. Prisoners in class B are permitted two visitors once every two weeks for a period of time not exceeding 20 minutes. Class C prisoners are granted two visitors once every two weeks for a period of time not exceeding 15 minutes. Class D prisoners, the highest security risk, are permitted one visitor once a month for a duration not exceeding 15 minutes. According to the ministry's Web site, class A and B prisoners are permitted to work in the prison in areas such as the cafeteria or cleaning. At this time, no credible sources suggest that

Part of a group of 150 former inmates leave a prison in Harare, Zimbabwe, on September 11, 2009. The inmates are among 1,500 prisoners being released across the country under a presidential amnesty program designed to ease overcrowding. (AP Photo)

movement between countries is legal for prisoners of Zimbabwe.

Megan Beckwith and Jennifer Janowski

Further Reading

Overseas Advisory Council. (2008). *Zimbabwe 2008 Crime & Safety Report:* https://www.osac.gov/Reports/report.cfm?contentID=80864.

U.S. Department of State. (2004). *International Religious Freedom Report 2004:* http://www.state.gov/g/drl/rls/irf/2004/35390.htm.

Zimbabwe Ministry of Justice, Legal, and Parliamentary Affairs. (2007). http://www.justice.gov.zw/zimba.html.

Zimbabwe Republic Police (ZRP). *Crime Statistics Report:* http://www.moha.gov.zw/.

Middle East and North Africa

Algeria

Legal System: Islamic/Civil
Murder: Low
Corruption: Medium
Human Trafficking: High
Prison Rate: Medium
Death Penalty: No
Corporal Punishment: Maybe

Background

Algeria is situated in the northern African region known as the Maghreb, with an estimated population of more than 33 million. It is about 2.4 million square kilometers in area and is the second-largest country in Africa after Sudan. Almost since the beginning of written history, Algeria has been conquered and recolonized by larger empires. As a result, the laws, culture, and criminal justice system have been the product of the amalgamation of different cultures over the centuries.

To maintain order within the country, several forms of policing have risen to prominence over the years. The type of policing enforced depended on who was exercising colonial or political control over the country. Although the Ottomans had their own system of government and law enforcement during their rule, the French National Gendarmerie system has had a far greater influence on modern policing in Algeria. As a result, there are three major organizational divisions in Algerian law enforcement: the Gendarmerie National, the Sûreté Nationale, and the Sûreté Militaire. The National Gendarmerie serves as a fully national police force that answers directly to one central authority, much like the current system in France. For the most part, the National Gendarmerie serves as the security and law enforcement force in the rural and remote mountain regions of the nation. The Sûreté Nationale (National Security) force is a police agency that was formed after the French left Algeria in 1962. This force focuses on urban areas and, like the National Gendarmerie, is based on the French system. The final branch of Algerian law enforcement is the Sûreté Militaire (Military Security or SM). The Sûreté Militaire is in charge of foreign and domestic intelligence, military offenses, and civilian espionage and subversion. For American audiences, they are similar to a combination of the FBI, CIA, and military police. It is a relatively large force with between 6,000 and 10,000 officers, and the group answers directly to a general who reports to the minister of national defense within the Ministry of the Interior. The use of the SM, which is also known as the Département du renseignement et de la sécurité (DRS), became somewhat controversial in the civil war following the invalidation of the 1991 election. Amnesty International has written reports on some of the agency's tactics. During the civil war, there were many reports of secret detention and the creation of situations that would facilitate the torture of prisoners and persons of interest. Additionally, controversy surrounds the use of the military as law enforcement, which stems from speculation about the military's involvement with terrorism in the country. For example, several individuals have accused the military of setting up false road blocks to allow terrorists to commit attacks. However, there is no concrete evidence that the SM were ever involved in any such attacks.

Others were concerned over the complete carte blanche that the military received to fight terror without regard for individual rights or civil liberties. Several reports indicate that the military slaughtered civilians in an attempt to root out suspected Islamic militants. Concerns have also risen regarding the secretive tactics used by the Military Security forces. For instance, members of the SM will go incommunicado while infiltrating the various terrorist organizations that have riddled the countryside from time to time. Because of this, it is often difficult to determine to what extent the officers have remained loyal to the state as opposed to joining the terrorist cause. Although there is some skepticism as to the SM's loyalties, the United States has put much faith into communicating with the Algerian military in recent years. Since the election of President Abdelaziz Bouteflika, American forces have been working in concert with Algerians to fight the war on terror and the threat of the Salafist Group for Preaching and Combat (GSPC).

Although 90 percent of the country lives within 20 percent of the Algerian landmass known as the Tell, there is still a need to police the other 80 percent of Algerian territory. These unique needs are addressed by the National Gendarmerie, the force that patrols the remote areas of the country. The gendarmerie is over 35,000 officers strong and is organized into battalions responsible for policing the 48 provinces known as *wilayat.* The battalions are highly mobile forces that are very well connected through well-developed communication systems. The gendarmerie officers are rigorously trained and well equipped. For instance, they are known to have at their disposal several light armored vehicles and helicopters for patrol and mobility in remote and inhospitable areas. Like the Military Security, the gendarmerie falls under the auspices of the minister of the interior.

Finally, the National Security (SN) force is the main police presence in Algerian urban areas. They exercise jurisdictional responsibility for the capitals of the wilayat and other major cities. They serve as the main police force for maintaining order, enforcing laws, and controlling crime. Within the SN, there are branches in charge of law and order, as well as judicial police that serve as the main investigators and detectives for crimes. Along with the Military Security forces, the SN assists in the control of public uprisings and are trained in riot control techniques.

Crime

Following independence, the Algerian government borrowed heavily from the French judicial system. Like the French, the Algerians use a codified system known as a penal code to outline crimes and corresponding punishments for those crimes. The Algerian penal code dictates a range of severity of punishment for particular crimes as a guideline. For example, unintentional fire setting that endangers others is punishable with a prison sentence between 6 months and 3 years and a fine of 10,000 to 20,000 dinars (approx. US$155–310). Also similar to the French system, the Algerian penal code classifies offenses based on the degree of seriousness of that offense.

Types of Crime

Offenses are classified, in order of seriousness, as a crime, délit, or contravention. As listed in the penal code, a "crime" is a very serious offense that is punishable by death or extremely long prison sentences. In the Algerian law system, a crime would be akin to *mala in se* offenses, such as rape and murder, in common law systems. Algerian crimes carry heavy penalties. Although the death penalty has not been used since 2003, many crimes are death-eligible offenses.

Firefighters begin removal of the remains of a car bomb that exploded in the center of Algiers on May 25, 1999. The explosion killed three people and wounded five others. (AP Photo)

Other punishments include 20 years to life in prison without the opportunity of parole. The punishment section of this entry further discusses the penalties that are available for Algerian offenses.

The second most serious offense is known as a délit. Délits are offenses that can be punished with shorter imprisonment sentences, fines, or both. An example of a délit in Algeria would be abandoning one's family for longer than two months without having a "good" reason to do so. As an Islamic nation, Algeria is very concerned with the well-being and preservation of families. As such, there are many offenses written into the penal code that address offenses against the family. In addition to offenses against families, délits include disruption of the public good. An example of a disruption of the public good would be threatening another individual either verbally or with images or other symbols.

The final degree of seriousness is that of contravention. In common law terms, a contravention is most comparable to a misdemeanor offense. There are varying degrees of seriousness within the category of contraventions. In Algeria, there are three levels of seriousness for contraventions. The most serious of offenses, the First Category offenses, include penalties of imprisonment up to two months and fines up to 1,000 dinars (US$16). Examples of First Category offenses would be animal baiting or unnecessarily killing of domestic or work animals.

Second Category offenses carry fines up to 500 dinars (US$8) and/or five days in prison. Individuals who deface buildings with graffiti face such a penalty. The Third Category of offenses carry fines between 30 and 100 dinars (between US$.47 and US$1.60) and include such crimes as neglecting to maintain, clean, or repair chimneys, ovens, or factories that use fire.

Various mitigating and aggravating circumstances are taken into consideration when classifying a crime, deciding culpability, determining guilt, and handing down sentence. Within this system of aggravating and mitigating circumstances, there are many distinctions made based on Islamic law. One might describe the Algerian penal code as based on the French system with influences from Islam. For example, within the Islamic law, a great deal of importance is placed on matters of family. As a result, there is a separate section of the penal code devoted to crimes and délits committed against family members. When determining the circumstances of a case of murder or manslaughter, there are stipulations within the code that allow for self-defense and circumstances that will reduce the sentence for a murder. However, the penal code clearly states that parricide cannot be mitigated, regardless of circumstance.

Special Crime Problems

Terrorism has been a major problem within Algeria over the last 20 years. Between 1970 and 2004, there were about 1,600 incidents of terrorism in Algeria. Using data from MIPT, NationMaster indicates that Algeria is ranked second in the world for the most terrorism when considering domestic terrorist attacks. Other reports put Algeria at approximately 19th overall for domestic terrorism between 1970 and 1997. There are also varying estimates of the number of lives lost during the civil war between 1992 and 2004, but a conservative estimate brings the total to around 100,000 deaths. Government reports were not forthcoming in the number of fatalities during the period and have given many different estimates of the number of deaths resulting from terrorism and violence in the 12-year span. The majority of those casualties were civilian targets.

These statistics are indicative of the grave problem that Algeria faced during the latter half of the 20th century and the first decade of the 21st century. The government understood the needs of the nation, and in 1995, Algeria added a special section to its penal code in an attempt to address these particular needs by aggressively combating the amount of terrorism that it faced.

Human trafficking is yet another crime problem that has received particular attention in Algeria in recent years. The UN's International Labor Organization defines human trafficking as a modern from of slavery in which individuals are bought and sold and coerced into performing sexual acts or involuntary labor. In 2006, Algeria was placed into the Tier 2 Watch List in the annual Tracking of Persons Report published by the U.S. State Department. The Tier 2 ranking indicates that Algeria does not fully comply with the minimum standards of protection against human trafficking and has failed to provide evidence of increasing efforts to combat human trafficking.

Drug Offenses

Unlike most of the North African countries, Algeria does not have a serious drug trafficking and production problem. Countries such as Morocco, Tunisia, and Egypt have long struggled with the task of curbing production and trafficking of marijuana and hashish. In fact, most of Europe receives its hashish from these North African countries. One of the potential reasons behind the hashish "problem" is the cultural usage of the drug. The Arabic and Berber cultures have a long history of using the drug in social settings. As a result, Morocco has become a famous destination for cannabis enthusiasts. Estimates put Morocco's production and sale of cannabis at approximately $4 billion per year. In recent years, there has been a crackdown on the transportation of hashish out of Morocco. The crackdown has sparked smuggling of the drugs into Algeria for sale in other regions of the world. In addition to the increased attention to drug smuggling, the global market has begun to focus on the role the drug money plays in the funding of terrorism. Although Algeria's role in the production and trade of the drug is minor at most, the terrorist group GSPC benefits from the sale of the drug through an elaborate and complex financial network. Also, according to the U.S. Department of State, Algeria has not been known to participate in extensive money laundering for the drug trade, but the State Department does recognize that Moroccans often use Algeria's border farmlands to grow their crops and to export them.

Statistics

For the most part, statistics on crime in Algeria are scarce. Those statistics that have been compiled are often questionable in regard to their reliability and validity. However, from what statistics are available, Algeria's murder rate for the period 2000–2004 was 1.4 murders per 100,000. It is also necessary to point out that a significant number of deaths from terrorism seem to be missing based on open source data that track terrorism fatalities. This may be the result of how the government counts murders versus terrorist attacks within the nation. Some crime analysts have noted that there was an increase in the number of offenses between 1999 and the early 2000s. However, this might not be an indicator of an upward trend but might instead be simply a reflection of an increased number of cars that can be stolen, a reporting artifact, or a change in reporting behavior on the part of crime victims or police. The following are the most recent statistics (crimes per 100,000 inhabitants) of reported offenses for major crime categories in 2000 as recorded by INTERPOL.

Murder and non-negligent manslaughter	1.49
Forcible rape	1.05
Robbery	10.58
Aggravated assault	42.58
Burglary	30.08
Larceny theft	106.59
Motor vehicle theft	6.34
Total	**259.76**

Although drug offenses have not been a large concern for Algerians over the past 20 years, there have been some modest drug seizures. Nonetheless, the level of drug enforcement activity has not approached the level of similar crackdowns in neighboring Morocco and Tunisia. Although Algeria has not experienced the same levels of illicit drug production, usage, or smuggling, analysts point to several potential risk factors for increased drug use. First, 70 percent of Algeria's population is 30 years old or younger. The youth of a population is often strongly correlated with crime and drug use in particular. Additionally, the high unemployment rate may be a factor that would contribute to drug use.

Finding of Guilt

The Algerian Constitution states that all arrestees are innocent until proven guilty. The Algerians, however, use the French tribunal system of judges as opposed to the American jury system. While in custody and awaiting trial, suspects are afforded a number of rights by law. For instance, upon arrest, individuals have the right to immediately contact their family. Although the Algerian Constitution makes this distinction, it is interesting from a Western perspective that no requirement for the presence of an attorney is mentioned, although free access to legal council is separately guaranteed. Suspects must also be released after 48 hours, and after that release, suspects have the right to receive a medical examination. In certain exceptional circumstances, the period of 48-hour detainment may be extended in accordance with the law. Interrogating a suspected terrorist would be considered an "exceptional circumstance."

Courts

Within the Algerian justice system, there are three different levels of courts. The lowest of the courts are known as the first instance courts and are administered on the *daira,* or district, level. There are 218 first instance courts that handle civil, commercial, and labor disputes as well as some low-level criminal cases. Above these courts are the *wilaya* courts.

These courts are divided into four different chambers for civil, criminal, administration, and accusation. The four chambers each have three judges and allow for appeals. *Wilaya* courts serve as the courts of appeal for the *daira* courts and are similar to the U.S. version of state courts, whereas *daira* courts are more comparable to county-level systems of justice. Within the *wilaya* system, there are courts of appeal. Appeals must be made on points of law and procedure as opposed to the interpretation of facts or additional information.

The court of final appeal in the Algerian justice system is the Supreme Court. It is the highest court in the land and located in Algiers. Like the lower *wilaya* courts, the Supreme Court is divided into four chambers. The Social Chamber of the Supreme Court focuses exclusively on issues of social security and labor disputes. The Public Chamber hears cases pertaining to civil and commercial disputes. The final two chambers deal with matters of criminal and administrative law. These chambers are, perhaps appropriately, named the Criminal Court and the Administrative Division, respectively. The Algerian Supreme Court does not issue legal decisions, and does not exercise jurisdiction over the actions of the Algerian government. Instead, the court only hears cases that are based on disputes over procedure. Finally, while not part of the civil court system, Military Tribunals were often used during the 1990's to try Islamist leaders, terrorists, and other criminal offenders. This was during a period in Algeria when the government declared a state of emergency and most individual rights were suspended. This included a suspension of sentencing guidelines as military tribunals were often known to issue harsh sentences, including regular use of the death penalty.

Punishment

The system under the greatest flux and reform is that of the penal system. Within Algeria, there are varying levels of punishment. Convicted offenders can receive punishment upon conviction ranging from fines to life in prison or a death sentence. As of this writing, there are no alternative sanctions specified in the Algerian penal code. Although there are still many death-eligible offenses on the records, there has not been an execution in Algeria since the institution of a moratorium in 2003. Before the moratorium, offenses that would qualify as death-eligible were crimes against the state such as treason and espionage and homicide.

One of the more interesting aspects of the Algerian penal code is the distinction of what crimes are labeled "excusable." Excusable offenses in the penal code often refer to violent criminal acts that are mitigated based on either victim characteristics, such as the victim's relationship to the perpetrator, or the nature of incidents that may have precipitated the attack. Within this category of "excusable" offenses, the Algerian belief in honor and family is apparent. As in many other nations, killing in self-defense is a case where one may be excused of homicide. More interesting cases, however, can be observed in cases where there has been an "attack on one's purity." For example, killing a spouse when he or she is caught in the act of committing adultery is excusable under the penal code. Castrating a man, if the crime is immediately provoked by a violent rape, is also excusable, as is killing or injuring an adult who is caught raping a minor (age less than 16 years old). However, parricide, or the killing of one's parents or grandparents, is never excusable. The distinctions between what is and what is not "acceptable" in the Algerian justice system paint an interesting depiction of the culture of the North African nation. It is clear that Algeria combines its past as a French colony with its cultural heritage as an Islamic nation.

Beyond the excusable offenses, the Algerian belief in family and morals is reaffirmed with the special section of the penal code that provides sanctions and definitions of crimes that are against "The Family" and "Good Morals." Many of the punishments attached to the crimes indicate a strong belief in the protection of children. Crimes such as abortion, family abandonment, and immoral or lewd acts are included, and punishments range from fines to imprisonment. As previously mentioned, abandoning one's family for longer than two months without a reason is punishable by imprisonment from two months to one year and a fine.

The dedication to the family and the sanctity of the family is also expressed in the gravity of incest in Algerian law. For instance, conviction for acts involving sexual relations between parent and child, grandparent and grandchild, or brother and sister is punishable by 20 years in prison. As the proximity of the bloodline decreases, so does the penalty. Sexual relations with a sibling's spouse are forbidden, as are relations with one's godparent, but these crimes result in a sentence of 5 years in prison, as opposed to 20. By contrast, under the U.S. Federal sentencing guidelines, incest between a father and a daughter where the daughter is less than 13 years old calls for a maximum prison sentence of 13 years. Additionally, abortion is strictly forbidden and carries a sentence of varying lengths in prison without parole, with a maximum of 5 years in prison as a possible sentence. Lewd public acts are forbidden and carry minor sentences or fines. However, if the "lewd act" involves homosexuality, the sentence is dramatically increased. Corrupting and contributing to the corruption of minors is also a fairly serious offense that carries a sentence of 5 to 10 years in prison.

Other offenses have varying levels of sentences. Sentences for rape range from 5 to 10 years for an adult and 10 to 20 years for raping a minor under the age of 16. However, if the perpetrator of the rape of an adult was in a parental role or other position of authority or power over the victim, the sentence is increased to 10 to 20 years in prison. If a parent or person of authority or power rapes a child less than 16 years old, that person faces life in prison. Depending on the circumstances surrounding a theft, robbery, or burglary, an offender runs the risk of being imprisoned for a month or less or up to 10 years in prison. If an offender is armed and commits robbery or burglary at night, he or she runs the risk of a death sentence. Within the penal code, there are many sentence enhancements for crimes that are committed at night.

Essentially, all of the sentences are relative to the circumstances surrounding the incident regarding the exacerbation or mitigation of a sentence. It is unclear whether the defendant's criminal history is taken into account during sentencing, but it is likely given the nature of the justice system.

In recent years, the government created a special section of the penal code to punish terrorists. Essentially, the sentences for terrorism act as enhancements for existing sentences. For example, if a crime originally held a penalty of life in prison, but the perpetrator committed that act as a form of terrorism, then the sentence would be increased to death. In the case of crimes with sentences of 10–20 years in prison, the perpetrator would receive life in prison. The section on terrorism goes so far as to punish creators of terrorist organizations with life in prison and members of the organization with sentences of 10–20 years in prison, even without committing any acts that threaten Algerian national security. The punishment for being involved in terrorist organizations also extends to any activity committed outside of Algeria. Thus, if a citizen joined Al Qaeda, he would be given the same punishment that he would have received had he joined Algeria's Armed Islamic Group. Financiers of terrorism, as well as any person generating or distributing terrorist propaganda, are also at risk for being sanctioned if convicted. Finally, if convicted of any terrorist involvement, the person must serve at least one half of his or her sentence before being paroled.

In an attempt to curb terrorism, President Bouteflika presented the Civil Concord Act in 1999 to the public for referendum. In this legislation, Bouteflika offered amnesty to terrorists who voluntarily ceased their terrorist activities and admitted to their terrorist actions. In return for their promises, the terrorists received lighter sentences than they would have been awarded upon conviction. The sole exceptions to this amnesty program were individuals who had committed rape or murder. Somewhat surprisingly, the referendum received approximately 97 percent approval by the populace. Even more surprisingly, reports estimate that approximately 80 percent of the extremists accepted the amnesty and have reintegrated into society.

The Prisons

In 2005, there were approximately 42,000 individuals in prisons across the nation, with prisons operating at about 140 percent capacity. This number includes individuals who had been sentenced to prison as well as individuals who were pretrial detainees. In terms of incarceration rate, Algeria had 127 inmates per 100,000 citizens.

There are currently two levels of imprisonment in Algeria. For low-level offenders, or individuals who have been convicted of civil offenses, there are provincial civil prisons. More serious offenders are sent to one of three state penitentiaries. Many of these offenders have committed crimes that are death-eligible, such as murder or rape, and also include convicted terrorists. The conditions within the prisons vary widely from rudimentary to more modern facilities. Inmates in the civil prisons are much better cared for than those inmates in the state penitentiaries. For example, inmates in civil prisons are usually taken to the hospital when seriously ill, are allowed weekly visitation from their families, and are allowed to receive food from outside the prison to supplement the nutritionally poor food provided by the prison. In contrast, the main penitentiary, El Harrach, has come under scrutiny by international human rights interest groups for its practices. The maintenance of health standards within Algerian prisons and the creation of alternatives for juveniles continue to be major humanitarian concerns among watch groups.

More recently, however, the Algerian government has been attempting to institute plans for modernization and reorganization of the prison system at all levels. This reform plan includes improvement of living conditions, organizational changes at the national and local levels, and overall modernization of both facilities and prison programs. This plan, as published, is general in nature but does include statements that indicate sweeping changes for the Algerian penal system. For instance, the Justice Ministry report states plans to replace decrepit prison buildings with newly constructed prisons that meet international standards, to focus on rehabilitative programs, and to increase the capacity of the prisons to meet the needs of a growing prison population and relieve overcrowding. Those who are planning or attempting research in this area should, then, observe the Algerian prison system closely to determine whether or not these changes are actually being implemented and whether they make any real difference. There does seem to be a real interest on the part of the Algerian government to pursue reform, given that they have recently hosted a prison reform conference in Algiers and allowed outside assessment by the International Centre for Prison Studies.

Amber Lesniewicz and Richard L. Legault

Further Reading

Amnesty International. (2006). *Algeria: Unrestrained Rowers: Torture by Algeria's Military Security:* http://www.amnesty.org/en/library/info/MDE28/004/2006.

International Centre for Prison Studies. (2006). Annual Report: http://www.kcl.ac.uk/content/1/c6/03/08/68/AnnualReport2006.pdf.

La modernisation de l'Administration Pénitentiaire. (2008). Ministère de la Justice, Organisation de la Justice, Système Pénitentiaire. Authors' translation: http://www.mjustice.dz/?p=sys_penl.

LaFree, G., I. Dugan, and S. Fahey. (2007). "Global Terrorism and Failed States." In *Peace and Conflict*, edited by J. J. Hewitt, J. Wilkenfeld, and T. R. Gurr. Boulder, CO: Paradigm Publishers.

Metz, Helen Chapan, ed. (1994). *Algeria: A Country Study.* Washington, DC: GPO for the Library of Congress.

NationMaster. (2007). *Algeria:* http://www.nationmaster.com/country/ag-algeria.

United Nations Office of Drugs and Crime. (2008). *Country Profile: Algeria:* http://www.unodc.org/egypt/en/country_profile_algeria.html.

World Law Guide. (2006). *Courts and Cases Algeria:* http://www.lexadin.nl/wlg/courts/nofr/oeur/lxctalg.htm#Administrative%20Courts%20(First%20Instance).

Bahrain

Legal System: Civil
Murder: Low
Corruption: Low
Human Trafficking: Medium
Prison Rate: Medium
Death Penalty: Yes

Background

Bahrain (official name: Kingdom of Bahrain) is an archipelago of 33 islands situated midway in the Persian Gulf with a total area of 691 square kilometers. The largest island, Bahrain Island, constitutes more than three-fourths the land mass and most of the 2008 estimated population of over 1 million, over half of whom are foreign nationals. In this former colony of Britain, the Constitution guarantees the king as the head of the kingdom. The prime minister is the head of the government and, along with the king, who is chief of state, appoint a council of ministers. The legislative branch consists of a bicameral parliament of a 40-member Council of Representatives and a 40-member Shura Consultative Council appointed by the king, the members of which serve four-year terms. The Council of Representatives, composed of elected officials, passes laws, while the Consultative Council reviews laws passed before they are sent to the king for final approval. The Supreme Court of Appeal is the apex court; it is independent, with right of judicial review, and decides on the constitutionality of laws and regulations.

Police

The earliest known history of the police in Bahrain goes back to 1869 when the first police patrols, called the *fedawewa,* were established. In 1920, the first Bahraini police force was set up, and the first law for police was issued. The police at the time consisted of the camel riders and cavalry men. The first motorbike division was established in 1937, followed by the traffic directorate in 1942. In 1996, an amiri decree was issued to reorganize the Ministry of Interior to establish various directorates and security sections. In 2004, another amiri decree was given to reorganize the Ministry of Interior with plans to improve public security and policing services. Among the goals are improvement in the recruitment and retention of officers, the use of scientific approach to problem solving, development of a national database and advanced network of communications, and improved cooperation with the public. An example of recent developments is the purchase of advanced Radar Auto Vision mobile CCTV systems for installation in Bahraini Police Force patrol cars, which helped in securing more than 700 prosecutions for traffic violations. Another example of improving relationships with the public include Bahraini Ministry of Interior personnel getting training on lessons to effectively interact with the media. These efforts have enhanced the Bahraini image both among the public and in the neighboring Arab states.

The overall responsibility for public security (Bahrain Public Security [BPS]), law, and order is vested with the Ministry of Interior, which has the primary responsibility to maintain public order and prevent and investigate crimes. In addition to the usual police functions, the mission of the force is to prevent sectarian violence and terrorist actions. Precise data on police personnel are not available for Bahrain. In 1992, there were an estimated 2,000 Bahraini national police officers, which increased to about 3,000 in 2006.

The Directorate of Criminal Investigation (DCI), which is responsible for investigation and prosecution of criminals, is associated with the BPS. The DCI has within its jurisdiction the Mobile and Stationary Forensic Laboratories, the Vice and Begging Squad, and the Narcotics Bureau, and it maintains the Juvenile Care Unit. The Public Security Flying Wing (which operates the helicopters) serves both the BPS and the DCI. The Directorate of the Coast Guard, which is responsible for coast guard work, is also within the jurisdiction of the BPS.

Bahrain's law enforcement authorities such as the vice squad and the Criminal Investigation

Directorate of the Ministry of Interior cooperate with other agencies such as the Municipal Council of the Capital Governorate. For example, raids are conducted by the police with the cooperation of these agencies on private apartments and hotels when residents report unlawful activities such as trafficking and prostitution. Yet research on domestic workers in Bahrain suggests that police authorities appear reluctant to investigate or effectively prosecute the reported cases of abuse of domestic workers. A Human Rights Watch report notes that domestic workers, who are often noncitizens, routinely face arbitrary detention and deportation as a result of disputes with their sponsors or lack of work permits, although the Constitution prohibits arbitrary arrest and detention with the exception of severe criminal cases involving treason.

The Bahraini Women Police force was established in November 1970, beginning with two female police officers. In 2006, there were an estimated 368 women officers. Women officers are assigned to police stations that have women police units to deal with female cases. They are also assigned to various other tasks, including cases dealing with domestic disputes; fingerprint sections to assist with women who come in for fingerprinting; traffic and the Immigration Directorate; security as it affects women travelers in the international airport; and the child protection office that deals with juvenile delinquency.

Police training for officers lasts six months. Basic training includes coursework in laws and regulations. In-house physical training is given by instructors at the Public Security Training Institute, and instructors from Bahrain University, the Civil Services Bureau, National Guard Headquarters, and the public prosecutor's office cover areas in their areas of specialization. Cadets receive a rank of MMT (assistant second lieutenant) upon successful completion of training and eventually get promoted based on the availability of vacancies and requirements. Besides in-house training, some cadets are sent abroad to various countries located in the region, such as the King Fahad Security College in Saudi Arabia, Kuwait Police College, Dubai Police College, Abu Dhabi Police College, and the Royal Police Academy in Jordan. For refresher courses, police officers are sent to police colleges or institutes in the United Kingdom, the United States, and France, among other countries.

Crime

The Ministry of Interior (MOI) lists a series of crimes with supporting penal codes: murder, treason, danger of fireworks, the "miscarriage" of chair power, fraud, hoax, money laundering, and flirting. Though rape is illegal, the ministry's Web site does not include it in the list. It should be acknowledged that marital relations are governed by sharia law, and thus spousal rape is not a legal concept within the law. Among the interesting concerns noted by the MOI is flirting. The penal code punishes offenders who harass young women over the phone (e.g., calling a young woman and telling her that he loves her or sending her MSM messages). Offenders face up to three months of jail and monetary fines.

The MOI Web site notes that the Bahraini penal code criminalizes soliciting for prostitution in public places, with penalties of up to two years' imprisonment. Other related offenses in this category are enticing or assisting a person to commit acts of immorality or prostitution; using coercion, threat, or deceit to force a person to commit prostitution; living off the money received from one's own prostitution or from the prostitution of another; and establishing or operating a brothel or an establishment for prostitution. Penalties are more severe if victims are 18 years and under. All forms of pornography are prohibited under sharia law, with no differentiation between adult and child pornography.

Bahrain recently enacted human trafficking laws, in 2008, with penalties of prison sentences and fines ranging from 2,000 to 10,000 Bahraini dinars (US$5,319 to US$26,731). The law also calls for the formation of a committee to combat human trafficking.

Local media and research suggest crimes against domestic workers are common. A common complaint from foreign women working as domestic workers is physical or sexual abuse. Though many cases are reported to local embassies and the police, most victims appear too frightened to sue their employers. There were reports that courts, however, allow victims who do appear to sue for damages or return home to their home countries, or both.

Current crime data from Bahrain are not available. The INTERPOL Web site has data available from 1996. The total number of crimes recorded in national crime statistics was 21,294, representing 3,686 crimes per 100,000 population (crime rate). During this year, there were 8 homicides (1.38); 235 (38.9) sex offenses including rape; 9 (1.6) serious assaults; 272 (47.1) thefts; 3,141 (543.7) breaking and entering; 2,156 (373.22) theft of motor cars; 332 (57.5) offenses related to drugs; and 238 (41.2) fraud cases. The U.S. State Department Web site notes that the crime rate in Bahrain is low and violent crime is rare. However, burglary, petty theft, and robberies do occur.

Courts

The legal system comprises customary tribal law (*urf*), three separate schools of Islamic sharia law, and civil law influenced by the British legal system. The Constitution provides for an independent judiciary and separate branch of government. The Minister of Justice and Islamic Affairs is the highest judicial authority, but the amir, who retains the power of pardon, is the highest judicial official.

The civil court system consists of summary courts and a supreme court. Summary courts of first instance are located in all communities and include separate *urf,* civil, and criminal sections. The Supreme Court of Appeal is the highest appellate court in the country. It hears appeals from the summary courts and decides on the constitutionality of laws and regulations.

Civil Courts

The civil law courts handle civil and commercial cases, including cases regarding the personal status of non-Muslims. The hierarchy of the civil courts is as follows: The courts of minor causes (the lower courts and the Court of Execution) are the first level and have one judge with jurisdiction over minor civil and commercial disputes. The High Civil Court of Appeal deals with larger civil and commercial disputes and personal status cases involving non-Muslims and is presided over by three judges. The Supreme Court of Appeal (or the Court of Cassation) is the final court of appeal for all civil matters and is composed of a chairman and three other judges appointed by decree.

Criminal Courts

The criminal law courts settle all criminal cases and are structured similarly to civil courts. The lower criminal court has one judge and rules on misdemeanor crimes; the higher criminal court deals with felony cases and has three judges and is also the place where appeals are made. The Supreme Court of Appeal (or the Court of Cassation) serves as the final appellate court for criminal matters.

Sharia Courts

The sharia law courts have jurisdiction over all issues related to the personal status of Muslims, both Bahraini and non-Bahraini, including matters relating to inheritance and wills. Sharia courts operate at two levels: the Senior Sharia Court and the High Sharia Court of Appeal. At each of the two levels there is a separate court for Sunni and Shiite Muslims to deal with all personal status cases brought by the respective populations. That is, there are Sunni courts at two levels, with jurisdiction over all personal status cases brought by Sunni Muslims, and Shiite courts with jurisdiction over cases brought by Shiite Muslims. The High Sharia Court of Appeal is composed of a minimum of two judges, and in cases of disagreement, the Ministry of Justice provides a third judge to attain a majority vote.

Special Courts

The Ministry of Defense maintains a court system for military personnel accused of offenses under the Military Code of Justice, and a similar court for police officers is maintained by the Ministry of Interior.

In 2000, the Higher Judicial Council was established for supervising the courts and the office of public prosecution. This council is chaired by the king. The king appoints the council members, who are drawn from a cadre of judges from the Supreme Court of Appeal, the sharia law courts, and the civil high courts of appeal.

The Constitutional Court was created in 2002 with jurisdiction over the constitutionality of laws. The Higher Judicial Council appoints a president and six members who serve nine-year terms and cannot be removed before their terms expire. Members of the government, including the king, can challenge the constitutionality of laws in this court. Decisions of the Higher Judicial Council are final and "binding on all state authorities."

Constitutional Safeguards

The Ministry of Justice is responsible for public prosecutors. Access to attorneys is not freely available. Civil and criminal trial procedures provide for an open trial with right to counsel and the right to appeal. Legal aid is made available when necessary. The Constitution states that "no person shall be arrested, detained, imprisoned, searched or compelled to reside in a specified place except in accordance with the provisions of the law and under the supervision of the judicial authorities." Criminal court proceedings do not appear to discriminate against women, children, or minority groups. In the early stages of detention, detainees and their attorneys must seek a court order to be able to meet. Detainees may receive visits from family members, usually once a month.

With the abolition of the State Security Act in 2001, courts refused police requests to detain suspects longer than 48 hours, and the police complied with court orders to release suspects. Judges may grant bail to a suspect. However, attorneys still require a court order to visit detainees in jail. In 2004, the government made efforts make the judicial process more transparent in the areas of recruitment of new judges as well as training of judges and prosecutors, establishment of an office of mediation, and steps to speed up court procedure.

Punishment

The Penal Code Law, article 333, provides for life imprisonment for cases dealing with premeditated murder. However, if it is well planned in advance or associated with other crimes, then the judge has the right to sentence the murderer to death. The same punishment applies to the killing of public employees during their working hours or to murdering people by explosive or poison products.

Article 49 of the penal code notes that the penalty for a felony is capital punishment or imprisonment for at least 3 years and deprivation of civil rights for a period exceeding 3 years but not more than 15 years. Article 50 of the same code lists the punishment for misdemeanors as imprisonment and a fine of amount in excess of 5 dinars and deprivation of civil rights for a period exceeding 3 years and not less than 1 year. The punishment for those who illegally take money from others is a jail term. The punishment is more severe if fraudsters steal public money or cheat their victims by changing their names or identities or use or sell properties owned by others. Offenders convicted of money laundering can receive up to 7 years in prison and a fine of BD1 million.

The Constitution prohibits torture and other cruel, inhumane, or degrading treatment or punishment. Following the reforms of 2001, systematic torture no longer takes place; however, there has been no attempt to investigate allegations of torture committed by government officials in the past.

Prisons

The corrections system is administered by the Ministry of Justice and Islamic Affairs through a director of prisons. The Kings College of London Prison Brief for Bahrain reports that there are two prisons in the sheikhdom, with a total population of 911 (rate of 155 per 100,000 population) in 1997 and 437 (60 per 100,000) in 2003. The 2004 UN Survey data report a prison population of 701 (95 per 100,000). The rocky islet of Jiddah houses the main state prison and has a capacity of 816 with a 2004 occupancy rate of 91 percent. Women prisoners are housed separately from men. In 1973, the juvenile care center was opened.

Mahesh K. Nalla

Further Reading

Al Ghaith, I., M. A. R. Al-Khayyat, and T. H. Al-Hassan. (2007). "Police Training and Education in Bahrain." In *Police Education and Training in a Global Society,* edited by Peter C. Kratcoski and Dilip K. Das. Lanham, MD: Lexington Books.

Human Rights Watch. (1997). *Routine Abuse, Routine Denial: Civil Rights and the Political Crisis in Bahrain.* New York: Human Rights Watch.

Strobl, S. (2006). "Not So Notorious: Bahraini Female Criminality in the Kingdom of Bahrain." *Al Raida* 23(113): 18–24. Institute for Women's Studies in the Arab World. Lebanon American University.

Strobl, S. (2008). "Post-Colonial Policing and the 'Woman' Question: A History of the Women's Police Directorate in Bahrain." In *Carceral Practices: Prisons and Policing in the Middle East and North Africa,* edited by L. Khalili and J. Schwedler. New York: Columbia University Press.

Strobl, S. (2008). "The Women's Police Directorate in Bahrain: An Ethnographic Observation of a Gender Segregated Unit and the Likelihood of Integration." *International Criminal Justice Review* 18(1): 39–58.

Strobl, S. (2009). "Policing Housemaids: The Criminalization of Domestic Workers of Bahrain." *British Journal of Criminology* 49: 165–183.

Egypt

Legal System: Civil/Islamic
Murder: Low
Burglary: Medium
Corruption: Medium
Human Trafficking: Medium
Prison Rate: Medium
Death Penalty: Yes
Corporal Punishment: No

Background

Situated in the northeastern corner of Africa, Egypt, officially known as the Arab Republic of Egypt, is the only land bridge from Africa to Asia. Although Egypt is on the African continent, it is considered an Arab country, and the official language is Arabic. With a total area of 1,001,450 square kilometers and a population of 81 million, the republic shares borders with Israel, the Gaza Strip, Libya, and Sudan and has coastline on both the Red Sea and the Mediterranean Sea.

Because of the various empires that have ruled Egypt throughout its long history, the Egyptian legal system has undergone various changes. Prior to the 1952 revolution, in which Egypt gained independence from Great Britain, the ruling parties enforced their own codes and laws as they saw fit. There were separate courts called sharia for Muslims, whereas other courts were reserved for the Christians. Since the revolution, Egypt has been governed by several constitutions, the last of which was adopted in 1971. With only three amendments to the Constitution in 1980, 2005, and 2007, this document still governs Egypt today. The Egyptian legal system is a civil law system that combines European and Napoleonic codes with Islamic or sharia law. Napoleonic code is essentially the criminal code that Egyptians were taught while Napoleon Bonaparte controlled the country.

The executive branch of Egypt is headed by the president, the chief of state, for unlimited six-year terms. The president appoints vice presidents, prime ministers, and the Council of Ministers. The president of Egypt also assumes the responsibility of commander in chief of all armed forces and has the power to declare war pending legislative approval. The president, as head of the party, controls the legislature with the power to dismiss the legislature at any time. The president can get the legislature to enact laws that he proposes or supports and has the power of veto any piece of legislation.

The legislative branch of the government is a bicameral system consisting of a lower house, the People's Assembly, and an upper house, the Advisory (Shura) Council. The People's Assembly is made up of 454 seats, 444 elected by popular vote and 10 appointed by the president for five-year terms. It is the job of the People's Assembly to draft and enact laws for the republic, as well as approve the yearly national budget. Furthermore, the People's Assembly is given, by decree of the Constitution, the power to monitor the executive branch.

The judicial branch of government consists of a variety of courts whose responsibility is to hear and rule on both civil and criminal matters. The highest court in the country is the Supreme Constitutional Court. Located in Cairo, the mission of the highest judicial body is to determine the constitutionality of laws and regulations, rule on disputes of jurisdiction, settle disputes in rulings of different judicial bodies, and interpret the laws and statutes issued by the executive and legislative branches. The Supreme Constitutional Court is not an appeals court, and individual defendants cannot appeal their cases to this judicial body.

Below the Supreme Constitutional Court in the Egyptian judicial hierarchy is the Court of Cassation, which serves as the highest court of appeals, and the misdemeanor courts of appeal are the first level of appeals. The courts of appeal review appeals of violations and misdemeanor cases submitted by either the defendant or the public prosecutor. Unlike the Court of Cassation, in a court of appeal, the basis of the appeal can consist of both factual findings and points of law. In addition, there are the courts of general and limited jurisdiction that serve as courts of first instance and are high-level trial courts in the judicial system. The courts hear lawsuits and other criminal charges brought forth by the public prosecutor or private parties. As a general jurisdiction court, the courts of first instance deal with criminal cases and civil matters where the sum of the dispute is greater than 10,000 Egyptian pounds. Cases that involve sums less than this are heard in trial courts of limited jurisdiction, also known as summary courts.

Police

The police force in Egypt is a major source of employment for the Egyptian people. According to figures published in 2006, the Arab Republic of Egypt employed 10,000 sworn and an additional 112,000 individuals serving in various capacities at that time. On top of that, a paramilitary force of about 300,000 officers is used to help with security, riot control, and other protective services. The Egyptian police force is organized in a national, centralized fashion. Under the guidance of the Ministry of Interior, the force is distributed throughout the provinces within the 26 governorates of the country. Governors and police chiefs in each jurisdiction control policing activities and carry out tasks as they are instructed by the Ministry of Interior. The overall structure of the national police force can be compared to that of a domestic military. The major general of police answers to the Ministry of Interior and, ultimately, the president.

To become a police officer, one must attend the Police Training College located near Cairo. During a three-month course, cadets are instructed on the finer points of policing and learn different procedures and practices pertinent to their job. This could include training in marksmanship, basic criminal and civil law, emergency response, and first aid. Those individuals looking to become officers (i.e., lieutenant) must graduate from the Police Training College with a two-year bachelor's degree in police studies. During their time at the school, candidates have the opportunity to take classes in a wide array of fields, including security administration, foreign language, first aid, cryptology, criminal investigation, and public relations.

Upon graduation from the training college, new officers are assigned to a new police division. If assigned to a basic police department, the tasks include keeping the peace, assisting in criminal investigations, and overall crime prevention. Besides general police departments, the national police force has a number of specialty divisions. Some of the notable ones include the Tourism and Antiquities

Police, the Port Security Division, the Immigration and Customs Division, and the Narcotics Division. These specialty divisions have a narrow scope of responsibility and focus specifically on their individual missions.

Crime

Classification of Crimes

As mentioned earlier, Egyptian law is a combination of European code and Islamic law. The Egyptian civil code is the source of laws and codes that govern the Egyptian people. Although this code is a variation of different legal systems, the French civil code seems to be the dominant influence, with Islamic law playing a lesser role. The secular code usually covers criminal matters such as murder, rape, robbery, and the like, whereas Islamic code deals with personal matters, family disputes, divorce, and other similar issues. However, in the past several decades, there has been a movement by Islamic fundamentalists such as the Muslim Brotherhood to adopt Islamic law completely. Although this has not taken place, in 1985, the People's Assembly began a review of the legal code and recommended changes to laws that conflicted with Islamic law. This action illustrates the struggle between secular and religious ideals within the government.

An officer of Egypt's Tourism and Antiquities Police patrols the pyramids at Giza. (Jack Versloot)

Today, the Egyptian criminal justice system comprises four different jurisdictions: military justice, administrative justice, emergency justice, and ordinary criminal justice. Military justice refers to the system that governs and brings to justice criminal offenders who are members of the military. In rare instances, civilians can be prosecuted in the military justice system. This usually occurs when crimes have been committed that affect state security and also when crimes occur during a state of emergency. The second jurisdiction, administrative justice, also does not deal with too many Egyptian civilians. The point of this jurisdiction is to provide an avenue of administrative review. Officials here are charged with reviewing presidential decrees and administrative decisions to determine their legality as they are brought forth by government employees. The third type of jurisdiction in the system is emergency justice. In this system, the president has the authority, per the Constitution, to declare a state of emergency. By doing this, the president assumes great power over the system. With the ability to skirt around the rights normally afforded to civilians, the president can order surveillance on citizens, searches and seizures, censorship of the media, the closure of businesses, and many other invasive procedures. There are also a number of powers given to the president for creating new courts and procedural rules within those courts. Although this power is supposed to be reserved for "emergencies," Egypt has been in a state of emergency since 1981 when President Sadat was assassinated.

Criminal Code

The criminal code in the ordinary criminal jurisdiction outlines three basic types of crimes. The first is a violation. This type of crime cannot carry a punishment of more than 100 Egyptian pounds. Violations can include disturbing the peace, unlawful discharge of a firearm, defacing property, and littering public waterways. The second type of crime is a misdemeanor. In Egypt, a misdemeanor is defined as any crime that carries a fine of greater than 100 Egyptian pounds but no more than three years in prison. Examples of misdemeanors include theft, perjury, aggravated assault, negligent homicide, and impersonating a public official. Last, the most serious types of crime are known as felonies. Intentional homicide, rape, mayhem, kidnapping, robbery, burglary, arson, and terrorism offenses are all defined as felonies in the criminal code. A typical punishment for the commission of a felony can range from imprisonment for three years to life in prison. For certain crimes, the death penalty is also an option.

Crime Statistics

Although Egypt is one of the few African countries that reports data to the United Nations Office on Drugs and Crime, there is no real way to verify the information that is being reported. The following are the crime statistics reported by the Egyptian government in response to the UNODC Crime Trends Survey: In 2005, Egypt reported 528 intentional homicides, which resulted in a rate of 0.72 per 100,000 people (WHO, however, reports a rate of 1.3 in 2004). There were also 261 assaults and 435 thefts in 2005. The only other two crimes reported by Egypt for the year 2005 were embezzlement and kidnapping. Their totals were 114 and 18, respectively. One interesting point is that for each of the crimes listed here, except for kidnapping, no more than 20 percent of each occurred within an urban area.

Other Crime Problems

Drug trafficking and subsequent use is a big problem in Egypt. The country has been pinpointed as a transit point for Southwest and Southeast Asian heroin and opium. The final destinations for the products are Europe, Africa, and the United States. Egypt also faces the problem of drug cultivation within the country. Both cannabis and opium are grown in various regions of the country. To combat this problem, the Egyptian government has undertaken a very aggressive drug control strategy. Under the direction of the Anti-Narcotic General Administration, the military, Coast Guard, customs department, and Ministry of Interior all work together to disrupt and intercept shipments. Over the past several years, the government has seen an increase in the amount of drugs seized each year. For example, in 2000, they seized 524 kilograms of cannabis, but in 2004, they seized 1,868 kilograms. The same can be said for opium: in 2000, officials seized 75 kilograms, but in 2004, they seized 114 kilograms. The biggest increase in seizures came from marijuana: almost a 50,000 kilogram increase from 2000 to 2004.

In a span of two years from 2004 to 2006, there were six terrorist attacks in Egypt. The attacks targeted not only a famous bazaar but also tourist buses and tourist resorts on the Red Sea. Although religious extremism has existed in Egypt for some time, this new wave of terrorism poses many challenges the government is forced to address. The Egyptian economy is geared around tourism, and when tourism drops due to fears of terrorist attacks, the strain on the economy is drastic. The Ministry of Justice has created a National Committee for Combating Terrorism that works closely with other nations to investigate and arrest suspected and known terrorists.

Finding of Guilt

Prosecutors and Judges

Prosecutors are considered both executive and judicial officials because they are granted both prosecutorial powers and the power of an examining magistrate. This means that prosecutors have the duty of investigating crimes, referring them to the court, and also prosecuting those cases that enter the system. As part of their powers, prosecutors can issue warrants for arrests or searches but also can make arrests in the role of a judicial officer. Because of this wide-ranging authority, the position of prosecutor is very powerful in the system. To become a prosecutor, individuals must be at least 21 years of age, hold a law degree, and be licensed to practice law. After selection, potential future prosecutors are required to attend a course at the National Center for Judicial Studies, which lasts for six months, and then pass various oral examinations. Once appointed as a prosecutor, the individual has tenure except in the case of gross negligent misconduct or failure to perform specific duties. Positions as a prosecutor are highly coveted because they are the stepping stone for obtaining judgeship.

Judges are also important actors in the process of finding guilt. Appointed by the executive branch and seated at all levels of the judicial system based on seniority, judges hold the responsibility of ensuring justice is preserved in a manner consistent with the Constitution and other judicial precedents. As of 2006, in Egypt there were 7,680 judges and magistrates, all male. This number includes all of the judges who preside over limited jurisdiction courts, general jurisdiction courts, the courts of appeal, the Court of Cassation, and the Supreme Constitutional Court. To receive appointment to a judgeship, individuals must hold a law degree and be a minimum of 30 years old. To serve on the courts of appeal, the minimum age requirement is 38, and in the Court of Cassation, the minimum age is 43. Judges are trained at the same National Center for Judicial Studies as prosecutors, in a variety of different subjects including criminal law, civil law, and criminal procedure. Judges at all levels also have lifetime tenure with respect to their appointments.

Arrest, Searches, and Seizures

The process of finding the guilt of an individual for the occurrence of a crime can be broken down in to two distinct phases. During this process, there are freedoms and individual rights afforded citizens, and these must be respected by government officials. The first phase is the pretrial. This phase covers the time from the first police interaction with the defendant up to the actual court date. To initiate the process of finding guilt, the defendant and evidence must first be brought into the system. This requires police and prosecutors to go out into the field, investigate crimes, collect evidence, and make arrests. These actions are regulated by specific rules regarding stops, arrests, and searches. In terms of stops, police are allowed to proceed with a search when the "circumstances warrant suspicion." This definition is very vague and is the product of decisions from the Court of Cassation. The same can be said for the act of frisking a suspect. Although there is no constitutional provision regulating this behavior, the courts have allowed them to be conducted when they are preventive in nature. This means police officers can search an individual for weapons or contraband that may be used to cause harm; however, there are a variety of rules that limit the scope and applicability of preventive searches.

Unlike the police procedures of stops and frisks, the power to arrest citizens is regulated by constitutional provisions. The Egyptian Constitution states, "Individual freedom is a natural right not subject to violation except in cases of *flagrante delicto,* and no person may be arrested, inspected, or detained or have his or her freedom restricted in any way or be prevented from free movement except by an order necessitated by investigation and the preservation of public security." To restrict someone's freedom, a warrant has to be issued by a judge or public prosecutor. Use of force is permitted to make an arrest or control unruly civilians. Defined as "military force," an officer is permitted to use deadly force on people who resist arrest or flee if they meet any of the following criteria: (1) the individual has been convicted of a felony or a misdemeanor that has an associated prison term of more than three months, (2) the individual is suspected of committing a felony or *flagrante delicto* misdemeanor, or (3) an arrest warrant has been issued for the individual. In certain situations that endanger public safety, deadly force may be used for crowd control. To use deadly force, the officer must first give a verbal warning and then a warning shot, before exacting deadly force against an individual.

The last police function the Constitution regulates in the finding-of-guilt process is that of search and seizure. In Egypt, there are three legal provisions addressing the legality of searches. The first is that private homes are protected against warrantless entry. For an officer to search a suspect's private dwelling, a warrant must be issued by a judge or judicial officer. Based on Court of Cassation rulings, the issuance of a warrant is valid only if there is sufficient evidence to indicate the individual has committed a crime. The second provision explicitly forbids warrantless surveillance of correspondence between individuals. Essentially, telephone calls, mail, electronic mail, and other forms of communication cannot be monitored without a proper warrant. Unlike warrants to search the homes of suspects, warrants to eavesdrop on communications between individuals must come from a magistrate or judge. A prosecutor does not have the authority to issue this type of warrant. The last provision of the Constitution regarding search and seizure simply ensures the protection of citizens' private lives and allows for legal action in the event of illegal searches and seizures.

Pretrial Process

Once an individual is taken into custody, the prosecutor has 24 hours to charge the suspect or he or she must be released. Typically, police officers or judicial officers do not question suspects. They simply turn the suspect over to the prosecutor after apprehension. During this time period, the prosecutor can question the suspect and attempt to build or strengthen a case. To formally charge a suspect, the prosecutor must file a summons stating the charges and deliver it to the defendant. Before trial, it may be necessary to hold preliminary hearings to settle disputes, obtain witness testimonies, and conduct other business. The pretrial process also involves pretrial motions and a period of discovery, in which both parties have the opportunity to examine all documents and evidence that the opponent plans to present to the court.

Trial

As previously noted, the nature of the charges determines what type of court the trial will take place in. Violations and misdemeanors are tried in summary courts with a single judge, and felonies are tried in a court with a three-judge panel consisting of judges pulled from the courts of appeal. The proceedings of the trial are fairly straightforward. They begin with the task of confirming the defendant's personal information and declaring the charges for the court record. The defendant is then given the opportunity to enter a plea. If the plea is not guilty, then the trial begins immediately. During the trial, the prosecutor has the first opportunity to introduce witness testimony. After the prosecutor is finished with questioning the witness, the victim, civil plaintiff, defendant, and responsible civil party may also question the witness. Upon hearing all of the witness testimony, the prosecution and the defense both present their closing arguments before the court renders its decision. If the defendant is found not guilty, then the court must release him or her from custody. However, if the verdict is "guilty," the court assigns punishment accordingly. Depending on the outcome of the trial, both parties have the right to appeal the decision of the court. Felony appeals are sent immediately to the Court of Cassation, whereas all other appeals follow the process outlined in the judicial branch section.

However, not every case brought into the system comes to conclusion with a full trial. There are a couple of options or dispositions available to the parties involved that can resolve a case without proceeding to a full criminal trial. The first is a simple guilty plea by the defendant. This usually occurs before the start of the trial, and the court determines appropriate punishment at that time. Another option is called a criminal writ. In cases where the charge is for a violation or other minor felony and the punishment is less than 1,000 Egyptian pounds, the prosecutor can call on the court to determine guilt based on the details of the investigation and the evidence collected. If the court determines the defendant is guilty, it can issue a criminal writ. This writ publicly declares the defendant innocent, but the defendant is responsible for the fine resulting from the writ. The defendant has the option to object to this ruling and send the case to trial, but if there is no objection, then the criminal writ is the final decision of the court.

A third option for avoiding a full trial in a criminal case is a conciliation or settlement between parties. Just like in criminal writs, this option is available only for violations and low-level misdemeanors. A conciliation takes place between the defendant and the prosecutor. When it happens, the two parties reach an agreement where the defendant pleads guilty and then is responsible for only a portion of the fine for the charged crime. Although this is not technically plea bargaining, one can see the parallels in the two processes. A settlement is an arrangement that is reached between the victim and the defendant. There are not currently any rules regulating this process other than that the agreement must be mutual.

Defendants' Rights

Throughout the criminal justice process, defendants are afforded a number of rights and protections. The following are some of the rights not previously discussed in the text, but which are still recognized as rights by the criminal code and the courts.

- An individual cannot be charged with a crime or punished when there is an absence of law forbidding that crime.
- One cannot be charged with a crime ex post facto. This means that laws cannot be applied retroactively and used to prosecute individuals who committed the act before the law was established.
- There is a presumption of innocence, and defendants have the right to a fair trial.
- Defendants have the right to counsel in all felony cases and misdemeanor cases where there is a possibility of imprisonment.
- Defendants have the right to remain silent and protect themselves from self-incrimination during court proceedings.
- If found innocent, those who were detained have the right to be compensated. Additionally, those who are found innocent on appeal have the right to public announcement of their exoneration in official newspapers and to be compensated for the situation.

Some of these rights are not expressly decreed in the criminal code but are recognized as rights by the precedents set forth in the Court of Cassation.

Conviction Statistics

The following are the conviction statistics for 2006, the most recent year for which data are available as reported by the government of Egypt to the United Nations Office on Drugs and Crime.

Persons brought to court	5,923,898
Grand total convictions	5,585,058
Adult* females convicted	694,320
Adult* males convicted	4,927,496
Juveniles convicted	36,578
Homicide convictions	3,123

**Legal adult is age 18.*

Punishment

Types of Punishments

If a criminal defendant is convicted of a crime, the court in which the trial took place will decide on a commensurate punishment. The general guidelines for punishment based on the crime are as follows: For a criminal violation, the punishment/fine cannot exceed more than 100 Egyptian pounds. A misdemeanor carries a fine of greater than 100 Egyptian pounds but no more than three years in prison, and the typical punishment for the commission of a felony can range from imprisonment for three years to life in prison. To determine the punishment within those guidelines, judges assess a number of factors including the severity of the crime and the defendant's prior criminal history. The ultimate punishment in Egypt is the death penalty. Although only two out of three judges are needed to convict and sentence felony offenders, the decision must be unanimous when sentencing someone to death. In addition, the sentence must be reviewed by the chief *muti,* Egypt's highest religious official, or the minister of justice.

Prisons

Criticized over the years by groups such as Amnesty International and Human Rights Watch for the conditions of its prison system, Egypt has also been the target of bad press for its use of the prison system to house political prisoners and other detainees for indefinite periods of time without a formal trial. The Egyptian prison system consists of an array of different prisons ranging from maximum-security prisons to slight-security and special-purpose prisons. As of 2002, there were 43 different prisons, jails, and correctional institutions in Egypt. These institutions held 61,845 prisoners, the vast majority of whom were male, and according to 2001 data, they were being monitored by a total of 9,455 employees. Prisoners are assigned to correctional institutions based on the severity of their crimes and any special needs or requirements they may have. For example, a low-level drug offender or white collar criminal will not be housed in the same area as murderers and terrorists. Reports regarding the condition of the prisons vary from source to source. According to a 1992 Human Rights Watch report, the overall prison conditions are not stellar. Although prisoners are allowed family visits and contact with outsiders, the system overcrowding has led to inadequate living conditions and medical care. Prisoners and international observers alike point out the existence of major sanitation issues, poor sleeping arrangements, and lack of quality food. Also, according to Middle East Watch, many inmates do not have the opportunity to engage in work and educational activities. Even though the 1992 report is somewhat dated, international human rights groups have continued to report on the poor conditions in Egyptian prisons. With a finite amount of resources at the government's disposal, it is unlikely there will be widespread prison reform in the near future.

Eric Wildey

Further Reading

Metz, Helen Chapin. (1990). *Egypt: A Country Study.* Washington, DC: GPO for the Library of Congress.

Reza, Sadiq. (2007). "Egypt." In *Criminal Procedure: A Worldwide Study,* edited by C. M. Bradley. Durham, NC: Carolina Academic Press.

United Nations Office on Drugs and Crime. (2005). *Country Profile: Egypt:* http://www.unodc.org.

Wahab, Mohamed S. Abdel. (2006). *An Overview of the Egyptian Legal System and Legal Research:* http://www.nyulawglobal.org/globalex/egypt.htm.

Iran

Legal System: Islamic/Civil/Common
Murder: Medium
Corruption: High
Human Trafficking: High
Prison Rate: High
Death Penalty: Yes
Corporal Punishment: Yes

Background

Iran (Persia) is a powerful force in the Middle East and has a long history dating back to 4000 BCE. It covers 1,648,000 square kilometers with a population of over 71 million people. The country is surrounded by the Caspian Sea, Armenia, Turkmenistan, and Azerbaijan to the north; the Persian Gulf and Oman Sea to the south; Afghanistan and Pakistan to the east; and Iraq and Turkey to the west. The official language of Iran is Persian (Farsi). The country also has a long history of the rule of law. Cyrus the Great drafted the first human rights document in 539 BCE. Freedom of movement, freedom of religion, and freedom of speech are some examples of the Cyrus conception of human rights.

Historically, the official religion of most Persians was Zoroastrian. However, with the invasion of Arabs in 641, Zoroastrianism was replaced by Islam. Iran had many dynasties throughout its history. The head of a dynasty had total power and was a symbol of justice. Hence, justice was rendered in the name of the king. The Qajar dynasty (1796–1925) played a major role in transplanting some Western ideas about justice-related matters by employing several Europeans advisors to reform the

Persian system. By the end of the Qajar dynasty, Iran had adopted its first Fundamental Law, which was based on the Belgium constitutional model, and later the Pahlavi dynasty adopted provisions of France's Napoleonic code. In January 1925, and following the French model, the first Iranian penal code classified three types of crimes: felony, misdemeanor, and violation.

In 1979, the Pahlavi dynasty was overthrown because of the Islamic Revolution. The new constitution was based on sharia (Islamic law). The leadership of the country appoints the head of the judiciary system (Principle 157). The Constitution accepts separation of powers; however, the leader oversees all three branches of the government. The system is primarily inquisitorial because courts act as fact finders for all types of crimes, which means the system is based on bench trials. However, there are two exceptions for bench trial: political crimes and libel crimes perpetrated by the media. Principle 168 of the Constitution indicates that with political crimes and libel crimes related to media, courts must proceed with an adversarial process in the presence of a jury.

An independent centralized court system follows the applicable penal and procedural regulations and makes independent decisions. Article 167 of the Constitution indicates that if a judge does not find the statute to make his decision in a specific case, he is obligated to refer to sharia. The Supreme Court also has a main role in making decisions regarding conflicting sentences and overturning unconstitutional or illegal decisions of the courts. Supreme Court decisions are regarded as law for the courts in similar cases. In sum, the main sources of law are the Constitution, statutes passed by legislature, sharia, and Supreme Court decisions.

Law enforcement agencies are under the executive branch of government. Prior to the revolution, the gendarmerie used to be responsible for rural areas and villages fewer than 5,000 inhabitants; also, the gendarmerie was responsible for maintaining the security of the roads. Police had jurisdiction over areas with more than 5,000. Before the Islamic Revolution, the shah of Iran also maintained a secret police known as SAVAK whose repressive tactics became notorious. After the Islamic Revolution, the SAVAK was abolished, and the Islamic Revolutionary Committee was added to maintain security and act as law enforcement. Eventually, the gendarmerie, police, and committee were combined to make the Islamic Revolution of Iran Police Force (IRIP). The force reports to the Ministry of Interior.

Crime and Punishment

According to the Constitution (Principle 4), all laws passed by Iran's Parliament should be compatible with Islamic law. That is why Parliament enacted the new penal code based on sharia. To satisfy this goal, Principle 96 of the Constitution established the Guardian Council whose primary goal is comparing statutes passed by parliament with sharia, to assure they are not against the Islamic regulations. The Guardian Council also is the only official authority to interpret the Constitution.

There is no general definition of crime in sharia; however, each act of commission or omission has its own definition, such as murder, rape, adultery, and so on. Most Islamic criminal law texts contain specific sections for each crime that consists of definition, procedure, law of evidence, and punishment for that crime. There are also some acts of commission or omission that are not discussed in sharia, however, which, because of societal change, are considered criminal behaviors. For instance, there is no concept of cyber crimes in Islamic law. Sharia left the door open for society's needs in the future, by the concept of *ta'azir,* that is acts of commission or omission that are not defined in Islamic law and could be defined by the legislature for the criminal justice system. Here is where the Iranian criminal justice system used the new ideas and standards to deal with those criminal behaviors that are not mentioned in sharia. To implement a policy, the legislature needs to have a general definition for the crime and make it known to the people. According to article 2 from section 1 of Islamic Penal Law (1991), "crime is any act of commission or omission which is against the law and punishable by law."

An unidentified woman, left, leaves the Irshad Judiciary Compound, north of Tehran, Iran, after receiving 70 lashes for taking part in a New Year's party wearing "indecent" clothing, January 3, 2001. Her mother, right, and an unidentified woman, center, walk with her. Police arrested more than 250 people, including foreigners, for attending the private party "indecently" dressed. In Iran, which strictly interprets Islamic laws, women must wear clothing that only shows their faces and hands. (AP Photo/Vahid Salemi)

Furthermore, the code does not divide the concept of crime as Napoleonic code (felony, misdemeanor, and violation). Instead, the sharia code is divided into four different types of punishments for different crimes: *hudud, qisas, diyat, and ta'azirat* (article 13). The code also added a fifth type of punishments called deterrent punishments, even though there are no such sanctions in the Islamic law.

Hudud is the plural of *hadd,* which means the criminal sanctions that sharia has determined for specific crimes. Usually, *hudud* are for serious crimes. Because Islamic law has provisions for these types of crimes in terms of the amount of punishment, the legislature followed the same standards in the code. The code provided different *hudud* for the following crimes: fornication, homosexuality, facilitating prostitution, false accusation of fornication or adultery, drinking alcohol, *dacoity* (armed robbery in which innocents are attacked or killed), and theft. Each of these crimes has specific punishments under the code. Some of them also have subclassifications. For instance, the code envisages different situations in which adultery could happen, from nonconsensual to consensual intercourse, and each has a specific punishment, from whipping to capital punishment through stoning.

Punishment for first-degree rape is capital punishment (article 82), and punishment for fornication is 100 lashes. Sometimes, the age of the victim could affect the amount of *hadd* as well. For instance, if a married woman has sexual intercourse with an underage boy, she has to suffer 100 lashes (article 82), but if the same person commits adultery with a mature man, the punishment could be stoning. It is interesting to note that sometimes the age of the offender can be considered as an aggravating circumstance to increase the amount of punishment. Article 84 indicates that if a married woman or man is old and commits adultery, he or she should suffer from whipping before being stoned to death. The idea of increased punishment based on aggravating circumstance is considered justified based on the general deterrent effect of punishment. Usually, society has higher expectations of elderly citizens because in most communities, elderly citizens are role models for youth. This means that by committing a crime, they are sending the wrong message to the society. That is why if an elderly citizen who is also married commits adultery, this is considered an aggravating circumstance that mandates more punishment than would adultery by someone who is young or not married. Basically, the code wants to send a message to elderly offenders that if they commit the same crime, they might be sentenced to a harsher punishment. Another type of *hadd* is *dacoity* (armed robbery). If the robber was armed and committed the robbery through creating public panic or endangering people's safety, he or she should be punished in one of the following ways, at the discretion of the judge: execution, hanging, amputation of the right hand and left foot, or exile.

There are also different types of *hudud* to which Iranian judges refer to find the right punishments within the provisions of Principle 157 of the Constitution. For instance, apostasy is a crime, and if a Muslim converts to another religion, including Christianity, he or she will face the death penalty.

Quisas

As Article 14 of the Islamic penal code mentions, *quisas* is a criminal sanction that mimics the offender's crime. *Quisas* is the same concept as *lex talionis* (the law of retaliation). The concept of an eye for an eye not only is mentioned in the Bible but also is part of Islamic law. Based on the same concept, the code contains the same provision for those found guilty of some specific crimes. The code accepted the law of retaliation for two different types of crimes, homicide and intentional inflicting of injury, and each type has its own subclassifications. The code divides homicide into three different types:

1. Premeditated murder for which the code prescribes life-for-life punishment. However, if the victim's family withdraws its complaint, the offender can escape capital punishment.
2. First-degree manslaughter.
3. Second-degree manslaughter. The code provides restitution provisions under *diya* (blood money, see next section) for first- and second-degree manslaughter.

The philosophy of *quisas* comes from retributive justice. Retributive justice believes that by committing crime, an offender inflicts harm against society. That is why the criminal justice system must impose the same amount of harm against the offender.

Diyat

Diyat is the plural of *diya,* which is an amount of money ("blood money") that the offender has to pay as punishment for crime in case of death or injuring people. *Diya* can be compared with the concept of restitution in the Western criminal justice system. Usually, for cases of unintentional killing of a victim, the offender has to pay *diya*. The code also has some provisions for converting *quisas* to *diya.* For example, if a victim or his or her family withdraws the complaint against the offender, the victim or family can ask for *diya* or simply forgive the offender without receiving any monetary compensation. It is imperative to note that in the Islamic criminal justice system, sometimes people have a right to forgive the offender. In a situation such as this, prosecutors do not have enough power to convict the offenders. Most of these cases happen regarding those crimes that are to be punished with *quisas* (the law of retaliation). Most offenders try to convince victims or their families to forgive them. Sometimes there are some social processes involved in this mediation. The offender or his or her family will participate in this process of forgiveness. As a result, the law of retaliation (an eye for an eye) is not applicable to such offenders. The amount of money that the offender has to pay for *diya* is based on the seriousness of the crime and also the part of the victim's body that is injured.

Ta'Azirat

Ta'azirat is the plural of *ta'azir*, a criminal sanction that is not mentioned in sharia; however, the state can pass some regulations through Parliament to adopt some punishments for acts of commission or omission. The basic philosophy behind *ta'azir* is the concept of new crimes in society. Islamic criminal law provides for those crimes that have existed throughout history. However, new types of crime will always occur in the future, and the criminal justice system must adopt new rules to respond to these criminal behaviors. Legislators use new ideas in criminal justice to enact some standards for these types of crimes. Policies such as probation, parole, mitigating or aggravating circumstances, necessity, self-defense, and so on are mostly used in *ta'azirat*.

Deterrent Punishments

Deterrent punishments are those punishments that are adopted by the legislature to discipline and maintain order in society (article 17). Because legislators already addressed these types of punishments under *ta'azir*, it seems unnecessary to have deterrent punishments as well. Therefore, the Supreme Court subsequently held that deterrent punishments mentioned in article 17 of Islamic penal code are for those offenders who commit intentional crimes, and *ta'azir* is not enough for them. Hence, imposing a maximum *ta'azir* punishment does not prohibit the judge from adding deterrent punishments to the sentence at his discretion.

There are no deterrent punishments in Islamic criminal law. According to the fourth principle of the Constitution, none of the statutes passed by legislature can be against sharia. Here is an important point about different interpretations of sharia. There are two main divisions of Islam, Sunni and Shia. Sunni mainly has been practiced in the Arab world. Persians mostly follow the Shiite school. Shiite doctrine holds that the prophet Mohammad chose his successor (his cousin Ali), and each successor chose the next one, called the imam.

According to the Shiite school, Islamic principles are divided into the following two parts:

1. *Primary principles,* which are those parts of Islamic rules adopted by the Koran, tradition (sayings and behavior of Prophet Mohammad and his successors), consensus, and reason.
2. *Secondary principles,* which are those changes that have been made to primary principles through high-ranking Shiite clergyman (ayatollah).

This means that the ayatollah has the authority to change some rules and regulations that initially belong to primary principles. Thus, adding deterrent punishments to the code is a legislative use of secondary principles.

There are also some other regulations under primary principles; however, the code changed them to be comparable with today's standards. For instance, under *quisas* (the law of retaliation), primary principles indicate that if an offender murders a person, he or she should be punished by capital punishment. However, if the victim's family forgives the offender through the process of restorative justice, the offender can be released instead of being punished. Legislators noticed that this option would release into society an offender who had committed a heinous crime. Applying this primary principle could create a big risk for society, especially if offenders become recidivists. To prevent this, the code indicates, in article 208, that in such instances, a court can impose between 3 and 10 years' imprisonment for the offender. As noted, these provisions are not in the primary principles of sharia, but by using the secondary-principles provisions of the Shiite school, legislators solved the problem. The code also accepts some of today's standards as secondary principles in the *ta'azir* category of punishments. For example, attempt, probation, parole, and some other concepts cannot be found specifically in Islamic law, but the code accepted them in *ta'azir,* which indicates that the legislature has a tendency to use today's standards through secondary principles.

Juvenile Justice System

In Shiite Islam, there is a belief that the imam is a guardian of children. Following this idea, in today's Iranian criminal justice system, juvenile justice exists based on the age of offenders. In section 4, article 49, the Islamic penal code indicates that children are free from criminal responsibility. If children commit an act that would be punishable if an adult did it, they will be trained or will be sent to correctional facilities. The code allows the courts to use their discretion in deciding whether to send the delinquent child to a correctional facility for rehabilitation or to let his or her parents supervise the child for training. In either case, the child is not criminally responsible.

The code also mentions that a child is not mature based on sharia, but because the legislation did not specifically mention until what age a person is considered a child, some problems have occurred. According to sharia, the age of maturity is 15 years for boys and 9 years for girls. However, there are instances in which delinquent children reach the age of 15 or 9 but are not mentally mature. It seems age of maturity differs from one person to another, depending on many circumstances; thus, there is no universal standard for the age of maturity. Therefore, some children who are already mature by sharia standards are not mature in reality. To solve the problem, the General Legal Affairs Administration of Judiciary System came up with a guideline: If a delinquent child is under the age of 18 but still is not mature, initially he or she will be prosecuted under the adult justice system. Depending on the punishment for the crime that the delinquent committed, the case will be sent either to juvenile court or to the criminal court of the province that has jurisdiction over the case. The legislature also recognized juvenile courts in the Act of Establishing General and Revolutionary Courts (2002).

Corrections

According to the Constitution (Principle 156), the corrections system is under the judiciary, and the judiciary system is required to provide policies to prevent crimes and rehabilitate offenders. As noticed in aforementioned discussions, punishments for *hudud, quisas,* and *diyat* are mentioned in sharia, which was used by Parliament to adopt the Islamic penal code. Most of those primarily principles of sharia are mentioned in the code. However, through the use of secondary principles, some of them have been changed to satisfy today's needs. In examining sharia, one will notice that imprisonment is mentioned for only three different offenses:

1. When a murderer kidnaps and kills the victim. The offender must be incarcerated for the rest of his or her life (life imprisonment) and is a subject for *quisas.*
2. Theft for the third time.
3. Apostasy of females.

There is no other crime in sharia to be punished by imprisonment. However, using imprisonment as a punishment was adopted by the system for a variety of *ta'azirat* and deterrent punishments. They are not mentioned in sharia, but today's standards are used to adopt some policies to deal with these types of crimes.

The penitentiary administration works under the supervision of the judiciary system. The administration supervises all of the correctional facilities in the country. All together there are 178 open, semi-open, and closed prisons; 23 juvenile correctional facilities, 28 after-care centers, and 18 work-therapy centers. In 1979, there were more than 13,903 prisoners in the country's correctional facilities, and in 2002 there were 160,000 prisoners.

Mohsen S. Alizadeh

Further Reading

Bjorken, Johanna. (2004). "Iran." In *Encyclopedia of Law Enforcement,* edited by Larry E. Sullivan. Thousand Oaks, CA: Sage Publications.

Jahangir, Amuzegar. (2007). *The Islamic Republic of Iran Constitution (Persian)*. 25th ed. Tehran: Didar Publications.

Nadjafi, Ali-Hossein. (2004). "Iranian Adult Corrections System: Constant Evolution." In *Adult Corrections,* edited by John Winterdynk, pp. 199–120. New York: Monsey.

Iraq

Legal System: Civil/Islamic
Corruption: High
Prison Rate: Medium
Death Penalty: Yes

Background

The Republic of Iraq has an estimated population of around 27,499,638, composed of Arabs (75–80%), Kurds (15–20%), and smaller minorities such as the Turkoman and Assyrians (5%). The vast majority of Iraqis are Muslim (97%), and of these, approximately 60–65 percent are Shia (Shiite), and 32–37 percent are Sunni (most Kurds are Sunnis). A small minority (3%) of Iraqis such as the Assyrians are Christian or have other religious affiliations.

Until March 2003, Iraq was under the dictatorial rule of Saddam Hussein, who was the head of the Sunni-controlled Arab Socialist Baath Party. A U.S.-led invasion by multinational coalition military forces overthrew Saddam and his ruling Baath Party. The invasion had far-reaching ramifications beyond turning Iraq into a democratic, federal, representative republic. In particular, for present purposes, it has meant that Iraq's police, legal, judicial, and penal systems have been overhauled in an effort to do away with injustices allowed under Saddam's regime and to establish the rule of law.

Since 2003, Iraq has been occupied by coalition forces, while insurgent and militia groups have entrenched themselves in parts of the country. At present, Iraq is considered the world's second-most unstable country, after Sudan, and is considered one of the world's most corrupt countries according to Transparency International.

During Saddam's rule, many changes were made to the police, judicial, and penal systems. The security and order of Iraq were mostly under the control of the military and security and intelligence agencies, and the civil police force played a minimal role. There was an emphasis on dealing with crimes affecting the internal and external security of the state and with crimes against moral decency. Torture and severe punishments such as amputation, branding, and the death penalty were allowed, even for nonviolent offenses. Furthermore, investigative, prosecutorial, and judicial systems were not considered to be independent.

Invasion by U.S.-Led Multinational Coalition Forces, 2003

In March 2003, Iraq was invaded by U.S.-led multinational coalition military forces. The main justifications for the invasion included the belief that Iraq was developing "weapons of mass destruction" and had not abandoned its weapons program in violation of the 1991 United Nations Resolution 687; that Iraq posed an imminent threat to the United States and its allies; that Iraq was cooperating with Al Qaeda and other terrorists; that Iraq had committed many human rights abuses; and that invasion could remove an oppressive dictatorial regime and establish democracy. Among other things, the invasion, which lasted from March 20 to May 1, 2003, led to the immediate political collapse of the ruling Baath Party and the later capture, trial, and execution of Saddam in December 2006, as well as other prominent figures.

The Coalition Provisional Authority (CPA) was created in May 2003 for the temporary administration of Iraq. In March 2004, the Transitional Administrative Law was introduced as the supreme law of the land. In June 2004, all governmental authority of Iraq was transferred to the Iraqi interim government. Following elections in January 2005, the Iraqi transitional government took over. A new permanent constitution was accepted in October 2005. Finally, after elections in December 2005 (where no Baath Party candidates were allowed to run because of their connection with the former regime), the new permanent Iraqi government took office in May 2006. The former Sunni control over Iraq had ended, and all three of Iraq's major ethnic groups (Shiite, Sunni, and Kurds) were represented in the new government. However, although Shiite and Kurdish communities supported the new Constitution, it was largely rejected by Arab Sunnis who had previously been the ruling group. Similarly, in the parliamentary elections, the votes were along ethnic lines. Although the sovereignty of Iraq was transferred to an Iraqi government, coalition forces still remain in Iraq and are working in partnership with the government to help rebuild Iraq and establish the rule of law.

As part of the reconstruction of Iraq, coalition forces made several changes to the police, legal, judicial, and penal systems. For instance, new police, security, and intelligence forces were recruited and trained; the third edition of the 1969 Iraqi penal code and the 1971 law on criminal proceedings were adopted and revised; the judicial and court systems were restructured; and the prison system was modernized. Additionally, basic rights regarding trial and punishment were established.

However, rebuilding the criminal justice system was severely hampered. First, much of the criminal justice infrastructure (buildings, equipment, and information) was looted or destroyed during the invasion. Second, the policy of de-Baathification introduced by the CPA immediately after the invasion meant that civil servants and criminal justice managers and professionals who were affiliated with the Baath Party (regardless of their level of support for Saddam's regime) were removed from their positions, thus leaving a large experience and skills gap in the operation of the criminal justice system (although later this policy was set to be reversed to some degree). Finally, the system has suffered from a lack of resources, including financial aid and expert advice, as a result of the limited investment made by coalition forces and other international bodies. The coalition forces and Iraqi government are also accused of corruption.

Although efforts are being made to establish the rule of law, during the invasion there was massive civil disorder and crime, supported in part by the fact that Iraqi police had left their posts and Saddam had earlier released thousands of convicted prisoners. Government buildings (including police stations, courthouses, and prisons) were looted or destroyed, public utilities were damaged, and violent crime soared. Since the invasion, insurgent and militia groups, including Al Qaeda, have formed and operate in Iraq. These have been responsible for much of the violent crime. There were 4,240 fatalities suffered by coalition forces from March 2003 to January 2008 according to the Iraq Index of the Brookings Institution. It is estimated that from June 2003 to January 2008, 7,829 Iraqi military and police were killed and that 103,567 Iraqi civilians were killed from May 2003 to December 2007 (although as will be shown later, estimates of Iraqi deaths vary dramatically). In addition, Amnesty International has reported evidence that coalition forces, the Iraqi police, and the Iraqi government have also committed violent acts against civilians and committed human rights abuses.

More recently, coalition forces have begun to hand over control of various provinces to the Iraqi government, and several coalition forces have pulled out of Iraq altogether, leaving primarily the U.S., British, and Polish forces. The government of Iraq became entirely responsible for leading security in the entire country pending the complete withdrawal of coalition troops.

Police

By the end of the invasion, most Iraqi police, intelligence and security services, border control guards, and military had left their posts. These were all initially formally dissolved by the CPA. Later, forces and services were reformed. For instance, the Iraqi Armed Forces was reestablished in August 2003 and is controlled by the Ministry of Defense. The military code was also revised. In addition, an Iraqi National Guard was established, and although under the Ministry of Defense, it supports the Iraqi police. The National Guard was not meant to be used in civil operations, but the need to tackle insurgency has meant that they are being used in this capacity.

The Iraqi National Intelligence Service was established in April 2004 to work with the Ministry of Defense and Ministry of the Interior to provide information on terrorism, insurgency, drugs, espionage, weapons of mass destruction, and organized crime. This service, however, now cannot arrest or detain anyone and is no longer allowed to report on domestic political issues or get involved in these.

Immediately after the invasion, the CPA had to reconstruct and transform the police in Iraq. This involved requesting existing personnel to return to duty, recruiting new personnel, and expelling any Baath loyalists or corrupt and unreliable personnel. The transformation also involved (re-)training the police to conduct routine patrols, make arrests, and investigate crimes (although magistrates mostly perform this function), as well as equipping and organizing the police. A police code of conduct was introduced. However, implementing a new police force in Iraq took considerable time, and the effort suffered from a lack of funding and agreement on the type of force required (e.g., to tackle community crime or counterinsurgency) and lack of direct, competent, and noncorrupt leadership from the Ministry of the Interior. As a consequence, the police were left unprepared for the violence they faced from insurgents, and insurgents have infiltrated the police force.

The Ministry of the Interior now manages the civil security forces. These comprise the Iraqi Police Service, the Iraqi National Police, and supporting forces such as the Department of Border Enforcement and the Facilities Protection Service. The Iraqi Police Service is mainly responsible for enforcing Iraqi criminal law, as well as performing daily station, patrol, and traffic control functions. In early 2006, a new Iraqi National Police was established (along the lines of a gendarmerie) to deal with insurgency operations, public disorder, and terrorism. Its personnel, however, include Shia loyal to militia groups. The Department of Border Enforcement consists of border police, customs, immigration, and nationality and civil affairs. Finally, the Facilities Protection Service protects government buildings and facilities. The Kurdistan Regional Government has its own security forces.

The U.S. Department of defense estimated that, as of January 2008, there were approximately 155,248 trained police (plus 41,399 national police) and 27,959 trained border enforcement personnel. In addition, there were 174,940 personnel in the army, 19,750 in the support forces, 1,370 in the air force, and 1,194 in the navy.

The Iraqi police and security forces are currently heavily supported by U.S. military teams, private contractors, and security companies. In addition, the Iraqi forces have benefited from the support of approximately 91,000 individuals who joined the Sons of Iraq (formerly called Concerned Local Citizens) to support the fight against insurgency by providing security to infrastructure and local-level intelligence. Some of these individuals are being trained and integrated into the Iraqi police, but it is unclear what the future of this group will be.

The work of the police in Iraq is difficult. They face violence from insurgents. For instance, individuals have been targeted at recruitment stations, while performing their duties, and after work on their way home. From June 2003 to January 2008, it is estimated that 7,829 Iraqi military and police were killed. Consequently, members have left the Iraqi police. Despite this, new recruits are readily found because of Iraqis' need to find employment.

Problematically, the new civil security forces have also been infiltrated by insurgents, who may commit crimes while working as part of the forces or steal uniforms and impersonate police officers when committing crimes. Indeed, the police in Iraq working under the Shiite-controlled Ministry of the Interior reportedly have links to Shia militia, and the Iraqi National Police in particular have been accused of using sectarian death squads against Sunnis, as well as kidnappings. The police have been accused of condoning attacks on people suspected of violating Islamic morality. Thus, it is apparent that the police in Iraq have not yet reached a sufficient degree of impartiality, responsibility, and accountability and are not yet working entirely within human rights obligations. Distrust of the police remains.

Crime

Classification of Crimes in the Third Edition of the 1969 Iraqi Penal Code

In 1969, the Baath Party adopted a new penal code that replaced the original code called the Baghdad Penal Code, which was introduced by the British in 1919. During Saddam's rule, the 1969 code was itself revised. Specific laws made it a crime to behave in a way that was deemed politically, economically, or socially disruptive. Thus, the definition of crime included acts that were harmful to the state. The number and range of crimes that carried the death penalty also increased to include several nonviolent crimes such as theft, prostitution, adultery, homosexuality, corruption, smuggling antiquities, and military desertion. Gender crimes such as sexual violence and honor killings (of female family members perceived to have brought dishonor upon the family) were not considered serious and were more or less condoned. In general, the penal code was very strict and especially biased against dissidents and women.

In July 2003, the CPA declared that the third edition of the 1969 Iraqi penal code would be re-adopted, with some revisions. In this code, criminal offenses are separated into those that are ordinary and those that are political. In addition, there are three categories of criminal offenses that increase in their level of seriousness: infractions, misdemeanors, and felonies.

The penal code separates offenses into those against the public welfare, those against the person, and infractions. Offenses against the public welfare include offenses against the external and internal security of the state; offenses against public authorities (e.g., against the Constitution, and public officials); offenses prejudicial to the court (e.g., affecting due process, perjury, and impersonating officials); offenses against the public confidence (e.g., counterfeiting and forgery of stamps and currency); offenses in breach of the duties of office (e.g., embezzlement); offenses that endanger the public (e.g., fire and explosives, flooding by a public utility, offenses affecting safety of public transport, telecommunications, and public health); social offenses (e.g., violating religious sensibilities, desecrating graves, offenses involving the family, drunkenness, gambling, and begging); and other offenses (e.g., prostitution). Drug offenses are not explicitly mentioned in the code.

Offenses against the person refer to those affecting the life and physical safety of others (e.g., murder, assault, intentional wounding, and abortion); offenses affecting the freedom of an individual include kidnapping, threats, and defamation, for example; and offenses against property include, for example, theft, breach of trust, deception, commercial offenses, damage to property, and killing animals. Although the penal code refers to theft, it does not use the terms burglary or robbery. Finally, infractions include offenses against the public highway, against the public peace, against public health, against property, and against the public decency and organizational offenses.

According to the new constitution, no law can be passed that contradicts the Constitution, the laws of Islam, or the principles of democracy. The penal code was further revised by the CPA. For instance, the death penalty was suspended for members of the Baath Party who commit certain offenses affecting internal state security, and imprisonment was suspended for anyone who publicly insults the president of Iraq. Legal proceedings can now be brought only with the written permission of the head of the Iraqi government for offenses of publication, offenses affecting external state security, certain offenses affecting internal state security, offenses affecting the Constitution, and certain offenses against public officials. No one can be prosecuted for working with coalition forces. In addition, some amendments were made to the maximum penalty carried by certain offenses, so that life imprisonment (remainder of person's natural life) now applies to kidnapping, destruction of public utilities, and rape and sexual assault (with 15 years for indecent sexual assault). The mitigating circumstances provided for kidnapping were repealed. The maximum penalty is now life imprisonment (remaining natural life) for theft of means of transport using force. The CPA announced that any individual publicly inciting violence and disorder or advocating changing Iraq's borders or a return to Baath Party rule would face immediate detention. Stiffer penalties would also be given to offenders originally granted amnesty by Saddam's regime in 2002 if they are convicted of a crime. There are now also increased sentences for individuals convicted of weapons violations after conditional release. Finally, gender-based crimes are being treated more seriously. For instance, judges and prosecutors from the Iraq Special Tribunal were trained to investigate, prosecute, and try crimes of sexual violence and honor crimes that affect women, so that legal precedents can be set on gender and women's rights. The statute used by the tribunal redefines rape as a serious gender-neutral crime and codifies other crimes such as sexual slavery and forcible prostitution.

Crime Statistics

Crime statistics from Saddam's regime are difficult to obtain, although it can be said that the severity of the regime tended to minimize general crime and that the nature of the laws and penalties probably served to fuel certain crimes such as those against women. In fact, the UN Special Rapporteur for Violence against Women reported that more 4,000 women were victims of honor killings from 1991 on.

The Border and Immigration Agency of the U.K. Home Office reports that, generally, the security situation in Iraq is poor. Crime is committed by organized gangs, members of the security forces, and insurgents. After the invasion in 2003, the coalition forces focused their efforts on securing oil fields and refineries, while violent and other property crime soared. Organized criminal groups trading in firearms, drugs, and stolen cars and who kidnap and blackmail have established themselves. Many crimes during that initial period were unreported because there were no police to report to. Similarly, because the country's borders were unmanned, there was opportunity for foreign criminals and terrorists to enter the country and for the smuggling of stolen antiquities, weapons, drugs, and other goods. These crimes would not have been detected. In fact, Iraq does not have any national crime statistics. However, in 2004, the Baghdad Police Department began to collect data on reported and detected crime.

The U.S. Department of Defense reports that property crime, including the destruction of government buildings and other public utilities, is pervasive. For instance, in Baghdad, major property thefts rose from 47 in 2003 to 284 in 2004. There were 466 attacks on Iraqi oil and gas pipelines, installations, and personnel from June 2003 to January 2008 according to the Iraq index. Throughout the country, there was also looting of archaeological sites and antiquities, although some stolen items from Iraqi museums and cultural heritage sites have now been recovered.

The definition and enforcement of Islamic morality, defended in the Constitution, has not been formalized, and so there are instances of private citizens, groups, and even Iraqi police taking the law into their own hands by punishing people (in particular, women and homosexuals) they suspect are guilty of immorality. Domestic violence remains prevalent. For instance, the WHO Iraq Family Health Survey 2006/7 found that 21.1 percent of married women said they had experienced physical violence in the preceding 12 months. Honor crimes against women in the Kurdistan region have also risen according to Amnesty International. Children are also being pushed into prostitution, drugs, and violence according to the U.S. State Department.

Drug abuse has also risen amid the increase in the availability of narcotics. Furthermore, there is evidence that some Iraqis are turning to growing drugs such as opium, which fund the insurgency.

Few kidnappings are brought to police attention often because families simply wish to pay the ransom. Nevertheless, more than 919 kidnappings were reported to the U.S. Embassy Baghdad Office of Hostage Affairs from 2004 to 2006. These included 347 Iraqis, and this figure is estimated to represent less than 10 percent of the actual kidnappings across the country.

In Baghdad, from May 2003 to April 2004, there was a rise in murders from 3.6 per 100,000 inhabitants before the invasion to more than 24 in 2004 according to a RAND study in 2005. These are conservative figures because they do not include deaths from insurgency and terrorism.

Generally, there has been a large increase in violent crime, including that by insurgent, militia, and terrorist groups. Several organizations have compiled statistics on the number of violent deaths in Iraq involving combatants and noncombatants during the invasion (March to April 2003) and since. However, whereas the deaths of coalition forces are reliably recorded, the tracking of deaths of others, including Iraqi forces, insurgents, and civilians, is less reliable. Furthermore, different methods for collecting data on Iraqi deaths have yielded different results, and there are several reasons (including lack of reporting and detection) to suggest that these deaths are undercounted.

The Commonwealth Institute estimated that during the invasion, there were a total of 12,150 Iraqi fatalities (plus or minus 2,150), including 3,750 (plus or minus 550) noncombatant civilians. These figures were based on a combination of journalistic surveys of hospital and burial records, media and nongovernmental reports, interviews with military personnel, and U.S. combat statistics. A report published in *The Lancet* estimated that after the invasion, as of July 2006, there were 654,965 (392,979–942,636) excess Iraqi deaths as a consequence of the fighting, with 601,027 (426,369–793,663) resulting from violence (e.g., gunshot, explosion, air strike, and car bomb). These data were based on a national cross-sectional survey of 1,849 randomly sampled household clusters from 16 governorates. By contrast, the Iraqi Family Health Survey Study Group also used a nationally representative survey of 9,345 households but estimated that there were 151,000 (104,000–223,000) violent deaths from March 2003 to June 2006. The Brookings Institute based its figures on UN reports, including hospital and morgue data, as well as data provided by the U.S. Department of Defense. It concluded that there had been 103,567 Iraqi civilian fatalities from May 2003 to December 2007. A survey of 2,414 adult Iraqis by Opinion Research Business estimated that there were 1,033,000 (946,000–1,120,000) civilian deaths between March 2003 and August 2007. According to the official military sources used by the Iraq Coalition Casualty Count, there were 4,321 fatalities of coalition forces from March 2003 to March 2008. Iraqi security forces and civilian deaths reported in the media totaled 39,797 from January 2006 to March 2008. The Iraq Body Count project cross-checks media reports and figures from hospitals, morgues, and nongovernmental organizations on violent deaths of civilian noncombatants (including some police and military). The figures are updated regularly, and as of February 2008, the project documented 82,591–90,115 deaths. Generally, the levels of civilian deaths fell by around 72 percent from July 2007 to February 2008.

Attacks by insurgents on coalition forces, Iraqi security, and civilians showed some decline over the period from May 2003 to July 2007 according to Global Security Operation Iraqi Freedom (OIF). However, there were still many attacks (e.g., around 140 in July 2007). Levels of violence in February 2008 were around 60 percent lower than June 2007 and similar to the levels in mid-2005, as reported by the U.S. Department of Defense. Iraqi forces and U.S. military deaths fell from January 2006 to February 2008. Finally, although incidents of sectarian violence rose from February 2005 to April 2006, ethno-sectarian deaths fell from January 2006 to February 2008.

Finding of Guilt

During Saddam's rule, the judicial system partly continued to follow the French model introduced prior to 1918 when Iraq was under Ottoman rule, partly followed the model introduced by the British who ruled subsequently until 1932, and partly followed Islamic law. The legal system was inquisitorial. Juries were not used in Iraq. The RCC chaired by Saddam was the highest legislative authority. The Ministry of Justice managed the courts and appointed all judges with the agreement of the president. There were courts of first instance (including magistrates' courts) dealing with misdemeanors and minor felonies, courts of sessions dealing with felonies and appeals from courts of first instance, and a Court of Cassation (Iraq's highest court) dealing with appeals. In addition, there was a security component to the court system (revolutionary courts) that dealt with crimes against the state and operated under a separate judicial system. Here, Baath Party members without legal training conducted closed hearings, and defendants had limited rights and faced harsh penalties. The prosecutorial system included the judicial investigator, the investigative judge, and the prosecutor. In practice, the judiciary was marginalized. There was no real independence of the judiciary, and the president could make laws and overturn any court decision, so the courts were used to protect the regime. Saddam granted immunity from prosecution to particular groups such as members of the Baath Party and men who committed rape and honor killings.

The justice system was overhauled after the invasion in 2003 in an effort to make the judiciary independent and operate under the rule of law and to make court proceedings follow those of modern Western courts. The system is, however, still inquisitorial, and juries are not used. In June 2003, the CPA established the Central Criminal Court of Iraq, which has jurisdiction over crimes committed in Iraq since March 19, 2003. This central court has two chambers: an investigative court and a trial court. The investigative court has jurisdiction over all criminal offenses and consists of one judge. The trial court consists of three judges and deals with matters (including felonies) referred to it by the investigative court. In addition, the Higher Juridical Council later established major crimes courts across Iraq as branches of the Central Criminal Court to deal with acts of terrorism. There is also a temporary court at the Rustafa complex in Baghdad. The hearings of the Central Criminal Court are public, although broadcasting from within the courtroom is prohibited. Judges' deliberations are confidential. There is a right to legal representation. There is a right of appeal from the decisions of both the investigative and trial courts, to the trial court and Court of Cassation, respectively. In 2004, there were 128 courthouses and 557 separate courts. The courts are organized into 17 appellate districts.

An Iraqi Special Tribunal was set up in December 2003 to deal with Iraqis accused of certain crimes committed in Iraq or abroad from July 17, 1968, to May 1, 2003. The crimes include genocide, crimes against humanity, war crimes, and violation of specific Iraqi laws (e.g., manipulating the judiciary, squandering public assets, and threat or actual war against an Arab nation). The tribunal also deals with gender crimes. The tribunal is independent. There is a trial chamber, an appeals chamber, and investigative judges, as well as a prosecutions department. Each chamber has permanent judges who do not overlap (i.e., five judges for the trial chamber and nine for the appeals chamber) and who may be Iraqi or foreign. The tribunal, which can set precedents, applies some of its own rules of procedure and evidence and principles of criminal law but otherwise uses the revised 1971 law on criminal proceedings and the revised 1969 penal code. The accused has rights similar to those in Western criminal courts operating under due process. Hearings are public. The verdict is based on a majority vote. Individual responsibility is assumed, and so punishment is applied to an individual. Only sentences compatible with those in existing Iraqi law (including the death penalty) can be imposed. The crimes of Saddam and other prominent members of the Baath Party have been tried in the Iraqi Special Tribunal.

After the invasion, the judiciary in Iraq became an independent branch of government, no longer reporting to the Ministry of Justice. A Judicial Review Committee was set up temporarily by the CPA in June 2003 to investigate the suitability of judges and prosecutors to hold office and to remove them where necessary. Although the committee was later abolished, its decisions remain. The Council of Judges was reestablished in September 2003 (after it was abolished in 1979) to supervise the judicial and prosecutorial systems in Iraq, independently of the Ministry of Justice. The Higher Juridical Council later assumed the role of the Council of Judges. The Ministry of Justice meanwhile drafts legislation and organizes judicial and prosecutorial training. In May 2004, the CPA made the judiciary (Council of Judges and Court of Cassation) financially independent of the Ministry of Justice. The Higher Juridical Council oversees and manages the budget of the court system, all court personnel, and courthouse security. The judiciary in the Iraqi Kurdistan National Assembly is organized slightly differently.

Effort was made to find attorneys and judges who were not Baath loyalists or who were not complicit in the abuses of Saddam's regime, as well as to reinstate judges unjustifiably dismissed by Saddam. The Iraq Index reported that as of November 2007, there were 1,200 trained judges (300 fewer than required). According to the CPA, judges should meet the following criteria: possess high moral character and reputation, not be affiliated with the Baath Party, have no criminal record or involvement, be an Iraqi National, have been a judge for at least five years with a demonstrated high level of competence, and be prepared to sign the oath of office. Judges and prosecutors have also been given training in human rights.

However, judicial work is dangerous, and judges and prosecutors have been attacked. Thirty-five Iraqi judges have been assassinated since 2003 according to the U.S. Department of Defense. A special area called the "Rule of Law Complex" has been set up in Rustafa to house judges and their families and hold trials in safety and security. More such areas are expected to be built around the country.

The Constitution defines basic rights regarding trial and punishment. These include equality before the law, independence of the judiciary, legal defense (including public defender/assistance), presumption of innocence, public trial, compensation, and protection against torture or inhumane treatment. The right to remain silent was added by the CPA. In addition, the courts apply the third edition of the 1969 Iraqi penal code as revised by the CPA and the Iraqi law on criminal proceedings of 1971 as revised by the CPA.

Iraqi Law on Criminal Proceedings of 1971 with Amendments

The law on criminal proceedings describes the initiation of criminal proceedings; investigation of offenses (e.g., investigating officers, notification of offenses, investigations conducted by the police, hearing witnesses, and search); methods to attend court (e.g., summons, arrest, bail, dealing with absconding, questioning the accused, and judges' post-investigation decisions); court process (e.g., types of court and their jurisdictions, defendants' court appearance, principles of trial, charge, court rulings, proceedings against those with diminished responsibility); appeals against judgments (including retrial); and implementation of penalties. The CPA made revisions to the provisions of bail, outlined rights of security detainees held by coalition forces, and altered use of the death penalty (which was later revised by the Iraqi interim government).

Briefly, initial investigations are conducted by examining magistrates or those acting under their supervision. The accused may attend court after being summoned or after being arrested (the latter always applying to those accused of offenses punishable by death or life imprisonment). Pretrial custody can be used under certain circumstances: An accused charged with an offense punishable by detention of three years or less or a fine must be released on a pledge with or without bail unless it is considered that he would obstruct justice or abscond. An accused charged with an infraction must be released unless he has no fixed abode. A person charged with an offense carrying imprisonment for a term of three years to life imprisonment may be held in custody for 15 days at a time or released on a pledge with or without bail if the judge does not consider the person will escape or prejudice the investigation. A suspect charged with an offense carrying a maximum penalty of life imprisonment can now be held without bail until trial. Similarly, a suspect charged with an offense carrying the death penalty may be held in pretrial custody for a longer period. The total period in pretrial custody should not exceed one quarter of the maximum sentence for the offense the accused is charged with. Bail should be set according to the type of offense and circumstances of the accused. A "bailsman" (bail bondsman) may be used. A remand in custody pretrial is deducted from the sentence, even if that sentence is a fine.

The accused must be questioned within 24 hours of his arrest, although he has the right to remain silent and to be legally represented. If the examining magistrate finds there is sufficient evidence for a trial, the accused is transferred to the appropriate court. The defendant has an opportunity to plead guilty, plead not guilty, or request a trial. There is a trial for each charge. (However, the court may issue a penalty without trial, which can later be contested and a trial set, for infractions not liable to a sentence of detention, where a request for compensation has not been submitted, and the defendant's action has been proven.) The trial may occur in the defendant's absence if he was notified but absconded or does not attend without legal excuse. Trial sessions are open unless the court decides otherwise to maintain security or decency (or if proceeding against a juvenile). Court proceedings are subject to written record. Offenders may be extradited in specific circumstances.

After the trial, the court can issue a verdict of guilty followed by a penalty, issue a verdict of not guilty followed by release, drop the charge due to insufficient evidence and release, or issue a judgment of diminished responsibility if the defendant is not legally responsible followed by release. Judgments may be made in absentia, and the defendant notified, who can object. Defendants have the right to appeal in the Court of Cassation (with death sentences being automatically appealed). Mentally ill defendants said to have diminished responsibility are given over to relatives on payment of a guarantee to undergo treatment.

Despite the legal rights and protections afforded by the law on criminal proceedings and by the Constitution, there is evidence that defendants are being denied a fair public trial according to the U.S. Department of State. They often lack an opportunity to get defense representation and face considerable delays.

Juvenile Justice

Saddam inherited a juvenile justice system from his predecessors that institutionalized juveniles. Although the Juveniles' Law 11 of 1962 included several features in common with modern juvenile systems, such as hearing cases in closed sessions, and emphasized the protection and treatment of offenders, this did not occur in practice. There was little effort to rehabilitate and reintegrate juveniles.

At present, the penal code sets out the liability of juveniles, and the law on criminal proceedings stipulates how juveniles are proceeded against. The code states that anyone under the age of 7 at the time the offense was committed cannot be tried. A juvenile is defined as someone who commits an offense between the ages of 7 and 18. Furthermore, if a juvenile is under 15 years at the time of the offense, then he is considered to be a child, and if he is between 15 and 18 years, then he is considered a young person.

Cases in juvenile courts are heard by a judge, lawyer, and social worker. The type of sentence is determined by the age of the offender. For example, a juvenile committing an infraction can be cautioned in court or fined. A child or young person committing a misdemeanor can be handed over to his or her guardians who must ensure the child's good behavior for a specified period, can be confined to a reform school or school for young offenders for a period of no more than three years, or can be fined. A child committing a felony can be sentenced to confinement in a reform school for two to five years, if the crime for an adult carries life imprisonment or the death penalty, or one to four years otherwise. A felony committed by a young person can result in confinement in a school for young offenders for 2 to 15 years if it carries life imprisonment or the death penalty, or from 1 year to half the maximum penalty otherwise. No person committing a crime between the ages of 18 and 20 can be sentenced to death (life imprisonment applies instead). Finally, young offenders may be confined in a school and children in a reform school, both for the purpose of training and correction for the period specified.

Effort is being made to develop policies and practices that will update and rejuvenate the juvenile system and integrate it with related agencies. It is anticipated that UNICEF will help in that capacity, with special training for juvenile judges, social workers, Iraqi lawyers, and juvenile police units.

Punishment

Types of Punishment—Sentencing According to the Third Edition of the 1961 Iraqi Penal Code

Since the invasion in 2003, sentences have been laid out in the third edition of the revised 1969 Iraqi penal code, and their implementation is described in the revised 1971 law on criminal proceedings. According to the code, the main sentences are death penalty, life imprisonment, imprisonment for a term of years, penal servitude, detention, fine, confinement in a school for young offenders, and confinement in a reform school. The death penalty involves hanging by the neck. Appeals of death sentences and life sentences are automatic. If the court upholds the decision, then the sentence must be carried out within 30 days. No one over 70 years of age should be executed. Life imprisonment means 20 years (or remaining natural life of person for certain offenses as amended by the CPA), and imprisonment cannot exceed more than 25 years in total. A person may be put to work during imprisonment. Penal servitude is for 3 months to 5 years. Detention is from 24 hours to 1 year, and a person must not be put to work. A sentence of detention less than 1 year may be suspended. A fine can be an additional sentence and may result in detention if it is not paid. The period spent in custody pretrial and during trial is deducted from a prison sentence or fine. The law on criminal proceedings allows a person given a custodial sentence to be granted a conditional discharge in certain circumstances.

In addition, the penal code lays out "incidental" penalties, "supplemental" penalties, and "precautionary measures." Incidental penalties are not necessarily stated in the sentence, and they may include withdrawal of certain rights and privileges (e.g., voting) and police supervision. Supplemental penalties also refer to the withdrawal of certain rights and privileges (e.g., holding public office and carrying arms), confiscation, and publication of the sentence. Precautionary measures may be imposed on a person who has committed a crime and who is considered a danger to public welfare (e.g., confinement in therapy unit, police supervision, driving disqualification, confiscation, and closure of business). Some of these penalties and measures may hold for a period after completion/termination of the primary sentence. Violations of some of these penalties and measures can result in detention or a fine.

The type of offense determines the severity of the punishment in the penal code. A felony is punishable by death, life imprisonment (i.e., 20 years), or 5 to 15 years' imprisonment. A misdemeanor is punishable by detention (with or without hard labor) for three months to five years or by a fine. Finally, an infraction is punishable by detention for 25 hours to 3 months or by a small fine.

Sentences are also determined by aggravating and mitigating circumstances. However, whereas the penal code does not list specific mitigating circumstances, it does refer to general aggravating circumstances such as having a base motive, the physical or mental vulnerability of the victim, use of violence, and the abuse of position of employment.

Torture and cruel, degrading, or inhumane treatment or punishment was prohibited by the CPA. The death penalty was suspended temporarily in June 2003 by the CPA, but it was reinstated by the Iraqi interim government in August 2004 for offenses against internal state security, offenses that endanger the public, attacks on transportation, premeditated murder, drug trafficking, and abductions. Anyone involved in terrorism may also receive the death penalty. Although there is an automatic right of appeal for those receiving the death penalty, there is no right to pardon or commutation of sentence (which was allowed under previous criminal procedure law). The death penalty is also used in the Kurdistan Regional Government area. According to Amnesty International, Iraq was fourth in the world for its frequent use of the death penalty in 2006, after China, Iran, and Pakistan. Since the new Iraqi government took control, 270 death sentences have been meted out, and at least 100 people have been executed (with at least 65 in 2006).

Prison

During Saddam's regime, the penal system was administered by the Ministry of Labor and Social Affairs. The prison at Abu Ghraib near Baghdad was the main prison and housed several thousand prisoners. In addition, there were three smaller prisons in the governorates of Al Basrah, Babylon, and Nineveh and detention centers around the country, as well as police cells. Standards in Iraqi prisons were poor, and prisoners suffered torture and other abuses. Precise imprisonment figures are difficult to obtain, but in 2003, the prison population was estimated to be 10,000, according to the Iraq Index. In October 2002, Saddam had given amnesty to most political prisoners in Iraq.

Today, the Ministry of Justice oversees the Iraqi Corrections Service (ICS), which is responsible for prisons, although detention facilities are also operated by other agencies such as the Ministry of the Interior and the Ministry of Defense. In addition, there have been reports of the operation of unofficial detention facilities by the Iraqi government and of holding cells on U.S. military bases such as Camp Cropper and Camp Bucca in Iraq. In 2005, the ICS operated 17 detention facilities throughout the country, and there were plans to build 3 more large prisons by the end of 2005, resulting in a total capacity of around 16,500 beds. The Kurdish regional authorities operated 7. The Ministry of Defense operated 30 "holding areas" or detention facilities. Although the precise number is unknown, the Ministry of the Interior operated over 1,000 facilities including police station holding facilities. The prison at Abu Ghraib in Baghdad remains the largest. The temporary prison at the Rustafa complex in Baghdad is also large, with approximately 6,647 (mostly untried) detainees as of February 2008. In addition, new facilities are being constructed that will provide education and skills training to help reintegration of offenders.

Prisoners in Iraq fall into three categories: prisoners of war, security detainees, and criminal detainees. The ICS prisons and detention centers hold criminal detainees who have violated the penal code (and so these do not include insurgents fighting coalition forces). Detainees may be on remand awaiting trial or serving sentences. There are a large number of untried prisoners because of the delay in investigating crimes. As of December 2007, there were approximately 26,000 people in U.S. custody and 24,000 in Iraqi custody, according to the Iraq Index. There were approximately 640 juvenile detainees at the Remembrance II Theater Internment Facility according to the U.S. Department of State. Around 80 percent of those held by the coalition forces are Sunnis. In February 2008, the Iraqi Parliament passed an Amnesty Law to consider amnesty for detainees who are charged with certain offenses and who are not already sentenced to death. This will reduce the number of people in custody.

The CPA made an effort to rebuild and modernize the prison system to meet international standards. Criteria for the management of detention and prison facilities in Iraq were outlined by the CPA. Prisoners of different categories (i.e., men and women, untried and convicted prisoners, persons imprisoned for debt or civil offenses and criminal offenses, and prisoners age under 18 and adults) should be kept separately. Prisoners who are determined to be mentally ill should be sent to a mental institution rather than detained in a prison, and during their stay in prison, they should be under medical supervision. There are a variety of other basic principles pertaining to quality of food, respect for religion, contact with families, and sanitary conditions.

However, the fact that many prisoners are being held in facilities not managed by the Ministry of Justice means that their well-being cannot be easily monitored or guaranteed. In fact, there are many reports of poor conditions in prisons run by the Ministry of Justice. For example, there is overcrowding, violence and other prisoner abuse, deaths in prison, children in adult prisons, unconvicted and convicted prisoners being held together, and people serving a longer time on remand than the potential sentence for the crime they are charged with. Conditions are particularly bad in detention facilities controlled by the Ministry of Defense and Ministry of the Interior, which have been infiltrated by Shia militias. Similarly, the conditions in prisons in the Kurdistan Regional Government area are also difficult. There have also been reports of the torture and ill-treatment of prisoners detained by the coalition forces, of which the most infamous were the abuses that occurred in Abu Ghraib prison in 2003. Finally, there is particular concern over the treatment of juveniles in detention.

New ICS corrections officers were recruited to work in a modern penal system (given that former officers were corrupt or otherwise unfit for duty). New recruits receive training covering topics such as corrections techniques, human rights, personnel management, and security. They will not normally be armed. Female staff will deal with women prisoners. Prisons will be inspected regularly. An Iraqi ombudsman for penal and detention matters has been established. Training and inspection are needed, not only because of the prisoner abuses documented in the past and more recently by U.S. military in Abu Ghraib prison, but also because although most corrections officers are Shiites, most prisoners are Sunnis.

Mandeep K. Dhami

Further Reading

Amnesty International. (2008). *Carnage and Despair. Iraq Five Years On:* http://www.amnesty.org/en/library/asset/MDE14/001/2008/en/3f78611b-f1e9–11dc-adcd-cdafd0ab0dfe/mde140012008eng.pdf.

BBC News. (2008). *Saddam's Life and Times:* http://news.bbc.co.uk/1/shared/spl/hi/middle_east/03/v3_iraq_timeline/html/default.stm.

Perito, Robert. (2003). *Establishing the Rule of Law in Iraq.* United States Institute of Peace Web site: http://www.usip.org/resources/establishing-rule-law-iraq.

Rathmell, Andrew, Olga Oliker, Terrance K. Kelly, David Brannan, and Keith Crane. (2005). *Developing Iraq's Security Sector.* Santa Monica, CA: RAND Corporation.

U.S. Department of State. (2008). *Iraq. Country Reports on Human Rights Practices—2007:* http://www.state.gov/g/drl/rls/hrrpt/2007/100596.htm.

Israel

Legal System: Common
Murder: Low
Corruption: Low
Human Trafficking: Medium
Prison Rate: High
Death Penalty: Yes
Corporal Punishment: No

Background

Political and Social Context

The state of Israel, established in 1948, is a parliamentary democracy, officially defined as a democratic and Jewish state. Its total area is about 22,000 square kilometers, and its population includes over 7 million residents. Although Jews make up more than three-quarters of the overall population, the country includes a substantial minority of Muslims (16.5%) and smaller numbers of Christians (2.1%, which include both Arab and non-Arab Christians) and Druze (1.7%). About 20 percent of Israelis are Arabs, a figure that includes Arab residents of East Jerusalem. About 66 percent of the Jewish population was born in Israel, whereas the rest came to Israel from numerous countries worldwide. Nearly half of the Jewish population is concentrated in the center of the country, whereas the Arab population is mostly centered in the north and south districts. Geographically, Israel is bordered by Syria and Lebanon in the north, Egypt in the south, the Mediterranean Sea in the west, and Jordan in the East.

The head of the state of Israel is the president; however, his role is mainly ceremonial. The Israeli Parliament (the "Knesset") is composed of 120 members who proportionally represent the different political parties. Elections for the Knesset are held every four years. The prime minister, who is the leader of the coalition government, is elected by the Knesset in a dual process. First, the president invites the leaders of political parties for discussions and assigns the one with the best chances of formulating the government with this task. The Knesset either approves or disapproves the new government established by the chosen party leader, and the leader who is eventually successful in formulating the government becomes the prime minister and holds much of the responsibilities associated with the government's activities.

Israel maintains the principle of separation of powers, whereby the Knesset constitutes the legislature; the government, led by the prime minister, holds the executive; and the Israeli courts hold the judicial responsibility. This last branch is composed of three levels of courts: magistrates' courts (or "peace" courts), which exercise authority over offenses punishable by a fine or by no more than seven years of imprisonment; district courts, which handle all cases that do not fall under the authority of the magistrates' courts, as well as appeals in relation to cases that were tried by these courts; and last, the Supreme Court, which handles appeals in relation to judgments of the districts courts and also serves as the High Court of Justice ("Bagatz"), where it provides judicial review of policies and actions of the state.

Legal System

The criminal legal system in Israel is adversarial. There is no jury and no preliminary hearing, and all cases are judged and ruled by professional judges. The burden of proof rests on the prosecution, which is usually the responsibility of the state prosecutor's office or, in minor cases, the police prosecution. The defendant has the right to be represented by an attorney during all stages of the criminal legal process, and in some cases, there is mandatory representation, and thus a defense counsel is appointed by the court.

The criminal legal process is governed by the criminal procedure law that was adopted by the Knesset in 1965 and reissued in a consolidated version in 1982. Its origins, however, may be traced back to the Criminal Code Ordinance of the British Mandatory Government of Palestine, which was introduced in 1936. It was based on the British common law and was modified to account for local circumstances. In 1977, a new integrated version was published in Hebrew, and in 1994, following ongoing revisions, a new draft of the major part of the penal law was adopted. This new version reflected Supreme Court decisions handed down over the years and included a revision of the basic principles of criminal responsibility, whereby subjective principles of culpability were emphasized.

In addition to the criminal procedure law, a second major statute related to the criminal process in Israel was the Criminal Procedure (Arrest and Search) Ordinance (New Version) 1969, which has been replaced by two laws that govern the pretrial procedures of arrest, bail, and searches. Today there are still numerous statutes related to the criminal law that were adopted during the British Mandate (and are thus called "Ordinance"), such as the Dangerous Drugs Ordinance (New Version) 1973.

The criminal legal system in Israel has evolved greatly since 1965, particularly with regard to defendants' rights. For example, the wiretapping law and privacy law prevent the admissibility of evidence that was obtained using illegal means. Although in certain notable court cases, the Supreme Court has upheld such exclusionary rules, the "fruit of the poisonous tree" doctrine is not part of the Israeli justice system. At the same time, there has been a shift toward the "crime control" model. For example, some statutory amendments are viewed as having an eroding effect on the "right to silence."

History, Organization, and Role of Police

Several Israeli policing scholars have noted that the origins of the Israel National Police are firmly rooted in the military. When the state of Israel was declared in 1948, the initial organizational structure and operational procedures of the Israeli police were based heavily on the model of the British Mandate Police, which was a colonial-military police. In turn, the responsibility for establishing the Israeli police was placed on the "Hagana" (the pre-state Jewish militia) and on the chief of the general staff of the IDF (Israel Defense Forces, the Israeli Army). The Israel police force was initially founded as a brigade in the IDF and depended on it for weapons, supplies, and manpower.

The police in Israel are organized at the national level. All police units are subordinated to the commissioner of police, who is appointed by the government on the recommendation of the minister of public security. Geographically, the Israeli National Police is divided into six districts: Northern, Tel-Aviv, Central, Judea and Samaria, Jerusalem, and

Southern. Each district (*machoz*) is again divided into two to four subdistricts (*mrchav*), and within the subdistricts are the local police stations. These three geographical levels also represent the hierarchy of command, and all are subordinated to the national commissioner and deputy commissioner. Another important national police entity is the Border Guard, which makes up about one-third of the estimated 28,000 sworn officers in the Israel National Police.

In addition to the districts, several important police units, which are also subordinated to the commissioner, form the National Headquarters in Jerusalem. It is composed of seven departments (patrol and security, organization and planning, traffic, community and civil guard, logistic support, human resources, and investigations and intelligence), which are expected to assist the police commissioner in developing policy, allocating resources, planning, coordinating, and supervising the various districts. Headquarters includes several additional units, such as legal advice, public relations, accounting, public complaints, and so on, which also answer directly to the police commissioner. Lastly, several police units operate on the national level and hold various responsibilities including important homeland security tasks.

The Israeli police force also has authority over the Civil Guard, which is the largest voluntary organization in Israel. The Civil Guard was established in 1974 following several major terror attacks that took place that year. Its volunteers directly assist police units in matters of homeland security throughout the country by carrying out activities such as patrolling, setting road blocks, and securing local and major events, schools, and public transportation. Further, Civil Guard volunteers assist in other police duties such as traffic control, investigations, identification of disaster victims, and rescue operations. In addition to the significant contribution in terms of manpower, the Civil Guard is considered an important vehicle for fostering police–community relationships.

In addition to the usual policing responsibilities of controlling crime and disorder, the Israeli police also are responsible for maintaining homeland security. This last responsibility was assigned to the Israeli police by the government in 1974, following the rise in Palestinian terrorism and a major terror attack in Maa'lot. This new responsibility forced the police to reorganize: the Civil Guard was established; the Border Guard began securing the airports and seaports; a year later, the Operations Division was established for the purpose of coordinating all operating forces and increasing their effectiveness; and a special unit for combating terrorism was established (the Ya'mam), along with a bomb-disposal unit.

The Israel National Police has been responsible for homeland security in Israel ever since, facing repeated threats and terrorist incidents. This extensive experience of the Israeli police has been generating much interest in recent years on the part of police forces worldwide.

Crime

Classification of Crimes

Crimes in Israel are classified into three categories: (1) contraventions, which are offenses punishable by imprisonment of no more than three months, or if the punishment includes a fine only, it cannot be larger than the fine imposed on offenses for which the maximum fine is not defined by law; (2) misdemeanors, which are offenses punishable by imprisonment of more than three months and up to three years, or if the punishment includes a fine only, it cannot be larger than the fine imposed on offenses for which the maximum fine is not defined by law; and (3) felonies, which are offenses punishable by more than three years of imprisonment.

In addition, the penal law classifies offenses into eight categories according to their type. Each offense includes a description of the offense components as well as the maximum penalty. The categories are as follows:

- Harm to the security of the country and foreign relations such as treason, espionage, and so on, punishable by life imprisonment or even death.

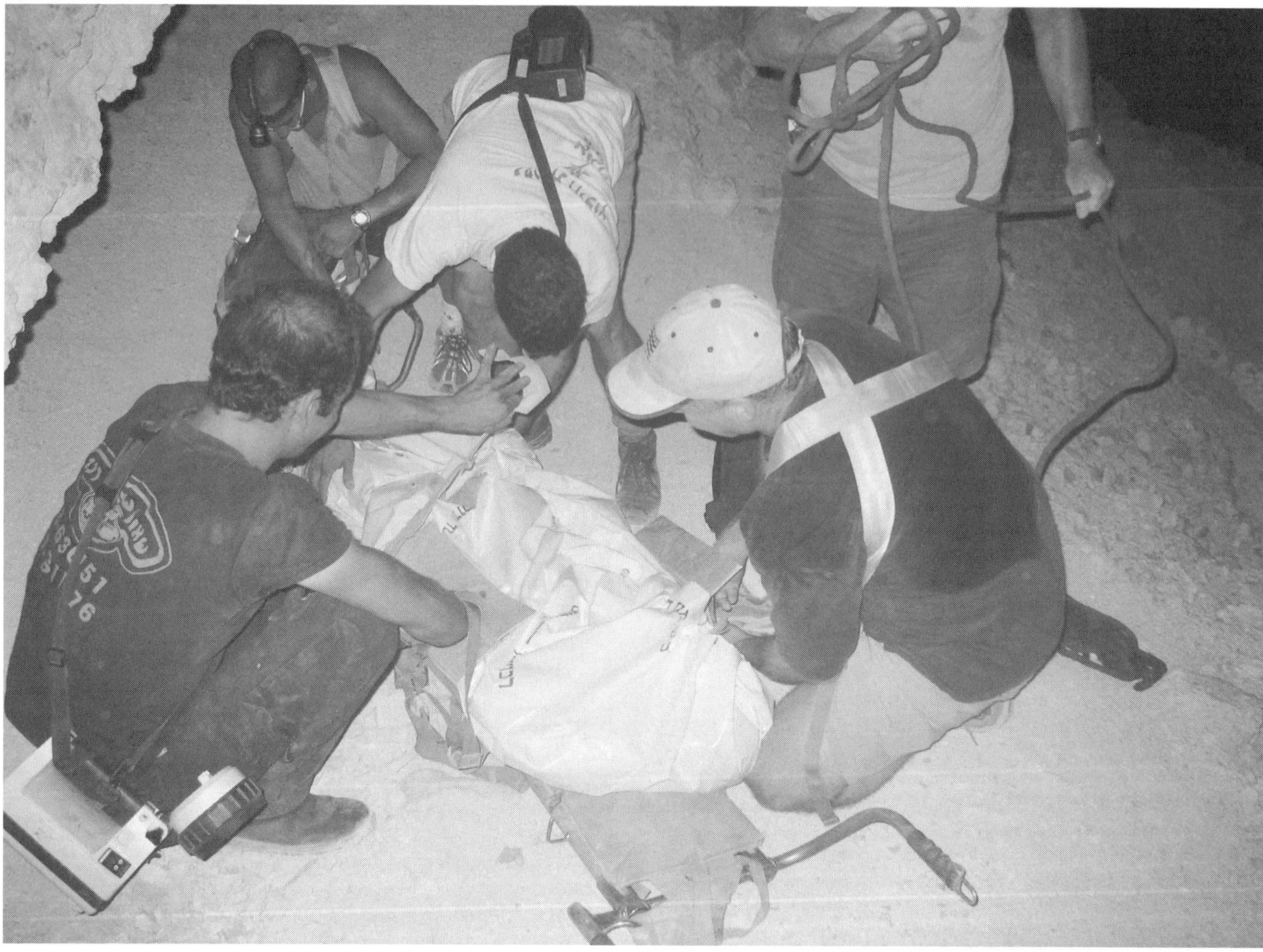

Members of the Israeli Eilat Rescue unit evacuate one of two Colombian women who died of dehydration in a canyon near the Israeli town of Eilat, September 13, 2006. Israeli police are investigating this as a case of human trafficking from Egypt into Israel. (AP Photo/Eilat Rescue Unit)

- Harm to the order of the government and society such as inciting racism, illegal demonstrations, disturbing the peace, insults to religious sensibilities or traditions, multiple marriages, prostitution, and some other sexual offenses.
- Harm to the order of the government and the law such as disruption of trials, attacks on police officers, bribery, and offenses carried out by public servants in the context of their employment.
- Harm to person such as murder, manslaughter, and causing death in an indirect manner. It also includes behaviors that endanger life or well-being, sexual offenses, offenses toward minors or the disabled, and assaults.
- Damage to property such as theft, robbery, burglary, the possession of an asset obtained through contraventions or misdemeanors, fraud, and extortion. These crimes constitute 55–60 percent of all offenses in Israel. Offenses of this nature, along with offenses that entail harm to another person's body, constitute the group of offenses that most occupy the criminal justice system in Israel.
- Forgery vandalism of banknotes, coins, bills, or stamps.

- Minor offenses such as blocking a public road, littering in a public area, and social disorders such as loud noise that disturbs the peace.
- Conspiracy by contacting another person to carry out contraventions or misdemeanors, providing means to carry out a contravention, and preparing an offense through the possession of explosives, a machine, or an instrument designed to carry out a contravention.

Counterterrorism

Counterterrorism activities, particularly preventing and thwarting attacks by terrorists, have become a major component in the daily routine of local police stations, often at the expense of other policing duties. These activities are carried out by all the units within the local station, Border Guard units, and Civil Guard volunteers as well as bomb-disposal units and include the collection of intelligence, setting roadblocks, carrying out observations, surveillance, security checks, and foot and car patrols. The challenges, benefits, and risks of combining the two fundamental tasks of fighting crime, particularly severe and organized crime, and combating terrorism have been raised in recent years by both scholars and practitioners.

Trafficking in Women

Trafficking in women has been considered a particular challenge to the criminal justice system in Israel over the past few years. The phenomenon began in Israel, as in Western Europe and North America, during the early 1990s, following the collapse of the Soviet Union and the breakdown of many of its social and economic systems. In July 2000, following the publication of the 2000 Amnesty International report, amendment 56 to the penal code was adopted, which defines the offense of human trafficking, prohibits trafficking in women for the purpose of prostitution, and provides a penalty of up to 16 years of imprisonment for this offense.

However, it was not until the U.S. Department of State published the Trafficking of Persons Report in 2001 that a significant change in policy and practice was adopted. This report determined that the State of Israel belonged to the third category of states—that is, it was considered one of the countries that did not fulfill minimal requirements of fighting the phenomenon of human trafficking and was therefore in danger of losing American financial aid. Consequently, dramatic changes in policy and practice were adopted: numerous women-traders and pimps were arrested; committees to examine the phenomenon in Israel were established; an emergency hotline for victims of trafficking was opened; and the prosecution changed its guidelines regarding bordellos where foreign women are found. For example, police data indicate that during the year 2002, the Israeli police opened 351 criminal investigations for the offense of trafficking in women, compared to only 1 case in 2000 and 25 cases during the first half of 2001. Indeed, in the 2002 Trafficking of Persons Report, Israel was moved up to the second category, which includes states that take initial measures to fight the phenomenon.

In the 2005 report, however, Israel was classified in a subcategory of the second category, reserved for countries that are in danger of losing their place in the second group. It was stated that the Israeli government has exhibited significant efforts to fight the phenomenon of human trafficking, but it has been lowered to the subcategory because of its inability to prove enhanced efforts over the last year.

Organized Crime

Trafficking in women in Israel is often considered part of the larger phenomenon of organized crime, which also presents a particular challenge to the criminal justice system in Israel. Recently, organized crime was brought to the center of public attention in 2003, following several events where hand grenades were tossed at police stations, in addition to eight innocent bystanders being murdered as part of turf wars between organized crime groups. A particularly horrific attack took place in December 2003, when in the center of Tel Aviv, at noon, a failed murder attempt of an organized crime group member resulted in the death of three bystanders.

The question of whether organized crime operates in Israel and to what extent has been raised since the 1960s and has resulted in several reports and governmental committees, including the Shamgar

Report (1971), the Bochner Committee (1976); and the Shimron Committee (1978). Much of the recent organized crime in Israel is traced to the wave of immigration that took place in the 1990s from Eastern Europe, particularly from the former Soviet Union. It has been recognized that some offenders, whose patterns of operation resemble classic organized crime patterns, infiltrated this immense wave of immigration and settled in Israel. These offenders are thought to be particularly active in the niche of trafficking in women. For example, one study found that between April 2001 and September 2004, 173 suspects were arrested for trafficking women by the Tel Aviv Police Central Unit. Of these suspects, 137 (approximately 80%) were immigrants from Eastern Europe and countries of the previous Soviet Union.

Recognition of the phenomenon led to the enactment of the Law of the Struggle against Crime Organizations, 2003. The law provides a definition of a "crime organization," determines heavy punishments of 10 to 20 years' imprisonment for those accused of leading or fulfilling certain roles in a crime organization, and sets the punishment of 10 years' imprisonment for a civil servant accused of using his or her position or authority to assist the activities of a crime organization. This law follows the Prohibition of Money Laundering Law, 2000, which was also legislated as part of the struggle against the phenomenon of organized crime.

Motor Vehicle Theft

The crime of motor vehicle theft has also been particularly challenging to the criminal justice system in Israel since the 1990s. This form of property crime is characterized by its strong relation to the unique economic and political situation in the region. About 70 percent of stolen cars in Israel are transferred to the Palestinian Territories (PT), where they are dismantled into used car parts that are subsequently sold within Israel. When borders with the PT were closed, after a terror attack, for example, significant decreases in motor vehicle theft in Israel were evident.

A recent phenomenon related to car theft is that of Israeli garages or car dealers transporting damaged Israeli vehicles to the PT, where they are repaired using stolen car parts. The vehicles are subsequently returned to Israel and sold as "ordinary" used cars. Beyond the financial loss, there is no supervision over the quality of the repair, and thus, vehicles are often returned to Israel and sold with significant safety problems that the new owners are not aware of. Motor vehicle theft in Israel is also related to terrorist activities. For example, car bombs that have exploded in Israel often have been made using stolen cars or license plates. Additionally, intelligence warnings indicate that tow trucks that transfer vehicles from the PT back to Israel may also carry terrorist devices.

Several measures have been taken over the last decade to try to control the phenomenon. After motor vehicle theft reached a peak in 1997, with 45,918 vehicles being stolen, a special unit within the Israeli police (Etgar) was established in 1998, and it operated until 2003, when it was shut down due to budget constraints. In 2006, the unit became operational again owing to financial assistance from private insurance and leasing companies. In July 2005, the law for "limiting the usage and registering activities with used car parts" was adopted. According to the law, any vehicle parts that are dismantled, assembled, imported, bought, sold, or transferred must be registered, including, for example, the details of the car part, the date, manufacture, the identity of the individuals involved in the transaction, and so on. If a law recently proposed in the Knesset is adopted, it will be illegal to repair cars in the Palestinian Territories, an offense punishable by up to three years' imprisonment.

Drug Offenses

The main legal basis defining drug-related offenses in Israel is the Dangerous Drugs Ordinance (1973). The amendments to the ordinance define almost 100 substances as "dangerous drugs," including hashish, opium, heroin, cocaine, and LSD. "Dangerous drugs" are illegal to use, entice minors to use, possess, or sell. The ordinance defines four types of drug-related offenses as illegal: (1) possessing and using dangerous drugs, offenses that are punishable by 3years of imprisonment; (2) dealing in dangerous drugs, which is an offense punishable by 10 years of imprisonment; (3) growing, manufacturing, and producing dangerous drugs, which are offenses punishable by 10 years of imprisonment; and (4) enticing minors to use drugs, which is a severe offense punishable by imprisonment for 25 years.

According to the Israeli Anti-Drug Authority, the phenomenon of drug use in Israel evolved during the 1980s from a marginal problem to a central trend influencing Israeli society. About 300,000 individuals in Israel abuse drugs, either occasionally or on a regular basis. Seventy thousand are teenagers between the ages of 12 and 18, who constitute about 11 percent of their age group. Twenty-five thousand of the total users are addicts. The Anti-Drug Authority reports that the growth in drug abuse among teenagers who attend school has leveled off and remains at around 11 percent. At the same time, however, the use of drugs, particularly hashish, marijuana, and Ecstasy, among 18- to 30-year-olds has been increasing.

The illegal drug market in Israel is estimated at about 6 billion NIS a year (equivalent to about US$1.5 billion) and includes approximately 100 tons of marijuana, 10 tons of hashish, 5 tons of heroin, 3 tons of cocaine, and more than 20 million tablets and doses of party drugs such as ecstasy and LSD. Numerous substitutes are also part of the drug market in Israel, including contact glue, air-conditioning gas, and laughing gas. Following the second war with Lebanon, the border with Jordan has become the major route for smuggling illegal drugs into Israel, particularly heroin, cocaine, and hashish. At the same time, Israel continues to be a "transit" country from Jordan to Egypt and Saudi Arabia. Much of the marijuana is smuggled across the border with Egypt, while Lebanon continues to be a transit country for heroin and cocaine and a source for hashish. A recent phenomenon is the smuggling of cocaine in liquid form, absorbed in clothes or concealed in wine bottles, from South America. Homegrown drugs for the purpose of retail sales are also part of the Israeli drug market.

Crime Statistics

The statistics detailed in the following list were reported by the Israeli police in their annual report for the year 2006. As a reference point, the population in Israel at the end of 2006 included approximately 7,116,700 residents.

- *Murder:* The Israel National Police reports 187 criminal cases opened for murder in 2006 throughout the country. Out of those, 107 are "cleared" cases—that is, cases in which an offender was identified. One hundred sixty-nine individuals were accused of murder, among whom 9 were adolescents.
- *Rape:* In 2006, 938 criminal investigations were opened for "rape using force or threat," out of which a suspect was identified in 692 cases. Six hundred thirty-one offenders were involved in this type of offense, out of which 70 were adolescents. For the second type of rape, 269 criminal investigations were opened for "rape and illegal coitus," out of which a suspect was identified in 194 cases. Two hundred twenty-four offenders were involved in this type of offense, out of which 94 were adolescents.
- *Robbery:* In 2006, the Israeli police opened 1,261 criminal cases for robbery and 1,033 for "robbery under severe circumstances." An offender was identified in 765 cases of the first type and in 580 of the second. Five hundred fifty-one offenders were accused of being involved in "robbery," out of which 161 were adolescents. Six hundred seventy offenders were accused of being involved in "robbery under severe circumstances," out of which 133 were adolescents.
- *Drug offenses:* 3,424 criminal cases were opened against individuals accused of dealing in, importing, or exporting drugs in 2006. "Cleared cases" constituted 3,072 of the total, which led to the identification of 2,305 offenders, out of which 351 were adolescents. An additional 519 criminal investigations were opened for growing, producing, or manufacturing drugs, out of which an offender was identified in 320 cases. Three hundred fifty-three individuals

were accused of this offense, out of which 29 were adolescents.

Finding of Guilt

Rights of Accused

A suspect in Israel is considered innocent until convicted by a court of law, following due process, in cases where the defendant's guilt has been proven beyond a reasonable doubt. The suspect has the right to remain silent and not incriminate him- or herself, while all matters between the suspect and his or her attorney concerning the suspect's representation are privileged.

If the suspect was arrested, the arresting officer must identify him- or herself, notify the suspect of his or her arrest and the reasons for the arrest, and provide a copy of the warrant if such exits. The suspect is then brought before the commanding officer of the police station, who determines if there was reasonable cause for the arrest and whether further detention is required. To extend an arrest, regardless of whether a warrant was issued, the detainee has to be brought before a magistrate no later than 24 hours from the initial arrest and no later than 12 hours if the suspect is a minor. If still in custody after 75 days, the prosecution has to decide whether to file an indictment or to release the suspect. A Supreme Court judge has the authority to provide additional 90-days extensions.

Every suspect or accused has the right to choose an attorney to represent his or her case. Because private attorneys are often expensive, if the defendant cannot afford one, the court has the right in certain cases to appoint an attorney free of charge, following the defendant's request or based on the court's initiative. The circumstances and types of assistance provided to defendants free of charge are detailed in the next section.

Once an indictment has been filed and prior to the trial, the accused and his or her attorney have the right to examine and copy the prosecution's material, a right that may be enforced by the court. Before the trial, some defendants with certain characteristics, such as those who hold high public office, may be granted an administrative hearing. This may be carried out upon the initiative of the prosecution before it has reached a decision as to whether to file an indictment, or it may be initiated by the defendant. For this purpose, an amendment to the procedural law has been adopted, whereby the defendant has to be notified immediately when the investigation file has been passed on from the police to the prosecution, before an indictment has been filed.

At the opening of a trial, immediately after the judge reads the indictment, the defendant may raise preliminary pleas, such as immunity or statute of limitations. If the defendant chooses not to do so, he or she may answer to the charge—that is, admit or deny some or all of the charges—and reveal any alibi that he or she may claim to have. If the alibi claim is not made at this point, it cannot be raised later unless authorized by the court. The defendant may choose not to raise any plea or keep silent altogether; however, this choice may be used as evidence against the defendant later on.

After the prosecution has presented its case, the accused may claim "no case to answer," that is, arguing that the prosecution has not produced basic evidence supporting the charge that the defendant has committed the alleged offenses. If the trial continues, at the stage when the defense presents its case, the accused has the right not to testify if he or she chooses not to do so. Additionally, at the defendant's request, the court will summon any witnesses, unless it believes that a specific witness cannot assist in clarifying the questions at hand.

After a verdict has been declared, the accused (as well as the prosecution) has the right to call additional witnesses to testify as to his or her character and to provide the court with any additional information that should be considered before the sentence is passed. Additionally, the accused (as well as the prosecution) has a basic right to appeal the court's verdict or sentence within 45 days. The appeal may be allowed in whole or in part, dismissed, or returned to the trial court with instructions.

Assistance to Defendant

A public defender system has existed in Israel since 1996, following the enactment of the Law of the

Public Defender in 1995. The goal of this office is to ensure adequate representation to all suspects, detainees, and accused, regardless of their financial means. The office includes a core team of in-house attorneys, who are employees of the Office of the Public Defender, and a large group of private lawyers hired as defense attorneys when needed. In the old system, the authority and responsibility for paying court-appointed defense attorneys lay in the hands of the courts, which often did not have the ability to supervise the professional standards of the defense. The public defender law, however, determines that any court decision to appoint an attorney will be handled by the Office of the Public Defender, and thus, the responsibility for payments as well as for the quality of the defense rests in the hands of the public defender, which has the organizational and professional ability to provide support and supervision.

Conditions that define the eligibility to be represented by a public defender attorney are detailed in section 18 of the Law of the Public Defender and take into account the type of legal procedure, the severity of the offense, and the financial status of the individual.

Investigations and Prosecutions

Generally speaking, the Israeli police force is the organization responsible for carrying out criminal investigations in Israel. Some exceptions include, for example, the military police, which has jurisdiction over criminal investigations within the military, or in some cases private or media investigators, whose initial inquires and collection of evidence may give rise to official police investigations. Additionally, if the alleged offense is a contravention or misdemeanor, the police may decide that the investigation will be carried out by another agency with investigative and enforcement powers, such as internal revenue investigators from the Ministry of Finance or environmental inspectors from the Ministry of Environment.

In certain cases, the police may decide that an investigation should be terminated and the suspect should not be indicted, usually owing to insufficient evidence or "lack of public interest." In cases of lack of public interest, the complainant will be notified and may appeal the decision to the attorney general's office.

Once the investigation is completed, and all relevant evidence has been gathered, the material is forwarded to the prosecuting agency, which will generally be the police prosecution unit (in cases of contravention or misdemeanors) or the district attorney's office (in cases of felonies). Other prosecuting agencies may include, for example, the Tax Authority or the military prosecution. The investigation file is then reviewed, and a decision is made as to whether further investigation is required (in which the case file will be returned to the police) or whether there is sufficient evidence to file an indictment.

Alternatives to Trial

In recent years, there have been several attempts to incorporate restorative justice and mediation programs into the criminal justice procedure in Israel, as alternatives to going to trial when the offender is a juvenile. These still represent, however, unusual and exploratory attempts.

How Are the Majority of Criminal Cases Resolved?

The large majority of criminal cases are closed before they reach the stage of an indictment. To begin with, at the investigation stage, many criminal cases that are considered "less serious" are defined by the police as "no prosecution" cases, which are consequentially not investigated. Police guidelines specify offenses that should not be investigated, such as perjury or false testimony in civil trials, unless directed by the courts. In actuality, many additional offenses, some with significant impact on quality of life and general sense of security, are almost never investigated. In 2006, 14.6 percent of cases opened by the police were disposed of as "no prosecution" cases.

The classification of cases is merely the first filter that files go through on the way to an indictment. Many of the cases that are investigated are closed at a later stage by authorized police officials. Files that remain open are passed on to a prosecutor (at either the police prosecution or the district attorney's office), who also may close the file due to lack of evidence or "public interest." Data from 2001 indicate that in about 55–60 percent of cases that are closed, the decision is made because of lack of sufficient evidence; in 20–25 percent, the reason for closure is "lack of public interest"; and lastly, some cases are closed because even the slightest evidence against the suspect could not be established, and thus it is determined that there is "no guilt."

Research has in fact shown that the large majority of cases that are investigated do not eventually reach the stage of an indictment. For example, only 7.7 percent of suspects identified in 1990 and 7.2 percent in 1995 were actually prosecuted. With regard to cases that reach indictment, preliminary data indicate that the large majority (approximately 75–80%) of cases tried in district courts are resolved with a plea bargain.

Incarceration before or Awaiting Trial

Incarceration before or while awaiting trial is permitted in Israel. At the outset, police officers have the authority to arrest an individual without a warrant if one or more of the following circumstances take place: there is a reasonable suspicion that an offense has been committed, and if not arrested or detained, the suspect may harm a person, the public, or the security of the state of Israel; the officer suspects that the individual may disrupt an investigation, tamper with evidence, or try to influence witnesses; or the individual has been released on bail but has violated the terms of his or her release or is a prisoner trying to escape.

Following the arrest, the detainee must be brought before the commanding officer of the police station, who determines whether the arrest was justified and whether the individual should remain in custody. Regardless of whether a warrant for the arrest was issued, the detainee must be brought before a judge no later than 24 hours following the initial arrest if the suspect is over the age of 14 and no later than 12 hours if the suspect is younger. The judge's decision as to whether to extend the detention period depends on the presence of evidence indicating that the detained individual, if released, will pose a danger to a person, to the public, or to the state of Israel; or on the judge's assessment that the suspect will tamper with evidence, try to influence witnesses, leave the country, or try to escape justice.

The courts may extend the detention period by up to 15 days at a time, though usually the period is extended by 5 days at a time. After 30 days, the police, with the consent of the attorney general, may request further extension. However, 75 days after the initial arrest, the prosecution must either indict the suspect or release him or her. A Supreme Court judge may order further 90-day extensions; however, this rarely takes place.

After an indictment has been filed, the prosecution may request that the suspect remain in custody throughout the trial. In making such a decision, the court considers three questions: (1) whether there is evidence against the accused that unless rebutted would suffice for a conviction; (2) whether there are reasons to believe that, if released, the accused may try to escape, tamper with evidence, influence witnesses, commit additional crimes, or endanger a person, the public, or the state of Israel (when the alleged offense is a severe one, such as rape, murder, etc., there is an assumption of such dangerousness); and (3), whether there are no alternatives to the detention, such as bail, house arrest, or handing over the suspect's passport to the police.

Criminal Court Judges: Numbers and Qualifications

Currently there are 15 Supreme Court judges in Israel. The Central Bureau of Statistics reports that in the year 2006, there were 121 district court judges and 353 magistrates' court judges.

Judges in Israel are appointed by the president, following the recommendation of the Judges Election Committee. This committee is composed of nine members, including the president of the Supreme Court, two additional Supreme Court judges, the minister of justice (who also serves as the chair of the committee), an additional minister, two members of the Knesset, and two representatives of the Israeli Bar Association. Thus, members of the Judges Election Committee represent all three powers of the state: the executive, the legislative, and the judicial, as well as the Israeli Bar Association. Attorneys who wish to be appointed judges complete an application and appear before a subcommittee, which submits its impressions and recommendations to the Judges Election Committee. A committee's recommendation to appoint a judge is based on a majority vote.

To be appointed a magistrates' court judge, a citizen of the state of Israel must adhere to the following preconditions:

- Be registered, or entitled to be registered, with the Israeli Bar Association.
- Have practiced law, held a legal position as a civil servant, or taught law at a university or law college for at least five years, out of which at least two were in Israel.

To qualify as a district court judge, an Israeli citizen must comply with the preconditions of a magistrates' court judge, but have 7 rather than 5 years of experience, out of which at least three must be in Israel, in addition to 4 years of experience as a magistrates' court judge. A Supreme Court judge must fulfill the same criteria, with no less than 10 years of experience, out of which at least 5 must be in Israel, and additionally have 5 years of experience as a district court judge.

The Juvenile Justice System

Minors, defined as 12- to 18-year-olds, are subjected to different treatments throughout the criminal justice process, owing to the emphasis of the juvenile justice system on individual treatment and rehabilitation, which gives rise to much flexibility, informality, and wide-based discretion.

First, as mentioned earlier, minors under the age of 14 may be detained for no more than 12 hours before being brought before a judge (in special circumstances, a senior police officer may order detainment for an additional 12 hours). A judge may order the continuation of the detainment for 10 days, followed by an additional 10 days (versus a total of 75 days for adult suspects—see earlier discussion). Minors may be detained only in special facilities, separate from adults. Parents or guardians must be informed immediately of the arrest and must be invited to be present during the questioning (unless there are special reasons not to do so).

The questioning of minors under the age of 14 who have been involved in sexual or violent offenses is carried out by special "child investigators." These special investigators are probation officers with university training in social work, employed by the Ministry of Welfare and Social Services. Their questioning incorporates a variety of methods such as picture drawing and role play. Leading questions in these types of investigations are allowed, and the entire process must be audiotaped.

When a minor has been detained or arrested, a youth probation officer must be informed. He or she will provide the police with a report on the minor and his or her background and family. This report may include a recommendation that the file be closed due to lack of public interest or because it may impede the minor's rehabilitation process. Thus, the Israeli police may, in cases involving suspects who are minors, close the file or put it "on hold." In such cases, the suspect is warned that the file may be reopened if he or she continues deviant behavior, and the suspect may be referred to further treatment by social services. If the minor complies, the file can be closed permanently and even removed from the records altogether. In any event, if the police do decide to press charges, they must do so no later than a year from the date of the offense. Prosecution at a later stage requires the approval of the attorney general.

Offenses where the suspect is a minor that do end up in court are dealt with by juvenile judges in special juvenile courts. Proceedings in these courts are not open to the general public, and all personal details of the minor are confidential. All minors who have been detained or accused are entitled to be represented by a public attorney, and the judge may order that the minor be supervised by a probation officer or sent for observation during the course of the trial. In cases where a child investigator carried out the questioning, the minor's testimony is presented by the investigator, along with the audio and sometimes videotape of the investigation. The same investigator may not deal with both the suspect and the victim in the same case.

If the court finds the minor guilty, the judge must receive a report from the probation officer before determining the sentence. The court then may convict and sentence the minor; order treatment; or make no order in cases of very minor or first-time offenses. In the majority of cases, treatment orders are made, which may include closed or open homes, probation, adult supervision, fine or financial compensation, or any other course of action that in the court's view is required for the minor's treatment and rehabilitation.

If the court convicts and sentences the minor, the normal sentencing options apply with several limitations: the death penalty is never allowed; minimum or mandatory penalties do not apply; imprisonment is available only if the minor is over the age of 14; and the option of a closed home is available instead of imprisonment, for a term that does not exceed the term of imprisonment available for that offense (this provision does not apply when a closed home is imposed as treatment).

Punishment

Types of Punishment

The types of punishment defined by Israeli law include the death penalty, imprisonment, "conditional imprisonment," "service work" (a type of imprisonment served in the community), "community service," fines, and probation. Courts in Israel are given much discretion in sentencing, and mandatory or minimal sentences are rarely imposed. Maximum sentences, however, are defined for any particular crime.

The death penalty under Israeli law is a possible punishment for the crimes of treason during wartime and crimes against humanity and genocide. It has been imposed only once in the history of the state of Israel, against Adolf Eichmann, the Nazi war criminal who was hanged in 1965.

The punishment for murder, which used to be death under the Criminal Code Ordinance inherited from the British Mandate, has been replaced with mandatory life imprisonment, which is also the mandatory punishment for kidnapping a child with the intent to endanger life. The punishment of life imprisonment is generally converted by the president to imprisonment of around 30 years, following a recommendation made by a specially designated committee. Such recommendations may be made only after the prisoner has served no less than 7 years of the life term. Offenses that under the British Mandate Criminal Code Ordinance were punishable by life imprisonment have been replaced with the maximum sentence of 20 years. Several severe offenses have been added to this category over the years, such as aggravated rape or enabling a minor to obtain drugs, which is an offense punishable by 25 years of imprisonment.

The punishment of "conditional imprisonment" (suspended sentence) is defined as a prison term, suspended for one to three years, that can be activated if the offender commits, within that time frame, an additional offense of a particular type as defined by the court. A conviction for a new offense may lead to an extension of the suspension period. Conditional imprisonment may be combined with a probation order, based on the ideology of combining the deterrence of the conditional imprisonment with the rehabilitation of the probation. Additionally, conditional imprisonment may require a financial obligation (a "suspended fine") to refrain from offending behavior during the designated timeframe.

"Service work" is considered a prison sentence, but one that is served in the community rather than in prison, and may replace a prison term of no more than six months. Its aims include reducing the overcrowding of the prisons as well as minimizing the harms caused by imprisonment.

Offenders engaged in service work are supervised by regional inspectors of the Israeli Prison Service, who according to the law must pay an unannounced visit to the service institute once a week and no less than twice a month. Violation of the service terms may result in their termination and the offender carrying out the rest of his or her sentence in prison. During the year 2002, more than 4,000 convicted offenders carried out service duty, in cycles, in 430 institutions.

"Community service" in some respects is similar to the common form of "service work," but the offender carries out services for the community in his or her free time. Community service is administered by the Probation Service and may be imposed without a registered conviction. These services are usually performed for no more than 250 hours, during a one-year period. A probation order may be added to this sanction.

Fines are common punishments for misdemeanors and contraventions, particularly in traffic law enforcement. Fines may also be imposed as an additional punishment to imprisonment, for example. Failure to pay the fine may result in imprisonment for the period of time specified in the sentence or determined by the law, which does not exceed three years. This sanction, however, rarely takes place. Courts may also order the offender to financially compensate the victim, up to a maximum sum revised periodically.

Probation can be ordered by the courts for a time period of six months to three years, with or without a registered conviction. Probation requires the consent of the offender and may be connected with an additional sanction such as conditional imprisonment or community service. If conditions set by the courts are violated, or an additional offense is committed within the determined time frame, an alternative sentence may be imposed.

In 2005, for most offenses, a suspended sentence was the most common type of punishment followed by imprisonment for offenses against the security of the state, bodily harm, sexual offenses, offenses against morality, and offenses against property. A fine was the next most common penalty for crimes against public order and for fraud. It is important to mention that often an offender will receive more than one type of punishment. The distribution of imprisonment for a variety of offenses in 2005 was as follows:

Against the security of the state	58.0%
Against public order	34.4%
Bodily harm	28.8%
Sexual offenses	51.9%
Against morality	40.1%
Against property	34.2%
Fraud	25.3%

Prisons

The Israeli Prison Service (IPS) is the national prison system in Israel. Its goal is to safely and suitably incarcerate prisoners and detainees, while maintaining their dignity, fulfilling their basic needs, and providing correctional capabilities to enhance the prisoners' ability to reintegrate into society upon release. The IPS operates 28 prisons and jails, including a prison for women (Neve Tirtza) and a prison for juveniles up to the age of 21 (Ofek). Additionally, many prisons operate wings intended for special populations, such as prisoners who require special protection; psychiatric wards; religious wings; drug-free wings; and wings for refugees, particularly from the Sudan, who have been entering Israel since 2005. The different prisons also vary in their security levels, ranging from minimum to maximum levels of security.

Since 2005, the IPS has been gradually taking responsibility over all prison and jail facilities in Israel, including those for "security prisoners" (inmates from the Palestinian Territories accused of terrorist activities), which were previously operated by the army. These additional "security prisoners" constitute a major increase to the prison population, which now includes more than 21,000 prisoners and detainees, out of which almost 10,000 are security prisoners. About 330 of all inmates are women.

The largest prison in Israel, both in size (400,000 square meters) and in population (over 2,200 prisoners), is "Ktziot" prison. It is located in the Southern District, south of the Gaza strip and east of the border with Egypt. Many of the inmates in this prison are "security prisoners" drawn from different terrorist organizations. Many were transferred to this prison after serving time in other prisons, in facilities of the SHABAK (General Security Agency) or in army jails throughout the country. Most are from the so-called new generation of terrorists, serving time for involvement in terrorist activities during the second Palestinian intifada. The prison also holds a wing of regular prisoners, who carry out maintenance duties. Additionally, since 2007, the prison has include a special separate wing for African refugees, mainly from the Darfur region in Sudan, who infiltrated Israel via the border with Egypt. Until 2006, when responsibility for the prison was transferred to the IPS, the Ktziot prison was run by the Israeli Army.

Work and Education Policies

Prisoners in Israel are legally obligated to work; however, according to Professor Leslie Sebba and other researchers, this provision is not strictly enforced owing to a lack of working opportunities. The majority of inmates do work, however, in the maintenance of the prison, including cleaning duties, cooking, and so on, for which they receive a small salary that allows them to purchase items in the prison canteen. Overall, work is encouraged as part of rehabilitation and acquiring good work habits and skills. Thus, professional courses are offered. Additionally, commercial companies set up small industrial units within prisons, which allow inmates to acquire important working skills while earning a salary. As part of reintegration into society, several months before their release, some prisoners (who qualify) may leave the prison, as a group, to work in a civil facility. The next stage is for the prisoner to leave the prison on his or her own, in civilian clothing, and return to the prison every evening after work.

The IPS also provides and enables formal education at all levels (from very basic reading and writing skills up to university-level education), as well as informal education. Formal courses are at least 12 weeks long and include 20 hours of class a week. Grades are passed on to the Ministry of Education, and official credentials are given. On a yearly average, 1,600 inmates in all prisons receive formal education. Informal education follows the format of a community center and includes a variety of courses and seminars in areas such as art, general knowledge, computers, tradition and holidays, health education, parenting, reading, and more.

Visiting Policies, Furlough, and Privileges

Three months after imprisonment, convicted prisoners are entitled to receive a visit once every two months, in the presence and within hearing range of a prison guard. As a privilege, visits may be granted once every two weeks. Additional visits may be granted in specific prison wings or under certain circumstance (such as the prisoner excelling in general behavior or at work, special family situation, etc.) and following the approval of the appropriate authority (wing or prison commander). Generally speaking, a visit may last no more than 30 minutes; however, much discretion is given to wing and prison commanders to extend this period. Each visit may include no more than three adults (not including the inmate) and the inmate's children, but the prison commander may approve two additional visitors. Usually a net or glass divider will separate the prisoner from the visitors, though in rehabilitation or advanced wings, visits are carried out in visiting rooms without separation devices.

Furlough from prison is not an automatic right of all prisoners but a privilege based on the discretion of the prison service and the Israeli police, while taking into account the inmate's security status, intelligence information, possible danger to the inmate's family, likelihood of involvement in criminal activity, and more. For example, sex offenders who renounce their guilt are not eligible for a furlough. Inmates who qualify may take their first leave after serving a quarter of their sentence, and no less than two months in prison. Their eligibility will be continuously reexamined, and if found eligible, they will be granted a furlough every month or every two months, for the time period of 6 to 96 hours. Some inmates who are not eligible for furlough may receive conjugal visits. Prisoners who are convicted of family violence or incest must go through a special procedure before conjugal visits are approved. "Security prisoners" are not eligible for this type of visit. If qualified, a prisoner may receive a conjugal visit once a month.

Extradition, Transfer, and Exchange of Prisoners

According to the Extradition Act (1954), an Israeli resident may be extradited to another country if the following criteria apply: the suspect committed an offense that under Israeli law is punishable by a year of imprisonment or more; the extradition request is for the purpose of prosecuting the suspect; the country requesting the extradition made a commitment that, if convicted, the sentence would be served in Israel; there is an extradition agreement between the requesting country and Israel, and the event at hand fulfills all conditions of the agreement.

In 1996, the Law for Transferring Prisoners to Their Countries of Origin (1996) was enacted. The purpose of this law was to allow Israeli citizens serving prison sentences abroad to carry out their sentence in Israel, while similarly enabling foreign citizens serving prison sentences in Israel to carry out their sentence in their country of citizenship. The law enabled the state of Israel to abide by international conventions and sign special agreements for transferring prisoners. Thus, the European convention for transferring prisoners was endorsed by the state of Israel in 1997 and became active in January 1998. Between 1997 and 2001, 95 Israeli citizens serving prison sentences abroad applied to be transferred to Israel, of which about 17 were actually transferred. During the same period, 13 foreign prisoners serving prison sentences in Israel applied to be transferred to their home countries, of which about 5 were actually transferred.

Security prisoners have been exchanged in the past in return for Israeli soldiers who were captured or kidnapped. A well-known example is the "Jibril Deal," which took place in May 1985. This deal between the state of Israel and the Popular Front for the Liberation of Palestine, the General Headquarters of Ahmad Jibril, included the release of 1,150 security prisoners serving time in Israeli prisons, in return for three Israel soldiers: Shai, Groff, and Salem, who were captured in 1982 during the Lebanon War. The Israeli government was severely criticized in the media, particularly for the large difference between the number of prisoners released and the number of soldiers returned and for releasing terrorists with "blood on their hands."

Tal Jonathan, Mimi Ajzenstadt, and David Weisburd

Further Reading

Friedmann, Robert R., ed. (1998). *Crime and Criminal Justice in Israel: Assessing the Knowledge Base toward the Twenty-First Century.* Albany: State University of New York Press.

Landau, Simha. (2003). "Violence in Israeli Society: Its Relation to Social Stress." In *Studies in Contemporary Jewry, vol. 19, Jews and Violence: Images, Ideologies, Realities,* edited by Peter Y. Medding, pp. 126–148. New York: Oxford University Press

Muhlbauer, Varda. (2006). "Domestic Violence in Israel: Changing Attitudes." *Annals of the New York Academy of Sciences* 1087: 301–310.

Sebba, Leslie. (2000). "Victims' Rights and Legal Strategies: Israel as a Case-Study." *Criminal Law Forum* 11(1): 47–100.

Jordan

Legal System: Common/Islamic/Customary
Murder: Low
Corruption: Medium
Human Trafficking: Medium
Prison Rate: Medium
Death Penalty: Yes
Corporal Punishment: No

Background

Following the breakup of the Ottoman Empire after World War I, Transjordan became a British Mandate. In 1946, the Hashemite Kingdom of Jordan became an independent nation. Jordan has been a hereditary constitutional monarchy since 1952, and the king is constitutionally above the law. As the head of state, the king enjoys very broad executive authority over the bicameral National Assembly and the armed forces.

According to article 99 of the Constitution, the courts are structured into three basic categories: ordinary civil courts, religious courts, the special courts. The legal and judicial systems are rooted in Islamic traditions and French codes.

The civil courts include magistrates' courts, courts of first instance, and conciliation courts for juvenile cases. They also include appellate courts such as the courts of appeal and the Court of Cassation as well as the high administrative courts. The judiciary is subject to executive influence through the Justice Ministry and the Higher Judiciary Council that the king appoints.

The religious courts are sharia courts for Muslims, and there are other tribunals for citizens belonging to other legally recognized religions. Constitutional articles 103–106 grant the sharia courts exclusive jurisdiction over personal status matters, such as religion, marriage, divorce, child custody, and inheritance involving Muslim citizens.

Jordan is not a multiparty democracy. Restrictive laws block the formation of true political parties, and elections are widely reported to be corrupted by government agents. The Constitution grants citizens the freedom to peaceably assemble and associate, but the minister of interior must certify nongovernmental organizations (NGOs) as lawful "societies" and has the power to dissolve them for alleged technical violations.

Censorship is prevalent, with about 20 laws concerned with press prohibitions. The press is heavily monitored and coerced, imported publications are censored or banned, and journalists have their foreign travel restricted and can be criminally fined and imprisoned.

Islam is the state religion, and over 90 percent of Jordanians are Sunni Muslims. Fewer than 5 percent are Christians, and not all religions are legally recognized. The Ministry of Religious Affairs and Trusts manages Islamic institutions and appoints imams to whom it pays regular salaries. The ministry also prohibits imams from engaging in what the ministry deems subversive political commentary.

About 90 percent of Jordanians are Arabs. Minority groups and refugees are said to suffer significant discrimination. This is particularly true for refugees. The regime has experienced difficulties in dealing with the estimated 500,000 to 750,000 Iraqi refugees fleeing war. They now constitute about 10 percent of Jordan's population. Discrimination is also a problem for the more than 1.7 million Palestinian refugees in Jordan who are now an outright majority in the country.

Given the traditional influence of both sharia law and tribal customs, it is not surprising that women experience systemic discrimination. Human rights groups have called on the regime to abolish a number of discriminatory laws such as the rape law. Indeed, until 2002, only men could legally file for divorce.

Criminal justice institutions contribute to the kingdom's bleak human rights environment through the well-developed system of special security laws, police, and courts. Together, these represent an exceptional system of control outside of the ordinary civil courts aimed at maintaining internal and external state security. They are subordinated to the executive's military authority.

Martial law in Jordan ended in 1989. But the 1954 Crime Prevention Law (CPL) has been revived. This law grants governors the authority to detain persons indefinitely on the pretext that those individuals are "a danger to the people." The governors preside over the country's 12 provincial governorates and answer to the king's minister of interior.

Police forces in Jordan have also been criticized for threatening human rights. For example, Amnesty International (AI) has reported that the public security police, operating under the auspices of the Ministry of Interior, have actually unlawfully killed citizens. But when the minister of interior had appointed public security police official to head its Commission of Inquiry to investigate the allegations, the commission exonerated its officers of any wrongdoing.

The General Intelligence Directorate (GID) is a military security agency directly linked to the prime minister. It is empowered to charge and remand security detainees and ultimately prosecute them in one of Jordan's special courts outside of civilian control under the State Security Law. There are various specialized courts, including the Supreme Council and the Court of Major Felonies, as well as the Police Court and the military-dominated State security court.

Crime

Jordan's 1960 penal code denotes a range of misdemeanor and felony criminal offenses. The minimum age of criminal responsibility was raised from 7 to 12. This is still the lowest age of criminal responsibility among the Arab states. According to the UN Tenth Survey of Crime Trends and Operation of Criminal Justice Systems, Jordan's homicide rate is low. In 2006, there were just 100 homicides per 100,000 civilians. The rate of intentional homicides resulting from firearms the prior year was just 0.47 per 100,000. Even in the country's largest city, Amman, there were just 1.84 per 100,000 civilians, or about 40 homicides in 2006.

Drug possession, use, and trafficking elicit severe penalties. However, the U.S. State Department does not regard crime to be serious in Jordan. It does warn that Western women traveling in Jordan are experiencing sexual harassments, though serious sexual assaults appear uncommon. Marital rape is not a crime in Jordan. There are no laws or shelters to protect domestic violence victims.

Jordanian women are also subjected to so-called honor crimes. Male relatives may assault and kill them for talking to unrelated males, having premarital sex, becoming pregnant outside of marriage, or marrying someone without family approval. There are about 25–30 "honor" killings annually. Article 340 of the penal code allows courts to treat killers leniently.

Jordan is regarded as both a destination and a transit country for men and women as forced labor, as well as for women in prostitution. The UN Human Rights Commission (UNHRC) reports that foreign workers experience slave-like conditions and exploitation, are regularly imprisoned and abused by employers, and suffer sexual and physical abuse. AI criticizes the government for failing to protect the 40,000 registered and 30,000 unregistered migrant workers from highly exploitive and abusive practices. Lacking victim protection service, authorities punish and deport victims instead of investigating and prosecuting offenders. The UNHRC also reports that Jordanian companies have also been forcibly transporting Asian workers to labor in American-occupied Iraq.

The U.S. State Department believes that the terrorism threat in Jordan from both transnational groups and less sophisticated local groups is high. Al Qaeda claimed responsibility for the November 9, 2005, bombings of international hotels in Amman killing 60 and injuring over 100. Afterward, authorities amended the new terrorism law to criminalize financing, interacting with, and recruiting for any terrorist group. It gave the military jurisdiction over terrorism cases and allowed surveillance of terrorism suspects as well as detention for up to 30 days.

Finding of Guilt

Three conciliation courts (Zarka, Irbid, and Amman) deal specifically with juvenile cases. According to the NCHR, the courts processed 1,985 juvenile cases in 2007, 21 of which were for females. They also note that juveniles are not guaranteed to have lawyers unless the charges carry a severe potential sentence such as death or life imprisonment at hard labor. Further, if juveniles are charged with having committed misdemeanors together with adults, juveniles are then charged in adult courts.

Prosecutors charging adults with serious interpersonal crimes such as murder or rape take cases to the Court of Major Felonies. This court was established in 1976. Reportedly, the court was established to guarantee speedy trials involving serious interpersonal crimes specifically to prevent blood feuds from erupting.

Defendants in the ordinary courts are constitutionally guaranteed basic due process rights such as the presumption of innocence, judicial review of pretrial detention, and fair trials based on evidence. The Constitution and the code of criminal procedure allow arrestees to be detained up to 48 hours without a warrant and up to 10 days without formal charges being filed in court. Courts routinely grant prosecutors 15-day extensions. Although the NCHR credits the country for making progress in providing for the right to have fair trials in the ordinary courts, they nonetheless point out that national legislation still does not fully guarantee judicial independence. Judges are subject to executive influence through the Justice Ministry and the Higher Judiciary Council, which the king appoints. As well, the judiciary has been slow to include women. Women have been judges only since 1996, and there were no women appeals court magistrates until 2007.

Yet arbitrary arrest and the violation of basic due process rights remain serious problems in Jordan because so many persons can be detained and adjudicated through the extraordinary state security police and court systems. Administrative detention under the CPL allows administrative governors to send security officers to arbitrarily detain and hold individuals while circumventing the ordinary court system and its constitutional due process guarantees. Unlike in the ordinary courts, authorities in the exceptional security system need not bring arrestees before a judge within 24 hours. Prosecutors can initiate proceedings without judicial review, and charges are not subject to review by an independent tribunal during the investigation.

According to HRW, authorities use administrative detention a good deal, averaging over 10,000 detainees annually. In 2006, there were reportedly 12,000. Administrative detainees commonly include prisoners whose sentences have expired and would otherwise have to be released, individuals arrested on suspicion of a crime but currently released on bail by judicial orders, offenders with prior criminal records, and victims threatened by tribal revenge or "honor" crimes. Even juveniles can be administratively detained.

The GID can hold detainees at Swaqa and its detention facility in Amman, which holds about 20 detainees. Detainees are prevented from receiving visits during at least the first week and are held in solitary confinement. Often, they are not even told with what crimes they will be charged. Military prosecutors can order the detention of civilians for up to six months, but some of the Islamist detainees have been detained for periods ranging from two-and-a-half to four years at a time.

Article 278 makes it an imprisonable offense to engage in speech or publication that the regime considers to be "offending the religious sentiments of people." The penal code also criminalizes *lese majeste* by allowing the prosecution of an individual deemed to be insulting the king pursuant to article 195.

Prosecutors from the courts of first instance decide whether to transfer those accused of violating politically suppressive laws and administrative detainees to the jurisdiction of a military prosecutor in the State Security Court (SSC), and by a 2001 temporary law, the prime minister may refer any case to the SSC. The SSC is a special three-member military court that has been operating since 1991. The court has jurisdiction over alleged crimes against internal or external state security, including those against "the dignity of the state and national consciousness."

Proceedings may be closed, and there are no appeals for misdemeanors resulting in imprisonment. There are no constitutional limits on pretrial detention in these cases, and defense attorneys are refused access to their clients until just before trial begins. The SSC also frequently fails to order in-depth investigations into allegations that detention and trials are unfair.

Torture is widespread in the context of administrative detention and the special security apparatus. The UN Special Rapporteur concluded that "torture is systematically practiced" by the GID and occurs in essentially all SSC cases. The International Commission of Jurists corroborates this conclusion, reporting that the use of torture and ill-treatment to extract "confessions" is routine in GID and the Public Security Directorate's (PSD) Criminal Investigations Department facilities.

Jordan has also been an active participant of the United States' rendition program in which American agents abduct individuals from various countries suspected of terrorist affiliations and then deliver them to security services in countries such as Jordan who will reliably extract "confessions" from them through torture. According to HRW, the GID, as proxy jailor, accepted at least 12 such abductees between 2001 and 2004 and successfully tortured them to "confess" to being Al Qaeda operatives.

Naturally, this contravenes international human rights agreements. Interestingly, the Jordanian government amended article 208 of its penal code to prohibit torture, actually defining it the same way as does the Convention against Torture. But it does not stipulate any penalties, and even though the Court of Cassation is responsible for addressing torture allegations when it reviews cases on appeal, it does not.

Punishment

A range of familiar punishments, such as fines, probation, imprisonment, and death, are available in the Jordanian courts. Juvenile offenders can receive probation, as 37 juveniles did in 2007 according to the NCHR.

Jordan retains and uses the death penalty. When juveniles between the ages of 15 and 18 are convicted of a crime normally warranting execution or life imprisonment at hard labor, the maximum penalty that they can receive is instead 4–12 years' imprisonment. Adult offenders committing violent crimes and terrorism offenses are eligible for the death penalty. But since 2006, it is no longer imposed for other ordinary crimes such as drug offenses.

The penal code and the 1952 military penal code both have provided for a high number of capital crimes. In 1988, the number of drug offenses eligible was greatly expanded. Crimes against the state's external security interests such as treason have carried with them mandatory death sentences. Various crimes against the state's internal security as well as homicides involving torture or "barbaric treatment" by roaming gangs of three or more armed persons have also been eligible for death.

Ordinary criminal courts of first instance can try capital cases, as can the Court of Major Felonies in rape and murder cases. By law, defendants in death penalty cases have the right to defense counsel. Death penalty convictions are reviewed by the courts of appeal and then the Court of Cassation. The SSC also has several capital offenses, such as security and drug offenses, within its jurisdiction. Since 1993, convicts in these SSC cases have had the right to appeal their cases to the Court of Cassation. The Court of Cassation then upholds the sentence and sends the condemned back to the SSC jurisdiction. The king must then approve all death sentences. He can also commute them.

According to article 358 of the code of criminal procedure, authorities are to execute convicts inside prison by hanging them at dawn. Until 1988, this took place in al-Mahatta prison in Amman. Since then, executions have occurred in the Swaqa prison south of Amman. Articles 359–362 deal with execution procedures. The condemned are not to be told of the time of their executions until 15 minutes beforehand.

AI estimates that Jordanian officials execute about 10 people annually. Various human rights groups have reported serious abuses in death penalty cases, particularly involving incommunicado detention and torture of individuals held by the GID and condemned to death by the SSC. Although King Abdullah has expressed his support for eventually abolishing the punishment, Jordanian authorities generally see the death penalty as a necessary sanction in Jordanian society and one justified by both Islamic sharia law and Arab tribal custom.

Prison

The PSD, operating within the Ministry of Interior, administers the prison system. According to the World Prison Population List, 8th edition, Jordan incarcerated about 7,500 prisoners, for a rate of about 123 prisoners per 100,000 civilians, in 2008. These prisoners were housed in 10 prisons designated for adults.

An estimated 46.1 percent are officially pretrial detainees. Human rights researchers also estimate that because of the extensive use of administrative detention, as many as 1 in 5 prisoners are actually an administrative detainee there indefinitely. In 2008, the PSD began to separate convicts from the pretrial and administrative detainees. The Qafqafa, Swaqa, and Muwaqqar prisons have been designated for the convicts, and the remaining adult prisons have been designated for the pretrial and administrative detainees. Officially 9.6 percent of prisoners are foreigners.

Just 3.6 percent of prisoners are females. They are incarcerated at the country's only prison for women, the Juwaideh women's prison in Amman. These include as many as 40 women administratively detained for "protective custody" because they have been threatened with "honor" crimes. HRW has called on officials to cease this punitive incarceration and instead protect these victims by providing them residence at the government's Wifaq Center or an alternative NGO shelter for at-risk women.

The Ministry of Social Development administers nine facilities for juveniles. Four are for males, two are for children needing protection and care, one is for females, and two are for beggars. Girls are detained separately at the Khansaa center for girls. Attempts are made to also separate juvenile detainees by age category. But pretrial and convicted juveniles are sometimes mixed because of facility limitations. There are holding cells available for boys in the Al Zohoon security post, Quwaysmish, and there has been a new one in the Aquba security center since 2007. But in the southern governorates, boys are detained along with the men because there are no separate facilities.

Jordan's prisons are generally near cities and larger communities. Some are older buildings, and some were built in the 1980s. Others, like the Juwaideh women's prison and Aqaba, are new. Officially, the PSD's prison system is only at 98.5 percent capacity. The NCHR disputes the official assertion, however, claiming that Jordanian prisons are actually above capacity. It is reportedly common to find prisoners sharing one bed or even renting out their beds or mattresses for money or services. Human rights investigators also conclude that the prisons suffer from poor conditions such as inadequate health, psychological, and food services, as well as insufficient allowances for recreation and the exercise of political rights. They also express concern that prisoners have too little access to their families and attorneys.

Human rights groups have expressed heightened concerns over the infliction of torture and ill-treatment upon Jordanian prisoners. In part, these concerns have been heightened by recent HRW investigative visits to Jordanian prisons. These include private interviews of randomly selected prisoners and officials.

Concerns were also raised following the recent deadly riots at the Juwaideh men's prison in 2007 and Swaqa prison in 2008. These were reportedly sparked by officers' abusive practices. There were no official investigations into the riots and their aftermaths.

Torture and corporal punishment commonly involve beatings with cables and sticks, metal or plastic pipes, or truncheons. As punishment for institutional infractions, prisoners are reportedly suspended from metal grates by their wrists and flogged. Islamists may be beaten en masse for allegedly threatening national security. *Falaqa,* or beating the soles of the feet, is reportedly common, as is the "salt and vinegar walk," which involves lacerating the feet and making the victim walk across a mixture of salt and vinegar to inflame the wounds.

The International Committee of the Red Cross visits the prisons every two weeks and submits its reports directly to government officials. Unfortunately, the internal mechanisms for detecting, investigating, and punishing torture and ill-treatment cases inside Jordan's prisons are inadequate. New prison directors are sometimes active participants in serious misconduct. For example, the new director at the troubled Swaqa prison reportedly ordered that the heads and beards of almost all the prison's 2,100 Muslim prisoners be forcibly shaved, a serious insult to a Muslim male—all on his first day on the job.

Prisoners can complain formally to the PSD's grievances officials. But these officials wear the same uniform as the prison officers, do not remove the alleged perpetrators from contact with the prisoners, and reportedly even threaten and intimidate prisoners who complain. The Public Security Law allows unit commanders such as prison directors to internally discipline subordinate officers for their misdemeanors instead of sending them to trial. An amendment made torture in the prisons a crime for the first time in 2007, and in 2008, the PSD assigned prosecutors to investigate abuses at seven prisons. But these prosecutors have still not prosecuted anyone under the law.

The special Police Court also has jurisdiction for investigating, prosecuting, and trying fellow officers accused of abuses. Police officials appoint officers to serve as prosecutors and judges. Only the most egregious cases have been taken up by the Police Court. When they have, invariably they have resulted in very lenient penalties. For example, after the deadly Swaqa prison riot, some guards were fined, the aforementioned prison director was fined the equivalent of US$180, and 12 guards were found not guilty because they were "just following orders."

In 2006, Jordan relented to demands and finally closed down the notoriously abusive al-Jafr prison south of Amman. Officials also took steps toward reform by hiring a U.S. consulting firm after the Swaqa prison riots that year. Taking the advice given by the Kerik International group headed by former New York City Police Commissioner Bernard Kerik, Jordanian officials opened a new "supermax" prison, Muwaqqar II, in 2008 to imprison its Islamist "national security" prisoners in 240 cells in 3 wings.

Paul Schupp

Further Reading

Amnesty International: http://www.amnestyusa.org.

Freedom House: http://www.freedomhouse.org.

Human Rights Watch: http://www.hrw.org.

National Centre for Human Rights: http://www.nchr.org.jo/.

Kuwait

Legal System: Civil/Islamic
Murder: Low
Corruption: Medium
Human Trafficking: High
Prison Rate: Medium
Death Penalty: Yes
Corporal Punishment: Yes

Background

The country of Kuwait, an Arab state located between Iraq, Saudi Arabia, and the Persian Gulf, is a democratic nation with a government divided into legislative, executive, and judicial branches. The amir (emir), titled "Head of the State" or "His Highness the Amir of the State of Kuwait," is a key person in the Kuwaiti government. To be eligible to become the amir, one must be a member of the Al-Sabah family and, in particular, must be a male descendent of Sheikh Mubarak Al-Sabah. The amir, along with the National Assembly, retains the government's legislative power. The executive power is held by the amir, the cabinet, and the ministers, whereas the judicial power is held by the courts.

Kuwait is divided into six governorates: Al Asimah (which is the capital), Hawalli, Al Ahmadi, Al Farwaniyah, Al Jahara, and Mubarak Al-Kabear. Kuwait offers freedom of religion to all persons. However, the government does designate Islam as Kuwait's official religion, which is reflected in its judicial system that includes religious courts. The country guarantees certain rights and freedoms to its people through the Kuwaiti Constitution. The Constitution was enacted in 1962 and is built on a foundation of the sovereignty of the state, public freedom, and equality before the law.

Among the amir's duties and capabilities is that which allows him to appoint the prime minister and ministers or, if necessary, dismiss them from their positions. In addition, he signs laws after they have been approved by the National Assembly. The amir is the head of the Kuwaiti defense forces. Furthermore, he retains the power to appoint judges to regular courts.

Before making judiciary appointments, the amir solicits recommendations for the positions from the Justice Ministry. Once the amir appoints a Kuwaiti judge, the judge holds that position for life. If a non-Kuwaiti person acquires a judicial appointment, his appointment may only be in renewable terms lasting from one to three years at a time.

Judicial System

The present Kuwaiti judicial system was brought about by legislation in 1959. Kuwait is separated into different administrative districts. The Kuwaiti judicial system is made up of a summary court in each of these administrative districts. Each of these summary courts is assigned one presiding judge. Although each summary court may be composed of more than one division, all of the divisions that fall within a particular summary court are under the jurisdiction of only the judge assigned to that court.

The summary court presides over all civil cases, leases, and commercial cases and is broken into several divisions. The first of these divisions is the Tribunal of First Instance. This court holds jurisdiction over administrative cases, civil cases, commercial cases, criminal cases, labor affairs, and personal status cases. The second of these divisions is the High Court of Appeals, which is divided into two chambers. The first chamber handles appeals regarding personal status cases and civil cases. The second chamber of the High Court of Appeals has jurisdiction over commercial case appeals and criminal case appeals. There is also a Court of Cassation, which deals with state security court appeals. The uppermost level of the Kuwaiti judiciary system is the Superior Constitutional Court, or the Supreme Court. This court is composed of five persons. Being the highest judiciary level, the Superior Constitutional Court holds jurisdiction over bylaws, the constitutionality of laws, the election of members of Parliament (MPs), and statutes. It also can determine the validity of MPs' membership and interprets the Constitution.

Crimes committed by or charged against members of the military or security forces are reviewed under separate circumstances. The Military Court handles these cases. Civilian cases also may be tried in the Military Court under conditions of martial law. The Military Court is separated into two "state security court panels." The State Security Court is made up of six individuals, three on each of the two panels.

In addition to those courts previously mentioned, the Kuwaiti judicial system allows for religious courts. There are two such courts, the Sunni and the Shia. Both courts handle family law issues. There is no appellate court for the Shia court. Any Shia decisions being appealed are handled by the Sunni court of appeals. Non-Muslim family law issues are handled in a separately established domestic court.

There are three different types of appeal for decisions rendered in the Kuwaiti courts. The first right of appeal would be to the Higher Court of Appeal. With this type of appeal, the entire case may be reheard. Second, a decision may be appealed to the Court of Cassation. In this instance, the case is reviewed to determine whether the decision may be dismissed based on the erroneous application of the law or whether the decision was inaccurately rendered. Third, a decision may be appealed via a request for a retrial in the same court, to make any necessary adjustments to the initial decision to amend any factual or legal mistakes. The amir is the final "court of appeal" regarding all issues. He has the authority to pardon or commute any sentence.

Police

The Kuwaiti government has established a police force with the goal of maintaining public order and preventing and investigating crime. The Kuwaiti police force is the single agency responsible for the enforcement of non-national security related issues. The police force falls under the control of the Ministry of the Interior, which is the ministry given the responsibility of security, law, and order within Kuwaiti society.

Information provided by the Ministry of the Interior regarding the Kuwaiti police force's utilization of a ranking system for the officers indicates that the system is similar to that of a military, which consists of several ranks from general through corporal. For an individual to obtain officer rank, he first must be selected for such, and he must attend a three-year program at the police academy. There are a total of 62 police stations currently listed on the Ministry of the Interior's Web site, located throughout the country.

The Kuwait Ministry of the Interior (MOI) has a host of vehicles, ranging range from motorcycles, cars, and sports utility vehicles to armed vehicles, boats, and helicopters, to aid in the performance of its duties. According to the Ministry of the Interior, its sea fleet is used in chasing smugglers and unwelcome intruders along the water borders of the country. Motorcycles are used to access places that are inaccessible to other forms of patrol, aiding in traffic control and participating in official processions. The MOI's armed vehicles are the frontline of convoys and are used to open gaps and remove barriers. Helicopters are used for the purpose of traffic control and transporting persons and cargo and are employed in search and rescue missions.

The Kuwaiti police force handles issues pertaining to the following areas: criminal investigations, traffic, emergencies, nationality and passports, immigration, prisons, civil defense, trials and courts-martial, terrorism, and issues in which collaboration with Iraq is suspected. Although the Kuwaiti police force handles a multitude of issues, women are permitted to work only in the areas of criminal investigation, inquiries, and airport security.

According to information provided by the Ministry of the Interior, the Criminal Sentences Execution Department of the Kuwaiti police force is located in Farwaniya. This department is responsible for carrying out sentences handed down to offenders by the court system.

Police actions are controlled by Kuwaiti law. Kuwaiti police are not permitted to make an arrest without first obtaining a written warrant from either a judge or state prosecutors. The only exception to this is in the occurrence of a "hot pursuit." Police are required to obtain sufficient evidence to substantiate the arrest of an individual, confirming individuals will not be subject to arbitrary arrest. Once arrested, police are allowed to hold an individual for up to four days without that person being charged for a crime, unless an order from an investigating officer indicating otherwise has been received. If such an order is issued, the accused may not be detained in protective custody for a period of more than three weeks. Once detained, the offender may be held for a maximum of six months from the arrest date unless the accused has been heard by the establishment handling the case and a review of the progress of the investigation against the accused has occurred.

According to the Country Reports on Human Rights Practices for 2007 issued by the U.S. Department of State, the Kuwaiti police force has problems with corruption, particularly regarding situations in which the police officer has a personal stake in the case. Furthermore, it was reported that the complaints and requests made to the police were not always taken seriously. Reported abuse of detained individuals further derogates the reputation of the police.

The state security department also falls under the jurisdiction of the Ministry of the Interior. Where the police oversee non-security related issues, state security handles issues in the area of overseas intelligence and national security. Its responsibilities include the investigation of security-related offenses, terrorism, and cases regarding suspected collaboration with Iraq.

Kuwait has established a National Guard whose responsibility is to provide backup for the military and the national police when necessary. Their duties also include guarding country borders, oil fields, and other locations susceptible to unwanted interference. Those guard members selected to become officers are required to complete their education at the Kuwaiti Military College. They receive further specialized training post-education.

External security involving the Kuwait army, navy, and air force is headed by the Ministry of Defense. Although the Ministry of the Interior has jurisdiction over internal security, the Ministry of Defense is responsible for defending the country. Once they turn 18 years of age, Kuwaiti males are obligated to give two years of service to the army, or one year if they have graduated from university. In addition to the members of the military, the

Ministry of Defense employs approximately 1,500 individuals.

Crime

Classification of Crimes

In Kuwait, in accordance with the rule of law, no act can be considered a crime or punished as such except as specified by the law. Furthermore, no person is to be retrospectively punished for an act committed prior to a law that establishes the act as a crime.

Kuwaiti criminal law originated in 1960. Ten years later, in 1970, the Kuwaiti criminal law was amended to the law currently practiced. Offenses in Kuwait are broken down into two categories, misdemeanors and felonies. A misdemeanor is defined as a crime that, by law, is punishable by up to three years in prison, a monetary fine, or a combination of the two. A felony is a crime punishable by over three years of prison, a monetary fine, or a combination of the two or by capital punishment.

There are several crimes within Kuwaiti jurisdiction that are classified as misdemeanors, including some types of physical assault and honor crimes. Crimes commonly classified as felonies include rape, murder, kidnapping, defamation and insult, vandalism, and drug crimes.

A misdemeanor may not be prosecuted if criminal action has not been taken within 5 years of the date the criminal act occurred. In the case of a felony, criminal action may be taken only within 10 years of the date the criminal action occurred. The age of criminal responsibility is 7 years old. Children under the age of 7 years may not be criminally prosecuted. Children between the ages of 7 and 15 years old are tried in the juvenile court system established by means of juvenile law. The juvenile court hears cases involving juveniles accused of criminal acts, misdemeanors, or felonies and juveniles who are considered to be "delinquent."

Human Trafficking

Human trafficking is a tremendous problem plaguing the country of Kuwait. According to the 2005 Trafficking in Persons Report issued by the U.S. Department of State, individuals are brought into Kuwait from many countries, including but not limited to Bangladesh, India, Indonesia, Pakistan, the Philippines, and Sri Lanka. These individuals are used mainly for labor purposes including domestic or household labor. Some are brought into acts of prostitution or are otherwise sexually exploited and verbally and physically abused while providing labor services. These individuals are provided with few, if any, means to escape these situations.

Human trafficking is a lucrative operation because it provides employers with inexpensive labor. The 2007 Country Reports on Human Rights Practices cite adult, female domestic laborers and uneducated, unskilled workers as the most common victims of trafficking within the country.

According to the same report, in some cases employers will pay for the transport of individuals to Kuwait for purposes of employment. Once these workers arrive in Kuwait, they often find that the employment conditions are less than what were promised to them. Leaving these exploitative situations can prove difficult because many of them have already become indebted to their employer. Even if they are capable of leaving, often their documents necessary for travel are withheld from them by their employers. In addition, it has been reported that the victims of trafficking are forced to work long hours and are sometimes prevented from even leaving their homes. They often do not receive adequate compensation for their services. Moreover, domestic employees in Kuwait are not protected under the Kuwaiti labor laws. Because many of the victims of human trafficking are being utilized for the purpose of domestic labor, they receive essentially very little legal guidance or protection from the government, further inhibiting their escape from these undesirable conditions. Furthermore, because there is very little protection for these individuals, if they are picked up for other crimes, the Kuwaiti government may detain, jail, or deport them. Some are even returned to the employment situation from which they came. In few cases, the government may provide these individuals with financial assistance.

The trafficking offenders are reportedly citizens and foreigners alike, as well as agencies involved in labor recruitment and individual employers. In its 2005 Trafficking in Persons Report, the U.S. Department of State indicated that the country of Kuwait was not in compliance with the minimum standards for the elimination of human trafficking. Although not considered in compliance with these standards, the Kuwaiti government has publicly denounced the act of human trafficking and did enact a law in 2004 in an attempt to preventing the use of children as camel jockeys, which is one of the utilizations of children being trafficked into the country. The government also created a task force to address labor problems, including domestic labor. As of 2007, a place of refuge has also been established for domestic employees who are attempting to escape from the problems typical of this type of employment.

Human trafficking is not directly punishable because Kuwait does not have laws specifically against the act. However, the practice is not supported by the government, and consequently, the government prosecutes human trafficking crimes using statutes already in place such as laws specifically against kidnapping, prostitution, rape, slavery, coercion, and forced labor. Punishment includes a prison sentence ranging from 3 to 10 years for kidnapping or "inducing prostitution," and capital punishment can be imposed as punishment for rape.

The Kuwaiti Ministry of the Interior initiated a labor contract that must be signed by all parties—the employer, the employee, and the employment recruitment agency—which presents specific guidelines regarding rules the parties are to follow, including a minimum wage that must be paid to the employee. Failure to abide by such a contract can result in prosecution under Kuwaiti law. The government is also attempting to control the trafficking situation by taking legal action against agencies and companies that violate labor laws.

As reported by the 2007 Country Reports on Human Rights Practices, statistics show 258 people were convicted of bringing persons into the country and not providing them with employment. There were 276 individuals convicted of selling residence permits to aliens unlawfully. There were also 19,908 violations of workers' rights convictions, all of which helped to combat the issue of trafficking.

Domestic Violence

Violent acts committed against women are also challenging crimes for Kuwait. Among these crimes are rape and physical assault, including domestic violence. The highest possible punishment for rape is the death penalty. However, according to the Country Reports on Human Rights Practices for 2007, offenders are not regularly arrested for rape charges, and some reports of rape cases are improperly handled by both the police and hospitals. Sources indicate that several rape victims have been foreign domestic employees.

According to the same report, police receive complaints of spousal abuse allegedly on a weekly basis. There is no specific law barring spousal abuse in Kuwait; however, these cases can be tried by charging the abuser with assault. The 2007 report indicated that most domestic violence or spousal abuse cases are not reported. Of the cases that are reported and in which abusers are convicted, penalties generally are not severe. The victim can file police reports and may also ask for formal charges to be issued against her spouse. As of the 2007 report, there were no domestic violence shelters, hotlines, or sources of reprieve available to victims. Adding to the problem, it is reported that even in situations where the abuse has been documented and witnesses can attest to the violence, abusers are not usually detained by the police.

Drug Offenses

Drug crimes continue to be problematic for Kuwait. Based on information provided by the Ministry of Justice, a large number of drug cases prosecuted are cases dealing with possession for personal use. However, some cases are referred to the courts to be heard for possession with intent to sell or manufacture drugs, or for growing narcotics with the intention of selling them. Information reported by the *Kuwait Times* indicates that the punishment for drug-related crimes can vary from a fine to a death sentence, with the death sentence being one of the least common forms of punishment.

Kuwait has established hospitals for treatment of drug-addicted individuals. In addition, a committee has been established for the purpose of examining drug addicts assigned to these institutions by order of the court. Very few individuals are sentenced to drug treatment programs when convicted of a drug-related crime.

Although information indicating narcotics are illegal in Kuwait is prominent, a list of specific drugs prohibited in the country is not readily available.

Prostitution

The criminal act of prostitution and crimes related to prostitution are problematic for Kuwait. Many foreign women are forced into prostitution. Typically, when prostitutes are caught, they are either deported to their home country or made to sign a "pledge of good conduct" before being released. Individuals running prostitution rings generally receive prison sentences.

Crime Statistics

Because Kuwait does not make available crime statistics, the only available data come from the INTERPOL International Crime Statistics, and the last available data for crimes known to Kuwaiti police are from 1997. These statistics were as follows:

Murder	16
Sex offenses, including rape	686
Rape	15
Serious assaults	2,609
Car theft	1,005
Fraud	1,767
Drug offenses	785

Although these statistics are very out-of-date, they do give some indication of the profile of crimes. INTERPOL reports that more than half of these crimes were committed by aliens. Women accounted for less than 20 percent of offenses.

The Ministry of Justice of Kuwait provides more recent statistics related to cases forwarded to and prosecuted within the court system. The last available statistics are for the year 2006. In 2006, 6,606 felony cases were received by the Ministry of Justice, and 6,633 were acted on. The ministry received 2,991 trade misdemeanors and acted on 3,344. Juvenile misdemeanors received by the courts equaled 2,012, ith 1,963 being acted on. Press misdemeanors received by the courts equaled 253 for the year, with 194 cases acted on. Of 1,194 false-checks misdemeanors, 1,176 were acted on. The number of drug cases received was 233, with 229 being acted on. This puts the total number of cases received by the Ministry of Justice at 13,289, with a total of 13,539 cases acted on.

Of the felonies received and acted on by the Ministry of Justice in 2006, 894 cases regarding murder and bodily assault crimes were considered. The courts received and acted on 299 kidnapping and illegal detention crimes, 477 defamation and insult crimes, 3,094 vandalism crimes, 346 bank crimes, and 1,058 drug and alcohol crimes. There were also 872 miscellaneous felonies received and acted on that were placed in a category titled "Other Crimes."

Rural and Urban Crimes

Because Kuwait is a largely urban area with only 4.4 percent of the country being classified as rural, it is difficult to distinguish between crimes that are common in urban areas and those that are common in rural areas. However, certain types of crime are more common in some areas of the country than others. For example, in third-country national (TCN) communities, a unique crime facing these communities is that of individuals pretending to be police officers. In these situations, a man in civilian clothes and vehicle attempts to stop a civilian, ask for his or her ID, and force that person to get into the offender's vehicle. Typically, the victim is brought to a remote area and beaten. Because Kuwaiti police officers are entitled to make traffic stops in their civilian attire and vehicles, it can be difficult to distinguish whether the stop is genuine.

The area of Jahra, a section of Kuwait City, is known for its high crime rate. Crimes within this area include vehicle vandalism, creating fires, and harassing aliens. It is thought that the high crime rate in this area may be due, in part, to tribal customs of the inhabitants of the area being more influential than police enforcement.

Finding of Guilt

Rights of Accused

All Kuwaiti criminal trials are open to the public unless the government decides that, to maintain public order or so as not to undermine the morals of the people, a trial must remain closed. Court decisions are rendered by judges. Trial by jury is not a right offered to the accused.

Individuals accused of committing criminal offenses in Kuwait are afforded many rights. An integral right afforded to all persons under the Kuwaiti Constitution is that all accused are considered innocent until proven guilty through means of a legal trial. Furthermore, the Constitution guarantees the right of equality to its citizens, so that no individual can be treated differently based on race, religion, age, sex, and so on in everyday dealings, while detained for accusation of criminal activity, or while in legal proceedings.

In Kuwait City, Kuwait, in 2009, a security van leaves the Justice Palace, where the country's law courts are located. (AP Photo/Gustavo Ferrari)

All individuals retain the right to trial and the right to counsel. In situations where the accused does not obtain counsel, counsel is assigned to accused by the court. In cases involving felony charges, the accused may have counsel with him or her throughout all parts of the legal course. Individuals who do not speak or understand the language being communicated within the courtroom are afforded the right to have an interpreter present. The right to remain silent is allowed to every defendant. The accused is not required to speak in his or her defense or against it. A defendant is also allowed to confront his or her accusers and is permitted access to case-related evidence. In addition, every individual is provided with the right to appeal a court decision. Finally, any wrongfully accused and detained individual is allotted the right to be compensated for hardship he or she has encountered caused by wrongful accusations by a witness or plaintiff.

Investigation and Prosecution

Individuals may be incarcerated while awaiting trial, within limitations. In Kuwait, an individual arrested for a criminal act must be delivered to the investigation authority within four days unless a written order is issued by the investigator indicating additional detention is required. During the initial four days the accused is being detained, the police have the right to refuse him visits, including those from counsel and family members. In addition, the accused cannot be detained any longer than six months without a court order commanding his detention. Furthermore, as established by Kuwaiti law, detained persons accused of a crime who have not yet been tried or convicted are to be kept separate from those who have been convicted of a crime and are serving a sentence. Therefore, there are separate quarters within a Kuwaiti prison for each of these two groups so as to keep them from intermingling.

Juveniles are prosecuted through a separate court system, the juvenile court. This court retains the power to commit a juvenile to institutions or health centers as the court finds necessary to address issues of health and rehabilitation and for the purpose of supervision of the minor. In the criminal justice system, juvenile offenders are kept apart from adult offenders and are housed in separate institutions. The country has also established a Juvenile Welfare Office whose purpose is to review problems of juvenile delinquency and their placement in facilities for rehabilitation, protection, and care. The Ministry of Social Affairs and Labor oversees the social welfare institutions under whose care delinquent juveniles are placed.

Many of the acts for which juveniles in Kuwait can be tried are the same acts for which adults can be tried. However, there are also additional restrictions placed on their actions by virtue of their age. Juveniles can be prosecuted for offenses including pornography, the purchase of drugs and/or alcohol, gambling, involving themselves with persons known to be criminals, running away from either home or school, and rebelling against their parents.

Punishment

Types of Punishment

Punishments typically issued to convicted criminals can be as little as a small fine and expand to include prison sentences and the death penalty. In some cases individuals may be sentenced to rehabilitation programs, specifically those cases involving drug use. The Kuwaiti government prohibits the banishment of any citizen from the country. Therefore, banishment cannot be used as a means of punishment for convicts. However, in the case of noncitizens who have been convicted of a felony, Kuwaiti law requires that they be deported on completion of their sentences. Furthermore, individuals can be stripped of their citizenship for committing an act that constitutes a felony within 10 years of becoming a Kuwaiti citizen.

Capital punishment is permitted and used in Kuwait. The death penalty can be imposed on an individual convicted of rape, murder, or drug offenses, among others. Although capital punishment is used, there are restrictions as to whom it may be inflicted upon. The law states that capital punishment may not be used as punishment for crimes committed by youth under 18 years of age. If an individual who has reached 15 years of age but not 18 is convicted of a crime otherwise punishable by death, the sentence must be reduced to an imprisonment of no greater than 15 years. In cases where a juvenile under 15 commits a crime that would otherwise be punished by a sentence of death or life in prison, a maximum sentence of 10 years may be imposed. The law also prohibits the use of capital punishment on pregnant women. It stipulates that if a pregnant woman commits and is convicted of a crime punishable by death, but goes on to birth a live newborn, her sentence must be reduced to life in prison.

Before executing a sentence of capital punishment, referral of the decision for appeal to a higher court is mandated. Every level of appeal must be exhausted before a death sentence may be executed. Finally, the amir must ratify a death sentence before the punishment may be imposed. He also retains the power to pardon or commute a sentence. From 2003 through 2007, the Kuwaiti government exercised capital punishment in the cases if 27 individuals.

Typical Crimes and Punishments

According to Kuwaiti law, abortion is a punishable crime. Kuwaiti law states that performing or attempting to perform, by use of any means, an abortion on a woman is a punishable act. The punishment for such an act is increased if the act is carried out by a medical or pharmacological professional. Intentionally preparing and distributing any substance that is used for the purpose of aborting a pregnancy is also punishable by way of a prison sentence and fine. Women who attempt to abort and in actuality abort a pregnancy are subject to punishment of up to 10 years' imprisonment and a fine.

Acts of prostitution are illegal and punishable in Kuwait. Any individual who assists another adult in the act of prostitution is subject to a punishment of imprisonment of two years or less, a fine of approximately 75 Kuwaiti dinars (KWD) (approx. US$250) or less, or a combination of the two. If the assistance is to a minor individual, meaning under the age of 18 years, the punishment is escalated to no more than a two-year prison sentence, a fine of no more than 150 KWD (approx. US$250), or a combination of the two. The punishment for a person who coerces or threatens another person to engage him or her in the act of prostitution faces a potential punishment of a prison sentence of five years or less, a fine of 375 KWD (approx. US$1,300) or less, or a blending of the two. If the same act occurs with a minor victim, the potential prison term increases to seven years or less, and the potential fine increases to 525 KWD (approx. US$1,800) or less. The law includes punishment of a maximum of two years' imprisonment and/or a fine of 150 KWD (approx. US$250) for any person who receives proceeds by persuading another person to participate in prostitution in exchange for a desired commodity. One who participates in the founding or maintenance of a location for the purpose of prostitution is punishable by a term three years or less imprisonment, a fine of 225 KWD (approx. US$783) or less, or a combination of the two. Finally if a person provokes the act of prostitution in a public place, he may be subject to a punishment consisting of a prison term of two years or less, a fine of 150 KWD (approx. US$520) or less, or a combination of the two.

Assault is prohibited by Kuwaiti law. The United Nations' *Initial Report of States Parties due in 1997* for Kuwait provides detailed information regarding different levels of assault and the punishment assigned to each level. According to this report, any individual who is convicted of beating, wounding, or causing bodily harm to another individual is subject to a punishment of imprisonment for no more than two years, a fine of no more than 150 KWD (US$520), or a combination of the two. If an individual commits an act that results in causing the victim "severe physical pain" or incapacitation "from using one or more of his organs in a natural way for more than 30 days," but the act did not inflict permanent damage to the victim, the offender's punishment will consist of a fine of no more than 375 KWD (US$1,300), a prison term of no more than five years, or a combination of the two. When serious injury is inflicted on an individual or individuals with the utilization of any instrument by another individual, the offender may be punished with a term of no more than 10 years' imprisonment and a fine of no more than 750 KWD (US$2,600). The same punishment may be applied if an individual causes irreparable harm to another individual in the sense that he or she becomes permanently deformed as a result of the act. Any other assault committed at a lesser level than those specifically listed is punishable by a fine of no more than 22 KWD (US$75), no more than three months in prison, or a combination of the two.

The law established that defamation of religion and criticism of the Constitution, the amir, the neutrality of the courts, or public prosecution are all criminal acts and are punishable. This law is commonly enforced, and as a result, some members of the press have been penalized for such acts. Homosexuality is considered a crime in Kuwait. Furthermore, there are penalties, including a fine, imprisonment, or both, for emulating the sex opposite of one's own.

The typical punishment for murder is dependent on the situation. If the killing can be determined to be an honor crime in which a female or her counterpart was murdered as a result of being caught in an adulterous act, or to be the killing of a daughter or sister for similar dishonorable acts, the killing may be construed as an honor crime, in which case the punishment should not exceed three years of imprisonment. In other situations, the act of murder may land an individual a life sentence in prison or the death penalty.

Prison

According to reports by the U.S. Department of State, in 2007 there were roughly 3,500 individuals being detained in the Kuwaiti prison system. This group consisted of either the accused awaiting trial or the convicted, serving previously issued sentences. Of the total population of detained individuals, approximately 10 percent were individuals awaiting trial, and 150 of the detained individuals were being held for having committed some form of state security offense.

Each prison is equipped with a health unit that provides health care to its inmates. All health units are supervised by a medical doctor. The responsibility of keeping prisoners in good health, including proper nutrition, exercise, and clothing, falls under his domain. The doctor is also responsible for preventing illness on a prison-wide basis. The medical doctor also ensures adequate prison food quality and sanitation of prison cells.

Kuwaiti prisons are segregated by characteristics of the prisoners. Persons accused of crimes must be kept apart from those previously convicted of crimes. Additional factors considered for placement of inmates are their age and their social and cultural background. In addition, an individual's openness to reform is measured. The type of crime for which they are serving time, their criminal histories, and their length of incarceration are also weighed in determining placement within the prison. Individuals who have received a sentence of the death penalty are alienated from all other inmates.

Each prison has an established committee made up of the warden of the prison and social work specialists, to oversee the social welfare of its prisoners and to assure that its prisoners' social and psychological needs are being taken care of, which includes the use rehabilitation programs. The warden of the prison also takes on the additional responsibility of making sure each prisoner is kept up-to-date on the status of his or her family and also of making sure a prisoner's family is kept aware of the prisoner's status and well-being in prison.

In addition to the warden and social work specialists, each prison has a religious figure. The duties of this religious figure are to encourage inmates to follow religious behaviors in the hope that this will have a rehabilitative effect on the inmates. Furthermore, prisoners are provided opportunities to attend classes to further their education. Prison libraries are accessible for prisoners to obtain reading material, and they may also opt to have books and newspapers brought to them from outside the prison, provided that the prisoner covers the cost and that the reading material is within the scope of materials allowed by prison policy. Other programs such as job skill training, training on the values of society, and drug rehabilitation programs also have been provided.

According to the 2006 Country Reports on Human Rights Practices issued by the U.S. Department of State for the country of Kuwait, some of the prison conditions were poor. It was reported that there was overcrowding. Despite a medical doctor being retained to address health conditions in the prison, including sanitation, it was reported that the sanitation conditions were less than satisfactory, and diseases were poorly contained. This was attributed to a lack of medical staff. Improper treatment of prisoners, including includes the abuse of prisoners and inaction on violence occurring between prisoners, was also reported. At the time of this report, a new prison for male offenders to alleviate the problem of severe overcrowding was determined to have met international standards for prisons.

Stephanie L. Stashenko

Further Reading

Kuwait Ministry Justice: http://www.moj.gov.kw.

Kuwait Ministry of the Interior: http://www.moi.gov.kw.

Kuwait Times Newspaper: http://www.kuwaittimes.net.

Lebanon

Legal System: Civil
Murder: Medium
Corruption: Medium
Human Trafficking: Medium
Prison Rate: Medium
Death Penalty: Yes
Corporal Punishment: No

Background

The republic of Lebanon is a western Asian country that borders Syria, Israel, and the Mediterranean Sea. The capital is Beirut, and the official language is Arabic, but English and French are widely spoken. Lebanon is a parliamentary republic. The total area of the country is 10,452 square kilometers, and the estimated population in 2009 is roughly 4 million, although the last official consensus was undertaken in 1932, with a population density of 440 per square kilometers. There are 18 recognized religious sects separated into three groups: 59.7 percent Muslim, 39 percent Christian, and 1.3 percent other.

Political and Social Context

The First Lebanese Constitution went into force in 1926 during the French mandate. The history of Lebanon has long been one of political and religious turmoil among periods of economic and cultural prosperity. The Israeli-Arab conflict that led to a huge inflow of Palestinian refugees, coupled with sectarian tension, led to the 1975 civil war.

The Palestinian forces then allied themselves with the leftist Muslim faction against the Lebanese president supported by Christian militias, Syrian military forces entered Lebanon upon the request of the Lebanese president in 1976. Israel invaded Lebanon in 1978 and occupied part of its southern land under the pretext of eliminating the military threat of the Palestinian Liberation Organization (PLO). Israel would occupy that land until 2000 (Lebanon maintains the position that Israel has still not withdrawn from all Lebanese territories). A UN Interim Force in Lebanon (UNIFIL) was deployed on the borders. It would be reinforced in 2006 and tasked to implement UN Security Council resolution 1701. During the period of the 1980s, which witnessed another Israeli invasion in 1982 that reached Beirut, fighting continued, leading to the killing of thousands of civilians and the assassinations of many high Lebanese officials and foreign diplomats as well. That period was marked as well by the presence of international forces and the rise of the Iranian-backed Hezbollah. By 1989, Lebanon witnessed the partition of Beirut into two governments: a Christian one in east Beirut and a Muslim one controlling the west of the city. Following further military confrontation, an Arab League delegation succeeded in gathering Lebanese Parliamentarians in Saudi Arabia, where the Taif accord was reached, which put an end to the civil war that reportedly claimed more than 150,000 Lebanese and 15,000 missing, whose whereabouts are still unknown. The Taif agreement introduced major amendments to the Lebanese constitution. These changes cut the wide executive power the Lebanese president enjoyed under the past constitution and vested it in the multisectarian council of ministers, which includes ministers (representatives) of all sects. Another significant amendment was the provision that an equal number of seats be reserved for Christian and Muslim members of Parliament. Currently, by virtue of custom, the Lebanese president should be Christian (Maronite), the speaker of Parliament should be Shiite, and the prime minister should be Sunni. The first elected president, Mouawad died in a car bomb explosion 18 days after his election. President Hrawi, his successor, remained in office until 1998. In March 1991, Parliament issued an amnesty covering all politically motivated crimes committed before its date of enactment, excluding those perpetrated against foreign diplomats and high officials.

In the aftermath of the Taif agreement, Lebanon entered the sphere of Syrian influence, with the presence of more than 40,000 Syrian troops in Lebanon. The Syrian military presence came to an end in 2005 following the assassination of the influential ex-prime minister of Lebanon, Rafik Hariri, when many Lebanese politicians accused Syria of being behind the assassination, sparking massive protests against the Syrian presence in Lebanon. This led to the formation of two opposing political campaigns: "March 14," which was anti-Syria and backed by Western powers, and "March 8," pro-Syria and backed by Iran and Syria. In 2007, UN Security Council resolution 1757 would establish the special tribunal for Lebanon, situated in the Hague, to prosecute those responsible for the killing of Hariri. Between 2005 and 2008, high tension prevailed among the two opposing campaigns amid car-bomb explosions that targeted March 14 politicians.

In 2006, Israel launched a strong aerial and ground attack against Lebanon after Hezbollah abducted Israeli soldiers on the borders between the two countries. The fighting between Israel and Hezbollah resulted in the death of roughly 1,500 Lebanese and 160 Israelis.

In 2007, fighting broke out between Lebanese armed forces and the extremist Islamic group Fatah Al Islam, which that controlled the Palestinian refugee camp of Nahr Al Bared in northern Lebanon. Around 168 soldiers and 226 militants were killed in the fighting during the 105-day siege of the camp. More than 400 soldiers were wounded and more than 200 militants were captured.

In May 2008, when fighting broke out in Beirut and Mount-Lebanon, political bickering reached its end between the groups March 14 and March 8. The Doha agreement between the Lebanese parties calmed the situation, and a national unity government was established to run the country. Currently, political tensions have eased and the country is in a state of relative stability. Arabic is the official language but English and French are widely spoken.

Police

The Lebanese national security system consists of the Lebanese Armed Forces (LAF), the Internal Security Force (ISF), the State Security Apparatus (SSA) and the General Security (Sureté Generale, or SG). The LAF has the power to arrest and detain suspects based on mere national security concerns. The authority of the ISF, a regular armed force, covers the whole Lebanese territory, including its regional waters and airspace. The SSA and SG are both charged with the collection of sensitive information about groups deemed to pose a threat to national security. The Sureté Generale, in particular, oversees the issuance of passports and residency permits, the screening and censoring of foreign periodicals, documentaries, television programs, movies, and so on, on the basis of their moral tenability and national security relevance.

As for the Internal Security Force, its functions include the following:

- Enforce rules on public and private morality.
- Protect citizens and their property.
- Protect civil liberties.
- Ensure the enforcement of specific laws and regulations.
- Execute warrants and other acts of the judiciary.
- Assist other public authorities in the performance of their duties.
- Guard public facilities.
- Guard prison inmates.
- Provide protection to diplomatic missions on Lebanese territory.

The Internal Security Force operates under the authority of the minister of the interior and is mainly subjected to military law. The ISF includes nine units:

1. The general staff of the ISF includes, among other things, a number of specialized bureaus responsible for studying sensitive issues and subsequently providing qualified advice to the force's director-general.

2. The Central Administration consists of administrative and technical sections in charge of the financial, supply, and equipment management of the Internal Security Forces and of the facilities it owns or controls.

3. The Social Services Administration is responsible for the publication of the ISF's own magazine and oversees its clubs as well as the implementation of cultural and social initiatives.

4. The Territorial Gendarmerie consists of all subsections operating outside of Beirut except for those that totally or partially refer to other lines of command: its posts are spread all over Lebanon.

5. The Mobile Unit is an ISF force equipped and trained to respond to security emergencies arising around the country in a way both rapid and effective; it includes all mobile battalions based in and outside Beirut.

6. The Beirut Police, which consists of a number of specialized divisions is the metropolitan police force in charge of enforcing the law within the city of Beirut. Because of a lack of personnel, many police operations are regularly carried out in conjunction with the military and under the command of a military officer, if not, in some cases, by the military alone.

7. The Judiciary Police includes the departments of crime combat, the detective department, the forensic police, and the tourism police.

8. The Apparatus for Security of Embassies, Administration and Public Institutions includes the forces charged with protection of embassies and other public administrations and institutions.

9. The Institution of ISF includes the academies of the police.

Heads of these departments are usually nominated based on sectarian allocation, though this is by virtue of custom, not enshrined in law. Whenever incidents pose a threat to national security, they are settled by the military. As any foreigner visiting Lebanon may notice right away, there are army checkpoints spread throughout the whole national territory.

Legal System

The current Lebanese criminal justice system has its roots in the period of Ottoman rule, the result of a combination of systems comprising, besides Ottoman Law, the so-called Canon Law and the codices based on the French model. Starting from 1516, and over the following three centuries, a relatively free interpretation of the Ottoman system was adopted; the ensuing French rule (1920 to 1943) then played a critical role in the development of the current system, albeit exerting no significant influence on Ottoman family law and on noncodified sources of personal law.

Central to today's system are codes coherent with the standards developed and adopted by civil law countries, rather than with the statutory law usual in countries of common law. Therefore, we can say that the Lebanese legal system is inspired by the French Legal system, and it is common for Lebanese judges to refer to French jurisprudence and case law in their judgments. As in the case of France, administrative law regulates the functioning of all branches of civil administration as *pouvoirs publics* based on statutory provisions and on the rulings of specialized courts of law.

The Constitutional Council was established in 1993 to review the constitutionality of laws and the legality of elections of the president, speaker, and members of Parliament. It is made up of 10 members nominated by Parliament (5) and the government (5). Recourse to the council is open to the president, speaker, prime minister, official heads of sects in personal status only, and 10 members of Parliament.

Hence, the Lebanese judicial system consists of two separate hierarchical structures, with a civil court system devoted to handling matters of criminal and civil nature and whose court of last resort is called Cour de Cassation, and an administrative court system whose Supreme Court is equivalent to the Conseil d'Etat (Majlis al-Shawra).

Depending on the pecuniary relevance of the case at hand, and on whether criminal prosecutors intend to present their case as a crime or as a felony, the courts of first instance may consist of either one or three judges. Above the Court of Appeal sits the Cour de Cassation, consisting of several chambers, which functions as the court of last resort for all cases of civil, commercial, and criminal matters; the judges, depending on their rank, are eligible to be appointed to the newly created Judicial Council (*Al-Majlis Al-Adli*) functioning as both a first- and a last-resort court (which is deemed as violating international legal standards that call for more than one stage of trial) in criminal and politically relevant cases that are considered especially sensitive by virtue of the threats to national security.

The code of criminal procedure was issued in 1948, with most of its articles deriving from the French Code d'Instruction Criminelle of 1808 (which in turn lasted through 1959), only to remain in force until 2001, when a new code was signed into law.

In general, whenever a case is filed against a suspect by the plaintiff or the district attorney's office, the investigating judge will initiate an investigation culminating either in the subject's acquittal or in his or her arraignment, which in turn will result in the defendant's trial by a court of law. In the case of felonies, the plaintiff, especially when no further investigations are needed, can go directly to the court of the single judge.

The procedural approach adopted by the Lebanese Code of Penal Procedure (LCPP) is mixed at best. The inquisitorial approach dominates the preliminary investigation phase, which sees the presence of the investigative judges who are entitled to question and detain suspects whenever they deem appropriate, except for the limitations set by the law itself. At this stage, investigations assume such a level of confidentiality that the defendant may even be unaware of being the subject of judicial attention.

During the second stage of the proceeding, the accusatorial approach's main landmarks become apparent, and the hearings are open to the public, in the presence of both the defendant and the district attorney (the district attorney does not appear before single-judge courts). The district attorney's presence and role in the Lebanese criminal system is, nonetheless, fully coherent with the inquisitorial paradigm, defining an offense not only by the damage that an individual victim or group of victims may sustain as a consequence of it, but also and mainly by the collective, general damage that it causes to society as a whole.

The eminently inquisitorial nature of the LCPP as modified in 2001 and its contiguity with the principles first expressed by the 1808 French Code d'Instruction Criminelle become even more evident if we consider the system's distinctions between the following three separate judicial bodies:

- The public prosecutor's office (*niaba aama*), in charge of initiating a proceeding.
- The inquisitorial bodies that investigate the case.
- The criminal courts that preside over the whole trial.

These three bodies make up "judicial justice," which, in turn and pursuant to the 20th Amendment of the Lebanese Constitution, is one of the three branches of the country's judiciary, the other two being "financial justice" and "administrative justice."

Coherent with the separation of powers principle, the Lebanese judicial, legislative, and executive branches of government are fully independent from each other. The hierarchy of sources relevant to Lebanese judicial justice consists of the following:

1. The Lebanese Constitution.
2. International treaties and conventions.
3. The Lebanese code of penal procedure.
4. The Lebanese code of martial laws.
5. The Lebanese Judicial Justice Act.
6. The Lebanese penal code.
7. The Lebanese code of civil procedure.
8. The Lebanese Public Officials Act.

The fundamental principles guiding the Lebanese judicial organization may be summarized as follows:

1. At the discretion of the Supreme Judicial Council, judges may be transferred from a court of civil law to a court of penal law, and vice versa.
2. Judges are by no means unremovable, and none of them may be permanently assigned to any court of civil or penal justice.
3. There is a distinction between ordinary and special courts.
4. Court judges are functionally, though not substantially, distinct from public prosecutors and initial inquisitorial judges, and all are subject to the same rules.

With regard to the public prosecutor's function, or *niaba aama,* article 6 of the LCPP describes it as "a judicial body vested with the duties and powers connected to the prosecution of penal offenses in the name of the Lebanese people and before penal justice authorities." The position enjoys remarkable independence. Following the Ottoman Code, the Lebanese legislature eventually exempted the *niaba* from the minister's control, vested the *niaba* chief prosecutor with the role of attorney general (AG), and left the minister with only residual power to request that the AG prosecute a crime brought to his office's attention, though the AG could, in turn, refuse to comply whenever he deems appropriate on the basis of "sound" and "valid" considerations (article 14, LCPP). The role of the *niaba* in Lebanese due process may vary based on whether *niabas* lend their contribution during the phase preceding prosecution, the initial investigation phase, the trial phase, or the ensuing sentencing and executory phases.

Courts

The Lebanese court system is shaped after the pattern laid out by the Napoleonic code (1808) and includes a separate order of specialized confessional courts exerting their jurisdiction on marital and hereditary affairs within the boundaries of their communities of origin and pertinence. There are Islamic sharia courts, either generically sharia or specifically Sunni and Shiite nature, and there are also Christian and Druze courts. Although the principle of independence of the judiciary is clearly stated by the 20th Amendment of the Lebanese Constitution, this power remains fully exposed to political influences, owing to the fact that senior positions in the judiciary system are filled by the political authority (council of ministers) like the head of the High Judiciary Council, the head attorney general, the head of Judicial Inspection, the head of the Conseil d'Etat, and the head of Court of Audit. Absent from the Lebanese Constitution is the principle of nonremovability of members of the judiciary.

The Lebanese courts of first instance, known by the name of Mahakim Bida'iyya, consist of three-member chambers, not withstanding the possibility for a single judge to preside over civil and penal trials (felonies) of minor relevance. The courts of appeals (Mahakim Isti'naf) handle both cases already handled by the courts of first instance and felony cases. There are seven of them, one in every district, with the exception of Mount-Lebanon, where there are two districts. The Supreme Court (Cour de Cassation) is the Lebanese court of last resort, situated in Beirut and divided administratively into nine chambers; its jurisdiction also encompasses disputes involving either an ordinary and a special court or two special courts. Special courts include the military/martial courts; the Audit Court, which oversees public spending and tax returns; the Publications Court oversees crimes committed by mass media (such as libel); the Higher Council exists to prosecute presidents and ministers, and the Judicial Council, a permanent tribunal consisting of five judges before which national security threats are discussed.

Trials before Lebanese courts are lengthy, and it is very common for a lease contract case brought before the courts to last for more than five years. Court hearings are adjourned for more than four months in many cases. Oral pleadings by attorneys before courts are not common in civil cases, but more common in criminal cases.

Crime

The Lebanese penal system defines misdemeanors, felonies, and crimes as offenses punishable by prison terms of 1 to 10 days, 10 days to 3 years, and 3 or more years, respectively.

Lebanon has long been plagued by bouts of virulent, hardly controllable terrorist activity, from car bombs all the way to aircraft hijackings, all but encouraged by the ineptitude of its security forces to enforce the rule of the law and by the apparent lack of political will on the part of the forces governing the country over the years.

During the years of the civil war, atrocities and grave crimes were committed on a large scale and went unpunished, especially after the Pardon Act. Genocide, crimes against humanity, and civil wars took place during those years and were perpetrated by both parties of the conflict.

Starting in October 2004, more than 30 bloody attacks by booby-trapped cars took place, with 12 of these definitely political assassinations.

As a consequence of the recent surge in political tensions, which have caused many to fear that another civil war may be in the making, there has been a sizable increase in arms trafficking, with many resorting to the black market in the hope of better protecting themselves from the dangers looming on the horizon, and with security forces fighting an anti-smuggling battle that seems to have been already lost. The price of a traditional AK-47 (Kalashnikov) increased from US$400 before 2005 to more than US$1,500 at the peak of the tension during 2007 and 2008.

Other forms of criminal activity heavily affecting the Lebanese people's perception of their own security include car theft and car-napping, with organized groups based in the northeast stealing motor vehicles that they then offer to return to their legitimate owners in return for a ransom.

The government has increased attention to the problem, and the practice seems far more under control. In charge of fighting corruption in the public sector is the Central Inspection Directorate, whereas private sector corruption falls within the purview of the district attorney's office. Corruption in public administration plagues the whole country's system, and no solutions or limitations are looming. The perception of corruption remains one of alarming proportions, with the 2007 International Corruption Perception Index putting Lebanon in a disheartening 99th position out of 180, and the 2001 UN Corruption Report estimated losses to the local economy at a staggering $1.5 billion, nearly 10 percent of the gross domestic product.

On April 20, 2001, in an effort to counteract the pervasive presence of money-laundering activities oftentimes operated in connection with the illegal drug business, Parliament passed Legislative Act Number 318 / 2001. Article 1 of the act defines the types of conduct it applies to, and article 6 foresees the creation of a Special Investigation Commission (SIC) as an independent legal entity with the Bank of Lebanon, the sole Lebanese agency officially entitled to collect confidential client information from within the banking system.

Despite a disturbing increase in the number of cases of domestic violence reported by the press, the Lebanese penal code still does not include a provision expressly aimed at fighting these acts, even though there is a penal provision generically punishing the battery of women with up to three years in jail. The special nature of these acts of violence, mainly perpetrated under the veil of domestic privacy and thriving on the victim's fear of losing everything she has, including her respectability, leads one to believe that the available statistics reveal only the tip of the iceberg. Furthermore, religious courts have no jurisdiction over this matter; they are only involved if the victim files a divorce lawsuit. The state of Lebanon offers free legal assistance, but no free medical care to female violence victims who cannot afford it. Another alarming side of domestic violence is that it is often directed against foreign domestic workers, mostly of Asian nationalities, who are more vulnerable than Lebanese women owing to the fact that they do not speak Arabic and are looked down upon.

Prostitution in Lebanon is illegal; however, it is widely practiced, as law enforcement is not efficient to curb it. Women from Eastern Europe form part of this secret prostitution and are often victims of abuse and exploitation by Lebanese pimps.

Despite the lack of any provision expressly prohibiting and punishing the practice of human trafficking, the Lebanese penal code generically states that "any person depriving another person's freedom either by abduction or by any other means shall be sentenced to a term of temporary hard labor. If the person abducted or kidnapped is also compelled to prostitution or is sexually assaulted, the term should not be less than seven years in prison." Forced prostitution is punished by from two months to two years in prison.

Foreign workers do enjoy the protection of Lebanese law as do Lebanese workers. However, foreign domestic workers almost lack any protection of their work rights. Their passports get seized by employment agencies upon their arrival at Beirut airport to make it easier for the police to chase down those who do not show up for work or who even disappear for good, which usually takes place under the pretense of criminal allegations falsely formulated by their employers. In 2009, the ministry of labor enforced a unified contract for domestic workers that protects them from abuse by the employers, but wide violations persist.

Owing to a significant decrease in illegal drug production starting from the early 1990s, Lebanon has recently been removed from the U.S. list of major illicit drug-producing countries, and the reason for this decrease ought to be ascribed to the Lebanese government's zero-tolerance approach to drug production. The efforts did not prove as effective, though, at curbing the massive amounts of opium poppy and cannabis still harvested in the remote Bekaa Valley, in spite of the many raids conducted by the police on that very area.

Furthermore, the ineffective and inefficient allocation and spending of funds provided by the

United Nations International Drug Control Programme (UNDCP) aimed at encouraging the transformation of illicit drug cultures into cereal cultures prevented these initiatives from yielding any appreciable results.

In 1998, the Lebanese Parliament passed an anti-narcotics act. The act prescribes, among other things, that drug traffickers be severely punished and that all resources and instruments connected or resulting from their operations be seized by the government. But the act lacks a provision allowing authorities to exercise any scrutiny on relevant banking records, casting serious doubts about its overall efficacy.

As for the chemical precursors needed to extract a number of illegal substances, and pursuant to DEA guidelines, the Lebanese Ministry of Health, the Ministry of Industry and Commerce, and the Lebanese Customs Department require that their importation be subjected to the issuance of specific authorizations and that the domestic production thereof be fully traceable at every stage of the process.

Drug use among Lebanese citizens has increased lately, triggering calls from prominent figures to crack down strongly on this crime. Besides a private program called "Oum al Nour" that enjoys some help from the government, there are very few drug-addiction prevention and rehabilitation initiatives in the country. As for the amounts sold to the end consumer, the decrease in hashish consumption has been more than compensated for by a surge in the demand for synthetic drugs such as amphetamines. To counter this trend, the Lebanese Narcotic Drugs and Psychotropic Substance Act was passed by Parliament on March 16, 1998.

As of 2010, and in spite of this act's uncompromising approach to the issue of narcotics possession regardless of the amounts at stake, no improvements of any appreciable relevance seem to have originated from this much-touted "new deal."

In addition to the creation of specialized detoxification and rehabilitation centers and of social rehabilitation programs (see article 182), this law now also contemplates the presence of a Drug Addiction Committee (article 199) that would consist of a presiding judge, a Ministry of Health physician, a social policy expert, a police officer with the narcotics division, and a member chosen by the National Council on Drugs (NCD). None of this has eventuated.

Another initiative worth mentioning is the so-called *sokun* ("silence") program, which aimed at shifting the whole perspective on drug-addiction issues from a punitive and repressive one to one centered on medical and psychological therapeutic care.

As for the substances listed as illegal, the law makes a fundamental distinction between those whose sale and consumption is illicit under any circumstance and those that may be possessed and used if authorized or prescribed.

In the year 2002, and to the effect of discouraging drug use, the government launched an all-round campaign that included placing into school textbooks educational resources meant to increase drug awareness. According to many nongovernmental organizations, the demographics of drug use in Lebanon have been gradually shifting toward younger age groups ever since the end of civil war, with the problem now mainly affecting teenagers and college students. From the end of the 1990s to the year 2004, the incidence of addicts age 24 or less in the general population resorting to the assistance of counseling and rehabilitation services increased dramatically, with heroin being the most widely consumed substance, followed by synthetic drugs such as amphetamines and Ecstasy.

There are only two male and one female rehabilitation centers in the whole country, with a total capacity of 70 residents and offering psychiatric, medical, and social assistance, but no drug replacement programs. However, several new facilities of this kind are currently under development, as in the case of the Zahleh, Bekaa Valley, and Mercy and Justice centers, the latter in the form of an NGO

Crime Statistics

In the virtual absence of government-provided statistical data, it is especially hard to fathom the extent and specificities of crime in Lebanon. The data provided by the Beirut-based ISF Directorate-General, gives a rough indication of the Lebanese crime situation within the time frame of 2005 to August 2008. The number of grand theft auto offenses dropped in 2006 only to increase again in 2007, with the 2008 number returning close to the 2005 level. A similar tendency seems to characterize the figures relative to recovered cars, with 75 vehicles retrieved out of 143 reported stolen (52.4%, the highest yearly percentage recorded since 2005). As far as homicide is concerned, the year 2008 featured the highest numbers ever recorded, especially if we consider that the fourth quarter had not yet been factored in when these numbers were provided: 198 killings, 74 of which were committed in May and 30 in July, in contrast to the slightly decreasing trend that had appeared in recent past years. The same seems to be true for the number of cases of substance trafficking and abuse. Although the 2008 monthly rate of the former substance trafficking reached the 2006 end-of-year watermark as soon as August 2008, with notable peaks in the months of April and June, the number of cases of substance abuse in the same final month of August was already as high as the number registered in record-year 2005 (44 versus 45 monthly rate cases).

The same negative tendency also seems to apply to robberies and qualified thefts. In fact, robberies reached the monthly rate of 42 cases at the end of August 2008 (versus 50 cases in the year 2005) and qualified thefts reached 145 cases in the same month (compared to 205 cases for 2005).

Conversely, a downward trend seems to characterize the misdemeanor arrest figures (1,265 monthly arrests as of August 2008, the smallest number in four years). It may be worth mentioning that the ISF data at issue do not allow for any recent/current trend analysis of the rape and aggravated assault prevalence, and the ISF definition of "qualified thefts" encompasses both burglaries and larcenies. The territorial distribution of the different offense types is variable at best, with a greater incidence of homicides in urban areas and of thefts in rural ones.

Finding of Guilt

Owing to the principle of due process, a suspect is to be brought before a judge within 24 hours of being arrested and by the officers carrying out the arrest, and the suspect may be held in custody without the authorization of the DA for a maximum of 48 hours (that could be extended to 72 hours upon the DA's approval) if at least one witness was present on the crime scene.

Under the 2001 LCPP, the same police officers are to be held responsible and punished for holding a suspect in custody if they did not take the suspect to be interviewed by a judge with 24 hours. If a suspect is held for the sole reason of engaging patrolling officers in a pursuit, he or she must be brought before a judge, who will, in turn, decide whether he or she is to be held in custody. The same code also provides suspects with a whole array of guarantees that have long been part of Western penal systems only, such as the right to legal assistance by an attorney, to medical attention whenever appropriate, to communication with loved ones, and to release on bail.

Although expressly prohibited by law, torture was applied on a wide scale to extort information and/or confessions from persons of interest during the times of Syrian presence, which ended in 2005, and especially within the 1991–2005 period; methods included bashing suspects and suspending them in the air with their arms tied behind their back.

According to the LCPP, a defendant must enjoy the assistance of an attorney during the whole trial process, regardless of his or her income status. However, the suspect can refuse the appointment of an attorney and the trial would proceed. There is no such thing as trial by jury in Lebanon, where crimes, even the most heinous and socially alarming ones, are tried before a mere three-judge court, and convictions may be appealed only before the three-judged Cour de Cassation or Supreme Court.

Hearings are held either publicly or behind closed doors; in either case, the defendant has the right to attend them, to consult with his or her attorney whenever necessary, to cross-examine witnesses if expressly authorized to do so, to get access to evidence relevant to the case at hand, and to appeal against a conviction or sentence. If put on trial for posing a threat to national security (most of the cases brought before this court are assassinations of political figures), the defendant must appear before the Judicial Council, under procedural conditions identical to those just described except that there is no appeal against the council's decisions.

Interestingly for a Middle Eastern country, the testimonial soundness of female witnesses is by no means deemed inferior to that of male witnesses. As for insane defendants whose trials end in a criminal conviction, they shall serve their sentence in a specialized correctional facility.

Before being tried, felony defendants may be held in custody for up to two months in normal cases, or four months in situations requiring complex investigation and trial preparation activities. As for criminal defendants and felony defendants whose records include at least one jail term in excess of one year, the time limits are 6 and 12 months, respectively, provided they did not commit murder, a drug-related crime, or any other of the offenses that the Lebanese system deems especially heinous and/or detrimental to national security, in which case there are no time limits to custodial incarceration. However, in practice, it is not uncommon to find suspects who have spent more than three years in prison without trial before a court.

In spite of the principle requiring that an arrest be based on a valid warrant, the practice of arbitrarily arresting and detaining people of interest still continues, especially in connection with operations conducted by military intelligence and in cases of espionage, betrayal, arms possession, and draft evasion. In 2004, the Lebanese Parliamentary Commission for Human Rights estimated that one-third of the 5,000 inmates sitting in Lebanese jails had not been convicted of any wrongdoing.

As for the organization of the judiciary, judge appointments and rotations fall within the purview of the Supreme Judicial Council and the minister of justice. The Supreme Judicial Council is composed of 10 judges; 7 of them are nominated by the political authorities, directly and indirectly. Hence, the political authority has clout over the judiciary. To be a criminal judge, one has to have a degree in law; have a criminal record clean of major felonies or crimes; be fluent in Arabic, French, and English; pass an exam; and attend a three-year training course held at the Ministry of Justice's Institute for Judicial Studies, upon completion of which he or she will become an assistant judge and be appointed to a civil or criminal court based on the Supreme Judicial Council's decisions. Remarkably, female judges constitute currently more than 50 percent of the total number of judges.

Juveniles

A new juvenile code was issued in 2002, which considers as juveniles persons below 18 years old. The new law envisions a number of educational, protective, and correctional measures all intended to guide juveniles at risk of becoming career criminals onto a path of personal and social recovery. The protective and educational measures apply to juveniles 7 to 12 years old; they may last for a definite period of time and consist of releasing the juvenile to the custody of his or her parents or relatives (relatives other than parents may come into play in the absence of parents or whenever the judge deems the parents' contribution less than useful). Correctional measures, on the other hand, include the juvenile's transfer to either a reeducational facility or a disciplinary institution, where, in addition to schooling, he or she will receive moral, religious, and physical education and be taught a job skill. If assigned to a disciplinary institution, juvenile detainees are housed in dedicated sections to prevent dangerous promiscuity with older inmates. In addition to this, specific treatment options are offered to juveniles with psychiatric or addiction problems.

Minors younger than seven years old are considered exempt from punishment (article 3) and must be released to the custody of a parent or relative; should a minor's rebel attitude make that approach appear unviable, he or she shall be sent to a reeducational facility and be housed there for at least 1 year or until 18 years old, which is also the first and only option available to treat minors between the ages of

12 and 15 who have committed a crime or a felony offense, and the third and last resort for minors of the same age group who committed only a misdemeanor offense. Minors stay subject to the monitoring of a social assistant who reports to the judge every three months on their situation.

The Special Tribunal for Lebanon

The assassination of prominent former prime minister Rafik Hariri, former economy minister Bassel Fleihan, 6 bodyguards, and 10 civilians on February 14, 2005, in a huge car bomb loaded with more than 1,500 kilograms of high-power explosives, led to an uprising that in turn forced Syrian troops out of Lebanon after some 29 years of rule over the whole country. As a direct consequence of the international community's resolution to bring to justice those responsible for this crime, the UN Security Council established a special investigative commission. Soon thereafter, the Special Tribunal for Lebanon, an international criminal court specially mandated with trying those suspected of having ordered and carried out the assassination, was established under chapter VII of the UN charter pursuant to UNSC Resolution 1664 (2007).

For the first time ever, a UN-appointed international tribunal "based on the highest standards of criminal justice" (UNSC Res. 1664) would be dealing with the trial for a crime committed against specific individuals rather than against an unspecified group of people and would be doing so by applying Lebanese criminal law (except for the death penalty and forced labor) as opposed to international criminal law (article 2 of the Special Tribunal's statute). Furthermore, its chambers consist not only of international judges but also of a number of Lebanese judges, a composition pattern similar to the one previously experimented with for the Special Court for Sierra Leone (article 8, SSTL).

So far, the tribunal, which is currently headed by a Canadian member in the role of prosecutor general, has issued eight reports, the first of which established a connection between the Syrian and Lebanese intelligence apparatuses and the assassination of Prime Minister Hariri and his economy minister, together with the aforementioned 6 six bodyguards and 10 bystanders, a view, needless to say, shared by many political observers and commentators. The Syrian regime along with pro-Syrian politicians in Lebanon, for their part, see the tribunal as instrumental to an American and French strategy to put pressure on Syria to withdraw its support for organizations such as Hamas and Hezbollah.

Punishment

Types of Punishment

The LPC foresees five separate ranges of punishment options depending on an indictable offense's qualification as a crime, as a felony of either a common or a political nature, or as a mere misdemeanor. Misdemeanors are usually punished by 1 to 10 days of arrest or fine. Major felonies and their punishments are shown in the following table.

It may be worth mentioning, though, that male perpetrators who kill their wives if they see them in the state of committing adultery or sexual intercourse are subject to especially lenient treatment. Despite a 1999 legislative initiative to strengthen penal treatment of such heinous practices, nothing seems to have changed as of this writing.

Concerning the death penalty, despite a 1998 moratorium, three executions were held in 2004, and 69 inmates remained on death row, according to the European Neighbourhood Policy program.

Since Lebanon became independent, 51 executions have taken place by either hanging or shooting; in a few cases, and for the sake of dissuasion, hangings were staged at the exact location where the crime leading to the execution had been perpetrated, which in turn led to vocal criticism from many political observers and human rights watch groups.

Other Punishments

Article 44 of the penal code mandates that, unless provided differently, the term duration for hard labor, imprisonment for a definite term, expulsion/deportation from the country, forced residency, and

OFFENSE	TYPE OF PUNISHMENT
Murder, first degree	Capital punishment (article 549)
Murder, second degree	15 to 20 years of hard labor but practically always punished with life in prison (article 547)
Murder, third degree	6 months' to 3 years' imprisonment (article 564)
Honor-motivated infanticide by the victim's mother	3 to 15 years imprisonment. More than 5 years' imprisonment if intentional (article 551)
Consensual homicide	Maximum of 10 years' imprisonment (article 552)
Instigation to suicide	Maximum 2 years of imprisonment if the victim actually commits suicide; 3 months' to 2 years' imprisonment if the attempt results in a permanent injury (article 553)
Theft	Ordinary theft: 2 months to 3 years imprisonment (article 636) or hard labor for life or for a definite term (dependent on circumstances)
Violent theft	Hard labor for a definite term of unspecified duration or at least 5 years of hard labor under particular circumstances
Sexual assault	Minimum 5 years' hard labor (minimum 7 years if the victim is under 15 years old)
Drug selling	Hard labor for life in addition to fine of 25 to 100 million Lebanese pounds (Act 673/1988, article 125)
Co-conspirator; Consumer of drugs	Prison term ranging from 3 months to 3 years and fine of 2 to 5 million pounds, regardless of the amount of illegal substance found in the person's possession. Alternatively, a 6-month rehabilitation program can be served instead of a prison sentence (only if this is the first such offense).
Assassination/terrorism	Death penalty.
Human trafficking	No provision beyond kidnapping expressly prohibiting and punishing the practice of human trafficking in the Lebanese penal code.

loss of all civic rights may not be less than three or more than 15 years; the specific type or form of forced labor imposed on any particular convict, to be performed either within or outside a correctional facility, must be suitable for his or her age and sex.

Expulsion and deportation orders must be complied with within 15 days of their issuance, and convicts caught on national territory again before their ban have expired are subject to a prison term ranging from a minimum coinciding with the amount of time left on the ban at the time of reentry to a maximum of twice that duration (article 47).

Forced residency (article 48) may not be served at the convict's domicile or place of residence; at the place where the victim or one of his or her first-, second-, third-, or fourth-grade relatives resides; or in the location where the offense was perpetrated.

Loss of civil rights (article 49) may also be integrated with an additional three-month to three-year prison term, which is always the case when a foreign national is convicted.

Disqualification from holding a civic office (article 50) is imposed, as a complementary punishment, on all convicts sentenced to forced labor or to a prison term.

Forced residency for felony convicts may last from a minimum of three months to a maximum of three years. A convict may at any time exercise his or her option to pay a fine by installments, provided the due date has not yet expired; if still unpaid as of 30 days after the sentence has become executed, the fine is converted into a prison term that may not exceed one year in duration (article 52, 53, and 54).

When the convict is a pregnant woman, the prison term is deferred until the sixth week following delivery; a similar rule applies to offenders who have a pregnant dependent family member under the age of 18, provided the latter has a fixed domicile (article 55).

Prisons

While the law provides that prisons should be under the supervision of the justice ministry, it is the interior ministry that controls it currently. According to a joint plan between the ministry of interior and ministry of justice, the authority over prisons will be actually transferred by 2012. According to the report of the director-general of ISF on August 26, 2009, published in the Annahr newspaper on September 25, 2009, the Lebanese prison population was at that time 5,324 inmates with an incarceration rate of 150 per 100,000 of the overall population of the country estimated to be four million inhabitants. The percentage of the detainees in Lebanese prison who are awaiting trial stands at a high rate of more than 66 percent, according to a report of the director-general of ISF on August 26, 2009. The percentage of foreign detainees who have served their sentence and are still in prison reaches 13 percent, according to the same report. This prolonged detention happens mainly because the state cannot afford to buy air tickets for foreigners who are also unable to afford them, so that they can be deported back to their countries of origin. Starting from 1993, occupancy rates featured an upward trend that still persists today. As for the inmate population's composition, 62.5 percent of those detained in a Lebanese correctional facility are in pretrial custody, which clearly exposes the local system's weaknesses. As of November 12, 2004, only 3.9 percent of inmates were female, and data collected on December 22, 2005, showed that minors and aliens accounted for 2.4 and 42.1 percent of the overall prison population, respectively.

There are 30 correctional facilities in the nation, 22 of which are penal facilities and 8 of which are functioning as temporary detention centers. As of December 12, 2005, overall correctional capacity was running at approximately 120.9 percent, which explains the many complaints external observers and inmates have voiced over time.

Decree Number 14310 of February 12, 1949, as amended by a number of ensuing legislative provisions, including the decree issued on March 30, 1995, provides a regulatory reference for everyday life within Lebanese correctional facilities, which applies to suspects under arrest, to convicted inmates, and to convicts sentenced to a term of hard labor (article 59).

Although inmates usually live in groups (article 61), some do live in solitary confinement subsequent to discretionary orders issued by the competent authority for a duration ranging between 3 and 15 years, to be materially served on a farm or at selected factories (article 77). Sentences may entail or not entail hard labor and may be as lengthy as life in prison (article 62); those who have to work and those who do not are segregated from one another even during outdoor time, regardless of the amount of courtyard space actually available.

All inmates have to keep their own cells clean, and only those distinguishing themselves for their good conduct may serve as cooks or as nurses, provided, needless to say, that the jail doctor and the jail director deem them fit for the job.

The elective work that inmates may do outside of their correctional facility and under the constant surveillance of prison guards may be only of a community service nature; aside from those sentenced to hard labor, no work duty may be imposed on any inmate unless he or she expressly asks for some, in which case the inmate will be burdened with it until the end of his or her sentence (articles 46 and 61). It falls to the jail doctor to ensure that jail work is carried out by healthy inmates in a clean and suitable environment.

Inmates are entitled to three hours of outdoor time each day, to be enjoyed under the direct supervision of prison guards, unless ordered differently by the jail director, and they may read books and magazines, but no newspapers (article 60).

Whenever transferred to court, to the visiting room, or to the interrogation room, inmates must always be escorted by prison guards; they may see their attorneys during daytime visiting hours as defined by the director or, exceptionally, by an appropriate judge. Inmates have to make use of their own blankets and other basics because prisons do not cover these items. Prisoners may receive presents, money, and correspondence only up to a certain limit; they may normally send off no more than two letters a week, a threshold that does not apply to attorney correspondence (article 63). Money from relatives may be spent only within a certain weekly amount, unless explicitly authorized otherwise by the Ministry of the Interior. Inmates may purchase a selection of items from prison stores located within their facilities and may pay for the goods by issuing stamp-like receipts previously signed by the jail director (article 65) under the condition that the inmates have no outstanding debt toward the government (article 66). Two times a year, on June 15 and December 15, inmates who have conducted themselves in an outstanding manner may see their residual sentence lengths reduced or even be released from prison (article 108). As of 2010, this provision is currently not implemented, but the ministry of justice has launched an initiative to enforce it.

As for alternative measures of punishment, Decree Number 1760 only contemplates monasteries for Christian juveniles and the Home of Muslim Orphans for Muslim juveniles.

Article 52 defines who may serve as part of a prison medical staff (doctors chosen by the Ministry of Interior in accordance with the Ministry of Public Health, registered public physicians, and if necessary, common practitioners) and mandates that, once a week, dentists be available for inmates to consult at a rate of one for every three hundred potential patients; doctors, for their part, have to be present three days a week (article 53, as unified by Decree Number 6394 of January 6, 1967). All doctors have to record their work and send the information to the prison director and to the public health minister once every three months (article 54). Jail doctors are assisted by army soldiers or by inmates featuring an outstanding conduct record. No psychiatric services are available (article 55).

Inmates suffering from particular conditions may be transferred to civil hospitals provided enough personnel are available to guard them throughout their stay (article 74). The real prison conditions as outlined by sources external to the department of corrections, differing from those portrayed by Lebanese legal provisions, reveal a situation characterized by systematic disregard for the physical and psychological health of inmates, along with indifference toward the inhumane practice of torture.

Despite the high number of deaths among prison inmates, the police usually abstain from investigating these occurrences and justify this by referring to the previously precarious health conditions of the deceased. Additionally, hygiene conditions are dreadful, and torture is used by prison guards to extort confessions or discipline "unruly" inmates. This is how the Lebanese Parliament's Human Rights Commission, which visited Zahle Penitentiary following the escape of 10 inmates on February 24, 2008, described it in their own words: "It is a prison for those sent to death, one of the worst prisons where it is unfit to be a ranch for animals, it requires radical solution." A new prison facility meeting international standards replaced the old one in Zahle starting in May 2010,

In April 2008, a protest that took place at Romyeh Penitentiary drew public attention to the inhumane living conditions of inmates, to the utter severity of punishments, and to the lack of security inside correctional centers. Due to the lack of enough human resources and guards and corruption, many inmates are not transferred to the courts for the hearings, and because courts adjourn hearings for more than two months at a time, these inmates end up spending more than three or four months before being brought to trial.

The condition of female inmates does not notably differ from that of men. The 2001 Amnesty International Report denounced conditions of dirt and heavy overcrowding and the constant occurrence of threats, beatings, and torture of a physical and psychological nature (Lebanon accepted the UN Convention against torture in 2000) amid repeated violations of the rights granted by the new 2001 LCPP.

The largest correctional facility of the Country is Romyeh, completed in 1964 and located five miles east of Beirut, which consists of four different blocks. According to the previously mentioned report of the director-general, Romyeh has an original capacity of 1,050 inmates, but more than 3,500 are detained there.

Under normal conditions, this prison hosts more than 3,000 convicts and suspects. It also includes a specialized juvenile section, which is usually so crowded that many juvenile offenders end up serving their sentence amid dangerous career criminals.

Work within correctional facilities is mandatory only for some inmates, while it is an option for others. Although the system does not provide inmates with any educational opportunities, an information technology (IT) training program has been in place for some years to prevent long prison terms from becoming unjustly prejudicial to a convict's future as a member of society.

Visits, including those by lawyers, must be authorized by the district attorney. Before being allowed to enter a correctional facility, all visitors must pass a security check; in the cases of transfers or exchanges of prisoners, this procedure applies only to foreign inmates.

Luisa Ravagnani, Carlo Alberto Romano, and Samer Abu Said

Further Reading

Bassiouni, M. C. (1985). *New Horizons in International Criminal Law.* Nouvelles etudes Pénales, 6.

Criminal Record: (2009): http://www.isf.gov.lb.

El-Gemayel, A. E. (1989). *The Lebanese Legal System.* Washington, DC: University Press of America.

Lebanon in Brief: (2009). http://www.pogar.org/activities/marrakech04/lebanon-rep-e.pdf.

Lebanon Tribunal: http://www.un.org/apps/news/infocus/lebanon/tribunal/.

Torture Prevention and Monitoring Project: (2009). http://www.lebanon-support.org.

Libya

Legal System: Civil/Islamic
Murder: Medium
Corruption: Medium
Human Trafficking: Medium
Prison Rate: Medium
Death Penalty: Yes
Corporal Punishment: Yes

Background

Libya, formally known as the Great Socialist People's Libyan Arab Jamahiriya, is 679,363 square miles in size, with a relatively small population of just over 5.5 million. It borders the Mediterranean Sea and lies between Egypt and Tunisia in northern Africa.

Libya was the stage for numerous battles between the Axis and Allied forces, and the country came under the control of the British and French after World War II. In 1951, it gained its independence through the United Nations, and a constitutional monarchy was formed under King Idris. The Al-Fateh Revolution in 1969 toppled the pro-Western King Idris. The leaders of the coup set up the Revolutionary Command Council (RCC), which ran the country, headed by a 28-year-old officer, Mu'ammar al-Qadhafi. The RCC, eventually replaced by the Arab Socialist Union, abolished the monarchy and declared the Libyan Arab Republic, which promoted Arab unity and the liberation of Palestine.

Judicial System

Prior to Italy invading the country in 1911, Libya had a dual judicial system, which distinguished between religious and secular matters. The majority of cases for Muslims—those involving individual personal status, such as marriage and inheritance—fell within the jurisdiction of religious courts, which applied Islamic law, or sharia. The courts, directed by an Islamic religious judge, a *qadi,* are organized into original jurisdiction and appellate levels. Cases involving secular matters, such as civil, criminal, and commercial law, were tried in a separate court system, which reflected Western influence in general and the Napoleonic code in particular. After the 1911 invasion, the Italians maintained the dual judicial system structure. The post-independent Libya attempted a merger of religious and secular legal systems in 1954, resulting in the subordination of Islamic law to secular law. Popular opposition led to a return to separate legal jurisdictions in 1958. However, in 1971, the Legislative Review and Amendment Committee was created to make existing laws conform to sharia in civil, criminal, and commercial law, as well as personal matters. A second postrevolutionary body, the Higher Council for National Guidance, was created in 1972 to present Islamic moral and spiritual values in such a way that they would be viable in contemporary Libyan society.

Police

The Libyan police force has an estimated 10,000 policemen and women (there is at least one women's police academy). Called the People's Security Force, the police perform the usual law enforcement functions such as investigating crimes, arresting criminals, and maintaining public order, but they are also responsible for the administration of prisons and assisting with passports and identity cards. Special police units are also assigned to counterespionage duties.

The original prerevolutionary mission of the Libyan police system was the same as those in many other Muslim and non-Muslim societies. The traditional concept of police, or *shurtah,* was a broad one. Domestically, the *shurtah* were primarily responsible for suppressing dissidence and insurrections as well as performing other internal security duties. The latter duties typically embraced the kinds of administrative and law enforcement functions often required of urban and rural police, such as the prevention of crime, investigation and arrest of criminals, and maintenance of public order.

After the 1969 military coup, Qadhafi reorganized the police force where military officers were temporarily integrated into key police administrative positions to guard against another coup attempt. All policing functions were consolidated under the Ministry of the Interior. In 1971, new separate agencies designed to handle civil defense and fire protection were provided for by law. Other units were also established by the Interior Ministry, such as the Central Department of Criminal Investigation, the Central Traffic Department, the Arab International Criminal Police Bureau, the Ports Security Department, the Police Training Department, and the Identity Investigation Department. A new police law in January 1972 not only spelled out the new functions of the police, but also gave them a new name: the Police at the Service of the People and the Revolution. In addition to the standard domestic functions, the new functions of the police were to take responsibility for the administration of the prisons, civil defense activities, and passport and nationality matters. Individual police units were under the jurisdiction of regional security directorates throughout the country, with primary responsibility for enforcing the laws and administering the police falling under the minister of the interior and his deputy.

There is a visible presence of uniformed police throughout the country, though the force appears to be understaffed, inadequately resourced, and ineffective. Sometimes the police forces are supported by members of the Libyan external and internal security personnel. Local police are supported by neighborhood volunteers, who have even less training and resources.

Finding of Guilt

Penal Code

Qadhafi's proclamation involved a reorientation of Libya's entire criminal code. Libyan legal and religious scholars attempted, in an extensive and slow-moving process, to minimize the obvious contradictions in the two systems. Amendments to the criminal code after 1973 addressed both moral issues related to Islamic beliefs and purely secular matters. Government announcements in 1973 and 1974 stated that lashings and imprisonment of adulterers, imprisonment of homosexuals for up to five years, and floggings for those transgressing the fast of Ramadan were issued as laws "in line with positive Islamic legislation." Any Muslim who drank or served alcoholic beverages could receive 40 lashes. Non-Muslims could receive fines or imprisonment for alcohol-related offenses, and fines and jail terms were set for possession of or trafficking in liquor.

The criminal code was further revised in 1975 to further strengthen state security. Actions such as revealing state or defense secrets, "scheming" with foreigners to harm Libya's military or political position, facilitating war against the state, infiltrating military reservations, and possessing means of espionage were made subject to harsh penalties, including life imprisonment and death. The number of actions that may result in execution has grown, including membership in political parties that oppose the principles of the 1969 revolution or economic crimes, such as damaging oil installations or stockpiles of basic commodities.

In 1994, the Purge Law was created to fight corruption, black marketeering, drug trafficking, and atheism, enforced by the government's "purification" committees since June 1996. Hundreds have been arrested arbitrarily on charges of corruption, dealing in foreign goods, and funding Islamic fundamentalist groups, and dozens of shops and firms have been closed.

In 1997, the government passed a law, pushed by Qadhafi, that provides for "collective" guilt. The Libyan General People's Congress approved a law that provides for the punishment of accomplices to a range of crimes, including instigating and practicing tribal fanaticism; possessing, trading in, or smuggling unlicensed weapons; and damaging public and private institutions and property. The 1997 law could find small or large groups, including towns, tribes, or families, guilty and subject to severe punishment such as denial of water, fuel, food supplies, and participation in local assemblies. The law, passed by the General People's Congress in March 1997, formally codified the government's previous threats of punishment for families or communities that aid, abet, or do not inform the regime of criminals and oppositionists in their midst. In May 1997, Qadhafi declared that if any member of a family was found guilty of an offense, the individual's entire family was to be considered guilty and punished as well. According to Human Rights Watch and the U.S. Department of State, Libya's human rights record remains poor, and it continues to commit numerous serious abuses.

Court Structure

Libya no longer has a dual court system. With the primacy of Islamic law and the merging of Islamic doctrine into the secular system, the dual religious-secular court structure was no longer necessary, and in 1973, the religious judicial system of *qadi* courts was abolished. The secular court system was retained, but its jurisdiction now included religious matters conforming to sharia, the religious jurisprudence. In 1987, the court system had four levels: summary courts (sometimes referred to as partial courts), courts of first instance, appeals courts, and the Supreme Court.

Courts in the lowest level, summary courts, are located in most small towns in Libya. In a summary court, a single judge hears cases involving misdemeanors. Misdemeanors are disputes involving amounts up to 100 Libyan dinars (LD, about US$78). Most decisions are final, but in cases where the dispute involves more than LD20, the decision can be appealed to the next higher level of courts, the courts of first instance.

Courts of first instance hear appeals from lower-level summary courts and have original jurisdiction over all matters in which amounts of more than LD100 are involved. A panel of three judges in each court rules by majority decision and hears civil, criminal, and commercial cases and applies sharia to personal or religious matters that were formerly handled by the *qadi* courts. The People's Court is a special court of first instance to which crimes against the state (alleged attempted forcible overthrow of the ruling regime or otherwise rallying opposition to it) are referred.

The three courts of appeals sit at Benghazi, Tripoli, and Sabha. A three-judge panel rules by majority decision and hear appeals from the lower courts. Sharia judges who previously sat in the Sharia Court of Appeals prior to the merging of the dual court system were assigned to the regular courts of appeals and continue to specialize in sharia appellate cases. Regardless of whether the People's Court acquits or convicts the defendants, both prosecution and defense have the right to appeal the judgment before the court of appeals in Tripoli. The decision of that court, too, can be challenged before the Libyan Supreme Court, whose judgments are final.

The Libyan Supreme Court is located in Tripoli and comprises five chambers: criminal, administrative, civil and commercial, constitutional, and sharia. A five-judge panel sits in each chamber and also rules by majority vote. The court is the final appellate body for cases coming from the lower courts. The Supreme Court can also interpret constitutional matters. All justices and the president (also seen as chairman) of the court are appointed by the General People's Committee; probably the general secretariat makes the actual selections. Before its abolition, the RCC made Supreme Court appointments.

Other Judicial Bodies

Some of the agencies involved in the administration or the enforcement of justice are situated outside the regular court system. For example, the Supreme Council of Judicial Authorities is an administrative agency that coordinates the various courts.

The People's Court

In 1971, a People's Court was established to try political, economic, and security crimes against the state. The People's Court also included an appeals court and a prosecution service, the Popular Prosecution Office. A member of the Revolutionary Command Council presided over the court, which also included one representative each from the armed forces, the Islamic University, the Supreme Court, and the police. Many of those tried were charged under violations of Law 71, which bans any person or group activity based on political ideology opposed to the principles of the 1969 revolution.

In January 1977, a new People's Court was formed to try political detainees for crimes against the state. Such crimes may be referred to a people's court, but plots and active conspiracies against the state are usually referred to special military courts created on an ad hoc basis for that purpose. The military courts and the people's courts have been criticized by human rights groups such as Human Rights Watch for routinely violating the legal rights of defendants in political cases. The Constitution provides "all necessary guarantees" for the defendant's defense and prohibits the subjection of the accused or imprisoned to "mental or physical harm." Realistically, however, and in spite of what the Constitution says, due process and individual rights of defendants are routinely ignored prior to, during, and after trials. Human Rights Watch interviewed five prisoners who were convicted under the People's Court. Four of the five complained of physical torture during the investigation, as well as due process violations, such as restricted access to lawyers representing them. Human Rights Watch asked the Libyan government on October 12, 2005, if it had conducted an investigation into the allegations of the prisoners, but as of January 10, 2006, the government had not responded. The General People's Congress voted in January 2005 to abolish the People's Court. A Libyan official told Human Rights Watch that the People's Court had performed a particular role after the 1969 revolution and that it was no longer required, due to changing circumstances. He did not specify which circumstances, or how they had changed.

The Revolutionary Courts

Special courts were established in 1980 to try political offenses. Such trials are often held in secret. The Revolutionary Courts normally abrogate many procedures and rights ensured by the traditional court system. The UN Special Rapporteur noted in 1996 a lack of fairness in capital trials. With the regime's blessing and encouragement, revolutionary committee members established courts that held (sometimes) public, occasionally televised trials of those charged with crimes against the revolution. A 1981 law prohibited private legal practice and made all lawyers employees of the Secretariat of Justice. Therefore, as of 1981, all lawyers worked for the government. In these courts, the accepted legal norms—such as due process, the right to legal representation, and the right of appeal—were frequently violated. According to Amnesty International, Libya held 77 political prisoners in 1985, of whom about 18 were held without trial or remained in detention, some incommunicado, after having been acquitted. Libya also sanctioned the murder of political opponents abroad, a government policy reaffirmed on March 2, 1985, by the GPC.

The security forces have the power to pass sentences without trial, especially in cases involving governmental political opposition. In the past, Qadhafi has incited local security forces to take extrajudicial action against suspected opponents. On May 6, 2004, 16 health professionals who were charged in 1999 with infecting 400 Libyan children with HIV were sentenced to death. Their defense attorney complained that he had been allowed to meet with his clients only twice since their incarceration.

Crime

The Libyan Criminal Code of 1954 identified crimes in increasing order of seriousness as contraventions, misdemeanors, and felonies. Under the Islamic sharia, though, an act could be, in increasing order of seriousness, mandatory, commendable, permissible, reprehensible, or forbidden.

Since he came to power in 1969, Qadhafi has regarded crime as an anomaly in complete conflict with his revolutionary goals and ideals, given that all Libyans are expected to contribute to the common good of society and its economic, social, and political development. Partially because of this, the government rarely publishes statistics on any crimes in the country. The U.S. Department of State rates Libya a medium threat for criminal activity. Notwithstanding the lack of specific statistics, crime has remained a problem in recent years with an understaffed, underfunded police department and a slow, inefficient legal system that has not demonstrated any effectiveness at preventing crime or prosecuting criminals.

Crime against foreigners is a growing problem in Libya, according to the U.S. State Department. The most common types of crime are auto theft and theft of items left in automobiles, as well as burglary. Pickpocketing and home invasion are also on the increase. The availability and increasing use of drugs and alcohol by both Libyans and non-Libyans have contributed to the increase in crime in the past few years. Women routinely face verbal harassment. Although physical violence is not common, there have been instances of assault against women, particularly women foreign to Libya. These assaults can range from sexual groping or assault/battery to attempted rape.

Although precise statistics are not available, residential burglary against foreigners is by far the most common crime reported to the Regional Security Office (RSO) by expatriates in Libya. Police officers are generally ill-equipped and poorly trained to investigate these incidents. Response time also varies and can be lengthy depending on the type of incident.

Trafficking in Persons

Libya is a transit and destination country for men, women, and children from sub-Saharan Africa and Asia trafficked for forced labor and sex; many victims willingly migrate to Libya en route to Europe with the help of smugglers, but may be forced into prostitution or work as laborers or beggars to try to pay off their $800–$1,200 smuggling debt. A U.S. State Department report notes that laborers from Egypt, Sudan, and Ethiopia are reportedly trafficked to Libya for the primary purpose of labor exploitation.

Pickpocketing

Pickpocket teams are known to operate in crowded venues of the cities, particularly hotels frequented by foreigners. Examples noted by the U.S. Department of State include the bus station adjacent to the Corinthia Hotel in Tripoli and the nearby Burj Al-Fatah Tower complex. Pickpocketing is carried out by teams of two and involves one pickpocket agent and one "security" person. The agent carries out the theft, while the accomplice waits poised to assist. Libyan victims who have resisted have reported being jabbed by a small pointed object on the opposite side from where their valuables are located—that is, the assailant is not meaning to cause grave bodily harm, as much as he is interested in getting the attention of the victim while the crime is perpetrated.

Vehicle Theft

According to the U.S. Department of State, vehicle theft is a problem, as is breaking into cars through auto windows and/or doors, particularly in the larger cities such as Tripoli. This type of crime is opportunity-driven and not specific to any particular nationality. Crimes of this nature almost always happen when an automobile has been left unattended in a vulnerable area. One U.S. Embassy employee was victimized after leaving an automobile unlocked on the street near his home. Thieves are primarily interested in car stereos. Other incidents have been reported by Corinthia Hotel staff, who park their privately owned vehicles along the unprotected Medina Wall. There were no reported incidents of carjacking in Libya during 2006.

Residential Crimes

According to the U.S. State Department, there were residential crimes (burglaries) reported by U.S. Embassy Tripoli personnel during 2006. Specific numbers were not available.

Punishment

Applying Islamic law to contemporary law and society sometimes presents problems in administering punishments. For instance, the administration of traditional Islamic physical punishments, such as the severance of a hand for the crime of theft, raises many issues. Argument arises over whether "severance" should mean actual amputation or simply impeding the hand from future crime by removing need and temptation. Literal religious interpretations are usually adopted, but their actual imposition as legal punishment is usually restricted by exemptions and qualifications, based (roughly) on Islamic tenets. In October 1972, though the government enacted a law providing for the amputation of the right hands of convicted thieves, this penalty has not been commonly imposed. A thief's hand would not be amputated, for example, if he truly repented of his crime or if he had committed the crime under some duress, such as to feed a starving family. Traditional sharia punishments such as limb amputation and flogging are seen as inhumane in Libya. Without formally rejecting sharia punishment, Libyan criminal justice utilizes modern forms of punishment instead, such as various terms of imprisonment. The death penalty is also regularly imposed, despite repeated appeals to Muammar Qaddafi by humanitarian groups such as Human Rights Watch and Amnesty International to abolish it.

The Death Penalty

Qadhafi has for years publicly stated that Libya should abolish the death penalty. In private, however, he either argues for it or at least does not argue against it. The "Green Book" revision of 1988 states that "the goal of the Libyan society is to abolish capital punishment"; however, the government has not acted in any way to abolish the death penalty, and the government's use of the death penalty has increased over the years. Many crimes, including political offenses and economic crimes, are punishable by death. A 1972 law mandated the death penalty for any person "associated with" a group opposed to the principles of the 1969 revolution, as well as for other acts such as treason, attempting to change the form of government by violence, and premeditated murder. A new criminal code was adopted in 1973, and it further criminalized certain acts against the security of the state and introduced the death penalty for "offenses against the principles of the revolution." After the attempted coup in 1975, the Libyan General People's Congress amended the criminal code, criminalizing as capital offenses conspiracy with foreigners against the state, divulgence of military or state secrets, and possession of devices to engage in espionage.

After an apparent increase in economic crimes nationally, in 1996 a law went into effect that applies the death penalty to Libyans who speculate in foreign currency, food, clothing, or housing during a state of war or a blockade and to crimes related to drugs and alcohol.

In 1997, two civilians and six army officers were executed after having been convicted in capital trials, the civilians by hanging and the army officers by firing squad. At least five others were given prison sentences, all convicted on charges of being American spies, committing treason, cooperating with opposition organizations, and instigating violence to achieve anti-revolutionary political goals. The UN Rapporteur on Extrajudicial, Summary, or Arbitrary Executions noted in 1996 that capital punishment is extensively imposed because of a lack of fair trial standards.

Penal System

The Libyan penal system is a responsibility of the Secretariat of the Interior and is administered by the judicial police. The judicial police agency is independent of the police and within the Ministry of Justice, not the Ministry of Public Security. Three institutions—the Central Prison at Tripoli, Kuwayfiyah Prison at Benghazi, and Jdeida Prison outside Tripoli—are known to exist, and smaller facilities in other cities are known to be part of the system. Prison conditions are poor. Qadhafi granted permission for visits by Amnesty International to several prisons in the late 1970s, but the necessary arrangements were never made by Libyan authorities. The prison system was reorganized under Law No. 47 in 1975, which (theoretically) changed the prisons from institutions of "punishment and terror" to ones where inmates were afforded "education and training" as part of a program to try to rehabilitate offenders.

Libyan security personnel routinely torture prisoners. In addition, Libya routinely prevents any human rights organizations from visiting prisons in the country. In April 1999, the UN Committee against Torture reported that it continued to receive allegations of torture by Libyan authorities. According to the United Nations, methods of torture reportedly used by the Libyan security forces include clubbing, applying electric shock, breaking fingers and allowing the joints to heal without medical care, suffocating with plastic bags, depriving inmates of food and water, hanging by the wrists, suspending from a pole inserted between the knees and elbows, burning with cigarettes, attacking with dogs, and beating on the soles of the feet.

Amnesty International (AI) reports that political detainees are held in cruel, inhumane, or degrading conditions and are denied adequate medical care, which has led to several deaths in custody. In July 1996, inmates protested poor conditions at the Abu Salim prison in Tripoli, run by the Internal Security Agency. According to an ex-prisoner interviewed by Human Rights Watch, the prisoners went on a hunger strike to protest the lack of medical care, overcrowding, and inadequate hygiene and diet provided at the facility. The prison held between 1,600 and 1,700 inmates at the time of the uprising. Security units were dispatched to suppress the uprising, and as many as 1,200 inmates were killed by security forces according to the witness, who worked in the prison kitchen. According to the former prisoner interviewed by Human Rights Watch and Libyan human rights groups abroad, the guards responded to the uprising at the prison by going from cell to cell, shooting prisoners as they went. The Libyan government claims that the police responded appropriately after the uprising and an escape attempt in which approximately 400 prisoners escaped, some of them leaving Libya. As of August 2005, the government officially had not released information about the incident or the names of the dead inmates but said it had established a committee to investigate the incident. The Libyan government does not permit regular prison visits by human rights groups or representatives. Hundreds of political detainees, many associated with banned Islamic groups, reportedly are held in prisons throughout the country (but primarily in the Abu Salim prison in Tripoli). Many are held for years without charge.

Jeffrey Dailey

Further Reading

Amnesty International. (2004, August). *Libya: Time to Make Human Rights a Reality:* http://www.amnesty.org/en/library/info/MDE19/007/2004/en.

Amnesty International. (2005, January). *Libya: Abolition of People's Court Is an Important Step.* Public Statement: http://www.amnesty.org/en/library/info/MDE19/001/2005/en.

Human Rights Watch. (2006). *Libyan Law and Human Rights* 18(1): http://www.hrw.org/en/news/2008/01/02/libya-serious-abuses-persist.

International Centre for Prison Studies. (2006). *Annual Report 2006.* London: Kings College, University of London: https://www.kcl.ac.uk/schools/law/research/icps/about.html.

Overseas Security Advisory Council—Global Security News and Reports. (2007, January 18). *Libya 2007 Crime and Safety Report: Crime and Safety-Middle East/North Africa:* https://www.osac.gov/Reports/report.cfm?contentID=62154.

U.S. Department of State. (2001). *Country Reports on Human Rights Practices—2000:* http://www.state.gov/g/drl/rls/hrrpt/2000/.

Morocco

Legal System: Islamic/Civil
Murder: Low
Corruption: Medium
Human Trafficking: Medium
Prison Rate: Medium
Death Penalty: Maybe
Corporal Punishment: No

Background

The Kingdom of Morocco constitutes a part of the Great Arab Maghreb. An official Arab state, at 172,402 square miles (446,550 square kilometers), it became independent from France on March 2, 1956. A bicameral legislature was formed in 1997, primarily as a result of political reforms. The Moroccan Constitution provides for a monarchy with a parliament and an independent judiciary. Ultimate authority rests with the king, who, in addition to being the head of the military as well as the country's religious leader, appoints the prime minister following legislative elections; presides over the Council of Ministers; appoints all members of the government; and, at his discretion, may terminate the tenure of any minister, dissolve Parliament, call for new elections, or rule by decree.

The legal system in Morocco is based on Islamic law and French and Spanish civil law systems. A series of constitutions, drafted in 1962, 1970, 1972, 1992, and 1996, preserve the monarchical nature of the Moroccan regime. Modeled after the French Constitution of 1958, the Constitution of 1962 granted even greater powers to the head of state. The Constitution created a bicameral parliament consisting of a chamber of representatives (two-thirds of which were directly elected) and a senate-like chamber of politicians nominated through electoral colleges. This parliament was considered relatively strong insofar as both chambers were to be consulted prior to the implementation of any royal legislative decree (article 72). However, Hassan II held the upper hand at all levels: the king had the capacity to dissolve the chamber of representatives (article 27) and thus to paralyze Parliament.

Since 1996, the bicameral legislature consists of a lower chamber, the Chamber of Representatives, which is directly elected, and an upper chamber, the Chamber of Counselors, whose members are indirectly elected through various regional, local, and professional councils. The councils' members themselves are elected directly. The powers of Parliament were expanded under the 1992 and 1996 constitutional revisions to include budgetary matters, approval authority, and the establishment of commissions of inquiry to investigate the government's actions. In addition, the lower chamber of Parliament may dissolve the government through a vote of no confidence.

Police

The Moroccan police force, known as the Sûreté Nationale, was created on May 16, 1956, after Morocco gained its independence. As part of Morocco's ambitious program to improve law enforcement efficiency, several new police services will be created by

2017 with 3,000 new policemen set to join the force. The plans call for almost 90 new provincial police districts, 131 police departments, 6 law and order enforcement units, 16 quick intervention squads, 10 mobile circulation units, 6 search and intervention police, several training centers, and a bomb sweeping unit. The police departments provide protection for Morocco's 16 regions, subdivided into 62 prefectures and provinces.

Judiciary

Article 82 of the Morocco Constitution holds that judicial authority is independent from both the legislative and executive powers. According to article 1 of the 1-74-388 law issued on July 15, 1974, it shall be composed of common laws, special courts, and specialized courts.

The Moroccan judiciary is independent. Given the support of the Moroccan Constitution's sanction, specifically article 82, the judiciary shall be independent from the legislative and executive powers. Additionally, sentences shall be passed and executed in the king's name (article 83).

According to the latest Constitution, the Supreme Council of Magistracy shall be presided over by the king and ensures the implementation of the guarantees granted to magistrates regarding their promotion and discipline (article 87).

The Courts

Article 1 of the 1-74-388 decree issued on Joumada II 24, 1394 (July 15, 1974), determines the judicial organization of the kingdom. Common law jurisdictions are Supreme Court, courts of appeal, first instance tribunals, and communal and district courts. Specialized jurisdictions are administrative tribunals and tribunals of commerce.

The judicial organization concerns all the tribunals and courts of the kingdom. The term "tribunal" indicates inferior courts such as the courts of first instance, and "court" refers to superior courts, such as the courts of appeal. According to article 82 of the kingdom's Constitution, the judicial authority shall be independent from the legislative power and the executive power

Drug Crime

According to the CIA, Morocco is one of the world's largest producers of illicit hashish; shipments of hashish produced in the country are mostly directed to Western Europe. The country is also a transit point for cocaine from South America destined for Western Europe and a significant consumer of cannabis.

Punishment

Death Penalty

Morocco is progressively moving toward settling the issue of capital punishment. According to the

Crowds gather at the Sidi Moussa jail, where 49 inmates were killed and about 80 injured when a fire broke out early on November 1, 2002. Located in El Jadida, 90 miles south of Casablanca, Morocco, the prison was known to be severely overcrowded. (AP Photo/Abdeljalil Bounhar)

Moroccan justice minister, this will be accomplished first by reducing the number of verdicts and then by ordering suspension of their execution before abolishing the practice once and for all. In Morocco, there is great disagreement about capital punishment, hence the need for continuing the debate on this issue, the minister said. He recalled a colloquium held by the Ministry of Justice in 2004, which recommended adopting a progressive approach in settling this issue, noting that following this meeting, the new penal code halved the number of crimes punishable by the death penalty from 22 to 11.

Since 1973 and 2007, 133 people were sentenced to capital punishment, two of whom were executed, the last case of which took place in 1993, the minister said, adding that the number of people sentenced to this penalty now amounts to 125. In Morocco, the death penalty, although still used as a sentence, is rarely actually carried out. Morocco was expected to ratify the abolition of this sentence by April 2008.

Punishment of Homosexuality

Homosexuality is criminalized under section 489 of the penal code (of November 26, 1962), which provides a penalty of between six months and three years' imprisonment and additional fines from 120 to 1,000 dirhams (about US$117) for "lewd or unnatural acts with an individual of the same sex."

Corrections

According to a report by the BBC in 2001, Morocco's 44 prisons are extremely overcrowded, with unhealthy conditions belonging to another age. The Moroccan Prison Observatory, an umbrella organization that incorporates a number of human rights groups, speaks of a prison regime immersed in corruption, violence, disease, and the sexual abuse of children as young as 12. According to the latest data from the International Centre for Prison Studies, t prison capacity in Morocco is at 155.1 percent. The number of penal establishments is as follows:

Penitentiary	1
Agricultural penitentiaries	4
Local prisons	38
Center for reform and education	1
Total detainee capacity	**36,500**

The BBC claims that at any one time, Moroccan prisons hold as many as 80,000 inmates, in a system designed for less than half that many. Although a few prisons are not full, others have so many people that the only place left to sleep is the toilets. Hygiene is minimal, medical care nonexistent, and disease rife. One example of this was the prison fire in 1997 at the Oukacha Prison complex in Casablanca that killed 28 inmates, in a cell designed to hold only 8 inmates. Located in the industrial area of Casablanca, the prison, one of the most modern in Africa, has a 33-foot-high wall for increased security. One of the most alarming aspects of the report deals with evidence that children as young as 12 are being kept in the prisons and are regularly being victimized. Legally, no one under the age of 16 is allowed to be in prison in Morocco. This is just one aspect of a comprehensive climate of corruption. Additionally, the only food available to inmates is that which is brought in by friends or relatives who must first pay a bribe to prison wardens.

A report from UPI from October 2008 notes that Al Qaeda inmates are seeking to dominate life in Moroccan prisons by using intimidation and the threat of death. This is particularly true in prisons around Casablanca, where the majority of Al Qaeda insurgents have been held, according to the Med Basin Newsline. Security sources told the news agency that opponents of the Al Qaeda inmates were intimidated or assaulted until they were transferred or accepted Al Qaeda's rule, which includes strict adherence to sharia law. Some who have opposed the Islamic militants, most of whom were convicted of terrorist offenses, have been strangled to death. According to the Med Basin Newsline, the Al Qaeda inmates also have succeeded in intimidating the prison authorities, who have allowed self-appointed investigators (inmates) to search prison cells for liquor or other contraband that violates Islamic law.

Jeffrey Dailey

Further Reading

National Portal of Morocco: http://www.maroc.ma.

Oufkir, Malika, and Michele Fitouss. (2001). *Stolen Lives: Twenty Years in a Desert Jail.* New York: Miramax Books.

Oman

Legal System: Islamic/Common
Murder: Low
Corruption: Low
Human Trafficking: High
Prison Rate: Medium
Death Penalty: Yes
Corporal Punishment: Yes

Background

A former British protectorate, Oman is a constitutional monarchy. It is the only Muslim country with an Ibadi (a sect of Shia) ruler and majority population (75 percent). In addition, 21 percent of the population consists of immigrant workers, primarily from South Asia. With only 3 million people, Oman is one of the most thinly populated countries in the world. The country is divided into six regions and two governates. Most of the country is desert with little or no rainfall, although coastal areas receive some rain. Oman is located at the Straight of Hormuz where the Indian Ocean meets the Arabian Gulf.

Arabic is the official language with English as a second language. In addition, Southern Arabian is spoken, a Semitic language distantly related to Arabic, and more closely related to languages found in Eritrea and Ethiopia. A minority of Omanis speak Swahili.

In the premodern era, tribes formed the dominant social and political structure as people organized to maintain and control irrigation systems (*aflaj*). Arabian Gulf tribes were united by an unwritten code of honor (*sharaf*) and loyalty (*shaff min dun*) in a patriarchal, hereditary social structure. Omani tribes are derived primarily from two competing blocks, the Hinawi and the Ghafiri. The ruling Al Bu Said family, of which Sultan Qaboos is a part, does not belong to either of these groups because the ruling family must be acceptable to both tribes.

Tribal leaders (*shaykhs*) first signed treaties with the British colonial power in the late 18th century. British control originally extended only to the coastal areas of Muscat and Salalah, with tribes in the interior maintaining their independence, under the leadership of imams. The intersection of tribal and religious leadership has long characterized the indigenous Omani approach to political organization. In the 1950s, tribal leaders (*shaykhs*) negotiated with the British-based Omani Petroleum Country to grant access to the country's oil resources. Today, oil income composes 80 percent of the country's gross domestic product.

Prior to 1970, Sultan Said bin Taymur kept the country closed, restricting foreign travel and education and maintaining Oman's protectorate status with the British. A bloodless coup aided by the British brought the sultan's son, Qaboos bin Said al-Said, to power in 1970. The country achieved its independence from Britain in 1971; however, senior positions in government continued to be staffed by British advisors until the 1990s. In recent years, Oman has developed its national administration and infrastructure in an effort to balance tribal, regional, and ethnic interests.

In 1996, the Basic Law of the state, Oman's first written constitution, outlined the governmental structure, including a bicameral legislature called the Council of Oman. The lower chamber is the Consultative Council (*majlis al-shura*), and the upper chamber is the Council of State (*majlis al-dawlah*). The sultan is the head of state, assisted by a council of ministers (*majlis al-wuzara*) who are appointed usually from the ranks of Muscat's merchant families. Since 1991, members of the *majlis al-shura* have been elected. Universal suffrage for people age 21 years and older was implemented in 2003. That year, 74 percent of those registered voted in national elections during which two women were elected to seats in the *majlis al-shura.* Currently, Oman has three women ministers.

Legal System

Legal thought draws heavily on *fiqh,* a doctrine that states that the ultimate law-giver is God. As such, humans, under the leadership of the sultan, strive to understand (*faqiha*) law. The Ibadi interpretation of sharia (Islamic law) dominates, and constitutional jurisprudence is performed regionally by the *wali* and *qadi,* a judge who has attained that position either by graduating from an Islamic law college or by studying and training with local religious experts.

Oman's criminal law borrows from English common law as well as sharia. A system of criminal law case precedents prevails. Despite the systematic and developed nature of the indigenous Islamic law, colonial powers dismantled those structures through gradual marginalization to exert their own social and political control. In postcolonial times in Oman, there has been only a partial return to Islamic legal structures. As such, and according to the Omani Constitution as well, no criminal law can be passed that runs counter to sharia law. However, Islamic law in practice rarely acts as the dominant influence on criminal justice. Crime in Islamic law falls into three categories: crimes against God (*hadd*), homicide and assault (*qisa*), and the remaining crimes (*ta'azir*). In theory, there is no discretion in punishment for *hadd* and *qisa* violations, which are explicitly spelled out in the Koran. For example, *qisas* are punishable by retaliation or blood money (*diya*). *Ta'azir* crimes, however, allow for judicial discretion in sentencing. In the Omani penal code, crimes are divided into two groups: *junha,* which are crimes punishable by less than three years' incarceration or fines, and *junaiyah,* which are crimes punishable by three years or more.

Crime and Punishment

According to INTERPOL data, the murder rate in 1997 was 0.91 per 100,000 people. The United Nations reports that the country had 1 murder per 100,000 people in 2003. Reported rape was 3.73, and aggravated assault was 1.87. The larceny rate was recorded as 12.2. Between 1995 and 2000, the murder rate fell by 3.2 percent from 0.94 to 0.91. The rate for rape decreased by 16.4 percent while aggravated assault increased 10.7 percent. The rate of larceny grew from 2.92 to 12.2, an increase of 317.8 percent.

According to a 2001 Ministry of Health report, there were unspecified increasing rates of children and teenagers abusing illegal substances in Oman and a number of cases involving child neglect, including drowning and other accidents. Human rights observers have noted that there has been a decline in children being exploited for use as camel-jockeys, a trend that was prevalent a decade ago.

Prostitution is illegal due to strict cultural norms, and authorities report that it is rarely found in Oman. Homosexuality is prohibited and punishable by up to three years in prison. Abortion under any circumstances is also illegal.

Female genital mutilation (FGM) is illegal in Oman and condemned by international health human rights standards. A few communities in the interior of the country and in the Dhofar region have had cases of FGM in recent years; however, it is believed to be declining annually.

Terrorism is criminalized under article 132 of the Omani penal code. In addition, the Comprehensive Security Agreement among the States of the Gulf Cooperation Council has provisions that criminalize terrorist behavior, such as providing weapons to terrorists. It is illegal to establish agencies, associations, political parties, or organizations that directly oppose the social, political, or economic systems of any other country. The penal code also prohibits the financing, arrangement, preparation, perpetration, or supporting of terrorist acts under the money laundering laws. Moreover, the law allows for the confiscation of funds and the freezing of assets shown to be the product of any unlawful act, including terrorism.

Oman is a destination country for South Asian migrants who are the victims of human trafficking schemes, including involuntary servitude as domestic workers and construction laborers. The Omani penal code further stipulates that anyone who conceals a person who has committed a crime, or who assists someone in escaping detection by authorities, is punishable under the law. According to executive respondents of the World Economic Forum's Global Competitiveness Survey, Oman is considered to have low levels of governmental corruption.

Finding of Guilt

Traditionally, crime and punishment were considered private matters to be handled within families and tribes. Intertribal allegations of crime, such as homicide, were handled by negotiation and, when this failed, blood feud (*diya*). The exception to this involved policing marketplaces. Men who policed and safeguarded the marketplaces in each district (*wilaya*) were known as *al-askar.* Modern-style policing was introduced in the country in the early 20th century by the British.

Today, the Royal Office handles the country's internal and external security. Under this umbrella, the Internal Security Service controls internal security while the Sultan's Special Force maintains border security and combats smuggling. The Royal Oman Police (ROP) manage airport security and immigration matters and oversee the coast guard. Police accountability is provided by the ROP's Directorate General of Inquiries and Criminal Investigation, which investigates claims of police abuse.

Policewomen compose 4.5 percent of the Royal Oman Police, approximately the same rate of female participation as in the United Arab Emirates and Qatar. Today they are employed as security screeners in airports and investigators in cases involving child and female offenders, and they provide assistance to women and children victims and witnesses. Policewomen entered the field at the time of independence from British power and were considered a part of the project of bringing Omanis into government positions.

Arrest and Detention

In Oman, the police do not need to procure a warrant to make an arrest. An individual can be detained for 48 hours without charges, after which the police must either refer the matter to public prosecution or release the suspect. If referred to prosecution, within 24 hours, a formal arrest must be made and court orders obtained to hold a defendant in pretrial detention. Typically, the court awards the prosecution 14 days for investigation.

Legal representation is provided to indigent defendants, although judges sometimes have to order this specifically, as well as remind police to allow attorneys and family members to meet with defendants. Oman's public prosecution office was created in 2000. Headquartered in Muscat, it has offices in 24 regions in the country. The office is responsible for investigating and bringing to trial court cases from initial processing until sentencing.

Courts and Trials

Oman boasts an independent judiciary, yet practically speaking, courts defer to the wishes of the sultan. Judges are appointed by the sultan and serve at his discretion. The sultan himself can act as a court of final appeal, an authority he primarily exercises over matters of national security. He has never overturned a magistrate court decision.

The judiciary is composed of magistrate courts and sharia courts and is managed by the Ministry of Justice. There are 42 courts of first instance in which judges hear criminal, civil, and commercial cases. Above these are six courts of appeal in which three judges hear each case. The Supreme Court is the highest court in Oman. It reviews decisions of the lower courts, provides oversight of judges, and decides matters of law and legal principles. Additionally, appeals can be made directly to the sultan, who has the power to pardon or mitigate sentences. Sharia courts handle cases involving family law and personal status, such as child custody, divorce, and inheritance.

Under the 1996 Basic Law, which outlines criminal procedure, Omanis have the right to a fair trial and legal defense for crimes punishable by over three years in prison. The presumption of innocence is a cornerstone of the law. Junaiyah cases are handled at the central magistrate court and are presided over by the president and vice president of the magistrate court as well as two judges. This panel also takes appeals coming from all the courts of first instance. The sultan has established rules of procedure pertaining to evidence and provisions for a public trial. For example, the police must state the charges against defendants, who have the right to present evidence and confront witnesses. The prosecution and the defense examine witnesses under the direction and participation of the judge, who decides all verdicts, often within one day of the end of a trial. For cases involving abuse of governmental authority, the *diwan* of the royal court reviews cases and has the power to award compensation to victims. The state security court hears cases about national security or high-profile criminal matters.

In 1997, the sultan created a committee to regulate the activities and appearances in court of all lawyers. Lawyers typically have studied at the College of Sharia and Jurisprudence for a three-year period. Afterward, students are employed in the Ministry of Justice or in the courts but can also choose to continue their education in sharia jurisprudence to become a deputy judge in an Omani court. Moreover, the Gulf Cooperation Council (GCC) has implemented a judge-inspection program in which announced and unannounced visits by legal experts will be made to courtrooms in the GCC countries (Kuwait, Saudi Arabia, Qatar, United Arab Emirates, Bahrain, and Oman). Judges' adherence to the laws in the countries will be the subject of the outside review.

Prison

At the age of 9, criminal responsibility attaches. However, minors between 9 and 13 years of age can be sentenced only to detention in a juvenile facility until he or she reaches 18 years of age. In Oman, punishments meted out by courts are primarily fines or incarceration. For example, in 2005, a state security court sentenced 31 people to between 1 and 20 years' imprisonment for attempting to overthrow Oman's sultan and create a purely Islamic state. Approximately 100 suspected religious extremists were arrested across Oman earlier that year.

Prisons are administered by the General Directorate of Prisons, which is a part of the Royal Oman Police. Prisons are located near Mabella and in Nizwa. Independent oversight of prisons is not generally allowed by the government; however, conditions reportedly meet international standards. According to the ROP, the objective of incarceration is rehabilitation and reform of prisoners. Each prisoner has a different color ribbon sewn on his or her clothes that represents the crime for which he or she was convicted. Prisoners participate in a variety of activities. Men's prisons have carpentry and farming, and women detainees have weaving and other traditional crafts. These items are sold at an annual exhibition that aims to inform the public about what prisoners can accomplish. In addition, Omani prisoners are encouraged to use their time to memorize the Koran.

The death penalty is a legal form of punishment for murder, but it is rarely used. Extradition of noncitizens facing criminal charges in another country is permitted except in the case of political asylum. Omani citizens cannot be extradited.

Staci Strobl

Further Reading

Al-Lamky, A. (2004). "Modernization and Child Neglect in Oman: Trends and Implications." *International Journal on Peace Studies* 21(3): 43–53.

Ballantyne, W. M. (1985). "The States of the GCC: Sources of Law, the Shari'a and the Extent to Which It Applies." *Arab Law Quarterly* (1)1: 3.

Crystal, J. (2001). "Criminal Justice in the Middle East." *Journal of Criminal Justice* 29: 469–482.

Kahn, A., and S. Laubach (2000). "Oman: Recent Developments." *Arab Law Quarterly* 15(1): 112–115.

Siegfried, N. A. (2000). "Legislation and Legitimation in Oman: The Basic Law." *Islamic Law and Society* 7(2): 359–397.

Palestinian Territories

Legal System: Islamic/Civil/Customary
Death Penalty: Yes
Corporal Punishment: Yes

Background

Occupied by the Ottoman Empire since the mid-17th century, "Mandate Palestine" was eventually claimed by the British following the end of World War I. Increasingly disenchanted by its imperial possession, the United Kingdom decided to withdraw from the Middle East in 1948, and Palestine was almost immediately seized by a combination of Jordanian and Egyptian forces. The territories' status again transformed dramatically with Israel's momentous defeat of the Arab nations in the 1967 Six-Day War, and the Jewish state's subsequent seizure of the Gaza Strip from Egypt and the West Bank from Jordan.

Although two decades of both internal and external tension ensued, Israeli control went relatively unabated during this time period. Although Yasser Arafat's Palestinian Liberation Organization

Palestinian police officers wave Palestinian flags as they are mobbed by cheering crowds upon arriving in the West Bank town of Jenin, on November 13, 1995. Thousands of Palestinians welcomed the police officers after Israeli soldiers pulled out before dawn. (AP Photo/Santiago Lyon)

launched a series of foreign attacks against the Jewish state, it failed to either mobilize international support or win any significant concessions. This changed dramatically with the first intifada (or uprising) of 1987, which began in the Jabailia refugee camp and spread dramatically throughout the territories. Met with the Palestinian peoples' increasingly violent demands for greater control and autonomy, the Israeli government agreed to finally consider the possibility of Palestinian statehood in the early 1990s. This eventually led to the signing of the 1993 Oslo Peace Accords and Palestinian governance over certain portions of the West Bank and Gaza Strip.

Established to gradually help steer its people toward eventual statehood, the Palestinian Authority quickly found itself plagued by both uncertainty and an inability to translate its demands into concrete reality. Following the collapse of the 2000 Camp David Accords, a second and even more violent intifada erupted, which both weakened the Palestinian Authority further and strengthened more radical groups such as Hamas. This culminated with Yasser Arafat's death in 2004 and Hamas's dramatic victory in the 2006 parliamentary elections. A potential coalition between the terrorist/resistance group and the Palestinian Authority quickly fizzled, with the former organization laying claim to the Gaza Strip and the latter to the West Bank.

Although the de facto ruler of the Gaza Strip, Hamas is still considered a terrorist organization by much of the outside world and has done little to dampen this image. An acronym for "Islamic Resistance Movement," Hamas was created in 1987 by Sheik Ahmad Yassin during the first intifada and was responsible for a string of suicide bombings across Israel. Although many of Hamas's central leaders have been assassinated by Israeli forces (including Sheik Yassin himself), the organization's horizontal structure has made it incredibly difficult to dismantle and defeat. The reasons for the group's success in the 2006 Palestinian parliamentary elections are likely twofold: Hamas has successfully acted as a sort of welfare organization to many Palestinians in need, and it has long exhibited a degree of discipline (and lack of corruption) wholly absent within the larger Palestinian Authority.

Demographic and Political Context

The Palestinian territories are generally considered to encompass three main areas: the West Bank, the Gaza Strip, and East Jerusalem. The West Bank is governed solely by the Palestinian Authority and contains a population of approximately 2,400,000. Mahmoud Abbas succeeded Yasser Arafat as president of the Palestinian Authority in 2004 and has generally steered a sort of middle path, fervently demanding Palestinian statehood while also agreeing to work with Israel against Hamas. Following the elections of 2006, the Gaza Strip has been almost exclusively governed by Hamas and is estimated to have a population of approximately 1,400,000. Although Gaza's de facto leader, Hamas is, as noted earlier, nevertheless considered a terrorist organization by Israel and the United States and is therefore rarely accepted internationally as an official governing body. Led politically by Prime Minister Ismail Haniya, Hamas refuses to recognize Israel's right to exist and continues to threaten the so-called Zionist entity with existential destruction. Following a brief but brutal war in Gaza from December 2008 to January 2009, the two parties declared unilateral cease-fires and (for the most part) have ceased aggressions. Although East Jerusalem remains under serious dispute, it is currently controlled entirely by Israel and consequently lies outside the scope of this entry.

Legal Context

The Palestinian territories are neither controlled nor unified by a single legal schema, a phenomenon that has become even more complicated following the electoral successes of Hamas. As one scholar has described, Palestine is essentially governed by three legal frameworks: (1) statutory legislation (or the laws "on the books"), (2) common law and precedent (often predicated upon sharia or Islamic law), and (3) tribal adjudication (know in Arabic as *al-qada al-ashari*). To make matters even more convoluted, statutory legislation generally consists of multiple legal traditions, including

Ottoman legislation (from before British control), British Mandate acts, various laws constructed by the Palestinian Authority, and even lingering Israeli military orders. Whereas the West Bank technically adheres principally to the Jordanian penal code of 1960, the Gaza Strip officially (at least before the rise of Hamas) shuns the pre-1967 Egyptian law. Further, there is little internal coherence to what criminal laws are applied in any given situation; adjudication is inherently politicized, and different offenders may receive entirely diverse sentences based on their given social status and geographical location.

Policing

Up until the early 1990s, the Palestinian territories were entirely policed by the Israelis. This changed dramatically with the 1993 signing of the Oslo Peace Accords and the establishment of a separate and (technically) autonomous Palestinian police force. The West Bank is specifically broken into three separate zones: Zone A (which encompasses the majority of West Bank towns) is placed entirely under Palestinian control and administration; Zone B (which contains around 40 percent of the Palestinian population) is dually policed by Palestinian and Jewish forces; and Zone C (which contains only a small percentage of the West Bank's Palestinians and the majority of Jewish settlers) is exclusively controlled and administered by Israel.

Although Palestinian policing has changed dramatically through the years, it has remained under the exclusive control of the PA president and his ministers. The civil police force received international aid and professional training throughout the 1990s and during this time period was generally considered a competent police force. This changed dramatically with the second intifada, however, and the subsequent low-level warfare between Israel and the Palestinian territories. Attempting to consolidate potential soldiers, President Arafat chose to integrate the Palestinian Civil Police into the general Security Forces (widely known as Fatah), and both groups were subsequently identified as enemy combatants by the Jewish state. In a matter of months, scores of Palestinian police officers were consequently injured or killed, many West Bank and Gaza police stations effectively destroyed, and the police's formally solid communication networks rendered virtually obsolete. Indeed, according to Human Rights Watch, despite the eventual dwindling in aggression, the current Palestinian police force has yet to recover from Israel's substantial assault; police units continue to lack "technical capacity," have neither the personnel nor the equipment to operate effectively, and are only recently beginning to rebuild their physical infrastructure.

Yet it would be inaccurate to trace present weaknesses in the Palestinian Civil Police to the Israelis alone. Many officers began their careers as resistance fighters and continue to act more as political henchman than neutral investigators (especially against suspected Israeli or Hamas collaborators). This is further complicated by the Palestinian president's unchallenged authority over the civil police and his ability to undermine or outright reject court rulings or decrees of lower magistrates he finds objectionable. Further, up until 2002, no clear legislation existed to govern the relationship between the police and the courts, and judicial decrees continue to be tenuously interpreted or strategically ignored by individual officers. Recognizing that an independent and effective police force is integral for upholding internal security, the United States and European Union have recently pledged both considerable financial aid and physical aid to the Palestinian police. What form this aid will take, however, and how quickly it will materialize remains to be seen.

Although it is difficult to determine the continually shifting status of the Palestinian Civil Police, it is nearly impossible to provide any definitive account of policing in the Hamas-controlled Gaza Strip. According to the latest Human Rights Watch Report, Gaza's internal security is currently broken into two main sections: the police and the Internal Security Forces. Whereas the former's task is to control and investigate everyday crimes, the latter is directly modeled after the Palestinian Authority's National Security Forces. Both organizations often blend into one another, however, and it remains unclear how extensively each was damaged in the

2008–2009 Israeli invasion. Further, the police force is often used purely as a political weapon and has been accused of intimidating and even murdering suspected Fatah or Israeli collaborators.

Crime

Classification of Crimes

Although a person's prosecution and punishment may vary considerably depending on whether they are located in Gaza or the West Bank, both regions recognize a similar litany of criminal offenses. Most serious are homicide, rape, sexual offenses, and assault. These are followed by theft, fraud, and drug-related crimes. Less serious, although still considered criminal matters, are road traffic accidents and so-called immoral offenses. Rape is not recognized within marriage, and acts of theft and fraud also include more serious offenses such as embezzlement and robbery. Immoral offenses are said to encompass any "violation of honor and ethical deterioration, including any ethical abuse, sexual abnormality or violation of a duty against another or the society in general," according to the Palestinian Central Bureau of Statistics, 2007. Although there is no separate juvenile justice system, offenders under the age of 18 are recognized as differing in culpability from more "mature persons."

Crime Statistics

The Palestinian Central Bureau of Statistics has attempted to record and schematize the territories' criminal statistics, but much of this data remains either rudimentary or incomplete. The most recent survey, performed from 2004 to 2005, sampled approximately 7,563 Palestinian households throughout the West Bank and Gaza Strip. Data revealed that approximately 11.3 percent reported being exposed to criminal offenses, with 1.2 percent exposed to theft and 1.5 percent exposed to property damage and assault. Individual Palestinians reported considerably higher levels of victimization, with theft/ robbery attempt around 20 percent and those exposed to threat/assault at about 13.1 percent. Nearly 60 percent of respondents reported having been harassed or assaulted by Israeli soldiers and settlers. The West Bank generally recorded lower rates of crime than the Gaza Strip, likely because of the formers' greater stability. The reported rates for homicide and sexual assault were 0.09 percent and 0.03 percent (per 1,000), respectively, although it is unclear how these statistics were gathered and calculated. The percentage of reported immoral offenses was not listed.

Violence against Women

Violence against women has proven particularly difficult for the Palestinian criminal justice system to effectively handle. According to a 2006 study by the Palestinian Central Bureau of Statistics, more than 60 percent of Palestinian women had encountered some form of abuse, with only a pittance of these cases properly recognized and addressed by the proper authorities. Perhaps most troubling were the high rates of domestic abuse and women's fear that reporting such incidents could lead to police apathy and even retaliatory attacks. Indeed, many of the existing laws actually encourage rather than deter violence against Palestinian females. Convicted rapists can often be exonerated if they agree to simply marry their victims, and women and girls who report rape or incest have been murdered by family members to remove this "horrible stain" from the family's reputation. So-called honor crimes are even more frequent against women suspected of engaging in improper behavior (such as talking to a man who is not her husband or direct relative) and frequently lead to lenient sentences or complete exemptions for the suspected perpetrator.

Drug Crimes

The increasing prevalence of substance abuse has also gained considerable attention. Although the Palestinian territories' number of drug users is believed to have increased substantially within the last few years, reliable statistics are frustratingly difficult to come by. According to one study, approximately 30,000 to 40,000 drug addicts are projected to exist in Palestine, with heroin accounting for the vast majority of addictions. Those who smoke marijuana are generally believed to be considerably younger, and synthetic narcotics such as

LSD and Ecstasy are reportedly becoming progressively popular among Palestine's youth. Because drug use remains taboo among Palestinian families, there is generally strong pressure to deny its existence. Interestingly, attitudes toward drugs can differ considerably based on their effects. Whereas stimulants such as cocaine are considered to be foreign and almost universally reviled, sedatives such as heroin or quaaludes are viewed as more "natural" and consequently less egregious. Drug use of any sort is rarely investigated by the police, however, and drug trafficking remains relatively (and fortunately) undeveloped.

Courts

General Overview

The Palestinian court system has proven significantly more stable than that of the civil police. This may be for a number of reasons. First, whereas the hodgepodge of Palestinian procedural laws offers only vague provisions regarding proper police structure and protocol, the court system has a more traditional hierarchy. Second, and perhaps more importantly, the courts have rarely been directly targeted by Israeli forces and have had to neither rebuild their infrastructure nor replace important personnel. Despite its relative stability, however, the Palestinian judiciary also suffers from a variety of setbacks. Judges are often seen more as political toadies than balanced arbitrators and are consequently distrusted by much of the Palestinian public. Second, the incredible convolution of Palestinian laws grants no clear rights to the accused, and therefore, the nature of appeals often remains ambiguous. Many citizens thus attempt to bypass judicial authority altogether and settle their disputes through tribal law rather than official adjudication.

The Palestinian Court Structure

The Palestinian justice system is inquisitorial, modeled primarily after the Jordanian and Egyptian systems of jurisprudence. Public prosecutors first investigate a crime, determine whether there is significant evidence to proceed to trial, and if so (generally) appear before a regular criminal court. Lowest are magistrate courts, which rule over all contraventions and misdemeanors and are composed of a single judge. One level up are first instance courts, which preside over felonies and are composed of a three-judge panel (usually chaired by the most senior among them). The Palestinian territories also contain three courts of appeals (although only two are presently functional), whose duty is to review objections filed in the first instance courts. Finally is the High Court, whose number of magistrates is left statutorily undetermined, but must be proportionate to the total amount of judges in Palestine. There is no distinct court for Palestinian juveniles, although punishments for minors are supposed to be both less severe and more attuned to rehabilitative goals. Although the preceding courts have technical control over all criminal offenses, the High-State Security Court has recently grown in prominence. Controlled entirely by the president of the Palestinian Authority (and set up by him on an ad hoc basis), this court generally presides over the most serious of cases, from those that carry the death penalty to accusations of treason or sabotage.

Specific Weaknesses

Although the function and structure of the Palestinian justice system is more straightforward than that of the police, it is also hampered by a number of serious deficiencies. First, there are not enough public prosecutors or judges to deal with the extraordinary number of cases that come before them. Lawyers can also be difficult to obtain and are often poorly trained and unprepared. Second, judges are almost always appointed by politicians and receive only minimal pay, which has led to a great deal of political and financial corruption. Third, although the Jordanian penal code guarantees certain (basic) rights to the accused, the intermingling of different (and even contradictory) Palestinian laws make it unclear how and when these are to be enforced. The amount of time served for a particular crime can also vary significantly based on the specific sentencing provision applied. Finally, courthouses receive only minimal funding from the state and subsequently lack many of the resources necessary to provide complete and comprehensive trials. Indeed, when asked in 2004, over 50 percent of the Palestinian people reported having no confidence in the judicial system "at all" and believed it neither reliable nor independent.

Tribal Justice and Sharia Law

Weaknesses in the Palestinian court system have led to the increasing popularity of tribal justice, which has long been practiced within certain segments of the Palestinian (and especially Bedouin) population. Although there are myriad forms of tribal adjudication, such practices generally involve a form of conciliation between the perpetrator and the victim conducted and mediated by a respected community member. Although tribal justice is generally quick and cost-effective, it has been criticized for leading to both archaic penalties and inconsistent resolutions. The official court system has nevertheless recognized certain tribal conciliations as legitimate forms of justice and has even accepted some minor judgments as legally binding.

Although tribal justice often entails elements of sharia (or Islamic) law, this form of jurisprudence has never actually enjoyed widespread practice in the Palestinian territories. The 2002 Palestinian Basic Law contains elements of sharia law, but it is more a potential constitution for a future Palestinian state than any sort of concrete procedural document. Although sharia law may grow more widespread with Hamas's seizure of the Gaza Strip, early reports of a purely Islamic-based jurisprudence have yet to be substantiated. Of course, many Palestinian legal schemas (such as the Egyptian and Jordanian penal code) claim foundational legitimacy only through their greater adherence to sharia because this is believed to provide a necessary framework for promoting a proper moral order.

Punishment

As described earlier, Palestinian criminal law is broken into a variety of different (and often conflicting) legal statutes and historical provisions. Although this makes it difficult to calculate the exact nature of particular offenses, especially unclear are many of the reasons for and actual rates of incarceration.

Penal Statistics

According to a survey conducted by the Palestinian Bureau of Statistics in 2006, approximately 3,934 individuals were imprisoned within the Palestinian territories (excluding East Jerusalem), with 2,529 held in the West Bank and 1,405 in the Gaza Strip. The most common offense recorded was theft (approximately 25.8%), followed by assault (approximately 17.3%), and "using or trading narcotic drugs" (approximately 10.7%). Murderers and rapists accounted for 3.2 percent and 0.4 percent of those incarcerated, respectively. Least common were those imprisoned for kidnapping (2%), immoral offenses (1.9%), disturbing public order (1.9%), and failing to meet financial obligations (1.8%, though the grounds for this offense go unexplained). Although the Palestinian Central Bureau of Statistics (PCBS) should be commended for its attempt to gather viable data, one must be extremely cautious when considering the preceding statistics. Left unrevealed is how these numbers were gathered, and the largest imprisonment category is simply labeled "Others." Further, the PCBS records only the rate of imprisonment, and it is therefore entirely unclear how many offenses were settled through either fines or more informal proceedings. Finally, these statistics exist prior to Hamas's takeover of the Gaza Strip and have likely changed considerably following this critical event.

Prison Conditions

Many Palestinian prisons date back to the Ottoman Empire and are therefore in incredibly poor physical condition. The second intifada resulted in the destruction of a number of major detention facilities, and those that remain often show substantial damage from years of Israeli bombing campaigns. Overcrowding is common in nearly every prison, and there are widespread complaints of physical abuse and even torture. Further, it is difficult to separate those persons incarcerated for purely criminal offenses from those there for political reasons. Finally and perhaps most troublingly, recent reports show that nearly 88 percent of those incarcerated have yet to be charged with any formal crime.

Capital Punishment

Of continuing controversy is the application of the death penalty within the Palestinian territories. Although the Jordanian penal code allows capital punishment for 17 separate offenses, in the West Bank, death is almost exclusively administered for the crime of murder. Traditionally, only the High-State Security Court can issue such a serious sanction, which then has to be reviewed and approved by the Palestinian president. Hamas has also shown considerable enthusiasm for capital punishment, often allowing "blood vengeance" to be carried out by victims' families. Although both the PA and Hamas claim the majority of death sentences are not politically motivated, this has been undermined by a number of state-sanctioned executions of collaborators on both sides. Further, political "murders" may not be openly endorsed by the authorities, but many are nevertheless believed to enjoy tacit approval by certain government figures.

Zachary Shemtob

Further Reading

Laquer, Walter, and Barry Rubin, eds. (2008). *The Israel-Arab Reader: A Documentary History of the Middle East Conflict.* 7th ed. New York: Penguin Books.

Lia, Brynjar. (2006). *A Police Force without a State: A History of the Palestinian Security Forces in the West Bank and Gaza.* New York: Ithaca Press.

Sacco, Joe. (2002). *Palestine.* Seattle, WA: Fantagraphic Books.

Persia. See Iran

Qatar

Legal System: Civil/Islamic
Murder: Low
Corruption: Low
Human Trafficking: High
Prison Rate: Low
Death Penalty: Yes
Corporal Punishment: Yes

Background

Qatar protrudes northward into the Persian Gulf for about 100 miles and has a maximum width of 50 miles. It shares its border with Saudi Arabia in the south and the United Arab Emirates toward the east and covers an area of 6,439 square miles. The capital of Qatar is Doha (Ad-Dawhah), which is the major administrative and commercial center of the country. Qatar was a poor British protectorate that derived its income from pearling. The economy was transformed with the discovery of oil and natural gas reserves in the 1970s. Consequently, the economy was crippled during the 1980s and 1990s as a result of the continuous siphoning off of petroleum reserves by the amir who came to power in 1972. In 1995, he was overthrown by his son in a bloodless coup. Due to its oil and natural gas, Qatar has one of the highest per capita incomes in the world. According to the 2007 estimates, Qatar has a population of 907,229. A majority of the population is in the 15–64 age group, with a median age of 31.9 years. The ethnic composition consists of 40 percent Arab, 18 percent Indian, 18 percent Pakistani, 10 percent Iranian, and 14 percent other.

Qatar is a sovereign state with executive power vested in the amir, who holds the post of prime minister. Most of the members of the government are members of the royal family. Their ancestry has been traced back to the Bani Tamim, one of the sharif tribes of ancient Arabia. The executive branch consists of a council of ministers and an advisory council of 35 appointed members. The advisory council represents businessmen, farmers, and landowners and reviews litigation that is given to them by the council of ministers. The amir appoints an 18-member council of ministers in addition to the aforementioned 35-member advisory council. The government does not allow political parties. There is a 29-member central municipal council that is elected by the people and that provides advice on municipal services.

On April 29, 2003, Qataris held a referendum to approve a new constitution. The Constitution was approved by 98 percent of the population. This new constitution became effective in 2005. Accordingly, it establishes a 45-member parliament in which 30 members are to be elected by the people and 15 members are to be appointed by the amir. It allows both men and women to vote and hold office. The first parliamentary elections were held in 2006–2007.

The government consists of 15 ministries, 7 councils, 20 authorities, and 9 institutions. The ministries include the Ministry of Justice, Ministry of Interior, Ministry of Labor and Social Affairs, Ministry of Defense, and a range of other ministries concerning education, finance, education, and foreign relations.

The seven councils consist of the following: Advisory Council, Council of Ministers, Supreme Council for Economic Affairs and Investment, Supreme Council for Family Affairs, Supreme Council of Information and Communication Technology, Supreme Education Council, and Supreme Judiciary Council. The 20 authorities include a wide range of organizations that administer charitable affairs, social security, and various other activities of government.

The nine institutions consist of the following: Aspire, Family Consultancy Center, Hamad Medical Corporation, Institute of Administrative Development, Kahramaa, Qatar Foundation for Child and Women Protection, Qatar General Post Office, Qatar Red Crescent, and Qatar University.

The Constitution stipulated that Qatar would be divided into 10 electoral districts. Each district was required to elect 4 candidates. From this pool of 40 candidates, the ruler would select 20, with 2 being drawn from each district. The selected 20 candidates formed the Advisory Council. It was incumbent upon the members to represent all the Qatari people and not merely their own districts. In 1975, the size of the Advisory Council was increased to 30 members.

Judicial System

Prior to the implementation of the Constitution, the ruler's legislative authority often overlapped or encompassed judicial functions, given that the ruler personally adjudicated disputes and grievances that came to him. The Constitution was an attempt to organize the judiciary. The secular courts were composed of a higher and lower criminal court, a civil court, an appeals court, and a labor court. In 1971, a civil code, a criminal code, and a code of judicial procedure were introduced. The secular courts have the authority to adjudicate on all cases that deal with the civil and criminal law. Because very few of Qatar's codes and judicial customs were applicable to the contemporary labor relations, a labor court was created in 1962.

Qatar's legal system has sources in sharia law, Ottoman law, and European law. Personal law is governed by sharia, but criminal law, though influenced by sharia, is not governed by it. The sharia courts and the secular courts are overseen by the higher Judicial Council. There are many lower courts, and there is a system of appeal courts. The final court of appeal is the amir.

One of the oldest elements of Qatar's judiciary is the sharia courts. These courts follow the precepts of the Hanbali school of Islam. The judges from this school follow a narrow and rigid interpretation of the Koran and the Sunna. Initially, these sharia courts had jurisdiction in all civil and criminal matters between Qatari nationals and other Muslim subjects. From 1960 onward, this jurisdiction came to be restricted by decree. In 1984, the sharia courts were restricted to adjudicate only in family matters, such as divorce, property, religious morality, and inheritance. A non-Muslim was tried in the sharia court only if married to a Muslim. During

1984, Qatar had three sharia courts with a total of six judges who also acted as notaries.

Finding of Guilt

The Constitution guarantees the legal presumption of innocence and also prohibits the use of ex post facto laws. According to the Constitution, judges are required to be independent in the exercise of their powers, and no party is permitted to interfere in the administration of justice. The judiciary was apparently independent not solely because of the constitutional guarantee but also because its jurisdiction was least likely to confront the power of the ruler. Adjudication in the secular courts was conducted on the basis of the ruler's past decrees, and the sharia courts were limited to questions of family life and personal behavior. There was no facility to judicially review the constitutionality of legislation or to make landmark judicial decisions that would challenge the ruler's plans or wishes.

Though there are sharia and civil courts in Qatar, only the sharia courts have jurisdiction in criminal cases. Because of a paucity of permanent security courts, these cases are tried by specially established military courts. Criminal cases are tried according to the sharia, and the proceedings of these trials are closed to the general public. Under the sharia system, lawyers merely prepare the accused for trial and do not play any formal role in the actual court proceedings. After the parties present their cases, and witnesses are examined by the presiding judge, the case is decided expeditiously. There is no bail; however, in minor cases, the accused can be released to the custody of a Qatari sponsor. Flogging as a method of punishment is prescribed and administered according to sharia, but physical mutilation has not been permitted since 1980.

The communications of suspects and security risks are routinely monitored by the police. Warrants are normally required for conducting searches, but these are not necessary when national security is involved. There are reports of security forces using torture and excessive force while investigating security-related and political cases. There are also some instances where suspects can be incarcerated without charge. According to the U.S. Department of State, there have been improvements in standards of police conduct. In 1991, there was a report of an incident in which a group of Qataris were detained without charge for two months for the unauthorized publication of articles and letters that were critical of the government. One of the members of this group happened to belong to the ruling family and was also reported to have been beaten.

Police

A police force of about 2,500 members has been controlled by the Ministry of the Interior since 1990. Responsibility for enforcement of the laws and arrest of violators rests with the local police forces. In 1991, the Criminal Investigation Department was replaced by the General Administration of Public Security, which was charged with the investigation of crime. The Mubahathat (secret police) are an independent part of the Ministry of the Interior that is responsible for dealing with espionage and sedition cases. The national army does not have the responsibility for maintaining internal security. However, in the contingency of serious civil disturbances, the army can be called in for assistance. The Mukhabarat constitutes a separate agency that has the task of providing intelligence and is under the jurisdiction of the armed forces. It endeavors to keep political dissidents under surveillance and to stop and arrest terrorists.

Crime

According to the eighth United Nations survey of crime and criminal justice systems, Qatar had a recorded homicide rate of 0.4 per 100,000 in 2002, and there were a total of 5,838 crimes. Of these crimes, 145 were acquitted, and 3,610 were convicted.

Because many men and women from South Asia and Southeast Asia willingly migrate to Qatar, there is a problem of human trafficking and involuntary servitude as domestic workers and laborers. There are also cases of commercial sexual exploitation. The most common offense is that of forcing workers to accept worse contract terms than those under which they were recruited. There are also problems regarding employers withholding pay, bonded labor, arbitrary detention, restrictions on movement, and sexual, mental, and physical exploitation.

Though the amirate has had little internal unrest, a potential source of instability emanates from the large number of foreigners who constitute a majority of the workforce. The state attempts to neutralize this threat by maintaining control over their activities and limiting the influence they have on the population. Just before the first Gulf War, many Palestinians, who worked in Qatar as businessmen and civil servants, were expelled after Kuwait was invaded by Iraq. Another potential source of instability and problems are Iranian Shiites because they are regarded as potential subversives. Foreigners also have complained of arbitrary police action and harassment and have of mistreatment upon arrest.

Punishment

According to the World Prison Population List, Qatar had a prison rate of 95 per 100,000 in 2003, of which 11.8 percent were women. It has a high population of foreign prisoners, with 55.6 percent of its prisoners being foreigners.

Farrukh B. Hakeem

Further Reading

Anthony, John D., and John A. Hearty. (1986). "Eastern Arabian States." In *The Government and Politics of the Middle East and North Africa,* edited by David E. Long and Bernard Reich. Boulder, CO: Westview Press.

Library of Congress "Qatar. Police and the Criminal Justice System." *Country Studies.* Federal Research Division. http://www.mongabay.com/history/qatar/qatar-police_and_the_criminal_justice_system.html.

Nyrop, Richard. (2008). *Persian Gulf States Country Studies.* Washington, DC: U.S. Government Printing Office.

Official Qatar site, Hukoomi Web site: http://www.gov.qa/wps/portal/homeEN.

Saudi Arabia

Legal System: Islamic/Civil/Common
Murder: Low
Corruption: Medium
Human Trafficking: High
Prison Rate: Medium
Death Penalty: Yes
Corporal Punishment: Yes

Background

The Saudi Arabian legal system and criminal laws are unique in many ways. Saudi Arabia is one of the few countries in the world that emphasizes a legal system based on Islamic law. This is not surprising given that Saudi Arabia is the birthplace of Islam and its Prophet and the location of two of the most sacred holy places—Mecca and Medina. Because of the emphasis on Islamic law, the country's secular laws are closely intertwined with religious laws that have the full force of the government behind them. Saudi Arabia has been an Islamic state, adhering to Islamic law, since its founding in 1926. Prior to 1926, and back to the 13th century, the Ottoman Empire ruled the country. The Ottomans, headquartered in modern Turkey, took over from Islamic caliphs who ruled from the seventh century CE. The modern Kingdom of Saudi Arabia resulted from the conquest of warring factions led by Sheikh Abdul Assiz, with the support of the British, after World War I. Since his death in 1953, a succession of Saudi kings has ruled the nation.

Islamic law is based on the rules of conduct revealed by God within two primary sources: sharia and the Sunna. The sharia (literally, "the way") are the body of rules of conduct revealed by God (Allah) to his Prophet (Muhammad) that direct people in how to live their life. The sharia is the current term used to describe the actual law that is practiced in Saudi Arabia, and it is considered the sole permissible source of legislation. For those who believe in Islam, it is important that the law be consistent with Islamic doctrine because the religion is considered as a way of life and not just a religious practice. In addition to the conventional issues of law, including property, contracts, and inheritance, sharia is concerned with many aspects of individual behavior, including dress, food, etiquette, and religious worship. The most important source of sharia is the Koran, the Muslim holy book. The Koran is not in whole or even in part a code of laws. Only a small percentage of the Koran includes any writings that may be construed as legal rules. Therefore, to deal with many legal matters not specified in the Koran, other sources of law are considered. Some of these are traditions derived from the statements and actions of the Prophet that were recorded in the Sunna.

The Sunna (also called the Hadith) is the second major source of Islamic law. It contains those decisions of the Prophet Muhammad that deal with issues not directly addressed in the Koran. It is important to mention, however, that in addition to the Sunna and sharia, there were, and remain, sources of law developed by different schools of Islamic law in the centuries after the death of Muhammad in CE 632. These were writings that stated the common consent of Islamic jurists (called *Ijm'a*) and cases decided through a process of reasoning by analogy (called *qiyas*). The latter is applied when a case or legal question is not clearly answered by the primary sources of the Koran, Sunna, or Ijma. When there is a conflict between traditional Islamic law and modern legal needs, a Judicial Council consisting mainly of a number of religious leaders will reconcile the matter. In addition, the king may supplement sharia through decrees when conditions require such extension.

There are actually four major schools of Islamic law, derived from religious leaders living in different areas and facing different problems in the two centuries following the death of Muhammad. These schools are Hanafi, Hanbali, Maliki, and Shafi'i. The main differences between these schools are in matters of emphasis, whether on tradition, judicial reasoning, or the elaboration of the Koran. Different countries tend to follow one or another school of Islamic law. The primary legal tradition in Saudi Arabia is the fundamentalist Hanbali school, named after the great theologian and jurist Ahmad Ibn Hanbal (CE 780–855). It is believed that the Hanbal school of Islamic law was adopted by Sheikh Abdul Assiz because that was the school adhered to by the Wahhabi (and Sunni) sect—the fundamentalist Islamic sect that he favored.

Because the country is governed according to the sharia, there is no separate and formal constitution, although some Saudis consider the Koran, the holy book of Islam, to be the constitution. In 1993, a document called the Basic Law (*nizam*) was introduced that articulates the government's rights and responsibilities. Although not a formal constitution and lacking some of the basic principles of other nation's constitutions, such as the rights of assembly and diverging religious expression, it fulfills many of the same purposes of such a document. Today, Saudi Arabia is an absolute monarchy governed by the Islamic law (sharia) and the Basic Law. The king is the prime minister and the guardian of Islam, and he appoints the Council of Ministers, which then selects the officials of the Ministry of Justice, which then presides over the sharia-based criminal justice system. In Saudi Arabia, the Council of Ministers makes decisions on the basis of majority vote, but the king must approve all final decisions. The criminal justice system is administered according to the sharia through religious courts whose judges (called *qadi*) are appointed by the king on the recommendation of the Supreme Judicial Council, which is made up of 12 senior jurists. The independence of the judiciary is protected by law. The king acts as the highest court of appeal and also has the power to pardon. Islamic law reflects the inquisitorial system through the strong cooperation between the judge and the investigator of the particular criminal offense and a lesser adversarial nature of defense attorneys.

World events, such as the terrorist acts of September 11, 2001, in the United States, have created complications for the Saudi government. Although Saudi Arabia remains a strong ally of the United States, economic and cultural ties with individuals and groups associated with terrorism have caused both countries to question the safety of Saudi and American interests in the region. Saudi Arabia has taken a number of steps to improve its internal security and support the fight against terrorism. Among the measures taken has been the implementation of international agreements to disrupt money laundering, the freezing of assets of individuals and groups believed to be linked to terrorist organizations, and working closely with the Untied States to root out terrorist networks. In addition, Western influences have begun to call for a liberalization of politics and social policies such as better treatment of women and more human rights for criminal offenders. However, religious extremists have moved strongly, even to the point of violence, to remove Western influences from the country. As a result, the Saudi government has now the difficult task of keeping internal peace while maintaining positive relations and upgrading its international reputation.

On October 31, 2003, a Saudi woman adjusts her veil in the food court of a Riyadh, Saudi Arabia, shopping mall. Saudi religious police patrol the malls to enforce strict segregation of the sexes and to ensure that women are properly covered. (AP Photo/Hasan Jamali)

Police

Saudi Arabia's highly centralized police force was formally developed by royal decree in 1950 by King Abd al Assiz. The minister of the interior, who is appointed by the king, is responsible for the administration of all police matters. The main police force is actually called the Department of Public Safety. Police in the Department of Public Safety handle most of the daily law enforcement functions in the country. The department is divided into the regular police and the special investigative police of the General Directorate of Investigation (GDI)—the *mubahith,* or secret police. The *mubahith* conduct criminal investigations and handle matters pertaining to domestic security and counterintelligence.

Saudi Arabia is divided into 14 provinces or emirates that make up the country's administrative divisions. Each of the provinces is run by a governor, but the police are directly administered by a general manager who controls the activities of the police within that area. The managers are responsible to the provincial governors, who are directly answerable to the director of public safety. The director is actually the head of the Saudi police and is a high-ranked official in the Interior Ministry. The director appoints most of the managers and officers of the local police forces. Under the provincial forces, there are also municipal forces.

In addition to the Department of Public Safety police, Saudi Arabia also has a "morals force," the religious police known as *mutawa* (or *mutaween*), which ensures that Saudi citizens live up to the rules of behavior derived from the Koran. This agency, also called Saudi Arabia's Commission for Promotion of Virtue and Prevention of Vice, has a membership of around 20,000 men; they are usually bearded men who wear traditional Arabic white robes (*kamees*). They are not armed and not trained as law enforcement personnel. Their roles are many and outlined in the commission's regulations, including to maintain strict separation of the sexes in Saudi public life, pressure women to wear the traditional long black robes and face coverings, and stop women from driving cars. The *mutawa* also ensures that businesses are closed during prayer hours, cover up advertising that depicts attractive women, and regulate alcohol use. They also have been known to disperse gatherings of women in public places designated for men and to prevent men from entering public places designated for families. One of the more surprising rules that the *mutawa* enforces is that women are not allowed to buy music from music stores; in fact, music in general is suspect in the highly puritanical Saudi society. Although the regulations do include a variety of behaviors describing what is "right and wrong," the *mutawa* are sometimes left to their own interpretation of the regulations. As a result, there are numerous reports of the mistreatment and harassment of many Saudi citizens, especially women, and foreign workers. Police have been known to be very aggressive in their investigation and arrest techniques.

When it comes to handling large crowds, the Saudis use what is called the Pilgrims and Festivals Police Force. This special force is used to control the large throngs that gather during the annual pilgrimage to the cities of Mecca and Medina. When these police are unable to handle problem situations, the National Guard and Saudi Army are called in.

Crime

Classification of Crimes

The Saudi government does not actually publish or disseminate a penal code, code of criminal procedure, or code of judicial procedure, and only a limited number of other laws exist in any published form. As mentioned previously, all legal decisions must be made under the auspices of Islamic (sharia) law, and all are subject to the approval of government-appointed religious leaders. However, that does not mean that there is no classification of crimes in Saudi Arabia. Crimes are classified according to whether they are acts against God or crimes against others and society. Crimes against God (*hudud* crimes) are very serious and seen as violations of "natural law"; they include theft, robbery, blasphemy, apostasy (voluntary renunciation of Islam or its rules), rebellion, and defamation, as well as drug offenses and sexual crimes such as adultery, sodomy, and fornication. These crimes are all tried in the sharia courts. As for punishments (called *hadd*) for these crimes, there are specific punishments implicit in the sharia.

All other crimes are private wrongs against individuals or against society and are called *ta'azirat* (or *tesar*) crimes. Those crimes include murder, manslaughter, or personal assault. If the crime is one that threatens a family's livelihood, as may be the case in murder, manslaughter, or assault, then *qisas* (retribution) or *diya* (compensation or fines) may be required. The blood money is given to the victim or the victim's family. In the case of *hudud* crimes, the state must initiate prosecution; in *ta'azirat* crimes, the victims or heirs theoretically must bring a complaint and serve as prosecutor. In practice, however; the state usually initiates these proceedings as well. Nor is the distinction between *hudud* and *ta'azirat* crimes as great as it seems, given that all criminal cases in Islamic countries are decided in government-run courts, and most punishments are fixed by the courts in accordance with religious or traditional rules. In cases where the punishments are not fixed, the judge (*qadi*) prescribes the sentence.

A third category of crimes deals with infractions not covered by the sharia such as personal disputes, labor law, trade law, corporate law, taxation, oil and gas, and immigration issues. These crimes and their punishments have developed over the years as Saudi Arabia has become more industrial and modern and, as a result, has needed additional codes of behavior to regulate public order and security. Until recently, these matters were handled administratively by secular tribunals set up by the king. But in 2007, a new legal decree was written called the Judiciary Law and Court of Grievances. The decree sets up specialized circuit courts that will address personal, trade, and labor disputes. It also calls for the development of new courts of appeals and a new High Court. The new High Court will replace the Supreme Judicial Council, which will now handle only some administrative matters such as judicial appointments. This new decree is seen as a significant development in the Saudi criminal justice system because it provides additional levels of courts and theoretically more legal guarantees for those seeking legal protection or redress.

Saudi Arabia does not have a separate juvenile justice system, so age is not an issue relative to criminal responsibility. Saudi authorities determine both whether a juvenile should be treated as an adult and the appropriate sentence for a juvenile based on the individual child's physical characteristics (e.g., having reached puberty) at the time of trial, sentencing, or execution of sentence. This is part of the judges' wide discretion to interpret the sharia. Strict punishments, the same as used for adults, remain the standard in Saudi Arabia. Included in this list are the imposition of the death penalty and corporal punishments that include amputation and flogging. In fact, corporal punishment is viewed as having a strong deterrent value, so it is often used in punishing juveniles.

Critics have charged that the Saudi method of dealing with juveniles is contrary to recent legal developments in international law relative to the treatment of juveniles. As a result, there has been a call within the international community and within Saudi Arabia itself to move the government to set a unified age of majority for both criminal and civil matters to 18. In 2008, Saudi officials responded by drafting a law that contained 24 articles, including provisions defining the term "child," prohibiting abuse in the home and in institutions, and prohibiting children's use in sexual exploitation, begging, and trafficking. However, the law has not yet been formally passed, and it is unlikely that the law will pass international standards because it still would not prevent judges from issuing death sentences for crimes committed while the offender was under age 18. Instead, it will require only that execution be postponed until the child turns 18. In January 2006, however, the government of Saudi Arabia informed the UN Committee on the Rights of the Child that it had raised the minimum age of criminal responsibility to 12 years for males. Young girls are not protected by any minimum age of criminal responsibility. Nevertheless, if true, this would represent a significant advance on previous practice, which had set the minimum age of criminal responsibility at 7 years.

Crimes Challenging to Saudi Arabia

Terrorism

Terrorism in Saudi Arabia revolves around religious factionalism. This should come as no surprise in a country where religion and religious orthodoxy are major preoccupations. As explained earlier, the prevailing religion in Saudi Arabia derives from the conversion in the late 19th century of King Abdul Assiz to the fundamentalist Wahhabi sect, which is tied to the Sunni branch of Islam. One of the deepest divisions within Islam is between Sunnis and Shiites. In Saudi Arabia, as well as in Bahrain, Oman, and Yemen in the Arabian Peninsula, radical Shiites have used terrorist tactics to destabilize the Sunni regimes, spread Shiite fundamentalism, and combat secularism and Western (especially Israeli) influences.

In recent years, the most serious acts of terrorism in Saudi Arabia has taken two forms. The first are attacks clearly directed at the United States. For example in June 1996, 19 people were killed and 500 wounded when a truck bomb exploded at the U.S. military base near Dhahran. More recently, in May 2003, suicide bombers in booby-trapped cars filled with explosives drove into the Vinnell, Jadewel, and Al-Hamra housing compounds in Riyadh, killing 9 U.S. citizens. The second are isolated terrorist attacks aimed at Saudi institutions and governmental offices. For example, in April 2004, a suicide car bomb exploded at Saudi Arabia's national police headquarters, killing 4 and wounding 125. In each of these cases, Al Qaeda was blamed for the attacks although there was no claim of responsibility by any group. The increasing volume of these kinds of incidents, along with some public dissent from citizens and foreign nationals who are unhappy with the American invasion and occupation of Iraq, has raised concerns about terrorism for Saudi authorities. In the past, because terrorists did not appear to be highly organized or to have much connection to each other, acts of terror were seen as isolated incidents. This is no longer the case, and it is now believed that terrorists are targeting not only foreigners but also the nation itself.

The Saudi police have begun a crackdown on terrorism including the 2003 investigation and arrest of people believed to be linked to bin Laden's terrorist network. Since May 2003, the Saudi government has claimed they have captured or killed most of Al Qaeda's Saudi-based senior leadership, operatives, and most wanted individuals. During 2007, the Saudi government announced the arrest of more than 400 terrorists and their supporters, including terrorist financiers and those advocating extremist ideology over the Internet. Government officials have indicated that more than 9,000 suspected terrorists and their supporters have been arrested since 2003, and more than 3,100 remain in custody.

Human Trafficking

Another crime that is known to occur in Saudi Arabia with some regularity and in violation of international law is human trafficking. Saudi Arabia is a destination country for trafficking of men and women. More specifically, men and women voluntarily come from numerous countries in Asia and Africa to Saudi Arabia for the purposes of gaining employment as domestic servants or other low-skilled laborers, but what results is involuntary servitude, commercial sexual exploitation, restrictions on movement, withholding of passports, threats, physical or sexual abuse, and nonpayment of wages. In addition, Saudi Arabia is also a destination country for Nigerian, Yemeni, Pakistani, Afghan, Chadian, and Sudanese children who after arrival are trafficked for involuntary servitude as forced beggars and street vendors. The government of Saudi Arabia does not fully comply with the international minimum standards for the elimination of trafficking. As a result of the lack of attention to this matter, the U.S. Department of State has designated Saudi Arabia as a Tier 3 violator of the standards set in the Trafficking Victim Protection Act of 2000 passed by the U.S. Congress. The Saudi government states that it does not believe that trafficking of persons is a problem because foreign workers come to the country of their own volition. The government similarly does not take law enforcement action against trafficking of persons for commercial sexual exploitation, nor does it take any steps to provide victims of sex trafficking with protection.

Crime Statistics

It is somewhat difficult to summarize the nature and extent of crime in Saudi Arabia. There are at least three reasons why this difficulty persists. First, crime is often underreported in Saudi crime statistics because the sharia promotes informal and nonlegalistic responses to criminal behavior. As a result, cases are often handled "unofficially" by the police and courts. This method of dealing with offenders exacerbates the problem of gaining verifiable data about the true extent of crime in Saudi Arabia. Second, there is the problem of determining crime rates over the course of the calendar year. The Arabic lunar calendar (Hijri) is based on the Islamic year, which has only 354 days rather than the Gregorian standard of 365. This slight difference over time makes crime measurement and comparisons problematic. Finally, it is well known that much of what goes on in the area of social policy and government in Saudi Arabia is not always released as public information. In this way, Saudi Arabia, like other countries that are not generous with sharing social data, believes that certain information such as crime data should not be made public. Saudis consider information about crimes and drug usage as state secrets and believe that withholding such information may be necessary for reasons of "internal security." Crime data are only one of the many areas in which we have limited knowledge about the Saudi criminal justice system.

In spite of the obstacles to measuring crime in Saudi Arabia, one can still state with confidence that crime is very low in comparison to most countries.

As with other countries with low rates, there is probably a combination of factors contributing to the low crime rates in Saudi Arabia. One possible explanation is that Saudi Arabia in some ways still is not a highly developed country and is certainly not highly urbanized, despite its great wealth per capita. For example, a sizable portion of the population continues to be nomadic Bedouins, who are unlikely to resort to a formal legal system to settle their disputes and resolve their crime problems. This way of living may be changing, however, as the country becomes more modernized and grows in relative wealth.

Another explanation offered by some criminologists and the Saudis themselves is that the harsh corporal punishments they employ, which are based on a philosophy of retribution, serve as effective deterrents to crime. For example, it is possible that the harsh punishments for drug traffickers, including the death penalty, may help to control the drug problem. A third explanation is that the low crime rate likely reflects the way the Islamic religion, most notably the sharia, permeates every aspect of society. There is no disconnect between Islam, the views of the government, and the society at large when it comes to behavior. Any violation of law is seen as an affront to not only the laws of society but also to the laws of God.

By any measure, and even in comparison to other Islamic countries, Saudi Arabia has a minuscule crime rate. Crime statistics compiled by the 8th United Nations Crime Survey reveal the most recent (2002) available statistics for Saudi Arabia, showing that the nation had an overall crime rate of 386.54 per 100,000 population, including a (completed) homicide rate of less than 1 (0.92) per 100,000 population. Rape (0.27) and auto theft (85.52) were also rare occurrences in Saudi Arabia. According to 2000 INTERPOL crime data, robbery rates in Saudi Arabia are also very low, at 0.14 per 100,000 population.

Although not as large a problem as in other countries, drug crimes have increased in recent years in Saudi Arabia. INTERPOL reported in 1988 that Saudi Arabia had a crime rate of 35.6 per 100,000 population for drug crimes. United Nations data for 2001 reflected an increased rate to 48.83 per 100,000. However, interestingly, the rate dropped to 5.74 in 2002. According to some sources such as the CIA, there has also been an increase in the consumption of heroin and cocaine in Saudi Arabia in recent years. However, because of the dearth of crime data made available from Saudi Arabia, it is difficult to obtain an accurate read on the extent or rate of crime.

Finding of Guilt

Rights of Accused

The question of rights of the accused in Islamic law has been debated by both Islamic and non-Islamic scholars. Saudis, in particular, have long felt that the "rights" of accused persons are not overly important in terms of formal procedure in Islamic law but exist more in terms of the need for justice and community welfare. In response to claims that they fall short of international standards, the Saudis have responded that the universal principles of the Koran protect humans better than current international treaties and conventions. Hence, legal officials have historically turned to this source for guidance with respect to criminal procedure. However, in recent years, two major developments have indicated a change in the way that the Saudis view the treatment of those accused of crime. In 2001, the Saudi government enacted a new code of criminal procedural law for those accused of the commission of crimes. The published document, called the *Protection of Human Rights in Criminal Procedure and in the Organization of the Judicial System* (hereafter called the criminal procedure law), addresses the treatment of offenders through each step of the criminal justice process from criminal investigation through the trial and dealings with those found guilty of crime. With the publication of this document, the international community hopes that the Saudis will address many of the human rights violations reported by such groups as Human Rights Watch and Amnesty International, as well as complaints lodged by individual citizens. Among the 225 articles of the criminal procedure law are the following:

- An arrested person "shall not be subjected to any bodily or moral harm" or to "any torture or degrading treatment."
- Any person arrested or detained shall "be advised of the reasons of his detention."
- Interrogation "shall be conducted in a manner that does not affect the will of the accused in making his statements."
- Notification of the reasons for detention should be prompt.
- Suspects have the right to contact their lawyer or legal representative to exercise their right of defense.
- The accused must be informed of charges, must understand the nature of the proof, and must have the opportunity to reply to the charges.

A second important development that may impact the future of Saudi criminal procedure occurred in January 2003 when the Saudi government for the first time allowed an official Human Rights Watch delegation to visit the kingdom. The reform of the criminal justice system was one of the main areas of discussion with Saudi ministers and other senior officials.

Investigation

The investigation and subsequent prosecution of criminal cases in Saudi Arabia are carried out during the initial (pretrial) stage by the Public Investigation and Prosecution Department. First, the criminal investigation officers conduct the necessary inquiries about the alleged offense, including obtaining evidence, conducting interviews of complainants and witnesses, and preparing the report that is sent to the Public Investigation and Prosecution Department, where the investigator determines whether the case should proceed to trial and what level of freedoms and rights should be given to the suspect. For example, here it is determined by the investigator whether a suspect should be remanded to custody while awaiting a formal trial. At this stage, proof and evidence are collected for the indictment brought before the examiner, and the results of the investigation will determine what level of crime the suspect will have to dispel at the trial stage. Thus, an investigation that results in more serious crime charges will undoubtedly lead to a more difficult case to defend against. Because of the importance of the role of the investigator, the criminal procedural law specifically states who shall conduct criminal investigations: members of the Public Investigation and Prosecution Department; police chiefs and their assistants; officers of the Border Guard, the Special Security Forces, the National Guard, and the Armed Forces; heads of governorates and administrative centers; captains of Saudi naval vessels and aircraft; public officials and persons vested with criminal investigation powers under the terms of special regulations; and heads of local Committees for the Propagation of Virtue and the Prevention of Vice.

Pretrial Detention

The issue of length of stay prior to formal adjudication is a controversial one in the Saudi criminal justice system. Technically, there are regulations governing questioning, arrest, and remand in custody. After the arrest, the investigator (also called the examiner) may remand the suspect to detention for 5 days. But the investigator is allowed to extend the detention after filing a request with the local branch of the Bureau of Investigation and Prosecution. The extension of the detention must not exceed the total of 40 days from the period of arrest. The suspect must be released by the end of 40 days unless another request is made to the Bureau of Investigation and Prosecution for another 30-day extension. These extensions should not last beyond 6 months. By the end of that period, the suspect should be released or sent to the appropriate court for adjudication.

If suspects are remanded in custody, they should not be detained where there are those already adjudicated, and the period of their remand in custody must be deducted from the period of their sentence if they are found guilty of the offense. The problem arises, however, in the application of these rules, especially as of late, with the growing number of terrorism examinations and prosecutions in

Saudi Arabia. Numerous accounts of Saudi citizens and foreign nationals being kept for long periods of time have been documented. Because of the emphasis on the need for confessions in Islamic criminal process, there are also serious suspicions and verbal accounts about the way confessions are retracted during the examination stages of the process.

Trials

Trials in Saudi Arabia are held without jurors and are generally closed. Justice is dispensed in Saudi Arabia solely by "*qadi* justice," that is by an Islamic judge who makes decisions on a discretionary case-by-case basis. The qadi receives his authority through adherence to the Koran and the legal traditions developed by various schools of legal jurisprudence. The judge has no need to justify exclusion of outsiders—they may be excluded to protect the privacy of the parties or for the sake of morals.

The standard of proof is high in Saudi Arabia, and the courts generally follow the stringent rules of Islamic law. The rules require a number of witnesses of particular kinds, and the accused is considered innocent until proved otherwise. For some *hudud* crimes (acts against God), which include apostasy, rebellion, theft, adultery, defamation, and drug offenses, the standard of proof is especially high—so high that it is not often adhered to in Islamic courts. For example, proving adultery requires the testimony of four witnesses (who must be male Muslims) or a confession. But confessions can be easily retracted, so such a standard of proof is not easy to obtain. For apostasy, which is the renunciation of Islam by a Muslim, two witnesses or a confession is required as proof. For crimes against persons, witnesses or confessions are also required as proof. Various types of homicide, assault, and fraud usually require two witnesses. Further, not just any witness is acceptable in the Islamic courts; non-Muslim testimony is not accepted, and witnesses must be male (although in some cases two females can be substituted for one male) and have sound mind and character.

Alternatives to Going to Trial

Plea bargaining in Saudi Arabia is available, although it is not applied nearly as much as in other countries such as the United States. In matters where offenders may be likely to receive some form of corporal punishment, the better alternative may be to plead guilty to the lesser offense to lighten the physical punishment. Many of the cases in which pleas are sought are in matters related to corruption or illegal business practices. In those matters, corporate officials request being charged for lesser offenses in exchange for paying large sums of money as fines.

The new criminal procedural law also provides for "special therapeutic measures" for mentally disturbed offenders. These therapeutic measures consist of confinement in hospitals for mental illnesses. In accordance with the provisions in the sharia, any person who is insane at the time of his commission of an offense cannot be held criminally responsible. However, if he becomes mentally disturbed after committing the offense, the offender must be transferred to a hospital for mental illnesses.

Courts

Under the king, the Saudi court system employs at least 700 judges. The largest part of the Saudi court system is the sharia courts, which have traditionally been organized into four levels: courts of the first instance (called summary and general courts), the Court of Cassation, and the Supreme Judicial Council. The summary courts, also called *musta'galah* courts, are convened by one judge (*qadi*) and are found in almost every town; where there are none, the general courts gain jurisdiction. Summary courts deal with minor domestic matters, misdemeanors, and small civil claims. The general courts, also called *kubra* courts, are convened generally by one judge. but in more serious matters, three judges preside. They have original jurisdiction over all criminal and civil cases that fall outside the jurisdiction of the summary court, such as those strictly regulated by a statutory law and cases that may require capital punishment and amputation and monetary damages (for crimes) exceeding one-third of the *diya* (blood money). The summary and general courts have jurisdiction over *ta'azirat* (discretionary punishment) cases and over *hadd* (Koranic prescribed punishment) cases. The general court cannot issue a death sentence by way of *ta'azirat* (discretionary) unless there is a unanimous vote by three judges. If there is a dissenting vote, the minister of justice will assign two additional judges (total five) who can issue the death sentence by a majority vote.

The Court of Cassation has traditionally served as a court of appeals for lower court judgments, and it consists of different divisions (criminal, civil, administrative). The head judge, called a president, oversees the selection of vice-president judges who are appointed on seniority basis. Three judges are involved in each division, headed by the president or a vice president, except in cases involving offenses punishable by death or amputation, in which case decisions are handed down by five judges. The Court of Cassation actually serves as an automatic review of the lower courts in cases where death, amputation, or serious flogging is involved.

The Supreme Judicial Council, also called the Higher Council of the Judiciary, provides the next level of the Saudi court system. This council has served as a level of appeal in addition to being the agency that makes regulations and policies for administering the court system of the country as a whole. Supervising the courts and serving as the main decision-making body for hiring, promoting, and transferring judges are major responsibilities. The court is composed of 11 members: a president and five full-time and five part-time members. Any verdict by the Supreme Judicial Council is subject to the review of the king.

With the 2007 reforms to reorganize the judicial system, the Saudis will soon include a new judicial arrangement abolishing the existing courts of appeals and establishing new courts of appeals in all 13 provinces. These courts will divide their caseloads among specialized labor, commercial, criminal, personal status, and civil circuits.

Qualifications of Judges

Not surprisingly, judges in Saudi Arabia require significant training and study in Islamic law. Aspiring lawyers and judges are required to attend religious preparatory schools for five years prior to attending the sharia institutes or colleges. After graduation, future judges must attend a judicial academy and an institute of public administration at which they will learn their craft, including two months of training in the commercial, labor, and criminal procedure laws and other relevant regulations. In addition to their educational legal training, Saudi Arabia assigns newly appointed judges to a court for a two-year probation period so that they can become acquainted with its working procedures. During the probation period, the judges are given simple cases and settlements that are referred to them by the court's presiding judge, who reviews and approves the judgments before they are handed down.

Juvenile Justice System

Saudi Arabia has few laws or regulations that explicitly address juvenile offenders. However, Saudi Arabia does have juvenile (only) courts staffed by sharia (adult court) judges. The kingdom also operates 13 social observation facilities used to hold Saudi and foreign boys ages 12 to 18 who are under investigation, facing trial, or being detained per a judicial order. There are also four welfare institutions used to hold girls and young women under age 30 who are under investigation, facing trial, or being judicially detained.

However, even with these special courts and facilities, there is in reality no clear "separate system" where juveniles are clearly treated differently than adults from the beginning to the end of the criminal justice process. The way the system for juveniles actually works is based on the broad discretion of criminal justice officials who use the basics of Islamic law (sharia and the Koran) to make legal decisions. Saudi officials determine to use many of the same criteria for arresting, detaining, and punishing juveniles as they do for adults. Consequently, some juvenile offenders are subject to arbitrary decisions that some would argue are in violation of individual rights. In Saudi Arabia's new law of criminal procedure passed in 2002, procedures were specified for adult offenders, and the law also specified that the investigations and trials of juvenile offenders, including young females, would be conducted in accordance with the set laws and regulations. However, the Saudi government has yet to issue laws and regulations specifically addressing arrest, investigation, trial, and sentencing procedures for juveniles.

Punishment

Types of Punishment

For those who commit serious offenses in jurisdictions with Islamic law, the punishments prescribed are in the Koran and are often very harsh, with emphasis on corporal and capital punishment. Under sharia law, imprisonment is in fact the punishment of last resort. But that does not mean that there are no other forms of punishment that are at least available for offenders, especially for lesser offenses. Some of the alternatives to corporal and capital punishment include the following:

- *Suspended sentences.* These can be used by judges in cases where the offense is not very heinous and the offender appears to have a sincere desire for rehabilitation and when their personal circumstances warrant consideration for such a sentence.
- *Probation.* Probation is provided for offenders in Saudi Arabia after they have served time in prison and when they have shown that they were willing to follow the rehabilitation program provided while incarcerated and that departure from prison would enhance that person's rehabilitation further. The Prison and Detention Regulations of the Kingdom, specifically article 25, provides for release on probation.
- *Release on health grounds.* Saudi Arabia has found that for humanitarian reasons, an offender can be released from prison based on health grounds.
- *Pardon.* An infrequent sentencing option, one used after sentencing or during the period of incarceration, is the pardon. The pardon is granted by the king and would most likely occur during the religious holiday of Ramadan. Interestingly, a number of prisoners facing the death penalty are pardoned by relatives of the murder victims and saved from execution.
- *Semi-liberty.* This is provided when an offender is sentenced to incarceration but is assigned to work outside the prison. The prisoner is permitted to leave every day in the morning but must return in the evening.
- *Prison.* Prison is not the conventional sentencing recourse in Saudi Arabia, but nevertheless, prisons do exist to house those awaiting trial and also those criminal offenders who are not deterred by the corporal punishments.

Death Penalty

Although there is an international trend away from the death penalty, Saudi Arabia is one of the countries that not only has retained its use but also has used it with considerable frequency. In fact, during 2007, Saudi Arabia was one of five countries, along with China, Iran, Pakistan, and the United States, that accounted for almost 90 percent of the known documented executions carried out throughout the world, according to an Amnesty International report.

The sharia allows for the death penalty for a variety of capital offenses such as adultery, sodomy, apostasy, drug trafficking, rebellion, and armed robbery. Executions are usually by public beheading, although executions for adultery may be by stoning. The severity of the punishment (*hadd*) is due to the fact that these crimes are seen as crimes against God (*hudud* crimes) and thus are very serious, seen as violations of "natural law." At the same time, murder and manslaughter as well as other crimes are considered not particularly as crimes against God, but more so against persons, so the punishment is more at the discretion of the court. With these crimes, called *ta'azirat* crimes, the courts can still call for the death penalty.

In cases such as murder or manslaughter, the victim's family can support the sentence and call for retribution (*qisas*) or mitigate the sentence and ask for monetary compensation (*diya*) or even a pardon. However, as mentioned earlier in this chapter, the real distinction between *hudud* and *ta'azirat* crimes is minimal. All criminal cases in Islamic countries are decided in government-run courts, and most punishments (*hadd*) are fixed by the courts in accordance with religious or traditional rules. In cases where the punishments are not fixed, such as with *hudud* crimes, then the judge (*qadi*) prescribes the sentence.

It is very difficult to know how many people in Saudi Arabia receive the death penalty because official statistics are not available. What we do know is provided by a variety of sources, most notably by human rights groups such as Amnesty International (AI), although AI has not been granted formal access to Saudi Arabia. The most recent data indicate that the Saudis executed at least 158 persons during 2007. The same sources indicate that the rate of executions for the beginning of 2008 was actually higher than in 2007. Additional information that is available tells us that the 158 executed in 2007 is almost double the number executed in 2005, when there were "only" 86 known executions.

What may be most troubling, however, about the use of the death penalty in Saudi Arabia is its use on juveniles. In January 1996, Saudi Arabia ratified the United Nations Convention on the Rights of the Child (CRC), undertaking not to execute anyone for offenses committed when they were less than 18 years of age. However, according to recent reports, child offenders continue to be sentenced to death, and in 2007, in some cases the punishment was carried out.

Prisons and Prison Inmates

According to the Eighth United Nations Survey on Crime Trends, the 2002 Saudi prison population was reported to be 28,612, with a rate of 132 per 100,000 persons in the population. Almost 6 percent (1,639) of the inmates were female, and almost 47 percent were foreign inmates. This 2002 rate is up from 1998, when 23,088 were incarcerated with a rate of 114 per 100,000, and a considerable increase from figures reported in 1994 that listed 7,939 inmates and a rate of 46 per 100,000. To house the almost 30,000 inmates, the Saudi government claims support for 104 adult correctional facilities. These totals probably do not include juvenile offenders who are detained in one of the 17 (13 male) special juvenile correctional facilities. Recent figures (2004) place around 13,000 juveniles in detention in that year.

There are many mixed reports about the conditions of prisons in Saudi Arabia. Anecdotal reports, often published by individual citizens or human rights organizations, frequently claim poor treatment of offenders relative to quality of prison conditions. However, according to the most recent (2005) Saudi Arabia Country Report on Human Rights Practices posted by the U.S. Department of State, "prisons and detention centers [in Saudi Arabia] were generally acceptable, according to international standards." However, problems do exist with some prisons that have "below-acceptable standards in hygiene, food, medical, and social services . . . jails remained overcrowded, and some detainees were allowed family visits only after a significant period of time after their initial incarceration."

The largest prison in Saudi Arabia is the Al-Ha'ir Prison, located 25 miles south of Riydah. The prison incarcerates offenders convicted of common criminal offenses and some Al Qaeda operatives who have been convicted of terrorism activities. Because of the growing number of those arrested and convicted of crime and terror-related activities, the Saudis have recently begun construction on five new high-security prisons, each able to accommodate 1,200 inmates. The prisons are designed to separate the common criminal from Al Qaeda and other terrorists. The prisons will also provide "rehabilitation" programs to terrorist insurgents through the use of dialogue and Islamic indoctrination. The buildings of the new prisons are also part of a larger movement by the Saudis to improve prison conditions and treatment of offenders, especially in light of allegations of abuse and prisoner maltreatment at facilities, in particular Al-Ha'ir Prison.

Harry R. Dammer

Further Reading

Al-Farsay, F. (1986). *Saudi Arabia*. London: Routledge and Kegan Paul.

Amin, S. A. (1985). *Middle East Legal Systems.* Glasgow: Royston.

Ansary, Abdullah F. (2008). *A Brief Overview of the Saudi Arabian Legal System.* Hauser Global Law School Program, New York University School of Law: http://www.nyulawglobal.org/globalex/saudi_arabia.htm#_edn240#_edn240.

Awad, A. M. (1982). "The Rights of the Accused Under Islamic Criminal Procedure." In *The Islamic Criminal Justice System,* edited by M.C.E. Bassiouni. New York: Oceana.

Lippman, Matthew, Sean McConville, and Mordechi Yerushalmi. (1988). *Islamic Criminal Law and Procedures.* Westport, CT: Praeger, pp. 42–46.

"Precarious Justice: Arbitrary Detention and Unfair Trials in the Deficient Criminal Justice System of Saudi Arabia." (March 2008). *Human Rights Watch.* Vol. 20, No. 3(E),: pp. 1–143: http://www.hrw.org/reports/2008/saudijustice0308/saudijustice0308web.pdf.

Sudan

Legal System: Islamic/Common
Murder: High
Corruption: High
Human Trafficking: High
Prison Rate: Low
Death Penalty: Yes
Corporal Punishment: Yes

Background

The Republic of Sudan is the largest country in Africa. Although Sudan's Arab population is only 39 percent, and the black African population is 52 percent, Arabs continue to control the government, military, and police forces. The Sudanese criminal code was formerly based on British law and the penal code of British colonial India. As a former British-Egyptian colony, the Sudanese legislative lawmaking assembly was established in 1948, in the aftermath of a weakened British empire following World War II.

Justice System

The legal structure of Sudan has been in constant transitional tribulation. Although attempts have been made to form a democratic nation with a constitution and parliament, this feat has never been fully realized because of ongoing economic problems, government corruption, and rebellion. Although a parliament theoretically exists, there is little southern representation, and most of the government has been appointed by President Bashir. Historical attempts to create a democracy in Sudan have been short-term and interrupted by numerous military coups. Today, Sudan is considered to be an authoritarian republic.

Legislature

The legislature consists of 24 representatives with some elected and some appointed by the president. Today, the legislative authority within Sudan is divided into two chambers. The Transitional National Assembly (Majlis Watani) consists of 450 appointed members who represent mainly the National Congress (NIF) ruling party and, in smaller number, the Sudan People's Liberation Army (SPLA) and other opposition political parties. The Council of States (Majlis Welayat) has 50 members who are indirectly elected by state legislatures. Members of the national legislature serve six-year terms. Friction between SPLA political representatives and members of the ruling National Congress are constant with noted police raids on SPLA offices in Khartoum.

Judiciary

In the aftermath of the 1991 military coup, the NIF organized a 15-member (reduced to 12 members in 1991) Revolutionary Command Council for National Salvation (RCC) under the leadership of President Bashir. The RCC declared a state of emergency across the country and granted itself broad policing powers. Bashir's government reintroduced sharia laws to the southern provinces by passing a new penal code known as the Criminal Act of 1991. Harsh punishments that included amputations and public stoning were reinstituted. By 1993, all non-Muslim judges in the south were replaced by Muslim judges from the north. Emergency tribunal and public order courts were established by the Bashir government in 2001 under a state of emergency. Due process is severely restricted in the emergency courts, and targeted behaviors include suspicion of prostitution, alcohol consumption, improper dress, and improper movements. Public order courts are administered by a single judge with preliminary jurisdiction over civil, criminal, and personal-matter cases when appropriate. There are 133 public court judges according to the Sudan judiciary. These judges also have appellate jurisdiction on judgments of magistrates who are third- and second-grade criminal cases judges. Trials in public order courts are often led by hostile prosecutors who are also junior military officers with little legal training. Presumptive guilt under sharia laws is common, and cases tend to be dealt with very quickly without adequate cross-examination of witnesses by the defense. Flogging remains active, usually consisting of 40 lashes for offenses consisting of sex and alcohol. Theft of anything valued over US$40 can result in the right hand being amputated. Public hangings have taken place for crimes such as armed robbery as well as adultery and homosexuality. However, convictions within the sharia courts for capital cases require large burdens of proof, preventing executions for many of the death penalty cases. Alongside public order courts are special security courts formed by military governors. These courts have three-member panels that include military and civilian judges. Although defense attorneys are permitted to sit with defendants, they do not normally address the court. Several hundred prominent politicians, academics, and journalists have been detained through the special security and public order courts.

Today's Sudanese judiciary is linked between civil and sharia branches. The civil branch includes a Higher Judicial Council that appoints all judges. Cases are tried mainly in the northern region of Sudan by Islamic judges (called *qadis*) who receive their training in Sunni Islamic legal schools. Under the 1973 Judiciary Act, civil cases are decided by provincial courts, courts of appeal, and the Supreme Court. Members of the Supreme Court are appointed by the president after advisement from the Supreme Council of the Judiciary. The Supreme Court reviews cases of the lower courts in civil, criminal, and personal matters in addition to theoretically providing interpretations of the Constitution when the Sudanese government recognizes its democratic institutions. The Supreme Court consists of 70 judges and operates through panels of three. Four circuits of the Sudanese Supreme Court operate outside the capital in the western, central, and eastern states. Decisions are reached by a majority and subject to revision only if the senior member of the three-judge panel deems that an infringement of Islamic (i.e., sharia) laws has taken place. If the chief justice determines a violation of Islamic law has occurred, the sharia branches of the judiciary convene with a five-member panel. The majority of this panel must not have participated in deciding the initial dispute. Formally, courts rely on statutes in determining guilt and punishment, and their formal decisions are published in the *Sudan Law Journal and Reports*. Legal statutes are published in the *Sudan Gazette*.

There are 28 judicial organs in Sudan, 3 in Khartoum and the rest distributed in the 25 states. Each state judicial organ has its own administrator, who is assisted by court presidents and senior officials. However, the court systems are not autonomous from the central government. The administrators of the court organs are appointed by members of the Supreme Court or courts of appeal. Appointed administrators preside over their organ's courts of appeal and judicial circuits in addition to distributing judicial work or deciding on judicial transfers. There are 130 appeal court judges who function in 28 appeal circuit courts distributed among 26 states, with each consisting of 3 judges. Decisions in the appeals courts are reached through a majority of opinion. Case appeals arise from public courts, preliminary judgments of first-grade judges in civil courts, and criminal/personal matter courts.

Informal legal practices or popular court justice is encouraged and exercised frequently throughout Sudan. There are 98 town courts, 897 rural courts, and 67 intermediate courts for civil and criminal proceedings. Members of popular courts are chosen by citizens in town and rural areas who are judged to be in good standing. Memberships include tribal chiefs known as sultans. Administrators of tribal courts consult with the heads of their respective judicial organs and executive authorities when trying to create new popular courts. Moreover, administrators of rural and town courts study local customs for the purpose of creating a unified legislative system of laws. The formal judiciary relies on community justice for solving disputes through tradition and reconciliation. The courts are located in regions without district courts. Customary laws vary throughout Sudan and are based on diverse customs, traditions, and tribal systems of justice that may not be consistent with the formal legal system or public policy.

Ethnic, religious, and political factors all play a role in the judiciary. Informally, communities rely on local chiefs, known as sultans, to resolve neighbor disputes. Because there is little standardization regulating informal justice in Sudan, and the country consists of a diverse ethnic and religious population, justice varies throughout tribes and communities. Formal courts and legal systems are utilized more fully in the northern region of Sudan. Although the Constitution calls for the judiciary to be unbiased and an independent fact finder, the reality is quite different. The Sudanese judiciary lacks independence, evident by the frequent dismissal of judges, attorneys, and law officers who work within the court system.

Judicial Treatment of Women

Despite the increased use of public order courts, the treatment of Sudanese women has not improved. For example, although rape accusations are prevalent, women who report rape are frequently blamed for being too complicit. Male witnesses are required to testify before a rape case can be proven before the court. If male witnesses are not available, the defendant has the option of bringing defamation charges against the complainant that can result in the woman receiving public flogging. Because of these rulings, judges frequently advise women not to bring cases alleging rape before the judiciary. Unmarried women who are pregnant or admit to having sexual relations have also been known to receive flogging of 80 lashes. In some villages, flogging is allowed to take place without formal judicial rulings. A religious body known as the Group to Enjoin Good and Forbid Evil has been authorized to flog offenders for suspected immoral behavior without due process.

Throughout the 1950s and into the 1970s, Sudanese women made great strides by gaining the legal right to vote, to decide on their own marriage partners, and to receive equal pay. During this period, women became physicians, judges, lawyers, engineers, diplomats, journalists, and professors. However, by the late 1970s, the Muslim Brotherhood (later the NIF) had successfully persuaded Sudanese leader Nimeiri to institute more conservative Islamic laws and violently shut down the Sudanese Women's Union (SWU). Female leaders and their husbands were arrested or killed. Sudanese women's rights have been further curtailed under the Bashir government, which has targeted not only disadvantaged minorities but also middle- and upper-class women. Today, law enforcement officers are allowed to exercise enormous discretion against women under strict interpretable Islamic laws. Women are forbidden from being seen in public with men other than family members or approved guardians. The 1991 Public Order Act, part of the Bashir regime's new penal code, was intentionally framed to challenge any social gathering with mixed genders. According to the legislation, these gatherings could be considered places for potential fornication, and the government can exclude women from any male-dominated public location. The "Family Law" portion of the 1991 Public Order Act requires women to obtain their husband's consent before visiting her family or friends. Other areas of Sudan have disallowed women to be on the streets at all during specific hours of the day.

Women are expected to act modestly and cover their bodies head to toe in an Iranian-style chador. Women who refuse to comply with the government regulations are subject to arrest and public flogging.

In July 2009, media attention was directed at a female journalist working for the United Nations who faced 40 lashes for wearing trousers. Ten other Sudanese women wearing trousers were given lashes at a Sudanese police station; however, UN workers are frequently given immunity.

The Sudanese media (government-controlled) advises women in chastity, male obedience, and being a good domestic. The National Islamic Front (NIF) argues that Islam is incompatible with females being employed outside of the home. Ironically, women head many Sudanese households because of males being involved in migrant farming labor, being soldiers in the government or rebelling factions, or being killed in the ongoing conflicts. Most of the widowed Sudanese women have been denied pensions after their husbands were killed in battle. The Islamic stance barring females from most outside occupations provides great conflict in families where the males are absent. Women attempt to make money through a variety of options. Some form groups attempting to sell tea, peanuts, and other food items from licensed public kiosks. However, sellers are frequently questioned and challenged by government officials regarding their licenses. Other women attempt to brew alcohol, a violation of Islamic laws, and often face prison and public flogging. Legal recourse against these women is considered hypocritical given that half of northern Sudanese males are suspected of consuming alcohol brewed by women in southern Sudan and the Darfur region. Reports indicate that Sudanese police officers have consumed alcohol at illicit drinking establishments and later returned to conduct raids at these locations. Police officers are frequently bribed to drop charges. Even more disparaging, Sudanese police have reportedly targeted women with sexual advances and, when denied, have hypocritically arrested the women on allegations of prostitution or illegally running a distillery.

Police

There are approximately 11,000 law enforcement officers in Sudan who are divided into regions led by regional commanders. Police patrol and response consists of foot and mounted brigades, with some patrolling on camels or mules. The ratio of officers in the population is about 1.5 per 1,000. Police operations are mainly directed toward traffic/riot control, animal theft, and tribal conflicts. Police officer cadets are known to receive two years of training at the Sudan Police College near Khartoum and four months of training at their respective provincial headquarters. The Sudan Police College also serves as a training school for the military. Police training includes general duties, criminal law interpretation, clerical duties, and specialized training in fingerprinting, use of small arms, and crime scene photography.

Several organizational changes in policing Sudan occurred during the Nimeiri administration. The Police Act of 1979 allowed for centralized command with direct reporting to the president. Today, the director-general of the police reports to the minister of interior. The Ministry of Interior centrally administrates policing in Sudan and exercises authority over applications for citizen travel using a committee composed of NIF loyalists, while exercising martial law (i.e., military police control) in government-controlled areas throughout Sudan. The Ministry of State Security, with the responsibility of collecting information on state security, also has its own police force. Central police headquarters is located in Khartoum and organized into divisions, with each commanded by a police major general. Each division is responsible for conducting criminal investigations, training, passport control, security, and public affairs.

The government's internal security force, known as the Popular Defense Forces (PDF), has been accused of numerous human rights violations while acting under extralegal authority of emergency powers through the security courts. The PDF's primary task is to carry out surveillance, and they are given the authority to arrest and imprison anyone considered to be a national threat. Often the popular police (public order) forces receive information from Salvation Popular Committees, established throughout Sudan, about how loyal local community members are to their national government. Enforcement from the PDF and public order police officers is often directed toward women's conformity to Islamic laws and potential rebel groups. Those arrested and incarcerated by the PDF are not entitled to due process.

Darfur—External Police Force

The main police presence in Darfur has come from the African Union Mission in Sudan (AMIS), originally called the Ceasefire Commission (CFC). AMIS was created in the aftermath of the Humanitarian Ceasefire Agreement in April 2004 between Sudan's government and the two rebel groups in Darfur—the Sudan People's Liberation Movement/Army (SPLM) and the Justice and Equality Movement (JEM). AMIS police advisers have had little impact in creating peace or addressing humanitarian needs. In late 2006, the United Nations sent supporting personnel to Darfur.

Sudanese security forces continue to detain displaced citizens from various refugee camps throughout Darfur. Estimates from the UN claim over 2 million people are gathered in refugee camps (referred to as internally displaced persons—IDPs) in Darfur, with 100,000 having been killed and 200,000 having died by hunger or disease between 2003 and 2007, since the conflict arose between Sudan and western rebel groups. AMIS police advisors are attempting to protect IDPs from Janjaweed ("men on horseback") militant attacks throughout the refugee camps. The Khartoum government has blamed the refugees for being the catalyst for the hybrid AMIS-UN contingency in Sudan, and international aid has been curtailed following reports that much of the aid never reaches the IDPs. Resistance from the Sudanese government and Sudanese Armed Forces (SAF) has kept AMIS police advisors (who are vastly understaffed and unequipped) out of several Darfur refugee camps. Moreover, the SAF continues to force relocation of many IDPs amid complaints from Amnesty International and international legal authorities.

The original mission for AMIS in Darfur did not include civilian police (CIVPOL) detachments. However, because of the resistance from the SAF, several meetings were held by the Peace and Security Council of the African Union, authorizing more than 1,500 civilian police officers to supplement the AMIS advisors already in Sudan. CIVPOL is internationally represented from police-contributing countries (PCCs) throughout Africa. AMIS also runs a training program for police advisors deployed to Darfur. Upon arrival, all officers undergo training introducing them to the conflict, AMIS policies and procedures, and expectations for police-advising duties throughout Darfur. After six weeks in Darfur, CIVPOL officers undergo collaborative training at El Fasher, CIVPOL headquarters, with the goal of pooling ideas and advice. Specific training has included case investigation, crime analysis, and gender-based violence.

Community Policing Attempts

Advisors have increasingly instituted models of community policing in Darfur through the leadership of CIVPOL. with a push toward grassroots social reconciliation. Historical distrust of the Arab-led government in Sudan has existed for centuries and has been heightened in the aftermath of the Darfur genocide. Community policing initiatives, if fully implemented, would allow law-abiding community members an opportunity to provide input to the justice process and assist in problem solving. Strategies for creating collaboration have included using CIVPOL female officers to arrange and lead regular women's forums inside refugee camps. The forums deal with child care and wellness during and following pregnancy. In addition, CIVPOL has organized community soccer and volleyball games with open invitations. Engagement of the community is critical for effective policing. In line with this principle, CIVPOL has moved toward a more broadly defined notion of safety and community building. Officers have run numerous educational sessions within the refugee camps. Examples include how to treat snake bites and how to prevent fires. A CIVPOL contingent from Uganda taught IDPs how to construct a clay stove that not only reduced fire risk but also used less fuel and wood. Darfur schools have been increasingly supported, and adult education centers have opened and are supported by AMIS trainers and equipment. As part of a joint peacekeeping consortium, AMIS and the UN have been working with Sudan to select, train, coordinate, and advise community police officers. These officers are expected to be more effective at gaining back Sudanese trust and operating according to internationally accepted standards.

The mandate authorizing CIVPOL does not give them express authority to enforce laws in Darfur or to protect civilians. Instead, CIVPOL employees are only supposed to monitor the Sudanese government police forces and assist other components that are attempting to create a secure environment. The CIVPOL officers reside with other African Union (AU) military advisors and are supposed to carry out investigations on alleged violations of the ceasefire agreement. Additionally, preventive escorts are arranged through CIVPOL to protect women and IDPs who leave the refugee camps to gather firewood for their stoves or to travel to surrounding markets to find food and water. Regular policing meetings are held with CIVPOL, military officers, humanitarian agencies, IDPs, and local police officers to coordinate proper security for the refugee camps. Victimization reports are brought to the attention of CIVPOL officers throughout their IDP camp patrols. Most of the female victims have been raped and are encouraged to file a criminal complaint with the Sudanese government's police force. However, AMIS human rights training has caused CIVPOL to shift its policies toward providing advice and counseling with more sympathy directed toward victims. As part of the CIVPOL mandate, reports are created on the outcome of cases prosecuted (or not prosecuted) through Sudanese police authorities. In mid-2004, the United Nation's Children's Fund (UNICEF) began to train Sudanese police on how to investigate sexual violence among child victims throughout Darfur. The initiative followed a visit to Sudan from UNICEF director Carol Bellamy, on which she heard testimonies of villages being burned, parents being killed, children being raped, and villagers being forced to flee. Jordan's police trainers have assisted in some of the training directed toward child victims of sexual violence.

The Darfur Peace Agreement has continually deteriorated despite the efforts of the AU, UN, and AMIS/CIVPOL. International recognition has found that these groups are not adequately resourced and do not have a sufficient mandate to operate or assist with an adequate justice system. Collaborative meetings to analyze staffing needs recommended additional support of AMIS/CIVPOL, and these recommendations were eventually supported by President Bashir. However, arguments were also presented to transition leadership assistance away from the AU and more toward a UN operation, and this has been rejected by the Sudanese government. The 2006 Addis Ababa meetings further strengthened the ceasefire, gave joint leadership to the AU and the UN, and allowed for varied support mechanisms to AMIS/CIVPOL from the UN, including additional UN police advisors. In 2006, the sixth African Union Summit took place in Khartoum, Sudan, despite threats from the AU to change locations. In lieu of the Khartoum summit, President Bashir advocated that he become chairman of the AU, replacing President Olusegun Obasanjo of Nigeria. Bashir's offer was rebuffed by AU administration. In February 2008, Tanzanian President Jakaya Mrisho Kikwete became chairman of the AU.

Crime

Although there is little information available about the type and extent of "traditional crime" such as property offenses and assault, these crimes are surely overshadowed by the genocide and ethnic cleansing–related crimes that have been largely prosecuted, amid great difficulty, through the International Criminal Court.

International Criminal Court (ICC)

The International Criminal Court (ICC) was established in 2002 with the purpose of prosecuting individuals for genocide, crimes against humanity, and war crimes. Darfur has become a target for ICC investigations. In March 2009, the court's chief prosecutor issued an arrest warrant for President Bashir for crimes against humanity. The arrest warrant, issued to the Sudanese government, is not expected to be executed. Over 100 governments have become members of the court, with the notable exception of China, India, Sudan, and the United States. In response to the formation of the ICC, President Bush signed the American Service-Members' Protection Act, allowing the United States to use military force to protect any Americans from future prosecution by the ICC.

The ICC has opened investigations into three other situations besides Darfur: Northern Uganda, Congo, and the Central African Republic. Although the court operates out of The Netherlands, proceedings can take place anywhere. In May 2007, the ICC's prosecutor in The Hague (Netherlands) issued arrest warrants for Sudanese humanitarian affairs minister Ahmad Muhammad Harun and Janjaweed militia leader Ali Kushayb for war crimes and crimes against humanity. The warrants followed a 94-page document that followed a 21-month investigation within 60 countries focusing on crimes committed in 2003 and 2004. (The ICC can investigate only crimes that have occurred after 2002.) Sudan has argued that the court lacks jurisdiction and that the men will remain in Sudan without extradition. The ICC does not have a police force and relies on targeted governments to carry out arrest warrants, which is not likely in Sudan given that the government rejects the ICC jurisdiction. Moreover, the Sudanese media, controlled by the government, has reported that the international community is using the ICC to plan future invasions of Sudan and that the United States is behind the court prosecutions.

A number of other obstacles exist for informing the Sudanese people about the process of international justice because the Khartoum government refuses open access to ICC personnel within Darfur refugee camps. Instead, ICC prosecution investigators and other outreach personnel operate in neighboring Chad, where Darfur refugee camps now exist, as a means for continuing to inform the Sudanese people about their mission. The goal of the outreach initiative is to inform the populous about international law and justice and solicit feedback from the Darfur community. The ICC has made progress in translating legal documents into Arabic as a means of providing the media with updates on court activities and broadcasting radio updates into the refugee camps. Despite these efforts, the Human Rights Institute of the International Bar Association (IBA) has argued that the ICC outreach in Sudan needs to increase significantly. However, much of the ICC investigatory efforts remain secretive so as to not endanger partners who are supplying the court with necessary legal information.

The United States is in a difficult position of supporting the UN stance on genocide and refusing to support the ICC. The Bush administration revoked the previous Clinton administration's treaty that helped establish the ICC on the basis that the court may attempt to exercise future frivolous legal actions against Americans abroad. The ICC's outreach to Darfur includes a focus on the rights of the victims throughout the proceedings, which includes a presentation of their view and concerns at all stages, regardless of whether they formally testify as witnesses. Consequently, members of the ICC prosecution have made limited contact with Darfur refugees in various camps to understand the extent of the genocide. The ICC prosecutors linked Khartoum with the Janjaweed (horseback) militias, claiming the Sudanese government bankrolled the genocide throughout Darfur. Additional warrants are expected from the ICC linking Khartoum to the genocide in Darfur.

As a response, in late 2005, Sudan established a special criminal tribunal and a national court for conflict-related crimes in Darfur to investigate and prosecute human rights abuses. Questions remain about how willing the tribunal will be to carry out prosecutions against those who hold positions in the government. The Sudanese government argues that the tribunals negate the authority of the ICC. In addition, the Sudanese government has sent a group of attorneys to London for training sessions on how to adequately represent and advocate for victims in Darfur during the tribunals. However, Amnesty International stated that the Sudanese-backed tribunal courts would fail unless there were legal reforms to ensure judicial independence and oversight from the government in Khartoum.

Prisons

Supervision of the Sudan Prison Service is carried out by the director-general of prisons. The central prisons are Kober in Khartoum, Shalla in Al Fashir

(Darfur), and Port Sudan on the Red Sea. With an organizational structure similar to that of the police, provincial authorities manage jails in their administrative jurisdictions. According to Justice Africa, a U.K.-based research group, and the U.S. State Department, Sudanese jails and prisons operate in overcrowded and harsh environments. Most of the prison property is without roofs, so prisoners use sheets to shade themselves from the sun. Rather than having individual cells, some Sudanese prisons consist of a large yard surrounded by four walls.

There have been reports of persistent beating and torture, but it is believed that this treatment has predominantly been inflicted by federal security officials and not provincial (local) prison guards. Sudanese prisoners frequently go without beds, clean drinking water, quality food rations, or proper hygiene. Relatives of prisoners are allowed to bring food and water to the prison, but officials arbitrarily deny prisoner visits. Prisoner treatment varies widely, with some prisoners restricted to shackles and others sentenced to day reporting and allowed home in the evening. High-ranking political prisoners are reported to enjoy better conditions than lower-class prisoners. Sudanese government administrators have frequently refused prison inspections by international agencies. Amnesty International has been allowed to visit a select group of prisoners in Kober following reports of prisoner torture. However, it is believed that Kober is in better condition than other prisons in Sudan, and the government self-selected this prison for Amnesty review.

The largest women's prison in Sudan, Omdurman, is filled mainly with women convicted of selling alcohol. Women prisoners reportedly have been raped by guards demanding sexual favors in return for allowing visitations. An estimated 75 percent of incarcerated women are pregnant or caring for young children, and one in five are widows. Female prison populations have grown considerably because of the sharia laws, with major overcrowding issues. In October 1994, the Sudanese government announced the release of most women incarcerated in the Omdurman women's prison as an act of clemency. However, it was suspected that the women were released after they rioted. Non-Muslim women are frequently given early release if they convert to Islam.

In September 2007, southern Sudan opened the Lologo Prison Regional Training Center for 550 former soldiers of the SPLA. Following the peace agreement with the Sudanese government, former soldiers sought employment and found jobs in the prison service. It is estimated that 1,500 former soldiers joined the Sudanese prison service. The training courses offer a three-month orientation and specialist training courses in management and medical care The establishment of additional prison service training centers is the start of a wider strategy to revise dilapidated infrastructures throughout the Sudanese prison system under a Multi-Donor Trust Fund (MDTF).

Brandon Kooi

Further Reading

African Union Mission in the Sudan: http://www.amis-sudan.org.

International Criminal Court: http://www.icc-cpi.int.

Jok, Madut. (2007). *Sudan: Race, Religion, and Violence.* London: Oneworld Publications.

U.S. Department of State. *Sudan's Report of Female Genital Mutilation (FGM):* http://www.state.gov/g/wi/rls/rep/crfgm/.

Xavier, John. (2008). *Darfur: African Genocide.* New York: Rosen Publishing Group.

Syria

Legal System: Civil/Islamic
Murder: Medium
Corruption: High
Human Trafficking: High
Prison Rate: Low
Death Penalty: Yes

Background

Syria was previously ruled as a French mandate after the ruling Ottoman Empire disintegrated

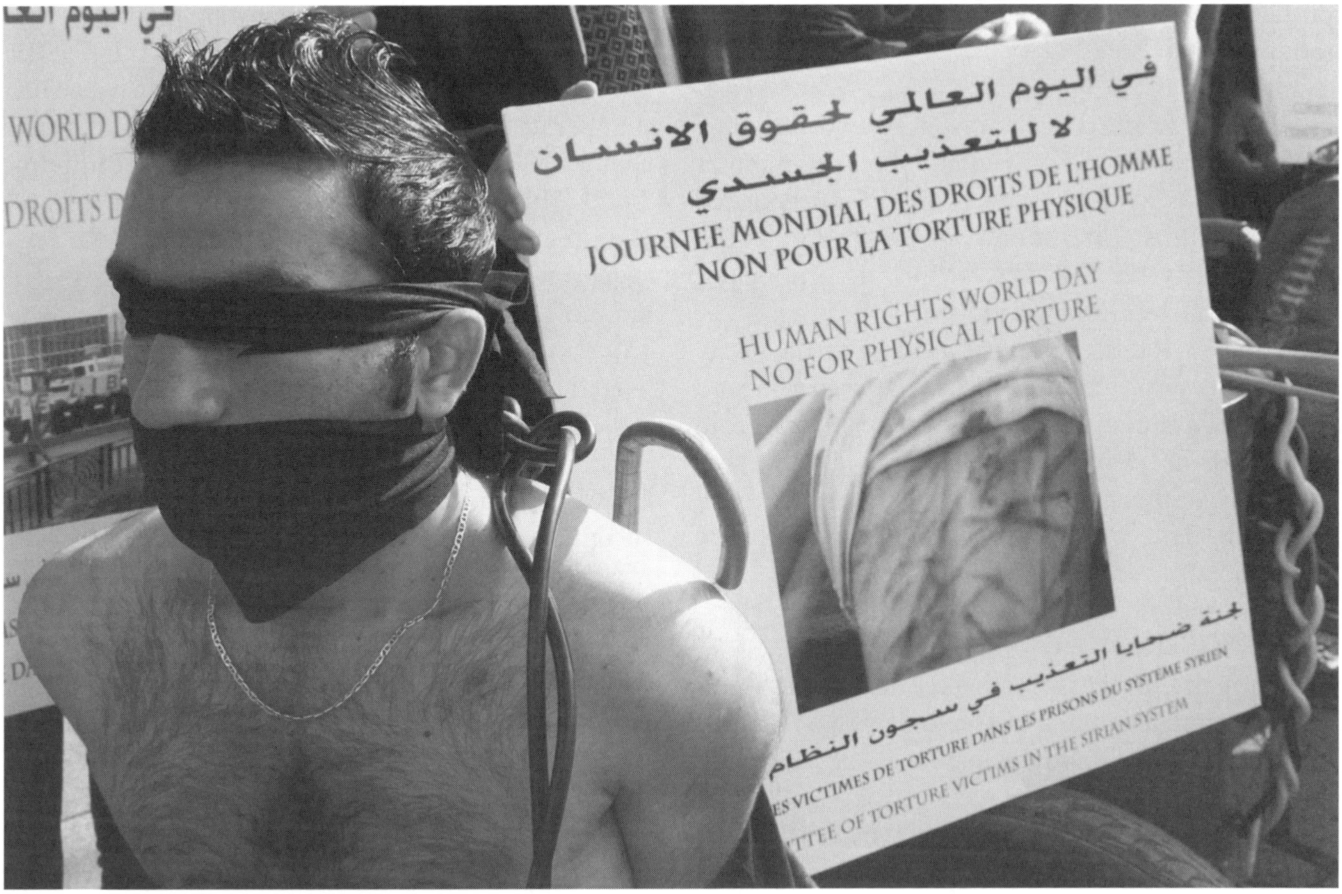

A blindfolded activist, opposed to the Syrian government, participates in a sit-in in Beirut, Lebanon, to protest Syria's use of torture on prisoners, December 10, 2009. The so-called Committee of Torture Victims in Syrian Prisons used props to illustrate the tools used by Syrian authorities to torture prisoners. Human rights groups have long accused Syria of torturing prisoners. (AP Photo/Bilal Hussein)

following World War I. Syria gained its independence in 1946 as a parliamentary republic, the Syrian Arab Republic. Civil, commercial, and criminal codes were promulgated in 1949, primarily based on French legal practices. Since then, the legal and judicial systems have been the resulting combination of these French and Ottoman traditions combined with Muslim sharia law and Arab tribal customs. Syria's ordinary courts operate in a three-tiered system under the auspices of the Ministry of Justice. Magistrate courts, courts of first instance, juvenile courts, and customs courts operate at the local level. There is also an intermediate tier of appeals courts. Above those, sits the Court of Cassation in Damascus, the highest court of appeal, which deals with disputes over jurisdiction and judicial matters. Syria also relies upon personal status courts based on sharia law to deal with family matters such as marriage, child custody, and divorce. The Druze and non-Muslim population have their own family courts.

The Baath Party's political dominance and its long-running conflict with Israel have greatly influenced the development of the country's criminal justice systems. Amid international conflict over Israel, Syria's two-year union with Nasser's Egypt ended in 1961. In 1963, the pan-Arab Baath Party seized power and has held it since. That same year, the regime instituted its Emergency Law, which suspended constitutional principles in the judicial systems when the executive deems it necessary to protect state security. The measure remains in effect today.

Although Syria is formally a parliamentary republic, in practice, it has not been so since the 1963 Baath seizure of power. The Baath Party dominates state and society, and power is highly concentrated among Baathist elites, drawn mainly from its Alawite minority sect, located within the presidency, cabinet ministers, and the military.

The 1973 Baathist Constitution vests the party with leadership functions in state and society and grants very broad powers to the president. From 1970 until his death in 2000, Hafez al-Asad was president, and his young son assumed power upon his death. True opposition parties are prohibited, and officially recognized non-Baath parties must vow to support the Baathist constitutional principles of "socialism" and "Arab nationalism."

Although the Constitution does not declare Islam to be the state religion, it does mandate that the president be a Muslim, and Islamic jurisprudence is the main source of legislation. A civil society with independent associations and political parties is almost nonexistent. Citizens have no right to peacefully assemble because all organizations much be licensed, and all nonreligious meetings must be registered in advance. Both requests are regularly denied.

As analysts at the American-based Freedom House observe, the problem of civil and political rights in Syria, given the nature of both political power and cultural traditions, is particularly pronounced for both women and minorities. Both groups face systemic discrimination. Although the Constitution grants women full participation in Syrian life, in practice they lack any meaningful legal or organizational protective measures. The nation's largest minority group, the Kurds, is also severely marginalized.

The regular police forces are organized within the Ministry of Interior. The emergency police operate through roving patrols and respond to 911 calls. The local neighborhood police deal with nonemergency community problems. There are also traffic and riot control police departments. But Syria's well-developed security forces are what really define Syrian criminal justice and social life more generally.

The Political Security Directorate (PSD), Syrian Military Intelligence (SMI), General Intelligence Directorate (GID), and Air Force Security (AFS) all operate independently. Only the PSD is formally under civilian control via the Ministry of Interior. Yet the 1963 Emergency Law remains in effect, and thus the minister presides as the president's delegated martial law governor. Under the permanent state of emergency, all citizens are subject to arbitrary arrest, detention, or exile.

Syria also relies on an exceptional security court system outside the ordinary courts. Accountable only to the minister of interior, these extra-constitutional courts are controlled by military officials according to military dictates. The Economic Security Court (ESC) hears cases involving economic crimes, and the Supreme State Security Court (SSSC) hears those dealing with national security.

These security courts and police forces have long contributed to the very poor human rights situation in Syria. Syria emerged from its long political isolation in 2008 when it was visited by a French presidential delegation. But as Amnesty International (AI) and Human Rights Watch (HRW) report, Syria still has a very grave human rights record marked by strict censorship, harassment of human rights activists, warrantless and arbitrary arrests, prolonged detention without trial, torture in detention, fundamentally unfair trials in the security courts, and a largely corrupt and inefficient police and judiciary.

Crime

The Syrian penal code was promulgated in 1949. At the local level, peace courts deal with minor law violations, while the courts of first instance deal with more serious crimes. Syria appears to have a low murder rate. According to the Ninth UN Survey of Crime Trends and Operations of Criminal Justice Systems, Syria had just 212 completed, intentional homicides in 2004, which is about 1.14 per 100,000 civilians. The U.S. State Department regards Syria as a low-crime country but warns that certain crimes such as ATM fraud, credit card theft, and the physical harassment of women appear to be rising.

The penal code affords women special protection from verbal and physical harassment and violence perpetrated by men. Rape is a felony punishable by at least 15 years' imprisonment. Prostitution is illegal, yet it is not considered to be widespread.

Still, women's rights advocates strongly criticize both Syrian laws and criminal justice authorities for regularly unequally protecting women. Although Syria has ratified the Covenant to Eliminate All Forms of Discrimination against Women (CEDAW) in 2003, it has done so with numerous serious reservations, and the penal code, Personal Status Act, and National Act are all said to have discriminatory provisions warranting repeal.

Under article 508 of the penal code, rapists can have their charges dropped if they marry their victims. Victims cannot effectively refuse since because families generally pressure them to agree so as to avoid public scandal. As well, so-called honor killings are tolerated. Article 548 of the penal code allows prosecutors to exempt offenders from further prosecution when they have killed their own female relatives whom they believe have had sex without their permission. When offenders are prosecuted, article 192 allows judges to reduce penalties for "honor" killings from the minimum 15 years' imprisonment to a maximum of 1 year.

Adultery is a crime, but here too genders are dealt with unequally. Evidentiary standards for proving female adultery are lower than they are for male adultery, which must actually have occurred inside the marital home. Women are punished with from 3 months to 2 years' imprisonment, whereas men can receive just 1 month to 1 year.

The Personal Status Code dealing with family and inheritance issues regards women as legal dependents of their male relatives, denying them full adult status in cases involving marriage, divorce, and child custody disputes. This customary status with respect to sharia law influences their status elsewhere even though they are formally entitled to equal status under the civil and criminal law.

Although abortion is criminalized in the penal code, marital rape is not, and there are no laws protecting women against domestic violence. According to Freedom House, there are no reliable statistics measuring these crimes. Male-dominated police departments, influenced by traditional customs, strongly discourage women from formally complaining and pursing arrests.

Indeed, nongovernmental organizations dedicated to women's rights are usually denied official licenses needed to operate independently, and it was not until 2007 that one was able to open the country's first hotline for abused women. A year later, the country opened its first officially licensed shelter for battered and abused women. Syria also has not ratified the UN Trafficking in Persons Protocol, and there is concern that the country is a destination and transit country in this trade. Critics assert that authorities have largely failed to deal with the problem, instead arresting, prosecuting, and deporting victims.

Although it does not appear to be a particularly serious problem in Syria, officials mete out severe penalties for drug crime. Drug possession is punishable with heavy fines or imprisonment. The death penalty may be meted out for growing, processing, and smuggling. However, this can be reduced to a minimum of 20 years' imprisonment.

Given its ongoing conflicts with Israel, as well as those in Lebanon and Iraq, Islamic terrorism is a concern. Syria has entered into several antiterrorism conventions. The penal code also imposes severe penalties of 15 to 20 years' imprisonment at hard labor for terrorism convictions. Thos convicted of engaging in terrorist acts that cause deaths through the destruction of buildings or vehicles are to be executed.

Finding of Guilt

Arrest procedures for most ordinary offenses are processed similarly to those in Western countries. Arrestees are processed and detained until trial dates are set. However, military prosecutors decide whether civilian defendants will be tried in the civilian courts or the military security courts. When civilian defendants go to the ordinary courts, investigating magistrates decide what cases go to trial.

Defendants have the right to be presumed innocent. They are also to have public trials except for juvenile and sex offense cases. They also have the right to choose their own attorneys, and courts appoint attorneys to defend indigent clients. At trial, defendants have the right to submit evidence and challenge their accusers. This former French mandate does not have jury trials. Judges preside and render verdicts. Convicts can appeal, but these tend to be difficult to win because courts do not keep verbatim transcripts, instead relying on presiding judges to summarize trial proceedings.

There do not appear to be reliable official statistics enumerating the number of Syrian court officials such as prosecutors and judges. The Baathist Constitution has included provisions, such as those in articles 131 and 133, formally guaranteeing judicial independence, making them autonomous and subject only to the law. However, the president clearly has great power in both the formulation and the implementation of law.

Circumstances are different with the extraordinary security courts, the SSSC and the ESC. Both military courts operate under the state of emergency, and neither acknowledges usual constitutional due process rights. Neither is independent of Baathist executive authority. As well, the military reportedly operates field courts outside of established courtroom locations, where it is believed that even fewer procedural rights are observed than in established security court sites.

Human rights observers continue to condemn these extra-constitutional courts for their persecution of political dissidents and severe human rights abuses. These courts combine with various suppressive laws that the authorities use to criminally charge political dissenters with "scheming with a foreign country, or communicating with one to incite it to initiate aggression against Syria" or belonging to a "secret organization," "publishing false news," " inciting sectarian strife," "broadcasting of false news," "taking action or making a written statement or speech which could endanger the state or harm its relationship with a foreign country, or expose it to the risk of hostile action," or simply "insulting the president." Authorities often prosecute and punish a wide range of individual behavior and group affiliations under these provisions in these courts systems.

According to HRW, authorities have tried thousands of people under these emergency conditions. These often have been communists, pan-Arab Nasserites, Iraqi Baathists, and most commonly, members of the banned Muslim Brotherhood. Those affiliated with Al Qaeda and individuals wishing to enter Iraqi as jihadists are also arrested and tried. Syrian Kurds, who are often denied citizenship, even when they are born in Syria, are often criminalized for expressing their ethnic identities or aspirations toward nationhood. Independent regime critics such as bloggers, those operating censored Web sites, and members of activist groups have suffered warrantless arrests, travel bans, and incommunicado through the security systems.

Although the penal code prohibits torture, it remains a standard practice that security services use to extract "confessions." Further, Syrian officials are actually legally protected from criminal prosecution for crimes they commit while on the job. If torture victims can identify their torturers, they must themselves file civil lawsuits against the perpetrators. Naturally, these fail.

Moreover, Syria has been a junior partner to the American government's so-called rendition program. In this program, American operatives abduct suspected "terrorists" and then deliver them to regimes such as Syria's, where security services hold them incommunicado and torture "confessions" from them. HRW documented Syria's involvement in at least 39 cases in 2007, one of which was the well-publicized case of Canadian Maher Arar.

Syrian agents have caused the "disappearances" of an unknown number of persons since the early 1980s. Despite official denial, human rights groups contend that there have been some 17,000 such "disappearances," mostly members of the Muslim Brotherhood and Syrian activists, but also many Lebanese citizens and stateless Palestinians. AI reports that when the security courts do try detainees, trials are fundamentally unfair, falling far short of international human rights standards.

Lawyers in security courts are forced to serve only "ceremonial" roles despite their competence or effort because they are denied access to their clients until the last minute and are only then allowed an extremely brief opportunity to learn about their cases. Judges regularly shout defendants down before summarily rendering their verdicts based on little or no evidence. Appeals are not allowed. In 2009, HRW counted 153 of what it calls "sham trials" since January 2007 and has called for the elimination of Syria's security courts. Some individuals have been detained for more than 20 years without trial, and Middle East Watch has concluded that fundamental reforms are needed if fair trials are ever going to be guaranteed in Syria.

Punishment

Apart from typical punishments such as fines and imprisonment, Syrian authorities retain, and use, the death penalty. It is available for such crimes as drug trafficking and terrorism. The penal code actually calls for the death penalty for members of the banned Muslim Brotherhood. According to Syrian journalist and death penalty abolitionist Nedal Naeiseh, this provision was introduced in 1980 after bloody clashes with the group. But now the law has been semi-suspended, with members instead receiving prison sentences.

Still, public hangings occur. AI reports that in 2007, for example, at least five persons were publicly hanged, and two of them were juveniles. They were reportedly hanged after unfair trials in field military courts without legal representation or appeal. The media reported that they had committed "various murders, and armed robberies, and had terrorized innocent citizens."

Syria appears to have a relatively small prison population and low prison rate. According to statistics provided by the Eighth World Prison Population List, Syria had a prison population of 10,599 in 2004, for a rate of 57 prisoners per 100,000 civilians. Pretrial or remand prisoners represent about half of the prisoner population. Females and foreigners make up 7.4 percent and 7.3 percent, respectively. There are separate facilities for men, women, and juveniles, although some juveniles have been incarcerated with adults.

The official prison system capacity of the 35 penal institutions is estimated to be 16,161. If true, this would make Syria unusual for having a prison system that is actually well *under* capacity when so many countries' prison systems are *over* capacity. But there are conflicting reports that cast doubt on official estimates. The International Committee of the Red Cross (ICRC) has reported that Syrian prisons are actually very overcrowded and face a shortage of beds. Syrian officials no longer allow the ICRC to inspect their prisons.

The Syrian Human Rights Committee asserts that the largest prison, Adra prison in Damascus, actually handles up to 10,000 prisoners despite being built in 1987 to house just 5,000. Further, despite being meant to house ordinary-crime convicts, Adra holds many political prisoners, mainly Muslim Brotherhood members, leftists, Palestinians, Islamist militants, and detained Syrian army soldiers.

HRW considers Syrian political prisoners to be "some of the most isolated in the world" in that they mostly have no contact at all with their families and suffer incarceration entombed inside windowless underground cells or crammed into giant communal cell blocks covered with open-mesh roofs, all while security services refuse to even acknowledge that they are in custody. This continues despite periodic amnesties in which many prisoners are released to commemorate Baathist national anniversaries. Inadequate medical care is also problematic, as is the severe restriction on politically sensitive literature including the Muslim Koran.

The penal code prohibits the use of corporal punishment. Yet it remains a disciplinary tool inside prisons. Forced labor also has been reported. The Syrian Human Rights Committee (SHRC) contends that prison officials use multiple methods of torture with impunity though it is illegal.

Tadmor (Palmyra) Prison had been particularly infamous for its frequent "extremely brutal abuses" since 1980. According to the SHRC, it was the site of the massacre of 1,000 Islamist prisoners on June 27, 1980. Since then, many political prisoners have been coerced into signing statements repudiating their past political activities as a condition of their being released. Thousands are believed to have been systematically murdered at Tadmor over the years.

Former Syrian defense minister Mustafa Talas told a German newspaper that he had ordered the murder of 150 Islamists *per week* for many years.

Although Tadmor closed in 2001, there are reasons to remain skeptical that human rights conditions inside Syria's prisons will improve. According to the Arab Organization for Human Rights, Abdul Karim Dhaon, an official at the Ministry of Health, wrote a report documenting the poor prison conditions. He was summarily arrested and imprisoned.

Paul Schupp

Further Reading

Amnesty International: http://www.amnestyusa.org.

Freedom House: http://www.freedomhouse.org.

Human Rights Watch: http://www.hrw.org.

The Jurist: http://jurist.law.pitt.edu.

Tunisia

Legal System: Civil/Islamic
Murder: Medium
Burglary: High
Corruption: Medium
Prison Rate: High
Death Penalty: Maybe
Corporal Punishment: No

Background

The Republic of Tunisia is located in the northernmost part of the African continent. It is surrounded by the Mediterranean Sea on the north and the east, by Libya on the south, and by Algeria on the west. The population of Tunisia is around 10 million, and Arabic and French are the major languages. This African nation is one of the smallest North African countries and also one of the richest. Politically, Tunisia is a multiparty, parliamentary democracy with a republican form of government. The Constitution of Tunisia was established in 1957, and it went through major amendments in 1998. The Tunisian legal system is based on French civil law and Islamic law.

The president is the chief of the executive branch of the state, and also the head of the state. The president is elected for a term of five years and can be reelected twice consecutively. The president has to be a Muslim and has to have been a Tunisian national for at least three generations. Other components of the executive office include the prime minister and members of the Cabinet. The Tunisian legislative branch consists of a unicameral Chamber of Deputies (Majlis al-Nuwaab), of 189 seats, and the Chamber of Advisors, which consists of 126 members. All members of the Chamber of Deputies are elected by popular votes and serve five-year terms. Eighty five members of the Chamber of Advisors are elected by municipal counselors, deputies, mayors, and professional associations and trade unions. The remaining 41 members are presidential appointees. All members of the Chamber of Advisors serve six-year terms.

The third branch of the government in Tunisia is the judiciary. The Constitution of Tunisia provides for an independent judiciary, though the president and the executive branch of the government can influence the judiciary. The president is the head of the Supreme Council of Judges. The executive branch appoints the judges. The court system consists of the civil and criminal courts and includes district courts, courts of first instance, courts of appeal, and the Court of Cassation. The district courts are the base of the Tunisian judicial structure, hearing civil cases of lesser value, and there are 51 of them. In these courts, a single judge hears the cases. The courts of first instance serve as the appellate courts for the district courts. Each region of Tunisia has a court of first instance, and it is composed of a panel of three judges. These courts hear all civil and commercial cases from small claims to claims involving large sums of money. The function of the courts of appeal is to serve as appellate courts for decisions made in the courts of first instance.

The Court of Cassation, or the Supreme Court, is the ultimate court of appeal in Tunisia. The High Court in Tunisia is above the Court of Cassation and is used to prosecute members of the government accused of high treason. Conflicts between the citizens and the state and public authorities are resolved at the Council of the State. There are also military tribunals within the Defense Ministry that try cases involving military personnel and civilians accused of national security crimes. A military tribunal consists of a civilian judge from the Supreme Court and four military judges.

Both the civil and the criminal court in Tunisia are influenced by the French system of judiciary and by Islamic law. The sharia courts were abolished in 1956, and since then, Tunisia has a unified judiciary structure. There has been a steady reform of Islamic legislations, such as abolishing polygamy, in Tunisia.

Police and Law

The police and the paramilitary National Guard are responsible for internal security in Tunisia. The police system operates in the capital city of Tunis and in few other urban areas. In the areas that are outside the urban areas, the police share or transfer their policing duties to the National Guard. Both the police and the National Guard are under the control of the president and the Ministry of Interior. The security forces in Tunisia have come under tremendous criticism because of allegations of human rights abuse, particularly in their involvement in suppressing speeches that are considered to be antigovernment or promoting ideas of terrorism. Freedom of expression is widely curtailed by the police, and there is also a special team of cyber police that monitors Web content.

As discussed previously, Tunisian law is based on French legal code and on Islamic law. From the time of independence in 1956, Tunisian law has promoted equality between men and women legally. The Code of Personal Status is a series of progressive laws that were introduced during that period and further reinforced by the amendments in 1993.

Tunisia was one of the first Arab nations to give equal rights to women. Polygamy along with prostitution is illegal in the nation, and women are guaranteed equal rights with men in matters of suffrage, marriage, and divorce. Women can also be elected members of the Chamber of Deputies in the legislative branch of the government.

Lesbian, gay, bisexual, and transgendered individuals face criminal prosecution in Tunisia. Under article 230 of the penal code, modified in 1964, individuals can face up to three years in prison for practicing homosexuality.

Tunisia established the Code for the Protection of Children in 1995 to strengthen laws on child abuse, abandonment, and exploitation of children. Even though child labor is banned in Tunisia, children are employed in the handicraft industry and as domestic help. Tunisia does not have a juvenile justice system, and corporal punishment is prohibited in the penal system. However, it is permitted in schools and at homes.

Crime

The crime rate in 2000 was 520.96 per 100,000 population. The homicide rate was 1.18, the rate of rape was 3.49, and the burglary rate was 80.31. According to the annual crime surveys, the rate for some index crimes—major assaults, rape, and burglaries—decreased between 1995 and 2000 in Tunisia. However, the rate for homicides has increased in recent years.

Drugs

Tunisia has no national survey data on drug abuse. The country is a part of all international drug conventions. There are no reports of significant production of drugs, and the government of Tunisia has claimed that it irradiated the production of cannabis. However, because of its strategic geographical location, Tunisia is high on the list for potential transit trafficking for cannabis to Europe, from its production center in Morocco. According to the United Nations Office on Drugs and Crime, there are reports that trafficking of heroin from Libya is also increasing in the country. However, because of the lack of data on drugs in Tunisia, these reports cannot be fully substantiated.

To control for drug-related corruption, Tunisia's 1992 drug law provides for sentences to be doubled if the drug enforcement officials, individuals involved in the administration and security of drug warehouses, are involved in drug crimes.

Finding of Guilt

The criminal court system in Tunisia is very similar in structure to the civil court system. Misdemeanor offenses are handled by the district courts, and all other criminal offenses, except felonies, are submitted to the courts of first instance for determination. Felony crimes are first heard by a grand jury. Felony crimes are submitted to the criminal courts division of the appeals courts after an indictment has been issued by a judge based on the findings of the grand jury (Chambre dMises en Accusation). Once a judge issues an indictment based on the grand jury proceedings, the case is submitted to the criminal court division of the appeals court. The criminal division of the Court of Cassation serves as the final appellate court for criminal matters. There is also a system of military tribunals with jurisdiction over military personnel and crimes related to national sovereignty.

The penal code of Tunisia prohibits the use of torture and other cruel and inhumane forms of punishment. However, human rights activists have reported that security forces in Tunisia, both the police and the paramilitary, have used coercive force to make detainees confess. According to Amnesty International, the courts in Tunisia are notorious for ignoring investigations of allegations of torture and mistreatment. The courts have also accepted confessions extracted under torture as evidence.

The government of Tunisia responded to the concerns of the United Nations and Amnesty International by amending the penal code. In 1999, it adopted the UN definition of torture and reinstated the rights of the detainees, such as medical rights and maximum detention period. However, these amendments are seldom followed in reality.

The police do not need warrants to arrest on charges of suspicions or for crimes in progress. Thus, arbitrary arrests and detentions that result from them are problems. Because of the penal code amendment in 1999, the maximum that an individual can be detained is three days, and the detainment can be renewed only once by the prosecutor, for a maximum of six days. The new amendment also required the arresting officers to inform the detainees and their family members of their rights. However, as mentioned before, the new amendment on the rights of detainees has often been ignored in reality, in the context of both common criminals and political detainees.

By law, the accused has the right to be present at trial, to be represented by counsel, to question the witness, and to appeal. Accused persons also have the right to request a trial in a different judge's court if they believe that the judge is not impartial. However, human rights activists have claimed that the judicial system in Tunisia is not fair, and sentences are harsher for defendants charged for political crimes. Human Rights Watch indicates that there is no definitive information regarding the number of political prisoners and that the number could be in the thousands.

Punishment

Overcrowding in prisons is a serious problem in Tunisia, with 40 to 50 prisoners typically placed in a single cell that is less than 200 square feet. Prison conditions are very poor, with serious sanitation problems, and do not meet international standards. For political prisoners, the conditions are much worse.

The government of Tunisia does not permit international organizations or the media to visit the prisons. In 2001, the government showed some interest in introducing prison reforms and transferred the authority of the prison system to the Ministry of Justice. However, there are no significant changes in the conditions of prisoners at the time of this writing. According to the Centre for Prison Studies, Kings College, London, Tunisia had 263 prisoners per 100,000 population in 2008.

Soma Chaudhuri

Further Reading

African Child Policy Forum. (2008). *The African Report on Child Wellbeing 2008: Tunisia:* http://www.africanchildinfo.net/site/.

Touchen, Dahmène,(2002). *Feature: A Guide to the Tunisian Legal System:* http://www.llrx.com/features/tunisia.htm.

United Nations Office on Drugs and Crime. Tunisia: http://www.unodc.org/egypt/en/country_profile_tunisia.html.

United Arab Emirates (UAE)

Legal System: Islamic/Common
Murder: Low
Corruption: Low
Human Trafficking: Medium
Prison Rate: High
Death Penalty: Yes
Corporal Punishment: Yes

Background

The United Arab Emirates consists of land and many islands in the Persian Gulf covering an area of about 51,460 square miles. It is bounded on the west and south by Saudi Arabia and on the west by Qatar. Toward its eastern border, it is bound by Oman. It has about 404 miles of coastline on the northern border that faces the Persian Gulf and the Gulf of Oman.

According to a 2009 estimate, the population is projected to be 5.06 million. Only about 19 percent of these are Emiratis; about 81 percent of the residents of UAE are non-Emiratis. This group of non-Emiratis consists of Arabs and non-Arabs. The Arabs consist of Palestinians, Egyptians, Jordanians, Yemenis, and Omanis. The non-Arab groups consist of Indians, Pakistanis, Bangladeshis, Afghanis, Iranians, Filipinos, and West Europeans. According to 2006 data, the nation has a workforce of 2.97 million, of which 93 percent of the workers are foreign, ranging in age from 15 to 64 years. Out of the UAE population, 3.08 million are males, and 1.4 million are females, according to the 2007 data. The 2009 estimate projects this to be 3.5 million males and 1.58 million females.

Political Context

Originally, each of the seven emirates of the UAE had separate treaty relationships with Britain and were referred to as the Trucial states until 1971; the British withdrew by the end of 1971, and six of the sheikhdoms came together to form the UAE on December 2, 1971; the seventh sheikhdom, Ras al Khaimah, acceded to the union in February 1972.

Government

From an administrative point, the country is composed of a loose federation of seven self-governing city-states—Abu Dhabi, Ras al-Khaimah, Dubai, Ajman, Fujairah, Sharjah, and Umm al-Quwain—with each having its own ruler. The government of the UAE consists of a federation of these seven emirates. As per the Constitution of December 2, 1971, each individual emirate retains considerable powers, including control over mineral rights (such as gas and oil) and revenues. Under this arrangement, federal powers have developed gradually. According to the Constitution, the president is the head of the state, and the president and vice president each serve five-year terms. The prime minister is the head of the government and is assisted by a Council of Ministers, a supreme council of rulers, and a 40-member Federal National Council (FNC). The FNC functions as a consultative body and has half its members elected and the other half appointed by the emirate rulers.

The political and financial power of each emirate is reflected in the provision of positions that are allotted in the federal government. Because the emirate of Abu Dhabi is the biggest oil producer, its ruler acts as the president of the UAE. The emirate of Dubai is the commercial center, and as such, its ruler is the vice president and prime minister. Each emirate retains substantial autonomy, although a significant percentage of each emirate's revenues is supposed to be devoted to the central budget of the UAE.

There are no political parties in the UAE, and the rulers exercise their powers based on their dynastic positions, and their legitimacy is obtained through a system of tribal consensus. As a result of modernization, advances in education, and the huge influx of the foreign population, there have been profound changes in the society. Limited elections, for the first time, were held in December 2006 to select half the members of the Federal National Council. As a result of these elections, there were significant gains for women. One woman was elected to the FNC, and seven other women were appointed as council members.

According to the Constitution, Arabic is the official language, and Islam is the official religion of the UAE. It also lists the fundamental rights and liberties of its citizens. The Constitution delineates a separation of powers between the executive, legislative, and judicial branches of the United Arab Emirates. There is a further separation of executive and judicial powers into federal and local jurisdictions. Some powers are exclusively reserved for the federal government, and the individual sheikhdoms exercise the residual powers.

In 1984, the separation of powers remained nominal, given that the Supreme Council of the Union (SCU) functioned as the highest federal authority in the legislative and executive capacities. The executive branch is made up of the SCU, the Council of Ministers, and the presidency. The SCU consists of the rulers of the seven emirates. This union elects from among its members a chairman and vice chairman, who both serve five-year terms. The SCU is responsible for the formulation of general policy, for the ratification of federal laws and decrees such as the annual budget and fiscal agreements, and for consent to the appointment of the prime minister and Supreme Court judges. The chairman of the SCU is the president of the UAE and also the head of state. The chairman also officiates as the supreme commander of the federation in the capacity as chairman of the Supreme Defense Council. The president convenes the SCU and appoints the prime minister, deputy prime minister, cabinet ministers, and other civil and military officials. The president also has the power to proclaim martial law. The Federal National Council (FNC) is below the Constitution. The FNC is the main legislative authority; however, its main role in the governmental process is limited to consultation. The ruler of each emirate appoints its members for two-year terms. For purposes of administrative implementation, the laws of the UAE are divided into two major categories: union law and decrees. Bills that are drafted by the Council of Ministers for deliberation by the FNC and then submitted to the president for assent and the SCU for ratification become union law upon promulgation by the president. Decrees are issued jointly by the president and the Council of Ministers between the sessions of the SCU.

The federal judicial system that was established under the Constitution has both a Supreme Court and a lower court. The president, with the approval of the federal supreme council, appoints the judges.

Division of Powers

According to article 120 of the Constitution, the federal government has exclusive legislative and executive jurisdiction over foreign affairs, national defense, internal security, federal finances and taxes, communications, highways and aviation, nationality, education, public health, public information, the census, currency, electric power, and weights and measures. The Constitution also assigns the federal government responsibility for legislation on labor relations; social security; banks; the penal code; civil and criminal proceedings in courts; printing and publications; copyrights; the protection of cultural, technical, and industrial property; the delimitation of territorial waters; and navigation of the high seas.

Crime

Legal System—Judiciary

As per article 94 of the Constitution, citizens are guaranteed an independent judiciary under the aegis of the Supreme Court of the Union. This body consists of a president and no more than five

The Dubai Courts in Dubai, United Arab Emirates, where a British couple accused of public indecency is to be tried, September 9, 2008. The couple is accused of having sex on a Dubai beach. (AP Photo/Aziz Shah)

judges who are appointed by the UAE president, upon approval from the SCU. The Supreme Court has been vested with the power of judicial review and original jurisdiction for adjudicating cases involving federal-emirate matters as well as disputes between emirates. The court also has been empowered to try cases of official misconduct that involve cabinet and other senior federal officials. There is also a provision for the establishment of union courts of the first instance to handle certain civil, commercial, criminal, and administrative cases; judgments from these courts are appealable to the Supreme Court. The local courts in each of the emirates have jurisdiction over areas that have not specifically been allotted to the union courts in the Constitution. In 1978, judicial authority was formally transferred from the emirates to the federal government.

According to the Constitution, sharia is the basis of all legislation. Legal codes are based on the sharia. There are four major schools of Islamic law—Hanafi, Shafii, Maliki, and Hanbali—and three of these four are present in the societies of the UAE. The majority of the indigenous population adheres to the Maliki legal school, but many of the residents of Fujairah observe the teachings of the Shafii school, and nearly one-half of the population of the city of Al Ayn are Wahhabis and therefore follow the precepts of the Hanbali school of law. According to observers, the belief is that if and when a legal code is adopted, it will conform to the Maliki school but will not be objectionable to the adherents of the other sects. During the 1980s, the judicial procedures were based on a synthesis of Anglo-Saxon, civil (European), and Islamic models. Many of the magistrates were Egyptian nationals.

Drug Trafficking

On account of laws that came into effect in January 1996, those convicted of drug trafficking are liable to get the death penalty. After January 2006, possession of even small amounts of illegal drugs has resulted in prison sentences of up to four years for foreign nationals who are transiting the UAE. Drugs normally taken under a doctor's prescription in the United States and even some of the common over-the-counter medications in the United States are regarded as narcotics in the UAE and are illegal to possess. A person is liable to arrest and prosecution if possession of medicines comes to the attention of the authorities. Poppy seeds are also on the list of controlled substances, and their possession and importation are strictly prohibited. Individuals who are found to possess even small quantities of controlled substances are subject to prosecution and liable to imprisonment for up to 15 years.

Terrorism

Laws were enacted in 2004 to criminalize the funding of terrorist organizations. On account of the law, the time that public prosecutors could hold terrorism suspects without charge was extended from 21 days to 6 months. Terrorism cases are referred to the Federal Supreme Court, which can extend the detention period indefinitely. In 2006, a cyber-crime law was passed to criminalize the use of the Internet to either promote terrorist ideologies or finance terrorist activities. The Dubai Ports Authority was the first Middle Eastern port to join in the U.S. Homeland Security Container Security Initiative in 2004. This program is aimed at preventing materials that could be used by terror groups from entering the United States in shipping containers. Pursuant to this program, U.S. customs officers and the Dubai Customs Intelligence Unit jointly screen suspicious cargo transiting Dubai's ports that are bound for the United States. To prevent money laundering for terrorist purposes, legislation was adopted in 2002 to give the Central Bank the power to freeze any suspected account for seven days without prior legal permission. All banks have also been cautioned to carefully scrutinize transactions that pass through the UAE from Pakistan and Saudi Arabia.

Human Trafficking

The trafficking of girls and women, to be eventually used as prostitutes and domestic servants, and of men, to be used as servants, laborers, and unskilled workers, continues in spite of promises by the government to end these practices. A federal law was enacted (UAE Federal Law 51 of 2006) to criminalize and combat human trafficking. Article 16 of the law lays down stiff penalties against traffickers that may range from one year to life in prison and fines of up to $275,000. This law was also specifically aimed at criminalizing the use of persons under age 18 as camel jockeys. Between 2005 and 2006, more than a thousand children who were identified by the UAE and the United Nations as victims of trafficking were repatriated to their home countries. There are social support and human rights offices in all police departments in the UAE to assist female and child victims of abuse. However, there is a perception that the government is not effective in protecting women from abuse.

Finding of Guilt

Court Structure

On account of its federal structure, the United Arab Emirates is unique in the Arab world. As of 1971, most judicial structures remained primarily at the emirate rather than federal level. In 1973, a Supreme Federal Court was created, and in 1978, some judicial matters were transferred from member emirates to that court. In 1983, a comprehensive law governing the federal judiciary was passed, creating a full-fledged federal judicial system. However, the member emirates retain significant and varying degrees of judicial autonomy. Laid on top of this federal structure is another distinction between civil and sharia judiciary. This gives the UAE quite an intricate judicial structure. There are two networks of civil court systems in the UAE: the federal system and the local systems. Although most emirates have given up civil jurisdiction from the local to the federal level, there are networks of sharia courts that still operate in each emirate. The federal court system has three levels: primary courts, appeals courts, and the Supreme Court. This system was set up on a framework proposed by the judiciary itself. The provisions of the UAE Constitution did not delineate how the federal system could establish a structure of federal courts beyond the Federal Supreme Court. The Ministry of Justice requested direction from the Federal Supreme Court regarding interpretation of the Constitution. The interpretation that was offered by the court paved the way for the three-tiered federal court system. The local systems are much older; they date back to the pre-independence era and in some cases even earlier. The local court systems generally consisted of two kinds of courts: sharia courts and rulers' courts. The sharia courts mostly operate on the assumption that they have general jurisdiction like the Saudi courts. The courts of the rulers of the member emirates originated out of the belief that settling disputes was an integral part of governing. These courts were formalized to different degrees, with some being staffed by professional judges and operating on the basis of codified law.

After the establishment of the federal system, all but two emirates (Dubai and Ras al-Khaimah) opted to cede their jurisdiction over civil, criminal, and administrative cases. Sharia courts continue to function, however, throughout the UAE.

In spite of the absence of any codification of personal status issues, there is not much dispute that personal status cases are to be dealt with in accordance with the Islamic sharia, and the sharia courts therefore are the main court in personal status matters.

All across the UAE (with the partial exception of Abu Dhabi), the relationship between the sharia courts and the civil courts (local and federal) has not been clarified in legislative texts. This fact may lead to some overlap of jurisdiction, though civil courts accept the jurisdiction of sharia courts in personal status cases. Further, civil judges are required to rely on the sharia in the absence of clear legislative texts.

The law of the Federal Judicial Authority establishes the rules of the sharia among the sources of authority over judges. This reduces the potential for conflict between the two judicial systems.

Prosecution System

The *niyaba* system operates in UAE. As such, investigation and prosecution of crimes is considered to be a judicial function. The attorney general heads the *niyaba* and is supervised by the Ministry of Justice. Qualifications for a *niyaba* position are analogous to those for a judgeship. The attorney general and members of the niyaba are appointed by the president of the UAE upon nomination by the minister of justice.

Integration of Administration in the Emirates

The main principle on which the rulers of the United Arab Emirates envisioned the development of political institutions was based on the concept of functionalism as espoused by the political scientist Enver Khoury. It was defined as a process that commenced with the integration of some noncontroversial areas such as social services and communications within the federal framework. Khoury believed that with the gradual development of a national identity, the individual emirates would gradually cede control over more controversial administrative and political sectors to the central government. He postulated that when the proposed federal system gained more responsibilities and power in the economic, social, and technical fields, this would lead to an enhancement of the political integration. There was an assumption that there would be convergence, due to functionalism, and not a growth of different identities. Up until the 1980s, this process of functionalism had reached a stage where crucial federal institutions such as the central bank and the central judicial structure had been set up. However, because of the rivalries and suspicions between the emirates, this process of integration has not gone any further. There were questions about the benefits of functionalism. Some of the emirates sought to opt for a restricted federalism wherein each of the emirates held on to its independence.

Interpretation of the Law

Article 7 of the UAE Constitution is referred to as the Constitutional Clause, and it deals with the position of sharia within the state legal system. According to the legislature, it is the theoretical basis for the Islamization of laws. However, this clause is ambiguous because it is amenable to varying juristic interpretations and has created tension and uncertainty within the state legal system and undermines its unification. With respect to interpretation of the Constitutional Clause, Arab jurists and legal commentators fall into two different camps—the Islamists and the Liberals. According to the Islamists, this clause elevates the sharia above all other sources of law. On the other hand, the liberals place the sharia on an equal footing with other sources of law. Though the Supreme Court has repeatedly held that recourse to Islamic sharia is a matter of policy within the purview of the federal legislature, the court has announced that all federal legislation should be derived from Islamic sharia. The court has adopted the position of the Islamists, according to which any legislation violating the sharia should be considered unconstitutional. Though there is strong evidence of an apparent conflict between the Constitution and the laws dealt with by the Supreme Court judgments, the court was reluctant to declare the laws unconstitutional. While interpreting and applying article 7 of the Constitution, the court distinguished between civil and criminal matters. While considering the legality of bank interest, the court considered the application of the sharia as a matter of policy to be left to the legislature, and not for the judiciary to decide. Regarding the application of the sharia in criminal matters, the court declared that the lower federal courts should apply the punishments prescribed by the sharia in *hadd* offenses. In practice, the UAE applies the sharia in the sphere of criminal matters only. It does not apply to commercial matters, especially with respect to commercial law. The sharia rules are applied regarding *hudud* offenses, but the sharia rules regarding bank interest are not. The reason for this seems to be a matter of practicality: the Supreme Court has stayed away from applying sharia where it would threaten orderly economic development and modernization of its institutions. However, the application of *hadd* punishments, by comparison, does not threaten any such disruption.

Sharia is the main source of law and applies to all family and criminal law matters. In criminal cases, the penal code is applied if the evidentiary standard required by sharia is insufficient. The UAE does not have a formal system for bail. Defendants are given legal counsel only after police have concluded their investigation. Though defendants are not guaranteed a speedy trial, they are entitled to a fair public trial and are presumed to be innocent until proven guilty. All trials are conducted before judges instead of juries. Trials that involve national security and issues involving public morality are heard only by the Federal Supreme Court and are not open to the public. There is an appeals process from all the courts. The military court system is used solely for trials of military personnel and is independent of the other courts.

Police

The police do not publish regular crime statistics. Police General Directorates throughout the emirates are supervised by the UAE Ministry of Interior. Each emirate maintains its own police force and is responsible for supervising its police stations. The total strength of the UAE police force is estimated to be 10,000 personnel. Police stations receive complaints from the public, make arrests, and transfer all cases to the public prosecutor, who forwards these cases to the courts for further processing. In 2007, the Ministry of the Interior announced plans to establish a new crime bureau, along with affiliated offices in the individual emirate police departments, to address problems such as money laundering, terrorism, and drug trafficking.

Human Rights

According to the annual report of the U.S. Department of State, the UAE has taken modest steps in the protection of human rights. However, there remain some concerns regarding many practices and policies. The UAE does not have democratically elected political parties or institutions. There are restrictions on free assembly and association, and the rights of workers are abused. However, this has been changing as a result of some high-level administrative reforms that got underway in 2004. Steps were taken to enhance public participation in government through the introduction of indirect elections to the country's parliament—the Federal National Council. Formerly, the 40 members of the FNC drawn from the seven emirates were appointed by the rulers. However, under these reforms, each ruler selected an electoral college for each emirate, with its members being at least 100 times the number of FNC members needed for each emirate (eight each for Abu Dhabi and Dubai, six each for Sharjah and Ras al-Khaimah, and four each for Fujairah, Ajman, and Umm al-Qaiwain). The respective electoral colleges were then tasked with electing half the FNC members, while the other half were appointed. This process got underway in 2006. In the resultant new FNC, there are 9 women out of a total of 40 members, representing 22.5 percent of the total.

Although the UAE Constitution guarantees freedom of speech and press freedom, in reality, these rights are limited. All publications are licensed by the government, and only approved editors are appointed. There are laws that regulate press content. Negative comments regarding Islam, the government, the ruling families, or UAE citizens by expatriates are punishable with imprisonment. Because the press normally practices self-censorship, this regulation rarely needs enforcement. With respect to cyberspace, the government restricts access to some Internet sites and also scrutinizes imported printed material for content. It places restrictions on the distribution of material that is considered to be excessively violent, pornographic, derogatory to Islam, or contrary to the foreign policy of the UAE government.

Punishment

Very strict punishments are meted out for morals offenses and violations of decency such as drug use, nudity, and gambling. The country has very strict drug laws with respect to illegal drugs/narcotics. There is very low tolerance for drug use. The standard minimum sentence for possession of drugs is incarceration for four years. Being increasingly concerned about illegal drugs in the mid-1990s, the UAE dramatically increased the penalties for smuggling, possessing, and using illegal drugs. This fact was illustrated in a high-profile case in 2001 when five Britons were arrested and tried on drug charges. Three of them were charged with importing drugs and faced the death penalty if found guilty. The group was charged with importing, possessing, and using cocaine and hashish. The case was heard in the sharia court of the traditional and conservative emirate of Ras al-Khaimah. Drinking or possessing alcohol without the requisite permit from the Ministry of the Interior also is illegal and subject to arrest and fines and/or imprisonment.

Open displays of affection are not permitted. Sexual activity outside of marriage is considered illegal in the UAE. In 2009, a British businesswoman was charged with having sex outside marriage, engaging in indecent behavior in public, and being drunk in public. Michelle Palmer was arrested in 2008 along with another Briton for having sex on a beach. She was faced with a sentence of up to six years in prison.

In another case in 2004, the police in the emirate of Sharjah arrested 61 Chinese men and women on charges of gambling. The group was arrested while they were engaged in casino-style gambling. This activity is illegal throughout the UAE. Not only were the members of the group liable to 2 years in prison or fines of up to $5,500 and deportation, but the tenant of the apartment was also liable to a punishment of up to 10 years in prison.

Prison

There is no information published regarding prisons or the number of prisoners in prisons in the UAE. According to the World Prison Population list, the prison population total in 1998 was 6,000, with a prison population rate of 250 per 100,000.

Farrukh B. Hakeem

Further Reading

Islamic Family Law: http://www.law.emory.edu/IFL.

Library of Congress. "United Arab Emirates" Country Studies—Federal Research Division:. http://lcweb2.loc.gov/frd/cs/cshome.html.

Official UAE Web site: http://uaeinteract.com.

Yemen

Legal System: Islamic/Civil/Common
Murder: Medium
Corruption: High
Human Trafficking: Medium
Prison Rate: Medium
Death Penalty: Yes
Corporal Punishment: Yes

Background

Located in the southwestern part of the Arabian Peninsula, Yemen comprises approximately 328,000 square miles of rugged, mountainous terrain in the north and coastal plains in the south. It is the poorest of the Arab countries and has a population of 22 million people, mostly Sunni Muslim, with a minority Shiite population in the north. Economically, the country relies on dwindling oil resources.

Historically, the country was split into north and south. The northern part of Yemen was part of the Ottoman Empire, and the south belonged to the British Empire beginning in the 19th century. In 1918, the north declared independence from the Ottomans and gradually became a republic, but the British remained in control of the south until 1967. In 1970, Marxists took over southern Yemen, and a civil war was waged between southern and northern Yemen, fueled by the Cold War. The Soviet Union backed the south, and the United States provided aid to the north. Yemen was subsequently unified in 1990.

Today, a low-level insurgency continues in the north, led by Shiites seeking to install a theocratic government. In August 2009, the government began an offensive against the Zaidi Shiite Houthi rebels in Saada and Amran provinces, involving airstrikes and artillery fire, killing many civilians.

Yemen is a constitutional republic and has a president and prime minister with a cabinet. There is a bicameral legislature made up of the Shura Council (appointed) and an elected House of Representatives. The Yemeni government is known for its corruption. At the same time, international observers note that the country has made substantial progress toward democracy and has cooperated with international efforts against terrorism.

Crime

Yemen's homicide rate averages 3 per 100,000 inhabitants yearly, according to information released by the National Statistical Office of Yemen in 2004. Crime is reportedly increasing each year in Yemen. According to statistics released by the Ministry of the Interior, 936 crimes were reported in the Sana'a governate in 2005, up 15 percent from the year before. Among the crimes, 307 were violent crimes. Experts believe that this grossly underrepresents the true figure of crime because nonreporting remains a problem. Two factors that the government believes contribute to the lack of reporting are the distance between police stations in rural areas and the public perception that the police will not do anything to help.

Because of the patriarchal nature of Yemeni society, many human rights experts have expressed concern over the prevalence of domestic violence. Among a sample of 111 women who live in Sana'a, one domestic violence victimization survey found that 50.9 percent of women had experienced verbal threats of violence from a male member of their family, and 54.5 percent had suffered physical abuse. In addition, 17.3 percent of the sample reported being sexually abused, and 28.2 percent had their freedom restricted. In 1996, according to official Yemeni records reported in the *International Review of Victimology,* 64 women were victims of shooting.

Yemen is known in the West as the site of the Al Qaeda bombing of the USS *Cole* in 2000, which killed 17 service personnel. In addition to Al Qaeda, there are two Yemen-based terrorist organizations operating in Yemen, the Islamic Jihad Movement and the Aden-Abyan Islamic Army. Other terrorist attacks in the country include a car bombing at the U.S. Embassy in Sana'a on September 17, 2008, which took 18 lives. In 2002, a French oil tanker was bombed, followed by the killing of foreign missionary doctors the same year. Yemeni extremists bombed a hotel in Aden in 1992, which killed a European tourist and a hotel employee.

Off the coast of Yemen, in the Gulf of Aden, pirates have been operating in increasing numbers. During the first half of that year, there were more than 40 attacks on other vessels, and 23 pirate vessels were seized by the government. In 2008, there were more than 60 attacks. Most often, the pirate vessels are from Somalia. Yemen's transportation minister announced that a regional center to combat piracy would be initiated in 2008 with the help of 20 other countries and the International Maritime Organization. A lack of naval and coast guard resources in Yemen has made it difficult for the country to protect against piracy activities. Problems with coordination of these efforts with the Yemeni army and policy have also been cited. Piracy in the Gulf of Aden has reportedly cost the country $350 million, including $200 million in losses taken by Yemeni fishermen who have stopped fishing in the pirate-infested waters for safety reasons. In addition, attempting to secure the Yemeni coastline has cost the government $150 million according to the *Yemen Post.*

Yemen is known for having the largest market for arms in the Middle East. It is estimated to have around 20 million guns within its borders. According to the Interior Ministry, 293,000 unregistered weapons were seized between July 2009 and August 2007, when a ban against carrying weapons was put in effect. Government corruption contributes to the viability of the burgeoning market that supplies arms to terrorist groups in the region, including Al Qaeda.

Kidnappings are relatively common. In the Saada governate in 2009, nine foreigners were kidnapped, and three were later found dead. The rest have not been found. Additionally, according to the U.S. Department of State, carjackings were on the rise in 2009.

It is traditional to chew khat leaves, a stimulant, in social settings. The drug is legal in Yemen but illegal in most other countries. An illegal market for marijuana and heroin is also present in Yemen.

Police

The Police Corps Act of 2000 states that the Yemeni police are intended to protect citizens' life and property; however, the national police force does not have control over all the rural spaces within Yemen. In some areas, tribal, customary forms of policing prevail, according to a report of the 2003 International Crisis Group.

Most major criminal investigations are handled by the Criminal Investigations Division (CID), which is housed in the Ministry of the Interior (MOI). Most high-ranking members of the ministry are related to, or tribally affiliated with, Yemen's president, Ali Abdullah Saleh. One wing of the MOI, which reports directly to the president, investigates government opposition leaders and has been criticized by human rights organizations. Yemen is a member of INTERPOL.

Yemen employs women as police officers and support staff as part of its mission to provide services to women and children. In 2000, policewomen numbered 1,476 and were represented among the ranks, although not at the highest rank of brigadier. The first policewomen were recruited into the national force in 1980. Yemen had 324 policewomen working in the capital, Sana'a, in 2000, including 59 who worked in the Ministry of Interior office, 46 in the supply office, 27 in civil affairs and registration, 26 in the women's prison, and 11 in the CID. Among their duties is acting as airport security screeners for women, interrogating women and children, liaising with INTERPOL, and completing the civil registration of women.

Legal System

Yemen's Constitution, ratified in 1991, provides for an independent judiciary. The judicial system is divided into three levels: first instance (*ibtida'iyya*), appeals, and the Supreme Court, located in Sana'a. The Supreme Court is a constitutional court in addition to being used for the adjudication of high officials and to handle election disputes and inter-jurisdictional court conflicts. There is also a separate military division of the court system. The executive branch's Supreme Judicial Council, whose members are appointed, exercises authority over other members of the judiciary.

Unlike many Arab Muslim countries, Yemen does not have a distinct personal status court. Cases of divorce and custody are heard in the general courts. There are, however, separate chambers within courts to hear juvenile criminal cases.

Journalism as Crime

Increasingly, journalists are being tried, convicted, and imprisoned for crimes related to writing articles that purportedly defame the government. Article 103 of the Press and Publications Law indicates that journalists must respect bans on the following:

> Anything which prejudices the Islamic faith and its lofty principles or belittles religions or humanitarian creeds; Anything which might cause tribal, sectarian, racial, regional or ancestral discrimination, or which might spread a spirit of dissent and division among people or call on them to apostatize; Anything which leads to the spread of ideas contrary to the principles of the Yemeni Revolution, prejudicial to the national unity or distorting the image of the Yemeni, Arab or Islamic heritage; and freedom of the individual by smears and defamation.

In 2009, the Supreme Judicial Council decided to set up a special court, the Press and Publications Court, for media-related cases. Members of the judiciary expressed concerned about the way the media was reporting on political violence in the south of the country, and seven newspapers were banned by the government that year. Journalists publicly protested the establishment of a separate court to try newspapers, publishers, and writers. Despite protests, the court tried its first case in July 2009. On July 15, 2009, Yemeni journalist Anis Mansour was sentenced to 14 months in prison for "separatism and attacking national unity" for his articles in the *Al-Ayyam* newspaper.

According to human rights reports, defense attorneys report regular unfair trials in which they do not have full access to the defendants' files. Some defendants have indicated that their confessions were obtained under torture.

Yemeni lawyers and judges are trained at the High Judicial Institute in addition to having law degrees. The institute, established in 1981, offers a three-year program in specialized and advanced legal training for practicing in Yemeni courts. There are female judges in Yemen, although the government has not released figures as to how many. In 2007, the Yemeni Parliament voted to ratify the International Criminal Court statute.

Punishment

In 2002, there were 14,000 people incarcerated in Yemen according to NationMaster, 2006. Under Yemeni law, nonmarital sex is punishable by 100 lashes and up to 3 years in prison. The sentence extends to 15 years if one of the parties is under 18 years of age. According to Amnesty International (2009), these sentences are frequent. Slandering the Yemeni president is punishable by up 2 two years in prison. Illegal drug exportation and importation can be punishable by the death penalty. For drug abuse in general, the punishment is a mandatory minimum of 25 years in prison.

A 2009 report from the National Forum on Human Rights revealed inhumane violations in Yemeni women's prisons. Although the deployment of women correctional officers is intended to safeguard women in custody, the report cites the frequent use of male guards for female prisoners as leading to sexual abuse of female inmates. In addition, the *Yemen Times* reports that houses and wings of police stations have been used for long-term detainment, and inmates have complained of unsanitary conditions, lack of food and mattresses, and juvenile inmates being held with adults. Yemen has capital punishment. In 2008, 13 people were executed.

Staci Strobl

Further Reading

Benjamin, D., and S. Simon. (2002). *The Age of Sacred Terror.* New York: Random House.

Brown, N. J. (2001). *Arab Judicial Structures: Yemen.* United Nations Office on Drugs and Crime: Programme on Governance in the Arab Region: http://www.pogar.org/publications/judiciary/nbrown/yemen.html#top.

International Crisis Group. (2003, January 8). *Yemen: Coping with Terrorism and Violence in a Fragile State.* Middle East Report No. 8: http://www.crisisgroup.org/home/index.cfm?id=1675&1=1.

NationMaster. (2006). *Middle East: Yemen: Crime:* http://www.nationmaster.com/red/country/ym-yemen/cri-crime&all=1.

U.S. Department of State. (2009, April 22). *Country Specific Profile: Yemen:* http://travel.state.gov/travel/cis_pa_tw/cis/cis_1061.html.

General Bibliography

Books, Periodicals, and Articles

Aas, K. (2007). *Globalization and Crime*. Los Angeles, CA: Sage.

Adeyemi, A. (1990). "Crime and Development in Africa: Case Study of Nigeria." In *Essays on Crime and Development,* edited by U. Zvekic, pp. 135–193. Rome: United Nations Interregional Crime and Justice Institute.

ADT. (2006). *Anti-Social Behaviour across Europe:* http://www.jdi.ucl.ac.uk/downloads/publications/journal_articles/cc4416AD_ANTI_SOCIAL_Report_UK_fv.pdf

Aebi, M.F. (2010). "Methodological Issues in the Comparison of Police Recorded Crime Rates." In *International Handbook of Criminology,* edited by S. Shoham, P. Knepper, and M. Kett, pp. 209–226. London: Routledge.

Aebi, M.F., K. Aromaa, B. Aubusson de Cavarlay, G. Barclay, B. Gruszczynska, H. von Hofer, V. Hysi, J.-M. Jehle, M. Killias, P. Smit, and C. Tavares. (2006). *European Sourcebook of Crime and Criminal Justice Statistics—2006.* 3rd ed. Den Haag: Boom Juridische Uitgevers.

Aebi, M.F., and N. Delgrande. (2009). *Council of Europe Annual Penal Statistics SPACE I: Survey 2007.* Strasbourg: Council of Europe.

Aebi, M.F., and A. Linde. (2009). *Review of the Current Situation in Respect of the Collection of Survey Data on Victimization.* Lausanne: Université de Lausanne.

Alvazzi del Frate, A. (2004). "The International Crime Business Survey: Findings from Nine Central-Eastern European Cities." *European Journal on Criminal Policy and Research* 10(2–3): 137–161.

Archer, D., and R. Gartner. (1984). *Violence and Crime in Cross-National Perspective.* New Haven, CT: Yale University Press.

Aromaa, K., and M. Heiskanen, eds. (2008). *Crime and Criminal Justice Systems in Europe and North America 1995–2004. Publication 55.* Helsinki, Finland: European Institute for Crime Prevention and Control, Affiliated with the United Nations (HEUNI).

Barak, G., ed. (2000). *Crime and Crime Control: A Global View.* Westport, CT: Greenwood Press.

Bayley, D.H. (2006). *Changing the Guard: Developing Democratic Police Abroad.* New York: Oxford University Press.

Beirne, P., and D. Nelken. (1997). *Issues in Comparative Criminology.* Sudbury, MA: Dartmouth.

Bennett, R. R. (1997a). "Excessive Force: A Comparative Study of Police in the Caribbean." *Justice Quarterly* 14: 651–686.

Bennett, R. R. (1997b). "The Determinants of Job Satisfaction among Police Constables: A Comparative Study in Three Developing Nations." *Justice Quarterly* 14: 295–323.

Bennett, R. R. (2004). "Comparative Criminology and Criminal Justice Research: The State of Our Knowledge." *Justice Quarterly* 21: 1–21.

Botchkovar, E. V., C. R. Tittle, and O. Antonaccio. (2009). "General Strain Theory: Additional Evidence Using Cross-Cultural Data." *Criminology* 47(1): 131–165.

Caldwell. J., ed. (1994). *Networking and AIDS in Sub-Saharan Africa: Behavioral Research and the Social Context,* pp. 101–116. Canberra: Australian National Universities.

Care, Jennifer, Tess Newton, and Don Paterson. (1999). *Introduction to South Pacific Law.* London: Cavendish.

Chevigny, P. (1995). *Edge of the Knife: Police Violence in the Americas.* New York: Free Press.

Dalgleish, D. (2005). "Pre-Colonial Criminal Justice in West Africa: Eurocentric Thought versus Africentric Evidence." *African Journal of Criminology and Justice Studies* 1(1): 155–169.

Delgrande, N., and M. F. Aebi. (2009). "European Prisons: Stability or Change?" *Criminology in Europe: Newsletter of the European Society of Criminology* 8(3): 1, 17–19.

European Journal of Criminology. Various issues providing country profiles.

European Journal on Criminal Policy and Research, in particular those on crime trends in Western and Eastern European Countries (Vol. 10[2–3], 2004) and prosecution and diversion within criminal justice systems in Europe (Vol. 14[2–3], 2008).

Fairchild, Erika, and Harry Dammer. (2001). *Comparative Criminal Justice Systems.* 2nd ed. Belmont, CA: Wadsworth.

Fiala, R., and G. LaFree. (1988). "Cross-National Determinants of Child Homicide." *American Sociological Review* 53: 432–445.

Findlay, Mark. (2000). *Criminal Laws of the South Pacific.* Suva: University of the South Pacific.

Friedrichs, D. (2007). "Transnational Crime and Global Criminology: Definitional, Typological, and Contextual Conundrums." *Social Justice* 34(2): 4–18.

Howard, G. J., G. Newman, and W. A. Pridemore. (2000). "Theory, Method, and Data in Comparative Criminology" (excerpted from *Measurement and Analysis of Crime and Justice. Criminal Justice 2000*) 4: 139–211.

International Journal of Comparative and Applied Criminal Justice. Published and copyrighted by the School of Criminal Justice, Michigan State University. ISSN 0192–4036.

Johnson, H., N. Ollus, and S. Nevala. (2007). *Violence against Women: An International Perspective.* New York: Springer.

Joireman, Sandra F. (2004). "Colonization and the Rule of Law: Comparing the Effectiveness of Common Law and Civil Law Countries." *Constitutional Political Economy* 15: 315–338.

Junger-Tas, J., I. Haen Marshall, and D. Ribeaud. (2003). *Delinquency in an International Perspective: The International Self-Report Delinquency Study.* The Hague, The Netherlands: Kugler Publications.

Karstedt, S. (2001). "Comparing Cultures, Comparing Crime: Challenges, Prospects and Problems for a Global Criminology." *Crime, Law, and Social Change* 36(3): 285–308.

Karstedt, S., and G. LaFree. (2006). "Democracy, Crime, and Justice." *Annals of the American Academy of Political and Social Science* 605: 6–23.

Kury, H., ed. (2001). *International Comparison of Crime and Victimization: The ICVS.* Ontario, Canada: de Sitter Publications.

Kyle, D., and R. Koslowski. (2001). *Global Human Smuggling: Comparative Perspectives.* Baltimore, MD: Johns Hopkins University Press.

Larsen, N., and R. Smandych, eds. *Global Criminology and Criminal Justice: Current Issues and Perspectives.* Peterborough, Ontario: Broadview Press.

Lee, M.R., and T. Earnest. (2003). "Perceived Community Cohesion and Perceived Risk of Victimization: A Cross-National Study." *Justice Quarterly* 20: 131–157.

Lo, Stefan H.C., Ian Dobinson, and Wing Hong Chui. "Sentencing for Drug Offences in Hong Kong: An Overview." *Hong Kong Law Journal* 34 (2005): 13–46.

Mawby, R., ed. (1996). *Policing across the World,* pp. 3–12. London: Routledge.

Messner, S. F., and Richard R. Rosenfeld. (2007). *Crime and the American Dream.* 4th ed. Belmont, CA: Thomson Wadsworth.

Nalla, M.K. (2009) "Democratic Policing: A Comparison of Police Officers' Perceptions of Their Role and Functions in Transitional Societies." *Journal of Criminal Justice and Security* 11(4): 520–535.

Nalla, M.K., and J. Johnson. (2009). "Are Police and Security Personnel Warming up to Each Other? A Comparison of Officer's Attitudes in Developed, Emerging, and Transitional Economies." *Policing: An International Journal of Police Strategies and Management* 32(3): 508–525.

National Institute of Justice, Office of Justice Programs, U.S. Department of Justice: http://www.ncjrs.gov/criminal_justice2000/vol4_2000.html.

Neapolitan, J.L. (1997). *Cross-National Crime: A Research Review and Sourcebook.* Westport, CT: Greenwood Press.

Newburn, T., and R. Sparks. (2004). *Criminal Justice and Political Cultures: National and International Dimensions of Crime Control.* Devon, UK: Willan.

Newman, Graeme R. (1999). *Global Report on Crime and Justice.* New York: United Nations Office of Drug Control and Crime Prevention.

Newman, Graeme R. (2008). *Comparative Deviance: Perception and Law in Six Cultures.* Reprinted with new introduction. Piscataway, NJ: Transaction Press.

Owomero, B. (1987). "Crime Rates and Development in Africa: Empirical Analysis of Data from Nigeria, Kenya, and Tanzania." *Indian Journal of Criminology* 15: 107–120.

Pridemore, W.A. (2008). "A Methodological Addition to the Cross-National Empirical Literature on Social Structure and Homicide: A First Test of the Poverty-Homicide Thesis." *Criminology* 46: 133–154.

Rafter, N.H., and F. Heidensohn. (1995). *International Feminist Perspective in Criminology.* Buckingham, UK: Open University Press.

Reichel, P.L. (2004). *Comparative Criminal Justice Systems: A Topical Approach.* Upper Saddle River, NJ: Prentice Hall.

Reichel, Philip L. (2008). *Comparative Criminal Justice Systems.* Upper Saddle River, NJ: Prentice Hall.

Robert, P., ed. (2009a). *Comparing Crime Data in Europe: Official Crime Statistics and Survey Based Data.* Brussels: VUBPRESS Brussels University Press.

Robert, P., ed. (2009b). *Evaluating Safety and Crime Prevention Policies in Europe.* Brussels: VUBPRESS Brussels University Press.

Savage, J., R.R. Bennett, and M. Danner. (2008). "Economic Assistance and Crime: A Cross-National Investigation." *European Journal of Criminology* 5: 217–238.

Schwabach, Aaron. (2003. Rev. 2006). *Non-Western Philosophies of Law.* In *Encyclopedia of Life Support Systems (EOLSS),* ed. Aaron Schwabach and Arthur John Cockfield, topic 6.31.1. Developed under the Auspices of UNESCO. Oxford: Eolss: http://www.eolss.net.

Sheptycki, J., and A. Wardak, eds. (2005). *Transnational and Comparative Criminology*. London: Glasshouse.

Stamatel, Janet P. (2006). "Incorporating Socio-Historical Context and Temporal Variation into Quantitative Cross-National Criminology." *International Journal of Comparative and Applied Criminal Justice* 30(2): 177–208.

Stamatel, Janet P. (2009a). "Correlates of National-Level Homicide Variation in Post-Communist East-Central Europe." *Social Forces* 87(3), 1423–1448.

Stamatel, Janet P. (2009b). "Contributions of Cross-National Research at the Beginning of the 21st Century." In *Handbook on Criminology and Deviance,* edited by Marvin Krohn, Alan Lizotte, and Gina Penly-Hall, 3–18. New York: Springer Science + Business Media.

Stamatel, Janet P. (guest editor). (2009, December). "New Methodological Directions for International and Comparative Criminology." *International Journal of Comparative and Applied Criminal Justice* 33 (2): 167.

Sung, Hung-En. (2004a). "Democracy and Organized Crime: Evidence from Fifty-Nine Countries." *Security Journal* 17(4): 21–34.

Sung, Hung-En. (2004b). "State Failure, Economic Failure, and Predatory Organized Crime." *Journal of Research in Crime and Delinquency* 41(2): 111–129.

Sung, Hung-En. (2006a). "Democracy and Criminal Justice in Comparative Perspective: From Crime Control to Due Process." *The Annals of the American Academy of Political and Social Science* 605(1): 311–337.

Sung, Hung-En. (2006b). "Structural Determinants of Police Effectiveness in Market Democracies." *Police Quarterly* 9(1): 3–19.

Sung, Hung-En, and Jack Reed. (2006). "Migration and Crime in Europe." In *Crime and Immigration,* edited by Joshua Freilich Graeme R. Newman, 95–120. Hampshire, UK: Ashgate.

Terrill, Richard J. (2009). *World Criminal Justice System: A Survey.* 7th ed. Southington, CT: Anderson.

Uildriks, N. (2009). *Policing Insecurity: Police Reform, Security and Human Rights in Latin America.* Lanham, MD: Lexington Books.

United Nations Office on Drugs and Crime. (2005). *Crime and Development in Africa.* Vienna, Austria: United Nations: http://www.unodc.org/pdf/African_report.pdf.

United Nations Office on Drugs and Crime. (2008). *Crime and Its Impact on the Balkans and Affected Countries.* Vienna, Austria: United Nations: http://www.unodc.org/documents/data-and-analysis/Balkan_study.pdf.

United Nations Office on Drugs and Crime and the Latin America and the Caribbean Region of the World Bank. (2007). *Crime, Violence, and Development: Trends, Costs, and Policy Options in the Caribbean.* Vienna, Austria: United Nations: http://www.unodc.org/pdf/research/Cr_and_Vio_Car_E.pdf.

Van Dijk, Jan. (2008). *The World of Crime: Breaking the Silence of Security, Justice, and Development across the World.* Thousand Oaks, CA: Sage.

Van Dijk, J., J. Kesteren, and P. Smit. (2007). *Criminal Victimisation in International Perspective: Key Findings from the 2004–2005 ICVS and EU ICS.* WODC: http://www.nicis.nl/kenniscentrum/binaries/nicis/bulk/onderzoek/2008/2/3/icvs2004_05report.pdf.

Weitekamp, E. G. M., and H. Kerner. (1994). *Cross-National Longitudinal Research on Human Development and Criminal Behavior.* Dordrecht, Netherlands: Kluwer Academic.

Zauberman, R., ed. (2009a). *Self-Reported Crime and Deviance Studies in Europe.* Brussels: VUBPRESS Brussels University Press.

Zauberman, R., ed. (2009b). *Victimization and Insecurity in Europe.* Brussels: VUBPRESS Brussels University Press.

Zimring, Franklin E., and David T. Johnson. (2008). "Law, Society, and Capital Punishment in Asia." *Punishment and Society* 10(2): 103–115.

Web Sites

BBC News Country Profiles: http://news.bbc.co.uk/2/hi/country_profiles/default.stm. This site is very good for background information on history, geography, and politics. It's also good for links to internal national sites and news media sites.

Cecil Greek's Criminal Justice Resources on International Criminal Justice: http://www.criminology.fsu.edu/p/cjl-world.php. There is a good variety of sources here, from common to the unusual, such as, for example, South Africa's Crime Mysteries.

CIA World Factbook: https://www.cia.gov/library/publications/the-world-factbook/index.html. The information in this book tends to be regurgitated in many Web sites, but it contains useful background information and is updated annually. Sometimes there are crime data, but usually descriptive, without statistics.

Council of Europe Annual Penal Statistics: www.coe.int/prison. Detailed data on prisons in Europe since 1983 can be found here.

The Council of Europe, European Commission for the Efficiency of Justice. (2008): *Evaluation of European Judicial Systems:* http://www.coe.int/t/dghl/cooperation/cepej/evaluation/default_en.asp.

Country Report of the Justice Studies Center of the Americas: http://www.cejamericas.org. This research and advocacy group publishes online country-specific analysis of legal systems and their operations in Latin America.

The Economist: http://www.economist.com/countries/index.cfm. This Web site offers much economic, historical, and political information on many countries and often useful information in its city guides.

European Society of Criminology: http://www.esc-eurocrim.org. This site provides a lot of relevant information on crime and punishment in Europe, including the programs of the annual conferences.

European Sourcebook of Crime and Criminal Justice Statistics: www.europeansourcebook.org. This site provides databases on police, prosecution, conviction, and correctional statistics since 1990 as well as some data on victimization.

International Centre for Prison Studies: http://www.kcl.ac.uk/depsta/rel/icps/home.html. This is a good source for international prison statistics.

International Court of Justice: http://www.icj-cij.org/.

Library of Congress Area Studies: http://www.loc.gov/rr/.

Nationmaster: http://www.nationmaster.com/index.php. This interesting interactive site allows comparative statistics of countries on a wide range of topics, including criminal justice. However, the crime statistics tend to be outdated.

The New York Times Countries and Territories: http://topics.nytimes.com/topics/news/international/countriesandterritories/index.html. These pages contain both general background information and links to recent media stories.

United Nations Interregional Crime and Justice Research Institute (UNICRI): http://www.unicri.it/wwd/analysis/icvs/data.php. A wide variety of information, particularly data for many countries participating in the International Crime Victim Survey (ICVS), is available.

United Nations Office on Drugs and Crime: http://www.unodc.org/. This site contains a wealth of information on crime, with extensive databases of crime statistics from the UN Surveys of Crime and Criminal Justice Systems.

U.S. Library of Congress Country Studies: http://lcweb2.loc.gov/frd/cs/. These are much more detailed than the usual country profiles, such as the CIA Factbook.

U.S. National Institute of Justice International Center: http://www.ojp.usdoj.gov/nij/international/. This site offers a variety of reports, articles, and descriptions of transnational and international crime and justice.

Wikipedia: http://wikipedia.org/. There is much information on countries, including interesting descriptions of crime and criminal justice issues. One has to be careful of the sources, but often there are links that lead to useful and reasonable resources. This is particularly good for tracking down internal national news media Web sites (i.e., local newspapers and TV stations) that almost always have news on local crimes.

World Criminal Justice Library Network: http://andromeda.rutgers.edu/~wcjlen/WCJ/mainpages/statres.htm. This site contains excellent statistical data from 80 countries. Internal national publications are usually the source.

World Factbook of Criminal Justice Systems. U.S. NIJ. Bureau of Justice Statistics: http://bjs.ojp.usdoj.gov/index.cfm?ty=pbdetail&iid=1435.

About the Editors and Contributors

General Editor

Graeme R. Newman is a distinguished teaching professor at the School of Criminal Justice, University at Albany, and the associate director of the Center for Problem-Oriented Policing. He has advised the United Nations on crime and justice issues over many years and in 1990 established the United Nations Crime and Justice Information Network.

Volume 1 Editor

Mahesh K. Nalla is professor of criminal justice at Michigan State University. His research interests include issues in public and private police in developed, emerging, and transitional economies.

Volume 1 Contributors

Mimi Ajzenstadt is an associate professor at the Institute of Criminology, Faculty of Law, and the Baerwald School of Social Work and Social Welfare and is the chair of the Lafer Center for Women and Gender Studies at the Hebrew University of Jerusalem.

Mohsen S. Alizadeh is an assistant professor at the Criminal Justice Division of Justice and Law Administration at Western Connecticut State University.

Joseph Appiahene-Gyamfi, PhD, is an associate professor and director of the criminal justice graduate program at the University of Texas–Pan American. He has published widely on issues of crime and punishment in Africa, with a focus on Ghana.

Sheila Atim-Scheijgrond works for the International Criminal Court in The Hague, Netherlands.

Megan Beckwith is currently pursuing her master's degree in criminal justice from Michigan State University. She obtained her Bachelor of Arts in criminal justice and Bachelor of Science in psychology in 2008 from Michigan State University.

Roberta Belli is a PhD candidate and graduate teaching fellow at the John Jay College of Criminal Justice. In 2004, she received her master's degree in internationalization of crime and criminal justice (LLM) at Utrecht University and was a law clerk in the International Criminal Court in The Hague, Netherlands.

Ashley G. Blackburn, PhD, is an assistant professor in the Department of Criminal Justice at the University of North Texas. Dr. Blackburn has published in journals including *Youth Violence and Juvenile Justice* and *The Prison Journal.*

Mark Bridge graduated with an MS in criminal justice from Michigan State University in 2008. He is currently a crime analyst for the City of Frederick Police Department in Frederick, Maryland.

Michael S. Caudy is a doctoral candidate in the Department of Criminology at the University of South Florida. He completed his undergraduate studies at the University of South Carolina in 2005 and earned his master's degree at the University of South Florida in 2007.

Soma Chaudhuri is an assistant professor at Michigan State University, holding a joint appointment with the Department of Sociology and the School of Criminal Justice.

Jeffrey Dailey is an assistant professor of criminal justice at Texas A&M University in Commerce, Texas. He has written several articles on policing and white-collar crime, and he coauthored *Community Supervision in Texas* (1996).

Harry R. Dammer is a professor and the chair of the sociology/criminal justice department at the University of Scranton (PA). His research interests include comparative/international criminal justice, community-based corrections, and religion in the correctional environment.

Anne-Laure Del Cerro, a native of Paris, France, works as a crime intelligence analyst at the John F. Finn Institute for Public Safety in Albany, New York. She is interested in the evaluation of international criminal justice systems as well as law enforcement agencies. She obtained her BA in 2007 at the University at Albany with Valedictorian Award.

Mandeep K. Dhami, PhD, is a professor at the Institute of Criminology, University of Cambridge. His recent publications have appeared in the *Canadian Journal of Criminology and Criminal Justice, Deviant Behavior, Criminal Justice and Behavior, Contemporary Justice Review*, *Law and Human Behavior,* and the *British Journal of Community Justice.*

Chelsea Diem graduated from Michigan State University in May 2009 with a BA in criminal justice with specializations in African studies and peace and justice studies. She is currently pursuing an MS degree in criminal justice from Michigan State University and expects to graduate in Spring 2011. Her interests are in family homicide and international criminal justice with an emphasis on African countries.

O. Oko Elechi is an associate professor of criminology and criminal justice at the Prairie View A&M University. He received his PhD from Simon Fraser

University, Canada. He has published widely in academic journals. He is the author of *Doing Justice without the State: The Afikpo (Ehugbo) Nigeria Model,* published in 2006.

Elisabeth Anne Filemyr has graduated with a BA in criminal justice and psychology from Michigan State University. She is working as a special agent for the Department of Defense and is currently pursuing an MS in criminal justice.

Kristan Fox is a doctoral candidate at Virginia Commonwealth University in criminal justice in the Wilder School of Government and Public Affairs. Her publications have appeared in the *Journal of Crime and Delinquency,* the *Journal of Criminal of Justice,* and the journal *Feminist Criminology.*

Michael Fox graduated with a BA in economics from William & Mary University, Williamsburg, Virginia. Although by trade a musician, he provides consulting in computer software, and his research interests include time series modeling.

Susan Gade is an academic specialist at Michigan State University. Susan received both a Master of Science degree and Bachelor of Arts degree in criminal justice from Michigan State University.

Michael Galezewski received his BS in criminal justice and BA in communication technologies from the University of Wisconsin–Platteville, graduating summa cum laude. He is currently pursuing his MS in criminal justice at Michigan State University.

Rhonda Gardner is a court management analyst. She is a graduate of Hollins College in Roanoke, Virginia, and is a candidate for a master's in criminal justice, with specialization in judicial administration, from Michigan State University.

Steve Grubbs graduated cum laude with a bachelor's degree in criminal justice from Tiffin University (OH). A police officer for the Westerville Police Department since 2000, he is currently pursuing a master's in criminal justice from Michigan State University.

Farrukh B. Hakeem, PhD, is an associate professor in the Department of Social Sciences, Shaw University, Raleigh, North Carolina. His main areas of research are comparative law, corrections, punishment, policing, and public health.

Jason Harris works as an executive team leader of assets protection for Target in Tampa, Florida. He is currently pursuing an MS in criminal justice at Michigan State University.

Ernest Harsch holds a PhD in sociology from the New School for Social Research in New York and is affiliated with the Institute of African Studies at Columbia University. He has written numerous journalistic and academic publications on Burkina Faso.

Raquel Hutts is a graduate of the State University of New York at Albany. She received her Master of Arts in criminal justice in December 2007.

Jennifer Janowski is a legislative analyst with the U.S. Department of Defense, Department of the Air Force. She has a degree in health sciences from Oakland University, Michigan, and is pursuing a degree in criminal justice from Michigan State University.

Pa Musa Jobarteh is a former commissioner of the Gambian Immigration Department. He holds a master's degree in criminal justice from Michigan State University, and a bachelor's degree in police studies from John Jay College of Criminal Justice of the City University of New York (CUNY). He previously worked as a fraud investigator before moving on to join the Gambian Immigration Department.

Joseph D. Johnson is a doctoral student in the Michigan State University School of Criminal Justice. His dissertation examines a community-driven violence prevention program that hires and trains ex-convicts, gang members, hustlers, probationers, and parolees.

Tal Jonathan is a PhD student at the Institute of Criminology, Faculty of Law, Hebrew University, Jerusalem, Israel.

Al Shek Kamara is an assistant inspector general in the Sierra Leone Police and has served as director of crime management and program manager for the SLP Justice Sector Development Program and as acting chief of immigration. He is the first African Visiting Scholar to the School of Criminal Justice at the Michigan State University in East Lansing, Michigan.

Brandon Kooi is the program chair of Criminal Justice at Aurora University. His research interests include community justice, problem-oriented policing, crime prevention, private security, and criminal justice educational issues. His book *Policing Public Transportation* was recently published by LFB Publishing, New York (2007).

Richard L. Legault is codirector of the Terrorism and Preparedness Data Resource Center (TPDRC) project at START and a DHS postdoctoral research fellow. He received his PhD from the School of Criminal Justice at the State University of New York at Albany in 2006, where he was also an assistant editor at the Sourcebook of Criminal Justice Statistics.

Amber Lesniewicz is the educational programs associate at the National Consortium of the Study of Terrorism and Responses to Terrorism (START). She has a degree in psychology and French from the University of Illinois and is pursuing a degree in criminology from the University of Maryland.

Ernest Mallya is an associate professor in public policy and administration at the University of Dar es Salaam and conducts research in the areas of public service delivery systems.

Dale Marsden is currently pursuing his MS in criminal justice at Michigan State University. He currently resides in Canada and is a member of the Ontario Provincial Police.

Meredith Matthews is currently pursuing a master's of science degree in criminal justice at the University of North Texas and expects to graduate in August 2008. She earned a Bachelor of Arts degree in music from Baylor University in May 2000.

Nathan Meehan is a PhD candidate at the School of Criminal Justice at the State University of New York at Albany. He received his BS from Northeastern University and Masters from University at Albany. At present, he is the lead crime analyst at the Schenectady Police Department, New York. His doctoral research is related to the impact of HIV/AIDS on the police in sub-Saharan Africa.

Michael E. Meyer, PhD, is a professor in the Department of Criminal Justice, University of North Dakota, and has published several articles in leading criminal justice and criminology journals. In 2003–2004, he was a Senior Fulbright Lecturer/Researcher in South Africa.

Angela R. Morris is an assistant professor at Campbellsville University, Campbellsville, Kentucky, and the president and founder of Peer-Polity Consulting International.

Mike Mudry graduated in 1997 from San Diego State University with a degree in social science and is working toward an MS in criminal justice from Michigan State. He has been working for Target Corp. in the security division for the past 24 years.

Mahesh K. Nalla is professor of criminal justice at Michigan State University. His research interests include issues in public and private police in developed, emerging, and transitional economies.

Seigo Nishijima is a PhD candidate in criminal justice at the State University of New York at Albany. His interests include comparative criminal justice and penology.

Gilberte Nkeshimana, born in Burundi, is a recent graduate in law from the University of the Great Lakes in Kiremba, Bururi. She obtained her degree in law in 2006. In 2007, she was employed as an interviewer in a project on rural welfare, economic activities, and violent conflict with the National Institute of Statistics in Burundi.

Ejakait (J. S. E.) Opolot is a graduate faculty member in the Department of Administration of Justice at Texas Southern University. He has widely published in international criminology periodicals and has also authored *Organized Crime in Africa* and *The Crime Problem in Africa: A Wake Up Call, Police Administration in Africa.*

Jessica Raber graduated from Albion College, Michigan, in 2007 with a major in sociology.

Luisa Ravagnani is a research fellow in criminology at the University of Brescia–Italy and expert judge at the Surveillance Court of Brescia. Her main research areas are detention, alternatives to prison, and comparative prison law.

James V. Ray received his BA from Ohio State University and his MA from the University of South Florida with a major in criminology. He is currently pursuing his PhD in criminology and is expected to graduate in the fall of 2010.

Nicole Reinsch is a substance abuse analyst with the State of Michigan and is currently pursuing an MS in law enforcement intelligence analysis from the School of Criminal Justice at Michigan State University (MSU). She received her BS in criminal justice and psychology from MSU in 2007.

Carlo Alberto Romano is a criminology professor at the University of Brescia–Italy. He is a member of the Italian Society of Criminology Directorate board and president of Carcere e Territorio Association (ONG, which works in the field of prisoner rehabilitation). He is also author of more than 140 publications with criminological topics.

Samer Abu Said is a Lebanese lawyer specializing in public, civil, and corporate law, formerly serving on the international staff of the International Committee of the Red Cross in North Darfur-Sudan. He is preparing his thesis for an MA degree in public international law from the Lebanese University, Faculty of Law and Political Sciences (Beirut), where he earned a bachelor's in general law.

Paul Schupp is an assistant professor in the Department of Criminal Justice at Niagara University. His primary scholarly interests are the sociology of punishment and the development of imprisonment patterns.

Zachary Shemtob is a PhD student at John Jay College of Criminal Justice in New York City.

Eric Smith graduated with a bachelor's degree in criminal justice from Michigan State University. A member of the New York Jets football team, he is currently pursuing an MS in criminal justice and is expecting to graduate during the Spring 2011 semester.

Stephanie L. Stashenko is a graduate student at the School of Criminal Justice, University at Albany, State University of New York.

Brian Stout is a senior lecturer in the Community and Criminal Justice Division at De Montfort University, Leicester, U.K. He is currently working on his doctoral research on the Child Justice Bill in South Africa.

Staci Strobl, PhD, of the Department of Law Police Science and Criminal Justice Administration, John Jay College of Criminal Justice, has published articles in international criminal justice journals related to gender and law enforcement. Her current research interests include the history of policing in the Arabian Gulf countries and the policing of minority Roma populations in Central and Eastern Europe.

Charles B. A. Ubah is an associate professor of criminology, criminal justice, law, sociology, and public policy at Georgia College and State University Milledgeville.

He has published in a wide variety of criminology and criminal justice journals and has been active in the African Criminology and Justice Association.

Veerle Van Gijsegem is currently a PhD fellow of the Research Foundation–Flanders. She has a master's degree in criminology and is a part-time assistant professor in the Department of Criminology at the Vrije Universiteit Brussel and a lecturer in the Department of Social Work at the Erasmushogeschool Brussel.

Philip Verwimp obtained his PhD in economics from the Catholic University of Leuven in 2003. He studied economics and sociology in Antwerp, Leuven, and Göttingen and specialized in political economy and genocide at Yale University. Together with Tilman Brück and Patricia Justino, he cofounded the Households in Conflict Network (http://www.hicn.org).

David Weisburd is a professor of law and criminal justice and the director of the Institute of Criminology at the Hebrew University Law School in Jerusalem and a distinguished professor and the director of the Center for Evidence Based Crime Policy at George Mason University in Virginia. He has published widely in criminology and is founding editor of the *Journal of Experimental Criminology.*

Eric Wildey is a graduate student at Michigan State University.

Index

Boldface numbers refer to volume numbers. A key appears on all verso pages.

1: Africa and the Middle East
2: The Americas
3: Asia and Pacific
4: Europe

1: Africa and the Middle East
2: The Americas
3: Asia and Pacific
4: Europe

1: Africa and the Middle East
2: The Americas
3: Asia and Pacific
4: Europe

1: Africa and the Middle East
2: The Americas
3: Asia and Pacific
4: Europe

1: Africa and the Middle East
2: The Americas
3: Asia and Pacific
4: Europe

1: Africa and the Middle East
2: The Americas
3: Asia and Pacific
4: Europe

1: Africa and the Middle East
2: The Americas
3: Asia and Pacific
4: Europe

1: Africa and the Middle East
2: The Americas
3: Asia and Pacific
4: Europe

1: Africa and the Middle East **2:** The Americas **3:** Asia and Pacific **4:** Europe

1: Africa and the Middle East
2: The Americas
3: Asia and Pacific
4: Europe

1: Africa and the Middle East
2: The Americas
3: Asia and Pacific
4: Europe

1: Africa and the Middle East **2:** The Americas **3:** Asia and Pacific **4:** Europe

Crime and Punishment around the World

Crime and Punishment around the World

THE AMERICAS

Volume 2

JANET P. STAMATEL AND HUNG-EN SUNG, VOLUME EDITORS
GRAEME R. NEWMAN, GENERAL EDITOR

ABC-CLIO

Santa Barbara, California • Denver, Colorado • Oxford, England

Copyright 2010 by Janet P. Stamatel and Hung-En Sung, Volume Editors

Graeme R. Newman, General Editor

All rights reserved. No part of this publication may be reproduced, stored in a retrieval system, or transmitted, in any form or by any means, electronic, mechanical, photocopying, recording, or otherwise, except for the inclusion of brief quotations in a review, without prior permission in writing from the publisher.

Library of Congress Cataloging-in-Publication Data

Crime and punishment around the world.
p. cm.
Includes bibliographical references and index.
ISBN 978-0-313-35133-4 (set : alk. paper) — ISBN 978-0-313-35134-1 (set ebook) — ISBN 978-0-313-35135-8 (vol. 1 : alk. paper) — ISBN 978-0-313-35136-5 (vol. 1 ebook) — ISBN 978-0-313-35137-2 (vol. 2 : alk. paper) — ISBN 978-0-313-35138-9 (vol. 2 ebook) — ISBN 978-0-313-35139-6 (vol. 3 : alk. paper) — ISBN 978-0-313-35140-2 (vol. 3 ebook) — ISBN 978-0-313-35141-9 (vol. 4 : alk. paper) — ISBN 978-0-313-35142-6 (vol. 4 ebook)
1. Crime. 2. Punishment. 3. Criminal justice, Administration of.
HV6025.C7115 2010
364—dc22 2010021159

ISBN (set): 978-0-313-35133-4
EISBN (set): 978-0-313-35134-1

14 13 12 11 10 1 2 3 4 5

This book is also available on the World Wide Web as an eBook.
Visit www.abc-clio.com for details.

ABC-CLIO, LLC
130 Cremona Drive, P.O. Box 1911
Santa Barbara, California 93116-1911

This book is printed on acid-free paper ∞

Manufactured in the United States of America

This volume set is dedicated to the memory of
Ali Sabeeh of Omara, Iraq, who, while preparing the entry on Iraq,
was kidnapped, tortured, and killed in October 2007

Editorial Advisory Board

Adam Bouloukos, Director of Outreach and Partnerships, UNOPS, Copenhagen, Denmark

Ronald V. Clarke, University Professor, Rutgers University

Adam Graycar, Professor, Australian National University

Martin Killias, Professor, University of Zurich

Jeremy Travis, President, John Jay College of Criminal Justice

Contents

Acknowledgments

The contribution made by the volume editors to this project has been inestimable. A project of this magnitude could not have been achieved without their unceasing efforts to find contributors for large and small countries alike, to manage their contributors' contributions, and to edit them into the style and format required by a publication of this type. They helped overcome a number of crises we met along the way. For this and for their always being on the receiving end of my constant emails, I express my sincere appreciation. I thank especially Janet Stamatel for producing the world and regional maps from my sometimes less than adequate databases.

Many authors have contributed to these volumes. Without them, of course, this project would not have been possible. The volume editors and I express our great admiration to our contributors and appreciation for their tolerance of our editorial demands, which oftentimes must have seemed unreasonable. We apologize if your chapter ended up a little shorter than you had wanted. We bear full responsibility for any misconceptions that may have occurred as a result of our at-times heavy editorial hand.

Finally, we thank the Editorial Advisory Board members for being there when we needed them.

—Graeme R. Newman
Albany, NY
December 31, 2009

General Introduction

We humans are fascinated by the diversity of cultures, climates, landscapes, and peoples. It is part of our deep human heritage that we have never been able to stay at home. Since the beginning of human time, our haplogroups have migrated far and wide, stumbling on new fauna and evolving with them, adapting to cold, hot, wet, and dry seasons and climates. Along the way, we have constructed societies and civilizations that have come and gone, none reaching perfection; each having tried its own solutions to the problem of order; each constructing rules, laws, customs, and ways of dealing with those who, for whatever reason, have broken with the sacred commandments of order. Somewhere along the way, no matter what the civilization or society, the idea of justice emerged, perhaps independently of the need for order and, indeed, every now and again in opposition to order. But whatever order's relationship to justice, one thing is certain: order is necessary for societies to survive. And embedded in this necessity is the inevitability that individuals will break laws, rules, and customs and will, as a matter of logic (and justice), be punished for it.

So law (so-called if it is written) and custom (embodying law and rules that may not be written but that are "practiced" and conveyed orally) is universal in all known societies. They are part of the "civilizing" process, which seeks to hold in check the tendency of humans to devour each other. It is true that great thinkers, philosophers, and even scientists have insisted—in the face of the overwhelming evidence of history that stands against them—that humans, if only given a chance, can or could work together for their common good without being coerced to do so. But we know of no society anywhere in which this utopian (if it is utopian) conception of human nature has produced a society without laws or customs and their concomitant punishments. And surely humans have had plenty of chances to construct such utopian societies. Yet each time they try, order takes over, because we know that individuals only grudgingly curb their own desires. They do not like the imposition of order, but they know that they cannot survive without it and its accoutrements. Or at least, we may say that life is much more comfortable if one gives into almost any kind of order. This observation probably applies even to the worst of tyrannical orders, for it is easier to remain in submission than it is to rise up and overthrow a very powerful authority. The 18th-century enlightenment thinkers upon whose ideas much of the world's criminal justice systems are based (whether civil or common) were clearly of the opinion that punishment was a necessary evil, a price paid for the

comfort of living in an ordered society. Its universality certainly attests to the truth of this assertion.

It should come as no surprise, therefore, that getting reliable information about such a touchy subject—essentially how a society, nation, or culture maintains order in the face of a populace that may secretly or even openly resent its imposition—is very difficult. Nations can be very secretive about their crime rates and their punishments, not to mention their procedures for finding guilt and their manner of interrogating suspects. Various organizations have set themselves up to monitor the most egregious violations of individuals in the name of order, such as Human Rights Watch and Amnesty International, but there is a far larger part of the maintenance of order and the processing of lawbreakers by nations and regional governments that also needs constant scrutiny. Violations of human rights in the name of order may easily be hidden inside the bureaucratic inertia and practices of even the most "enlightened" societies. To admit to having a very high rate of murder or incarceration—perhaps one of the highest—of its citizens is not something of which a nation can be especially proud. Such statistics say something about that nation, though what that something is, unfortunately, can be easily misinterpreted. For example, some countries may be criticized for having very high imprisonment rates, but their retort may be that this is because they have very high crime rates, to which it may be asked, but why do you have such high crime rates? The reply may be, "Because we have strict laws that are strictly enforced, which is for the good of our citizens, who are kept safer than those in other countries whose administration of criminal justice is too lax." Provided here is just a taste of the controversies and disagreements concerning the differing levels of crime and punishment in diverse countries, as well as the puzzling relationship or lack thereof between prison rates and crime rates. The riddle can be stated thus: more punishment should reduce crime, but more crime requires more punishment.

One would think that the costs in public relations to a nation would be far too high to allow for the publication of crime and punishment statistics. So it is an amazing achievement that the United Nations World Crime Surveys, whose mission is to collect the official statistics on crime and justice from member nations, have shown steady and significant increases in the number of countries submitting their statistics since they were first collected in the 1970s. From a handful of countries in the beginning, the number providing crime and punishment statistics had grown to about 50 as of 2005. That is the positive spin. In fact, this is only 50 out of 190 member UN nations, and there are signs of decreasing reporting by countries in recent years, according to Jan Van Dijk, author of *The World of Crime* and former UN expert on international crime and justice.

Although it is true that nations are reticent to make public their crime and punishment statistics for reasons of public image, there are many technical difficulties in making comparisons of officially collected crime and justice statistics across countries. Many of these difficulties are serious, and *the reader is warned to use considerable caution in making such comparisons across countries*. These technical difficulties include the following:

- Different legal definitions of offenses make it difficult to compare specific offenses across nations.
- Different reporting and recording practices of the police who generally have first official contact with a crime make comparing statistics from one country to another unreliable without knowledge of these practices.
- Different legal systems may affect the finding of guilt, recording and classification of offenses, and recording of arrests and convictions.
- Inconsistent classifications of crime records and frequent changes over time make it difficult to compare trends in crime or punishment.
- Different bureaucracies and government departments within each nation that collate and publish crime and punishment statistics may produce different statistics. For example, city- or state-level collection of crime rates or prison rates may differ from collection at the federal level, as in the United States.
- Inadequate infrastructure for collecting and processing crime and justice reports, including information technology, may hinder the amount or accuracy of criminal justice data.
- Lack of professionally trained crime analysts and statisticians may limit the reliability and depth of statistical data available.
- Local events or conditions may inflate crime and punishment statistics, such as genocidal events that may or may not be recorded as murders.
- Changing government policies about making crime and justice statistics public may affect trends and the amount and type of data made available. There have been instances where countries have revealed crime and justice statistics to the United Nations, but not to their own citizens. The reverse is also true. There was a time, for example, when the Soviet Union routinely collected crime statistics for its internal use but officially denied to the United Nations that there was any crime at all in the Soviet Union, because there could be no crime in a true communist society.
- In large populous countries, there may be vast differences within those countries. For example, the levels of crime and punishment vary enormously throughout the United States; some states still retain the death penalty, and many do not. There may also be huge differences in amounts and kinds of crime between urban and rural regions. There may even be different legal systems operating within the same country, such as, for example, Quebec in Canada or the several customary, Islamic, and civil law systems operating in Timor-Leste.

If one must make comparisons—and most people are unable to resist it—the best way to overcome these pitfalls is to make sure that one knows as much as possible about the historical and social context within which the statistics are collected. *Crime and Punishment around the World* provides just that context. This encyclopedia describes in detail the crime and punishment practices of each country and, in some instances, specific regions. The four volumes offer a glimpse of the ways in which all the nations around the world try to solve the basic problem

they all face: what to do with those who break the law? They have all enacted either customary or written criminal laws. They have all inherited their criminal laws from their ancestors near and far, not infrequently from other nations that either usurped them or overtook them through migration. They have all developed procedures for the finding of guilt of the accused, and all, of course, follow up the finding of guilt with legislated or customary punishments. These are all essentially the product of their legal systems.

World Legal Systems

For more than 1,000 years, the Roman Empire encompassed just about all the region around the Mediterranean and stretched as far north as Great Britain. Law was probably its major weapon against the peoples it subdued, bringing with it order and a stable means of commerce. Its concepts would form much of the basis of canon law and eventually much of the civil law of Europe. Furthermore, much of the Islamic and customary law of the countries surrounding the south and east of the Mediterranean was deeply affected by Roman law because those peoples were also subjects of the Roman Empire at various times for over 1,000 years. Those countries of Europe that retained more of the Roman law and its procedures would later come to be known as "civil law" countries. Those European countries that managed to put aside Roman law came to be known as "common law" countries. And those of North Africa and the Far East retained Islamic and customary law systems.

Civil law systems account for over 50 percent of the world's legal systems, although many such systems are mixed with other legal systems because of local and historical circumstance. In fact, as a result of constant reforms, it is likely that there are no purely civil law systems left in the world. Most countries have incorporated various aspects of the adversarial system. The main characteristics of civil law systems are the following:

1. Systematically written legal codes are the prime source of authority in legal decisions and procedures.
2. Their procedures are often (though not entirely) based on what is sometimes called the "inquisitorial system"—reaching back to the days of the Roman Catholic Inquisition—in which the process of finding of guilt is conducted by a judge or magistrate who both investigates and conducts the final trial. These trials are usually, though not always, conducted before a magistrate or panel of magistrates.

Probably the prime examples of European civil law systems are those of France and Germany and, to some extent, Italy, which has recently incorporated aspects of the adversarial system.

Common law systems account for another 20 percent of the world's legal systems. These are commonly referred to as "adversarial systems" because the finding of guilt is not conducted by the magistrate who decides and investigates the case as in civil law; rather, a prosecutor (or sometimes an investigating police officer) investigates the case and prepares the case for a trial by judge and jury

(although juries are not always required). The two significant features of common law systems are the following:

1. Cases are decided based on precedent, which views previous cases and decisions as a cumulative wisdom and authority.
2. Cases are a courtroom drama in which the prosecutor is pitted against the defense.

It should be noted, however, that in modern legal systems of common law, there are legal codes that systematize the law, and these may or may not be based on the codification of past legal practice. In the United States, for example, every state, in addition to the federal system, has its own written code. Cases are decided, however, based not only on how well the offender's acts match the written code but also on the cases that came before it—that is, precedent. One sees this tradition played out in the U.S. Supreme Court, which arduously scrutinizes past decisions to conclude whether a particular case was decided correctly or not, in accordance with the supreme law of the land, the U.S. Constitution. The popular view that contrasts these two legal traditions is that civil law is focused more on finding a probably guilty person guilty, whereas common law is focused more on defending a possibly innocent person from a guilty verdict. Both systems do, however, adhere to the presumption of innocence of the accused until proven guilty. The most typical examples of common law systems are those of the United Kingdom, the United States, and Australia.

Islamic legal systems account for about 10 percent of the world's legal systems, although there are probably no purely Islamic systems anywhere in the world. This is because of the early Roman influence on all countries surrounding the Mediterranean and because of the imperialism of the West during the 16th through 20th centuries. In its pure form, the Islamic system of law follows the exact law of God, as interpreted by experts (Mullahs), deriving from the Koran, the Bible, and other sacred texts. Islamic law is often called sharia—the path to follow. Perhaps the most contrasting feature of Islamic law is that it is more a way to live one's life than a set of prohibitions laid down by a state authority as in Roman law and its progenitors. Thus, not only does it include prohibitions, some of which are set out in the Ten Commandments, but it also includes exhortations to lead a good life (e.g., love thy neighbor). No such positive exhortations are found in other Western legal traditions, whose defining principle is prohibition. The procedural rules of Islamic law are those of human reasoning and consensus. One of the problems that faces legal theorists in Islamic law is that there are many offenses that are not specifically covered in any of the sacred texts. For example, sodomy is not mentioned in the Koran or Sunna (another sacred text), but adultery is. So the judge may reason that the two offenses are similar and the punishments prescribed for one may apply to the other. In practice, however, many cases are decided also on custom and precedent, given that in many Islamic countries, tribal customs concerning redress of wrongs (e.g., feuding and vengeance) have developed alongside Islamic and other kinds of law. The majority of countries with Islamic legal systems therefore also have customary law as a major component, especially in dealing with day-to-day infractions. Finally, most Islamic law

countries also have a considerable dose of civil law, especially in the field of commerce, though it has been necessary even there for such countries to develop ways to get around the Islamic prohibition of usury, defined rather broadly.

Customary law is the law that has arisen through oral tradition among tribes and cultures where law is not written down but rather communicated across generations by tribal elders. Village or regional chieftains are usually, though not always, the main repositories of such legal wisdom, and the finding of guilt usually occurs within an informal meeting of interested parties. In many countries of Africa and southern Asia, these kinds of local meetings occur and settlements are reached based on the hearing of all sides of the complaints. Depending on the culture, shamans or others thought to hold special powers may be brought in as expert witnesses and sometimes as judges. However, the most important attribute of customary law is its specificity to the local region or village. These traditions can be very deep and resistant to change or imposition from outside influences. Perhaps a prime example in the 21st century is that of the tribal villages in the mountains of Pakistan and parts of Afghanistan that have defied state authority for hundreds of years. Instead, these tribal areas have their own chiefs and their own informal ways of settling infractions and disputes.

Socialist legal systems are those that have arisen on top of civil law systems, for the most part. Certainly this was the case in the Soviet Union and continues to be the case in Cuba and other communist countries, although China is perhaps an exception. Yet even there, the customary legal system was usurped by Western powers in the 19th century and abolished by the revolution of 1949. However, the emergence in the 1980s of China as an industrial and trading nation required that it develop a legal system that would make commerce possible and more efficient. The result has been that its legal system is based essentially on civil law, with criminal law that codifies edicts of the State and procedures that are largely reflective of the inquisitorial system.

Finally, although there are probably no countries that are purely of one or the other legal system, there are quite a number of countries whose legal systems are mixtures of some or all of the preceding. Many African and some South Asian countries are mixtures of customary, civil, common, and Islamic law. Such countries would include, for example, India, Afghanistan, and maybe Egypt.

How Does Your Country Measure Up?

Although for the reasons recounted earlier, comparing the crime and punishment of countries to each other is a very difficult procedure, it is nevertheless important to get a rough idea of how one country compares to the rest of the world. It is probably one of the main reasons people refer to world encyclopedias of any kind, to get a sense of how one fits in the universe.

To provide a very rough glimpse of how a country's crime and punishment compare to the rest of the world, we have provided a snapshot of some major indicators of crime and punishment for each country at the start of each country essay. We have chosen these indicators because they are readily available and offer a reasonably approximate way of ranking countries along a continuum. Of

the crime indicators, murder is chosen as probably the most reliable for making comparisons because its definition is roughly similar across nations, and in most cases, the statistics have been adjusted to fit the UN standard definition of murder for countries reporting their murder rates. Nevertheless, many countries do not report their murder rates. Prison rates are also reasonably reliable for making comparisons, although they too involve great technical difficulties in measurement, considering that the counting of inmates may occur on different days of the year, and a simple accounting on a particular day does not give any indication of the flow of prisoners in and out of the prison over a given period of time. The snapshot indicators provided for each country or region when available are as follow:

- *Type of Legal System*
- *Murder*—murders per 100,000 people
- *Burglary*—those victimized by burglaries per thousand people
- *Corruption*—levels of perceived corruption
- *Human Trafficking*—how much the country is doing to control human trafficking
- *Prison*—number of prisoners per 100,000 population
- *Death Penalty*—whether the country has the death penalty
- *Corporal Punishment*—whether corporal punishment is available to the criminal justice system

Legal System

The types of legal system were compiled from the United Nations *Global Report on Crime and Justice,* supplemented by information from individual country Web sites and from the University of Ottawa Civil Law Section Web site on World Legal Systems at http://www.droitcivil.uottawa.ca/world-legal-systems/eng-tableau.php.

Murder

These are officially reported statistics on murder supplied by countries to the United Nations World Crime Surveys, supplemented where necessary by individual country information plus homicide statistics from the World Health Organization. Most of the statistics were taken from the revised listing supplied by Jan Van Dijk in his book *The World of Crime,* in which he reported the average murder rates for 1998–2002, supplemented by more recent United Nations surveys. Additional data from INTERPOL and individual country sources, where available, sometimes for a slightly different period of years, were also included. However, such small differences should not matter because we know that murder rates are fairly stable over time. The countries are ranked from highest to lowest murder rate (murders per 100,000 people) and then divided into quartiles, with the middle two quartiles classified as "Medium" and the two outer quartiles labeled "High" and "Low." The world distribution of murder rates can be seen in Map 1, Murder around the World.

Burglary

Obtaining reliable rates of property crime, the most common of which is usually referred to as theft, is especially difficult when relying on officially recorded statistics because definitions and enforcement practices vary enormously across nations. We have therefore included measures of victimization of individuals by burglary. These measures are derived from the International Crime Victim Surveys (ICVS), which are interviews or questionnaires asking samples of a population whether they have been victims of particular offenses over a particular number of years (usually the past year). In this case, the samples were households, and the survey was conducted in many countries, although *limited only to urban populations*. Therefore, they do not, of course, represent the country or region as a whole, though they do, perhaps in the case of burglary, represent most of the population of a given country that there are, generally, many more households in urban settings than in rural settings. These data are taken from Van Dijk's *World of Crime.* Countries were ranked according to their burglary rates (number of victimizations reported per 1,000 people) using quartiles, divided into High, Medium, and Low, with Medium defined by the two middle quartiles.

Corruption

The ways in which crime and punishment are eventually perceived by the public and administered by the State are affected by the level of corruption in a particular country. We have therefore included a measure of corruption, a kind of crime that is neither a violent crime nor, strictly speaking, a property crime. Rather, it is a crime against justice itself. There is also the advantage that data on perceived corruption in countries are much more available, thanks to the source of our data, Transparency International at http://www.transparency.org/policy_research/surveys_indices/cpi. This Corruption Perception Index (CPI) is based on the ranking of "180 countries by their perceived levels of corruption, as determined by expert assessments and opinion surveys" according to Transparency International. We have taken these rankings, added some additional countries in some cases where they were not included in the survey, and then divided them into Low, Medium, and High, using quartiles once again.

Human Trafficking

This measure is taken from the U.S. Department of State three-tier listing of countries it classifies as making a strong effort to control human trafficking, making some effort, or making very little effort. The classifications are taken from the U.S. Department of State *Trafficking in Persons Report 2008*, found at http://www.state.gov/g/tip/rls/tiprpt/2008/index.htm. The classification scheme is derived from the U.S. Trafficking Victims Protection Act of 2000 (TVPA), which defines the minimum standards for the elimination of trafficking. It should be noted, however, that our ratings of "High" "Medium," and "Low" in the rates of human trafficking are only very rough because they assume that countries that comply with the U.S. anti-trafficking standards of enforcement will therefore have low levels of human trafficking. This is not always true. The United States,

for example, is rated as low for human trafficking because it complies with the TVPA anti-trafficking act; however, we know that it is a major destination country for trafficked humans. The classifications are as follows:

- *Low Amount of Trafficking* (Tier 1): Countries that fully comply with the U.S. Department of State standards for anti-trafficking enforcement.
- *Medium Amount of Trafficking* (Tier 2): Countries that do not fully comply with the minimum standards but are making significant efforts to bring themselves into compliance.
- *Medium Amount of Trafficking* (Watch List): Countries on Tier 2 requiring special scrutiny because of a high or significantly increasing number of victims, failure to provide evidence of increasing efforts to combat trafficking in persons, or an assessment as Medium based on commitments to take action over the next year.
- *High Amount of Trafficking* (Tier 3): Countries that neither satisfy the minimum standards nor demonstrate a significant effort to come into compliance. Countries in this tier are subject to potential non-humanitarian and non-trade sanctions.

Prison

The prison rate assessments are derived from the International Center for Prison Studies, King's College, London, and found at http://www.kcl.ac.uk/schools/law/research/icps. The rates are of prisoners per 100,000 population, and countries are ranked from high to low and divided into High, Medium, and Low using the quartile method described previously. These were the most up-to-date and thorough statistics available as of 2008. The world distribution of prison rates is depicted in Map 2: Imprisonment around the World.

Death Penalty

About 65 percent of countries have abolished the death penalty either by legislation or in practice. A few have essentially abolished it while retaining it for especially heinous crimes, although it may not have been used for many years. These countries are classified as "maybe" in our assessment of whether the death penalty is available to countries. Thus, the classifications for whether countries have the death penalty as an available punishment are "Yes," "Maybe," and "No." The information has been taken from the Web site *Info Please* at http://www.infoplease.com/ipa/A0777460.html, which in turn has taken its statistics from Amnesty International. The world death penalty distribution may be seen in Map 3: Death Penalty around the World.

Corporal Punishment

The assessments as to whether countries have available to them the use of corporal punishment, either as a sentence for a crime or for use within the prison system for disciplinary purposes, is based on information provided by the Web site http://www.endcorporalpunishment.org/pages/frame.html, which assesses

mainly the legislative steps that countries have taken to prohibit the use of corporal punishment. The Web site covers the use of corporal punishment in homes and schools as well as in the criminal justice system. Its assessments of countries are based almost entirely on whether legislation has been passed prohibiting corporal punishment either as a sentence in criminal justice or as a means of discipline in prisons. The legal situation is often ambiguous because, as with the death penalty, many countries retain the possibility of corporal punishment's use either as a sentence or in prisons but rarely or never resort to it. Thus, there is a category of "maybe" for those countries. Perhaps surprisingly, less than 20 percent of the world's countries have prohibited by legislation the use of corporal punishment either as a sentence for a crime or for use in prison discipline. Like the death penalty, our classification of the availability of corporal punishment is "Yes," "No," or "Maybe." The world use of corporal punishment is presented in Map 4: Corporal Punishment around the World.

Regions of the Four Volumes

The four volumes are broken up into the following regions:

- Volume 1: Africa and the Middle East
- Volume 2: The Americas
- Volume 3: Asia and Pacific
- Volume 4: Europe

There are any number of ways to classify countries into regions of the world. We have mostly relied on a geographical classification based on the United Nations Statistics Division classification system (http://unstats.un.org/unsd/geoinfo/default.htm). But this method is far from satisfactory. Although geography (relatively speaking) remains the same, the borders of countries do not, mostly as a result of political conflict and other factors such as migration. Furthermore, the definition of what makes a country a country is also very difficult because there are many instances where "principalities" (e.g., San Marino) and "independent nations" (e.g., the Navajo Nation in the United States) exist inside larger nations or countries. The complex histories of colonialism and migration have resulted in particular countries containing a vast variety of peoples, cultures, and social arrangements, such that calling them a "country" or even "nation" gives a misleading impression of a cohesive national system governed by one set of laws. Bosnia and Herzogovina are perhaps a prime recent example of this difficulty.

Given the shifting boundaries and definitions of countries and the social, cultural, and political diversity contained in them, allocating such countries to broad regions of the world is obviously even less precise. The final allocation of countries that were hard to classify—Turkey, for example—was admittedly somewhat arbitrary. We finally placed Turkey, along with Georgia, in Asia, not Europe. And we located countries of the Middle East (itself a very difficult region to define in both geographical and political terms) along with Africa in Volume 1. A number of the countries classified in the Middle Eastern region could just

as easily be placed in Asia, and others are geographically located in North Africa. And the variety of countries found in the Asia and Pacific volume is also vast in terms of both geography and culture; New Zealand and Australia, for example, have much more in common with Europe, from a historical and cultural point of view, than they do with their near and distant neighbors in Asia (although this is probably changing). Thus, comparing regions on any number of crime and punishment factors is fraught with even greater difficulties than comparing individual countries. Some commonalities and patterns, however, do emerge when one peruses the world maps that are provided. It is likely, as editors to the respective volumes point out, that these patterns reflect the colonial past of these regions, although there are no doubt other explanations related to local culture, migration patterns, and political history.

About the Contributors

We have drawn on a variety of authors to contribute to these four volumes. In some cases, these authors are professionals who work for their governments, but in other cases (the majority), these authors are independent scholars. The objectivity of reports written by those who work for governments may perhaps be questioned, but on the other hand, government officials have much greater access to information and statistics than do outsiders. With a couple of important exceptions, all governments, by and large, have a monopoly on crime and punishment information. The exceptions are the international crime-victim surveys described earlier that are conducted mostly apart from governments, because they do not necessarily depend on officially recorded statistics by criminal justice officials. However, more government departments are conducting their own victimization surveys because some governments in the past have been embarrassed by the findings. Various nongovernmental watch groups, such as Amnesty International and Transparency International, also collect crime and punishment information and it is part of their mission to apply value judgments and criticism to governments and their administrators. As editors, we have tried in these chapters, as far as possible, to avoid either advocacy on behalf of the government's interest or criticism of governments, although in some cases the criminality and punitive practices of governments cannot be ignored.

—Graeme R. Newman
University at Albany

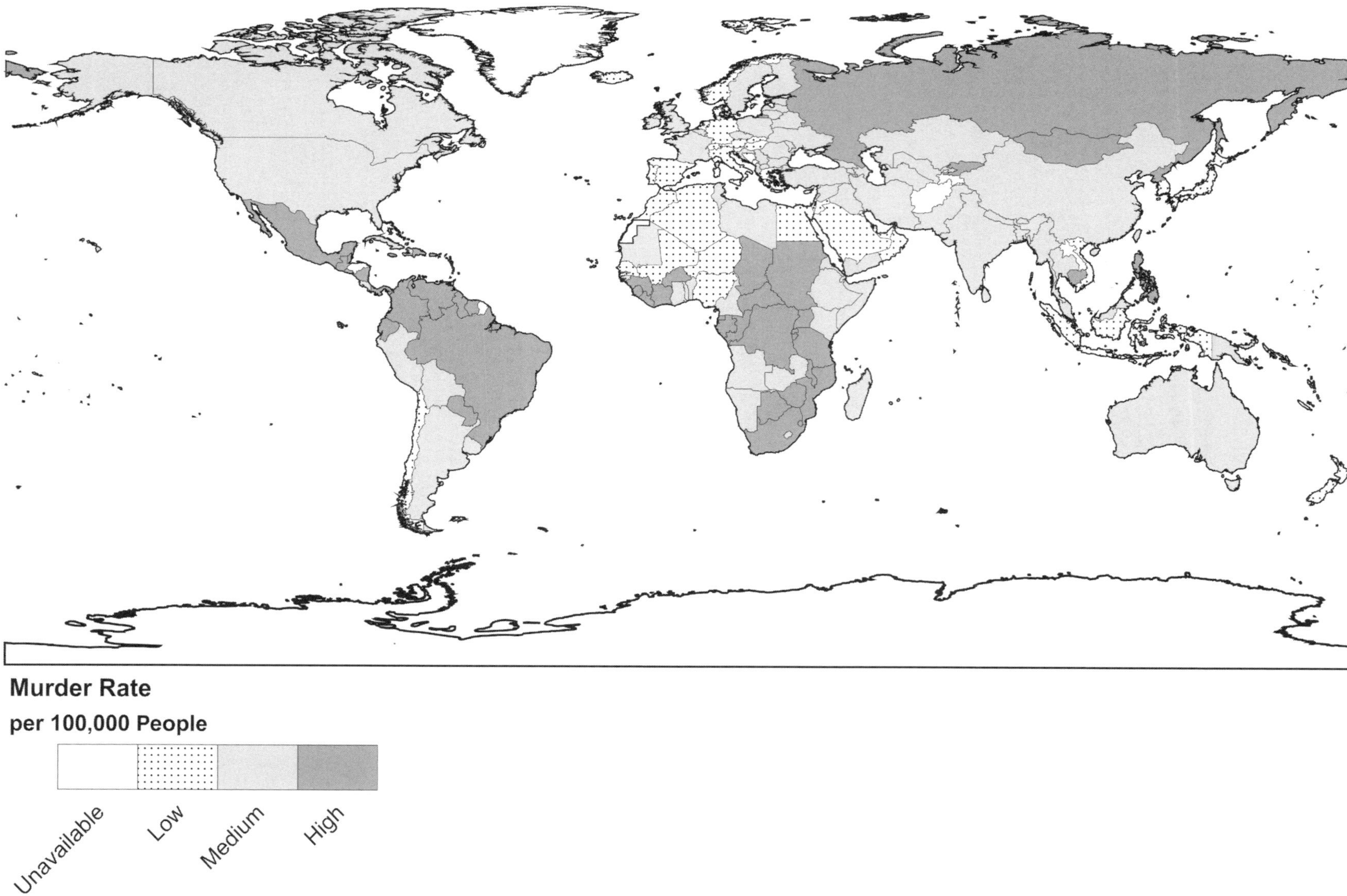

Murder around the World

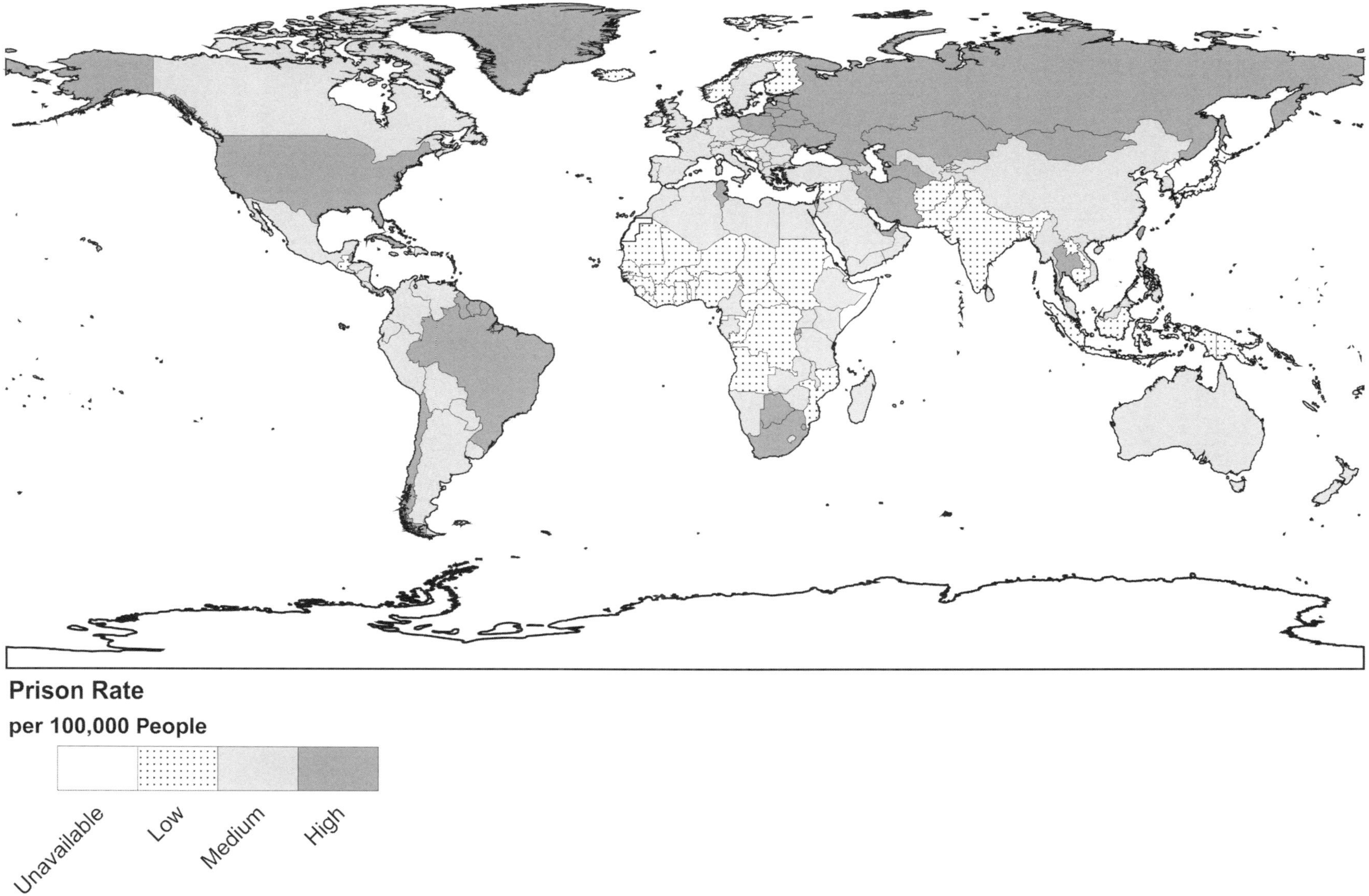

Imprisonment around the World

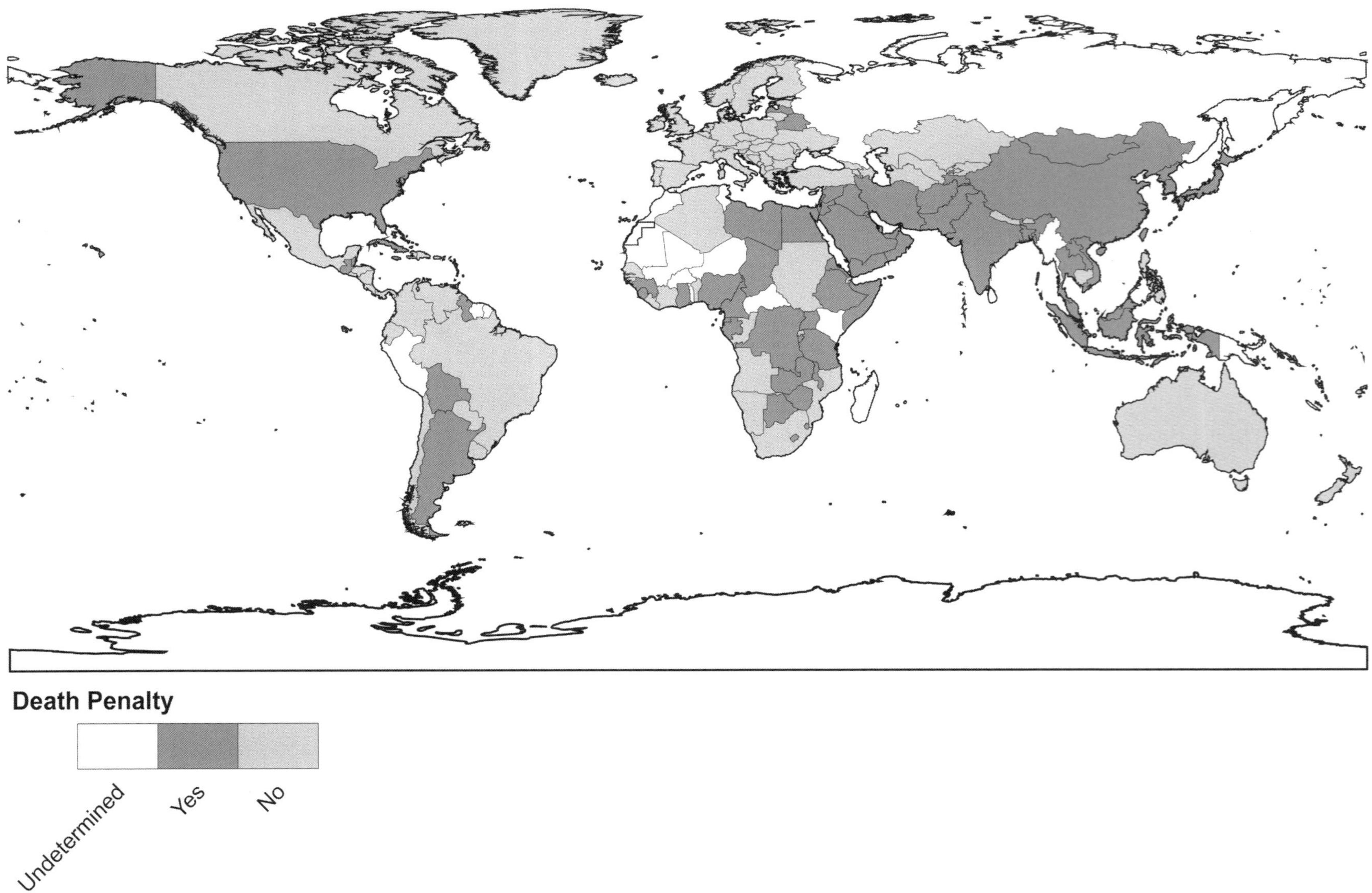

Death Penalty around the World

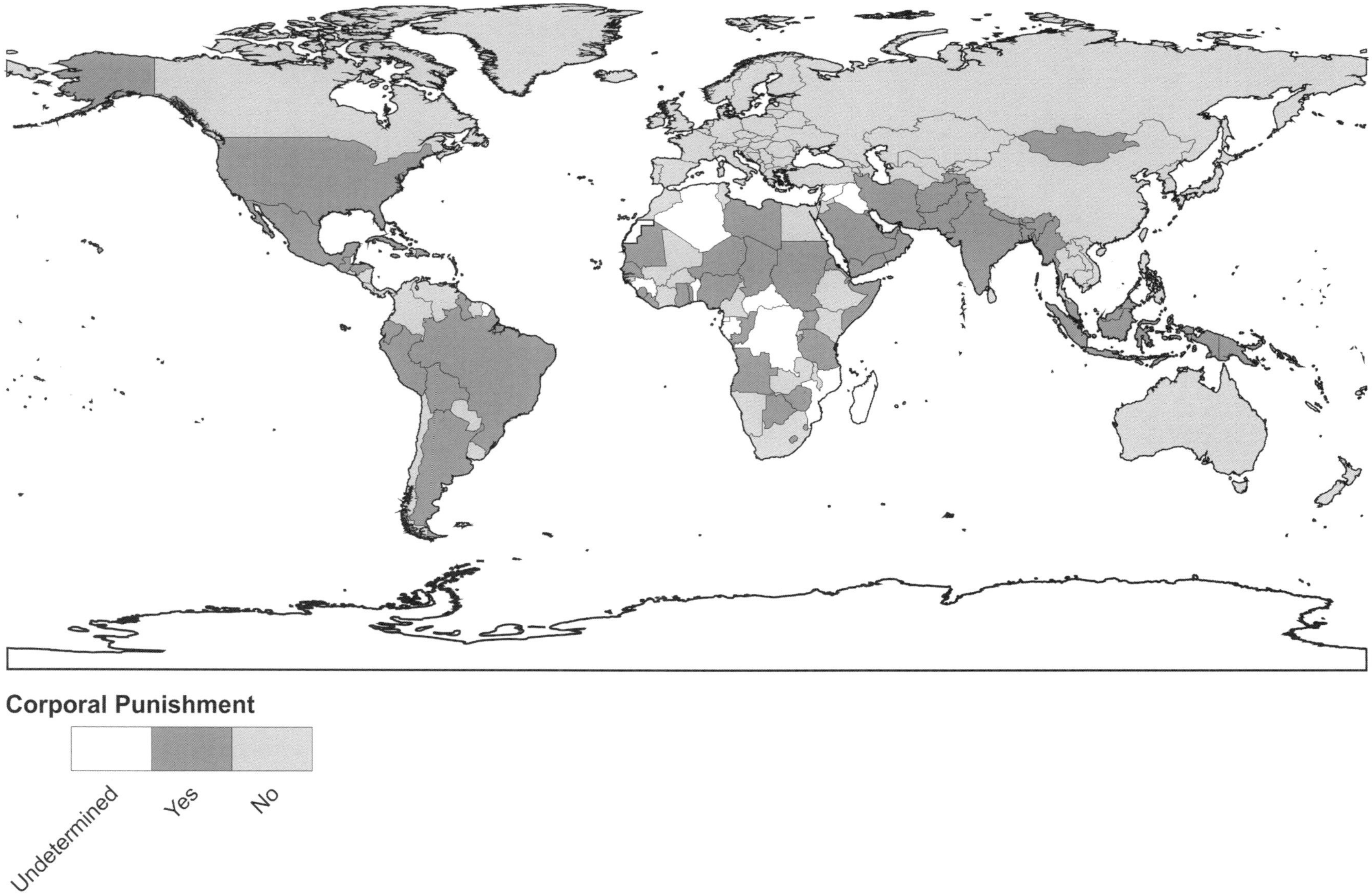

Corporal Punishment around the World

Introduction

The Americas volume of *Crime and Punishment around the World* encompasses North, Central, and South America, as well as the Caribbean islands. The Navajo Nation of the United States is also included in this volume. With respect to crime and punishment, the Americas are often categorized as having both high violent crime rates and high imprisonment rates. Although the maps in this volume show that these assessments are somewhat accurate, the range of the physical sizes of these countries obscures some of the diversity in crime and punishment patterns. For example, the relatively low homicide rates in Bermuda, Montserrat, and even the much larger country of Chile and the low imprisonment rates of Guatemala or the British Virgin Islands are overshadowed by larger countries with higher rates on these indicators.

It is difficult to compare the geographically large and populous countries of Argentina, Brazil, Canada, Mexico, and the United States with the smaller countries of Central and South America or the relatively tiny islands of the Caribbean. Experts typically control for size variations by comparing rates per 100,000 people, but this adjustment does not capture the different social dynamics in large versus small countries that contribute to or inhibit crime or the variability in informal and formal resources for social control and punishment. The country descriptions provided in this volume capture these nuances, which are easily overlooked in statistical snapshots.

We encourage readers to appreciate the differences among the countries in this volume and to avoid gross generalizations or oversimplifications, but also to notice the interesting patterns that emerge when connecting information across countries. Here we highlight five themes that we consider particularly noteworthy for understanding crime and punishment in the Americas.

Colonial Legacy

All the countries in the Americas share a colonial history, although the legacies differ depending on the colonizing countries, the length and extent of colonization, and the level of acceptance of the imposed order by indigenous populations. The "New World" was colonized by Norse, British, Spanish, Portuguese, Dutch, French, and other Europeans as early as the 11th century and lasting through the 20th century, and many of the smaller countries still retain territorial or dependency status. This colonial legacy has shaped contemporary crime and criminal justice issues in these countries in a number of ways.

First, the legal systems of these countries were adopted from those of the colonizing countries. For example, the common law system of Great Britain was retained in most of Canada, the United States, Belize, Jamaica, and Trinidad and Tobago, among other countries. In contrast, the civil law systems of Spain, Portugal, France, and the Netherlands permeate Central and South America, as well as many Caribbean countries. In several places, the imported legal systems have been adapted to fit local conditions. For example, customary laws and indigenous legal mechanisms coexist with national legal systems in many countries, including Bolivia, the British Virgin Islands, Greenland, and the United States.

Second, the colonial history has created quite heterogeneous populations in most of the countries in the Americas. Such diversity makes it difficult to achieve normative consensus and build strong informal social-control mechanisms to inhibit criminal activities, and it may also create inequalities and subcultures conducive to criminal behavior, as found in the examples of Barbados, Jamaica, and Brazil. This heterogeneity also poses challenges for the police, courts, and correctional institutions because citizens are sensitive to the identities of those exercising power over them.

Third, for some dependent nations, the colonial legacy has created multilevel criminal justice systems, whereby some criminal activities are regulated at the local level and others are handled at a higher level of government (e.g., the Navajo Nation within the United States) or even in another country (e.g., Britain's overseas territories). Additionally, laws imposed by the parent system may not be well received within the dependency. For example, there has been some debate in the Turks and Caicos Parliament regarding introducing corporal punishment and the death penalty as penal options, but this is unlikely to happen because it is an overseas territory of Great Britain, which does not permit these types of punishments.

The Role of Geography

The countries in this volume nicely illustrate the important role that geography—in terms of both relative location and physical characteristics—plays in crime commission, prevention, and detection and the overall functioning of the criminal justice system. In most of these entries, the sections on drug crimes and human trafficking highlight how geography facilitates the movement of goods from production or origin countries to consumption or destination countries. The entries on the Caribbean countries demonstrate the challenges of monitoring the movement of people and goods along vast waterways, coastal borders, and unregulated airspace with limited personnel and financial resources. In many countries, physical characteristics, such as land use, dense forests, and access to waterways, heavily influence the extent and types of trafficking problems.

Another less obvious way that geography affects crime and the criminal justice system is through natural disasters. Central America and the Caribbean islands are especially vulnerable to hurricanes, tropical storms, and volcanoes that hamper government infrastructures, including the criminal justice system. These disasters also contribute to economic downturns, migration, and other social disruptions that can increase criminal activity. The chapters on Dominica,

Nicaragua, and Montserrat provide poignant examples of how such disasters have affected the functioning of criminal justice systems.

Globalization

The entries in this volume provide many examples of how crime commission and criminal justice responses have been affected by globalization. International and transnational crimes, especially various forms of trafficking, have motivated countries to pool resources to deal with global criminal justice issues. There are several examples of multinational task forces to fight such crimes as drug trafficking and money laundering. Much of this cooperation involves common legislation and pooling resources for police training and operations. The small islands of the Caribbean, in particular, have initiated several cooperative arrangements to share criminal justice expertise and resources, such as the fairly recent creation of a Caribbean Court of Justice.

Globalization has also increased the sharing of new ideas and best practices for criminal justice systems. Practices that are common in many developed Western countries are being considered in other countries to alleviate problems such as court case backlogs and prison overcrowding. For example, Paraguay has recently established a Mediation Office to relieve court dockets, and the Bahamas is considering using electronic monitoring and community service for less serious offenders to reduce prison overcrowding.

An old form of globalization, and a new form of colonialism to some critics, is the critical role of the United States in reshaping judicial systems and criminal procedures across Latin America. Through the U.S. Agency for International Development (USAID) under the Department of State, Washington has provided an enormous amount of funding, technical assistance, personnel training, equipment transfer, and political backing or pressure to initiate and maintain criminal justice reform. USAID usually begins with the identification of political parties, government agencies, and nongovernmental organizations supportive of system revisions for the enhancement of human rights, control of illicit drugs, promotion of anticorruption, protection of public safety, and good governance in general. Because the isolation of the judicial system from undue political, societal, or economic influences constitutes the unifying thread of these progressive political agendas, the United States has been fairly successful in promoting and accomplishing important institutional changes in these emerging democracies. The result is the widespread adoption of American-born adversarial trial practices (e.g., oral and public proceedings, the jury, professionalization of prosecutors, etc.), crime control policies (e.g., community policing), and community outreach programs (e.g., drug-abuse reduction and education programs) in a continent with a long history of civil law traditions.

Dynamic Social Systems

The entries in this volume also highlight how national criminal justice systems change not only in response to crime problems but also to accommodate other social changes. The most notable changes for this region are political. Many Central and South American countries have experienced prolonged periods of political upheaval since their independence. Despite the historical legacy of colonialism that is still apparent, laws, social conditions, and criminal justice systems are all shaped by existing political structures. For example, recent electoral changes in Mexico have been accompanied by reforms in policing, anticorruption initiatives, and efforts to improve the efficiency of the criminal justice system. Likewise, the chapter on Cuba nicely illustrates how laws have been shaped by the socialist government and how both crime and the criminal justice system are changing in the post-Castro era.

The diversity and multiplicity of social changes have also created forces that are pushing criminal justice systems in different, and sometimes conflicting, directions. For example, the search for a police accountable and responsive to the citizenry has led to the introduction of community-oriented or problem-solving policing practices aimed at the improvement of citizens' satisfaction with the police in Brazil, Colombia, Guatemala, and Honduras. But the rampant activities of drug syndicates and violent street gangs have triggered the militarization of police operations and the distorted application of quasi-counterinsurgency tactics in the same countries, which have brought about an array of complaints about a severe erosion of civil rights. How these emerging democracies should prioritize their criminal justice needs and sail through the dilemmas posed by divergent social forces remains a thorny problem whose resolution requires participatory deliberation from the public, a commitment from the government to stamp out institutional hurdles against the rule of law, and sustained foreign assistance that is substantively meaningful and geopolitically neutral and credible.

Fear of the Return of Authoritarianism

Between the 1960s and 1980s, coup d'états led by the military, who justified their rule as a way of bringing political stability for the nation or rescuing it from the threat of communism, swept Latin America. The typical military dictatorship in Latin America was ruled by a committee composed of several officers, often from the military's most senior leadership, but in other cases, less senior, as evidenced by the term "colonels' regime." The judiciary and supporting criminal justice agencies were deprived of their autonomy and often forced to collaborate in systematic violations of human rights. Illegal arrests, criminal investigations for the purpose of political harassment, unsubstantiated prosecutions, the selection of prosecutors and appointment of magistrates based on ideological loyalties, suspension of habeas corpus, torture, and extrajudicial executions were some common aberrations of the formal apparatus of social control.

During the 1990s and 2000s, judicial reforms seized Latin America following the reemergence and consolidation of democratic governance. These reforms often began with constitutional redesigns that gave more influence and resources to the Supreme Court to strengthen the independence of the judiciary and introduce adversarial elements (e.g., replacing judges of instruction with prosecutors, limited use of juries, etc.) into criminal proceedings to enhance the chance of the accused to have access to a fair and open trial. The demilitarization of police forces is also frequently seen as an essential ingredient in the democratization of the system. The penal apparatus remains the weakest link in the chain of criminal justice rebirths. Few alternatives to incarceration have been implemented, and existing prisons are still infamous for overcrowding, violence, and substandard management. Overall, progress in the rule of law is facilitated by an ongoing political competition among risk-averse parties. Whereas the society at large demands these institutional revisions as a protection against the return of authoritarian practices or dictatorial regimes, political parties find in an independent and functioning judiciary an effective check on the power of their rivals. The implementation of judicial reform serves the ruling party as an insurance policy, in that a strong judicial branch reduces the risks faced by a ruling party once it loses power and becomes the opposition.

Acknowledgments

Many of the entries in this volume provide unique insights on crime and punishment because of the professional expertise and firsthand knowledge of the authors. Some of the shorter entries rely primarily on secondary sources, but compiling that information is still a challenging task despite the assistance of the Internet. We are grateful for the efforts of all of the contributors in making this volume as comprehensive as possible.

—Janet P. Stamatel
University at Albany;
Hung-En Sung
John Jay College of Criminal Justice

Country Key to the Americas Maps

American Samoa	AS	Guadeloupe	GP
Anguilla	AI	Guatemala	GT
Antigua and Barbuda	AG	Guyana	GY
Argentina	AR	Haiti	HT
Aruba	AW	Honduras	HN
Bahamas	BS	Jamaica	JM
Barbados	BB	Martinique	MQ
Belize	BZ	Mexico	MX
Bermuda	BM	Montserrat	MS
Bolivia	BO	Netherlands Antilles	AN
Brazil	BR	Nicaragua	NI
British Virgin Islands	VG	Panama	PA
Canada	CA	Paraguay	PY
Cayman Islands	KY	Peru	PE
Chile	CL	Puerto Rico	PR
Colombia	CO	St. Kitts and Nevis	KN
Costa Rica	CR	St. Lucia	LC
Cuba	CU	St. Pierre and Miquelon	PM
Dominica	DM	St. Vincent and the Grenadines	VC
Dominican Republic	DO	Suriname	SR
Ecuador	EC	Trinidad and Tobago	TT
El Salvador	SV	Turks and Caicos Islands	TC
Falkland Islands (Islas Malvinas)	FK	United States	US
French Guiana	GF	Uruguay	UY
Greenland	GL	U.S. Virgin Islands	VI
Grenada	GD	Venezuela	VE

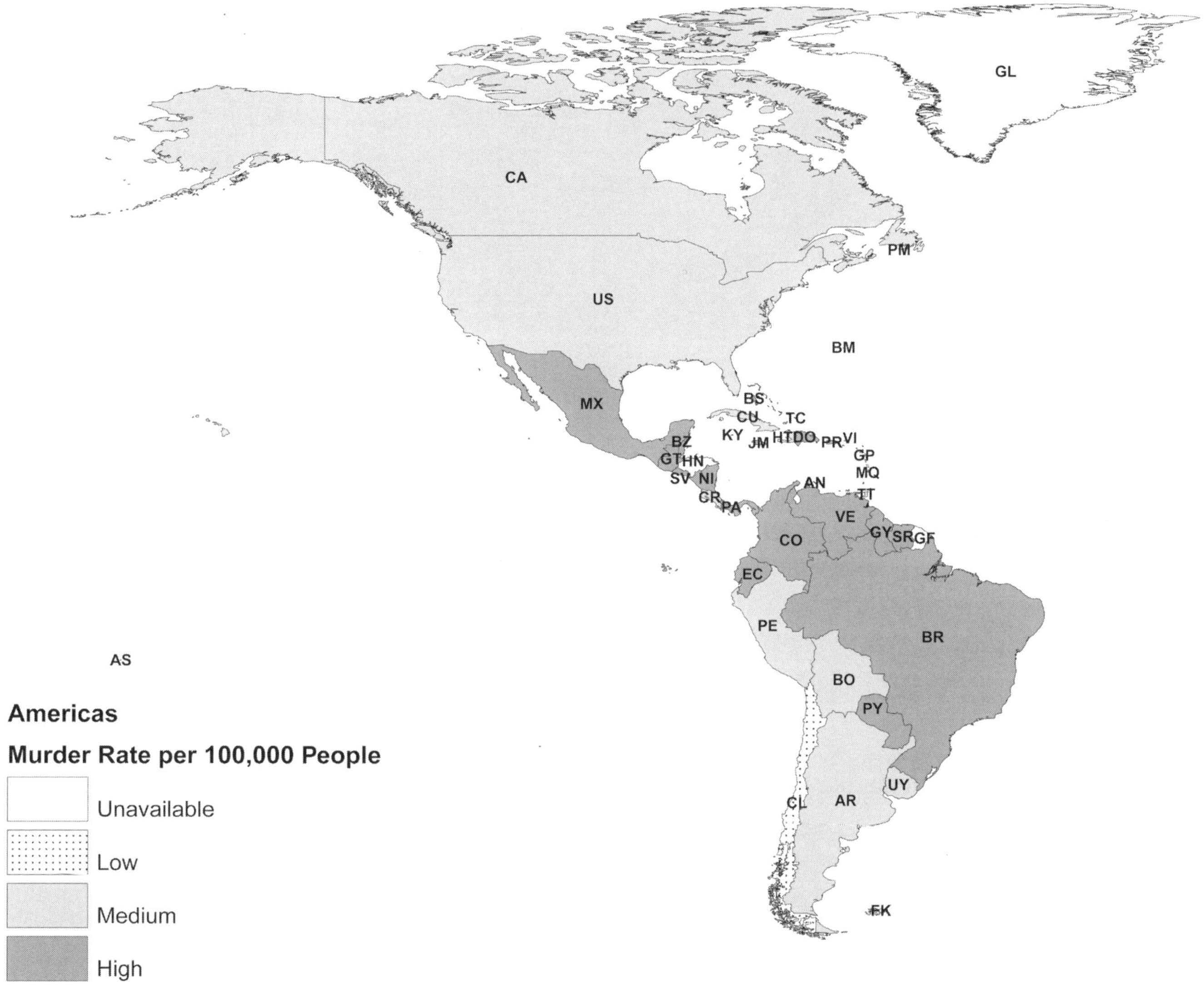

Murder in the Americas

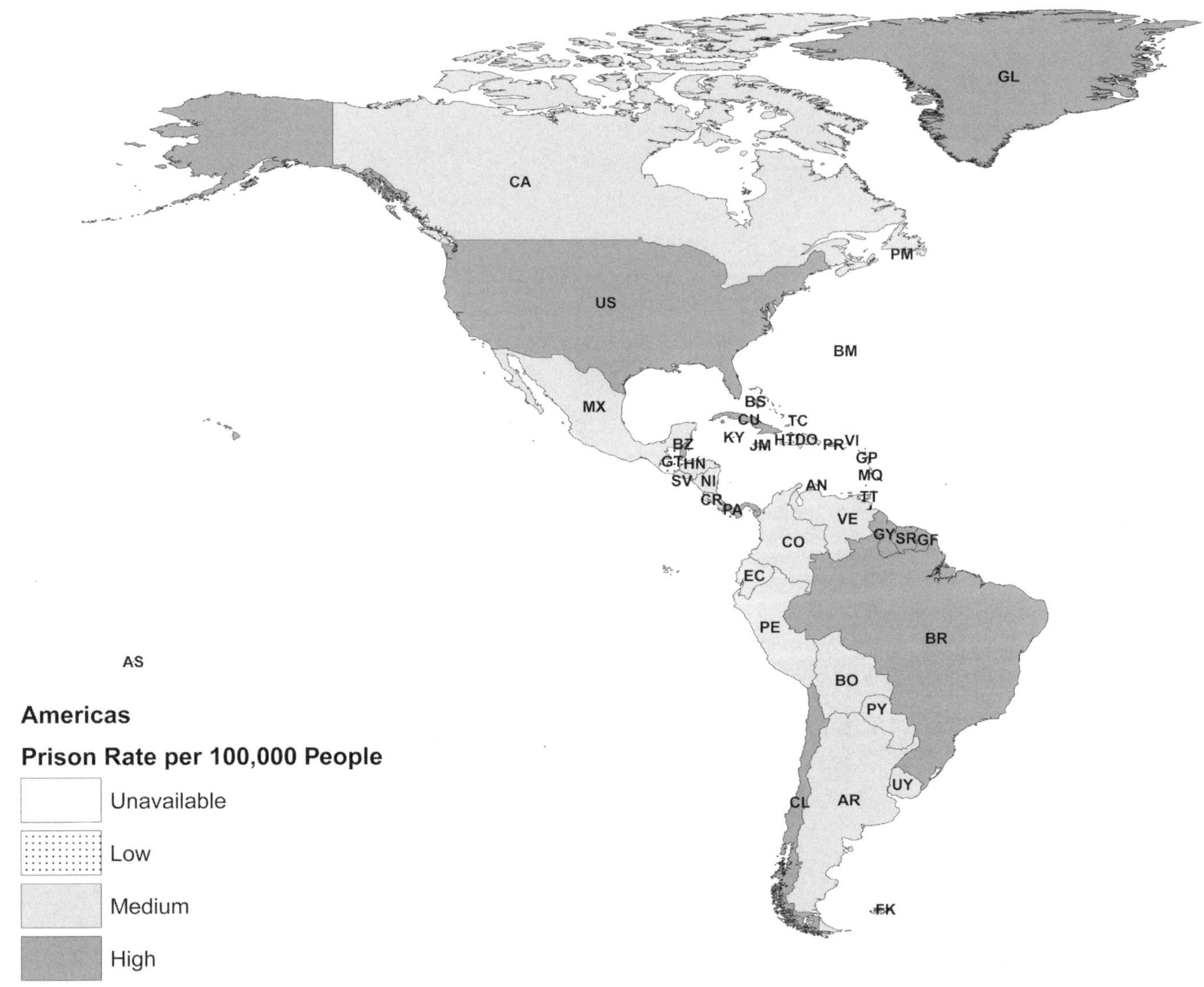

Imprisonment in the Americas

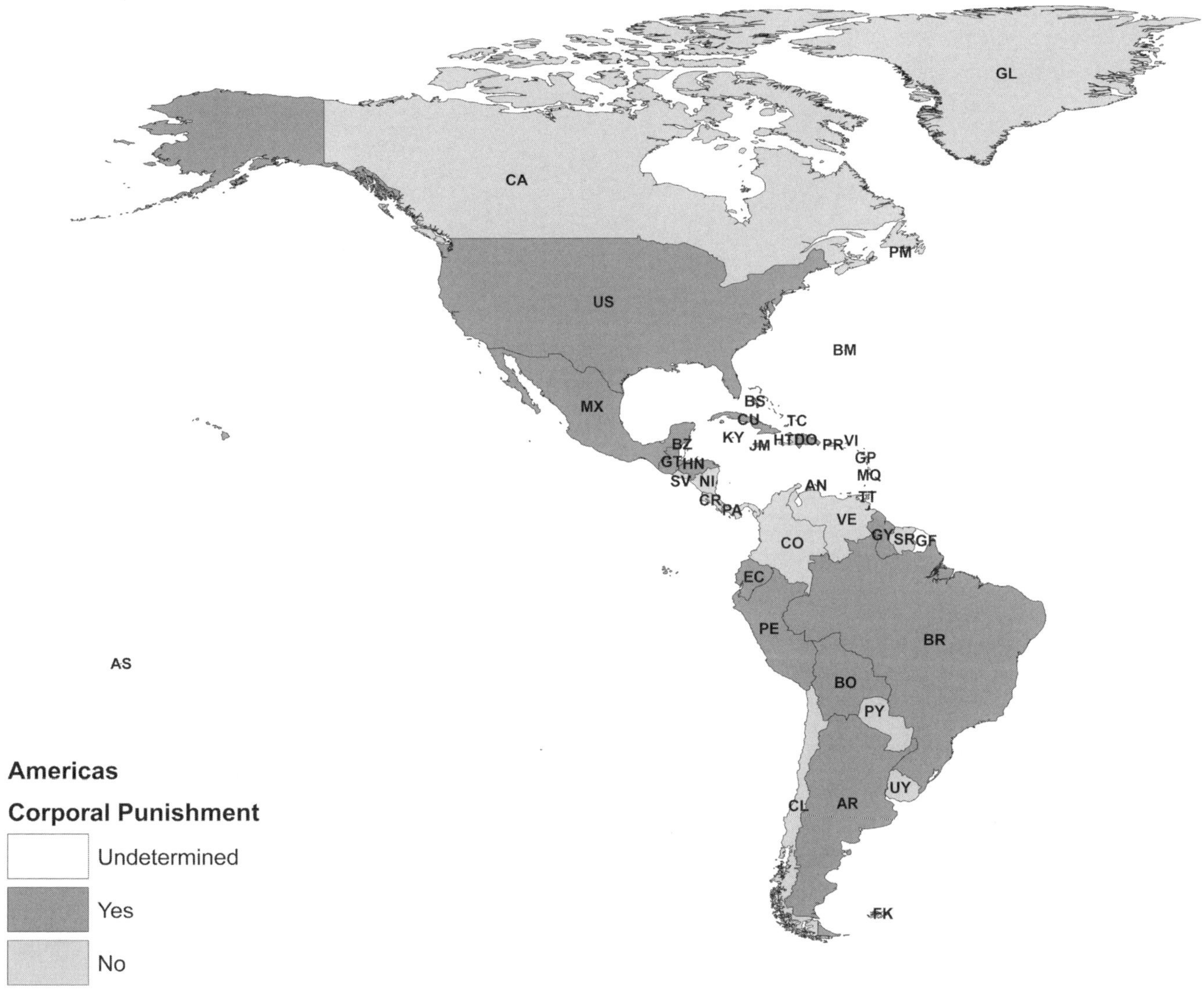

Corporal Punishment in the Americas

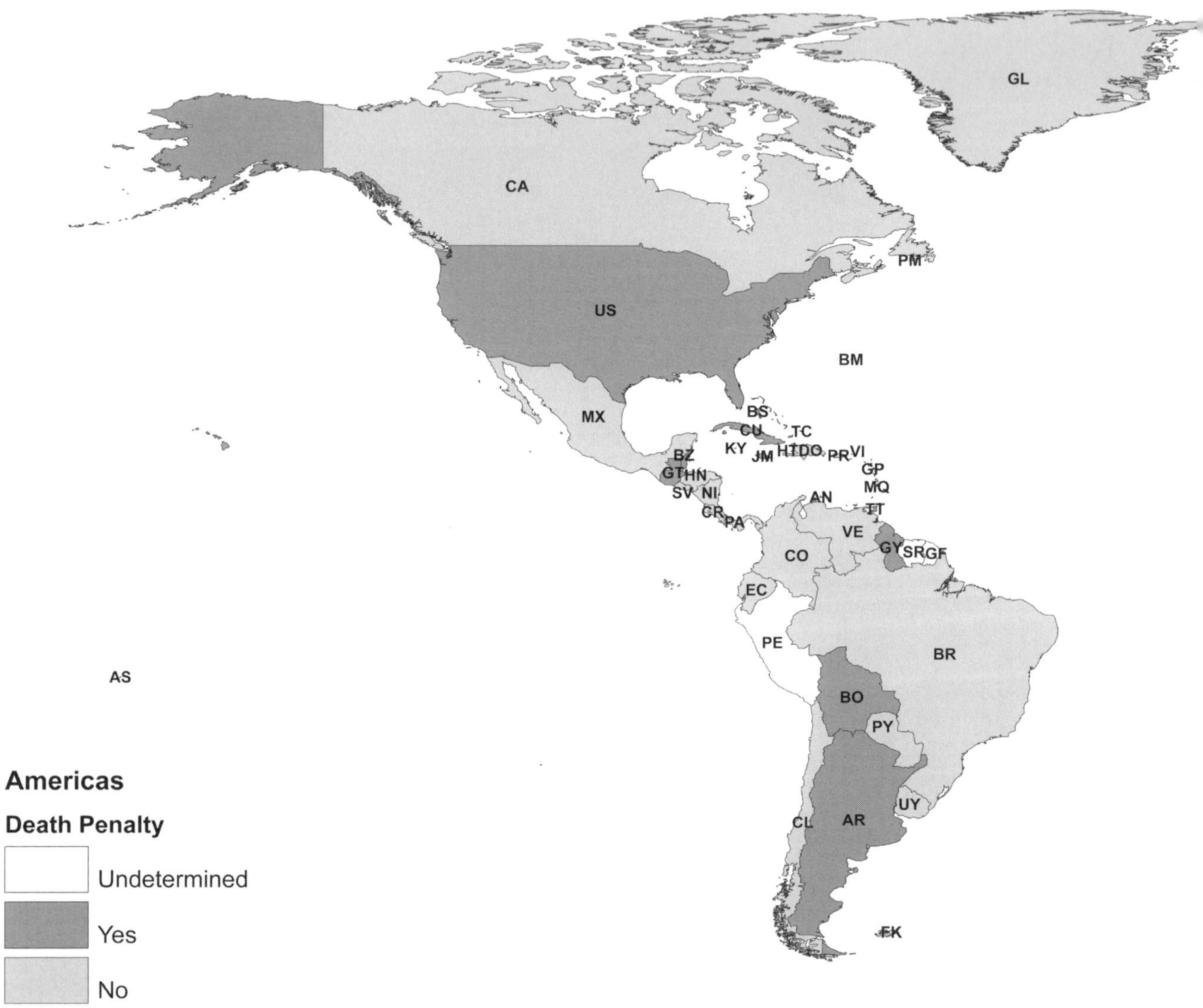

Death Penalty in the Americas

The Americas

Anguilla

Legal System: Common
Prison Rate: High
Death Penalty: No
Corporal Punishment: No

Background

Anguilla is the most northern of the Leeward Islands in the eastern Caribbean Sea. Apart from the main island of Anguilla, the territory includes a number of smaller islands and cays with no permanent population. Anguilla's land area covers 91 square kilometers, and the population is about 9,000 people. The official language of Anguilla is English, but some inhabitants speak a Creole language derived from a mixture of African and English languages.

Before the Europeans inhabited Anguilla, the Arawak Indians had settled there. It was first colonized in 1650 by English settlers who believed the land would be beneficial for cultivation. However, the dry climate, thin soil, and hurricane season severely hampered agricultural development. During the 1830s, the British recommended the union of St. Kitts, Nevis, and Anguilla, much to the dismay of the Anguillan people. In 1962, the federation of the West Indies collapsed, and St. Kitts, Nevis, and Anguilla were made into an associated statehood. Anguilla wanted to be free of this statehood, sparking the Anguilla Revolution. The British intervened and developed a peacekeeping committee, but debates regarding Anguilla's succession continued until December 19, 1980, when Anguilla became a separate overseas territory.

As an overseas territory, Anguilla recognizes Queen Elizabeth II as the chief of state who is represented by an appointed governor. The governor has powers with respect to legislation, external affairs, offshore finance, defense and internal security, and the public service. The 1982 Constitution provides for a governor, an Executive Council, and a House of Assembly. Anguilla is an associate member of the Caribbean Community (CARICOM) and of the Organization of Eastern Caribbean States (OECS).

Legal and Criminal Justice System

In Anguilla there is a High Court of Justice with a resident High Court judge, whose jurisdiction is original and unlimited. This judge presides over both civil and criminal matters. There is also a Magistrate's Court, whose jurisdiction is statutory. Both courts are located in the capital of Valley.

The Magistrate's Court deals with a large quantity of minor legal matters. Some of these matters include civil claims up to EC$15,000 (approx. US$5,714), the issuance of search warrants, bail applications, traffic violations, and the trial of minor criminal charges. Minor criminal offenses tried in the Magistrate's Court are known as summary offenses. More serious offenses, known as indictable offenses, are usually tried in the High Court. There are cases in which an indictable offense may be tried in a Magistrate's Court if certain conditions are met. The Magistrate's Court is also responsible for hearing preliminary inquiries. A preliminary hearing is held whenever a person is charged with an indictable offense that cannot be tried summarily. An example of such an offense would be rape or murder. The Magistrate's Court must review the evidence and decide whether the accused will be tried in the High Court.

The Eastern Caribbean Supreme Court (ECSC) was established in 1967 by the West Indies Associated States Supreme Court Order. It is a superior court of record for nine member states, including Anguilla. The court has unlimited jurisdiction in the member states. The ECSC sits in two divisions: the Court of Appeal and the High Court of Justice Trial Division. Each member territory has its own high court. A three-judge panel of the Eastern Caribbean Court of Appeal sits in Anguilla during rotations within the territories that make up the Eastern Caribbean Supreme Court. The headquarters of the Eastern Caribbean Court of Appeals is in Castries, Saint Lucia. The court interprets and applies the laws of the member states and decides on criminal and civil matters. The ECSC also listens to appeals from the decisions of the Magistrate's Court and the High Court. There is a final right to appeal to the Privy Council in the United Kingdom.

The Common Law Act, originally enacted in 1705, adopted the English common law, subject to any modifications thereof. In 2000, Anguilla's laws were revised and consolidated, resulting in the Revised Statutes and Regulations of Anguilla. The courts also rely heavily on the jurisprudence of the Commonwealth as a whole, including the wider Caribbean, although only the jurisprudence of the Eastern Caribbean Supreme Court and of the Privy Council is binding on them.

Police

The Royal Anguilla Police Force is responsible for maintaining law and order on the island. It was formed after the withdrawal of the London Metropolitan Police in February 1972. It is headed by the commissioner of police and is made up of approximately 100 officers. Since 2001, there has been a focus on community policing and developing relations with community organizations. There have also been efforts to improve the qualifications of recruits and to diversify the police force.

Crime

Classifications of Crime

According to the Anguilla criminal code, an offense is triable summarily when the maximum term of imprisonment for the offense is two years or less. An offense is triable on indictment when the maximum term for imprisonment is more than two years. The criminal code of Anguilla maintains that ignorance of the laws of the land is not an excuse unless knowledge of the law is an expressed element of an individual's defense. If an individual has a mistake of fact that is honest and reasonable but that leads to a certain act or omission of an act, that person will not be held criminally responsible.

The Anguilla criminal code distinguishes between an individual successfully committing a criminal act and attempting a criminal act for certain crimes. For other crimes, where the law does not distinguish between attempted and completed crimes, a person may be subject to the same punishment that he or she would receive if he or she had successfully completed the crime attempted.

Drugs and Money Laundering

Anguilla, along with other U.K. Caribbean overseas territories, has established offshore banking institutions. This has created a problem for the country because drug traffickers have tried to use these facilities to launder money. In response, the British government has increased regulation over its financial services sector. The introduction of guidelines for the issuance of new bank licenses has helped restrict licenses to subsidiaries of well-established banks with effective parent-bank supervision.

Anguilla has been noted as a transshipment point for South American narcotics destined for the United States and Europe. Illicit drugs transit the eastern Caribbean mostly by sea in small quick vessels, larger fishing vessels, yachts, and freight carriers.

There is also some narcotics shipment through airdrop in this region. Recently, there has been an increase in the use of sailing yachts to transport drugs from the Caribbean to Europe. Penalties for possession, use, and trafficking in illegal drugs are severe. Once convicted, offenders can be faced with heavy fines and long jail sentences.

Crime Statistics

The only justice statistics available are those from the annual police report. Crimes are reported by the police, but prosecutions are conducted through the court system and are then recorded manually in the police records. The records from the police are not given to the statistics department because of the confidential nature of the data. The police department currently needs a computer system for administrative and statistical purposes. They currently use a system known as the Overseas Territories Regional Criminal Intelligence System (OTRCIS), which is problematic because the police department is dependent on those in Miami to make any changes to it so that different information can be captured and reports produced.

Despite those challenges, Anguilla's statistics department published some information regarding crime and justice that was reported by the Caribbean Development Bank. These statistics show that there was a steady increase in property crime between 1995 and 2001, though assault and robbery remained stable. Of the 206 reported burglaries in 2001, 61 cases were cleared. Numbers of crimes reported to police for 2001 were as follows:

Thefts and other stealing	227
Burglary (house and store)	206
Criminal damage	23
Assault and robbery	34
Drugs	20
Sexual offense	16
Firearm	5
Other	21

According to data collected by the Anguillan statistics department, the murder rate in Anguilla has been increasing in recent years. In 1995, the homicide rate was about 10 per 100,000. This increased to more than 16 in 2002 and 2003 but declined to 8 per 100,000 in 2004.

Finding of Guilt

Rights of the Accused

The Anguilla Constitution maintains that a person charged with a criminal offense shall be given a fair hearing within a reasonable amount of time and that the hearing will be given by an independent and impartial court established by law. The accused has the right to be informed orally and in writing of the nature of the offense for which he or she is being charged. Any person who is charged with a criminal offense is believed to be innocent until proven guilty and must be granted adequate time to prepare a defense.

The rights of the accused also include the right to an interpreter, free of charge, to anyone who cannot understand the English language. An individual may not have a harsher punishment imposed on him or her retroactively because of an increased penalty for a specific crime. A person may not be found guilty of a crime that did not, at the time it took place, constitute such an offense. Once a person has been acquitted or convicted of a particular crime, that person cannot be tried for that crime again. An accused person also shall not be compelled to give evidence at his or her trial.

Juvenile Justice

According to the Juvenile Act, Anguillan courts are required to have regard for the welfare of juveniles (persons under 16 years of age) and are authorized to take steps to remove a juvenile from an undesirable surrounding. Under the Juvenile Courts Act, a juvenile cannot be tried in a Magistrate's Court. The act established a juvenile court separate from others where members of the public are excluded to protect the juvenile. The juvenile court can issue orders that commit the juvenile to the care of a willing adult. They are also authorized to put a juvenile and his or her parents on probation. Once the juvenile is in the care of an adult, these adults are subject to the same liabilities as the juvenile parents. If a juvenile runs away from those to whose care he or she has been committed, the juvenile may be apprehended without a warrant. Juveniles are placed in a "place of safety" while awaiting juvenile court decisions. The construction of a Juvenile Rehabilitation Center in Anguilla was almost completed as of 2009, and a manager for the Juvenile Center has been hired. The rest of the staff will be recruited from the Department of Probation.

Punishment

Types of Punishment

According to the Anguilla criminal code, there are many forms of punishment that may be imposed on offenders, including imprisonment, fines, probation, and community service. In a case where an individual may be subject to punishment by fines, imprisonment, or both, it is in the court's discretion as to which punishment should be applied. In situations where there are no express provisions related to the fine, the amount is unlimited but cannot be excessive. When the sum of money to be paid may not exceed EC$200 (approx. US$76), the period of imprisonment may not exceed 14 days. When the sum of money to be paid exceeds EC$2,000 (approx. US$756), the period of imprisonment may not exceed six months. The Anguilla courts may take mitigating factors into account, such as age, character, antecedents, health, mental condition, nature of the offense, and extenuating circumstances. Even if it was determined in trial court that the charge has been proven, a court can dismiss the charge after taking into account a variety of these factors.

For the crime of attempting to commit rape or aiding in a rape, a person is liable to imprisonment for seven years upon conviction. A person who is convicted of procuring or attempting to procure a woman into prostitution is liable to imprisonment of three years. Any person who is convicted of wounding another person is liable to imprisonment for two years upon conviction. Any person who is convicted of murder is liable to imprisonment for life. When a person participates in unlawful use of firearms, he or she is liable to imprisonment for five years. Infanticide is an offense that is treated as manslaughter according to the Anguilla criminal code. In 1999, the death penalty was abolished in Anguilla, along with all of the small British dependencies.

Since 1993, the punishment for most criminal convictions in Anguilla was a fine. According to the statistics department, 49 percent of convicts in 2003 were fined instead of having other punishments such as imprisonment. Of the total criminal offenses in 2002, there were 12 imprisonments, 176 fines, and 68 other penalties. In 1995 and 1996, the number of persons imprisoned remained constant with only four persons. These years contained the lowest number of prisoners from 1992 to 2004.

Probation

The Department of Probation in Anguilla was first established in 2005 and has served more than 100 clients so far. Over 95 percent of adults on probation are employed, and all juveniles in the probation system are attending school. The Department of Probation in Anguilla describes probation as an alternative in which defendants aged 10 years or over are supervised in the community by a probation officer. The probationer is permitted to carry out normal daily activities as well as maintain employment and reside at home. A sentence of probation can be no less than 12 months and no longer than 3 years.

A few of the terms for probation include a curfew, home visits by probation officers, and community service. The Department of Probation coordinates regular curfew checks to confirm compliance, and often probation officers conduct checks with the Royal Anguilla Police Force. Probationers cannot leave Anguilla without written permission from their chief probation officer.

The probation officer has many responsibilities including preparing pre-sentencing reports when ordered by the court; accepting offenders on probation; providing supervision, guidance, and enforcement of the probation order; becoming friendly with the probationer and seeking his or her confidence; and acting as a confidant to the probationer. It is interesting to note the positive relationship a probation officer is asked to maintain with his or her probationer. The Department of Probation has also worked in collaboration with Her Majesty's Prison and other departments to develop draft legislation for the parole of prisoners.

Prison

The Ministry of Social Development is responsible for all matters related to the probation and prison system. Her Majesty's Prison is Anguilla's sole prison. The head of prison administration receives the title of superintendent of prisons. According to the International Centre for Prison Studies, in September 2007, the total prison population including pretrial detainees was 55. Juvenile and minors represented 3.6 percent of the total prison population, and there were no women in prison. Foreign prisoners made up 7.3 percent of the prison population.

Jessica Gentile

Further Reading

Banks, Victor F. (2008). *Time for Consolidation: Coping with the Growing Pains of Transformation.* Budget Address: http://www.gov.ai/story.php?id=227.

Eastern Caribbean Supreme Court: http://www.eccourts.org/.

Government of Anguilla: http://www.gov.ai/.

Halcrow Group Limited. (2004). *Caribbean Development Bank Government of Anguilla Country Poverty Assessment.* (2002). London: Halcrow Group Limited.

Hope-Ross, Penny. (2004, July 1). *A Strategic Plan for the Statistical System of Anguilla 2005–2009.* Government of Anguilla: http://unstats.un.org/unsd/dnss/docViewer.aspx?docID=2199.

Peters, D. C. (1992). *The Democratic System in the Eastern Caribbean.* Westport, CT: Greenwood Press.

Antigua and Barbuda

Legal System: Common
Murder: Medium
Prison Rate: High
Death Penalty: Yes
Corporal Punishment: Yes

Background

Antigua and Barbuda is an island nation located between the Caribbean Sea and the North Atlantic Ocean. The country consists of three islands: Antigua, Barbuda, and the uninhabited Redonda. Together the islands make up a small area of land about 442.6 square kilometers. The total population of Antigua and Barbuda is approximately 84,522.

In 1981, Antigua and Barbuda became an independent state within the British Commonwealth of Nations. At the same time, the country was also inducted into the Organization of Eastern Caribbean States (OECS) and to the Caribbean Community and Common Market (CARICOM). The country is a constitutional monarchy with a parliamentary system of government. Queen Elizabeth II is the head of state, and she is represented by a governor-general who acts on the advice of the prime minister and the cabinet.

Legal and Judicial Systems

The supreme law of Antigua and Barbuda is its Constitution, which was made by royal prerogative under the 1981 Antiguan Independence Act of the United Kingdom. The country's Constitution guarantees many basic fundamental human rights, such as the right to freedom of speech, freedom of the press, freedom of religion and association, the presumption of innocence, and freedom from discrimination based on race, political opinion, religion, and so forth. The Constitution also recognizes the separation between the executive, legislative, and judicial branches of government. The primary source of law in Antigua and Barbuda is legislation. Common law is still very much alive in the country, and there is reliance on the doctrine of judicial precedent.

The judicial branch in Antigua and Barbuda consists of the magistrates' courts for minor offenses and the High Court for major offenses. Beyond those courts, a case may proceed to the Eastern Caribbean States Supreme Court. The members of this court are appointed by the Organization of Eastern Caribbean States (OECS). Any appointments or dismissals of magistrates of the Supreme Court require unanimous approval from the heads of government in the OECS system. The prime minister of Antigua and Barbuda acts on the recommendation of the attorney general in making decisions regarding this judicial body.

The final court of appeals for Antigua and Barbuda is the Judicial Committee of the Privy Council, located in London, England. Under certain circumstances, a defendant has the right to appeal a lower court's ruling to the Privy Council. These circumstances include civil proceedings where the matter under dispute has a value of EC$1,500 (approx. US$562) or above, civil proceedings involving questions about property rights, proceedings that are centered around the nullification of a marriage, proceedings that involve constitutional questions and interpretations, and any other cases that may be prescribed.

The only specialized judicial body in Antigua and Barbuda is the Industrial Court. This court has the ability to hear and determine trade disputes, to enjoin a trade union or other organization from taking or continuing an industrial action, and to hear any complaints brought in accordance with the Industrial Court Act. This court has special privileges, such as not having to follow regular evidentiary procedures and allowance to act without regard to technicalities and legal form. The Industrial Court basically determines its own procedures, although its decisions can be appealed to the Court of Appeals in certain scenarios. There are no military or political courts.

Role of Police

Security forces consist of the Royal Police Force of Antigua and Barbuda and the small Antigua and Barbuda Defense Force. The police force is organized, trained, and supervised according to British law enforcement practices. It is made up of about 600 persons. The uniformed men and women do not normally carry firearms. Many officers come from other islands to work for the Royal Police Force, thus adding to the impartiality of policing a small community. The divisional headquarters is in St. John's. The police force is responsible for law and order maintenance and is also responsible for the seaward defense of the state.

Crime

Classification of Crimes

Indictable offenses include felonies or the more serious offenses. The maximum penalty for such an offense is usually at least 12 months. Non-indictable offenses are known as summary offenses. Generally, the punishment is a reliable indication of the type of offense. Usually, if the punishment is a fine or 6 months' imprisonment or less, then the offense is summary. In many circumstances, the statute creating the offense will specify whether it is punishable on summary conviction.

All criminal proceedings must start in the magistrates' courts whether they are for indictable or summary offenses. Magistrates hold preliminary hearings regarding indictable offenses to determine whether a prima facie case of guilt has been made and to decide if a case should be determined by a trial by jury. An indictable offense must be tried in the High Court unless there is a specific scenario that allows a magistrate to hear the case. The magistrates' courts can hear certain types of more serious cases at the option of the accused, the prosecution, or the court. If an offense is summary, then the magistrate is responsible for trying the matter without the participation of a jury. Usually a magistrate, not a justice, sits in the magistrates' courts. A magistrate is usually a trained lawyer and is the judge of both fact and law in summary courts.

The age of criminal responsibility in Antigua and Barbuda is 8 years of age. Under the Juvenile Act, a person under the age of 16 is considered a juvenile. The Juvenile Act asserts that every court shall have a distinct regard for the welfare of a juvenile during criminal procedures.

Steadroy McDougal is escorted by prison officers to the High Court in St. John's, Antigua, on September 27, 2000. McDougal is accused of the 1998 murders of his ex-girlfriend and her boyfriend. (AP Photo)

Drug Trafficking and Money Laundering

The Misuse of Drugs Act in Antigua and Barbuda breaks controlled drugs up into three classes. Class A drugs include cocaine, desomorphine, hydrocodone, morphine, opium, oxycodone, and many more. Class B drugs include cannabis, codeine, amphetamine, and others. Class C drugs include benzphetamine, mephentermine, phentermine, prolintane, and others. Antigua and Barbuda is considered a minor transshipment point for narcotics, particularly cocaine, on their way to the United States and Europe from South America. Certain locations including secluded beaches and uncontrolled marinas provide excellent locations to conduct drug transfer transactions.

The islands are also significant offshore financial centers. In 1997 and 1998, the country passed anti–money laundering legislation to help regulate the offshore banking sector, which was facing difficulties because of laundered money from drug trafficking. Additionally, the Antigua and Barbuda government has asked a number of agencies to work with the Caribbean Financial Action Task Force (CFATC) to review the country's financial systems and ensure that they meet international standards.

Domestic Violence

Domestic violence against women is another serious problem in Antigua and Barbuda. The legal system tends to be relatively lenient when addressing this issue. The police are reluctant to get involved, and many women opt not to testify because of fear of retaliation. Domestic violence legislation was passed by parliament in 1999. Domestic violence was classified as any act of violence, verbal or physical abuse, perpetrated by a member of a household upon a member of that same household that may cause physical, mental, or emotional harm to the abused party.

The Domestic Violence Act of 1999 made orders of protection available to the court that prohibited a victim from being in an area where a specified person might be. Although there are no legal restrictions on women's roles in society, tradition lends little support for activities outside the home. Nongovernmental organizations in Antigua and Barbuda advocate for women's rights and help provide support for women who have been abused. The Directorate of Women's Affairs helps provide programs for women concerning health, crafts, and business skills.

Crime Statistics

Although there are relatively few publicly available statistics, it seems that the overall consensus is that crime has been increasing in Antigua and Barbuda within the last years leading up to 2009. According to the Judicial Studies Center of the Americas, the courts received 3,526 criminal complaints in 2004. It was reported that only one crime resulted in the death of one or more victims and that there were 24 reports of robbery or theft. In 2007, Antigua and

Barbuda had 19 murders. The Foreign Office also has reported an increase in gun crime.

In a study published by the OECS Judicial and Legal Reform Project in 2002 that analyzed 2,898 cases heard by the magistrates' courts, 21 percent involved crimes against the person, 24 percent involved crimes against property, 13 percent were drug offenses, 11 percent were traffic violations, 3 percent were firearm offenses, less than 1 percent involved the use of firearms against persons, and 28 percent were unspecified criminal offenses. It should be noted that these statistics represented a first attempt at compiling data for this country, and there may be gaps in the information and possibly flaws in the records.

Finding of Guilt

Rights of the Accused

The police in Antigua and Barbuda do not need a warrant to arrest a person suspected of committing a crime. However, criminal defendants do have the right to a judicial determination of the legality of their detention. The police must bring a person being detained before a court within 48 hours of his or her arrest or detention. The Antigua and Barbuda Constitution includes a right to bail and states that excessive bail should not be required. The bail system was recently modified to require those accused of more serious crimes to appeal to the High Court for bail, taking this responsibility away from the lower-court magistrates.

Criminal proceedings in Antigua and Barbuda are adversarial and guided by the principles of immediacy and the use of oral hearings. The Antigua and Barbuda Constitution states that criminal defendants should receive a fair, open, and public trial. Prosecution is the responsibility of the Office of Criminal Prosecution, which forms part of the Ministry of Justice and Legal Affairs; however, in some cases, the police can investigate and even serve as prosecutors.

Antigua and Barbuda allows capital punishment, and only in these cases does the government provide legal assistance at public expense to persons without the means to retain a private attorney. Otherwise, the country does not have an institutionalized legal aid system. There is currently a proposal to open a legal aid office under the jurisdiction of the Ministry of Justice and Legal Affairs.

Juveniles

Juveniles are given special treatment during criminal proceedings. The Juvenile Courts Act requires the establishment of one or more juvenile courts in the magisterial districts of Antigua and Barbuda. The same act forbids the public from juvenile courts to protect the juvenile. The Juvenile Act prohibits juveniles, while being detained for any reason, from associating with an adult who has been charged with any offense other than an offense with which the juvenile is jointly charged. When a juvenile is charged with an offense jointly with an individual above the age of 16, it is permissible for the charge to be heard in a magistrates' court.

Punishment

Types of Punishment

Antigua and Barbuda has a wide range of possible punishments, including prison sentences, fines, probation, community service, and parole. In August 2002, the first statistical profile of criminal cases tried by the magistrates' courts was published for Antigua and Barbuda by the Judicial Studies Center of the Americas. The study analyzed 2,898 cases and showed that 36 percent of convictions involved a fine and imprisonment. The average fine was EC$1,523 (approx. US$583), and the average prison sentence was 1.3 months. Of the cases studied, 16.4 percent resulted in an acquittal or reprimand. In 13 percent of the cases, prison sentences were given for an average of 4.3 months. In addition, 6 percent of cases required paid compensation, and in 4.2 percent of cases, the convicted person was put on parole. Last, the sentence in 4.3 percent of cases was community service. This data set represents a first attempt at compiling statistics in this subregion. There are substantial gaps in the information, given that not all jurisdictions keep systematic, ongoing records of case-flow data. Additionally, the Industrial Court offers mechanisms for reaching out-of-court settlements in labor disputes and industrial cases.

Antigua and Barbuda allows corporal punishment for certain crimes. According to the Corporal Punishment Act, a court may pass a sentence of corporal punishment by whipping or flogging in addition to other punishments that may be administered upon the conviction of numerous crimes, including the following: wounding a person by means of a deadly or destructive instrument, being armed with any offensive weapon or instrument, robbing a person and using personal violence at the time or immediately after the crime is committed, and assaulting any person with the intent to rob that person. The punishments of whipping and flogging may not be administered to any female regardless of age.

Punishment for drug-related offenses is relatively severe in Antigua and Barbuda. Summary offenses typically result in two years' imprisonment and a fine between EC$20,000 and EC$500,000 (approx. US$7,490–$18,727), whereas indictable offenses typically result in seven years' imprisonment and a fine.

Prison

Her Majesty's Prison is Antigua and Barbuda's sole prison for the islands. In 2005, it was reported that the prison held 194 inmates; 188 were men, and 6 were women, for an imprisonment rate of 239.5 per 100,000 inhabitants. Of the individuals in the prison, 81 were of indigenous descent. The United States' 2005 *Country Report on Human Rights Practices* stated that the prison was in poor condition. The prison did not have the proper bathroom facilities, and slop pails were used in 122 prisoners' cells. Part of the reason for the overcrowding was the passage of a law in 2004 that limited a judge's power to issue protection orders other than pretrial custody for certain types of crimes. Magistrates had limited ability to grant bail to certain individuals. The prison staff at her Majesty's Prison complained to the press about the poor conditions and included the fact that there was an increase in the number of prisoners who had HIV and AIDS.

Jessica Gentile

Further Reading

Eastern Caribbean Supreme Court: http://www.eccourts.org/.

Kritzer, H. M. (2002). *Legal Systems of the World: A Political, Social, and Cultural Encyclopedia.* Santa Barbara, CA: ABC-CLIO.

Lazarus-Black, M. (1994). *Legitimate Acts and Illegitimate Encounters: Law and Society in Antigua and Barbuda.* Washington, DC: Smithsonian Institution Press.

Organization of Eastern Caribbean States: http://www.oecs.org.

Sanders, R. (2002). *Antigua Vision.* Royston, Hertfordshire: Hansib Publications Limited.

Seetahal, D. S. (2001). *Commonwealth Caribbean Criminal Practice and Procedure.* London: Cavendish Publishing Limited.

Argentina

Legal System: Civil
Murder: High
Burglary: Medium
Corruption: Medium
Human Trafficking: Medium
Prison Rate: Medium
Death Penalty: Yes
Corporal Punishment: Yes

Background

Argentina has an area of 2,780,403 square kilometers and had a population of 38,970,611 inhabitants as of 2006. In 2005, 91.8 percent of the population lived in urban areas. There are more than 400,000 members or descendants of the first generation of some indigenous people, representing just over 1 percent of the total population. The country ranked 36 in the 2006 United Nations Human Development ranking (the highest among Latin American countries). In 2005, the unemployment rate was11.5 percent, and 2.8 percent of the population over 15 years were illiterate.

Argentina's Supreme Court is located in the Palacio de Justicia in Buenos Aires. (Beatrice Murch)

Argentina is a federal democracy divided into 23 autonomous provinces and the city of Buenos Aires, seat of the federal government. The Constitution provides for a tripartite organization of government, with an executive branch, a legislative branch, and a judiciary. The president, elected by direct vote, heads the executive branch and is the dominant player at the federal level. The Congress is composed of two houses, with a 72-seat Senate and a 257-seat Chamber of Deputies, which constitutes the legislative branch. Under the federal structure, each province enacts its own constitution and elects its own governor and legislator.

Political and Cultural History

In May 1810, residents of the city of Buenos Aires reacted to the overthrow of King Ferdinand VII by Napoleon in Spain with the creation of the first autonomous government among Spanish colonies in the Americas. However, it was not until 1816 that the fledgling nation formally declared independence from Spain. The Argentinean Constitution developed in 1853 was based in large part on the U.S. Constitution and established the nation as a representative and federal republic. Between 1880 and 1930, Argentina experienced a dramatic social restructuring triggered by a significant increase in newly arrived immigrants from Europe and the ensuing population explosion and rapid economic development brought about by the rapid growth of the cattle and agricultural industries. In fact, by 1914, roughly one-third of the population was made up of immigrants, and the country itself became a major player in the world economic system. The global economic crash of 1929 began a period of economic instability and a series of coups that continued for nearly 50 years.

In 1977, the military took control of the country after the failed presidency of Isabel Peron. The new military government initiated a campaign to end growing guerilla activities. This campaign, termed the "War on Subversion," would ultimately be known as the "Dirty War" because of the disappearances of some 10,000 to 30,000 people. Under the leadership of General Leopoldo Galtieri, Argentina went to war against Great Britain over the Malvinas (Falkland) Islands in 1982. The subsequent humiliating defeat of the Argentine forces combined with continued disappearances of suspected dissidents led to not only a loss of the islands but also public outcries against the legitimacy of the military government. On December 10, 1983, Raul Alfonsin assumed the presidency after winning the majority vote in the presidential elections that marked the return of democratic institutions. His administration initiated the trial of the juntas, prosecuting some of the top generals of the previous military regimen for violations of human rights committed during the Dirty War, and created the National Commission on the Disappearance of Persons to document these abuses. Alfonsin encountered fierce resistance from the military, and his rule was plagued by economic turmoil and destabilized by repeated military uprisings. Eventually, he supported the passing of two laws, the Ley de Obediencia Debida (Law of Due Obedience) and the Ley de Punto Final (Full Stop Law), which in practical terms blocked further investigations and provided amnesty to most Dirty War criminals. Both pardon laws were repealed by the Congress in August 2003, which allowed for the reopening of cases that involved crimes against humanity. To this date, top generals from the 1976–1983 military dictatorship are still being tried for their violations of human rights. General Videla was under house arrest until October 2008 when he was sent to a military prison.

Upon the expiration Alfonsin's term of office in 1989, Carlos Menem stepped into the executive office. Although Menem brought the rampant inflation and unemployment under control, his administration was scarred by continuous and scandalous allegations of corruption. Despite their failings in consolidating the rule of law, both Raul Alfonsin and Carlos Menem were instrumental in helping the country's transition from military to civilian rule and in setting Argentina back on a course toward political stability. This transition was codified and made permanent through the revision of the National Constitution in 1994. Among the most salient points of the constitutional reform are the reduction of the length of the presidential term from six to four years, the reelection of the president for two consecutive terms, and the removal of the requirement for the president to be a Roman Catholic.

To prevent the repetition of the human rights abuses committed during the Dirty War, the 1994 constitutional amendments included the addition of key legal safeguards available to Argentine citizens: *amparo,* the power of a magistrate to pronounce the unconstitutionality of a decision by state authorities or private citizens that impinges on a right protected by the Constitution; habeas corpus to protect the right of physical freedom when it is threatened, limited, modified, or injured; and *habeas data,* mandating that any information referring to a citizen and recorded in public or private registers be kept confidential and accurate.

The Legal System

Argentina is a civil law country and employs an inquisitorial method for exposing evidence in trial, with the judge playing a very active role in criminal proceedings. The administration of justice is divided into federal and provincial systems, and each system has lower courts, courts of appeal, and supreme courts. The highest judicial authority of the country is vested in the Supreme Court of Justice, which has nine members. The president names both the justices of the Supreme Court, with the consent of the Senate by two-thirds of its members present, and other judges of the lower federal courts from a binding proposal of three candidates submitted by the Council of Magistracy. There are no prior investigations on the legal and other relevant history of the nominees; nor are there public hearings or bar association reports. The Senate receives a résumé drafted by the nominees themselves, and the review of the nominations is conducted in a closed session by the judiciary committee. Recommendations by the committee are then presented and voted on by the entire chamber. The lack of transparency in the process of judicial appointments has been a permanent focus of concern among judicial monitors. Each province appoints its own judges to the provincial courts. Judges at all levels enjoy lifetime tenure conditioned on good behavior. In 2004, Elena Inés Highton de Nolasco was approved to become the first woman justice in the country's Supreme Court.

Military justice has jurisdiction over military crimes committed by military officials. But civilians may become subject to military jurisdiction for offenses committed during times declared as states of siege.

The Defensor del Pueblo, or People's Defender, and the Ministerio Público, or Public Ministry, are among the most important institutions created by the 1994 constitutional reforms. The People's Defender, similar to the Scandinavian ombudsman, protects the right of the citizenry in issues related to human rights, social security, public services, health, education, and the environment. It operates with complete autonomy, receives no instructions from any government authority, and initiates investigations proactively or in response to citizen complaints. The People's Defender also supervises the administration of public agencies and is empowered to investigate government officials or agencies when credible allegations arise of human rights infringement, abuse of power, malign neglect, discriminatory practices, and other government misconduct. The office has judicial standing, and its actions have parity to judicial proceedings. The defender is appointed by Congress with the vote of two-thirds of the members present of each chamber for a nonrenewable term of five years. He or she enjoys all the immunities and privileges of legislators. The Public Ministry instead is an independent body that promotes the defense of the public interests of the community in coordination with the other government authorities.

Crime

Crime Classification

As prescribed in the Argentine penal code, the major categories of criminal offenses against individual citizens include (1) crimes against a person (e.g., murder or injuries in quarrel, duel, assault with weapon, and abandonment of a person); (2) crimes against honor (e.g., calumnies or slander, libel or defamation, crimes against sexual integrity, and crimes against marital status); (3) crimes against an individual's freedom (e.g., violation of domicile or trespassing, violation of correspondence, crimes against freedom of work and association, crimes against freedom of assembly, and crimes against freedom of press); and (4) crimes against property (e.g., theft, robbery, extortion, scams and frauds, usury, and usurpation).

Additional categories include (1) crimes against society and public safety (e.g., fires and other damages, crimes against the security of transportation and communication, piracy, crimes against public health, and adulterating drinking water, food, or medicine); (2) crimes against public order (e.g., incitement to commit crimes, illicit association, public intimidation, and vindication of a crime); (3) crimes against national security (e.g., treason and crimes that threaten the peace and dignity of the nation); (4) crimes against public authorities and the constitutional order (e.g., sedition); (5) crimes against public administration (e.g., abuse of authority and violation of the duties of public officials, bribery and influence peddling, embezzlement of public assets, business dealings incompatible with the exercise of public functions, extortion, false testimony, concealment and laundering of assets derived from criminal activities); and (6) crimes against public trust (e.g., counterfeiting, falsification of documents).

On June 24, 2008, the Argentine Congress promulgated an innovative law that sanctions information technology crimes. Law number 26388, set to be part of article 77 of the Argentine criminal code, defines the following behaviors as crimes: distribution and possession with the intent to distribute of child pornography, e-mail violations, illegal access to information system, distribution of viruses and damage to information systems, aggravated crimes against information systems, and interruption of communications.

Crime Statistics

Crime is a serious problem in Argentina, but one that is becoming better managed and under control. Recent crime trends show that the catastrophic economic collapse of 2001 led to a subsequent breakdown of social order in 2002, when the overall crime rate peaked at 369.7 offenses known to the police per 100,000 inhabitants, according to the Instituto Nacional de Estadistica y Censos. However, as the economy recorded a robust recovery in subsequent years, the overall crime rate also decreased at a gradual, yet steady pace, to hover around 332.9 offenses per 100,000 inhabitants in 2005. Intentional homicide dropped most significantly, from 9.47 offenses per 100,000 inhabitants in 2002 to 5.24 offenses per 100,000 inhabitants in 2006. The fact that 20.6 percent of the population in the urban areas remained below the poverty line in 2008, down from over 50 percent in the immediate aftermath of the 2001 economic crisis, suggests that public safety still rests on a fragile social fabric.

Street crime is becoming increasingly more violent and often is perpetrated with a firearm: it is estimated that there are anywhere between 800,000 to 2 million unregistered weapons in Argentina. Although criminal activities are high in comparison to countries of similar social development, they are concentrated in urban areas, especially Greater Buenos Aires, Cordoba, Rosario, and Mendoza. Urban crime includes pickpocketing/purse snatching, scams, mugging, express kidnapping, residential burglary, home invasion, thefts from vehicles (smash and grab), sexual assaults/rape, car theft, and carjacking. The wealthier neighborhoods of metro Buenos Aires suffer high rates of property crime, with some high-income areas often registering as many complaints as some of the poorer and supposedly more dangerous parts of town. Highway robbery is not uncommon and largely affects commercial vehicles. Between 2002 and 2005, the rate of property crime declined by 18 percent, from 2,485.6 offenses per 100,000 inhabitants to 2038.7 per 100,000 inhabitants.

Unlike property crimes and other forms of violent offenses, sex offenses appear to show a stability that is resilient to changes in socioeconomic circumstances. The rate of sex crimes known to the police fluctuated minimally around 27.5 offenses per 100,000 inhabitants during the 2002–2005 period. Argentina is still considered a transit country for drugs, but local consumption is increasing, with growing demands for cocaine and other derivatives by middle-class youths. Drug crimes rose dramatically in recent years, from 42.4 offenses per 100,000 inhabitants in 2002 to 61.7 percent per 100,000 inhabitants in 2005.

Finding of Guilt

Players in the Criminal Justice System

Argentina has a federal system of government. The competence of the justice system in Argentina is divided into two jurisdictions: the provinces and the federal jurisdictions. Although procedures may vary depending on the level of jurisdiction, each provincial state has autonomy to administer and organize its judicial system. Overall, both federal and provincial state judicial systems are divided into two types of courts: the civil court and the criminal court. Provincial states have in addition the labor forum or courts that deal with labor legislations.

An understanding of this division is important because, in Argentina, depending on the legal classification of crime, whether it falls under the federal or provincial jurisdiction, criminal case procedures are conducted under federal or judicial provincial courts (Criminal Procedural Code [CPC], articles 22–33). In this regard, under the federal level, individuals accused of crimes that violate federal law are prosecuted by the public prosecutor, a member of the Public Prosecutor's Office (in the United States, this corresponds to the Attorney's General Office). Amid many responsibilities, the public prosecutor has the primary role of acting as the plaintiff and the attorney for the federal state interests. Under the provincial level, the public prosecutor, or el *agente fiscal,* is responsible for conducting the public criminal cases (CPC, article 5). It is important to note that in Argentina, the prosecutor acts not only as the accuser in public criminal matters but also as a guarantor (fiscal) of the law and of the legality of the procedure. Thus, the prosecution may intervene in all stages of the investigation and review at any time the proceedings (CPC, article 198).

Another player in the Argentine criminal justice system, whether at the federal or provincial level, is the lawyer, or *abogado.* According to the CPC, chapter 7, lawyers have some obligations once they have accepted to proceed with the defense. Article 106, for instance, says that the defense lawyer is obliged to defend once he or she has accepted the case, except when there is valid excuse. Additionally, the Argentine procedural code asserts that no more than two lawyers are allowed to defend the accused.

Criminal Investigation and the Prosecution

The criminal investigation in Argentina is initiated in a variety of ways. The CPC, article 174, permits any individual, whether he or she is the victim of a crime or has knowledge that a crime has occurred, to report it to the judge, the public prosecutor, or the police. Some individuals, however, according to the CPC, are obliged to report a crime (article 177), including public officials in the exercise of their functions—for example, public prosecutors, judges, police, and any individual whose job is related to the exercise of medical profession. If the announcement of a crime is given to a judge, he or she will immediately transfer the information to the public prosecutor, who is the authority responsible for bringing public criminal prosecution under the CPC. This does not exclude the criminal judge, who in Argentina law has an active role, from beginning an investigation within his or her judicial power. The judicial police are the primary investigators in the Argentine criminal justice system. Although their functions are under the supervision of the Public Prosecutor's Office, the police have autonomy to initiate an investigation anytime they have knowledge that a crime has occurred. The police force's roles include (but are not limited to) receiving the report of a crime, interrogating witnesses, and collecting information or material as evidence of crime.

The procedures so far explained pertain to crimes that do not depend on private initiation. The Argentine criminal code has classified some crimes as private offenses that require the victim or legal representative for the initiation of a criminal procedure. Crimes that depend on private initiation include sexual crimes; minor injuries, except if committed with intent; slander and libel; and other minor offenses, all enumerated in the Argentine criminal code. Private crimes are then reported via *querellas,* a petition that an individual uses to describe the offense to the designated authority, whether the police, the public prosecutor, or the judge. Given the initiation and termination of the investigation, the public prosecutor in possession of evidence and information on the crime committed will file a report, which will contain who the accused is, what criminal offense he or she has committed, and further investigation the prosecutor believes necessary for the criminal procedure. If the accused does not have a lawyer or cannot afford one, it is during the arraignment phase that the judge will assign to the accused a public defender, who is also a member of the Public Prosecutor's Office.

Rights of the Accused

Argentina's penal code and criminal procedure code delineate the rights of the accused in the criminal justice system. In this regard, it is important to note that the understanding of the rights of the accused under the Argentine criminal justice system is somewhat different from that of the common law system. During the investigation conducted by the police, the accused cannot be questioned by the police without the police first explaining to the accused that he or she has the right to an attorney and can refuse to answer any question, but that if he or she decides to answer, the accused is not required to swear to say the truth and cannot be coerced to confess to the crime he or she is accused of committing.

If an arrest is made, police may detain suspects for up to 10 hours without an arrest warrant as long as the authorities have probable cause to believe that the suspect may have committed the crime or is about to commit a crime. The police can also detain the suspect for a crime if his or her identity is unclear or has not been determined. Although police can withhold the suspect for 10 hours, he or she has the right to promptly appear before a criminal lower-court judge who will determine whether to proceed with the investigation and to maintain the suspect into custody.

In the arraignment stage, in which the judge is involved, the judge has to inform the accused what crime he or she is accused of and what evidence exists against him or her, as well as inform the defendant that he or she has the right to remain silent, which will not be used as presumption of culpability. The accused has the right to an attorney, and if one is not available, the judge can assign a public defender to represent him or her before the criminal court. The procedural code also requires that the public defender meet with the defendant regularly to inform him or her of the status of the case. It is important to note that while awaiting conclusion of the investigation or while undergoing trial, individuals who have been indicted can be detained for up to two years. It is at the discretion of the judge, with request of the defendant, and after informing the public prosecutor, to release the defendant.

Trials are public, and a panel of judges decides guilt or innocence. As a reaction to the abuses and excesses of past military regimes, Argentina has been moving from an inquisitorial procedure driven by closed and written proceedings toward a more participatory adversarial system based on oral and public proceedings. Trials in the federal and provincial criminal courts are oral, which replaces the old system of written submissions. Argentina's Constitution of 1853 instituted the right to a jury trial, but no regulation has ever provided for juries. Legislators have long debated whether to adopt the jury trial. The first experiment came in 2005 when the province of Cordoba adopted lay participation in criminal trials through mixed tribunals composed of eight jurors and three professional judges. Also in the same year, and for the first time in 60 years, the nation's Supreme Court addressed the question of trial by jury and dictated that mixed tribunals were a valid and probably preferable alternative to trial by jury. It is still unclear whether the Cordoba experiment is just an anomalous exception or the beginning of a trend.

The Criminal Judges and the Criminal Courts

In Argentina, a specific body called the Council of Judges has the role of creating a list of judges. This council, created by the Constitution, is composed by members of Congress, the Supreme Court, and professional organizations. Its function is to evaluate applicants to the courts based on an objective basis. The reason for such a diverse composition, with representatives of the judicial power, legislators, and lawyers elected by their peers in their respective jurisdictions, is to ensure that the evaluations of the candidates are objective and fair. The list of the candidates is then given to the Senate for confirmation.

Judges in the Argentinean justice system do not have a mandatory retirement, meaning that they can hold their position until they decide to resign. Life tenure notwithstanding, they can be removed from office under certain circumstances stated in the Constitution. For instance, after committing a serious fault in their duty, or committing any crime, judges can be tried by special courts and, if condemned, removed from office. The special courts composition varies depending on the position the judge held. If the case of impeachment is against a member of the Supreme Court, the special court will be composed of the entire Senate. However, if the case is against a simple judge, a special jury will be created.

This process ensures their right to defense. The Senate and special jury decide only whether the judge should or should not be removed from office.

Juvenile Justice System

The age of criminal responsibility is 18 years old or older, which means that individuals who have not yet reached 18 years old can be tried only by the Juvenile Justice System. Legislation in Argentina provides individuals under the age of 18 with special protection. An example is Law 26.061, which states that the government must guarantee both children and adolescents, in addition to all the rights provided by the national Constitution, the following rights: (a) to be heard before a competent authority; (b) to have his or her opinion primarily considered at the time of the decision; (c) to have specialized legal counsel, which should be paid by the government in case of economic barriers, from the beginning to the end of the judicial or administrative proceeding; and (e) to appeal before the superior courts if needed.

Argentina has participated in the Convention on the Rights of the Child, a treaty it signed that helps to guarantee children around the world basic social and economic rights. According to child advocates, however, in spite of the enactment of Law 26061, the juvenile justice system still needs to be fully reformed to implement the mandates of that law and of the convention. The current law, 22.278 of 1980, as amended by Law 22.803, on the "criminal regime of minors," does not provide a punitive juvenile regime that considers the special needs of children and adolescents. Law 22.278 is based on the doctrine of "irregular situation" and does not make a clear distinction between children in need of care and protection and those in violation of the law. Under the current law, a judge can order the detention of children without due process based only on their social situation, and this decision cannot be appealed. There is a 2005 draft bill on juvenile justice pending congressional approval that would fulfill these commitments. It establishes limits on juvenile criminal responsibility and procedures to be followed, in accordance with article 40, paragraph 3, of the Convention on the Rights of the Child.

Punishment

The Argentine Ministry of Justice and Human Rights is in charge of penal and correctional policy and practices. The 1994 constitutional reform permitted strong influence from French jurisprudence, which manifests itself most openly in the codification of solutions to crime as opposed to merely punishment in the penal code. But the lack of resources available for the rehabilitation of offenders renders the goal of effective social reintegration largely unaccomplished.

Types of Punishment

A range of punishments is meted out by the Argentine criminal justice system depending on the severity of the crime. For offenders classified as adults, the main penal option is deprivation of liberty through imprisonment. The sentences for imprisonment can be life sentences or a specified amount of time. Other possible punishments include fines, house arrest, reparations, and compensation for losses. In September 2008, Argentina effectively abolished the death penalty by ratifying the Second Optional Protocol to the International Covenant on Civil and Political Rights and the American Convention on Human Rights to Abolish the Death Penalty. The last judicial execution on record in Argentina was carried out in 1916.

The standard sentence for murder is a minimum of 8 years and up to 25 years to life. However, this may vary depending on certain aggravating circumstances, such as if extreme cruelty or torture was employed, if it was a murder for hire, or the victim or offender was a police officer. A sentence of 3 to 6 years will be imposed if the act was committed out of passion or if the intention was not to kill but only to harm. A sentence of 1 to 4 years will be imposed if an individual persuades another or helps another to commit suicide. A sentence of 5 to 10 years will be imposed if an individual causes the death of another because of professional negligence of some kind.

Abortion is deemed a criminal offense and can carry sentences ranging from 3 to 10 years if it is performed without the consent of the pregnant woman and 1 to 4 years with the consent of the pregnant woman. Abortion is allowed if the pregnancy is the product of rape and the pregnant woman is not of sound mind. A sentence of 6 months to 2 years is imposed if a woman who is raped has an abortion but is in good mental health.

Sentences for the crime of rape also may vary depending on the particular circumstances of the rape. A sentence of 6 months to 4 years will be imposed if there is the threat of rape through the threat of violence or intimidation. A 4- to 10-year sentence will be imposed if the act of rape is actually committed. A sentence of 8 to 20 years will be imposed if any of the following circumstances apply: serious mental or physical damage was caused during the act; the act was committed against a family member; the individual who committed the rape was carrying a sexually transmitted disease and knew it; the rape was committed by two or more people or the perpetrator was armed; the accused is a police officer; or the victim is a minor.

Crimes involving theft, burglary, or robbery are dealt with in articles 162 through 185. The basic sentence for simple theft could result in a sentence ranging from one month to two years. A sentence of six years is applied for the following: when the theft involves agricultural equipment or fertilizer, is a case of automobile theft, or if the theft takes place during a fire or natural disaster. A sentence of one month to six years may be imposed if physical force or violence is used in the commission of the theft. If the theft leads to the death of the victim, a sentence of 10 to 25 years may be imposed. A sentence of 5 to 15 years may be imposed in the following cases: if the victim is injured by the perpetrator or if the robbery was carried out with a weapon. (If a firearm is discharged in public, the minimum and maximum sentencing periods will rise by a third.)

These sentences for murder, rape, and theft/robbery are not the complete list of sentences that may be meted out, but they do provide a general overview of the range of possible outcomes. Argentina's civil law contains details about nearly every possible scenario that may arise in the commission of the various crimes.

Prisons

The Federal Penitentiary Service under the purview of the Ministry of Justice and Human Rights holds in custody and guarantees the safety of defendants awaiting trial or disposition in detention and implements custodial sentences of convicted offenders. This institution is responsible for the management of correctional facilities and related services as well as the rehabilitation of offenders sentenced to custodial sentences in the territory of the Federal Capital and in the provinces under the jurisdiction of the national government. The service manages a total of 28 prisons, 2 penitentiary complexes, and 10 municipal jails throughout the national territory. The correctional system was staffed with 4,399 full-time personnel in 2004. The adult correctional population throughout Argentine prisons totaled 54,472 in 2006. Whereas the prevalence of crime increased by 37 percent between 1997 and 2006, the prison population expanded by 83 percent during the same period. The reliance on incarceration to deal with the problem of violence and crime shows no sign of wavering.

Correctional Law N 24.660, article 106, dictates that work is a right and an obligation of inmates. The Argentine criminal code also prescribes that male adult inmates are required to work (article 9), except for those who suffer from some sort of mental illness or disability or are 70 years old or older (article 7). In these special cases, a specific type of work is provided by the penitentiary administrative system.

The purpose of incarceration, according to Argentine correctional law, is to rehabilitate inmates. The law, in this regard, has laid out basic rights and privileges for inmates. Education is a right, and thus, the correctional facilities are required to provide appropriate accommodations for the learning process. Interestingly, Argentine correctional law provides compulsory education to illiterate inmates and those who have not attained the minimum level set by law. Moreover, correctional facilities have to provide to inmates a library adequate to fulfill their academic formation, and the library is also to serve a recreational function. Inmates' rights also include medical assistance, spiritual practices, and social relations. It is considered part of the socialization process that inmates maintain their family relations. Thus, Argentina correctional law prescribes that inmates must have the right to periodically communicate, in written or verbal form, with family, friends, relatives, and curators and lawyers.

Female inmates and young adults between 18 and 21 years old have special establishments. Female inmates are to be supervised exclusively by female personnel. Appropriate accommodations for pregnant women and childbirth are to be provided. The inmate is authorized, according to the law, to keep her child until he or she is four years of age. After that, some assistance is given to find someone to take care of the child. For young adults, special institutions or separate or independent areas of adult facilities are provided to lodge them. The law also requires for young adults compulsory education, professional qualification, and maintenance of the family bonds.

According to Amnesty International, conditions of incarceration are harsh in most prisons and detention centers, and inmates are ill-treated. Prisoners are reportedly seriously injured in fires in prisons and police stations, allegedly because of lack of help. In response to the problems of overcrowding, maltreatment by correctional staff, and violence that plagued Argentine prisons and detention centers, the Supreme Court, in a landmark ruling in 2005, ordered all correctional facilities in the country to abide by the United Nations Standard Minimum Rules for the Treatment of Prisoners. Despite slight improvements in the province of Buenos Aires, the national picture remains dire. For example, the number of detainees diverted from the overflowing prison system to police lockups declined between 2006 and 2007. Yet again, the number of detainees held in police lockups in July 2008 exceeded the number in 2007. The habit of sending criminal suspects to prison to await trial is driving prison overcrowding: in 2008, nearly 77 percent of the prison population was made up of defendants awaiting trial or disposition.

Extradition

The first law on the extradition of foreigners was enacted in Argentina in 1885 and was replaced by the 1997 Law of International Cooperation in Criminal Matters. The country is obliged to grant extradition of a criminal alien only if there is an international agreement with the state requesting the extradition. When there is no treaty, Argentina is empowered to agree to extradition but is not obliged to grant it. Argentina maintains bilateral extradition treaties with 18 countries and is a signatory to 4 multilateral extradition treaties. Argentina is one of the few countries in the world that allow the extradition of their own citizens to other countries for offenses committed in foreign lands. The Congress is the only power authorized to determine, by a special law, where trials are to be held in the case of crimes committed by Argentine citizens outside the national territories in violation of international law.

Clarissa F. Dias and Hung-En Sung

Further Reading

Chavez, Rebecca Bill. (2004). *The Rule of Law in Nascent Democracies: Judicial Politics in Argentina.* Palo Alto, CA: Stanford University Press.

Finkel, Jodi S. (2008). *Judicial Reform as Political Insurance: Argentina, Peru, and Mexico in the 1990s.* Notre Dame, IN: University of Notre Dame Press.

Nouzeilles, Gabriela, Graciela Montaldo, and Robin Kirk, eds. (2002). *The Argentina Reader: History, Culture, Politics.* Durham, NC: Duke University Press.

Aruba

Legal System: Civil
Prison Rate: High
Death Penalty: No
Corporal Punishment: No

Background

Aruba is an island nation located in the Caribbean Sea, just northwest of the Netherlands Antilles. The island is roughly 74 square miles, with a population of approximately 103,065. Spanish explorers discovered the island in 1499, and the Dutch gained control in the 1630s. For the majority of the time of

Dutch control, Aruba was part of the Netherland Antilles, a neighboring island group. During the latter part of the 20th century, however, Aruba began a journey for independence apart from the Antilles. In 1986, Aruba officially broke away from its neighboring islands and became a semi-independent nation within the kingdom of the Netherlands.

Political Context

The government is a constitutional monarchy with a parliamentary system. A governor is appointed by the monarch to act as the representative head of state. The governor is not expected to openly remark on political topics but is appointed to supervise the island government to make sure that an action is not taken that is contrary to guarantees, rights, or guidelines put forth by the Netherlands.

A one-house legislature called Staten consists of 21 members who serve four-year terms and are elected by the citizens of Aruba. The Staten elects a prime minister and deputy prime minister, who head the Council of Ministers. Both the legislature and the Council of Ministers are responsible for the creation of legislation and must agree to pass legislation.

Role of Police

The Korps Politie Aruba (KPA) is the main police force for Aruba. It is headed by a police commissioner and has four main precincts located in Oranjestad, Noord, San Nicolaas, and Cruz. According to the KPA, the total number of police in 2006 was 425: 337 men and 88 women. Aruba's police force deals with issues relating to public safety and traffic, and it also conducts criminal investigations under the supervision of the public prosecutor. Aruba also jointly maintains a coast guard with the Netherlands Antilles, which is used to help fight drug trafficking, a common problem for both nations.

Crime

Crime Classification

The legal system of Aruba is modeled after the Dutch legal system, which breaks the classification of criminal offenses into two categories: crimes and infractions. The legislature decides which offenses fall under each of these two categories. Crimes are considered more serious offenses than infractions. Traffic offenses, however, fall under another category called administrative offenses, which are handled by the police, not the courts.

Drug Trafficking

Aruba is relatively close to nations that have high rates of organized crime and drug production. Drug trafficking throughout the island has historically been a common problem because of this location. Unlike destination nations such as the United States, drugs are not trafficked to Aruba for the purpose of sale, but instead the island is used as a portal to funnel drugs to destination nations around the world. In the mid-1990s, the prevalence of drug trafficking through Aruba was so common that the U.S. government considered Aruba to be one of the major illegal drug-transit nations in the world. Today the problem of drug trafficking has been reduced; however, it still is a challenge to the nation. Drugs are easy to obtain in Aruba, which is considered to have caused a considerable amount of the population to become drug users. The government of Aruba considers drug-related crimes to have been the second most frequent offense between the years 2003 and 2006.

Human Trafficking

The expanding economy in Aruba, created by a booming tourism industry, has created many jobs on the island. One drawback to this demand for labor is that it also may have led to an increase in illegal trafficking of people to fill the demand for labor on the island in both legitimate fields, such as construction, and illegitimate fields, such as prostitution. Although it is unclear as to how many individuals are actually brought illegally into Aruba, the U.S. Department of State has suggested that more effective methods to counteract the trafficking problem need to be put in place and utilized by Aruba.

Crime Statistics

Aruba's Central Bureau of Statistics (CBS) provides some annual crime statistics. In 2007 there were 4,945 burglaries, 459 car thefts, 333 assaults, and 863 acts of vandalism (cars, buildings, schools, etc.). Aruba's Department of Public Health reported two deaths in 2004 from homicide, injury purposely inflicted by another person, war, and/or legal intervention. The Aruba police department reported the number of drug seizures in 2006 was 109 for cocaine, 12 for heroin, and 340 for XTC pills.

Finding of Guilt

Rights of the Accused

Under the Constitution of Aruba, all individuals are innocent until proven otherwise, and they have a right to a fair trial, held within a reasonable time span. Any individual in custody of the police prior to being questioned must be informed of his or her right to a lawyer, and if the individual earns less than the nation's minimum wage, a lawyer will be made available to him or her. There is one exception to this right to legal counsel: if the prosecutor has serious suspicion that a suspect's contact with a lawyer will prevent justice. If the prosecutor finds this to be the case, then access to a lawyer can be prevented for up to eight days.

Investigation and Prosecution

The public prosecutor is mainly responsible for the supervision of criminal investigations and the prosecution of suspected criminals. Although the police often accomplish the actual fact-finding associated with investigations, the prosecutor's duty to supervise the investigation is mainly to make sure the requirements set forth by the law are not violated. The prosecutor also has the choice to drop cases prior to going to trial. Individuals who have a stake in a dropped case can appeal such a decision to the Joint Court of Appeals. The prosecutor can also attempt to settle the case prior to going through the court system through what are called transactions. Transactions can be a variety of stipulations put on the offender that require him or her to pay a fine, give personal property to the government, provide compensation for actions through work or financial means, and so on.

Pretrial Incarceration

Individuals who are suspected of committing a crime can be brought into police custody for questioning for up to 16 hours prior to being brought before a judge. This time limit can, however, be extended by the prosecutor if it is deemed necessary for the success of the investigation. It is legally possible to keep an individual in police custody for up to 3 days and 16 hours prior to bringing him or her before a judge. If the prosecutor requests the holding of the criminal in detention, and the judge agrees, an individual may remain in police custody for another 8 days. The prosecutor can, after this period, request that the judge place the suspect in pretrial incarceration for 60 days if it is deemed necessary. In cases dealing with serious offenses, the pretrial incarceration is renewable up to two times, 30 days each time.

Courts

The organization and management of the Aruba judicial system is jointly shared with its neighbors the Netherlands Antilles. There are three levels of courts. The first level is called the Court of the First Instance. In this court each case is dealt with by one judge who decides the outcome. The decision of this court can be appealed to the next level, which is the Joint Court of Appeals. This second level is shared with the Netherlands Antilles. A board of judges decides cases at this level. The decision of the Joint Court of Appeals can be appealed one final time. Cases that make it to this third level are sent to the Netherlands and go before the Supreme Court, and this court is concerned only with reviewing the case's legal history to ensure the law was applied correctly in the lower levels.

Criminal Court Judges

To qualify to become a magistrate, applicants must be 35 years or older and have a law degree from the Netherlands, Aruba, or the Antilles. Many of the judges presiding over cases in the Antilles and Aruba are actually judges from the Netherlands who are only in Aruba and the Antilles on a temporary basis, because of a shortage of magistrates from Aruba and Antilles. Criminal court judges who serve in both Aruba and the Antilles are appointed by the monarch for life.

Juvenile Justice

The age of criminal responsibility in Aruba is currently 12 years. Those younger than 12 cannot, in accordance to the law, be punished or prosecuted for an offense. Aruba uses the same justice system for a juvenile (individuals between 12 and 18) that is used for adults with some modifications, such as allowing parents to visit a juvenile while in police custody, holding concealed trials for all youth under 16 as well as in some cases where the youth is under 18 to protect the identity, and so on. Although some may see these modifications as minor, the courts' special treatment of juveniles is more evident in terms of sentences.

Although youthful offenders 12 and older can be held criminally responsible, the law requires the application of special punishments, often much less severe than adult punishments, for individuals under the age of 18. Although a youth's age is important in sentencing, a youth's level of maturity is also taken into account for those 16 and older. If a youth is older than 16 and is deemed to have a sufficient level of maturity, then an adult-level punishment can be administered. This also applies conversely to individuals 21 and younger; individuals in this range can receive a youth-level punishment if they are deemed to have an insufficient maturity level.

Punishment

Types of Punishment

There are two types of consequences for committing criminal offenses, called measures and penalties. Measures are meant not to intentionally punish an individual but rather to protect the community and can be issued upon an individual even if the person has not been found guilty of committing a criminal offense. Examples of measures would be confiscating property, such as illegal or dangerous weapons; confiscating funds from illegal activities; and committing mentally ill individuals who are considered to be a danger to mental health facilities.

Penalties are retributive in nature and are used as punishments against a guilty individual for committing a criminal act. Both prison sentences and fines would be examples of penalties utilized in Aruba. The severity of these different forms would be based on the seriousness of the offense being punished. The death penalty is no longer used in Aruba; therefore, a life sentence is the most severe penalty in Aruba and is relatively rare. Less severe prison sentences can range from 1 day to 20 years depending on the offense.

General Description of Prison

Because Aruba is small in size, the nation has only one prison facility, called the Korrektie Instituut Aruba, or KIA. The KIA has a maximum inmate population of 310 inmates. The KIA also has relatively new facilities created specially to deal with female and youth inmate populations, along with up-to-date medical facilities. Although the KIA has recently expanded the size of the facility, along with including special areas for certain inmates, it is relatively understaffed. According to a Council of Europe Report, as of 2007, the total number of individuals working at the KIA was 172, much lower than the required 208 staff needed to properly run the prison. This low number of KIA employees has caused the prison not to be able to effectively use some of the new areas of the prison.

Under Aruban law, inmates in the KIA are required to work if they are so instructed by prison staff, although the law accepts forms of training and education as exceptions to the labor requirement. The KIA offers vocational along with educational programs and employment opportunities for the majority of inmates. The physical limitations of the facility and its grounds, however, limit the number of activities offered and the number of inmates who can participate in certain activities. The KIA typically gives inmates the privilege of at least three telephone calls a month for a maximum of 10 minutes per call.

Robert B. Fletcher III

Further Reading

Aruba Police Force: http://www.kparuba.com/.

Aruba's Official Government Web site: http://www.overheid.aw/.

Blickman, T. (1999). "The Rothschilds of the Mafia on Aruba." In *Transnational Crime,* edited by N. Passas, pp. 123–162. Farnham, Surrey, UK: Ashgate Publishing Company.

Kritzer, H. M. (2002). *Legal Systems of the World: A Political, Social, and Cultural Encyclopedia.* Santa Barbara, CA: ABC-CLIO.

Tak, P. J. P. (2003). *The Dutch Criminal Justice System: Organization and Operation.* Den Haag: Boom Juridische Uitgevers.

The Bahamas

Legal System: Common
Murder: High
Prison Rate: High
Death Penalty: Yes
Corporal Punishment: Yes

Background

The Bahamas is a Caribbean country composed of 700 islands and more than 2,400 inlets spread over 80,000 square miles of ocean and extending east by 50 miles from the Florida coast. The country's capital, located in Nassau, New Providence, is where 60 percent of the country's 303,611 citizens reside. Another 46,994 live on Grand Bahama Island, with the remaining citizens living on one of the 17 inhabited "Family Islands." In addition, there are approximately 30,000 to 50,000 Haitians living on the islands of New Providence, Abaco, and Eleuthera, either legally or illegally.

American colonists loyal to the British Crown settled in the Bahamas during the American Revolution. They brought with them their slaves, the ancestors of 85 percent of today's Bahamian citizens. In the 1960s, after more than 300 years of British colonial rule, the country's black citizens engaged in organized acts of civil disobedience to gain political control of the Bahamas. In 1964, the Bahamas was granted self-government over its internal affairs by the British government. On July 10, 1973, black Bahamians peacefully established a constitutional parliamentary democracy with regular elections.

Government

As a Commonwealth country, its political and legal traditions follow those of the United Kingdom, guaranteeing certain fundamental rights such as the right to a fair trial and protection against arbitrary arrest or detention. The Constitution of the Bahamas establishes a federal government by providing for the executive, legislative, and judicial branches. The legislative branch has the power to make laws, the executive branch has the power to carry out and enforce the laws, and the judicial branch has the power to interpret the laws and judge whether they apply in individual cases. Following the Westminster model, the executive branch is directly responsible to the other branches of government.

Courts

All actions of the government, its citizens, and the law are subject to the review of the courts to ensure they adhere to the Constitution. The judiciary of the Bahamas is made up of the magistrates' courts, the Supreme Court, and the Court of Appeal. Most major cases are heard in the Supreme Court, the only court where the defendant is provided with a trial by jury. Justices of the Supreme Court and magistrates' courts are appointed by the governor-general, acting on the advice of the Judicial and Legal Service Commission. The justices have unlimited jurisdiction in all general, civil, and criminal matters. Their decisions can be appealed to the Court of Appeal, which is the highest tribunal court. The justices of the Court of Appeal are appointed by the governor-general on the recommendation of the prime minister. The Privy Council, located in London, is the highest court in the judicial system and is the final Court of Appeal.

The magistrates' courts are the courts of first instance and handle crimes that have a maximum sentence of five years. There are 17 magistrates' courts in the Bahamas. The governor-general appoints the chief magistrate and two deputy chief magistrates with the advice of the Judicial Legal Service Commission. A magistrate has jurisdiction to try all summary offenses, investigate all charges of indictable offenses, hear and determine any civil case where the amount to be recovered or the value of the property in dispute does not exceed $5,000, and hear juvenile and domestic matters.

The Supreme Court is the second-highest court of the country. It consists of a chief justice along with 11 other justices. The chief justice is appointed by the governor-general on the recommendation of the prime minister. Justices of the Supreme Court are appointed by the governor-general with advice from the Judicial and Legal Service Commission. The Supreme Court has unlimited original jurisdiction in civil and criminal causes and an appellate jurisdiction conferred on it by the Supreme Court Act of 1996, which includes appeals from the magistrates' courts.

The Court of Appeal consists of a president who presides over four justices of appeal, plus the chief of the judiciary who is an ex-officio member. The court has jurisdiction to hear and determine appeals from judgments, orders, and sentences made by the Supreme Court. The Court of Appeal also has jurisdiction to hear and determine appeals from matters in a magisterial court with respect to indictable offenses if the court had no jurisdiction in the matter, made an unreasonable decision, passed a sentence based on a wrong principle, involved illegalities that affected the merits of the case, or handed down a sentence that was too severe or too lenient.

Police

The Royal Bahamas Police Force (RBPF) is responsible for the internal security of the country, and the smaller Royal Bahamas Defense Force (RBDF) is responsible for its external security. The RBPF is modeled after the traditional British constable system and acts as a small paramilitary force headed by a police commissioner. The commissioner, appointed by the governor-general, is supported by a deputy commissioner and several senior assistant commissioners and assistant commissioners. It operates with approximately 2,200 personnel as well as 200 members in its Police Reserve Unit. The police force is organized into three districts: New Providence (where 75 percent of all its officers are assigned), Grand Bahama, and the Family Islands.

The police force is divided into several different branches, including the Drug Enforcement Unit (DEU), Central Detective Unit (CDU), Criminal Records Office (CRO), Fire Branch, Security and Intelligence Branch (SIB), Harbor Patrol, Mobile Division, Police Reserve, Forensics, Research and Planning, Community Policing/Relations Unit, Urban Renewal Division, and Complaints and Discipline Unit. The Bahamas Police Academy is located in Oakes Field, Nassau, New Providence and provides a 26-week training program along with continuing education classes for all potential regular police, fire police, police reservists, beach wardens, and local constables. All officers are armed with modern small arms.

The RBPF receives significant funds from the U.S. Department of State's International Narcotics Control (INC) program. The INC program trains police units throughout the world to conduct sophisticated drug-trafficking and money-laundering investigations and offers maritime interdiction training. Funding allowed the police force to implement an Automated Fingerprint Identification System (AFIS), allowing it to improve its operations in fingerprinting and criminal records research. Over the years, expenditures for the Royal Bahamas Police Force have been increased annually. The government allocated $117,467,000 to the force in 2008 and earmarked $121,932,000 for 2009.

The Constitution prohibits arbitrary arrest and detention by police officers. Law enforcement officials must conduct arrests openly and, when required by law to do so, obtain warrants authorized

A Royal Bahamas police officer boards a vessel near a possible drug drop zone in the Bahamas, April 6, 2006. (AP Photo/ Wilfredo Lee)

by a judge. However, they are not required to secure a warrant in such serious cases as suspected narcotics or firearms offenses when probable cause exists.

Although the RBPF is generally well-regarded by citizens, there have been charges of corruption. For example, in December 1998, the RBPF Drug Enforcement Unit (DEU) arrested two police officers from the RBPF Drug Canine Unit at Nassau International Airport for working with a cocaine trafficking ring. Over the past several years, police officials proven to be involved in narcotics-related corruption have been successfully prosecuted and incarcerated. Police officials acknowledge that officers have occasionally abused their power but pledge to address any further drug-related corruption swiftly and to the fullest extent of the law.

There have also been charges of police abuse of suspects, many of which have involved beatings by officers to extract confessions from detainees. For example, in 2004, a 19-year-old detainee claimed police stripped him, handcuffed him to a tree, and beat him with a metal pipe to extract a confession before charging him with attempted armed robbery. Human rights watchers and members of the public continue to express concern over such instances of police abuse against suspects. Police officials, while denying systematic or chronic abuses, acknowledge that police on occasion act improperly and pledge to address any wrongdoing by police officers. Police policy requires that an officer involved in a shooting or killing of a suspect automatically be placed under internal investigation. During 2006, police underwent training in human rights issues, including in-house training for officers on use of force, human rights, internal investigations of complaints against police, and corruption.

According to the U.S. Department of State, there were 253 complaints against officers in 2005 and 283 in 2006. Of these 283 cases in 2006, authorities resolved 99, with 59 remaining before a tribunal and another 125 still under investigation at year's end. Of the resolved cases, 16 were handled informally, and the remainder were dismissed or withdrawn as unsubstantiated. Following investigations into complaints against the police during 2006, including unethical conduct, assault, wrongful arrest, and excessive use of force, authorities dismissed 3 officers and brought criminal charges against 15 officers, all of which were pending at year's end.

Although police officials insist that their investigations are generally fair and thorough, local human rights observers doubt the force's ability to investigate itself impartially. In cases of alleged abuse and misconduct, human rights advocates believe that many incidents of improper police behavior go unreported. In response to such concerns, an independent civilian was appointed by the cabinet in 2001 to oversee the Police Complaints and Corruption Branch. The Police Complaints and Corruption Branch, which reports directly to the minister of national security and consults with the police commissioner, is responsible for investigating all allegations of police brutality. The unit determines whether enough evidence of abuse or misconduct exists in a particular case to warrant disciplinary action within the police system or, in some cases, criminal prosecution by the attorney general. Local attorneys and human rights advocates, however, still express concern that the Complaints and Corruption Branch lacks the independent authority needed to impartially investigate allegations of abuse and misconduct and that perceived lack of impartiality discourages the full reporting of complaints.

The government reports that it plans to complete the upgrade of a police communication system; increase the number of officers to 2,500; provide upgraded local and international training for junior and senior officers in criminal investigation, forensic, ballistic, and crime scene investigation techniques; enhance insurance coverage for police officers; enhance fairness in promotion policies; establish an independent civilian police board to hear appeals from disciplinary decisions by the commissioner of police; and accelerate community policing programs throughout the country.

Crime

Age of Responsibility

In the statute, an adult is any person age 18 years and older, a juvenile is a young person older than the age of 7 but younger than the age of 18, and a child is defined as any person under the age of 14.

Crime Statistics

An abbreviated 2007 crime report was released to the media by the RBPF Research Planning Unit. *The Bahama News* reported that crimes against persons rose by 37 percent over the preceding year (1,532 in 2007 versus 1,112 in 2006), and crimes against property rose by 10 percent. The murder count rose from 60 in 2006 to 79 in 2007. Although there were no recorded cases of attempted murder in 2005 or 2006, there were seven recorded cases in 2007. Rape cases jumped from 72 in 2006 to 135 cases in 2007, with attempted rapes also increasing (23 in 2006 versus 36 in 2007). Charges of unlawful sexual intercourse also rose from 208 in 2006 to 240 in 2007. In 2006, there were 548 armed robberies, 188 robberies, and 12 attempted robberies. In 2007, these statistics rose to 817 armed robberies, 195 robberies, and 19 attempted robberies. Property crimes saw a smaller rise from the 2006 numbers: 325 burglaries (363 in 2007), 1,531 shoplifting charges (1,542 in 2007), 1,323 stealing charges (1,326 in 2007), 948 thefts from vehicles (1,006 in 2007), and 1,176 stolen vehicles (1,187 in 2007).

Although the government conducts intensive public education programs aimed at child abuse, the crime remains a serious problem. According to the Bahamian Ministry of Social Development, there were 672 cases of child neglect reported to officials in 2007. The government report also noted that there were 356 cases of physical abuse, 286 cases of child sexual abuse, 159 cases in need of care and protection, 24 cases of child abandonment, 21 cases of incest, and 20 cases of emotional abuse to a child.

The Royal Bahamas Police Force (RBPF) attributed most murders, home invasions, and robberies to drugs and domestic violence. The drug transit issue is intimately related to many of the nation's socioeconomic problems, including a rising crime rate and a substantial increase in drug addiction. These problems have been fueled by a high unemployment rate (11,365 unemployed, or 6.9 percent of the labor force in 2000), particularly among the nation's youth.

Drug Offenses

According to the U.S. State Department, the Bahamas is a major transit country for cocaine and marijuana bound for the United States from South America and the Caribbean. It is not considered a significant drug producer or a producer or transit point for drug precursor chemicals. Located only 50 miles from the Florida coast, the Bahamas has been considered an ideal base for international smuggling. With its many uninhabited islands, a growing stream of tourists, and uncontrolled airstrips, the country has become a critical point on the drug routes from Jamaica and Colombia to the United States.

The country participates actively as a partner in Operation Bahamas and Turks and Caicos (OPBAT), a multiagency international drug interdiction cooperative effort established in 1982. Between 2004, and November 2005, OPBAT had seized 840 kilograms of cocaine and 9.0 metric tons of marijuana. Marijuana seizures doubled between 2004 and 2005, whereas cocaine seizures decreased as a result of the breakup of the largest drug trafficking organization in the Bahamas, headed by Samuel "Ninety" Knowles.

The government generally cooperates closely with the United States to stop the flow of illegal drugs through its territory, to target Bahamian drug trafficking organizations, and to reduce the domestic demand for drugs within the Bahamian population. However, unreliable jury pools and weaknesses in the drug laws resulted in several major Bahamian drug dealers evading conviction in the 1990s. The Bahamas has been warned by the United States that it must improve the effectiveness of its court system in gaining convictions against major drug dealers and trafficking organizations by strengthening its drug trafficking laws and improving the prosecutorial capabilities of the police. The country generally cooperates with the United States on extradition requests, based on the 1994 U.S.-Bahamas Extradition Treaty, but with mixed results. There are several such extradition requests pending in the Bahamian court system.

Money Laundering

Money laundering is also a problem in the Bahamas as a result of drug trafficking. The financial needs of drug traffickers, evaders, and money launderers have been met by the offshore banking industry. Its bank secrecy laws, the role of the country as a regional financial center, and the existence of a largely unregulated international business corporation (IBC) sector made the Bahamas a natural choice as a center for money laundering and other financial crimes.

Violence against Women

In 2008, the United Nations General Assembly expressed grave concern about the high incidence of violence against women in the form of domestic violence and sexual assault. In a 2007 United Nations report, the Bahamas was found to have the highest rate of reported rapes in the world, with 135 rape cases reported in 2007, compared to 72 cases in 2006. Additionally, the report found that more than 16 percent of the 2007 murders were found to be the result of domestic violence. Sexual violence within a marriage is not a crime.

Trafficking in Persons

There are no laws that specifically address trafficking in persons, but the law prohibits prostitution and the procurement of persons for purposes of prostitution, either in or outside the country, by force, threats, intimidation, or the administration of drugs. The maximum penalty for prostitution is five years' imprisonment, and procurement for the purpose of prostitution brings eight years' imprisonment. Local observers complain that the law does not protect trafficking victims who might be fearful of pressing complaints as a result of the country's current emphasis on immigration enforcement.

There have been reports that persons are trafficked within, to, or from the country, but the full nature and extent of the problem is undetermined. A 2002 report by the International Labor Organization estimated that 35 children were involved in commercial sexual activities, and the government acknowledges that the estimate is generally reflective of current levels of exploitation. The lack of a legal prohibition renders it difficult to assess accurately the extent of trafficking within the vulnerable illegal immigrant communities, especially Haitian communities. Although child labor laws exist, observers acknowledge that a small number of children have been involved in the worst forms of child labor, including slavery/bondage, sexual exploitation of children through incestuous relationships, illicit or unlawful activities, hazardous activities, and commercial sexual activities.

Finding of Guilt

Rights of Accused

Upon arrest, the accused person must appear before the magistrate within 48 hours (or by the next business day for cases occurring on weekends or holidays) to hear the charges being brought against him or her. Police can apply for a 48-hour extension upon simple application to the court and can request even longer extensions when they are able to show sufficient need. The government does not provide legal representation to defendants who cannot afford an attorney unless they are charged with a capital crime. There are currently nearly 600 lawyers qualified to practice before the Bahamas bar. The Constitution of the Bahamas provides the right to a fair trial, and an independent judiciary is charged with enforcing it. Defendants are presumed innocent until proven guilty in a court of law and are permitted to question witnesses and can view all government evidence against them. They also have the right to appeal to a higher court.

Bail and Remand

The country has a bail system, but individuals who cannot post bail are often held on remand indefinitely. Although the Constitution states that suspects can be held for a "reasonable period of time" before trial, human rights advocates complain that the heavy backlog of cases and court delays result in excessive pretrial detention that can extend two to four years or more. This lengthy remand can act as a strong disincentive to request a trial, given that a guilty plea can actually mean less incarceration time for the defendant, whether guilty or innocent. In 2003, Amnesty International estimated that 41 percent of inmates could not afford legal representation. Human rights activists maintain that this lack of representation might result in quicker convictions for the government, but only because the evidence is unchallenged by defendants who cannot afford an attorney. A lack of representation also contributes to excessive pretrial detention because defendants lack the means to push their case forward to trial.

The law prohibits bail for repeat offenders as well as those accused of certain violent crimes. Judges will sometimes authorize cash bail for foreigners accused of minor offenses. Generally, these individuals plead guilty and pay the fine rather than face detainment in the Bahamian prison system and lengthy delays in the court system. Those who go to trial can face indefinite incarceration. For example, according to the U.S. Department of State, in March 2006, the Court of Appeal awarded damages to a man from Japan who had been illegally detained and held in the Bahamian prison system without due process and without a trial since 1992. Human rights activists claim that a lack of transparency in the country's criminal justice system, along with a lack of legal representation, allows detained individuals such as the Japanese man to become lost within the criminal justice system.

In an attempt to address these delays, the Bahamian government instituted the Swift Justice Initiative with the goal of bringing all cases to trial within a two-year time frame. Although it passed through the legislature with the hope of lessening trial delays and easing the burden on witnesses, the initiative is not without its critics. In November 2006, the Court of Appeal issued two rulings regarding the initiative, finding undue government influence on the judiciary process. In one ruling, the judges maintained that the Swift Justice Initiative reduced judicial independence by assessing judges on their conviction rates and speed. The second ruling found that the mechanism for the governmental control of judicial salaries also interfered with judicial independence, hampering the court's ability to adjudicated cases in a fair manner. These concerns were echoed by other judicial and legal officials, including the president of the Court of Appeal and the president of the Bahamian Bar Association. In response, the government holds that judicial independence is still protected under the initiative and has appealed the ruling.

Despite measures to improve efficiency, complaints persist of excessive pretrial detention, outdated record keeping, delayed justice for victims, and a failure to update new laws in the books. Some judges have been brought in from abroad to help alleviate court backlogs. Though familiar with English common law, these foreign judges lack experience regarding Bahamian law and procedures. There are isolated complaints of deviations from normal, fair court proceedings—particularly in civil matters—but there are no indications that this is a widespread problem.

Punishment

Types of Punishment

The Bahamian Penal Code defines various crimes and establishes a penalty for each. There are five categories of punishment for offenses: (1) death, (2) imprisonment, (3) fine, (4) payments of costs, (5) payment of compensation, or various combinations of these. The court also has the option to place an offender under the supervision of the Probation Department. For those crimes that do not contain a specified punishment, seven years' imprisonment is given for a felony and two years for a misdemeanor. Some examples of punishments for first offenses, as specified by the penal code, are the death penalty for murder, treason, and piracy; life imprisonment for attempted murder and manslaughter; 20 years' imprisonment for arson of a dwelling or building, burglary, and use of deadly means of harm; 14 years to life for robbery; 14 years for housebreaking; 10 years for forgery and common theft; 6 months for trading in prostitution; and 3 months and a fine for keeping a brothel. For second and subsequent offenses, the penalties are increased.

Death Penalty

The death penalty has been the mandatory punishment for murder in the Bahamas since British rule. As of 2006, according to *The Bahama News,* the Bahamas had hanged 50 men since 1929. In 2006, approximately half of the 28 men on death row had been there for five or more years. In March 2006, the Privy Council, the highest court of appeal for the Bahamas, abolished the mandatory death sentence for murder as being in breach of the Constitution. The attorney general announced that resentencing hearings would be held for all death row inmates. The death penalty still has wide public support in the country, and several new death sentences have been issued since the court decision, although no executions have taken place.

Prison

More than one out of every 200 Bahamians is incarcerated, making its rate of imprisonment the eighth highest in the world, according to Amnesty International. Bahamian prisons are operated by the Prisons Department of the Ministry of National Security. Fox Hill is the only prison in the country.

In 2005, a new Central Intake Facility was opened, housing 60 inmates. It is used to assess and classify incoming inmates and recidivists for a period of between 7 and 14 days for the purpose of reception, orientation, sentence planning, and housing unit assignment. Bahamian officials maintain that inmates are assessed in a number of critical areas, including escape risk; correctional, educational, medical, social, and psychological history; and special needs.

Individual sentence plans are developed for inmates based on their strengths, weaknesses, vulnerabilities, interests, and long-term goals from a psychological, social, and educational position. Sentence plans are designed to ensure that each inmate is exposed to job skills, positive work habits, self-esteem enhancement, and life skill expansion while confined.

Prison officials have instituted some technical and vocational programs, and correctional officers have undergone instruction to become certified trainers. Training facilities are equipped with computers, and the prison offers some educational and literacy programs for prisoners. Approximately 500 of the 900 eligible prisoners participate in training and work release programs. Women prisoners do not have access to the work release programs available to male prisoners. Outside organizations providing aid, counseling services, and religious instruction are reported to have regular access to inmates. Inmates are also allowed approved visitations from family members on the designated visiting days.

Prison Classifications

Bahamian prisoners are housed in one of nine housing classifications: (1) super maximum security, (2) maximum, (3) high medium, (4) medium, (5) minimum security, (6) mental health supervision, (7) juveniles, (8) remand, and (9) women. Inmates sentenced to death or serving life imprisonment sentences, in addition to those who are serving sentences of 20 years or longer and those who are considered escape risks, are housed in the super maximum-security housing unit. Those serving sentences for dangerous, violent offenses such as rape and armed robbery with violence and drug offenses, in addition to multiple recidivists, are housed in the maximum-security housing unit. High-medium supervision applies to inmates convicted of armed robbery (where no violence was involved), manslaughter, child abuse, assault, conspiracy, extortion, incest, arson, auto theft, and drug possession (small quantities). Inmates serving life sentences, but who have qualified to be moved from the super maximum-security unit, are also housed there. Medium supervision applies to persons convicted of robbery, burglary, house and shop breaking, bigamy, gambling, forgery, perjury, fraud, and concealed firearm possession. Inmates convicted of such crimes as vagrancy, trespassing, civil offenses, loitering, littering, resisting arrest, public nuisance, offensive language, stealing, and poaching are housed in the minimum-security unit. Inmates are required to wear specially colored arm bands that serve as identification badges for institutional purposes and in the event of an escape.

The maximum-security building has a separate section for juvenile offenders aged 16 to 18. There is occasional mixing of juvenile with adult inmates depending on the severity of their crimes. Offenders younger than 16, along with children made wards of the court by their parents because of "uncontrollable behavior," are held at the Simpson Penn Center for Boys and the Williamae Pratt Center for Girls.

Prison Problems

Male prisoners placed in the maximum-security unit are crowded into poorly ventilated cells that generally lack regular running water, toilets, and laundry facilities. Most prisoners lack beds, sleep on pieces of cardboard placed on concrete floors, and are locked in small cells 23 hours per day, often amid human waste. Maximum-security inmates are allowed outside for exercise four days a week for one hour per day. Inmates complain of inadequate medical care and treatment.

Women prisoners are held separately from males. The prison's female population is around 40 inmates, considerably less than the female unit's full capacity of 200. Although their facilities have running water, women are detained in solitary confinement and suffer from a lack of women's health care. There have been repeated, unconfirmed, serious allegations of sexual abuse and rape that remain uninvestigated by the authorities.

With at least one death reportedly resulting from inadequate medical care and several reported suicides at the prison, Amnesty International reported that access to physical and mental health care is chronically lacking. There are high rates of infectious diseases. It is reported that prisoners suffering from AIDS, HIV, or tuberculosis (TB) do not receive adequate medical care or drugs. Thirty-two percent of the prison intake population is infected with TB, 20 percent are admitted with HIV, and seven prison deaths from AIDS-related complications have been reported by Amnesty International, although prison authorities estimate that only 8 percent of the population is infected with HIV, according to the U.S. Department of State.

Overcrowding among male prisoners is a major problem. In *The Bahama Journal,* Devaney (2007) reported that the country's prison is at 129.2 percent occupancy and the prison population is growing. The men's maximum-security block, originally built in 1953 to hold 450 inmates, holds more than 725. The entire prison system, designed to house 1,350 inmates, stands at 1,359. Further, Devaney stated that the prison remand area, built to hold 358 prisoners awaiting trial, is insufficient to hold the 587 prisoners awaiting trial, leaving many pretrial detainees confined in cells with convicted prisoners in the maximum-security unit. Of the 587 on remand in 2007, 404 had been placed there in 2007, 106 had been remanded since 2006, 39 had been remanded since 2005, 17 had been remanded since 2004, 15 had been remanded since 2003, 5 had been remanded since 2002, and 1 had been remanded since 2001. More than 200 persons were serving time for relatively minor, nonviolent, nondangerous crimes. Twenty-five inmates were sentenced and incarcerated for vagrancy, 19 for using obscene language, 12 for breach of the Road Traffic Act, 4 for breach of the Fisheries Act, 2 for loitering, and 7 for overstaying their time in the Bahamas.

Another cause for the overcrowding is the detainment of Haitians and Cubans for immigration violations. Haitians are frequently denied bail on the basis that they pose a significant flight risk. The country's proximity to Haiti and Cuba has made it a haven for economic refugees, adding to the social and economic problems in the Bahamas. Several have been repatriated, but many are detained for deportation in less than humane facilities. Attempts are made to repatriate illegal Haitian immigrants within 48 hours, but cases of individuals being held for long periods of time are reported. For instance, authorities held seven Cuban nationals at Carmichael Road Detention Center for more than two years, including five of whom, according to the Department of Immigration in the office of the UN High Commissioner for Refugees (UNHCR), were determined to have a legitimate fear of persecution if sent back to Cuba. International observers claimed that the length of detention for these detainees was excessive.

In 2007, Amnesty International reviewed the prison system and found reports of abuse, including excessive use of force, by members of the security forces. For example, a male prisoner who had been recaptured following a prison escape involving the death of a prison guard was shot dead while handcuffed as he was being transported back to Fox Hill Prison in January of 2006. A prison officer was found guilty of his murder by a Coroner's Court jury, but the verdict was deferred pending a constitutional review, and he was allowed to remain on duty with pay. Prison officials maintain that there was no unlawful abuse of the escaped inmate, despite prisoner claims and photographic evidence. Immigrants, largely Haitian, also continue to be ill-treated within the prison system.

The government increased training on use-of-force guidelines adopted in 2005, working with foreign experts on humane prisoner-control techniques. Local attorneys and human rights observers assert that the prison's Internal Affairs Unit, established in 2005, lacks the independent authority needed to impartially investigate allegations of abuse and misconduct within the prison system. In 2006, there were numerous complaints of abuse by prison guards, but the Internal Affairs Unit recommended that only one officer be prosecuted for the abuse of an inmate.

Other Sentences

Although the Constitution of the Bahamas prohibits torture and other cruel and degrading treatment or punishment, law enforcement and corrections officials have been known to beat and otherwise abuse suspects and prisoners. Corporal punishment was abolished in 1984 but was reinstated in 1991 for specific offenses. According to Bahamian law, sentences of flogging cannot exceed 24 strokes, and whipping has a maximum of 12 strokes. Caning is permitted at police stations but only if performed by a high-ranking official. Cat-o'-nine-tails are allowed at prisons but have not been used for several years, according to prison officials.

The government is considering plea bargaining, the use of electronic bracelets, community service, and compulsory education and skills programs to free up the courts and the prison system. Violent and dangerous repeat offenders would not be eligible for plea bargaining or diversionary programs. Officials are calling for the changes because of the high level of repeat offenders who leave the system not rehabilitated and unable to successfully reintegrate into society. With 1 out of every 232 Bahamians, predominantly young men, in the country's prison system, the country sees the depletion of its human capital and seeks ways to support their integration into mainstream society and legitimate enterprises.

Barbara J. Nowak

Further Reading

Block, Alan. (1991). *Masters of Paradise: Organized Crime and the Internal Revenue Service in the Bahamas.* Edison, NJ: Transaction Publishers.

Devaney, Clunis. (2007, October 18). *National Security Minister Addresses Issues of Crime and Prison Reform.* Nassau, The Bahamas: Commonwealth of the Bahamas Press Release.

Hanna, Chaswell, Altida Khalfani, and Kemuel Knowles. (2007). *The Story of the Royal Bahamas Police Force.* Nassau, New Providence: Royal Bahamas Police Force.

Johnson, Howard. (1996). *The Bahamas: From Slavery to Servitude, 1783–1933.* Gainseville: University Press of Florida.

Lex Bahamas: Bahamian Online Legal Resource Centre. (n.d.). "Overview of the Bahamian Legal System": http://www.lexbahamas.com/overview_of_the_bahamian_legal_s.htm.

Nowak, Barbara. (2001). "Keeping It Better in the Bahamas: A Nation's Socioeconomic Response to Juvenile Crime." *Journal of Black Studies* 31(4): 483–493.

Official Web site of the Government of the Bahamas: http://www.bahamas.gov.bs.

Barbados

Legal System: Common
Murder: High
Corruption: Low
Prison Rate: High
Death Penalty: Yes
Corporal Punishment: Yes

Background

Barbados is the most easterly of the Caribbean islands, 14 miles in width and 21 miles in length, occupying a total area of 66 square miles. It is home to about 300,000 residents, and it is visited by thousands of tourists each year. It first became known to the European world via a Portuguese explorer in 1536 before being colonized by the British in 1627. Barbados became independent from the United Kingdom on November 30, 1966, and committed itself to universal suffrage and parliamentary democracy based on the British system.

Political Context

Under the Constitution of Barbados, the governor-general, appointed by the government, represents the monarch, and the cabinet headed by the prime minister has responsibility for the day-to-day governance of the country and control of power. Barbados adopted the Westminster system of governance, which is found and practiced in the United Kingdom. It is a parliamentary democracy led by a prime minister, which means that the political party with the largest number of seats in Parliament forms the government, and the leader of that party automatically assumes the mandate of prime minister.

The Parliament of Barbados has two parts, namely the House of Representatives and the Senate. The House of Representatives has 28 members who are elected by universal suffrage for five-year terms. The Senate has 21 members. The governor-general appoints 12 members on the advice of the prime minister, 2 on the advice of the leader of the opposition, and 7 at his or her discretion. The government is responsible for criminal justice policies. The usual practice is for Parliament to debate and pass new laws and amendments, with the approval of the governor-general in some cases.

Legal and Criminal Justice System

Barbados has a fair and open legal system dating back to the early period of the post-independence era in the mid- to late 1960s. Under its Constitution, Barbados has an independent legal system including the police and the judiciary. The latter is particularly independent in terms of its decisions, although judges of the Supreme Court, the highest court inside Barbados, are usually appointed by the governor-general, as recommended by the prime minister in consultation with the leader of the opposition. The Constitution provides for a judiciary comprising magistrate courts and a Supreme Court. The number of magistrate courts and their authority are established by statute.

The Supreme Court consists of two parts, namely the High Court and the Court of Appeals. The High Court and the Court of Appeals have four judges each. The chief justice serves on both the High Court and the Court of Appeals. Some analysts and commentators may see a potential conflict of interest in this situation, especially as cases move hierarchically from one court to the next, but it appears to work well in Barbados. The leading political parties accept this practice, and there are other judges on both courts to resolve or overrule any potential conflict of interest arising from the chief justice sitting on the benches of the two courts.

Barbados has been strongly influenced by Britain, not only by adopting the Westminster system of governance but also by making the Judicial Committee of the Privy Council in London the country's highest court and, thus, the court of last resort. Dissatisfied parties can seek redress at the Privy Council, but all decisions of the council are final and binding on all concerned.

The Police

The Royal Barbados Police Force is organized according to three geographic divisions, namely the Northern, Southern, and Bridgetown divisions. There are three other countrywide divisions—the Operations Support Division, the Administrative Support Division, and the Criminal Investigations Division.

Because Barbados is a small country, the divisions support each other mutually. There have been instances where criminal activities were carried out across geographical divisions and where investigations spread across the whole country involving all three divisions. There is also the traffic arm of the police, which maintains law and order on the country's roads, attends to traffic offenses and accidents, and arranges for the prosecution of people involved in serious traffic offenses.

There is considerable cooperation between the police and the country's army. The army has been called in to help quell prison riots and breakouts and to help catch or rearrest dangerous criminals who have escaped from lawful custody. For example, serious riots occurred in the country's only prison, Glendairy Prison, in 2005. The prison burned down as a result of the major riots, and the army provided support in dealing with the riots, although armies from neighboring countries also came in to help.

Crime

Crime Types and Classifications

The Barbados legal system distinguishes between major and minor crimes, each with further subclassifications. The seriousness of the crime defines the category in which it falls. Serious life-threatening crimes and property crimes involving huge damages are usually classified as major crimes, whereas less serious offenses are classified as minor. Further distinction is made between "crimes against persons" and "crimes against property." Both major and minor crimes generally fall within these two broad categories.

With regard to major crimes, there is further distinction between non-sex-related crimes (classified as "A") and sex-related crimes (classified as "B"). Type A offenses, falling under the category of major crimes against the person, include murder, serious bodily harm, endangering life, kidnapping, robbery, and so on. Type B offenses classified as major crimes include rape, indecent assault, assault with intent to rape, and so on. Minor crimes against the person include assaults, wounding, harassment, and the like.

Major and minor crimes against property are also classified as "A" and "B." Type A major crimes against property include burglary, sacrilege (disrespect of and damage to something which is regarded as sacred), and other related crimes and attempts. Type B major crimes against property include arson, attempted arson, and criminal damage. Type A minor crimes against property include theft and theft-related crimes (motor vehicle, home, wallets, and bags, etc). Fraud-related crimes constitute Type B minor crimes, although corporate fraud may be classified as a major offense.

In addition to the major and minor crimes just discussed, certain specific crimes are clearly distinguished as "other crimes" and subclassified under four categories. Drug crimes are subclassified as Type A, firearms and ammunition crimes as Type B, escaping lawful custody as Type C, and public order breaches and all other summary crimes as Type D.

Drug Crimes

Drugs are a major problem in Barbados, as in the wider Caribbean. A large number of major and minor offenses involve drugs and the use of illegal drugs in one way or another, explicitly or implicitly. Many crimes occur because the perpetrators have used drugs or were involved in crimes against the person or property to obtain drugs or to seek money or something to sell to obtain money to buy drugs. The Barbados legal system classifies as criminal activity the possession and use of illegal drugs, the sale of illegal drugs, and the smuggling, trafficking, and distributing of illegal drugs.

All sorts of drugs are illegally available in Barbados. The main drugs include marijuana, heroin, and cocaine, as well as party drugs such as GHB and Ecstasy. It is criminal to sell and use any of these drugs. The problem is that Barbados is a small island, and the police cannot patrol or be at every part of the coast at the same time. Drug smugglers have made it a point to use boats, canoes, and other vessels to bring the illegal drugs to remote and isolated beaches of the country, from where the drugs find their way to the populated parts of the country if the drug dealers are not caught by the law enforcement agencies.

Juvenile Offenders

Most offenders under 16 years old are classified as juvenile offenders and placed in boys' and girls' industrial homes after conviction, whereas offenders aged 17 years and over are usually classified as adult offenders and sentenced to prison terms to be served in the adult correctional facility. The juvenile detention centers, called the Government Industrial Schools in Barbados, are located at Dodds and Summervale.

Crime Statistics

Not only is crime a major problem in Barbados, but the incidence and prevalence of crime are also rising. According to police statistics, between 1990 and 1999, reported incidents of motor vehicle theft increased from 35 to 282, drug offenses increased from 555 to 984, and robbery increased from 352 to 443; however, violent crimes decreased from 383 to 340, and burglary decreased from 2,736 to 2,071. Despite this decrease, burglary was the most frequently reported crime to the police during this period (34.7 percent of all offenses in 1999), followed by other types of theft (16.3 percent of all offenses in 1999). Most of the theft and burglary offenses were committed to raise money to finance drug habits, as reported consistently in the courts by various prosecutors and admitted by offenders.

More recent police data from the first quarter of 2006 (January to March 2006) provides further insights into the nature and pattern of crime. With regard to the contribution of each category to the overall crime level, property offenses are outstanding. The category of major crimes against property was the single-largest contributor to the overall level of crime in the first quarter of 2006 (29.01 percent), followed by the category of minor crimes against property (24.77 percent).

Thus, crimes against property (major and minor) constituted more than half the number of all crimes in Barbados in the first quarter of 2006 (53.9 percent). Of the five broad categories of crime in Barbados, minor crimes against the person were the third-single-largest contributor to crime, and other crimes constituted the fourth-single-largest contributor in the first quarter of 2006 (15.76 percent). The category that made the smallest contribution to the overall level of crime was major crimes against the person, contributing about 10 percent.

In terms of specific types of crime, burglaries, sacrilege, and other related crimes (23.11 percent); theft and other theft related crimes (22.73 percent); and assaults, wounding, and harassment (20.43 percent) made the strongest contributions to crime levels in the first quarter of 2006. Escaping lawful custody (0.25 percent), firearms and ammunition crimes (0.89 percent), fraud-related crimes (2.04 percent), and rape, indecent assault, and assault with intent to rape (2.17 percent) made the weakest contributions to overall crime level during this period. The small contribution of sex-related offenses (classified as major crime against the person in Barbados) is particularly interesting, given the usually large number of reported cases in the Barbados press. In addition, it is worthy to note that each of the categories of drug offenses, murder, manslaughter, endangering life, kidnapping, and robbery offenses contributed less than 10 percent to the crime level in the first quarter of 2006, even though they usually constitute some of the most serious types of crimes in the country. The patterns and trends in crime observed in the 1990s continued in 2006. For example, burglary and theft of all sorts continued to be the main areas of criminal activity in the first quarter of 2006 as they were in the 1990s.

Of more concern to most people in Barbados, as reported in the press, is the possession and willful use of firearms by perpetrators of crime during criminal activity. According to police statistics, there were 7 reported cases of firearm-related murder in 1999 and six in 2000, but firearm-related robbery and robbery with assault increased from 75 in 1999 to 138 in 2000, shooting at someone or endangering life increased from 35 in 1999 to 61 in 2000, and unlawful possession of a firearm increased from 61 in 1999 to 73 in 2000.

Crimes Committed by Foreigners

Based on Barbados police statistics, the *Caribbean Net News* reported that of the 2,831 suspects arrested and charged with various offenses in Barbados between January and November 2005, 75 were Guyanese, 36 were Vincentian, 30 were Jamaican, 20 St. Lucian, and 8 were from Trinidad and Tobago. Further breakdown shows that 29 British nationals were arrested and charged with diverse offenses, together with 10 Americans and 5 Germans. Some other nationalities are also represented, but in very small numbers.

Social Context of Crime

Although Barbados is a wealthy country with a fairly high gross domestic product per capita, large segments of the population are unemployed or live on little income. A society where most young people have nothing to do increases the potential of youth to commit crime. There is widespread drug use involving expensive drugs and a cultural practice that encourages males to buy expensive gifts for their girlfriends in a very promiscuous society, both of which support thefts and burglary of all kinds. The girls tend to associate with the males who are able to provide those gifts, making it likely for the males to commit crimes to get the needed money.

Finding of Guilt

Rights of the Accused

The accused have many rights, including a fair trial, the right to seek legal advice without representation if required, the right to legal representation, the right to appeal the decision of any court in the legal system inside the country, and the right to decide and make a plea (guilty or not guilty) in consultation with their legal representative. Indeed, aggrieved parties can appeal all the way to the Privy Council in London for a final and binding decision, if the Privy Council decides that a case for appeal hearing has been established.

In Barbados, the accused do not usually have the legal right to plea bargain as such, and definitely not in the way it works in Western countries. However, plea bargaining occurs in practice when the accused try to negotiate with prosecutors and magistrates in court. The large number of cases, especially those involving robbery, burglary, and theft, means that speedy trial is not usually possible. Most cases have to wait for trial and are slotted in and attended to as court time permits. While awaiting trial, some accused are released on bail and ordered to reappear at a specified date and time, whereas other accused persons are remanded in custody and taken to Glendairy Prison.

Trial by Jury and Bail Practices

In Barbados, the right to a trial by jury does not exist for most offenses. The jury system is used only in serious offenses such as murder, where it is required. For other offenses, the usual procedure is trial before a magistrate who decides and makes a finding of guilt or otherwise. Most offenders, especially those involved in minor crimes, tend to represent themselves, because free legal assistance is not readily and widely available.

The criminal justice system of Barbados allows for the accused to be granted bail if certain conditions are met and if the presiding magistrate is satisfied that the risk to the community is minimal. For most nonserious offenses, suspects would be expected to seek or apply for bail and be granted it. The decision to grant bail rests with the presiding magistrate. Defense attorneys and prosecuting officers usually make submissions for and against bail, respectively, and the magistrates make the final decision after assessing risks to the community and related factors. Offenses such as minor crimes against property (theft and theft-related crimes and less serious fraud-related crimes) and minor crimes against the person (assaults, wounding, harassment) are more likely to attract bail.

Bail conditions are becoming increasingly tougher, and many offenders, especially repeat offenders, are finding it very difficult to be granted bail. Most magistrate courts have consistently made it clear that no bail application would be entertained for offenses involving the use of firearms, irrespective of the nature of the offense, thus underscoring the seriousness of crimes involving firearms and ammunition in Barbados.

It is normal practice to decline bail for offenders involved in major crimes against the person (murder, serious bodily harm, endangering life, kidnapping, rape, etc.), major crimes against property (arson, criminal damage, etc.), and other serious crimes (escaping lawful custody). Firearms and ammunition and drug charges are also most likely to be refused bail. Like most legal and criminal justice systems around the world, the decision to grant or refuse bail appears to be made primarily on the basis of risk to the community and the seriousness of the offense, although each bail application or case is assessed and determined on its own merits and risks.

Alternatives to Trial and Other Procedures

Once criminal investigations conclude that the law has been broken in one way or the other, going to trial is inevitable. Negotiated settlement without going to trial does not usually happen in criminal cases. Medical or other forms of supervision are ordered by the courts pre- or post-trial, and the police cannot order the suspects or accused to undergo any form of medical supervision without due process in a court of law. Similarly, offenders requiring treatment that relates to their criminal activity (e.g., mental disorders such as schizophrenia) will still have to first go through due process in court.

Most criminal cases in Barbados go before the magistrate courts. Each magistrate court is presided over by one magistrate who hears evidence and arguments from both sides—the prosecutors and defense attorneys (or self-represented defendants, as applicable). There are four judges each in the High Court and the Appeals Court, the two courts that constitute the Supreme Court of Barbados. The magistrates and judges are very qualified to practice law and have the requisite experience to sit on the bench. Most possess a bachelor's or higher degree in law coupled with many years recognized experience in legal practice in the public or private sector.

Juvenile offenders are usually treated as young offenders. Juvenile offenders are remanded in custody or sentenced to a term of detention after conviction, and they are kept in one of the two main industrial or detention homes for young offenders. There are separate juvenile detention homes for boys and girls, but they all have the objective of getting juvenile offenders, especially those who commit serious crimes and repeat offenders, off the streets and out of the community. The juvenile industrial homes or detention centers also work toward stopping and preventing juvenile offenders from graduating into adult offenders.

Punishment

Throughout the history of independent Barbados, the single-most widely used form of punishment for convicted offenders has been incarceration. For decades, diverse forms of sentencing such as fines, corporal punishment, public punishment, probation, home detention or house arrest, probation, reparations, compensation/restitution, and periodic detention were hardly used or not even known in the country's criminal justice system. Today most offenders are still sentenced to various prison terms, which are served in the country's only prison, namely Glendairy Prison.

Crime Types and Sentencing Patterns

As is expected, the type of sentence meted out depends on the seriousness and type of crime. Murder convictions generally attract capital punishment or life imprisonment. Although provisions exist for the imposition of capital punishment, as of 2008, no convicted criminal sentenced to death had been executed in Barbados in the previous five years, though Barbados continues to be a strong advocate of the death penalty. Barbados vehemently opposed a moratorium on the death penalty recommended by a United Nations General Assembly Panel in November 2007.

The incidence and prevalence of rape is high in Barbados, and punishment for rape and other serious sexual assault offenses has become increasingly severe. On average, offenders convicted of rape, for example, can expect to be sentenced to between five and seven years in prison, although higher sentences may be given depending on the circumstances and/or whether a weapon was used in committing the crime. Sometimes rape cases are difficult to determine in Barbados, a problem that is exacerbated by the culture of widespread promiscuity and the fact that many reports of rape are made after the victim's partner has become aware that sexual intercourse has taken place between the victim and the accused, thus prejudicing the case against some suspects.

Another area of concern to law enforcement authorities in Barbados is escaping lawful custody. This is considered a very serious crime in Barbados, attracting what many may consider harsh sentences. The sentencing pattern has evolved over the years as criminals have become more sophisticated in the way and manner they plan and execute their escapes, bringing a lot of embarrassment to the law enforcement authorities. A few high-profile criminals have escaped from lawful custody, undermining the confidence residents have in the criminal justice system of Barbados.

To serve as a serious deterrent and to keep drug traffickers and major users off the street and out of the community, punishment for drug crimes continues to be severe. Convicted drug offenders can expect a sentence of 5 to more than 10 years, with convicted drug traffickers receiving sentences at the higher end of the range, especially if a firearm is involved in perpetrating the crime.

Firearms and ammunition crimes have been considered serious crimes in Barbados for many years. The incidence and prevalence of firearms and ammunition crimes have been so high that a culture of fear prevails in many parts of the country. The country has responded accordingly with severe sentences. In the early 2000s, for example, magistrates made it clear to criminals that no bail would be granted to any person or persons arrested on suspicion of firearms and ammunition crimes, regardless of their individual circumstances. In addition, convicted criminals involved in firearms and ammunition crimes have been given long and severe sentences (five to seven years on average and higher in some cases). Even so, it goes without saying that these measures have not been successful in preventing firearm and ammunition crimes, and weapons continue to be used in perpetrating crimes, including some minor thefts.

One area where sentencing has varied significantly is theft, robbery, and burglary. The level of punishment in these cases by and large depends on the magistrate, the nature of the offenses, whether a weapon was involved, and whether the culprit has previous convictions for similar offenses. Thefts that are not serious, including pickpocketing and shoplifting, may attract a sentence of a few months. More serious burglary and robbery offenses, aggravated by the use of a weapon and/or threatening and/or wounding, can attract longer prison terms of three to more than five years on average.

Minor offenses tend to attract less severe sentences, although most still attract custodial sentences. Minor crimes against the person, such as minor assaults, harassment, wounding, and so on, can attract sentences of a few months up to three or more years in prison, again depending on the circumstances of each case and previous convictions. Minor crimes against property, such as theft and theft-related crimes and minor fraud crimes, also attract less severe sentences similar to or less than those meted out to criminals convicted of minor crimes against the person, depending on various factors surrounding each case. It should be further noted that other crimes, such as public order breaches, are treated with seriousness in Barbados, but sentences have varied over the years, with each incident or offense being considered on its own circumstances and merits.

Prison

Although prison numbers are not readily available and are not usually published, there is some evidence to suggest that the daily number of prisoners averaged between 900 and 1,050 during the few years prior to 2008, including sentenced prisoners serving their time and those on remand awaiting trial. Indeed, at the time of the prison riots in 2005, the prison housed about 1,000 inmates, including 51 females and 949 or so males.

There is only one prison in Barbados, called Glendairy Prison, which is also known as "Her Majesty's Prison." Built in 1855, the old Glendairy Prison held both male and female adult prisoners, including those tried and sentenced to prison, as well as those suspects on remand while awaiting trial. The old facility was located at Station Hill in the Parish of St. Michael. Inadequate amenities, overcrowding, and congestion constituted major problems during the operation of the old prison. In 2004, the prison superintendent indicated that the old Glendairy Prison was built to house a maximum of about 350 inmates, but that it was housing more than 1,000 inmates, making life inside very uncomfortable and putting extreme pressure on the inmates and staff of the correctional facility.

Successive governments were faced with resolving the problems at Glendairy Prison, as the number of inmates continued to rise and conditions inside deteriorated unabated. They also had to deal with the difficulty of developing and implementing policies and practices that would provide a balance between punishment and humane treatment of prisoners, bearing in mind the difficult living conditions in the prison. These difficulties have been exacerbated by the fact that criminal activity continues to be perpetrated in such a manner as to instill fear among residents. Governments are aware that any effort to reduce punishment of offenders would not meet the expectations of residents and would quite possibly result in residents' loss of confidence in law enforcement provisions.

There have been many controversies involving the old Glendairy Prison. For example, sodomy is so widespread in Glendairy Prison that some prisoners see it as a logical source of sex and a normal way of life. This has generated a national debate as to whether condoms should be made freely available to inmates of the correctional facility. The incidence and prevalence of HIV/AIDS have been high in Barbados, and the use of condoms is proven to reduce infection of HIV.

Another controversy surrounds the availability and use of mobile phones within the prison. Crime lords have been known to operate from within the confines of Glendairy Prison. The instrument of communication with accomplices outside the prison is the mobile phone. These phones have been used by prison inmates to order and arrange attacks, to intimidate victims and witnesses, and to foster a continuous perpetration of crime, especially by drug moguls who ply their trade from within the prison using the cellular phone to provide instructions to accomplices living in the community.

In addition, circulation of drugs within the prison has sometimes precipitated arguments and fights among inmates, causing serious bodily harm to those involved in some cases. The availability of illegal drugs serves as a catalyst to enhance and support gang activity within the prison, with the main problem being that the gang activities continue when the inmates are released and returned to the community, resulting in reoffending. This is one main reason why recidivism is so high in Barbados.

Like the situation with illegal drugs, there is a marked presence of illegal weapons in Glendairy Prison. Despite the improving security measures adopted and implemented within the facility by officials, weapons including knives and firearms continue to be found in the facility, creating major concerns for inmates and prison wardens. There have been instances where Glendairy Prison inmates have used weapons to leash attacks on fellow inmates; to forcibly sodomize other inmates, using the weapons to threaten their victims; and even to attack prison wardens and officials.

Prison Unrest

Glendairy Prison has experienced many instances of prison unrest over the years, including in the form of fights among individual inmates, rival gang attacks, and attacks on prison wardens and related officials, as well as minor disturbances and protests against prison policies and/or practices, especially when a new policy or practice is introduced that has the potential to curtail the benefits prisoners enjoy in the corrections facility. Of all the reported disturbances and unrests, the one that caused the greatest destruction was the prison unrest of 2005.

The 2005 Glendairy Prison riots began on Monday, March 28, and are perhaps the most prominent event in the history of Glendairy Prison, in terms of casualties and damage to property. A second fire was set on Wednesday, March 30, causing further havoc and homelessness for the inmates. Although the cause was initially unclear, it was generally believed that an undesired act of sodomy by one inmate on another had resulted in an open fight among several inmates. The attempted sodomy was reported to a warden, and when no specific action was taken to protect that inmate and other victims of forced sodomy, the inmates took matters into their own hands in a manner never seen before in Barbados. However, forced sodomy is so rampant inside Glendairy Prison that some commentators argued that it could not have initiated the riots. In trying to identify the exact cause of these riots, one should not lose sight of the fact that the inmates had been under a lot of stress and pushed to the limit from the overcrowded and harsh prison conditions and were probably ready to explode at the earliest opportunity and from any cause.

The fight spread among other inmates and flowed into a major broad-based disturbance. The prison was set on fire, causing extensive damage to the roof, and two buildings housing the kitchen, bakery, and the library were virtually destroyed and rendered unusable. The situation appeared disastrous, given that Barbados has only one adult prison. The government and prison officials had to decide and act quickly.

A decision was made to evacuate both male and female inmates to undisclosed locations on the island for security reasons. It must be stressed right from the outset that the riots were well contained within a short time, thanks to the effective actions of prison officials, government policies, and regional cooperation. For example, the decision of the government to erect an internal perimeter fence inside Glendairy Prison a few months before the riots paid off and prevented inmates from escaping. No inmate escaped, all inmates were accounted for, and at no stage was the community at serious risk.

Although damage to prison property was the main highlight, it is worthy to note that there were human casualties as well. One male inmate was killed, and 13 people, including 6 prison officials, were taken to the country's main hospital, Queen Elizabeth Hospital. One inmate had to undergo surgery after he was severely beaten by fellow inmates for attacking a prison official. One prisoner received two gunshots to the hip, and a few others were treated for burns to the scalp and rope burns around the neck indicating an attempted strangulation. As expected, the fumes caused severe problems for inmates and prison officials with preexisting asthmatic conditions. As details emerged, it became clear that many inmates had endured injuries that were not severe enough to require hospital treatment.

The old dilapidated Glendairy Prison was burned and uninhabitable as a result of the prison riots of 2005. It has since been replaced by a new prison, also called Glendairy Prison. The new Barbados prison is located at Dodds in the Parish of St. Philip and has better facilities than the previous prison. It started housing prisoners early in 2007.

A significant outcome of the Barbados prison riots was the special powers given to law enforcement authorities in the country as a result, especially the police and the military. The Parliament of Barbados passed legislation that gave the police and the military greater powers to deal with criminals and prisoners and oversee the detention centers, although such powers were initially seen to be temporary. An amendment to the Prisons Act allowed the police and soldiers to carry guns in prison and to use them to foil escape attempts and control riots, if necessary. It also gave them the power to challenge, guard, transport, and search without the requirement of having prison wardens around, powers that had never been seen before in Barbados.

Prison Programs

Rehabilitation and employment programs are available to inmates of Glendairy Prison. However, participation in these programs is not automatic, and inmates have to earn the right or privilege to participate in most of the programs, especially the employment programs. Even so, most drug offenders are usually allowed to take part in the drug rehabilitation programs.

Rehabilitation programs take various forms, but most are targeted at inmates convicted of drug and drug-related offenses. The distinct feature of the drug rehabilitation program in Glendairy Prison is that only inmates who have served a substantial portion of their sentence and are about to be released into the community are eligible for participation. The main objective is to make them drug-free and to help them cope with drug problems on reentry into the community and avoid reoffending.

The Inmate Drug Rehabilitation and Counseling Program is prison-based and available to both male and female inmates. There are about five main components, namely education, treatment, prerelease counseling, individual counseling, and connection with or referral to community-based rehabilitation services on release. Inmates who participate in the program are provided with drug-related education, given treatment as appropriate for their drug addiction or problem, and counseled about potential problems, temptations, and issues before their reentry into the community. Individuals who are considered likely to have difficulties resettling are provided with individual counseling. This type of counseling is tailored to the needs of the particular individual to facilitate his or her return to the community, as well as prepare him or her for life outside Glendairy Prison. Individuals who are not able to participate in the group prerelease counseling services are also provided with opportunities for individual counseling.

Glendairy Prison's Inmate Drug Rehabilitation and Counseling Program operates under the auspices of a program coordinator. Participants are introduced to concepts of addiction and are encouraged and taught how to undertake self-assessment. More importantly for successful reentry into the community, participating inmates are prepared to survive relapses through the provision of specific program components that deal with relapse prevention. Pressure is put on inmates to redefine the thinking and previous lifestyle that brought them to the prison. They are made to assess and reassess the cost of their drug use and its consequences—financial, human, material, and otherwise.

Yet another salient feature is the focus on spirituality, which tends to bring humility and an element of sadness and remorse to a number of participating inmates. The Glendairy Prison Rehabilitation and Counseling Program adopts and uses some of the approaches of community-based drug and alcohol rehabilitation programs. A case in point is the emphasis put on the 12-step recovery model usually used by groups such as Alcoholics Anonymous and Narcotics Anonymous.

On release, all participants are referred to or connected with a community-based rehabilitation agency to enable them to continue with further rehabilitation and to assist with their successful resettlement. Despite all of these practices, recidivism or reoffending involving illegal drugs is high in Barbados.

All other inmates receive prerelease counseling and individual counseling where necessary. They are also exposed to education and crime-prevention activities. Some of the inmates are connected with community agencies to assist with their resettlement into the community after their release from prison.

Prison Employment Programs

Like many prisons elsewhere, there are provisions for inmates of Glendairy Prison to have access to employment during the period of their detention. As alluded to previously, inmates do not have automatic access to employment and have to earn the privilege to work during the period of their incarceration. Different types of work are available, including cleaning, assistance in the kitchen, and the inhumane job of carrying the "poo bucket." With the building of the new Glendairy Prison, some of the nasty jobs have been phased out. Pay levels for prison inmate jobs have been low, rising from a few Barbados dollars to about 10 Barbados dollars. Needless to say, most jobs in prison attract low pay levels elsewhere as well, and thus, the situation in Barbados is not entirely unique to the country.

David Achanfuo Yeboah

Further Reading

Barbados National Task Force on Crime Prevention. (2004). *Crime and Justice Bulletin 4: Prisoners in Glendairy Prison.* Bridgetown: National Task Force on Crime Prevention.

Brathwaite, Farley, and Yeboah David. (2004). "Victims of Crime in the Criminal Justice System of Barbados." *Journal of Criminal Justice* 32(2): 431–442.

Royal Barbados Police: http://www.barbadospolice.gov.bb/.

Yeboah, David A. (2002). "Crime and Its Solutions in Barbados." *Journal of Criminal Justice* 30(5): 409–416.

Belize

Legal System: Common
Murder: High
Corruption: Medium
Human Trafficking: Medium
Prison Rate: High
Death Penalty: Yes
Corporal Punishment: Maybe

Background

Belize is a thinly inhabited country located between Mexico and Guatemala and bordering the Caribbean

Sea. Its population of 310,000 residents occupies an area of 22,966 square kilometers, which is about the size of the state of Massachusetts. About half (48 percent) of Belizeans live in rural areas, and nearly 25 percent reside in the largest city and former capital of Belize City. The comparatively low life expectancy at birth (68 years) and the very high fertility rate (3.4 children per woman) have converged to render Belize a very young nation: youths younger than 14 years of age constituted more than 34 percent of the population in 2009.

Ethnic diversity and linguistic plurality characterize the Belizean society. Mestizos of mixed Mayan and European descent represent 44 percent of the population, Creoles of Afro-European ancestry account for 30 percent, Mayan Amerindians top 11 percent, Garifunas or Afro-Amerindians constitute 6 percent, and the remaining 9 percent include Europeans, East Indians, Chinese, Middle Easterners, and North Americans. English is the official language and spoken by all, and a Creole dialect is spoken by most. Spanish is the native tongue of half of Belizeans and used as a second language by another one-fifth. Mayans still speak their indigenous languages within their own groups. About half of the population is affiliated with the Roman Catholic Church, and the other half follows various brands of the Protestant faith.

Tourism and exports of marine products, citrus, cane sugar, bananas, and garments form the backbone of Belize's small economy. The gross domestic product per capita, adjusted for purchasing power parity, reached US$8,400 in 2009, and 34 percent of the population lived under the poverty line. Because of persistent economic hardships, the country has developed a chronic dependence on foreign aid assistance. About 77 percent of Belizean adults are literate, and over 8 percent of the labor force was unemployed in 2007.

Several Mayan city-states prospered in what is today the territory of Belize until their decline at the end of the 10th century. The British and Spanish wrangled over the territory for more than a hundred years until Belize formally became the crown colony of British Honduras in 1862. In the 20th century, various constitutional reforms were passed to enlarge the representativeness of the government. Full internal self-government of Belizeans under a ministerial cabinet was granted in 1964. Territorial disputes between the United Kingdom and Guatemala delayed the full independence of Belize until 1981.

Belize is a parliamentary democracy and a Commonwealth realm. The government is organized into executive, legislative, and judicial branches. The British Monarch is head of state and represented in the country by the governor-general appointed by the monarch. The governor-general names the prime minister and appoints the cabinet on the advice of the prime minister. The prime minister, usually the leader of the majority party or coalition prior to the legislative elections, is chief of government. Cabinet ministers are members of the majority party in the National Assembly and usually hold elected legislative seats concurrently with their ministerial appointments. The National Assembly performs legislative duties and consists of a House of Representatives and a Senate. The 31 members of the House are popularly elected to a five-year term, and the governor-general appoints the Senate's 12 members to a five-year term on the advice of the opposition party, major church bodies, trade and commerce chambers, and other civic groups.

The judicial branch is formed by local magistrates, the Supreme Court, and the Court of Appeal. In 2001, Belize joined with most members of the Caribbean Community (CARICOM) to create a Caribbean Court of Justice (CCJ), which began operations in April 2005. It has largely replaced the Judicial Committee of the Privy Council in London as the highest court of appeal, which still hears appeals from the Court of Appeals from Belize under certain circumstances. The CCJ is a hybrid institution acting both as a municipal court of last resort, hearing appeals from common law courts within CARICOM jurisdictions, and as an international court with compulsory and exclusive jurisdiction in the interpretation of the Treaty of Chaguaramas, which gave birth to the Caribbean Community and Common Market (CARICOM's first official name) in the first place. The Belizean judiciary has not accepted compulsory International Court of Justice (ICJ) jurisdiction.

Legal System

The Belizean legal system comprises several departments and offices, including the Judicial Branch, the Attorney General's Ministry, the Director of Public Prosecutions, the Legal Advice and Services Center, the Ombudsman, and the police. The judiciary is headed by the three-member Supreme Court, which has the authority to settle constitutional disputes and is the trial institution with unrestricted jurisdiction over criminal matters through the subordinate summary jurisdiction courts and civil matters through the subordinate district courts. The chief justice is appointed by the governor-general on the advice of the prime minister after consultation with the leader of the opposition party; the other two justices are also appointed by the governor-general on the advice of the judicial and legal services section of the Public Service Commission. The Court of Appeals, integrated by a president and three justices of appeals, has unrestricted jurisdiction over civil and criminal appeals. At the bottom of the judicial system are the magistrate courts found in each of Belize's six district capitals. Magistrate courts have ample jurisdiction over summary offenses and limited jurisdiction in more serious offenses. The Family Courts Act of 1988 created district family courts to processed juvenile offenders.

In 2005, 19,500 cases were filed in the Belizean judicial system; 78 percent of them were criminal cases, 21 percent civil cases, and 1 percent family matters. Of these filed cases, 17,092 cases (88 percent) were disposed: 79 percent of the disposed cases were criminal, 20 percent were civil, and 1 percent were family law cases. A total of 26 judges were employed by the system in 2007: 7 justices in the Supreme Court, 4 judges in the Court of Appeals, and 15 judges in the magistrate courts.

The Attorney General's Ministry represents the executive branch in the legal system and advises the government on legislation and provides legal counsel to government offices in civil matters. The attorney general has the rank of a minister and is required to possess five years of experience as a practicing lawyer or to have served in a court with criminal and civil jurisdiction in Belize or another Commonwealth member country. The director of public prosecutions initiates and monitors the prosecution of all criminal offenses occurring within the national territory. This office is administratively a part of the Attorney General's Ministry, but the Constitution establishes that it is autonomous and not subject to the oversight or control of any authority. The director works with crown counsels who follow the director's orders and prosecute offenders of serious crimes (such as homicide, armed robbery, and rape) and appear before the Supreme Court throughout the criminal proceedings. Civil prosecutors and police handle minor crimes that are prosecuted in the magistrates' courts. In 2006, there were a total of 15 crown counsels and civil prosecutors, who initiated prosecution against 90 defendants in 77 separate criminal cases.

The Legal Advice and Services Center was established in 1981 to provide legal defense to indigent defendants without the economic means to hire private counsel. The center was first supported by funding from an international consortium led by the U.S. Agency for International Development (USAID). Today, the center is funded completely by the Belize Bar Association. Services are provided by private attorneys appointed by the Supreme Court's Records Office. Eligible private citizens involved in criminal, family, small claims civil, and other types of cases can request service. In 2006, public defense or other legal services were provided to 124 new cases by the center; 19 (15 percent) were criminal cases.

The ombudsman is in charge of the protection of civil liberties; appointment by the governor-general notwithstanding, the ombudsman acts as an independent check on governmental abuses of power. The most frequent complaints made against criminal justice authorities involve allegations of misconduct and abuse by members of the police and of the Department of Corrections.

The civil police force under the Ministry of Home Affairs is in charge of order maintenance, peace preservation, protection of life and property, crime prevention and detection, law enforcement, arrest of crime suspects, and criminal investigation. The governor-general is constitutionally authorized to use the police as a paramilitary force to defend

Belize in a state of war or emergency, at which point all police officers become subject to military legislation and command. The Belizean police regularly work with the director of public prosecutions in the pursuit of crime suspects and the investigation of crime. They also transport inmates to and from court. The Belizean police force manages special task divisions, including narcotics, criminal investigations, the Special Unit, and the Office of Internal and Disciplinary Affairs. In 2008, members of the Belizean police force numbered 1,240.

Juvenile Justice

The family courts established by the Family Courts Act 1990 handle the trial and sentencing of juvenile offenders. The lead judge of a family court is trained in youth welfare, social work counseling, and paralegal studies, and the remaining judges are trained in law. Family courts have jurisdiction over juveniles who are in need of care and protection, as well as juvenile offenders. Juvenile matters are heard twice a week. Probation officers usually attend the juvenile court sessions. Separate from other courts, family courts occupy buildings where other social service agencies are conveniently housed. In jurisdictions where a family court is not available, summary juvenile courts following the same procedures are made available.

Once a child is arrested, the arresting officer must seek out his or her parents before interrogating the child. In the absence of a parent, the child must be questioned in the presence of a probation officer. After the judge explains the charge in simple language, the juvenile may or may not admit the offense. If the offense is admitted, the judge will hand down sentence only after the receipt of a presentencing or social inquiry report on the juvenile. If the charge is not admitted, the case has to be decided by evidence. The juvenile has the right to cross-examine witnesses, to present evidence, and to call witnesses. If the charge is proved, the judge will again rely on a presentencing report for sentencing.

The 1994 Criminal Justice Regulations provide community service as a form of punishment for offenders over 14 years, yet because of lack of coordination, staff training, and public support, this option is underutilized. Detention in segregated units within the Hattieville Prison remains the most widely used measure; education, training, and counseling programs are offered on-site, but solitary confinement and corporal punishment are also adopted as disciplinary sanctions. Non-drug, nonviolent first-time offenders can be diverted to community-based rehabilitative settings.

Most juvenile offenders engage in property offenses, especially larceny, burglary, and robbery; some are involved in the peddling of illicit drugs. Minors, especially girls, are often recruited by and used in pornography and prostitution. There is an emerging problem of street gangs, with a resulting increase in gang-related violence among youths. Its stably serious status over time notwithstanding, juvenile delinquency suffered its worst deterioration in the 1990s, a decade when the number of juvenile offenders serving time in prison quadrupled, according to a UNICEF report.

Crime

Classification of Crime

Crime is generally defined as any behavior that is prohibited by law and that may result in penal punishment. The criminal code and the Summary Jurisdiction (Offences) Act revised in 2000 classify crimes as either punishable on conviction on indictment or punishable on summary conviction. Indictable offenses are more serious offenses that are heard by the Supreme Court and can be tried on an indictment only after a preliminary hearing to determine whether there is a prima facie case to answer. In trials for indictable offenses, the accused normally has the right to a jury trial, unless the individual waives that right. Summary offenses are nonserious offenses that make up the vast majority of court cases, that are heard by the summary jurisdiction courts and the magistrate courts, and that can be proceeded with summarily, without the indictment and right to a jury trial. They are subdivided into petty misdemeanors and petty offenses and are punishable by shorter prison sentences and smaller fines. The current minimum age of criminal responsibility is 12.

Crime Statistics

Crime and violence are major social problems that have resisted government's control interventions. Major crimes including murder, rape, robbery, burglary, and theft grew by 8.1 percent between 2007 and 2008. The number of reported murder cases increased by 191 percent, from 47 to 103, which placed Belize's murder rate at 34 per 100,000 inhabitants. In fact, the murder rate in Belize has continued to rise at an average pace of 5 percent per year since 2003. The number of robberies, burglaries, and thefts known to the police also jumped from 3,003 in 2007 to 3,248in 2008, representing a 12.7 percent increase in just a year. There were more crimes and more offenders carrying guns while they were committing the crime. The number of guns seized in firearm-related offenses rose from 127 in 2007 to 194 in 2008, showing a 52.3 percent increase. The most recent peak in firearm-related offenses was recorded in 2003, when 198 guns were seized.

Drug Abuse and Trafficking

Drug abuse is a growing problem and particularly alarming among the youth and in certain tourist enclaves. Whereas heroin is largely unknown and its user population negligible, there is a fairly significant group of cocaine users: data reported by the United Nations estimate that 0.9 percent of the population between ages 12 and 65 had consumed cocaine in 2005. Marijuana has historically been the substance with the largest market share: 8.5 percent of adult Belizeans had used cannabis. The prevalence rate for annual use of amphetamine and Ecstasy was estimated at 1.4 percent and 0.3 percent, respectively. Of all these substances, only marijuana is domestically cultivated and processed.

Belize is a transit point for cocaine and heroin between Colombia and Mexico and the United States. Extensive uninhabited jungles, miles of inland waterways, unguarded coastline facing hundreds of islets, and an underequipped and corrupt law enforcement apparatus converge to make Belize a very attractive transshipment center. In 2008, authorities seized 16.2 kilograms of cocaine, 0.7 kilogram of cocaine, 275.5 kilograms of marijuana, 50,050 marijuana plants, and 100,892 marijuana seeds. Proceeds from drug dealings in the amount of $112,510 were also seized. A total of 1,539 drug arrests were made in 2008, but very few are expected to end in successful convictions and punishment because prosecutors and judges are not provided with the resources to handle such a large volume of complex criminal cases. The importation of pseudoephedrine and ephedrine was prohibited in 2008 to prevent the transformation of Belize into a major manufacturer and exporter of amphetamine and/or methamphetamine.

Belize is a signatory of the 1961 Single Convention on Narcotics Drugs, the 1971 UN Convention on Psychotropic Substances, and the 1988 UN Drug Convention. It has also ratified the Caribbean Regional Agreement on Maritime Counter Narcotics.

Human Trafficking

Belize is a source, transit, and destination country for men trafficked for the purpose of forced labor and for women and children trafficked for commercial sexual exploitation. Most victims are Belizean minors trafficked to cater to the domestic demand from the sex industry and "sugar daddies." The "sugar daddy" phenomenon refers to situations where poor rural families offer their young daughters to provide sexual favors to wealthy older men in exchange for school fees, money, and gifts. Local communities and law enforcement agencies are reluctant to identify middlemen and consumers of these sexual services as human traffickers. Cross-border import of women for forced prostitution involves victims from Guatemala, Honduras, and El Salvador; other women enter Belize as migrant workers in search of jobs but are later pressured into commercial sex after unsuccessful employment bids. Labor trafficking most likely involves males from neighboring countries and East and South

Asian countries such as China, Nepal, and India. Victims are deceived by false promise of high-pay employment, and once inside Belize, their passports are routinely confiscated by criminal syndicates as a way to restrict their movement and subject their labor to slavery-like conditions. Both local and foreign criminal organizations have been engaged in these illegal businesses.

Belize criminalized all forms of human trafficking through the 2003 Trafficking in Persons Prohibition Act, which imposes penalties of up to five years of imprisonment and a parallel monetary fine. These punishments appear severe enough but are not commensurate with punishments applied to other serious criminal offenders such as rapists, who can receive a penalty of eight years to life imprisonment. Whereas criminal investigations and prosecutions are often initiated against suspected traffickers of people, the conviction rate of these cases is extremely low. In 2007 and 2008, of the 11 known human trafficking prosecutions, none resulted in a conviction. Whereas the complicity with traffickers by law enforcement agents seems to be the main determinant of some failed prosecutions, the lack of specialized training and adequate resources constitute the main cause of the overall ineffectiveness of the Belizean criminal justice system to combat the problem.

When it comes to related victim services, the performance of the government of Belize is impeccable. The Ministry of Human Development and Social Transformation operates two shelters for adult trafficking victims with a full range of services including health care, psychological counseling, and integration assistance; child victims are housed and taken care of in foster care institutions for minors. In 2008, 11 victims of labor trafficking received shelter assistance, victim services, and work permits, and another 60 were repatriated to their countries of origin. During the same period of time, neither the government nor nongovernmental organizations had received reports of victims being jailed or penalized for illegal entry, tax evasion, or working without permit as a direct result of being trafficked. Foreign victims who would face retribution or hardship in their home countries are regularly provided temporary residency and other temporary legal alternatives to expulsion. Despite these guarantees, victim cooperation in prosecutions against human traffickers has not been encouraging because of fear of mistreatment or stigma.

Finding of Guilt

Criminal Procedure

All criminal cases begin with an arrest. The police must inform a detainee of the cause of detention within 48 hours of arrest and bring the person before a magistrate to be charged within 24 hours. Public prosecutors have the responsibility of enhancing the evidentiary strength of a case and formally pressing criminal charges against suspected perpetrators of crime. With respect to charges laid out on indictment, there is a preliminary hearing to determine whether there is a prima facie case justifying a trial. All court proceedings are adversarial, oral, and public. At the end of the trial, a defendant may be found guilty or acquitted. Verdicts are given by trial juries formed by ordinary citizens, and sentences are handed down by the presiding judge.

Rights of the Accused

Police must obtain court-issued warrants to conduct searches or arrests, except in cases of hot pursuit, when there is probable cause, or when the presence of a firearm is suspected. The Constitution prohibits arbitrary arrest and detention and extends to the accused the rights to be presumed innocent, to be protected against self-incrimination, to a public trial, and to appeal. Defendants have the right to be present at each hearing or session of their trial unless the judge concludes that the safety of the defense, the victim, or a witness is at a very high risk. The right to legal counsel is guaranteed only in capital cases. Although the Belizean courts are known for their independence and constitutional loyalty, the Belizean police are frequent violators of the search and arrest rules.

Punishment

Penal sanctions provided in the criminal code include fines, community services, alternatives to incarceration sanctions, and imprisonment.

Prison

The first Belizean prison, with a 300-bed capacity, was constructed in Belize City in the early 1900s. In the late 1980s and early 1990s, the irreversible dilapidation of the prison building, the overcrowding that stretched its population to 250 percent of the designed capacity, and the safety concern from the U.S. Embassy, which was located right next door to the correctional facility, converged to prompt the relocation of the only prison to Hattieville, a town established as a refugee camp after the 1961 Hurricane Hattie made many people homeless in Belize City. (The Belize Central Bank Building now sits at that site of the old prison, and the old prison building has been renovated as a museum.) Lack of funding and political will derailed the grand vision of a modern prison geared toward rehabilitation of incarcerated offenders. Inmates from the old prison were mobilized to build the new facility, and authorities cut corners everywhere to save money and meet the deadline. The end product is a large prison with substandard structural integrity, which was later coupled with inappropriate security, sanitation, and service components. Inmates were relocated to the Hattieville Prison in 1993, when the construction had not been completed yet. It began as a prison without sewage facilities and potable water, where cells were flooded most of the time and no kitchens were available. These initial missteps were followed by allegations of endemic corruption and mistreatment of prisoners. The government decided to push a radical reform by handing over the management of the Hattieville Prison to a not-for-profit organization made up of concerned members of the Rotary Club of Belize, the Kolbe Foundation.

The transfer of management took place in August 2002, under a contract in which the Belizean government promised to reimbursed Kolbe US$6 per day per inmate to cover meal and board costs. Kolbe immediately moved to complete the building and furnish of the correctional complex, added new service facilities, and subcontracted medical and psychiatric services to serve the prison population. Inmates were classified and segregated into remand, minimum-security, maximum-medium, supermax, female, and youth units. Solitary confinement is used as a measure for internal discipline. A prison radio station was also set up. The first sign of improvement came in the form of reduced escapes: there were 93 escapes during the two years prior to the takeover by Kolbe; the number went down to 12 in the two years following the change.

Christian ministries have become the pillars of Kolbe's rehabilitation interventions in Hattieville Prison. In addition to the involvement of local Roman Catholic and Protestant groups and churches, Kolbe has also introduced the U.S.-based Prison Fellowship, whose Inner Change Freedom for Belize program celebrated its sixth anniversary of operations in the Belizean prison in February 2009. Faith-based drug-abuse treatment services are offered vis-à-vis regular literacy, education, and vocational training programs. Prison work at Hattieville maintains a growing volume of business transactions with the outside community and supports a woodwork shop, a tailor shop, a welding shop, a jewelry shop, a cement block factory, and a farm.

With funding and technical assistance from the Wager Foundation, a not-for-profit organization headquartered in the U.S. state of Wisconsin, a 75-bed segregated unit for juvenile males ages 17 or younger was established in 2004. This juvenile rehabilitation program is a boot-camp/school hybrid where strictly regimented daily routines are integrated with counseling and educational support. A separate unit for women inmates is located 200 yards outside the large compound for male offenders; conditions in the women's unit are considerably more humane and tolerable than those in the men's units. The Belizean correctional system does not imprison juvenile females charged with or convicted of crimes but places them under the care of social services authorities.

The size of the Belizean prison population stood at 1,334 on January 6, 2008, which translates into an incarceration rate of 455 inmates per 100,000 persons. The number of people who had been admitted into the Hattieville Prison increased from 1,880 in 2002 to 2,452 in 2007, and the proportion of convicted offenders among inmates decreased from 47.7 percent (897) in 2002 to 44.3 percent in 2007. In 2007, over 13 percent of all inmates were foreigners, and 46.1 percent were aged 25 years or younger. Women and juveniles represented 2.2 percent and 4.4 percent of the prison population, respectively.

Death Penalty

The death penalty is permitted in some murder cases. The last execution was carried out in 1985, when Kent Bowers was hanged at Hattieville Prison despite a petition for clemency reportedly signed by 2,500 people. There have been several attempts in recent years to expand the types of murder punishable by death and to restrict the number of allowable appeals. Given the serious threats from crime and violence, popular support for death penalty remains high. Although numerous death sentences have been handed down since 1985, none have been carried out because of the Judicial Committee of the Privy Council's refusal to allow execution of people convicted of murder who had spent more than five years pursuing their various appeal options: according to a 1993 JCPC ruling, these persons should have their sentences commuted to life imprisonment. With the inauguration of the Caribbean Court of Justice in 2005, observers believe that the de facto moratorium on death penalty may come to an end.

Hung-En Sung

Further Reading

Gillett, Georgia Brown. (2002). "Belize." In *Legal Systems of the World: A Political, Cultural, and Social Encyclopedia,* edited by Herbert M. Kritzer, pp. 151–153. Santa Barbara, CA: ABC-CLIO.

Grant, C. H. (2008). *The Making of Modern Belize: Politics, Society and British Colonialism in Central America.* New York: Cambridge University Press.

Philips, Sir Fred. (2002). *Commonwealth Caribbean Constitutional Law.* London: Routledge-Cavendish.

Reid, G. Michael. (2006). "Belize." In *World Police Encyclopedia,* edited by Dilip K. Das and Michael J. Palmiotto, pp. 84–92. New York: Routledge.

Bermuda

Legal System: Common
Murder: Medium
Prison Rate: High
Death Penalty: No

Background

Bermuda is a group of islands in the Atlantic Ocean located east of the United States and north of the Caribbean. It consists of 6 principal islands and 120 smaller islands. Bermuda is one of the most densely populated areas in the world with an estimated population of 67,837 people in 2009. It is also one of the wealthiest countries in the world with a gross domestic product per capita of US$69,900 in 2004.

Bermuda is an overseas territory of the United Kingdom. The government is based on the Westminster model of parliamentary democracy and consists of a head of state, governor, deputy governor, cabinet, legislature, and judiciary. The head of state is Queen Elizabeth II, who appoints the governor and commander-in-chief.

Police and Military

The Bermuda Police Service consists of approximately 382 full-time police officers. Additionally, the police maintain a group of reserve officers and use them as needed. The main role of the police is the prevention and enforcement of the law. The Bermuda military, or Bermuda Regiment, serves more of a community role than it does national security. The national security of the country is mainly the responsibility of the British government. Nevertheless, the Bermuda Regiment's main functions include military conscription, disaster relief, traditional/ceremonial activities, military training, and the development and training of Bermuda's youth. The Bermuda Regiment annually selects, by ballot, young men to draft into the military. If selected, the individuals are required to fulfill their duty of serving in the Bermuda Regiment. The military is seen as a tool for developing the skills and discipline of the youth of Bermuda, as well as exposing them to a diverse setting where teamwork is essential.

Crime

Classification of Crime

The criminal statutes and codes of Bermuda can be found in the amended Criminal Code Act of 1907. Crimes are classified into two different levels. Summary offenses include less serious actions, such as speeding and driving without a license. Indictable offenses are those acts that are considered to be more serious in nature, such as murder, rape, and robbery. Several types of offenses can be tried in court as a summary offense or as an indictable offense depending on the level of severity of the act.

An individual under the age of 8 is not criminally responsible for any act or omission. Individuals aged 8 or older are considered to have reached the "age of criminal responsibility," and they are liable to face criminal charges for any illegal acts. A person is considered a juvenile until reaching his or her 16th birthday. After age 16, an individual is considered an adult within the criminal justice system and can be tried for an offense as an adult. The Family and Youth Court is responsible for handling hearings concerning juveniles.

Crime Statistics

The crime rate in Bermuda is classified as moderate, yet the new millennium has seen an overall increase in criminal incidents. The fact that Bermuda is a popular tourist destination has led to a high rate of property crimes on the islands. According to the Bermuda Police Service's (2009), *Crime Statistics Archive,* crimes reported to the police for 2007 were as follows:

Murder/manslaughter	3
Attempted murder	3
Assault with grievous bodily harm	52
Wounding	64
Sexual assault	45
Sexual exploitation of a young person	8
Firearm offenses	12
Robbery	123
Theft from person	166
Handbag/attempted handbag snatch	16
Theft from unattended vehicle	199
All burglary	1,119
Taking without owners' consent (all vehicles)	1,009

Drug Offenses

All of the statutes and laws relating to drug-related offenses can be found in the Misuse of Drugs Act of 1972. It is a crime to take part in any drug activities, including but not limited to possessing, producing, selling, and trafficking illegal substances within Bermuda. In addition to these activities, the use of marijuana for medicinal purposes is prohibited on the islands. There is no legal defense for the voluntary use of illegal substances within Bermudian criminal law. The government goes to great lengths to punish those involved in these activities to the fullest extent of the law in an attempt to keep illegal drug activities to a minimum on the islands.

The Bermuda Police Service has a unit devoted strictly to preventing and investigating drug-related crimes. The police and customs also work closely with other nations, including the United States, to combat drug activity on the islands. Drug-related arrests and seizures are included in the police service's annual reports, which provide departmental statistics on these offenses. There were a total of 526 arrests for drug offenses in 2006, the majority of offenders being male. There were a total of 812 seizures of drugs that included cannabis, cocaine, diamorphine, cocaine freebase, cannabis resin, cannabis plants, and methamphetamines.

Finding of Guilt

Rights of the Accused

The Bermudian Constitution was introduced in June 1968 and has been amended twice. The Constitution guarantees the fundamental rights of the citizens of Bermuda, including the rights to life, freedom of expression, and freedom of movement.

Each individual arrested and charged with an offense is presumed innocent until proven guilty or until he or she pleads guilty. Upon arrest, an individual is entitled to have the charges brought against him or her read in a language that is understandable to the common person. In addition, following arrest or detention, an individual has the right to be informed of his or her rights, such as the rights to remain silent, to seek legal advice and/or legal representation, and to have one person informed about his or her arrest and location. Once a person has been notified of his or her rights and has had the

On November 26, 1998, members of the jury view Whale Bone Bay in Hamilton, Bermuda, where the rape and murder of Rebecca Middleton took place in June 1996. Middleton was killed while vacationing with a high school friend, a native of Bermuda. The suspects were arrested, but not convicted. The results of this case are considered controversial. (AP Photo/David Skinner)

charges read, he or she then has the right to a fair trial within a reasonable amount of time by an independent and impartial court. The accused person should also be given sufficient time and facilities to prepare his or her defense.

Pretrial confinement is allowed, and the time served is taken into consideration by the judge or magistrate when imposing a sentence or punishment. Accused persons are permitted to defend themselves, to obtain a legal representative of their own choice at their own expense, or to have legal representation appointed by the court at the expense of the public.

The right protecting Bermudians from arbitrary arrest or detention is guaranteed within their Constitution. If an individual is unlawfully arrested or detained, then he or she is entitled to compensation from the individual who unlawfully arrested or detained him or her. Accused persons also have the right to question the witnesses against them, to have an interpreter if they cannot understand the language being spoken in court, and to have their trial heard before a jury when being charged with an indictment offense in the Supreme Court. The accused also have the right to appeal.

The Judiciary

The judiciary consists of the Magistrates' Court, the Supreme Court, the Court of Appeals, and the Registry of the Supreme Court. The Magistrates' Court handles less serious criminal cases, traffic violations, arrests and search warrants, juvenile delinquency cases, preliminary inquiries, and civil litigations of BM$25,000 (US$25,000) or less. The magistrate is the sole decision maker in these cases. The Supreme Court is responsible for handling the more serious criminal cases, legal business matters and international business matters, civil litigations of BM$25,000 or more, and appeals from the Magistrates' Court. The Supreme Court tries cases in the presence of a judge and jury. The Court of Appeals is in charge of hearing all of the appeals from the Supreme Court and is the highest court in Bermuda. It sits three times a year. The administrative functions of the judiciary are the responsibilities of the Registry of the Supreme Court. In addition to the criminal and civil courts, there are several other specialized courts that are used to make the criminal justice process as efficient as possible, including Traffic Court, Drug Court, Family Court, Youth Court, Plea Court, and Commercial Court.

Prosecution

The prosecution of the accused is the primary responsibility of the Department of Public Prosecution, which is located under the Office of the Attorney General and Ministry of Justice. The department works closely with other criminal justice agencies, such as the Bermuda Police Service, to ensure that all of the evidence dealing with each case is presented in court. The Bermuda Police Service usually conducts the investigations of the crimes and then passes the information on to the prosecutor. The public prosecutors try to work hand-in-hand with the police to ensure that they are fully informed about the facts of each case.

Defense

The Legal Aid Office, which is located under the Office of the Attorney General and Ministry of Justice, is responsible for representing those persons who cannot represent themselves or afford legal representation. To use this service, an accused person must first qualify and submit an application to the Legal Aid Committee. The committee then makes a decision as to whether the accused warrants the use of public counsel. To qualify for legal aid, a person must meet certain financial criteria and be charged with a qualifying offense. Legal aid is available for those accused in the areas of criminal, civil, or family law. It is available for criminal matters in the Supreme Court and the Court of Appeal and sometimes in the Magistrates' Court at the discretion of the committee or where the charges carry a sentence of five years' imprisonment or more.

Alternatives to Trial

The accused have the option of taking a plea deal instead of going to trial. Plea bargaining is a common occurrence within the Bermudian criminal justice system. The process of arraignment and entering a plea is handled within the Plea Court. A person accused of an indictable offense may also submit a request to the Supreme Court to remove the indictment prior to going to trial if there is prejudice involved or if the charges are defective. The court can also order that the charges be amended if they are not legally sufficient.

The Drug Treatment Court affords those accused of an eligible drug offense an alternative to going to criminal trial. Offenders may receive a sentence of mandatory drug treatment along with probation instead of receiving a prison sentence.

The Bermudian criminal justice system also includes an insanity defense option for those who qualify as mentally insane. For an individual to be considered insane, he or she must not be capable of understanding his or her actions, not be able to control his or her actions, and not be capable of knowing that the acts that he or she committed were against the law. It is the burden of the defense to prove the existence of all three elements to successfully prove that the accused is insane. If an individual is acquitted on grounds of insanity, the court will order the individual to be kept in strict custody until the governor sees him or her fit to be released. The decision to keep an insane person in custody and when to release such a person is the decision of the governor and the Advisory Committee on the Prerogative of Mercy.

The court may conditionally or absolutely discharge an offender of his or her offense instead of convicting him or her. Additionally, the court may require the offender to follow certain stipulations, such as a probation order and/or other set conditions, such as not committing another offense. If the accused fails to uphold any aspect of this agreement, the accused may then be punished for his or her offense to the fullest extent of the law.

Punishment

Types of Punishment

The common forms of punishment include probation, community service, fines, restitution, reparation, and imprisonment. Within the specialized courts such as the Drug Treatment Court, an offender may be ordered to enroll in a drug treatment program. Bermuda used to have the death penalty; however, it was abolished in December 1999. Corporal punishment is also prohibited as a sentence, and it is not allowed as a disciplinary measure in penal institutions. In contrast, corporal punishment is allowed within schools and is lawful within the privacy of citizens' homes.

The most severe punishment for the accused is a life sentence of imprisonment. Prison was traditionally used as a common form of punishment, but because of high recidivism rates, the Bermudian criminal justice system now uses imprisonment as a last resort. The Bermudian judiciary has shifted from punishment-oriented sentences to those that focus on changing the offender. The goal now is to impose a sentence that will have more of a rehabilitative effect on the offender so that he or she will become a productive citizen within society.

Parole is also utilized within Bermuda for certain sentences. Parole may be granted after the offender has served the required minimum of his or her overall sentence. There are a couple exceptions to the sentences handed down by the courts. For example, if an offender is found to be a "persistent offender," then the person is eligible to receive police supervision upon completing his or her original sentence.

Typical Sentences

Offenders of premeditated murder are usually sentenced to life imprisonment without the eligibility for release until the person has served at least 25 years of the sentence. Offenders of murder can be sentenced to life in prison with a minimum of 15 years served prior to being eligible for parole.

Common assault is classified as a summary offense, and a person can receive a sentence of imprisonment for 12 months. Assault causing bodily harm is classified as a misdemeanor offense. If a person is convicted of this offense under the summary jurisdiction, he or she can receive a sentence of imprisonment of 2 years, and conviction on an indictable offense can result in up to 4 years' imprisonment.

Sexual assault is classified as a felony and can bring a sentence of 20 years' imprisonment if the person is convicted for an indictable offense and 5 years if convicted under summary jurisdiction.

Theft within Bermuda is triable only as a summary offense if the dollar amount stolen is BM$1,000 (US$1,000) or less. If the dollar amount of theft is greater than BM$1,000, and the person is convicted under the summary jurisdiction, the sentence could include a fine of BM$10,000 or 5 years' imprisonment, or both. The same crime on an indictable conviction can result in a fine of BM$100,000 or 10 years' imprisonment, or both. If a person is charged with a robbery offense upon a summary conviction, he or she can be sentenced to a fine of BM$10,000 or 5 years' imprisonment, or both, and an indictable conviction can result in 20 years' imprisonment. Burglary upon conviction under summary jurisdiction can bring a sentence BM$10,000 or 5 years' imprisonment, or both. Conviction on an indictable offense of burglary that was committed on a building that is a dwelling or where there is habitation can result in a 14-year prison term, and burglary on any other building can result in 10 years' imprisonment.

Drug offenses are considered very serious crimes and can result in harsh penalties. Production and/or possession of a controlled substance with the intent to sell or distribute on an indictable conviction can result in a sentence of up to imprisonment for life, a fine of BM$1 million or three times the street value of the controlled substance (whichever is greater), or fine and imprisonment. The same crime upon a summary conviction can bring a sentence of up to 10 years' imprisonment, a fine of BM$500,000 or three times the street value of the controlled drug (whichever is greater), or fine and imprisonment. Possession of a controlled substance by an individual as an indictable offense can result in imprisonment of 5 years or a fine, or both, if it is the first offense of this nature for the individual. If it is not a first-time offense for the individual, then it can result in up to a 10-year prison term or fine, or both. If the offender is convicted of possession under a summary offense, he or she is liable to receive a 12-month prison sentence or BM$1,000 fine, or both. Additional information on the penalties associated with drug offenses can be found in the Misuse of Drugs Act 1972.

Prison

The principal functions of the Department of Corrections include custody and rehabilitation of offenders. The criminal justice system in Bermuda views imprisonment as a last resort. Recidivism rates within Bermuda are high, and therefore, the Bermuda Department of Corrections places a strong emphasis on rehabilitating offenders. This is achieved by providing inmates with a variety of training, educational, and rehabilitation programs. These include educational programs (such as math and English), computer literacy, arts and crafts, carpentry, masonry, and plumbing. There are four main correctional facilities on the islands of Bermuda: Westgate Correctional Facility, Farm Facility, Co-Educational Facility, and Transitional Living Centre. Each facility is responsible for a different type of inmate population and for creating an atmosphere that is conducive to the rehabilitation of the offenders.

The Westgate Correctional Facility is a male inmate facility that can hold prisoners in maximum-, medium-, and minimum-security conditions. It was designed to hold approximately 208 prisoners. The Farm Facility is an adult minimum-security prison for those inmates who have been found to be a low security risk. It is used for helping offenders make the transition back into society. It was designed to hold approximately 93 inmates. Inmates are required to go on a work release on a daily basis as well as to perform charity work while at the Farm Facility. The Transitional Living Centre is similar to the Farm Facility. The facility is more of a halfway house and is capable of holding up to 15 inmates at a time. It provides inmates with job placement so that they may become productive and law-abiding citizens upon reentry. The Co-Educational Facility is responsible for females and juveniles.

Prison statistics from the Department of Corrections show that Bermuda's correctional system is operating at a full capacity. As of 2006, there were

343 prisoners for an imprisonment rate of 532 per 100,000 and a 93 percent occupancy level. Of those prisoners, 19.2 percent were pretrial detainees, 10.5 percent were female prisoners, and 5.6 percent were juveniles.

Christopher M. Bzduch

Further Reading

Bermuda Government: http://www.gov.bm/.

Bermuda Online: http://www.bermuda-online.org/.

Bermuda Police Service: http://www.police.bm/.

British Foreign and Commonwealth Office: http://www.fco.gov.uk/en/.

Kurian, G. T., ed. (2006). "Bermuda." In *World Encyclopedia of Police Forces and Correctional Systems,* pp. 218–219. 2nd ed. Vol. 1. Farmington Hills, MI: Thomson Gale.

Lexadin. (2009). *The World Law Guide: Legislation Bermuda:* http://www.lexadin.nl/wlg/legis/nofr/oeur/lxweber.htm.

Bolivia

Legal System: Civil/Adversarial
Murder: Medium
Burglary: High
Corruption: Medium
Human Trafficking: Medium
Prison Rate: Medium
Death Penalty: Yes
Corporal Punishment: Yes

Background

Bolivia is a tropical, landlocked country in central South America. It is a unitary or centralized republic divided into nine departments. Two cities officially stand as the capital of Bolivia: Sucre is the seat of the Supreme Court and known as the constitutional capital, whereas the executive and the legislative branches of government are located in La Paz, the administrative capital. In 2006, 9,672,000 inhabitants populated the 1,098,580 square kilometers of the country. Sixty-four percent of the population lived in urban areas, and nearly three-fourths were aged 34 or younger in 2005. Bolivia's indigenous population numbers more 4 four million. About 95 percent of the population profess Catholic faith, although pre-Columbian pantheistic and animistic rituals are widely practiced in indigenous communities.

In 2004, with an unemployment rate of 6 percent, 63.9 percent of Bolivia's population lived in poverty, and 34.7 percent in extreme poverty. The 2005 gross domestic product per capita was US$1,033, making Bolivia one of the poorest countries in the Western Hemisphere.

Constitutional History

Bolivia is commonly known as the most politically unstable country of South America. Overcoming 193 coups d'états between its independence in 1825 and 1981—averaging a change of government once every 10 months—and dependent on more than 56 foreign aid organizations, the Republic of Bolivia has long been vulnerable to corruption.

The Constitution that founded the Republic of Bolivia in 1825 as an independent nation established a centralized government with three branches: executive, legislative, and judicial. This first constitution was inspired by those of the United States of America and the French Republic, yet it was never adopted. It was revised a year later by the liberator Simon Bolivar Palacio. This newly revised constitution instituted a lifetime presidency with four clear strata of governing powers: the president, an independent judiciary, a tricameral congress, and an electoral body. This Bolivarian constitution was said to reflect Simon Bolivar's mistrust of the social and economic elite and his fear that these rival factions would fight against each other for control over the new nation. As such, his constitution institutionalized a strong, centralized, and lifetime presidency. Despite this foresight, the incongruity between the state's national aspirations and its actual power over Bolivia's disparate regions and populations made for a short-lived constitution.

By 1831, the concept of "lifetime presidency" was abolished as the Constitution introduced bicameralism and presidential power limited to renewable four-year terms. In fact, from 1831 to 1873, Bolivia was subjected to the whims of change of transient *caudillos* who were political-military leaders at the head of an authoritarian power dictating constitutional charters almost as regularly as the changes of government. Following the end of "caudillo politics" and after losing its access to the sea to Chile (War of the Pacific, 1879–1880), Bolivia's most durable constitution was approved (1880). The basic premises of representative democracy were introduced: bicameralism was put into effect, and the legislative powers of Parliament finally became significant grounds for political debate.

For the next 58 years, Bolivia's political stability was commensurate with the boom of tin exports and the rise of tin entrepreneurs in national politics and ended with the tumbling of global demand for tin, the overthrow of President Salamanca Urey in 1934, and the devastating loss of the Chaco War (1932–1935) to Paraguay. The Great Depression that began in 1929 accentuated the friction between elite leaders and their middle-class followers and led to widespread disdain for the political establishment and increased social tensions that culminated in the return of the military back into politics in 1935. The next 17 years (1935–1952) were characterized by populist social, economic, and political reforms pioneered by military officials and civilian intellectuals. The role of the state in the country's economic organization expanded considerably, whereas unions of miners and peasants were formed to become the foundation of new political parties that in due course played central roles in the 1952 revolution.

In 1952, tin miners rose against tin entrepreneurs, and the Nationalist Revolutionary Movement examined alternative forms of political organization. After much debate, universal suffrage was finally adopted in 1961 via a new constitution, as was the nationalization of the mines, and agrarian reform. During the process, the indigenous peasantry was freed from labor obligation and given land and the right to vote, making them a major force in the Bolivian politics.

General Barrientos Ortuno eventually overthrew the Movimiento Nacionalista Revolucionario (MNR) in 1964 and introduced a new era in the Bolivarian constitutional development. Under the terms of his 1967 Constitution, currently in force, Bolivia was set to be a unitary republic that retains a democratic and representative democracy. Article 2 stipulates that sovereignty resides in the people, that it is inalienable, and that its exercise is delegated to the legislative, executive, and judicial powers. The 1967 Constitution recognizes Roman Catholicism as the official religion while also guaranteeing the right to publicly worship all faiths.

In 1990, indigenous communities from the eastern lowlands organized a massive protest march to La Paz to present two specific demands: first, explicit acknowledgement of the ethnic and cultural diversity of the country in line with the 1967 Constitution; and second, realization of the right to land enshrined in the statutes. These demands were met by constitutional reform in 1994. The multiethnic and multicultural character of Bolivia was officially recognized. But the indigenous groups were not content with the nominal recognition of the "pluricultural state." They insisted on the actual enforcement of principles spelled out in the Constitution. Such implementation began only when Evo Morales, the country's first fully indigenous head of state, was elected president of the country in 2006.

A constitutional referendum was requested by President Evo Morales and held in January 2009, which introduced seismic changes to the political and social organization of Bolivia. The new Constitution was enacted in February 2009 and radically empowered the indigenous majority and mandated a fundamental land reform. Major reforms included the possibility of reelecting a president to a second term, expanded indigenous rights, decentralization of national government power and increased autonomy of local governments, nationalization of key natural resources, full recognition of indigenous systems of justice, replacement of the congressional appointment of judges with popular election of judges, termination of the privileged status of Roman Catholicism, and prohibition of land ownership beyond 5,000 hectares. Within the next two years, the Bolivian Congress would enact new laws and the national government would create new agencies implementing issues relating to the passage of the new Constitution, including the establishment of a constitutional court and an autonomous ministry to oversee indigenous rights and take input from the citizenry.

The Legal System

The organization of Bolivia's judicial power is heavily influenced by Spanish law and the Napoleonic code (i.e., French civil code). The main judicial bodies are the Supreme Court of Justice, the Constitutional Tribunal, the Judicial Council, the National Agrarian Court, the superior district courts, the National Labour and Mining Court, and provincial and local courts to try minor cases. The Supreme Court is the highest court of the republic and consists of 12 ministers who are organized into four specialized chambers of three justices each. Two chambers deal with civil cases, a third deals with criminal cases, and the fourth with administrative, social, and mining cases. The ministers are nominated by the president, confirmed by the Congress for 10-year, nonrenewable terms, and seated in their headquarters in the city of Sucre. Exclusive rights are given to the Supreme Court and the superior district courts to change and repeal sentences or decisions made by lower courts, and the Constitutional Tribunal handles appeals on constitutional issues. Bolivia's judicial system adopted many changes to keep its judiciary processes independent of external influence; however, political pressures and corruption are consistent and longstanding problems. In 2003, Bolivia had 98 superior district judges (*vocals*), 451 district judges (*de partido*), and 281 instructing judges. Among the latter two groups, 68 percent of the judges served in criminal courts, and the remaining 32 percent served in civil, family, juvenile, or agrarian courts.

There are some other specialized judicial bodies. Bolivia maintains controlled substances courts supported by antinarcotics police to process illicit drug cases. Legislation enacted in 1997 created the office of People's Defender as a high commissioner of the Congress. The office is actually an autonomous agency playing the role of human rights ombudsman: it oversees the legality of decisions made by all state institutions and safeguards against violations of human rights.

Despite the presence of the formal judicial structure, private systems of dispute resolution have always existed in the forms of traditional indigenous legal mechanisms. The influence of Spanish rule and the long dominance of liberalism and westernization notwithstanding, indigenous practices and legal concepts remain influential. The constitutional reform of 2009 granted indigenous systems of justice the same status as the existing official administration of justice.

Internationally, Bolivia shares the commitments of the United Nations (UN) and the Organization of American States (OAS), whose charters advocate protection and respect for human rights. In line with these values, Bolivia has undertaken to uphold the Universal Declaration of Rights of Man and the American Declaration of the Rights and Duties of Man, as well as many other international legal codes such as the Convention on the Prevention and Punishment of the Crime of Genocide, the International Convention on the Elimination of All Forms of Racial Discrimination, and a host of others. Despite these international commitments, Bolivia has not accepted the compulsory jurisdiction of the International Criminal Court.

Code of Criminal Procedure

Bolivia's current code of criminal procedure was ratified in 1972, revoking the penal procedural code enacted 74 years earlier, and was significantly revised in 2001. Prior to 2001, Bolivia belonged to the statute-bound civil law tradition and had an inquisitorial system of justice. Trial examinations were lengthy and conducted behind closed doors as the judge accumulated evidence—predominantly in the form of written briefs. Defendants had few rights and were not automatically presumed innocent.

After 2001, the written system was changed into an oral adversarial system of justice. Bolivia's present system emphasizes case law, similar to the

British common law tradition, and focuses on individual cases. Enacted in 2002, the Public Ministry Law established a new function for the prosecutor in the Bolivian legal system. Thereafter, judges were no longer in charge of running investigations against a defendant; the state's inquiry was set to be conducted by prosecutors. The judge's role was limited to acting as a moderator between the prosecution and the defense. Defendants are presumed innocent until proven guilty. Whereas the old written trials fronted an opaque and protracted process that generated various opportunities for corruption, the switch to adversarial oral trials reduces the monopolistic concentration of discretionary power on one single person, the judge, and makes the trial process more transparent, with the presentation of evidence and arguments in one place and at the same time. This profound change was accompanied by a parallel national training of judicial personnel, law enforcement forces, nongovernmental organization workers, and students of law in the new code of criminal procedures, with a particular emphasis on the protection of civil liberties and human rights.

Different criminal cases are now handled by different judicial procedures. For example, in cases of misdemeanor, the defendant appears before a judge in the lower court, and it is the judge alone who decides the defendant's fate. In felony cases, in contrast, a verdict is determined by two judges and a jury of three citizens.

Crime

Classification of Crime

Bolivia's penal code clearly distinguishes felony offenses from misdemeanor offenses. Felonies are defined as being performed voluntarily and with a spirit of malice. Misdemeanors, on the other hand, are defined as being committed devoid of malice. Bolivia's penal code allows three types of sentences applicable to criminals found guilty of either felony or misdemeanor, including corporal restraint or confinement of the offender (i.e., imprisonment); noncorporal and nonphysical penalties such as the deprivation of a civil right, surveillance, and/or probation; and financial penalties such as fine.

Age of Criminal Responsibility

A clear distinction has been made in the Code for Children and Adolescents between criminal responsibility and social liability. The latter is applicable for youth between 12 and 16 years of age, and when in conflict with the law, they appear before a juvenile court. Criminal liability, on the other hand, is recognized for adolescents between 16 and 18 years of age and is not distinguished from adults under the criminal code.

Drug Offenses and Their Control

Bolivia is largely known for its widespread cultivation of coca, the main ingredient of cocaine. The use of the coca leaf is both licit and illicit depending on its sociocultural use (i.e., traditional or processed). Coca-growing is an agricultural and cultural activity that has historically been oriented in a legitimate manner toward consumption, to use in medicine and in spiritual rituals of the Andean peoples. The issue of coca has therefore generated a very heated international debate.

At the international level, Bolivia is a signatory of the 1961 UN Single Convention on Narcotic Drugs (as amended by the 1972 Protocol), the 1971 UN Convention on Psychotropic Substances, and the 1988 United Nations Drug Convention. On July 19, 1988, the Bolivian Congress passed the Coca and Controlled Substances Act (Law 1008) under strong pressure from the U.S. government. The law in question defined the legal characterization of coca cultivation, its transformation, and trafficking. However, because of the longstanding licit sociocultural and religious usages of coca among the indigenous peoples, Law 1008 permitted the legitimate cultivation and consumption of coca in three geographical zones, with a quota of 12,000 hectares for licit cultivation. The law divided Bolivia into legal, transitional, and illicit zones of coca cultivation. But because of the draconian penalties mandated by the law and its ruthless enforcement by a growingly militarized security apparatus that resulted in human rights violations and civilian deaths, the abolition of Law 1008 became a rally cry among the targeted indigenous regions.

A soldier of the FELCN (Bolivia's Special Force to Fight Drug Trafficking) stands guard as a cocaine factory is burned in the tropical region of Croce Andino, Bolivia, on December 27, 2005. (AP Photo/Dado Galdieri)

Indigenous *cocalero* (coca-leaf grower) movements from the Chapare and later from the Yungas started mobilizing and claiming their cultural and spiritual rights to coca.

In general, drug offenses under domestic law include those commensurate with article 3 of the 1988 UN Convention against Illicit Traffic in Narcotic Drugs and Psychotropic Substances, which addresses the production, manufacture, extraction, preparation, offering, offering for sale, distribution, sale, delivery on any terms whatsoever, brokerage, dispatch, dispatch in transit, transport, importation, or exportation of any narcotic drug or any psychotropic substance. Article 17 of the Bolivian penal code states that the punishment for drug-related offenses should not exceed 13 years of imprisonment. However, most other crimes in the penal code carry a maximum sentence of 10 years.

Crime Statistics

According to crime statistics reported by the National Institute of Statistics of Bolivia, the general crime drop that began in the late 1990s started to reverse in 2006. Theft remains the most prevalent form of crime, followed by homicide. Common crimes reported to police for 2007 were as follows:

Against corporal integrity and health	740
Against rights to family assistance	3,421
Fraud and other	1,013
Homicide	4,566
Theft	9,079
Robbery	1,791
Aggravated robbery	1,982
Rape and sexual assault	740

Although crime is among the most significant of concerns for people in Latin America, according to data from *Latinobarometro* 2008, the continent-wide public opinion survey, only 1 percent of Bolivians consider crime as the biggest problem in the country. However, the apparent lack of concern with the issue does not mean that the country does not suffer from violence or is free from crime. As a matter of fact, 33 percent of the respondents reported having been victims of crime in the past 12 months, and on a violence scale of 0 to 10 (where 0 represents a very peaceful country and 10 a very violent one), survey respondents gave Bolivia a score of 6.2, higher than that received by Colombia. However, the fear triggered by crime-induced violence and insecurity was pale in comparison with the pain resulting from weak governance, political instability, and economic hardships.

Finding of Guilt

Rights of the Accused

As required by the Constitution, Bolivia adheres to the principle of presumption of innocence and the rights to a speedy trial, to an attorney, to confront witnesses, to present evidence on one's own behalf, to due process, to an appeal, and to confront legal charges with government prosecutors before a formal court process is initiated. However, these rights are not always respected. Bolivia's penal code also includes a statute of limitations. An accused cannot be prosecuted for a felony committed longer ago than 10 years plus 1 day. An offender must be brought to justice within 10 years of the date of the offense.

A National Public Defender Service was established by Law 2496 of 2003, providing the poverty-stricken accused with defense attorneys at public expense if needed. However, in reality, attorneys were not always available, despite the presence of traveling attorneys from the mobile public defenders program established to reach the more remote parts of the country. That program has proved somewhat effective, but the demand is so great that even these defenders remain overburdened.

In line with democratizing Bolivia's judicial process, the government increased the number of public defenders, legal assistants, and social workers supporting rural public defense by more than 40 percent, achieving a total of approximately 167 in the year 2000. Initially, the National Public Defender Service tried to involve public defenders in arrest cases at the earliest possible stages and attempted to provide information about human rights to citizens, but defenders were overloaded, and by 2006, the Bolivian government had reduced the team to 72 workers as a result of budget shortfalls. There continues to be a significant shortage of public defenders in rural areas. As of 2006, according to the Inter-American Commission on Human Rights, only 3 percent of municipalities had a public defender.

A Human Rights Office and a Public Defender Office were also set up in Chimore—a rural area of the Chapare known for its elevated coca eradication activities—as a pilot project by the Ministry of Justice. These offices were considered appropriate channels for the observance and protection of human rights and to aid in the appropriate administration of justice in this high-risk area. Moreover, in response to a long history of neglect and exploitation of the indigenous peoples in Bolivia, pluralist, multiethnic, and multicultural values became key elements in Bolivian politics.

Military Justice

When a military officer is accused of a crime related to his service, he is subjected to an investigation within the military justice system. The commander of the affected unit appoints an officer to conduct this investigation and to document his findings in a report. This report is then forwarded to a judicial advisor who finds the military member in question innocent or guilty. In the case of "major infractions," the lawsuit is advanced to a military court. Generally, senior-level influences tend to aid in the avoidance of rulings that would embarrass the military. At times, there is conflict regarding military and civilian jurisdiction, especially in human rights denunciations. In 2004, a constitutional court decision provided that military personnel should be tried in civilian courts for human rights violations.

Juvenile Justice

In pursuance with the new Juvenile Code of 1992, a juvenile court system was established within the broader criminal justice system. By law, young offenders age 16 to 18 are legally responsible and have the right to legal protection and guarantees and to receive necessary legal assistance. However, despite the prescriptions of the Juvenile Code and the Law against Domestic and Family Violence advocating the humane treatment of children and the prohibition of corporal punishment, such codes fail to protect children adequately because they contain provisions that prohibit violence *only* when it can be shown to be abusive, which can be interpreted as tolerating certain forms of severe disciplinary measures. Hence, much violence directed toward the most vulnerable members of Bolivian society remains undetected.

Article 208 of the Juvenile Code requires that juvenile cases be heard and tried via youth courts. The youth court judges are given responsibility to hear cases of juvenile offenses, of material or of moral neglect, and of danger or maltreatment suffered by juveniles. They have the power to pronounce abandonment of a minor; to settle cases concerning acts endangering the health or physical or moral development of a minor; to place youth in the care of his parents,; and to determine appropriate measures for the treatment, care, and protection of minors in circumstances envisaged in the code. Follow-up and preventive measures are also set for abandoned youth placed in institutions regarding possible irregularities infringing the rights of the child. Despite weekly inspections of police stations and institutions, set to be conducted by specifically appointed persons, for the protection, assistance, and rehabilitation of minors, the summary record of the UN Committee on the Rights of the Child report of its 52nd session in 2009 clearly stated that amenities are still inadequate, often placing youth in adult detention centers.

Punishment

Typical Punishment for Murder

Prior to 1997, the Bolivian penal code prescribed the death penalty for murder, especially parricide. However, the penalty contradicted article 17 of the Constitution, which states that "cases of assassination, parricide and treason against the state [are] punished by 30 years of prison, without the right to pardon." In 1997, Law 1768 formally replaced the death penalty with the 30-year jail sentence consistent with the Constitution. Additional penalties include absolute legal incapacity (loss of civil rights) and special legal incapacity (loss of some civil rights).

Typical Punishment for Rape

In Bolivia, physical and sexual violence against women is rampant yet underreported. In 1997, Law 1678 was promulgated and modified the penal code to include "sexual violence" as a crime punishable by law, but the problem persists. Bolivia houses a paternal and male-dominant culture where women and young girls, especially of lower economic means, have accepted a passive role toward men. Although the Office on Drugs and Crime reported 134 "total recorded rapes in city" and 7 "rape suspects" in 2006, the Center for the Information and Development of Women reports that 70 percent of women were physically and/or psychologically abused and that this number still "did not reflect the full magnitude of the problem of violence against women" because most women did not report the daily aggression they faced.

The code of criminal procedures makes rape and sexual crimes against minors public crimes. Forcible statutory rape against a child under 14 years of age is penalized by law with 10 to 20 years in prison. In cases involving consensual sex with a minor (between the ages of 14 and 18 years), the penalty is 2 to 6 years' imprisonment. Forcible rape of an adult, depending on circumstances, is punishable by 4 to 10 years' imprisonment.

Typical Punishment for Theft, Burglary, and Robbery

According to the Bolivian penal code, article 331, theft, burglary, and robbery are punishable by imprisonment for between 1 and 5 years. Aggravated robbery, on the other hand, is liable to be punished by 3 to 10 years, depending on the circumstances (e.g., with a weapon, number of participants, area in which act was committed, etc). For the indigenous Aymara community in the Andes and Altiplano regions and the Quechua community in the rural areas, the most serious crime is often considered to be theft of agricultural products and farm animals. With remote police presence in mountainous and rural areas, the guilty party often has been dealt with by the community by means of mockery, intimidation, stoning, exile, and even death.

Death Penalty

A constitutional amendment abolished capital punishment in 1961. But it was reinstated in 1971 for terrorism, kidnapping, and crimes against government and security personnel. In 1973, the Supreme Court of Justice upheld the constitutionality of the controversial article 109 that went into force in 1973, which mandates the death penalty, by firing squad, for any citizen who takes up arms against the nation, joins its enemies, or collaborates with the enemy in the event of a foreign war. In 1981, the death penalty was extended to drug trafficking. In 1997, the death penalty was abolished for ordinary crimes. A death sentence could not be carried out, however, until the president decided against commutation. The president could commute the death penalty in favor of the second-most severe punishment, which was 30 years at hard labor, with no recourse to pardon or clemency. The last execution in Bolivia was carried out in 1974.

Indigenous communities in areas with little state presence impose punishments that reportedly have included the death penalty for members who violated traditional norms of morality and ethics, although the Constitution prohibits the death penalty for ordinary crimes defined in the penal code. How the conflict between the official recognition of communitarian justice by the 2009 constitutional reform and the constitutional prohibition of the death penalty will be settled remains unknown.

Prison

Penitentiary centers are used to house defendants awaiting trial or disposition and convicted offenders serving custodial sentences. The number of correctional establishments decreased from 89 in 2003 to 67 in 2006; because of rampant human rights problems, some of the worst prisons were closed down over the years. In 2005, Bolivia's total prison population (including pretrial detainees) included 7,710 inmates in facilities designed to hold 4,700 prisoners. With an estimated national population of 9.3 million, the prison population rate was at 83 inmates per 100,000 of the nation population. As per the International Centre for Prison Studies, almost all countries have a proportion of women prisoners lower than 12 percent, with a norm of about 6 percent; in Bolivia, 16.7 percent of the prison population are women.

In terms of offenses, 80 percent of the inmates are serving sentences for drug-related offenses, whereas in terms of legal status, defendants awaiting trial or disposition represent 75 percent of the total prisoner population—hence, only about 25 percent of all prisoners are actually serving a sentence. Overcrowding in penal institutions is alarming; for example, the population exceeds capacity by 500 percent at the men's facility of San Pedro Prison in La Paz, by 300 percent at the women's prison in La Paz, and by 345 percent in Mocovi Prison. Prison escapes are frequent; with the exception of the maximum-security prison Chonchocoro in El Alto, correctional authorities control only the outer security perimeter of each prison. Prisoners typically control the insides of the prison walls, allowing for criminal gangs to operate from their cells without interference.

Most inmates live with their families within prison walls, have jobs (e.g., selling food, doing laundry, shining shoes, cutting hair, and performing maintenance), and elect leaders to enforce laws and to manage the general finances. The wives and children of the inmates are free to come and go, often working or attending school outside the prison walls. Legally, children under 6 years of age are allowed to remain with their parents in prison, but in reality, children all the way up to the ages of 12 to 15 years often stay. This creates an interesting social phenomenon. Younger children are cared for by the day cares available inside the prison walls. Without the income of their husbands, the wives are often unable to financially sustain themselves and their children in the city. Moreover, this family connection often provides an important psychosocial support for the prisoner. Financially, wives often bring items into the prison and help provide an alternative income by selling these items in small market stalls or directly from their cells.

Typically, inmates are required to work to pay for their cells and to provide for their own food. Cells are rented for the duration of the inmate's sentence with a mandatory entrance fee of approximately US$500 and a subsequent cell rental cost ranging from US$1,000 to US$1,500, which makes detention unaffordable for many. However, if a prisoner is wealthy, he or she can either pay his or her way out of jail or live in a comfortable cell and have people working for him or her (i.e., in a kiosk, small store, or restaurant).

Visiting hours run according to the institutions' set curfews. All visitors must pay an entrance fee. In fact, tourism within the prison provides an important income for the inmates. In bigger prisons, inmates work as tour guides and sell handmade crafts to the visitors. There is even a hotel within the San Pedro Prison for visiting guests, as well as a hospital and a church. However, San Pedro's doors have recently been closed to visitors because of the illegal coca base, paste, and cocaine market within the prison. Aside from tourism, political candidates often visit prisons to conduct campaigns aimed at winning the support of incarcerated offenders. Unlike many other countries, Bolivian inmates maintain their right to vote in national elections.

In June 2006, President Evo Morales indicated that it was unacceptable that certain inmates enjoyed privileges as a result of their financial, political, or social status because according to article 5 of the penal code, criminal law does not recognize any jurisdiction or personal privilege. Hence, an initiative was set to enforce this rule and eliminate privileged spaces for the wealthy in Bolivia's prisons.

Juveniles

Although statutes specify that adolescents between 16 and 21 years old should be separated from the adults, as a result of insufficient resources in juvenile corrections, they are often sent to adult prison. In 2006, 706 convicted juvenile detainees (16 to 21 years old) lived with adult prisoners in prisons and were prime targets for abuse. For youth aged 12 to 16 charged with social liability, there are a few juvenile detention centers or reformatories in the country. Youths from 12 to 16 years of age can be detained indefinitely in juvenile institutions for known or alleged offenses, for their protection, or merely based on the recommendations of a social worker without any judicial review of such orders.

The few juvenile institutions that exist tend to be understaffed and poorly run. There is a deep concern over the unhealthy conditions of these custodial institutions, and civic groups have started to demand for experimentation with noncustodial sanctions for youths as alternatives to custodial dispositions. Worse, in 2004, there were more than 730 children and adolescents, including 450 boys and 280 girls, living with their convicted and sentenced parents in adult prisons because they did not have other legal guardians and had nowhere to go. Although basic education and medical care were provided to these youths, the prison environment posed a very serious threat to their developmental well-being.

Extradition

Bolivian law regulates extradition in both its substantive and its procedural codes. Article 3 of the criminal code determines that

> no person subject to the jurisdiction of Bolivian law may be delivered by extradition to another state, unless otherwise provided for under an international treaty or convention of reciprocity. The Supreme Court shall decide whether the extradition has a legal basis or is unfounded. In the case of reciprocity, extradition may not proceed if the act for which it is sought does not constitute a crime pursuant to the law of the state requesting the extradition and that of the state asked to grant it.

Two requirements must be met for proceeding with extradition. First, there must be a treaty or agreement of reciprocity, duly approved by national legislation. Second, the act must constitute a crime in both Bolivia and the country requesting extradition. The code of criminal procedure regulates the procedure governing all extradition matters; it indicates the steps to be taken by the Foreign Ministry of the Republic and gives the Supreme Court the power to decide on the viability of the matter.

Claudia Zambrana

Further Reading

Linera, Alvaro Garcia, Marxa Chaves Léon, and Patricia Costas Monje. (2005). *Sociología de los Movimientos Sociales en Bolivia: Estructuras de movilización, repertorios culturales y acción política.* La Paz, Bolivia: Diakonia/Oxfam, Plural editores.

Thoumi, Francisco E. (2003). *Illegal Drugs, Economy and Society in the Andes.* Washington, DC: Woodrow Wilson Center Press.

Youngers, Coletta A., and Eileen Rosin. (2005). *Drogas y Democracia en América Latina: El impacto de la política de Estados Unidos.* Buenos Aires, Argentina: Editorial Biblos.

Brazil

Legal System: Civil
Murder: High
Burglary: Low
Corruption: Medium
Human Trafficking: Medium
Prison Rate: High
Death Penalty: No
Corporal Punishment: Yes

Background

With a total area of 3,265,075 square miles and approximately 183 million inhabitants, Brazil is the world's fifth-largest country both in area and in population. It is also the world's ninth-largest economy, with a gross domestic product (GDP) of roughly 1.8 trillion in 2007. According to official statistics, about a third of Brazilian citizens are below the poverty line, and the unemployment rate is 8 percent. The country presents a high concentration of people in urban areas. The average urbanization rate in Brazil is over 82 percent, reaching more than 90 percent in some states, such as São Paulo.

The Federative Republic of Brazil is composed of 26 states and a federal district, divided politically and geographically into five different regions. Comprising seven states, the North region covers the major part of the Brazilian territory and is dominated by the Amazon River basin as well as the Brazilian portion of the rainforest. The Northeast includes nine states and features the country's lowest life expectancy and highest poverty levels. From an economic perspective, the Southeast is Brazil's most important region, and it holds in its four states most of the country's industrial production and the highest concentration of population. Brazil's largest cities—São Paulo and Rio de Janeiro—are located in this area. The South, composed of three states, is the country's smallest region and has increasingly developed its industrial base. Last, the Midwest includes three states and the Federal District, which contains the country's capital, Brasília. Although the transfer of the capital from Rio de Janeiro to the region in 1960 has contributed to the area's development, most of the region's economy is based on cattle-breeding and agriculture, especially soybean production.

Brazil shares its borders with all but two South American countries: Ecuador and Chile. Its extensive borders with drug-producing countries in the continent, as well as its vast waterways, air, and road infrastructure, facilitate smuggling routes for drug trafficking.

Governance

The country follows a tripartite model of governance. The judicial branch is formed by the Supreme Federal Tribunal (with 11 ministers); the Higher Tribunal of Justice (at least 33 members); five regional federal tribunals (with seven judges); the higher electoral tribunals (with 27 members); the higher military tribunals (15 members nominated by the president and selected from the army, navy, and air force, as well as civilians); and finally, the state and the federal district tribunals. The most important role of Brazil's Supreme Federal Tribunal is to rule on the final interpretation of the Constitution; the tribunal can also declare void the acts decreed by the Congress. The legislative branch is bicameral: the Federal Senate (81 seats) and the Chamber of Deputies (513 members) form the National Congress. Last, the executive branch is headed by the country's president (elected democratically every four years with reelection allowed only once) and includes several ministries, secretaries, departments, and agencies.

The legislative process in Brazil is complex. Bills can originate from the president's office, the Supreme Federal Tribunal, or the Higher Tribunal of Justice or can be introduced by federal deputies, the general prosecutor, senators, state assemblies, or citizens. Every bill is submitted to technical, material, and formal scrutiny by at least one of the standing committees of the Chamber of Deputies or Senate. If approved, a bill is subject to voting in a plenary assembly and can be amended. After endorsement by the originating instance, the bill is evaluated by the country's president, who sanctions or vetoes it entirely or in part. However, a presidential veto is not decisive; a congressional vote can override it.

Legal History

The history of Brazil's legal system can be traced to its colonization by the Portuguese in 1500. It encompasses four major periods: a colonial period, during which Portugal's laws extended over the colony; an imperial era, following Brazil's independence in 1822; the Old Republican era, which inaugurated the democratic system in Brazil; and the era beginning with the 1940 penal code, which to date still represents a considerable portion of Brazilian penal law.

During the colonial period, the Portuguese law codes were the only ruling documents on which the Brazilian legal system relied. Four legal ordinances, issued respectively by King Afonso V (1500–1512), King Manuel I (1512–1569), King Sebastião I (1569–1603), and King Filipe II (in effect from 1603 to 1830), marked the period in which law and religion were practically indiscernible, and sins and moral offenses made up most of the punishable crimes. The punishments were often cruel and included mutilation, branding, and torture. The death penalty was widely applied and took various forms (by hanging or "natural death," preceded by torture, or *morte cruel*; or by fire followed by dismemberment of the cadaver, or *morte atroz*).

In 1830, eight years after Brazil declared its independence from Portugal, the Imperial Criminal Code was passed into law. Highly influenced by Jeremy Bentham's utilitarian doctrine, as well as by the liberal principles of the Enlightenment, the code proscribed political persecutions and reserved the death penalty for crimes committed by slaves. In 1832, the first criminal procedure code was promulgated, which completed the Brazilian penal legislation of the period.

In 1890, following the abolition of slavery and the establishment of Brazil as a republic, a new penal code was drafted and passed into law. Known as the Republican Penal Code, the document abolished the death penalty and instated the correctional penitentiary regime.

Finally, in 1940, a new penal code (Código Penal Brasileiro) was drafted and became effective two years later. To this date, the 1940 code is still the fundamental piece of Brazilian penal legislation. Civil, commercial, and civil procedure laws compose the three other principal codes in which Brazilian law is prescribed.

In 1984, following three major reforms in 1963, 1969, and 1978, the General Part of the Penal Code (Parte Geral do Código Penal) was substantially modified to include the Penal Execution Laws (Leis de Execução Penal), a number of seemingly unrelated regulations ranging from crimes against the environment to electoral as well as postal service laws. The bulk of the 1940 penal code (with its reforms) was then incorporated into what is now called the "Special Part" (*Parte Especial*) of the penal legislation.

Just as Brazilian's legal history has been profoundly affected by that country's colonization process, so have its criminal justice system and the official mechanisms of social control. For example, the trial process in Brazil still retains an inquisitorial component, inherited from Portugal's continental law-based system. In addition, Brazil's state police force, the Polícia Civil, finds its roots in the Police Commissariat (Intendência Geral de Polícia), founded in 1808 by Brazil's Prince D. João VI to contain slave insurgency.

Political and Social Context of the Criminal Justice System

Brazil remained a colony for 322 years after the Portuguese landed there in 1500. Following its independence in 1822, the country conserved a monarchal form of government until 1889 when the republic was proclaimed, and a constitutional system similar to the American model was established.

During most of the duration of the republic, two states—São Paulo and Minas Gerais—dominated the political leadership in Brazil. This bipartisanship came to an end with the 1930 revolution, which brought about the first electoral code. Among several inroads toward democracy, the code extended voting rights to women.

The period between the end of World War II and 1964 was a politically unstable one in the history of the country and culminated with the establishment of the Brazilian military regime. Formally resumed in 1985, Brazil's re-democratization reestablished party pluralism, and a new Constitution was promulgated in 1988. Fernando Collor de Mello became the first president to be democratically elected since the military coup d'état. He was later impeached because of his involvement in several corruption scandals.

Corruption in Brazil is not circumscribed to the political circle and directly affects the criminal justice system. To illustrate, the judiciary has increasingly been the focus of streamlining actions by the current president, Luiz Inácio Lula da Silva. In December 2004, the National Congress passed a constitutional amendment aimed at guaranteeing uniformity of jurisprudence. The amendment also established a National Council of Justice (Conselho Nacional de Justiça) as an external oversight mechanism over the judiciary.

Corruption is also prevalent in all levels of the police forces. The average Brazilian policeman makes the equivalent to US$300.00 per month. Bribes and hit jobs (i.e., murder for money) complement this meager income. Not only corruption but also discriminatory practices contribute to high levels of public distrust in the police force. For example, a study conducted by the Instituto Superior de Estudos Religiosos (ISER, or Superior Institute for Religion Studies) reveals that in 1999, blacks and mulattoes were more likely to die during confrontations with police (70.2 percent) than whites (29.8 percent). Brazil's former secretary of public security, Luiz Eduardo Soares, has stated that "the fight against racism [in Brazil] is also a fight against a corrupt and violent police."

The legal control of crime and violence in Brazil also suffers from many other failings, especially with respect to violations of human rights. Torture of offenders and suspects, discrimination against certain groups' rights (women, children, landless peasants, etc.), ill treatment of prisoners, and the undeniable existence of police extermination groups are just a few examples. In an attempt to counter such violations and impunity, in 1997, then-president Fernando Henrique Cardoso created a National Department for Human Rights (Secretaria Especial de Direitos Humanos). Currently, the department's agenda focuses, among other themes, on the minimization of illegal slavery and sexual exploitation of children and adolescents. Besides government initiatives, civil society groups, such as Rio de Janeiro's Viva Rio and São Paulo's Violence Study Unit continually bring the issues of violence, crime, and human rights violation to public attention, thereby pressing for public policy and legal reforms.

Crime

Classification of Crimes

The Special Part of the penal code prescribes the following types of felony ("delicts" or "crime") offenses. Felonies are punished with imprisonment, fines, or restriction of certain rights (e.g., suspension of professional license), depending on the offense.

1. *Crimes against persons* consist of six major offenses. "Crimes against life" include three forms of homicide (simple, which is equivalent to the American definition of murder; unintentional, which parallels the American notion of manslaughter; and aggravated, in which, for instance, death is caused to cover other crimes). "Personal injury crimes" comprise major and minor assaults. "Crimes of endangerment of life and health" include, among other offenses, intentional exposure to venereal disease and the abandonment of newborns. "Crimes against honor" (e.g., defamation) and those qualified as "vendetta" (e.g., taking part in feud brawls) are also proscribed. Finally, kidnappings, forced labor, and other types of "crimes against personal freedom" are also prohibited.
2. *Crimes against property* consist of theft, robbery, blackmail, extortion, and embezzlement, among others.
3. *Crimes against immaterial property* concern copyright violations and the like.
4. *Crimes against the organization of labor* include abusive strikes, lockouts, and others.
5. *Crimes against religious sentiment and respect for the deceased* regard religious persecutions, violation of graves, and so on.
6. *Crimes against social norms* include forcible rape, child abuse, prostitution, trafficking in persons, and so on.
7. *Crime against family* include bigamy and child neglect. In 2005, the code was reformed to exclude adultery as a crime. Until then, the argument of legitimate defense of the honor was widely used in trials involving unfaithful wives killed by their husbands. In a symbolic gesture, Brazil's president Luiz Inácio Lula da Silva signed the law reform on March 8, the International Women's Day.
8. *Crimes against public safety* include, among others, arson, sabotage, and the intentional release of harmful germs.
9. *Crimes against public peace* concern inciting crimes and participating in organized crime.
10. *Crimes against public trust* involve several types of counterfeiting.
11. *Crimes against public administration* are those regarding corruption, abuse of power, tax evasion, and so on.

The penal code also outlines several misdemeanors (*contravenções*), such as unlawful production and commerce of weapons, animal cruelty, gambling, peddling, solicitation, and other acts. Misdemeanors are punished with imprisonment or fines, depending on the offense.

Age of Criminal Responsibility

The age of criminal responsibility in Brazil is 18. However, prompted by the brutal murder of a 6-year-old boy by minors in Rio de Janeiro in 2007, Brazilian legislators are currently considering a reduction in the age of criminal responsibility from 18 to 16 for common offenses and to 13 in the case of heinous crimes.

Children, defined as persons younger than 12 years of age, cannot be criminally charged. Juveniles, or those between 12 and 17 years of age, are not subject to the penal code. Instead, their offenses are regulated by the Statute of Children and Adolescents (Estatuto da Criança e do Adolescente), a law passed in 1990. Juveniles are also subject to judicial actions under the jurisdiction of a special court system, the Childhood and Youth Justice System (Justiça da Infância e da Juventude).

The Statute of Children and Adolescents determines that juvenile offenders cannot be sentenced to imprisonment. According to the law, these offenders are subject to the following punishments: verbal warning, financial reimbursement to the victim, community service, probation, and detention in designated custodial institutions. Though designed to protect the welfare of accused juveniles and promote rehabilitation, the statute has undesirable effects. The degree of impunity provided by the law makes children and juveniles ideal couriers for drug trafficking.

Drug Offenses

In 2006, Brazil sanctioned a new law redefining drug offenses and prescribing measures of prevention, treatment, and social reintegration, as well as punishments. Among other accomplishments, the law instituted the National Anti-Drug System (SISNAD), a centralized agency in charge of coordinating and organizing antidrug efforts. Three other main changes were brought about by this law. First, it decriminalized possession and production of drugs in small quantities, exclusively for personal consumption, offenses that are now punished by 5 to 10 months of community service, mandatory participation in educational programs, verbal warnings, and/or fines. The proceeds of the fines are destined for the National Anti-Drug Fund and invested in treatment and prevention programs. The law also prescribes a tougher punishment for drug trafficking (prison sentences with a minimum of 5 years and a maximum of 15 years). And finally, the law provides changes in several aspects of the criminal procedure (e.g., pretrial detention is limited to 30 days for investigation of the charges).

As stipulated by this law, any substances or products capable of causing dependency are considered "drugs." Illegal drugs—or those for which use, possession, production, and any form of trade are legally proscribed—change constantly and are regulated by resolutions made by the National Agency of Sanitary Vigilance (ANVISA). The most recent document was issued in 2007, and it enumerates more than 100 different substances that are subjected to special control by Brazilian authorities. The list includes common illegal drugs such as cocaine, heroin, MDMA (Ecstasy), marijuana, and certain inhalants as well as the base-substances and/or plants from which other illegal drugs can be manufactured (e.g., peyote cactus).

Crime Statistics

According to a study by the United Nations Regional Office on Drugs and Crime, Brazil is among the most violent nations in the world. Different sources report slightly different figures concerning homicide rates in Brazil. The National Coroner's Office (considered to be one of the most reliable by researchers in that country) reported 23.5 homicides per 100,000 in 2000. The data published by the National Secretary of Public Security is slightly higher: 27 homicides per 100,000 for the same year. There is a consensus that the rates are steadily increasing; in 1980, for instance, homicide rates according to the SENASP (Secretaria Nacional de Segurança Pública) were 11 per 100,000. It is worth noting, though, that homicide rates have decreased substantially in the city of São Paulo between 2000 and 2004. A few scholars have attributed this to the efforts of partnerships between community and police, as well as revitalization projects.

Homicides are spatially concentrated in urban areas: 50 percent of the homicides are concentrated in 27 cities, and 50 percent take place in the remaining 5,480 municipalities. Some cities, such as Diadema in the state of São Paulo, present rates of more than 120 homicides per 100,000 inhabitants. Such figures are comparable to those from areas undergoing civil war. Victims of homicides in Brazil are mainly young people between 15 and 25 years of age, and these incidents often involve use of firearms. In 2000, gun-related rates were 18.6 per 100,000 (or, in other terms, roughly 61 percent of homicides involved use of a firearm). Nonetheless, in a referendum held in 2005, the Brazilian population rejected gun control.

In 2001, according to the SENASP, more than 14,000 reports of rape were registered, a rate of 16.8 per 100,000 people. In 2003, the rate declined slightly to 15.9 per 100,000.

The United Nations Center for International Crime Prevention (CICP) published data placing Brazil among the nations with the highest robbery incidence, with a rate of 400 robberies per 100,000 in 2000. In 2004, the rate of robberies reported to the police increased to 506.5 per 100,000; and in 2005, the figures reached a historical apex of 511.5 per 100,000.

In 2001, more than 700,000 larceny-theft reports were filed in Brazil, which corresponds to 964.1 per 100,000. In 2002, the rate was 1,053.1 per 100,000, and in 2003, it increased slightly to 1,201.6 per 100,000. These data account for reported burglaries (*arrombamento*) and motor-vehicle thefts as well. According to official statistics, 370,120 vehicles were reported stolen in 2002—for a rate of 218 vehicles per 100,000 people. SENASP also reports that the rates for aggravated assault have been steadily increasing: 327.4 per 100,000 in 2001; 345 per 100,000 in 2002; and 350 per 100,000 in 2003.

Overall drug consumption in Brazil has steadily increased in the past years, as stated in the 2007 World Drug Report by the United Nations Office on Drugs and Crime (UNODC). For instance, the report documents an increase in the proportion of Brazilians who consume cocaine (0.4 percent of the adult population in 2001and 0.7 percent in 2005, the latest trend year for which data are available). The 2005 data correspond to roughly 860,000 cocaine users between the ages of 15 and 64 years. Additionally, the report stated that the consumption of marijuana also had increased (from 1 percent in 2001 to 2.6 percent in 2005). Brazil is also the largest opiate market in South America, with an estimated 600,000 people, or 0.5 percent of the general population, age 12–65, being users.

Finding of Guilt

Criminal trials in Brazil are typically composed of two phases. The first part is inquisitorial and presided over by a judge who questions the parties involved, as well as witnesses. In the case of crimes against life (e.g., homicide, abortion, suicide assistance, etc.), the prosecutor or the defense counsel may request the second phase of the trial to be handled by a jury court (*tribunal do júri*). The jury court is composed of a judge and 21 prospective jurors, later narrowed down to a group of 7 who will actually participate in the trial, often questioning defense witnesses if they wish to do so. The jury system was instituted in Brazil in 1822, and much like in the United States, the pool of prospective jurors is randomly drawn from the adult population of the district in which the court operates. Though plea bargaining, as practiced in the United States, is not allowed by law in Brazil, there is a functional equivalent used to manage overwhelming caseloads (*confissão delatória* and *delação premiada*).

The legal rights of the accused are guaranteed by the 1988 Constitution. These rights can be summarized as follows: to be informed specifically and clearly of the charges; to be assisted by family, attorney, or legal aid following arrest; to be assisted, during the preliminary investigation, by a defense attorney or public defender; not to give self-incriminating evidence; to request investigation of the facts or circumstances that might establish innocence; to report directly to a judge; to be informed of the content of an investigation; to habeas corpus, particularly if the accused is threatened with violence, coercion, or abuse; not to be tortured or treated in a cruel, inhumane, or degrading manner; not to be subjected to investigative or detention techniques that alter free will or volition, even when consented to; not to be tried in absentia; and to jury decision by secret ballot in cases of prosecution of crimes against life. The right to bail was modified in 1990 with the introduction of the Law of Heinous Crimes (*Lei dos Crimes Hediondos*). This law establishes that judges cannot allow bail when a person is accused of homicide, rape, kidnapping, or aggravated assault, among other crimes. All other crimes are eligible for bail, set by the trial judge.

One of the implications of the Law of Heinous Crimes is that the majority of criminal defendants do not even have the right to request provisional liberty, which results in excessive pretrial detention. Very often, lengthy pretrial detention is also combined with extensive criminal proceedings. Though information on the national average length of trial proceedings is absent, the situation in some states seems worse than in others. To illustrate, in the Northern state of Pará, 7 of every 10 prisoners were still awaiting trial in 1999.

The slowness of the justice system in Brazil may also be caused by the relatively low rate of judges per number of inhabitants. To illustrate, a report by the National Council of Justice issued in 2006 revealed a rate of 6 judges per 100,000 inhabitants; by comparison, in Austria, for instance, the proportion is 21 judges per 100,000. The different levels of the justice system require different qualifications from judges. Though all of them must have a law degree and a minimum of three years of experience in the criminal justice system, lower-court judges are admitted through public exams, whereas higher-court judges must be appointed by the president and confirmed by the Senate.

Punishment

Types of Punishment

The kinds of punishment typically used in Brazil include fines, reparations and/or compensation for victims, temporary interdiction of rights, detention, and imprisonment. Verbal warnings, treatment, community service, and mandatory participation in prevention programs are also applied in drug convictions, minor crimes, and juvenile adjudications. In cases of imprisonment, the maximum sentence per conviction is 30 years. The calculus of the sentence starts with a number of years specified in the penal code, which can be increased or decreased depending on the mitigating and aggravating circumstances of the crime in question. Inmates are eligible for parole after serving one-third of the sentence in the case of first-time offenders and after serving one-half for recidivists. Those convicted of heinous crimes must serve at least two-fifths of their sentence to qualify for parole.

Murder convicts can be punished with 6 to 20 years of imprisonment. However, this length can be decreased by one-sixth to one-third if the judge determines the existence of mitigating circumstances (e.g., relevant social or moral motive); an increase in years in prison can also be carried out if the judge determines the existence of aggravating circumstances (e.g., murder preceded by torture). Imprisonment is also the typical punishment for rape (6 to 10 years), as well as for theft, burglary, and robbery (4 to 10 years, subject to change if mitigating or aggravating circumstances are present).

Brazil is an abolitionist nation for ordinary crimes. In fact, the 1988 Federal Constitution proscribes the institution of death penalty in a clause that cannot be altered by the Congress (*cláusula pétrea*). Capital punishment is applicable only in case of declared war.

Alternatives to imprisonment, such as community service, have received increased support from the Brazilian government, given the growth of the inmate population between 1994 and 2006. In 1999, the National Center of Support and Oversight of Alternative Punishment and Measures (Central Nacional de Apoio e Acompanhamento de Penas e Medidas Alternativas) was established, with the goal of implementing such alternatives to incarceration. The result was a remarkable rise in the number of people serving alternative sentences: from 197 in 1987 to roughly 300,000 in 2006.

Prisons

In 2007, as reported by the Brazilian Justice Department, the number of inmates in Brazil reached a total of 422,590 distributed through state and federal penitentiaries, as well as local jails. This corresponds to a rate of roughly 227 inmates per 100,000 inhabitants. Still, according to the department, the country's prison system can adequately house only 275,000 inmates. The deficit is an indicator of just how overcrowded Brazilian cells are, which has led to numerous claims of human rights infringement by activist groups such as Human Watch International and Amnesty International, among others.

The annual cost per inmate is roughly US$6,000. Official 2007 data provide the following information about the prison population: Nearly 40 percent of the inmates did not complete high school. Twenty-seven percent of Brazilian prisoners are serving 8 years or less, whereas roughly 4.5 percent are serving sentences between 20 and 30 years. A considerable number of offenders were convicted for simple or aggravated robbery (27 percent), drug offenses (15 percent), burglary (13 percent), and homicide (11 percent). Women account for merely 6 percent of the total inmate population, and most prisoners (58 percent) are between 18 and 29 years old.

In 2007, according to data published by the National Department of Penitentiaries, Brazil's penal system presented a total of 402 correctional facilities, 41 prison farms, 38 halfway houses, 1,030 local jails, and 25 custodial hospitals. Still according to official statistics, the state of São Paulo houses one of every three Brazilians who are in prison. The state also used to house the largest prison system in Latin America—the Casa de Detenção or Carandiru. Founded in the 1920s, Carandiru had a population of approximately 8,000 inmates in the late 1990s. The prison complex was demolished in 2002, 10 years after 111 of its inmates were killed by the military police during a riot.

The national law regulating inmates' rights and duties require all convicted prisoners to work. However, despite the law's mandates, the country's penal facilities do not offer sufficient work opportunities to occupy all prisoners. The situation is even more precarious in police lockups, where the only job opportunity is janitorial work. Inmates are typically employed by private companies, which hire prisoners to produce items such as notebooks, toys, or license plates. The National Prison Fund (FUNPEN), in charge of managing prison labor, operates sewing and carpentry workshops in a few prisons. By law, each working inmate should be paid three-quarters of the national minimum wage monthly, or approximately US$180.00 per month. A report by Human Rights International has found that very few prisons actually pay inmates salaries near that amount, and most commonly, inmates in manufacturing jobs are paid according to the number of pieces produced. The report points out that several prisons did not pay inmates at all. Under federal law, inmates are also entitled to an education, including vocational and professional training. However, the opportunities offered in reality are also scarce in this area.

Brazilian inmates are entitled to visitation rights, and a few prisons allow for conjugal visits. The degree of security check of visitors varies from prison to prison. In maximum-security prisons, such as the Campo Grande Penitentiary, all visitors must undergo a thorough strip search, and in case of suspicion that the visitor is in possession of weapons or any other contraband, a medical team is summoned to conduct a body cavity search.

Extradition of prisoners to other countries is allowed in Brazil. To illustrate, Brazil's Supreme Court authorized in March 2008 the transfer of Juan Carlos Ramirez Abadia, one of Colombia's most-wanted drug lords, to the United States. The extradition rested on the condition that Abadia would not face the death penalty and would not serve more than 30 years in prison—the maximum sentence per conviction prescribed by the Brazilian penal code. The drug trafficker was arrested in São Paulo in 2007. As one of the leaders of the Norte del Valle Cartel, Abadia was wanted on drug smuggling, murder, and racketeering charges in the United States.

Giza Lopes

Further Reading

Caulfield, Sueann. (2000). *In Defense of Honor: Sexual Morality, Modernity, and Nation in Early-Twentieth-Century Brazil.* Durham, NC: Duke University Press.

Hecht, Tobias. (1998). *At Home in the Street: Street Children of Northeast Brazil.* New York: Cambridge University Press.

Hinton, Mercedes S. (2006). *The State on the Streets: Police and Politics in Argentina and Brazil.* Boulder, CO: Lynne Rienner Publishers.

UNODC Regional Office of Brazil. (2005). *Country Profile.* United Nations Office on Drugs and Crime: http://www.unodc.org/pdf/brazil/COUNTRY%20PROFILE%20Eng.pdf.

British Virgin Islands

Legal System: Common
Prison Rate: Low
Death Penalty: No

Background

The British Virgin Islands (BVI) comprise the islands of Tortola, Virgin Gorda, Anegada, Jost Van Dyke, and around 50 other islets, cays, and rocks. They are situated to the north and east of the U.S. Virgin Islands, from which they are separated at their closest point by a stretch of water known as The Narrows. Bounded at the north by the Atlantic Ocean and the south by the Caribbean Sea, the islands cover a total land area of around 59 square miles, of which the largest, Tortola, accounts for 21. The estimated total population of the islands stood at 24,491 in July 2009 with around 9,000 living in the capital, Road Town, on Tortola. According to the 2004 census, 83.4 percent of the population is black. The islands are considered a self-governing overseas territory of the United Kingdom.

Legal History

British proprietorship over the British Virgin Islands is generally dated from 1672, the year that Colonel William Stapleton took possession of Tortola from the Dutch. It was not until 1773 that permission was granted from Britain to establish an independent legislature, the islands having been governed until that time from Antigua by the governor of the Leeward Islands. Legislation to establish courts was passed in 1783, and in 1859, an inspector of police and two policemen were appointed, an additional officer being added in 1860. Rural constables existed but were not salaried.

The judiciary—consisting of unpaid justices of the peace, a chief justice, and a stipendiary magistrate—had been abolished piecemeal by 1872. A circuit court was established based out of the Supreme Court of the Leeward Islands, though this too was abolished in 1902 when the legislature—which had by this time been reduced to an appointed, rather than elected, body—was disbanded altogether. Authority over the islands was again vested in the governor of the Leeward Islands, and the administration of justice was left in the hands of an untrained commissioner-magistrate.

A legislative council was restored in 1950, with a Constitution and full self-government arriving in 1967. From the 1970s, the islands began to develop as an important offshore financial center when U.S. companies began taking advantage of a double-relief tax treaty. When the treaty was revoked unilaterally by the United States in 1981, the islanders reacted with the International Business Companies Act (IBCA) in 1984—an oft-copied piece of legislation that exempted companies from local taxation provided they did no business with local residents.

New incorporations came slowly at first but increased in number following the U.S. invasion of Panama in 1991. In 2000, according to a KPMG report, the British Virgin Islands accounted for no fewer than 41 percent of new incorporations in offshore financial centers worldwide, making it the world leader in new incorporations. The IBCA was repealed in 2006 following international pressure from the Organisation for Economic Cooperation and Development (OECD) and other bodies. Such is the importance (and litigiousness) of the financial services industry in the BVI that a commercial court was founded in 2009 to preside over litigation concerning commercial claims and to refine procedure and practice in relation to such claims. The building of the court was expected to be completed by the summer of 2009, at an estimated cost of almost 4 million U.S. dollars.

Today, the law of the British Virgin Islands is a combination of English common law and local legislation. Criminal trial proceedings are accusatorial in nature. The 13-member House of Assembly of the British Virgin Islands, the local legislative body, produces legislation unique to the islands. In addition, law can be created in the islands by "orders-in-council"—legislation ordered and promulgated by the British government. Orders-in-council have recently been used to enact controversial legislation such as the abolition of the death penalty for murder and the decriminalization of homosexuality.

Police

Founded in 1967, the Royal Virgin Islands Police Force (RVIPF) is responsible for policing the islands. The organization has three subdivisions, known respectively as "community policing," "specialist operations," and "management services," each headed by a superintendent. The community policing unit is responsible for police deployment, community relations work, the suppression of firearms violations, and traffic control. The special operations division is responsible for criminal investigations, intelligence and forensics, the investigation of financial crime, and the suppression of drug trafficking (in part by marine and air patrols). Management services is staffed largely by civilian personnel and provides administrative support. In 2000, the RVIPF employed a total of 212 people, including 92 constables, 41 sergeants, 19 inspectors, and 11 traffic wardens (BVI Developmental Planning Unit 2000).

The 2007 Constitution required that policing be overseen by a five-member Police Service Commission. The commission is intended to advise the governor on appointments to the police and on matters of discipline, though the governor may disregard its advice where he or she feels it "would prejudice Her Majesty's service." The first commission was appointed in February 2009.

Crime

Classification of Crimes

Offenses in the British Virgin Islands are divided into those that are triable on "indictment only" and those triable "summarily." Indictment-only offenses are tried following a preliminary hearing to determine whether a prima facie case exists, and the right to a jury trial generally attaches. "Summary" offenses may generally be tried without a jury in the Magistrate's Court. Certain offenses may be triable "either way," though depending on the seriousness of the case in question, the Magistrate's Court may not be permitted to try particular cases.

Under section 12 of the 1997 Criminal Code Act, children under the age of 10 cannot be held liable for "any act or omission." Children under the age of 14 are similarly protected, though the presumption that they do not know the difference between right and wrong is rebuttable. Generally, youth 16 years of age and under are dealt with under the Youth Courts Act of 2005.

Drug crime and drug smuggling remain a considerable problem in the British Virgin Islands. The British Foreign and Commonwealth Office (FCO) warns that "problems associated with drug trafficking are potentially the most serious threat to stability." The FCO goes on to report that the BVI are an ideal stopping point for traffickers making their way to Puerto Rico and the U.S. Virgin Islands, both of which are access points for the United States. Penalties for the use of drugs within the BVI, including cannabis, are stiff.

Crime Statistics

Annual crime statistics are reported by the RVIPF. In 2006, counting procedures were reformed to count criminal incidents rather than criminal charges, as had previously been the case. In total, exactly 1,503 crimes were recorded by the Royal Virgin Islands Police Force in 2006, the most recent year for which data are available. Twenty percent of these were categorized as offenses against persons, 52 percent as against property, and 28 percent as other types of offenses (including customs, narcotics, weapons, public order, and fraud offenses). Major offenses reported against the person included 4 murders and 1 attempted murder, 3 rapes, 6 indecent assaults, and 5 cases of unlawful sex with a minor. Of the 40 assaults reported, 14 were recorded as having inflicted "grievous" bodily harm, whereas the remaining 26 inflicted only "serious" bodily harm.

Of the 283 burglaries reported on the islands in 2006, 43 percent were of houses, 12 percent were commercial, and 10 percent were of "boats used as a dwelling." These latter burglaries are characterized by especially low clearance rates (3%) compared to those in land-based residences (12%) and commercial properties (18%). The RVIPF refers to clearance rates as "detection rates." The RVIPF recorded exactly 100 drug offenses in 2006, the majority of which (68%) were for the unlawful possession of cannabis. Ten percent were for possession of a variety of drugs with intent to supply, and 9 percent were for the unlawful cultivation of cannabis.

Finding of Guilt

No statement on the fundamental rights and freedoms of British Virgin Islanders existed prior to the enactment of a new constitution in 2007. Section 16 of the 2007 Constitution specifies that individuals have the right to be presumed innocent, to be informed of the nature of the charges against them, to be given adequate time for the preparation of their defense, to retain legal representation, to examine witnesses brought against them, to obtain witnesses to testify on their own behalf, and to be provided with an interpreter. Individuals have the right to be tried by jury when charged on indictment. Legal representation is to be provided at public expense "where he or she is unable to afford to retain a legal practitioner and the interests of justice so require." Section 16 also contains protections against double jeopardy and self-incrimination, affirmations of the rights to appeal and to a speedy and public trial, and a provision allowing for compensation to victims of miscarriages of justice.

The authority to prosecute criminal cases is vested in the person of the director of public prosecutions, appointed by the governor on the advice of the Judicial and Legal Services Commission—a five-person commission dominated by high-ranking jurists. The Constitution specifies that this individual must be admitted to practice law in the British Virgin Islands with seven years' experience. All judges are appointed by the chief justice of the Eastern Caribbean Supreme Court (ECSC). The ECSC is, for most purposes, the highest court of appeal in the BVI, though for certain cases, further recourse may be available to the Judicial Committee of the Privy Council in London.

The annual reports of the ECSC provide much of the available data on the performance of BVI courts. Of its 82 judgments passed in 2007, 15 concerned the BVI. The BVI Magistrate's Court, which deals with most low-level (summary) cases, received 1,138 filings in criminal matters in 2007, 50 percent of that year's filings in the court, the remainder being civil and other matters. Seven hundred and six criminal cases were disposed in the Magistrate's Court in 2007, representing 37 percent of all dispositions. A separate system for trying juveniles exists for all persons 16 years old or younger, as described in the Youth Courts Act of 2005.

Punishment

Types of Punishment

The BVI Criminal Code, passed into law in 1997, specifies the punishments for most criminal offenses. Under section 22 of the code, seven types of punishment are allowable, and an eighth category provides for "any other punishment expressly provided for by law for the time being in force." The seven categories explicitly noted include imprisonment, fines, payment of compensation to injured party, suspended sentences, release on recognizance, probation, and forfeiture of the articles involved in an offense. The Criminal Justice (Alternative Sentencing) Act of 2005 expanded sentencing options to include alternatives such as required attendance at treatment or training programs.

Where imprisonment is imposed, the criminal code specifies the upper limit on the sentence for which an offender is liable, with the exception of murder, where a life sentence is required. Suspended sentences are intended for exceptional cases only and may be imposed only where the term of imprisonment that would otherwise have been imposed would not have exceeded two years. Offenders who commit another imprisonable offense within one to two years of the order (as specified by the court) may then face the imposition of the original sentence, at the court's discretion. Offenders released on their own recognizance are required to "keep the peace and be of good behavior" and can be required to offer financial sureties to ensure compliance. Compensation to the injured party may be ordered in addition to any other punishment imposed in any case. In certain cases, it is also possible to order the convicted offender to pay the costs of prosecution. Sentences are cumulative unless the court specifically mandates they run concurrently.

Section 150 of the act specifies that the penalty for murder is life imprisonment. Under section 23 of the same act, no shorter term may be applied. For convictions of all other types, shorter terms than the maximum may be awarded. For rape, the offender is liable to a maximum of life imprisonment (section 117). The punishment for theft depends on whether the individual was convicted summarily or on indictment. Summary convictions render offenders liable to a sentence limited to 2 years; convictions on indictment increase the maximum possible to 10 years (Section 209). Offenders convicted of robbery are liable to life imprisonment (Section 210). Offenders convicted of burglary are liable to a sentence not exceeding 14 years, except in aggravated cases. Aggravated burglary occurs when the offender was in possession of an offensive weapon and renders those convicted liable to life imprisonment (sections 211, 212). The death penalty for murder was abolished in 1991 by an order-in-council.

Prison

The only prison in the BVI is located at Balsam Ghut on the eastern end of Tortola, where it is overseen by a superintendent who is directly accountable to the governor. It was constructed between 1996 and 1997. At the time of its construction, it contained 68 cells with separate compounds for high-security and female prisoners. It is also equipped with workshops, laundry and cooking facilities, and a basketball court. A new immigration detention center, with a reported capacity of 36 men and 24 women, was opened at the prison in 2008.

On May 26, 2008, 117 people were held in prison at Balsam Ghut, including remand (pretrial) detainees. Of the total population, 2.6 percent were under 18 years of age. The International Centre for Prison Studies at Kings College, London, calculates that this translates into an incarceration rate of 488 individuals per 100,000 head of population. This figure is up from a total of 43 prisoners, or a rate of 215 per 100,000 population, in 1999.

Inmates are not required to attend classes, though a 2000 report stated that educational opportunities were available in academic subjects (English, mathematics, social studies, and computer studies, among others) and certain vocational skills (tailoring, carpentry, and silkscreen printing). The prison is described as "based on a 'farm-camp' concept," and participation in agriculture is regarded as an essential part of the prison's rehabilitative regime. A work release program also allows prisoners to earn money working for a civilian employer: prisoners considered to be a low security risk are permitted to work outside the compound, performing such work as the cleaning of cemeteries, playgrounds, and government buildings. In-prison craft work projects also allow prisoners to earn money. Prisoners are allowed an hour of recreation daily.

Andrew Davies

Further Reading

British Virgin Islands Gazette (authoritative source): http://www.bvigazette.org/.

BVI Developmental Planning Unit: http://www.dpu.gov.vg/

Dookhan, I. (1975). *A History of the British Virgin Islands 1672–1970.* Epping: Caribbean Universities Press.

Eastern Caribbean Supreme Court. (2009). *Annual Report 2007–2008:* http://www.eccourts.org/publications/annual_reports/AnnualReport2008.pdf.

Royal Virgin Islands Police Force. (2009). *Crime Statistics 2006:* http://www.rvipolice.com/statistics/Annual%20Crime%20Statistics%202006.pdf.

Canada

Legal System: Common/Civil
Murder: Medium
Burglary: Low
Corruption: Low
Human Trafficking: Low
Prison Rate: Medium
Death Penalty: No
Corporal Punishment: No

Background

Canada is the world's second-largest country, extending from the Atlantic Ocean in the east to the Pacific Ocean in the west and northward into the Arctic Ocean. Although Canada is vast, most of the territory is too rugged to sustain viable communities. In fact, the vast majority of the 33 million Canadian population lives in a strip of land of 200 kilometers from the U.S. border.

Canada is often characterized as one of the most advanced countries in the world. Although it is ranked only ninth in the world in terms of wealth, it has undoubtedly high living standards. On the Human Development Index (based on measures of literacy, life expectancy, and per capita GDP), it is ranked fourth after Iceland, Norway, and Australia.

The Supreme Court of Canada in Ottawa, Ontario. (Howard Sandler/Dreamstime)

Canada has been occupied by aboriginal people for more than 10,000 years. The Inuit, inhabitants of the northernmost regions of Canada, are believed to have come from Russian Siberian tribes who crossed the Bering Strait during the last Ice Age, whereas Natives of the more temperate zones are of different lines of descent. Today, between 2 and 4 percent of Canadians are Natives, but it is believed that a much larger proportion of descendants from the early colonists have mixed happily with Natives.

The European settlement of Canada can be traced to John Cabot from England in 1497 and Jacques Cartier from France in 1534, although there had been some visits from Vikings before that. Following wars between Britain and France that extended to the Americas, the French territories were ceded to Britain in 1763. With the Constitution Act of 1867, Canada was formed as a federal dominion of four provinces, therefore providing its independence. As time went by, additional provinces and territories were accredited, and autonomy from United Kingdom was increased.

Canada has always been a land of immigration, with first the French and English. In the 20th century, there were important waves of immigration from European countries such as Italy, Portugal, and Germany. However, in more recent decades, immigrants have been coming to Canada from all over the world, such as from Algeria or Haiti to Quebec, from Pakistan and India to Ontario, and from various Asian countries to all over the country and particularly to British Columbia.

Government

Now comprising 10 provinces and 3 northern territories, Canada is a parliamentary democracy and a constitutional monarchy with the queen of England as head of state and the prime minister as head of government. Although executive authority is formally and constitutionally vested in the monarch, the queen of England and her representative play a predominantly ceremonial and apolitical role and have no real powers. In line with Canada's federalist structure, the Constitution divides governmental responsibilities between the federal government and the 10 provinces. Canada's 3 territories have fewer constitutional responsibilities than the provinces and some structural differences. For example, the legislative assembly of Nunavut has no parties and operates on consensus.

There are three levels of government in Canada: federal, provincial, and municipal. At the federal level, the government is responsible for voting laws and assuming certain duties such as immigration, defense, international aid, and so on. Provincial governments assume responsibility for such services as health care, education, transportation, and so on. City governments handle local affairs. The administration of the criminal justice system in Canada is divided between those three levels of government working in cooperation with and complementing each other.

Legal System

The Constitution is the supreme law of Canada and consists of an amalgamation of codified acts, passed by the Parliament of Canada and by provincial legislature, and uncodified conventions and traditions. In 1982, the adoption of the Canadian Charter of Rights and Freedom in the Constitution Act affected the operations of the criminal justice agencies. The charter is the constitutional guarantee of collective and individual rights and provides rights such as freedom of religion and of beliefs, freedom of expression, freedom of association, and so on. It protects many rights in the domain of justice: rights to life, rights to be protected from unreasonable search and seizure, rights to legal counsel, rights against self-incrimination, rights not to be subject to cruel and unusual punishment, and so on.

All Canadian laws formally derive their power from the Constitution, which also enumerates the subject matters on which either level of government (federal or provincial) may legitimately enact legislation. The Constitution established criminal law as the sole jurisdiction of the federal government, whereas the provinces have exclusive control over civil law (also called private law), which encompasses numerous areas of law involving disputes between parties (individuals, corporations, and government). Even if provincial governments cannot enact criminal law legislation, they do have the power to promulgate quasi-criminal or regulatory offenses in a variety of administrative and other areas, and every province has done so with myriad rules and regulations across a broad spectrum. The administration of justice and penal matters is under the jurisdiction of the provinces, so each province administers most of the criminal and penal laws through provincial and municipal police forces.

The Canadian legal system has its foundation in the British common law legal system. Interestingly, the province of Quebec still retains a civil law legal system for civil law matters because its roots go back to the French colonial era. Common law systems place great weight on the precedents of court decisions, which are considered "law" with the same force of law as statutes. By contrast, in a civil law legal system, court decision precedents are given less weight, and scholarly literature is given more.

The Criminal Code of Canada is the codification of most of the criminal offenses and procedure in Canada. The criminal code was enacted in 1892 and has been revised numerous times. The current version dates back to the 1985 consolidated statuses. Other important Canadian criminal laws are the Firearms Act, the Controlled Drugs and Substances Act, the Canada Evidence Act, the Food and Drugs Act, the Youth Criminal Justice Act, and the Contraventions Act. Although the national criminal code applies everywhere, criminal justice agencies are mostly administrated at the provincial level, with the exception of the national police and the correctional services of Canada handling prisoners with longer sentences. The criminal justice system is based on the trilogy of law enforcement, the courts, and correctional services.

Police Services

There are currently three major types of police organizations in Canada: municipal, provincial, and federal. Constitutionally, police organizations are a provincial responsibility, but most urban areas have been given the right to have their own police forces. Most cities have a municipal police service, and many city services can coexist in larger metropolitan areas. However, in recent years, there has been a trend toward merging smaller, adjoining police services. In the provinces of Quebec, Newfoundland, and Ontario, there is a provincial police service covering the territories not under the jurisdiction of a municipal police service and offering more specialized services to local law enforcement agencies.

In the other provinces and territories, the Royal Canadian Mounted Police (RCMP), known as the Mounties, provide the same services as the Sûreté du Québec, the Royal Newfoundland Constabulary, and the Ontario Provincial Police. The RCMP also has a nationwide role in enforcing various federal statutes, but it is mainly concerned with drug importation, organizing police services in aboriginal communities, managing database information services, and so on. The Canadian Security Intelligence Service deals with terrorism matters and other international threats to the safety of Canadians. There are also other parallel private police services, mainly dealing with ports, railroads, and airports and having the same power as other government forces. In Canada the army and government militias play no role in law enforcement matters.

According to Statistics Canada, in 2007 there were 64,000 sworn police officers in Canada, for a rate of 206 police officers per 100,000 Canadians (or 1 police officer per every 512 citizens). This police-population ratio has been pretty constant since 1972. However, in recent decades, there has been a large growth in the number of private security personnel.

Recently, one of the goals of law enforcement agencies has been to reflect the diversity of the community served. Therefore, there have been efforts to integrate more women and minorities into the police forces across Canada. Less than 1 percent of police officers were women in the early 1970s, but in 2007, women accounted for 18 percent of the total and 21 percent of the patrol officers. According to Statistics Canada, the total police services expenditures in 2007 were C$10 billion (approx. US$8.6 billion), or C$300 (approx. US$259) per citizen.

Crime

Classification of Crimes

A person may be prosecuted criminally for any offense found in the criminal code or any other statute containing criminal offenses. There are three types of offenses in criminal law: summary conviction offenses, indictable offenses, and hybrid offenses. The most minor are summary conviction offenses. These offenses are heard by a judge and are punishable by a fine of no more than C$2,000 (approx. US$1,732) and/or six months in jail. The most serious are the indictable offenses. The available penalties are greater for indictable offenses than for summary offenses, and the person charged with an indictable offense has the choice of being heard by only a judge or by a judge and a jury. Most offenses defined by the criminal code are hybrid offenses, which allow the prosecution to choose to prosecute the offense as a summary or an indictable offense. It is important to note that until the crown elects how to prosecute the offense, it is treated as indictable.

Crime Statistics

Since 1962, information on crimes known by the police in Canada has been relayed from local jurisdictions to the Canadian Centre for Justice Statistics, an agency of Statistics Canada, and compiled as the Uniform Crime Reports (UCR). With these data, the trend of homicide in Canada shows an important increase from the late 1960s to the end of the 1970s. According to Statistics Canada, the homicide rate in 1960 and 1965 was 1.4 per 100,000. Then 1970 appears to have been a period of social transformation with major changes in values. Many commentators have blamed the boost in crime on the arrival of very large cohorts of teenagers and young adults born in the postwar baby-boom period. The homicide rate peaked at 3.03 per 100,000 in 1975. Since a bump at 2.69 in 1991, it has declined and stood at 1.80 per 100,000 in 2007.

In the UCR system, crimes are grouped into the larger categories of violent crimes, property crimes, and other forms of crimes. In addition, infractions against the various drug laws and infractions related to traffic behaviors are computed separately. Following are selected crime rates per 100,000 people for 2006 from Statistics Canada:

Arson	41
Assaults	735
Burglary	768
Drug-related crimes	295
Fraud	284
Motor-vehicle theft	487
Robbery	94
Sexual aggression	68
Theft	1,941

In 2006, there were 2,572,770 crimes declared or known to the police for a population of just 32,623,000 people. Hence, 1 of every 12 Canadians officially experienced some form of victimization during that year. However, given the fact that a large majority of crimes are either not known by the victim or known but not declared to the police, it is obvious that the real incidence of crime is much higher than what official statistics shows us. Every five years, Statistics Canada conducts a national victimization survey of about 25,000 respondents. The 2005 survey shows that 24 percent of Canadians had experienced in the last 12 months one of the 11 types of crimes portrayed in the survey, 7 percent having been the victim of a violent crime and 12 percent having been the victim of a simple theft.

Finding of Guilt

Court System

The court system of Canada is made up of many courts differing in levels of legal superiority and separated by jurisdiction. Some of the courts are federal in nature, whereas others are provincial, territorial, or municipal. The provinces have jurisdiction over the administration of justice in their territory. Almost all cases, whether criminal or civil, start in provincial courts and may eventually be appealed to higher-level courts. As with all common law countries, Canadian law adheres to the doctrine of stare decisis, meaning lower courts are bound by and must follow the decisions of higher courts. However, decisions made by a province's highest court (provincial courts of appeal) are not binding on other provinces, although they are considered persuasive. Only the Supreme Court of Canada, created by Parliament in 1875, has the authority to bind all courts in the country with a single ruling. This intricate interweaving of federal and provincial powers is typical of the Canadian Constitution.

Investigation and Prosecution

Once the police have been informed of a crime, a police officer will proceed to an investigation. When the investigation is over, a police officer will appear before a judge to declare under oath that he or she has reasonable motive to believe that the person has committed a crime only if the prosecution has agreed. The judge will examine the case before giving his approval to charge the suspect with a crime. If a person has been arrested for having presumably committed a crime, he or she has to be charged within one day or be released.

During this appearance, the suspect will plead guilty or not guilty to the charges levied. Once charged by a prosecutor, the suspect will appear within three days before a provincial court in which the judge will decide whether the accused should remain in custody before trial. During the trial, the prosecutor must prove that the accused has engaged in a criminal conduct (as defined by the criminal code and known as the *actus reus* or "external element") accompanied by a criminal state of mind (known as the *mens rea* or "fault element") on a standard of "beyond reasonable doubt." The specific elements of each offense can be found in the wording of the offense as well as the case law interpreting it. Specified external elements are typically required in an act of accusation: there must be an "act" committed under some "circumstances" and sometimes having a specific "consequence" caused by the action. If there is a total absence of proof on one of the essential elements of the offense, the case will be dismissed. In Canada, a person accused of a felony has a right to trial before a judge alone or to a trial before a judge and jury, in which the judge applies the law and the jury appreciates the facts. Relatively few high-profile cases are heard by a judge and jury. In almost all courts, legal aid is provided to individuals who have limited monetary resources.

Court Case Processing

Data on adult criminal courts from Statistics Canada show that the most frequent crimes processed in courts are driving while intoxicated, simple assault, and simple theft (respectively, 12 percent, 9 percent, and 8 percent of all infractions). Criminal courts in Canada rely heavily on plea bargaining to speed up the process. Yet a common problem with courts in Canada is that the average time between arraignment and a decision is 192 days. Although this situation is well known, attempts and reforms to speeds things up have not been successful given that criminal cases have become more and more complicated with time. The federal government has now decided to increase the number of judges in provincial superior courts across the country to keep pace with the increasing demands on the justice system. Contrary to what has happened in civil law matters and in the treatment of juvenile offenders, alternatives to the traditional judicial process, such as mediation, diversion, or restorative justice programs, have not yet been fully implemented. Although there are many pilot projects on justice alternatives, there is still much resistance from victims of criminal acts and pressure from the media impeding development in that sector. Juveniles are treated by a separate justice system in which diversion programs are an important part.

Victim Services

In recent years, various services for victims of crimes have been developed, including legal representation, victim impact statements, and compensation. Legal representation of victims refers to the obligation of the attorney general to take reasonable measures to ensure that the victim is provided with advice and representation by a lawyer.

Victim impact statements are written accounts prepared by crime victims detailing the physical, financial, emotional, or psychological impact that a crime has had on their lives. In effect, they enable crime victims to say, in their own words, how their lives have been affected by the convicted criminal's acts. The criminal code broadly defines who a victim is for the purposes of a victim impact statement (e.g., in cases of homicide). Completed statements are presented to the court following conviction, but prior to sentencing. In Canada the federal Department of Justice began testing various models of victim impact statements in the mid-1980s. In 1995, amendments were made to the criminal code requiring the court to consider a victim impact statement where one has been submitted. The procedures related to the preparation and submissions of these statements vary by province/territory.

In Canada, financial compensation for victims of violent or personal crimes is administered by the provinces, according to their own rules and standards. This overview provides information generally applicable to all provincial programs; however, some programs may offer more services and benefits than those mentioned here. Claimants are generally victims of violent or personal crimes and dependents of homicide victims. Generally, a victim must report a crime to the police within a year of its occurrence to be eligible, but exceptions can be made. Also, citizens of foreign countries are eligible to apply for compensation. Medical expenses, mental health expenses, lost wages for incapacitated or disabled victims, rehabilitation expenses for disabled victims, services to replace work in the home previously performed by the victim, funeral expenses, and loss of support for dependents of victims are generally covered by provincial compensation programs. The maximum award benefits range between C$5,000 to C$25,000.

Punishment

Types of Punishments

Once a person has been found guilty of committing a criminal offense, sentencing is the sole responsibility of the judge. A wide range of sanctions can be imposed: absolute discharge, conditional discharge, probation, restitution, fines, community service, conditional sentence, intermittent imprisonment, and imprisonment. In some cases, the judge can decide to designate a person convicted of a violent crime under the dangerous offender provision. Here, the offender will be kept imprisoned until he or she is considered no more at risk of violent reoffending. The death penalty was officially abolished in 1976, although there had been no executions since 1962.

The fundamental principle of sentencing is that the sentence must be proportionate to the gravity of the offense and the degree of responsibility of the offender. A sentence should also be increased or reduced to account for any relevant aggravating or mitigating circumstances relating to the offense or the offender. Finally, an offender should not be deprived of liberty if less restrictive sanctions may be appropriate in the circumstances. The judge considers sentence propositions by the prosecutor and the defense attorney and uses guidelines from the criminal code and jurisprudence to impose a sentence. He or she might also require a presentence report that would be written by a probation officer describing, among other things, the person's criminal history, employment history, family situation, and substance abuse. Given the seriousness of the crime and the person's criminal history, as well as other factors, the judge provides a sentencing decision.

In Canada, a majority of people accused of a crime are later found guilty given that police and prosecutors will carry charges only when the evidence is strong. In most cases, the defendant will eventually plead guilty on lesser charges or on the basis of a sentence agreement between the prosecutor and the defense attorney that will in most cases be ratified.

Correctional Services

In Canada, the administration of correctional services is shared between the federal and provincial or territorial governments. Offenders sentenced for two years or longer in prison are the responsibility of federal correctional authorities, whereas offenders receiving sentences of less than two years in prison, community sentences such as fines, community service work, or probation, as well as suspects in custody while waiting trial, are under provincial and territorial correctional authorities.

There are three levels of security within the Correctional Service of Canada (CSC): maximum, medium, and minimum. Case management is completed by institutional parole officers (IPO) within institutions and by community parole officers in the community. The IPO completes a comprehensive assessment of the offender's criminality and formulates an "offender security classification report" and a "correctional plan." However, for offenders who receive a life sentence, there is a mandatory two-year residency at a maximum-security institution, regardless of the offender's behavior.

Most inmates are released on parole after serving a third of their sentence or are subjected to community supervision after serving two-thirds of their sentence. However, in some special cases, an inmate can be released and be subjected to community supervision after serving a sixth of his or her sentence. A parole board has complete responsibility for making liberty decisions at the point in the court-imposed sentence where an offender is allowed to live in the community on conditional release. In the case of first-degree homicide, the duration of imprisonment is fixed by law at 25 years, but special circumstances may lead to a release after 15 years. In the case of non-premeditated homicide, the judge may decide on a given period of time before the person may ask for a conditional release.

Statistics from 2002–2003 illustrate the range of sentences for major crimes. For homicide, 87.7 percent of offenders were incarcerated for an average of 10.8 years, 6.5 percent received a suspended sentence, and 8 percent were granted probation. For robbery, 71.9 percent of cases resulted in incarceration for an average of 624 days, 8.1 percent of sentences were suspended, and 54.2 percent included probation. In contrast, for theft cases, 38.8 percent involved incarceration for an average of 30 days, 4.8 percent were suspended, and 50.3 included probation. For drug possession, 13.6 percent were incarcerated for an average of 10 days, 1.2 percent of cases were suspended, and 29.3 percent included probation.

According to Statistics Canada, there are approximately 32,000 adults imprisoned on any given day (two-thirds are condemned, and the others are awaiting trial) and a total of 120,500 adults under some form of community surveillance. An analysis of the characteristics of persons admitted in prison in five provinces for 2005–2006 shows interesting results. First, women represent 10 percent of all prisoners admitted in detention, and Natives are largely overrepresented relative to their percentage in the general population. Overall, 94 percent of all those admitted to prison are drug users or have alcohol dependency, and 70 percent of the total have employment difficulties. As of 2009, the use of imprisonment in Canada had not changed much in the previous four decades. The total adult incarceration rate has fluctuated between 129 and 150 prisoners per 100,000 adults since the 1970s.

In Canada, aboriginals make up about 5 percent of the total population but constitute an important segment of the population in several provinces/territories: 85 percent in Nunavut (mainly Inuit), 50 percent in the Northwest Territories, 25 percent in Yukon, and 15 percent in Manitoba and Saskatchewan (mainly Indians). In those provinces/territories, aboriginals constitute a much larger proportion of the criminal justice clientele than their weight in the population. For example, aboriginals account for more than 60 percent of all inmates in Saskatchewan and Manitoba. In the past years, the Justice Ministry and the Correctional Service of Canada have been developing national policies and initiatives aimed at addressing the overrepresentation of aboriginal offenders in the criminal justice system. However, the high rate of alcohol abuse and violence among aboriginals is likely to remain a problem given the isolation and poverty of many first-nations communities.

The number of offenders diagnosed with mental health disorders at admission has also been increasing in the last decades. In 2005, 12 percent of male and 26 percent of female offenders were identified with very serious mental health problems, and there was an increasing prevalence of learning disabilities and low-functioning capacities among offenders.

Another current problem in Canadian prisons is drug consumption. About four out of five offenders now arrive at a federal institution with a serious substance abuse problem, with one out of two having committed their crime under the influence of drugs, alcohol, or other intoxicants. In this context, drugs become very valuable inside facilities, sometimes increasing to more than five times their street value. Drugs become a source of power, criminal influence, and currency, and many incidents of violence can be attributed to drug trade activities. In Canadian prisons, state-of-the-art equipment and techniques are used to identify individuals who attempt to smuggle in drugs. The CSC also regularly searches cells, buildings, grounds, and inmates and has a program in place where randomly selected inmates are asked to provide urine samples for drug testing. A range of effective substance-abuse programs, like methadone maintenance treatment for heroin users, is also used to help inmates deal with their addictions.

Inmates of correctional facilities worldwide are at greater risk of contracting HIV infection than the general population because they are more likely to engage in high-risk behaviors such as intravenous drug use, nonsterile tattooing, and unprotected sex. These risky behaviors sometimes continue while incarcerated. Studies in Canada estimate the prevalence of reported HIV cases in provincial and federal offenders to be between 2 percent and 8 percent of the inmate population, and thus nearly 10 times the reported prevalence of 0.2 percent in the general Canadian population. Although many inmates enter the correctional system already infected, others who are uninfected continue to engage in risky behaviors while in prison, placing them at risk of infection. Inmates also have an approximately 30 times higher rate of hepatitis C. The CSC offers its inmates the opportunity to discover their HIV infection status, to be counseled on the meaning of their test result, and to be educated on ways to reduce their risk of acquiring and transmitting HIV. Medical treatment for HIV-infected inmates is a cornerstone of this broad-based approach and uses universally accepted standards of care.

In Canada, many changes have been made over the years in the criminal justice system. Some of the legislation passed recently promotes harsher punishments for offenders and could have an impact on the Canadian incarceration rate. For example, in 2008, the federal government passed the Tackling Violent Crime Act, which changes, among other things, the sentences for persons caught driving under the influence of alcohol and/or drugs. Those offenders will now face a maximum life sentence if they cause death and a maximum 10-year sentence if they cause bodily harm. They will also face a higher maximum penalty on summary conviction of 18 months compared to 6 months previously.

Marc Ouimet and Marie-Eve Boudreau

Further Reading

Carrigan, Owen. (1991). *Crime and Punishment in Canada: A History.* Toronto: McClelland and Stuwart.

Ekstedt, John W., and Curt T. Griffiths. (1984). *Corrections in Canada: Policy and Practice.* Toronto: Butterworth.

Griffiths, Curt T., Brian Whitelaw, and Richard B. Parent. (1999). *Canadian Police Work.* Scarborough, Ontario: ITP Nelson.

Hagan, John. (1991). *The Disreputable Pleasures: Crime and Deviance in Canada.* Toronto: McGraw-Hill.

Ouimet, Marc. (2005). *La criminalité au Québec durant le vingtième siècle.* Québec: Les presses de l'Université Laval.

Cayman Islands

Legal System: Common
Murder: Medium
Prison Rate: High
Death Penalty: No
Corporal Punishment: No

Background

Situated in the Western Caribbean about 150 miles south of Cuba and 180 miles north of Jamaica is the island trio of Grand Cayman, Cayman Brac, and Little Cayman. These are the Cayman Islands, an overseas territory of Britain. The name "Cayman" is derived from the Carib word for marine crocodile. The three islands have a total land area of about 100 square miles.

Population

The history of the Cayman Islands began 500 years ago when Christopher Columbus and his men came upon two very small and low islands in 1503. What first drew visitors—French, Spanish, Dutch, and English—to the Cayman Islands was the abundance of green turtles that provided invaluable food for military forces and ordinary mariners, as well as early settlers on other Caribbean islands. It was only about 300 years ago, between 1670 and 1730, that people began permanent settlement in the Cayman Islands. Legend has it that early settlements were formed by runaway white soldiers and servants from Jamaica, shipwrecked sailors, and buccaneers seeking a quieter life ashore.

Population growth was very gradual until the mid-20th century, but thereafter, there were notable changes in Cayman's population. In 1900, early census figures counted 5,000 residents. In 1943, the population was 6,690—a mere increase of approximately 2,000 persons over a 43-year period. However, between 1960 and 1980, the population of the Cayman Islands doubled from 8,511 to 17,757, and it more than doubled again by 1999, to 39,600 residents.

This astonishing growth was due more to immigration than to natural increase in the local Caymanian population. Fifty-nine percent of Cayman's residents in 1999 were foreign-born and hailed from 100 different countries, with the largest number emigrating from Jamaica. The latest census figures show a resident population of 53,886 in 2007.

Economic Growth

The rapid increase in population during the second half of the 20th century and into the 21st century was mirrored by and directly linked to the remarkable economic growth that took place in the Cayman Islands during this same period. The tourism sector was one of two economic wands that almost magically transformed the islands in the last third of the 20th century from the traditional, homogeneous, undeveloped "islands [that] time forgot" into a booming economy with a GDP of CI$951.9 million by 2006 (approx. US$1.13 billion).

The second magic wand was Cayman's financial industry, which quickly surpassed tourism in economic value to become the country's main revenue earner. Although Cayman provided an attractive environment for offshore banking—one that was stable, secure, well regulated, and discreet—few, if any, Caymanians had any previous experience in high finance. Much of the impetus and expertise had to come from outside.

Political and Legal History

In 1655, an English expedition landed in Jamaica and captured that island from the Spanish, who had been in possession of it since 1494. It has been said that through the Treaty of Madrid in 1670, the Cayman Islands were ceded to the British along with Jamaica. In 1962, Westminster Parliament enacted the Jamaica Independence Act, but the act excluded Cayman Islands from the definition of Jamaica. Consequently, after August 6, 1962, sovereignty by Great Britain over Jamaica ceased but was retained over the Cayman Islands. Moreover, the West Indies Act, which came into force in April 1962, vested in Her Majesty in Council full power to provide for the government of the Cayman Islands. This power was exercised to create a new Constitution Order for the Cayman Islands that came into operation to coincide with the independence of Jamaica. Under the 1962 Constitution Order, powers formerly exercised by the governor of Jamaica as governor of the Cayman Islands were conferred upon an administrator appointed by the Crown. There were further replacement Constitution Orders after 1962, but it is the 1972 Order that currently governs the Cayman Islands' Constitution.

Under this Constitution, legislative powers are vested in the Legislative Assembly, which includes members of an executive council. The executive powers are vested in a governor and an executive council. However, given the subordinate status of these islands as a British colony, the executive arm of government is subject to the control of the Crown. The governor of the Cayman Islands is appointed by the Crown. He is obliged to act in accordance with royal instructions, and he holds office at Her Majesty's pleasure. The Crown also retains ultimate control over the other arms of government. For example, Her Majesty has a power of disallowance of any laws enacted by the local legislature, and the Privy Council of the United Kingdom is the final domestic court of appeal for the Cayman Islands.

The Role and Organization of the Police

The Royal Cayman Islands Police Service (RCIPS), which is for the most part an unarmed police force, undertakes the traditional policing role of keeping the peace and preventing and detecting crime. There is no standing army in the Cayman Islands; hence, national security falls within the purview of the RCIPS and the British government.

Despite the fact that the Cayman Islands have a duly elected government, a cabinet, and a leader of government business, it is quite clear that the governor is a formidable figure in the Cayman Islands. The governor has powers to initiate investigations, as he sees fit, into alleged misconduct on the part of any public figure or into any department that falls under his purview, and these include the police force and the judiciary. Recent evidence of this is the action taken by the governor of the Cayman Islands on March 27, 2008, when he announced that the police commissioner, the deputy commissioner, and a senior detective chief superintendent were being put on required leave to allow an investigating team from the Metropolitan Police Service to proceed with their inquiries into allegations against them.

The police service in Cayman is made up of approximately 350 police and auxiliary officers, and it is supported by 67 civilian members of staff and a team of special constables. Roughly 40 percent of the RCIPS's overall staff is non-Caymanian, primarily men and women from other Caribbean islands and from Britain. The commissioner of police is recruited from the United Kingdom. There has been only one short-lived exception to this practice: a Caymanian held the post between September 2003 and September 2005.

The RCIPS has decentralized its operations across the three islands. There is one police station in Cayman Brac and one in Little Cayman, and there are five stations in Grand Cayman—one in each of the five districts into which this largest island is divided. Each police station is headed by a chief inspector. In addition to the response officers who are based at each police station and the neighborhood policing officers who address existing concerns in their respective communities, there are a number of special units. These include the Criminal Investigation Department, the Financial Crimes Unit, the Traffic Unit, the Drugs Task Force, the Marine Support Unit, the Family Support Unit, the Uniform Support Group (providers of firearm support), and the K9 Unit. The RCIPS is also supported by training and forensic officers.

The police, through its Marine Support Unit, have responsibility for the interdiction of vessels involved in drug smuggling and for search and rescue at sea. In recent years, in addition to responding to fishing vessels in distress, there has been the challenge of boats loaded with Cubans attempting to make illegal entry into the Cayman Islands at various spots along much of Grand Cayman's unprotected coastline. In these situations, the Marine Unit of RCIPS escorts them into safe harbor and hands them over to the Immigration Department, which takes responsibility for their fate. A joint Marine Support Unit is currently being formed in conjunction with the Department of Customs and the Department of Immigration and will have responsibility for security and safety at sea.

Crime

Classification of Crime

There are three basic distinctions in terms of the classification of offenses in the Cayman Islands. Category A offenses are indictable and are tried only in the Grand Court (e.g., murder, rape, robbery, arson). Category B includes both indictable and nonindictable offenses and can be adjudicated in either the Grand Court or a summary court before a magistrate (e.g., burglary, indecent assault, gang activity, theft). Category C offenses, less serious crimes, are tried only in the magistrates' summary courts, where as a rule the maximum sentence handed down is two years (e.g., unlawful use of firearms, insulting the modesty of a woman). There are, however, exceptions to this rule, an example of which is a magistrate exercising his or her jurisdiction under the Misuse of Drugs Law (2000 Revision). The judicial officer is allowed to impose penalties of 20 years and a fine of unlimited amount and 30 years with a fine of unlimited amount for a range of supply-type offenses involving two ounces or more of hard drugs.

Age of Criminal Responsibility

The Youth Justice Law (2005 Revision) provides for a separate court for young persons to be tried for offenses. A child under 10 years old cannot be held criminally responsible. A child under the age of 14 can be held criminally responsible only if it can be proven that he or she had the capacity to know that the act was wrong at the time it was committed. Additionally, a male child under the age of 12 is presumed incapable of having carnal knowledge.

Illicit Drugs

The importation, trafficking, and use of illegal drugs, particularly marijuana, cocaine in its various forms, and "designer drugs," are cause for concern. As detailed in the Misuse of Drugs Law (2000 Revision), there are several offenses under which an individual may be charged. However, typical drug charges include importation or possession with intent to supply, possession or consumption of a controlled drug, cultivating ganja, and possession of a drug utensil.

With the introduction of the Drug Court in Cayman in 2007, provision has been made for persons charged with certain types of drug or drug-related offenses to receive rehabilitative treatment instead of facing criminal proceedings and court sanctions. An offender is eligible for consideration by the Drug Court if the person is not under the age of 17, appears dependent on the use of drugs, and is charged with a relevant offense, including drug offenses of simple possession and consumption and offenses of theft, handling of stolen goods, robbery, or burglary that appear to be motivated by drug dependency. However, drug possession with intent to supply where the offender was not also a consumer of the drug and offenses involving violent conduct or sexual assault are not relevant offenses, and their perpetrators are not eligible for consideration in the Drug Court of the Cayman Islands.

The Caribbean has been for some time now a haven for drug traffickers, and the Cayman Islands is no exception. The island character permits entry into and use of Caribbean territories from the surrounding sea at literally hundreds of different points. The geographical location allows for proximity to drug-producing nations, namely Colombia, Honduras, and Jamaica. The Cayman Islands is essentially in a drug-trafficking vortex situated between a major drug producer (i.e., South America) and a major drug consumer (i.e., North America).

Closely linked to the challenge of drug trafficking is the importation of illegal firearms. Illegal and unlicensed guns, which are at times used in committing crimes locally, are often included in shipments of drugs coming to the Cayman Islands from Nicaragua, Honduras, Jamaica, and so on.

Taking of Marine Life

The Cayman Islands probably have the most robust marine conservation laws in the entire Caribbean. Obviously developed to specifically curb destructive practices, there are laws to prevent the taking of certain sea creatures outside of the approved fishing season (e.g., lobster, turtles, conch, etc.) and to prevent damage to underwater flora and fauna. For example, anyone who takes or receives lobsters from Cayman waters between the months of March and November is guilty of an offense. Taking more than three lobsters in any one day during the open season is also an offense. Similar restrictions apply to conch, Nassau groupers, whelks, and other species in need of protection. There are also areas designated as marine parks that are closed to members of the public. No fishing is allowed in these areas, and entry is restricted to those who are licensed by the Marine Conservation Board. The regulations under the Marine Conservation Law are strictly enforced and carry a heavy penalty. Persons found guilty of any offense under this law are liable on summary conviction to a fine of CI$500,000 (approx. US$592,500) and to imprisonment for 12 months. In addition, the court may confiscate any vessel or equipment that was used or was intended to be used in the commission of the offense.

Financial Crimes

The Cayman Islands has emerged to be the world's fifth-largest financial center. With almost 300 banks registered and around 1 trillion U.S. dollars on deposit and booked through the Cayman Islands, banking is undoubtedly big business. Grand Cayman is now home to 426 bank and trust companies. It is the number one jurisdiction for hedge funds in terms of both funds formed there and net assets held by these funds. As of June 2008, there were 10,037 funds registered with the Cayman Islands Monetary Authority (CIMA), including many of the world's largest multibillion-dollar hedge funds. Cayman is the leading domicile for health care insurance companies, and with 740 companies registered, it is the second-largest offshore center for captive insurance in the world. In addition, the management of private and commercial trusts is important business, with 135 trust companies registered in Cayman.

The Cayman Islands' government has spared no effort over the years in ensuring that there are strict laws and regulations in effect to maintain the integrity of the financial services sector. In 1984, the Cayman Islands signed the Narcotics Agreement with the United States and Great Britain and, two years later, a Mutual Legal Assistance Treaty. Through these instruments, the governments agreed to share information about known drug traffickers and money launderers and to provide assistance to apprehend offenders. Cayman undertook to give information about the flow of money from suspect sources, under strict conditions that would not breach the general rule of confidentiality.

For example, the Cayman Islands has always subjected its hedge fund investments to one of the toughest anti–money laundering regimes, in terms of due diligence required on those forming and investing in these funds, as well as in the reporting requirements for any suspicious activities. The Cayman Islands' banks are also bound by strict money laundering laws that, together with "know-your-customer" (KYC) regulations, are recognized as meeting or even exceeding those of all major onshore jurisdictions. It is noteworthy that in 1995 the Cayman Islands became the first member of a Caribbean Financial Action Task Force to voluntarily put its financial services and practices under the scrutiny of a panel of legal, financial, and law enforcement experts. The panel indicated that the Cayman Islands' progressive attitude countering money laundering demonstrated that such policies were compatible with a developing offshore financial center. In September 1996, through the Proceeds of Criminal Conduct Law, the Cayman Islands also became the first British-dependent territory to adopt a more stringent attitude and policy against international financial criminals.

Crime Statistics

Property crime and other crimes of acquisition, including the very lucrative offense of drug trafficking, are the most common crimes committed in Cayman as a whole. There is very little crime on the sister islands of Cayman Brac and Little Cayman compared to Grand Cayman. Within Grand Cayman, there is a higher incidence of crime in George Town, the capital, because of a greater concentration of residences, hotels, and people (residents and visitors) in town and the surrounding areas. According to the Overseas Territories Recording Crime Intelligence Services, in 2007, the RCIPS recorded 3 murders, 13 rapes, 3 armed robberies, 561 burglaries, 478 thefts, 10 cases of possession of cocaine/crack with intent to supply, and 28 cases of possession of ganja with intent to supply.

Finding of Guilt

The legal system in the Cayman Islands is accusatorial, which facilitates a keen contest between the prosecution and defense in the presentation of legal arguments to the court. Unlike the inquisitorial system, the presiding judicial officer remains aloof of any investigative or evidence-gathering processes. Instead, the primary role of the judge or magistrate is adjudication—to direct the jury (where applicable) on matters of law and make a judicial determination based on the facts and law.

Rights of the Accused

Accused persons are innocent until proven guilty. For culpability to be proven, the evidence presented in the case against the accused must establish guilt beyond a reasonable doubt. The accused has a right to elect trial by judge and jury or by judge alone for indictable offenses. Accused persons have a right to a fair and speedy trial and may plead guilty to lesser offenses where those offenses are established on the facts. The prosecution determines whether pleas to lesser offenses are acceptable.

The Legal Aid Law (1999 Revision) provides for assistance to persons who are charged with scheduled offenses and offenses that can be tried in the Grand Court but who do not have the means to instruct an attorney to advise or represent them. Under these circumstances, the court shall grant a certificate entitling such persons to free or subsidized legal services throughout the proceedings of their case and in any appeal. Scheduled offenses include but are not limited to arson, assault causing grievous bodily harm, burglary, carnal knowledge offenses, rape, manslaughter, and murder. Persons charged with offenses punishable with imprisonment for 14 years or more are also eligible for legal aid.

Investigation and Prosecution of Cases

The police conduct investigations into most crimes. Other departments that conduct their own investigations into specific matters include the departments of Immigration, Customs, Pensions, Planning, Labor, and Health Insurance, the Office of the Auditor-General, and the Office of the Complaints Commissioner. The police prosecute traffic offenses. All other offenses are prosecuted by the attorney general's office.

Alternatives to Trial

Negotiated settlement and dispute resolution are not alternatives to going to trial in the Cayman

Islands, and although there is no formal system of plea bargaining, pleas can be offered by defense counsel who may also seek a "goodyear direction" from the court. This U.K. case precedent permits a trial judge to give an early indication of possible sentence if a plea was to be offered to a particular offense.

The majority of criminal cases in the Cayman Islands go to trial. Incarceration before and while awaiting trial is allowed. If an individual is charged with an offense and has not been granted bail, he or she will be remanded to prison. The length of pretrial detention varies but is typically six to nine months.

The Court System

The courts administer justice in keeping with the Constitution, the laws of the islands, and the common law that has been developed through precedent set by the decisions of local, British, and other Commonwealth courts and reflected in the written judgments of cases. Although the common law applies, it can be modified by locally enacted laws. Some laws are made by the United Kingdom for the Cayman Islands through an order-in-council. In some cases, this imposes on the overseas territory a legal position that might otherwise not be initiated by the local Legislative Assembly, given prevailing sentiments in the islands on a particular issue. For example, by way of the Caribbean Territories (Criminal Law) Order 2000, homosexual acts in private for consenting persons over age 18 in all U.K. overseas territories were legalized.

The judicial system of the Cayman Islands consists of four levels of jurisdiction. The three summary courts, which have both criminal and civil jurisdiction, are presided over by a chief magistrate and two other magistrates. Appeals are to the Grand Court, which also has an original jurisdiction equivalent to that of the English High Court of Justice in all its divisions. Presiding over the Grand Court is a chief justice and three puisne (associate) judges. Appeals from the Grand Court go to the Court of Appeal, which is composed of distinguished jurists from the wider Caribbean and elsewhere in the Commonwealth. The final appellate court for the Cayman Islands is the Privy Council in London.

There is no shortage of judicial officers in Cayman, the majority of whom are from Jamaica but now reside in Cayman. To date, there are no Caymanian-born magistrates or judges. Grand Court judges must be qualified to practice as a barrister or solicitor in England or the Commonwealth and have practiced for not less than 10 years. Magistrates must be qualified to practice as a barrister or solicitor in England or the Commonwealth and have practiced for not less than 5 years.

Juvenile System

The Juveniles Law provides a system for dealing with young persons in need of care and protection and who are considered to be incorrigible. The Youth Justice Law (2005 Revision) provides for a separate court for persons under the age of 17. It should be noted that no young person can be dealt with by the court without the intervention of a social worker who will provide a social inquiry report on the background, school record, and home circumstances of the young person. A number of options are available to the Juvenile/Youth Court in responding to children who are either juvenile delinquents or "victims" of some negative circumstances and must be placed in a safe environment. With respect to juvenile and young offenders, judicial officers have the following sentencing options: probation, admonish and discharge, conditional discharge, fines, parental fines, community service, fit person order, juvenile and youth rehabilitation orders, and as a last resort, Eagle House, which is tantamount to a youth prison.

Punishment

Types of Punishment

Fines, prison, probation, compensation, suspended sentences, and community service orders are the forms of punishment typically used in the Cayman Islands. The Alternative Sentencing Law of 2006, which is soon to be implemented as of this writing, will provide for other types of sentences such as curfew orders, exclusion orders, suspended sentences with supervision, electronic monitoring, and victim restitution.

The typical punishment for murder is imprisonment for life, which means the offender's natural life. However, this rigid policy on the sentence of "life" is currently being revisited with a view to introducing a tariff system. The typical punishment for rape is 12 to 14 years' imprisonment, with a maximum penalty of life imprisonment. The typical sentence for serious theft and burglary is 3 to 8 years, and for robbery it is 5 to 10 years, depending on compounding factors such as possession of an illegal firearm with intent to commit an indictable offense, causing grievous bodily harm, and other such offenses. Therefore, although the maximum sentence for these crimes is 14 years' imprisonment, sentences vary depending on the seriousness of the offense, the use of a weapon, the use of a firearm, the extent of violence involved, and the loss to the victim.

The most serious drug offense in the Cayman Islands is the trafficking of hard drugs (e.g., importation/possession of cocaine with intent to supply), and its perpetrators are usually sent to prison for 8 to 12 years, depending on the quantity. The maximum sentence is 20 years' imprisonment.

The death penalty was abolished in the Cayman Islands by way of a 1991 U.K. order-in-council that nullified any law in force in Cayman with respect to the death penalty. It stipulated that no person convicted for the crime of murder shall be sentenced to death but shall be sentenced to imprisonment for life instead. In 2000, the legislature of the Cayman Islands amended its penal code to reflect the abolition of the death penalty.

Prison

There are three institutions of penal incarceration: Her Majesty's Prison (HMP) Northward for adult males, Fairbanks for females (adult and uncontrollable teenagers), and Eagle House for young males. According to the Office of the Commissioner of Corrections and Rehabilitation, the daily average population in these facilities is 203 adult males, 12 male youth, and 15 females. The Cayman Islands has a very high rate of imprisonment of 429 inmates per 100,000 population.

The biggest prison is the one designated for adult males, HMP Northward. It is located on the main island of Grand Cayman, as are the other two facilities. There are a number of challenges associated with the management of Northward prison. First, the public has direct access to the perimeter fence, and this introduces a considerable security risk. There is no outer cordon. In fact, a public road passes right behind the fence at the back. One can therefore drive directly up to the fence in the front or back of the facility and toss an item or package over the fence, although it is a high fence. This has been a means by which contraband has entered the facility. Second, Northward prison is 50 percent overcrowded. The facility's stated capacity is 135, and the daily average is over 200 adult male inmates.

Third, the population at the prison is mixed. Pretrial detainees, long-term convicts, short-term inmates, the mentally ill, and those remanded for sentencing are not necessarily housed separately. There is, however, a maximum-security wing and caged area called the Basic Unit for those who display violent conduct and pose a security a risk as well as for those who are certified mentally ill and are a risk to themselves and others.

Fourth, there are parts of the physical compound of Northward prison that are in bad condition and cannot be used. Buildings condemned by civil engineers had to be recently demolished. However, as revealed during an interview with the Commissioner of Corrections and Rehabilitation, approval has been granted for the construction of a new prison at Northward. This will see the closure of both Eagle House and Fairbanks as separate prisons and the relocation of their populations to separate and secure facilities within the new Northward prison compound.

Although work is compulsory by law for inmates, there are not enough work programs ongoing to involve all inmates, so a number of them are actually idle during the day. In addition to prison domestic duties, some inmates are involved in a fairly substantial farm program, and others work in the woodwork shop, in physical plant maintenance, or in small construction projects at one of the three facilities. It should be noted, however, that although work is compulsory for inmates, their participation in sentence planning is not. Therefore, if an inmate does not wish to undergo training and/or rehabilitation, there is no obligation.

Inmates are entitled to weekly visits from family and friends. Privileges include recreation, phone calls, and out-of-cell activities such as gym time, football, and basketball.

Prisoner Exchange or Transfer

Although there is no evidence of prisoners being exchanged between Cayman and other countries, prisoners can be transferred. Provided that the particular country has agreed to accept their citizens who are incarcerated in foreign jurisdictions, Cayman authorities would repatriate those inmates. For example, in 2008, a Canadian citizen who was serving a life sentence for killing his girlfriend was transferred to a Canadian prison to serve the remainder of this sentence.

Jamaicans constitute the largest proportion of foreign-born inmates at HMP Northward. In the past, the Cayman Islands Prison Service transferred a number of Jamaican prisoners to finish their sentences in their homeland, but the Jamaican authorities stopped the practice. There was also a case of five prisoners being sent to serve their sentences in Britain because they posed a security risk in the local prison. These inmates were believed by authorities to be the main instigators of the 1999 prison riot at HMP Northward during which time prison officers were injured and the inmates took charge of the facility. Their removal was therefore seen as expedient.

Yolande C. Forde

Further Reading

Barker, Deborah. (2007). *Criminal Litigation in the Cayman Islands.* 2nd ed. Cayman Islands: C.I.L.S. Academic Press.

Craton, Michael. (2004). *Founded upon the Seas—A History of the Cayman Islands and Their People.* Kingston, Jamaica: Ian Randle Publishers.

Davies, Elizabeth. (1989). *The Legal System of the Cayman Islands.* Oxford: Law Reports International.

Forde, Yolande. (2006, June). "Pre-Disposing Factors to Criminality in the Cayman Islands." Report submitted to the Government of the Cayman Islands. http://www.education.gov.ky/pls/portal/docs/PAGE/MEHHOME/EDUCATION/CURRICULUM/SENREPORT/FULLREPORT/SENCONSULTATIONREPORTFINAL.PDF.

Government of Cayman Islands. Economic and Statistics Office: http://www.eso.ky.

Judicial Administration and Portfolio of Legal Affairs Information: http://www.caymanjudiciallegalinfo.ky.

*The author is grateful to the attorney general, the solicitor general, the acting commissioner of police, the commissioner of corrections and rehabilitation, and the chief magistrate of the Cayman Islands, as well as the law librarian and her assistant, Rev. Mary Graham, and Doralyn Stewart.

Chile

Legal System: Civil
Murder: Low
Burglary: High
Corruption: Low
Human Trafficking: Medium
Prison Rate: High
Death Penalty: No
Corporal Punishment: No

Background

The Republic of Chile is a democratic country with a population of 16.8 million inhabitants. Its territory of 302,778 square miles occupies a long coastal strip, with the Andes mountains on the eastern border and the Pacific Ocean to the west. The terrain and the climate divide the country into three regions: arid desert in the north, subtropical and fertile valleys in the central portion, and volcanoes and lakes bathed in yearlong cool and damp weather in south.

Nearly 90 percent of the population lives in urban areas, with more than one-third of Chileans concentrated in the metropolitan region of Santiago, which is the capital city of the republic. Whites and those of mixed white/Amerindian heritage constitute the ethnic majority (95 percent), whereas the Mapuches remain the largest aboriginal group. Although the Roman Catholic Church still dominates the religious landscape, evangelical Protestants have rapidly expanded their influence in Chile and now make up 15 percent of the population.

This previously impoverished South American country has built a successful market economy and now actively participates in global trade. Exports account for 40 percent of the gross domestic product: as of 2009, Chile had signed 57 bilateral or regional trade agreements with other countries or regions, more than any other economy in the world. The sustained economic growth in the two decades prior to 2009 has raised the median income to US$15,000. Yet about 18 percent of Chileans still live below the poverty line, and income inequality is significant. Ninety-five percent of adults are literate, and life expectancy hovers around 77 years of age.

Before the arrival of the Spanish in the 16th century, northern Chile was part of the Inca Empire, and central and southern Chile was controlled by the Mapuche Indians. Chile became formally independent of Spain in 1810, but the Spanish forces were not decisively defeated until 1818. Chile fought against Peru and Bolivia in the War of the Pacific (1879–1883), from whom it annexed its present northern territories. Immediately after the war, the victorious Chilean Army launched the bloody pacification of the Araucanian region to completely and permanently subjugate the Mapuche Indians.

After a series of elected governments, the three-year-old Marxist government of Salvador Allende was overthrown in 1973 by a military coup led by Augusto Pinochet, who left more than 2,900 Chileans dead and missing during his 17-year military dictatorship. In contrast to its ironhanded political rule, the Pinochet administration pursued decidedly laissez-faire economic policies, which laid down a solid foundation for Chile to move away from economic statism and toward a vibrant market economy attractive to domestic and foreign investment. Freely elected president Patricio Aylwin was installed in 1990. Sound economic policies coupled with the consolidation of democratic governance and political stability have since transformed Chile into the most prosperous, free, and well-governed country in South America.

The Constitution promulgated in 1980 instituted a government with executive, legislative, and judicial branches. The executive power is headed by the president, who is elected by popular vote for a single four-year term and serves as both the chief of state and the head of government. Legislative duties rest with the bicameral National Congress, which consists of the 38-seat Senate and the 120-seat Chamber of Deputies; both senators and deputies are elected by popular vote, with the former serving eight-year terms and the latter serving four-year terms. The judiciary is led by the Supreme Court of Justice and does not accept the jurisdiction of the International Criminal Court.

Legal System

The Chilean legal system is created and empowered by the Constitution. Neither the president of the republic nor the Congress may, under any circumstance, exercise judicial functions such as taking over pending cases; revising the grounds for, or contents of, the decisions; or reopening closed cases.

The Supreme Court exercises the highest judicial authority and is composed of 21 justices appointed by the president of the republic from a short list of five candidates nominated by the court itself. These appointments are subject to Senate review and approval. Sixteen of the 21 Supreme Court justices must come from the judiciary, and five must be practicing attorneys from the nonjudicial sector.

The chief justice is chosen by his or her peers for a two-year period. Proceedings may involve full bench sessions or special chambers. One of the most basic duties of the Supreme Court is to act as an annulment court to promote consistent interpretation of the law. Unlike countries with Anglo-Saxon legal systems, court rulings in Chile, including those of the Supreme Court, are binding only over the cases to which they apply. However, the jurisprudence of annulment hearings sets important precedents for the application of the law in similar cases, contributing to a more uniform and just application of the law. Through a specialized agency called the Judicial Branch Administrative Corporation, the court supervises administrative, disciplinary, and financial issues of all courts except the Constitutional Tribunal, the Electoral Review Board, and the regional electoral boards.

A separate seven-member Constitutional Tribunal possesses broad powers to judge the constitutionality of laws passed by the Congress as well as treaties submitted by the executive power for legislative review and approval. It can also declare unconstitutional any decrees issued by the president of the republic and rule on the constitutionality of a plebiscite. The tribunal resolves disputes among government ministers, legislators, and the executive and can rule on complaints presented by the president or members of either of the legislative chambers, provided that at least one-fourth of the members agree to register a formal grievance. It is made up of three Supreme Court justices plus two attorneys named by the National Security Council, one by the president of the republic, and one by the Senate. A five-member Electoral Tribunal, formed by four Supreme Court justices and a former speaker or deputy speaker of the Senate or the Chamber of Deputies, decides on disputes emerging from national referenda and presidential, congressional, and municipal elections. In 2006, 236 cases were filed before the tribunal. Of these filed cases, 46 percent (108 cases) were ruled admissible.

Broadly speaking, Chilean courts can be grouped into six categories. First, there are 17 appellate courts, not including the Supreme Court, that review trials and decisions made by lower courts and act as courts of first instance for habeas corpus and other civil rights protected by the Constitution. The remaining five categories include 522 first-instance courts of all or mixed jurisdictions. Trial courts have jurisdiction over civil, criminal, and family matters, which are in turn followed by juvenile courts that deal with alimony, guardianship, and adoption of minors as well as the processing and rehabilitation of juvenile offenders. Labor courts are present only in larger urban areas, whereas military courts process and decide on cases involving members of the armed and/or police forces as plaintiffs or defendants in time of peace or war. Last, there exist local courts regulating traffic and motor vehicle violations, consumer affairs, and small claim disputes. As of 2006, permanent judicial staff numbered more than 7,900 individuals, including 1,023 judges.

The Public Ministry or Public Prosecutor's Office is an independent body tasked with the responsibilities of leading the investigation of criminal incidents, initiating formal prosecutions against criminal suspects, and protecting crime victims and witnesses during the trial process. With national jurisdiction, this office sets the prosecutorial agenda across the country and supervises the regional administration of resources and operations. The national public prosecutor is the highest-ranking prosecutor and responsible for all prosecutorial activities across the country, whereas the national executive director oversees the logistic coordination. The Public Prosecutor's Office (PPO) is divided into 16 regional offices—one for each of the 12 regions and 4 in the metropolitan region. Each regional office is headed by a regional public prosecutor who is in turn aided by the assistant prosecutors. Each regional office is organized around six functional units, including Management Evaluation, Oversight and Development, Human Resources, Administration and Finance, Technology, Victim and Witness Assistance, and Local Public Prosecutors. A regional executive director coordinates these units under the leadership of the regional public prosecutor. Local public prosecutor's offices led by chief prosecutors are staffed with assistant prosecutors and are accountable to the regional public prosecutor. In 2006, the Chilean national prosecutorial apparatus processed

784,151 filed cases with a staff of 3,620 full-time employees, including 16 regional public prosecutors and 647 assistant prosecutors.

Legal counsel is a constitutionally guaranteed right of every Chilean citizen. Prior to the criminal procedure reform of 2005, all law students were mandated to provide free defense services to indigent defendants through a compulsory six-month legal aid internship supervised by the Ministry of Justice. The quality of this public defense service was predictably extremely low. The 2005 reform established the Public Defender's Office and prohibited legal representation of criminal defendants by law students. Trained attorneys permanently employed or temporarily contracted by the Public Defender's Office now assist indigent defendants in criminal cases; some provide mediation services for out-of-court settlements in civil cases in a few urban centers. The Public Defender's Office is structured around a national office located in Santiago, 14 regional offices, and 120 local offices, and it employs nearly 600 attorneys.

The Ministry of Justice (MOJ) is headed by a minister appointed by the president of the republic; it bridges the executive and judicial branches and administers support services to facilitate the administration of justice. MOJ officials devise criminal justice policies and public safety programs, ensure access to free legal aid, manage correctional facilities, plan and implement rehabilitation activities for prison inmates, maintain national databases for identification of persons, and monitor services for minors requiring guardianship or with custodial, behavioral, or legal problems. To achieve these objectives, the ministry is divided into functional units, including the Medical Examiner's Office, the Prison Guard Administration, the National Children's Service, the Public Defender's Office, the Civil Registry and Identification Service, the Office of the Superintendent of Bankruptcy, and the Judicial Assistance Corporation.

Police

Two national corps of police exist in Chile for the maintenance of law and order: the uniformed Carabineros and the plainclothed Police of Investigations. The Carabineros are the armed police created to deter crime through visible patrol and community outreach and to perform general law enforcement duties. All Carabineros have received combat training and are designed to become part of the armed forces to play an active paramilitary role during wartime or a state of emergency. It is widely recognized as one of the best trained and most scrupulous police forces in Latin America.

In contrast, the Police of Investigations are geared toward technical and scientific support in the investigation of crimes and prosecution of criminals. Members of the Police of Investigations begin their service after one year of professional training and work closely with prosecutors and judges in the gathering, analysis, and presentation of evidence. Special units have also been established to combat drug trafficking and organized crime, to control the movement of people across national borders and entry points, to monitor the legal stay of foreigners in the country, and to represent Chile before INTERPOL. As of 2006, there are more than 34,200 sworn officers in both the Carabineros and the Police of Investigations.

Juvenile Justice

A new juvenile justice system composed of 45 juvenile courts was approved by Congress in 2004 and began its operations in 2007. The new Juvenile Criminal Responsibility Law sets the age of criminal responsibility at 14 and embraces rehabilitation and reintegration of juvenile delinquents as the core mission of the system. This mandate is supported by a network of intervention programs and correctional facilities that include professionals and specially trained staff to offer treatment, education, and human services to youths supervised by the judiciary. Many noncustodial sentences are available to the sentencing judge to be applied to minors and include assisted release, community service, restitution, fines, and warnings. All sentences are enforced and monitored by an investigative judge. In 2007, the entire juvenile justice system disposed 1,182 juvenile cases, of which 132 cases involved robbery and 124 cases involved theft.

Crime

Classification of Crime

The criminal code of Chile was enacted in 1874 and significantly revised in 1928. It was modeled after the continental codes of Austria, Belgium, France, and Spain. The code is broken down into two sections. The first section spells out general principles of legal jurisdiction relating to the definition of crime, criminal intent and complicity, chronic offenders, punishments, and mitigating and aggravating circumstances. The second section discusses specific crimes and their corresponding penalties. In this respect, the courts are charged with ensuring that the penalty is proportional not only to the crime but also to the offender's ability to understand and exercise his or her responsibility.

Criminal offenses are classified into three fundamental groups: felonies (*crímenes*), misdemeanors (*delitos*), and violations (*faltas*). Crime is defined as a willful act of commission or omission for which the law imposes punishment. Criminal responsibility is specifically excluded in cases in which defendants are insane or less than 14 years of age. Minors 14 to 18 years of age are not criminally responsible unless it can be proven that they acted with full understanding of the illegality of their acts. Criminal responsibility is also waived for violent acts committed in the defense of one's own person, property,

Unidentified members of the Chilean Army guard seven tons of cocaine found onboard the ship *Nativa* from Panama, in Arica, Chile, January 17, 2000. This is the largest drug seizure in Chile and the second largest in the world, with a value of some $430 million. (AP Photo/La Estrella)

or rights or in defense of those of one's spouse or those of a third party. Also excluded are violent acts committed accidentally in the exercise of a legal act, violent acts committed in the exercise of public duty, violent acts committed under duress or fear, and the killing or wounding of the accomplice of an adulterous spouse. Criminal responsibility is also waived in the case of crimes of omission owing to a legal or irresistible cause.

Crime Statistics

Crime rates are low in rural and suburban areas and are moderate in Santiago, Valparaiso, and other major cities. Violence and crime have, in fact, fallen in Chile in recent years or, at the very worst, remained constant. In 2008, the overall crime rate was 2,714.4 offenses reported to the police per 100,000 inhabitants. Grand larceny accounted for 38.2 percent of all reported crimes and attained a rate of 1,035 offenses per 100,000 inhabitants. It was followed by theft (596.6 offenses per 100,000 inhabitants), assault (588.7 offenses per 100,000 inhabitants), and robbery (331.1 offenses per 100,000 inhabitants). The homicide rate of 1.6 offenses per 100,000 inhabitants placed Chile among the Latin American countries with the lowest incidence of deadly violence.

Chile has successfully implemented annual crime victimization surveys with national coverage; this data program provides crime statistics that include offenses not reported to the police or not recorded by the police. Overall, households reporting crime victimizations decreased from 43.0 percent in 2003 to 35.3 percent in 2008. In 2008, the most common forms of crime were theft and grand larceny, which affected 9.4 percent and 7.8 percent of Chilean households, respectively. The rates of robbery (6.5%) and burglary (6.2%) ranked third and fourth, respectively. Violent offenses such as assault (2.5%) represented a small fraction of the total volume of crime victimizations. Although car theft (1.8%) was relatively rare, theft of car parts (18.2%) was widespread. Among all victimized households, nearly one-third (32.4%) suffered repeated or chronic victimizations.

Data surely indicate that Chileans have a growing fear of crime. Indeed, they worry about it more than almost everyone else in the region—a surprising finding in a society that prides itself on being a haven of safety in a dangerous continent. Evidence from citizen surveys reveals that although in 2003, 20.1 percent of Chileans said they felt very unsafe walking in their neighborhood at night, the figure had climbed to 25.0 percent in 2008. Although survey respondents tended to attribute crime and delinquency in the country primarily to the failure of parental involvement and monitoring (24.3%), most blamed the lack of Carabinero patrol presence as the main determinant of insecurity in their own neighborhood (33.9%percent).

Drug Abuse and Trafficking

Chile has historically remained relatively unaffected either by drug trafficking or by extensive drug abuse, despite its proximity to the major Andean producers of cocaine and heroin. However, epidemiological data suggest that although this general depiction is still true, some important changes have taken place in recent times: Chile is becoming the fourth-largest consumer of cocaine and the largest consumer of marijuana among South American countries. According to statistics compiled by the United Nations, the prevalence of opiate use, including heroin, went up moderately from 0.3 percent to 0.4 percent of the adult population between 1995 and 2006, whereas the prevalence of cocaine use grew from 1.3 percent in 1998 to 1.7 percent in 2006. The largest increase was observed among cannabis users, from 4.7 percent of the adult population in 1998 to 7.5 percent in 2006. New synthetic drugs have also made inroads to the Chilean scene in recent years: 0.4 percent of the adult population were identified as amphetamine users and 0.1 percent as Ecstasy users in 2006.

Chile's extended and deserted borders with Peru, Bolivia, and Argentina and busy seaports and airports make it an appealing transit country for shipments of cocaine from the Andean region to Europe, with small consignments going to the United States as well. The country is also an exporter of precursor chemicals for use in cocaine processing in Peru and Bolivia. Chile is a signatory of the 1961 UN Single Convention on Narcotic Drugs, the 1971 UN Convention on Psychotropic Substances, and the 1988 UN Drug Convention. Therefore, it is legally obliged to criminalize and fight against the production, trafficking, and use of illicit drugs and to collaborate with other countries in this endeavor. Sixty-three new cases of drug trafficking were initiated in Chilean courts in 2007, and 172 offenders were convicted and sentenced for drug trafficking.

In 2008, Chile revised its penal code to bring punishments for trafficking cannabis into line with punishments for trafficking cocaine and heroin. Before this change, offenders convicted of cannabis trafficking did not receive the same harsh sanctions under the law as those convicted of trafficking cocaine or heroin. The change is a response to the increase in both domestic use of cannabis and massive importation of cannabis from Paraguay. Pressure from an ever-growing number of drug offenders also forced criminal justice authorities to adopt therapeutic concepts and practices previously unknown to the Chilean jurisprudence and justice system. As of 2008, there were 18 drug courts in Chile modeled after U.S. drug treatment courts providing detoxification and recovery services to drug-abusing offenders under judicial supervision. These problem-solving innovations are being monitored and evaluated by the Public Prosecutor's Office.

Human Trafficking

Chile exports, transfers, and imports men, women, and children trafficked for the purposes of commercial sex and labor exploitation. Domestically, most victims are Chilean women and girls from rural areas who accept deceitful job offers and afterward are sold into forced prostitution and involuntary domestic servitude in urban centers. Some are traded to Argentina, Peru, Bolivia, and Western Europe. Women from neighboring countries such as Argentina, Bolivia, Peru, Colombia, and Paraguay, in addition to Asian countries such as China, are lured to Chile with false employment promises and subsequently induced into sexual or labor exploitation. More recently, Chile's mining and agricultural developments have attracted foreign male and/or underage victims from Bolivia, Peru, Colombia, Ecuador, and China. Many Chinese victims are originally consensually smuggled through Chile en route to Mexico, Brazil, and the United States, but some become lured or forced into illicit and degrading businesses with fraudulent promises of hefty pay and generous benefits.

Chilean authorities have sustained continuous law-enforcement pressures on traffickers of women and minors but have largely ignored the trading of male adults in recent years. This differential control is determined by the fact that whereas Chilean criminal law prohibits cross-border trafficking of persons for sexual exploitation and punishes violators with 3 to 20 years of imprisonment, human trafficking for labor servitude, as well as internal trafficking of persons for prostitution, remains legal in the country. As of this writing, legislative efforts are still underway to promulgate a comprehensive anti-trafficking code that effectively clamps down all forms of trafficking of persons.

The government maintains 14 rescue and assistance centers for minor victims of sex trafficking and provides them with specialized services. These nonresidential centers are enabled to service nearly 700 children and adolescents simultaneously, and they work closely with civic groups that operate shelters to satisfy the temporary housing needs of many minor victims. For adult victims, a witness protection program is available to help victims of sex trafficking, sexual assaults, and domestic violence. Adult victims with housing and other needs are often referred to not-for-profit shelters, where they receive health care, counseling, and support. To enhance the chance of success in the investigation and prosecution against cross-border sex traffickers, Chilean authorities encourage foreign victims to stay in Chile's territory during trials and allow them to apply for permanent residency after the proceedings are completed. However, the application for the status of permanent resident can be denied for various reasons, and some foreign victims still face mandatory deportation to their country of origin after the end of their legal proceedings. Services and privileges are available to minor victims of sex trafficking and/or adult victims of cross-border sex trafficking exclusively; persons traded for forced servitude and adult victims of domestic sex trafficking are not legally defined as victims of human trafficking.

Finding of Guilt

The pre-2005 criminal process was based on the procedural code of 1857 derived from Spanish law and was plagued with serious problems of efficiency and fairness. Under the old inquisitorial system, victims had to be detained a long time before seeing a magistrate and receiving legal aid from the government, and while defendants often had to undergo lengthy jail detention in isolation from their families, they remained unaware of the status of the proceedings against them. Backlogs and delays seriously eroded the quality of justice delivered to the citizenry.

Reforms began to be implemented in a few small jurisdictions in 2000 and included measures such as the abolition of pretrial detention in minor criminal cases, the replacement of detention with noncustodial controls prior to the final disposition of cases in many major criminal cases, the adoption of oral proceedings, the provision of competent and professional legal counsel to indigent defendants, and the creation of victim and witness protection programs, among others. Chile completed its transition from an inquisitorial to an adversarial judicial system in 2005. For criminal offenses committed prior to the implementation of the 2005 judicial reforms, court proceedings remain inquisitorial rather than adversarial. The statute of limitations to press charges is 10 years. At 2008's end, judicial authorities had already closed four of the six inquisitorial criminal courts in the Santiago Metropolitan Region, and all pre-reform cases faced extensive waits for trial. Although the change is still being consolidated, poll results indicate that the public is embracing the new system, which appears to have sped up the resolution of cases.

Only law enforcement officials are authorized by law to arrest or detain citizens suspected of having committed a crime, and they must immediately notify a prosecutor of an arrest. The prosecutor must initiate informal investigation and make sure that the detained suspect is present at the detention control hearing. Detention control hearings occur twice a day and are aimed at a judicial determination of the legality of the detention within 24 hours of arrest. Detainees must be informed of their rights, including the right to legal counsel and the right to remain silent during interrogation. Public defenders are provided if detainees cannot afford private counsel. Family members of the detainees must be notified of the arrest and detention of their relative. Violations of any basic right of the detainee can lead the judge to declare the detention illegal and to order the immediate release of the detainee at the hearing. The judges can set bail, grant conditional release, or remand the detainee as necessary to the criminal investigation or for the protection of public safety.

The new criminal procedure code transfers the responsibility for investigating crimes from the judge of instructions to the prosecutor in direct collaboration with the police. The judge now plays the role of an impartial rule enforcer to determine the truth of the case in the contest between the prosecution and the defense. Prosecutorial preparations for trial are monitored by an investigative judge, who has the duty of settling any dispute related to the rights of the accused. During this phase of fact-finding, the prosecutor is required to obtain judicial permission for every investigative activity that is needed for the preparation of the case and that could infringe on the rights of the defendant. The indictment serves as a control over inquiry and scrutiny initiated by the prosecutors, whose scope of exploration is restricted by the charges clearly and precisely stated in the indictment.

Once the prosecutor completes the investigation at the end of this fact-finding phase, he or she may recommend that the judge dismiss the case or formally charge the defendant in court. If the defendant is formally charged, he or she is given time and legal counsel, if needed, to prepare the defense. A preliminary hearing is usually held before the judge prior to the initiation of the trial.

During this hearing, the judge convenes both parties to consider the admissibility of evidence, the appropriateness of applying alternative sanctions should the defendant become convicted, and the possibility of adopting abridged procedures if the case is minor in nature. If traditional penalties remain the option, and abridged procedures do not apply, the case is adjourned for full adjudication, and a written and open document is issued specifying the charges to be considered at trial, the parties involved in the contest, the tribunal and magistrates with jurisdiction over the case, and the evidence that has been declared admissible in court.

The trial is held in a collegiate court presided over by three professional judges. All admissible evidence should be presented at this point. The court has some limited powers to accept new evidence and examine witnesses once both sides have cross-examined them. After the analysis of the evidence, the court listens to closing arguments, offers the defendant an opportunity to make a final statement, and then retires to deliberate and reach a decision. Once the verdict is delivered, a period is set for submitting the grounds for the decision and sentencing. Only cassation appeals may be brought to challenge a definitive ruling. Court records, rulings, and findings are generally accessible to the public.

Punishment

The Chilean system of criminal punishments was standardized in 1930 and has since been administered by the Ministry of Justice. As per existing statutes, the correctional system emphasizes the rehabilitation of offenders over other penal goals. Criminal sentences for convicted offenders can be broadly classified into custodial sanctions and community-based alternatives. "Custodial sanctions" refers to the incarceration of detainees awaiting trial or disposition and convicted offenders sentenced to imprisonment. As of September 2009, 50,133 adult Chileans were detained or serving sentence in closed correctional institutions. Community-based alternatives include probation supervision (*libertad vigilada del adulto*), parole (*remisión condicional de la pena*), and nighttime reclusion (*reclusion nocturna*). As of September 2009, 45,907 convicted offenders were serving sentence under some kind of community-based alternatives; of these offenders, 67.6 percent were under parole supervision, 21.8 percent were under probation supervision, and the remaining 10.6 percent were under nighttime reclusion.

The Prison System

Chile constructed its first penitentiary, which was also the second-oldest prison in South America, in Santiago in 1847. (This facility is still in use and known as the Center for Preventive Detention of Southern Santiago.) Both the architectural design and managerial philosophy of this first prison followed the individual cellar approach of the Pennsylvanian model. Other correctional presidios were built in the following years to solve the problem of a growing convict population. However, these earliest correctional facilities were operated by provincial authorities independently of the federal government and of each other, which resulted in huge disparities in living conditions and administrative styles across institutions.

The penal code of 1930 placed all correctional institutions under the unified administration of the Ministry of Justice and ordered the construction of the model Maipo prison in Santiago, with a capacity for 1,000 inmates and equipped with a segregated unit for tubercular inmates, as well as the building of another 40 smaller facilities across the country. The penal reform of 1930 was progressive in nature and instituted prison-based educational and vocational training in a wide range of disciplines and skills. Work inside prison walls is mostly geared toward the instruction of technical expertise in electrical equipment and carpentry and is often remunerated.

The gendarmerie, subordinated to the leadership of the Ministry of Justice, is responsible for the operation and security of Chilean prisons. As of 2009, there were more than 150 correctional facilities holding 50,133 inmates; 78.0 percent (39,094) of these inmates were convicted offenders serving their sentences. Both the correctional facilities and the inmates are classified and matched. Prisons are categorized according to the length of sentences of their inmates: certain facilities specialize in the custody of inmates with an incarcerative sentence of 60 days or less, some receive inmates sentenced to 60 days to 5 years of imprisonment, and others house inmates with sentences ranging from more than 5 years to life.

Inmates are assessed according to their needs and risks, including external appearance (i.e., language skill, presence of tattoos, and other body marks), human capital (i.e., educational achievement, employment history, vocational aspiration, etc.), community ties, and criminal history. Each inmate receives a score on his or her risk of recidivism or criminal commitment (*compromiso delictual*): about half of the prison population are diagnosed as high risk, and nearly one-fourth are deemed of medium-high risk. Most Chilean inmates experience their incarceration through a four-stage progression. Newly admitted inmates spend their first month in solitary confinement with maximum restrictions. Afterward, they move to the yearlong second stage characterized by a greater amount of social contacts and increased responsibility: inmates leave solitary confinement, are allowed to communicate with friends and family members, and engage in prison work. Once in the third stage, inmates receive much more generous pay for their work and enjoy greater autonomy: they only have to return to their cells at night. Conditional release represents the final stage. Each of these four stages can be extended or reversed according to the performance of the inmate.

Security in Chilean prisons shows a contradictory picture. On the one hand, the gendarmerie appeared to have significantly control over prison breaks. In 1995, 1 out of every 100 prison inmates escaped from their captivity; by 2008, the ratio had decreased to less than 0.01 escapes for every 100 inmates. But on the other hand, prison violence and deaths are as rampant as they were at the end of the 20th century Overcrowding has been blamed as the fundamental cause of the malaise in Chilean prisons. The reliance on incarceration as the main penal option for the punishment of serious criminals has inflated Chile's incarceration rate to 305 inmates per 100,000 inhabitants. The explosion of the Chilean prison population was most dramatic between 2003 and 2009, when it increased by 31.0 percent, from 38,266 to 50,133. There is no sign of abatement to the growth. The current population of 50,000 inmates represents an excess of 51.5 percent over the system's originally designed capacity of 33,000 beds. This major crisis has resulted in violence perpetrated by both inmates and gendarmerie guards, substandard sanitary conditions, and overstretched subsystems of medical, social, and human services.

In 2003, the Chilean government began gradually introducing private capital and resources to assist with the construction and/or management of some facilities as well as with the rehabilitation of offenders. The goals are to save taxpayers money, to improve prison conditions, and to reduce recidivism. Although official expectations are high, public pessimism lingers.

Death Penalty

The death penalty was first abolished in 1930. But between 1930 and 2001, execution by firing squad was reinstated for murder of a family member, kidnapping of children or violence against them, and kidnapping of adults that caused the death or murder of police agents. In May 2001, President Ricardo Lagos signed the permanent abolition of capital punishment into law. The penal code has commuted the death penalty to life imprisonment, which now means imprisonment for 40 years.

Hung-En Sung

Further Reading

Blanco, Rafael, Richard Hutt, and Hugo Rojas. (2006). "Reform to the Criminal Justice System in Chile: Evaluation and Challenges." *Loyola University Chicago International Law Review* 2(2): 253–268.

Hilbink, Lisa. (2007). *Judges beyond Politics in Democracy and Dictatorship: Lessons from Chile.* New York: Cambridge University Press.

Marangunic, Antonio, and Todd Foglesong. (2004). *Charting Justice Reform in Chile: A Comparison of the Old and New Systems of Criminal Procedure.* New York: Vera Institute of Justice.

Colombia

Legal System: Civil
Murder: High
Burglary: High
Corruption: Medium
Human Trafficking: Low
Prison Rate: Medium
Death Penalty: No
Corporal Punishment: No

Background

Colombia has a population of around 43 million inhabitants, 75 percent of whom live in urban areas. It is a multiparty democracy that has been facing a 43-year internal armed conflict between the government and illegal armed forces, consisting mainly of two leftist guerrilla groups, the FARC (Revolutionary Armed Forces of Colombia) and the ELN (National Liberation Army), and paramilitary groups. The guerrillas have moved into the drug business, which along with their illegal revenue from kidnappings is the main source of their financing.

During the first term of recently reelected President Alvaro Uribe, a peace process was promoted by which an illegal right-wing armed group, the AUC (United Self-Defense Forces of Colombia), was demobilized. A 2005 congressional law known as the "Justice and Peace Law" offered former AUC members reduced sentences for confessing their crimes and compensating their victims. Interestingly enough, those confessions have revealed links between the paramilitaries and well-known politicians, many of whom are now behind bars.

Although in May 2008, the Colombian government extradited to the United States 13 of the main paramilitary leaders who were participating in that peace process, as a result of their drug trafficking activities, these extradited detainees have continued testifying and confessing from their American jails to Colombian prosecutors and judges via satellite communication. Some of their testimony has continued to link Colombian politicians to paramilitary activities.

The Colombian unemployment rate is around 10 percent, the illiteracy rate is 9.6 percent, and based on the basic needs index, 27.6 percent of Colombians live in poverty. Although the poverty rate has declined in recent years, the drama of internally displaced people continues because of the domestic armed conflict. Based on official data, the Colombian government has registered more than 1.8 million displaced people since 1995, though "the Office of the UN High Commissioner for Refugees (UNHCR) estimated that more than 2.5 million persons in the country had been displaced at some point during the past 15 years."

In spite of all these difficulties experienced by the "suffering Colombia," there is another Colombia with nice brick buildings, green avenues, high-class restaurants, a cosmopolitan environment, sophisticated academicians, gifted entrepreneurs, a middle class, and wonderful natural resources.

Legal System

The Colombian legal system is rooted in its Spanish colonial past and based on the preponderance of written law following the tradition of the civil law. Colombia declared its independence from Spain in 1810 and gained total autonomy in 1819 after the patriotic troops led by General Simon Bolivar defeated the last Spaniards. Until 1837, the criminal law primarily consisted of the India Laws enacted by the Castilian Crown in Spain for its American settlements during the colonial era. On June 27, 1837, the first penal code was enacted. It was partly based on the French Penal Code of 1810 and the Spanish Penal Code of 1822. During a series of civil wars, six constitutions were promulgated between the 1830s and 1860s. In 1873, a federal criminal code was promulgated and was effective until 1890, when a new penal code was enacted following the adoption of the centralist Constitution of 1886. Although the 1873 code was lenient, the 1890 code was significantly more punitive, as was the 1837 code that inspired it. For example, the 1863 Constitution and the 1873 code prohibited capital punishment, but the 1886 Constitution restored it.

In 1936, a new penal code was introduced, clearly influenced by the Italian criminological positivism then in vogue. The main tenets of this school of legal thinking were that crime was determined by social and biological factors, that society had the right to defend itself from criminal harm with minimum consideration for the rights of the offender, and that criminals were ill and dangerous people in need of treatment. Almost half a century later, Colombian legal experts, now persuaded by the German dogma, were of the opinion that this code had become old-fashioned and pushed for a new code that was eventually promulgated in 1980. However, the turmoil caused by a parasitic violence born of partisan civil wars in the first half of the 20th century, and later perpetuated by leftist guerrilla groups, right-wing paramilitary gangs, and drug trafficking cartels into the new millennium, gave rise to several laws that addressed political or collective violence, usually issued by the president under state-of-siege powers.

For more than 100 years, Colombia lived under the umbrella of the 1886 Constitution and its several amendments, until 1990. In that year, an impetuous student movement prompted by the 1985 seizure of the Main Justice Palace and the killing of 11 of the Supreme Court justices by the now-demobilized M–19 guerrilla group, as well as the 1990 assassination of Colombian leader Luis Carlos Galan, then a presidential candidate, pushed for a new constitution as a means for solving the perpetual malady of violence and hopelessness. The new Constitution, enacted in 1991 and portrayed as a tool for preventing violence, prohibited the Congress from vesting the president with the power to issue codes or statutes, because during most of the 20th century, it was the president who issued the majority of criminal laws, either with the authority of the Congress or by using the extraordinary powers granted him when he declared the state of siege.

Among the new institutions that were created by the novel 1991 Constitution, three have had a major impact on the application of criminal law: the Constitutional Court, the Ombudsman, and the Attorney General. The Constitutional Court, the Supreme Court, and the Council of State marked a significant shift toward a less formalistic manner of legal interpretation that is highly sensitive to human rights and international humanitarian law issues. Under the new regimen, the Constitutional Court can exercise judicial review and declare laws unconstitutional, and any citizen whose fundamental constitutional rights have been violated can file with any lower court without the need to be represented by a lawyer.

Three other superior judicial bodies exist at the same level as the Constitutional Court: the Supreme Court, the Council of State, and the Superior Council of the Judicature, which has two chambers: the Disciplinary Chamber and the Administrative Chamber. All justices of these high-level courts are elected for an eight-year term. Currently, there are a total of 76 justices on these supreme judicial bodies.

Meanwhile, the new Attorney General's Office, which is part of the judiciary, presided over a mixed criminal system, in which cases were prosecuted mainly by written means, and in which prosecutors, during the investigation phase of the process, were allowed to obtain evidence without the involvement of a judge and to decide, usually without the involvement of a judge, on the defendant's pretrial detention. The trial judge was empowered to decide on the basis of the evidence in the prosecutor's records without allowing defendants any real opportunity to confront witnesses. However, in 2002, a constitutional amendment authorized the adoption of an accusatory system, which was adopted by Congress in 2004. This law provided for the implementation of the new system in a staggered process, and as of January 2008, all new criminal cases were being handled under accusatory principles.

Crime

Following the teachings of German criminal law doctrine, for conduct in Colombia to be regarded as criminal, (a) it must be clearly specified in a law, (b) it must be wrongful or unlawful, that is, without legal justification (i.e., self-defense), and (c) the person must be culpable (i.e., legally guilty). Culpability comes into play when a person is blamed for having been conscious of the illicitness of his or her behavior and for, though being able act otherwise, nevertheless committing the wrongful act.

Classification of Criminal Offenses

In Colombian law, the actual phrase used to refer to criminal offenses generally is "punishable conduct." Crimes (*delitos*) and misdemeanors (*contravenciones*) are subcategories of punishable conduct. Misdemeanors are mainly governed by the Police Code of 1970, and most of the common crimes are contained in the penal code of 2000. There is no hard and fast rule for distinguishing between crimes and misdemeanors; such distinction is within the discretion of Congress to make, meaning that when Congress considers that a specific offense is not very serious, it may punish it as a misdemeanor.

Misdemeanors

In 2007, the Colombian Congress tried to enact a Small Claims Act (SCA) to define and punish offenses involving property losses not exceeding 10 times the country's monthly minimum wage. Some of the proposed offenses included larceny, larceny by trick, fraud, embezzlement, false pretenses, illegal issuance and transfer of checks, interruption of possession, and damage to property.

However, unlike the regular procedure for crimes, in the failed Small Claims Act, there was no participation of a prosecutor in the adjudication process for misdemeanors. Furthermore, criminal offenses included in the Small Claims Act of 2007 were treated as crimes punishable by prison terms, and because the adjudication process did not include the prosecutor, the Constitutional Court found that this criminal adjudication system violated the Constitution. Therefore, the majority of what the unsuccessful Small Claims Acts considered to be misdemeanors were transformed back into the category of crimes.

The National Police Code of 1970 defines several misdemeanors that are less serious than those contained in the unsuccessful SCA of 2007. These include conduct that adversely affects public spaces or urban zoning, breach of the public peace and order, violation of the rules governing the operation of vehicles and businesses, and so on. Penalties provided for such conduct are usually public or private admonition, required commitment to observe good conduct, business lockouts, and fines. Indeed, this is an example of the so-called repressive nature of the police.

Crimes

Colombia makes no distinction between serious and less serious crimes. All conduct proscribed by the penal code as crimes are indictable. The most common crimes are homicide, robbery, kidnapping, drug trafficking, bribery, domestic violence, rape, failure to pay child support, forgery, conspiracy, arson, perjury, and rebellion.

Age of Criminal Responsibility and Juvenile Justice

The penal code (Law 599 of 2000) is applicable to adults, meaning people over the age of 18. For people between 14 and 18 years of age, whom the law regards as "adolescents," the applicable law is the Infancy and Adolescence Code (Law 1098 of 2006). There is no criminal responsibility for minors under the age of 14, no matter how serious the offense they might have committed. If a person younger than 14 commits a crime, he or she is subject only to administrative measures aimed at guaranteeing the minor's rights. These offenders must be provided with educational opportunities and protection. The Colombian Institute for Family Welfare (ICBF, for its Spanish name) is in charge of providing such assistance.

Moreover, the legal treatment of minors between 14 and 18 years of age can never be the same as adults. Juveniles cannot be prosecuted as adults, no matter the type of crime. Plea bargaining agreements between the prosecutor and the minor are not allowed in the juvenile criminal system, although the prosecutor may decide not to prosecute adolescents who have been members of illegal armed groups if the minor was under certain social, economic, psychological, and cultural conditions that forced him or her to join such a group. Special judges preside over the trials of juvenile delinquents. There is also a specialized team of prosecutors and counselors in charge of their cases.

In terms of punishments for juveniles, incarceration is allowed in only two types of cases: First, if the defendant is between 14 and 18 years of age, and the crime is voluntary homicide, kidnapping, or extortion, the juvenile found guilty may be incarcerated for between two and eight years. Second, for other crimes (for example, rape), the juvenile can be incarcerated only if he or she is 16 years old, and the crime would result in a minimum sentence of six years of imprisonment if committed by an adult, in which case the punishment could be incarceration from one to five years. Moreover, in these two types of cases, pretrial detention is exceptional and available only in situations where there is a risk of evasion by the juvenile, or a risk that he or she may destroy evidence or harm the victim, the person who has reported the crime, a witness, or the community.

Drug Offenses

The main punishment for criminal offenses related to the drug trade is a prison term generally ranging from 4 to 30 years, depending on the seriousness of the crime, the quantity of drugs involved, and the personal conditions of the defendant. The drugs prohibited include marijuana, cocaine, morphine, heroin, and any drug that produces dependency. Colombian law does not define drugs in terms of origin or specific chemical structure, although police experts use standard protocols to determine when a confiscated substance is a prohibited drug.

The use of a minimum personal dose of an otherwise prohibited drug is not punishable in Colombia as long as it is not consumed in public or in the presence of minors. The dose for personal use is defined by the law. The personal dose for marijuana is no more than 20 grams, for hashish 5 grams, for methaqualone 2 grams, and for cocaine and any other substance made from cocaine (e.g., crack) 1 gram. However, according to a decision recently rendered by the Supreme Court, even if the amount of illegal drugs found on someone is more than one personal dose as defined by law, if the evidence indicates that the person was carrying the drugs for his or her personal consumption, then such conduct is not unlawful because no harm or danger was caused to others. In any case, although consumption of a personal dose is legal, its sale is illegal.

The decriminalization of personal consumption of drugs was a result of a ruling by the Constitutional Court in 1994. A divided court ruled 5–4 in favor of not using the criminal law as a way to punish such private activity. Since then, there have been many attempts to introduce a constitutional amendment to recriminalize the personal use of drugs, but none of these attempts has been successful.

Crime Statistics

Colombia is known for suffering an extremely serious problem of violence. Yet the rate of violent crimes has been declining steadily and significantly in recent years, as can be seen in the number of violent crimes recorded by the Colombian National Police in 2002 and 2007:

	2002	2007
Murder	28,837	17,198
Kidnapping	2,986	521
Extortion	2,512	1,082
Terrorism	1,645	383

In contrast, the number of street robberies, burglaries, and commercial thefts experienced a noticeable growth in recent years, whereas car theft, motorcycle theft, bank robbery, and highway banditry dropped considerably, as is apparent from the following statistics of crimes reported to the Colombian National Police:

	2002	2007
Street robbery	33,431	50,847
Burglary	16,093	17,601
Commercial thefts	11,984	14,904
Auto theft	17,303	8,478
Motorcycles theft	12,974	9,708
Livestock theft	1,822	1,704
Bank robbery	257	70
Highway banditry	1,436	565

Sex crimes have been on the rise at a very alarming rate, and children and young teenagers appear to be especially vulnerable to sexual violence.

Although part of the increase in sex crimes could be accounted for by better reporting resulting from an improved police-citizen relationship, change in reporting and recording practices cannot completely explain, for example, the period 2002 through 2007, during which there was an increase of 90 percent in rape of minors 14 years or younger, of 357 percent in other sexual abuses against minors, of 50 percent in rape of victims aged older than 14, of 128 percent in other sexual abuses against victims older than 14, and of 468 percent in sexual abuses against disabled people.

In rural areas, the most common crimes are those associated with coca and poppy crops. In 2007, more than 218,000 coca hectares and almost 368 poppy hectares located in rural areas were sprayed or manually eradicated. Still, coca cultivation is estimated at around 76,000 hectares, based on data provided by the United Nations Office on Drugs and Crime. The internal conflict with guerrillas exists mainly in rural areas, although guerrilla militias sometimes hide in urban areas. Other type of crimes such as street robbery, auto theft, and bank robbery are common in urban areas.

Finding of Guilt

Constitutional Principles

Articles 28 and 29 of the Colombian Constitution set out the general principles to be followed in all criminal cases. They prescribe that nobody can "be interfered with in his/her person or family, sent to jail or arrested, or have his/her home searched except pursuant to a written order from a competent legal authority, subject to due process and for reasons previously established by law." They provide that from the time a person is arrested, he or she is entitled to "be placed at the disposition of a competent judge within the following 36 hours," so that the judge may evaluate the legality of the arrest. In addition, there are no prison terms for debts, and all crimes, including murder, have a statute of limitations. Due process of law is applicable to all judicial and administrative cases, and no one may be subject to a judicial process unless it is conducted in accordance with existing written law before a competent court that follows preestablished formalities. The presumption of innocence is also established in the Constitution, as is the right to legal counsel during the pretrial investigation and the trial. Moreover, no one in Colombia may be subject to double jeopardy for the same behavior.

Furthermore, based on article 93 of the Constitution, the Colombian Constitutional Court and all of the other courts in Colombia recognize that international human rights treaties or agreements ratified by the Colombian Congress have the same status as the Constitution itself. As explained previously, a new modern oral accusatory system is being implemented throughout the entire country. The influence of U.S. law on the new Colombian accusatory system is notable.

Rights of the Defendant

Every criminal defendant has a constitutional right to a trial. Though the constitutional amendment of 2002 established the possibility of trials by jury, the criminal procedure code of 2004 does not regulate them because the existence of outlaw elements in the society still presents risks to jurors, and the country needs to consolidate the monopoly of legitimate state force before a jury system can be implemented with security. This means that currently only bench trials are permitted, and jury trials remain a mere expectation.

Though defendants cannot be compelled to testify against themselves, they have the right to testify. If they choose to do so and lie, remain silent, do not answer some or all of the questions asked, or fail to tell the complete truth, they cannot be prosecuted for perjury, according to a Constitutional Court ruling.

The Right to Counsel

The 1991 Constitution created the office of the Ombudsman for the first time in Colombia as an independent and autonomous office not part of the executive, legislative, or judicial branches. In 1992, Congress enacted Law 24 to create the Ombudsman Office and its Public Defender Directorate. Since then, the number of public defenders has increased substantially. The staff of the Public Defender Directorate has also increased considerably since the adoption of the accusatory system. For example, in 2007, more than 1,795 public defenders were part of the permanent Public Defender Directorate's staff and served the majority of defendants in criminal cases. Indeed, at least 74 percent of arrested defendants in criminal cases under the new accusatory system have been assisted by public defenders, and when all cases (with or without the arrest of the defendant) are considered, this percentage increases to 85 percent.

A defendant is entitled to counsel upon his or her arrest or after being summoned to the first hearing. The defense attorney must be afforded reasonable time and means to prepare the defense. He or she has to personally assist the defendant. Moreover, he or she has the right to examine evidence against the defendant, obtain court subpoenas to call witnesses, and conduct direct examination of defense witnesses and cross-examination of prosecution witnesses.

Victims' Rights

Since a landmark Constitutional Court ruling in April 2002, which was influenced by the United Nations Declaration of Basic Principles of Justice for Victims of Crime and Abuse of Power, a national crusade for victims' rights in the criminal justice system has become more vigorous. Although other Constitutional Court rulings addressed victims' rights before 2002, this ruling substantially increased victims' opportunities to participate in criminal pretrial and trial procedures. The court stated that victims' rights are not merely those of an economic nature and that victims are entitled to the right to know the truth, the right to justice in the particular case, and the right to reparations.

Moreover, since this court decision, the new 2004 criminal procedure code and other rulings of the Constitutional Court have given victims more specific rights to participate in the criminal process. Victims are entitled to be informed of the status of the cases from the very moment that they come into contact with the authorities (police, prosecutors, or judges).

Victims are also entitled to present, reject, or require evidence or its discovery. However, they are not entitled to conduct direct examinations, cross-examinations, or impeachments or to interpose objections during the trial. Nevertheless, if the judge renders a guilty verdict, the victim has up to 30 days to seek compensation, and the sentencing can be imposed only after such period. In addition, victims have the right to be heard in plea bargaining negotiations between the defendant and the prosecutor and also when the latter, with the court's permission, is not going to prosecute.

Regarding the demobilization of paramilitaries and members of other illegal armed groups in exchange for reduced sentences, a process that the Colombian government of President Uribe has encouraged based on Law 975 of 2005, the Constitutional Court has ruled that victims of paramilitary atrocities are entitled to seek compensation from defendants' assets, including not only illicit assets subject to forfeiture but also legal ones.

Criminal Investigation

In criminal cases, the judicial police are responsible for the investigation under the direction of the prosecutor appointed by the Attorney General's Office. "Judicial police" is a legal concept meaning the authorities who collaborate with the judicial officers in the criminal investigation and the arrest of criminal suspects. Once a crime has occurred, the judicial police perform the initial investigative acts that must be urgently carried out (also known as "urgent acts"), such as visits to the crime scene, visual inspections of the crime scene, corpse inspections, interviews, the collection of evidence, and taping of the crime scene.

It should be noted that the Colombian judicial police do not consist of a single organism. Rather, several offices discharge duties as judicial police; among the most common are the members of the national police and the National Administrative Department of Security specially designated to perform such duties and the technical investigation body of the Attorney General's Office. In theory, they have to discharge their duties in accordance with the policies established by the Attorney

General's Office and under the direction of the designated prosecutor.

Once the prosecutor receives the judicial police report, he or she designs a methodological program of investigative goals and tasks that the judicial police team has to perform. However, the police need a judge's authorization to conduct search and seizure operations on private property. To conduct wiretapping and electronic surveillance, the judicial police need a prior written order issued by the competent prosecutor. Once the operation is conducted, a hearing must be held before a guarantee judge within the subsequent 24 hours to examine the legality of the judicial police procedure. A guarantee judge is a public official in charge of some pretrial hearings designed mainly to evaluate the legality of decisions made during the criminal investigation such as arrests, searches and seizures, bail hearings, and so on.

However, if a suspect is caught in the act (*in flagrante delicto*), the police may arrest him without an arrest warrant. In this case, the police have to contact the prosecutor, who has up to 36 hours from the time of the arrest to bring the suspect before a guarantee judge for a ruling on the legality of the arrest. For other types of arrest, a prior arrest warrant signed by a guarantee judge is needed, although in very exceptional circumstances, the prosecutor may sign that warrant if it is clear that a judge is not available and if there is a serious risk that the defendant may be a threat to society, destroy evidence, or flee.

If the prosecutor determines that, based on the evidence the judicial police have collected, it is reasonable to infer that the suspect is the principal or an accomplice of a crime, the prosecutor must file charges against the suspect. If pretrial detention is allowed for the crime allegedly committed, the prosecutor, in the bail hearing, may ask the guarantee judge to hold the defendant in custody.

In the case of suspects who are caught *in flagrante delicto,* it is common for three hearings—that is, the bail hearing, the hearing to decide on the validity of the warrantless arrest, and the oral filing of the complaint—to be held all at once, in what is known in legal jargon as the "combo" hearing. Thereafter, the prosecutor has up to 30 days to file the indictment, which will be the basis for the trial.

Plea Bargaining

When the 2002 constitutional amendment establishing the accusatory system was proposed in the Colombian Congress, one of the main changes projected was the adoption of plea bargaining as a legal measure intended to simplify and speed up the administration of criminal justice. However, the criminal procedure code of 2004, enacted to implement the accusatory system, and rulings of both the Constitutional Court and the Supreme Court have limited the use of plea bargaining because the deeply rooted culture of compulsory prosecution remains.

Colombian prosecutors do not enjoy true prosecutorial discretion because in most cases, when deciding whether or not to prosecute, they are subject to court authorization. First, a decision not to prosecute, which in Colombian legal language is known as "application of the principle of opportunity," is prohibited in cases of drug trafficking, terrorism, international humanitarian law crimes, and crimes against humanity.

Moreover, Colombian law establishes a specific and extensive list of legal grounds for which the decision not to prosecute is allowed. Before a decision not to prosecute is made, the law allows for the possibility of suspending the criminal proceeding for a test period of up to three years when the defendant has so requested to compensate the victim. Besides the decision not to prosecute having a specific list of detailed legal grounds, if the legal sentence to be imposed for the crime is more than a six-year prison term, only the attorney general (or the attorney general's designee) is entitled to make such a decision. However, the Constitutional Court, holding that the decision not to prosecute is an exception to the principle of compulsory prosecution, has ruled that even when suspending a procedure, the prosecutor needs judicial approval.

Moreover, in the case of intentional murder, intentional personal injury, kidnapping, and sexual assault against minors, neither plea bargaining nor parole measures are allowed. In practice, the termination of criminal cases on the basis of a decision not to prosecute occurs in less than 1 percent of all terminated cases.

A better outcome has been experienced via guilty pleas resulting from plea bargaining in crimes against adults. In these agreements, the defendants plead guilty in exchange for reduced charges or reductions in sentences. For example, if the defendant pleads guilty in the hearing in which the prosecutor formally presents a complaint against him or her, the defendant is entitled to a reduction of up to half of the sentence that otherwise would have been imposed. But unlike the decision not to prosecute, a guilty plea involves the imposition of a sentence. It is estimated that more than half of criminal cases are terminated because of guilty pleas entered by defendants in the hearing in which the prosecutor formally presents a complaint to a judge.

Pretrial Detention

After a Constitutional Court ruling in 2001, a set of requirements for pretrial detention were imposed. The Constitutional Court ruled that formal and evidentiary requirements are not sufficient for imposing pretrial detention because the judge in charge of making this decision must also take into consideration whether pretrial detention is constitutionally justified in the specific case. The court held that pretrial detention is constitutional if it is necessary to preserve evidence, to protect witnesses, or to avoid a serious risk of harm to society posed by the release of the defendant on bail, or when it is clear that the defendant will flee. The new criminal code adopted this doctrine, and in addition to the formal and legal requirements related to the seriousness of the investigated crime, it demands that the judge who orders pretrial detention verify that this exceptional measure is needed to avoid the obstruction of the due exercise of justice, or because the defendant is a danger to society, or that it is probable that the defendant will not return to court or will not obey the sentence.

Among those crimes for which pretrial detention is allowed are genocide; homicide; crimes against international humanitarian law; forced disappearance; kidnapping; aircraft piracy; torture; illegal displacement; trafficking in people; sex trafficking of adults by force, fraud, or coercion; sex trafficking of children; rape and sexual assault; child pornography; domestic violence; robbery; violation of economic copyrights; counterfeiting and forgery of currency and public documents; money laundering; conspiracy; terrorism; drug trafficking; bribery and corruption of public officials; pandering; perjury; espionage; insurrection; and sedition.

For other crimes, pretrial detention is not allowed unless such crimes have been committed in concurrence with other crimes for which it is allowed. Among these are manslaughter, injuries that have not caused permanent disability, abortion, injuries to a fetus, inducement to commit suicide, cloning of human beings, nonconsensual artificial insemination, burglary with no stealing, trade in wiretapping devices, violation of workers' rights to freedom of association, defamation and slander, failure to pay legal child support, nonaggravated larceny, writing checks without sufficient funds, trespassing or taking over real property, damage to property, false impersonation, tampering with the quality of consumer goods, illegal exploitation of natural resources, arson, improper use of privileged information, and violent picketing.

Pretrial home detention may be imposed for defendants who are older than 65 or seriously ill in the opinion of official experts, or when the defendant is a pregnant woman during the last two months of pregnancy and up to six months following childbirth. It is also allowed in the case of a man or woman who is the head of a family with children younger than 18 or with older children with disabilities. In addition, this kind of detention is allowed when the judge determines that, based on the personal, labor, social, or family conditions of the defendant, the purposes of detention can be achieved by detaining the defendant at home. However, this form of detention is prohibited in certain cases, such as (a) crimes of voluntary homicide, personal injury, sexual assault, and kidnapping if the victim is a minor and (b) when the case is to be tried before a special circuit judge (mainly cases involving complex crimes such as drug trafficking or genocide).

Organization of the Judiciary

The judiciary in Colombia is hierarchically structured. At the bottom are the municipal judges, and above them are the circuit judges and specialized circuit judges. They work as sole adjudicators and do not sit on panels or *en banc*. Most of the time, they act as trial judges.

To be appointed a municipal judge, the candidate must be an attorney with at least two years of experience after getting his or her law degree. Municipal judges are in charge of trials of minor offenses, such as personal injury, crimes against property valued at no more than 150 times the country's monthly minimum wage, domestic violence, failure to pay child support, and crimes that require that the injured person file a criminal complaint for the matter to be prosecuted.

Special circuit judges are in charge of complex crimes such as drug trafficking, genocide, forced disappearance, crimes against international humanitarian law, aircraft piracy, torture, money laundering, unjust enrichment, terrorism, murder of public servants, and so on.

Circuit judges are in charge of trials of most serious crimes (for example, the majority of homicides, crimes against property valued at more than 150 times the country's monthly minimum wage, rape, violation of intellectual property, etc.). To be appointed a circuit judge, in addition to having a law degree, the candidate must have at least four years of experience after the awarding of a law degree.

Above these single judges are the district courts of appeals, whose headquarters are usually located in department capitals. Judges in these courts must be attorneys with at least eight years of professional experience. They decide on final rulings of municipal judges and on final and interlocutory orders of circuit and special circuit judges. Courts of appeals sitting as trial courts hear cases against judges, prosecutors, or inspectors who appear before a judge or a prosecutor because such defendants have the right to be tried in a special jurisdiction.

In Colombia, there are 32 judicial districts, each with a court of appeals that hears criminal cases. In addition, there are 4,285 judges, including 971 multiple-jurisdiction municipal judges, 435 criminal municipal judges, 342 criminal circuit judges, 88 multiple-jurisdiction circuit judges, and 67 judges in charge of execution of punishment and security measures.

As noted previously, there is a special type of judge called a "guarantee judge" who presides over hearings on bail and other judicial authorizations that affect a defendant's rights or the legality of arrests and searches and seizures. Some municipal judges discharge their duties as guarantee judges, and the appeals of their decisions are heard by circuit judges. In cases that are directly tried by the Supreme Court, the Bogotá Court of Appeals performs the function of a guarantee judge. Finally, for the execution of punishment, there is a special category of judges called judges for execution of punishment and security measures.

All regular judges below the level of the Supreme Court, as well as their clerks, are appointed from among the best-qualified candidates in an open public contest. Unlike the justices of the Supreme Court, the other Colombian judges, once appointed, may retain their positions on a permanent basis until they are discharged as a result of a disciplinary or criminal action, or until they attain the age of mandatory retirement, which is 65. Also, it is important to note that Colombian judges usually have much more experience than the required minimum.

Separate from the ordinary judiciary are martial courts in charge of trying members of the army, navy, air force, and police force who commit acts related to military service. This means that if they violate human rights or international humanitarian law, which are nonmilitary offenses, they are tried not by a martial court, but rather by an ordinary court.

Sitting atop all of the judges and courts of appeals mentioned here is the Supreme Court, which has three chambers: one civil (with seven justices), one labor (with seven justices), and one criminal (with nine justices). Justices of the Supreme Court hold their positions for an eight-year term or until they reach the age of mandatory retirement. They must be duly licensed attorneys with at least 10 years of professional experience.

The Supreme Court also has appellate jurisdiction over the rulings made by the courts of appeals when the latter act as trial courts and investigative and trial jurisdiction when the defendant is a congressman. It also has trial jurisdiction when the defendant is the president of the republic, after the House of Representatives has brought charges against him or her and the Senate has declared that there are grounds for the president to be tried by the Supreme Court. In addition, the Supreme Court has trial jurisdiction over certain high officials, such as the inspector general, the ministers of the president, the ombudsman, the comptroller general of the republic, ambassadors and chiefs of diplomatic or consular missions, governors, magistrates of the courts of appeals, generals of the army, and admirals of the navy, among others. In the case of these high officials, only the attorney general himself, and not any of his delegates, can legally conduct the investigation.

The *tutela* action, established by article 86 of the 1991 Constitution, entitles any person (human being or entity) to file an informal petition with any court, no matter its jurisdiction, alleging the violation or endangerment of fundamental rights, when the petitioner does not have another means of judicial recourse or is in need of an immediate temporary device to avoid irreversible harm. The judge has to decide on the petition within 10 business days, and if the judge rules that the petitioner's fundamental rights have been violated or threatened, he or she has to issue a protective order that must be complied with no later than 48 hours after its issuance.

The *tutela* action may seem quite straightforward, but because it is possible that judicial decisions themselves violate fundamental rights, this constitutional relief may be sought against those decisions, as well. In its early days, the Constitutional Court was hesitant about nullifying via *tutela* actions the final judgments entered by its brethren courts, but it has since affirmed its authority to overrule any other court's final judgment, including those entered by the Supreme Court, the Council of State, and the Superior Council of the Judicature. The Constitutional Court examines *tutela* decisions in three-justice panels, although if the matter is of high importance or a unified doctrine is needed, the review may be conducted *en banc*.

Lately, high courts such as the Supreme Court of Justice and the Council of State have refused to obey Constitutional Court rulings invalidating their judgments. This is not to say that overturning a Supreme Court or Council of State final decision via a *tutela* action is an easy step, but to show that this quarrel among high Colombian courts (a problem known as "clash of trains") is not only a nuisance for the judiciary itself but also a source of uncertainty for the public because nobody knows when the adjudication process has come to an end.

Punishment

Types of Punishment

Imprisonment and fines are the main forms of punishment in Colombia. For the most common crimes such as murder, rape, theft, burglary, and robbery, the typical punishment is prison. For example, homicide is punishable by 17.3 to 37.5 years of imprisonment, aggravated homicide by 33.3 to 50 years, rape by 12 to 20 years, and robbery by 6 to 14 years.

Neither the death penalty nor life in prison is allowed under the Colombian Constitution. Actually, the death penalty was totally abolished in 1910. Corporal punishments are also banned. The maximum prison term is 60 years in case of multiple offenses, and for single offenses no punishment more than a 50-year prison term is legally possible. However, there are many parole options, and in the nation's criminal history, no defendant has actually served the maximum sentence.

Colombian law provides different community supervision options. One is home confinement, which can be applied when the minimum prison term for such a crime is of five or fewer years and the judge concludes on the basis of the personal, familiar,

A man pleads with police after being stopped on suspicion of robbery in Bogota, Colombia, September 15, 1995. Police anticrime activity has been increased since President Ernesto Samper declared a state of emergency aimed at fighting violent crime. Crime statistics for 1994 showed 26,000 homicides committed in Colombia, making it the most violent nation that is not at war in the world. (AP Photo/Richard Rogers)

labor, and social conditions of the convicted that the individual will not be a danger to the community and will not flee. In such a case, the defendant has to pay bail as a guarantee of good behavior.

The convicted defendant may also be freed on probation (not in home confinement) if the sentence actually imposed is no more than a three-year prison term, the defendant has paid all pending fines, and the judge determines that imprisonment is not needed based on the defendant's criminal record, his or her personal conditions, and the nature of the crime. In such a case, the judge may suspend the prison sentence for a test period ranging from 2 to 5 years.

If the imposed sentence is no more than an eight-year prison term, and the defendant has no criminal record for the last five years, he or she may be freed on bail with the use of a monitoring bracelet. This option is not available for defendants convicted of certain crimes, such as forced disappearance, torture, kidnapping, forced displacement, trafficking in persons, sexual assault, extortion, conspiracy, money laundering, terrorism, and drug trafficking.

Convicted felons who are serving a prison term may be considered for parole once they have served two-thirds of their sentences if they have exhibited good behavior in prison, compensated the victims (when the defendant's economic situation makes it feasible), and paid any pending fines. In addition, for each two days of work or education (either studying or teaching), the convicted felon reduces his or her prison term by one day.

Prisons

The National Institute for Penitentiaries and Jails operates 139 correctional facilities, including prisons, jails, and other confinement settings, through six regional directorates. There are 96 combined facilities with separate prison and jail compounds, 13 jail-only facilities, 11 prison-only facilities, and 11 women-only facilities, among others. A few prisons are classified by their levels of security. The prison with the largest number of inmates is the Modelo Prison in Bogotá, which houses more than 5,500 convicted offenders, although its regular capacity is no more than 2,900 inmates. This prison is dirty and overcrowded and has been known for its high incidence of violence. Correctional operations are regulated by the Prisons and Jails Code of 1993, which provides a legal framework for the protection of human rights and civil liberties within correctional facilities. Nevertheless, the implementation of these principles of good prison governance is far from satisfactory.

As of September 2008, Colombia had almost 70,000 inmates, of whom roughly 46,000 were convicted felons; the remaining were defendants under pretrial detention. Male inmates represented 94 percent of the entire prison population. Visits are permitted and usually take place on weekends. There is no compulsory work or study, but work and education may reduce a prisoner's sentence.

Colombia has signed agreements with Venezuela, Spain, Panama, Costa Rica, and Ecuador regarding the return to Colombia of Colombian prisoners serving sentences in those countries, but their usage has been limited because of the overcrowded conditions of Colombian prisons, which leaves no place for them.

Orlando Munoz-Neira

Further Reading

Bernal-Cuellar, Jaime, comp. (2003). *Lecciones de Derecho Penal. Parte Especial.* Bogotá: Universidad Externado de Colombia.

Corporación Excelencia en la Justicia: http://www.cej.org.co (click "biblioteca").

Martinez-Rave, Gilberto. (2006). *Procedimiento Penal Colombiano.* Bogotá: Editorial Temis.

Velasquez-Velasquez, Fernando. (2007). *Manual de Derecho Penal. Parte General.* 3rd ed. Bogotá: Comlibros.

Costa Rica

Legal System: Civil/Adversarial
Murder: Medium
Burglary: High
Corruption: Medium
Human Trafficking: Medium
Prison Rate: Medium
Death Penalty: No
Corporal Punishment: No

Background

Legal System

Prior to 1841, Costa Rica was governed by a variety of Spanish colonial laws. In that year, the General Code of 1841 combined in one statutory body legal codes pertaining not only to both civil and criminal matters but also to aspects of substantive and procedural law.

The promulgation of a new penal code in 1880, and the ratification of the penal procedural code in 1910, allowed criminal legislation to become independent from civil law, additionally leading to the separation of penal substantive law and the norms regarding procedure in the application of penal law. In terms of procedural application of criminal law, the Penal Procedural Code of 1910 was inquisitorial, that is, marked by a predominance of written statements and secrecy by which processes were conducted, with the impossibility for the prosecution or the defense to challenge or refute rival arguments. This process produced a degeneration of the system with frequent violations of human rights. In 1973, a new procedural code was adopted, which forced criminal justice to evolve into a two-pronged system with both inquisitorial and accusatorial features. The system remained inquisitorial during the early stages of the criminal justice process, including the investigation of criminal charges and instruction of causes that were written and kept private, whereas the latter stage of the process was accusatorial in nature, with public trials, so that both the prosecution and the defense could contest each other's arguments.

In 1996, the penal procedural code that is currently in practice was officially adopted. This code is adversarial in nature, does away with judicial instruction, favors spoken and reciprocal arguments by all parties involved, and redesigns the right to a defense for the accused, such as including victim statements during criminal processing. This code also establishes the Public Ministry as the authority responsible for criminal investigation and clearly delineates cases that require the intervention of the Public Ministry for the initiation of criminal prosecution (crimes of public action or complaint by the victim and crimes of public action punishable by private instance) and cases where no action is required (crimes of private action), and it also expands the diverse causes for extinction of a punishable act along with alternatives to criminal prosecution.

Among the reforms that occurred during the 1990s, the abolition of preventive incarceration stood out as one of the most important because under the procedural penal code of 1973, preventive incarceration functioned as an advance on a sentence of incarceration, which under all scrutiny was illegal. Another transformation of the system was the constitutional reform of 1989, which created La Sala Constitucional, or the Constitutional Chamber, making it possible for citizens to appeal whenever they felt that a fundamental human right had been violated. The Sala Constitucional also has the capability to order the release of inmates awaiting trial in overcrowded prisons by exercising constitutional control over rulings that originally denied them release from prison. Another significant modification of the system was in the practice of pretrial detention, which became the subject of more rigorous monitoring after 1993; these regulations were later formally codified in the Procedural Penal Code of 1998. A final noteworthy change to the system was the adoption of the Juvenile Penal Justice Law in 1996, which along with the Procedural Penal Code of 1998, implemented robust guarantees aimed at protecting the rights of defendants under the age of 18.

With regard to substantive penal legislation, it is important to emphasize that a series of fundamental reforms preceded the penal code of 1971 and the penal code that is currently in effect. These include the permanent abolition of the death penalty in 1871; the adoption of a taxonomic scheme to classify punishable acts in 1924, which divided them into two major groups, *delitos* (crimes) and *faltas o contravenciones* (violations); the introduction by the penal code of 1941 of treatment measures for persons with mental illnesses or drug addictions, or those unable to understand the illicit character of their acts; the limitation of maximum prison time to 30 years; and the inclusion of conditional suspension of a sentence and conditional liberty.

The penal code enacted in 1971 was intended to shift the criminal justice system from an organization primarily tasked with social repression to a body committed to restoring justice and harmony. This commitment was evident by the reduction of the maximum prison penalty from 30 years to 25 years and the emphasis on rehabilitation and social reintegration as the key correctional goals. There was also an increase in the benefits provided to those sentenced for a crime: the conditional execution of the sentence, judicial pardon, the possibility of pardon granted by the Council of the Government, and amnesty for political crimes.

Contrary to this earlier revival of rehabilitative ideals, modifications made to the penal code in 1994 were characterized by an increase in punitive rigor. The maximum prison sentence was elevated from 25 years to 50 years, sanctions for homicides and certain sexual crimes were increased, and new acts became classified as criminal. These changes have all inflated the prison population, which in the period from 1992 to 2004 increased from 103 to 202 persons incarcerated per 100,000 residents.

Courts

The courts are responsible for the preparatory and intermediary processes that precede a trial, including providing resources for appeal in matters of *contravenciones* (violations). Penal tribunals are responsible for overseeing the trial stage of the criminal justice process and can consist of one presiding judge or a panel of several judges, depending on the nature of the case. A single judge is employed when a defendant has admitted to the act committed and pleaded guilty, when the court is dealing with cases of simple infractions and violations punishable with a non-incarcerative sentence, when the court is dealing with crimes that warrant a sentence no greater than five years in prison, or when the court is dealing with illicit drug violations; in these cases, the trial is brief and does not require all stages of an ordinary oral and public trial. The collegiate tribunals come into play when the defendant fights for his or her innocence and the trial follows all stages of an oral and public trial.

Special tribunals also exist, including the Tribunal de Casación (Tribunal of Annulment) and the Tribunal de Casación Penal (Tribunal of Penal Annulment). The Tribunal of Annulment is composed of five magistrates from the Supreme Court of Justice, and its function is to exercise control over the application of sentences specified by collegiate penal tribunals. The Tribunal of Penal Annulment is composed of three judges whose function is similar to those performed by the Tribunal of Annulment, but the Tribunal of Penal Annulment intervenes only in sentences dictated by a single judge.

There are mixed tribunals and courts that carry out joint functions; that is, they simultaneously attend to more than one matter, for example, both criminal and civil cases, as determined by the number entering the judicial system. Moreover, the judicial system also includes courts solely dedicated to matters relating to the execution and fulfillment of punishment (i.e., *juzgados de ejecución de la pena,* or courts for execution of punishment).

The requirements for judgeship include holding Costa Rican citizenship and having full exercise of the rights afforded to citizens. The age requirement is 30 years, and judges must possess the title of attorney in law legally recognized in Costa Rica and must have practiced the legal profession for more than six years, except public officials with a legal practice of no less than three years. In 2007, there were 189 criminal court judges.

Crime

Classification of Crimes

The Costa Rican penal code divides punishable acts into two broad categories: *delitos* and *contravenciones.* The former refers to those illicit acts considered to be grave, for example, murder or rape. The latter refers to acts perceived as less grave and includes minor injuries or indecencies. *Delitos* can be punished with the privation of liberty, whereas *contravenciones* are punishable only by monetary fines, which the defendant must pay to the public institution.

Delitos are described under the first title of the second book of the penal code and are grouped according to the legal virtue they protect: life, honor, sexual integrity, family, liberty, scope of privacy, property, good faith in business, public safety, public tranquility, national security, public powers and the constitutional order, public authority, the administration of justice, the duty of the public functions, public faith, and human rights. *Contravenciones* are described in the first title of the third book of the penal code and can also be divided according to the legal virtues they protect: violations against persons, good customs, inviolability of land, estates or businesses, public order, and public security.

Not all *delitos* are included in the penal code because in the last 30 years, the categories of acts considered criminal have been expanded in new statutes. These new laws regulate a variety of specific matters, such as the environment, taxes, public administration, and consumption among others. In like form, special laws have been created that regulate all actions relating to drugs (Law 8204 of 2002). This last law establishes that the trade, consumption, industrialization, manufacturing, refinement, transformation, extraction, analysis, preparation, cultivation, production, importation, exportation, transport, prescription, supply, storage, distribution, and sale of illicit psychotropic substances or their derivatives are strictly limited to activities and necessary quantities needed for medical treatment, toxicology and chemical analysis, training of animals used by police for the detection of illicit substances, analysis of pharmaceuticals in medical or athletic matters, and authorized production of medical products. Only persons legally authorized can intervene in any matters relating to said substances. Personal consumption of drugs or possession of illicit substances is strictly prohibited.

Age of Criminal Responsibility

Article 17 of the penal code; articles 1, 2, 5, and 6 of the Juvenile Penal Justice Law; and the Childhood and Adolescent Codes establish the age of criminal responsibility at 18 years. Persons accused of crimes who are 18 years or older are prosecuted according to the penal code, and those under the age of 18 are prosecuted according to the Juvenile Penal Justice Law.

Crime Statistics

Criminality has shown an upward trend in Costa Rica during the last quarter of a century; the overall crime rate is fundamentally explained by trends in property crime. Robbery using force, larceny, robbery of a means of transportation, and robbery exerting violence on a person are emphasized because these categories make up 90 percent of the total crimes against property recorded during the 1980–2005 period.

Property crimes using force and larceny constitute the most frequent crimes: 42 percent and 24.5 percent, respectively, according to the *Estadísticas Policiales.* Crimes for infractions of the psychotropic laws also stand out, registering a rate of 27.4 cases per 100,000 residents between 2000 and 2005. Most reported crimes occur mainly in urban areas. In comparison to property crime, the average rate of homicides between 2000 and 2005 was 6.36 cases per 100,000 residents, a rate in line with the country's historic average. Rates per 100,000 residents of crimes reported to police in 2005 and the robbery rate in 2004 were as follows:

Property crimes using force	344.5
Larceny-theft	198.1
Robbery (2004)	158.6
Motor vehicle theft	121.2
Drugs	24.4
Forcible rape	12.9
Criminal homicide	6.9

Finding of Guilt

Prosecution

Criminal prosecution is the responsibility of the Public Ministry, which also directs criminal investigations with the aid of the judicial police. When information is obtained about a criminal act, the police proceed to investigate the incident, meet with and interview suspected authors and accomplices of the crime, collect evidence to build the factual foundation for prosecution, and produce a report that informs the prosecutor of the results of their investigation.

The prosecutor then has the duty of evaluating preliminary proceedings conducted by the judicial police, with the purpose of deciding whether to continue with the investigation or to solicit from a judge of the intermediate stage (judges of guarantee) one of the following options: to disregard the accusation or police action because no crime was found to be committed; to file a prosecutorial charge if there is a punishable crime but no suspect was found; to discharge the person being charged and drop charges against the person if there is no viable evidence of his or her guilt; to file for a partial or complete discontinuance of any criminal prosecution; to apply an abridged criminal process, which is viable only when the accused pleads guilty; to negotiate a reconciliation between parts; or to suspend and impose conditions to the accused or take any other step oriented in finalizing the prosecution process.

If the prosecutor decides to continue the investigation after deciding that there is enough evidence to charge a suspect of participating in the punishable act, the prosecutor can order any action permitted by law with the objectives of building a foundation for the formal prosecution and validating criminal charges to be presented before a judge in the intermediary stage. When the accused is detained for a flagrant crime, and criminal proceedings have been followed according to the law in building the case against that person, the prosecutor can immediately draw up the charges.

Prior to the preparation of charges, the prosecutor must summon the accused so that the person can provide his or her statement. If the accused is detained, the prosecutor must take any statements the person makes immediately or at the latest within 24 hours of the arrest. During this time, the accused is informed of the rights that he or she is afforded. If the accused decides to make a statement upon his or her arrest, only the Public Ministry and not the judicial police can legally obtain that statement.

The attorney general of the republic, under the Ministry of Justice, can prosecute crimes including crimes against national security, public tranquility, public powers or the constitutional order, the environment, land zones or public property, and the duties of public functions; illicit taxes or the violation of customs law; and crimes violating the organic law of the Central Bank of Costa Rica and the law against the illicit accumulation of wealth by public servants. The attorney general is qualified to initiate and exercise direct criminal prosecution without subordination to the Public Ministry.

Once the charge against a suspect is announced, there is a preliminary hearing before a judge of guarantees. The judge of guarantee will then order the case to the penal tribunal, which is the entity responsible for conducting the trial and dictating sentencing.

Rights of the Accused

According to article 39 of the Constitution of Costa Rica, there is no sentence that is legally effective unless the accused are given the opportunity to defend themselves and reject, by any legal means, the charges formed against them. The accused has the right to be heard within a reasonable time by a judge or tribunal in regard to the charges formed against them ("right to petition"). The accused has the right to be informed, prior to the imposition of the sentence, of the content of the charges and the relation between the criminal act and elements of evidence. The accused has the right to participate actively in the judicial process and can demand the appearance of witnesses, experts, and other persons to interrogate and cross-examine them. This right is used especially during the trial stage where both parties have the opportunity to consider and argue the evidence in front of an impartial tribunal. The accused has the right to personally defend himself or herself and can count on the assistance of a defense attorney of his or her choice. The accused also has the right to communicate privately with his or her attorney. If the accused does not choose to defend himself or herself and does not choose an attorney, the accused has the right to be provided with a public defender paid for by the state.

The right to a defense cannot be renounced and must be available to the accused from the first moment of criminal investigation, allowing him or her to understand any judicial or police action that singles out the individual as a possible suspect of a crime or a possible participant in a crime. It is the duty of the judicial police, the Public Ministry, and of the judges to inform the accused immediately and in a comprehensible manner of his or her rights as listed here and, in addition, the right to abstain from making any statements or declarations, the right not to be submitted to methods that induce or alter free will or compromise his or her dignity, the right to prevent any medium that impedes free movement, and the guarantee that no prejudice is inflicted during any procedural stage of prosecution by the tribunal or the Public Ministry.

Detention can be mandated prior to trial or before a sentence is ordered, but only in those cases where danger exists that the accused will escape to avoid prosecution or sentencing or when there is a risk that he or she will obstruct the investigation. The judge can also prescribe pretrial detention to prohibit the accused from committing further crimes. Nevertheless, the procedural code does not establish criteria regarding what constitutes an eminent threat. In any case, any time that pretrial detention is prescribed, there must be an order from a competent tribunal.

Pretrial detention is solicited by the Public Ministry before a judge of guarantee and at most can be used for up to only 12 months. If an extension of detention is required, the Public Ministry must petition before the Tribunal of Penal Annulment, and the maximum extension that can be granted is for an additional period of 12 months. Pretrial detention can also be ordered when a trial has already occurred and the convicted person is awaiting sentencing, in which case detention has the possibility of being expanded for up to 6 months. If the criminal matter at hand is complex in nature, the length of detention can be expanded in the following ways: when a trial is underway, the maximum time for detention is 18 months, with the possibility of being extended for another 18 months; and when a trial has already concluded and the convicted is awaiting sentencing, the detention can be extended up to 8 months.

Alternatives to Trial

There are three alternatives to trial in accordance to the penal procedural code: conditional suspension of the process or trial, integral reparation of damages, and reconciliation. The conditional suspension of the process or trial refers to a procedural instrument that ceases criminal prosecution and orders the implementation of restorative justice with the accused having to repay damage within a period of no less than two years and no more than five. The accused is also subject to the regulations established by article 26 of the procedural penal code, which can consist of mandated medical treatment under special circumstances. Once the penalty is carried out to the satisfaction of the judge, the prosecution is terminated without further legal consequence. The tribunal also has the power to revoke any alternative to trial and pursue full criminal prosecution against the accused. The conditional suspension of the process is applied only when the crime in question carries a prison sanction that does not exceed three years or when the convicted person can be sanctioned by punishment that does not deprive the person of his or her liberty.

It is important not to confuse the conditional suspension of the process with the conditional suspension of a sentence, given that the latter seeks to provide conditional release from prison when a sentence is brief. The conditional suspension of a sentence also differs from conditional suspension of the process in that the former allows prisoners to complete the remainder of the prison sentence in freedom as long as that prisoner does not relapse. Conditional suspension of a sentence is a benefit and not a right and depends on an evaluation of several factors by a judge of penal execution and the fulfillment of the following legal requisites: the prisoner must have completed half of the total sentence, the prisoner must not have a criminal record with convictions that warrant prison time for more than six months, and the prisoner must hold a report from the National Institute of Criminology that attests to his or her good behavior. Conditional suspension of a sentence and conditional liberty are also different from the conditional suspension of the process because they imply actions that occur once a trial has completed, whereas the conditional suspension of the process is an alternative to trial.

Integral reparation of damage is an alternative applied to crimes that are not violent in nature, including nonviolent crimes against persons and crimes that are not intentional. The objective of this alternative consists of total compensation to the victim for the damages caused. Examples of nonviolent crimes that warrant integral reparation include larceny, fraudulent administration, and unlawful and irregular appropriations. Nonintentional crimes can include involuntary manslaughter, abortion, reckless lesions, and injuries, among others.

Reconciliation consists of an agreement made by all parties in the conflict to desist from pursuing adjudication in court. Reconciliation is used as an alternative to trial in cases involving *contravenciones* (minor violations) or in cases involving crimes that do not require the intervention of the Public Ministry, including crimes against a person's honor (injuries, defamation, and calumny). Some crimes that require a formal complaint from the victim so that the Public Ministry can initiate penal action can also be resolved through reconciliation, for example, consensual sexual relationships with a person over the age of 12 and under the age of 15, rape of a person over the age of 15 who has not been deprived of reason or is unable to resist aggression, sexual aggression that is not aggravated, minor injuries and minor criminal acts, and crimes that qualify for a conditional suspension of sentence. For a reconciliation to take place, the tribunal must authorize the agreement between the parties and declare any prosecutorial action extinct.

A trial can also be avoided when the accused admits his or her criminal acts, and the Public Ministry and the affected party accept a brief process. Once these conditions are met, the matter is sent to the tribunal of trial so that they can dictate a sentence without holding a formal trial, unless the judge believes the parts must be heard, in which case the judge will assign an oral audience. This is the brief process described earlier.

It is important to emphasize that the majority of the cases that come before a tribunal are resolved through trial. For example, of the 12,529 cases registered in 2006 in the diverse penal tribunals of the country, 106 were resolved by reconciliation, 83 were resolved through the conditional suspension of the process, 33 were resolved through integral reparations of damages, and 6,487 were resolved through sentencing. Of this last number, 918 were resolved though brief processing.

Juvenile Justice

Persons under the age of 18 are not subject to the regulations of the penal code, but to the Juvenile Penal Justice Law. This legal body, which came into effect on February 6, 1996, is applied to persons between the ages of 12 and 18 years that commit acts categorized as *delitos* or *contravenciones* by the penal code or any special laws. This legislation, however, is not valid for boys and girls under the age of 12. In these cases, a judge is obligated to send the child to the Patronato Nacional de la Infancia, or the National Trust for Infancy, a government entity that is service-oriented and nonpunitive in nature, responsible for matters of childhood and adolescence in the country. This child welfare agency can implement the institutionalization of a minor in any of the juvenile centers established for the purpose of care and reform only under the explicit order and continuous monitoring of a judge of juvenile penal execution, who will control the imposed sanction.

The Juvenile Penal Justice Law is guided by the penal code to determine acts categorized as crimes; however, it is autonomous in terms of general dispositions, procedures, execution, and control of sanctions. In fact, these latter duties are completely different from those established by the penal code. The sanctions are subdivided into three categories: orders of orientation and supervision, socio-educative sanctions, and sanctions that involve deprivation of liberty.

Orientation and supervision could include a warning carried out in a verbal manner by a competent authority, assisted liberty, community service, or reparation of damages to the victim. Socio-educative sanctions establish a determined place of residence or a change of residence for the juvenile and often demand that the juvenile stop associating with determined persons. These sanctions prohibit the minor from visiting bars, clubs, and other specific providers of entertainment and require the minor's matriculation in a center of formal education or any other institution whose objective is to teach a vocation. Sanctions also require the minor to maintain employment and abstain from consuming alcoholic beverages, hallucinogenic substances, narcotics, or any toxins that can produce an addiction or habit. Under socio-educative sanctions, the institutionalization or treatment of the minor in a public health center or a private rehabilitation center for substance abuse treatment can be ordered. The third set of sanctions corresponds to the deprivation of liberty, institutionalization during leisure time, or institutionalization in specialized centers different from those reserved to persons over the age of 18.

Specialized judicial entities that focus on the juvenile population are responsible for criminal matters involving underage offenders and operate independently from judicial entities that prosecute adults over the age of 18. The Juvenile Penal Court is responsible for dictating sentences, whereas the Juvenile Penal Tribunal resolves appeals of sentences dictated by the Juvenile Penal Court, submitted by minors. The Tribunal of Penal Annulment resolves matters resulting from appellation decisions made by the Juvenile Penal Tribunal. The Public Ministry also operates a special unit dedicated to matters of juvenile law that works alongside the Juvenile Penal Execution Court, which is in charge of controlling the execution of sanctions imposed on minors.

Punishment

Types of Punishment

For those acts classified as *delitos,* the penal code establishes three types of punishment: principal punishments (prison, exile, fine, or civic disenfranchisement), accessory punishments (absolute and special disenfranchisement), and lending services of public utility. The punishment of exile is applied only to foreign nationals and is practically in disuse. It consists of their expulsion from the national territory and prohibits them from returning during a period allotted by the sentence. A fine obligates the accused to pay a sum of money to a public institution within 15 days following sentencing. If the convicted persons cannot pay the fine imposed as part of a sentence, the judge can convert the fine into community service payable to the state or to public institutions. If the convicted person has the means to pay the imposed fine but abandons the payment schedule settled by the court, the penal code establishes that the sentence can be turned into one day of prison for every day of the payment schedule that is not paid.

Absolute disenfranchisement consists of the loss of employment, loss of public office by election or appointment if the convicted person holds such title, ineligibility to obtain another public position, loss of public commissions, the deprivation of active and passive political rights, the inability to practice profession or trade, and the inability to practice the legal representation of minors and the administration of goods. Absolute disenfranchisement can be imposed for a period of time from 6 months to a maximum of 12 years. Special disenfranchisement consists of the privation or restriction of one or more rights and can be imposed simultaneously with principal punishments. It can be imposed for the same period of time as absolute disenfranchisement.

A prison sentence is the punishment applied with the highest frequency and has a maximum limit of 50 years. Prison sentencing is regulated by international norms to which Costa Rica subscribes, including the Standard Minimum Rules for the Treatment of Prisoners adopted by the United Nations in Geneva in 1955 and the American Convention on Human Rights. Both international conventions concur with Costa Rican national legislation in regard to the use of prison sentences for the purpose of rehabilitation.

Prison

Crimes such as homicide, rape, and robbery are punished with prison sentences, and the lengths of these sentences vary depending on mitigating and aggravating factors surrounding the crime. For example, simple homicide warrants an expected prison sentence minimum of 12 years and a maximum of 18 years. When an act is classified as intentionally causing death to a known person, a prison sentence can fluctuate between 25 and 35 years. When homicide is accompanied by mitigating factors (e.g., the original intent of the assailant was not to cause death but to inflict bodily damage), a prison sentence can vary from 1 to 6 years.

Simple rape carries a penalty that can range from 10 to 16 years in prison. The prison sentence for rape against a family member or when aggravating factors exist (e.g., when damage is produced to the health of the victim) can vary from between 12 and 18 years of incarceration. In the case of robbery, if the action is carried out with use of force, the total sentence ranges from 3 months to 6 years. If violence is inflicted on a person in the course of a robbery, the prison term can range from 3 to 9 years, and if the robbery is aggravated, for example, by use of a firearm, the prison sentence can range between 5 and 15 years.

Prison Population

In Costa Rica, the General Directorate of Social Adaptation, an entity of the Ministry of Justice, is the institution responsible for serving the offender population under different forms of criminal justice supervision: conditional suspension of the process, alternative sanctions, juvenile sanctions, and adult incarceration. With respect to this last one, the country has 15 prisons, and as of October 31, 2007, these prisons housed a total of 7,898 persons, of whom 23 percent had not been sentenced (pretrial detention). One percent corresponds to juvenile penal justice, with nearly one-third of this juvenile population located in the Center for Institutional Attention La Reforma. Only 6 percent of the entire correctional population was female.

In regard to the rights of the persons deprived of liberty, Costa Rican legislation establishes that prisoners enjoy the same individual, social, and economic rights as the rest of the population save for the rights that are incompatible with incarceration. In addition, prisoners receive professional attention from a interdisciplinary team that helps them to acquire understanding and to develop skills that will be useful in life, for example, a clear comprehension of social and personal aspects that caused the prisoner to lapse into criminal behavior, with the goal of preventing the person from becoming involved in new criminal acts.

Work is conceived as a right and not as an instrument of punishment for those who are incarcerated. Therefore, forced labor and other disciplinary sanctions that go against the dignity and human rights of a prisoner are prohibited. Activities and routines are programmed to achieve the goal of social reintegration of those incarcerated and include vocational training in technical professions. For every two days of work completed, one day of prison is deducted from the sentence. The same rule applies in the case of persons who are being held as part of pretrial detention, but the benefit is granted only once the prisoner is given a firm sentence.

Prisoners are granted three types of visits: general, conjugal, and special. The first refers to visits from relatives or friends, which the prisoner can have at least once a week for a period of no less than three hours. Conjugal visits give the prisoner the right to intimate contact with the person of his or her choice, as long as the chosen partner is not of the same sex. Each conjugal visit lasts no less than four hours and can be granted once every 15 days. Special visits are conceded outside the general visiting hours, depending on the gravity or urgency of the circumstance; they must be authorized by the director of the correctional facility, and each special visit cannot exceed one hour, with the exception of cases marked by law. Visits from international human rights organizations to Costa Rican prisons are regularly authorized.

Extradition

Last, current legislation prohibits the extradition of Costa Rican nationals. This means that if a foreign country solicits the extradition of a Costa Rican national (whether by birth or naturalization) because the person has committed a crime in that country, the solicitation will be denied. Nevertheless, if the crime for which the person is being prosecuted exists in the national legislation, that person will be processed in the Costa Rican tribunals under the laws of the country.

If extradition petitions are requested for a foreign national, these petitions will be processed if they follow strict guidelines. For example, the crime for which the order is made cannot be political and must be of a common type with equivalents regulated under Costa Rican legislation. Furthermore, if the crime is punishable with the death penalty in the country soliciting extradition, this order will be rejected because Costa Rica, a subscriber to various international humanitarian agreements, opposes capital punishment. In October 2007, only five people were incarcerated under the request of a foreign nation and were waiting to be transferred to the country that requested the order of extradition to face the criminal prosecution for the crime with which they were charged.

Rodolfo Calderón and Eduardo González

Further Reading

Fournier, Fernando. (2001). *Historia del Derecho*. 3rd ed. Costa Rica: Editorial Juricentro.

González, Daniel. (1997). *Reflexiones sobre el Nuevo Proceso Penal*. Costa Rica: Colegio de Abogados y Asociación de Ciencias Penales.

Instituto Nacional de Estadística y Censos. (2007). Estadísticas Vitales. INEC: http://www.inec.go.cr.

Ministerio de Justicia. (2008). Estadísticas: http://www.mj.go.cr/Estadísticas.htm.

Poder Judicial. (2007). Estadísticas Policiales: http://www.poder-judicial.go.cr/planificacion/estadisticas/.

Cuba

Legal System: Civil/Socialist
Murder: Medium
Corruption: Medium
Human Trafficking: High
Prison Rate: High
Death Penalty: Yes
Corporal Punishment: Yes

Background

The Socialist Republic of Cuba is an archipelago of 11 million inhabitants located in the Caribbean

Sea 90 miles southeast of Key West, Florida. Geographically, Cuba consists of one large island that is home to the majority of the country's population, the much smaller Isle of Youth, and hundreds of minor, mostly uninhabited islets. Cuba has a population of approximately 11 million people, about 10 percent of whom (2.2 million people) live in the capital city of Havana. Cuba was a colony of Spain for 400 years, and as a consequence, Spanish remains the country's national language. About 45 percent of Cubans identify themselves as Catholic, and another 5 percent are Protestant; however, in daily life, these religions are less prominent than Santeria, an Afro-Cuban spiritual practice that blends African beliefs and religious practices with Catholic ones.

History

The white man's history of Cuba began when Christopher Columbus claimed the island for the king of Spain in 1492. For centuries prior to contact, Cuba had been inhabited by the Taino-Arawak Indian peoples, whom Columbus sought to enslave in service of the Spanish empire, thus beginning a brutal conflict that ultimately led to the near-extinction of Taino-Arawaks on the island.

In the mid-1800s, Cuban nationalists began a series of armed struggles for independence. In 1898, as the revolutionaries were nearing victory, the United States inserted itself into the Cuban war of independence, inaugurating what came to be known as the Spanish-American War. As a result of winning this

Police patrol the streets of Colon, Cuba. (Barnaby Dorfman)

wider conflict, the United States obtained a peace treaty from Spain that gave the United States sovereignty over Cuba. In 1902, the United States withdrew its armies from Cuba, but only after a fledgling Cuban government accepted a constitution that gave the United States the authority to intervene in Cuba's domestic affairs whenever U.S. interests on the island were threatened. The terms of the U.S. withdrawal also granted the United States the right to use Cuba's Guantanamo Bay as a naval station, an arrangement that has remained a sore spot for the Cuban government into the 21st century. Since the onset of the U.S. war on terror, for many people outside the United States, the U.S. prison camp at Guantanamo has become synonymous with illegal detention, torture, and violations of human rights.

In the late 1950s, a number of political organizations opposed to the government of military strongman and President Fulgencio Batista joined together in an armed rebellion. After a series of internal debates within these movements and conflicts among them, Fidel Castro emerged as the overall leader of the revolutionary coalition. On January 1, 1959, the Cuban revolution toppled the U.S.-supported Batista government, beginning a political process that would eventually lead to the proclamation of Fidel Castro as Cuba's president and "maximum leader." This also led to the transformation of Cuba into a socialist state with a centrally planned economy and a democratic-centralist government in which each level elects representatives to the next highest level, rather than direct election to any position other than the Cuban equivalent of city councils.

In 2008, Fidel Castro resigned. The new president of Cuba, Raul Castro, indicated that he would continue many of the socialist policies and practices established under the leadership of his brother, Fidel. He also signaled, however, somewhat greater receptivity to expansion of internal private markets. In 2008, for instance, the Raul Castro government liberalized public access to cell phones and the Internet for those who could pay for these services with U.S. dollars or their economic equivalent in pesos. Although this is a significant liberalization of communications access in Cuba, relatively few Cubans living on the island had sufficient income to take advantage of these changes.

Cuban and U.S. Relations

The government of the United States has maintained an active policy of "regime change" against Cuba longer than it has toward any other country in the world. For half of a century, the U.S. government has sought to isolate Cuba economically, undermine its socialist political economy, and return Cuba to its former position as a client state with close economic and political ties to the United States. The resignation of Fidel Castro did little to change this policy.

Given the historic and contemporary geopolitical hostility between Cuba and the United States, any analysis of Cuba faces the challenge of piercing the miasma of propaganda and political rhetoric on both sides of the U.S.-Cuba divide. In addition, the U.S. government has long prohibited expenditure of federal funds to support scholarly research in Cuba. Whether self- or foundation-financed, U.S. scholars who arrive in Cuba can do so only after negotiating complicated and burdensome procedures required by the U.S. Office of Foreign Assets Control to obtain permission to travel to Cuba. The alternative is to risk a US$10,000 fine and up to five years in prison. At the time of this writing, Cuba is the only place in the world that a U.S. citizen can be punished for simply visiting.

Current Political Organization

The government of Cuba is divided into executive, legislative, and judicial branches. The executive branch consists of a Council of State and a Council of Ministers. The president of the Council of State serves as the president of Cuba. The national legislative branch consists of a unicameral body known as the National Assembly of People's Power. The Supreme Court of Cuba serves as the nation's highest judicial branch of government and as the court of last resort for all appeals from provincial-level courts.

Below the national level, Cuba is divided into 14 provinces and numerous municipalities, each with its own elected Assembly of People's Power. Politically, Cuba is a one-party, socialist state organized according to Marxist-Leninist principles of democratic centralism. This means that primary political leadership is provided by the Communist Party of Cuba and that those elected to base-level representative bodies, such as a municipal assembly, choose from among themselves who will serve in the provincial assembly. This process is repeated when provincial representatives choose who will sit in the National Assembly and when the National Assembly selects the executive officers of the government, including the president.

Role of the Police

Cuba's police, known as the Policía Nacional Revolucionaria (PNR), operate under the supervision of the Internal Order and Crime Prevention division within Cuba's Ministry of the Interior (MINIT). In addition to policing, the Internal Order division of MINIT also supervises fire protection and corrections.

The PNR is responsible for uniform policing, criminal investigation, crime prevention, juvenile delinquency reduction, and traffic control. The PNR is organized into numerous provincial police divisions, each with its own chief of police. Mirroring Cuba's larger system of democratic centralism, these departments are subject to oversight by provincial-level (county) governments, which are in turn responsible to the national directorate of the PNR.

To the extent that Cuban policing is linked to repression of prohibited political activities, these controls originate from the Security Directorate of MINIT, which has responsibility for protecting against sabotage, espionage, and other actions deemed a threat to state security, or as byproduct of Cuba's system of citizen involvement in social control.

Cuba has long relied on citizens to perform nightly watch patrols (*la guarida*) in neighborhoods and around workplaces and on neighborhood associations known as Committees for the Defense of the Revolution to promote compliance with civil responsibilities such as water and electricity conservation, inoculations, proper garbage disposal, and in some cases, reporting "suspicious" activity. If suspicious activity reported to the PNR is deemed to be political in nature, it will typically be transferred from the Internal Order division of MINIT to the Security Directorate for investigation.

Crime

Classification of Crimes

Crimes in Cuba are divided into felony and misdemeanor offenses. Felony crimes are those with a potential sentence exceeding one year of imprisonment or a fine of more than 300 *cuotas*. *Cuotas* are units of a fine that have variable value. Thus, one person may be subject to a fine of 100 *cuotas* at one peso each whereas another may be subject to the same fine but at a rate of two pesos per *cuota*. The resultant numerical inequality—100 versus 200 pesos for the same offense—is designed to ensure that people with differing levels of economic resources experience similar levels of punishment. For this reason, some Cuban judges will set the value of a *cuota* equivalent to a person's hourly wage.

Felony-equivalent crimes in Cuba encompass a standard array of offenses against persons or property including murder, rape, assault, death or injury by vehicle, robbery, burglary, larceny, vehicle theft, arson, and drug trafficking, as well as various offenses designed to address specific problems associated with a socialist economy. Except for murder, rape, and robbery, most offenses under the Cuban legal code have less serious, misdemeanor equivalents.

Cuba's 1988 penal code revision redefined a crime as an act that both violated the law *and* caused significant social harm. Acts that violated the law but caused only limited harm were redefined as infractions that would be handled by paying a fine. For example, one case that this author researched involved a man charged with stealing five five-gallon containers of cooking oil from the factory where he worked. The defense attorney convinced the judicial panel that the theft did not meet the standard for "crime" because it did not cause significant harm. The court agreed and ruled that his offense was, indeed, an infraction. However, because the judges were sitting in a criminal court panel that did not have jurisdiction over infractions, they released the man with only a warning.

Cuba's socialist system of production and distribution has also led to new categories of wrongdoing and new crime-control priorities. The system of rationed and planned distribution enabled Cuba to achieve higher overall levels of nutrition, public health, housing, and education than are found in many developing nations, but it also created barriers to satisfying desires that exceeded the minimum provisions. As a result, for over a generation, both private individuals and those in charge of economic operations often turned to underground markets operating outside the planned distribution system as a means of connecting sellers and buyers of desired commodities. The manager of a clothing factory, for instance, might trade cloth in an underground market for parts to repair a broken machine—parts that very well might have been stolen from another factory. A worker in a chicken-processing plant might routinely steal a few birds to sell to friends and neighbors. In the pre-1993 era, when possessing U.S. dollars was illegal, a street hustler (*jinetero*) might exchange Cuban pesos for U.S. dollars with foreign tourists and then use them to buy goods in tourist stores for personal consumption or for resale on the black market. In response, the Cuban legal system devotes considerable energy to identifying and prosecuting black-market offenders and others who disrupt Cuba's socialist system of production and distribution.

Although Cuba's legal system focuses more on those involved in organized black-market operations than on end consumers, the illegality of buying and selling in the underground market means that many otherwise law-abiding Cubans find themselves committing at least minor crimes on a regular basis as they try to supplement what is available through the formal distribution mechanism. Even those who enforce the laws against underground markets have admitted to making black- and gray-market purchases. Cubans will often note that their economic system, even after a degree of post-Soviet market liberalizations, forces them to live a double morality (*doble moral*), underscoring the particular contradiction between socialist distribution and socialist legality in Cuba.

Crime Incidence

There is little available statistical data on rates of street crime in Cuba. The country does not regularly publish official crime statistics and does not participate in the periodic United Nations Survey of Crime Trends and Operations of Criminal Justice Systems. As a result, most available information regarding crime in Cuba is based on ethnographic information, analyses by nongovernmental organizations, and reports by citizens and travelers to the country. Taken together, these data sources suggest that rates of ordinary street crime in Cuba are low compared to other developing countries and that in some categories, such as interpersonal violence, rates compare favorably with those of developed nations. Cuban citizens typically report having relatively little fear of being victims of property crimes, although some have suggested that increases in inequality since the dollarization of the economy have led to a noticeable growth in property crimes.

These current reports are consistent with this author's own research. In 1989, the author obtained a list of rates for serious street crimes in Cuba through a contact in the Cuban Ministry of Justice. These data showed rates of reported crimes to be very low by U.S. standards in almost every category except for assault. In 1992, *Granma,* the official newspaper of the Cuban Communist Party, published rates of major crimes that were consistent with the data the author received.

Although street crime is not a major concern in the day-to-day life of Cubans, an increasing reliance on tourism as an important source of foreign currency has spurred the growth of associated crimes, particularly those related to sex work. One of the successes of the Cuban revolution was the near elimination of the open, public prostitution that had circulated in and around the casino-oriented tourist community in the 1930–1960 era. Since the 1990s, as Cuba expanded its tourist industry through the construction of new beach hotels and other tourist amenities, sex tourism has reemerged in Cuba as one of the downsides of a tourist economy.

By the beginning of the 21st century, Cuba had become a popular destination for European men, particularly Italians and Spaniards (but also some Americans willing to risk illegal travel to Cuba) seeking the companionship and sexual favors of young, healthy, relatively educated Cuban women. Rather than exchanging quick sex for a fixed price, these women, known as *jineteras,* frequently accompany men for the duration of their stay as a way of gaining entrance into expensive clubs and shops, as well as receiving cash and other gifts. This semiunderground industry involves more than the women willing to serve as companions and "minor wives" to visiting foreigners with U.S. dollars. In some cases, taxi drivers direct potential customers to prostitutes or clubs where women are likely to be available. Other Cubans with rooms or apartments to rent make them routinely available to *jineteras* and their "boyfriends." In an attempt to control this growth of sex tourism, and particularly an emergent organized criminal underground in the sex trades, the Cuban government instituted laws specifically targeting individuals whom the government defined as "parasites" of the sex trade. Under Cuba's penal code revision of 1999, anyone who induces someone into the commercial sex trade or who benefits from this trade (e.g., pimp, madam, owner of a hotel or dwelling used for sex) can be sentenced to prison for a period from 4 to 10 years, depending on circumstances and prior record.

In addition to crimes associated with sex tourism, the increase in foreign visitors has created the context for growth in several other crime categories. The tourist industry is a fertile ground for redirecting many of the material goods that tourism requires—good food, alcohol, color televisions, air conditioners, and so on—into domestic underground markets. Tourists are also lucrative targets for theft. Unlike Cuba's earlier days, when tourists reported having Cubans return their lost purses or wallets with nothing removed, today tourist Web sites warn those going to Cuba to take basic precautions against theft, although they also typically indicate that tourists have little to fear in the way of interpersonal violence. Lastly, there is more widespread availability of illegal drugs in Cuba's youth underground than in the later decades of the 20th century, which appears to be associated with increased travel into Cuba.

Finding of Guilt

Socialist Legality

The concepts that inform Cuba's legal system reflect the island's history as a Spanish colony, a U.S. satellite, and a centrally planned socialist state. Cuba's history as a Spanish colony left the island with deep civil law traditions similar to those found in Europe. After the 1959 revolutionary victory, the Cuban legal system continued to emphasize written codes rather than court-based precedent as the source of law. Although Cubans may win appeals in high-level courts, rulings of this type do not change existing law the way they can under common law systems. Significant changes to Cuba's legal system, as in most civil law states, come about through the formal revision of legal codes.

In addition to residues from its prerevolutionary history, the Cuban legal system has been shaped by nearly 50 years of legal development guided by Marxist theory, as well as three decades of close relations with the former Soviet Union and its allies. These factors have produced a legal system that relies on concepts of "socialist legality."

One of the most striking features of Cuba's system of socialist legality is that it is specifically designed to weigh substantive measures of justice along with juridical ones. This approach directs judicial actors such as judges and lawyers to find legal outcomes that reflect the concrete reality of the harm done and the lives affected, rather than requiring judges to adhere to narrow legal definitions. In one case that this author researched, a man was accused of stealing two chickens from a processing plant, bringing one home for his wife to cook, and selling the other on the black market for 200 pesos. The three-person municipal court (two citizens and one trained jurist) found the man guilty and levied a fine of 100 pesos. The judges explained that they assessed a fine that was less than the amount of money the offender had earned by selling the chicken because the accused was poor, so a 200-peso fine would amount to excessive punishment for the crime, particularly because the social harm resulting from stealing from a factory was less than if he had stolen from a private individual.

A second important element of socialist legality as practiced in Cuba is the view that the law should be used as a deliberate tool for socialist development rather than merely a framework that individuals and institutions can use to protect or promote their own interests. In the 1980s, for instance, government policy governing the distribution of highly desired but scarce consumer items such as automobiles, motorcycles, air conditioners, and color televisions required that these items be first allocated to workplaces based on the level of their overall productivity and then to workers in those places based on their performance as judged by a council of coworkers. The controlled distribution of desired goods led to a flourishing underground market in these items, bringing together individuals in positions to divert these items to the underground economy and individuals with the money to purchase them but no institutional opportunities to do so. In accordance with Cuba's concepts of socialist legality, involvement in the black market for high-ticket items was more than theft; it was a significant undermining of the entire system of socialist distribution, and as a result, many of these offenses carried particularly long prison terms.

The third aspect of Cuba's socialist legality promotes the use of "social courts" rather than formal tribunals to resolve a variety of private disputes or conflicts that do not involve criminal matters. Thus, as will be discussed later in this entry, many disputes that would end up in formal courts in the United States are often handled within the arenas where the problem occurred, such as workplaces and neighborhoods.

Fourth, Cuba's socialist legality emphasizes direct citizen involvement in both the adjudication and the prevention of crime. Two of the most significant examples of this involvement are the use of citizens as lay judges in municipal and civil courts and the requirement that citizens take part in citizen safety patrols (*guardia*) in their neighborhoods and workplaces.

Rights of the Accused

Persons accused of crimes in Cuba have the right to legal representation, a court trial, and consideration of release before trial. In the 1970s, as part of formalizing its system of socialist legality, Cuba established a national system of law collectives known as *bufetes colectivos*. The *bufetes colectivos* were designed to provide the full range of legal services at affordable prices determined by the government. Although state-provided attorneys remain the norm, in the post-Soviet era, some attorneys now work as private legal counselors who, though not appearing in court, can provide legal advice and guidance to citizens with legal troubles, including those facing criminal charges.

According to Cuban procedural law, a person who has been arrested should not be detained longer than 24 hours unless the case has been submitted to a police investigator, who must then submit it to a judicial prosecutor (*fiscal*) within three working days. The *fiscal* then has three working days to dismiss the case, release the suspect pending trial, or submit to the court that will eventually hear the case a justification for keeping the suspect in custody until trial. The court, in turn, has three days to approve detention or order release. In sum, according to Cuban law, a person accused of a criminal offense may be held for a total of 10 workings days prior to a formal decision to release or detain before trial, but not longer than that. Defendants who are released prior to trial may be released on their own recognizance, to the oversight of some social organization such as a workplace or a union, or they may be released on payment of bail.

Prosecution

Cuba also utilizes an inquisitorial system of criminal procedure. Among other things, this means that prosecutors, on one side, and attorneys for the defense, on the other, are expected to determine the truth of the matter at hand regardless of whether doing so will help them win their respective cases. To further this ideal, the Cuban prosecutorial system is organized according to a civil service model rather than an electoral one, thus reducing the significance of a prosecutor's win-loss record as a factor in career advancement. During the author's research in a Cuban law collective, he learned of several instances where prosecutors received disciplinary letters because they were winning nearly all of their cases, which the office of the attorney general (*fiscal*) interpreted as paying too much attention to winning rather than fact-finding.

Defense

Intermingled with Cuba's civil law traditions are elements of the Anglo-American adversarial system, including a version of habeas corpus and a greater separation of courts and prosecutors than was typical in many other socialist legal systems. Consequently, Cuban lawyers enjoy somewhat greater latitude in defending their clients than did attorneys in the former Soviet Union and its socialist allies. A key feature of this difference is that Cuban attorneys may submit evidence directly to courts without obtaining the prior approval of prosecutors. The result is that Cuban attorneys typically have achieved higher levels of acquittals for their clients in criminal cases than attorneys in other socialist countries. In a study of a large law collective in central Havana, this author found an overall acquittal rate of approximately 15 percent for all the criminal cases handled over a five-year period, considerably higher than the 1 percent acquittal rate typical of the former Soviet Union and East Germany.

Judicial Organization

Each municipality and province in Cuba has a system of courts. Cuba's municipal-level tribunals serve as courts of first instance for lesser crimes and minor civil matters. Three-judge panels, composed of two lay judges and one trained jurist with a law degree, hear cases in these courts. Lay judges are ordinary citizens who are elected to serve in a judicial capacity for a limited period of time and who, after their election, complete a brief legal course to prepare them for their duties as a judge. Provincial courts handle felony-level crimes, divorces, and civil disputes, and appeals from municipal courts. These higher-level courts utilize five-judge panels consisting of three trained judges and two lay jurists. Appeals from provincial courts are heard in one of the sections (*salas*) of the Supreme Court. The Cuban legal system also includes a system of military courts that adjudicate offenses committed by members of the country's military while serving in government posts.

In addition to this extensive system of formal courts to handle crimes and other problems, Cuba's pursuit of socialist legality led to the promotion of nonjudicial forums for dispute resolution. Conflicts between neighbors, for instance, are often directed to block-level Committees for the Defense of the Revolution for settlement. Similarly, disputes between workers and between workers and supervisors are frequently referred to workers' councils rather than municipal or provincial courts, just as disputes resulting from Cuba's socialist system of housing allocation are typically handled by municipal housing authorities rather than municipal or provincial civil courts.

Legal Education

By the 1980s, Cuba had a well-defined system of socialist legal education, with law schools at the University of Havana and throughout the country's university system. Unlike the United States, where legal education is a postgraduate course of study, in Cuba, like many civil law states, law is a five-year, postsecondary program. Upon graduation, law students are expected to perform a two-year social service internship, such as providing legal counsel for poor clients or working for some agency or ministry.

As in many civil law states, the role of providing legal counsel to the public and that of being a judge are relatively distinct career paths. Lawyers wishing to provide direct service to the public will orient their training and social service in this direction, seeking positions in law collectives or other agencies. Those who seek a career path as jurists will work with and through the Ministry of Justice to obtain positions first in municipal courts or other lower-level dispute-resolving bodies and later in provincial courts.

The economic crisis experienced by Cuba as a result of the disappearance of the socialist trading bloc and the escalation of the U.S. embargo had a serious impact on the career paths of many Cuban attorneys and jurists. As the country's domestic economy became tied to the U.S. dollar, Cuban lawyers and even law professors increasingly left their positions for less skilled but more lucrative jobs in the tourist industry or other sectors of Cuba's post-Soviet economy, where they could earn at least a portion of their income in foreign currency. Some attorneys, frustrated with their increasingly downward mobility in a marketizing economy, immigrated to Europe or the United States, and interest in law as a career declined.

Punishment

Types of Punishments

The Cuban penal code provides for the usual range of penal sanctions ranging from fines and probation to incarceration or execution. In 1988, Cuba underwent a major liberalization of its penal code that lowered many penalties and expanded opportunities for supervised work as part of probation. In 1999, largely in response to citizen dissatisfaction with penal policies that many citizens felt were "soft on crime," Cuba again revised its penal code, this time increasing criminal penalties.

The new code instituted life imprisonment as a possible sanction in place of the death penalty and simultaneously expanded the crimes that could be punished by death. Previously, the maximum prison sentence for any crime had been 30 years, and the death penalty had been largely reserved for crimes involving homicide or treason. Under the revised code, however, the death sentence can be applied for certain crimes involving particular aggravated circumstances.

For instance, the base maximum penalty for trafficking a large amount (*cantidades relativamente grandes*) of illegal drugs is 8 to 20 years' imprisonment. The death penalty, however, can be applied in a drug trafficking case if the offense is committed by a government official using government property, or if it involves using youth under the age of 16. Similarly, although the crime of rape without any aggravating circumstances is punishable by a prison sentence between 4 and 10 years, if a rape involves serious injury to the victim or was committed against a person under the age of 14, execution is a possible sanction.

Although Cuba's code permits the use of execution for a number of offenses not involving homicide, this appears to be more symbolic than routine. Between 2000 and 2008, Cuba executed only three individuals, all associated with a hijacking that resulted in the death of a police officer. In April 2008, Cuba's new president, Raul Castro, commuted the death sentences of all those on death row to life imprisonment.

Prison

The Directorate of Jails and Prisons under the Cuban Ministry of the Interior operates a penal system of 550 detention and correctional facilities, consisting of local jails; two types of adult correctional institutions, prisons and *granajas*; and reform schools for juveniles less than 16 years old. Adult prisons are typically walled or fenced facilities. *Granajas* are open farms used primarily for those convicted of misdemeanors or lesser felonies. Juvenile offenders are housed in school-like facilities that emphasize education. With the exception of several large, older prisons, the majority of penal institutions in Cuba are relatively small, typically housing 100 offenders or fewer.

Cuba's rate of imprisonment fell in the late 1980s and early 1990s as a result of penal liberalization. In the latter part of the 1990s, these numbers began to rise as the country experienced both an increase in crime and the institution of harsher penalties. In 1990, Cuba's rate of imprisonment was estimated at around 190 persons per 100,000. By 2006, this figure had risen to 457 per 100,000, the seventh highest in the world, although nearly 40 percent lower than the U.S. prison rate of 738 per 100,000 that same year.

Reports of prison conditions in Cuba's prisons vary widely. Available research, however, suggests that overall conditions in Cuba's prisons are similar to those in many developing countries, with food, sanitation, and health care falling below prison practices in more affluent nations. The Cuban prisons that this author visited in the late 1980s and mid-1990s were closer to the living standards of ordinary working-class Cubans than, for instance, U.S. prisons were to ordinary working-class living standards in the United States. This, however, does not make them pleasant places. Prisoners have reported losing considerable weight while incarcerated because of limited diets, and many have complained of illnesses resulting from unsanitary or unhealthy living conditions, such as exposure to extremes of heat and cold.

Various human rights organizations have reported that prisoners incarcerated for antigovernment activities experience harsher treatment and greater deprivations of liberties than ordinary offenders, particularly in terms of contact with the outside world. One of the reasons for this is that political prisons are sometimes held in special units overseen not by regular prison guards, but by members of the State Security section of the Ministry of the Interior.

Healthy prisoners are expected to work in prison industries or farms that supply products for state agencies. These workers are typically paid the same rate as ordinary laborers. If a prisoner is married or has children, a portion of his or her salary will be provided for the maintenance of dependents. In recent years, as the purchasing power of the peso has declined substantially, the ability of wages and remittances to improve the lives of prisoners and their families has similarly declined. According to Cuban penal policy, both male and female prisoners are permitted conjugal visits from a spouse or long-term paramour once every two months, although this frequency can be increased for good behavior.

Raymond Michalowski

Further Reading

Brenner, Phillip, Marguerite Rose Jimenez, John M. Kirk, and William M. Leo Grande, eds. (2007). *A Contemporary Cuba Reader: Reinventing the Revolution*. New York: Rowman & Littlefield.

Evenson, Debra. (1994). *Revolution in the Balance: Law and Society in Contemporary Cuba*. Boulder, CO: Westview Press.

Michalowski, Raymond. (1995). "Between Citizens and the Socialist State: The Negotiation of Legal Practice in Socialist Cuba." *Law and Society Review* 29(1): 65–101.

Zatz, Marjorie. (1994). *Producing Legality: Law and Socialism in Cuba*. New York: Routledge.

Dominica

Legal System: Common
Murder: Medium
Corruption: Low
Prison Rate: High
Death Penalty: Yes
Corporal Punishment: Yes

Background

Dominica is often misunderstood to mean the Dominican Republic, a Spanish-speaking island that borders Haiti, between the islands of Cuba and Puerto Rico. Dominica, to the contrary, is an English-speaking island located 30 miles south of Guadeloupe and 30 miles north of Martinique, in the northern end of the Windward island chain of the Lesser Antilles, in the Caribbean.

Dominica is 290 square miles, and its 71,242 residents (2001), who are mostly (95%) from the Africa diaspora, speak English and Creole as their first and second languages, respectively. Carib Indians, the indigenous people, make up about 4 percent of the population, and 1 percent are from other racial backgrounds.

Dominica is often referred to as the "Nature Island of the Caribbean" because of its natural beauty and lush greenery. Approximately 60 percent of the land is under forest, and it is one of the most mountainous countries in the world, second only to Switzerland. In 1492, Christopher Columbus sailed into the Caribbean while searching for Asia. In 1493, he became the first known European to land at Dominica. Throughout its post-European "discovery," Dominica shifted as a possession of the French and British, depending on which nation's fortunes were on the wane.

In 1748, there was an agreement between the English and the French to leave the island to the Caribs. The 1763 Treaty of Paris assigned Dominica to Britain, but the treaty was broken when the French made two subsequent failed attempts to recapture Dominica in 1795 and 1805. Thereafter, until 1967, the island remained a British colony and, later, a self-governing associated state. November 3, 1978, marked the nation's full independence from Britain. Dominica is now officially known as the Commonwealth of Dominica, although it maintains republic status within the British Commonwealth.

Over 20 years of census counts (1981–2001), the population of Dominica declined by 3.5 percent (73,795 in 1981 to 71,242 in 2001). Much of the population decline has been attributed to emigration. Fifty percent of Dominica households have at least one family member residing overseas, and over 30 percent of households as of 2009 have had members migrate over the previous 10 years. Forty percent of Dominica migrants relocate to other Caribbean islands; 40 percent to North America; and most of the remainder to Britain. This high emigration has mainly been in reaction to the failing agriculture sector and lack of significant growth in other sectors, such as the tourism and offshore banking that have resulted in population stabilization and increase in other islands. Because most emigrants are adults in their prime working age (20–34), this contributed to the 40 percent decrease in the number of live birth rates in Dominica over the decade prior to 2009. The male and female populations are almost evenly distributed, with 49.8 percent male and 50.2 percent female. According to Halcrow Group Limited, 46 percent of the Dominica population in 2002 was under the age of 25, of which 62 percent had not reached the age of 15.

Crime

Classification of Crimes and Crime Statistics

At the time of this chapter's writing, credible Dominica crime statistics were not available for years prior to 1983. Interviews with reliable police sources have indicated that the turmoil that characterized everyday life in Dominica soon after independence in 1978, after Hurricane David in 1979, and during coup attempts prior to 1983 had profound effects on the reporting and recording of crimes that occurred in the nation. Therefore, official crime data prior to 1983 are not discussed here. Crime statistics referenced in this entry were obtained from the Dominica Statistical Division and from official police sources. Crimes in Dominica are recorded under two broad categories: indictable (more serious) and summary (less serious) matters. Indictable crimes include abduction, abortion, arson, assault, buggery, burglary, drug importation and trafficking, forgery, grievous bodily harm, incest, indecent assault, infanticide, kidnapping, murder, rape, robbery, and theft. Summary crimes include assault, battery, child abuse, disorderly conduct, malicious damage, possession of drugs, traffic offenses, vagrancy, and wounding.

Between 1983 and 2007, indictable (serious) crimes reported to the police increased by 129 percent (600 in 1983 and 1,371 in 2007). Because the population in Dominica dropped from about 73,273 in 1983 to an estimated 71,278 in 2007, these crime figures translate to 8 indictable crimes reported for every 1,000 residents in 1983, and 19 per 1,000 residents in 2007. This is a 138 percent increase in the nation's indictable crime rate over those two decades. It is important to note that although indictable crimes trended downward in 2007 compared to 2002, there was a slight 4 percent increase from 2004 to 2005.

Burglaries mostly determined the trends in total indictable crimes over the two decades examined. This is because burglaries have accounted for such a large proportion of total indictable crimes on the island, and other crimes account for such small proportions. Over the 25 years between 1983 and 2007, burglary accounted for 93 percent of all crimes in

1983 and was at its lowest rate in the years 1992 and 2005, when burglaries accounted for 71 percent of all indictable crimes. Robberies account for the next largest proportion of indictable crimes reported in the nation. Although no robberies were reported in 1983, 104 were reported in 2005, accounting for 7 percent of indictable crimes reported for that year. This is the greatest proportion of total indictable crimes that robbery accounted for over the two decades.

Grievous bodily harm, vehicle theft, deception, major theft, and sex crimes (indecent assaults, rape, and unlawful sexual intercourse) account for most of the other indictable crimes, and some have increased in proportions over the last decade. Each of these categories of crime accounted for between 1.5 and 5.5 percent of indictable crimes in any given year over the two decades.

Crime and the Dominican Economy

Over the two examined decades in Dominica, a 1 percent increase in total gross domestic product (GDP) rates per capita in a given year was related to a 2.2 percent increase in total indictable crimes and a 2.6 percent increase in burglaries two years later. This means that the significant relationship between crime and GDP indicators exist on a two-year lag. Economic factors require sufficient time to take effect.

Among the 13 major GDP sectors, two sectors—(1) construction and (2) banking and insurance—are most responsive to significant changes in crime rates. Those sectors also have a positive relationship with crimes. For instance, every 1 percent increase in the construction sector has been significantly matched with a 0.6 percent increase in total crimes and a 0.6 percent increase in burglaries two years later. A 1 percent increase in the banking and insurance sector has been significantly matched with a 1.5 per cent increase in total crime growth rates and a 1.3 percent increase in burglaries two years later.

The term "more money more crime" does not mean less money will lead to less crime. Economic growth, especially employment creation, is important and encouraged for a variety of obvious reasons. However, based on these findings, one researcher argued that policy makers should not rely primarily on economic developments to reduce crime problems in Dominica. Instead, considering the trends from the previous two decades in Dominica, economic developments should be expected to accompany increased crime rates. This becomes possible because economic growth often disproportionately benefits some persons and not others, and relative deprivation and inequality increase in the process. Many of the problems that lead to criminal involvement in the first place are often ignored in the process of economic growth. As societies advance economically, additional criminal opportunities arise, and new forms of victimization also emerge. Therefore, mechanisms for crime reduction must be important components of economic developmental plans; otherwise, crimes will almost inevitably be fueled by economic growth.

Thus, concurrent with efforts aimed at increasing economic developments, which should include gainful employment, serious commitments must be made to independently address factors that will have direct impacts on reducing crime in the nation. These factors may include promoting moral development, reducing drug and alcohol addictions, reducing relative deprivation, reducing inequalities, increasing solidarities with the state, and considerably improving police, prison, courts, and other criminal justice services so that punishments can be swift, certain, and severe enough to fit the crimes committed, but also rehabilitative.

Finding of Guilt

Because Dominica is a democratic nation, the doctrine of proof beyond a reasonable doubt is used in the courts to determine guilt and innocence. Dominica maintains an adversarial system where a prosecutor tries criminal cases on the behalf of the state. In Dominica, the due process for the accused is similar to that of most democracies. When a person is suspected for having committed a crime, a complaint is made by the victim to the police, who then conduct investigations. The accused can be represented by her or his private attorney or have one provided by the court when such cannot be afforded by the accused. Dominica has a legal aid system that is maintained by the bar association. Certain lawyers are available to provide representation for indigent persons accused of crimes.

Indictable matters are typically heard in the High Court and summary matters in the Magistrate Court. It is not mandatory for magistrates to be attorneys. Adult defendants have the right to trial by jury, which follows the process of jury selection similar to that of other democratic nations.

A person can be charged for a crime from the age of 12, but the legal age for trial as an adult is 18. Juvenile cases are heard before a magistrate in the same courtroom spaces as adult cases are heard. However, juvenile cases are heard in a different environment, with the magistrates and police dressed in civilian clothing and the public excused.

Punishment

Punishment for crime is determined by a confluence of factors that include prior offending, severity of the offense, admission of guilt, age of the offender, and plea bargaining. Punishments for indictable and summary offenses are categorized in a way similar to felonies and misdemeanors, respectively, in other countries. Summary offenses typically carry less than one year in prison, and indictable offenses are punishable for one year or more of incarceration. Aside from imprisonment, community service and probation are other forms of sanctions administered by the social welfare department and probation office accordingly. Both adults and youth can receive community service or probation based on the nature of the offenses committed.

Prison

On September 16, 2003, the first ever national crime symposium was held in Dominica under the theme "Working in Partnership for Crime Prevention and Control." The prison superintendent at that time, Algernon Charter, indicated that there were 266 inmates (263 men and 3 women) incarcerated in the prison. He added that the mission of the prison service was to ensure public safety and to humanely look after prisoners and help them become useful members of society after release.

The superintendent also discussed the three main challenges faced by this institution: drug offenses and drug-related offenses, sexual offenses, and theft/burglary. A vast majority of the inmates are incarcerated either for drugs (mainly crack/cocaine and marijuana) or for other drug-related offenses such as theft, grievous bodily harm, and battery. As a result of tough economic conditions in Dominica, these individuals participate in the drug trade to obtain lucrative financial gains. It is often difficult to convince some of these individuals that other options are available to them. The trafficking of drugs into prison is another problem because while inmates serve time, they develop friendships with each other, and upon release from prison, some have returned to the area to toss drugs over the fence to their friends. Friends and family members of inmates also transport drugs to them concealed in fruits and other items. Incarceration for sexual offenses—that is, rape, indecent assault, carnal knowledge, and buggery (male homosexual intercourse)—has also increased considerably. Sex offenders generally do not perceive themselves as criminals and are often the best behaved and most industrious of that population.

Most inmates serving time for economic street crimes such as theft, burglary, and robbery are from the lower socioeconomic strata of society. Their economic conditions and drug habits, developed over time, often result in their involvement in such crimes as a way of supporting their lifestyles.

Rehabilitation in Prison

In 2003, the prison superintendent stressed that to manage the prison population and achieve the mandates of its mission, the following creative programs were established, with an explicit emphasis on rehabilitation: auto-body repair and spray painting, auto-mechanics, arch welding, pottery, agriculture (farming and animal husbandry), leather craft, tailoring, embroidery, carpentry/joinery, construction, and music.

Not all inmates are eligible for these rehabilitative liberties because some are considered too high a risk for escape. Inmates are categorized into four areas: Category A inmates (such as certain deportees and most wanted criminals) must not be allowed to escape from prison because of their high profile as notorious criminals. Their escape would cause severe embarrassment to the state, which would be perceived as incapable of managing any inmates of their profile. Category B inmates are those who would escape from custody at all costs. Category C inmates must work under direct supervision because they will be easily influenced by their peers. Category D inmates work on their own with scant supervision. Most of the inmates who are engaged in labor are Category C and D inmates.

Contemporary efforts at rehabilitating Dominica prison inmates are not limited to labor and occupation but also include spirituality, adult education, entertainment, and maintaining family ties. In 2003, four of the six students who took the Junior Secondary Program Examinations passed, and attempts are being made to have inmates sit for the Caribbean Examinations Council (CXC), an exam that students complete at the end of high school to increase their chances for employment or for acceptance into college programs in academic or technical fields. Every year, inmates participate in a Calypso competition where they sing songs as well as play instruments.

Inmates are encouraged to continue strong bonds with their close relatives and friends and are sometimes allowed to visit such persons when they are severely ill. Inmates who are released from prison (albeit very few) have also received assistance from prison staff to network with willing and prospective employers. Prison officials have also assisted inmates to receive donations of tools from local agencies so that they can apply the newly acquired skills once released from incarceration.

Prison Overcrowding

The problem of prison overcrowding is widespread internationally, and Dominica is no exception. Although the Dominica state prison is designed to accommodate about 200 inmates, there are times when about 275 inmates are housed in the institution. Although the main security block should house no more than 12 inmates, about 18 are held there at any given time. All inmates in the block are from Category A. Charter stressed that this issue was of great concern to the staff.

After Hurricane David in 1979, the prison management acquired a building known as the Old St. Luke's Hospital and refurbished it for the purpose of inmate rehabilitation. However, although that facility was designed to accommodate 44 inmates, it typically housed about 59 inmates. These aspects of prison overcrowding have considerable physical, financial, and human resource implications for the institution.

In a 2003 interview, journalist Felix Henderson spoke with then Dominica Attorney General Henry Dyer, who explained that the Dominica government is concerned about prison overcrowding. He said part of the problem was that Dominica has no rehabilitation center for juveniles, who are instead housed in the state prison with adult offenders. Dyer said that his office was deliberating how they could expand the prison to accommodate more inmates and that they treat this need as a priority although the nation was is financial difficulties. The plan, Dyer said, is to rely more on community service.

Financial and Medical Conditions

The financial and medical conditions of the Dominica State Prison raise several questions about the nation's commitment to rehabilitating offenders. Ethnographic research conducted at the prison in 2003 and 2004 indicated that staff members engaged in creative methods of fund-raising and were frequently pleading with the national government for financial and medical assistance, often resulting in little support if any response at all. These pleas to deaf ears threaten the efficiency and security of the prison. Charter explained that in the 2002–2003 fiscal year, $92,000 was subtracted from the prison budget. In addition to this, the maintenance and personnel emoluments of staff were reduced, making prison management more difficult. In the 2003–2004 financial year, no budgetary allocations were changed, but provisions were made for 275 inmates.

The prison also lacks a medical officer attached to the facility and a medical unit within it. The Dominica State Prison does not have an infirmary where inmates can be quarantined in the event of an outbreak of a communicable disease. The prison administration is concerned about the potential ramifications for prison officers and their families. The inmates who are frustrated and complain about the dehumanizing conditions at the prison often place a strain on the human resources of the prison because they constantly threaten to hold the staff at hostage and make good on their plans to escape.

Although the colonial emphasis on hard labor is still prominent at the Dominica State Prison, efforts are being made to improve some inmates' education and skills while incarcerated and to prepare them for employment upon release. The emphasis on spiritual development and continued family unification is promising. However, counseling services are not systematic, juveniles are housed with adults, space is limited, and medical attention is lacking. These limitations are further complicated by the historical lack of adequate response and support from the national government, often because of its focus on other priorities, and limited financial conditions. Considering the reviewed historical and legal foundations of the Dominica prison system, and the contemporary conditions as explained by the superintendent's address in 2003, the stage is set to analyze conditions of recidivism at that institution and in the Dominica society in general.

Peter K. B. St. Jean and L. Daisy Henderson

Further Reading

Andre, Irving W., and Gabriel J. Christian. (1992). *In Search of Eden: The Travails of a Caribbean Mini State.* Toronto: Pond Casse Press.

Halcrow Group Limited. (2003). "Commonwealth Development Bank Government of the Commonwealth of Dominica Country Poverty Assessment Final Report. Volume 2 of 2: Appendices." London: Halcrow Group Limited.

Honychurch, Lennox. (1995). *The Dominica Story: A History of the Island.* London: Macmillan Education Ltd.

St. Jean, Peter K. B. (2007). "Explaining Strained Community-Police Relations in a Racially and Ethnically Homogenous Community: Grand Bay Dominica." *Journal of Ethnicity in Criminal Justice* 5:1–27.

St. Jean, Peter K. B. (2006). *Lessons from Grand Bay: Prospects for Maintaining Low Crime in Dominica, Nature Island of the Caribbean.* Brampton, ON: Pond Casse Press.

Dominican Republic

Legal System: Civil/Common
Murder: High
Corruption: Medium
Human Trafficking: Medium
Prison Rate: Medium
Death Penalty: No
Corporal Punishment: Yes

Background

The Dominican Republic is a unitary state composed of 34 provinces and 1 national district. Its total area is 48,730 square kilometers. According to official estimates, its population reached 9,249,970 inhabitants in 2005 and was expected to grow by 8.8 percent over the following five years. Two-thirds of the population live in urban areas, and two-thirds of the population are aged 34 or younger. Nearly half the population is below the poverty line. Dominican Republic is ranked 94th in the world human development ranking and is seventh among Latin American countries.

The political organization of the country is based on the Constitution of the republic, last amended in

Hundreds of people holding banners that read "stop the violence" at a rally against crime and violence in Santo Domingo, Dominican Republic, July 26, 2006. The Dominican government deployed some 6,000 soldiers and police across the country to crack down on crimes ranging from drunk driving to gun violence. (AP Photo/Ramon Espinosa)

1994. The government is democratically elected and has three independent powers: the executive branch, the legislative branch, and the judicial branch. The Constitution has always recognized basic civil rights and political freedoms, but these liberties have often been violated by political strongmen. Although the supreme law acknowledges private property rights, to this day, the Dominican government still retains the discretionary authority to expropriate private land.

The country occupies the eastern two-thirds of the island of Hispaniola and shares this territory with the neighboring nation of Haiti. Quisqueya, as the island was originally called by the Taino Indians, was explored by Christopher Columbus in 1492 on his first voyage to the Americas. Although Hispaniola was claimed by Spain, the French began to settle in the western part of the island in the 16th century, and Spain ceded the western third of the island to France in 1697. In 1795, Spain ceded Santo Domingo to France, giving France control of the entire island. Following the French Declaration of Human Rights in 1789 during French and Haitian rule, the French Napoleonic codes were adopted as the official legal framework of the island, and the French judicial system was adopted.

In 1844, after several attacks on the Haitian armies, an underground group called La Trinitari succeeded in securing independence for the eastern half of the island. The newly independent nation was named La República Dominicana (The Dominican Republic), and in 1855, the French penal code was formally adopted by the new nation. After continuous periods of political strife, the United States occupied the Dominican Republic for a period of eight years starting in 1916, during which time the Dominican law and judicial system were kept intact. The Dominican criminal justice system at this time operated under a continental or inquisitorial model.

General Rafael Leónidas Trujillo established a military government that lasted from 1930 to 1961. This was a period of progress for the Dominican Republic, with advances in education, welfare, and reduction of the national debt. However, Trujillo ruled with extreme violence to eliminate his opponents and was responsible for the murder of 17,000 to 35,000 Haitians in the Parsley Massacre, which was carried out in 1937 to sanitize the borderlands of Haitian inhabitants. During his reign, basic rights guaranteed by criminal procedure codes were systematically ignored.

After Trujillo's assassination in 1961, the Dominican Republic began a lengthy journey toward democratic consolidation with a brief interruption by a civil war and another U.S. intervention in 1965. During its turbulent political history, the Dominican Republic provided few basic rights to its citizens when it came to the practice of criminal justice. In 1966, however, the revised Constitution granted basic rights to its citizens, including the right to due process, the right to a public trial, the right to be advised of all charges, and the right against self-incrimination.

Crime

Unlike the Unites States, where classification and punishment for crime can vary from state to state, the Dominican Republic's penal codes apply to the entire nation in a uniform manner. Dominican penal law divides infractions of the law into *contravenciones, delitos,* and *crimenes. Contravenciones* are minor violations of the law and the least serious of the three. *Delitos* involve more serious infractions of the law but are not as serious as *crimenes,* which are punishable by the highest penalties. *Delitos* are in a sense much like a misdemeanor, and *crimenes* are similar to a felony. The penal codes classify crimes as they fall into the following distinct categories: crimes against national security, crimes against the Constitution, crimes against public peace, crimes against persons, and crimes against property.

Crimes against National Security

Crimes against national security are grouped into crimes that constitute an external threat and crimes that constitute an internal threat. External threats are defined by the Dominican penal codes as any act that threatens the safety of the republic, whether by taking arms against the nation or by plotting with foreign bodies, whether entire governments or individuals, to bring war on the Dominican government. Acts that constitute an internal threat are those that seek to bring instability or war from within the Dominican Republic without the aid of a foreign body. Crimes under this category include attempts on the president's life and taking up arms with the purpose of causing revolt or civil war.

Crimes against the Constitution

Crimes against the Constitution include those that by use of violence or threats hinder the practice of rights guaranteed to citizens or threaten any of the laws established by the Constitution. This category covers acts like falsifying electoral ballots, electoral fraud, misuse of authority by public officials, some types of political corruption, and impeding the exercise of free speech, religion, and other basic rights.

Crimes against Public Order

The Dominican penal code enumerates crimes that can lead to public disorder. Crimes of falsification include counterfeiting of money, knowingly using false money, and falsification of official state seals, public credit documents and bank bills, passports and private documents. This section of the penal codes also makes criminal the use of power by public officials in a manner that injures the public such as receiving and acting on bribes to the benefit of only a few. Crimes against public order include acts of resistance and disobedience committed against public authority, acts of rebellion, and damages to public monuments. Finally, the penal code enumerates minor infractions under this category that include vagrancy and panhandling in public spaces.

Crimes against Persons

Homicide and Murder

Dominican penal codes define homicide as a voluntary act of ending another person's life, and murder is defined as a premeditated act of murder. Premeditation is defined as the formation of a plan prior to the act of murder to commit that act and can include surveillance of the victim for some time in one or more places. Acts that fall under the category of murder and homicide include parricide and infanticide and any act of poisoning with the purpose of causing death.

Injuries That Do Not Lead to Death

Injuries or blows to a person that do not result in the death of that person are defined under a separate category. Injuries considered under this category include mutilation, amputation, loss of use of any body part, loss of sight or an eye, and any injuries causing illness or incapacitation from work. These crimes all fall under the category of *crimenes,* but are prosecuted to a lesser degree than are those crimes that purposefully lead to murder.

Involuntary Murder, Injuries, and Excusable Crimes

Involuntary murder, according to penal codes, occurs when a person's imprudence, carelessness, or negligence causes the death of another. These crimes are subject to more lenient sanctions than murder, which purposefully seeks to cause death. When violence is threatened and homicide is committed in answer to that violence, the act of ending the person's life is excused by the law. Homicide is also permissible in defense of one's home, in defense of self, or in defense of another.

Sexual Crimes

Rape is defined by penal law as any act of sexual penetration that is committed using violence, constraint, threat, or surprise. Rape is punished severely, and sanctions increase when rape against a person of diminished capacity occurs, including persons with physical or mental handicaps or children and adolescents. Intimate partner rape is also prosecuted by law. Incest is punishable by the law and includes any sexual act that an adult engages in with a child or adolescent to whom they are related by natural or adoptive parentage. Minor sexual crimes include sexual harassment by persons in positions of authority and exhibition of genitals in public places.

Property Crimes

Robbery is the focus of the property crimes section of the Dominican penal codes. Robbery is defined as any fraudulent means of obtaining that which does not belong to a person. Robbery is sentenced according to the circumstances surrounding the robbery. The highest penalties for robbery are given when a robbery is committed at night; when a robbery is committed by two or more persons; when the perpetrators of robbery carry weapons, whether they are visible or concealed; and when property is damaged by instruments used as part of the robbery.

Drug Offenses

Drug offenses are considered serious crimes in the Dominican Republic and are punished harshly. Possession of any amount of a controlled drug or substance is a punishable offense, with incarceration being the normal sanction. Because of the Dominican Republic's Caribbean location, the government has strictly enforced drug laws, originally passed in 1988, to protect the country from becoming an international gateway for drugs originating in South America and being transported to North America and Europe. Illicit drugs and controlled substances are classified under five distinct categories according to their potential for addiction.

Drug Crime Sanctions

Illicit importation or exportation of controlled substances to and from the Dominican Republic can be punished by 5 to 20 years in prison and a fine of no less than 250,000 DOP (Dominican pesos, approx.

US$6,775). If the final destination of the controlled substances trafficked is the Dominican Republic, punishment increases to 30 years in prison and no less than 1,000,000 DOP. When two or more persons assemble with the purpose of importing or exporting controlled substances, they can face 3–10 years in prison and a fine of 10,000 to 50,000 DOP. The use of an establishment for the sale or use of controlled substances carries a penalty of 3–10 years, a 10,000 to 50,000 DOP fine, and the closing of the establishment for three years.

The three categories of offenses are possession, distribution and sales, and trafficking. Marijuana possession is defined as the possession of 20 grams or less. Distribution and sales is defined as possession of more than 20 grams but less than 1 pound of marijuana. Trafficking is defined as possession of 1 pound or more of marijuana. Cocaine possession is defined by the possession of 1 gram or less of cocaine. Distribution and sale is defined by the possession of more than 1 gram but less than 5 grams of cocaine. Trafficking is defined as possession of more than 5 grams of cocaine. Ecstasy is not mentioned in the penal codes but is currently placed in the same category as cocaine.

If any persons are caught with LSD or any other hallucinogen, regardless of the quantity found on the person, they will be prosecuted as traffickers. The penalty for possession is 6 months to 2 years in prison and a fine of 1,500 to 2,500 DOP. For the crime of distribution and sale, the penalty can range from 3 to 10 years in prison and a fine of 10,000 to 50,000 DOP. Trafficking brings the heaviest penalties with a prison sentence that can range from 5 to 20 years and a fine of 50,000 DOP or more.

Crime Statistics

Crime statistics are made available by the *procuraduria fiscal del distrito nacional* (attorney general). The most recent statistics made available covered the period starting in January 2008 and ending in September 2008. Crimes that are reported are recorded by the national police and by the National Institute of Forensic Science. For the crime of homicide and violent deaths in 2008, up to September 1, 807 cases were reported, an increase of 21.5 percent from 2007. The highest number of homicides occurred in Santo Domingo, which reported 525 cases, followed by Distrito Nacional, with 215 cases reported. This demonstrates that violent crimes are concentrated in the two most densely populated jurisdictions. The lowest number of homicide cases was reported by Santiago Rodriguez, with only 2 cases on record by September 2008. Statistics also were made available regarding the circumstances surrounding homicides. Homicides committed as a result of other crimes including drug-related homicides, kidnapping, homicide that occurred in the course of a motor vehicle theft, homicide as a result of an attempted robbery, and homicide as a result of robbery totaled 602 cases, or 33.3 percent of the total for the period between January and September 2008. Accidental homicide, homicide due to legal action, homicide due to stray bullets, homicide as a result of domestic violence, personal and familial disputes that end in homicide, and unknown reasons for homicide totaled 1,205 cases, or 66 percent of the total. Men were victims in 1,650 (91.3 percent) of all homicide cases as compared to 157 cases (8.7 percent) involving women victims.

For property crimes during the period January 2008 to July 2008, 37 cases of fraud, 849 cases of aggravated robbery, 316 cases of simple robbery, 2 cases of car theft, and 40 cases of arson were reported. For sexual crimes, 121 cases of sexual aggression, 5 cases of attempted rape, 73 cases of rape, 14 cases of sexual harassment, 4 cases of incest, and 1 case of exhibition of genitals were reported.

Finding of Guilt

Investigation

The duty to conduct an initial investigation of all criminal acts falls on the national police of the Dominican Republic. The national police force was established in 1936 as a centralized force under the executive branch. Prior to 1936, various police forces existed, operating in individual towns. Following centralization, all local police forces were disbanded. In 1999, the National Police Center for Criminal Investigation was established with the purpose of investigating any criminal act committed under its jurisdiction. The center divides the task of investigating crimes into eight departments: the Homicide Department, the Department of Monetary Crimes, the Department of the Investigation of Crimes Involving High Technology, the Department of Search and Capture of Fugitives, the Department of Stolen Vehicle Recovery, and the Department for the Registration and Control of Deportees. Currently, the Center for Criminal Investigation is directed by General Rafael O. Bencosme Candelier. In 2002, the Deportee Unit was established because of the large influx of deportees to the Dominican Republic.

The 2002 criminal procedural code modified the criminal procedure by establishing an adversarial system, replacing the old inquisitorial framework that was previously in place. The new procedural code distinguishes the process of investigation from that of the trial, with the first coming under the jurisdiction of the prosecutor and the second under that of the judge, who is responsible for safeguarding basic rights and ensuring the legality of the investigative actions of the prosecutor.

The criminal investigation begins with the preparatory stage, where the Public Prosecutor's Office and the victim consider charges and prepare the case. The prosecutor gathers all available evidence and assesses whether there are grounds for a trial. Then comes the preliminary hearing, in which both the substance and the legality of the prosecutorial investigation are examined by the investigative judge, who can allow and push the charges, order a summary procedure or a stay of proceedings, issue a restraining order, or approve the settlement agreed to by the parties. The judge may also dismiss the charges if he or she finds that there is insufficient evidence to incriminate the defendant or if the defendant cannot be held criminally responsible.

The trial is oral and public. The trial courts are presided over by a single judge if the crime involves punishment of up to two years in prison or a panel of three judges when the sanction requires more than two years of imprisonment. In cases involving criminal charges that carry a sentence of more than 10 years' imprisonment, separate hearings for determining guilt or innocence and for sentencing are held. The defense can always appeal the disposition of the trial.

The enforcement of judgment takes place when the judge issues a final ruling. In this case, the sentence enforcement judge supervises the implementation of the terms of the sentence and guarantees the rights of those convicted. This judge also inspects prisons, ensures compliance with conditions for dismissal, requests sentence reviews, and hears matters related to the parole of those convicted.

Rights of the Accused

Both the Constitution of the Dominican Republic and the criminal procedure codes afford several basic rights to citizens charged with a crime. Beginning with the presumption of innocence, every person charged in the Dominican Republic is presumed innocent and is treated as such until it is proved otherwise. It is the prosecutor's job to refute the innocence of the accused. The accused has the right to be informed of all the charges against him or her and has the right to examine all the evidence that as been gathered for prosecution. The person who is charged with a crime has the right to know the identity of the arresting authority and must be treated humanely during arrest and detention. Excessive use of force or violence against the accused is against any law of the Dominican Republic.

Any person accused of a crime must be assisted by legal counsel from the very beginning of the judicial process. Any statement made by the accused will not be considered legal as evidence unless the accused has made the statement in the presence of his or her defense attorney. The accused has the right to choose his or her defense attorney, and if the accused person cannot afford a defense attorney, the state has the obligation of providing one. The accused person also has the right to meet with his or attorney under strict privacy.

The right against self-incrimination is also guaranteed to the person accused of a crime. The person has the right to remain silent throughout the judicial process, and his or her silence cannot be taken as an incriminating element. The accused person is also guaranteed the right to a public trial to be held within a reasonable time frame. Persons being accused of any crime cannot be exposed to the media in a manner that can damage their reputation or expose them to danger. Every person accused of a crime who enters the criminal justice system is guaranteed equality under the law. This means that judges cannot take into account any extralegal factors when deciding on the guilt or innocence of the accused person. Particular circumstances of the criminal act can be taken into account such as aggravating and mitigating circumstances, but race, religion, sexual orientation, gender, political ideas, and economic or social conditions cannot be considered in judging guilt or innocence.

The Dominican Court System

The Dominican Republic's court system is modeled after the French system, as were the criminal penal codes. Because the country follows civil law, rather than common law, judges preside over trials and decide on the guilt of the accused. The court system is arranged in a hierarchical manner with the Supreme Court being the highest court in the land.

The Peace Courts

The peace courts of the Dominican Republic are at the first level of the judicial branch. Each province in the Dominican Republic is equipped with a peace court. There are 31 provinces and therefore 31 peace courts. These courts are designed to hear civil cases, cases involving *contravenciones* (minor violations), and traffic infractions involving motor vehicles. The judges presiding over these courts are *jueces de paz* (judges of the peace) and have the duty of hearing the case and delivering a verdict.

The Courts of First Instance

A court of first instance is the first court to preside over serious criminal offenses that sanction two or more years in prison. Only one judge presides over a case and decides the verdict. These judges are known as *jueces de primera instancia* (judges of first instance). The courts of first instance divide cases according to the type of case being heard. For example, all criminal cases passing through this level of courts would be reviewed in one chamber, and all civil cases would be reviewed in another. At this level of the judicial branch, you can also find *jueces de la instruccion* (judges of instruction). These judges are responsible for overseeing preparatory procedures and hearing preliminary audiences with the accused prior to trial. *Jueces de ejecucion penal* (judges of penal execution) have the duty of setting appropriate sentences for every decided case.

The Court of Appeals

The Court of Appeals is responsible for hearing cases that have already been heard by the courts of first instance. This court is composed of a panel of five judges who are responsible for deciding whether to affirm or refuse the original verdict set by the court of first instance. The decision rendered by this court can still be appealed in the highest court of the Dominican Republic. The Court of Appeals can also hear cases regarding the recusal of judges from lower courts.

The Supreme Court of Justice

The Supreme Court is the final court of appeal in the criminal justice system and is also the highest court in the country. The Supreme Court is responsible for hearing cases and deciding whether to affirm or contest the verdict rendered by the lower courts, but unlike the Court of Appeals, the Supreme Court hears only cases in which interpretation of the law is necessary. The Supreme Court also presides over procedures of extradition and recusals of judges of the Court of Appeals.

The constitutional reform of 1994 eliminated congressional appointment of judges and created the National Magistrates Council, which is invested with the power to designate judges of the Supreme Court, who in turn appoint the rest of the judicial staff. Administratively, the Supreme Court is entrusted with the responsibility of organizing and overseeing the functioning of all the courts. This has been a daunting task given the ever-growing judicial demand and the limited resources allocated to the courts.

The Juvenile Justice System

Penal law 136-03 establishes a separate judicial process for juveniles apprehended for the commission of a crime, providing children and adolescents with basic rights and protections not afforded to adult offenders. Once criminal responsibility has been established, the penal system seeks to apply a reasonable sanction with the principle of rehabilitating the child or adolescent. The child's best interest is at the heart of the juvenile justice system and is determined with consideration for the opinion of the child, the child's stage of development, and international codes for children's rights along with other factors. Administration of justice is carried out by special courts that focus on children and adolescents. The police responsible for investigating crimes committed by children and adolescents also have a specialized branch trained to deal with this population of offenders.

Age of Criminal Responsibility

The age of criminal responsibility in the Dominican Republic is 18. Children from the age of 13 to 18 are prosecuted under the juvenile justice system. Children under the age of 13 are not legally responsible under the law. Children under the age of 13 cannot be detained, their liberty cannot be denied, and they cannot be sanctioned by any authority.

Rights of Children and Adolescents

The rights afforded to children and adolescents accused of a crime are similar to the rights afforded to adults. However, children's identities and criminal records are protected to a greater extent. Juveniles have the right to be informed of all charges against them and have the right to be informed of all evidence gathered for the prosecution. Juveniles also have the right to counsel and will be provided one if their family cannot afford an attorney. Immediately after arrest, a child has the right to contact family and legal counsel to inform them of the arrest. The child can meet with his or her attorney under strict privacy. The child also has the right against self-incrimination, and the child's decision to remain silent cannot be taken as an admission of guilt. The adolescent offender has the right to prevent his or her identity from being published and to have his or her record sealed. Pretrial jail time is to be served at a special facility for juveniles and is used only when charges against the juvenile involve the most serious crimes.

Sanctions under the Juvenile Justice System

Socio-Educative Sanctions

Socio-educative sanctions are usually prescribed when the crime committed by the juvenile is minor. These sanctions can consist of a warning or community service at hospitals, schools, parks, or any place that does not place the child at physical or psychological danger. Sanctions also include assisted living, which consists of mandatory compliance by the juvenile with any condition placed by the court for a maximum of three years. Restitution for any damages caused can also demanded by the court.

Orientation and Supervision

Sanctions in the category of orientation and supervision are usually prescribed to juveniles who have committed *delitos* or crimes that are more serious in nature but that do not warrant the maximum penalties. If the juvenile is sentenced to these sanctions, the court can assign the juvenile a place of residence where the juvenile can be monitored. The court can also require the juvenile to enroll in an education program or vocational training. Mandatory medical treatment in either a public or a private rehabilitation center is required if the juvenile is addicted to drugs.

Deprivation of Liberty

Deprivation of liberty is a sanction reserved for juveniles found guilty of serious crimes. Sanctions that deprive children of their liberty can take the form of house arrest and detention in juvenile centers. House arrest can be prescribed for no more than six months during which the juvenile may not leave his or her place of residence. Arrest during free time is a type of house arrest in which the child may leave his or her place of residence for school, but during free time such as evenings and weekends, the child must return and remain at home. Incarceration is the ultimate deprivation of liberty in which a child is removed from his or her home and placed in a detention center for juveniles. A child may be sentenced to incarceration when found guilty of homicide, causing permanent physical injury, rape, aggravated robbery, kidnapping, sale and distribution of narcotics, or any crime that carries a sentence of five or more years. Juveniles from the age of 13 to the age of 15 can be sentenced to only one to three years of prison. Juveniles ages 16 to 18 can be sentenced to one to five years of prison.

Punishment

Punishment is prescribed according to the severity of the infraction of the law. For acts that constitute a *contravencion* (minor violation), punishment warranted is known as *pena de policia* (punishment of simple police). Punishments prescribed are minor and include restitution for damaged property, fines, and at most five days in jail. Infractions of the law that constitute a *delito* warrant punishments under the classification of *penas correcionales* (correctional punishments). Punishment under this category can warrant jail time that exceeds five days. Other punishments ordered under *penas correcionales* include exile; confinement; temporary prison; interdiction of civic, civil, and family rights; and fines.

Infractions that constitute a *crimen,* the most serious of all crimes, warrant punishment classified under *penas aflictivas e infamante* (afflictive and defaming punishments). Punishments under this category include *reclusion mayor* (major reclusion) and *reclusion menor* (minor reclusion). Those punished by major reclusion are subject to having their civic, civil, and political rights taken away. Those sentenced to incarceration under major reclusion will be removed from society and placed in a Dominican prison to serve the time allotted by the court.

Civic degradation can be prescribed as a punishment under major reclusion. This punishment involves removing the convicted person from his or her daily functions including employment and public office if he or she holds such a position. The person can be stripped of their right to vote or to be elected to public office and lose the right to be a witness in another's trial. Civic degradation also prohibits the convicted person from carrying weapons, belonging to the National Guard or the Dominican Army, or being employed as a teacher or professor in any educational institute. Civic degradation can be accompanied by a prison sentence and cannot exceed a period of five years.

The Dominican Republic does not have life sentences and follows the rule of no accumulation. This means that if a person is charged with several crimes and is convicted on all charges, that person may not serve a separate sentence for each crime. Instead, the highest sentence the person can be subject to is the sentence that is mandated by the court. The maximum sentence in the Dominican Republic is major reclusion of 30 years. Aggravating and mitigating circumstances can be taken into consideration by judges deciding on a sentence, but ranges for sentences are set by the criminal penal codes.

For the crime of murder, the mandated sentence is 30 years of major reclusion, the highest penalty allowed by law. Homicide that precedes or accompanies the commission of other crimes is also punishable by 30 years of major reclusion. Another crime that warrants the maximum penalty is torture when used on children, adolescents, or other persons with special vulnerabilities such as age, handicap, and mental or physical deficiencies. When torture is committed against a judge, an attorney, or any person in public service, or when it is employed against a witness or victim with the purpose of impeding that person's testimony, it also warrants the maximum penalty of 30 years. Sexual aggression when preceded or accompanied by homicide warrants a punishment of 10–20 years of major reclusion and a fine of 100,000–200,000 Dominican pesos. Injuries caused to a person that leave them incapacitated for 21 or more days carry a punishment of 6 months to 2 years of prison and a fine of

500 to 5,000 Dominican pesos. Rape carries a penalty of 10 to 15 years of major reclusion and a fine of 100,000 to 200,000 Dominican pesos. Rape of a child, adolescent, or person with a special vulnerability carries a penalty of 10 to 20 years of major reclusion. Robbery can carry a penalty of 5 to 20 years of major reclusion and can be punished by the maximum penalty of 30 years under major reclusion if aggravating factors listed by the penal codes exist, including robbery committed at night, robbery committed by two or more people, or robbery in which the perpetrators carry weapons.

The Death Penalty

The death penalty existed early in the history of the Dominican Republic and was applied to what were considered to be the most severe of crimes, including murder and treason. In 1966, the Constitution of the Dominican Republic was revised, and the death penalty was abolished, along with torture and any other punishment that could bring physical harm to the person. But the rise in crime rates that the Dominican Republic has suffered in recent years has brought the debate of the death penalty and life imprisonment back to the forefront. Though the people of the nation have shown support for capital punishment, it remains unconstitutional.

Prison

Criminal procedure codes mandate that every judicial district have a prison that will hold pretrial detainees and a separate prison to hold persons who have already been convicted and sentenced. The law requires that these two populations be kept separate even in cases where both these populations are located within the same facility. But prison overcrowding has led to the combined housing of the pretrial detainee population and the convicted offender population. The law also requires that every facility have separate accommodations for male prisoners and female prisoners. Currently, the prison population is composed of 96 percent males and 4 percent females. The governors of the provinces are responsible for the overall conditions of the prisons located within their respective jurisdictions, which includes security and hygiene conditions; however, detailed administration of the prison is the responsibility of the prison warden or director. Prison personnel, including the warden and his staff, are appointed by the governor of each province.

Wardens and prison guards are charged with maintaining the security of the prison, preventing escapes by prisoners, and providing a humane environment for prisoners within their facility. Wardens must keep the governor of the province informed of all prison activities, the state of the prison population, and any escape of prisoners, and in the case of a prisoner's death, the warden must inform the governor and the attorney general of the occurrence within 24 hours. Behavioral issues and violence directed by prisoners at prison staff or at other prisoners can be punished with a period of isolation from the general prison population. Security is the top priority of the prison system, and prison staff must work to prevent prisoners from escaping, in addition to keeping prisoners secure from other prisoners and from existing prison conditions that can cause the inmates harm. Security at 11 prisons, including La Victoria, Monte Plata, and 15 de Azua, are under the direction of the national police. Security for other prisons, including San Pedro de Macoris, San Francisco de Macoris, and Neyba, falls under the direction of the National Army.

Currently, the Dominican Republic operates 34 prisons within its national territory. Two of these prisons are maximum-security prisons, two facilities are centers of rehabilitation, two of the prisons are under special jurisdiction because they are located in the federal district, and the rest of the prisons are public prisons. The current prison population is numbered at 13,500 prisoners by the Direccion General de Prisiones.

Services provided within prisons include education, which is usually coordinated by the prison along with institutions that operate outside the prison system. Some of the institutions providing education and vocational training to Dominican prisoners include the Institute of Technical Professions, the Secretary of Education, the Vocational Schools of the Armed Forces, and local churches.

According to the Direccion General de Prisiones, there are 1,369 prisoners enrolled in literacy and basic education classes. Vocational training is available in the areas of woodwork, blacksmith, upholstery, electricity, and tailoring.

Criminal procedure codes mandate that every judicial district must have a prison doctor. Currently, there are 46 doctors who work within the Dominican prison system. Specialists include gynecologists, psychologists, neurologists, dentists, and health care providers specializing in sexually transmitted diseases. Any required hospitalization takes place at state hospitals where prisoners are guarded by the national police. If the prisoner wishes to be treated at a private hospital or medical facility, he or she must receive proper authorization and must cover the cost of the medical treatment.

Legal assistance is one of the most important services provided within Dominican prisons. Available at each facility are professionals whose job is to assist prisoners with any legal process or with the filing of any legal documents and to inform prisoners of any important deadlines. Visitation privileges are among the most valued by Dominican prisoners. Families who visit are allowed to bring hygiene products and food, although some articles of food can be confiscated by prison authorities. Prison visitations are allowed to all prisoners; however, the U.S. Department of State reports that corruption in the prison system is widespread and that prisoners find themselves having to pay for visitation privileges and for access to vocational and education programs, and in some cases, prisoners had to pay prison officials to be allowed to attend scheduled court hearings.

The New Penitentiary Model

The Dominican Republic has been known for its inhumane practices within the prison system. Overcrowding, unsanitary conditions, and corruption have become major issues within the walls of Dominican prisons. The prison population, now reaching 13,500 prisoners, far exceeds the number of beds available within the entire system, which is estimated at 6,300 beds. La Victoria, the largest prison in the system, has the capacity to hold 1,000 inmates, yet it has only 354 beds available, and the actual population at that facility is 3,500 prisoners. Many prisoners are forced to sleep in makeshift beds or accommodate themselves on cell floors. The majority of prisoners in the system (51.1%) have not yet been sentenced and are awaiting trial, deliberation of verdicts, or sentences. Only 23.6 percent of prisoners have already been sentenced, and 24.9 percent are awaiting appeals on their sentences.

Following several unfortunate instances in which prisoners lost their lives because of the poor conditions of prison facilities, and with mounting pressure from national and international human rights groups, the Direccion General de Prisiones and the Procuraduria General have developed the New Penitentiary Model, to be implemented nationwide. This model involves plans to construct new facilities and improve existing facilities to ease overcrowding and advance the living conditions of those deprived of their liberty. A new facility has already been planned and is to be built in Santo Domingo, with the capacity to hold 200 prisoners. As for existing facilities, 11 have already been targeted for reparations and expansion of living facilities.

Angela Marcela Navarro

Further Reading

Código de Procedimiento Criminal de la Republica Dominicana. (1987). Santo Domingo: Republica Dominicana.

Codigo para el Sistema de Protección de los Derechos Fundamentales de los Niños y Adolescentes. (2003). Santo Domingo: Republica Dominicana.

Código Penal de la Republica Dominicana. (2007). Santo Domingo: Republica Dominicana

Dirección General de Prisiones: http://www.procuraduria.gov.do/PGR.NET/Dependencias/Prision/Index_GaleriaPrision.aspx.

Policía Nacional de la Republica Dominicana: http://www.policianacional.gov.do/system/index.php.

Pons, F. M. (1998). *Dominican Republic: A National History.* Princeton, NJ: Markus Weiner Publishers.

Procuraduría General de la Republica Dominicana: http://www.procuraduria.gov.do/PGR.NET/Index.aspx.

U.S. Department of State. (2008). *Country Reports on Human Rights Practices: Dominican Republic.* Washington, DC: U.S. Government Printing Office.

Ecuador

Legal System: Civil
Murder: High
Corruption: High
Human Trafficking: Medium
Prison Rate: Medium
Death Penalty: No
Corporal Punishment: Yes

Background

Ecuador is a nation with a rich history extending over thousands of years. Located in the northwest of South America, this country received its name from the equator across which the country lies. The pre-Columbian-era Ecuador was settled by native tribes that grew to establish large cities along the southern coast by 500 BCE. Ecuador and the civilizations that had established themselves in the region came under the dominion of the Inca Empire in 1463. By 1532 the territory had been claimed for the Spanish Crown. Ecuador quickly became one of Spain's central colonies and remained so for 300 years.

At the beginning of the 19th century, most Spanish colonies in the Americas had begun their struggle for independence from the Crown. Ecuador, joining this movement, attempted its independence in 1809. This early revolt was subdued quickly. In 1820, the Free Province of Guayaquil under Joaquin de Olmedo declared itself free from Spanish rule. This precarious autonomy was not consolidated until 1822, when Simon Bolivar sent his general Antonio Jose de Sucre to Guayaquil to fight and win the decisive battle of Pichincha, which led to the formal and permanent independence of the territory of Guayaquil.

The newly freed Guayaquil joined La Gran Colombia under the leadership of Simon Bolivar. But Bolivar's dream of establishing a nation similar to the United States to the north eventually came to an end. In 1830, leaders in Guayaquil decided to leave the union as Venezuela had done. They named their independent nation Ecuador, with the capital at Quito. Rule of Ecuador was ceded to Venezuela, under whom the Magna Carta of Ecuador was written. A succession of dictators ruled the country until 1875, when Eloy Alfaro, a liberal who reestablished civil rights including freedom of speech, was installed as the president. During his presidency, the criminal codes establishing such concepts as criminal intent and rights of defense and definitions of crimes including homicide, robbery, and fraud were adopted. These codes have remained almost intact to this day. The 1912–1925 period is known as an era of economic liberalism, when banks took control of public business and almost the entire country. In 1934, Jose Maria Velasco Ibarra became president of Ecuador and went on to hold five nonconsecutive terms in office until he was overthrown by a military government in 1972. Velasco's terms as president were interrupted by conflict with the neighboring country of Peru, civil strife within Ecuador, and brief periods under other elected presidents. Democracy was restored in 1978 with the drafting of a new constitution, and since this time, the country has been led by elected officials.

Legal System

The Ecuadorian penal system for most of its history has been inquisitorial in nature. This means that judges supervised all aspects of the criminal justice process from investigation to management and presentation of evidence, processes of a trial, and dictation of the sentence. All judicial processes under the inquisitorial model are traditionally carried out in written form. In 1998, the Constitution was modified, and there was a move to change the traditional penal system from an inquisitorial model to the adversarial system. Beginning in June 2001, the adversarial system was put into effect. Under this system, criminal processes are debated by two sides, the prosecutor representing the state and the defense representing the defendant, publicly and orally. This shift has experienced some opposition.

In Ecuador, the criminal justice apparatus comprises the court system (which includes the Supreme Court, the Constitutional Court, the National Judicial Council, the high courts and appellate tribunals, and the lower courts), the Public Prosecutor's Office, the Attorney General's Office, the Ombudsman, and the Judicial Police. Ecuador has a large and active community of legal professionals. The national Federation of Bar Associations and the provincial bar associations assess and certify qualifications of attorneys as well as maintain disciplines among members. All individuals wishing to practice law must register with and become subject to the oversight of a bar association.

Crime

Classification of Crime

Ecuadorian penal law defines an infraction of the law as an act that is punishable under the law. Therefore, persons cannot be punished for an act not listed in penal codes as a punishable act. The Ecuadorian penal code does not allow retroactive criminal legislation that changes the legal consequences of acts committed prior to the enactment of the law. Penalties are set according to the severity of a crime; however, if the penalty for a crime is changed from the time the crime was committed to the time of sentencing, the judge is to execute the lesser punishment. Extensive interpretation of the law by judges is prohibited. Judges must function by the letter of the law, and in complicated cases that require extensive interpretation, the judge must adopt the definition of the law most favorable to the defendant. Ecuadorian law, like that of many other countries, assumes that individuals are educated in the basics of the law and therefore cannot claim ignorance of the law as a valid defense.

Like other Latin American countries, Ecuadorian law divides crimes into *delitos* and *contravenciones,* with the former covering more severe crimes and the latter covering minor infractions. The law also defines different levels of intent. An *infraccion dolosa,* or a deceived infraction, is that in which the actor of the crime intends to cause harm. An *infraccion intencional,* or intentional infraction, is that in which an act or the omission of an act was planned. and the resulting consequence was desired by the actor. An *infraccion preterintencional* is an act or an omission of an act that causes more harm than what the actor intended. And finally an *infraccion culposa* is an act in which the actor could have foreseen a consequence, but the consequence was not the intent of the actor and rather was produced by the person's negligence or lack of skill, or simply by not observing the law.

Several actions under Ecuadorian law are not legally considered criminal, even though they may cause harm to a person. These nonpunishable harmful acts include any act that is ordered by the law itself or by a competent authority, or acts a person is pushed into by a force that could not be resisted. If a person injures another person in the act of self-defense, then the act is not considered a crime if the person defending himself or herself was presented with legitimate aggression that he or she did not provoke. The same applies in the defense of another person. If a person's property is invaded, the person has the right to defend his or her property. and any injuries caused to the perpetrators will not be considered criminal. The penal code also absolves any person who kills, injures, or assaults his or her spouse after having witnessed the spouse in an act of adultery.

Crimes against National Security

Crimes against national security include crimes that threaten the nation with foreign invasion. Crimes under this category include conspiracy to induce a foreign nation to declare war on Ecuador; facilitation of the entrance of foreign enemies into the country; surrender of national territories, properties, and military equipment to a foreign enemy; and provision of material aid such as soldiers, guides, money, vehicles, munitions, and weapons to a foreign enemy. Under this section of the penal code, persons can also be criminally charged for giving false leads or intelligence to the Ecuadorian Armed Forces, concealing enemy soldiers, and destroying arms, munitions, and other property with the purpose of aiding a foreign enemy. Impeding national troops from receiving aid, arms, equipment, instructions, or news is also a punishable crime.

Crimes against Peace and Dignity of the State and Crimes against Interior Security

These crimes include any attempts made against the welfare of a foreign nation. Crimes under this category include hostility against a foreign nation without the consent of the Ecuadorian government and attempts on the life, liberty, or welfare of the president or representatives of a foreign nation. Crimes against interior security include revolts against the government, attempts to depose the established government or impede Congress from meeting, or the provocation of civil war. Promoting discord among the citizenship and taking up arms against each other with or without the intent to overthrow government are also punishable under this section of the penal codes.

Crimes of Sabotage and Terrorism

Crimes of sabotage apply to persons who are in a position to lend aid or persons who have the duty to provide help, but refuse to give aid to someone in need. The penal code specifies that any doctor, nurse, pharmacist, or health care practitioner who refuses care or abstains from providing care to a person in need can be prosecuted and punished for his or her inaction. Any person who withholds any material or equipment that can be used in rescue in case of a fire, flood, shipwreck, or any other calamity will also be prosecuted and charged criminally. Crimes considered terrorism under Ecuadorian penal law include fabrication, acquisition, theft, use or introduction into the country of weapons or munitions, explosives, explosive material, toxins, or substances and materials used in the preparation of explosives. Terrorism also includes destruction or invasion of banks, marketplaces, housing units, schools, hospitals, military spaces, or police spaces by guerilla groups, gangs, or terrorist cells, whether armed or unarmed, under any patriotic, social, economic, political, religious, or racial pretext.

Crimes against Constitutional Guarantees and Racial Equality

Ecuadorian penal law provides its citizenry protection of their constitutional rights, including the right to exercise such political rights as voting, the right to practice any religion tolerated by the state, and the right against arbitrary or illegal imprisonment by the order of public officials. The law also prohibits crimes against prisoners such as prohibiting their communications for long periods of times or holding prisoners without a court-mandated sentence and provides the rights to petition, assembly, and freedom of expression. Racial discrimination is also prohibited under this section of the penal code. Crimes of this nature include promoting ideas based on racial superiority, promoting any type of racial discrimination, engaging in acts of violence against a race, and financing and assisting any racist activities.

Abortion

Ecuadorian law prohibits abortion. Crimes that could be prosecuted under this law include causing a woman to abort by giving her food, drink, or medication to cause the abortion or using violence to cause the abortion. Voluntary abortion by a woman with her consent is also a punishable act. Abortion is not punished if the procedure is performed by a medical doctor under two special circumstances: first, if the pregnancy causes serious risk to the health of the mother and the health risk cannot be avoided; and second, if the pregnancy is the result of rape or if the pregnant woman is mentally challenged.

Homicide and Murder

Simple homicide is defined by the Ecuadorian penal codes as an act in which the perpetrator has the intention to end the life of another person. Murder is defined as any homicide in which any of the following circumstances exist: premeditation, reward for the killing, killing following torture of the victim, defenseless victim, temporal-spatial concealment (e.g., the crime was committed at night or in a desolate area), attempt at concealment of the act or avoidance of prosecution, and killing to conceal another crime. Other crimes that fall under this category include murder of a newborn baby by the mother or grandparents of the child to conceal a dishonor, aiding a person in suicide, and unintentionally causing the death of a person because of neglect or recklessness.

Assault and Battery

Crimes under this category include any injury caused by striking another person that could incapacitate him or her from work temporarily or permanently or cause the person sickness, mutilations, or loss of an organ. Unintentional injuries caused by neglect or recklessness are also prosecuted under this section of the penal code.

Abandonment

Abandonment of a child is listed a punishable act and varies depending on several factors. Factors taken into account in the prosecution of child abandonment include whether a child was abandoned in a populous or a desolate area, if the abandonment was by the natural parents or the legal guardians of the child, and whether the child suffered injuries or death as a result of being abandoned.

Abuse of Arms

Ecuadorian penal law states that using any firearm against a person or aggression with any other weapon is a punishable crime even if this does not result in an injury.

Sexual Crimes

Penal code defines three types of sexual crimes. Attempt against modesty (*atentado contra el pudor*) is defined as any indecent act that does not involve copulation that can offend a person regardless of the person's sex. Rape (*violacion*) is defined as any carnal access with partial or complete penetration through the vaginal, anal, or oral orifice, of a person of either sex. Rape by deception (*estrupo*) is defined as copulation with a woman by employing seduction or deception to gain her consent. Rape of a boy by his father or any male adult in a position of authority, such as a public official, a teacher, a professor, or any other person responsible for the boy, is labeled by penal law as homosexualism. Promoting or facilitating prostitution is also listed by Ecuadorian penal code as a punishable act.

Property Crimes

Property crimes are divided into several sections under the penal code. Theft is defined as the fraudulent taking of another's property without the use of violence or threat. Robbery is defined as an act that employs violence or threats against a person to fraudulently take that which belongs to the person, whether violence or threats occur before the act of taking property, during the commission of the act, or after the act has been committed. Property crimes also include theft and robbery of cattle, extortion, and other types of fraud.

Drug Offenses

Ecuador, along with other countries in the Andean region, is considered to be a high-traffic country for narcotics and illegal substances. This has to do with the nation's location and its shared border with Colombia and Peru, two of the largest producers of cocaine and heroin. Ecuador ratified laws against narcotics and psychotropics with the purpose of combating production, sale, and use of illegal substances. However, rampant corruption within government ranks and inadequate training of national police have hindered the battle against drugs. Cocaine seizures have been on the rise, with 5.8 metric tons seized in 2004 as compared to 2.5 metric tons seized in 2003, and 4.4 metric tons seized in 2005 as compared to previous years.

Drug offenses are strictly punished in Ecuador and carry the maximum prison sentence allowed by law. They are punished even more harshly than some crimes against persons, including homicide and rape. The following crimes are sanctioned with a maximum penalty of 12 to 16 years of incarceration: cultivation of plants that can be used to extract substances subject to prosecution; trafficking of illegal substances (whether via sale, purchase, distribution, imports, or export); transportation of illegal substances by water, land or air; and possession of illegal substances for personal use.

Crime Statistics

Property crimes constitute the majority of crimes reported in Ecuador. In 2007, 64 percent of all reported crime was property crime. When broken down by province, those most affected by this type of crime were Pichincha and Guayas, two large urban centers. The crime of robbery includes both armed robbery and burglary, and in 2007, it was reported at higher levels than theft. There were more reports of robbery against individuals (8,511 cases) than robbery against private residences (3,595 cases) and robbery against commercial entities (4,040 cases). Crime statistics for other crimes are available for 2005, which show that there were 21,963 reported violent offenses or crimes against persons, not including sexual crimes, representing 12.3 percent of the total volume of crime. Nearly 5 percent (8,680 cases) of all reported crimes were sexual crimes, less than 2 percent (2,933 cases) were crimes against constitutional guarantees, and less than 1 percent (1,179 cases) were drug crimes. The 109,140 property crimes reported to the police accounted for 61 percent of all crimes known to the police during this same year.

Finding of Guilt

Rights of the Accused

In the Ecuadorian legal system, no person can be found guilty, nor can they be judged of their guilt, by any official other than a competent judge as determined by the law. Competent judges must have a law degree accompanied by three years or more of experience in the practice of law. Ecuador practices the presumption of innocence; all defendants are innocent until proven otherwise. Defendants have the right against self-incrimination and can remain silent without their silence being considered a sign of guilt. Similar to double jeopardy, Ecuador upholds *unico proceso,* which means that a defendant cannot be processed or sentenced for the same crime twice. The defendant has the right to be informed of all aspects and processes relating to the case and must be informed of his or her rights as guaranteed by the Constitution. Defendants have the right to defense counsel and must choose someone to represent them before any formal proceedings begin and before any statements are taken. If the defendant does not choose an attorney, the presiding judge must assign a public defender to the defendant. The defendant also has the right to defend himself during legal proceedings and has the right to be present at and to intervene in all proceedings. Preventive prison can be ordered by a judge if there is evidence that the suspect is responsible for the crime in question, while the prosecutor continues to gather evidence and build the case.

Criminal Proceeding

Prior to 2001, criminal proceedings were conducted by the presiding judge, as is characteristic of the inquisitorial system. Following the change to the adversarial model, a public prosecutor from the Public Ministry is responsible for representing the state in criminal proceedings. The prosecutor, with the help of the judicial police, is responsible for investigating all aspects of a crime. When sufficient evidence is gathered, the prosecutor can officially charge a person for the crime in question. Preliminary proceedings are then held and are used by both the prosecutor and the defense to bring forth issues regarding criminal charges and competence and legality of proceedings, as well as to make any pretrial motions. If a judge finds that there is sufficient evidence and a well-founded case against the defendant, then the proceedings move into trial. The trial phase is held before a judge, and both sides, the prosecutor and the defense, argue their case. Both parties can present evidence, witnesses, and experts to support their case. The presiding judges can cross-examine the defendant, the victim, witnesses, and experts who take part in the trial. The judge dictates the verdict and the sentence. Any party that is not in accord with the sentence mandated by the judge has the right to contest the sentence through any means allowed by the law.

Juvenile Justice

As of 2007, there were 33 chambers of juvenile justice across Ecuador. Ecuadorian law defines a child as any person who has not yet reached 12 years old. A juvenile is defined as a person between the ages of 12 and 18. The age of criminal responsibility in Ecuador is 18. When the age of the child or juvenile is in question, the law presumes that a person is a child before presuming the person is a juvenile and presumes that the person is a juvenile before presuming he or she is over the age of 18. Juveniles who commit crimes are not taken before judges who normally conduct criminal proceedings, nor are they subject to sanctions listed by penal law. Special judges for children and juveniles review juvenile cases and consider the circumstances surrounding the crime, the youth's personality, and his or her behavior within the family and in the community to suggest the most appropriate response. Juveniles who commit crimes listed under the penal code are subject to socio-educative sanctions.

Juveniles accused of committing a crime have the right to be informed of all processes regarding their case, including why an investigation is being conducted, and the identity of authority that ordered the investigation. The juvenile also has the right to remain silent, the right to a translator if the language is not understood, the right to an attorney, and the right to contact family. Attorneys representing the juvenile must be retained immediately after the juvenile's apprehension. If the juvenile cannot afford an attorney, one must be assigned to guarantee the juvenile a professional defense. The juvenile has the right to examine evidence, to be heard anytime during proceedings, and to cross-examine witnesses and experts. Judges can mandate that a juvenile remain in his or her home under supervision, that the juvenile be placed in the care of a person or entity who will keep the judge informed of the individual's progress, that the juvenile report to the judge periodically, that the juvenile not leave the country, that the juvenile not gather in certain locations determined by the judge, or that the juvenile not communicate with persons whom the judge prohibits the juvenile from communicating with. Privation of liberty for the juvenile accused of a crime exists in exceptional cases. Children are absolutely exempt from prosecution for crimes listed under the penal code. If a child is caught in the commission of a crime, the child will be returned to his or her parents or legal guardian, and if the child has neither, he or she will be assigned to a social entity that cares for children.

Punishment

Ecuadorian penal law lists the different types of punishments that can be applied depending on the act in question. The sanctions that apply to a *delito* include major reclusion, which is a prison sentence to be served at a penitentiary that can range from 4 to 8 years or from 8 to 12 years. In severe cases, this sentence can range from 12 to 16 years in prison, known as extraordinary major reclusion. Minor reclusion is a prison sentence also to be served in a penitentiary that can range from 3 to 6 years or from 6 to 9 years. In severe cases, extraordinary minor reclusion can be warranted and ranges from 9 to 12 years of prison time. Those who are older than 60 years of age cannot be sanctioned with reclusion. Ecuadorian law has special privileges for persons who are responsible for a crime but who have special health conditions. Persons over 60 years of age convicted of a crime punishable by incarceration will not serve their sentence in a penitentiary, but in another location established as an improvised center of detention, like a home. Women who are pregnant and are convicted of a crime that warrants prison time cannot be incarcerated until 90 days after birth. Sanctions for *delitos* also include supervision by a capable authority, limitations in the practice of one's profession, a lifetime ban on obtaining a position in public office, and deprivation of certain political and civil rights. There are several cases that warrant the suspension of political and civil rights for a term of three to five years even if a prison sentence is less than three years. Sanctions that apply to the commission of a *contravencion* include jail time from one to seven days and a fine. Sanctions common to all violations of the law whether, it be a *delito* or a *contravencion,* include fines. Under penal law, persons responsible for the commission of a *delito* must pay for the procedural costs and damages caused to the victim.

Legally admissible mitigating circumstances at sentencing are listed as follows: threats or injuries caused to the defendant prior to his criminal action, age of 60 years or older, intention to pay reparation, voluntary surrender to the authorities, exemplary behavior after the commission of a crime, prior prosocial behaviors and commitments, reasonable justification for the criminal act based on a moral or conventional value, and willing and/or truthful confessions during investigation. Regarding crimes against property, mitigating circumstances may further include extreme poverty or public calamity that made it difficult for the defendant to find legitimate employment at the time of the commission of the crime.

Aggravating circumstances at sentencing are premeditation; treachery; reward for the commission of the crime; and use of flooding, arson, and poison, mines, derailing a train, or other means that place people other than the intended victim at unnecessary risk. Other aggravating circumstances include the use of fraud, the viciousness and savagery of the crime, the use of torture or any other method that can prolong the suffering of a victim, the physical or mental incapacity of the victim, and the abuse of power in the commission of a crime. Using public disorder or calamity to perpetrate a crime; falsifying titles, names, or insignia given to public authority to facilitate the commission of a crime; committing a crime where a religious ceremony is taking place; committing crime in an isolated area or at night; committing crime as member of a gang; perpetrating a crime with violence; being a fugitive for a previous crime; or committing crime against a foreign diplomat can also prompt the judge to impose a more severe penalty on the convicted offender.

When there are two or more mitigating circumstances and no aggravating circumstances, extraordinary major reclusion can be reduced from 12 to 16 years to 8 to 12 years. Ordinary major reclusion can be reduced form 8 to 12 years to minor reclusion of 6 to 9 years. Major reclusion that ranges from 4 to 8 years can be reduced to minor reclusion of 3 to 6 years. Extraordinary minor reclusion of 9 to 12 years can be reduced to minor reclusion of 6 to 9 years, and minor reclusion of 3 to 6 years can be reduced to 1 to 2 years in a correctional facility

Ecuador does not apply life in prison, nor is the death sentence practiced. The maximum penalty a person can be sentenced to is extraordinary major seclusion, which ranges from 12 to 16 years. This punishment is typically reserved for murder. Murder of parents, spouse, or children also warrants extraordinary major reclusion. Simple homicide is punished with major reclusion of 8 to 12 years. Murder of a newborn by the mother or grandparents of the child warrants 3 to 6 years of minor reclusion. The sanction for aiding a person in his or her suicide is 1 to 4 years in prison, regardless of success or failure of the suicide. Injuries that cause unintentional death can be punished with 3 to 6 years of minor reclusion, whereas unintentionally causing death because of neglect or carelessness is punished with 3 months to 6 years of prison. Purposefully causing a woman to abort during pregnancy carries a penalty of 3 to 6 years of minor reclusion, and unintentionally causing an abortion with violence carries a penalty of 6 months to 2 years in prison. Voluntary abortion by the mother given her consent warrants a sanction of 1 to 5 years in prison, and employing any method to cause an abortion that results in the death of the mother carries a penalty of 3 to 6 years of minor reclusion.

Injuries that do not result in death are sanctioned according to the damage caused to the victim. If the injuries result in incapacitation from work for more than 3 days but fewer than 8 days, the perpetrator of the injuries can be punished with 15 days to 3 months in prison and a fine. Injuries causing incapacitation for more than 8 days but less than a month are sanctioned with 2 months to 1 year of prison and a fine, and injuries causing incapacitation that lasts more than 30 days but less than 90 are punished with 6 months to 2 years of prison and a fine. Assault causing permanent injuries or a serious effect on the health of the victim, mutilation, or the loss of an organ is punished with 2 to 5 years in prison. Unintentional injuries caused by recklessness or neglect are punished with 8 days to 3 months in prison.

Indecent sexual acts that do not involve copulation, defined as attempts against modesty, are punished with 1 to 5 years in prison if the victim is under the age of 14 and with 3 to 6 years of minor reclusion if the victim is under 12 years old. Any indecent sexual act that incorporates violence or threats is punished with 3 to 6 years of minor reclusion. These same acts are punished by 4 to 8 years of major reclusion if the victim is mentally or physically impaired and is under the age of 14, and major reclusion of 8 to 12 years if the mentally or physically impaired victim in under 12 years old. Rape of a minor is punished with 3 months to 3 years of prison if the victim is over 14 years old but under the age of 18, and 2 to 5 years in prison if the victim is under 14 years old but over the age of 12.

Soliciting sexual favors for oneself or a third party from a subordinate in the workplace is considered sexual harassment and is punished with 6 months to 2 years in prison. Rape with partial or complete penetration is punished with major reclusion of 4 to 8 years if the victim is under 14 years old, if the victim was defenseless or incapacitated, or when violence or threats of violence were used on the victim. If rape causes severe damage to the victim's health or if death occurs as a consequence of the rape, it is punished with 12 to 16 years of extraordinary major reclusion. An additional 4 years of prison is added to the sentence if the perpetrator is the parent or sibling of the victim, if the rape is committed by a public official who abused the power of his position to commit the rape, if the perpetrator is a health care professional responsible for the well-being of the victim, or if the perpetrator is aided by other persons.

Theft without violence or the threat of violence is punished by 1 month to 3 years in prison, taking into account the value of the stolen property. The sanction for theft increases when the crime occurs in the occasion of a fire, explosion, flood, shipwreck, railroad accident, riot, or any other disaster or public commotion, and if the stolen property includes tools, instruments, or animals that the victim needs in his profession, art, or job, or if the victim is needy and lives in poverty. Robbery is punished with 1 to 5 years in prison. This sanction can be increased to 3 to 6 years of minor reclusion if violence instigated as part of the robbery produces temporary injuries; if the robbery is committed with the use of weapons, at night, in a desolate area, as a gang, or in a public space; and finally if during the course of the robbery, a wall, fence, roof, floor, door, or window is perforated to commit a robbery. If two or more of the conditions mentioned exist, then minor reclusion can be increased to 6 to 9 years. If violence exerted as part of a robbery causes a permanent injury, it will be punished with major reclusion of 8 to 12 years, and if death results as a consequence of violence exerted during the robbery, it can be sanctioned with extraordinary major reclusion of 12 to 16 years.

Prisons

In Ecuador, prisons philosophically serve two functions. The first is to prevent or dissuade the individual from committing a new crime, and the second it to rehabilitate and prepare the offender for social reinsertion. However, these tasks have proven difficult because of overcrowding and violence that breeds in the prison environment. Ecuador currently operates 35 prisons across 17 provinces. Of these prisons, 10 are assigned to men, 4 are assigned to women, 20 hold a mixed population, and 1 serves as a provisional detention center. As of 2008, there were 12,000 inmates held across the Ecuadorian prison system, a figure Cuidad Segura found to be far above capacity. The largest prisons in Ecuador are the Garcia Moreno in Quito and Costal Prison in Guayaquil.

Although rehabilitation programs are mandated by the government, prison staff falls short, and funding for such programs is unavailable.

According to Cuidad Segura, lack of funding has also led to an inadequate food supply and elementary medical attention with only 42 doctors operating across the entire prison system, 130 social workers, and no psychologists. Work programs are available, and prisoners have the right to work while they serve their sentence for very small wages. Prisoners have visitation rights, although abuse by prison officials can lead to the cancellation of these rights. Corruption within the system has led to bribery of prison guards for prisoners to secure better conditions or simply to obtain their visitation rights.

Angela Marcela Navarro

Further Reading

Bermeo, Rodrigo. (2002). "Ecuador." In *Legal Systems of the World: A Political, Social, and Cultural Encyclopedia,* edited by Herbert M. Kritzner, pp. 457–463. Santa Barbara, CA: ABC-CLIO.

De la Torre, Carlos, and Steve Striffler, eds. (2009). *The Ecuador Reader: History, Culture, Politics.* Durham, NC: Duke University Press.

El Salvador

Legal System: Civil/Common
Murder: High
Corruption: Medium
Trafficking: Medium
Prison: Medium
Death Penalty: No
Corporal Punishment: No

Background

El Salvador is the smallest country in Central America and the only one that has no coastline on the Caribbean Sea. It is populated by 7.2 million inhabitants, 61 percent of whom live in urban areas. Mestizos, or people of mixed European and Amerindian ancestry, represent the largest ethnic group (90%), followed by whites (9%) and Amerindians (1%). About 80 percent of Salvadoran adults are literate, and nearly one-third of the population lives below the poverty line.

The country achieved independence from Spain in 1821 and now has a democratic and republican form of government led by a president, a unicameral Legislative Assembly, and a judiciary structured under the Supreme Court. It has the smallest territory and the largest population among all Central American countries. The country is divided into 14 departments and has remained stable since the end of the bloody civil war (1980–1992), which was fought between the rightist government backed by the Ronald Reagan administration of the United States and the Farabundo Martí National Liberation Front (FMLN) supported by Cuba and the Soviet Union. The conflict cost 75,000 lives and ended when an international peace accord initiated and completed a successful process of demobilization of guerrilla forces and civilianization of a militarized state apparatus.

Legal System

The current Salvadoran legal system is based on civil and Roman tradition and has emerged from the civil war as a part of broader reforms implemented to secure lasting peace among rival social and political groups, to strengthen democratic processes, to increase state capacities, and to guarantee basic human rights.

This judicial branch focuses on the interpretation and enforcement of constitutional and legal provisions on constitutional, criminal, civil, commercial, agrarian, labor, and administrative matters. It is headed by the 15-justice Supreme Court of Justice, which is structured into four chambers: Constitutional, Criminal, Civil, and Administrative. The Legislative Assembly elects justices for a nine-year term; elected justices may be reelected and renewed every three years. When it comes to criminal justice issues, the Constitutional Chamber hears and resolves cases related to orders of protection and habeas corpus, whereas the Criminal Chamber studies cassation requests and appeals from second-instance courts.

Under the Supreme Court are the appellate courts, followed by trial courts and justices of the peace. Twenty-six appellate courts are distributed in nine cities and divided into civil, criminal, traffic, labor, family, juvenile justice, and mixed courts. The 201 trial courts process sentences; investigations; traffic matters; prison security; commercial, civil, labor, rent-related, military, family, and juvenile sentencing Finally, there are 322 peace courts in 14 cities throughout El Salvador. This judicial machine is staffed by more than 500 judges on the bench, which can be translated into a judges-to-citizen ratio of 1 judge for every 11,000 population.

El Salvador's Constitution establishes the Public Ministry and its three divisions: the Public Prosecutor's Office, the Public Defender's Office, and the Human Rights Ombudsman's Office. Each of these divisions is autonomous and has its own administrator elected by the Legislative Assembly and its own budget and administration. The Public Defender's Office is represented by the defender general and has 17 branch offices across the country. The office is tasked with the provision of legal services to indigent defendants unable to hire private legal counsel, to fulfill the constitutional requirement of protecting the right of the people to a qualified defense. Public defenders represent their clients in adult and juvenile hearings, from the initial investigative stages to the execution of the sentence. In 2006, nearly 76,000 defendants were represented by the office.

The Public Prosecutor's Office is in charge of the protection of public safety and the defense of the law through the investigation of criminal events in collaboration with the National Civil Police and exercise of criminal prosecution. The prosecutor general is the legal head of this office and is aided by the assistant prosecutor general, assistant prosecutor for human rights, and general secretary, each of whom has a group of advisory and support units. Prosecutors are organized under the Anti-Narcotics Unit, the Financial Investigation Unit, the Human Trafficking Unit, the Anti-Organized Crime Unit, and the Anti-Corruption and Complex Crimes Unit; they are empowered to direct the National Civil Police and other public security agencies in the investigation of punishable crimes.

The Human Rights Ombudsman's Office is a permanent and independent agency created to protect, promote, and defend regarding human rights. The Ombudsman's Office has national jurisdiction and is responsible for investigating cases of human rights violations ex officio or in response to a complaint, assisting the victims of said violations, monitoring the situation of those detained, promoting reforms for progress in this area, and related tasks. The ombudsman may request assistance and/or reports from government agencies, civil officials or authorities, military officials, or public security agents.

The National Civilian Police (PNC) was established in 1993 to replace the notorious National Guard, National Police, and Treasury Police, which were directly involved in the brutal repression of the left-wing guerrillas, and now has about 16,000 officers. The first members of the PNC were trained through the International Criminal Investigative Training Assistance Program and subsequently through the National Public Security Academy supported by the U.S. Department of State's Bureau for International Narcotics and Law Enforcement Affairs. The PNC is responsible for maintaining public security across the country, but in rural areas, the military participates in some PNC patrols and antinarcotics efforts.

Crime

Several factors have converged to maintain a very high rate of crime and violence in El Salvador. Its geographic location renders the Salvadoran territory a transit route favored by drug and human traffickers, the endemic and stark wealth disparities have raised a large army of dissatisfied and unemployed youths, the understaffing of criminal justice agencies drastically reduces the crime-control capacity of the public safety apparatus, and a recent history of armed conflict has facilitated the availability of deadly weapons and of psychosocial predispositions to their use.

Minors watch television at the Border Police precinct after being held at the border town of Hachadura, El Salvador, October 7, 2003. Some 10 minors were rescued by border police after traffickers intended to cross them into Guatemala en route to the United States. (AP Photo/Victor Ruiz Caballero)

By 1995, lives lost to criminal homicide exceeded the average annual number of war deaths during the second half of the civil war, making El Salvador the most violent society in the region. In 2006, 3,927 homicide cases were known to the police, which translated to a rate of 58.1 homicides per 100,000 inhabitants. About 78.2 percent of these homicides involved firearms, and only 9.3 percent of all homicides took place in the capital city of San Salvador. The concentration of violent offenses in less urbanized cities and departments is unique to El Salvador. La Libertad and Sonsonate are the two jurisdictions that have enjoyed high socioeconomic development, and yet they have suffered the highest homicide rates in the country. As the main seaports on the Pacific coast, connected by the Pan American Highway, these two departments are critical transshipment centers preferred by international drug traffickers and thus are exposed to an unusual level of violent incidents. Armed robbery, major assault, kidnapping, rape, theft, and fraud are common threats to Salvadoran residents.

Gang Violence

El Salvador has hundreds of violent street gangs with more than 30,000 active members. Violent and well-armed street gang growth continues in El Salvador, with Los Angeles's 18th Street and MS-13 ("Mara Salvatrucha") gangs being the largest and most influential in the country. During the civil war, large numbers of Salvadorans sought refuge in the United States. There, they congregated in Hispanic urban neighborhoods, particularly those in Southern California. These impoverished areas have a long history of serious gang problems, and the new immigrants found themselves targeted by local gangs. Partly as a defensive reaction, many young Salvadorans either joined the existing gangs or formed their own. When the United States began to tighten its immigration policy in 1996, many Salvadoran gang members were deported to their homeland. All deportees were first housed in the Guezaltepeque Prison, in northern El Salvador. Quickly and unexpectedly, U.S.-style gang culture flourished in the Salvadoran prison system, and recruitment began on the streets in El Salvador. Both L.A.'s 18th Street and MS-13 soon became the largest gangs in El Salvador and spread to the Honduras and Guatemala.

Salvadoran gangs focus on narcotics and arms trafficking, murder for hire, carjacking, and violent street crime. Gangs composed of unemployed youth roam freely, day and night, targeting affluent areas for burglaries, and gang members are quick to use deadly force if resistance is offered. They were once concentrated in urban areas but are now showing up in the most remote corners of El Salvador. In addition to committing crimes in urban streets, gang members are now terrorizing rural farmers and stealing their crops. It is estimated that 60 percent of all intentional homicides are carried out by street gangs. The U.S. government has assigned a Gang Advisor to assist the government of El Salvador with combating the gang problem. Additionally, the Federal Bureau of Investigation has established a transnational anti-gang unit with the PNC, based in San Salvador.

Drug Abuse and Trafficking

El Salvador is a signatory of the 1971 UN Convention on Psychotropic Substances and the 1988 UN Drug Convention and thus is obligated to criminalize and combat drug production, trade, and consumption domestically and internationally. El Salvador remains a transit country for cocaine and heroin from the Andean region of South America, en route to the United States. Estimates indicate that approximately 400 metric tons of cocaine flow through the Eastern Pacific. Salvadoran authorities continued to conduct maritime and land interdiction of cocaine and heroin along the nation's coastline and overland routes, as well as to investigate narcotics-related money laundering operations. Yet despite visible efforts, success has been very limited. In 2008, the PNC seized 1.35 metric tons of cocaine, 430 kilograms of marijuana, and 8.4 kilograms of heroin. The government also confiscated $1.5 million from suspicious bank accounts and cash drug transactions.

Transnational street gangs are involved in retail-level drug sales but not major wholesale trafficking. Although investigators have not yet uncovered serious problems with production or trading of precursor chemicals, investigations suggest that signs of deterioration are present. For example, a recent audit of one of El Salvador's principal pharmaceutical laboratories showed 2 million ephedrine pills missing from the inventory.

Overall drug abuse has remained moderate and relatively stable in El Salvador. According to estimates by the United Nations, the prevalence of opiate and cocaine abuse among adults aged 15 or older did not change in any significant way between 1997 and 2005, with 0.1 percent using them in 1997 and 0.4 percent in 2005. Amphetamines and cannabis are the two most popular illicit drugs and are used by 3.0 percent and 2.7 percent of Salvadoran adults, respectively. To reduce the demand for illicit drugs, several government agencies are tasked with the responsibility of addressing the issue. The Ministry of Education provides lifestyle and prevention training in public schools and sponsors after-school activities. The PNC operates a Drug Abuse Resistance Education (D.A.R.E.) program directly imported from the United States, where the model has proved to be of minimum, if any, impact. The National Council of Public Security promotes gang member demobilization and conducts drug-abuse prevention outreach toward El Salvador's gang population. The civic society is mostly engaged in the treatment and rehabilitation of drug abusers; local faith-based treatment programs and counseling programs administered by recovering addicts are the most visible players.

Human Trafficking

El Salvador sends, trades, and receives women and children trafficked for the purposes of sexual and labor exploitation. Human trafficking in El Salvador is mostly domestic. Young women and girls are sold from rural areas to urban centers for commercial sex, whereas some adults and children are trafficked internally for forced agricultural labor and apparel assembly. Most foreign victims are women and children from neighboring countries, such as Honduras and Guatemala, and other nearby Spanish-speaking countries, such as Nicaragua, Mexico, and Colombia; these foreign victims travel to El Salvador in response to job offers but are subsequently forced into prostitution or domestic servitude. In recent years, trafficked Salvadoran women also have been found in brothels, pubs, and massage parlors during law enforcement raids in Guatemala, Mexico, Belize, the United States, Spain, and Italy.

The Salvadoran penal code criminalizes all forms of human trafficking and prescribes punishments of up to 8 years in prison. Since the enactment of El Salvador's anti-trafficking statute in 2004, some prosecutors have avoided its application and chosen to charge trafficking-related crimes under the country's rape statute, which carries a punishment of up to 20 years in prison, to secure stiffer penalties against offenders. In 2008, Salvadoran criminal justice authorities brought charges in 15 cases of human trafficking and obtained 8 convictions, with sentences ranging from 4 to 10 years' imprisonment. Such results compare with 46 prosecutions initiated and 5 convictions secured in 2007. Enforcement efforts have focused mostly on trafficking for commercial sexual exploitation and on only a very small number of cases related to forced labor.

Supported by foreign assistance, the Salvadoran government also engages in the assistance of victims of human trafficking. The country's federal agency for children and adolescents operates a national network of 11 shelters to provide safe housing, around-the-clock medical care, psychological counseling, and vocational training to victims of child abuse, including trafficking victims. However, most government assistance and services are directed to child victims of human trafficking and are not readily accessible to adult victims, especially males. Furthermore, government support services rarely extend beyond shelter care and do not provide greater reintegration assistance. Law enforcement agents actively encourage collaboration from trafficking victims: in 2008, 57 victims participated in the investigation and prosecution of their traffickers, although many more refused to offer assistance because of social stigma or fear of reprisals. Victims are not prosecuted or punished for illegal acts committed as a direct result of their victimizations. Although extant statutes do not offer a formal alternative to deportation to a country where a trafficking victim may face hardship or retribution, criminal justice and social service officials have requested and obtained residency status for some victims on a case-by-case basis.

Finding of Guilt

Criminal Justice Procedure

Despite the Salvadoran penal justice's long inquisitorial tradition, a new criminal procedure with strong oral and adversarial components was introduced in 1998 to avoid some of the gross human rights violations committed in the past. The new procedure dictates that the National Civil Police be involved in the investigation of criminal offenses under the direct order of the Public Prosecutor's Office.

Allegations of criminal events are usually reported to PNC agents, who initiate first investigations by questioning victims, witnesses, and suspects and gathering physical evidence. Salvadoran courts accept the rule that interrogation without the presence of counsel is coercive and that any testimony obtained in such a manner is inadmissible during trial. As a result, PNC authorities generally delay questioning until a public defender or an attorney arrives. Family members are also allowed prompt access to detained suspects.

The Constitution allows the PNC to detain a suspect for 72 hours before bringing the person to court, after which the judge may order detention for an additional 72 hours to determine whether an investigation is warranted. Although the Salvadoran Constitution prohibits arbitrary arrest and detention, there are frequent complaints that the PNC has indeed arbitrarily arrested and detained persons. In 2007, the Human Rights Ombudsman's Office received 193 complaints of arbitrary arrest or detention, including 121 illegal detentions.

Once the Public Prosecutor's Office receives a written complaint from the police, a request for intervention is sent to a peace court judge. This petition formally initiates the judicial engagement and begins with a preliminary hearing in which the judge decides whether the defendant will be taken into custody and whether the case requires further investigation and legal action. The criminal justice process is composed of three key stages: the preliminary stage of investigation, the intermediate stage of analysis, and the adversarial stage of trial. Upon the presentation of the charges and supporting evidence by the prosecutor to the investigating judge, the preliminary hearing is convened for motions and discovery. The judge may opt for alternatives to trial or accept evidence and order a trial. After all contending parties have been informed of the judicial decision of moving forward with the procedure, the investigative judge submits all documents and evidence to the trial court and ensures the appearance of the accused. The law permits up to six months for investigation of serious crimes before requiring either a trial or dismissal of the case.

Within 48 hours of receiving the respective notifications, the presiding judge of the trial court will schedule the first oral, public trial hearing, which must take place between 10 days and 1 month after this date and which requires the continued presence of the judges and parties.

The rights of the defendant to attend all court sessions, cross-examine witnesses, and present witnesses and evidence are guaranteed by the Constitution. Although the Constitution further provides for the presumption of innocence, protection from self-incrimination, the right to legal counsel, freedom from coercion, and government-provided legal counsel for the indigent, some of these legal rights and protections are occasionally violated in practice.

All trials are public. When both the prosecution and the defense have concluded their arguments, the judges deliberate to decide on the disposition of the case. In principle, the law provides for trial by jury in select cases, especially in those involving charges of environmental pollution and certain misdemeanors. In these exceptional jury trials, juries determine the innocence or guilt of the accused, but only judges decide the sentence. An overwhelming majority of criminal cases are processed through bench trial in El Salvador. Whereas a jury's verdict is final, a bench verdict can be appealed. In either jury trial or bench trial, if a verdict of not guilty is reached, the court will immediately set the defendant free; if the defendant is found guilty, the parties have the opportunity to present arguments on the sentence. All convicted offenders have the right to be informed of their sentences within five days of the end of their convictions.

There exists a Program for the Protection of Victims and Witnesses to secure the safe participation of Salvadoran citizens in the adjudication of criminal cases involving violent street gangs. In 2008, 2,347 new requests for protection were submitted to the program, and at the year's end, 3,110 witnesses or victims were under some kind of police protection. Unfortunately, intimidation and violence against witnesses by criminal gangs has created a solid climate of their impunity from prosecution.

Judicial misconduct is a serious problem that erodes the credibility of the courts to achieve a fair and efficient administration of justice. During 2008, the Public Prosecutor's Office investigated 73 judges and 9 magistrates for corruption; the Supreme Court received 169 complaints from private citizens against judges for alleged irregularities and penalized 3 judges for improper conduct. During the same year, 203 complaints against prosecutors for misconduct were submitted to the Public Prosecutor's Office, resulting in the dismissal of 1 prosecutor and the suspensions of 13 others for corruption and other serious infractions.

Juvenile Justice

The official age of criminal responsibility is 16. Offenders aged 15 or younger are considered juvenile offenders, whose processing and care are regulated by the Juvenile Offenders Act. The juvenile justice system is authorized to dispense a wide range of coercive rehabilitative measures on youths under its supervision including mandatory counseling to custody in a juvenile detention center.

To put the destabilizing threat of youth gangs under control, the National Council for Public Security implemented a Safe Country plan dubbed the Super Heavy Hand policy in 2004. Units of the armed forces patrolled with the civilian police to monitor children of disadvantaged backgrounds who were blamed for making a disproportionate contribution to the rampant criminal violence. Although of the 300,000 suspects detained under the security policy between 2000 and 2006, fewer than 6 percent were under 16, 43 percent of these minor detainees were held without evidence of criminality. Authorities have attempted to lower the age of criminal responsibility to 12, but such a proposal has encountered fierce resistance from human rights organizations and other civic groups.

Punishment

According to the 1983 Constitution, Salvadoran prisons are established first to rehabilitate criminal offenders and then to punish them in a way commensurable to the harms they have inflicted on the society. The institution responsible for prison policy is the General Directorate of Prisons, which reports to the Ministry of Government. It has the mission of ensuring the safety and well-being of all prison inmates and designing rehabilitation and social reintegration programs. The Penitentiary Law governs sentence enforcement and security measures stipulated in the penal code, as well as other sentences contained in special laws. The subordinate bodies that coordinate policy planning, service delivery, personnel training, and other logistic support for the accomplishment of the stated mission include the Directorate, the National Criminological Council, the Regional Criminological Councils, and the Penitentiary Academy.

The correctional system includes 22 facilities classified by the type of criminal offenders that they house. At the end of 2008, there were 19,814 prisoners held in the 22 correctional facilities and 2 additional secure hospital wards, with a combined designed capacity for 8,227 individuals. In other words, Salvadoran prisons are used at 241 percent of their capacity. Overcrowding poses a serious threat to inmates' health and security, and the rapid growth of the prison population has not yet leveled off. Of these inmates in 2008, 64 percent (12,702) had been convicted, and 36 percent (7,112) were in pretrial or presentence detention. Because of a lack of holding cells, pretrial and presentence detainees are often remanded in regular prison units together with violent convicts. Salvadoran law permits release on bail for detainees who pose no flight risk or whose release would not jeopardize the investigation of the case. Because it may take several years for a case to come to trial, some prisoners are incarcerated longer than the maximum sentences for their crimes. In such situations, detainees could request a Supreme Court review of their continued detention.

Current or former gang members known to correctional authorities made up 34 percent (6,801) of the entire prison population in 2008. Gang members are classified as high-risk inmates and are routinely segregated from the regular prison population. They continue to exercise influence through intimidation, violence, and bribery within the prisons and the judicial system and are a constant source of tension and violence. In a 2007 gang-on-gang battle, 21 inmates were killed in the notorious Apanteos Prison, which resulted in the conviction of nine inmates for homicide and the administrative punishment of many other incarcerated gang members. Gang leaders reportedly conduct criminal activities and order smuggling of weapons, drugs, and cellular telephones from their cells, at times with the complicity of prison guards. Corruption among prison personnel is widespread, and control efforts have been ineffective. In 2008, authorities convicted one prison guard, dismissed charges of wrongdoing against three others, and continued criminal investigations against an additional two guards.

In 2008 there were 561 juvenile offenders housed in four juvenile detention facilities with a combined capacity of 763 beds. Despite added investment in programs and services, gang activities in juvenile-holding facilities remain a serious threat to the goal of rehabilitation.

Hung-En Sung

Further Reading

Call, Charles T. (2007). "The Mugging of a Success Story: Justice and Security Reform in El Salvador." In *Constructing Justice and Security after War,* edited by Charles T. Call, pp. 29–68. Washington, DC: United States Institute of Peace Press.

Dodson, Michael. (2002). "El Salvador." In *Legal Systems of the World: A Political, Social, and Cultural Encyclopedia, Volume 2,* edited by Herbert M. Kritzer, pp. 468–474. Santa Barbara, CA: ABC/CLIO Press.

United Nations Office on Drugs and Crime. (2007). *Crime and Development in Central America: Caught in the Crossfire*. Vienna, Austria: UNODC.

Falkland Islands

Legal System: Common
Murder: Low
Prison Rate: Low
Death Penalty: No

Background

The Falkland Islands are an archipelago in the South Atlantic Ocean classified as a British sovereign territory. There are two main islands and 776 smaller islets; the total area of 12,173 square kilometers is slightly smaller than the state of Connecticut. As of 2008, 3,140 people reside permanently on the islands. The economy of the Falkland is built on fisheries, sheep farming, and tourism and has yielded a gross domestic product per capita US$35,400.

The Falklands were first discovered by English explorers in 1594, but the first landing by English sailors did not take place until nearly a century later in 1690. The first permanent settlement was established by the French in 1764 and taken over by Spain in 1766. The ensuing disputes over the control of the islands among Great Britain, Spain, and later the newly independent Argentina quieted down in 1833, when the British Crown formally colonized the Falklands by establishing a naval garrison in Port Stanley. Despite the de facto occupation of the islands by the British, Argentina pursued its claim of sovereignty and invaded the islands in April 1982. The British government under the premiership of Margaret Thatcher responded with an expeditionary force that recovered the Falklands by force in June 1982.

The governor represents the Crown and the British government to the islands, and conversely, he or she represents the citizens to the Crown and is responsible for the management of all foreign affairs and defense and ensures the integrity and the justice system. The chief executive and the six-member executive council are responsible for the daily management and delivery of government services on the Islands. The 10-member Legislative Assembly presided over by the governor meets twice a month to pass legislation with respect to local order, peace, and good governance; however, all legislation passed is subject to the approval of Her Majesty the Queen.

Legal System

The Falkland Islands' legal system, as is the case of any British sovereign territory, is independent of the United Kingdom; however, the civil and criminal laws are explicitly drawn, with some allowances for local needs, from the English statute law. The British Foreign and Commonwealth Office ultimately oversee the police and judiciary, like all of the government functions in the Falklands. In fact, the supreme authority over the Falklands is vested in Her Majesty the Queen, and on her behalf, this authority is managed through the aforementioned appointed governor. The governor rules with the advice and assistance of the locally elected chief executive, executive council, and Legislative Assembly.

The chief justice of the islands, who is a nonresident, oversees the judiciary of the Falklands. The highest court in the island's judiciary is the Supreme Court. The court employs four lawyers, one of whom is the attorney general. The court system is streamlined. A panel of justices of the peace (JPs) oversees the Summary Court. JPs are not required, by law, to be lawyers; rather, they must be "upstanding members of the community." The JPs deal with low-level criminal cases in addition to civil matters (such as marriage licensing).

A local magistrate, who must be a trained attorney, manages the judiciary. He is responsible for hearing the majority of civil and criminal cases, including family, admiralty, and commercial disputes. The magistrate is also the islands' coroner and is responsible for investigating any unexpected or violent deaths that occur. The nonresident chief justice of the islands is appointed by the governor and typically visits the island once annually for the purpose of hearing complex felonies. Criminal cases that must be heard before the Supreme Court include murder, manslaughter, rape, piracy, treason and arson with the intent to endanger life, appeals from the magistrate's court, or cases involving the constitutional rights of the accused.

Policing and local prison responsibilities are given to the Royal Falkland Islands Police (RFIP). The RFIP was created with the enactment of the Constables Ordinance 1846, and along with the Police Ordinance Act of 2000, the RFIP is required to follow all of the procedural and legal guidelines established by the British Home Office for all local constabularies throughout England and Wales. Within the organization of British policing, the RFIP is affiliated with the Devon and Cornwall Constabulary. The Devon and Cornwall Constabulary is responsible for policing the southwestern counties in England.

The RFIP, full-time, employs 18 sworn officers and 3 administration staff (1 to oversee the jail and 2 for administration); however, all Royal Air Force and Marine personnel who are stationed in the Falklands are sworn deputies who can be called up to aid in civil matters at the direction of the governor. The RFIP is headed by a chief inspector. The chief inspector is responsible for the administration of both the public safety and the island's prison. RFIP officers do not carry firearms.

The Falklands criminal justice system is explicitly an extension of the English system; the sections that follow deal only with local deviations from that system. For a more detailed accounting of the English system, the readers are encouraged to familiarize themselves with the British entry elsewhere in this encyclopedia.

Crime

Classification of Crimes

The Falklands crime classifications are the same as in England. The age of criminal responsibility is 10 years old.

Crime Statistics

There are no official crime statistics available for the Falkland Islands; moreover, the Home Office Web site states that there is "no crime" in the islands. This is meant in the context of serious violence or drug offenses. The most likely reason for the lack of official statistics is that the police do not necessarily address crimes as much as they provide public safety. Second, they are not required, due to their political relationship with Britain, to provide such data to the Home Office. The Falklands are invited by the United Nations to submit their crime data to the annual UN Crime Survey; however, they have never provided that data. Last, most crime problems are very low-level offenses that are addressed directly by the justices of the peace. This has to do with the island geography and small population of the Falklands. As such, policing services are centralized in the capital, Stanley, and the JPs are relied on to adjudicate and maintain order in the majority of the townships and villages.

According to newspaper accounts, drunken brawlers, teenage vandals, and the occasional skinny-dipper appear most in the officers' notebooks. The last murder to occur in the Falklands was in 1985, and since 1998, the most notable criminal events have been three rapes and one arson.

A Recent Major Crime

In December 2008, an estimated 1.5 million dollars' (U.S.) worth of cocaine disappeared from a specially sealed cell at the only police station in the Falklands. The 29 packets of cocaine were being held as evidence pending trial. The drugs were seized off of a foreign fishing vessel that was moored in Stanley, the capital. The two suspects in that case were being held at the station awaiting trial; however, they were allowed to roam the corridor at night to use the bathroom and the kitchen. That same corridor gave access to the cell that was used to store the cocaine, as well as access to the weapons used by the RFIP. According to newspaper accounts, there is large gap between the door and the floor of the cell used to store the evidence. The magistrate's court found that the one of the two defendants had taken advantage of his "freedom to roam," discovered the drugs, and simply put his hand through the "substantial gap" and removed 23 of the 29 packets over the course of several days. Authorities believe that the offender flushed away the evidence as a means of disrupting his felony drug transshipment charge.

Finding of Guilt

Adjudications for offenses follow the English common law system. Most criminal offenses, which are adjudicated by the justices of the peace, result in a fine or some form of community service. For more serious cases, involving the magistrate's court, incarceration before or during trial in the islands' 13-person jail is possible. For felony sentences where guilt is found, the individual is incarcerated in an English prison.

Punishment

Types of Punishment

Most punishments in the Falklands involve a fine or some kind of public service. The severity of the vast majority of cases does not warrant any greater punishment. All felony offenses are adjudicated and sentenced under the same rules and procedural guidelines as in England. The death penalty was abolished for homicide in 1965 and for all other offenses by the mid-1970s. Adults who are convicted of murder receive a mandatory life sentence; however, only in rare cases do offenders actually spend the rest of their life in prison. A person who is sentenced to life is parole-eligible after 14 years, and many are released at that time. That said, there is no requirement of parole because a life sentence is, technically, indeterminate. A life sentence is possible for offenses such as rape and robbery.

Prison

There is one jail in the Falklands. It is located in the police station, which is in the capital, Stanley. The jail has 4 cells and is capable of holding 12 to 13 people.

Vincenzo A. Sainato

Further Reading

Cawkell, Mary. (2001). *The History of the Falkland Islands*. Shropshire, UK: Anthony Nelson Ltd.

Falkland Islands government: http://www.falklands.gov.fk//index.html.

Falkland Islands Information Portal: http://www.falklands.info/index.html.

Greenland

Legal System: Civil
Murder: Medium
Prison Rate: High
Death Penalty: No
Corporal Punishment: No

Background

The Danish realm includes the largest island in the world, Greenland. It represents an area of 2,170,000 square kilometers. Most of Greenland is covered with a polar ice cap, but still, there are about 57,000 inhabitants on the island. On the ice-free coast, the capital of Nuuk (Godthåb) has approximately 15,000 inhabitants in a municipality that is two and a half times as large as Denmark. The Greenland Home Rule Government is located in Nuuk, and Greenland is also represented by two members in Folketinget (the Danish Parliament) in Copenhagen.

The Greenland judicial system differs from the Danish system in many ways. In Greenland, the administration of justice is handled by ordinary citizens, working as district judges, lay judges, and defense counsel. Only when a case is brought to the High Court in Nuuk are legally trained prosecutors, judges, and defense counsel brought into the process. The Greenland Criminal Code also does not mention punishment at all and has no penal limits. It offers a number of special sanctions, from which the court can choose the sanction that seems best suited to prevent the offender from relapsing into crime.

The duties of the Greenland police are similar to those in the Danish realm. According to the first section of the Act on Police Activities, the purpose of the police is to maintain safety, security, peace, and order in society. The police are also required to focus on prevention, assistance, and law enforcement. They are to ensure that the law and other regulations are complied with and take necessary actions to prevent crime, but one of their main fields of responsibility is to handle the prosecution of cases.

Crime

Classifications of Crime

The Greenland criminal code is structured differently than other European penal codes. Instead of a general and specific part, its first part is simply about crime and contains rules and regulations that are similar for all types of crimes. The second part is about the legal consequences of crime and contains rules concerning prosecution and other measures. These measures refer mostly to punishment but are used to point out that punishment is just one of the social reactions warranted by the code.

The Greenland Administration Act of Justice and the criminal code were drafted and written shortly after World War II, reflecting the strong social values of the time. Greenland went through a radical and rapid social change soon after, which led to a large increase in criminal activity. Compared to other countries, criminality is especially characterized by relatively many acts of violence, including sexual offenses, homicides, and attempted homicides. Recently, cannabis-related crime and economic crimes have also become problematic. There has been a smaller amount of other drugs, such as cocaine, heroin, and amphetamine, but this problem has not been investigated too well.

Crime Statistics

There are 17 police districts in Greenland. About 31.6 percent of all crimes are committed in the police district around Nuuk. The police in Nuuk handle around 700 cases a year, compared to an average of 100 cases a year in other areas. Most crimes in Greenland are committed by offenders aged 15 to 39. The age of criminal responsibility is 15. Homicides are about three times more common in Greenland than in the rest of Denmark, possibly because knives and other sharp weapons are part of the daily life in Greenland. But it has to be pointed out that homicide statistics include negligent road fatalities, negligent homicide, and bodily harm resulting in death, distinctions that are not included in homicide statistics concerning the rest of Denmark.

Finding of Guilt

The magistrates' courts with three lay judges hear all types of cases in the first instance. Cases range from simple theft to homicide. They also deal with civil cases, family law, divisions of estate, and so on. At a hearing in the courtroom, a local police officer handles the prosecution, and a counsel chosen by the local people is assigned to the accused. The counsel does not necessarily have any legal knowledge. Only at the High Court in Nuuk does the accused have the right to a lawyer.

All types of crimes may be the subject of public prosecution. In assessing the seriousness of the offense, consideration is always given to the harm, danger, and violation involved, as well as to what the offender knew or should have known at the time of the offense. In assessing the information about the offender, consideration is given to the offender's general, personal, and social circumstances, as well as to circumstances before and after the offense and the offender's motives for committing the offense.

The accused is entitled to make a statement before his or her case is heard. A reason must be given for all denials and decisions that go against the accused. The accused also has the right to get a copy of all written material and to make a statement before the decision is made. Furthermore, he or she has the right to receive advice about possibilities for appeal. Personal freedom is inviolable according to the Danish Constitutional Act, which also applies to Greenland. Anybody who is taken into custody has the right to appear in front of a judge within 24 hours. If the accused cannot be released immediately, the judge has to decide as soon as possible whether the accused is to be imprisoned or released on bail. The nature and amount of such a bail shall also be determined.

If a person intentionally or by gross negligence endangers the body or property of another, he or she shall be responsible for his or her actions. This is especially relevant for intoxication, and the responsibility even extends to those who cause intoxication in others. Intoxication and its consequences can be much more severe in Greenland because of its geographical and climatic conditions. Road traffic legislation is also quite strict in Denmark in general. Driving under the influence of alcohol or drugs is treated as a very serious offense. The rules are strictly and immediately enforced, and violations can result in heavy fines or even jail sentences.

Punishment

Types of Punishment

Greenland has its own court system, which is composed of the High Court of Greenland and 18 magistrates' courts. In the magistrates' courts, decisions are made by a magistrate and two lay judges, who do not necessarily hold law degrees. If special legal knowledge is needed in a case, it may be taken over by the High Court. Appeals from the magistrates' courts go to the High Court. Major cases are heard in the High Court of Greenland, and appeals from this court go to the High Court of Eastern Denmark.

General measures available to the court, according to the criminal code, are imprisonment, probation order with or without supervision, warning, fine, compulsory work or education, and other restrictions of freedom or action. A commitment to an institution or another suitable home can be ordered in connection with the specific measure. The court can choose freely among the measures and also, if necessary, combine them. For juveniles and mentally ill offenders, there are some special sanctions available.

Imprisonment is used three times more often in Greenland than in other Nordic countries. A sentence of imprisonment is either life or a limited time from 7 days to 16 years. A juvenile offender under the age of 18 cannot be sentenced to more than 8 years of prison. Furthermore, not only psychological but also physical diseases can result in a sentence of medical treatment, something that is very specific to Greenland.

Prison

Prison sentences are served in the three open prisons in Greenland, in police detention, or in the hostels of the Probation Service. The prisons in Greenland have room for 76 inmates. About 75 percent of inmates are placed in the prison in Nuuk. The rest are placed in the two smaller prison units in Aasiaat and Qaqortoq. Inmates are treated quite well in Greenland. They are generally not cut off from the community. For example, work and leisure-time activities often take place outside the prison.

The Herstedvester Institution in Denmark is the only place that has a special unit for Greenlander inmates. The institution has capacity for 13 inmates but currently houses 22. The government takes special measures to keep these prisoners in touch with their culture. For example, they employ Greenlandic staff or offer Greenlandic food. However, according to the European Committee for the Prevention of Torture and Inhuman or Degrading Treatment or Punishment, many of these inmates still feel that they are facing a double punishment by not being able to serve their sentences in Greenland. As such, there are plans to build a new facility for these inmates in Nuuk. Despite the very serious nature of the offenses committed by the inmates housed in the Herstedvester Institution, violent conflicts, disciplinary sanctions, and relapses into crime occur fairly rarely compared with prisons in other countries.

Anna Gustafson

Further Reading

Danish Police: http://www.politi.dk/en/About_the_police/duties/.

Danish Prison and Probation Service, Kriminalforsorgen: http://www.kriminalforsorgen.dk/English/DanishPrisonAndProbationService/Greenland.html.

Government of Greenland: http://uk.nanoq.gl.

International Work Group for Indigenous Affairs: http://www.iwgia.org/sw15471.asp.

Jensen, Henrik G. (1986). *Criminal Justice in Greenland.* Copenhagen: University of Copenhagen (Fulfillment for thesis: Simon Fraser University, Ottawa, 1992).

Royal Danish Ministry of Foreign Affairs: http://www.um.dk/publikationer/um/english/factsheetdenmark/greenland/html/chapter01.htm.

Sermitsiaq English News: http://sermitsiaq.gl/english/.

Grenada

Murder: Medium
Corruption: Low
Prison Rate: High
Death Penalty: Maybe
Corporal Punishment: Yes

Background

The state of Grenada is not a single island but several islands jointly referred to as the Grenadines. The three largest islands are Grenada, Carriacou, and Petite Martinique. Grenada is the second-southernmost of the island group known as the Lesser Antilles, north of the twin-island Republic of Trinidad and Tobago. It has a land area of 344 square kilometers and a coastline of 121 kilometers.

Grenada has a population of 90,343 residents, with nearly 5 percent residing in the capital city of St. George's. Although English is the official language, many Grenadians also speak French patois. Overall, blacks make up 82 percent of the population, followed by 13 percent mixed black and European, 5 percent European and East Indian, and a small faction of Arawak/Carib Amerindian.

Grenada relies heavily on tourism as its main source of foreign exchange, especially since the construction of an international airport in 1985. Although Grenada has rebounded from the devastating effects of Hurricanes Ivan (2004) and Emily (2005), it incurred huge financial debts from the

Members of the Royal Police Force stand at attention during a parade in Granada's capital St. George's. (Bibikow/StockphotoPro)

rebuilding process. From 2007 to 2008, Grenada's economy enjoyed a modest 3.1 percent annual growth rate, only to be offset by the dampening effects of inflation, which reached 3.7 percent. The latest available unemployment figures paint an even grimmer picture; 12.5 percent of Grenadians were looking for work, perhaps a partial reflection of a staggering poverty rate that claims nearly 32 percent of its citizens.

Political History

The state of Grenada achieved independence from England in 1974. Afterward, it adopted a modified Westminster parliamentary system based on the British model, with a governor-general appointed by and representing the British monarch and a prime minister. The country experienced political turmoil for the first decade of independence, including an intervention by U.S. and Caribbean forces in 1983. By the 21st century, Grenada had achieved a level of economic and political stability that made it one of the most democratic states in the Caribbean. As of July 2008, attorney Tillman Thomas, representing the National Democratic Congress, was elected Grenada's new prime minister.

Legal System

When Grenada gained independence in 1974, it also became a member of the British Commonwealth. Consequently, Grenada accepted the rule of common law, as well as a democratic system with ties to Great Britain. Its Constitution guarantees basic rights and protections to its citizen from arbitrary governmental intrusions. Included among these rights is the freedom of speech, freedom from religious persecution, rights to property ownership, the protection from arbitrary arrest, and the right to travel in and out of the country.

Although Grenada's legal system was based on the common law system, it was also receptive to other legal systems, derived from Hindu, Muslim, and Indian law. These traditions and customs are incorporated into the legislation and reflect the cultural, social, political, and economic needs of its citizens. As members of the Commonwealth Caribbean countries, government power is divided among the executive, legislature, and judiciary, although there are tendencies to rely heavily on the form, structure, substance, and content of the law as expressed in England.

The Judiciary

The Constitution provides for an independent judiciary, which is a provision generally respected by the government, that is part of the Eastern Caribbean legal system. As of 2003, Grenada had 7 judges, 50 attorneys, and 1 prosecutor. Grenada's judicial system mirrors other adversarial proceedings in both structure and arrangements. Inferior courts, regarded as courts of summary jurisdiction, are made up of magistrates' courts, petty sessional courts, and coroner's courts. They have a dual function—investigative and trial—in criminal matters. However, their jurisdiction is limited to civil offenses. There are also specialized courts or tribunals, which may be inferior, intermediate, or superior courts. Among these are juvenile, family, divorce, administrative, gun, revenue, and industrial courts.

The Grenada Supreme Court, located in St. George's, consists of a High Court of Justice and a two-tier Court of Appeals. The High Court is the trial court or court of first instance. It has original, unlimited, and appellate jurisdiction over all matters that arise from the inferior courts, whether criminal or civil. The Court of Magisterial Appeals hears appeals from magistrates' courts, which exercise summary jurisdiction. The Itinerant Court of Appeal hears appeals from the High Court. Three resident judges hear cases in the Supreme Court. An appeals court is staffed by a chief justice who travels around the Eastern Caribbean islands to hear cases. To exhaust all legal proceedings, defendants can make final appeals to the Privy Council in the United Kingdom. The council advises heads of state of a respective nation, typically, but not always, in the context of a monarchic government. Beyond issuing orders-in-council and granting royal charters, it functions as a court of appeal for British courts in present and former overseas territories.

Established in 1967, the Eastern Caribbean Supreme Court (ECSC) is the highest court for its nine independent member states, which include

Grenada, Antigua, Dominica, Nevis, Barbuda, Saint Kitts, Saint Lucia, Saint Vincent, and the Grenadines. The chief justice of the ECSC is the residing head of the judiciary. The reigning monarch of the United Kingdom appoints the chief justice on the recommendations of the member states' prime ministers. The establishment of the Organization of Eastern Caribbean States (OECS) enabled the court to function more smoothly in its administration, composition, financial resources, accountability, and judicial establishment. The ECSC has ensured the rule of law and public respect, both locally and internationally, for its role as the principal arbiter in serious criminal, major civil, and all constitutional disputes, with limited rights of appeal to the Privy Council from decisions of the Court of Appeal. The ECSC replaced the Judicial Committee of the Privy Council as a court of final appeal for most matters.

Since its adoption, the relatively new Caribbean Court of Justice (CCJ) has been designated as a court of last resort for member states of the Caribbean Community. Grenada was among the eight nations that ratified the treaty to establish the CCJ in 2003. It was inaugurated on April 16, 2005, in Port of Spain, Trinidad and Tobago. It had a long gestation period, commencing in 1970 when a Jamaican delegation proposed its establishment in substitution for the Judicial Committee of the Privy Council. The Caribbean Court of Justice is designed to be more than a court of last resort for member states of the Caribbean Community. In addition to replacing the Judicial Committee of the Privy Council, the CCJ is vested with an original jurisdiction with respect to the interpretation and application of the Treaty Establishing the Caribbean Community. In effect, the CCJ was designed to exercise both an appellate and an original jurisdiction.

Policing

The Royal Granada Police Force has a history of personal and political manipulation in Grenada. Under then prime minister Eric Gairy (1974–1979), the establishment of personal paramilitary units undermined the authority and professionalism of the force. After Gairy's ouster in 1979, Maurice Bishop (1979–1983) set about restructuring Grenada's security system along with its governmental, political, and economic systems. Following the assassination of Bishop in 1983, Grenada's leadership changed hands six times before election in 1995 of the Rt. Hon. Dr. Keith Mitchell, who was the state's longest-serving prime minister. In July 2008, attorney Tillman Thomas became the newly elected prime minister and, by default, the minister of national security of Grenada.

In the immediate wake of the action by the U.S. military and the 350-member Caribbean Peace Force (CPF) in 1983, units of these forces handled police and security duties on the island. The last of the U.S. military police personnel departed Grenada in June 1985. The remnants of the CPF pulled out shortly thereafter, leaving the new and inexperienced RGPF to fend for itself. Although the title of the organization is traditional, the force had been reconstituted and its members retrained and reequipped since the U.S.-Caribbean intervention of 1983.

Today the Royal Grenada Police Force (RGPF) is responsible for enforcing criminal, immigration, and maritime laws in Grenada. It is also responsible for seaport security and fire services. As of 2005, the national police force consisted of 830 sworn officers, including 200 rural constables. The force also includes an 80-member paramilitary special services unit (SSU) and a 30-member coast guard. The U.S. Army and the U.S. Coast Guard provide periodic training and material support for the SSU and the coast guard. The force has a hierarchical chain of command that resembles most military organizations.

Despite limited resources, the Royal Grenadian Police Force is generally effective in responding to complaints. Beyond prohibiting arbitrary arrest and detention, the Constitution also prohibits police use of brutal and excessive force. Although individual cases of police corruption and abuse have been reported, these practices are not very common. In the event police are suspected of illegality, an internal investigation follows. If allegations are sustained, the police commissioner can discipline officers up to the rank of sergeant with a wide variety of penalties, including dismissal. Only the Public Service Commission can discipline officers with the rank of inspector or above.

Crime

Classification of Crimes

Crimes are divided into summary offenses and indictable offenses. Serious crimes, also known as indictable-only offenses, such as murder and rape, must be heard in court before a judge and a jury. On the other hand, lesser crimes or summary offenses, which are punishable by no more than six months' imprisonment in the case of an adult, are heard by two or more lay magistrates without a jury.

Crime Statistics

According to the United Nations Office of Drugs and Crime, as of 2007, Grenada's crime rate was 10,177 per 100,000 persons. In comparison to other Windward Islands, this is relatively high. According to statistics provided by the Royal Grenada Police Force, personal crimes are less frequent than property crimes. Between 2001 and 2005, there were 10 homicides reported to the police per year, on average. The use of threatening language and common assault were the most frequent personal crimes, and theft was the most frequent property crime for this period. According to the Royal Grenada Police Force, the following crimes were reported to the police in 2005:

Murder	11
Rape	23
Indecent assault	67
Assault with a deadly instrument	165
Wounding	217
Common assault	908
Stealing	1,352
Stealing from domicile	351
Housebreaking	193
Burglary	58

Tourists have been victims of armed robbery, especially in isolated areas, with thieves frequently stealing credit cards, jewelry, foreign passports, and money. Muggings, purse snatchings, and other robberies generally occur in areas near hotels, beaches, and restaurants, particularly after dark. Among citizen victimizations, however, crimes appear more personally injurious. Chop wounds to the hands that sever the wrist, physical assaults to other parts of the body, and stabbings in general have come to characterize the violent nature of some crimes in Grenada. Many are of the opinion that the recent rise in violent crime is directly related to an increased number of gangs and illegal drug-related activity.

Drug-Related Crimes

Drug trafficking in Grenada is a problem because coastal waters facilitate the transshipment of cocaine and marijuana en route to U.S. and other markets. Marijuana remains the drug of choice among Grenadian users, and it is widely believed that marijuana is smuggled through Grenada from both St. Vincent and Jamaica. According to the Grenada Drug Information Network (GRENDIN) annual report for 2003, local officials estimate about 75 percent of the marijuana remains on the island. The remaining 25 percent is destined for other markets, primarily Barbados and the Republic of Trinidad and Tobago. There is also a small amount of marijuana cultivation in Grenada, primarily for local consumption. The Royal Grenada Police report that possession of marijuana is the most frequent drug offense that comes to their attention. GRENDIN asserts that the drug situation in Grenada is closely linked to the drug trade in the Caribbean and by extension the international drug trade. Consequently, the drug trade is also linked to arms trafficking, money laundering, and other crimes. According to the Royal Grenada Police Force, the following drug-related crimes were reported to the police in 2005:

Possession of marijuana/cannabis	292
Possession with intent to supply	124

Possession of cocaine	59
Trafficking of controlled drug	27
Cultivation of marijuana	25

According to police, there are no drug processing labs in Grenada (i.e., those used to produce methamphetamines, opium, or morphine). However, the increase in violence and gang activity associated with the drug trade, including armed robbery and kidnapping reported earlier, continues to cause concern. Petty crimes, including theft and break-ins for cash to pay for drugs, are equally problematic. In an ongoing effort to stem the flow of illegal narcotics into the country, Grenada is a party to the United Nations Convention on Transnational Organized Crime and its three protocols. An extradition treaty and a Mutual Legal Assistance Treaty are in force between the United States and Grenada.

Because of its collaboration with the U.S. Drug Enforcement Administration, Grenada has achieved reasonable successes in its interdiction efforts. According to the U.S. Department of State, from January through October 15, 2007, the police arrested 382 people on drug-related charges, 356 men and 26 women. Of those arrested, 375 were Grenadian, 2 were from St. Vincent and the Grenadines, 1 was from Trinidad and Tobago, 1 was from St. Kitts and Nevis, one was from Guyana, and 2 were from the United Kingdom.

According to the U.S. Department of State, in 2007, Grenadian authorities seized approximately 935.8 kilograms of cocaine, 9,824 marijuana plants, 260 kilograms of marijuana, and 1,686 marijuana cigarettes. Regular rural patrols contribute significantly to deterring large-scale cultivation of marijuana on the island. Cultivation usually consists of around 50 or fewer plants in any one plot. Approximately seven acres of marijuana were eradicated during the period.

Government Response to Crime

Fear of crime among Grenadians is very real and appears to be a response to an increase in violence among young people. As a result, crime reduction strategies were developed on the theory that the confluence of television, music, and the media's coverage of negative incidents contributes largely to the perception of high crime.

Since 2005, the primary concerns about crime in Grenada have included older and more recent trends in criminal activity. An increase in domestic violence poses a concern for authorities because it appears to coincide with an increase in sex crimes, including incest, rape, and child molestation. Beyond the increase in conventional crimes—such as murder, wounding, kidnapping, and pickpocketing—law enforcement authorities are also confronted with similar increases in organized crime, specifically financial crimes and those that involve money laundering. Added to these concerns are the ongoing threats and devastating effects of terrorist activity, which has created a need for special legislation that would permit wiretapping and other undercover operations. Lastly, though this is in no way an exhaustive list, the increase in trafficking of illegal drugs through Grenada has created a greater need for increased international support and cooperation that would enhance air and maritime patrol capabilities to intercept enterprises that use Grenada as a transshipment point.

According to former prime minister Keith Mitchell, the overall crime situation in Grenada is compounded by the bad influences that deported criminals from first-world countries have on the local criminal element. The confluence of these factors has led to a culture of disrespect for government and law enforcement agencies. Therefore, the government recognizes and appreciates the need to change its response to crime.

To facilitate these changes, the government of Grenada recently embarked on a major recruitment drive to attract 170 new recruits into the police service, bringing it closer to acceptable levels of efficiency and competence. It also increased budgetary allocations for police by EC$5 million (approx. US$1.8 million). Furthermore, the prime minister proposed to increase the salary and fringe benefits for law enforcement and correctional officials. The increase in officer salary represents a raise of 1.9 percent, where monthly salaries will move from EC$21,372 (approx. US$8,000) per month in 2006 to EC$23,556 (approx. US$8,820) per month in 2008.

Finding of Guilt

Rights of the Accused

Under the laws of Grenada, police can detain persons on suspicion without a warrant, but they must bring formal charges within 48 hours. To safeguard and protect the rights of those accused, a judicial determination of the legality of detention must be made within 15 days after arrest on a criminal charge. After such determination, police must either formally arraign or release a detained person within 60 days. In the interim, bail is made available to all persons charged, except those charged with capital offenses. In the very rare instance that someone is charged with treason and/or sedition, bail is accorded only on the recommendation of the governor-general. Furthermore, with the exception of persons charged with a killing and foreign-born drug suspects, the courts usually grant most defendants bail while awaiting trial. In most cases, and consistent with due process, detainees are provided access to a lawyer and family members within 24 hours of apprehension.

The law also provides for the right to a fair and public trial, where there is a presumption of innocence. The law protects persons against self-incrimination and requires the police to explain a person's rights upon arrest. The accused has the right to remain silent and to seek the advice of legal counsel. A defense lawyer has the right to be present during interrogation and may advise the accused how to respond or not to respond to questions. In a trial setting, the accused has the right to confront his accuser. This entire process begins with a first appearance that is held in a magistrates' court.

Public Defense

As of 2001, Grenada was the only Eastern Caribbean country that had an established legal aid system within its judiciary. The legal aid system institutionalized in Grenada provides legal aid not only in criminal cases but also in civil cases and those involving family matters. The Eastern Caribbean system makes provision for legal counsel only in capital cases.

The court requires and appoints attorneys for indigents only in cases of murder or other capital crimes. In other criminal cases that reach the appellate stage, the court appoints a lawyer to represent the accused if the defendant was not represented previously or reappoints earlier counsel if the appellant no longer could afford that lawyer's services. Assizes are held three times a year for a two-month period.

Resolution of Cases

The Judicial Study Centers of America's (JSCA) *Report on Judicial Systems in the Americas (2002–2003)* provides a statistical profile of the 4,159 criminal cases processed in Grenada in 2002. Based on this report, 14 percent of the cases were crimes against property, 17 percent traffic disputes, 9 percent drug offenses, and 7 percent use of firearms against persons. The type of crime was not identified in a small percentage of cases. Sixty-one percent of cases were resolved in pretrial hearings, whereas 26 percent were struck, 10 percent were dismissed for lack of merit, and 3 percent of the charges were withdrawn. Of the 2,566 cases resolved by pretrial hearing, 51 percent of the defendants pleaded guilty, and 34 percent of the defendants were found guilty. Six percent of the hearings were still in progress, and 2.3 percent were remanded to trial. Arrest warrants were issued for defendants in 671 cases, whereby 78 percent of the arrest warrants had been executed, and 22 percent remained pending. Unfortunately, 92 percent of case records did not provide information regarding legal counsel. Of those cases where information was provided, 7 percent of defendants had a defense attorney, and 1.14 percent had no legal counsel. Thirty-three percent of sentences involved both a fine and incarceration. According to the same report, the average fine was EC$430 (approx. US$161), and the average prison sentence was 0.74 months. Of the 10 criminal convictions that were appealed, 9 were filed by defendants and 1 was filed by the prosecutor.

Constitutional Due Process

The Grenada Constitutional Order of 1973 established the Constitution of Grenada, prescribed its form of government, and guaranteed certain fundamental rights and individual freedoms. As expected, the Constitution prohibits discrimination based on race, place of origin, political opinion, color, creed, or sex. These rights were among those protected by the Universal Declaration of Human Rights that was adopted by the United Nations in 1948, of which Grenada is now a part.

Grenada's rules of criminal procedure are remarkably similar to those of the United States and the United Kingdom. Its Constitution provides for the right to a fair trial, and police are required to explain a person's rights upon arrest. The accused also has the right to remain silent and to seek the advice of legal counsel. The law allows for a defense lawyer to be present during interrogation and to advise the accused how to respond or not to respond to questions. The accused has the right to confront his accuser and has the right of appeal.

Punishment

Types of Punishment

Criminal law in the Commonwealth Caribbean territories, including Grenada, is essentially English. Although the laws of Grenada were revised in 1990, the criminal code as reflected in the 1958 revised edition remains in force. Nonetheless, crimes that occur in other Caribbean nations are very similar to crimes that occur within Grenada. Criminal definitions, however, tend to vary, as the following examples illustrate.

In Grenada, rape is defined as "the carnal knowledge of a female of any age without her consent," and carnal knowledge is deemed complete upon proof of the least degree of penetration only. Criminal laws concerning same-sex intimacy in Grenada are noticeably different from other democratic nations. For example, according to the criminal code, same-sex intimacy is regarded as "unnatural." Section 435 of the criminal code notes that the offense of "unnatural crime" is committed by way of sexual intercourse *per anum* (i.e., anal penetration). Moreover, if any two persons are guilty of "unnatural connexion," or if any person is guilty of "unnatural connexion" with any animal, every such person shall be liable to imprisonment for 10 years. These laws are easily engineered to target and prosecute lesbians and gay men and, more generally, all nonreproductive sexual behavior. Within Grenada, the laws governing abortion are equally strict. For instance, those who intentionally and unlawfully cause abortion or miscarriage are liable to imprisonment for 10 years.

Grenada laws concerning organized crime are interesting as well. According to the criminal code, the penalty on a summary conviction of money laundering is a fine up to EC$500,000 (approx. US$187,230) or a prison term not exceeding five years or both. In instances resulting in an indictable conviction, offenders are sentenced to a term of 10 years or an unlimited fine, or both. A person convicted for a predicate offense can also be tried for money laundering, because according to Grenadian law, it is defined as an autonomous crime. Predicate offenses include illicit drug trafficking, trafficking of firearms, kidnapping, extortion, corruption, terrorism and its financing, and fraud. On summary convictions, imprisonment for a maximum of five years or a maximum fine of EC$500,000 (approx. US$187,230) or both may be imposed. On indictable convictions, maximum imprisonment of 10 years or an unlimited fine or both may be imposed.

Prison

According to the U.S. State Department Human Rights Report, as of 2006, Grenada's prison population, including pretrial detainees and remanded prisoners, totaled 334 persons. A small fraction were female prisoners (0.8 percent), who shared space with pretrial detainees (17.3 percent) and foreigners (2.1 percent). Located in St. George's, Richmond Hill Prison is the island's only state prison and was originally designed to hold 98 prisoners. As of this writing, the prison was 258 percent above capacity. Although the relatively smaller number of prisoners appears manageable, one of the consequences of overcrowding is that juveniles are housed with adults in the general population.

According to the Bureau of Democracy, Human Rights, and Labor, torture and other cruel, inhumane, or degrading treatment or punishment is prohibited by the Grenadian Constitution. Flogging, however, is occasionally used as punishment for sex crimes. Otherwise, the law stipulates a sentence of 15 years' imprisonment for a conviction of any nonconsensual form of sex. Sentences for assault against a spouse vary according to the severity of the incident.

In accordance with the Grenadian criminal code, corporal punishment is legal as a disciplinary measure in penal institutions, and some provisions of the criminal code allow for the whipping of male offenders aged 7 to 15 as part of their sentence. In alternative care settings, however, corporal punishment is prohibited in institutions licensed by the Grenada Bureau of Standards by licensing requirements.

Death Penalty

Prior to 2001, a death sentence was mandatory for anyone convicted of murder, and hanging was the traditional method of execution. Actual executions, however, were rare, and none have taken place since 1978, when Charles Ferguson was hanged after he was convicted for murder. Recent challenges to the constitutionality of the death penalty have produced significant rulings. In the case of *Hughes and Spence v. the Queen of England* (2001), the Court of Appeals ruled that the mandatory death penalty was unconstitutional, inhumane, and degrading punishment. Furthermore, convicted persons must be afforded an opportunity to address the court after conviction, to argue that they should be given a lesser sentence than death (i.e., life imprisonment or a fixed term). This ruling applies to all the Organization of East Caribbean States (OECS) jurisdictions because they all have similar constitutions.

Eight years prior to this ruling, the Privy Council ruled that prisoners convicted of capital crimes and not executed within five years suffered "inhuman or degrading punishment" and should have their death sentences commuted. According to the *New York Times,* some countries and local governments, in response to public pressure, began speeding up appeals procedures to beat the five-year deadline. In response, defense lawyers began using all of their skills to drag out the appeal process to gain eligibility for commutation for their clients, a strategy that has annoyed a vast majority of Caribbean residents.

Lee E. Ross

Further Reading

Caribbean Net News: http://www.caribbeannet news.com.

Embassy of the United States. (n.d.). *Barbados and the Caribbean:* http://barbados.usembassy.gov/

Government of Grenada: http://www.gov.gd/a_z_gov.html.

Grenada Constitution. (1973). http://pdba.georgetown.edu/Constitutions/Grenada/gren73eng.html.

Judicial Study Centers of the Americas: http://www.cejamericas.org.

Steele, Beverley. (2003). *Grenada: A History of Its People*. Oxford, UK: McMillan Publishing.

Thorndike, T. (1985). *Grenada: Politics, Economics and Society*. Boulder, CO: Lynne Rienner Publishers.

United Nations Office of Drugs and Crime: http://www.unodc.org/pdf/barbados/caribbean_report_crime-trends.pdf.

La Guadeloupe

Legal System: Civil
Prison: Medium
Death Penalty: No
Corporal Punishment: No

Background

History of the Legal System

The history of the legal system of this French department is primarily linked to its colonial status since its discovery. La Guadeloupe became known to Europeans via Christopher Columbus in 1493. This nation was ruled by Spanish authorities until 1635, when it became a French colony. Slavery trade began immediately, and the island was owned from 1643 to 1664 by a governor, Charles Houel, who was named "Marquis de Guadeloupe" by Louis XIV and was in charge of the application of the law. Details about the criminal justice system during this period are scarce. The law was mostly used to police the slave trade, highlighted by the enactment of the "Code Noir" in 1685. The laws grouped under this code were used to legitimize a widespread practice. This code forbade Protestants or Jews to own slaves. Corporal punishments as well as the use of the death penalty against slaves were also regulated; the criminal justice system was therefore used to guarantee the status quo on slavery. Multiple military tensions appeared in the 18th century, and Guadeloupe only obtained its full independence as a colony in 1775. The French Revolution of 1789 led to the instability of the department and then to the abolition of slavery in 1794. Reforms of penal procedures and the creation of the penal code began in 1791. The laws of the Guadeloupe were extremely similar to those of metropolitan France; slavery was, however, briefly reestablished in 1802. Documents dated from 1828 reveal that the criminal justice system of Guadeloupe was regulated by the French civil code, the civil procedural code, and the French penal code. The judicial police force was administered by the *gardes champetres, gardes forrestiers,* and police guards; prisons were administered locally, and one prison was located in the Guadeloupe. The analysis of additional documents revealed the existence of the gendarmerie in Guadeloupe as early as 1823. A law passed December 30, 1823, led to the creation of specialized units of the gendarmerie. In 1830, the gendarmerie was composed of 1 captain, 2 lieutenants, 5 "marechaux du logis," 70 gendarmes, 88 civilians, and 10 "brigadiers." These individuals were in charge of law enforcement in the colony. As of January 24, 1857, the gendarmerie at Guadeloupe was composed of 166 men; there were 179 men and 1 lieutenant in the territory as of 1861. Slavery was finally abolished by law on April 27, 1848. Guadeloupe has been represented in the French Parliament since 1871 and its criminal justice system has been shadowing the French metropolitan criminal justice system. The judicial system has been undergoing modernization since 2007; the French *carte judiciaire* was redrawn, and legal jurisdictions were modified. This modernization is now complete and consists of a centralization of all courts on the territory.

The legal system in Guadeloupe is inquisitorial and is similar to the French legal system. It was introduced by the Ordonnance of Colbert in 1791 and was based on the code of penal procedures written under Napoleon. This justice apparatus was officially implemented in Guadeloupe after its departmentalization in 1946.

Social and Political Context

The French National Police and the Gendarmerie Nationale as well as other agencies composing the French criminal justice system are currently facing important social challenges. Economic and social circumstances have been deteriorating in the first decade of the 21st century. A general strike erupted in January 2009. Most of the law enforcement officers were mobilized to control riots and prevent vandalism and other property damages. Unfortunately, the death of a union member, who had been mistaken for a police officer, in February 2009, caused a rise in social tensions. Four groups of the Mobile Gendarmerie, 280 gendarmes, were therefore sent from metropolitan France to secure the territory. Such eruption of violence led French president Nicolas Sarkozy to visit Guadeloupe on June 26–27, 2009, where he met with the elected officials of all French overseas departments. He highlighted the need for a profound analysis of the reasons for social unrest and for the development of solution to inherent societal problems. Eight themes were identified, including the need for an evolution of local agencies such as law enforcement agencies. The president asserted that he would "keep the promise of equality" to all French citizens living in Guadeloupe. Laws related to the changes in Guadeloupe are currently being drafted, and major changes in institutions located in Guadeloupe are expected; such modifications may have an impact on the criminal justice system.

Police and Gendarmerie

As in other French departments, Guadeloupe is policed by two separate agencies: the national police and the gendarmerie. The national police are mainly responsible for law enforcement in urban areas. The police mission statement is based on two articles of the French Constitution. The 1st article indicates that personal safety is an inherent right of humankind; the 12th article highlights the need for a public force to be created for the good of all. The national police are therefore responsible for the safety of all citizens, public peace, and justice. The national police are also accountable for information gathering, the reduction of illegal immigration, maintenance of public order, the fight against drug trafficking and organized crime, and finally the prevention of terrorism. There are currently more than 900 police officers in Guadeloupe; these officers are mainly located at Pointe-a-Pitre, Basse-Terre, les Abymes, and the Gossier. The national police force is undergoing constant modernization; the use of scientific and technical progress is now inherent to policing. The national police have been undergoing structural changes since 2003, and manpower is currently being geographically redistributed to answer to the needs of the community. Finally, as indicated by the Ministry of Interior, the national police are a "symbole de la reconnaissance de la nation," a symbol of national recognizance.

The gendarmerie is the other agency responsible for the maintenance of public order as well as public safety. There are more than 600 gendarmes located in Guadeloupe. These individuals are part of the 161 groups named "brigades de gendarmerie territoriales." There are 3,503 members of the Gendarmerie Nationale in nonmetropolitan areas of France. Six hundred and eighty-six individuals are located in Guadeloupe; there are 30 operational officers, 2 technical and administrative officers, 531 officers, 18 civilians, and 105 volunteers. These individuals belong to multiple units that have specific roles in the territory. Certain officers are in charge of surveillance; others are responsible for airport safety. It is important to note that the Gendarmerie Nationale is a military group attached to the French military; civilians, officers, gendarmes, and volunteer compose this law enforcement agency. One commander is in charge of all the territory, and members are divided into mostly rural areas; the current bases are located in Saint-Claude, Petit-Bourg, Saint-Barthelemy, Saint-Francois (nautical branch), and les Abymes. Finally, the Gendarmerie Nationale is in charge of the safety of all diplomatic visitors and ambassadors who reside or visit this French department.

Crime

Classification of Crime

Crimes are classified into five types of infractions of the law: against individuals, against material goods, against the state, organized crime, and victimless crime. Crimes against persons include homicide, rape, and torture. Infractions against goods include robbery and theft. Finally, terrorism and treason are considered as crimes against the state.

All infractions are divided into three levels based on its characteristics, circumstances, and seriousness. Crimes are the most serious infractions and include murder, rape, armed robbery, and drug trafficking. Under article 131-1 of the French penal code, these crimes incur a minimum of 10 years of incarceration.

Delits, the second type of serious infractions, incur imprisonment of less than 10 years, fines, and community service; they include theft and drug dealing. *Delits* are the equivalent of misdemeanors. Finally, petty infractions include traffic violations. According to article 131-13 of the penal code, fines will be determined according to the seriousness of the offense.

The age of responsibility is 18 years old. Individuals under 13 years old are deemed irresponsible, and juveniles between the ages of 13 and 16 are processed by the juvenile justice system. However, juveniles who commit serious crimes can be handled by the adult criminal justice system. Most convicted juvenile delinquents are sentenced to education and vocation programs. Incarceration is used only for juveniles who present a threat to public safety and whose rehabilitation is deemed improbable.

Challenges

Guadeloupe is geographically located between marijuana-producing countries and consumption markets located in Europe and North America. Indeed, this department is considered a *plaque tournante* of drug trafficking in the Caribbean; 55 percent of the cocaine produced in South America travels via the Caribbean, including Guadeloupe. Customs data indicate that there was a 22 percent increase in drug-related arrests in the French Caribbean departments (Guadeloupe, Martinique, Guyane) from 2001 to 2002; a 34 percent increase was noted from 2002 to 2003. Drugs, especially marijuana and cocaine, are transported via postal, naval, and aerial services from the Guadeloupe to European countries. Cocaine, for example, is liquefied and transported in rum bottles; a man recently died on October 5, 2009, from accidentally consuming liquefied cocaine from a friend's alcohol bottle. Drug trafficking has, as expected, a high number of negative consequences on Guadeloupe. Drug-related arrests saturate law enforcement agencies and sociomedical structures; indeed, drug dealers often pay smugglers with drugs and therefore supply addiction.

Drug trafficking is now presenting a risk to national security. The national police and the gendarmerie are now cooperating with INTERPOL and other agencies so as to control and decrease the amount of drugs imported from South America to Europe through Guadeloupe. The present increase in drug-related arrests in Caribbean countries such as Guadeloupe and Martinique is therefore illustrating the increased local efforts to deter and reduce drug trafficking and drug use in Caribbean territories.

Drug Offenses

As illustrated in the preceding section, drug use and trafficking have been problematic issues for the last decades. There was a 22 percent increase of drug offenses in Guadeloupe from 2007 to 2008. There were 1,778 arrests for drug-related offenses in 2008. One thousand and seventy-nine individuals were arrested for drug use, and 85 offenders were arrested for drug sale and trafficking. One hundred and twenty-four individuals were arrested for various offenses of drug laws. In Guadeloupe, as in metropolitan France, drugs are classified into four categories: stupefying substances, psychotropic substances, medications, and dangerous substances. Stupefying drugs are heroin, cocaine, Ecstasy, and cannabis. The production and distribution of these substances are prohibited by article 3421-1 of the French Code of Public Health. Penal measures may be avoided by arrestees if they obtain psychological and medical help. Provocation to drug trafficking can lead to five years of imprisonment and fines up to 75,000 euros (article L3421-4 of the Code of Public Health). Drug use can lead to up to 1 year of imprisonment, and possession of stupefying substances with intent to sell will incur a maximum sentence of 10 years of imprisonment. Drug dealing may be punished by a maximum of 5 years of imprisonment (article 222-38 of the penal code). Finally, the organization of drug trafficking can result in prison sentences up to 30 years and fines up to 7,500,000 euros under article 222-34 of the penal code. The lengths of imprisonment listed here can be doubled if these substances are sold to minors or in educational areas.

Crime Statistics

As indicated by the French minister of the interior, crime rates in Guadeloupe are slightly higher than in metropolitan areas; the rate of violent crime is increasing and is among the highest of the French departments. There were 63 homicides in 2008; Guadeloupe has the second-highest homicide rate of all French departments. There were 116 rapes, including 71 rapes on minors; sexual assaults have been fortunately decreasing, and the 2008 rape rate represents a 15 percent decrease from 2007. Guadeloupe also has the third national rank regarding robberies; there were indeed 235 robberies in 2008, a 33 percent increase from 2007. Burglaries, however, decreased by 3 percent, with 2,610 incidents in 2008. Finally, drug offenses are widespread in Guadeloupe; indeed there were 1,778 arrests for drug-related offenses.

Finding of Guilt

Rights of the Accused

The code of criminal procedures states that the accused individual must be immediately informed of the crimes or infractions for which an investigation is necessary. If the accused is unable to read or understand the charges pending, an interpreter or any other methods will be used to facilitate communication with this individual.

This individual is also allowed to contact family members, roommates, and employers by phone during the first three hours of detention (article 63-2 of the code of criminal procedure). The accused also has the right to be examined by a physician and can be granted another visit if the detention lasts longer than 24 hours. A prosecutor or judicial agent can also contact medical serves if deemed necessary. Article 63-5 of the code of criminal procedure also assures that physicians are the only individuals allowed to conduct body searches.

Once detained, the accused have the right to have a self-obtained lawyer or a state-appointed lawyer called *avocat commis d'office* (article 63-4 of the code of criminal procedure). The meetings between lawyers and accused are confidential but cannot last longer than 30 minutes. If the detention lasts more than 36 hours, the accused has the right to another meeting with a lawyer.

Assistance Provided to the Accused

L'aide juridique, or legal aid, is available through the French public defender services. This aid is available only to individuals who cannot afford a private defender (article 63-4 of the code of criminal procedure). The accused must prove a lack of financial means. The Bureau d' Aide Jurisdictionelle, a group composed of magistrates and counselors, decides whether this legal aid will cover the amount of legal representation partially or entirely. However, this aid does not cover additional expenses related to the trial or fines imposed to the convicted individual.

Alternatives to Trial

Individuals who are deemed mentally incapable during the completion of their crimes may be referred to psychiatric services instead of incarceration. Article 122-1 of the criminal code declares the accused free from criminal liability if a court-appointed psychiatric expert deems that the accused was mentally incompetent during his or her criminal activity. There are alternatives to trial for drug offenders and juveniles as well. However, the majority of offenses are resolved by trial. Plea bargaining, dispute resolution, and guilty pleas are not allowed under French law.

Pretrial Incarceration

The accused may be incarcerated if accused of an offense for up to three years pretrial. The average length of preventive detention is four months. These individuals are not incarcerated with convicted offenders; they are housed in separate correctional facilities.

Investigation

The beginning of an investigation is led by law enforcement officers. However, prosecutors or *juges d' instruction* (in the most serious cases) seek to establish whether prosecution of an individual is justifiable. All investigations are supervised by the judiciary.

Judges are also required to investigate and obtain evidence incriminating an accused individual. Those judges are *a charge et a decharge,* meaning that they are responsible for finding evidence linking a suspect to a particular crime. These judges can also seek evidence proving the innocence of the accused. Indeed, defendants are not allowed to conduct their own investigation. Also, the judges can transfer their judiciary powers to police officials using a *commission rogatoire.* Finally, judges have the right to emit search, seizure, and arrest warrants. They can also meet with suspects at any time and can order preventive detention.

The Courts

There are multiple courts in Guadeloupe. Following the reorganization of the criminal justice system in the three years prior to 2009, courts are now mainly located in two geographical poles: Basse-Terre and Pointe-a-Pitre. Civil matters are handled by the *tribunal d'instance* and the *tribunal de grande instance.* There are currently two of these types of courts, respectively located in Basse-Terre and Pointe-a-Pitre. The instance court handles civil matters (under 10,000 euros). This court is headed by one judge assisted by a clerk. This professional magistrate is in charge of all aspects of civil justice during proceedings; this magistrate is also in charge of handling citizenship requests and civil matters involving minors. The court of *grande instance* handles cases (over 10,000 euros) such as divorces and matters of real estate law. This court is headed by three magistrates who are professional judges; they handle procedural law and sentencing.

A commercial court and the Conseil des Prud'Hommes, in charge of litigation regarding work contracts, are located at Basse-Terre and Pointe-a-Pitre; an administrative court handling cases involving the department or the state is located at Basse-Terre. Traffic violations and infractions are handled by police courts located at Marie-Galante, Saint-Martin, Pointe-a-Pitre, and Basse-Terre. The *tribunal correctionnel* or correctional courts processes the *delits.* Finally, the criminal court, or Cour d'Assises, processes criminal cases. This court is composed of a judge-president and two assessors. These magistrates passed a specific national exam and attended law school to belong to this court. There is one assize court in each French department including Guadeloupe. This court is located at Basse-Terre and is held once every 3 months for a maximum of 15 days. The judges generally travel from metropolitan France to hear these criminal cases. Finally, two appellate courts are available in Guadeloupe. The Cour d'Assises d'Appel handles appellate cases and is located in Basse-Terre; it meets on a case-by-case basis. A civil appellate court is also located at Basse-Terre and processes civil and correctional cases. As illustrated here, Basse-Terre has become the most important judicial pole in Guadeloupe; restructuring, however, may change the geographical repartition of the different courts.

Juveniles

The French juvenile criminal system was created in February 1945. Its primary goals are the reinsertion and rehabilitation of offenders between the ages of 13 and 18 years. Juveniles are handled by a separate system including specialized judges and magistrates. Also, specific facilities were created, preventing juvenile offenders from having contact with the general inmate population. Juveniles judged as adults, however, can be housed in the general inmate population. Finally, each department is responsible for its juvenile system. The family court of Guadeloupe therefore handles all cases involving juvenile offenders.

Punishment

Types of Punishment

There are numerous types of punishment in the French criminal justice system. These include fines, electronic monitoring, suspended sentences, probation, community service, reparations, postponement of sentence, incarceration, and half-imprisonment (day in the community, night in a correctional facility). Illegal immigrants can also be expulsed from the French territory if they are convicted of any type of infraction.

Homicide

The typical punishment for murder is up to 30 years of imprisonment. If the murder is connected to other crimes, facilitates another crime, or targets witnesses, the sentence can be increased to life in prison without possibility of parole. Premeditated murder is punishable by life imprisonment. If a murder is committed against an individual under

15 years old or is accompanied by a sexual assault or torture, the defendant will have to serve a minimum of 30 years in prison. Also, the murder of disabled individuals and pregnant women will result in life in prison. Finally, the murder of a public official or witness in a criminal case will also be punished by up to life in prison.

Rape

Rape is punishable by up to 15 years in prison. If this offense causes mutilation or permanent disability, the sentence will be increased to up to 20 years in prison. Also, the rape of a minor or a natural ascendant or a rape involving the use of a weapon will be punishable by 20 years of imprisonment. Finally, the death of a rape victim or the torture of a rape victim will lead to life imprisonment.

Theft

Larcenies are punishable by up to 3 years of imprisonment as well as a fine of 46,000 euros (article 311-3 of the penal code). Violence against the victim will increase a potential sentence to up to 5 years of prison and/or 100,000 euros in fines. Theft can also be punished by up to 7 years in prison if two aggravating circumstances such as violence against the victim and degradation of private property occur during the commission of the crime. The presence of three aggravating circumstances could lead to up to 10 years of imprisonment. Finally, the use of weapons during theft or larcenies committed by groups can lead to imprisonment of up to 30 years for all offenders involved.

Drug Offenses

The most serious drug offense consists of the management and organization of a drug trade: production, fabrication, export, transportation, offer, and sale of narcotics. This offense is punishable by life imprisonment and up to 8,000,000 euros according to article 222-34 of the penal code. Articles 222-35 and 222-36 also state that the production and fabrication of drugs can lead to 20 years of imprisonment if committed alone. The fabrication and production of controlled substances by an organized group can lead to incarceration terms up to 20 years.

The Death Penalty

The death penalty was abolished in all French territories on October 9, 1981. Corporal punishment is also illegal.

Prisons

There are two correctional facilities in Guadeloupe: the center of La Baie-Mahault and the facility of Basse-Terre. The largest penitentiary center of Guadeloupe is located at la Baie-Mahault. This facility was opened in 1996 and is located near swamps, 10 minutes from the international airport of the Pole-Caraibes. This facility has the only psychomedical center located in Guadeloupe; it can house 504 inmates divided into different sections. There are 27 cells for women, 188 cells for adult men, 17 cells for minors, 232 cells for pretrial detention, and finally, 8 cells for semi-liberty inmates. Eight individuals can also be detained in the "service medico-psychologique regional" (SMPR).

The penitentiary of Basse-Terre, located in the city of Basse-Terre, can hold up to 130 offenders. This facility works in coordination with the center of la Baie-Mahault and houses only individuals on pretrial detention or offenders whose incarceration does not exceed one year.

Certain imprisonment guidelines are applied to all French correctional facilities, including the prisons located in Guadeloupe. Individuals placed on preventive detention are allowed a minimum of three visitations per week. Other inmates are allowed a minimum of one visit per week. Visitors of inmates must bring identification documents.

French inmates have numerous privileges, which include receiving mail, keeping certain personal items, watching television, and having access to sport facilities. Inmates are also allowed to work, but work is not mandatory. They can be paid up to 2.26 euros/day. Inmates also receive social security benefits while incarcerated (up to four years).

Finally, French inmates can vote during their imprisonment.

As in metropolitan France, inmates are not required to work or attend classes. However, multiple educational programs are offered to all inmates in the facility of la Baie-Mahault. Inmates can participate in sawing, construction, agriculture, and sport classes. Offenders are also offered programs such as electronic maintenance and business creation. Finally, inmates have access to rehabilitation and reading classes. The length of these classes ranges from 3 to 24 months; these classes welcome up to 20 inmates per session.

Extradition

A law passed on March 10, 1927, asserts that only non-French citizens can be extradited from any French territory, including Guadeloupe. According to article 2 of the law, the extradition is permitted only if the individual is charged with or convicted of a crime. The accused individual must have been sentenced to two months or more of imprisonment or must be facing up to two years of imprisonment if extradited. As indicated in article 5 of the law, the individual will not be extradited if he or she is French or is being extradited for political reasons. Finally, the individual cannot be extradited but then punished for a crime other than the one for which he or she has been extradited.

Anne-Laure Del Cerro

Further Reading

Bell, John, Sophie Boyron, Simon Whittaker, Andrew Bell, Mark Freedland, and Sylvia Hargreaves. (1998). *Principles of French Law.* New York: Oxford University Press.

Bellenus, Rene. (1998). *L'Esclavage en Guadeloupe et en Martinique du XVIIème au XIXème siècle.* Pointe-a-Pitre: Editions Jasor.

Institut National de la Statistique et des Etudes Économiques, France. *Justice:* http://www.insee.fr/fr/themes/tableau.asp?reg_id=0&ref_id=NATTEF05305.

Kock, Gerald, and Richard S. Frase. (1988). *The French Code of Criminal Procedure.* American Series of Foreign Penal Codes 29. Littleton, CO: Fred B. Rothman.

Ministère de l'Intérieur, de l'Outre-mer et des Collectives Territoriales, France. *La Guadeloupe:* http://www.outre-mer.gouv.fr/.

Site de l'Etat en Guadeloupe, France. *Securite Publique:* http://www.guadeloupe.pref.gouv.fr/sections/les_actions_de_l_eta/securite_publique.

Guatemala

Legal System: Common/Civil
Murder: High
Corruption: Medium
Human Trafficking: Medium
Prison Rate: Low
Death Penalty: Yes
Corporal Punishment: Yes

Background

The Republic of Guatemala is located in Central America and shares borders with Mexico in the north, Honduras and El Salvador in the south, and Belize in the northeast. It is also bordered on the west by the Pacific Ocean and on the southeast by the Caribbean Sea. There are 22 departments, or states, in Guatemala, which are further subdivided into more than 300 municipalities.

Although profoundly impacted by the Guatemalan Civil War, which was fought between the years 1960 and 1966, making it the longest civil war to occur in Latin America, the country has emerged relatively stable over the decade prior to 2009. Recent immigration trends and continued sophistication of global technologies have all affected the cultural trajectory of Guatemala. The projected population estimate for Guatemala for mid-2008 was just over 13 million persons. Current estimates show that 1.2 million Guatemalans, approximately 10 percent of the global Guatemalan population, reside in the United States. About 60 percent of these are undocumented, although figures from the U.S. Census do not necessarily reflect this estimate.

The Guatemalan justice system, like much of Latin America, was historically based on a codified civil law or inquisitorial model of criminal justice. Often contrasted with the common law system prevalent in the United States, the civil law model of justice has its roots in both French and Italian legal systems. In 1992, Guatemala became the first country in Central America to completely reform its criminal procedural code, which became effective in 1994. In the 15 subsequent years, the Guatemalan legal system experienced a number of reforms that have dramatically transformed the former inquisitorial model to an accusatory model. There are major differences between the two, and there is some evidence to suggest that attorneys and other legal actors in Guatemala have experienced some difficulties in adjusting to the new system. Perhaps the most significant area of change has been in the role of the judges, who are now less active, and the prosecutors, who have much greater responsibility in investigating and providing evidentiary arguments. Indeed, the shift toward oral trials has been an adjustment for all participants.

Crime

Classification of Crimes

There are two basic categories of crimes in Guatemala: *faltas* and *delitos. Faltas* are the less serious type and include crimes such as public drunkenness, minor assaults, petty thefts, animal cruelty, and so on. Serious crimes in Guatemala are referred to as *delitos. Delitos* include such charges as homicide, serious assaults, rape, robbery, and thefts of larger amounts. Prison terms for *delitos* range from 1 month to 50 years. *Delitos* can also include fines as small as 10 but not exceeding 200,000 *quetzales* (10 *quetzales* are approximately equivalent to US$1). Normal confinement periods for *faltas,* referred to as the penalty of arrest, are from 5 days to 60 days. Under no circumstances can a perpetrator charged with a *falta* be held in confinement for more than 1 year according to the Guatemalan penal code, article 480.

Fines that a judge may impose depend on which type of crime the offender is convicted. According to the penal codes, fines should be reasonable considering the economic capacity of the offender, including considerations of their income, housing expenses, employability, and familial responsibilities. Normally, fines must be paid within three days of the judgment, but payment plans may be approved in certain situations. Failure to pay fines may lead to incarceration.

Although not considered to be a fine per se, individuals who do not pose great threat to society and who are sentenced to less than five years in prison, not including habitual offenders and those convicted of robbery or serious larceny, can have their prison term commuted by paying an amount as ordered by a judge. This adjustment in the confinement sentence is regulated to cost between a minimum of 5 *quetzales* (approx. US$0.62) and a maximum of 100 *quetzales* per day of sentenced incarceration.

Several different classification levels are possible for inmates sentenced to confinement in Guatemala. Besides traditional prisons, sentenced persons may be required to serve time in inpatient psychiatric facilities, agricultural or industrial work camps, vocational or educational work centers, or other specialized treatment facilities. Certain types of restraining and limited freedom orders that prohibit offenders from visiting or making contact with certain areas or individuals can also be imposed. House arrest is also a sanction option.

The Guatemala penal code clearly defines *delitos* and their corresponding penalties. A charge of simple homicide carries a penalty of 15 to 40 years in prison. Other types of crimes that result in the death of another person carry a range of penalties. For example, a homicide committed during an act of emotional rage carries a sentence of 2 to 8 years. Assisting a suicide has a penalty of 5 to 15 years. A woman convicted of infanticide, defined as the killing of a child between birth and 3 years old by a mother with intimate motives affected by indubitable psychiatric strain, has a possible prison sentence of 2 to 8 years. A person found guilty of assassination will be subject to the death penalty.

Guatemalan antidrug police prepare over 7,000 pounds of cocaine for incineration in Guatemala City, October 8, 2003. (AP Photo/Rodrigo Abd)

Injurious crimes, violent acts harming another person but not intended to cause death, may carry a charge of 3 to 10 years. Certain specific violent acts, such as castration or other sexual mutilation, have penalties of 5 to 12 years. A variety of other injury crimes are specified in great detail in articles 146 and 147 of the Guatemalan penal code. Kidnapping offenders will serve between 1 and 3 years in prison.

Rape is defined as forcing a woman either physically or through some other manner to have sex against her will. Incidents of sex with females under age 12 are also considered rape. Incidents of rape involving multiple attackers; situations where the perpetrator is a parent, teacher, or other appointed guardian; and circumstances where the victim suffers great bodily harm are considered aggravated, and offenders are subject to penalties of incarceration between 8 and 20 years.

Larceny and theft charges carry penalties of 1 to 6 years depending on the circumstances and amount of the theft. Aggravated thefts, which include looting during times of public crisis, conspiracies, crimes against travelers, and thefts of firearms, include penalties ranging from 2 to 10 years in prison. Aggravated robbery, defined as any intended theft involving a weapon or threat of physical violence, carries a penalty of 6 to 15 years. Other types of crimes that are considered aggravated robberies include attempted robberies using a disguise or mask; train, boat, airplane, or automobile robberies; and attacks involving banks or industrial, commercial, or other businesses.

Faltas are less serious crimes that have corresponding less punitive consequences. Persons charged with *faltas* may be held in a local confinement facility or more commonly in a prison. The confinement period for a *falta* charge, known as the *pena de arresto,* normally does not exceed 60 days. For example, if an individual were to cause an injury to a person, causing the injured person to be unable to work for up to 10 days, that individual would face between 20 and 60 days in confinement. This same charge would be placed against any person convicted of finding an abandoned or unattended child under the age of 12 and failing to deliver him or her to safety. Similarly, failing to help an injured person in need of assistance would be considered a *falta* punishable by 20 to 60 days in prison. A person who mistreats his or her domestic partner could face 15 to 40 days of incarceration. If, however, this mistreatment results in more serious injuries, the perpetrator may receive a more punitive charge.

Damage to property such as vandalism is also considered a *falta.* Damage to a victim's property with a value less than 100 *quetzales* (approximately US$10) carries a charge of 20 to 60 days. Less serious types of fraud including interpreting dreams, divination, and fortune telling can also be subject to criminal penalties under the penal code. A person who accidentally kills or wounds another person's animal is normally required to recompense the injured party at the common value of the animal. Other lesser charges such as public drunkenness have possible penalties ranging between 10 and 50 days.

Crime Statistics

Between 2004 and 2006, the number of arrests for criminal offenses made by the Guatemalan National Civilian Police decreased by 26 percent, from 50,259 to 37,340. Violent crimes continued to be the most serious threat to public safety.

Violent Crime

Guatemala is struggling with an increasing violent crime rate. In 2006, the Inter-American Commission on Human Rights reported that the murder rate in Guatemala, 70 homicides per 100,000 people, was the highest in Latin America. This report is supported by official police figures for violent deaths: approximately 5,885 Guatemalans suffered violent deaths in 2006. Five hundred more persons died violently in 2006 than in 2005. The violent death rate had increased by 60 percent since 2003. In a recent span of five years, special attention underscored the rise in female murder victims between 2001, when 303 women were murdered, and 2006, when the total climbed to 603. The situation in Guatemala is often cited as an example of femicide. More than 2,500 unsolved murders of girls and women have occurred in Guatemala since 2001. Guatemala's murder conviction rate is in the single digits, with some reports claiming that the clearance rate for murder is less than 2 percent. As a result of this lawlessness and the resulting allegations of corruption and incompetence, in early 2007, the International Commission against Impunity in Guatemala (CICIG) was established in an effort to improve the situation.

In 2007, the United Nations Development Programme (UNDP) produced a statistical report on violent crimes in Guatemala. Composed of six victimization surveys, the report helped to explain local perceptions and attitudes toward issues of violent crime. Interviews were conducted in 639 households in Guatemala City; 2,725 people above the age of 18 were included in the sample. In 37.3 percent of the homes, at least one member of the family reported being affected by crime in the preceding six months. Eighty percent of these cases were muggings, robberies, or theft. A considerable majority of these crimes (74.9 percent) were not reported to the police. There were several reasons for this failure to report crimes to the police. The majority of the respondents (59%) said it was useless to report crimes; 13.1 percent did not feel that the crimes were serious enough to report; and 9.7 percent said they did not report crimes committed against them because they were afraid of reprisals.

The lowest violent crime rates in the country are found in rural areas inhabited by indigenous people; these areas are also the poorest parts of Guatemala. Violence generally occurs in municipalities that are less poor and have lower indigenous populations. The high prevalence of violence is in part exacerbated by several cultural traits. Guatemala is one of fewer than a dozen countries in the world that continue to have "honor defense" statutes according to the United Nations. In the case of rape, for example, the honor defense presumes that a woman's honor is restored when she marries the man who raped her. Marriage is also considered reparation for the victim.

The results of the UNDP study show that men in Guatemala City are more affected by crime than women are; however, men feel safer than women. Furthermore, the study shows that a considerable majority of both victims and perpetrators are between the ages of 18 and 35. There is a general uneasiness among the people in Guatemala as a result of unchecked violent crime. According to one of the surveys, 61.5 percent of the respondents mentioned that they worried about crime more than anything else; the second most common answer was unemployment, which was mentioned by 14.7 percent of the respondents. As the report suggests, quality of life is decreased if a person must constantly worry about safety. In the poorest neighborhoods of the capital, extortion is common; people often have no choice but to leave their homes, jobs, and old lives to avoid being murdered.

Drugs, Gangs, and Crime

Guatemala is a major stop on air, road, and maritime routes by which illegal narcotics, especially cocaine, travel from South America through Mexico to the United States. Approximately 150 tons of cocaine are transported through Guatemala annually; it is estimated that 10 percent of that stays in Guatemala to be consumed locally. Guatemala was a source of opium poppies in the late 1980s and early 1990s, but the majority of the poppy crop has been eliminated by manual and aerial eradication operations that were conducted between 1990 and 1996. In 2004, Guatemala eradicated over 5.4 million poppy plants, or 181 hectares, yet poppy cultivation is once again a problem. The United States National Drug Threat Assessment maintains that in 2004 Guatemala could potentially produce 1.4 metric tons of heroin, whereas Colombia had the potential to produce 3.8 tons. The U.S. and Guatemalan governments are continuing to focus on narcotics-related threats in Guatemala. These threats include cocaine transshipment, government corruption, diversion of precursor chemicals, money laundering, increase in domestic drug abuse, and controlling cultivation of opium poppy and marijuana crops.

Drug-related convictions are common in Guatemala, although a relatively low percentage (1.2 percent) of Guatemalans aged 15–64 had used cocaine during the past 12 months in 2006, according to a UNODC report. Drug trafficking is a problem that continues to garner a serious portion of Guatemala's criminal justice resources. Recently, Guatemala has become a more important transit point in cocaine trafficking, giving criminals in Guatemala a greater amount of economic clout. Trafficking of pharmacological drugs, "stupefying" drugs, and all other types of illegal drugs or material used to make illegal drugs may be sanctioned with penalties ranging from 3 to 5 years in prison plus fines from 500 to 5,000 *quetzales.* Trafficking charges are considered aggravated if the activity occurs nears a school, involves minors, occurs across international boundaries, or involves professionals in positions of influence (i.e., medical doctors, chemists, pharmacists, dentists, teachers, ministers, midwives, nurses, etc.).

Another factor important to the overall crime situation in Guatemala is the increase in members of youth gangs, or "*maras.*" Some sources estimate that these gangs have more members than the 19,000-strong police force; more conservative estimates approximate somewhere in the neighborhood of 14,000 youth gang members in Guatemala. Government officials estimated that there were approximately 111 gang members per 100,000 people in the population in 2005. There were a total of 434 gangs identified in the same year, with memberships totaling 14,000 and a mean gang member size of 32 individuals. In Central American countries, only Honduras has more gang members. However, the true effect of these *maras* may not be as great as some authorities fear. In several perception and attitude surveys conducted by the United Nations, interviewees said that they believe that common thieves, not members of *maras,* are responsible for most of the crimes in their neighborhoods. Another UN study appears to similarly question the overall impact of gangs in Guatemala. An analysis of 427 intentional homicides that occurred in January 2006 found that only 58 incidents, or 14 percent, had an apparent connection to gang activity. Others argue that criminal gang activity is bolstered by the influx of criminal deportees from the United States who have few social ties. A total of 8,722 individuals have been deported from the United States to Guatemala since 2000.

Finding of Guilt

Because of the recent criminal justice initiatives launched by the USAID, the World Bank, the Inter-American Development Bank (IDB), the United Nations Development Program (UNDP), and others, the Guatemalan criminal justice system's police, courts, and corrections department have been in constant flux over the past decade.

Police

The Guatemalan National Civil Police (PNC) has about 19,000 officers nationwide, a rate of 119 per 100,000 in the population, the second-lowest rate in Central America behind Honduras. Compare this to the rate of 326 per 100,000 in the United States. Many families choose to hire private security guards for their homes because of the sense of vulnerability resulting from surging violent crime rates. It is estimated that there are about three times more private security guards in Guatemala than there are police officers. Private security guards are employed by 10.9 percent of households in Guatemala City. The especially high number of private security guards may also provide evidence of a widespread lack of trust in the justice system, which many feel has been infiltrated by organized crime. Efforts to improve law enforcement in Guatemala have also been seriously undermined by discontinuity of leadership. According to a 2007 UN report, between the years 2000 and 2002, there were four ministers of government, seven national police directors, and nine directors of the antinarcotics police in Guatemala. This turnover was partly due to corruption, which is a major obstacle. In fact, in 2004 and 2005, 4,000 Guatemalan national police officers were dismissed under allegations of corruption—20 percent of the overall police force. Transparency International's Global Corruption Barometer annual reports completed in 2005, 2006, and 2007 show that the public believes that the police are the most corrupt sector of Guatemalan society.

The national police often suffer from shortages in logistical supplies such as vehicles and fuel. There have been some improvements in this regard in recent years. Also, police officers are not trained sufficiently in many areas. The government is currently pursuing officers who are involved in illegal activities; the number of administrative or legal actions taken against officers is increasing. There are problems with crime scene control; common problems are destruction of evidence and contamination of crime scenes. Most crime scene investigations are conducted by court prosecutors because of a lack of trained investigators. Even so, these investigators often must use public transportation to conduct interviews.

Arrest

A person who is legally accused of a crime in Guatemala may be arrested or detained by the police. The Guatemalan Constitution requires that a person who is arrested be notified immediately, orally and in writing, as to the cause of his or her arrest. Every detainee must be explained his or her rights in an understandable way promptly following arrest. Detainees' specific right to have an attorney present at all police and/or judicial proceedings is guaranteed by the Constitution. Any interrogation of suspects by police must be conducted by a judicial authority, normally within the first 24 hours of arrest, and only judicial authorities have the right to order imprisonment.

Persons arrested in Guatemala may be detained only at legally designated public locations. Similarly, trials or other legal proceedings are not allowed to take place at secret or otherwise nonpublic locations.

Probable cause is required in Guatemala before a legal arrest can occur, and there is a presumption of innocence for all arrested persons. All parties involved, the prosecutor, the detainee, the victim, and defense attorneys, have the right to obtain and have access to all evidence and procedural documents. Finally, the Guatemala Constitution provides that defendants cannot be forced to incriminate themselves in any testimony. Spouses and legal relatives are also excused from being forced to testify against a defendant. Guatemalan citizens have the right to privacy, and search warrants must be obtained in writing before police can search a property. Similarly, a warrant must be obtained before any communication can be recorded or seized, including all written materials, telephone, cable, radio, and other correspondences available through various technologies. After a warrant is obtained, the citizen, or the citizen's appointed representative, has the right to be present during the search. No searches are allowed before six in the morning and after six in the afternoon. Finally, all Guatemalan citizens have the right to file a petition in court, individually or collectively, should they feel that their rights have been violated.

Courts

The Republic of Guatemala has three main branches of government: the executive, the legislative, and the judicial. The judicial branch of government enforces the laws and procedures according to the Guatemalan Constitution, the laws of judicial organization, civil codes and civil trial rules, and the corrections system. The Guatemalan court system has four levels. The highest court is known as the Supreme Court. Lower courts include the Second Instance Court, the First Instance Court, and the local justices of the peace. The Supreme Court is the highest court and is responsible for the national administration of justice, including developing budgeting priorities and assigning human resources. The Supreme Court makes decisions on constitutional matters. The Guatemalan attorney general represents the country and defends state interests in legal matters. The state attorney for human rights serves as a delegate to the National Congress and is assigned to investigate and prosecute reported human rights abuses. The Ministry of Government is responsible for civil security, including the administration of the national penal system and the National Civil Police. Finally, the Institute for Public Penal Defense is available to provide legal aid to citizens seeking public defense.

Prosecution

Criminal prosecution proceeds through three stages: a probable cause hearing, an oral trial, and an appeals procedure. The process sometimes takes over a year to complete. According to the Guatemalan Constitution, the defendant is presumed innocent; the prosecutor must prove that the defendant is guilty beyond a reasonable doubt. No person can be detained unless an official charge has been levied against him or her. An arrest warrant must be issued by a court to arrest a suspect, unless the individual is caught while committing a crime. Once an individual is arrested, the Guatemalan Constitution requires that the court review the case within six hours and that the defendant appear before a judge or justice of the peace within 24 hours.

All persons in Guatemala have the right to have a defense attorney, and one will accompany them to the pretrial detention hearing. At this first appearance hearing, the judge decides whether the individual must remain in custody to await trial. Many charges, including all drug-related offenses, require pretrial detention, but there are some alternatives to incarceration, including bond and house arrest, although, according to the Guatemalan Institute of Comparative Studies in Penal Science, these alternatives are used in less than 5 percent of all cases filed. A person accused of a crime in Guatemala can be charged with either a *falta* or a *delito* offense. According to the Guatemalan criminal code, pretrial detention should not exceed one year if the charge is a *delito,* or the amount of time under one year that the defendant would be sentenced to if convicted.

Following this initial pretrial hearing, the prosecutor will conduct a preliminary investigation that must be completed within three months. During this three-month period, the prosecutor attempts to gather sufficient evidence to determine whether the defendant is responsible for the alleged crime. Any time extension beyond the initial three months requires court approval for individuals in state custody, and the prosecutor must provide sufficient cause to continue the investigation. For situations where the defendant is out on bond or under house arrest, the court automatically allows for a time extension while the prosecutor conducts the preliminary investigation. All Guatemalan citizens have the right to file a petition of habeas corpus on behalf of individuals who are missing or have been illegally detained. Such petitions do not have to be filed by a Guatemalan attorney, as is required for many other types of petitions.

Bureaucratic processes significantly affect how long it takes for an individual to go to trial. In some cases, a trial date may not be set until over a year after the crime was committed. The system is largely paper-driven, and there is evidence that reliance on written documents, especially handwritten ones, may substantially affect how quickly cases are heard. According to the Institute of Comparative Studies in Penal Science, it can take several weeks before a suspect can be moved from a detention facility to the courthouse. Another concern is the difficulty that arises as a result of many witnesses not showing up for court, and an improved witness notification system is sorely needed. This failure of witnesses to appear causes almost half of all trials to be postponed.

The prosecutor has an incredibly important role in the Guatemalan justice system. The prosecutor plays an integral part in the process of the investigation as well as in evidence gathering. Prosecutors are also responsible for conducting interviews and working closely with law enforcement officials, especially local police who do not have the capacity or training to conduct more extensive investigations. Whereas judges may have a far more active role in a purely civil law system, the court's involvement in Guatemala is largely supervisory and limited to authorizing searches, seizures, and arrest warrants.

Plea Bargaining

Individuals are eligible to have their case handled by plea bargain if the offense that they are charged with carries a penalty of five years in prison or less. The accused and their lawyer must agree to the plea bargain, and it must be approved by the court. The Guatemalan "abbreviated procedure" was originally applicable to crimes punishable by a maximum of two years but has now been extended to those punishable by no more than five years (§ 464 CCP-Guatemala, as amended in 1997). Similarly, the "abbreviated procedure" in Guatemala also allows for suspension of imposition of prison sentences up to three years and commutation of sentences up to five years. In Guatemala, around 25 percent of all convictions were achieved via "abbreviated procedure" from 1996 to 1998.

After the preliminary investigation is completed, the intermediate phase begins. At this stage, the prosecutor must establish probable cause before the court to continue the case. The judge will determine whether the evidence is sufficient to continue to oral trial. This intermediate phase hearing is the first time that the defense attorney is allowed to contest and exclude any evidence obtained illegally or any witness statements collected under conditions of duress. Once the prosecutor has presented the initial evidence, and the defense attorney has had an opportunity to challenge it, the judge issues a written opinion either allowing the case to proceed to oral trial or ordering the case to be provisionally closed. The judge may also stay the case pending additional evidence.

If the case goes to trial, both the defense and the prosecutor will produce witness and evidence lists. The court will then issue subpoenas as necessary to compile all of the necessary evidentiary requirements of both sides. Also, either party can at this point file any petitions for recusals or other objections to any evidence or setting venue. The oral trial is held before a three-judge panel, and all evidence is presented. At this time, all witness statements are reviewed, and opportunities to cross-examine are allowed. Once all the evidence is presented, the three-judge panel will issue a written finding of guilt or innocence, which provides justification for their decision based on specific evidence presented. If there is a finding of guilt, the panel of judges also determines the sentence for the convicted individual. The Guatemalan Constitution does allow for an appellate process, but normally, appeals consider only issues of procedural law and do not review details of the case.

Court System Reforms

There have been two main periods of judicial reform in Guatemala. The first period, largely sponsored by the U.S. Agency for International Development (USAID), occurred in the mid- to late 1980s. This program, which was divided into two projects, one handled by Harvard and one by USAID, was financed from 1987 through 1991, during the continuing civil war. Although there were changes in the legal system as a result of these reforms, they did not meet their established goals, and when the project ended, there was little or no follow-up by the Guatemalan counterparts. The second period of foreign aid for legal development was sponsored by USAID, the World Bank, the Inter-American Development Bank (IDB), the United Nations Development Program (UNDP), and others. Starting in the mid-1990s, there have been real improvements in the Guatemalan judicial system as a result of this initiative. The criminal code has been reformed to include due process protections and the right to a public defender. Investigations and prosecutions have been assigned to the Public Ministry (judges formerly handled much of this); trials have been made more open and public. There have been some changes in the appointment and training of new judges; there is improved access to the justice system, especially for the indigenous.

The main objective of this second project was to create an effective, accessible, and credible justice system that would apply laws consistently and fairly and inspire public confidence. According to the 2004 Global Corruption Barometer Report, a study done by Transparency International, 37 percent of respondents felt that judges are susceptible to bribery. Before the USAID project, less than 30 percent of the country had any judicial coverage; as a result of the project, there were approximately 500 judges in the Guatemalan court system (one per 22,000 inhabitants) in 2006. Nearly one-fifth of the judgeships statewide are held by females. Every municipality in the country now has at least one justice of the peace, half of whom are women. Another important reform has been the method by which judges are selected. All judges are hired solely on the basis of competitive examinations, and the Code of Ethics established in 2001 strictly establishes expected conduct.

This judicial reform project, which is also being expanded to El Salvador, Honduras, and Mexico, has made a number of significant improvements in the Guatemalan judiciary system. Two regional-level justice centers and one departmental-level justice center have been opened, and nearly 200 new justice of the peace courts have been implemented under the project. These improvements have increased the ratio of judges to approximately 6 judges per 100,000 people in the population. In 2003, two mobile courtrooms, located inside buses, traveled around the country to provide free mediation, dispute resolution, and information services to people in remote areas. In the first year of its operation, the service benefited more than 6,000 people; 63 percent of those were women. Additionally, 25 mediation centers have opened and are providing mediation services in indigenous languages, which is consistent with the targeted emphasis on cultural sensitivity training throughout the justice system. Since 2001, more than 22,000 disputants have sought mediation, of which almost half have reached agreement. Finally, this project has underscored the need for improved use of technology. Two dozen criminal records offices are now networked across the country, and the General Archive of Protocols Office has been automated and decentralized. These innovations have allowed unprecedented transparency, speed, and access to information.

Judicial Qualifications

In Guatemala, the requirements for becoming a judge or magistrate are set forth in the Constitution. Judgeship appointments are issued by the Supreme Court. To be eligible for an appointment, a person must be a native Guatemalan citizen in good standing and also be a registered attorney. A normal appointment lasts five years, although judges can be reappointed for a second term. During an active appointment, a judge may not be removed from office unless appropriate legal steps have been followed. There are 13 Supreme Court justices in Guatemala. Supreme Court justices must be at least 40 years old and are elected by the Congress of the republic for five-year terms. The representative committee in charge of nominations is made up of university rectors and deans of recognized law schools throughout the country and equal numbers of representatives from the General Assembly of the Association of Lawyers and Notaries and judges from the Court of Appeals. This committee nominates 26 candidates. The election of candidates requires a two-thirds vote of the members of the nominating commission. Finally, appeals court judges must meet all the requirements of lower-court judges but must be at least 35 years of age. They also must have served five years as a judge in the First Instance Court. They are elected in a process similar to that for Supreme Court justices, requiring a nomination process by a similar judicial commission of twice as many people as there are judgeships. Election to the Court of Appeals requires a two-thirds vote by the members of the commission.

Punishment

Guatemala's incarceration rate is 68 prisoners per 100,000 adults in the general population. It is possible that this low incarceration rate is due to failure to obtain convictions rather than policies designed to decrease prison numbers. Article 19 of the Guatemalan Constitution defines the laws of confinement and the rights of prisoners held in the prison system. The stated purpose of the Guatemalan prison system according to the Constitution is the social rehabilitation of offenders. The Constitution provides clear language disallowing any type of coercion, abuse, extortion, torture, or other cruel treatment to detainees. In April 2003, there were a total of 8,307 individuals in state custody, for a total incarceration rate of 71 prisoners for every 100,000 people in the population. Approximately 90 percent of all incarcerated individuals are males ages 18 to 35 who have not yet completed their primary education. Based on national statistics, 39 percent of inmates are already sentenced, and the remaining detainees are awaiting trial or otherwise being processed. The percent of individuals convicted, compared to the overall number of individuals incarcerated, has varied considerably over the years. In 1996, 74 percent of those incarcerated were not sentenced. In 1999, this figure had dropped to 64 percent, and by 2002, the rate was at 47 percent, but it increased one year later to 61 percent.

There are 17 prisons located throughout the country, including 3 federal facilities. The Guatemalan prison system is crowded. Designed to accommodate 6,824 persons, the prison system currently houses 8,307 and is thus 22 percent above recommended capacity.

The Guatemalan prison system employs around 1,650 employees, of which 917 are prison guards. The remaining employees are administrative and professional staff. Additionally, there are 22 medical doctors, 27 nurses, and 2 dentists who each work four hours a week to meet the needs of the prison population. In 2005, the national penal system had an operating budget of 141,626,033 *quetzales* (equivalent to just over US$18 million).

At the end of 2006, the Guatemalan prison system had a total of 8,359 persons incarcerated, of which 3,952 (47 percent) were already sentenced, and the remaining 4,307 (52 percent) were presentence detainees being held on *delito* charges. One hundred arrestees were being held on *falta* charges only.

According to the administrative offices of the national penitentiary system (Dirección General del Sistema Penitenciario), the number of prison beds as of the end of 2005 totaled 7,044 spaces distributed throughout 18 different facilities. Six of these facilities are dedicated as facilities for sentenced inmates, and the other 12 are mostly dedicated to unsentenced individuals. The National Civil Police operate an additional 27 smaller detention centers with approximately 450 beds. There has been a concerted effort since the mid-1990s to combine and regionalize the various prison facilities in the country. Historically, there were as many as 45 different prison facilities.

Prisoners are eligible for a reduction in their overall sentence for "good time." Article 44 of the penal code allows prisoners who have served three-fourths of their sentence to be released on a type of parole. If any new offenses are committed prior to the offender completing his or her original term of sentence, the offender is required to complete the remaining sentence in prison while awaiting the additional potential penalties of the new offense.

Prisoners are required to work while incarcerated according to the penal code. This work, however, is paid labor, although remuneration can occur in several different ways. The types of jobs assigned to inmates take factors such as age, gender, training, and physical condition into account to ensure appropriate assignments. Inmates over 60 years of age and those with physical impairments or illnesses are not required to do mandatory labor. Wages for prison work may be applied to retribution fees resulting from any damages caused by the inmate. Funds may also be applied to any account charges that the inmate may have occurred during his or her incarceration for food and other personal items. Earnings may also be invested to help the inmate improve his or her productivity. Some inmates also choose to conserve their pay in a type of savings fund for use upon their release. Many inmates remit a portion of their earnings to their families.

The Guatemalan prison system faces a number of structural challenges. First, the available programming and efforts toward rehabilitation are sorely lacking. There is little consistency between the stated goals of the penitentiary system and what steps are being taken to achieve them. In short, programming infrastructure is inadequate. Second, overcrowding is a perpetual problem that exposes other aspects of an inadequate infrastructure. Much of this crowding is driven by drug possession charges and lesser misdemeanor charges. Third, some observers have noted the precarious lack of basic services in some facilities, including lack of consistent access to potable water (93 percent of facilities report water shortages), lack of showers (1 for every 57.4 inmates), lack of commodes (1 for every 32.2 inmates), food shortages and poor-quality food, and lack of telephone communications. Furthermore, medical services to inmates are limited, with many facilities offering four hours of medical appointments each week.

Additional sources of concern for Guatemalan prison authorities are how to effectively manage vulnerable populations including those with mental illness, women, and indigenous populations and high-risk populations including gang members. According to the Guatemalan Institute for Comparative Studies in Penal Science, in 2006, there were 49 cases of torture reported in five different prison facilities. These same five facilities also had at least 42 reported cases of less serious mistreatment. Experiences of female inmates, especially in detention centers operated by the National Civil Police, are also precarious; there are numerous reports of sexual abuses.

Nearly one-fourth of all Guatemalan inmates are indigenous, and most of them are not primary Spanish speakers. There is some evidence to suggest that these indigenous inmates are often required to accept menial work assignments to survive while in prison. Mentally ill inmates are offered little in the way of treatment while incarcerated. The prisons in Cantel, Pavón, and El Boquerón have no services at all for inmates suffering from mental illness.

Gang members are held under some of the most restrictive and tortuous conditions. They experience food restrictions and are not allowed to receive books or other reading materials. Some are forced to sleep on the floor in tightly restricted spaces. Medical attention is inadequate, and most suffer from a variety of skin diseases. Finally, gang members and other special populations have inconsistent and arbitrary access to make official complaints about their situations. Corruption in regard to access to privileges within the facilities is common, especially preferential treatment and placement for inmates able to afford bribes. Corrupt prison employees also allow for contraband and other controlled substances to be introduced into the facility.

Death Penalty

Although the Guatemalan Constitution does not allow the death penalty for female defendants, those over age 60, political prisoners, or those facing extradition, the law does allow state executions for kidnapping, rape of children younger than 10 years old, and some drug trafficking-related offenses. However there has been a de facto moratorium on the death penalty for several years, with the last execution occurring in 2000. The de facto moratorium began during the presidency of Alfonso Portillo (2000–2004), after the Guatemalan Congress overturned an 1892 law allowing presidential pardons. Because of the repeal of this law, the government was left with no options to allow death sentences to be commuted or otherwise pardoned. In December 2007, Guatemala voted in favor of a global moratorium on the death penalty before the United Nations General Assembly; however, in early 2008, the Guatemalan Congress voted to approve Decree 06-2008, which would allow presidential pardons to resume. In March 2008, President Álvaro Colom Caballeros vetoed the bill.

Acceptable forms of execution in Guatemala include firing squads and lethal injection. In 1996, the execution of two men by firing squad was televised. Another execution was carried out in 1998, also televised, and two were carried out in 2000 by lethal injection. In 2007, nine people had their death sentence commuted to 50-year prison terms after the Inter-American Court of Human Rights (IACRH) ruled that the conviction charges did not meet the definition for crimes eligible for the death penalty. There are currently 21 people on death row in Guatemala.

Juvenile System

According to article 8 of the Guatemalan Civil Code, the age of criminal responsibility is 14, although the legal age of adulthood is 18. According to Guatemalan law, when someone under 14 is accused of a crime, he or she must be referred by police to the Guatemalan equivalent of the Attorney General's Office (Fiscalia de Menores). The Attorney General's Office decides whether to press charges and prosecute the child or to send the child to some rehabilitation or other diversionary program. If the decision is made to prosecute, the case is forwarded to the Court of Children and Youth (Juzgado de Niñez y Juventud), which will send the child to a pretrial detention facility or prison; there the child will await trial and sentencing. Upon sentencing, children may be placed in a facility for youthful offenders because juveniles are not allowed to be housed with adult detainees. Children under 12 years old cannot be prosecuted for crimes, and thus, younger and younger children are targeted for youth gang membership.

Wayne J. Pitts

Further Reading

Fuentes, J. (2005). "Violent Conflict and Human Development in Latin America: The Cases of Colombia, El Salvador, and Guatemala." Human Development Report Occasional Paper No. 10 of 2005. New York: United Nations Development Programme.

Guatemalan Institute for Comparative Studies in Penal Science (El Instituto de Estudios Comparados en Ciencias Penales de Guatemala—ICCPG). Source of information on criminal justice in Guatemala: http://www.iccpg.org.gt/.

Sieder, Rachel, Megan Thomas, George Vickers, and Jack Spence. (2002, January). *Who Governs? Guatemala Five Years after the Peace Accords.* Cambridge, MA: Hemisphere Initiatives.

United Nations Office on Drugs and Crime. (2007, May). *Crime and Development in Central America: Caught in the Crossfire.*

Guyana

Legal System: Common/Civil
Murder: High
Corruption: Medium
Human Trafficking: Medium
Prison Rate: High
Death Penalty: Yes
Corporal Punishment: Yes

Background

Guyana, the land of many waters, is a member of the British Commonwealth located on the northern coast of South America. The Guyanese territory has been disputed over the years by the English, Dutch, French, and Spanish, all of which exerted their own influences over the nation and its legal system. The British Empire eventually retained control of Guyana, and to this day, Guyana is the only country in South America that uses English as its official language. Guyana's population, which stands at 772,298 as of 2008, is composed of a variety of ethnic groups. Although a large part of the population (43%) is of East Indian origin, and 30 percent is of African origin, Guyana is also home to a mixed population (17%), an Amerindian population (9%) and a minority population of Chinese and Portuguese (1%).

Guyana's government is divided into three separate branches that function under a system of checks and balances. Guyana's National Assembly, a unicameral entity, serves as the legislative branch of government. The assembly was formed after Guyana's independence in 1966 and is responsible for promulgating the laws of the country. The executive branch is headed by the president of the republic, who appoints a prime minister and other ministers as part of his cabinet. The judicial branch is responsible for interpreting the law and administering justice. The highest court of Guyana is the Court of Appeal.

Guyana was first chartered by the Spanish Crown as early as 1499, but it was the Dutch who first settled the territory, establishing the colony of Essequibo in 1616. In 1627, the Dutch settled their second colony, Berbice, in the Guyanese territory, and in 1741, Demerara, the third major colony in Guyana, was settled. Under Dutch colonial rule and the administration of the Dutch West India Company, these colonies became producers of vast amounts of tobacco and sugar. Amerindians were used as laborers on these plantations. One of the unintended consequences suffered by the natives of Guyana was their decimation as a result of diseases brought over by Europeans. To maintain their sugar and tobacco production, the Dutch began to import African slaves, who lived under the cruelest conditions. After the complete abolition of slavery in 1838, Guyana began to import indentured servants who mostly came from India. In the 20th-century racial tensions between the Afro-Guyanese and the Indo-Guyanese, populations broke into violence as a result of political uproar.

Under the rule of the Dutch, Guyana had followed the Roman-Dutch code system. This system forged together Roman law, also known as civil law, and Dutch law, which followed Germanic legal traditions. In 1814, the colonies of Guyana were ceded back to Britain, but the Roman-Dutch system remained the dominant legal system in Guyana until 1916. During the early 20th century, the British began to expand their influence on Guyana. The common law system of Britain provided better flexibility and protection during a time when British judges were imported into the Guyanese legal system.

The common law adversarial system in which the defense contests charges made by the prosecutor, who represents the state, was officially adopted in 1917. Roman-Dutch law, however, continued to be applied on legal matters such as land law. Guyana achieved independence in 1966 and drafted a constitution pronouncing the democratic status of the country. In 1964, Forbes Burnham became the prime minister of Guyana. During the 1970s, Burnham began rallying for changes to the Constitution. In 1980, a new constitution was drafted and enacted, replacing the Constitution of 1966.

The 1980 Constitution strengthened the power of the executive branch and that of the president, an office to which Burnham was elected that same year. The role of the prime minister was significantly diminished. The Constitution of 1980 secured Guyana's status as a republic of the British Commonwealth and restructured the country's economic philosophy from capitalism to socialism. Burnham's government was suspected of several acts of violence against the opposition, including the People's Progressive Party, led by Cheddi Jagan, and the Working People's Alliance.

Burnham died in 1985 and was succeeded by Desmond Hoyt. In 1992, free elections resumed in Guyana, and Cheddi Jagan was elected to the office of president. Jagan died in 1997 and was succeeded by his wife, Janet Jagan, who was elected president in December of that year. Janet Jagan stepped down in 1999, and since then, Guyana's president has been Bharat Jagdeo. As of 1995, 12 amendments have been added as part of the Constitution. Although the Constitution provides for a fair trial, due process is not always a guarantee because of inadequate resources, a backlog of cases, and the executive branch's significant influence on criminal sentences.

Crime

Classification of Crimes

Like most common law countries, Guyana separates crimes into felonies and misdemeanors. Felony crimes are the most serious of crimes and include murder, assault, robbery, and rape; they are also referred to as indictable offenses. These crimes are punishable by lengthy prison sentences. Misdemeanors are punished less severely than felonies because they are considered less grave. The lesser crimes are also known as summary offenses.

Crimes in Guyana fall under the following categories: crimes against person and reputation, offenses against right of property and rights arising out of contracts, forgery and similar offenses, crimes against public order and the administration of justice, and crimes against religion, morality, and public convenience.

Crimes against Person and Reputation

This category of crimes includes defamation, assault, causing bodily injury, rape, incest, bigamy, abduction, and homicide. These offenses are divided into subsections specifying the types of crimes that fall under each category. For example, under the incest and rape category, crimes are charged differently when incest is committed by a male as opposed to a female or when a victim is under 12 years old or mentally handicapped. Under the homicide subcategory, the law differentiates between manslaughter, infanticide, and murder.

Crimes against Right of Property and Rights Arising Out of Contracts

Crimes under this category include malicious injury to property, larceny, fraud, robbery and extortion, housebreaking, and burglary. Under the category of malicious injury to property, the law differentiates between injury to growing things such as trees or vegetation; injury to animals such as cattle; injury to machinery, specifically agricultural machinery; injury to the public or private work area; injury to naval property such as ships, vessels, or beacons; injury to buildings such as private dwellings, public buildings, or places of worship with the use of fire or explosion; and injuries to other things including works of art. Larceny is divided into several subsections including simple larceny, larceny of vegetation and animals, larceny of written instruments, and miscellaneous larcenies, which include larcenies committed by a public officer.

Forgery and Similar Offenses

These crimes include forgery of official seals and public and judicial documents, forgery of deeds and private documents, forgery of debt and stock documents, and forgery of government bonds, bank notes, and miscellaneous documents, including employment documents. Falsification of coins and the possession of false money are punishable crimes under this category.

Crimes against Public Order and the Administration of Justice

Rioting, treason, perjury, bribery and corruption, and escape from prison are all subject to prosecution under this section of the criminal laws of Guyana.

Crimes against Religion, Morality, and Public Convenience

This category of punishable crimes includes blasphemous slander, disturbing a congregation, preventing a religious leader from performing service, and a series of vague offenses such as publishing obscene documents, committing indecent acts, gross acts of indecency with a male person, attempts to commit unnatural offenses, and keeping a disorderly house.

Drug Crimes

Penalties for drug crimes vary depending on the severity of the crime. Possession and use of marijuana, opium, heroin, or cocaine is subject to a fine and a prison sentence that can range from a year to 10 years. Penalties for drug trafficking can range from 3 to 5 years, and in severe cases, persons found guilty of trafficking can be sentenced to life imprisonment. Bail is usually denied in drug trafficking cases, and those charged with this crime are usually subject to pretrial detention. To be prosecuted for drug trafficking, Guyana law states that a person must be in possession of at least 2 grams of heroin, 1 gram of cocaine, 55 grams of opium, 3 grams of morphine, or 15 grams of cannabis. The cultivation of illegal crops carries a prison sentence of 3 to 5 years, and the government may seize any land or equipment used in cultivation.

Drug Abuse and Traffic

Guyana's proximity to some of the world's largest cocaine producers has made this country a gateway to the North American and European drug trades. However, drugs trafficked through Guyana enter the United States at very low rates, and impact on the American illegal drug market is minimal. Progress in efforts to combat the drug trade and traffic in Guyana has been slow because of inadequate and underfunded law enforcement initiatives. Cocaine and marijuana are the main drugs trafficked through Guyana. Marijuana is trafficked to a lesser extent and tends to be sold within Guyanese borders more than it is trafficked abroad. Seizures of cocaine dropped from 167 kilograms in 2007 to 40 kilograms in 2008. Although cocaine seizures have decreased, eradication of marijuana crops doubled from 15,280 kilograms destroyed in 2007 to 34,000 kilograms destroyed in 2008.

The United Nations World Drug Report estimated that about 2.6 percent of the population, between ages 15 and 64, used cannabis in 2006. Cannabis was the most prevalent drug in Guyana as of 2009, and its use among the population has increased in recent years. About 2.5 percent of the population uses opiates, and some increase in use has been reported. It is estimated that 0.1 percent of the population, between ages 15 and 64, are consumers of Ecstasy. Amphetamines are not as prevalent as cannabis, and consumption has remained stable over the past few years.

Human Trafficking

Men, women, and children have been trafficked for sexual exploitation outside of Guyana to neighboring countries including Brazil and Suriname and the Caribbean islands of Barbados and Trinidad and Tobago. Still, the majority of human trafficking victims are traded within Guyana's borders. Victims tend to be poor, uneducated teens enticed with promises of employment. Although the country has not fully complied with the Trafficking Victims Protection Act of 2000, progress in observing international guidelines has been made, ranking Guyana as a Tier 2 country. Under the Trafficking of Persons Act of 2005, all forms of human trafficking can be punished with a prison sentence ranging from three years to life imprisonment.

Age of Criminal Responsibility

The age of criminal responsibility in Guyana is 17; offenders under the age of 17 are defined and treated as juveniles. Guyana law defines a child as any person under the age of 14. By law, no child under the age of 10 can be charged or found guilty of a criminal offense. Juveniles charged with crimes must be processed through a separate juvenile court system.

Crime Statistics

Official crime statistics are lacking for Guyana, and the Guyanese police force has been criticized for failure to keep arrest records and records of crimes reported. The Guyana Bureau of Statistics provided some data for major causes of death by gender. The most recent statistics showed that 83 men and 22 women died as a result of homicide in 2007, and

27 men and 13 women died as a result of other types of violence. Rape and attempted rape continue to be underreported, but it is estimated that the majority of rapes are non-stranger rapes; that is, they are perpetrated by someone known to the victim.

Rights of the Accused

Warrants

The Constitution provides citizens with protection against unreasonable searches. Legal searches are conducted by police officers after a warrant is secured from a magistrate who reviews evidence and decides whether a search is justified. Nevertheless, international human rights organizations have investigated claims of unlawful search and seizures by police officers that have resulted in disciplinary action. Arrests can be carried out without a warrant by a law enforcement officer if that officer witnesses a crime or has reasonable suspicion that a crime has been committed or will be committed.

The Right against Arbitrary Arrest or Detention

The Constitution provides the right to liberty and protection against arbitrary detention. However, 29 complaints were filed in 2008 against police officers for improper conduct including unlawful arrests and unnecessary use of violence. Disciplinary action was taken against several officers.

The Right to Be Informed of Criminal Charges and the Right to an Attorney

All persons arrested and detained by law enforcement must be informed of the reasons for their arrest and detainment within a reasonable time. Although Guyana guarantees the right to an attorney to represent defendants during legal proceedings, the attorney must be paid for by the accused person. Unlike other common law nations, the government of Guyana does not guarantee the right to have an attorney provided when the accused cannot afford one, unless the case in question is a capital case. Georgetown is the only city that operates a legal aid clinic, which usually deals with cases of domestic violence and women's rights.

The Right to a Fair and Public Trial and Trial by Jury

Misdemeanors and other minor crimes are heard in the magistrates' courts, which are presided over by a judge. There are no juries in these courts. Felonies or indictable crimes are heard by the high courts, where the accused is provided with the right to a trial by jury. To qualify as jurors, persons must be Guyanese citizens with no criminal convictions and must be between the ages of 18 and 60. Potential jurors must be able to speak, read, and write English.

Torture and Inhumane Treatment

Both the Constitution and the criminal procedure laws provide the accused the right against cruel and inhumane treatment prior to and upon arrest. Guyanese officials, especially law enforcement officers, have often come under scrutiny for violation of legal and human rights. In November 2008, it came to light that the Guyana Police Force tortured a 14-year-old detainee, burning parts of his body and denying him access to an attorney for four days. Two police officers were arrested and investigated for these allegations. In October 2008, a detainee under police custody was killed after suffering blunt force trauma to the head. In February 2007, a man was allegedly killed by a member of the Guyana Police Force. Criminal charges against the officer were recommended after an inquest into the matter.

Bail and Pretrial Detention

Persons accused of a misdemeanor that warrants a penalty of less than two years' imprisonment or a fine are entitled to bail. They can be released on their own recognizance or can be mandated to provide collateral to secure their return to court. Failure to appear at any scheduled court hearing will result in bail revocation, and an arrest warrant will be issued. Persons charged with felonies that warrant more than two years' imprisonment can be detained throughout the course of criminal proceedings at the discretion of a judge.

Finding of Guilt

Prosecution

Criminal prosecutions are the responsibility of the director of public prosecutions. Prosecutors working under the director have the discretion to choose which cases to prosecute and which cases to dismiss. The director is also responsible for ensuring the rights of the accused, investigating criminal charges, and representing the state in criminal cases.

Plea Bargaining

Plea bargaining is a fairly new practice in Guyana. It was introduced as a way to combat backlogged court dockets and as a tool for prosecutors to utilize against drug traffickers. No data is available on the percentage of cases that are resolved through plea bargaining.

Court System

Guyana's court system includes magistrates' courts (the lower courts), high courts, and the Court of Appeal, which is the court of last resort. The magistrates' courts have jurisdiction over criminal and civil cases and are responsible for supervising criminal cases involving minor offenses and criminal cases that involve a penalty of up to five years' imprisonment. Trials that take place in magistrates' courts are heard by a judge. There are a total of 23 magistrates' courts, which are located in all 10 regions of Guyana.

The high courts serve as courts of first instance and hear civil cases and the most serious criminal cases, which are those that carry a penalty of more than five years in prison or capital cases. Unlike in the magistrates' courts, defendants tried in the high courts have the right to a trial by jury. The high courts also serve as appeals courts and hear cases decided in the magistrates' courts. The high courts are presided over by a chief justice and 11 other judges. There are 13 high courts in Guyana.

The Court of Appeal is the highest court of Guyana. The chancellor of the judiciary and three other judges preside over this court. The Court of Appeal functions like the Supreme Court in the United States, deciding on cases heard in the lower courts and setting precedents to guide future decisions.

According to the Report on Judicial Systems in the Americas, there are currently 3.5 judges per 100,000 inhabitants. The chancellor of the judiciary, the chief justice of the high courts, and the chief magistrates are selected by a committee appointed by the president. To qualify as a judge, a law degree is necessary as well as five years of experience as a barrister. With five years of experience, a barrister can be appointed as a magistrate by the president.

Juvenile Justice

Juveniles are afforded special protections to which adults are not entitled. To protect the juvenile's identity, only parties to the case at hand are allowed in juvenile courts. The names, address, school, and photos of juveniles processed through the courts are strictly prohibited from being leaked by the media or any other person. Any person who releases the identity of a juvenile offender is subject to a fine. Juveniles may be released on their own recognizance to await legal proceedings. Judges have the discretion to deny bail if the juvenile is accused of homicide, if the court deems that detaining the juvenile is in his or her best interest, or if there is reason to believe the juvenile will evade justice if released. If a juvenile is detained prior to being convicted, the juvenile must be kept in a holding facility separate from adults.

All juvenile cases are remanded to juvenile courts, save juveniles charged in homicide cases. Parental permission is unnecessary to hear a case in juvenile court. Juveniles have the right to be informed of the charges against them and can decide with the help of parents whether they want their case heard by a judge or a jury. Juveniles have the right to make statements to the court and to provide evidence in their defense. If a juvenile admits guilt, he or she may provide the court with a statement of mitigating circumstances. Juveniles can be sentenced to detention in a facility specified by the court if they are found guilty of homicide, manslaughter, or intent to cause serious injury. Less severe crimes can be punished by detention in a reform school or institution.

Punishment

The most typical forms of punishment in Guyana are fines, compensation for injury caused, and imprisonment. Other types of sanctions, including whipping and flogging, are also allowed by law but are not as commonly applied.

Assault

A crime of assault that results in little harm can be punished with one year of imprisonment. Conspiracy and assault against an employer with the intent to raise wages is punishable with two years' imprisonment. Assault with the intent to commit a felony can be punished with a two-year prison sentence. Indecent assault on a female and assault with the intent to cause harm merit a prison sentence of five years. The intent to cause bodily harm with a firearm can be punished with life imprisonment.

Incest, Carnal Knowledge, and Rape

Incest that occurs when the female victim is the granddaughter, daughter, sister, or mother of the perpetrator is punishable by 7 years' imprisonment. If consent is given by the female to engage in an incestuous relationship, she can also be punished with a 7-year prison sentence. Attempted incest is punished with 2 years of prison. The act of "carnally knowing" a girl between ages 12 and 13 warrants a penalty of 10 years' imprisonment. When the victim is under the age of 12, this same offense warrants a penalty of life imprisonment. Carnal knowledge of a mentally handicapped female is punished with 5 years' imprisonment. Any person who acquires or attempts to acquire a female for the purpose of prostitution can be punished with a prison sentence of up to 10 years. Attempted rape in punished with 10 years' imprisonment, and rape warrants a penalty of life imprisonment. Spousal rape is yet to be recognized by the laws of Guyana.

Homicide

The penalty for manslaughter ranges, but it may be punished with a sentence of life imprisonment. Aiding and abetting a suicide can also merit a penalty of life imprisonment. Attempted suicide can be punished with two years' imprisonment. Murder is prosecuted as a felony and warrants capital punishment. Conspiracy to commit murder is punishable with 10 years' imprisonment. Attempted murder that involves the use of poison, serious bodily injury, explosives, firearms, or strangulation can also be punished with life imprisonment. Self-defense that results in the death of another person is justifiable and merits no punishment.

Property Crimes

Harm caused to property, whether by fire or explosives, can carry a sentence ranging from seven years' to life imprisonment depending on the damage caused. Simple larceny is punishable with three years' imprisonment, although circumstances surrounding the case can increase severity of the punishment. The sentence for grand larceny varies depending on the value of the stolen object and the circumstances of the case, but the crime of larceny can warrant life imprisonment. Embezzlement and simple robbery both carry a penalty of 14 years' imprisonment, and robbery with the use of force or violence can be punished with life imprisonment. Burglary penalties vary but can also warrant life imprisonment depending on the severity of the crime.

Capital Punishment

Although Guyanese law continues to allow the death penalty, capital punishment has been abolished in practice. Guyana has not executed any prisoners since the 1970s. According to criminal offense law, capital punishment is justified in cases in which the intent to end a person's life is clearly present. One interesting exception to capital punishment is women who are pregnant at the time of their conviction. If a woman's crime merits the death penalty, her sentence is commuted to life imprisonment.

Prisons

The minister of home affairs is responsible for the administration of prisons in Guyana. Currently, there are five prisons operating in the country. Correctional facilities are managed by the director of prisons, who is assisted by the deputy director and the superintendent of prisons. As of 2006, Guyana's prison population stood at 1,955 persons incarcerated. This makes the prison rate approximately 260 prisoners per 100,000 of the national population. The largest prison complex is in Georgetown, which houses 700 prisoners in a facility with a capacity for only 500. The Mazurani prison, located on the bank of the Essequibo River, is the second-largest correctional facility in the country. Female prisoners are housed at the New Amsterdam prison located on the northeastern coast of Guyana.

Rehabilitation programs, though available, are underfunded and deficient. International human rights groups have investigated and reported the conditions of correctional facilities in Guyana. Because of mandatory prison sentences for drug offenders, the Guyanese prison system has seen an increase in the prison population. Overcrowding and deteriorating facilities have contributed to inhumane practices, including poor medical care and inadequate meals. HIV/AIDS has become widespread in the prison system. Juveniles, at times, are held with adults, though this is prohibited by law, and females awaiting trial in regions without a women's prison were held in the same facility as men. Several reports of torture within prison walls have surfaced. In July 2008, a prisoner was beaten and tortured, and he later succumbed to his injuries. Two senior officials were charged with manslaughter in this case.

Exchange of Prisoners

Persons accused or convicted of an offense in Guyana can be returned to Guyana by request if they are fugitive in a Commonwealth nation or a nation that holds an extradition treaty with Guyana. If a person accused or convicted of a crime abroad is found as a fugitive in Guyana, that person may be returned to the country seeking his or her extradition if the country belongs to the Commonwealth or if the country holds an extradition treaty with Guyana. Guyana will not return fugitives of other countries if they are accused of political crimes; if they are being persecuted because of their race, religion, sex, or political inclinations; or if it is clear to Guyanese authorities that the person would face an unfair trial if returned to the country seeking extradition.

Angela Marcela Navarro

Further Reading

Carey, H. (2002). "Guyana." In *Legal Systems of the World: A Political, Social, and Cultural Encyclopedia,* Herbert M. Kritzner, pp. 636–642. Santa Barbara, CA: ABC-CLIO.

Guyana Office of the President: http://opnew.op.gov.gy/index.php?option=com_content&view=frontpage.

Guyana Police Force: http://www.guyanapoliceforce.org/.

U.S. Department of State. (2009). *Guyana:* http://www.state.gov/r/pa/ei/bgn/1984.htm.

Haiti

Legal System: Common
Murder: High
Corruption: High
Prison Rate: Low
Death Penalty: No
Corporal Punishment: No

Background

The Republic of Haiti is located on the island of Hispaniola in the Caribbean. Haiti covers the western third of the island, and the Dominican Republic covers the remaining two-thirds. The island has a total area of 27,750 square kilometers, and the population is 9,035,536 people. Haiti's official languages are French and Creole.

The original inhabitants of Hispaniola were Taino Amerindians, most of whom died after Christopher Columbus landed on the island and Spanish settlers took over. In 1697, the Treaty of Ryswick was signed, by which Spain ceded its control over the land to France. Thousands of slaves were shipped to the French colony from Africa to do the hard labor of growing and harvesting crops. In the late 1700s, slaves began attempts at retribution against the landowners for the maltreatment they had suffered. The rebellion against France continued to grow in strength until approximately half a million slaves successfully revolted. Haiti officially declared its independence on January 1, 1804.

Haiti has yet to have a long period of stability. Between 1843 and 1915, there were 22 different men in control of the government. The United States stepped in from 1915 to 1934. Subsequent governments were plagued by violence and corruption. The United Nations Stabilization Mission in Haiti, or MINUSTAH, provided assistance on June 1, 2004, to help secure and stabilize the government and protect Haitian human rights. It is still currently active. Current president Rene Preval has been in office since May 14, 2006, and Prime Minister Michele Pierre-Louis was appointed by the president on September 5, 2008. The National Assembly is the legislative branch of government and consists of a 30-member Senate and the 99-seat Chamber of Deputies. All members of the National Assembly are elected by popular vote.

Legal and Criminal Justice System

Haiti adopted the French criminal code and code of criminal procedure. The judicial branch in Haiti is divided into four levels. The lowest level consists of the justices of the peace. These judges issue warrants, rule on minor cases, take depositions, and refer cases to higher justices. The next level consists of the courts of first instance, which handle more serious cases. Judges from these courts can refer cases to the courts of appeals. There are 15 appellate court justices. The highest court is the 11-member Court of Cassation. Its purpose is to hear cases that question whether a case was conducted following procedural law and/or that question its constitutionality.

Police

There is one centralized police agency called the Haitian National Police (HNP). The police officers of HNP have the sole responsibility for law enforcement and maintaining order. As of 2007, the HNP consisted of 7,700 members. Corruption and misconduct were major problems for the HNP until as recently as 2005. For example, officers have been known to kill civilians and have the charges dismissed. Because of the United Nations involvement with MINUSTAH, unnecessary killings by police officers have declined.

Many nations have sent police personnel to provide aid to the United Nations (UN) and its stabilization mission in Haiti since June 2004. Countries aiding the UN include the United States, France, Spain, Brazil, Turkey, and Egypt. There are currently just over 2,000 police personnel from 40 different nations.

Crime

Drugs and Money Laundering

It is illegal to both sell and use a variety of drugs, including hallucinogens such as LSD and cannabis, stimulants such as cocaine and amphetamines, and opiates such as heroin. Drug trafficking, production, manufacturing, and distribution are some of the most serious drug-related offenses with a criminal sentence of 5 to 20 years with a fine of HTG$500,000 to $10,000,000 (approx. US$12,603–$25,208). Cocaine is trafficked through Haiti on its way from South America to the United States. The U.S. Department of State estimated that 67 metric tons of cocaine were trafficked through Haiti in 1999 alone.

At the start of the new millennium, Haiti began using the Law on Money Laundering from Illicit

New York police chief Raymond Kelly, center, walks with Jean Nesly Lucien, Haitian national police director, at Admiral Killic Coast Guard Base in Port-au-Prince, Haiti, April 29, 2002. A six-member panel of U.S. drug experts, including Kelly, arrived in Haiti to help this impoverished Caribbean country coordinate its fight against drug trafficking and money laundering. (AP photo/ Daniel Morel)

Drug Trafficking and other Crimes and Punishable Offenses as its anti–money laundering legislation. Prior to this time, Haiti had no laws against money laundering. In 2002, the National Committee to Fight Money Laundering was formed. Its purpose is to promote, coordinate, and recommend policies to aid in the prevention, detection, and suppression of the laundering of assets from illicit trafficking of drugs and other serious offenses.

Crime Statistics

According to the World Health Organization, Haiti's homicide victimization rate in 2004 was 5.3, although according to the United Nations Office on Drugs and Crime, other sources note that the intentional homicide rate reported to the police could be as high as 33.9. In 2007, the United Nations reported that there were 487 homicides in Haiti, which is a rate of about 5.6 per 100,000 people.

MINUSTAH also has collected statistics about kidnappings. They reported that from 2005 to 2006, there were a total of 1,356 reported kidnappings, but only 237 in 2007. The most recent statistics from June 2008 reported a total of 160 kidnappings for the first half of the year.

Finding of Guilt

Rights of the Accused

Haiti's Constitution outlines the rights of individuals in the criminal justice system. An individual may not be arrested or detained unless caught in the act of committing a crime or by written order of a legally competent official that states the reason for the arrest. An individual must appear before a judge within 48 hours to confirm that the arrest was made legally. The police must also notify the arrestee of his or her right to counsel in all phases of the investigation.

Due to the extreme overload and corruption in the criminal justice system, many individuals have not been granted these and other constitutional rights. Approximately only 10 jury trials are held annually per first instance court. This denies most Haitians their right to a jury trial. Many corrupt judges also deny criminal defendants their right to be present at trial, the right to confront witnesses against them, and the right to present witnesses and evidence on their own behalf. Although defendants are allowed the right to legal counsel, most Haitians cannot afford it. The government is not required to pay for it; therefore, many defendants do not get a fair trial in court.

Preventive Detention

Haitians are permitted to be incarcerated while awaiting trial. These individuals make up the vast majority of the current prison population. According to the U.S. Department of State, 84 percent of prisoners are awaiting trial. Some of these people may eventually be granted bail by an investigative judge because bail hearings are not automatic. Bail is typically granted for only minor cases and humanitarian grounds such as a need for medical attention.

Juvenile Justice System

In 2003, the Convention on the Rights of the Child and its related committee published specific concerns that it had in relation to children in Haiti. One concern surrounded the juvenile justice system. Such a system exists in only two places in Haiti, Cap Haitien and Port-au-Prince. The committee wished to reform the juvenile justice system by establishing juvenile courts, limiting the amount of time allowed in detention and incarceration, improving the conditions of detention and imprisonment, and providing children with basic services such as schooling.

Punishment

Types of Punishment

Haiti has a wide range of possible punishments that a convicted defendant may receive, including hard labor, forced labor, incarceration, banishment, and loss of civil rights. Convicted persons can also receive fines as their sole punishment or as part of their sentence. No convicted person can be sentenced to death according to article 20 of Haiti's 1987 Constitution.

A person convicted of murder will typically receive a punishment of forced labor for life. If the crime of murder is accompanied by another crime or has been preceded by another crime, then the punishment is typically increased to hard labor for life. However, if a man kills his wife whom he caught cheating in his home, he is excused of the murder. This same justification does not hold true for women. If a man is convicted of rape, the maximum penalty he will receive is 10 years' imprisonment. If the rape is a gang rape or was premeditated, aggravated assault, the sentence is increased to 15 years of hard labor. The typical punishment for theft can range anywhere from 1 to 5 years of incarceration.

Prison

Haitian prisons have become known worldwide for their horrendous conditions. There is a lack of basic necessities such as food, water, and shelter. Severe overcrowding in the prison cells is also a problem. These conditions lead to malnutrition and allow for infectious diseases to run rampant throughout the prisons. A majority of all prison inmates, around 84 percent, have not been convicted of a crime and are being held in prison while awaiting processing. The average wait time to court is 20 months. The Health and Human Rights Prison Project (HHRPP) aims to improve prison conditions by providing appropriate health care for inmates. Another of its goals is to decrease the number of prison inmates who are there for pretrial detention purposes by providing legal counsel to these detainees.

The prison system in Haiti is called the Direction de l'Administration Pénitentaire (DAP). The current director is Jean Roland Célestin, who oversees 21 prisons. The National Penitentiary is the largest prison in Haiti and is located in the nation's capital, Port-au-Prince. According to the International Centre for Prison Statistics, as of February 27, 2009, there were 8,345 people in prison, including pretrial detainees, which is well above the maximum capacity of the prison system of 2,448 people. Female prisoners made up 4.9 percent of the prison population and juveniles made up another 4.9 percent. There is a separate penitentiary in Port-au-Prince for children who are under the age of 16 and male. Females of all ages are housed together in the prison.

Vanessa Schrader

Further Reading

Globalex. *Researching Haitian Law:* http://www.nyulawglobal.org/Globalex/.

Institute for Justice and Democracy in Haiti: http://www.ijdh.org/index.html.

l'Entraide Judiciaire en Matière Pénale et d'Extradition: http://www.oas.org/juridico/mla/fr/hti/fr_hti_penal.html.

MINUSTAH, United Nations Stabilization Mission in Haiti: http.www.un.org/Depts/dpko/missions/minustah/.

U.S. Department of State. *Haiti:* http://www.state.gov/g/drl/rls/hrrpt/2006/78895.htm.

Honduras

Legal System: Civil
Murder: Medium
Corruption: Medium
Human Trafficking: Medium
Prison Rate: Medium
Death Penalty: No
Corporal Punishment: Yes

Background

Honduras is a small Central American country bordering the Caribbean Sea to the north, Guatemala and El Salvador to the west and southwest, the Pacific Ocean to the southeast, and Nicaragua to the southeast. About 7.8 million Hondurans live in this land of 112,000 square kilometers. The population is very young due to a high growth rate of nearly 2 percent and a moderate life expectancy of 69 years; people aged 65 years or older represent less than 4 percent of the Honduran society.

Exports of banana and coffee, two agricultural products vulnerable to volatile price fluctuations in the global market, constitute the backbone of the economy. Despite admirable economic growth achieved in the 2000s, the gross domestic product adjusted for purchasing power parity remains at $4,400. Real unemployment rate is believed to have approximated one-third of the labor force, and half of the population lives under the poverty line. Poverty and an extremely unequal distribution of wealth are two of the most visible socioeconomic features of this developing country.

Once a colony of the Spanish Crown, Honduras declared its independence in 1821. It was briefly annexed by Mexico before it joined the short-lived United Provinces of Central America in 1823. The fragile federation broke down in 1838. Honduras' agriculture-based economy was dominated in the 1900s by U.S. multinational companies that maintained vast banana plantations along the north coast. Foreign capital, plantation life, and conservative politics held sway in Honduras from the late 19th century until the mid-20th century. A military coup in 1963 initiated two and a half decades of mostly military rule, which did not end until a democratically elected civilian administration came to power in 1982. During the 1980s, Honduras became embroiled in the regional conflict by supporting anti-Sandinista guerrillas combating the Marxist regime in Nicaragua and allying itself with the U.S.-backed Salvadoran government in fighting leftist armed groups. Ever since the return of the democratic rule, the Honduran society and its civic institutions have been marred by endemic poverty, rampant violence and crime, and massive natural disasters (the 1998 Hurricane Mitch left nearly 6,000 deaths, 1.5 million displaced people, and US$3 billion in damages).

The 1982 Constitution provides for a powerful executive, a unicameral National Congress, and a judiciary named by the Congress. The president is both chief of state and head of government and is directly elected to a four-year term by popular vote. Administratively, Honduras is organized into 18 local departments, and municipal executives are democratically elected for four-year terms. The 128-seat unicameral Congress exercises the legislative power, and its members are selected in proportion to the number of votes each party receives and serve a four-year term. The judicial branch is led by the Supreme Court of Justice, formed by a president or chief justice and 14 magistrates chosen by Congress for a seven-year term. Other judicial bodies include courts of appeal and several courts of unique or mixed jurisdiction—such as labor, tax, and criminal courts.

Criminal Justice System

The Honduran legal system is rooted in Roman and Spanish civil law traditions with a growing influence of Anglo-Saxon common law. It accepts International Criminal Court jurisdiction with some reservations. Structurally, the legal system is structured around courts and is supported by the Ministry of Government and Justice, the Public Ministry, the Public Defense Service, and the National Preventive Police.

In addition to the duties described in the previous section, the 15-member Supreme Court is mandated by the 1982 Constitution to manage and oversee the judicial power, to appoint judges to the appellate courts and the ordinary courts, and to hear criminal processes involving ranking state officials with the approval of the Congress. The 12 appellate courts handle sentence appeals emerging from first instance courts as well as requests for protection of individual rights against the acts of local governments. Trial courts are first-instance tribunals that accept and process cases in civil, criminal, labor, family, juvenile, housing, and administrative matters. There were 77 trial courts in 2008. They also serve as a second-instance review for the appeal of rulings handed down by the peace courts. The 330 peace courts, in turn, have jurisdiction over civil cases involving small claim disputes, certain criminal cases involving misdemeanor offenses, and domestic violence cases. In 2006, a total of 66,728 new cases were filed in the entire Honduran court system, and 39,231 cases were disposed and closed in the same year. These cases were processed by 48 magistrates in the appellate courts, 294 judges in trial courts, and 244 judges of peace courts.

The Public Ministry is functionally the Public Prosecutor's Office with national jurisdiction and is operationally independent of all branches of government. It is tasked with the investigation and prosecution of criminal offenses, the enforcement of criminal sentences, and the oversight of compliance with constitutional principles by local law enforcement agencies. The ministry represents, defends, and protects the interests of the public before the courts. Public prosecutors are legally treated as delegates of, and thus subordinated to, the attorney general of the republic. However, the attorney general may at times initiate new prosecutions or intervene in ongoing adjudications directly and personally in exceptional cases on behalf of societal interest. Internally, the Public Ministry also maintains the Directorate of Forensic Medicine to provide pathological and psychiatric analysis and evidence in support of crime investigation and prosecution.

The Public Defense Service is led by the national public defender appointed by the Supreme Court and provides free legal counsel to indigent defendants unable to hire private defense. This public and free legal aid service is only available in criminal matters; it begins when charges are filed and ends with the completion of criminal proceedings. The public defender in each specific case can either be appointed by the judge or be requested by the defendant or his or her family. In 2006, 232 public defenders staffed the service.

The National Preventive Police, the largest police force in Honduras, is directed by the Ministry of Security and involved in virtually every aspect of public safety (such as outreach and patrol) and in many stages of the criminal justice process including arrest, investigation, transport of defendants, and prison security. The number of officers serving in the National Preventive Police and the General Directorate of Criminal Investigations, which conducts criminal investigations and forensic analyses in support of the prosecution of criminal offenders, almost doubled from 7,000 in 2005 to 13,500 in 2008. This rapid expansion was attained at a cost. Misconduct and abuse of power are widespread in the police; the Ministry of Security reported that in 2008, 268 police officers were prosecuted for criminal offenses ranging from abuse of authority to drug trafficking, rape, and homicide. The Public Ministry also announced that during the same year, another 312 reports involving violations of civil rights such as excessive use of force, unlawful detention, and extortion were filed against the police with the Special Prosecutor for Human Rights, of which 163 cases were investigated and 43 were substantiated.

Juvenile Justice

The legal instrument governing the treatment and protection of minors is the 1996 Children and Adolescents' Code, which defines juveniles as those youths between the ages of 12 and 18 years. Juveniles are criminally responsible but processed by a separate system of juvenile justice. Official statistics show that the majority of crimes committed by Honduran juveniles are offenses against property such as theft, larceny, and vandalism. Relatively few engage in violent crimes such as homicide and rape. There is a worrisome growing trend involving juveniles in crimes against public security, specifically the offense of illicit association for being a member of a street gang. In 2003, 92 percent of all juveniles arrested by the police were detained at the moment their crime was being committed; the remaining 8 percent were arrested under a court order.

The Honduran Constitution establishes specialized children's courts to deal with juvenile delinquents and child protection matters. There are 14 children's judges serving in 10 children's courts across the territory. Regular trial judges attend juvenile cases in some rural areas not covered by children's courts. Children's judges are professional lawyers with training or work experiences in the area of child welfare and are selected by the chief justice of the Supreme Court.

During the investigation of a juvenile case, the prosecutor can request a number of measures on behalf of the minor, including guidance and social support, imposition of rules of conduct, obligatory residence, assisted liberty, and detention. Most juvenile detainees are street children or gang members, so minors receiving noncustodial controls during the pretrial period often run away and do not turn up for trial. Because of a recent increase in gang delinquency, about half of the juveniles incarcerated in correctional facilities for boys are still awaiting trial. Children's judges are encouraged to divert juveniles from formal trial to conciliation meetings with the harmed party, to judgment of opportunity (i.e., letting the minor go with a warning but without formal punishment), or to remission to community programs. These diversionary rules are not very frequently implemented because most juveniles in the system are serious offenders not qualified for diversion.

Although abbreviated procedures and negotiated sentences are available, most serious juvenile offenders are routinely sent to reformatories for the time necessary for their rehabilitation and for a maximum of eight years. There are four juvenile correctional facilities in Honduras; two of them are closed institutions guarded by heavily armed officers. In July 2004, the four centers housed approximately 400 juveniles, with convicted and unconvicted residents mixed in these settings. Physical and sanitary conditions are poor, and solitary confinement and denial of family contacts are used as disciplinary measures in some facilities. Basic educational and vocational trainings are provided, but they fall short of triggering systematic rehabilitation because most of these programs are manned by insufficient or undertrained staff.

Crime

Crime Statistics

High rates of violence and crime are permanent social maladies in Honduras. Predatory gang activities and violent gang warfare, especially from rival gangs MS-13 (Mara Salvatrucha) and Mara 18, have instilled desperation and eroded community fabric among Hondurans. It is estimated that in 2005 there were 36,000 gang members in this country of 7.8 million population. That is, there are more than twice as many gang members as police officers. The lack of capable manpower, training, equipment, and other resources has hampered police control.

In 2008, the rate of homicide cases known to the police reached 57.9 cases per 100,000 inhabitants, which represented a 56.5 percent increase over the rate of 37.0 cases per 100,000 inhabitants in 2005. Seventy-eight percent of the 4,473 homicide victims were killed by firearms, and males ages 25 to 29 constitute the most vulnerable demographic group, with a rate of 254.9 homicides per 100,000 members of the group.

Most gang members are alienated urban males between the ages of 15 and 24, a demographic group that accounts for a disproportionate portion of street crimes and violence. They are involved in a large number of killings, mostly of each other. But it would be unwise to assume that incarcerating gang members will solve the crime problem in Honduras. To begin with, given the size of the gang population, doing so would overwhelm the Honduran government. Even if incapacitation of this dangerous population is achieved, a new generation of gangs and gangsters would likely spring up, so long as the socioeconomic disadvantages that created the problem in the first place remain intact. Also, evidence suggests that the youngest members of street gangs account for a relatively small share of crime. In Honduras, data reveal that less than 5 percent of all criminal offenses in the country are committed by youths under 18 years of age. This young age range characterizes a large percentage of gang membership. Therefore, the finding suggests that chronic or violent criminals are made in a relatively lengthy socialization process in which preventive interventions that offer realistic life opportunities could be promising.

The unfavorable geographic location of Honduras between the world's cocaine suppliers (i.e., Colombia) and its main consumers (i.e., the United States) has enormously expanded its exposure to foreign organized crime pressures. Lamentably, Honduras is especially vulnerable to intrusion by criminal syndicates because of socioeconomic pressures, lack of law enforcement capacity and integrity, and a history of armed conflicts. The resulting crime and disorder feed back into the social system to further weaken institutions and morale. A 2005 survey by the World Bank found that 61 percent of surveyed Honduran firms perceived crime as a major constraint on their businesses. Another 2005 study estimated that 52 percent of Honduran GDP is generated by shadow economies vulnerable to predation from organized crime. Without prompt and effective responses, crime and violence are likely to continue undermining the economic development and the rule of law in Honduras.

Drug Abuse and Trafficking

According to the epidemiological statistics compiled by the United Nations, consumption of illegal drugs is still low in Honduras. In 2005, 15 percent of the population between 12 and 35 years of age were estimated to have used opiates, including heroin, in the previous year. Prevalence rates of cocaine and marijuana use were at 0.9 percent and 1.5 percent, respectively. Users of synthetic drugs such as amphetamines and Ecstasy numbered 0.8 percent and 0.1 percent of the 12–35 population, respectively.

Honduras has historically been a transit country for Andean cocaine and small amounts of Colombian heroin destined for the United States and Europe by land, sea, and air. The most notorious development in recent years was the growth in the influx of precursor chemicals through Honduras, after enactment of tighter regulations on the chemicals in neighboring countries. In 2008, the government of Honduras confiscated 3.5 million pseudoephedrine pills and more than 5 tons of precursors such as sodium sulphate and soda ash. Another 13 metric tons of pseudoephedrine were intercepted in the United States en route to Honduran territories to be diverted to Mexican drug cartels. A total of 721 persons were arrested for connection to drug trafficking in 2008. Marijuana is the only known drug cultivated or produced in Honduras. It is planted in small remote farms throughout the country to cater to the modest domestic demand.

Honduras is a signatory of the 1988 UN Drug Convention, the 1971 UN Convention on Psychotropic Substances, and the 1961 UN Single Convention. Major Honduran seaports comply with the screening requirements set forth in the International Ship and Port Facility Security codes, and the government actively participates in the Inter-American Drug Abuse Control Commission.

Human Trafficking

Honduras is both a major source country and an important transit port for the trafficking of persons for the purpose of commercial sexual exploitation. Most transactions are domestic. Honduran women and children victims are usually enticed by fraudulent employment promises from rural villages to urban centers and tourist enclaves, such as Tegucigalpa, San Pedro Sula, and the Bay Islands. Some Honduran women and children are trafficked to surrounding and nearby countries such as Guatemala, El Salvador, Mexico, Belize, and the United States in response to the huge demands from the sex industry. Most foreign victims of forced prostitution in Honduras are from adjacent countries; others are economic migrants or smuggled aliens victimized en route to the United States. A growing trafficking concern now focuses on reports of child prostitution in the tourist hub of the Bay Islands and some criminal gangs' forcing children to conduct street crime.

Human trafficking for the purpose of sexual exploitation is legally prohibited in Honduras and carries custodial punishments of between 8 and 13 years of incarceration with increments by one-half under aggravated circumstances. In 2008, prosecutors initiated 82 anti-trafficking investigations and 18 prosecutions and obtained 11 convictions. However, trafficking of persons for forced servitude is not criminalized in Honduras. Very little is known about the extent of the problem of labor trafficking, which is known to be serious in neighboring countries, and even less is known about who the victims are.

The Honduran government's involvement in the assistance and care of victims of sex trafficking is very limited. The bulk of support for victims of sex trafficking is shouldered by nongovernmental organizations, which are also actively engaged in the prevention of human trafficking with some government help.

Finding of Guilt

In 2002, a new criminal procedural code went into effect in Honduras, replacing the inquisitorial, written proceedings with an adversarial model that introduced oral procedures and vested investigative and prosecutorial functions in prosecutors.

Under the new framework, the Honduran criminal procedure comprises three stages: the preliminary stage, the intermediate stage, and the trial stage. The preliminary stage encompasses the first 24 hours following arrest, the 6-day investigative period, and the initial hearing. According to the Honduran criminal procedure code, an arrestee can be detained for up to 24 hours while the authorities investigate or gather evidence to support the accusation made against that person. The suspect may be detained at local premises of the National Preventive Police or the General Directorate of Criminal Investigations. Within 24 hours of the arrest, the police must either set the detainee free or turn the case over to a prosecutor at the Public Ministry. Upon receipt of the case, the prosecutor must review its evidentiary strength and decide whether or not to further investigate the case in preparation for formal adjudication. The prosecutor may request that the court grant an extension of up to 6 days to gather witnesses and additional evidence. At the end of the 6-day investigative period, the detainee will appear in the initial hearing before a judge, who will review the merit of the case and decide either to dismiss the case or to proceed with the adjudication. If the court decides to proceed with the case, it will also decide whether the detainee will remain in jail, be placed under house arrest, be released under personal recognizance, or be released on bail.

The intermediate stage entails the arraignment hearing. Once the prosecutor concludes an investigation, he or she may petition that the judge allow a full prosecution of the case, temporarily suspend prosecution, order abbreviated procedures, or dismiss the case. If the prosecutor decides to bring the full weight of prosecution on the defendant, he or she must formalize the charges, and the defense attorney can respond to them directly in the arraignment hearing. Afterward, the judge orders that the bench trial be initiated and the materials forwarded to the trial court, which is composed of three magistrates and no jury.

Benchmarks in the trial stage include the trial itself, verdict, and sentencing. The presiding judge of the trial leads the oral and public proceedings during which the prosecution and the defense must present the arguments outlined in the written materials that they have submitted. The accused is then given a chance to speak, after which prosecutorial evidence is presented. Once both parties have made their closing statements, the three judges deliberate. The verdict is rendered immediately after the end of the deliberation. The sentence is pronounced at a separate hearing within 30 days of the pronouncement of the verdict.

Because trial is allowed to be delayed for up to two years from the time of the arrest, unnecessarily lengthy pretrial detention and court backlogs exacerbate judicial inefficiency. In 2007, according to the Supreme Court of Honduras, of 271,000 cases filed with the General Directorate of Criminal Investigations, only 6,000 reached trial. Yet, of these 6,000 trial cases, 80 percent ended in convictions and sentences.

Rights of the Accused

The Honduran penal code provides that police may apprehend and detain a Honduran citizen only with a court order, unless the arrest is requested by a prosecutor, made during the commission of a crime, made when there is evidence that a person has committed a crime and is trying to evade prosecution, or made when the person is caught with evidence related to a crime. The detainee has the right to be informed by the police of the grounds for the arrest as well as the right to be brought before a judge within 24 hours of the arrest. All detainees have the right to prompt access to family members and/or a defense attorney of their choosing; if indigent, the detainee should have immediate access to state-provided legal aid. The Constitution promises the presumption of innocence to all citizens and guarantees the rights of the accused to a fair public trial, to an initial hearing by a judge, to bail, to legal counsel, and to post-conviction appeal. In practice, all these rights are often neglected.

Punishment

Prisons

Honduras has a peculiar gendered and bifurcated organization of its penitentiary system; some commentators even conclude that there are actually two separate penal systems: one for male offenders and the other for female offenders. The National Directorate of Penal Establishments under the Ministry of Government and Justice (MGJ) manages national penitentiaries for male inmates serving a prison sentence of three years or longer, departmental prisons for male inmates serving a custodial sentence of less than three years, and local jails for male inmates awaiting trial/disposition or serving a custodial sentence of up to 90 days, whereas the National Board of Social Welfare under the Ministry of Work is in charge of supervising female inmates housed in the Female Center of Social Adaptation in the Locality of Tamara, which was constructed in 1974 as the only facility available to women. Although the administration of these two subsystems is entrusted to different state agencies, the legal mandate and the stated mission of both are unified under the 1985 Law of Rehabilitation of Offenders, where the purpose of incarceration is set as aimed at the preparation of inmates for future social reinsertion through needs assessment and rehabilitative services. Female inmates generally live under conditions similar to those of male inmates, but unlike their men counterparts, women do not have conjugal visit privileges. Children up to age two are allowed to stay with their mothers in captivity.

There are a total of 26 correctional facilities in Honduras, 9 of which are penal farms. Although the amount and quality of resources available to penitentiary authorities have not changed in any significant way, the number of inmates under their supervision increased by 218.8 percent between 1986 and 2005, from 3,636 to 11,592. The current incarceration rate of 161 inmates per 100,000 places a nearly unbearable burden on the very limited budget of the government, which has been forced to operate the entire prison system at 200 percent of its designed capacity. This situation is created and worsened by an ever-growing crime rate and an extremely inefficient court system: in 2008, 53 percent of Honduran inmates were detained defendants awaiting trial or trial disposition. Pretrial detainees regularly are housed together with convicted offenders in mixed quarters.

The first direct consequence of overcrowding and restricted resources is the abandonment of the progressive ideal of transforming prison inmates for a productive lifestyle. Existing prison-based remedial services are insufficient to reverse the human and social deficits of most inmates. Furthermore, physical and sanitary conditions in most settings are deplorable to the point of breeding resentment and hostility among inmates. Health care and psychiatric attention are barely existent, and medicines, basic amenities such as soap and towels, and even extra food must often be supplied by family members or procured with personal means from outside the institution. Sport and other recreation activities are generally scarce, except at the women's facility.

Prison violence, particularly inter-gang warfare, and deadly accidents have become the hallmark of overcrowded Honduran prisons. For example, in May 2004, a morning fire ignited by a short-circuited refrigerator at the congested San Pedro Sula prison in northern Honduras consumed a cell-block housing gang members, killing 103 and injuring 25 others. Some inmates were believed to have been shot dead by guards who were afraid of a massive escape during the chaos. Prison managers have tried to classify inmates into three groups—*maras* (active gang members), *pesetas* (former gang members), and *paisas* (those who have never been in a gang)—and to segregate inmates from opposing gangs in different facilities or in different units of the same facility to reduce prison violence. Yet no sign of major improvement has been seen. In 2003, an inter-gang fight at La Porvenir prison outside Tegucigalpa triggered a shootout and riot that left close to 100 inmates dead. In April 2003, 69 inmates were killed in a penal farm outside La Ceiba called La Granja. In April 2008, 9 inmates died in the San Pedro Sula prison; eight days later, 18 of the inmates who were transferred from San Pedro Sula to another facility to the north of Tegucigalpa for protection were hacked to death. According to official statistics, at least 109 inmates lost their lives while incarcerated at the hand of rival gangs between January 2006 and October 2008.

Inmates with mental disorders and those with infectious diseases such as tuberculosis are frequently housed with the rest of the prison population in shared quarters. All inmates are vulnerable to brutal and inhumane treatment by correctional officers, but homosexual inmates are most likely to suffer sexual violence by fellow prisoners, which is condoned, if not tacitly encouraged, by prison staff. Despite these many problems, Honduran prisons are quite transparent and generally open to visits by independent local observers and international human rights organizations, who have been working with the government to promote needed prison reforms.

Death Penalty

The last judicial execution was carried out in 1940, and capital punishment was formally and completely abolished in 1956. However, in response to the pervasive fear of violence and crime among the citizenry, several presidential candidates in recent electoral campaigns have expressed support for the reinstatement of death penalty through national referenda if given a chance.

Hung-En Sung

Further Reading

Pine, Adrienne. (2008). *Working Hard, Drinking Hard: On Violence and Survival in Honduras.* Berkeley: University of California Press.

Prillaman, William. (2002). "Honduras." In *Legal Systems of the World: A Political, Social, and Cultural Encyclopedia,* edited by Herbert Kritzer, Vol. 2, pp. 656–661. Santa Barbara, CA: ABC-CLIO.

Ungar, Mark. (2006). "Honduras." In *World Police Encyclopedia,* edited by Dilip K. Das and Michael J. Palmiotto, Vol. 1, pp. 361–368. New York: Routledge.

Jamaica

Legal System: Common
Murder: High
Corruption: Medium
Human Trafficking: Medium
Prison Rate: Medium
Death Penalty: Yes
Corporal Punishment: Yes

Background

Jamaica is an island located in the Caribbean Sea approximately 90 miles south of Cuba and almost 600 miles south of the Florida panhandle. It is approximately 146 miles long and 50 miles wide. Formerly a British colony, Jamaica gained independence from the United Kingdom on August 6, 1962. With a population of approximately 2.7 million persons, Jamaica is the largest English-speaking country in the Caribbean. Over 90 percent of the population is black with the rest of the population comprising persons of Chinese, East Indian, European, and mixed heritage. The capital of Jamaica, Kingston, is located in the southeastern corner of the island. Jamaica has two cities, Kingston and Montego Bay.

Government

Jamaica is a constitutional parliamentary democracy patterned on the British Westminster model. The queen of England is Jamaica's head of state and is represented by a governor-general. The prime minister is the member of the Jamaican Parliament who

Jamaica's prime minister P.J. Patterson, center, signs the document ratifying the agreement establishing the Caribbean Court of Justice (CCJ), June 9, 2003, at Jamaica House in Kingston, Jamaica. The ratification paves the way for the CCJ to become the final court of appeal instead of the Privy Council in England. Looking on are Owen Arthur, left, prime minister of Barbados, and Ralph Gonsalves, prime minister of St. Vincent. (AP Photo/Collin Reid)

commands confidence of the majority of the members of the House of Representatives. The prime minister chairs the cabinet of ministers, which initiates government policies and is responsible for the general direction and control of the government. The legislative arm of government is a bicameral Parliament consisting of the Senate (21 members) and House of Representatives (60 members).

The judicial arm of government is made up of the Judicial Committee of the Privy Council that sits in London, England; the Court of Appeal; the Supreme Court; and the resident magistrate's courts. There is a Judicial Service Commission that makes recommendations on the appointment and removal of judges and exercises disciplinary control when necessary. The Judicial Service Commission consists of the chief justice, the president of the Court of the Appeal, the chairperson of the Public Service Commission, and three other members appointed by the governor-general on the advice of the prime minister in consultation with the leader of the opposition.

The head of the judiciary is the chief justice, whose office is made secure by the Constitution. The governor-general appoints both the chief justice and the president of the Court of Appeal on the advice of the prime minister after consultation with the leader of the opposition. At the Supreme Court and Court of Appeal levels, judges' positions, salaries, and conditions of service are secured by the Constitution.

Evolution of the Legal System

Originally colonized by Spain, Jamaica was conquered by England in 1655, and the common law was introduced via a proclamation of the Crown on December 14, 1661. The sources of law in Jamaica include the Constitution, legislation, common law and judicial precedent, custom, equity, and increasingly, international law and the law of regional treaties.

The operation of judicial precedent in Jamaica has been impacted by the structure of the court system and the hierarchy of courts. Judgments of the Privy Council hold the most authority in the hierarchy of courts in Jamaica, and decisions of the Privy Council are binding on all courts. The Caribbean Court of Justice (CCJ) was established on February 14, 2001, and was designed to replace the Privy Council of England and to be the final court of appeal for the member states of the Caribbean Community (CARICOM), of which Jamaica is party. In recent years, there has been significant debate concerning the establishment and jurisdiction of the CCJ. In 2005, the Judicial Committee of the Privy Council ruled that the acts of Parliament seeking to establish the CCJ as the final court of appeal in Jamaica were unconstitutional and therefore void.

Criminal Justice System

Prior to 2001, the Ministry of National Security and the Ministry of Justice were one unit. Currently, they are separate ministries with their own missions, administrative units, and budgets. The Ministry of Justice is composed of the courts, the Chief Parliamentary Counsel, the Attorney General's Department, the Office of the Director of Public Prosecutions, and the Legal Reform Department. The Ministry of Justice protects the constitutional rights of the citizens, maintains the independence of the judicial system, carries out legal reform, provides the means of redress when people are abused by the state, and executes legal directives imposed by the courts.

The Ministry of National Security exercises the overall responsibility for the security and defense of Jamaica. It has under its auspices the Jamaica Defense Force, the Jamaica Constabulary Force, and the Department of Correctional Services. It is responsible for the Private Security Regulations Authority (PRSA), which registers private security guards and security companies, and the Firearm Licensing Authority (FLA), which regulates firearm licenses in the country. The Ministry of National Security also has a number of social programs in collaboration with other ministries that are aimed at building social cohesion and enhancing community safety in the island. Among them are the Citizen Security and Justice Program, the Community Security Initiative, the Safe Schools Program, and the Parish Crime Prevention Program.

The Police

The Jamaica Constabulary Force (JCF) was founded in 1845. The Island Special Constabulary Force (ISCF) is the main auxiliary body of the JCF. Its main roles and responsibilities include traffic management, municipal policing, acting as court orderlies, preventing and controlling public disorder, enforcing environmental and larceny laws, and maintaining the security of government departments, agencies, the residence of judges, and other officials.

The commissioner of police is the head of the police force and is responsible for the overall command and superintendence of the JCF. The senior management groups, which are organized into activities described as portfolios, are below the rank of the commissioner. The Administration and Support Services portfolio is responsible for the coordination of the administrative machinery of the force. The Operations portfolio is responsible for services such as the control and regulation of traffic, community safety and security, firearms and coastal security, the mobile reserve, and community relations. The Crime portfolio comprises three main units: Criminal Investigation Bureau (CIB), Serious and Organized Crime, and Narcotics. The Intelligence portfolio oversees the National Intelligence Bureau and Operation Kingfish, a special anticrime initiative that focuses on the major organized criminal networks in Jamaica. As of March 2008, the strength of the JCF stood at 8,195 members, of which some 6,000 were below sergeant rank. The ratio of police to citizenry was 1:315 persons.

The JCF is separate from the Jamaica Defense Force (JDF), which is the country's military. The JDF is composed of an Infantry Regiment and Reserve Corps, an Air Wing, a Coast Guard fleet, and a supporting Engineering Unit. The JDF functions to defend the country in the event of aggression, as well as to assist the police and other agencies in the event of civil disturbances or major disasters. The JDF also performs surveillance of Jamaica's territorial waters to prevent the smuggling of narcotics into the country.

Crime

Classification of Crime

There are three classifications of offenses: those triable only on indictment, those triable only summarily, and those triable either way. An indictable offense is a serious breach of the law that is tried by a judge and often a jury. Indictable offenses include felonies and misdemeanors and are tried in a Supreme Court. Summary offenses are tried by resident magistrates and/or justices of the peace and do not need to be tried with a jury. Both statute and common law determine which offenses are summary or indictable or triable either way. The following well-known offenses are indictable and usually tried by a jury in Jamaica: murder, manslaughter, rape, carnal abuse, robbery with aggravation or violence, arson, abduction, and kidnapping. In some cases, the summary trial of an indictable offense is allowed. The Judicature Resident Magistrates Act confers authority on a resident magistrate to hear an indictable offense in a resident magistrate's court. To proceed with such a case, the resident magistrate must hold the power to deliver punishment that is adequate for the offense that was charged. The age of criminal responsibility is 12 years old.

Under the Dangerous Drugs Act, illegal drugs in Jamaica include cocoa leaves, ganja (also referred to as marijuana), raw opium, prepared opium, morphine, and cocaine. It is unlawful to import, export, produce, cultivate, or deal in any of these. Breaches of this law may be an indictable or a summary offense.

The Firearms Act controls the importation, exportation, transshipment, manufacture, sale, purchase, disposal, possession, and use of firearms and ammunition in Jamaica. Firearm offenses, except for murder and treason, are tried in a specialized court known as the Gun Court, which was established in 1974 by the Gun Court Act.

Crimes that are seen as a particular challenge to the country include murder, shooting, rape, robberies, drug trafficking, illegal firearm trafficking, and increasingly, kidnapping.

According to data from the Jamaican Constabulary Force, the homicide rate per 100,000 residents was 8.1 in 1970. It grew to 41.7 in 1980, declined until about 1990, and then started rising again, reaching 63.2 in 2005. It was 59.1 in 2007. In 2002, the *Report of the National Committee on Crime and Violence* outlined the root causes of violence. These included an over-centralization of power that leaves communities without the wherewithal to solve their own problems, excesses in policing that have fractured the relationship with communities, political tribalism that has bred a dependency syndrome in many of the nations' citizens and divided communities along party lines, nontraditional community leadership that has its roots in tribal politics and the drug culture, and finally, protracted economic hardships that have denied many citizens an opportunity to earn a livelihood. Other issues bearing weight on the high rate of crime and violence include the high availability of firearms and other weapons, the drug culture, corruption in government institutions, and the weak financial status of civil society organizations.

Jamaica is faced with a lack of social and economic progress in some communities, and the culture of violence that has developed has led to the public having high levels of fear. The criminal justice system depends on the cooperation of citizens as witnesses and jurors, but the fear of retaliation impedes citizens' willingness to participate, thereby affecting the proper functioning of the system. This is due in part to the fact that Jamaica has a cultural idea of "informer fi dead," which means that any person known to give information to the authorities with respect to a crime should die. This phenomenon is prevalent in urban Jamaica and has been reinforced by instances in which witnesses have been killed before being able to offer testimony in a case.

Crime Statistics

According to the Statistics Department of the Jamaica Constabulary Force, for the calendar year 2007, there were 5,728 reported major offenses against persons, which included murder, rape, carnal abuse, shootings, and robbery. There were 1,583 reported murders, 1,441 reported shootings, 670 reported rapes (female victims only), 427 reported cases of carnal abuse, and 1,598 reported cases of robbery. For other offenses against persons, there were 50 reported suicides and 4,036 reported cases of felonious wounding. Major offenses against property included 331 reported cases of burglary, 611 reported dwelling-house breakings, and 525 other breakings. There were 2,259 reported breaches of the Firearms Act and 9,452 breaches of the Dangerous Drugs Act. Other offenses included 783 reported cases of fraud and 100 reported cases of arson.

The implements used to commit murder in 2007 included guns (1,246), knives (194), machetes (59), and other implements, such as blunt objects (83). Of the 1,598 robberies, a gun was used in 1,149 cases, and a knife was used in 244 cases, and a combination of a knife and a gun was used in 71 cases. During 2007, the JCF recovered 648 stolen firearms, and a total of 97 firearms were reported stolen. In 2007, the main types and quantities of drugs seized by the police included marijuana (37,439 kilograms), cocaine (98.2 kilograms), crack (2.6 kilograms), hash oil (41 kilograms), and Ecstasy (1,023 tablets).

Finding of Guilt

Rights of the Accused

The Constitution provides that any person charged with a criminal offense has the right to a trial by an independent and impartial court. The trial should be commenced within a reasonable time from the date of the criminal charge. A person is presumed innocent until he or she is proven guilty or until he or she has pleaded guilty to the offense. Every person who is charged with a criminal offense must be informed of the nature of the offense in a language that he or she can understand, and adequate time and facilities to prepare their defense must be given. A person charged with a criminal offense has the right to defend himself or herself in person or by choosing legal representation. All persons charged have the right to examine the witnesses called by the prosecution and to have witnesses in their defense by the same conditions afforded the prosecution. If necessary, they also have the right to an interpreter if English is not understood. A person should not be charged with a criminal offense when at the time the act was committed, it did not constitute a criminal offense. Also, no penalty should be imposed for a criminal offense that is more severe than the maximum penalty that might have been imposed at the time the offense was committed. A person may not be charged for a criminal offense for which he or she already stood trial and was convicted, acquitted, or pardoned.

The Constitution provides that any person who is arrested or detained shall be informed as soon as reasonably practicable of the reasons for the arrest or detention in a language that he or she can understand. Once arrested, a person should be brought without delay to a court and tried within a reasonable time. The Office of the Public Defender investigates circumstances in which it is alleged that a person's constitutional rights have been violated.

Legal Aid

The Legal Aid Council provides services to persons who are being detained before a court appearance and provides legal advice to persons detained or accused of an offense. It may also make representation for bail at the place of remand and represent the accused on their first appearance in court. A legal aid certificate may be granted after it has been verified that the accused has insufficient means to secure legal services. Legal aid may be denied if the accused is charged with an "excepted" offense, which includes certain offenses under the Money Laundering Act and the Dangerous Drugs Act. Although the Legal Aid Act makes provision for legal aid in civil matters, at present, it is granted only in criminal matters.

The Legal Aid Council is administered by a board composed of a chairperson and not less than 13 and not more than 15 members. It maintains a panel of attorneys who are willing to offer their services to persons in need of legal aid. Presently, there are 295 attorneys on the panel. During the 2006–2007 fiscal year, 1,137 persons were given legal aid assistance, which accounts for a 22 percent increase over the previous year.

Prosecution and Investigation

Criminal cases are prosecuted by the director of public prosecutions (DPP). According to the Constitution, the DPP has the power to institute and undertake criminal proceedings against any person who has committed an offense against the law of Jamaica. He or she also has the right to take over and continue criminal proceedings that may have been initiated by another person or authority as well as the power to stop criminal proceedings at any stage of the process as long as a judgment has not yet been rendered. The DPP advises the police and government departments on criminal matters and prosecutes criminal cases in the Supreme Court, Gun Court, and the resident magistrate's courts. The DPP also supervises coroners under the Coroners Act. The position of DPP may be filled only by a person who has the qualifications to be appointed as a judge in the Supreme Court, and the position may be held until the DPP is 60 years old or until 65 years with permission from the governor-general.

Police officers are granted the right to lay charges and prosecute in police cases under the Constabulary Force Act. The act provides that any member of the police force may lay a charge, and police officers may appear before a resident magistrate or justice of the peace and inquire into the charges laid and examine the witnesses. Although police officers have the right to prosecute cases, police prosecutors are subject to the overall control of the DPP because of the constitutional power granted the DPP to take control of all criminal prosecutions. The investigation of cases is handled primarily by the police.

The clerk of the courts may also prosecute cases in the resident magistrate's courts. The clerk is a trained lawyer who is empowered to prosecute cases by the Judicature Resident Magistrates Act. The clerk of the courts may prosecute trials for both indictable and summary offenses as the minister of justice directs. It is also the duty of the clerk of the courts, with the assistance of the principal officer of the constabulary, to prepare any indictable case for hearing and to procure the attendance of the witnesses for both the prosecution and the defense.

Justices of the peace are authorized to hear certain cases that fall within the jurisdiction of the resident magistrate's court. They are persons of unquestionable integrity who seek to promote and protect the rights of the individual. Under the Justice of the

Peace Jurisdiction Act, they have the power to issue summons, to issue warrants for an arrest, and to consider applications for bail. For criminal offenses, justices of the peace may hear only summary cases, and this may be done only with two justices of the peace sitting together. The maximum penalty imposed by a justice of the peace is JMD$2,000 (about US$24), and the maximum term of imprisonment imposed cannot exceed three months.

Power of Arrest

Police officers are given the power of arrest under the Constabulary Force Act. If a warrant is made for the person's arrest, the warrant does not have to be in the officer's possession at the time of the arrest, but on the demand of the person apprehended, the warrant must be shown to the person as soon as possible. It is lawful in Jamaica for a police officer to arrest a person without a warrant.

Any person who is apprehended by a member of the constabulary force must then be taken to a police station or lockup, and the officer or sub-officer in charge may grant bail to the person in accordance with the Bail Act. If a person refuses or is unable to provide a security that is required as a condition for bail, that person may then be detained in custody until he or she can be brought before a justice of the peace. If the person is in the custody of the police force without the warrant of a justice of the peace, then that person is also eligible to be granted bail unless the person is in custody on a charge of murder or treason.

Bail

The Bail Act provides that an accused person may be released on bail, and this may be granted by a court, a justice of the peace, or a police officer. A person who is charged with an offense must not be held in custody for longer than 24 hours without the question of bail being considered. A person who is charged with murder or treason may be granted bail only by a resident magistrate or a judge. Bail may be denied a defendant if the court, the justice of the peace, or the police officer believes that if the person is released on bail, he or she would fail to surrender to custody, commit an offense while on bail, interfere with witnesses, or otherwise obstruct the course of justice. Other factors taken into consideration include the seriousness and nature of the offense, the defendant's character, the defendant's associations and community ties, the defendant's record, or any other relevant factor. If the defendant is refused bail, he or she has the right to be given the reasons why bail was refused. The defendant must also be notified of the right to appeal the decision. The penalty for absconding bail is a summary conviction and a fine up to JMD$500,000 (about US$5,800) or a term of imprisonment up to two years.

Criminal Courts

The highest court in Jamaica is the Judicial Committee of the Privy Council, which sits in England. Next is the Court of Appeal, which hears disputes of judgments made by the Supreme Court and the resident magistrate's courts in all civil and criminal matters. It consists of the chief justice, who is an ex-officio member, a president, and up to six judges. The chief justice cannot sit in a case in the Court of Appeal unless four other Court of Appeal judges are sitting in the case and the president of the Court of Appeal invites the chief justice to sit. A judge of the Court of Appeal must be an attorney-at-law for at least 10 years and holds the office until attaining the age of 70. Currently, there are seven judges on the Court of Appeal.

The Supreme Court is a superior court of record and exercises unlimited jurisdiction in civil and criminal matters. Its criminal cases are handled by circuit courts after committal by resident magistrates. The Supreme Court consists of the chief justice, a senior puisne judge, and at least 20 other puisne judges. Circuit courts are the criminal jurisdiction of the Supreme Court and are convened in each of the parishes in the country. The total number of criminal cases disposed of within the criminal division of the Supreme Court 2006–2007 was 523. The highest number of cases (29 percent) originated from the Home Circuit Court.

The resident magistrate's courts have limited jurisdiction in both civil and criminal matters. They do not hold trial for the criminal offenses of murder, treason, and rape except for a preliminary inquiry. In such an inquiry, the resident magistrate's court will determine whether there is sufficient evidence for the accused to stand trial in a Supreme Court. There are 14 resident magistrate's courts, one in each parish, and each is presided over by a judge known as a resident magistrate. A resident magistrate must be an attorney-at-law for at least five years before consideration for appointment. There are between 40 and 50 resident magistrates and no less than 9 at any one time. Petty sessions courts hear minor criminal cases and are presided over by justices of the peace.

Trial

The majority of criminal cases in Jamaica are resolved through trial. In 2006–2007, a total of 296,695 criminal cases were filed in the resident magistrate's courts. Of that number, 244,101 were disposed. In the criminal division of the Supreme Court, 1,632 cases were filed, and 523 cases were disposed. There were 340 new cases filed in the Court of Appeal in 2006–2007 and 893 cases brought forward from the 2005–2006 period. During the 2006–2007 year, the Court of Appeal disposed of 412 cases. Approximately 55 percent of the cases disposed of were criminal matters. In 2007, there were 17 cases from Jamaica that received a judgment by the Judicial Committee of the Privy Council in England.

Alternatives to Trial

Alternatives to trial currently include the use of mediation services offered by the Dispute Resolution Foundation (DRF), which is a private voluntary foundation established in July 1994. The DRF encourages the use of alternative dispute resolution techniques to resolve conflict and has established Peace and Justice Centers throughout the island. On September 18, 2006, the Supreme Court of Jamaica instituted the automatic referral of cases in the civil jurisdiction to a court-appointed mediation referral agency. The Dispute Resolution Foundation is the only mediation referral agency at the moment, and jurisdiction has not yet been granted in criminal proceedings.

Juveniles

There is a separate system for juveniles, and special provisions are made for the trial and punishment of a juvenile. A juvenile in Jamaica is a person who is under 18 years of age. From arrest to trial to sentencing, juveniles follow a different set of rules.

The Jamaica Constabulary Force established a juvenile unit within the Community Relations Branch of the force. There are four main methods used by the police when handling juvenile offenders. These include an outright release without further action; a voluntary program of counseling with the assistance of social services; police counseling treatment consisting of mainly supervision, which must be agreed to by the parent or guardian of the offender; and finally, arrest and referral to the Children's Court.

Once a juvenile is detained at a police station, he or she must be kept separate from adults and prevented from associating with adult prisoners. After being charged, a juvenile is expected to be released to his or her parent or guardian. In circumstances where the juvenile is charged with murder or other grave crimes, there is reason to believe that the ends of justice would be defeated, or it is necessary to remove the juvenile from association with a reputed criminal or prostitute, then a juvenile may not be granted bail. If a juvenile is not released on bail, he or she must be kept in a juvenile remand center until he or she is brought to court. The parent or guardian of the juvenile arrested is required and warned to attend court and when necessary may be summoned to court.

The Children's Court has the all the powers of the resident magistrate's courts, and all proceedings in relation to a child are to be heard in the Children's Court. This includes cases involving juveniles as both victims and offenders of crime. If a juvenile is charged jointly with a person who has attained 18 years, the case is not heard in the Children's Court. Once brought before the court, it is the duty of the court to explain to the child, in as simple language as possible, the reason for the child being in court and that the child is entitled to the assistance of a children's advocate. The law provides that no person shall be present at the Children's Court except members and officers of the court, any authorized person defined by the Child Care and Protection Act, parties to the case, the parties' attorneys-at-law, witnesses and other persons concerned with the case, bona fide representatives of newspaper or news agencies, and any other persons as the court may specially authorize to be present. The proceedings of the Children's Court are restricted, and the names of the victims and offenders are not usually publicized. Where a child is charged with an offense, the case is typically conducted through a summary trial unless the juvenile is charged with an indictable offense, such as murder.

Punishment

In general, penalties are determined by the statute that created the offense. Punishments include a term of imprisonment, monetary fines, community service, corporal punishment, curfew order, attendance order, or mediation order. The death penalty is the punishment for murder and treason. A term of imprisonment is the typical punishment for serious offenses, and the length of the term will be determined by the type of crime committed. In less serious offenses, monetary penalties may be charged.

Life imprisonment is the typical sentence for murder, attempted murder, rape, or firearms trafficking. Drug production or trafficking can result in a fine or imprisonment up to 35 years or both. Imprisonment with hard labor up to 21 years is typical for robbery with use of an offensive weapon, whereas other robberies typically get imprisonment with hard labor up to 15 years. Imprisonment up to 21 years is typical for burglary, and other housebreaking generally gets imprisonment up to 10 years. Imprisonment up to 10 years is also typical for conspiracy to commit murder and attempted rate with use of a weapon. Illegal possession and use of a firearm could result in imprisonment up to five years and/or a fine up to JMD$100,000 (about US$1,170).

Monetary Fines

A fine is the most typical and frequent form of punishment imposed on offenders in summary offenses. A period of imprisonment may also be imposed for default on the payment of fine including if it was only partially paid or not paid on time. The maximum amount of the fine is typically set by statute, but the court will decide on the amount to be paid based on factors such as the means of the defendant, the nature of the offense, the age of the defendant, and previous convictions.

Imprisonment

For indictable offenses, imprisonment is a typical form of punishment meted out to the convicted person. The maximum term of imprisonment is determined by the statute governing the offense. It is not the norm for imprisonment to be imposed for a summary offense. A term of imprisonment is the typical punishment for offenses such as trafficking in illegal drugs, certain offenses against the person, and certain breaches of the Firearms Act. Parole may be granted and is governed by the Parole Act. An inmate may become eligible for parole after one-third of the sentence is served or after a period of 12 months, whichever is greater. For a person convicted of murder after February 18, 2005, and sentenced to imprisonment for life, he or she may become eligible for parole after a period of 10 years or a period specified by the court. A parole order may be revoked if the parolee breaks the rules of the parole order set forth by the court.

Probation

Probation is governed by statute and is granted depending on the type of offense and the seriousness of the offense, as well as the character, mental health, age, and home surroundings of the offender. The Probation of Offenders Act stipulates that probation should last for a term of one to three years. Probation orders may include conditions such as abstaining from alcoholic beverages or living within a certain court district. Probation may be revoked if an offense is committed during the probationary period or if the probationer fails to comply with the conditions of the probation.

Other Sentences

The community service order is now an alternative to serving a term of imprisonment in Jamaica. The convicted offender serves the entire sentence or a part of the sentence by performing unpaid work in the community for a period of time determined by statute. The Criminal Justice Reform Act specifies that community service orders may run concurrently, and in the case where they are made to run consecutively, they may not exceed a maximum of 480 hours. The community service may not conflict with the offender's religious beliefs or with the times that the offender works, is in school, or is attending an educational program. Community service orders cannot be given for offenses that involve violence or the use of a firearm.

Exceptional circumstances may cause a suspended sentence to be delivered and include factors such as good character, the mental health of the defendant, or whether or not a defendant's personal circumstances may make it difficult to serve the sentence in prison. If a defendant commits another offense during the period of a suspended sentence, the sentence may be activated. Typically, a suspended sentence is imposed on a term of imprisonment that is not more than three years.

An attendance order is another form of punishment that may be imposed on a person who is over the age of 18 years and who has been convicted of an offense other than murder. Rather than imprisonment, the court may require the convicted person to attend a day training center for a certain number of hours over a specified period.

A curfew order may be imposed for any offense other than murder and on a person who has attained the age of 18 years. The requirements of a curfew order must not conflict with the offenders' religious beliefs or interfere with the times that he or she would normally work or attend an educational institution. In some instances, electronic monitoring requirements may be added to the curfew order.

A mediation order may be delivered by an approved mediator of the court. The court will typically place a limit on the time in which the mediation should be concluded and specify a time by which a report on the mediation needs to be submitted. Typically, the court will require that the parties involved appear before the court to discuss whether the matter has been resolved by mediation. If the matter was resolved, the court will then either dismiss the charges against the person charged or incorporate the terms of the mediation agreement, if any, into an agreement reached by the court. If the matter was not resolved, the court will proceed to try the case.

Corporal punishment remains part of the law under the savings clause and the Crime (Prevention of) Act, which specify that flogging administered with a cat-o'-nine tails and whipping with a tamarind switch are both still allowed. The savings clauses of the Jamaican Constitution specify that any form of punishment that was valid before independence shall remain so after independence. It is open to the legislature to abolish corporal punishment by an act of Parliament, but the legislature has not done so to date. Corporal punishment may not be imposed on a female or on a male under the age of 16 years. Corporal punishment in Jamaica has not been used in recent times.

Death Penalty

The death penalty is allowed in Jamaica. The mandatory sentence of death for capital murder was held to be unconstitutional by the Judicial Committee of the Privy Council in 2004 in the case of *Lambert Watson v. The Queen.* Following that decision, the Jamaican Parliament amended the Offenses against the Person Act to indicate those categories of murder that could, on the discretion of the judges, give rise to the death sentence. Accordingly, the death penalty may be sentenced if a person is convicted of the murder of a member of the military forces, a member of the police force, a member of the correctional services, a judicial officer, or a justice of the peace all while executing their duties; a juror, present or past; or a witness to or party in a pending or concluded civil or criminal case. The death penalty may also be imposed for murder that occurred in the course of committing a robbery, burglary or housebreaking, arson to a dwelling, a sexual offense, paying to cause or assisting to cause the death of another, or any other act of violence that by its nature creates a state of fear in the public.

Pregnant women may never be sentenced to the death penalty. In fact, no women have been executed pursuant to death penalty law in Jamaica since its independence. A person convicted of murder who has received the death penalty has the right to appeal the sentence. The person may appeal to the Court of Appeal, and in some instances, his or her appeal may also be heard by the Judicial Committee of the Privy Council.

The method of execution in Jamaica is hanging, and there have been no executions since 1988. The highly publicized case of Earl Pratt and Ivan Morgan versus the attorney general for Jamaica and the superintendent of prisons was heard by the Judicial Committee of the Privy Council in 1993, which ruled that Pratt and Morgan had suffered cruel, inhumane, and degrading punishment because they had served 14 years on death row. Since that ruling, the practice has been to commute death row sentences to life sentences if the prisoner has served more than 5 years on death row.

Punishment of Juveniles

A juvenile may not be sentenced to imprisonment in Jamaica; rather, a juvenile must be placed in the custody of a juvenile correction center. Where a child has been found guilty of any offense before a Children's Court, that court may make an order to dismiss the case; send the offender to a juvenile correctional center; order the parent or guardian of the offender to pay a fine, damages, or costs; or commit the offender to the care of any fit person, whether a relative or not, who is willing to undertake the care of the child. The court may also make an order of probation under the Probation of Offenders Act or order the parent or guardian of the offender to enter into a recognizance for the good behavior of such offender.

A juvenile may never receive the death penalty. Persons under age 18 convicted of murder would be sentenced to "detention during the Court's pleasure," which means in effect that they remain in custody until the court opts to have them released.

Prison

The Department of Correctional Services oversees the prison system. The mission of this department is to contribute to the safety and protection of society by keeping offenders secure and facilitating their rehabilitation and reintegration as law-abiding citizens while developing a professional and committed staff. The aim of the programs of rehabilitation is to assist inmates to live productive lives upon release. The functions of the department are determined by statute and imposed by the courts.

The Department of Correctional Services is composed of a head office in Kingston, seven adult correctional centers, and three juvenile correctional centers. Correctional services throughout the island include probation, aftercare, parole, and prevention offices. There are six adult male prisons and one adult female prison. Of the three juvenile correctional centers, two hold male juveniles and one holds female juveniles. There is also one adult remand center and one juvenile remand center.

The overall holding capacity of all prisons in Jamaica, including both adult and juvenile centers is 4,247 inmates. According to the Department of Correctional Services, the actual prison population as of January 2008 was 4,861 inmates. The most common offenses for admittance to the adult services were drug offenses, breaches of the Firearm Act, larceny, felonious wounding, and other minor offenses.

The Tower Street Adult Correctional Centre is the island's biggest prison. It was formerly known as the General Penitentiary and is located in Kingston. According to the Department of Correctional

Services, the holding capacity is 850, and it presently houses 1,620 inmates. Overcrowding can lead to unhygienic conditions that foster the spread of disease, as well as tensions and riots. In 2007, 197 violent incidents occurred in the adult correctional institutions, with the majority occurring in the Tower Street facility.

In 2006, the department acquired land and a building in Montpelier, St. James, which will be used to establish a juvenile correctional center. In 2008, it expects to complete the predesign of a new 5,000-bed facility and to initiate phase one of the Montpelier Project.

Work Programs for Inmates

Inmates are not required to work or attend classes; instead, inmates may volunteer to participate in various rehabilitation programs. The rehabilitation programs aim to reduce the rate of reoffending and promote behavioral changes among the inmates, so that once released, they can readjust to the norms of society. The programs also aim to eradicate illiteracy among the inmates and to help them acquire marketable skills in various areas.

There are four main types of rehabilitation programs: education, agricultural practices, vocational, and life skills. Of the inmates involved in rehabilitation programs, approximately 50 percent are participants in the educational programs. These programs include education in information technology; the School Bench Project, which trains and certifies inmates in furniture making; and the Rehabilitation Thru Music program, which creates opportunities for inmates to record songs and produce music videos while they are incarcerated.

Visiting Policies for Prisons

All inmates are given the opportunity to communicate with visitors. Special visits may be given in certain circumstances with the discretionary approval of the superintendent. Visiting privileges are granted for five-minute periods, but the length of time for discretionary visits is decided by the superintendent. Visitors are subject to being searched. Lawyers are also subject to search when visiting their clients, a point that has prompted some degree of discussion.

Prisoner Exchange Programs

As of this writing, Jamaica has agreed to a memorandum of understanding with the United Kingdom for the development of a prisoner exchange program. This is a one-off agreement that proposes that approximately 40 Jamaican-born offenders currently incarcerated in the United Kingdom will be transferred to Jamaica. The aim of the program is to promote family reunification and reduce the hardship placed on Jamaican families whose family members are serving time far away from home. Offenders convicted of violent crimes such as murder, rape, or shooting are not eligible to participate in the program. The transfer of prisoners will depend on space availability in the Jamaican prisons as well as the prisoners' agreement to participate in the program. To date, the necessary domestic legislation to instigate the program has not yet been ratified, and no prisoners have been transferred to Jamaica as yet.

Glendene Lemard

Further Reading

Antoine, Rose-Marie. (2008). *Commonwealth Caribbean Law and Legal Systems*. 2nd ed. London: Routledge-Cavendish.

Harriott, Anthony, ed. (2003). *Understanding Crime in Jamaica: New Challenges for Public Policy*. Kingston: University of the West Indies Press.

Ministry of Justice Web site: http://www.moj.gov.jm/.

Ministry of National Security. (2002). *Report of the National Committee on Crime and Violence.* Kingston: Ministry of National Security.

Vasciannie, Stephen. (2002). *International Law and Selected Human Rights in Jamaica*. Kingston: Council of Legal Education.

Martinique

Legal System: Civil
Prison Rate: Medium

Background

History of the Legal System

Martinique was first encountered by Christopher Columbus in 1502. The island became a French territory in 1635 under the Compagnie des Isles d' Amerique created by Richelieu. A general prosecutor and a judge governor were in charge of the legal system of the island until 1685. The criminal justice system of Martinique was organized around the slave trade. The Code Noir, for example, forbade cruelty against slaves and also regulated the use of physical force to punish the slaves.

Martinique was occupied by England from 1794 to 1802, a period during which revolutionary movements emerged on the island. However, the colony was transferred back from England to France in 1802, allowing for slavery to be regulated under the laws of the French government. A general captain was then responsible for the defense of the colony, and a grand judge was responsible for the administration of justice. No real changes were noted in the judicial system from 1830 to 1848. A series of laws enacted on April 27, 1848, abolished slavery.

After 1848, the criminal justice system was marked by centralism with the application of law entirely submitted to the authority of the governor, annihilating the local powers. Republican institutions were implemented from 1870 to 1885, and the citizens of Martinique obtained republican rights such as voting. Law passed on July 27, 1881, granted freedom of press.

The current criminal justice system shadows the French system that evolved after the French Revolution. The law of March 19, 1946, proclaimed Martinique as a French department. The territory is now divided in four districts: Fort-de-France, Trinite, Le Marin, and Saint-Pierre. All national legislation is applicable to the department but can be modified to situations specific to Martinique. As a French department, Martinique is a member of the European Union and benefits from specific measures that adapt communitarian law to the particular characteristics and constraints of the region. The legal system in Martinique is inquisitorial and is similar to the French legal system. It was introduced by the Ordonnance of Colbert in 1791 and was based on the code of penal procedures written under Napoleon. This justice apparatus was officially implemented in Martinique after its departmentalization in 1946.

The French criminal justice system has been undergoing modernization since 2007. Indeed, the map of the judicial system was modified to assure an effective distribution of magistrates. Two decrees were signed on February 15, 2008, to modify the location of the *tribunaux d'instance* and *de grand instance.* As of January 1, 2011, all jurisdictions will have undergone dramatic changes. This reform will also affect commercial courts.

There are currently three *tribunaux d' instance* in Martinique, located at Fort-de-France, Lamentin, and Cayenne. As of 2011, all courts will be located at Fort-de-France; the courts located at Lamentin will be closed. A *maison de la justice et de droit* (house of justice and law) will be created at Fort-de-France; two *antennes de justice* (judicial antennas) will be created at Fort-de-France as well as at Sainte-Marie. These changes will lead to a better administration of justice as well as economical savings.

Finally, the riots that occurred in Martinique in February and March 2009 in response to economic hardships could lead to a restructuring of economic and administrative institutions. As of this writing, the French prime minister is scheduled to visit the territory in the near future and will advocate for radical changes in the institutions of the island. Changes can therefore be expected in all governmental institutions, including the criminal justice system.

Police and Gendarmerie

Similarly to other French territories and to metropolitan France, Martinique is policed by two different law enforcement agencies. The Police Nationale is mainly responsible for urban areas and has five main roles, including the protection and safety of individuals, material goods, and institutions. The police are also in charge of the control of immigration movements, illegal work, organized crime, and drug trafficking. This agency is furthermore responsible for the protection of the territory against terrorism. As of 2008, there were 837 police officers in Martinique, 3 percent less than in 2007.

The national police branch in Martinique is named La Direction Departementale de la Securite Publique. This agency has been undergoing restructuring since 2003. Manpower is being redistributed to answer emerging criminal activity such as drug trafficking. The national police personnel are divided between two districts. The Circonscription de Fort-de-France is a tourist area where community policing was introduced in 2003. The police department in the area is responsible for 110,000 inhabitants. Police officers are redeployed to sensitive areas such as sport and medical facilities. The second antenna, the Circonscription du Lamentin, is mainly composed of dangerous areas where delinquency has increased due to high population movements. The officers located in this area are responsible for 9,500 inhabitants.

The other agency accountable for public order is the Gendarmerie Nationale. This agency is under the control of the Ministry of Defense, and it is composed of military personnel and civilians. These officers are responsible for maintaining law and order in rural areas. The Gendarmerie d'Outre-Mer has 531 officers in Martinique who are in charge of the protection of 85 percent of the population, dispersed on 98 percent of the territory. The main gendarmerie center is located at Fort-De-France, and two other antennas are located in Trinite and le Marin. These officers are divided into 26 brigades.

Crime

Classification of Crime

Crimes are classified into five types of infractions: against individuals, against material goods, against the state, in organization, and without victim. Crimes against persons include homicide, rape, and torture. Infractions against goods include robbery and theft. Finally, terrorism and treason are considered as crimes against the state.

All infractions are divided into three levels based on their characteristics, circumstances, and seriousness. Crimes are the most serious infractions and include murder, rape, armed robbery, and drug trafficking. These crimes incur a minimum of 10 years of incarceration. *Delits,* the second type of serious infractions, incur imprisonment of less than 10 years, fines, and community service. They include theft and drug dealing. Finally, petty infractions include traffic violations. Fines are determined according to the seriousness of the offense.

The age of responsibility is 18 years old. Individuals under 13 years old are deemed irresponsible, and juveniles between the ages of 13 and 16 are processed by the juvenile justice system. However, juveniles who commit serious crimes can be handled by the adult criminal justice system. Most convicted juvenile delinquents are sentenced to educational and vocational programs. Incarceration is used only for juveniles who may present a threat to public safety and whose rehabilitation is deemed improbable.

Challenges

Drug use and drug trafficking have become significant challenges to Martinique society because of its geographic location. As exposed by multiple research agencies, drug use is widespread among juveniles and is often related to social conditions such as poverty. The recent redeployment of the Police Nationale is mainly aimed at reducing drug offenses. Between 2006 and 2007, there was a 42 percent increase in drug-related arrests.

Drug Offenses

In Martinique, as in metropolitan France, drugs are classified into four categories: stupefying substances, psychotropic substances, medications, and dangerous substances. Stupefying drugs are heroin, cocaine, ecstasy, and cannabis. The production and distribution of these substances are prohibited by the French Code of Public Health. Penal measures may be avoided by arrestees if they obtain psychological and medical help. Provocation to drug trafficking can lead to five years of imprisonment and fines up to €75 (approx. US$106). Drug use can lead to up to one year of imprisonment, and possession of stupefying substances with intent to sell will incur a maximum sentence of 10 years' imprisonment. Drug dealing may be punished by a maximum of five years of imprisonment. Finally, the organization of drug trafficking can result in prison sentences up to 30 years and fines up to €7,500,000 (approx. US$10,648). The lengths of imprisonment listed here can be doubled if these substances are sold to minors or in educational areas.

Crime Statistics

According to the Institut National de la Statistique et des Etudes Economiques (INSEE), there were 21,444 infractions reported in 2007. There were 49 homicides, 286 sexual offenses including rape, and 2,607 burglaries. There were also 1,602 drug-related arrests and 10,832 larcenies. Generally, criminal activity has been declining during the last few years. However, there was 14.52 increase in juvenile delinquency from 2006 to 2007.

Finding of Guilt

Rights of the Accused

The code of criminal procedures states that the accused individual must be immediately informed of the crimes or infractions for which an investigation is necessary. If the accused is unable to read or understand the charges pending, an interpreter or any other methods will be used to facilitate communication with this individual.

The individual is also allowed to contact family members, roommates, and employers by phone during the first three hours of detention. The accused also has the right to be examined by a physician and can be granted another visit if the detention lasts longer than 24 hours. A prosecutor or judicial agent can also contact medical services if deemed necessary. Physicians are the only individuals allowed to conduct body searches.

Once detained, the accused has the right to have a self-obtained lawyer or a state-appointed lawyer. The meetings between lawyers and accused are confidential but cannot last longer than 30 minutes. If the detention lasts more than 36 hours, the accused has the right to another meeting with a lawyer.

Assistance Provided to the Accused

Legal aid is available through the French public defender services. This aid is available only to individuals who cannot afford a private defender. The accused must prove a lack of financial means. The Bureau d' Aide Jurisdictionelle, a group composed of magistrates and counselors, decides if this legal aid will cover the amount of legal representation partially or entirely. However, this aid does not cover additional expenses related to the trial or fines imposed to the convicted individual.

Alternatives to Trial

Individuals who are deemed mentally incapable during the completion of their crimes may be referred to psychiatric services instead of incarceration. The criminal code declares the accused free from criminal liability if a court-appointed psychiatric expert deems that the accused was mentally incompetent during his or her criminal activity. There are alternatives to trial for drug offenders and juveniles as well. However, the majority of offenses are resolved by trial. Plea bargaining, dispute resolution, and guilty pleas are not allowed under French law.

Pretrial Incarceration

An individual may be incarcerated before trial for up to three years. The average length of preventive detention is four months. These individuals are not incarcerated with convicted offenders; they are housed in separate correctional facilities.

Investigation

The beginning of an investigation is led by law enforcement officers. However, prosecutors or *juges d' instruction* (in the most serious cases) seek to establish whether the prosecution of an individual is justifiable. All investigations are supervised by the judiciary.

Judges are also required to investigate and obtain evidence incriminating an accused individual. Those judges are *a charge et a decharge,* meaning that they are responsible for finding evidence linking a suspect to a particular crime. These judges can also seek evidence proving the innocence of the accused. Defendants are not allowed to conduct their own investigation. Also, the judges can transfer their judiciary powers to police officials using a *commission rogatoire.* Finally, judges have the right to emit search, seizure, and arrest warrants. They can also meet with suspects at any time and can issue a preventive detention order.

Courts

There are multiple courts located in Martinique, and they are staffed by more than 30 magistrates (judges) and 8 prosecutors. The *tribunals d' instance* handle civil matters under €10,000 (approx. US$14,205) and notary law. There are currently three of these courts located at Fort-De-France, le Lamentin, and Cayenne. The *tribunal de grande instance* handles family laws and civil matters over €10,000. The *tribunal de police* handles violations; one magistrate is assigned to the processing of fines. There are two local judges, located in Fort-de-France and le Lamentin, who are responsible for *delits* as well as civil matters that do not exceed €4,000 (US$5,683). There is also a juvenile court, composed of one judge and two assessors located at Fort-De-France. An administrative court, a commercial court, and a *conseil des prud'hommes* are also located in Fort-de-France and handle administrative, commercial, and work-related matters. There is an appellate court and an appellate administrative court located in Fort-de-France. Finally, a criminal court, or *cour d'assises,* composed of a president (a judge) and two assessors, processes crimes. These judges are magistrates who received law school education and passed national exams. There is one assize court in each French department, including Martinique. This court meets at Fort-de-France and is held once every three months for a maximum of 15 days. Its members are highly trained magistrates who often travel from metropolitan France to hear criminal cases.

Juveniles

The French juvenile criminal system was created in February 1945. Its primary goals are the reinsertion and rehabilitation of offenders between the ages of 13 and 18 years. Juveniles are handled by a separate system including specialized judges and magistrates. Also, specific facilities were created, preventing juvenile offenders from having contacts with the general inmate population. Juveniles judged as adults can be housed in the general inmate population. Finally, each department is responsible for its juvenile system. The family court of Martinique therefore handles all cases involving juvenile offenders.

Punishment

Types of Punishment

There are numerous types of punishment in the French criminal justice system. These include fines, electronic monitoring, suspended sentences, probation, community service, reparations, postponement of sentence, incarceration, and half-imprisonment (day in the community, night in a correctional facility). Illegal immigrants can also be expelled from the French territory if they are convicted of any type of infraction. The death penalty was abolished on October 9, 1981. Corporal punishment is also illegal.

A suspension of punishment can be announced by a court after the conviction of the offender (*sursis*). This suspension may be ordered when a defendant has not been previously condemned for a criminal act and is applicable in particular circumstances (e.g., vehicular manslaughter). The suspension becomes void after five years of its application.

In the case of reoffending, the offender must accept the suspended sentence as well as his or her new penalty, which cannot be merged. The convict is placed under the control of a judge of application of punishments. There were 146,000 individuals in January 2007 whose sentences were suspended. Most of them had suspended sentences coupled with penal measures such as probation, electronic monitoring, or community service.

Typical Punishments

The typical punishment for murder is up to 30 years of imprisonment. If the murder is connected to other crimes, facilitates another crime, or targets witnesses, the sentence can be increased to life in prison without possibility of parole. Premeditated murder is punishable by life imprisonment. If a murder is committed against an individual under 15 years old or is accompanied by a sexual assault or torture, the defendant will have to serve a minimum of 30 years in prison. Also, the murder of disabled individuals and pregnant women will result in life in prison. Finally, the murder of a public official or witness in a criminal case will also be punished by up to life in prison.

Rape is punishable by up to 15 years in prison. If this offense has caused mutilation or permanent disability, the sentence will be increased to up to 20 years in prison. Also, the rape of a minor or a natural ascendant, or a rape involving the use of a weapon, will be punishable by 20 years of imprisonment. Finally, the death and/or the torture of a rape victim will lead to life imprisonment.

Larcenies are punishable by up to 3 years of imprisonment as well as a €46,000 (approx. US$65,364) in fines. Violence on the victim will increase a potential sentence to up to 5 years of prison and/or €100,000 (approx. US$14,208) in fines. Theft can also be punished by up to 7 years in prison if two aggravating circumstances such as violence on the victim and degradation of private property occur during the commission of the crime. The presence of three aggravated circumstances could lead to up to 10 years of imprisonment. Finally, the use of weapons during larcenies committed by groups can lead to a conviction up to 30 years for all offenders involved.

The most serious drug offense consists of the direction and organization of a drug trade: production, fabrication, export, transportation, offer, and sale of narcotics. This offense is punishable by life imprisonment and up to €8,000,000 (approx. US$11,366,011) in fines. The production and fabrication of drugs can lead to 20 years of imprisonment if committed alone. The fabrication and production of controlled substances by an organized group can lead to incarceration terms of up to 20 years.

Prisons

There is only one correctional facility on Martinique. It is located in the city of Ducos (15,000 inhabitants) and can board up to 490 inmates. This detention center is divided into two sections. The first building groups individuals with short sentences (40 cells) and individuals on semi-liberty, working during the day, sleeping at the facility (24 cells). The other building has 426 cells, including 152 spots for adult males and 34 spots for adult females. The facility can house 25 juveniles. The detention center can board 150 inmates, and *la maison centrale* can welcome 50 individuals.

Certain imprisonment guidelines are applied to all French correctional facilities, including the prison located at Ducos. Individuals placed on preventive detention are allowed a minimum of three visitations per week. Other inmates are allowed a minimum of one visit per week. Visitors of inmates must bring identification documents.

French inmates have numerous privileges, which include receiving mail, keeping certain personal items, watching television, and having access to sport facilities. Inmates are also allowed to work, but work is not mandatory. They can be paid up to €2.26/day (approx. US$3.21). Inmates also receive social security benefits while incarcerated (up to four years). Finally, French inmates can vote during their imprisonment.

Inmates at Ducos have access to several educational programs. A graphic communication class, a carpentry class, and a cooking class are respectively offered for 6 months to 12 inmates. A business development class lasting 10 months is also offered. Finally, the Ducos facility is equipped with a psychological and medical services center.

Extradition

The law of March 10, 1927, asserts that only non-French citizens can be extradited from any French territory. Extradition is permitted only if the individual is charged with or convicted of a crime. The accused individual must have been sentenced to two months or more of imprisonment or must be facing up to two years of imprisonment if extradited. The individual will not be extradited if he or she is French or is being extradited for political reasons. Finally, the individual cannot be extradited and then punished for a crime other than the one for which he or she has been extradited.

Anne-Laure Del Cerro

Further Reading

Bell, John, Sophie Boyron, Simon Whittaker, Andrew Bell, Mark Freedland, and Sylvia Hargreaves. (1998). *Principles of French Law.* New York: Oxford University Press.

Bellenus, Rene. (1998). *L'Esclavage en Guadeloupe et en Martinique du XVIIème au XIXème siècle.* Pointe-a-Pitre: Editions Jasor.

Kock, Gerald, and Richard S. Frase. (1988). *The French Code of Criminal Procedure.* American Series of Foreign Penal Codes 29. Littleton, CO: Fred B. Rothman.

Ministère de l'Intérieur, de l'Outre-mer et des Collectives Territoriales, France. *La Martinique:* http://www.outre-mer.gouv.fr/?presentation-martinique.html.

Préfecture Région Martinique, France. *Défense et Sécurité:* http://www.martinique.pref.gouv.fr/pages/ddsp.html.

Mexico

Legal System: Civil/Common
Murder: High
Burglary: Medium
Corruption: Medium
Human Trafficking: Medium
Prison Rate: Medium
Death Penalty: No
Corporal Punishment: Yes

Background

Vibrant indigenous cultures of the Olmecs, Mayas, Toltecs, and Aztecs existed long before the Spanish conquest by Cortes in 1519 and settlement thereafter. Like much of Latin America, Mexico spent nearly 300 years under Spanish colonial rule (and brief French occupation) and only truly gained its independence after the 1910 revolution and the ratification of the Federal Constitution on February 5, 1917. For much of the 19th century, the country's political and economic life was polarized by contentious debates between liberals and conservatives, between republicans and monarchists, and between federalists who favored state autonomy and those who supported centralized government. The Institutional Revolutionary Party (PRI) was created in 1929 to provide a platform for peaceful contests among factions representing competing interests with a long history of hostile or even violent disputes. The PRI controlled the Mexican national government and the country's politics at all levels for 71 years. This monopolistic rule ended in July 2000 when Vicente Fox Quesada of the National Action Party (PAN) defeated his PRI rival in the presidential election widely seen as the freest and fairest in Mexico's history. President Fox was succeeded by Felipe Calderon in 2007.

Mexico is the most populous Spanish-speaking country in the world and has a population of 111.2 million inhabitants. Amerindian-Spanish mestizos and Amerindians account for 60 percent and 30 percent of the population, respectively. Caucasians account for nearly 9 percent. About 76 percent of the people live in urban areas; the migration of idled labor from impoverished rural areas in southern regions and the populous central plateaus to industrialized urban centers and the areas along the U.S.-Mexico border is still ongoing. Between 14 and 40 percent of Mexicans lived in poverty in 2008, depending on the definition of poverty; yet the gross domestic product adjusted for purchasing power parity per capita reached US$14,200 in 2008, a high performance by Latin American standards. Mexico has achieved important improvements in the human development of its citizens in recent decades and attained an adult literacy rate of 91 percent and life expectancy at birth of 76.1 years in 2008.

Federal and state governments in Mexico are divided into the legislative, the executive, and the judicial branches. The president, elected by popular vote for a single six-year term, is both the chief of state and the head of government and has the exclusive authority of appointing the entire cabinet, with the exception of the attorney general whose appointment requires approval of the Senate. The National Congress is bicameral and consists of the 128-seat Senate and the 500-member Chamber of Deputies. Ninety-six of the Senate's 128 members are elected by popular vote, and the remaining 32 seats are proportionally allocated according to each party's popular vote; by the same token, 300 members of the Chamber of Deputies are directly elected by popular vote, and the rest are proportionally allocated. The Supreme Court is the highest court and is responsible for maintaining the institutional order created by the Constitution, keeping the balance of powers between government branches through its rulings, and settling serious disputes in final instances. The court has two chambers, each staffed with five justices. The First Chamber handles criminal and civil cases, and the Second Chamber has jurisdiction over administrative and labor matters. The chief justice does not sit in either chamber. All 11 Supreme Court justices are appointed by the president with the consent of the Senate. Administratively, the country is divided into 31 states and 1 federal district.

Legal System

Mexico's current legal system is mixed. It is based primarily on Spanish civil law with some French law, some Roman-Germanic tradition (codification), and some American common law influences. Most recently, there have been major adoptions of the U.S. trial procedures in parts of Mexico. It also has a small number of indigenous criminal justice systems. However, many important distinctions separate the systems. For example, unlike the United States, Mexico does not constitutionally provide jury trials, nor does it adhere to the principle of stare decisis—the doctrine that courts are bound to previous legal precedents.

Mexico's criminal justice system is plagued at all levels by inefficiency and corruption. This malady is, in large part, due to over 71 years of nearly unchallenged rule by the Revolutionary Institutional Party (PRI), during which patronage and corruption, political and otherwise, became entrenched in Mexico's government, social institutions, and society as a whole. Only recently, in 2000, did the presidency change party hands with the election of Vicente Fox Quesada of the National Action Party (PAN), who pledged numerous corruption reforms. However, he left office in 2006 with little to show for his reform efforts.

A federal republic, Mexico is composed of 31 sovereign states that control most criminal justice matters, except those specifically identified by the Federal Constitution. Each state is divided into numerous local municipalities. The Federal District is divided into 16 delegations. Each state possesses its own civil and criminal courts (sometimes called common courts); there are also federal courts and a special jurisdiction for matters involving the military. Mexico maintains an appeals process, and appellate cases are decided by a three-person superior tribunal within each state. These court jurisdictions handle the bulk of all civil and criminal cases. Substantive and procedural laws are very similar at the state and federal level. Structurally, the Supreme Court heads the federal judicial branch, which also encompasses an Electoral Court, the Federal Judicial Council, collegiate and unitary circuit courts, and district courts. As of 2006, there were 180 collegiate courts and 70 unitary courts performing appellate duties in the federal system, and 295 federal district courts served as first-instance tribunals. A total of 248,724 cases were filed and 246,703 cases disposed during the same year. Similarly organized court systems are found in each of the 31 states. Working with these federal and state courts are the Attorney General's Office, state attorney's offices, the Federal Public Defender's Office, state public defender's offices, the National Human Rights Commission, state human rights commissions, and the police.

Police

Although there are various police agencies at the local, state, and federal levels in Mexico, they generally fall into two categories: the uniformed preventive police (*policía preventiva*) and the plainclothed investigative police (*policía judicial*). The federal police consist of the Federal Agency of Investigations (AFI), which was created in 2002 to replace the notoriously corrupt Federal Judicial Police. As in most countries, crime prevention and criminal investigations largely remain local responsibilities. In addition, the national government operates a Federal Highway Patrol, which is responsible for patrolling Mexico's federal highways, the Mexican Immigration Service, and Customs Service.

There are about 400,000 sworn police officers working in approximately 3,000 separate agencies at both federal and local levels across Mexico. The Federal District of Mexico employs approximately 90,000 officers in an urban setting of approximately 25,000,000 citizens. The largest agency in Mexico City is the Protection and Transit Directorate (traffic police), with over 29,000 officers. These officers have only local jurisdiction and focus on Mexico City's high crime areas. Mexico's state and local police usually work out of a 200-person precinct, or *delegación.*

Traditionally, the preventive police perform the traditional police patrol function. They provide law enforcement visibility and perform order-maintenance functions. Generally, unless a crime is in progress, the preventive police are not expected to necessarily respond, and they are not charged with investigation. In fact, investigation of a crime, even when a preventive officer has stopped a crime in progress, is turned over to the judicial police and the Public Ministry under the command of the State Attorney General's Office (Procuraduría General). However, several states are now experimenting with police and judicial reforms to address this division between the two agencies. Depending on the jurisdiction, the judicial police may enforce both federal and local laws where no local law enforcement agency exists. In addition to the judicial police, each Public Ministry oversees its own group of investigators who work directly for the public prosecutors and the state's forensics experts.

Juvenile Justice

As a federal republic, Mexico has 32 juvenile justice legislations and systems that regulate illegal acts committed by minor children. The age of criminal responsibility in federal courts is 18, but children as young as 11 can be charged with a criminal offense, but with a rehabilitative focus. For most states, the age of criminal responsibility ranges from 16 to 17, with some childreń being charged with adult offenses between ages 10 and 11. The common thread unifying these various federal and state systems is the understanding that formally children are not capable of understanding their legal responsibilities. Consequently, the system becomes one of child welfare in which magistrates are substituted by counselors and sentences become security measures. In this paternalistic environment, processed juveniles do not have the right to legal counsel for defense, nor do they have the right to call witnesses or present evidence during the adjudication process.

A decision to free juveniles apprehended by the police or to continue adjudication must be made within 120 hours of the arrest. The juvenile process includes the investigation, initial disposition, screening and assessment, final disposition, delivery of treatment and rehabilitation services, evaluation of intervention effects, treatment conclusion, and further follow-up. Almost all teenagers mandated to juvenile facilities come from disadvantaged families. More males than females are caught and processed by the Mexican juvenile justice system, which has resulted in a serious shortage of rehabilitative resources for girls, who are sometimes in turn forced to stay in units originally designed for boys. The lack of a clear and meaningful scheme of offender classification often leads to the confinement of juveniles of varying ages and delinquent involvement in the same unit or cell. Conditions in most juvenile facilities are poor with a frequent lack of adequate space, health care services, and security, which renders the achievement of the rehabilitative goals of juvenile justice administration an elusive dream.

Crime

Classification of Crime

In Mexico, crimes are classified into serious offenses and nonserious offenses. Seriousness of crime can be determined by two alternative methods. First, it can be clearly codified in the criminal statute; second, it can also be determined by specifying a punishment beyond which a crime is considered as serious and below which a crime is deemed nonserious. For example, in Mexico City, offenses are codified as serious if they are punishable by a prison sentence of 5 years or longer.

Crime Statistics

Criminal violence is rampant across the country. The U.S.-Mexico border region, including cities such as Tijuana, Ciudad Juarez, Nuevo Laredo, Nogales, and Matamoros, is infested with brutal warfare among drug cartels and between criminal organizations and the police. Once largely limited to urban areas, particularly Mexico City, skyrocketing violent crime rates have begun to spread to Mexico's rural and resort areas where even beheadings have occurred. In the town of Juarez, just across the Rio Grande from El Paso, Texas, almost 500 women have disappeared, or their dead, mutilated bodies have been found, in the past 15 years. In its attempt to control violence, the government of Mexico has even mobilized military units to man checkpoints on highways and to conduct preventive patrols. Occasional outbursts of politically motivated violence occur from time to time in the southern states of Chiapas, Guerrero, and Oaxaca. Ordinary street-crime rates seemed to be highest in Mexico City, Tijuana, Ciudad Juarez, Nuevo Laredo, and Acapulco and the states of Sinaloa and Durango, with approximately 25 percent of all crimes occurring in the Federal District.

Accurate crime statistics for Mexico are difficult to locate because crimes may not be reported to any of several public agencies (one government estimate is that 75 percent of crimes go unreported), the decentralized organization of the police has effectively fragmented the data-collection capability of the system, and there is no standard procedure for recording, categorizing, or disseminating crime data. However, the national legislature has recently made important efforts to provide more accurate and comprehensive crime data, including overhauling the previous data-collection procedures and partnering with several public and private institutions to collect more accurate information about crime and the criminal justice system of Mexico.

According to the statistics published by the United Nations Office on Drugs and Crime, 166,397 defendants were brought before Mexico's federal and state criminal courts in 2004. Of these, 146,894 (88.3%) defendants were convicted, and the remaining 19,503 (11.7%) people were acquitted. Of all convicted offenders, 5,567 (3.8%) were for homicide; 24,395 (16.6%) were for assault; 5,570 (3.8%) for rape; 51,824 (35.3%) for robbery; 10,962 (7.5%) for drug offenses; and 3,286 (2.2%) for fraud and embezzlement. Although there were only 440 people convicted of kidnapping, accounting for just 0.3 percent of all convicted offenders, kidnapping, including the kidnapping of foreigners, remains a hallmark of the deterioration of public safety as well as a source of deep public fear. So-called express kidnappings, which consist of attempts to obtain quick cash in exchange for the release of a hostage, have taken place in almost all of Mexico's large cities and appear to be quite indiscriminate in their target selection.

Although drug abuse appears to have remained relatively low (0.8% of the adult population had used cocaine, and 0.1% had consumed heroin in 2006,

A Tijuana police officer detains a suspect as part of the "Safe Community" program in a neighborhood in east Tijuana, Mexico, July 15, 2008. (AP/Wide World Photos)

according to United Nations estimates), the amount of drugs processed and transported in or through Mexico to the United States remains high. Estimates vary, but the U.S. government estimates that Mexico supplies approximately 25 percent of all heroin used in the United States and between 50 and 80 percent of all marijuana. And due to the crackdown on Caribbean drug routes, at least half of all cocaine that enters the United States travels through Mexico: after being transported to Mexico from places such as Colombia, it is then shipped by vehicle and crosses into the United States, a process made somewhat easier by NAFTA and the additional tens of thousands of trucks that enter the United States each day. The United States and Mexico have launched numerous joint efforts to combat narco-trafficking, but substantive success has been elusive.

Besides the relatively free flow of drugs, Mexico's drug gangs have become so powerful as to control whole towns along the northern border where they operate with near immunity. Mexico's drug gangs are also known to employ "Zetas," former military commandos, trained in the School of the Americas, to protect drug shipments and eliminate competitors. The drug gangs have little or no fear of law enforcement and have even gunned down police chiefs in broad daylight.

Recent Reforms

To combat both corruption and citizen mistrust, there have been important structural reforms in Mexican law enforcement and the judicial system at the federal, state, and local levels. As mentioned earlier, in 2002, the federal government of Mexico established the Federal Agency of Investigations (AFI) to replace the infamous Federal Judicial Police (PJF). Other more general reform attempts include the creation of a national system of public safety, joint U.S.-Mexico efforts to fight organized crime, a national crusade against delinquency, and the creation of a federal secretary of pubic safety. At present, combating the drug trafficking along Mexico's northern border has become a priority, so Mexico has even shown a willingness to utilize the military in what have traditionally been civilian police operations.

In addition, starting on October 1, 2008, two states, Morelos and Chihuahua, have implemented major reforms aimed at improving street-level crime control, increasing investigative efficiency, and combating corruption. These states are to act as laboratories for what is expected to be a nationwide reorganization. Preventive policing and investigations will no longer be divided between agencies. Preventive police, like police in most of the Western world, not only will handle the patrol and order-maintenance functions, but also will participate in the investigations and any additional police matters related to any crime to which they respond.

Perhaps the most radical change in the history of Mexico's legal system is taking place in the courts—with the help of the U.S. Agency for International Development (USAID) and federal and state prosecutors' offices from different parts of the United States. The adjudication process in Morelos and Chihuahua will be transitioning from what was formally a completely written adjudicative process to an adversarial system with oral arguments and testimony based on the U.S. model. With a strong basis in the restorative justice model, this process is also expected to add a "speedy trial" element to what has been a notoriously slow process and to lead to a greater use of bail. Also, defendants will be considered "innocent until proven guilty," and cases will now be heard by a three-judge panel rather than a solo judge. The belief is that this will help combat corruption because three judges will be harder to bribe than one. Jury trials have not been incorporated because of cost concerns.

In March 2004, the federal government presented an initiative to Congress to improve the safety of the Mexican society as well as the fairness and efficiency of its criminal justice system. A series of criminal procedure changes and a new federal criminal procedure code were proposed by the administration of President Fox. The goal was to create a criminal process that would be predominantly adversarial and oral, especially in its preliminary investigations and court proceedings. These federal reform efforts stalled during the Fox presidency, but his successor, President Calderon, passed the reform legislation in 2008, which has set a timetable of eight years for full implementation.

Finding of Guilt

Rights of the Accused

The Mexican Constitution (article 20) provides both substantive and procedural protections for the accused. Defendants have the right to a speedy and public trial and to call witnesses, to inspect all evidence available for defense, and to offer exculpatory evidence. The Constitution also protects the right to face one's accuser, but with the limited exceptions of cases involving victims who are minors or the crimes of rape and kidnapping.

For a confession to be legal, the accused must be over 18 years of age and have full knowledge of the criminal charges, the confession may not be coerced, and any confession must be made before a Public Ministry official or a judge with the assistance of the defendant's attorney. In addition, a defendant must be informed of his rights at the beginning of the criminal process. Defendants have a right to counsel at each stage of the criminal proceedings, and if the defendant cannot afford an attorney, the state provides a public defender. A defendant's detention may not be extended if he or she is incapable of providing restitution to the victim, and he or she may have any pretrial detention counted as "time served" and deducted from any subsequent jail or prison sentence.

Mexico does not offer pretrial diversion programs per se, but in cases where crimes are minor, or the parties involved reach a settlement, or the victim concedes pardon for the transgression, preliminary investigations can be avoided, or the Public Ministry may settle cases when the facts are not considered sufficient to identify a crime. A case may also be dismissed if the victim withdraws the complaint. In a procedure known as "overseeing the case," the Public Ministry may encourage parties to find an extralegal solution to the dispute. This procedure is utilized in cases where evidence is limited, or the voracity of the victim's claim is suspect. No official statistics exist to measure the number of cases that are dismissed.

Criminal Procedure

Investigation of criminal activity falls exclusively under the Public Ministry and the Procuraría (also sometimes referred to as a Procurador). During the initial inquiry, a complaint or other procedural requirement is needed to initiate an investigation. The ministerial police force, often called the judicial police, responds to initial complaints, conducts initial investigations, and controls crime scenes. Although judicial police are not supposed to take suspects' depositions or make formal arrests without a judicial warrant—except in cases of crimes caught in commission—suspects are often arrested without a warrant, and judges tend to turn a blind eye to such oversights. Once in custody, the accused must appear in front of a judicial officer within 48 hours, or 96 hours if there is suspicion of drug activity. At this point, the accused are informed of their rights and the charges against them. Within 72 hours of arraignment, the magistrate must either release or remand the accused to custody. In some cases, the Public Ministry may request that a defendant be held for up to 30 days until the initial inquiry is complete and may request a subsequent 30-day extension. In drug cases, detention may be extended for up to 90 days. With few exceptions, suspects have a right to conditional/pretrial release. However, in cases where the accused has prior offenses and/or presents a danger to society, the Public Ministry may ask that release be denied. Judges are expected to weigh several factors in the decision, including seriousness of the crime, aggravating and mitigating circumstances, the defendant's prior criminal record, and his likelihood of compensating damages to the victim. Upon accepting release, defendants agree to make restitution and pay trial expenses. There are no official statistics on how often conditional release is used, but the large numbers of individuals who cannot afford bail are considered a primary cause of Mexico's overcrowded prisons.

Mexico does not have a recognized plea bargain system, and article 14 of the Mexican Constitution protects citizens' rights not to be deprived of life, liberty, or property without a court trial. However, in some cases where a defendant turns "state's witness" (e.g., organized crime) and provides substantial assistance to the government, he can receive as much as a two-thirds reduction in his sentence. In all other cases, for there to be a conviction, a trial must be completed. The entire process from trial through appeals generally takes a year or more, and many individuals are held beyond the constitutional limits to their detention.

It is the responsibility of the judge to determine proper sanctions for offenders. The judge takes into consideration a variety of circumstances to determine sanctions that include, but are not limited to, the defendant's criminal record, the seriousness of the offense committed and the level of involvement by the defendant, damage caused to victims or society, circumstances under which the violation was committed and reaction afterward, and the offender's biographics. The judge is also bound by law to follow the Mexican penal code, which stipulates mandatory minimum sentences for certain crimes. After the judge considers all these variables, a punishment or method of rehabilitation will be decided on.

Punishment

Mexican law allows for the following punishment: incarceration, community treatment, suspension of rights, suspension or termination from job, forfeiture of illegal assets, and treatment under free conditions.

Death Penalty

Prior to 2005, the death penalty was a legal sanction for serious crimes; however, it was rarely applied. These crimes include aggravated murder, arson, hostage taking, pirating, treason, and certain crimes committed by military officials. The last case of the death penalty for a civilian crime occurred in 1937. The last person executed was José Isaías Constante Laureano, in 1961. Constante was put to death by firing squad for murdering a fellow soldier and his commander. At the time the death penalty was abolished, there were eight military members on death row. Although the death penalty has been abolished by constitutional amendment, recent surges in violent crime have led some to call for its reinstatement, and at least one survey by major political parties showed public opinion at 85 percent in favor. In fact, the high rate of crime and violence due to the illegal drug trade has the Mexican legislature considering ways to reinstate capital punishment.

Prison

The criminal law provides a range of prison sentences for each crime punishable with incarceration. Sentences are usually short, in most cases not longer than seven years. The actual time that must be served is usually three-fifths of the announced sentence, assuming good behavior. Those sentenced for less than five years may buy out further time in jail by payment of a bond.

Correctional facilities are divided into prisons, at both the federal and state level, and jails. Jails house offenders prior to a trial and also those convicts serving time for less serious crimes. Mexico's prisons are a function of the executive branch in Mexico's government. Federal prisons hold offenders who have committed serious offenses. As of July 2000, there were 446 prisons in Mexico. There are three maximum-security prisons and one minimum-security prison, and the remaining facilities are considered medium-security.

The three maximum-security prisons are all similar in design. The first federal maximum-security prison was built in 1991 in Almoloya de Juarez. The second was built in 1993 in Puente Grande, and the third in 2000, located in Matamoros. The prisons at Almoloya de Juarez and Puente Grande have a capacity for over 700 inmates each. The majority of the inmates are between the ages of 30 and 34, come from low economic standing, and have minimal education. Maximum-security inmates receive education at the basic through technical levels and can receive certificates for their achievements. Almoloya has special treatment and observational facilities. Almoloya also has a separate high-security wing for solitary confinement to house more violent and dangerous inmates.

Mexico's minimum-security prison is a sharp contrast to the maximum-security prisons. There are no barbed-wire fences and very few guards. Instead, this institution is located on the Islas Marias, and the ocean serves as its boundaries. This federal penal colony opened in 1905 and has a capacity for 2,500 inmates, making it the largest correctional facility in Mexico. In this facility the inmates participate in rehabilitation services ranging from recreational activities to work. Inmates perform a variety of jobs, mainly in agriculture. The average inmate is between the ages of 35 and 39, comes from the middle economic class, has a moderate educational background, and is a first-time offender. Inmates' families are allowed to live on the island with the inmate. The facility provides training services for the families of inmates.

Mexico also has one psychological treatment facility for convicts who have a permanent or temporary mental illness. This psychosocial rehabilitation center was built in 1994 and designed to hold 48 inmates. However, in 2000, the facility was holding 176 inmates. The typical inmate in this facility is between the ages of 30 and 34, is of low socioeconomic standing, is a chronic offender, and is serving an irrevocable sentence.

The system was built to accommodate 121,635 inmates. The prison population stood at approximately 218,000 inmates in 2008. Mexico's penitentiary system is facing a serious overcrowding problem. The overcrowding of the prison system has led to increased violence, privacy issues, and a poor diet for inmates. Of the total inmates, approximately 96 percent are male. There are more than 2,000 prison guards in the system. This is not enough guards to provide adequate supervision, and as a result, guards are often the target of violence.

The prison system in Mexico aims to achieve rehabilitation. Under law, prisons must provide work, training, and education for all their inmates. Inmates can even receive wages for their work. If inmates are exceeding expectations in their duty, it can lead to a reduced sentence time. Inmates are also given the right to education. Every prison must have a library. All inmates are given education in the following areas: ethics and civics, art, physical education, and hygienic responsibilities.

In addition to receiving the opportunity to work and receive education, inmates are afforded some other rights. They are allowed guests and the option to use telephones and mail service. Guests include friends, family, authorities, chaplains, defense attorneys, and counselors. Families often bring in food to supplement the prison diet. As a result, visits are monitored to prevent the entrance of prohibited goods. More recently, inmates have been allowed conjugal visits. Wealthy inmates also have the opportunity to purchase certain comforts such as additional food, televisions, and sports equipment. It is not unheard of for a wealthy inmate to receive a rare air-conditioned cell. In many prisons, senior inmates have had considerable control over their environment and other inmates, displacing correctional authorities and creating general insecurity, leading to inmate deaths, often at the hands of other prisoners.

Mexican authorities allow independent monitoring of prison conditions by human rights organizations. The International Committee of the Red Cross (ICRC), the National Human Rights Commission (CNDH), and state human rights commissions make frequent visits to detainees. In 2008, the CNDH made 240 prison visits: 97 in response to complaints, 43 in response to requests from local civic groups, and 100 in conjunction with the National Mechanism to Prevent Torture. Also, the CNDH opened 357 complaint cases following allegations of abuses of prison inmates, ultimately confirming 126 of the complaints.

Extradition of Prison Inmates

Prisoners are allowed to be transferred both to and from other countries. Mexico has entered into extradition treaties with the following countries: Argentina, Australia, Belize, Brazil, Canada, Chile, Colombia, Cuba, Dominican Republic, Ecuador, El Salvador, England, France, Greece, Guatemala, Honduras, Italy, Korea, the Netherlands, Nicaragua, Panama, Peru, Portugal, Spain, the United States, Uruguay, and Venezuela. As of 2001, there have been 223 prisoner transfers completed. One hundred twenty-seven of those transfers were Mexicans transferred from foreign countries. Fifty-four of those transfers were foreigners transferred back to their home countries.

Juvenile Corrections

In 1985, Mexico agreed to the United Nations Standard Minimum Rules for the Administration of Juvenile Justice, better known as the Beijing Rules. These broad guidelines outline substantive social policy dedicated to promoting juvenile welfare and minimizing formal, state intervention. The hope is to avoid the harm often associated with the formal processing and punishment of juvenile offenders. Anyone between the ages of 11 and 18 is defined as a youth and falls under specific guidelines of the Act for the Treatment of Minor Violators in the Federal District on Common Matters and for the Entire Republic in Federal Matters. This law was passed by Mexico's Congress in 1991 and was designed to provide a more therapeutic approach to the rehabilitation by placing the juvenile offenders in a more administrative rather than legal process and stressing education, counseling, and job training. Success has been, at best, limited, and as late as 2005, juvenile offenders were still being placed in adult prisons. Remarkably, the Mexican legislature took the drastic step of changing the Constitution to remove the juvenile process from the executive to the judicial branch and required various due process guarantees and mandatory treatment.

Anthony LaRose and Erin Maloney

Further Reading

The Advocates. (n.d.). "Mexico: General Information": http://www.mnadvocates.org/Mexico.html.

Jucios Orales: Por una Justicia Rápida y Transparente. (2008): http://www.forojuiciosorales.com/.

Morris, Stephen D. (1999). "Corruption and the Mexican Political System: Continuity and Change." *Third World Quarterly* 20(3): 623–643.

Programa de Apoyo Para el Estado de México: http://www.proderecho.com/.

Reames, Benjamin. (2008). "Paths to Fairness, Effectiveness, and Democratic Policing in Mexico." In *Comparative Policing the Struggle for Democratization,* edited by M.R. Haverfield and Ibrahim Cerrah, pp. 97–119. Thousand Oaks, CA: Sage Publications.

Montserrat

Legal System: Common
Murder: Low
Prison: Low
Death Penalty: No

Background

Montserrat is one of the Leeward Islands in the Eastern Caribbean, lying 27 miles southwest of Antigua and 40 miles northwest of Guadeloupe. The island's area of 102 square kilometers (39 square miles) is entirely volcanic and very mountainous. Named after a monastery in Spain by Christopher Columbus in 1493, the island became a British colony in 1632. Africans were brought into Montserrat by the mid-1600s as part of the trans-Atlantic slave trade. After a couple of short occupations by the French during the 17th century, it has been a British territory since 1783.

Montserrat was a small but thriving open economy before its most recent series of volcanic eruptions beginning in 1995. The volcano destroyed approximately two-thirds of the island, including the capital of Plymouth and the W. H. Bramble Airport. The population has also changed significantly. The two years of 2006 and 2007 show negative net migration figures of –379 and –177, respectively. The country is now totally reliant on aid from the United Kingdom.

The chronic nature of the volcanic disaster and the challenges of building the new society created in its wake have generated a fragile socioeconomic climate and have affected every facet of life on this island, including the justice system. The system was plagued by the movement of the court seven times in three years. There have been challenges in securing records and gaps in personnel because of the migration of legal professionals and sometimes witnesses, which has led to serious delays in the hearing of cases.

Political Context

The country is an internally self-governing overseas territory of the United Kingdom. The government consists of a governor appointed by the Crown, an Executive Council that has the general control and direction of government, and a Legislative Council of 11 seats. Nine members are popularly elected, and the attorney general and financial secretary are ex-officio. The governor retains responsibility for internal security (including police), external affairs, defense, public service, and offshore finance.

The government is formed from the political party with the largest number of elected members and led by a chief minister. Voting "at large" was introduced in 1996 when the volcanic eruption destroyed the majority of constituencies. In December 1989, Montserrat's Constitution was consolidated into one document and came into force on February 13, 1990. A constitutional review process began in 1999 and is still continuing with a timetable of completion by 2010. The current review of the Constitution grapples with contentions about the definition of "Montserratian." This is a sensitive matter given the dramatic dispersal of the population and the open-door policy of migration from CARICOM countries.

The CARICOM is an organization of 15 independent Caribbean nations and 5 associated dependent territories. Montserrat is a full CARICOM member although it is still a dependent territory. CARICOM's main purpose is to promote economic integration and cooperation among its members. It also devises and institutes special projects for the less-developed countries within its jurisdiction. It operates as a regional common market for many of its members. It also operates the Caribbean Court of Justice (CCJ), which serves as the final court of appeal for many CARICOM members and also handles regional trade disputes.

Montserrat issued an invitation to citizens of CARICOM to come to the island to help with its rebuilding after the 1995 volcanic eruption. However, the arrival into Montserrat of fairly large numbers of migrants from other Caribbean countries is new and has interesting implications for the way life is lived on the island, given that the pre-volcanic population operated as close knit, family-centered village enclaves. The post-eruption displacement of Montserratians who remained on the island from these traditional village communities into shelters and hastily constructed temporary housing adds to the intrigue about social interactions in the "new" Montserrat. There are also a small number of Montserratians returning from voluntary evacuation to the United Kingdom, and criminal deportees from the United States are being returned to the island.

Socioeconomic Context

Only the northern section of the island is now inhabited. The government functions from Brades, which is in the Carr's Bay/Little Bay vicinity on the northwest side of Montserrat. There are projections of possible renewed fortune from geothermal energy and the construction of a new town as replacement for the devastated commercial center. The island's sustainable development plan of 2007 suggested significant emphasis on ecotourism as a source of economic renewal. Development of the agricultural sector is also viewed as a key source of income, although it will be difficult because of the lack of suitable land for farming and the vulnerability of crops to volcanic emission of gas and ash falls. The economic growth rate for the three years from 2004 to 2006 was 5.82, 4.36, and 7.56 percent, respectively. Montserrat currency is the Eastern Caribbean dollar, and its per capita income for 2006 was EC$22,803 (approx. US$8,737).

Housing is a major difficulty for people living in Montserrat, although there has been an intense commitment to the rebuilding of housing since the destruction of the vast majority of homes by the volcanic eruption. Pre-volcano housing was primarily privately owned and substantially built through self-help labor, but in the current situation, many people are renting accommodations that are perceived to be expensive. Notwithstanding, the government of Montserrat has been encouraging residents to purchase their homes through grants, loans, and other solutions. Some housing solutions involve settlements in typical social housing projects without adequate spaces for children and young people to play or for adult entertainment. Typically, the bulk of the migrant population lives on the margins of safety in proximity to the volcano, where housing is cheapest.

The provision of social services in Montserrat is fairly modern given the economic limitations of the island. Education is free up to secondary school, and so are health services for children, vulnerable groups, and those over 60. There is a modest social welfare provision, which has been extended to a larger number of vulnerable people since the chronic volcanic situation. The government of Montserrat found it necessary to make this provision because a scarcity of land and housing without traditional vegetable garden space forced those who were reliant on subsistence agriculture to become dependent on welfare support.

Those who are employed are also enduring hardships because many are burdened with paying rent for their current housing as well as paying a mortgage for properties that were abandoned in the areas affected by the volcano. Migrants to the island are believed to be in similar situations of socioeconomic distress because of low earnings in Montserrat, high living costs, and commitments to repatriate funds to family left in their countries of origin.

Social welfare and community services are administered by a department within the Ministry of Health and Community Services, which all members of the community can access when in dire need. This department deals with juveniles, who are defined as children 10 to 16, with 10 being the age of criminal responsibility. The Community Services Department is also the base for the one probation office providing services in Montserrat.

Policing

The Royal Montserrat Police Service is led by a commissioner who is responsible to the governor. The service has 77 members who have been recruited from a variety of countries within CARICOM, about 10 percent of whom are women. There are nine divisions within the service: general office and administration, training, immigration, marine, beat and patrol, traffic, family center, criminal investigation, and the Salem police station, which is a generic police station outpost. Community policing is the key approach of the Montserrat police force and has been found appropriate for the small, close-knit society.

Crime

Crime Classification

Montserrat's criminal justice system emulates the English system where the nature and seriousness of the offense are the most significant factors taken into consideration in criminal matters. All offenses are classified as triable only on indictments in the High Court, triable only summarily in the Magistrate Court, or triable either way. The decision on where (Magistrate or High Court) and how (summarily or indictment) depends on the nature or circumstances and the seriousness of the charge and whether the defendant pleads not guilty. Not-guilty pleas in most cases imply that the case needs to be proven and as such requires a court trial.

Offenses are also classified by statute or legislation. Summary offenses are comparatively less serious crimes, such as motoring offenses and common assaults. All summary offenses are made by statute. Offenses triable only on indictments are very serious matters that include murder, rape, robbery, and wounding with intent. Some offenses can be triable-either-way and they include burglary, assault, and occasioning actual bodily harm and can include theft depending on whether the value of the item stolen is over EC$2,000 (approx. US$766).

Crime Statistics

According to the British Foreign and Commonwealth Office, Montserrat has a low level of crime. Statistics available from the commissioner of the Royal Montserrat Police indicate that in general, crime levels are rising. All crimes including minor offenses rose from 1,088 in 2006 to 1,317 in 2007. This is a sharp rise given a relatively small population. Minor offenses including larceny, criminal damage other than arson, and nonpayment of fines and licenses make up more than 55 percent of the total crimes of the island. Serious crimes account for the other 45 percent. Assaults and domestic violence are among the most frequent crimes. Some examples of the numbers of crimes reported to police in 2007 are as follows:

Assault	136
Burglaries	70
Dangerous drugs	39
Domestic violence	160
Grievous bodily harm	6
Murder	0
Rape and sexual offenses	2
Theft	35
Wounding	5

Laws protecting minors exist, but there is likely underreporting of offenses against minors. In particular, anecdotal evidence suggests that there is underreporting of sexual offenses involving young people. In some instances where reports have been made to the police by social agencies and where there have been investigations, these cases have come to naught because of the failure of parents to cooperate. Parents and their families sometimes claim that investigations and court hearings exacerbate the victimization for their child in such a small society. There are also claims in the popular media (Calypso) that there have been instances where parents make up the case or settle the situation in their own way, sometimes accepting money payoffs, particularly where the perpetrator is rich and powerful.

Finding of Guilt

Criminal Investigations

The police investigate all criminal matters in Montserrat. At the moment, there is no fraud squad, no financial crime task force, no special branch or drug squad as found in other territories of a similar size. The police may seek the assistance of the Community Services Department (social services) when dealing with juveniles or domestic violence.

Prosecutions are undertaken by a senior police officer, and the decision to prosecute is made by the police and endorsed by the magistrate. The Attorney General's Office prosecutes serious summary matters in the Magistrate Court and all indictable matters in the Supreme Court.

The Montserrat prosecution process was outlined by a superintendent of police in an interview. The Montserrat Constitution establishes that a person is deemed innocent until proven guilty before the courts. It is the duty of the prosecutor to prove his or her case in a criminal matter.

On arrest, a person is given a copy of the charge(s) and informed of his or her rights to consult with a lawyer in private, to three meals a day, to writing materials, and so forth. Once charged, the individual is fingerprinted and photographed, and a description is taken as well as confirmation of the individual's parents' names or next of kin and nationality. After being processed by the police, the individual is taken before the Magistrate Court as soon as possible. The individual may also be granted police bail. A superintendent or a senior officer above that rank is allowed to grant bail with surety for that individual to appear at court at the next working day.

On appearing before the magistrate, the charge is put to the individual, and he or she is asked to plea based on the nature of the offense. If the offense is summary, and the person pleas, then it is fixed by the magistrate. If the offense is indictable, then the person is not called on to plea because this is a matter for the High Court. The prosecutor, who is a police officer, states whether he or she supports or objects to the granting of bail, and the magistrate makes the decision. The magistrate also states the sum of the bail and whether the individual needs sureties.

When an individual is taken before the courts in a summary matter, and the individual pleads not guilty, there is a trial in which the prosecutor presents its case by calling witnesses. On the closing of the prosecution's case, the magistrate informs the defendant of three options. The defendant may be remanded in the dock and say nothing, may take the stand and give sworn evidence, or may remain in the dock and give unsworn evidence. If the defendant is represented by counsel, at his or her own expense, the counsel lets the magistrate know which option will be taken. These options are also put to the individual even if he or she is unrepresented.

If the defendant chooses to give unsworn evidence, then he or she testifies without cross-examination. If the individual gives sworn evidence, then he or she is cross-examined by the prosecutor. If the defendant chooses to say nothing, then no questions can be asked. The defense is also allowed to present its case, if it has any witnesses.

On completion, the prosecutor and the counsel address the magistrate about the case, and in the end, the magistrate makes a decision as to whether the person is guilty or not. When the individual is found guilty, the magistrate determines the sentence based on the specification of the offense and the punishment as stated by statute or discretion. If fined, then the person may have to pay the money forthwith or may be given a period of time, depending on the amount of money. If the individual is being incarcerated, he or she is taken to Her Majesty's Prison.

The magistrate may also discharge the offender without punishment. When the court thinks that the charge is proven, but believes, after considering the character, antecedents, age, health, or mental condition of the accused, or the trivial nature of the offense, or the extenuating circumstances in which the offense was committed, it is not expedient to inflict any punishment, the court may, without proceeding to conviction, make an order dismissing the charge.

Courts

Montserrat's legal system is based on the British legal system (English common law), with criminal cases being heard by the assizes and civil cases being heard by the High Court. The system is administered by the Eastern Caribbean Supreme Court, the Court of Summary Jurisdiction, and the Magistrate Court. In both criminal and civil cases, there is the right of appeal to the Court of Appeal with the ultimate right of appeal to the Privy Council in England.

The Supreme Court Montserrat Circuit is a court of assizes and is part of the Eastern Caribbean Supreme Court (ECSC). The ECSC consists of 10 other Caribbean countries, and the judge assigned to Montserrat visits for criminal matters three times a year (March, July, and November). There is a backlog in criminal cases (some serious) because the judge sits for an average of only two weeks in each assizes.

There is one magistrate on the island appointed by the governor to exercise the jurisdiction of the Magistrate Court after consultation with the chief justice. The magistrate is a trained lawyer. This court deals with all summary matters, all preliminary inquiries, and a number of civil, family, labor, license, and coroner matters.

In Montserrat, there is no right to trial by jury in the Constitution. However, a jury system is part of the democratic process, and the jury is made up of a group of 12 Montserratians who are aged 21 to 65, who either own or have land in trust, and who earn at least EC$2,000 (approx. US$762) per annum. The latter is the absolute minimum earned even by those receiving social assistance. The only exceptions are people with criminal convictions.

Juvenile Court

The age of criminal responsibility is 10 years, and the definition of "juvenile" is given to children 10 to 16 years old. Children who are charged with adults, despite the availability of a Juvenile Court, appear in the High Court and are tried with adults. The Juvenile Court happens as often as there are cases. Two juvenile assessors (male and female) are appointed by the government for two years at a time. Assessors are chosen because they have a background in working with children and belong to the Christian Council, an association of various religious denominations dedicated to ecumenism and social justice. There must be one assessor sitting with the magistrate for a decision to be made on a case.

There is no provision in the law for sentencing juveniles, and there is no institution for juvenile offenders. The court ensures the involvement of a social worker and seeks a behavioral report from the school. The emphasis is on guidance. Assessors speak to the juvenile in private. The majority of juveniles are secondary school pupils and males. Assessors may also recommend the enforcement of curfews or that the child be supervised by a probation officer.

There is an alternative system to court proceedings called a community settlement, which the police administer. It may involve parents, sometimes opting through the court to replace stolen items or pay for medical attention where there has been wounding. The emphasis here is to prevent the child from having a criminal record. The child does not have a voice in the process.

There has been mounting concern in recent years about what should be done with repeat offenders. Sometimes they do not show up to court. It is assumed that the court does not exercise sufficient authority in relation to juveniles because of the absence of laws for sentencing. Assessors have observed that offenses are committed in the early mornings or at night (1–2:00 A.M.) when children should be under parental supervision; therefore, questions have been posed about the quantity and quality of parental supervision.

Rights of the Individual

The criminal justice process as laid out in the Montserrat Constitution establishes that a person is deemed innocent until proven guilty before the courts. It is the duty of the prosecution to prove its case in a criminal matter as laid down in the Criminal Procedure Code, Revised Edition, shown as law as of January 1, 2002.

An individual is entitled to request bail. The amount of bail in any case is to be decided by the court, and any court may, in its discretion, accept a deposit of cash in lieu of giving security. When any person is apprehended without warrant between eight o'clock in the evening and five o'clock in the morning, such person is taken to a police station, and it is lawful for the police officer in charge to take bail by recognizance, with security, for the appearance of such person before the magistrate on a day to be mentioned in such recognizance to be dealt with according to law.

Bail is not granted in cases of capital felony, accusation of treason, murder, or genocide, or in any charge of an offense punishable by life imprisonment. Bail may be refused in cases where the court is satisfied that there are substantial grounds for believing that the defendant, if released on bail, would fail to surrender to custody, commit an offense while on bail, or interfere with witnesses or otherwise obstruct the course of justice. Bail may also be refused if the offense is an indictable one, if it appears to the court that the person was on bail in criminal proceedings on the date of the offense, if the court is satisfied that the defendant should be kept in custody for his or her own protection, if a child or young person should be protected, or if it appears to the court that it could be impracticable to complete the inquiries without keeping the defendant in custody.

Punishment

Types of Punishment

The following kinds of punishment may be imposed by a court on persons convicted of offenses: imprisonment, fine, payment of compensation to injured party, finding security to keep the peace and be of good behavior or to come up for judgment, probation under the Probation of Offenders Act, and any other punishment expressly provided by law.

A magistrate can impose a custodial sentence of only up to two years, except where a person is charged with drug trafficking and elects to have his or her case tried by the magistrate, who can then impose a maximum sentence of 10 years' imprisonment.

Fines and imprisonment are the most common form of punishment in Montserrat. Capital punishment was last given in 1969 but was removed from the statutes in 1989. The last person sentenced to death was in 1985, and this sentence was later commuted to life in prison.

Legislation

Both the Prison Act 1952 and the Prisons Ordinance Regulations make provision for all persons who are serving a sentence of 30 days or more to be granted automatic remission of one-third of their sentence on account of good conduct and industry. In addition, there are five other pieces of legislation that affect and inform punishment in Montserrat. The first is Penal Code No. 12 of 1983, which provides for seven noncustodial sentences: fines, forfeiture, compensation, costs, bind-over, conditional discharge, and absolute discharge. A bind-over is a court order imposed by either a magistrate or a judge that requires a person to carry out some act. A person may be bound over to appear in court at a particular time if bail has been granted or, most commonly, be bound over not to commit some offense (for example, causing a breach of the peace).

The second legislation is the Probation of Offenders Act, which empowers the court to impose probation orders up to a maximum of three years. In addition to placing the offender under supervision, the court may attach to the order any condition that the court regards as necessary to prevent the commission of further offenses. The power to impose a probation order exists whether or not a conviction has actually been recorded against the offender. Should the offender breach any condition of the order, then the court has the ultimate power to revoke the order and sentence afresh.

The third statute, Juveniles Ordinance No. 20 of 1982, provides for sanctions such as a probation order, a care order, committing the juvenile into the care of any fit person, and a parental responsibility order, which puts the onus for ensuring that the young person obeys the law on the adult parent(s).

The fourth legislation, the Community Service Orders Act 1994, enables the court to order an offender to perform community service. The maximum number of hours that the court can order is determined on the basis of 32 hours in the month. Whether the order is made by the High Court or the Magistrate Court, the supervising court is the Magistrate Court. If the order is breached, the offender can be sentenced afresh. Under the Community Service Orders Regulation No. 50 of 1996, the community development officer is assigned the responsibility of soliciting from the head of each government department, charitable organization, or nongovernmental organization (NGO) a description of the work that they need to be done and that could suitably be performed under a community service order.

Finally, the most recent legislation, the Parole Bill, was enacted in 2004. Prisoners can apply for parole when they have served one-year imprisonment or one-third of their sentence, whichever is more. The parole board hears applications for parole and makes recommendations to the superintendent of prisons. Persons serving a sentence of life imprisonment can apply for parole when they have served 15 years or more.

Noncustodial Penalties

The introduction and broadening of the parameters of noncustodial punishment in Montserrat is not only recent, but the debates are at present most topical in the current jurisprudence. The only judge and the single magistrate on the island have registered their concern that the means to supervise and enforce community orders (as alternatives to custodial sentences) were unavailable and inadequately resourced. The lack of a probation officer specifically dedicated to working with offenders was seen as a very real disadvantage to an "alternatives to custody" approach to sentencing.

In response to these concerns by the court, the Community Development/Social Services Department confirmed that contact is maintained on a regular basis with potential work providers from within both the private and the public sector. Where community service orders have been made, the overwhelming majority were successfully completed. However, supervision by the Community Development Department in terms of counseling offenders and preparing reports for court hearings placed a real strain on the department's resources. The department stated that it did not have the personnel to dedicate any one person to that type of work.

Prison

During the years of the most recent volcanic crisis (2003–2006), there was not a conventional prison service, and those sentenced to terms in excess of 12 months were accommodated in prisons in other Caribbean countries, namely the British Virgin Islands (BVI) and the Turks and Caicos Islands (TCI). There are 21 people presently imprisoned either on remand or serving sentences of imprisonment on the island. Seven are still serving those sentences in the TCI and two in the BVI. Those prisoners are serving long sentences.

The new prison on the island was constructed in 2004 and is presently furnished to accommodate 52 inmates, 32 general males, 10 high-security males, 8 females, and 2 young offenders. It is the only penal institution in Montserrat. The current prison population is 13 persons, all male adults, of whom 7 are serving long-term sentences of five or more years. The average prison population has been 13 in recent years. Between 2006 and 2008, 14 persons were sent to prison, of which 11 were Montserratians, 2 Guyanese, and 1 Dominican.

As of July 2008, the prison housed 11 convicted prisoners and 2 remanded inmates for a variety of criminal offenses. Age differentiation in the prison population shows that prisoners are mainly between 17 and 45 years. One juvenile was convicted of attempted murder in 2008, but due to a lack of a law for the sentencing of juvenile offenders and a facility to house them, a noncustodial sentence was imposed that included curfew and community supervision.

Women in prison are a rarity in Montserrat society. As of 2009, it has been reported that within the last two years, there were five women charged with serious offenses who have spent short periods in prison on remand; one female was charged with murder was convicted of manslaughter; one was charged with attempted murder, but has not gone before the court as of this writing; another was charged with trafficking of cannabis on two occasions in the two years prior to 2009 and has spent brief periods in prison; another woman was charged with forgery and theft; another was charged with handling stolen goods; and, finally, another was charged with criminal damage.

There is no special place for mentally ill persons. If they violate the criminal law, they are sent to prison under "Queen's Pleasure." There are two such prisoners presently in prison who have already served 12 years.

Prison Programs

The Montserrat prison has no professionally run programs, for example, dealing with substance abuse or anger management, although the government employs a psychologist who provides counseling to at least one prisoner. The superintendent of prisons expressed that he is conscious that the lack of professionally led programs is undesirable and indicated in his view that a probation officer, who could assist professionally with the rehabilitation of prisoners in preparation for their release back into the community, is a priority.

There is no facility for testing for drugs in Montserrat, either within the prison itself or as part of any community order. Abuse of Class A drugs is not presently seen as problem in Montserrat. Use of controlled drugs seems to be limited to cannabis.

At Her Majesty's Prison Montserrat, the general rule is that all inmates must be engaged in some form of work. This can include woodwork and craftmaking, agriculture, gardening, and block-making. Community work is also available to meet the requests from other government departments, needy agencies, and individuals in the community who need assistance of varying kind. Prisoners are allowed to undertake work release programs. This involves an inmate being allowed out of the prison to engage in paid work with a view to earning a small income and to enhance skill development. The terms and conditions of this program of employment vary based on the skills and abilities of the inmates concerned.

Educational programs are run in the prison for inmates based on the assessed needs at the time. There is a great demand for educational programs because more than half of the inmate population is illiterate. Interested inmates are assessed, and specific programs are designed for them. This program relies totally on the goodwill of volunteers.

Prisoners' religious needs are met by two prison chaplains who conduct religious counseling in the prison and coordinate the religious activities in the prison. Before the volcanic crisis, a number of religious representatives would visit the prison and conduct religious counseling and services on a regular basis. The numbers have dwindled, and presently, there are two organizations that attend the prison to conduct counseling and religious services. They are the Adventist Church prison ministries group, who visit every Saturday afternoon, and the Men's' Fellowship of the Brade's Pentecostal Church, who visit on Sunday afternoons. They both conduct services and Bible discussions with inmates.

Prisoners receive medical treatment on a regular basis. When an inmate is admitted to prison, he or she undergoes a medical check by a medical officer, and a medical file is created on that inmate. In case of an emergency, the inmate would be taken to the casualty department of the single hospital on the island. Prisoners are escorted to see a doctor at either of the two local clinics (Cudjoe Head Clinic or John's Clinic). Inmates can make a request to see their own private doctor at their expense.

Incentives are used to reward and encourage inmates who work well and conform to the prison rules and regulations. The awarding of incentives is determined by the resources available, the deed that is done, the security category of the inmate, and the needs of the inmate. Some incentives that are employed allow prisoners to undertake and to receive payment for work (payments are made in keeping with prison procedures) and to receive extra letters from relatives.

Visits to the prison are regulated under the Prison Act 2002, which provides first for the maintenance and closing of prisons and second for the confinement and treatment of prisoners. It also makes provision for a Prison Visiting Committee, constituted by the governor and consisting of justices of the peace in Montserrat and six other members of the local community. Appointments, duration, and manner of conduct and organization of this committee are all prescribed by the rules. For example, members are required to pay frequent visits to the prison and hear any complaints that may be made by the prisoners; to consider periodically the character, conduct, and prospects of each prisoner; and to report to the governor any matter that they consider expedient to report. Any member of the Visiting Committee may at any time enter the prison and have free access to every part of it and to every prisoner.

Lystra Hagley-Dickinson

Further Reading

Allen, K. (2007). "Access to Justice." An address delivered by Kenneth Allen QC to a Prison Visitors Conference for the British Overseas Territories, Brades, Montserrat, May 8.

Barnes, V. C. (2001, June). "The Montserrat Volcanic Disaster: A Gender Analysis of Psychosocial Effects and Coping." *Journal of Eastern Caribbean Studies* 26(2): 33–53.

British Foreign and Commonwealth Office: http://www.fco.gov.uk.

Saunders, A. (2005). "The Administration of Justice in Montserrat and the Impact of the Volcanic Activity." A public lecture delivered at Brades, Montserrat, Caribbean, at the invitation of the Montserrat Police Service during the annual Police Week Activities by the Honorable Mr. Justice Adrian Saunders, Judge of the Eastern Caribbean Court of Justice, November 3.

Sullivan, Oris. (2007). "Prisoner Rights." Presented at the Prison Visitors Conference for the British Overseas Territories, Brades, Montserrat.

*The author acknowledges with thanks the major contribution of Dr. Clarice Barnes, who was instrumental in undertaking the local research and interviewing key local authorities for this essay.

Navajo Nation

Legal System: Customary/Common
Murder: High
Death Penalty: Yes

Background

With 180,462 residents in the 2000 census, the Navajo Nation is the largest Native American tribe in the United States. The reservation covers 27,000 square miles in the states of Arizona, New Mexico, and Utah. The Navajo Nation is akin to a federalist state or country. Though it is technically a "domestic dependent nation" of the United States, the tribe still maintains its sovereignty and has its own elected government officials who enact and execute tribal laws and policies. The Navajo Nation does not have a constitution, but it has a comprehensive Tribal Code that spans six printed volumes.

The Navajo Nation has a three-branch government system. The executive branch is headed by a president and vice president, who are elected by popular vote and serve four-year terms. Since 1990, the legislative branch has been headed by the speaker of the Navajo Nation Council, who is chosen by the members of the Navajo Nation Council and who serves a two-year term. The current Navajo Nation Council consists of 88 delegates who are elected to four-year terms by registered Navajo voters. The Navajo Nation is divided into 110 chapters, or local levels of government similar in some respects to states or counties. Navajo Nation Council delegate representation is proportional to voting district population in the chapters.

In addition to council delegate representation, the residents of each chapter also elect chapter officials, including a president, vice president, and secretary/treasurer, who work in cooperation with their council delegates. These chapter officials oversee local policy. Certified chapters enjoy a fair amount of autonomy and may enter into agreements with other chapters, the mainstream Navajo Nation government, the U.S. federal government, or individual counties or states. The chapter officials execute leases and sales of property, control land use, and may decide whether their chapter will collect taxes.

Courts

The Navajo Nation judiciary consists of a Supreme Court with three full-time justices, district courts, family courts, and peacemaker courts/program in each of 10 judicial districts, two of which were just recently added. Because the judiciary is "required to incorporate traditional teachings" into their rulings, all judges must speak Navajo and English in addition to understanding Navajo culture, the Navajo clan system, and Navajo religion. Though bound by the confines of U.S. federal law, Navajo courts rely on tribal precedent and decisions from other jurisdictions in arriving at rulings. The judicial system may be classified as a common law model adapted to customary Navajo law.

The Navajo Nation Supreme Court hears appeals from the district and family courts. The Supreme Court is the tribe's highest judicial authority for both criminal and civil cases. The court relies on tribal and federal precedent as well as *Diné Bi Beenahaz'áanii,* a body of law composed of Navajo traditional, customary, natural, and common law ideas. Justices on the Navajo Nation Supreme Court are not required to have law degrees, and historically, at least one of the three members has lacked a formal legal education. The current Supreme Court consists of two women (Louise Grant and Eleanor Shirley) and Chief Justice Herb Yazzie.

The courts of general jurisdiction are the district and family courts. As would be expected, the family courts hear cases related to domestic relations and children. The district courts hear criminal and civil cases. At first deceptively simple, criminal and civil

Attorney Donovan D. Brown, senior acting chief prosecutor for the Navajo Nation, right, organizes his notes before a special session of the Navajo Nation Supreme Court, held at Harvard University in Cambridge, Massachusetts, to decide if the Navajo Nation has jurisdiction over Sioux activist Russell Means, February 6, 1999. Means, who lived on Navajo land for 10 years, claims the Navajo Nation court has no jurisdiction to prosecute him for allegedly beating his father-in-law in 1997 in Arizona's Navajo Nation. (AP Photo/William B. Plowman)

jurisdiction in the Navajo Nation is rather complex because it is intensely regulated by U.S. federal law. Jurisdiction depends on the type of crime and status of both alleged offender and victim.

A third court system could be appropriately termed a court of voluntary jurisdiction. The peacemaker courts/program is a court-annexed restorative justice program that has attracted a lot of international interest over the past decade because it is considered both a forerunner and frontrunner in the restorative justice movement.

Policing

The Bureau of Indian Affairs (BIA) is a federal agency founded in 1824 to manage the lands held in trust by tribes and to oversee the education of Native Americans. The agency is an important one that dominates relations between the U.S. federal government and individual tribes across the country. Much of tribal justice, from police to courts to corrections, is overseen and/or funded by the BIA, making that agency one of the most important federal agencies when discussing crime and punishment on reservations. The BIA coordinates a tribal police academy and a judicial training program in addition to working to improve tribal corrections systems and detention facilities.

In addition to services provided by U.S. federal law enforcement officers, especially the officers with the BIA, law enforcement is provided by two tribal agencies: the Navajo Department of Public Safety (NDPS) and the Navajo Law Enforcement Rangers. In existence since 1872 in some fashion or the other, the Navajo police were at first annexed to the U.S. military, which provided the first official legal oversight for the Navajo Nation. In traditional times, police services were provided by local headmen or elders, who worked as peacemakers with victims and offenders to fashion restorative responses to crimes that satisfied both victims and society.

The Navajo Department of Public Safety is the primary law enforcement agency serving the reservation. Controlled by the BIA until 1959, NDPS operates in seven districts and is headquartered in the tribal capital, Window Rock, Arizona. Their primary responsibilities include investigation of crimes and general protection of the public. They engage in preventive patrols but seldom foray into what is termed "the backcountry" (i.e., the woodlands and plains areas of the Navajo Nation), performing most of their work in the many communities that dot the reservation. NDPS has a number of units/teams, including patrol, traffic, K-9, tactical operations, dive team, internal affairs, and recruitment/training. NDPS is the largest tribal police agency in the United States.

According to the U.S. Department of Justice, in 2000, there were 321 full-time sworn officers or an average of 2 per 1,000 residents and 1 per 100 square miles. In 2006, there were 54 criminal investigators associated with the NDPS's Criminal Investigations Department. Like many other tribal police agencies, NDPS operates under a 638 contract (named for Public Law 93-638), meaning the tribe receives funding from the BIA to operate its police force, but it is controlled by the tribe itself. Funds from the 638 contract are supplemented by grant monies and some funding from the tribe.

The second Navajo law enforcement agency is the Navajo Rangers, part of the Navajo Nation Department of Resource Enforcement. The Rangers' duties include enforcement of Navajo environmental laws; search and rescue; livestock inspection; settlement of livestock disputes; investigation of livestock thefts; and protection of archeological and paleontological sites, cultural artifacts, and minerals (e.g., oil and gas), including patrol of the backcountry to prevent depredation of those areas. The Rangers have the responsibility of investigating natural resource crimes and enforcing federal statutes that apply to the environment, forest, and fish and game regulation. The Rangers are the only tribal policing agency authorized to perform cultural law-enforcement duties (i.e., protection of cultural items such as traditional medicine bundles and cultural areas such as burial sites). The Rangers also serve as supplemental officers, augmenting the general crime fighting efforts of NDPS. In 2007, there were 26 Rangers divided into three districts. Their headquarters are in Window Rock, Arizona, which is a short distance from the NDPS headquarters. The Rangers are funded by the tribal government. They have also been successful in obtaining competitive federal grants to enhance their provision of law enforcement services.

In addition to the two tribally operated agencies, the Navajo Nation benefits from the law enforcement provided by the Federal Bureau of Investigation (FBI) and the Bureau of Indian Affairs. Both of these federal agencies investigate crimes and enforce the law on the Navajo reservation. They have jurisdiction over federal crimes and any cases that are not under tribal jurisdiction because of the type of crime or status of the victim or offender, as discussed in the following section.

Crime

Classification of Crimes

Given its status as a domestic dependent nation, the Navajo Nation uses the same legal classification for offenses as does the United States. Misdemeanors are those crimes for which an offender can be sentenced to a maximum of one year or less in jail. Felonies are more serious offenses and can result in longer terms of incarceration and other serious sanctions, including the death penalty. Full criminal responsibility attaches at age 18.

The Navajo Nation, like other tribal governments in the United States, is in a unique position with reference to jurisdiction over crime. The Major Crimes Act has transferred jurisdiction over serious felonies from tribes to the federal government since its passage in 1885. In 1968, the Indian Civil Rights Act (ICRA) was enacted by Congress to transfer important guarantees of the Bill of Rights to criminal justice processes in tribal courts. It also states that tribal governments cannot impose sentences more severe than one year in jail and/or a fine of $5,000. That constraint essentially means that tribes are limited to adjudicating misdemeanors. The situation is complicated further if the federal government declines to prosecute a case, leaving such actions to the tribe, which is forced to try sometimes serious offenses as misdemeanors (i.e., aggravated assaults as simple ones, rapes as minor sexual assaults, etc.).

The status of the alleged offender and victim also matter in deciding whether a tribe has jurisdiction over an offense. Since the General Crimes Act (also known as the Indian Country Crimes Act) was enacted in 1817, Native Americans who commit certain serious crimes against non-Indians have been transferred out of the tribal courts and into the federal justice system. Tribal courts also do not have criminal jurisdiction over non-Indians. In fact, the only time tribal jurisdiction is fairly certain is when a Native American is alleged to have committed a misdemeanor crime against another Native American in Indian Country, which includes all tribal lands and allotments.

The jurisdictional puzzle is made even more complex when one considers that the Navajo Nation has a region called the "checkerboard area" resulting from small noncontiguous pieces of the eastern part of the reservation being converted to private ownership, as well as the existence of public and railroad lands there. Depending on one's precise location in the checkerboard area, one can be on tribal, state, or federal land. The cross-deputization of law enforcement officers has helped ensure that the maze's confusion is not exploited by criminals who would otherwise escape apprehension if the wrong agency were to respond to a call for service.

Challenging Crimes

Many crimes pose a challenge to the Navajo Nation, but drug and alcohol offenses pose a particular difficulty. Though the reservation is technically dry (meaning all forms of alcohol are illegal to possess, consume, or distribute), the prevalence of bootlegged alcohol keeps the social work, health, and justice systems quite busy. In addition to offenses directly tied to alcohol (e.g., possession and consumption), the substance is linked as an accelerant to the most common violent offense on the reservation, domestic violence, as well as other forms of offending. In fact, according to testimony provided to the U.S. Senate, approximately 60 percent of the U.S. Uniform Crime Reports Part 1 offenses on the reservation in 2003 involved offenders who had used alcohol.

It has become popular for some chronic alcoholics who cannot obtain alcohol to mix water or fruit juice and liquid hairspray in a concoction locally referred to as "ocean." Because it contains methyl alcohol and other toxic ingredients, ocean is highly dangerous and has been linked to central nervous system impairment. It is also popular among Navajo drinkers in Gallup, New Mexico, an off-reservation community near the reservation, because that city is dry on Sundays.

More recently, drugs have become an issue for the Navajo Nation, with increased numbers of tribal members using methamphetamine and other illicit drugs. When compared to alcohol, however, drugs are far less common and were involved in only 2 percent of part 1 offenses in 2003.

Crime Statistics

Given the tribe's large size, the Navajo Nation courts are much busier than other tribal courts, disposing of more than 75,000 cases a year. More than half of the cases are civil matters, but there are still a significant number of criminal cases dealt with in the Navajo Nation court system. According to the U.S. Department of Justice, there were 31,507 criminal cases and 46,876 civil cases filed in 2001. According to 2006 court statistics, a total of 81,326 cases were disposed of in the Navajo Nation courts.

Serious offending is relatively uncommon on the Navajo reservation. The vast majority of crimes in Indian Country would be classified as nonserious acts. Though much more research is needed to fully describe the nature and type of crimes committed on tribal lands, the few available studies have been consistent in their findings, revealing that the most common arrests are for drunkenness and other liquor violations.

The most common part 1 offenses involve family violence (e.g., domestic violence and child abuse) and aggravated assault fueled by alcohol consumption. According to the Senate Committee on Indian Affairs, in 2003, there were 51 offenses of homicide-manslaughter; 121 forcible rapes; 2,554 offenses of child abuse; 12,253 offenses of domestic violence; 29 strong-arm robberies; 20 aggravated assaults with a firearm; 244 aggravated assaults with other weapons; and 6,250 other aggravated assaults. Over 40 percent of each of these offenses was alcohol-related. Juveniles committed 33 of the forcible rapes, 202 acts of child abuse, and 386 offenses of domestic violence.

By far the most common non-part 1 offense is drunkenness. According to the Senate Committee on Indian Affairs, in 2003, there were 1,124 offenses of drug abuse/possession; 4,091 cases of driving while intoxicated (DWI); 3,598 violations of liquor laws; and 22,119 cases of drunkenness. Juveniles committed 384 of the drug abuse/possession offenses, 94 DWIs, 151 violations of liquor laws, and 637 acts of drunkenness.

Finding of Guilt

Rights of the Accused

The major rights of the accused in the Navajo Nation nearly mirror those provided to defendants in the mainstream United States. In 1958, the Navajo Nation adopted its own Bill of Rights, patterned on the U.S. model. Guarantees of the rights to due process, to trial by jury, to assistance of counsel, to freedom of religion and speech and press, to assembly and seek redress, and to bear arms were granted to defendants in the Navajo Nation in addition to rights against unreasonable searches and seizures, double jeopardy, self-incrimination, excessive bail, and cruel or unusual punishment. In 1968, the Indian Civil Rights Act (ICRA) was enacted by Congress to transfer important guarantees of the Bill of Rights to criminal justice processes in tribal courts, and the Navajo Nation was forced to adopt that legislation although its own Bill of Rights was already in place. In addition, the ICRA was less complete than the Navajo Nation Bill of Rights because it did not guarantee freedom of religion, the right to bear arms, or the assistance of counsel. Now defendants in the Navajo Nation get the rights guaranteed by both the ICRA and their own Bill of Rights.

Defendants who face the specter of incarceration are provided with assistance from the public defenders office if they cannot afford an attorney on their own because of the tribe's Policy on Appointment of Counsel and Indigency adopted in 1993. The public defender's office is not well funded, however, and has only five full-time public defenders on staff. DNA—People's Legal Services (*Dinebeiina Nahiilna be 'Agha'diit'aahii,* "Attorneys working for the revitalization of the people") is a nonprofit organization that provides free legal assistance to low-income individuals who need assistance in civil matters, including vehicle and property-repossession cases. DNA also provides aid to those who need help seeking a protection order from domestic violence.

There are also a host of private attorneys who are affiliated with the Navajo Nation Bar Association (NNBA), a professional organization founded in 1978 to promote education and professionalism among attorneys who serve in the Navajo Nation courts. Native Americans are not required to have completed a law school education to join the NNBA but must pass a bar exam and have some form of education beyond high school (i.e., law school, a bachelor's degree, paralegal or advocacy training, training offered by the NNBA, or completion of an apprenticeship program approved by the NNBA). Non-Indians who wish to affiliate with the NNBA must have a law degree before they are eligible to sit for the bar exam.

Defendants who are transferred to the state or federal justice systems get whatever protections and rights that are available to those charged in the respective system (i.e., U.S. Bill of Rights, any rights accorded to those charged in a state court, right to public defender or assistance from a legal aid society, etc.).

Investigation and Prosecution

Crimes that fall under the jurisdiction of the tribe are investigated by the Navajo Department of Public Safety (NDPS), the Navajo Department of Criminal Investigations (affiliated with NDPS), or another appropriate law enforcement agency (e.g., the Navajo Law Enforcement Rangers). Crimes that fall under the jurisdiction of the state or federal justice systems are investigated by the appropriate authorities. Cases transferred to the federal courts, for example, would be investigated by the Federal Bureau of Investigation or Bureau of Indian Affairs investigators, whereas those in the state courts could be investigated by state police or local sheriff's department.

Prosecution of cases that fall under tribal jurisdiction is carried out by the Navajo Nation Prosecutor's Office, which employed 22 full-time prosecutors in 2002. The prosecutor's offices are headed by the chief prosecutor and serve 10 districts mirroring the geographical district boundaries used by the courts.

Peacemaking

Many cases are eligible to be referred by the prosecutor's office to an alternative dispute resolution process known as peacemaking. The Peacemaker Court/Program was launched in 1982 as a modern version of the traditional form of dispute resolution employed in the Navajo Nation since prehistoric times. In the traditional form of peacemaking, a *naat'áanii* (headman or elder) would be asked to help the parties in a dispute come to a reasonable solution that both found acceptable. When what we would now call crimes occurred, the *naat'áanii* would help the victim and offender fashion a response that restored the victim and helped protect the community from future victimization. This traditional form of justice continued into the 1980s, when it was revitalized by the Navajo Nation Judicial Branch in a court-annexed program.

In the modern version of peacemaking, victims of crime or those who seek redress in civil-type matters can ask a court liaison to appoint a peacemaker to help them restore peace in their relationships or lives. The peacemakers are chosen by their communities based on their character, problem-solving skills, and leadership abilities. The cases take between 2 and 12 hours to resolve because everyone who attends is allowed to speak until they no longer wish to speak. The parties may bring many family members or involved individuals to the session, or a requestee seeking redress to some harm the requestee feels he or she has wrongly experienced may simply ask a respondent (who could be termed the "defendant" in mainstream courts) to come participate in the session. The peacemakers sometimes tell traditional stories to help identify key issues in a nonthreatening way so that the parties may talk about their problems indirectly by instead talking about how characters in the stories should have acted. Some modern Christian peacemakers tell Bible stories for the same purpose. The peacemaker does not fashion a response for the parties but instead guides them toward deciding one on their own, using traditional teaching and knowledge to inform the parties and the process. Often, the parties will mutually decide on appropriate *nályééh* (restitution) for anyone harmed by the respondent and will design a response that also includes protection against future victimization (e.g., referral to a batterers' or anger management program). Although peacemakers in olden days were typically given tangibles (e.g., a sheep) in addition to a meal for their time and assistance, their modern counterparts are paid a small stipend by the parties.

Peacemaking was given a major boost in 2000, when the Navajo Nation Council enabled the transfer of most criminal cases into peacemaking as part of a move toward incorporating more traditional Navajo customs and cultural ideas into the modern justice system. There are currently 242 peacemakers registered with the court-annexed program and countless other individuals who still serve as *naat'áanii* for the traditional form of peacemaking.

The Navajo Peacemaking Court/Program has been viewed as a model by other tribes and countries. The program has many international visitors every year who observe and document the system in action in hopes of bringing parts of the process back to adapt into their own court procedures. Recidivism has been found to be lower for those who go through peacemaking when compared to defendants processed in the mainstream courts.

Courts

With reference to criminal cases, the vast majority of matters in the tribal courts result in guilty pleas. More than 90 percent of defendants plead guilty rather than contest their guilt. Traditional Navajos are likely to plead guilty because of cultural pressures to admit fault even if one is not guilty of the offense charged. The *Navajo Nation Times,* the tribal newspaper, sometimes runs stories educating Navajos about their rights to trial because the ideas are foreign to traditional individuals. It is not uncommon for Navajo defendants to plead guilty but to add that they "didn't do it" (the crime).

Criminal cases that go to trial are heard in the district courts, which employed 15 full-time judges in 2002, although there are currently slots for 16 judges. Judges are appointed and must meet the specified qualifications. As of 2003, successful candidates for Navajo Nation judge must be at least 30 years of age, be a member of the Navajo Nation Bar Association, have no felony convictions, have no misdemeanor convictions in the five years prior to being considered for a judgeship, possess at least a two-year associate's degree, have at least four years experience in a law-related position, possess knowledge of Navajo Nation courts and laws, speak both Navajo and English, have knowledge of Navajo culture and ceremonies, be in good mental health, possess a driver's license, and not be addicted to drugs or alcohol. In addition, candidates must pass a written test and ethics screening process, possess management skills, and submit four references attesting to their good character. Candidates for the position of Supreme Court judge must have a four-year bachelor's degree, and existing district court judges are given preference in selection for the high court. All judges, including those appointed to the Supreme Court, serve two-year probationary periods before being confirmed to a lifetime appointment during good behavior. Newly appointed judges must attend training.

In addition to the judges, the courts employ a number of commissioners who hear domestic violence and other routine cases and make recommendations to the court, which are typically signed into action by the judge overseeing the commissioner. Defendants whose charges could result in incarceration may elect to be tried by a jury of six of their peers.

Native American juveniles on reservations face particularly problematic issues because of the onerous reality of the Federal Juvenile Delinquency Act (FJDA). Enacted in 1938 and woefully behind the times, the FJDA combines with the Major Crimes Act to order the transfer of Native American juveniles from their tribal justice system to the federal courts if they commit a felony. Under the FJDA, tribal youth aged 15 or older who commit serious crimes such as murder, rape, or robbery on tribal lands are transferred to the federal courts, as are youth aged 13 to 14 whose tribes consent to the transfer. But because the FJDA was designed for the most sophisticated and incorrigible youth, Native juveniles charged with relatively nonserious property crimes can find themselves transferred to the federal system with its harsher sentences and its lack of good time, parole, and aftercare. In addition, because the sentences imposed under the FJDA are usually limited to five years, transferred youth are likely to be certified to the adult system, where they are twice as likely as their counterparts who retain their juvenile status to be sent to prison. Due to the FJDA and Major Crimes Act, nearly two-thirds (61 percent) of juveniles held in federal detention are Native American, according to the U.S. Bureau of Justice Statistics.

Juveniles are adjudicated in the Navajo Nation justice system, and some are incarcerated in its two juvenile detention facilities. At midyear 2007, 16 youth were held in Navajo Nation juvenile facilities. Cases that do not fall under tribal jurisdiction are processed in the appropriate state or federal court and are subject to the rules of those systems with respect to rights and processes.

Punishment

A wide range of sanctions are available in the Navajo Nation. In olden days, the typical sanctions were restorative in nature, with rare usage of the death penalty for those suspected of witchcraft. Such alleged offenders were often tossed off cliffs to their untimely deaths. Sometimes offenders would be asked to make symbolic restorative payments through donated labor, much like today's community service sanctions. Those offenders may be asked to chop wood for the elderly or perform other important tasks for those who needed societal assistance. Just being known as a wrongdoer and having rumors told about oneself was enough of a sanction to keep most offenders in line. Trials in olden days were called *'ahwiinít'í* ("they talk about you" or "where they talk about you") and were the cause of great shame because traditional Navajos did not like being talked about.

After the introduction of courts by the U.S. federal government, Navajos were introduced to jail as a sanction. Their first experience with Americanized courts and sanctions occurred during their years of captivity at Bosque Redondo, where the Navajos were rounded up and imprisoned between 1864 and 1868. One day a week was set up for court hearings, and that day became known as *Ghol Di* (also seen spelled as *Gooldi*) by the Navajos, who now refer to their courts as *Dine Bi Ghol Di* in honor of that first name assigned to them long ago. Some historical accounts on the reservation note that the choice of the words *Ghol Di* was an attempt to say "Jail Day" because that sanction was nearly universally imposed on the bewildered Navajos who appeared in the court on a variety of cultural charges, such as practicing their religion or traditions. Others trace the name to a transliteration of *Hwéeldi* ("the place of suffering"), the name given by the Navajos to their place of captivity at Bosque Redondo. Either way, going to *Ghol Di* meant getting punished. The Navajo word for judge is *'ánihwii'aahii*—"he who issues punishment"—another phrase that betrays the Navajos' feelings about the justice system that was imposed on them. Once a foreign sanction, now jail is quite commonly imposed by the tribal courts, though the terms tend to be quite short.

The Navajo Nation operates six adult detention facilities and one juvenile facility. Three of the adult facilities are used for holding new arrestees, and the other half were designed to house inmates serving sentences. Navajo Nation defendants may be detained before trial, and the vast majority (89 percent) of those incarcerated at midyear 2007 were unconvicted individuals. The typical adult inmate serves eight days because the courts are forced to release inmates serving sentences to make room for newly sentenced offenders in their overcrowded system, and 8 percent of arrestees are not even able to be booked because of a shortage of jail space, so they are simply arrested and released. The tribe has space to hold 179 adults and 36 juveniles, but that includes space for both sentenced inmates and those awaiting trial. According to the Bureau of Justice Statistics, at midyear 2007, there were 212 adults and 24 juveniles held in Navajo Nation detention facilities, and two of the six adult facilities were operating above 150 percent capacity in June 2007.

Offenders serving time in the Navajo Nation at midyear 2007 included assaulters of various types and those convicted of offenses involving drugs or alcohol. Seven percent were serving time for assault or domestic violence, 3 percent had been convicted of rape, and an additional 7 percent were convicted of other assault offenses, meaning that one-fourth of incarcerated offenders are in Navajo Nation jails for violent offenses. About one-tenth had been jailed for DUI/DWI (6 percent) or drug offenses (3 percent). The remaining inmates were there for other offenses, or their offenses were not reported on the midyear survey of inmates.

Most of the offenders serving time in Navajo Nation jails are male. The vast majority (89 percent) of the adult inmates at midyear 2007 were male, as were more than half (56 percent) of the juvenile detainees. This is not surprising given the higher proportion of men involved in crime when compared to women.

Due in part to the very limited jail space and a cultural distaste for incarceration for all but the worst offenders, intermediate sanctions are the most common sanction doled out in the tribal courts. Intermediate sanctions available in the Navajo Nation include fines, community service, counseling, and drug and alcohol treatment. Probation is also quite common, especially when linked with mandated counseling or treatment. According to court statistics, 6,948 individuals were on probation in the Navajo Nation in 2006.

As mentioned previously, the Indian Civil Rights Act (ICRA) limits tribal courts to imposing sentences of only one year or less in jail and/or a fine of US$5,000. That means that sanctions for even severe offenses such as murder, rape, serious burglary, or serious drug offenses would be one year in jail combined with a fine. Though the federal justice system has exclusive jurisdiction over serious charges such as these, the rate at which the federal system declines felony cases committed on tribal lands amounts to roughly two-thirds of all cases presented to the authorities. Federal prosecutors cite the reliability of witnesses being affected by their consumption of alcohol as one of the reasons they decline to pursue charges; however, many factors can affect their decision not to prosecute when they feel their chances of winning in court are uncertain. Unfortunately, the affected tribes have little recourse other than charging defendants with whatever misdemeanor charges they can assemble. In some cases, those who commit serious crimes, including murder, spend only a couple of months in a Navajo Nation jail. Tribes across the country, including the Navajo Nation, lament that they are unable to pursue felony charges against violent offenders when the federal government decides the case might not result in an automatic win.

Death Penalty

Those Navajos alleged to have committed serious felonies and charged with a federal crime face lengthy prison sentences or the death penalty if they are convicted. Though the death penalty is an option for Native Americans processed in the federal courts for crimes committed in Indian Country, it is rarely sought. Tribes are given the option of "opting in" to the death penalty, which the Navajo Nation has not. The first Native American to be sentenced to death in recent times was a Navajo double murderer, Lezmond Mitchell, who was sentenced to die in 2003. The prosecutor assigned to his case initially refused to seek the death penalty before being overruled by then attorney general John Ashcroft.

Prison

Technically, prison is not an option for those sentenced in the tribal courts given that the these courts do not have jurisdiction over felonies and cannot impose sentences longer than one year in jail. Defendants can be and are jailed, however, as discussed earlier. Two percent of inmates in the Navajo Nation jails were being held on felonies at midyear 2004.

Prison is an option for those sentenced in the state or federal courts. however, because both of those jurisdictions have authority to sentence offenders to more than one year in jail. Those processed in the federal system, including juveniles processed under the Federal Juvenile Delinquency Act, are quite likely to receive prison terms.

Jon'a Meyer

Further Reading

Becker, B. N., and P. Spruhan. (1998–1999). "Profile of the Law of the Navajo Nation." *Tribal Law Journal:* http://tlj.unm.edu/tribal-law-journal/articles/preview/navajo/index.php.

Bureau of Indian Affairs: http://www.doi.gov/bia/.

Lowery, D. L. (1993). "Developing a Tribal Common Law Jurisprudence: The Navajo Experience, 1969–1992." *American Indian Law Review* 18: 379–438.

Navajo Nation Judicial Branch. (1993). *A Public Guide to the Courts of the Navajo Nation.* Window Rock, AZ: Navajo Nation Judicial Branch.

Nielsen, M. O., and J. W. Zion. (2005). *Navajo Nation Peacemaking: Living Traditional Justice.* Tucson: University of Arizona Press.

Yazzie, R. (1994). "'Life Comes from It': Navajo Justice Concepts." *New Mexico Law Review* 24: 175–190.

Netherlands Antilles

Murder: Medium
Prison Rate: High
Death Penalty: No
Corporal Punishment: No

Background

The Netherlands Antilles consists of five islands located in the Caribbean Sea. They are divided into two groups. The Windward Islands are located in the north, and they include Saba, St. Eustatius, and St. Maarten. The Leeward Islands, which are in the south of the sea, include Bonaire and Curacao. The total breadth of the Antilles territory spans nearly 600 miles.

Historically, the Arawacs inhabited the Leeward Islands, and Caribs inhabited the Windward Islands. After being settled by the Spanish in the 1400s, and then conquered by the Dutch West Indies Company, today many Dutch Antilleans report having a mixed racial/ethnic heritage. Over 85 percent of the 186,000 people who reside in the Antilles consider themselves mixed black, and the remainder of the population report their ethnicity as Latin American, white, and/or East Asian. Although Dutch is the official language, *Papiamento,* a local dialect derived from Spanish, Portuguese, Dutch, and English, is widely spoken. Many nationals also speak English and Spanish fluently.

Political and Social Context

The first constitution of the Netherlands Antilles was adopted in 1865. It stated that the Antilles were a federated state associated with the Kingdom of the Netherlands. In 1954, a revision to the Constitution changed the way in which the islands were governed and created the opportunity for each island to have its own political relationship with the Netherlands. At this time, the islands of the Antilles, along with Aruba, gained their independence from the Netherlands. In 1986, Aruba seceded from the Antilles and formed closer ties with the Netherlands. The Antilles, on the other hand, headed toward a greater level of independence. In the 1990s, several conferences were held to further clarify the nature of the relationship between each island and the Netherlands. Nearly 90 percent of the people in the Antilles voted to permanently dissolve the official bonds between the islands and the Netherlands.

As of July 2008, the Netherlands Antilles are still considered an autonomous nation of the Kingdom of the Netherlands. However, the relationship between the islands and the Netherlands is currently undergoing renegotiation, and the islands are expected to disband in 2010 and no longer be part of the Netherlands territories at all.

Government and Judiciary

Much of what occurs in the Antilles is subject to the jurisprudence of each individual island. Although there is an overarching government that supervises the Antilles and a heavy reliance on the Netherlands for financial and military support, most legal and political issues are dealt with at the island level. Currently, the queen of the Netherlands oversees international issues facing the Antilles. Each island has a president who reports to the Kingdom of the Netherlands and oversees local issues.

The queen appoints all judges in the Netherlands Antilles. These individuals have generally received their legal training in the Netherlands. They are often not Dutch Antilleans but rather relocated to the Antilles as a result of their appointment. Many have lived in the Antilles for only a limited time, thus resulting in limited knowledge and experience with the experiences of Antillean citizens.

Policing

The organizational structure of the police in the Netherlands Antilles has historically been fraught with corruption and clouded by inefficient bureaucracy and complex arrangements of police duties and responsibilities. As a result of these problems, the legislature in the Netherlands passed the 1993 Police Act, which attempted to restructure the police.

Prior to the enactment of the Police Act, police in the Netherlands Antilles were divided into two groups. The first group, the municipal police force, was responsible for patrols, criminal investigations, vice, juvenile offenders, traffic affairs, immigration, and administrative issues. The second group, the national police, was responsible for providing law enforcement services to rural areas and special services to help ensure safety on the coast, on waterways, and at airports.

After the passage of the Police Act, officers were assigned to different regions rather than to specific duties. This was intended to streamline the police organization, weed out corruption, and make the police more efficient in responding to criminal activity. Moreover, it set forth a direct chain of command with officers reporting to local government officials rather than to the minister of defense or other high-level officials. The Police Act also clarified the roles and responsibilities on the islands for police from the Netherlands and the Antilles.

Despite these organizational changes, in 2002, the Dutch government was concerned that the law enforcement system in the Netherlands Antilles was suffering from a shortage of personnel and lacked the necessary resources to adequately enforce the local law. With the help of the Netherlands, which provided most of the financial resources, training, and equipment, police in the Netherlands Antilles have increased their effectiveness in crime control and reduced the amount of corruption within the police organization.

The roles and responsibilities for police in the Netherlands Antilles are limited to domestic issues, whereas the Netherlands handles all international law enforcement. The local police are responsible for detective and investigational work for criminal cases. Police have the power to arrest a suspect, keep that person in police custody, and seize evidence or property. Senior police officers, who are appointed to act as auxiliaries to the court, can use more aggressive investigative approaches than their junior associates, such as coercion. The full spectrum of investigative techniques afforded to the police is more limited in the Netherlands Antilles than in many other countries. For example, there is limited surveillance authority because excessive surveillance is thought to infringe on individual privacy. Also, there is very limited use of force by officers in their investigations.

Crime

Classification of Crimes

Crimes in the Netherlands Antilles are classified by the legislature based on perceived seriousness and harm. Prohibited acts are classified as felonies or infractions (transgressions). Crimes that involve physical harm to another person are often classified as felonies. This includes murder, intentional homicide, or other violent acts such as assault. Additionally, some crimes relating to personal property may also be classified as felonies. Actions that are less serious in nature but still violate law may be considered a transgression. For example, individuals who violate traffic laws may be cited. Such transgressions are usually handled by an administrative court, where there is no judge or legal proceeding. Individuals are cited rather than expected to report to the authorities and pay a fine. In most cases, there is no right to appeal the fine or culpability.

The classification of crimes in the Netherlands Antilles significantly impacts judicial procedure in so far as the type of offense ultimately determines the type of judge who will preside over a case and the court in which the case will be heard. For example, transgressions are tried in a different court from felonies, and a police judge or an appointed person hears the case rather than a criminal court judge. Individuals who are considered experts in the law may be appointed to serve on the judiciary regardless of their credentials as a lawyer or professional training.

Drug Offenses

Some drugs in the Netherlands Antilles are decriminalized for personal use; however, the sale and use of most substances is considered a serious criminal offense. The National Criminal Intelligence Service of the Netherlands determines which drugs should be classified as "soft" drugs versus "hard" drugs. Such determinations dictate criminal justice policy and enforcement of drug legislation. Currently, drugs such as heroin, cocaine, and amphetamines are classified as "hard" drugs, and marijuana and hashish are classified as "soft" drugs.

Crimes Challenging the Country

Like many of the other islands in the Caribbean Sea, the Antilles have witnessed a significant rise in the amount of drug-related crime over the past few decades. For example, the United Nations Office on Drugs and Crime reported that in 1991, only 590 kilos of cocaine were seized; in 2001, more than 1,043 kilos were seized; and in 2004, over 9,000 kilos were seized. In 2004, the Netherlands Antilles ranked eighth in the world for cocaine seizures and was among the world's leaders with respect to the amount of drugs seized per capita.

In addition to crimes involving the drug trade, the Netherlands Antilles are experiencing problems with human trafficking and illegal immigration. According to the United Nations Report on International Human Rights, the country has been receiving and exporting men, women, and children for sexual exploitation, domestic servitude, and forced labor to the countries' construction and agricultural industries. This report specifically sited Curacao and St. Maarten as culprits in human trafficking for the sex trade in Peru, Brazil, and Colombia. Furthermore, the report argued that more than 500 foreign women may be working as prostitutes, many against their will. Recent efforts in collaboration with the Kingdom of the Netherlands have attempted to curtail these abuses, the success of which has yet to be determined.

The Netherlands Antilles provides a certain degree of latitude for individuals who are engaged in the sex industry. For example, all islands in the Antilles have legal brothels that are regulated by the government. The government issues permits for "dancers" that allow women to work in the facilities for up to three months. During their time as employees, women are subject to regular medical checkups. The brothels are limited in the number of workers they are allowed to have at any given time. However, a significant amount of sex work occurs outside of the brothels and involves many of the women trafficked for the sex industry. Prostitutes can be found in local bars, discos, and clubs. These women, who work in unregulated facilities, do not have access to regular medical checks and are often subject to abuse, sexually transmitted diseases, and deplorable living conditions.

Crime Statistics

Each island is responsible for tracking criminal events, victimizations, and arrests. Accordingly, the smaller islands with fewer resources are less proficient in systematically collecting and disseminating data on criminal events. Unlike the smaller islands of Saba and St. Eustatius, which do not have publicly available data on crimes reported to the police, the islands of Bonaire, Curacao, and St. Maarten have been collecting data in earnest for the past few years.

The most recent data available from the Central Bureau of Statistics Netherlands Antilles suggest that theft is the most widely reported crime. For example, in 2003, St. Maarten recorded 1,086 incidents of qualified theft, 397 of theft, and 165 of theft with violence. There are relatively few instances of homicide. In 2003, there were 2 homicide cases reported to the police on Bonaire and fewer than 20 cases reported on St. Maarten.

Finding of Guilt

The criminal justice system in the Netherlands Antilles is modeled after the inquisitorial criminal procedures used in the Netherlands. Accordingly, judges in the criminal court play an active role in determining the facts of a case rather than acting as an impartial moderator between the state and the accused. A judge is free to ask questions of witnesses, and the accused and can also act as the driving force behind evidence collecting efforts. Judges also ultimately determine guilt or innocence.

Rights of the Accused

In the Netherlands Antilles, individuals who are accused of a criminal offense are not afforded many of the rights that are often taken for granted in other countries. This includes the right to trial by jury, judicial expediency, and the option to plea to lesser charges. The incorporation of lay members of the community is generally left out of judicial procedure. An appointed judge decides all cases serious in nature. Moreover, the notion of a speedy trial can be hampered by the laborious pretrial process, which allows individuals to be held without trial for months at a time. The option to plea to lesser charge is determined by the police or judge and is not afforded to all offenders. Although fines are gaining popularity in their use, it is up to the state to determine when and how they will be applied.

Court-appointed attorneys are provided under very limited conditions and only at specific times in the judicial process. There is no right to court-appointed assistance in the pretrial phase of the investigation unless the individual has been deprived of liberty as a result of detention. In such cases, attorneys are provided when offenders are unable to secure assistance for themselves.

Criminal Investigation and Prosecution

Criminal investigations are conducted by the police and at the will of the presiding judge. Cases can be investigated through traditional police practice where a complaint is levied. Investigations can also be conducted by the police in accordance with, and under the direction of, the presiding judge during the pretrial and trail phase of a case when questions remain unanswered or evidence is needed.

Prosecutors are actors of the state, and they are the only actors who have the power to make a decision about dropping cases, settling cases out of court by means of transaction, or issuing a writ of summons. In general the amount of prosecutorial discretion has increased over the past decade but still remains largely regulated by the code of criminal procedure.

In some cases, prosecutors decide not to take a case to trial but rather recommend the case be settled by transaction. In such cases, the accused may or may not admit to the charges, but rather than going through with a trial and having the charges on his or her court record, the accused agrees to a set of conditions laid out by the prosecutor. Most cases that are settled in this way require the individual to pay some predetermined fine that corresponds to the criminal charge.

Pretrial Procedures

Prior to a trial, the police have a significant amount of latitude with respect to detaining suspects. For example, in cases where an individual is caught in the act of committing an offense, police have the ability to keep the suspect and question him or her for up to six hours. After the initial interrogation, senior-level police officers can make the determination to release the suspect, pending further investigation, or keep the suspect in police custody for an additional six days. After the six days of police custody have expired, the suspect can be further detained at the will of the presiding judge. This detention can last for several months; however, every 30 days, the suspect has the right to be heard by a judge. Additionally, the suspect has access to an attorney during this time and can challenge his or her detention prior to trial.

Criminal Responsibility

To determine guilt, causation and culpability must be established. Causation suggests that the person who is accused of committing an offense or harm to another person actually participated in an event in which some foreseeable action could result in the harm of a person or property. More specifically, causation is not limited to one individual purposefully harming another, but also includes any individual behaving in such a way that there is a reasonable possibility that injury to someone could occur given the behavior of the accused.

Culpability, or responsibility, is divided into two subgroups. First, culpability can be determined based on intent. Intent suggests that the accused meant to cause harm, violate the law, or act in a fashion that is likely to result in harm. The second form of culpability includes negligence. Conscious negligence is argued to have occurred when an individual takes a risk that is likely to result in harm but justifies his or her actions to engage in such behavior based on faulty logic. Unconscious negligence is argued to have occurred when the offender acts thoughtlessly or was not aware that certain behaviors or actions can result in harm, but should have been.

In some cases, the finding of guilt can be averted because the accused has provided a reasonable defense or an excuse. The law does not distinguish between a justification under the law and an excuse. The result, when compelling evidence is provided, is the same—an acquittal. Some examples of justifications or defense strategies include self-defense, public obligation, and obeying the order of a competent authority.

In contrast to a defense or justification for committing an offense, some individuals opt to present the court with an excuse of culpability. This may include insanity, duress, and absence of blameworthiness. Insanity in the Dutch system is defined as a mental state in which one cannot be found criminally culpable because of a mental disorder or mental disease. The excuse of duress can be used if the accused is found to have acted as a result of external pressures that created a situation in which he or she could not resist their actions. The excuse of absence of blameworthiness was derived from case law in the Netherlands and suggests that the accused did not know his or her actions were illegal. This excuse must be reasonable to the court but allows for the accused to be found inculpable due to ignorance of the facts or the law.

Age of Criminal Culpability

Children who are not yet 12 years old are thought to be too young to be criminally responsible for their actions; however, they can be mandated to attend juvenile court on civil matters. There are special laws that pertain to children between the ages of 12 and 16. For juveniles between the ages of 16 and 18, juvenile law is still applicable; however, under some conditions, adult law can be applied. The decision to proceed in adult court and under adult law is subject to the circumstances of the case, the seriousness of the offense, and the character of the offender. These factors also come into play with individuals between the ages of 18 and 21. Offenders under age 21 may be tried in juvenile court if the offense is less serious in nature and if the characteristics of the offense and the offender are such that adult law would be inappropriate. The transfer of children to adult court is very rare.

Victims' Rights

The role of the victim under Dutch law and in the Netherlands Antilles is extremely limited. The only time the victim's experience is taken into consideration is during the trial and then only if he or she is called as a witness. There is no right to speak at trial or to offer an impact statement to the judge as a means of swaying opinion in favor of one punishment or another. Victims also do not have the right to counsel or to appeal a court's decision. Additionally, in criminal cases, victims have no right to privately pursue prosecution. The right to prosecute is solely a matter of state discretion. If, however, the state decides not to move forward with a prosecution, the victim can file an appeal to the court. Rarely are these appeals granted.

Punishment

The criminal justice system classifies penalties for adults as either punishments or measures. Punishments are designed to affect offenders and society at large through deterrence. A measure does not require that an individual be found guilty of an offense and is intended not to cause hardship to the accused, but rather to restore a sense of safety and security to society.

The determination of imposing a punishment or a measure is generally left to the discretion of the presiding judge or senior investigating police officer. Ultimately, these decisions are made within the context of the recommendations found in the penal code and are specific to the court in which the case is decided.

Punishments

The death penalty has not been used since 1950, and it has been illegal for all Dutch Antillean citizens, both civilian and military, since the 1980s. In the case of murder, the code suggests a punishment of life imprisonment, confinement for up to 20 years, or a fine of €45,000 (approx. US$57,355). In contrast, assault, which is considered to be a less serious offense, is defined as a physical harm to another that is punishable by a term of imprisonment not to exceed two years or a fine of €11,250 (approx. US$14,345).

There are several different types of punishment that can be imposed on an individual who is found criminally responsible for his or her actions. These punishments generally include task penalties, community service, fines, and/or incarceration. In some special cases, where offenders also have an underlying metal health problem or drug addiction, they may also be remanded to a treatment facility. As discussed before, there is a significant reliance on fines as a central form of punishment in the Netherlands Antilles. However, there has been increasing interest in more creative sentencing practices, which include those focused on ways to rehabilitate offenders.

Task penalties are a unique way in which the Dutch system tries to rehabilitate offenders while at the same time minimizing reliance on incarceration and detention. These types of punishments may include electronic monitoring or penitentiary programs, which are specific to the needs of the offender as determined by the courts. The notion of task penalties dates back to the 1970s, when a committee dedicated to alternative penal sections debated alternative systems of correction and advised the Dutch government on various ways to reduce crime and prison sentences while at the same time minimizing recidivism.

In addition to task penalties, the court can also impose various forms of community service. These programs have tried to replace short-term detentions for nonviolent and nonserious offenders with activities that specifically relate to restoring the community and rehabilitating offenders. It is important to note that although the court can impose community service, legislation has been passed that states community service cannot be used as a replacement for a suspended prison sentences or fine.

In many cases, the courts have opted to use fines as a means of punishment rather than incarceration. This form of punishment considerably increased after the passage of the Financial Penalties Act. This specific form of legislation allowed judges to more liberally apply fines in cases where incarceration had been previously used.

Measures

The goal of a measure is not to sanction the individual but rather to ensure community safety and security. There are several different kinds of measures that can be imposed, ranging from the seizure of one's personal property to fines or state-mandated drug treatment or psychiatric care.

The criminal code specifies that objects that are thought to be harmful to individuals or the public can be removed from circulation without trial or arrest. For example, objects discovered during a police investigation that may relate to some kind of criminal activity or possession of which is illegal can be seized by the police regardless of whether there is enough evidence to try the person whose possessions are seized or whether they are found guilty by the court.

Another measure that can be administered by the courts is the confiscation of money that was obtained through illegal activities. This measure, which is predominately used to punish individuals and corporations involved in organized or white-collar crime, targets the purse strings of those suspected of illegal activity. In such cases, individuals can be forced to pay the state treasury fines that equal the amount of money that is suspected to have been gained through illegal transactions. Although individuals and corporations do not have to be found guilty for these measures to be imposed, the court is responsible for assessing and estimating the amount of profits earned through illegal endeavors to determine the amount of money that is to be paid back to the state treasury.

Although the measures describe here arguably are intended to recoup the costs of criminal activity or protect the community from objects in circulation that can be harmful if not seized, other measures imposed by the court are directly intended to help the accused. For example, the court may impose a measure that is intended to force the accused to undergo treatment for psychiatric illnesses or drug addition.

Psychiatric Illness and Drug Treatment

In the case where an individual is found not guilty because criminal culpability is lacking due to an underlying metal illness or deficit, the court can require the accused be remanded to psychiatric treatment for up to one year. For the court to impose such a measure, it must be determined that the accused is a threat to himself or herself or to the community at large. This determination is not made by the judge per se, but rather requires an extensive investigation into the offender's psychiatric state by at least two psychiatrists who are required to submit an evaluation to the court prior to sentencing.

In addition to requiring the accused to undergo psychiatric treatment, the court also has the power to enact an entrustment order. This measure can be imposed for crimes that are more serious in nature and result in a more extensive hospitalization than specified in the psychiatric treatment order. Generally, the entrustment order is applied in cases where the accused is found to be responsible regardless of his or her mental handicap. Under the entrustment order, the accused can be remanded to hospital care at a state-run facility for a term of up to two years. In special cases, the court can extend the hospitalization beyond the two-year term limit when extraordinary conditions suggest this would be in the best interests of the accused and the community.

In less severe circumstances than those described under the psychiatric hospital order and the entrustment order, individuals can be required to seek out and undergo outpatient hospital care. This measure is often imposed alongside other penalties, such as probation.

The Dutch system provides judges with the power to force the accused into drug treatment. These treatment facilities are designed to provide long-term and intense drug treatment regimens to individuals with habitual problems related to drugs. Some of the services that are offered by state-run drug treatment faculties are counseling, nursing care, education, and employment training. Offenders who are sentenced to mandatory drug treatment have their daily activities monitored by officers of the court from the probation department who specialize in drug rehabilitation.

Juveniles

Since 1995, the police, in addition to judges, have had the discretion to handle juvenile cases through transactions rather than traditional trials. In cases where juveniles are accused of engaging in relatively minor offenses including vandalism and shoplifting, police officers can require the accused to participate in crime prevention programs that are intended to curtail criminal activity in young people before it becomes more serious in nature. Ultimately, the goal of such penalties is to change the behaviors of the accused and have them understand the harm that was caused by their actions.

The maximum length of a detention term for a juvenile is much lower than that which is specified in Dutch law for adults. For juveniles under the age of 16, the maximum term that can be imposed is 12 months. The term is doubled for those who are over the age of 16. Juveniles, in addition to being subject to alternative systems of justice and punishment, are also provided with alternative facilities for detention. In these facilities, the notion of rehabilitation is stressed even more than it is for adults. Juveniles are provided with the opportunity to engage in community service to repair the damage their actions caused, and they are also afforded educational opportunities and job training.

Prisons

There are three institutions in the Netherlands Antilles that currently house 780 prisoners. Bon Futuro Prison is the largest prison in the Netherlands Antilles and can house up to 362 prisoners. Pointe Blanche is much smaller and can house only 130 inmates, and the third facility in Bonaire is even smaller, with only 51 spaces. All facilities are equipped to hold both male and female inmates. Females account for roughly 11 percent of the prison population. According to the International Centre for Prison Studies, Bon Futuro is at 172 percent capacity, and Point Blanch is at 108 percent.

Bon Futuro has recently undergone extensive renovations in response to a recent visit from the European Committee for the Prevention of Torture and Inhuman or Degrading Treatment or Punishment. This committee described the newly renovated facility as having a large yard with open and shaded areas that is equipped with tables for the prisoners to congregate around. Moreover, the prison currently allows for the total out-of-cell time per day to be more than eight hours. Access to equipment for exercise and sport on the yard is limited; however, there is a prison gym.

Prior to the renovations, several complaints were brought forth by prisoners that resulted in the initial visit from European Committee for the Prevention of Torture and Inhuman or Degrading Treatment or Punishment. During this visit, shortcomings were noted by this committee, which resulted in a widespread effort to urge the government of the Netherlands Antilles to improve the "inhumane" conditions at Bon Futuro prison, as well as the cells located at the police stations on the islands of St. Maarten and Bonaire. Of central concern were the issues of overcrowding, sanitary conditions, quality of food, and outdated ventilation systems.

Members of this committee also noted what appeared to be widespread corruption among police and other officials, as well as reports of mistreatment of prisoners by guards at Bon Futuro. In prior years, the committee had attempted to convince the government that there were reports of violence among prisoners, which included instances of sexual assault. These efforts initiated a government-led investigation, which resulted in ample evidence being found that suggested some of the prison guards on Curacao and St. Maarten regularly assisted inmates by facilitating drug and firearm smuggling. Additional evidence suggested that prison guards allowed violent breakouts to occur and ignored sexual assaults in the prisons. The results of the investigation empowered the Justice Minister to suspended 175 of the 202 guards and replace them with regular police.

Assistance to implement the renovations was provided by the Dutch government, which earmarked money to build a new juvenile wing and a maximum-security facility and assisted with other improvements to Bon Futuro. Additionally, the Netherlands has also offered assistance with training prison guards.

Jennifer L. Christian

Further Reading

Government of the Netherlands Antilles: http://www.gov.an/ccg/home.nsf.

Tak, P. J. P. (2003). *The Dutch Criminal Justice System: Organization and Operation*. Den Haag: Boom Juridische Uitgevers.

U.S. Department of State. (2010) *Background Note: Netherlands Antilles:* http://www.state.gov/r/pa/ei/bgn/22528.htm.

Nicaragua

Legal System: Civil
Murder: High
Corruption: Medium
Human Trafficking: Medium
Prison Rate: Medium
Death Penalty: No
Corporal Punishment: No

Background

After declaring independence from Spain in 1821, Nicaragua experienced decades of unrest as the United Kingdom and the United States struggled over control of a transit canal route across Nicaragua. What followed were frequent U.S. military interventions into Nicaragua and a tendency for Nicaraguan politicians to ask the United States to settle domestic disputes. To support President Adolfo Díaz, U.S. marines landed in Nicaragua in 1912. Shortly afterward, under the 1916 Bryan-Chamorro Treaty, Nicaragua became a protectorate of the United States. Opposition to U.S. intervention led to guerrilla warfare against the ensuing U.S.-supported military dictatorships, even after the U.S. marines withdrew in 1933. Anastasio Somoza and his family ruled Nicaragua from 1936 until 1979, when a massive popular insurrection, led by the Sandinista National Liberation Front, overthrew the Somoza dictatorship.

The Sandinistas established a government based on mass organizations of workers and farmers, abolished the existing Constitution, and promulgated the Fundamental Statute of the Republic of Nicaragua, which created the basic governmental institutions of Nicaragua, and the Statute on the Rights and Guarantees of Nicaraguans, which extended equal protection and equal obligations of all Nicaraguans. This comprehensive scheme of civil liberties, economic rights, and privileges of citizenship was later incorporated into the new Constitution. In 1981, the U.S. government ended its economic aid to the Sandinista government and began to support the counterrevolutionary military forces, known as the Contras, in their war to overthrow the Sandinista government. In 1984, elections were held, and Sandinista Daniel Ortega won the presidency. The Contra war intensified for the next few years.

In 1990, the Sandinista government was electorally defeated by a broad anti-Sandinista coalition when Violetta Barrios de Chamorro became president. The U.S. trade embargo was lifted, and the Contras stopped fighting. Although Chamorro attempted to create a cooperative political environment, tense relations with the Sandinistas and business groups threatened to destabilize the government. Business groups felt that the pace of Chamorro's economic reforms was too slow, whereas the Sandinistas were upset that their earlier achievements were being dismantled. Furthermore, widespread governmental corruption led to the disillusionment of Nicaraguans with their government and its institutions. In 1996, José Arnoldo Alemán Lacayo, leader of the conservative Liberal Alliance, was elected to office and was followed in 2001 by another Liberal Constitutionalist Party (PLC) member, Enrique Bolaños Geyer. Bolaños led an anticorruption campaign against Alemán, which resulted in Alemán's conviction for embezzlement and other crimes. A power struggle erupted between the National Assembly's Liberal party members, in alliance with the Sandinistas and President Bolaños. In 2006, Sandinista Daniel Ortega was again elected president.

For nearly 30 years, Nicaragua has been in the midst of a complex process of political, economic, social, and legal transition. Almost 70 percent of Nicaragua's 5.7 million people live in poverty, with the rural population being particularly vulnerable. Nicaragua's economy and infrastructure, greatly damaged by the Contra war and later by Hurricane Mitch in 1998, are slowly recovering, but Nicaragua continues to experience widespread underemployment, extreme poverty, and severe income inequality. The gross domestic product adjusted for purchasing power parity was US$2,800, and the literacy rate was just over 67 percent in 2008.

The Nicaraguan government is divided into three branches: executive, legislative, and judicial. The president leads the executive power and is both chief of state and head of government: he or she rules administratively through the Council of Ministers. The president is elected on the same ticket with the vice president by popular vote for a five-year term and can serve a second term as long as it is not consecutive. The legislative power is exercised by the 92-member unicameral National Assembly. Ninety members are popularly elected by proportional representation to serve five-year terms, one seat is reserved for the previous president, and one seat is for the runner-up in the previous presidential election. In addition to its legislative duties, this National Assembly also elects the 16 justices that form the Supreme Court of Justice; justices serve five-year terms.

Courts

The single unified court structure, duties, and procedures remain largely unchanged from the 1894 Organic Law of the Courts and various decrees issued since the law has been enacted. The Organic Law established a judicial system that is composed of a Supreme Court, six courts of appeal, district courts, and local courts.

The highest court is the Supreme Court of Justice, which has territorial jurisdiction over the entire country and subject matter jurisdiction over all issues except labor disputes. Recently, the Supreme Court has been expanded to include 16 justices who are elected by the National Assembly from recommendations by the president of the republic and members of the National Assembly in consultation with civil associations. Justices, who have functional immunity, serve for a five-year period and can be reelected.

To serve as a Supreme Court justice, a candidate must have Nicaraguan nationality and be an attorney of good morals who has been in practice for at least 10 years or has served as an appellate court judge for five years. A judge must be at least 35 years old but less than 75 years old and not have been suspended from legal practice. The candidate must be fully entitled to his or her political and civil rights and not be an active or recent member of the military. Finally, he or she must have lived in the country continuously for four years prior to the date of election, except if performing a diplomatic mission, working in an international agency, or completing a course of study abroad.

The function of the Supreme Court of Justice is to administer justice, which includes resolving appeals from the district and local courts, the recourse of amparo for violation of the rights established in the Constitution and the Law of Amparo, the recourse of unconstitutionality of laws and governmental administrative functions, and international affairs. The Supreme Court's Criminal Chamber consists of six justices who hear, process, and resolve all criminal matters under its jurisdiction. In 2005, the Supreme Court's Criminal Chamber issued 121 rulings as compared to 44 in 2000, 39 in 2001, 43 in 2002, 42 in 2003, and 112 in 2004. Finally, the number of decisions on appeals for legal protection (*amparo*) issued by the Constitutional Court grew by 86 percent in 2005.

Directly subordinate to the Supreme Court of Justice, the six courts of appeal have jurisdiction over a particular geographical region of the country. At least five magistrates in each court of appeals handle civil, labor, and criminal cases. The chief justice of the court of appeals is appointed by least two-thirds of the members of the court to serve a one-year term and may be reelected. Court of Appeals justices hear appeals from the district courts, recourses of amparo, and jurisdictional disputes between lower-court judges.

Immediately below the courts of appeals are the district courts, which hear both criminal and civil cases. As of June 2006, there were 136 district courts: 31 in Managua, 23 in the central zone, 18 in the west, 13 in Las Segovias, 10 in the south, 13 in the north, 5 in the South Atlantic, and 7 in the North Atlantic. The district courts are divided by subject matter into single courts as well as civil, family, criminal, labor, and other special courts. District court judges, who are elected by the full Supreme

Court, preside over criminal trials and sentencing in departments and autonomous regions. District court judges hear criminal cases, criminal case appeals from the local courts, disciplinary actions, and administrative matters.

The lowest courts are the local courts, which hear criminal cases and small commercial cases. Each municipality has at least one local court, with a single judge elected by the full Supreme Court. The 186 local courts are organized by subject matter, which include single courts, a civil court, a family court, a criminal court, and a labor court. These courts are the first step in the criminal judicial process, but the judges do not conduct criminal trials and cannot sentence. Their role is a preliminary one.

Historically, the Nicaraguan judicial system has been characterized by widespread corruption. Under the Somoza dictatorship, bribery was common, as were arbitrary arrests, house-to-house searches, and summary executions carried out by Somoza's National Guard. Consequently, public confidence in the judicial system was very weak. After the Sandinistas took power in July 1979, most of the judges who had been in office during the Somoza era fled the country, leaving a manpower gap in the judicial system.

Supporting the courts are the Attorney General's Office, which represents the executive branch and government interests; the Public Ministry, an independent agency staffed with 260 prosecutors nationwide that investigates crimes and exercises criminal prosecution; the Public Defender's Office; and the Human Rights Ombudsman. The entire legal system continues to be prone to political influence and corruption. Often a judge's sympathies, pressure from political leaders, or acceptance of bribes influence his or her judicial findings. Inexperienced and undereducated lawyers and judges, passive prosecutors, an underfunded and understaffed Public Defender's Office, and arcane legal codes create additional burdens to the system. To help combat these problems, in 2006, the judicial branch began several projects that included expanding the infrastructure of public defender's offices, building infrastructure for implementing the criminal procedure code, and drafting a plan for sustainability and modernization of the public records system. Between 2002 and 2006, the budget of the Attorney General's Office rose by 153 percent, whereas between 2004 and 2007, the budget for the court system and the Public Ministry (the Public Prosecutor's Office) increased by 95 percent and 194 percent, respectively.

Crime

Classification of Crime

The current criminal code was passed in 1974 under the Somoza dictatorship and is substantially the same as the original 1879 criminal code, which divided punishable crimes into misdemeanors and felonies. In 2000, the National Assembly began writing a new penal code, but its approval has been delayed by extended political disagreements.

Murders in Nicaragua are classified as homicides and assassinations, which are divided into completed acts, attempts, and blocked attempts. Further, homicides can be intentional, culpable, and culpable vehicular homicides. Parricides and infanticides and their attempts are separate crimes. Murder is punishable from 1 to 25 years, depending on the relationship between the victim and offender as well as the circumstances of the homicide. The murder of one's parents, children, close ascendants, or close descendants (legal or common law) can result in 10 to 25 years in prison. If the victims are adoptive parents or children, the punishment is 6 to 14 years. If the offender kills his or her spouse in the heat of passion when surprised by adultery, the punishment is 2 to 5 years in prison. Deliberate, intentional homicide of a nonrelative is punishable by 3 to 6 years. Assassination, which is premeditated, cruel, murder for hire, by suffocation, arson or poison, with treachery, or in the course of a burglary, is punishable by 15 to 30 years. For murder of an unrelated child less than 7 years old or of an infant, the punishment is 15 to 30 years. No crime is punishable by more than 30 years in prison.

Felony assault laws do not penalize the offender for his or her actions, but for the effects of those actions. The damage can be physically visible, such as a wound, or can be any alteration in health to the person. This includes mental humiliation or threats.

The sentence imposed after conviction, which can range from one to six years, depends on the severity and location of the injury. The new law provides that the offender receive the maximum sentence if the injuries are a result of domestic violence.

In August 1996, the National Assembly passed the Law on Aggression against Women, which is designed to establish a basis for prosecuting crimes against women. The Law to Prevent and Punish Domestic Violence, or article 230, was enacted as the result of a strategic alliance between politicians, government officials, community leaders, researchers, and legal and health professionals. To protect domestic violence victims, a judge can order the following: (1) prohibition or restriction of the presence of the aggressor within 100 meters from the victim's home or workplace; (2) the ability of the victim to return home if forced to leave because of violence or intimidation; (3) medical, psychological, or psychiatric assistance for the victim; (4) rehabilitation for the aggressor; (5) biological, psychological, and social examination/assistance for any children involved; (6) compensation for any possible damages; (7) seizure of any weapons in the aggressor's possession; and (8) prohibition on all forms of harassment, including electronic, that disturb the victim's tranquility. Punishment for a domestic violence conviction ranges up to five years' imprisonment. The law also allows for restraining orders when a woman fears for her safety.

Although abortion has been illegal in Nicaragua, there has been an exception for therapeutic reasons if three doctors agreed that there was a risk to the woman's life. In 2006, with support of Sandinista Daniel Ortega (who later became president), the law was amended to criminalize abortion even if the woman's life is in danger. A woman who obtains an abortion faces up to 4 years in prison. During the new law's first 11 months, there were 82 documented deaths of women who had had illegal abortions. Although the health ministry issued protocols that doctors should respond to obstetric emergencies, including post-abortion care, many doctors and other health officials are frightened to administer such aid for fear of being prosecuted. Punishment for medical personnel who perform an abortion is 5 to 10 years in prison.

Prostitution is not illegal, but its promotion is banned, as is human trafficking, which carries a prison sentence of 4 to 10 years. Nicaragua is a source country for trafficking of women and children for sexual exploitation.

In 1999, a National Forum against the Sexual and Commercial Exploitation of Children and Adolescents was established to publicly fight for children's rights. Violence against children is a significant problem, with one of five boys and one of three girls being a sexual abuse victim. Ten percent of those victims are younger than 13 years old. Several public forums on child exploitation and human trafficking were held, and anti-trafficking publications were publicly distributed. Abandoning a minor child 7 years old or younger can result in 3 to 5 months' confinement. If the child dies as a consequence of abandonment, the sentence is 5 to 10 years in prison.

People convicted of participating in a duel face 1 to 6 months' confinement if there are no injuries. If there is an injury, the punishment is 6 months to a year. Sexual assault and abuse, which includes marital rape, is punishable by 2 to 15 years' imprisonment depending on the type of assault. If the sexual assault is aggravated, 10 years is added to the proscribed sentence. False imprisonment for up to 8 days is punishable with 1 to 6 months' confinement plus a fine. If there is violence, coercion, or withholding of food, the sentence is 2 to 5 years. Kidnapping with violence, coercion, or withholding of food brings a 4- to 7-year sentence. Sequestering or kidnapping a woman or child under the age of 14 will add 1 to 2 years to the proscribed sentence.

As for crimes against property, robbery sentences range from 9 months to 10 years depending on the value of the stolen property. If there is violence or intimidation during the robbery, the sentences range from 6 years for minor injuries to 30 years if the victim dies. Extortion carries a sentence of 2 months to 2 years, and identity theft/swindling and defrauding are punishable from 6 months to 6 years depending on the value lost. Arson and other destruction carry sentences of 3 to 8 years if there are no injuries and 10 to 21 years if a death occurs. If the destruction is to residential property, the sentence is doubled but cannot exceed 30 years.

There are also crimes against business interests, including defrauding creditors, usury, and crimes against the national economy, with sentences that range from 6 months to 10 years. Crimes against public transportation range from 9 months for causing deterioration to 6 years for causing an accident. Punishments for crimes against public health range from 3 to 10 years. If injuries or death occur, the sentence is increased to 4 to 12 years for injuries and 10 to 21 years if a death occurs.

Criminal Responsibility

A person is exempt from criminal responsibility if any of the following are present: mental illness or serious alteration of consciousness with the inability to appreciate or determine the criminal nature of the act; 10 years old or younger; over 10 years old, but less than 15 years old if the act was without knowledge and intelligence; and acts in self-defense or defense of another person. The code also allows for mitigating circumstances of criminal responsibility and aggravating circumstances of criminal responsibility. Under the 1998 Law of the Child and Family, the Attorney General's Office investigates crimes committed by and against juveniles.

Incidence of Crime

Although Nicaragua is relatively safe, violent crime is increasing in the cities, with street crimes somewhat common. There is some gang activity, including robbery, assault, and stabbings, in poorer neighborhoods. According to the national police statistics, 108,930 crimes were committed in 2004. The crime rate increased from 1,731 crimes per 100,000 population in 2003 to 1,934 per 100,000 population in 2004. This was an increase of 19 percent from the previous year and 25 percent from 2000. Half of those crimes were property crimes, and 36 percent were crimes against individuals. Seventy-two percent of crimes against people were assaults, 4 percent were rapes, and 1.65 percent were homicides. Thirty percent of the property crimes were thefts, and 26 percent of property crimes were aggravated thefts, 10 percent of property crimes were robberies and violent thefts, and 4 percent of property crimes were fraud.

Despite the increase in overall crime, murders declined by 4.5 percent from 2000 to 2002. In 2002, there were 554 murders, which is a rate of 9.7 per 100,000 population. For forcible rape, the rate was 25.23, and the assault rate was 452.2. The overall rate for crimes against individuals was 627.48. The property crime rate was 880.91; aggravated theft rate was 227.56; theft with intimidation was 80.89; robbery and violent theft rate was 85.72; and fraud rate was 39.41.

There is a growing narcotics problem, especially the availability and use of cocaine. It is estimated that 0.9 percent of the population of ages 12 through 65 had consumed cocaine in 2006, and 1.1 percent had used cannabis during the same year. The larger problem, however, is drug trafficking. Because of Nicaragua's open access to the Atlantic and Pacific Oceans and the Pan American Highway, transnational drug trafficking syndicates have taken advantage of these infrastructures to transport illicit substances and illegal proceeds through the country via land, air, and maritime routes, which has effectively turned Nicaragua into a major transshipment nexus for South American cocaine and heroin heading for North America. A large quantity of narcotics is shipped by boat via Bluefields, Puerto Cabezas, and the Corn Islands regions. Lack of resources and technical capabilities and corruption in law enforcement agencies notwithstanding, cooperation between the judiciary and military intelligence groups yielded a significant growth in drug seizures and dismantlement of criminal groups in recent years. In 2008, the government of Nicaragua confiscated nearly 19.5 metric tons of cocaine and also conducted the first seizure of pseudoephedrine, a chemical precursor for the manufacturing of methamphetamine, in the country.

Finding of Guilt

Criminal Process

The criminal process begins with the arrest by police. In 1979, a professional national police force replaced the National Guard. The national police force, under the control of the Ministry of Government, is responsible for internal security, but it shares this responsibility in rural areas with the army.

The law prohibits arbitrary arrest and detention. Police must obtain a judicial warrant before detaining a suspect, and a prosecutor is required to accompany the police when the arrest is made. The police must then notify the detainee's family members within 24 hours of the arrest. The suspect can be held for a maximum of 48 hours so that the police can collect evidence prior to bringing the detainee before a judge. The judge then orders the accused released or transferred to jail. After the first 48 hours, the suspect has the right to bail, legal representation, and visits from family members. Because the laws regulating police practices have changed dramatically, actual police procedures often conflict with current law. Although the Constitution criminalizes torture, there is credible evidence that the police continue to beat and physically mistreat arrestees, often to obtain a confession. Further, the national police statistics indicated that approximately 21 percent of prisoners had not yet been convicted in 2006, compared with 16 percent in 2005.

After the initial arrest, the criminal process shifts into the judicial system, which has its roots in the continental European civil law tradition. The 1998 Organic Law of Judicial Power and its reforms regulate the judicial system. Justice administration guarantees the principles of equality, legality, and protection of human rights. In December 2002, a new criminal procedure code was adopted. The former written, inquisitorial system was replaced with a more oral, public, adversarial model. Under the former inquisitorial system, the local court judge reviewed all the relevant evidence in the case and amassed a written record. After a thorough investigation was conducted, the judge made a determination as to whether a crime was committed and whether the defendant was the offender. If those determinations were made, the case went to trial, where the prosecutor and defense attorney presented written evidence prior to the judge determining guilt or innocence of the accused.

The new adversarial process relies on prosecutors instead of judges and magistrates to file charges. The preliminary investigative stage is initiated either by a formal complaint from the victim or by the prosecutor's order. The investigatory phase ends with the charges being withdrawn, the charges being dropped for lack of evidence (temporarily or permanently), a decision not to prosecute, or formal charges being brought before the court. There are then pretrial proceedings to determine whether a trial is needed. A preliminary hearing must be held within 10 days to determine whether the case will go to trial or be dismissed.

Following the pretrial stage is a public trial, and the defendant is presumed innocent until proven guilty. He or she has the right to a jury trial with 12 jurors, the right to a lawyer, and the right to confront and question witnesses. The judge presides while the attorneys present oral arguments to a jury. Although jury trials have been restored, the jury system has not proven effective, partly because prospective jurors evade jury duty, thus delaying trials. If convicted, defendants have the right to appeal. Finally, the sentencing takes place. If the defendant is unable to afford a lawyer, one will be appointed by the court free of charge.

Prior to the 1998 Organic Law of Judicial Power, the presiding judge also appointed attorneys to represent indigent defendants pro bono, but many attorneys were able to pay a small fine instead of representing these clients. In 1999, a Public Defender's Office, which represents 70 percent of all defendants, was created to represent defendants who do not have the economic resources to hire private counsel. There are a total of 92 public defenders (13 in Managua), 61 percent of whom are women. In 2006, 6,883 defendants were represented, which was more than double the number represented two years earlier. The law allows the Public Defender's Office to intervene at the request of any person, including the defendant, family member, friend, acquaintance, or any other person or official. However, the earlier system remains in effect in areas that do not have public defenders.

Although the new system allows the accused enhanced access to the process, this radically different process may result in longer trial delays as the judicial system adjusts. Among the problems are staffing shortfalls for public defenders and prosecutors, who play a leading role in trials under the new system.

The standard for admissibility of evidence at trial is undergoing a transition in Nicaragua. Traditionally, the appraisal system was used. This system gave a specific value to each type of evidence. For example, documentary evidence was more valuable than testamentary evidence. In 1982, Nicaragua adopted the *sana critica* standard. Gradually, the criminal justice system is moving toward this evidentiary system, under which the judge uses logic to determine admissibility of evidence. Hearsay evidence is allowed as long as four responsible witnesses testify to the hearsay. Unlike common-law evidentiary rules that make predetermined judgments about which classes of evidence are not admissible, the *sana critica* standard permits the judge to make exclusionary decisions on a case-by-case basis. Although some illegally obtained evidence can be admitted into evidence, letters, documents, and other private papers seized illegally are not admissible. As the judicial process transforms, these evidentiary rules may change.

Alternative Dispute Resolution

Nicaraguan law provides for three forms of alternative dispute resolution (ADR): negotiation, mediation, and arbitration. Under the 2002 code of criminal procedure, alternative dispute resolution is available for certain victims after the defendant has admitted guilt. ADR can provide mediation, the withdrawal of charges, a plea, a shortened procedure, and a stay of proceedings. However, mediation is limited to cases of negligence, misdemeanors, petty crimes, and breaking and entering.

Recourse of Amparu

The system of *amparo* has its roots in the law of colonial Spain and was transported to Latin America in the 19th century. Traditionally, there are three interpretations of the meaning of *amparo. Amparo* is used as a remedy or means of challenging judicial decisions and to designate a type of injunction, which was usually used to protect real property rights. In addition, *amparo* is a procedural instrument for securing individual rights. This function, which comes from the complaint hearings of Aragon, was directly applied to the Spanish colonies, where *amparo* has been broadly expanded.

The Constitution of 1950, the Regulatory Statute of 1950, and the Constitution of 1974 provided relief against all violations of fundamental individual rights by acts of authorities. The rights of personal liberty, habeas corpus, and challenge to unconstitutional statutes were all included in Nicaragua's *amparo.* After the Sandinista Revolution, *amparo* was incorporated into the Fundamental Statute of the Republic of Nicaragua, the Statute on the Rights and Guarantees of Nicaraguans, and the 1987 Constitution.

Amparo is relief, through judicial decision, against all acts of authorities affecting the fundamental rights of individuals, including the right of personal freedom. The goal of *amparo* is to maintain the effectiveness of rights and guarantees that are formally guaranteed in the Constitution. It is used when a person is detained or threatened with detention by an authority, when detained by an individual, and when not detained, but a sentence of imprisonment has been set.

When a person is detained or threatened with detention by an authority, any citizen or resident of Nicaragua can appear before a court of appeals and petition for *amparo* for the detainee. The petition can be formally written, oral, by telegram, or by letter. The court then decides the facts, which include the name and official position of the detainer and the location of the detainee. If the petition for *amparo* is denied, it can be appealed to the Supreme Court of Justice. If it is granted, the court then prepares a Decree of Exhibition, which names an executor judge to investigate the facts. The executor judge can be any citizen but is usually a lawyer. He or she goes to the accused authority, who must answer immediately. The executor judge orders the authority to present the detainee and any documents or actions taken by the authority.

There are several situations that may occur. The authority can say that the detainee is not under his or her charge. If the whereabouts of the detainee are unknown, the court orders the attorney general to investigate to determine his or her whereabouts. If the person is being detained by the police, he or she must appear before the police judge within 24 hours. The police judge then has seven days to investigate and go to the attorney general, who determines whether a case exists against the detainee.

If the person is being detained by a criminal court judge, that judge has 10 days to go forward or to dismiss the case. If more than 10 days have passed, the executor judge can order the liberty of the detainee. If the judge does not obey, he or she can be tried for contempt of court. The executor judge makes a decision on the basis of what is found during the investigation. He or she then presents the findings to the court, which makes the final determination. The court usually accepts the findings of the executor judge as true and rules on that basis. Under the new Nicaraguan Constitution, *amparo* used for individual freedom cannot be restricted during a state of emergency, except for crimes against the national security.

Punishment

As of July 11, 2006, the country had 6,139 prisoners in its nine prisons and jails, which was an incarceration rate of 108 inmates per 100,000 inhabitants. This compares to 3,692 prisoners (including pretrial detainees) in 1996, a rate of 80 per 100,000 inhabitants, and 5,610 prisoners (including pretrial detainees) in 2001, or a rate of 98 per 100,000 inhabitants.

Prison conditions are harsh. According to the government's National Penitentiary System, the prison system is severely underfunded and understaffed. Prisons are overcrowded and lack adequate medical supplies and medical specialists. Forty-nine percent of prisoners sleep on concrete beds or mattresses directly on the floor. The quality of prison food remains poor, and malnutrition is a problem in police holding cells and local jails. As a result, many prisoners must rely on food, medicine, and medical

Alleged members of the Sinaloa drug cartel are transferred back to jail after appearing in court in Tipitapa, 18 miles north of Managua, Nicaragua, June 29, 2007. (AP Photo/Esteban Felix)

attention from visitors, religious groups, and charitable organizations.

The Bluefields prison, described as obsolete, deplorable, and inhumane by the general director of the prison system, has only four toilets and two showers for more than 100 prisoners in a prison built for 40 prisoners. Occasionally, prison authorities release prisoners if they can no longer feed them. Many of the jails and holding cells have deteriorated infrastructure, inadequate electric and sewage systems, and lack of potable water. Holding cells are often poorly ventilated, unhygienic, and overcrowded.

Women make up 3.8 percent of the prison population. There are two all-female prisons. In addition to the women's prison in Managua, a women's prison opened for 60 prisoners in Estelí in March 2008. Elsewhere, women are guarded by female custodians in separate wings of male prisons. The women's prison system and the Public Defender's Office work together to ensure proper functioning of the women's prisons.

Juvenile Inmates

The juvenile prison population has been declining. The percent of prisoners who were juveniles between the ages of 15 and 18 declined from about 4 percent in 1999 to 2 percent in 2007. Although juveniles are usually held in separate wings from adult prisoners, a small detention facility for juveniles recently opened. It employs a psychologist, a social worker, and a sociologist.

According to a recent survey by the Human Rights Ombudsman's Office, the police did not inform more than 21 percent of the juveniles the reason for their detention at the time of their arrest, mistreated 47 percent of the juveniles, and held 48 percent of the detained juveniles for more than three days or more before seeing a judge. Half of the juveniles surveyed were not aware that they had been assigned a defense attorney, and 24 percent were incarcerated with adults.

Jo-Ann Della Giustina

Further Reading

Blandino, Magda. (n.d.). *Guide to Legal Research in Nicaragua.* New York University Law Global Web site: http://www.nyulawglobal.org/globalex/Nicaragua.htm.

Justice Studies Center of the Americas. *Report of Justice: Nicaragua.* CEJA Web site: http://www.cejamericas.org/reporte/muestra_pais.php?idioma=I NGLES&pais=NICARAGU&tipreport=REPORTE2&seccion=TASADELI.

Maclure, Richard, and Melvin Sotelo. (2004). "Youth Gangs in Nicaragua: Gang Membership as Structured Individualization." *Journal of Youth Studies* 7: 417–432.

Rocha, Jose Luis. (2007) "Mapping the Labyrinth from Within: The Political Economy of Nicaraguan Youth Policy concerning Violence." *Bulletin of Latin American Research* 26: 533–549.

Panama

Legal System: Civil
Murder: High
Burglary: Medium
Corruption: Medium
Human Trafficking: Medium
Prison Rate: High
Death Penalty: No
Corporal Punishment: No

Background

The Republic of Panama is located in Central America, bordered by Colombia, Costa Rica, the Caribbean Sea, and the Pacific Ocean. With a unitary, republican, and democratic form of government, the country is organized into 9 provinces that are further subdivided into 75 municipalities, 3 indigenous territories, and 620 townships. Panama is an isthmus that has a total area of 78,200 square kilometers. In 2009, it had a population of 3.4 million inhabitants and a life expectancy of 74 years for men and 80.2 for women. Mestizos of mixed African, Amerindian, and European ancestry represent the largest ethnic group (70 percent), followed by West Indians (14 percent), Caucasians (10 percent), and

Amerindians (6 percent). Whereas Spanish is the official and dominant language, English is widely spoken by the West Indians and by many members of the upper middle class. Nearly 84 percent of the population profess the Roman Catholic faith. The urbanization rate is as high as 73 percent, with more than half the population living in the Panama City-Colon metropolitan region. About 32 percent of Panamanians live in poverty, and 6.3 percent of the labor force was unemployed in 2003. The literacy rate surpasses 90 percent. Six-year primary education is mandated for all children.

History

The first indigenous residents of Panama were the Cuevas and the Coclé Amerindians. Unlike the empires of the Incas or the Mayan city-states, the Cuevas and the Coclé never organized themselves above the level of villages, which were headed by autocratic chieftains assisted by councils of elders. But these earliest tribes were destroyed by disease and fighting when the Spanish arrived in the 1500s.

Panama first became known to Europeans in 1501 when Rodrigo de Bastidas landed there, but it was explored and settled by Christopher Columbus in 1502. In an expedition led by de Bastidas, Vasco Nunez de Balboa crossed the Central American isthmus and became the first European to see the Pacific Ocean. Panama was quickly transformed into the traffic circle and bazaar of Spain's empire in the New World. Precious metals from South America were shipped to Panama City, transported across the isthmus, and loaded aboard ships for Spain. The isthmus remained under the Spanish imperial rule for three hundred years (1538–1821).

Panama declared its independence from Spain in 1821 and joined the Great Colombia—a confederation composed of Colombia, Venezuela, Ecuador, and Panama. A presidential decree of 1825 provided that Spanish laws in force in the colonies up to 1808 would be a supplementary source of jurisprudence to the Colombian laws enacted by autocratic executive and subordinate legislatures in Bogota. The isthmus tried several times to secede from the union but failed in most of these attempts. A brief independence was achieved between 1863 and 1885 when Panama declared itself the Sovereign State of the Isthmus, enacted a separate constitution, and elected its own assembly. The assembly audaciously replaced Spanish laws with an autonomous set of civil and administrative codes, which later inspired other Colombian states to follow suit. The use of the Spanish legal instruments did not end until the 1873 enactment of the national Colombian Civil Code, which finally abrogated the Spanish law along with all previously promulgated codes.

The Panamanians' aspiration to become an independent state was fulfilled by geographic destiny. A trans-isthmian canal had captivated public imagination since the beginning of Spanish colonization. Between 1880 and 1890, Ferdinand de Lesseps tried and failed to construct a sea-level canal on the site of the present Panama Canal. But the ambition of the French developer was inherited by the United States, which in 1903 prompted the independence of Panama and in 1904 forced the Hay/Bunau-Varilla Treaty on the newly formed republic. The bilateral accord gave de facto sovereign rights to the United States in a zone roughly 10 miles wide and 50 miles long, where a canal would eventually be built and administered by the United States in perpetuity. A common-law area subsisted in the Panama Canal Zone: courts within the zone applied U.S. federal laws until new treaties between the two countries abolished these practices in 1979.

Between 1903 and 1968, Panama developed a constitutional democracy led by an oligarchy with strong business ties. The constitutions of 1941 and 1946 guaranteed universal social rights and created the explicit duties of the welfare state; these constitutional mandates were subsequently realized by the passing of the Labor and a Health Code as well as the enactment of a progressive tax code. Beginning in the 1950s, the Panamanian military began to revolt against the hegemony of the political establishment, and in 1968, the National Guard succeeded in removing the popular President Arnulfo Arias Madrid from power after numerous attempts. The commander of the National Guard, General Omar Torrijos, immediately formed a military government to replace the civilian regime. Torrijos suspended most constitutionally guaranteed freedoms, abrogated all political parties, and fired most judicial civil servants. Through the new constitution in 1972, he created a single-party legislature and granted the head of the National Guard the exclusive authority to name cabinet ministers and Supreme Court justices. Although Torrijos's rule was ruthless and corrupt, his magnetic personality, populist social programs, and nationalist stance against the United States secured broad public support for his regime.

Torrijos's death in 1981 changed the facade but not the essence of Panama's political life. The 1983 constitutional reform, which abolished the most dictatorial clauses of the previous constitutional reform, continued to proscribe a dominant role for Panama Defense Forces in the political life of the country. By this time, General Manuel Noriega had emerged as the undisputed strongman in firm control of all state institutions. Noriega was not capable of maintaining a broad support base and suffered a devastating defeat in the presidential elections of May 1989, in which Panamanian voters overwhelmingly supported the opposition leader Guillermo Endara. Noriega swiftly annulled the outcome of the election and launched a new round of repression against dissenters. In December 1989, the U.S. military directly intervened in Panama to remove Noriega from power and to restore democratic institutions.

The Electoral Tribunal quickly reinstated the results of the May 1989 election, and Endara was inaugurated as the new president in December 1989. Endara created a new police force entrusted with the mission of conducting law enforcement under the principles of democracy and the rule of law. Whereas visible improvement in human rights was achieved by this criminal justice reform, much less satisfactory was its impact on crime control. Subsequent administrations of Ernesto Perez Balladares and Mireya Moscoso were marred by allegations of widespread corruption, and in 2004, Martin Torrijos, son of the former military dictator, won the presidency on a platform of a zero tolerance for corruption. New anticorruption legislation was passed to improve the transparency of government, and a National Anti-Corruption Council integrating ranking officials and civic figures was formed. The number of political appointees decreased, and the percentage of technocrats increased in Torrijos's government. Despite these systemic efforts, corruption remains a severe problem in the Panamanian political life.

Government

Panama is a representative democracy with three branches of government: executive and legislative branches elected by direct vote for five-year terms and an independently appointed judiciary. Presidential and legislative elections are universal and mandatory for all citizens 18 years and older. Presidential elections do not require a simple majority, and Panama's last three presidents were elected with the support of only 30 to 40 percent of voters. Weak popular mandates have seriously undermined government effectiveness. The president is both head of state and head of government and appoints cabinet ministers and the directors of several regulatory entities at his or her discretion. Since the fall of Noriega, and the end of the 21-year military dictatorship, Panama has successfully completed four peaceful transfers of power to opposing political factions. Several executive bodies play an important role in the administration of criminal justice, including the Ministry of Government and Justice manages the Public Force, which is responsible for national defense and public safety, and the Directorate of Corrections, which administers all penitentiaries and penal issues.

The legislative branch consists of a 74-member unicameral National Assembly. It enacts laws and hears cases during impeachment proceedings. Although Panama's political arena is dominated by two major parties, the National Assembly is elected by proportional representation in fixed electoral districts, which allows the representation of many smaller parties, many of which are propelled by personal charisma of their leaders more than political beliefs or ideals.

The judicial power is headed by a nine-member Supreme Court and covers all district tribunals and municipal courts. Supreme Court justices jointly arbitrate constitutional litigations; groups of three justices form four chambers: Civil, Criminal, Contentious-Administrative, and General Affairs. The Supreme Court is also responsible for constitutional review of legislations and policies: With the presence of the national attorney general or the solicitor general, the plenary hears and rules on the constitutionality of the form and/or substance of decrees, laws, resolutions, agreements, and other acts that are brought before the court by any citizen or citizen group. Decisions or rulings by the court cannot be appealed. The nine justices are appointed by the consensus of the cabinet and confirmed by the National Assembly. Justices serve for 10 years and elect their president every two years. There are currently also five Chamber secretaries, 12 administrative offices, an Internal Auditing Service, and a Judicial and Informatics Academy. An autonomous Electoral Tribunal supervises voter registration, the election process, and the activities of political parties. The rest of the judicial branch is composed of superior courts, with 38 judges and 10 court secretaries distributed at the district level, the circuit courts and municipal courts, and the public defender's offices in each province.

Crime

Classification of Crimes

The criminal code of the Republic of Panama classifies breach of public order, harm to public security, violation of public trust, indecency, injury of person, and damage of property as felonies (*delitos*) or misdemeanors (*faltas*), depending on the seriousness of the offense. Despite the clear differentiation defined between felonious and misdemeanor offenses, the handling of convicted offenders allows great flexibility. Punishments also are applied on convicted offenders according to the seriousness of the crime, but in virtually all cases, the code ascertains maximum and minimum sentences within which a judge exercises his or her discretion to dispense a punishment that fits the crime. In assaults against state agents, much harsher sentences are made available.

Crime Statistics

In 2006, Panama recorded a national average of 11.04 homicides per 100,000 population, according to the United Office of Drugs and Crime 2005–2006 survey. Violence in Panama is mainly an urban problem with large cities suffering a homicide rate (29.90 per 100,000) nearly three times as high as the national average. Yet the most alarming development in Panama's public safety is the recently observed steep upward trend in most crime categories. Between 2001 and 2005, the overall crime rate increased by 83.85 percent; excluding rape, whose dramatic growth in official statistics appeared to be driven by a steady change in victims' reporting behavior, drug offenses and major theft reported the greatest jump during the five-year period, by 50.32 percent and 69.50 percent, respectively, according to the United Nations survey. The homicide rate remained stable, whereas dramatic drops were seen for robbery and major assaults. These longitudinal patterns suggest that there is a pressing need to find effective strategies to curb the rise of drug-related and property offenses. As of 2006, the number of crimes per 100,000 population recorded by police were as follows:

Drug	85.82
Auto theft	18.83
Major theft	545.33
Robbery	38.14
Rape	24.09
Major assault	36.29
Homicide	11.04

Drug Problem

Panama functions as a major transit country in the global distribution of illicit drugs. Its strategic geographic location and developed port infrastructures facilitate transshipment of cocaine and heroin from the Andean countries to the United States and Europe. Criminal syndicates take advantage of Panama's rapidly expanding international hub airport of Tocumen, the containerized seaports, the Pan-American Highway, numerous unguarded airfields, and unprotected and exposed shorelines on both the Atlantic and the Pacific to smuggle drugs and weapons, which has not shown signs of abatement. Drug trafficking is most out of control between the secluded and lawless Darien province and Colombia.

The flow of cocaine and heroin has contributed to increasing domestic drug abuse. About 0.2 percent of Panama's adult population abuse opiates, including heroin, and 1.2 percent abuse cocaine, according to the United Nations Office on Drugs and Crime 2008 World Drug Report. Panama does not produce significant amounts of drugs or precursor chemicals. Although only limited volumes of cannabis are cultivated locally, a staggering 4 percent of adult Panamanians consume cannabis. Other drugs that are being sold and used in the country include amphetamines (0.4 percent) and Ecstasy (0.6 percent).

Although the recent Torrijos regime actively cooperated with the United States on security and law enforcement issues, its collaboration with regional neighbors in drug control was perceived as less vigorous. In 2007, Panamanian law enforcement seized 60 metric tons of cocaine—the largest confiscation of illicit drugs in recent history. Panama is a signatory of the 1988 United Nations Drug Convention, which entails the responsibility of criminalizing the possession of psychoactive substances and participating in the international regime of control.

Human Trafficking

Panama is a source, transit, and destination country for women and children trafficked for the purpose of commercial sexual exploitation, according to the U.S. Department of State's *Trafficking in Persons Report 2008*. Domestic demand for sex workers drives the flow of modern slavery and involves most victims: Girls and boys are traded within the Panamanian territory into the sex trade. Other women are exported to Jamaica and Europe to cater strong demands for Panamanian prostitutes, whereas children and youths from rural areas may be trafficked internally to large cities and sold as very efficient labor. Colombian, Dominican, and other Central American victims are trafficked into Panama. Some Colombian women enter Panama with the intention to find employment in Panama's legalized sex industry through the country's *alternadora* visa program. The *alternadora* visa legally permits foreign women to participate in and contribute to Panama's booming sex economy. Nevertheless, some Colombian women who hold *alternadora* visas are deceived by criminal organizations as to the true nature of employment and later become victims of involuntary servitude and forced prostitution.

Human suffering from sex and labor trafficking will not decline in Panama unless authorities intensify law enforcement efforts against major traffickers and decide to terminate the *alternadora* visa program. More cross-border collaboration with Colombia and Central American neighbors will also be needed to strengthen assistance to and protection for foreign trafficking victims and to devise an effective empowerment strategy to prevent vulnerable women and at-risk youth from becoming new victims.

Finding of Guilt

Criminal Procedure

A gradual progression from the inquisitorial system to a mixed criminal procedure system with clear elements borrowed from the adversarial tradition is currently underway. The Panamanian procedural code supports a two-phase criminal adjudication process: the first stage encompasses a summary proceedings stage for preliminary investigation, which is mainly written, and the second stage consists of an oral trial that is public or plenary.

The preliminary investigation is initiated and conducted by prosecutors, who produce and submit a written report known as a *vista fiscal* at the end of their summary investigation. In the *vista,* the prosecutor may request an order to prosecute the accused or ask for a final or conditional stay of proceedings, as appropriate. If the prosecutorial inquiry is complete and conclusive, the process advances to the intermediate stage, and the court proceeds to a decision on the merits of the case. At this point, and at no other time, the court may broaden the scope of the investigation.

An indictment may follow the prosecutorial presentation of charges and their call to trial to signal the beginning of the criminal trial. During the indictment, the courts may also formally request the collection of specific evidence or testimony deemed essential to the legal battle. Trial hearings are oral and public; during these hearings, the judge is authorized to direct the debate and examine the parties involved. To conclude the trial, the judge will close the discussion and issue a formal statement. If the defendant is convicted, sentence is then handed down. Both the accused and the prosecutor have the right to appeal.

A trial by jury is available to defendants in serious public safety cases such as those involving deaths caused by public hazards, or those involving deaths resulting from sabotaged transportation or communications systems. Juror service is compulsory and uncompensated. The defendant can waive the right to trial by jury.

Rights of the Accused

The Panamanian Constitution provides that arrests must be carried out with a warrant issued by the appropriate authorities and that suspects are to be brought before a judge within 24 hours. In theory, defendants can be detained during the pretrial period for only an acceptable length of time, which is defined as up to two months for the preliminary investigation and up to four months for the follow-up investigation phase, depending on the number of suspects. All defendants enjoy the right to appeal.

These constitutional guarantees are generally safeguarded by the criminal justice system in practice, with the exception of pretrial detention. According to 2002 statistics, about 55 percent of the prison population was made up of pretrial detainees, and the average period of pretrial custody was 12 months. In fact, pretrial detention in excess of the maximum sentence for the alleged crime was common. Yet no complaints about systematic violation of human rights in the administration of justice have been made by major international watchdogs such as Amnesty International and Human Rights Watch in recent years, and Freedom House has ranked Panama as one of the Central American countries most successful in promoting political freedoms and protecting civil rights among the citizenry. According to a 2006 Inter-American Development Bank survey, 46 percent of Panamanians believe that the justice system protects citizens' rights but fails to punish criminals.

Juvenile Justice

Youths under 18 years of age are considered juvenile and processed by separate juvenile courts. Juvenile offenders who are convicted by a court are cared for in a special system that provides protection and education and attempts to rehabilitate minors before they come of age. Institutionalization is seen as the intervention of the last resort, and the progress of institutionalized children is regularly reviewed by a juvenile judge. When juvenile offenders reach the age of majority at 18 years, the sentence imposed by the juvenile court is terminated. If they are to remain in detention for special reasons, they will be transferred to special institutions, still under the supervision of the juvenile justice system.

Punishment

Types of Punishment

Typically, sentences or sanctions for convicted offenses carry upper and lower limits in which the judiciary has discretion. However, regardless of prison sentence, labor is a requirement. With regard to punishment, the most severe penalty an individual may receive is a 20-year sentence. Neither capital punishment nor corporal punishment is utilized. *Reclusion* is a severe sanction in which the sentence may range from 30 days to 20 years, whereas the simple sentence, *prision,* ranges from 30 days to 18 years. Parole is determined based on the seriousness of the offense; offenders sentenced to *reclusion* are parole-eligible after serving approximately three quarters of the sentence. and *prision* offenders are eligible after serving two-thirds. Hence, both *reclusion* and *prision* are sentences received for felony offenses.

Misdemeanor offenses may receive a sanction of *arresto,* in which the sentence is typically less than 18 months and may be served within a local holding facility. Offenders who commit offenses that do not require custodial detention include *confinamiento.* With this sanction, the offender is limited in his or her physical movement. The offender may be required to remain in the place of residence and may also be required to stay away from the physical location in which the offense or offenses occurred. The length of *confinamiento* is typically left to judicial discretion. *Multas* are sanctions that require some payment to the criminal justice or judicial system. *Multas* may be a single sanction, or it may be used in combination with *reclusion, prision,* or *arresto.* An offender may receive *arresto* for failure to pay *multas.*

Within the Panamanian criminal court system, offenders who are deemed fit to remain in the community may receive a sanction of *condena condicional. Condena condicional* is a suspended sentence in which an offender is allowed to remain in the community with certain, fixed conditions. Typically, this sanction may be used for first-time offenders. Additionally, offenders who commit serious felony offenses are generally not eligible for this sanction as a matter of public safety. Some conditions of *condena condicional* may include reporting changes in life situations to the court (change in address, marriage, employment); the offender may be required to visit the court, or criminal justice personnel may conduct site visits to monitor offender whereabouts and behavior. If an offender violates a condition of *condena condicional,* the suspended sentence may be imposed.

Prisons

The modern Panamanian prison system was initiated in 1940 with the creation of the Directorate of Corrections. In 1942, Panama reorganized its prison management following recommendations by experts from the U.S. Federal Bureau of Prisons who were surveying prisons in the United States and elsewhere. The key new practice conceived in this encounter with American officials was the classification of inmates by age, offense, gender, and mental health status and the matching of inmate profiles with institutional specializations of correctional facilities.

Currently, each provincial capital has a prison where both pretrial detainees and sentenced offenders are housed. Oftentimes, hardened criminals are mixed with first-time offenders, a practice that encourages abuse and undermines the goal of rehabilitation. Prisoners are afforded training and programming to better equip them to reenter into society to avoid recidivism. The prison system purports to reject physical and emotional abuse of prisoners. Female prisoners are housed separately from male prisoners. Female correctional facilities are typically operated by nuns with a focus on discipline and humaneness; they tend to deliver much better care and services than male facilities. Likewise, juveniles are housed separately from adults and provided with educational and counseling in segregated units or facilities to nurture their human capital and to ameliorate the effect of stigmatization.

Between 2000 and 2006, Panama's prison population grew by an average of 5 percent a year, according to the Justice Studies Center of the Americas. In total, the entire prison population increased by 37 percent during the six-year period. By 2006, Panamanian prisons were operating at 138 percent of their functional capacity. Women represented 6.8 percent of all inmates in 2006, and 41 percent of the entire population have been convicted of a crime,; the remaining 59 percent are awaiting sentencing. These figures suggest that the overstretched pretrial detention remains unsolved. Inmate populations as of 2006 were 10,849 males and 791 females.

Traqina Emeka and Hung-En Sung

Further Reading

Meditz, Sandra, and Dennis M. Hanratty, eds. (1987). *Panama: A Country Study.* Washington, DC: GPO for the Library of Congress.

Pearcy, Thomas L. (2006). *The History of Central America.* Westport, CT: Greenwood Press.

Rico, J. M. (1979). "Crime and Criminal Justice in the Caribbean." *Revue Interrnationale de Criminologie et de Police Technique* 32: 345–356.

Paraguay

Legal System: Civil
Murder: High
Burglary: High
Corruption: High
Human Trafficking: Medium
Prison Rate: Medium
Death Penalty: No
Corporal Punishment: No

Background

Paraguay, located in the interior of South America, is approximately 407,000 square kilometers, with a population of about 6 million people, 95 percent of whom self-identify as mestizo (Spanish and Native American) decent. This heritage makes Paraguay the most racially and culturally homogeneous state in Latin America. Guaraní, the language of the indigenous people, is more commonly spoken, but most governmental and business transactions are conducted in Spanish.

The government itself is nominally democratic with elected officials serving in a system of divided powers. Paraguay has a long history of political problems exacerbated by despotic rulers, entrenched corruption, economic frailty, and complex international issues. In the modern era, Paraguay has sought to strengthen its global position through a series of alliances, both with immediate neighbors and throughout the hemisphere. Today, Paraguay is a member of the Tri-Border Area (TBA), along with its neighbors Argentina to the southwest and Brazil to the east (Cavallaro et al. 2003). Paraguay also holds membership in the United Nations (UN), the Organization of American States (OAS), and the Latin American Integration Association, and is a signatory of the 1947 Inter-American Treaty of Reciprocal Assistance (Rio Treaty) (Cavallaro et al. 2003).

Paraguay is strongly shaped by its colonial legacy, but its human history extends much further than the Spanish *Entrada.* Guaraní-speaking indigenous tribes were the land's earliest inhabitants. As a matter of fact, Guaraní remains the most widely used language in Paraguay today, after Spanish. Unlike many of the other South American colonies, Paraguay had little gold or silver, making it less attractive to the Spanish Crown. From 1608 until their expulsion from the Spanish dominions in 1767, the Jesuits maintained an extensive establishment in the south and east of Paraguay. In 1811, Paraguay revolted against Spanish rule and became one of the first independent states in Latin America.

Paraguay has long been ruled by dictators, but none was more influential than General Alfredo Stroessner. Stroessner took control of Paraguay on May 4, 1954, when he deposed President Federico Chaves. Stroessner retained control until a 1989 military coup led by General Andres Rodriguez removed him from power.

Given the brutal and secretive machinations of the Stroessner government, it is difficult to speak with much authority on the subject of criminal justice in Paraguay before 1990. As the following sections illustrate, matters have generally improved, but a number of major hurdles remain before the administration of justice in Paraguay can be characterized as broadly fair, humane, or modern. Moreover, in those cases where information is missing, it is often difficult to tell whether the gap exists because of benign neglect in reporting or willful opacity.

Although one hopes that the bleak conditions of the Stroessner regime are a thing of the past, a 2003 assessment from the Paraguayan Attorney General's Office is hardly encouraging. In their article appearing in the *International Review of Penal Law,* M. Rika and M. Miyamae state, "Values have been inverted. The honest is considered a fool and the majority of public servants wish to attain positions of direction to take advantage, not to serve citizenship" (p. 527), and they report the assistant attorney general's observation that corruption is not only accepted by the public but expected: "A public servant that performs his functions honestly is generally an exception and is considered a fool by the majority of the citizens."

Government and Court Structure

The "highly centralized" Paraguayan government underwent fundamental change with the 1992 adoption of a new constitution. Among the most significant changes is a division of governmental powers between the concurrently elected bicameral Congress (80-member Chamber of Deputies and a 45-member Senate) and the office of the president. Members of Congress are elected through a system of proportional representation. The deputies are elected by individual department and the senators through national election. Each of the 17 departments is also headed by an elected governor.

In general terms, the Paraguayan judiciary bears a strong resemblance to French and Argentine court systems. The highest judicial body in Paraguay is the five-member Supreme Court. This court has both appellate and original jurisdiction. In Paraguay, there are four appellate tribunals: civil/commercial, criminal, labor, and juvenile. The nation also has special courts for civil, criminal, and commercial cases. Many less serious cases may be resolved by a localized system of justices of the peace. There is also a military court system specific to the armed forces.

Each district in Paraguay has a judge appointed by the central government. These courts are intended to function as lower courts of original jurisdiction. Federal judges and magistrates are appointed by the president for a five-year term. These terms coincide with the presidential term, such that the Supreme Court judges and lesser tribunals are always named by the sitting executive. All Supreme Court appointments are subject to the approval of the Council of State. As per the 1992 Constitution, selection of judges is done by an independent body working with both the Congress and the executive branches.

The U.S. Agency for International Development (USAID) reports that substantial efforts are being made to combat corruption throughout the Paraguayan government. With particular regard to the judiciary, the USAID notes, "A Judicial Code of Ethics was approved and is being implemented by the Supreme Court. Selection criteria, exams and a computerized registry for judges, prosecutors and public defenders have been developed and are also being implemented." Lending an internal perspective to the reforms, the assistant attorney general concludes, "It is possible to say that many mistakes have been made, but in global analysis, results are quite positive and encouraging" according to the Rika and Miyamae report. According to the Organization of American States Commission on Human Rights report on Paraguay (2001), among the promising changes is the legislative change from an "inquisitorial" criminal procedure, wherein the judge sought evidence and issued rulings on it, to the current "accusatory" process, in which the Public Ministry is assigned the function of collecting the evidence and formulating the indictment, and the judge is limited to judging.

Crime

Crime Statistics

As an extension of the difficulties noted previously, reliable crime statistics are extremely difficult to obtain for Paraguay because police agencies did not compile comprehensive statistics during the Stroessner regime. Despite the fact that Paraguayan justice agencies are now beginning to collect data, there is still no coordinated data collection system in place. As such, the best available information about crime in the region comes from international nongovernmental initiatives such as the Pan American Health Organization (PAHO) and the International Crime Victim Survey (ICVS).

Homicide rates are considered by many to be the best available proxy for violence in a country. Murders are typically the most reported crimes, and as such, they can provide the most reliable measure of violence. The homicide rate in Paraguay has seen a modest increase since 1996, though 2006 did see a substantial drop in the police rate and the total number of reported homicides (13.7 compared to a high of 19.4 in 2004).

The ICVS can be considered another relatively reliable measure of crime statistics. The United Nations has collected data continuously since 1989, and more than 80 countries have taken part in the survey. It should be noted, however, that these victimization rates are for major cities of the country, not for the country overall. Paraguay ranks the highest in burglary rates, with 8.2 percent of those surveyed reporting their victimization. Car thefts and thefts from vehicles were low at 2 percent 8 eight percent, respectively. Rates of robbery in Paraguay were 6.7 percent, sexual assault was relatively low at 2.7 percent, assault with force was the lowest at 1.1 percent, and assault without force was also low at 2.0 percent.

Although published statistics are difficult to obtain for Paraguay, reported and resolved crimes were published in the *Reporte sobre la Justicia en las Américas 2004–2005.* The raw numbers for select crimes reported in 2002 show that breaking and entering makes up the single largest category of reported crimes, with 1,977 reported. The reported number of murders (890) is substantially lower than the number estimated by PAHO (1,198). This helps to underscore the difficulty in obtaining reliable information. Differences in the homicide rate notwithstanding, the raw data reveal approximately 655 reported vehicular homicides, 289 reported rapes, 10 abductions, 175 assaults, and 1,612 reports of persons causing intentional harm.

Though a relatively infrequent occurrence, abduction/kidnapping is perceived by many, both within Paraguay and outside of the country, to be a significant problem. One high-profile 2005 case involved the kidnapping and murder of Cecilia Cubas, daughter of former Paraguayan president Raul Cubas. Public outcry from the case was so strong that Congress increased the penalty for kidnapping to a maximum of 30 years. According to a report published in *ABC,* a Paraguayan newspaper, recently the governments of Switzerland and Italy warned their citizens against traveling to Paraguay, in part because of kidnapping fears. The U.S. State Department has recognized the increase in kidnapping incidents, but the Bureau of Consular Affairs maintains that kidnapping targets are primarily wealthy members of the Paraguayan business community and their families.

Finding of Guilt

Criminal Procedure

The criminal adjudication process begins with the prosecutorial preliminary investigation in which it is determined whether there exists sufficient evidence to press charges against a suspect and to put the person on trial. The investigation may be triggered by a complaint by a citizen to the police or prosecutor, or by a complaint made directly by the victim before the supervisory judge (*juez penal de garantías*). The national police and the judicial police serve as the collaborators of the Public Prosecutor's Office, and the national police work closely in this stage of the criminal process. Next, the supervisory judge examines the substance and legality of the investigative procedures in an oral and public hearing. At this stage, the processing of the case may end in a withdrawal of charge, plea bargain, conditional stay of proceedings, protective measures, or dismissal of charges.

The trial is oral and public and encompasses preparation, corroboration and deliberation, and sentencing. The trial judge decides on the outcome by ruling on the innocence or guilt of the defendant and the sentence to be applied. The accused has the right to challenge and appeal the ruling. The courts enforce the sentence through criminal enforcement judges (*jueces penales de ejecución*) who have the responsibility of ensuring the execution of the sentences as well as the protection of the constitutional rights of the sentenced offender.

Guarantee of Rights and Criminal Process

Article 17 of the Paraguayan Constitution clearly delineates a number of procedural rights afforded to all individuals involved in processes where criminal sanction is possible. Among the statutory guarantees are the following: the right to be presumed innocent, the right to a public trial, protection against double jeopardy, the right to have counsel, the right to a public defender for indigent defendants, the right to notification of charges, the right to review evidence, and the right to indemnification in the case of governmental errors.

That said, those things that are codified and those that are practiced appear to markedly diverge. Cavallaro and his co-researchers cite a particularly telling observation made by Paraguayan Attorney General Ruben Candia: "The presumption of innocence has been imported into Paraguay like some small Chinese shoes that have been put on our big feet, which obviously do not fit. This model was imported and 'forced' upon us . . . [it] does not fit our conduct and culture."

The Paraguayan Constitution also provides protections against cruel and degrading punishments (e.g., torture). Here, too, there appears to be a strong disconnect between the theoretical and the practical construction of justice. According to the U.S. Department of State, several citizens have been killed needlessly either in the midst of a police action or while in police custody. The U.S. Department of State outlined two such examples in its 2007 Human Rights Report for Paraguay. In the first of these, police allegedly killed six suspected kidnappers during a police raid in Minga Guazu, Alto Parana Department. The second speaks to a more generalized corruption and abuse of power: "Members of the National Commission for Citizen Security (CONASEG), which coordinates the public security efforts of government ministries, agencies, and civil groups, have been accused of killings, robberies, assaults, and protecting traffickers. Several members were under investigation . . . none had been prosecuted by year's end." These reports strongly echo the sentiments of Paraguay's Attorney General Candia that many so-called foreign ideas about criminal justice simply do not mesh with Paraguayan sensibilities.

As if the preceding account of judicial problems were not sufficiently grim, the Paraguayan court system is also notoriously overburdened. In an effort to relieve the congestion, the judicial branch established a special Mediation Office that aids parties in settling their case outside of court (*Reporte sobre la Justicia en las Américas 2004–2005*). The Mediation Office employs six professional mediators and nine private mediators, as well as a coordinator and an assistant coordinator (*Reporte sobre la Justicia en las Américas 2004–2005*). To date, it is unknown whether mediation is widely used as an alternative to court because the program is still in its infancy.

National Police

As of 2005, Paraguay's national police force had a total of 13,567 officers, or 223.5 per 100,000 inhabitants (*Reporte sobre la Justicia en las Américas 2004–2005*). The police are organized under the police command (*comando*), which is responsible for supervision, planning, coordination, oversight, and resource allocation; general departments (*direcciones generales*), and departments (*direcciones*). The *comandante de la policía nacional* is appointed by the president and has the rank of general commissioner (*comisario general comandante*). The national police force is composed of four general departments, including the Department of Order and Security, the Department of Police Institutes and Training, the Department of Logistics, and the Department of Police Services (*Reporte sobre la Justicia en las Américas 2004–2005*).

According to a report by the Policía Nacional del Paraguay, Paraguayan police officers undergo formal training at the national police academy, the Instituto Superior de Educación Policial (ISEPOL). Unlike at the police academies in the United States, students of the ISEPOL may participate in a variety of curricular tracks leading to both undergraduate and advanced degrees. Programs vary in length from one to three years.

The role of the national police in Paraguay has changed considerably with the newly revised criminal code. The police no longer have the sole authority to conduct criminal investigations. That duty has been assigned instead to prosecutors, with the police serving a largely ancillary role. Given that the police function as an autonomous agency apart from their investigative functions, this new restructuring has caused some obvious strain between the police and prosecutors.

Enmity with the prosecutors aside, the police in Paraguay face measurable challenges. Chief among these are a steadily declining public confidence combined with a public reluctance to enlist their help and an outright fear of the police. Beyond these concerns, the police at an organizational level appear plagued with numerous implacable problems. As documented by multiple sources, including the U.S. Department of State Country Reports on Human Rights Practices, the police in Paraguay have a long-standing tradition of brutality and excess that exists in the context of an organizational culture that is resistant, if not impervious, to change.

Despite significant changes in Paraguayan laws and leadership, the U.S. Department of State Country Reports on Human Rights Practices document the ongoing police practice of using torture for the purposes of extracting confessions, punishing escapes, and general intimidation. During visits to multiple police departments throughout Paraguay, the special rapporteur on torture and other cruel, inhumane, and degrading treatment or punishment from the United Nations notes that torture is still widely practiced by the police, particularly when an individual is first taken into police custody. The special rapporteur recounts that police in Ciudad del Este use a variety of torture techniques. including "beating, stripping detainees naked, placing plastic bags over their heads and squeezing their testicles."

Punishment

Types of Punishment

According the Library of Congress country study of Paraguay, various punishments are available for criminal offenses, including incarceration, confiscation of property and land, exile, and disqualification. Inmates are incarcerated in jails or prisons, depending on the level of their infraction, and those inmates serving terms in jails often perform involuntary labor as part of their sentence. Disqualification can entail the loss of public office or involve the stripping of some rights of citizenship, such as the right to vote or receive pension benefits. The death penalty was abolished in 1967, and according to the advocacy group Global Initiative to End All Corporal Punishment of Children, corporal punishment is prohibited by law both as a criminal punishment and as a sanction inside prisons. All this said, one is again confronted with the fact that those things mandated by law and those things that actually occur are routinely, often violently different. As evidence of this divergence, it is notable that capital punishment was banned during the height of the Stroessner regime. Even today, there appears to be little in the way of meaningful oversight regarding consistent or equitable distribution of criminal sanctions at any level of government. As such, to even attempt many of the most general descriptions regarding "typical sentences" or a schedule of penalties is at best a dubious task. One area, however, that does provide relatively more reliable insight (due in large measure to external observation) is the Paraguayan correctional system.

Prisons

In his article appearing in *Human Rights Quarterly*, M. Ungar notes that correctional populations have steadily increased in Paraguay and that the prison population has been growing since 1995. According to the International Centre for Prison Studies, the majority of those currently incarcerated (69.2%) are pretrial detainees. Female prisoners make up a small minority of those currently incarcerated (5.1%), juveniles account for less than 1 percent of correctional populations, and 5.7 percent of the prison population is made up of foreign prisoners.

Pretrial detainees account for the majority of those held in correctional institutions because alternatives to detention, namely bail, have been extremely limited by the criminal code. Case-processing time has further exacerbated the overcrowding of most Paraguayan prison institutions. Article 136 of the criminal procedural code extends the time limitation on case proceedings from three years to a maximum of four. This change was implemented to give officials more time to investigate and prosecute cases, but the practical effect has been to further stretch the capacity of the prison system beyond that which it is capable of holding. According to Freedomhouse.org, Paraguayan law further contributes to the pretrial detention problem because it is legal to hold those accused of crimes without a trial until the minimum sentence has been served, a practice that, according to the U.S. Department of State, is quite common.

The U.S. Department of State notes that there are 20 correctional institutions in Paraguay, which have the capacity to hold approximately 2,863 inmates. Tacumbú Prison in Asunción is the largest prison with an official capacity of about 900 inmates. This institution is horrifically overcrowded, currently holding about 3,000 inmates. According to the International Centre for Prison Studies, the total occupancy of the Paraguayan correctional system as of 2003 was vastly overcrowded at 178.5 percent.

Given that the Paraguayan correctional system operates at almost twice its designed capacity,

Inmates at Tacumbú Prison in Asuncion, Paraguay, February 15, 2010. Judges in Paraguay are demanding the closure of the notoriously overcrowded prison where six men share cells for two, and suspects awaiting trial must survive among convicted drug traffickers and murderers. The prison holds 3,100 people in a space meant for 1,200. (AP Photo/Jorge Saenz)

the prisons have failed to adhere to most international standards of incarceration. According to the U.S. Department of State Human Rights Report, all prisoners held in the Paraguayan system suffer from overcrowding, unsanitary living conditions, and mistreatment. The report noted that inmates in the maximum-security wing of the Ciudad del Este Regional Penitentiary suffered from overcrowded conditions and lacked light, ventilation, and basic hygiene. This wing is referred to as the "black hole," and the chances of an inmate contracting tuberculosis because of the conditions are quite high.

During a visit to several prisons in Paraguay, Manfred Nowak, the special rapporteur on torture and other cruel, inhumane, and degrading treatment or punishment from the United Nations, noted a number of problems in the majority of Paraguay's prisons. In both old and new prison facilities, essentials such as food, health care, and leisure and rehabilitation activities are largely absent. This leaves most inmates in the unenviable position of having to rely on family members to provide these basic services or, in the case of poor inmates with no family, doing without. For those inmates with financial means, it is possible to pay prison staff for basic necessities. The failure of authorities to provide for inmates and the low salaries paid to prison staff have led to corruption that is endemic in the entire prison system. Additional problems stem from a lack of security in most prisons. For example, the 3,000 prisoners held in the Tacumbú facility are watched by no more that 40 guards, well below the 120 that the UN standards recommend.

Consistently horrid prison conditions have prompted inmates to riot on numerous occasions. BBC news reported in 2000 that 2 juvenile inmates were killed and 30 injured in a fire during a protest over food. Another BBC news report in 2001 noted that 25 inmates were killed and more than 250 were injured at the Ciudad del Este facility when inmates started a fire to protest the shooting of an inmate.

Laurie Gould and Matthew Pate

Further Reading

Cavallaro, James, Jacob Kopas, Yucan Lam, Tomothy Mayhle, and Soledad Villagra de Biedermann. (2008). *Security in Paraguay: Analysis and Responses in Comparative Perspective.* Cambridge, MA: Harvard University Press.

Jaenike, William F. (2008). *Black Robes in Paraguay*. Minneapolis, MN: Kirk House Publishers.

Lopez, Abalberto. (2005). *The Colonial History of Paraguay: The Revolt of the Comuneros, 1721–1735.* New York: Transaction Publishers.

McSherry, J. Patrice. (2005). *Predatory States: Operation Condor and Covert War in Latin America*. Lanham, MD: Rowman & Littlefield Publishers.

Saeger, James Schofield. (2007). *Francisco Solano López and the Ruination of Paraguay*. London: Rowman & Littlefield Publishers.

Peru

Legal System: Civil
Murder: Medium
Burglary: High
Corruption: Medium
Human Trafficking: Medium
Prison Rate: Medium
Death Penalty: No
Corporal Punishment: Yes

Background

Peru is a South American country with a territorial extension of 1,285,215.60 square kilometers located between Colombia, Ecuador, Brazil, Chile, and the Pacific Ocean. The Peruvian territory comprises three very different geographic regions: the coast; the Andean zone, or sierra; and the jungle, or Amazon. Peru has a multiethnic and multicultural population of 28,220,764 people. Although the official language of the country is Spanish, part of the population living in the Andean and Amazon regions speak Quechua and other indigenous languages.

The Peruvian criminal justice system is composed of a single and independent Judicial Power integrated by all levels of courts, the Public Ministry that oversees the Public Defense and the National Penitentiary Institute, and the Peruvian National Police under the Ministry of the Interior. The judicial apparatus is organized around the Constitutional Tribunal, the highest interpreting body of the Constitution, and the Academy of the Magistrate, the autonomous body responsible for the formation and improvement of judges and prosecutors. As mandated by the Constitution, the public defender is responsible for protecting the constitutional and fundamental rights of the people and for supervising public services for the citizenry, including justice services.

Prior to its formal independence from Spain in 1821, Peru was an important colony and viceroyalty of Spain. Spain's influence on the country is evident its history and culture and in the Peruvian penal justice system. Like other Latin American nations, the Peruvian criminal justice system has been strongly influenced by the continental model and the European inquisitorial model, in a historic rather than modern version. In Peru, the Prosecutorial Public Ministry, autonomous from the Judicial Power, was only recently created in 1979 and did not become effective until 1981.

Legal System

Like many other countries in the Latin American region, Peru's criminal justice system is experiencing a shift from a mixed inquisitorial model to an accusatorial and adversarial system. Beginning in 2006, Peru began a gradual implementation of a new penal procedural code based on the central principles of oral litigation and equality between parties (prosecution and defense) before an impartial judge, public and oral proceedings, speedy legal processing, decongestion of the penal system, and the increased visibility of the victim throughout the penal process. The new penal procedural code has been adopted by a growing number of judicial districts of the country and will be implemented in the capital city of Lima by 2013. As of December 2008, the new criminal justice code was in use in 5 out of the 29 judicial districts of the country (Huaura, La Libertad, Moquegua, Tacna, and Arequipa).

The Peruvian criminal justice system has been operating in a democratic and republican structure that has survived repeated challenges from dictatorships, authoritarian tendencies of popularly elected administrations, and organized political violence. In the 1980s and early 1990s, economic and social crises gave birth to and nurtured two subversive groups that violently confronted the state: Sendero Luminoso and the Túpac Amaru Revolutionary Movement (or MRTA). The prolonged violence left thousands of victims among civilians, members of the armed forces, and members of the subversive groups.

In 1992, the brutal civil strife and the deep distrust of the government were used as a justification for a self coup by then president Alberto Fujimori, who shut down Congress, suspended the Constitution, and purged the judiciary with widespread popular and military support. The measure led to the limitation of individual guarantees and established special summary penal procedures for dealing with crimes regarded as terrorism and offenses against the state. *Sumarieda* (speedy penal processes without the guarantee of impartiality or the exercise of the right to a defense) became the general rule regulating criminal justice processes.

Beginning in the mid-1990s, activity by terrorist groups was significantly reduced and became limited to distant regions in the Peruvian jungle. Peru also began to reenter the international community and to rekindle the largely dormant economy. The ensuing economic growth triggered a lasting revitalization. Currently, Peru is recognized as one of the nations with the largest projections of growth in the region. Poverty and extreme poverty, concentrated in rural areas, were reduced to 39.3 percent and 13.7 percent, respectively, in 2007.

There are still signs of weakness in the judicial branch and public safety organs of the Peruvian state. Public distrust of the justice system has surpassed 80 percent, popular anger is directed at the delays in civil and criminal proceedings, formalism of the process, unpredictability of judicial decisions, corruption of judicial officials, and lack of coverage and coordination mechanisms in rural and Amazonian zones. According to the regional survey Latinbarometer 2007, confidence in the judicial power and the police hovered at 30 percent and 39 percent, respectively; and a 2008 survey of the Pontifica Universidad Catolica de Peru found that only 17 percent of the respondents reported confidence in the legal system. Insecurity, coupled with negative portrayals by the mass media and recurrent prison riots, is another crisis that fuels public perceptions of an utterly inefficient criminal justice system. In 2008, the Peruvian prisons were utilized at 169.1 percent of their designed capacity, a figure that represents an increase of more than 80 percent from 2002 (137.8%).

Positive results in terms of speediness of the process, transparency, respect for the right to legal counsel, decongestion of the judicial system, and reduction in the number of persons detained without a sentence have been reported in those districts where the new penal procedural code has been put into effect. Given these encouraging preliminary outcomes, much hope is placed in the consolidation of the new criminal processing and the subsequent emergence of a new legal culture.

Crime

Classification of Crimes

The current Peruvian penal code has been in effect since 1991. Illegal behaviors in Peru are classified into *delitos* (crimes) and *faltas* (misdemeanor). *Delitos* are serious crimes such as homicide, robbery, theft, or crimes against sexual liberty, and *faltas* are illicit acts that are less grave in nature, such as attempts against customs or tranquility of the neighborhood. Sanctions for *delitos* include deprivation of liberty among others, and *faltas* are punished with fines and community service.

Crimes in Peru are classified and denominated according to the public good the law seeks to protect. Major categories of punishable crimes include crimes against life, crimes against body and health, crimes against honor, crimes against liberties, crimes against the estate, crimes against trust and good faith in business, crimes against public safety, crimes against the environment, and crimes against humanity, among others.

The seriousness of a crime and its punishment can be aggravated by special circumstances during the commission of the offense. For example, simple homicide is considered grave when the perpetrator is a close relative of the victim (father, mother, or spouse) or if it is effected with cruelty or for reward. Crimes against property (such as robbery and theft) are considered grave when they are committed by organized groups or when violence is employed against persons or properties. Crimes against sexual liberty are aggravated when they are committed with the use of weapons; committed against children, adolescents, or persons with physical or mental disability; or perpetrated by the parents or siblings of the victim. When crimes present aggravating circumstances, sanctions that involve the privation of liberty can be increased to a life sentence (e.g., in the case of rape of a child under the age of 10 and property crimes that result in death or serious injury to the victim). In Peru, the death penalty is not practiced, but sentences can run consecutively to a maximum of 35 years. As of 2006, recidivism and chronic offending can be taken into account as aggravating circumstances at sentencing.

Juvenile Criminal Responsibility

In Peru, the legal age of 18 determines penal procedures and sanctions applicable to those accused of a crime. Persons under the age of 18 are processed by a special procedural and sentencing system typified in the Code for Children and Adolescents, whereas those who are adults are subject to the penal code. When a child above the age of 14 commits a penal infraction, socio-educative sanctions are applied; these include reprimand or warning, assisted liberty, community service, restricted liberty, and admission to a treatment facility. If the child is under the age of 14, measures of protection (i.e., care in child's own home, participation in support programs, incorporation into a substitute family, and admission to a special protection facility) are applied.

Judges, prosecutors, and defense attorneys specializing in family matters are involved in the penal proceedings against children and adolescents. Adolescents can be detained only by judicial order or if they are caught in the commission of a crime. All processes against adolescent transgressors are realized with intervention of the family prosecutor and the defense. If the infraction committed is not serious, it is typical that the judge commits the adolescent to the custody of his or her parents. In the case of serious crimes (e.g., rape or armed robbery), judges can subject the adolescent to preventive detention in a juvenile center for rehabilitation, operating under the Judicial Power. To sentence a minor, the judge must take into account the seriousness of the reported acts, the damage caused, the degree of the adolescent's responsibility, and a report provided by a multidisciplinary team composed of a psychologist, a doctor, and a social worker.

Penal Processes for Drug Offenses

In Peru, drug crimes are punished with a sentence of 5 to 35 years of imprisonment, depending on the seriousness of a crime. The most severe sentences are mandated when a person forces another person, whether by violence or threat, to cultivate cocaine, poppy, and marijuana plants. Harsh sentences are also handed to leaders of organized groups dedicated to drug trafficking. Sentences are also severe when drugs are sold to minors or when the offender is a member of an organization dedicated to this crime.

In Peru, the cultivation, fabrication, commerce, and trafficking of illicit drugs are prohibited by law. Importing and exporting illicit chemical precursors are also sanctioned. Possession of drugs for personal use is not punishable, as long as consumption of the drug takes place immediately and the amount of the drug possessed does not exceed 5 grams of basic cocaine paste, 2 grams of cocaine hydrochlorate, 8 grams of marijuana, or 2 grams of derivatives.

Because of Peru's geographic location in a region with a dense Amazonian jungle and various harbors with access to the Pacific Ocean, cases of illicit crop cultivation and trafficking of illicit drugs abound; these psychoactive goods are commercialized mainly through harbors and airports. The most common sanctions in these cases are preventive incarceration and deprivation of freedom. As of December 2008, there were 11,386 persons incarcerated for illicit drug traffic: 9,334 men and 2,052 women, both citizens and foreign nationals. Of this number, 1,876 had been sentenced, and 9,510 had only been accused of the crime.

Crime Statistics

The main sources for criminal statistics in Peru are the police statistics. The police periodically publish statistics on their Web site (http://www.pnp.gob.pe). The Public Ministry and the Judicial Power also publish statistics regarding judicial processes for committed crimes. Statistics gathered by the Peruvian National Police show than in 2007 there were more than 144,000 reported crimes, with robbery, theft, and injuries reported most frequently. Detailed statistics follow. In 2007, 2,934 homicides were reported, which represents a rate of 10.4 homicides per 100,000 persons. There were 7,223 reported sexual violations, representing a rate of 26 violations per 100,000 persons. A total of 41,606 robberies were reported in 2007, which translates into a rate of 147 robberies per 100,000 persons. This figure is added to 45,228 thefts (without violence), which represent a rate of 160 thefts per 100,000 persons.

In 2007, the Peruvian National Police executed 12,040 interventions connected to drug crimes: 3,719 police interventions for illicit traffic, 1,583 for commercialization, and 6,738 for consumption. During this same year, 721 drug couriers, both Peruvian citizens and foreign nationals whose objective was to transport drugs to other countries, were detained.

Peru is a country with vast rural regions. The most frequently occurring crimes in these zones are theft of animals and crimes relating to property of land and family crimes (domestic violence, failure to provide food). The Constitution of Peru provides protection for indigenous or rural justice so long as it does not violate fundamental rights. In urban zones, the crimes with the highest incidence of occurrence are robbery and theft (such as robbery of cellular phones in the street and in homes).

Finding of Guilt

Rights of the Accused

The new penal procedural code considers the right to the presumption of innocence and equality of means to both parties throughout the entire penal process. It dictates the right to a defense beginning at police investigation. The accused has the right to rely on an attorney of his or her choice in all police actions, detention, and penal processes. The principal rights of the accused are the following:

a. The right to know all charges against them; and in case of detention, the reason for this measure must be expressed, and the accused must be presented with the order of detention.
b. The right to assign a person or institution to be contacted and informed of their detention. This communication must take place immediately after apprehension.
c. The right to have a defense attorney beginning with the early stages of investigation.
d. The right to withhold a statement, and if the accused choose to provide a statement, they have the right to have their defense attorney present during the statement and in all activities that require the defense's presence.
e. The right against coercive or intimidating measures and the right against methods and techniques that can alter free will or to suffer any restriction not authorized by law.
f. The right to be examined by a legist doctor or by any other health care professional when health conditions require this.

Judicial Organization

The new penal procedural code establishes the following jurisdictional penal organs. First are the courts of preparatory investigation, responsible for hearing issues raised by parties in the preparatory investigation phase, such as deciding on preventive measures that can be applied to the accused during this phase (preventive detention). These courts are also responsible for proceedings regarding anticipated evidence and management of the intermediate phase and execution of sentences.

Second are the courts of decision that can be either collegiate or unipersonal. Collegiate courts are composed of three judges responsible for crimes punishable with a prison term over six years. The unipersonal courts are responsible for judging other minor crimes. Both the unipersonal and collegiate courts are responsible for directing the judgment phase and for resolving incidences of crime assigned to them respectively. In addition, unipersonal courts must be familiar with prison benefits and sentence appeals from the peace courts (community or local courts). Unlike Bolivia, Nicaragua and some provinces in Argentina, Peru does not make use of a jury system.

The Penal Process

The new penal process is divided into three phases. The first stage involves preparatory investigation headed by the prosecutor, with the objective of gathering elements of conviction to allow the prosecutor to decide whether to charge the accused with a crime. This stage gives the accused an opportunity to prepare a defense, demanding that fundamental rights are respected. This phase is subject to the control of the judge of preparatory investigation. The second stage is the intermediate phase directed by the judge of preparatory investigation who hears requests by prosecutors or any other parties in regard to suspension of the cause. Judgment or sentencing constitutes the concluding stage, directed by the unipersonal penal judge or the collegiate tribunal composed of three judges, who have the responsibility of reviewing evidence of the accusation while respecting the exercise of defense and contradiction, with the purpose of making a sound judicial decision.

Penal Prosecution and Early Termination of the Judicial Process

In Peru, penal prosecution of a crime is the responsibility of the prosecutors under the Public Ministry. Prosecutors have a broad discretion and can apply early termination to decongest the often backlogged system. In regard to discretional faculties, the new procedural penal code establishes that prosecutors can choose not to prosecute accusations or complaints if the acts are not considered crimes or if the charges have a small possibility of leading to a successful conviction in court.

In regard to early termination, prosecutors can apply the "principle opportunity" and reparative agreements. The principle opportunity refers to the prosecutor's abstention of penal action (1) when the accused has been greatly affected by the consequences of the crime, so long as it does not involve a serious crime; (2) when dealing with crimes that do not seriously affect the public interest; or (3) when extenuating circumstances exist and no public interest is seriously compromised.

The application of the principle opportunity requires reparation of damages and harm caused or a reparatory agreement between the accused and the victim when the conditions 1 and 2 exist. The reparatory agreement is proposed by the prosecutor, on his or her own or by request of the accused or the victim, and is appropriate in minor injuries, simple theft, theft of cattle, and common illicit appropriation, among other crimes.

Unlike other Latin American countries, in Peru, the principle opportunity can be used by prosecutors even after criminal proceedings have begun (but before a formal accusation is presented). A hearing before the judge of preparatory investigation is held in the presence of the accused and the victim, and the judge will then decide on terminating the legal process.

Negotiated Terminations and Mechanisms of Procedural Simplification

With regard to negotiated terminations, the new penal procedural code establishes three possibilities: immediate process, anticipated termination, and anticipated conclusion. The immediate process is applicable when the accused has been caught in the commission of the crime and has been detained, when the accused has confessed to the commission of a crime, or when elements of conviction gathered during investigation and previous interrogations of the accused evidence that the accused committed crime. This process is solicited by the prosecutor from the judge of preparatory investigation, who then decides if the requirement exists for immediate process. If immediate process is granted, the prosecutor forms the accusation or charges, which are then sent to the penal tribunal (collegiate or unipersonal) by the judge of preparatory investigation so that the tribunal can dictate the criminal procedure process and summon the accused to trial.

Anticipated termination occurs when an agreement exists between the prosecutor and the accused about the sentence and civil reparations and any other consequences of the crime. Anticipated termination must occur before a formal accusation is filed by the prosecutor. If necessary, a private audience will convene where the judge will explain to the defendant the agreement reached, the consequences of the agreement, and the limitations presented by arguing responsibility.

Anticipated conclusion occurs during the trial audience, after the accused has been informed of his or her rights. The judge will ask the accused if he or she admits to being the author or a participant of the crime in question, and whether the accused accepts responsibility for the civil reparations that are a consequence of the crime. If the accused, after consulting with his or her defense attorney, responds affirmatively, the judge will declare anticipated conclusion of the trial and will proceed to sentencing. The sentence is in this case a product of the agreement reached by all parties, unless the judge believes that no crime was committed or that the accused is innocent.

Public Defense

The public defender, operating under the Ministry of Justice, is responsible for providing free legal counsel to those accused of a crime. The public defender employs attorneys specialized in the new penal procedural code, who are available 24 hours a day to attend to the needs of those detained or urgent cases. Public defenders go to police precincts and participate in audiences. In August 2008, the public defender had 637 attorneys, which represents a rate of 2.3 public defenders per 100,000 persons.

Preventive Detention

One measure of procedural coercion is preventive detention. The new penal procedural code mandates that preventive detention should be mandated only in exceptional cases, when the following requirements are met: (a) well-founded and grave elements of conviction exist that lead to a reasonable belief that the accused can be linked to the crime as a perpetrator or participant; (b) the sanction warranted by the crime is more than four years of incarceration; (c) there is reasonable belief that the accused, according to his or her history and other circumstances of the case, will attempt to elude justice (flight risk) or obstruct the investigation into the truth (danger of obstruction).

One of the most serious problems plaguing the Peruvian justice system is the high level of persons who are incarcerated without being sentenced. Traditionally, preventive detention has been the most frequent cautionary measure taken by judges. To address this problem, the new code dictates that preventive detention should not be used for more than 9 months. In complicated cases, the limit of preventive detention is no more than 18 months.

Under the new procedural code, preventive detention is decided in oral public audiences where the parties (prosecutor and defense) can debate this measure. In the judicial districts where the new code is already in use, the application of preventive detention has been reduced in a significant manner, and the number of sentenced prisoners has also increased. It is projected that this reform will produce important positive results in Peru's new procedural system.

Punishment

Types of Criminal Sanctions

Sanctions in Peru are classified as (a) deprivation of liberty (temporary: minimum 2 days and maximum 35 years; life term); (b) sanctions of restricted liberty (exile for citizens and expulsion from the country for foreign nationals); (c) sanctions that limit rights (community service, limitation to days off, disqualification) and; (d) fines (money that must be paid to the Peruvian state, based on days-fine).

Despite the diverse possibilities in sentencing, the most frequently used sanction is deprivation of liberty. However, it is usual for judges to suspend this sentence for crimes that are less serious in nature, stipulating certain conditions (periodically signing in a judicial notebook, not frequenting specific locations, keeping a distance from the victim, and not leaving the country).

In rural areas, it is common that community leaders apply their own justice, with sanctions such as public apologies or labor on the victim's territory. However, there are times when these authorities are excessive, and corporal punishment is applied to persons suspected of committing crimes, especially with suspected robbers. In these cases, the police must intervene and rescue the accused.

In cases of homicide, rape, and aggravated robbery, privation of liberty is common. Homicide is sanctioned with a prison term of 6 to 20 years. Rape is sanctioned with a prison term of 6 years to life. Sanctions for injuries are from 2 years to 15 years depending on the gravity of the crime (aggravating circumstances include domestic or familial violence).

Prisons

According to the Instituto Nacional Penitenciario (INPE), in December 2008, the Peruvian prison population figured at 44,060 inmates with an incarceration rate of 156 inmates per 100,000 people. Of the total number of inmates, 41,122 (93%) were men, and 2,938 (7%) were women. Of the total number of inmates, 28,522 (65%) were processed, and 15,538 (35%) were sentenced. At the national level, there are 81 penitentiaries. There are special penal institutions for prime offenders (such as the penal institution "San Jorge" in Lima), but in reality, overcrowding makes real separation of inmates difficult, especially in the capital city of Lima where overcrowding in prison reaches 225 percent.

Prison work is voluntary and paid. All prisoners have the right to work. Work is considered beneficial for the rehabilitation and reentry of inmates and can be used to shorten the length of stay: two days of work reduce one day from the sentence. Education is another activity that is considered part of penitentiary treatment and can lead to a reduction of a sentence. For every two days of treatment, one day is reduced from the sentence. Inmates have access to basic education, secondary education, and through long-distance learning and correspondence, a postsecondary education.

All inmates have the rights to receive visits from family members and attorneys, to receive conjugal visits (priority given to spouses), and to spend time in the yard. The correctional institution arranges these visits according to the infrastructure of the prison and the number of inmates. Hours of recreation or of yard time are based on classification of the inmate (dangerous inmates, low risk inmates, etc.).

The new penal procedural code establishes that foreign nationals sentenced to prison in Peru can serve their sentence in their native country. Peruvian citizens convicted of crimes abroad can choose to serve their time in Peru. For this exchange to occur, there must be an existing agreement between the countries involved. The decision belongs to the central government. In February 2008, the Peruvian government began coordinating with embassies of different countries for the purpose of having convicted persons serve their time in their native countries, especially foreign nationals sentenced for illicit drug traffic.

Nataly Ponce Chauca

Further Reading

Instituto Nacional Penitenciario: http://www.inpe.gob.pe.

NGO Justicia Viva: http://www.idl.org.pe.

Poder Judicial: http://www.pj.gob.pe.

Policía Nacional del Perú: http://www.pnp.gob.pe/.

Ponce Chauca, Nataly. *La Reforma Procesal Penal en Perú. Avances y Desafíos a partir de las experiencias de Huaura y La Libertad.* Centro de Estudios de Justicia de las Américas: http://www.cejamericas.org.

Puerto Rico

Legal System: Civil/Common
Murder: High
Corruption: Low
Prison Rate: High
Death Penalty: No
Corporal Punishment: No

Background

The Spanish-American treaty of 1898 ceded the island of Puerto Rico to the United States. The current judicial system in Puerto Rico, organized under the Puerto Rican Department of Justice, has its origins in the 1899 Executive Order 12, issued under the military regime established by the U.S. Congress. The Department of Justice, under the jurisdiction of the military governor, administered the prisons and jails and supervised the judges and the judicial system in general. The military governor also appointed the head of the insular police, whose main function was to maintain law and order. After the abolition of the military regime in 1900, Puerto Rico was governed under two different constitutional laws passed by the U.S. Congress. The Foraker Act of 1900 provided for a governor appointed by the U.S. president, a legislative branch, and a judicial branch. In addition, the Foraker Act allowed Puerto Ricans to send a delegate to the U.S. Congress to voice the concerns of the Puerto Rican people, but without the right to vote in legislative matters. The Jones-Shafroth Act of 1917 granted U.S. citizenship to residents of the island and contained a Bill of Rights that was modeled after the U.S. Constitution. Under both acts, the federally appointed governor retained control over the police, the Puerto Rican Supreme Court, and the Department of Justice. Moreover, the U.S. Congress had legislative authority over Puerto Rico, and the decisions of the Puerto Rican Supreme Court were subject to review by thc U.S. Court of Appeals for the First Circuit.

For many years, Puerto Rican and American politicians debated the political and constitutional status of the island. In response to the increasing demand for political participation by the Puerto Rican people, in 1947, the U.S. Congress passed legislation authorizing the popular election of the governor, and Luis Munoz Marin became the first popularly elected governor of Puerto Rico. In 1950, under pressure from the United Nations, the U.S. Congress passed Public Law 600, which provided for the drafting of a constitution by the Puerto Rican people. Two years later, the U.S. Congress and the president approved the Constitution of the Commonwealth of Puerto Rico.

Justice System

The current Department of Justice was officially created as an executive branch subject to the authority of the legislative branch. The department is responsible for providing legal advice to the governor, the legislative branch, municipalities, and the heads of government agencies. The department also represents the government in civil and criminal cases, investigates and prosecutes accused people, and promotes public safety. In 1956, the Puerto Rican legislature created the current Puerto Rican police department under the same name, whose main functions were to protect the public, maintain public order, protect private property, and fight crime. Although the police department remained under the authority of the governor, the Puerto Rican legislature created the position of police superintendent, who was nominated and appointed by the governor with the consent of the Puerto Rican Senate. In 1967, the Puerto Rican legislature created the Agency for Criminal Investigations, a highly specialized and scientifically oriented agency whose main functions included investigating high-profile cases, white-collar crimes, homicides, and robberies. Until 1969, the Puerto Rico Department of Revenues was in charge of investigating and prosecuting drug trafficking and drug dealing cases; however, in 1969, the Puerto Rican legislature transferred this task to the Puerto Rico police department.

In addition to the local judicial system, the U.S. federal judicial system operates in Puerto Rico. Federal law enforcement agencies such as the Federal Bureau of Investigation (FBI) and the Drug Enforcement Administration (DEA) enforce federal laws. This dual system of justice has produced great social and political tension in Puerto Rico. In 1978, in what is commonly known as "The Cerro Maravilla Incident," two pro-independence activists were killed during an ambush operation conducted by the local police force. The preliminary investigations conducted by the Puerto Rico Department of Justice, the U.S. Justice Department's Civil Rights Division, and the FBI concluded that despite the inconsistencies in the police officers' testimonies, they acted in self-defense. After seven years of investigation, in 1984, 10 officers were indicted and found guilty of perjury, destruction of evidence, and obstruction of justice; 4 of the 10 were convicted of second-degree murder. In 1992, Drew S. Days III, former chief of the U.S. Department of Justice's Civil Rights Division, publicly admitted that the FBI had acted negligently and unprofessionally during the investigation of the case.

More recently, the September 23, 2005, killing of Filiberto Ojeda Ríos, a leftist leader of the pro-independence group Los Macheteros, by FBI agents in Puerto Rico prompted some Puerto Rican people to question the political relationships between Puerto Rico and the United States. While awaiting trial for his alleged involvement in the Wells Fargo 1983 robbery in Hartford, Connecticut, where 7.2 million dollars were stolen, Filiberto Ojeda Ríos cut off the electronic ankle monitor and became a fugitive. In July 1992, Ojeda was tried in absentia in Connecticut and found guilty on 14 counts related to the Wells Fargo robbery, fined $600,000, and sentenced to 55 years in prison. After years of investigation, the FBI located Ojeda Ríos, and on September 23, 2005, without informing the Puerto Rican government and law enforcement authorities, an FBI's sniper observer team from Quantico, Virginia, traveled to Puerto Rico and captured and killed Ojeda Ríos. The Office of the Inspector General (OIG) conducted an investigation to determine the facts and circumstances of the shooting incident and concluded that the three shots fired by the FBI agent at Ojeda Ríos through the kitchen window did not violate the Deadly Force Policy. Further, the OIG concluded that the decision not to notify Puerto Rico officials of the operation was justified and reasonable because of concerns about leaks that could compromise the operation. Pro-independence leaders labeled the FBI operation a political assassination and a manifestation of the oppressive colonial system imposed by the federal government in Puerto Rico since 1898.

In addition to this political tension, the U.S. war on drugs has created tension between Puerto Rico's local law enforcement agents and federal agents regarding the role of the local government in this effort. Since 1994, Puerto Rico has been designated a High Intensity Drug Trafficking Area (HIDTA) by the DEA. Federal agents believe that Puerto Rico is very attractive to drug traffickers because of its geographical location, being only 450 miles from the South American coast, and its strong economy and high level of transient visitors, given that about 2,000,000 cruise ship passengers and more than 9,000,000 tourists visit annually. Of the drugs smuggled through Puerto Rico, the DEA has estimated that Puerto Rico's drug consumption is about 30 percent of the drugs transshipped and that less than 1 percent of the cocaine smuggled to the continental United States in 2006 traveled through Puerto Rico.

Given the island's political relationship with the United States, Puerto Rico has played an important role in the coordination and implementation of federal anti–drug trafficking policies in Latin America and the Caribbean. However, the success of the war against drugs in Puerto Rico and the region has been the subject of great debate and controversy. For example, in 2002, Asa Hutchinson, the chief administrator of the DEA, accused DEA agents working in San Juan of misreporting their drug seizure and arrest figures.

Crime

Classification of Crimes

The Puerto Rico penal code sets the age of criminal responsibility at 18 except in those cases defined under the code for minors. There also is a lack of criminal responsibility in cases of insanity and involuntary intoxication. Article 16 of the Puerto Rican criminal code classifies crimes as either felonies or misdemeanors. The punishment for felonies is a prison term, and the punishments for misdemeanors may include both fines and prison. A typical prison sentence is 99 years for first-degree murder; 9–15 years for second-degree murder or rape; 3–8 years for robbery, voluntary manslaughter, aggravated burglary, or money laundering; and 6 months to 3 years for negligent homicide, performing or soliciting an abortion, aggravated battery, child abandonment, or identity theft. Misdemeanors such as child neglect, prostitution, simple burglary, or vandalism typically result in a fine of $5,000 or incarceration up to 90 days.

Based on the federal schedule for controlled substances, the government of Puerto Rico has classified controlled substances into five schedules. Schedule I includes any opiates, opium derivatives, and hallucinogenic substances that have a high potential for abuse, have not been accepted for medical use in the United States, and are unsafe for use under medical supervision (e.g., heroin, codeine, morphine, marijuana, peyote). Schedule II comprises those substances that have a currently accepted medical use in the United States or a currently accepted medical use with severe restrictions. However, the abuse of the drug or other substances may lead to severe psychological or physical dependence. These drugs are produced directly or indirectly by extraction from substances of vegetable origin, by chemical synthesis, or by a combination of extraction and chemical synthesis (e.g., opium derivatives, opium poppy and poppy straw, coca leaves). Schedule III includes any material, compound, mixture, or preparation that contains any quantity of substances having a stimulant or depressant effect on the nervous system (e.g., amphetamine, methamphetamine, codeine). Schedule IV drugs have a low potential for abuse relative to Schedule III drugs, are accepted for medical use in the United States, and produce limited physical or psychological dependence (e.g., barbital, chloral hydrate, phenobarbital). Schedule V drugs have a low potential for abuse relative to Schedule IV drugs, have a medical use, produce limited physical or psychological dependence relative to drugs in Schedule IV, and have a limited amount of narcotic drugs mixed with non-narcotic active medicinal ingredients.

Under Puerto Rico's penal code, it is illegal to knowingly or intentionally manufacture, distribute, dispense, transport, or conceal a controlled or adulterated substance. The penalty for violation of the laws regarding Schedules I and II narcotic drugs is imprisonment for a fixed term of 20 years, which can be increased to 30 years if there are aggravating factors and reduced to 10 years if there are mitigating factors. If the person has one or more prior drug convictions, the sentence increases to 35 years in prison. Violation of the laws governing Schedule I drugs, non-narcotic, carries a sentence of imprisonment for a fixed term of 12 years—20 years if there are aggravating factors and 5 years if there are mitigating factors. Having a prior drug conviction increases the imprisonment term to 25 years. In the case of violation of the laws regarding Schedule III drugs, the penalty is a fixed term of imprisonment of 7 years, with a maximum of 10 years if there are aggravating factors and a reduced sentence of 5 years if there are mitigating factors. Having a prior drug conviction increases the incarceration term to 15 years. Violation of the laws regarding Schedule IV drugs nets a prison sentence of 3 years, with a maximum of 5 years for aggravating factors and a minimum of 2 years in case of mitigating factors. A prior drug conviction will increase the sentence to 6 years. Violation of the laws regarding Schedule V drugs carries a fixed sentence of 2 years, with a maximum of three years and a minimum of 1 year, and having a prior drug conviction will double this sentence. Finally, if a person transfers or administers, induces, aids, or conspires to induce a minor to use a controlled substance, the punishment is up to twice the penalties provided under the penal code.

Crime Statistics

Over the past few decades, Puerto Rico's image as the "Enchanted Island" has been overshadowed by violent crime. The Puerto Rico Police Department, in accordance with the standards established by the National Incident-Based Reporting System (NIBRS), collects data regarding offenses reported to the police. In 1992, the violent crime rate peaked at about 900 offenses per 100,000 residents and then began a steady decline, reaching 227 offenses per 100,000 residents in 2006. The property crime peaked in 1985 at about 2,779 offenses per 100,000 residents followed by a steady decline thereafter, reaching 1,354 per 100,000 in 2006. The burglary rate followed a similar pattern, reaching its peak in 1985 with 1,205 burglaries per 100,000 residents, but declining to 424 per 100,000 in 2006. From 1989 through 1994, the murder rate increased sharply, peaking in 1994 with 27 murders per 100,000 residents. Puerto Rico's 2006 murder rate of about 18.8 per 100,000 residents is almost four times that of the United States as a whole, which has 5.7 murders per 100,000 residents. Finally, the rape rate has been steadily declining since 1977, when it reached 26 rapes per 100,000 residents, and was down to 3 per 100,000 in 2006. Geographically, the rape rate is higher in the central and southern municipalities of Villalba (13.4 per 100,000 residents), Ponce (10.5 per 100,000 residents), Yauco (8.3 per 100,000 residents), Peñuelas (6.9 per 100,000 residents), and Salinas (6.2 per 100,000 residents).

Overall, violent crime is relatively higher in urban areas, particularly in the metropolitan area of San Juan (i.e., San Juan, Bayamón, Guaynabo, Cataño, Carolina, and Trujillo Alto) and some of its adjacent municipalities. The San Juan metropolitan area accounted for 49 percent of murders, 62 percent of robberies, 43 percent of forcible rapes, and 40 percent of burglaries in 2007. However, the adjacent municipalities of Loíza and Río Grande showed relatively high murder rates, 97.3 and 53.5 per 100,000, respectively.

The DEA has estimated that about 80 percent of homicides in Puerto Rico are related to drugs. A 2005 survey by the Office of National Drug Control Policy, U.S. Sentencing Commission, of 6,017 adult convicts incarcerated under the jurisdiction of the Puerto Rico Department of Corrections and Rehabilitation indicates that 63 percent (3,819) of the respondents had a drug-related problem. Among incarcerated juvenile offenders, 46.8 percent of the 250 surveyed reported having a drug-related problem. At the federal level, the Office of National Drug Control Policy and the U.S. Sentencing Commission have reported that in 2006, 51 percent of the 567 federally sentenced defendants in Puerto Rico had committed drug offenses, and 57 percent (167 defendants) of these involved powder cocaine, particularly cocaine trafficking.

Finding of Guilt

The Bill of Rights of the Constitution of the Commonwealth of Puerto Rico protects against illegal searches and seizures, prohibits the death penalty, and guarantees due process and equal protection under the law, the right to speedy and public trial, jury trial, the right against self-incrimination, the right be informed of the charges, the right to cross-examine witnesses, the right to have assistance of counsel, the right to be presumed innocent, and the right to reasonable bail. The Puerto Rican Bill of Rights also limits incarceration prior to trial to no more than six months. In 1995, the government of Puerto Rico created the Office of Pretrial Services to protect the constitutional right of the defendant to pretrial release and to reduce the effect of social and economic inequality in the criminal justice system. The pretrial release program offers the following options: release in custody of a third party, release on personal recognizance, conditional release, and release on deferred bail. The Legal Assistance Society provides legal representation to indigent defendants in criminal cases. During the 2006–2007 fiscal year, the Legal Assistance Society handled 12,451 cases; in 22.3 percent of the cases, the courts found no probable cause, and in 13.6 percent of the cases, the charges were dismissed. Puerto Rican defendants also are covered under the Bill of Rights of the U.S. Constitution, and indigent defendants qualify for the services of the Federal Public Defender for the District of Puerto Rico. According to the federal judiciary, in 2007, 50 percent of the 1,603 criminal cases handled by the federal courts in Puerto Rico were plea bargained, and only 7.4 percent were dismissed. About 82 percent (1,204) of the convicted offenders received an incarceration sentence.

The Puerto Rican judicial system consists of three court levels. The highest level is the Supreme Court of Puerto Rico, whose members are appointed by the governor with the advice and consent of the Senate. This is the court of last resort and is composed of a chief justice and six associate justices who sit together as a panel of no fewer than three justices in San Juan. The composition of the Supreme Court can be changed only by law upon request by the Supreme Court. Members of the Supreme Court are required to be citizens of the United States and of Puerto Rico, to have been admitted to the practice of law in Puerto Rico at least 10 years prior to their appointments, and to have resided in Puerto Rico at least 5 years immediately prior thereto. The Supreme Court may hear, in the first instance, petitions for habeas corpus, mandamus, injunction, and any other causes and proceedings as determined by law.

The second level is the Court of Appeals, and it has the authority to review cases decided by the Court of First Instance. This court is located in San Juan and consists of a panel of three to seven judges appointed by the president of the Puerto Rico Supreme Court. The third level is the Court of First Instance, and it consists of 253 superior and 85 municipal judges appointed by the governor with the consent of the Senate. The Superior Court judges serve a 12-year term, and the municipal judges serve a term of 8 years. This court holds its meetings in San Juan, Bayamón, Arecibo, Aguadilla, Mayagüez, Ponce, Guayama, Humacao, Caguas, Aibonito, Utuado, Carolina, and Fajardo, and it is authorized to hear any type of civil or criminal case and cases involving violation of municipal ordinances. In addition to these courts, there are eight drug-court programs in Puerto Rico that provide rehabilitation services to drug users and abusers who have been charged with nonviolent offenses related to their drug dependency. The drug courts handle cases involving possession of a controlled substance with intent to distribute, simple possession of a controlled substance and drug paraphernalia, theft, burglary, forgery, and illegal possession of autos and auto parts.

The Puerto Rican juvenile justice system operates under the 1986 Puerto Rico Minors' Act. The system's mission includes providing for the care, protection, development, habilitation, and rehabilitation of minors and promoting public safety. Accused juveniles have the right to a fair and impartial trial and due process of law, to have contact with their relatives at all times, and to obtain legal counsel in the presentation of their defense. Juveniles between 15 and 18 years of age who are charged with first-degree murder or who have been previously charged with a felony as an adult are tried as adults. According to police statistics, from 1990 through 2005, the rate of police intervention with juveniles under the age of 18 for robbery and burglary steadily declined. For example, the number of police-juvenile contacts per 100,000 juveniles was 120.7 in 1990 but declined to 20.5 in 2005. On the other hand, police-juvenile contacts for rape and murder increased during the late 1990s, but they have declined in recent years. For example, the police-juvenile contact rate for rape was 3.9 in 1990, 7.8 in 1996, and 0.9 in 2005.

Punishment

Types of Punishment

Puerto Rico's penal code provides the following penalties: imprisonment, therapeutic commitment, house arrest, fine, suspension or revocation of license, restitution, probation, and community service. First-degree murder carries a prison sentence of 99 years, manslaughter carries a sentence of no less than 3 years and no more than 8 years in prison, and involuntary manslaughter incarceration has a sentence of between 6 months and 3 years in prison. When involuntary manslaughter is committed by a person driving a motor vehicle under the influence of alcohol or a controlled substance, the sentence is imprisonment for a fixed term of 1 year. Rape carries a sentence of 8 to 15 years in prison. If the offender is under the age of 18 and the victim is under the age of 16, and the offender is tried as an adult, the presumptive sentence is between 3 years and 8 years in prison.

Prisons

According to the Puerto Rico Department of Corrections, there are 30 correctional institutions in Puerto Rico. The total number of prisoners in Puerto Rico in 2007 was 12,334 (11,949 in prison and 385 inmates in treatment and medical centers). More than 50 percent of the prison inmate population consists of relatively young inmates (52 percent are less than 30 years of age); 66 percent are recidivists; 67 percent have a sentence of more than five years in prison ; 80 percent were unemployed at the time of the offense; 90 percent use alcohol or illegal drugs frequently. The incarceration rate peaked in 1998 with 624 inmates per 100,000 residents over the age of 18 and has since declined to an incarceration rate of about 500 in 2006. The two largest correctional institutions in Puerto Rico are the Correctional Complex of Ponce, with about 8,000 inmates housed in 20 facilities, and the Bayamon Correctional Complex, with 3,939 inmates (2006). In addition, the Metropolitan Detention Center (MDC) in Guaynabo is a federal detention center that holds approximately 1,500 male and female inmates. There were also about 18,000 probationers and parolees in 2007, with an estimated annual probation and parole revocation rate of about 7 percent, or 1,275 revocations.

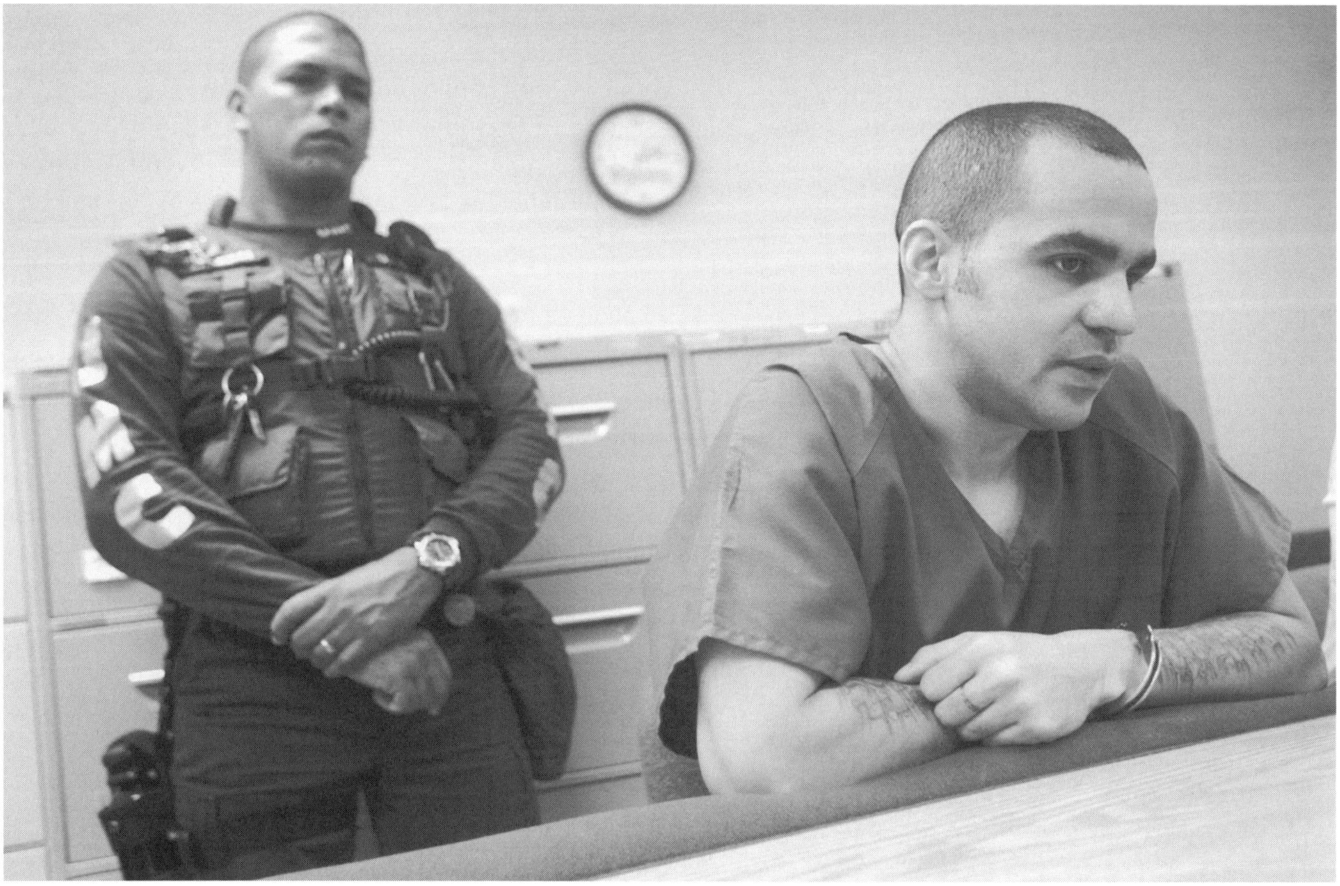

Watched by a prison guard, Puerto Rican detainee Juan Martinez Cruz sits handcuffed in an interview room at Las Cucharas Penitentiary, in Ponce, Puerto Rico, June 1, 2006. Martinez is accused of killing a man in a Philadelphia bar in 2000. His lawyers are fighting extradition to Philadelphia in the Puerto Rican Supreme Court on the grounds that he could face capital punishment, which is illegal in Puerto Rico. (AP Photo/Brennan Linsley)

The Administration of Juvenile Institutions (AJI) is responsible for the direct operation of nine male juvenile centers and a female center with an average annual population of 800 and 70 offenders, respectively. In 2007, approximately 2,471 juveniles received services from the AJI, including mental health services (1,460) and vocational education (2,123). This represents a 48 percent increase from 1997 (1,660 offenders). Of the 250 incarcerated juveniles tried as adults in 2005, 99 percent were male, 98 percent committed their offense in urban areas, 99 percent were drug users, and 20 percent were serving time for murder.

The visiting rules and regulations in adult institutions provide for a maximum of six persons at a time. Upon being admitted at a correctional institution, the inmate submits a list of names of the people he or she wants to be included in the list of visitors. Children under the age of 12 do not count as visitors as long as they do not occupy a seat and if they are on the lap of a visiting adult; any visitor in a wheelchair counts as one of the six authorized visitors. The inmate has the right to change the list of visitors every four months. An inmate's close friend who wants to be included in the inmate's list must not be listed on the visiting list in another institution. Visitors who are not part of the list of the inmate's immediate family and who have prior criminal records have to provide evidence that three years have elapsed since the date of their last conviction.

Inmates sentenced to less than 15 years in prison may receive credit for good behavior of up to 12 days per month, and those sentenced to 15 years or more may get a credit for 13 days per month. These incarceration privileges do not apply to those sentenced to 99 years or more; they do not qualify for sentence reduction for good behavior. In addition, inmates receive credit for time served while waiting for trial and for participating in institutional work or educational programs. Regardless of the length or type of inmates' prison terms, the Puerto Rico Electoral Law grants the right to vote to adult inmates.

In 1991, the government created the Employment and Training Enterprises Corporation, which is responsible for providing training, entrepreneurial development, and employment experiences for the adult and juvenile correctional clientele in the production of office furniture, pillows, beds, and mattresses. The corporation's main function is to coordinate activities with public agencies, corporations, municipalities, and for-profit or nonprofit public or private persons or entities, by contracts or collaborative efforts, that would help improve the participants' employment and self-employment skills. According to the Puerto Rico Department of Correction, in 2007, the corporation employed 1,405 correctional clients and sold about 3.8 million dollars in products to governmental agencies and the general public.

To help alleviate prison crowding and to promote the rehabilitation of the offenders, the Puerto Rico Administration of Corrections provides diversion services and reintegration programs such as the Social Adaptation Homes (halfway houses) and the ticket of leave (*pases extendidos*) for educational or medical purposes. Those convicted of murder, rape, incest, sodomy, child sexual abuse, or repeat drug offenders are excluded from these programs. In 2004, legislators amended the Puerto Rico Organic Law of the Administration of Corrections (Law 116) to the effect that some qualified incarcerated inmates are required to serve at least 20 percent of the prison sentence imposed before they can benefit from these post-release services. By increasing the time served from 10 percent to 20 percent, the government expected to reduce offenders' recidivism and promote public safety. To facilitate the reintegration of incarcerated offenders into the community, the Department of Corrections offers job fairs, provides letters of recommendation for employment, and assists inmates in finding housing and medical services.

The Puerto Rico law of extradition makes the governor responsible for arranging the arrest and delivery of any person who resides on the island and who has been charged in another state with any crime. Similarly, the governor may request the extradition to Puerto Rico of any person who has been charged with any crime in Puerto Rico and who is imprisoned or awaiting trial in another state. In 2002, the governor of Pennsylvania requested the arrest and extradition of Juan Martínez Cruz, who at the time was living in Puerto Rico, on charges of murder and illegal possession of weapons. Upon his arrest, the Court of First Instance denied the extradition to

Pennsylvania on the grounds that it would be unconstitutional to extradite the accused to Pennsylvania if he faced a possible death sentence because the death penalty is prohibited by the Constitution of Puerto Rico. The Appeal Court affirmed the lower court's decision. However, in 2006 in *The People of Puerto Rico v. Juan Martinez Cruz,* the Puerto Rico Supreme Court reversed the appeal court decision against the extradition of Juan Martinez Cruz because it imposed limits on the use of the death penalty by the government of Pennsylvania and made the island a potential sanctuary for criminals trying to escape the death penalty in the United States.

Alfredo Montalvo-Barbot

Further Reading

Centro de Estudios de Justicia de Las Americas: http://www.cejamericas.org/.

Departamento de Corrección y Rehabilitación de Puerto Rico: http://ac.gobierno.pr/correccion/.

Malavet-Vega, Pedro. (2007). *El Sistema de Justicia Criminal en Puerto Rico*. Ponce, PR: Ediciones Lorena.

Policía de Puerto Rico: http://www.gobierno.pr/PoliciaPR/Estadisticas/.

Saint Kitts and Nevis

Legal System: Common
Murder: High
Prison Rate: High
Death Penalty: Yes
Corporal Punishment: Yes

Background

The islands of St. Kitts and Nevis are located in the Leeward Islands in the Caribbean, approximately 225 nautical miles southeast of Puerto Rico. The two islands have a landmass of 269 square kilometers and a coastline of 135 kilometers. As of July 2006, the population on both islands was estimated to be 42,696 (31,515 on St. Kitts and 11,181 on Nevis). The majority of residents are of African descent. Although English is the official language of the federation, inhabitants of St. Kitts and Nevis commonly use a Creole language. Tourism is the greatest source of revenue of the federation.

History

Christopher Columbus landed on St. Kitts in 1493 on his second voyage to the region and named the island St. Christopher after his patron saint, which was later shortened to St. Kitts. Christopher Columbus also discovered Nevis on his second voyage, which he named Nevis because of its resemblance to a snowcapped mountain called Nuestra Senora de las Nieves in Spanish, meaning "Our Lady of the Snows." The Treaty of Paris awarded both islands to Britain in 1783.

The two islands, along with Anguilla, were incorporated into a single British dependency. They became part of the West Indies Federation from 1958 to 1962. After two rebellions in 1967 and 1969, Anguilla seceded from St. Kitts and Nevis and became a separate British dependency. The government of St. Kitts and Nevis attained full independence on September 19, 1983. It became a member of the British Commonwealth and Organization of the Eastern Caribbean States (OECS) and the Caribbean Community and Common Market (CARICOM).

Political Structure

The federal Parliament is the highest decision-making institution in the country. It is located in St. Kitts, although Nevis operates under a local government and has some degree of autonomy. Queen Elizabeth II is the head of the state, and she is represented by a governor-general, whose powers are largely ceremonial. The governor-general acts on the advice of the prime minister and the cabinet and also appoints three senators, two on recommendation of the prime minister and one on the recommendation of the leader of the opposition.

The Constitution gives Nevis the right to secede from the federation, and its attempts in 1996 and 2004 to secede failed on both occasions. Some Nevisians believe that Nevis would be better off politically if it took full responsibility for its own affairs. In addition, some Nevisians believe that St. Kitts disproportionally receives most of the economic resources. For example, St. Kitts is the headquarters for many of the businesses in Nevis; cargo entering Nevis is taxed in St. Kitts; and most importantly, most of the economic development takes place in St. Kitts.

Criminal Offenses

Crime has become a major problem for the government of St. Kitts and Nevis. In 2007, the Royal St. Christopher and Nevis Police Force recorded 222 crimes against the person, 53 against morality, 1,457 against property, and 120 against lawful authority, for a total of 1,852 crimes committed in that year. In 2007, there were 16 murders, but only 7 were solved. The federation also reported a reduction of 9 percent in the number of crimes committed between 2006 and 2007. Between 2003 and 2007, property crimes constituted 79 percent of all crimes, offenses against person were 11 percent, and offenses against morality were 3 percent. Among major crimes, break-ins and larcenies are the most frequent. In 2007, the following numbers of crimes were reported to the police:

Breakings	735
Larcenies	407
Robberies	119
Woundings	162
Malicious damage/arson	115
Firearms and drugs	115
Other	147

Homicide

According to the Royal St. Christopher and Nevis Police Force, there were 5 murders in 2002, 10 in 2003, 11 in 2004, 8 in 2005, 17 in 2006, and 16 in 2007. Although crime was down in St. Kitts and Nevis for the first six months of 2008 as compared to the same period in 2007, there were already 13 murders in St. Kitts during those 2008 months, sparking a public outcry against gun violence in the country. Even though the number of murders for each year is relatively small, the rate of murder based on population size may be relatively high in comparison to many developed countries. Based on the number of murders for the first six months of 2008, St. Kitts and Nevis would have a murder rate of 30.4 per 100,000 people.

Sexual Offenses

In St. Kitts and Nevis, many sexual offenses, including rape, incest, and unlawful carnal knowledge, require actual sexual intercourse as the material element of the offense. Sexual intercourse is also limited to vaginal penetration by a penis. Several of the sexual offenses apply only to acts committed by men against females and exclude intercourse that is initiated by a woman or a man with young boys. The offenses of rape and unlawful carnal knowledge are, therefore, currently gender-specific and offer no protection to boys and young men.

Regarding child sexual abuse, the criminal provisions that prohibit unlawful carnal knowledge impose a maximum penalty of five years' imprisonment for a child under the age 16 but above the age of 14. There is a sanction of life imprisonment for unlawful carnal knowledge of a girl under the age of 14.

Rape is an underreported crime everywhere in the world, and high rates of rape reflect a very serious problem. According to the Royal St. Christopher and Nevis Police Force, 6 rapes were reported in 2003, 9 in 2004, 11 in 2005, 10 in 2006, and 7 in 2007. It is interesting to note that the offense of rape in St. Kitts and Nevis carries a harsher penalty (up to life imprisonment) than the offense of unlawful carnal knowledge of a girl under the age of 16 but above the age of 14. This clearly indicates a disparity in the punishment for these two offenses.

The government has passed a series of laws, including the Law Reform Act, that provide stiffer penalties for rape, incest, sodomy, indecent assault, or any offense involving children. The act also prohibits reporting information that could identify the defendants in sexual offense cases, which is especially significant in a small society such as St. Kitts and Nevis where people tend to know each other. According to the United Nations Children's Fund, sexual offenses in St. Kitts and Nevis account for almost one-third of all cases that were prosecuted in the courts between September 2006 and September 2007.

A behavioral surveillance survey conducted by the country's chief medical officer and reported in the *Sun St. Kitts Nevis* in June 2008 revealed that many children studied in 2005–2006 were introduced to sex as early as age 10. The study, which was conducted among 980 youths aged 15 to 24 years, indicated that the perpetrator was often an adult male acquaintance of the family. The police data also indicated that twice as many girls under the age of 16 in comparison to females over the age of 16 years were the victims of sexual offenses. Many of the perpetrators were high-profile individuals.

The Department of Probation and Child Protection Services, as the de facto child protection agency in St. Kitts and Nevis, also collects statistical information on this subject. The United Nation's Children's Fund reported that there were 136 cases of child abuse in 2006. Of these, 62 percent were neglect, 20 percent physical abuse, 8 percent sexual abuse, and 10 percent other types of child abuse. However, the data reflect only those cases that the agency received and investigated. Given the poor state of reporting by other agencies to the department, there is no centralized data collection, and this, in turn, undermines any accurate assessment of the true extent of child abuse in the federation.

The Probation and Child Welfare Board Act of 1994 mandates that certain individuals have a duty to report child abuse cases. Mandatory reporting of child abuse is, therefore, expressly enshrined in the legislation. The provision, however, does not expressly require parents or guardians to report, nor does it address the sanctions to be imposed if there is a failure to report. In addition, the legislation also imposed a limitation period on the prosecution of cases involving unlawful carnal knowledge of girls between 14 and 16. The unlawful conduct must be prosecuted within 12 months after the commission of the offense.

Illegal Drugs

Like many countries in the Caribbean, the islands of St. Kitts and Nevis have become transshipment sites for cocaine from South America to the United States. According to the International Narcotics Control Strategy Report for 2007, drugs are transferred out of St. Kitts and Nevis primarily by small sailboats, fishing boats, and go-fast boats bound for Puerto Rico and the U.S. Virgin Islands. The trafficking organizations, which operate in St. Kitts and Nevis, are linked directly to South American traffickers, some of whom reportedly are residing in St. Kitts. Marijuana is grown locally for consumption and for export.

The government officials of St. Kitts and Nevis reported that they seized 29 grams of cocaine and approximately 7.5 kilograms of marijuana and made 105 arrests from January through October 2007. The officials also claimed that they eradicated approximately 6,243 marijuana plants in 2005; 31,000 in 2006; and 161,500 in 2007. According to the government, this figure does not represent an increase in cultivation, but rather an increase in eradication efforts.

The government of St. Kitts and Nevis has made attempts to control the flow of illegal drugs in it territories. In 1996, it developed a five-year master plan for drug control, which was refined in November 2000. Also in 2000, it passed the National Council on Drug Abuse Prevention Act (NCDAPA), which provides for the prevention and abatement of the misuse and abuse of drugs, the rehabilitation of victims of misuse and abuse of drugs, and a centralized coordination of antidrug activities in St. Kitts and Nevis. The government also established the National Council on Drug Abuse Prevention unit (based on the NCDAPA). This unit is responsible for coordinating demand reduction and drug-related statistical data. It engages in the Inter-American Uniform Drug Use Data System (SIDUC) and the Uniform Statistical System on Control of the Supply Area (CICDAT). The government also has a drug squad, but its effectiveness is affected by lack of resources.

The government has also ratified the Convention against Transnational Organized Crime and the Inter-American Convention against the Illicit Manufacturing of and Trafficking in Firearms, Ammunition, Explosives, and Other Related Materials. The most recent amendment to the Firearms Act of 1967 was completed in 2003. National laws, which require that firearms be marked at time of manufacture and on importation, have been enacted. Drug-demand reduction programs, such as D.A.R.E., Operation Future, and the National Drug Council, are available to schools and society in general. The Florida Association of Volunteer Agencies/Caribbean Action (FAVA/CA), supported by the State Departments Bureau of International Narcotics and Law Enforcement (INL), carried out in 2002–2003 a successful demand reduction and prevention sustainability program in St. Kitts. There are, however, no drug rehabilitation clinics in the federation, and persons seeking such treatment have to be sent to St. Lucia.

Juvenile Delinquency and Youth Crime

Juvenile delinquency is an emerging problem in St. Kitts and Nevis. In 1990, juveniles committed only 1.2 percent of the total number of offenses in St. Kitts and Nevis, but by 1998, this had increased to 17 percent. Juvenile delinquency decreased between 2003 and 2004 but increased significantly between 2004 and 2005. According to the police, the most common offenses were crimes against property, with 54 percent in 2003, 66 percent in 2004, 66 percent in 2005, 64 percent in 2005, and 52 percent in 2007.

The National Drug Council on Drug Abuse Prevention conducted a national drug survey in secondary schools to determine the prevalence of substance use/abuse among students from levels 8 (average 13 years), 10 (average 15 years), and 12 (average 17 years) throughout the two islands. A total of 1,927 students participated in the survey; 410 (21.3 percent) attended schools on Nevis, and 1,517 (78.7 percent) attended schools on St. Kitts. The results showed that the lifetime prevalence of alcohol, cigarettes, and marijuana was 72 percent, 22 percent, and 17 percent, respectively, and the prevalence of use at the time of the survey was 28 percent, 3 percent, and 4 percent, respectively. The use of alcohol was also more prevalent among the male students than among their female student counterparts, with 78 percent versus 70 percent, respectively. Cigarette usage was 31 percent among males and 16 percent among females, and marijuana usage was 23 percent among males and 12 percent among females. Overall, the lifetime prevalence of tranquilizer (3 percent), solvent (3 percent), and cocaine (0.5 percent) use was low.

In 2002, a National Youth Tobacco Survey was conducted throughout the federation to assess smoking, exposure to environmental (second-hand) tobacco smoke, knowledge and attitudes, and other factors that make school children susceptible to tobacco use. The questionnaires were self-administered to 1,756 students, and 1,000 (56.9 percent) participated. Both female (57 percent) and male (43 percent) students, ranging in age from 11 to 17 years, participated. Most of the respondents were from Forms 1 to 4 (age 13 and 15 years). Generally, both boys and girls started experimenting with tobacco at 10 or 11 years old.

The security minister of St. Kitts and Nevis, the Honorable Dwyer Astaphan, stated recently that youth gangs and youth-gang violence are major threats to national security in St. Kitts and Nevis and that the causes for youth involvement in gangs and violence needs to be examined. He further pointed out that he had several meetings with youths, including on television and radio, to help the community to understand the impact of the problem. He blamed the gang problem on men who father children but do not take care of them. Moreover, he argued that the problem of crime in St. Kitts and Nevis is related to the closure of the sugar care industry.

According to the Honorable Astaphan, the youth gangs in St. Kitts and Nevis are well organized. They sell drugs; are involved in prostitution, extortion, and contract killing; and recruit children eight to nine years old. He pointed out that the strategies to combat this problem are based on aggressive intelligence-gathering and aggressive problem-solving. He also reported that the federation had implemented a number of programs to promote a structured social setting to assist gang members and certain categories of people with their self-esteem and job acquisition. The minister stressed that the local police would enforce curfews for people less than 16 years because there is no need for them to be in bars and nightclubs where liquor is sold given that the drinking age is 18 years.

Domestic/Family Violence

By far the greatest problem affecting women in St. Kitts and Nevis is the growing number of women who end up dead because of domestic and relationship-related violence. In addition, it is estimated that less than 10 percent of domestic violence incidents are reported to the authorities, and surveys suggest that one in three women have been victims of domestic violence. To address the issue of domestic violence, the government has made an attempt to assist women fleeing from violence by providing "safe homes," but the period of stay is limited. Often, the very women whom the safe homes are trying to protect refuse to testify against their spouses/partners. This refusal stems from fear of further abuse and the reliance of these women on their abusive partners for maintenance and shelter. Although free legal advice is available, many women are unaware of this service, but there is no legal aid. Because of the small size of the islands, it is very difficult to institute a shelter for women because it may be difficult to maintain anonymity.

In 2000, the St. Kitts and Nevis government passed the Domestic Violence Legislation, which criminalizes physical harm, psychological suffering, incest, indecent assault, and rape, but which does not address spousal rape. It provides for penalties of up to EC$13,500 (approx US$5,152) or six months in prison. Penalties include imprisonment for life for statutory rape or incest with someone under 16 and up to 20 years' imprisonment for incest with a person 16 or older. Although many women were reluctant to file complaints or pursue them in the courts, the Ministry of Gender Affairs reported 25 cases of domestic violence during 2007. However, there were no prosecutions or convictions for domestic violence during 2007.

Special measures have been taken to raise awareness and inform law enforcement officials of the issue of domestic violence. The Ministry of Gender Affairs has offered counseling for victims of abuse and conducted training on domestic violence and gender violence for police officers, officials of fire departments, nurses, school guidance counselors, and other government employees. In addition, the ministry's permanent secretary has participated in a weekly radio program to discuss gender issues, including domestic violence. Zero Tolerance and Life Free of Violence campaigns have been launched, and a Women's Empowerment Conference was held for victims of domestic abuse, as well as abuse counselors. Law enforcement officers have also made positive changes in the treatment of victims of sexual assault. St. Kitts and Nevis is presently contemplating the establishment of a Family Court, specifically to deal with family matters.

Responses to Crime

The government of St. Kitts and Nevis has recognized the seriousness of crime and violence and is exploring policy responses at the national level to address the problem. The approach in both islands has been between law enforcement and preventive measures, with the majority of government programs falling into the first category.

The government has developed a zero-tolerance approach to crime. This approach allows law enforcement officers, who might otherwise exercise their discretion in making subjective judgments regarding the severity of a given offense, to impose a predetermined punishment. The zero-tolerance approach includes ongoing patrols in areas known for high criminal activity, the maintenance of high police presence in vulnerable areas, and random stops and searches. The St. Kitts and Nevis federal cabinet has recently pledged the necessary financial support for more anticrime initiatives. The federation is also planning to implement a closed circuit television program, where a number of cameras would be erected in some sensitive areas so that people will understand that what they do will be seen. There are also plans to establish a forensic lab in the federation so that it could service the Northeastern Caribbean and end dependence on Barbados, Trinidad, Jamaica, and the U.S. Federal Bureau of Investigation. The government also wants to establish a Police Development Center, which will train not only enlisted officers but also recruits and members of private security firms.

The government has also enhanced technical and managerial training to its police officers and has introduced community policing. It has intensified the search and stop activities of the security forces and has stiffened the penalties for criminal activities, especially with respect to gun-related crimes. The government also intends to solicit technical assistance from the government of Canada with a view to further strengthening the managerial, as well as the crime prevention and crime detection, capabilities of the security forces.

The St. Kitts and Nevis government recently sponsored a resolution on crime and violence at the General Assembly of the Organization of American States (OAS) in Medellin, Colombia. The resolution, which was cosponsored by the CARICOM States and supported by all member states of the Western hemispheric body, places the issue of crime and violence squarely on the agenda of the OAS, which has now resolved to take certain actions regarding the increased crime rate in the region. The St. Kitts and Nevis minister of foreign affairs, Dr. Timothy Harris, who presented the resolution, highlighted the necessity for a criminal justice–focused approach in particular circumstances and the importance of a preventive public health approach in fighting crimes. He argued that the public health approach does not replace criminal justice and human rights responses to violence but rather complements their activities and offers them additional tools and sources of collaboration.

Finding of Guilt

The St. Kitts and Nevis Constitution basically outlines the criminal justice process and the basic rights and freedoms of residents of the islands. The present Constitution came into effect in 1983 when the two countries became independent.

Police

The St. Kitts and Nevis Police Force consists of 370 officers (72 officers in Nevis), with 27 auxiliary members. Police may arrest a person based on the suspicion of criminal activity, and warrants are not required. The law requires that persons detained be charged within 48 hours or be released. If charged, the police must bring a detainee before a court within 72 hours. When a person is arrested or detained, that person should be informed of reasons for his or her arrest or detention within 48 hours.

There have been several incidents of questionable police conduct in St. Kitts and Nevis. For example, in 2007, the police shot and killed two persons in two separate incidents. In June 2007, the police also shot and wounded one man who reportedly attacked the police and another man when he attempted to run away from them. In July 2007, four defendants, who were on trial for robbery, accused a police officer of abusing them during police custody. The police allegations and the case were deferred to the 2008 court session because the case ended in a hung jury. In December 2007, the Police Disciplinary Tribunal found Constable Alister Huggins guilty of "discreditable conduct" for stealing money during a search at a Rastafarian community. The tribunal sentenced Huggins to be confined to barracks for 28 days, and he faced criminal charges at year's end. According to the U.S. Department of State, in 2007, senior police officers investigated 170 complaints against the police. Of these, 3 cases were dismissed, 35 cases resulted in warnings, 12 were deemed false or unproven, 4 were withdrawn, and, as of 2008, 20 were pending action, and 96 cases were still under investigation.

Rights of the Accused

The judicial system is modeled on the British system, and its jurisprudence is based on English common law. The court system is composed of one high court and four magistrates' courts at the local level, with the right of appeal to the Eastern Caribbean Court of Appeal. Final appeal may be made to the Privy Council in the United Kingdom. Free legal assistance is available for indigent defendants in capital cases only. The federation has a bail system, and family members, attorneys, and clergy are permitted to visit detainees regularly.

The St. Kitts and Nevis Constitution outlines the rights of the defendants in the court. Every person accused of a crime must receive a fair, speedy, and public trial, and these requirements generally are observed. The length of remand varies according to offense and charges; persons may be held for days, weeks, or months. The Constitution also states that a person who has been found guilty or been acquitted of a crime cannot be tried a second time except on the order of a superior court in the course of appeal or review proceedings relating to the conviction or acquittal. The Constitution also indicates that a person cannot be tried for a criminal offense if he or she shows that he or she has been pardoned for that offense. A person who is tried for a criminal offense shall not be compelled to give evidence at the trial. According to the U.S. Department of State, at the end of 2007m there were 26 prisoners in pretrial detention and 34 waiting a preliminary inquiry.

Punishment

Typical Punishment

In the past, the federation offered very few alternatives to incarceration. However, in December 2003, the legislature empowered the courts to pass noncustodial sentencing such as discharges, suspended sentences, probation orders, and community service orders. Probation has been used for juveniles and adults for crimes such as carrying an offensive weapon or wounding with intent. The court also can order, as a condition of probation, for a juvenile to observe a curfew. Fines are used for such offenses as possession of cannabis, and failure to pay the fine would result in imprisonment of several months based on the quantity of illegal drugs. Fines are also used for disorderly conduct by fighting, being armed with an offensive weapon, or driving under the influence of liquor.

In St. Kitts and Nevis, corporal punishment is legal; a court can order that an accused person receive lashes if found guilty. In fact, in November 2007, the court sentenced a 12-year-old boy found guilty of possessing an illegal firearm to receive 10 lashes as punishment.

Prisons

There are two prisons in the federation. Prison conditions are generally poor and severely overcrowded. The prison on St. Kitts, which was built in 1840, and the low-security prison in Nevis are often overcapacity, forcing some prisoners to sleep on mats on the floor. The government permits prison visits by independent human rights observers. In addition, the Ministry of National Security has appointed "visiting justices" who volunteer to oversee the treatment of prisoners. The prisons offer voluntary work and educational programs to the prisoners, but resources remain limited. The prison staff periodically receives training in human rights. In 1994, 150 inmates set fire to the prison, and many escaped, forcing the government to call for help from the regional security and police forces to restore order and capture the escapees.

Female inmates are segregated from male prisoners. Likewise, pretrial detainees and juveniles are held separately from convicted prisoners and constituted less than 1 percent of the prison population in 2007. Prisoners are required to work if their sentence was more than 30 days and stipulated "hard labor." They received a small stipend for this work, paid upon discharge. The prison in St. Kitts, which is designed to hold 150 prisoners, held 182 prisoners on October 31, 2007. Likewise, the prison in Nevis, which is designed to hold 20 prisoners, held 44 inmates by October 31, 2007.

According to the International Centre for Prison Studies (ICPS), the rate of imprisonment in St. Kitts and Nevis was 295 per 100,000 population in 1995, 288 in 1998, 441 in 2001, 559 in 2004, and 588 in 2007. Moreover, based on these rates of incarceration in St. Kitts and Nevis, ICPS argued that the federation ranked third in the world, behind United States and Russia, for 2007, with 751 per 100,000 population and 613 per 100,000 population, respectively.

Death Penalty

The death penalty is still in use in St. Kitts and Nevis. In April 2004, the government tried, convicted, and sentenced to death, by hanging, a convicted murderer. Prior to that, the last hanging took place in July 1998. The use of the death penalty by the government of St. Kitts and Nevis has been strongly criticized by Amnesty International.

Janice Joseph

Further Reading

Caribbean Net News: http://www.caribbeannetnews.com.

Federation of Saint Kitts and Nevis Constitutional Order. (1983). http://www.constitution.org/cons/stkitts-.htm.

The Royal St. Kitts and Nevis Police Force: http://www.police.gov.kn.

United Nations Office on Drugs and Crime. (2003, July). *Federation of St. Kitts and Nevis National Report:* http://www.unodc.org/pdf/barbados/st_kitts_and_nevis_2002.pdf.

U.S. Government of State. (2007). *Background Note: Saint Kitts and Nevis:* http://www.state.gov/r/pa/ei/bgn/2341.htm.

Saint Lucia

Legal System: Civil/Common
Murder: High
Corruption: Low
Prison Rate: High
Death Penalty: Yes
Corporal Punishment: Yes

Background

The island of St. Lucia is a Commonwealth located in the Caribbean Sea, north of Trinidad and Tobago. It has a total area of 616 square kilometers, and the population is about 160,267. The majority (82.5 percent) of residents are black, with another 11.9 percent classified as mixed. The remaining 5.5 percent of the population consists of East Indian residents or others who have not been specified. English is the official language of the nation, but French Patois is also spoken.

To this day, the history of St. Lucia seems to be up for dispute. It was believed for a long time that Christopher Columbus was the first European to land at St. Lucia, but that claim has since been disproved. The one undisputed fact about St. Lucia and its history is that the first attempt at settlement by Europeans occurred on August 23, 1605. The island remained in flux for centuries, as it was repeatedly fought over by the French and English during the 17th and early 18th centuries. As a result of these continual conflicts, the island's possession changed hands 14 separate times. Finally, St. Lucia was ceded to England in 1814.

On March 1, 1967, St. Lucia became an Associated State of Great Britain, which brought with it the right to oversee internal affairs while the country's defense and foreign affairs would still fall within Britain's responsibility. This system remained until February 22, 1979, when St. Lucia became an independent member of the Commonwealth of former British Empire Territories.

Government

St. Lucia is a parliamentary democracy. Queen Elizabeth II serves as the country's head of state and is represented by a governor-general, whom she appoints. Most of the power in the country is held by the prime minister and the cabinet, who usually represent the majority political party. The Parliament of St. Lucia has two houses, a 17-member House of Assembly and an 11-member Senate.

St Lucia's judicial system is independent of its political system. District courts and a high court constitute the legal system of the country. District courts are known as the courts of summary jurisdiction. These bodies have criminal and civil authority, although they handle only petty offenses and civil matters up to roughly XCD$1,850 (approx. US$690). The High Court has unlimited authority in criminal and civil matters. Appeals from these lower courts are sent to Eastern Caribbean Court of Appeals, and if a case cannot be resolved there, it is then sent to the Judicial Committee of the Privy Council in London, which serves as the court of last resort.

Police

The Royal Saint Lucia Police Force is the only security force within the country. The force has a northern and a southern division, with a total of 13 police stations located around the island. As of September 2003, 947 officers were employed by the force. Although St. Lucia lacks a military, there is a Special

Services Unit of the police force that receives paramilitary training and a coast guard unit.

Crime

Classification of Crimes

St. Lucia's original criminal code was written in 1920 but was revised as recently as 2004 to serve the current times. Sections within the code include Offenses against the Person (homicide, assault, sexual offenses), Offenses against Property (theft, forgery, bankruptcy fraud, extortion, damage to property), Offenses against Public Order (treason, libel, and intimidation), Offenses against the Administration of Justice (contempt of court or fabricating false evidence), and summary offenses (stealing something valued at less that XCD$500 [approx. US$187] or wasting of police time). Crimes within these sections can be either indictable or summary offenses, but one must find the offense within the code to determine what sentence is appropriate. In addition, arrest and bail, search and seizure, trials, appeals, punishment, imprisonment, fines and compensation, pardon, remission, and reward are also covered within the code.

Crime Statistics

The country makes annual crime statistics available through the Royal St. Lucia Police's Web site. As of late May 2009, crime statistics were available about all crimes island-wide that had been reported to the police from 2000 until 2007. According to this information, no capital murders were reported to the police in 2007. Additionally, 27 noncapital murders were reported, with 25 of them accepted by the police for investigation; 17 were solved, leading to a 68 percent clearance rate for noncapital murders. Thirteen males were apprehended for noncapital murder, and only three females were arrested for the same crime.

In the same time period, 77 rapes were reported, with 69 accepted by the police and 18 of them solved, resulting in a 26.08 percent clearance rate for rape in 2007. All 12 individuals who were arrested for committing rape were males.

Armed robbery statistics show a different picture regarding crime in St. Lucia. In 2007, 72 armed robberies were reported, with 70 of them being accepted for investigation. According to the available statistics, only 2 robberies were solved for the entire year. The resulting clearance rate was only 2.8 percent.

Contrary to robbery, cocaine trafficking has been handled much more effectively by the police. All 14 cases that were reported were also accepted for investigation and solved. It is also interesting to note that of the 17 individuals who were apprehended for trafficking, 6 of them were women, compared to 11 men.

St. Lucia's Royal Police had 12,145 total crimes reported to them in 2007, with 11,454 accepted for further inquiry. The total clearance rate was reported as 34.35 percent. The most frequent crime that was reported within the country was stealing, with 1,774 cases reported and 1,677 accepted.

Finding of Guilt

Rights of the Accused

The Constitution of St. Lucia outlines the fundamental rights and freedoms of citizens. All citizens who are accused of a crime are to be presumed innocent until they are proven guilty. The accused have the right to a fair hearing within a reasonable time by an independent and impartial court that has been established by the law. Following arrest, they should be informed as soon as reasonably practicable in language that they understand regarding the charges against them.

Adequate facilities and time shall be given to the accused to prepare their defense. Despite this right, the criminal code states that one has a right to state-appointed counsel only in capital murder cases. In all other cases, accused persons are allowed to either represent themselves or hire their own attorney. Also, there is the right to examine witnesses presented by the prosecution and to have witnesses to testify on the behalf of the accused. An interpreter will be provided by the state if such services are required.

The accused has a right to be present at trial, unless the offender's presence would hinder the ability of the court to determine guilt. If acquitted, a person cannot be tried for the same crime twice. Additionally, one does not have to be a witness against oneself during a trial. Court proceedings are open to the public; however, the court may close proceedings if a public trial would prejudice justice, would harm public morality, would harm the private lives of the parties involved, involves persons under 18, or is related to defense, public safety, or public order. If any question arises in court about the proceedings, the presiding judge may refer the case to the High Court of St. Lucia.

The criminal code states that every case involving an indictable offense that is decided before the court shall be tried and decided by a judge and a jury. The accused has the right to remain silent, which cannot be used against the offender in the determination of guilt or innocence. Offenders are advised of the rights under section 589 of the criminal code, which allows them to meet with a legal practitioner. Accused persons also have the right to have an attorney present during the questioning, but that right can be waived.

Punishment

Types of Punishment

Capital murder in St. Lucia is punishable by death. Those under the age of 18 cannot be put to death if they are found guilty of capital murder. An offender who commits noncapital murder either can be imprisoned for life or can be sentenced to death under certain circumstances. For instance, if the convicted offender has previously been found guilty of another

Francis Phillip, left, and Kim John react to a judge's sentence of death by hanging, St. Lucia, April 30, 2003. The two men were charged with murdering a St. Lucian priest and an Irish nun during an attack on a church, in which they doused parishioners with gasoline and set them alight. (AP Photo/Timothy James)

murder, he or she can be sentenced to death. Also, if the offender is found to be guilty of more than one murder during the same crime, he or she also can be sentenced to death. Despite the death penalty's continued mention within the criminal code, the United Kingdom outlawed the death penalty in all of its territories, including St. Lucia. Now the death penalty occurs only if a rare case arises.

The punishment for rape can be life imprisonment. The criminal code of St. Lucia states that if a husband or wife commits rape against his or her spouse, the offender can be sentenced to up to 14 years in prison. Anyone under the age of 12 cannot be found guilty of rape.

Punishment for robbery and burglary can be up to 20 years in prison. If an offender is found guilty of having committed aggravated burglary with a firearm, an imitation firearm, any weapon of offense, or an explosive, they can be sentenced to life imprisonment.

St. Lucia prohibits the use of torture or other cruel, inhumane, and degrading forms of punishment. Additional forms of punishment include fine, probation, or an extramural sentence where the offender works under the supervision and control of a public authority. Curfew orders can be placed on individuals so that they are required to be at certain locations at certain times. Also, a subsection of the criminal code is devoted to combination orders, where the offender is put in a probation program and required to serve an extramural sentence. When children are tried summarily in noncapital cases, they are subject to a maximum prison term of six months, or a XCD$500 (approx. US$187) fine.

Prisons

St. Lucia has one prison, the Bordelais Correctional Facility, which is located near Dennery, on the eastern part of the island. The International Centre for Prison Studies reported that as of September 2005, the total prison population of St. Lucia was 503. The operating capacity of the prison is listed at 500, giving the impression that the prison is crowded. Only 1.7 percent of the prison population is female, and a juvenile training school reported having 14 juveniles under the age of 18. Finally, the prison population rate was reported to be 303 per 100,000, a high figure.

Frank Hemming

Further Reading

Government of St. Lucia: http://www.stlucia.gov.lc.

Permanent Mission of St. Lucia to the UN. (n.d.). *History of St. Lucia:* http://www.un.int/stlucia/consularservices/history.htm.

Royal St. Lucia Police Force: http://www.rslpf.com.

Saint Vincent and the Grenadines

Murder: High
Corruption: Low
Prison Rate: High
Death Penalty: Yes
Corporal Punishment: Yes

Background

The country of St. Vincent and the Grenadines is part of the Windward Islands that make up the archipelago surrounding the Caribbean Sea. St. Vincent is the largest of more than 30 islands that make up the nation, covering roughly 390 square kilometers (150 square miles). The Grenadines extend 72 kilometers (45 miles) to the southwest, like a kite's tail. Throughout this entry, references will be made to St. Vincent, which includes all of these Grenadines islands, unless otherwise specified.

According to the United Nations, the population is estimated at 120,000, with about a quarter of the people living in the capital, Kingstown, and its suburbs and 8 percent living on the Grenadines. St. Vincent has a high rate of migration, and population growth remains a major problem. The ethnic mix consists of 66 percent African descent, 19 percent mixed race, 2 percent Amerindian/black, 6 percent East Indian, and 4 percent European.

St. Vincent is one of the 53 member states of the Commonwealth Caribbean, an association of countries that were once part of the former British

Empire. The country is governed by a constitutional monarchy and representative democracy. Queen Elizabeth II is head of state, and she is represented by a governor-general. The legislature is unicameral, with a House of Assembly of 21 members. The leader of the majority party in the House of Assembly becomes prime minister and selects and heads a cabinet.

Crime

Crime Classifications

Offenses are classified as triable only on indictment in the High Court, triable only summarily in the magistrates' courts, or triable either way. Summary offenses are comparatively less serious crimes, such as motor vehicle offenses and common assaults. All summary offenses are made by statute. Offenses triable only on indictment are very serious matters that include murder, rape, robbery, and wounding with intent. Offenses that can be tried either way include burglary, assault causing actual bodily harm, and other offenses of relative seriousness depending on the facts. Theft, for example, can range in seriousness depending on the value of the item stolen or the circumstances surrounding the theft.

Crime Statistics

Newspaper reports provide irregular reports of crime data, focusing mainly on murder, assaults, wounding, burglaries, and theft. According to *The Vincentian,* the total number of crimes reported to the police was 10,228 in 1997 but 7,096 in 2007. Two types of crimes that seem to cause the most concern are homicide and rape. Media from the island and external sources suggest that the increase in homicides on the island is of an unacceptable proportion. The regional Caribbean newspaper cited in several articles that 25 homicides took place in 2005, compared with 12 in 2003. Official statistics available from the World Health Organization showed that St. Vincent had a homicide victimization rate of 13 per 100,000 people in 2002, which was higher than the world average for that time and higher than many other Caribbean nations.

The other high-volume crime in St. Vincent is rape. Newspapers report tourists being raped, and even the prime minister has been accused of rape. A local human rights group called the St. Vincent and the Grenadines Human Rights Association (SVGHRA) reported that the police investigated 50 cases of rape in 2006 and 47 in 2007. According to their report, in 2007 there were an additional 8 cases of attempted rape, and of the 47 cases investigated, 18 went to trial.

Rape, including spousal rape, is illegal in the country, but domestic violence is not criminalized. The Domestic Violence (Summary Proceedings) Act of 1995 provides protection for victims, and cases involving domestic violence are normally charged under assault, battery, or other similar laws. However, access to the legal protection of the courts is limited for the majority of women who are poor. Additionally, the SVGHRA reported that the police generally ignored complaints of domestic violence. Despite the reluctance to involve the police or to press charges after making a complaint to the police, victims can seek assistance from the Gender Affairs Division of the Ministry of National Mobilization, as well as social development and nongovernmental organizations (NGOs). These agencies provide referral and information services to victims.

There are no battered women's shelters in St. Vincent. The Marion House, an NGO, deals with issues relating to domestic violence and sometimes takes in victims, but by no means can it respond to the general needs of domestic abuse victims. There are no halfway houses, and victims usually rely on family members to help them escape abusive situations.

Drugs and Money Laundering

The U.S. State Department International Narcotics Control Strategy report for 2008 stated that St. Vincent both produces a lot of marijuana and has a lot of marijuana users. Efforts have been made to tackle marijuana cultivation. The report also stated that officials seized 1,559.7 kilograms of marijuana, arrested 335 persons on drug-related charges, and convicted 257. The sale of cocaine as an illegal drug, more than its use, is another area of concern for the country because it forms part of the south-to-north drug import-export chain. A report of the United Nations Children's Fund provided data suggesting that marijuana was the drug of choice among young people aged 14–19 in St Vincent. Although the report did not provide any data for the number of children involved in illegal drug use, it stated that from 1998 to 2003, 14 children under 15 years and 265 aged 15–19 were arrested for possession of drugs. The report also stated that only 20 of the young people arrested were girls.

The country is party to many international conventions in the fight against drug misuse, including the 1961 United Nations (UN) Single Convention as amended by the 1972 Protocol, the 1971 UN Convention on Psychotropic Substances, the 1988 UN Drug Convention, and the Inter-American Convention against Corruption. St. Vincent has also signed, but not ratified, the Inter-American Convention against Trafficking in Illegal Firearms, the Inter-American Convention against Firearms, and Inter-American Convention against Terrorism.

The country has taken steps to curb money laundering, and the Financial Action Task Force (FATF) on Money Laundering, a Caribbean intergovernmental body dedicated to tackling the issue, has removed St. Vincent and the Grenadines from its list of noncooperative countries. Progress has been made in combating money laundering in recent years, in part as a result of measures to block terrorist financing. The FATF has been a major factor in Caribbean countries improving their policies to combat money laundering. The country has also established an International Financial Services Authority Financial Intelligence Unit (FIU), as the regulatory body that registers and licenses international financial entities and practitioners. The FIU was established in 2002, and it functions as a specialist agency to receive and analyze any suspicious transaction reports of money laundering and to investigate money laundering and other serious financial crimes. It plays a key role in ensuring that the financial services sector is not facilitating terrorism and money laundering activities. All financial institutions must abide by the Proceeds of Crime and Money Laundering Act, 2001.

Finding of Guilt

The criminal justice system in St. Vincent relies on four main agencies: the police, prosecution, courts, and prisons. As in other English-speaking Caribbean countries, the judiciary in St. Vincent is rooted in English common law. Hence, the criminal justice proceedings have much in common with the English system based on the adversarial principle that requires the police to identify a suspect from the evidence available and, if there is sufficient evidence against the person, to prosecute that person and establish the person's guilt.

Policing

The criminal justice process commences when an arrest is made by the police. Generally, the police have the power to arrest, to enter private premises to make an arrest, to search and seize a person who is arrested, and to stop and question persons in the course of an investigation. The person arrested is entitled to be informed of the reason for his or her arrest. The reason for arrest has been given statutory recognition in the fundamental human rights sections of the St. Vincent's Constitution, so the person also has the right to an attorney.

In St. Vincent, the police may arrest without warrant any person found committing an offense punishable by imprisonment, but a private citizen may only do so if the offense carries a penalty of at least three years in prison. There are not many private citizens' arrests recorded in the country.

The Royal St. Vincent and the Grenadines Police Force is made up of six police divisions, and there are 22 police stations throughout St. Vincent and the Grenadines' population centers. It is the only security force in the country, and it includes a Coast Guard, a small Special Services Unit with some paramilitary training, and the Fire Service. There are approximately 850 members of the police force, all of whom are law enforcement officers who could be rotated among the various parts of the force. The police report to the minister of national security, a portfolio held by the prime minister. The government operates an Oversight Committee to monitor police activity and hear public complaints about alleged police misconduct. The committee reports to the minister of national security and to the minister of legal affairs and actively participates in investigations.

Allegations made by the SVGHRA suggest that there is a high percentage of convictions based on confessions. The association asserted that most confessions, including false confessions, resulted from unwarranted police practices, including the use of physical force during detention, illegal search and seizure, and failure to properly inform those arrested of their rights. It complained that on the whole, the government failed to adequately investigate allegations of abuse or punish those police officers responsible for such abuses. Figures obtained from SVGHRA indicated that there were 101 incidents of questionable police misconduct in 2006 and 2007, 69 of which were assaults, 14 of which were charges of disrespect, and 28 of which were negligence, harassment, or threats.

The SVGHRA reported that police officers investigate all such complaints and submit their findings to the police commissioner. By the end of 2007, authorities had brought disciplinary charges against six police officers, and in 2006, only one officer had charges brought against him. One matter in 2007 was referred to the director of public prosecution (DPP), whereas all others were reported as hearings pending or still under investigation as of 2008.

The SVGHRA also commented on the situation of arrest and detention, indicating that the police apprehended persons openly, and detainees were allowed to seek judicial determinations of their status after 48 hours if not already provided. They found that the bail system was generally effective. The association reported that most detainees were given prompt access to counsel and family members, although in some instances, access delays occurred.

The Director of Public Prosecution (DPP)

The Constitution outlines the post of the director of public prosecution (DPP) as having the power to institute and undertake criminal proceedings against any person before any court other than a court-martial in respect of any offense against the law. The DPP can take over and continue at any point in criminal proceedings that may have been instituted by any other person or authority. The DPP can discontinue at any stage before judgment is delivered any such criminal proceedings by any other person or authority.

Although these provisions seem to give the DPP full control over criminal proceedings, there are specific limitations to that power. The minister heading the Ministry of Legal Affairs, who is elected or nominated by the ruling political party and who is also the attorney general (AG) in St. Vincent, may exercise some control over the Office of the DPP. Although the AG may have more or less administrative powers of control over the DPP, the DPP still acts independently in the actual control of criminal proceedings. In St. Vincent, the privilege of charging an offender lies within the domain of the police, but the DPP is in charge of all prosecutions.

Courts

The Constitution provides for an independent and impartial judiciary, and the government respects this provision in practice. There are 13 courts in three magisterial districts on the mainland of St. Vincent and scattered on some of the major smaller islands. The Lower Judiciary includes the magistrates' courts and the family courts, with the High Judiciary consisting of the High Court and the Court of Appeal. Appeals can be made through the Eastern Caribbean Supreme Court. The court of last resort is the Judicial Committee of the Privy Council in London. All of the Lower Judiciary is located in St. Vincent, including the family courts, which are juvenile courts and courts of summary jurisdiction for domestic violence matters. These are the courts through which many sexual offenses are dealt with at the preliminary stage. They are also the forum where the majority of child custody cases and their maintenance matters are heard.

Of the High Judiciary, the High or Supreme Court is called the Eastern Caribbean Supreme Court, which was established in 1967 by the West Indies Associated States. It is a superior court of record for nine member states, namely Antigua and Barbuda, Dominica, Grenada, St. Kitts and Nevis, St. Lucia, St. Vincent and the Grenadines, and three British overseas territories: Anguilla, the British Virgin Islands, and Montserrat.

The Eastern Caribbean Supreme Court has unlimited jurisdiction in the member states, in accordance with the respective Supreme Court acts. The Courts Order empowers the chief justice and two judges of the Supreme Court, selected by the chief justice, to make rules of court for regulating the practice and procedure of the Court of Appeal and the High Court. Additionally, national legislation in the countries served by the court confers rule-making authority on the chief justice in relation to matters outside the Court of Appeal and the High Court. One judge of the Supreme Court resides in St. Vincent.

Prior to 2003, the court of final appeal, particularly in the matter of the capital offense of murder, which carries the death penalty, was the Judicial Committee of Her Majesty's Privy Council in London. The establishment of a regional judicial tribunal—the Caribbean Court of Justice (CCJ)—is designed to be more than a court of last resort for member states of the Caribbean. It is vested with an original jurisdiction over the interpretation and application of the Treaty Establishing the Caribbean Community. In effect, the CCJ is designed to exercise both an appellate and an original jurisdiction.

Even though only a minority of defendants qualify for jury trial, the jury system remains the cornerstone of the criminal trial in St. Vincent, as in all the Commonwealth countries. To qualify as a juror, a person must be an adult and a resident or citizen and must satisfy other requirements as stated for jury service. The number of jurors that make up a jury in St. Vincent is 9 in the trial of a noncapital case and 12 in the trial of a capital matter.

In St. Vincent, the period of limitation for all offenses where the punishment is only by fine or imprisonment for 6 months or less is, except if longer times are specifically provided, 12 months from the date the matter arose or when it came to the knowledge of a competent complainant. This means that a summary offense, if committed against a child or otherwise incapacitated person, could still be prosecuted outside the limitation time if it was brought to the attention of a "competent" complainant, such as a parent, after 12 months from the date of the incident. This would indicate a specific protection for young and other incapacitated persons in the country's criminal legislation.

Magistracy

Similar to the adversarial system in the United Kingdom, St. Vincent sees the majority of activities of due process taking place in the magistrates' courts. Unlike British jurisdictions, magistrates, not justices, sit in the magistrates' courts in St. Vincent. The magistrate is usually a trained lawyer who sits as a one-person tribunal and is the judge of both fact and law in the summary courts. Issues surrounding jurisdiction, including district boundaries, are regulated by the St. Vincent Magistrates Act, which also sets the period of statutory limitations for prosecution of summary offenses.

The St. Vincent government magistracy is concerned with the dispensation of justice in the hearing of criminal, quasi-criminal, and civil matters summarily in the three magisterial districts. The department is also concerned with the holding of preliminary inquiries, coroner's inquests, and liquor license sessions. There are five magistrates attached to the magistracy. It is also worth noting that it was only in 2007 that a private lawyer was appointed as a special coroner to deal specifically with coroner's inquests.

As stated earlier, there are two levels of court system in St. Vincent, and broadly speaking, it is the seriousness of the offense that determines the distribution of cases between the magistrates' courts and the High Court. In the High Court, offenses are triable only summarily, and in the magistrates' courts, they are triable either way. St. Vincent statute provides that some indictable offenses in given circumstances may be tried summarily in the magistrates' courts. These are usually referred to as matters "triable either way."

All summary offenses are tried in the magistrates' courts. However, there are four instances in which indictable offenses may be tried summarily in St. Vincent. The first is where the offenses are "scheduled" or specified by statute. The second is where the offense itself may be charged indictably or summarily. The third is where the inquiring magistrate feels that the evidence established a summary offense of a "like kind." The fourth is where a juvenile (usually a person under 16) is charged with a noncapital offense. Generally, all matters of various types (e.g., traffic, criminal, civil, application for liquor licenses) are heard in magistrates' courts.

Family Court

Family courts are presided over by a judge, called the president, who effectively also serves as a magistrate when called on to do so. The jurisdiction of the family courts is much broader than a juvenile court. Most of the matters that come before the courts pertain to the maintenance of children and spouses, domestic violence cases, custody or access to children, matters involving juveniles, and sexual offenses. They also handle criminal cases for minors up to age 16, which is the age used to describe a "child" or "young person."

Although the legal minimum age for criminal responsibility is eight years, the St. Vincent Juveniles Act makes provisions for certain special procedures for arraigning and trying juveniles who commit offenses. There are special procedures before, during, and after trial. For example, a juvenile who is detained in a police station must be kept separate from adult prisoners and should be released into the care of a parent or guardian if he or she cannot be brought before a magistrate immediately or for any offense not involving homicide or other grave crime, or this would defeat the ends of justice. If a juvenile is not released on bail, he or she must be remanded in a children's home or other place of detention that is not a prison.

Juvenile justice does not occur without its problems. Key among them are that juvenile justice protections are not afforded to all persons under age 18, public perceptions are negative, and facilities for young people are inadequate. Low status and priority undermine the effectiveness of family courts in the region, and in St. Vincent, the status of the court is that of an inferior court. Public perception holds that juvenile crime is a serious problem, and the solution is thought to be harsh punishments. A UNICEF study noted that in many of the states in the region, including St. Vincent, there are no remand facilities for juveniles. If they are not released on bail, they are remanded in police stations, where they sleep on benches in full view of the general public and other adult detainees. These issues remain unresolved; however, it is fair to state that juvenile justice is much less adversarial and is in fact structured, if not in reality, more along the lines of a social welfare ethos.

Punishment

Types of Punishment

Sentencing options range from absolute discharge to the death penalty. The most common forms of sentences are fines, probation, or imprisonment. Sentencing maximums vary depending on whether the procedure is indictable or tried summarily. Generally, summary offenses carry a maximum penalty of six months' imprisonment or a suitable alternative fine. The jurisdiction specifies an increased sentence where an indictable offense is tried summarily. This is particularly the case with such offenses as possession of illegal narcotics, trafficking in illegal narcotics, and illegal possession of firearms, all of which are subject to special provision in statute. The maximum penalty for any possession of illegal drugs charge is five years or EC$15,000 (approx. US$5,725), and the court even has discretion to send the matter for sentence to the High Court if it feels that heavier punishment is necessary.

In St. Vincent, the power of absolute discharge is contained in the Probation Act and so is open for use by a judge. Probation is a kind of supervisory sentence that is used more for juvenile than adult offenders, although there is no prohibition on its use for adult offenders. Since the passage of the original probation legislation, statutes have been introduced to provide for combination orders consisting of community service and probation orders or other forms of community sentencing and probation. Common forms of sentencing include probation, community services (if the offender is an older juvenile), being placed on a bond, and fines. Many juvenile offenders are also recommended for counseling. There appears to be no organized supervision when juveniles are carrying out community service activities and no programs other than counseling to rehabilitate young offenders.

Probation orders ought not be for more than three years, and if the order is breached during that time, the defendant will be brought before the court for sentencing in accordance with statute. In St. Vincent, probation is permitted instead of punishment and also without any conviction being recorded, but the latter is only for cases that are treated summarily.

Corporal punishment is part of the law of St. Vincent (i.e., the flogging with the cat-o'-nine-tails or a whipping with a tamarind or birch rod). Corporal punishment is not prohibited in the home, in schools, or in alternative care settings but is permissible in the penal system both as a sentence and as a disciplinary measure. However, there is no report of its use as a sentence in recent times, since 1997 when in the case of *Peters v. Marksman,* the High Court of St. Vincent and the Grenadines declared that it was not justifiable and enforceable in international laws. The court found that flogging with the cat-o'-nine-tails in St. Vincent violated article 1 of the UN Declaration on the Prevention of Crime and Treatment of Offenders. The family court may order corporal punishment for a child, but this has not occurred during the tenure of its last president whose contract was not renewed in 2006.

Very serious offenses such as possession or trafficking of narcotics, possession of firearms, rape, and murder attract very long sentences of imprisonment. In the case of rape, the sentence could be 8 to 10 years and a possible sentence of life imprisonment, although this is rare. In the case of murder and treason, there is a mandatory sentence of the death penalty. St. Vincent's political policy is still very much in support of the death penalty even though the last sentence of death by hanging was executed on the February 13, 1995.

Prison

Imprisonment is the usual mode of punishment for an offender convicted of an indictable offense. The prison rules specify that an offender earns an almost automatic remission of up to one-third of any term of imprisonment to which he or she is sentenced. For example, an offender sentenced to 36 months in prison may serve only 24 months, unless he or she forfeits the remission by bad conduct.

St. Vincent has two prisons, one for males and another for females. In January 2006, the government opened a new facility called the Belle Isle Prison Farm that allows inmates to learn and work on the farm on a daily basis. The male establishment is called Her Majesty's Prison and was built in 1872. It is a walled prison, situated in the center of Kingstown, the country's capital. It is bounded on the south by the yard of the High Court and on the west and east by a densely populated residential and business area. The government claims that the prison was initially built to house 70 prisoners, but after renovations, it can hold up to 300 inmates.

The female prison is situated at Fort Charlotte, which is two miles from the male prison. The building that is used to house the female prisoners was originally used as a garrison. Its official capacity is 50 female prisoners as stated by the International Centre for Prison Studies (ICPS). For the past three years, there has been an average of 10 inmates accommodated in the female prison.

Prison conditions are poor. Reports have indicated that the antiquated buildings, overcrowding, and poor sanitation cause serious health and safety problems. A 2001 prison report from the SVGHRA indicated that the main prison was ridden with crime due to endemic violence and cited understaffing, underpaid guards, uncontrolled weapons and drugs, an increase in HIV/AIDS, and prevalence of unhygienic conditions, such as missing toilets. The report also noted that police and guards conducted sporadic, infrequent, and inefficient searches of the prison. Furthermore, the prison guards routinely beat prisoners to extract information regarding escapes, violence, and crime committed in prison.

The United Nations General Assembly Special Session on HIV/AIDS (UNGASS) report of 2008 noted that St. Vincent remains a low-HIV-prevalence country with an estimated 0.4 percent prevalence in the general population. In April 2005, 344 male inmates (92 percent of inmates on the survey days) were tested for their HIV serological status. The seroprevalence rate for all inmates tested was 4.1 percent. Half of these HIV-positive inmates were between the ages of 20 and 29 years.

ICPS data show that the total prison population and the prison rate per 100,000 of the national population are increasing. The rate was 294 in 1992, 390 in 1998, 338 in 2005, and 317 in 2007. In 2006, approximately 80 prisoners (21.8 percent) were classified as pretrial detainees or remand prisoners. There are no data on how long someone can stay in prison under this classification. There were 27, or 7.4 percent, prisoners classed as foreign prisoners, but no details as to their individual nationalities were available. Juveniles, minors, or young prisoners made up a total of 63 (17.2 percent) of the prison population; these included pretrial detainees and young offenders (16–21 years), who were held with convicted prisoners. A UNICEF report from 2006 found that juveniles were sometimes sent to prison when a lesser punishment could have been applied. It also found that the "approved schools" provided for in the Juvenile Act did not exist, and as a result, convicted children over 16 were sent to an adult prison.

Boys under the age of 16 are held at a separate center: Liberty Lodge Boy's Training Center. However, this was retained mostly for boys who could no longer stay at home due to domestic problems. The SVGHRA reported that of the 30 boys in the center in 2007, the majority were there because of domestic problems, and only a small number were charged with committing a crime.

The superintendent of prisons provides for a social worker and psychologist to work with the prisoners. There is a rehabilitation program that allows inmates to receive contracts and jobs with local entrepreneurs. A school program offers courses in carpentry, tailoring, baking, and mechanical engineering. Prisoners are allowed visitors based on their classification. Penal prisoners are allowed one visit per week. Remand prisoners and appellants are allowed two visits per week. Visiting hours are 9:30 A.M. to 11:45 A.M. and 1:00 to 2:30 P.M. Monday to Friday and 9:30 A.M. to 11:45 a.m. Saturday. There are no visits on Sundays and public holidays. All visits for female prisoners are conducted at the male prison through appointments.

Lystra Hagley-Dickinson

Further Reading

Bell Antoine, Rose-Marie. (2008). *Commonwealth Caribbean Law and Legal Systems.* 2nd ed. Oxford, UK: Routledge-Cavendish.

Griffith, Ivelaw L. (2004). *Caribbean Security in the Age of Terror: Challenge and Change.* Kingston: Ian Randle Publishers.

Official Government Web site of St. Vincent and the Grenadines: http://www.gov.vc.

Seetahal, Dana. (2007). *Commonwealth Caribbean: Criminal Practice and Procedure.* London: Cavendish Publishing.

St. Vincent and the Grenadines Human Rights Association (SVGHRA). *Annual Reports 2006 and 2007.*

United Nations Office on Drugs and Crime and the Latin America and the Caribbean Region of the World Bank. (2007, March). *A Joint Report on Crime, Violence, and Development: Trends, Costs, and Policy Options in the Caribbean* (Report No. 37820).

U.S. State Department International Narcotics Control Strategy, 2007 and 2008: http://www.state.gov/p/inl/rls/nrcrpt/2008.

Suriname

Legal System: Civil
Murder: High
Burglary: Low
Corruption: Medium
Human Trafficking: Medium
Prison Rate: High
Death Penalty: Maybe
Corporal Punishment: No

Background

Suriname is situated in northern South America, flanking the Atlantic Ocean in the north, French Guiana in the east, Guyana in the west, and Brazil in the south. This independent country has the smallest territory and population on the South American continent, with a surface area of 163,270 square kilometers and 481,300 inhabitants in 2009. Most of the population is concentrated in the urban region along the coastline, with nearly half living in the capital city of Paramaribo. The territory is administratively divided into 10 districts.

The East Indian community represents the largest ethnic group and accounts for 37 percent of the population. These East Indians are known in the country as Hindustanis and are descendants of contract workers from northern India who were introduced in the late 19th century. About 31 percent of the Surinamese are Creoles, whose ancestors were West African slaves and Dutch colonizers. The Javanese (descendants of contract workers from Java, Indonesia) and the Maroons (descendants of West African slaves who escaped to the inland) make up 15 percent and 10 percent of the population, respectively. Individuals of Amerindian, Chinese, and European origin make up the remaining 7 percent of the Surinamese. This ethnic diversity leads to a rich assortment of religious traditions in Suriname: Hinduism (27 percent) and Protestantism (25 percent) attract the largest numbers of followers, whereas Roman Catholicism (23 percent) and Islamism (20 percent) also command significant influence. Animism based on indigenous beliefs is practiced by 5 percent of the population. Although Dutch is the official language, English is widely spoken.

The mining industry has dominated the Surinamese economy, supplying bauxite, gold, and crude oil to the West for the past 100 years. The export of wood and wood products, rice, bananas, fish, and shrimp also plays an important role. Suriname was one of the wealthiest countries in Latin America and attained a much higher level of education, economic well-being, and public health than its neighbors in the 1960s and 1970s; but coups d'état and misguided policies in the 1980s and 1990s coincided with the termination of development funding from the Netherlands and the United Nations to force a long-term stagnation in its economic and social development. In 2008, Suriname achieved a gross domestic product adjusted for purchasing power parity of US$4.3 billion, which translated into a GDP per capita of approximately US$8,900. The economy and standards of living are highly vulnerable to the volatility of mineral prices in the global market. Between 10 and 14 percent of the workforce was unemployed during 2004–2008. Suriname is classified as a country of medium human development by the United Nations, with a life expectancy of 70 years and a literacy rate of 90 percent.

Suriname is the most ethnically diverse society in the Western Hemisphere. Each ethnic community maintains its own languages, cultural heritage, and institutional affiliations. Even support for political parties, to a large degree, follows ethnic threads. Informal ties in the community are structured around class and ethnic identities: members of the elite from all ethnic backgrounds interact intensely and mingle freely; but outside of the privileged classes, work, friendship, and family connections tend to develop within ethnic enclaves. All groups have equal access to education and job opportunities.

History

The Amerindians first occupied Suriname around 5,000 BCE. The first European explorer, the Spaniard Alonso de Ojeda, arrived in 1499, and the British settled in and colonized present-day Suriname in 1651. The Dutch initiated their long dominance in 1667 when they signed the Peace of Breda with the British and officially annexed Suriname as a possession of the Netherlands. This geopolitical arrangement remained unchanged for 308 years, until the declaration of Suriname as an independent state in 1975.

The Dutch Crown sold the territory to the West Indian Company in 1682, which transformed Suriname into a plantation-based colony. About 300,000 black slaves from West Africa were trafficked into Suriname in the 17th and 18th centuries to supply the labor needed to develop the plantations of sugar, coffee, indigo, and timber. Over the years, a large number of slaves broke from the forced servitude and took refuge in the jungle of the inland. These freed slaves, known as Maroons, established autonomous settlements and had frequent violent clashes with the European owners of plantations along the coastline. The abolition of slavery in 1863 triggered another seismic change in the demography of the land as tens of thousands of contract workers were hired from China, India, and Indonesia to provide the agricultural and mining labor. This massive wave of labor immigration did not end until the eve of World War II.

The postwar decolonization movement made its first impact in 1948 when universal suffrage was granted to allow the Surinamese to elect members of parliament. Ethnic political parties quickly emerged to compete in general elections. Then in 1954, the establishment of a parliamentary body with functioning ministers further consolidated the constitutional autonomy for self-government. In 1973, a coalition of Creole, Javanese, and Hindustanis forces won the parliamentary elections and laid down the blueprint for the full independence of Suriname from the Netherlands, which was realized in the proclamation of a new constitutional democracy two years later. However, one-third of the citizenry left Suriname to relocate to the Netherlands prior to the formal independence of the country because they feared that an independent Suriname would not sustain the stability and prosperity gained under the Dutch colonial rule.

Economic underperformance and erratic policies severely weakened the first democratically elected government led by Henck Arron. In 1980, a dispute over the legality of labor union between the military and the civilian administration ended in a coup orchestrated by noncommissioned army officers. The military regime suspended the Constitution, declared a state of emergency, dissolved parliament, changed the country into a socialist republic, and ruled by military decrees. The extrajudicial execution of 15 prominent civilians in 1982 prompted the unilateral discontinuance of a critical aid program funded by the Netherlands. The event signaled the beginning of the socioeconomic stagnation of the Surinamese development. The worsening social conditions led to, and were further deteriorated by, the emergence of the guerrilla group Jungle Commando in east Suriname in the mid-1980s. Ruthless counterinsurgency warfare, subsequently investigated by the United Nations, which concluded that many innocent victims had been summarily executed, depleted the last political capital of the besieged military regime, which was obliged to align with the old civilian oligarch. In September 1987, a new constitution was ratified, and two months later, a multiparty coalition defeated the party backed by the ruling military in general elections. The military overthrew the civilian administration in 1990 and briefly held onto the power. But strong pressures from the international community forced the return of popular elections in 1991, which were won by the four-party New Front coalition. The democratic governance has ruled since, and the ruling coalition expanded to eight parties in 2005.

Government

Suriname adopted a tripartite form of state organization with some unique features. The executive power is led by the president, who serves as both the chief of state and the head of government. Rather than receiving the governing mandate from direct popular vote, both the president and the vice president are elected by a two-thirds majority in the National Assembly for five-year terms. But if no presidential candidate is elected by the National Assembly after two votes, a simple majority in the nearly 900-member United People's Assembly, formed by all National Assembly representatives and regional and municipal delegates, will decide. The elected president is accountable to the National Assembly. There are no term limits for the chief executive post, and no constitutional venue provides for the impeachment or removal of the president, who appoints the 16-member cabinet of ministers and commands the armed forces.

The National Assembly, a unicameral parliament with 51 members elected by popular vote for a five-year term, heads the legislative branch. In addition to the election of the president and the enactment of law, the National Assembly also nominates members of the Constitutional Court to the president for final confirmation.

The Court of Justice tops the judicial branch, which also includes the cantonal courts, the lower courts, and the Constitutional Court. The Court of Justice is an appellate court for civil and criminal cases decided in lower courts and cantonal courts and also serves as the first-instance court for cases against lawyers and public notaries. Up to early 2009, it consists of 11 full-time and 3 part-time justices who are appointed for life by the president of the nation in consultation with the National Assembly. There are three cantonal courts appointed to specific geographical districts with jurisdiction over civil and criminal litigations. Each cantonal court is led by a single judge whose decisions require confirmation by the Court of Justice. Two lower courts exist in Suriname. The first is the Martial Court, with jurisdiction over cases involving members of the armed forces, and is presided over by military judges. The second lower court is the Medical Discipline Court, which hears and decides on cases against physicians, pharmacists, pharmaceutical companies, and other health professionals and businesses. Article 144 of the 1987 Constitution mandates the creation of an independent Constitutional Court to oversee the constitutionality of government actions, but this court has yet to be established.

Suriname is a member of the Caribbean Court of Justice, which is the highest judicial authority within the Caribbean Community, and accepts compulsory jurisdictions of the International Court of Justice and Inter-American Court of Human Rights.

Crime

Classifications of Crime

The legal classification of criminal offenses is provided by the penal code of 1910 enacted under Dutch rule, which has remained largely intact. All criminal acts are categorized as either felonies or misdemeanors. Felonies are indictable serious offenses listed in the second chapter of the penal code; misdemeanors are instead less serious nonindictable offenses defined in the third chapter of the penal code. Felonies include attacks against state security and assaults against the dignity of the head of state, public disorder, violence against other human beings, contempt of public authorities, perjury, falsification of currency and/or stamps, falsification of documents, breaching of confidentiality, deprivation of personal freedom, theft and poaching, blackmail, peculation and fraud, criminal use of shipping and aviation, and corruption. Misdemeanors are also related to general safety of persons and goods, public disorder, disobedience of public authorities, violations against public decency, withholding assistance from people in need, and other minor offenses.

Crime Statistics

Crime, including violent offenses, is common in Suriname, particularly in the capital of Paramaribo. Insecurity and violence are especially rampant in the Palm Garden neighborhood of Paramaribo, where police presence is negligible. In 2004, Suriname recorded an overall crime rate of 5,220 offenses per 100,000 inhabitants, according to the United Nations Office of Drug Control. Property offenses such as theft (3,086 offenses per 100,000 inhabitants), burglary (495 offenses per 100,000 inhabitants), and embezzlement (140 offenses per 100,000 inhabitants) were the driving factor behind the general crime rate. Whereas the homicide rate of 10 offenses per 100,000 inhabitants falls within the average range among developing countries, attempted homicide victimizations (74 offenses per 100,000 inhabitants) and rape victimizations (51 offenses per 100,000 inhabitants) are especially high. The rate of drug offenses was 35.8 per 100,000 population.

Illicit Drugs

Suriname is a transshipment nexus linking major Andean producers of cocaine and local distribution networks in Europe, Africa, and the United States. Despite signing the 1988 United Nations Drug Control Convention, Suriname has not met the treaty requirement of implementing all necessary antidrug legal tools, including laws regulating precursor chemicals for the manufacturing of illicit psychoactive substances. Surinamese authorities also face important institutional barriers to the effective enforcement of the existing drug-control statutes such as lack of properly trained drug enforcement agents, insufficiency of material resources, understaffed border patrol and drug control units, and corruption among police and military officers. These deficiencies resulted in very few sizable drug seizures in 2007 and 2008 in this country well known for large volumes of drug shipments via commercial air flights, transatlantic sea cargos, and land- or river-based border-crossing.

Domestic demand for illicit drugs is low because Suriname has maintained a very limited population of substance abusers. According to United Nation statistics, cannabis is the most popular drug, with 2 percent of Surinamese aged 15 or older reporting having used it, and the prevalence rate of opiate, including heroin, consumption was the lowest (0.08 percent). The proportions of cocaine and amphetamine abusers in the population were 0.5 percent and 0.6 percent, respectively. Despite this mild picture, the National Anti-Drug Council under the Ministry of Health is implementing the bold National Drugs Master Plan (2006–2010) to reduce both supply of and demand for drugs. Since 2007, this multiyear initiative has been expanded to involve the business community, religious groups, and nongovernmental organizations to play a greater role in drug-abuse prevention and support for recovering addicts. If adequately funded and carefully executed, this program is likely to bring about a healthier community and a stronger civil society.

Human Trafficking

Suriname is a popular destination market as well as a busy transit country for the cross-border trafficking of adults and children for commercial sex and forced labor. There is no general prohibition on prostitution. Only in restricted circumstances is prostitution illegal, but related laws go unenforced in practice. Whereas the demand for Brazilian, Colombian, and other Latin American women in the clubs and brothels of Paramaribo has always existed, Chinese women reportedly are the most recent victims of sexual exploitation in massage parlors and brothels. Traffickers receive about US$500 from club owners for every imported foreign woman. Some foreign girls and women transit Suriname en route to Europe. The seemingly unlimited supply of underage girls and boys from impoverished families has given a steady rise in the internal trafficking of youngsters to cater to the booming sex industry surrounding male-dominated mining camps in the inland. Very often, the transition from working as a juvenile newspaper vendor or shop attendant on the streets of Paramaribo to becoming a victim of child prostitution is smooth and seamless.

Men smuggled from coastal provinces of China are subjected to debt bondage in Suriname and are forced into involuntary labor in supermarkets and at construction sites. Haitian migrants, typically en route to French Guiana, sometimes are forced to work in Surinamese agriculture.

Suriname has been accused of not fully complying with the minimum standards for the elimination of human trafficking, particularly the cross-border trade of humans; however, it has sustained a moderate level of law enforcement actions against trafficker syndicates and started to implement victim assistance and prevention efforts with significant pressures and participation from civic groups. Legislation proposals have been drafted to stop deporting victims to their countries of origin, where retribution is likely, and to provide them with emergency residency permits instead. Human trafficking is punishable with 5 to 12 years of incarceration, plus heavy monetary fines. However, the high level of poverty afflicting the youths, the de facto tolerance of the sex industry, and the corruption of immigration and custom officials are likely to restrict the success of these anti-trafficking efforts.

Finding of Guilt

Rights of the Accused

Unless caught in the act of committing a crime, Surinamese people can be arrested only with properly issued warrants and must be promptly informed of the charges against them. Crime suspects may be detained by the police for up to 14 days if the offense carries a punishment of more than four years of incarceration. Incommunicado pretrial detention is allowable. The accused must be brought before a prosecutor to be formally charged during the

14-day period, but if additional time is necessary to examine the case, the prosecutor and the judge of instruction may add a maximum of 150 days to the detention. There is no bail option for pretrial detainees, who have the right to counsel of their choosing in principle, but the right may be revoked if the prosecutor believes access to counsel could harm the investigation.

The Constitution provides for the right to a fair and public trial in which defendants have the right to counsel; both rights are generally respected in practice. The accused are presumed innocent and can always appeal their verdict. Defendants and their attorneys have access to evidence held by the prosecutor before trial and are permitted to cross-examine witnesses presented by the prosecutor during trial. They also have the right to present their own witnesses and evidence to support the innocence of the accused. All trials are bench trials. Publicly funded private counsel is available to indigent defendants. However, there are only 14 court-appointed attorneys for both civil and criminal systems in Suriname, and they often appear at the trial itself without previously meeting with the defendant.

Criminal Procedures

Suriname has an inquisitorial criminal procedure in which the judges have the authority to collect their own evidence in a case. Prosecutors generally initiate the investigation and prepare criminal cases with technical assistance from the judicial police. Citizens can also file a case by presenting a petition to the courts, and a judge will determine whether a formal investigation is warranted. Prosecutors make the decision to bring a case before the court or to drop it from the process depending on its evidentiary strength. The written dossiers are prepared during the investigative phase prior to the formal trial, and the trial is mostly intended to clarify uncertainties in the dossier. Plea bargaining is nonexistent; most criminal cases are disposed by trial, with convictions handed down by one of the seven criminal court judges. These judges do not function exclusively as criminal court judges but also preside over civil court hearings.

Juvenile Justice

In Suriname, persons between the ages of 0 and 21 are legally considered minors. According to article 56 of the Surinamese penal code, children 10 years and younger cannot be prosecuted. A minor who commits a criminal act before the age of 16 can be withdrawn from his or her legal guardian and placed under foster care, without any additional legal sanction. The judge can also decide to provide this minor with an official reprimand as punishment. In case of a felony, the judge can commit the offending minor to a youth custody center. Minors aged 16 or older can receive a conviction as an adult, with the provision that the maximum punishment will be reduced to one-third of the original sentence, and a death sentence or life sentence will be converted into a maximum sentence of 15 years. Juvenile custodial units for boys between the ages of 10 and 18 are located within adult prisons and tend to be relatively adequate. Education is mandatory for the youth delinquents in custody: primary schooling and junior secondary education are provided. There is no separate facility for girls under the age of 18, who are housed within the women's section of one of the other adult prison complexes. All juvenile inmates have access to sports and recreational activities.

Punishment

Types of Punishment

The penal code makes six punishments available to sentencing judges: death penalty, incarceration, monetary fines, disfranchisement of political rights, community services, and confiscation of private properties. Although the penal code provides for the death penalty through hanging, no judicial executions have reportedly been carried out since 1927. Political rights vulnerable to penal disfranchisement include the right to serve in public functions, the right to serve in armed forces, the right to vote, the right to nominate electoral candidates, and to the right to practice law as a counsel. Community services are usually added as a supplement to incarceration, and the sequestration of private properties relates only to goods used to commit the offense or goods gained by committing the offense.

Prisons

Suriname has three major penitentiaries at Hazard, Santa Boma, and Duisburg, with two segregated units for juvenile offenders under the administration of the Ministry of Justice and Police. The adult penitentiaries are mixed facilities and house all types of inmates, from pretrial detainees to maximum-security inmates. In addition, there are 23 detention cells at police stations throughout the country, designed to hold suspects for up to 42 days. Unfortunately, these overcrowded settings have been utilized as regular custodial facilities for convicted offenders when space is unavailable in the three national penitentiaries. By 2005, the Suriname prison population totaled 1,600 inmates, which represented a national incarceration rate of 356 inmates per 100,000 population, according to the International Centre for Prison Studies, 2009. About 55 percent of all Suriname inmates were detainees awaiting trial or disposition. Among sentenced offenders serving time for their offenses, 9.7 percent were juveniles convicted as adults, and 19.3 percent were foreigners, according to the United Nations Office on Drugs and Crime.

Prison conditions by and large do not meet international standards. Prisoners also mistreat each other, and violence among prisoners is usually left unpunished by the authorities. Some prison facilities have been renovated to improve health and safety conditions in recent years. However, most correctional facilities, especially older units, remain seriously overcrowded, with as many as four times the number of detainees for which they were designed. Sentenced female adults receive training in sewing and poultry farming, and agricultural, animal husbandry, and technical work opportunities are available for sentenced male inmates. Only detainees have access to sport and recreational activities.

Extradition

The Act of Extradition governs the surrender of a suspected or convicted alien criminal to foreign countries. No Surinamese can be extradited out of the country. Requests are processed and reviewed by the Ministry of Justice and Police and can be denied when there is a suspicion that the petition for extradition is intended to prosecute or to penalize the suspect because of the person's religious or political convictions, nationality, or race or ethnicity. Deportation of incarcerated illegal aliens is permitted. But the extradition of a detained or sentenced inmate is possible only if the individual is a citizen of a country with which Suriname has a bilateral convention regarding admission of their court decisions. Exchange of prisoners is prohibited as well.

Milton Castelen and Hung-En Sung

Further Reading

Munneke, H. F., and A. J. Dekker. (2002). "Suriname." In *Legal Systems of the World: A Political, Social, and Cultural Encyclopaedia,* edited by Herbert M. Kritzer, pp. 1547–1556. Santa Barbara, CA: ABC-CLIO.

Walmsley, Roy. (2009). *World Prison Population List.* 8th ed. London: International Centre for Prison Studies.

Westoll, Andrew. (2008). *The Riverbones: Stumbling after Eden in the Jungles of Suriname*. Toronto: Emblem Editions.

Trinidad and Tobago

Murder: Medium
Corruption: High
Prison Rate: Medium
Death Penalty: Maybe
Corporal Punishment: Yes

Background

Trinidad and Tobago is an English-speaking twin-island state. It is the southernmost country in the Caribbean archipelago of islands, northeast of Venezuela and south of Grenada in the Lesser Antilles. It has a population of approximately 1.3 million people and covers 5,128 square kilometers (or 1,979 square miles). Ninety-six percent of the population live on the main island of Trinidad, and the remaining 4 percent live on the smaller island of Tobago.

Both islands were originally settled by Amerindians of South America. Trinidad was claimed by Christopher Columbus in 1498 for Spain. There were many European wars for the island that included the French, Dutch, and British. The island of Tobago also had a similar past. Trinidad was ceded to Britain in 1802. In 1889, the islands of Trinidad and Tobago were made into a single colony. Partial self-government was instituted in 1925, and from 1958 to 1962, the nation was part of the West Indies Federation. Trinidad and Tobago gained its independence in 1962 from England and gained its republican status in 1976.

The population is composed mainly of those of African and Indian descent, at approximately 40 percent each, and about 20 percent mixed, with small proportions of Caucasian, Chinese, Syrian/Lebanese, Portuguese, and so on. The people also have a wide variety of religious backgrounds.

Government

Trinidad and Tobago is a parliamentary democracy whose republican Constitution dates from August 1, 1976. The country's legal system is based on English common law. The country's chief of state is a president, elected to a five-year term of office by an electoral college comprising members of the House of Representatives and the Senate. The head of government is a prime minister, usually the majority party leader in the House after elections are held.

The doctrine of separation powers, inherited from the British Westminster system, provides for the executive, the legislature, and the judiciary. The executive is made up of a cabinet of ministers led by the prime minister. The legislature consists of a bicameral Parliament comprising the House of Representatives and the Senate. The House has 41 members elected to five-year terms by popular vote. The Senate has 31 appointed members serving terms up to five years. Apart from this national parliamentary composition, Tobago has a unicameral House of Assembly with 12 members serving four-year terms as a function of local government.

The chief justice, as head of the judiciary, has overall responsibility for the administration of justice. The judicial system's jurisdiction, practices, and procedures follow closely those of the High Court of Justice in England. The Constitution established the Supreme Court of Judicature, consisting of a High Court of Justice and a Court of Appeal. There is also a lower judiciary called the Magistracy. The Supreme Court is housed in four locations: the capital of Port-of-Spain, San Fernando, the island of Tobago, and the northwestern Trinidadian suburb of Chaguaramas.

The High Court and the Magistracy exercise original jurisdiction in both civil and criminal matters. The Magistracy (in its petty civil division) deals with civil matters that involve sums less than TT$15,000.00 (approx. US$2,500). It exercises summary jurisdiction in criminal matters and hears preliminary inquiries in indictable matters, thereby determining whether a matter is to be held over for trial in the assizes. The Magistracy is divided into 13 districts. The High Court hears indictable criminal matters, family matters where the parties are married, and civil matters involving sums over the petty civil court limit. Civil actions and proceedings are usually heard by only one High Court judge but may be tried by a jury of nine members. A High Court judge with a jury of 9 to 12 members tries criminal offenses. Minor offenses are handled by district courts, including traffic courts. The judicial system also includes the Industrial Court and Tax Appeal Board.

Appeals from the Magistracy and the High Court go to the Court of Appeal, and appeals from the Court of Appeal go to the Privy Council in England, sometimes as of right and sometimes with leave of the court. The Court of Appeal judges are referred to as justices of appeal, and High Court judges are referred to as either judges of the High Court or *puisne* (associate) judges.

The Supreme Court *puisne* (associate) judges sit in the following divisions: criminal, civil, and matrimonial. In the civil division, there are civil open courts and civil chamber courts. The masters of the High Court have the jurisdiction of judges in civil chamber courts except for certain areas in which their jurisdiction is expressly limited by statute. Though providing the seat for the Caribbean Court of Justice, Trinidad and Tobago has not yet accepted the Caribbean Court of Justice as its appellate court for criminal matters because of the refusal by the opposition to give its support for the special majority needed for adoption.

Qualifications of Judges

The chief justice is appointed by the president after consultation with the prime minister and the leader of the opposition. The Judicial and Legal Services Commission is charged with the task of appointing justices of appeal, High Court judges, masters of the High Court, magistrates, registrars of the Supreme Court, and the administrative secretary to the chief justice, all of whom are judicial officers.

A High Court judge should have at least 10 years' standing as an attorney-at-law. High Court judges who have sat on the bench for at least 3 years and attorneys-at-law of at least 15 years' standing are eligible for appointment to the Court of Appeal. All judges are appointed with security of tenure and hold office during a period of good behavior until the age of 65. Temporary judges are appointed for fixed periods, mainly to assist in reducing the backlog of cases.

Criminal Justice System

Generally, the criminal justice system operates free from interference by the executive, although the executive has direct control over the police and corrections; that is, they both fall under the Ministry of National Security. The judiciary does not fall under any government ministry, but it depends on

Members of the Regional Judicial and Legal Service Commission pose during the installation ceremony on August 21, 2003, in Port-of-Spain, Trinidad. The 10-member panel was installed to select judges for a new Caribbean Court of Justice. (AP Photo/Shirley Bahadur)

the executive for all of its funding. Recently, there have been claims from some members of the criminal justice system, as well as from opposition parties, of governmental attempts to interfere in the criminal justice system, especially with regard to the police and the courts. One example was the attempt by the prime minister in 2006 to impeach the chief justice for alleged misbehavior in public office. The matter was eventually won by the chief justice. This was the first time in the history of the Commonwealth countries that efforts were made to impeach a sitting chief justice.

In the seven years up to 2008, the criminal justice system has also witnessed police investigations, charges, arrests, court trials, and imprisonment of several members of Parliament, on both the government and opposition sides. Added to this is the frequent revelation of police officers, defense force personnel, and prison officers being involved in a wide range of criminal activities, including murder, drug trafficking, kidnapping, robberies, and rapes. As a result, the criminal justice system has been subjected to intense public debate.

Policing

The country is served by the Trinidad and Tobago Police Service (TTPS), which falls under the Ministry of National Security. The TTPS has national jurisdiction. There are approximately 8,000 police officers, a number that results in a police-citizen ratio of 1:162. The TTPS is also served by a set of officers called the Special Reserve Police (SRP), which supplements the regular police workforce.

The country is divided into nine police divisions. These are further subdivided into approximately 70 police stations and 5 police posts. Further, there are several specialized units, such as the Homicide Bureau, Fraud Squad, Traffic Branch, Organized Crime and Narcotics Unit/Firearms Interdiction Unit, Forensics, Crime and Problem Analysis, Community Relations, and Training Academy.

An independent body appointed by the president, called the Police Service Commission, looks over the efficiency and effectiveness of the roles, functions, and performance of the commissioner of police and the deputy commissioners of police and, by extension, the entire police service. Another independent body, the Police Complaints Authority, hears complaints about the conduct of police officers. It also monitors the investigation of complaints and determines disciplinary measures where appropriate.

There is also another policing unit called the Special Anti-Crime Unit of Trinidad and Tobago (SAUTT), which also comes under the Ministry of National Security. This unit was established in 2003 to support the TTPS, as well as to advance law enforcement in Trinidad and Tobago. The unit comprises personnel from both the police service and the defense force.

The military is called the Trinidad and Tobago Defense Force. Its various units include the Trinidad and Tobago Regiment and the Trinidad and Tobago Coast Guard, which includes the Air Wing Operations. The military falls under the Ministry of National Security. Its strength is approximately 2,000 members. There are several joint police and military operations in Trinidad and Tobago. These occur with regard to anti-narcotic operations, street patrols, raids, searches, and so on. In fact, there is an established Inter-Agency Task Force for these purposes.

Crime

Classification of Crimes

Crimes can be either indictable or nonindictable. Crimes are further categorized into three groupings: serious crimes, minor crimes, and minor offenses. Serious crimes are all crimes that carry a penalty of five or more years, for which prosecutions have been instituted in the High Court. Examples include murder, rape, incest, felonious wounding, kidnapping, treason, robbery, burglaries and break-ins, larceny of over TT$2,000.00 (approx. US$328), trafficking of dangerous drugs over a certain quantity, and so on. Minor crimes are all crimes carrying a penalty of less than five years for which prosecutions have been instituted in a magistrate court or in the High Court. Examples include indecent assault, unlawful wounding and inflicting, possession of firearm and ammunition, larceny of under TT$2,000 (approx. US$300) trafficking of dangerous drugs within a certain quantity, and so on. Minor offenses are all offenses for which prosecutions have been summarily instituted in a magistrate court. Examples include loitering, assault by beating, armed with a weapon, breaches of the peace, malicious damage of TT$1,000 (approx. US$150) and under, cruelty to animals, and gambling and betting.

Age of Criminal Responsibility

The age below which a child is conclusively presumed to be unable to commit an offense is 7 years under the common law. However, legislation raising the age of criminal responsibility to either 10 or 12 is being considered by the relevant authorities.

Crime Statistics

The latest crime statistics available from the Trinidad and Tobago Police Service are for the year 2007. The provisional statistics show the number of crimes that were "reported" and the number of crimes that were "detected." "Detected" does not mean convicted or solved. It means that for this crime, a person has been arrested after police investigations.

In 2007, there were 391 murders reported and 74 detected, which is a 19 percent detection rate. For rape, incest, and sexual offenses, 759 incidents were recorded, and 474 were detected, for a 62 percent detection rate. For burglaries and break-ins, 4,851 incidents were reported, and 537 were detected, which is an 11 percent detection rate. For narcotics crimes, 589 incidents were reported, and 587 were detected, for a 99 percent detection rate.

Between 2000 and 2007, total serious crimes increased by 11 percent, total minor crimes decreased by 11 percent, and total minor offenses decreased by 10 percent. The year 2007 had the highest number of murders ever for Trinidad and Tobago. For a relatively small country, with a population of approximately 1.3 million persons, having an average of more than one murder per day is high. Closer examinations of the situations of murders suggest that there is a notable connection between murders, gang warfare, and drug trafficking. Rape, incest, and sexual offenses increased by 38 percent from the 2001 to 2007, and wounding and shooting increased by 32 percent, which coincides with an increasing use of illegal firearms. Narcotic offenses increased by 22 percent. The geographic location of Trinidad and Tobago, close to the South American continent, makes it a strategic transshipment point for the main suppliers of cocaine from South America to the consumers in North America and Europe.

During the same period, robberies increased by 18 percent, larceny by 18 percent, and kidnapping by 4 percent. The year 2005 had the highest number of kidnappings in the country's history, with 240 (19 per 100,000 residents). Trends suggest that small- and medium-size business owners and their families are the main targets of kidnapping for ransom.

The most typical crimes in urban areas are robbery, wounding and shooting, murders, narcotics, possession of arms, and ammunition. The most typical crimes in rural areas are larceny, burglary, breakings, rapes, incest, and sexual offenses. Further, robberies tend to increase in certain months. For example, during the Carnival season (January to March annually), the police find an increase in robberies. This is especially the case in certain urban areas where some *mas* (masquerade) players need to acquire money to purchase carnival costumes and to attend music concerts and other festivities. Also, during the Christmas season, when there are a lot of commercial activities in the urban centers, robberies also increase.

Drug Offenses

The two major illegal drugs are marijuana and cocaine. Persons can be charged with trafficking and possession, as well as with using these drugs. There have also been a small number of incidents with trafficking of heroin. Along with illegal drugs, illegal firearms and ammunitions are also trafficked.

Trinidad and Tobago does not produce cocaine. However, marijuana is grown and produced in Trinidad and Tobago for trafficking as well as for local consumption. Any quantity of cocaine or marijuana is illegal to traffic, possess, and use, and convictions for these offenses carry prison sentences. The courts are very strict when it comes to sentencing for drug offenses.

Finding of Guilt

All criminal cases start with the filing of a complaint in the summary court. Minor offenses are tried before the magistrate. For more serious offenses, the magistrate holds a preliminary inquiry. If there is sufficient evidence, the accused goes to trial before a judge and jury of the High Court.

In the Constitution, there is the explicit right to a fair trial. An independent judiciary vigorously enforces this right. All criminal defendants have the right to an attorney. The judiciary is independent of the other branches and free from outside interference. Criminal defendants are presumed innocent and are afforded the right to representation by counsel.

Rights of Accused

Some crimes, such as the use of obscene language, can be tried only in a magistrate court. Other crimes—for example, murder, rape, kidnapping—can be tried only in a High Court with a judge and jury. For some other crimes—for example, dangerous drugs—the accused has the right to elect whether he or she wants the matter to be tried by a magistrate or a High Court judge and jury. The accused has no right to a speedy trial. The accused must follow the case management system for his or her matter before the court.

Defense

The accused has the right to an attorney, and if he or she cannot afford one, one will be appointed to him or her. The accused does not have the right to choose an attorney that is allocated by the state. The Legal Aid and Advisory Authority appoints an attorney for the accused upon application. This authority provides legal advice and court representation from a panel of attorneys before coroners, magistrates, and judges and juries, in matters of probation, family law, civil law, and criminal law where costs are defrayed wholly or partly out of monies provided by an act of Parliament. This act aims to make legal aid and advice readily available to persons of little and moderate means. The Legal Aid and Advisory Authority is a unit of the Ministry of Legal Affairs. Any member of the public can visit any of the nine branches across Trinidad and Tobago. There is a TT$10.00 (approx. US$1.64) application fee.

In matters before a magistrate court or in proceedings before a High Court or Court of Appeal, a magistrate or judge must decide whether an accused is eligible for legal aid or representation. In High Court civil matters, eligibility is based on the applicant's means and the merits of the matter.

Investigation and Prosecution of Cases

The police service conducts the investigation of criminal cases. For some crimes, the police may prosecute in the magistrate courts only. The police officer must be of a certain rank. Further, police officers are also allowed to conduct preliminary inquiries in the magistrate courts.

For all High Court matters, attorneys from the Office of the Director of Public Prosecution (DPP) prosecute while the police perform the investigation of the cases. There is also a provision whereby the DPP's office can retain the services of private attorneys to represent the state on court matters.

Criminal Law Department

The Criminal Law Department is headed by an independent public officer, the director of public prosecutions (DPP), who has the power to initiate and undertake criminal proceedings against any person before any court with respect to any offense against the laws of Trinidad and Tobago, to take over and continue any such criminal proceedings that may have been instituted by any other person of authority, and to discontinue at any stage before judgment is delivered any such criminal proceedings instituted or undertaken by himself or any other person or authority. The DPP may allow an attorney-at-law in private practice to prosecute on application.

The mission of the department is to serve the state by representing it in criminal matters before the courts in Trinidad and Tobago and where necessary abroad. Further, it provides advisory services on matters of a criminal nature to government departments and agencies. The objectives of this department are to appear in all criminal matters at all levels, to advise all departments (police, customs, immigration, town and county, and price control) in criminal matters, to represent police officers on cross charges, and to assist the police in prosecution where difficult points of law are involved in the magistrate courts.

Alternatives to Trial

In Trinidad and Tobago there are alternatives to going to trial, such as "out of court" settlements or plea bargaining, the latter rarely being used. This is where the accused and the prosecutor can bargain an agreement for a plea of guilty to a lesser offense, or they can make an agreement whereby the accused testifies against other accused persons for a reduced sentence or immunity, for example.

For certain crimes, magistrates may offer the accused and the victim the opportunity to refer their matter to mediation. A trained mediator will try to resolve the main contention between both parties. If both parties do not agree to go to mediation, then the matter is tried by the court. Both parties must agree to abide by the decisions of the mediation process. The magistrate sets a time limit to have the matter settled by mediation, and if the matter is not resolved within the time frame, the mediator can ask the magistrate for an extension if he or she believes that some additional time is required. If the time allocated expires, and the matter is not resolved, the matter is returned to the court for trial.

When the accused is deemed to be medically unfit to stand trial, he or she is sent via the courts to a medical institution for diagnosis and treatment. It is also possible, when the accused are deemed to be medically unfit, to have their cases discharged.

Incarceration Before or While Awaiting Trial

There are two criminal acts in which the accused does not have the right to seek bail—murder and treason. For all other crimes, the accused can apply for bail. After the accused has been arrested and charged by the police, he or she can apply for bail. If he or she cannot afford bail or until he or she obtains bail, the accused is incarcerated. If the accused has several matters pending before the courts or has a lengthy criminal record, he or she may be refused bail. An accused has a right to appeal to a High Court judge if he or she is not granted bail by a magistrate.

If an accused is held in prison before conviction, that is, while awaiting trial, he or she is placed in a separate section in the prisons called remand. Upon conviction, the prisoner is transferred to another section in the prison for convicted persons.

System for Juveniles

There is no statutorily defined juvenile court. However, appropriate arrangements are made in a magistrate court to facilitate the trial of matters directly affecting juveniles. In comparison to adults, the names of accused juveniles are not allowed to be portrayed in the media.

Punishment

Types of Punishment

Several forms of punishment are listed on the books. These include fines, prison sentences, probation, treatment, corporal punishment/flogging, house arrest, reparations, compensations, community service, and others. They are used to varying degrees. The most frequently used punishments are prison sentences and fines.

Typical Punishments

The punishment for murder is execution by hanging. However, there have been a number of judgments by the Privy Council in London, England, that have placed restrictions and limits on its implementation. As a result, many persons who have been convicted of murder are serving lifetime sentences in prison. As of 2009 there had been no executions in the previous five years.

The typical punishment for rape is a relatively long prison sentence between 15 and 25 years for each conviction of rape. It should be noted that there have been some questionably inconsistent sentences where convicted rapists have been given relatively short sentences that produced much public outcry. There have also been sentences where judges have prescribed long prison terms accompanied by corporal punishment. The typical punishment for serious theft, burglary, and robbery is a relatively long prison sentence, from 5 years to 15 years. For the most serious drug offenses, the typical punishment will be life imprisonment.

Probation

Probation is a suspended jail sentence where instead of serving time in prison, the criminal is returned to the community for a period in which he or she has to abide by certain conditions set forth by the court under the supervision of a probation officer. General conditions may include maintaining employment, abiding by a curfew, living where directed, abstaining from unlawful behavior, following the probation officer's orders, not absconding, and refraining from contact with other individuals, who may include victims of the original crime, potential victims of similar crimes, potential witnesses, or those who partnered with the offender in the earlier crime. Usually, the offender is supervised by a probation officer, to monitor his or her performance during the probation period. The probation officer helps the offender adapt to living in the community and behave in a lawful and responsible way. Trinidad and Tobago does not yet have a parole system. This is being considered by the relevant authorities.

Prison

The prison population in 1988 was 2,855. It rose steadily and peaked at 4,474 in 1998, which was a 57 percent increase. After 1998, there was a gradual decline to 3,851 in 2007, representing a decrease of 14 percent. The prison population per 100,000 residents was 296 in 2007.

There are seven prisons; six are for convicted persons, and one is for remand. These prisons are the Carerra Convict Prison, the Port of Spain Prison, the Maximum Security Prison, the Golden Grove Prison for male convicts, the Golden Grove Women's Prison, and the Tobago Prison and the Golden Grove Prison for remand.

There are three juvenile institutions for convicted juveniles. The first institution is the St. Michael's School for Boys, which caters to males between the ages of 10 and 16 years. The second institution, St. Jude's School for Girls, serves 10- to 16-year-old girls. Males 16 to 18 years old are sent to the Youth Training Center. Girls aged 16 to 18 years are sent to the women's adult prison.

The biggest prison in Trinidad and Tobago is the maximum-security prison. It is located in Arouca in the main island of Trinidad. It can accommodate approximately 2,000 prisoners. It has state-of-the-art security systems. The facilities and physical infrastructure at this prison are better than the other prisons. There is no problem of overcrowding in this prison, in stark comparison to the other prisons. The prison has classrooms, recreational facilities, a library, sports facilities, a computer laboratory, religious facilities, a kitchen, a dining hall, and a sick bay.

Characteristics of Prisoners

A study conducted by the author and colleagues in 2003 reported the following characteristics of adult prisoners in Trinidad and Tobago: The majority of the prisoners were males, and almost 30 percent of the prisoners were between 17 and 26 years old, and approximately 35 percent were between 27 and 36 years old. The majority of prisoners were Afro-Trinidadians followed by prisoners who were Indo-Trinidadians and mixed ethnicities.

Most prisoners were single (84%). Fifteen percent were married, and some 60 percent had children. The vast majority of prisoners had a low socioeconomic background. The highest proportion of prisoners resided in the northern region of Trinidad (46%). This was followed by those who lived in the southern region of Trinidad (31%) and the central region of Trinidad (17%). Five percent lived on the island of Tobago, and 1 percent were foreign nationals.

The same study also found that a majority of the prisoners (56%) were recidivists. These prisoners would continuously return to prison to serve sentences for committing other crimes upon release. Thirty-nine percent were in prison for the first time, and 5 percent had "other" statuses, such as awaiting appeal, prohibited immigrants, adjourned cases, and so on. The highest proportion of prisoners was imprisoned for narcotic-related crimes, followed by larceny-related crimes, and then personal crimes.

Twenty-five percent of prisoners were serving sentences of less than 1 year, 23 percent were serving 1 to 3 years, and less than 5 percent were serving more than 20 years. Overall, 94 percent had sentences of hard labor, and 6 percent had other types. Of this 94 percent with hard labor, 73 percent had only hard labor, 12 percent had hard labor or a fine, 6 percent had hard labor and a fine, and 3 percent had hard labor and strokes (whipping).

Labor and Vocational Activities in Prisons

Although most prisoners' sentences may stipulate hard labor as part of the sentence, this typically involves cleaning up the surroundings, ensuring a regular supply of water on the compound, kitchen duty, agriculture, rearing animals, and the like. It is not compulsory that prisoners work on the prison compound. Depending on the attitude and disposition of the prisoners, as well as the availability of prison staff to supervise them, prisoners may be called on to do work.

Some prisoners are allowed to work outside or away from the prison compound itself. For example, they do cleaning jobs at various coast guard and army sites. Prisoners who work are paid a small stipend by the prison service. They receive such monies when they are ready to be discharged. Because of the shortage of prison officers to supervise prisoners when they are out of their prison cells doing work, this aspect of working is limited to a relatively small number of prisoners. This number varies from prison to prison.

Prisoners are allowed to attend classes that are offered on their prison compound. These classes are taught by prison officers, volunteers, ex-prisoners, and even other prisoners. Some class categories or topics include academics, skills and training, religion or spirituality, counseling, literacy, pottery, tailoring, electrical, and computers. In fact, there are several instances whereby prisoners were able to undertake national and international examinations while in prison and were quite successful. Further, many prisoners have been able to gain entry into local and foreign universities after passing classes and examinations from the prison.

Visiting Policies and Privileges

The visitation policies of the various prisons are slightly different from one another. However, the general policy is that if an inmate is serving a longer sentence, he or she has a longer length of time for the visit. Generally, each inmate will be allowed one visit every four to six weeks with a maximum of three persons for any visit. The shortest time allowed for a visit is 15 minutes, and the longest time is 45 minutes.

The actual area set aside for visits varies from prison to prison. In some prisons, prisoners are allowed to interact with the visitors, whereas in others, they communicate via telephone lines and a glass window between prisoner and visitor. Conjugal visits are not allowed.

Some of the other privileges that prisoners can access include mail and the ability to attend the funerals of very close relatives under the escort of a prison officer. Prisoners are also allowed to receive toiletries and food items from family and friends when they visit them. Female prisoners who give birth to babies while in prison, or who have recently given birth to babies just before entering prison, are also given special visitation privileges to take care of the newly born.

Ramesh Deosaran

Further Reading

Deosaran, R., ed. (2007). *Crime, Delinquency and Justice: A Caribbean Reader.* Kingston, Jamaica: Ian Randle Publishers.

Deosaran, R., I. K. Ramdhanie, and V. Lall. (2003). "Crime Statistics, Analysis and Policy Action in Trinidad and Tobago." Special Research and Policy Reports on Crime Statistics, Community Policing and Police Performance in Trinidad and Tobago. *Caribbean Journal of Criminology and Social Psychology* 8 (1-2): 1–60.

The Judiciary of the Republic of Trinidad and Tobago: http://www.ttlawcourts.org.

The Ministry of National Security, Trinidad and Tobago: http://www.nationalsecurity.gov.tt

Trinidad and Tobago Ministry of Legal Affairs: http://www.legalaffairs.gov.tt

Turks and Caicos Islands

Legal System: Common
Murder: High
Prison Rate: High
Death Penalty: No
Corporal Punishment: No

Background

The Turks and Caicos Islands (TCI) are part of the British overseas territories in the Caribbean. The TCI are part of the Bahamas chain. The 40 TCI atolls (or cays) cover some 430 square kilometers (193 square miles). Six of the TCI islands are permanently inhabited: Grand Turk, Salt Cay, South Caicos, Middle Caicos, North Caicos, and Providenciales. Grand Turk is home to the territorial capital, Cockburn Town. Providenciales, often called "Provo," is the business and tourist center and remains the most populous island. The major languages are English and Creole.

Population

The total population counted 33,202 in 2006, with an estimated indigenous "Belonger" population of 11,750 (34 percent) and 21,452 "non-Belongers" (66 percent). The estimated population for 2007 was about 34,862. In 2007, about 400 to 500 illegal "boat people" per week were coming to the TCI.

Non-Belongers consist mostly of immigrants from Haiti and the Dominican Republican, as well as American, Canadian, British, and other European expatriate residents and workers. Though Belongers are not fully defined in law, the TCI Constitution makes frequent reference to them. For example, a person seeking appointment to office in public or government service must be a Belonger. The governor grants Belonger status on the basis of the length of time that applicants have stayed in the TCI, the contribution they have made to the country, and how they have assimilated into the community. In each case, the governor should consult with the secretary of state.

The majority of the population is of African descent, the rest being of mixed race. About 14,000 former TCI islanders live in the Bahamas, and some return for seasonal work. The TCI's population is mostly Protestant Christian.

Economy

The main economy is based on tourism and offshore financial services, with the United States and Canada being the leading sources of those businesses. The TCI are a "zero tax" jurisdiction. The islands have no income, capital gain, wealth, gift, or inheritance taxes. The TCI have no tax treaties with any other jurisdictions. The major sources of government revenue include stamp duties, customs receipts, and fees from offshore financial activities. The U.S. dollar is used as the local currency. The TCI have no central bank or monetary authority. There are no restrictions on movement of funds into or out of TCI.

The TCI have a structure for financial supervision that encompasses banking, insurance, mutual funds, investment brokers, trusts, trustees, companies' registrations, and company service providers. The banking sector, consisting of seven banks, is small but pivotal in the financial structure of the TCI. Specialized insurance, in the form of producer-owned reinsurance companies (PORCs) is a major and growing line of business in the offshore financial sector. TCI trusts and corporate vehicles for offshore clients provide the basis for an active trust and company service-provider sector. Recently, the TCI have seen an upsurge in cruise ships and their registration on Grand Turk. The economic and financial structure of the TCI and the corporate vehicles available under TCI law make it vulnerable to money laundering. A variety of money laundering cases involving TCI have been prosecuted or are under investigation.

Annual tourism amounted to over 200,000 visitors in 2007, particularly with holiday makers from Canada. This is one of the reasons the Canadian government has made continuous efforts to annex the TCI over the past years.

History

There has been a considerable amount of political conflict surrounding the ownership of the Turks and Caicos Islands, not only within the Caribbean, such as Bermuda and the Bahamas, but also within the British Empire. The Spanish explorer Juan Ponce De Leon first put these *cayos* (small islands) on the map in 1512. Over time, the Turks islands were occupied by the French, Spanish, and British, in turn.

Between the 17th and 20th centuries, the Turks were occupied by Bermudans, federated with the Bahamas, and later annexed to Jamaica. When Jamaica gained independence in 1962, the Turks and Caicos Islands became part of the Federation of the West Indies. On May 31, 1962, the TCI became a British Crown colony with its own administrator, but in 1965, the governor of the Bahamas took over governance of the TCI. When the Bahamas gained independence from the United Kingdom in 1973, the TCI once again became a constitutional self-governing part of the British overseas territories.

In 1976, the TCI were granted their first full Constitution establishing an elective form of government. This Constitution was suspended in 1986. A new Constitution followed in 1988, which was eventually superseded by the Constitution of 2006.

Following an investigative report by Sir Robin Auld, a former lord justice of appeal, the Turks and Caicos Islands were handed over to direct rule by the British government at Westminster, London, in April 2009. The Turks and Caicos Constitution was suspended, and its first minister's position was disbanded. The Auld Report blamed "clear signs of political amorality and immaturity and general administrative incompetence." New democratic elections are scheduled for 2011.

Governance

Today, TCI is an internally self-governing overseas territory (OT) of the United Kingdom with a ministerial system of government. The British monarch, Queen Elizabeth II, is the sovereign of all OTs, represented by respectively appointed governors. The United Kingdom's Foreign and Commonwealth Office overseas all OTs' policies and supports the appointed governors. The governor of TCI retains responsibility for internal security, external affairs, defense, public service, and offshore finance. The governor appoints the judiciary, as well as the attorney general and the chief secretary.

The ministerial system of government of the TCI has a premier as head of government. The TCI's Executive Council consists of three ex-officio members plus five appointed members by the governor chosen from among the members of the Legislative Council. The TCI cabinet is made up of the governor, the premier, six ministers, and the attorney general. The TCI parliament is referred to as the House of Assembly and consists of the speaker, 15 elected members, 4 appointed members, and the attorney general.

Legal System

TCI's legal system is based on English common law; however, some customary laws still exist from Jamaica and the Bahamas. Most of the laws derive from ordinances passed in the legislative council and, to a lesser extent, from legislation specially extended to TCI by the United Kingdom. In the case where statutory law does not apply or requires interpretation, the common law applies. The attorney general is responsible for all legal advice to the TCI government and for all prosecutions, law revision, and law reform.

The court system is made up of the magistrates' courts, the Supreme Court, and the Court of Appeal, all of which sit in the TCI. The Supreme Court is vested with the same jurisdiction and powers as the High Court of England and Wales. Powers to pardon lie with the queen but are exercised by the governor.

The judges of the Supreme Court must be qualified barristers or solicitors, from the United Kingdom, any part of the Commonwealth, or Ireland, or they must be a member of the Faculty of Advocates or a Writer to the Signet of Scotland. All judges are appointed by the governor. The TCI Court of Appeal consists of a president and two justices of appeal, determined and appointed by the governor on his discretion.

The Judicial Committee of the Privy Council, part of the Ministry of Justice in London, is the court of final appeal for the U.K. overseas territories and Crown dependencies. The committee, usually made up of five judges, has complete discretion over whether to grant special leave, mostly granted in criminal cases, but it is sometimes granted in civil cases where the local Court of Appeal has for any reason refused leave. The TCI Court of Appeal sits for two weeks twice a year, hearing criminal and civil appeal matters. There were two appeals pending before the Privy Council Judicial Committee in 2007.

Crime

Classification of Crimes

TCI's criminal justice system is adversarial in nature, based on English criminal law. Classification of criminal offenses follows English procedural and criminal justice legislation. Less serious crimes are referred to as summary offenses, and serious ones are known as indictable offenses. Similar to English criminal procedure, all criminal offenders are brought in the first instance before a TCI magistrates' court, to decide where the defendant should be tried. Rules of evidence also follow English law supplemented by local statutory instruments.

Drugs and Money Laundering

By far the most serious offenses in the TCI today involve international organized crime, such as drug trafficking and money laundering, because the TCI are one of the main transshipment points for illicit drugs for South American narcotics destined for the United States and Europe. Money laundering offenses extend to proceeds derived from all serious (indictable) offenses, and self-laundering is covered. Corporate bodies can also be held liable for money laundering. However, one problem lies in the fact that money laundering is criminalized by four separate TCI statutes. The International Monetary Fund Report of 2005 suggested that the TCI urgently needed to harmonize and unify all applicable money laundering offenses by removing the distinctions between drug and non-drug money laundering and by consolidating all legislation regarding money laundering into one statute for the TCI and other OTs.

TCI domestic laws enable a range of drug-related mutual legal assistance. Various bilateral U.K. and U.S. money laundering statutory instruments deal with and allow for judicial cooperation concerning the financing of terrorism in overseas territories. All OT mutual assistance must be channeled through the governor and the attorney general's chambers for non-U.S. related cases or through the chief magistrate for U.S.-related cases. No formal arrangements authorize TCI law enforcement authorities to conduct cooperative investigations or coordinated seizure and forfeiture actions with other jurisdictions. However, such cooperation is said to exist.

In February 2003, the executive of the International Monetary Fund (IMF) conducted a large-scale investigation into the TCI's economic and financial structure linked to off-shore finance and money laundering. The report established that by the end of 2002, there were a large number of foreign banks and insurance companies on TCI. There were eight licensed banks, of which six were national banks and two were offshore banks with no banking operations in TCI. Three banks conducted a largely retail banking business and account for the bulk of bank assets and deposits. Total bank on-balance sheet assets were \$480 million. There were two offshore banks carrying on banking business in Panama and Venezuela. There were 3,013 licensed insurance companies, and there were no details available as to the total assets.

The 2005 IMF report concluded that English common law and banking regulations were inadequate to deal with fraud and money laundering happening in the TCI. The IMF found large inconsistencies in banking legislation and regulatory guidelines regarding disclosure and money laundering. There was a total lack of transparency. Many banks and insurance companies did not produce annual reports, making fraud and money laundering easy for those in the know. The IMF strongly recommended that the U.K. government make efforts to put in place additional regulatory resources, indicating that if this did not happen immediately, TCI would continue to be exposed to the risk of its financial and corporate services being misused for illegal purposes.

INTERPOL, the world's largest police organization facilitating international police cooperation, has a permanent sub-bureau on the TCI. INTERPOL's Anti-Money Laundering Unit cooperates with Europol's Financial Crime Unit in the fight against money laundering and terrorism financing by placing specific liaison officers in the TCI as points of contact for its Camden Assets Recovery Inter-Agency Network (CARIN). CARIN is an informal international network for tracing, freezing, seizing, and confiscating the proceeds from criminal activities. The Proceeds of Crime Act 2002 provided the U.K. Assets Recovery Agency with unique powers to confiscate assets within the EU and its overseas territories, thereby helping to reduce transnational organized crime.

Crime Statistics

The official TCI tourism Web site informs visitors that crime on the islands is "the lowest in the Caribbean," but recorded police statistics show that violent crime is on the increase, mostly linked to drug trafficking from Latin America to the U.S. mainland via Miami. Most property crimes are committed on Providenciales and Grand Turk by inter-islanders. The Royal Turks and Caicos Police Force has been strengthened and increased in size as a result of additional British government overseas aid funding in 2003, which accounts for the increase in arrests and charges ("clear up rates"). Five Cays and Chalk Sound now have sub-police stations to conquer organized illegal drug trafficking into Miami.

Police statistics for 2006 showed a decrease in crime by 17 percent in Providenciales, whereby 287 fewer crimes were reported compared with the previous year. However, there was a sharp increase in recorded crime on Grand Turk, accounting for a quarter of all crime committed on TCI, with an increase of 148 percent in 2006 compared with the previous year. The latter can be attributed to increased police resources on Grand Turk as well as new stop-and-search powers. In 2003, some 505 persons were arrested and charged. This figure decreased to 467 in 2005 and rose again to 557 in 2006. Police clearance rates have averaged 30 percent since 2005. Providenciales, the holiday island, continues to report the largest proportion of crime (67% in 2007).

Like in England, Wales, and Northern Ireland, the age of criminal responsibility is 10 years, and adult crime begins at age 18. Juvenile delinquency is a large social problem, mainly linked to the Haitian boat-people crisis, with large influxes of children being dumped on the TCI and trafficked to other Caribbean islands or sold to Florida. The number of teenage boys involved in crime has increased dramatically, though there are still low prosecution results, something that continues to worry the TCI government. In 2005, 14 boys were charged with property offenses compared with 69 in 2006, which is a 40 percent increase. Most of them are repeat offenders. Three teenage girls were arrested and charged in 2005.

Most reported crimes are tourist- and vehicle-related, making up 17 percent of the total crimes reported in 2006. There were 263 reported "motor-vehicle interferences" in 2005. This decreased in 2006 to 120, a decline of 54 percent. The offense of "taking a motor vehicle without authority" decreased from 115 to 59 over the same period, a drop of over 50 percent. There were 34 firearms offenses in 2006. Of the 38 robberies reported in 2006, 74 percent involved the use of firearms, and 35 occurred on Providenciales. A gun amnesty was held in 2007 in an effort to combat gun-related crime in the TCI. The *TCI Free Press*'s annual public opinion poll of 2006 showed that the fear-of-crime element had decreased, with locals feeling "safer" because of an increased police presence on the islands. In 2005, 82 non-Belongers were charged with at least one criminal offense, and 128 were charged in 2006. Police and government reports state that most crimes are committed by illegal immigrants from neighboring Haiti.

Finding of Guilt

All criminal investigations and prosecutions are instigated by the attorney general (AG). Pretrial detention on remand is commonplace, directed from the magistrates' court on Provo Island. A defendant does not have the *prima facie* right to bail, as would be the case in an English court. Alternative sanctions, such as community service orders, do not yet exist; consequently, there is no probation service. Trial of indictable (serious) offenses has been by judge and jury in the main courthouse of Grand Turk, although this burned down in October 2007.

Since January 2008, video-conferencing facilities have existed at the Providenciales Magistrates' Court. The direct court video system links the justices' bench straight into HMP Grand Turk, aiming to make considerable savings in the prison's budget because it reduces the number of inmates who are being transported to and from the court by air for short hearings. The system is used mainly for bail and further remand hearings, and each hearing typically takes about 10 minutes of court time. Full trials and preliminary inquiries still require the inmate to appear in court in person. The TCI are awaiting another new magistrate's court plus a new Supreme Court, both of which will service HMP Grand Turk.

Punishment

Types of Punishment

Due to deep-rooted Christian values and beliefs on the TCI, crime is still associated with sin, impurity, and evil. Local Belongers strongly believe in retributive justice in that the criminal must be punished severely for his wrongdoing and misdemeanors. Prison sentences tend to be long, and the local population thinks this a suitable sacrifice toward an aggrieved deity. Generally, the court makes no distinction between the sentencing of a male, female, or juvenile offender for similar crimes. Accommodation is usually in the one prison, which is HMP Grand Turk.

The death penalty was abolished in 1991 under the Abolition of Death Penalty for Murder–Caribbean Territories Act 1991 for treason and piracy-related offenses. The TCI Parliament has frequently debated the reintroduction of corporal punishment and the death penalty, although it is fair to say that these options will not be available as long as the TCI remain a British overseas territory. For this reason, sentencing punishment tends to be more severe than in England for similar offenses (though there are some exceptions), whereby non-Belongers are often doubly punished. Tourists convicted of drunk driving are immediately expelled from the islands, preceded by remand in custody without bail. Penalties for possession, use, or trafficking in illegal drugs are severe; convicted offenders can expect long jail sentences and heavy fines. Engaging in sexual conduct with children and using or disseminating child pornography in a foreign country are offenses punished by imprisonment under the Sexual Offenses Act of 2003. Homosexuality was an illegal act until the Caribbean Territories (Criminal Law) Order of 2000 legalized homosexual acts between two consenting adults in private.

Corporal punishment was still in existence until 1998 and was used in the old local prison principally on juveniles, even though torture by public officials in the course of their duties had officially been abolished in 1988. When the European Torture Commission of the Council of Europe visited the TCI in 1998, the inspectors took particular interest in the management of prisoners at HMP Grand Turk. The commission noted with concern that prisoner beatings by staff were commonplace, and the report strongly recommended the removal of corporal punishment from the TCI's statute books. The Torture Commission stated that corporal punishment was no longer acceptable in a modern society and that the maltreatment of prisoners in the new HMP Grand Turk was contrary to the European Convention. Subsequently, on March 25, 1998, the TCI's Legislative Council passed new legislation and removed all references to corporal punishment.

The Supreme Court and magistrates' courts of the TCI have a limited sentencing range available, which is not always in line with English law on the U.K. mainland. For example, the maximum sentence for indecent assault in England is 10 years and for assault 5 years, and in the TCI, it is 2 years.

Prison

Following reports by the English chief inspector of prisons, Judge Stephen Tumim, in 1988 and 1991 documenting poor prison conditions on Grand Turk, the old prison was eventually demolished, and HMP Grand Turk was built in 1997, following the designs of London's Pentonville Prison of 1842 with its traditional radial star-shaped design. Though the prison was initially designed to hold 104 inmates, HMP Grand Turk held 113 prisoners, including remands and juveniles, in December 2006.

Since its inception, the prison has experienced problems with racial integration among staff and prisoners, and the causes can still be attributed to historical events. Very few local prisoners tend to populate the prison; the majority of inmates are from neighboring Jamaica, Haiti, or the Dominican Republic. On arrival, many demand separate living units, often to the detriment of female prisoners. After the volcanic eruptions on Montserrat in 1998, prisoners were evacuated from HMP Montserrat to the new prison at HMP Grand Turk. The Montserratians demanded separate accommodations, objected to local TCI guards, and also objected to some Jamaican prison officers. This resulted in separate Montserratian prison guards being flown hundreds of miles to guard their own prison population. Although this was seen as only a temporary measure, this arrangement of taking long-term prisoners from Montserrat continued until 2005. Eventually, the Grand Turk prison administration refused to take any more foreign prisoners because of overcrowding.

Today, the majority of prisoners are either remanded or convicted in connection with illegal drugs or money laundering trade. As a result of long and harsh prison sentences, the relatively small prison has become overcrowded, housing adult males and females, as well as some young offenders, in a very confined space.

Race relations among staff continue being a problem. The 2000 European Torture Commission's report urgently recommended that the TCI government pass specific legislation that would prohibit racial discrimination, which was openly practiced at HMP Grand Turk as well as by other official authorities on the TCI. Though the 2006 TCI Constitution provided for separate accommodation for juvenile prisoners, the prison still accommodates unconvicted juvenile prisoners from time to time. Child protection legislation is still in need of reform, including with regard to corporal punishment in schools.

Following the European Torture Commission Report of 2000, U.K. government aid was released to construct a separate juvenile detention and rehabilitation center, by converting the old police headquarters at Cockburn Town. By 2006, the facility was to become part of the Department of Social Development, and this safe holding facility was to provide 16 units for convicted juvenile males under 18. Due to a large organized petition by Grand Turk residents, followed by a public demonstration, construction of the juvenile rehabilitation center was halted by the TCI cabinet in 2007. This means that juveniles are still being held at HMP Grand Turk, thereby arguably violating the Constitution of 2006.

HMP Grand Turk came under further scrutiny and criticism by the law enforcement agency in 2006, following a number of security breaches and serious riots at the prison. All disturbances were related to illegal drugs and followed the arrest in July 2006 of a prison officer, who had worked at the prison for over two years and was found with 90 grams of cannabis hidden in his vehicle. After he pleaded guilty to the charge of possession with intent to supply, he was fined $3,500 and deported back to Jamaica.

In 2005, HMP Grand Turk introduced some correctional industries (prison workshops) outside its perimeters, including apprenticeships in carpentry and tailoring, funded by a public outreach program. Members of the community assist with the rehabilitation of some less dangerous prisoners, with limited educational and vocational training facilities also offered. A small prison shop outside the prison walls sells prisoner-made furniture. Of the 30 percent of prisoners on remand in 2007, only very few were permitted to participate in rehabilitative constructive regimes. Maximum-security and mentally ill prisoners are excluded from programmed activities, though some long-term inmates were involved in the construction of a new building to accommodate improved facilities for learning and counseling programs inside HMP Grand Turk. By April 2007, the prison's superintendent had introduced sentence planning for long-term inmates, which reviewed prisoners' progress every six months.

Juvenile offending remains on the increase with little room for juveniles at the local prison. The Department for Social Development tries, wherever possible, to send young convicted offenders outside the TCI for rehabilitation in the absence of a juvenile detention facility. In 2007, seven male juvenile offenders were accommodated at the Jamaican Juvenile Rehabilitation Center, part of the Jamaican Department of Corrections. Three juveniles were at a Seventh-Day Adventist facility in West Virginia, and a further 18 young males were accommodated at HMP Grand Turk. A U.K. government report of 2006 noted that sending juvenile convicts outside the TCI for punishment created an unnecessary expense and that, furthermore, the TCI government was losing sight of the care and rehabilitation of its young offenders.

Ursula Smartt

Further Reading

International Monetary Fund. (2005, January 26). *Turks and Caicos Islands: Assessment of the Supervision and Regulation of the Financial Sector—Review of Financial Sector Regulation and Supervision.* IMF Country Report No. 05/24. Washington, D.C.

Sadler, Herbert, E. (1997). *Turks Islands Landfall—A History of the Turks and Caicos Islands.* Kingston, Jamaica: United Cooperative Printers.

Smartt, Ursula. (1999, March). "Constitutionalism in the British Overseas Territories of the Caribbean." *European Journal of Crime, Criminal Law and Criminal Justice* 7(3): 300–314.

The Turks and Caicos Department of Economic Planning and Statistics: http://www.depstc.org

The Turks and Caicos Free Press: http://www.tcifreepress.com

The Turks and Caicos Island Government: http://www.turksandcaicosislands.tc/.

The Turks and Caicos National Museum: http://www.tcmuseum.org

United States of America

Legal System: Common
Murder: Medium
Burglary: Low
Corruption: Low
Human Trafficking: Low
Prison Rate: High
Death Penalty: Yes
Corporal Punishment: Yes

Background

Because the United States was once a colony of Great Britain, the American criminal justice system was steeped in the same legal traditions found in that country. However, the application of these traditions shifted and adapted to the social, political, and geographical differences between the two nations. Some of the key elements retained from the British tradition that are still found in the American criminal justice system are the application and importance of common or case law, a guarantee of a trial by a jury of "peers," and protection from double jeopardy, or being retried on the same charge.

Although the United States has a body of statutory laws comprising the formal codification of laws and the consequences of their violation, judicial decisions are also based on prior cases and precedent, or case law. In fact, there is an obligation for the courts to adhere to their own prior decisions and those of higher courts as long as the legal issues are substantively similar. The result is a system that can respond to the evolving nature of crime, as well as minimize differential application of criminal law.

In the adversarial system of the United States, a judicial authority, which is an impartial third party, renders legal decisions after two disputing parties have pleaded their case. In the application of criminal law, the two disputing parties are the state and the accused. Although there is usually a wronged victim in a violation of criminal law, the criminal justice system contends that any violation of criminal law "injures" society as much as it does an individual victim. The state pursues the determination of guilt or innocence on behalf of itself and the victim—usually with the cooperation of the victim.

The government of the United States can be thought of as a series of nesting boxes with each level of government covering increasingly larger geographic areas and their inhabitants. Each layer within this federalized system has responsibilities of its own, as well as responsibilities to its subordinate governmental entities. Given these political divisions, the criminal justice system of the United States is not a monolithic structure. When reading this entry, it is important to keep in mind that there will be exceptions from the norm found throughout the criminal justice system.

Crime

Classification of Crime

In the United States, wrongs are generally classified as either crimes or torts. A crime is an act punishable by law. The government, on behalf of the particular victims, exacts the consequences for these acts in a variety of ways, from fines to imprisonment. On the other hand, the remedy for the commission of a tort would most likely be the payment of monetary damages directly to the individual, as opposed to the government.

Crimes that are the most severe are considered felonies. These acts are typically punished by imprisonment of more than one year or possibly death. Examples of felony crimes are murder, rape, robbery, aggravated assault, burglary, and arson. However, as is the case with many aspects of the American criminal justice system, what crimes are classified as felonies can vary from state to state. Crimes that are not considered as serious as felonies are labeled misdemeanors. The punishment for a misdemeanor would include fines, the forfeiture of property, briefer forms of confinement (usually for less than one year), or probation. Some of the typical crimes associated with misdemeanors are petty theft, assault with no injury (simple assault), breaking and entering, and disturbing the peace, among others.

Age of Criminal Responsibility

The American criminal justice system has a separate response for juveniles who commit acts that would be considered criminal if committed by an adult. Individuals who have reached their 17th or 18th birthday (depending on the state) are considered adults and are tried in criminal court. However, for those under this age, the behavior is considered delinquent and is handled by the juvenile justice system. The youngest age at which a child might be considered delinquent varies depending on the state. This minimum age is based on the idea of the youngest age at which an individual could distinguish right from wrong and is usually in the range of 8 to 12 years of age.

The age of criminal responsibility is the youngest age at which an individual could be held responsible for his or her acts, meaning that he or she would be tried in a criminal court, as opposed to being considered delinquent. This age varies from state to state but has become increasingly younger in recent years. One would typically find it to be 14 years of age. At least one state (North Dakota) has set the age of criminal responsibility to be as young as 7 years old, and Michigan will allow a child of any age to be tried as an adult for a crime.

Drug Offenses

Although many crimes clearly have victims who have suffered injury to either their person or their possessions, there is a class of offenses where the victim is not clear. Often they are referred to as "victimless" crimes or crimes against society. A significant portion of these crimes against society involves drug offenses.

In the United States, drug offenses primarily focus on those substances whose legal uses are "controlled" by law. Hence, one often hears the term "controlled substance" as another phrase for potentially illicit drugs. Whether the use of the substance is legal depends on the age of the user or the situations in which it was used.

The Comprehensive Drug Abuse Prevention and Control Act (1970) categorized drugs in terms of possible medical uses, the risk for abuse, the risk of addiction or dependence, and the impact on society. Schedule I drugs are considered to have no established medical usage and present a high risk for abuse. There are virtually no circumstances in which a Schedule I drug may be legally used. Examples would include substances such as heroin, LSD, Ecstasy, and marijuana and its variants. Schedule II drugs have a high risk for abuse but also have established medical benefits in certain circumstances. In this case, the legal use of Schedule II drugs is highly regulated. Examples of these drugs are opium, morphine, codeine, cocaine, PCP, barbiturates, and certain stimulants like Ritalin. Many of the drugs on Schedule II, once diluted, would be considered Schedule III drugs. These are drugs that typically can be obtained through a doctor's prescription. Finally, Schedule IV and V drugs are considered to have a very low risk of abuse and are commonly prescription medications with traces of narcotics or some other controlled substance higher on the schedule.

Crime Statistics

There are two primary methods by which the level of crime is measured. First, there is a nationally representative survey of households to assess the level of victimization called the National Crime Victimization Survey. Second, there are data collected directly from law enforcement agencies reflecting the number of crimes that were reported to, or have come to the attention of, law enforcement called Uniform Crime Reporting (UCR). Often the UCR statistics are referred to as official crime statistics because of the nature in which they were collected.

The UCR program captures the number of offenses reported to law enforcement for eight major offenses, also known as Part I offenses. These are murder/nonnegligent manslaughter, forcible rape, robbery, aggravated assault, burglary, larceny-theft, motor vehicle theft, and arson. The UCR program collects arrest figures, rather than the number of offenses reported, for an additional 21 offenses. The FBI is responsible for managing and publishing the statistics collected through this program. The primary motivation for the creation of the UCR program by police chiefs in the late 1920s was to provide a uniform and comparable manner to record the level of criminality in a particular jurisdiction. As such, there are specific definitions and rules for each of the offenses within the statistical collection.

The category of murder and nonnegligent manslaughter is defined by the UCR as "the willful (nonnegligent) killing of one human being by another." According to the FBI, in 2006, there were an estimated 5.7 murders and nonnegligent manslaughters for every 100,000 inhabitants in the United States. This is equivalent to 17,034 murders in the United States for 2006. Although most other offense categories include both attempted and completed crimes, there are no attempted murders included in these counts because they would be considered aggravated assaults.

Forcible rape is defined by the UCR as "the carnal knowledge of a female forcibly and against her will." The definition is very particular and does not encompass a wide range of acts of sexual assault and abuse. It narrowly refers to a man having sexual intercourse with a woman. The restrictions imposed in terms of the types of acts, as well as the gender of the victim, should be kept in mind when reviewing the reported statistics.

According to the FBI, in 2006, the estimated forcible rape rate was 30.9 rapes per 100,000 inhabitants. Based on an estimated 92,455 forcible rapes, there were 60.9 per 100,000 females. Overall, 91.9 percent of the rapes reported to law enforcement were considered rape by force. The remaining 8.1 percent were classified as attempted rapes. The resulting rates are 56.0 rapes by force per 100,000 females and 4.9 rape attempts per 100,000 females.

Based on the classification rules of the UCR program, the most serious property offense is burglary. Burglary is defined by the UCR as "the unlawful entry of a structure to commit a felony or theft." According to the FBI, in 2006, an estimated 729.4 burglaries occurred per 100,000 inhabitants, with an estimated property loss value of $4 billion. For these 2,183,746 burglaries, 66.2 percent were burglaries of residential structures. Further analysis of reported burglaries revealed that 6.6 percent of offenses were attempted forcible entries, with the remaining 93.4 percent reflecting completed forcible entries and unlawful entries combined.

Although drug offense reports are not collected in the UCR program, the number of persons arrested for drug offenses is available. Drug abuse violations include a range of infractions such as production, distribution, and use of controlled substances. Based on reported data from the FBI, there were 636.8 arrests per 100,000 inhabitants for drug abuse violations. Of the 1,889,810 estimated arrests for drug abuse violations in 2006, 82.5 percent were

The body of a victim lies covered on the street in front of a car that plowed through a crowded farmers market in Santa Monica, California, July 16, 2003. George Russell Weller, driver of the car, was convicted of 10 counts of vehicular manslaughter with gross negligence. (AP Photo/Damian Dovarganes)

for possession of a controlled substance. The remaining 17.5 percent included sale or manufacturing of a controlled substance.

Crime in Urban and Rural Areas

In cities of 250,000 population or higher, the most common violent crime in 2006 was aggravated assault. According to the FBI, aggravated assaults accounted for approximately 53 percent of the reported violent crimes, which is equivalent to 501.3 aggravated assaults for every 100,000 in population. Murder and nonnegligent manslaughter were the least common violent crimes.

In 2006, reported property crimes were more common than violent crimes. The most frequent property crime in cities of 250,000 or more inhabitants was larceny-theft, which encompassed most types of nonviolent thefts of property. For every 100,000 in population, there were 2,829.0 larceny-thefts reported, which translates into approximately 61 percent of property crimes. The second most frequently reported property crime in urban areas was burglary, followed by motor vehicle theft.

The UCR program does not define what "rural area" means. However, it does collect statistics from agencies that serve small towns (less than 10,000 in population), as well as county agencies for nonmetropolitan areas. In terms of the relative frequency of both violent and property crimes, rural areas experience crime much in the same way that urban areas do. However, the overall frequency of these crimes is typically lower.

Finding of Guilt

Investigation

The responsibility for investigating criminal offenses resides with law enforcement. Federal law enforcement agencies are tasked with the responsibility to investigate and enforce federal laws. Jurisdiction for federal agencies is principally determined by which laws they enforce. For example, the Drug Enforcement Agency's jurisdiction is the enforcement of federal drug violations.

Beyond federal law enforcement, state and local jurisdictions are normally a function of geography. Usually, law enforcement agencies whose primary jurisdiction is a city or town are referred to as a police department and headed by a chief that is hired by a governmental agency (such as a city council). Those agencies whose primary responsibilities are to unincorporated areas of a county are called sheriff's offices. A sheriff, who heads such an office, is in many instances elected to that position rather than appointed.

A law enforcement agency gets involved in the investigation of a crime in two primary ways. A crime comes to the attention of law enforcement via a report (by a victim or a witness), or it is observed by a law enforcement officer. Once the agency determines that there is sufficient evidence of a crime, it will proceed with an investigation to resolve the question of who will be held criminally responsible. An investigation involves a systematic inquiry into the circumstances and information surrounding the criminal event. This can include gathering physical evidence, interviewing witnesses, and interviewing possible suspects. Although the key duty of law enforcement is to investigate criminal acts, there are times that prosecutors can influence the direction of an investigation. As such, these powers are not completely separate in the United States.

Rights of the Accused

In the American criminal justice system, the accused are guaranteed certain protections under the Constitution and the law. The Fourth Amendment protects individuals from unwarranted searches and seizures of property. In addition, it provides that there must be more than just a suspicion of wrongdoing, often referred to as probable cause, before a court issues a warrant for a search or seizure.

The Fifth Amendment guarantees that individuals do not need to answer accusations without an indictment, nor can they be required to engage in self-incrimination. The government cannot assume property or deny liberty without due process in a court of law. The Fifth Amendment also prevents an individual from being tried more than once for the same criminal act (double jeopardy). An exception to the concept of double jeopardy is if the criminal acts violate both federal and state laws. In those cases, an individual can be tried in both state and federal jurisdictions for the same acts.

The Sixth Amendment guarantees a speedy and public trial by jury, the right to confront accusers, the right to legal representation, the right to information on the nature of the criminal charges, and the right to obtain information from the prosecution that establishes the innocence of the accused. The Eighth Amendment prohibits extreme punishments in the form of excessive bail and fines or cruel and unusual punishment.

The U.S. Supreme Court had the opportunity to consider many of the rights of the accused in the 20th century. Most famously in *Miranda v. Arizona,* the Supreme Court ruled that the accused must be informed of these rights upon arrest. If not, evidence collected after arrest, especially by the admission of the accused, may not be admissible in the trial. Because of situations such as *Miranda v. Arizona* in which the Supreme Court interpreted the Constitution, the rights of the accused may include additional nuances that grow out of the Fourth, Fifth, Sixth, and Eighth Amendments.

Adjudication

Presiding over the legal process is the trial judge. It is the judge's responsibility to ensure that both the prosecution and the defense observe the rules of the legal process. If there is a violation of the intent of the law or the process of adjudication, this becomes the basis of an appeal of the original decision. In some cases, the judge will also be the individual to render the legal decision rather than a jury. Just as often, a jury or a group of citizens asked to render a decision about the guilt or innocence of the defendant will hear cases related to serious offenses. According to court statistics collected by the Bureau of Justice Statistics, of the 5 percent of convictions that resulted from trials, 2 percent were jury trials, and 3 percent were bench trials.

The prosecuting attorney or district attorney has the responsibility to represent the government in the pursuit of criminal charges against the defendant. Defense counsel is also guaranteed in the American criminal justice system. If a defendant is unable to pay for an attorney, then one will be made available by the state. Depending on the location, this representation could come in the form of a public defender, assigned counsel, or contract attorney. Public defenders are salaried attorneys whose job is to represent indigent defendants through either a nonprofit or a state-run organization. Assigned counsel and contract attorneys are private attorneys who accept indigent clients on a case-by-case basis (assigned counsel) or whose firm maintains a contract to provide such defense. The court jurisdictions in most states do not rely on one method solely, but have a mixed system for defense of the indigent.

Once an arrest has been made in connection with a criminal act, defendants are brought before a judge for the first appearance. It is at this first appearance that the charges are read to the defendants, and they are informed of their rights, including the right to an attorney. The judge determines whether the defendants will be released on bail or on their own recognizance. Bail is, in essence, collateral that defendants provide to guarantee their appearance at trial. The judge could also determine that the defendant will be held without bail based on the seriousness of the crime, the risk to the community, or the risk of flight by a defendant.

Sometime after the first appearance, either the case is brought before a grand jury, or a preliminary hearing is held to determine whether to return an indictment, or formal accusation of a crime, on the defendant. A grand jury is a panel of typically 23 citizens convened to hear the facts of the case and decide whether they support an indictment. Grand juries do not usually use a highly formal process in their efforts to question witnesses and in other manners of fact-finding. The grand jury process is used by the federal courts and in about half of the states. The remaining states rely on preliminary hearings. At least two states use both a grand jury and preliminary hearings to decide on an indictment. A judicial authority conducts preliminary hearings after the prosecution submits a complaint or information on the case. The preliminary hearing, though not as involved as a full criminal trial, is very similar to a trial in its proceedings.

Assuming that the judge or grand jury issues an indictment, the defendant is arraigned, or appears before a judge to enter a plea. The acceptable pleas are guilty, not guilty, or no contest. The results of a guilty plea and a no contest plea are essentially the same. The main difference is that the defendant does not admit guilt by pleading no contest. Therefore, the defendant would not be as vulnerable to a civil suit. If the defendant pleads guilty or no contest, he or she is then sentenced; otherwise, the defendant is tried to determine guilt. According to the Bureau of Justice Statistics, the vast majority of felony convictions (95 percent) are the result of a guilty plea. The remaining are the result of either a jury trial or a bench trial.

Guilty pleas, however, are not always for the original charge. The Bureau of Justice Statistics estimated that up to 90 percent of all guilty pleas are a result of a plea bargain, which is an agreement that a defendant will plead guilty in exchange for a reduction in charge or lesser sentence. Plea bargains are often negotiated between the prosecution and the defense because of the burden of time and expense that would result from the trial process. In addition, some communities are using alternative dispute resolution centers to handle minor offenses, usually upon referral from the court or under court supervision.

U.S. Court System

In the United States, the courts are organized based on their jurisdiction. There are courts that serve local and state jurisdictions and courts that serve the federal jurisdiction. The two jurisdictions traditionally do not interfere with each other unless there is a violation of due process as guaranteed by the U.S. Constitution. In those cases, the federal court system would assume jurisdiction over the state's case.

Within the federal court system, each state has one or more district courts that serve as the court of original jurisdiction (meaning it hears the case first) for federal crimes within their area. There are currently 94 U.S. district courts, including three that serve the territories and outlying areas. In addition, there are specialized federal courts of original jurisdiction that hear cases related to such things as international trade, veterans' appeals, and military review. Once a case has been heard in a court of original jurisdiction, one of the parties in the case can appeal it to the U.S. Court of Appeals. The current 13 U.S. courts of appeal and the U.S. Court of Military Appeals form the federal appellate jurisdiction, which has the right to review and revise a lower court's decision. Finally, the U.S. Supreme Court is considered the court of last resort within the federal court system. The U.S. Supreme Court hears final appeals of the decisions of lower courts, including the U.S. courts of appeals. Although the U.S. Supreme Court can choose whether to hear an appeal, the U.S. courts of appeals have mandatory jurisdiction, meaning that the U.S. courts of appeal must accept a nonfrivolous appeal, if filed.

The organization of the state court system also includes courts of original jurisdiction and courts of appellate jurisdiction. Trial courts of original jurisdiction for the states can be further divided into trial courts with general jurisdiction and those with limited jurisdiction. Limited jurisdiction courts would include those courts that hear only particular types of cases such as traffic courts, family courts, and municipal courts. General jurisdiction courts would hear a wider range of cases for a particular state. According to the Bureau of Justice Statistics, as of 2004, there were 26,557 trial court judges within the state court systems in the United States. Approximately 67 percent served in a court of limited jurisdiction, and 33 percent served in a court of general jurisdiction. Although all states have a court of last resort as part of their appellate jurisdiction, there are 39 states that also have an intermediate appellate court that hears cases before they would be remanded to the court of last resort. Typically, both the court of last resort and the intermediate appellate court have some discretion over whether to accept a case.

The qualifications to be a trial or appellate judge can vary based on jurisdiction or state. At a minimum, most trial judges for courts of general jurisdiction and appellate jurisdictions are required to have a law degree. There may also be additional residency, age, or legal credential requirements. For judges of courts of limited jurisdiction, it may not be a requirement to have a law degree to sit on the bench. The selection of trial court judges can also vary by jurisdiction. In the state court systems, trial judges can be either elected or appointed. In some states, judges are first selected by a commission or appointed by the governor, but they subsequently go through a retention election to determine whether they keep their appointment. Federal judges are nominated by the president of the United States and confirmed by the U.S. Congress. Assuming there is no judicial indiscretion in the course of their tenure, federal judges have their appointment until they choose to resign.

In recent years, there have been some changes to state court organizations. Some states have sought to simplify or reform their court system. This has usually involved the dissolution of many of the courts of limited jurisdiction in favor of courts of general jurisdiction. As of 2004, 10 states had implemented this simplification and reform of their state system. In addition, problem-solving courts have gained popularity. Problem-solving courts seek to blend the traditional judicial process with other types of treatment and supervision to address certain issues, more as social problems than as criminal matters. The most common problem-solving courts address such issues as domestic violence, drugs, mental health, and reentry into society by convicted offenders.

Juvenile Justice System

There is a separate system to address violations of the law by juveniles, or those under the age of 18. Although the remainder of the criminal justice system uses a formal adversarial system, the juvenile justice system was created with the thought that the courts would serve almost as a caring parent to help a youth engaging in delinquent acts. Once the police or some other authority has taken a juvenile into custody, the juvenile system decides whether to (1) release the youth to his or her parents' care, with possible additional follow-up by an outside agency, or (2) recommend an adjudicatory hearing. An adjudicatory hearing seeks to determine whether the allegations against the juvenile are supported (roughly equivalent to a guilty verdict). After an adjudicatory hearing, there is a dispositional hearing, which would be similar to a sentencing hearing for an adult. The disposition in these cases focuses on the goal of rehabilitating the youth by possibly providing a variety of services, including counseling or community service. If the offense is serious, or if it appears that the juvenile is resistant to the methods of the juvenile system (based on repeat offenses), it is possible for jurisdiction to be waived by the juvenile court. The juvenile would then answer to the charges in adult criminal court.

Punishment

Types of Punishment

Once a defendant has pleaded guilty to the charges or has been convicted, there are several options for punishment available in the American criminal justice system. The most common punishment is some version of incarceration. Seventy percent of all convictions result in incarceration in a prison or jail. Prisons are typically used for sentences longer than a year and are administered by the state or federal governments. Jails, on the other hand, usually hold those sentenced to less than a year of incarceration. The administration of jails can be the responsibility of the state or, more typically, a county or local government. The administration of both prisons and jails can be contracted to private firms. These privately operated facilities are gaining in popularity. There are also alternative facilities, such as juvenile detention, that, depending on the structure of the facility, may also be considered an incarceration facility.

After incarceration, the next most common sentence is probation, which is a form of conditional release of the convicted defendant. The defendant's activities and behaviors will be monitored by the court through a probation officer. If the defendant fails to meet the expectations laid out at the time of sentencing, probation can be revoked, and the defendant will be sent to prison or jail. In essence, probation serves as a suspended sentence that will be honored as long as the probationer maintains good behavior. In about 28 percent of all sentences, probation is imposed. However, as the offenses become less violent and less serious, probation becomes a more common alternative to incarceration.

A recent innovation to the idea of incarceration in the United States is house arrest, sometimes called community corrections. Technology has enabled many communities to allow those convicted of a crime to serve their sentence in their own home, with strict monitoring of their movements. Although similar to the idea of probation in terms of releasing the defendant into the community, the defendant convicted and sentenced to house arrest does not have the same freedom of movement as a probationer. House arrestees typically wear an electronic device that enables authorities to know where the arrestees are or when they have moved outside of their prescribed area. They may be given some latitude to go to work, but beyond that, their movements are severely limited. Community corrections may also include day reporting centers and community residential centers. Although very similar in terms of the types of intense counseling and services provided, day reporting centers provide these services in a nonresidential format rather than the residential format of community residential centers. These methods could be described as a mixture of intense probation and house arrest.

Incarceration and probation account for the vast majority of sentences in the United States, but a range of other options are available in addition to or instead of the traditional sentences. Fines or restitution can be imposed as the sentence or part of an overall sentence. Fines would be payable to the court or federal, state, or local government, whereas restitution is given directly to the victim to compensate for damages incurred during the crime. According to the Bureau of Justice Statistics, in 2004, an additional penalty of a fine or restitution was imposed on 51 percent of the felons sentenced. In addition to the financial aspect, the restitution process usually includes some aspect of mediation between the convicted offender and the victim.

A common option, especially for crimes related to drugs or alcohol, is to sentence defendants to treatment. Treatment can take the form of counseling, rehabilitation, or mental hospital confinement. According to the Bureau of Justice Statistics, in 2004, approximately 9 percent of felons convicted were given an additional sentence of treatment. That percentage increased significantly for those convicted of rape (11 percent), other sexual assault (17 percent), motor vehicle theft (19 percent), and drug possession (19 percent).

Finally, publicity is another option that has gained popularity in certain communities or has been imposed by legislation. Some communities publish the names of defendants for such crimes as driving under the influence of drugs or alcohol or for soliciting a prostitute. The idea is to impose shame on the individual in addition to what might be the traditional punishment for the offense. There are also recent efforts to require individuals who are convicted for certain types of offenses to register with local authorities. This information is then made available to the community. The most notable example of this is sex offender registries. These were established in many states by the mid-1990s. With the passage of Megan's Law in 1996, that information was permitted to be released to the community, thus providing additional and continuing publicity surrounding a conviction received for a sex offense.

The typical punishment for those convicted of violent offenses such as murder or rape is incarceration, based on 2004 data on state court sentencing from the Bureau of Justice Statistics. Of those convicted for murder and nonnegligent manslaughter, 91 percent were sentenced to either prison or jail. Only 7 percent of those convicted of murder were sentenced to probation. Rape also saw a high proportion of incarceration. Nearly 90 percent of those convicted of rape were sentenced to prison or jail, and only 9 percent received probation. Of those convicted of robbery, 87 percent were sentenced to incarceration, and 12 percent were sentenced to probation. Incarceration is less common for property and drug crimes. Seventy-five percent of those convicted of burglary and 69 percent of those convicted of drug trafficking offenses were sentenced to prison or jail. Twenty-four percent of those convicted of burglary and 28 percent of those convicted of drug trafficking received probation.

Sentencing

The length of time in incarceration also obviously varies from crime to crime. Based on a study of violent felons in large urban counties in the years 1990 through 2002 conducted by the Bureau of Justice Statistics, the average length of sentence for a murder conviction was 308 months. The average sentence for rape was 152 months, and robbery saw an average sentence of 100 months. Whether the entire sentence is served depends on the location and whether it uses indeterminate or determinant sentencing.

Indeterminate sentencing allows for a sentence range to be imposed on the defendant. Then, depending on the behavior of the prisoner, an early release could be allowed if a panel of community representatives and criminal justice professionals (or parole board) believes the inmate has had sufficient rehabilitation. Given communities' recent dissatisfaction with the early release of certain prisoners, there has been a trend toward determinate sentencing in many states. With determinant sentencing, there is no provision for early release of the prisoner as decided by a parole board. Sometimes determinant sentences set a mandatory minimum for a particular offense.

The United States also allows for the imposition of the death penalty, most typically for homicides in which there were aggravating factors. According to the Bureau of Justice Statistics, 38 states and the federal government currently have capital statutes. By far the most common form of execution is lethal injection. All but one capital punishment state (Nebraska) use lethal injection as a form of execution. In addition, execution by electrocution (nine states), lethal gas (four states), hanging (three states), and firing squad (three states) are also allowed. In the years 2003 to 2007, 279 prisoners were executed in the United States. In 2005, the U.S. Supreme Court decided that the execution of juveniles for capital crimes was in violation of the Eighth and Fourteenth Amendments.

Prison

As of the end of 2006, there were an estimated 2,385,213 prisoners incarcerated in the United States. This population includes those under the jurisdiction of federal and state prisons, jails, customs and military facilities, and juvenile facilities. According to the Bureau of Justice Statistics, of the 1,570,861 inmates held by state or federal authorities, only 12.3 percent of the prisoner population were in the federal system. The vast majority of prisoners (87.7 percent) were held in state-funded facilities.

Based on the most recently available Census of State and Federal Correctional Facilities, there were 1,668 federal, state, and privately operated correctional facilities in 2000. This figure included facilities such as prisons, prison hospitals, prison farms, boot camps, and other centers associated with prison facilities. It did not include facilities such as jails or regional detention centers or those facilities in which the populations were not predominately federal or state inmates. State governments operated approximately 79 percent of the correctional facilities, and almost 16 percent were operated by private entities under contract to federal or state governments. The remaining 5 percent were federal facilities.

Prison facilities are also described by the level of security imposed on the inmate population. Most of the prisons in the United States are classified as minimum- or low-security (48.8 percent). The inmates of minimum-security facilities are considered to be low risk and therefore receive more privileges and freedoms than do prisoners at higher levels of security. The next most common facilities are medium-security (31.3 percent). Compared to minimum-security facilities, those rated at a medium-security level would have increased safeguards put in place, with fewer privileges available to the inmate population because of increased risk. The highest level of security is the maximum-security or even "super-max" facility. These facilities house the highest-risk inmate population and impose the greatest limitations on the inmates. A little less than 20 percent of the facilities in the United States are considered maximum-security.

In addition to the security concerns addressed by facility management, the inmate population is regulated in terms of the activities or work afforded to inmates and the means of communication allowed with outside entities. Based on the individual inmate and the risk associated with the activity, inmates can routinely be involved in work programs, such as regular maintenance on the buildings and grounds of the facilities, agricultural work, prison industries, or public works projects. The most recent figure estimates that 92 percent of the federal and state facilities and 73 percent of privately operated facilities had some version of work program available for inmates. Although participation in work programs is not necessarily required, there is a general interest in keeping the inmate population occupied during their time of incarceration. Other programs available to inmates of American facilities include educational programs (in 90 percent of state and federal facilities and 80 percent of privately operated facilities) and counseling programs (in 96 percent of state and federal facilities and 91 percent of privately operated facilities).

Visitation and communication with the inmate population is usually encouraged, albeit highly regulated. Facilities monitor communications between the inmate population and outside entities by reviewing mail and other correspondence or authorizing telephone calls to only certain phone numbers, for example. Visitation is typically allowed only on particular days and at specific times during the day. Visitors are expected to comply with a host of policies regarding which behaviors are appropriate and what objects are prohibited.

The size of a prison facility can be measured in several ways. The design capacity of a facility refers to the optimal size of the inmate population for the size and design of the facility. The rated capacity is the number of beds allocated to the facility as determined by a rating official. Usually, the rated capacity is larger than the design capacity. The largest correctional facility by rated capacity is the Correctional Training Facility in Soledad, California. Based on the 2000 census figures, the Correctional Training Facility had an estimated rated capacity of 7,223. The Correctional Training Facility is classified as a general confinement facility. Its inmate population is entirely adult males.

Parole

Parole is the conditional early release of an inmate from incarceration. Although in some ways similar to probation, parole differs from it in key points. The conditions imposed on parolees are more stringent than those for probationers. In addition, the decision to release an inmate on parole is made by a parole board, not a judge. Continuing oversight is also provided by the parole board rather than the presiding judge, as is the case for probation. Those states that continue to use parole see it as a means to encourage reintegration and rehabilitation of the inmate. It can also be seen as a deterrent to future crime because of the threat of having parole revoked and being reincarcerated. Parole has other practical benefits as well. It can offer a means to alleviate overcrowding in prison facilities, and it can also offer a way to mitigate any disparity in sentencing due to race or class, for example. Although most correctional facilities offer credit for good behavior toward an early release, some states have abolished parole.

Extradition

The United States allows for the transfer of individuals to other countries to face criminal charges. This happens before the adjudication process rather than after. To consider extradition to another country, the United States must have entered into a treaty with the other nation specifying the conditions that would dictate a transfer. Older treaties, typically those from before 1980, are list treaties, which provide a list of particular offenses that would make an individual eligible for extradition. More recent treaties are written to be dual criminality treaties. Rather than a list of offenses, an individual would be eligible for extradition if the offense is punishable in both the United States and the other country by at least one year in prison.

Cynthia Barnett-Ryan

Further Reading

Binder, Arnold, Gilbert Geis, and Dickson D. Bruce Jr. (2001). *Juvenile Delinquency: Historical, Cultural, and Legal Perspectives*. 3rd ed. Cincinnati, OH: Anderson Publishing Co.

Champion, Dean J. (1998). *Corrections in the United States: A Contemporary Perspective*. 2nd ed. Upper Saddle River, NJ: Prentice Hall.

Schmalleger, Frank. (1999). *Criminal Justice Today: An Introductory Text for the 21st Century*. 5th ed. Upper Saddle River, NJ: Prentice Hall.

U.S. Department of Justice, Bureau of Justice Statistics: http://www.ojp.usdoj.gov/bjs.

U.S. Department of Justice, Bureau of Justice Statistics. (2009). *Sourcebook of Criminal Justice Statistics Online*. 31st ed.: http://www.albany.edu/sourcebook.

U.S. Department of Justice, Drug Enforcement Administration: http:/www.usdoj.gov/dea.

U.S. Department of Justice, Federal Bureau of Investigation. *Uniform Crime Reports:* http://www.fbi.gov/ucr/ucr.htm.

U.S. Department of Justice, National Institute of Justice: http://www.ojp.usdoj.gov/nij.

United States Virgin Islands

Murder: High
Prison Rate: High
Death Penalty: No
Corporal Punishment: No

Background

On March 3, 1917, after more than 240 years of Danish rule, the United States purchased the United States Virgin Islands (USVI) from Denmark for 25 million dollars in gold. Formerly known as the "Danish West Indies" and currently nicknamed "America's Caribbean Paradise," the USVI is made up of three primary islands (St. Thomas, St. Croix, and St. John), the smaller inhabited Water Island, and approximately 50 surrounding and uninhabited keys and islets. The capital of the USVI is Charlotte Amalie, which is located on the island of St. Thomas. Collectively the islands are part of the northeastern West Indies.

Today the political status of the islands is an organized "unincorporated" territory of the United States. Although the secretary of interior is administratively responsible for the coordination of federal policies for the USVI, Congress has the constitutional authority to make all "needful rules and regulations" pertaining to the islands. The USVI maintains a dual government (e.g., federal government and territorial government). To differentiate between the two and for the sake of clarity in this entry, the phrase "federal level" is used in reference to federal matters, and the phrase "local level" is used when referring to territorial matters.

According to the 2000 census, the population count of the USVI was 108,612, with blacks/African Americans constituting the bulk (71 percent) of the islands' population. Hispanics (14 percent) are the second-largest racial/ethnic group, followed by whites (11 percent). According to Virgin Islands historian Harold Willocks, the territory is also home to a sizable portion of Palestinians, who first migrated to the Virgin Islands via Puerto Rico and New York, and East Indians, who are believed to have arrived from India via Jamaica, Curacao, and the Canary Islands.

History of the Legal System

To ensure a smooth transfer from Danish rule to American sovereignty, the Congressional Act of 1917 mandated that the Danish colonial style of government was to remain in effect. Accordingly, the judicial system of the USVI was established under the Danish colonial laws of 1906. The judicial system at that time consisted of several courts, including an ordinary town court, a special court, a criminal court, a police court, a dealing court, a reconciling court, and a court of appeals. The Danish system of operation continued until the adoption of the Code of General and Special Laws for the Municipality of St. Thomas/St. John and the Municipality of St. Croix. Known as the Judicial Codes of 1920 and 1921, these codes superseded all Danish laws and brought the USVI under an American system of common law.

On June 22, 1936, Congress passed the Organic Act of the Virgin Islands of the United States. In dealing with the enumeration of courts, the act consolidated the three subjudicial district courts created under the judicial codes of 1920 and 1921 into one district court with two divisions. One division was to cover the municipality of St. Croix and its surrounding cays and islets. The other division was to encase the municipality of St. Thomas/St. John and the surrounding cays and islets. Perhaps one of the most significant features of the act is that it extended the Bill of Rights to the residents of the USVI.

Almost 20 years later, the Revised Organic Act of 1954 was enacted, and with it, additional changes to the USVI judicial system and its structure were instituted. One important feature of the act is that it now serves as the Virgin Islands Constitution. Another important provision is that it delegated to the secretary of interior the responsibility for consolidating, codifying, and revising the local laws and ordinances in the Virgin Islands. The act further instructed that the anthology be titled the "Virgin Islands Code" and that it be accessible as a public document. Because many of the existing laws at that time were enacted under Danish rule, the compilation of the Virgin Islands Code was considered a pivotal and much-needed endeavor in reforming the antiquated local laws.

The empowerment of the local legislature to create inferior courts was made possible by the passage of the Organic Act of 1936. An early pivotal step in the establishment of the local judiciary entailed the abolishment of the three police courts that were created under the Judicial Codes of 1920 and 1921. In their place, two municipal courts were created: one for the municipality of St. Thomas/St. John and the other for the municipality of St. Croix. In 1965, the structure of the local judiciary was altered when the two municipal courts were combined to form a single court titled the Municipal Court of the Virgin Islands. In 1976, the court was renamed and given the title Territorial Court of the Virgin Islands. A third name changed occurred in 2004 when the local court assumed jurisdiction over all violations of local law and received its current and official title, the Superior Court of the Virgin Islands. The last major structural change to impact the local courts in the Virgin Islands occurred on October 29, 2004. On that historical date, the governor of the Virgin Islands signed into law the Virgin Islands Supreme Court Bill. The bill went into effect on January 1, 2005, making the Virgin Islands the last jurisdiction in the nation to establish its own appellate court. On January 29, 2007, the Supreme Court of the Virgin Islands commenced reviewing decisions of the Superior Court.

Courts

The territory utilizes a dual court structure consisting of federal courts and territorial courts. The federal level is a three-tier system consisting of a district court, a circuit court of appeals, and a U.S. Supreme Court. The District Court of the U.S. Virgin Islands was created under Article I of the U.S. Constitution and thus is considered a legislative court as opposed to a constitutional court. As a result of the judicial boundaries created by the Organic Act of 1936, the district court in the USVI has two subdivisions. One division is located on the island of St. Thomas and serves both St. Thomas and St. John. The other subdivision is located on the island of St. Croix. Each division consists of one district judge and one magistrate. District court judges are nominated by the president and confirmed by the Senate. Because it is a legislative court, judges serve a period of 10 years. Magistrates are selected by the chief justice and serve a period of 4 years. Decisions appealed from the district court are heard in the Third Circuit Court of Appeals, located in the state of Pennsylvania. Further appeals are heard in the U.S. Supreme Court located in Washington, D.C. According to the U.S. Sentencing Commission, in 2006, less than 1 percent (117) of the 72,585 offenders sentenced according to the sentencing guidelines in the U.S. federal courts were from the district of the Virgin Islands. More recent statistics show that for the 2007 fiscal year, there were 497 cases filed and 1,724 cases pending.

On the local level, the territorial court structure is a two-tier system consisting of a court of general jurisdiction known as the Superior Court of the Virgin Islands and an appellate court officially titled the Supreme Court of the Virgin Islands. The Superior Court has two divisions. One division serves the islands of St. Thomas/St. John and the other the island of St. Croix. There are nine judges, five for the division of St. Thomas/St. John and four for the division of St. Croix. The judges are appointed by the governor with the advice and consent of the legislature of the Virgin Islands. To be qualified for judgeship in the Superior Court, nominated judges must be a member in good standing of the Virgin Islands Bar Association and must also have been a practicing lawyer for at least five years immediately prior to their nomination. The judicial candidate must have been practicing law in the territory for at least three of those last five years.

The Superior Court reported that there were 34,088 cases filed in that court during the 2007 fiscal year. Seventy percent of the filings (23,520) involved traffic offenses. The second-largest category of cases filed in the territory pertained to family, marriage, and probate issues. Collectively, they constituted 17 percent (5,784) of the cases. Less than 5 percent (1,939) of the cases pertained to criminal matters. The remaining cases filed were civil in nature (1,355), included infractions such as littering (318), involved juveniles (297), or dealt with conservation (76).

Appeals from decisions made in the Superior Court are heard in the newly established Supreme Court of the Virgin Islands. The Supreme Court consists of a chief justice and two associate justices. The presiding justices are nominated by the governor, with the advice and consent of the Virgin Islands legislature. The initial term of office is 10 years, and upon reappointment, the justices serve for life. The court began hearing cases in January 2007. During its first year in operation, the Supreme Court reported that 221 cases were filed. Of those, 12.7 percent (28) involved criminal matters. The remainder of the cases involved bar governance (104) and civil (89) matters.

Currently, further appeals are heard in the Third Circuit of the U.S. Circuit Court of Appeal. Decisions from the Circuit Court of Appeals are appealed to the U.S. Supreme Court. However, in compliance with the Revised Organic Act of 1954, cases that were pending prior to the Supreme Court's commencement date are to retain the old procedure. In the old procedure, an appellate division within the District Court of the U.S. Virgin Islands heard all appeals from the Superior Court. Appeals from decisions in the appellate division were then to be heard by the U.S. Court of Appeals for the Third Circuit. Further appeals were then heard in the U.S. Supreme Court. The Revised Organic Act further stipulated that in the Supreme Court's first 15 years of operation, decisions from the Supreme Court of the Virgin Islands will be heard by the U.S. Court of Appeals for the Third Circuit and, if further appeals are necessary, by the U.S. Supreme Court. Every five years throughout the oversight period, the U.S. Congress will review the progress of the Virgin Islands Supreme Court. If within the review process, Congress determines that "sufficient institutional traditions" have been developed, it will begin allowing decisions from the Supreme Court of the Virgin Islands to be directly reviewed by the U.S. Supreme Court.

Questions on the exact location of the Supreme Court trigger conflicting responses and much controversy in the territory. The local law responsible for establishing the Supreme Court of the Virgin Islands "legislatively" placed the court on the island of St. Croix. However, citing the Revised Organic Act of 1954, which mandated that the headquarters of government branches be physically located in the capital of the USVI, a judicial decision has determined that the Supreme Court of the Virgin Islands is "properly" located on the island of St. Thomas. Although the issue remains somewhat unsettled, at present the administrative offices of the Supreme Court are located in St. Thomas, with justices' chambers on the island of St. Croix.

Police

The Virgin Islands Police Department (VIPD) was established in accordance with the Virgin Islands Code. The primary responsibility of the department is law enforcement. Organizationally, it is a department of service, regulation/enforcement, and social control. The USVI can best be described as a centralized police force because there is one police commissioner who serves as head of the police forces in the territory. Attached to the Office of the Commissioner is the Law Enforcement Planning Commission (LEPC). Assisting the police commissioner is an assistant commissioner and a support staff consisting of a deputy commissioner of support staff, a legal advisor, a public information officer, and a grants manager. A victim/witness advocate is also designated for the St. Thomas/Water Island division, the St. John division, and the St. Croix division. Under the assistant police commissioner is one chief of police who serves the islands of St. Thomas/St. John and another for the island of St. Croix. Below the chief of police are three deputy chiefs, one for each of the three islands. The deputy chief of police supervises the lower-level officers on their respective islands. Collectively, there are 478 sworn police officers in the territory. There are also a variety of specialized units. Among them are a fleet management unit, a street enforcement unit, a youth investigation unit, a K-9 unit, a marine unit, a hazardous device unit, a school security unit, a criminal investigation unit, a domestic violence unit, an auto theft unit, a major crimes unit, and a forensics unit. In addition to the specialized units, the Virgin Islands Police Department (VIPD) also maintains a communication bureau, a traffic bureau, a criminal division, a patrol division, and a court liaison. In compliance with the mandates of Act No. 6036, the Narcotics Strike Force was placed under the VIPD solely for budgetary purposes.

In addition to local law enforcement, there are a number of federal law enforcement officials and agencies stationed in the Virgin Islands. Some of those include the Federal Bureau of Investigation (FBI), the U.S. Marshals, Immigration and Naturalization Services (INS), Alcohol, Tobacco and Firearms (ATF), the U.S. Coast Guards, the Drug Enforcement Agency (DEA), and the Internal Revenue Service (IRS) task force. Other federally sponsored programs include Highway Safety, High Intensity Drug Traffic Area (HIDTA), Project Safe Neighborhoods, and the Safe Street Violent Crime Initiative (SSVCI).

Crime

Classification of Crimes

The age of criminal responsibility in the USVI is 14. However, Virgin Islands statute dictates that individuals over the age of 7 but under the age of 14 can be held culpable and legally responsible for a crime if they knew at the time of the offense that their actions were wrong. Crimes in the USVI are classified according to misdemeanors or felonies. Misdemeanors are the lesser of the two offenses and carry a penalty of a fine not to exceed $200 and/or an imprisonment of 365 days or less. All offenses that carry a penalty of imprisonment of more than one year are classified as a felony. Unless a law prescribes a different punishment, offenses classified as a felony carry a penalty of one to five years' imprisonment. Conviction of a second felony committed within 10 years after completion of serving the first felony conviction will result in life imprisonment.

Statistics submitted to the FBI Uniform Crime Report classify criminal offenses according to Type I or Type II offenses. Type I offenses, also known as index offenses, consists of the more serious crimes of homicide, robbery, forcible rape, burglary, larceny, motor vehicle theft, and arson. In the territory, aggravated assault is considered a misdemeanor as opposed to a felony. All other offenses are classified as Type II. Because the USVI maintains a dual style of government, crimes in the USVI can also be distinguished as a federal offense or a local offense. Federal crimes are offenses that violate laws promulgated by the U.S. Congress, whereas local crimes are offenses that violate the laws promulgated by the legislature of the Virgin Islands.

Crime Statistics

The territory has a reputation for strongly enforcing its immigration laws. In the USVI, the most challenging criminal offenses on the federal level are immigration violations. According to the U.S. Sentencing Commission, in the 2006 fiscal year. over half of all defendants sentenced in the Virgin Islands district court were convicted of an immigration offense. During that same time period, almost 18 percent were sentenced for drug crimes, almost 8 percent for fraud, 6 percent for firearms, and less than 1 percent for robbery or larceny offenses.

With respect to violations of local law, the most challenging offense is third-degree burglary. Statistics collected by the Virgin Islands Police Department show that for the 2006 fiscal year, there were 5,482 Part I offenses in the territory. Almost three-quarters of the Part I offenses reported to local law enforcement officials were property offenses, with burglary (2,206) and grand larceny (1,344) being the most frequent. The remaining Part I offenses in the territory were crimes committed against person. In 2006, there were 40 reported homicides and 69 rapes.

The reported number and types of offenses vary from island to island. For example, although the district of St. Thomas/St. John reported 7 cases of arson in 2006, the district of St. Croix reported 48 cases of arson. However, over 60 percent (1,352) of the 2,206 reported burglary offenses in the territory came from the district of St. Thomas/St. John. The reported cases for the more serious offenses of homicide and rape were split fairly even across St. Thomas/St. John and St. Croix.

The Caribbean region is experiencing concentrated law enforcement inquiries into its drug trafficking activities. After immigration offenses, drug offenses are by far the second-largest category of federal convictions in the USVI. The Federal Sentencing Commission disclosed that for the District of the Virgin Islands in 2006, over half (52.4 percent) of the drug cases involved powder cocaine, 19 percent concerned marijuana, and 14.3 percent involved crack cocaine.

Although a report by the High Intensity Drug Traffic Area (HIDTA) revealed that as much as 90 percent of the cocaine flow from South America to the Central America occurs via Eastern Pacific and Western Caribbean routes, the Virgin Islands, despite being a part of the Eastern Caribbean region, are considered a drug transshipment point to the U.S. mainland. In an effort to help fight the drug problem in the territory, in 1994, the territory was officially designated a High Intensity Drug Traffic Area. Participation in the HIDTA program provides additional federal resources that will enable the territory to adequately respond to the drug activities plaguing its area. Aside from drug and immigration offenses, there are also growing concerns among law enforcement officials that the territory may be home to terrorist sleeper cells. Therefore, the territory is part of the joint terrorism task force. Members of the task force are highly trained individuals whose primary responsibility is to monitor, investigate, and protect the territory against terrorist activities.

Finding of Guilt

According to the Virgin Islands Bar Association, there are approximately 1,000 registered attorneys in the territory. On the federal level, the prosecution of cases is handled by the U.S. attorney, and the attorney general prosecutes cases on the local level. Unless the defendant waives the appointment of counsel, all indigents are entitled to an attorney in cases that carry a possible penalty of incarceration. Defense counsels are expected to represent their clients at every critical stage of the court proceedings. There is a public defender system on both the federal and local levels. In addition to the public defender system, the territory also uses an assigned counsel system in which a superior court judge can assign a counsel from a list of private attorneys maintained by the court. The use of the public defender's office is the first line of defense. However, Virgin Islands statute dictates that if the assigned counsel system is also used, it cannot be used in more than 15 percent of the cases involving indigents.

Within a few hours to a few days of an arrest, the suspect is granted an initial appearance before the court. At this early stage, the suspect is informed of the charges, reminded of his or her constitutional rights, appointed an attorney if one has not yet been appointed, and receives a bail hearing. If a continuance motion is granted, the suspect may be detained for up to three days pending a bail hearing. Although incarceration before or awaiting trial is generally allowed, suspects charged with serious offenses, such as first-degree murder, first-degree rape, first-degree robbery, first-degree burglary, kidnapping for ransom, and drug trafficking, may be denied bail. Factors considered in setting bail include prior record, the nature and circumstances of the present charge, the strength of the evidence, family ties, employment and financial resources, character and mental condition of the suspect, danger to society, and the likelihood that the suspect will appear for trial. Detention orders are accompanied by written findings of fact and the reason for this outcome. Suspects who are denied bail are placed on an expedited calendar, and the case is given priority over cases involving suspects who are free on bail.

Congress has extended to all defendants in the territory the rights of the accused provided in the Fourth, Fifth, Sixth, Eighth, and Fourteenth Amendments to the U.S. Constitution. These rights include, but are not limited to, protections against unreasonable search and seizure, the exclusionary rule, protections against self-incrimination, protections against double jeopardy, the right to face one's accuser, the right to a public trial, the right to be tried by an impartial jury, protection against excessive bails and fines, protection against cruel and unusual punishment, and the right to due process.

According to the U.S. Sentencing Commission, in 2006, almost 90 percent of the offenders sentenced in the District of the Virgin Islands had their cases resolved by a plea agreement. Eighty-three percent of those sentenced received a term of incarceration. The remaining defendants received punishment ranging from prison and community service (2.6 percent) to probation and confinement (3.4 percent) or solely probation (11.1 percent). In the Superior Court of the Virgin Islands (e.g., the local court), slightly over half (54.88 percent) of criminal defendants invoked the use of a jury trial.

The territory has in place a number of diversionary programs and alternative sanctions. Offenders charged with offenses other than murder, kidnapping, assault in the first or second degree, rape in the first and second degree, and arson in the first degree can be diverted to a pretrial intervention program. Pretrial diversion may be ordered at the initial appearance or anytime thereafter. According to statute, not only must the offender's participation be voluntarily, but the offender must also, in the presence of the committing officer, voluntarily waive the applicable statute of limitations and the right to a trial during the period of diversion. To be eligible for diversion to community supervision program or services, the offenders must have no prior conviction after the age of 17. Additional eligibility standards prescribe that the offender be free of outstanding warrants, continuances, appeals, or pending criminal cases. A recommendation from officials at the community supervision program outlining how the offender can benefit from such a program is also required. Defendants who have been diverted to the Superior Court's Pretrial Intervention Program are required to pay a $200.00 administrative fee for the monitoring and supervision services being provided.

Punishment

Types of Punishment

The territory uses a variety of sentencing options. The most commonly used sentencing options are probation and fines. According to the monthly statistical report, at the end of November 2007, there were 1,430 individuals under probation supervision. Considerably smaller than the probation figures, Correctional Compliance Coordinator Dwayne Benjamin explained that on any given day, there are approximately 75–100 detainees and 350–400 adjudicated inmates held in correctional facilities throughout the Virgin Islands. Restitution, electronic monitoring, and parole options are also utilized. The typical punishment for the more serious offenses such as murder, rape, burglary, robbery, and drug offense is incarceration. Banishment, public punishment, and corporal punishment are not practiced in the territory. Although the death penalty is not imposed in the USVI, defendants receiving life sentences are by Virgin Islands statute defined as "civilly dead."

With the exception of inmates who are sentenced to life imprisonment without the possibility of parole, all inmates sentenced for a definite term or terms of 180 days or more (including life sentences) are eligible for parole. To be eligible, an inmate must have a good record of conduct and the recommendation of the director of the Bureau of Corrections. The recommendation from the director of the Bureau of Corrections must, in turn, be supported by the recommendation of a psychiatrist and/or psychologist. With affirmative recommendations, the inmate may be released on parole after serving one-half of his or her imposed sentence, after serving 15 years of a sentence over 29 years, or after serving the minimum sentenced required by law. The Board of Parole, however, can fix an even earlier eligibility date for a prisoner's release based on a recommendation from the director of the Bureau of Corrections. Again, the director's recommendation must be supported by the recommendation of a psychiatrist and/or psychologist. Also required for an earlier release date is a two-thirds affirmative decision by the members of the parole board. If an earlier release date is granted, the inmate can be release after serving one-third of his or her term or after serving 10 years of a sentence over 29 years, including life sentences.

Jails/Prisons

The USVI maintains a separate system for juveniles. The Youth Rehabilitation Center is located on the island of St. Croix. According to Superintendent Catherine Tyrell, on any given day, there are approximately 30 juveniles held at the center. The juveniles range from 13 to 18 years of age. With respect to adults, there are two local jails, both of which are located on the island of St. Thomas. One jail houses both male and female detainees, and the other is home to adjudicated males serving one year or less. The only prison facility in the territory is the 600-bed Golden Grove Correctional Facility and Detention Center located on the island of St. Croix. Prison overcrowding is not a problem in the territory because approximately 20 percent of the prison beds at the Golden Grove facility go unoccupied on any given day. Because there are no jails on the island of St. Croix, a section of the prison is designated as a detention center for those awaiting trial.

Inmates at the Golden Grove facility are classified and separated according to minimum, medium, and maximum level of security. Inmates can also be given "protective custody" status if they are defined as "preys" and "predators." The classification level that inmates receive is initially based on the seriousness of the offense and, later, the behavior and demeanor of the inmate. Inmates of all levels of security are housed in the same facility. Within the facility, levels of security are divided by units. Each unit is equipped with day rooms, exercise rooms, and telephones. Although there are televisions, there is no access to cable networks. Daily newspapers are delivered each morning to interested inmates. Common areas, such as the dining room, are shared by all units. All units also share the prison law library, which is equipped with computers. Inmates, both detainees and adjudicated, are allowed to have visitors. Attorneys are entitled to unlimited amount of visitation hours with their clients. All others (e.g., family, relatives, friends, etc.) are allowed a maximum of three hours per visitation. Although spousal visits are welcome, conjugal visits are not allowed.

Currently, there are no federal detention facilities in the territory. However, federal detainees can be separately housed at all three facilities located throughout the Virgin Islands. Once the cases have been heard and adjudicated, sentenced defendants are transferred via private aircraft to the Metropolitan Detention Center (MDC) Guaynabo in San Juan, Puerto Rico. Interviews with members of the courtroom work group disclosed that the islands' lack of a federal detention facility creates challenges for the federal administration of justice in the USVI. Defense attorneys, for example, spoke of the extra burden they faced flying to and from Puerto Rico to engage in face-to-face interviews with their clients. U.S. marshals must confront the logistical problems associated with transporting inmates. At times, judges are hampered by the backlog of cases brought on by delayed or canceled flights.

The territory is continuously taking steps aimed at improving the education and job skills of its inmates. A number of programs are already in place that are designed to give inmates an opportunity to earn a high school diploma or equivalency, earn a college degree, learn the English language, and receive job training. As a supplement to existing programs, a bill was recently passed by the Virgin Islands legislature that would give rise to a much-needed reading program for jail and prison inmates. The program is being established on the principle that it will increase the self-esteem of inmates, which in turn will facilitate a decrease in the territory's recidivism rates.

Although the Bureau of Corrections may require inmates to work, the scarcity of jobs makes employment a challenge for all. Through an agreement with the Department of Public Works, the Bureau of Corrections can utilize the services of inmates for road beautification, landscaping, the maintenance of public buildings, and other similar tasks. Inmates' participation, however, is voluntary, and no inmates are allowed to work more than eight hours per day. By Virgin Islands statute, the inmates retain at least 20 percent of the income they receive. The remaining 80 percent is deposited in an account that can be used for restitution to the victim, payment of court-ordered fines, child support, payments on outstanding debts, and reimbursement to the territory for the lodging, food, transportation, and other expenses incurred as a result of the inmates' charges and conviction. Work release is available to inmates with less than three years of their time remaining. The awarding of work release gives inmates the privilege of leaving the institution on a daily basis to fulfill employment or education obligations. Furloughs are another type of privilege that can also be extended to inmates. Inmates serving time for first-degree murder and rape are ineligible for work release.

Defendants convicted of immigration violations can be deported back to their country of origins. However, illegal immigrants who commit violent crimes are required to serve their sentence prior to their deportation. No prisoners in the USVI are exchanged or transferred to other countries. However, the USVI is part of the Interstate Compact. Participation in the Interstate Compact makes it feasible to transfer Virgin Islands' prisoners to prisons on the U.S. mainland. Currently, the USVI Department of Justice Bureau of Corrections has a contract with the Virginia Department of Corrections. The existing contracts allow for the transferring of USVI inmates with disciplinary problems and/or those who require a higher level of security (i.e., in a super-max facility) to the Virginia Department of Corrections. Currently, there are as many as 25 inmates fitting this description who as a result are now being housed in facilities in the state of Virginia. As part of the contract agreement with the Virginia Department of Corrections, the Virgin Islands Bureau of Corrections retains financial responsibility for the transportation and housing of its off-island inmates.

Gayle Iles

Further Reading

Coeffelt, Soraya Dias. (2001). "The United States Virgin Islands at the Judicial Crossroads: Is it Time for a Supreme Court of the United States Virgin Islands?" Master's thesis, University of Nevada-Las Vegas.

Iles, Gayle. (2006). "America's Forgotten Paradise: An Assessment of Sentencing Decisions and Outcomes in the United States Virgin Islands." PhD dissertation, University of Nebraska-Omaha.

Leary, Paul, ed. (1992). *Major Political & Constitutional Documents of the United States Virgin Islands. 1671–1991.* St. Thomas: University of the Virgin Islands.

Official Web site of the Government of the U.S. Virgin Islands: http://www.governordejongh.com/.

Willocks, Harold, and Myron Allick. (1997). *Massacre in Paradise: The Untold Story of the Fountain Valley Massacre.* Published by Authors.

Uruguay

Legal System: Civil
Murder: Medium
Corruption: Low
Human Trafficking: Medium
Prison Rate: Medium
Death Penalty: No
Corporal Punishment: No

Background

The Eastern Republic of Uruguay is a constitutional democracy administratively divided into 19 departments with limited autonomy. It is the tiniest Spanish-speaking country in South America, with a surface area of 68,000 square miles. In 2008, the Uruguayan population was 3.3 million inhabitants, 1.6 million (48.5 percent) of whom made up the active workforce. About one-third (1.3 million) of Uruguayans reside in the capital city of Montevideo, and the remaining residents are distributed in 20 major townships; the urbanization rate of the country hovers around 92 percent. European descendants represent the largest ethnic group (93 percent), and two-thirds (66 percent) profess the Roman Catholic faith. The nation has a literacy rate of 98 percent.

Uruguay had a gross domestic product of 32.3 billion in 2008, 60 percent of which was accounted for by the service sector. Agriculture and agriculture-related industry were responsible for 16 percent and 10 percent of the economy, respectively. Economic growth recovered after the banking crisis and economic collapse of 2001 and averaged 8 percent annually between 2004 and 2008. The GDP per capita adjusted for purchasing power parity reached US$12,200 in 2008. As of 2006, over 19 percent of Uruguayans lived under the poverty line, and 3.9 percent struggled in extreme poverty. In 2008, Uruguay's unemployment rate dropped to 7.6 percent from the 19.4 percent recorded in 2003. The country has achieved third-highest level of human development in Latin America, second only to Argentina and Chile.

Unlike most Latin American countries, Uruguay is characterized by high levels of educational attainment, a vibrant middle class in urban centers, comparatively small income inequality, a well-trained labor force, and high degrees of welfare spending. The typical Uruguayan living standard measures favorably in comparison with that of most other nations in the continent. Since the late 1980s, nearly 500,000 Uruguayans have left the country, migrating mainly to Argentina and Spain. Outflows to the United States also increased considerably. With the low birth rate, high life expectancy, and growing emigration of younger people combined, Uruguay is an aging society, which also distinguishes it from other Latin American societies.

History

The Charrua Indians, expelled from Paraguay by the Guarani Indians, were the only occupants of present-day Uruguay before the arrival of the Europeans in 1516. However, the fierce resistance from these aboriginals coupled with the lack of silver and gold in the region rendered the settlement of Spanish colonizers sparse in the area before the 1800s. The strategic importance of Uruguay increased significantly after the Portuguese sought the expansion of Brazil's frontiers. But it remained largely a farmland where the Spanish introduced cattle, and the export of beef and leather became a critical source of income and wealth.

The rise of breeding industry and the establishment of Montevideo as a military stronghold in the early 18th century initiated a lasting competition between Montevideo and Buenos Aires, the capital of Argentina, for commercial and political influence in the region. Yet the small size of both its territory and its population had largely determined its destiny as an interstice in the constant clashes first between the British, Spanish, and Portuguese colonial empires and then between the newly independent powers of Argentina and Brazil. In 1811, Uruguay gained autonomy from Spanish rule after a successful rebellion led by Jose Gervasio Artigas. However, in 1821, Uruguay, then known as the Provincia Oriental del Rio de la Plata, was surrendered to Brazil by Portugal. A series of violent uprisings against the new colonial rule ensued, and in 1825, Uruguay declared independence from Brazil and joined the regional federation led by Argentina.

Strictly speaking, Uruguay did not become a truly independent state until 1828, when the military clash between Brazil and the Argentinean-Uruguayan alliance prompted the intervention of Great Britain to broker the Treaty of Montevideo. The British, whose trade interests in the region were growing exponentially, convinced both Argentina and Brazil to renounce all territorial claims over Uruguay so that a pro-Britain buffer state could emerge. Its first Constitution was promulgated in 1830. The rest of the 19th century witnessed intrusions by expansionist neighbors, politico-economic upheavals, and massive immigrations of Europeans. Jose Batlle y Ordoñez used the two terms of his presidency (1903–1907 and 1911–1915) to set Uruguay on the course of institutional modernization through extensive political, social, and economic reforms such as welfare initiatives, state intervention in the economy, and a diverse executive.

In 1965, the U.S. Office of Public Safety, in close collaboration with USAID and CIA, began training Uruguayan police and intelligence in counterinsurgency techniques to meet the challenge posed by the growing urban guerrilla movement. Social and political instabilities had already forced a number of constitutional amendments by 1966, and a revamped Constitution was introduced in 1967. A state of emergency was declared in 1968, followed by a further suspension of civil liberties in 1972, to allow the armed and security forces to combat guerrilla groups with the greatest freedom and the least legal restraints. In 1973, amid increasing economic hardships and constant threats from left-wing revolutionary groups, the armed forces shut down the General Assembly and created a civilian-military government to bring about peace and stability through harsh repression and systematic abuses of human rights. Uruguay returned to civilian rule in 1984 after a constitutional proposal by the regime was rejected in a 1980 plebiscite, and military-backed parties and politicians suffered a complete defeat in internal elections held in 1982.

Julio Maria Sanguinetti served as the first democratically elected president after the military rule, and from 1985 to 1990, his administration undid the institutional anomalies to strengthen the democratic governance. To promote reconciliation in a society torn apart by years of armed struggle between the right and the left, Sanguinetti secured public support in a referendum for a contentious amnesty for former leaders in the military regime charged with human rights violations and sped the release of former guerrillas. Several radical groups (leftist parties, student groups, and labor organizations, etc.) that were banned or suppressed during the military dictatorship had since surfaced and been reintegrated as legitimate players in the Uruguayan politics. By 1985, all political parties were legalized by the government, and to date, there are no citizens incarcerated for political reasons or political groups banned for their views in the country.

In October 2004, Tabare Vázquez won the presidential elections, and his party achieved parliamentary majority. The Vázquez administration implemented its campaign promise to revisit the human rights violations committed during the 1973–1985 military dictatorship and unearthed critical forensic evidence supportive of prosecutorial actions. As of 2009, the criminal justice system continued to probe these past flagrant human rights abuses. Like its neighbor Argentina, Uruguay has vacillated between a forceful quest for transitional justice and a deep desire for lasting social reconciliation for the past 25 years. This ambivalence has left its imprint in the administration of justice.

Legal System

The Uruguayan legal system includes a code of civil law. As a colony, it was first ruled by the Spanish Law of the Indies, and once independent, Uruguay tailored its law after the Napoleonic code. The current Constitution, which was approved in 1967 and then subsequently amended four times in 1989, 1994, 1996, and 2004, has established that all the laws of the land should be written and passed by Parliament and then enacted by the president of the republic. The Constitution organizes the state into three separate powers (i.e., executive, legislative, and judicial branches) and provides for basic human rights, including the right to life, honor, freedom, security, work, and property, as well as freedoms of religion, speech, and assembly and habeas corpus.

The nation's president leads the executive power and is both chief of state and head of government. President and vice president are elected on the same ticket by popular vote for five-year terms and are not allowed to serve consecutive terms. The Council of Ministers is appointed by the president and approved by the national legislature. The legislature consists of the General Assembly, which comprises the 30-member Chamber of Senators and the 99-member Chamber of Representatives; in both Chambers, members are elected by popular vote to serve five-year terms.

The judicial power is vested in the Supreme Court of Justice and other tribunals instituted by law. The Supreme Court is formed by five justices appointed by the General Assembly with a two-thirds majority; justices serve for 10 years, and the presidency of the court rotates yearly among the five members. It has the authority to review and alter any decisions made by the appellate and first-instance courts and is the only body empowered to declare laws passed by the General Assembly unconstitutional. Additionally, all decisions on issues involving diplomats and treaties with foreign countries, the execution of the rulings of foreign courts, and interactions among government agencies fall under the purview of the Supreme Court. The president of the Supreme Court of Justice has the power to participate in meetings of the committees of both chambers of the General Assembly and has a voice in discussion but is not allowed to vote.

The courts of appeal decide on appeals of rulings and sentences by the first-instance courts in civil, criminal, family, and labor matters. There are a total of 15 courts of appeal; all of them are located in Montevideo but have national jurisdiction. Each court of appeal has three sitting judges. First-instance courts have departmental jurisdictions, and each hears cases in family, administrative, civil, commercial, criminal, and labor laws. There are 89 first-instance courts in Montevideo and 81 in the remaining 18 departments. There are 170 justices of the peace, each appointed for a four-year term, presiding over peace courts in Montevideo and other departments, rural peace courts, and misdemeanor courts. Justices of the peace are constitutionally mandated to attempt a settlement or resolution between parties in a hearing before a case enters court for trial.

Crime

Classification of Crimes

Almost all the crimes in Uruguay are classified similarly to other countries in the region. Its penal code was first enacted in 1889 and comprehensively amended in 1934. The entire criminal law is divided into three parts. The introductory part deals with general principles of the law and the definition of offenses, which are classified into felonies and misdemeanors according to the severity of the social harm caused by the criminal behavior. It also stipulates various penal options, which range from imprisonment in a correctional facility to banishment, dispossession of political rights, annulment or suspension of professional credentials, and monetary fines. This first part also discusses legitimate mitigating factors in a criminal adjudication, such as age, mental health status, and state of consciousness. The second part focuses on felony offenses, which comprise crimes against state sovereignty, political institutions, social order, public administration, and public health. The rest of the articles in this second part revolve around offenses against persons and property. The concluding part centers on misdemeanor offenses. Uruguay is one of the first Latin American countries to define and penalize hate crime. A 1989 amendment to the penal code provided sanctions against violence or the incitement of hatred or any form of violence against other people based on race, color, religion, or national or ethnic origin.

Throughout Uruguay's history, several other statutes have been enacted to criminalize new forms of activities deemed harmful to the community and public safety. For example, a drug law was passed in 1974 to combat the commercial sale and use of psychoactive substances and to penalize the trafficking and consumption of illicit drugs.

One of the most unique anomalies of the Uruguayan system is the concept of "extinction of crime by marriage" expounded in article 116 of the penal code. Specifically, punishment for the offense of rape is nullified by marriage between the offender and the victim. Related offenses that fall under this statute are violent indecent assault, statutory rape, and abduction/kidnapping.

The Ministry of Interior periodically reports on the prevalence and trends of six major categories of crime, similar to the index crimes in the Uniform Crime Report of the United States. These categories are homicides, injuries, sexual offenses, robberies, thefts, and damages. Despite the multiplicity of offenses defined in the penal code, all criminal offenses are captured and summarized under these categories in governmental tabulation of crime statistics.

Crime Statistics

In general, crime and violence are not high in Uruguay by Latin American standards. The volume of offenses is greater in urban areas, especially in the capital city of Montevideo, than in the countryside. In Montevideo, areas frequented by tourists and disadvantaged neighborhoods suffer the highest rates of crime. Residential burglaries constitute a major public safety issue in the areas of Carrasco and Pocitos, where there are important concentrations of affluent families and resident foreign diplomats. Recent trends in official crime statistics show a bifurcated development: between 2000 and 2006, violent offenses categorized under the labels of homicides and injuries declined by 16.3 percent and 7.2 percent, respectively, whereas property offenses identified as robberies and thefts rose dramatically, by 34.6 percent and 71.8 percent, respectively. Record-high rates of unemployment and the unprecedented drop in Uruguayans' purchasing power resulting from the economic breakdown of 2001 may partly account for the property crime wave. Sex victimizations appear to be stable in recent years. According to the Departamento de Datos, Estadisticas, y Analisis, of the Uruguay Ministry of Interior, crimes recorded by police in 2006 were as follows:

Homicides	144
Injuries	6,897
Sex offenses	738
Robberies	6,764
Thefts	77,170
Damages	8,753

Drug Abuse and Related Offenses

Uruguay is neither a major drug-producing country nor a major nexus of transshipment. However, free trade zones afford relative anonymity for the movement of licit and illicit merchandise. Its strategic maritime location and unguarded land borders with Brazil and Argentina further aggravate its vulnerability to drug trafficking. Efforts to strengthen port security and customs services were progressing slowly as of 2007, limiting inspection of containers at maritime ports and cargo shipments at the international airport.

Overall, consumption of illicit drugs is moderate. About 0.2 percent of Uruguayans aged 15–64 abused opiates, including heroin, according to United Nations Office on Drugs and Crime 2008 World Drug Report in 2008. The increasing local demand for the very addictive and accessible cocaine-based derivative known as "pasta base" is a rising concern. Regular users of cocaine make up 1.4 percent of the population aged 15–64. Yet users of cannabis or marijuana constitute the largest group of drug consumers, with a prevalence rate of 5.2 percent. Synthetic drugs such as various forms of amphetamines (0.3 percent) and Ecstasy (0.2 percent) are making inroad into the Uruguayan population.

Uruguay is a signatory of the 1988 United Nations Drug Convention and thus is required to criminalize drug trade and use and collaborate in the global drug control. In 2007, the government of Uruguay confiscated 657 kilograms of regular cocaine and 84 kilograms of "pasta base" in both national and international antidrug operations, but there was no heroin seized, and no cocaine labs were destroyed in the same year. In addition, the processing of drug cases in Uruguay is distinguished by a very high attrition rate. For example, the government made 1,923 drug-related arrests in 2007, but only 486 convictions and 13 imprisonments resulted from these arrests.

Human Trafficking

Because prostitution is legal for adults and is widespread in major cities and tourist resorts, trafficking of women and children for prostitution occurs to cater to the demand. Victims are mostly women and girls, and some boys, who are trafficked, sometimes with the consent and assistance of their families, within the borders of Uruguay to areas frequented by domestic and foreign tourists for sexual exploitation. Others fall into the hands of international criminal syndicates and are sold to brothels in Spain and Italy. According to officials from the International Organization for Migration, traffickers have a net profit of US$13,000 per year on each woman they exploit in the region.

The involvement of minor children in child prostitution and child pornography is particularly alarming. The large number of missing and/or street children provides a large pool of minor candidates for the sex industry. The Ministry of Interior has estimated that about 3,100 minors lived or worked on the streets of Montevideo and surrounding area in 2003, and in the month of June 2004 alone, law enforcement authorities in inland Uruguay received 72 requests to locate missing children, 15 of whom were girls. In 2008, after detecting a growth in online child pornography material produced in the provinces of Maldonado, Salto, and Artigas and broadcasted through servers based in central Europe, Interpol joined Uruguay's Ministry of Interior to promptly investigate and prosecute five cases of child pornography. This social malady has yet to come under effective control.

Forced labor is another factor driving human trafficking. Parents strained by extreme economic hardships reportedly trade their own children for domestic and agricultural servitude in rural areas. UNICEF projected that over one-fourth of children working as domestic servants in Uruguay were less than 10 years old. When minors live and work away from their adult caregivers or guardians, they become vulnerable to sexual and physical abuse as well as economic exploitation.

Uruguay has recently stepped up its anti-trafficking efforts. An anti-trafficking law was enacted as part of a broad immigration reform in December 2007 to ban all kinds of trafficking in persons and to impose punishments of up to 16 years in prison, which surpasses the harshness of sanctions set down for rape. Statutes also prohibit forced labor, trafficking of minors, and child pornography, allowing punishments of up to 12 years in prison. These powerful legal tools notwithstanding, the government of Uruguay has been accused of not doing enough to eliminate the problem because the invocation of these anti-trafficking laws is uncommon, and the number of related convictions is even rarer, according to the U.S. State Department.

Finding of Guilt

The Criminal Procedure

The code of criminal procedure regulates the process of criminal adjudication, which is primarily written. One oral hearing is permitted when the defendant has been taken into custody in *flagrante delicto,* has made a confession or pleaded guilty, or has committed a nonserious or misdemeanor offense that allows for a succinct investigation and expedite ruling, but in practice this oral hearing is rarely convened.

The principles of due process, double jeopardy, territoriality, and official procedure guide the criminal process. The courtroom contest involves the judge, the prosecution, and the defense. The Uruguayan criminal procedure has evolved to a mixed system made up of an inquisitorial phase (preliminary and investigative stages) and an accusatory phase (the trial stage). During the preliminary and investigation stages, the judge may present charges, although the prosecutor also has the right to play the role. And during the accusatory phase, the prosecutor presses the charges forward or requests a stay. All trials in Uruguay are public in the sense that they are open and announce a public statement of the charge. Nevertheless, written arguments by both the prosecution and the defense are submitted to the judge, and these written statements are unavailable to the public. The defense attorney has the right to access and review all written documents submitted to the court. For crimes that carry a sentence of more than three years, appeals are automatic.

Rights of the Accused

The Uruguayan Constitution requires the issuance of a written warrant by competent authorities for the arrest of criminal suspects unless the suspect is caught in the act of committing the crime. The suspect can be held incommunicado for 24 hours and be brought to answer charges before a judge, who has to decide whether to free the person or press charges against the person. The accused has the right to legal counsel, and public defenders are regularly appointed to represent indigent defendants who cannot afford counsel. In cases where the accused is charged with a crime that carries a penalty of at least two years, the individual can be detained during the investigation of the case. A bail bond is granted only if the individual is not deemed a danger to society or a flight risk. The Uruguayan Constitution provides neither protection against self-incrimination nor right to trial by jury.

Juvenile Justice

A separate juvenile justice system was established in 1934 through a code for minors. Offenders under the age of 18 come under the jurisdiction of juvenile courts in Montevideo. In 2005, these juvenile cases represented 11.6 percent of all cases processed by the Uruguayan administration of justice (including civil, family, criminal, and labor cases). Specialized institutions are entrusted with the task of rehabilitating and educating youths under the care of the juvenile justice system. The National Institute for Minors oversees and operates all facilities that deal with minors in Uruguay. Juvenile offenders who have committed very serious crimes are incarcerated in juvenile detention centers whose design and management are patterned after those found for traditional cell-based adult prisons. Those juveniles who are deemed low risk are placed in halfway houses geared solely toward rehabilitation and reintegration.

Punishment

Most criminal offenses are punished with custodial sanctions and/or monetary fines. The death penalty was abolished by Constitution in 1907, and the last recorded execution took place in 1905. Less ordinary penal sanctions include exile to foreign countries and internal banishment or forced relocation. Despite the constitutionality of the use of exile as a criminal punishment, it has been very rarely applied in the criminal justice process. Sadly, most recent cases of forced exile occurred during the 1973–1985 military rule when hundreds of Uruguayan citizens, including many well-respected public figures such as the journalist Eduardo Galeano and the novelist Juan Carlo Onetti, were driven out of their own homeland, not as a punishment for any crime committed but as a governmental response to their political views or involvement in social activism.

Prison

The Uruguayan prison system was first developed in the early decades of the 19th century, and by the 1870s, humane treatment of prison inmates had become an openly stated goal of the country's correctional management. The revision of the penal code in 1882 and the subsequent report from a study commission led to the adoption of the hybrid Pennsylvania-Auburn model of penitentiary administration. As a result, mandatory labor and the implementation of graduated sanctions with rewards and penalties aimed at modeling prosocial behaviors became the core of the rehabilitation process. The progressive movement of prison reform continued into the 20th century with the creation of specialized facilities or units for defendants awaiting trials, women offenders, inmates with mental health problems, and colonies for educational and vocational training.

Currently, the National Directorate of Prisons under the Ministry of Interior oversees and manages all federal prisons and departmental jails. Defendants awaiting trial and/or sentences are temporarily detained in departmental jails. Once they are convicted and sentenced to incarceration, these offenders are transferred to one of the three main federal prisons or to the work colony at San José (the Educational Colony of Work). Of the three federal prisons, two are for men (Prison No. 1 and Prison No. 2), and the third is for women (the Establishment for the Correction and Detention of Women). The largest prison in Uruguay is the COMCAR prison in Montevideo, which is located in the Santiago Vasquez district on the outskirts of the city. The work colony is divided into maximum-, medium-, and minimum-security units on a premise of 1,800 acres. Attempts at rehabilitation take place at the work colony where agricultural work is mandated for all inmates. Work is mandatory for all sentenced inmates serving time as well as detainees awaiting trial in all correctional facilities. The latter are paid a symbolic wage upon release. Prerelease facilities for inmates due for release exist to accommodate the special needs of these offenders preparing for reentry, whose families are permitted to stay with them until the final discharge.

Although Uruguay pioneered the modern administration of prisons in Latin America, and its Constitution prohibits torture or cruelty against prisoners, the country has been severely criticized in recent years for inadequate maintenance, poor administration, and abuses of inmates' civil rights. Overcapacity and understaffing created sanitation, social, and health crises of unimaginable proportion. Experts from the United Nations reported that because of the lack of access to medical care, many inmates had to hurt themselves to get a chance to see a doctor. Others relied on visitors for sufficient food to obtain the required daily nutritional intake, whereas 35 percent of the inmates are believed to be infected with tuberculosis. Inmate-on-inmate violence remained rampant, partly contributed to by insufficient separate, high-security units for violent offenders.

According to data provided by the Ministry of Interior, between 2000 and 2006, the size of the Uruguayan prison population increased by 52 percent, from 4,368 in 2000 to 6,638 in 2006, averaging an annual increment of 8 percent. The recidivism rate among prison inmates as measured by the percent of inmates being repeat offenders rose from 49 percent in 2000 to 55 percent in 2006.

Amilcar Herbert and Hung-En Sung

Further Reading

Departamento de Datos, Estadisticas, y Analisis. (2006). *Observatorio Nacional sobre Violencia y Criminalidad de Uruguay.* Montevideo: Ministerio del Interior.

Gillespie, Charles Guy. (2006). *Negotiating Democracy: Politicians and Generals in Uruguay.* New York: Cambridge University Press.

Scheina, Robert. (2009). *History of Uruguay: Early and Modern Uruguay.* Mauritius: Alphascript Publishing.

Winslow, Robert, and Sheldon Zhang. (2008). *Comparative Criminology: A Global Perspective.* Upper Saddle River, NJ: Prentice Hall.

Venezuela

Legal System: Civil/Common
Murder: High
Corruption: High
Human Trafficking: Medium
Prison Rate: Medium
Death Penalty: No
Corporal Punishment: No

Background

Venezuela is a country of approximately 27.5 million inhabitants, located on the northern coast of

South America. It has been peopled for many thousands of years by Amerindian tribes, including the Wayuu, the Warao, and the Yanomami. Christopher Columbus first saw the South American mainland on his third voyage to the Indies in 1498, and Spanish colonization began in earnest during the 16th century. Three racial groups met and mixed in this process: the Amerindians, who already inhabited the territory; the Caucasians who colonized it; and the Africans who were brought in as slaves up until the 1850s.

From 1498 until the early 19th century, Venezuela was part of the Spanish empire. The movement for independence began in 1810 and finally came to fruition in 1821. Venezuela was ruled by autocrats until well into the 20th century, with the first elected government taking office in 1948. This was short-lived, but electoral politics were firmly established in 1958 with the overthrow of the military dictator Marcos Pérez Jiménez. There have been attempted coups during the years since then (the most recent in 2002), but none have been successful.

Currently, Venezuela is the world's ninth-largest producer of oil and the fifth-largest exporter. Rapid increases in oil revenues, both in the 1960s and 1970s and in very recent times, have caused some marked distortions in the economy and fostered corruption and mismanagement. Thus, despite vast oil revenues, the gross domestic product is only slightly above the average for Latin American countries, and only about one-seventh that of the world's wealthy nations. One-third of the population is classified as poor (household income does not cover basic expenditures) and one-tenth lives in "extreme poverty" (income does not cover the cost of food). Unemployment hovers around the 17 percent mark, and approximately half of the economically active population work in the informal sector (characterized by low wages, lack of job security, and no welfare benefits).

Economic problems led to serious rioting in 1989, in what became known as the *Caracazo* (after the capital city, Caracas, where most of the violence was concentrated). This was a series of disturbances that took place over several days in which more than 300 civilians died, at least 45 of them at the hands of the police and military forces. The *Caracazo* and its brutal aftermath fueled discontent among radical military officers, and in February 1992, some of them attempted a military coup. This was unsuccessful but, coming after the relative calm of the 1970s and 1980s, galvanized the country. One of its leaders, Lieutenant Colonel Hugo Chávez, achieved instant national fame for a short speech to his comrades in arms, delivered on television immediately after his arrest. Along with co-conspirators, Chávez was convicted of military rebellion and imprisoned; however, the government released him in 1994, and he immediately began political activities aimed at seeking the presidency in 1998. Dissatisfaction with the traditional parties was very high, and Chávez won the presidency with a landslide majority.

Immediately on entering office, Chávez dissolved the Congress and called for a Constituent Assembly to draft a new constitution. The new constitution (approved at the end of 1999) partially reshaped the institutional landscape of the country, particularly the Congress and the judiciary. Following reelection in 2006, Chávez announced plans to reform the Constitution yet again and set the country on the path to "Twenty First Century Socialism," but these plans were rejected in a referendum held in December 2007.

Legal Tradition

As a former colony of Spain, Venezuela obviously has its legal roots in Europe. The most recent version of the criminal code, enacted in 2005, contains many articles from former versions (particularly that of 1926), although it has been modified to account for contemporary circumstances (particularly penalizing aggressive opposition to the government). Nevertheless, the term criminal "code" is something of a misnomer because the code itself does not codify all crimes, and there is a long tradition in Venezuela of promulgating additional criminal legislation through separate laws. Notable in this regard are the Anti-Corruption Law (1982), the Drug Law (1994, most recently reformed in 2005), the Environmental Crimes Law (1992), the Law on Women's Right to a

Life Free From Violence (1998, 2007), and the Law against Organized Crime (2005).

Until around 1999, criminal procedure in Venezuela was inquisitorial (investigation and adjudication undertaken by judges, frequent use of preventive detention, written proceedings, limited access to case files for the defendants and their attorneys, no juries). However, like many other Latin American countries, Venezuela adopted the adversarial model (in July 1999), which produced a paradigm shift in the criminal justice system. The primary responsibility for investigations was transferred from the judges to the public prosecutors; the use of preventive detention was greatly restricted; proceedings were conducted on an oral basis; and lay co-judges and juries were instituted for more serious crimes. This change, which took arrest powers away from the police and drastically reduced the number of suspects in preventive detention, coincided with a significant increase in crime rates. The popular perception was that the new legislation had done nothing to stem the rise in crime and may have done something to fuel it. Additionally, it proved difficult to convene juries to try the most serious crimes, thereby producing long delays in proceedings. Thus, calls to reform the procedure code were soon being made (by politicians, the police, and the public), and in 2001, changes were made that increased the scope for arrest and preventive detention and eliminated juries (although lay co-judges are still used in more serious cases). Further reforms were made in 2006 and 2008.

Crime

Classification of Crimes

The criminal code distinguishes between crimes, which are punishable by imprisonment, and misdemeanors (*faltas*), which are punishable by arrests or fines. In the code, crimes are classified by major types, as follows:

- Crimes against national sovereignty and national security: treason and espionage; crimes against national and state government; crimes against international law.
- Crimes against liberty: crimes against political, personal, and religious freedom, etc.
- Crimes against public administration: embezzlement, extortion, corruption, misuse of authority, aggressive words or acts against public officials. (Corruption is also defined in the 1982 anti-corruption law.)
- Crimes against the administration of justice: failure to provide legal assistance, simulating crimes, false testimony, collusion, concealment, flight, etc.
- Crimes against public order: conspiracy to commit crime; incitement to crime; manufacture and carrying of weapons, incitement to civil disorder and resistance.
- Forgery: false currency; forged seals, fiscal stamps, documents, passports, licenses, etc.
- Crimes against public and private interests: arson, causing floods, etc.; against public health and nutrition.
- Crimes against public morals and the family: rape, seduction, prostitution, corrupting minors, adultery, bigamy, etc.
- Crimes against persons: homicide, battery, abortion, abandoning children, slander, etc.
- Crimes against property: theft, robbery, extortion, kidnapping, fraud, etc.
- Drug crimes (defined in a separate law):
    - Trafficking, distribution, supply, manufacture, preparation, refining, alteration, extraction, preparation, production, transport, storage, organization, financing, or aiding in the trafficking of substances or raw materials prohibited by the law.
    - Planting, cultivation, harvesting, preservation, storage, organization, or financing and in general, any illicit act of acquisition, trafficking, supply, storage, and distribution of seeds, plants, or parts of plants that contain any of the substances prohibited by the law.
    - Illegal possession of substances, raw materials, seeds, plants, or parts of plants that contain any of the substances prohibited by the law.

- Laundering money derived from drug offenses.
- Providing drugs to a minor.
- Providing a vehicle or premises for drug use.
- Incitement to drug use.

Substances that are subject to criminal law are those listed in international agreements and ratified by Venezuelan law, such as the Convention against Illicit Traffic in Narcotic Drugs and Psychotropic Substances, 1988, and any other substance defined as narcotic or psychotropic by the Venezuelan Ministry of Health. The drug law creates a distinction between drug users and those involved in the production, distribution, possession, and sale of drugs. The former are sentenced to treatment, whereas the latter are punished.

In Venezuela, misdemeanors are divided into the following:

- Public order: for example, failure to obey an order, begging, disorderly behavior.
- Public safety: improper manufacture and sale of arms, faulty construction practices, illegal elimination of waste materials, etc.
- Public morals: betting and gaming, insobriety, offenses to public decency, etc.
- Public protection of property: for example, unlawful possession of weights and measures, unlawful copying of keys.

State police codes also include many of the same misdemeanors, which are similarly punishable by arrest or fine.

Crime Statistics

In 2007, a total of 156,258 serious crimes were recorded by the police. Of these, property crimes were by far the most common, with the different types of theft and robbery accounting for nearly 70 percent of the total. Violent crime is less common, although it is a source of serious social concern. Of particular note is the category "resisting authority," which refers to civilians killed in allegedly armed confrontations with the police. As human rights organizations have frequently pointed out, many of these encounters take place away from public view, and some may involve execution-style killings by the police; thus, the extent to which these incidents represent legitimate use of force rather than police violence is particularly hard to determine. (In 2007, more than 1,500 people were killed in this way.) Kidnappings have also become sufficiently frequent to earn a place in the police statistics, with at least 279 victims during 2007.

It is well known, of course, that not all crimes are reported to the police, and the "dark figure" of crime is generally larger than that which is officially recorded. Estimates from surveys of crime victims in Venezuela indicate that between 30 and 40 percent of common crimes are reported to the police. Reporting rates for serious crimes, such as kidnapping and vehicle theft/robbery, are over 80 percent, whereas the rate for less serious crimes such as simple theft hover around 20 percent.

As important as the total number of crimes committed is their frequency relative to the population (i.e., the crime rate) and the extent to which this is changing over time. In 2007, there were 569 serious crimes per 100,000 inhabitants. This rate has decreased by nearly 20 percent since 2000. However, within this overall picture, violent crimes and property crime show different trends. Property crimes decreased by nearly 30 percent, from 552/100,000 in 2000 to 394/100,000 in 2006. As the predominant type of recorded crime, property crimes naturally exerted a strong influence on the total crime rate.

By contrast, the rate of violent crime increased by about 20 percent between 2000 and 2006. Within this group of crimes, homicides showed a particularly dramatic increase, from 33/100,000 in 2000 to 48/100,000 in 2007—an increase of almost 50 percent. In Caracas, more than 2,700 people were killed in 2007, making it one of the most violent cities in the Americas, with a murder rate of 130/100,000. In addition, the figures for homicide do not include deaths through "resistance to authority," alluded to previously. These killings by the police occurred at a rate of 5.7/100,000 during 2007.

Although information is unavailable on the rates and types of crime committed in urban and rural areas, inspection of the crimes recorded for each of the 23 states and the metropolitan district (Caracas) indicates that, overall, property crime predominates everywhere. However, in the rural regions of the country, simple thefts are somewhat more prevalent, as are assaults. By contrast, vehicle theft/robbery and kidnappings tend to be concentrated in the more urban regions of the country.

Finding of Guilt

Rights of the Accused

Article 125 of the criminal procedure code (CPC) sets out a number of legal rights for persons accused of crimes:

1. To be informed specifically and clearly of the charges.
2. To call family members, an attorney, or a legal aid association to advise of arrest.
3. To assistance, during the preliminary investigation, by a defense attorney or public defender.
4. To an interpreter, should one be necessary, without charge.
5. To request that the prosecutor investigate facts or circumstances that might establish innocence.
6. To declare directly to a judge.
7. To request that the investigation proceed and to be informed of its content, except where parts have been temporarily declared confidential.
8. To request a speedy revocation of preventive detention.
9. To adhere to the constitutional precept of silence or to declare while not under oath.
10. Not to be tortured or treated in a cruel, inhumane, or degrading manner.
11. Not to be subjected to investigative or detention techniques that alter free will or volition, even when freely consented to.
12. Not to be tried in absence, except in cases permitted by the Constitution.

Apart from these, the CPC establishes the following other important requirements and opportunities regarding the accused:

1. *Trial by judicial panel.* Currently, the CPC provides for a bench trial (i.e., trial by a professional judge) in misdemeanor and criminal cases where the maximum prison sentence is no greater than four years. The other, more serious cases are tried by a judicial panel comprising one professional and two lay judges. Lay judges are selected from voter rolls.
2. *Sentence reduction for a guilty plea.* There is no provision for plea bargaining in Venezuela. However, if the accused pleads guilty at the preliminary hearing, the judge must move immediately to sentencing and must reduce the sentence accordingly. The maximum reduction permitted for violent offenses is one-third, but for other offenses and depending on circumstances, the reduction can be up to one-half (article 376, CPC).
3. *Appeals.* The CPC allows the accused to appeal procedural decisions (e.g., concerning bail or preventive detention) and adjudication (finding of guilt). If the appeal is upheld, the case is sent for retrial in the same jurisdiction, but before a different judge or judicial panel.

Legal Assistance for the Accused

Accused persons may name up to three private attorneys, or if they do not have the necessary financial resources, the court will appoint a public defender to represent them. If there is no public defender in the jurisdiction, the court can name a private attorney to serve the accused without fee.

The Public Defender's Office is administratively attached to the Supreme Court. In 2001, there were 517 public defenders, 356 of whom were working in the adult criminal justice system and 161 in the juvenile justice system. Public defenders find that they have very high caseloads and complain that it is impossible to give more than cursory attention to most offenders.

Responsibility for Investigation and Prosecution of the Case

In establishing an adversarial procedure to replace the former inquisitorial system, the new CPC assigned the primary responsibility for investigating and prosecuting cases to the public prosecutor. The Public Prosecutor's Office (known as the Ministerio Público or Fiscalía) is an independent body with offices in each judicial circuit. In 2001, there were a total of 498 prosecutors: 55 covering national cases, 24 senior prosecutors, 116 prosecutors in Caracas, and 303 in the states. Each prosecutor has one or two assistant prosecutors.

The prosecutors are, firstly, responsible for criminal investigation and case preparation. In this, they are assisted by the police, with whom they must establish a close and effective working arrangement, while at the same time exercising oversight of police activity. In Venezuela, there are numerous police agencies, among which the following are particularly relevant:

1. *Judicial police*. This is the principal police agency charged with investigating crime. It is the primary agency to which the public reports crimes, and—with certain exceptions—crimes reported to (or detected by) other police agencies must be passed on to the judicial police as soon as possible. Attached to the Ministry of Interior and Justice, it has about 8,200 officers.
2. *State police.* Each state has its own police force, which is responsible for public order, crime prevention, and preliminary arrest and criminal investigation. In total, there are some 58,000 state police officers.
3. *Municipal police.* Approximately 100 municipalities have their own police forces (with a total of almost 11,000 officers). Their functions are very similar to those of the state police. Starting in 2009, the state and municipal police forces will be partially integrated as a national police force.
4. *National Guard.* Attached to the Ministry of Defense, the National Guard has general responsibilities for public order and specific responsibilities in relation to drug trafficking, contraband, and environmental crimes. It has about 32,800 officers.

Although these and other police agencies may undertake their own investigations of crimes, as soon as arrest becomes a necessity or a possibility, the case must be referred to the prosecutor. If the police make an arrest in the course of their activities, they must refer the case to a prosecutor within 12 hours. If the police wish to make an arrest in connection with an ongoing investigation, they must seek the approval of the prosecutor, who in turn must request a warrant from a criminal court. The prosecutor will direct the judicial police in the preparation of a case that will be taken to court. This includes undertaking interrogations and inspections and, with authorization from the court, interception of telephone calls and searches of houses or other premises. Judicial warrants for these activities are valid for 30 days and renewable on request.

Once a case has been prepared, the responsibility for taking it through the court system rests with prosecutors. Criminal courts in Venezuela are divided into three types, which correspond to the investigation, adjudication, and sentencing and sanction of the offender. Prosecutors are heavily involved in the control and trial phases of the process, requesting warrants, continuations, dismissals, and the like; presenting evidence and cross-examining defense witnesses; and making opening and closing statements. They are also notified of key decisions relating to the sentence as it is being served but generally involve themselves little in this aspect of the criminal justice system.

In 2002, the Public Prosecutor's Office initiated 220,000 new cases, and in 2005, the number of new cases was 300,000—an increase of about one quarter. This figure covers all kinds of crime and misdemeanors and is therefore much larger than the totals of serious crime reported previously. According to the attorney general, in 2005, each prosecutor (and their assistants) had to deal with an average of 2,808 cases. With such caseloads, priority is obviously given to cases for which there is an arrestee or a suspect who has been accused. It is not surprising that many cases remain open or inactive: in 2005, about 58 percent of cases were closed (through discretionary closure, dismissal by the court, or adjudication), but 42 percent of cases remained open. However, this latter figure was a major improvement over earlier years: in 2002, just 15 percent of cases were closed while the rest remained open. The marked increase in closure rates between 2002 and 2005 is probably due more to changes in administrative procedure (i.e., a decision to treat pending cases as closed almost immediately if there is little or no chance of proceeding to prosecution) than to marked increases in prosecutorial efficiency.

Alternatives to Going to Trial

Apart from dismissal, there are a number of ways in which a case may be resolved without trial:

1. *The opportunity principle.* The prosecutor can ask the court to close a case if it is a trivial or highly infrequent crime; when the accused had very minor participation in the crime; in crimes of negligence, in which the accused has suffered grave physical or moral injury; when conditions would be met for granting probation; when the punishment would be extremely light; or when the case involves organized crime, and the accused cooperates with the investigation (article 37, CPC).
2. *Restitution.* Restitution made by the offender to the victim(s) is applicable for crimes that affect property and for crimes of negligence that have not caused death or permanent serious physical harm, when the victim(s) and accused have agreed to restitution. The offender must offer some kind of monetary compensation to the victim and agree to perform work or some other activity for them or may simply apologize for the offense. The important thing is that the victim agrees to the proposal.
3. *Diversion.* This option is open to persons accused of crimes that carry a maximum prison sentence of three years. The accused must admit to having committed the crime and offer reparations to the victim. If diversion is granted, the adjudicatory procedure is suspended, and the offender is placed on probation for a period of one to two years.
4. *A guilty plea.* As mentioned previously, if the accused pleads guilty, investigation and/or adjudication are immediately suspended, and a sentence is imposed. Offenders can be given a reduction of between one-third and one-half of their sentence for entering a guilty plea.

Case Processing

Pertinent information was provided by the public prosecutor for the year 2000. Dismissals represented the most frequent outcome, accounting for 42 percent of cases. These were followed by cases declared as "pending further action" (almost one-third of the total). Diversion was used in only 1 percent of cases, but reconciliation (which was at that time permitted in cases of family or intimate violence) was used somewhat more frequently (3.2 percent). Formal charges were filed in 6,137 cases, of which 1,458 (5.4 percent of all cases, 23.7 percent of cases charged) resulted in guilty pleas. The other cases (4,679) proceeded to trial, although the outcome was not recorded.

Incarceration Before, or While Awaiting, Trial

Preventive detention can be used when the offense is punishable by imprisonment, when there are grounds for accusing the suspect, and when there is a reasonable presumption that the accused will flee or attempt to obstruct any part of the investigation (article 250, CPC). Risk of flight is determined by the circumstances of the accused (taking account of employment, family circumstances, and residence), by their behavior during the current case (or a previous case), and by the magnitude of harm caused through the crime.

Unless the accused is caught "in the act," preventive detention must be requested by the prosecutor and decided by a judge within 24 hours of the prosecutor's motion. When preventive detention is ordered, prosecutors have 30 days (with an additional 15 days if requested) to file charges or make some other case decision. If no action has been taken, the accused can be released or subjected to a cautionary measure.

Cautionary measures are as follows: house arrest; supervision by a designated person or institution; reporting to the court or other institution; prohibition on leaving the country, or the jurisdiction where the trial will be held; prohibition on attending certain meetings or frequenting certain places; prohibition on communication with certain individuals (without impinging on the right to defense); restraining order (domestic violence and rape); and bail. Such measures are applicable only when the potential prison sentence does not exceed five years and the accused has no prior convictions. However, they are rarely used. For example, in 2001, the Ministry of the Interior and Justice reported that, nationwide, only 71 accused were subject to cautionary measures.

According to figures from the Ministry of the Interior and Justice, in 1998 (the year before the current CPC was implemented), an average of 14,573 offenders were in preventive detention, representing 60 percent of the total incarcerated population. By 2000, this figure had fallen to 6,418 (42 percent of the total). However, with the loosening of the guidelines in 2001 and perhaps a more conservative approach among judges in the face of high levels of social concern about crime, the number of accused on preventive detention has increased. By late 2007, 11,933 accused were in preventive detention (equivalent to 57 percent of the total incarcerated population). After 10 years under the new procedure code, preventive detention may be back to where it was under the inquisitorial system.

Criminal Court Judges: Number, Qualifications

According to information from the Supreme Court, in 2008, there were 621 criminal court judges. The urban states, with large populations and higher crime rates, have larger numbers of judges than the rural states. Interestingly, women dominate this profession: 62 percent of judges are female. Qualifications necessary for serving as a professional judge and additional criteria used in selecting judges are as follows: Venezuelan nationality, lawyer, at least five years' professional experience or graduate credential and at least two years' experience, good moral standing, no civil or political interdiction, no union activity or political party affiliation, satisfactory physical and mental health, willing to submit to periodic investigations of family wealth, computer skills. The appeals courts and Supreme Court require a minimum of 10 years' experience. Appointment is by competitive examination, organized by the Executive Direction of the Judiciary, attached to the Supreme Court.

To serve as lay judges, citizens must be at least 25 years old and have completed secondary education. They must live in the jurisdiction where the case is being tried, have no criminal record, and have no physical or mental condition that would impede their role. Government officials and lawyers cannot serve in this capacity.

Juvenile Justice

In 1990, Venezuela set in motion the reform of its juvenile justice system when it signed and adopted into law the International Convention on Children's Rights. Following this, intensive work and consultation by legal scholars and children's advocates led to the development and implementation of a new law in 1998 called the Organic Law for the Protection of Children and Adolescents. This replaced the preexisting Minors Law and instituted a change from a paternalistic to a due process model of juvenile justice.

In relation to crime, juveniles are governed by the same laws as adults, and there are no status offenses. However, juvenile preventive detention, adjudication, sentencing, and sanctions are organized through separate institutions that deal only with juvenile cases. The National Institute for Minors runs the juvenile detention centers, including both preventive detention and postsentencing detention, and also provides professional and administrative support for other actions taken with juvenile delinquents. Special juvenile courts oversee the preliminary, trial, and supervisory stages of case processing. According to the Supreme Court, in 2008 there were 151 juvenile (criminal) judges, 82 percent of whom were female.

The law makes an important distinction between children (under 12 years old) and adolescents (12 to 17 years old). Children are considered to be free from responsibility for their criminal acts. Adolescents are held responsible for their criminal acts. The juvenile court operates with the same professionals (judges, prosecutors, public defenders, etc.) and most of the same procedures (e.g., oral trial) as criminal courts, except that juvenile proceedings are not public. If children are found to have committed a crime, they must be assigned to a protective measure, such as improved family care and supervision, foster care, adoption, or treatment. Adolescents can be assigned to one of the following measures: warning, community service (not more than eight hours a week for a maximum of six months), probation (maximum two years), day center (must attend during the part of the day when not at school; maximum one year), and detention. For 12- to 13-year-olds, the minimum period of detention is six months, and the maximum is two years. For 14- to 17-year-olds, the minimum period is one year, and the maximum is five.

Detention can be used only for serious violent crimes, drug trafficking, and vehicle theft or robbery; for repeat juvenile offenders when the maximum (adult) prison sentence for the instant offense is at least five years; and for offenders who have violated other measures (in which case detention can be no more than six months). Detention must be served in special juvenile facilities. If a juvenile offender in detention reaches the age of majority, he or she is to be transferred to an adult facility but must always be kept separate from adult offenders. Supervisory judges can "exceptionally" authorize offenders to stay in juvenile detention centers until they are 21.

Punishment

Types of Punishment

A long-standing feature of the criminal code, dating from at least 1926, is a fairly elaborate classification of the types of punishment. Articles 9 and 10 of the current code set out the following "corporal" and "non-corporal" penalties:

- *Corporal penalties:* Incarceration (penitentiary), incarceration (prison), arrest (police jail), penal colony, confinement, and deportation.
- *Non-corporal penalties:* Supervision by public authorities, civil interdiction, political interdiction, prohibition from engaging in certain trades or professions, termination from work, suspension from work, fines, cautions, loss of instruments or weapons with which the crime was committed, payment of legal costs.

Clearly, corporal penalties relate to some kind of incarceration or deportation, whereas non-corporal penalties affect the rights, activities, or patrimony of the convicted offender. Many of the non-corporal penalties are designed to be attached to corporal penalties; for example, confinement is supposed to be accompanied by suspension from work.

In the criminal code, the punishment for the majority of crimes is imprisonment, and precise sentencing guidelines are set. For example, the punishment for robbery is specified as 6 to 12 years of imprisonment. Judges must impose the midpoint sentence (in this case, 9 years), unless there are mitigating circumstances (e.g., offender between 18 and 21 years of age) that would justify the minimum term or aggravating circumstances (e.g., premeditation, the use of disguise) that would justify the maximum term. Fines are also specified quite frequently as the sanction for less serious crimes, and to avoid the effects of inflation, they are expressed in "tributary units" (TUs). For example, unauthorized hunting on private land carries a fine of 10 to 25 TUs. The current value of a TU is about 20 U.S. dollars.

Recent criminal laws have also incorporated a variety of other sanctions, most of which are supplementary to imprisonment. For example, the Environmental Crimes Law cites community work as a possible primary sanction for individuals together with, among other sanctions, professional suspension, prohibition from contracting with government, and publication of the sentence in the national press (at the offender's expense) as supplementary sanctions. Companies are subject to fines, closure, and other measures. Similarly, article 66 of the drug law provides for confiscation of property related to, or deriving from, drug crimes.

Despite this conceptual creativity, imprisonment has always been, and continues to be, the primary criminal sanction in Venezuela. As seen previously, the criminal code distinguishes several types of imprisonment: in penitentiaries, prisons, penal colonies, and so on. Prisoners on preventive detention are supposed to be held in separate institutions called judicial internment centers, which are not even mentioned in the criminal code. Because the criminal courts are organized at state level, each state needs an internment center, and—in theory at least—the system of prison facilities for convicted offenders should be independently organized at national level. However, lack of funding (or the political will to invest in confinement facilities) means that separate systems were never created. In some states (e.g., Sucre), the judicial internment center has been made to double as a prison; in others (e.g., Zulia), the "national prison" has been made to double as a judicial internment center. In addition, there are strong pressures from inmates and their families to ensure that time is served in the state where they live. Thus, despite its formal title, the prison in each state is likely to hold accused persons on preventive detention, convicted offenders from that state, and convicted offenders from other states (who have been sent there for a variety of reasons). With no internal segregation of prisoners by legal status, the experience of incarceration is the same for inmates on preventive detention as it is for convicted offenders (underlining the particular problem of "prisoners without trial"), and the character of penal institutions is very similar across the country. There is, therefore, no real difference between serving a sentence in a judicial internment center and serving a sentence in a penitentiary.

Probation has existed in Venezuela since 1980 but has never been an option available at sentencing and is not mentioned in the criminal code. Instead, it is considered to be a post-conviction option that can be requested by the offender once in prison. The conditions for granting probation have been made somewhat stricter in recent years, and currently, it is available only for first-time offenders with a sentence no greater than five years who can show that they will have employment on being released from prison. Probation can be granted for between one and three years, and probationers must comply with a set of conditions, such as maintaining employment, reporting to a probation officer, and seeking authorization before traveling away from their area of residence. The most recent figures are from 2001, when the Ministry of the Interior and Justice reported that there were 3,502 offenders on probation (17 percent of all offenders serving sentences). Restrictions on granting probation imposed since then most likely mean that the number and proportion of offenders on probation have decreased in recent years.

Other early-release mechanisms have also been available to prisoners since 1981. Thus, they can apply for work release after completing a quarter of their sentence. Under this arrangement, prisoners leave the facility to work during the day and return in the evenings. Transfer to an open prison facility, with a more relaxed regime, can be applied for after a third of the sentence is completed. Once again, offenders are expected to go out to work during the day and spend nights and weekends in the facility. Parole is available to prisoners who have completed two-thirds of their sentence. To apply for any of these "benefits," as they are known in the Venezuelan criminal justice system, prisoners cannot have had a conviction for the same crime within the last 10 years, nor can they have committed any crime while in prison. In addition, the 2005 reform of the criminal code expressly prohibited the possibility of probation or these "benefits" for offenders convicted of rape, murder, robbery, and kidnapping. However, following massive hunger strikes by prisoners, in 2008 the government Ombudsman persuaded the Supreme Court to consider revoking this restriction.

Finally, to help shorten prison sentences and encourage self-betterment among prisoners, in 1993, a new law permitting the Judicial Redemption of

Sentences for Work and Study was enacted. This allows inmates to earn one day of remission from their sentences for every two days spent in work or study within the prison. Remissions are not automatically deducted from prisoners' sentences but must be applied for from the court that is overseeing the prisoner's sentence. Such applications are often accompanied by a request for one of the three "benefits" mentioned previously.

Typical Punishments

The maximum prison sentence that can be given is 30 years, for certain cases of homicide; however, the average sentence for homicide is much lower. In general, the average sentences given for all the crimes in the table are located toward the lower end of the range prescribed by law. In the case of drug offenses, this means that the average sentences for "large scale" drug trafficking (over one kilo of marijuana, 100 grams of cocaine, or 20 grams of heroin) are not markedly greater than those given for small-scale drug trafficking.

The Death Penalty

The death penalty was abolished in Venezuela in 1863 and has never been reinstated. Some commentators equate the contemporary killings at the hands of the police with the death penalty (and death squads have been found to operate in several states since the late 1990s). Likewise, lynching has increased in frequency over the last 10 years, and it was estimated that there were 75 incidents between October 2007 and September 2008, with 15 fatalities. However, neither police killings nor death at the hands of the community can be considered equivalent to the carefully restricted categories and carefully prescribed procedures that inhere in most death penalties.

The Prisons

As of September 2008, there were 24,069 inmates held in prison facilities, including 14,825 individuals on preventive detention (59 percent). A total of 9,244 inmates were serving a sentence, of whom 6.8 percent were women. They were housed in 30 prison facilities distributed throughout the country. There is a prison facility in all but three states (which must rely on facilities in neighboring jurisdictions), and a few states have more than one facility, particularly those with large populations. There is a dedicated women's facility in Caracas, but elsewhere, female inmates as housed in annexes to the male prison. The largest prisons are the Western Penitentiary Center in Táchira State (2,201 inmates), the Judicial Internment Center close to the city of Valencia (2,167 inmates), and the National Prison in Maracaibo (1,580).

Prison Life

The key to understanding the experience of incarceration in Venezuela is the weak presence of authorities within the facilities. Perimeter security is provided by the National Guard, whose task it is to prevent escapes, check for the entry of contraband into the prison, and quell internal disorder. The interior of the prison is staffed by personnel from the Ministry of the Interior and Justice. The director and other administrative and professional staff usually occupy offices close to the main entry. Beyond that, most prisons have several communal dormitory blocks and exercise areas that are nominally patrolled by civilian guards. However, the ratio of inmates to guards is very high: one researcher found that in the Mérida State facility, there were 17 inmates to every guard, but that at any one time, there could be as many as 65 inmates per guard.

With such small numbers of guards, most of whom are unarmed, much of the internal control of the prisons has long been in the hands of the inmates. Although the assignment of inmates to dormitory blocks is undertaken by the staff, it is not done on any legal or programmatic basis. Middle-class and professional prisoners will, if they are lucky (or can pay), be assigned to the best dormitory (for the prisons are rather like small cities with stratification between the richer and the poorer). Other prisoners will be assigned to a dormitory based on their geographic origin (prisoners from within and outside the state tend to be kept apart).

Venezuelan justice minister Hilarion Cardoza, right, gives money to a prisoner at the Las Planta Prison in Caracas, Venezuela, June 16, 1997. Justice officials spent the day conducting a census of the country's 33 prisons, labeled among the most violent and chaotic in Latin America. (AP Photo/Jose Caruci)

However, once assigned to a dormitory, it is up to the newly arriving prisoner to find a place to sleep, purchase a mattress (if he has money), and so on. For this, he must contact the inmate, or group of inmates, that runs the dormitory. In some prisons, there is a building tender system in place, in which selected prisoners function to keep order within the dormitory and preserve relatively harmonious relations with the prisoners in other dormitories. In doing this, the tenders have the full support of the prison administration and are able to reap benefits in terms of special privileges. In other prisons, the building tender system has broken down, to be replaced by gang-like groups that establish themselves in each dormitory and sustain relatively hostile relationships with other dormitories.

Whichever system of internal control is in place, the prison guards are largely confined to the role of turnkey, opening and closing doors and gates at set times of the day. Although relationships with the guards can be important for the prisoners, of far greater importance are the relationships with other prisoners. Where building tenders operate, the inmate must make sure that he does not fall out of favor because he might be subject to corporal punishment or expelled from the dormitory. Where gangs exist, the inmate must make sure that he does not stray into "enemy" territory and, with his companions, must be constantly on the alert for potential attacks.

Thus, violence is a key facet of prison life in Venezuela. In 2008, more than 400 prisoners lost their lives in prison violence (which gives a staggering rate of 1,896 deaths per 100,000 inmates), and almost twice that number were seriously injured. A study completed for the Ministry of the Interior and Justice in 2005 revealed that 71 percent of deaths and 49 percent of serious injuries were caused by firearms, which reveals the level of weapons trafficking in prisons.

Another facet of the weak administrative presence within prisons is the poor infrastructure and deficient provision of services. Many prisons have dilapidated buildings with scant sanitary facilities, and the provision of food is patchy and inconsistent. The 2005 study for the Ministry of the Interior and Justice found that in some prisons the contracted suppliers had ceased to deliver food, forcing the authorities to seek stopgap alternatives with local and regional organizations. Although precise data collection was difficult, it was estimated that the volume of food prepared in most prisons covered only about 60 percent of the prisoners, leaving the rest to fend for themselves. In general, it appeared that most prisoners could count on only one meal per day and that they were only getting 75 percent of daily nutritional requirements. Added to the shortage of food are the failure to provide bedding or clothing and the inadequate medical and dental facilities at most facilities.

In light of the foregoing conditions, families and friends are a vital support for prisoners, and fortunately, visiting policies are liberal. All facilities are open for visits twice a week (midweek and weekend). At that time, prisoners are permitted to see as many friends and family as are willing to visit them, who can bring in much-needed food, clothing, medicines, and materials for work. Visitors are allowed into the dormitory areas for a period of four to five hours. At these times, gang rivalries are put on hold, and the prison takes on something of the air of a market or carnival as children play, couples hold hands, and prisoners try to sell their wares to visitors. Conjugal visits are also allowed but are arranged throughout the week in a separate annex.

The government has acknowledged the woeful condition of the country's penal establishments by developing a plan for "humanizing prisons." Under this plan, in July 2008, a new model—"Penitentiary City"—was inaugurated in the city of Coro, and there are plans for building three additional facilities in the states of Carabobo, Lara, and Miranda, together with 25 community treatment centers around the country.

Work and Study in Prison

The Penitentiary Regime Law, last reformed in 2000, declares that prisoners have both the duty and the right to work. As in many prison systems, however, there are serious obstacles to providing full, meaningful, and reasonably paid work for all (or even most) prisoners. First, the character of the Venezuelan economy (heavily dependent on revenues from the oil industry) and the recent political shift to the left have stunted the growth of stable large-scale enterprises of the kind that could develop prison labor initiatives. Second, the longstanding neglect of prison infrastructure has led to a considerable deterioration in the condition of workshops: in 2005, less than half of them were fit for purpose, and nearly a quarter were being used by inmates as sleeping areas. Third, the prison estate itself is able to absorb only a portion of inmates in institutional labor (cooking, maintenance, etc.) and pays extremely low wages (equivalent to less than US$200 per year). Fourth, in prisons where inmates are essentially divided into warring gangs, movement within the facility is extremely limited, and the threat of lethal violence generally confines individuals to their dormitory area.

In 2005, only 41 percent of all prisoners were working. Only 3 percent of these were under the government's Institute for Prison Work, and about 34 percent were employed by prison administrations. The rest (63 percent) were self-employed, many as artisans making products to be sold inside or outside the prison, some as food and drink vendors within the establishment. The government has recently taken some measures to bring down the figure of nearly 60 percent of prisoners who are not working, including five agricultural projects developed in conjunction with the Food and Agricultural Organization of the United Nations and the provision of occupational training to about 5 percent of prisoners. However, it remains to be seen how much real progress can be made.

In 2005, just over a fifth of prisoners were enrolled in education programs, most of them in the government's national education "missions," which have been extended to the prisons. Of these, 11 percent were in literacy programs, 16 percent in primary education, 36 percent in secondary education, and 8 percent in university education. The remaining 29 percent were in "traditional" educational programs. Problems stemming from administrative disorganization and high levels of violence within many facilities limit the number of inmates that take up these activities. Sport, however, is particularly popular: in 2005, 40 percent of prisoners participated in a sports team, mainly in some form of soccer. Cultural activities are also important: in 2005, there were 143 different groups in existence (membership equivalent to 15 percent of the prison population), with music and theater being the most popular activities. The recently created Penitentiary Symphony Orchestra, with members from four different prisons, has attracted considerable public attention.

International Exchanges and Transfers of Prisoners

Prisoner transfer treaties exist with Colombia, Spain, Holland, and Denmark. Although there is no bilateral treaty with the United States, U.S. ratification (in 2001) of the Inter-American Convention on Serving Criminal Sentences Abroad (1993) would allow the transfer of prisoners between the two countries. Venezuela has also made a request to the European Union to subscribe to the Strasbourg Convention on the Transfer of Sentenced Persons (1983). If the request is approved, Venezuela could exchange/transfer prisoners with members of the European Union. No figures exist on the number of prisoners transferred to or from Venezuela in each year, but the number is likely to be very small. Meanwhile, bilateral negotiations on prisoner transfer are being held with various countries, including the United Kingdom and France. Talks with the latter have been complicated by the fact that a prisoner transfer treaty could allow the repatriation of Carlos Ilich Ramírez (alias The Jackal), a Venezuelan terrorist serving a life sentence in France.

Neelie Pérez Santiago and Christopher Birkbeck

Further Reading

Birkbeck, Christopher. (2002). "Venezuela." *World Factbook of Criminal Justice Systems.* Washington: Bureau of Justice Statistics: http://www.ojp.usdoj.gov/bjs/pub/ascii/wfcjsvz.txt.

Birkbeck, Christopher, and Pérez Santiago, Neelie. (2006). "The Character of Penal Control in Latin America: Sentence Remissions in a Venezuelan Prison." *Criminology and Criminal Justice* 6(3): 289–308.

Briceño-León, Roberto. (2006). "Violence in Venezuela: Oil Rent and Political Crisis." *Ciencia & Saúde Coletiva* 11(2): 315–325: http://www.scielo.br/pdf/%0D/csc/v11n2/30420.pdf.

Kane, Frank, and John Tilsley. (2006). *In the Shadow of Papillon. Seven Years of Hell in Venezuela's Prison System.* Edinburgh: Mainstream Publishing.

General Bibliography

Books, Periodicals, and Articles

Aas, K. (2007). *Globalization and Crime*. Los Angeles, CA: Sage.

Adeyemi, A. (1990). "Crime and Development in Africa: Case Study of Nigeria." In *Essays on Crime and Development,* edited by U. Zvekic, pp. 135–193. Rome: United Nations Interregional Crime and Justice Institute.

ADT. (2006). *Anti-Social Behaviour across Europe:* http://www.jdi.ucl.ac.uk/downloads/publications/journal_articles/cc4416AD_ANTI_SOCIAL_Report_UK_fv.pdf

Aebi, M.F. (2010). "Methodological Issues in the Comparison of Police Recorded Crime Rates." In *International Handbook of Criminology,* edited by S. Shoham, P. Knepper, and M. Kett, pp. 209–226. London: Routledge.

Aebi, M.F., K. Aromaa, B. Aubusson de Cavarlay, G. Barclay, B. Gruszczynska, H. von Hofer, V. Hysi, J.-M. Jehle, M. Killias, P. Smit, and C. Tavares. (2006). *European Sourcebook of Crime and Criminal Justice Statistics—2006.* 3rd ed. Den Haag: Boom Juridische Uitgevers.

Aebi, M.F., and N. Delgrande. (2009). *Council of Europe Annual Penal Statistics SPACE I: Survey 2007.* Strasbourg: Council of Europe.

Aebi, M.F., and A. Linde. (2009). *Review of the Current Situation in Respect of the Collection of Survey Data on Victimization.* Lausanne: Université de Lausanne.

Alvazzi del Frate, A. (2004). "The International Crime Business Survey: Findings from Nine Central-Eastern European Cities." *European Journal on Criminal Policy and Research* 10(2–3): 137–161.

Archer, D., and R. Gartner. (1984). *Violence and Crime in Cross-National Perspective.* New Haven, CT: Yale University Press.

Aromaa, K., and M. Heiskanen, eds. (2008). *Crime and Criminal Justice Systems in Europe and North America 1995–2004. Publication 55.* Helsinki, Finland: European Institute for Crime Prevention and Control, Affiliated with the United Nations (HEUNI).

Barak, G., ed. (2000). *Crime and Crime Control: A Global View.* Westport, CT: Greenwood Press.

Bayley, D.H. (2006). *Changing the Guard: Developing Democratic Police Abroad.* New York: Oxford University Press.

Beirne, P., and D. Nelken. (1997). *Issues in Comparative Criminology.* Sudbury, MA: Dartmouth.

Bennett, R.R. (1997a). "Excessive Force: A Comparative Study of Police in the Caribbean." *Justice Quarterly* 14: 651–686.

Bennett, R.R. (1997b). "The Determinants of Job Satisfaction among Police Constables: A Comparative Study in Three Developing Nations." *Justice Quarterly* 14: 295–323.

Bennett, R.R. (2004). "Comparative Criminology and Criminal Justice Research: The State of Our Knowledge." *Justice Quarterly* 21: 1–21.

Botchkovar, E.V., C.R. Tittle, and O. Antonaccio. (2009). "General Strain Theory: Additional Evidence Using Cross-Cultural Data." *Criminology* 47(1): 131–165.

Caldwell. J., ed. (1994). *Networking and AIDS in Sub-Saharan Africa: Behavioral Research and the Social Context,* pp. 101–116. Canberra: Australian National Universities.

Care, Jennifer, Tess Newton, and Don Paterson. (1999). *Introduction to South Pacific Law.* London: Cavendish.

Chevigny, P. (1995). *Edge of the Knife: Police Violence in the Americas.* New York: Free Press.

Dalgleish, D. (2005). "Pre-Colonial Criminal Justice in West Africa: Eurocentric Thought versus Africentric Evidence." *African Journal of Criminology and Justice Studies* 1(1): 155–169.

Delgrande, N., and M.F. Aebi. (2009). "European Prisons: Stability or Change?" *Criminology in Europe: Newsletter of the European Society of Criminology* 8(3): 1, 17–19.

European Journal of Criminology. Various issues providing country profiles.

European Journal on Criminal Policy and Research, in particular those on crime trends in Western and Eastern European Countries (Vol. 10[2–3], 2004) and prosecution and diversion within criminal justice systems in Europe (Vol. 14[2–3], 2008).

Fairchild, Erika, and Harry Dammer. (2001). *Comparative Criminal Justice Systems.* 2nd ed. Belmont, CA: Wadsworth.

Fiala, R., and G. LaFree. (1988). "Cross-National Determinants of Child Homicide." *American Sociological Review* 53: 432–445.

Findlay, Mark. (2000). *Criminal Laws of the South Pacific.* Suva: University of the South Pacific.

Friedrichs, D. (2007). "Transnational Crime and Global Criminology: Definitional, Typological, and Contextual Conundrums." *Social Justice* 34(2): 4–18.

Howard, G.J., G. Newman, and W.A. Pridemore. (2000). "Theory, Method, and Data in Comparative Criminology" (excerpted from *Measurement and Analysis of Crime and Justice. Criminal Justice 2000*) 4: 139–211.

International Journal of Comparative and Applied Criminal Justice. Published and copyrighted by the School of Criminal Justice, Michigan State University. ISSN 0192–4036.

Johnson, H., N. Ollus, and S. Nevala. (2007). *Violence against Women: An International Perspective.* New York: Springer.

Joireman, Sandra F. (2004). "Colonization and the Rule of Law: Comparing the Effectiveness of Common Law and Civil Law Countries." *Constitutional Political Economy* 15: 315–338.

Junger-Tas, J., I. Haen Marshall, and D. Ribeaud. (2003). *Delinquency in an International Perspective: The International Self-Report Delinquency Study.* The Hague, The Netherlands: Kugler Publications.

Karstedt, S. (2001). "Comparing Cultures, Comparing Crime: Challenges, Prospects and Problems for a Global Criminology." *Crime, Law, and Social Change* 36(3): 285–308.

Karstedt, S., and G. LaFree. (2006). "Democracy, Crime, and Justice." *Annals of the American Academy of Political and Social Science* 605: 6–23.

Kury, H., ed. (2001). *International Comparison of Crime and Victimization: The ICVS.* Ontario, Canada: de Sitter Publications.

Kyle, D., and R. Koslowski. (2001). *Global Human Smuggling: Comparative Perspectives.* Baltimore, MD: Johns Hopkins University Press.

Larsen, N., and R. Smandych, eds. *Global Criminology and Criminal Justice: Current Issues and Perspectives.* Peterborough, Ontario: Broadview Press.

Lee, M.R., and T. Earnest. (2003). "Perceived Community Cohesion and Perceived Risk of Victimization: A Cross-National Study." *Justice Quarterly* 20: 131–157.

Lo, Stefan H.C., Ian Dobinson, and Wing Hong Chui. "Sentencing for Drug Offences in Hong Kong: An Overview." *Hong Kong Law Journal* 34 (2005): 13–46.

Mawby, R., ed. (1996). *Policing across the World,* pp. 3–12. London: Routledge.

Messner, S. F., and Richard R. Rosenfeld. (2007). *Crime and the American Dream.* 4th ed. Belmont, CA: Thomson Wadsworth.

Nalla, M.K. (2009) "Democratic Policing: A Comparison of Police Officers' Perceptions of Their Role and Functions in Transitional Societies." *Journal of Criminal Justice and Security* 11(4): 520–535.

Nalla, M.K., and J. Johnson. (2009). "Are Police and Security Personnel Warming up to Each Other? A Comparison of Officer's Attitudes in Developed, Emerging, and Transitional Economies." *Policing: An International Journal of Police Strategies and Management* 32(3): 508–525.

National Institute of Justice, Office of Justice Programs, U.S. Department of Justice: http://www.ncjrs.gov/criminal_justice2000/vol4_2000.html.

Neapolitan, J.L. (1997). *Cross-National Crime: A Research Review and Sourcebook.* Westport, CT: Greenwood Press.

Newburn, T., and R. Sparks. (2004). *Criminal Justice and Political Cultures: National and International Dimensions of Crime Control.* Devon, UK: Willan.

Newman, Graeme R. (1999). *Global Report on Crime and Justice.* New York: United Nations Office of Drug Control and Crime Prevention.

Newman, Graeme R. (2008). *Comparative Deviance: Perception and Law in Six Cultures.* Reprinted with new introduction. Piscataway, NJ: Transaction Press.

Owomero, B. (1987). "Crime Rates and Development in Africa: Empirical Analysis of Data from Nigeria, Kenya, and Tanzania." *Indian Journal of Criminology* 15: 107–120.

Pridemore, W.A. (2008). "A Methodological Addition to the Cross-National Empirical Literature on Social Structure and Homicide: A First Test of the Poverty-Homicide Thesis." *Criminology* 46: 133–154.

Rafter, N.H., and F. Heidensohn. (1995). *International Feminist Perspective in Criminology.* Buckingham, UK: Open University Press.

Reichel, P.L. (2004). *Comparative Criminal Justice Systems: A Topical Approach.* Upper Saddle River, NJ: Prentice Hall.

Reichel, Philip L. (2008). *Comparative Criminal Justice Systems.* Upper Saddle River, NJ: Prentice Hall.

Robert, P., ed. (2009a). *Comparing Crime Data in Europe: Official Crime Statistics and Survey Based Data.* Brussels: VUBPRESS Brussels University Press.

Robert, P., ed. (2009b). *Evaluating Safety and Crime Prevention Policies in Europe.* Brussels: VUBPRESS Brussels University Press.

Savage, J., R.R. Bennett, and M. Danner. (2008). "Economic Assistance and Crime: A Cross-National Investigation." *European Journal of Criminology* 5: 217–238.

Schwabach, Aaron. (2003. Rev. 2006). *Non-Western Philosophies of Law.* In *Encyclopedia of Life Support Systems (EOLSS),* edited by Aaron Schwabach and Arthur John Cockfield, topic 6.31.1. Developed under the Auspices of UNESCO. Oxford: Eolss: http://www.eolss.net.

Sheptycki, J., and A. Wardak, eds. (2005). *Transnational and Comparative Criminology*. London: Glasshouse.

Stamatel, Janet P. (2006). "Incorporating Socio-Historical Context and Temporal Variation into Quantitative Cross-National Criminology." *International Journal of Comparative and Applied Criminal Justice* 30(2): 177–208.

Stamatel, Janet P. (2009a). "Correlates of National-Level Homicide Variation in Post-Communist East-Central Europe." *Social Forces* 87(3), 1423–1448.

Stamatel, Janet P. (2009b). "Contributions of Cross-National Research at the Beginning of the 21st Century." In *Handbook on Criminology and Deviance,* edited by Marvin Krohn, Alan Lizotte, and Gina Penly-Hall, 3–18. New York: Springer Science + Business Media.

Stamatel, Janet P. (guest editor). (2009, December). "New Methodological Directions for International and Comparative Criminology." *International Journal of Comparative and Applied Criminal Justice* 33 (2): 167.

Sung, Hung-En. (2004a). "Democracy and Organized Crime: Evidence from Fifty-Nine Countries." *Security Journal* 17(4): 21–34.

Sung, Hung-En. (2004b). "State Failure, Economic Failure, and Predatory Organized Crime." *Journal of Research in Crime and Delinquency* 41(2): 111–129.

Sung, Hung-En. (2006a). "Democracy and Criminal Justice in Comparative Perspective: From Crime Control to Due Process." *The Annals of the American Academy of Political and Social Science* 605(1): 311–337.

Sung, Hung-En. (2006b). "Structural Determinants of Police Effectiveness in Market Democracies." *Police Quarterly* 9(1): 3–19.

Sung, Hung-En, and Jack Reed. (2006). "Migration and Crime in Europe." In *Crime and Immigration,* edited by Joshua Freilich Graeme R. Newman, 95–120. Hampshire, UK: Ashgate.

Terrill, Richard J. (2009). *World Criminal Justice System: A Survey.* 7th ed. Southington, CT: Anderson.

Uildriks, N. (2009). *Policing Insecurity: Police Reform, Security and Human Rights in Latin America.* Lanham, MD: Lexington Books.

United Nations Office on Drugs and Crime. (2005). *Crime and Development in Africa.* Vienna, Austria: United Nations: http://www.unodc.org/pdf/African_report.pdf.

United Nations Office on Drugs and Crime. (2008). *Crime and Its Impact on the Balkans and Affected Countries.* Vienna, Austria: United Nations: http://www.unodc.org/documents/data-and-analysis/Balkan_study.pdf.

United Nations Office on Drugs and Crime and the Latin America and the Caribbean Region of the World Bank. (2007). *Crime, Violence, and Development: Trends, Costs, and Policy Options in the Caribbean.* Vienna, Austria: United Nations: http://www.unodc.org/pdf/research/Cr_and_Vio_Car_E.pdf.

Van Dijk, Jan. (2008). *The World of Crime: Breaking the Silence of Security, Justice, and Development across the World.* Thousand Oaks, CA: Sage.

Van Dijk, J., J. Kesteren, and P. Smit. (2007). *Criminal Victimisation in International Perspective: Key Findings from the 2004–2005 ICVS and EU ICS.* WODC: http://www.nicis.nl/kenniscentrum/binaries/nicis/bulk/onderzoek/2008/2/3/icvs2004_05report.pdf.

Weitekamp, E. G. M., and H. Kerner. (1994). *Cross-National Longitudinal Research on Human Development and Criminal Behavior.* Dordrecht, Netherlands: Kluwer Academic.

Zauberman, R., ed. (2009a). *Self-Reported Crime and Deviance Studies in Europe.* Brussels: VUBPRESS Brussels University Press.

Zauberman, R., ed. (2009b). *Victimization and Insecurity in Europe.* Brussels: VUBPRESS Brussels University Press.

Zimring, Franklin E., and David T. Johnson. (2008). "Law, Society, and Capital Punishment in Asia." *Punishment and Society* 10(2): 103–115.

Web Sites

BBC News Country Profiles: http://news.bbc.co.uk/2/hi/country_profiles/default.stm. This site is very good for background information on history, geography, and politics. It's also good for links to internal national sites and news media sites.

Cecil Greek's Criminal Justice Resources on International Criminal Justice: http://www.criminology.fsu.edu/p/cjl-world.php. There is a good variety of sources here, from common to the unusual, such as, for example, South Africa's Crime Mysteries.

CIA World Factbook: https://www.cia.gov/library/publications/the-world-factbook/index.html. The information in this book tends to be regurgitated in many Web sites, but it contains useful background information and is updated annually. Sometimes there are crime data, but usually descriptive, without statistics.

Council of Europe Annual Penal Statistics: www.coe.int/prison. Detailed data on prisons in Europe since 1983 can be found here.

The Council of Europe, European Commission for the Efficiency of Justice. (2008): *Evaluation of European Judicial Systems:* http://www.coe.int/t/dghl/cooperation/cepej/evaluation/default_en.asp.

Country Report of the Justice Studies Center of the Americas: http://www.cejamericas.org. This research and advocacy group publishes online country-specific analysis of legal systems and their operations in Latin America.

The Economist: http://www.economist.com/countries/index.cfm. This Web site offers much economic, historical, and political information on many countries and often useful information in its city guides.

European Society of Criminology: http://www.esc-eurocrim.org. This site provides a lot of relevant information on crime and punishment in Europe, including the programs of the annual conferences.

European Sourcebook of Crime and Criminal Justice Statistics: www.europeansourcebook.org. This site provides databases on police, prosecution, conviction, and correctional statistics since 1990 as well as some data on victimization.

International Centre for Prison Studies: http://www.kcl.ac.uk/depsta/rel/icps/home.html. This is a good source for international prison statistics.

International Court of Justice: http://www.icj-cij.org/.

Library of Congress Area Studies: http://www.loc.gov/rr/.

Nationmaster: http://www.nationmaster.com/index.php. This interesting interactive site allows comparative statistics of countries on a wide range of topics, including criminal justice. However, the crime statistics tend to be outdated.

The New York Times Countries and Territories: http://topics.nytimes.com/topics/news/international/countriesandterritories/index.html. These pages contain both general background information and links to recent media stories.

United Nations Interregional Crime and Justice Research Institute (UNICRI): http://www.unicri.it/wwd/analysis/icvs/data.php. A wide variety of information, particularly data for many countries participating in the International Crime Victim Survey (ICVS), is available.

United Nations Office on Drugs and Crime: http://www.unodc.org/. This site contains a wealth of information on crime, with extensive databases of crime statistics from the UN Surveys of Crime and Criminal Justice Systems.

U.S. Library of Congress Country Studies: http://lcweb2.loc.gov/frd/cs/. These are much more detailed than the usual country profiles, such as the CIA Factbook.

U.S. National Institute of Justice International Center: http://www.ojp.usdoj.gov/nij/international/. This site offers a variety of reports, articles, and descriptions of transnational and international crime and justice.

Wikipedia: http://wikipedia.org/. There is much information on countries, including interesting descriptions of crime and criminal justice issues. One has to be careful of the sources, but often there are links that lead to useful and reasonable resources. This is particularly good for tracking down internal national news media Web sites (i.e., local newspapers and TV stations) that almost always have news on local crimes.

World Criminal Justice Library Network: http://andromeda.rutgers.edu/~wcjlen/WCJ/mainpages/statres.htm. This site contains excellent statistical data from 80 countries. Internal national publications are usually the source.

World Factbook of Criminal Justice Systems. U.S. NIJ. Bureau of Justice Statistics: http://bjs.ojp.usdoj.gov/index.cfm?ty=pbdetail&iid=1435.

About the Editors and Contributors

General Editor

Graeme R. Newman is a distinguished teaching professor at the School of Criminal Justice, University at Albany, and the associate director of the Center for Problem-Oriented Policing. He has advised the United Nations on crime and justice issues over many years and in 1990 established the United Nations Crime and Justice Information Network.

Volume 2 Editors

Janet P. Stamatel is an assistant professor in the School of Criminal Justice and the Department of Informatics at the State University of New York at Albany. She received her PhD in sociology from the University of Chicago. Her research interests include cross-national crime comparisons, the consequences of macro-level social changes, and information use in criminal justice.

Hung-En Sung, PhD, is an associate professor of criminal justice at John Jay College of Criminal Justice. His scholarly work revolves round drug control policy and comparative analysis of crime and justice.

Volume 2 Contributors

Cynthia Barnett-Ryan is a survey statistician with the Federal Bureau of Investigation (FBI). In her work with the FBI, she is responsible for conducting research for the criminal justice and intelligence communities. Views in this entry are those of the author and do not necessarily reflect the views of the FBI or the U.S. Department of Justice.

Christopher Birkbeck, PhD, is a reader in criminology at the School of English, Sociology, Politics and Contemporary History, University of Salford (Manchester, United Kingdom). Dr. Birkbeck has published articles in Spanish and English on a variety of criminological topics, which currently include the use of force by the police, penal trajectories, and Venezuelan criminology.

Marie-Eve Boudreau is a PhD student at the School of Criminology, Université de Montréal. Her main area of research is the judicial treatment of spousal violence cases.

Christopher M. Bzduch graduated from the State University of New York at Albany with a BA in criminal justice in May 2009. He works as a criminal investigator for the New York State Office of Tax Enforcement: Petroleum, Alcohol, and Tobacco Bureau.

Rodolfo Calderón, PhD, is an associate professor of sociology at the University of Costa Rica. He is currently working on a book titled *Transgressors and Globalization: A Sociological Study of Crime in Costa Rica.*

Milton Castelen is an attorney practicing both criminal and civil law and a member of the National Bar Association. He has taught at the COVAB—the nursing school of Suriname—and at the training institute for health care workers for the Surinamese hinterland.

Jennifer L. Christian, PhD is an assistant professor at California Lutheran University in the departments of criminal justice and legal studies and sociology. Currently, she is working on several manuscripts from her dissertation on the intersection of public opinion, media, and elite discourse on health and crime policy.

Andrew Davies is a doctoral student at the School of Criminal Justice at the State University of New York at Albany. He has received master's degrees from SUNY Albany and Oxford University in related fields. His interests are in state criminal justice policy making and the psychology of victimization.

Anne-Laure Del Cerro, a native of Paris, France, works as a crime intelligence analyst at the John F. Finn Institute for Public Safety in Albany, New York. She is interested in the evaluation of international criminal justice systems as well as law enforcement agencies. She obtained her BA in 2007 from the State University of New York at Albany with Valedictorian Award.

Jo-Ann Della Giustina, JD, PhD, is an assistant professor of criminal justice and the director of the Prison and Jail Initiative at Bridgewater State College. She is an expert in intimate-partner femicide, and her areas of research interest include women and crime, domestic violence, community issues and crime, search and seizure law, and media and the law.

Ramesh Deosaran is a professor emeritus of criminology and social psychology and is currently program professor at the University of Trinidad and Tobago. He has published more than 400 scholarly papers and journal articles and is author or editor of 14 books and research monographs. The research assistance of Ian Ramdhanie (BSc, MSc) is gratefully acknowledged by the author.

Clarissa F. Dias is a doctoral student in the department of political science at Georgia State University. She is a native of Brazil, where she received her law degree. Dias also holds a master's degree in criminal justice from Georgia State University.

Traqina Emeka, PhD, is an assistant professor of criminal justice at the University of Houston Downtown. Professor Emeka has researched and published in the areas of juvenile delinquency, health issues of female inmates, and adult certification of juveniles.

Robert B. Fletcher III received his bachelor's degree in criminal justice at the State University of New York at Albany in 2009. He is currently working on his master's degree from the same institution.

Yolande C. Forde is a criminologist and the director of Global Consulting Services (ycforde@caribsurf.com). She specializes in policy-directed research and policy initiatives related to border security, transnational organized crime, crime reduction strategies, correctional reform, and legal and judicial reform in the Caribbean region. She provides technical assistance to international development agencies (IDB, World Bank, etc.) and to regional governments in a number of areas within her professional expertise.

Jessica Gentile received her master's in criminal justice at the State University of New York at Albany. She currently works at a law firm that specializes in criminal defense, and she plans on pursuing a PhD in criminal justice.

Eduardo González is a judge in the Republic of Costa Rica. He has also worked for several years at the Judicial School of the Poder Judicial in Costa Rica. His research interests focus on public policies regarding crime prosecution as well as the functioning of justice administration.

Laurie Gould is an assistant professor at the University of Texas at Arlington in the criminology and criminal justice department. She has published on a variety of topics, including the use of strategic planning by state correctional agencies and the availability of jail visitation information.

Anna Gustafson holds a Bachelor of Law degree from Abo Akademi University in Finland. She is working towards a master's degree in law and is currently working at the district court of Parainen.

Lystra Hagley-Dickinson (BSc, Hons; MSc; PhD) is a senior lecturer in criminology, the research and enterprise lead for the Department of Social Sciences, and an associate of the research institute of Children Childhood and Youth (CCY) at the University of Northampton. Born in Trinidad and Tobago, she has worked and published in the Caribbean and has pursued careers in government, the European Union, and the community and voluntary sectors.

Frank Hemming received his bachelor's and master's degrees in criminal justice from the State University of New York at Albany. His contribution is dedicated to his father for his unending support, advice, and love.

L. Daisy Henderson, a native of Dominica, is a doctoral candidate in the Department of Sociology, State University of New York at Buffalo. Her research focuses on race and ethnicity, family, and immigration.

Amilcar Herbert is a graduate student at John Jay College of Criminal Justice. Prior to migrating to America in 2001, Mr. Herbert had served for nine years in the Trinidad and Tobago Police Service as a criminal investigator, close protection specialist, and training school instructor.

Hung-En Sung, PhD, is an associate professor at John Jay College of Criminal Justice. He has published extensively about substance abuse among offenders and comparative criminal justice.

Gayle Iles is an assistant professor of criminal justice at the University of Tennessee–Chattanooga. Her research interests include sentencing disparities and international comparative criminal justice systems.

Janice Joseph, PhD, is a professor in the criminal justice program at Richard Stockton College of New Jersey. She is also the editor of the *Journal of Ethnicity in Criminal Justice* and serves on the editorial boards of several criminal justice journals. She has published books and numerous articles on delinquency, gangs, domestic violence, stalking, sexual harassment, and minorities and crime.

Anthony LaRose, PhD, is an associate professor of criminology and criminal justice at the University of Tampa. Dr. LaRose was a 2004 Fulbright Scholar, and his research background includes police value systems, ethics in the criminal justice system, and comparative studies of American and Mexican legal systems.

Glendene Lemard, PhD, is a research assistant professor at the University of Massachusetts, Amherst. Her areas of specialization are global health, international development, and violence prevention in developing countries.

Giza Lopes is a PhD student at the School of Criminal Justice, State University of New York at Albany, and assistant editor at the *Sourcebook of Criminal Justice Statistics*.

Erin Maloney is a senior honors student at the University of Tampa. She has won numerous academic scholarships, and her research focus is on domestic and dating violence in Latin America.

Jon'a Meyer is an associate professor of criminology and director of the criminal justice program at Rutgers University, Camden, New Jersey. She received her PhD in social ecology at University of California–Irvine. She has published on many topics, including Native American legal systems, restorative justice, sentencing, and criminal courts.

Raymond Michalowski is Arizona Regents' Professor of criminal justice at Northern Arizona University. He has published many books and articles on criminological theory; international human rights; immigration and border policy; social justice; and corporate, environmental, and political crime.

Alfredo Montalvo-Barbot is an associate professor of sociology and criminology at Emporia State University, Emporia, Kansas. He has conducted research on crime in Puerto Rico and on the constitutional development of Puerto Rico.

Orlando Munoz-Neira is a Colombian attorney licensed to practice law in the State of New York. He holds an LLM degree from the University of Virginia. Currently, he is the manager of a justice program of an international cooperation agency in Colombia. His opinions in this article are his own and do not represent the opinions of his current or prior employers.

Angela Marcela Navarro received her master's degree in criminal justice from John Jay College of Criminal Justice. She has participated in studies on the involvement of undocumented immigrants with in American criminal justice system and published on the reentry process of immigrants who have been deported to their native countries after serving time in U.S. prisons. Navarro is currently pursuing her law degree from the Law School of the City University of New York.

Barbara J. Nowak is an associate professor of social work at Albany State University in Albany, Georgia. Her research focus is on crime, delinquency, and international social problems.

Marc Ouimet received his PhD in criminal justice from Rutgers University in 1990. He is now full professor at the School of Criminology, Université de Montréal. He teaches courses in crime analysis, delinquency theories, and statistics. His main area of research is the analysis of crime rates across time and space.

Matthew Pate is a doctoral candidate in the School of Criminal Justice at the State University of New York at Albany. He has published on topics as varied as the Alger Hiss affair, court review of search and seizure practices, and Neighborhood Watch program evaluation.

Neelie Pérez Santiago is a research professor at the Instituto de Ciencias Penales of the Universidad Central de Venezuela. Professor Pérez Santiago has researched on sentence remissions and is an expert in the Venezuelan criminal justice system.

Wayne J. Pitts, PhD, is an assistant professor of criminal justice at the University of Memphis. Professor Pitts holds a doctoral degree from the University of Mexico, and his research interests revolves around immigration, occupational stress for law enforcement, sex offender supervision, substance abuse and crime, and research methods.

Nataly Ponce Chauca is a Peruvian attorney with a master's degree in Latin American studies. She works as a researcher at the Justice Studies Center of the Americas, in Santiago, Chile, and specializes in crime prevention, public safety, and human rights issues.

Lee E. Ross, PhD, is an associate professor in the Department of Criminal Justice and Legal Studies at the University of Central Florida. He has published in a variety of academic journals, including *Justice Quarterly, Journal of Criminal Justice, Journal of Crime and Justice, Journal of Criminal Justice Education,* and *Sociological Spectrum,* among others.

Vincenzo A. Sainato, PhD, is assistant professor of criminal justice at Loyola University–New Orleans. His research crosses a wide spectrum of subject areas, including economic development and crime, technology and criminal justice, critical incident analysis, crime prevention, and cybercrime.

Vanessa Schrader graduated from the State University of New York at Albany in May 2010 with a BA in criminal justice and a BA in psychology. She will be pursue an MS in accounting at the State University of New York at Albany. She has an interest in forensic accounting.

Ursula Smartt is a consultant specializing in comparative criminal law and criminal justice systems and media law. She has been an independent international prison researcher and penal policy adviser to a number of governments for more than 20 years and has published widely in this field.

Peter K. B. St. Jean, a native of Dominica, is an assistant professor in the Department of Sociology at the State University of New York at Buffalo. His research focuses on crime, violence, cities, family, Caribbean Studies, and quality of life.

David Achanfuo Yeboah is manager of the Health Statistics Centre, Queensland Health, Brisbane, Australia. A Commonwealth scholar and United Nations fellow, Dr. Yeboah has been a senior fellow at the University of the West Indies, Barbados, and an associate professor at Deakin University, Australia, and Zayed University, United Arab Emirates.

Claudia Zambrana is a doctoral candidate in criminology at the University of Montreal. She is also a research assistant at the Centre of International and Comparative Criminology, University of Montreal. Zambrana has researched the impact of globalization on drugs and crime and drug laws in Bolivia.

Index

Boldface numbers refer to volume numbers. A key appears on all verso pages.

1: Africa and the Middle East
2: The Americas
3: Asia and Pacific
4: Europe

1: Africa and the Middle East **2:** The Americas **3:** Asia and Pacific **4:** Europe

1: Africa and the Middle East **2:** The Americas **3:** Asia and Pacific **4:** Europe

1: Africa and the Middle East **2:** The Americas **3:** Asia and Pacific **4:** Europe

1: Africa and the Middle East
2: The Americas
3: Asia and Pacific
4: Europe

1: Africa and the Middle East
2: The Americas
3: Asia and Pacific
4: Europe

1: Africa and the Middle East
2: The Americas
3: Asia and Pacific
4: Europe

1: Africa and the Middle East
2: The Americas
3: Asia and Pacific
4: Europe

1: Africa and the Middle East
2: The Americas
3: Asia and Pacific
4: Europe

1: Africa and the Middle East
2: The Americas
3: Asia and Pacific
4: Europe

1: Africa and the Middle East
2: The Americas
3: Asia and Pacific
4: Europe

1: Africa and the Middle East **2:** The Americas **3:** Asia and Pacific **4:** Europe

1: Africa and the Middle East
2: The Americas
3: Asia and Pacific
4: Europe

Crime and Punishment around the World

Crime and Punishment around the World

ASIA AND PACIFIC

Volume 3

DORIS C. CHU, VOLUME EDITOR
GRAEME R. NEWMAN, GENERAL EDITOR

ABC-CLIO

Santa Barbara, California • Denver, Colorado • Oxford, England

Copyright 2010 by Doris C. Chu, Volume Editor

Graeme R. Newman, General Editor

All rights reserved. No part of this publication may be reproduced, stored in a retrieval system, or transmitted, in any form or by any means, electronic, mechanical, photocopying, recording, or otherwise, except for the inclusion of brief quotations in a review, without prior permission in writing from the publisher.

Library of Congress Cataloging-in-Publication Data

Crime and punishment around the world.
p. cm.
Includes bibliographical references and index.
ISBN 978-0-313-35133-4 (set : alk. paper) — ISBN 978-0-313-35134-1 (set ebook) — ISBN 978-0-313-35135-8 (vol. 1 : alk. paper) — ISBN 978-0-313-35136-5 (vol. 1 ebook) — ISBN 978-0-313-35137-2 (vol. 2 : alk. paper) — ISBN 978-0-313-35138-9 (vol. 2 ebook) — ISBN 978-0-313-35139-6 (vol. 3 : alk. paper) — ISBN 978-0-313-35140-2 (vol. 3 ebook) — ISBN 978-0-313-35141-9 (vol. 4 : alk. paper) — ISBN 978-0-313-35142-6 (vol. 4 ebook)
1. Crime. 2. Punishment. 3. Criminal justice, Administration of.
HV6025.C7115 2010
364—dc22 2010021159

ISBN (set): 978-0-313-35133-4
EISBN (set): 978-0-313-35134-1

14 13 12 11 10 1 2 3 4 5

This book is also available on the World Wide Web as an eBook.
Visit www.abc-clio.com for details.

ABC-CLIO, LLC
130 Cremona Drive, P.O. Box 1911
Santa Barbara, California 93116-1911

This book is printed on acid-free paper ∞

Manufactured in the United States of America

This volume set is dedicated to the memory of
Ali Sabeeh of Omara, Iraq, who, while preparing the entry on Iraq,
was kidnapped, tortured, and killed in October 2007

Editorial Advisory Board

Adam Bouloukos, Director of Outreach and Partnerships, UNOPS, Copenhagen, Denmark

Ronald V. Clarke, University Professor, Rutgers University

Adam Graycar, Professor, Australian National University

Martin Killias, Professor, University of Zurich

Jeremy Travis, President, John Jay College of Criminal Justice

Contents

Acknowledgments

The contribution made by the volume editors to this project has been inestimable. A project of this magnitude could not have been achieved without their unceasing efforts to find contributors for large and small countries alike, to manage their contributors' contributions, and to edit them into the style and format required by a publication of this type. They helped overcome a number of crises we met along the way. For this and for their always being on the receiving end of my constant e-mails, I express my sincere appreciation. I thank especially Janet Stamatel for producing the world and regional maps from my sometimes less than adequate databases.

Many authors have contributed to these volumes. Without them, of course, this project would not have been possible. The volume editors and I express our great admiration to our contributors and appreciation for their tolerance of our editorial demands, which oftentimes must have seemed unreasonable. We apologize if your chapter ended up a little shorter than you had wanted. We bear full responsibility for any misconceptions that may have occurred as a result of our at-times heavy editorial hand.

Finally, we thank the Editorial Advisory Board members for being there when we needed them.

—Graeme R. Newman
Albany, NY
December 31, 2009

General Introduction

We humans are fascinated by the diversity of cultures, climates, landscapes, and peoples. It is part of our deep human heritage that we have never been able to stay at home. Since the beginning of human time, our haplogroups have migrated far and wide, stumbling on new fauna and evolving with them, adapting to cold, hot, wet, and dry seasons and climates. Along the way, we have constructed societies and civilizations that have come and gone, none reaching perfection; each having tried its own solutions to the problem of order; each constructing rules, laws, customs, and ways of dealing with those who, for whatever reason, have broken with the sacred commandments of order. Somewhere along the way, no matter what the civilization or society, the idea of justice emerged, perhaps independently of the need for order and, indeed, every now and again in opposition to order. But whatever order's relationship to justice, one thing is certain: order is necessary for societies to survive. And embedded in this necessity is the inevitability that individuals will break laws, rules, and customs and will, as a matter of logic (and justice), be punished for it.

So law (so-called if it is written) and custom (embodying law and rules that may not be written but that are "practiced" and conveyed orally) is universal in all known societies. They are part of the "civilizing" process, which seeks to hold in check the tendency of humans to devour each other. It is true that great thinkers, philosophers, and even scientists have insisted—in the face of the overwhelming evidence of history that stands against them—that humans, if only given a chance, can or could work together for their common good without being coerced to do so. But we know of no society anywhere in which this utopian (if it is utopian) conception of human nature has produced a society without laws or customs and their concomitant punishments. And surely humans have had plenty of chances to construct such utopian societies. Yet each time they try, order takes over, because we know that individuals only grudgingly curb their own desires. They do not like the imposition of order, but they know that they cannot survive without it and its accoutrements. Or at least, we may say that life is much more comfortable if one gives into almost any kind of order. This observation probably applies even to the worst of tyrannical orders, for it is easier to remain in submission than it is to rise up and overthrow a very powerful authority. The 18th-century enlightenment thinkers upon whose ideas much of the world's criminal justice systems are based (whether civil or common) were clearly of the opinion that punishment was a necessary evil, a price paid for the

comfort of living in an ordered society. Its universality certainly attests to the truth of this assertion.

It should come as no surprise, therefore, that getting reliable information about such a touchy subject—essentially how a society, nation, or culture maintains order in the face of a populace that may secretly or even openly resent its imposition—is very difficult. Nations can be very secretive about their crime rates and their punishments, not to mention their procedures for finding guilt and their manner of interrogating suspects. Various organizations have set themselves up to monitor the most egregious violations of individuals in the name of order, such as Human Rights Watch and Amnesty International, but there is a far larger part of the maintenance of order and the processing of lawbreakers by nations and regional governments that also needs constant scrutiny. Violations of human rights in the name of order may easily be hidden inside the bureaucratic inertia and practices of even the most "enlightened" societies. To admit to having a very high rate of murder or incarceration—perhaps one of the highest—of its citizens is not something of which a nation can be especially proud. Such statistics say something about that nation, though what that something is, unfortunately, can be easily misinterpreted. For example, some countries may be criticized for having very high imprisonment rates, but their retort may be that this is because they have very high crime rates, to which it may be asked, but why do you have such high crime rates? The reply may be, "Because we have strict laws that are strictly enforced, which is for the good of our citizens, who are kept safer than those in other countries whose administration of criminal justice is too lax." Provided here is just a taste of the controversies and disagreements concerning the differing levels of crime and punishment in diverse countries, as well as the puzzling relationship or lack thereof between prison rates and crime rates. The riddle can be stated thus: more punishment should reduce crime, but more crime requires more punishment.

One would think that the costs in public relations to a nation would be far too high to allow for the publication of crime and punishment statistics. So it is an amazing achievement that the United Nations World Crime Surveys, whose mission is to collect the official statistics on crime and justice from member nations, have shown steady and significant increases in the number of countries submitting their statistics since they were first collected in the 1970s. From a handful of countries in the beginning, the number providing crime and punishment statistics had grown to about 50 as of 2005. That is the positive spin. In fact, this is only 50 out of 190 member UN nations, and there are signs of decreasing reporting by countries in recent years, according to Jan Van Dijk, author of *The World of Crime* and former UN expert on international crime and justice.

Although it is true that nations are reticent to make public their crime and punishment statistics for reasons of public image, there are many technical difficulties in making comparisons of officially collected crime and justice statistics across countries. Many of these difficulties are serious, and *the reader is warned to use considerable caution in making such comparisons across countries*. These technical difficulties include the following:

- Different legal definitions of offenses make it difficult to compare specific offenses across nations.
- Different reporting and recording practices of the police who generally have first official contact with a crime make comparing statistics from one country to another unreliable without knowledge of these practices.
- Different legal systems may affect the finding of guilt, recording and classification of offenses, and recording of arrests and convictions.
- Inconsistent classifications of crime records and frequent changes over time make it difficult to compare trends in crime or punishment.
- Different bureaucracies and government departments within each nation that collate and publish crime and punishment statistics may produce different statistics. For example, city- or state-level collection of crime rates or prison rates may differ from collection at the federal level, as in the United States.
- Inadequate infrastructure for collecting and processing crime and justice reports, including information technology, may hinder the amount or accuracy of criminal justice data.
- Lack of professionally trained crime analysts and statisticians may limit the reliability and depth of statistical data available.
- Local events or conditions may inflate crime and punishment statistics, such as genocidal events that may or may not be recorded as murders.
- Changing government policies about making crime and justice statistics public may affect trends and the amount and type of data made available. There have been instances where countries have revealed crime and justice statistics to the United Nations, but not to their own citizens. The reverse is also true. There was a time, for example, when the Soviet Union routinely collected crime statistics for its internal use but officially denied to the United Nations that there was any crime at all in the Soviet Union, because there could be no crime in a true communist society.
- In large populous countries, there may be vast differences within those countries. For example, the levels of crime and punishment vary enormously throughout the United States; some states still retain the death penalty, and many do not. There may also be huge differences in amounts and kinds of crime between urban and rural regions. There may even be different legal systems operating within the same country, such as, for example, Quebec in Canada or the several customary, Islamic, and civil law systems operating in Timor-Leste.

If one must make comparisons—and most people are unable to resist it—the best way to overcome these pitfalls is to make sure that one knows as much as possible about the historical and social context within which the statistics are collected. *Crime and Punishment around the World* provides just that context. This encyclopedia describes in detail the crime and punishment practices of each country and, in some instances, specific regions. The four volumes offer a glimpse of the ways in which all the nations around the world try to solve the basic problem

they all face: what to do with those who break the law? They have all enacted either customary or written criminal laws. They have all inherited their criminal laws from their ancestors near and far, not infrequently from other nations that either usurped them or overtook them through migration. They have all developed procedures for the finding of guilt of the accused, and all, of course, follow up the finding of guilt with legislated or customary punishments. These are all essentially the product of their legal systems.

World Legal Systems

For more than 1,000 years, the Roman Empire encompassed just about all the region around the Mediterranean and stretched as far north as Great Britain. Law was probably its major weapon against the peoples it subdued, bringing with it order and a stable means of commerce. Its concepts would form much of the basis of canon law and eventually much of the civil law of Europe. Furthermore, much of the Islamic and customary law of the countries surrounding the south and east of the Mediterranean was deeply affected by Roman law because those peoples were also subjects of the Roman Empire at various times for over 1,000 years. Those countries of Europe that retained more of the Roman law and its procedures would later come to be known as "civil law" countries. Those European countries that managed to put aside Roman law came to be known as "common law" countries. And those of North Africa and the Far East retained Islamic and customary law systems.

Civil law systems account for over 50 percent of the world's legal systems, although many such systems are mixed with other legal systems because of local and historical circumstance. In fact, as a result of constant reforms, it is likely that there are no purely civil law systems left in the world. Most countries have incorporated various aspects of the adversarial system. The main characteristics of civil law systems are the following:

1. Systematically written legal codes are the prime source of authority in legal decisions and procedures.
2. Their procedures are often (though not entirely) based on what is sometimes called the "inquisitorial system"—reaching back to the days of the Roman Catholic Inquisition—in which the process of finding of guilt is conducted by a judge or magistrate who both investigates and conducts the final trial. These trials are usually, though not always, conducted before a magistrate or panel of magistrates.

Probably the prime examples of European civil law systems are those of France and Germany and, to some extent, Italy, which has recently incorporated aspects of the adversarial system.

Common law systems account for another 20 percent of the world's legal systems. These are commonly referred to as "adversarial systems" because the finding of guilt is not conducted by the magistrate who decides and investigates the case as in civil law; rather, a prosecutor (or sometimes an investigating police officer) investigates the case and prepares the case for a trial by judge and jury

(although juries are not always required). The two significant features of common law systems are the following:

1. Cases are decided based on precedent, which views previous cases and decisions as a cumulative wisdom and authority.
2. Cases are a courtroom drama in which the prosecutor is pitted against the defense.

It should be noted, however, that in modern legal systems of common law, there are legal codes that systematize the law, and these may or may not be based on the codification of past legal practice. In the United States, for example, every state, in addition to the federal system, has its own written code. Cases are decided, however, based not only on how well the offender's acts match the written code but also on the cases that came before it—that is, precedent. One sees this tradition played out in the U.S. Supreme Court, which arduously scrutinizes past decisions to conclude whether a particular case was decided correctly or not, in accordance with the supreme law of the land, the U.S. Constitution. The popular view that contrasts these two legal traditions is that civil law is focused more on finding a probably guilty person guilty, whereas common law is focused more on defending a possibly innocent person from a guilty verdict. Both systems do, however, adhere to the presumption of innocence of the accused until proven guilty. The most typical examples of common law systems are those of the United Kingdom, the United States, and Australia.

Islamic legal systems account for about 10 percent of the world's legal systems, although there are probably no purely Islamic systems anywhere in the world. This is because of the early Roman influence on all countries surrounding the Mediterranean and because of the imperialism of the West during the 16th through 20th centuries. In its pure form, the Islamic system of law follows the exact law of God, as interpreted by experts (Mullahs), deriving from the Koran, the Bible, and other sacred texts. Islamic law is often called sharia—the path to follow. Perhaps the most contrasting feature of Islamic law is that it is more a way to live one's life than a set of prohibitions laid down by a state authority as in Roman law and its progenitors. Thus, not only does it include prohibitions, some of which are set out in the Ten Commandments, but it also includes exhortations to lead a good life (e.g., love thy neighbor). No such positive exhortations are found in other Western legal traditions, whose defining principle is prohibition. The procedural rules of Islamic law are those of human reasoning and consensus. One of the problems that faces legal theorists in Islamic law is that there are many offenses that are not specifically covered in any of the sacred texts. For example, sodomy is not mentioned in the Koran or Sunna (another sacred text), but adultery is. So the judge may reason that the two offenses are similar and the punishments prescribed for one may apply to the other. In practice, however, many cases are decided also on custom and precedent, given that in many Islamic countries, tribal customs concerning redress of wrongs (e.g., feuding and vengeance) have developed alongside Islamic and other kinds of law. The majority of countries with Islamic legal systems therefore also have customary law as a major component, especially in dealing with day-to-day infractions. Finally, most Islamic law

countries also have a considerable dose of civil law, especially in the field of commerce, though it has been necessary even there for such countries to develop ways to get around the Islamic prohibition of usury, defined rather broadly.

Customary law is the law that has arisen through oral tradition among tribes and cultures where law is not written down but rather communicated across generations by tribal elders. Village or regional chieftains are usually, though not always, the main repositories of such legal wisdom, and the finding of guilt usually occurs within an informal meeting of interested parties. In many countries of Africa and southern Asia, these kinds of local meetings occur and settlements are reached based on the hearing of all sides of the complaints. Depending on the culture, shamans or others thought to hold special powers may be brought in as expert witnesses and sometimes as judges. However, the most important attribute of customary law is its specificity to the local region or village. These traditions can be very deep and resistant to change or imposition from outside influences. Perhaps a prime example in the 21st century is that of the tribal villages in the mountains of Pakistan and parts of Afghanistan that have defied state authority for hundreds of years. Instead, these tribal areas have their own chiefs and their own informal ways of settling infractions and disputes.

Socialist legal systems are those that have arisen on top of civil law systems, for the most part. Certainly this was the case in the Soviet Union and continues to be the case in Cuba and other communist countries, although China is perhaps an exception. Yet even there, the customary legal system was usurped by Western powers in the 19th century and abolished by the revolution of 1949. However, the emergence in the 1980s of China as an industrial and trading nation required that it develop a legal system that would make commerce possible and more efficient. The result has been that its legal system is based essentially on civil law, with criminal law that codifies edicts of the State and procedures that are largely reflective of the inquisitorial system.

Finally, although there are probably no countries that are purely of one or the other legal system, there are quite a number of countries whose legal systems are mixtures of some or all of the preceding. Many African and some South Asian countries are mixtures of customary, civil, common, and Islamic law. Such countries would include, for example, India, Afghanistan, and maybe Egypt.

How Does Your Country Measure Up?

Although for the reasons recounted earlier, comparing the crime and punishment of countries to each other is a very difficult procedure, it is nevertheless important to get a rough idea of how one country compares to the rest of the world. It is probably one of the main reasons people refer to world encyclopedias of any kind, to get a sense of how one fits in the universe.

To provide a very rough glimpse of how a country's crime and punishment compare to the rest of the world, we have provided a snapshot of some major indicators of crime and punishment for each country at the start of each country essay. We have chosen these indicators because they are readily available and offer a reasonably approximate way of ranking countries along a continuum. Of

the crime indicators, murder is chosen as probably the most reliable for making comparisons because its definition is roughly similar across nations, and in most cases, the statistics have been adjusted to fit the UN standard definition of murder for countries reporting their murder rates. Nevertheless, many countries do not report their murder rates. Prison rates are also reasonably reliable for making comparisons, although they too involve great technical difficulties in measurement, considering that the counting of inmates may occur on different days of the year, and a simple accounting on a particular day does not give any indication of the flow of prisoners in and out of the prison over a given period of time. The snapshot indicators provided for each country or region when available are as follow:

- *Type of Legal System*
- *Murder*—murders per 100,000 people
- *Burglary*—those victimized by burglaries per thousand people
- *Corruption*—levels of perceived corruption
- *Human Trafficking*—how much the country is doing to control human trafficking
- *Prison*—number of prisoners per 100,000 population
- *Death Penalty*—whether the country has the death penalty
- *Corporal Punishment*—whether corporal punishment is available to the criminal justice system

Legal System

The types of legal system were compiled from the United Nations *Global Report on Crime and Justice,* supplemented by information from individual country Web sites and from the University of Ottawa Civil Law Section Web site on World Legal Systems at http://www.droitcivil.uottawa.ca/world-legal-systems/eng-tableau.php.

Murder

These are officially reported statistics on murder supplied by countries to the United Nations World Crime Surveys, supplemented where necessary by individual country information plus homicide statistics from the World Health Organization. Most of the statistics were taken from the revised listing supplied by Jan Van Dijk in his book *The World of Crime,* in which he reported the average murder rates for 1998–2002, supplemented by more recent United Nations surveys. Additional data from INTERPOL and individual country sources, where available, sometimes for a slightly different period of years, were also included. However, such small differences should not matter because we know that murder rates are fairly stable over time. The countries are ranked from highest to lowest murder rate (murders per 100,000 people) and then divided into quartiles, with the middle two quartiles classified as "Medium" and the two outer quartiles labeled "High" and "Low." The world distribution of murder rates can be seen in Map 1, Murder around the World.

Burglary

Obtaining reliable rates of property crime, the most common of which is usually referred to as theft, is especially difficult when relying on officially recorded statistics because definitions and enforcement practices vary enormously across nations. We have therefore included measures of victimization of individuals by burglary. These measures are derived from the International Crime Victim Surveys (ICVS), which are interviews or questionnaires asking samples of a population whether they have been victims of particular offenses over a particular number of years (usually the past year). In this case, the samples were households, and the survey was conducted in many countries, although *limited only to urban populations*. Therefore, they do not, of course, represent the country or region as a whole, though they do, perhaps in the case of burglary, represent most of the population of a given country that there are, generally, many more households in urban settings than in rural settings. These data are taken from Van Dijk's *World of Crime.* Countries were ranked according to their burglary rates (number of victimizations reported per 1,000 people) using quartiles, divided into High, Medium, and Low, with Medium defined by the two middle quartiles.

Corruption

The ways in which crime and punishment are eventually perceived by the public and administered by the State are affected by the level of corruption in a particular country. We have therefore included a measure of corruption, a kind of crime that is neither a violent crime nor, strictly speaking, a property crime. Rather, it is a crime against justice itself. There is also the advantage that data on perceived corruption in countries are much more available, thanks to the source of our data, Transparency International at http://www.transparency.org/policy_research/surveys_indices/cpi. This Corruption Perception Index (CPI) is based on the ranking of "180 countries by their perceived levels of corruption, as determined by expert assessments and opinion surveys" according to Transparency International. We have taken these rankings, added some additional countries in some cases where they were not included in the survey, and then divided them into Low, Medium, and High, using quartiles once again.

Human Trafficking

This measure is taken from the U.S. Department of State three-tier listing of countries it classifies as making a strong effort to control human trafficking, making some effort, or making very little effort. The classifications are taken from the U.S. Department of State *Trafficking in Persons Report 2008,* found at http://www.state.gov/g/tip/rls/tiprpt/2008/index.htm. The classification scheme is derived from the U.S. Trafficking Victims Protection Act of 2000 (TVPA), which defines the minimum standards for the elimination of trafficking. It should be noted, however, that our ratings of "High" "Medium," and "Low" in the rates of human trafficking are only very rough because they assume that countries that comply with the U.S. anti-trafficking standards of enforcement will therefore have low levels of human trafficking. This is not always true. The United States,

for example, is rated as low for human trafficking because it complies with the TVPA anti-trafficking act; however, we know that it is a major destination country for trafficked humans. The classifications are as follows:

- *Low Amount of Trafficking* (Tier 1): Countries that fully comply with the U.S. Department of State standards for anti-trafficking enforcement.
- *Medium Amount of Trafficking* (Tier 2): Countries that do not fully comply with the minimum standards but are making significant efforts to bring themselves into compliance.
- *Medium Amount of Trafficking* (Watch List): Countries on Tier 2 requiring special scrutiny because of a high or significantly increasing number of victims, failure to provide evidence of increasing efforts to combat trafficking in persons, or an assessment as Medium based on commitments to take action over the next year.
- *High Amount of Trafficking* (Tier 3): Countries that neither satisfy the minimum standards nor demonstrate a significant effort to come into compliance. Countries in this tier are subject to potential non-humanitarian and non-trade sanctions.

Prison

The prison rate assessments are derived from the International Center for Prison Studies, King's College, London, and found at http://www.kcl.ac.uk/schools/law/research/icps. The rates are of prisoners per 100,000 population, and countries are ranked from high to low and divided into High, Medium, and Low using the quartile method described previously. These were the most up-to-date and thorough statistics available as of 2008. The world distribution of prison rates is depicted in Map 2: Imprisonment around the World.

Death Penalty

About 65 percent of countries have abolished the death penalty either by legislation or in practice. A few have essentially abolished it while retaining it for especially heinous crimes, although it may not have been used for many years. These countries are classified as "maybe" in our assessment of whether the death penalty is available to countries. Thus, the classifications for whether countries have the death penalty as an available punishment are "Yes," "Maybe," and "No." The information has been taken from the Web site *Info Please* at http://www.infoplease.com/ipa/A0777460.html, which in turn has taken its statistics from Amnesty International. The world death penalty distribution may be seen in Map 3: Death Penalty around the World.

Corporal Punishment

The assessments as to whether countries have available to them the use of corporal punishment, either as a sentence for a crime or for use within the prison system for disciplinary purposes, is based on information provided by the Web site http://www.endcorporalpunishment.org/pages/frame.html, which assesses

mainly the legislative steps that countries have taken to prohibit the use of corporal punishment. The Web site covers the use of corporal punishment in homes and schools as well as in the criminal justice system. Its assessments of countries are based almost entirely on whether legislation has been passed prohibiting corporal punishment either as a sentence in criminal justice or as a means of discipline in prisons. The legal situation is often ambiguous because, as with the death penalty, many countries retain the possibility of corporal punishment's use either as a sentence or in prisons but rarely or never resort to it. Thus, there is a category of "maybe" for those countries. Perhaps surprisingly, less than 20 percent of the world's countries have prohibited by legislation the use of corporal punishment either as a sentence for a crime or for use in prison discipline. Like the death penalty, our classification of the availability of corporal punishment is "Yes," "No," or "Maybe." The world use of corporal punishment is presented in Map 4: Corporal Punishment around the World.

Regions of the Four Volumes

The four volumes are broken up into the following regions:

- Volume 1: Africa and the Middle East
- Volume 2: The Americas
- Volume 3: Asia and Pacific
- Volume 4: Europe

There are any number of ways to classify countries into regions of the world. We have mostly relied on a geographical classification based on the United Nations Statistics Division classification system (http://unstats.un.org/unsd/geoinfo/default.htm). But this method is far from satisfactory. Although geography (relatively speaking) remains the same, the borders of countries do not, mostly as a result of political conflict and other factors such as migration. Furthermore, the definition of what makes a country a country is also very difficult because there are many instances where "principalities" (e.g., San Marino) and "independent nations" (e.g., the Navajo Nation in the United States) exist inside larger nations or countries. The complex histories of colonialism and migration have resulted in particular countries containing a vast variety of peoples, cultures, and social arrangements, such that calling them a "country" or even "nation" gives a misleading impression of a cohesive national system governed by one set of laws. Bosnia and Herzogovina are perhaps a prime recent example of this difficulty.

Given the shifting boundaries and definitions of countries and the social, cultural, and political diversity contained in them, allocating such countries to broad regions of the world is obviously even less precise. The final allocation of countries that were hard to classify—Turkey, for example—was admittedly somewhat arbitrary. We finally placed Turkey, along with Georgia, in Asia, not Europe. And we located countries of the Middle East (itself a very difficult region to define in both geographical and political terms) along with Africa in Volume 1. A number of the countries classified in the Middle Eastern region could just

as easily be placed in Asia, and others are geographically located in North Africa. And the variety of countries found in the Asia and Pacific volume is also vast in terms of both geography and culture; New Zealand and Australia, for example, have much more in common with Europe, from a historical and cultural point of view, than they do with their near and distant neighbors in Asia (although this is probably changing). Thus, comparing regions on any number of crime and punishment factors is fraught with even greater difficulties than comparing individual countries. Some commonalities and patterns, however, do emerge when one peruses the world maps that are provided. It is likely, as editors to the respective volumes point out, that these patterns reflect the colonial past of these regions, although there are no doubt other explanations related to local culture, migration patterns, and political history.

About the Contributors

We have drawn on a variety of authors to contribute to these four volumes. In some cases, these authors are professionals who work for their governments, but in other cases (the majority), these authors are independent scholars. The objectivity of reports written by those who work for governments may perhaps be questioned, but on the other hand, government officials have much greater access to information and statistics than do outsiders. With a couple of important exceptions, all governments, by and large, have a monopoly on crime and punishment information. The exceptions are the international crime-victim surveys described earlier that are conducted mostly apart from governments, because they do not necessarily depend on officially recorded statistics by criminal justice officials. However, more government departments are conducting their own victimization surveys because some governments in the past have been embarrassed by the findings. Various nongovernmental watch groups, such as Amnesty International and Transparency International, also collect crime and punishment information and it is part of their mission to apply value judgments and criticism to governments and their administrators. As editors, we have tried in these chapters, as far as possible, to avoid either advocacy on behalf of the government's interest or criticism of governments, although in some cases the criminality and punitive practices of governments cannot be ignored.

—Graeme R. Newman
University at Albany

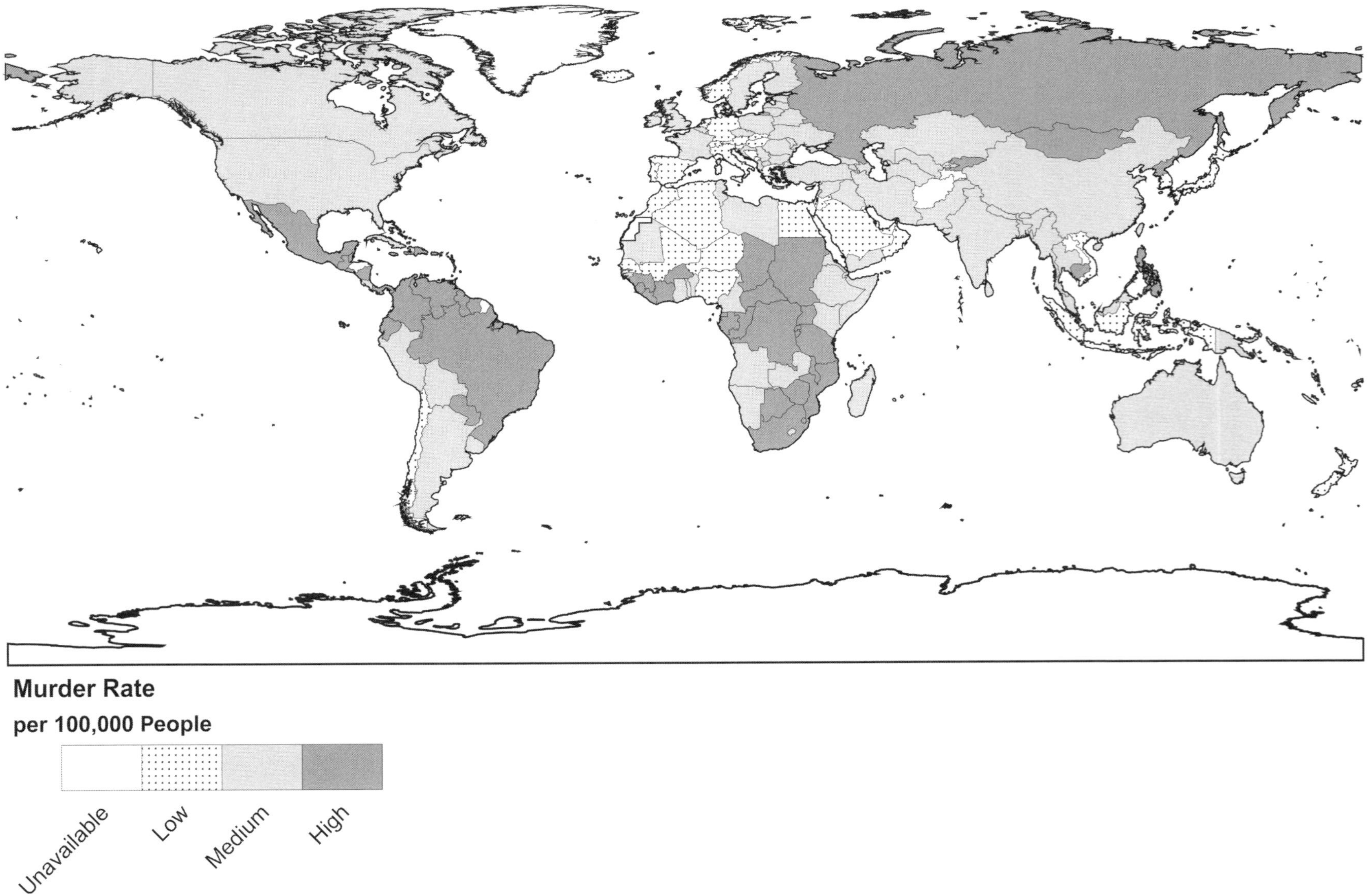

Murder around the World

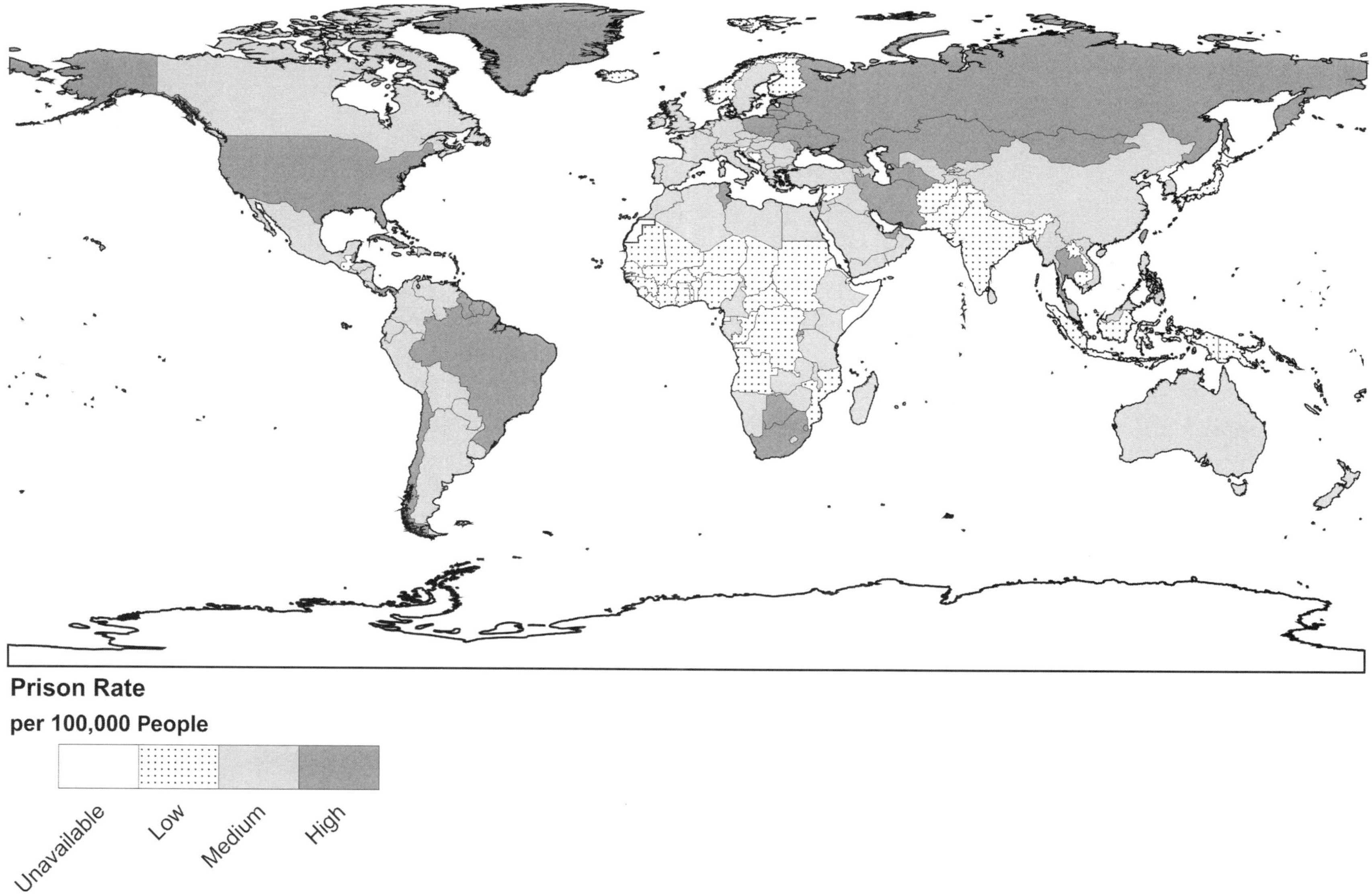

Imprisonment around the World

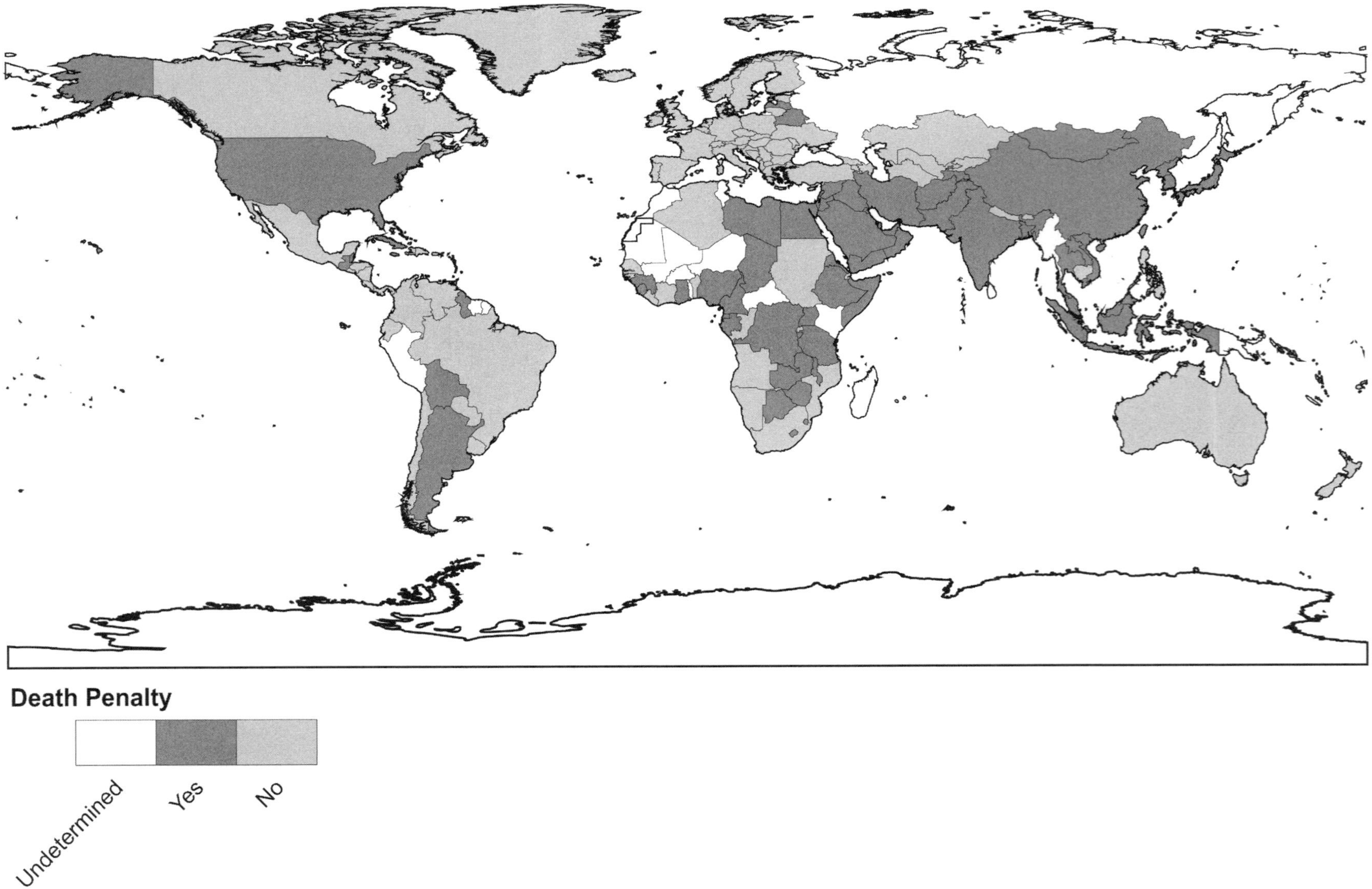

Death Penalty around the World

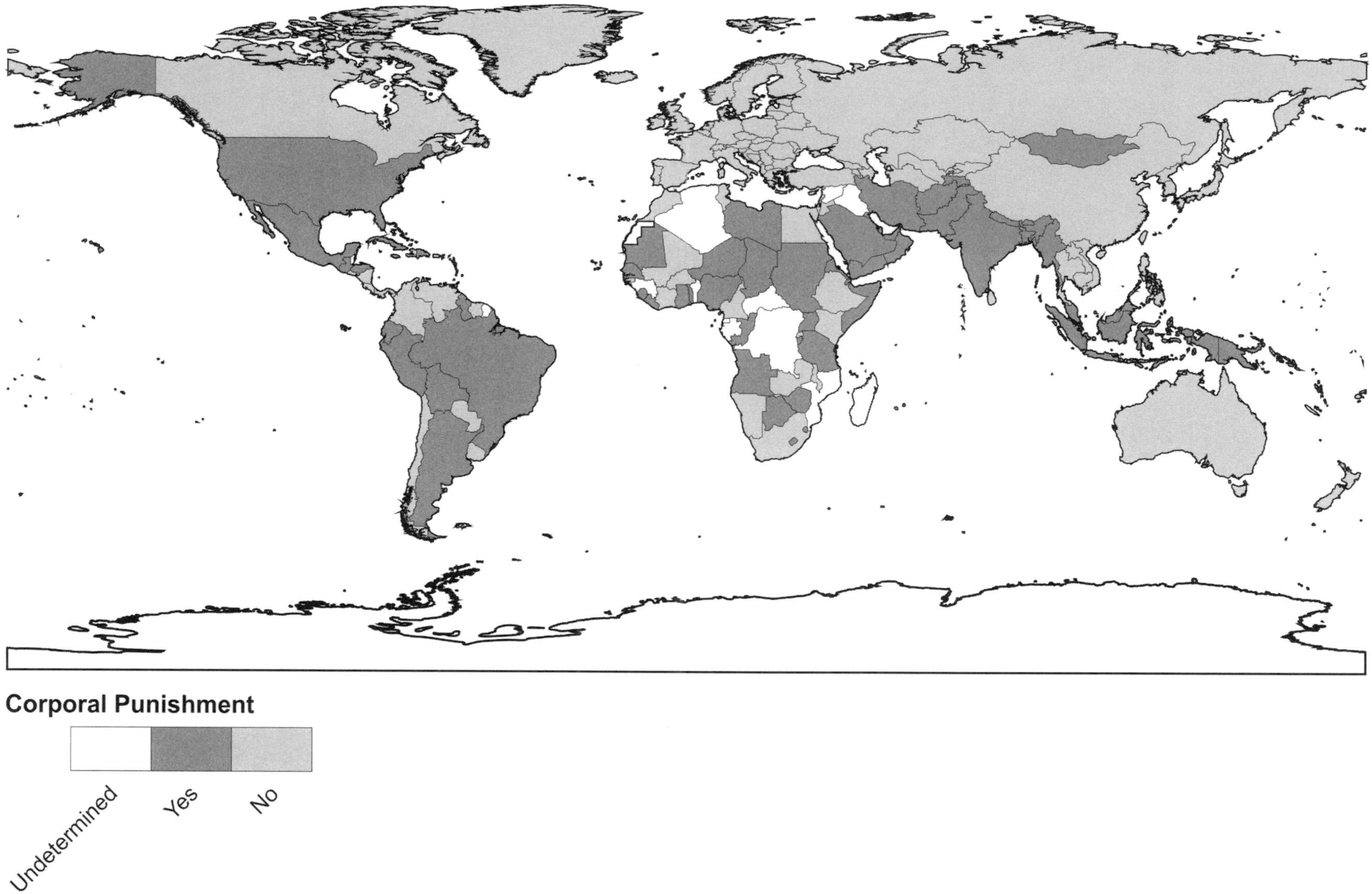

Corporal Punishment around the World

Introduction

Asia and the Pacific comprise the largest region in the world, which is home to more than half of the world's population. Three out of the four most populous countries in the world—China, India, and Indonesia—are located in Asia. Asia/Pacific includes the largest number of countries in the world. The growing role of Asia/Pacific in the world makes documenting the criminal justice practices and philosophies within the region essential.

Volume 3 of *Crime and Punishment around the World* contains individual chapters for each of the following countries (regions): Central Asia (Kazakhstan, Kyrgyzstan, Tajikistan, Turkmenistan, and Uzbekistan); Eastern Asia (China, Hong Kong Special Administrative Region of China, Japan, Mongolia, Macao Special Administrative Region of China, Republic of Korea [South Korea], Democratic People's Republic of Korea [North Korea], and Taiwan), Southern Asia (Afghanistan, Bangladesh, Bhutan, India, Maldives, Nepal, Pakistan, and Sri Lanka), Southeastern Asia (Brunei Darussalam, Cambodia, Indonesia, Lao People's Democratic Republic, Malaysia, Myanmar, Philippines, Singapore, Thailand, Timor-Leste, and Vietnam), Western Asia (Armenia, Azerbaijan, Georgia, and Turkey), and Oceania (Australia, Melanesia, Micronesia, New Zealand, Norfolk Island, Polynesia, Pitcairn, and Tonga). The individual chapters for each of the subregions of Oceania—Melanesia, Micronesia, and Polynesia—encompass the following islands:

- *Melanesia:* Fiji, Papua New Guinea, Solomon Islands, and Vanuatu
- *Micronesia:* Guam, Kiribati, Nauru, Northern Mariana Islands, Marshall Islands, Palau, and the Federated States of Micronesia
- *Polynesia:* Cook Islands, French Polynesia, Niue, Samoa, Tokelau, Tuvalu, and Wallis and Futuna Islands, with separate chapters for Pitcairn and Tonga in Polynesia

Some countries from Asia that may be classified as "Middle East" are included in Volume 1 of *Crime and Punishment around the World,* which covers Africa and the Middle East. Those countries include Iran, Iraq, Israel, Jordon, Kuwait, Lebanon, Oman, Palestine, Qatar, Saudi Arabia, Syria, United Arab Emirates, and Yemen. In addition, Cyprus is included in Volume 4: Europe.

With the rapid changes in communication, technology, and transportation, crime is no longer a problem limited by national borders of individual countries. Transnational crimes such as human and drug trafficking, money laundering, credit card skimming, hijacking, terrorism, and acts of piracy pose challenges to the international community. To overcome these challenges, multinational collaboration has become an inevitable trend. The form of collaboration usually starts with neighboring or regional countries since the sharing of adjacent borders poses difficulties for individual countries in their attempts to prevent and control crime. This volume covers information regarding human trafficking, drug crimes, and the most challenging crimes (faced by states) for individual countries in the region. While this volume does not provide direct comparisons among countries, its in-depth information regarding crime and punishment covering almost all of the countries (or territories) in the region does provide a good opportunity for those interested in gaining a broad understanding of the region's crime problems and criminal justice practices.

The layout of the book starts with the section on history and context (legal system, criminal justice system, and role of police). Political and historical backgrounds are also included since they are related to the development of legal and criminal justice systems. Sections on crime (classification of crimes and crime statistics), criminal justice procedures (investigation, trial stages, and sentencing), and punishment follow. Some important themes discussed in the country essays are described below.

Legal Systems

The legal systems in a number of Asian countries are linked to European colonialism. Civil and common law systems, the two predominant legal systems, were brought into Asia largely through European colonization. Countries colonized by the British, such as India, Malaysia, and Singapore, were largely influenced by common law traditions. On the other hand, civil law was introduced through such colonizers as the Dutch in Indonesia. Additionally, some countries in the region (e.g., Thailand and Japan) never had external legal systems imposed on them through colonization; they chose civil law tradition as the basis of their legal system.

Some countries classified under one legal system can also borrow ideas from other systems. The imposed legal system through colonization can also co-exist with indigenous traditions. As a result, the legal classification of some countries can be described as integrated or combined systems. India is one of the examples with a combination of common, Islamic, and customary laws. There are great varieties of political, social, and historical backgrounds among nations in Asia/Pacific; thus, the legal systems in the region tend to be versatile. Overgeneralization may miss some of the unique features.

Crime

While crime statistics are included for each country (territory) if data were available, those statistics should be interpreted with caution. Some of the statistics were based on police records while some represent number of convictions. In addition, categories included in the total number of crimes may vary from nation to nation. For example, since professional negligence in traffic accidents comprises a considerable amount of the crime in Japan, the inclusion of professional negligence in traffic accidents in statistics may distort crime trends in Japan. Thus, it is important to keep these caveats in mind while making interpretations of crime statistics.

Although great variability exists (see the accompanying maps below), nations in the region share some commonalities in crime problems that they find challenging. Many countries in the region state drug crimes are a prominent challenge to them. A number of countries in Asia take rigid positions against drug-related offenses and adopt severe penalties. In some countries, such as China, India, Indonesia, Laos, Myanmar, Singapore, Sri Lanka, Taiwan, Thailand, and Vietnam, the harshest punishment for the most serious drug offenses includes the death penalty.

Death Penalty

Correctional systems around the globe can be distinguished by whether the death penalty is used as an available punishment. Zimring and Johnson (2008) indicated that Asia has been the center of death penalty concerns. They claimed that those who study the death penalty must study Asia since Asia is the site of at least 85 percent of the world's executions. Albeit there is a higher prevalence of death sentences and executions in Asia compared to other regions in the world, variability of death penalty policy and practices exists among nations. As indicated in this volume, a number of countries (territories) (e.g., Armenia, Australia, Bhutan, New Zealand, Hong Kong, and Macao) have by legislation abolished the death sentence for all types of crime. Some of the countries in the region were classified as having the death penalty as an available punishment but they had not carried out any executions for a long period of time. For example, in Brunei, the death penalty is allowed; however, in practice Brunei has not carried out any executions since 1957. Likewise, in Laos the death penalty is allowed but not carried out in practice. On the other hand, there are countries (e.g., China, India, Japan, Malaysia, Mongolia, Singapore, Thailand, and Vietnam) that retain the death sentence and also carry out executions in practice. To get more detailed information regarding distinctions between death penalty policies and recent practices among nations, readers are encouraged to refer to the section on punishment in the chapters. The map below also shows the distribution of the death penalty for each country in this region.

Prison

While prison rate assessments are available in the snapshot as well as in the map on page xxxv, readers should be cautioned about making direct comparisons. The prison rates are computed based on number of prisoners per 100,000 population. While this measure is a popular way of making comparisons and is constantly employed by researchers, plain comparisons with relative incarceration rates may be inaccurate at times and can pose some problems. For example, in some countries, there is no distinction between jails and prisons. As indicated in the Bangladesh chapter in this volume, all penitentiary institutions are referred to as jails in that nation. Of its total population in jails, only about 29 percent were convicted prisoners and the remaining 71 percent were either awaiting trial or detained for investigation. Thus, more comprehensive information about the prison system in a given country may help to make more accurate interpretations of prison rates. More in-depth information about inmates and prisons is included in this volume, which can help readers to get a comprehensive picture.

Acknowledgments

I am grateful to all the contributors. The preparation of this volume would not have been possible without their hard work and endless efforts.

—Doris C. Chu
Arkansas State University

Country Key to Asia and Pacific Maps

Afghanistan	AF	Nepal	NP
Armenia	AM	New Caledonia	NC
Australia	AU	New Zealand	NZ
Azerbaijan	AZ	Niue	NU
Bangladesh	BD	Norfolk Island	NF
Bhutan	BT	North Korea	KP
Brunei Darussalam	BN	Northern Mariana Islands	MP
Cambodia	KH	Pakistan	PK
China	CN	Palau (Pacific Islands)	PW
Cook Islands	CK	Papua New Guinea	PG
Federated States of Micronesia	FM	Philippines	PH
Fiji	FJ	Pitcairn Islands	PN
French Polynesia	PF	Samoa	WS
Georgia	GE	Singapore	SG
Guam	GU	Solomon Islands	SB
Hong Kong	HK	South Korea	KR
India	IN	Sri Lanka	LK
Indonesia	ID	Taiwan	TW
Japan	JP	Tajikistan	TJ
Kazakhstan	KZ	Thailand	TH
Kiribati	KI	Timor-Leste	TL
Kyrgyzstan	KG	Tokelau	TK
Laos	LA	Tonga	TO
Macao	MO	Turkey	TR
Malaysia	MY	Turkmenistan	TM
Maldives	MV	Tuvalu	TV
Marshall Islands	MH	Uzbekistan	UZ
Mongolia	MN	Vanuatu	VU
Myanmar (Burma)	MM	Vietnam	VN
Nauru	NR	Wallis and Futuna	WF

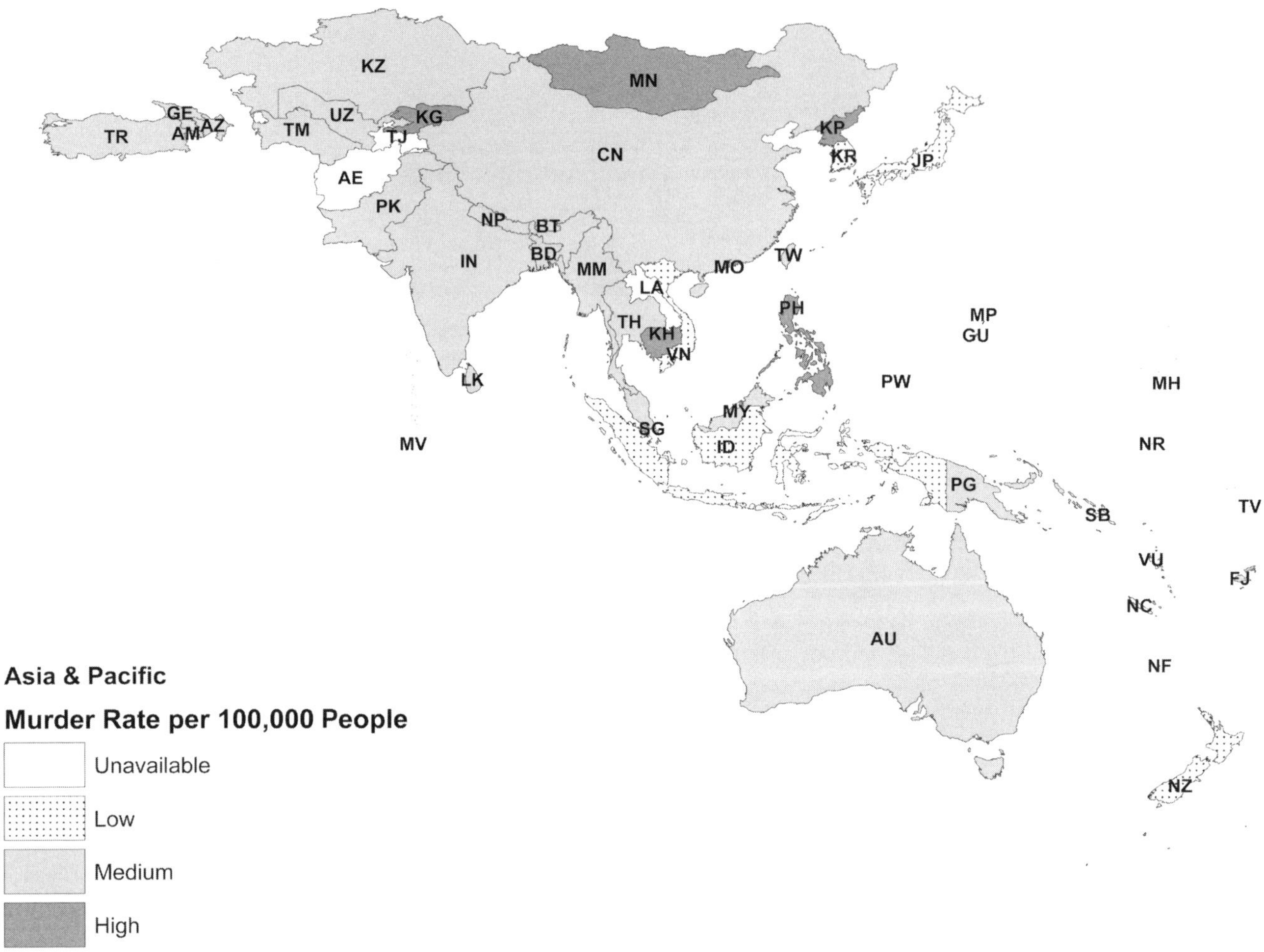

Murder in Asia and Pacific

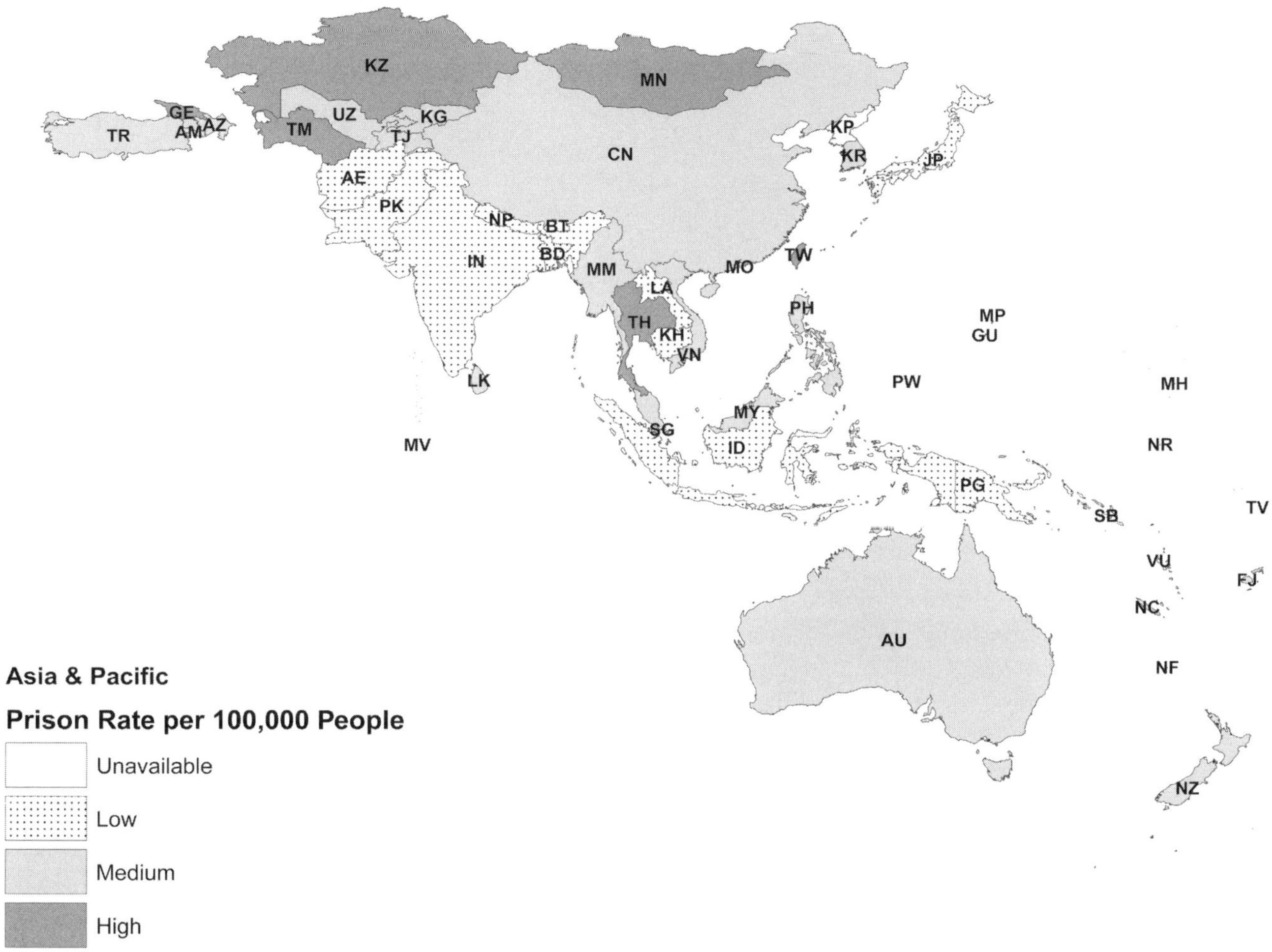

Imprisonment in Asia and Pacific

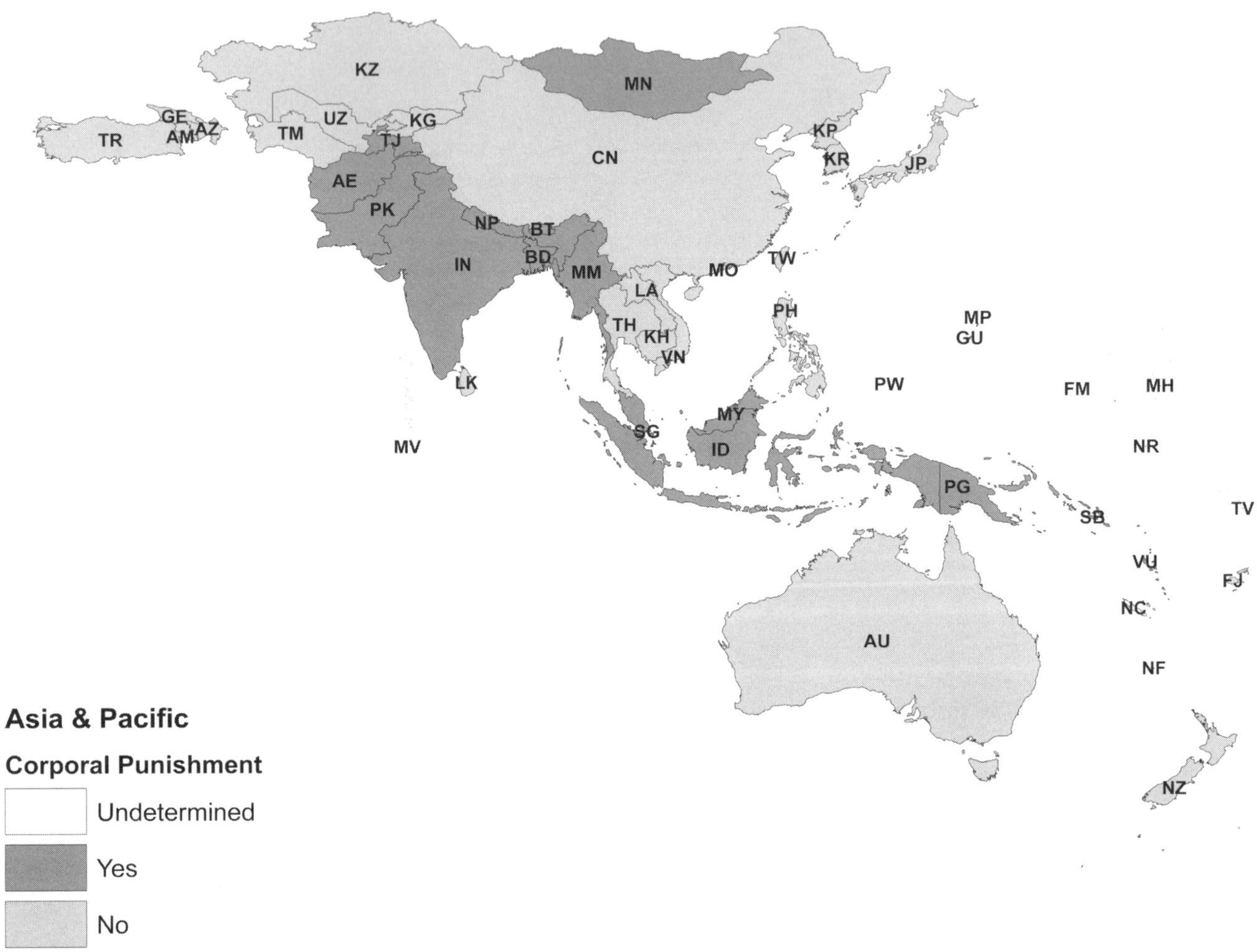

Corporal Punishment in Asia and Pacific

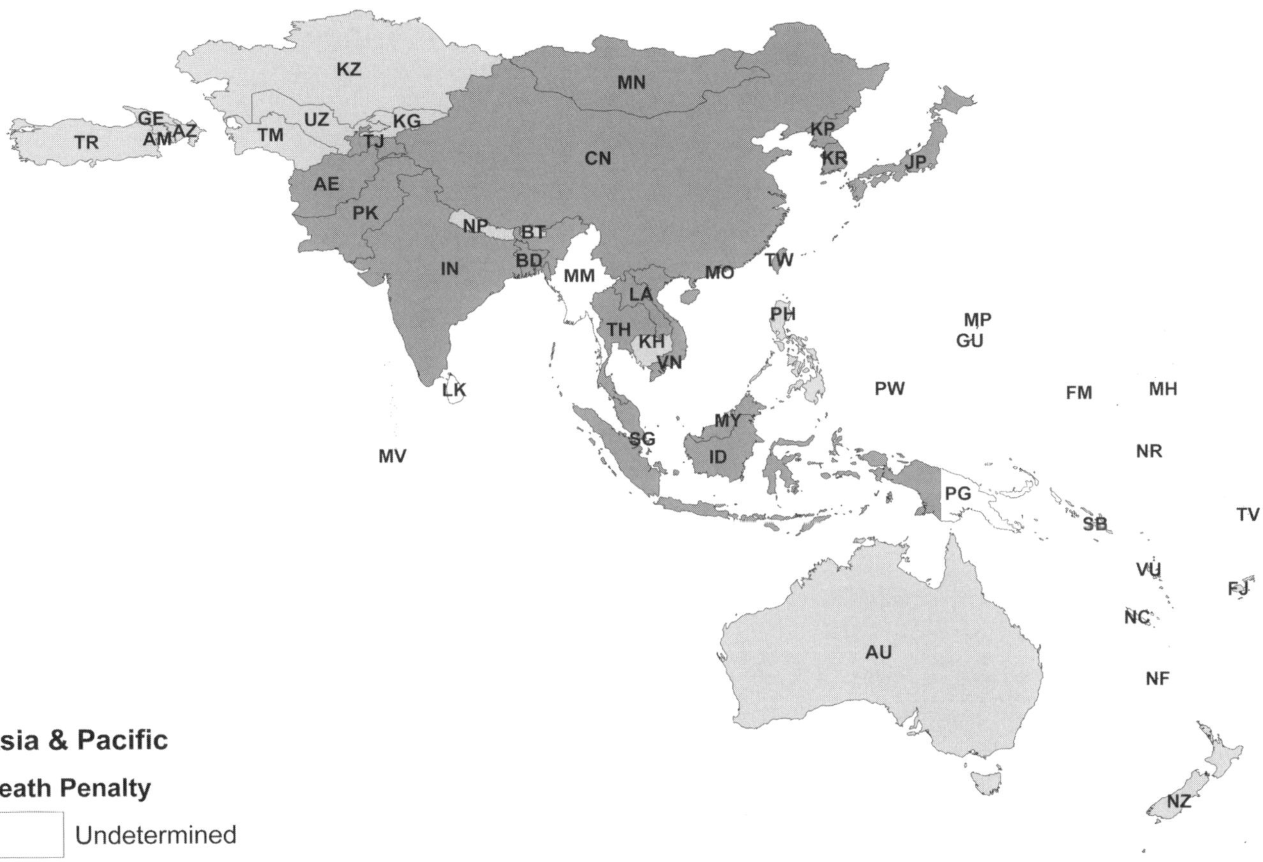

Asia & Pacific

Death Penalty

Undetermined

Yes

No

Death Penalty in Asia and Pacific

Asia

Afghanistan

Legal System: Islamic/Civil/Common/Customary
Corruption: High
Human Trafficking: Medium
Prison Rate: Low
Death Penalty: Yes
Corporal Punishment: Yes

Background

Afghanistan is a landlocked country bordered by China, Pakistan, Iran, Tajikistan, Turkmenistan, and Uzbekistan. The population numbers approximately 28.7 million, with an estimated 2 million refugees in Pakistan and 800,000 in Iran. The biggest ethnic group is the Pashtun people followed by Tajik, Hazara, Uzbek, Aimak, Turkmen, and Baloch.

The Afghan legal system undertook several reconstructions during the 20th and early 21st centuries. Several constitutions have been implemented to coincide with regime changes, while the formal justice system has been influenced at specific times by widely different ideological, theological, and legal schools of thought. During the early 20th century the Hanafi school of Islamic jurisprudence provided a foundation for the state criminal justice system, in parallel to customary dispute resolution mechanisms. The 1950s and 1960s were a time of great change as attempts were made to modernize the state, and a new constitution was adopted in 1964. This constitution elevated state law over Islamic law. The codification of state law continued until 1978 and many laws, which still stand today, such as the Penal Code, were enacted during this time.

In 1978, the president was assassinated in a coup d'état by the Afghan Communist Party. Soviet forces invaded in 1979 on the pretext of defending the Afghan Communist Government from Islamic rebels. The Communist regime enacted a Soviet-style judicial system along the lines of Marxist legal school of jurisprudence. Much of the progress made since the 1950s was quickly lost under Communist rule.

In 1989, Soviet troops withdrew from the country and in 1992 the Soviet-backed president was overthrown by mujahideen and other rebel groups; Islamic law was reinstated as the primary source of law. By 1994, Afghanistan was in a state of anarchy characterized by general lawlessness and violent conflicts between various former warlord commanders and criminal organizations to exert influence over areas including the profits from illicit commerce. The emergence of the Taliban out of the conflicts offered the Afghan peoples, tired of fighting and exhausted by famine and drought, peace and a modicum of stability. A far right, patriarchal interpretation of Islamic law was the only source of law during the Taliban era and was enforced with brutality and a complete disregard for basic concepts of human rights.

The Taliban were opposed, and eventually overthrown, in 2001, by an alliance of Afghan factions, supported financially and militarily by a coalition of foreign forces. A new constitution was adopted by the *Loya Jirga* in January 2004. In 2004 and 2005 presidential and parliamentary elections were held

Afghan National Police trainees listen to a speech by their instructor at the police academy in Kabul, Afghanistan, May 22, 2004. (AP Photo/Emilio Morenatti)

in accordance with democratic principles. With regard to the presidential election, 10.5 million Afghan peoples registered to vote and Hamid Karzai was elected from 18 candidates with a majority of 55 percent. Since then the slow process of redrafting the body of legislation and reforming the fractured institutions has been underway.

The erratic journey of the Afghan national police force may be illustrative of the history of the criminal justice system in full. A national civilian force was built during the 1960s modernization drive. This force was based upon the European model and supported by West and East Germany. During the Soviet-backed Communist regime the *Khedamat-e-Atlaat-e-Dawlati* (KhaD), an Afghan alternative to the Soviet Union's *Komitjet Gosudarstvjennoj Bjezopasnosti* (KGB), was created. The police and KhaD were used in the internal power politics of the Afghan Communist Party, which often resulted in violent armed clashes. The police force disintegrated as a civilian force. Reform was attempted again in 1989 with the support of Germany; however, this was halted due to the conflicts between former warlord factions. The only criminal justice institution the Taliban administered was the despotic Vice and Virtue Ministry, which was mandated only to enforce the Taliban's far right, patriarchal interpretations of Islamic law.

Current Status of the Criminal Justice System

Years of conflict and regime changes left a confused and contradictory body of legislation; in 2001 there were 2,400 separate laws originating from different regimes, and therefore legal schools of thought, that overlapped and conflicted with one another.

The post-2001 reforms, at first glance, are promising. The 2004 Constitution is a progressive document defending democracy, human rights, and the rule of law. A more critical view is that the status of Islam in the Constitution could be used by the far-right Islamic factions operating within the state to repress the movement toward a greater realization of civil and political rights. The Constitution provides in article 3 that Afghanistan's religion is Islam and that no law can violate any Islamic principle. Articles 130 and 131 also state that if no law exists on a subject then the provisions of Hanafi or Shiite jurisprudence will be applied, which makes Islamic law a secondary source of law.

However, the Penal Code gives Islamic law primacy in certain areas of criminal law such as the punishments of those guilty of murder, adultery, and theft. To many the punishments enacted through Islamic law are unjust and can be perceived as contrary to Afghanistan's human rights commitments. One example is of a student who allegedly downloaded and distributed information on the role of women in Islamic culture. He was sentenced to death by a district court for apostasy; the decision is currently being appealed at the Kabul Appeals Court. However, in the Islamic faith, these punishments come from the Koran and sunna texts and are thus sacred. In sum, the conflict between Islamic law and codified law, coupled with overlapping and contradictory legal codes, makes Afghan law, at present, too complex and lacking in clarity and consistency. With regard to the institutional infrastructure, decades of violent conflict corroded an already weak criminal justice system, limiting not just the material resources but also the pool of professional and trained coercive, legal, and support personnel from which criminal justice systems are founded upon. At present, the judicial process is slow and open to corruption. The administrative infrastructure is poor with a lack of effective record keeping, inadequate storage facilities, and a lack of resources to effectively track the progress of cases. Many buildings are not fit for court, with inconsistent power supplies and no areas for attorneys and clients to privately converse. In many provinces, district courts are convened in rented houses or take place in an impromptu manner in provincial court buildings. Furthermore, the educational infrastructure to support the system is inadequate. With regard to the coercive arm of the state, the Afghan National Police (ANP) are employed by the Ministry of the Interior and comprise the Afghan Uniformed Police; the Afghan Border Police; the Afghan Civil Order Police (a rapid reaction force intended to maintain civil order in Afghanistan's largest cities, created in response to the ineffectiveness of the uniformed police to control riots in Kabul in 2006); Afghan Highway Police; and Counter-Narcotics Police of Afghanistan. There is also a separate Special Narcotics Force, an elite paramilitary force that reports directly to the president and carries out high-level interdiction raids.

There is no agreement on the number of police officers operating in Afghanistan. Estimates range from 62,000 (of which 12,000 are border police) to 82,000. The real number could be half this estimate due to desertion, injury, "ghost names," and the general ineptitude of many officers. In 2008, according to the International Crises Group, only 511 of these officers were female. The lower estimate of 50,000 is equal to 180 operational officers per 100,000, which is very low compared to other states in the region such as Jordan (600/100,000) and Kyrgyzstan (340/100,000), and Western states such as Germany (292/100,000). However, some Afghan experts maintain that even this low number is unsustainable without the financial support of the international community. An alternative to the unsustainability of the ANP was the creation of an Auxiliary Police Force in 2006 to patrol Southern and Eastern Provinces and support counterinsurgency operations. The force was 11,270 strong, recruited locally and came under the control of tribal *Jirgas*. It was perceived by many Afghans and ANP officers as unprofessional and ineffective, and by many as a policy by a Pashtun president to re-arm Pashtun militias. For these reasons the force was disbanded in 2008.

Another major problem with the ANP is that of the blurring of the boundaries between its role as a civilian and military force. However, in a state such as Afghanistan, the lines between military and civilian are blurred; the cultivation of opium is within the civilian sphere, yet many farmers are protected by large, well-armed militia. The ANP is lacking many necessary resources and sufficient training. The 2006 Kabul riots are illustrative as the ANP was ineffective in quelling the civilian dispute; many ran from the scene. Furthermore, there appeared to be no prior intelligence or chain of command, while the officers lacked necessary equipment such as protective gear, pepper spray, and water cannons.

More troubling is that the force is perceived by many Afghans as inefficient and largely corrupt. Many have reported that the police steal from travelers on state highways. Furthermore, the ANP was accused of numerous human rights violations including torture, illegal detention, and arbitrary arrest in 2006. However, strategic reform was underway, at the time of writing, including placing two officers trained to monitor human rights violations in each province, while the respected Afghanistan Independent Human Rights Commission began providing training to officers.

The continued inefficiencies and lack of consistency in the Afghan legal system may point to why, at present, it is estimated that between 80 and 90 percent of the peoples of Afghanistan choose to use informal dispute mechanisms, according to a report of the Istituto Superiore Internazionale di Scienze Criminali (ISISC). The most common of these are the customary conflict resolution mechanisms referred to as *Jirgas* (in Pashtun tribes) or *Shuras* (in non-Pashtun tribes); due to the similarities between the two mechanisms *Jirga* shall refer to both. The *Jirga* is a customary legal system in which interpretations of Islamic law and local customs are enacted to arbitrate and prevent conflict that has the potential to harm the community. The rules and procedures differ from tribe to tribe; however, all are centered on a belief in "restorative justice" that primarily seeks to restore peace to the community rather than seeking retribution for crimes. The central tenet is that the offender is shamed and then accepted back into society with the victim agreeing to a truce. However, one researcher, Verna Lieble, has also described how many Pashtuns choose to ignore the results of the *Jirga*, opting instead for personal vengeance.

At present the Afghan criminal justice system as a whole is also perceived by many as corrupt, inefficient, expensive, and slow (many Afghans cannot afford the bribes to have cases referred to court). The lack of legal infrastructure means many rural people have to make long journeys on roads that are considered unsafe due to threat from insurgents, bandits, and corrupt/criminalized police officers. When at court the process can be slow, due to frequent delays caused by administrative problems.

Conversely, customary mechanisms are conducted by respected elders with reputations for fairness who reach decisions using "accepted" and established local traditions and values. Many Afghans are illiterate and unable to complete legal paperwork, and due to a lack of legal education, are ignorant of the formal law; yet they are aware of their rights and duties under their tribes' customary laws.

However, the negative aspects are that it is a patriarchal system where women are not allowed to witness the process that can, in many tribes, legitimately give them away as a form of dispute settlement or compensation; much customary law was constructed by men, for men. The UN Special Rapporteur on Women objects to the Pashtun *Jirga* tradition of arranging a marriage between a female member of the defendant's family to a male member of their victim's family. The rationale is that the marriage will bind the families and prevent further disturbance; in practice it reduces women to the property of men, a commodity to be traded. Furthermore, in many areas insurgents and former warlords violently take seats to increase their illegitimate authority.

Finding of Guilt

Formal System

Afghanistan's formal court system is developing based on the Constitution, the 2005 Law on Organization and Jurisdiction of Courts of the Islamic Republic of Afghanistan, and the 2004 Interim Criminal Code for Courts. Afghanistan is also a signatory of the International Covenant on Civil and Political Rights and commits, in the preamble of the Constitution, to observe the Universal Declaration of Human Rights. Thus, Afghanistan is obliged to uphold the judicial rights contained within these international instruments. However, the practical application of law lags far behind the actual legislation.

The Afghan Judiciary, mandated by the 2005 Law on Organization and Jurisdiction of Courts of the Islamic Republic of Afghanistan, is hierarchically structured, with the Supreme Court at the top. Each of Afghanistan's 34 provinces has a provincial court that is required to have within its jurisdiction: a Central Provincial Primary Court, Juveniles Court, Commercial Primary Court, Family Issues Primary Court, and District Primary Court. District courts have jurisdiction over petty, misdemeanor, and felony crimes. Appeals are referred first to the provincial court and then to the Supreme Court.

The 2005 Narcotics Law allows for the creation of special Narcotics Tribunals within the Kabul Provincial Court, which operate and are bound under the 2005 Law on Organization and Jurisdiction of Courts and the 2004 Criminal Code for Courts.

The 2005 Juvenile Code article 3 mandates that a juvenile primary court must be held in the capital city of all of Afghanistan's 34 provinces to protect and prosecute juveniles. An example of the conflicting nature of Afghan legislation is that Juvenile Code article 7 defines a child as a juvenile under 18 years old, while article 10 states that children below 12 are not criminally responsible. Penal Code articles 70 to 73 offer a different classification with minors being aged between 7 and 13, teenagers aged between 14 and 17, and children under 7 being exempt from prosecution.

There currently exist 34 provincial courts and 408 primary courts, although only 81 percent of these are functioning. Juvenile courts are situated in the provincial capital as are some primary courts, due to a lack of resources. This makes them inaccessible to many rural people who may have to make long journeys on poor roads that are considered unsafe due to the insurgency, bandits, and/or criminalized police officers.

Under the 2004 Criminal Code for Courts, all primary courts are assigned three judges, although it is possible for one judge to sit for security reasons or a lack of resources. Penal action for the prosecution of all crimes is introduced to the court by the primary *Saranwal* (prosecutor) who investigates whether a crime has been committed and who is responsible. At this stage the *Saranwal* can either indict the suspect, or if there is not sufficient evidence, the case may be dismissed (a more senior *Saranwal* or the victim may file a complaint against this decision). A notification of the deeds must then be served to the suspect at least three days before the trial. If the suspect cannot be found, then the notification is issued to a police-appointed defense council who acts on the suspect's behalf and the defendant is tried in absentia. The suspect and defense have the right to examine all documents collected in the *Saranwal*'s investigation. The accused has a right to remain silent during the process. The judge's decision can be petitioned by the *Saranwal*, sentenced person, relative, or the defense council. The petition is evaluated by a committee headed by a Supreme Court judge and two appellate judges.

Under the Constitution all citizens of Afghanistan have equal rights and duties before the law, and all are considered innocent until proven guilty (a right which, as shall be discussed shortly, is seldom adhered to with regard to rape); the basic right of due process is provided for under article 27. All are provided with the right to be immediately informed of the nature of the accusation upon arrest.

Article 31 of the Constitution provides all with the right to appoint a defense attorney and those charged with a criminal act are entitled to defense from a state-appointed attorney. The right to confidentiality between attorney and client is also provided for in this article. Article 19 of the Criminal Code for Courts sets the eligibility for state assistance as the accused, or suspect, being "financially unable to appoint a defense attorney." It further states that the defense council must be informed of any searches, confrontations, line-ups, expert examinations, or interrogations during the investigation so that they can be present.

Unfortunately, there is a void between legislation and practice in Afghanistan. Legal representation is scarce to the point of being unavailable. There are just 250 lawyers registered with the Ministry of Justice to provide free legal aid to cover a population of 28.7 million. In many provinces there is no access to free legal aid at all. Legal aid in Kabul appears to have improved since 2001; however, few lawyers are present during interrogation and trial, contrary to the Constitution and the Criminal Code for Courts. Furthermore, many defense attorneys are contacted on the day of the trial, instead of the five days prescribed by the Criminal Code for Courts; this leaves them little time to produce an effective case.

Under article 30 of the Constitution, statements or confessions obtained by means of compulsion are invalid; the confession must be voluntary and the confessor must be of sound mind. However, several women interviewed by a UN researcher in Pol-e-Charki Prison, Kabul, maintained that they were made to sign confessions at police stations without a defense attorney present. The women interviewed were illiterate and ignorant of their rights and duties before the law. Furthermore, many reported promises of release after signing; these confessions therefore should have been considered invalid under Afghan law.

At present the Supreme Court employs 1,700 judges, while the Attorney General's Office employs 2,500 *Saranwals.* The Law on Organization and Jurisdiction of Courts, article 58, states that to qualify as a judge an individual must hold a BA degree in law or Islamic law, or a diploma in religious studies from a recognized center and have completed the state practical judicial training course. In practice, the make-up of Afghan judges' education does not conform to this provision:

- 44 percent of judges hold degrees in Islamic law.
- 21 percent have attained no higher than a high school education.
- 16 percent have qualifications from nonuniversity programs.
- 12 percent hold degrees in law.
- 8 percent hold nonlaw degrees.

With regard to *Saranwals,* in Kabul 37 percent have university law backgrounds, while in the provinces only 20 percent hold law or Islamic law degrees. Clearly, there is a huge void between the rights and procedures expressed under state law and the ability of the state to enforce them. Under these conditions it is little surprise that the majority of Afghans prefer to use informal dispute resolution mechanisms.

Informal System

Ali Wardak, an expert on Afghan customary law, notes that mediation tends to be split between spheres of authority within Afghan society. This starts with the family, where all "private" matters, such as domestic violence and divorce, tend to be resolved; the oldest male family member has the greatest influence. Conflicts outside of this private sphere are resolved in *Jirgas* at either the village or tribal level depending on the potential disruption the dispute may cause. For instance, disputes over land rights or murders, which may have the potential to disrupt the tribe, will be under the jurisdiction of the tribal *Jirga*. The *Jirga* is composed of the elite of village or tribal elders who are considered to embody certain qualities that make them good sources of judgment, including hospitality, belonging to a honorable family, a record of bravery in violent conflict, while they must be eloquent orators and have a proven record of fair and effective judgment at *Jirgas.*

These men sit in an inner circle with a respected religious leader. An outer circle is formed in which all males of the tribe can observe the proceedings; this is thought to act as a transparency mechanism. The elders then pass judgment using their interpretations of the customary laws of their tribe. The laws tend to be a mixture of custom, practice, and interpretations of Islamic law. The laws and customs vary from tribe to tribe. The formal and customary systems do in some cases interact. In Kandahar Province criminal cases are forwarded to tribal *Jirgas* by the state and then returned to the prosecutor's office if the case cannot be resolved.

Islamic Law

If Islamic law is used as the source of law to decide a case, then all *Hudud* and *Qissass* offenses must be witnessed by two sane adult Muslim *men*, four in the case of *Zena*. It is argued that the harshness of the punishments deters offenders and that the standard of proof is very high and must, according to the sunna, be proved beyond reasonable doubt. Thus, a lot depends on the honesty of the two/four male witnesses.

Under Islamic law a child under seven years old is unpunishable, while from the ages of 7 to 15, the family or tribe is held responsible. After 15 the individual is criminally responsible. The individual can also use the defense of insanity and coercion into the crime.

Crime

State Law

Crime in Afghanistan is currently classified by the 1976 Penal Code, Book 2, under the following three levels of seriousness:

- *Felonies,* which include embezzling public funds; counterfeiting; the torture of individuals by public officials; arson; murder; kidnapping, with coercion or fraud, of a teenager; kidnapping of an adult women; adultery; highway robbery.
- *Misdemeanors,* which include bribery; the use of illicit narcotics or alcoholic drinks; illegal detention of an individual (extended to a felony if accompanied by torture, coercion, or if the individual is a state employee); kidnap of a minor; kidnapping of a male adult; crimes pertaining to the unlawful slaughtering and hurting of animals.
- *Obscenities,* which include causing disturbance or inconvenience by blowing a horn "or producing uproar or hubbub"; releasing a lunatic "who terrifies people" on public roads; public nudity; and cruelty to domesticated pets.

Rape is not clearly defined in the Penal Code; it is implied in various articles that refer to *Zena* (adultery or sex outside of marriage), including article 429(1) which states: "A person who, through violence, threat, or deceit, violates the chastity of another (whether male or female)." However, it is noted by a UN report that victims of rape are generally treated as committing the crime of *Zena* until able to prove their innocence.

Under the Penal Code, article 61, individuals are protected from prosecution if murder is committed in defense of fear of death or serious injury; the act of, or fear of, adultery or homosexuality; human kidnapping; defense against larceny; or defense against unauthorized entry into a residential home at night. Article 62 does though limit the action in that if legal recourse was possible, then it reverts back to being classified an illegal act. It could be argued that this article implicitly makes homosexuality a prohibited act by its inclusion; however, we are unaware of any penalties formally set in the legislation.

The use, production, trafficking, possession, and retailing of illicit narcotics is prohibited under the 2005 Counter-Narcotics Law. This law lists the substance prohibited under national law in the following four classification tables:

1. "Prohibited drugs of abuse with no medical use"—this includes heroin, opium poppy seeds and straw, MDMA (Ecstasy), and cannabis.
2. "Strictly controlled plants and substances with a medical use" (which are considered high-risk drugs of abuse)—this includes cocaine and opium.
3. "Controlled plants and substances with a medical use" (considered drugs with a risk of abuse)—this includes codeine and GBH.
4. "Substances frequently used in the manufacture of narcotic drugs and psychotropic substances (precursor chemicals)"—this includes ethyl ether and ephedrine.

Islamic Law

Article 1 of the Penal Code differentiates between crimes under the jurisdiction of the code and those to be administered according to Islamic law. The code covers *Tazir* crimes, ones that are considered less serious under Islamic law and can therefore be left to the discretion of nonreligious judgment. Crimes not covered are those that under Islamic law entail nonflexible punishments, once proved by a just trial. These crimes are classified as follows:

- *Hudud* (crimes that threaten the existence of Islam), which include *Sariqah* (theft); *Hirabah* (armed robbery or armed rebellion); *Zina* (adultery and sex outside of marriage); *Qadhf* (an unsupported accusation of *Zina*); *Sharb al-Khamr* (intoxication); and *Riddah* (apostasy).
- *Qissass,* which are intentional crimes committed against an individual's person and could include murder, manslaughter, or bodily harm.

If there is a lack of evidence to try the individual under Islamic law, then the case is reclassified as a *Tazir* crime and comes under the jurisdiction of the Penal Code.

Drugs

The illicit narcotics trade, or more specifically the illicit opium trade, is one of the most high profile and damaging crimes in Afghanistan. It is also indicative of the deficiencies in the criminal justice system.

Afghanistan is by far the world's largest producer of illicit opium—it is estimated that of 8,870 metric tons of illicit opium produced globally in 2007, 8,200 was produced in Afghanistan: a 92 percent share of the market. The nearest rival is Burma, which was able to produce only 460 metric tons. This record-breaking output is cultivated over a 193,000-hectare area.

During 2008, 98 percent of all opium was confined to the areas in the west and south, which are classified as high or extremely risky by the United Nations Department of Safety and Security (UNDSS). Most districts are inaccessible to UN and nongovernmental organizations and under the authority of insurgents and/or organized criminal networks, who have violently opposed eradication measures by the state in the past. The major growing areas of production levels include Helmand, Kandahar, Uruzgan, Farah, and Nimroz. According to the United Nations Office of Drug Control (UNODC), 2.4 million Afghans, or 9.8 percent of the population, were involved in the trade in 2008.

The increased cultivation has had a direct effect on neighboring states, many of whom are used as trafficking routes and as a result have witnessed a rise in opium abuse; the highest levels of opium and heroin consumption in the world occur along the trafficking routes out of Afghanistan.

The consumption of opiates in Afghanistan is above the global average. In 2005, it was estimated that within Afghanistan 150,000 people had consumed opium (0.6 percent of the population) while 50,000 (0.2 percent) had used heroin, 520,000 (2.2 percent) had used hashish, and 160,000 (0.7 percent) of the population had consumed alcohol (a prohibited intoxicant). In general, rural populations are more likely than urbanites to consume opium, heroin, and hashish, while alcohol is more widely used by urban populations.

Corruption

Corruption in Afghanistan facilitates the illicit narcotics trade. Police and local state officials are bribed to not eradicate opium crops, according to a UNODC report, while high-level offenders are immune from arrest and prosecution due to connections with the political and criminal justice elite. This is illustrated by the practice in some areas of posts for police chiefs in poppy-growing districts being auctioned off to the highest bidder. They can reach as much as US$100,000 for a six-month appointment: an appointment that legitimately pays approximately US$360 over the six months.

Corruption in Afghanistan runs deeper than the involvement of drug trafficking networks. Afghanistan is an overall hugely corrupt nation; in the World Bank's report, "World Governance Indicators," Afghanistan is placed in the lowest 1 percentile: the only state considered less able to control corruption is Somalia.

A consequence of ongoing violent conflict, the existence of former warlords (many of whom profited from the illicit opiate trade during their conflicts with Soviet and Taliban forces) in state institutions and their illegitimate authority in rural areas, the lack of state influence in many areas, and ineffective institutional constraints on corruption is that a culture of impunity has arisen in which criminal networks are protected by corrupt state employees at all levels.

Connected to institutional corruption is the criminalization of the police, which appears to be a problem of epidemic proportions. There are reports of the police facilitating kidnapping and creating ad hoc, unofficial tollbooths on national roads. In 2007, 35 police officers were removed after a group of truckers went on strike over the payment of such tolls on the Herat-Delaram highway. The corruption and criminalization of state employees is arguably the most damaging crime in Afghanistan, for as long as it, and the impunity it offers, continues, the state will be unable to counter other high-level crimes such as the trade in illicit narcotics.

Insurgency

Many prominent crimes in Afghanistan can be linked to the ongoing insurgency. The insurgency claimed 6,500 lives in 2007. A worrisome development is that civilian targets such as schoolteachers, religious leaders, and politicians who support human rights are increasingly being targeted. This strategy has resulted in the closure of 370 schools, which has prevented almost 220,000 individuals from receiving an education, and the death of many perceived progovernment religious leaders and state employees, including nearly 900 police officers and 140 teachers and students in 2007. Another insurgent-linked crime is kidnapping by the Taliban and other militia. In the second half of 2006, 190 kidnappings were reported for political or criminal purposes. The actual level is likely to be much higher, according to a U.S. State Department report. The United Nations reports that the number of insurgent-based security incidents increased significantly in 2008.

Human Trafficking

The U.S. State Department notes that Afghanistan is a source, transit, and destination country for men, women, and children forced into sexual, military, and commercial servitude. Human trafficking, forced servitude, and prostitution can be linked to the illicit opium industry as opium seed is offered on a credit basis by criminal organizations. If a debt cannot be repaid, for instance after a poor harvest, then it is not unknown for poor farmers to repay the debt with female members of the family.

Violence against Women

Violence against women is a persistent problem. According to the U.S. State Department Human Rights Report, women suffer at the hands of their family members, police officials, and the general tolerance of violence in their communities. And, as noted above, women who report their rape risk being charged as adulterers, or *Zina*. The Afghanistan Independent Human Rights Commission documented 1,651 crimes against women in 2006; of these, 558 were in the form of "severe beatings," 213 were forced marriages, 50 were murder cases, and 34 were cases of rape (though rape is not a codified crime). The true number is likely significantly higher.

The Ministry of the Interior in 2006 reported 134 cases of rape against women and 103 against male children in 2006. An extension of this problem is that of former warlords and their militias raping male and female children and women; during 2005, 21 such cases were reported according to a U.S. State Department report. Again the true number is likely significantly higher. It is also reported that forced marriages and abductions are common crimes committed by former warlords and their militia.

Other

A 2006 study by the Centre for Strategic International Studies interviewed 1,000 Afghans; the major conclusion was that the majority of all crimes are unreported. The results indicated increase in theft in both rural and urban areas and a rise in burglaries in Kabul. Kidnapping for ransom has also increased dramatically and is thought to be widespread.

Punishment

State Law

The Penal Code, articles 23 to 26, state that:

- Felonies are punishable with the death sentence or continued (16–20 years) or long (5–15

years) imprisonment. The death penalty is defined as "the hanging of convicted person on gallows until death."
- Misdemeanors are punishable with a prison term from three months to no more than five years, or a cash fine of more than 3,000 afghanis.
- Obscenities are punishable with a prison term of between 24 hours and three months, or a cash fine of up to 3,000 (US$63) afghanis.

In October 2007, 15 Afghanis were executed, by firing squad (not hanging as called for in the Penal Code) at Pol-e-Charki Prison, Kabul. The offenses included murder, robbery, and looting. Prior to this, the last execution in Afghanistan was in April 2004, according to Amnesty International.

A unique characteristic of the Penal Code is that *Zena*, if unpunishable by Islamic law, is considered an offense punishable with a long prison term. Many women who abscond from home are also tried for *Zena*. A UNODC study, which interviewed 56 women in Pol-e-Charki Prison in Kabul, found that 50 percent were detained for committing "moral crimes," which appear to consist of a wide interpretation of what constitutes *Zena*; most puzzling is that one woman was charged with "attempted adultery."

The 2005 Narcotic Law, Chapter 4, sets forth penalties, primarily the following:

- Trafficking; the punishment is reliant on the amount, and the substance, trafficked. A guideline is set at a maximum of life imprisonment and a fine of between 1,000,000 (US$21,022) and 10,000,000 (US$210,227) afghanis for trafficking heroin, cocaine, or morphine. The minimum sentence is up to three months' imprisonment and a fine of between 5,000 (US$105) and 10,000 (US$210) afghanis for the trafficking of any other substance contained in the tables. Furthermore, employers or organizers of traffickers are set penalties three times as severe as the maximum penalty, not exceeding 20 years.
- Drug laboratories, manufacturing and storage; an individual who allows his or her property to be used for the purpose of manufacturing, cultivating, processing, storing, concealing, or distributing illicit narcotics can be sentenced to between 10 and 20 years' imprisonment and fined between 50,000 (US$1,052) and 1,000,000 (US$21,022) afghanis.
- Drug-related corruption and intimidation is punishable by 5 to 10 years and a fine of twice the amount of the bribe.
- Cultivation; for the cultivating of one *jerib* (0.4 hectares) of opium or coca bush the penalty is between six months and one year of imprisonment and a fine of between 10,000 (US$210) and 50,000 (US$1,052) afghanis. This is increased by one month imprisonment and a 5,000 (US$105) afghani fine per 100 square meters in excess of one *jerib*. In addition the crops shall be destroyed without compensation.
- Consumption of illegal drugs; the consumption or possession of heroin, morphine, or cocaine is punishable with six months to one year in prison and a fine of between 20,000 (US$420) and 50,000 (US$1,052) afghanis. All other substances are punishable with between three and six months' imprisonment and a fine between 10,000 (US$210) and 25,000 (US$315) afghanis for opium or 5,000 (US$105) to 10,000 (US$210) afghanis for all other illicit substances. Possession of more than 1 gram of heroin, morphine, or cocaine and 10 grams of opium or hashish are punished as trafficking.

The Penal Code also gives the court the power to: quarantine individuals into mental health hospitals or other relevant health institutions for a period of no less than six months; restrict individuals movement or residence to prevent repetition of the crime; delicense individuals from their trade or profession or from driving for a limited amount of time; and close properties used to commit a crime. Article 35(2) of the Narcotics Law also allows for the extradition of nationals in accordance with international and bilateral international agreements.

Juvenile Punishment

The Juvenile Code article 10(2) states that children between the ages of 7 and 12 can, instead of penal punishment, be given a warning, confined to a rehabilitation center, or be supervised by social service. Children between 12 and 18 can be punished with long, medium, and short imprisonment as long as it does not exceed one-third of the maximum term given to adults. The death penalty is prohibited, yet continued imprisonment is allowed if it does not exceed half the maximum applied to adults. If the imprisonment is less than three years, then it may take place in a rehabilitation center. One year probation can also be applied in exchange for imprisonment if the term would be less than three years.

Islamic Law

The Penal Code does not offer punishments for *Hudud* or *Qissass* crimes, as under Islamic law these punishments are inflexible. The judge has no discretion once a crime is proved, as punishments are set by the Koran or sunna. *Hudud* punishments consist of the following:

- *Sariqah,* which is punishable with the amputation of a hand.
- *Hirabah,* which is punishable with death, crucifixion, cross-amputation (one hand and one foot), or banishment.
- *Zina,* adultery is punishable with death by stoning, sex outside of marriage with 100 lashes.
- *Qadhf,* which is punishable with 80 lashes
- *Sharb al-Khamr,* which is punishable with 40 lashes.
- *Riddah,* which is punishable with death.

The central concept of *Qissass* is that of *lex talionis* (an "eye for an eye"). Under Islamic law the victim (or victim's family) is entitled, under the supervision of the authorities, to inflict a proportional punishment of similar magnitude to the crime. However, this right may be waived, in which case the offender is pardoned by the wronged party in exchange for a *Diat* (fine).

There have been no recent reports of the official sanction of stoning or flogging (which would suggest minimal or unreported enforcement of *Hudud* punishments). Cases in state courts involving murder and rape have been reported in which the judges have allowed the victim to enforce the execution of the guilty party themselves, or receive a form of compensation (which would conform to *Qissass*). However, all capital punishment must be authorized by the president.

Informal Systems

Punishments differ between tribes and regions, yet certain characteristics permeate all tribes, cultures, and regions, including the belief in restorative justice, with the apology of the perpetrator of the crime being central to this. According to the International Legal Foundation, punishments can include the following:

- The penalty for murder in most regions ranges from the paying of a fine to the victim's family, to the death sentence, or the binding of the families through the giving of a woman from the perpetrator's family to marry a male from the victim's family (a custom condemned by some tribes especially those in Nuristan Province).
- The punishment for *Zena* between two married persons tends to be the death sentence for both parties.
- In Pashtun tribes, if a man rapes a women, he is killed.
- The punishment for theft tends to be centered on returning the goods. However, rules differ as to whether an extra punishment should be enacted. Hazaras pay no extra fine other than an apology, while in the Nuristan Province the extra fine can be anywhere between two and five times the worth of the object and a sheep must be slain at the house of the victim.
- With regard to domestic violence, in the Pashtun regions if a husband beats a wife, the husband must pay the wife's father a fine or in the case of murder, the father may kill the perpetrator.

Furthermore, many rural areas of Afghanistan are controlled by former militia warlords and insurgents, including, but not exclusively, the Taliban. The illicit punishments handed out by such groups are largely undocumented. However, the punishments enforced by the Taliban during its rule may be reflective of its contemporary method of punishment. From 2000 to 2001 the Taliban officially banned the cultivation of the opium poppy. The punishments for disobeying this order included public humiliation; prison sentences of two years or more; and corporal punishment such as lashings, public beatings, and executions. In 2006, more than a dozen Afghan and foreign nationals were beheaded for "crimes" such as espionage and support of the Karzai Government.

Prison

The 2005 Law on Prisons article 12 states that every province shall have a detention center (for holding accused individuals pretrial) and a prison (for holding those convicted of a crime). Each district must also have a detention center. Article 23 obliges all prisons and detention centers to be built in accordance with Islamic principles and the United Nations Standard Principles and Terms, while all remaining facilities must be adjusted. Articles 24 to 28 oblige the state to offer a minimum standard of living, including all individuals having a bed and bedding, adequate hygiene, healthy food, clean drinking water, and the opportunity to walk outdoors in the open air for a minimum of two hours a day; a free health service must also be provided. Well-equipped libraries are required to help detainees to study, worship, and for recreation. Prison administrators are required to operate educational and vocational training centers approved by the Ministry of Education. Prisoners are afforded the right to be remunerated for any work they carry out while incarcerated. Detainees and prisoners have the right to contact with their families; these meetings must be in places controlled by the prison or detention center staff. Article 37 also provides for up to 20 days home leave and up to seven days on compassionate grounds.

The formal prison population has significantly increased in recent years from approximately 600 in 2002 to more than 10,000 in 2007 (in addition to more than 500 juveniles), an increase of more than 1,600 percent in five years, according to the ISISC. As the other arms of the Afghan justice system become more efficient, then this number will likely increase. An alternative estimate by the International Center for Prison Studies for 2007 was 9,600. This estimate states that 2.8 percent of the population was female, 4 percent juveniles, and 0.9 percent foreign nationals.

The current prison infrastructure is unable to cope with such numbers. The flagship prison is Pol-e-Charki, in Kabul, which has been described by a UN official as overcrowded, lacking sufficient power and clean water, with a security situation described as "shaky," largely due to corruption and lack of prison staff. Yet for all these negatives the UN official maintains that "Pol-e-Charki is a great prison compared to the other prisons in the country. . . . Most are uninhabitable."

The Afghan Ministry of Justice has noted that of the 34 official prisons, 42 percent are in rented homes. The U.S. State Department reports that in some districts shipping containers are used to house convicts and that in many areas where no detention facilities exist, women are forced into slave labor for the families of village elders. Furthermore, it is noted with regard to juvenile offenders that in 12 provinces, as separate facilities did not exist, children were detained alongside adults. Due to this children are exposed to physical and sexual exploitation and abuse.

James Windle and Graham Farrell

Further Reading

Conference on the Rule of Law in Afghanistan. (2007): http://www.rolafghanistan.esteri.it/ConferenceRol.

International Crises Group. (2008). Policing in Afghanistan: Still Searching for a Solution: http://www.crisesgroup.org.

Ruben, Barnet. (2006). *Afghanistan's Uncertain Transition from Turmoil to Uncertainty*. New York: Council on Foreign Relations.

United Nations Office of Drugs and Crime: http://www.unodc.org/.

Wardak, Ali. (2004). "Building a Post-War Justice System in Afghanistan." *Crime, Law and Social Change* 41(4): 319–341.

Armenia

Legal System: Civil
Murder: Medium
Corruption: Medium
Human Trafficking: Medium
Prison Rate: Medium
Death Penalty: No
Corporal Punishment: No

Background

A former republic of the Soviet Union, Armenia is a landlocked mountainous country located in the southern Caucasus. One of the world's oldest civilizations, Armenia was the first country to officially adopt Christianity as its religion in 301. However, the current republic was established in 1991 when the country declared its independence from the Soviet Union. The capital of Armenia is Yerevan.

At present, Armenia is a unitary, multiparty, presidential representative democratic republic. Legislative power is entrusted to the Parliament of Armenia. Executive power is exercised by the government while judicial power by the courts.

Armenia is very homogenous. According to the April 2006 data, the population of Armenia was 3,215, 800 with ethnic Armenians making up 97.9 percent of the population. The largest minority groups are the yezidis and Russians. Other minorities include Greeks, Kurds, Assyrians, and Georgians.

History of the Legal System

The history of Armenian criminal law and legal system takes its origins from the first Armenian kingdoms, where judicial power was executed solely by the kings. Later, in the 12th to 13th centuries Mkhitar Gosh's "Codex" and Smbat Sparapet's "Law Book" were introduced. These codified acts contained provisions regulating the age of criminal responsibility, the system of punishments, and evidence.

After many centuries of living under the rule of conquerors and having no state system, in 1918, the First Armenian Republic was created. The government of the newly established country founded a Ministry of Interior and created a police force. A law on police was adopted on April 21, 1920, regulating its structure, jurisdiction, and responsibilities. According to the law, the Ministry of Interior was divided into units ("commissariats") administered in provinces and districts, as well as in Yerevan. In the villages the responsibilities of the police were carried out by the Ministry of Interior officers ("commissars"). In the 1920s, the government of the First Armenian Republic developed the judicial system based on the transformation of the Russian Empire's Court System into the Armenian legislation. The Prosecutor's Service was attached to the Court System.

On November 29, 1920, Armenia was declared a Soviet republic. In 1961, the Criminal Code and Criminal Procedure Code of the Armenian Soviet Republic were adopted, modeled on the Criminal Code of the Russian Soviet Republic. The structure of the Armenian Soviet Republic judiciary system was identical to that of the other Soviet republics. In general, the police and prosecutor's office were responsible for fighting crimes and investigating the cases. Afterward, the cases were handled by the Courts of the First Instance ("national courts"). The Supreme Court of the Armenian Republic had the authority to review the cases solved by the First Instance courts. As to the jails, they were under the control of the Ministry of Justice. All these institutions were acting under the respective bodies of the USSR.

After the collapse of the Soviet Union and the establishment of the new republic, Armenia was faced with the necessity to adopt new legislation and reconstruct the main administrative bodies. During the first years of independence, the legislation of the previous Soviet Union was in force. On July 5, 1995, the Constitution of Armenia was enacted upon the referendum. In 1998, the Parliament of Armenia (which is called National Assembly) approved the Criminal Procedure Code, while the Criminal Code of the newly established Armenia was adopted only on April 18, 2003. The Criminal Code set criminal responsibility for such new offenses as terrorism, money laundering, illegal banking, human trafficking, and so forth. One of the achievements of the code was the introduction of a system of alternative sanctions and abolition of the death penalty, which had been in the Soviet Criminal Code.

Being a civil law country where the legal system is based entirely on written law, Armenia also adopted laws regulating the structure of the judiciary and law enforcement bodies. On November 8, 1996, the president of Armenia signed a decree entitled On Judiciary Reforms of the Republic of Armenia. In 1998, the Armenian Parliament passed laws on Formation of Courts, On the Status of Judges, On Prosecution, On the Solicitor Service, On Compulsory Implementation of Judiciary Acts, and On the Service Providing the Compulsory Implementation of Judiciary Acts.

In correspondence with the new legislation, a three-staged judiciary system replaced the two-staged court system, which was inherited from Soviet times. The new judiciary system started to function consisting of the primary-level Courts of First Instance, followed by the Courts of Appeal and Court of Cassation (the supreme judicial body of the Republic of Armenia except for constitutional matters). As a part of judiciary reforms taking place in the country, on April 18, 2007, the Judicial Code of Armenia was introduced, which provided for the creation of specialized courts, in particular, the Criminal and Civil Courts (Northern, Southern, and Yerevan City). However, in 2008, these specialized criminal courts were abolished.

All the reforms relating to the judiciary are carried out by the Ministry of Justice. The functions of the ministry include, but are not limited to, providing legal advice to the president, governmental bodies, or the legislative branch; providing assistance in developing the legislation of Armenia; administering punishments imposed by the courts; and ensuring the compulsory enforcement of judicial acts of the courts of the Republic of Armenia. As a part of judiciary reforms and as a requirement for Armenia's ascension into the Council of Europe, in 2001, the Penitentiary Service of the Republic of Armenia, which functioned under the jurisdiction of the Ministry of Internal Affairs, was transferred to the jurisdiction of the Ministry of Justice of the Republic of Armenia.

Radical reforms were carried out also in the prosecutor's office and police. In the beginning of the 1999, according to the law On Prosecutor's Office, the prosecution system was divided into the General Prosecutor's Office, Prosecution Offices of the Provinces, of the Yerevan City, of the Yerevan City Districts, as well as into the Prosecutor's Offices of the Military Units. The prosecutor's office is authorized to initiate criminal prosecution, including criminal case, as prescribed by law; wield control over the legality of preliminary investigation and inquiry; support the prosecution on criminal cases in courts; present state interests protection suits to the court; appeal the acts, verdicts, sentences, or the decisions of the court; and supervise the implementation of punishment and other means of enforcement measures. In 2007, one of the functions of the prosecutor's office, investigation of crimes, was taken from the unit and handed to the newly established Special Investigations Service.

As to the police, one of the first changes encountered by this body in 1992 was the creation of internal police forces and the elimination of neighborhood police (the latter to be re-established in later years). Special units to combat organized crime and drug trafficking were created. In the same year, Armenia joined the International Criminal Police Organization (INTERPOL). This helped establish closer cooperation between the police officers of Armenia and foreign countries. In November 1996, the Ministries of Internal Affairs and State Security were combined into one. However, in 1999, they again were divided and continue to function independently.

On April 16, 2001, the Armenian Parliament passed the law On Police and on June 30, 2002, the law On Police Service. According to the last document, the Armenian police became a law enforcement body adjoined directly to the government of Armenia. The main responsibilities of the police include law enforcement, investigation of crimes, crime prevention, social control, and protection of the public.

The activities of the police are directed by the chief of police appointed by the president of Armenia. The structure of the Armenian police is represented by the Central Body, Yerevan Police Department, 10 regional departments (one per each marz/region) and 54 police districts. It also includes the Police Force, Police Academy, and Police Training Center. The Central Body heads the police command staff and is composed of Headquarters, Combating Organized Crime Main Department (including the Trafficking in Drugs and Human Beings Division), Criminal Investigations Main Department, Investigative Main Department, Public Order Department, Personnel Department, Information Center, Public Relations and Press Department, Finances and Economic Affairs Department, Administration, Department of Road Inspection, Passports and Visas Department, State Protection Department, Criminal Forensics and Legal Affairs Department, as well as the National Central Bureau of INTERPOL.

Crime

Detailed definitions of crimes are prescribed by the Criminal Code of Armenia. Therefore, a person cannot be accused as a criminal for the willful committal of a socially dangerous act, if the latter is not established as a crime by the Criminal Code.

Crime in Armenia is multifold. Nowadays the most frequent types of offenses are corruption, tax evasion, assault, and theft. Due to the extremely high level of hidden corruption, crimes are not accurately reflected in official crime statistics. In the last two decades, corruption has become a particular challenge for Armenian society. However, the cases that receive international resonance are based on political motives. One of the offenses took place on October 27, 1999, when six armed men attacked the Armenian parliament and killed the Armenian prime minister and seven other high-ranking officials. The leader of the group, Nairi Hunanyan, accused the government of being corrupt and leading Armenia into political and economic ruin. On October 28, the attackers surrendered and freed the hostages after they were allowed to speak on national television and were promised a fair trial. The court said the criminals had acted on their own and were not guided by outsiders. The criminals were sentenced to life imprisonment. However, many people believe that some political forces, which remained unrevealed and unpunished, were behind the 1999 Armenian parliament shooting.

Classification of Crimes

The age of criminal responsibility in Armenia is 16. However, juveniles who reached the age of 14 before the committal of the crime are subject to criminal responsibility for several types of crimes: murder, rape, violent sexual acts, kidnapping, grave assault, theft, robbery, extortion, hooliganism, joyriding, theft or extortion of weapons, drugs, damaging transportation or communication systems, destruction or damage of property in aggravating circumstances.

Article 19 of the Armenian Criminal Code classifies crimes into four categories: not very grave, medium gravity, grave, and particularly grave offenses. The gravity of the offense is evaluated based on the punishment provided for the particular crime by the Criminal Code of Armenia. Not very grave crimes such as libel, insult, forgery or use of forged documents, false crime reporting, and tax evasion are the least serious of the four offenses and are punished either with a punishment other than imprisonment or with imprisonment not exceeding two years. Medium-gravity intentional crimes such as joyriding or inducting a person into the use of drugs are punished by a term of imprisonment not exceeding five years. Crimes of negligence receive different levels of punishment but usually do not rise above medium gravity so that the categories of grave and very grave crimes include only intentional crimes. Theft, fraud, robbery, drug sale, production, trafficking, assault, and bribery usually are in the list of grave crimes. The Criminal Code provides a maximum punishment not exceeding 10 years of imprisonment for grave crimes. Particularly grave crimes such as murder, money laundering, terrorism, and treason are the most serious crimes. The usual punishment for these crimes is imprisonment for more than 10 years or life imprisonment.

Starting from 2008, no criminal responsibility is provided for the consumption of drugs in Armenia. Nevertheless, criminal responsibility and imprisonment for the term of three to seven years is set for the illegal cultivation, production, sale, supplying, possession, transportation, theft, or extortion of any type of drugs. The punishment can be increased to 15 years if there are aggravating factors. A person voluntarily submitting drugs to police is exempted from criminal responsibility for illegal production, sale, possession, supplying, and transportation of drugs. Special provisions are provided for abetting or involving a person in the use of drugs, as well as for the organization and maintaining of dens for the use of drugs.

Crime Statistics

For many decades Armenia had an image of a country with extremely low crime. During the last several years, the rise of property and violent crimes, as well as drug-related and corruption offenses, has challenged this conception.

According to Armenian police data, the crime rate peaked in 1992 at 473 offenses per 100,000 residents and then began a decline and reached 304 offenses per 100,000 population in 2006. In 2007, there were 8,428 criminal offenses in the country; 43.6 percent of offenses reported to the police were property offenses and 11.6 percent, violent crimes. In spite of the fact that, according to the Corruption Perception Index for 2007, Armenia was ranked 99 out of 179 countries, only seven cases of bribery were registered by the Armenian police. This figure is enough to make anybody think that official crime statistics are misrepresented. According to unpublished data from the Armenian police, the crimes recorded for 2007 were as follows:

Homicide	104
Assault	521
Rape	8
Robbery	199
Theft	2,712
Joyriding	137
Embezzlement	69
Fraud	432
Drug offenses	1,080
Bribery	7
Hooliganism	241
Traffic offense	408
Illegal turnover of weapons	180
Money counterfeiting	57
Other crimes	2,273
Total	**8,428**

Though, according to official data, the trends of such crimes as theft, robbery, rape, and homicide have remained more or less steady over the last 10 years, an enormous change was registered in drug-offense rates. Mitigation of the control over the borders with Turkey and Iran, which used to be strictly closed during the Soviet era, in recent years has contributed to the increase in drug-related offenses. From 1999 through 2007, the drug-offense rate increased sharply, peaking in 2007 with 33.6 drug offenses per 100,000 population.

The reported number and types of offenses vary within the country. In 2007, the highest crime rate was registered in Yerevan (the capital of Armenia) with a rate of 452.7 per 100,000 population, and the lowest rates were registered in Gegharkunik (208.3), Armavir (231.8), and Vayots Dzor (253.5) regions. This distribution has remained almost unchanged since the year 2000.

Both violent and property crimes are relatively higher in urban areas. Thefts, robberies, and frauds are more frequent in metropolitan areas, while assaults are common in rustic areas. According to the unpublished data provided by Armenian police, the homicide rate is higher in Tavush (17.4 per 100,000 population), Syunik (16 per 100,000 population), Yerevan (8.8 per 100,000 population), and Lori (8.1 per 100,000 population). Syunik, Shirak, and Lori have relatively high assault rates, 7.9, 8.8, and 7.3 per 100,000 population, respectively. Thefts are more frequent in Yerevan (118 per 100,000 population), Lori (112.6 per 100,000 population), and Tavush (111 per 100,000 population).

Law enforcement officials and experts are increasingly concerned about juvenile involvement in crime. In 2002, 4.9 percent of the total crimes reported to police were committed by juveniles while in 2007 the percentage reached 6.7 percent. For the given years, the amount of the assaults committed by juveniles increased from 3.6 percent to 6.7 percent, and for thefts the data were 5.3 percent and 16 percent, respectively.

Finding of Guilt

The Constitution and Criminal Procedure Code of Armenia endow the accused with many rights, which include, but are not limited to, protection against unreasonable search and seizure, protection against double jeopardy, protection against self-incrimination, the exclusionary rule, the right to be informed of the charges, the right to be presumed innocent, the right to a public and fair trial, protection against cruel punishments, the right to due process, equal protection under law, and the right to have assistance of counsel.

Starting from the moment of arrest, the accused have the right to have a private or public defender. The latter one is expected to represent the client at every stage of the case proceedings. According to the Criminal Procedure Code of Armenia, the participation of the defender is mandatory in the following cases: the accused undergoes a speedy trial, the accused expressed a wish to have a defender, the accused has difficulties in exercising the right to defense due to physical or mental disorders, the accused does not have sufficient command of the Armenian language, the accused is a juvenile or a person drafted for military service, there are discrepancies in the interests of the accused, meanwhile one of them (the accused) has a defense attorney.

The persons charged with committal of a crime can remain in a status of arrestee for no more than 72 hours. At this stage, the suspects are informed of the charges, have their constitutional criminal-procedural rights explained to them, and are given the opportunity to choose their defender. When 72 hours of an arrest are over, the suspect either has to be freed or must be detained based on the court's decision. Usually, pretrial detention may be executed for a committal of a crime, for which the person can be imprisoned for more than a year. The detainment carried during pretrial proceedings shall not last longer than two months. However, the time of pretrial detention may be extended up to one year due to the complexity of the case. In Armenia, bail is an alternative to the pretrial detention for those who are accused of committing a crime categorized as not grave or medium gravity. As follows, suspects charged with serious offenses, such as murder, rape, robbery, aggravated theft, aggravated assault, kidnapping, and drug trafficking will be denied bail. The court also may deny the release of the accused in those cases where the identity of the accused is not established or when the accused does not have a permanent place of residence, and where the suspect has attempted to hide from the authority that carries out the criminal proceeding.

In Armenia, there is no separate system for juveniles. Though Criminal and Criminal Procedure Codes of Armenia provide several privileges for juveniles, offenses committed by juveniles and adults are handled within the same justice system. Depending on the type of crime committed, the investigation of the case may be conducted by the police, Ministry of Defense, Tax or Customs Service, National Security Service, or Special Investigations Service. In general, police investigators are responsible for the investigation of the majority of crimes including homicide, theft, robbery, drug offenses, and so forth. When the investigation is over, the case either will be dropped or it may be brought before a court. In Armenia, any person charged with a crime may be found guilty only by the verdict of the court. As a rule, when a plea bargain takes place, the case undergoes a speedy trial. In that case, the sentence does not exceed two-thirds of the maximum punishment provided for the charged offense by the Armenian Criminal Code.

The Armenian judicial system consists of three court levels: Universal Jurisdiction Courts of First Instance, Court of Appeals, and Court of Cassation. All the judges in Armenia are appointed by the president of Armenia with the advice of the Justice Council. To become a judge, one has to earn at least a bachelor's degree in law, work as an attorney at least for two years prior to nomination, and graduate from judicial school. There is no special term period during which a person can serve as a judge. However, judges' powers must be terminated upon reaching retirement age.

There are 16 Universal Jurisdiction Courts of First Instance in Armenia with 147 judges in total. Each court has a chairman and judges, who hear any type of civil or criminal case. The second level is the Court of Appeals. There are two courts of appeal in Armenia: the Criminal Appeal Court and the Civil Appeal Court. The Court of Appeals has the authority to review cases resolved by the Court of First Instance. It consists of 16 judges, including the chairman. Each case is reviewed at the Criminal Appeal Court in a panel of three judges. The highest level of the courts is the Court of Cassation. Based on a complaint in cases stipulated by law, the Cassation Court reviews judicial acts of the Court of Appeals. The Cassation Court has two chambers: the Civil Chamber and the Criminal Chamber. The latter consists of six judges, who must participate in any session of the Cassation Court.

Punishment

Armenia's Criminal Code provides the following penalties: a fine; a prohibition to hold certain posts or practice certain professions; public works service; deprivation of special titles or military ranks, categories, degrees, or qualification class; confiscation of property; arrest; service in a disciplinary battalion; imprisonment; or life sentence. These penalties fall into three categories: basic, supplementary, and mixed punishments. Public works, fine, arrest, service in disciplinary battalion, imprisonment, and life sentence are used only as basic punishments. Deprivation of special titles or military ranks, categories, degrees, or qualification class and confiscation of property are applied only as supplementary punishments. Prohibition to hold certain posts or practice certain professions is a mixed punishment and is imposed both as basic and supplementary punishment. Only one basic punishment can be assigned for one crime. One or more supplementary punishments can be added to the basic punishment. Public punishment, banishment, and corporal punishment are not practiced in Armenia. The most commonly used sentencing option is incarceration followed by fines and parole.

According to the statistical data provided by the Criminal–Executive Department of the Armenian Ministry of Justice, at the beginning of 2008, there were 2,922 individuals serving their term in prisons. The typical punishment for murder, rape, robbery, theft, and serious drug offenses is imprisonment. Life imprisonment is practiced for aggravated murder, international terrorism, and genocide, crimes against humanity. The death penalty is not imposed in Armenia.

All convicts serving their term of imprisonment are eligible for parole. To be eligible, the convict must meet two main requirements: have a good record of conduct and actually serve the minimum sentence required by law. The latter one is one-third of the convict's imprisonment term for a not grave or medium gravity offense, half of the punishment for a grave offense, and two-thirds for a particularly grave offense. For some offenses such as aggravated murder, aggravated rape, or aggravated robbery, the inmate has to serve three-fourths of the imprisonment term. The actual term of imprisonment served by a person cannot be less than three months. For juvenile convicts, the minimum sentence required by the law is set to one-fourth, one-third, and half of the imprisonment term for not grave and medium gravity, grave, and particularly grave offenses accordingly. People who were sentenced to life imprisonment can be freed on parole after serving 20 years of incarceration.

Prisons

According to the Criminal–Executive Department of the Armenian Ministry of Justice, at the beginning of 2008, there were 12 correctional institutions in Armenia. In 2008, one more was established, and at present the number of correctional institutions has reached 13.

Based on the level of isolation, the following types of correctional institutions are distinguished: "open," "semiopen," "semiclosed," "closed," and medical penitentiary institution. Assignment of the convicts is based on the seriousness of the offense committed, and, later, the behavior of the inmate. The inmates needing the minimum state of security serve their sentence at penitentiary institutions of the open type, while those sentenced to life imprisonment or imprisonment exceeding 10 years are at closed-type jails. The majority of the penitentiary institutions, except Kosh, Sevan, and Erebuni correctional institutes, provide sections for keeping pretrial detainees.

On January 1, 2008, the total number of prisoners was 3,539 (3,278 in prison and 261 convicts in medical correctional institutions). The majority of the prison inmate population, 53 percent, consists of convicts under the age of 30. Only 4 percent of the prisoners are women, and 1.4 percent are juveniles.

The largest correctional facilities in Armenia are Nubarashen, Kosh, and Erebuni penitentiary institutions. Nubarashen serves as the biggest pretrial detention center where inmates awaiting trial are kept (as of January 1, 2008, 407 of 770 prisoners kept at Nubarashen jail were pretrial detainees), while Kosh and Erebuni prisons' population consists only of adjudicated convicts.

Usually, several levels of isolation (divided by units) are housed in the same facility. Nubarashen jail provides all levels of security, while Kosh Prison serves as a correctional institution of open, semiopen, and semiclosed type. Kosh jail has day rooms, library, and telephones. There are televisions in the day rooms, but there is no access to cable networks. The convicts can make phone calls, but not in unlimited amounts. Inmates are allowed to have visitors. Attorneys can have an unlimited amount of visitation hours with their clients. The others (family, relatives, friends, etc.) can have a limited number of short-term or long-term visitations. The latter one is provided only for the family or close relatives of the prisoner. The duration of short-term visitation is four hours, and the long-term visitation lasts three days. Short-term visits are allowed during the daytime (from 10:00 A.M. until 5:00 P.M.) in special rooms occupied for that purpose. The convict can have short-term visitation once per month, and long-term visitation is allowed once per two months. The number of visitations for those serving a life sentence in prison is reduced to three and one, correspondingly. The visiting rules in correctional institutions provide for a maximum of three adult persons at a time for short-term and two adults for long-term visitations. Juveniles under age 18 do not count as visitors. However, the list of juvenile visitors is restricted to the brothers, sisters, children, or grandchildren of the prison inmates.

Criminals serving their term in prison may be granted a privilege to have extra short-term visits, receive extra parcels, or make additional phone calls for good behavior. Good conduct is required to be eligible for parole or to be transferred to a correctional center with a lower level of isolation. Short-term furloughs usually not exceeding seven days are another form of privilege granted to prisoners and detainees.

Though the correctional institution may require inmates to work, scarcity of jobs makes employment actually impossible. To provide jobs for the prison inmates, the Armenian government founded the fund Assist the Prisoner. In Yerevan in 2006, the market hall Prison Art was opened, which gave the prisoners the opportunity to have their handicrafts sold and the money transferred to their personal accounts. Upon their consent, the prisoners also can be engaged in voluntary works aimed at the maintenance of correctional institution facilities or territories. This occupation cannot exceed two hours per day.

Penitentiary establishments take measures to provide necessary conditions for the education of both juvenile and adult inmates. Secondary and vocational education is offered by the correctional institutions free of charge, while higher education can be provided by correspondence at prisoners' own expense.

Prisoners who serve their punishment in Armenia and who have been charged in another country with any crime can be delivered there. The main requirement is the existence of signed multilateral or bilateral treaties between Armenia and the requesting state. At present, such treaties exist between

Armenia and Russia and many countries of Europe, the Newly Independent States (NIS). No extradition agreement was signed with the United States. However, the transfer of the criminal from Armenia to the United States or any country having no signed agreement with Armenia can be done based on mutual goodwill. An example of prison inmates being transferred to another country is the case of two citizens of Kazakhstan charged with drug smuggling. Drug smugglers planned to take more than 700 grams of heroin to Greece from Tashkent, but the flight was interrupted in Armenia when one of the smugglers went into a coma as the result of the dissolving of the container of heroin he had swallowed. The criminals were sentenced to 10 years of imprisonment. However, in 2008, they were transferred to Kazakhstan upon their request.

Anna Margaryan

Further Reading

Gabuzyan, Ara. (2007). *Problemi prestupnosti v Respublike Armenia v perekhodniy period* (The Problems of Criminality in the Republic of Armenia in the Transitional Period). Yerevan.

Gabuzyan, Ara, and Anna Margaryan. (2004). *Tendenzen der Kriminalität in Armenien in der Übergangszeit. Strafrecht and Kriminaltät Entwicklungen in Mittel-und Osteuropa* (Trends of crime in Armenia during the transition. Criminal justice and crime at developments in Central and Eastern Europe). Bochum.

Margaryan, Anna, and Ara Gabuzyan. (2009). "Armenia." In *Juvenile Delinquency in Europe and Beyond: Results of the Second International Self-Report Delinquency Study,* edited by Josine Junger-Tas, Ineke Haen Marshall, Dirk Enzmann, Martin Killias, Majone Steketee, and Beata Gruszczynska. New York: Springer.

Official Web site of the Judiciary of Armenia: http://www.court.am.

Official Web site of National Statistical Service of the Republic of Armenia: http://www.armstat.am.

Official Web site of the Public Prosecutor Office of the Republic of Armenia: http://www.genproc.am.

Azerbaijan

Legal System: Civil
Murder: Medium
Burglary: Low
Corruption: High
Human Trafficking: Medium
Prison Rate: Medium
Death Penalty: No
Corporal Punishment: No

Background

On the eve of the Soviet Union's dissolution, the Republic of Azerbaijan re-established its independence with passage of the Constitutional Act on Restoration of State Independence, October 18, 1991. With this act, Azerbaijan instituted a presidential republic with a separation of federal powers into legislative, executive, and judicial branches, governed by a system of civil law.

The new constitution of 1995 called for political and individual rights as well as the independence of the judiciary. Since its signing of a memorandum of understanding with the Organization for Security and Co-operation in Europe (OSCE) on the July 17, 2000, Azerbaijan has been obligated to respect the rule of law and observe human rights standards as established in the Copenhagen, Moscow, and Budapest Documents of 1990, 1991, and 1994, respectively. Following its successful bid to join the Council of Europe (CoE), Azerbaijan since January 2001 has been obliged to amend its legislation to conform to CoE standards. After joining the CoE, Azerbaijan ratified in 2002 the European Convention on the Protection of Human Rights and Fundamental Freedoms. As a party to the convention, violations can be brought to the European Court on Human Rights when all domestic avenues have been exhausted.

Legal System

Domestically, district and municipal courts principally serve as trial courts for criminal, civil, and juvenile cases, while the Supreme Court, the head of the judiciary, largely performs appellate reviews. The Supreme Court consists of 12 members appointed by the Chamber of Deputies to serve five-year terms. The court is divided into four chambers with three justices in each. Two chambers are charged with reviewing civil cases, a third chamber handles criminal cases, and a fourth reviews administrative, social, and mining cases. In addition to performing appellate reviews, the High Court has original jurisdiction on questions concerning charges against top officials or state contract disputes.

Responding to indications that the Supreme Court is acquiescent to the authority of the president, the Council of Europe offered financial assistance to facilitate further reform of Azerbaijan's judicial system toward a more democratic example. Although Azerbaijan's Constitution presumes innocence in criminal cases, calls for public trials, and upholds a defendant's right to legal counsel, reports continue that judges are subject to political influence and sometimes may take bribes, according to the Fund for Peace, 2009.

Among the array of crimes addressed by the Penal Code of Azerbaijan, thefts and frauds are the most clearly defined. In the first six months of 2007, for example, 8,676 crimes were officially registered. Of these, approximately 18 percent were premeditated murders while robberies and muggings accounted for 15 percent; 6 percent were reportedly burglaries; 24 percent consisted of cattle theft; and car theft actually dropped by 11 percent during this period, according to a BBC report.

Public prosecutors generally handle prosecutions and supervise investigations by common law enforcement agencies. To practice criminal law, defense attorneys must first obtain membership to the Collegium of Advocates, or the Azerbaijan Bar Association, a quasigovernmental entity that limits its enrollment. Membership is currently obtained through an unclear process that combines a Soviet legacy with an ill-formed mechanism for admitting new members. Further, the Collegium remains under the influence and power of the prosecutor's office. Thus, despite almost 20 years of independence and ongoing attempts to move the legal system further away from the influence of the previous Soviet system, prosecutors maintain an imbalance of power that can influence the outcome of cases.

Although the 2004 Law on Advocates, a revision of the previous 1999 Law on Advocates and Advocate Activity (itself intended as a revision of the 1980 Provision on the Advokatura of the Azerbaijan Soviet Republic), in principle designed to restructure the Collegium's monopoly control over which licensed lawyers can serve as criminal defense attorneys, in practice the Collegium has not been required to establish a clear and transparent mechanism for admitting new members. Consequently, the original 350 members admitted under the 1980 Provisions on the Advokatura, and another 150 subsequently admitted, preserve their monopoly control over criminal defense. Given the low number of criminal defense attorneys available to the public, approximately 500 for a population close to 8.5 million, it appears that Azerbaijan does not have sufficient criminal defense resources to serve its citizens. At the same time, the Collegium's dependence on the prosecutor's office leaves advocates susceptible to the influence of police, investigators, the prosecutor's office, and political authorities.

While legislatively Azerbaijan's judiciary is independent of political control, in practice judges remain largely subject to the executive branch, leading to presumptions of likely corruption and influence peddling. Judges, acting on the instruction of executive branch officials, regularly sentence detainees to jail within hours of their arrest without providing access to a lawyer.

Crime

Even as Azerbaijan's oil-based economic development continues to expand, incidences of officially reported crimes have been increasing over previous years. According to official Ministry of Internal Affairs statistics for 2008, the total number of reported crimes, 21,692, was an increase of 16 percent over 2007 levels. More than 7,500 of these reported crimes involved personal injury, with close to 6,500 concerning theft and robbery and approximately

6,000 committed against public security. While official statistics suggest that 816 crimes were committed against state authority, what constitutes such a crime is contested by a range of national and international commentators. Official statistics published in 2008 by Azerbaijan's State Statistical Committee suggest that in 2007, there were 18,667 crimes with 17,734 convictions.

Human trafficking violations reached 394 reported incidents in 2008, an increase of 111 since 2007. Reported drug possession, distribution, and selling charges reached 3,767, compared to 3,224 in 2007. The Border Control intercepted 350.5 pounds (159 kg) of illegal drugs while the Ministry of Internal Affairs confiscated 1,435 pounds (651 kg) within the country.

On the other hand, 2008 also marked an apparent decline from 2007 in certain officially reported crimes, ranging from bribery (a reported decrease of 50%) and car theft (down 33%), to sexual assault (down 26%) and willful homicide (down 4.5%), as reported by the Ministry of Internal Affairs.

While violence against women remains problematic throughout the country, and legislation provides for criminal prosecution of domestic violence and punishment for acts of rape (including spousal rape), comprehensive statistics concerning the scope of the problem are sketchy. Officially, there were 34 reported instances of rape and attempted rape in 2007, compared to a 12-year high reportedly set in 1995 of 70, according to an Organisation for Economic Cooperation and Development (OECD) 2009 report.

Finding of Guilt

Four years after the Republic of Azerbaijan declared its independence, the Police Law was passed in 1995, formally instituting a centralized state police system. The country's initial internal Special Forces unit, the Detachment of Police of Special Purposes (OPOR), played a significant role in early 1990s political and public life. However, after this military unit mutinied in the nation's capital in 1993, its command was disbanded and subsequently Azerbaijan's internal security forces were placed under the control of the Ministry of Internal Affairs rather than the Department of Defense. Empowered to contain protests, processions, and unauthorized activities, these forces were called upon by the central government to keep a check on protests surrounding the results of the 2003 presidential elections.

Police, the prosecutor's office, and magistrates each can instigate identity checks and arrests; the prosecutor's office and police can further order questioning of citizens. Police have the power to detain individuals for 48 hours but with a judge's order can hold individuals in custody longer; police do not require a court order to conduct searches of persons and premises. With a court order, police are empowered to tap private telephone lines as well as bug public locations.

Azerbaijan adheres to the presumption of innocence, a tenet ensured in principle by article 63 of the Constitution, the Criminal Code of Procedure, and the Code of Administrative Offences. In practice, according to a study commissioned by the Baku Office of the Organization for Security and Co-operation in Europe (OSCE) in 2006, the Prosecutor General, the Minister of Internal Affairs, representatives of the Presidential Apparatus, and the heads of other administrative bodies frequently refer to suspects in high-profile cases as "criminals" without a final court decision and will discuss evidence publicly.

After a decade or so of the media's growth and diversification, since assuming the presidency following his father in 2003, the government of President Aliyev has been increasing its formal and informal restrictions on freedom of expression. Consequently, the largely government-controlled media has been complicit in its broadcast of unproven allegations and accusatory speeches with apparently little regard for fact checking, further complicating the constitutionally protected right to the presumption of innocence.

The Constitution ensures that every citizen who has been detained, accused, or arrested for a crime has the right to legal representation at each stage of his or her legal proceeding. The Constitution's article 61 guarantees the right of every citizen to have access to a lawyer from the moment of detention,

Police officers detain an opposition activist while dispersing an unsanctioned rally against President Ilham Aliev in downtown Baku, Azerbaijan, December 18, 2005. (AP Photo/Aida Sultanova)

accusation, or arrest for a crime, while article 67 directly provides that each accused, arrested, or detained individual will be advised of his or her rights immediately. The Law on Advocates and the Criminal Procedure Code each provide that an advocate and client will be given adequate time to meet in private. According to a study by ABA-CEELI (2005), however, for the most part neither jails, courthouses, nor police stations have or provide for private and separate meeting rooms. Further, consultations between client and advocate are commonly conducted either in the presence of law enforcement personnel or members of the court. While the Constitution provides the right of access to an advocate from the moment of arrest or detainment, individuals may be held for several days without access to a defense attorney, or until the accused has signed a confession. Although the Constitution's articles 57, 60, and 65 guarantee the general right of appeal, the appeal's process in practice can be somewhat unclear, and the actual timeframe varies on a case-by-case basis.

Prison

Azerbaijan's prison system, administered by the Chief Department for the Execution of Court Decisions and overseen by the Ministry of Justice, consists of more than 50 penal institutions ranging from those for juveniles to maximum-security units. Like many other penal systems in Eurasia, Azerbaijan employs congregate rather than single-occupancy cells. Azerbaijan's penal institutions are divided according to population. For example, certain facilities house juveniles while others are dedicated to former police officers and members of the civil service; one is reserved for women, and another for tuberculosis patients.

The total prison population as of 2007 was 18,259 consisting of approximately 10 percent women, 4 percent repeat offenders, and almost 70 percent from the ranks of the unemployed. Of those convicted of a crime and serving time in 2007, sentences of two to five years were most common. There were 18 individuals sentenced to life imprisonment.

The Parliament on June 24, 2008, voted to approve penitentiary legislation that called for the improvement of penal detention standards. These improvements included, among others, more family visits, allowance of food parcels brought in from the outside, and a reduction in the number of inmates per cell for those serving life imprisonment. Capital punishment was abolished in Azerbaijan in 1998, following a moratorium on executions applied in 1993.

Jeremy Tasch

Further Reading

ABA-CEELI. (2005). *The Legal Profession Reform Index for Azerbaijan*. Azerbaijan: American Bar Association and Central European and Eurasian Law Initiative.

Abdullahzade, Cavid. (2007). "The Status of International Treaties in the Legal System of Azerbaijan." *Review of Central and East European Law* 32: 233–256.

"Human Rights Center of Azerbaijan Individual UPR submission—Azerbaijan, September 2008." (2008): http://209.85.229.132/search?q=cache:aJYe60n5bCYJ:humanrightshouse.org/noop/file.php%3Fid%3D10010+Human+Rights+Center+of+Azerbaijan+Individual+UPR+submission+-+Azerbaijan,+September+2008&cd=1&hl=az&ct=clnk&gl=az&client=firefox-a.

"Life Imprisonment and Conditions of Serving the Sentence in the South Caucasus Countries." (2009). A Project of the Global Action to Abolish the Death Penalty, DDH/2006/119763: http://www.penalreform.org/edith/South%20Caucasus%20Life%20Term%20feb%2009.pdf.

Ministry of Internal Affairs. (2009): http://www.mia.gov.az/?/en/content/29162/.

Bangladesh

Legal System: Common/Islamic
Murder: Medium
Corruption: High
Human Trafficking: Low
Prison Rate: High
Death Penalty: Yes
Corporal Punishment: Yes

Background

Bangladesh became an independent nation in 1971. It is located in South Asia and is nearly surrounded by Indian territory except for a small strip in the southeast, where it borders Myanmar. Formerly, Bangladesh was a part of British India and then of Pakistan from 1947 through 1971. The total land area is 147,570 square kilometers (56,977 square miles) and its population is 153,546,896 as of July 2008, which makes it the seventh most populous country in the world. The main religion in Bangladesh is Islam, and Bangla is the primary language. Muslims account for 88 percent of the total population, Hindus 10.5 percent, less than 1 percent Buddhist or Christian.

Bangladesh has experienced an unstable political climate since its independence. This political instability has often resulted in emergency declarations of martial law, undermining the legal regime of personal liberty. The impact of such political regimes on the criminal justice system has been clearly demonstrated in the administration of courts and corrections (justice) in Bangladesh. For example, the increased use of preventive detention under the present emergency rule has caused unprecedented growth in prison population. Also, it produced an increasing number of convictions in special courts.

The imposition of emergency on January 11, 2007, has significantly altered the political history of Bangladesh. Over the years enactment of special laws such as Special Powers Act, Anti-Terrorism Act, Public Safety Act, Speedy Trial Act, and more recently, Emergency Powers Ordinance 2007 and Anti-Terrorism Ordinance 2008 have greatly affected the administration of law and order as well as the protection of basic human rights in Bangladesh. At the same time, these legislative initiatives by the government have increased the punitiveness of the criminal justice system. The United Nations Development Programme (UNDP) 2002 report states that Bangladesh is facing a significant level of human insecurity with regard to access to justice, enforcement of laws, misuse of authority and abuse of power by some people. A study by Bangladesh Rural Advancement Committee (BRAC) found that "the administration of justice is underfunded, painfully slow and inefficient which results in excessive delays." At the same time, the justice system is not accessible to a great majority of the population due to costs and time associated with litigation, lack of legal awareness, and fear of interaction with the police.

After assuming state power on January 11, 2007, the caretaker government worked to ensure a good governance and corruption-free society. To implement this political agenda the government had adopted more than 60 ordinances and policies on legal and institutional reforms during the tenure of the government. The major ordinances and policies that were adopted by the caretaker government include separation of the judiciary from the executive and formation of the Supreme Judicial Commission to ensure the appointment of neutral and competent judges, National Human Rights Commission, Anti-Terrorism Ordinance, and Bangladesh Attorney Service.

Since corruption became a great concern for the government, it reconstituted the Anti-Corruption Commission (ACC) to fight corruption effectively. More than 70,000 cases were filed with the ACC during the last 18 months. As a part of crackdown on rampant corruption, the military-backed interim government had detained immediate past prime minister Khaleda Zia and her two sons and another former prime minister, Sheikh Hasina. Both the prime ministers had to face charges of corruption and extortion. The ACC filed a large number of corruption cases against the top politicians. Accordingly, more than 160 political leaders, including former ministers and parliament members, had been detained, and many of them received jail sentences ranging from 3 to 13 years. Although the caretaker government made significant advances in its drive to bring corrupt politicians to justice, toward the end of its rule almost all the detained political leaders, including the two former prime ministers, had been released from the jail just to ensure the participation of the two major political parties in the national election held on December 29, 2008. It is important to mention that the caretaker government made reform in many constitutional bodies. For example, reform in the election system ensures that corrupt and convicted politicians could not take part in the election. And the government became more lenient toward corruptive and convicted politicians who were allowed to participate in the election.

It appears that the caretaker government could not sustain the political pressure from the two major political parties, though many believed that the prosecution of corrupt politicians and other reform activities would bring a new political era. However, after the national election in which the Awami League came to state power with overwhelming victory, the newly elected government has already discarded many reform activities initiated by the caretaker government. Most importantly, some of the ordinances and bills were not even endorsed by the new Parliament. As a result, the political culture of Bangladesh remained largely unchanged due to unwillingness of the political parties.

Legal System

Bangladesh inherited a colonial legal system from the British and Pakistani rule, thus the legal system is founded on English common law. Nevertheless, most laws in Bangladesh are statutory laws passed by the legislature and interpreted by the higher courts. The procedural laws offer an adversarial system of proceedings in which prosecution has to prove the guilt of the accused and the accused is presumed innocent until found guilty after trial. On the other hand, in a civil case the burden is divided between the litigating parties. All laws of the country are subordinate laws made by the elected Parliament in compliance with the principles of the Constitution.

The judicial system remained the same until the enactment of the Constitution of Bangladesh on December 16, 1972. The two levels in the court system include the subordinate courts and the Supreme Court. The subordinate courts are divided into two broad classes: civil courts and criminal courts. The civil courts are created under the Civil Courts Act of 1887. There are five tiers of civil courts, which have jurisdiction to try all suits of a civil nature. There are two classes of criminal courts, Courts of Session and Courts of Magistrate. There are four tiers of judicial magistrates: chief metropolitan magistrate in metropolitan area and chief judicial magistrate to other areas, magistrate of the first class, second class, and third class.

The Supreme Court is divided into two sections: the High Court and the Appellate Court. The High Court hears original cases and assesses cases from the lower courts. The Appellate Court has jurisdiction to hear appeals of judgments, decrees, orders, or sentences of the High Court or any other body. Verdicts of the Appellate Court are binding on all other courts. The High Court may proclaim any law incompatible with the fundamental rights as null and void. The Supreme Court is not only autonomous, but also acts as the keeper of the Constitution. In addition to interpreting laws made by Parliament, the Supreme Court can also enforce fundamental rights of the citizens.

In addition there are administrative tribunals to decide service disputes of public servants and some special courts and tribunals such as family court, Artha Rin Adalat (Money Loan Court) to decide money claims of the banks and other financial institutions, Nari-o-Shishu Nirjatan Daman Adalats to decide cases of crimes committed against children and women.

Parliament can enact laws, but that must be consistent with the provisions of the Constitution. It appears that almost all the substantive laws creating rights and obligations are those endorsed during the British period, and are still in action with alterations over time. For example, the existing Criminal Codes and Procedures in Bangladesh result from the period of British rule, as modified by Pakistan and Bangladesh. Likewise, the fundamental documents such as the Bangladesh Penal Code, first promulgated in 1860 as the Indian Penal Code; the Police Act of 1861; Bengal Jail Code of 1864; the Evidence Act of 1872; the Code of Criminal Procedure of 1898; the Criminal Law Amendment Act of 1908; the Official Secrets Act of 1911; the Muslim Personal Law (Shariat) Application Act, 1937, relating to Muslim family affairs, are still in operation in Bangladesh.

Politicization of Police

The state exercises strong control over police agencies. As a consequence many policy decisions regarding police are instigated for political purposes. Evidence indicates that politicians even manipulate preparation of charge sheets and final reports; as a result the "fall out" rate of arrest is high. Most importantly, the investigations of sensational cases have been redirected according to the will of the ruling party.

It may be noted that after assuming state power each successive government brought major changes in different tiers of the police administration, including the appointment of new police chiefs. For example, during the tenure of Bangladesh Nationalist Party (BNP) government (October 2001–October 2006) a total of 65 senior (of them 6 additional inspector generals, 19 deputy inspector generals, and 4 additional deputy inspector generals) and 950 lower-ranking police officers were forced to retire, while 796 members of the police force were dismissed during the same period on political grounds. Similarly the new Awami League government also brought major changes in the police administration.

In sum, the extent of politicization has been reflected in appointment, promotion, and academy training of the police officers.

To improve the quality of police services in 2007, the caretaker government drafted a new police ordinance aiming at freeing police from extraneous influences and making them more accountable to the people. The ordinance entitled Bangladesh Police Ordinance, 2007 will replace the existing 148-year-old Police Act. The goal of the new ordinance includes making police more service-oriented and people friendly and protecting human rights. Under the new ordinance any interference in police work will be treated as a criminal offense. Unfortunately, the caretaker government did not pass the draft ordinance and the new political government has yet to pass the ordinance as well.

Separation of Judiciary

Although the Constitution grants an independent judiciary, the lower courts have remained a part of the executive branch since independence. In 1999, the Supreme Court gave a 12-points directive for separating the judiciary from the executive organ of the state. The directive came following a case—popularly known as the Masder Hossain case filed in 1995. Despite the repeated pledge, the successive political governments did not take any steps for separating the judiciary. Finally, on November 1, 2007, the interim government implemented the court's directive for the separation of judiciary. Accordingly, all magistrates at subordinate courts started exercising their judicial functions under the authority of the Supreme Court that contributed to significant changes in the structure of criminal courts in Bangladesh. Moreover, the existing Code of Criminal Procedure 1898 has been revised. Truly, this is the major achievement of the past caretaker government.

Crime Control and Human Rights

There have been allegations that two specific laws facilitate endemic human rights violations in Bangladesh: (1) the Special Powers Act, 1974 (SPA) and (2) the Emergency Powers Rules of 2007. The SPA allows arbitrary detention for long periods of time without charge, and Section 54 of the Code of Criminal Procedure facilitates torture in police or army custody. The limited safeguards provided in the act allow the government to abuse it to control freedom of expression and to suppress political opposition. Political parties have repeatedly promised to repeal the law when in opposition, but the law has been maintained so far. Each year, thousands of people are capriciously in custody under SPA, which rebuffs them from resorting to judicial remedies.

The legal experts argue that a number of provisions in the Emergency Powers Ordinance and Emergency Powers Rules (EPR) 2007, providing death penalty and life-term imprisonment for violating these provisions and also any rules with retrospective effect, are against the fundamental structure of the country's Constitution. For example, Rule 10(2) states that "all crimes committed under this law shall be cognizable, non-compoundable and non-bailable." Also, Section 6(1) of the Emergency Powers Ordinance 2007 provides blanket impunity for all actions to state actors.

In sum, the Emergency Powers Rules (EPR), enforced by the government in January 2007, suspended many basic rights, including freedom of press, freedom of association, and the right to bail. There were widespread allegations that in the prosecution of anticorruption cases in the newly established Special Judges' Courts instead of regular courts, the due process rights of the accused were not maintained properly. Meanwhile, the present government has withdrawn a large number of corruption cases against the leaders of the ruling political party, arguing that all the cases were politically motivated.

Police

The police in Bangladesh are a centralized national force. The Ministry of Home Affairs controls its functions while the operational responsibilities are vested in Police Headquarters. The inspector general is the chief executive of the police departments.

Bangladesh police follow the British police system of the colonial era with some minor modifications. The Police Act of 1861 oversees the police administration, whereas operational parts are directed by the Police Regulation of Bengal (PRB), 1943. In addition, the Home Ministry has the authority to issue administrative regulations on personnel and police operations.

The main branches in the police department include Traffic, Special, and Detective branches. In addition to that, there is the Central Investigation Department (CID), which deals with the high profile and serious cases, and Rapid Action Battalion (RAB). In recent years, Highway Police and Trafficking of Human Beings (THB) units have been introduced. Policing activities are carried out from a central office known as police station (Thana) in both urban and rural areas. There are presently 599 police stations in Bangladesh. The officer in charge (OC) of a police station is responsible for maintaining law and order and prevention and detection of crimes in his jurisdiction. The metropolitan police, a separate wing within the police department, are responsible for policing the major cities of the country.

Police officers are classified as gazetted and nongazetted, roughly equivalent to commissioned and noncommissioned officers in the military services. The top four managerial positions are inspector general of police (IGP), additional inspector general, deputy inspector general (DIG), and superintendent of police (SP). The nongazetted category consists of inspector, sub-inspector (SI), and assistant sub-inspector (ASI). The superintendent (SP) of a district and officer in charge (OC) of a Thana are the two most powerful officers in the police administration. The lower echelons of the police are known as constables and constitute more than 70 percent of the police force. According to Police Headquarters, as of June 2008, the total manpower of Bangladesh police was 123,000.

Rapid Action Battalion (RAB): Policing by Military

In the face of the rising crime problem, especially organized crime, the government has created a specialized unit of police called the Rapid Action Battalion (RAB) in June 2004, based on the Armed Police Battalions (Amendment) Act, 2003. It is a composite force drawing its personnel from the police, paramilitary forces, and the various branches of the armed forces. Presently, 12 battalions of RAB are working throughout the country. In comparison to the police, RAB staff are better trained, well paid, and well prepared.

The main functions of RAB include crime fighting, elimination of illegal arms, arrest of wanted criminals, controlling organized crime (e.g., women and child trafficking), Islamic militancy, and money laundering. Since its inception, RAB has played a very effective role in improving the law and order situation in the country. Its success stories include apprehension of top leaders of Islamic militants like Jamatul Mujahidin of Bangladesh (JMB), Horkatul Jehad, and some most wanted gang leaders. Despite wider public acceptance, its involvement in "extra-judicial killings," popularly known as "crossfire," has generated wide controversy among politicians and members of civil society groups at home and abroad. The U.S.–based Human Rights Watch reports that over the past four years, RAB members have killed more than 540 people as of June 2008.

Crime

Classification of Crimes

The major categories of crimes and their punishments are listed in the Penal Code and Schedule II of the Code of Criminal Procedure 1898, the country's most significant and comprehensive penal decree. Among the listed classifications of more serious crimes are activities called offenses against the state, offenses affecting life, such as murder. Among other categories of felonies are offenses against the public tranquility (meaning unlawful assembly), rioting, and public disturbances; offenses relating to religion; and offenses against property, such as theft, robbery, and dacoity (robbery by a group of five or more persons). The age of criminal responsibility in Bangladesh is 16 years.

Crime Statistics

Bangladesh experienced a sharp increase in crimes in the early 2000s. A study by Kashem for the Bangladesh Center for Criminological Research found that over the years, the patterns of murders have changed significantly in terms of premeditation and brutality. And the use of firearms in committing crimes, especially murder, has increased in the past decade. The data provided by the Police Headquarters indicate that between 2000 and 2007, the number of reported crimes has increased by 44 percent in Bangladesh. While, during the same period, violent crime such as murder has increased by 13.6 percent. According to crimes recorded by police in 2007, there were 157,200 reported crimes and an overall crime rate of 91.5 per 100,000 population. The most typical crimes recorded by police in rural areas are theft, robbery, cruelty to women for dowry, while in urban areas the most typical crimes are burglary, mugging on the city streets, drug-related crime, and extortion at the city markets and business establishments. Most recent crime statistics (2007) are as follows:

Dacoity (gang robbery)	1,047
Robbery	1,298
Murder	3,863
Seedy Trail Act	1,980
Rioting	263
Cruelty to women	14,250
Child abuse	967
Police assault	278
Burglary	4,439
Theft	12,015
Arms Act	1,746
Explosive Act	232
Narcotics	15,622
Smuggling	5,202
Kidnapping	774
Others	93,224

Controlling Muslim Militancy

In recent years the rise of religious militancy is a big challenge for the law-enforcing agencies of Bangladesh. It appears that since 1999, attacks by Islamist militants have been increasing. They have targeted opposition politicians, scholars, journalists, members of the judiciary, religious minorities, and so forth. Law-enforcement agencies have identified 29 Islamic organizations for suspected involvement in militancy. Of them only two major militant groups, namely, Jama'atul Mujahideen (JMB) and Harkatul Jihad-al-Islami (Huji), are active. Interviews of senior police officers suggest that controlling religious militancy is a difficult task, as the issue is linked to policy choice of the government. Most importantly, the law-enforcement agencies cannot get tough on them because of the religious issue. One leaflet of these organizations entitled *"Islamer Prokrito Salah"* ("Real Salah +9of Islam") says that "jihad or military program or armed struggle is a must to establish the rule of Islam." Using the verses of the holy Koran, it is reported that "if anyone leaves jihad or armed struggle, they shall not be accepted to Allah as a *momen* (devout/real Muslim)." Citing this example, one senior official of a law-enforcement agency observes: "As long as the government allows such campaigns or activities and does not prohibit such propaganda, we cannot consider it as an offence." That is, existing laws are inadequate to fight against militancy. The government has so far banned four Islamist militant organizations. But police could not trace the many leaders of these militant groups because their activities are largely confined to mosques and madrassas (religion-based educational institutions).

Women and Child Trafficking

Trafficking in human beings (THB) has been increasing in Bangladesh. The major factors behind the trafficking have been identified as poverty, illiteracy, landlessness, overpopulation, and low levels of income. There are no reliable statistics; however, according to United Nations Children's Fund (UNICEF) since 2004, between 10,000 and 29,000 children are used for the purpose of prostitution in Bangladesh. In fact, the actual number of THB cases is higher than the recorded ones by the police. According to a U.S. State Department report (2005), Bangladesh serves as both the source and transit country for men, women, and children. They are used "for the purpose of sexual exploitation, involuntary domestic servitude, child camel jockeying, and debt bondage." The U.S. State Department Trafficking in Persons Report 2008 revealed that Bangladeshi women and children were engaged in forced labor and prostitution in India and Pakistan. While boys have been used as camel jockeys in the Middle Eastern countries such as United Arab Emirates and Saudi Arabia, most of them were trafficked to these countries through fraudulent job offers by some Bangladeshi recruitment agencies.

In a country like Bangladesh, clearly, the social consequences of trafficking are extremely serious, especially for the women and girls who are sold for the purpose of sexual exploitation. According to police officials, the investigation of trafficking cases is complex and time-consuming. Additionally, the police and judicial departments do not have sufficient capacities in prosecuting trafficking cases, which is a major obstacle in controlling trafficking. Recently, within the police department, a specialized THB unit has been set up to strengthen the fight against different types of trafficking.

Cybercrime

Although cybercrime is still not alarming in Bangladesh, the growing number of Internet users poses a great threat to the country. So, Bangladesh police are now improving their capacity to combat cybercrime. They have identified the following sites: (1) illegal prostitution promotion sites; (2) use of the Internet for transmitting false and malicious information; and (3) use of the Internet for women and child trafficking. Interviews with police officers suggest that due to a lack of resources, trained investigators, and equipment, presently it would be very difficult for the police to control cybercrime in Bangladesh. Furthermore, in the absence of digital forensic laboratories for investigation and detection of cybercrime, the investigative capability of the police is limited. In identifying the major obstacles to controlling cybercrime, police executives argue that cybercrime is not a cognizable offense. On the other hand, the lack of legislation to extradite the offender is one of the major obstacles in dealing with this problem. The establishment of a Cyber Appellate Tribunal is essential. At the same time, the level of Information Communication Technology (ICT) knowledge of judges must be increased for successful prosecution of cybercrimes.

Finding of Guilt

Jury trial does not exist in Bangladesh. In the subordinate courts a single judge hears all the cases while in the Supreme Court, a judicial panel comprising two to three judges conducts the majority of the trials. Trials conducted under the SPA and the Women and Children Repression Prevention Act are analogous to normal trials, but these are tried without the prolonged deferments as observed in other cases. Under the provisions of the Speedy Trial Act (STA) and the Women and Children Repression Prevention Act, special tribunals hear cases and issue judgments. Cases under these laws have to be investigated and tried within specific time restrictions. For example, the Women and Children Repression Act, 2000 (Nari O Shishu Nirjatan Daman Ain, 2000) specifies a speedy investigation (generally within 60 days; with permission of the Tribunal within 90 days to 120 days—Section 18) and trial (within 180 days—Section 20).

Rights of Accused and Legal Aid

The rights of the accused include the right to be represented by counsel, to review accusatory material, to call witnesses, and to appeal verdicts. State-funded defense attorneys are seldom afforded, and there are few legal aid programs to offer financial assistance to poor plaintiffs. There is no mandated provision of counsel for accused indigents, but the government does appoint lawyers to represent individuals tried in absentia. In rural areas, individuals frequently do not have legal representation. In urban areas, legal counsel usually is offered if individuals can find the funds. Nevertheless, there are accusations that sometimes detainees and suspects in police custody were denied right of legal counsel.

Legal aid in many countries, for example, the United States, United Kingdom, and India, has

Prisoners look out from a prison van at the court premises in Dhaka, Bangladesh, August 4, 2009. Bangladesh launched a campaign to formally establish village courts in 500 rural administrative councils to settle small-scale disputes outside formal courts. (AP Photo/Pavel Rahman)

developed largely through private initiatives. The voluntary organizations such as legal aid societies, social service organizations, law school clinics, and bar associations have been playing an important role for the poor. In Bangladesh as well, some leading nongovernment organizations (NGOs) have come forward to provide legal aid, sometimes with the active assistance of different donor agencies. Among the most prominent organizations are Bangladesh Legal Aid and Service Trust (BLAST), Ain O Salish Kendro (ASK), Bangladesh National Women Lawyers' Association (BNWLA), and Madaripur Legal Aid Association. Most of these NGOs render legal aid schemes to cover a particular area of the country, but some have been offering legal assistance all over the country. For example, BLAST has been providing legal assistance to the poor through legal aid clinics in the country. These organizations offer training, mediation, legal awareness, and counseling schemes to help indigent people solve their legal problems. Besides that, since 1996, BLAST has been conducting a number of public interest litigations aimed at improving the legal empowerment of poor and marginal people.

Under the Legal Aid Act of 2000, the government formed a National Legal Aid Organization to provide legal aid to poor litigants. Between 2001 and 2007, legal aid has been provided in 56,211 cases (civil and criminal) in 55 districts. Also, legal aid has been provided in 1,020 jail appeal cases.

Problems of the Court System

A major problem of the court system is the devastating accumulation of cases, and prolonged trial process. Consequently, many accused persons are held in prison for many years. It is alleged that corruption occurs in the judicial process, prohibiting many persons from attaining a fair trial. A survey by the World Bank in 2005 found that the performance of judiciary was the worst among the participating countries in the survey. The average civil case in the district court in Bangladesh takes nearly five years to resolve, excluding the time taken for the appeals process. In some cases, especially land-related litigation, it is more than 15 to 20 years from filing in the trial court to decision by the appeal court.

The data provided by the Supreme Court revealed that as of January 1, 2008, more than 1.6 million cases are pending in Bangladesh. Of them, the Appellate Division of the Supreme Court has 8,834, the High Court has 262,345, and the judicial magistracy has 602,173 cases. However, the disposal rate of cases has significantly increased since the separation of judiciary.

Between November 2007 and April 2008, a total of 307,322 cases were disposed of. It appears that the rate of disposal of criminal cases in the courts of magistrates has increased by 51 percent in December 2007, as compared to the cases disposed of by the judicial magistrates in November 2007. Interviews suggest that the lengthy trial process and the shortage of judges in the court systems cause enormous delay in disposing of cases. To bring transparency to the judiciary, modern technology has been introduced in the management of court and cases in recent years.

Prosecution

Bangladesh does not have an enduring prosecution service. The attorney general is the major law officer of the government. He or she is aided by the additional attorney general, deputy attorney generals, and assistant attorney generals. They stand for the state in the Supreme Court and conduct cases at courts on behalf of the state. Currently, there are 77 attorneys, including the attorney general for dealing with cases for the state.

Additionally, at the subordinate courts, the prosecution division consists of public prosecutor (PP), government pleader (GP), and special public prosecutor (SPP). Law officers are attended by assistants, whose numbers differ based on the number of courts in their jurisdiction, and the size and population of the district. They correspond to the state in the subordinate civil and criminal courts in the district and perform cases in these courts on behalf of the state.

Law officers are appointed on the basis of their political affiliations. The recruitment process depends on the political selection of the ruling political party. Consequently, whenever a new party holds the power, all prosecutors are removed from their posts, and a new group substituted.

Interviews with the court officials suggest that one of the major problems of this political appointment is that in many cases younger and less-experienced lawyers are being appointed using their personal and political connections. It is noteworthy that a large number of these prosecutors often have insufficient knowledge of law and experience in legal practice. On the other hand, senior lawyers are unwilling to serve as prosecutors because of the lack of facilities and low payment.

To improve the state of prosecutorial service, the past caretaker government has created the Government Attorney Department for dealing with cases in courts and performing other duties on behalf of the state. Under the new ordinance, the Attorney Department would directly recruit the law officers (prosecutors) through competitive examination with transparency, neutrality, and responsibility. But the new government did not endorse the ordinance in Parliament. As a result, the process of political recruitment remained unchanged.

The use of police officers as prosecutors is another distinctive feature of government prosecution service. Under Sections 492(2) and 495 of the Code of Criminal Procedure, the government allocates police to conduct the prosecution in the magistrates' courts, which deal with approximately 70 percent of all cases in the country. Typically, a police officer at the rank of sub-inspector handles the prosecution of cases before the court, even if these officers do not have law degrees or sufficient training in prosecution. Interviews with police officers, however, suggest that since police investigate the cases, they can plead the case better than the regular prosecutors to prove charges against the accused.

Investigation

The most common preliminary step in the quest of justice is to file a complaint either with a police station or magistrates' court in the jurisdiction where the offense allegedly happened. Complaints filed with police are classified as GR cases: those on the Government Register. Nevertheless, in many cases filing complaints with police stations is hard for the poor and politically weak, particularly if the complaints relate to wealthy and politically powerful persons. In such cases, the other selection is to file a complaint straight to a magistrates' court. Such cases are categorized as CR cases: those on the Complaint Register. In either category of cases, police investigate, collect evidence, and take essential steps.

It has been argued that successful prosecution of criminal cases requires a thorough and professional police investigation. A study by Kashem and Saadi reported at the Asian Association of Police Studies in 2007 found a "high fall out" rate. Between 2002 and 2006, the average conviction rate for the police-submitted charge sheets was about 34 percent. The study also reported that political influence in police investigative work and improper use of the public prosecutors for personal benefit or some other reasons are largely responsible for this low conviction rate. The police chief (IGP) recently pointed out that police submit charge sheets in about 50 to 60 percent of the cases, while the rest end up in final reports (closing the inquiry without trial).

The prosecutions of criminal cases in Bangladesh are heavily dependent on oral evidence and confession instead of physical evidences. Research on police investigations suggests that the amendments of various legal provisions in the Evidence Act of 1872 are essential to rectify the existing investigative practices of police. Specifically, changes in the rules regarding confessional and self-incriminating statements by the suspects before the police or magistrates are essential for efficient investigations of criminal cases. The lack of specially trained evidence technicians for crime scene processing also affects the quality of police investigation in Bangladesh.

Alternatives to Trial

Alternative Dispute Resolution (ADR)

Plea bargaining does not exist in the court system of Bangladesh. Thus, in the face of the judicial system's million-case backlog, the government has been experimenting with the Alternative Dispute Resolution (ADR). ADR is a process to settle disputes through a consensual method chosen voluntarily by the parties. Three main types of ADR consist of negotiation, mediation (including conciliation), and arbitration. The Ministry of Law in 2001 began a pilot program offering ADR in various civil cases through mediation or arbitration. Since then, ADR is becoming a popular mode of dispute resolution by the litigants of civil cases. The concept of alternative dispute resolution in the form of mediation in family disputes was first introduced in the Family Court Ordinance of 1985. Accordingly, exclusive family courts were established in June 2000. Also, the judicial mediation program in the district-level family courts has been implemented in some selected jurisdictions, for example, in Dhaka and Chittagong. It is known that in view of the time and costs associated with traditional lawsuits, many favor ADR. Most importantly, it provides an opportunity for community involvement or participation in the dispute resolution process. Based on government reports, extensive use of mediation in civil cases has accelerated the administration of justice. The report, however, also pointed out that the majority of the general public and many lawyers at subordinate courts are not aware of this alternative method of dispute resolution.

Village Salish

Salish is an informal justice institution through which the rural poor attempt to resolve their conflicts in Bangladesh. Widely practiced at the village level, salish involves the resolution of a conflict by a method other than traditional litigation. Built on traditional models of popular justice, the salish is conducted by religious leaders, or other community figures of the village. The outcome of village-based salish mediation includes shaming and fines. However, it appears that the existing process of shaming through salish in many cases is disintegrative rather than reintegrative.

Truth Commission: A New Version of Guilty Plea in Bangladesh

In the wake of the massive load of corruption cases and prolonged legal processes and convictions by courts, in May 2008, the caretaker government established the Truth and Accountability Commission (TAC) as an alternative for dealing with high-profile corruption suspects. TAC provided an opportunity for a graft suspect to admit his or her culpability and to be instantly penalized monetarily instead of going through prolonged legal processes. In other words, any person who earned wealth through corruption could avoid jail (get clemency) by confessing crimes, disclosing his or her wealth statement, and depositing ill-gotten wealth to the commission voluntarily. Many government officials, politicians, and business persons applied for voluntary disclosure. The commission heard cases within 14 days of submission and delivered its verdict in 30 days. Failure to comply with TAC rulings will result in five years' imprisonment. People convicted by TAC will be barred for five years from contesting in elections to any public office toward the end of the caretaker government.

Juvenile Justice System

The administration of juvenile justice in Bangladesh is governed by two exclusive acts, the Children Act, 1974 and the Probation of Offenders Ordinance, 1960 (amended in 1964). The Children Act contains both procedural and substantive components. The procedural component entails establishment of a separate juvenile court for children, whereas the substantive component depicts offenses committed by children and prescribes penalties. That is, the Children Act handles the trial, custody, protection, punishment, and treatment of juvenile offenders. Juveniles were required by child laws to be detained in juvenile correctional facilities such as juvenile development centers or safe homes and can only be tried in the juvenile courts or court duly empowered to try the juvenile cases. Accordingly, a number of separate juvenile courts and three child development centers have been established in the country. According to the Children Act, after arrest, a police officer can release the juveniles on bail or produce before the magistrates' court to release the juveniles on probation. However, in most cases, police have been producing delinquent children before the court and the court is sending them to prison instead of safe homes or the juvenile development centers where these juveniles are incarcerated with adults. Though in some cases age determination is a major problem for the police officer to process the juvenile offenders, in many cases police deliberately or negligibly claim a higher age of the child and forward the child to adult courts to avoid extra work. A recent press report revealed that about 412 juveniles are detained in different prisons across the country for years, violating the Children Act. It should be noted that the court has the discretion to send the juvenile offenders to juvenile development centers directly.

Punishment

Following the Western model of corrections, a number of Asian countries (such as India, Sri Lanka, and Pakistan) have introduced probation, parole, home leave, work release, and suspended sentences in recent years. Thus, it is evident that as compared to other Asian countries, the Bangladeshi correctional system is still lagging behind. The major causes may be attributed to nonavailability of funds for correctional programs, lack of political supports, and lack of research on corrections. Although the Jail Commission Report of 1978 recommended the establishment of the system of probation, parole, and work release in Bangladesh, these recommendations have yet to be implemented, which means imprisonment is the only sanction for offenders. The certainty of punishment, the likelihood that a criminal will be punished for a serious crime, and the amount of time a criminal is likely to spend in prison are higher today than they had been in the 1990s. This is primarily due to enactment of various anticrime laws over the years, and more recently, the emergency rule from January 11, 2007, to December 2008. The typical punishment for various types of offense as prescribed in the Penal Code and the Code of Criminal Procedure, 1898 (as amended up to October, 2007) are shown as follows:

- Dacoity (gang robbery): transportation for life or rigorous imprisonment for 10 years, and fine.
- Murder in dacoity: death, transportation for life or rigorous imprisonment for 10 years, and fine.
- Robbery or dacoity, with attempt to cause death or grievous hurt: rigorous imprisonment for not less than seven years.
- Robbery: rigorous imprisonment for 10 years, and fine.
- Theft: imprisonment for three years or fine or both.
- Rape: death or life imprisonment.
- Offenses against the state: punishable by death or imprisonment for 20 years.
- Violence against women (acid throwing): death or life imprisonment.

Death Penalty

Article 35(5) of the Constitution of the People's Republic of Bangladesh precisely states that no person shall be subjected to cruel, inhuman, or degrading punishment. But the courts have been imposing the death penalty for various offenses. According to the data provided by the Prison's Directorate, as of July 1, 2008, the total number of death row population in Bangladesh was 1,012. And between 2004 and 2008, Bangladesh executed a total of 31 prisoners.

Prison

The nomenclature in Bangladesh makes no distinction between jails and prison. All institutions are referred to as jails in Bangladesh. The prison system of Bangladesh had its inception in the legislation of the Prison Act of 1894, which was basically derived from the England Prison Act of 1877. The correctional system is administratively centralized. The jail is the only correctional institution in Bangladesh, which holds inmates who are awaiting trial, undergoing trial, and serving sentences. Jails are controlled by the Ministry of Home and their operational responsibilities vested in the Prisons' Directorate. Bangladeshi jails are still administered under the century-old colonial Prison Act. Presently, there are 67 jails, which vary greatly in size, as well as many other characteristics. They are divided into two categories: central and district jail. They are generally distinguished by their degree of security that relates to perimeter control and internal gates and bars, and the types of population they hold. As of 2008, there were 12 central jails and 55 district jails. Imprisonment is of two types: rigorous and simple. Persons admitted under sentence of rigorous imprisonment are required to work, while persons serving simple imprisonment have no such liability.

Prison Population

Since imprisonment is the only legal sanction, this conservative ideology of punishment is responsible for the present crisis in corrections in Bangladesh. In the absence of any population-reduction strategy, a substantial increase in prison populations has been observed in Bangladesh. Evidence suggests that the use of imprisonment as a sanction for crime has accelerated rapidly after the 1990s. Since then, the number of offenders incarcerated in jails has increased every year from about 39,530 in 1993 to more than 87,000 in 2008. The prisons are becoming no more than warehouses. It seems that part of the growing problem of prison crowding is attributable to the shift in sentencing policy over the 1990s; for example, enactment of the Anti-Terrorism Act of 1993, Public Safety Act of 2000, and Speedy Trial Act of 2002, and more recently, the Emergency Powers Ordinance of 2007.

According to the data provided by the Prison's Directorate, the prison population increased by about 55 percent between 1993 and 2008, reaching 87,011 as of July 1, 2008, which is more than 300 percent of official prison capacity. Bangladesh has the capacity to accommodate 27,386 inmates in jails across the country. Of the total population, only 25,173 (about 29%) were convicted prisoners and the remaining were under-trial (70.7 percent) or detained for investigation. Almost all the institutions are housing far more inmates than the design capacity. The daily population of Dhaka Central Jail on July 1, 2008, was 10,424.

It appears that overcrowding of the under-trial prisoner is the main problem for the prison systems. In most cases, cells were so packed that prisoners had to sleep in shifts. More than anything else, it is the war on corruption that has caused this dramatic increase in prison population, especially during the regime of the immediate past caretaker government (2007–2008). Additionally, the courts and legislatures did indeed get "tougher" on offenders during this period and is the reason for the stunning growth in prison populations. In the face of serious overcrowding in jails recently, the government has decided to release some selected nonviolent offenders who already served half of their prison terms of seven years or less.

Prison Programs

The jails in Bangladesh are primarily custodial institutions. The goal of imprisonment is to incapacitate and punish the offenders. Jail conditions seem consistent with that goal. Thus, no aspects of imprisonment in Bangladesh seem to be linked to rehabilitating prisoners. The problem of overcrowding has seriously affected both the safe running of the prison system and the rehabilitation of individual offenders. Institutional treatment programs such as individual or group counseling is totally absent. Educational and vocational programs that exist in the jails suffer from inadequate funding and administration. As a result, the existing prison programs cannot serve as an important tool in gaining marketable skills for the prisoners in their postimprisonment life.

Visiting Policies and Privileges

Prisoners do not have access to telephones and law libraries. In general, prisoners are not entitled to have a newspaper, except division prisoners that are subject to censorship. Visits from approved family members are allowed at specified intervals. According to the Jail Code, the ordinary inmates can write one letter every month and the division prisoner can write twice a month. Prison authorities do sometimes grant a short furlough for few hours to the Division I prisoner for emergency occasions such as a death in the immediate family. There are no dayrooms or dining facilities for the inmates in jails. The concept of conjugal visits is unknown in Bangladesh. It is important to mention that political prisoners are a privileged class and immune from the harsher confinement conditions. Despite the limited resources of the prison system, this category of prisoners receives better treatment in terms of housing, food, visitation, and other facilities than the ordinary prisoners.

Alternative to Imprisonment

The Bangladeshi penal system provides just one alternative measure—probation. Where a person is convicted of an offense punishable with imprisonment for not more than two years, the court may, after considering the age and character of the offender and the nature of the offense, make a probation order. The penal laws of Bangladesh do not provide the system of parole.

Exchange of Prisoners

Prisoners can be exchanged to other countries such as Myanmar and India. In August 2006, Bangladesh and Myanmar signed an agreement to exchange prisoners from their respective countries. And very recently, Bangladesh and India agreed to exchange each other's prisoners.

Mohammed Bin Kashem

Further Reading

BLAST: Bangladesh Legal Aid and Services Trust: http://www.blast.org.bd.

Kashem, Mohammed B. (1996). "Jails in Bangladesh." *International Journal of Comparative and Applied Criminal Justice* 20(1): 31–40.

Kashem, Mohammed B. (2004). "The Social Organization of Police Corruption: The Case of Bangladesh." In *Police Corruption: An International Comparative Perspective,* edited by Dilip K. Das and Rick Sarre, pp. 237–246. Lanham, MD: Lexington Books.

Ministry of Law, Justice and Parliamentary Affairs. Legal and Judicial Capacity Building Project: http://www.minlaw.gov.bd/ljcbp.htm.

Strengthening Bangladesh Police. Police Reform Program: http://www.prp.org.bd.

Bhutan

Legal System: Customary/Common
Murder: Low-Medium
Corruption: Low
Death Penalty: No
Corporal Punishment: Yes

Background

Bhutan, meaning "Land of the Thunder Dragon," is a small kingdom-state located in the eastern Himalaya Mountains of southern Asia. Landlocked between India to the south and the Tibetan region of China to the north, Bhutan has an area of 47,000 square kilometers (18,147 square miles), and its terrain is predominantly mountainous. Bhutan has been popularly described as the "last Shangri-la" or the only remaining Buddhist kingdom in the Himalayas. These narratives represent Bhutan as "a fairy-tale kingdom," locked in ancient culture and tradition, untouched by modernization and globalization. Though these idyllic representations are exaggerated, indeed, Bhutan remained largely isolated from the rest of the world well into the early 1960s when Bhutan's third monarch, King Jigme Dorji Wangchuck, began the process of cautious modernization. Since then, Bhutan opened its doors to regulated tourism in 1974, became a member of the South Asian Association for Regional Cooperation (SAARC) in 1985, and lifted a nationwide ban on television and the Internet in 1999.

The rugged terrain of Bhutan makes transportation and communication between Bhutanese communities challenging. In fact, there were no telecommunications or roads in Bhutan until the 1960s. Though some roads and highways have since been constructed with the help of migrant workers from India, even today, a number of communities can only be reached by walking. Therefore, despite gradual modernization efforts, the Bhutanese people still remain largely isolated from one another and from the rest of the world. This seclusion is further enhanced by the government's strict regulation of tourism and other forms of foreign influence to preserve the kingdom's traditional culture.

Today, Bhutan continues to be one of the poorest and most underdeveloped countries in the world. The vast majority of the Bhutanese people (more than 90%) live in rural communities and a large majority of the labor force (more than 60%) is employed in the agriculture or forestry industries. The government of Bhutan, however, has objected to assessment of the nation's material wealth as a measure for overall quality of life. In 1998, the government abandoned Gross Domestic Product (GDP) as the primary measure of national prosperity and replaced it with Gross National Happiness (GNH), which prioritizes social, cultural, and spiritual well-being over material wealth.

The Bhutanese government is very committed to preserving its national heritage and cultural traditions; however, Bhutan continues to take steps toward development and modernization. Bhutan is in the midst of social and political changes that have significant implications for the nation's crime rates and the criminal justice system. Historically, Bhutan has reported very low crime rates; however, crime rates appear to be increasing in the last decade. Considering that the "first-ever crime wave" in the nation corresponds to the introduction of television, a number of Bhutanese officials have suggested a relationship between television and increasing crime, drug use, and the deterioration of traditional family values.

As Bhutan has opened itself to foreign influence, it has also become particularly concerned about maintaining its cultural and religious traditions.

As a result, since the late 1970s, the government of Bhutan has instituted many policies to forge a unified Bhutanese identity. Some of these policies are considered restrictive and even repressive of minority groups within the country and have caused some human rights groups to accuse Bhutan of ethnic cleansing. According to critics, the long-standing repressive policies may have incited recent terrorist attacks across the country.

At the same time, the nation has made significant strides toward more democratic governance, including the adoption of a new Civil and Criminal Procedural Code in 2001, a new Penal Code in 2004, and the codification of basic rights in a new Constitution in 2008.

Government

During the 19th century, Bhutan was under decentralized rule by a number of independent principalities that were in continuous competition and civil war. After several years of conflict, between the years of 1882 and 1885, Ugyen Wangchuck of Trongsa was finally able to unify the many decentralized local governments across Bhutan and achieve a peaceful truce among the parties. On December 17, 1907, respected community leaders of Bhutan selected Ugyen Wangchuck to be the first hereditary king of Bhutan and, thereby, established the Kingdom of Bhutan as an absolute monarchy.

Bhutan's modern political history is unique from most other nations in that it is one of the few nations in which the movement for democracy has been largely from the top-down. Though the monarchy continues to be very popular among the people of Bhutan and the majority of the general public has not been enthusiastic about political transition, Bhutan's last few monarchs have been eager to institute gradual democratization. King Jigme Dorji Wangchuck, Bhutan's third monarch, started the democratization movement in 1953 when he established the nation's first legislature, the National Assembly, to promote a more democratic and inclusive form of governance.

The National Assembly, under the guidance of King Jigme Dorji Wangchuck, enacted the first comprehensive codified law code in 1959. The law code, known as the *Thrimzhung Chhenmo*, or, the Supreme Law, codified the civil and criminal laws of Bhutan. Though many sections have been amended by subsequent legislation, the *Thrimzhung Chhenmo* is considered to be the foundation for Bhutan's legal system. During his reign, King Jigme Dorji Wangchuck also created a Royal Advisory Council in 1965 and established a Council of Cabinet Ministers in 1968.

In 1998, King Jigme Singye Wangchuck, Bhutan's fourth monarch, introduced significant political reforms in the government and transferred many of his administrative powers to the Council of Cabinet Ministers. One of his most significant reforms is that King Jigme Singye Wangchuck established a procedure by which the National Assembly could impeach the monarch by a two-thirds majority vote. During King Jigme Singye Wangchuck's rule, the National Assembly enacted the Civil and Criminal Court Procedure of Bhutan in 2001 and the Penal Code of Bhutan in 2004. These legal codes established the appropriate protocols for civil and criminal procedures and outlined the classification of crimes and punishment for civil and criminal offenses. The codification of the court procedure and penal code were significant reforms for Bhutan's justice system.

In 2006, King Jigme Singye Wangchuck abdicated the throne in favor of his son, King Dasho Jigme Khesar Namgyal Wangchuck, who became the fifth monarch of Bhutan. During King Dasho Jigme Khesar Namgyal Wangchuck's reign, on March 24, 2008, the country's first-ever national elections took place, and Bhutan finally made the anticipated transition from an absolute monarchy to a constitutional monarchy. A draft constitution that had been unveiled during his father's rule in 2005 was adopted after the elections, and the Supreme Court of Bhutan was established as the highest court of the land with the chief justice at its head.

Cultural Context

Bhutan's government prefers to portray the nation as homogenous; however, Bhutan is actually a multiethnic, multireligious society with three major ethno-linguistic groups: the Ngalung, the Sarchhop, and the Lhotshampa. The Ngalung, who migrated from Tibet in the 17th century and live predominantly in the northwestern region of the country, practice Drukpa Kagyu Buddhism and speak Dzongkha (an offshoot of Tibetan). The monarchy of Bhutan belongs to the Ngalung ethnic group. The Sarchhop, a native Bhutanese ethnic group, live predominantly in the eastern region of Bhutan, practice Nyingmapa Buddhism, and speak a native Bhutanese dialect. The Lhotshampa, an ethnic group of Nepalese descent, live predominantly in the southern region of Bhutan along the Indian border, practice Hinduism, and speak Nepali.

The Bhutanese government, dominated by the Ngalung ethnic group, has instituted a policy of *driglamnamja* or "one nation, one people" and passed a number of laws in an effort to assimilate the Bhutanese population according to Ngalung cultural values and traditions. The government has been criticized for ethnic and religious discrimination against minority groups, particularly the Lhotshampa. The Bhutan Marriage Act of 1980, for example, restricted marriage with non-Bhutanese and denied Bhutanese citizens who married non-Bhutanese state support such as land, loans, education, and health benefits. The act was discriminatorily applied to the Lhotshampa population to curb marriages with noncitizen Nepalis living in Bhutan.

Furthermore, in 1985, the government passed a Citizenship Act that stipulated that Bhutanese citizens would be required to prove their residency in Bhutan for more than 10 years. Considering that members of the Lhotshampa ethnic group were more likely to include immigrants from Nepal, documentation of 10 years' residency in Bhutan was more difficult for the Lhotshampa. The Citizenship Act also stipulated that citizens could lose their nationality if they left their farmland or broke the law. Again, these laws were targeted at the Lhotshampa, to limit their freedom of movement and political participation.

In the 1990s, political tensions led the government of Bhutan to force more than 100,000 Lhotshampa and ethnic Nepalis out of the country into refugee camps in Nepal. Those refugees are still living in refugee camps awaiting a resolution that will allow them to come home. The refugee crisis will be discussed in more detail later.

The long-standing ethnic conflict may help explain the fact that demographic data about the Bhutanese people are inconsistent and controversial. According to the government census of 2005, Bhutan has an estimated population of approximately 672,425, but other reports, such as numbers from the United Nations and the CIA, indicate that the population may be as high as 2 million. The discrepancies in population estimates may be due to the ongoing refugee crisis involving the Lhotshampa, since some population estimates do not include the refugees or ethnic Lhotshampa still residing within Bhutanese borders whereas others do. Conflicting numbers indicate that approximately 47–85 percent of the population are either Ngalung or Sarchhop and follow the Buddhist tradition, and approximately 15–53 percent, the ethnic Nepalese, follow the Hindu tradition.

The religious and cultural traditions of Bhutan, both Buddhist and Hindu, serve to reinforce the predominant social value that all forms of life are to be considered sacred. The people of Bhutan are generally known to be a peaceful people and the overall crime rates in Bhutan remain very low, though Bhutan has seen some escalation in crime over the last decade. Though crime does not seem to be a major problem, there is insufficient data to conduct a systematic review of the nature and extent of crime in Bhutan. Nevertheless, it is perhaps fair to say that Bhutan's most long-standing "criminal justice" problem has to do with the ethnic conflict and refugee crisis that has plagued the nation for almost two decades.

Legal System

Bhutan's legal system is based largely on Buddhist tradition, English common law, and the Indian legal system. Lower courts exercise original jurisdiction on cases within their territorial jurisdiction and appellate courts review appeals cases from the lower courts. The Supreme Court was established as the highest court of Bhutan with the adoption of the Constitution in March 2008 and will be presided over by the chief justice of Bhutan. Prior to 2008, the Bhutanese legal system had a three-tier court system. The High Court, established in 1968, was the highest court of Bhutan. The High Court is made up of three benches that each consist of a minimum of two judges. The *Dzongkhag,* or district courts, are the next level of courts. The first district court was established in 1961, and there are currently 20 across Bhutan. The *Dungkhag,* or local court, was established in 1978, and there are currently three local courts in Bhutan.

The registrar general of the High Court heads the administrative division of the courts and is appointed by the chief justice for a period of three years. The registrar general serves at the pleasure of the chief justice for one term. Recent procedural reforms in the administration of the court system have reduced the cost of litigation in Bhutan, and the National Assembly has asked the High Court to develop guidelines to limit the fees of *jabmis* (counsel) to make litigation more affordable and accessible to all citizens. The time to disposition for the majority of all legal cases, and virtually all criminal cases, is within 108 days.

The Bhutanese legal system is based on the adversarial principle, though there are some elements of the inquisitorial system as well. The courts are supposed to be impartial participants in the proceedings, and judges are responsible for ensuring procedural fairness during trial. Defendants may choose to defend themselves or may select a *jabmi* to represent them in front of the court. In cases in which the defendant is indigent and cannot afford to retain the services of a *jabmi,* the court can appoint legal counsel for the defendant. The litigants or their counsel may present relevant information to the court and answer questions posed by the judges. The courts are charged with deciding cases based on the facts submitted by the parties. Defendants are presumed to be innocent. For criminal cases, the prosecution has the burden of proof to prove guilt beyond a reasonable doubt. For civil cases, the plaintiff has the burden to prove his or her case by a fair preponderance of the credible evidence.

Police

Bhutan's security forces include a national militia, the Royal Bhutan Army, and the Royal Bhutan Police. The national militia was established in 1958, and shortly thereafter the Royal Bhutan Army was established in 1963. In 1965, the Royal Bhutan Police was established on September 1, and this date continues to be commemorated and celebrated annually as Police Day. The Royal Bhutan Police serves as the national police force and is organizationally inferior to the Royal Bhutan Army. The nation's first police officers were a few hundred army personnel who were reassigned to the new police force. By the late 1970s the police force had expanded to more than 1,000 constables and officers, and by the mid-1990s the police force had grown to about 5,000.

Police recruits, at a minimum, are required to have completed a sixth-grade education, and the Royal Bhutan Police is the only security force in Bhutan that recruits women. Until 1981, all new recruits were trained at the Police Training Centre in Zilnon Namgyeling, Thimphu District. In 1981, a new police training center opened in Jigmiling, Geylegphug District, and police officers are now trained at that location as well. The police training curriculum includes weapons training, tae kwon do, physical training with and without arms, legal training, simple investigation techniques, check-post duties, traffic control, and public relations. Some officers are chosen for advanced training in criminology, traffic control, and canine corps and are sent to India for those training programs.

Police officers are required to perform a variety of functions that go beyond standard policing practices. Officers serve as border guards, corrections officers, firefighters, and first aid providers. Some critics have noted that there may be issues of conflict of interest in requiring police officers to participate in such a diverse set of functions; however, the government of Bhutan has not been particularly concerned with specializing these functions or separating the police from these other service and enforcement functions.

The Royal Bhutan Police has been cognizant of development and modernization programs and has made gradual adaptations to those changes. Construction of roads and the increasing number of motor vehicles in use has resulted in increasing numbers of traffic accidents. In response to the changing circumstances, the Royal Bhutan Police established a mobile traffic court staffed by police personnel and a judicial official to facilitate on-the-spot legal decisions.

In 2007, the Royal Bhutan Police established a new Women and Child Protection Unit in the capital, Thimpu. This new unit is one of the first steps in developing women and child friendly police and judicial procedures. The unit is run by women police officers in collaboration with the National Commission for Women and Children (NCWC) and provides a safe environment for female victims and witnesses to come forward. It is the first unit of its kind in the country and, based on support from the United Nations Development Program, will likely be replicated in other regions in the near future.

A procedural code has also been established that stipulates that police officers may not arrest an individual without an arrest warrant or specific cause and that an arrestee must be brought before the court within 24 hours, not including travel time from the place of arrest. These reforms are relatively new, and, in practice, these legal protections are not systematically applied, primarily because of deficiencies in police training and some gaps in the procedural codes that will hopefully be addressed in the next few years.

Crime

Classification of Crimes

Bhutan's Penal Code came into effect on August 11, 2004. The Penal Code consolidated and clarified existing legal codes on the culpability and punishment for criminal acts committed in Bhutan. According to the Penal Code, the age of criminal responsibility for adult offenders is 18. Juvenile offenders cannot be held responsible for any criminal acts committed under the age of 10; however, juveniles between the ages of 10 and 18 may be held responsible for criminal acts and sentenced to appropriate punishment, though punishment is scaled lower for juveniles than adults.

The Penal Code classifies criminal acts into four categories ordered by severity of offense: felony, misdemeanor, petty misdemeanor, and violation. Felony crimes are the most serious category of criminal offenses and are further classified into four degrees of severity.

First-degree felonies are the most serious offenses and include such crimes as murder, treason, terrorism, defilement of national monuments, and the illegal manufacturing of weapons of mass destruction. Second-degree felonies include such crimes as the illegal transaction of a controlled substance, the rape of a child under the age of 12, and the trafficking of a minor for prostitution. Third-degree felonies include such crimes as gang rape, the trafficking of adult women for prostitution, torture that causes physical disability, extortion, and armed robbery. Fourth-degree felonies include such crimes as rape, the illegal sale or purchase of a firearm, the unauthorized opening of another person's mail, trafficking of humans for labor, child molestation, torture that does not cause physical disability, the illegal sale of national or cultural heritage property, robbery, burglary, and arson.

Misdemeanor crimes include such crimes as eavesdropping through unlawful wiretapping, patronizing a prostitute, assisting in suicide, sodomy, and abortion. Abortion is legal only under the following circumstances: the mother's life will be put at risk to carry the unborn child to term, the child is the product of rape or incest, or the mother is of unsound mental condition. Otherwise, abortion is illegal and is treated as a misdemeanor crime, as are "unnatural" sex acts such as sodomy.

Petty misdemeanor crimes include such crimes as battery, sexual harassment, pollution, illegal hunting and fishing, abandonment of a person in danger, failure to report a crime, and gambling. Violations include such crimes as disorderly conduct, assault, public intoxication, and the use of tobacco. Bhutan banned the use of tobacco in 2004 and is currently the only nation to have completely banned smoking in public.

Human Rights Issues

The government of Bhutan has passed a number of laws to give life to the "one nation, one people" policy and to preserve Bhutan's traditional culture. For example, in 1989, a royal decree made it compulsory to wear the national dress at formal gatherings and government institutions, including schools, to preserve and promote Bhutanese culture. For men, they must wear the "gho" or a wrap-around, coat-like, knee-length garment with a narrow belt. For women, they must wear the "kira" or an ankle-length dress made of a rectangular piece of cloth held at the shoulders with a clip and closed with a woven belt at the waist over a long-sleeved blouse. Failure to the wear the required dress results in fines of three days' wages (approximately equivalent to US$10 to US$55) or up to a month in prison.

The government has also established a language policy requiring use of the official language, Dzongkha, in schools and public offices, a policy that has marginalized the Nepali-speaking minority. Furthermore, religious freedom is minimal, and the law forbids religious conversions and penalizes those who attempt to convert others. The government has also enacted a number of laws pertaining to marriage and family life. The Marriage Act of 1980 legislated punitive measures against Bhutanese who marry non-Bhutanese nationals. From the day of such a marriage, the Bhutanese citizen is denied promotion in government services, is ineligible for employment in national defense, cannot run for election, and is deprived of many privileges, including land, loans, education, and medical treatment.

In 1990, the government also imposed a policy of compulsory birth control. If a couple has more than two children, the government may compel one of the parents to undergo a sterilization operation. These drastic birth control measures, however, have been implemented discriminatorily against minorities, and, according to critics, violate human rights. Meanwhile, polygamy is legal in Bhutan on the condition that the first wife gives permission to her husband to take a second wife. Divorce is also legal and fairly common in Bhutan, and the legal code favors women in matters of alimony and child custody.

Crime Statistics

Bhutan has not reported any crime statistics to the United Nations and the official crime statistics are not available to the public. Most reports, including estimates from the U.S. Department of State and the Central Intelligence Agency, suggest that there is relatively little crime in Bhutan. Of crimes committed in Bhutan, the vast majority tends to be nonviolent crimes. Violent crime rates are estimated to be very low; however, there is not sufficient data for precision. Homicide rates for 2004 are estimated to be between 2.4 and 4.3 homicides per 100,000 population, according to the United Nations Office of Drug Control. Although Bhutan has not experienced a serious crime problem, according to news reports, crime has been gradually increasing in the last decade.

Bhutan's courts have made public the number of cases reviewed by the courts over the last 15 years. Based on the official data, there has been a general trend of rising numbers of cases filed in the courts over the last decade. For the years 1991 and 1992, the courts decided a total of 3,136 cases. These numbers grew to a total of 8,804 cases in 2002, 10,376 cases in 2006, and 11,501 cases in 2007. The numbers, however, do not indicate the type or severity of the cases, though some reports indicate that the majority of cases were related to loans, land disputes, and marital issues. The judiciary of Bhutan is working toward technological improvements to automate its record keeping so that it is able to generate better case tracking statistics and improve the overall judicial system.

According to news reports, April 2002 was likely the "first-ever crime wave" in Bhutan. There were several incidents of fraud, violence, and even murder. Some residents of Bhutan blame increasing problems with crime, drugs, and alcohol on television. The government of Bhutan lifted the ban on television in June 1999. Bhutan opened its first and only local television station shortly thereafter, and international television channels also became available for viewing via satellite dishes. There is significant concern in Bhutan that exposure to satellite television has resulted in harmful cultural changes, especially among the youth population.

Based on qualitative research, an independent group of Bhutanese academics found a correlation between exposure to satellite television and cultural changes, including increased participation in crime, corruption, and less conventional romantic relationships. Some critics have even asserted that television can be blamed for increases in drug use and family break-ups. Whereas the Bhutanese people have traditionally shied away from killing even insects, now they are exposed to extreme violence as well as ultraliberal sexual mores on television. In addition, discos and nightclubs have recently opened and are considered to be threatening the traditional values and peaceful culture of Bhutan.

There are no official statistics on drug use in Bhutan; however, the government recognizes it as a growing and potentially serious problem. Bhutan is an active participant in regional initiatives to combat drug trafficking and substance abuse and is a signatory on the SAARC Convention on Narcotics Drugs and Psychotropic Substances (1990). Bhutan also joined International Criminal Police Organization (INTERPOL) in 2005.

Bhutan has no pharmaceutical industry and relies on the import of licit drugs from India. Bhutan's trade relationship with India allows for free and unregulated trade between the neighboring countries. The relatively open and insecure borders between Bhutan and India make Bhutan vulnerable to international drug trafficking across the border. Anecdotal data suggest increasing use of amphetamines smuggled in from India, and there are some estimates of approximately five to six deaths from morphine overdoses each year. Use of heroin and injecting drug use, however, is considered to be minimal. Before the introduction of television, cannabis plants, which grow freely in Bhutan, were used to feed pigs. In recent years, however, the police have arrested hundreds for smoking marijuana.

According to official sources, most drug users in Bhutan are young males under the age of 25. As a result, there is significant concern about young people's propensity for drug use as well as their risk for HIV. As of 2005, there were 144 officially reported cases of HIV in Bhutan and some estimates indicating that there could be approximately 500 people living with the disease by the end of that year. Concerns about increasing levels of drug use and HIV prompted the National Assembly, in 2005, to pass the Prevention and Control of Drug Abuse Act and create a new Narcotics Control Agency. The National Assembly specifically called for joint efforts by the government and local communities to enhance preventive education measures and to collaborate for improvements in the quality and availability of effective treatment, rehabilitation, and social reintegration when prevention fails.

Violence against Women

Bhutan ratified the Convention on the Elimination of All Forms of Discrimination against Women (CEDAW) in 1981 without any reservation and has drafted a National Plan of Action for Gender (NPAG) that was spearheaded by the National Commission for Women and Children and will be rolled out from 2007 to 2013.

Though the actual extent of the problem is not known since most cases of family violence go unreported, anecdotal evidence suggests that domestic violence is a problem in Bhutan. In response to the problem of domestic violence and gender violence in general, Her Majesty Queen Ashi Sangay Choden Wangchuck started a nonprofit organization for women called Respect, Educate, Nurture and Empower Women (RENEW) in 2004. RENEW seeks to be the leading institution in shaping the role of women in Bhutanese society, and its mission is to empower disadvantaged girls and women to be independent and socially and economically productive members of society.

According to RENEW, reported cases of assault against women and girls that were prosecuted in court grew from 56 in 2000 to 99 in 2003. Police reports indicate that of the 347 cases of assault against women and girls that went to court from 2000 to 2004, 43 percent involved the woman's intimate partner. The problem is exacerbated by the fact that there are currently no emergency shelter or support services available in Bhutan for women trying to escape from violent and abusive relationships or situations. Many women, especially those who are financially dependent on their husbands, have nowhere to go for counseling, therapy, or information on how to become independent.

RENEW's Web site also reports that although accurate statistics are not yet available in Bhutan, hospital staff and the police are seeing increasing incidence of sexual and physical abuse of women and girls. As the government has made public education more widely available and has encouraged the schooling of girls, more and more girls are sent to schools away from their families. A serious issue of concern is the sexual abuse of girls and young women who are sent away to schools. Many educators who responded to a limited confidential study on female students in their schools replied that sexual abuse of girls is a problem.

The government of Bhutan is also concerned about the problem of human trafficking. Bhutan is known to be an origin and transit location for human trafficking. Bhutanese women are often trafficked to neighboring Nepal, and children are trafficked through Nepal and India to Pakistan.

Finding of Guilt

The Civil and Criminal Code of Bhutan ensures equal justice under the law without discrimination on the basis of sex, race, religion, or any other reason. Citizens accused of crimes are to be tried by ordinary courts, not by any ad hoc tribunals. In criminal proceedings, the accused are afforded the right to a trial by judicial panel on the appropriate court's current bench, and the trails are intended to be fair and public trials. In some circumstances, there may be exceptions made regarding public trials when there are concerns about public order, national security, or privacy of the parties. Defendants may plead their cases or defend themselves in person or may select a *jabmi,* legal counsel, for assistance. Defendants may waive their right to have a *jabmi* if they do so competently and intelligently. While there is no separate court system for juveniles, juvenile offenders may have their parent or guardian present with them during trial proceedings and may have their privacy protected by the court. Only indigent defendants who cannot afford to secure their own legal counsel may be offered free legal services by the court. If a defendant is not satisfied with the decision of a court, he or she may file an appeal within 10 days of the initial judgment.

Punishment

Types of Punishment

The Penal Code's stated objective is to reinstate dignity to victims of crime and increase the possibilities for rehabilitation of offenders. Those who are convicted of criminal offenses may be imprisoned, released on probation, made to pay fines to the state, made to pay compensation as restitution to victims or victims' families, or a combination. Mutilation as punishment was abolished in 1965. Exile was once an official punishment; however, it is no longer used as a form of punishment. Furthermore, capital punishment was abolished by royal decree on March 20, 2004. The Penal Code is largely based on the rehabilitative ideal, though in recent years, some policy makers have advocated for harsher punishments, particularly for sexual crimes.

Juveniles under the age of 10 are not held responsible for criminal conduct. Juveniles between the ages of 10 and 18 are held responsible for their acts and are liable to punishment, though juveniles receive punishment scaled lower than adults for similar offenses. In fact, juveniles are to receive a minimum of half the sentence that would otherwise be imposed if the offender had been an adult when committing the crime. In 1997, the Youth Development and Rehabilitation Center was established for juvenile offenders with the primary goal of rehabilitation. Nevertheless, in some cases in which a juvenile may face imprisonment, the court may choose to assign an alternative sentence. Children are a high priority in Bhutan, and the country was one of the first to ratify the Convention on the Rights of the Child in 1990 and has since been investing steadily in services to benefit children. Bhutan's justice system tends to be more lenient toward juvenile offenders and is primarily concerned with rehabilitating them.

Felony crimes are the most serious category of criminal offenses and are punishable with a minimum of three years of imprisonment to a maximum of life imprisonment. First-degree felonies are punishable with a minimum of 15 years of imprisonment to life imprisonment. Second-degree felonies are punishable with 9 to 15 years of imprisonment. Third-degree felonies are punishable with 5 to 15 years of imprisonment. Fourth-degree felonies are punishable with three to five years of imprisonment. Misdemeanor crimes are punishable with a minimum of one year of imprisonment to a maximum of three years. Petty misdemeanor crimes are punishable with a minimum of one month of imprisonment to a maximum of one year. Violations are punishable with fines for up to 90 days at the national minimum wage rate. Offenders convicted on a repeat offense are punishable with enhanced sentences. Typically, these offenders are sentenced as if they had committed a crime one degree higher than their actual offense.

The Penal Code does allow the court to consider mitigating and aggravating circumstances. Mitigating circumstances include that the defendant has no criminal record, the defendant committed the crime under extreme mental or emotional distress, the crime was committed accidentally, the victim consented to the criminal conduct, the crime was conducted because the defendant believed there was reasonable justification for the act, the defendant was only an accomplice in a crime committed by someone else and his or her participation was minor, the defendant acted under duress, or, at the time of the offense the defendant's capacity to appreciate the wrongfulness of the conduct or to conform to the requirements of the law was impaired on account of mental disability or intoxication. Aggravating circumstances include that the defendant had previously been convicted of a crime, the defendant committed another crime at the same time as the current offense, the defendant knowingly created a grave risk of death or serious bodily injury to another person, the defendant negligently caused bodily injury to another person with a deadly weapon, the crime was essentially heinous, atrocious, or cruel and represents exceptional depravity on behalf of the defendant.

In some circumstances, and according to the court's discretion, the court may make an order that the defendant pay a fine or perform community service in lieu of imprisonment. Typically, these considerations are afforded to nonfelony offenders provided that the offender is not a recidivist or habitual offender.

According to the Penal Code, those who are found to be mentally insane may be sentenced to civil commitment in lieu of imprisonment. There are, however, no mental hospitals or community residential facilities in Bhutan, and forensic cases are typically kept in police custody. Residential facilities that are available include a 50-bed facility for juvenile delinquents, a 15-bed facility for drug detoxification and rehabilitation, and a 5-bed residential facility for the elderly. Furthermore, according to the Ministry of Health, a residential facility for victims of domestic violence and rape is currently under construction.

For some felony cases, the court may order the defendant to pay compensatory damages to the victim or victim's family in addition to imprisonment. For example, for some murder and rape cases, the court may order compensation to the victim or victim's family for up to 10 years. Similarly, for most property or monetary crimes, such as bribery and fraud, the court punishes offenders based on value-based sentencing and attempts to compensate the victim with comparably valued damages. The monarch retains the power to grant amnesty or commute any criminal sentences.

Prisons

In Bhutan, prisons are under the jurisdiction of the police. Police officers administer the prisons and serve as correctional officers. Bhutan does not publish prison figures and according to the *World Prison Population List* (8th edition), there are currently no reliable statistics available on the number of prisoners incarcerated in Bhutan's prison system. In the 1990s prison conditions were widely known to be poor, with inadequate hygiene, unhealthy food, and prevalent overcrowding that allegedly resulted in the deaths of detainees. The government ended the use of shackles in 1992 as a result of pressure from Amnesty International. Representatives from the International Committee of the Red Cross (ICRC) began visiting prisons in 1993, and, according to ICRC, prison conditions in Bhutan are now satisfactory. Furthermore, the opening of a new prison camp in Chemgang and a new prison in the capital city, Thimpu, in 1994 improved the conditions of detention.

Medical treatment in prisons is provided by the Basic Health Unit (BHU). These units are normally staffed by a medical officer, health assistant, assistant nurse, and two nonmedical staff members. Health records of the individual prisoners are kept and minor illnesses of the prisoners are treated at the BHU. The medical officer visits the BHU on one occasion a week for custom check-ups of prisoners. In terms of mental health services, Bhutan's prisons offer very little. According to the Bhutan Ministry of Health, less than 4 percent of prisoners suffer from psychosis or mental retardation. Therefore, the need for mental health services is not dire. Nevertheless, Bhutanese prisons have at least one prisoner per month in treatment contact with a mental health professional. As for training, some police officers (21%–50%) and a few (1%–20%) judges and lawyers have participated in educational activities on mental health in the last five years.

The Refugee Crisis

Opposition to the government's "one nation, one people" policy and the cultural protection laws resulted in mass demonstrations in September and October 1990. Up to 18,000 protesters participated in the demonstrations and the government moved decisively to suppress the movement. Demonstrators were labeled as "ngolops" (antinationals) and the National Security Act of 1992 made antinational activities into criminal offenses. From 1989 to 1992, police and army forces arrested thousands of ethnic Nepalese suspected of supporting a rebellious movement. Some were detained and others simply disappeared.

The government has denied accountability for any disappearances; however, in the past several years, the government has freed from detention at least 1,666 ethnic Nepalese under official amnesties. According to local human rights groups, widespread human rights abuses were reported during 1989–1992 and were likely committed as part of an effort to drive out ethnic Nepalese. These policy initiatives suggest that the government tacitly condoned the abuse of ethnic Nepalese.

Several thousand people were imprisoned for months in what some allege to have been substandard conditions. The United Nations High Commission for Refugees detailed 2,200 allegations of torture in the government prisons of Bhutan. Victims reported severe beating and kicking, exposure to extreme heat and cold for long periods, scalding, light depravation, electric shocks, *chepwa* (pressing the thighs between iron rods or logs), nails in the flesh, hanging people upside down, and rape of women.

Military officers were stationed in the southern districts and allegedly forced village headmen and others to provide local teenagers for sexual favors. According to the *Coalition against Trafficking in Women Factbook on Global Sexual Exploitation* (1999), in 1991, an estimated 12,000 Bhutanese women refugees fled to western Nepal as a result of sexual violence perpetrated by the Bhutanese military.

The Human Rights Organization of Bhutan (HUROB), the People's Forum for Human Rights, Bhutan (PFHRB), and the South Asia Human Rights Documentation Center (SAHRDC) published dozens of sworn statements from victims of torment and rape who escaped to refugee camps in Nepal. Human Rights Watch alleges that children were forced to commit atrocities against their families and neighbors so as to ensure that they would be stigmatized and unable to return to their communities.

Bhutan is, in fact, the source of more refugees fleeing their homeland to escape persecution than almost any other country in the world. Bhutanese refugees live in seven refugee camps in Nepal, and their numbers range from 100,000 to 130,000. Several nongovernmental organizations (NGOs) offer rehabilitation services to victims of torture for those refugees. Meanwhile, the Bhutanese government has instituted a resettlement program that brings people from other parts of the country and settles them on the land formerly owned and occupied by the refugees. In essence, the government policy is a deliberate attempt to make it more complicated and difficult for refugees to return to Bhutan. By 2003, 70 percent of the land of those in exile had been resettled. Those who resettled were given cash incentives for the move.

About 13 percent of the population of Bhutan, or approximately 82,000, were considered to be nonnationals and were ineligible to vote in the historic 2008 elections. A few months before the elections, on January 20, 2008, coordinated bomb blasts in Thimpu and three other locations generated political shock in Bhutan. The police suspected Nepal-based exile groups, and the previously unknown United Revolutionary Front of Bhutan claimed responsibility for the attacks. The organization expressed the grievance that the move toward democratization should be inclusive of all Bhutanese. More bomb blasts occurred in February and March 2008. Certainly, if Bhutan wants to move into a new era of democratic governance, it will need to take steps to resolve the refugee crisis and the treatment of minorities within its borders.

Julie Ahmad Siddique

Further Reading

Giri, B. R. (2004). "Bhutan: Ethnic Policies in the Dragon Kingdom." *Asian Affairs* 35: 353–364.

Lamsang, Tensing. (2008, April 12). "A Decade of Crime in Bhutan." *Kuensel:* http://www.kuensel-online.com/modules.php?name=News&file=article&sid=10194.

National Portal of Bhutan: http://www.bhutan.gov.bt/government/index_new.php.

Rizal, D. (2004). "The Unknown Refugee Crisis: Expulsion of the Ethnic Lhotsampa from Bhutan." *Asian Ethnicity* 5: 151–177.

Brunei Darussalam

Legal System: Islamic/Common/Customary
Murder: Low
Prison Rate: Medium
Death Penalty: No
Corporal Punishment: Yes

Background

During the 14th and 16th centuries, Brunei was ruled by a powerful sultanate. In 1847, the sultan concluded a treaty with Great Britain and Brunei Darussalam officially became a British protectorate in 1888. In 1906, the Residential System was established, which allowed for a system of indirect British rule or protection for Malay states. A British resident was appointed to represent the British government. He advised the sultan in all matters, with the exception of Malay customs, traditions, and religion. However, the resident had no police or army support from Britain, and no specific set of guidelines to follow, so the sultans and followers resisted change for several centuries of traditional rule. The resident's success or failure depended on his relationship with the sultans and his Malay chiefs.

In 1959, Brunei Darussalam received its own constitution and self-governance. In 1967, Sultan Haji Sir Muda Omar Ali Saifuddien, gave up his throne and his son Penigran Muda Mankota Hassanal Bolkiah became the 29th ruler of Brunei Darussalam. After giving up his throne, Omar Saifuddien became the defense minister and Brunei received full internal independence, in 1971, with the exception of defense and external affairs. Then in 1984, Brunei Darussalam gained full independence. Subsequently, the sultan became known as the prime minister, finance minister, and home affairs minister. He presided over a cabinet of 6, and this cabinet increased to 11 members in 1986. His Majesty Sultan Haji Hassanal Bolkiah remains sultan today.

Located in southeastern Asia, neighboring Malaysia, Brunei Darussalam is situated on the northwest island of Borneo. Brunei Darussalam is divided into four districts, Brunei/Muara, Tutong, Belait, and Temburong. Bandar Seri Begawan is the capital of Brunei. Brunei Darussalam has a total area of 5,765 square kilometers (2,226 square miles). As of July 2008, Brunei has a total population of 381, 371. Not long after Brunei received full independence, Brunei joined the Association for Southeast Asian Nations (ASEAN). Many of the citizens were resistant, first to the changes that came with independence and second on becoming a member of ASEAN. Brunei went back and forth between different powers for many years. Merging with a larger entity would have ensured Brunei's political survival; however, political groups and the monarchy wanted to keep Brunei as a separate entity. This was primarily because Brunei had become oil-rich, and Brunei officials, particularly the monarch, wanted to remain in power and continue to control its oil, and wealth. With the emergence of full independence, Brunei Darussalam became the center of media attention on its National Day of celebration not only because of its extravagance as one of the richest nations, but also the spectacle of the sultan's 1,778-room palace, which was reported to have cost $300–$500 million. With the formation of the new government, governmental responsibilities were given to other members of the sultan's family, revealing a clear commitment to remain a ruling monarchy. With this form of government, losing touch with the population and corruption were risks. Other government officials saw an opportunity, because for the leaders it was sometimes hard to distinguish between personal and governmental funds, thus providing opportunities for corruption.

Police

Established in 1921, the Royal Brunei Police Force has several departments, each with its own function. For example, the Department of Administration and Finance's function is the administration of personnel and preparation of the Royal Brunei Police Force's annual budget. The total workforce consists of 3,594, plus 204 civilian employees, which include gardeners, cleaners, technicians, clerical staff, and confidential secretaries. Some of the other departments include the Department of Operation, Department of Criminal Investigation and Intelligence, Department of Logistic, Department of Traffic Investigation and Control, and the Commissioner of Police Secretariat and Public Relations. Also, under the Department of Operation, are the Immigration Department, Royal Customs and Excise, Royal Guards, Airport Police, and the Narcotic Control Bureau. Not only does Brunei have a police force of its own, but it is also affiliated with two international police forces. Those two international police forces are the Association of South East Asian Nations Police (ASEANAPOL) and International Criminal Police Organization (INTERPOL). The reason for these memberships is to maintain good international relations.

Crime

Since the Special Investigation Unit was formed in 1993, it has handled 32 cases, which include murder, suspicious death, armed robbery, and arson. Fourteen of the 32 cases have been solved while the others are still under investigation. In 1997, it solved five murder cases. Although there are no signs of terrorism, the government monitors terrorist groups to prevent terrorism. A Women and Child Abuse Unit has also been set up under the Investigation unit. Its responsibilities include investigating women and child abuse, rape cases, and to prevent and suppress prostitution.

Drug Offenses

According to the United Nations report on Drugs and Crime in 2001, the number of drugs entering and leaving Brunei is minor; however, there has been an increase in the number of drug-related arrests. The types of drugs have also changed over the years. In the 1990s heroin, cannabis, and cough mixture were the most dominant drugs, while methamphetamines, also called Syabu, were minor drugs. In 1997, the amount of heroin seizures was calculated at 1.35 grams, which is less than 2 grams, and had decreased to 0.0011 grams by the year 2000. Syabu seizures in 1997 amounted to 122.82 grams and increased in 2000 to 1,649.73 grams. In 2000, there were 54.39 grams of cannabis seized. Most drug users arrested in 2000 were between the ages of 21 and 30 years old. The Misuse of Drugs Act Chapter 27 is the principal legislation for drug trafficking and possession. For possession of drugs of a certain amount, the penalty could be the death penalty, although there have been no executions in Brunei since 1957. In 1996, the annual prevalence of abuse, among the population of 15- to 64-year-olds, for cannabis was 0.02 percent. In 1998, it was 0.01 percent for opiates, and in 2006, it was 0.3 percent for amphetamines. Amphetamines and cannabis, in 2006, were the primary drugs of abuse among those treated for drug problems. The number of people treated in Brunei for drug problems was 57; of those, 98.2 percent were treated for amphetamine abuse and 1.8 percent were treated for cannabis, according to the United Nations Office on Drugs and Crime's "2008 World Drug Report." There are two drug rehabilitation facilities, which assist approximately 250 voluntary and involuntary residents. The names of the facilities are the Al-Islah Rehabilitation Centre and the Al Islah Intoxicating Substances Rehabilitation Centre. These facilities are under the control of the Prisons Department and the Ministry of Home Affairs. There are three ways of admission, court order, minister's order, and voluntary order. Detoxification treatment is for a period not exceeding 14 days. After conviction by the court and release from prison or rehabilitation, an individual must be enrolled in a supervision scheme.

Crime Statistics

Crime statistics for Brunei Darussalam are hard to find because not all of the official records of crime statistics are up to date or made available. As reported by http://www.bruneiresources.com. in 2003, the total number of criminal cases was 4,075; in 2004, the number was 4,796; and in 2005, it was 2,207. For the entire time period, by far the major portion of cases reported to police were for property crime, followed by crimes against the person and drug crimes.

According to news reports, crime rates in Brunei have been decreasing for many years. According to these news reports, crime statistics released by the Royal Brunei Police Force in 2004 were the highest since 1996; however, in 2005 there was a drop in the number of crimes reported to police and another drop again in 2006, a drop of 170 cases was calculated for the two years. Brunei has an estimated population of 381,371 people as of July 2008, and the crime ratio was 593 crime cases to 100,000 people, based on crimes recorded by police. Miscellaneous crimes dropped 21 percent during 2005 and 2006, overall crime dropped 4 percent, the rate of apprehensions and arrests dropped 3.4 percent, and fraud cases decreased by 183 percent. The crimes that showed an increase were cases of house break-ins and burglaries. There was an increase of 145 break-ins and burglaries. Most of the break-ins occurred in the Brunei Muara district. Car thefts also increased by 6 percent, and out of the 169 stolen vehicles (mainly Toyota brand), 106 were recovered. The number of arrests increased by 0.05 percent in 2006, and 10.5 percent of those arrested were below the age of 18 and generally involved in thefts and burglaries. The United Nations report on drug statistics for 2001 showed a 21 percent increase in drug-related arrests, an average increase of 46.5 arrests per month to 56.4 between 1999 and 2000. The majority of drug-related arrests were male, but the number of females has increased. In 2007's statistics, 4,519 crimes were reported. The Royal Brunei Police Force handled 3,370 of those cases. In total, there were 1,136 arrests made and 1,046 criminal cases solved.

Finding of Guilt

Criminal Prosecution

There are two court systems in Brunei Darussalam, a national system that deals with laws in the Constitution, and another system that deals with Islamic law. The National System is composed of three courts, the Subordinate Court, the Intermediate Court, and the Supreme Court. Most cases appear in the subordinate court, which is also called the magistrates' court. In the intermediate court, the more serious criminal and civil matters are seen. However, the intermediate court does not handle capital offenses. The Supreme Court includes the High Court and the Court of Appeals. This court also tries cases that carry capital sentences. The other court system is the Syariah Courts. This court coincides with the Supreme Court and only handles matters of Islamic law.

Criminal prosecutions and proceedings are under the direction and control of the attorney general, who is also the public prosecutor. Occasionally, His Majesty will appoint a deputy public prosecutor who is under the direction of the public prosecutor. The police conduct investigations, and they have the power of search and seizure; however, they must document what has been seized. The owner of the property, who must be present during the search, as well as the officer, must sign the document. The officer may also question witnesses, and witnesses then write and sign their statement. The officer then reads the statement to the witness, who then signs it. These statements can be submitted as evidence in a trial. When an officer interviews a potential defendant, the officer is required to read the defendant his or her rights. Silence is not a right in Brunei Darussalam since the courts may see this as a detrimental factor for the defendant. Once a suspect is arrested, he is either placed in remand or released on bail. If remanded by the magistrate, the defendant cannot be retained for more than 15 days. If the court ordered the arrest, there is no time limit. Preliminary inquiries are held for offenses against the state, in addition to murder or any offense that carries a death sentence. The magistrate at this stage determines if there is enough evidence to submit the case to the High Court; however, drug trafficking and rape cases go straight to the High Court, while other cases are tried summarily in the magistrate court. Charges against a defendant may be dropped any time before a judgment is made, and only the prosecution can withdraw the charge.

Defendants have the right to counsel, if they cannot afford counsel the court does not provide one unless it is a capital case. In noncapital cases, defendants may act as their own counsel. Defendants also have the right to a speedy trial and the right to confront their accusers. The number of judges presiding over the trial varies; it can be either one judge or a panel of judges. At the trial, the defendant is read the charge and asked to enter a plea of either guilty or not guilty. If the plea is guilty, it is recorded, and he or she may be convicted on that plea; however, the judge makes sure the defendant know the consequences of his or her plea. If the plea is not guilty, a trial will be held and witnesses and evidence will be seen before a judge. If the defendant is found not guilty, the court appoints an acquittal. If the defendant is found guilty or has pleaded guilty, the court then sentences the defendant. Defendants are allowed to appeal. However, the appeal will be heard in the High Court. If the defendant appeals the High Court's decision, the Court of Appeal hears the appeal.

The magistrate court handles civil court proceedings, and the cases viewed involve matters between people concerning breaches of contracts and compensation. These trials are heard in public; however, the magistrate may request that the hearing be in the presence of the parties alone. The High Court cases are initiated by writ, summons, motion, or petition. In these cases, if a defendant wants to avoid a hearing, he or she may pay the court the amount of money a plaintiff claims. If the plaintiff accepts the money, notice must be given to the defendant. In High Court cases, offers to settle and summary judgments may be made.

Juvenile Offenders

Originally, the age of criminal responsibility was seven years old; however, after some controversy, the law was changed to 12 years of age. The courts have limited powers when dealing with juveniles. Under the Criminal Procedure Code, the court may impose several alternative sentencing options, instead of imposing fines or imprisonment on a youthful offender. Those alternative sentencing options include: (1) discharging after admonition, (2) delivering the offender to a guardian, nearest relative, or another person who is responsible for the juvenile for a period not exceeding 12 months, (3) ordering the offender to be released on probation of good conduct on the entering into a bond, and to appear and receive judgment if and when called upon by the court, and (4) in the case of the High Court, committing the offender to custody in the detention facility of Jerudong Prison, for one to five years. Other alternatives are to inflict a fine of $1,500 on the offender's guardian should the court consider that the guardian has contributed to the misconduct through neglect of care or other reasons. Offenders under the age of 18 may not receive the death penalty.

Punishment

Some of the most common punishments in Brunei Darussalam are expulsion from the country, caning (whipping), death penalty (no longer inflicted), life imprisonment, fines, and payment of compensation. In sentencing hearings, where the death penalty may be imposed, there must be two judges present, and they both must agree with the decision. Women who are pregnant are not sentenced to the death penalty; instead, they receive life imprisonment. Life imprisonment means the defendant will spend the rest of his or her life in prison. Besides life imprisonment, prison terms can carry long sentences. Caning has been in use since 1988, and is a mandatory punishment for 42 different criminal cases. An adult who is sentenced to caning or whipping usually receives a maximum number of 24 lashings. Defendants below the age of 18 receive a maximum number of 18 lashings. Women and men above 50 years old, and those sentenced to death, are exempt from caning. Canings must be conducted in the presence of a doctor, who for medical reasons can stop the caning at any time. Offenders prefer this method to long-term punishment. Fines are assessed according to the relevant law, and if there is no relevant law, the court may decide on the appropriate amount. In addition to the punishments imposed, the court can also order the defendant to pay compensation, if he or she can afford it. If a defendant can pay the compensation amount but defaults on the payment, the result is imprisonment or additional imprisonment.

Caning is used as a punishment in nearly 80 percent of criminal convictions. Under Brunei's penal code, murder is punishable by death. Those convicted of rape are sentenced up to 30 years in prison and shall be punished with caning, as well. Those who have sexual intercourse with a woman less than 14 years of age without her consent could receive a prison term not less than 8 years but not more than 30 years, and shall be punished with caning not less than 12 strokes. For theft, a criminal could be punished with imprisonment for a term up to three years, with a fine, or with both. Other types of theft could see up to seven years in prison. Theft that causes harm, fear of harm, or death could see as much as 15 years in prison and receive a caning. Those who commit robbery could receive as much as 30 years in prison and, with whipping, no less than 12 strokes.

There are very severe penalties for illegal drug offenses. For possession of certain amounts of narcotics, there is a "mandatory" death penalty. Possession of heroin, Ecstasy, and morphine derivatives of more than 15 grams; cocaine of more than 30 grams; cannabis of more than 500 grams; Syabu or methamphetamine of more than 50 grams; or opium of more than 1.2 kilograms carries the death penalty. Possession of lesser amounts is considered minor drug possession, and charges are known to carry a 21-year sentence and/or heavy fines. There is a presumption clause, which states that anyone in possession over a certain amount of controlled drug is assumed to be trafficking. Drug trafficking of other amounts of narcotics is punishable with a minimum of 1 to 30 years in prison, and 1 to 15 strokes of whipping. Prostitution is illegal, and women who move to Brunei solely for prostitution are deported. As noted above, in Brunei, the death penalty is allowed; however, Brunei can be considered abolitionist in practice because it has not executed anyone since 1957, and is believed to have a practice of not carrying out executions.

Sharia law is only applied to Muslims. Sharia law punishes individuals who commit crimes against the Islamic law; however, it does not apply to non-Muslims. It provides punishment for moral crimes such as adultery, fornication, alcohol use, as well as many other crimes. These crimes are included in a group of punishment called "hudud" crimes. These crimes are considered crimes against Allah. Under the sharia law, robbery crimes are punishable by cutting off the hand of the thief, while fornication by unmarried persons and alcohol consumption are punishable by caning. Being stoned to death is the punishment for adultery. Other crimes, such as murder and assault, are punished severely, with murder being punished by the death penalty, and assault being punished using the "eye for an eye, tooth for a tooth" principle. Through negotiation, in an Islamic court, an individual can escape such punishments by providing compensation.

Prison

Until 1998, Brunei only had one prison. The Jerudong Prison was established in 1954. This prison was built to accommodate all categories of prisoners, ranging from those sentenced to one day of prison to life terms and death penalties. The purpose of the prison is to rehabilitate offenders into law-abiding citizens, as well as protect society by holding and guarding criminals. Rehabilitative programs were established to reintegrate offenders back into society. Religious and social counseling, physical training, and vocational courses are just a few of the opportunities provided by the programs. It is mandatory that prisoners work to build ethics and discipline. The rehabilitative process uses a Progressive Stage System, which has five stages. In the first stage, a prisoner is allowed to send and receive one letter every two months and get one 15-minute visit every two months. This is for prisoners serving less than six months. In the second stage, a prisoner is allowed to send and receive one letter every two months; however, this is for prisoners serving more than a six-month sentence. With good behavior, they can be promoted to the third stage. In the third stage, the prisoner is allowed to send and receive letters every three weeks. Prisoners are also allowed to receive earnings and can have 20-minute visits every six weeks. In the fourth stage, the prisoner is allowed to send and receive one letter every two weeks and have 30-minute visits every month, but only with good behavior. In stage five, called the Special Stage, prisoners are honored with a special blue uniform. Prisoners can send one letter every month and receive unlimited amounts of letters and have a 30-minute visit every two weeks. There are no reported cases of police misconduct with prisoners, and the prisons are said to meet the minimum international standards. In 1998, a new prison was established to accommodate the increasing numbers of prisoners. Overcrowding is not a problem in the prisons. Prisoners are allowed visits from their family, and they are allowed to bring food into the prison. The number of inmates incarcerated during 2003 was 443 prisoners. In 2005, there were 492 prisoners. The percentage of female inmates was 7.5 percent. In 2007, the United Nations Development Program reported that the total number of prisoners was 529, with only eight female prisoners.

Pamela Shultz

Further Reading

About ASEAN. ASEAN Secretariat. Association of Southeast Asian Nations: http://www.aseansec.org.

The Government of Brunei Darussalam Official Web site: http://www.brunei.gov.bn.

Laws of Brunei. Chapter 22 Penal Code. Attorney General's Champers Web site: http://www.agc.gov.bn/LOB/PDF/Cap22.pdf.

Legal Procedure in Brunei Darussalam. Legal Systems in ASEAN. ASEAN Law Association Web site: http://www.aseanlawassociation.org.

Sharp, A. M. (2006). "Brunei Darussalam." In *The World Police Encyclopedia,* edited by D. K. Das and M. Palmiotto, pp. 131–134. New York: Routledge.

Cambodia

Legal System: Civil
Murder: High
Burglary: High
Corruption: High
Human Trafficking: Medium
Prison Rate: Low
Death Penalty: No
Corporal Punishment: No

Background

Cambodia is a small Southeast Asia nation bordered by Laos in the north, Vietnam in the east,

Thailand in the west, and the Gulf of Thailand in the south. During the last quarter of the 20th century, Cambodians have suffered civil war, foreign aggression, and genocide. At peace since 1998, one of the characteristics of the population, which was about 13 million in 2005 and growing at a rate of 2.4 percent per year, is its youthfulness: 60 percent are under 25 and 40 percent are less than 15 years old. Cambodia comprises 24 provinces, 84 percent of the population reside in rural areas, many subsisting on less than US$1 a day. Close to 60 percent of the remaining 16 percent of urban dwellers reside in the capital Phnom Penh. The population is 95 percent Buddhist and ethnic Khmer.

For centuries the Khmer were ruled by revered god kings; most famously, during the Angkorian period, in which cultural brilliance between the 9th and 13th centuries has not been surpassed. Cambodia suffered recurring territorial and political conflicts with its Vietnamese and Thai neighbors, until the modern period when Cambodia was engulfed in the imperialist pursuits of French colonialism. In 1863, Cambodia was established as a French Protectorate, which lasted until independence in November 1953.

In 1954, Cambodia became a constitutional monarchy led alternatively as king or prime minister by Prince Norodom Sihanouk. In the 1960s, Cambodia was gradually enmeshed in the civil war in neighboring Vietnam. In 1970, Sihanouk was ousted by a U.S.-supported coup led by General Lon Nol. Cambodia was declared a republic and entered a period of civil war, which was rendered even more destructive by the heavy and illegal U.S. bombing targeting Vietcong supply routes inside the country. This conflict boosted the popularity and power base of groups opposed to the Lon Nol regime, among whom the dominant groups were royalists and a revolutionary movement known as the Khmer Rouge led by Pol Pot. In 1975, the Khmer Rouge (KR) defeated the republican army and entered Phnom Penh. Once in power, the KR emptied the cities, and established a Chinese-backed utopian regime of agrarian revolutionary terror, which killed (through starvation and murder) close to 3 million people and ended in 1979 with a military occupation by the Vietnamese. The Vietnamese army of occupation installed a socialist regime called the People's Republic of Kampuchea (PRK), led successively and briefly by a number of former KR defectors, and six years later by Hun Sen, himself a former KR defector. In 1989, when Vietnam withdrew its troops from Cambodia, the regime was renamed the State of Cambodia (SOC). In 1979, a second civil war (with strong nationalist anti-Vietnamese overtones) commenced. The combatants comprised PRK/SOC forces supported by Vietnam and the Soviet Union on one side, and KR and royalists forces supported by the United States and China on the other. In 1991, a United Nations intervention resulted in a peace settlement known as the Paris Accords and the establishment of the United Nations Transitional Authority in Cambodia (UNTAC).

In 1993, UNTAC oversaw the adoption of the present constitution and implementation of the first free elections. The royalist party (FUNCIPEC) won a majority but, in the hope of preserving a fragile peace between former warring factions, was forced into an inherently unstable governmental alliance (a joint prime ministership) with the Cambodian People's Party (CPP) led by Hun Sen. This precarious peace was indeed seriously threatened by armed clashes between the CPP and royalist forces in 1997, which led to a significant number of casualties and the end of the co-prime ministership with the defeat of the royalists' military capability. After the second elections of 1998, the CPP/FUNCIPEC governmental alliance was eventually reinstated, but with a greatly weakened FUNCIPEC. However, this arrangement was accompanied by continued periods of political uncertainty and violence. Remaining pockets of KR resistance ended in 1998, which also coincided with the death of Pol Pot.

Efforts to bring to justice the leaders of the KR responsible for the genocide and atrocities of the revolutionary period have been long delayed by a government reluctant to disturb pragmatic arrangements that encouraged defections from the KR. At the time of writing, a tribunal of Cambodian and international jurists is leading a trial against the few remaining aging leaders of the KR. After four rounds of national elections in 1993, 1998, 2003, and 2008, the CPP has consolidated its dominance over government, and its leader, Prime Minister Hun Sen, has steadily increased his grip on power.

History of the Legal System

Before the Protectorate, the Cambodian legal system was essentially a customary law system with widespread use of mediation and reparation to settle local disputes and crime. During the Protectorate, an official legal system patterned after the laws and courts of France was imposed (hence inquisitorial in relation to the criminal law). After the Protectorate and until 1975, the official legal system and informal practices in use during the Protectorate were maintained. The Khmer Rouge regime of terror (1975–1979) destroyed the legal system, judicial officials were murdered, and traditional informal mediation practices were undermined.

During the PRK/SOC regime (1979–1991), a Soviet-style legal system was imported from Vietnam and staffed according to political allegiance rather than expertise in the field of law and criminal justice. Many police were trained in Vietnam and Russia and focused mostly on internal security and intelligence rather than on law and order and crime control. Regarded as a security agency of the government with minimal commitment to civilian peacekeeping, the police and the whole criminal justice system (CJS) had a very low standing in the community. Recourse to the formal justice system was rare as people continued to use traditional mediation and resolution to deal with crimes and conflicts at the commune and village level. While a court system, styled as People's Revolutionary Courts, had been re-established in May 1980 and formalized by the enactment of the Constitution of June 1981, judges and prosecutors were generally unqualified, poorly educated, and subject to military control. There was no independent appellate body. Any review of verdicts and sentences pronounced by the courts was thus in the hands of the executive branch. Further developments, such as the enactment of the Law Concerning the Organization of the Courts and Prosecutors and the establishment of the Institute of Public Administration and Law (IPAL) in 1982, the People's Supreme Court in 1985, or even the new SOC Constitution in 1989, did not bring any significant changes to the system and its standing in the community.

Since the Paris Accords in 1991, the official system has remained inquisitorial and is primarily based on a civil law mixture of French-influenced codes from the period of UNTAC, royal decrees, and acts of the legislature, with influences of customary law and remnants of communist legal theory. However, most cases continue to be dealt with informally at the village or commune level. In addition to a new constitution, 2007 saw the passage of the Law on Criminal Procedure, which defines the roles and functions of the police, courts, and prisons. Agencies in the Cambodian CJS include the Ministry of Interior (MOI), the National Police Department, the *Gendarmerie Militaire,* and the Department of Prisons. The Ministry of Justice (MOJ) is responsible for the court system, and the Supreme Council of Magistracy for the management of judges and prosecutors.

Some international donors such as the Australian government (AusAID) have focused their aid on rebuilding a legitimate Cambodian CJS. However, in spite of several years of ongoing assistance, many Cambodian people continue to regard the current CJS as having little legitimacy, because in the three branches of the system (police, judiciary, and corrections), regime capture (lack of independence) and corruption is endemic.

Role of Police

The Cambodian Police comprises the Gendarmerie and the Cambodian National Police (CNP). The Gendarmerie is primarily a military police force and does not have the rural policing function that it generally plays in France and francophone countries. However, in its 2007 reports, the Cambodia Criminal Justice Assistance Project (CCJAP) noted the overlapping of functions between the CNP and the Gendarmerie: the latter has become increasingly visible deploying to district level in rural areas as well as in towns and cities, performing "national security" roles. The new Criminal Procedure Law provides the Gendarmerie with the same powers of arrest held by the judicial police, although such powers have long been exercised by them under the general provision for arrest in the UNTAC penal code.

The structure of the Cambodian National Police includes a number of central departments such as Traffic, Training, Scientific and Technical, Human Trafficking and Child Protection, Public Order Police, Border Police, Security Police, and judicial police. In all provinces the CNP structure is replicated at the various administrative strata down to the commune level (Police Post). However, the provincial commissioners must comply with the national policies and procedures laid down by the MOI, which is responsible for salaries and operating expenses but takes direction from the deputy governor (who, in theory but rarely in practice, is responsible for infrastructure and other resources) about provincial policing priorities.

The role of the judicial police and its Central Department of Criminal Police is similar to the role performed by traditional policing agencies in many other countries (i.e., mediation, complaint handling, investigation, and arrests). One of the functions of the Scientific and Technical Office, under the control of the judicial police, is to record and classify reported crimes as well as offenders and fingerprints. According to the law, the judicial police can also act as prosecutors and are often appointed to conduct investigations, but in this role they have limited powers of arrest and must seek authority from a prosecutor. As in most inquisitorial systems, the investigating judge appointed to the case can conduct further inquiries.

However, CCJAP points out that poor training of the police force and the judiciary often prevents the proper application of and compliance with the laws of Cambodia. For instance, many police interrogations end up in confessions with little supporting evidence. As part of its regular monitoring of prison conditions in Cambodia, the Cambodian League for the Promotion and Defense of Human Rights (LICADHO) conducted interviews with prisoners in 18 prisons, and found that from 1999 to 2006 between 450 and 163 inmates had been tortured in police custody. However, it is worth noting that in 1999 reports of torture in police custody represented 13.7 percent of the population of the surveyed prisons but that they have steadily fallen to represent only 1.8 percent by 2006.

Other problems reported by CCJAP, affecting the CNP in general and the judicial police in particular, are poor management and supervision and lack of strategic planning and equipment: According to CCJAP, the creation of the Offices of Human Trafficking and Child Protection under the responsibility of the judicial police is a positive response, but its effectiveness is impaired by a "lack of proper definition of function, staffing requirements, training requirements, and a plan for how these Offices will actually function."

Decades of conflicts have resulted in an overstaffed National Police Department, which was used to absorb demobilized military personnel with little sense of their civilian mission and the provision of services to the community. This contributes to a widespread feeling of mistrust, reflected, for instance, in the very low reporting rates of criminal victimization to the police. Given the level of corruption in the police and in most other institutions, there is also cynicism about impartiality and fair treatment by such agencies. For instance, it is not rare for the judicial police to seek between 20–50 percent of the cost of a stolen motorbike up front before they begin an investigation. While street-level police corruption of this kind has generally decreased between 2000 and 2007, in many locations public cynicism about police corruption has grown despite reductions in its incidence.

It is difficult to obtain reliable information about the number of CNP in Cambodia. CCJAP estimated more than 65,000 police in 1996 and 64,000 in 2001. There was a national plan to reduce the 1996 staffing by 24,000 in five years, but by 2000 the numbers appear to have reduced by only 11,630. In 2001, the judicial police had between 8,000 and 9,000 officers, but only 800 were female. More recent estimations (2007) put the CNP number at 70,000. Yet, a report by the National Police Commissioner (dated January 22, 2007) indicated that the total number of the national law enforcement officers as of November 2006 was 50,824 (1,993 females), comprising middle-rank officers of 12,658 (789 females) and local law enforcement officers of 38,166 (1,204 females).

Crime

Police crime statistics provided by the MOI distinguish between a "serious crime situation," also referred to as a "felony," with four categories: robbery (threat/nonfatal and robbery-murder), murder (successful and attempted), terrorism (kidnapping, confinement, grenade attack, organized crimes), and sexual offenses (rape, rape-murder, human trafficking); and a "minor crime situation," also referred to as "misdemeanor," with five categories: theft (stealing and pickpocketing), fraud/breach of trust, battery with injury, use of illegal weapon, and others. While article 21(1) of the UNTAC code stipulates that children under the age of 13 must not be placed in detention, there is no age of criminal responsibility in Cambodia.

Kem Sokha, Director of the Cambodian Center for Human Rights, below, and his deputy director put palm prints on the black cloth hung on a truck to symbolize "no corruption," Phnom Penh, Cambodia, September 4, 2006. Cambodian police have prevented prominent human rights groups from holding anticorruption demonstrations. (AP Photo/Heng Sinith)

Corruption is endemic in Cambodia and affects many government and nongovernment institutions and businesses. However, street-level corruption by officials has abated since 2000. For instance, two sweeps of the United Nations International Crime Victim Survey (UNICVS) conducted in three provinces in 2000–2001 and 2006–2007 showed that the estimated rates of rent seeking by officials had reduced from 27.8 percent to 18.2 percent in Phnom Penh, and from 15.6 percent to 12.9 percent in Kampong Cham. In the third province, Kandal, the rates (18.3%) had not changed. The actual experience of corruption had also decreased in respect to police (except in Kandal). In Phnom Penh, the proportion of victims of police corruption reduced from 10.1 percent in 2000 to 5.7 percent in 2005 and represented 31.2 percent of all victims of corruption compared to 36.5 percent in 2000. In Kampong Cham the proportion reduced from 4.5 percent in 2000 to 2.5 percent in 2006 and represented 20.2 percent of all victims of corruption compared to 29.1 percent in 2000. In Kandal, however, the experience of corruption by police officers had increased, from 3.5 percent in 2000 to 4.4 percent in 2005 and represented 24.1 percent of all victims of corruption compared to 18.9 percent in 2000. In the three provinces, the most frequently cited offenders by victims of corruption both in the first and second sweeps were elected commune officials. It is more difficult to estimate the extent of corruption by the elites, but it is clear that many high-ranking government officials have amassed fortunes unrelated to their legitimate salaries.

Commercial fraud affecting ordinary consumers is still widespread, although the rates have declined between 2000 and 2006, from 39.6 percent to 25.4 percent in Phnom Penh, 31.8 percent to 18.7 percent in Kandal, and 29.8 percent to 22.0 percent in Kampong Cham. Human trafficking, including children, for illegal labor and prostitution in neighboring countries (e.g., Vietnam and Thailand), is often cited as a serious criminal activity. However, there is a scarcity of empirical research on the extent and dynamics of this illegal trade.

A recent report by the national police commissioner indicates that drug trafficking (heroin and particularly methamphetamines) is rising and that "the demand for illegal drugs among youth, students, and other citizens has remarkably increased." The report mentions that in 2006 the quantity of heroin and methamphetamines (ice) trafficked to Cambodia was three times higher than in 2005.

While the rates of robbery, including robbery-murder, have declined since 1992, the number of robbery-murders is still relatively high. In rural Cambodia, livestock theft is the most prevalent crime and can have dramatic consequences for both the victim(s) (i.e., serious impoverishment) and the offender(s) (i.e., high risk of being killed by villagers if caught in the act). Given that more than 80 percent of the Cambodian population makes a meager living through farming activities, this crime affects a large number of citizens.

Drug Offenses

The production, use, and sale of illegal drugs are a criminal offense in Cambodia, although drug use appears to be classified as a misdemeanor and trafficking as a felony. The same types of drugs (e.g., heroin, cocaine, cannabis, methamphetamines, Ecstasy, etc.) as in most Western countries have been declared illegal. According to article 98, personal consumption, and production for the unique purpose of personal consumption, of any of the prohibited drugs is punished by a fine ranging from US$25 to US$250. Article 36 stipulates that the offense of selling or providing any of these drugs to a person for his or her personal consumption "shall be punished to imprisonment from one month to one year and with a fine from 1,000,000 (about US$250) to 5,000,000 riels (about US$1,250), or to either one of the two penalties." Article 86 provides a more severe penalty of one year to five years in prison and with a fine of about US$2,470 if the drugs are made available to minors.

Any other drug offenses for the eventual intentional purpose of trafficking incur a penalty from 5 to 20 years' imprisonment with fines up to 50,000,000 riels (about US$12,500). In his January 2007 report, the national police commissioner commented that Cambodia had been used as a safe haven for the transit and distribution of illegal drugs from the Golden Triangle to other countries in the regions.

Crime Statistics

The official national statistics of crime recorded by the police in 2007 and provided by the Ministry of Interior (MOI) are presented below (rates per 100,000):

- Murder: 2.32
- Attempted murder: 0.75
- Robbery-murder: 0.55
- Rape-murder: 0.09
- Grenade attack (considered lethal): 0.11
- Combined homicide (murder, robbery-murder, rape-murder, and grenade attack): 3.07
- Robbery: 4.32
- Rape: 1.80
- Theft: 8.93
- Drug trafficking (based on number of arrested offenders provided by national police commissioner in 2006): 3.94

At this stage we need to emphasize that in Cambodia there is an enormous "dark figure" of crime. The two sweeps of the United Nations International Crime Victim Survey (UNICVS) revealed that most victims of crime do not report their victimization to the police, who in addition only record a fraction of the reported offenses. For example, if we compare the rates based on police records in 2005 with the estimated rates based on the UNICVS in Phnom Penh, very large differences are observed. Instead of a rate of 29 for nonfatal robbery based on police records, a rate of 1,831 per 100,000 is estimated by the UNICVS; for nonfatal rape, instead of 0.7 based on police records, a rate of 92 per 100,000 is estimated. Again, for assault with injury, instead of 6.5 per 100,000 based on police records, 1,465 per 100,000 is estimated by the UNICVS; for all theft (including vehicles, livestock, burglary, and pickpocketing) instead of 18.4 per 100,000 based on police records, the UNICVS estimated a rate of 33,700 per 100,000, and for fraud instead of 0.62 per 100,000, 25,366 per 100,000. The same order of magnitude in the difference between rates based on police records and the UNICVS was found in Kandal and Kampong Cham in 2000 and 2005.

Although actual crime rates are far higher than the official crime rates, they have dramatically reduced since 1998. Analyses of press reports, interviews with judicial police, and hospital data confirm the declining trends of the rates of homicide, and the UNICVS sweeps show a significant decrease in both property and violent crime.

Crimes in Rural Areas

As mentioned earlier, the UNICVS shows that livestock theft is the most prevalent crime in rural areas. In 2001, in two of the surveyed rural provinces, Kampong Chhnang and Kampong Speu, the one-year prevalence rates of livestock theft were close to 35 percent and reached 25 percent in Kampong Cham. In 2006, the rate had declined to 11 percent in Kampong Cham, but was still one of highest rates apart from fraud and corruption (Kampong Chhnang and Kampong Speu were not surveyed in 2006). On the other hand, police statistics show that rates of homicide tend to be higher in many rural areas compared to the capital Phnom Penh.

Crimes in Urban Areas

Until 2005, the rate of robbery was significantly higher in the capital Phnom Penh than in other provinces. For instance, of all the robberies recorded nationally by the police over seven years (1996–1999 and 2001, 2003, 2005), a third occurred in Phnom Penh whose population during the same period was only about 9.5 percent of the national population (hence, an average rate of 33.16 per 100,000). However, in 2006 the number of robberies (including robbery-murders) recorded in Phnom Penh by the police had significantly declined to reach a rate of only 14.79 per 100,000, which was lower than the rates in a few semirural and rural provinces (Sihanoukville, Kong Kep, and Pailin). The UNICVS also revealed that, although reduced, the prevalence of robberies as well as street-level fraud and corruption was higher in Phnom Penh than in Kandal and Kampong Cham. UNICVS (but not police statistics) showed higher rates of burglary in Phnom Penh, and both police statistics and UNICVS showed higher rates of pickpocketing in Phnom Penh than in rural areas.

Finding of Guilt

Rights of the Accused

Although the principle of presumption of innocence is enshrined in the Cambodian constitution, the way the inquisitorial system is practiced in Cambodia mostly ensures that a person is presumed guilty by the time he or she appears before the court. Guilt or innocence tends to be determined during a pretrial stage, which takes place before prosecutors whose enquiries are not open to the public. The Law on Criminal Procedure does specify a number of basic rights for the accused, such as the right to be informed of the imputed criminal act, the right to answer or not to answer the investigating judge without the assistance of a lawyer or defender chosen by the accused, the right to communicate privately with defenders, and the right to appeal a court decision. However, there is no provision for the right to remain silent and to have an attorney present during police interrogations. There is no trial by jury in Cambodia or a right to plead guilty to a lesser offense. As for a speedy trial, it is not a right provided to the accused but a provision of the Law on Criminal Procedure allowing the prosecutor to send an accused direct to trial (i.e., without relying on the work of the investigating judge) when the offense is a misdemeanor incurring a penalty of no more than a year of imprisonment or a misdemeanor incurring more than a year of imprisonment in the case of flagrante delicto (i.e., when the accused was caught red-handed in the act).

Assistance to the Accused

Because the criminal justice system and the legal profession were decimated during the Khmer Rouge dictatorship, there is a scarcity of trained and competent lawyers in Cambodia. In theory, and according to the Law on Criminal Procedure, an accused person has the right to be assisted by a lawyer or a "defender" as soon as the prosecutor lays charges and during interrogations conducted by him or her or the investigating judge, up to and including the trial. Article 76 of the Law on Criminal Procedure stipulates that the automatic appointment of a lawyer shall be made by the presiding judge (other provisions mention the investigating judge rather than the presiding judge) in the following cases:

- The victim is a minor without defense.
- The accused person is a minor without defense.
- The accused person is mute, deaf, blind, or has a mental disorder.
- The accused person is not able to afford a defender.

Funded by U.S. donors, the Cambodian Defenders Project (CDP) was set up in the mid-1990s to train a group of defenders whose role was to represent those accused of crimes in the court. They formed themselves into an organization that now provides legal aid from offices in Phnom Penh and a number of provincial towns. In 2001, it comprised 30 lawyers, 30 supporting staff, and 17 law interns. According to CCJAP, defenders were sometimes regarded with suspicion by judges, prosecutors, and court clerks and even forbidden to appear; however, as trained lawyers, they raised the standard of court procedures. Yet, CCJAP reported that despite being paid decent salaries, "some of them have succumbed to the pervading corruption found in the court system." Legal Aid of Cambodia (LAC) was set up shortly after the establishment of the CDP, as the latter split into two distinct groups. Funded by several European assistance projects, in 2001 LAC had offices in Phnom Penh and nine provinces and was staffed by 18 lawyers and 18 legal assistants.

In addition to the CDP and LAC, in 1995 a statute established the Cambodian Bar Association and stipulated that only members of the association could practice law in Cambodia. The association, which in 2000 had 216 members, includes lawyers in private practice and those in the legal aid/defender bodies. Although generally not offering legal services, a number of NGOs specialized in justice issues (e.g., Cambodian League for the Promotion and Defense of Human Rights [LICADHO], Cambodian Human Rights and Development Association [ADHOC], Cambodian Law and Democracy Project, Cambodian Legal Resources Development Center, Cambodian Women's Crisis Center) provide training and advice to CJS personnel and advocate on behalf of the rights of victims and accused persons.

Prosecution and Case Investigation

Because of the legacy of the French Protectorate, particularly in relation to the inquisitorial nature of the criminal justice procedure, there are a number of similarities between the prosecution of criminal cases in France and Cambodia. A notable similarity is the extensive role of the *juge d'instruction* (investigating judge). Two distinct, yet closely collaborating, groups therefore conduct the prosecution and investigation of a criminal case: prosecutors and investigating judges. Each province has a public prosecutor department whose role is to supervise the case brought by the judicial police. In principle, the usual route for the prosecution, investigation, and adjudication of a criminal case starts with the judiciary police. The latter receive denunciations or complaints relating to crimes, misdemeanors, and minor offenses; gather evidence; may decide on the detention of suspects for a maximum of 48 hours; and then make reports to the prosecutor of the competent jurisdiction. Then, the duty of the prosecutor is to immediately open a judicial inquiry, that is, to make a charge called "introductory requisition," which indicates the offense in accordance with the law, and, unless it is a flagrante delicto offense (in that case prosecutors can proceed with the investigation by themselves), send it to the investigating judge. According to article 38 of the Law on Criminal Procedure, there is at least one judge responsible for investigating criminal cases in each provincial court. Investigating judges are given extensive powers to conduct their inquiry. They may reach different conclusions as to the charge laid by the prosecutor and must therefore maintain a close communication with the latter. When both the investigating judge and the prosecutor are satisfied that there is a case to answer, the prosecutor refers the case to the competent provincial or municipal "criminal tribunal."

In principle, there is an absolute incompatibility of office between a trial judge and a representative of the prosecution department or the investigating judge. In practice, due to customary traditions and a profound distrust of the corrupt and costly official judicial system, most victims do not report crimes to the police but to village and commune chiefs. However, village and commune chiefs only play an informal role in conflict mediation geared toward reparation and compensation rather than a formal prosecuting or investigating function.

Alternatives and Outcomes of Prosecution

Apart from this informal system, which appears to process and "solve" many cases, there are no formal alternatives to going to trial, and the official system does not include provisions such as plea bargaining or any kind of medical or other types of supervised or unsupervised treatment. The majority of criminal cases, apart from the most serious ones, are therefore "resolved" through the informal system. Serious cases go to trial, in principle, following the procedure mentioned above (in practice, due to lack of proper training and corruption, many aspects of this procedure are not observed). There is no trial by jury; after hearing the prosecution and the defense, the presiding judge (or trial judge) decides on guilt or innocence, and if the accused is judged guilty, decides the penalty to be imposed.

Incarceration before or awaiting trial is allowed and regulated by the UNTAC Criminal Code. Article 14(4) stipulates that time held in detention without trial should be no more than four months, which can be extended to six months by a judge with appropriate reasons given. Article 21(1) specifies that accused persons must be tried no later than six months after arrest, that children under the age of 13 must not be placed in detention, and for children between the ages of 13 and 18, no longer than one month, which can be doubled if the child is charged with felony. However, CCJAP reported that very often the courts do not comply with these rules and that many accused persons were kept in detention before trial for longer periods than required by law.

Scope of the Criminal Courts

There are 22 courts in Cambodia, one in each province and one in each of the two municipalities (Phnom Penh and Sihanoukville). There is also one Appeal Court and one Supreme Court, both located in Phnom Penh. On January 1999, a total of 89 judges, 47 prosecutors, 368 court clerks, and 233 other officials were attached to these courts. Currently, there are about 250 judges in place.

In 2001, no training institution existed for the magistracy and court clerks, and apart from uncoordinated and inadequate programs provided by some NGOs, training courses for judges and prosecutors before or after appointment were virtually nonexistent. While some judges had received university education, very few were legally qualified, including the majority of provincial courts presidents and prosecutors. Even the president of the Appeal Court was not a qualified lawyer; the only exception was the president of the Supreme Court, the highest court in Cambodia. There have also been changes in a number of Supreme Court judges, increases in the pay of judges, improved training, and further oversight of judges by the Council of Magistrates.

Juvenile Justice

There are no separate courts for juveniles in the Cambodian CJS, and juvenile cases are processed and eventually heard in provincial courts in the same way as adults. The law, however, requires that penalties for juveniles be half of those for adults and prohibits the detention of minors younger than 13 years; two rules, which according to LICADHO, the judges normally apply. Despite the absence of juvenile courts and separate prisons, no specialist training in relation to the treatment of juveniles as victims, witnesses, or offenders is provided to officials in the court system. As there are no alternatives to imprisonment for minors, in 2007, the latter represented 5.5 percent of the prison population, a rate that has steadily increased since 1999 (3.9%). The same prison rules (e.g., recreation time) apply for adults and juveniles and no schooling is provided.

Punishment

Officially, degrading treatments such as corporal and public punishment are not allowed in Cambodia. Fines and prison are the most common types of punishments imposed by the courts. According to CCJAP, there is a lack of alternatives to imprisonment. Noncustodial sentences are limited to fines, suspended sentences, and conditional release. There are no legal provisions for community work orders, supervised probation and parole systems. The courts can also impose reparations and compensation, but their greatest use probably occurs in the informal system.

Punishment for Serious Crime

Murder

Capital punishment has been abolished in Cambodia since 1989 and no legal executions have taken place since then. Nevertheless, the law imposes heavy penalties of imprisonment for serious crime. Limited details about the length of prison sentences are provided by the MOI. Article 31 of the Criminal Code stipulates imprisonment for a term of 10 to 20 years for murder.

Rape

Article 33 specifies a prison sentence of 5 to 10 years, which cannot be suspended (but can, under article 68, be reduced by half for offenders under 18). However, according to a report by LICADHO, judges often apply the law "incorrectly and inconsistently, giving convicted rapists suspended sentences when the law prohibits it."

Theft, Burglary, and Robbery

The Criminal Code classifies burglary as robbery. Article 34 stipulates a prison term of six months to five years for theft, depending on the circumstances; for robbery a prison term of 3 to 10 years that varies according to the amount of force or weapon used.

Drug Trafficking

As noted earlier, long prison terms and heavy fines are prescribed by the Criminal Code, and it seems that these long prison sentences are indeed often inflicted. Travel advisories of various foreign governments warn travelers of the severe prison sentences inflicted for drug trafficking.

Prisons

CCJAP reported a national figure in March 2001 of 5,500 detainees and prisoners (300 females and 250 juveniles). There were 1,300 prison officers (75 females). The smallest prison housed 100 inmates and the largest (one of the national prisons, Correctional Center I [CC-I]), 1,350. On January 26, 2001, CC-I (which is an adult male-only correctional facility) had 1,314 inmates (796 convicted males and 518 males awaiting trial, 122 of the latter held beyond the legal six-months period) and was staffed with 100 officers. According to the national prisons data collected by the Department of Prisons in the Ministry of Interior, there were 6,346 prisoners in Cambodia in January 2004; of these, 266 were child prisoners and 47.7 percent of these children were pretrial detainees.

The National Prison Agency attended the Asia and Pacific annual conference of Correctional Administrators and reported 6,778 prisoners in mid-2004 (a rate of 47 per 100,000 population). In January 2006, figures provided to LICADHO by CCJAP indicated a total number of 9,373 prisoners in Cambodia. During the last 13 years, the estimated rates of imprisonment have escalated significantly from 21.6 to 73.7 per 100,000. The estimated proportions of female prisoners have ranged between 4.7 percent in 1995 and 6.9 percent in 2006 of the prison population (about 5.9% in 2007). As reported earlier, between 1999 and 2007, the proportions of incarcerated juveniles have risen from 3.9 percent to 5.5 percent of the prison population.

In 2007, 25 prisons (3 national and 22 provincial/municipal prisons) operated in Cambodia. The Department of Prisons' headquarters is located in the MOI in Phnom Penh. Two of the national prisons, CC-I and CC-II, are situated 12 kilometers (7.5 miles) from Phnom Penh, and CC-III near the Vietnamese border. Most Cambodian prisons are overcrowded. In its survey of 18 prisons, LICADHO reported a housing capacity for 6,410 prisoners, but in 2004 these prisons on average operated at 123 percent, and in 2006, at 138 percent of their capacity. In CC-I, which is considered to be one of the better prisons compared to provincial facilities, between 22 and 25 men may share a cell that is about 64 square meters (688.90 square feet). Since 1999, CC-II houses only female and juvenile prisoners. In 2006, 256 females and 285 juveniles, as well as 14 babies and infants living with their mothers in prison, were incarcerated at CC-II (operating at 155% of its capacity). CC-II is the only facility of this sort in Cambodia. All the other prisons, apart from the all-adult male CC-I, house both male and female prisoners in more or less well-separated quarters.

In addition to overcrowding, health problems are frequent in Cambodian prisons. The Prisons Department is allocated only 1,500 riels (about US$0.38) per prisoner per day to cover not only the cost of feeding the prisoners, but also transportation, sanitation, cooking fuel, water, electricity, and administration. According to LICADHO, the daily nutritional requirements stipulated in article 4.1 of Prison Procedure, would cost, even using the lowest-quality ingredients, at least 1,700 riels (about US$0.41) in the Phnom Penh Market. Because of widespread corruption in the prison system, inmates with enough money can purchase nutritious meals while many others are malnourished and suffer from poor health.

The number of deaths in the prisons monitored by LICADHO varied from 43 in 2002 to 100 in 2005, that is, between 0.8 percent and 1.2 percent of the prison population. The highest rates of death in custody occurred in provincial facilities. Prison escapes are common. In its survey, LICADHO reported 72 escapees in 2005 and 53 in 2006 (respectively 0.87% and 0.60% of the population of the 18 surveyed prisons). Most of them involved group escapes. In 2005 and 2006, respectively, 25 percent and 23 percent of these escapees were killed during their attempts, and only 31 percent and 45 percent were recaptured (i.e., 44% in 2005 and 32% in 2006 were successful escapes).

Correction Center I (CC-I), which is a new prison located (10 kilometers) from the capital city and one of the only three prisons under the direct management of the General Department of Prisons, is the largest correctional facility in Cambodia with a capacity for 1,500 prisoners. Built on (10 hectares), CC-I houses only adult male prisoners. Like most Cambodian prisons, CC-I is overcrowded and in 2006, with 2,132 inmates, it operated at 142 percent of its maximum capacity and employed more than 150 staff.

Although security in CC-I is exceptionally tight, in June 2006, a group of 12 prisoners managed to escape and only one of them was recaptured. The number of deaths in custody was 17 in 2002, 13 in 2003, 22 in 2004 (1.4% of CC-I population), and 18 in 2005 (in 2006, CC-I did not provide information on prison deaths to LICADHO).

The prison employs an administrative system that centralizes all decisions in the hands of the wardens. Officially, family visits are on every Saturday and public holidays from 7:30 A.M. to 10:30 A.M. and 2:00 P.M. to 4:00 P.M. While Prison Procedure (no. 8, article 4.1[n]) "expressly forbids the collection of goods or money from visitors by any prison official for the privilege of visiting a prisoner" and stipulates that "all prisoners have the right to receive visits from families or friends for at least one hour each week at times designated in the prison rules by the prison chief," in CC-I the no-fee rule seems to be respected only during official family visit days. Thanks to corruption, it is possible to visit prisoners any day but visitors have to pay a fee of at least 5,000 riels (about US$1.25). The places where the visits occur and the privileges accorded during the visits also depend on the amount of bribes visitors are willing or can afford to pay. No payment is required if the visit happens via a phone in a room where visitors and prisoners are separated by glass and iron bars. In another room, where they are only separated by iron bars and can touch each other, a payment of between 10,000 riels (about US$2.50) and 40,000 riels (about US$10) is necessary. A "gold-class" visit area, away from the inner core of the prison where cells are located, allows visitors and prisoners to sit together on a concrete lounge, but for this privilege visitors have to pay a minimum of US$10. Unlike many other Cambodian prisons, and despite a level of overcrowding that often results in more than 20 inmates having to share a 64-square-meter (688.90-square-foot) cell, CC-I only allows prisoners to go out of their cells for a short period of time once a week or two. However, prisoners who can bribe officials are allowed to leave their cells every day for a long period of time to do minimal work around the interior compound.

In 2001, CCJAP mentioned plans to assist in the development of vocational training, literacy, and numeracy programs for detainees. Some of these programs may have been implemented in the prison located in the site where CCJAP has focused its attention, but in the main, as reported in 2003 by the 23rd Asian and Pacific Conference of Correctional Administrators "[n]o formalized programs exist within prisons for the rehabilitation of prisoners to return to society at the end of their sentence."

Between November and December 2007, one of the authors visited seven major Cambodian prisons and found that most of them did not have workshops, and when they did, these workshops were small and did not provide any significant skills, mainly sewing for females, and carpentry and gardening for males. While generally inmates are not officially required to work, an informal trade system exists where there are many jobs that can be done by prisoners for prison staff or other prisoners in exchange of money, food, or privileges.

Two other privileges include prison transfer and reduction of prison terms. An official reason for prisoners requesting a prison transfer is to be close to their homeland and make family visits more convenient. Because prison conditions, such as building environment and rules, vary greatly in Cambodia, unofficial reasons would include moving to a better facility. The transfer process requires approval from the heads of the relevant prisons and the general director of the Prison Directorate. The payment of bribes would expedite this process.

Normally, each prison has a committee chaired by the warden, which monitors and reviews prisoners' behavior and performance and can propose a sentence reduction or abolition. By law, the committee must submit such request to the king. For prisoners sentenced up to a year maximum, the request can be made after half the sentence has been served, and for those sentenced to more than a year, after at least two-thirds has been served. This privilege provides ample opportunities for corrupt conduct, as members of prison committees, especially wardens, can make significant income from relatively wealthy prisoners who in exchange would be proposed for a sentence reduction. Many more "unofficial" privileges in relation to cell allocation, treatment by prison guards, food rations, relative freedom within the prison, recreation, opportunity to make money, and sex are available for those who can pay their way in the corrupt prison system. A prisoner transfer agreement was signed with Australia in October 2006. At the same date, no such agreement existed with the United Kingdom. The Cambodian government also signed an extradition agreement with Thailand in 1999, China in 2000, and Laos in 2005.

Roderic Broadhurst, Thierry Bouhours, and Chenda Keo

Further Reading

AusAID. (2001). "Cambodian Criminal Justice Assistance Project: Feasibility Study Phase II." Unpublished report. Canberra: AusAID.

Broadhurst, Roderic, and Thierry Bouhours. (2009). "Policing in Cambodia: Legitimacy in the Making?" *Policing and Society* 19(2): 174–190.

Cambodian League for the Promotion and Defense of Human Rights (LICADHO): http://www.licadho-cambodia.org/.

Chandler, David. (2007). *A History of Cambodia*. 4th ed. Boulder, CO: Westview Press.

Royal Cambodian Embassy in Washington, Constitution of the Kingdom of Cambodia: http://www.embassy.org/cambodia/cambodia/constitu.htm.

China (People's Republic of China)

Legal System: Civil/Socialist
Murder: Medium
Burglary: Medium
Corruption: Medium
Human Trafficking: Medium
Prison Rate: Medium
Death Penalty: Yes
Corporal Punishment: No

Background

China is a socialist country under the uniform leadership of the Chinese Communist Party (CCP). It has a total land area of 9.6 million square kilometers (3.7 million square miles) and about 1.3 billion people, which amounts to one-fourth of the world population. Administratively, China has 4 municipalities directly under the leadership of the central government, 23 provinces, 5 autonomous regions, and 2 special governing zones (i.e., Hong Kong and Macau). China has a civil law system with only statutory law, not case law. It also has substantial elements borrowed from the former Soviet Union and inherited from traditional Chinese law.

Written statutes and customary laws can be found in each Chinese dynasty or regime. The law promulgated in the Tang dynasty in the seventh century C.E. is one of the oldest legal codes that provided a foundation for the later legal codes in Song, Yuan, Ming, and Qing dynasties. The law created by the emperor had legal power for all residents except the emperor himself. The emperor could determine the guilt of accused individuals, dictate the penal sentence, or change the decisions by lower judicial authorities.

Efforts had been made to modernize the legal system during the late Qing dynasty at the beginning of the 20th century and continued until it was overthrown in 1911 when by the Kuomintang. The regime enacted a Constitution (1912, 1923, 1947), Civil Law (1929), Criminal Law (1928, 1934), Civil Procedure Law (1931, 1935), and Criminal Procedure Law (1928, 1935). All these laws had a strong Western orientation.

When the Chinese Communist Party (CCP) took control of China in 1949, it abolished the laws enacted by the Kuomintang regime. During the 1950s, several major laws were adopted. The first socialist Constitution was adopted by the National People's Congress (NPC) in 1954. In the same year, the legislation Reform through Labor on rehabilitating offenders was passed. In 1957, the first Police Law was adopted. The NPC had also drafted Criminal Law, Civil Law, Criminal Procedure Law, and Civil Procedure Law, which reflected the communist ideology during the time period.

The Cultural Revolution initiated by Mao in 1966 is viewed as a lawless period in which the criminal justice system was entirely paralyzed. In 1978, the Third Plenary Session of the CCP 11th Central Committee officially ended the Cultural Revolution and started reconstruction of the legal system. In the following year, the Second Session of the Fifth National People's Congress passed the Criminal Law and the Criminal Procedure Law. The Criminal Law was further amended in 1997 and again in 2002, and the Criminal Procedure Law was revised in 1996.

China's criminal justice system has four major components including police, procurators, courts, and correctional institutions. The Supreme People's Court, along with the Supreme People's Procurator, is the highest judicial agency in China. It has the power and authority over the administration of justice in the Basic People's Courts and People's Tribunals, Intermediate People's Courts, and Superior People's Courts. In theory, all courts and procurator offices should have independent legal and judicial power and authority. However, their judiciaries are subject to the Communist Party's directives and guidance. The Ministry of Public Security and the Ministry of Justice of the Chinese central government control and manage China's police forces and correctional institutions, respectively. All these government agencies are under the uniform leadership of a special central committee of the Communist Party on comprehensive management of public security and safety, which is led by a member of the Central Standing Committee of the party.

The Chinese police system has five components including the public security police, state security police, the prison police, judicial police in the People's Procurators, and judicial police in the People's Courts. Under the uniform leadership of the Ministry of Public Security, police forces in the five components have a similar administrative system in ranking and adopt the same police uniforms and badges. However, each component functions independently and performs specifically designed tasks. Historically, the public security police are the major police force in China.

The administration of the public security police is a combination of the power of central and local governments. All the police forces fall under the uniform leadership of the Ministry of Public Security (MPS) of the central government. At the same time, they are also subject to control and directive of provincial and local governments. Each province, county, city, and town has police departments, and the grassroots police agency is the neighborhood police station. The MPS also has special police units including railroad police, transportation police, civil aviation police, and forestry police.

Crime

China adopted its Criminal Law in 1979 and amended it in 1997 and 2002. According to the law, crime is any human act that endangers society and is subject to punishment. However, an act that endangers society may not be deemed a crime if the circumstances are obviously minor and the harm of the act is not serious. Such an act shall be referred to as an unlawful act. China's Criminal Procedure Law (1996) defines the procedures in investigating and prosecuting criminal behaviors. In contrast, any unlawful acts are defined by administrative laws and regulations, punished by administrative agencies, and subject to administrative penalties.

The Criminal Law defines 10 categories of criminal offenses: (1) threatening and harming national security such as treason, espionage, and mass rebellion; (2) endangering public security and safety such as arson, explosion, poison, and trafficking of guns or ammunition; (3) endangering economic order such as fraud, smuggling, and embezzlement; (4) infringing upon citizens' legal and civil rights, such as homicide, aggravated assault, rape, and forcing women into prostitution; (5) infringing upon citizens' property such as robbery, stealing, and extortion; (6) damaging public safety and security such as disrupting public affairs, harboring criminals, concealing stolen goods, and gambling; (7) endangering national interests such as destroying national defense facilities and disrupting military tasks; (8) corruption and bribery such as using official power to receive personal payment and bribing government officials to gain personal interests; (9) malfeasance such as abuse of official power and authority and betrayal of state secrets; and (10) violation of military duty and administration such as stealing and betrayal of military secrets.

The age limit of full criminal liability is 16 years old. However, a person who is in the age range of 14 to 16 shall bear full criminal responsibility if he or she commits homicide, aggravated assault, robbery, arson, repeated theft, or any other crime that seriously undermines public safety and security. The severity of punishment can be reduced because of age. Death penalty is not applicable to a minor under the age of 18. If a minor is not criminally liable because of his or her age, his or her parents or guardians should have legal responsibility to provide discipline to the minor. When it is necessary under certain conditions such as incapable parental guardianship, the minor may be referred to a shelter or a rehabilitation program operated by the local government.

Most crimes have surged in China since the early 1980s. Bribery and official corruption have been a major challenge to the Chinese government and the criminal justice system. With regard to the street-level offenses, property crimes such as bicycle theft and household burglary have become more prominent.

In 1990, the NPC adopted legislation on drug prohibition that outlaws any drug possession, manufacture, transportation, and sale. The criminal penalty for drug-related offenses ranges from fines to the death penalty. The 2002 amended Criminal Law has similar legal stipulations. Illicit drugs defined in these legislations include opium, heroin, morphine, marijuana, cocaine, and other addictive drugs. The most prevalent illicit drugs are heroin and opium as reported in China. Official reports indicate that China has more than 1 million registered drug users, about 600 mandatory drug treatment centers with 110,000 beds, and about 250,000 drug users receive treatments in the centers each year. Law enforcement agencies cracked down on 500,000 drug-related criminal cases and confiscated 51 tons of heroin, 14.8 tons of opium, and 1,464 tons of other drugs between 1998 and 2003. Also, there are about 100,000 drug trafficking–related criminal cases each year.

The numbers of criminal cases and convictions handled in Chinese courts have gradually increased since 1980s. In 1987, approximately 300,000 criminal cases were tried and more than 300,000 individuals were convicted. In 1999, courts tried about 540,000 criminal cases and convicted 539,335 cases. Property offenses accounted for 44 percent of all the tried criminal cases in that year. In 2005, a total of 684,897 criminal cases were tried in courts and 683,997 were convicted. Property crimes also accounted for about 44 percent of all convicted criminal cases in this year. In 2006, 889,042 suspects were convicted by courts at all levels across the country and 153,724 received sentences longer than five years, including life imprisonment and death penalty. A common practice of Chinese courts is to adjudicate approximately 40 percent of the offenders to five or more years' imprisonment, life imprisonment, or the death penalty.

Finding of Guilt

Criminal procedure in China is divided into three legal stages as defined in the Criminal Procedure Law (CPL): investigation, prosecution, and trial. There are three corresponding institutions in charge of each of these stages: the investigative agencies, mainly police agencies, the procuracy, and the courts. The police, the procuracy, and the courts exercise their powers independently and function free of any interference by any other administrative agencies, public organizations, or individuals (CPL, Art. 5). The relationship between these three legal institutions is that they divide responsibilities, coordinate their efforts, and check on each other to ensure effective and efficient enforcement of the law (CPL, Art. 7).

In collaboration with the procurator, police agencies are responsible for criminal investigation and evidence collection after a criminal incident is reported. The process involves preliminary investigation to assess the reported criminal activity, filing a criminal case upon discovering criminal evidence (CPL, Art. 83), issuing an order to require a suspect to appear in the police station for questioning, detaining a suspect if incriminating evidence is found, and arresting a suspect upon confirmed evidence. The police agency provides recommendations based on its investigation and collects evidence for prosecution. It sends the recommendations along with their investigation files and evidence to the procurator office at the same administrative level for review. The procurator office reviews the case and police reports to make a decision whether or not the suspect should be prosecuted. If a prosecution decision has been made, the procurator will initiate a court hearing. The court reviews the case to determine a court hearing in which the suspect is formally brought to a trial. There are few alternatives to going to a full trial such as plea bargaining.

Under Chinese law, a suspect has no right to remain silent. He or she has a duty to answer questions truthfully when asked by investigators but may refuse to answer questions that are irrelevant to the case (CPL, Art. 93). There is no legal duty for the suspect to assist police investigations under Chinese law. It is an offense only when a person knowingly gives false testimony in criminal proceedings, which is punishable by a maximum sentence of three years' imprisonment.

Police agencies have discretion to recommend a case to a reeducation-through-labor (*laojiao*) committee (a branch of local government), which may send the offender to a reeducation-through-labor

A cook shovels rice into a bowl, right, as another stirs food in a wok at the Masanjia reeducation-through-labor camp in northeast China's Liaoning Province, May 22, 2001. The camp has been nominated as a model correctional facility because of its success in "transforming" practitioners of falun gong, the spiritual movement that China banned in July 1999. (AP Photo/John Leicester)

camp for rehabilitation up to three years. The committee reviews the recommendation and makes a final decision without judicial proceeding. Although the individual has a right to challenge the decision in court after it has been imposed, the chance to repeal is usually small. According to an official report, approximately 230,000 offenders were accommodated in 280 reeducation-through-labor camps in 1998.

If a suspect is detained, police must conduct an interrogation of the detainee within 24 hours after he or she was held. If no grounds are established for detention, the suspect should be released immediately. For arresting a suspect, a police agency should request a warrant from the prosecutor's office within three days after the detention. The prosecutor shall make a decision whether or not a warrant should be issued. If a warrant is not issued, police shall release the detainee immediately. Also, the period for holding a suspect in custody may not exceed two months. However, it may be extended to one more month for cases with complex circumstances.

Due process rights are provided in China's 1982 Constitution, but the application is limited. According to the 1996 Criminal Procedure Law, all trials are open to the public with an exception for cases that involve state secrets, juveniles, or personal privacy. Cases are typically processed rapidly and the conviction rates are high. There is a bail procedure in which a defendant may be granted bail with a guarantor to await trial without custody or to stay home under security surveillance. Specifically, a female defendant or a defendant who is pregnant, who has an infant, or who has serious illness, may be granted bail.

Court System

There are four levels of courts that have legal authority to process and adjudicate criminal cases. They are the Supreme People's Court, the Superior People's Courts, the Intermediate People's Courts, and the Basic People's Courts. The Supreme People's Court serves as the highest judicial branch of the state for serious criminal cases and cases that have appeals against the decisions from the Superior People's Court and the People's Military Court. Cases with appeals brought by the Supreme People's Procurator are also handled by the Supreme People's Court. In addition, the Supreme People's Court has the authority to supervise and monitor the operation of lower courts. There are more than 3,000 Basic People's Courts at the county level, about 20,000 people's tribunals located in towns and villages, 376 Intermediate People's Courts, and 31 Superior People's Courts at the provincial level. There are a total of about 200,000 judges at different levels of courts.

In 1995 China promulgated the Judge Law, which contains 17 chapters and 42 articles. According to the law, the minimum qualifications of being a judge are that the individual shall be a citizen of the People's Republic of China; be at least 23 years old; accept the Constitution of the People's Republic of China; have high political, professional, and moral standing, and be in good health. The educational requirement is a law degree from a higher education institution. An individual may be qualified with a nonlaw degree from a higher education institution if he or she has solid knowledge and understanding of laws and two years of working experience in the legal system. Working experience in the legal system is not a requirement for those who have a master's or a PhD degree in law.

Courts' presidents at various levels are elected by the People's Congress at the corresponding administrative levels and the tenure of a president is the same as that of the People's Congress. The elected president nominates the vice president, members of the judicial committee, presiding judges, deputy presiding judges, and general judges for appointment by the Standing Committee of the People's Congress at the same level. Primary and assistant judges are recruited through civil examinations.

Rights of the Accused

Chinese law has no clear stipulations on the presumption of innocence and the burden of proof. The concept itself has been criticized as capitalist. Since China's socialist legal system has adopted the principle of "deciding a case according to facts," presumptions of innocence and any related procedural rules are not a significant component in the criminal law, but there are certain stipulations that protect suspects and defendants' rights—rights to legal representation, cross-examination, against torture and forced confessions, and so forth. In a rigorous pursuit of "truth," legal stipulations protecting the rights of the accused are often swept aside. The 1996 Criminal Procedure Law (CPL) gives the court exclusive authority to determine the guilt or innocence of the accused. Article 12 of the CPL provides that no one shall be guilty of a crime without a judgment of the people's court.

In 1996, the National Peoples' Congress adopted new legislation in an effort to reform the criminal procedure and the legal profession. It was the first time that the new legislation recognized that lawyers represented their clients, not the state. Under the new legislation lawyers may establish their private law firms. As the 1996 Criminal Procedural Law defines it, the accused has the right to defend himself or herself. Also, a defendant may authorize the following people to represent him or her in defending: (a) lawyer; (b) representative from a social organization, or from the defendant's work unit; or (c) a close relative or guardian of the defendant. The defendant also has several other legal rights: (1) the right to know the nature of the accusation, (2) the right to participate in proceedings using his or her native spoken and written language, (3) the right to request new investigation during the court hearing, (4) the right to ask questions of witnesses,

(5) the right to make a final statement after closing the cross-examination, and (6) the right to request members of the judicial panel, the court clerk, the public prosecutor, expert witness, or interpreters to withdraw from the case proceeding. After a judicial decision has been made, the accused also has the right to appeal and the right to file a petition for the legal decision. If the defendant cannot have a representative, the court has authority to assign one to the defendant.

Criminal Procedure

As defined in the 1996 Criminal Procedure Law, a criminal case is commonly tried by a legal panel consisting of three judges or a judge with two representatives elected from local residents. The legal panel has authority to decide whether or not the defendant is guilty and the possible penalty. Such a legal panel is the basic unit in a court. It is not a permanent legal body but organized to adjudicate an individual case. The number of a legal panel must be odd. Minor criminal cases can be handled by a single judge rather than a legal panel. However, cases in a second trial must be tried by a legal panel. The chief judge in a panel is appointed by the court's president or the division chief in the court. A president or division chief shall be the chief judge if he or she participates in a trial.

The parties to litigation may use the trial supervision procedure to challenge the final decision. Such a challenge may be made to an appellate court or a higher court. After reviewing the complaint, the chief judge in an appellate court or a higher court may request a judicial committee to make a decision whether or not the appeal is valid and a retrial is necessary. The appellate court may order a retrial when it is necessary. However, the retrial cannot suspend the enforcement of the court decision that has been challenged.

Juvenile Offenders

The first juvenile court in China was initiated as part of the Basic People's Court of Changing District in the city of Shanghai in 1984. Since then, more than 3,300 juvenile courts have been established nationwide. A juvenile offender who is under the age of 18 may be referred to a juvenile court. There is no waiver procedure by which a juvenile can be transferred to an adult criminal court. A juvenile court shall act as a "parent" and the trial in a juvenile court is closed to the public. Education is a major component of the juvenile court proceeding. In 2005, juvenile courts processed 82,721 cases that were involved with suspects who were under the age of 18.

Punishment

Five major penalties and three supplemental penalties are provided in the 2002 Criminal Law. The major penalties are (1) surveillance (*Guan Zhi*); (2) detention (*Ju Lu*); (3) fixed term imprisonment (*You Xi Tu Xing*); (4) life imprisonment (*Wu Qi Tu Xing*); and (5) death penalty (*Si Xing*). Supplemental penalties include fine, deprivation of political rights, and expropriation.

Surveillance is a penalty for minor offenses. For such a penalty, the offender remains in the community under the surveillance of a law enforcement agency. The offender is required to report to the agency on a regular basis. The length of such a penalty may be three months to two years. Detention is a penalty also for minor offenses for which the offender is confined in a detention center rather than a prison. He or she is allowed to go home for one or two days each month and can be paid for work in the center. Such a penalty may be held for one to six months. Offenders who have a fixed term imprisonment may serve their prison time for 6 months to 15 years. However, the term may be up to 20 years if other penalties are added on.

In Chinese law, the death penalty is used only for the most serious crimes such as murder, rape, or serious property crimes. It cannot be applied to juvenile offenders under the age of 18 or women who are pregnant at the time of adjudication. If the death penalty is applied but the offender may not deserve immediate execution in terms of the offense seriousness, a two-year suspension of execution may be applied to the offender. The 1979 Criminal Law defined 26 offenses punishable by the death penalty. In

1997 the Amended Criminal Law raised the number to 65. China relied solely on firing squads to execute offenders for death penalty in the past. Recently, it began using lethal injections, particularly in high-profile cases such as the execution of gangsters and corrupt officials. The Chinese authority is planning to increase the use of lethal injections to make executions "more humane."

There is a verification system for death penalty cases. The People's Court Organization Law and the Criminal Procedure Law provide that all death penalty cases, unless handled by the Supreme People's Court, shall be reported to the Supreme People's Court for verification and approval. The Supreme People's Court, if necessary, may authorize the Superior People's Courts at the provincial level to exercise that power for death penalty cases involving homicide, rape, robbery, explosives, or other serious offenses. Death penalty cases with a two-year suspension of execution ruled by intermediate courts shall be verified and approved by higher courts. Death penalty cases ruled by intermediate courts shall be first verified and approved by higher courts before being submitted to the Supreme People's Court for approval.

The 1996 Death Penalty log published by Amnesty International on China reported that 6,145 people were sentenced to death and convictions were known in 4,490 cases. Of the 4,490 death penalty cases, 66.4 percent involved violent crime such as murder, rape, and robbery, 2.9 percent were economic and corruption-related cases such as graft and fraud, and about 13 percent, drug trafficking–related. Recently, the 2007 Amnesty International report estimated that at least 1,010 people were executed and 2,790 sentenced to death during 2006.

The Ministry of Justice of the Chinese central government controls all prisons across the country. There are five main types of correctional institutions: (1) prisons, (2) reform-through-labor camps, (3) juvenile rehabilitation centers, (4) detention centers, and (5) jails. It was estimated that there were about 1,250 prison units including reform-through-labor camps in 1998. Also there were about 2,000 jails of various sizes, some of which might hold sentenced prisoners for a year. Official reports indicate a total number of 5.92 million prisoners between 1979 and 1998. The overall ratio of custodial personnel to prisoners is no more than one for every five prisoners, and there were about 300,000 such personnel in the Chinese prison/reform system. The rate of imprisonment seems to be 160 per 100,000 population.

Inmates who are healthy must work during incarceration. Since 1981, inmates began to be included in China's national education program, which requires correctional institutions to provide both educational and vocational programs to inmates. Each program has a director, instructors, and curriculums. Inmates usually study in the program for about two hours per day. Inmates who have completed the program requirements receive certificates that are equivalent to those issued in normal educational institutions.

Inmates have a right to receive letters from family members, relatives, and friends and send letters to them. Family members are encouraged to provide help for inmates' rehabilitation, and they are permitted to visit and meet with the inmates twice a month. However, special visits and meetings may be set up for family members to provide help and assistance to inmates' correction and rehabilitation. Inmates have a right to maintain their health. They receive medical treatment in correctional institutions or in community hospitals when they are ill. They also receive a routine medical check once a year. Group therapy and counseling is also available to inmates for their mental health. During incarceration, inmates have a right to file petitions to procurators or courts. Any prisons shall set up a complaints' box and designate a special staff member to collect complaints.

There are noninstitutional services to offenders. During the suspension of execution of sentence or after release on parole policy, agencies provide supervision over the offenders. Probationers and parolees are turned over by police agencies to a community-based organization such as a help group (*Bangjiao*). The police officer who has the responsibility for the safety and security of the community supervises and monitors the offenders' daily life, work, and other routines, and helps them to become law-abiding citizens. Meanwhile, the police officer shall maintain regular contacts with the neighborhood committee (a semiofficial organization that manages community daily affairs) in an effort to monitor a probationer's or parolee's behavior.

Lening Zhang

Further Reading

Borge, Bkken, ed. (2005). *Crime, Punishment, and Policing in China*. Lanham, MD: Rowman and Littlefield.

Jianhong Liu, Lening Zhang, and Steven Messner, eds. (2001). *Crime and Social Control in a Changing China*. Westport, CT: Greenwood Press.

Supreme People's Court of the PRC: http://en.chinacourt.org/.

Troyer, Ronald, John P. Clark, and Dean J. Rojek. (1989). *Social Control in the People's Republic of China*. New York: Praeger.

Zhang, Lening, Steven F. Messner, and Jianhong Liu, eds. (2008). *Crime and Criminal Justice in China: The Current Knowledge Base and Prospects for Future Research*. A Special Issue of *Crime, Law and Social Change: An Interdisciplinary Journal* 50(3).

Note: The author thanks Hong Lu for her valuable comments on an early draft of the chapter.

Georgia

Legal System: Civil
Murder: Medium
Burglary: Medium
Corruption: Medium
Human Trafficking: Low
Prison Rate: High
Death Penalty: No
Corporal Punishment: No

Background

After the Russian Revolution in October 1917, Georgia declared its independence on May 26, 1918. On June 11 of that year, a commission was created to write the first Georgian Constitution, which went into effect in February 1921, four days before the occupation of the country by the Russian army on February 25, 1921. Under the influence of the Soviet Union, the first Constitution as the Socialist Republic of Georgia was adopted. The Constitution was revised in 1937 and again in 1978, as Georgia was a part of the Soviet Union. As the decline of the Soviet Union approached (the end of the 1980s), more and more national-oriented politicians were elected for Parliament.

After the collapse of the Soviet Union, the newly elected Parliament of Georgia declared independence on April 9, 1991, and changed the Constitution of 1978. After the civil war in 1992, a military council was established, and the Constitution of the independent Georgia of 1921 went into force once again. In 1995, a new Constitution was passed, which continues today but was revised by the governing parties after the Rose Revolution in 2003. At the present time, a new constitution is in preparation. According to the Constitution, Georgia is a democratic republic with a strong president system and a centralized administration.

From 1801 on, Georgia was, with the exception of the period from 1918 to 1921, part of the Russian Empire and did not have its own law. However, like the Georgian Constitution, the Penal Law is clearly influenced by the Soviet model. The first Penal Law of Georgia is from 1922, the time of the Soviet Union. Between 1928 and 1960, the Penal Law was revised fundamentally under Soviet influence. The General Part of the Georgian Penal Law was largely adopted from the Russian Penal Law. Like other Soviet Republics, Georgia had no possibility to change basic principles of the Soviet Penal Law. The last version was in power with changes, which were partly arranged by the Georgian Constitutional court. Not until July 22, 1999 was the first new Penal Law of independent Georgia decided, and it was put into effect on June 1, 2000. This version is valid today, though with some fundamental changes.

The new Penal Law, especially the General Part, was influenced strongly by the German Penal Law. Special protections of human rights were formulated, which was not the case in the Russian law. The Russian Penal Law protected the property of the state more than private property. Thus, theft was divided into two parts: theft of public property (art. 91) and theft of private property (art. 150). Theft of public property (state property) was punished more severely than theft of private property.

In the Special Part of the Penal Law, some important improvements were made such as new definitions of crimes that took into account the political and social changes of society. There are also influences from Anglo-American law that especially affect Procedural Law. This is the case for the ongoing revision of the new Procedural Law of Georgia.

The first Procedural Law of Georgia derives from 1923, the second from 1960, and it has been frequently changed since then. The current valid Procedural Law was put into effect in 1998. According to this law, the legal system is mixed, which includes accusatorial and inquisitorial parts. The duty of opposing sides in the trial is to present their proof to the judge. The judge has the right to collect evidence independently, but should be reserved in doing so (art. 439 Penal Law).

The new development in Penal Law is strongly influenced by members of the Georgian universities. The first university was established in Georgia in 1918, Tbilisi State University (today known as the Iv. Javakhishvili State University of Tbilisi). Until the 1990s this was the only university in the country teaching law. Tbilissi today has 3 state universities and more than 20 private ones, which also offer law instruction. In addition to the universities, the Institute for State and Law in Tbilissi had a strong influence on the development of law. The institute was established in 1957, and today it is part of the Ministry of Education. The institute has Departments of Theories and Methods of Law, International Law and History of Law, Civil Law, and also a separate Department of Penal Law and Criminology.

Crime

Classification of Crimes

According to article 12 Penal Law of Georgia, a crime can be classified as less severe, severe, and very severe. Less severe criminal offenses are negligent or intentional crimes that are punished by a prison sentence of up to 5 years. Severe criminal offenses are intentional crimes that are punished from 5 to 10 years or negligent crimes punished by a prison sentence of more than 5 years. Very severe crimes are intentional crimes punished by a prison sentence of more than 10 years or life imprisonment.

After the Rose Revolution of 2003, the Georgian Penal Law was severely changed on the grounds of a new penal law politics—"Zero Tolerance" against criminals. The punishment was extended to the preparative actions of crimes; the definitions of crimes were changed and the probation restriction became much sharper. Those changes resulted in a strong increase of prisoners to more than 18,000 as of the end of 2008, which is triple that of 2003 (6,274). Also, the number of acquittals reduced sharply. In 2005 there were 83 acquittals but only 30 in 2008. The attitudes of the judges have apparently changed with the political climate. According to a 2003 survey, 65 percent of the judges perceived that the Georgian population felt that only imprisonment is a real punishment.

Police play an important role in implementing the politics of Zero Tolerance. After the Rose Revolution, the police were drastically reformed, and the very high corruption rate among the police was reduced. Special seminars for education in this topic were held; the salary of policemen was increased, and the job they were doing was controlled more rigidly. It resulted in a clear reduction in corruption and better police work. Today, police are a part of the Ministry of Internal Affairs, which also includes the Department of State Security. The ministry has special departments, which include, for example, Criminal Investigation Division, Traffic Police, Information-Analytical Division, Division for Extraordinary Emergency Cases, Division for Protection of the Constitution, and National Bureau of INTERPOL. There are subdivisions of the ministry in different regions of the country (like the capital Tbilissi, Adjaria, Guria, Batumi, or Kobuleti).

Crime Statistics

Georgia provides limited statistics about crime and punishment, most of which are produced by the police and courts or the special departments in the respective ministries. The central problem of these statistics is their lack of validity. According to police crime statistics, in 2008, there were 44,644 crimes (964 per 100,000 inhabitants). The real number of crimes is estimated to be much higher. Research into this problem is only just beginning. In 2008, 263 murders were registered, but only half of them were cleared. This low clearance rate may be attributed to mistakes by police. In addition, the clearance of these cases was often hindered by high-ranking members in government because their own interests were connected to these cases. Only 100 rapes in 2008 were registered, and 66 percent could be cleared. In the same year, 14,814 thefts were registered, and from these, only 24 percent were cleared. According to article 177 Penal Law, a severe theft is defined as when the loss is more than 150 Lari (about €60 or US$88). On the basis of this definition, nearly every fourth theft or nearly every second property crime is defined as severe. There were 8,699 registered drug cases, which, in quantity, is second only to property crimes. The relatively high number of drug crimes is attributed to the relatively high number of poor people, who often try to get more money by dealing with illegal drugs. The low clearance rate is also influenced by the lack of trust in the crime prosecution administration. This influenced the reporting rate, which resulted in an enormous dark figure (i.e., unreported) of crime.

Most registered crimes are property crimes and illegal drugs. Crimes like money laundering, terrorism, and corruption reduced noticeably on the grounds of specific measures of prosecution. Money laundering and corruption, especially, is done by organized groups which, as single cases show, have connections with parts of the government. The prosecution of these crimes is made more difficult because of the lack of special police squads. In 2007, 120 police officers were accused of corruption. Since then, there were no official cases of money laundering.

Due to a dramatic increase in the official registered crime rate, the courts are overloaded. In 2008, there were 15,367 new penal cases of criminal proceedings that were brought to the courts of the 11 regions in the country. Among these cases, 6,435 cases (42%) were registered at the courts in Tbilissi, 1,771 cases (12%) were registered at the courts in Imereti, 1,604 cases (10%) in Adjaria, and 1,581 cases (10%) were registered in Kvemo Kartli. At the beginning of 2008, there were 6,715 pending cases from the prior year. As of 2008, 18,161 cases were finished (decided).

A big problem today is the high traffic accident rate, which is influenced by bad road conditions and an increasing number of fast freight cars. To control the traffic, more and more video cameras have been installed. There were no less than 500 in Tbilissi and 65 in Batumi. Another problem is that the group of organized criminals from the Soviet era, the "Thieves in Law" (the majority of organized crime ringleaders in Russia are said to be Georgian compatriots) who have been active in Georgia, needs to be reduced considerably.

Juvenile Crime

The age of criminal responsibility in Georgia is 14 years old. However, children of 12 years and above can be punished by criminal courts if they commit a very severe crime. These are based on article 33 Penal Law: murder, homicide, robbery, theft in public spaces (article 178 Penal Law)—the offender commits the theft, for example, in a bus or on the street. These crimes are seen as very severe and thus punished more harshly. Examples of severe crimes include if the damage is not less than 150 Lari (about €60 or US$88), severe bodily injury, rape, or having a weapon with the person. Having a bigger knife with the person in cases of juveniles (under 21 years) is considered a crime (article 238 I Prime Penal Law). According to a new regulation of the Penal Law, which was put into force on July 1, 2008, children between 12 and 14 years old are not allowed to be incarcerated in a regular prison. At present, they can only be punished by a fine because of the country lacking special institutions (such as foster homes) for offenders aged 12 to 14. The only chance to help them is in schools. However, they are not prepared for these problems. Special educational or treatment programs for these children are nonexistent.

Finding of Guilt

With few exceptions, crimes are, according to article 62 Procedural Law, investigated by officials of the Ministry of Internal Affairs. The investigator has to charge the person within 48 hours, and within an additional 24 hours, a court has to make a decision. The investigation of the crime has to be finished within four months. During this time the investigator has to coordinate with the prosecutor to accuse the crime before court or to release the suspect if he or she is in pretrial detention. The accused is seen as innocent unless he or she is proven guilty by the court. According to the Procedural Law, the suspect has the right to have a defender and also have the chance to defend himself or herself. The person under suspicion must have a defender if the person is a juvenile, if a lifelong sentence is imposed, if the person does not speak the language of the court, if the person cannot defend himself or herself because of psychological or physical problems (illness), or if there is a procedural agreement between the person under suspicion and the prosecutor. As a result of justice reform, the prosecutor is located in the Ministry of Justice. The Minister of Justice is also the general prosecutor of the country.

The duty solicitor is paid by the state. There is no alternative to the penal procedure in criminal cases. The penal procedure can be shortened if there are agreements between the defendant and prosecutor. The possibility to do agreements during the penal procedure was introduced in 2006. According to the Procedural Law, it is within the capacity of the prosecutor. The prosecutorial statistics show that, as of today, such agreements are done in about half of the criminal procedures. Agreements regularly end with fines. There are no limitations for procedural agreements (plea agreement) so that the prosecutor can use them in all cases. Pretrial detention is used in nearly half of the charges. In 2008, the prosecution presented 8,197 cases to the responsible courts and asked for a pretrial detention. Almost all of these cases, 96 percent, were approved by the court. This suggests that judges have less independence in comparison to prosecutors.

Beside the Courts of the First Instance, there are two Courts of Appellation (in Tbilissi and Kutaisi) and a Supreme Court in Tbilissi. The judges of the First Instance are not specialized with the exception of those in Tbilissi. There are three specialized courts for civil law, administrative offenses, and penal law in Tbilissi. In the other regions of Georgia, the judges are not specialized as they hear different parts of law at the same time as penal lawyers.

The judges in Georgia are appointed by the High Council of Justice. According to the Constitution, a judge can be a person who successfully completed the study of law, is at least 28 years old, has professional experience of five years or above, and has passed an examination for judges. As of 2009, Georgia has 273 judges (144 males and 129 females). There are about 85 penal judges in the First Instance, 21 in the Second Instance, and 5 in the Third Instance courts. There are no specialized courts for juveniles. Judges who treat with cases of juveniles must have, according to the Code of Criminal Procedure, a proof of their qualification in pedagogy and juvenile psychology. This proof is regularly obtained by participating in a weekend seminar. Nevertheless, it is questionable if the judges can get the necessary knowledge from these seminars.

Punishment

Types of Punishment

According to article 40 of the Code of Criminal Procedure, punishments include the following groups: fine (art. 42); disbarment from profession or removal from office (art. 43; according to art. 41, these two sanctions can be given as a main punishment but also as an additional punishment); community service (art. 44); labor camp (art. 45); work reduction for members of military (art. 45; in practice, very seldom used); restriction of freedom (art. 47); time-limited custodial sanction (art. 50); lifelong custodial sanction (art. 51; all these sanctions are main sanctions); confiscation of personal property (art. 52; is an additional sanction). The death penalty was abolished in 1997. According to the statistics of the Supreme Court of Georgia, sanctions usually used are custodial sanctions (including probation) and fines.

According to article 45 Administrative Offence Act, first-time illegal drug users or offenders who possess only small quantities of drugs are punished by a fine of 500 Lari (about €220 or US$295) or 30 days in custody. In case of recidivism, according to article 273 of the Code of Penal Law, the offender is punished by a custodial sanction up to one year or with a fine or community service up to 180 hours. According to article 260, an offender who cultivates drugs or materials for producing drugs without special permission, buys, stores, transports, sends, or deals with such materials is punished by a custodial sanction up to 11 years. According to article 260 III, the punishment is from 8 to 20 years or with life imprisonment if the amounts of drugs are large (e.g., 1 gram of heroin) or if the offense is committed by organized groups. According to article 261, the punishment is a fine, labor camp up to two years, or with a custodial sanction up to three years if the offender unlawfully cultivates psychotropic plants or substances, produces, buys, stores, transports, sends, or deals with these materials.

In the first three months of 2009, 223 juveniles were registered as offenders. Among these, 1 person is 12–13 years old, 63 persons are 14–15 years old, and 159 persons are 16–17 years old; 110 were accused of theft, 24 of robbery, and 10 of murder. The punishments for these juveniles are as follows: 122 were punished by probation, 80 were punished by a custodial sanction of under 10 years, and 12 were punished by a custodial sanction of 10 to 15 years.

In 2008, 20,804 criminal procedures were initiated. The sentences included 10,601 probation sanctions, 8,846 time-limited custodial sanctions, 1,010 fines, and 10 life imprisonments. Other additional sanctions were also given, which included 3,278 disbarments from profession or removals from office, and 79 confiscations of personal property.

Additionally, 321 persons were punished in cases of murder, 4,111 in cases of theft, and 593 in cases of robbery. The typical sanction for murder is a time-limited custodial sanction of 7 to 15 years (art. 108); in severe cases, a custodial sanction up to 20 years or life imprisonment (art. 109) can be imposed. In cases of rape, severe theft, burglary, robbery, or drug crimes, regularly time-limited custodial sanctions are imposed. In cases of severe drug crimes, a life imprisonment can be given (art. 260). In the new Georgian Penal Code, life custodial sanction is the most severe punishment for crimes such as murder, rape, serious drug crimes, crimes against the safety of the state, treason, threat of the state of law or the inner security.

Prison

Imprisonment is regulated by the Law of Arrest, July 22, 1999, and by the rules of Procedure Law on Penalties and Probation, June 20, 2001. As of the end of 2008, there were 18,664 prisoners, a rate of 403 per 100,000 population. This represents a 280-percent increase since 2004, when there were just 6,654 prisoners. In comparison to Western industrialized countries, the prison rate is very high. Nevertheless, it is, in comparison to former Soviet countries, only medium. Of the prisoners, 16 percent are pretrial detainees/remand prisoners, 4.1 percent are females, 1.5 percent are juveniles/minors/young prisoners, and 0.9 percent are foreign prisoners. There are 67 (0.4%) who have a lifelong custodial sanction. Georgia has 17 prisons with an official total capacity of 18,700 places. That means that the prisons currently are fully occupied. With regard to incarcerated women, the number of female prisoners increased from 184 (2004) to 764 in 2008 (a growth of 415%). For juveniles, the increase is from 84 (2004) to 279 in 2008 (a growth of 332%). Also, the number of probationers has dramatically increased from 8,652 in 2006 to 23,500 in 2008 (a growth of 272%).

The reason for the increasing overcrowding of prisons is the high percentage of custodial sanctions of all criminal sanctions. For example, in Georgian Penal Law, the minimum penalty for theft with a loss of 151 Lari, that is, €60 or US$89, is three years' imprisonment. The judges are bound to the minimum sanction. There is little use of alternative sanctions. Custodial sanctions and probation are usually imposed. In cases of probation, an additional fine is regularly given. If the fine cannot be paid, the sanction must be served as custodial sanction.

As shown by the Parliamentary Reports of the Public Defender, the situations in the prisons of West Georgia are worse than in the eastern part of the country (Tbilissi or Rustavi). In some of the overcrowded prisons, there are not enough places for inmates to sleep in their cells. Thus, prisoners have to take turns to sleep. In general, prisoners have the obligation to work. Officially there are educational programs for prisoners. However, they are not practiced regularly because of a lack of facilities. Prisoners can have visits from outside. Foreign prisoners can be extradited according to article 6 of the Penal Code on the grounds of special regulations.

The bigger and newer prisons of Georgia are in Tbilissi (3,729 places for prisoners) and in Rustavi (2,022 places). Many of the existing prisons are totally outdated. Currently, two new, big prisons with 3,500 places are under construction (Region Kacheti and Guria). Among the 17 prisons, one is a prison for juveniles (with 167 places in Tbilissi), one is a prison hospital and a prison for prisoners with tuberculosis (with 537 places in Mzcheta). The exact number of prisoners with tuberculosis is not available. According to nonofficial estimations, about one-sixth of all prisoners have tuberculosis; about 1,000 prisoners are in treatment.

Helmut Kury, Moris Shalikashvili, and Edisher Phutkaradze

Further Reading

Courts: http://www.supremecourt.ge/default.aspx?sec_id=40&lang=2.

Crime data: http://www.police.ge/en/statistika.aspx.

Falishvili, A., ed. (2002). *Strafprozessordnung Georgiens. Ein Lehrbuch.* Tbilissi. (Criminal Procedure Code of Georgia).

Kury, Helmut, and Khatuna Kapanadze. (2004). *Strafvollzug und Sanktionen in Georien aus westlicher Sicht. Kartuli Samartlis Mimoxilva,* 2–3, pp. 280–306. (Penal System and Sanctions in Georgia).

Parliament of Georgia. Constitution of Georgia: http://www.parliament.ge/index.php?lang_id=ENG&sec_id=68.

Phutkaradze, Edisher. (2007). *Strafrechtliche Sanktionen und ihre Anwendung in der Praxis der georgischen Gerichte. Osteuroparecht* 2, pp. 96–99. (Application of Criminal Sanctions in Georgia).

Prisons: http://www.dep.gov.ge.

Public Defender of Georgia. (2009). *State of Human Rights in Georgia.* Parliamentary Reports of the Public Defender. Tbilissi.

Turava, Merab. (2008). *Strafrecht. Allgemeiner Teil.* Tbilissi, 7. Auflage. (Penal Law. General Part).

Hong Kong

Legal System: Customary/Common
Murder: Low
Burglary: Low
Corruption: Low
Human Trafficking: Low
Prison Rate: Medium
Death Penalty: No
Corporal Punishment: No

Background

Hong Kong, officially known as the Hong Kong Special Administrative Region of the People's Republic of China (hereafter referred to HKSAR), is a territory located on China's south coast on the Pearl River Delta. It faces the South China Sea in the east, west, and south, and borders China's Guangdong Province in the north. The total land and sea area of Hong Kong is about 1,092 square kilometers (422 square miles), and as of July 2008, it had a population of 7,018,636, making it one of the most densely populated areas in the world. As of 2006, the Hong Kong population was mostly Chinese (95%) but also 1.6 percent Filipino, 1.3 percent Indonesian, and 2.1 percent other ethnicities. Consequently, the spoken language is primarily

Cantonese, one of the Chinese dialects, but the official languages are both Chinese and English.

Hong Kong was ceded to the United Kingdom in 1841 by China, a result of a series of Anglo-Chinese wars and their "unequal" treaties, including the Treaty of Nanjing in 1842, Convention of Beijing in 1860, and the Second Convention of Beijing in 1898. The two major constitutional documents handed down by the Queen were the Hong Kong *Letters Patent* and *Royal Instructions*. These outlined the constitutional arrangements, including the powers and responsibilities of the governor and different branches of the government. The governor of Hong Kong was appointed by the Queen, and he was assisted by a group of senior civil servants, including a chief secretary, financial secretary, attorney general, and a group of secretaries responsible for various functions such as education, health, social welfare, and transport. Some of these key positions were British expatriates and others were recruited locally as senior civil servants to work for the colonial Hong Kong government.

On July 1, 1997, Hong Kong's sovereignty was returned to the People's Republic of China. Until 1997, its legal system and criminal justice institutions were largely modeled after the British system, and despite its return to the Chinese administration, Hong Kong has maintained a high degree of autonomy from China in all issues except foreign and national defense affairs. Like England and Wales, Hong Kong still has no written statement of the principles of criminal justice. However, the principles underpinning criminal justice procedure and administration are outlined in various legal documents and ordinances such as the *Basic Law*, *Hong Kong Bill of Rights Ordinance* (Cap. 383), *Police Force Ordinance* (Cap. 232), and *Criminal Procedure Ordinance* (Cap. 221). Article 8 states that the laws previously in force in Hong Kong, that is, the common law, rules of equity, ordinances, and customary law shall be maintained, except for any that contravene the *Basic Law*, which are subject to any amendment by the legislature of the HKSAR. Until 2047, which will be 50 years after its break from British rule, the previous capitalist economic and social systems will remain intact. China's socialist system, therefore, is not practiced in the HKSAR.

In many respects, since the 1997 handover, the Hong Kong criminal justice system has still preserved the British political, social, and economic systems; however, several remarkable changes to the government have been made. First, the governor is now replaced by a chief executive who is elected by a representative Election Committee in accordance with Annex I of the *Basic Law*, and then appointed by the Central People's Government in Beijing. The chief executive is responsible for implementing the *Basic Law*, signing bills and budgets, promulgating laws, making decisions on government policies, and issuing Executive Orders. Second, the attorney general is now called the "secretary for justice." The secretary for justice, now appointed by the Central People's Government upon nomination by the chief executive, is the principal legal advisor to the chief executive, the government, and the individual government departments and agencies. Third, the Court of Final Appeal, headed by the chief justice, was established to replace the United Kingdom's Privy Council as the highest appellate court. Other than this change, the judiciary enjoys its independence and is not subject to the interference of the chief executive and Executive and Legislative Councils. Other features of the government have remained basically the same.

The legal system of Hong Kong is different from the legal system of Mainland China. The sources of Hong Kong law are mainly the common law and rules of equity, supplemented by local ordinances enacted by the local legislature of the HKSAR, international treaties, and the *Basic Law*. Due to the colonial origin, the Hong Kong legal system is based on the common law systems used in England and Wales and other commonwealth countries. The law of Hong Kong relies extensively on the rule of law and the independence of judiciary. The rule of law has been regarded as a cornerstone of Hong Kong's success as a leading international commercial and financial center since colonial days. The rights and freedom of citizens are protected, and the rule of law is upheld by the independence of the judiciary. Article 85 of the *Basic Law* emphasizes that "The courts of the Hong Kong Special Administrative Region shall exercise judicial power independently, free from any interference."

In addition to the rule of law and the independence of judiciary, the two major principles of criminal justice in Hong Kong are adversarial justice and the due process rights of defendants. These principles determine how guilt should be established and whether a suspect, defendant, or convicted person has rights to be treated fairly by the law enforcement agencies and authorities. As opposed to the inquisitorial system, the adversarial system relies on the skill of advocates or lawyers who represent their clients and the prosecutors to determine the truth of the case in the trial where the judge or jury is the adjudicator. In criminal trials in Hong Kong, and generally all of the common law countries, the burden of proof lies in the hands of the prosecution, and the standard of proof is "beyond the reasonable doubt." Several provisions in Hong Kong law are concerned with the due process rights of the suspects. For instance, article 28 of the *Basic Law* specifies that no one shall be subjected to arbitrary or unlawful arrest, detention or imprisonment, and arbitrary or unlawful search of the body of any resident or deprivation or restriction of the freedom of the person shall be prohibited. As highlighted by the Department of Justice, "A number of principles of defence, which are in accordance with article 14 of the *International Covenant on Civil and Political Rights* (which has been applied to Hong Kong by the *Hong Kong Bill of Rights Ordinance* [Cap. 383]), have been incorporated in the *Criminal Procedure Ordinance* (Cap. 221), *Legal Aid in Criminal Cases Rules* (Cap. 221D), or absorbed into the common law." To be specific, the rights that are preserved by laws in Hong Kong are equality before the courts, the right to a fair and public trial by a competent, independent and impartial tribunal established by law, the presumption of innocence, the right to legal representation, the right to be tried without undue delay, the right to call witnesses and secure their presence in court, the right to have the free service of an interpreter, the right to remain silent in court, and the right to appeal against conviction and/or sentence.

Police

The Hong Kong Police Force was first established in the mid-19th century by the British government, and developed into a paramilitary colonial force to suppress patriotic protests. Following the independence of India and then Pakistan in 1947, most of the rank-and-file police officers in these two countries returned home, and an increasing number of locals began taking up the position. In the 1970s the colonial administration was committed to dealing with police corruption within the police organization by adopting a shift in governance style, and turned the paramilitary style of policing to the police force, which focused on maintaining public order and fighting crime. In addition to these two focuses, the contemporary police force adopted the model of community policing, which explicitly stresses the police-public cooperation by promoting community interaction and support since the 1990s.

Crime

Hong Kong is regarded as one of the safest cities in the world in terms of its overall recorded crime per capita in the *Seventh United Nations Survey on Crime Trends and the Operations of Criminal Justice Systems*. Two main types of crime measurement have been used to study the nature and extent of crime and victimization in Hong Kong, official statistics and crime victimization surveys. In addition to these, there are regular surveys of public opinion, which tend to show a high degree of public confidence in the police and the anticorruption body. Also, self-reported studies on delinquency and drug abuse among young people have been conducted to examine both reported and unreported criminal and delinquent behavior, though these studies are not carried out on a regular basis. Admittedly, none of these measurements are without problems, but they are able to give us a rough picture of the trends, nature, and prevalence of crime as recorded by the authorities and reported by crime victims.

According to annual departmental reports, the Hong Kong Police Force classifies crimes into 10 types, which are listed as follows, including the numbers recorded by police for 2007:

Violent crime against person	12,513
Violent crime against property	2,421
Burglary and theft	41,453
Fraud and forgery	5,967
Sexual offense	995
Serious narcotics offense	2,769
Offenses against lawful authority	763
Serious immigration offense	765
Miscellaneous crimes	11,876
Preventive crime	1,274
Grand total	**80,796**

It can be seen that the most common type of crime reported to the police was burglary and theft in both years. The annual police departmental review indicates that the largest number of crimes reported were classified as "other miscellaneous thefts," followed by shoplifting. The total number of recorded crimes increased from 76,771 in 1999 to 81,125 in 2007, and crime reports on fraud and forgery drastically increased by 37.4 percent between 1999 and 2007.

Of the total crimes reported, 45.6 percent were detected. The detection rate for attempted murder, manufacturing of dangerous drugs, other serious narcotics offenses, possession of arms and ammunition, and unlawful pawning offense was 100 percent in both years. The specific forms of crime that have had the lowest rate are burglary with breaking (7.7%) and criminal damage (19.3%).

In addition to detection, one of the key responsibilities of the police force is to arrest suspects of crime when appropriate. In 2007 the total number of persons arrested was 43,000, of which approximately 25 percent were females. In general, the major group of those arrested were young adults. Persons were arrested most often for burglary and theft (9,369 men, 5,325 women), closely followed by violent crimes against the person (7,657 men, 1,737 women).

While the Hong Kong Police force deals with crime statistics, other law and order statistics such as money laundering, drug abuse, corruption reports, number of consumer protection investigations, number of illegal immigrants appended, and penal population in institutions are compiled by different law enforcement agencies. For instance, the Joint Financial Intelligence Unit is run by staff of the Hong Kong Police Force and the Hong Kong Customs and Excise Department, and it deals with reports of suspicious financial activity and transaction reports related to terrorist property. Its statistics show that the number of persons convicted of money laundering has increased from 49 in 2004 to 179 in 2007, and the value of assets restrained has also increased from HK$68,818,082 in 2004 to HK$723,764,771 in 2007 (the equivalent then to US$887,798 to US$93,389,002). In addition to the Hong Kong Police Force and the Customs and Excise Department, several key government departments are responsible for maintaining law and order, fighting crime, enforcing the law, and rehabilitating offenders. These include the Department of Justice, the Immigration Department, the Independent Commission against Corruption, the Labour Department, the Fire Services Department, the Legal Aid Department, the Social Welfare Department, and the Correctional Services Department. Each of these law enforcement agencies provides and compiles updated information about the work they are responsible for, thereby giving the public some idea of the volume of crime, and number of convictions and sentences given on an annual basis.

Crime victimization surveys have been conducted seven times in Hong Kong under the auspices of the Fight Crime Committee to measure and estimate the risk of criminal victimization. They were taken in 1978, 1981, 1986, 1989, 1994, 1998, and 2005. The aim of these surveys is to provide the administration of criminal justice with information on the nature and extent of crime, as well as the reasons for reporting or not reporting to the police, data not otherwise available from official records. A total of 20,100 households within a representative and random sampling were interviewed in the latest survey conducted in 2005, with a response rate of 83 percent. The scope of this survey was limited to two types of crime, namely crimes of violence (e.g., indecent assault, wounding and assault and criminal intimidation) and crimes against household (e.g., theft of vehicle and criminal damage to property). The estimated number of crime victimizations in

2005 was 358,800, which showed an increase of 1.9 percent when compared with 352,200 of 1998. It is not surprising to note that persons aged between 12 and 19 had the highest overall victimization rate of 46.7 per 1,000 among all ages, and females aged 12 and over (37.0 per 1,000 persons) are more likely than males of the same age (33.4 per 1,000 persons) to experience victimization. About 19.1 percent of crime victimizations were reported to the police in 2005, which is a much lower percentage than in 1998 (29.3%). The three major reasons for reporting to the police were "the victims hope to catch the offenders" (51.5%); "reporting was a prerequisite of getting a replacement of documents or claiming insurance" (13.4%); and "the victim's duty as a citizen to report to the police" (13.1%). The three major reasons for not reporting to the police were "the victims suffered not much" (30.3%); "the case lacked evidence" (23.9%); and "reporting procedures are too cumbersome" (9.7%). The Census and Statistics Department has emphasized that the reliability of these findings depends upon the willingness of respondents to cooperate and their honesty, and therefore these findings should be treated with care.

Finding of Guilt

Arrest and Prosecution

The two major actors in the pretrial stage of the criminal justice system are the police and the prosecutor, which are often referred to as the "gatekeepers" of the criminal justice system. According to the *Police Force Ordinance* (Cap. 232), police officers are given the power to stop, search, and arrest a person; request to see the person's proof of identity; and interrogate a person if he or she is under suspicion of committing or involvement in crime. Among other powers, a police officer, usually in the senior rank, can decide if there is sufficient evidence to lay a charge against a suspect, whether or not it is necessary to seek the advice of the Department of Justice about his or her decision to prosecute and can exercise discretionary power to divert a suspect from prosecution. On behalf of the secretary for justice, the Prosecutions Division of the Department of Justice has the overall responsibility for the conduct of prosecutions in Hong Kong, and its primary duty is to determine if a particular case or class of cases should be prosecuted by the government. The Hong Kong Police Force and other relevant law enforcement organizations such as the Department of Immigration and Customs and Excise Department seek advice from the Prosecutions Division when involved in prosecuting serious or complicated cases. In this respect, both the police and prosecutor make important decisions regarding the treatment of a suspect or defendant after being arrested and before appearing before the judge or jury.

Even though police may arrest offenders, this does not mean that they will necessarily be prosecuted. Once a crime is reported or detected, the police must investigate the circumstances of crime scene to see whether evidence is sufficient to lay charges against the suspect. There are generally three possible outcomes after the police investigation is completed. The first outcome is that the case is discharged due to the fact that it lacks sufficient evidence. The second outcome is that the case will not be prosecuted simply because it is petty in nature. These cases, especially those aged between 10 and 18, will escape prosecution by instead being issued a caution under the Police Superintendent's Discretionary Scheme. To be eligible for cautioning, juvenile and young suspects voluntarily confess to their criminal behavior, and most important, are usually first-time or second-time offenders. The third outcome is that the case is prosecuted. The suspect is required to appear at court on a certain date, and while waiting for the court hearing may be required to be on police bail or remanded in custody.

It is also important to note that on some occasions the prosecutor may advise the police or law enforcement agencies not to continue the prosecution in the pretrial process. According to the Department of Justice, two issues that determine whether or not to prosecute are the strength and sufficiency of evidence to justify the institution of proceedings and the public interest test. On behalf of the Secretary for Justice, the prosecutors should not be subject to any instructions or directions from the executive. In general practice, all prosecutions at the summary level that are simple cases are often processed by the police force or other law enforcement agencies instead of getting the secretary for justice involved.

Trial

Once the decision to prosecute has been made by the police, either court prosecutors or lawyers from the Prosecutions Division of the Department of Justice are in charge of initiating, conducting, and finalizing prosecutions. Court prosecutors deal mainly with the majority cases before magistrates, whereas the lawyers from the Prosecutions Division appear before magistrates in important cases and in the trials held in the district court and Court of First Instance.

In Hong Kong, the criminal trial courts consist of the magistrates' court, district court, and Court of First Instance; and the criminal appeal courts consist of the Court of First Instance, Court of Appeal, and Court of Final Appeal. Each of these courts takes its powers from its enabling ordinance. All criminal cases start in the magistrates' court where a defendant first appears. The case is then either dealt with in the magistrates' court or transferred to the district court or the Court of First Instance, depending upon the decision made by the magistrate.

The prosecutor plays a significant role throughout criminal proceedings. As a minister of justice, the prosecutor must be firm and fair and should not press for a conviction at court. More specifically, *The Statement of Prosecution Policy and Practice* states that the prosecutor is as independent as the judge. In addition, the prosecutor must assist the court to avoid an error in the appeal. If there is an appeal against conviction or sentence, the duty of the prosecutor is to ensure that a just disposal of the appeal is achieved.

As discussed earlier, one of the rights of the defendant is the right to legal representation or access to justice in both pretrial and trial stage. It is indeed guaranteed by the provisions of the *Basic Law* and *Hong Kong Bill of Rights Ordinance* (Cap. 383). In Hong Kong, both the Duty Lawyer Service and the Legal Aid Department provide legal representation in criminal cases to any person who needs legal services for pursuing or defending a legal action and is unable to have access to a lawyer due to lack of means. The Duty Lawyer Service is subsidized by the HKSAR government but operated independently by the Law Society of Hong Kong and the Bar Association. The Duty Lawyer Scheme within the Duty Lawyer Service provides legal representation to defendants who are charged and brought before all magistrates' courts and Juvenile Courts. The defendant has to pass both the means and merit tests to be eligible for Duty Lawyer Scheme and must be able to pay a handling charge of HK$400 (the current equivalent of US$51.6). The Department of Justice reports that in 2007, a total of 38,640 defendants were assisted under the scheme, involving 1,549 barristers and solicitors to provide legal assistance. Likewise, the Legal Aid Service is funded by the government, and lawyers of the Legal Aid Department are responsible for assessing the applications for legal aid based upon the means and merit tests. The financial resources of the applicant should not exceed the limit of legal aid, which is HK$165,700 (the current equivalent of US$21,380). The merit tests refer to the Director of Legal Aid's decision regarding the desirability in the interests of justice to grant the applicant legal aid. Those who have been granted legal aid would then be assigned to the lawyers from the Legal Aid Department or solicitors or barristers in private practice. Legal aid covers all criminal cases in the district court, the Court of First Instance, and all appeals against decisions of magistrates and to the Court of Appeal and Court of Final Appeal. Those who are not granted legal aid may choose to represent for themselves in the trial or hire a legal counsel for legal representation at their own expense. In an adversarial system, the defense lawyer has a duty to act according to the best interest of the defendant in the pursuit of justice throughout the criminal proceeding.

The magistrate and judge, who is regarded as an "umpire," play a significant role in the courtroom, as they determine whether or not the accused is guilty. This indeed is not an easy task because the decision may affect how the suspect is further processed in the formal justice system. Therefore, the magistrate or judge is expected to be neutral, impartial, and knowledgeable of the law and procedure in trial. Magistrates are appointed because of their professional legal training and work experience as solicitors or barristers.

All summary cases are tried before one magistrate or one judge in the district court or the Court of First Instance. Trial by a judge, sitting with a jury of seven people, is reserved for the most serious criminal cases such as murder, manslaughter, rape, armed robbery, and certain drug offenses in the Court of First Instance. Depending on the number of jurors in a trial, the judge will urge a jury to strive for a unanimous verdict or a majority verdict of five to two or seven to two. To be eligible to serve as a juror, a person must have reached the age of 21 but not yet 65, be of a sound mind and have no hearing or visual impairments that might prevent him or her from serving as a juror, be of good character, and have sufficient knowledge of the language used in the court proceedings. The majority of the criminal cases tried in the magistrates' court in Hong Kong are conducted in Chinese, whereas English is commonly used in higher courts such as the Court of First Instance and Court of Appeal.

The conviction rate is one of the key performance indicators of the Prosecution Division of the Department of Justice. The division is proud of its relatively high conviction rates, which were, in 2007, 76.6 percent in the magistrates' court, 90.5 percent in the district court, and 93.4 percent in the Court of First Instance.

Punishment

After finding guilt, another important function of the court is to impose appropriate sanctions or punishments to the individual for a criminal offense. The ultimate aims of sentencing are to reintegrate offenders into the community and to turn them into law-abiding citizens. There is a range of sentencing measures available for the magistrate or judge to choose from, depending upon the levels of court. There are three main types of sentencing options, namely unsupervised (such as fines and binding over order), supervised (such as probation order and community service order), and custodial sentences (such as detention center order and imprisonment). Corporal punishment and the death penalty were abolished in Hong Kong in 1989 and 1993, respectively. In trying to arrive at a fair and just sentence, the sentencing magistrate or judge has to take several factors into consideration, including the seriousness of crime, the harm done to the victim, mitigating and aggravating factors, constitutional rights of the offenders, and the interests of the public. Different ordinances usually specify a maximum penalty for different forms of crime. For instance, Section 118(1) of *Crimes Ordinance* (Cap. 200) stipulates that a man who rapes a woman shall be liable upon conviction or indictment to imprisonment to life. The *Dangerous Drugs Ordinance* (Cap. 134) also specifies the maximum penalties of various drug-related offenses. Lo, Dobinson, and Chui, writing in the *Hong Kong Law Journal,* provide a comprehensive overview of the sentences handed down by the courts over the past decade for various offenses involving drugs such as cannabis, opium, heroin, cocaine, methaqualone (mandrax), methamphetamine hydrochloride (ICE), and methylenedioxy methamphetamine (MDMA or Ecstacy). In those cases involving juvenile and young offenders, information about their character, physical and mental conditions, schooling, employment, and family circumstances are collected by the sentencing magistrate or judge through a number of reports. The social enquiry, suitability, or presentence reports prepared by probation officers, prison officers, psychiatrists, and medical officers also contain their recommendations regarding the type of sentence that is appropriate for the offender.

The right to an appeal or a review of the conviction and sentence is also granted according to Hong Kong law. For instance, article 11(4) of the *Hong Kong Bill of Rights Ordinance* (Cap. 383) states that everyone convicted of a crime shall have the right to the conviction and sentence being reviewed by a higher tribunal. The three types of court with appellate jurisdiction over criminal matters in Hong Kong are the Court of First Instance, Court of Appeal, and Court of Final Appeal. Examples of the grounds for appeals against conviction and sentence are cases involving the question of fact and law and inappropriate as well as excessive punishment.

Corrections

The ethos of rehabilitation is the dominant sentencing theory and the main intervention method of dealing with offenders in Hong Kong, other than retribution, deterrence, incapacitation, and restoration. In the posttrial stage, governmental departments who work with offenders in the community and prison are the Social Welfare Department and Correctional Services Department. While the former administers two community sentences, including probation order and community service order, the latter is responsible for operating and managing correctional institutions in Hong Kong. In contrast to other noncustodial sentences such as fines, disqualification, and compensation, the two community sentences involve both an element of active participation by the offender and close supervision or monitoring by a designated authority figure from the Probation Section within the Social Welfare Department. The intended goal of the community sentence is to "help offenders reintegrate into the community as law-abiding citizens" through counseling, proper supervision, and social skills training. Probation is the most common form of community sentences in Hong Kong, as can be seen in the listing of cases by the Social Welfare Department for the 2005–2006 period:

Probation supervision	2,907
Community service order	883
Probation home and hostel	109
Reformatory school	32
Community Support Services Scheme:	
(Youth members)	624
(Parents members)	298
Postrelease Supervision of Prisoners Scheme	526

The Social Welfare Department operates probation homes for juvenile offenders aged between 10 and under 16 who are required by the court to receive residential training as a part of the probation sentence. Reformatory school is a custodial sentencing option for young offenders under the *Reformatory Schools Ordinance* (Cap. 225). The Community Support Services Scheme is available for those offenders aged under 25, and their parents, under Probation Order, Community Service Order, or Reformatory School Order.

The community sentence is a nonpunitive approach, targeting first-time, nonviolent offenders who pose little threat to society, and is considered as an alternative to custody. Major justifications for community sentences are diversion or deinstitutionalization, reintegration (or rehabilitation), and reparation. The Social Welfare Department is staffed by registered social workers to promote prosocial behavior among those being given community sentences. The *Probation of Offenders Ordinance* (Cap. 298) details the responsibilities and core tasks of probation officers and how an offender should be supervised in legal terms. The probation order applies to all ages of 10 or above. It must clearly specify the period of probation, which should be no less than one year and no longer than three years. An empirical study with 115 adult probationers aged between 18 and 35 found that the probation service places an emphasis on an individualized casework treatment approach to the probationer. Section 4(1) of the *Community Service Orders Ordinance* (Cap. 378) enables the court to order that those convicted of an offense be punishable with imprisonment, for any number of hours with a maximum of 240 within a period of 12 months. The court shall not make the order against an offender unless the offender consents to the making of such an order, and the court is satisfied after considering a social enquiry report as to the offender's suitability to be made the subject of such an order. The offender on community service order has to make reparation to the public through unpaid work and learn to be responsible for the harm caused to others.

Prisons

The custodial sentence requires the offender to be locked up in the correctional institution. According to the sentencing tariff, prisons are suited to those who have committed serious offenses. In contrast to the social welfare approach adopted by the

Social Welfare Department, the Correctional Services Department is a disciplinary force, administering a detention center; drug addiction treatment centers; rehabilitation centers; training centers; and minimum, medium, and maximum security prisons for offenders aged 14 years of age or above. In addition, its halfway houses offer temporary shelter for young offenders during their adjustment period after release. The total population in major penal institutions in 2007 was 10,946, of which 2,178 were females. Breakdown of prisoners in different types of institutions were as follows:

Prisons	8,238
Drug addiction treatment center inmates	608
Training center inmates	270
Detention center inmates	123
Rehabilitation center inmates	187
Remanded persons	1,790

Since January 1998, the Correctional Services Department has set up a Rehabilitation Division to oversee the rehabilitation services for offenders, which comprises five major units: Rehabilitation Unit for Assessment and Supervision, Rehabilitation Unit for Welfare, Counseling and Supervision, Education Unit, Vocational Training Unit, and Psychological Services Section. While the vocational training unit is available to those prisoners under the age of 21, industrial employment is available for inmates covering 13 trades such as garment making, leather products, sign making, metalwork, bookbinding, and printing. About 6,000 inmate workers are currently engaged in these types of industrial work every day, and these products are then supplied to government departments and tax-supported bodies. The Correctional Services Department has identified four important factors that contribute to the successful offender rehabilitation in an inclusive society: quality custodial services, comprehensive rehabilitative services, offender's motivation and determination to change, and community support. In this respect the department is committed to finding strategies to improve the quality of the correctional services. Depending upon the custodial sentence, the length of statutory supervision or postrelease supervision varies, and the provision of aftercare services is not always required. Various schemes such as the Release Under Supervision Scheme, Pre-release Supervision of Prisoners Scheme, Conditional Release Scheme, and Supervision after Release Scheme ensure that the necessary continued care and support is given to those who are released from the penal institution. Regular face-to-face contact and home visits are arranged to ensure a gradual transition from institution to the community.

Emerging Issues

In this concluding section, three controversial issues surrounding the contemporary criminal justice system are discussed, with the aim of highlighting the current concern of the public and policy makers in Hong Kong. These three issues are the proposal of introducing sex offender registers, the proposed use of coercive drug testing in the high school, and the reluctance of grant the prisoner's right to vote.

In July 2008, the Law Reform Commission of Hong Kong consulted the public's opinion on setting up a sex offender register to protect children and vulnerable adults, including the mentally disabled, from being abused. The major intention of the register would be to allow the public, especially employers in child-related activities, to have access to the history of sexual offenses of their prospective job applicants and employees. As indicated in the consultation paper, the inclusion of sexual offenders on the register would be based upon the designated offenses. While the details of what should be contained in the sex offender register and how it is going to be used are yet to be finalized, different public polls indicate a favorable response to the proposal. It is anticipated that the Law Reform Commission of Hong Kong is likely to recommend further action to set up the register. However, the sex offender register would most likely not be used as a means of imposing harsher punishment or posing obstacles or barriers to the rehabilitation of sex offenders.

Another area of concern among the law enforcement agencies is the increasing number of youth drug abuse, and consequently the government has proposed drug testing in high schools. The latest drug-abuse statistics indicate a changing trend in drug abuse among young people; they initiate substance abuse earlier and have more access to psychotropic substances such as ICE, cocaine, and club drugs such as Ecstasy and Ketamine. In view of these changes, a special task force has been set up, chaired by the secretary for justice, to identify strategies to tackle this social problem. One of the key recommendations was to introduce new legislation for compulsory drug testing of a person reasonably suspected of having consumed dangerous drugs in schools. The intention is to identify children aged between 11 and 16 who abuse drugs, so that early intervention and treatment programs can be delivered to these at-risk children, young people, and their families. Despite the possible infringement of civil liberties of young people, the government is very keen to pilot this drug-testing measure on a random basis to deter young people from abusing drugs. However, a number of liberal groups have questioned the legality of this coercive measure and the plan to implement it is yet to be seen.

The last issue concerns the right to vote among prisoners. In late 2008, a few prisoners applied for a judicial review to challenge the ban on their right to vote, which began to arouse people's attention to the importance of this issue. In fact, some have argued that laws in Hong Kong should be amended to remove the barrier to voting faced by the prisoner and ex-prisoner. One of the central arguments is that article 26 of the *Basic Law* states that permanent residents shall have the right to vote and the right to stand for election in accordance with the law. Voting is a fundamental right of democracy and promotes citizen participation in choosing the people to represent them in the political system. In this view, Hong Kong should follow other jurisdictions such as the United Kingdom, Europe, Australia, and Canada to practice criminal disenfranchisement in more limited ways. On December 8, 2008, a High Court judge ruled that prisoners and people being held in custody should have the right to vote, and this ruling restored more than 4,000 prisoners the right to register and to vote in the election. However, the government may appeal against this decision, and has not yet finalized a plan to amend the law nor looked for measures to allow people detained in penal institutions to register to vote or to vote in the coming elections.

Wing Hong Chui

Further Reading

Chui, Wing Hong, and Tit Wing Lo, eds. (2008). *Understanding Criminal Justice in Hong Kong*. Cullompton, Devon: Willan.

Jackson, Michael. (2003). *Criminal Law in Hong Kong*. Hong Kong: Hong Kong University Press.

Jiao, Allan. (2007). *The Police in Hong Kong: A Contemporary View*. Lanham, MD: University Press of America.

Jones, Carol, with Jon Vagg. (2007). *Criminal Justice in Hong Kong*. London: Routledge-Cavendish.

Lo, S.H.C., I. Dobinson, and W. H. Chui. (2004). "Sentencing for Drug Offences in Hong Kong: An Overview," *Hong Kong Law Journal* 34 (1), 13–45.

Whitfort, Amanda. (2006). *Criminal Procedure in Hong Kong: A Guide for Students and Practitioners*. Hong Kong: LexisNexis.

Web Sites

Basic Law of the Hong Kong Special Administrative Region of the People's Republic of China: http://www.info.gov.hk/basic_law/flash.html.

Correctional Services Department: http://www.csd.gov.hk/.

Department of Justice: http://www.doj.gov.hk/.

Hong Kong Police Force: http://www.police.gov.hk/.

Independent Commission against Corruption: http://www.icac.org.hk/.

Legal Aid Department: http://www.lad.gov.hk/.

Security Bureau: http://www.sb.gov.hk/.

Social Welfare Department: http://www.swd.gov.hk/en/index/index.html.

India

Legal System: Common/Islamic/Customary
Murder: Medium
Burglary: Low
Corruption: Medium
Human Trafficking: Medium
Prison Rate: Low
Death Penalty: Yes
Corporal Punishment: Yes

Background

Rich in cultural and religious diversity, India's democratic and pluralistic commitment comport well with a multifaceted legal and criminal justice system. These factors, socioreligious diversity, and an unrelenting democratic ideology, are the two keystones of Indian jurisprudence.

Ancient India was essentially Hindu-ruled and religious principles formed the basis of legal thought. The *Arthashastra* and the *Manusmriti,* for example, are Indian scholarly treatises dating from 400 BCE and 100 CE, which were instrumental in the development of legal doctrine. In ancient Indian monarchial society, the king's authority was derivative from the guiding principles of *Dharma,* which were unquestionably expected to be upheld. Today, India's political governance adheres to Federalist ideology, combining shared rule with self-rule.

Legal System

The Indian Constitution, drafted in 1950, was based on the principles of English common law and incorporated important American court decisions. Among the inalienable rights guaranteed by the Indian Constitution are equal rights to all citizens; a prohibition of discrimination on the basis of race, ethnicity, gender, caste, and religion; and universal franchise, thereby making the Indian electorate the largest in the world. India's Constitution is an admixture of laws originating from traditional India, Europe (Ireland, Britain, and France), and the United States. The Constitution is the most significant source of the contemporary Indian legal and criminal justice system. On the whole, Indian laws are in compliance with accepted international law such as the United Nations guidelines on human rights law, environmental laws and international treaties, and international trade laws, including those on intellectual property. The Legal System in India has four subsystems, Legislature, Enforcement (police), Legal System, Adjudication (courts), and Corrections (prisons, community facilities).

The Indian legal system is a mix of adversarial and accusatorial legal systems. Despite India's Federalist system and the existence of both central (i.e., Federal) and state laws, each with its predefined spheres of application, there exists a single integrated system of courts, which administers both the central and the state laws. Catering to India's pluralistic society, the Indian Constitution and laws respect and preserve the tenets of both Hindu and Muslim jurisprudence. Politically, the president of India and state governors act according to the advice of the Council of Ministers. In rural areas, an informal justice system known as *Panchayat* or by some other similar name—meaning "rule of the people"—operates to resolve civil, family, and criminal disputes of petty and local nature.

Indian civil law is complex, as it is tailored to adhere to the individual laws of each religious group represented in India's diverse ethnic and religious society. Indian laws are adapted to various religions that are locally represented in different states or communities of India, that is, Hindus, Muslims, Christians, Sikhs, and followers of other religions. A notable exception to this *religio-legal* pluralism is the state of Goa, where a Portuguese uniform civil code is in place, whereby all religions have a common law regarding marriages, divorces, and adoptions.

The first Indian Penal Code (IPC) was adopted in 1860. This code defined crime and prescribed appropriate punishments for crimes. In 1861, a Code of Criminal Procedure was enacted and added to the IPC. This Code of Criminal Procedure established the rules to be followed in all stages of investigation, trial, and sentencing in the criminal justice system. This code was repealed and a new code was established in 1974. These two codes, along with parts of the Indian Evidence Act of 1872, form the essence of India's criminal law. A large number of special and local laws such as the Arms Act, Prohibition Act, Immoral Traffic (Prevention) Act, and so forth, address various other antisocial activities.

Crime

The established laws on crime prevention and punishment are embodied in the following three principal statutes, which are universally applicable in the entire country:

1. The Indian Penal Code of 1860
2. The Code of Criminal Procedure of 1973 (Cr.P.C.)
3. The Indian Evidence Act of 1872

A woman protests the sexual abuse of women in New Delhi, India, July 12, 2005. (AP Photo/Saurabh Das)

There are a number of "special laws" dealing with particular subjects and local laws that have been enacted from time to time by the Union/state legislatures to meet the specific challenges of crime prevention needs. Inasmuch as these special laws serve local needs and interests, they remain subordinate to the Constitution of India.

Classification of Crimes

Inasmuch as separate state legislation overlaps with the subject matter of federal statutes relating to criminal liability for acts such as smuggling, illegal use of arms, and corruption, all local legislation must be in compliance with the relevant federal statutes. Furthermore, all federal and local statutes, in turn, are still subordinate to the Constitution.

Outside the subject matter jurisdiction of the IPC or similar areas attributable to the Central government as expressed in the provisions of the Constitution, each state has the freedom to draft its own laws on subjects that are considered state subjects. With the exception for laws governing local taxation rates, the citizens of each state must abide by existing central laws passed by the Parliament of India.

The Criminal Procedure Code (§§ 2(c), (l) Cr.P.C.) divides crimes into the following two categories:

1. *Cognizable* offenses are those in which a police officer, on probable cause, can make an arrest without a warrant. Under the IPC of 1860, all major crimes like theft, burglary, robbery, cheating, assaults, homicide, and so forth are considered cognizable offenses. The police officers can investigate and make an arrest without a warrant in a cognizable crime. The police officer also has the discretionary power to evaluate and redefine the reported offense in the complaint. For instance, the officer may not find sufficient corroborating evidence to believe and hence reduce the gravity of the complaint to make it a noncognizable offense.
2. *Noncognizable* offenses are those in which a police officer lacks the authority to make an arrest without a warrant in noncognizable crimes. A noncognizable criminal incident is

defined as a minor infraction of the law where a police officer can make an arrest only by the order of the court. As such, the remedies for noncognizable offenses are generally distributed at the discretion of the court, in actions pursued by the affected parties themselves. Absent magisterial permission, law enforcement officers do not generally initiate investigation in noncognizable crimes.

The following special crimes are defined in acts other than the IPC:

1. Arms Act, 1959
2. Narcotic Drugs and Psychotropic Substances Act, 1985
3. Gambling Act, 1867
4. Excise Act, 1944
5. Dowry Prohibition Act, 1961, and Prohibition of Child Marriage Act, 2006
6. Explosives and Explosive Substances Act, 1884, 1908
7. Immoral Traffic (Prevention) Act, 1956
8. Railways Act, 1989
9. Registration of Foreigners Act, 1930
10. Protection of Civil Rights Act, 1955
11. Indian Passport Act, 1967
12. Essential Commodities Act, 1955
13. Terrorist and Disruptive Activities Act, 1987
14. Antiquity and Art Treasure Act, 1972
15. Dowry Prohibition Act, 1961
16. Child Marriage Restraint Act, 1929
17. Indecent Representation of Women (P) Act, 1986
18. Copyright Act, 1957
19. Sati Prevention Act, 1987
20. SC/ST (Prevention of Atrocities) Act, 1989
21. Forest Act, 1927
22. Other crimes (not specified above) under Special and Local Laws, including Cyber Laws under Information Technology Act (IT), 2000

Age of Criminal Responsibility

Under the IPC, the age of criminal responsibility is established at the age of seven. However, any act, which would otherwise be criminal, committed by a child 7–12 years old, is free from liability if the presiding judge is convinced that the child had not attained sufficient maturity of understanding the nature and consequences of his or her conduct when the offense in question was committed.

Drug Offenses

The Narcotic Drugs and Psychotropic Substances Act (NDPSA) of 1985 promulgated by the Union government is the main legislation dealing with drug offenses. The act defines narcotic drugs as coca leaf, cannabis (hemp), opium, straw, and manufactured drugs, which includes all coca derivatives, medicinal cannabis, opium derivatives, and poppy straw concentrate. Psychotropic substances are those listed in the Schedule of the Act and include, among others, LSD, DET, and MDA.

The NDPSA prohibits cultivation of coca plants and the possession, sale, purchase, and use of coca leaves in violation of the act and in contravention of any license granted under it. A similar prohibition is imposed by the act for psychotropic substances. Officers empowered under the NDPSA include those of the Union government (Central Excise, Narcotics, Customs) and the state government (including Revenue, Drug Control, Excise, and the Police).

Crime Statistics

The National Crime Records Bureau (NCRB) of the Union Ministry of Home Affairs in New Delhi publishes annual records of crime in India. Since 1999, the total number of complaints received by police has been recorded. These data include records of oral or written complaints, distress calls, or those initiated by police, and are a telling portrayal of the volume of crime in India and the sizable workload of police. In 2005, Indian police received 64,670,600 complaints compared to 76,200,949 received in 2004. The means of notifying police were distributed as follows: 39.7 percent—written complaints, 15.2 percent—oral complaints, 37.7 percent—complaints initiated by police, and 7.4 percent—distress phone calls. Significantly, nearly 77.7 percent of these complaints were registered as cognizable offenses, comprising 18.23 million cases under the IPC and 32.04 million cases under the Special and Local Laws (SLL). In addition to the decrease in the number of annual complaints, there was a decline in the IPC/SLL ratio (1:1.92 in 2000 to 1:1.76 in 2005) and the total crime (summation of IPC and SLL) rate (a decrease of 12.4% and 17.9% in 2001 and 2004, respectively).

According to the IPC, there were 32,719 murders recorded in 2005 and 28,031 murder attempts reported. The majority of murder victims were between the ages of 18 to 30 and male. There were also 18,359 rapes reported in 2005. According to the IPC, rape is defined as sexual intercourse by a man with a woman against her will, without her consent, or with her consent, if her consent has been obtained by putting her or any person in whom she has an interest in fear of death or harm. Finally, there were 15,750 kidnapping incidents reported in 2005, the majority of victims between the ages of 18 and 30 and women. Other cognizable crimes reported to police for 2004 were recorded as follows:

Robbery	18,458
Burglary	92,490
Theft	273,045
Auto theft	80,682
Riots	59,971
Criminal breach of trust	14,176
Counterfeiting	1,529
Arson	8,637
Dowry death	7,026
Molestation	34,567
Sexual harassment	10,001
Cruelty to women by husband/relatives	58,121
Trafficking girls	89
Causing death by negligence	69,423
Cheating	51,939

Under the main legislation dealing with drug offenses described above, the NDPSA, a total of 29,421 cases were registered in 2005. This number represents an increase of 6.6 percent relative to 2004 records (27,608). All statistical indicators suggest that drug offenses are increasing in incidence. The increase in drug offenses interestingly parallels the decline in the total crime rate. While total crime rate has declined, 10- and 5-year trend analysis of drug offense data show a 46 percent and a 15 percent increase, respectively. Interestingly, 35.0 percent (10,283) of the total cases are attributable to just one state in India, Uttar Pradesh.

Finding of Guilt

Rights of the Accused

Pursuant to the Code of Criminal Procedure of 1973, the accused are afforded constitutionally guaranteed protections. Alternatively, those arrested under special security legislation (SSLL) may not be afforded such protections. Before searching for and seizing evidence, police officers are generally required to secure a warrant from a magistrate. An individual taken into custody has certain rights including the right to be advised of the charges brought against her or him and to seek counsel. Notwithstanding the elaborate procedural and substantive safeguards that are maintained for protecting the rights of the accused, implementation of such rules is not always equitable. The extent of protected rights is often dependent on the class and social background of the accused.

From a procedural standpoint, individuals taken into custody by police are required, within 24 hours of arrest, to appear before a magistrate. The judge or magistrate retains the discretion to release the accused on bail. While under trial, a defendant is protected against self-incrimination. Criminal cases generally take place in open trials; however, closed trials also occur in limited circumstances. Decisions made by lower courts can be appealed to higher courts following established appellate procedures.

Pursuant to the Indian Constitution, inalienable, fundamental rights endowed upon citizens are enforceable in the Constitutional Courts (High Court and the Supreme Court). Article 21 of the Constitution of India states, "No person shall be deprived of his life or personal liberty except by a procedure established by law." The Supreme Court has given a wider interpretation to this fundamental right and stated that any procedure to curtail liberty has to be a "just, fair, and reasonable procedure." Under the Indian Constitution and the Criminal Procedure

Code (Cr.P.C.) of 1973, the accused are afforded several fundamental rights, including a presumption of innocence until proven guilty. The accused has the right to a speedy trial. In addition, the Indian Code of Criminal Procedure includes provisions for additional rights of defendants, including the right to an expedited and efficient judicial process as well as legal assistance if the defendant is indigent.

Under the Criminal Justice System in India, law enforcement officers are often the first persons of contact with the victim and accused. Complaints about criminal incidents are received and processed by law enforcement officers who act as gatekeepers to the criminal justice system. A police officer determines if a criminal incident has taken place and only she or he is empowered to investigate the case. The Code of Criminal Procedure delineates exact procedures for recording the complaint and subsequent investigation of the alleged offenses.

Section 154 of the Criminal Penal Code requires that a criminal complaint made to the police is recorded by the station house officer in writing. This section stipulates that whenever a citizen informs the police, or the police learn otherwise about the occurrence of a cognizable crime, the station house officer (SHO) shall institute a First Information Report (FIR), which initiates the criminal investigation.

Courts

Each state is divided into judicial districts presided over by a district and sessions judge, who is the highest judicial authority in a district. Below her or him, there are courts of civil jurisdiction, known in different states as subjudges, civil judges, and the like. Similarly, criminal judiciary comprises a chief judicial magistrate and judicial magistrates of first and second class.

The Indian Code of Criminal Procedure provides for the following three sets of magistrates for the subordinate criminal courts:

1. Executive magistrates, whose duties include issuing warrants, advising the police, and determining proper procedures to deal with public violence.
2. Judicial magistrates, who are essentially trial judges.
3. Petty criminal cases are sometimes settled in panchayat courts for rural areas, whereby civil and criminal disputes of petty and local nature are resolved.

Jury Trials

In 1960, the Indian government abolished jury trials, as it was believed that jury trials are unfair to the poor. It is believed that jury trials are susceptible to media and public influence.

Punishment

The punishment meted out to the convicted is in proportion to the crime committed. Under the Penal System of India, there is a range of punishments imposed on the convicted. These punishments are divided into six categories. These punishments range from monetary fines to capital punishment. The six categories of punishment are listed below.

1. Fines
2. Forfeiture of property
3. Simple imprisonment
4. Rigorous imprisonment with hard labor, solitary confinement
5. Life imprisonment
6. Death penalty

Failure to pay fines can result in imprisonment. Solitary confinement, albeit rare, is employed for serious and dangerous offenders. Although the death penalty is one of the aforementioned six categories of punishment, it is infrequently applied. The death penalty is reserved for crimes such as treason, terrorism, political assassination, and multiple murders. Death and life sentences may be discretionarily commuted. When death penalty is prescribed, the method of execution is by hanging.

Prisons

Under the Constitution of India, the states and territories are charged with the task of custody and correction of criminals. Various statutory provisions, including the Prisons Act of 1894, the Prisoners Act of 1900, and the Transfer of Prisoners Act of 1950, have established the procedural and administrative roles of the state and local agencies in managing prisons. An inspector general of prisons administers prison affairs in each state and territory.

The Indian Ministry of Home Affairs oversees law enforcement and correctional administration at a Central government level. Pursuant to such authority, the ministry is responsible for policy formulation and planning services in addition to providing an active supervisory role related to state penal roles. Particularly, the Central government aids the states in the maintenance of internal security measures, modernization of law enforcement infrastructure, and oversees correctional administration in the states. The government also provides facilities and support for ad hoc advanced training in forensics and technological advancements in criminal science.

Indian prisons meet the basic requirements of human rights protection. Some prison administrators, however, concede that the prevailing conditions of poverty in Indian society contribute to recidivism because a prison sentence guarantees minimal levels of food, clothing, and shelter.

Prison conditions vary from state to state. The states that have more resources have better facilities. These prosperous states have better rehabilitation programs as compared to the states that are not politically or economically wealthy. The poorer states provide the most minimal facilities and barest accommodations. Male and female prisoners are housed in separate prisons. Conditions for holding prisoners also vary according to classification.

Plea Bargaining

A recent June 2006 amendment to the Criminal Procedure Code of India confers a provision for plea bargaining in certain cases. The relevant section of the statute, Chapter XXI A, allows plea bargaining to be used in criminal cases where the prescribed maximum punishment is below seven years. Exceptions include cases where the victim is (1) a minor under the age of 14; (2) where the victim is a woman; or (3) where the crime is likely to affect the socioeconomic condition of the country. There are also provisions in the amendment aimed at policing the plea bargaining process, to ensure that the compliance of the accused is not predicated on coercive or corrupt tactics.

Compensation to Victims of Crime

Inherent as a critical keystone of the Indian Criminal Justice System is the dual desire to punish and reform criminals. An equally compelling motivation is to award both compensatory and punitive damages to the victim. A reconciliatory attempt to pursue these objectives is reflected in the Code of Criminal Procedure, 1973, § 357 and the Probation of Offenders Act, 1958, § 5. These statutory provisions empower the court to provide compensation to the victims of crime. All courts are empowered to exercise such provisions and award adequate compensatory damages to the victim, particularly when an accused is released on probation or when the parties settle a dispute. Indigent victims of illegal detention by governmental authorities may recover compensatory damages under article 21 of the Constitution of India.

Suman Kakar

Further Reading

Hazra, A. K., and Bibek Debroy, eds. (2007). *Judicial Reforms in India: Issues and Aspects*. New Delhi: Academic Foundation (Publishers) in Association with Rajiv Gandhi Institute for Contemporary Studies.

Kalpana, Kannabiran, and Ranbir Singh, eds. (2008). *Challenging the Rule(s) of Law: Colonialism, Criminology and Human Rights in India*. New Delhi: Sage.

Rajgopal, P. R. (1988). *Violence and Response: A Critique of the Indian Criminal Justice Process*. New Delhi: Centre for Policy Research, Uppal Publishing House.

South Asia Human Rights Documentation Centre. (2007). *Handbook of Human Rights and*

Criminal Justice in India: The System and Procedure (2007). South Asia Human Rights Documentation Centre. Delhi: Oxford University Press.

Indonesia

Legal System: Civil/Islamic/Customary
Murder: Low
Burglary: Medium
Corruption: Medium
Human Trafficking: Medium
Prison Rate: Low
Death Penalty: Yes
Corporal Punishment: Yes

Background

Indonesia, the largest archipelagic state in the world, located in Southeast Asia, comprises approximately 17,508 islands. Its total area is about 1,919,440 square kilometers (735,355 square miles). Indonesia is a heterogeneous and multiethnic country, with a Muslim majority; however, constitutionally it is not an Islamic state. The estimation of population in 2009 is around 240 million. Most of the population (about 65%) lives on Java Island, in which Jakarta (the capital city of Indonesia) is located. Java is the fifth largest island in Indonesia.

Prior to Indonesia's independence in 1945, the Indonesia legal system was a dual legal pluralism. During the preindependence Dutch Colonial era, the Western people and certain Asian nationalities, especially the Chinese, were acknowledged as similar in status as the Western people and were subject to the formal Western civil law system, while the indigenous people were subject to its customary (*adat*) law. Since its independence, both legal systems (Western as well as adat) have been applied to all Indonesian citizens. The use of the Dutch legal system was based on the Indonesian Constitution 1945 that stipulates that before the new law could be enacted, the previously existing law would still be applied until the new one was enacted, and adat law (even canonical law) has also been adhered to by various ethnic groups.

Under the Soekarno regime, the authority of the judicial bodies was under control of the executive body. The president had the right to direct the work of the judicial bodies and select and promote the judges. Article 19 of Law Number 19/1964 stipulates that the president could interfere at any stage of the judicial process for the sake of the ongoing revolution. Under the ideology of Guided Democracy, the rule of law and the concept of "state based on law," the radical-populist ideology emphasized substantive rather than procedural justice. This policy was ended in 1970 after the successor of Soekarno, General Soeharto, took over. The new order continued until 1998. The first fundamental change in the legal system was the replacement of Law Number 19/1964 by Law Number 14/1970 that reverted back to the judicial bodies as autonomous bodies. However, the judicial bodies did not really have their independence, since the selection and promotion of the judges and the budget was still under the control of the executive. The police, as the first institution that operated in the criminal justice system, were placed under the coordination of the Indonesian Army. Finally, when the Soeharto regime collapsed in 1998, based on Law Number 4/2004, the judicial bodies had their own independence in administering their own arrangements, such as budgeting, selecting, and promoting of the judges of first and appellate courts and nominating candidates of the judges of the Supreme Court to Parliament.

In 1981, the Indonesian government successfully established a new law on the Administration of Criminal Justice (Law Number 8/1981), replacing the Dutch Administration of Criminal Justice, while the Administration of Civil Justice had still been using the Dutch law. The adat law jurisdiction was limited to civil cases of its relevant ethnic groups, while canonical law, especially Islam law jurisdiction, was limited to marital and inheritance cases. After the fall of Soeharto in 1998, which brought about the reformation and regional autonomy era, the Aceh Province was granted authority to apply Islamic law (*syariah*) to its followers in that area.

In the area of criminal justice, there is a sharp distinction between the Dutch law and the new Indonesian law in terms of the system. The Dutch legal system applies the inquisitorial system, while the Indonesian Administration of Criminal Justice 1981 applies the accusatorial system. The principles of the new law put forward the idea of presumption of innocence, rather than presumption of guilt, and provide wide ranges of protection for the rights of the suspect.

Since 1990, the Indonesian police have become an independent organization responsible directly to the president. The Indonesian National Police (INP) or Kepolisian Negara Republik Indonesia (POLRI), a national organization, is financed, directed, and organized by the central government. By 2004 the INP staffed approximately 285,000 people, serving for approximately 220,000,000 citizens. The functions of the INP as stipulated by Law Number 2/2000 focus on public security and order maintenance; law enforcement; protection, guardians, and services to the public. Based on Presidential Decree Number 70/2002 concerning the INP Organizational Structure, the top of the organization is INP Headquarters (Markas Besar Kepolisian Republik Indonesia/MABES POLRI). The implementation of the police functions is carried out by the following four organizational bodies at the MABES level:

1. The Board of Intelligence and Security (Badan Intelijen Keamanan/BAINTELKAM)
2. The Board of Criminal Investigation of Crimes (Badan Reserse Kriminal/BARESKRIM)
3. The Board of the Maintenance of Internal Security (Badan Pembinaan Keamanan/BABINKAM)
4. The Mobile Brigade (Brigade Mobil/BRIMOB)

As the Indonesian National Police is a national organization, the operational activities at province level are carried out by regional police, namely POLDA (Kepolisian Daerah). At the district level, the operational activities are carried out by POLRES (Kepolisian Resor). Under the POLRES are the smallest operational units, namely POLSEK (Kepolisian Sektor), equivalent to police precinct; the jurisdiction of POLSEK is equal to a subdistrict. Since Java Island and Madura Island are the most densely populated islands, there are subregional police, namely POLWIL (Kepolisian Wilayah), under the POLDA to coordinate the operation of several POLRES in its jurisdiction. POLDA Metropolitan Jakarta Raya, POLDA Yogyakarta, and POLDA Banten, nevertheless, have no POLWIL units. Every provincial capital city, except Jakarta, has POLTABES (Kepolisian Kota Besar), whose organizational ranks are similar to the POLWIL in Java.

At the POLSEK level, there are five units to support the POLSEK tasks; each is led by the chief of unit, namely Unit Intelijen dan Pengamanan/Intelkam (Police Intelligence Unit), Unit Reserse (Criminal Investigation Unit), Unit Samapta Bhayangkara/Shabara (Police Patrol Unit), and Unit Binamitra (Community Policing Unit). Unit Intelijen dan Pengamanan (Police Intelligence) has the state security and intelligence function.

Unit Lalu-lintas (Traffic Police Unit) is complementary to the POLSEK, depending on the needs of the area. The office location is usually separated from the POLSEK office. This unit is accountable to the traffic police section at the POLRES level and responsible for the enforcement of traffic law and highway patrol. At the POLRES level, the traffic unit is also responsible for issuing driving licenses, motor vehicle licenses, and registrations.

Crime

Classification of Crime

According to the Indonesian Criminal Code (*Wetboek van Straftrecht*), which was inherited from the Dutch Indian Colonial, criminal actions are divided into two categories. The first category, as stipulated in Book II of the Criminal Code, is regarding criminal actions classified as crimes (*misdrijven*), while the other category at Book III of the Criminal Code regards criminal actions classified as offenses (*overtredingen*). Book II of the Criminal Code stipulates either treason or felonies, while Book III of the Criminal Code stipulates misdemeanors only. The punishment inflicted for treason and felonies ranges from imprisonment (a maximum of 20 years), life sentence to capital punishment, while the punishment inflicted for misdemeanors is mainly in the form of fines. Book I of the Criminal Code stipulates the definitions of terms, types of punishment, procedures to be followed in criminal cases, and specific attempts, accessories, mitigating as well as incriminating circumstances that may affect the severity of a sentence. Outside the Criminal Code, there is some law stipulating certain criminal offenses, such as corruption, environmental crimes, terrorism, drug trafficking, and other forms of transnational crimes.

Treason comprises crimes against state security (killing of the president and vice president, separatism, rebellion, revealing state defense secrets); crimes against the honor of the president and vice president; crimes against friendship states, statements, and diplomats; crimes against the implementation of civil rights and duties; individual fighting; crimes against public security and property security; crimes against public officials; false oath; counterfeiting of notes and state seals; counterfeiting of documents; crimes against civil status, and so forth. Felonies comprise crimes against public order; crimes against decency; abandonment of people in need of help; causing humiliation; discovering occupational secrecy; crimes against persons; crimes against human lives (i.e., murder); crimes against the body (i.e., assault, rape), including negligence; crimes against property (i.e., larceny, robbery); blackmail and extortion; embezzlements; deceptions; vandalism; crimes in the course of an occupation; crimes in the course of ship navigation and seamanship; crimes against aviation infrastructures; and aiding crimes.

According to the Law of Juvenile Justice (Law Number 3/1977), the minimum age of criminal responsibility is eight years old. A juvenile between 8 years and 18 years old who commits criminal offenses should be brought to Juvenile Court. Currently, there is a discussion to reform such a minimum age of criminal responsibility to be at least 15 years old.

Crimes that are particularly challenging to Indonesia are human trafficking, terrorism attacks, and drug offenses. The International Organization of Migration (IOM) (with the assistance of IOM Indonesia) has reported that between March 2005 and January 2008, of 3,042 victims, 88.9 percent were female and only 11.1 percent male, 74.0 percent were adult and 25.8 percent children, and 0.2 percent infants.

Marked by the suicide bombing of Bali I on October 22, 2002, some terrorism attacks in Indonesia since 2002 have become issues of transnational crimes. Since that bombing, there have been three incidents of suicide bombing, which include a suicide bombing in the Hotel Marriott on August 5, 2003, a suicide bombing attack at the Australian Embassy in Jakarta on September 9, 2004, and a suicide bombing attack known as Bali II on October 1, 2005.

The seriousness of the drug offenses is marked by the increasing number of drug-related prisoners and the involvement of international networks in drug trafficking. Several actions that are defined as crimes in relation to drug offenses are illegal possession of drugs, illegal drug use, drug trafficking, and drug production. Trafficking and production of drugs could be punished with death penalty.

Since 1998, which is noted as an era of reformation, corruption has been considered one of the most serious crimes. A special state commission named the Anti Corruption Commission (Komisi Pemberantasan Korupsi) was established in 2004, whose special task is to investigate and to prosecute corruptors in a Special Anti Corruption Court.

Crime Statistics

Crime statistics collected by the Bureau of Planning and Administration of the Indonesia National Police for 2007 were as follows:

Murder	1,236
Rape	2,224
Violent attack	18,799
Robbery	10,140
Motor vehicle theft	32,042
Drug-related offenses	9,254

From 2001 to 2007, the homicide rate declined by 44 percent, though rape increased by 78.2 percent. Violent attacks and robbery fluctuated over the same period. Motor vehicle theft and drug offenses increased substantially over the period.

Police performance as indicated by crime clearance between 2001 and 2007 was relatively steady at the level of between 51 percent and 59 percent.

Finding of Guilt

Article 1 of the Criminal Code stipulates that no one shall be punished if there is not any law that has been breached. This stipulation is in line with the presumption of innocence principle, in which the accused should be regarded as innocent until the court finds him or her guilty. In this sense, the accused has the right to remain silent since he or she was arrested by the police and during the trial. It is the duty of the attorney to prove the guilt of the accused. There is no jury system used in Indonesia. However, to preserve objectivity of the trial, the criminal trial is conducted by a judicial panel that consists of three judges. The judges' verdict must be based on at least two pieces of evidence and ultimately based on their firm conclusion as to the guilt of the accused. Even though the accused has the right for a speedy trial, such a right is obstructed by the provision of pretrial detention up to 120 days that may be requested by the police and the public prosecutor.

Basically the accused has the right to be assisted by a lawyer before and during the trial. However, free legal aid is only available for the poor who are accused of legal offenses punishable with at least five years' imprisonment. Lawyers who provide free legal aid for the poor receive a very small financial compensation from the government budget. As a result, the provision of legal aid is not attractive to the professional lawyers, and only the young lawyers or apprentice lawyers have the interest to do this job.

The investigation of crime is conducted by the police. Law Number 8/1981 on the administration of criminal justice stipulates that the role of the criminal investigator is divided into two sorts of officials, namely: (1) "investigator," an official of the national police or a certain official of the civil service who by law is granted special authority to conduct an investigation; and (2) "junior investigator," an official of the national police who is granted authority by this law to perform a preliminary investigation. These investigators have two somewhat different tasks. The investigation conducted by the investigator is a series of acts regulated by legal procedure for the gathering of evidence to clarify whether an offense has occurred and to locate the suspect. The preliminary investigation, then, is a series of acts by a junior investigator to seek for and to find an event that is presumed to be an offense to determine whether or not an investigation may be carried out by means regulated in this law.

The specified tasks for the investigator consist of accepting a report or complaint from a person about the existence of an offense; taking the first step at the crime scene; ordering a suspect to stop and examine the suspect's identification; carrying out an arrest, detention, search and seizure; examining and seizing documents; fingerprinting and photographing a person; summoning a person to be heard or examined as a suspect or a witness; calling in an expert required in connection with the examination of a case; terminating an investigation; taking other acts in accordance with law.

An investigator does not have a duty to prosecute the suspect before the court. The investigator should deliver the dossier of a case to the public prosecutor. The delivery of the dossier of a case to the public prosecutor shall be accomplished as below.

At the first stage, the investigator shall deliver only the dossier of a case; where the investigation is deemed to have been completed, the investigator shall cede responsibility for the suspect and the physical evidence to the public prosecutor. The prosecution of the suspect is the duty of the public prosecutor based on the dossier of a case submitted by the investigator. The prosecutor may terminate the case if it is not provided with sufficient evidence or did not substantiate a criminal case. If the prosecutor proceeds with the case, the prosecutor must submit the case before the court as soon as possible.

Basically, there is no alternative other than going to trial. However, there is a provision stipulating that the police have the right to terminate the investigation, and the public prosecutor has the right to terminate the prosecution. Such rights spark criticism from lawyers and nongovernmental organizations who are concerned with the judicial process; they suspect such a procedure may easily lead to corruption. There are many cases involving financial scandals in the Central Bank (Bank Indonesia), to which the attorney general has released decisions terminating prosecution, which were harshly criticized by the public. In the illegal drug use cases, there is a provision that the judges should send the users to treatment. However, up to 2008, there has been no judge's verdict that applied such a provision. Some judges have argued that they have insufficient information regarding medical facilities that exist for treatment of drug users. Actually, there are many narcotics treatment institutions that were built to fulfill the provision of the antinarcotics law. And since 2008 the National Anti Narcotics Board (Badan Narkotika Nasional) has had a narcotic rehabilitation center that provides medical treatment for drug users.

Most of the accused in criminal cases brought before the court are usually found guilty and are sentenced to imprisonment. For trivial cases and first offenses, the judges will release a probationary verdict. Pretrial detention, or incarceration before trial, is allowed by the law of criminal justice procedure, and the judges will calculate the length of detention as part of the imprisonment. The judges have discretionary authority to impose a lesser punishment.

The court system consists of four branches, namely general courts, religious courts, military courts, and administrative courts. The criminal court is part of the general court. There is no specialization of the judges, whether he or she is a criminal judge or civil judge. There are 3,015 judges in the general courts. To be a judge, a person should hold a law degree and be admitted to the judge training program for approximately one year. Postgraduation, they are not directly appointed to be a judge. They have to be apprentice judges for one year, acting as district court registrars before finally being appointed judges of district court.

The juvenile trial is conducted by a special judge of the district court who has an interest in juvenile problems. The trial is conducted informally. The judge, the attorney, and the social worker do not wear uniforms, and the child should be accompanied by his or her parents. It is compulsory to attach a social report of the child provided by the social worker. The child can be brought before the juvenile court if he or she is between 8 and 18 years old.

Punishment

Types of Punishment

The provision of punishment as stipulated in the Criminal Code comprises the death penalty, life sentence, imprisonment, fines, publication of the sentence, and probation. Punishments listed in the Criminal Code are allowed the maximum. However, the judges have discretionary authority to impose lesser punishment. The victim of crime has the right to sue the offenders before the court during criminal examination. The provision of reparation and compensation to the victims applies only to the gross violation of human rights, if the judge's verdict explicitly orders the offender to do so. Law on the elimination of domestic violence (Law Number 23/2004) stipulates the protection and reparation of victims of domestic violence and that such protection and reparation should be conducted by the government.

The punishment for an intentional murder ranges from 20 years of imprisonment to life sentence to death penalty. A murder committed along with other incriminating offenses may be punished with life sentence or a maximum of 12 years' imprisonment. A murder without full intent may be punished with a maximum of 12 years' imprisonment. A planned infanticide by the mother is punishable with a maximum of nine years' imprisonment, while an infanticide without a plan is punished by a maximum of seven years' imprisonment.

The maximum punishment for a forcible rape to a woman is 12 years of imprisonment. A rape to an unconscious or vulnerable woman is punishable with a maximum of nine years' imprisonment. The law on the elimination of domestic violence (Law Number 23/2004) stipulates that a marital rape shall be punished with a maximum of 12 years' imprisonment or fines of IDR 36,000,000 (about US$3,600).

A punishment imposed for a theft with incriminating factors is a maximum of nine years of imprisonment. A theft that causes death to the victim or the witness shall be punished with a maximum of 15 years of imprisonment, while a burglary that causes death with incriminating factors shall be punished with a maximum of 20 years of imprisonment. The incriminating factors of the burglary may vary, which include committing at night, committing in closed/locked properties, being committed by two or more people in a group, breaking and entering, and causing injury or death.

There are two laws related to drug offenses, namely, Law on Narcotics Crimes and Law on Psychotropic Crimes. The types of punishment depend on the offense committed, and the types of drugs. The most serious drug offenses are production and trafficking, which shall be punished by death penalty.

The death penalty is one of the forms of punishment stipulated in the Criminal Code. Some criminal sanctions that are not stipulated in the Criminal Code also impose the death penalty. The law on narcotics is an example. Several drug offenders have been executed. The execution method is shooting to death by a group of police officers usually in a remote area. The public prosecutor who prosecutes the case before the court must be present at the execution. There have been 12 prisoners executed between 2004 and 2008. This includes, in 2008, the three masterminds of the Bali I bombing—an event that drew international attention.

Prison

The directorate general of corrections has revealed that, as of August 2008, the total number of inmates (prisoners and detainees) was 137,144, consisting of 130,895 males (95.44%) and 6,249 females (4.56%). The number of prisoners was 81,127 (59.2%), while the detainees numbered 56,017 (40.8%). The number of male prisoners was 77,531 (95.57%), and female prisoners was 3,596 (4.43%). The number of male detainees was 53,364 (95.26%), and female detainees was 2,653 (4.74%). The number of juvenile inmates was very low, with the total number of 2,837 (2% of the total inmates), which consisted of 2,760 boys (97.28%) and 77 girls (2.72%). The number of foreign inmates was 549 (0.4% of the total inmates), consisting of 424 (0.31% of the total inmates) prisoners and 125 detainees (0.09% of the total inmates). Among the foreign inmates, there were 537 males (97.81%) and 12 females (2.19%). The number of death row prisoners was 99 (0.07% of the total inmates), and life sentence prisoners was 153 (0.11% of the total inmates). The number of drug-related inmates was 38,427 (28.02% of total inmates), consisting of 27,062 prisoners (19.73% of total inmates) and 11,365 detainees (8.29% of total inmates). Among the drug-related inmates, there were 35,832 males (93.25%) and 2,595 (6.75%) females.

The daily average number of inmates based on the capacity of the detention centers between 1995 and 2002 has shown that the problem of overcrowding has existed since 2002. By 1995, the daily average number of inmates was 47,047, with the total accommodation capacity of 64,047 inmates (72.81% occupation rate), while in 2002 the daily average number of inmates was 67,960, with the total accommodation capacity of 64,345 (105.62%) inmates.

There were 408 prisons and detention centers in 2008, consisting of 220 prisons and 188 detention centers. In fact, the detention centers also accommodate prisoners, whereas the prisons accommodate detainees as well. Although most of the biggest prisons are located in the capital cities of provinces, there is a small island in south central Java, namely, Nusa Kambangan, that is used to hold various types of prisons. Most of them were built during the colonial era and were known as the deadly prisons. Nowadays, there are a maximum security prison, medium security prison, and minimum security prison (open prison) located in Nusa Kambangan. The special narcotics prison, super maximum security prison, and one open prison were recently built.

Formally, every prisoner should participate in working activities. However, due to overcrowding in most prisons, only several prisons provide working activities programs. As a result, the working activities and other treatment programs could not be implemented. The wards of the prison concentrate mainly on maintaining the security of the prison. An exception to this is the newly built narcotics prison where the treatment of drug users is still being implemented.

Every inmate has the right of a visitation. The visit permit for the prisoners' relatives can be obtained at the prison site; the visit permit for detainees, however, must be obtained from some institutions in charge of the detention, for example, the police, the prosecutor, or the judges, depending on the examination steps undergone by the particular detainee. There are several rights that may be granted to the prisoners, for example, parole or home visits, if the prisoners show good behavior. Remission of the sentences may also be granted annually.

Even though there are many foreign prisoners, there is no provision for transfer of prisoners yet. This situation may affect the rights of foreign prisoners, since most of the foreigner prisoners' visas will be overdue after their release, and thus they shall be referred to immigration quarantine, or sent back to their home countries immediately at their own cost. Poor foreign prisoners or prisoners from poor countries in particular face this problem.

Muhammad Mustofa

Further Reading

Atmasasmita, R. (1996). *Bunga Rampai Hukum Acara Pidana. (Reading in the Administration of Criminal Justice).* Bandung: Alumni.

Lev, D. S. (1978). *Judicial Authority and the Struggle for an Indonesian Rechtsstaat.* Reprinted from *Law and Society Review* 13(1) (Fall): 37–71.

Leyser, J. (1954). "Legal Developments in Indonesia." *The American Journal of Comparative Law* 3(3) (Summer): 399–411.

Rosenberg, R., ed. (2003). *Perdagangan Perempuan dan Anak di Indonesia (Trafficking of Women and Children in Indonesia).* Jakarta: ICMC.

Japan

Legal System: Civil/Common
Murder: Low
Burglary: Low
Corruption: Low
Human Trafficking: Medium
Prison Rate: Low
Death Penalty: Yes
Corporal Punishment: No

Background

Japan comprises five main islands (Hokkaido, Honshu, Shikoku, Kyushu, and Okinawa), with additional remote small islands, and is located in the east of the Eurasian continent. The Japanese population is approximately 128 million people, and the land size is about 145,920 square miles. Thus, the population density in Japan is approximately 877 people per square mile. The capital of Japan is Tokyo, located near the center of Honshu Island.

Historically, Japanese culture was heavily influenced by China and other countries located in the eastern part of the Eurasian continent. For example, the techniques to crop and cultivate rice, the Japanese people's main diet, were imported via the continent approximately 3,000 years ago. Furthermore, the Japanese language has its origin in China. The influence of Western culture in Japan can be observed primarily after the 16th century when a group of Christian missionaries arrived in Japan.

In terms of economy, Japan may be most notable in its rapid economical development after World War II. The annual economic growth rates during the 1960s and 1970s were more than 10 percent on average, while they were approximately 2–3 percent after 2000.

Sociodemographic Characteristics

Japanese society is homogeneous with 99 percent of the country's population being ethnic Japanese and having the same historical background. Japan is often viewed as a group-oriented society rather than an individualistic society. Japanese society is also characterized by the hierarchical system, which is observed in the language and behavior exhibited by Japanese people in business and personal contexts. This is grounded in cultural traditions of Confucianism, which stresses respect and honor toward an elder.

Political System

The Japanese government is often considered a centralized government, and because of this, Japanese scholars view the federal, state, and local governments as exercising their political power equally over their constituents. The contemporary Japanese political system has been influenced by the prewar political system based on the 19th-century German and British parliamentary models. Its political system has also been affected by the Constitution of Japan, which was established in 1947 and largely influenced by the U.S. government during the post–World War II occupation.

The government is fundamentally divided into executive, legislative, and judicial branches. The Constitution also guarantees the separation of state power. In particular, the executive power resides in the Cabinet and the legislative power resides in the Diet, while the judicial power resides in the Supreme Court and other lower courts. As the head of the judicial branch, the chief justice stands at the same rank as the prime minister, who is the head of the Cabinet (the executive branch). To preserve fairness in the criminal justice system, the status of the judges is protected by the Constitution, and they can only be removed from their jobs by public impeachment.

Legal System

Under the Constitution, there are five main legal codes: the Civil Code, the Penal Code, the Code of Civil Procedure, the Code of Criminal Procedure, and the Commercial Code. The Japanese justice system has changed dramatically since the Meiji Restoration of 1868. The Penal Code and Code of Criminal Procedure, which were based on French models, were publicly promulgated in 1880. Under these codes, offenses and punishments for the offenses were specified, all citizens were treated equally, and the justice system was centralized. However, this system did not incorporate the defendant's presumption of innocence and frequently used capital punishment as a means to solve criminal cases.

The Japanese criminal law and prison law were revised in 1907 to reflect German law, but the rights of the accused did not become a main issue until post–World War II. The system became adversarial, and the judge decided a case based on evidence presented by both sides. The juvenile law was not reformed until 1947.

Crime

Classification of Crime

The primary legal code that defines crime and punishment in Japan is the Penal Code. The current Penal Code was enacted in 1907, although the code has continued to be revised as Japanese society underwent changes over time. For example, as a special class of crimes, crimes against the Imperial family were abolished as a result of the postwar reconstruction of Japanese society. Furthermore, articles that imposed harsher punishments for individuals who had committed bodily injury, fatal injury, or murder against their family members were deleted in 1995. Although the vast majority of crimes (e.g., homicides, rape, robbery, assault, and larceny) are defined by the Penal Code, it is important to note that other legal codes, often categorized as Special Codes, also define crimes. Examples of Special Codes are the Traffic Law, the Stimulants Control Law, the Firearms and Sword Control Law, and Anti-prostitution Law.

There are several sources of official crime statistics in Japan. The White Paper on Police is published annually by the National Police Agency, while the White Paper on Crime is published by the Ministry of Justice. Although both white papers report the number of reported crimes and the number of cases cleared, additional information is presented by each white paper. For example, the White Paper on Police often discusses emerging trends in crime and recent police activities. The White Paper on Crime, on the other hand, discusses topics in corrections and rehabilitation, as the Ministry of Justice is responsible for correctional and rehabilitation services. Additionally, the Annual Report of Judicial Statistics, published by the Supreme Court, summarizes information on the number of criminal cases, as well as their dispositions.

The White Paper on Police categorizes crimes as felonious offenses, violent offenses, larceny offenses, intellectual offenses, moral offenses, and other offenses. Felonious offenses include murder, robbery, arson, and rape. Violent offenses include assault, bodily injury, intimidation, extortion, and unlawful assembly with dangerous weapons. Larceny offenses include both burglary and nonburglary thefts. Intellectual offenses include fraud, embezzlement, counterfeiting, official corruption, and breach of trust. Moral offenses include gambling and sexual offenses (including indecent assault and indecent exposure). The number of crimes reported to police in 2005 were as follows:

Felonious offenses	11,360
Murder	1,392
Robbery	5,988
Arson	1,904
Rape	2,076
Violent offenses	73,772
Assault	25,815
Bodily injury	34,484
Intimidation	2,479
Extortion	10,978
Assembly with dangerous weapons	16
Larceny offenses	1,725,072
Burglary	244,776
Theft of vehicles/bicycles	556,987
Nonburglary theft	923,309
Intellectual offenses	97,500
Moral offenses	12,085
Other offenses	349,504
Total offenses	**2,269,293**

Of the four felonious offenses, robbery constituted the most frequent offense category. Additionally, there were 1.1 homicides per 100,000 people. Of the five categories of violent offenses, bodily injury comprised the biggest category, followed by assault.

Larceny offenses (including both burglary and nonburglary) were reported, with the highest frequency among felonious, violent, larceny, intellectual, and moral offenses. Of larceny offenses, 53 percent were nonburglary thefts; 33 percent were thefts of bicycles, motorcycles, and vehicles; and 14 percent were burglaries.

As for the proportion of cases cleared by the police, the clearance rate for homicide stood out at about 97 percent. The clearance rates for homicide had been consistently high throughout the modern history of the Japanese criminal justice system. The clearance rates for other felonious and violent offenses were also relatively high, ranging from approximately 50–70 percent. Compared to other offense types, clearance rates for larceny offenses are relatively low at 25 percent.

The total number of crimes known to police, derived from Penal Codes and Special Codes, excludes 855,644 cases of professional negligence in traffic accidents, which was 27.4 percent of the total number of crimes known to police. As professional negligence in traffic accidents comprises a substantial amount of the crimes in Japan, a failure to exclude it from statistics often distorts crime trends in Japan.

The trends of crimes in Japan between 1945 and 2005, excluding professional negligence in traffic accidents, stayed around 1,500,000 cases per year for a long time after World War II, until it increased sharply in the late 1990s. The number of crimes peaked in 2002 at about 2,854,000. While such a rapid increase in the level of crime might give an impression of worsening safety conditions in Japanese society, several scholars cautioned for such an interpretation. In particular, as a reaction to several police scandals in the late 1990s, the National Police Agency issued a guideline for police officers taking police reports. As a result, police officers were required to process many minor consultation issues as part of their police reports. Thus, it is quite possible that this administrative change is one of the reasons why the number of crimes known to police increased sharply in this time period.

Organized Crime Groups and Drug Crimes

Despite relatively low levels of crime in Japan, of particular challenge to the safety of citizens and law enforcement activities are organized crime groups, known as *yakuza*, and youth motorcycle gangs, known as *bosozoku.* According to the White Paper on Crime, there were about 43,300 regular members and 43,000 associate members of the Japanese mafia (*yakuza*) in 2005. The number of incidents of disputes between rival groups was 18, and guns were used in 11 of them. Although the number of disputes among *yakuza* and the usage of guns may seem low, these statistics need to be interpreted within the context of Japanese society.

The Japanese government imposes a very strong gun control policy. Although citizens are allowed to own hunting guns, they are required to go through strict background checks. For example, when citizens apply for a permit of owning hunting guns, police officers not only check the criminal history of the applicants through their database, but also ask neighbors of the applicants about behavioral and social problems associated with the applicants. The possession of handguns is illegal, as defined by the Firearms and Sword Control Law. The police confiscated 489 handguns in 2005. Because of the strict gun control policy, the number of shooting incidents is relatively low in Japan. There were 76 incidents of shooting in 2005, which was a substantial decrease from about 200 shooting incidents in 2001. Ten people died of shooting in 2005.

Furthermore, according to the White Paper on Crime in 2001, there were 23,399 *bosozoku* (youth motorcycle gangs) members in 1,165 groups. Group size varied, but 6.5 percent of them had 30 or more members. Among crimes committed by juveniles, approximately 25 percent of murders, 10 percent of robbery and bodily injury, 6 percent of intimidation/extortion, and 1 percent of larceny were done by *bosozoku* members. In addition to the fact that substantial numbers of juvenile offenses were committed by members of motorcycle gangs, it is notable that their behaviors affect the quality of life of law-abiding citizens. For example, motorcycle gang members typically get together at night on weekends and ride their specially customized motorcycles to make loud noises. Furthermore, motorcycle gangs often become recruitment places for *yakuza* (Japanese mafia) members, providing generational ties across criminal groups.

In addition to violent offenses, the *yakuza* is closely involved in illicit drug markets. Major illegal drug types in Japan include methamphetamine, cocaine, heroin, synthetic drugs (e.g., MDMA), opium, and cannabis. The major criminal codes defining these illegal drugs are Opium Law, Stimulants Control Law, Cannabis Control Law, and Narcotics Control Law. According to these criminal codes, selling, possessing, trading, producing, and using drugs are considered crimes. Of these illegal drugs, the majority of offenders are charged with violation of the Stimulants Control Law that mainly regulates methamphetamine (13,549 offenders in 2005), followed by violation of the Opium Law (2,063 offenders in 2005).

Although the number of drug offenses in Japan is relatively low compared to other offenses such as larceny offenses, the law enforcement agencies tackle the crimes very seriously as illegal drugs are considered as major money sources of organized crime groups. For example, of the arrested offenders in drug crimes, approximately 50 percent were members of *yakuza* groups. Furthermore, the majority of these offenders were charged with trading and possession of illegal drugs, indicating their close involvement in the illicit market. In addition to the police and related agencies investigating and preventing drug offenses, the correctional agency operating prisons provides specialized rehabilitation programs for inmates convicted of drug offenses.

The general public's attitudes toward illegal drugs are quite different from those held in the Western world. For example, more than 90 percent of the general public identified methamphetamine and marijuana as "very scary things" in a government survey in 2005. Moreover, discussions about legalizing marijuana use, even for medical purposes, are rare. Additionally, Japan as an island nation helps law enforcement agencies relatively easily prevent drugs from being smuggled in by limiting entry points. Various law enforcement agencies, such as the police, customs officers, and the Japan Coast Guard, cooperatively work in preventing drugs from being smuggled in.

Crimes Committed by Foreigners

In 2005, 14,786 foreign nationals were arrested, which accounted for a total of 43,622 crimes (Penal Code offenses excluding the professional negligence in traffic accidents). More than 80 percent of these offenders were from Asian countries. In 2005, based upon the nationality of foreign offenders, the top country was China (40.2%), followed by Korea (12.6%), the Philippines (8.0%), Brazil (6.0%), and Thailand (3.8%).

Japan has an international treaty with the United States and Republic of Korea. The treaty allows Japan to transfer American and Korean criminals to their home countries upon request of a criminal justice agency. Furthermore, the transferring of other foreign national criminals can also be done if mutual cooperation is expected from their corresponding governments. Finally, there are several penal institutions that provide special accommodations for prisoners with foreign nationality.

Police

The police are a primary agency in charge of crime prevention, as well as criminal investigation. As both activities are key roles of the police at the local level, the Police Law enacted in 1947 highlights local autonomy of policing, although one legal system governs the whole nation.

The organization of Japanese police forces can be divided into two levels: national and prefectural levels. The police organization at the national level is called the National Police Agency, while there are 47 prefectural police headquarters, one in each prefecture, at the local level. Both at the national and prefectural levels, the police are administratively supervised by their respective public safety commissions (the National Public Safety Commission is above the National Police Agency and the respective Prefectural Public Safety Commission is above each prefectural police headquarters). The members of the public safety commissions are all civilians. These safety commissions were implemented after World War II to safeguard democratic administration and ensure political neutrality in police operations. They were deemed necessary as the authoritative power of the police had been abused by the national government during the war.

At the national level, the National Police Agency acts as a central agency to supervise all prefectural police, and it controls national policies related to police matters. The vast majority of law enforcement activities are, however, conducted at the local level. This is clearly indicated by the number of personnel belonging to the National Police Agency and the prefectural police. There are 1,700 police officers and 4,500 civilians working at the National Police Agency, while 250,000 police officers and 29,000 civilians are employed at the prefectural police offices. The Tokyo Metropolitan Police Department, which employs about 42,000 police officers, is the largest among prefectural police offices. Nationwide, there are about 11,600 female officers. Female officers are expected to play a larger role than their male counterparts in tackling juvenile delinquency, sex crimes, and child abuse.

A unique feature of the Japanese policing is its application of the police box system, known as *koban*. The police box (*koban*) system is implemented nationally and, in many neighborhoods, more than one police officer is assigned to a police box around the clock. Officers use the police box as their base camp for foot patrols and as their office for writing reports. Furthermore, officers are responsible for visiting each household in their neighborhood. Therefore, officers can get to know neighborhood residents and communicate with them regarding safety information, such as recent crime incidents in the area as well as basic crime prevention tips. Officers stationed at the police box can act as agents to strengthen informal social control in neighborhoods, in addition to their formal patrols.

Finding of Guilt

Justice System and Rights of Accused

A number of actors play parts in the current Japanese criminal justice system. The police are considered as the principal law enforcement agency in crime prevention and criminal investigations. The public prosecutor also participates in investigations, especially at later stages, and takes part in prosecuting criminals at the court. Japanese criminal trials employ the adversary trial system to balance the finding of the truth and protect the rights of the accused.

Historically, the modern Japanese criminal justice system was established in the late 19th to the early 20th centuries with considerable influence from the French and German criminal justice systems. Under this modern criminal justice system, however, the rights of the accused were greatly limited. For example, the presumption of innocence was hardly maintained in criminal trials, because the same judge was involved in pretrials (similar to an arraignment) and formal trials. Furthermore, the police often abused their power to gain confessions.

The current Japanese criminal justice system can be considered as a hybrid of the continental European and the Anglo-American criminal justice systems. After World War II, the American government became closely involved in the postwar reconstruction of Japan. At the heart of the reconstruction was passage of a constitution that fully acknowledges fundamental human rights. Among the 103 articles in the Japanese Constitution, more than 10 are concerned with the rights of the accused and proper application of criminal procedures. These include due process of law in criminal procedures; strict judicial requirements for warrants of search, seizure, and arrest; the right to defense counsel; the right to remain silent; the right to a fair and speedy trial; the right to a public trial; the right to examine/cross-examine witnesses; evidential rules of confession; the protection against double jeopardy; and the right to monetary compensation by the state if detained but subsequently found not guilty.

As the Constitution lays the foundations of the Japanese judiciary, the Code of Criminal Procedure further articulates the rights of the accused, legal restrictions of criminal investigations, prosecutions, and criminal trials. For example, the adversary system is adapted at the trial stage. Furthermore, as a safety measure against abuse of police authority, strict requirements of judicial warrants for compulsory investigative measures (i.e., search, seizure, and arrest) are noted in both the Constitution and Code of Criminal Procedure. In fact, the first article of the Code of Criminal Procedure articulates the purpose of this code is to balance the fundamental rights of human beings, finding of the truth, and proper and swift application of criminal laws.

When discussing the rights of the accused in the Japanese criminal justice system, it is important to note that the system differentiates the rights of a suspect and those of a defendant (the accused). The suspect may be under the custody of the police and under investigation, although he or she has not been charged with a crime yet. That is, prosecution has not been initiated for the suspect. Once the public prosecutor initiates prosecution (indictment), the status of the suspect changes to the defendant (the accused). The rights of the accused are broader than those of the suspect. One example of different rights between the accused and the suspect is the right to the public defender. In principle, a public defender funded by the state cannot be assigned to a suspect. It is important to note, furthermore, that much of the police investigation, including interrogation (or questions and interviews), is conducted voluntarily in Japan. That is, the police often ask a person of interest to come down to the police station for an interview. Although the person has the right to refuse such a request, any refusal may raise further suspicions. Furthermore, privately funded defense attorneys cannot be present during the interrogations.

The accused, on the other hand, has the right to hire legal counsel for his or her defense, as guaranteed by the Constitution. If the accused cannot afford to hire one, public defenders can be assigned whose expenses are paid by the state. For offenses that carry the death penalty, the accused needs to have defense counsel (either privately funded or a public defender) for a trial to proceed. Unlike the United States, the defense counsel cannot be present at the time of interrogations conducted by the police and the public prosecutor. Nonetheless, the accused has the right to have interviews with his or her legal counsel without the presence of any officials from the police. According to the Annual Report of Judicial Statistics by the Supreme Court of Japan, about 98 percent of the accused persons in the district and summary courts have been assisted by defense counsel. Of these, about 25 percent of the accused persons tried at the district courts retained their own defense counsel, while 75 percent were assisted by public defenders. In the summary courts, about 90 percent of the accused were assisted by public defenders.

Another difference between the rights of the suspect and the accused is regarding bail. When the police arrest a suspect, the public prosecutor needs to decide within 72 hours whether to file a request for detention, if deemed to be necessary for further investigation. A judge, then, decides if the detention of the suspect is necessary based on evaluation of the following criteria: (1) there are reasonable grounds to suspect that the suspect has committed the alleged crime; (2) the suspect does not have a fixed residence; (3) there are reasonable grounds to suspect that the suspect will destroy evidence; and (4) there are reasonable grounds to suspect that the suspect will escape. In principle, the period of pretrial detention is only for 10 days, with a possible extension of another 10 days if there are unavoidable circumstances. The public prosecutor has to decide by the end of the detention period whether or not to file an indictment against the suspect. For a maximum of possibly 23 days (72 hours + 10 days + 10 days), bail is not allowed for the suspect. That is, before the filing of the indictment (or the initiation of prosecution), the arrested suspect needs to be in the physical custody of the police and the public prosecutor, as long as a judge determines detention is judiciary warranted.

Once an indictment is filed, the detention of the accused continues automatically. As initiation of prosecution changes the status of the suspect to that of the accused, however, he or she may apply for bail. The Code of Criminal Procedure stipulates that the request for the bail should be granted, unless there are reasonable grounds to suspect that the accused will destroy evidence, the accused is charged with a serious offense, or the accused is likely to commit another crime once released. Despite such a principle stated in the Code of Criminal Procedure, only 13.4 percent of the detained defendants tried in the district courts were granted bail in 2005. While the majority (64.3%) of defendants tried in the district courts were detained between one and three months, a substantial portion (25.3%) of defendants were detained for longer than three months.

Public Prosecutors

The organizational structure of the public prosecutor offices is similar to that of the courts, with the Supreme Public Prosecutors Office as its highest hierarchical structure, followed by High Prosecutors Offices, District Public Prosecutors Offices, and Local Public Prosecutors Offices. There were approximately 2,350 public prosecutors (including 900 assistant public prosecutors), as of 2003. Qualifications of the public prosecutor are the same as the judges and the defense counsel. These qualifications include that they have passed the national bar exam, that they have gone through training at the Legal Training and Research Institute, and that they have passed the final examination upon completion of the training.

The public prosecutors take part in all aspects of criminal investigators, although initial criminal investigations are primarily conducted by the police. The public prosecutors' tasks are to interrogate the suspect, file a request for detention, and initiate prosecution. A broad degree of discretion is allowed for the public prosecutor as to whether or not to prosecute the suspect. The public prosecutor makes such a decision after considering a variety of factors, including a suspect's age, personality, home environment, past criminal history, behavior after the crime, indication of remorse, the gravity of the crime, and motivations to commit the crime, among others.

Including the Penal Code offenses and Special Code offenses, the police cleared approximately 68 percent of cases in 2005. All cleared cases, except for minor offenses specified by the public prosecutors, were transferred to the public prosecutors who conduct further investigations. Based upon the evaluation of evidence and the gravity of crimes, the public prosecutor decided whether or not to prosecute offenders. Of the total number of offenders processed to the public prosecutor, only a small fraction was prosecuted for formal trials (7%). A substantial amount of offenders (34%) were processed to the summary courts via summary procedures that involved examinations of documents and no open court sessions. Summary procedures could be initiated if crimes were punishable with fines less than 500,000 yen (approximately US$5,000) and if the accused did not challenge the charges. Noteworthy of mention is that the public prosecutor suspended prosecutions for a large number of offenders (46%). The public prosecutor decided to suspend prosecutions by weighing several factors, such as offenders' age, prior records, personality, gravity of offenses, circumstances surrounding criminal acts, and conditions subsequent to criminal acts (e.g., financial restitution to the victims, victims' suffering, etc.).

Courts

The Japanese judiciary has five types of courts: the Supreme Court, High Courts, district courts, family courts, and summary courts. The first two courts are considered to be appellate courts, while the last three are the Court of First Instance with different jurisdictions by types of case. The Supreme Court is regarded as the court of last resort and is located in Tokyo. The Supreme Court has jurisdiction over cases making the second appeal. Grounds for appeal to the Supreme Court are limited to a violation of the Constitution, an erroneous interpretation of the Constitution or laws, and a conflict with Supreme Court precedents. High Courts have jurisdiction over cases making the first appeal (an exception to this is crimes related to insurrection that are first tried at High Courts). Grounds for appeal with the High Courts are clearly specified in the Code of Criminal Procedure. These include, but are not limited to, an error in fact-finding, an excessively harsh or lenient punishment, and an error in the interpretation of laws.

District courts are the Court of First Instance where the public prosecutor files an allegation, except for cases whose first jurisdiction resides in family courts and summary courts as specified by laws. The judgment at district courts is based upon a single-judge panel, with a few exceptions, for example, criminal cases that are punishable by the death penalty or imprisonment for life. In such a serious criminal case, a three-judge panel is used to form a judgment. There are 50 district courts (one for each of the 47 prefectures and an additional three in Hokkaido Island due to its large land size) with 203 branches in total.

Family courts were established based upon a postwar judicial reform to specialize in domestic relations cases and juvenile delinquency cases. Thus, they have the first jurisdiction over disputes taking place in a family context, such as the determination of guardianship and marital disputes. Furthermore, family courts also have the first jurisdiction over juvenile delinquency cases, as well as cases that endanger the welfare of children. As the United States was actively involved in the postwar reconstruction of the Japanese criminal justice system, the philosophy behind this separate court system for juvenile delinquents is similar to that of the United States, namely, that juveniles need guidance and help instead of punishment. Thus, the emphasis is placed more upon rehabilitation and less upon punishment. Furthermore, more emphasis is placed upon offenders and less on offenses. Based upon this philosophy, not only juveniles who have committed a delinquent act, but also juveniles who are considered prone to commit a delinquent act in the future can be brought to the family court. Unlike criminal courts, family court proceedings are conducted in a closed court. Although the initial investigation may be conducted by the police before the case is referred to a family court, the investigation of delinquent acts is also conducted by family court probation officers. Judgments made in the family court take into account not only juveniles' delinquent acts, but also their personality, family relationships, and home environment. Psychiatrists are also called upon to provide medical evidence for juveniles' psychiatric conditions. Oftentimes, juveniles may be placed in a juvenile classification home for scientific and medical evaluations. Based upon the evaluation of these wide varieties of factors, the family court judges may adjudicate the juveniles and place them under probation or in juvenile training centers. In the case of serious offenses, however, the current Juvenile Law allows family court judges to transfer juveniles aged over 14, who have committed a serious crime, to adult criminal courts.

Summary courts have territorial jurisdictions over criminal cases that are punishable by fines and habitual gambling crimes. As a general rule, the summary courts cannot impose imprisonment with or without labor. Exceptions to this rule are some larceny offenses where the summary courts can impose imprisonment with labor for not longer than three years. A substantial number of criminal cases are handled by the summary courts, indicating the importance of the summary courts in effective administration of the criminal justice in Japan. For example, while 77,507 of adult offender cases were tried at the district courts and 386 at the family courts, 730,792 cases were handled by the summary courts in 2005, according to the White Paper on Crime 2006. Approximately 98 percent of cases processed by the summary courts involved summary procedures that only involved examinations of documentation and no open trials. Such summary procedures can be initiated if the crimes are punishable by fines less than 500,000 yen (approximately US$5,000) and if the accused does not contest the charges against him or her.

There are 15 Supreme Court judges, 1,597 judges, 915 assistant judges, and 806 summary court judges in lower courts (assistant judges can only participate in a multijudge panel), as of 2006. Although many judges predominantly handle either civil or criminal trials, statistics are not available with regard to how many judges handle predominantly criminal cases.

In principle, the judges have to have the same qualifications as the public prosecutors and the defense counsel, such as that they have passed the national bar exam. Exceptions to these qualifications are that Supreme Court judges can be selected from distinguished legal scholars and that summary court judges can be selected from individuals with distinguished knowledge and expertise in legal matters.

Punishment

Types of Punishment

The Japanese criminal court can impose a wide range of punishments, including the death penalty, imprisonment with or without labor for an indeterminate or determinate term, penal detention, and fines. The most severe form of punishment in the Japanese criminal justice system is the death penalty. The method of execution is by hanging. Recent issuances of death penalty sentences have varied, being 5 in 2001, 3 in 2002, 2 in 2003, 14 in 2004, 11 in 2005, and 4 in 2006. The numbers of prison inmates executed also varied by year: 2 in 2001, 2 in 2002, 1 in 2003, 2 in 2004, 1 in 2005, and 4 in 2006. Although the Code of Criminal Procedure requires that convicted offenders sentenced to the death penalty be executed within six months of the final court decision, many inmates on death row spend more than six months in prison. A particular issue concerning the death penalty in Japan is that the Minister of Justice needs to sign a document and authorize an execution. This means that the actual execution is, to some extent, at the discretion of the Minister of Justice. Some ministers may be reluctant to sign the paper and thus effectively halt the death penalty, although the court may have imposed such a penalty. For example, Justice Minister Seiken Sugiura publicly announced in 2005 that he would not sign the document during his term in office.

The Penal Code states that a homicide is punishable by the death penalty, imprisonment with labor for an indefinite term, or imprisonment with labor for a definite term of longer than five years. Of these available sentencing options, the majority of homicide cases were ended with sentences for 5–10 years (29.3%) and 10 years and more (26.7%), while a substantial proportion of sentences were suspended (17.1%).

Robbery is punishable by imprisonment with labor for a term longer than five years. The two robbery cases that resulted in the death penalty were robbery resulting in death. The most frequent forms of punishments for robbery were imprisonment for 5–10 years (34.8%) and 3–5 years (32.8%).

A prison cell for several inmates at Tokyo's Fuchu prison, January 24, 1997. The Japanese-style futons, or sleeping mats, are tidily folded and the cell is kept clean and orderly according to the rules. Exercise is forbidden in cells, tobacco is banned, television viewing is controlled, and prisoners' faces must be visible while they sleep. (AP Photo/Wahyu)

Bodily injury is punishable by imprisonment with labor for not more than 15 years or a fine of not more than 500,000 yen (approximately US$5,000). The typical punishment for bodily injury was imprisonment for 1–3 years, although a large portion of such sentences were suspended.

Theft is punishable by imprisonment with labor for not longer than 10 years or a fine of no more than 500,000 yen (approximately US$5,000). Similar to bodily injury, the typical punishment for theft was imprisonment for 1–3 years, although a large portion of such sentences were suspended.

Rape is punishable by imprisonment with labor for a definite term of longer than three years. The data available through the Supreme Court of Japan combine sentences of rape and other sexual crimes. A large proportion of offenders are given suspended sentences, which is a typical characteristic of the Japanese criminal justice system.

Punishments for illicit drugs vary by types of drugs (e.g., opium and methamphetamine) and charges (e.g., possession, trade, and cultivation). For offenders who were convicted of the Stimulants Control Law, which covers various drugs including methamphetamine, a typical punishment was imprisonment for 1–3 years. A notable characteristic of sentences for these drug offenders was that the majority of offenders were imprisoned, as opposed to receiving suspensions like other types of crime.

A unique characteristic of Japanese criminal trials is that plea bargaining is not allowed, although many defendants do not contest charges against them. Admission of guilt is often used as an indication of remorse and can be grounds for a lenient sentence. Furthermore, whether financial compensation was made by the accused can also be grounds for a lenient sentence. Thus, oftentimes, the defense counsel presents evidence of mitigating circumstances surrounding the accused to obtain lenient sentences during court hearings.

Finally, the most frequent form of punishment given out by the courts was fines (89%). It is notable that only a very few defendants were found not guilty in the Japanese criminal justice system (66 defendants or about 0.05% of the defendants prosecuted for formal trials in 2005). This could be largely due to the wide discretion given to the public prosecutor regarding their decisions to prosecute. That is, prior to prosecutions, the public prosecutor carefully selected cases that required penal punishments. Another characteristic of the sentencing patterns in the Japanese criminal justice system was that sentences were suspended for a large number of convicted offenders. In 2005, sentences were suspended for 55,000 defendants, while 34,000 were imprisoned.

Prisons

There are two departments that are responsible for corrections and rehabilitations. The Correction Bureau of the Ministry of Justice is the prime agency providing correctional services for both adults and juveniles. As of 2006, there were 74 penal institutions (59 prisons, 8 juvenile prisons, and 7 detention houses) with 113 branches (6 prison branches and 107 detention house branches). Additionally, there were 53 juvenile training schools. Detention houses mainly hold arrested suspects and defendants awaiting trials. Although these arrested suspects and defendants awaiting trials are also held in prisons, they are segregated from prison inmates in such a case. The average number of people housed in the penal institutions in 2005 was 77,932 (11,131 of whom were arrested suspects and defendants awaiting trials). A vast majority of people housed in penal institutions were males (about 94%). Out of 74 penal institutions, 56 (76%) exceeded their capacities in 2005. As the number of prison inmates has been increasing since the late 1990s, the total capacity of penal institutions has been exceeding 100 percent since 2001.

The Correction Bureau employs a classification system to identify penal institutions and correctional treatment programs that are best suited for rehabilitation of prison inmates. The classification system evaluates inmates based upon their criminal history, their personal characteristics (e.g., sex, age, mental illness, citizenship), and types of correctional programs (e.g., vocational training, drug rehabilitation, organized crime rehabilitation, sex crime rehabilitation, moral teaching, and traffic safety). Inmates are evaluated at the beginning of their sentences, and regularly afterward, to identify correctional treatment programs suited for individual needs. For example, first-time offenders placed in prisons are classified as Class A, while career criminals held in prisons are classified as Class B. Juvenile offenders placed in the system are classified as Class J. Women incarcerated in prisons are classified as Class W. Foreign nationals incarcerated in prisons are considered Class F.

The Rehabilitation Bureau of the Ministry of Justice is the primary agency responsible for administering rehabilitation programs for parolees and individuals under probation. To serve the goal of rehabilitating ex-offenders, the bureau is actively involved in all aspects of rehabilitation services, for example, adjusting an inmate's family and surrounding environments prior to parole, and supervising halfway houses and volunteer probation officers. In the Japanese criminal justice system, voluntary probation officers play a crucial role in rehabilitation and supervision of parolees and probationers. Voluntary probation officers have their expenses paid by the government, but receive no other compensation as they supervise and assist probationers and parolees in their rehabilitation. Volunteer probation officers evaluate home and work environments of these ex-offenders prior to their parole and make adjustments if problems that may affect their rehabilitation exist. The importance of volunteer probation officers can be illustrated by sheer comparisons of the number of professional probation officers (approximately 1,400) and volunteer probation officers (approximately 50,000).

Finally, at the correction and rehabilitation stage, approximately 53 percent of inmates were paroled before the completion of their sentences. For juvenile offenders placed in juvenile training schools, 98 percent were granted paroles before completing their terms. Of 55,000 defendants whose sentences were suspended, 5,000 were suspended with paroles.

Juvenile Offenders

Adult and juveniles are distinguished at the age of 20 in the Japanese criminal justice system. Individuals over the age of 20 who violate the Penal Code are prosecuted and tried at adult criminal courts, although adult offenders who are charged with endangering the welfare of children can also be brought to the family court, as the focus here is on the children as the victims of the crime.

This separate court system for juveniles is established based upon the philosophy that juveniles are still amenable. Juveniles are considered to be in need of help and guidance. Thus, when deciding the best dispositions for juveniles, stronger emphasis is placed on rehabilitation than on punishment. To adequately rehabilitate juveniles, various factors are considered, including but not limited to, family environment, personality, past delinquency history, gravity of offenses, and association with other delinquents. To assess proper treatments for juveniles, the courts may place them in a juvenile classification home for scientific and medical evaluations for a maximum of four weeks. Rather than the adversary trial system, characteristics of the juvenile justice system include a focus on rehabilitation rather than punishment, closed-court hearings, and cooperative hearings among parties involved to determine appropriate measures in the best interest of the accused juveniles.

When a juvenile commits a serious offense, however, a family court judge may decide to refer him or her back to the public prosecutor so that the juveniles can be tried at an adult criminal court. It is important to note that the Juvenile Law states that juveniles younger than the age of 14 cannot be held responsible for criminal acts. Furthermore, in practice, the family court only transfers juveniles, who are older than 16 and committed a serious offense such as murder, to an adult court. In deciding whether or not a juvenile should be transferred to the adult court, the family court judge examines a variety of factors, such as the motivation for the crime, the circumstances surrounding the case, the gravity of the crime, personality, age, and the home environment. When juveniles are transferred to the adult criminal court, trial procedures for adult criminals are applied to the accused juveniles. When juveniles are tried in the adult criminal court, the death penalty cannot be imposed upon juveniles younger than the age of 18. Juveniles who were tried in the criminal court could be placed in juvenile prisons for their rehabilitation.

Finally, it is important to note that, under the Japanese criminal justice system, juveniles who are considered prone to delinquent behavior and likely to commit a crime in the future can also be referred to the family court by the police and child welfare agencies. For example, juveniles with a history of running away and intimate associations with known adult offenders can be considered as juveniles prone to delinquent behavior and referred to the family court by the police, the public prosecutor, and social workers at child welfare agencies.

Out of about 216,000 cases refereed to the family court in 2005, the majority of cases were dismissed, 19 percent of which had hearings and 56 percent of which had no hearing. Only 2 percent of juveniles processed to the family court were sent to juvenile training schools, while a substantial portion of juveniles were placed under probation (17%). Juvenile training schools offer a variety of vocational training, education, and rehabilitation services. As of 2006, there were 53 juvenile training schools in Japan.

George Kikuchi and Yoko Baba

Further Reading

Leonardsen, Dag. (2004). *Japan as a Low-Crime Nation*. New York: Palgrave Macmillan.

Ministry of Justice: http://www.moj.go.jp/ENGLISH/index.html.

National Police Agency: http://www.npa.go.jp/english/index.htm.

Parker, Craig I. (2001). *The Japanese Police System Today: A Comparative Study*. Armonk, NY: M. E. Sharpe.

Supreme Court of Japan: http://www.courts.go.jp/english.

Thornton, Robert Y., and Katsuya Endo. (1992). *Preventing Crime in America and Japan: A Comparative Study*. Armonk, NY: M. E. Sharpe.

Kazakhstan

Legal System: Civil
Murder: High
Corruption: High
Human Trafficking: Medium
Prison Rate: High
Death Penalty: No
Corporal Punishment: No

Background

Kazakhstan, the largest of the countries in central Asia, has a population of approximately 15 million people. In 1936, Kazakh became a republic of the Soviet Union and in 1991, with the dissolution of the Soviet Union, Kazakhstan came under the rule of a new president. In 1995, the country adopted its own constitution as an independent nation.

Kazakhstan has taken on a legal system similar to that of the Soviet era. This legal system consists of the National Security Committee, the Ministry of Internal Affairs, and the Office of the Procurator General. Each of these sections of the legal system maintains its own individual responsibilities in law enforcement and protection. The National Security Committee handles all intelligence and counterintelligence affairs. The Ministry of Internal Affairs oversees the militia (also known as the police), the investigation of criminal activity, fire protection, automotive inspection, and preservation of order. Lastly, the Office of the Procurator General handles the prosecution of criminals.

The Kazakh legal and judiciary system is broken down into three components: district, provincial, and federal. In general, the district courts handle most of the criminal cases. The provincial courts hear appeals from the lower-level district courts. Finally, the federal Supreme Court, made up of 44 members and the highest court in the country, is mainly an appeal court for the provincial courts. Each level of the court system is overseen by the executive branch of the government and the judges are appointed by the president. In addition to the three courts, the country's Constitution allows for a Constitutional Council, which handles all constitution matters. The Constitutional Council is composed of seven members. The president appoints three of the council members. The legislature appoints the other four. The president holds the right to veto all decisions rendered by the Constitutional Council. There is no form of appeal for a decision issued by this council.

Role of Police

Kazakhstan's police force, which is headed by the Ministry of the Interior, was staffed at approximately 20,000 in 2005. Although they were previously headed by a military official, the police have been operating under a civilian minister since 2003, which has effectively removed them from military control and placed them under civilian jurisdiction.

There are different categories of police within the country. The secret police are used by the Kazakhstan government to attempt to suppress opposition to the government. The country has a separate agency, known as the Financial Police Agency, which reports directly to the prime minister. This agency manages the investigation of financial crimes such as money laundering. The regular police force of Kazakhstan handles all other issues. They are known for corruption and brutality, according to mongabay.com.

Because of the many different units, it is often unclear under which jurisdiction a crime should be handled. Due to this uncertainty of jurisdiction and the well-known problem of corruption, individuals feel that they must watch out for each other. Civil responsibility is taught within the school system to aid in the deterrence of crime.

Presently, the Kazakhstani police agencies are facing a shortage of staff and the existing staff is lacking a strong degree of professionalism. These problems are said to be due to the low pay rate provided to the officers and the discontinuation of amenities that were allowed as compensation for law enforcement services, such as apartments. Law enforcement positions are becoming difficult if not impossible to fill.

The country is attempting to combat this problem by developing schools for policing whose purpose is to teach potential officers the elements of police work, the Constitution of the republic, and criminal and administrative codes. This education is provided free of charge to the trainees. In return, the trainees help their high school teachers keep order within the schools. Once they graduate from the schools, they are guaranteed credit toward acceptance into the police academy and toward furthering their education outside of the law enforcement realm.

Crime

Classification of Crimes

Article 9 of the Criminal Code of the Republic of Kazakhstan defines crime as a "publicly dangerous act." Article 10 further divides crimes into those of "lesser gravity, crimes of medium gravity, grave crimes, and especially grave crimes."

Crimes of lesser gravity include intentional acts for which the punishment is two years or less of "deprivation of freedom" or negligent acts for which the consequence is no longer than five years of imprisonment.

Crimes of medium gravity are those for which the punishment does not go beyond five years of deprivation of freedom. This category also includes negligent crimes whose punishment is imprisonment for a period of time greater than five years. The category of grave crimes consists of acts for which the maximum punishment does not exceed 12 years of imprisonment.

Especially grave crimes are defined as those crimes punishable by imprisonment for more than 12 years. Especially grave crimes include attempt on the life of a person administering justice or preliminary investigations; attempt on the life of the president; murder with aggravating circumstances; planning, preparation, or conduct of aggressive war; sabotage; state treason; terrorism; use of prohibited means and methods of conducting war; genocide; and mercenary participation in armed conflict.

Article 15 states that the age of criminal responsibility is 16 years; however, exceptions may be made for murder; rape; kidnapping; theft; robbery; brigandage; extortion; aggravated car theft; terrorism; capture of a hostage; theft or extortion of arms, ammunition, explosive materials, and explosion devices; hooliganism under aggravating circumstances; vandalism; theft or extortion of drugs or psychotropic substances; and a range of other crimes. Individuals who are psychologically lacking and therefore not completely aware of the danger of their acts cannot be held criminally liable.

The rate of juveniles being detained for criminal behavior is very high. Some believe this may be due to the country implementing the same laws and regulations for minors as they do for adults and they are tried under the same judicial system. Within the country of Kazakhstan, some types of crime are particularly troublesome; in particular, domestic violence and rape, which severely impact the women of the country. In domestic violence situations, the Kazakh police are only permitted to handle physical violence. They do not deal with any sexual or economic violence occurring within the family environment.

The grave crime of rape is handled in a private manner. This makes the prosecution of an individual for rape charges extremely difficult. Since the affair is a private matter, it is the responsibility of the victim to obtain legal counsel and pursue the prosecution of the offender. For aggravated rape, the trial may be public and prosecutors can pursue the case. However, they may also choose to decline, in which case the responsibility to seek justice returns to the victim. Another problem plaguing Kazakhstan is that of white-collar crimes such as embezzlement, tax fraud, and power abuse. However detrimental they are to the country, they are an ongoing affair of frequent occurrence.

Human trafficking is one of the most prevalent crimes found throughout Kazakhstan. It is the third-most profitable crime in the country, according to Freedom House. Kazakhstani people are trafficked not only within the confines of the country but also to other areas such as the United Arab Emirates (UAE), Germany, Greece, Israel, Russia, and Turkey. A factor that partially enables the act of trafficking is the lack of compliance with the standards for the elimination of trafficking on the part of the government. According to the *Trafficking in Persons Report 2007 U.S. Government Report* issued by the Office to Monitor and Combat Trafficking in Persons, Kazakhstan has been placed on the Tier 2 watch list for failing to provide substantiation of their initiative to combat human trafficking.

Drug Offenses

The drug problem in Kazakhstan originated with the dissolution of the Soviet Union. The country became a primary route for drugs in course from Afghanistan to consumers in Russia and Europe. Lax customs controls have made Almaty, a major city in Kazakhstan, a crossroads for the trade of opiates and cannabis from southwest Asia as well, according to a Library of Congress report. The country has now also become a user of the drugs and a major source of cultivation of cannabis since excellent growing conditions for cannabis and opium poppies can be found throughout the country. The extreme poverty throughout central Asia makes drugs appear to be a worthwhile business. In addition, the corruption in agencies such as the police and excessive amount of migration throughout the area only aid in the trafficking of drugs. These factors and its proximity to Afghanistan make drug trafficking a lucrative business for many, and a large crisis for Kazakhstan.

Crime Statistics

Statistics on crime for the Republic of Kazakhstan are available through the United Nations Office on Drugs and Crime. During 2005 it was reported that 625.7 kilograms (1376.5 pounds) of heroin were seized, an increase from the 457.7 kilograms (1,006.9 pounds) seized during 2004. Relatively consistent with the amount of heroin was the quantity of opium seized in Kazakhstan. In 2005 the reported amount of opium obtained was 668.9 kilograms (1,471.6 pounds), compared to 352.8 kilograms (776.2 pounds) in 2004. By far, the most troublesome quantities of drugs seized within the country are that of cannabis. In 2005 officials obtained 21,732.6 kilograms (47,811.7 pounds) of cannabis, which remained at a relatively steady quantity from the previous year of 21,348.6 kilograms (46,966.9 pounds).

Information reported to the United Nations Office on Drugs and Crime by the Kazakh's Ministry of the Interior provides the 2005 statistics on drug-related crime within the country. The country reported 9,741 registered drug-related crimes, which amounts to 65.7 drug-related crimes per 100,000 people. There were a reported 7,429 drug-related convicts in 2005, for a rate of 50 per 100,000 people.

Statistics reported to the United Nations Office on Drugs and Crime by the Kazakh's General Prosecutors Office indicated, in 2005, 146,347 crimes were registered, which equals a rate of 986.8 crimes per 100,000 people. There were a reported 57,902 convicts, which provides a rate of 388.5 convicts per 100,000 people.

Statistics show, within the first six months of 2006, there were a reported 68,900 crimes committed in Kazakhstan. The republic saw 873 murders, 6,092 robberies, and 27,934 thefts. According to this information, the total rate for reported criminal activity in Kazakhstan for the first half of 2006 is 464 per 100,000 people.

Finding of Guilt

Rights of the Accused

Kazakhstan's Constitution encompasses generally recognized international human rights standards with which all criminal proceedings must strictly comply. This Constitution encompasses the widest possible range of civil, political, economic, social, and cultural rights of citizens. The Code for the Execution of Criminal Penalties further outlines the specific rights of convicted criminals and offers them protection both socially and legally.

Article 14 of the Constitution states that everyone is equal before the law and that "(n)o one shall be subject to any discrimination for reasons of origin, social status, property status, occupation, sex, race, nationality, language, attitude towards religion, convictions, place of residence or any other circumstances." Everyone has the right to secrecy of personal savings and investments, letter exchange, telephone conversation, postal, telegraph, and other communication. Restrictions of these rights are only allowable during criminal proceedings in accordance with procedures directly established by the law.

According to the Criminal Procedural Code of the Republic of Kazakhstan, a person suspected or accused of a crime has the following rights: to immediately be given the basis for his or her detention as well as the legal qualification of the crime of which he or she is suspected or accused; to receive from the body of criminal prosecution an immediate explanation of his or her rights; to have a public trial by an independent, competent, and impartial tribunal; to be present at his or her trial; to be heard in court; to provide explanations and testimony with regard to suspicions or accusations that exist against him or her in a language of which he or she has a command; to utilize the assistance of a translator at no cost; to be presumed innocent; to abstain from giving self-incriminating testimonies or explanations; and to present evidence and call witnesses in his or her defense. It was not until 2007 that trials by jury were implemented, although the law did allow for such trials long before this time. Only serious murder cases are brought before a jury.

Accused individuals have the right to legal counsel and to have unlimited, private, confidential meetings with their legal representatives from the moment of their initial detention. Furthermore, the defendant has the right to have his or her defense counsel present during questioning and other investigative acts. Defense also has the right to participate in preliminary hearings, judicial discovery, and court debates.

At any point in the criminal proceedings, suspects or accused individuals have the right to refuse counsel, which signifies the individual's intent to perform his or her own defense. However, in cases in which the defendant is a minor, faces 10 or more years' imprisonment, does not speak the language of the court, or has a mental or physical disability, the law dictates that he or she must have legal representation.

If accused individuals cannot afford legal representation, the Constitution guarantees qualified, government-provided legal representation free of charge.

After their case has been heard, individuals have the right to file complaints concerning acts and decisions of the court, procurator, investigator, or inquest officers. Each convicted person has the right to challenge his or her sentence and have his or her sentence revised by the upper court. They also have the right to ask for pardon or mitigation of punishment.

Kazakhstan has very low acquittal rates—less than 1 percent. Some believe this is the result of the power of the prosecutors, passivity of judges, and the powerlessness and low quality work of the defense bar.

Investigation and Prosecution

Procedures for initiating and conducting criminal prosecution are outlined in Kazakhstan's Code of Criminal Procedure. These guidelines are strictly followed to ensure all suspects are given an impartial hearing.

Preliminary investigations, researching circumstances of cases, carrying out criminal prosecution, and implementing sanctions and court decisions are the responsibility of the investigator. Once these tasks are completed, finished criminal cases are sent to the procurator.

The burden of proof, which consists of collecting, evaluating, and utilizing evidence rests with the procurator, or prosecutor, who exercises the supervision of the legality of such activities as interrogation, investigation, and court decisions. The prosecuting party must be represented by a state procurator or a private procurator when the court is considering each criminal case. In criminal proceedings in which the procurator represents the state, the procurator must be present at all stages of the main trial. Procurators wield a large amount of power in Kazakhstan because they, rather than judges, have the right to issue arrest, search, and detention warrants. They also have the power to protest and suspend judicial decisions.

Corruption of prosecutors is a real concern in Kazakhstan. To elicit bribes, procurators will intervene in civil or commercial matters in which the state has no interest in the outcome, according to an American Bar Association report. Furthermore, procurators will fail to provide protection to citizens who are unable to afford to prosecute privately or whose cases do not seem important to the local authorities. The inquest officer is responsible for performing pretrial procedures associated with criminal cases and is obliged to comply with the instructions of the court, procurator, body of preliminary investigation, and the body of interrogation.

Court System

The court system in Kazakhstan remains objective and impartial and has interest only in upholding the law, not in prosecution or defense. It functions at three levels: local courts, regional courts, and the Supreme Court. Local courts, or *rayon* courts, handle petty crimes such as pickpocketing and vandalism. As of 2004, there were approximately 260 *rayon* courts in Kazakhstan with 1,851 judges. There are also 16 economic courts, which handle commercial disputes. Regional courts, or *oblast* courts, are separated into civil, criminal, and supervisory sections. These courts handle more serious offenses, such as murder and grand larceny, as well as appeals from local courts. These courts, with 572 judges, sit in each of the country's 14 *oblasts*, plus in the cities of Almaty and Astana. The Supreme Court handles appeals of lower-level court decisions. The Supreme Court is divided into civil, criminal, and supervisory sections. It has 44 members and hears cases in panels of nine or three judges depending on the seriousness of the case.

Supreme Court justices are elected by the Senate, upon the proposal of the president, based on a recommendation by the High Judicial Council, which is composed of the chairpersons of the Constitutional Council, Supreme Court, Prosecutor General, Minister of Justice, two Senate deputies, six judges, the Secretary of the High Judicial Council, and others appointed by the president. Judges in oblast courts and rayon courts are appointed by the president, based on the recommendation of the High Judicial Council and the Minister of Justice. All judges in Kazakhstan serve life terms. The president determines how many judges there are as well as their rate of pay.

All judges must be citizens of Kazakhstan, have graduated from a law school, be at least 25 years old, and have two years of prior legal experience. Oblast-level and Supreme Court judges must have five years of prior legal experience, including a minimum of two years serving as a judge. The appointment of rayon-level judges is based on examination and criteria such as grades throughout law school and reputation in the community. The appointment of oblast-level and Supreme Court judges does not depend on examination, but other criteria such as experience, professionalism, and reputation are considered. All judges are required to attend the Judiciary Academy for initial training (Bhavna), and additional training sessions are offered within each individual court and through the Union of Judges of Kazakhstan.

Pretrial Incarceration

Pretrial detention is permissible in the Republic of Kazakhstan. Suspects may be held in custody for no more than 72 hours before being officially charged with a crime. During the investigation process, detainees are held in investigatory jails. At their request, when appropriate, accused individuals may be allowed to work inside the jail during their detention and receive appropriate wages after various deductions specified by law.

A person may not be held in pretrial detention for more than two months. However, this period may be extended up to 12 months if it is found to be impossible to complete the investigation in a shorter time period. Any person detained must be immediately notified of the reason for his or her detention as well as the legal description of the offense of which he or she is suspected or accused.

Detainees are afforded various rights, such as the right to courteous treatment; the right to receive letters and parcels; the right to religious practices; the right to private and confidential meetings with legal counsel, representatives of trade unions, and other voluntary associations acting as defense counsel; as well as with relatives and other persons participating in the case as counsel.

If it is believed that a suspect is attempting to elude the preliminary inquiry, hamper investigations, or that he or she is likely to continue committing crime during judicial proceedings, preventative measures can be taken. These include disallowing the suspect to change addresses without permission, placing a minor under supervision, bail, house arrest, or arrest.

Punishment

Types of Punishment

Incarceration is the most common punishment used for criminal cases in the Republic of Kazakhstan, but fines, probation and community service, or social work, are alternative forms of punishment that can be applied to individuals who are convicted of lesser offenses. In 2006, 51 percent of convicted individuals were sentenced to confinement, 7 percent were fined, 2 percent were sentenced to correctional work, 38 percent received a suspended conviction, and less than 1 percent were sentenced to execution (the death penalty was abolished in 2007).

Colonies in Kazakhstan were once self-supporting through prison labor. All prisoners were expected to produce something during their incarceration. However, this is not the case in Kazakhstan today. Now, convicted individuals are held in corrective facilities known as "colonies," in which they are given the opportunity to be rehabilitated through socially useful labor, education, vocational training, and public pressure.

Since the new Code for the Execution of Criminal Penalties in 1998, convicted individuals have been categorized based on the seriousness of their offense. The conditions of their incarceration are based on this distinction. These categories are normal, relaxed, rigorous, and privileged. Eligibility for parole is also based on this distinction. Convicted persons may be eligible for parole after serving one-half, one-third, two-thirds, or three-quarters of their sentence, depending on their classification.

A large-scale prison reform program was begun in 1998 with support from the International Centre for Prison Studies, Penal Reform International, the Royal Netherlands Tuberculosis Association, and the Polish Prison Administration. This project had two main parts. The first involved introducing human rights and strategic management programs within the regional prison administration and prison colonies. The second aspect of the reform focused on the problem of tuberculosis among the prison population. This project was a success in that it brought a substantial amount of professional training to the employees of the penal system and improved prison conditions, including altering the psychological climate within the prisons by improving staff and prisoner relations. Staff behavior was also better managed after this program's introduction. This program was so successful in its initial three years that it was extended for another three years at the end of 2000. The Prison Committee had developed its own five-year plan of reformation, which included addressing such issues as overcrowding, staff to inmate ratios, staff training, treatment of tuberculosis, insufficient work for prisoners, and a need for programs that better prepare inmates for their release from prison to ensure they do not recidivate and can lead healthy and productive lives.

In 2004, several amendments were made to the criminal statutes of Kazakhstan. These amendments were intended to temper the criminal punishment system, reduce the number of offenses punished by incarceration, and simplify investigating procedures. Changes included the introduction of plea bargaining and increasing the use of fines in place of imprisonment. Some petty crimes, including assault, assault while under the influence, and causing harm through negligence, were decriminalized and reclassified as administrative offenses.

Juvenile Justice

Although there is not a separate juvenile justice system in Kazakhstan, there are specific chapters and articles within the criminal codes that pertain specifically to juvenile crime and punishment, and juveniles are held in separate facilities. Sentences used in juvenile cases include fines, forfeiture of the right to undertake certain activities, community service, correctional work, arrest, and deprivation of liberty. Juveniles may also be sentenced to any of the following educational measures: warning; placement under supervision by a parent, guardian, or specialized state body; restitution; restriction of leisure time; or placement in a special correctional or clinical-educational institution. Minors accused of committing a crime enjoy better food and living conditions than adults. They are also entitled to daily walks (of no less than two hours) and to watch movies and television. Some of the premises are also equipped for sports. In general, juvenile colonies provide more opportunities for activities outside the premises than are available in adult colonies, and juveniles are allowed more contact with family.

Youth penal colonies are categorized into four types: ordinary, mitigated, privileged, and severe. Offenders generally begin their sentence under "ordinary" circumstances and may be transferred based on their behavior. Offenders who are well behaved and show effort toward both work and education programs may be transferred after three months to "mitigated" circumstances.

Under ordinary circumstances, inmates are allowed two long and six short visits per year, and they are housed in a dormitory within the colony. If held under mitigated circumstances, the offenders are still housed within the colony's dormitory, but the inmates are allowed twice as many visits per year and may be allowed to enjoy these visits outside the colony. As the inmates' release date draws near, they may be transferred to "privileged" circumstances under which they are allowed to sleep outside the colony under supervision. Juveniles held under privileged conditions are allowed further visitation and can use money without restriction and wear civilian clothing and footwear. If sentenced to "severe" circumstances, the inmates are only allowed four short visits per year and are isolated within the colony unless working or studying. These inmates are those convicted of an intentional crime with aggravating circumstances.

Juveniles can earn privileges or rights based upon their behavior, volunteer work, and academic studies. These rights include the right to attend cultural or sporting events outside the educational colony, with facility supervision, and the right to leave the colony with family supervision. Convicted juveniles also have the right to receive mail and parcels; the right to practice religion and attend services; and the right to have telephone conversations with relatives. Juveniles are also given the opportunity to perform volunteer work in the community to aid in the reintegration of the offenders after their sentence.

Typical Punishments

The severity of sentences in Kazakhstan is often based on factors surrounding the offense. For example, assault and battery have a maximum sentence of 10 years in prison, including cases of domestic abuse, but if the act inflicts physical pain but has no long-term effects, punishments can be as insubstantial as a fine, 180 hours of social work, or one-month imprisonment.

According to the 1998 Criminal Code, rape is typically punishable by imprisonment from three to five years. However, many circumstances can increase this sentence. Repeat offenders can be sentenced to 5 to 10 years. Rapes in which the victim is underage or infected with a sexually transmitted disease (other than HIV) as a result of the rape, as well as gang rapes, are also punishable by 5 to 10 years.

Prostitution is punishable only by warning or fine. However, more severe punishments can be used for individuals convicted of forced prostitution,

prostitution connected to organized crime, or operating brothels or prostitution rings.

Prison

As of the beginning of 2007, the prison population in Kazakhstan was 348 per 100,000, according to the International Centre for Prison Studies. Seven percent of these inmates are female and 1.9 percent are juveniles. The prison rate is down slightly since 2004 when there was a rate of 386 per 100,000. In 2001, this rate was at 549 per 100,000, its highest point since 1990.

The Ministry of Justice is responsible for sentenced prisoners. It currently manages 95 penitentiary institutions. These include 18 pretrial detention centers holding 15,855 detainees and 77 correctional colonies for sentenced prisoners, which house 70,630 prisoners, three of which are for women and three of which are for juveniles. Women account for just over 4 percent of the total prison population. There is a special unit within one women's prison where female minors are held. As of 1999, this unit held 100 girls.

Improved living conditions have been created for pregnant women and women with children who receive specialized medical care and better food and creature comforts, as required by the government. Furthermore, they may not be penalized by being placed in a punishment cell. Unless a woman has been convicted of a particularly heinous crime, she may be allowed to serve a delayed sentence if she is pregnant or has children under the age of eight. As of 1999, there were 36 women imprisoned with their children under the age of three. In these cases, the children are housed in a separate area of the prison and the mothers are allowed to communicate with them and participate in their care.

Prisoner Rights

Convicted persons have been guaranteed the right to practice their religion, and virtually all corrective establishments have their own prayer rooms and mosques. Those held in colonies are entitled to 12 working days of paid release from work per year. Those held in corrective establishments may be authorized to leave their establishment short term, for a period not exceeding seven days for purely personal reasons (the death or serious illness of a close relative), or long term, for the period of annual paid release from work.

Transfer of Prisoners to Other Countries

According to the Republic of Kazakhstan's Constitution and international agreements, foreigners and stateless individuals who commit offenses in other territories and then are seized in Kazakhstan can be extradited to that territory for criminal prosecution or to serve their sentence. However, individuals who have been granted asylum in Kazakhstan may not be extradited. Asylum may be granted to individuals or families who fear persecution in the country of their citizenship because of their race, nationality, political actions, or religious beliefs.

One condition for the extradition of offenders to another country is the existence of an international treaty with the Republic of Kazakhstan. If the country does not have such an agreement, the decision of extradition is handled through the diplomatic service of the Republic of Kazakhstan.

Kristen Lee Hourigan and
Stephanie L. Stashenko

Further Reading

Governance: Basil Institute on Governance, Asset Recovery Knowledge Center, the Constitution of the Republic of Kazakhstan. Basil Institute on Governance Web Site: http://www.assetrecovery.org/kc/resources/org.apache.wicket.Application/repo?nid=1d1292dd-80c2-11dd-aec8-83823fa6e881.

Legislationline. "Law No. 167 of 16 July 1997 of the Republic of Kazakhstan the Criminal Code of the Republic of Kazakhstan." Legislationline Web Site: http://www.legislationline.org/upload/legislations/25/c8/ca1cfb8a67-f8a1c2ffe8de6554a3.htm.

United Nations Office on Drugs and Crime. Country Fact Sheet: Kazakhstan—2006. United Nations Web Site: http://www.unodc.org/uzbekistan/en/fact_kaz.html.

Kyrgyzstan

Legal System: Civil
Murder: High
Burglary: High
Corruption: High
Human Trafficking: Medium
Prison Rate: Medium
Death Penalty: No
Corporal Punishment: No

Background

From 1936 to 1991, the country was a constituent republic of the Soviet Union. At that point, it became the independent Republic of Kyrgyzstan. It ratified its first Constitution in 1993, formalizing the country as a democratic republic, sovereign, and subject to the rule of law. It is hard to believe that for a while after independence, many had considered Kyrgyzstan to be an "island of democracy" in Central Asia. But the Soviet Union's disintegration deprived the new country of its chief source of economic sustenance, and the move toward a market-based economy has devastated this largely impoverished nation.

Political turmoil and widespread popular disaffection eventually ousted the first president, Askar Akayev, from office during 2005's so-called Tulip Revolution. While Akayev fled to Kazakhstan, his successor, Kurmanbek Bakiyev, took over. Bakiyev's mandate was to disperse political power, open space for the development of civil society actors, and end the pervasive private and public sector corruption. Unfortunately, this mandate quickly came to naught. Bakiyev and his Ak Jol Party centralized governmental power in their own hands. The powerful presidency coincides with a powerful pro-regime bloc in Parliament. The constitutionally formalized separation of powers across branches does not exist.

Amnesty International (AI) continues to condemn the government's efforts to severely restrict the space for human rights defenders and independent civil organizations. Likewise, Reporters without Borders consistently ranks Kyrgyzstan as one of the worst countries regarding press freedoms. Not only has Bakiyev's regime reneged on its promise to convert its state media to independent public media, the regime has condoned an environment in which journalists critical of the regime and its official corruption are criminally prosecuted, harassed, and subjected to physical violence, even culminating in assassination. Corruption continues to be endemic. Transparency International regularly lists Kyrgyzstan among the most corrupt nations in the world.

The 2006 Constitution formally prohibits any type of discrimination against any social group including ethnic minorities, women, and religious affiliates. About 70 percent of the population is ethnic Kyrgyz, with most minorities being either Uzbek or Russian, 15 percent and 10 percent, respectively. Three-quarters of the population is reportedly Muslim, while one-fifth is Russian Orthodox. The regime has always been secular, however, and human rights investigators such as Human Rights Watch (HRW) report on the state's aggressive stance toward even nonviolent Muslim celebrations. As well, the UN Committee on the Elimination of Racial Discrimination (CERD) reported in 2007 that the government has still failed to adequately deal with the clashes between Kryzyz and Dungan countries in 2006 and has failed to properly protect refugees fleeing violence from the Uzbek government.

Legal System

The nation's legal tradition is based almost exclusively on Tsarist and Soviet civil law traditions. In part, this is manifested in the procuracy, which continues the Soviet tradition of the strong *Prokuratura*. The procuracy continues to be a unified, national entity with a strict hierarchy that expresses state power centralized in the executive branch. The Prosecutor General's Office operates above the provincial, or oblast, prosecutors' offices. Below is a separate prosecutors' office for the City of Bishkek, the country's capital and largest city, the military prosecutors' office, as well as interdistrict, or inter-rayon, city, and rayon (district) prosecutors' offices.

There are also equal-status specialized prosecutors' offices.

In the political turmoil that has continued since the country's first Constitution in 1993, governments have amended the Constitution in 1996, 1998, 2001, and again in 2003. In 2006, a second Constitution was ratified and quickly amended. These often legally specious actions have largely occurred through dubious political procedures. Chapter 6 of the original Constitution deals with the court system and the judiciary, as do the 1999 Law on Advocacy Activity, 1999 Constitutional Law on the Status of Courts, the 2001 Constitutional Law on the Status of Judges, and the 2003 Law on the Supreme Court and Local Courts. The 1997 Criminal Code and 1999 Criminal Procedure Code govern the criminal proceedings.

The Constitutional Court is the highest judicial body. It is responsible for protecting the Constitution. It rules on the constitutionality of legislation, decides disputes regarding Constitutional interpretation, and issues opinions on the validity of presidential elections, proposed Constitutional amendments, and on the removal from office of the president and judges of both the Constitutional and Supreme Courts. The Constitutional Court, composed of a chairperson, a deputy chairperson, and seven judges, suffers from low public confidence because of its close service to whatever presidential regime reigns at the moment.

The Supreme Court is the highest body for civil, criminal, and administrative matters. It is divided into civil, criminal, and commercial sections. It hears appeals from the lower courts, and a panel of three judges hears ordinary appeals. A presidium of nine judges hears important appeals. A plenum issues opinions on court practices. These are binding on the lower courts and remind some legal observers of the hierarchical nature of Soviet courts, in which higher courts attempt to discipline and harmonize activities in the lower court.

The Courts of General Jurisdiction deal with civil and criminal matters at three levels that correspond with the country's administrative divisions into 7 provincial oblasts, 43 district rayons, plus the City of Bishkek. The Oblast Courts operate as Courts of Second Instance. They are formally divided into civil and criminal divisions. Cases are heard by a panel of three judges.

The Rayon Courts operate as Courts of First Instance. The majority of cases are heard by a single judge. The courts are not divided into sections. But judges tend to specialize in either civil or criminal cases.

The Military Court system is authorized to hear criminal cases involving members of the military and other bodies including the National Security Service, the Ministry of Interior (MoI), and the Criminal Penitentiary System of the Ministry of Justice (MoJ). There are five Garrison Courts and a Court of Appeal.

The judiciary is not truly independent from executive power. The National Council of Justice, which is part of the presidential administration, is responsible for proposing, selecting, and certifying judges for the local courts. Of its 14 members, only 5 are judges. The president exerts powerful control over judicial appointment. He nominates judges for the Supreme and Constitutional Courts and his Parliament approves them. The same is true for some of the lower court judges. The president also determines how many judges the country will have, where they will be posted, and how much they will be paid. Judicial corruption is widespread among the subordinated and low-paid judges.

Over 90 percent of judges are Kyrgyz, as are 72 percent of lawyers. Just one-third of judges are females, and these are disproportionately relegated to work civil cases. Prevailing stereotypes hold that female judges should not be entrusted with important criminal cases, particularly violent crime cases. In 2005–2006, the Office of the Prosecutor General reported that just 8.8 percent of the influential prosecution service was minority. Only 12 percent of prosecutors were women, and although some do hold senior or supervisory positions, the very senior positions are male.

Police

According to 2002 World Health Organization data, there were 16,727 police in Kyrgyzstan or 3.25

police per 1,000 civilians. Investigating agencies include the Ministry of Internal Affairs, the National Security Service, the Financial Police, the Transportation Service, and the Drug Control Agency. The police forces have not been free from corruption and brutal misconduct. As the American-based Freedom House (FH) reports, Customs Officers in Osh are especially corrupt, providing cover for drug smugglers, allowing the free flow of drugs from Tajikistan and elsewhere.

In 2002, while citizens in Jalal-Abad peacefully protested arbitrary arrest practices, police shot them with live ammunition. This event sparked massive protests that helped set the stage for the Tulip Revolution a few years later. But police still harass human rights defenders, political opponents, members of the LGBT community, and Muslims. Bishkek police carried out warrantless raids on the Labrys community shelter in 2008 to harass the LGBT community there, perpetuating what HRW calls an "atmosphere of prejudice."

In 2009, the Supreme Court heard cases of 32 defendants who were accused of organizing demonstrations in Nookat. According to credible reports, the police actually attacked celebrants while they peacefully attended the Islamic Eid al-Fitr. Reportedly wielding guns and batons, police arrested celebrants and subjected them to torture by using plastic bags and gas masks to semisuffocate them, beating them upon the soles of their feet, and forcing them

Police officers detain opposition members gathered for an antigovernment assembly in central Bishkek, Kyrgyzstan, November 16, 2002. (AP Photo/Gyaz Tokombayev)

to stand in their underwear in cold rooms with their feet in water for up to three days.

In 2002, the National Ombudsman was created by the Law on Peoples' Rights Defenders. It has been mandated to be an independent advocate for private citizens and NGO rights. Interestingly, it is believed that because the Ombudsman was clearly positioning himself for a presidential campaign, public faith in the institution suffered. Yet in 2004 alone, the National Ombudsman received about 15,000 complaints.

Crime

According to a 2009 Radio Free Europe report, Interior Minister Moldomusa Kangantiev declared, "Crime is on the rise in Bishkek," and he promised that, "We are stepping up our efforts. Armed policemen will work during night shifts." According to the 8th UN Survey of Crime Trends and Operations of Criminal Justice Systems in 2002, there were 413 murders, 88 by youth. There were also 1,497 robberies.

However, the minister's alarm does seem to be a function of the country's continued political turmoil rather than the high rates of common crime. Indeed, the mass riots and looting of earlier protests, endemic corruption, officially abetted organized crime, and occasional political assassination seem to have engendered a sense of disorder and political fatigue among even those who once had faith in the new regime's willingness to fight corruption.

Corruption

Although Criminal Code Section 8 details the prohibition against fraud and other economic crimes, authorities seem very reluctant to investigate and prosecute such cases. Corruption is tied to other crime problems that challenge the country. For example, Kyrgyzstan is a transit country for drugs being trafficked through Tajikistan and elsewhere bound for Europe. Still, it appears that drug use within the country is relatively low. According to the World Drug Report 2009, the annual prevalence of use among the population aged 15–64, was just 0.80 percent. Cannabis use is more common, with 6.4 percent in this age group. There are no reliable statistics for cocaine, amphetamines, or Ecstasy use. There were 879 drug abusers in treatment in 2007. Of those in treatment, opiates and cannabis were the primary drugs of choice for 77.3 percent and 19.4 percent, respectively.

Human Trafficking

Human trafficking has also challenged the nation's criminal justice system. According to a 2009 U.S. State Department report, Kyrgyzstan has been a source, transit, and to a lesser extent, a destination country for men and women for forced and sexual labor. Both men and women are trafficked to Russia and Kazakhstan, while women are trafficked to the United Arab Emirates, Kazakhstan, and several other countries for sexual labor. Domestically, the city of Osh is believed to be a growing destination for female sex workers.

The government is believed to be improving its response in several ways, including providing more locally available information for at-risk people, making space available for NGOs to run victims shelters, as well as doing more to repatriate Kyrgyz nationals. In 2008, the government and NGOs identified 161 victims, down from 331 in 2007. NGO shelters helped 34 victims, and the government did not prosecute the victims. In 2008, there were 92 investigations, up from 33 in 2007. Officials prosecuted eight defendants and convicted six in 2008. Still, there are concerns about the complicity of low-level government officials and that police accept bribes from traffickers.

Domestic Violence

Violence against women and girls is clearly very prevalent. In 2003, human rights activists successfully achieved the ratification of the Law on Social-Legal Protection from Domestic Violence. This recognizes domestic violence as a specific offense and provides for the use of orders of protection in these cases. It also prohibits sexual violence against marital partners.

The Ministry of Internal Affairs registers 8,000 to 10,000 emergency family crisis calls annually. Each month, 40 to 50 domestic violence victims are hospitalized in the Bishkek City Hospital alone. Officials registered 4,135 cases of violence between 2005 and 2006. Yet only 63 domestic violence cases reached the courts, resulting in just 18 court orders. In 16 of these, courts only issued warnings of administrative arrest or criminal proceedings. Critics warn that authorities have not bothered to enforce orders of protection, keeping victims in risk. Indeed, authorities do not consider violence against women and girls to be serious prosecutable crimes.

This has been particularly true of bride-kidnapping. This is a common crime in Kyrgyzstan. HRW reports that at the end of each school year, a "literal hunt for young girls starts all over the country." Gangs of men kidnap young girls and take them to their presumptive grooms' homes. There, strangers beat and rape them and force them into marriages and do not allow them to return home. According to HTW, "Many Kyrgyz officials portray bride-kidnapping as a harmless ritual, a voluntary practice. But women all over the country paint a very different picture." For them, it is a violent and traumatic experience, one that is so prevalent because it is perpetrated with impunity. Only 27 cases were initiated under article 155 in 2005, up from a mere 15 the prior year. Human rights observes argue that official inattention to crimes like these reflects the disproportionately small representation of women in decision-making positions throughout the country's political and criminal justice systems. Not surprisingly, those victims who do seek help prefer to contact NGO crisis services rather than state officials.

Finding of Guilt

The Constitution provides that an individual has the right to criminal defense, either by oneself or by a defense lawyer from the moment of arrest. But the Criminal Procedure Code delays this to the moment of first interrogation or actual arrival at the investigating institution. Investigators are supposed to advise detainees of their rights at the time of their detention. But this does not always happen, and they sometimes pressure them to waive this right. Juveniles, processed through the same system as the adults, cannot waive this right. Also, lawyers have to get permission from the investigators before gaining access to their clients.

Indigent arrestees also have the Constitutional right to free legal aid. However, defendants must prove their eligibility through time-consuming procedures. The pay is so low, attorneys find the work distasteful. As well, defense attorneys must actually receive documentation from prosecutors or judges attesting to how much time the defense attorneys actually spent in court working on their indigent clients' cases or else they will not be compensated. Understandably, many defense attorneys do not participate in the program.

There is a general shortage of lawyers. In 2004, there were 1,192 advocates for a population of 4.8 million. There are two types of defense lawyers: advocates and nonadvocates. Advocates represent clients in both criminal and civil cases. Nonadvocate lawyers work civil but not criminal cases. To practice, lawyers need law degrees and licenses from the MoJ. Commonly, investigators will appoint defense attorneys to defendants who do not have their own attorneys. This has led to the proliferation of so-called pocket lawyers who are dependent upon investigators to supply them with clients. This tends to undermine the vigor with which they defend clients, sometimes even leading them to aid the prosecution.

In practice, there are many obstacles to effectively implementing the principle of equality of arms between prosecution and defense. Investigators hamper defense access to evidence, as well as make it more difficult for the defense to present evidence during trial. The Criminal Procedure Code grants defendants the right to confer privately with their attorneys. But this is typically impossible simply because many facilities lack sufficient space.

The powerful procuracy also unbalances the presumptive equality of arms. Prosecutors do not just prosecute defendants. They also supervise the legal propriety of the proceedings, being that they are responsible for ensuring the uniform implementation of legislative acts. If prosecutors dislike judges' rulings, they may place complaint letters in the judges' files. These files are later reviewed when the judges come up for reappointment. They are also responsible for exercising appropriate supervision over criminal investigations. But it is believed that they often fail to do so, enabling the police to illegally collect evidence and forcibly extract confessions.

The public widely perceives that the procuracy is subject to improper influence from both prosecutorial and outside authorities, despite prohibitions against such influence. Also, supervisors limit the discretion of subordinate prosecutors due to the procuracy's highly bureaucratic, hierarchical nature. In 2007, there were 720 prosecutors working in 67 offices, all with law degrees.

The Constitution guarantees the presumption of innocence. There are obstacles in practice. For example, there is a notable lack of courtrooms, so trials are often held in judges' offices. This makes it impossible to ensure public accessibility to trials. Old courts still keep defendants caged during trials even when they are charged with minor, nonviolent crimes.

The Constitution prohibits the use of ill-gotten evidence. But there is no definition of inadmissible evidence or detailed rules on the appropriate procedures for excluding inadmissible evidence. So the use of illegal evidence is routine.

The Constitution also prohibits the use of torture and ill-treatment and inhuman or degrading investigation techniques. Still, prosecutors are reluctant to have such allegations investigated. Thus, maltreatment occurs frequently.

Judicial proceedings are extremely long, severely undermining the right of speedy trial completed within a reasonable amount of time. This is particularly problematic for defendants in pretrial detention. Courts commonly remit cases for supplementary investigation instead of rendering final verdicts. This too slows proceedings, and it casts doubt upon the certainty of judicial decisions and the principle of equality of arms.

The Constitution grants defendants the right to appeal their convictions. But judges frequently fail to seriously re-examine cases, let alone overturn convictions. Because trial records are recorded by court clerks who keep handwritten notes, trial records are often unhelpful at appeal. Here, too, judges frequently just send cases back to the lower courts for further investigation instead of rendering final verdicts. Again, this casts doubt on the certainty of judicial verdicts and lengthens proceedings.

The Law on Attestation Procedure of Judges of the Local Courts 1999 governs judicial selection in those courts. Judges must have law degrees, professional legal experience, and be of a certain age. As noted earlier, the Attestation Commission, operating under MoJ, recommends judicial nominees to the president who actually appoints them.

Judicial candidates must first pass an oral exam and the commission members vote by secret ballot to determine whether or not candidates pass. The general perception is that this process lacks objectivity. Unfortunately, those candidates who successfully become judges will draw low salaries and have no mandated ethics training. Many will become part of a practice that legal observers call "telephone justice." This is said to occur in politically sensitive cases. Executive authorities directly influence judicial rulings, and senior judges directly influence their juniors on how to rule in particular cases. In sum, practices such as these all culminate in very high percentages of cases ending in conviction. According to Department of Court statistics, more than 98 percent of cases between 1998 and 2002 resulted in convictions.

Punishment

The Criminal Codes makes relatively severe punishments available, if courts wish to mete them out. By law, human trafficking may incur sentences ranging from 3 to 20 years' imprisonment. However, in 2008, four of the six convicted human traffickers received suspended sentences, while the other two were imprisoned for three to eight years. The prescribed penalty for bride-kidnapping is a fine in the amount of 100–200 times the country's minimum wage or up to five' years imprisonment. Such penalties are infrequently imposed, though. Likewise, although the Criminal Code articles 134, 299, and 373 provide for criminal punishment for criminal acts of discrimination, authorities rarely invoke these provisions.

This contrasts sharply with the severe prison terms inflicted upon those arrested during the Nookat protests in 2008. Courts convicted them of "incitement to cause or participate in mass unrest," "separatism," "attempting to overthrow the constitutional order," and "spreading ethnic or religious strife." Their prison sentences range from 9 to 20 years.

There has also been concern regarding severe punishments for juvenile offenders. There is no separate juvenile system, and thus no alternative penalties tailored specifically to juveniles. As well, there is a notable lack of rehabilitative or vocational juvenile programming. Commissions on minors' affairs are set up within local administrations. These bodies can take those minors aged 11–14 who have not been processed through the criminal courts and place them in so-called special schools for difficult children.

The death penalty has also been a normal part of penal punishment in Kyrgyzstan. In 1998, authorities declared the first moratorium on its use. They extended it several times. The International Helsinki Federation for Human Rights reports that despite this, judges had still continued to hand down death sentences because there were loopholes in the law, and judges were able to ignore the new Constitution's provisions relating to these cases. By 2007, there were 167 unofficially condemned persons waiting on makeshift death rows in the basements of investigation agency jails since there are no specially designated death row facilities in Kyrgyzstan.

However, in 2007, the Criminal Code was finally amended to abolish the death penalty. Executions are to be replaced with life sentences. The amendments also reduce some prison sentences for some crimes. Still, in this region, decisions pertaining to matters such the death penalty are not always final.

In 2006, a UN Special Rapporteur expressed concern about the general failure to provide sufficient alternatives to extremely long prison sentences. The MoJ administers the prison system. According to the World Prison Brief, in 2009, there were 6 pretrial detention facilities and 11 prisons in the system. The prison population was 7,199 prisoners, giving the country an imprisonment rate of 133 prisoners per 100,000 citizens.

Within the prison population, 27.6 percent were pretrial/remand detainees. Females and foreigners constituted 3.9 percent and 1.9 percent, respectively. Juveniles were only 1.2 percent of the prisoner population. But juveniles face long pretrial detention periods while being held in adult facilities.

The official capacity is 14,445 prisoners. Reportedly, the occupancy rate is a manageable 49 percent. This claim is not credible. If true, Kyrgyzstan, with its high levels of corruption, poverty, and conviction rates, could be said to have countered the worldwide trend toward severely overcrowded prisons, a trend that is particularly pronounced in Central Asia and former Soviet republics. Human rights investigators have strongly encouraged criminal justice proposals within Kyrgyzstan, in part because they argue that the poor country cannot continue to sustain its high levels of imprisonment and overcrowding humanely.

The International Committee of the Red Cross (ICRC) visited 44 prisons and detention facilities in 2007. They expressed concern about the lack of judicial guarantees for detainees in police custody. The government did agree to set up an interministerial working group to improve policy custody conditions.

The ICRC also made recommendations for improving confinement conditions for females, foreigners, and juveniles. They also found it necessary to provide prisoners with mattresses, hygiene and cleaning products, stationery, as well as jackets to survive the cold Kyrgyz winters. Tuberculosis has also been problematic. Unfortunately, when officials began to interfere with their regular visitation procedures, the ICRC ended its visits, casting doubt on the likelihood of significant reforms.

Paul Schupp

Further Reading

Bishkek, Kyrgyzstan: 2006 Crime and Safety Report: http://www.osac.gov/Reports/report.cfm?contentID=40853.

Constitution of Kyrgyzstan: http://www.coe.int/T/E/Legal_Affairs/Legal_co-operation/Foreigners_and_citizens/Nationality/Documents/National_legislation/Kyrgyzstan%20Constitution%20of%20the%20Kyrghyz%20Republic.asp.

Ryan, Tricia. (2007, August 11). "'Our Women Are Really Very Patient': The Construction of Domestic Violence as a Problem in Kyrgyzstan." Paper presented at the annual meeting of the American Sociological Association, New York City: http://www.allacademic.com/meta/p184186_index.html.

Soltobaev, Aziz. (2000, August 30). *Central Asia: Tajikistan-Kyrgyzstan Drug Route*. American University in Kyrgyzstan, Economics Department. *CACI Analyst:* http://www.cacianalyst.org/?q=node/496.

United States Department of State. (2009, June 16). *Trafficking in Persons Report 2009—Kyrgyz Republic:* http://www.unhcr.org/refworld/docid/4a4214ac2d.html.

Laos (Lao People's Democratic Republic)

Legal System: Civil
Corruption: High
Human Trafficking: Medium
Prison Rate: Low
Death Penalty: Yes
Corporal Punishment: No

Background

Lao People's Democratic Republic (Lao PDR) is a landlocked country in southeast Asia. The republic was created in 1975 toward the end of the Indo-China War. The country suffered immensely from the war and became the most bombed country in the world. Still classified as a "least developed country," Lao PDR aims at moving out of that class by 2020. The population, according to the last census carried out in 2005, is 5.6 million.

The Lao Constitution declares in article 2 that the country is a people's democratic state. The National Assembly appears as the supreme instrument of state power in terms of the Constitution. But this must be viewed in context of the political regime. Article 3 states that the Lao People's Revolutionary Party is the leading nucleus of the political system. The party thus has a leading role recognized by the Constitution.

The People's Supreme Court is the highest court of the land. Below it are the three Regional Appellate Courts (for the Northern, Central, and Southern regions). There is a provincial court for each of the 17 provinces and for the capital city of Vientiane, which is referred to as the Vientiane Municipality Court. Each district should have a district court but due to lack of judges, there are only 102 district courts for the 141 districts, up from 63 in 2006. In all courts, cases are taken up before three-judge panels.

District courts have a limited civil and criminal jurisdiction. The provincial courts have original civil and criminal jurisdiction as well as appellate jurisdiction in respect of judgments of district courts. From provincial courts, an appeal lies to the appellate court on questions of law or fact. The Supreme Court has an appellate jurisdiction in respect of judgments of appellate courts, but only on matters of law.

The president of the Supreme Court is appointed and is removable by the National Assembly. Before 2003, all other judges of the country were appointed by the Standing Committee of the National Assembly on the recommendation of the government. An amendment to the Constitution effected in 2003 provides for the vice president of the People's Supreme Court to be appointed or removed by the president of the state on the recommendation of the president of the Supreme Court. Other judges of the Supreme Court and judges of all other courts are appointed, transferred, and removed by the Standing Committee on the recommendation of the president of the Supreme Court. The administration of courts was transferred from the Ministry of Justice to the Supreme Court, another welcome development.

Under article 86 of the Constitution, the Office of the Supreme Public Prosecutor (OSPP) has the duty to monitor the correct and uniform implementation of laws and regulations by all state institutions, mass organizations, local administrations, civil servants, and citizens. Under article 3 of the Law on Prosecutors, the OSPP monitors and inspects the enforcement of laws by the investigation and interrogation authorities and in places of detention, prisons, and rehabilitation centers.

The departments of Police, Forests, Customs, Income Tax, and Immigration are the main law enforcement agencies. The police are a powerful organization, and there are complaints that, sometimes, even directions of prosecutors are ignored by the police. The police appear to be more powerful in the provinces, being closer to the local authorities. Officials, however, insist that while there may be officers who abuse their powers, this is not a general phenomenon and that violations are not condoned.

The Lao legal system is basically a civil law system. In recent times, certain features of the common law system have also been incorporated. Decisions of the Supreme Court are now binding on all other courts. Article 5 of the Law on People's Courts, adopted in 2003, reads:

> The judgment of the People's Supreme Court on a matter that is not (or is not clearly) defined by the laws shall be considered as a court precedent, which the people's courts shall comply with until such matter is regulated by a law.

The system of criminal law is inquisitorial. Article 8 of the Law on Criminal Procedure declares the principle of presumption of innocence. Article 28 recognizes several rights and obligations of accused and defendants. One of the obligations is to "give statements or clarifications in relation with the accusations." There is thus no right to silence.

The Legal Sector Evaluation (LSE) of 2003, commissioned by the United Nations Development Programme (UNDP) with the support of the Lao government, noted several inconsistencies with internationally accepted norms in criminal trials. Evidence is not formally led through witnesses. Trials are conducted in effect by judges with prosecutors being quite passive. There is no presumption of innocence in practice. Defendants are found guilty based solely on alleged confessions, without confessions even being proved to be voluntary and true. Senior judges and officials at consultative workshops held during the evaluation have stated that the instances cited were mostly aberrations due to inexperience and inadequate training of judges and did not represent the state of the law in the country.

In 2004 the Criminal Procedure Law was amended to provide that a conviction shall not be based principally on confessions made by the accused or defendant. In practice, however, many judges continue to use confessions as the sole basis for convictions. New laws do not always find their way, especially to lower courts, and there is little information on amendments to laws. Lack of training of judges and passiveness of prosecutors and lawyers are contributory factors.

Crime

Classification of Crimes

Article 8 of the Penal Law divides offenses into the following three categories:

1. "Minor offenses" are offenses punishable by public criticism or fine. Examples: forbidden gambling (article 83), hooliganism (article 84), violation of traffic security (article 85), and failure to perform obligations toward minor children, parents, or spouse (article 127).
2. "Major offenses" are offenses punishable by reeducation without deprivation of liberty and imprisonment from three months to 10 years and fine. Examples: money laundering (article 64), disclosure of state or administrative secrets (article 71), unlawful production, possession, and use of weapons or explosives (article 76), battery (article 90), unlawful arrest and detention (article 99), theft and forceful misappropriation of state or collective property (article 108), robbery of personal assets (article 118), and corruption (article 174).

3. "Crimes" are offenses punishable by imprisonment from five years onward or by the death penalty. Examples: treason (article 56), rebellion (article 57), and murder (article 88).

Minor crimes are taken up by district courts. All other criminal cases are tried by provincial courts. Lao law does not contain a provision that explicitly lays down the age of criminal responsibility. Article 53 of the Penal Law, titled "Measures towards Children," permits courts to require the offender to request a pardon from the offender, order compensation payable by the parents or guardians, or send the child to the parents or guardians or to administrative authorities or social organizations for reeducation. But for a court to do so, there has to be a finding of guilt. To further complicate matters, article 4 of the Law on Criminal Procedure provides that investigations may not be opened and criminal proceedings may not be continued in cases involving "acts threatening the society by children less than fifteen years of age" and that in such cases, educational measures shall be applied. The question again arises as to how educational measures could be applied without a finding of guilt.

Drug-related offenses, money laundering, and human trafficking are the crimes that are particularly challenging to Lao PDR. Opium has been almost eradicated from the country. Yet, the use of other drugs appears to be increasing. An increase in cases of theft has been seen, and most suspects in such cases were drug addicts.

The production, sale, distribution, possession, importation, export, transportation, or the transit through the Lao People's Democratic Republic of narcotics such as heroin, amphetamines, any ingredient used in the production of heroin or amphetamines, opium, and marijuana is punishable under article 146 of the Penal Law.

Persons who are found to have consumed, or purchased for consumption, less than three grams of heroin, morphine, cocaine, amphetamines, or other psychotropic substances are regarded as victims and sent for treatment. So are smokers of marijuana.

There are reports of drug traffickers using close relatives and friends, even small children and pregnant women, making detections difficult. People from ethnic groups with a low understanding of criminal liability were also being used. Capacity of police officers in identifying and analyzing drugs is low. Lack of equipment for anti-trafficking units is a major drawback.

The country is ranked as being high among countries of origin of human trafficking. Money laundering is an issue of concern, illegal proceeds being mainly derived from corruption and drug trafficking. There have been only a relatively few prosecutions for human trafficking and still less for money laundering.

Crime Statistics

Statistics, official or otherwise, are not available in respect of crimes committed. Nor are statistics of arrests and detentions available. In the rural areas, the most typical serious crimes are drug-related crimes, theft, illicit felling of timber, human trafficking, and smuggling of immigrants, while motor traffic offenses constitute the most typical minor offense. Most suspects in cases of theft are drug addicts. Drug-related crimes top the list of serious crimes in urban areas, with theft, money laundering, and human trafficking also making the top grade. Violations of motor traffic laws are the most common minor offense.

It is not to be assumed that these categories top the lists in terms of prosecutions too. As stated earlier, there have been relatively few prosecutions for money laundering and human trafficking.

Some statistics from the Supreme Court relating to criminal cases are available. In 2008 there were a total of 2,801 cases in provincial courts. It may be presumed that trials account for 80–90 percent of the cases in provincial courts and that the percentage of convictions is more than 95 percent.

Finding of Guilt

Rights of the Accused

The Constitution contains a chapter on Fundamental Rights and Duties of Citizens. Article 42 is the only provision related to criminal procedure:

> The right of Lao citizens in their bodies, honour and houses are inviolable. Lao citizens cannot be arrested or searched without the order of the Public Prosecutor or the people's courts, except if otherwise provided by the laws.

The Law on Criminal Procedure recognizes several rights of accused and defendants. Article 5 assures the inviolability of citizens' rights and freedom. The equality of citizens before the law and courts is guaranteed by article 6, while article 7 guarantees the right of a defendant to defend himself or herself. The presumption of innocence is declared by article 8. Trials are ordinarily held in public.

All criminal cases, in the district courts as well as in provincial courts, are tried by three-judge panels. Trial by jury is not available. No express provision related to acceptance of a plea of guilt to a lesser offense is found; neither is there such a practice. There is no express legal provision guaranteeing speedy trial. In practice, trials do not drag on.

Right to Representation, Legal Assistance

An accused or defendant has the right to be represented by an attorney, a representative of an organization, a guardian, or a close relative. A lawyer is appointed by court in cases where capital punishment may be given, when the accused or defendant is a child less than 18 years of age, is deaf or is a mute or mentally deficient person, and when the accused or defendant does not understand the Lao language. The trial begins immediately after the accusation is read out. The trial is not adjourned for the defendant to prepare his or her defense and/or retain a lawyer.

Investigations and Prosecution

Investigations into alleged offenses are conducted by agencies such as the police and departments of Customs, Forestry, Income Tax, and Immigration. The opening of an investigation shall be reported to the public prosecutor. The prosecutors ensure the lawful performance of investigations. At the conclusion of an investigation, the case file is forwarded to the prosecutor.

Under the Law on Criminal Procedure, prosecutors play an important role in arrest and detention pending trial. Under article 62, an arrest can be made only upon a warrant issued by a prosecutor or a court. In what are described as "flagrant" and "urgent" cases, article 63 provides for arrest without warrant. All arrests have to be reported to the prosecutor. Detention pending the institution of criminal proceedings in a court requires a warrant in writing from the prosecutor.

According to article 61 (Detention), a suspect may be detained for 48 hours, on the order of the head of the investigation agency or a public prosecutor, for the purpose of carrying out further investigation if there is "sufficiently firm information" that such suspect has committed a criminal offense for which the law provides imprisonment as punishment. "Where there are firm indications supporting the order to open an investigation" and if provisional detention is seen necessary, an application shall be made to a public prosecutor. In the absence of "firm indications," a request shall be made for release. The public prosecutor decides whether the suspect should be released or detained.

Article 62 is titled "Arrest" and deals with arrest with a warrant issued by a prosecutor or a court. For the issue of a warrant for arrest, there should be "firm evidence" that the suspect has committed an offense punishable with imprisonment. Other factors such as "possible escape by the suspect, destruction of evidence, repeated offense, physical attack against the victim, witness or possible physical attack by the victim or other persons against the suspect" shall also be considered. A person arrested shall be notified of the warrant and the reasons for arrest. The arrest shall be reported to the prosecutor within 24 hours, a statement taken from the suspect within 48 hours at the latest, and an application made to the prosecutor for release or provisional detention. The prosecutor shall decide on release or detention within 24 hours. Arrests may be made without a warrant in "flagrant" and "urgent" cases.

Violations of these provisions are common. The LSE referred to a district prosecutor who discovered during a prison inspection that only 10 out of 80 prisoners had been detained upon a proper order from his office. From information received by concerned parties, it appeared unlikely that the situation would be remedied in the near future, the LSE observed. There are no reports of improvement.

Detention and Release Pending Trial

Article 65 of the Law on Criminal Procedure provides for "provisional detention," explained as "temporary detention prior to the court's final decision to carry out investigations." Provisional detention requires a warrant from the public prosecutor and is issued considering the same factors considered in issuing a warrant for arrest under article 62. A person placed under provisional detention shall be detained separately from other prisoners. The period of provisional detention shall not ordinarily exceed three months. Where further investigation is deemed necessary, the public prosecutor may extend the period of provisional detention, each time for three months at the request of the head of the investigation agency. The total period of provisional detention shall not exceed six months in the case of a misdemeanor and one year in the case of police matters. Misdemeanors and police matters are not defined. The Penal Law categorizes offences as minor offenses, major offenses, and crimes. At the end of such period, the public prosecutor shall order the accused person's immediate release if there is insufficient evidence to prosecute the case. The period of provisional detention is reduced from the term of imprisonment if the accused is ultimately convicted and sentenced to imprisonment.

Provisional release is release pending the conclusion of the trial and is governed by article 66. Only a person accused of a minor offense can be so released. Provisional release is not permitted in cases of offenses referred to, again, as police matters.

In article 74, the public prosecutor shall study a case submitted by an investigation agency or a court and shall within 15 days issue any of the following instructions: instructions on further investigations where investigations are incomplete; suspension of the proceedings; closure of case. When investigation or restrictive measures applied by investigation officers or court officers are inadequate in the circumstances of the case, the public prosecutor may modify, cancel, or terminate such measures. Where there is sufficient evidence, the public prosecutor shall order that the accused person be prosecuted.

When the case file is received by a court, a judge assigned by the president of the court studies the file and on his recommendation, the court may return the case file to the public prosecutor for further investigation or for more offenses or defendants to be added. If the court is satisfied that a proper investigation has been carried out, a date is fixed for a court hearing.

The lack of clarity in the Law on Criminal Procedure on the procedure to be followed has a major impact on the quality of criminal justice. Also, there is no law on evidence.

Alternate Dispute Resolution

The country has a long and healthy tradition of settlement of disputes at village level. Village Mediation Units (VMU) were set up pursuant to the Decision of the Minister of Justice No. 304/MOJ, dated August 7, 1997. New guidelines were issued by Decision No. 08/MOJ, dated February 22, 2005. Minor civil and criminal disputes first go before a VMU. If not settled, mediation is again attempted by the District Justice Office, which refers disputes that are not mediated to the appropriate court. VMUs have been set up in around 85 percent of the 10,944 villages in the country.

VMUs are administered by Provincial and District Justice Offices. Overall responsibility for VMUs lies with the Department of Judicial Administration of the Ministry of Justice. A VMU has five to nine members. The head of the village (*Nai Ban*) is ex-officio president. The Lao Women's Union and the Lao Front for Reconstruction are represented. The other members are appointed by the authorities in coordination with the *Nai Ban* and the said representatives. Overall, about 90 percent of cases coming before VMUs are settled. The rate of settlement in rural areas is high, rural people being more compromising. In urban areas, people appear more concerned about prestige.

No statistics regarding the percentage of criminal cases resolved by guilty pleas are available. Even when a defendant pleads guilty, courts go into details about the circumstances of the crime, questioning witnesses and defendants as in a trial.

The Lao law does not contain an explicit provision that permits a court to take into consideration the fact that a defendant has pleaded guilty at the earliest possible stage in deciding the sentence to be awarded. But article 40 of the Penal Law lists the circumstances that would reduce penal responsibilities and permits courts to take into consideration other factors not provided in this article but which would commonly be considered relevant in reducing penal responsibilities.

The Law on People's Courts provides that the Supreme Court, appellate courts, and provincial courts should each have separate criminal and juvenile chambers. There is no such requirement for district courts. Due to the shortage of judges, judges of provincial courts serve in more than one chamber.

Due to lack of judges, justice officials also used to serve as judges in the past. The LSE reported that, in 2003, only 66 of the 158 functioning judges in district courts had formal appointments, the others being officials. In 2006, district courts had 96 judges, all formally appointed. The figures for 2008 are not available, but the number should be much more, considering the fact that 102 of the 141 districts have their own district court, up from 63 in 2006. Supreme Court officials state that officials do not function as judges anymore. Provincial court judges are sometimes sent to district courts to make up the three-member panels required by law.

All judges should have had a formal legal education, being graduates of the Faculty of Law and Political Science of the National University of Laos or of a recognized university or the former Vientiane Law School. Some of the judges in the higher courts have had no basic legal education and had been appointed to the judiciary when a degree in law was not a requirement.

Punishment

Categories of Punishment

Article 28 of the Penal Law lists the various punishments that can be inflicted. Punishments are categorized into principal penalties and additional penalties.

Principal penalties include the following:

- Public criticism—ordinarily by criticism of the offender in court; may be by publicity.
- Reeducation without deprivation of liberty.
- Deprivation of liberty. Life imprisonment shall not be imposed on an offender who was less than 18 years old or was in a state of pregnancy when the offense was committed.
- Death penalty—by shooting—shall not be imposed on an offender who was less than 18 years old the time the offense was committed or on a woman offender who was in a state of pregnancy at the time the offense was committed or who is pregnant at the time the court makes its decision. A woman who is pregnant shall not be executed.

Additional penalties include the following:

- Fine (which may be the principal penalty in certain cases).
- Confiscation of items connected to the offense.
- Confiscation of property.
- Suspension of the right to vote and to be elected.
- House arrest—forbids the offender from leaving a place of residence or from entering areas specified by court.

In addition to penalties, a court may request the relevant authorities to withdraw driving licenses or other permits; to relieve the offender from performing or to forbid the offender from performing a function or duty; to withdraw orders, medals, or titles; or to deport the offender.

The execution of a sentence of imprisonment, reeducation without imprisonment, or fine as the principal penalty may be suspended for a period of five years. If during such period, the offender is not convicted of any other offense, the sentence shall not be executed. In the event of a subsequent conviction resulting in the offender being sentenced to imprisonment, the new penalty as well as the one that has been suspended will be executed. The suspension of the execution of a penalty may be in whole or in part. A person who has committed an offense while serving a sentence for a previous offense or within a period of five years after serving a sentence for the same or similar offense, an offender sentenced to three years of imprisonment or more, or an offender sentenced for a "crime" (an offense punishable with imprisonment from five years onward or by the death penalty) cannot benefit from a stay of execution of penalties.

Compensation for Victims of Crime

Article 29 of the Law on Criminal Procedure states that a victim of a crime is entitled to compensation. A civil plaintiff has the same rights as a victim. A feature of the Lao criminal process is that parties who are entitled to damages or liable to pay damages under civil law are also entitled to participate in criminal trials. This is salutary as the need to file separate civil actions is obviated. However, the law does not lay down the procedure to be followed for a victim or civil plaintiff to present evidence and satisfy the court as to the compensation payable.

Selected Serious Offenses

Article 88 of the Penal Law deals with murder. A person who intentionally causes the death of another person is punishable with 10 to 15 years of imprisonment and fine. Where the accused is a professional killer, where the killing has been barbarous, where the victim was a pregnant woman, and so forth, life imprisonment or death penalty may be imposed. Where the killing was in response to a grave provocation by the victim, the sentence is three to five years' imprisonment. Under article 20, an act of legitimate defense does not amount to an offense.

The penalty for rape, in the absence of the aggravating circumstances, is three to five years of imprisonment and fine, less than in most other jurisdictions. As article 128 stands, only intercourse "against the will" of the woman in the given circumstances would amount to rape. The following situations, caught up in the definition of rape in many jurisdictions, will not constitute rape under Lao law. For example: A man has sexual intercourse with a woman who is sleeping or is unconscious. The intercourse is without her consent but not against her will.

Theft (simple) is punishable with three months to two years of imprisonment or reeducation without deprivation of liberty and fine. Theft by mugging shall be punished with six months to three years of imprisonment and fine. Where theft is committed through "forced entry or by damaging fences, doors, cases, cupboards and others," the offender shall be punished with six months to three years of imprisonment and shall be fined. Where the offender is a professional thief or a member of an organized group or where the loss is substantial, the offender punishment is three to five years of imprisonment and fine. Attempted theft is also similarly punishable.

Punishment for robbery is four to eight years of imprisonment and fine. Where the offender is a professional robber or a member of an organized group or where severe injuries or loss of life or substantial damage is caused, punishment is 8 to 15 years of imprisonment and fine. Preparation or attempt to commit robbery shall also be punished. There is enhanced punishment for theft and robbery of assets of the state and collectives.

Imprisonment is the typical punishment for drug offenses. All drug offenses are punishable under article 146 of the Penal Law. The prohibited acts include the production, sale, distribution, possession, importation, export, transportation, or the transit through the Lao People's Democratic Republic of narcotics such as heroin, amphetamines, any ingredient used in the production of heroin or amphetamines, opium, and marijuana. As seen earlier, the death penalty can be imposed for more serious crimes. Execution is by shooting. According to officials, the death penalty is not carried out in practice.

Prisons

There is very little official information available. There are more than 50 prisons and detention centers. The prison in Samkhe village in Vientiane probably houses the largest number of inmates. Foreign prisoners are mostly said to be in the prison at Phonthong village in Vientiane.

Jayampathy Wickramaratne

Further Reading

Wickramaratne, Jayampathy, Miomir Serbinson, and Xaynari Chanthala. (2004). *Evaluation of the Implementation of the Rule of Law in Lao PDR, 1997–2003, Lessons and Challenges*. Vientiane: United Nations Development Programme.

Macao

Legal System: Civil
Murder: Medium
Corruption: Low
Human Trafficking: Medium
Prison Rate: Medium
Death Penalty: No
Corporal Punishment: Maybe

Background

Macao is located at the southern coast of Mainland China. It is approximately 60 kilometers (37 miles) west of Hong Kong and 145 kilometers (90 miles) south of Guangzhou (Canton). The total area of the territory is only about 30 square kilometers. It consists of a small peninsula, which borders the Guangdong Province of China, and a much larger outlying island.

In recent decades, Macao has been witnessing a considerable expansion of population due to massive influx of immigrants from Mainland China and elsewhere. In fact, this city is basically an immigrant society. More than half of the residents were not born in Macao. Thousands of legal immigrants come from the other side of the north border every year. These new arrivals are mostly of low educational background.

By the end of 2007, the population in the Macao Special Administrative Region (SAR) was estimated to be about 538,100, and the density was larger than 18,000 per squared kilometer. It has become one of the most densely populated regions in the world. The percentages of male and female population were 49.38 percent and 50.62 percent, respectively.

Before December 1999, Macao was a territory under Portuguese colonial rule. In 1845 Portugal declared Macao a free port in an attempt to compete with the rapidly rising British colony of Hong Kong. A century passed, and the Chinese Communist Party established the People's Republic of China (PRC) in Beijing in 1949. The new Chinese government declared that all the previous treaties signed by the Manchu government with Portugal to be invalid. However, as with Hong Kong, Macao was left to retain its status quo for a few more decades. The "Joint Declaration on the Question of Macao" was signed in Beijing in 1987. After about 440 years of Portuguese occupation since the mid-16th century, the government of the PRC resumed its sovereignty over Macao in December 1999 and transformed the small city into another Special Administrative Region in the same manner as Hong Kong.

According to the Joint Declaration on the Question of Macao and the three principles provided by the Basic Law of Macao—"One country, two systems," "Macao people governing Macao," and "A high level of autonomy"—the Macao SAR is entitled to preserve its own capitalist socioeconomic system for at least 50 years, and to retain administrative and legislative autonomies, independent judicial powers, and final adjudication powers. National defense and diplomatic affairs are the only two areas of exception that are exclusive responsibilities of the central government of the PRC. The new governor of SAR is called the chief executive, who is accountable to both the central government of the PRC and the people of Macao SAR.

Today, Macao is regarded as a wealthy region with very low unemployment. Official figures show that this small city has become an economically fast-growing city in the coastal region of southern China. Although tourism is often claimed to be the backbone of Macao's economy, the casino industry is the one that really occupies a pivotal role in the economic vitality of the region. A major part of the SAR government's revenue is actually produced by casino taxes.

Legal System

Due to its Portuguese heritage, the overall legal system of Macao, including the criminal justice system, can be regarded as broadly based on Portuguese law, and therefore of basic characteristics of the continental legal system of Europe. In other words, Macao is typically a civil law legal system where legislation is the chief source of law. Case law is not a major source of law in Macao.

The Basic Law of the Macao Special Administrative Region of the People's Republic of China consists of 145 articles and 3 annexes. After the handover, this Basic Law, which was adopted by the National People's Congress as the constitutional law for Macao, took effect immediately on December 20, 1999. In compliance with the central government's "one country, two systems" policy, most of the legal codes in Macao remain unchanged after the handover, except for a small portion of the existing laws and regulations that has been identified as contradictory to the Basic Law of the Macao SAR.

The most authoritative framework of the legal system in Macao at present is composed of five significant codes: the Civil Code, the Commercial Code, the Code of Civil Procedure, the Penal Code, and the Code of Penal Procedure. They are collectively known as the "Five Big Codes" in Macao. In addition, there are a number of other codes such as those in the field of administrative law.

Macao SAR has been entitled to exercise a high degree of legislative autonomy. The sole legislature of the SAR, the Legislative Assembly, enjoys the power to make, amend, suspend, and repeal laws. Currently, the Legislative Assembly is composed of 29 members, being 12 from direct elections, 10 from indirect elections, and 7 as nominated by the chief executive. All laws enacted locally shall be reported to the central government for the record.

The Penal Code of Macao is one of the five most important codes. Although it was enacted by the Legislative Assembly of Macao, it is generally recognized that the contents, legislative philosophy, and the fundamental principles of this code have been deeply influenced by the criminal jurisprudence theories and thoughts of Portugal.

There are four fundamental principles in this Penal Code:

1. The Principle of Minimum, Necessary, and Appropriate Intervention of Criminal Law
2. The Principle of No Crime without a Law, No Penalty without a Law
3. The Principle of No Penalty without a Fault
4. The Principle of Humanization of Legal Consequence of Crime

Crime

Classification of Crimes

The Penal Code of Macao classifies crime into the following five major categories:

1. *Crimes against the person* include homicide, manslaughter, all types of abortion, all types of physical abuse, kidnapping, rape and child molestation, libel, slander, defamation, crimes against privacy such as trespassing and hacking.
2. *Crimes against property* include theft, burglary, robbery, embezzlement, fraud and blackmail; crimes against property rights include intended bankruptcy, piracy.
3. *Crimes against peace and humanity* include inciting to war or genocide, racial discrimination, and so forth.
4. *Crimes against social order* include bigamy, abduction of minors, forging of currency, arson, explosion, pollution, hijacking, dangerous driving, and participation in triad societies or terrorist organizations, and so forth.
5. *Crimes against the country* include inciting to collective disobedience, insult to national emblem, usurpation of public office, disobedience of legal orders, perjury, abuse of authority, violation of confidentiality, corruption, bribery, and so forth.

Trends in Crime

By general impression, Macao has a relatively moderate level of crime. This perception is supported by the official statistics. There has been a 30.25 percent increase in recorded crime in the period 2003 through 2007. More than half of the recorded criminal cases for these five years were property crimes, especially in 2003 (54.89%) and 2005 (54.23%). Instead, crimes against the person, which are generally regarded as more serious than property crimes, accounted for about one-fourth of all cases in the same period of time. Among these crimes against the person, assault was the most frequent type of offense, whereas homicide was the least frequent form of crime. According to the Macao Yearbook, crimes recorded by the police in 2007 were as follows:

Theft, burglary, and robbery	5,726
Homicide	11
Assault	412
Sexual offense	75
Crimes of social disturbance	1,420
Crimes against the territory	888
Others	1,018

In addition to the official record compiled by the police, the Public Prosecutions Office of Macao in the same period (2003 to 2007) reported cases filed that showed similar trends for the same period. Statistics for different types of crimes as reflected in cases filed for 2007 were as follows:

Illegal immigration and related crime	1,476
Physical assault	1,431
Violation of personal freedom	302
Drug-related crime	157
Illegal gambling and loan sharking	216
Sexual assault	47
Organized crime	31
Murder	24
Others	3,496

Although Macao has long enjoyed a relatively low crime rate, it did encounter a short period of trouble when Macao approached the end of Portuguese colonial rule. Things got worse when the monopolized casino company STDM changed its style of business administration from the centralized management to the new subcontracting system in the early 1990s. Triad members (organized crime) had the chance to infiltrate casino by controlling the selling of gambling chips and loan sharking. As time went on, disputes over power and monetary profit between the competitors became intense. Violent means were employed by triad societies to settle the disagreements. There were gunshots and bomb attacks on triad members, attempted assassinations of judicial officials, and kidnappings of some wealthy people; even a member of the Legislative Assembly was seriously threatened by the gangland violence.

In the eyes of the international media, Macao turned into a center of organized crime just a few years before the PRC resumed its sovereignty over the territory. Eventually, by means of arresting and penalizing the triad boss and stationing the People's Liberation Army in the territory, Macao quickly resumed its peace and social order in the postcolonial era.

Police

Before the handover of Macao back to the Chinese government, the public order of this Portuguese colony was maintained by two separate police systems: the Public Security Police and the Judiciary Police. The Public Security Police was primarily responsible for the maintenance of daily public order. The Judiciary Police specialized in crime prevention and investigation. After the establishment of Macao SAR government, the police system went through a substantial restructuring. An integrated police department, the Unitary Police Service, has been formed to lead and direct all the police operations. The two above-mentioned systems, the Public Security Police and the Judiciary Police, come under the direct central command of this Unitary Police Service.

This central department, the Unitary Police Service, is primarily responsible for planning and giving advice on all police operations. There are five units within UPS:

1. The Intelligence Analysis Centre
2. The Operations Planning Centre
3. The Department for Resource Management
4. The Computer and Information Technology Unit
5. The Information and Public Relations Office

Under the leadership of the commissioner-general, the Public Security Police is responsible for ensuring the fundamental public order of the territory. In 2007, the number of staff members in Public Security Police was more than 3,500. There are altogether 10 ranks in the Public Security Police ranging from the commissioner-general to constable.

Within the structure of Public Security Police, there is one management board heading nine subordinate units: Resource Management Department, Information Department, Operations Department, Immigration Department, Traffic Department, City Police Department, Islands Police Department, Tactical Police Unit, and Logistic Support and Services Division. Besides, the Public Security Police has its own police school to manage the recruitment and training of police officers.

Another police system is the Judiciary Police. It is a criminal investigation sector that has six subordinate units: Criminal Investigation Department, Management and Planning Department, Forensic Science Laboratory, INTERPOL Macao-China, Criminal Intelligence Division, and the Department for the Investigation of Gaming-related and Economic Crimes. Like Public Security Police, the Judiciary Police has its own police training school to recruit and drill the new blood in criminal investigation.

INTERPOL Macao-China is a special unit in the Judiciary Police. It is also a subbureau of the Chinese National Central Bureau of ICPO-INTERPOL. Upon the request of overseas INTERPOL offices, it provides operational assistance in Macao, including issuing international arrest warrants, exchanging crime information, and detaining international fugitives. Through the operation of this unit, the Macao police system establishes cooperative relations with overseas security authorities.

Another special unit is the Department for the Investigation of Gaming-related and Economic Crimes. The duty of this unique police unit is to prevent and investigate gaming-related offenses and many other crimes committed in casinos and gaming venues. Its set-up reflects the prosperity of the casino industry in this city. Macao is literally a *casino state* in the Far East. It has often been called the "Monte Carlo of the Orient" or "Las Vegas of the Orient." Many studies have shown a substantial positive association between organized crime and the gambling industry. In this socioeconomic context, the establishment of the unit is deemed to be necessary.

Customs

The Macao Customs is another law enforcement sector in Macao's public security system. An independently administered unit apart from the police, it is responsible for exercising its authority to lead, implement, and supervise measures related to customs laws and policies. Macao Customs performs its policing duties such as combating customs fraud, curbing and stamping out unlawful trafficking, safeguarding intellectual property rights, and monitoring external trade activities to protect Macao's international reputation.

Macao Customs puts much emphasis on interregional and international cooperation. Because the territory consists of a small peninsula and an outlying island, patrolling the coastal waters is an essential part of Macao Customs' duties. The Customs Service Fleet, which takes up the responsibility of this marine patrolling, has gained the cooperation of the Guangdong Provincial Public Security Department and other mainland customs departments of the PRC. Joint operations at sea are frequently conducted to maintain order along the coastal waters.

The Commission against Corruption

Because of the seriousness and prevalence of corruption in the territory before the handover, the Macao SAR government needed to set up a special law enforcement unit to combat the crime of corruption and carry out ombudsman functions. Modeling the Independent Commission against

Corruption in Hong Kong, this new unit is independent from the police and other law enforcement teams and accountable only to the chief executive. The unit is called the Commission against Corruption of Macao (in Portuguese: *Commissario contra a Corrupcao—CCAC*).

CCAC, as an independent law enforcement team, makes no laws itself. Its power and duties are prescribed in article 59 of the Basic Law. Moreover, CCAC makes no prosecution in its own right. After investigation, the cases are transferred to the Public Prosecutions Office for prosecution.

Regarding the organizational structure, the CCAC has one cabinet and two subordinate bureaus—the Anti-corruption Bureau and the Ombudsman Bureau. Each bureau has its own investigation department and is responsible for the control of different negative bureaucratic behavior in public administration. All staff are recruited separately from other departments to maintain its independency.

According to the latest annual report of the CCAC, altogether 736 complaint cases were recorded in 2007. This figure represents a 12.4 percent decrease compared with the record in 2006 and an even more drastic decrease of 33.6 percent compared with the record in 2005. This is also the lowest number of complaints received since the Macao SAR was established. The decrease of complaints related primarily to the drop-off of criminal offenses and the overall improvement of integrity in Macao, especially the upgrading of public administration services.

Finding of Guilt

According to the Code of Penal Procedure of Macao, there are two categories of criminal proceedings—the ordinary process and the special process. The ordinary process includes the trial by the Collegial panel and Sole-judge bench. The special process can be the simple process or the correctional process. The simple one is used to try offenders who are punishable by a prison term of not more than three years, whereas the correctional one is used to try trivial criminal offenses.

The penal procedure can be divided into seven phases—registration of cases, investigation, preliminary hearing, adjudication, ordinary appeal, extraordinary appeal, and execution. The phase of adjudication itself can be divided into three stages—the antecedent action such as pretrial examination; hearing of evidence, which means the holding of a court hearing; and the ruling that is the consequence of judgment on a case made by a court.

The prosecution adopts different approaches to try different categories of criminal offenses. For public offenses, the prosecution determines whether it is necessary to institute legal proceedings regardless of the will of the victims. But for the quasipublic offenses and private offenses, whether the prosecution decides to institute legal proceedings depends on whether the victims or their agents will lodge a complaint to the prosecution.

The power of investigation into criminal cases mostly belongs to the prosecution, and partly belongs to the examining magistrates. For criminal police authorities, they are entitled to participate in the investigation with the authority extended by the prosecution or courts.

Although the law legalizes the means of collecting evidence that meet the requirement of modern society, such as monitoring of telephone conversation, it provides for very strict restriction on the application of these means to safeguard basic rights and freedom of citizens.

Police must present persons remanded in custody to an examining judge within 48 hours of detention. Cases must come to trial within six months of an indictment. However, judges can refuse bail in cases of serious crime.

The Public Prosecutions Office

The Public Prosecutions Office is the only official judicial organ in the judiciary of Macao that possesses the power of prosecution. The office is independent from other departments and institutions and is free from any political interference. The Public Prosecutions Office has equivalent status to that of the courts, though they are working together closely in the judiciary of Macao.

The head of the Public Prosecutions Office, the public prosecutor-general, shall be a permanent resident of the Macao SAR. Nominated by the chief executive, the candidate needs to be appointed by the central government. Public prosecutors (also known as judicial officers in this office) are nominated by the public prosecutor-general and appointed by the chief executive.

According to the incumbent public prosecutor-general, Mr. Chio-ming Ho, the Public Prosecutions Office of Macao has the following powers and functions:

1. To represent the Macao SAR government in the courts.
2. To monitor the application of law.
3. To safeguard public interests.
4. To supervise criminal investigation and ensure successful criminal prosecutions.

Furthermore, the Public Prosecutions Office has established a judicial framework entitled "One Institution, Three Levels of Assignment." One institution refers to one unified body within the structure of the office, as opposed to the three levels of the office corresponding to the three tiers of courts.

Judiciary

Under the Basic Law and the Macao SAR Judicial Organization Framework Law, there are two independent judiciary bodies in Macao. The first is the court system, which is responsible for the exercise of the power of adjudication. The second system is the Public Prosecutions Office that possesses the power of prosecution in the judicial ambit of Macao SAR.

The Basic Law stipulates that judges of the courts at all three levels shall be appointed by the chief executive. The public prosecutor-general as the head of the Public Prosecutions Office shall be nominated by the chief executive and appointed by the central government of PRC. The rest of the prosecutors of the Public Prosecutions Office are appointed by the chief executive. In 2006, there were altogether 29 judges in all three levels of courts, plus another 29 magistrates in the Public Prosecutions Office.

Courts

The courts of Macao SAR are clearly structured into three levels. This hierarchical court system embodies the power of final adjudication granted by the central government of the People's Republic of China.

1. The Court of First Instance

The president of the Court of First Instance is appointed by the chief executive from the local judges of that level of court. The term of office of this presidency is three years. The court consists of both the Lower Court and the Administrative Court.

The Lower Court is composed of three Civil Courts, three Criminal Courts, one Court for Minor Civil Cases. It also has two Examining Magistracies. There are two distinctive ways for the Lower Court to adjudicate over legal proceedings: (a) Collegial panel is the form of hearing conducted by a group of judges, and (b) Sole-judge bench is a hearing conducted by a single judge. Offenses punishable by a term of imprisonment not less than three years are generally heard by the Collegial panel. The rest of criminal offenses are normally tried by a Sole-judge bench. Currently, the Lower Court has altogether 18 judges for the two different ways of legal proceedings—4 presidents of Collegial panel and 14 judges of Sole-judge bench. The Examining Magistracy, with a team of two judges, hears criminal cases at various stages of investigation. During the criminal hearing process, the Examining Magistracy performs investigative judicial functions, conducts preliminary trials, and decides whether to send a case for a full trial. In addition, the magistracy can carry out judicial work related to detention, imprisonment, and rehabilitation.

The Administrative Court has two judges to adjudicate in cases in the form of either a Collegial panel or a Sole-judge bench. They hear disputes of the following three main types: public administration, taxation, or customs. The Administrative Court is not entitled to hear criminal cases.

2. The Court of Second Instance

The Court of Second Instance (or the Court of Appeal) is the court of the middle rank. At present, it has five judges. All of them are appointed by the chief executive. The president serves a term of three years. The main functions of the Court of Second

Instance include hearing appeals against the Court of First Instance, hearing jurisdictional conflicts between different parts of the Court of First Instance, deciding whether criminal cases should be retried, and reviewing and confirming other judgments made by courts or arbiters outside Macao.

3. The Court of Final Appeal

The Court of Final Appeal is the court of the highest rank in Macao SAR with the power of final adjudication. It currently has three judges. The president of the Court of Final Appeal shall be appointed by the chief executive among the local judges of that level of court. The appointee shall be a Chinese citizen who is a permanent resident of the Macao SAR. The term of office of this presidency is three years. Like the Court of Second Instance, the Court of Final Appeal functions in chambers and in sessions and holds a general meeting once a week.

Punishment

There are two types of legal consequences prescribed by the Penal Code: penalties and security measures.

Penalties

Because of the humanistic approach of the criminal law of Macao, the application of penalty to the convicts should be intended for the prevention of crime and the correction of the offenders. Punishment should be applied as a means to achieve these two objectives simultaneously. Under this philosophy, death penalty and life imprisonment have long been abolished.

According to the criminal law of Macao, there are two types of penalties—the principal penalty and the accessory penalty. The execution of penalties must be in sequence. The principal penalty has to be completely executed before the accessory punishment could be carried out.

The principal penalties consist of sentence to imprisonment and sentence to fines. In Macao's criminal justice system, a substitution practice has been effectively operating within the two principal penalties for a long period of time. Under specific circumstances, the sentence to fines could substitute for imprisonment when the judges consider that the objective of crime prevention can still be met. Besides, the original sentence must not be more than a six-month imprisonment. On the other hand, if convicts fail to pay the fine without a reasonable explanation, they still have to serve the prison terms.

Prison terms are set by days, months, or years. The shortest term is one month. In general, the longest term will be 25 years. Under specific circumstances, the term may be set to 30 years maximum. Judges may set the prison term longer than 25 years when applying concurrent punishment for several crimes at one time. Prison terms for the most common serious crimes according to the Penal Code are as follows:

Murder	10 to 20 years
Aggravated murder	15 to 25 years
Manslaughter	A maximum of 3 years
Aggravated manslaughter	A maximum of 5 years
Forcible rape	3 to 12 years
Robbery	1 to 8 years
Blackmail	10 to 20 years

Fine as a penalty for crime is applied through two stages. First, the judge has to determine the number of days for the fine that is correspondent with the extent of criminality. Second, the judge has to decide the value of the fine for each day, ranging from 50 to 10,000 Macao patacas (1 U.S. dollar is equivalent to 8 patacas), according to the financial capabilities of the convict. The product of the two figures will be the actual amount of fine payable by the convict.

Accessory penalty is applied to the convict in the form of deprivation of his or her right to engage in certain public activity or to hold a certain job position. The application of accessory penalties in addition to principal penalties appears only under specific circumstances. It is not a necessary consequence of the conviction.

Security Measures

According to article 18 of the Penal Code of Macao, all subjects under the age of 16 are legally presumed to be unable to recognize the illegality of their actions and to make a decision on their actions. This clearly indicates that the age of criminal responsibility in Macao is 16 years of age. Under this criminal legislation, minors cannot be incriminated and criminal penalties cannot be applied. Security measures, such as verbal admonition, provisional internment for observation, attended liberty and internment, are the only legal consequences that can be applied to minors. When the wrongdoers reach the age of 18, these security measures will become inapplicable to them.

Besides the minors, another group of wrongdoers who also cannot be incriminated are those who are psychologically abnormal. According to the criminal law of Macao, persons with mental abnormality lack the subjective abilities to comprehend their own actions. If they engage in activities that constitute criminal offenses, preventive measures need to be taken to protect them and the recipients against potential danger and damage to legal interests and rights. These preventive actions are normally taken in the form of security measures.

Probation and Parole

According to the criminal law of Macao, the court can apply probation to those offenders who have committed less serious crimes. Probation is the suspension of a sentence of imprisonment. A convicted criminal who needs to serve a jail sentence not more than three years and demonstrates substantial evidence of remorsefulness can be placed on probation. He or she can return to the community under the supervision of a probation officer. The criminal has to abide by certain conditions set forth by the court for a probation period of one to five years. Based upon the assessment of the performance of the convicted during the probation period by the probation officer, the court can withdraw the application of probation and send the criminal back to the prison.

Parole is a special correctional program in the Macao penal system. It is the supervised release of a prison inmate before the completion of his or her sentence. According to the criminal law of Macao, the inmate must have served at least two-thirds or six months of his or her sentence. In other words, parole would not be applied to those with a sentence of less than nine months. The second condition for application of parole is the demonstration of substantial evidence of remorsefulness from the convicted. The final condition is the demonstration of substantial evidence of not posing potential danger to the society by the parolee after the release. Monitored by a parole officer, the parolee will be assisted to reintegrate into the normal society on an earlier date.

Prison

Macao Prison has a long history that can date back to ancient dynasties of Imperial China. However, the modern one was only built in 1990 on an outlying island. It is a crucial part of the Macao criminal justice system. Its function is to execute court-imposed custodial sentences. The principle of punishment in Macao is to help criminals reintegrate into society and lead a normal life after discharge from prison. Because of that, the prison is responsible for the discipline and rehabilitation of the inmates during their period of confinement.

The prison has employed a unisex policy of administration. Men and women have separate sections. Some special zones are set up for detention of inmates who might need absolute or limited isolation from other prisoners. The maximum accommodation of the prison is 1,050 inmates. In 2007, there were a total of 812 persons in prison, of which about 10 percent were female and 25 percent were prisoners on remand.

The prison offers a wide range of courses from primary school level to secondary school level. Academic placement tests are also provided to assess the prisoners' educational abilities. For those inmates who have already completed secondary school education, they are entitled to apply for distance learning correspondence courses.

Vocational training workshops have been set up where professional tutors are recruited to teach inmates different vocational knowledge and skills. Moreover, the prison has established partnerships with a number of tertiary institutes in Macao to offer professional programs to equip inmates with a variety of job skills and thus pave their way to return to society in the future. Inmates can obtain professional certificates after the completion of courses and become certified technicians or skilled workers.

In addition to these occupational training opportunities, inmates who have children under 16 years old are entitled to join a program called "the Child Support Program." In company with a social worker, inmates in this program are allowed to meet their children on Sundays to maintain and strengthen their parent-child relationships. This is another humanistic mechanism of paving the way for their return to normal life.

Social Rehabilitation Department

The Macao SAR government has set up a Social Rehabilitation Department under the Legal Affairs Bureau to provide rehabilitation services to released inmates. The provision of these services corresponds with the spirit of Macao's criminal justice system of assisting offenders to rectify the wrongdoings and reintegrating them into society. The services include psychological counseling, financial aid, and employment support. The assistance can be extended to the family of the ex-convicts.

Besides the services toward released inmates, the department is also responsible to implement noncustodial sentences to those offenders who have been convicted of minor offenses. These noncustodial sentences include suspended sentences, probation, labor service as a substitute for paying fine, and compulsory abstinence from drug abuse. In 2007, the Social Rehabilitation Department reported that there were 119 offenders on probation, 83 serving suspended sentences, 7 on community service orders, and 2 drug-addiction rehabilitation cases.

Furthermore, this department provides rehabilitation services not only to adults but also to juveniles. These services include compiling presentencing reports to the courts, conducting educational and vocational training programs, offering psychological counseling, and monitoring them on their school attendance behavior. The department reports that in 2006 there were more than 450 juvenile cases annually, of whom 412 were in follow-up education and 23 were serving suspended sentences.

Reformatory for Juvenile Delinquents

The Reformatory for Juvenile Delinquents is an institution operating under the governance of the Legal Affairs Bureau of the Macao SAR government. It holds young persons who have violated Macao's criminal law. All clients are referred by the courts. Its mission is to help these juvenile delinquents remedy their cognitive, psycho-emotional, and behavioral problems. It also aims to enhance their ability for self-care and independence, strengthen their capacity to think and learn, and equip them with basic life skills so that they can adapt better to society in the future.

In general, the reformatory as an institution accepts juvenile delinquents aged 12 to 16. But once an adolescent has been accepted as an inmate, he or she can stay in the institution until the age of 21. The reformatory has established two different areas for boys and girls with a team of counselors working around-the-clock in each area, respectively. Other professionals such as psychologists, social workers, and occupational training instructors work together to take care of the inmates' psychological, interpersonal, and occupational needs. In 2007 there were 42 boys in reformatory and 4 girls. This was a 30 percent decline compared to 2006.

The reformatory also provides formal education programs up to secondary school level to the inmates. It also helps arrange for the inmates to study at other vocational training centers. Besides educational opportunities, the reformatory has developed a community service scheme to help juvenile delinquents understand better about the larger society and develop a stronger sense of social responsibility. Under this scheme, inmates are required to participate in a number of voluntary work teams to provide social services to the community such as assisting nonprofit organizations in organizing various community activities.

Samson Chi-fai Kwan

Further Reading

The Basic Law of the Macao Special Administrative Region of the People's Republic of China. The Government Printing Bureau of the Macao Special Administrative Region Web site: http://bo.io.gov.mo/bo/i/1999/leibasica/index_uk.asp.

Centro de formacao Juridica e Judiciaria. (2007). P*roceedings of the International Conference on Criminal Procedure Law Challenges in the 21st Century.* Macao: Centro de formacao Juridica e Judiciaria.

Chio, Kuok-keong. (1998). *A Study of Penal Law of Macao.* [in Chinese]. Macao: Macao Foundation.

Leong, Candy Veng-mei. (2004). "Macau Casinos and Organized Crime." *Journal of Money Laundering Control* 7(Spring): 298.

Malaysia

Legal System: Islamic/Common/Customary
Murder: Medium
Corruption: Medium
Human Trafficking: Medium
Prison Rate: Medium
Death Penalty: Yes
Corporal Punishment: Yes

Background

Malaysia consists of Peninsular Malaysia, which comprises 11 states (Perlis, Kedah, Penang, Perak, Selangor, Negeri Sembilan, Melaka, Johor, Pahang, Kelantan, Terengganu), and Sabah and Sarawak. The population in Malaysia is about 25 million. The male population makes up 51 percent of the population, while the female population is 49 percent. The population consists of diverse ethnic groups and religions. The three main ethnic groups in Malaysia include Malays (53.4%), Chinese (26%), and Indians (7.7%). The other indigenous groups, besides the Malays, live mainly in Sarawak and Sabah (e.g., Iban, Bidayuh, Melanau, Kadazan, Bajau, and Murut) and make up 11.7 percent of the population. Other small ethnic minority groups, such as the Portuguese and Siamese descendents, make up the rest of the population (1.2 percent). The religions practiced in Malaysia entail Islam (60.4%), Buddhism (19.25), Christianity (9.1%), Hinduism (6.3%), and others (5%). Islam is the official religion of the country.

Malaysia is a democratic country with a constitutional monarchy. The ruling party is the *Barisan Nasional* (National Front), which is a coalition of the United Malays National Organization (UMNO)—the dominant party, Malaysian Chinese Association (MCA), Malaysian Indian Congress (MIC), and a few smaller parties.

Legal History

Malaysian legal history begins with the arrival of Francis Light from Britain in Penang in 1786, followed by the cessation of Melaka in 1824. Before then, there were kingdoms and sultanates dispensing Islamic law, traditional law, and customary law, notably the *Undang-undang Melaka* (the laws of Melaka), which existed around 1422 to 1458.

When the English first arrived in Penang, they did not bring any legal system with them as their main concern was trade. At that period, British rule in Penang is said to be a period of "legal chaos." The First Charter of Justice, based on the law of England at the time, which was founded upon the common law, was introduced into Penang in 1807. Through the charter, a Court of Judicature was established. English law in Malaysia, therefore, started in Penang. The Second Charter of Justice was introduced to Melaka and Singapore in 1826, and the Third Charter of Justice was introduced in 1855. The application of English law was confirmed by the Privy Council (in England) in 1875. As the trading business developed, English law spread from Penang, Melaka, and Singapore to other states. However, there was no statutory introduction of English law in these other states until 1937, although it had been practiced widely. The Civil Law Enactment of 1937 gave statutory authority for its application.

As for criminal law, the Indian Penal Code 1860 and criminal procedure were formally adopted by Penang and Melaka in 1871. In 1884, Perak formally adopted the Indian Penal Code. The codes gradually spread to other states through British officers and Malay magistrates. By 1889, Negeri Sembilan, Selangor, Perak, and Pahang had accepted British authority and the British Residential system, where each ruler or *sultan* had to accept a British Resident. The *sultans* were the sovereign rulers, but actual government was in the hands of the British Residents. In 1896, all four states formed the Federated Malay States. The Federated Malay States formally adopted the Indian Penal Code in 1905. The other states, which did not join the Federated Malay States, were known as the Unfederated Malay States. In 1948, the Federated Malay States, the Unfederated Malay States, and the Straits Settlements of Penang and Melaka joined up to form the Federation of Malaya. The Federation of Malaya gained independence from British colonial rule in 1957. A new federal constitution was introduced, which became the supreme law of the country. The federation, together with Sarawak and Sabah, which were under British colonial rule in 1946, and Singapore, formed Malaysia in 1963. Singapore separated from Malaysia in 1965.

At present, every state has its own government and constitution regulating the government of that state. Malaysia, as a whole, has a written constitution called the Federal Constitution. It is the supreme law of the country. Under the Constitution, Parliament has the legislative authority of the central government. The Parliament consists of the *Yang di-Pertuan Agong* (the King), a Senate or *Dewan Negara,* and a House of Representatives or *Dewan Rakyat*. Parliament enacts laws for the whole of Malaysia. However, if the laws enacted by Parliament are inconsistent with the Federal Constitution, the courts of law may declare them void. The legislature of a state may also make laws with respect to matters specified in the State List. The list covers matters such as Islamic law, personal and family law of Muslims, Malay customs, offenses by Muslims, sharia courts, local government, local services, and offenses against the state law. However, article 75 of the Federal Constitution provides that if any state law is inconsistent with the federal law, the federal law shall prevail.

Police

The first modern police force in Malaysia started on March 25, 1807, after the introduction of the First Charter of Justice in Penang. Most of the officers then were of British origin. Similar independent police organizations were soon introduced to other states. After the Japanese occupation in Malaya ended on April 1, 1946, the Straits Settlements Police, the Federated Malay States Police, and the Unfederated Malay States Police merged together to form the Malayan Union Police with its headquarters in Kuala Lumpur.

During the Malayan Emergency that took place between 1948 and 1960, the police, together with the military, played a huge role in defeating the communist insurgency. The *Yang di-Pertuan Agong* awarded the police force with the title *DiRaja* (Royal) on July 24, 1958. On September 16, 1963, the police force in Malaya, Sabah, Sarawak, and Singapore merged together to form the *Polis DiRaja Malaysia* (Royal Malaysia Police) and was led by an inspector-general of police.

Sources of Malaysian Law

Malaysian law can be classified into written and unwritten law. Written law refers to federal and state constitutions and legislation enacted by Parliament and the state assemblies. Unwritten law comprises principles of English law applicable to local circumstances, previous judicial decisions, and local customs accepted by the courts.

Another source of Malaysian law is Islamic law, which only applies to Muslims. The Federal Constitution provides that the states have power to administer Muslim law. The courts that enforce Muslim law are the sharia courts. It covers mainly family matters (e.g., marriage and divorce) and division of property and assets of a deceased person.

The Judicial System

The doctrine of binding judicial precedent in English law is practiced by Malaysian courts. Decisions of higher courts bind lower courts and some courts are bound by their own decisions.

Before January 1, 1987, the Privy Council, which sits in England, was the final court of appeal in Malaysia. Appeals to the Privy Council on criminal and constitutional matters were abolished on January 1, 1978. The highest court of appeal after that was the Supreme Court until June 23, 1994 where the Federal Court took over as the highest court of appeal.

Courts

The hierarchy of Malaysian courts is as follows. The superior courts consist of the Federal Court (the highest court of appeal), the Court of Appeal, the High Court in Malaya (in Peninsular Malaysia), and the High Court of Sabah and Sarawak. The subordinate courts consist of the Sessions Court, Magistrates' Court, *Penghulu's* Court (in Peninsular Malaysia only), and the Native Court (in Sarawak and Sabah only). The head of the judiciary is the chief justice.

Penghulu's Court

The *penghulu's* court is the lowest level of the subordinate courts in Peninsular Malaysia. It is presided over by a *penghulu,* or headman, appointed by the state government for a *mukim* (district). Disputes are normally settled informally and of a civil nature. For criminal cases, the *penghulu's* court can only try minor offenses against persons of an Asian race and that can be punished by a fine not exceeding 25 ringgit (about US$7). Any person charged with an offense before a *penghulu's* court may elect to be tried by a magistrates' court.

The Sultan Abdul Samad Building in Kuala Lumpur is home to Malaysia's judicial branch and is the location of the Federal Court and other high courts. The architecture reflects Malaysia's predominantly Muslim population. (Sandra Prietz/Dreamstime)

Magistrates' Court

The magistrates' court, presided over by a first-class or a second-class magistrate, deals with minor civil and criminal cases. A first-class magistrate is a member of the judicial and legal service of the Federation and, therefore, legally qualified. A second-class magistrate is appointed by the *Yang di-Pertuan Agong*. Under Section 85 of the Subordinate Courts Act 1948 (Revised 1972) (SCA), a first-class magistrate may try all offenses for which the maximum term of punishment provided by the law does not exceed 10 years' imprisonment, all offenses punishable with fine only, and offenses under Sections 392 (robbery) and 457 (lurking, house-trespass or house-breaking by night) of the Penal Code. Section 87 of the SCA states that the first-class magistrate may pass the following sentences:

1. Not exceeding five years' imprisonment.
2. A fine of not more than 10,000 ringgit (about US$2,788).
3. Whipping up to 12 strokes.
4. A combination of any of the above sentences.

However, in the case of Dangerous Drugs Act 1952, the magistrate may impose a fine not exceeding 100,000 ringgit (about US$27,884) on offenders.

A second-class magistrate may try offenses for which the maximum term of imprisonment does not exceed 12 months or offenses punishable with a fine only. Under Section 89 of the SCA, the second-class magistrate may pass the following sentences:

1. Not exceeding six months' imprisonment.
2. A fine of up to 1,000 ringgit (about US$279).
3. A combination of the above sentences.

The magistrates' court also orders adjournments, bails, remands, warrants to search places, apprehensions of criminals or offenders, transfers of proceedings to sessions courts, and holds inquiries of death.

Juvenile Courts

Juvenile courts, presided over by a first-class magistrate and assisted by two lay advisers (one of whom shall, if practical, be a woman), deal with persons who have attained the age of criminal responsibility, that is, 10 years old, but below 18 years old. A child is a person under the age of 14 years, while a young person is between 14 and 18 years of age.

The juvenile courts can try all offenses except those punishable by death. The court is closed to members of the public, unlike the other courts where the public generally may have access. The newspaper is prohibited from revealing the name or any particular information that may lead to the identification of any child or young person in the proceedings.

The offender who was found guilty may be sent to a juvenile institution or a school to be given corrective or rehabilitation education. If the offense does not involve homicide, the court may discharge him or her on condition that he or she executes a bond, with or without sureties, to be of good behavior and to come up for sentencing when called upon. Appeals by the offender may be made to the High Court. A death sentence cannot be imposed on juveniles; instead, the person will be detained during the pleasure of the *raja* or *sultan* (ruler of the state) or the *Yang di-Pertuan Agong*.

Sessions Court

The sessions court, presided by a sessions court judge, is the highest of the subordinate courts. It deals with both criminal and civil cases. Its criminal jurisdiction extends to all offenses other than those punishable with death.

Native Courts

The native courts exist only in Sarawak and Sabah and are empowered to try civil and criminal matters relating to native laws or customs. In Sarawak, the native courts are statutory courts established by the Sarawak state law and not by federal law. They administer a system of laws entirely different from that of the High Court and the subordinate courts in Sarawak. The native court system consists of three courts: the district native court, the native officer's court or chief's court, and the headman's court. The headman's court consists of a headman and two assessors. It has the power to impose a fine not exceeding 50 ringgit (about US$13.93). The native officer's or chief's court consists of a native officer or chief and two assessors. It has the power to impose a term of imprisonment not exceeding six months and a fine not exceeding 100 ringgit (about US$27.88). The district native court, comprising a magistrate, a native officer, and two assessors, possesses the widest jurisdiction. It may impose a term of imprisonment not exceeding two years and a fine not exceeding 200 ringgit (about US$55.74).

The Resident's Native Court and the Native Court of Appeal exercise only appellate jurisdiction. The Native Court of Appeal is presided over by a judge with powers similar to those of a High Court judge and nominated from the High Court by the *Yang di-Pertua Negeri* (rulers in Sarawak and Sabah). The district native court is not subordinate to the High Court. The High Court also has no jurisdiction to entertain the motion of any applicant from the district native court.

In Sabah, jurisdiction is exercised at the native court with the district officer acting in a supervisory cum appellate capacity. All proceedings are subjected to scrutiny by the district officer who may quash or vary the proceedings, or direct a rehearing if he or she considers that such proceedings have been irregular or improper. An imprisonment sentence cannot be imposed without the endorsement of the district officer. In his or her appellate capacity, the district officer hears appeals from any order of a native court. An appeal from any order of the district officer lies to a Native Court of Appeal presided over by a judge of the High Court. The Court of Appeal also comprises the Resident of the residency in which the original proceedings took place and one native chief duly appointed.

High Court

There are two High Courts in Malaysia presided over by two chief judges. They are the High Court in Malaya (in Peninsular Malaysia) and the High Court of Sabah and Sarawak. The jurisdiction of the High Court is original, appellate, and supervisory. In its original jurisdiction, it has unlimited criminal and civil powers. In criminal cases, they can only be brought to the High Court after the offenders have been properly committed for trial after a preliminary hearing in the magistrates' courts. All cases punishable by death are tried at the High Court. In the exercise of its appellate jurisdiction, the High Court hears civil and criminal appeals from the magistrates' and sessions courts. As such, the High Court may, in the interest of justice, call for the records of any proceedings in the subordinate courts at any stage of such proceedings. It may also remove the case to the High Court or give such directives to the subordinate courts as it deems necessary.

Court of Appeal

The Court of Appeal constitutes the president of the Court of Appeal and up to 10 Court of Appeal judges. The Court of Appeal case is heard by three judges or such greater uneven number of judges. Its jurisdiction covers both criminal and civil offenses. In criminal cases, the Court of Appeal has jurisdiction to hear and determine any appeal against any High Court decision. Appeals are decided in accordance with the opinion of the majority of judges composing the court. Where an appeal has been heard and disposed of by the Court of Appeal, it has no power to review the case.

Federal Court

The Federal Court is the highest court in Malaysia and consists of the chief justice, the president of the Court of Appeal, the chief judge of Malaya, the chief judge of Sabah and Sarawak, and six Federal Court judges. Every proceeding in the Federal Court is heard by three judges or such greater uneven number of judges as the chief justice may in any particular case determine. Its jurisdiction covers both criminal and civil offenses. In criminal cases, the Federal Court has the jurisdiction to hear and determine any appeal of the Court of Appeal in its appellate jurisdiction in respect of any criminal matter decided by the High Court in its original jurisdiction. An appeal may be made against acquittal, conviction, or against sentence on a point of law or fact.

Finding of Guilt

Criminal Procedure

There are many laws governing the administration of criminal justice or criminal procedure in Malaysia, but the foremost statute is the Criminal Procedure Code (CPC). All offenses under the Penal Code and offenses in statutes may be tried according to the CPC. However, if a specific statute lays down a special mode of trial or investigation, then that statute will prevail over the CPC; for example, search in relation to drug offenses would have to be conducted according to the provisions of the Dangerous Drugs Act 1952. Besides local statutes, the CPC allows reference to be made to English law whenever appropriate.

Arrest

There are generally four categories of persons who may effect the arrest: (1) the police officer, (2) the *penghulu* (headman), (3) the private person, and (4) the magistrate or justice of the peace. Section 23 of the CPC allows a police officer to arrest a person without a warrant. The *penghulu* may arrest in situations similar to those of a police officer. After the arrest, the *penghulu* has to hand over the person to the nearest police officer or to the nearest police station without unnecessary delay.

Investigation

After the police have arrested the persons or after a police report has been made by a complainant, the police will decide on whether to proceed with investigation. In the course of investigation, Section 117 of the CPC allows the police to detain the arrested person, but he or she must be produced before a magistrate within 24 hours, exclusive of time taken for any journey, if the police want to detain him or her longer than 24 hours. The magistrate may extend the period of detention to a maximum period of not exceeding 15 days.

Prosecution

Once the police investigation is completed, the investigating officer is required to forward to the public prosecutor a report in the form set out in the procedures to institute or not to institute prosecution in court. However, the public prosecutor may issue an order in writing directing that no report be forwarded to him or her in cases of a character to be specified in the order and may at any time vary or revoke the order.

According to Section 376(1) of the CPC, the attorney general will be the public prosecutor and will control and direct all criminal prosecutions and proceedings under the CPC. The solicitor general will have all the powers of a deputy public prosecutor and shall act as public prosecutor in the absence of or inability to act of the attorney general. The powers of the public prosecutor are numerous. The public prosecutor may appoint deputies who will be under his or her general control and direction.

Crime

Criminal Offenses

Where criminal offenses in Malaysia are concerned, the Penal Code and the Criminal Procedure Code are the main references, although there are many other laws governing the administration of criminal justice. The Penal Code offenses broadly include, but are not limited to, the following:

1. Offenses against the state and armed forces; unlawful assembly and rioting; bribery and corruption; counterfeiting, forgery, giving false evidence.
2. Offenses affecting the public health, safety, convenience, decency, and morals, and offenses relating to religion.
3. Offenses affecting the human body, for example, murder and rape.
4. Offenses against property.
5. Offenses relating to marriage, for example, enticing or taking away or detaining with a criminal intent a married woman.
6. Defamation, criminal intimidation, insult, and annoyance.
7. Attempts to commit offenses.

The Malaysian police classify crimes according to the Malaysia Crime Index, which divides them into those of violence and those against property. Violence includes murder, attempted murder, rape, gang robbery with firearms, gang robbery without firearms, robbery with firearm, robbery without firearm, and voluntarily causing hurt. Property crimes include van/lorry/heavy machinery thefts, car thefts, motorcycle thefts, snatch thefts, housebreaking and thefts during the day, housebreaking and thefts during the night, and other thefts. For 2007, there were 35,158 violent crimes recorded by police, of which 588 were murders. There were 174,440 property offenses. From 2001 to 2007, the number of murders has remained relatively stable, while there has been a gradual increase in property offenses, the rate increasing more steeply in 2006 and 2007.

Punishment

Sentencing

Sentencing in Malaysia aims at retribution, deterrence, and rehabilitation. A convicted offender may be given more than one sentence. The sentences include (1) death by hanging; (2) imprisonment; (3) whipping; (4) fines; (5) compensation orders and costs; (6) police supervision; (7) good behavior bonds; and (8) orders in relation to juveniles. Two other sentences that are not meted out by the courts, but by the minister, are restricted residence and banishment.

The death sentence may be imposed by the High Court, Court of Appeal, or the Federal Court. The sentence is assigned to grievous offenses such as murder, kidnapping, possession of firearms, and trafficking in dangerous drugs. One exception where the death penalty cannot be imposed on an offender convicted of an offense punishable with death is a woman pregnant with a child. A sentence for imprisonment for life will then be imposed. Another exception is juvenile offenders. However, under Regulation 3(3) of the Essential (Security Cases) Regulation 1975, a juvenile offender who is charged with a security offense, such as possession of firearms, can still be sentenced with the death penalty.

Imprisonment may be divided into three categories: (1) imprisonment for life, (2) imprisonment for a definite period, and (3) imprisonment in default of payment of fine.

Whipping of a maximum of 12 strokes may be imposed by the first-class magistrates, while there is no limit placed on the other courts. However, Section 288 of the CPC restricts the number of strokes to 24 for an adult (aged 16 years and above) and 10 for a youthful offender (between 10 and 16 years). The rattan used for adults will not be more than half an inch in diameter, while for youthful offenders, whipping will be inflicted in the way of school discipline with a light rattan. Under civil law, whipping cannot be imposed on non-Muslim females, males sentenced to death, and males who are older than 50 years. It is generally imposed where there is evidence of use of violence or brutality such as rape and robbery committed with the use of weapons. Whipping for offenses that do not involve violence (purportedly for deterrence) include criminal misappropriation of property, criminal breach of trust, and cheating. As of December 2009, the caning of women for adultery is also administered for Muslim women (under Sharia Law). All strokes imposed must be executed at one time. It cannot be executed in installments. Before the sentence is executed, a medical officer has to be present to certify that the offender is fit to undergo such punishment. If, during the execution of the sentence, a medical officer certifies that the offender is not in a fit state to undergo the remainder of the sentence, whipping will finally be stopped.

As for fines, the first-class magistrates' court can impose a fine of a maximum of 10,000 ringgit (about US$2,790) unless there are exceptional circumstances where the court may impose the maximum specified for a particular offense or unless a specific statute says otherwise.

For compensation orders and costs, the court may order the convicted offender to pay the costs of prosecution, or such part of it as the court directs, and compensation to victims of offenses to be fixed by the court. The scale for imprisonment in default of payment is generally less than 25 ringgit (about US$7) for one month's imprisonment, 25–50 ringgit (about US$7 to $14), for two months' imprisonment, and in any other case, four months' imprisonment.

Police supervision for offenses punishable by two or more years may be imposed if the offender has been convicted of an offense previously and it is one punishable with imprisonment for a term of two or more years. The High Court or sessions court can issue the period of police supervision to be not more than three years, commencing immediately after the expiration of the sentence passed on him or her for the last of such offenses. Magistrates' courts can issue the period of police supervision to be not more than one year.

The juvenile courts may admonish and discharge the offender; require a bond of good behavior; commit to the care of a relative or other fit person; order a parent or guardian to execute a bond to exercise proper care and guardianship; make a probation order; commit to an approved school or Henry Gurney School (rehabilitation school); order to pay a fine, compensation, or costs; and order imprisonment subject to that allowed by a sessions court.

Children cannot be sentenced or ordered to be imprisoned for any offense. A young person may be sentenced or ordered to be imprisoned, provided he or she cannot be suitably dealt with in any other way whether by probation, fine, or committal to a place of detention, approved school, or Henry Gurney School, or otherwise. In prison, he or she should not be allowed to associate with adult prisoners.

Section 12(3) of the JCA provides that the words "conviction" and "sentence" will not be used in relation to juveniles dealt with by the juvenile court. Instead, a conviction is construed as "a finding of guilt" and a sentence is "an order made upon a finding of guilt." As they cannot be convicted, they do not possess "previous convictions" in the form of offenses committed before reaching 18 years of age. Should juveniles be tried in courts other than juvenile courts, they may be convicted. For example, if a juvenile is charged for murder and is tried in the High Court, the High Court may convict him or her or sentence him or her.

Restricted Residence and Banishment

Under the Restricted Residence Act 1933, the minister may order a person to reside in a particular area, either for life or for a term to be specified by the minister. The grounds for such an order have not been made clear. The only guide offered by the law to the minister is a suggestion that the person so confined is given to seditious activities, incitement to violence, or breaches of the peace. Those arrested under the law of restricted residence are exempted from being produced before a magistrate within 24 hours of arrest.

Under the Prevention of Crime Act 1959, members of secret societies, drug traffickers, traffickers in women and girls, and certain habitual criminals, together with persons banished under the Banishment Act 1959, may be arrested and made the subject of an inquiry by a person appointed by the minister for that purpose. If the inquiry officer so recommends, and the minister agrees, the name of the person so arrested is entered on a special register. Under Section 18 of the Prevention of Crime Act 1959, if, for example, a person so registered is found "near any place in which any act of violence or breach of the peace is being or has just been committed," he or she will, unless he or she can satisfactorily account for his or her presence there, be guilty of an offense. Another peculiarity of the act is that if the person so registered commits any one of a number of specified offenses under the Penal Code, the Societies Act, and the Corrosive and Explosive Substances, and Offensive Weapons Ordinance of 1958, he or she will be liable to imprisonment for a term twice as long as the maximum prescribed for the offense and also to whipping.

Sharia Law and Punishment

Sharia laws, which only apply to Muslims, are legislated at state level by the various state governments with the exception of the federal territories sharia laws, which apply to the three federal territories of Kuala Lumpur, Labuan, and Putrajaya. The sharia laws for these three federal territories are legislated at federal level by the federal Parliament. Although the laws are invariably derived from Islamic teachings, the contents of the laws, and the list of offenses and the types of punishments provided for by these laws, are generally similar save for some detailed procedures, minor differences in definitions, and the scale and types of punishments for the offenses committed. For purpose of illustration and discussion in this article, the federal territories sharia laws, incorporating Sharia Criminal Offences (Federal Territories) Act 1997, Sharia Criminal Procedure (Federal Territories) Act 1997, and Sharia Court Evidence (Federal Territories) Act 1997, will be used as the main source of reference.

Under Sharia Criminal Offences (Federal Territories) Act 1997, sharia crimes are divided into five distinct categories, namely:

1. Offenses relating to *Aqidah* (religious belief)
2. Offenses relating to the sanctity of the religion of Islam and its institution
3. Offenses relating to decency
4. Miscellaneous offenses
5. Abetment and attempt

Sharia Punishments

Although the act provides the punishments of fine, imprisonment, whipping, or any combination of the three punishments listed for all the offenses discussed earlier, the act also provides some leeway for the court to institute "rehabilitation measures" toward the offenders. The Islamic Council, through a *Gazette* notification, may appoint a place or institution to be an approved rehabilitation center for the purpose of rehabilitating offenders guilty of committing offenses under the act. Persons found guilty of committing offenses relating to *Aqidah* (religious belief) and persons found guilty of committing some of the offenses relating to sanctity of the religion of Islam and its institutions may be subjected to this rehabilitation measure. The period of counseling or rehabilitation would be specified by the court order, but would not exceed six months. If the sentence of imprisonment is imposed together with counseling or rehabilitation, the period of counseling or rehabilitation and imprisonment combined should not exceed the aggregate of three years.

For female offenders who are guilty of committing offenses relating to decency, they can be ordered to be committed to an approved rehabilitation home for women for a period as may be specified by the court. This period, however, would not exceed six months. This punishment can be meted out either in lieu of, or in addition to, the punishment for the offense committed.

The Carrying Out of Sentences

Generally, the carrying out or execution of punishments for offenses committed under sharia law is almost similar to those punishments meted out for offenses committed under civil law in regard to imprisonment and fines, treatment of juveniles, and suspension, remission, or commutation of sentence. There are some slight variations in regard to administration of whipping.

The whipping rod and prior examination of the offender is carried out as in civil law. In executing the sentence, the person appointed will use the whipping rod with average force without lifting his hand over his head so that the offender's skin is not cut. After inflicting the stroke, he will lift the rod upward and not pull it. The whipping may be inflicted on all parts of the body except the face, head, stomach, chest, or private parts.

During the execution, the offender will wear clothes according to Islamic law. If the offender is male, the whipping will be inflicted in a standing position. If the offender is female, the whipping will be inflicted in the sitting position. If, during the execution, the government medical officer certifies that the offender can no longer receive the strokes, the whipping will be postponed until the offender is certified fit to undergo the balance of the sentence.

If the offender is sentenced to whipping only, he or she will be dealt with as if he or she is sentenced to imprisonment until the sentence is executed. For those who are old or suffer illness and certified by the government medical officer to be unable to undergo the whipping, either fully or partly, the court may consider reasonable execution.

Death Penalty

From 2002 to 2006, 280 local male prisoners, 3 local female prisoners, 46 foreign male prisoners, and 3 foreign female prisoners were hanged.

Prison

In Malaysia, offenders could be sent to the following institutions depending on their age and the type of offense they have committed:

1. Prison
2. Henry Gurney School
3. Detention center
4. Rehabilitation center
5. Detention depot

At present, there are 48 institutions for convicted offenders. There are plans to build more prisons in Malaysia to house the increasing number of offenders in the country. The annual admission of convicted prisoners has increased from 49,243 in 2002 to 72,615 convicted prisoners in 2006; an increase of almost 50 percent. Annual admission of convicted female prisoners is much less compared to the convicted male prisoners. Convicted female prisoners made up about 12 percent of the total convicted prisoner population.

The biggest prison at present is in Kajang. The construction work of the prison started in 1975. The female section of the prison was opened on March 1, 1984. At the time, the male and female prisons were managed by the same prison officials. In the early 1990s, it was decided that the female prison should be separated from the male prison so that it could be managed more efficiently. As such, by January 1, 1993, the Kajang Female Prison was made autonomous from the Kajang Prison, which now housed only male inmates. In 2006, the Kajang Prison housed 21,058 male inmates. The Kajang Female Prison, which is, at present, the biggest female prison in Malaysia, housed 11,403 female inmates.

Under the Rehabilitation and Treatment Section of the Prison Department, the rehabilitation programs include education and living skills, and the treatment programs offered include health, treatment (e.g., rehabilitation programs for drug users and counseling programs), and religious education (for Muslims, Christians, Hindus, and Buddhists).

Juvenile and young offenders are encouraged to continue their school education. Contract teachers are employed to teach them, and all necessary facilities are provided so that they could study comfortably. Adult offenders could also continue their studies if they wish to do so. Besides this, adult offenders are also taught living skills so that they could find employment and integrate back into society when they leave the prison. They are taught skills pertaining to industries such as construction, farming and livestock, food production, clothing, and furniture. These skills could be taught in the prison or in joint venture programs with local companies.

Joint venture programs with local companies to provide skills to the prisoners started in 1981. These companies provide the place, raw materials, machines, and supervisors for this training. They also pay a salary to the prisoners involved in the training and provide them with insurance policies. The Prison Department will, in turn, have to send prison officers to accompany the prisoners while they are on training.

The Vocational and Industry Section of the Prison Department was officially set up on January 1, 2007, to plan, produce, promote, and sell quality products of prisoners. Its aim is to set up viable industries within the prison compound. This will provide jobs and salaries to prisoners as well as enable them to obtain skill training certificates that will be beneficial to them when they leave the prison.

Visiting Policies

The Prison Department encourages visits to the prisons from the society to deter them from wrongdoings. The visits will also contribute to the rehabilitation process of the prisoners. Those who could apply to the Prison Department to visit the prisons include uniformed groups (e.g., police and the military), voluntary organizations and nongovernmental organizations that could contribute to the rehabilitation process of prisoners (e.g., religious organizations), students from higher education institutes, and youth organizations.

Families of prisoners are encouraged to visit the prisoners to help strengthen family relationships and reduce pressure or stress on the prisoners. A prisoner initially admitted into the prison is entitled to receive a visit from close relatives within four weeks after his or her admission.

Usually spouses, close family members, and close friends of the prisoners are allowed to apply to visit the prisoners. Duration of the visit is 45 minutes and only five persons are allowed. If there are more than five family members present, they will have to take turns within the 45 minutes. A child below 10 years is not counted as a visitor. During the visit, food, drinks, and essential items required by the prisoner may only be purchased from the prison canteen.

Prisoners are also permitted to celebrate their religious festivals based on their religious belief as stated in their records. Family members could visit them in conjunction with these festivals. On these occasions, family members are allowed to bring food for the prisoners that could only be consumed during the visiting time.

Others who could apply for visitation include the police, lawyers, and welfare bodies handling the prisoners' cases.

The prisoners could be allowed, with the consent of the director-general of prisons, to visit a critically ill close relative or on the occasion of death. Approval could only be considered if the application is made by a close relative and consented to by the prisoner. However, a prisoner who has been allowed to visit a critically ill relative will not be allowed to visit him or her again upon his or her death. A prisoner about to be hanged may be visited by his or her family members face to face for the last time one day before the hanging takes place.

Prisoners in Malaysia cannot be exchanged or transferred to other countries because Malaysia does not have any extradition treaty. Likewise, Malaysians who committed crimes under Malaysian law cannot be extradited back to Malaysia from other countries.

Yik Koon Teh and
Ahmad Ghazali bin Abu Hassan

Further Reading

Hickling, R. H. (2001). *Malaysian Law: An Introduction to the Concept of Law in Malaysia.* Kuala Lumpur: Pelanduk Publications.

Lee, Mei Pheng. (2005). *General Principles of Malaysian Law.* Kuala Lumpur: Oxford Fajar Sdn. Bhd.

Mimi Kamariah Majid. (1995). *Criminal Procedure in Malaysia.* Kuala Lumpur: University of Malaya Press.

Prison Department of Malaysia: http://www.prison.gov.my/pride/.

Teh, Y. K. (2006). "Female Prisoners in Malaysia." *Journal of Offender Rehabilitation* 43(1): 45–64.

Maldives

Legal System: Islamic
Murder: Low
Corruption: Medium
Prison Rate: High
Death Penalty: Maybe
Corporal Punishment: Yes

Background

Maldives is a small island nation situated in the Indian Ocean on a major marine route. The name "Maldives" is derived from the Sanskrit term *maladvipa*, meaning "garland of islands." The location of Maldives, with close neighbors Sri Lanka and India, has had a major impact on world trade. For instance, in ancient times, the Maldives' islands provided the unit of currency, the cowrie shells, for Asia and parts of the East African coastal areas. Additionally, very recently, the islands of the Indian Ocean, including Maldives, played a crucial role in Eastern-Western conflict as it served as a route through which much oil from the Persian Gulf states passed in shipment to markets elsewhere.

Geographically, Maldives is made up of 1,200 coral islands that form a double chain of 27 atolls. Maldives has a total land area of 300 square kilometers (115 square miles) and has a population of about 385,925. The people represent a composition of Sinhalese, Dravidian, Arab, Australasian, and African groups who speak a Dhivehi language. The majority of Maldivians are Sunni Muslims and attend religious, Koranic schools. Maldives' official religion is Islam and all citizens adhere to Islamic religion. In fact, the practice of a faith other than Islam is forbidden. The country reports a 98 percent literacy.

Maldivian law has revolved around the sultanate, a position that began under Dutch control and later turned to British protection. The Maldives became independent in 1965 and three years after independence, it became a republic (1968). Politically, Maldives had a single party until 2005. Following the political riots of 2004, the Maldivian Malé political parties were legalized. The president of Maldives, Maumoon Abdul Gayoom, had been elected to six successive terms by single-party referendums, and he consequently dominated the political scene on the islands for approximately 30 years.

A constituent assembly, the Special Majlis, in June 2008, developed and instituted a new constitution, which was ratified by the president in August 2008. In October 2008, the Maldives held its first-ever presidential elections under a multicandidate, multiparty system, representing a significant accomplishment for the island nation. In this election, Gayoom was defeated by Mohamed Nasheed, a political activist who had been jailed several years earlier by the former regime.

Notwithstanding the fact that Maldives ascribes to civil law, Islamic sharia law is applied in the majority of cases. Pursuant to Islamic law, women have limited rights. A striking example is in the weight accorded to the testimony of a woman—pursuant to Muslim practice, the testimony of one man is equivalent to that of two women. Furthermore, the rights of laborers are limited as well. Specifically, they may not form unions or participate in any strike. Maldivian law does not recognize any freedom of the press or speech. Nor does the government usually respect such rights. Nevertheless, in 1994, a Press Council was established to protect journalists. This granted some limited freedom of the press.

Political System

The Maldivian government is parliamentary in nature. Combined with this, the Maldivian government also incorporates a strong executive. The revised 1968 Constitution of Maldives purports to enlarge the centralized role of the presidential government. The president of the Maldivian government has the authority to appoint members of the Cabinet, the judiciary, and 8 members of the 50-member Parliament. In addition, pursuant to the Maldivian Constitution, the president assumes additional discretionary influence as the "Supreme authority to propagate the tenets of Islam." The Maldivian government is run by the president who is elected for a renewable five-year term by the legislature, or Majlis.

Constitution

Pursuant to Maldivian law, the courts exist as an extension of the executive branch. The minister of justice, an appointed official under the president, is responsible for overseeing the nation's court systems. The organizational and hierarchical structure of the governmental power is based on the 1968 Constitution and the subsequent revisions of 1970, 1972, and 1975. The constitutional directives provide for a highly centralized, presidential form of government, wherein religious and other powers reside in the president. For instance, the Constitution vests final authority for the propagation of Islam in the president, who in turn is empowered to appoint all judges who interpret and apply the sharia in the adjudication of civil and criminal cases.

The basic constitutional rights of people are broadly phrased under Maldivian law. These fundamental rights, however, are subject to being exercised within the framework of the Islamic, or sharia, law. The Maldives Constitution, article 38 in the Penal Code, allows the jailing or banishment "for any gesture, speech or action that instills malice or disobedience in the minds of Maldivians against lawfully formed government."

Internal and External Dissensions

Security threats to Maldives have existed mainly in the form of internal dissensions rather than external threats. In May 1980, President Maumoon Abdul Gayoom disclosed details of efforts related to an abortive coup against his regime. Gayoom ascribed the internal threat to the actions of former president Ibrahim Nasir, supported by nine British ex-Special Air Services mercenaries. Nasir denied this allegation but in April 1981, the authorities sentenced Ahmed Naseem, former deputy minister of fisheries and brother-in-law of Nasir, to life imprisonment for plotting to overthrow Gayoom. In 1983, Gayoom encountered another unsuccessful coup attempt. Attempts to extradite Nasir from Singapore failed.

In November 1988, Abdullah Luthufi, a former Maldivian businessman, spearheaded a mercenary force of approximately 150 Sri Lankan Tamil separatists. These forces invaded Maldives and attempted a coup d'état. The president requested the intervention of the Indian government. India responded with a cordial offer of a 1,600-member unit to Maldives. With the help of the Indian military assistance, the coup attempt was immediately aborted. The four Maldivians and 12 Sri Lankans who participated in the coup attempt had their death sentences commuted to life imprisonment by President Gayoom.

Government

Within the parliamentary structure, the legislative assembly, also known as the Majlis, has 50 members: two from Malé, two from each of the 20 administrative atolls, and eight appointed by the president. The president appoints the speaker of the Majlis, who acts as an *ex officio* member. Inasmuch as the Majlis sessions are open to the public for viewing and participation, only elected members can exercise the right to vote. Maldivians enjoy a universal right of suffrage for those aged 21 years and over. The procedure for electing a president is as follows: (1) the president is nominated in a secret ballot by the Majlis, and (2) the president is then elected by a majority vote at a national referendum for a five-year term. The president exercises significant power in the appointment of all cabinet members, ministers, and judges. The High or Supreme Court consists of a chief justice and four judges.

The Maldivian executive branch is composed of the following three branches:

1. The president's office
2. The attorney general's office
3. The 17 ministries and associated entities

The executive branch is responsible for the execution and implementation of all official national government programs. The ministries of government, the attorney general's office, and the High Court are subservient to the president's discretion. The sitting president wields power over financial matters and is the governor of the Central Bank.

Crime and Justice

Maldivian society is extraordinarily homogenous: there is but one religion (Sunni Muslim) and one language, Dhivehi. This uniqueness is reflected in its social milieu, and as a result, there is very little reported crime, social strife, or conflict. Notwithstanding a history of some civil unrest, these dissensions were predominantly rooted in power struggles within the controlling government. Also contributing to this unrest was the often tumultuous relationship between Maldives and the British government prior to the latter's withdrawal in 1976.

Defense and Security System

Maldives is a relatively safe place; the country has not faced any external threats since its independence. Maldives maintains a single security unit, the National Security Service, which employs approximately 1,800 personnel. These military employees maintain security and perform army, police, and maritime duties. Owing to the geographically disparate and noncontiguous nature of the atolls, it is unfeasible to employ military personnel on every island. This is also reflected in the inability of the coast guards to protect every atoll and its surrounding area.

Age of Criminal Responsibility

Under Maldivian sharia law, the minimum age of criminal responsibility is seven years. This age delineation also applies to certain property-related crimes, intentional killing, and narcotics offenses.

For all other criminal offenses, children can be held criminally liable at the age of 14.

Laws Pertinent to Children

The rights of children are represented in Maldivian law, which serves to protect them from abuse, both physical and psychological. The Maldivian Ministry of Gender, Family Development, and Social Security have the vested authority to enforce the law as it relates to children. Notwithstanding the fact that reliable data are lacking, some reports indicate that incidents of child abuse, including sexual abuse, are gaining more prevalence in the Maldives. From a punitive perspective, the penalties for sexual abuse of a minor include imprisonment for up to three years up to a more severe punishment including banishment. Notwithstanding the fact that some protections for children exist under Maldivian law, child labor remains a problem, primarily in traditional areas of Maldivian subsistence, such as agriculture, fishing, and small-scale commercial activities and family businesses. Virtually nonexistent are reports of child labor in the industrial sector.

Drug Trafficking, Money Laundering, and Trafficking in Persons

Maldives has a relatively minor drug problem, but it is one that appears to be on the growing trend. The Maldivian government is cognizant of the growing problem and has fully cooperated with the United States on fighting this issue. The skewed age distribution of the Maldivian population, wherein children under 16 are disproportionately overrepresented, raises the suspicion of UN International Drug Control Program officials of the high growth potential for drug use in the country. The Maldivian police, however, can regulate and prevent the sale of drugs on the streets of the capital and most populated city, Malé. Maldivian police have stated that the nation's approximately 25,000 foreign workers may be responsible for most of the trafficking.

The Maldivian government took charge of this growing problem in November 1997 with the development of a Narcotics Control Board (NCB) pursuant to the executive authority of the president. The NCB primarily is responsible for rehabilitation of addicts and coordinates the efforts of NGOs and other individuals engaged in counternarcotics activities.

Distinct laws have been enacted to address the problems with narcotics trade, terrorism, and corruption: For instance, Law No. 17/77 on Narcotic Drugs and Psychotropic Substances prohibits consumption and trafficking of narcotics. The law also prohibits laundering of proceeds from narcotics trade. Law No 2/2000 on Prevention and Prohibition of Corruption prohibits corrupt activities by both public and private sector officials. Pursuant to this law, all proceeds must be forfeited, and this law also empowers judicial authorities to freeze accounts pending a court decision.

Law No. 10/90 on Prevention of Terrorism in the Maldives deals with related aspects of money laundering and terrorist financing. Provision of funds or any form of assistance toward the commissioning or planning of any such terrorist activity is unlawful. There have been no known or reported cases of terrorist financing activities through banks in the Maldives.

Crime Statistics

Maldives has a relatively low crime rate. However, the highly protected and regulated infrastructure of the Maldivian legal system makes the acquisition of reliable data or statistics a difficult task. As such, there exists very little information on actual crime rates. INTERPOL, however, provides some information.

Based on the analysis of the INTERPOL data, for murder, the rate in 1997, the most recent year available, was 1.2 per 100,000 population. For rape, the rate in 1997 was 3.2. For robbery, the rate in 1997 was 20.4. As for aggravated assault, the rate in 1997 was 7.2 for Maldives. With regard to burglary, the rate in 1997 was 37.2. The rate of larceny for 1997 was 659.2 for Maldives. The rate for motor vehicle theft in 1997 was 0. The rate for all index offenses combined was 728.4 in 1997.

Violence against women, such as domestic violence, has a generally low prevalence in Maldives.

There is, however, a dearth of effective records on this subject matter, especially due to the private nature of the conduct. Notwithstanding the lack of official records, according to the U.S. Department of State, Maldivian police officials have reported that they received few complaints of assaults against women, such as rape and other violent crimes. Sharia law provides that the penalty for rape is flogging, imprisonment for up to five years, or banishment.

Finding of Guilt

The police initiate investigations after having received written complaints from citizens, police officers, or government officials. The police can also initiate investigation on suspicion of criminal activity. However, Maldivian police are not required to obtain arrest warrants to investigate a person. The attorney general is responsible for referring cases to the appropriate court. The attorney general's decision is predicated on the results of the police inquiry. In general, details of a case are not released until it is certain and there is sufficient evidence to indicate that the charges are likely to be upheld.

Detention

Pursuant to older laws in the Maldives, suspects could be detained for long periods without being charged. However, revisions to the Maldivian laws and Constitution explicitly prohibit arbitrary arrest and detention. Current Maldivian law dictates that, "a suspect may be detained in prison, remain free, or be placed under house arrest for 15 days during investigations, depending upon the charges." However, in the majority of cases, the suspect will be released if not brought to trial within 15 days. Although this aspect of criminal procedure is established, the president may elect to unilaterally extend pretrial detention for an additional 30 days. Criminal defendants, who are released pending trial, are subject to geographical constraints, in that they may not leave a specific atoll. Fundamental due process under Maldivian law necessitates that within 24 hours of an arrest, an individual must be told of the grounds for the arrest. Subsequent to this, a suspect can be held for seven days. If no judicial proceeding is initiated within a period of seven days, the matter is then delegated to an anonymous three-member civilian commission. The members of this commission are appointed by the president, and the commission is empowered to authorize an additional 15 days of detention. Maldivian law affords no provision for bail.

Legal Aid

Maldivian law does not have any general provision of legal aid for criminally charged defendants. However, recent strides may change the law. For instance, a recent law that became effective in December 2002 provided for legal assistance, albeit limited, to people accused of a criminal offense. This particular law affords civil litigants with the opportunity to appoint a lawyer. This law is exclusively limited to civil cases, in which the litigants, both plaintiff and defendant, are private individuals. However, Maldivian courts do not recognize a right to legal representation for the indigent. Similarly, during police interrogation, there is no right to legal counsel. Despite this, detainees are often granted limited access to family members during the interrogation process.

The Judicial System

The judicial infrastructure of Maldives exists with a High Court and eight lesser courts, which are situated in Malé. Serving as the superior-most court of law in Maldives, the High Court exercises jurisdiction over politically sensitive cases. Another task that the High Court fulfills is that it mostly acts in its appellate capacity, or as a court of review. The lesser courts that are lower in hierarchy have jurisdiction over matters such as debt, theft, or property claims. Other islands aside from Malé that make up the chain of atolls of Maldives have generic courts that exercise broad subject-matter jurisdiction.

There are three courts in Maldives: One court for civil matters, one for criminal cases, and one for family and juvenile cases. Malé also has a High Court, which is independent of the Justice Ministry. The High Court can exercise discretionary jurisdiction over a broad range of cases. The court often chooses to certify, and thereby accept, jurisdiction over politically sensitive matters. Additionally, the High Court serves as a court of appeals, in that it can review a lower court's decision for reversible error. The president has the vested authority to subsequently assemble a five-member advisory council to review High Court rulings. Such ad hoc councils effectively serve a pseudo-appellate/supervisory capacity. Furthermore, the president has the vested authority to affirm judgments of the High Court, to order a second hearing, or to overturn the court's decision. This vests the president with supreme authority over judicial decree.

Maldivian judges and magistrates who are fluent in Islamic, civil, and criminal law conduct trials in public. Maldivian law affords no right to jury trials, and as such none are provided. Pursuant to the Maldivian Constitution, however, an accused is presumed innocent until proven guilty. As such, the Constitution affirms the notion of due process, but qualifies such a right—an accused person has the right to defend himself "in accordance with Shari'a." Pursuant to this obligation, during a trial, the accused may call witnesses and be assisted by a lawyer (for a civil dispute). Judges can question the concerned parties and attempt to establish the facts of a case.

Owing to the supremacy of sharia under Maldivian law, civil law is necessarily subordinate. As such, sharia applies in all situations not within the purview of civil law as well as in certain matters of cultural/religious significance such as divorce and adultery. There is no general judicial provision upholding a right to legal counsel for matters relating to matrimonial and criminal cases. The predicate for such a legal stance is that sharia law mandates that all answers and submissions should come directly from the parties involved, and hence the use of advocates infringes on Islamic law. Notwithstanding this general bar, the High Court allows legal representation for parties in all cases, including those in which lower courts denied such a right. Pursuant to Maldivian interpretation of Islamic customary practice, the testimony of two women equals that of one man in matters within the jurisdiction of sharia, such as for adultery, financial matters, and inheritance. In other cases, however, the testimony of men and women are equivalent.

Courts

Maldivian courts do not employ any jury trials. Sitting judges interpret Islamic law and determine how the specific provisions apply to the case at hand. Trials are open to the public. The Maldivian court system was entirely restructured in 1997. In particular, the following three categories of lower courts supplanted the previously existing judicial infrastructure:

1. Madani (Civil) Court
2. Jinaaee (Criminal) Court
3. Aaelee (Family/Juvenile) Court

Under Maldivian jurisprudence, a litigant or other party to a legal action can appeal against the judgment of a lower court (the Criminal Court). This appeal is usually made to the chief justice at the High Court and subsequently to the president who may independently conduct a separate review of the legal merits of a case. The president's decision in such a case, however, is final.

Punishment

Owing to the Islamic-centered legal system of Maldives, the law recognizes crime under the Islamic code, or sharia. There is no formal criminal code. Under Maldivian Islamic sharia law, the following six crimes are recognized:

1. Unlawful sexual intercourse
2. False accusation of adultery
3. Theft
4. Highway robbery
5. Drinking intoxicants
6. Apostasy (conversion from Islam to another religion)

Judges under Maldivian law possess significant discretion in determining how justice is meted out. Much like any other legal system, Islamic law works in a similar fashion in terms of outlining the law and correlative punishments, but it is distinct in that it also incorporates religious rules and rituals.

A telling portrayal of classical Islamic law is the punishment for a nonvirgin who has sex out of wedlock. The punishment would be death by stoning. Further, theft or simple larceny would result in the amputation of a hand.

Penal System

The Maldivian penal system is predicated on Islamic law with admixtures of English common law, primarily for commercial matters. In general, Maldivians follow the sharia or Islamic law, both for law codification as well as for punitive matters. For certain offenses, the courts may order convicted criminals to be beaten. More frequently, the Maldivian courts limit punishment to the following:

1. Fines
2. Compensatory payment
3. House arrest, imprisonment
4. Flogging
5. Banishment to a remote island

Banishment

At the core of Maldivian law, as mentioned earlier, is Islamic sharia law, but admixed with this are elements of the civil law enactment of 1968 and its subsequent amendments. The product of this addendum was a modified sharia law, which excludes excessive punishments such as amputation and stoning to death. Notwithstanding the prohibition against cruel and unusual punishment, the modified code still sanctions floggings and the sentencing of banishment to a remote island.

Current Maldivian enactments limit the banishment sentence to a range of eight months to one or two years. The punishment entails that the prisoner is left to survive on an island with the indigent peoples on that island. The prisoner has to attain, usually by laborious efforts, sufficient money to supplement the paltry per diem allotment distributed by prison authorities. The predicament is worst for women who are banished since they are highly susceptible to harassment and sexual abuse by the village men.

The offenses for which banishment may be imposed on Maldivian citizens are usually those that are religious in nature (i.e., Islamic law violations):

1. Drinking alcohol
2. Extramarital sex
3. Theft
4. Eating in public during the fasting month of Ramadan

Owing to the highly protected and regulated infrastructure of the Maldivian legal system, data or detailed statistics are lacking on the number of banishment cases. However, some reports, albeit unofficial, indicate the prevalence and incidence of banishment as a punitive outcome. A report depicts that in 1988, there were 1,224 convictions, of which 806 people were banished. One-third of those banished were reportedly women, according to Kirsten Ellis in her book *Odyssey Illustrated Guide to the Maldives,* published in 1993. Another report provides more recent statistics: a report in *Haveeru daily online* quotes the Department of Corrections (Maldivian prison department) in stating that in 2002, 647 people were banished to outer islands. The report, however, notes that the source had not provided information on the nature of the offense committed.

Flogging

Maldivian law permits flogging as a punitive outcome. This form of punishment is in accordance with the Maldivian courts' construction of suitable forms of punishment under sharia law. In most matters, flogging is publicly performed, usually in front of the court building. For defendants with great public importance, this "public" requirement is waived. In such cases, the flogging is conducted in the court room and then announced to the general public that it has been successfully carried out.

Death Penalty

Under Maldivian law, the death penalty is a potential punitive outcome for egregious offenses. Since 1958, however, all death sentences have been commuted to lesser sentences, such as life imprisonment or banishment. In fact, the death penalty has not been actually implemented in any case in the Maldives since the 1950s. This is despite the fact that the death penalty continues to persist under the country's legal system, which is an admixture of common and sharia law. Those convicted of murder may be sentenced to death; however, these convictions have almost invariably been commuted to life in prison by the president. A notable example that received considerable media attention was the 2005 conviction of eight former Maldivian government security officers. These eight governmental employees were sentenced to death for the 2003 killing of prisoner Hassan Evan Naseem, which triggered significant political upheaval and mass protests. The president commuted the sentences to life imprisonment in January 2007.

Prisons

Maldives has three main prisons. The prison population, although fluctuating, approximates 300 at the country's main facility. Inmates are segregated based on gender, age, and type of crime. For instance, women are imprisoned separately from men, children are imprisoned separately from adults, and persons arrested for drug use are sent to a "drug rehabilitation center" on a space available basis.

Suman Kakar

Further Reading

Library of Congress Country Studies—Maldives: http://lcweb2.loc.gov/cgi-bin/query/r?frd/cstdy:@field(DOCID+mv0006).

President's Office, Strategic Communications Unit, Malé, Republic of Maldives: http://www.maldiviandetainees.net/RelevantLegalDocuments/Proposed_Constitutional_Amendments_20050214.pdf.

U.S. Department of State—Maldives: http://www.state.gov/g/drl/rls/hrrpt/2004/41741.htm.

Mongolia

Legal System: Civil
Murder: High
Burglary: High
Corruption: Medium
Human Trafficking: Medium
Prison Rate: High
Death Penalty: Yes
Corporal Punishment: Yes

Background

Mongolia is a large landlocked country covering an area of 604,103 square miles with a population of only 2,612,900. The end of the Soviet Union in 1990 and the collapse of the Council for Mutual Economic Assistance (COMECON), whose member states were Mongolia's main trading partners, forced Mongolia into a difficult and rapid transition to democracy and a market economy. After having been an independent but still satellite state of the Soviet Union for 70 years, Mongolia's peaceful Democratic Revolution of 1990 culminated in the ratification of a new democratic constitution in 1992. Even in 2009, about 40 percent of the population still maintains a nomadic lifestyle. About two-thirds are under the age of 30 and approximately 1 million people, that is, about two-fifth of all Mongolians, live in the capital city of Ulaanbaatar.

Legal System

Mongolia's social, political, and legal structures were modeled along the lines of those in place in the Soviet Union and other Eastern Block countries. In the years before becoming a democracy, Mongolia benefited particularly from intensive assistance from the German Democratic Republic (GDR). After the collapse of the Soviet Union, the now-unified Federal Republic of Germany almost immediately substituted most of the assistance previously provided by the GDR, including assistance for legal reform. As a result, the Mongolian legal system today looks very much like the German legal system with some elements that are more frequently present in common law systems, such as inclusion of some adversarial processes, a high commitment to strong judicial branch administration, and independence of the courts and prosecutors' services.

Mongolia's justice system shares the challenge of having to adjust to rapid and fundamental societal changes with the rest of the government and society. Limited resources, lack of infrastructure, higher caseloads, and increasingly complex cases before criminal and civil courts escalate the demands on an already strapped justice system. As a result, public trust in the rule of law is not well established, and critics often question the fairness of the justice system, despite the passage of significant legal reforms and considerable changes in justice sector operations, especially in the prosecution service and the courts.

At the same time, many positive changes can be observed today. Supported by extensive international assistance, all courts and most prosecutors' offices are automated, case management software assists in tracking cases, managing caseloads, and providing management information. All courts have public access terminals where everybody can check on the status and outcome of a case; courtrooms have been redesigned and policies changed to provide for more equality among the parties and for public access, particularly media access, to the courts. All judges and prosecutors have access to the latest laws, many via a uniform information network. On the other hand, assistance for the police, the "public face of the justice system," has been limited.

Police

Mongolia's police are a national force, organizationally located within the Ministry of Justice and Home Affairs. Public order, crime control, and some emergency response functions are at the core of the police's mandate. There are more than 7,000 officers located throughout Mongolia (51% are low-ranking officers, including patrol and beat officers; 49% are mid- and high-ranking officers). The Mongolian Police is still a strictly hierarchical organization. At the same time, police are completely separate from the military and General Intelligence Agency. Boarder control and customs are also outside its mandate.

Supported by a few small grants from the Open Society Foundation, the Mongolian Police embarked in 2001 on a program to experiment with community policing in a few small neighborhoods in Ulaanbaatar and three rural areas. These projects successfully brought the community and police closer together, resulting in improved procedures and mechanism to address community issues. When funding ceased, the police continued these efforts at least in the existing pilot sites. Renewed international donor interest in these efforts promises support for expansion of community policing throughout the country starting in 2008.

Crime

Classification of Crimes

Mongolian law distinguishes four categories of crimes—minor, less serious, serious, and grave. Based on the Mongolia Criminal Code as amended in 2007, these are defined as follow:

- *Minor crimes* are punishable by a fine equal to 5 to 50 times the minimum wage, or 100 to 250 hours of forced labor, or by incarceration for one to three months. Minor crimes are specified in 64 articles of the Criminal Code and include a broad range of crimes—for example, minor theft, infliction of a minor bodily injury (i.e., causing a short-term detriment to health or a slight loss of the ability to work), evasion of treatment of a venereal disease, engaging minors in heavy drinking, drug abuse, prostitution, vagrancy, or begging.
- *Less serious crimes* are punishable by a fine equal to 51 to 250 times the minimum wage, by 251 to 500 hours of forced labor, by incarceration for three to six months, or imprisonment for up to five years. There are 251 different articles that outline less serious crimes and include offenses such as illegally crossing the border, negligent manslaughter, torture, and sexual intercourse with a minor.
- *Serious crimes,* of which there are 73, are punishable by a fine equal to 251 to 500 times the minimum salary or imprisonment for 5 to 10 years. This includes serious theft cases, rape, kidnapping, among others.

- *Grave crimes,* defined in 38 articles, are punishable by imprisonment of 10 to 15 years or in extraordinary cases of up to 25 years or by death. This includes murder, serious organized and gang crimes.

Age of Criminal Responsibility

The age of criminal responsibility in Mongolia is 16. Exceptions are offenders aged 14 to 15 who committed select serious cases, such as homicide, deliberate infliction of a severe bodily injury, rape, robbery, aggravated theft, deliberate destruction or damage of property, and aggravated hooliganism. For first-time offenders of a minor or a less serious crime who are under the age of 18, the court may apply probation or an alternative measure of coercion of educational character instead of formal punishment. Such alternative can be payment of compensation for any damages caused, if the juvenile has his or her own source of income, or working for a NGO or specific individual, which can be the victim, if appropriate. Sentencing to a special educational facility is another alternative for juveniles aged 14 to 16, if other less invasive alternatives have not been successful. According to information provided by the Supreme Court Research Center, typically half or more juveniles receive alternative sentences.

Drug Crimes

Considering that illicit drug use is still a rare occasion in Mongolia, drug possession is currently not punishable. Illicit production, manufacturing, and distribution of narcotic and psychotropic drugs

A Mongolian police officer drags a drunken man, dressed in only a blanket after being given a cold shower, back to his cell at a police station in Ulan Bator, Mongolia, November 16, 1998. (AP Photo/Greg Baker)

may be considered a less serious crime if smaller quantities are involved; it is a serious crime if larger quantities are involved, or there are other aggravating factors (i.e., gang or organized crime activity, serious endangerment of the population). The schedule indicating what are considered illicit narcotics and psychotropic drugs in Mongolia is developed by the Department of Health.

The drug of choice in Mongolia is alcohol. Alcoholism and poverty both going hand in hand with high unemployment rates, are the root causes of crime in Mongolia. The main crimes are property crimes, mainly theft, assaults, and other crimes resulting in bodily injuries, including the much underreported but serious problem of domestic violence. At least one-quarter of all crimes reported to the police are committed under the influence of alcohol. While violent crimes seem to be increasing and are at least of increasing concern to the population, especially in the urban areas, Mongolia remains a relatively low-crime country employing a relatively harsh justice regime of crime control.

Crime Statistics

Data provided by the Information and Research Division of the Mongolian General Police Department in February 2008 indicate increases in the minor crimes categories and decreases in the more serious crimes recorded by police. The top three categories of crimes recorded by police are theft (36.5% of all cases in 2006), infliction of bodily harm (19.6% of all cases in 2006), and traffic violations (7.8% of all cases in 2006). Cases of theft in rural areas include significant numbers of cattle theft, and cases involving bodily harm are frequently related to alcohol abuse, including significant numbers of brawls while under the influence of alcohol. Reflecting the above-mentioned limited occurrence of illicit drug use, the official statistics do not include any drug-related crimes. Crimes recorded by the police for 2006 are as follows:

Minor crimes	6,168
Less serious crimes	8,961
Serious crimes	2,715
Grave crimes	409
Murder	311
Rape	314
Robbery	455

The crimes most typically recorded in urban areas are theft, vandalism, traffic crimes, intentional infliction of severe bodily injury, and robbery. The crimes typically recorded in rural areas are theft (especially of livestock), brawls, and vandalism.

Finding of Guilt

Following the continental European legal tradition, Mongolia does not have jury trials. At the current time, minor cases are heard by a single judge; in other cases, the Mongolian law requires that a panel of at least three judges hears the case. This requirement was introduced as part of major changes to the Criminal Procedures Code in 2002 to ensure a fair trial. In rural jurisdictions with limited numbers of judges available, this requirement not only increased cost and the burden on individual judges who have to cover multiple panels, it also delayed trials due to insufficient availability of judges. As a result, future changes to the Criminal Procedures Code may again allow a single judge to hear not just minor but possibly also less serious cases. Mongolia complies with international requirements to provide for a speedy trial, and cases generally come to trial within a few months.

Right to an Attorney

Defendants have a right to an attorney starting at the time an investigation begins, and certainly at the time an arrest is made. However, the right of the attorney to be actually present during arrest and detention decisions was only recently added to the Criminal Procedures Code. More importantly, there exists no public defender system in Mongolia; instead private attorneys are assigned by the court to those who cannot afford their own attorney. Further, the right to have an attorney present does not mean that the state has to provide an attorney in all cases. Article 40 of the Mongolian Criminal Code specifies that the participation of an attorney is mandatory and the state is required to provide an attorney only when the defendant is mute, deaf, blind, and/or due to a physical or mental handicap not able to defend himself or herself; if the defendant is a minor, does not have command of the Mongolian language; if the death penalty may be applied; or if a co-defendant has a defense counsel.

The 2002 Law on Advocacy states that it is mandatory for each member of the Mongolian Advocate's Association to defend two indigent people per year. The state is required to pay the attorney fees when their participation is mandatory and the defendant cannot afford his or her own counsel. The fees the state pays attorneys are, however, extremely low. The very fact that the state has started to finance legal aid is a sign of progress. However, since most criminal offenders are poor, more state funding is needed for legal aid. Considering that Mongolia's state budget is still very limited, significant increases are not expected in the near future. With international assistance, a few legal aid centers have been created in the capital and others are planned to be established in each of Mongolia's 21 state capitals.

Investigations and Prosecutions

Investigation of cases is generally the responsibility of the police. Exceptions are crimes committed by police, prosecutors, or judges, which are investigated by members of a Special Investigative Unit that was created in 2003 under the prosecutor general's office. Other exceptions are state corruption cases, which are investigated by staff of the Anti-Corruption Agency (created in 2007), and select cases that involve state security matters, such as espionage, treason, assault on public figures, and similar cases, which are investigated by staff of the General Intelligence Agency.

Prosecutions are conducted by members of the national prosecution service. Mongolian prosecutors have very little discretion, but, according to article 205.7 of the Mongolia Criminal Procedures Code (CPC), they may dismiss a case for lack of evidence or if the following occur:

- A suspect, accused, or defendant committed a minor crime for the first time and has voluntarily revealed and compensated the damage caused or corrected the harm caused.
- The actions investigated are no longer considered of socially dangerous nature.
- The suspect, accused, or defendant committed a minor crime for the first time, reconciled with the victim, and redressed the damage caused.
- The suspect, accused, or defendant was mentally ill when committing the crime.

Otherwise, cases are generally settled through a trial. Changes to the CPC introduced in 2007 simplified proceedings that can be applied in select minor cases if the accused has confessed and the parties have no further disputes. Simplified proceedings still require a court hearing, even though an abbreviated one. Negotiations or dispute resolutions are not available in criminal cases, even though judges are allowed to encourage the parties to settle their dispute before commencing the trial. Other alternatives to a trial do not exist except in cases involving juveniles. There is no plea bargaining.

Pretrial Detention

Pretrial detention is allowed, generally following international principles, that is, there must be a reason justifying pretrial incarceration, such as circumstances that indicate the likelihood of reoffending, endangering the investigation, or likelihood of not appearing for the trial. The decision to hold someone in pretrial detention is made by a judge following a request by a prosecutor who generally follows the recommendation of an investigator. Police may arrest persons suspected of a crime and hold them for up to 72 hours before a decision is made to prosecute or release them. Still, according to a U.S. State Department report, arrest without a warrant is fairly common. The report cites a survey of detainees conducted by the Mongolia National Human Rights Center in 2006, which found that 919 out of 978 persons detained in the main pretrial detention center near Ulaanbaatar were arrested under the "pressing circumstances" exception to the requirement that a court warrant should be obtained prior to arrest. In addition, the length of time suspects can be held in pretrial detention has raised concerns. The maximum period of court-ordered pretrial detention was finally reduced in 2007 from 24 months to 4 months for less serious crimes, 12 months for serious crimes, and 24 months for grave crimes. Further, the court now has to review the decision to detain the suspect every month. Detainees may be released on bail with approval of a prosecutor. According to the law, juveniles under 16 cannot be held in pretrial detention and those older than 16 are to be held separately from adults. Outside of Ulaanbaatar, this usually means just in a different cell, since separate facilities for juveniles are not available.

Mongolia's Judiciary

In 2007, there were a total of 429 judges in Mongolia. Judges are not specifically assigned to handle criminal cases only, except those serving at the Highest Appeals Court, the Capital City Court, and at the Supreme Court. No separate juvenile courts exist in Mongolia. To become a judge or prosecutor, a law degree from a Mongolian law faculty is required and candidates must have passed a special qualification exam, which can only be taken after two years of legal practice.

Considering the relatively low standard at Mongolia law schools, the prior low qualification requirements, and low salaries of judges, it is not surprising that the regard for judges and public opinion of the judiciary in Mongolia is not very high. Public perception of the judiciary has improved somewhat over the past years. Still, many perceive that judges are not well versed in critical substantive areas of the law (particularly economic law and human rights) and accusations of favoritism and corruption are frequent. Critics point out that the high proportion of women in the judiciary (approximately 70% in the countryside and 50% in Ulaanbaatar) indicates the profession's low prestige. Increasing judicial salaries, along with new selection requirements, is aimed at raising the status and professionalism of the judges serving in Mongolia's courts.

Punishment

Types of Punishment

The predominant punishment applied in Mongolia is a prison term. Information provided by the prosecutor general's office in February 2008 showed that during the first half of 2007, a total 4,657 individuals were convicted. Of these, 3,206 or 68.8 percent were sentenced to prison. Not all of them had to serve their prison term, however; 1,150 individuals (35.8%) received a conditional prison sentence, for 444 (13.8%) the execution of the prison sentence was postponed, and 65 persons were released after an amnesty.

Further, 1,431 offenders received other types of punishment: 332 (23.2%) were punished by a fine, 384 (26.8%) were sentenced to forced labor, and 715 (49.9%) were sentenced to other forms of detention. Of those sentenced to prison, 138 were sentenced to a term of up to 1 year, 1,396 to a term of 1–3 years, 442 to a term of 3–5 years, 784 to 5–8 years, 163 to 8–10 years, 197 to 10–15 years, 58 to 16–20 years, and 28 to a term of 20–25 years.

Information provided by the general prosecutors' office indicates that the typical punishment for murder and rape is prison. Robbery and serious theft also resulted in prison time often; of the 840 individuals convicted for these crimes in 2007 in Ulaanbaatar alone, 389 were sentenced to prison.

Corporal punishment is not part of the sentencing options in Mongolia. Nevertheless, every year reports from human rights organizations, such as Amnesty International, decry the unofficial use of corporal punishment in Mongolia's detention centers and prisons, and every year prisoners die as a result of abuse, neglect, and the generally terrible conditions in most of Mongolia's prisons.

According to a 2006 United Nations Development Programme (UNDP) report, 259 individuals were sentenced to capital punishment (death sentence) between 1990 and 2000. In comparison to the first five years of that decade, a 60 percent reduction in the use of capital punishment sentence was registered from 1996 to 2000. However, information on the use of capital punishment is classified, official data are not released, and, as the UNDP report states, prison conditions for those sentenced to capital punishment are atrocious, and family members are never notified of executions. The method of execution is a shot in the neck. Changes to the Criminal Code introduced in 2002 prohibit capital punishment for women, men over the age of 60, and individuals who had not reached the age of 18 at the time the crime was committed.

Prisons

According to information provided by the Court Decision Enforcement Department (CDED) in February 2008, there were 5,934 offenders sentenced to prison, 165 persons sentenced to arrest, and 1,824 individuals in detention centers on December 15, 2007. Compared to the end of 2006, the number of individuals sentenced to prison increased by 15.1 percent, the number of persons sentenced to arrest increased by 47.2 percent, and the number of detainees increased by 14.4 percent. Only 27 foreigners were serving their sentence in Mongolian prisons. Of these, 14 were from Russia, 9 from the People's Republic of China, and 1 each from the Czech Republic, Azerbaijan, Armenia, and Great Britain.

There are 21 penal institutions under the authority of the Court Decision Enforcement Department (CDEA): 1 high security prison, 2 special regime, 8 strict regime, and 10 normal regime prisons. In addition, there are 14 arrest centers and 29 detention centers. The CDEA also has a Central Prison Hospital with 120 beds, a Tuberculosis Hospital with 50 beds, and a Central Detention Center Hospital with 45 beds. On average, the Central Prison Hospital has 1,900–2,050 in-patients and 3,700–5,000 prisoners, and detainees get medical aid and services annually. Information provided by the prosecutor general's office of Mongolia, which has some oversight functions over the prisons in Mongolia, indicates that on November 25, 2007, there were 62 individuals held in high security prison, 842 in special regime prison, 2,438 in strict regime prison, 2,501 in normal regime prison, and 180 persons in arrest centers.

The biggest prison is located in Baganuur District, about a two-hour drive from the capital of Ulaanbaatar. This is a strict regime facility housing more than 1,000 inmates. A 2007 report of a prison visit by a member of the International Federation of Red Cross and Red Crescent Societies indicated that more than half of the male inmates there, mostly between 18 and 30 years old, were expected to serve a prison term of more than 15 years. Health issues, especially tuberculosis, are a major problem here and in most Mongolia prisons and detention centers. The Red Cross provides health education and medical services but also all-important assistance for transitioning to the outside world. The conditions here are not the worst of all prison facilities in Mongolia but still shocking to foreign visitors. Quarters are cramped and while reports of abuse have declined over the years, the conditions are still bleak. For most of the nonworking hours, prisoners are not assigned to cells but to compartments that are about 10 feet long, 6 feet deep, and only high enough to sit in. Up to six prisoners may be in one of these compartments that are stacked high along the walls.

According to the Law on Court Decision Enforcement and related procedures, prisoners are required to work. The CDED is required to ensure that labor safety standards for prisoners meet the requirements of the Mongolia Labor Law. Hours of work and rest for the prisoners in normal regime prison and juveniles are in accordance with the labor law. Whenever possible, prisoners are to be provided with the opportunity to be assigned work that is related to their professional skills and working abilities. However, lack of such work is not a ground for release from the work requirement. On average, around 45 percent of all prisoners are working. They can participate in training to obtain skills needed in related professions and may also have an opportunity to be enrolled in other educational courses; for example, courses leading to general and/or higher education, as well as other professional skills training, enabling them to work as construction carpenters, decorators, bricklayers, painters, welders, and plumbers. Those passing all courses are awarded certificates issued jointly with the relevant certifying organizations. Moreover, regular courses to increase literacy (reading and writing), computer skills, and English language are conducted at prisons and prisoners are enrolled on a voluntary basis.

The normal regime prisons may send their inmates to work under supervision on CDED farms or may contract them out. In addition, the prisoners in normal regime prisons may provide services, such as cleaning or maintenance, at other prisons, arrest, and detention centers. Prisoners in special or strict regime facilities can work only at their own facility under the supervision of a security guard. For them, the hours of work and rest can differ from the labor law.

All prisoners may receive a compensation based on the quantity and quality of work performed. The rates need to reflect standard wages. If prisoners performed work on an outside contract, the employer transfers the wages to the account of the prison. The prison takes certain deductions from the money earned; the rest is transferred to the prisoners' account. Prisoners have the right to spend 10 percent from this account each month. The remaining money will be given to them at the time of release. All prisoners are allowed a limited number of phone calls and can make money transfers. The number of calls allowed will vary with the security level of their confinement.

Visits with family members and others are regulated by internal policies and regulations developed in conformity with the Law on Court Decision. Prisoners in normal regime prisons are allowed 4 short-term visits and 8 long-term visits per year and may receive packets and letters. Short-term visits are less than 3 hours, and long-term visits are less than 72 hours. Prisoners in strict regime facilities are allowed 3 short-term and 2 long-term visits annually and may receive 3 packets and 2 letters per month. Those in high security prisons are allowed 2 short-term visits per year and 1 letter per month.

According to the Law on Court Decision, the prisoners also have the right to:

- Know about the circumstances and regulations of the punishment imposed, related rights, obligations, and restrictions;
- File complaints to the official or institution they are serving in;
- Get legal assistance;
- Write a book, produce scientific writings, and create works of art at their own expense;
- Be provided with food of a certain amount of calories, clothes, an adequate cell, and get medical assistance;
- Subscribe to a limited number of newspapers, magazines, and use the library of the prison;
- Be entitled to get a pension or other benefits continuously;
- Receive humane treatment from the prison personnel;
- Protection of their personal security.

Prisoners who have properly fulfilled their assigned duties and have not committed disciplinary breaches may be granted a leave of up to 30 days once in a quarter. Prisoners in prisons with normal regime may be granted leave of up to seven days in case of serious illness or death of relatives or if a considerable loss has occurred to the family due to natural calamity or other disaster. The chief prison administrator may grant such leave if a request is issued by the local governor or a hospital. On average, around 265–300 convicts enjoy this right annually, a very low percentage.

Considering that relatively few foreigners live in Mongolia and that the number of foreign temporary workers and visitors remains low, it is not surprising that few foreigners get in conflict with the law. As a result, the number of foreigners Mongolia has transferred is few. Some sentenced offenders have been transferred to Russia and Kazakhstan following the Berlin Protocol on Exchange of Convicts from May 19, 1978. If foreigners are accused of crimes, they are more frequently either kept in Mongolian prisons or deported before a trial.

Heike Gramckow

Further Reading

Gramckow, Heike. (2007). "The Long Winding Road: Judicial Sector Reform in Mongolia." *International Judicial Monitor* 2(1). Judicial Monitor Web Site: http://www.judicialmonitor.org/archive_0207/sectorassessment.html.

Tseveen, Odgerel, and Battsetseg Ganbold. *The Mongolian Legal System and Laws: A Brief Overview.* Globalex Web Site: http://www.nyulawglobal.org/globalex/Mongolia.htm.

United Nations Development Programme. (2006). *Democratic Governance Indicators: Assessing the State of Governance in Mongolia*. Ulaanbaatar,

Mongolia: http://www.undp.org/oslocentre/docs07/DGI-Mongolia.pdf.

The World Bank. (2007). *The Enabling Environment for Social Accountability in Mongolia*. Report No. 32584–MN. Washington, DC: The World Bank.

Note: Assistance in data collection was provided by Suheemaa Dugersuren and Gantulga Yonkhor, staff members of the Mongolian Judicial Reform Project (JRP). The staff of the Mongolian General Police Department, the Prosecutor General's Office, the Supreme Court Research Center, and the executive secretary of the General Council of Courts were instrumental in providing translations and access to data.

Myanmar (Burma)

Legal System: Common/Customary
Murder: Medium
Corruption: High
Prison Rate: Medium
Death Penalty: Maybe
Corporal Punishment: Yes

Background

The British Empire ruled this country—then known as Burma—as part of its Indian colony until Burma became the independent nation Union of Burma in 1948. The country's legal and judicial origins lie in its 1947 Constitution. This constitution incorporated key liberal democratic principles, such as the presumption of innocence, habeas corpus, and the right to due process and fair trials, as well as Britain's common law tradition with the development of case law and the use of an independent judiciary of competent, impartial legal arbiters. It also provided the structure and procedures around which the Burmese legal and judicial systems would be organized. Courts would be organized from local townships and districts all the way up to the country's Supreme Court.

Throughout the 1950s, these principles of individual justice remained relatively vital, with the use of writs and the exercise of habeas corpus protections common. Yet, the constitutional protections for regionalized ethnic minority groups were much weaker and provoked discord. Successive military coups, beginning with the so-called caretaker regime under General Ne Win in 1958 and again in 1962 by the self-styled Revolutionary Council began what would prove to be a successful systematic dismantling of the British common law tradition underpinning Burma's constitutional system, a dismantling intellectually orchestrated by Dr. Maung Maung. This successfully eliminated the judiciary's independence and its legal competence. In 1974, a military dictatorship calling itself Socialist Republic of the Union of Burma seized power and eliminated the professional judiciary and its case law, appointing party apparatchiks to preside over the ironically labeled "People's Courts." As a result, the legal and judicial system could no longer serve as independent countervailing forces to the military dictatorship's endemic corruption and systematic criminality.

In 1988 the military junta, calling itself the State Law and Restoration Council (SLORC), butchered thousands of Burmese opponents to seize state power and reinstate the previously corrupted constitution and its lawless judiciary. It changed the country's name to the Union of Myanmar a year later, a national renaming that continues to engender divisions so strong that dissidents continue to refer to their stolen country as Burma. And once it had solidified its dominance over the country, the SLORC chose an even friendlier name for itself, the State Peace and Development Council (SPDC), while systematically draining the nation of its wealth and vitality.

Still, the junta did allow elections in 1990, elections that it fully expected to win. The SPDC was stunned when the National League for Democracy (NLD) led by Daw Aung San Suu Kyi defeated it in a landslide victory, despite the violence aimed to prevent such a victory. Thanks to the postelection crackdown and the annulment of the displeasing election results, the SPDC has since managed to retain dictatorial control over Myanmar. Despite skepticism, the junta announced that it would unilaterally impose its so-called Seven-Step Road map to Disciplined Democracy, free of democratic involvement. This included unilaterally imposing the

A Myanmar man is arrested by plain clothes police officers during a protest against fuel price hikes in Yangon, Myanmar, on August 28, 2007. (AP Photo/Democratic Voice of Burma)

2008 Constitution that officially legalized military rule. The junta is expected to hold elections in October 2010, though regime opponents will boycott the elections, contending that the elections will be a sham.

Throughout the country's history, both uniformed and "plainclothes," police forces have supported military juntas. The current secretive regime does not seem inclined to publish reliable statistics detailing the manpower numbers of its police force, and there have no public investigations into the country's police activities and few official statements. So there is no official acknowledgment of just how much the Burmese people fear and despise them. As a neo-colonial police force presided over by a military junta, they are guided by an institutional mentality of self- and regime-service rather than public service and upholding the rule of law.

The police are fully subordinate to Myanmar's army, the 400,000-strong *Tatmadaw*. To prepare for a reemergence of mass protests such as those that had erupted in 1988, the head of the SPDC, Senior General Than Shwe, formed what the junta calls the Union Solidarity Development Association (USDA) to serve as "plainclothes" proxies for uniformed security forces to attack and intimidate dissidents. The USDA and the so-called *swan-ar-shin,* or "masters of force," are not the typical self-directed paramilitary forces seen elsewhere. Rather, they are hierarchically organized and trained units, who remain on call for township-level authorities and whose activities are closely orchestrated by the junta. One of their most infamous accomplishments was the Depayin massacre. The Burma Lawyers' Council in Thailand estimates that as many as 5,000 of these militia attacked Daw Aung San Suu Kyi's motorcade during her 2003 tour.

Human rights watchers and dissident legal analysts report that Myanmar's police forces are fundamentally flawed. Routine violence, favoritism, incompetent investigations, pursuit of personal interest, and profiteering remain standard operating procedure. Police corruption is endemic. Officers regularly initiate criminal investigations, not because crime victims request that they do so. Rather, police seize arrest powers as opportunities to extort bribes in the form of money, personal property, or sex from their victims. Or else they make arrests because persons able to do so use the police to further personal vendettas or steal property from their neighbors.

Dissident criminal justice analysts assert that Myanmar's police force does not receive the professional training and supervision that genuinely modern police forces in other countries do. Myanmar's police therefore do not possess the skills needed to actually perform meaningful criminal investigations. Thus, the Asian Legal Resource Centre concludes that unlawful detention and torture remain an "indispensible part of criminal inquiries." Worse, the fundamental inability of police to competently investigate crimes, even if officials were inclined to do so, functionally guarantees that the junta remains totally unaccountable for its own criminality and corruption. Consequently, while the police force needs to be wholly dismantled and modernized, it is in the regime's interest to ensure that this does not happen.

Crime

Myanmar has a Penal Code, though there are no discernible classifications for crimes such as felony versus misdemeanors elsewhere. The Penal Code refers to a range of ordinary crimes against person, property, and public order. With respect to criminal responsibility, there is no statutory definition for adult criminal responsibility, though children are considered to be those individuals under age 16, while youths are considered to be those individuals between the ages of 16 and 18.

Myanmar's secretive rulers do not participate in the UN's Survey of Crime Trends and Operations of Criminal Justice Systems, so the typical crime data do not appear to be readily available. In the absence of any official statistics, the junta has been inclined to promote the image of Myanmar as a socially conservative, predominantly Buddhist society that enjoys very low levels of crime and violence. However, journalistic sources, dissident legal commentators, and human rights defenders strongly dispute this official image, condemning authorities for doing little to control crime and the regime itself of engaging in much of the crime and violence.

For example, officials assert that there are very few missing children in Myanmar, and thus the police force does not need a special department solely responsible for policing the crime. Yet this denial may stem in part because such a large number of the abducted children are taken by the military itself, which exploits them as military "porters" as physical and sexual laborers. As Human Rights Watch estimates, children may account for as much as 35–45 percent of the SPDC's new recruits.

Indeed, the police and army appear to be either directly or indirectly involved in most crime and violence. It is reported that police regularly victimize civilians, and initiate criminal investigations against them, not because actual crime victims file complaints, but because locals have bribed the police to do so often in efforts to carry out vendettas or various criminal schemes. Special drug-squad police regularly accost civilians for bribes, frequently beating and killing them. State-controlled media regularly ritually denounce civilians who complain that police or military officials have abused them. Instead, official media assert that complainants are of ill-repute while their officers have demonstrated excellent discipline and have acted according to proper regulations.

Further, the Myanmar Penal Code contains a number of provisions to counteract citizen complaints to police and aggressively deter them from doing so, making any official crime statistics even more unreliable. Provisions allow prosecutors to criminally charge complainants for bringing "false charges" against their neighbors or officials.

Provisions threaten charges, punishable by prison sentences, for filing "false information with intent to cause a public servant to use his lawful power to the injury of another person" as well as accusations deemed to be "criminal defamation" done for "intentional insult with intent to provoke breach of peace; statements conducing to public mischief."

Invoking these provisions means that police do not need to conduct investigations, for which they are unqualified, and cases can be resolved expediently. As well, others learn that criminal complaints are dangerous for the complainant and that crimes committed by police and state officials will be committed with impunity. Not surprisingly, authorities in this highly authoritarian state commonly determine that victims of both ordinary crime and officer abuse are indeed defaming others in attempts to disrupt security and imprison the troublemakers accordingly.

As part of Indochina's "Golden Triangle," Myanmar provides large quantities of harvested opium each year. Officially, the Central Committee for Drug Abuse Control (CCDAC), which the Directorate of Defense Services Intelligence (DDSI) effectively controls, leads Myanmar's counternarcotics operations. The CCDAC includes personnel from the police, the army, and military intelligence with 18 drug enforcement task forces around the country in major cities and along key transit routes near the country's borders with China, India, and Thailand.

In 1999, the junta initiated its 15-year plan to eliminate opium crop production by 2014. The UN's Office on Drug and Crime's 2008 Opium Survey in Myanmar, which it conducted in conjunction with the dictatorship's officials, reported that the dictatorship has considerably decreased the country's opium production, which was reportedly potentially 410 metric tons (451 US tons) in 2008. It also reported that the overall prevalence of adult heroin users in the country that year was a low 0.12 percent of the population and somewhat higher for males than it was for females.

U.S. drug control analysts tend to be less sanguine about the levels of opium production, though they seem to agree on the level of local heroin users. The U.S. State Department believes that the CCDAC has inadequate resources with which to achieve its stated mission. U.S. authorities have declared that Myanmar's counternarcotics efforts by 2008 have "failed demonstrably," with the country producing 90 percent of Southeast Asia's opium, making it the second-largest opium producer in the world.

Although the ruling junta, which traffics in the country's other lucrative extractive industries, does not appear to be systematically involved in the drug trade, powerful local army personnel are reported to be. As well, it is believed that the junta's published statistics greatly underestimate the extent of Myanmar's black market overall, which includes significant trade in methamphetamines and counterfeit pharmaceuticals, suggesting that money laundering is also more substantial than the junta suggests.

Sources agree that about 90 percent of Myanmar's opium crops exist in its Shan State, with additional production occurring in the Kachin and Kayah State. These states represent the political aggregation of specific regionalized ethnic groups. There has been significant ongoing armed conflict between rebel Karen National Union (KNU) forces and the *Tatmadaw* and its allies, the Democratic Karen Buddhist Army (DKBA), a loose coalition of thugs and drug-runners.

This conflict and the drug trade have corresponded with widespread problems of civilians being extorted by armed forces, the taking of slave laborers, and other crimes against humanity such as torture and extrajudicial killings, as well as the trafficking of women and children for foreign labor. This has all led to continued problems of migrating persons forcibly displaced from the regions. In 2007, for example, there were an estimated 3 million internally displaced persons in Myanmar in addition to the many millions fleeing the country.

Finding of Guilt

Those accused of crimes in Myanmar have no actionable rights in the criminal court systems. The Burma Lawyers' Council concludes that in practice authoritarian policies have systematically led to the "emasculation of the principles of fair trials and due process," effectively reducing the courts to merely legalistic facades. The accused are regularly arrested without warrants and held incommunicado without access to family members or attorneys. Because there is no modern police force trained to perform actual criminal investigations and provide prosecutors with evidence, criminal cases are not investigated and prosecutors need not actually establish cases with evidence. Instead, pretrial detention under police custody, coupled with confessions extracted with torture, provide prosecutorial material.

Under the Myanmar Penal Code, courts can grant bail in cases where police are not legally authorized to do so. But in practice, bail decision making is chaotic and unprincipled, made by authorities without respect to their legal authority. Bail is frequently set at monetary levels exceeding the legally permissible maximum.

Although dissident commentators report that there still remains a coterie of competent and dedicated defense attorneys and human rights advocates attempting to defend defendants within the court system, in practice, criminal defendants cannot assert due process rights or even predict how their cases will be resolved. The junta's own Judiciary Law of 2000 formally acknowledges the right to public hearings with various exceptions. Yet the courts regularly deny defendants public hearings.

According to Amnesty International, trials fall far short of international standards for fair trials, with authorities regularly making prejudicial pretrial statements about cases, abrogating the presumption of innocence, and holding trials in secret with or without defendants present. The 1947 Constitution had mandated that Supreme Court judges had to have at least 15 years' experience as advocates in that court before becoming judges. But successive military juntas have done away with any such competency standard. Instead, judges are selected for their willingness to comply with military dictates. Although the junta abolished military tribunals in 1992, the judiciary remains firmly under military control, and the Judiciary Law of 2000 has further legalized judicial dependence.

Defendants may legally appeal their convictions. Appeals can be made from township court to district or division court, up to the Supreme Court and then defendants may apply for special appeal. But appeals inevitably fail.

Successive juntas have also instituted a series of suppressive laws that have effectively criminalized all forms of political dissent. These are ostensibly designed to prohibit "subversive acts" that officials deem to threaten the "stability" and "security" of both their "State" and their "Union." In particular, the regime regularly invokes the Emergency Provision Act of 1950 and arrests dissidents for the peaceful exercise of their natural rights to free expression, association, assembly, and movement, and commonly subjects them to secretive political trials in its special criminal courts. These, in place since 1962, still have broad authority to process all manner of Myanmar's "insurgents" and "traitors" and represent what the Asian Legal Resource Centre describes as a "completely sealed off parallel system" to the ordinary courts. Firmly controlled by the military, these courts do not allow defendants to appeal to the ordinary courts.

Punishment

The Penal Code allows for a range of familiar criminal punishments in the ordinary criminal courts such as fines, imprisonment, transportation for life, and the death penalty. Although reliable official statistics do not appear to exist, it seems that a large majority of ordinary criminal convictions results in the imposition of monetary fines. As well, human rights watchers have reported that it is relatively common for police to effectively adjudicate cases of serious interpersonal crimes such as murder and rape by coercing victims to accept monetary restitution from offenders in lieu of seeking a prison term for their attackers. However, for the serious political prisoners processed through the special criminal courts, there are three penalties available: at least three years' imprisonment at hard labor, full life imprisonment, or death.

The World Prison Population List, eighth edition, reports statistics for Myanmar's prison system collected from the junta's Correctional Department in its Ministry of Home Affairs. It reports that in

2007, Myanmar's prison population was an estimated 65,063 with an imprisonment rate about 126 per 100,000 population. Pretrial detainees represent about 15 percent of the prison population, while juveniles and foreign prisoners represent about 1.6 percent and 0.6 percent, respectively.

The Correctional Department administers 94 prisons. These include 22 maximum, 7 medium, and 10 minimum security prisons. The system also includes about 50 prison labor camps of various sorts. Depending upon the facility, prisoners are forced to work in rock quarries, engage in livestock breeding, work on rubber plantations, or perform agricultural labor, railway construction, or engage in other construction work. There is also a women's prison and two rehabilitation camps, one of which is specifically designated for drug addicts.

But the junta's centerpiece prisons are Mandalay and the infamous Insein Prison in Yangon, formerly Rangoon. Many of the junta's estimated 2,100 political prisoners, including Suu Kyi, are incarcerated here. Although the official capacity is between 5,000 and 6,000, the actual prison population at Insein is estimated to be more than 10,000.

Bo Kyi, current secretary of the Burmese Assistance Association for Political Prisoners, who was himself imprisoned in Insein, describes it as the "darkest hell-hole in Burma." Concrete cells are 8 feet by 12 feet without sleeping mattresses, toilets, or showers. Tuberculosis and scabies, dysentery and mental disorders are rampant. Guards regularly torture prisoners and criminal convicts are frequently used to discipline political prisoners. Torture through stress positions and morning "exercises" are commonly inflicted, and conditions inside the prison have become so bad that the International Committee of the Red Cross has stopped its prison inspections throughout Myanmar in protest. For many, incarceration inside Insein is a death sentence.

Paul Schupp

Further Reading

Amnesty International: http://www.amnestyusa.org.

Asian Legal Resource Centre: http://www.article2.org.

Burma Lawyers' Council: http://www.blc-burma.org. This organization aims at restoring the rule of law.

Human Rights Solidarity, a publication of the Asian Human Rights Commission. Article 2, International Covenant on Civil and Political Right.

Human Rights Watch: http://www.hrw.org.

Nepal

Legal System: Common/Customary
Murder: Medium
Corruption: Medium
Human Trafficking: Medium
Prison Rate: Low
Death Penalty: No
Corporal Punishment: Yes

Background

Cloaked by the majestic Himalayan Mountains, Nepal is a developing nation that borders India and China. While Nepal has a total land area of 147,181 square kilometers (56,827 square miles), slightly larger than the state of Arkansas in the United States, the country has a population of 29,519,114 (July 2008 est.). Nepal shares porous borders with India and China, a fact that has translated into increased growth in interborder trafficking of goods, drugs, and people. Nepal's unique form of government—a combined form of parliamentary democracy and constitutional monarchy—is reflected in its mixed legal system. Having been crippled by political instability for a long time, Nepal's current pursuit of politico-legal activism is poised to restructure the Nepalese legal system.

Origins of Legal and Criminal Codes

The ancient laws of Nepal can be traced back to the rule of Nepalese king Amshuverma (sixth century C.E.). Under King Amshuverma's rule, the first laws of administration, land reform, and monetary system, albeit unwritten, were introduced. Subsequent kingdoms introduced written laws, including the *Manav Nyayashastra* introduced by King Jayasthithi Malla (1382–1395). Translated as "Civic Laws," the *Manav Nyayashastra* was a legal and social code strongly influenced by contemporary Hindu principles. Another example is King Ram Shah's *Chhabish Thiti* (26 Commandments).

A more formalized written law, the *Muluki Ain* (Civil Code), was introduced in 1854 by Prime Minister Jang Bahadur Rana. Modeled after both the Napoleon Code and the Common Law System, this civil code formally established the reign of the Royal Court. This code remained in effect until 1950.

The roots of the Nepalese Independent Judiciary can be traced back to the *Pradhan Nyayalaya* (Supreme Court) of 1950, the forerunner of the modern Nepalese Supreme Court. The judiciary was granted independence from the king and supremacy over matters of law. However, the role of the Supreme Court as the supreme "guardian of the law" was ephemeral, since in 1963, the king regained his power. Under his newly claimed authority, the king superseded the three branches of the government—the executive, legislative, and partially the judiciary—and declared the Supreme Court as *Hukum Pramangi* (Order of the Crown). This heightened royal power remained in effect until 1990, when the revolution sought to establish democratic principles, foremost among which was an independent judiciary. However, this was also short-lived. In 2002, Parliament dissolved and the king reclaimed his sovereignty, a rule that lasted from 2005 to 2006.

Although Nepal's current criminal justice system is predicated on the essentially democratic ideals envisioned by the Constitution, the monarchy was responsible for the administration of the criminal justice system until 1990. During this era, the Nepalese army played a significant role, along with the implementation of the one-party *panchayat* system. In 1990, however, the *panchayat* system was supplemented with an independent criminal justice system with a multiparty interim government. Along with political changes, 1990 brought swift legal changes to Nepal. The Nepalese Constitution of 1990 upheld and established the legal notion of a fair and an impartial criminal justice system.

The Communist Party of Nepal (Maoists) staged a revolution in 1996 and seized judicial power. More recently, on November 21, 2006, the Nepalese government executed the Comprehensive Peace Agreement, an agreement formally ending the Maoist insurgency that began in 1996. As a result of the ensuing violence and political unrest, an interim nonpartisan constitution was drafted and adopted on January 15, 2007. This 2007 Constitution is expected to integrate formal democratic principles and establish the sovereignty of the people. The newly created interim constitution embraced democratic philosophies and norms, such as nonpartisanship, fundamental civil liberties, basic protections and freedoms, right of franchise, and other edicts that establish the authority of the rule of law. As such, it replaced the king as the head of state with the prime minister. The newly established constitution underscores several fundamental liberties, that is, equality and a fair and balanced criminal justice system.

Most recently, the king was ousted following the April 2008 general elections and the first meeting of the Constitution Assembly. Following these elections, Nepal was declared a secular, Federal Democratic Republic by the Constitution Assembly on May 28, 2008, and the king was replaced by leaders of the Communist Party of Nepal (Maoist) (CPNM).

In conclusion, the *Muluki Ain* (The Legal Code) of 1854, as mentioned above, was introduced by the first rana prime minister, and remained in effect until the early 1990s. Amended several times, the *Muluki Ain* was entirely revamped in 1963. It attempted to harmoniously integrate royal rule and local customs. The entire treatise was called the *Ain Sangraha*.

The revised code fostered the notion of democracy and equality before the law. This was significant in that it endeavored to end legal favoritism based on caste, creed, and sex. The code revolutionized local customary law by permitting divorce, intercaste marriages, and abolishing laws that allowed discrimination based on caste. The *Muluki Ain* created a uniform family law that was applicable to all and engendered the ideal of caste-blind equality. In the absence of the code's specificity, community customs shaped the decision. This has produced a unique and complex legal system.

Legal System

The ancient Nepalese legal system has been inquisitorial, plural, and also follows civil law. Pursuant to the 1990 political upheaval and ensuing changes, the role of the judiciary broadened. With it, independent judicial review of executive and legislative branch decisions became established as a legal norm. Judicial independence, during this era, fostered the growth and autonomy of the Supreme Court, largely independent of monarchical intrusion (at least theoretically). Under the 1990 Constitution, some substantive procedural protections for criminal defendants were implemented, namely, the right to counsel, protection from double jeopardy, and protection from retroactive application of laws.

Courts

The Nepalese legal system is an admixture of Hindu legal and English common law traditions. On the whole, Nepal's legal system is influenced by Tibet, China, and India, and an interlude of British colonial guidance. Nepal's Hinduism is a testament of India's influence, and this defines its culture and caste-structured society.

The ancient *Muluki Ain* prior to its 1963 revision had no specific interpretation of law. The magistrates and justices subjectively interpreted laws. Court procedures were not uniform and no writs of habeas corpus were issued. The accuser was placed in jail along with the accused. There was no provision for a speedy trial and/or swift administration of justice. The burden of proof rested with the accused, who was presumed guilty until proven innocent. There were no jury trials. Although the ancient rules dictated that the accused could not be convicted of a criminal charge without confessing, torture was often used as a means of obtaining confessions. Courts under the *Muluki Ain* had executive and judicial powers along with final decision-making authority vested in the prime minister.

The feudal-based legal system envisioned by the *Muluki Ain* was overthrown in 1951 pursuant to the reforms enacted and the Constitution of 1948. This divested the prime minister of judicial authority. The statutory enactment of the Supreme Court Act of 1952 established the Nepalese Supreme Court as the highest judicial body, modeled after the Indian Supreme Court. Under this new Supreme Court, special traveling courts were established. These courts traveled to different districts to provide citizens easier access to justice. These courts were courts of general jurisdiction, and as such, were empowered to audit public accounts, hear complaints of all kinds, make arrests, hold trials, and impose sentences.

Jurisdictionally, each district has a Court of First Instance that affords legal redress for the aggrieved plaintiff in contemporary Nepal. The jurisdiction of the courts is divided by subject matter, such as civil, criminal, a court of appeals, and 14 zonal courts. Additionally, there are five regional courts and a Supreme Court. The Supreme Court is empowered to issue writs of habeas corpus and decide on the constitutionality of laws. The Supreme Court of Nepal has both original and appellate jurisdiction. The original jurisdiction of Supreme Court oversees 4 regional, 15 zonal, and 75 district courts. In Nepal, there are 5 development regions, 14 zones, 75 districts, 3,995 village development committees, and 36 municipalities. Nepal has not accepted compulsory International Court of Justice (ICJ) jurisdiction.

Originally, the Supreme Court justices were appointed by the king. Inasmuch as the Supreme Court is considered as the court of last resort, the king had power of "executive clemency," whereby the king had discretionary authority to grant pardons and suspend, commute, or remit sentences of any court. The Supreme Court is composed of a total of 14 justices—a chief justice, six other associate justices, and seven alternate judges in reserve.

The Nepalese Supreme Court

Nepalese Supreme Court Justices hold offices until the age of 65. They can be impeached by a two-thirds majority of the House of Representatives on the grounds of incompetence or improper conduct or dishonesty. The chief justice and other justices reserve the right to resign from office at any time. The Supreme Court has the power to hear petitions and appeals, review and revise judgments, and to try certain cases. It also administers the Court of Appeal and all the district courts and disseminates the Supreme Court decisions.

Under Nepalese judicial and criminal justice systems, there is no distinction between criminal and civil courts other than some basic procedures. The Nepalese Constitution classifies courts into three categories:

1. The Supreme Court of the Kingdom of Nepal
2. The Court of Appeal
3. The District Courts

Various types of benches determine the judicial power of the Supreme Court. Examples include the following:

1. Single Bench formed of a single justice, concerned with the procedure of cases.
2. Division Bench composed of two justices, hearing the appeals filed after the decision of the Court of Appeal and other revisions of court decisions.
3. Full Bench composed of three or more justices to render the final decision upon the cases that do not have unanimity in the decision of the division bench or other cases.
4. Special Bench composed of three or more justices to hear petitions concerning the constitutionality of the law.

The Full Court

The Full Court is commonly known as the meeting of all the justices present including the chief justice. It is a high-level policy-making body of the judiciary. The Full Court is basically responsible for the formulation of policies relating judicial administration. Policy decisions formulated by the Full Court are basically carried out by the Registrar (*ex officio* secretary of the Full Court) of the Supreme Court. Major functions of the Full Court are as follows:

1. To recommend new legislation relating to the administration of justice and any amendment or change required in such law.
2. To consider the policy issues relating to administration of justice and court management.
3. To approve the annual report of the Supreme Court.
4. To award the title of Senior Advocate.
5. To consider on matters referred to the Full Court either by the chief justice or any of the justices.

Nepalese Military Courts

In Nepal, there are separate military tribunals that generally deal with military personnel. Generally, civilians are not tried in the military courts. There is no jury system. Special tribunals hear cases involving terrorism or treason under the treason act. Nepal's military court system was modeled after those of the Indian Army and was composed of courts-martial. The king was the head and presiding authority for the courts-martial. The four divisions of the courts-martial were (1) general, (2) district, (3) summary general, and (4) summary.

An *ex officio* member of the general court-martial was an officer of the Department of the Judge Advocate General. This division of the court-martial was authorized to levy any sanctions pursuant to army regulations. A district court-martial, however, had the vested authority to levy any sanctions other than the death penalty.

Police

The Nepalese police force is under the general supervisory authority of the Ministry of Home Affairs. The cabinet is vested with the authority to appoint the inspector general of police and other senior administration of the police force. The police are classified into the following five categories:

1. The Nepal Public Police Force
2. The Armed Police Force
3. The Guard Police Force
4. The Riot Police Force
5. The Traffic Police Force

Historically, Nepal kings (*rajas*) essentially carried out police and judicial functions. Outside the capital, however, the central government appointed local governors, also known as *bada hakim,* run by the *panchayat* system. (The *panchayat* system is a consular assembly of village leaders.) This *panchayat* maintained order in their local communities, similar to Indian rural law. Local custom informed and molded the administration of police and judicial function. As such, cultural and social position, that is, caste, had a strong influence on judicial and police treatment. Aggrandizement of polito-social power by the central government was a main point of contention with the tribal groups. This federalism argument belied local disregard for central government policy.

During rana-rule, there was no centralized police system. Rather, crime and punishment were matters of local concern, handled by the *panchayat* system. An anti-rana revolt began in 1950, which sparked the modernization of the Nepalese police system. Indian police aided the Nepalese officials in restructuring the police force and the creation of infrastructure for the Nepalese criminal justice system.

In 1955, King Mahendra enacted the Nepal Police Act, which was instrumental in the modernization of Nepal's police system. This statutory law effected major structural and functional changes in the Nepalese punitive system and improved its efficiency. Pursuant to the Nepal Police Act, Nepal was divided into geographical zones, also known as "ranges."

The Nepalese Constitution provides that Ministry of Home Affairs and its appointed "chief district officer" shall be responsible for maintaining law and order at the district level. The *panchayat* informal system was replaced by village and municipal development committees charged with local administrative and judicial functions. The *chowki hawaldar* (local police officer) replaced the village leaders and was responsible for the maintenance of law and order at the local level. The *chowki hawaldar,* in turn, reports to the *thana* (station inspector). On a larger scale, all *chowki hawaldars* work under the direction of *thanas,* the chief district officer.

Hierarchically, the Nepalese Police Force was the highest police agency that was under the control of the Ministry of Home Affairs. The inspector general of the Nepalese Police Force directed the Central Police Headquarters, which had different divisions, as follows: (1) criminal investigation division; (2) intelligence, counterintelligence, motor transport, and radio sections; (3) a traffic policy branch; and (4) a central training center.

Crime Investigation

Since the Nepalese legal system is an admixture of accusatorial and inquisitorial legal systems, criminals are prosecuted before the judiciary by the police and the office of the attorney general. Under the contemporary police system in Nepal, the Crime Investigation Department (CID) executes the crime investigatory functions of the police. The CID works as a unit under the Nepal Public Police Force at the Nepal Police Headquarters and is directed by an assistant inspector general of police.

The hierarchical organization of the CID is divided across 5 regions, 14 zones, and the 75 districts of Nepal. Regional police offices (for each region of Nepal) are directed by a deputy inspector general of police. Each zone has its "zonal police offices," which are under the direction of senior superintendents of the Nepalese police force. The district-level police offices are subsequently directed by the zonal or regional superintendents of police or deputy superintendents of police, respectively. District police offices pursue investigative capacities within their territory. For cases of national concern, the regional police offices act as a liaison between district units and the Central Crime Investigation Department at Nepal Police Headquarters.

The CID is classified into the following eight specialized divisions based on the nature of crimes:

1. Crime Investigation Groups
2. National Level Dog Section
3. Narcotic Control Unit
4. Crime Investigation School
5. Crime Research Branch
6. Foreign Branch
7. Anti-Terrorist Branch
8. Scientific Resources Coordination Branch

These divisions serve the investigatory and organizational capacity of the CID.

The Anti-Terrorist Branch is classified into internal and external terrorist sections. The Scientific Resources Coordination Branch deals with criminal behavior, fingerprinting, photography, and forensic science. The Crime Research Branch includes the following subdivisions:

1. The Central Women's Cell
2. Records Section
3. Research Section
4. Crime Investigation Information Section
5. White Collar Crime Section

Some of these subdivisions are products of recent legislation enacted to further democratic principles.

Crime

Age of Criminal Responsibility

The age of criminal responsibility in Nepal is 10 years. Pursuant to Nepalese law, children above the age of 16 are regarded as adults. As such, they are subject to the same penalties as adults and must face the consequences of their actions. In Nepal children between 16 and 18, or those who are jointly charged with adults, can be tried in an adult court under ordinary procedures. The police officers have broad discretionary powers and can apprehend children on various grounds, including vagrancy, indecent behavior or prostitution, being a public nuisance, "incorrigible," or exposed to moral danger.

The New Civil Code (*Naya Muluki Ain*) classifies children into three different categories by age:

1. Age of complete innocence
2. Age of quasi-responsibility
3. Age of complete responsibility

Currently, in Nepal, children's cases are heard by a panel that includes a magistrate and social workers.

Crime Statistics

Few data are available on crime in Nepal. According to the advisory for travelers put out by the U.S. government and the U.S. Embassy in Nepal, the rate of violent crime in Kathmandu is low, but crime, such as robbery and home invasion by armed gangs, in Kathmandu and in adjacent areas has been rising since April 2006.

Limited data are available on certain types of crimes in Nepal from various United Nations surveys. The rates of crime in 2006, per 100,000 population, are reported as follows:

Intentional homicide	1.84
Intentional homicide with a firearm	0.30
Assault	3.79
Rape	0.76
Robbery	0.54
Thefts	1.95
Burglary	0.10
Fraud	0.30
Drug offenses	0.80
Illicit drug traffic crimes	0.80
Human trafficking	0.21
Participation in organized criminal groups	0.12

These crime data are adapted from the 10th United Nations Survey on Crime Trends and the Operations of Criminal Justice Systems (2009) conducted by the United Nations Office on Drugs and Crime, Centre for International Crime Prevention. There were 4,082 total recorded crimes in Nepal during 2005 as compared to 4,134 in 2006, producing crime rates of 15.07 and 14.96, respectively. There were a total of 564 intentional homicides completed during 2005 as compared to 509 during 2006, producing rates of 2.08 and 1.84, respectively. The assault rate in 2005 was 3.86 as compared to 3.79 in 2006. The rates for burglary, fraud, drug offenses, illicit trafficking in drugs, human trafficking, and organized crime do not display any significant changes from 2005 to 2006.

Drugs

Nepal is not a significant producer of narcotic drugs. Despite its proximity to the major heroin source countries of Myanmar and Afghanistan,

Nepal has not been a major transit route. However, its relatively porous borders and easy travel between Nepal and neighboring countries may facilitate transit routes for drugs and other illegal activities, although the rates for these crimes do not appear to be especially high, according to the United Nations data.

Punishment

Death Penalty

Nepal abolished the death penalty for ordinary crimes in 1990, and in 1997 the death penalty was completely abolished. The last execution to take place in Nepal was in 1979. Generally, the death penalty was used for treason, mutiny, desertion, inciting panic, and surrender of troops, arms, or garrisons to the enemy with a finding of cowardice. During the time of war, punishment for dereliction of military duties was twice as severe as for the same offense committed in peacetime. Officers and citizens were strictly forbidden to have any contact with foreign diplomats and attachés. Only a few high-ranking officers in army headquarters were permitted to interact with foreigners solely on official matters. Failure to observe this rule could result in disciplinary action.

The disciplinary powers allowed officers and noncommissioned officers were more extensive than in the U.S. military service. Unit commanders could impose up to 30 days' confinement in prison or restriction to barracks. The most common forms of company punishment included extra guard duty, suspension from duty or from supervisory assignments, fines of up to 14 days' pay, detention of pay until a financial or property loss was compensated, reprimand, and warning. Junior commanders could demote officers with the rank of *hudda* (sergeant) or lower.

Corporal Punishment

In Nepal, corporal punishment is used on children up to the age of 16 years under the Child Act (Sections 11 and 15) and the general prohibition of cruel treatment in Section 7. In 1964, the Act to Repeal Some Criminal Cases and Remitting Punishment abolished a number of cruel punishments, including shaving of the head (*Mudne*), pricking with needles (*Khopne*), applying hot metals to the body (*Damal Garne*), and feeding faeces (*Abhaksha*). Following this act, the main sanctions available to the courts were fine and imprisonment. The Compensation for Torture Act (article 31) and the Constitution (article 14) prohibit torture and inhuman and degrading treatment. There is no explicit prohibition of corporal punishment as a disciplinary measure in penal institutions, but Section 7 of the Children's Act and the 2005 Supreme Court decision prohibit corporal punishment.

Prisons

Prior to 2001, offenders as young as 10 years old could be handcuffed. In 2001, the Supreme Court ordered the banning of handcuffing young offenders. Section 15 of the Children's Act prohibits the use of handcuffs, fetters, and solitary confinement of children.

In Nepal there is no separate place for juveniles either in police custody or in prison despite the fact that the Children's Act of Nepal clearly prohibits housing children alongside adult criminals in the same facility. The Prisons Act (1962) attempted to instill humanitarian treatment in Nepalese prisons. Prisons for females are very crowded and are attached to men's prisons. Most female prisoners awaiting trial are housed in crowded prisons adjacent to prisons for men. Pregnancy during imprisonment in Nepalese prison is a common occurrence. In Nepal, the mentally ill are also housed in prisons.

Nepal does not have a department of corrections, and as such, there is no separate prison officer cadre and no minimum ratio for staff to prisoners. The civil servants are frequently transferred from department to department to administer different departments, including prisons.

Suman Kakar

Further Reading

International Civil Defense Directory—Nepal Web Site: http://www.icdo.org/pdf/struc/nepal-en.pdf.

The Library of Congress Country Studies. CIA World Factbook—Nepal: http://www.celrrd.

org/2.1/strengthening_of_criminal_justice_system.php.

Strengthening the Criminal Justice System—From the ADB Regional Workshop in Dhaka, Bangladesh, May 30–31, 2006 Web Site: http://www.adb.org/Documents/Books/Strengthening-Criminal-Justice-System/strengthening-criminal-justice-system.pdf.

The United Nations Office on Drugs and Crime, Centre for International Crime Prevention: http://www.unodc.org/documents/data-and-analysis/Nepal.pdf.

Youth and the Criminal Justice System Context and Practices within Asia: http://www.pficjr.org/Resources/documents/Youth%20and%20the%20Criminal%20Justice%20System.pdf.

North Korea (Democratic People's Republic of Korea)

Legal System: Civil/Customary/Socialist
Human Trafficking: High
Death Penalty: Yes
Corporal Punishment: Yes

Background

Criminal law and the criminal justice system have a long history in Korea. Early criminal codes specified formal penalties for murder, the infliction of physical injury, and theft. Later, a centralized, systematized, and bureaucratized criminal justice system emerged, and criminal law was specifically written down and more articulated. During this period, a professionalized criminal justice system—including police and a judicial bodies—was developed. However, a division of labor between military, police, and judicial functions did not exist. Also during this time, criminal law was well developed and regulated many aspects of criminal matters including treason, defeat in warfare, surrender to the enemy, murder, theft, killing livestock, adultery, abuse of a government official's authority, and embezzlement.

During the Joesun dynasty (from 1390 to 1910), the criminal justice system was professionalized, and in 1894, the French criminal justice and legal system was imported into the nation and the modern police force was created independent of the judicial body. This Westernized system continued until the Japanese occupation in 1910. During this period, Korean criminal law and its criminal justice system were heavily impacted also by German influences, which were imported by the Japanese.

After the Korean liberation in August 1945, North Korea underwent a two-year Soviet military governance during which time the Japanese criminal justice system and criminal law were altogether rejected and the new socialist criminal justice system and law were strongly enforced. Before the establishment of the North Korean state, the police force was created by Korean communists, primarily led by Kim Il-sung and his group, and backed by the Soviet army. The main functions of this police force were to defend the communist temporary governing body, punish the anticommunist population, and keep the peace. With the birth of the new state in 1947, North Korean criminal law was heavily influenced by socialist law to serve and protect the communists and Kim Il-sung's dictatorship regime. After the creation of its own regime, armed forces were separately created, and thus the police were relieved of their military function.

Since the creation of the North Korean state, the political history of this country and related criminal law can be divided into four important time periods. During the first period (August 1945–April 1956), Kim Il-sung's leading communists concentrated on attacking and destroying all other noncommunist political groups and individuals. The North Korean police and other criminal justice bodies played important roles in arresting and punishing these enemies of communism. During the second period (April 1956–May 1972), the North Korean state consolidated Kim Il-sung's one-man dictatorship. All other communist groups, individuals, and the general population not supporting Kim Il-sung were summarily executed or sent to labor camps for life without any judicial proceeding. The North Korean police again played a significant role in this political campaign. The police were separated from the Interior Ministry and became the independent, extremely powerful Ministry of Social Security. The third period (May 1972–July 1994) witnessed Kim Il-sung's regime attempt to abdicate the throne in favor of his first son, Kim Jung-il. Kim Il-sung faced fierce political opposition for this hereditary succession of power. The North Korean criminal justice system and police played a crucial role in completing this succession process and defending Kim Il-sung's regime. A great number of the elder Kim's political rivals and members of the general population were arrested, executed, or sent to labor camps without judicial proceeding. Kim's regime reshuffled its criminal justice agencies to strengthen its political control over political rivalries and the general population. The Ministry of Social Security was renamed as the Department of Social Security and developed into the current general police organization in North Korea. A suborganization was separated from the Ministry of Social Security and became an independent political police and intelligence organization called the National Political Protection Agency. The last period (July 1994–present) saw three major issues threaten Kim Jung-il's regime: the collapse of the former Soviet Union, a significant economic recession and famine during most of the 1990s, and the death of Kim Il-sung, who was revered as a god. His successor and son, Kim Jung-il, named his father as an eternal president of the nation.

Upon these crises, Kim Jung-il reengineered his ruling structure and relied heavily on the North Korean military and other coercive state agencies. He proclaimed the "military first" policy. Based on this principle, the National Defense Commission was created as the practically ultimate authority of North Korea, including all other nonsecurity matters as well as national defense. Then, Kim Jung-il became the chair of the National Defense Commission, and thus he was able to rule his country.

In North Korea, criminal justice agencies and other security bodies exist to protect a personal ruler and his regime or to execute his will over his subjects. This essence is imbued with socialist principles. In the socialist legal tradition, the primary function of criminal justice is to protect the communist state, punish individuals opposing communist principles or states, and reeducate the population as communist persons. Accordingly, the North Korean criminal justice agencies and other security agencies have all those purposes—but never the protection of individual rights and properties. Thus, judicial independence for checking the abuse of power of state agencies is ignored. Criminal justice agencies and other security agencies have free hands over individual suspects in criminal justice proceedings.

Finally, when understanding crime and the criminal justice system in North Korea, it is crucial to distinguish between formally stated principles and actual practices. Unlike other countries, formally stated principles in North Korea have propaganda purposes for foreigners. The Constitution and criminal law in North Korea may include principles of due process, human rights, personal protection, separation of powers, and rules of evidence; however, those principles are never seriously considered. Actual practices in real life are set by Kim Jung-il's or other high-ranking state officials' arbitrary decisions. For this reason, when examining crime and punishment in North Korea, one needs to focus on actual practices, not formally addressed missions and principles.

Crime

The North Korean government does not release statistics on crime. In principle, crime is a product of class conflict in the capitalist state and, according to socialism, is primarily committed by the capitalist state and bourgeoisie in the process of protecting its ruling system and to oppress the proletariat. Being a socialist state, North Korea basically stands on the ground that there is no crime in the country.

North Korea's complete government control over its people and thorough seclusion from the outside world are other reasons for the scarcity of information regarding crime in this country. No foreign scholars, organizations, or mass media can enter this country to develop independent reports on crime. Independent foreign media sources are completely shut out. Thus, there is little way to secure an accurate picture of crime in North Korea.

Despite this enormous challenge, there are ways to gain an impression of the extent of crime in

North Korea by using alternative sources. Those sources include interviews with North Korean defectors; Web site information provided by government, media, NGOs, or Christian missionary groups helping North Korean defectors; intelligence; a human rights' report; and rare news reports.

Classification of Crime

In general, two different types of crimes exist in the socialist legal tradition: political crimes and conventional crimes. Political crimes are usually considered grave offenses. These crimes include crimes against socialist principles, the socialist state, or the Communist Party. Conventional crimes are grave or minor offenses, such as murder, theft, rape, assault, and traffic violations. There are four different types of political crimes: those against rulers, against the nation, against communism/socialism, and crimes of border-crossing without state permission.

The first type of offense is a particularly serious crime in North Korea. In any nation, an attempt to assassinate or plot against the head of state is a serious crime. However, in North Korea, crimes against rulers also include seemingly harmless or trivial acts such as a criticism or an insult against rulers including both the current leader Kim Jung-il and the deceased leader Kim Il-sung. For example, stepping or sitting on a picture of rulers in the newspaper, tearing a ruler's picture apart, having a dirty portrait of a leader, or a verbal insult against a leader can be serious political offenses.

The second type of crime, treason, is far more broadly defined than in any other country. This crime also reflects a bitter rivalry against South Korea. This type of crime includes aiding or abetting a South Korean agent or civilian; praising South Korea or its system, politics, economy, or culture; and attempting to escape to South Korea. Also, seemingly harmless and trivial acts can be included in this type, such as singing South Korean pop songs and watching South Korean television or movies.

The third type of crime is against socialist principles. Socialism is eagerly preached in North Korea and any criticism, rejection, or idleness on these principles can be grave political offenses. Examples of these serious types of crime against socialism can be verbally criticizing socialism or praising capitalism. Running a private business is a grave offense that threatens the socialist system. Stealing or obtaining agricultural products such as corn, rice, or potatoes can also be political offenses, in addition to not reporting to one's assigned work without government permission.

The last type of political offense arose during the 1990s, when North Korea underwent a great famine. As a result, its state distribution system collapsed, and many North Koreans illegally crossed the North Korea–Chinese border or the North Korea–Russian border to search for food, money, jobs, and a better opportunity. Initially, the North Korean government took draconian measures against illegal border crossings because it felt threatened by this development. All border trespassers, if caught, were severely punished. However, in the late 1990s and early 2000s, there were so many North Koreans crossing the border that the North Korean government reluctantly eased its sanction on border-crossing criminals. It classified border trespassers into two categories: the simple border crossing offenses and the serious border crossing offenses. The North Korean government severely punishes the latter, while it less harshly punishes the former as simple border crossing offenses are for pure economic reasons. Border trespassers simply work in Russia or China to make money or obtain food and then return to North Korea later. Some trespassers may engage in border trade, buy items in Russia or China, and then sell them in North Korea. The serious border crossing offenses are illegal border crossings beyond pure economic reasons and usually involve South Korea or Christianity. For example, illegal border crossing with an intention to enter South Korea or other Western democratic countries falls into this category. Also, conversion to Christianity or contact with a South Korean or a Christian missionary after crossing the border is included in this category.

Conventional crimes can be sorted into felonies and misdemeanors. Felonies seem to include murder, theft, rape, robbery, burglary, assault, smuggling, organized crime, drug trafficking, bribery, embezzlement, and corruption. Murder is punishable by the death penalty and even homicide by traffic accident can be punishable by the death penalty. Theft, rape, robbery, burglary, and assault are punishable by imprisonment of one year or longer. Smuggling, bribery, embezzlement, and corruption can be also punishable by one year or more prison sentence. Misdemeanors may include traffic violations, adultery, and domestic violence—all considered trivial offenses. Domestic violence exists but is widely ignored by the authorities as an insignificant matter. Adultery exists and was a common crime among women in the past whereupon female offenders were lightly sanctioned. Traffic violations include drunken driving, smoking while driving, and failure to maintain a clean vehicle in Pyongyang, the capital city. Also, in Pyongyang, there exist certain hours in a day during which one can drive: driving outside these permitted hours can be a traffic violation. Such acts are generally punishable by fine or driving license suspension or revocation. Additionally, prostitution, juvenile delinquency, organized crime, and drug trafficking also exist in North Korea.

Prevalence of Crime

After analyzing interviews and reports, it seems reasonable to estimate that a variety of crime has been rapidly increasing in North Korea since the early 1990s. Most of these crimes are either a direct byproduct of the economic crisis in this society (theft, robbery, prostitution, black market activity, smuggling, and border crossing), or are secondary byproducts such as murder, assault, domestic violence, juvenile delinquency, gang violence, organized crime, rape, and corruption. Many of these crimes occur in and around the black market (*Jangmadang* in Korean). An interviewee noted that crime is rampant in most parts of North Korea. Generally, people feel unsafe; when a wife works outside to make a living, a husband stays home to protect their property.

Due to the great famine of the 1990s and a continuing economic collapse, the state stopped providing the necessities of life and paying salaries for the majority of the civilian population, except for a few of the loyal ruling class. People stole food, goods, and machinery from the state factories or farms to sell on the black market. Also, famine forced a great number of people to leave their homes and wander in search of food. These people easily transformed into criminal offenders or victims. Also related to this famine was prostitution, which rapidly increased as starving women sold their bodies to provide for themselves and their families. Desperate people easily turned to violence and an increase in murders, assaults, and battery resulted from personal disputes. Youth gangs were formed and harassed and extorted people in and around the black market. Meanwhile, police took full advantage of black markets and accepted bribes. A North Korean informant claimed that the police were the real criminals and true gangsters.

Crime in North Korea has distinct dynamics in four different geographic regions: Pyongyang, large cities in the provinces, border areas, and the countryside. In Pyongyang, crime is minimal as only state-selected people can live and work in this capital city with residential permission dependent on one's loyalty to the North Korean regime and the Communist Party. Thus, residents in Pyongyang are usually the elite ruling class of the nation. Visitors need government permission before entering the city; once inside, the police tightly control the security of the city to squelch potential riots, coups, or assassinations. Accordingly, it is not surprising to see low crime in this capital city. Yet, even in this environment, gang activity and other crimes have reportedly been increasing. Crime seems widespread in large cities in the provinces with most crimes occurring in and around the black market areas. Stealing, gang activities, and violent attacks are frequent in these areas. Also, prostitution thrives at railroad stations or near travelers' inns. Among large cities in the provinces, crime is particularly rampant in border cities or port cities. Border areas have also experienced a rapid increase of crime as a great number of people illegally cross borders. Smuggling is also active with various smuggled items such as used cars, televisions, cigarettes, clothing, and cosmetics from Russia and China. These smuggled items and their transporters are often targets of theft, as smugglers usually carry large amounts of cash or goods and are robbed or murdered. Agricultural product theft is rampant in the countryside due to starvation and the collapse of the state distribution system. People steal crops and vegetables from the state farm or storage. Oftentimes, women engage in "on the spot" prostitution with government officials to acquire agricultural products.

Organized Crime

Organized crime, corruption, and gang activity are widespread in North Korea due to loosening government controls driven by the economic crisis. Usually, these organized gangsters prey on the general population in the form of black market merchants and small-time border-crossing smugglers who oftentimes pay for police protection. In the upper levels of organized crime, criminals may work for highly placed government figures in such activities as drug trafficking. They are hired by the North Korean government and work as its secret representatives trafficking drugs manufactured by the North Korean government.

Meanwhile, throughout the North Korean government, organized corruption is rampant. Police officers and soldiers steal or extort from the civilian population. They are rarely punished unless they are caught at the scene of the crime. Also, other forms of corruption, including embezzlement, selling and buying of government offices or ranks, various favors such as Communist Party membership, residential rights in Pyongyang, travel permission, reduced punishments or release of prisoners, and abusing one's authority, are widespread among government officials.

Lastly, transnational organized crime activities are worth mentioning. Unlike other countries, North Korea as a state commits transnational organized crime activities. According to a report, it is increasingly clear that not only are key figures within the North Korean regime involved in transnational organized crime, but that the state itself has criminalized itself as a matter of policy. In this respect, North Korea is metamorphosing into a true "criminal state." These criminal ventures include not only drug trafficking, but also counterfeiting U.S. currency, illicit trade in endangered species, human trafficking, fraudulent antiques, counterfeit CDs and tapes, cigarettes, and radioactive materials. Particularly in drug trafficking, the state encourages illicit opium cultivation and manufacturing heroin and methamphetamines. It was reported in a United Nations conference in 2001 that the profit from narcotics trafficking netted North Korea U.S. $300 million per year.

Police and the Criminal Justice System

Apart from the already noted ultimate mission of the North Korean criminal justice system to protect its leader, the Communist Party, and the socialist state, the criminal justice system is also composed of the standard police, courts, and prisons. Among them, police or other law enforcement agencies play the most important roles and have far greater power than other components of the criminal justice system. They can literally arrest anyone on their own discretion and detain the arrestee for up to almost a year without any formal proceeding. They also run their own prison system. In some cases, the police or other law enforcement agencies enjoy judicial decision-making power such as conviction, sentencing, and execution.

Two major policing agencies exist in North Korea: *Inmin Boan Sung* (People's Security Department) and the *Gukga Ahnjeon Bowee Boo* (National Security Protection Agency). The People's Security Department is a general police agency equivalent to the Ministry of the Interior in the former Soviet Union. This agency deals not only with ordinary crime and criminals in principle but, depending on circumstances, may deal with political crime and criminals. *Gukga Ahnjeon Bowee Boo* (or simply *Bowee Boo*) is a combined agency of intelligence and political police equivalent to the KGB in the former Soviet Union. The primary function of this agency is spy activity overseas, antiespionage within the territory, and prosecuting political criminals in the country. Although its jurisdiction is limited to only political criminals in principle, its actual police power covers a large portion of population in North Korea because political crime is so broadly and arbitrarily defined.

Inmin Boan Sung, the North Korean police, was created in 1945 as *Jungchee Boan Guk* (Political Security Agency) and later became an independent ministry, *Sahoe Ahnjeon Sung* (the Ministry of Social Security). In 2000 it was renamed as *Inmin Boan Sung* (the Ministry of People's Security). Officially, the North Korean police is a ministry of the cabinet and thus under the command of the prime minister. Yet, in reality, the prime minister has no commanding power over the police except for traffic-related administration. The police take no orders from the cabinet and directly report to Kim Jung-il.

The structure of the North Korean police is along military lines and composed of three geographical tiers: the central organization in the capital city of Pyongyang, provincial organizations existing in each provincial administrative unit, and the *Boonjoo So* existing in the lowest level of administrative unit. The central organization in Pyongyang controls all suborganizations and units in the North Korean police and includes 15 departments such as internal affairs and seven independent agencies such as foreign affairs, education, and transportation. Provincial departments are under the central administration's chain of command and have two tiers: provincial headquarters and the lower-tier departments, which are located in cities of provinces or districts of three special cities. For the lowest level of North Korean police, *Boonjoo So* is structured under each lower-tier provincial department and under the lowest level of the North Korean administrative unit. It is said that about 4,000 *Boonjoo So* are established all over North Korea.

The total size of North Korean police is estimated between 180,000 and 200,000 for a total population of roughly 23 million people. Their structure includes 21 different ranks (the same as the military) with two tiers: an upper rank of generals and officers and a lower rank of petty officers and soldiers. In the lower level, an individual police officer must spend between 8 and 10 years mandatory service period, as in the military. After spending this mandatory service period, a police officer may be discharged or apply for Inmin Boan Sung Political University to become a ranking officer. Entering this university is very competitive and extremely selective. Students spend four years in this university and become a ranking officer after graduation.

In general, the police are feared, hated, and despised among the general population; yet, it is very popular to become a police officer among North Koreans. People want to have good and friendly relationships with a police officer due to the almost unlimited power of the police.

Bowee Boo is another important police organization in North Korea, as it is considered an intelligence agency, a counterespionage agency, and the political police. In general, it is a more powerful organization than the North Korean police. *Bowee Boo* was under the direct command of the North Korean president, Kim Il-sung, up until his death in 1994 when Kim Jung-il presumably took command. Like the North Korean police, the structure of *Bowee Boo* also follows the basic structure of other North Korean administrative units: a centralized organization under a strict chain of command with its nucleus in the capital city of Pyongyang commanding all other suborganizations dispersed in local administrative units. *Bowee Boo* is primarily responsible for counterespionage and political crime and identifies, investigates, and arrests foreign spies or members of the domestic population opposing (or even complaining) about North Korean leaders, the North Korean state, communism, the Communist Party, and the regime. This agency has several other functions including operating its own prison camps and responsibility for border patrol and protection, immigration control, customs and smuggling control, airport and seaport protection, and personal protection for Kim Jung-il and other high-ranking government and party figures.

The total size and recruitment practices of *Bowee Boo* are not known; however, it does operate its own educational facility for agents called *Gugka Bowee Boo Jungchee Daehak* (National Security Protection Agency Political University). Only Communist Party members can enter this university to spend five years receiving military training and studying politics, psychology, philosophy, and socialist economics. Successful graduates become agents in *Bowee Boo* or ranking officials in the Communist Party or other government organizations. In this university, everyone including teachers, trainers, and staff—but not students—is military personnel. Upon graduation, a student receives a military rank.

Like the police, *Bowee Boo* is widely feared and hated by most North Koreans. Usually, it is more feared than the ordinary police; however, *Bowee Boo* as a profession is very popular. Many people want to be a *Bowee Boo* agent but the selection process is very competitive. This popularity is probably due to the enormous political power and access to wealth by means of corruption attached to this profession.

Besides the police and the political police, other components of the criminal justice system such as prosecutor, court, and lawyer exist in North Korea; however, their roles or powers are limited and minimal, because many cases are directly processed by the police or the political police.

Regarding structure, the prosecutor is not under the administrative body but instead the legislative body. The *Choigo Inmin Hoeu* (Supreme People's Assembly) is the legislative body of North Korea and is controlled by Kim Jung-il in practice. Under the chain of command of the central prosecutor's office, provincial prosecutors' offices exist in the intermediary-tiered three special cities and nine provinces. Under these provincial offices, local prosecutor's offices exist in districts of special cities, cities of provinces, and *goons* (equivalent to counties in the United States). The head of a provincial or local prosecutor's office is appointed by the head of the central prosecutor's office. The structure of the court is similar to that of prosecutor.

Lawyers do exist in North Korea, but have extremely limited roles. In principle, anybody can be the criminal defender (the role of a lawyer in trial) without any license or education. Individual or private law firms do not exist, as all lawyers are paid by the state and are members of the lawyer's committee, which takes cases in bulk and distributes them. There are about 500 lawyers in North Korea, of which approximately 200 are professional lawyers with the remainder being part-time lawyers having other professions such as college professor or legal researcher.

Since extremely few numbers of prosecutors, judges, and lawyers exist in North Korea, most North Koreans think no such people exist in their country because they never met anyone with such a profession. To become a prosecutor, judge, or lawyer, one only needs to major in law at the university. Once graduated from the university majoring in law, the new graduate should work in a lower-level job such as court clerk for several years. After that, one can be appointed as a prosecutor or judge by the state. Regarding the licensing of lawyers, a bar exam was established in 1993; however, retired prosecutors and judges or persons with five years or more work experience in the legal field can become lawyers without passing the license exam. Generally, these legal professions are not popular among young North Koreans.

Finding of Guilt

In North Korea, either the police or the political police play the most important role in determining guilt for both political crime and conventional crime, as such a finding is based on the police's arbitrary decision after hearing confessions extracted through torture. In political crimes, cases bypass the formal criminal procedure of prosecution, trial, and conviction and are exclusively handled by the police or the political police. Criminal suspects can be identified and arrested by *Bowee Boo* or the police, who have their own detention facility for their arrestees called *Gamok* (jail) or *Guryu Jang* (detention center). These are holding facilities for criminal suspects who can be detained in such facilities for up to several months without any legal charge or prosecutor, judge, or lawyer recognition or intervention. *Bowee Boo* or the police can interrogate or torture their suspects until obtaining confessions, whereupon *Bowee Boo* makes a judicial decision as to guilt. When the police determine guilt by confession, they usually transfer their detainees to *Bowee Boo* for political crime cases. When *Bowee Boo* finds guilt, they execute their detainees in a secret trial or an open trial if the case is serious. No judges, prosecutors, or lawyers are present in any of those trials. In less serious cases, *Bowee Boo* usually sends the guilty person to a prison camp for forced labor without a determined sentencing period. Family members of the guilty party are also sent to the prison camp for forced labor with no determined sentencing period.

In conventional crime cases, *Inmin Boan Sung* is the most important authority in the determination of guilt. Formally, these criminals are supposed to stand trial before a judge—but this is in principle only. Many criminal cases never reach the point of trial or even the prosecutor but instead are decided and punished by the police. The finding of guilt in conventional criminal cases is not much different from political crime cases, except that the cases are handled by the police, not by the *Bowee Boo*. The police find and arrest a criminal suspect and detain him or her in their holding facility. Without any outside interference—as in political crime cases—the police detain their arrestee for up to several months. The police constantly interrogate and torture their suspect until obtaining a confession. Once the police have a finding of guilt based on the confession, the detainee stands on one of two public trials: an open trial before the public, where police officers read the criminal charges and related criminal codes and convict the accused; or, in the other case, a formal criminal trial can be held. Once the police pass the case to the prosecutor, the prosecutor handles the case and makes a decision for either going to trial or returning the case to the police. The prosecutor can rarely reduce the charges set by the police. In trial, the prosecutor, judge, lawyer, and *Inmin Chamsimwon* (equivalent to the jury in the United States) are present. The lawyer does nothing to defend the criminal defendant, as his only job in the trial is postconviction when he provides the defendant the options: "I consent" or "I have no objection." The jury is selected from a population with strong loyalty to the Communist Party and supports the prosecutor in the trial. The prosecutor makes a statement, and the judge makes a final decision on conviction and sentencing. Although the judge has autonomy to make a decision in trial on paper, he usually confirms the prosecutor's charge because his performance is censored by the North Korean state or the Communist Party. Formally, an appeal is guaranteed if the defendant is dissatisfied with the conviction—but in principle only, as no appellation seems realistic in practice.

Punishment

Four different types of punishments have been identified in this country: the death penalty, imprisonment, forced labor, and fines. Among them, prison and forced labor are usually combined; however, forced labor as a separate punishment also exists. The death penalty is widely practiced even for nonheinous crimes and can be issued by a judge in a formal trial and immediately executed by the police. A murder conviction usually receives the death penalty; however, these formal death sentences seem relatively rare in this totalitarian state as in most cases, people can be simply executed without any formal trial or in an ad hoc open trial. When one attempts to steal agricultural products or government property, military or the police guarding that state property may simply shoot and kill a thief on the spot. The National Security Protection Agency or the police can execute their arrestee based on their own administrative decision. An open trial is basically held in open market, under a bridge, a sandy field along the river, or other open spots. The audience is forced to gather and to watch the trial. The chief of the local police department has the authority to decide an execution, which is then carried out by the police who shoot or hang the criminal in front of the assembled population. Execution is also common in prison, not only for prison riots or escape attempts, but also for rule violations or simple disobedience.

Imprisonment is another common type of punishment in North Korea. Political criminals and their family members can be imprisoned. Usually in this case, there are no formal trials or hearings as criminals and their families are literally kidnapped by the political police, *Bowee Boo,* and directly sent to prison camps run by the political police. No definite term of imprisonment is given, which means, in practicality, life imprisonment. In case of conventional criminals, a definite term of imprisonment is given. Inmates serve their sentence in prisons run by the police. Unless an inmate is sick, every inmate is subjected to slavelike labor. No exception is tolerated by the prison staff.

Forced labor is another type of punishment that is also widely practiced in prison. Inmates are forced to work in agriculture, construction, mining, or industry with no payment. Forced labor is also applied to those who are convicted of less serious crimes. These offenders are sent to labor-training camps, *Rodong Dalryeonn Dae,* where they are forced to work during their defined time in this facility.

Fines as a type of punishment are limited to traffic violations. Although North Korea has a very small number of vehicles, traffic regulation is strict and its punishment is harsh. Fines for traffic violations vary from 10 won to 50 won (US$0.01 to 0.05).

Prison

As detailed earlier, no separate and independent correctional agencies exist in North Korea. Instead, prisons are administered by either the National Security Protection Agency or the police and can be categorized into two different types: prisons for political criminals and their families run by the National Security Protection Agency and prisons for conventional criminals run by the police. Meanwhile, prisons can be divided by the length of detention. This can be also divided by two types: prisons for a long-term confinement (one year or longer) and prisons for a short-term confinement (less than a year) as shown in the following table.

	Administered by National Security Protection Agency	Administered by Police
Long-term confinement	Prison for political criminals and their family members	Prison for conventional criminals
Short-term confinement	Detention center for political criminals	Detention center for conventional criminals

The type of prison for political criminals and their family members is called *Gwalli So* ("controlling facility") or *Tkbyeol Dokjae Guyeok* ("special dictatorship zone"), both resembling the Soviet gulag. The incarcerated are expelled from society and confined in a specially designated area for life as they are considered "hostile" in accordance with the state's classification of the entire population into three categories: the core class (loyalists), the unstable class (potentially swayed against the regime), and the hostile class (dangerous). This type of prison can be one prisonlike building or composed of very large sprawling encampments located mostly in the valleys between high mountains and in the northern provinces. One part of the prison is self-contained, closed compounds for the alleged political criminals, and the other is a closed and fenced-in village for family members of the alleged political criminals. The two parts are completely separated and no communication or contact is permitted. There are between 5,000 to 50,000 prisoners per *Gwalli So*, totaling some 150,000 to 200,000 prisoners throughout the nation. The prisoners live under brutal conditions in permanent situations of deliberately contrived semistarvation.

Another type of prison, for conventional criminals, is more like a typical correctional institution. This facility is designed for persons convicted of serious crimes, that is, the equivalent of felony offenses. This type of prison is called *Gyohwa So* ("correctional facility"). Some of the *Gyohwa So* resemble large penitentiaries: a single, large compound surrounded by high walls and barbed or electrified wire fencing with several buildings for manufacturing production, prisoner housing, and offices for guards and prison officials. Other *Gyohwa So* are large, barbed-wire-enclosed encampments—located in the valleys of high mountains—composed of prisoner villages where prisoners engage in mining or logging. In many aspects of day-to-day prison life, this type of prison resembles the first type of prison as inmates are forced to do hard, often heavy, and dangerous labor while provided food rations insufficient to sustain even sedentary life. The combination of hard labor and inadequate food provisions results in rapid weight loss, industrial or mining work accidents, malnutrition-related diseases, and death. Prison hospitals and clinics are essentially places where the sick and injured are sent to await death. Loss of life occurs at such high rates that many of the *Gyohwa So* are perceived by prisoners as death camps (like political prisons) in that prisoners expect to die before the completion of their set sentences.

The other two types of prisons are detention centers run by the *Bowee Boo* and those run by the regular police. They essentially have no practical differences and both are of two types: a short-term *Jipgyeol So* and a *Rodong Dalryeonn Dae*. The latter is an even shorter-term detention center, set up to accommodate the overflow from the established detention centers caused by the large numbers of famine-related criminals in recent years, and is more localized than *Jipgyeol So* and not specified in the criminal statute. Generally, these detention centers deal with petty criminals convicted of what would be considered, in other countries, misdemeanor offenses or petty infractions, such as the large number of North Koreans who illegally crossed the border and were repatriated from China. Also, many petty offenders are held in this facility under such offenses as leaving one's village or traveling within the country without authorization, not showing up at one's designated worksite, or leaving the country. Despite its short-term confinement, the living and working conditions of these detention facilities are not much different from regular prison. Inmates are forced to do hard labor such as farming, mining, and manufacturing work in harsh conditions. Guards' treatment of inmates is harsh and brutal and, again, there is a lack of medical care. As a result of all these, the death rate among detention facilities is unusually high despite the short term served.

Minwoo Yun

Further Reading

The Daily NK: http://www.dailynk.com/english/.

Hawk, David. (2003, October 22). *The Hidden Gulag: Exposing North Korea's Prison Camps*. Washington, DC: U.S. Committee for Human Rights in North Korea.

Koreascope: http://www.koreascope.org.

Ministry of Unification, Republic of Korea: http://unikorea.go.kr/english/.

Pakistan

Legal System: Islamic/Common
Murder: Medium
Corruption: Medium
Human Trafficking: Medium
Prison Rate: Low
Death Penalty: Yes
Corporal Punishment: Yes

Background

The Islamic Republic of Pakistan is the sixth-most populous nation in the world and the second-biggest Muslim country with an estimated population of about 177 million and an area of 340,133 square miles. Geographically, Pakistan shares borders with Afghanistan to the northwest, China to the north, India to the south and east, and Iran to the west. In the south it is located on the Arabian Sea very near to the mouth of the Persian Gulf. Historically a part of India, over the years, it was ruled by rulers of various denominations but primarily by Hindus, Muslims, and the British. Before the British formally colonized this territory in 1857, Muslims had been ruling this area for about 1,145 years. In 1947, after independence from Britain, Pakistan appeared as a new nation on the world map with about 98 percent Muslim population.

But the majority Muslim population did not at all mean a theocratic state to be "ruled by priests with a divine mission." Quaid-e-Azam Mohammad Ali Jinnah (1876–1948), the founding leader of Pakistan, and completely a secular man, clearly enunciated his vision even three days before Pakistan actually was established. In his address to the first constituent assembly, on August 11, 1947, he said: "You are free; you are free to go to your temples, you are free to go to your mosques or to any other place of worship in this State of Pakistan. You may belong to any religion or caste or creed that has nothing to do with the business of the State." To further emphasize his point, in February 1948, he elaborated: "We have many non-Muslims-Hindus, Christians and Parsis—but they are all Pakistanis. They will enjoy the same rights and privileges as any other citizens and will play their rightful part in the affairs of Pakistan." So to start with, Pakistan adapted the Government of India Act (1935) as the first constitution of Pakistan, which was secular. The current constitution of Pakistan was framed in 1973 by the elected government of Prime Minister Mr. Zulfiqar Ali Bhutto—altogether a secular politician educated in UC Berkley. The only clause worth mentioning of the Constitution concerning Islam was that nothing in the law was going to be repugnant to the basic tenets of Islam. Different rulers from time to time made some amendments to the Constitution, but the citizens always want to revert to the original constitution of 1973, which was passed unanimously by all the constituent units of Pakistan.

Under the Constitution of 1973, Pakistan is a parliamentary democracy with the president as the head of state and the prime minister as the head of government. It has a two-house Parliament with a 100-member Senate and a 342-member National Assembly. Administratively, Pakistan is divided into four provinces and some federally administered tribal areas. Four provinces include the Punjab, Sind, Baluchistan, and North West Frontier Province (NWFP), administered by the respective provincial assemblies headed by the chief ministers aided by some provincial ministers. Some areas along the border with Afghanistan, since the British time, have enjoyed a special status, having relatively more independence as compared to the areas under the provincial governments. These tribal areas are called Federally Administered Tribal Areas (FATA) and are administered by the president through the provincial governor of NWFP. Capital territory Islamabad is also under the federal government. Northern areas of Gilgit and Baltistan until recently were ruled by the federal government, but in 2009 they elected their assembly and the assembly has elected the first chief minister and the governor is nominated by the federal government.

Crime and Justice

Criminal Law

Mainly the secular nature of the Constitution, amended with some Islamic provision, is reflected in the procedural and substantive law of the country as well. Pakistan's secular laws are based on British common law. The Criminal Procedure Code dates back to 1898 while the Pakistan Penal Code was legislated in 1860—both of them promulgated in the British period. In the same way, Prisons Act and Prisoners Act have been in force since 1894 and 1900, respectively. However, supposedly, to Islamize the law of evidence, General Zia-ul-Haque, the military ruler of Pakistan, replaced the Evidence Act passed by the British Parliament in 1872 with *Qanoon-e-Shahadat* (the Law of Evidence) Order in 1984. In addition to the Criminal Procedure and Pakistan Penal Code, there are some local and special laws. Local laws are specific to some geographic region: for example, Frontier Crime Regulations, 1901 is implemented in just the FATA area. And special laws deal with some specific subject: for example, Anti-Terrorism Act, 1997 is meant to deal with the terrorism cases.

Crime

In Pakistan, murder, attempt to murder, culpable homicide, rape, grievous hurt, hurt, kidnapping, abduction, assault on public servant, and suicide are grouped as crime against the person, while crime against property includes dacoity (robbery in which accused are five or more), robbery, burglary, cattle theft, theft, and cheating. Violations of Arms Act (1965), Prohibition Order (1979), and other miscellaneous laws are counted under the category of local and special laws. In 2008, a total of 581,919 crimes were reported to the police out of which 96,312 (16%) crimes were against person, 111,979 (19%) against property, and 373,628 (64%) under local and special laws. Terrorism, although generally a crime against the person, is categorized as violation of the special laws. According to the Global Terrorism Database, maintained by the University of Maryland, from 1970 to 2007, 2,590 cases of terrorism occurred in Pakistan, in which 5,840 people were killed and 11,597 injured. No doubt this figure is very conservative.

Although most of the laws are either adapted or promulgated by the federal government, a minimum of actual law implementation is with the federal government itself. It administers (policing, adjudication) the capital Islamabad and FATA. Federal Investigation Agency (FIA), under the federal government, investigates immigration cases, and some important terrorism cases, whereas the National Accountability Bureau (NAB) conducts investigations into corruption of federal government departments. National Highways and Motorway Police is also controlled by the federal government. Some other law enforcement agencies controlled by the federal government include rangers (border security force), coast guards, frontier constabulary, and political administration in FATA. Federal government also issues policy guidelines to the provinces on important crime control and public order issues.

Broadly speaking, crime prevention, investigation, adjudication, correction, compensation of the victims, and maintenance of public order rests with the provinces. Provinces have an elaborate system for most of these functions, especially for policing, adjudication, and corrections.

Women and Children

Women and children are two weaker sections of the society and once they come into contact with the criminal justice system, they merit special treatment. Pakistan is signatory to a number of rights of child and women's rights' instruments such as the Universal Declaration of Human Rights, Convention on the Rights of the Child (CRC), Stockholm Declaration and Agenda for Action against Commercial Sexual Exploitation of Children, Convention for the Suppression of the Traffic of Persons and of the Exploitation of the Prostitution of Others, and Convention

Pakistani women participate in a protest against gang rape, July 6, 2002, in Lahore, Pakistan. A tribal council ordered a teenage girl to be gang-raped because her 11-year-old brother was seen with a woman not related to him, a crime punishable by death in some remote regions of Pakistan. (AP Photos/K.M. Chaudary)

on the Elimination of Discrimination against Women (CEDAW). However, women continue to remain the victims of murder, domestic violence, human trafficking, physical and sexual abuse, kidnapping, rape, acid thrown and burn, and honor killing. Women are also victims of Hudood Laws, which most of the people consider as discriminatory.

At different times, the government has taken some steps for the promotion and protection of women's rights, which includes amendments in the West Pakistan Family Ordinance 1964. Also, the former prime minister, Benazir Bhutto, inaugurated the women police station on June 2, 1994. The general public received it very well, particularly the women in Karachi. Now women police stations exist in almost all parts of Pakistan.

Pakistan in 1990 ratified the United Nations (UN) Convention on the Rights of the Child (CRC) and in 2000, Pakistan issued Juvenile Justice System Ordinance (JJSO). It was necessary to keep the fundamental difference between the juvenile justice system and the criminal justice system. The rehabilitation of juveniles is considered to be the primary goal of the juvenile justice system, while that for the adults has been retribution. The introduction of JJSO came to an sudden halt when, on December 6, 2004, the Lahore High Court revoked the JJSO with effect for the whole country. In February 2005, the Supreme Court of Pakistan stayed the Lahore High Court judgment. While the appeals are pending in the Supreme Court and the JJSO has been temporarily restored, Amnesty International urges the government of Pakistan forcefully to make the case for child rights when the appeal comes up for hearing. What makes the situation more critical is that out of Pakistan's population of 177 million, almost half, or 49 percent, are under the age of 18 years while 22 percent are adolescent (10–18 years).

Police

Until 2002, the police were administered through the Police Act (1861) and the Police Rules (1934). Finding these laws outdated, and to make the police operationally neutral and free from extraneous influences, the federal government promulgated a new Police Order in 2002 that replaced the Police Act of 1861. Now the police are organized geographically on the police station level, subdivision level, district level, region level, and the province level. The police station is the basic geographical unit of operation and consists on average of about 100 police commanded by an inspector of police, while the province is commanded by an inspector general, and the police strength varies according to population of the province. For example, the inspector general of Punjab Police commands about 170,031 police.

The Police Order of 2002 also provides for the functional specialization of police into two major functions: operations and investigations. Operations staff is responsible for preventing crime, registering cases, serving as first responders to crime in case of need, and maintaining public order. Investigation staff is deputed to investigate cases, arrest the accused, and pursue the cases in court with the help of the prosecution branch.

Some support and logistic branches of police are provided under the law. For example, the Criminal Investigation Department (CID) collects, analyses, and transmits intelligence concerning terrorism, mainly at the provincial levels but with some regional offices as well. It also interrogates the arrested terrorists and keeps their records, while another support staff called Special Branch concerns itself with crime and political intelligence. Traffic Branch, in liaison with the district police officers, manages traffic flow and issues tickets on traffic violations. Telecommunication and Transport supports the other police branches with logistics support on wireless networks and purchase and major repair of vehicles.

Finding of Guilt

Courts

The judicial system in Pakistan is a mix of secular and Islamic courts, including a Supreme Court, provincial High Courts, district courts, subdivisional courts, and federal sharia courts that administer Islamic law. In addition, there are some special purpose courts like anti-terrorism courts. The lower courts at the subdivision level are presided over by civil judges-cum-magistrates who, along with civil cases, try criminal cases as well. They are empowered to try cases in which punishment is up to

14 years of rigorous imprisonment. Above them are the sessions judges who sit at the district level, or in case of additional sessions judges, at the subdivisions level. They have the power to try cases leading to capital punishment.

Every province has its High Court with a jurisdiction conferred on them by the Constitution (articles 175(2) and 199 of the 1973 Constitution) or by law. Generally, they are the first level of appeal against the judgments of civil judges and the sessions judges. They hear different writ petitions like writ of habeas corpus and take actions on matters of vital importance to the public. The Supreme Court of Pakistan is the apex court in Pakistan's judicial hierarchy—the final arbiter of legal and constitutional disputes. The court consists of one chief justice and 16 other judges. Although its permanent seat is in Islamabad, the capital, it has a number of branch registries where cases are heard. Its legal powers are outlined in the Constitution.

The Anti-Terrorism Court (ATC) was established in Pakistan to try terrorism cases by the 1997 Anti-Terrorist Act. Later on the act was amended on October 24, 1998, by the Anti-Terrorism (Amendment) Ordinance to bring it more in line with the Constitution. On August 25, 1999, through the Pakistan Anti-Terrorism (Amendment) Ordinance, the government generalized the ATC system to all of the country.

To strengthen the judicial system, reform efforts were made in 1958, 1967, 1978, 1993, and 1997. The major problem with the court system was found to be the high backlog of cases. The following causes and factors responsible for the delays in trial of criminal cases were identified: unsatisfactory service of processes and the nonattendance of witnesses, shortage of judicial and ministerial staff, delay on the part of investigating agencies and delay in writing and delivering judgments, frequent adjournments and dilatory tactics by the lawyers and the parties, and unattractive service conditions of subordinate judicial officers. Some of the legal and administrative measures were recommended to upgrade the system. The recommendations generally included increases in the number of judicial officers, provision of courtrooms and allied facilities, restructuring the service condition of judicial officers, timely submission of cases for prosecution, taking effective measures to ensure attendance of witnesses, liberalizing the provisions of bail, to check and control frequent adjournments, separation of the functions of civil and criminal courts, and strict supervision on court management. Access to the Justice Program initiated and sponsored in 2001 by the Asian Development Bank is on its way to remove some of the problems identified earlier.

Prosecution

In all criminal cases in Pakistan, the state is deemed to be the complainant of the case. However, the victims appear as witnesses and if they could afford a lawyer, they are allowed to engage their own lawyers. In the initial days before 1980, police officers served as prosecutors in the magisterial courts and the district attorneys prosecuted cases in sessions courts. But in the early 1980s, all the prosecution was taken over by the offices of the district attorneys. However, under the Access to Justice Program, the government of Punjab has established a separate Public Prosecution Department through the Punjab Criminal Prosecution Service (Constitution, Functions and Powers) Act 2006. The province of Sindh, in July 2006, established its own prosecution service under the ordinance called the Sindh Criminal Prosecution Service (Constitution, Functions and Powers) Ordinance 2006. The provinces of Baluchistan and NWFP have also independent prosecution services.

Punishment

Pakistan's prison system has existed since the British era and the basic infrastructure is present in almost all the district headquarters. However, in the newly established districts, the prisons have been built or are being built. Separate facilities are seldom available for convicts, and under trial prisoners, and for children and women. An old and chronic problem of prisons is the overcrowding caused partly by cumbersome and technical provisions of procedure and partly because of nonobservance of provisions. According on a report published in 2006, Pakistan has more than 95,000 people in custody for criminal offenses, of which approximately 67 percent (about 63,600) are pretrial detainees. Out of the more than 31,400 convicts, nearly a quarter—more than 7,000 individuals, including almost 40 women—have been sentenced to death, and are either involved in lengthy appeals processes or awaiting execution after all appeals have been exhausted.

Under a ruling from the Federal Sharia Court, family rooms are being built in prisons to provide facilities for the convicts to spend some days with their spouses. Some high-security prisons are also being constructed to keep the terrorists separate from the ordinary prison population. The need for measures to lessen the population of the prisons through reforms in the jail administration and restorative justice programs has been recommended many times. Probation services, although existing for a long time in Pakistan, are almost nonconsequential.

Death Penalty

The number of persons sentenced to death in Pakistan and executed is increasing every year, with 394 accused sentenced to death and 15 hanged in 2004 and 309 sentenced to death and 134 hanged in 2007. Pakistan currently has 26 criminal offenses that allow for the death penalty—as opposed to just two, for murder and treason, at the time of independence in 1947. Several of these laws were enacted to deal with some exigencies. The list of 26 offenses includes many crimes that cannot be justified as a "most serious crime," as required for the death penalty under the International Covenant on Civil and Political Rights. Therefore, scholars recommend that there is an urgent need for a review to remove the death penalty as a sentence for many of these crimes. They further recommend a review of the laws and witness requirements for such crimes and provision for defendants' access to a competent counsel.

Syed Ejaz Hussain

Further Reading

Chaudhry, M. A. K. (1997). *Policing in Pakistan.* Lahore: Vanguard.

Cohen, Stephen P. (2006). *The Idea of Pakistan.* 2nd ed. Washington, DC: Brookings Institution Press.

Usa, Ibp. (2009). *Pakistan Justice System and National Police Handbook,* 6th ed. (World Strategic and Business Information Library). Washington, DC: International Business Publication, USA.

Wasti, Tahir. (2008). *Islamic Law in Practice: The Application of Qisas and Diyat Law in Pakistan,* Yearbook of Islamic and Middle Eastern Law, Vol. 13 (2006–2007).

Philippines

Legal System: Civil/Common
Murder: High
Burglary: Low
Corruption: High
Human Trafficking: Medium
Prison Rate: Medium
Death Penalty: No
Corporal Punishment: No

Background

The Philippine legal system is a mixed common and civil law system, incorporating elements from Spanish civil law, American common law, Muslim law, and customary law. Philippine private laws, including laws on persons and family relations, law on sales, property, and contracts, are primarily civil law in nature. Philippine's constitutional law, criminal law, business law, taxation, banking, and evidence are influenced by American common law.

The practice of codifying laws in the Philippines started as early as 1521 when Spain colonized the Philippines. During Spanish colonization from 1521–1898, Spain introduced codification of laws, enacting codes such as the Spanish Civil Code (to govern civil, family, and property relations) and the Penal Code (to govern criminal acts). When the Americans colonized the country from 1898–1946, the system of codification was continued. However, the United States also introduced the common law system under which decisions of the Philippine Supreme Court were treated as binding. Thus, although legal codes were still widely used, court decisions interpreting the codes also had the binding effect of law. The Americans also revised the Spanish codes and enacted a new Revised Penal Code (1930) and a new Civil Code (1950).

The practice of using both statutory law (written instruments from the legislative branch) and case law (binding court decisions) continued after the Philippines gained independence on July 4, 1946. Under the newly established government, laws enacted by Congress were (and are still) called Republic Acts. During the martial law period (1972–1981), President Ferdinand Marcos issued more than 2,000 presidential decrees that also had legal and binding effect. The issuance of presidential decrees was terminated in February 1987 when the 1987 Constitution was ratified.

At present, several codes are in use, including the 1930 Revised Penal Code and the Civil Code. The Revised Penal Code defines criminal acts, provides for criminal liability, and establishes the penalties for different crimes. The Revised Penal Code distinguishes penalties into capital (death or *reclusion perpetua*), afflictive (six years to life imprisonment), correctional (one month to six years), and light (up to 30 days). These penalties are imposed in relation to the classification of the crime. Thus, serious crimes have capital or afflictive penalties. Less grave crimes have correctional penalties. Light crimes have light penalties. The 1987 Constitution, however, prohibits the death penalty unless allowed by Congress through duly enacted laws.

Government

The Americans granted the Philippines independence on July 4, 1946, pursuant to both the 1935 Constitution and the 1934 Tydings Mcduffie Law. The 1935 Constitution provided for three separate branches of government: the executive headed by the president; the legislative consisting of a bicameral Congress; and the judiciary, consisting of the Supreme Court, and all lower courts. Efforts to amend the 1935 Constitution were initiated through a Constitutional Convention that convened on June 1, 1971. While the convention was still in session, President Ferdinand E. Marcos declared martial law. The Constitutional Convention completed its draft constitution, which was then submitted for ratification through citizens' assemblies on January 17, 1973.

Although the 1973 Constitution was ratified and a parliamentary form of government was authorized, a parliamentary government was not set up due to a transitory provision of the 1973 Constitution. Instead, President Marcos established military tribunals and abolished Congress. President Marcos lifted martial law in 1981. He then abolished military tribunals and authorized the holding of elections wherein he emerged as winner. The Constitution was again amended in 1984 and elections were held for the elective seats in Parliament.

Subsequent political developments, including the assassination of opposition member Senator Benigno Aquino, forced President Marcos to call a special presidential election on February 7, 1986. The National Movement for Free Elections results showed that Sen. Aquino's widow, Corazon Aquino, was leading the elections by a landslide. Ferdinand E. Marcos and Arturo M. Tolentino, however, were officially declared winners for the positions of president and vice president. This led to a peaceful and spontaneous uprising by the people ("People Power") and eventually led to the ouster of President Marcos on February 25, 1986.

Post-EDSA Revolution (1986–Present)

The events subsequent to the People Power Revolution and the ouster of President Marcos led to the revival of a democratic republic. When President Marcos fled the country, Corazon C. Aquino took her oath of office as president. Immediately thereafter, she issued several proclamations, including the following: (1) Proclamation No. 1, where she and Vice President Laurel assumed power; (2) Proclamation No. 3, which provided for a new government and a Provisional or Freedom Constitution; and (3) Proclamation No. 9, where a Constitutional Commission was established.

The Constitutional Commission was tasked with drafting a new constitution, which was ratified on February 2, 1987. The Constitution provided that the president and vice president elected during the February elections would have a maximum six-year term. The 1987 Constitution also established a republican form of government composed of three independent branches (executive, legislative, and judiciary).

The military (Armed Forces of the Philippines [AFP]) is under the control of the Department of National Defense. But the civilian police (Philippine National Police [PNP]) is under the control of the Department of Interior and Local Government.

Police

Attempts to restructure the police started as early as the mid-1970s. Prior to this, the Philippine Constabulary was solely responsible for law enforcement at the national level. Local law enforcement (city and municipal police officers), on the other hand, maintained peace and order at the local level and were under the supervision of the National Police Commission. This system created problems including territorial jurisdiction, lack of uniformity and coordination, intrapolice disputes, and political partisan involvement in police employment. Another major problem was the use by local incumbent politicians of the police as private armies to intimidate political opponents. To resolve these issues, the 1973 Constitution provided for the integration of police, fire, and jail services nationwide.

The Integrated National Police was organized to ensure public safety, protect lives and property, enforce laws, and maintain peace and order throughout the nation. It was given powers to prevent crimes; arrest, detain, and rehabilitate criminal offenders; prevent and control fires; investigate crimes; and bring offenders to justice. However, in practice, the Philippine Constabulary handled serious crimes or cases involving separate territorial jurisdictions, while the Integrated National Police handled less serious crimes and local traffic, crime prevention, and public safety.

The structure and functions of the Philippine Constabulary and Integrated National Police were reorganized and integrated into the Philippine National Police (PNP). The PNP was created as a police force that is national in scope and civilian in character. The PNP is administered and controlled by the National Police Commission.

Organization of Police

According to law, the chief of the PNP is supported by the following administrative and operational units:

1. Administrative Support Units, which consist of (a) Crime Laboratory, to provide scientific and technical investigative aid; (b) Logistic Unit, to procure, distribute, and manage all logistical requirements, including firearms and ammunition; (c) Communications Unit, to establish an effective police communications network; (d) Computer Center, to design, implement, and maintain a database system; (e) Finance Center, to provide finance services; and (f) Civil Security Unit, to provide administrative services and general supervision over all organized private detectives, watchmen, security guard agencies, and company guard forces.
2. Operational Support Units, which include (a) Maritime Police Unit, to perform all police functions over Philippine territorial waters and rivers; (b) Police Intelligence Unit, for intelligence and counterintelligence functions; (c) Police Security Unit, to provide security for government officials, visiting dignitaries, and private individuals authorized to be given protection; (d) Criminal Investigation Unit, to monitor, investigate, and prosecute all crimes involving economic sabotage and other organized crimes. The Criminal Investigation Unit shall also investigate all major cases involving violations of the Revised Penal Code and organized crime groups, unless the president assigns the case exclusively to the National Bureau of Investigation (NBI); (e) Special Action Forces, to function as a mobile strike force or reaction unit to support local police forces in controlling civil disturbance, counterinsurgency, hostage-taking rescue operations, and

other special operations; (f) Narcotics Unit, to enforce all laws against dangerous and other prohibited drugs and substances; (g) Aviation Security Unit, to secure the country's airports against offensive and terroristic acts; (h) Traffic Management Unit, to enforce traffic laws and regulations; (i) Medical and Dental Centers, to provide medical and dental services for the PNP; and (j) Civil Relations Unit, to promote community and citizens' participation in maintaining peace, order, and public safety.

Crime

The Revised Penal Code classifies crimes into nine categories depending on the right or interest violated:

1. Crimes against national security and the laws of nation such as treason and espionage, piracy, and so forth.
2. Crimes against the fundamental laws of the state such as arbitrary detention or expulsion, violation of dwelling, dissolution of peaceful meetings, and crimes against religious worship.
3. Crimes against public order such as rebellion or insurrection, coup d'état, crimes against legislative bodies.
4. Crimes against public interest such as forgery, impersonation, false testimony; monopolies in restraint of trade; unfair competition.
5. Crimes against public morals such as gambling and betting, offenses against decency, obscene publications and exhibitions, vagrancy and prostitution.
6. Crimes committed by public officers consisting of various forms of bribery and corruption.
7. Crimes against persons such as parricide, murder, homicide, infanticide and abortion, kidnapping, abandonment of helpless persons and exploitation of minors, threats and coercion.
8. Crimes against property such as of robbery, theft, swindling, arson, and other crimes involving destruction and malicious mischief.
9. Crimes against chastity such as adultery, rape, and seduction, corruption of minors and white slave trade, libel and slander.

In President Gloria Macapagal Arroyo's State of the Nation Address for 2006 and the 2007 State of the Nation Address Technical Report prepared by the Presidential Management Staff, she identified three major criminal activities that are currently being targeted: terrorism, organized crimes, and illegal drugs.

Republic Act No. 9372 (the Human Security Law) was enacted to combat terrorism. As of July 2007, 840 communist terrorists and 107 members of the Abu Sayyaf Group (a terrorist organization funding its activities through kidnapping and other illegal activities, such as drug trafficking) were arrested or killed. Government reports claim that terrorist activities decreased by 41.3 percent from 11,930 in 2001 to 7,003 in 2005. To emphasize its seriousness in curbing the threat of communist insurgents, the government allocated Philippine pesos (PhP) 1 billion (the current equivalent of US$21.5 million) to the Armed Forces of the Philippines, the Philippine National Police, and other related agencies tasked with eradicating the Communist Party of the Philippines–New People's Army by 2010. Although military operations have been ongoing, the Communist Party-New People's Army continues to exist. Avelino Razon, Philippine National Police chief, stated that the New People's Army (NPA) rebels have only 5,700 members (the lowest level in 20 years) as of 2007, due to military destruction of 13 suspected insurgency bases. In January 2010, the Armed Forces of the Philippines issued an official news release stating that at least 566 NPA rebels surrendered during the past year. The report further stated that "the large number of surrenders during the past year is attributed to the healthy partnership of the Philippine Army with the local government units and, most importantly, the cooperation of the residents in the area. With this drop in the number of NPA strength in the country, there is not a doubt that the June 2010 deadline of significantly weakening the NPA rebels shall be met."

During the first half of 2007, law enforcement officers seized illegal drugs valued at PhP 1.74 billion (the current equivalent of US$38,280,000). As of July 2007, a total of 9,761 pushers and users were arrested, leading to the filing in various courts of 7,107 drug-related criminal cases. This is in contrast to the efforts of the government for the entire year of 2006, wherein a total of illegal drugs valued at PhP 2.9 billion (the current equivalent of US$63,800,000) were confiscated and 9,739 drug cases were filed in court.

Under existing Philippine law, dangerous drugs and controlled substances are defined in accordance with international law instead of being defined by local statute. Thus, dangerous drugs are defined as to "include those listed in the Schedules annexed to the 1961 Single Convention on Narcotic Drugs, as amended by the 1972 Protocol, and in the Schedules annexed to the 1971 Single Convention on Psychotropic Substances." "Controlled Precursors and Essential Chemicals" are defined as to "include those listed in Tables I and II of the 1988 UN Convention Against Illicit Traffic in Narcotic Drugs and Psychotropic Substances."

Under the Dangerous Drugs Act of 2002, dealing in dangerous drugs is punishable by a penalty of life imprisonment to death and a fine from 500,000 pesos (the current equivalent of US$11,000) to 10 million pesos (the current equivalent of US$220,000). Dealing in controlled substances is punishable by a penalty of imprisonment ranging from 12 years 1 day to 20 years and a fine from 100,000 pesos (US$2,222) to 500,000 pesos (US$11,000). The Dangerous Drugs Act of 2002 also provides for situations where the penalty is higher, such as if the transaction occurs within 328 feet (100) meters of a school, or minors are used as runners.

Crime Statistics

For the year 2006, the Directorate for Investigation and Detective Management Division of the PNP reported the following number of street crimes: 6,196 murder incidents, 3,299 homicide cases, 2,589 rape cases, 7,313 robbery incidents, and 9,988 cases of theft. These crimes totaled 29,385 for the year 2006 and the PNP reported an efficiency rate averaging 82 percent representing the total number of crimes solved.

The National Statistical Coordination Board, on the other hand, reported that the total number of crime incidents per 100,000 population increased from 81.9 in 2006 to 115.6 in 2007. Out of the total crime incidents, index crimes increased from 47.8 in 2006 to 65.5 in 2007 per 100,000 population. Non-index crimes also increased from 34.1 in 2006 to 50.1 in 2007 per 100,000 population.

Based on official reports from the Bureau of Jail Management and Penology (BJMP), the most typical crimes in rural areas are theft and various crimes against persons such as homicide, physical injuries, and rape. Theft in rural areas accounted for more than 50 percent of the total crimes reported as of July 2007. Similarly, the incidence of homicide, physical injuries, and rape accounted for more than 50 percent of the total crimes reported as of July 2007.

The most common crimes in urban areas are robbery and drug-related offenses, with the National Capital Region accounting for almost 49 percent of the total reported incidence of robbery reported as of July 2007 and almost 40 percent of the total reported incidence of drug-related offenses reported as of July 2007.

Finding of Guilt

Section 14, article 3 of the 1987 Philippine Constitution guarantees the following rights of the accused: (1) presumption of innocence; (2) to be heard by himself or herself and counsel; (3) to be informed of the charges against him or her; (4) speedy, impartial, and public trial; (5) right to confront witnesses; and (6) compulsory process to secure attendance of his or her witnesses and evidence. In addition, the Rules on Criminal Procedure guarantee that the accused is not compelled to be a witness against himself or herself and has the right of appeal.

In addition to the above rights of the accused, the 1987 Philippine Constitution has adopted the judicial ruling in the United States concerning Miranda rights in the case of *Miranda v. Arizona*, 384 U.S. 436 (1966). Section 12, article III of the 1987 Constitution provides for the rights of any person under custodial interrogation. Custodial investigation is questioning initiated by law enforcement officers after any individual is placed under custody or "deprived of his freedom of action in any significant way." The 1987 Constitution requires law enforcement officers to inform a suspect of the right to remain silent and to have competent and independent counsel. The Constitution also provides that, if the suspect cannot afford the services of counsel, he or she must be provided with one. These rights to remain silent and to counsel cannot be waived except in writing and in the presence of counsel.

Prosecution and Defense

The Public Attorney's Office (PAO), an attached agency under the Department of Justice, is responsible for providing indigent litigants free legal assistance, including defending the accused at trial. The precursor of the PAO is the Citizen's Legal Assistance Office (CLAO). Under these laws, the CLAO was mandated to represent, free of charge, indigent persons. With the enactment of the Administrative Code of 1987, CLAO was renamed the Public Attorney's Office and the title Chief Citizen's Attorney was renamed Chief Public Attorney.

The law provides that for offenses punishable by imprisonment for at least four years, two months, and one day, a preliminary investigation is required and a complaint must be filed only with any of the following officers: provincial or city prosecutors and their assistants, judges of the municipal trial courts and municipal circuit trial courts, national and regional state prosecutors, and other officers as may be authorized by law. For all other offenses, the complaint or information may be filed directly with the municipal trial courts and municipal circuit trial courts, or the complaint may also be filed directly with the office of the prosecutor.

Upon the filing of the complaint, a preliminary investigation is conducted by the prosecutor's office to determine whether there is sufficient grounds to believe that a crime has been committed and the respondent is probably guilty, and should be held for trial.

On the basis of the complaint and any accompanying affidavits, the investigating officer may either dismiss the case or issue a subpoena to the respondent. The respondent is given the opportunity to present his or her counteraffidavit, the affidavits of his or her witnesses, and other supporting documents. Thereafter, the investigating officer may set a clarificatory hearing. If he or she finds cause to hold respondent for trial, the investigating officer will prepare and file the information with the proper court.

The ombudsman also has the power under the 1987 Constitution to investigate any alleged illegal act of any public official, employee, or government agency. The ombudsman has authority to conduct preliminary investigations and to file with the *Sandiganbayan* (the Anti-Graft and Corruption Criminal Court) investigations against public officers and agencies. This power of the ombudsman is concurrent to that of other investigative authorities such as the police and prosecutors when the accused is a public official with salary grade of lower than 27.

Accused Is Higher-Level Public Officer

The ombudsman has primary jurisdiction to conduct preliminary investigation of all complaints against higher-level public officials such as governors, mayors, diplomatic officials, highly ranking military and police officers, top executives of government corporations, members of Congress, and members of the judiciary. The ombudsman is allowed to deputize and designate regular prosecutors to assist him or her in the case.

Dispute Resolution

A law passed by Congress on April 2, 2004, established the Alternative Dispute Resolution Law. Mediation and other forms of alternative dispute resolution such as evaluation of a third person, minitrial, and mediation-arbitration are allowed under this law. In addition, all international commercial arbitrations are required to be governed by the Model Law of International Commercial Arbitration adopted by the United Nations Commission on International Trade Law on June 21, 1985, and recommended and approved on December 11, 1985.

Based on a study conducted by the Supreme Court of the Philippines with the assistance of the United Nations Development Programme (2006), a significant portion of criminal cases at the regional trial court and lower trial court levels are either archived (33.80%) or dismissed (33.69%). Only approximately 23 percent of the cases filed actually go to trial, with 18.06 percent of the cases resulting in convictions and 4.53 percent resulting in acquittals. The study further suggests that a significant portion of criminal cases are not brought to trial due to settlement between parties. On the other hand, a substantial portion of cases are archived due to failure of the prosecution to gather enough evidence such as eyewitnesses to proceed with the case. Similarly, at the Sandiganbayan, 75 percent of the criminal cases filed against various government officials result in acquittals.

Rights of Detained Persons

Incarceration before or awaiting trial is allowed, if the accused or detainee has not posted bail. A person under legal custody can only be released when he or she has posted and been granted bail. Philippine Rules on Criminal Procedure provide that bail can be posted to secure the release of a person under legal custody. Bail is a right: (a) before or after conviction by the metropolitan trial and municipal trial or circuit courts of an offense punishable by not more than six years' imprisonment; and (b) before conviction by the regional trial court for an offense not punishable by death, *reclusion perpetua,* or life imprisonment. Bail, on the other hand, is discretionary: (a) before conviction by the trial court of a capital offense, when the evidence of guilt is not strong; and (b) after conviction of an offense not punishable by death, *reclusion perpetua,* or life imprisonment.

As for persons legally detained, the Revised Rules on Criminal Procedure provide that any person under legal detention shall not be released or transferred except when there is a lawful court order or when he or she has posted and been granted bail. Thus, a person who is detained lawfully under a warrant of arrest cannot be released or transferred to another place unless there is a valid court order or is admitted to bail.

Courts

There are as many criminal court judges as there are judges of the various courts in the Philippines including the Municipal Court, Metropolitan Court, Municipal Circuit Trial Court, Regional Trial Court, Sandiganbayan, Court of Tax Appeals, and Sharia courts. All of these courts exercise jurisdiction over specific criminal cases defined by existing laws.

Under Philippine law, metropolitan trial courts, municipal trial courts, and municipal circuit trial courts have jurisdiction over the following offenses: (a) violations of city or municipal ordinances committed within their respective territorial jurisdictions, (b) all offenses punishable by not more than six years' imprisonment regardless of the amount of fine and other accessory penalties, and (c) where the sole penalty for the offense is a fine (and not imprisonment), offenses punishable by not more than 4,000 pesos (approximately US$83.26) fine.

Regional trial courts are granted exclusive jurisdiction over the following: (a) all criminal cases not within the exclusive jurisdiction of any other court, tribunal, or body; and (b) where the sole penalty for the offense is a fine (and not imprisonment), offenses punishable by a fine of more than 4,000 pesos (approximately US$83.26) for private persons and not more than 6,000 pesos (approximately US$124.89) for public officers and employees.

The Anti-Graft Court (Sandiganbayan) has jurisdiction over cases involving corruption by government officials with rank of Grade 27 or higher under the Compensation and Position Classification Act of 1989.

The Court of Tax Appeals (CTA) has jurisdiction over violations of the National Internal Revenue Code, Tariff and Customs Code, and other laws enforced by the Bureau of Internal Revenue or the Bureau of Customs. However, if the amount of taxes and fees claimed is less than 1 million pesos (around US$22,000) or there is no specific amount claimed, the regular courts have jurisdiction and their decision is appealable to the CTA.

The sharia courts are special courts created under Presidential Decree No. 1083 (Code of Muslim Personal Laws). These courts have exclusive jurisdiction over all violations of the code.

These judges must be qualified to hold the positions in said respective courts, as defined by law. A regional trial court judge, under Philippine laws, must be a natural-born Philippine citizen, at least 35 years old, and for at least 10 years have been engaged in the practice of law or held Philippine public office that requires admission to the practice of law. A judge of a metropolitan or municipal trial or municipal circuit trial court must be a natural-born Philippine citizen, at least 30 years old, and for at least 5 years have been engaged in the practice of law or held Philippine public office that requires admission to the practice of law.

Juvenile Law

The Juvenile Justice and Welfare Act 2006 was signed by President Gloria Macapagal-Arroyo, effective in May 2006. The law introduced a new juvenile justice system and provides a framework for victim reparation for the crime; reconciliation of the offender, the victim, and the community; and reintegration of offender into society.

Under the new law, a child 15 years old or under at the time of the commission of the offense is exempt from criminal liability, but subject to an intervention program. A child above 15 years but below 18 years is also exempt from criminal liability and subjected to an intervention program, unless he or she has acted with discernment, in which case such child shall be subjected to the appropriate proceedings. The exemption from criminal liability does not include exemption from civil liability.

Chapter Two of the law outlines diversion procedures. Individuals responsible for the juvenile justice program are required to conduct mediation, family conferencing, conciliation, and appropriate indigenous modes of conflict resolution having in mind the best interest of the child. The chapter provides for the creation of diversion contracts and the procedure to follow if the contract is not completed. Diversion can be used at all stages of the juvenile proceeding.

Punishment

Under Philippine law, the principal penalties that may be imposed are: (a) afflictive penalties, consisting of *reclusion perpetua* (up to 30 years in prison), *reclusion temporal* (12 years and 1 day to 20 years), and *prision mayor* (from 6 years and 1 day to 12 years); (b) correctional penalties, consisting of *prision correccional* (from 6 months and 1 day to 6 years), *arresto mayor* (from 1 month and 1 day to 6 months), suspension, and *destierro;* and (c) light penalties, consisting of *arresto menor* (from 1 day to 30 days), and public censure. Fines and bond to keep the peace may also be imposed in addition to any of the above penalties.

Philippine law also provides that any person sentenced to *reclusion perpetua* shall be pardoned after undergoing the penalty for 30 years, unless such person by reason of his or her conduct or other serious cause is considered by the chief executive as unworthy of pardon. The law provides further that any person sentenced to *destierro* or banishment shall not be allowed to enter the place or places designated in the sentence, nor within a specified radius of 25 to 250 kilometers (15 to 155 miles) from the place designated. The penalty of *arresto menor* may be served under house arrest. The law states that *arresto menor* may be served in the municipal jail or in the house of the defendant himself or herself under the surveillance of an officer of the law, depending on the discretion of the court.

Accessory penalties consist of perpetual or temporary absolute disqualification from public office, suspension of the right to vote and be voted for, suspension from a profession, forfeiture or confiscation of instruments and proceeds of the offense, and payment of costs.

Any person who kills a member of his or her family is guilty of parricide and shall be punished with the penalty of imprisonment ranging from 20 years and 1 day to 40 years to death. Any person guilty of murder shall be punished by imprisonment ranging from 17 years, 4 months and 1 day to 20 years to death, depending on various aggravating circumstances. The crime of rape is punished by *reclusion perpetua* (imprisonment of 20 years and 1 day to 40 years).

The penalty imposed under Philippine law for theft corresponds with the value of property stolen. The law imposes imprisonment of *prision mayor* in its minimum (6 years and 1 day to 8 years) and medium periods (8 years and 1 day to 10 years), if the value of the item stolen is more than 12,000 pesos (US$265) but does not exceed 22,000 pesos (US$488), but if the value of the item stolen exceeds the latter amount, the penalty shall be *prision mayor* in its maximum period (10 years and 1 day to 12 years), and one year for each additional 10,000 pesos (US$222), but the total of the penalty that may be imposed shall not exceed 20 years. On the other hand, imprisonment of *prision correccional* in its medium (2 years and 4 months to 4 years and 2 months) and maximum periods (4 years, 2 months, and 1 day to 6 years) is imposed if the value of the thing stolen is more than 6,000 pesos (US$133) but does not exceed 12,000 pesos (US$266). The penalties for theft decrease as the value of the property stolen decreases.

Robbery with violence against or intimidation of persons is punished with the penalties of: (a) *reclusion perpetua* (imprisonment of 20 years and 1 day to 40 years), when by reason or on occasion of the robbery, the crime of homicide is committed; (b) from *reclusion temporal* in its medium period (14 years, 8 months, and 1 day to 17 years and 4 months) to *reclusion perpetua* (imprisonment of 20 years and 1 day to 40 years) when the robbery is accompanied by rape or intentional mutilation; (c) *reclusion temporal* (12 years and 1 day to 20 years), when by reason or on occasion of the robbery, physical injuries are inflicted; and (d) *prision mayor* in its maximum period (10 years and 1 day to 12 years) to *reclusion temporal* in its medium period (14 years, 8 months, and 1 day to 17 years and 4 months).

The law punishes both importation and sale of dangerous drugs and controlled substances. Importation of any dangerous drug, regardless of quantity and purity, including opium poppy or substances derived from opium (even for floral, decorative, and culinary purposes), is punishable by life imprisonment to death and a fine ranging from 500,000 pesos (US$11,000) to 10 million pesos (US$220,000). Importation of any controlled precursor and essential chemical is punishable by a penalty of 12 years and 1 day to 20 years' imprisonment and a fine ranging from 100,000 pesos (US$2,200) to 500,000 pesos (US$11,000). Selling or transacting in dangerous drugs is punishable by life imprisonment to death and a fine ranging from 500,000 pesos (US$11,000) to 10 million pesos (US$220,000). Selling any controlled precursor and essential chemical is punishable by imprisonment from 12 years and 1 day to 20 years and a fine ranging from 100,000 pesos (US$2,200) to 500,000 pesos (US$11,000). Penalties are increased for selling to minors or close to a school.

Death Penalty

The death penalty was abolished on June 24, 2006. Although the 1987 Constitution prohibits death penalty "unless otherwise provided by law," Congress subsequently enacted Republic Act No. 7659, which imposed the death penalty for specific "heinous crimes." In 1999, lethal injection was approved as the method of execution through Republic Act No. 8177. On March 24, 2000, President Joseph Estrada suspended all executions. On April 15, 2006, the death penalties for about 1,230 death row inmates were commuted to life imprisonment. Republic Act No. 9346, later signed by President Gloria Macapagal-Arroyo on June 24, 2006, abolished the death penalty. The penalties of life imprisonment and *reclusion perpetua* (indeterminate sentence, 30-year minimum) replaced the death penalty.

Prison

In 2005, jails managed by the Bureau of Jail Management and Penology (BJMP) in Manila, Philippines, operated at 390 percent of designed capacity, compared with 323 percent in 2003. As of December 2005, the BJMP reported a total of 61,331 inmates in its centers. The number of inmates in BJMP centers dropped to 60,732 as of December 2006 and 60,209 as of July 2007. The Bureau of Corrections reported a total of 29,000 inmates in its national prisons as of 2005 and 30,468 as of 2007.

As of November 2007, there are 1,132 city, district, and municipal jails nationwide that are under the administrative control of the BJMP, and there are 7 national prisons under the administrative control of the Bureau of Corrections (BuCor). The BJMP is an agency of the Department of Interior and Local Government, while the BuCor is an agency of the Department of Justice. The BJMP has operational and administrative control over 1,132 city, district, and municipal jails. In reality, only 417 jails (2 female dormitories, 2 youth centers, 152 district jails, 84 city jails, and 177 municipal jails) are actually under control of the BJMP, since 63 percent or 715 jails are still being operated by the Philippine National Police.

The BuCor was created under the Reorganization Act of 1905 (Act No. 1407 dated November 1, 1905). It was charged with the safekeeping of all prisoners in prisons and all penal settlements, or those institutions under its custody.

The country's biggest prison is the National Bilibid Prison in Muntinlupa, Rizal Province. The prison houses inmates serving life imprisonment or long-term imprisonment. Prior to its existence, inmates were housed at the Old Bilibid prison in Manila. Commonwealth Act No. 67 provided for the construction of a new national prison in Muntinlupa. All inmates in the Old Bilibid Prison in Manila were transferred to this location. The building with a capacity of 3,000 prisoners was officially named the New Bilibid Prison on January 22, 1941. The prison reservation area consisted of 587 hectares (1,451 acres), part of which was arable. The prison compound area consisted of 300 x 300 meters or a total of 9 hectares (22.24 acres) and was surrounded by three layers of barbed wire.

From the 1970s to the present, the New Bilibid Prison has served as the national maximum security compound, containing death row convicts, inmates sentenced to life imprisonment, persons accused of numerous pending cases, inmates with multiple convictions, and inmates sentenced to more than 20 years' imprisonment. In the late 1960s, the prison's security fences were reinforced with concrete slabs. The height of this concrete wall was later increased in the 1980s. Also, another facility was constructed about 2.5 kilometers (1.5 miles) away from the main building. This facility was named Camp Sampaguita or the Medium Security Camp.

Inmates are required to work in the national prisons and penal farms. In the Correctional Institution for Women, women prisoners were allowed to do embroidery, poultry, piggery, and cultivation of crops, flowers, and fruits. In the Iwahig Penal Colony, a merit system was established in 1906 for the prisoners. They could choose from among the following vocational activities: farming, fishing, forestry, carpentry, and hospital paramedical work. In 1955, the government allowed the distribution of colony lands (maximum of six hectares or equivalent of 14.83 acres) for cultivation by colonists. Four years later, a committee created to study the state of national prisons recommended the division of prisoners in Iwahig into two groups: the settlers and colonists. Based on this committee recommendation, settlers who engaged in farming for their own benefit could cultivate the land awarded to them by government. The government also furnished the initial capital requirements for tools, dwellings, and farm animals. The settlers, however, were required to reimburse household expenditures from earnings from their farm products. Upon release from the colony, they receive monetary amounts credited in their favor, after deducting the expenses reimbursable to the government.

The San Ramon Prison and Penal Farm were established in southern Zamboanga through a royal decree promulgated in 1869. Inmates were required to do agricultural work. During the Spanish-American War in 1898, prisoners in San Ramon Prison were released and the buildings destroyed. The prison was later reopened and in 1912; Gen. John Pershing, chief executive of the Department of Mindanao and Sulu, classified the institution "as a prison and penal colony." After a few years, the colony became self-supporting, with 75,000 coconut trees contributing to its income. Various crops such as rice, corn, papaya, and other crops were also harvested. The Philippine Coconut Authority later took over management of the coconut farm from San Ramon.

The Davao Penal Colony requires inmates to do handicrafts. According to the Bureau of Corrections, the facility established a carpentry shop and the shop became known for the fine workmanship of prisoners. Sales of handicrafts were made through the institutions and inmates were compensated depending on the availability of funds.

The Sablayan Penal Colony (located in Occidental Mindoro) and the Leyte Regional Prison (in Abuyog, Southern Leyte) similarly follow the same agricultural and rehabilitative programs of the other penal farms described earlier.

Visiting hours are allowed for inmates and detainees. Each jail has its own visiting hours. Visiting time in Makati City Jail, for example, is limited from 9 A.M. to 12 noon.

Exchange of Prisoners and Extradition

Prisoners may be exchanged or transferred to other countries. Under Presidential Decree No. 1069 and the 1994 RP-US Extradition Treaty, extradition of persons who have committed crimes in a foreign country is allowed.

In the landmark case of *Government of the United States of America v. Hon. Purganan and Mark Jimenez* (G.R. 148571, September 24, 2002), the Supreme Court was confronted with several issues under the RP-US Extradition Treaty. This case involved a request by the U.S. Department of Foreign Affairs to the Philippine Department of Justice for the extradition of Mark Jimenez to the United States. The request contained the grand jury indictment, the warrant of arrest issued by the U.S. District Court, Southern District of Florida, and other supporting documents for said extradition. The papers alleged that Mark Jimenez was charged in the United States with attempt to evade or defeat tax; fraud by wire, radio, or television; false statement or entries; and election contributions in name of another. The Supreme Court in this case ruled that an extraditee is not entitled to notice and hearing before a warrant for his arrest can be issued. The Supreme Court further ruled that the respondent of the extradition request is not entitled to post bail or to gain provisional liberty while extradition proceedings are pending.

Claire Angelique Nolasco and Rolando V. del Carmen

Further Reading

American Bar Association. (March 2006). *Judicial Reform Index for the Philippines:* http://www.abanet.org/rol/publications/philippines_jri_2006.pdf.

Bureau of Jail Management and Penology. (2007). *Data and Statistics:* http://www.bjmp.gov.ph/data.html.

Philippine National Police. (2007). *National Crime Statistics:* http://www.pnp.gov.ph/index.html.

Public Resource Management Consultants. (March 2006). *Conduct of Further Study on Operations and Linkages of the 5 Pillars of Justice Final Report:* http://apjr.supremecourt.gov.ph/pubreports/Conduct%20of%20Further%20Study%205%20Pillars%20of%20Justice.pdf.

Santos-Ong, Milagros. (2009). *Philippine Legal Research:* http://www.nyulawglobal.org/globalex/Philippines1.htm.

Singapore

Legal System: Common/Islamic
Murder: Low
Corruption: Low
Human Trafficking: Medium
Prison Rate: High
Death Penalty: Yes
Corporal Punishment: Yes

Background

Singapore consists of the main island of Singapore and 63 offshore islands in Southeast Asia. The main island city-state is located at the southern tip of the Malayan Peninsula between Malaysia and Indonesia. Singapore has a heterogeneous population of 4,839,400 as of June 2008, consisting of 74.7 percent Chinese, 13.6 percent Malays, 8.9 percent Indians, and 2.8 percent of people who are Eurasians or of other races.

The modern criminal justice system in Singapore is organized around the British model of law and jurisprudence, as Singapore was its colony between 1819 and 1959. English law (statutes and common law) as it stood then was formally received as the law of Singapore on November 27, 1826, by virtue of the Second Charter of Justice, but its application was subject to local circumstances with a view to adapting the application of English law to the native cultures of the Malay, Chinese, and Indian peoples. Between 1826 and 1872, English criminal law applied to all the inhabitants of Singapore as supplemented by local legislation. Criminal procedure was based on Indian legislation, which itself was partly based on English criminal practice. The Penal Code was enacted in 1872, and as it was considered a local statute, the condition of the Second Charter of Justice that English law be applied to suit local conditions and cultures ceased to apply. Between 1873 and 1888, several statutes on criminal procedure were enacted to update the existing criminal procedure to be consistent with the Penal Code, which abolished the distinction between felonies and misdemeanors. The current Criminal Procedure Code (Cap. 68) was enacted in 1900. These three statutes on criminal justice remain in force in Singapore in substantially the same form as when they were introduced.

Many of the functions the contemporary criminal justice system in Singapore perform are similar to those of the British. Chapter 235 of the Singapore Police Force Act stipulates the function of the Singapore Police Force's role as maintaining law and order, preserving public peace, preventing and detecting crime, and apprehending offenders. Consequently, from a legislative viewpoint, there is nothing conspicuous about the way in which Singapore categorizes its major crimes. The nation's criminal code consists of 23 chapters and 511 sections, which classifies approximately 330 different types of criminal activity in six broad categories.

The Singapore Police Force (SPF) comprises 12 staff departments and 11 line units, which include the Volunteer Special Constabulary, Traffic Police, Airport Police, District Police Divisions, Security Command, Commercial Affairs Department, Police National Service Department, Gurkha Contingent, Special Operations Command, Police Coast Guard, and Training Command. Presently, the SPF has an operationally ready strength of 12,516, comprising 7,826 regular officers, 1,206 civilian officers, 3,484 National Service Full-time (NSF) personnel, 20,852 Operationally Ready National Servicemen (NS), and 1,049 Volunteers Special Constabulary (VSC) officers. The Singapore police come under the Ministry of Home Affairs while the military institution is under the jurisdiction of the Ministry of Defence. Though the two institutions are structurally and legally separated through the administration of the Police Force Act (Cap. 235) and Singapore Armed Forces Act (Cap. 295), it is now commonplace for the police and military to organize joint operations or be involved in joint patrolling of key installations following the 9/11 terrorist attacks in New York.

The Singapore model of policing is akin to the authoritarian typology: its centralization under the direct and almost exclusive authority of the executive power makes it a *state* police. As a consequence of this direct connection with the political, it is characterized by a function of political or "high" policing where the police function is institutionally and explicitly attributed to maintaining a *particular* conception of social order. The Singapore state's credence in prioritizing *order* over *justice* is best exemplified in the crime control model of justice that drives the operation of the criminal justice process. This is witnessed particularly in the Misuse of Drugs Act and Prevention of Corruption Act where the laws operate on the basis of the presumption clause—in that a person is deemed guilty unless otherwise proved.

Despite the authoritarian character of the Singapore state, it is equally important to acknowledge that its model of formal policing attests to the Anglo-Saxon model of "community" policing based on the idea of "policing by consent." This categorization fundamentally flows from the assumptions that policing in Singapore is high on accountability; undertaken with public consent that does not mean acquiescence but a broad tolerance indicating a satisfaction with the service and enforcement roles of policing; its organizational structure allows the public to express their policing wants and needs; and last but not least, the SPF's professional culture is epitomized by the officer on the street, close to the community, and patrolling the beat with the consent of the general public. The 40-percent citizen-initiated arrests in the major crimes of outrages against modesty, robbery, housebreaking, motor-vehicle theft, rape, and murder for the year 2005 and the success of community policing are attributed to the so-called community model of policing adopted by the government.

The crime control model has its roots in the political and social upheavals in the immediate preindependence and postindependence years that called for the need for a robust formal control machinery to ensure social order in the newly formed multiracial and multireligious state. The period marked the intensification in the use of the Internal Security Act (ISA) and the Criminal Law (Temporary Provisions) Act of 1955 to ensure an orderly transition to eventual independence. While the latter primarily empowered the executive to incarcerate the common criminal indefinitely, the former, which has its roots in the Emergency Regulations of 1948 introduced by the British in Malaya and Singapore, dealt with the problem of communism, subversion, and racial and religious extremism. These regulations allowed the police to arrest anybody suspected of having acted *or being likely to act* in a way that could threaten security, without warrant, hold them incommunicado for investigation, and detain them indefinitely without the detainee ever being charged with a crime in a court of law. The priority of the criminal justice system then was to address *public order offenses*. The use of the ISA and Criminal Law was primarily designed to contain the twin problems of communism and communalism and the violence associated with Chinese secret societies in Singapore, which rose phenomenally in the immediate postwar period. The Maria Hertogh riots of December 1950, the 1964 communal riots between the Malays and the Chinese in Singapore sparked off during a religious procession on the birthday anniversary of the Prophet Mohammed, and the 1969 race riots in Kuala Lumpur are reminders of the traumatic origins of Singapore. The national priority of economic and political stability diffused into the ideology and practice of the criminal justice system in the aftermath of Singapore's separation from Malaysia in 1965.

Crime

Classification of Crimes

Crimes in Singapore are classified into six classes. Class I: crimes against persons, which include murder and causing grievous hurt; Class II: violent property crimes, which include robbery, extortion; Class III: housebreaking, motor theft, and related crimes; Class IV: theft and related crimes; Class V: commercial crimes such as cheating, fraud, forgery, among others; Class VI: miscellaneous crimes that are subdivided into A: seizable offenses and B: nonseizable offenses. Seizeable offenses are those in which the police may act without an order from a magistrate and without a warrant of arrest may apprehend the suspect.

The Children and Young Persons Act of 1949 defines the "child" as being a person below the age of 14 years and a "young person" as being a person who is between 14 and 16 years of age. Offenders who belong to these age categories are tried in the juvenile courts, except in situations where the juvenile is charged for a capital offense or jointly tried with an adult for a capital offense where the case is heard in the High Court. The law specifying the age of criminal responsibility states that "nothing is an offence which is done by a child under 7 years of age or if the child is above seven and under 12 years of age who has not attained sufficient maturity of understanding to judge [of] the nature and consequence of his conduct on that occasion (Penal Code, Cap. 224, s. 82 & 83). In practice, however, case laws dictate that this presumption might be rebutted by a showing by the prosecution that the offender had sufficient mental capacity to distinguish right from wrong. The issue of nonculpability also applies to an act of a person of unsound mind where the law states that "nothing is an offence which is done by a person who, at the time of doing it, by reason of unsoundness of mind, is incapable of knowing the nature of the act, or that he is doing what is either wrong or contrary to law."

In light of the above classification, some crimes have come to be viewed as particularly challenging to the country. For instance, the great cost of investigating white collar crimes (WCC) such as occupational crime (e.g., insider trading, credit card fraud, among others) and corporate or organizational crime (e.g., price fixing, antitrust laws, among others) and the lack of statistical information on WCC pose a great challenge to authorities. Nevertheless, the Commercial Affairs Department (CAD), as a specialized and nontraditional police department, was conferred a new status as a law enforcement agency, which allows it to better deal with WCC. A more recent challenge is that of terrorism and the subsequent escape of a Jemaah Islamiyah (JI) detainee, Mas Selamat Bin Kastari, on February 27, 2008.

In the area of drug offenses, the Misuse of Drugs Act provides for strict and mandatory punishments where it empowers the police with extensive powers of search and arrest. An important feature of this law is that it does not distinguish between drug trafficking and possession (and for purposes of personal consumption), as any person found to have the proscribed drug in his or her possession is deemed to be involved in trafficking—the most serious of offenses in the drug law. For example, the Misuse of Drugs Act states that "any person who is proved to have had in his possession more than (a) 100 grammes of opium; (b) 3 grammes of morphine; (c) 2 grammes of diamorphine; (d) 15 grammes of cannabis; (e) 30 grammes of cannabis mixture; (f) 10 grammes of cannabis resin; (g) 3 grammes of cocaine; (h) 25 grammes of methamphetamine . . . whether or not contained in any substance, extract, preparation, or mixture shall be presumed to have had that drug in possession for the purpose of trafficking unless it is proved that his possession of that drug was not for that purpose."

The Misuse of Drugs Act distinguishes between three classes of controlled drugs—A, B, and C-which warrant different punishments. Some of the commonly abused drugs in Singapore belonging to the A category include buprenorphine, opium, heroin, cannabis, Ecstasy, methamphetamine, and ketamine (previously a Class B drug). The respective punishments the different classes of controlled drugs warrant are listed in the following table.

CLASS A	CLASS B	CLASS C
Maximum 20 years and 15 strokes	Maximum 20 years and 10 strokes	Maximum 10 years and 5 strokes
Minimum 5 years and 5 strokes	Minimum 3 years and 3 strokes	Minimum 2 years and 2 strokes

A death sentence is prescribed under the Misuse of Drugs Act for possession of larger quantities of cannabis, cocaine, heroin, methamphetamine, and morphine.

Crime Statistics

According to the official crime statistics provided by the SPF, Singapore's crime situation registered an improvement in 2007. The overall crime reported in 2007 fell from 33,263 to 32,545 cases when compared to 2006. In addition, the overall crime rate also fell from 742 to 695 per 100,000 population in 2007, which was the third-lowest in 10 years. Of the six classes of crime, only commercial crimes recorded a significant increase of 330 cases (from 3,159 to 3,489 cases in 2007). Violent property crimes increased slightly, while crimes against persons and miscellaneous crimes did not register any significant change. Housebreaking and related crimes fell, from 1,201 to 925 cases in 2007. Theft and related crimes, which generally constitute more than half of overall crime each year, fell for the second year running from 20,301 to 19,522 cases in 2007. The SPF has attributed Singapore's overall crime rate—which is the third-lowest in 10 years—to the firm police-community partnership that has been forged over the years.

Finding of Guilt

The accused person is presumed innocent until proven otherwise and must be notified of the grounds of arrest. The accused person has the right to (1) consult and be defended by a legal practitioner of his or her choice, and (2) to remain silent in the course of a police investigation (Constitution, Art.9 [3]). Nevertheless, one must be reminded of the presumption clause—in that a person is deemed guilty unless otherwise proven, which contradicts the presumed innocence integral to the accused's rights. The available forms of assistance provided to accused persons include the Legal Aid Bureau of the government that provides legal aid for civil cases; the Law Society of Singapore that provides legal aid in noncapital cases; and in the cases of crimes carrying the death penalty, the Registrar of the Supreme Court in the government's behalf assigns a lawyer for the defense.

In minor cases, an officer will go to the scene of a crime to investigate the offense and to arrest any alleged offenders. Officers are also authorized to have special powers to initiate investigations of serious offenses. When a police investigation discloses an offense, the Attorney General's Chambers (AG) has the discretion to initiate a criminal prosecution. Upon completion of that investigation, the prosecutor will initiate the criminal prosecution and the case will be prepared for trial. The charge notifies the accused of the offense. The accused may be tried in a magistrates' court, a district court, or High Court depending on the seriousness of the offense. After a review of the case, the magistrate issues a summons or a warrant of arrest to the accused. An examining magistrate then conducts an investigation to determine if the case against the accused justifies proceedings in the High Court. All criminal cases are tried by a single judge, with the exception of capital offense trials, which are conducted by courts consisting of two High Court judges. In short, all criminal proceedings for the state are represented by the public prosecutor. The AG Chamber has the sole prosecutorial discretion and is responsible for all criminal prosecutions. To ease the workload of the AG's office, deputy public prosecutors adopt the role of supervising specially trained police prosecutors to conduct the prosecution of lesser crimes.

The alternatives to going to trial must also be noted. In 1991, the Singapore International Arbitration Centre (SIAC), an institution administering arbitration, was established. Committed to complete impartiality and transparency in all that it does for parties, the SIAC seeks to meet the demands of the international business community for a neutral, efficient, and reliable dispute resolution institution in a fast-developing Asia. Broadly, it helps parties in three ways: first, the appointment of arbitrators when they cannot agree on an appointment; second, the management of the financial and other practical aspects of arbitration; and, third, the facilitation of the smooth progress of arbitration.

In 1994, the Court Mediation Centre, whose primary function is to pull all the mediation processes in the various courts that come under the Subordinate Courts together, was first introduced as an alternative (civil) avenue of dispute mediation. Subordinate Courts is divided into 4 divisions—the Criminal Justice Division, Civil Justice Division, Family Justice Division, and Juvenile Justice Division. The Court Mediation Centre handles the mediation of civil, family, small claims, and criminal matters (i.e., relational disputes and juvenile matters). In May 1998, the Court Mediation Centre was renamed as the Primary Dispute Resolution Centre (PDRC).

In line with the development of alternative dispute mediation, the Singapore Mediation Centre (SMC), a nonprofit organization guaranteed by the Singapore Academy of Law, was incorporated on August 8, 1997, and officially launched by the Honourable Chief Justice Yong Pung How on August 16, 1997. Fundamentally, the SMC is dedicated to promoting the amicable and fair resolution of dispute and aims to create an environment where people can cooperate to find enduring solutions to conflicts by broadening awareness of, and providing access to, constructive means of dispute resolution. Since then, mediation is routinely conducted in the Ministry of Community, Youth and Sports' Maintenance of Parents Tribunal (Cap. 167B), small claims tribunals, the Family Court, and the juvenile courts. In addition, the Subordinate Courts have also harnessed the "e@dr" or "eAlternative Dispute Resolution" scheme to allow for parties to resolve their disputes on the Internet via an e-commerce transaction.

On certain legal grounds, incarceration before or awaiting trial is allowed. On arrest, an individual may be searched and brought to a police station for questioning. Pending questioning, that individual may be detained in a lock-up for a maximum period of 48 hours from the time of the arrest. If the officer wants to detain that individual for more than 48 hours, the officer must bring him or her to court. If the police or other officers do not wish to detain an individual for more than 48 hours, they may let him or her go on a personal promise or put the person on police bail to make sure he or she goes back to the station or attends court when told to do so.

Based on the Subordinate Courts' Annual Report 2006, there are about a total of 51 judges, all working in the Criminal Justice, Civil Justice, and Family and Juvenile Justice Divisions. There are also 14 judges on the Supreme Court Bench. Supreme Court judges are appointed by the president, who acts on the advice of the prime minister and the chief justice. A person is qualified for appointment as a judge of the Supreme Court if he or she has for an aggregate period of not less than 10 years been a qualified person within the meaning of Section 2 of the Legal Profession Act or a member of the Singapore Legal Service, or both. District court judges and magistrates are appointed by the president on the recommendation of the chief justice. All judges must first be "qualified persons" under the Legal Profession Act.

The Juvenile Justice Division marks a separate system for juveniles in Singapore. The Juvenile Court was created by the Children and Young Persons Act of 1949. This act prescribes the method for processing juvenile delinquents between 14 and 16 years old. The focus is on counseling and community intervention to resolve issues involving juveniles between 14 and 16 years of age, a form of restorative justice nonetheless. If remanded, juveniles are either placed in an approved home for two to three years or placed on statutory supervision for a specified period, not exceeding three years, under the supervision of a social worker.

Punishment

Types of Punishment

The kinds of punishment typically used include banishment, caning, compensations, corporal punishment, fines, forfeiture of property, house arrest, prison, probation, public punishment, publicity of punishment, reparations, treatment, and the death penalty. The punishments and the crimes for which they are prescribed are as follows:

Murder, piracy, kidnapping, and various drug offenses	Death
Attempted murder	Imprisonment 10 years to life
Culpable homicide	Imprisonment for life; imprisonment 10 years plus fine or caning
Theft	Imprisonment up to 3 years, or with fine, or with both
Rape	Imprisonment up to 20 years, plus fine or caning
Robbery	Imprisonment 2 to 10 years, 20 years if gang robbery; plus 6 strokes, more if committed at night, not less than 12 strokes if armed

Since Singapore was a British colony, capital punishment has been a legal form of punishment and is still present today. Legally, the Penal Code provides for the death sentence for at least 10 offenses including the crimes of murder, endangering a person's life during an act of piracy, and "offences against the President's person"; these typically carry a mandatory death sentence. However, in recent years, the death penalty is only known to have been imposed for drug trafficking, murder, and firearms offenses, all of which carry a mandatory death sentence. According to the Criminal Procedure Code, the death penalty may not be imposed on pregnant women or on youth offenders who are aged below 18 at the time of the offense. In addition, four other acts also provide the imposition of the death penalty: first, the Misuse of Drugs Act (MDA) provides for a mandatory death sentence for at least 20 different drug offenses; second, the Internal Security Act (ISA) stipulates a death sentence for certain offenses involving firearms, ammunition, or explosives; third, the Arms Offences Act provides for a mandatory

Candles are lit during a vigil held for Ngyuen Tuong Van, an Australian national, just hours before his execution in Singapore, December 2, 2005. The Singapore government rejected repeated appeals for clemency for Nguyen, who was convicted of trafficking almost 14 ounces of heroin through Singapore's Changi Airport. Photos of Ngyuen Tuong Van are seen on the table. (AP Photo/Wong Maye-E)

death sentence for anyone, including accomplices, using or attempting to use firearms or trafficking in arms; and fourth, the Kidnapping Act provides for the death penalty for kidnapping for ransom.

According to the *Prison Service Annual,* the average daily population in penal institutions and drug rehabilitation centers (DRCs) in 2006, excluding inmates placed on special programs, was 12,643 and 216, respectively. The number in drug rehabilitation centers has declined dramatically since 1995. In contrast the prison population reached a peak of some 16,000 in 2003 but has declined in recent years. Eighty-nine percent of inmates of penal institutions are men, 11 percent women. Eighty-two percent of drug rehabilitation centers are men, the rest women.

Currently, the types of prisons and DRCs in Singapore are Changi Prison Cluster A, Changi's Women Prison, Khlasa Crescent Prison, Admiralty West Prison, Queenstown Remand Prison, Tanah Merah Prison, Sembawang DRC and Selarang Park DRC, and the Kaki Bukit Prison School meant for youth offenders. Singapore's biggest prison is the Changi Prison Complex (CPC), which has been an ongoing project that commenced in 2000. This complex marks the consolidation of all existing medium-security and maximum-security facilities and the construction of four clusters of institutions, support facilities, and prison headquarters, which will be implemented in phases. Strategically, the use of high-rise complexes addresses the problem of limited land space to accommodate up to 23,000 prisoners. The infrastructure, design, and technology of CPC would enable economies of scale, additional capacity, enhanced security, more focus on rehabilitation, more employment opportunities as well as better management in general.

Part of the inmates' incarceration and rehabilitation experience includes work programs and education. The work program, administered by Singapore Corporation of Rehabilitative Enterprises (SCORE), includes linen services, food services, subcontracting services, industrial space leasing and digital media services. In addition, vocational and employability training is also made available. Educationally, inmates have access to the Institute of Technical Education (ITE), general education (secondary level, 1 to 3), General Certificate of Education (GCE) for Ordinary ("O") and Advanced ("A") levels, moral education, religious counseling, and enrichment activities such as sports and music, among others. These education programs are administered by the Kaki Bukit Prison School.

The visiting policies of prisons state that only family members are allowed. Friends and others will be subjected to approval by the authorities in charge. The frequency of visits is once every two weeks or once every month. Items that are allowed to be brought in or bought from the institution for inmates include reading materials (maximum three), spectacles, dentures, medication, and hearing aids. Televisits in the form of videoconferencing visits at prison link centers (PLCs) are also approved.

The Extradition Policy states that prisoners can only be exchanged or transferred with nation-states that have signed treaties with Singapore. The extraditing of political offenders is impermissible. For declared Commonwealth countries, an "extraditable" crime is an offense (wherever committed) against the law in force in Singapore and the maximum penalty for which is death or imprisonment for a period of not less than 12 months. For Malaysia, the offense would be an offense punishable on conviction with imprisonment for six months or more under the law of Malaysia.

Narayanan Ganapathy and Anil Singh Sona

Further Reading

Chan, Wing Cheong, and Andrew Phang. (2001). *The Development of Criminal Law and Criminal Justice in Singapore*. Singapore: Singapore Journal of Legal Studies, Faculty of Law, National University of Singapore.

Ganapathy, Narayanan. "Criminal Justice Policy: Social Order, Risk and the 'Governmental Project.'" In *Social Policy in Post-Industrial Singapore,* edited by C.K. Tong and K.F. Lian, pp. 247–278. Leiden and Boston: Brill.

Ganapathy, Narayanan. (2002). "Rethinking the Problem of Policing Marital Violence: A Singapore Perspective." *Policing and Society* 12(3): 173–190.

The Subordinate Courts of Singapore: http://app.subcourts.gov.sg/subcourts/index.aspx

Yeo, Stanley M.H., Neil Morgan, and Wing Cheong Chan. (2007). *Criminal Law in Malaysia and Singapore*. Singapore: LexisNexis.

South Korea (Republic of Korea)

Legal System: Civil/Customary
Murder: Low-Medium
Burglary: Medium
Corruption: Low
Human Trafficking: Low
Prison Rate: Medium
Death Penalty: Yes
Corporal Punishment: No

Background

The modern legal system of the Republic of Korea took shape after the Kabo Reforms (1894–1895). Previously, kings in an oriental monarchy system ruled Korea while governmental agents oversaw judicial matters, which included the prosecution and punishment of offenders. In 1894, the Office of Legal Affairs, the modern judicial branch, was established to handle legal affairs, prosecution, and court functions. This separation of judicial operations from the government administration was recognized as a major step toward the foundation of the modern legal system. After the end of Japanese colonial rule (1910–1945), the Ministry of Justice was created as part of the executive branch, separated from the judiciary, through the Government Organization Act on July 17, 1948. Today, the Korean legal system consists of a highly centralized and hierarchical organization. Accordingly, police and the prosecutorial system have been under centralized and inclusive state control.

Political and Social Context

The Korean criminal justice system cannot fully be understood without considering the authoritarian and repressive features of the political regimes of the era of industrialization between 1960 and 1980. The degree of authoritarianism and repression fluctuated within and across regimes until the first civilian president was elected in 1992. Under authoritarian rule, the criminal justice apparatus was tightly controlled by the regime. In line with the investigation and prosecution process, for example, public prosecutors are quasijudicial officials who independently carry out their authorities and duties. According to the "principle of identity," however, public prosecutors belong to the executive branch and must follow orders from their superior. This hierarchical structure has sometimes allowed regimes to affect prosecutorial decisions in favor of their own interests. Furthermore, military regimes forcefully obtained compliance from the judiciary by using a punitive nonreappointment and transfer system. As a result, criminal justice practices may have been affected more by political forces of that era than by economic and organizational factors.

Criminal Justice System

Police

The police organization is the largest government department of professional civil servants in South Korea. The national police organization, in a modern sense, was established in 1945 after the end of Japanese colonial rule when the Korean police modeled their organization after the structure and practices of the Japanese.

The Korean police are directed by the Ministry of Home Affairs (or the Ministry of Public Administration and Security). Police functions have been organized under the National Police Agency, which is an independent organization with a commissioner general, a vice minister–level official, as its head. The National Police Agency has nine provincial and seven metropolitan police agencies as special local administrative headquarters. Each provincial and metropolitan police office directs many police stations and substations. As of 2008, there were 239 police stations, 813 police offices, and 579 police boxes under the police stations. In 2007, South Korea employed 147,651 police officers. Of these, 96,324 were sworn officers. The population per police officer was 509.

When a crime is committed, a police officer initiates an investigation. However, although crime control is a police function, the police do not have exclusive authority during criminal investigations. Police officers are required to report to the appropriate prosecutor, who guides and supervises "judicial police officers" on the investigative process.

Public Prosecutor's Office

The public prosecutor's office has vast authority and discretionary power over criminal justice matters. Public prosecutors initiate and complete criminal investigations, during which they supervise and direct judicial police officers and have exclusive power to request various warrants for searches, seizures, and detentions. After investigative authorities conclude that sufficient evidence exists against a suspect and decide to prosecute, the suspect becomes the "accused" and the prosecutor creates a deposition, deciding whether the case amounts to a crime. Prosecutors can choose to indict or not indict a suspect. They may choose to suspend the prosecution of offenders whose crime is relatively minor, who do not have long criminal records, or who show remorse for their behavior.

There are 62 prosecutors' offices nationwide, which include 1 supreme prosecutor's office, 5 high prosecutors' offices, 18 district prosecutors' offices, and 38 branch offices. The public prosecutor's office is attached to the Ministry of Justice. The supreme prosecutor's office is responsible for commanding and supervising the investigations and operations of all other prosecutors' offices in South Korea. The prosecutor general is in charge of all duties within the supreme prosecutors' office and directs all civil servants of prosecutors' offices. High prosecutors' offices handle High Court criminal proceedings, civil and administrative litigation in which they represent the government and government agencies, and appeals against nonprosecution decisions of district prosecutors' offices and branch offices. District or branch prosecutors' offices are divided into investigative and prosecutorial departments, allowing investigators, prosecutors, and staff to work as a team. As of March 2008, there were 1,680 prosecutors in South Korea.

Public prosecutors must pass the judicial examination and complete a two-year training course at the Judicial Research and Training Institute. Upon completion of training, graduates may choose, in principle, to become a judge, a public prosecutor, or a private attorney. Actual selection does not seem to be determined only by the preference of the applicants. Judgeships are generally reserved for the top students. Public prosecutors and private attorneys tend to be regarded as the second choice. The total number of registered attorneys has risen from 3,845 in 1996 to 9,280 in 2007. The president appoints and assigns public prosecutors upon the recommendation of the minister of justice.

Courts

Unless otherwise stipulated by the Constitution, the courts have the power to judge all civil, criminal, and administrative disputes in South Korea. The judiciary system consists of three basic levels: the Supreme Court, the High Court, and the District Court with its branches.

As the highest judicial organization in South Korea, the Supreme Court hears appeals against decisions of lower courts. It has exclusive jurisdiction concerning the validity of presidential and parliamentary elections. Finally, the Supreme Court has the power to review the constitutionality or legality of orders, rules, regulations, and actions taken by administrative entities. One chief justice and 12 justices, including the minister of the National Court Administration, comprise the Supreme Court. Its chief justice, who is appointed by the president with the consent of the National Assembly, serves six years and cannot be reappointed. Other Supreme Court justices are appointed by the president upon the recommendation of the chief justice. Their term is also six years, but reappointment for one other term is possible.

High Courts typically consist of one chief judge and several other judges. Currently, there are five High Courts in Korea. Judgments from High Courts are rendered by a panel of three judges. Appeals against judgments or rulings from a panel of three judges by district courts or the Family Court, or by the Administrative Court, are heard by High Courts. There were more than 313 High Court judges in 2007. District courts have primary jurisdiction over most cases and are usually presided over by a single judge. A three-judge panel is mandatory, however, in criminal cases punishable by death or more than one year of imprisonment. District courts can be assisted by one or more branch courts, overseen by a single judge, to alleviate a portion of the district court's caseload. Additionally, municipal courts hear criminal cases involving less than 30 days' penal detention or a fine not exceeding 200,000 Korean won (approximately US$200 as of June 2007). In 2007, there were 18 district courts, with 43 branch courts and 101 municipal courts. On average, district court judges preside over 170 criminal trials per year, which include the penal code and many special laws.

South Korea also established specialized courts to alleviate the burden on the judicial system. The Constitutional Court handles cases concerning constitutional issues. Laws or articles decided unconstitutional by the Constitutional Court lose their legality from the day the decision is given. The Family Court hears domestic relations and juvenile offense cases. However, South Korea currently has only one Family Court, located in Seoul.

Passing the judicial examination is the first qualification for judgeship. After two years of training at the Judicial Research and Training Institute (JRTI), those who choose judgeship as their career usually start their service in district courts. Every two years, district court judges generally rotate from Seoul to provinces or from one province to another. As a result, about 700 judges are moved to other provinces annually. In 2007, there were 2,294 judges in South Korea.

Crime

Classification of Crimes

The *Analytical Report on Crime,* published by the Supreme Public Prosecutor's Office, contains the most comprehensive compilation of statistical data on crime, police activity, and dispositions of public prosecutors in Korea. The report divides crime into two broad categories: offenses that violate the Criminal Code and offenses that violate many Special Laws.

According to the Criminal Code, offenses are classified into seven subcategories: violent crimes, property crimes, forgeries, crimes committed by government officials, crimes against public morals, crimes of negligence, and others. Of these, violent and property crimes comprise approximately four-fifths of all Criminal Code Offenses (CCO). The violent crime category includes criminal homicide, robbery, arson, rape, assault, aggravated assault, intimidation, kidnapping, and illegal confinement. Of these, homicide, rape, robbery, and arson have been regarded as the most serious crimes in South Korea. On the other hand, property crimes consist of larceny-theft, stolen property, fraud, embezzlement, malfeasance in office, and destruction of property. In recent years, larceny-theft, fraud, and assault were the three most frequently committed CCOs in South Korea. In 2007, for example, one out of four CCOs reported to the police was larceny-theft, followed by fraud (22.0%), assault (11.5%), and aggravated assault (11.0%).

Violations of Special Laws (VSL) include various laws regulating all aspects of society. In 2000, there were approximately 200 Special Laws. Typical examples of these laws include the Road Traffic Act, the Special Act on Disposition of Traffic Accidents, and the Act Concerning Punishment for Violent Acts (APVA), which deals with minor forms of assault. Violations of these three laws comprise approximately 80 percent of all violations of Special Laws.

In relation to drug crime in South Korea, the abuse of marijuana in and around American military bases became a major social problem during the 1970s. Since the beginning of the 1980s, methamphetamine (*hi-ro-ppong*) has been one of the most serious drug problems in South Korea. The abuse of a variety of drugs such as marijuana, cocaine, methamphetamine, heroin, and many types of pharmaceutical drugs, as well as the use of chemical solvents (e.g., model glue, paint thinners, and butane gas) among teenagers, become a large concern in recent years. To address drug problems, Korea enacted three major laws prohibiting the abuse of drugs: the Narcotic Act of 1957, Cannabis Control Act of 1976, and Psychotropic Medicine Control Act of 1979. Of these, violations of Psychotropic Medicine Control Act occupied almost 80 percent of all drug crimes in 2007, while the Narcotic Act comprised 9 percent, and the Cannabis Control Act comprised 11 percent.

Crime Statistics

Data on crime, arrests, and prosecutions come in large part from the *Analytical Report on Crime*. An annual publication of the *White Paper on Crime,* published by the Legal Research and Training Institute, it may be used in part to calculate crime and arrest rates. Data on convictions and incarcerations are available in the *Judiciary Yearbook,* which is published annually by the Administrative Office of Courts.

The total number of crimes occurring in Korea has increased 3.8 times over the past three decades, from 513,165 in 1978 to 1,965,977 in 2007. The crime rate, which is defined as the total number of crimes that take place per 100,000 people, has also increased approximately 2.9 times over the same period, from 1,388 in 1978 to 3,988 in 2007. During the past decade (1998–2007) in particular, the total number of crimes that occurred in South Korea increased 11.3 percent. The crime rate also increased 4.5 percent over the same period. The total number of crimes steadily increased to 810,416 in 1985, 1,171,380 in 1990, 1,399,085 in 1995, 1,867,882 in 2000, and 1,893,896 in 2005.

Criminal Code Offense (CCO)

Violent and property crimes consist of approximately four-fifths of all CCOs in South Korea. The total number of CCOs increased 86.9 percent, from 452,260 in 1998 to 845,311 in 2007. CCOs increased every year until 2003 with 857,488, after which the total number of CCO crimes declined from 2004 to 2006, then increased again in 2007.

There has been a steady increase in most serious crimes (homicide, rape, robbery, and arson) during the past decade. However, there have been only minor changes in the crime rate of homicide since 1998. Murder increased 1.2 times, from 966 cases in 1998 to 1,124 cases in 2007. There was a steady increase in the incidence of rape (including sexual assault) during the same time period. With the exception of 2002, rape increased every year from 7,886 in 1998 to 13,634 in 2007. In the case of robbery, the number of crimes dropped from 5,407 in 1998 to 4,712 in 1999, after which it showed a steady increase until 2003 with 7,327 cases. It then showed a decreasing trend, reaching 4,470 in 2007. Arson showed a steady increase until 2003 with 1,713 cases, but then began to fluctuate.

The total number of property crimes experienced minor changes over the past decade. These crimes increased from 338,943 in 1998 to 469,654 in 2007, which is a 40 percent increase. However, this increase has not been consistent; the number of property crimes in South Korea declined from 1998 to 1999 and from 2003 to 2005. Major property crimes in 2007 consisted of larceny-theft (45.3%), fraud (39.6%), destruction of property (8.2%), embezzlement (5.1%), malfeasance in office (1.1%), and stolen property (0.7%). In general, there has been a steady increase in larceny-theft, stolen property, and destruction of property crimes. South Korea experienced a sharp increase in stolen property crimes (i.e., receiving, selling) over the last decade. There has also been a drastic increase in larceny-theft cases since 1999 with the exception of the year 2004. The number of cases rose from 82,584 in 1999 to 212,530 in 2007. Stolen property also increased from 1,581 in 2004 to 3,050 in 2007. Fraud and embezzlement has remained somewhat stable and shown patterns of minor increase and decrease over the last decade.

Violations of Special Laws (VSL)

In terms of the number of incidents of crime, offenders who violated Special Laws were more numerous than those who violated CCOs. For example, while the total number of CCOs was 845,311 in 2007, the total number of violations of Special Laws was 1,120,666. The number of incidents of VSL rose to 1,432,307 in 2001, showed a sharp decrease from 2002 to 2006 (1,001,190 in 2006), and then rose again to 1,120,666 in 2007. The number of drug crimes has risen from 8,350 in 1998 to 10,649 in 2007. However, this has not been a steady increase. After a sharp increase in 1999 to 10,589, the number of crimes remained relatively stable until 2003, when the number of crimes dropped to 7,546. After this sharp decline, drug crimes again remained stable until 2007, when they experienced a sharp increase in 2007.

Finding of Guilt

Investigative Process and Rights of the Accused

The legal system of South Korea is adversarial in nature. When a crime is reported or detected, police officers initiate an investigation and search for the suspect. When it comes to the age of criminal responsibility, a person who is 14 years old or above is criminally liable for his or her crime. The suspect has the right to remain silent and can refuse to answer questions by the police or prosecutor. In principle, police investigators fall under the supervision of public prosecutors, who have the original authority to initiate and complete criminal investigations, and should follow their orders. However, in practice, the police initiate most investigations (over 90%). In cases concerning complex offenses or white-collar crimes, the prosecutor usually initiates the investigation *ex officio* or without previous investigation by police officers.

South Korean chief justice Yun Young-chul, center, presides over a hearing on the impeachment of President Roh Moon-hyun at the Constitutional Court in Seoul on April 30, 2004. (AP Photo/KIM Jae-hwan)

When detention is necessary for an arrested suspect, the police should have a warrant, which must be sought by the public prosecutor and issued by a court judge (Criminal Procedural Law, article 201). Because the ability to obtain a warrant lies solely with public prosecutors, the police must ask prosecutors, who then must decide whether or not to request a warrant from the court. However, in cases where the suspect is caught committing a crime or exigent circumstances exist, the suspect may be arrested immediately and a warrant may be obtained within 48 hours after the arrest.

If investigative authorities seek a warrant of detention, the suspect or a concerned party (i.e., defense counsel or family member) can request an examination of the suspect by the judge before deciding whether to issue the warrant. The public prosecutor or police officer must inform the suspect of this right at the time of arrest. In addition, the judge may examine the suspect before deciding to issue a warrant of detention for a suspect who is not under arrest. The judge takes into account the result of the examination as well as records submitted by investigative authorities to determine whether circumstances justify detention.

Once a suspect is detained with a warrant, police officers should transfer the case, its documents, and evidence to the public prosecutor's office (*Song-Chi*) within 10 days. After a review of legality, the court can order the release of the accused if there is a valid argument for the request. The court may release the accused on bail, which can be substituted for a written undertaking or a surety insurance policy, at the request of the accused or *ex officio.* When release is granted, the court often orders defendants to remain within the physical boundaries of their neighborhoods or homes.

After receipt of a case, the public prosecutor may continue and complete the investigation and decide whether or not to pursue a trial. When there is not sufficient evidence, prosecutors often decide to dismiss the case (nonprosecution). Nonprosecution includes "suspension of prosecution," "free of suspicion," "does not constitute a crime," and "no right for prosecution." The percentage of nonprosecution was 45 percent of all cases reviewed by prosecutors in 1980; it increased to 62 percent in 1990, and then dropped to 38 percent in 2007. Customarily, about 10 percent of offenders who are brought to the public prosecutor's office receive a "suspension of prosecution." Excluding these cases, public prosecutors decide which of the remainder will resume to trial.

There are two kinds of prosecution: summary indictment and formal trial proceedings. When public prosecutors request a summary indictment, the court relies only on documentary evidence prepared by public prosecutors and the presence of the accused is not required. The chief candidates for summary trial proceedings are offenses punishable by fines of $250 or more. On the other hand, formal trial proceedings are reserved for severe offenses and repeat offenders, whose crimes are punishable by incarceration or death. However, the accused can request a formal trial proceeding within seven days of receiving a summary order notification. In 2007, 24.7 percent of all CCO cases in South Korea were disposed by summary trials, while only 7.6 percent proceeded to formal trials.

Court Trial Process

The trial process in criminal courts for less serious crimes is usually presided over by a single judge in district or branch courts. In 2007, about 85.6 percent of 312,317 cases were tried before a single judge. On the other hand, cases punishable by a minimum of one-year incarceration or more, including the death penalty, are tried by a collegial court of three judges. In certain cases, depending on the brevity and expeditiousness of the proceedings, the speedy-trial procedure is applicable. This option is available for minor offenses punishable by no more than 200,000 Korean won (around US$200). The chief of police, not the prosecutor, refers these cases to the court. One judge presides over this trial in a public place other than the police station. Speedy-trial sentences are supervised by the chief of police and reported to the prosecutor.

Defense attorneys are mandatory for minors or individuals more than 70 years old, the mute, the mentally incapable, and for those who commit crimes punishable by more than three years' imprisonment. When the accused is too poor to afford a private defense attorney, a public defender may be appointed at the request of the accused.

At the adjudication stage the public prosecutor, defense attorney, and judge interrogate the accused about the commission of the crime. Investigation of the material evidence and cross-examination of witnesses are also conducted and the public prosecutor makes a statement about proper application of the law and recommends the type and severity of punishment. The hearing concludes with the judge rendering a verdict. A confession alone cannot produce a guilty verdict. If the judge renders a judgment of not guilty, the accused may receive compensation if he or she has been placed under detention. Both the accused and the prosecutor can appeal the decision of the court within seven days from the date of the judgment. When delivering the sentence following a conviction, judges generally impose a less severe sentence than that recommended by the prosecutor.

The Supreme Court established the Sentencing Commission on May 2, 2007, to implement fair and objective sentencing practices. The commission was given authority to establish or revise sentencing guidelines. Judges must respect the sentencing guidelines established by the commission in rendering decisions (i.e., category and period of sentencing), although these guidelines are not legally binding.

South Korea established a Family Court on October 1, 1963, to handle domestic relations and juvenile offense cases. However, because South Korea currently has only one Family Court, located in Seoul, all functions related to the Family Court in other jurisdictions are performed by the district court.

Beginning January 1, 2008, South Korea adopted the Lay Participation system, which allows citizens to act as jurors in criminal trials. The jury's verdict and sentencing opinions do not have a binding effect on the judge's decision.

Punishment

There are four major types of criminal sanctions classified in the Criminal Law: life sentence (e.g., death penalty), imprisonment sentences (e.g., penal detention, imprisonment, penal servitude), financial sentences (e.g., confiscation, minor fine, fine), and status sentences (e.g., suspension of status, deprivation of status).

Of these, fine, probation, and imprisonment are the three most typical punishments in South Korea. In 2007, half of all original sentences included imprisonment. Of these, 17 percent of sentenced offenders were incarcerated, while 32 percent received suspension of execution under probation. Another 34 percent of offenders were ordered to pay a fine. Detention cannot exceed 30 days of confinement, during which detainees are generally placed in a local police jail. Penal servitude contains forced labor while imprisonment does not. However, those who receive imprisonment can work upon request.

South Korea still has the death penalty as a criminal sentence for serious murder, but few criminals have been sentenced to the death penalty in recent years (20 cases in 2000, 12 in 2001, 5 to 8 each year during 2002–2006, and 0 in 2007). However, there has not been a single execution for those sentenced to death penalty during the past decade.

Even when a criminal receives a guilty verdict, judges can suspend the imposition of the sentence for offenders who commit crimes punishable by not more than one year of imprisonment. Unless the offender commits other crimes punishable by more than a suspension of status for two years, the sentence for the original crime looses its validity.

Judges may also impose the appropriate penalty, but postpone the execution of punishment for a given period of time. About one in three imprisonment sentences earned a "suspension of execution" in 2007. If an offender commits other crimes punishable by imprisonment after receiving a suspension of execution, the suspension is revoked and the offender must serve the imposed sentence for the original crime.

Prison

There has been a steady decrease in the number of prisoners in South Korea during the past decade. The total number of inmates in prisons and jails declined from 67,883 in 1998 to 46,313 in 2007, which is a 31.8 percent decrease. The greatest change occurred in the number of suspects housed in jails, which dropped 66 percent from 2,930 suspects in 1998 to 996 in 2007. Jails experienced a 49.7 percent decrease in the number of defendants during the same time period. Prison inmates also declined 16.6 percent over the past decade. Overall, the total number of inmates has shown a steady decrease with a few exceptions (e.g., inmates in prisons in 1998, the number of suspects in 2000 and 2002, and the number of defendants in 2003, 2004, and 2006).

The Korea Correctional Service (KCS) under the direction of the Ministry of Justice oversees the administration and operation of correctional facilities in South Korea. The KCS utilizes a system of incarceration and supervision to segregate inmates from society while still providing educational and rehabilitation programs to increase the chance of successful reentry into society after release. Work and self-improvement opportunities are organized by the KCS in an effort to assist offenders in becoming law-abiding citizens after their release.

Correctional facilities in South Korea can be divided into two categories: prisons, which secure sentenced inmates for all security levels, and detention centers (or jails), which mostly house defendants awaiting trials and remand inmates.

Inmates are provided the opportunity to learn and improve basic academic skills. A variety of classes from collegiate courses to vocations programs are offered by the KCS to meet the diverse educational needs of inmates. Additionally, the KCS encourages inmates to choose a single religion to cultivate morality through the purification of the mind by religious devotion. The KCS has recently created a video monitoring system that allows inmates to have medical checkups via remote medical staff and visitation with family members without a correctional officer present.

Inmates awaiting trial are generally allowed visitors every day, including holidays, Saturday afternoons, and Sundays. However, the number of visits allowed per month for convicted offenders varies depending on the classification level of the inmate.

Although the maximum visits allotted per month are four, exemplary inmates are often allowed to see their families on an unlimited basis per month. Unless the institution prohibits it for security or rehabilitation reasons, inmates are allowed to write letters to anyone outside the facility as long as the inmate pays the postage. Inmates may also make telephone calls to their families after purchasing a phone card and agreeing to a screening of the phone conversation.

Four correctional institutions in South Korea established Conjugal Visitation Houses in June 1999, which allowed exemplary long-term inmates to stay with their spouses or families in a house for one night. This opportunity sustained the relationship between inmates and their families. Exemplary inmates are also eligible for the furlough program after serving at least one year of their sentence and passing at least one-third of their sentence term. Inmates are often allowed to spend 72 hours on a weekend or holiday with their families to maintain family ties and adjust to society life after release.

By March 2008, the KCS included 4 regional headquarters and 47 correctional institutions: 32 prisons, 10 jails (detention centers), 1 vocational training correctional institution, and 4 correctional branches. Each of the regional headquarters performs intermediate supervision by directly overseeing local correctional institutions within its jurisdiction and administers front-line correctional facilities. The KCS employs more than 17,000 professionals (14,500 correctional officers and 2,500 defense guards) throughout South Korea.

Probation and Juvenile Justice

The Korean probation system was established as a juvenile corrections program in 1989. Due to the implementation of the Criminal Act in 1995, the court can now sentence adult offenders to probation, community service, or an attendance center when suspending the imposition or execution of a sentence. South Korea currently has 16 probation offices, 5 parole examination committees, and 28 branch offices. If a juvenile is sentenced to probation or released on parole, a probation officer supervises the juvenile and supports rehabilitation, executes community service and attendance center orders, and prepares presentence investigation reports for the Family Court. A Parole Examination Committee decides whether juveniles housed in juvenile training schools should be released on parole.

There are 16 juvenile protection facilities, which include 1 juvenile classification and examination center (JCEC), 9 juvenile training schools, and 6 juvenile delinquency prevention centers, which handle rehabilitation programs for juvenile delinquents. Training schools accommodate and protect juvenile delinquents by providing educational, vocational, and character-building opportunities. The first juvenile training school was established in 1942, and a revision of the Juveniles Act required the incorporation of the regular school system into juvenile training schools in 1989. The curriculum of juvenile training schools has now changed to run specialized education programs, which focus on practical English and computer skills, in an effort to provide juvenile delinquents with a more practical education. Schools are equipped with multimedia language labs and computer rooms and employ competent teachers to provide students with vocational training.

Hee-Jong Joo

Further Reading

Korea Correctional Service. Korea Correctional Service Web site: http://www.corrections.go.kr.

Korean Department (or Ministry) of Justice. Korean Ministry of Justice Web site: http://www.moj.go.kr.

Korean Institute of Criminology. Korean Institute of Criminology Web site: http://www.kicjp.re.kr.

Korean National Police Agency. Korean National Police Agency Web site: http://www.police.go.kr/eng/index.jsp.

Supreme Court of Korea. Supreme Court of Korea Web site: http://eng.scourt.go.kr/eng/main/Main.work.

Supreme Prosecutor's Office. Supreme Prosecutor's Office Web site: http://www.spo.go.kr.

Sri Lanka

Legal System: Civil/Common/Customary
Murder: High
Corruption: Medium
Human Trafficking: Medium
Prison Rate: Medium
Death Penalty: Maybe
Corporal Punishment: Yes

Background

Sri Lanka is an island nation situated off the southeast coast of India. It was known as Ceylon until 1972. According to the CIA World Factbook, Sri Lanka has a population of 21,128,772, and a total land area of 65,610 square kilometers (25,332 square miles). Sri Lanka gained sovereignty from colonial British rule in 1948 and has since developed as an independent nation subscribing to a republican form of government.

As set forth in the Constitution, adopted in 1978, the legislative arm of the Sri Lankan government resides in Parliament, also formerly known as the National State Assembly or the House of Representatives. The legislative or parliamentary branch of the Sri Lankan government is composed of members who are elected by democratic vote. The president of Sri Lanka constitutes the head of the Sri Lankan Republic, and this office is also democratically elected. The executive arm of the Sri Lankan government is represented by the president and his or her cabinet. Hierarchically, the president oversees the executive affairs of the state, and the president's deputy is the prime minister, who leads the ruling party in Parliament. Subsuming the law-making capacity of the Sri Lankan government, the Parliament is hence also termed the legislature. The Sri Lankan unicameral Parliament is composed of 225 seats, and members are elected by popular vote on the basis of an open-list, proportional representation system by electoral district to serve six-year terms. Notwithstanding the fact that the president possesses the authority to summon, suspend, or end a legislative session and dissolve Parliament altogether, the Parliament is vested with the exclusive law-making capability.

Legal System

The Sri Lankan legal system is reflective of its culturally and religiously pluralistic society. As such, the Sri Lankan criminal justice system accommodates and incorporates diverse jurisprudential philosophies that reflect its complex colonial history and rich society. Hence, the Sri Lankan legal system is a complex admixture of old English common law, Roman civil law, Islamic law, and customary international laws. The essential tenets of Sri Lankan criminal law rules of criminal procedure are predicated on old English common law roots. According to the earliest known written records, Roman-Dutch law was the initial formal law administered in Sri Lanka. Amidst political unrest, this Roman-Dutch law has remained the framework for Sri Lankan general and common law.

Criminal Justice

Under Sri Lankan criminal law, the accused is presumed innocent until proven guilty. Within the Sri Lankan executive branch of government, the attorney general is the principal law-enforcing agent of the state. Subservient to the attorney general, the district attorney and state counsels conduct criminal prosecutions. Most of these cases are adjudicated in the magistrates' courts by the charging officer.

In keeping with the British common law tradition, the police play a heightened role in the prosecution of crimes. The police, first and foremost, are exclusively charged with the investigative capacities and prosecution of ordinary criminal cases. The public prosecutors for criminal cases are usually the state councils or the state attorneys themselves. These prosecutors are given the task of prosecuting serious crimes that are generally tried in the High Court.

The Penal Code

The original Penal Code of Sri Lanka was put into effect in 1833. Since this initial codification of criminal law in Sri Lanka, numerous developments have taken place. The original 1833 Sri Lankan Penal Code was based on the corresponding Indian law. A few decades after the institution of this Penal Code, procedural requirements were much needed. This was met with the establishment of the first Criminal Procedure Code in 1882, 1898, 1973, and amended by the Judicature (Amendment) Act of 1979.

General Exceptions to Criminal Liability

The principal general exceptions to criminal liability recognized by the Sri Lanka Penal Code are insanity, intoxication, necessity, duress, and private defense.

Age of Criminal Responsibility

A defendant above and including the age of 6 years can be charged with criminal responsibility. Defendants between the ages of 6 and 12 years are not punished unless there has been a judicial determination at the discretion of the magistrate that the defendant has attained sufficient maturity. Competency to stand trial is also a judiciary-determined standard.

The codes of criminal procedure (Code of Criminal Procedure Act of 1979 and the Judicature Act of 1978) serve as the jurisdictional basis of judiciary administration. Socially relevant laws cater to the local customs and mores of the Sinhalese, Tamils, and Muslims. Each of these groups is geographically and socially diverse.

Police

The Sri Lankan police force is a centralized system that emulates that of the British police system. The Sri Lankan police department is directed by the inspector general of police. This official oversees all personnel and deputies. Emulating Scotland Yard, the Sri Lankan Central Investigation Department conducts complex and sensitive investigations.

Sri Lankan police are authorized to use deadly force only in specific situations wherein there is an imminent danger to life or limb. The Sri Lankan police have the authority to arrest any person with or without a warrant. Under Sri Lankan law, a person arrested is required to appear before a judicial magistrate within 24 hours in case of arrest without a warrant or be released on bail. Pursuant to these laws, the magistrate may order detention of the person arrested for a maximum of 15 days. Upon proof of probable cause, the police are required to obtain a search warrant from a magistrate before property can be seized. Notwithstanding this general rule, in specific circumstances, the police have the authority to seize illegal possessions without a warrant.

Crime

Classification of Crimes

The Sri Lankan Penal Code and Criminal Procedure Code define and classify crimes, describe the punishments for crimes under the code, and general exceptions to criminal liability. Crimes are classified in two main categories, and further subdivided into 21 categories.

The broad classifications of crimes are as follows:

1. *Grave crimes:* crimes that are indictable
2. *Minor crimes:* crimes that are nonindictable

The distinction between grave and minor crimes is somewhat analogous to the delineation among index and nonindex crimes in American criminal law. Within the grave crime classification, there are 21 subclassified crimes that are organized into seven categories.

1. Crimes against the state
2. Crimes against public tranquility
3. Crimes affecting the human body
4. Crimes against property
5. Crimes relating to religion
6. Sexual and marital crimes
7. Crimes relating to coins and government stamps

Crime Statistics

The Sri Lankan police collect and publish the main data on crimes reported to the police. The total number of crimes reported for 2007 was 56,454, of which theft of various kinds accounted for over half the crimes reported to the police, followed by roughly one-third crimes against the person. There are also some striking regional differences with the highest levels of homicide/suicide found in Jaffna, but the highest total crimes found in Nugegoda and Mt. Laviniya. None of the Colombo districts display exceptionally high rates; in fact, the South Colombo district has one of the lowest levels of crime.

The level of crime can also be measured according to the number of those convicted of crimes, in contrast to cases reported to police. This statistic measures *offenders,* whereas the police-recorded statistics measures *offenses*. According to the Department of Sri Lanka Prisons, there have been slight differences in the total number of convicted persons sent to prison over the years between 2004 and 2007. For example, there were 26,113 male and 785 female prisoners with a total of 26,898 convicted persons in 2004 as compared to 30,292 male and 1,014 female prisoners with a total of 31,306 in 2007.

Drug Crimes

The sale and use of specific dangerous substances is prohibited under the Poisons, Opium and Dangerous Drugs Ordinance. Under Sri Lanka law, it is a crime to sell and use drugs termed "harmful substances." These are cannabis, opium, heroin, morphine, hashish, hashish oil, cocaine, LSD, and psychotropic substances. The number of admissions for drug crimes has increased considerably over the 10-year period 1996–2007, although it appears that the proportion of total admissions that are for narcotic-related offenses has not increased.

Finding of Guilt

Judicial Process

The Sri Lankan Constitution affords the accused certain rights and immunities. In addition to the presumption of innocence, the accused has the following rights:

1. The right to notification of the charges
2. The right to answer to the charges
3. The right to present witnesses
4. The right to confront and cross-examine opposing witnesses
5. The right to legal representation
6. The right to a trial by jury in cases involving indictable grave offenses

Jury Trials

In Sri Lanka, the accused are also afforded the right to a trial by jury for any indictable grave crime. The accused person also has the option of pleading guilty to a lesser crime. All criminal trials are open to the public. Indigent persons are afforded legal representation by the government under Sri Lankan law. Pursuant to Sri Lankan criminal law, grave crimes, including murder, attempted murder, and rape, are tried at the first instance in the High Court. Such a case is handled as a bench trial or a jury trial. The jury is composed of seven jurors, randomly selected from the jury list.

Courts

The Court of Appeal hears appeals for criminal convictions and the Supreme Court exercises final appellate jurisdiction. In addition, the Supreme Court retains special jurisdiction for alleged violations of fundamental constitutional rights and freedoms. In the Sri Lankan criminal justice system, the magistrates' court has subject matter jurisdiction over grave criminal matters, while the primary court adjudicates minor criminal cases.

Pursuant to the Sri Lankan Constitution, the judiciary is independent and autonomous, in relation to the other branches of government. The judiciary in Sri Lanka is constituted by the Supreme Court, Court of Appeal, High Court, and a number of subordinate courts. The justices of the Supreme Court, Court of Appeal, and High Court are all appointed by the president. The Supreme Court is made up of 11 justices including the chief justice. In contrast, justices of the lower courts are appointed by the Judicial Service Commission. This commission is the administrative arm within the Supreme Court and consists of the three Supreme Court justices headed by the chief justice. Justices can be impeached for misconduct following an inquiry conducted by the president and the Parliament.

Analogous to American law, the Supreme Court affords the appeal of last resort for both criminal and civil cases. As such, the Supreme Court has the authority to review judicial and legislative decisions. The Attorney General's Department has authority over all government institutions as well as state corporations, statutory boards, and business undertakings fully owned by the government.

Juvenile Court

In Sri Lanka, there is one juvenile court at Bambalapitiya in Colombo.

Punishment

Types of Punishment

Punishments prescribed under the Penal Code are as follows:

1. Death
2. Imprisonment (simple and rigorous)
3. Whipping
4. Forfeiture of property
5. Fine
6. Probation
7. Suspended sentence
8. Community service
9. Institutional treatment

Disenfranchisement is used occasionally for offenses committed while holding public office. Corporal punishment, public punishment, banishment, and exile are not used or available under the law. By far the most common punishment for serious crimes is imprisonment. In 2003, 6.7 percent of the total convicted persons were sentenced to under a month as compared to 8.4 percent in 2007. Similarly in 2003, 1.4 percent of the total convicted were sentenced to more than 10 years as compared to 1.7 percent in 2007.

Death Penalty

Sri Lankan law permits the application of death penalty for certain crimes. Following a previous ban on capital punishment, the death penalty was reintroduced in 1960. Albeit rarely employed, the most frequent method used for death is hanging. Since 1997, there has not been any death sentence actually carried out. In 1997, there were 58 convicts sentenced to death and in 2007, there were 176 convicts sentenced to death. In 1997, 34 convicts had their death sentences commuted to imprisonment and in 1998, 16 had their death sentences commuted to imprisonment. All other convicts sentenced to death during 1997–2007 are under appeal awaiting execution or final decision for commutation of execution.

Probation

Probation has been in effect since 1944 in Sri Lanka but is infrequently employed.

Prisons

The Sri Lankan Central Government has jurisdiction over prisons. The commissioner of prisons oversees the Department of Prisons. Prison headquarters are located in the capital of Sri Lanka, Colombo. All prisons function pursuant to the Ministry of Justice and Law Reforms, Sri Lanka. Sri Lankan law classifies prisons into seven categories as follows:

Closed prisons for convicted prisoners	3
Remand prisons	18
Work camps	8
Open prison camps	2
Correctional centers for youthful offenders	2
Training schools	1
Lock-ups	25

Pursuant to the Sri Lankan Constitution, executive clemency, parole, and good time credit earned for good behavior can be used to remit sentences.

Sri Lankan law provides for the institution of educational and vocational programs for prisoners serving their sentence in prison. All prisoners are entitled to visitation and medical assistance. Prisoners in Sri Lanka can be released under three different schemes: (1) a work release scheme, (2) a license scheme (parole), and (3) a home leave scheme.

Suman Kakar

Further Reading

Code of Criminal Procedure Act of 1979. Colombo: Government Printing Office.

Cooray, A. (1996). "Sri Lanka: Oriental and Occidental Laws in Harmony." In *Studies in Legal Systems: Mixed and Mixing,* edited by E. Ötücü, E. Attwooll, and S. Coyle, pp. 71–88. London: Kluwer International.

Derrett, J. D. M. (1956). "The Origins of the Laws of the Kandyans." *University of Ceylon Review* 14: 149.

Nadaraja, T. (1972). *The Legal System of Sri Lanka in Its Historical Setting,* pp. 183–188. Leiden: E. J. Brill.

Taiwan (Republic of China)

Legal System: Civil/Customary
Murder: Medium
Corruption: Low
Human Trafficking: Medium
Prison Rate: High
Death Penalty: Yes
Corporal Punishment: No

Background

Taiwan, officially known as the Republic of China (ROC), lies off the southeastern coast of mainland Asia, across the Taiwan Straits from Mainland China. It consists of a main island and numerous islets. Its total land area encompasses about 36,000 square kilometers (13,900 square miles) with an estimated population of 23,037,031 as of December 2008. Today, people of Han extraction make up approximately 98 percent of Taiwan's population, while the remaining 2 percent are of Austronesian ancestry. Coinciding with a decrease in government ownership of major industries, the nation underwent tremendous economic growth beginning in the 1980s and today is recognized as one of East Asia's economic "Tigers," exporting products to countries around the world. Its estimated GDP—per capita in 2007 was $30,100, which ranked 40th in the world. Politically, it is a multiparty democratic republic. Elections for national and local officials are held every four years.

Legal System

Taiwan's current legal system is based on civil law and Western philosophies of jurisprudence. Prior to 1895, laws in Taiwan were dominated by Chinese legal traditions. However, Taiwan's legal system was gradually introduced to a subverted concept of Western law during Japan's colonial occupation (1895–1945), and then by the Chinese nationalist government during the second half of the century (1945–2000). The modernization/Westernization of law by these two regimes has dramatically but not entirely changed the legal system in Taiwan. The original motivation for Japan and China to adopt Western laws in their own lands was simply an attempt to compete with Western countries, not to protect people's human rights. Both regimes had imposed special criminal codes in their own lands to suppress social movements, demonstrations, and freedom of speech. When they imposed themselves on Taiwan, each regime enacted new criminal codes and intentionally ignored existing laws. Their goal was to eliminate any possible threat and thus to secure their ruling.

The legal system of the Kingdom of Prussia was adopted by Japan, and later adopted by the Chinese nationalist government. As a result, continental European law, particularly German law, became prevalent in Taiwan, even though the term "Western Law" could equally refer to common law. Additionally, because many Taiwanese scholars attended advanced studies in Germany and Japan and later helped to update the legal system in Taiwan, the continental European legal tradition has persisted on the island.

The criminal justice system in Taiwan unsurprisingly looks much like the German criminal justice system. At least before 2003, the criminal process was purely inquisitorial. The judge played the key fact-finding role during each case at trial. The prosecutor assisted the judge in a search for the truth. However, in reality, the prosecutor seldom appeared in court and when he or she did often played a very passive role in the truth-finding process. The defendant was thus forced to argue his or her case against the judge. To improve this situation, in 2003 and 2004, the Code of Criminal Procedure was dramatically restructured. It now has several elements that are crucial to the accusatorial system, such as cross-examination, the hearsay rule, and the exclusionary rule. The purpose of adopting cross-examination was to give the prosecutor a more substantial role in court. Additionally, to further the interest of justice, plea bargaining was introduced as a legal procedure, as was deferred prosecution. Legislators called the new mixed system a "refined accusatorial system." However, in essence, the new mixed system is more like a "refined inquisitorial system," because the judge still has the ultimate responsibility to find the truth and thus to decide the case.

In fact, the Code of Criminal Procedure has been modified or amended quite frequently in the past two decades. In 1997, legislators revised the laws concerning the right to counsel and pretrial detention. They also added a law to protect the defendant's right to remain silent and the right to counsel. In 2001, the laws concerning search and seizure were revised. Under these new laws, only the court can issue a search warrant. The police can make a warrantless search only under certain urgent circumstances or secure voluntary consent from an individual prior to the search.

The reform of Taiwan's criminal procedures can be attributed to a gradual democratization that began in the 1980s. Taiwan had been under authoritarian rule since the nationalist government declared martial law on May 19, 1949. Under martial law, free assembly, association, demonstration, and the right to petition were prohibited. Criminal laws and criminal procedure were used by the nationalist government to suppress political dissents. Therefore, abolishing or modifying those special criminal codes and empowering defendants with the enactment of new criminal procedure was central in the process of democratization. After martial law was lifted in 1987, numerous legal provisions that unreasonably restricted the civil and political rights of individuals have been reexamined, modified, or even abolished. The discretion afforded to police and prosecutors has been considerably restricted, including the police's ability to make a stop and frisk on the open road without probable cause. Various measures were also taken to ensure the independence of the judiciary, and to elevate the public confidence of the judiciary.

In 2000, Taiwan underwent its first peaceful transfer of political power when the Nationalist Party lost control of government to the Democratic Progressive Party. In 2008, the nationalist candidate Ma Ying-jeou won the presidential election and became the 12th president of Taiwan. Even though control of government transferred back to the Nationalist Party, the election was free and democratic.

Police

The police system in Taiwan is centralized and defined by the Police Act, which states that the police shall perform the following duties: (1) maintain public order, (2) protect social security, (3) prevent hazards, and (4) promote citizens' welfare.

The National Police Agency (NPA) was established in 1972 and is responsible for the administration of all police services in Taiwan. The NPA comprises administrative support units and operational units. The administrative support units include a command center, a planning committee, and various support units within divisions (e.g., police administration, public order, education, household registration, foreign affairs, civil defense, traffic, economic affairs, logistics, internal affairs, and general affairs). The operational units, under direct supervision of the NPA, include eight bureaus, namely, criminal investigation, aviation police, highway police, railroad police, and four harbor police bureaus at Taiwan's principal ports: Keelugn, Tiachung, Kaohsiung, and Hualien, and seven security police corps. While

Protesters attempt to break the line of police on December 23, 2008, in Taipei, Taiwan. The protestors want authorities to penalize businesses that force employees to take unpaid leave. (Chunche/Dreamstime)

the missions of the above units are national in scope, they also provide direct or indirect support to Taiwan's two municipal police jurisdictions and its various city (county) level police forces.

As of February 2008, Taiwan employed 67,802 police officers, which includes 13,997 officers assigned to administrative support and operation units, and 53,805 officers assigned to municipal and city (county) level police bureaus. The two municipal police bureaus operate under the jurisdictions of the largest city, Taipei, and the second-largest city, Kaohsiung City. In addition, there are 23 city (county) level police bureaus nationwide. Officers are tactically posted in police bureaus, precincts, or substations. To date, there are 154 police precincts and 1,604 police stations in Taiwan.

Before martial law was lifted in 1987, police officers in Taiwan were assigned to a wide assortment of duties, which may not be considered normal police practice in other countries; for example, the management of census records, provision of customs services at the nation's seaports and airports, prevention of disasters, fire fighting, and so forth. In recent years, several agencies had been separated from the police organization. This has allowed the police to concentrate on issues like crime and traffic control. The agencies that were separated from the NPA include the National Fire Agency (1995), Coast Guard Administration (2000), Airborne Service Corps (2005), and the National Immigration Agency (2006).

Crime

Classification of Crimes

Offenses are normally classified into three groups: (1) offenses against the person, (2) offenses against the society, and (3) offenses against the state. In the criminal code, offenses against the person include

69 different types of offenses, such as homicide, assault, abortion, restraining one's liberty, obstruction of reputation and credit, intrusion to privacy, larceny, robbery, embezzlement, kidnapping, property destruction, and so forth. Offenses against the society include 70 different types of offenses, such as arson, driving while intoxicated, forging documents and seals, counterfeiting securities, public indecency, gambling, manufacturing, selling, and using narcotics. Offenses against the state consist of 61 various types of offenses, including armed rebellion, treason, bribery, malfeasance in office, obstruction of justice, obstruction of governmental operations, disorderly conduct, interference with voting, destruction of evidence, perjury, malicious accusation, and so on.

The age of criminal responsibility in Taiwan is 14. Those who are older than 14 are held accountable for their behaviors. However, in cases where individuals are between 14 and 18 years of age or those who are older than 80, the judge can exercise discretion and reduce their sentences, if warranted. Although offenders who are less than 14 are not punishable by the criminal law, those who are older than 12 can be remanded to juvenile court and placed on probation.

In view of the above categorization of crime, some of the latest methods involved in crime have posted a great challenge to authorities in Taiwan. Since 2003, fraud crime has been rampant and become a major concern for society. According to the statistics provided by NPA, in 2008, there were 42,910 fraud cases reported to the police, which recorded an increase of 6.35 percent (or 2,562 cases) compared to the figures of 2007. Since 2006, telephone-based fraud has been a frequently used tactic by criminals. Perpetrators often impersonate police or court officials and ask victims to follow their orders to transfer money to certain accounts. Considering the number of accounts and the huge amounts of money that can be quickly accessed by the perpetrators, this crime has tremendous real and potential damaging effect on banking security and people's confidence in the criminal justice system. The government has focused its efforts on increasing public awareness of the latest methods involved in fraud crime. To help prevent people from being victimized by this type of fraud, NPA officials staffed a special task force and established a 24-hour toll-free anti-fraud hotline.

Drug Crimes

Drugs have also been a major concern for society in Taiwan. Drug crimes have always been punished harshly in Taiwan. Since the Criminal Code was promulgated in 1935, it has been illegal to manufacture, transport, or to sell narcotics. Violators could be incarcerated up to seven years. However, because of the dangers illegal drugs posed to society, a special code, the Statute for Eradicating Narcotics, was enacted in 1955. This statute enhanced the punishment for drug violations. From 1955 to 1992, it was punishable by a mandatory death sentence, to manufacture, transport, or to sell narcotics and opium. However, the harshness of the statute often presented the court with sentencing difficulties. For example, anyone who merely sold a small portion of narcotics was to be sentenced to death. This situation aroused public criticisms. Therefore, in 1992, a new statute was enacted that provided another possible punishment for the court—the life sentence.

Because of increased drug use and high recidivism rates, the policy against drug crimes has changed from punishment to treatment. In 1998, the Statute for Eradicating Narcotics was renamed—the Statute for Narcotics Hazard Control (SNHC), which classified violation into three types: the first degree, the second degree, and the third degree. The Statute for Narcotics Hazard Control places an emphasis on treatment and rehabilitation rather than punishment. In 2003, this statute was revised again when narcotics violation were classified into four types: (1) first-degree narcotics includes heroin, morphine, opium, cocaine, and the like; (2) second-degree narcotics includes poppy straw concentrate, coca, marijuana, amphetamine, pethidine, pentazocine, and the like; (3) third-degree narcotics includes secobarbital, amobarbital, nalorphine, and the like; and (4) fourth-degree narcotics includes allobarbital, alprazolam, and the like.

The punishment for drug-related crimes is differentiated according to the type of narcotics and the kinds of criminal activity involved. For example, to manufacture, transport, or sell first-degree narcotics, an individual can be punished by death or a life sentence with punitive fines up to 10 million NTD (approximately US$296,200). To manufacture, transport, or sell fourth-degree narcotics, an individual can be sentenced from 3 to 10 years in prison with punitive fines up to 3 million NTD (about US$ 88,860).

According to article 10 of the SNHC, using first- or second-degree narcotics is punishable. The SNHC mandates individuals arrested for using first- or second-degree narcotics to complete a two-month detoxification program. Prior to completion of the detoxification program, the individual will be assessed if he or she is required to participate in a six-month to one-year compulsory substance abuse treatment. The assessment is primarily based on a diagnosis of the individual's tendency of drug dependence. If an individual uses narcotics again within five years, he or she will get the punishment the law prescribes. According to article 10 of the SNHC, an individual can be sentenced from six months to five years in prison for using first-degree narcotics and up to three years' imprisonment for using second-degree narcotics. To encourage drug users to rehabilitate, for those who voluntarily go to the hospital or other facilities for detoxification treatment before they are discovered by criminal justice system, the hospital is exempt from reporting the case to law enforcement.

Crime Statistics

According to crime statistics compiled by the Criminal Investigation Bureau of the NPA, the overall number of crimes reported to the police declined from 512,788 (in 2006) to 491,815 in 2007. The overall crime rate dropped from 2,247 in 2006 to 2,146 for every 100,000 population in 2007. According the official crime statistics recorded by police, there were 881 murder cases and 1,530 murder offenders in 2007, which registered a murder rate of 3.8 per 100,000 population. It also indicates a decline in murder rate compared to 4.0 per 100,000 population in 2006. In addition, there were 2,487 rape cases and 2,405 rape offenders in 2007. Theft has been a prominent crime in Taiwan. In 2007, there were 241,091 larceny and automobile theft cases and 42,053 offenders, with a registered offender rate of 1,052 per 100,000 population. With regard to drugs, there were 52,835 drug offenses and 53,681 offenders in 2007. Thus, figures show a decline in the crime rate across different types of crime in 2007 compared to the figures in 2006. Since Taiwan is densely populated and urbanized, there are few differences in the type of crime between urban and rural areas.

Finding of Guilt

The finding of guilt can be divided into three stages: investigation, prosecution, and adjudication. Different authorities are in charge of each stage: the police and the prosecutor investigate crimes, the prosecutor (but not exclusively) pursues the cases, and the court hears and decides the cases.

Investigation

According to the Code of Criminal Procedure in Taiwan, the prosecutor has the main responsibility in criminal investigation. Whenever the prosecutor is alerted to a possible crime, he or she has the obligation to start the investigation. The police are the prosecutor's assistants. The prosecutor can give orders to the police, asking them either to make an arrest or to conduct a search. But in reality, the police are the main criminal investigators. About 70 percent of criminal investigations were initiated by the police. The police often conduct the criminal investigation on their own. When the police gather enough evidence, they must transfer the case to the prosecutor. But if the prosecutor is dissatisfied with the result of the police investigation, the prosecutor can return the files and the evidence to the police and ask the police to conduct further investigation within a certain period of time.

Prosecution

At the stage of prosecution, the prosecutor also plays a crucial role. He or she alone can decide whether and how to pursue the case, including prosecuting the case, deferring the prosecution, or dropping the case. As long as the decisions by the prosecutor are made in compliance with the Code of Criminal Procedure in Taiwan, these decisions need not be approved by the head prosecutor before they become effective.

The decision made by the prosecutor generally decides whether a case can be tried by the court. According to the statistics offered by the Ministry of Justice in Taiwan, about 99.99 percent of the criminal prosecutions are brought by prosecutors. For example, in 2007 of 186,991 prosecutions, 185,874 were brought by the prosecutors, while 827 were brought by private persons. But the prosecutor does not monopolize the prosecution. According to the Criminal Code in Taiwan, the prosecution of certain crimes, such as theft between family members, needs to be approved by the victim. Besides, the victim can bring the charge against his or her perpetrator, too. According to the Code of Criminal Procedure in Taiwan, the victim and the victim's close family members, such as the victim's spouse or his or her guardian, are allowed to bring private prosecution against the offender. In private prosecution, the victim takes over the role of prosecutor and bears the burden of proof. To make private prosecution more efficient, a 2003 amendment requires that anyone who wants to bring a private prosecution must have a lawyer to represent him or her at trial. The legislators added another restriction on the private prosecution in 2003: if the prosecutor has already initiated a criminal investigation, no private prosecution is allowed, unless the case can only be indicted upon the victim's complaint.

Adjudication

There is no jury trial in Taiwan. Criminal cases are tried exclusively by professional judges. Under the relevant regulation, every district court, High Court, and the Supreme Court must establish civil courts and criminal courts. Criminal cases are thus handled by criminal courts in different levels of courts. Unfortunately, there are no official statistics about the number of the criminal court judges in Taiwan. Statistics provided by the Judicial Yuan only tell us how many judges are in different level of courts. As of 2007, there were 1,172 judges in all district courts, 344 in High Courts, and 65 in the Supreme Court.

Criminal court judges must be Taiwanese citizens. They have to pass a special exam for judges and prosecutors first, and then receive professional training. After training, they will be assigned to district courts or district prosecution offices based on their wishes and grades during the training. A newly trained judge is generally assigned to the criminal court first, simply because there are more vacancies there. A substantial number of senior criminal court judges prefer civil courts, for they believe the pressure as a criminal court judge is higher. These senior judges apply for reassignments, and thus leave more vacancies in criminal courts. Fortunately, many senior judges also stay in criminal courts and pass their experiences to the junior judges.

According to the relevant regulation, every district court, High Court, and the Supreme Court must establish civil courts and criminal courts. Criminal cases are exclusively handled by criminal courts in the different levels. In addition to civil courts and criminal courts, the Juvenile Accident Act (JAA) requires that every district court must establish juvenile courts. The objectives for juvenile procedure are to reform and to protect the juvenile. The juvenile court takes persons ages 12 to 18 years old who are accused of crime(s) or delinquent acts. According to JAA, the juvenile procedure must not be open to the public, and the personal information of the juvenile defendant must be removed from the court judgment. In 2007, the juvenile courts handled 44,156 cases, about 9 percent of the district criminal courts' load in the same year.

Rights of Defendants

In the past two decades, the protection of the defendant has been greatly improved. The issues that received most attention are (1) the right to counsel, (2) pretrial detention, (3) the presumption of innocence, (4) the right to remain silent, and (5) the right to confrontation.

Right to Attorney

The right for the defendant to have legal assistance was the first issue that caught the legislators' attention, even before martial law was lifted. In 1982, the first bank robbery in the history of Taiwan took place. Twenty-three days later, the police arrested the suspect, and the suspect confessed to his crime in the police station. But, later he committed suicide to protest his innocence. This event shocked the conscience of society. The legislators immediately revised the law to allow the defendant to have a lawyer to protect him or her any time in the criminal process. In 1997, the legislators further gave any government official the legal obligation to inform suspects/defendants of their right to attorney before interrogation.

In addition to legal assistance before trial, the Code of Criminal Procedure mandates the court to provide legal assistance at trial in certain circumstances, if the defendant does not hire a lawyer for himself or herself. Circumstances include when the defendant is charged with serious crimes, or if the defendant is mentally challenged. In 2006, the legislators amended the law to provide more legal assistance to a mentally challenged defendant. According to the new law, the prosecutor is obligated to provide the defendant legal assistance even during the investigation. Additionally, in a plea bargaining procedure, if the defendant is willing to accept a sentence longer than six months' imprisonment, the court is obligated to provide legal assistance.

Pretrial Detention

Over the past two decades, pretrial detention has probably been the most controversial issue concerning the criminal process. In 1995 and 2008, the Council of Grand Justices—the constitutional court in Taiwan—has made two constitutional interpretations concerning the pretrial detention. Interpretation No. 392 withdrew the prosecutor's discretion to detain the suspect. Interpretation No. 653 gave detainees the legal right to appeal to the administrative court, if they want to object to their treatment in detention.

Currently, the Code of Criminal Procedure in Taiwan allows two kinds of pretrial detention: general and preventive detention. For general detention, the prosecutor has to file a motion to initiate a proceeding and prove in front of the judge(s) by preponderance of evidence that the defendant is highly probable (1) to be convicted of the crime charged by the prosecutor, and (2) to flee or to tamper with evidence, including destroying evidence, or instigating perjury. If the defendant is charged with a very serious crime—offenses punishable by the death penalty, life sentence, or incarceration for more than five years—the defendant is assumed to have a high risk of flight or evidence tampering. The prosecutor also has to prove that the pretrial detention is absolutely necessary to prevent the defendant from flight or tampering with evidence. For preventive detention, the prosecutor needs to file a motion to initiate the detention proceeding and prove in front of the judge(s) by preponderance of evidence that the defendant is highly probable (1) to be convicted of the crime charged by the prosecutor, and (2) to repeat any one of the following crimes: arson, sexual assault, larceny, mugging, restraining one's liberty, or extortion. The prosecutor similarly has to prove that the pretrial detention is necessary to prevent the defendant from repeating her or his crimes. According to statistics offered by the Ministry of Justice in Taiwan, the rate that the court approves the prosecutor's motion of pretrial detention is about 85 to 86 percent, at least in the past four years.

The Presumption of Innocence

The rule of presumption of innocence is a fundamental right for the defendant in every criminal trial. This right should have come to Taiwan with the adoption of the Western criminal procedure. But in the past, the extent to which this rule been respected in practice remained a big question. To highlight its importance, in 2003, the legislators explicitly put this rule in the Code of Criminal Procedure.

The Right to Remain Silent

The right to remain silent is another fundamental right the defendant should have in the criminal procedure. This right derived from the privilege against self-incrimination. The defendant can refuse to testify on the grounds that the answer would incriminate him or her in a criminal offense other than the current one. No adverse inference can be drawn from the defendant's silence. In 1997, the legislators revised the law and gave government officials the legal obligation to inform the suspect/defendant before interrogation of the right to remain silent.

The Right to Confrontation

How to protect the defendant's right of confrontation is another issue that has caught the attention of many people in the past few years, including the legislators, the Grand Justices, and the Supreme Court in Taiwan. In 2003, the legislators introduced the hearsay rule to exclude the out-of-court statements that cannot be cross-examined during the trial. They also introduced the rules of cross-examination, not only hoping to force the prosecutor to participate actively in the trial, but also hoping to improve the truth-finding process. In addition to the efforts by the legislators, in July 2004, the Council of Grand Justices issued Interpretation No. 582, which has given the defendant the right to confront any witness, even if the witness is the accomplice. This interpretation deliberately corrected an old practice among the courts. In fact, even the courts themselves have changed their attitude toward the defendant's right to confrontation. In the last two years, the Supreme Court in its decisions set up more procedural restrictions on the application of the hearsay exceptions, which shows that the importance of the right of confrontation is gradually recognized in Taiwan.

Alternatives to Trial

In the past decade, the number of criminal cases has increased dramatically. But the number of judges has not increased correspondingly. The caseloads for judges and prosecutors are already heavy. When the legislators have added more safeguards to protect the rights of the defendant, which has made the criminal procedure more complicated and take more time, how to alleviate the caseloads for the court without sacrificing the rights of the defendant has also become an important issue in the past decade. The legislators have introduced the summary procedure, the plea bargaining procedure, and the deferred prosecution to alleviate the caseloads for judges.

Summary Judgment

The summary procedure has existed in Taiwan's Code of Criminal Procedure since the code was promulgated. But the pressure of the caseload has forced the legislators to expand the application of this procedure. Currently, if the case is not serious (i.e., the court can only sentence the defendant to probation, a short prison term that can be commutated to a fine, detention, or punitive fine) and if the defendant has already confessed during the investigation, or if there is enough evidence to convict the defendant, the prosecutor is given the discretion to ask the court to make a summary judgment. In the summary procedure, many procedural rules, including the hearsay rule, do not apply. The summary judgment that the judge needs to render in this procedure is quite simplified, which has made the procedure rather appealing to the prosecutor as well as the court. In 2007, about 41 to 42 percent of cases have been handled in the summary procedure.

Plea Bargaining

In addition to the summary procedure, the legislators also introduced the plea bargaining procedure to the criminal justice system in Taiwan. According to the new amendments to the Code of Criminal Procedure in 2004, those who are not charged with serious offenses can ask for making a deal with the prosecutor. But before the prosecutor and the defendant begin their negotiation, the prosecutor must consult with the victim and get the court's approval. In the bargaining procedure, the prosecutor will generally recommend a more lenient punishment, such as a shorter prison time or lesser punitive fines, to the judge, in return for the guilty plea from the defendant. According to the legislative notes, count and charge bargaining are not allowed in Taiwan, because legislators as well as many scholars are convinced that it violates many important principles to let the defendant plead guilty to lesser offenses. Once the defendant makes a deal with the prosecutor, there will not be an open trial for his or her case. Many procedural rights, such as the right to confrontation, are automatically waived by agreeing to enter the sentence bargaining procedure. Therefore, before making the judgment as recommended by the prosecutor, the court has to make sure that the defendant makes the deal voluntarily.

Compared to the summary procedure, the plea bargaining procedure includes more types of cases, which can supposedly further alleviate the caseloads for the prosecutor and the judges. Nevertheless, statistics show that plea bargaining is rarely used in Taiwan. Only about 2 percent of cases were handled in the plea bargaining procedure in 2007. Researchers point out that this is because the plea bargaining procedure takes more time for the prosecutor than the summary procedure. Most of all, whether it is fair for the victim or the society to make a deal with the defendant is still a controversial issue in Taiwan. Prosecutors in Taiwan prefer using either the summary procedure or deferred prosecution.

Deferred Prosecution

Learning from Germany and Japan, in 2002, the legislators added a new system of "deferred prosecution" to the Code of Criminal Procedure in Taiwan. The purposes of introducing this new system are multiple. Most importantly, it could alleviate the caseloads. By deferring the prosecution, it allows for the defendant's pretrial rehabilitation, possibly abnegating a trial. According to the new laws, if the defendant is not involved in a serious offense, and not prosecuting the defendant would not obstruct the public, then the prosecutor can impose some obligations on the defendant, such as community service or money donations, and defer the prosecution within a period of time. If the defendant fulfills all the obligations that the prosecutor has assigned to him or her and does not commit another crime within a certain period of time, then his or her case will not be prosecuted by the prosecutor. Statistics show that about 13 to 14 percent of cases were handled with deferred prosecution.

Punishment

According to the criminal code, there are five kinds of punishment in Taiwan: death penalty, life sentence, timed imprisonment, detention, and punitive fine. Timed imprisonment refers to incarceration of a term from two months to 15 years. But if the case has any mitigating or aggravating factor, the judge has the discretion to decrease the defendant's sentence to less than two months for the former or to increase his or her sentence up to 20 years for the latter. Detention refers to the short-term imprisonment for one day to two months. However, the judge is allowed to increase the detention time up to four months, if necessary.

According to the statistics provided by the Ministry of Justice in 2008, about 60 percent of convicts are sentenced to timed imprisonment. Of those sentenced to timed imprisonment, about 60 percent received a term of less than six months, and more than 85 percent are sentenced for less than two years. But not all of those sentenced serve the prison time. Those who received sentences of less than six months can convert their prison time to punitive fines, if their prosecutors do not oppose.

According to the statistics provided by the Judicial Yuan in 2007, the main district court punishment for intentional killing is to be sentenced to a term of imprisonment from 10 to 15 years. The typical punishment for rape is incarceration for three to five years. The typical punishment for theft is detention and incarceration for six months to one year. The typical punishment for robbery (with force) is incarceration for 7 to 10 years. Typical punishment for the most serious drug offense—that is, manufacture, transport, or sale of first or second degree of narcotics—is incarceration for 7 to 10 years.

Death Penalty

The offenses that are punishable by death have been changed a lot in the past decade. Before 2000, the death penalty remained mandatory for 65 different offenses. This situation has been harshly criticized as unconstitutional. Therefore, from 2000 on, the legislators have begun to revise these laws. By the end of 2006, the death penalty became discretionary for all capital offenses. During the same period of time, the legislators rescinded the law allowing the use of the death penalty for minors. The number of offenses carrying a death penalty has also been reduced. Currently, offenses such as sedition, hijacking, pirating, kidnapping, manufacturing or sale of narcotics, and intentionally killing are all punishable by death. Nevertheless, due to the pressure from the abolitionist groups, only offenders who have taken a victim's life will be sentenced to death.

The death penalty has existed in Taiwan for a very long time, while its application has varied in different periods. According to an investigation by the International Committee for Human Rights in Taiwan, from 1982 to 1985, at least 102 individuals were sentenced to death and at least 32 people were actually executed. Executions increased dramatically after martial law was lifted in 1987, with 69 people executed in 1989, 78 in 1990, and 59 in 1991. Since 1993, nevertheless, the number of executions has decreased. In the last five years, less than 10 people have been executed, with 3 people executed in 2004, and 3 in 2005. From 2006 to 2008, there was no execution in Taiwan at all, even though the death penalty has never been officially abolished. By the end of 2008, there were still 31 inmates on death row. Some of them have been there for a long time. This de facto abolition is attributed to the relentless efforts by capital punishment abolitionist groups in Taiwan. Activists have successfully made the abolition of the death penalty an important human rights issue for the Taiwan government. In 2003, the Taiwan government unveiled a draft of the Human Rights Basic Law, which includes provisions for the gradual abolition of the death penalty. However, even though this de facto abolition has been applauded by human rights groups, both international and domestic, it has upset a lot of people in Taiwan. Criticisms mostly come from supporters of the death penalty, which are the majority of Taiwanese people.

Prison

According to the Department of Corrections (DOC), Ministry of Justice, there were 77 correctional institutions as of 2008, including 24 prisons, 3 training institutes, 2 juvenile reform schools, 2 juvenile correctional high schools, 19 detention centers, 18 juvenile detention houses, and 9 drug abuser treatment centers. The prisons serve to execute criminal sentences against convicted offenders, while the training institutes hold prisoners who were sentenced to mandatory work programs and to disciplinary programs. The juvenile reform schools hold offenders who were sentenced by a juvenile court to receive reformatory education. As for juvenile correctional high schools, they provide schooling for juveniles who were sentenced to prison terms, detention, or correctional punishment. The detention centers hold suspects during investigation as well as defendants prior to the trial, while the juvenile detention houses hold those under 18 years of age who were under investigation or trial. The drug abuser treatment centers were established to hold drug abusers for substance treatment programs.

Based upon the statistics provided by DOC, there were 34,991 (31,427 males and 3,564 females) people admitted into correctional institutions in 2007. As of March 2008, the daily number of inmates incarcerated was 54,620, which includes 50,340 male and 4,280 female inmates. The biggest prison, Taiwan Taichung Prison, is located in the central part of Taiwan. As of March 20, 2008, 5,144 inmates were held in Taiwan Taichung Prison.

It is mandatory for inmates to work or attend training programs. If inmates refuse to follow, a penalty will be imposed. For example, according to article 19 of the Prison Camp Act, for an inmate with disciplinary violation or being slow at work, the following punishments may be imposed through the verdict of a prison committee's meeting: (1) admonishment, or (2) suspension of outdoor activities for one to seven days.

In Taiwan, there is a progressive stage system that regulates inmate's visitation and correspondences. According to article 56 of the Prison Serving Progressive Treatment Act, inmates' privileges on visitation and mail correspondence should be regulated based upon their different grades:

1. Grade IV prisoners: once each week
2. Grade III prisoners: once or twice each week
3. Grade II prisoners: once every three days
4. Grade I prisoners: no restriction

Prisoners at Grades II through IV can only receive visits at the visitation rooms, while prisoners at Grade I may receive visits at any approved locations (article 57 of the Prison Serving Progressive Treatment Act). In addition, prisoners at Grades I through II do not have to be monitored during their visits (article 58 of the same act).

According to article 3 of the Enforcement Rules of the Prison Serving Act, if the convicted offender had a foreign nationality or did not have a nationality, he or she should be moved to a designated prison if deemed necessary. As defined by law, international prisoners can be transferred back to their own countries in compliance with a mutual treaty of prisoners' exchange. Nevertheless, in practice, there has been no such treaty signed as of yet. To date, there have been no transfers.

Chia-Wen Lee, Charles K. M. Chang, and Doris C. Chu

Further Reading

Ministry of Justice, Taiwan: http://www.moj.gov.tw/mp095.html.

National Police Agency, Taiwan: http://www.npa.gov.tw/NPAGip/wSite/ct?xItem=36854&ctNode=11349.

Vaughn, M. S., F. Deng, and L. J. Lee. (2003). "Evaluating a Prison-Based Drug Treatment Program in Taiwan." *Journal of Drug Issues* 33: 357–384.

Tajikistan

Legal System: Civil
Corruption: High
Human Trafficking: Medium
Prison Rate: Medium
Death Penalty: Yes
Corporal Punishment: Yes

Background

Since 1929, Tajikistan had been a separate, subordinate republic of the Soviet Union. Following the Soviet Union's breakup in 1991, Tajikistan formally declared its independence. Unfortunately, the country endured a brutal civil war from 1992 and 1997. Government forces, led by old-guard former Soviet elites, fought against the United Tajik Opposition (UTO), a loose confederation of Islamists and others. The conflict killed an estimated 50,000 and displaced an estimated 1.2 million people before regional powers and the UN brokered a cease-fire and power-sharing agreement in 1997, implemented in 2000.

The 1994 Constitution formalized the country as a parliamentary republic that is secular, unitary, and sovereign. The president and the bicameral legislature, the Supreme Assembly, are to govern by the rule of law and respect civil rights. In reality, the polity is much more authoritarian than democratic.

Emomali Rahmon, a leading governmental figure during the civil war, has been president since 1994 and has essentially been entrenched as president-for-life through successive elections that Human Rights Watch (HRW) concludes were "marred by flagrant fraud" and fell well short of international standards for fair elections. He and his People's Democratic Party (PDP) possess nearly total control of the government, and the notion of separation of powers is nonexistent. Media restrictions and reprisals for criticizing the government or drawing attention to pervasive official corruption are prevalent. Reprisals include harassment and even prosecution for criminally defaming the president, which under article 137 of the Criminal Code is punishable through exorbitant fines or up to five years' imprisonment.

As the American-based Freedom House (FH) observes, Rahmon's and the PDP's power base is rooted in the country's Kulob region, based upon traditional, patriarchal clan-based figures who exercise power through patronage and networks composed of common ancestral ties. The ruling elite have mobilized around nationalism and the primacy of Tajik culture since the civil war that experienced ethnic cleansing and an exodus of ethnic Russians. Tajiks represent about 80 percent of the population, with Uzbeks as a significant minority of about 15 percent, and the rest being primarily Russians and Kyrgyz. About 85 percent are Sunni Muslims, while 5 percent and 10 percent are Shia Muslims or members of other predominantly Christian affiliations, respectively.

The liberalized economy, combined with the resurgence of patriarchal discourses and practices, themselves rooted in traditionalist and religious doctrines, have made women and children extremely vulnerable. Previously outlawed by Soviet authority, practices such as bride prices, early and polygamous marriages, and unregistered religious marriages have returned.

Legal System

The legal system is based upon the civil law and does not provide for the judicial review of legislative acts. Since independence, and particularly following the civil war, Tajikistan has adopted or amended several laws. These include several that are directly related to criminal justice such as the 1998 Criminal Code, 1998 Family Code, 1999 Civil Code, and the 2001 Penal Enforcement Code.

The 2001 Constitutional Law on the Courts of Tajikistan was adopted to consolidate and systematize previous laws. The ordinary court system includes Rayon and city courts. These act as Courts of First Instance in civil, criminal, and administrative cases. These courts can refer cases involving constitutional questions to the Constitutional Court.

Other ordinary courts include Oblast Courts, the Court of the Badakshan Mountainous Autonomous Region, and the City Court of Dushanbe, which is Tajikistan's capital and largest city. These can act as courts of cassation or first instance of civil, criminal, and administrative cases. The presidium of each of these courts supervises activities.

Military courts at the garrison level function as courts of first instance. These, along with the Military Chamber of the Supreme Court, are part of the ordinary court system. Military courts consider both criminal and civil cases, provided that at least one of the crimes or accused individuals falls within military jurisdiction. A military judge and two officers drawn from the service ranks hear cases. There is also a system of special economic courts. The Higher Economic Court is the highest jurisdictional body for the resolution of economic disputes.

The Supreme Court is the highest jurisdictional body. It supervises the activities of the military courts at the garrison level, the Court of the Badakshan Mountainous Autonomous Region, the regional courts, the Dushanbe City Court, city courts, and district courts in civil, criminal, administrative, and other cases. It acts as a court of first instance in criminal cases. The court also includes three divisions (*collegia*) addressing civil, criminal, and military jurisdiction cases.

The Constitutional Court was established in 1995 to protect constitutional provisions. It mainly deals with constitutionality of legal acts and disputes between state organs relating to their competencies. It also hears individual complaints from citizens who allege violations of their constitutional rights and freedoms resulting from the implementation of potentially unconstitutional laws.

The Council of Justice (CoJ) was established in 1999, ostensibly to grant judicial independence, moving the judicial administration from the Ministry of Justice (MoJ) to the CoJ. The CoJ is a collegiate body responsible for organizing work of courts (excluding the Constitutional Court, the Supreme Court, and the Higher Economic Court) regarding resources, finances, and logistics. The CoJ has seven members, only one of whom is a judge (the chairperson of the Supreme Court). Three members are appointed by presidential decree, as are the chairpersons and deputies and judges of the Rayon and city courts. The CoJ proposes, and the president approves, judges for the Oblast Courts, the Court of the Badakshan Mountainous Autonomous Region, and the City Courts of Dushanbee. The president proposes, and the upper chamber of Parliament, the National Assembly, ratifies the chairperson and judges of the Supreme Court.

Consequently, the CoJ effectively subordinates the judiciary to the president and his administration. Judicial corruption is widespread. However, in 2007 alone, the government arrested five justice system officials. This resulted in two judges and two notaries being convicted.

Police

Nearly all police agencies operate under the auspices of the Ministry of Interior (MoI). The MoI shares law enforcement responsibilities with the Drug Control Agency (DCA), the Agency on State Financial Control and Fight against Corruption (Anti-corruption Agency), the Tax Committee, the Customs Service, and the State Committee for National Security (SCNS). The SCNS is responsible for intelligence matters and controls the Border Service. Law enforcement agencies often have overlapping responsibilities and typically defer to the SCNS.

According to a 2008 UN Special Rapporteur, there are few specialized police departments that formally record and investigate domestic violence claims. Traffic police have been known to pocket fines paid for traffic violations. Police and security forces have been notorious for brutal practices since the civil war, especially regarding behavior occurring inside police-controlled facilities.

Victims of police abuse may complain in writing to the abusive officers' supervisors. Naturally, most do not. In 2007, the government arrested just 67 officials for criminal violations, 29 of which were for corruption. Radio Free Europe reported that one of those cases was resolved in a Dushanbe court. Two police officers were each sentenced to two years' imprisonment for torturing a 16-year-old boy during a robbery investigation, subjecting him to beatings and electric shocks. Another officer was fined US$1,700 for failing to intervene. Overall, the FH concludes that the police forces remain unreformed and a serious threat to human rights.

Crime

It is difficult to accurately gauge common crime levels since there are no official statistics available.

Domestic Violence

A 2009 UN Special Rapporteur concluded that crime rates among children and adolescents are low. However, some investigators reaffirmed the widely held belief that domestic violence against women and children is quite high and culturally accepted, so that it is largely unreported and unacknowledged. Human rights investigators believe that about 8 of 10 acts of violence occur within the home. The 2009 Special Rapporteur estimates that between one-third and one-half of all women regularly suffer some form of familial violence, with about 20 percent experiencing both physical and sexual violence. Also, probably between 20 and 60 percent of children endure familial or school violence. There is no specific law pertaining to domestic violence or violence against women.

Institutional responses are insufficient. The Institute for War and Peace Reporting suggests that in 2009, suicide among abused women had become an epidemic. Victimized girls are often detained in hospital wards or "special schools." Likewise, victimized boys may be incarcerated in closed institutions.

Human Trafficking

Men, women, and children are all victimized by crimes involving the exploitation of migrant labor and human trafficking. Men and boys are subjected to forced labor in Russia and Kazakhstan. In 2009, the Military Commission chief in the Sughd Province and two associates were sentenced to one year of imprisonment at forced labor when they were convicted of forcibly conscripting young men into military service. It appears to be common practice for military officials to illegally "hunt" young men to fill the army's shrinking ranks.

In 2004, as a result of the Interministerial Commission on Combating Trafficking in Persons, the Law on Fight against Human Trafficking was adopted. These are believed to be positive developments. Articles 130 and 132 of the Criminal Code address this crime. Still, reports persist of officials being involved in trafficking of women and children. The Committee against Torture (CAT) has expressed concern over a notable absence of information on the sentences actually being handed down for these crimes.

Women are most likely to be trafficked to Russia and the United Arab Emirates (UAE) for sexual labor. In 2000, 300 went to the UAE. According to the International Organization for Migration (IOM), there were 45 mostly successful cases against traffickers in 2005, and 107 victims were repatriated. The Tajik General-Prosecutor's Office opened 24 criminal cases of child trafficking in 2007, and it had repatriated 80 women over the prior four years. The IOM operates two victim shelters in Dushanbe and Khujand.

Terrorism

The government has heightened its sensitivity to Islamist terrorism. This appears to be a function of the regime's long-running secular policy of hostility toward Islamist political opposition as well as the lucrative interest that the United States has shown in Tajikistan's Afghan border as a base of military operations following the 9/11 terror attacks in New York City. Disaffected with the 1997 cease-fire agreement, many UTO fighters joined the Islamist Movement of Uzbekistan (IMU). Former president George W. Bush later linked IMU with Osama bin Laden. Rahmon's regime has outlawed the IMU as well as the Hizb ut-Tahrir (Freedom Party), equating both with "Islamic extremism" as both seek to establish Islamic law in the region. Articles 189 and 307 of the Criminal Code prohibit "extremist organizations" and "religious incitement." In 2008, the U.S. State Department noted concern that the regime has seized upon the prosecution of "extremism" as a valuable pretext for policing and harassing a broad spectrum of regime opponents and political dissidents. In 2009, Radio Free Europe reported that seven Hizb ut-Tahrir activists were imprisoned from three years and seven months to nine years and seven months for belonging to the illegal group.

Corruption

Endemic corruption is the heart of the country's crime problem. It continues to affect all spheres of private and public life. The State Financial Control and Anticorruption Agency initiative has consolidated nearly all governmental anticorruption functions. Officials claim that the initiative successfully dealt with 300 corruption cases, recovering US$24 million in 2007. There were criminal cases against 20 police officers and several court employees.

Drug Trafficking

Drug trafficking also appears to be a major source of corruption. Since late 2001, there has been a massive upsurge in cultivation and trafficking from Afghanistan through Tajikistan. The FH reports that Tajikistan has one of the highest rates of both drug trafficking and interdiction in the world. However, local use appears to be relatively low. According to the 2009 World Drug Report, the annual prevalence of opiate use as a percentage of the population aged 16–64 was 0.54 percent. Cannabis use prevalence was 3.4 percent. In recent years, there were 589 persons in drug treatment at any one time, about 99.2 percent of these for opiate abuse.

Finding of Guilt

The Constitution and the Criminal Procedure Code provide for the protection of important rights of arrestees, detainees, and criminal defendants. However, in practice, the criminal justice process is quite authoritarian and severely violates due process rights at all stages.

By law, police cannot enter a private home without authorization from a prosecutor unless a delay would hurt national security. If they do, they must inform a prosecutor within 24 hours. But as the U.S.

State Department reports, police frequently ignore the law, and they violate prohibitions on monitoring private communications. Police have also been known to knowingly arrest and frame innocent persons to clear cases.

Constitutional article 19 says that individuals are entitled to legal counsel assistance from the moment of arrest. But article 49 of the Criminal Procedure Code delays this from the moment of arrest to 24 hours after arrest, and in practice, this only occurs once the arrest is actually registered, which may take days. Also, a UN Special Rapporteur observes that this is further obstructed by the requirement that the lawyer receive permission from the official in charge of investigating the case and sometimes also the head of the remand center.

Many detainees are unaware of their right to counsel and are sometimes forced or persuaded to sign a declaration renouncing this right. There is no explicit constitutional guarantee to free legal assistance for indigent arrestees. In practice, two collegia of advocates and NGOs such as the League of Women Lawyers, the Bureau on Human Rights and Rule of Law, and the Human Rights Centre provide counsel.

Article 412 of the Criminal Procedure Code requires notification of arrest to the family in juvenile cases. But it does not specify the time delay and is regularly disregarded in practice. While they detain arrestees, police frequently harass families to pressure detainees to confess. Articles 6, 90, 413, and 415 of the Criminal Procedure Code provide guidance for pretrial custody. In general, prosecutors can impose remand custody for offenses punishable by a year or more imprisonment. Pretrial detention is supposed to be an exception. But in practice, prosecutors frequently use it without sufficient justification. By article 221, detainees can appeal. They rarely do, and courts tend to agree with prosecutors. By article 92, pretrial detention should not exceed two months.

Under exceptional circumstances, district prosecutors can extend detention up to three months. Then a regional prosecutor or a prosecutor of the Badakshan Mountainous Autonomous Region can extend detention for up to six months. The general prosecutor and the senior military prosecutor can extend it up to nine months. In exceptional circumstances, if the detainee is accused of a grave crime, it can be further extended up to one year and three months.

Constitutional article 20 and Criminal Procedure Code article 8 formally enshrine the presumption of innocence, as well as the principle of equality of arms between prosecution and defense. But in practice, these are undermined due to the overarching might of the prosecutor, and the media frequently refer to suspects in inflammatory ways, such as labeling them "criminals." Trial courtrooms are even equipped with holding cages in which to display defendants during proceedings.

The Law on Advocacy has been downgraded from a constitutional law to an ordinary law. So it is inferior to the Constitutional Law on the Prosecutor's Office. Powerful prosecutors have authority to supervise the propriety of judicial proceedings while they prosecute suspects. They have powerful arrest and remand authority. The law gives prosecutors the authority to issue arrest warrants, indirectly initiate legislation, to "protest" against judicial decisions, and temporarily defer the execution of judicial decisions, as well as other powers.

According to both the Constitution and the Criminal Procedure Code, defense lawyers have a right to access relevant evidence, but this is not always requested. The prosecutor or the investigating officer has de facto power to deny access until the investigation is completed. Courts have rejected defense requests to call witnesses that are not already on the prosecutor's list. Further, based on Criminal Procedure Code article 233, common practice is to return cases for complementary investigation rather order defendants' release. There are even cases where the defendants have only learned of the charges against them when their trials began.

Courtrooms are in poor condition, often requiring judges to hold trials in their own offices, and they are in short supply. Facility limitations make it difficult for interested parties to observe. Public access to trial records is not guaranteed.

There is no separate juvenile system. Thus juvenile defendants are processed according to the same procedures under the same laws as are adults. During the investigation, a pedagogue's presence is mandatory, and at trial, the presence of a defense lawyer is supposed to be mandatory.

The presiding judge, with the aid of two "peoples' assessors" with unclear qualifications, determines guilt or innocence. Judges often favor even uncorroborated testimony from police, especially SCNS, and discount physical evidence that contradicts it. Judges mainly base their decisions upon prosecutorial arguments. Judges hesitate to independently pronounce judgments for fear that prosecutors will retaliate against them by charging them with corruption, accusing them under article 349 of the Criminal Code of knowingly rendering an illegal verdict. Prosecutors bring and win such cases.

The legal codes provide insufficient protection for defendants in the event of torture. Torture is still regularly used to determine guilt, despite rulings by both the Constitutional and Supreme Courts against doing so. Judges still base their decisions on confessions even when defendants withdraw them while alleging torture. According to the CAT, there is no legislation for effective, independent mechanisms that would enable torture victims to even complain and seek redress. As well, victims are denied the access to independent medical examinations. Worse, there is concern that recent amnesty laws have immunized perpetrators of torture and ill-treatment committed between 1995 and 1999, thereby entrenching impunity.

Like judges, witnesses fear prosecutors. They too may be prosecuted, and there is no witness protection system. Not surprisingly, acquittal rates are quite low. In 2005, only 1.7 percent of cases ended in acquittal.

Judges

Since the CoJ is responsible for selecting judges, a *collegium* composed solely of judges was established within it, and in 2003, the Training Centre for Judges was as well. According to Constitutional article 85, judges must be at least 25 years old and have at least three years of experience in the legal profession. At the Oblast level this is 30 years old and five years' experience, while at the Supreme Court level, judges must be at least 30 years old and have five years' experience. The age requirement is the same for Constitutional Court judges, but the experience requirement rises to 10 years.

Since Tajikistan's independence, the number of law faculties has grown to its current eight. In 2005, there were 286 judges total at the Oblast, Rayon, and City Court levels. Female and minority representation in the judiciary and legal profession apparently diminishes with the status level of the position. In 2005, of 334 judges, only 66 were women. While 30 percent of advocates were women, only 10 percent of prosecutors were. About 16 to 19 percent of advocates were ethnic minorities, while just 5 percent of prosecutors were.

The standards governing admittance into the legal profession are unclear, and there is need for a single, self-governed, independent body responsible for administering all issues related to the profession and its training and standards. There are currently three principal lawyers' organizations, or *collegia,* and there is concern that allowing the MoJ to retain licensing authority potentially threatens the profession's independence relative to executive power. The executive already exerts a good deal of authority over the removal of judges. The general prosecutor can initiate criminal investigations against judges and try them in the Supreme Court. The CoJ can propose the removal of a judge. The Qualification Collegium of the CoJ reviews it and submits its opinion to the president who then decides. The president also has constitutional authority to propose the removal of judges from the Constitutional, Supreme, and Higher Economic Courts. The National Assembly dominated by the president's party then removes the judges.

Punishment

Since independence, Tajikistan has had a secretive system of penal punishment to match its authoritarian criminal justice process. In particular, human rights organizations have criticized its use of the death penalty. Historically, officials have used it frequently, convicting defendants in the Supreme

Court or by secret trials that have been flagrantly unfair. The condemned have been executed in secret as well. The proceedings and executions have been so secretive that attorneys and family members have not known if and when the condemned had been executed or where their bodies have been discarded.

However, in 2004, the president declared a death penalty moratorium and signed it into law. This commuted previous sentences to 25 years' imprisonment. A year later, the Criminal Code was amended to establish life imprisonment as a death penalty alternative. As well, women and children who previously were eligible for execution may no longer even be subject to life imprisonment. In 2007, the International Helsinki Federation for Human Rights expressed its support for the moratorium. But it fears that given the historical treatment of anything related to the death penalty as a state secret and the nature of regional politics, if these reforms are not solidified into a total elimination of the death penalty option, changing political wills may simply overturn the moratorium.

Prison

In 2002, administrative authority for the prison system was successfully transferred from the MoI to the MoJ, in a move that international observers widely desired. However, the MoI still retains authority over pretrial detention facilities. The penal system includes 19 facilities. Six of these are pretrial facilities while 13 are prisons.

According to the World Prison Brief, the prisoner population was 7,350 in 2008, which gave the country an imprisonment rate of 109 per 100,000 civilians. Fifteen percent of these were pretrial/remand prisoners, while 4.9 percent were foreigners. Females comprise a small fraction of the prisoner population, just 1.6 percent in 2008.

There is no separate juvenile prison system. Human rights investigators report that authorities frequently detain children found on the streets, even if they have not committed a particular crime, and often detain them with adults rather than giving them some alternative placement. Police can use the Temporary Isolation Centre for children detained in Dushanbe.

Officially, the prison capacity is 11,950, with room for 2,500 and 9,450 pretrial/remand detainees and convicted prisoners, respectively. Officials therefore report that the system is at 44 percent and 66 percent capacity for its pretrial/remand and convict prisoner populations, respectively. This would leave the overall system at just 61.5 percent of its capacity. No outside investigators have corroborated this figure. Indeed, prison officials have been quite secretive, and according to the UN Special Rapporteur, the prisons remain inaccessible to independent monitoring. The International Committee of the Red Cross has not visited since 2007.

The CAT reports that the prisons suffer from poor conditions, particularly overcrowding, poor sanitation, staffing shortages, and a lack of medical attention. They also expressed concern about the high number of deaths in custody. Tajikistan's Center for Human Rights and the FH have both echoed this overall assessment.

The president signed an amnesty for prisoners who had been held on charges dating back to the civil war. Some 400 were released. But potentially severe sentences can keep prisons filled. For example, those convicted of sexual harassment may face two-year sentences. Those convicted of trafficking in persons could face from 5 to 15 years, while rape convicts may serve up to 20 years in prison. In 2008, officials accepted custody of a detainee transferred from America's Guantanamo camp, and more may follow. Such detainees may be expected to serve long sentences. Already, particularly long sentences have been meted out to women convicted of killing their partners, such as those imprisoned at the Nurek women's prison for terms of 7 to 20 years.

Paul Schupp

Further Reading

Conciliation Resources. *Key Elements of the Tajikistan Peace Agreement:* http://www.c-r.org/our-work/accord/tajikistan/key-elements.php.

Social Institutions and Gender Index (SIGI). Gender Equality and Social Institutions in Tajikistan: http://genderindex.org/country/tajikistan.

United Nations. Constitution of the Republic of Tajikistan. Dushanbe. (1994): http://unpan1.un.org/intradoc/groups/public/documents/untc/unpan003670.htm.

United Nations Development Fund for Women. Tajikistan: Women Demand Law to Criminalize Domestic Violence. (2008): http://www.unifem.org/gender_issues/voices_from_the_field/story.php?StoryID=366.

United Nations Development Programme. (2007). Annual Report. Tajikistan. Project on Promoting Transparency and Accountability: http://74.125.47.132/search?q=cache:luLab00PwpUJ:www.undp.tj/files/project_profiles/PTA%2520PHR/Annual%2520Project%2520report%2520PTA%2520–2007.doc+"Corruption+in+Tajikistan:+ Public+Opinion"&cd=5&hl=en&ct=clnk&gl=us.

Thailand

Legal System: Civil/Common
Murder: High
Corruption: Medium
Human Trafficking: Medium
Prison Rate: High
Death Penalty: Yes
Corporal Punishment: No

Background

The Kingdom of Thailand was established in the mid-14th century and was recognized as a nation in 1783. It is the only country in Southeast Asia that was never colonized by a European power. This fact is shown in the country name, Thailand, meaning the land of freedom. Thailand has a total area of 514,000 square kilometers (198,457 square miles), with a population of 65,493,296 (as of July 2008) and comprises 76 provinces. Thailand has a bicameral National Assembly, consisting of the Senate and the House of Representatives.

The judiciary and justice system in Thailand was created around the mid-1200s to mid-1300s by King Ramkhamhaeang the Great during the Sukhothai Period (1238–1350). The period for the emergence of the modern judiciary and legal system in Thailand was between 1868 and 1910. It was during this period and under the reign of King Chulalongkorn the Great (1853–1910) that the Ministry of Justice was established. Because of historical antecedents of the Thai justice system, the modern Thai legal system is a mixture of both the civil and common law elements. Two European colonial powers (England, the representative of common law, and France, the representative of civil law) asserted their influence over Thailand, since to maintain its independence, Thailand had to allow the European legal system to be established for a certain period of time that had a jurisdiction for all legal cases that involved a European person. Because of this practice, Thailand later adopted and embraced both legal systems, resulting in the modernization or Westernization of Thailand at the turn of the 20th century. However, the processes of adjudication follow the civil law tradition, which is an inquisitorial system. Judges in Thailand take a position to question involved parties as well as advising lawyers and witnesses. The biggest change in the Thai legal system in the late 20th century was the enactment of a new constitution in 1997. This new constitution set the framework of laws and administrative procedures. Among other goals, it protects individual liberties, restricts the power exercised by state officers against individual rights, and advocates an independent judiciary. Many procedures in criminal law have been altered. For example, the 1997 Constitution decreases the time period of booking and detention during the arrest and investigation processes by the police from 7 days for serious crimes to 72 hours. It also transfers the authority to issue an arrest warrant and search warrant from the police authority to magistrates or judges.

Police

The Royal Thai Police is a centralized police system. All of the police personnel are sworn officers, which number approximately 240,000. The police-population ratio is about 1 to 260. All police officers in Thailand are under the command of the commissioner general of the Royal Thai Police. According to the Criminal Procedure Code, the police in Thailand are the primary mechanism for conducting criminal investigations. The Royal Thai Police is a militaristic-style, service-oriented police organization and is divided into three main components: general-staff units, operation units, and support units. The general-staff units are responsible for collecting information, filtering materials submitted to management, planning, and giving support and advice to high-ranking officers. All of the general staff-units are located in Bangkok, the capital of Thailand, including the finance division, police aviation division, traffic, and civil service planning division, among others.

Royal Thai Police dressed in riot gear prepare for an antigovernment demonstration on March 13, 2010. (Dreamstime)

The operation units are the main groups that are generally responsible for crime prevention and suppression. These units consist of various bureaus located throughout the country, including a total of 1,500 police stations in Thailand. The responsibilities of these units are making arrests and investigating criminal cases, maintaining public order, controlling traffic, and maintaining security along the border areas, enforcing drug laws, acquiring and managing intelligence concerning national security, providing security for His Majesty the king and the royal family. The bureaus in the operation units include Metropolitan Police Bureau, the Provincial Police Regions 1 to 9, Border Patrol Police, Narcotics Suppression Bureau, Special, Police Immigration Bureau, and Office of the Royal Court Security Police. Lastly, the support units are in charge of promoting and supporting police work in the areas of education, training, medical services, and scientific functions. The Police Cadet Academy, Office of Forensic Science, Office of Information and Communication Technology, and Office of Surgeon-General are all part of the support units.

Crime

Classification of Crimes

The criminal code of Thailand does not clearly classify criminal behaviors into types of offenses. It only defines petty offenses to cover any illegal act punishable by a jail time of no more than one month and/or a fine of no more than 1,000 baht (about US$32). Felonies then refer to criminal acts, which are not included in petty offenses. The criminal code stipulates five penalties for violating the code: death penalty, imprisonment, detention, fines, and forfeiture of property to the state.

Based on Thailand's criminal code, there are 12 groups of offenses that can be considered as felonies.

1. Crimes against the security of the kingdom, including crimes against the royal family, treason, espionage, acts that damage friendly relationships with foreign countries, and acts of terrorism (which were added into the criminal code in 2003).
2. Crimes relating to public administration (offenses against public officials and official misconducts).
3. Crimes relating to justice (perjury, offenses against the police and the judiciary and their orders, destruction of evidence, and misconducts of the judiciary and the persons who carry their orders).
4. Crimes against Buddhism.
5. Crimes against public order and safety including gang-related activities.
6. Acts against public order and safety (e.g., arson and acts to sabotage public transportation).
7. Offenses of counterfeiting money, seals, and other documents.
8. Crimes against trade (using false weights and measures, distorting information about goods on sale, and violating trademarks).
9. Sexual offenses, including procuring business and pornography.
10. Crimes against the person, including abortion and neglect of child and elderly person.
11. Crimes against liberty and reputation (e.g., criminal threatening, kidnapping, libel, and illegally disclosing information by public officials).
12. Crimes against property.

Petty offenses in the criminal code of Thailand cover a wide range of violations classified as misdemeanors. These offenses include the following:

1. Refusal to disclose a real name and address or falsely give a wrong one to an official.
2. Refusal to follow an order of an authorized official.
3. Damaging any sign or announcement posted by an authorized official.
4. Carrying weapon openly to a village, city, or public pathway.
5. Creating loud noise that is threatening or disturbing public.
6. Fighting in public and disturbing the community.
7. Shooting a gun that uses gun powder in public.
8. Showing or drawing a weapon during a fight.
9. Drunk in public.
10. Inflicting a cruel killing upon or torturing an animal.
11. Public nudity.
12. Carelessly causing an injury to a person without any intention.
13. Assault resulting in minor injury.
14. Disposing a body of dead animal, which may cause disturbing smell on a pathway.
15. Torturing a child under 15 of age or elderly person whose life depends on the person who commits the offense.

Children under 7 years of age are not subject to criminal penalties. Children between ages 7 and 14 may not be punished, but judges may give instructions or require their parents to come to the court to ensure that there will be no repeated violations. The court may then send the child to a vocational training school, release on probation, or restrict the child to his or her home. When juveniles older than 14 but not older than 17 years of age commit delinquency, judges may give a sentence in one-half of the penalties of fines or a period of confinement prescribed by the code. Finally, judges may give a sentence in one-half or two-thirds of the penalties for the offenses committed by juveniles older than 17 but not older than 20 years of age.

Challenging Crime Problems

Although various crime problems plague the country, the two major problems are drug use and human trafficking. According to Thai laws, narcotics are illegal substances. However, reliable information about the use of the substances in Thailand is not available because very few large-scale studies on this matter have been conducted. Most studies surveyed students to learn about their drug use.

It was estimated that the number of drug users in Thailand was 450,000 in 1980, according to an East-West Center working paper, and it had risen to 3 million in 2002. Methamphetamine (as opposed to heroin, opium, and marijuana) is their primary substance of consumption. One survey estimated that 29 percent of 1,736 students in the sample of a Thai vocational school reported having used methamphetamines. Glue and other solvents have recently gained popularity among children in the country. Thailand's drug problem among adolescents and children is considered a serious issue and could definitely stymie the development of the country.

The International Labor Organization, a specialized agency of the United Nations, estimated that 12.3 million people are in forced labor, bonded labor, forced child labor, and sexual servitude at any given time around the world. Although Thailand's effort to suppress human trafficking is ranked favorably, it still needs to address this issue more effectively. One obvious indication of the problem is the presence of more than 20 UN agencies and nongovernmental organizations in Bangkok dealing with matters of human trafficking. Thailand is located in the center of many other developing countries, such as Myanmar, Cambodia, Laos, and China. Therefore, its suitable location has been used as a transit point in trafficking men, women, and children for sexual exploitation and forced labor. Thai and hill tribe women and girls along the Thai border are sexually exploited both domestically and internationally. Organized crime groups use Thailand as a transient place for transferring women and girls to other foreign destinations, including Bahrain, Canada, Europe, Japan, Malaysia, Middle East, Singapore, South Africa, and the United States. Many types of businesses use women and girls to sell sex, such as bars, karaoke, strip shows, and sex-massage.

The main reason driving the flow of human trafficking in and to Thailand is the economic disparities. Boys and young men, many from Myanmar and Cambodia, are the main sources for labor work in begging gangs. Many young men and women from Myanmar, Laos, and Cambodia migrating illegally to Thailand have been exploited as they are drawn into many small-sized businesses, such as small labor factories, as well as for household work.

Currently, the Thai government responds to the problems by setting its priority to safeguard the welfare of Thai women and children. In 1996, the criminal law was amended to increase penalty for a person engaging in sexual activities with a minor. The law also aims to control the sexual exploitation of minors by criminalizing people involved in a sex trade, such as customers, procurers, pimps, owners, and operators of brothels. Moreover, the law also targets the parents who sell their children to profiteers. The problem of human trafficking for labor exploitation in Thailand, however, still does not receive much attention from the government, as well as law enforcement agencies. Labor exploitation in Thailand has been found mostly in fisheries and the seafood and garment industries. The main reasons law enforcement agencies are lethargic in addressing these issues are the lack of understanding of the problems and the lack of collaboration and coordination between and among the agencies involved. Several interventions are suggested to better address these issues, including providing proper police investigative training and more coordination between criminal justice agencies and other stakeholders, supporting and protecting the survivors to bring their cases to the courts, and amending laws to focus more on comprehensive trafficking.

Drug Offenses

The Narcotics Act of Thailand enacted in 1979 criminalizes the production, importation, exportation, disposing, or possession of narcotics unless a license is obtained from a licensing authority. Another law involving narcotics is the Psychotropic Substances Act 1975. This law intends to control the psychotropic substances, including gamma hydroxybutyrate (GHB), ephedrine, ketamine, dormicum, phenyl cyclohexyl piperidine, psilocybine, psilocine, and amineptine. It is illegal to possess or consume these substances without a license or prescription. Finally, the Emergency Decree on Prevention against Abuse /Using of Volatile Substances 1990 was promulgated to prevent the use of volatile substances, an increasing problem among teenagers. The volatile substances controlled by this law are thinners, lacquers, and synthetic or organic adhesive. However, the law does not prohibit the possession of volatile substances because they are still used in many legitimate activities, such as painting and construction.

Crime Statistics

The statistics of crime cases recorded by the Royal Thai Police for 2006 were as follows:

Murder	4,687
Nonnegligent manslaughter	336
Negligent manslaughter	277
Rape	5,308
Robbery	1,244
Extortion	246
Drug offense	110,904

The crime rates of violent crimes were 14 per 100,000 population. Crimes against persons and crimes against property were 69.74 and 123.17, respectively. The rates were calculated based on the country's population of 62,418,054.

The most typical crimes in the rural areas of Thailand are the stealing of agricultural tools and equipments as well as animals used for agriculture (e.g., cows, water buffalos, tractors, and irrigation pumps). Statistics in 2006 show that the majority (47.7%) of the stealing of agricultural tools and equipments occurred in Provincial Police Region 6, which covers provinces in the lower northern part of Thailand, while these types of crimes did not happen at all in a big city like Bangkok. In the same year, cases of stealing of animals used for agriculture were highest in Provincial Police Region 5, the upper northern part of the country; similar cases did not occur at all in Bangkok that year.

For the urban areas, common crimes are drug abuse and trafficking, prostitution, and possession or distribution of pornographic materials. In 2006, more than a quarter (28.9%) of the arrests of all drug offenses took place in Bangkok. In the same year, 83 percent of all arrests made under the auspices of the Prevention and Suppression of Prostitution Act occurred in Bangkok, while the number of arrests involving pornography taking place in Bangkok was 53.5 percent of all arrests.

Finding of Guilt

Rights of the Accused

The Thai Constitution guarantees to the accused the presumption of innocence and the right to defend himself or herself, including the right to have a counsel and other standard treatment of human rights protection. No judgment of conviction shall be delivered unless and until the court is fully satisfied that an offense has actually been perpetrated and that the accused has committed that offense. In case of doubt, the benefit will be granted to the accused.

In criminal justice procedure, a person shall have the right to an uncomplicated, convenient, quick, thorough access to justice procedure. Basic rights in judicial process must at least guarantee an open court hearing; right to factual information and sufficient cross-examination of documents; right to present facts, witness, or evidence, and express his or her dissent or disagreement with judges or arbitrators; right to require full quorum of judges or arbitrators in the hearing of his or her case; and right to hear the clarification of court decision, judgment, or order. Children, youths, women, and disabled persons are eligible for special protection during judicial procedure.

The Thai Criminal Procedure Code (CPC) also empowers the court to declare evidence obtained through illegal means (the exclusionary rule) inadmissible at trial. However, in practice, this rule is seldom applied by the court because the law of search and seizure gives the police so much power that almost all searches and seizures are deemed legal.

Legal Assistance for the Accused

The Constitution of Thailand and the CPC guarantee the right of the accused to counsel during pretrial stages, as well as during the preliminary hearing and trial. The laws stipulate that the court appoint a lawyer for the accused who does not otherwise obtain one and faces a possible prison term.

A court-appointed lawyer is granted to criminal defendants to prevent oppression by both private and public prosecutors. The defendants, however, have a right to proceed without counsel when they choose to do so, and a judge may not force a lawyer upon them if they insist on conducting their own defense. The court will pay a fee, specified by the Regulation of the Ministry of Justice, to court-appointed lawyers.

In August 2006, the Ministry of Justice established a "justice fund" to facilitate legal advice and a lawyer, out-of-court settlement, and other legal expenditures to defendants who are innocent and unable to bear legal expenditures. Eligibility to receive a justice fund depends on the financial means of the individual and the merit of the case being defended.

In addition to legal assistance provided by the government, several private institutions such as the Institute of Legal Education, Thai Bar Association, Office of the Attorney General, the Law Society of Thailand, and the Legal Clinic of Thammasat University also offer legal assistance to the criminal defendant.

Investigation and Prosecution

According to the Thai CPC, criminal investigation rests solely on the responsibility of the police, who play the role of "inquiry officials." The court has no role in the fact-finding process both during pretrial and throughout the trial period. Thai laws do not empower public prosecutors to initiate investigations nor institute the case themselves. The prosecutors begin their role after receiving investigation files from the police. After reviewing the file and the police recommendation on whether the case should be prosecuted, prosecutors may decide to prosecute the case and file the charge directly to the Criminal Court of First Instance. The fact that prosecutors do not take part in the investigation process at the beginning causes the problems of check and balance of powers and distortion of evidence and witness. Several cases of wrongful convictions have been found due to the unjust fact-finding process by the police.

Alternatives to Going to Trial

As a viable alternative to the formal criminal justice process, the Thai justice system has recently adopted a restorative justice initiative aiming to reduce not only the heavy court workload but also prison overcrowding. The restorative juvenile justice initiative, also known as the Family and Community Group Conferencing (FCGC) initiative, occurred in 2004 because of Section 63 of the Act for the Establishment of and Procedure for Juvenile and Family Court 1991 that allows public prosecutors to use their discretion to drop charges and refer cases for a restorative process.

The FCGC is a restorative justice process that aims to repair harm. The FCGC allows young offenders to talk about their offenses and show their remorse for committing the crime harming the victim. Family members participate in the process of deciding an appropriate response to their juvenile's offending behavior. In addition, the FCGC provides a crime victim the opportunity to be a part of the process in dealing with the offense. Victims and young offenders determine a mutually acceptable response to repair the material, psychological, and social damages caused by the crime. The community also has an opportunity to take part in the process to support the child and parents and to bring the child back to the community. To be eligible to participate in the FCGC process, juveniles must meet these four criteria: (1) the penalty for the offense must be less than five years' imprisonment; (2) the child must be a first-time offender; (3) the child must admit responsibility for the offense and show his or her intention to repair the harm; and (4) the victim must give consent to use the FCGC approach.

Outcomes of Criminal Cases

In general, conviction rates are very high in Courts of First Instance. Acquittal rates are about only 2 to 3 percent. At the appellate levels, conviction rates are much lower. Based on statistics in the 1990s, criminal cases submitted to the Courts of Appeal resulted in approximately 55 percent conviction versus 45 percent acquittal rate. In the Supreme Court, conviction rates were even slightly lower than those decided in the Courts of Appeal. The same statistics also reported types of punishment the convicted offenders received. It showed that of all the offenders convicted, about 58 percent were fined, 30 percent had their punishment suspended, and 10 percent received imprisonment between one month and three years.

Incarceration before Trial

Thai law allows incarceration before or when an accused is awaiting trail. The law requires the police take the arrestee to the police station immediately after arrest. The police can keep the arrestee no more than 48 hours from the time of his or her arrival at the police station, with extensions of up to three days permitted. If the inquiry is not complete and a longer detention period is necessary, the police must bring the alleged offender to the court and submit a motion for a detention warrant. The court can grant a remand to detain the alleged offenders for additional periods (up to a maximum of 82 days for serious offenses).

The Courts of Justice and Judges

Compared to other criminal justice agencies in Thailand, the Courts of Justices has been viewed as the most honorable and most trustworthy agency in the eyes of the public. The Courts of Justice in Thailand is divided into three tiers: (1) the Courts of First Instance; (2) the Appellate Courts; and (3) the Supreme Court. For adjudication, Courts of Justice have power to hear and adjudicate cases relating to criminal, civil, bankruptcy matters, including all other cases that are outside the jurisdiction of other types of courts. When a jurisdictional problem arises, the Commission on Jurisdiction of Courts chaired by the president of the Supreme Court will decide the outcome.

The Courts of First Instance are divided into general courts, juvenile and family courts, and specialized courts. The General Courts are ordinary courts with the authority to try and adjudicate both criminal and civil cases. Some of the general courts are civil court, criminal court, provincial courts, and municipal court. The Juvenile and Family Courts are set up separately and are explained later. The Special Courts (including the labor court, the tax court, the intellectual property and international trade court, and the bankruptcy court) deal with other criminal and civil issues.

The appellate courts comprise the Court of Appeal and nine Regional Courts of Appeal. Each of the Courts of Appeal hears an appeal against the judgment of the lower criminal and civil courts. The Supreme Court is the highest and final court of appeal whose jurisdiction covers all civil and criminal cases. The Court's members are president, vice presidents, the secretary, and a number of justices. The president of the Supreme Court also acts as the chief of the Courts of Justice. The Supreme Court judges are appointed from the appellate court judges with qualified experience, knowledge, and seniority. Generally, like the appellate courts, at least three judges of the Supreme Court are required to form a quorum.

In Thailand, judges are professionals like police officers and prosecutors. There are four types of judges: career judge, senior judge, associate judge, and *Datoh Yutithum* (or *Kadis*). For a person to serve as a career judge, one must be a Thai citizen who is at least 25 years old with more than two-years' working experience in a legal professional career and who passes both a Thai Bar Association examination and a competitive examination given by the Judicial Commission. After passing this competitive recruitment process, the applicants are required to be a judge trainee for one year before the Judicial Commission renders its approval and officially defers to His Majesty the King for royal appointment.

Lay judges or associate judges are ordinary citizens who are selected for their knowledge and expertise in a special field so that they can assist a career judge in adjudicating cases. Courts that need the presence of lay judges include the Juvenile and Family Courts, the Labor Court, or the Intellectual Property and International Trade Court. There also are different qualifications for lay judges. For instance, lay judges are a temporary position, and they will get appointed in a position for a term of a certain number of years depending upon which specialized court they are in.

Datoh Yutithum (or Kadis or Islamic judge) is a special type of judge serving jurisdictions in the four southern provinces of Thailand (Pattani, Narathiwat, Yala, and Satun). In accordance with the Act on the Application of Islamic Law in the Territorial Jurisdictions of Pattani, Narathiwat, Yala, and Satun Provinces, the Islamic Law on Family and Succession shall supplant the Civil and Commercial Code in rendering judgment in civil cases regarding family and succession of Muslims. In such cases where both parties are Muslims, a Kadi (who is an expert in Islam) is required to help a career judge adjudicate the case. A Kadi must be at least 30 years old, proficient in the Thai language at the prescribed level, and conversant with the Islamic laws relating to family and succession. As of April 2007, there were 3,805 judges in Thailand, comprising 3,332 judges, 246 assistant judges, and 227 senior judges.

Juvenile Justice System

Thailand uses the Act for Establishment of and Procedure for Juvenile and Family Court of 1991 to regulate all the juvenile cases and family affair issues. For the age of criminal responsibility, a child younger than 7 years of age is not to be punished for committing an illegal act. The act divides the juvenile's age into two groups. The first group is a child whose age is between 7 and 14 years old. The child may be exempted from penalty with certain conditions imposed by the court. The second group is a young teen whose age is between 14 and 18 years old. The jurisdiction of the juvenile court is, therefore, over the juvenile offender whose age does not exceed 18 years.

Under the act, the rights of juveniles are protected throughout the juvenile justice process. When a child is taken into custody, the police are required to immediately notify the director of the Observation and Protection Center (OPC) and parents, as well as guardians or the person with whom the child lives. The police must complete the initial inquiry within 24 hours and then send the child to the OPC. After the OPC receives the juvenile, the OPC's director can decide whether to detain the juvenile at the center until adjudication or to release the juvenile to his or her parents or guardian with or without bail.

At the OPC, the probation officer assigned to a case must gather information about the case by interviewing with the child and his or her parents, as well as his or her schoolteachers. To protect the child, the law requires the presence of a counselor, a public prosecutor, a psychologist or social worker, and parents during this administrative procedure. After finishing the investigation, the probation officer must submit a case report to the public prosecutor for adjudication consideration.

The law empowers the prosecutor to use discretion to either adjudicate or drop charges based on information in the investigation report and the recommendation given by the director of the OPC, which is a unique characteristic of the juvenile justice system.

The law also protects the child during the adjudicatory hearing. The hearing must be closed to the public, and only the witnesses and relevant persons involved with the case are allowed to be present. The photo or personal data of the juvenile are strictly confidential and are unavailable to the public. The hearing must be carried out in a simple way that is easy for the juvenile to comprehend.

The judge panel consists of two career judges and two associate judges whose backgrounds and experience are related to young people and family affairs with the condition that one of the associate judges must be a female. If the juvenile is found to be delinquent, the court may choose one of the following: (1) placing in a detention center or a commitment program or a psychological counseling center until a time before the juvenile becomes 24 years old; (2) probation under certain conditions as an alternative to paying a fine; or (3) suspending the punishment for a certain period of time.

Even if the judges found the child to be nondelinquent, for the juvenile's best interest, the act stipulates that the judges may still put the juvenile on probation under certain conditions. The Ministry of Justice appoints the OPC's director who reports to the chief judge of the Juvenile Court.

Punishment

Types of Punishment

The death penalty is the most severe type of punishment and is reserved for the most heinous crime. The current method of execution is lethal injection. In practice, only a small number of prisoners have been executed. The statistics from the Department of Corrections revealed that 48 prisoners were executed in Thailand from 1990 to 2006. The majority of the prisoners who received the death sentence have had their sentences converted to life imprisonment.

Imprisonment is the most common form of punishment in Thailand. The lengths of imprisonment range from a minimum of one day to a life term. As stated by Thai law, a term of imprisonment is a determinate sentence, which means that the convicted offender must serve the full sentence handed down by the court.

Confinement is a less severe type of punishment than imprisonment and death sentence. The sentence to confinement is usually given to those who committed petty offenses and to those offenders who failed to pay fines.

Fine is another type of sentence applicable to petty crimes. When offenders are ordered to pay a certain amount of money to the authority for their crimes and fail to do so, the court can convert a fine to confinement.

Forfeiture of property is the last form of punishment. The court may issue an order to forfeit any items, weapons, and assets that the offenders used to commit an offense or acquired as a result of crime.

The Typical Punishment for Murder

Penalties for murder include death penalty, lifetime imprisonment, or incarceration between 15 to 20 years. In deciding which type of punishment to sentence, the court usually takes into consideration the surrounding circumstances and other aggravating factors such as defendant's intention, murder victim, and murder method.

The Typical Punishment for Rape

According to the Penal Code of Thailand, penalties for rape are death penalty, lifetime imprisonment, or incarceration between 4 and 20 years, and fines ranging from 8000 baht (about US$250) to 40,000 baht (about US$1,250), depending upon the surrounding circumstances and other factors such as defendant's intention, victim's relationship with the offender, or the method used to commit rape. If the rape victim is dead, the offender is subject to death penalty or life imprisonment.

The Typical Punishment for Serious Robbery

The law stipulates that every person who shall commit (1) robbery by the use of a dangerous weapon, (2) robbery where a victim is injured, or (3) robbery where the victim is a person who is severely impaired or an elderly person shall be guilty of first-degree robbery and shall be imprisoned from 5 to 10 years, or may be imprisoned for life, or fined not more than 20,000 baht (about US$625). The punishment, however, can be more severe under various aggravating circumstances.

The Typical Punishment for the Most Serious Drug Offense

The penalties for drug offenses vary considerably, ranging from diversion to death penalty. Thailand's narcotic act classifies drugs into five categories. Those who were found to be in possession of the most dangerous category of drugs, including no less than 20 grams of heroin, amphetamine, methamphetamine, Ecstasy or LSD, are subject to 1 to 10 years in prison and fined large amounts of money. The most severe penalty for heroin and methamphetamine traffickers is capital punishment, which is imposed as a deterrence mechanism. For instance, on March 31, 2000, the criminal court sentenced two men to death when they were found guilty of possessing 470,000 methamphetamine tablets with intent to supply. The government also passed the Narcotics Addict Rehabilitation Act of 2002 aiming to divert from the criminal justice system drug addicts, drug users, and those who support their habits by selling small amounts of drugs. Under this new law, drug users are considered as "patients" in need of rehabilitation rather than criminals and will receive treatment instead of prosecution. To be eligible for treatment, the drug users must be involved in a small amount of drugs either as users, sellers, or in possession.

Death Penalty

After an eight-year moratorium of the death penalty in 1995, the Department of Corrections has resumed executions. Surveys of the public's attitudes toward the death penalty indicated that 90 percent of Thai citizens still favor the death penalty and consider the death penalty not only as a necessary and effective tool for dealing with the high rates of serious crimes, but as a deterrence mechanism. Under the Thai Criminal Code, the death penalty is mandatory for felony offenses such as murder or attempted murder of any member of the royal family or for any offense likely to endanger the life of a king, murder of a public official or anyone assisting a public official in performing his or her duty, murder committed in perpetrating another offense or in an attempt to escape punishment, matricide or patricide, premeditated murder, or murder by torture. However, it cannot be imposed on juveniles under the age of 18 or women who are pregnant when on trial.

The number of executions has been relatively low for several reasons. First, the Thai Criminal Code assures a convicted prisoner the right to appeal to the appellate courts. Second, every convicted prisoner has the right to petition to the king for individual royal pardon, as well as collective royal pardon on special national anniversaries. If collective royal pardon is granted, the death sentence shall be reduced to life imprisonment. Therefore, in practice, only a small number of executions have been carried out. From 2001 to 2006, there were only 26 executions, compared to 58 executions in the 1970s, 53 executions in the 1980s, and 21 executions in the 1990s.

The Department of Corrections has changed the methods of execution several times. Prior to 1934, beheading the death row inmates was the method of choice. Later, from 1934 to October 2001, as a result of the amendment of the Thai Criminal Code, any prisoners sentenced to death were to be shot to death by a firing squad. From October 19, 2001, to present, the Department of Corrections has replaced the firing squad with lethal injection. The first executions in Thailand by lethal injection took place on December 12, 2003. This involved three male prisoners who had been convicted of drug offenses and murder. As of July 31, 2007, there have been no further executions.

Prison

According to the Department of Corrections 2007 statistics, there have been significant changes in the prison population in Thailand over the last decade. In 1997, the inmate population was 125,870, and it had climbed up to 244,240 in 2001 and reached the highest level of 245,801 in 2002. The number of inmates then started to descend sharply and went down to 151,586 in 2006. The rapid increase of prison population during the late 1990s was mainly attributed to the Thai government's war on drug policy that resulted in a considerable number of drug-related offenders going into prison. Later, the government enacted the Narcotic Addict Rehabilitation Act of 2002, with the main purpose to diverting drug offenders (i.e., drug users) from the criminal justice system into treatment programs, thus reducing the prison population, as well as the courts' caseload. In 2004, the government also declared the Royal Pardon Decree to commemorate the Queen's Sixth Cycle Birthday, resulting in many of prisoners' receiving shorter sentence terms or being released.

In 2004, there were 11,288 correctional officers (9,240 males and 2,048 females). Among all officers, 570 (5%) work at the headquarters, while the other 10,460 officers (95%) perform their work in prison facilities. The prisons have a normal capacity for housing about 105,748 inmates, which indicates a long-time problem of prison overcrowding. The ratio between the number of correctional personnel and inmates is about 1 to 12 in 1997, 1 to 22 in 2002, and 1 to 13 in 2006.

As of 2007, there were 140 prisons throughout Thailand under the supervision of the Thai Department of Corrections, including 26 central prisons, 4 remand prisons, 24 correctional institutions, 55 provincial prisons, 27 district prisons, 2 houses of confinement, 1 house of relegation, and 1 medical prison. Central prisons are responsible for housing convicted prisoners whose prison terms are between 10 years and 30 years. Bangkwang Central Prison, located in a small suburb north of Bangkok called Nonthaburi, is the only maximum-security prison in Thailand that houses death row inmates, lifers, and those with more than 30-year sentences. Because of its classification, Bangkwang Central Prison is the biggest prison for high-sentenced and dangerous prisoners and is the most well-known in Thailand. In terms of size, Klong Prem Prison, which is also located in Bangkok, is the biggest one.

Remand prisons are used to detain offenders during their trial period. Upon conviction, the convicted offenders will be transferred to central prisons based on the type of sentences. At present, Thailand has three remand prisons (Bangkok Remand Prison, Thonburi Remand Prison, and Minburi Remand Prison), and one remand prison located in Chonburi Province (Pattaya Remand Prison).

Correctional institutions have been built to house and provide suitable treatment for particular groups of inmates, including young offenders, women, drug addicts, and the open institutions. As of 2007, a total of 24 correctional institutions were in operation, which included 4 correctional institutions for young male offenders, 6 women's correctional institutions, 7 correctional institutions for drug addicted offenders, and 7 open correctional institutions.

Provincial prisons and district prisons are responsible for detaining offenders who are awaiting trial, including convicted offenders with less than 10 years of imprisonment. Provincial prisons are found in all the provinces that have a criminal court, but district prisons serve a criminal court only in major districts.

A House of Confinement accommodates offenders with the sentence to confinement and those who failed to pay fines. A House of Relegation is the institution that keeps habitual offenders whom the court believed are less likely to be rehabilitated. The courts also may choose to confine the offenders for a certain length of time as a security measure as stipulated in the Penal Code.

The medical prison was built to provide health care for ill prisoners who require long-term treatment, and it is the only medical detention facility located in Bangkok with a capacity of 350 beds. Each correctional facility, however, can provide necessary medical assistance to its inmates with minor illness. For inmates with serious illness, the corrections agency can transfer those inmates to the medical prison in Bangkok or a nearby hospital.

All inmates have to work while serving time in a correctional facility. In addition, article 51 requires that the correctional institution provide inmates aged under 25 years old with appropriate education and vocational training and order awaiting-trial offenders to work for the institution for prison hygiene and sanitation purposes.

Regarding education and vocational training in prisons, the Department of Corrections has launched an adult education school in every prison as part of its rehabilitation program effort. Inmates have access to various kinds of education (including religious courses) and vocational training that will help to equip them with sufficient knowledge, as well as essential skills needed after their release. In collaboration with the Department of Non-Formal Education, the various courses offered in prison schools are certified and accredited by the Ministry of Education. Inmates who passed these courses receive a certificate, which can be used to apply for a job after release. The prison administration accommodates inmates' religious needs through course offerings in Buddhism, Islam, and Christianity.

The Department of Corrections receives support and cooperation from private and public agencies in teaching inmates needed skills for today's market. The emphasis is to enable inmates to open their own business upon release. After completing these courses, inmates receive a certificate issued by the

Ministry of Education. Every year, the Department of Corrections holds the Annual Prison Products Exhibition in Bangkok, where products derived from vocational training programs in prison will be for sale. Thai prison products are also currently sold online under the "e-prison product" through the Department of Corrections Web site. About 50 percent of the net profits from product sales go to inmates.

For visitation, the corrections facility usually allows inmates to have a visit during office hours on weekdays at least once a week. There is a limit of 30 minutes per visit, but it does not limit the number of visitors. The visiting room has the iron bar barrier with 1-meter distance between inmates and visitors. During the visit, the law allows correctional officers to hear their conversations, patrol around visiting areas, search visitors, and terminate the visit if necessary. Inmates are allowed to receive permitted items from visitors, except for cash, which needs to be deposited in the inmate's account.

In addition to general visitation mentioned above, the prisoners who are classified as good class or higher are entitled to have a contact visit twice a year. As the Department of Corrections values the importance of family bonding and close ties among family members, it allows inmates to have family contact visits and conjugal visits. The conjugal visit policy has been implemented since 1993. In 2004, 781 inmates received conjugal visits in 13 open correctional facilities throughout the country. For family visits, a group of no more than five persons is allowed to enter the prison and stay in the designated areas with an inmate. During this special two-hour family visit, the inmate can talk freely and have a meal with his or her family members.

Prison privileges are also available to inmates based on their behavior, which is classified according to six different categories: excellent, very good, good, fair, bad, and very bad. Upon conviction, inmates will be classified as fair, but they will be classified as bad if they have a prior conviction history in the past five years. Privileges include promotion to a higher classification, being appointed as a trustee, receiving a furlough, being considered for parole, receiving good conduct allowance, and being sent to engage in public work outside the prison and earn sentence remission.

Thanks to Resolution 13 adopted by the United Nations Congress on the Prevention of Crime and the Treatment of Offenders, held in Caracas, Venezuela, in 1980, Thailand has been part of an international agreement of transferring and exchanging of inmates with 24 countries. The objective of the bilateral treaties is to facilitate the transferring of qualified foreign or Thai nationals committing crimes in foreign countries to return and serve the remaining sentences in their own countries. These 24 countries are France, Spain, Canada, Italy, the United States, Sweden, the United Kingdom and Northern Ireland, Finland, Germany, Portugal, Austria, Israel, Poland, Denmark, Hong Kong, Switzerland, Norway, Philippines, Estonia, Czech Republic, Australia, Nigeria, Netherlands, and Mali. As of 2006, Thailand has transferred 726 foreign nationals back to their respective countries, and 8 Thai nationals have been transferred from other countries to Thailand.

Unisa Lerdtomornsakul, Prapon Sahapattana, and Sutham Cheurprakobkit

Further Reading

Kittayarak, Kittipong. (2003). The Thai Constitution of 1997 and Its Implication on Criminal Justice Reform. Asia and Fareast Institute for the Prevention of Crime and the Treatment of Offenders Web site: http://www.unafei.or.jp/pdf/no60/ch06.pdf.

Naigowit, Prapan. Criminal Justice in Thailand: http://www.iap.nl.com/speeches_asia_conference_2003/criminal-justice-inthailand-by-prapun-naigowit.html.

Royal Thai Police. Office of Information and Communication Technology: http://www.royalthaipolice.go.th/.

Sungkawan, Decha. Thai Community-based Correctional Programmes for Narcotics Addicts in Response to the 2002 Rehabilitation Act: A System Approach: http://www.unafei.or.jp/english/pdf/PDF_rms/no64/ch08.pdf.

Suriyawong, Vitaya. Thai Correctional System Profile: http://www.acpf.org/Asia/Thailand/CorrectionThaiVitaya(E).html.

Timor-Leste

Legal System: Civil/Customary/Islamic
Corruption: High
Human Trafficking: Medium
Prison Rate: Low
Death Penalty: No
Corporal Punishment: No

Background

Timor-Leste (East Timor) is located to the north of Australia. Inhabited by peoples from Melanesia and continental Asia, the island of Timor became a Portuguese colony in 1702. For many decades, Portugal's position with regard to Timor-Leste was one of "benign neglect" and the vast majority of Timorese were relatively untouched by colonial powers, continuing to live without basic services under traditional rulers in mountain communities.

In 1974, following a coup in Portugal, the Portuguese government began an immediate process of decolonization, leaving a power vacuum in Timor-Leste. Three principal parties—Fretilin (Front for an Independent East Timor), UDT (Timorese Democratic Union), and Apodeti (Timorese Popular Democratic Association)—developed and following a short civil war, Fretilin emerged as the leading party. The ensuing period of "peace" was short-lived. For various reasons—including local oil reserves, an ideological commitment to fight supposed communists, and a political demand to retain control over islands in the region—Indonesian officials began a campaign of destabilization. Fretilin leaders declared the independence of Timor-Leste at the United Nations on November 28, 1975. Nine days later, the Indonesian government launched an attack. The subsequent occupation lasted almost 25 years.

Following years of resistance to this occupation, Timor-Leste finally garnered international attention in the 1990s. The Santa Cruz massacre of November 12, 1991, presented a significant shift, with smuggled footage of the Indonesian shooting and beating to death of about 270 people in a Dili cemetery broadcast to the world. From this time, the campaign for self-determination in Timor-Leste gained a momentum that eventually could not be stopped by the Indonesian government. On January 27, 1999, it announced that the Timorese people could choose between autonomy or independence in a referendum. Despite increased violence against the Timorese population, to "encourage" votes in support of Indonesia, 78.5 percent voted for independence on August 30, 1999.

Crimes during Occupation

The Commission for Reception, Truth and Reconciliation estimates that up to 183,000 people were killed during occupation. Timorese people died in massacres, bombing raids, and killing sprees as well as in strategic military operations wherein civilians were used as human shields against Fretilin resisters. Thousands were forcibly displaced from their homes and land and slowly starved to death in so-called resettlement camps, and individuals thought to be sympathetic to Fretilin and their military wing, Falintil, were similarly exiled on the island of Ataúro, where they suffered illness and starvation. Alongside these killings, Timorese people were routinely raped, tortured, ill treated, and detained without trial.

The criminal justice system was an integral part of this repression. Indonesian police as well as the military operated everywhere in the region. Soon after the start of occupation, special commands were established throughout Timor-Leste. Provincial, district, and subdistrict police units worked alongside military police, riot control brigades, elite counterinsurgency forces, intelligence task forces, combat team regiments, and military commands so that all aspects of life were policed and controlled.

East Timorese experienced little protection from this treatment through the courts. Trials to convict those East Timorese who were suspected of supporting Fretilin were often closed and relied on "evidence" from informants. Presiding judges would commence trials by speaking about their support for Indonesia. Timorese defendants would not have adequate access to defense counsel and rarely understood legal procedures.

Indonesian criminal justice officials were also assisted by Timorese auxiliaries. Local people worked within the Indonesian army and police; many also participated in militias, intelligence units, and civil defense forces. In these roles, they provided a means by which Indonesian officials could distance themselves from the violence and avoid international scrutiny, while presenting the idea that they were a neutral force in a country made volatile by internal conflict.

The complicity of Timorese people in repression was particularly significant during 1998–1999, in the time before, during, and after the referendum. During this period, the Indonesian military funneled millions of dollars to militia commanders who were paid a salary to recruit, coordinate, and mobilize local members. Militia members were used to intimidate the population, to convince the Timorese to vote in favor of Indonesian rule and, in the wake of the vote for independence, to engage in swift retribution. Guided by and operating alongside Indonesian officials (a point still denied by Indonesia), they caused massive destruction. A UN multinational military force eventually landed on September 20, 1999, and, over the following months, a fragile peace was established. In May 2002, the country finally joined the United Nations as a sovereign state.

Recent Insecurities

The worst violence of the postindependence period began in early 2006, sparked by the dismissal of 593 soldiers. These members of the F-FDTL (Falintil-Forças de Defesa de Timor Leste) had petitioned the government for better pay and conditions, finally deserting their posts in protest. Many soldiers alleged widespread discrimination in the armed forces, based on supposed distinctions between westerners (*loromonu*) and easterners (*lorosa'e*). Despite the ethnically and historically arguable nature of these categories, this rhetoric fueled disputes between the F-FDTL and the Policia Nacional de Timor-Leste (PNTL) that ultimately spilled onto the streets, beginning with shootings and rioting at a demonstration on April 28, 2006.

The desertion of Major Alfredo Alves Reinado, then head of the military police, and 17 of his men, deepened the conflict. A self-appointed spokesperson for the aggrieved *loromonu*, Reinado used media channels to decry government inaction and pledged support for the political camp of President Xanana Gusmão. His ambush of F-FDTL troops in the outskirts of Dili, in which one soldier was killed and seven wounded, put further pressure on an embattled Fretilin administration. Skirmishes between various loosely defined civilian and armed forces groups overtook the capital, with 2,200 international troops then arriving to quell the violence.

Facing opposition within his own party, and rising public anger against his governing Fretilin party, Mari Alkatiri—accused of inflaming the violence—was forced to step down as prime minister on June 26, 2006, in favor of a compromise candidate, diplomat and Nobel laureate José Ramos Horta. Shortly after, Reinado and his followers, called by President Gusmão to disarm and participate in a national dialogue, were arrested and imprisoned, having continued to stockpile weapons. Though calm had been restored with the aid of newly deployed Australian, Malaysian, New Zealand, and Portuguese forces, a humanitarian emergency had been precipitated.

Over the course of these events, more than 100,000 people moved into camps and makeshift homes around the country. Poor living conditions in the camps heralded ill health and a reported increase in violence against women and children. Despite attempts to mobilize youth, the aftermath of the 2006 crisis eroded Fretilin's historical dominance of Timorese politics. The 2007 elections saw Ramos Horta ascend to the presidency and a coalition headed by Gusmão's CNRT party take government. Disputes over the constitutionality of this arrangement prompted renewed violence across the country, and the destruction of properties owned by the Catholic Church, which was seen as having unduly interfered.

In recent times, Reinado—having escaped with his followers from a Dili prison—became a symbol of generalized discontent. Having evaded recapture by international forces, he broke cover on February 11, 2008, and was killed in an exchange of fire outside the president's residence in which Ramos Horta was also shot and wounded. Soon after, an attack was made on Prime Minister Gusmão, who escaped.

Despite claims of a coup attempt, the motivation for these assaults remains largely unknown. Fearing a backlash, a state of emergency was declared and a curfew imposed for several months. At the time of writing, Reinado loyalists—following a formal surrender—are on trial for their role in the events of February 11, 2008.

Building the New State of Timor-Leste

Following the 1999 vote for independence and the related violent retribution from Indonesian officials and their militias, Timor-Leste was faced with the challenge of building most things—homes, churches, hospitals, roads, schools—again. In criminal justice terms, police stations, court buildings, and prisons had all been decimated; the vast majority of legal personnel had left the country, there was not a single judge in the territory; there were only a handful of police officers with very basic skills; and the written records of the previous regime had been destroyed. Further, as Timorese people had traditionally been excluded from judicial work, most individuals did not have the professional skills or training to work in the legal system.

The task of building new criminal justice institutions has been made more problematic by poverty. With a population of just under 1 million, half of which are under 18, Timor-Leste is one of the poorest countries in the world, and it is also getting poorer. Life expectancy is just 55.5 years, almost 50 percent of the population is illiterate, many adults do not possess work skills, and unemployment is high (among young people, there is a 40% unemployment rate). Basic health, housing, clothing, education, and transport needs are not met for most of the population. While the funds that will inevitably flow from the production of oil and gas from the Timor Sea will assist to change this situation, in the short term the building of criminal justice institutions has been dependent on international assistance.

In this context, the United Nations has engaged in a number of missions in Timor-Leste, beginning in 1999 and continuing through 2009. In terms of criminal justice, each UN mission has had a mandate to provide law enforcement and security and to assist in the development of new criminal justice institutions. Accordingly, UN staff members have had dual duties not only to operate criminal justice institutions but also to build capacity among local staff. Given the violence endured by the Timorese population, the UN also established that it would bring to justice those perpetrators involved in gross human rights violations during the Indonesian occupation.

Legal System

The legal regime in Timor-Leste incorporates a number of distinct and sometimes competing influences. The first regulation, issued by the United Nations Transitional Administration (UNTAET) in the postindependence period, determined that all previously operating statutes would continue to be upheld except where superseded by forthcoming interim UN regulations or ultimately by domestic law. This overlapping of legal authority has rendered some confusion, with Indonesian law, carried over from occupation, often applied even where it appears inconsistent with subsequent legislation or with the human rights and treaty obligations entered into by Parliament.

Aside from constitutional underpinnings and other ad hoc legislation, the basic framework of the legal system remains predominantly Indonesian in origin. Despite the passage of domestic penal and civil procedure laws in 2003 and 2006, respectively, until recently, the law itself remained as it had been under occupation—one exception being the end of capital punishment, according to UN dictate.

A Timorese penal code was passed in 2009, following considerable public debate. One area of concern related to criminal defamation offenses, which have been used in other jurisdictions as a means of quashing political dissent. The decriminalization of procuring and performing abortions was also bound to be controversial in such an overwhelmingly Catholic country. A clause was passed in the original statute allowing exception from prosecution in cases of medical emergency. An amendment swiftly followed, however, that imposes onerous practical conditions, the constitutional validity of which is, at the time of writing, under examination.

The process of drafting and interpreting law has been made more complex by the governmental choice of Portuguese as the principal language of administration. Though measures of fluency vary, surveys suggest that less than 7 percent of Timorese speak Portuguese—likely fewer would ably negotiate the technical lexicon of the legal profession. This seemingly counterintuitive political decision has been connected to the occupation-era exile of the initial Fretilin leadership in Mozambique and other Lusophone nations. Portugal, the former colonial power, retains a large aid presence and holds significant influence in legislative development and judicial training. This linguistic divide certainly hampers the ability of the public to navigate the legal system. No formal channel presently exists for the dissemination of laws, and much of this duty has fallen to the United Nations and civil society. Nongovernment organizations such as the Asia Foundation are progressively translating statutes into Tetum, the dominant indigenous language, to provide greater local understanding and hopefully access to justice.

Crime

District courts operate as courts of first instance, hearing crimes that include, among others, the following: crimes against the security of the state and president, crimes concerning state duties and state rights, crimes against public order, endangering persons or property, crimes against public authority, perjury and false testimony, counterfeiting, forgery, crimes against decency, abandonment, defamation, causing death or bodily harm by negligence, theft, extortion and blackmail, embezzlement, fraud, damage to property, crimes committed by officials, and receiving stolen property.

In addition, there are misdemeanors that include, among others: misdemeanors concerning the security of persons, property, and public health; relating to public order; against public authority; relating to descent and marriage; relating to destitute persons; relating to morals; and relating to officials.

Crime Statistics

Since 2002, official crime rates (as available) have been relatively low, perhaps in part reflecting a continued recourse to traditional methods of dispute resolution. The authors of *The PRIME System: Measuring the Success of Post-Conflict Police Reform* report that the total reported crimes decreased each year between 2002 and 2005, from 5,234 in 2002 to just 1,558 in 2005. Conversely, reports of gender-based violence have increased, perhaps as a result of increased societal awareness. Indeed, during 2005, such cases represented more than half of all filed complaints to police in some districts, according to the United Nations Integrated Mission in Timor-Leste in 2007. Traffic violations have risen, related to an influx of cars to Dili roads. Recent violence can also be expected to result in a sharp rise in criminal complaints since mid-2006, and rates may increase further if current high unemployment rates, and limited opportunities for young people, do not abate.

Comprehensive statistics on the number of arrests and convictions are not publicly available, and institutional records are often incomplete. Recent documentation from the Office of the Prosecutor-General suggests a greater than two-to-one conviction rate, though this may relate to the prioritized lodgement of cases with strong testimonial evidence. Prison records divulge an emphasis on violent crime, with 87 of Timor's tiny prison population—comprising in 2007 just 132 postsentence inmates—incarcerated for murder. These include some individuals sentenced under the UN serious crimes process. A further 27 were recorded as serving terms for sexual offenses, and 69 are reported as being in pretrial detention for illegal weapons possession or disturbing the peace, resulting from post-2006 crises.

Particular Challenges

External donor states, such as Australia, have lately focused their attention on crimes in Timor-Leste that may have implications for their own security, such as terrorism, immigration offenses, drug smuggling, and human trafficking. The level of such transnational criminal activities is, however, believed to be relatively low in Timor-Leste, although there has been recent concern about the numbers of women forced into sex work from Timor-Leste and abroad as a result of unemployment, internal displacement, and the increased presence of international workers in the region.

Some international groups have also claimed an increase in the manufacture and use of illegal amphetamines, a problem believed to be linked to the incidence of violent clashes between local youth, or martial arts gangs. These issues are exacerbated by the smuggling of goods over Timor's largely porous border with Indonesia. Though a Border Patrol Unit has been formed, it has been plagued by political maneuverings and allegations of corruption. The passage of the Special Crime Prevention Operations Law in 2006 was intended to provide broader powers to stamp out organized crime, but little reportable effect can yet be attributed to this, perhaps due to a shift in police priorities related to outbreaks of violence and the recent state of emergency.

The struggle to address the justice needs of women is made difficult by a legacy of violence and a largely patriarchal cultural heritage. These factors have combined to produce an alarmingly high rate of gender-based violence, with a 2003 study finding that nearly half of the female respondents had experienced physical abuse from a partner over the previous year, according to a report by the Dili International Rescue Committee. Such incidents are rarely reported, with matters commonly resolved within families or by traditional processes in which women have only a superficial role.

The United Nations introduced gender officer roles within the mission as well as a discrimination policy. Accusations of sexual misconduct among its members have, however, tarnished this record. The Timorese government has undertaken its own efforts, establishing an Office for the Promotion of Equality. The Women's Network of Timor Lorosa'e, the East Timor Women's Communication Forum, and the Women's Justice Unit of the Judicial System Monitoring Programme, among others, advocate for reform and provide services to vulnerable groups.

Timor's legal system has been much criticized for its handling of such cases. Though there have been successful prosecutions under the UN serious crimes process for sexual offenses dating from the preindependence period, a sense of impunity persists. Constitutional and international sources of law are infrequently considered by the courts, even as irrelevant facts such as the chastity of a victim are included in judicial reasoning. Custodial terms are generally at the lower end of the discretionary spectrum, and suspended sentences are common. Cause for optimism exists, however, in the establishment of a police Vulnerable Persons Unit and a rise in reporting that may reflect greater awareness of gender-based violence as a crime. In 2007, 157 such cases entered the Prosecutor-General's Office, up from 75 in 2006. Even allowing for a suspension of judicial activity due to the 2006 crisis, existing records show a rise not only in the reporting of sexual crime and domestic assault, but also in court decisions, according to the Judicial System Monitoring Programme.

Timor-Leste's legal framework remains ill equipped to promote justice and equality for women. Yet, a domestic violence law soon to be considered by Parliament, and anticipated debate on witness protection, are positive signs.

Courts and Commissions for Serious Crimes

A range of truth and justice initiatives have been implemented to deal with the serious crimes committed over the previous 25 years.

The Ad Hoc Human Rights Court

The Indonesian government established this court in 2000. Despite proclaiming a commitment to justice, the government and the Attorney General's Office consistently failed to support the court to bring Indonesian officials to account. Commencing work in March 2002, it focused its investigations on just 3 (Liquiça, Suai, and Dili) of Timor-Leste's 13 districts, for events that occurred during just two months, April and September 1999. Of the 18 defendants brought to trial, 12 were initially acquitted and 6 convicted of crimes against humanity. Following various appeals, the 6 had their convictions overturned. The last man to be released (Eurico Guterres, the Timorese leader of the Aitarak militia) ran for Parliament in the last Indonesian election.

The Serious Crimes Process

In June 2000, the UN established the serious crimes process in Dili. The Special Panels for Serious Crimes (SPSC) was a hybrid tribunal that brought together international and national judges to try serious criminal offenses. The SPSC took universal jurisdiction over charges of genocide, war crimes, and crimes against humanity. Prosecutors initially considered serious crimes from 1975; however, the Serious Crimes Unit (SCU) subsequently changed policy to focus all attention on cases from January–October 1999. Completing trials by May 2005, the final statistics for the serious crimes process are quite impressive for an internationalized court: 95 indictments against 440 accused were filed; 55 cases were tried and 84 defendants were convicted (with three acquitted and one ruled unfit to stand trial).

The serious crimes process faced criticisms in respect of departures from international standards of fairness and due process. For instance, in 2003, the SCU had only eight investigators, each with responsibility for more than 300 murders across multiple districts. Similarly, the defense team was impossibly small and had no access to a reliable IT system. Further, although the courts operated across four languages (Indonesian, Portuguese, English, and Tetum), translators were not always present.

The serious crimes process failed to deal with high-ranking perpetrators. The 84 convicted men were all minor players (in 2009, just one remained in prison). There are 339 indictees who remain at large principally within Indonesia, with many continuing to serve in the Indonesian armed forces. This issue has consistently undermined the success of this process. In February 2008, the UN and the Timorese government established a new agreement to prosecute outstanding serious crimes cases. In 2009, there does not appear to be much political will—or resources—to make this happen.

The Commission for Reception, Truth and Reconciliation (CAVR)

The Commission for Reception, Truth and Reconciliation (CAVR) started work in January 2002. With a remit to determine an official truth regarding human rights violations between April 1974 and October 1999, the commission also had the duties of supporting the reintegration of individuals who had harmed their communities, promoting reconciliation, and referring serious crimes matters to the SCU.

The CAVR's final report, *Chega!* (meaning "no more," "stop," or "enough"), was released onto the Internet in December 2005. It shows that, although Timorese people engaged in violence, the conflict was one precipitated and sustained by international influences. While Indonesian officials were principally responsible for serious crimes, the CAVR concluded that most UN members also failed to stop Indonesian activities or to provide support to Timor-Leste. Further, the United States, the United Kingdom, and Australian administrations provided significant aid and trade, as well as military and political support, to Indonesia. Despite its significance, this report has not yet been discussed by either the Timorese government or the UN Security Council.

One unique aspect of the CAVR was the Community Reconciliation Process (CRP). Local leaders and CAVR staff conducted CRP hearings in affected communities, and following discussions, made reconciliation agreements through which perpetrators had to make amends, often by making an apology, paying a fine, or undertaking community work. Following these acts, the perpetrator gained immunity from any court action. The incorporation of customary law—specifically the traditional practices of "lisan" or "adapt" (see below)—encouraged wide community participation. An estimated 40,000 people attended these hearings, and while there were criticisms of the CRP (particularly when perpetrators were less than honest about their past actions), they enjoyed wide popular support.

The Commission of Truth and Friendship

The Commission of Truth and Friendship (CTF) was formed by the governments of Indonesia and Timor-Leste in 2005. Billed as an attempt to forge friendlier relations between the two governments, the main objective of the CTF was to establish a definitive and unifying truth with regard to the events of 1999. This mandate was criticized for repeating the work of previous truth and justice measures, and the CTF has also faced intense opposition due to its ability to recommend amnesty for those perpetrators who fully cooperated in revealing the truth. The Catholic Church and victims' groups repeatedly argued that this heralded a potential official immunity from prosecutions; similarly, the UN declared that it would not cooperate with the CTF as these terms did not comply with human rights standards.

Overall, truth and justice initiatives for Timor-Leste have, thus far, failed to bring serious human rights violators to account. These measures have been, as the UN Commission of Experts (CoE) argued in 2005, "manifestly inadequate." In light of these failings, the CoE recommended that the UN create an ad hoc international criminal tribunal. This position, echoing the continuing demands of Timorese grassroots organizations, has not been met with a warm reception from Timorese leaders.

Domestic Courts

There are four district courts in Timor-Leste, located in Dili, Baucau, Oecusse, and Suai. The highest tribunal is the Dili-based Court of Appeal. The Office of the Prosecutor-General initiates indictments and prosecutions and the Ministry of Justice is responsible for the administration of the courts and the Public Defenders Office as well as the prisons. There is no separate system for juveniles. Serious offenses—those which may result in a prison term of five years or more—are heard before a panel of three judges while lesser crimes are heard before a single judge.

All courts in Timor-Leste are run jointly by national and international staff. The first group of 27 national judges, prosecutors, and public defenders (including nine women) was appointed in July 2007, following their completion of a prolonged training program. A further 12 (including three female) national workers were expected to join them in 2008. There is currently no accreditation program for the approximately 80 private lawyers who operate in Timor-Leste, an issue that has resulted in the variable quality of workers.

The Dili District Court conducts hearings on a daily basis. Staffed by six judges (three international, three national), four prosecutors (two international, two national), and nine public defenders (six international, three national), it is by far the best resourced and managed court. Between January–September 2007, this court registered 706 criminal cases and issued 304 decisions, according to the Judicial Monitoring Program. Many of these cases dealt with the violence that erupted in 2006.

Before 2006, the Baucau District Court operated on an ad hoc basis. It currently handles daily cases, although there have been recent intermissions due to the burning of court buildings during the conflict of 2007. With three judges (one international, two national), two prosecutors and several public defenders, this court decided 109 criminal cases between January and July 2007. Some of these cases dealt with matters from as long ago as 2002.

In Oecusse, the district court conducts hearings once or twice a month. There are no permanent judicial staff presently located at this court and legal workers (one judge, one prosecutor, and one defender) travel from their residence in Dili to hear cases. Attempting to hear approximately eight cases per month, the court registered 33 criminal cases between January–September 2007. At the Suai District Court, hearings are held three times a month, again by a single judge, prosecutor, and public defender who travel into the region from Dili. Between January–April 2007, the court handed down judgments in 10 minor cases.

During 2007, the Court of Appeal had six judges (three international, three national). There has been confusion about the authority of the national judges, who also serve on the Dili District Court. Between January and September 2007, the Court of Appeal registered 44 criminal cases and decided 34 cases.

The Courts Registry is dependent on international clerks. The UNDP recently asserted that there are no national clerks trained for this work and that there is still no effective case-management system. Since 2000, there have been consistent reports that thousands of case files have been lost, and there are numerous examples of cases in which final written judgments have not been recorded.

From its inception, the court system in Timor-Leste has been severely affected by a lack of material resources. In January 2006, the UNDP launched a US$10 million project to strengthen the justice system. This program builds on a previous (2003–2005) project that was critiqued for its lack of action with regard to the training and mentoring of local staff.

Recent conflict in Timor-Leste has also taken a significant toll on the court system. This violence meant that many international staff left the territory and trials were postponed. Court offices were looted and files, forensic evidence, computers, translation equipment, and transport were stolen. The increase in violent crimes has also burdened the system with further complex cases.

Impact of Weak Resources on the Rights of Defendants

The shortage of court staff has had repercussions throughout the system. For instance, the law requires judicial warrants to be issued prior to police searches and arrests. Given the scarcity of judges, this provision has been frequently violated. Similarly, government regulations require a first judicial hearing within 72 hours of an arrest so that judges can review the lawfulness of detention, assess the strength of evidence, and decide on matters of pretrial detention. Invariably, detainees have been forced to wait long periods for this first hearing, an issue that has become particularly acute outside Dili. In many instances, it appears that the police have taken to releasing detainees after the 72-hour period, when a hearing cannot be arranged in good time.

Timorese law also provides the right to a fair trial. Under the Penal Procedure Code, defendants enjoy the presumption of innocence; they have the right to be present during trial and the right to legal representation; they may present witness testimony and evidence; they have access to prosecutorial evidence; and they have the right to appeal. Due to staff shortages, however, these rights are often negated.

The lack of resources and poor administration have also resulted in situations in which defendants, victims, and witnesses have not attended court hearings. There are numerous reasons for this, including the fact that individuals are often not informed of trial dates. Those who live outside Dili often have no transport options and police officers—who also lack vehicles and fuel—are similarly incapable of delivering civilians to courtrooms.

The issue of funding has inevitably impacted on the speed at which cases can be processed, and there is a significant backlog within the courts—in Dili alone, the backlog of cases was reported, by the United Nations Integrated Mission, to have increased from 1,658 in January 2007 to 2,413 cases in July 2007.

Training Issues

The training of court personnel has, as detailed above, been a particular issue of concern. A range of problems has been associated with the transfer of skills, including that mentoring has been dependent on the individual personalities or skills of international judges; differences in the legal backgrounds of international staff have made training difficult; and internationals have focused on maintaining basic services rather than mentoring.

Yet, the biggest obstacle to training has been the Portuguese language. With national law now written in Portuguese, the Judicial Training Centre conducted its operations in Portuguese. Perhaps unsurprisingly, all trainee judges, prosecutors, and defenders failed their first written examinations during 2005, making them unable to hear and present cases in the district courts. This situation was widely attributed to language difficulties rather than issues of competence or understanding.

The Relationship between the Police and the Courts

In the move to independence, approximately 3,000 police (PNTL) officers were recruited and trained by UN Civilian Police Officers. From the start, the establishment and training of the PNTL was lacking in effective management, planning, and policy development, culminating in a police force that lacked critical skills and proficiency. While some officers had a degree of professionalism, UN police advisors detailed that over half of the new recruits were incompetent. Indeed, the police began to gain a reputation for ill-treatment and abuse. For instance, PNTL officers were accused of meting out their own punishments—by illegally detaining citizens or abusing them—instead of pursuing cases through the courts.

With the majority of cases presented to the newly established Office of the Provedor (Ombudsman) focusing on human rights abuses and maladministration by PNTL members, Timorese people have not always been keen to report crimes. Moreover, the PNTL have not always pursued investigations either from a lack of ability to deal with complex cases or as a consequence of differential attitudes to certain sections of the population (an issue particularly felt with regard to crimes of physical or sexual violence against women and children). Problems of inadequately trained police officers, and their difficulties in making initial assessments of evidence, has also been linked to the high rate of cases struck out by the courts.

During the 2006 conflict, the PNTL disintegrated, particularly in Dili. Allegations ensued that some police officers were involved in criminal activity and mob violence. Such claims were reasserted during the recent "state of siege" that followed the attacks on the president and prime minister. UNMIT, under an Australian command, took over policing responsibilities and every member of the PNTL was to undergo a new registration, screening (to check previous involvement in criminal activity), and mentoring (over six months) program. At the end of 2007, 3,110 national officers had registered and undergone screening, 1,274 officers remained under UN supervision and just 186 had been fully certified and were able to operate independently. Increasingly, community policing responsibilities are being handed back to PNTL.

Punishment and Prisons

The Indonesian code offers limited sentencing options for judges. Potential sentences include community service (that is relatively underused), fines, and jail terms. The draft Timorese code adds verbal "admonition" for young offenders.

The postindependence leadership of Timor-Leste made grand claims for the reestablishment of the prison system, emphasizing the need to rehabilitate prisoners. The destruction of facilities during Indonesian withdrawal, and the lingering influence of a regime marked by abuse and torture, has made this a substantial challenge.

Institutional provisions were made with the assistance of the United Nations Transitional Administration (UNTAET). Immediately postindependence, the UN maintained a Civilian Detention Centre in Dili. Detainees were transferred to newly reconstructed facilities as they became available from 2000. Reconstruction first took place at Becora in Dili, where three new cellblocks now provide capacity for 260 prisoners, and at Gleno, in Ermera district, which can house up to 100. A further prison has been established at Baucau, although ongoing renovations forced relocation of the 22 prisoners located there in late 2007. Prisons now fall under the portfolio of the Ministry of

Justice and are administered by the National Directorate for Prison Services and Social Reinsertion.

Prison populations appear to be diminishing, as is the proportion of detainees awaiting trial (as opposed to serving a sentence). Data collected in December 2007 by local human rights network Forum Tau Matan put the total number of prisoners at 232 (including 4 women and 3 juveniles), of whom 47.8 percent were awaiting trial. This compares favorably with figures collected by the Office of the UN High Commissioner for Human Rights in 2003, which reported a total of 320 prisoners (including 1 woman and 6 juveniles), of whom 70.9 percent were yet to be sentenced. Despite improvements, delays in accessing justice are still of concern, with 45 detainees in Timor's main prison having waited more than six months for a hearing date. Courts often sentence only to time served.

Alongside prisons, criminal suspects are also detained at district police locations. In 2007, the UN Police Vulnerable Persons Unit reported that over the last reporting year, 1,272 persons were held in police custody for up to 72 hours. Observer groups claim cells are often unsuitable, with a lack of access to sanitation and bedding. Police often receive no budget for food or transport related to persons in custody, resulting in a reluctance to detain or in privations for detainees. Compounding this is a mentality among certain police members that substandard conditions are an appropriate way of "teaching [presumptive] criminals a lesson."

Conditions within the prisons appear to be more appropriate. Accommodation and sanitation standards have generally been held to comply with international standards. Medical services are provided by nurses at each location, and generators guarantee power supply. Nevertheless, concerns were raised in 2004 over the disrepair of infrastructure and inconsistent water supply at Gleno. Additionally, outbreaks of violence in 2003 saw the Becora prison administration complex burned down—this was replaced the following year.

Prisoners have access to a small range of recreational and vocational opportunities. Various charities and nongovernmental organizations intermittently run carpentry workshops and classes on tailoring, construction, and weaving. The United Nations Development Programme is piloting a literacy scheme, and UNICEF provides writing materials and sporting goods for young people in detention. Social workers are sometimes available, and family members and independent observers are allowed access to prisoners, although this is discretionary. Detainees whose families cannot visit them use Red Cross messages to maintain or reestablish contact.

Prior to the opening of the newly refurbished prisons, more than 30 Timorese wardens were recruited. The New Zealand government, in particular, sent experts and equipment to support the training and daily activity of these first staff. Four-month training courses have regularly been run for new guards, variously providing human rights training and workshops in self-defense and non-lethal incapacitation methods. However, there are continuing claims that some guards remain poorly trained. Staff recruitment has been an issue and insufficient human resources have been blamed for the limits on prisoner movement, as well as the 2003 prisoner attacks on prison infrastructure. In 2004, 112 personnel were reported as working across the three prisons; this rose to 168 by 2006. The ratio of prison officers to inmates is now reported to be reasonable by regional standards. There have been relatively few reports of staff violence against prisoners; those that have emerged highlight violence in the first 72 hours of detention. Worryingly, there is no formal complaints mechanism.

Security is an ongoing problem and there have been several cases of mass prisoner escape. In 2002, 181 prisoners broke out from Becora. Many escapees protested at Parliament over the poor conditions in the prison and the delays in reaching trial; they voluntarily returned to confinement. In 2006, 57 inmates fled, including now-deceased rebel leader Alfredo Reinado. A further escape in 2007 is being investigated by a government commission.

While male and female prisoners are segregated, the system yet fails to deal effectively with minors who commit crimes. No legislation currently exists to regulate the status of underage suspects, and there is no definitive minimum age for criminal responsibility, as required by the Convention on the Rights of the Child. Without clear legal guidance, reports are emerging of police simply releasing offenders younger than 17, even those detained in relation to serious offenses such as rape or arson.

Concerns have also been raised over the housing of juveniles with serious and/or habitually violent criminals, again contrary to international law obligations. Incidents have been reported of child inmates being beaten or brutalized by other prisoners. In some cases, advocacy groups such as Forum Communicacoes Juventude, with support from UNICEF and local defense lawyers, have successfully lobbied for minors to be released into protective care. Similar alarm is felt over the reported lack of understanding or treatment for mental illness in detention facilities, especially as high rates of post-traumatic stress disorder are reported.

Alternatives to Formal Justice Provisions

Perhaps 70 percent of the country's population live outside of the urban and regional centers where court facilities are located. This fact, coupled with frustration at the slow process of state reconstruction, may have bolstered local support for various customary mechanisms for maintaining peace and good order, known broadly as "lisan" or otherwise by the Indonesian "adat." This traditional approach to dispute resolution offers advantages in terms of being more embedded in community tradition, not to mention being relatively quick and cheap. Critics have, however, pointed to its potential for abuse and to its frequent dissonance with more globally accepted standards of justice, especially in relation to the status of women.

Under the United Nations Transitional Administration in East Timor, there was little consultation on customary law and legal process. There appeared to be a prevailing sense that it was anathema to the development of a modern legal sector. Certainly, no more than symbolic recognition was given to lisan in the Constitution and the province of law was explicitly given to formal instruments of state.

Despite this apparent denial of legitimacy, frontline personnel such as outposted UN police were, in the absence of guidelines on how to constructively engage with lisan, discovering its usefulness as a means of deescalating conflict and keeping order. A survey conducted by the Asia Foundation across all districts found that a staggering 94 percent of respondents had confidence in the lisan system, which is effectively to say that its presence and dependability are articles of faith for local peoples. Notably, though, 75 percent acknowledged that it could use some reform.

There have been several attempts in Timor to pilot legal structures fusing elements of customary practice with court-based proceedings. For example, the Oecusse Diversionary Justice Program drew on Western juvenile justice principles to diminish the risk of recidivism among young offenders, using social authority to reinforce legal messages and preferring community work sentences over custody. It settled 23 land disputes and three criminal disputes with the aid of local elders before the term of the pilot was completed. Similarly, the UN Land and Property Unit undertook negotiations to refer some title and boundary cases to traditional forums. The CAVR process also used "nahe biti" ceremonies to facilitate the reintegration of ex-militia personnel. Meaning to unroll, or lay out the mat, "nahe biti" can be considered analogous to Western notions of mediation, conciliation, and arbitration.

Elizabeth Stanley and Andrew Marriott

Further Reading

Commission for Reception, Truth and Reconciliation. (2005). *Chega! The Report of the Commission for Reception, Truth and Reconciliation in Timor-Leste*. Dili: CAVR: http://www.cavr-timorleste.org/en/index.htm.

Globalism Institute Timor-Leste Research Library: http://www.timor-leste.org/index.html.

Hohe, Tanja, and Rod Nixon. (2003). *Reconciling Justice: "Traditional" Law and State Judiciary in East Timor*. Dili: United States Institute of Peace.

Judicial System Monitoring Programme Web site: http://www.jsmp.minihub.org/.

Shoesmith, Dennis, ed. (2007). *The Crisis in Timor-Leste: Understanding the Past, Imagining the Future.* Darwin, Australia: Charles Darwin University Press.

Stanley, Elizabeth. (2008). *Torture, Truth and Justice: The Case of Timor-Leste*. London: Routledge.

Turkey

Legal System: Civil
Murder: Medium
Burglary: Medium
Corruption: Medium
Human Trafficking: Medium
Prison Rate: Medium
Death Penalty: No
Corporal Punishment: No

Background

Before converting to Islam, the Turks were ruled by a single ruler (*hakan*) and his family. The ruler gathered his high-rank commanders and administrators twice a year to decide about the issues concerning the state, including peace and war. Laws consisted of the decisions made in those gatherings; traditions were not in written form and religion did not play a significant role in state or legal affairs.

Starting from the 10th century, the Turks adopted Islamic criminal law, while in some Turkish states traditions were used more than the Islamic legal system. Especially during the Ottoman period (1299–1922), the Islamic legal system, which depended on the Holy Koran and the interpretations of its verses, was strictly used and traditions were applied only on the points where the Koranic resources did not explain them. However, especially during the reign of Sultan Suleiman the Magnificent, a tendency to codify those new rules in thick books (*Kanunname*) developed. In the Islamic legal system, there are some principles that are used in modern criminal justice systems. Some of those principles are:

1. Individuals are innocent until proven guilty: The general principle is that people are born into this world innocent and free of debt. Crimes and loans emerge later; therefore, whoever claims that a person has committed a crime or has not paid a loan is required to prove that allegation.
2. Suspicion is used in favor of the accused. Toward the end of the 19th century, Westernization of the criminal system began. The foundation of the Turkish Republic in 1923 was followed by the Turkish Penal Code of 1926, which was partly a translation of the Italian Penal Code of 1889. That code was replaced with the new Penal Code in 2005. The Criminal Procedures Code of 1929 was a translation of the German Procedures Code of 1877. This code was then replaced with a more up-to-date one in 2004. One major reason for the adoption of those two laws was Turkey's unification efforts with the European Union.

The modern legal system that was used with the inauguration of the republic is the continental European civil law system; and therefore, the type of criminal procedures system is "mixed" or "cooperative" where judges may not initiate prosecution on their own, but the initiation of a public prosecutor is needed. In this system, judges have an efficient position during the procedures; however, the defendant (and/or his or her representatives) and the prosecutor may also actively contribute to the judicial process. Judges are not bound by the evidence presented, but they also may search for new evidence. In this system the pretrial period is confidential, whereas trials are open to the public.

Police

Law enforcement in Turkey is carried out mainly by two institutions: the police and the gendarmerie. While the jurisdiction of the police is urban or municipal areas, the gendarmerie enforces law in rural areas, but their responsibilities and authorities are basically the same. The police are completely the civilian part of law enforcement. On the other hand, the gendarmerie is a part of the Turkish Army and connected to the Commander in Chief in terms of its military duties, education and training, while it is connected to the Ministry of Interior (like the police) in terms of its responsibilities regarding public order. The role of the military in politics and maintenance of public order has historically been very important.

The Turkish police, like the gendarmerie, have a centralized structure of administration. At the center (the capital city of Ankara), the General Directorate of Security functions under the Ministry of Interior and has extensions in 81 districts throughout Turkey. As of 2009 the number of police officers in Turkey was more than 250,000. Regardless of where they work, all police officers work under the authority of the General Directorate.

The structure of the police at the center is quite similar to that in districts. Both at the central headquarters and in districts, there are specialized departments, such as antiterrorism, antismuggling, and organized crimes, public order, riot control, in city and highway traffic, juvenile, intelligence, and so forth, along with support units. The police have no structural connection with the military except for the instances of martial law and state of emergency. Naturally, cooperation between the gendarmerie and the police is provided for cases that have extensions with both cities and rural areas.

Crime

Classification of Crimes

In the rescinded Turkish Penal Code of 1926, the classification of offenses as "felony" and "misdemeanor" existed; however, the current Penal Code does not categorize offenses. Following the current trend in the continental European criminal system, the Law on Misdemeanors adopted in 2005 transferred most misdemeanors in the previous code to the jurisdiction of the administration. While such punishments as imprisonment, juridical fines, and other juridical precautions may be awarded to violators of crimes in the Penal Code, only administrative fines and measures may be applied against violators of misdemeanors. Crimes in the context of the Penal Code are more serious ones, such as genocide, murder, torture, rape, assault, threat, and violation of freedoms. On the other hand, misdemeanors listed in the Law on Misdemeanors are less serious ones, such as begging, gambling, unlawful use of public places, violation of public order by making noise, and smoking in prohibited areas.

Age of Criminal Responsibility

Criminal responsibility begins after age 12; and children younger than that age may not be punished or investigated for any offenses. Punishments given to minors between 12 and 15 are deducted by 50 percent if they have the ability to discern; otherwise, they go unpunished. For minors between 15 and 18, punishments are deducted by one-third with the maximum limit of 12 years of imprisonment.

Crimes Challenging Turkey

Terrorism could be considered as the most serious problem for Turkey. The country has been suffering from revolutionary and separatist movements for many years, but it was the worst in the 1990s when the Kurdish separatists (PKK) were active in the southeast of the country. Around 32,000 people are believed to have been killed during the surge of the PKK terrorism. The leader and founder of PKK, Abdullah Ocalan, was arrested on February, 15, 1999, and has been held under solitary confinement as the only prisoner in an island prison in the Sea of Marmara. He was first sentenced to death; however, when the death penalty was abolished in Turkey, his punishment was commuted to lifelong aggravated imprisonment.

In terms of ordinary crimes, no crime is as disturbing for the public as terrorism. Among such crimes, however, are traffic-related misdemeanors committed on Turkish roads by Turkish drivers and casualties are to such an extent that they are referred to as "traffic terrorism."

Drug Offenses

For drug-related offences, Turkey is seen as a transit country; however, numbers regarding usage are on the rise. Drug offenses in the Turkish Penal Code

Police forensic officers examine and collect evidence in front of the Neve Shalom Synagogue in Istanbul, Turkey, November 16, 2003. (AP Photo/Burhan Ozbilici)

include illegal production, inducting, exporting, selling, giving, transporting, storing, and possessing sedative or stimulative substances. If the substance is heroin, cocaine, morphine or morphine-based, the punishment given to violators is increased by half. Although use of sedative and stimulative substances is prohibited and punished by the code, the law does not identify any substance as requiring an increased punishment.

Crime Statistics

An overview of crime statistics at the national level as of 2006, according to the Turkish Bureau of Statistics (http://www.tuik.gov.tr/Start.do), is as follows. (Crimes that are reported to the police and investigated by the prosecutor and/or the police have been included. Those numbers have been taken from the Ministry of Justice database.)

Total number of murders:	5,788
Premeditated killing of people:	3,991
Imprudently killing of people:	1,797
Total number of sex-related crimes:	6,836
Serious property offense total:	7,714
Theft:	6,603
Robbery:	1,111
Serious drug offenses total:	2,198

Finding of Guilt

Rights of the Accused

In general there are two alternative ways that can be followed by the accused: going to trial and reconciliation. While the former alternative is the most common and has been used since the acceptance of the rescinded Criminal Procedures and Penal Code, the latter was introduced by the new codes adopted in 2004 and 2005, respectively. Other than going to trial and reconciliation, there are no other ways for the defendant, prosecutor, or victim, such as going to trial by jury, plea bargaining for lesser offense, and so forth. Reconciliation is limited to certain offenses listed in the Penal Code, such as causing minor injury, minor thefts, causing minor property damage, and so forth. If a reconciliation agreement is reached between the offender and the victim, the case is automatically dropped. No other way of reconciliation agreement (e.g., between the offender and the prosecutor) is possible.

Rights of the accused are taken very seriously in Turkey, as illustrated by the example of a case that occurred in the city of Manias on December 26, 1995. The police arrested 16 youths, most of whom were high school students. The allegation against them was that they were members of an illegal leftist terrorist organization. However, the case is not known by the allegation against the youth, but the allegations that the police tortured them during their arrest. The case has been the symbol of the struggle for the protection of human rights and required a long time to be resolved. At the end of the trials, the youth were found not guilty, but a police captain and officers were found guilty and were punished by a total of 85 years of imprisonment. The officers were also dismissed from the police force. The officers' punishments ranged from 2.5 years to 12.5 years.

Assistance Provided in Defense

Starting with the arrest by law enforcement officers, the accused must be made aware of his or her rights, which are as follows:

- Knowing the accusation: The accused is given information about the accusation and his or her rights at the time of the arrest.
- Right to remain silent: The accused is not legally required to give information except that regarding his or her identification.
- Directing the prosecution: The accused may provide information about the allegation and submit evidence.
- Informing others of the arrest: Law enforcement officers contact a person (either a family member of the accused or a person he or she determines) and make him or her aware of the arrest. If the arrestee is a foreign national, his or her country's consulate is given information unless the arrestee wishes otherwise and puts his or her consent in written form.
- Right to remain unblemished during the investigation phase: The investigation phase is confidential and the accused is deemed innocent until proven guilty.

In the light of those rights and principles, the accused is expected to defend himself or herself. The right to defend starts with the time of the arrest when the arresting officer notifies the arrestee that he or she may benefit from aid of a defender of his or her own choice. The arrestee is assigned a public defender free of charge upon his or her request if he or she states that he or she is unable to hire one. For juveniles it is a legal obligation to assign a defender regardless of his or her or his or her parents' demand.

Prosecution and/or Investigation of the Case

In general it is the public prosecutor who conducts the prosecution. Immediately after being notified about a violation of law, the prosecutor has to investigate the allegation either directly or through the use of law enforcement in his or her jurisdiction. There is a hierarchical structure between prosecutors and law enforcement in terms of prosecution of an allegation or its investigation: law enforcement officers must follow the prosecutor's command. Except for emergencies, law enforcement has no authority to initiate or continue criminal investigation without approval of the prosecutor. Magistrates may also be involved in criminal investigation and prosecution in case the prosecutor is not reachable or the decision for arrest of the suspect is needed during the investigation.

Resolution of the Majority of Criminal Cases

Due to the general character of prosecution in Turkish criminal prosecution, most cases end up in trials. As mentioned above, only a small portion of offenses are closed with the agreement of reconciliation between the victim and the offender.

Incarceration before or Awaiting Trial

In the Turkish Penal System, incarceration is allowed both before and during trial, and the decision of incarceration must be given by a judge. At the investigation phase, it is the magistrate court judge who decides the incarceration, while it is the judge(s) of the court where the case is handled during the trial phase. For incarceration to be decided, there are certain requirements in the Turkish Penal Criminal Procedures Code.

Number of Criminal Court Judges

In addition to the specialized ones such as military courts, there are three types of criminal courts in Turkey depending on the severity of the punishment required for the alleged action: (1) the Magistrate Criminal Court handles cases that require up to two years of imprisonment; (2) the High Criminal Court handles cases that require aggravated lifelong imprisonment, lifelong imprisonment, and those requiring imprisonment for more than 10 years; and (3) the Criminal Court of First Instance handles cases that are outside of the responsibilities of the other two criminal courts. There is only one criminal judge in each of the Magistrate Criminal Courts and the Criminal Courts of First Instance, while there are three in the High Criminal Court.

Qualifications of Judges

According to the Law on Judges and Prosecutors, all criminal judges must be selected from people having a law degree, which requires successfully completing a four-year law school (bachelor's degree) in Turkey or a respected law school abroad with the requirement that some additional courses are successfully completed. If a person with that degree wishes to be a criminal judge, he or she has to pass an exam and complete the following two-year candidacy. There are four degrees for criminal judges, and each criminal judge may be assigned to positions depending on the degree possessed. To determine his or her qualifications, each criminal judge is graded depending on the speed of the trial, whether there were unnecessary delays, wording of decrees, whether some sample decrees have been taken into consideration, and so forth.

Separate System for Juveniles

In Turkey there is a separate system to deal with juvenile offenders, and the system shows several differences with the common procedures. While for adult offenders the investigation can be carried out by both the police and the prosecutor, only the prosecutor may carry out the investigation against juvenile offenders. A defender is assigned to the minor even if he or she does not ask for one; minors are kept separate from adults; all the procedure is confidential; and handcuffs or similar devices may not be used. If the prosecutor deems it necessary, a social worker may also be called to be present and provide psychological aid during investigation at any phase. As mentioned above, punishments are deducted for juvenile offenders, and the limit of 12 years of imprisonment may not be exceeded.

Punishment

Types of Punishment

Punishments in the Penal Code are divided into two types: sanctions and security measures.

Sanctions

In some instances the sanction of the crime committed can require quite a short time of imprisonment, or the sanction could be mentioned as payment of a certain or calculable sum of money. If the judge of the case decides the payment of some money as the sanction or converts the short period of imprisonment into payment of money, then the sanction is called "judicial fine." The condition of conversion is that the term for imprisonment must be between 5 and 730 days. The judge determines a multiplier for each day according to the economic and personal conditions of the indicted. Then the number found is multiplied by the number of the days of imprisonment determined as the punishment.

Lifelong aggravated imprisonment requires the prisoner to serve lifelong in principle; however, prisoners serving lifelong aggravated imprisonment may be released on parole after staying in prison with good behavior for 30 years. The difference between this type of punishment and life imprisonment is the regime followed during the execution of the punishment: the inmate may be deprived of some rights, and the conditions of living differ.

Although lifelong imprisonment requires the inmate to serve lifelong, if he or she is on good behavior, after 24 years he or she may be released on parole. Compared to those who have been punished with lifelong aggravated imprisonment, these prisoners have more privileges in prison and have better living conditions. Imprisonment is called "limited time" if the imprisonment is between 1 month and 20 years.

Security Measures

The convicted may be deprived of some certain rights listed in the Penal Code, such as prohibition from public service, deprivation of political rights, losing rights of parenthood of a child, prohibition of being managers or controller of public institutions or political parties, and prohibition of carrying out a certain profession.

If a material item has been used during the commitment of a crime in particular, or it has been prepared to be used in the commitment of a crime but has not been used, or some benefit has been provided by the commitment of the crime, the judge may decide to confiscate the item or the benefit provided.

If a foreign national has been convicted of a crime and the person has been put on probation, he or she is deported. If the convicted foreign national has been put in prison, he or she is deported after the end of serving his or her term in prison.

Since the insane do not have the ability to discern, they are not punished for their violations. In case of violation, they are hospitalized in high-security institutions for their treatment until they are recovered from that ailment.

Within the context of those measures, protective and supportive measures, consultation, education, training, care, and sheltering are listed in the Law on Protection of Minors.

Typical punishment for intentional murder is lifelong imprisonment, for rape between 7–12 years of imprisonment, for serious theft between 3–7 years of imprisonment, and for serious burglary between 10–15 years of imprisonment.

The death penalty was abolished in August 2002 for any type of crime. Before that, all decisions of death penalty had to be approved by the National Assembly to be executed. Since the assembly had not approved any death penalty decision after October 1984, it was practically abolished even before 2002.

Prisons

According to the official Web site of the Ministry of Justice (http://www.cte.adalet.gov.tr), as of December 1, 2008, there were 103,296 inmates in 384 prisons in Turkey. Of those people, 44,038 were convicted and 59,258 were arrested. The biggest prison is located in Silivri, Istanbul (it is also the sixth biggest prison in Europe), which is an "L" type prison with a total capacity of 6,000 inmates. In that prison all rooms have windows (double layer, transparent); all inmates live in individual rooms; inmates may use courtyards or common living spaces in day time; all entrances are equipped with sensitive doors, X-rays, and devices for retina scans. In that prison there is one warden, assistants to the warden, an accountant, and an adequate number of administrative officers, medical doctors, dentists, psychologists, social workers, teachers, secretaries, paramedics, guards, technicians, nurses, laundrymen, repairmen, and workers. Each common living place is equipped with a television antenna input, a small kitchen, an electric outlet, and an emergency button.

Inmates in Turkish prisons are not required to work; however, inmates having served in prison for at least one year could be allowed to work inside the institution as long as they are in good standing. Inmates cannot be asked to work in personal businesses of prison administrators and other staff. On the other hand, juvenile inmates may not be allowed to work in any case. Inmates who work at prisons are allowed to get wages and social privileges in turn for their labor. Inmates are offered classes for the development of their personality, rehabilitation, and gaining skills that prepare them for their postincarceration lives. Inmates can be visited by their family members listed in the law and have access to free health care.

Prisoners of foreign nationality can be transferred to their countries for execution of their crimes and the conditions to be met are listed in the Penal Code. However, a prisoner having Turkish nationality may not be transferred to other countries with the exception that the crime committed falls within the jurisdiction of the International Court of Justice.

Erkan Sezgin and Sener Uludag

Further Reading

Justice and Prison Statistics (Adalet ve Ceza İnfaz Kurumu İstatistikleri): http://www.adli-sicil.gov.tr.

Law on Execution of Punishments and Security Measures (Ceza ve Güvenlik Tedbirlerinin İnfazı Hakkında Kanun): http://www.mevzuat.adalet.gov.tr/html/1433.html.

Law on Protection of Minors (Çocuk Koruma Kanunu): http://www.mevzuat.adalet.gov.tr/html/1527.html.

Ministry of Justice Statistics (Adalat Bakanlığı İstatistikleri): http://www.cte.adalet.gov.tr.

Özbek, V. O., P. Bacaksiz, and K. Doğan. (2006). *Knowledge on Criminal Law* (Ceza Hukuku Bilgisi). Ankara: Seckin Publishing.

Özbek, V. O., N. Kanbur, P. Bacaksiz, and K. Doğan. (2007). *Knowledge on Criminal Procedures Law* (Ceza Muhakemesi Hukuku Bilgisi). Ankara: Seckin Publishing.

Regulation on Visiting Convicted and the Arrested (Hükümlü Ve Tutukluların Ziyaret Edilmeleri Hakkında Yönetmelik).

Turkmenistan

Legal System: Civil/Islamic
Murder: Medium
Corruption: High
Prison Rate: High
Death Penalty: No
Corporal Punishment: No

Background

Turkmenistan has been an independent nation since October 27, 1991. Prior to that time, it was incorporated into larger countries or empires, including the Union of Soviet Socialist Republics (USSR), the Russian Empire, and the Persian Empire. Contemporary Turkmenistan shares a border with Iran to the southwest, Afghanistan to the southeast, Uzbekistan to the northeast, Kazakhstan to the northwest, and the Caspian Sea to the west. While the majority of the 5 million people in the country are Turkmen, they identify with a variety of nomadic tribes. There are five major tribes—Ersary, Goklen, Teke, Yasr, and Yomut—each of which has a distinct origin and dialect. Most Turkmens are Muslims.

During the 66 years in which Turkmenistan was part of the Soviet Union, it followed the communist model for politics, economics, and ideology. When the communist government of the Soviet Union collapsed in 1991, the First Secretary of the Turkmenistan Communist Party, Saparmurad Niyazov, became the first president of the newly independent Turkmen nation by winning an uncontested election on June 21, 1992. Unlike other postcommunist countries in this region, Niyazov did little to reform the Soviet political and economic systems. Instead he consolidated power and wealth into his own hands, isolated Turkmenistan from the international community, and ruled through a combination of fear and a cult of personality.

In a 1994 referendum, Niyazov's term was extended an additional five years, precluding the presidential election scheduled to take place in 1997. In 1999, he was elected President for Life and continued to rule until he died of cardiac arrest on December 21, 2006. He was succeeded by his vice premier, Gurbanguly Berdimuhamedow, who won the 2007 presidential election.

Government Structure

The Constitution of Turkmenistan, adopted May 18, 1992, is the supreme law of the land. While it states that there are three separate branches of government—executive, legislative, and judicial—in reality the executive branch has centralized and virtually unrestrained power. The Constitution also claims that Turkmenistan operates under the rule of law, but the president has overridden the law on numerous occasions.

The legislative branch is composed of two parliamentary bodies, the Mejlis (National Assembly) and the Halk Maslahaty (People's Council). The Mejlis is composed of 50 officials elected by popular vote to serve five-year terms. Although the Mejlis previously functioned as the country's supreme legislative body, amendments to the Constitution in August 2003 subordinated it to the People's Council, a body composed of 2,500 delegates. The president serves as Chairman for Life of the People's Council and Supreme Leader of the Mejlis. Thus, for all practical purposes, the president of Turkmenistan is the head of both the executive and legislative branches.

The judicial branch is composed of three separate levels—the Supreme Court, six regional courts, and 61 district and city courts. The Constitution states that judges are independent. They are only subordinate to law and are guaranteed immunity from criminal and civil liability. To ensure this independence, the Constitution specifies that judges may not hold other paid positions or take part in political associations during their term. However, judges at all levels are appointed by the president. They serve five-year terms that may be renewed indefinitely. The president also has the sole authority to dismiss judges, thereby making the judiciary subordinate to the executive branch.

Legal System

The legal system in Turkmenistan is still strongly influenced by the Soviet model plus Islamic law. The Soviet Union created the socialist legal system, which was rooted in the civil law tradition, but adapted to conditions specific to communism. In particular, it was characterized by a large number of public laws related to the regulations of the state, especially economic functions. The legal system was also used to administer political justice and consolidate power for government leaders. Although the Soviet Union tried to ban all religions, Turkmenistan reclaimed its Islamist heritage with independence. As a result, the legal system is also influenced by Islamic law, which recognizes rules of behavior as revealed by God rather than created by people.

Policing

Turkmenistan's criminal justice system remains much as it was during the Soviet era. The structure and practices of policing are no exception. The various security forces in Turkmenistan operate independently of the military. The Ministry of Internal Affairs maintains jurisdiction over the national police force, continuing to direct the operations of police departments throughout the country as it did during Soviet times. Given that the Office of the Procurator General fulfills all investigative needs, the role of the police is generally restricted to the routine maintenance of public order and to performing administrative tasks. The Ministry of National Security retains most of the same functions as the Soviet-era Committee for State Security (KGB). Its primary responsibility is to ensure that the government remains in power. The criminal police, operating through the Ministry of Internal Affairs, work closely with the Ministry of National Security on national security issues. In addition to the above-discussed ministries, the president's personal security force also performs policing functions. According to Freedom House, the Presidential Guard is composed of 2,000 to 3,000 former security agents and it is not subordinate to any of the other security services. As with the Ministry of National Security, it operates with impunity.

Turkmenistan's security agencies have traditionally been viewed as instruments of state repression, and accusations of police abuse are rampant. According to the Department of State Report on Human Rights Practices in 2007, Turkmenistan's human rights problems include the torture and mistreatment of detainees, incommunicado and prolonged detention, and arbitrary arrest and detention. The abuse and torture of suspects for confessions are also widespread. While President Berdimuhamedow created a commission to review citizens' complaints of abuse by law enforcement agencies, it is questionable whether members of law enforcement were being held accountable. Notably, in July 2007, the chair of the Supreme Court, who served as the leader of the police complaints commission, was fired and later arrested, in part for failing to assure that cases of abuse were properly reviewed.

Crime

Classification of Crimes

Turkmen law distinguishes four categories of crime: light, average, serious, and grave. These categories indicate the severity of the criminal act and the maximum punishment that may be applied in the form of deprivation of freedom. Light crimes are punishable by a maximum sentence of 2 years; average crimes can go up to 8 years; serious crimes carry up to 15 years; and grave crimes up to 20 years. Prior to 1999, grave crimes were also punishable by death.

Under Turkmen law, an individual may not be held criminally responsible if he or she failed to reach the age of majority prior to committing the crime under consideration or if he or she was legally insane at the time of the crime. The age of majority is 18; however, 14- to 16-year-olds may be subject to criminal liability in some cases. Juveniles charged with more serious crimes, such as intentional murder, rape, and robbery, may be held criminally responsible for their actions. The criminal code defines sanity as the ability to appreciate the nature and quality of one's actions (or inaction) at the time of the crime. While individuals, such as the mentally ill, may be deemed not responsible under Turkmen law, the court retains the authority to mandate treatment. With regard to alcohol and drug use, intoxication does not relieve one of criminal responsibility; however, the court may consider the reason for one's intoxication, degree of intoxication, and the influence of intoxication on one's criminal act at sentencing.

Drug Trafficking

Although Turkmenistan is not a significant producer or source country for illegal drugs, its geographical position makes it attractive to drug smugglers. According to the International Criminal Police Organization (INTERPOL) in 2008, an estimated 24 percent of all Afghan heroin is smuggled along the Silk Route, which runs through Kazakhstan, Kyrgyzstan, Tajikistan, Turkmenistan, and Uzbekistan. Turkmenistan's vulnerability to drug trafficking is largely due to the 744-kilometer (462.3-mile) border that it shares with Afghanistan and the 992-kilometer (616-mile) border that it shares with Iran, both of which are rugged and remote, making them difficult to police. Turkmenistan is primarily a transit country for Afghan narcotics, including opium and heroin, bound for Russia, Western Europe, and heroin to Turkey.

Turkmenistan's counternarcotics activities are carried out by the Ministry of National Security, Ministry of Internal Affairs, State Customs Service, Border Guards Service, and Prosecutor General's Office under the supervision of the State Counternarcotics Coordination Commission. Vowing to wage a large-scale war against drugs, President Berdimuhamedow implored these law enforcement agencies to devote all of their time and resources to combating the drug trade at a meeting of the cabinet of ministers in June 2007. Although Turkmenistan's government has shown a commitment to counter narcotics, it lacks the requisite equipment, training, and resources to tackle a problem of this magnitude. According to the United Nations Office on Drugs and Crime, law enforcement officials in Turkmenistan seized more than 1,000 kilograms (2,200 pounds) of illegal narcotics in 2005.

Domestic Drug Use

Domestic drug abuse, specifically of opium and marijuana, is on the rise in Turkmenistan. According to the Silk Road Studies Program and the Central Asia-Caucasus Institute, the number of registered drug users has increased from around 3,000 in 1995 to 13,000 in 2002. This is not surprising given the increased presence of narcotics resulting from the drug trade. The Turkmenistan Helsinki Foundation, a human rights group operating out of Bulgaria, estimated that Turkmenistan has the highest number of regular drug users per capita in Central Asia. In an effort to combat this problem, the Turkmen Ministry of Health runs seven drug-treatment facilities where narcotics addicts can receive confidential drug treatment. This is imperative since drug addiction is a prosecutable offense that may result in jail time, though drug addicts are traditionally sentenced to treatment if convicted. In addition to drug addiction, a Library of Congress Report has suggested that the presence of illegal drugs has resulted in an increase in street crimes related to drug addiction. Likewise, the Bureau of International Narcotics and Law Enforcement Affairs cited President Berdimuhamedow as reporting in March 2007 that the number of drug-related crimes was on the rise.

Corruption

Corruption has also proved challenging for Turkmenistan. Transparency International gave it a score of 1.8 on its Corruption Perception Index (CPI) for 2008. With scores ranging from 0 "highly corrupt" to 10 "highly clean," this ranking indicates that Turkmenistan is one of the most corrupt nations in the world. Of the 180 countries receiving a CPI ranking in 2007, only 13 received lower rankings than Turkmenistan. Though corruption takes many forms, Turkmenistan is mainly beset by problems of embezzlement and bribe taking. This is not surprising given the low salaries of law enforcement officials and the broad extent of their power. Numerous reports from human rights organizations have suggested the involvement of police and other high-level officials in bribe solicitation and narcotics smuggling.

In 2002 former president Niyazov embarked on a campaign against corruption among the elite, during which more than 200 state workers were arrested. Although the government is ostensibly addressing the problem of corruption by regularly purging the government of corrupt officials, human rights organizations such as Freedom House have suggested that authorities exploit such campaigns to remove potential rivals and that they merely serve as a pretext for maintaining the current power structure.

Crime Statistics

Relatively little information is available concerning the prevalence of crime in Turkmenistan. Although the government does not publish any crime statistics, the Overseas Security Advisory Council (OSAC) reported in 2007 that the overall crime rate is reasonably low. The center of Ashgabat was noted for being particularly low in crime because of the high police presence in the area. However, the OSAC reported that Turkmenistan's burglary rate is rather high, likely due to the common practice among residents of keeping money at home rather than in a bank.

Some statistics concerning the frequency of crime are available from international organizations. For example, the World Health Organization Mortality Database reports that the rate of registered homicides has hovered around 2 to 3 per 100,000 population for the period 1981 through 1998, with the male rate approximately double that of females. According to the Ninth United Nations Survey on Crime Trends and the Operations of Criminal Justice Systems, police recorded 373 intentional homicides in 2004 or 8.06 intentional homicides per 100,000 population.

The United Nations Children's Fund (UNICEF) also supplies information related to the incidence of crime in Turkmenistan. The UNICEF TransMONEE database, which contains data on the situation of children in Central and Eastern Europe, the Commonwealth of Independent States, and the Baltic States, provides estimates for Turkmenistan's juvenile crime rate and total crime rate. The juvenile crime rate was 45 per 100,000 population in 2002 and the total crime rate was 169 per 100,000 population in 2002. These statistics should be interpreted cautiously given how little information about crime in Turkmenistan is made public.

Finding of Guilt

The Office of the Procurator General supervises criminal investigations. The procurator general is appointed by the president to a five-year term. All regional procurators are also appointed by the president, although staff at lower levels is appointed by the procurator general.

Rights of the Accused

The Turkmen Constitution guarantees equality of citizens before the law regardless of gender, religion, or nation of origin. It protects against arbitrary arrest and detention and violations of the home. It guarantees the right to remain silent, right to a public trial, and the right to appeal court decisions and sentences. The law also provides for rights of due process, including the right to call witnesses; the right to self-representation; the right to an attorney, court-appointed if necessary; access to government evidence; and the right to be free from double jeopardy.

While Turkmenistan has guaranteed a number of rights to the accused, these rights are often disregarded in practice. For instance, the Constitution recognizes the right to professional legal assistance at all stages of the legal process; however, a number of sources, including the U.S. Department of State and the Library of Congress, have indicated that there is a shortage of independent defense attorneys in Turkmenistan. This problem is likely exacerbated by the fact that the Ministry of Justice has forbidden the establishment of an organized bar. Human rights organizations have also alleged that Turkmen authorities frequently deny the accused access to defense attorneys. Defendants have also been prevented from confronting their accusers, have often not enjoyed a presumption of innocence, and have been denied their right to a public trial. Defendants and their attorneys have also been denied access to accusatory materials and have been prevented from entering exculpatory materials into evidence.

While the Constitution stipulates that evidence may not be acquired using psychological or physical force or by unlawful means, Freedom House and other human rights organizations have observed that convictions are commonly based on coerced confessions, extracted through the use of torture and psychotropic substances. At times, state-sponsored television networks have been used to present suspects publically "confessing" their guilt. This practice was especially prominent following the attempt on President Niyazov's life in November 2002. The International Helsinki Federation for Human Rights has suggested that torture and humiliation were used to obtain these publicized declarations of guilt.

Although the state also guarantees equal protection under the law, numerous reports indicate that members of religious minorities, especially Baptists, Protestants, and Jehovah's Witnesses, are subjected to harassment by authorities. The International Religious Freedom Report released by the Bureau of Democracy, Human Rights, and Labor reported that adherents to minority religions were threatened with fines, loss of employment, and imprisonment in 2007.

Protections against arbitrary arrest and detention are also regularly violated. A warrant is not required for arrest. The chair of the cabinet of ministers, a position filled by the president, must approve those that are issued. Turkmen law dictates that suspects may be detained for up to 72 hours without a formal arrest warrant. Law enforcement officials are required to obtain an indictment within 10 days of arrest to continue holding a suspect. Bail is not an option in Turkmenistan. Once a bill of indictment is issued, the detainee's right to counsel attaches. Turkmen law dictates that pretrial detention should last no longer than two months or, in exceptional cases, one year. However, the various limitations on pretrial detention are often exceeded. Authorities hold suspects for an average of two to three months before trial in pretrial detention facilities. Reports indicate that detainees are sometimes held incommunicado, leaving family members in the dark concerning their whereabouts. Some of the more egregious violations of the protection against arbitrary arrest and detention occurred subsequent to the attack on Niyazov's motorcade in November 2002. In the months that followed, authorities detained several hundred suspects in addition to some of their families and friends.

The Turkmen Court Structure

Turkmenistan does not use a jury system. All cases are tried by a panel of judges or, in some cases, by an individual judge. The basic structure of Turkmenistan's court system has remained essentially unchanged since the Soviet era. It is composed of three separate levels—the Supreme Court, 6 regional courts, and 61 district and city courts. The Supreme Court, which is composed of 22 members, including a president, judges, and associate judges, hears cases of national importance only. The Supreme Court is separated into civil, criminal, and military chambers. The regional or appellate level is composed of five provincial courts (i.e., the Provincial Court of Ahal, Balkan, Dashhowuz, Lebap, and Mary) and a separate court for the capital city of Ashgabat. Lastly, the district and city courts, located within the provinces, hear cases concerning civil, criminal, and administrative matters. Criminal cases involving members of the armed forces are also tried in the district and city courts. Beyond these three levels, there are military courts, in which disciplinary cases are tried and those criminal cases involving crimes committed by and against military personnel, and the Supreme Economic Court, which settles disputes between enterprises and state agencies, as did the State Arbitration Court of the Soviet era.

Information regarding Turkmenistan's juvenile justice system is not widely available. A report by the UN Committee on the Rights of the Child indicates that persons under 18 are subject to the same criminal procedures as adults, that children may be held up to six months pending trial, that youth offenders are not always separated from adults, that confessions are sometimes extracted by force, and that deprivation of liberty is not always used as a last resort.

Punishment

Types of Punishment

The Constitution of Turkmenistan originally provided for capital punishment, but it was amended on December 29, 1999, by presidential decree. In its current form, the Constitution stipulates that no one may be deprived of his or her right to life. Prior to its abolition, the death penalty was reserved for the most serious crimes, such as intentional homicide, rape, genocide, treason, espionage, terrorism, and the illegal production, processing, acquisition, storage, and transportation of narcotic drugs for the purpose of sale. Today, the maximum sentence for these crimes is life imprisonment without possibility of parole, pardon, or amnesty. President Niyazov proposed life imprisonment as the new maximum shortly after the attempt on his life in 2002. Before that time, the 1998 Criminal Code of Turkmenistan allowed for prison sentences between 6 months and 20 years.

On January 16, 2003, the National Assembly passed a decree allowing for life sentences in cases of treason. Under the new law, one may be classified as a traitor for harming or threatening to harm the president, questioning the authority of the president and his policies, and generally opposing the state. Other serious crimes are punishable by up to 25 years in prison. Sentences depend upon the level of violence involved and the offender's record. In addition to confinement, Turkmen law allows for other penalties, including house arrest and internal and external exile. Exile is typically a punishment reserved for political opponents and former government officials.

Prison

According to the Ninth United Nations Survey on Crime Trends and the Operations of Criminal Justice Systems, the total number of prisoners in Turkmenistan was 14,015 in 2004 and the prison population rate was 302.71 per 100,000 of the national population. Turkmenistan has 19 incarceration facilities, including traditional prisons, education-labor colonies, and correctional-labor colonies. All prisons are run through the Ministry of Internal Affairs.

One of the more controversial prison facilities in Turkmenistan is Ovadan-Depe, an incarceration center located just outside of Ashgabat in the Kara-Kum ("black sands") desert. Ovadan-Depe, meaning "Picturesque Hill," was built in 2003 at the insistence of former president Niyazov to house his political opponents, mostly former state officials and persons implicated in the 2002 attack on his life. Niyazov had a hand in designing the prison and personally oversaw its construction. Reports suggest that he would take newly appointed state officials on visits to the facility as a warning of what would become of them if they were to question his authority. Accounts of the prison indicate that inmates live in terrible conditions and are subject to torture.

On December 21, 2006, Niyazov's death triggered a riot at Ovadan-Depe. After news of his death reached the prison, inmates demanded to be set free, banging on the prison bars with their dishes. Soldiers with trained dogs were sent in to take control of the situation; however, their presence merely encouraged the prisoners. In the end, the prison administration enlisted military aid to suppress the revolt. The Turkmenistan Helsinki Foundation for Humans Rights reported that 23 people were killed after servicemen with machine guns arrived on the scene. President Berdimuhamedow has since indicated that the prison will be demolished.

Though unique in its inception and prison population, conditions at Ovadan-Depe are not exceptional when compared to those at other detention centers in the country. Prison conditions in Turkmenistan are generally poor. According to human rights organizations, the abuse of prisoners is a consistent problem. Countries have denied extradition requests made by Turkmenistan for this very reason. One high-profile case of prisoner abuse concerns the death in custody of Ogulsapar Muradova, a reporter for Radio Free Liberty and an activist for the Turkmenistan Helsinki Foundation. Muradova was convicted of illegal arms possession and antistate activities in August 2006 during a closed trial in which she was refused legal assistance. Amnesty International suggests that the charges against her were fabricated. On September 13, shortly after receiving a six-year prison sentence, Muradova was found dead. Although authorities maintain that she died of natural causes, witnesses said her body showed signs of torture. As of yet, there has been no independent investigation into her death.

Aside from prisoner abuse, a number of other factors contribute to the generally poor conditions of Turkmenistan's detention centers. Prison facilities are badly overcrowded and unsanitary, producing outbreaks of tuberculosis (TB) and other infectious diseases. What's more, inadequate medical care has prompted some concern that inmates are released prior to their being tested and treated for TB, thereby putting the larger community at risk for this disease. According to the World Health Organization, TB case identification rates in general rose in Turkmenistan from 58.6 per 100,000 population in 1980 to 79.3 in 1997. Food and water supplies are also insufficient. The Department of State Report on Human Rights Practices in Turkmenistan observed that inmates must often depend on family members to supplement their diets. Notably, those convicted of treason are forbidden from receiving provisions from their relatives.

Access to prisoners by relatives and international organizations is frequently limited. According to Human Rights Watch, regular access to incarcerated family members is generally denied and some are held incommunicado. Visiting policies and privileges commonly depend upon one's crime of conviction, with political prisoners having the most restricted visitation rights. Organizations such as the International Committee of the Red Cross, which has engaged in activities designed to fight drug-resistant tuberculosis in Kyrgyzstani prisons and to reduce the TB mortality rate in Azerbaijani prisons, have also been denied access to Turkmenistan's incarceration facilities.

Mass prisoner amnesties became a common occurrence under Niyazov's regime and have continued to be a regular event under the direction of Berdimuhamedow, largely due to prison overpopulation. There were four prisoner amnesties in 1999 alone, one of which involved pardoning more than 10,000 inmates. Before their release, prisoners were required to pledge that they would refrain from criminal activity and be loyal to the *Ruhnama,* Niyazov's "Book of the Soul," during a televised event. In the same year, a law was passed regarding annual amnesty and pardoning that mandated an amnesty take place each year at the end of Ramadan, a Muslim holy month. While mass prisoner amnesties cut down on the overcrowding in Turkmenistan's incarceration facilities, relief is short-lived due to the high number of arrests and lengthy prison sentences.

The majority of the prisoners eligible for amnesty are petty felons. Those convicted of more serious crimes, including rape, murder, and terrorism, are officially barred from receiving pardons. Freedom House has suggested that, with the exclusion of political prisoners, such individuals are routinely freed after the payment of bribes. Therefore, it is not surprising that amnesties are generally followed by a rise in crime. For example, according to Freedom House, an amnesty in October 2005 was reportedly followed by an increase in the incidence of muggings and burglaries. Roughly two-thirds of the prison population (8,145 inmates) were released during that amnesty. Two mass pardons have occurred since Berdimuhamedow became president. Eleven prisoners were released on August 9, 2007, and 9,013 on October 9, 2007. Although these pardons did not include a significant number of political prisoners sentenced under Niyazov's regime, a few high-profile inmates, including environmental activist Andrey Zatoka and three Jehovah's Witnesses who had refused mandatory military service, were pardoned.

Jennifer Lynn Owens and Janet P. Stamatel

Further Reading

Cummings, Sally N. (2003). *Oil, Transition and Security in Central Asia.* London: Routledge.

Open Society Institute. Turkmenistan Project, a Division of the Open Society Institute's Central Eurasia Project: http://www.eurasianet.org/turkmenistan.project/index.php?page=about&lang=eng.

Siever, Eric W. Law and Environment Eurasia Partnership (LEEP). (1992, May 18). "Constitution of Turkmenistan." University of Texas at Arlington. (Translated in 1997). http://www.uta.edu/cpsees/TURKCON.htm.

Stalbovsky, Oleg, and Maria Stalbovskaya. A Research Guide to the Turkmenistan Legal System: GlobaLex: http://www.nyulawglobal.org/globalex/turkmenistan.htm.

Uzbekistan

Legal System: Civil
Murder: Medium
Corruption: High
Human Trafficking: Medium
Prison Rate: Medium
Death Penalty: No
Corporal Punishment: No

Background

The Republic of Uzbekistan has a population of 27,780,059 as of July 2007, approximately 37 percent of this being urban and 63 percent rural. Common to Central Asia, the populace of Uzbekistan is quite young. It continues to be protected and supported by Russia even after gaining its independence from Soviet rule.

On December 8, 1992, the republic replaced the Constitution of the Uzbek Soviet Socialist Republic, adopted in 1976, with a new Constitution oriented toward the development of private property and an open market economy. The new Constitution introduced a separation of powers into the legislative, executive, and judicial branches. The Constitution outlines the human rights provisions in 23 separate articles, comprising over 18 percent of the entire Constitution. These include protection of basic rights, including the right to life and personal inviolability; freedom of speech; protections against torture, arbitrary arrest and incarceration, forced labor; as well as the right to legal defense and a public judicial process. However, according to the World Organization against Torture (OMCT)—Europe and the Legal Aid Society human rights assessment in 2005, these changes have been largely cosmetic.

Policing

The law enforcement system is led by the Ministry of Interior. Information regarding its personnel and budget is a state secret; therefore, there are no accurate data on the number of officials within the ministry. Human rights organizations estimate the total number reaching 200,000. This is nearly three times the size of the army. The responsibilities of this ministry include maintaining public law and order, firefighting, automotive inspection, passport services, and extension of visas for foreign citizens. Special units include those developed to combat terrorism and corruption and internal military units made up of troops trained to handle mass disorder and terrorism. The ministry enjoys a direct relationship with the president's office. The public does not have the opportunity to oversee its activities because the mass media is given no access.

The Library of Congress estimates that the Uzbeki police force is made up of about 25,000 individuals who are trained according to Soviet standards. Recently, the U.S. Department of Justice also began programs in the country to train law enforcement agents in Western techniques. The chief intelligence agency in Uzbekistan, the National Security Service (NSS), which is mainly staffed by former KGB personnel, is made up of approximately 8,000 paramilitary troops. Police are under direct control of the Ministry of Interior (MoI). Corruption, organized crime, narcotics, and other national security issues are handled by the NSS, which is run by a chairman who answers directly to the president.

The Bureau of Democracy, Human Rights, and Labor reported in 2008 that, although human rights training is incorporated into the training of all officers, one of Uzbekistan's most difficult problems is the corruption of law enforcement personnel. According to the World Bank's Worldwide Governance Indicators, corruption is a severe problem in this country. There have even been cases in which false charges have been raised by law enforcement officers against individuals believed to have knowledge of corruption.

Bribery of police agents as well as arbitrary detainment of citizens is commonplace. Bribery is even widespread within traffic enforcement. In a recent survey, reported by the Library of Congress, the majority of Uzbek citizens stated that bribery is a routine occurrence in not only police departments, but also in courts and in the office of the state procurator. Such abuses are investigated and disciplined internally, but the government rarely punishes law enforcement agents involved in such undertakings. Narcotics and the trafficking of weapons are also believed to be sustained and supported by law enforcement and government officials. In this same survey, 25 percent of responding police agreed that other officers were in the practice of taking bribes or involved in the sale of narcotics.

Bribery is not restricted to law enforcement and political figures. Judges are also often influenced by bribes when deciding civil suits. Common services in Uzbekistan also often come at a price. In the survey mentioned above, more than two-thirds of respondents stated that bribes were necessary to receive services that are intended to be provided for all citizens free of charge. For example, in 1993, it was determined that the cost of admission to a prestigious institution cost nearly twice the average annual salary in Uzbekistan.

Finding of Guilt

Procurator/Prosecutor

The Procurator's Office functions to ensure consistent and accurate application of the law and to protect the rights and freedoms of citizens, including due process. It carries out investigations for many types of crimes and represents the state in prosecution. It is a centralized system of supervision, prosecution, and surveillance led by the procurator general. The procurator operates independently from the government, abiding only to the law. However, in practice, this office is controlled and influenced by the executive power, as the procurator general is appointed by the president for five-year terms.

According to the Criminal Procedure Code (CPC), prosecutors oversee the inquiry and pretrial investigation of each case. Their responsibilities include ordering arrests; supervising investigation in regard to measures of restraint, search, and seizures; pretrial investigations; monitoring telephone and other communications; recommending sentences; and forwarding criminal cases to court. At trial, the prosecutor conducts the prosecution; expresses his or her opinion on the application of Criminal Code provisions, sentencing, and other issues including

Alleged participants in an uprising in the city of Andijan sit behind bars during a trial in Tashkent, Uzbekistan, November 14, 2005. (AP Photo)

dismissing the case if he or she concludes that court findings show the defendant is not guilty.

Investigation

Investigative agencies include the police; military commanders; national security service officials; head of punishment enforcement systems, penitentiary facilities, convict colonies, correction colonies, investigative isolation wards, and prisons; fire security officials; border guard agents; captains of seagoing vessels; and customs agents. Heads of these agencies have the power to initiate, or refuse initiation of, criminal cases and begin the process of inquiry. Under their supervision, inquiry officers conduct investigations into criminal cases as well as assist investigators throughout their investigations.

Investigators of the prosecutor's offices, internal affairs agencies, and the NSS conduct pretrial investigations. Investigators have the power to initiate and discontinue criminal cases, detain and interrogate suspects, conduct investigations, prosecute, and impose measures of restraint. They also have the right to object to the decisions of prosecutors including classification of the offense, scope of the charge, imposition of detention as a measure of restraint, or dismissal of a case.

Public Accusers and Public Defenders

Representatives from public organizations or communities are elected to act as public accusers or public defenders in court hearings. During court proceedings, public accusers and public defenders have the power to review case files, introduce evidence and participate in its examination, and file motions. Public accusers have the right to substantiate accusation while public defenders have the right to justify the crime or show mitigating circumstance.

Local Self-Governance

Issues can also be settled at the local level through the use of local self-governance organs. These are known as Mahalla Committees (*mahalla* meaning community). Decisions made in this capacity can be based on local interests, customs, and traditions as well as on national and spiritual values. Powers of these Mahalla Committees are kept separate from state power. However, in practice, state interests are upheld, as the chair of the Mahalla is paid by the state.

One of the key principles of the Mahalla Committee is the preservation of families. These committees act as courts on family issues. This dedication to the family comes at a cost, though, as it is considered unacceptable for one member of a family to press charges or raise claims against another. Therefore, Mahalla Committees will deny abused wives permission to file a divorce, instead sending them home to their violent husbands. This is a clear violation of the law of Uzbekistan as well as a violation of the right to legal defense.

Judicial System

There are a number of types of courts in the Republic of Uzbekistan, categorized by the nature of the cases each handles. These include the constitutional court, which reviews laws, decrees, and judicial decisions to ensure compliance with the Constitution; the Supreme Court with general jurisdiction, which handles cases of national significance; the Higher Economic Court, as well as economic regional and city courts; supreme civil courts as well as civil courts operating on the city, district, interdistrict, and provincial levels; supreme criminal courts as well as criminal courts operating on the city or district level; and martial courts.

The legal system of Uzbekistan is based on the civil law system. The three branches of government act independently, and the judicial branch also operates independently from political parties and other community associations. However, the courts exercise little independence in practice, taking direction from the executive branch, particularly the General Prosecutor's Office.

Judges are greatly influenced by the process of appointment and dismissal. After examination to prove qualifications, candidates are selected by the Judicial Qualification Commission under each court to then be interviewed by the Higher Qualification Commission. This commission is greatly influenced by the president, as all members of the commission are appointed by the president and are accountable to him. After candidate recommendation from this commission, final approval comes directly from the president. All terms last only five years. The removal of Supreme Court judges must be confirmed by Parliament, which is also greatly influenced by the president. This entire process is known for being nontransparent and almost entirely subjective. These processes are not only found in the Supreme Court, as judges in lower instance courts are also appointed by this process. In this way, the courts remain under complete control of the executive branch of government.

Trial

Most trials are officially open to the public, although, in practice, access is often restricted. To gain access, it is necessary to obtain written permission from the court chairman or from the Supreme Court. This permission is both difficult to obtain and time-consuming. The government also limits the access of international observers at trials.

Uzbekistan does not hold jury trials. Instead, a panel of three judges is selected to preside over each trial. These panels are chosen either by committees of worker collectives or neighborhood committees and consist of one professional judge and two people's assessors. According to the CPC, the people's assessors are entitled to all judicial powers but rarely participate in any active role, and the professional judge usually defers to the recommendations of the prosecutor on all matters, including those that are of a legal nature. For this reason, the role of the courts is often seen as of rather low standard. Judicial errors are numerous and defects in the work of the investigator and procurator are often left unnoticed. Beyond this, the possibility of acquittal is rarely considered.

Juveniles

In the past, Uzbekistan has had a separate law enforcement department to handle minors' issues—the Inspection on the Issues of Minors, which was part of the Ministry of Interior, and there was a similar department on minors' issues in the Procurator's Office. Since 2001, these departments were abolished and their functions were transferred to local inspectors and special commissions within institutes of local self-governance. Currently, there are no special requirements for the arrest and detention of juveniles. Likewise, there are no separate courts for juveniles.

Rights of the Accused

There are a number of rights specifically outlined within the CPC. These include the right to be free from violence, torture, or other cruel or degrading treatment as well as from acts or decisions degrading dignity, violating privacy, endangering health, or causing unjustified suffering. The law also protects the inviolability of dwellings and the confidentiality of correspondence and communications including mail and conversations both in person and over the telephone. These rights can only be legally violated in circumstances specifically outlined in the criminal code.

The law mandates that all detainees be questioned within 24 hours and be afforded the right to remain silent. Formal charges must be made within 72 hours of detention, although the prosecutor has the option to extend this period for an additional seven days. After this extension, the individual must either be charged or released.

As outlined in the CPC, once accused, an individual has the right to be informed of charges against him or her; to give testimony and provide explanations about the charges and circumstances of the case; to file motions and challenges; to introduce evidence; and to participate in investigative actions, with the permission of the inquiry officer or investigator. During criminal proceedings, through the use of interpreters, participants have the right to use a language over which they have a command for all communications including making statements, giving testimonies, and filing complaints. Appeals do not result in the reversal of convictions, but it is not uncommon for sentences to be reduced or suspended after appeal.

All suspects have the right to defense from the moment of apprehension or announcement of their recognition as a suspect and to have unlimited confidential meetings with defense counsel in private. It is the responsibility of the inquiry officer, investigator, prosecutor, or court to inform the accused of his or her rights and ensure the individual has the opportunity to secure defense. If it can be shown that the suspect cannot afford the expense of this defense, the cost is covered by the state.

The rights of the defense counsel are also outlined in the CPC. These include the right to be informed of charge against the defendant; to participate during questioning and interrogations of the defendant, witnesses, experts, and specialists; to introduce evidence; and to file motions, challenges, and complaints. Individuals have the right to serve as their own defense. However, in certain circumstances, it is mandatory that the suspect be aided by legal counsel. These include cases in which the defendant is a juvenile, has mental or physical disabilities, or has no command of the language. Legal defense counsel is also mandatory in cases regarding a capital crime.

According to the 2007 Country Reports on Human Rights Practices, the above rights are generally observed in high-profile human rights and political cases. However, according to the Bureau of Democracy, Human Rights, and Labor, guilty verdicts are often the product of confessions and witness testimonies obtained through torture, threats to family members, or other types of coercion. Furthermore, this report claims that although the government is legally required to provide citizens with the opportunity to examine court documents and decisions, in practice, this information is not made available. This is in part due to the broad definition used for information considered classified, and thus protected, by the state.

Other violations of rights are also commonly found within the criminal justice process. Inquiry officers and investigators often will not inform detainees of their rights but will have the individuals sign a form stating that they were informed of their rights. Also, although the law dictates that suspects be either charged or released within a set period of time, authorities will go so far as to file false charges against an individual to keep the person in custody beyond this time period.

Defense lawyers often play a role of intermediary between the investigators, prosecutors, and judges, holding little influence on the judicial process in the absence of a jury. They often have limited access to case files and evidence and, in many cases, the defendant is not allowed to meet with legal counsel before being questioned by the prosecutor, at times under torture, according to the World Organization against Torture. When lawyers claim that confessions were brought about through coercion or torture, judges often refuse to investigate. According to the Country Reports on Human Rights Practices, state-appointed counsel is often incompetent and their involvement in the case is frequently limited to submitting confessions and mercy pleas.

Human Rights Violations

The Constitution of the Republic of Uzbekistan outlines extensive human rights protections to Uzbek citizens. Legislation in the mid-1990s also enhanced individual rights. However, these rights are not evenly protected, and the government continues to suppress political movements, fabricate charges to justify the arrest of figures opposing the government, and ban independent media as well as unsanctioned public meetings and demonstrations.

In 1996, the president founded the National Human Rights Center of the Republic of Uzbekistan. Headed by a director appointed by the president, the center's functions include the preparation of national reports on human rights protections, ensuring cooperation between the Republic of Uzbekistan and international and national human rights organizations. Yet in 2003, the publication of the UN Special Report (UNSR) on torture drove the Uzbek government to develop further a strategy for the protection of human rights. The only concrete measure resulting from this plan has been a single revision made to the Penal Code to include an article redefining torture and outlining its liability. Only a few offenders have been punished for the use of torture since this amendment.

Human rights violations have especially victimized two target populations:

1. Muslim groups; members of religious organizations considered terrorist groups; human rights groups; opposition parties; and journalists reporting on the views of these groups.
2. Vulnerable people, such as women, children, socioeconomically marginalized individuals, and those accused or convicted of criminal activity.

The most common violations of human rights are torture, arbitrary arrest, and restriction of freedom of speech. These rights are often violated by the same forces set up to protect them. Many reports have been made by international human rights organizations regarding cases of violence and torture in prisons, pretrial facilities, and local police and security service precincts in Uzbekistan. The government in Uzbekistan insists that torture is not systematic but the UN Committee against Torture (CAT) has concluded that torture and abuse were a systemic problem in Uzbekistan.

Crime

Crime Statistics

Uzbek police and security services do not supply official crime statistics for the country, so crime rates are not specifically known. Estimates vary, one such estimate by the United Nations Office on Drug Crimes claims that the total crime rate in 2005 was 300 crimes committed per 100,000 people, and another by the Embassy of the Republic of Uzbekistan puts this figure at only 146 crimes per 100,000 people as of June 2006. The embassy reports low incidents of many crimes compared to neighboring countries. However, according to the Uzbekistan 2007 Crime and Safety Report of the Overseas Security Advisory Council, violent crime is on the rise. Theft, robberies, and violent crimes are not uncommon, and it is believed that this is in part due to the economic conditions of the country. Also, each year thousands of prisoners are set free by government amnesty. Reports showed that in 2005, approximately 28,000 prisoners were pardoned. These individuals then find themselves without assets or stable income and often will return to a life of crime to survive.

Classifications of Crime

Crime is defined in the Criminal Code of the Republic of Uzbekistan as any culpable socially dangerous act causing or inviting a real danger, either by action or inaction. Crimes are classified by character and degree of social danger. Four categories are used: insignificant social danger, less serious, serious, and especially serious. Those classified as crimes with insignificant social danger are any intentional crimes punishable by imprisonment up to three years as well as crimes committed unintentionally and punishable by imprisonment up to five years. Less serious crimes are intentional crimes punishable from three to five years and unintentionally committed crimes punishable by imprisonment more than five years. Intentional crimes punishable by 5 to 10 years' imprisonment are classified as serious crimes and those punishable by more than 10 years are considered especially serious crimes.

In Uzbekistan, only individuals aged 16 years or older and deemed sane at the moment of commission of the crime are subject to liability. One exception to this is in the case of intentional aggravated killing. For this crime, individuals as young as 13 can be held liable. Insane individuals by law are those who, due to a chronic or temporary mental disorder, could not be aware of the character of their actions and control them. If the court recognizes an individual as insane when committing a socially dangerous act, it can apply compulsory medical measures. Being under the influence of alcohol, narcotics, or other substances affecting cognitive functioning is not grounds to discharge an individual from criminal liability.

Types of Crime

The Uzbekistan Criminal Code defines the following major crimes:

- *Assault* is an intentional infliction of serious bodily injury endangering life, disfiguring the body, causing illness, interrupting a pregnancy, causing the loss of eyesight or hearing, or causing disability. Such acts are punishable with imprisonment from three to five years. An offender can be sentenced to up to 10 years if there are various aggravating circumstances.
- *Rape,* sexual intercourse committed by force or threats of abuse, is punishable with three to seven years' of imprisonment. This sentence can be raised to 10 years if there are multiple victims or multiple offenders, and up to 15 years if there are other various aggravating factors. Although the law prohibits rape, cases are rarely reported to the press, as cultural norms discourage women and their families from speaking openly about this topic. Marital rape is implicitly prohibited under the rape laws but never has such a case been known to be tried in court.
- *Robbery* is punishable with correctional labor up to 5 years' imprisonment and up to 15 years with aggravating factors, especially if organized.
- *Theft* is defined in the criminal code as "larceny in secret" and is punishable with a fine up to 50 minimum monthly wages, correctional labor up to two years, arrest up to six months, or imprisonment up to three years. A larger sentence can be ordered in cases of pickpocketing or in cases in which the offender illegally entered a dwelling.
- *The intentional killing of another person* is punishable by imprisonment from 10 and 15 years. Aggravated intentional killing is punishable with up to 25 years' imprisonment. The intentional killing of a newborn child committed by the mother during childbirth or immediately thereafter is punishable with imprisonment up to three years.

Drug Crime

Use of narcotic, psychotropic, or other substances that affect intellectual ability is punishable with correctional labor up to three years or imprisonment up to three years. A second offense is punishable with up to five years' imprisonment. Individuals convicted of lesser drug offenses may be relieved of the penalty for their crime if they voluntarily surrender the substances.

Manufacture and Sale

The illegal raising of opium, oil poppy, cannabis, or other plants that contain narcotic or psychotropic substances is punishable with a fine from 25 to 50 minimum monthly wages, correctional labor up to three years, or imprisonment up to three years. Punishment may be increased up to 20 years' imprisonment according to the size of operation and type of drug and amount.

Trafficking

Uzbekistan's central location makes it a prime area for narcotics trafficking. Since independence, border security has become more lax, allowing more drugs to be brought in and out of the country across the Afghanistan border, bound for Russian and Western European markets, according to the CIA World Factbook. At the same time, it is estimated that each year between 2,000 and 3,000 hectares (4,942 and 7,413 acres) of opium poppy is grown domestically. Cannabis is also increasingly problematic as it grows wild in Uzbekistan.

Since the 1990s, drug sales have been increasingly connected to arms sales and funding of armed groups in neighboring Afghanistan and Tajikistan. Consequently, drug-related crime has risen significantly in Uzbekistan. In 2005, it was estimated that there were 31 drug-related crimes per 100,000 people. Since the 1990s, rates of domestic drug use have also sharply risen. In 1994, it was estimated by the Ministry of Health that the country had about 44,000 drug addicts. As of 2005, it was estimated that there were 74 registered drug abusers per 100,000 people. More than 64 percent of these individuals were heroin users. In 2005, there were 467 reported heroin seizures in Uzbekistan, 108 opium seizures, and 445 cannabis seizures, according to the United Nations Office on Drug Crimes.

Domestic narcotics processing was first recognized as a problem in 1995 when several kilograms of locally produced heroin were seized by authorities. In this year, the National Commission on Drug Control was established in Uzbekistan to raise public awareness and improve coordination between the National Security Service, the Ministry of Internal Affairs, and the State Customs Committee—all sharing jurisdiction in this arena. A new criminal code also outlined harsher penalties for drug-related crimes and the government's eradication program was significantly expanded.

Punishment

Measures of Restraint

There are several different measures of restraint. These include allowing release on bail, recognizance to show good conduct, and personal surety. The court can also order a suspect into pretrial detention for the duration of the investigation. If a suspect is released on bail, the amount of bail is determined by the inquiry officer, investigator, prosecutor, or court. Bail can be paid with money, valuables, or immovable property. If the suspect violates the obligations of bail, the bail is transferred to the government and a more severe measure of restraint is applied.

The most restrictive measure of restraint is pretrial detention. Detainees are kept in areas separate from the general population of individuals serving their prison terms. Within the areas used specifically for detainees, men are kept separately from women and juveniles from adults. Individuals believed to be especially dangerous recidivists are also kept separate from the others. In the cases in which the crime committed is classified as serious or very serious, defendants are held in prisons or in cells within investigation isolation wards. In some instances, defendants charged with the same offense or a series of interconnected offenses will be kept in separate premises. This measure of restraint is not used in cases of juvenile defendants or if the defendant is over the age of 60, severely ill, or has a psychiatric disorder.

Defendants held in custody may be kept in detention facilities for no longer than 10 days. In the event that it is impossible to deliver the detainee to the investigation isolation ward within 10 days, the person may be kept in detention facilities for no longer than 30 days. Defendants can be held in investigation isolation wards for no longer than three months. After this time, it is necessary to seek approval for continued custody if it is impossible for the investigation to be completed in this time frame. The maximum allowable time frame with extensions is one year. This extension can only be granted by the general prosecutor. If there is a conviction, the court credits one day of commitment to a disciplinary unit or three days of correctional labor for each day of pretrial detention.

Penalties

There are a number of possible punishments that can be ordered by the courts including fine, correctional labor, arrest, and imprisonment. Military servicemen are penalized by suspension from office or commitment to a disciplinary unit. An additional punishment of the deprivation of certain rights can be used as additional penalty or as the primary punishment.

Fines range from 5 to 600 times the minimal monthly wages. Correctional labor can be ordered with terms ranging from six months to three years. If ordered to correctional labor, 10 to 30 percent of the offender's salary is turned over to the state. The place of employment for correctional labor is determined by agencies in charge of the execution of the penalty. This form of punishment is not used for individuals who are pregnant, disabled, or on military service.

Imprisonment is defined as isolation through the commitment to a prison or to what is known as a "colony of execution of penalty." Imprisonment can be ordered for a time period of six months to 20 years.

Colonies are categorized into three types: settled, general security, and high security. Settled colonies are used for individuals convicted of less serious crimes or those crimes deemed not socially dangerous. Those convicted of intentional less serious and serious crimes are held in colonies of general security, and high-security colonies are reserved for individuals convicted of especially serious crimes or those offenders who have been convicted of a crime for which they have previously been imprisoned. Also held in high-security colonies are those prisoners for whom, by an act of pardon, capital punishment was commutated to imprisonment.

Compulsory medical measures may be also be ordered in cases in which the offender is found to be insane at the time of the act or has become mentally diseased before the sentence has been rendered or during the term of his or her sentence. The purpose of these measures is both treatment and prevention of further crime. These measures may include outpatient supervision and psychiatric treatment or in-patient treatment in a psychiatric institution. Compulsory medical measures may also be ordered for those suffering from alcohol, drugs, and toxic substances addiction.

The courts also have the option of ordering a conditional conviction. If the court determines that a person sentenced to imprisonment, committed to a disciplinary unit, suspended from office, or sentenced to correctional labor may be corrected without serving the sentence, the court may decide not to execute the imposed penalty. This may be determined because of the nature and degree of the crime, the personality of the offender, or other circumstances of the case. In such a case, the individual will be placed under supervision for a period of probation. If during that period of supervision, there emerge no reasons for revocation of the conditional conviction, the original penalty will not be executed. Probationary periods range from one to three years. During this time, the offender may be ordered to compensate the victims of the crime, find employment, or enroll in an educational program. The individual may also be required to undergo alcohol or drug rehabilitation or be restricted from going to certain places. Conditional conviction cannot be ordered in cases of especially serious crimes or repeat offenders unless the offender is a juvenile, disabled, female, or over the age of 60.

Conditional early release may also be ordered if the offender has completed one-third of a sentence for a less serious crime, one-half of a sentence for a serious crime, or two-thirds of a sentence for an especially serious crime. Conditional early release is not allowed in cases in which capital punishment was commutated to imprisonment or in cases in which the offender is considered a dangerous recidivist or is known to participate in an organized criminal group. It is also not allowed in cases of aggravated intentional killing, rape, crimes against the Republic of Uzbekistan, smuggling of weapons of mass destruction, or smuggling of drugs.

A first-time offender who commits a minor or less serious crime may be relinquished entirely from liability for the crime if the offender has undone the damage caused by the act; surrendered to authorities and admitted his or her guilt; repented for his or her behavior and reconciled with the victim; and assisted in the detection of the crime. Crimes for which this discharge of liability is possible include intentional infliction of medium or trivial bodily injury, infliction of intentional serious bodily injury in the heat of passion, infliction of unintentional serious or medium bodily injury, professional negligence, neglect of the helpless, failure to take care of a minor or disabled person, insult, infringement of copyright, larceny by embezzlement, fraud, theft, and the intentional destruction or damage of property.

Capital Punishment

Capital punishment through firing squad was once allowed as penalty for an intentional aggravated killing, aggression, genocide, and terrorism. The death penalty could not be imposed on men over the age of 60 or below the age of 18 or on women. Although exact numbers cannot be found, Mothers against the Death Penalty and Torture estimates that, in the recent past, well over 100 people were executed each year in Uzbekistan. Families of those sentenced to execution were given no notification by the government of the sentence, the date of execution, or the burial place. This was deemed cruel and inhuman by the UNSR on torture. Furthermore, it was noted in the Country Reports on Human Rights Practices that local and international observers reported that those sentenced to death often did not have adequate legal defense and were not given adequate opportunity to appeal their sentence after conviction.

As of January 1, 2008, legislation was adopted abolishing the death penalty and replacing it with terms of imprisonment ranging from 20 years to life, which by Uzbek law is equivalent to 25 years. This legislation mandates that prisoners sentenced to life must serve 20 years before making their first appeal. It also limits lifetime imprisonment to those individuals convicted of premeditated murder and terrorism. Those offenders sentenced to life imprisonment are held under incredibly harsh conditions and allowed only one short meeting with family and one telephone call each year during the first 10 years of the sentence, according to Kuban Abdymen writing for the Inter Press Service in 2008. He also reports that after the death penalty was abolished, Amnesty International requested that Uzbek authorities release details regarding the past operation of the death penalty, including the sites of burial, but this information has not yet been obtained. However, according to Penal Reform International, some human rights activists have estimated that about 1,000 prisoners were on death row when the punishment was abolished.

Juvenile Punishment

There are two types of correctional facilities used for juveniles: general and high security. Upon a male juvenile's first offense, he will be sentenced to a general security facility. After subsequent offenses, he will serve his sentence in a facility of high security. Female juveniles, on the other hand, are always held in colonies of general security.

When determining sentencing, the court will consider such things as the minor's level of development, personality, life conditions, and reasons for commission of the crime. If sentencing a juvenile to imprisonment or correctional labor, the court may decide to impose a conditional conviction in much the same manner as it would for adult offenders. If it is determined that correction is possible without penalty, for reasons related to the nature of the crime, the individual's personality, or other circumstance, the court may discharge a first-time juvenile offender from liability if the crime was of a minor social danger. If it is determined that, due to underdevelopment, the juvenile was unable to fully understand the consequences of his or her action, the court is obliged to consider substituting compulsory measures for the penalty. These measures may include offering an apology to the victims of the crime, compensating the victims for damages caused by the crime, or commitment to an educational colony.

Punishments for juveniles include fine, correctional labor, arrest, and imprisonment. Fines can range from 2 to 20 minimal monthly wages; correctional labor (imposed only on employable juveniles) can range from one month to one year; and arrest periods can range from one to three months. Juveniles can be sentenced to a maximum of 10 years' imprisonment for the most serious offenses.

Like their adult counterparts, juveniles may be eligible for conditional early release from imprisonment or correctional labor under certain circumstances. After completing one-quarter of the sentence for a less serious crime, one-third of the sentence for a serious crime, or one-half of the sentence for an especially serious crime, conditional early release may be allowed.

Prisons

According to prison officials reporting to the United Nations Office on Drug Crimes, as of 2004, there were 168 prisoners per 100,000 people in Uzbekistan. As of 2007, approximately 34,000 inmates were held at 53 detention facilities throughout the country.

Prison conditions are very poor and potentially life-threatening, as tuberculosis and hepatitis are widespread. Accurate numbers of infected prisoners cannot be found as international health organizations and other outside monitors are not granted access to assess the situation. Reports of severe abuse are commonplace and prison overcrowding remains a problem. In many cases, prisoners are held for extended periods of time without any communication with family or attorneys. Many prisons do not have enough food or medical supplies for the inmates, and prisoners must often rely on visits from relatives to obtain food and medicine.

Religious and Political Prisoners

In the Country Reports on Human Rights Practices published by the Bureau of Democracy, Human Rights, and Labor, it was reported by human rights activists that political prisoners and members of banned religious extremist groups were held in specially demarcated sections of prisons under harsher conditions, subjected to more horrid treatment than other prisoners as well as undergoing particularly severe interrogations. In a 2003 interview with an Uzbek political prisoner reported by the UN Office of Humanitarian Affairs, it was stated that, during his sentence, political prisoners were treated much more harshly than other inmates, being tortured, humiliated, left in the cold of winter without outerwear, forced to perform tasks that were filthy and degrading, and given rotten food and undrinkable water. Those inmates known for opposing the government are even subjected to beatings from other inmates who are persuaded, and at times even paid, by authorities to inflict such treatment. Further reports stated that prisoners convicted of religious extremism are often not released after completing their sentences. This is accomplished by fabricating claims of crimes committed while imprisoned, thus extending prison terms. The international NGO, Human Rights Watch, claims that more than 15 political prisoners have been tortured to death in prisons in Uzbekistan since 2000.

A large number of inmates in Uzbekistan are political prisoners. Although it is impossible to know the exact number, human rights activists believe that the number of political prisoners sentenced each year is more than the number of these prisoners given amnesty or released after completion of their sentence. The majority of these prisoners are being held on charges of anticonstitutional activity, involvement in illegal organizations, or preparation or distribution of material threatening of public safety. Others are convicted of extortion and hooliganism, especially human rights activists or journalists who are penalized to repress their freedom of speech.

Extraditing Offenders

Citizens of the Republic of Uzbekistan, as well as those permanently residing in Uzbekistan, are held liable for crimes committed outside the republic if a court in the country where the crime was committed has not sentenced them. An Uzbek citizen cannot be extradited for a crime committed on a foreign state's territory unless in accordance with international treaties or agreements.

Kristen Lee Hourigan

Further Reading

Abdymen, Kuban. (2008). *Death Penalty: Uzbek Abolition Draws Line under Past.* Inter Press Service: http://ipsnews.net/news.asp?idnews=40819.

Combating Crime in CIS Countries: Through Lens of Statistics. Embassy of the Republic of Uzbekistan Web site: http://www.embuzisr.mfa.uz/modules.php?op=modload&name=News&file=article&sid=2221.

IRIN News: UN Office for the Coordination of Humanitarian Affairs: Interview with Former Uzbek Political Prisoner Jora Murodov, September, 16, 2003. Muslim Uzbekistan Web site: http://muslimuzbekistan.net/en/centralasia/genocide/detail.php?ID=514.

Vietnam

Legal System: Civil/Socialist
Murder: Low
Corruption: Medium
Human Trafficking: Medium
Prison Rate: Medium
Death Penalty: Yes
Corporal Punishment: No

Background

The Socialist Republic of Vietnam, with an area of 331,114 square kilometers (127,844 square miles) has a population of more than 82 million. It consists of 59 provinces, which are subdivided into towns, districts, and villages, and 5 municipalities. Hanoi is the political capital of Vietnam, and Ho Chi Minh City is considered the center for economic and industrial development. In the last 20 years, Vietnam experienced tremendous social changes as a result of renovation (or *doi moi* in Vietnamese), which moved the country's economy toward the market system, facilitated urbanization, and increased consumerism.

Up until the late 1980s, the political and economic organizations in Vietnam had certain features in common with those in the Soviet Union and the socialist states of Eastern Europe. Under this system, the ruling party, the Vietnamese Communist Party, exercised a monopoly of control over the state bureaucracy, armed forces, and mass organizations. Party members were appointed to overlapping leadership positions in the government bodies. Consequently, the party penetrated and controlled all legal agencies, set their goals and objectives, determined their structures, and approved their leading personnel.

Since 1986, Vietnam has formally embarked on a program of renovation that involved the restructuring of the economy and the reforms of political and legal institutions. The most dramatic reform occurred in 1992 with the creation of a new constitution that recognized five economic sectors, including the private sector. The 1992 Constitution emphasized the democratization of society and its institutions through legal and constitutional reform and the development of a new legal framework to regulate domestic economic activities and foreign investment. The 2001 amendment to the 1992 Constitution increased the role of the National Assembly and accelerated the reform of the state apparatus. Despite many changes in the Constitution, the Socialist Republic of Vietnam remains a one-party state under the leadership of the Vietnamese Communist Party.

Legal System

The current Vietnamese legal system follows the Roman-Germanic, or Continental tradition, with French, Chinese, and socialist inheritances. The first penal code since the country reunification was enacted in 1985, followed by the Criminal Procedure Code enacted in 1988. Within more than 10 years, five revisions were made to the Penal Code (1987, 1991, 1993, 1997, and 2000) and four to the Criminal Procedure Code (1990, 1992, 2000, and 2003). The Penal Code reflected the country's political system as socialist in the East European style of socialism. Consequently, it was closer to East European than to the West European variant of the Continental tradition. French influence was found in the inquisitorial style of criminal investigation and trial. The influence of the socialist system is evident by a lack of separation of powers as seen in the United States and other Western cultures. Chinese culture, particularly Confucianism, has its imprint on the definition of crime, determination of crime seriousness, and the severity of treatment based on Confucian principles of hierarchical social relationships. For example, crimes committed against family members, particularly parents and grandparents, are considered more serious than if they are committed against strangers. Prior to 1985, legal analogy, the practice whereby a person could be punished for an act analogous to an offense made criminal by legislation, had been used in Vietnam due to a lack of criminal laws. This practice has been eliminated by the Penal Code.

The Police

In Vietnam, crime detection and fighting, law enforcement, and peacekeeping activities are treated collectively under the heading of "public security." Four clusters of agencies with different organizations in urban and rural areas are responsible for crime prevention and the maintenance of public order and internal security. The People's Security Force or the People's Police (*Cong An Nhan Dan*), which is a law enforcement agency in the same sense as the term used in the West, operates primarily in urban areas. Its responsibilities include maintaining public order and security, protecting public property as well as lives and property of individuals, and preventing crime. The People's Police are authorized to arrest, temporarily detain and release suspects, and search people and their homes and belongings. Since the mid-1980s, responsibilities of the People's Police have also included traffic control, residence registration, immigration and border control, counterespionage, and counterreactionary activities. In 1997, the antinarcotic police force was established at the central level with 21 provincial branches to deal with increased illegal drug activities. The second cluster of law enforcement is the plainclothes or secret police.

In rural areas, the People's Public Security Force (*Luc Luong Anh Ninh Nhan Dan*) is responsible for both law enforcement and internal security. In addition, each village administrative committee has a security section composed of trusted party members who are concerned with surveillance and detection of suspects. The security section receives considerable amount of information from local residents who are encouraged by the Constitution to participate in law enforcement and crime prevention. Villages also maintain their own local watchmen for patrol and guard duties. The last cluster is the People's Armed Security Force (*Luc Luong Vu Trang Nhan Dan*), a quasimilitary organ that operates mainly in villages and rural areas and is concerned with both crime and antistate activities. Although official information about the size of law enforcement is considered a national secret by Vietnamese government, it was estimated in 1987 that the People's Army Security Force had at least 500 personnel in each province with a total of more than 20,000. The responsibilities of the People's Armed Security Force tend to overlap with those of the People's Public Security Force because no sharp division exists between the internal security duties of the People Armed Security Force and those of the civilian People's Public Security Force.

The Procuracy

The Vietnamese Constitution provides for a prosecutorial system (also called the procuracy or *Kiem Sat* in Vietnamese) to oversee the compliance with the law by ministries and other state bodies and to exercise the power of public prosecution in both criminal and military courts. Thus, within the legal system, the procuracy plays a double role, working as a prosecutor while also reviewing the work and decisions of the court.

Since the application of renovation policies in 1986, the organization of the procuracy has received increased attention from the government. After a series of reforms within the context of renovation and consistent with the Constitution, the prosecutorial system now consists of a three-level hierarchy that matches the three levels of court. At the top of the hierarchy is the Supreme People's Procuracy (*Vien Kiem Sat Nhan Dan Toi Cao*), which contains 22 subordinated bodies, including specialized tribunals for criminal, civil, economic, and administrative cases. The Supreme People's Procuracy is headed by the procurator general (chief prosecutor). This office is independent from the Ministry of Justice, and the chief prosecutor answers directly to the National Assembly. About 150 prosecutors and legal specialists work in the Supreme People's Procuracy Headquarters in Hanoi. Two branch offices in Danang and Ho Chi Minh City have 200 staff. The chief prosecutor and prosecutors at the Supreme Court level are appointed by the National Assembly. The Supreme People's Procuracy is in charge of prosecuting extremely serious or complex cases that are initially tried by the criminal tribunal of the Supreme People's Court (e.g., mass homicide; government officials charged with corruption offenses that could result in the death penalty).

Below the Supreme People's Procuracy are procuracies in 53 provinces with more than 1,500 procurators. Provincial procuracies are responsible for prosecuting criminal cases that fall outside the jurisdiction of district people's courts (e.g., serious crime against national security). The third level consists of 600 local procuracies, which are located in rural districts, provincial capitals, large towns, and urban districts. Local procuracies are staffed by more than 3,000 district procurators. Women account for 40 percent of all prosecutors at the provincial and local level. Each local procuracy is headed by a local procurator general who reports to the Supreme People's Procuracy in Hanoi and local people's councils via the provincial procuracy. Normally, district procuracies are in charge of prosecuting offenses punishable by imprisonment for no more than seven years. Provincial and district prosecutors are appointed by the chief prosecutor.

The Court

Vietnam has a three-tiered judicial system. At the top is the Supreme People's Court (*Toa An Nhan Dan Toi Cao*) headed by the chief justice who is appointed by and reports to the National Assembly. The Supreme People's Court, which is the highest court of appeal and review, consists of a Council of Judges, a Committee of Judges, and six specialized divisions, including a criminal division. The Board of Judges and the Committee of Judges have particular responsibilities with regard to developing and disseminating new laws and policies. The Board of Judges is responsible for reviewing decisions of the Committee of Judges, guiding courts on the application of laws, guiding the conduct of trials, and drafting bills for submission to the National Assembly. The Committee of Judges is responsible for reviewing decisions by lower courts, guiding courts in the implementation of resolutions issued by the Board of Judges, and approving the chief justice's reports prior to their going to the National Assembly. In addition, the Supreme People's Court issues guidance to lower courts, either as circulars or as statements.

Under the Supreme People's Court are provincial people's courts, people's courts in the cities that are directly under the central government (e.g., Hanoi, Hai Phong, and Ho Chi Minh City) as well as people's courts in districts, precincts, and towns. In 2004, nearly 4,000 judges served at the district-level people's courts. People's courts at all three levels can be courts of first instance. The Supreme People's Court can be a trial court for cases that have national level of importance. Courts at higher levels have to review decision of lower courts and guide them in making correct decisions. Essentially, decisions are reviewed to see whether they protect the people's democratic regime; protect social order, public property, and legitimate interests of the people; and contribute to the construction of a socialist society.

There are two main types of judicial officers working within the Vietnamese court system: judges and people's assessors (lay judges or jurors). In 2004, Vietnam had 3,700 district judges. Prior to 1992, judges were elected by the National Assembly and local People's Committees. As the selection of judges could have negative influences on judicial independence, changes were made to the recruitment and administration of judges. Since 1992, judges have been appointed, rather than selected. In 2002, the authority over local courts was transferred from the Ministry of Justice to the Supreme People's Court. Both movements were aimed at increasing judicial independence. However, due to a lack of the separation of powers among branches of government, and due to the influence of the party on the outcomes of cases that involve perceived threat to the state or the party's dominant position, there is little evidence that these changes can help achieve judicial independence. The second group of judicial officers in the Vietnamese court system includes people's assessors. The use of people's assessors was introduced to Vietnamese courts in the late 1940s after Ho Chi Minh declared independence from France. The role of the people's assessor was to assist judges to reach a decision that reflected the will of the people. Originally, people's assessors were explicitly connected to the socialist revolution. This practice still exists today, as people's assessors are recruited among members of local committees affiliated to the party.

Crime

Classification of Crimes

Crime is defined as an act that not only contains the elements prohibited by the Penal Code but also that causes harm to the state, the socialist economy, and/or the rights of citizens. Crimes are classified under nine categories as follows:

1. Crimes against national security with the punishment ranging from three years of imprisonment to a death sentence. These crimes are broadly defined to include nonviolent acts in opposition to the socialist regime, such as "making, storing and/or circulating documents and/or cultural products with contents against the Socialist Republic of Vietnam."
2. Crimes against persons and human dignity, which include murder, rape, assault, assisting suicide, and spreading HIV, are crimes against human life and health. Slander and defamation are also crimes against human dignity, as are illegal arrest and search. The seriousness of crimes against persons is determined by the age of the victim, family relationships, and the influence of cultural practices. Murder is punishable by long prison terms or death, but murder of a newborn is treated more leniently. In this case, the offender will face noncustodial reform for up to two years or three months and two years of imprisonment. Various aggravating circumstances are also recognized and result in increased punishment.
3. Property and economic crimes, which are divided into two groups. The first group is crimes against ownership rights, including robbery, kidnapping for ransom, extortion, theft, vandalism, swindle, and embezzlement. The second group includes a wide range of behaviors in violation of economic and business rules and regulations, from smuggling, illegal production, illegal business, tax evasion, speculation, loan sharking, and counterfeiting to making false management reports and advertisements. The Penal Code distinguishes the severity of punishment between theft from the state, which receives harsher penalty, and theft from individuals, which receives a less severe penalty.
4. Crimes against marriage and family institutions include incest, mistreatment of parents, bigamy, child stealing, organizing and arranging child marriages.
5. Drug crimes, which include growing plant-bearing narcotic substances; illegal production, transportation, storing, and trading drugs; organizing drug use (e.g., drug houses or opium dens); and harboring illegal drug use (leasing or renting property used in organizing drug use). Long prison terms or life

sentences can be applied to those who are convicted of producing, transporting, storing, or trading drugs, and the death penalty can be used for drug crimes involving large amounts of drugs (e.g., 600 grams of heroin or cocaine powder). On the other hand, drug users and drug addicts are considered victims, rather than criminals, and they are required to undergo compulsory medical treatment in rehabilitation and reeducation centers. Relapse into drug use is punishable up to five years of imprisonment.

6. Crimes against public safety and public order, which include violations of vehicle and road safety, hijacking, computer-related crime, gambling, prostitution, pornography, and money laundering. The law only prohibits promoting and procuring prostitution (clients), who can face imprisonment up to five years. Being a prostitute is not considered a crime; they are seen as victims rather than criminals and are required to undergo treatment and job training. Both engaging in gambling and organizing gambling are criminal behaviors. Light sentences, including warning, noncustodian reform, fines, or a prison term up to two years can be applied to gamblers, but harsher sentences (fines or a prison terms up to five years) can be applied to gambling organizers. Although abortion is legal in Vietnam, the Penal Code indicates that illegal abortion is a crime punishable by imprisonment up to five years. However, the Penal Code does not explain what constitutes illegal abortion.
7. Violations of administrative orders and regulations, which include evading military service, deliberately and unintentionally disclosing state secrets, forging documents, violations of media production and distribution regulations, and illegally entering or leaving the country, are punishable by imprisonment of several months to several years.
8. Position-related crimes and violations of judicial duty, which are crimes resulting from abuse and misuse of authority such as corruption, bribery, embezzlement, disclosing state secrets, and losing state documents. A desire to curb widespread corruption has led to the creation of harsh sentences for corruption-related offenses. Embezzlement of state property worth VN$500 million (US$33,000) or more and receiving bribes worth VN$300 million (US$20,000) or more are punishable by life in prison or a death sentence, in addition to possible fines and confiscation of the bribed property. Crimes related to the violations of judicial duty are punishable with up to 10 years of imprisonment.
9. Environment crimes (pollution), crime against peace and humanity, and war crimes. Punishment ranges from prison terms for pollution to death for war crimes.

The Extent of Crime and Crime Statistics

Limited statistics from the government's news agency show that between December 2006 and October 2007, more than 43,000 cases of various crimes were reported to authorities, but the true figures may be much higher. Research conducted in the mid-1990s indicated nearly 70,000 crime incidents per year, with half of these crime incidents occurring in Hanoi and Ho Chi Minh City, and more than 70 percent of apprehended criminals were between the ages of 14 and 28.

Since the implementation of renovation programs, crime incidents have increased substantially. Changes in the country's economy resulting from a movement toward the market system, rapid urbanization, and a lack of emphasis on the rule of law have created an environment for illegal behaviors to flourish. For the period between 1990 and 1997, murder increased 25 percent and robbery 18 percent. Other serious violent crimes, including assault and robbery, and gang activities are on the rise. In 2007, an estimate of 250 gangs with more than 1,200 members were located and had activities in Ho Chi Minh City, a crime hot spot, in addition to other thousands of mobile gangs whose members frequently moved from one locality to another. Since 1990, there has been an increase in several types of crime that rarely occurred before, such as killing and assaulting for hire, assaulting teachers, and child prostitution. Illegal behaviors associated with the market system, such as tax evasions, false advertisement, and violations of business management regulations, are also on the rise.

Despite increases in violent crime, the most common crimes in the renovation era are property and economic crimes. Between 1990 and 1997, trading illegal products increased 56 percent. The widespread availability of counterfeit goods, including fake fertilizers that have caused harm to many farmers, is a massive problem. Smuggling is a big business in Vietnam with many items, including television sets, videos, and automobiles, coming across the long borders with China, Cambodia, and Laos, or arriving by sea. The smuggling of hardwood timber out of Vietnam has been a big business and a major cause of the destruction of Vietnam's forests.

Corruption is a widespread problem in Vietnam. Party cadres and members have committed numerous violations of economic rules and regulations. An estimate of 26 percent of party members have violated economic regulations, and this figure could be as high as 45 percent in Ho Chi Minh City. Given the low pay for government officials, it is not surprising that bribery of officials is a major problem. The lenient sentences imposed on convicted officials are among reasons that corruption has not been curtailed. The lack of an independent judicial system is another reason. Judges and members of the jury (people's assessors) are often under strong pressures from the local party organization or governments.

Besides increases in economic crimes, drug crime is one of the top concerns among government officials. From 1990 to 1997, drug crime incidents increased 110 percent. In the six years between 2001 and 2007, law enforcement agencies arrested 119,286 drug offenders involved in 76,443 drug cases (an average of 20,000 arrests per year), and the court tried 55,663 drug cases involving 77,348 offenders (an average of 10,000 cases per year). The growing of opium poppies and the distribution of heroin have constituted the most serious drug problem in Vietnam. Law against drugs in Vietnam is considered one of the harshest in the world, and it is not uncommon for young men who are caught transporting or selling drugs to be executed, but drug trade, trafficking, and usage have not decreased. In 2007, the number of drug addicts was estimated around 170,000; another unofficial estimate indicated that the number of heroin users alone was 160,000, and these numbers are expected to rise in coming years.

Finding of Guilt

Legal and Procedural Safeguards

Although certain concepts in Western laws such as "proof beyond reasonable doubt" have no equivalent in the Vietnamese system, the Constitution and the Criminal Procedure Code contain a number of provisions that set out guarantees and respect for the rights of the defendant. The Criminal Procedure Code places the burden of proof on the state. Other protections and safeguards include the presumption of innocence; protection from illegal arrest, search, and seizure; the right to legal counsel; the right to an impartial criminal proceeding; and the right to appeal. The role of a jury in the criminal justice process in Vietnam is not the same as it is in the United States where a jury can decide either guilt or sentence or both. In Vietnam, both jurors and trial judges make decisions on guilt and sentences, and the law provides guarantee for the participation of the jury in criminal proceedings.

Actual practices do not often match up with laws in the book, however. Government officials often avoid or nullify these rights and guarantees. A lack of knowledge about the law, unfamiliarity with the rights guaranteed in the recent Constitution, and judicial incompetence have reinforced the reluctance of judicial officials to recognize these basic rights and safeguards. In addition, the continuous control by the party over the state also serves as a barrier to compliance with the rule of law.

Investigation

According to the Criminal Procedure Code (article 110), criminal investigations are carried out by the People's Police. Under some situations, other investigating bodies may be involved, such as the People's Procuracy or the People's Army. The procurator has a supervisory role to ensure that investigations are conducted in compliance with the law and in a manner that does not infringe on the rights of the defendant. When there are grounds to believe that a person has committed a crime, the investigating body will file a criminal case against the defendant. The document must clearly state the time and the place of the filing decision and the details of the offense charged. A copy of the document must be sent to the defendant and advise him or her of his or her rights and obligations. These rights include the right to request a change of persons who conduct the criminal proceedings on the grounds of conflict of interests and the right to retain counsel of his or her own choice.

During the investigation, investigating officials may conduct search and seizure and/or order arrest and preventive detention. Arrest and search warrants are issued by a procurator, an assistant to a procurator, a judge, or an assistant to a judge. After making an arrest, the police must question, interrogate, and obtain statements from the suspect immediately. However, there are exceptions to the requirement of arrest warrant. The police can make arrest without warrant when they believe that a crime is in progress or if a suspect is accused of rape, murder, attempt to overthrow the government, or other serous crimes, or if the police believe that the suspect may destroy evidence or flee. Additionally, a warrantless physical examination of a person under arrest may take place when there is strong grounds to believe that this person is hiding on his or her body something that should be seized.

Bail and Preventive Measures

The decision to grant bail is made by either a procurator, a judge, or a chief of law enforcement at the provincial level based on the seriousness of crime committed and the likelihood that the defendant will flee. Release awaiting trial can be obtained through sponsorship by relatives, friends, an agency, or a business or by depositing a sum of money or a property. Due to a lack of emphasis on the principle of separation of powers, the rules on bail and preventive measures, which give procurators and chiefs of law enforcement the authority to decide on bail or pretrial detention, cause serious conflicts of interest and are inconsistent with the International Covenant on Civil and Political Rights (article 9.4).

Criminal Defense

The Constitution (article 132) and the Criminal Procedure Code (article 11) guarantee the right to criminal defense. Although the law guarantees the right to legal counsel, the implementation of the law raises several important issues. First, defense lawyers must have approval from criminal justice officials to do their job. Second, defense lawyers are not always able to participate in all critical stages of the criminal process. In principle, defense lawyers can assist all suspects after arrest and during the initial investigation by the police. In reality, investigative agencies often question or interrogate the suspects without the presence of legal counsel, and in only few cases are lawyers able to participate from the beginning of the investigation.

Lawyers and attorneys are placed under the control and administration of the Ministry of Justice. Barristers (legal advocates), solicitors (legal consultants), and lay advocates can defend before Vietnamese courts. As of 2007, nearly 3,700 lawyers belonged to 61 provincial bar associations. These lawyers had diverse legal training in different legal systems, including USSR, French, and Vietnamese, and many lawyers have training that cannot be applied to new situations in Vietnam. The shortage of legal counsel poses serious problems to the exercise of the right to legal counsel for many groups. Prior to 2007, defendants did not have a right to an appointed attorney except in capital cases and cases in which the suspects were mentally ill or under the age of 20. Thus, indigent defendants who did not fall into one of these three categories were most likely to go through the criminal justice process without the benefit of legal counsel. A new law on legal aid, which was enacted in June 2006 and took effect in January 2007, expands the list of persons eligible for legal aid service to include the poor, war veterans, lonely elderly, people with disability, orphans, and ethnic minorities living in economically disadvantaged areas (article 10 of Law on Legal Aid). In principle, judges and the procuracy can ask a provincial bar association to select an attorney if the suspect does not have one. Members of bar associations have a constitutional duty and are supposed to be dedicated to helping criminal defendants. For the most part, however, the provision of legal aid is not systematic. In 2007, an estimated 3,400 lawyers served in 64 legal aid centers at the city and provincial levels, providing legal consultation, legal defense in court, and legal counsel outside the court for those who were eligible. This number was considered too small to meet the demand. In many provinces, only 2 to 10 lawyers agreed to work for legal aid. Young lawyers who received the most recent legal training often refuse to work for legal service in remote areas due to low salary and poor working conditions.

The quality of legal counsel is also influenced by the level of professionalism. Laws in Vietnam were not codified until recently. By 2002, several legal information databases were established in the Office of the National Assembly, the Government Office, and the Ministry of Justice, but each legal database was incomplete, was not linked to the Internet, and was not well maintained. Consequently, there is no comprehensive and accessible compendium of national legal databases and court decisions for lawyers as well as other legal professionals to consult. In addition, the power of the party and its members at all levels, as well as a lack of respect for the rule of law, render professional skill less important. For many Vietnamese lawyers, the most crucial aspect of successful advocacy work is a good relationship with judges. It is not uncommon in Vietnam for legal counsel to visit a judge before a hearing to explain the evidence, and it is not unusual for judges in tort cases to be offered a fee linked to the case outcomes.

Criminal Prosecution

The chief procurator, or his or her deputy, has the authority to file and dispose of cases. When the procuracy receives a file from the investigating body, it must decide whether to prosecute the defendant and issue an indictment decision, remand the case for additional investigation, or suspend the case either temporary or permanently. This decision must be taken within 30 days, but in case of necessity, the procurator general is allowed one extension of no more than 30 days. This prosecutorial rule raises concerns about the violation of human rights because the detention period can be imposed twice without the benefit of a court hearing and because a person can be detained for 60 days without formal charges against him or her. In reality, many persons arrested for involvement in prodemocracy activities have been detained for several months or years without being formally charged. Within 30 days of the issuance of the prosecutorial decision, the procuracy must send the case to the court. Due to substantial increases in court cases in recent years, there has been a significant increase in delay at the investigative, prosecutional, and adjudicative stages.

Criminal Trials and Appeals

The people's courts are authorized to try cases of criminal offenses committed on Vietnamese territory. Upon receiving a case from the procuracy, the court has 45 days to three months to decide whether to proceed with a trial, remand the case for additional investigation, or suspend the case temporarily or permanently. In complicated cases, the president of the court may allow a 30-day extension. Once the court decides to proceed, the trial must begin within 15 days to 30 days from the decision.

Normally, a professional judge hears a criminal case with two lay judges called people's assessors who are representatives from the local people's committee. If the accused is charged with an offense punishable by the death penalty, the trial court will consist of two professional judges and three lay judges. Each of the professional and lay judges has an equal vote on all questions before the court. In the Vietnamese judicial system, a trial judge is not only an adjudicator who listens to the procurator and the defense counsel, but he or she also poses questions to the witnesses and the defendant. When there are differences among members of the bench, a verdict is rendered by the majority.

Under the Criminal Procedure Code, persons other than witnesses for the prosecution or the defense are allowed to participate in criminal trials. In addition, persons who have civil claims arising out of criminal incidents may take part in criminal trials. The Criminal Procedure Code also includes the participation of various social organizations and private citizens, such as the Fatherland Front, the Trade Union, the Association of Farmers, the Youth Union, and the Federation of Women. Under the Constitution, these social organizations and citizens have the right and duty to contribute to the fight against crime by participating in the criminal justice process. During trials, judges cannot dismiss charges, but they can only find the defendant not guilty if conviction is not warranted.

Plea bargaining is not often used to shorten the criminal justice process. If the accused admits guilt during the court proceeding, his or her statement will be recorded in the file, and the court will continue as usual. The right to remain silent is not recognized as a legal safeguard, but the accused's silence is not taken to imply an acknowledgment of guilt. In reality, it is rare for the accused to remain silent because he or she is expected to tell about the case.

Trials are supposed to be public, except in special cases where the trial can be closed, but court outcomes must always be publicly disclosed. In recent years, the trials of major corruption cases involving high-ranking government officials and political cases involving individuals who had engaged in pro-democracy activities were closed to the public, and members of the international press were allowed to watch trials televised live in a separate room.

Judgments and court decisions acquire legal force 15 days after the trial. Within this period of time, the accused and the civil parties in a criminal case may appeal, and the procurator may file a protest against the judgment or court decision to the next higher court. The Vietnamese court system that gives people's courts at all three levels the jurisdiction to act as trial court of first instance creates a problem for appeal. This happens when a case is tried as first instance in the Supreme People's Court (e.g., extremely important or serious cases), because there is no higher tribunal to which the accused may appeal. A conflict of interest arises because of the ability of the Supreme People's Court to both try and review cases, making the practice inconsistent with international criminal law (article 14.5 of the International Covenant on Civil and Political Rights).

Until recently, specific qualifications were not set for those who could be elected to judgeship, except for the requirement that candidates should have several years of working in governmental agencies before their appointment, but a law degree was not necessary. After being elected, judges were expected to take continuing legal education via short courses offered by the Supreme People's Court or the Ministry of Justice. In most part, those who led the training and developed curriculum were trained in socialist legal systems. A lack of competence among trial judges is evident in large numbers of judgments and decisions deemed incorrect by courts of appeal. In the context of renovation, new recruitments are expected to have a law degree. As the teaching of law only began in the 1980s, there are not many qualified graduates for judgeship.

The organizational structure of the legal system and the overall power of the party over the state exert a great deal of influence on judicial independence. Under the Constitution, courts are accountable to the National Assembly, and this reflects their subordination to political authority led by the party. In addition, the Fatherland Front, an organization affiliated with the party, plays an integral role in the selection of judges at all levels. Moreover, judges may be removed at the end of a five-year probationary period following their appointment. Judges are also under much influence from the electorate at the local level. Not only are members of the court connected to the party, but the party also influences their decisions. Senior figures in the party are able to suggest directly to a court how particular cases ought to be decided. If a judge refuses to cooperate with the party's direction, he or she will face the possibility of dismissal. Corruption is worse at the provincial, district, and village levels where local party leaders are the most powerful persons.

Alternatives to Trial

The use of alternatives to trial is common in Vietnam. By 2002, there were 120,000 conciliation groups with 427,000 conciliators working at the grassroots level. The capacity of conciliation groups and the conciliators to mediate and conciliate is often poor due to a lack of knowledge about basic legal principles and citizens' fundamental rights. The Ministry of Justice at the provincial levels is responsible for legal education for conciliators, but officials responsible for the training tend not to have the professional skills necessary for carrying out this task. Consequently, conciliation processes are not always consistent with basic legal principles and do not always secure citizens' fundamental rights. In 2003, the Program on Legal Education and Dissemination was created, hoping to strengthen the capacity and efficiency of the conciliation groups and conciliators.

Juvenile Cases

According to the Penal Code (article 12), the age of criminal liability begins at 14 years. Children under the age of 14 who commit criminal acts are dealt with by administrative measures, which may involve working off the offense or being sent to a reeducation center. Young persons who are between the ages of 14 and 16 will be held responsible for very serious and serious crimes. Persons who are 16 years old or older will bear responsibility for all crimes they have committed.

Special procedures are applied to persons aged 14 to 20. First of all, defense counsel or other approved representatives must be present in case proceedings. In addition, investigators, procurators, and judges who conduct an investigation, a prosecution, and a trial involving a juvenile offender must have necessary knowledge of psychology and education as well as experience in the field of juvenile delinquency. The Criminal Procedure Code indicates that one of the lay assessors of the trial court must be either a teacher or a representative of the Ho Chi Minh Youth Union.

Consistent with the emphasis on reeducation and rehabilitation, more lenient sentencing provisions are applied to juvenile offenders. Neither the death penalty nor life imprisonment is used for juvenile offenders. Fifteen years is the maximum term of imprisonment for an accused between 14 and 16 years of age, and 20 years for those between 16 to 20 years of age. If a juvenile under the age of 18 is sentenced to prison, he or she must be housed separately from adult offenders. Imprisoned juveniles are entitled to education training during their prison terms. In reality, the detention of juvenile offenders in Vietnam has not fully complied with international standards, particularly the Convention on the Rights of the Child, as reported by the International Center for Criminal Law Reform and Justice Policy (University of British of Columbia).

Punishment

In recent years, an increase in crime resulting from changes in Vietnam's economic and political circumstances and the urgent demand for crime suppression has led to an increase in the severity of punishment. Rehabilitation through labor is a prominent feature of penology in Vietnam, and at the same time, sentences for major offenses have become much more severe in recent years.

Types of Punishment

Types of punishment typically used in Vietnam include warning, fines, house arrest, probation, compulsory treatments, confiscation of property, imprisonment, and death. In addition, deprivation of certain civil rights, including prohibition against employment in certain occupations, prohibition against holding certain governmental positions, and residential restrictions as a consequence of a criminal conviction are parts of criminal punishment determined by criminal courts.

In pursuit of rehabilitation, the Penal Code makes extensive provision for reeducation without detention. The Penal Code authorizes suspension of the prison sentence if it is deemed more rehabilitative than serving the sentence in prison. Suspension of a prison sentence is permitted only if the sentence is for five years or less. The court grants a probation period between one to five years and entrusts the convicted person to his or her employment organization or a social organization in the local area where he or she resides for the purpose of oversight and education. These groups serve the role of probation officers. This type of penalty permits a person convicted of minor offenses to continue working under the condition that his or her employer and/or coworkers must agree to take responsibility for his or her rehabilitation. A 5- to 20-percent salary deduction as a penal fine is also imposed, and the arrangement may exist for two years. Reeducation without detention is considered more beneficial than incarceration because it can avoid costs associated with incarceration, including expenses for construction of prison buildings, salaries paid to guard personnel, and prison management. It also serves the socialist aim of transferring some governmental functions to social organizations. A similar type of punishment called "correctional task" permits a convicted person to continue his or her previous employment under a condition that his or her wages will be deducted to certain amounts as a penal fine for a period of time.

Current penal law requires in-custody drug treatment from one to two years for drug addicts who are 12 to 18 years old. For those who are older than 18, besides the time in custody for treatment, they are also subject to administrative penalty, such as prohibition against employment in certain occupations or prohibition against holding certain government positions. However, drug treatment centers in the country only have ability to house one-third of drug addicts who are in the custody list (about 170,000 in 2007). Media reports indicate that a substantial majority of those who finished drug-treatment programs (80% to 85%) relapsed and used drugs again. More severe punishments, including life imprisonment and death, have been applied to those who engaged in trading, storing, and transporting drugs.

Detention for reeducation is permitted by law in Vietnam through processes administered outside the court. Decrees and regulations at the national and provincial levels permit detention through administrative processes without a court trial. Officially, this type of detention is not considered a criminal penalty, although it can last for years. For example, a regulation issued by Ho Chi Minh City in 1987 provides up to two years of detention for counter-revolutionary elements who refuse to be reeducated. A circular issued by the Democratic Republic of Vietnam in 1961 was used to detain without trials hundreds of thousands of former civil and military personnel of the Republic of Vietnam in reeducation camps across the country for three months to 15 years.

Prison

Detailed information on Vietnam's prison system is not easy to access. A report from Human Rights Watch has indicated that "Vietnamese officials unnecessarily withheld basic information such as the number and location of labor camps, prisons, and temporary detention centers; . . . general statistics on detainees." Information from the International Centre of Prison Studies at King College (University of London) showed that the prison population in Vietnam increased 120 percent during a 10-year period from 43,000 inmates in 1996 to 98, 556 inmates in 2006. Female inmates account for 12 percent of the prison population. Information from other sources suggests that at least 150 prisons and reeducation camps exist across the country, and that each of the 59 provinces and five major cities has at least one prison with various capacities, according to a Library of Congress report. Hoa Lo Prison, the most notorious prison located in Hanoi, also known as the Hanoi Hilton where American prisoners of war were detained, has been demolished, and prisoners have been moved to other prisons located outside the city or even prisons in other provinces. Other major prisons in Vietnam include Chi Hoa Prison located in Ho Chi Minh City, Thu Duc Prison located outside Ho Chi Minh City, and a branch of Hoa Lo Prison located in Hai Phong

City. Each major city also has several detention centers where individuals are held awaiting trial.

Unlike prisons, reeducation camps tend to be located in remote rural areas or deep in the jungle. Camps are divided into subsections, which are several miles apart. Larger camps are under the jurisdiction of the Ministry of Public Security (formerly the Ministry of Interior), and smaller camps are under the jurisdiction of the Ministry of Defense. Major reeducation camps are located in several provinces, including Son La, Ha Nam, Dong Nai, Phu Yen, Nghe An, Ha Tinh, and Thanh Hoa. In addition, there are also many detention centers, which are under the control of local authorities.

Due to a lack of research on prisons in Vietnam, information about detention conditions comes mainly from reports by human rights organizations and testimonies by former prisoners and detainees. Prison conditions have been reported as short of international standards, with poor sanitary conditions, heavy labor, and grossly inadequate medical care. Abuse, such as the beatings by prison guards and the use of dark cells for solitary confinement, does exist. Generally, relatives of inmates and detainees are allowed to visit periodically, and these visits are often essential to provide inmates and detainees with food, medicines, and other supplies, or money to buy these items. In principle, prisoners are entitled to complain about unlawful treatment, but those who make their complaints known to the outside world are likely to experience retaliations through restricted family visits or solitary confinement.

Death Penalty

The Penal Code lists the number of offenses punishable by the death sentence at 29. These include crimes against the state, murder, armed robbery, drug trafficking, sexual abuse of children, and a string of economic crimes, such as embezzling state property worth 500 million dong (equivalent to US$33,000) or more, or receiving bribes worth the same values. In recent years, the death penalty was mainly applied to major drug trafficking and corruption cases. As drug trafficking became widespread, government officials perceived that the death penalty would have the deterrent effect. The death sentence can be applied for those who traffic, trade, and store 600 grams or more of powder heroin or cocaine (or 20 kilograms of opium resin or coca plasma).

Under the Criminal Procedure Code, the state is obliged to carry out the death sentence as soon as possible once the appeal for clemency has been turned down. In practice, persons condemned to death are usually kept on death row for at least a year before being executed. Executions in Vietnam are often carried out in public and at dawn by a firing squad of five. The convicted are blindfolded and tied to a stake. Relatives are not informed beforehand, but they are asked to collect the belongings of the executed two to three days after the death. To defuse criticism by Western governments and international human rights organizations on its use of the death penalty, the Vietnamese government has classified death penalty statistics as a "state secret." A decree signed in January 2004 makes it an offense for publishing and disseminating information on death sentences and executions.

Human rights organizations have indicated that at least 214 persons were executed within four years, from 2002 to 2005, with the highest number (82 executions) in 2004 and the lowest number (27 executions) in 2005. It was also suggested that the low number in 2005 might result from the 2004 government decision to consider statistics on the death penalty a state secret, and the actual numbers of executions may be much higher than those reported by human rights watch organizations. In fact, a report by a Vietnamese magazine, *Thanh Nien,* which is an official magazine of the Youth Union (ThanhNien News.Com), estimated that around 100 persons were executed each year for drug offenses. In 2006, government officials admitted that the deterrent effect of the death penalty was not as strong as expected, but the imposition of the death sentence did not seem to slow down. Within two months, November and December 2007, 43 heroin traffickers were sentenced to death in the country. In January 2008 alone, the Ho Chi

Minh City Court sentenced three members of a drug-trafficking ring to death.

Hoan N. Bui

Further Reading

Nicholson, Penilope (Pip). (2010). "Judicial Independence and the Rule of Law: The Vietnamese Court Experience." *The Australian Journal of Asian Law* 3: 37–58.

Quigley, John. (1988). "Viet Nam's First Modern Penal Code." *New York Law School Journal of International and Comparative Law* 9: 143–193.

Quin, Brian J. M. (2003). "Vietnam's Continuing Legal Reform: Gaining Control over the Courts." *Asian-Pacific Law and Policy Journal* 4: 432–468.

Vietnamese Penal Code, Vietnamese Criminal Procedure Code, and Vietnamese Law on Legal Aid (English Version) Web Sites: http://vbqppl3.moj.gov.vn/law/en/1991_to_2000/2000/200001/200001040005_en/lawdocument_view; http://vbqppl3.moj.gov.vn/law/en/2001_to_2010/2003/200311/200311260010_en/lawdocument_view; http://vbqppl3.moj.gov.vn/law/vi/2001_to_2010/2006/200606/200606290017.

Pacific

Australia

Legal System: Common
Murder: Medium
Burglary: Medium
Corruption: Low
Human Trafficking: Low
Prison Rate: Medium
Death Penalty: No
Corporal Punishment: No

Background

Australia is an island continent with a landmass of 7.69 million square kilometers (2.97 million square miles). While Australia is the largest island in the world, it also is the smallest continent. Australia is home to nearly 22 million people, most of whom live within 100 kilometers (62 miles) of the coast. Australia's criminal justice system has a federal structure, with six state jurisdictions, two territories, and a limited commonwealth jurisdiction. The federation was formed in 1901 from separate British colonies. The first of these colonies was the penal settlement of New South Wales, established in 1788. Contemporary Australia is a stable, prosperous liberal democracy with regular free elections and a Westminster tradition of responsible government through ministers. Criminal law is largely the province of the states and territories. Federal police and courts have province over crimes against the commonwealth and commonwealth laws, such as fraud and drug importation, and make use of state prisons. The criminal court system is primarily adversarial.

The overflow of British prisons in the late 18th century, and the desire to relocate the worst elements of the "criminal classes," led to the selection of Australia as a British penal colony. Crime was a major social problem in the penal and frontier periods of the 19th century. In the latter part of the century, crime was mitigated by the professional organization of policing and social factors such as a growing middle class of farmers, artisans, and skilled laborers. Lower crime rates continued through the 20th century. However, consistent with many Western countries, rapid rises in offenses reported to police occurred from the 1970s.

With a small federal police force and no local police, policing is carried out by large state forces. Military involvement in policing is limited to an emergency or disaster support role. Police departments follow a common four-part structure, with frontline patrol services; detectives who engage in follow-up investigations; a wide range of specialist squads such as water police, traffic, juvenile aid units, and scenes of crime (forensics) officers; and nonsworn civilian support staff.

Crime

Criminal law in Australia has followed two main traditions. Queensland, Western Australia, Tasmania, and the Northern Territory enacted criminal codes, based on a draft written in the 1890s. The criminal law of the remaining states (New South Wales, Victoria, and South Australia) is based on common law (i.e., diverse statutes and previous case decisions). Over time, criminal codes have been subject to modifications through precedent-setting cases as well as parliamentary additions and amendments. The Commonwealth adopted a criminal code in 1995. This was intended to serve as a national model for all jurisdictions. However, adoption of the model has so far failed to eventuate. Criminal law remains fragmented, although all jurisdictions share the following common broad categories:

- Against property—e.g., theft, robbery, vandalism, fraud.
- Against the person—e.g., murder, manslaughter, assault.
- Against morality—e.g., prostitution, drug offenses.
- Against the state—e.g., corruption.
- Against public order—e.g., public drunkenness, unlawful assemblies.

An Australian Customs Service officer holds shark fins found on a suspected illegal fishing boat in the waters off Cape Wessel in the Northern Territory of Australia on April 5, 2006. (AP Photo/Australian Customs Service)

The primary classification of crimes in Australia also follows a nomenclature common to many Western democracies. The terms "summary" and "indictable" offenses are favored over "misdemeanors" and "felonies." Summary offenses are less serious offenses usually heard by a magistrate, whereas indictable charges concern more serious charges usually heard before a judge and jury. Age of criminal responsibility begins at 10, with a juvenile court system applying up to age 16 (for Queensland and Victoria) or 17 or 18 (for all other states and territories). Jurisdictions also have hierarchies of offenses where the seriousness of offenses is linked to the severity of penalties. Since 1993 the Australian Bureau of Statistics (ABS) has reported national figures on crimes reported to or detected by police for each calendar year. These data cover offenses categorized according to the Australian Standard Offence Classification (ASOC). The 16 ASOC offense divisions, listed below, are ordered to reflect the seriousness of offense, with homicide at the top and "miscellaneous offenses" (such as sanitation offenses and defamation) at the bottom.

1. Homicide and related offenses.
2. Acts intended to cause injury.
3. Sexual assault and related offenses.
4. Dangerous or negligent acts endangering persons.
5. Abduction and related offenses.
6. Robbery, extortion and related offenses.
7. Unlawful entry with intent/burglary, break and enter.
8. Theft and related offenses.
9. Deception and related offenses.
10. Illicit drug offenses.
11. Weapons and explosives offenses.
12. Property damage and environmental pollution.
13. Public order offenses.
14. Road traffic and motor vehicle regulatory offenses.

15. Offenses against justice procedures, government security and government operations.
16. Miscellaneous offenses.

The Australian Bureau of Statistics reported the total figure of 1,062,621 offenses reported to the police in 2006, which can be compared to Australia's population at the time of approximately 20.7 million. Murder accounted for only 0.02 percent of offenses compared with much less harmful volume crimes such as "other theft" (including shoplifting) at 48.70 percent. However, it also should be kept in mind that although a serious crime such as sexual assault, for example, accounted for only 1.71 percent of the total, in reality this was 18,211 incidents reported in a category where there is substantial underreporting.

For many decades Victoria has had low recorded crime rates and the Northern Territory has had very high crime rates. Crime can also vary enormously by local area. For example, some communities have up to six times the rate of offenses of other communities. Australia also has the common problem of a "dark figure" of unreported crime. Reportage of burglary is around 74 percent and motor vehicle theft around 90 percent. However, surveys indicate reportage of assault is low, around 31 percent, and very low for robbery, around 38 percent, according to the Australian Bureau of Statistics.

Time series data of crimes reported to police show that Australia has followed a fairly typical pattern of steep rises from the early 1970s, peaking around the 1990s or turn of the century, with declines in many crime categories. Consistent national crime statistics have only been collated since 1993. Prior to this, national figures were taken from the annual statistical reports by the state and territory police forces, which were often highly inconsistent. Nonetheless, the sources have a degree of internal consistency and retain value for comparative purposes. They indicate that from 1973–1974 to 1995–1996, the rate of stealing increased 120 percent, burglary increased 123 percent, motor vehicle theft increased 92 percent, robbery increased 243 percent, and serious assault increased 558 percent. At the same time, the homicide rate declined by 8 percent.

In the 1990s, increases in recorded crime rates began to slow down, many peaking around the turn of the century, with declines setting in, mainly in property crimes. For example, total unlawful entry with intent (UEWI) peaked in 1998 at 2,319.5 offenses per 100,000 population and dropped to 1,271.2 in 2006. Motor vehicle theft peaked in 2000 at 725.2 and fell to 364.6 in 2006. Other theft peaked in 2001 at 3,607.0 and fell to 2,511.8 in 2006. Robbery offenses peaked in 2001 at 137.0 and fell to 83.9 in 2006. The murder rate has been fairly stable reaching 2.0 in 1999 and dropping to 1.5 from 2004 to 2006. Increases in reported sexual assault slowed from around 2003 but continued to increase slowly to 88.4 in 2006. Assault increased fairly steadily, standing at 829.4 in 2006.

The downward trend in crime is supported by the results of the International Crime Victims Survey (ICVS), which has been conducted in Australia four times since 1989. The most recent survey was in 2004. The percent of respondents who reported being a victim of one or more of 10 types of crimes in the preceding year increased from 23.3 percent in 1989 to 24.0 in 1992 to a peak of 25.2 percent in 2000, and then dropped to 17.3 percent in 2004. (The latter is a projected figure from 16.3 percent for nine crimes. The sexual assault question was considered inconsistent with previous years and countries.) Of note is the fact that ICVS uses a category "assaults and threats," rather than just assaults. The responses for this category were 5.2 percent in 1989, 4.7 percent in 1992, 6.4 percent in 2000, and 3.8 percent in 2004.

Fear of crime, or a sense of safety, is also an important part of the official national picture in Australia. In the ICVS survey for 2004 the majority of Australians felt either very safe or fairly safe in their neighborhoods after dark. However, males were more likely to feel very safe (44%) or fairly safe (42%) walking alone after dark than females (21% and 38%, respectively). Women (39%) were much more likely to feel unsafe walking alone after dark than men (13%).

Trafficking in, and use of, illicit drugs are considered major crimes in Australia. Two sources are reported on here: arrest data and usage surveys. The Australian Crime Commission monitors drug arrests made by all police departments. Total arrests increased from 73,959 persons in 2001–2002 to a peak of 80,020 in 2003–2004, down slightly to 77,333 in 2004–2005 and back up slightly to 78,533 in 2005–2006. Of note is a change in proportions, from 75.2 percent for cannabis in 2001–2002 down to 71.0 percent in 2005–2006, heroin down from 4.4 percent to 2.9 percent, and "amphetamine-type stimulants" up from 10.8 percent to 15.1 percent. The National Drug Strategy Household Survey asks persons questions about drug use in the past 12 months. The most recent data show a pattern of rise and fall, and partly mirror the arrest pattern. Responses regarding any illicit drug use increased from 15.3 percent in 1991 to a peak of 22.0 percent in 1998, back to 15.3 percent in 2004. Similar to the arrest data, cannabis use declined from 13.7 percent in 1991 to 11.3 percent in 2004, and heroin declined from 0.4 percent to 0.2 percent. At the same time, methamphetamine (speed) increased from 2.6 percent to 3.2 percent, and Ecstasy use increased from 1.1 percent to 3.4 percent.

In Australia, like all countries, the very large majority of offenders are male. Criminal convictions indicate that about 80 percent of crime, and about 90 percent of violent crime, is committed by males. The average for the three most violent crimes (homicide, sexual assault, and robbery) is even higher for males, around 95 percent. For the least violent crime category—deception (primarily "fraud")—the split is higher for females, although females are still in a minority, at 33 percent. For victims of recorded crimes, the gender differences are more complicated. Males make up the large majority of victims of murder, attempted murder, robbery, and assault—approximately 65 percent. But females make up the very large majority of sexual assault victims (82%) and kidnapping/abduction victims (63%). Race also is a significant variable in offending and victimization. Indigenous persons make up just under 2 percent of the population but a much greater proportion of persons arrested and jailed. According to the Australian Institute of Criminology, the imprisonment rate is approximately 16 times the nonindigenous rate; and indigenous women are 44 times more likely to be hospitalized for assault than nonindigenous females.

Australia's prosperity, its social and political stability, its foreign entanglements, and its fragile ecosystem make it vulnerable to a range of other crimes including people smuggling, terrorism, money laundering, the illegal importation of pests and diseases, and Internet-based crimes. People smuggling peaked as a problem around 2000–2001 when more than 4,000 persons arrived illegally by boat. Subsequently, a controversial system of rapid interdiction and offshore detention of asylum seekers virtually eliminated the problem. There have been no deaths from terrorist attacks on Australian soil since the heightened terror alert of September 11, 2001. However, Australia's participation in the Iraq and Afghanistan wars has made it a target for attacks by Muslim terrorists both offshore and domestically. The worst example was the 2002 Bali bombings in which Australians made up 89 of the 202 fatalities. In February 2008, in a home-grown terror case, the trials began of 17 Muslim men from Melbourne and Sydney accused of planning attacks on critical infrastructure. The most recent estimate for money laundering was that AU$2.8 billion (about US$1,992,368,000) had been laundered in 2004, with most of the money coming from fraud. Most offshore banking havens for Australian criminals were in Asia.

One of the biggest security challenges for Australia is border protection. At airports alone each month, in 2004–2005 about 45,000 quarantine items were seized. Nonetheless, audits indicate that 21 percent of prohibited items passed through airports undetected and 31 percent of prohibited items passed through mail centers. Illegal foreign fishing also represents a serious threat to the environment and commercial fishing. In 2005–2006 Customs and Navy apprehended 367 vessels engaged in illegal fishing.

The Australian Computer Crime and Safety Survey provides data on Internet crime and organizations. The 2006 Australian Computer Crime and Security Survey found that 22 percent of responding organizations had experienced damaging "electronic attacks" in the year. Average losses per organization were AU$241,150 (about US$171,593). The survey also found that the number of organizations free from damaging attacks increased dramatically from 28 percent in 2002 to 73 percent in 2006, probably as a result of the application of better security software and security procedures. Although in 2006 only 10 percent of respondents said they were "managing all aspects of security well," this was an improvement from a low of 5 percent in 2004.

Finding of Guilt

The Australian court system is complex, with variations between jurisdictions. Nonetheless, there are a number of common characteristics. For example, in all jurisdictions a hierarchy of courts deals with varying levels of seriousness of cases and appeals. These are magistrates (or local) courts, intermediate (or district) courts (in larger jurisdictions), and supreme courts. A federal high court presides over appeals from supreme courts. Australian jurisdictions lack standing commissions to investigate possible miscarriages of justice. However, apart from the appeals process, there are various procedural safeguards designed to protect the accused. The presumption of innocence puts the onus on the prosecution to prove their cases "beyond reasonable doubt." Committal procedures for indictable offenses entail an appearance before a magistrate where the evidence is scrutinized. The magistrate can dismiss charges if the evidence appears inadequate. Additional protections include the right to legal representation, the right to silence, and the right to trial by jury for more serious offenses. Despite the expansion of fixed or mandatory sentencing, discretion in sentencing is a mainstay of the work of judges and magistrates.

In addition to these courts, specialist courts deal with specific types of offenses or clientele, such as juvenile or children's courts, drug courts, and indigenous courts. Prosecutions in lower courts are conducted by police prosecutors, whereas higher court cases are conducted by public prosecution lawyers in departments of justice (administratively separate to the courts). Legal defense is provided by private and public lawyers. Australia has an extensive system of publicly funded legal aid that applies an income-based "means test" to applicants.

As noted, Australian criminal law has adopted an adversarial system in which the prosecution and defense attempt to "win" a contest, "played" within rules, to convince the magistrate or jury of the justice of their case. Plea bargaining is a regular practice, and police and prosecutors will drop some charges in return for a plea of guilty on others. Although justice is meant to be swift, extensive delays in bringing matters to court are a major problem. For example, in 2005–2006, the Australian Institute of Criminology reported that only 32 percent of matters finalized in the higher courts took less than 13 weeks to finalization. Twenty percent took more than 52 weeks. Remand time in prison is also highly variable, and a source of some controversy.

The very large majority of cases are minor and dealt with by magistrates' courts—97 percent. Of the defendants appearing in the higher courts, 20 percent are either never adjudicated or are acquitted, and 12 percent of defendants in the magistrates' courts are not sentenced because of nonadjudication or acquittal. However, of those cases adjudicated, the very large majority of cases—91 percent and 96 percent, respectively—result in a guilty verdict. Also of note is the fact that 81 percent of defendants who are proven guilty in the higher courts receive custodial sentences, whereas in the magistrates' courts an even larger proportion of defendants (91%) received noncustodial sentences.

The Australian criminal justice system is a site of change and controversy. One such area is preventive detention—or selective incapacitation. It was once considered anathema to imprison a person without a conviction for a past offense. However, the problem of serious repeat offenders prompted Queensland in 2003 to introduce legislation allowing for the indefinite detention of offenders deemed "dangerous"; and several other jurisdictions have since adopted similar legislation.

Punishment

The last time the death penalty was applied in Australia was in 1967, and the last state to abolish the death penalty did so in 1984. Australia does not have a mandatory sentencing regime. Instead, judges (sentencing in the higher courts) and magistrates (sentencing in the lower courts) are guided by a criminal code act, a penalties and sentencing act, and by case law, which sets out sentencing precedents. It is important to note that there is a great deal of variation in sentencing outcomes across crime types both within and across Australian jurisdictions. However, some patterns are discernible. For instance, throughout much of the 1980s and throughout all of the 1990s, sentences for violent offenses such as murder and assault have become tougher. There also has been an increasing trend toward the use of parole-type sentences. It would appear, however, that this trend toward tougher sentences has not effected any declines in violent crime rates. In fact, it would appear that sentencing outcomes and crime rates remain independent.

A major feature of Australia's prison system and source of criticism is the increase in imprisonment. In the 23 years between 1984 and 2006 the national total increased from just under 9,500 to more than 25,500. The rate of increase in the numbers of prisoners was higher than the increase in the general population: 88 persons were imprisoned per 100,000 in 1984 compared to 163 in 2006. From 1984 to 2005, remand rates more than tripled from 10 per 100,000 to 35. At the same time, the rate of imprisonment of juveniles has declined sharply from 65 per 100,000 in 1981 to 30 in 2006.

As indicated earlier, an additional concern is the persistent very high rates of imprisonment of indigenous men. The first national census of prisoners conducted by the Australian Institute of Criminology in 1982 showed that approximately 10 percent of the Australian total were of indigenous heritage. The most recent survey showed that in 2006 they comprised 24 percent of the total (while just under 2% of the population). In the early 1980s, women were 2.5 percent of all prisoners, but comprised 7 percent in 2006.

Imprisonment rates vary considerably between jurisdictions. The high rate of imprisonment of indigenous people in the Northern Territory—with an overall indigenous population of approximately 25 percent—in large part accounts for the fact the territory has over three times the national rate of imprisonment. Western Australia, with the highest state imprisonment rate, imprisons just over twice as many persons as Victoria, with the lowest rate.

Noncustodial sentences entail a number of options. Offenders can be given community work orders or allowed to live in the community under supervision. Under these arrangements, offenders may be required to stay at home outside work hours, with monitoring by correctional officer visits and/or electronic "bracelets." They can also be ordered to pay fines, including compensation payments to victims. Periodic detention involves offenders staying in secure facilities for varying periods of time each week, such as for weekends or outside work hours.

Another key feature of Australian criminal justice is the increasing use of restorative justice interventions in response to crime. Like New Zealand, Australia is a world leader in the use of restorative justice principally in cases of youthful offending. Restorative justice takes the form of youth justice conferences where offenders and their victims come together to discuss the impact of the crime and what young offenders can do to make up for harms they have caused. Key aims of restorative justice include making offenders accountable, meeting the needs of victims, reparation, and restoration.

There are three referral pathways to a restorative justice conference. Young offenders, who have admitted to their offending, may be referred to a restorative justice conference by either the arresting police officer or a youth court magistrate. If referred by a magistrate, the referral may be the court outcome (e.g., the sentence), or the young offender may be referred to a conference before sentencing. In the latter case, the outcome of the conference will serve to inform final sentencing outcomes.

A restorative justice conference typically lasts about 60–90 minutes. This is very unlike typical youth court appearances, which are usually very brief (e.g., about 20 minutes in duration). In a conference, the facilitator (the "convenor") opens with general introductions and explains what the conference is meant to achieve and what everyone is expected to do.

In addition to the convenor, attendees include the arresting police officer or representative, the young offender, the victim, and support people for the offender and victim (e.g., parents of young offenders and partners of adult victims). After introductions, the convenor asks the young offender to explain the circumstances leading up to the offense. Then the victim is asked to describe the impact of the offense and is given an opportunity to ask the offender questions about motive. This "storytelling" phase of the conference serves to provide the offender and victim with a shared understanding of the offending and its impact. During this phase, victims can regain a sense of security because they receive answers to important questions they have about the offense. Victims often receive apologies during the storytelling phase, which also are important to them. Support people are given an opportunity to comment on the offending and its impact. Finally, once everyone has had an opportunity to speak, all participants negotiate ways that the young offender will make up for harms caused. This is the outcome of the conference, or the "agreement." Common agreements include verbal and written apologies, performing some work for the victim and/or the community, or monetary restitution.

Advocates claim that restorative justice initiatives should reduce crime. However, the empirical literature on restorative justice and reoffending has produced mixed results. This is largely because restorative justice takes many forms as we observe different jurisdictions around the world. In Australia, research on restorative justice and reoffending demonstrates that it has the potential to reduce crime. However, it still is not clear what features of restorative justice effect changes in offending behavior.

Tim Prenzler and Hennessey Hayes

Further Reading

The Australian Component of the International Crime Victim Survey: http://www.wodc.nl/onderzoeksdatabase/icvs-2005-survey.aspx.

Australian Institute of Criminology. The statistics section of its Web site has a variety of crime data in different formats for different jurisdictions and aggregations, both current and historical: http://www.aic.gov.au/stats/.

Australian Institute of Criminology. *Australian Crime: Facts and Figures.* The annual series is an AIC publication of about 100 pages in booklet form packed with vital statistics about crime and criminal justice: http://www.aic.gov.au/publications/facts/.

Bronitt, S., and B. McSherry. (2005). *Principles of Criminal Law.* 2nd ed. Sydney: Thomson Law.

Hayes, H., and T. Prenzler, eds. (2009). *An Introduction to Crime and Criminology.* 2nd ed. Sydney: Pearson Educational.

Melanesia

FIJI ISLANDS

Population in 2007: 837,271
Legal System: Common
Murder: Medium
Human Trafficking: High
Prison Rate: Medium
Death Penalty: No
Corporal Punishment: No

NEW CALEDONIA

Population in 2008: 244,600
Legal System: Civil
Prison Rate: Medium
Death Penalty: No
Corporal Punishment: No

PAPUA NEW GUINEA

Population in 2000: 5,171,548
Legal System: Common/Customary
Murder: Medium
Burglary: High
Corruption: High
Human Trafficking: High
Prison Rate: Low

Death Penalty: Maybe
Corporal Punishment: Yes

SOLOMON ISLANDS

Population in 2008 (projection only): 506,992
Legal System: Common/Customary
Corruption: Medium
Prison Rate: Low
Death Penalty: No
Corporal Punishment: Yes

VANUATU

Population in 1999: 186,678
Legal System: Common/Customary
Corruption: Medium
Prison Rate: Low
Death Penalty: No
Corporal Punishment: Yes

Background

Melanesia is one of the three major sociogeographical groupings most widely recognized in relation to the Pacific (the other two being Polynesia and Micronesia, which are considered elsewhere in this collection). While there is some discussion as to where the boundaries of Melanesia lie, for the purposes of this section, it is taken to comprise the following countries and territories: Papua New Guinea (PNG), Solomon Islands, the Republic of Vanuatu, Fiji Islands, and New Caledonia. With the exception of New Caledonia, all of these are independent states. New Caledonia is a French territory. Fiji became independent in 1970, Papua New Guinea in 1975, Solomon Islands in 1978, and Vanuatu in 1980. New Caledonia was annexed by France in 1853. In 1984 the French national assembly passed a law that granted internal autonomy to New Caledonia, and this came into effect through the operation of an "Organic Law" in 1999. In 1998 the Noumea Accords postponed discussions about independence for the territory until 2013.

The Westminster system of government operates in all except New Caledonia. At the time of writing, Fiji Islands is governed by a military regime following the 2006 coup (the third since independence), and although elections were scheduled for early 2009, it now seems unlikely that these will take place leaving open to question if or when democratic rule will be restored to that country. Papua New Guinea, Solomon Islands, Vanuatu, and Fiji Islands are members of the Pacific Islands Forum, and they also form the Melanesian Spearhead Group (MSG). The MSG was formed in 1986 and its Secretariat was established in Port Vila, Vanuatu, in 2008. The membership and affiliations of this grouping illustrate some of the controversial issues that arise in relation to nationhood within the region. At the inception of the MSG in 1986, observer status was granted to the people of Kanaky (New Caledonia) as represented by the Front de Liberation National Kanak et Socialist (FLNKS). Subsequently in September 2007, the Australian West Papua Association (based in Sydney) called upon MSG leaders to grant the same status to the Melanesian people of West Papua (currently under Indonesian rule). This call was taken up by the government of Vanuatu, which made a push for this at the MSG leaders' meeting in 2008, but it was blocked by Sir Michael Somare, prime minister of Papua New Guinea.

Language and Culture

Melanesia is a part of the world characterized by extreme cultural and linguistic diversity; this marks a significant point of difference between Melanesia and both Polynesia and Micronesia whose populations are, generally speaking, more homogenous in nature. For example, in Papua New Guinea (PNG), more than 700 different languages are spoken, including two national languages (English and Tok Pisin), and Vanuatu has the highest density of languages per capita in the world with approximately 112 languages (including 3 national languages—Bislama, English, and French) spread across a population of just under 200,000 people (according to the 1999 census).

Economy and the Significance of Aid

With the exception of New Caledonia (whose economy is skewed by virtue of its being a French territory), the countries in Melanesia are ones with small developing economies and whose populations are low earning as compared with those in other parts of the world. In terms of donor partnerships, Australia is the largest player in Melanesia, although other assistance is provided by New Zealand, the European Union, China, Japan, Taiwan, and others, including numerous arms of the United Nations. In 2006, Vanuatu signed a compact with the Millennium Challenge Corporation (USA) in relation to major infrastructure projects worth US$66 million, making Vanuatu the only Pacific island country to have benefited from this funding opportunity. Donor partners have emphasized governance and strengthening of law and justice agencies within their aid assistance programs, with perhaps the most significant of these in terms of size and impact being the Regional Assistance Mission to Solomon Islands (RAMSI), led by Australia and the Enhanced Cooperation Programme in PNG.

Papua New Guinea is the largest single recipient of Australian aid and the estimated expenditure for the period 2003–2009 in relation to law and justice in PNG is AU$200 million. In PNG, the Enhanced Cooperation Programme places seconded Australian personnel in in-line positions in several key agencies, including the Office of the Public Prosecutor. This program was originally designed to include a policing element with Australian Federal Police (AFP) officers actually policing the streets of Port Moresby and performing other key in-line roles. This component was excised following a dispute between the governments of PNG and Australia over the issue of immunity from prosecution for AFP posted officers. AusAID (the aid agency for the government of Australia) also funds a Law and Justice Sector Program in PNG to provide multiagency support as well as the Justice Advisory Group, which works with senior officials in the agencies of the sector to enhance coordination and cooperation. The government of New Zealand (through NZAid) provides funding to assist with the strengthening of law and justice in the Autonomous Region of Bougainville through activities such as the Bougainville Community Policing Project.

Mention has already been made of RAMSI in Solomon Islands, which has a "whole of government" approach and operates extensively in the law and justice sector, particularly in the area of correctional services. Although this is a regional assistance program, AusAID is the most significant in terms of amount of funds contributed. As part of the work done within the RAMSI Law and Justice Program, AusAID has contributed to work done to improve security and professionalism within the Solomon Islands Correctional Services authorities. NZAid also contributes to the RAMSI Law and Justice Program, primarily by funding expatriate High Court judges and magistrates to work within the court system of Solomon Islands. NZAid also supports a Save the Children project focused on protecting the rights and interests of young people within the justice system and on reducing youth crime.

In Vanuatu, AusAID funds a Legal Sector Strengthening Project that provides support (through advisers and assistance with training) to the State Law Office, the Office of the Public Prosecutor, the Public Solicitor's Office, and the State Prosecutors' Office (within the Vanuatu Police Force). This project is now in its third phase. AusAID also funds the Vanuatu Kastom Governance Partnership and provides support to the Vanuatu Women's Centre, which has a particular focus on the impact of violence against women. Within the realm of correctional services in Vanuatu, the New Zealand government funds an institutional strengthening project within the Department of Correctional Services (previously located within the Vanuatu Police Force) and plans to be involved in building a new prison farm outside Port Vila. This construction project was scheduled for 2009. As of May 2010, a site has been identified and set aside but the building project has yet to begin.

On a regional basis, the government of Australia funds the Pacific Regional Policing Initiative (PRPI), which is concerned with the standardization and improvement of police training in Pacific island countries, including those in Melanesia (with the exception of New Caledonia). The government of New Zealand also provides a funding contribution to this program. The government of New Zealand provides core funding to the Pacific Islands Chiefs of Police Secretariat, which brings together police commissioners from 21 Pacific island countries and is co-funder (with AusAID) of the Pacific Judicial Development Program.

Legal Systems

It is certainly the case that the colonial powers, and in particular the United Kingdom and Australia (in relation to PNG), have left their mark on the laws of Melanesian countries and may continue to exert some influence in the jurisprudential development in this part of the world. However, the countries of Melanesia have a plurality of legal sources or resources that both lend color to their sociolegal environments and create numerous ambiguities and complexities.

Constitutional Documents

All of the countries of Melanesia have constitutional documents that were adopted at independence. In relation to criminal procedure, these documents are important as they contain provisions relating to rights and freedoms, some of which take on particular significance within the context of the criminal justice system. For example, a suspect's right to be informed of charges in a language that he or she understands is recognized by article 2(c) of the Constitution of Vanuatu. Constitutional issues have been and continue to be very frequent bases of litigation in the courts of Melanesia, as is the case elsewhere in the Pacific island region. A key area in this context is the availability of legal advice and representation. Such a right, where it exists, is of importance at the trial (or other hearing) stage of the criminal justice process and, more problematically, at the pretrial stages, particularly during periods of detention and/or police questioning. The question of resources is one that is central in this context. As we have already seen, the countries of Melanesia have small economies with limited amounts of available public funds, which are subject to many pressures and demands. Therefore, it is problematic as to who should bear the cost of legal representation for suspects who cannot afford to pay for such representation themselves. Each country has a public solicitor (or equivalent), but these agencies are both underresourced and overworked, leaving them often unable to meet the demands for their services.

In Vanuatu, the right to legal representation is contained in article 5(2)(a) of the Constitution. However, this right is limited to cases where a person has been charged with a "serious offence." It is not clear from either the Constitution or the Criminal Procedure Code (Cap. 136) how a "serious offence" should be defined. It may be that a serious offense should be deemed to be the same as a cognizable offense, that is, one for which it is possible for the police to make an arrest without having first obtained a warrant. Such offenses are listed in a Schedule to the Criminal Procedure Code (Cap. 136). In Fiji, the right of a charged person to defend himself or herself in person or to be represented at his or her own expense by a legal practitioner is encapsulated in S.28(1)(d) of the Fiji Constitution Amendment Act 1997. Significantly, S.27 of the act makes specific reference to the rights to be accorded to arrested and detained persons (before the charging stage); the right to consult with a legal practitioner is recognized in this context. In both Fiji Islands and PNG, the right to appeal against conviction or sentence is given constitutional recognition.

Locally Enacted Legislation

All of the countries of Melanesia, with the exception of New Caledonia, have an Anglo-Welsh legacy in the realm of criminal law and procedure as in many other areas. Unlike other areas of law (such as family law and land law), criminal law and criminal procedure law in Melanesian countries is largely codified. PNG is unique in having one code that covers matters of substantive criminal law and procedural issues. In Solomon Islands and Fiji, there is a principal act concerned with criminal law. These documents set out offenses and the relevant penalties. They also often include interpretation sections and statements of criminal liability and available defenses. Some minor offenses may be contained in other pieces of legislation such as the Minor Offences Act of Fiji (Cap. 18) and the Public Order

Act of Vanuatu (Cap. 84). In relation to criminal procedure, a codified approach is also favored, so in these jurisdictions there is a separate codified document that covers matters of criminal procedure. Other versions of these codes exist elsewhere in the world. The penal codes of Fiji Islands and Solomon Islands largely resemble the criminal codes of Queensland and Western Australia. By contrast, the Vanuatu Penal Code (Cap. 135) is a recent (i.e., postindependence) and original code, enacted in 1981. This code exhibits the influence of the Anglo-Welsh common law approach to criminal law but does not appear to reflect the effect of the French contribution to the country's administration during the period when the New Hebrides (the preindependence name of Vanuatu) was administered as a condominium by the governments of the United Kingdom and France.

(English) Statutes of General Application

During the colonial period, statutes of general application applied in colonies as well as in the home jurisdictions of the colonial powers. Over time, a cut-off date was nominated by the colonial power. This designated the date after which legislation enacted by the colonial power ceased to apply in the colony in question. As the colonies attained independence, these dates were maintained. For example, in Solomon Islands the cut-off date in relation to statutes of general application enacted by the English Parliament is January 1, 1961. Pre-1961 legislation continues to apply (in the absence of relevant local legislation or express provisions to the contrary) unless it is considered unsuitable to local circumstances. In relation to criminal law and procedure, the difficulties associated with the applicability of received legislation that are prevalent in other areas of law are not so marked, as this is an area of law in which there is a great deal of comprehensive locally enacted legislation. In fact, in most situations throughout Melanesia, there will be no need to refer to legislation from outside the jurisdiction because locally enacted statutes will cover the relevant circumstances. This point was considered in the Solomon Islands' case of *R. v Ngena [1983] SILR 1*. The court held that the Homicide Act 1957 of the United Kingdom no longer applied in Solomon Islands (even though it had been enacted prior to the cut-off date) as all issues relating to homicide were dealt with in the Penal Code.

The Impact of Case Law

There is more than one type of case law available as a source of law in the countries of Melanesia. The availability of these sources and their relative importance may not always be easy to ascertain and may vary from jurisdiction to jurisdiction. The general rules of precedent apply in the courts of the countries of the region.

The law of England and Wales is considered to have a particular significance to the courts of the region in the context of interpretation of relevant legislative provisions, owing to the historical importance of the United Kingdom as a colonial power. For example, in the jurisdictions of Fiji and Solomon Islands, it is specified that, in the absence of local definitions and interpretations, the Penal Code should be interpreted in accordance with "English criminal law." However, it is important to remember that most jurisdictions have a cut-off date in relation to the common law of England and Wales, that is, the date on which such law ceased to be binding in that jurisdiction. For example, in Schedule 3 to the Constitution of Solomon Islands, it is stated that English case law should cease to be binding on the courts of Solomon Islands with effect from July 7, 1978. From this point onward, the only relevance that decisions of the courts of England and Wales may have is as persuasive authority. In relation to case law more generally, there may be some question as to whether one type of case law is considered more significant than another. The courts of the region have previously been engaged in a consideration of whether the principles laid down in Anglo-Welsh cases should be considered as more important than those in cases from other common law jurisdictions, in particular, Australia and New Zealand. However, this debate has receded more recently as the courts and lawyers in the region have more access to case law from other Pacific island countries, and it is certainly the case in the Supreme Court of Vanuatu that the judges would expect lawyers to present decisions from their Melanesian neighbors as persuasive authority rather than cases from a country such as the United Kingdom or Australia.

Customary Law and Practice

Of particular significance is the role of customary law and practice in the field of criminal law and procedure. It is not possible to generalize about customary law and practice across the region as there are often quite significant differences between different countries and indeed between different parts of the same country. Within Melanesia a general rule of thumb is that each language group will have its own set of customary laws and practices and, as we have already seen, the number of language groups in this part of the Pacific is extremely high. While it is the case that customary law is enunciated and enforced by chiefs or other community leaders outside the introduced/adopted court system, there are also instances of the introduced/adopted formal system taking account of customary principles in particular areas.

All of the countries of Melanesia (with the exception of New Caledonia) make some provision, usually in a constitutional document, for customary law to be recognized as a source of law. For examples, see article 95(3) of the Constitution of Vanuatu and S.75 of the Constitution of Solomon Islands. However, these provisions do not provide any guidance as to how the weight of customary law decisions (where such can be identified) or principles should be compared with the weight of statutory provisions or decisions of the courts.

The impact of customary law in relation to issues of criminal law and procedure is possibly more limited than is the case in other areas of law, most notably land law. The impact of customary law varies on location—it is much more significant in rural areas than in urban areas where people have better access to the police and the courts and where there is an increased likelihood of the authority of chiefs or other traditional leaders having been diluted through exposure to different ideas or the pressures of city life. In the villages of rural Melanesia decisions as to wrongdoing and punishment in relation to all except the most serious (and there may not always be consensus as to what is the "most serious") offenses will be made by chiefs, village councils, or other bearers of traditional authority. Offenses against custom are not demarcated into "civil" and "criminal" wrongs and may often include transgressions that might appear to outsiders as no more than (perfectly legal) deviations from an accepted social norm (such as wearing the wrong sort of clothes). The processes associated with establishing that a wrongdoing has occurred, how blame is to be apportioned, and what punishment is to apply are very often commenced, conducted, and concluded without any recourse to the police or the formal court system, although it may be the case that there will be some involvement of the quasiformal courts, such as the Island Courts of Vanuatu or the Local Courts in Solomon Islands.

Crime

In the countries of Melanesia (with the possible exception of New Caledonia), it is hard to obtain crime statistics that are current and/or accurate for a number of reasons, but predominantly because of a lack of available resources and/or expertise in this area within policing organizations. These problems are exacerbated in relation to statistics compiled by policing posts situated in remote areas that would almost certainly have to be compiled by hand and then somehow transported to the capital or administrative center for collation. Added to this is the problem of the "dark" figure of crime—that is, crime that occurs that is not reported to the police. This phenomenon is one that arises in all parts of the world. A particular characteristic of the "dark" figure of crime that applies in relation to Melanesia (and indeed anywhere where strong "traditional" cultures persist) is that some wrongdoings that would be reported to the police in other parts of the world are not reported in these countries; rather, they are dealt with through traditional forms of dispute resolution as administered by chiefs, village elders, or other community leaders.

Recently, bureaus of statistics and national statistics offices have made use of online media to publish a range of statistics including those that relate to crime. In this endeavor they have been assisted with a regional project operating under the auspices of the South Pacific Community entitled "Pacific Regional Information SysteM" (PRISM). However, it remains a challenge for these Web sites to be kept current, and there are ongoing problems associated with obtaining reliable raw data from the law enforcement agencies within country. Available data are as follows:

- *PNG.* In 2003, per 1,000 inhabitants, there were 3,037 crimes against the person and 6,061 crimes against property recorded by police (PNG National Statistical Office).
- *Solomon Islands.* In 2003, there were a total of 1,051 crimes against the person and 1,395 crimes against property reported to police (Solomon Islands National Statistics Office).
- *Fiji.* In 2007 there were a total of 3,343 offenders recorded for crimes against the person and 5,358 persons recorded for crimes against property. The majority of offenders were male. In that same year there were 58 cases of rape recorded. (Fiji Islands Bureau of Statistics; "Fiji Facts and Figures as at 1 July 2008.")
- *Vanuatu.* In 2004, there were a total of 287 crimes against the person and 457 crimes against property reported (Vanuatu National Statistics Office).

Police try to stop looters at the Taurama shopping center in Port Moresby, Papua New Guinea, after a demonstration at Murray Army Barracks turned violent, March 19, 1997. (AP Photo/Mike Bowers)

There are attempts made by external agencies to assess levels of crime or disorder in the countries of Melanesia, but the figures they produce need to be treated with some caution as they have been compiled at some distance removed from the firsthand data in country. However, it is often the case that these statistics are easier to obtain than statistics in any collated or published form from policing organizations of the countries concerned. An example of this type of "remote" survey is that produced by the Overseas Security Advisory Council (OSAC), which produces information on security issues for the American business market. Its Fiji review of 2007 indicated that crime is rising in that country, with a 3 percent increase in reported offenses in the period covering the last nine months of 2007 as compared with the previous year. Property offenses are the most commonly occurring (58%) with offenses against the person being the second-most common type of offense to be recorded (24%). As with all statistics, a certain amount of unpacking is required. In this instance the OSAC report refers to "Fiji" whereas the majority of this criminal activity is likely to occur in urban areas such as Suva, Nadi, and (to a lesser extent) Lautoka, Lami, and Ba.

From the information that is available and bearing in mind all the limitations of those data that have previously been identified, it is evident that the most common type of offense to be reported to the police is one relating to property—predominantly theft. What theft looks like can vary from country to country. It remains the case that in Vanuatu, street crime continues to be rare whereas it is much more established as a criminal activity in Fiji and PNG, particularly in the capitals (Suva and Port Moresby, respectively) and other highly populated urban areas. Until relatively recently, thefts from houses in Vanuatu tended to take the form of items being taken from outside the house (e.g., on the veranda) or break-ins that were committed while the house was unoccupied. However, this trend is changing with an increase in home invasion crimes and an attendant increase in crimes of violence committed against occupants who challenge intruders. In Fiji, PNG, Solomon Islands, and Vanuatu, crimes of domestic violence are very common, although they are largely underrepresented in the available crime statistics owing to underreporting. In all of these countries, there has been an increase in urban drift since independence with a growth of squatter settlements on the outskirts of the capital cities and other areas of (relatively) large urban population. This trend is often believed to be a significant contributory factor to rising crime levels. It is certainly the case that levels of unemployment tend to be higher in these settlements than elsewhere in the community and these locations are often the site of flashpoints such as intercommunity disputes that may become very violent very quickly.

Papua New Guinea has an entrenched severe law and order problem arising out of *raskol* activity, which occurs in all urban centers but especially in Port Moresby and Lae, which are the most populous. There is a great deal of violent crime in Port Moresby, exacerbated by the ready availability of firearms, many of which have been stolen from police and defense force armories. Port Moresby is one of the most dangerous capital cities in the world. The social, psychological, and economic impacts of this ongoing and seemingly intractable situation are significant on individuals, businesses, communities, and the country as a whole. In addition, law enforcement authorities are often called upon to deal with interethnic disputes that often become violent, especially in the troubled Southern Highlands Province, centered on Mt. Hagen. Elections also tend to provide a flashpoint for violent clashes in PNG. Furthermore, the law, order, and security situation is not helped by frequent turf war–type disputes between the police and the PNG Defence Force.

The state of law, order, and community safety was relatively unremarkable in Solomon Islands until 1999, which marked the start of growing ethnic tension between the indigenous people of Guadalcanal (the island on which the capital Honiara is located) and the people of Malaita living there, many of whom were descended from Malaitans who had been brought to Guadalcanal during the colonial period and whose families had integrated and intermarried with those on whose land they resided. The tensions became increasingly violent and, as in PNG, the situation was made worse by the relatively widespread availability of firearms (some of which were left over from World War II and others of which had been transported across the notoriously porous border between the north of Solomon Islands and Bougainville, the semiautonomous island province of PNG). In 2003, at the invitation of the Solomon Islands government, Australia put together a regional (military-led) assistance mission entitled "Operation *Helpem Fren*"—the Regional Assistance Mission to Solomon Islands (RAMSI). The military aspect of RAMSI has been scaled back over time with more use being made of civilian police officers drawn from several countries around the region, including the other Melanesian countries (except New Caledonia). Having reestablished basic security and law and order within Honiara and elsewhere, the support provided by RAMSI is now more of the "institutional strengthening" kind to provide assistance to the machinery of government, including law enforcement agencies, the courts, and correctional services.

Police

Policing organizations in the countries of Melanesia are subject to a number of pressures including limited resources (as is the case in relation to all aspects of service delivery by governments including education, health, and infrastructure), cultural expectations and restrictions, and changing patterns of crime at local, national, and international levels.

Policing Challenges

The populations of Melanesian countries are growing in comparison with their economies, and there are many well-documented cases of urban drift, which in turn leads to a breakdown in social cohesion, a dilution of traditional authority (such as the power of the chiefs to control the behavior of young people), resulting in increased criminality (predominantly property offenses but including other types of offenses) in urban areas. Policing resources tend to be stretched thinly, thus reducing their ability to deal with this "normal" criminality and rendering them almost ineffective in cases of "acute" situations such as riots, interethnic violence, prison breaks, and so forth. For example, in Fiji Islands the police strength in 2005 was enumerated at 4,076 including 1,565 special constables. This means that the number of police officers to serve each 1,000 members of the population is estimated at 4.93. However, this does not reflect the fact that at any one time a number of members of the police force will not be available for operational duties because they are on leave, involved in training, or seconded to an overseas posting such as RAMSI or a UN peacekeeping mission.

The countries of Melanesia have geographies that have adverse impacts on the effectiveness of policing organizations. For example, approximately 80 percent of the population of Vanuatu live in rural areas, many of which have minimal infrastructure, very poor communications, little or no access to electricity or telephones, making it extremely difficult for members of these communities to feel adequately provided for by policing organizations. This has a particular impact on women who are the victims of sexual crimes or domestic violence as the chances of them being able to talk to a woman police officer about what has happened to them are seriously reduced if they live in rural or remote areas (this is compounded by the fact that women are generally underrepresented in policing organizations in Melanesian countries, especially as operational officers). It is almost certainly the case that crime of all types, and particularly crimes committed against more vulnerable groups such as women or young people, are dramatically underreported in rural areas.

As has already been noted, the countries of Melanesia (with the exception of New Caledonia) have small, developing economies and are financially somewhat fragile. There are limited resources available for all services provided (whether in theory or practice) by government and government agencies, including those responsible for law, order, and security. Additionally, there is ample evidence (both anecdotal and otherwise) of resources being used inefficiently and/or being misappropriated.

Overseas Assistance to Policing Organizations

For many years, law enforcement agencies in most Melanesian countries have benefited from on the ground support provided by advisers from overseas, usually Australia. The Defence Cooperation Programme places Australian Defence Force personnel in advisory positions within a country's defense force or the paramilitary wing of the police service in countries where no defense force exists (such as Vanuatu). More recently, the growth of the International Deployment Group within the Australian Federal Police (AFP) has seen its personnel being used to fill advisers' positions within programs established to provide institutional strengthening or capacity development to policing organizations. For example, the Vanuatu Police Force Capacity Building Project in Vanuatu (funded by AusAID, the aid agency for the government of Australia) is delivered in country by a team drawn from the International Deployment Group of the AFP. The AFP has also been instrumental in setting up Transnational Crime Units throughout the Pacific, including within Melanesia (in Vanuatu, for example) to which they provide ongoing support by way of resources, training, and mentoring. These units focus their attention on combating transnational crimes such as trafficking of drugs, people, and firearms as well as terrorism. They tend to be very well resourced as compared with the police forces of the region more generally, and there is some debate as to the level of contribution this type of activity makes to the day-to-day security and safety of people who live in Melanesia.

Punishment

All of the countries in Melanesia have life imprisonment available as a penalty in relation to very serious crimes such as murder. However, the reality is that most convicted criminals serve relatively short sentences and it is not uncommon for prisoners to be released before they have served their full sentence. In Vanuatu, it was previously common practice for the president to pardon large numbers of prisoners at Christmas and on the anniversary of independence, but this has not happened more recently following community concerns about the impact of this practice on (apparently) rising crime rates and community safety.

As with other areas we have considered, it is the case in relation to prison populations that reliable and current statistics are difficult to obtain. As of 2007, according to the Fiji Islands Bureau of Statistics, the prison population was 841, of which 87 percent were males. Length of terms being served were as follows:

Offenders serving 1–6 months	310
Offenders serving 6–12 months	152
Offenders serving 12–21 months	165
Offenders serving 2–5 years	146
Offenders serving 5 years–life	68

Custom and Sentencing

In PNG the use of customary compensation in criminal cases has been enshrined in legislation by virtue of the Criminal Law (Compensation) Act 1991. Vanuatu refers to the incorporation of the customary concepts of reconciliation and compensation in the Criminal Procedure Code (Cap. 136), more particularly in Sections 118 and 119.

The Death Penalty

The death penalty is not practiced in the countries of Melanesia. It was abolished in Solomon Islands in 1966, in Vanuatu in 1980, and in France (and therefore in New Caledonia) in 1981. In Fiji Islands it was abolished for ordinary crimes in 1979. This means that the penalty still remains available for crimes committed against the state or in times of war. So, for example, George Speight who was the leader of the 2000 coup was sentenced to death, but his sentence was subsequently commuted. Papua New Guinea abolished the death penalty in 1950, but it was reintroduced in 1991 as a response to increasing crime and community concerns about the breakdown in law and order. However, no executions have been carried out since that time and Amnesty International describes the situation in PNG as "abolitionist in practice." In April 2007, the Minister for Justice announced that there would be no return to executions and also stated that he would work toward completely abolishing the death penalty. In the same year, three men who had been under sentence of death since 1997 had their sentences commuted to imprisonment for life following an appeal court finding that the trial judge had erred in his belief that he was required by law to impose the death penalty.

Tess Newton Cain

Further Reading

Fiji Islands Bureau of Statistics. "Fiji Facts and Figures as at 1 July 2008": http://www.stats fijigov.fj/FFF08.pdf.

Institut de la Statistique et des Etudes Economique. "Key Figures": http://www.isee.nc/anglais/key figures/keyfigures.html.

National Statistical Office of Papua New Guinea. "Population and Social Statistics": http://www.spc.int/prism/country/pg/stats/Pop_Soc_percent20Stats/popsoc.htm.

Solomon Islands National Statistics Office. "Solomon Islands Projected Population by Province 1999–2014": http://www.spc.int/prism/country/sb/stats/Social/Popcen/Projection.htm.

Vanuatu National Statistics Office. "Social Statistics": http://www.spc.int/prism/country/vu/stats/SOCIAL/soc-index.htm.

Micronesia

Legal System: Common/Customary
Prison Rate: Medium
Death Penalty: No
Corporal Punishment: Yes (Kiribati only)

Background

Micronesia, which lies in the North and Central Pacific Ocean, is composed of more than 2,100 tropical islands spread across an area of approximately 7,770,000 square kilometers (3,000,000 square miles) of the Pacific Ocean. Its total dryland area, however, is only about 2,706.5 square kilometers (1,045 square miles). It is one of the three ethnogeographical subregions of Oceana, in addition to Melanesia and Polynesia. Politically, it includes seven independent nations and territories: the Republic of Belau (Palau), the Commonwealth of the Northern Mariana Islands (CNMI), Guam, the Federated States of Micronesia (FSM), the Republic of the Marshall Islands, the Republic of Kiribati, and the Republic of Nauru.

Geographically, the CNMI and Guam, which are both U.S. territories with distinctive political relationships to the United States, are part of the Marianas archipelago consisting of 21 islands in the northwestern part of Micronesia. Guam has the largest land area of any of the islands (214 square miles) and it also has the largest population of Micronesia, with about 185,793 people. The CNMI has the fourth-largest population at 69,221. The Republic of the Marshall Islands is an independent nation with a Compact of Free Association with the United States and consists of more than 1,200 islands concentrated in the eastern part of the region. It has a population of about 50,840 people. FSM and Palau, which are also independent nations with a Compact of Free Association with the United States, are part of the Caroline Islands archipelago in the southern part of Micronesia, stretching from the east (south of the Marshall Islands) to the west (south of the Marianas). The entire archipelago contains a total of 957 islands, islets, and reefs. FSM has the second-largest population, at 107,008. Palau has the second-smallest population, next to Nauru, with 19,907 people.

These two territories and three "freely associated states" collectively form what has been called "American Micronesia" because of their historical and present ties to the United States as a result of World War II (except for Guam, which was ceded to the United States in 1898 following the Spanish-American War). Most of American Micronesia shares a similar political and legal history dominated by foreign powers—first by the Spanish from the 16th century until the late 19th century, followed by the Germans until the start of World War I, and the Japanese until the end of World War II. With the exception of Guam, which was already a U.S. territory, the islands were then politically formed into the Trust Territory of the Pacific Islands (TTPI) in 1947 and placed under an American administration. As the UN's sole "strategic trust," it was essentially closed off to any outside influence other than that of the United States. This American influence is reflected in the governmental systems of the political entities that eventually emerged from the TTPI as most of the governments have adopted an American presidential model, with the exception of the Marshall Islands, which adopted a parliamentary model.

The republics of Kiribati and Nauru, which occupy the southeast border of Micronesia, are both independent nations that are geographically a part of Micronesia but are not associated with the United States. The Republic of Kiribati consists of 169 islands and three archipelagoes—the Gilbert Islands, including Banaba (Ocean Island), the Line Islands, and the Phoenix Islands. It has the third-largest population, with 92,533 people. In 1888 the Gilbert and Ellice islands were made a protectorate of the United Kingdom and later a crown colony in 1916. The islands remained in British control until their independence in 1977. The Republic of Nauru is an independent nation west of Kiribati that consists of a single island. It is the smallest political unit in Micronesia, and it also has the smallest population at 9,086 people. Prior to its independence in 1967, Nauru was a UN Trust Territory administered by Australia and was additionally influenced by earlier British and German administrations. Both Kiribati and Nauru have adopted a parliamentary form of government.

Due to limited resources and technology in most of Micronesia, detailed statistics monitoring crime trends, law enforcement personnel, and correctional facilities are either unavailable or not updated on a regular basis. Moreover, much of the information that is available is not readily accessible on official government Web sites. However, each of the nations and territories has a national statistics office that coordinates with the Secretariat of the Pacific Community (SPC) to publish available statistical information in an online database called the Pacific Regional Information SysteM (PRISM). Although the reporting system is not uniform across the countries in terms of the types of data collected and the methodologies used, it often provides the most current, albeit basic, statistical information about crime in the member country. Other information regarding the components of each member country's criminal justice system must be sought elsewhere. A summary of available information for each of the U.S. territories and independent nations of Micronesia follows.

Republic of Belau (Palau)

Legal System

Palau is an independent republic composed of 16 states. It is characterized by a common law legal system and the sources of law for the nation are the Constitution, the Republic of Palau National Code (PNC), initiatives enacted by the people, custom and common law. Palau currently has a Compact of Free Association with the United States under which the United States maintains a military presence in the territory and has additional operating rights in exchange for U.S. economic aid and defense of the nation. The compact declared the self-governing status of Palau and mandated the renegotiation of certain terms, such as those relating to economic aid. It was finally approved by the Palauan people after eight referenda and an amendment to the Palau Constitution. The compacts entered into force in 1994, making Palau the last district in the Trust Territory of the Pacific Islands to officially gain independence.

Under the Palau Constitution, the national government is composed of an executive, legislative, and judicial branch. The executive branch consists of the president, vice president, and the Council of Chiefs. The Council of Chiefs advises the president on issues involving custom, tradition, and the Constitution. The council is composed of a traditional leader from each state. Legislative power is vested in the Palau National Congress, also called the *Olbiil Era Kelulau* (OEK). The OEK is a bicameral legislature with a Senate consisting of 13 members elected nationally and a House of Delegates consisting of a single member per state. The judiciary consists of the Supreme Court, which has a trial and appellate division; the Court of Common Pleas, which usually handles minor civil cases and criminal cases if the maximum fine is US$2,000 or less, or five years' imprisonment or both; and the Land Court. The Office of the Attorney General is under the purview of the Ministry of Justice and is responsible for prosecuting crimes. The office prosecutes approximately 500 criminal cases per annum. There is also an Office of the Public Defender, which is a part of the Ministry of State.

Policing

The Bureau of Public Safety is divided into six divisions—the Patrol Division, Division of Correction and Rehabilitation, Division of Criminal Investigation and Drug Enforcement Section, Division of Fish and Wildlife Protection, Division of Marine Law Enforcement, and the Division of Fire and Rescue. In 2009, there were a total of 158 police officers (141 male, 17 female) and 17 civilian personnel.

Classification of Crimes

Title XVII of the Palau National Code (PNC) classifies crimes as felonies or misdemeanors, where felonies are crimes or offenses punishable by imprisonment for more than a year, and misdemeanors are all other crimes.

Crime Statistics

In 2008, police handled two cases of murder in the first degree, three cases of involuntary manslaughter, and one rape. There were a total of 10 assault crimes (assault and battery with a dangerous weapon, assault and battery, and assault). The most reported crimes were grand larceny, with 149 cases, and burglary, with 72 cases.

Rights of the Accused

Article IV, Section 7 of the Palau Constitution lists the fundamental rights of the accused, which include, among others, the presumption of innocence until proven guilty, the right to be informed of the charges against oneself, the right to a speedy and public trial, the right to a compulsory process of obtaining favorable witnesses, and the right to have counsel at all times, including the right to have counsel assigned by the government for indigent defendants.

Title 18, Chapter 4 of the Palau National Code enumerates the rights of defendants: the right to a copy of the charges before trial, the right to the assistance of counsel, the right to apply for further time to prepare a defense, the right to bring witnesses to trial and to have witnesses summoned by the court, the right to give evidence on one's behalf if one so chooses, the right to have proceedings interpreted when one is unable to understand them otherwise, and the right to request the appointment of an assessor in trials in the event that one has not been appointed.

Types of Punishment

There is no death penalty in Palau. Under Title 17 of the code, types of punishment include fines, orders requiring specified residence, restitution, compensation, forfeiture, closing of business, labor without imprisonment, and probation. Custom is accorded "due recognition" in the imposition or suspension of the execution of sentences and the granting of probation. The punishment for homicide varies according to its classification: (1) murder in the first degree has a penalty of life imprisonment; (2) murder in the second degree has a minimum penalty of 5 years' imprisonment and a maximum of life imprisonment; (3) voluntary manslaughter has a maximum penalty of 10 years' imprisonment; and (4) involuntary manslaughter has a maximum of 3 years' imprisonment or a fine not to exceed US$1,000, or both. The punishment for rape is imprisonment for a maximum of 25 years. There is a limitation of punishment for acts that are considered crimes solely based on custom, which is a maximum fine of $100, or six months' imprisonment, or both.

Prison System

Prison administration is the responsibility of the Division of Corrections, which is under the Ministry of Justice. There is one prison facility, which is located in Koror. In 2009 there were a total of 97 prisoners (91 male, 6 female). Of these, 8 were in long-term custody (7 male, 1 female).

Commonwealth of the Northern Mariana Islands (CNMI)

Legal System

The Commonwealth of the Northern Mariana Islands (CNMI) is a U.S. territory characterized by a common law legal system. The political relationship between the United States and the CNMI is governed by the Covenant to Establish a Commonwealth of the Northern Mariana Islands in Political Union with the United States (the "Covenant"). The covenant together with the applicable provisions of the U.S. Constitution, treaties, and laws of the United States (as specified in the covenant) are the supreme law of the land. Applicable federal laws and provisions of the U.S. Constitution are enumerated in article V and include the first nine amendments of the U.S. Constitution. These rights include the right to a jury trial, the privilege against self-incrimination, and prohibitions of excessive bail and cruel and unusual punishment.

The covenant also granted U.S. citizenship for the people of the CNMI (article III) and vested judicial authority in the courts established by the Constitution and laws of the CNMI (article II). Article IV established the federal district court for the Northern Mariana Islands with jurisdiction over all causes arising under the Constitution, treaties, and laws of the United States, regardless of the amount involved in the dispute. Other sources of law are the CNMI Constitution and some pre-Commonwealth laws (such as Trust Territory and Marianas District laws).

Under the CNMI Constitution, legislative power is vested in a bicameral legislature consisting of a House of Representatives with 14 members popularly elected for two-year terms, and a Senate with 9 members popularly elected for four-year terms. Twelve of the 14 representatives are from the island of Saipan, which has the largest population and is the seat of the Commonwealth's capital. The number of senators is equally divided among three senatorial districts: Saipan (including the northern islands, which have minor populations), Tinian and Aguiguan, and Rota. The executive branch is headed by a governor who is popularly elected for a term of four years.

The judicial branch consists of the Superior Court, which has original jurisdiction over all criminal cases, and the CNMI Supreme Court, which is the highest appellate court in the CNMI and has appellate jurisdiction over Superior Court judgments. Its decisions are reviewable only by the U.S. Supreme Court. In 2006, 274 criminal cases were filed in the Superior Court and 4 in the Supreme Court.

Policing

The Department of Public Safety (DPS) is responsible for local law enforcement. DPS is headed by a commissioner and is divided into the Police Division, Fire Division, Criminal Investigations Division, and the Department of Motor Vehicles. There are stations on the islands of Saipan, Tinian, and Rota. The Criminal Investigations Division is charged with the investigation of all crimes within the CNMI's jurisdiction and applicable federal laws. It is divided into the Juvenile Police Unit, the Drug Enforcement Task Force (DETF), Domestic Violence Intervention Unit, Special Homicide Activities Resolution Project (SHARP), Theft Apprehension Select Coalition (TASC), Human Trafficking Intervention Coalition, and the General Crimes Unit.

Classification of Crimes

Title VI of the Commonwealth Code (6 CMC) deals with crimes and criminal procedure in the CNMI.

Offenses are classified as either felonies, which are punishable by imprisonment for at least one year, or misdemeanors, which are punishable by not more than one year's imprisonment.

Crime Statistics

In 2004, police made arrests for 1 homicide, 1 rape (sexual assault in the first degree), 6 robberies, and 104 thefts. The top four crimes for which police made an arrest were assault crimes (450), disturbing the peace (334), driving under the influence (236), and reckless driving (254).

Rights of the Accused

Article I, Section 4 of the Commonwealth Constitution enumerates the fundamental rights of the accused in criminal prosecutions, which includes the right to assistance of counsel, the right to be confronted with adverse witnesses and to have a compulsory process for obtaining favorable witnesses, the right to a speedy and public trial, the right to be protected against giving self-incriminating testimony, and the right to be protected against double jeopardy, excessive fines and bail, and cruel and unusual punishment.

Title VI, Section 6105 lists the rights of persons arrested, which include the right to see counsel, family members, or employers at reasonable intervals and for a reasonable time at the place of detention; the right to the services of the public defender, free of charge; the right to be either charged or released within 24 hours. Section 6105 also requires the police to inform those in custody of the right to remain silent and the right to have the police call counsel before questioning.

Types of Punishment

Capital punishment is expressly prohibited under article 1, section 4 of the Constitution. Title VI of the Commonwealth Code lists available sentences, which include imprisonment, fines, orders requiring specified residence, restitution, compensation, and probation. The sentence for homicide varies depending on whether the homicide is classified as murder (unlawful killing with malice aforethought) or manslaughter (unlawful killing without malice aforethought). Murder is divided into first-degree and second-degree murder, and the sentence for first-degree murder is imprisonment for at least 10 years, up to life imprisonment. The sentence for second-degree murder is imprisonment for at least 5 years, up to life imprisonment. Manslaughter is divided into voluntary and involuntary manslaughter. The sentence for voluntary manslaughter is imprisonment for a maximum of 10 years, and a maximum of 5 years for involuntary manslaughter. Sexual assault is divided into four degrees. The most serious sexual assault offense—sexual assault in the first degree—is punishable by imprisonment for a maximum of 30 years, a $50,000 fine, or both. Local customs may be considered in sentencing as mitigating or aggravating factors.

Prison System

Prison administration is conducted by the Division of Corrections (DOC), which falls under the Department of Public Safety (DPS) and is headed by the commissioner. There is only one prison facility, which is located on Saipan. According to the International Center for Prison Studies, the prison population in October 2008 was 131.

Guam (Guahan)

Legal System

The Territory of Guam (Guam or Guahan) is a U.S. territory characterized by a common law legal system. The ultimate source of U.S. control over Guam comes from article II of the 1898 Treaty of Paris in which Spain ceded Guam to the United States after the Spanish-American War. In 1950, the U.S. Congress passed the Organic Act of Guam granting, among other things, U.S. citizenship to Guamanians and establishing the form and structure of the government. The Organic Act thus essentially functions as Guam's constitution. Under the act as amended, the executive branch is headed by the governor, who is popularly elected for a term of four years. The legislative branch, called the Legislature of Guam, consists of a unicameral legislature with a maximum of 21 legislators, called senators, who are elected for two-year terms. In 1996 the number of senators was reduced to 15.

Judicial authority is vested in the federal District Court of Guam and the Guam judiciary. The judicial branch consists of the Supreme Court of Guam, which is the highest court (excluding the District Court), the Superior Court, and lower local courts. In 2005 adult and juvenile drug courts were recognized as courts of record by the judiciary. With regard to criminal matters, the District Court previously exercised jurisdiction over felonies, while jurisdiction over misdemeanor cases were handled by either the Island Court or the Police Court. In 1974 the Judicial Reorganization Act abolished both the Island and Police courts and created the Superior Court to exercise jurisdiction in all cases arising out of the laws of Guam. Between September 30, 2005, to September 30, 2007, the Superior Court handled 3,129 criminal cases.

Policing

While the United States is responsible for the military defense of the island, the Guam Police Department is responsible for local law enforcement. There are a total of 19 villages on Guam that are divided into four precincts. The department is headed by the chief of police, followed by the police commander, who oversees the Operations and Investigations bureaus, and the deputy chief of police, who oversees the Support Bureau. In 2007, the Guam Police Department employed 309 full-time sworn officers (6.5% female, 93.5% male) and 66 civilians (72.7% female, 27.3% male). There is an average of 1.8 full-time employees per 1,000 inhabitants.

Classification of Crimes

Guam criminal law is based on the Model Penal Code advocated by the U.S. National Conference of Commissioners on Uniform State Laws. It is particularly influenced by the California Penal Code. The Criminal and Corrections Code falls under Title 9 of the Guam Code (9 GCA). Crimes and offenses are classified as felonies, misdemeanors, petty misdemeanors, and violations. Felonies are subdivided into first-, second-, and third-degree felonies, while misdemeanors and petty misdemeanors are crimes that are not subdivided into degrees and do not have specified sentences authorized upon conviction. Violations are not considered crimes and are offenses for which the penalty is limited to a fine or forfeiture.

Crime Statistics

According to the Federal Bureau of Investigation (FBI) Uniform Crime Report (UCR) for Guam, a total of 1 homicide, 208 forcible rapes, 108 robberies, and 117 aggravated assaults were reported to the police in 2007. The total number of violent crimes had increased slightly from the previous year, from 410 in 2006 to 434 in 2007. Unlike violent crime, the total number of property crimes reported in 2007—burglary, larceny-theft, motor vehicle theft, and arson—reflected a downward trend, from a total of 4,651 in 2005, to 4,177 in 2006, and finally to 4,077 in 2007. The sharpest decrease in property crimes was in the number of burglaries, which fell from 1,292 in 2006 to 1,058 in 2007.

Rights of the Accused

Under the Organic Act, the rights of the accused in criminal prosecutions include the right to a speedy and public trial, to be informed of the nature and cause of the accusation, to be confronted with the witnesses against oneself, to have a compulsory process for obtaining witnesses in one's favor, and to have the assistance of counsel for one's defense. The rights of defendants in criminal proceedings are elaborated in Title 8, Chapter 1 of the Guam Criminal Code and also includes the right to appeal and the right for indigent defendants in criminal cases to have counsel appointed at public expense at all stages of the proceedings.

Types of Punishment

There is no death penalty on Guam. Title 9, Chapter 80 of the Guam Code specifies five types of sentences: (1) imprisonment by a term required by law, (2) imprisonment and an additional parole, (3) a fine or restitution authorized by law, (4) probation, and (5) a combination of a fine, restitution, probation, and/or imprisonment. Unless otherwise specified by law, first-degree felonies are generally punishable by a sentence of imprisonment for at least 5 years, and no more than 20 years. Second-degree felonies carry sentences of at least 3 years, and no more than 10 years. Third-degree felonies carry sentences that do not exceed 5 years. Prison terms for first-time offenders have a shorter range; for example, first-degree felonies carry sentences of at least 3 years, but no more than 15 years. Extended sentences are allowed and could increase the term for a first-degree felony to life imprisonment, a second-degree felony to between 5 and 20 years, and a third-degree felony to between 3 and 10 years.

There are four types of criminal homicide recognized in the Criminal Code, each with a different sentence: aggravated murder, murder, manslaughter, and negligent homicide. Aggravated murder, murder, and manslaughter are all first-degree felonies, while negligent homicide is a third-degree felony. Chapter 16 of the Code provides specific sentences for aggravated murder and murder. For aggravated murder the sentence is life imprisonment without possibility for parole, work release, educational programs outside the prison, or a suspended sentence. The sentence for murder is similar to aggravated murder, except that there is possibility for parole after 15 years.

Criminal sexual conduct is covered under Chapter 25 of the Code and is subdivided into four degrees. First-degree criminal sexual conduct is a first-degree felony punishable by a minimum of 15 years to a maximum of life imprisonment without possibility of parole. Second-degree criminal sexual conduct is also a first-degree felony, but without the ability to participate in work release or outside educational programs. Third-degree criminal sexual conduct is punishable as a second-degree felony, and fourth-degree criminal sexual contact is punishable as a third-degree felony, unless the person is a first-time offender, in which case the crime is punishable as a misdemeanor.

Prison System

There are four major prison facilities: the Adult Correctional Facility (ACF), the Hagåtña Detention Facility, the Women's Facility, and the Community Corrections Center (C3). The ACF houses immigration detainees, minimum, medium, and maximum security inmates. In May 2009, the ACF had a total population of 411. The Hagåtña Detention Facility houses local pretrial detainees and U.S. federal marshal detainees. Its population in May 2009 was 119. The Women's Facility is the only detention facility for women, and it had a population of 27 women in 2009. Finally, the Community Corrections Center houses inmates who are eligible for work credit, work release, and educational release. Its population was 22 in May 2009.

Federated States of Micronesia (FSM)

Legal System

The Federated States of Micronesia (FSM) is an independent nation composed of four states: Pohnpei, Yap, Chuuk, and Kosrae. It is characterized by a common law legal system at both the national and state levels. Sources of law are the FSM Constitution, state constitutions, national, state and local legislation, treaties, customary law, Trust Territory laws, and common law. The FSM currently has a Compact of Free Association with the United States under which the United States maintains a military presence in the territory and has additional operating rights in exchange for U.S. economic aid and defense of the nation. The compact was approved by the majority of FSM citizens in a plebiscite held in 1983 and became effective in 1986.

The FSM Constitution is the supreme law of the land. It established three branches of government, with the executive branch headed by a president who is elected by the legislature for a term of four years. Legislative powers are vested in the Congress of Micronesia, which is a unicameral legislature composed of 14 senators. Each state has 1 senator elected for a four-year term, and the remaining 10 senators are elected for two-year terms and are apportioned according the population of each state.

The highest court is the Supreme Court, and there is currently no other national-level court.

Because the FSM is a federal system, each state has an independent government and adheres to its own laws in addition to the national Constitution and national laws. All four states have a constitutional government with an executive, legislative, and judicial branch. The state of Yap is the westernmost state of the FSM. It has an executive branch headed by a governor and a unicameral legislature with 10 members. The highest state court is the State Court of Yap. The state of Chuuk has the largest population in the FSM, with about 53,000 people. The executive branch is headed by a governor, and the legislature consists of the Senate with 10 members and the House of Representatives with 28 members. The highest state court is the Chuuk State Supreme Court. The state of Pohnpei has the largest land area and is also the seat of the national capital. The state executive is the governor, and the Pohnpei Legislature consists of 23 senators. The Pohnpei State Court is the highest state court.

Policing

At the national level, the attorney general of the FSM is the highest law enforcement official and oversees the Division of Security and Investigation (DSI), which is the national government's police force.

Classification of Crimes

The National Criminal Code is found in Title XI of the FSM Code (11 F.S.M.C.) and is generally based on the Model Penal Code. Prior to 1991, the national government was responsible for prosecuting "major crimes," which were defined as crimes punishable by imprisonment for at least three years or resulting in the loss of property or services amounting to a minimum of US$1,000. In 1991 the FSM Constitution was amended, transferring jurisdiction over most crimes to the states and giving the national government jurisdiction over "national" crimes as defined by the Congress (article IX, § 2). National crimes are crimes that are "inherently national in character" as specified in Title IX of the FSM Code, or crimes that are "otherwise against the Federated States of Micronesia." Crimes are classified as either felonies or misdemeanors, where felonies are crimes that are punishable by imprisonment for more than a year and misdemeanors are defined as all other crimes. The states likewise classify crimes as either felonies or misdemeanors.

Crime Statistics

Detailed statistics about crime by type of offense are not available. However, according to the FSM's 2008 Statistical Yearbook, a total of 877 criminal cases were filed in the courts of each state—102 in Yap, 125 in Chuuk, 450 in Pohnpei, and 200 in Kosrae. With regard to offenses reported to the police, there were 75 felonies reported in Chuuk, 266 in Pohnpei, and 29 in Kosrae.

Rights of the Accused

The national Constitution contains a Declaration of Rights similar to the U.S. Bill of Rights, and protects, among other rights, the right to a speedy public trial and the right to the assistance of counsel. Title XII of the FSM Code (12 F.S.M.C.) covers criminal procedure and enumerates the rights of defendants, which include the rights to have a copy of the charge prior to trial, to consult counsel prior to and during the trial, to bring witnesses or have witnesses summoned in defense, and to have proceedings interpreted. With regard to arrested individuals, public officials are required to inform them of their rights, such as the right to remain silent and to be informed of the criminal charges. The rights of the accused in the different states are similar.

Types of Punishment

Capital punishment is expressly prohibited under article IV, Section 9 of the Constitution. Under Title XI of the code, national crimes are punishable by imprisonment, fines, restitution, reparation or service to the victim of the crime or the victim's family, community service, and confinement to a particular geographical area. The code also recognizes customary law in matters of crime and criminal responsibility as well as in sentencing. The national crime with the highest penalty is treason, which is punishable by a minimum of two years' imprisonment and a maximum of life imprisonment.

The types of punishment for crimes in each state are similar and include fines, imprisonment, restitution, probation, hard labor without imprisonment, closing of business, and specified residence. Homicide is not uniformly classified across the states and the punishment for the different types of homicide varies somewhat. For example, Kosrae divides homicide into murder, which has two degrees, and involuntary manslaughter. The punishment for first-degree murder is a maximum of 20 years' imprisonment, a $20,000 fine, or both. In Chuuk, homicide is divided into murder, manslaughter, and criminal homicide. The punishment for murder is a minimum of 5 years' imprisonment and a maximum of life imprisonment. The minimum punishment for murder in Yap, which also divides homicide into murder and manslaughter, is 5 years, and the maximum is also life imprisonment. The punishment for the highest form of sexual assault is similar across the states. For example, in Chuuk, the punishment is a maximum of 9 years' imprisonment, a $10,000 fine, or both; whereas in Yap, the punishment is a maximum of 10 years' imprisonment, a $10,000 fine, or both. States also have a limitation on the punishment of acts that are made criminal solely by custom. For example, in Chuuk and Yap, there is a maximum fine of $100, imprisonment for a maximum of 3 months (Chuuk) or 6 months (Yap), or both.

Prison System

Prison administration falls under the Division of Corrections and Rehabilitation, which is headed by the chief. There are four facilities, one located in each of the four states. In 2007, the total number of prisoners was 96, with an average of 89 for every year since 2000. The majority of prisoners (44% or 46%) were detained in Pohnpei.

Republic of the Marshall Islands

Legal System

The Republic of the Marshall Islands is an independent nation characterized by a common law legal system. It has a Compact of Free Association with the United States that was approved by the Marshallese people in a plebiscite held in 1983 and that became effective in 1986. Sources of law are the Marshall Islands Constitution, adopted legislation from the Trust Territory Code, and legislation enacted by Parliament, or Nitijela, treaties and compacts, customary law, and common law. Although it was formerly under an American administration as part of the Trust Territory of the Pacific Islands, the Republic of the Marshall Islands ultimately adopted a quasiparliamentary governmental structure as more congruous with the actual political experience of the people.

Under article IV of the Marshall Islands Constitution, legislative power is vested in the Nitijela, which is a unicameral parliament with 33 members who are popularly elected for four-year terms. Article V vests the executive power in the cabinet with 10 ministers who are collectively responsible to the Nitijela. The cabinet consists of the president, who is the head of state and a member of the Nitijela, and other members of the Nitijela who are appointed as ministers. The president is elected for a four-year term by a majority of the Nitijela. The Constitution under article III also provides for an advisory body composed of traditional leaders called the Council of Iroij. With respect to the cabinet, the council's advisory role is not restricted to matters relating to customary law. With respect to the Nitijela, however, the council's advice is limited to matters affecting land and custom. Neither the cabinet nor the Nitijela is required to follow the council's advice, although the Nitijela must reconsider any bill returned to it.

Article VI of the Constitution vests the judicial power in the Supreme Court, a High Court, a Traditional Rights Court, and such district courts, community courts, and other subordinate courts as are created by law. The Supreme Court is the highest appellate court. The High Court is a court of general jurisdiction over matters of law and fact, and it has both original jurisdiction over cases properly filed and appellate jurisdiction over cases filed in lower courts. With regard to criminal matters, the district court has original jurisdiction concurrently with the High Court in criminal cases involving offenses for which the maximum penalty does not exceed US$4,000 or imprisonment for a term of less than three years, or both. The district court also has appellate jurisdiction over decisions made by the community court. There are 24 community courts in local government areas that have concurrent jurisdiction with the High Court and district court in criminal cases where the maximum penalty does not exceed a $400 fine or six months' imprisonment, or both. Finally, the Constitution provides for the Traditional Rights Court, which has jurisdiction limited to questions related to land matters and matters depending wholly or partly on customary law.

Policing

The Marshall Islands has a national police force under the Department of Public Safety, which is part of the Ministry of Justice. There are also local police forces on the different atolls. The RMI Statistical Yearbook for 2004 reported a total of 137 national police officers on three different atolls and a total of 466 local police officers.

Classification of Crimes

Under the Criminal Code, which is Title 31 of the Marshall Islands Revised Code (31 MIRC), crimes are classified as felonies or misdemeanors. Felonies are offenses punishable by imprisonment for more than a year. All other crimes are classified as misdemeanors. If a crime is punishable by imprisonment for less than a year, it is considered a petty misdemeanor. All other crimes are classified as misdemeanors.

Crime Statistics

In 2004, there were a total of 2,074 offenses reported to the national police. Of these offenses, there was 1 of murder, 3 cases of rape/attempted rape, 100 cases of burglary, and 295 total assault crimes (aggravated assault, assault, assault and battery, assault and battery with a dangerous weapon). The most reported offenses were disturbing the peace (773) and drunken disorderly conduct (408). These numbers only reflect those offenses known to the national police and do not include those criminal cases that were handled by the local government police.

Rights of the Accused

Under the Bill of Rights (article II of the Constitution), the rights of the accused in criminal trials include the right to be informed promptly and in detail of the nature of the accusations, the right to a speedy and public trial before an impartial tribunal, the right to have adequate time and facilities for the preparation of a defense, the right to counsel, including the right to have counsel appointed if the interests of justice so require.

Section 137 of the Criminal Procedures Act (32 MIRC) lists the rights of defendants in criminal proceedings. These rights are similar to those in other Micronesian states and include the right to have in advance of trial a copy of the charge, the right to consult counsel, the right to present witnesses on one's behalf and to have them summoned by the court, and the right to have proceedings interpreted if the defendant would not be able to understand them otherwise. The rights of the arrested (32 MIRC § 120) are also the same as for other Micronesian states.

Types of Punishment

The death penalty is prohibited as cruel and unusual punishment under article II, Section 7 of the Constitution. Part XXIX of the Criminal Code specifies the types of punishment, which include fines, orders requiring specified residence, restitution, compensation or forfeiture, closing of business, labor with or without imprisonment, and probation. The punishment for homicide varies according to its classification under Part XIV of the Criminal Code.

The penalty for murder in the first degree is life imprisonment. For murder in the second degree, the penalty is a minimum of 5 years' imprisonment and a maximum of life imprisonment. For voluntary manslaughter, the penalty is a maximum of 10 years' imprisonment, and for involuntary manslaughter, the penalty is a maximum fine of $1,000 or 3 years' imprisonment, or both. Sexual offenses are divided into four degrees, and the highest penalty is for sexual assault in the first degree, which is a maximum of 25 years' imprisonment. The maximum penalty for a property crime or burglary is 10 years' imprisonment. As with the other Micronesian states, there is a limitation of punishment for acts that are made crimes solely because they violate native customs—a maximum fine of $100 or 6 months' imprisonment, or both. There is also a recognition of custom in the imposition or suspension of sentences and the granting of probation.

Prison System

Prison administration is the responsibility of the Correction Division under the Department of Public Safety. There is a single prison facility, which is located in Majuro, the capital of the RMI. In 2006, there were 47 prisoners.

Republic of Kiribati

Legal System

The Republic of Kiribati (formerly the Gilbert Islands) is an independent nation with a parliamentary form of government. It is characterized by a common law legal system. Sources of law include the Constitution of Kiribati, statutes (acts of the Maneaba [legislature], certain UK statutes), common law, and custom. The republic gained its independence from Great Britain in 1979 through the Kiribati Independence Order, which also provided a written constitution. Under the Constitution of Kiribati, executive authority is vested in the cabinet, which consists of the Beretitenti (president), the Kauoman-ni-Beretitenti (vice president), ministers appointed by the Beretitenti from among the Maneaba, and the attorney general. The Beretitenti is both the head of state and head of government and is nominated from among the Maneaba and elected by a national vote. Thus, the parliamentary system adopted by Kiribati also incorporates to a certain extent the American model.

Legislative authority is vested in the Maneaba ni Maungatabu, which consists of 41 members who serve four-year terms. Thirty-nine members are elected by popular vote, one is nominated by the Rabi Island Council in Fiji to represent Banaba, and one member serves *ex officio.* The judicial branch consists of magistrates' courts, a High Court, and the Court of Appeal. Constitutional cases involving Banabans may be appealed directly to the Privy Council in England. With regard to criminal matters, the magistrates' courts have jurisdiction over cases in which the maximum punishment is a fine of $500 or 5 years' imprisonment, or both. The High Court has unlimited original jurisdiction in criminal cases and has jurisdiction over certain criminal cases from the magistrates' courts. The Court of Appeal has appellate jurisdiction over criminal appeals.

Policing

The police force is headed by the commissioner of police and prisons, followed by three superintendents who are responsible for crime and security, prisons, and administration. The commissioner reports to the Office of the President. In 2006, there were approximately 300 police officers and 40 correctional officers.

Classification of Crimes

Under the Penal Code (Cap. 67), offenses are classified as either felonies or misdemeanors. Felonies are offenses punishable by imprisonment for at least three years, and misdemeanors are all other crimes.

Crime Statistics

The most recent crime statistics available are from 2000, which reveal a total of 1,337 crimes reported. Of these crimes, 311 were classified as crimes against the person and 588 as crimes against property.

Rights of the Accused

Section 10 of the Constitution lists the rights of every person charged of a criminal offense: the right to be presumed innocent until one is either proved guilty or has pled guilty; the right to be informed of the charges as soon as reasonably practicable; the right to defend oneself or through counsel at one's own expense; the right to be given adequate time to prepare a defense; the right to examine adverse witnesses and to call witnesses on one's behalf; the right to have the assistance of an interpreter free of charge if one cannot understand the language used by the trial court. The Criminal Procedure Code (Cap. 17) further elaborates on the procedural rights of defendants.

Types of Punishment

Under the Penal Code, the penalty for murder is life imprisonment (§ 193). The penalty for manslaughter as well as for rape is up to life imprisonment (§§ 192 and 129, respectively). The penalty for burglary is up to 14 years' imprisonment. Other types of punishments include fines, corporal punishment, community service orders, probation orders, residence orders, and police supervision for a maximum of 5 years.

Prison System

Prison administration is the responsibility of the Kiribati Prison Service under the Office of the President. The head of the prison system is the commissioner, who is also the head of the police force. In 2007, there were a total of 88 prisoners in four prison facilities, including one facility for females.

Republic of Nauru

Legal System

The Republic of Nauru (formerly Pleasant Island) is an independent nation with a parliamentary form of government. It is characterized by a common law legal system, and its sources of law include the Constitution of Nauru, legislation (postindependence acts of the Nauru Parliament, subordinate legislation such as regulations, preindependence colonial ordinances, and certain statutes in force in England on January 31, 1968, British common law, and custom). Formerly a UN Trust Territory under the administration of Australia, the Republic of Nauru gained its independence on January 31, 1968. The Constitution of Nauru was adopted two days earlier, on January 29. Under the Constitution, executive authority is vested in the cabinet, which is collectively responsible to Parliament. The cabinet consists of five members appointed by the president, who is elected by Parliament for a three-year term. The president is both the head of state and the head of government. The Nauruan Parliament is a unicameral legislature consisting of 18 members (MPs) who are popularly elected for three-year terms.

The judicial branch consists of the Supreme Court, the District Court, and Family Court. The Family Court was established by the Family Court Act of 1973 and consists of members appointed by the president. Its jurisdiction is limited to issues provided for in the Maintenance Ordinance (1959–1967) and the Adoption of Children Ordinance (1965–1967). The District Court was established by the Courts Act of 1972, and it consists of magistrates appointed by the president. It has jurisdiction over all civil cases where the amount in controversy does not exceed $3,000. With regard to the criminal matters, the Courts Act does not specify any substantive criminal jurisdiction for the District Court.

The Supreme Court of Nauru has original jurisdiction over the interpretation or effect of constitutional provisions. It also issues advisory opinions to the cabinet on questions involving the Constitution. With regard to criminal matters, the Supreme Court has jurisdiction over appeals from decisions of the District Court. Furthermore, the High Court of Australia has jurisdiction to hear appeals from the Supreme Court for any final first instance judgment and for certain cases with leave of the trial judge or the High Court. There are a number of situations in which appeals to the High Court of Australia are not permitted, such as appeals involving the interpretation or effect of the Nauruan Constitution or appeals from decisions that are final according to statute. Although the High Court may review criminal cases, it rarely does so.

Policing

The Ministry of Justice oversees the Nauru Police Force. As of July 2009, there were a total of 76 Nauru police officers. Other law enforcement officials with specific enforcement duties include 18 immigration officers and 5 customs officers. Because prison administration is also handled by the Nauru Police Department, 18 corrections officers and 10 reserve officers are counted as part of the police force. The government is currently in the process of creating a separate Department of Corrections.

Classification of Crimes

The Republic of Nauru has adopted the Queensland (Australia) Criminal Code. Under the code, offenses are classified as either regulatory or criminal. Criminal offenses are further classified as crimes or simple offenses. Crimes consist of every offense defined in the code, every indictable offense, and every offense declared under an act to be a crime.

Rights of the Accused

Under the Constitution, the rights of the accused include the presumption of innocence until proved guilty, the right to be informed of the charges against oneself and to be given adequate time and facilities for the preparation of a defense, the right to have an interpreter free of charge if one cannot understand the language used by the court, the right to counsel and to have counsel appointed where "the interests of justice so require," and the right to examine witnesses against oneself and to be able to call witnesses in one's favor.

Types of Punishment

Under the Queensland Code, there is a mandatory penalty of either life imprisonment or an "indefinite sentence" for murder and a maximum penalty of life imprisonment for manslaughter. The maximum penalty for rape is life imprisonment. The penalties for the different degrees of sexual assault range from a maximum of life imprisonment for the most serious offense to 7 years' imprisonment. The penalty for property crimes of stealing and dishonest appropriation ranges from 7 to 14 years' imprisonment.

Prison System

Prison administration is the responsibility of the Nauru Police Department headed by the director of police. As of July 2009, there were a total of 24 male prisoners serving terms ranging from three months to life, and 9 prisoners in remand.

Estelle Hofschneider

Further Reading

Bird, R., A. Matich, and Dianne Thompson. (2008). *Law of the Pacific Islands: A Guide to Web Based Resources:* http://www.llrx.com/features/pacific.htm.

International Centre for Prison Studies: http://www.kcl.ac.uk/schools/law/research/icps.

Ntumy, M., ed. (1993). *South Pacific Islands Legal Systems.* Honolulu: University of Hawaii Press.

Pacific Islands Legal Information Institute (PacLII): http://www.paclii.org/.

Pacific Regional Information SysteM (PRISM): http://www.spc.int/PRISM/index.htm.

New Zealand

Legal System: Common
Murder: Low
Burglary: Medium
Corruption: Low
Human Trafficking: Low
Prison Rate: Medium
Death Penalty: No
Corporal Punishment: No

Background

New Zealand is a relatively isolated nation with a population estimated to be 4.25 million persons. The country has long been known for benefits conferred by a compassionate welfare system that cares for victims of crime, disease, and disaster. Today, the significant reduction of the island's demographic homogeneity, particularly by an influx of migrants from the Pacific region, and the continuing migration to the cities from rural areas, combined with economic pressures, has led to a curtailing of some of the more generous subsidies to those in need. Nonetheless, the spirit that has been responsible for the country's communitarian policies is reflected in significant ways in a criminal justice system that makes particularly strenuous efforts, both in its laws and in its operational programs, to salvage and reintegrate those who have committed criminal offenses.

In the 19th century, the indigenous Maori population was overwhelmed by British settlers, who took formal command of the country under terms of the Treaty of Waitangi that was signed on February 6, 1840, a day that now is a national holiday, though the legality of the treaty has been recently questioned. The Treaty of Waitangi meant that the laws in England would now prevail in New Zealand.

Police

The first police in New Zealand arrived in 1840 with the landing party that established New Zealand as a British colony. Magistrates were authorized two years later to appoint men who were accorded powers existing in the common law of England for investigating crimes and making arrests. At first, the police served partly as law enforcers and partly as a militia. Four years onward, an ordinance called for the establishment of a constabulary force that would contain sufficient numbers of fit and able men to preserve the peace and prevent robberies and other felonies and apprehend offenders. The Police Act of 1886 mandated the formation of the country's first national police force, and in 1968 a new Police Act eliminated the word "Force" from its name, declaring that from then forward the organization should be known as the "New Zealand Police," a move reflecting the less confrontational style of enforcement that the authorities favored.

The New Zealand Police are commanded by a commissioner with headquarters in the national capital in Wellington and are subdivided into 12 districts, each led by a district commander with the rank of superintendent. Each district has three operational branches: general duties, criminal investigation, and road policing. Special units handle matters such as intelligence, forensics, diplomatic protection, and maritime enforcement. There are also some 400 community policing stations in the country. At the beginning of 2008, there were 10,300 employees in the police force, of whom 75 percent are sworn enforcement officers, with Maoris making up about 10 percent of that contingent. Some 80 percent of the officers are men.

Applicants for police positions must have at least four years of high school education, must pass proficiency tests in mathematics and literacy, and need to undergo fitness tests and a psychological assessment. They cannot have a record of serious law breaking, a category that includes drunken driving.

New Zealand police constable Mike Smith, foreground, falls to the ground after being shot with a Taser gun by Sergeant Darrin Putt in a demonstration of the device at the Police College in Wellington, New Zealand, August 29, 2006. (AP Photo/NZPA, Ross Setford)

The training of recruits and advanced courses for sworn officers are conducted at the Royal New Zealand Police College in Papakowhai, a suburb of Puawai City, located 22 miles north of Wellington. Each year, there are usually six new recruit classes, called "wings," with about 40 to 100 members in a wing. The entry-level course takes five months and successful graduates then serve two years as probationary constables during which time they are given 10 different work assignments and must prepare a paper for a university class.

Strategic Tactics Group

The New Zealand police often are extolled for the fact that they do not carry firearms but rather rely on armaments such as batons and pepper spray. Senior police officers routinely carry an assortment of weapons in the locked trunk of their car and police who anticipate violence may have a holstered gun that they will be careful to tuck out of sight under their jacket or sweater. There also is a well-armed Special Tactics Group (STG) that is trained in the use of weapons in preparation for dealing with emergencies such as terrorist attacks, riots, or domestic disputes that can turn dangerous for enforcement interveners.

The work of the STG squad, which is manned by about 50 officers, was expanded considerably with the passage in 2002 of the Terrorist Suppression Act. The major enforcement focus has been on deterring the financing of groups deemed likely to mount terrorist actions, but after Parliament in November 2007 called for the creation of lists of suspected terrorist individuals and organizations, the SGT has played a more forceful role in rounding up persons it believes pose a terrorist threat.

A major antiterrorist raid was carried out by the police in the vicinity of the larger New Zealand cities in October 2007 at sites said to be "terrorist training camps" and "anarchist group homes." The raids were conducted by more than 300 armed police officers and focused on Maoris and on environmental activists. Numerous guns and grenades were seized and one of the alleged leaders of the movement was found with a semiautomatic shotgun and several Molotov cocktails. Thereafter, the police infiltrated the camps and did extensive videotaping of what went on.

Monitoring Police Behavior

In 1988, Parliament established the Police Complaints Authority (PCA) to handle grievances filed against the police and to investigate controversial police actions. Toward the end of 2007, the entity was renamed the Independent Police Conduct Authority (IPCA) to seek to convey more authoritatively that the agency was not, at least formally, beholden to the police.

The IPCA is charged with the investigation of police involvement in situations in which death or serious injury occurred. They also entertain allegations by citizens or other civilians of serious police misconduct and examine situations in which a suspect died while in police custody. The most recent tally shows that about 300 complaints regarding police misconduct had been filed with the authority during the previous year. The authority is appointed by the governor-general and reports to Parliament and to the attorney general. The staff numbered 18 persons in 2008, with investigators largely former police offices, a situation that has given rise to claims that its work tilted in favor of the police rather than complainants.

The New Zealand police sought early on to take steps to establish a national collection of DNA profiles on the basis of a 1978 recommendation by the Criminal Law Reform Commission on Bodily Examination and Samples as a Method of Identification. But the idea met with strong resistance and did not come to fruition until the passage of the Criminal Investigations (Blood Samples) Act in 1995. The act established a national DNA data bank with samples required from persons convicted of specified offenses and criminal suspects who voluntarily yielded DNA samples. In 2003, the Criminal Investigations (Bodily Samples) Amendment to the original act added the use of bucal, or mouth, swabs to obtain DNA samples. The collection had built to 64,199 DNA profiles by the end of 2006 with additions averaging about 800 to 1,000 a month. To date, more than 50 previously unsolved cases have been cleared on the basis of DNA evidence.

Objections to the program remain strong, based on principles of privacy. The Auckland Civil Rights group has maintained that the system represents a slippery slope that will eventuate in a mandatory program that would represent an unacceptable assault on the civil liberties of New Zealanders.

Crime

Criminal offenses in New Zealand are divided into six categories. The first includes purely summary offenses that are tried before a judge alone in a district court. These offenses, which are relatively minor, carry a penalty of three months or less.

Electable offenses can be tried summarily or on indictment in a district court, whichever the accused chooses. The offenses involved carry a possible penalty of more than three months' imprisonment. Typical offenses in this category are simple assault and the possession or use of marijuana.

Hybrid offenses are tried summarily in the district court following an indictment. The category includes most offenses against the person and against property. Offenses that also are tried in district court following an indictment, but require a jury, include corruption, bestiality, aggravated assault, and arson.

Arson cases in New Zealand are disproportionately committed by young persons. Typically, about 65 percent of New Zealand's arsonists are under 17 years of age with 40 percent being under 14. The majority of young persons and adolescents who set fires are dealt with by the New Zealand Fire Service by means of a youth intervention program.

The law against bestiality—sexual activity involving a human and an animal—derives from early religious orthodoxy. In New Zealand the offense can incur a maximum seven-year penalty. In 1989 a bill introduced in Parliament sought to eliminate the behavior from the roster of crimes and redefine it as a mental health problem but failed of passage. Some judges, however, have taken a milder view of bestiality. In *Police v. Sherry* in 1991, the court observed in a bestiality case that "the community is now more lenient and understanding of unusual sexual practices that do not harm others."

A fifth category embraces offenses that are to be heard in the High Court following an indictment. The High Court, however, can return these matters to a district court after taking into account the gravity of the offense, the complexity of the case, and the interests of justice. These offenses include rape, grievous bodily harm, and kidnapping. Finally, murder and manslaughter charges must be heard in the High Court before a judge and jury.

Crime Statistics

The seven categories of criminal offenses under New Zealand law about which statistics are reported are listed here in descending order in terms of the number of reported violations: (1) dishonesty offenses, (2) drug and antisocial offenses, (3) violent offenses, (4) property damage, (5) property abuse, (6) administrative offenses, and (7) sexual offenses.

In the 2007–2008 reporting year, there were 112 homicides, and only for this offense may we reasonably compare it to the totals for earlier years: in 2006–2007, there were 96 homicides and the year before 105.

The three categories of assaults—serious (21,096 cases), grievous (5,009), and minor (14,921)—show a combined total of 41,026 reported or discovered incidents. Robberies, involving force or fear, stood at a total of 2,629; kidnapping and abduction at 242.

Dishonesty Offenses

Dishonesty offenses accounted for more than half of New Zealand's crime in the 2007–2008 fiscal year with a rate of 51.97 per 100,000 population. The category includes five subdivisions: (1) theft, which accounts for about half of the dishonesty violations; (2) burglary, which makes up 26 percent of the total; (3) car theft and related offenses (3%); (4) fraud (1%); and receiving stolen goods (less than 1%). A fifth category, concerned with what are called "miscellaneous dishonesty," has shown insignificant totals over the past decade.

Sexual Offenses

For statistical purposes, with the totals in parentheses, sexual offenses break down into sexual attacks (2,364); sexual affronts, which include indecent performances and "obscene exposure" (596); immoral behavior (353); immoral behavior/miscellaneous (174); and abnormal sex, such as incest and bestiality (35).

Drug Offenses

Drug and antisocial crimes constituted 14 percent of the country's total crime. Acts defined legally as "disorder" were responsible for 42 percent of the offenses in this category, with cannabis use accounting for 26 percent of this amount.

Drug usage in New Zealand tends to be viewed from a public health perspective. Cannabis is the most popular drug in New Zealand and domestic cultivation is widespread so that there is no need to smuggle it into the country. LSD (lysergic acid diethylamide), a hallucinogen, is the next most common drug of choice and is mostly imported; New Zealand has one of the world's highest rates of LSD usage, although a 2005 survey by the Illicit Drug Monitoring System indicated that recourse to LSD has been declining recently. More than 80 percent of those who use LSD are males and their median age is 24. Use of Ecstasy, Fantasy, and other so-called designer drugs is believed to have contributed somewhat to a drop in LSD use. These drugs often are traded in nightclubs and at electronic music performances and are primarily found in urban areas.

There is little use of cocaine or heroin in New Zealand, perhaps largely because of the high price that they command. The country has a program of needle exchange for those who inject opiates intravenously that has contributed significantly to a reduction in cases of hepatitis and in AIDS/HIV infections. These drugs commonly pass through New Zealand for transshipment to other markets, most notably Australia.

Miscellaneous Offenses

Other crime totals for 2007–2008 include the 53,794 offenses defined as destruction of property, 11,030 acts recorded as "against justice," 272 immigration crimes, and 3 instances declared to violate racial laws. The Sentencing Act of 2002 had incorporated hate crimes in its embrace, increasing the sentences possible for crimes directed against persons because of their race, ethnicity, sexuality, or religion. Some have objected that act did not include gender or disabilities as a protected category.

Crime Victim Survey

New Zealand has carried out two crime victim surveys, the first in 1996 and the most recent in 2001. The 2001 national survey was based on a sampling of 5,000 persons who were 15 years or older. Of that total, 38 percent declined to participate in the interviews, a figure that rose to 57 percent among Maoris. Seventy percent of the respondents indicated that they had not been victimized during the previous 12 months, while 12 percent reported that they had been the victim of a crime five or more times in that period. Victims disproportionately were young, Maoris, especially Maori women, students, beneficiaries (welfare recipients), single parents, the unemployed, and persons living with flatmates (roommates).

Forty percent of the offenses tabulated by the victim survey had been reported to the police. A majority of the respondents said that they had no fear of venturing forth in their neighborhood after dark, although this was less true for women than men, and even less true of women over 60. Overall, the major crime concern expressed during the interviews was the fear of being injured or killed in a traffic accident by a drunk driver. The lowest levels of concern were about assault by a known person, or being assaulted because of race, or being racially harassed on the street.

Organized Crime

Serious attention was first paid to organized criminal activity in New Zealand in the late 1980s when it became a matter of police concern that groups of Asian immigrants had criminal connections in their home countries. Typical organized crime activities are fraud, illegal drug dealing, and extortion.

In 1991, the police formed Asian Crime Units to monitor and deal with triad gangs that were involved with drugs, credit card frauds, the forging of passports, extortion, counterfeiting, motor vehicle theft, and the fencing of stolen goods. In addition to the triads, other Asian organized crime groups in New Zealand included Vietnamese migrants who entered as refugees after what they called the American War. Some became involved in gambling, prostitution, and the importation of heroin. There also has been an influx of *boryokdua,* organized criminals of Japanese origin. The government has tightened immigration restrictions in an attempt to cut off the flow of criminals from overseas sites.

White-Collar Crime

New Zealanders take pride in the fact that their country is listed in the *Corruption Perception Index* as the third-least corrupt nation—after Denmark and Finland—among the 183 countries considered by Transparency International, a nongovernmental agency with a secretariat in Berlin. Corruption is defined as "the abuse of entrenched power for private gain."

In regard to corporate misdeeds, prior to the 1980s less than a handful of serious fraud prosecutions were launched in the country and the penalties were lax. The crash of the stock market in 1987, however, focused public and legislative attention on illegal maneuvers in the business world. The result was the creation in 1990 of the Serious Fraud Office (SFO) to deal with business wrongdoing. The office had a curious beginning when the leading candidate to head it, a New Zealander who was the senior prosecutor for the commercial fraud unit in Hong Kong, was found to have received millions of dollars in bribes from companies to help them avoid prosecution. He ultimately received an eight-year prison term. The Serious Fraud Office had special powers unusual in New Zealand law enforcement. It reported directly to the attorney general, bypassing both the police and the courts. Nor could the attorney general interfere in any decision the office director took in regard to whether or not to prosecute a case. In late 2007, however, the government announced that it would amalgamate the SFO into a new force, the Organized Crime Agency, that would be operated by the police. The move was justified by the claim that the behaviors—white-collar and organized crime—had similar profiles and that the SFO had been notably unsuccessful in obtaining convictions in recent well-publicized cases. Skeptics regarded the move as a concession to corporate New Zealand and a bureaucratic move by the police to expand their reach and power.

Criminal Law

Criminal law was first codified by the Criminal Code Act of 1893 and revised in 1908. The main statute concerned with serious crimes is the Crimes Act of 1961. Among other things, this law declared that only criminal statutes enacted in New Zealand could be charged, that as Section 9 of the act stated: "No one shall be convicted of any offense at common law."

New Zealand has no written constitution. It sought to compensate for this absence by passage of the Bill of Rights Act of 1990, which established, among other things, the right to a fair trial, a speedy hearing, security against unreasonable searches and seizures, and the right to legal counsel and freedom from torture or degrading treatment. The Bill of Rights also incorporates the Treaty of Waitangi. The reach of the Bill of Rights as a supreme source of law is a subject of ongoing juridical and political wrangling.

Misuse of Drug Act

The Misuse of Drug Act divides illegal drugs into several groups. Class A includes cocaine, heroin, lysergic acid, and, a bit oddly, thalidomide. Drugs listed in Class B are morphine, opium, hashish, methadone, and other manufactured drugs such as amphetamines. Class C includes cannabis fruit, plants, and seed, cocoa leaf, and barbiturates. In 2008, the government added to the Class C list benzpiperzein and phenylpiperazeine, drugs known to their users as "herbal highs" and "dance pills," that were earning their sellers more than $5 million each year.

A 2004 report indicated that drugs classified as amphetamine-type stimulants (ATF) were competing with cannabis for market share. Listed as ATS synthetic drugs were methamphetamine, Ecstasy, and crystal methamphetamine ("ice"). One in 10 New Zealanders aged 18–19 had used one of these drugs during the previous year, with the profits from their sale being concentrated in a small number of organized gangs. Twenty-one percent of persons arrested admitted to using an ATS drug during the previous month, and 9 percent just before committing their offense. Contrary to cannabis smokers, two-thirds of whom obtained their drug from a dwelling, about half of the ATS users carried out their business by mobile phone. Polydrug use was found to be common in the ATS study sample. Users were disproportionately male and showed high level of full-time employment, with their ranks including professionals earning mid-level incomes. Ninety-three percent considered methamphetamine more harmful than cannabis, and an overwhelming majority said that it was "very easy" or "easy" to obtain ATS drugs.

Penalties for dealing drugs are substantially more serious than those for using. For dealing in Class A drugs, the maximum sentence is life imprisonment; for Class B, 14 years; and for Class C, 10 years. For possession or use of Class A drugs, a person may receive a maximum sentence of six months; for other classes, the maximum is three months' imprisonment. Beefing up the antidrug laws is the Proceeds of Crime Act of 1991, which allows the seizure of assets when a person has been convicted of an offense punishable by more than 5 years' imprisonment and when a High Court judge determines that the assets have been accumulated as a result of crime.

Possession of Weapons

The Arms Act of 1983, with later amendments, regulates the possession of weapons. Permits are issued by the police after the applicant undergoes a background check and passes a test that deals with responsible firearms use. The law requires that all firearms not in use must be locked in a secure rack or cabinet. Recent figures show that there are about 250,000 registered gun owners in New Zealand, and estimates are that there are slightly more than 1 million weapons in the country. In 2005, there were 624 episodes of violence in which weapons played a part.

Prostitution/Sex Work

Notably absent from the current criminal laws in New Zealand is the interdiction of prostitution or, as it is often called these days, sex work. The Prostitution Reform Act (PRA) of 2003 represented a reversal of the traditional legal position on prostitution both in New Zealand and in the major countries of the world. Before 2003, there was widespread availability of sex partners for pay in New Zealand, including escort services and massage parlors. The PRA was introduced as a private member's bill, that is, not as a political party motion, and members of Parliament were accorded the privilege of voting their conscience rather than following their party's dictate. The bill decriminalized all aspects of prostitution, including streetwalking, soliciting, living off the earnings of a prostitute, and the operation of brothels. Today, sex workers freely advertise their wares on billboards, the Internet, late-night television, and in the newspapers.

The new legislation mandated that to remain within the law sex workers had to be 18 or older, and it allowed local jurisdictions to impose reasonable restrictions on commercial sex. A study conducted by the Otego University's Christchurch School of Medicine and Health Sciences concluded that the new approach had not increased the population of prostitutes in the country. In 2006, three years after the new law became effective, doing research in tandem with the New Zealand Prostitutes' Collective, the Christchurch team counted 100 prostitutes at work in the city. Before the passage of the decriminalization act, 106 prostitutes were believed to have been at work in the city.

Young Offenders

The ethos of New Zealand's criminal justice approach is symbolically characterized by the replacement of the term "juvenile delinquent" by "youth offenders." Under New Zealand law, no person under the age of 10 can be charged with a crime. A youngster under 14 can be held criminally responsible as an adult only if the offense is murder or manslaughter. Otherwise, between the ages of 14 and 17, the accused is dealt with under laws pertaining to youth offenders. New Zealand's Children and Young Persons and Their Families Act of 1989 stands as a pioneering measure that has been copied in several other countries. The act decrees that persons admitting delinquent behavior or having been found guilty can participate in a conference procedure either before formal charges are filed or before sentencing.

For the 14- to 17-year age group, about two-thirds of the cases are settled by means of the wide discretion enjoyed by the police. While practices vary considerably among different districts, nationwide about two-thirds of those youngsters dealt with by the police are diverted, a process that typically involves a written, or, less often, a personal apology to the victim, or, in most other instances, community service. The outcomes often include the imposition of curfews and restitution orders and in some instances donations to charity and enrollment in training programs. Restorative justice conferences involve the young person's family, which can include friends, teachers, and, if it is a court-referred case, a lawyer. Members of the community also may participate as well as the victims of the behavior and their supporters. The conferences may be held in the offender's home, or, for Maoris, in a meeting house, but most often they are convened in a room in the offices of the Department of Child, Youth and Family Services. A youth justice coordinator or facilitator, who often is a social worker, chairs the conference. The youth service coordinator is responsible for liaison with the police, arranging the conference, delivering services, and providing resources. The conference's decision generally is reached after a recess period during which the youth and his or her family decide on their recommendation. The entire group then is expected to reach a consensus. Since the inauguration of the conferencing process in New Zealand, court referrals and institutional placements have declined sharply. On the other hand, research indicates that two-thirds of the youths who go through a family conference proceeding are recommitted and about 20 percent are imprisoned within five years after the conference experience.

Youth Gangs

Two major gangs, both largely made up of Maori members, dominate the scene in New Zealand today, headquartered largely in southeast Auckland. They are the Mongrel Mob and Black Power. Allegiance to one or the other is often decided by birth, and the two groups are in a continual state of feuding warfare. The former got its name from a magistrate who called them a "pack of mongrels." Between them they are estimated to have about 2,600 members, divided among 145 "chapters" whose core is a "pad" or clubhouse. *Time* magazine in the summer of 2007 described New Zealand as having a "strong, unique and brutal street-gang culture." Of late, with the imprisonment of many members, the turf on which gang wars are being fought has been relocated into the prisons.

Gang members in New Zealand after initiation are "patched," a process that is marked by their adoption of prominent facial tattoos. Typical Mongrel Mob garb includes baseball caps, baggy pants, and colored scarves. They may wear German World War II helmets and greet each other with the Nazi salute: *Sig Heil*! Their vocabulary echoes that of their gang counterparts in south-central Los Angeles.

Youth Court

Section 4 of the law establishing the Youth Court indicates its mission: "To promote the well-being of children, young persons, and their families and family groups." The Youth Court, before pronouncing sentence, must first submit the case for family conferencing, and a large majority of cases are resolved by the conference group.

Youth Court procedures follow those of an adult tribunal with some minor modifications. If the alleged offender desires a jury trial, the case will be transferred to a district court. Similarly, if the judge deems that it serves the interests of justice, the case will be moved to a trial court.

Adult Courts

New Zealand has a four-tier court system: district courts, a High Court, a Court of Appeal, and a Supreme Court. In extremely rare cases (only 10 times in 166 years), a case might have been presented on appeal to the Privy Council in London, but this route was eliminated in 2004 when New Zealand constituted its own five-member Supreme Court.

Trials are adversarial contests between the prosecutor and the defense. Judges are appointed by the governor-general who in theory is responsible to the Queen of England but in practice answers to the New Zealand prime minister and Parliament. The country has the unusual legal stipulation that members of Parliament may not publicly criticize a judge.

Juries

Juries are used in less than 1 percent of the criminal cases heard in New Zealand. They are made up of 12 persons between the ages of 20 and 55 who are selected from the election rolls. Maoris first were allowed to serve on juries in 1962, women in 1976. The Jury Act of 1981 restricted considerably those who automatically were exempt for jury service. Nonetheless, only 26 percent of the persons summoned for jury duty appear, and half of these are dismissed by the registrar before or on the day of the trial. Particularly likely to be dismissed are teachers, the self-employed, and mothers who have children at home.

Victims of Crime

Victims have no role in criminal prosecutions except as witnesses, although a victim-impact statement is required before sentencing but cannot include the victim's view on the proper punishment. Crime victims may themselves mount a prosecution if the government declines to do so. The inclusion of a victim-impact statement in the sentencing phase of a criminal trial is controversial in New Zealand. A victim-impact statement usually provides an element of satisfaction and surcease for the victim's family, but it raises questions about the fairness of introducing such emotionally charged material into court proceedings. Critics maintain that the testimony of the survivor varies according to how articulate and how angry that person might be.

Crime Victim Compensation

No review of criminal justice in New Zealand could be complete without reference to the fact that the country led the way in the inauguration of a program of compensation to crime victims, an approach that now is duplicated in all major countries in the world. Legislation creating the Crime Injuries Compensation Tribunal was passed in 1963. The government rejected the rationale that it was responsible for the control of crime and that therefore it should be held responsible for losses incurred by those who suffered from criminal acts. Instead, it equated the program to workmen's compensation where liability resulted with no fault being laid on the employer.

Not long thereafter, in 1974 New Zealand again took the worldwide lead by amalgamating its crime victim compensation program into an integrated approach that included all other losses and injuries suffered by residents from workplace accidents, crimes, sports, and automobile injuries as well as other untoward events that might give rise to a tort action. In 2005, the government added "treatment injuries" to the roster of circumstances that would qualify for compensation.

The Accident Compensation Corporation is a state monopoly, no-fault operation funded by taxes on all New Zealand residents. This social welfare approach has drawn sharp criticism from those most disadvantaged by it, in particular, insurance companies and lawyers who specialized in tort cases.

Prisons

The New Zealand Department of Corrections administers the country's prison system. There are

20 prisons that can accommodate 8,459 persons at any one time. Of the 20 prisons, 17 are for men and 3 for women, who make up 6.2 percent of the prison population. Capacity limits range from 59 inmates at Duniden Prison to 1,034 at Waikeira Prison, a facility that extends over 1,200 hectares (2,964 Acres). As of 2008, New Zealand's prisons were overcrowded and the government was struggling to accommodate the fourth-highest per-capita prison population in the world—185 inmates per 100,000 population. The only countries with higher incarceration rates are the United States, Mexico, and Poland. The financial cost of keeping so many persons locked up keeps rising. It was NZ$660 million (about US$3,480,770,359) in 2006 and jumped to NZ$778 million (about US$4,095,866,950) the following year.

Maoris comprise about half of New Zealand prisoners, although they constitute only 15 percent of the country's population. Maoris have a deep cultural sense of revulsion and fear in regard to being held in correctional captivity. John Pratt, in his definitive study of the early history of New Zealand's prisons, tells of a Maori chieftain who was sentenced to two months in prison and said that he would rather be executed than suffer the humiliation and indignity of a prison term. Today, to try to adapt the prisons to their Maori inmates, New Zealand has erected a Maori prayer house within the Spring Hills Correctional Facility and has inaugurated programs based on Maori culture. In 2007, a seven-year program ticketed at a cost of NZ$1.5 million (about US$789,506) was launched to increase prison staffs by adding Maoris, Pacific Islanders, Asians, women, and persons between the ages of 18 and 20.

New Zealand's correctional authorities stress rehabilitation. The Integrated Offender Management regime, introduced in 1985, advocates a "psychotherapeutic" approach focusing on the "rehabilitative needs" of prisoners. It is arguable how successful this treatment emphasis has been, presuming that what is advocated is what is done. Nonetheless, the rhetoric can be impressive. The Tongariro/Rangipo Prison, for example, which first opened in 1926, covers 848.6 hectares of forest, farmlands, river reserves, and native forest. It houses up to 662 prisoners, who primarily are from Auckland. It also includes a special unit for the custody of illegal immigrants. Work available to inmates includes deer, sheep, and cattle farming. Timber is milled on site, and there is a manufacturing plant that turns the lumber into marketable products for both domestic use and export. The assumption is that persons who are incarcerated possess little work experience and few vocational skills so that plans call for 60 percent of the inmate population to be enrolled in vocational programs. That figure stood at 43 percent in June 2007 and 17 percent the previous year. There are 140 prison-based industries that provide practical work experience. Prisoners who are low-security risks or nearing their release time can be eligible for community-based jobs.

The Corrections Act of 2004 dictates that prisoners are entitled to a bed, food and drink, private visitors, legal advisors, physical exercise, and educational programs. They are permitted at least one preapproved private visitor a week for at least 30 minutes. A minimum of three yearly family visiting days are also allowed. With the exception of security surveillance, visits are not recorded by sound or visual equipment without the prior approval of the head of the prison, the prisoner, and his or her visitor. Inmates may send and receive mail, which is censored, and make personal telephone calls once a week of up to five minutes. They also may make calls to an outside agency and a legal advisor.

No correctional institutions have been constructed since the 1980s, but in 2005 the first of several new-style facilities was opened under the terms of the Regional Prison Development Project. The buildings are large, secure enclosures, with a single point of entry. Where it is deemed feasible, emphasis is placed on duplicating features of free-world structures. Separate units are set in large, open spaces and clustered around centrally located services such as kitchens, industry areas, and program rooms. Based on their security classification, prisoners are assigned to a zone and can follow a daily routine, such as work, education, training, and medical appointments, within that zone.

Private Prisons

New Zealand has experimented only once with the growing worldwide use of private prisons. The Auckland Central Remand Prison was one of the country's two maximum-security institutions. The privately operated facility, located at Mt. Eden and operated by the Australian Correctional Management Company, was said by Greg Newbold, a sociology professor at the University of Canterbury who served a five-year term in the maximum-security Paremoreno prison for a drug offense, to be more humane and more orderly than government-operated prisons. The facility was notable for its amenities, including a well-equipped gymnasium, snooker tables, and bathrooms attached to each cell.

A five-year contract had been negotiated with the private prison company by the conservative National Party government. When the Labour Party assumed the reins of the government in 2000, the contact was not renewed. It was claimed, among other things, that the for-profit correctional organization would seek to increase the number of inmates rather than releasing them as rapidly as possible and advocating alternative methods of rehabilitation. Margaret Wilson, the Acting Commissioner for Corrections, pinpointed the ideological rationale for the government's action: "Prisons by their very nature involve the use of highly coercive power against individuals. The Government believes that it is inappropriate for private sector organizations to wield such power."

No research was undertaken to determine the performance of the private prison in comparison with an equivalent state-run facility, in part because it is exceedingly difficult to match satisfactorily the populations and sites and also because for many it would be ethically impermissible to randomly assign prisoners to a facility only on the basis of an experimental design.

Corina Oliver and Gilbert Geis

Further Reading

Dunstan, Stephen, Judy Paulin, and Kelly-Ann Atkinson. (1995). *The Composition of New Zealand Juries.* Wellington: Policy and Research Division, Department of Justice.

Hill, Richard S. (1986–2005). *The History of Policing in New Zealand.* 5 vols. Wellington: V. S. Ward.

Newbold, Greg. (2007). *The Problem of Prisons: Corrections Reform in New Zealand since 1840.* Wellington: Dunmore.

Paulin, Judy, Wendy Searle, and Trish Knaggs. (2003). *Attitudes to Crime and Punishment in New Zealand Society.* Wellington: Ministry of Justice.

Pratt, John. (1992). *Punishment in a Perfect Society: The New Zealand Prison System.* Wellington: Victoria University Press.

Norfolk Island

Legal System: Common
Murder: Low
Prison Rate: Low
Death Penalty: No

Background

Discovered by Captain James Cook in 1774, Norfolk Island is located 1,676 kilometers (1,041 miles). east of Sydney, Australia. Its capital is Kingston and it covers about 34 square kilometers (13 square miles), which is mostly steep terrain and rocky cliffs, with poor access to the sea. The population is about 2,500. Norfolk Island is of particular interest to criminologists because of its colorful past as a convict settlement. The first settlement occurred in 1788 when the British sent a small convict party to develop the island as a source of flax and wood from the Norfolk pine, both commodities that England needed to bolster its relentless colonization of countries around the world. It would remain a convict settlement, supplying food and other materials to the starving Sydney penal settlement until 1805 when it was abandoned. The flax had proven too difficult to use and the pine unsuitable for ship building. And the island itself was deemed too difficult and costly to maintain. It was abandoned completely from 1814 until 1825 when the second convict settlement was established.

The second penal colony tells an unhappy story. The remoteness of the island was this time seen as a great advantage, and it was chosen for this very reason as a place where the most terrible of all convicts in Sydney and elsewhere—the worst of the worst—were selected to be sent. The idea was that the experience on the island would be a "hell in paradise," the worst punishment short of the death penalty. The cat-o-nine-tails was a common punishment for disciplinary infractions. This lead-weighted lash broke the skin after the first few strokes. Twenty lashes were common. If too much flesh was torn off and the convict appeared unconscious, the punishment was stopped and resumed at a later date after the offender had recovered and was well enough to bear remaining lashes. It was thought that harsh, unrelenting punishment was the only way to control such an angry, incorrigible mob of convicts. But it seemed that the more severely the convicts were punished, the worse they became. There were mutinies in 1826, 1834, and 1846—though to little end since there was no way to escape the isolated island. The typical punishment was to be hanged.

The dismay of British authorities must have been considerable to allow an individual, Alexander Maconochie who had very different views of how to manage a penal colony, to become commandant of this island of hell. In 1840 Maconochie began one of the most famous experiments in penal reform in the history of penology, based on two radical principles: the aim of punishment should be reform not retribution, and that imprisonment should focus on a series of tasks that, if completed successfully, would lead to release. Thus, incentives, such as moving from one level of incarceration to a less harsh level after fulfilling socially useful tasks (called the "mark system"), were introduced into penological thinking. This penal experiment lasted but a few short years and was greatly criticized from its beginning as too lenient. The climax came when, during a Queen's birthday celebration, there was a riot when many inmates got drunk and one of the convicts (a murderer) ran off with Maconochie's daughter (though where he could run to is a puzzle). Maconochie was replaced in 1844, and things reverted to the standard punishments of the past with convict uprisings and retributive hangings. The penal settlement was abandoned in 1855. Maconochie's legacy remains, revered by penologists and reformers as the "father of parole."

In 1856, the Queen offered Norfolk Island as a place of refuge for the Pitcairn Islanders (themselves originating as a community from the mutineers of the *Bounty*) who at the time were starving. They briefly settled in Norfolk Island, but many returned to Pitcairn when they realized that the Queen had not ceded Norfolk Island to them completely and that they must remain under the government and laws of Britain. Today, approximately half of Norfolk Islanders are descendants of the *Bounty* mutineers.

Government

Norfolk Island was transferred to the administrative territory of Australia in 1913, and the Norfolk Island Act of 1979 established Norfolk Island as a self-governing Territory of Australia, with a legislative assembly consisting of nine members elected every three years and an executive council of ministers. Laws must be approved by the administrator. However, as recently as 2006, a group of Norfolk Islanders rejected Australian citizenship, insisting that Australia recognize Norfolk Island as a completely separate and independent entity from Australia.

The court system is composed of the Supreme Court and the Court of Petty Sessions. The Supreme Court deals with serious crimes and the Petty Sessions deals with minor crimes punishable by fines and other civil matters. Its decisions may be appealed to the Supreme Court. The three magistrates who sit on the bench are appointed either from the island itself or from the Australian Capital Territory courts.

The Norfolk Island Police provides professional and ancillary service by arrangement with the Australian Federal Police. The police force fulfills all the regular duties such as investigation, responding to calls for service, traffic coordination, policing of liquor licenses, issuing of gun licenses, dog control, and assistance to national park rangers. However, recent announcements by the Australian government have suggested that it will be "taking back" certain operations from Norfolk Island to cut down on costs. These would include immigration, customs, and quarantine.

Crime

Crimes are generally defined by the Australian Commonwealth Criminal Code. There are no official or unofficial crime statistics available. The general impression of travel sites and blogs is that the level of crime is very low. In fact, according to BBC News, there had been no murders on the island since 1856, until New Zealander Glenn McNeill was found guilty of stabbing to death a restaurant worker in March 2002. After a lengthy trial, in 2007 he was sentenced to 24 years in prison, with a minimum of 18 years. Because the island has no prison, McNeill is serving his sentence in New South Wales, Australia. The Australian government provided $70,000 to cover the cost of the trial. Another high-profile killing, technically not a "murder," was the shooting to death of a member of the Norfolk Legislative Assembly, "Toon" Buffett (a Pitcairn descendant) in 2004, by his son who was found mentally unfit to stand trial. He is currently held in Sydney's Long Bay Prison Hospital.

Punishment

Information on typical punishments in modern-day Norfolk Island is sparse. The Kingston police have one modern jail holding cell. A statement of accounts published in the Norfolk Island Government Gazette No. 30 reported that for the fiscal year 2001–2002, AUD29,000 (approximately US$24,000) were collected in court fees and fines and AUD15,000 (approximately US$12,750) in road traffic fines.

Graeme R. Newman

Further Reading

Clarke, Marcus. (1970). *For the Term of His Natural Life.* Adelaide: Rigby, Seal Books Edition.

Morris, Norval. (2003). *Maconochie's Gentlemen: The Story of Norfolk Island and the Roots of Modern Prison Reform.* Oxford, UK: Oxford University Press.

Norfolk Island. Bloodless Genocide: A Political History of the Pitcairn People in Norfolk Island from 1856 to 1996: http://www.pitcairners.org/bloodless_genocide2.html.

Norfolk Island Act 1979: http://www.aph.gov.au/House/committee/ncet/NorfolkGov/Norfolk Island79.pdf.

Pitcairn Islands

Legal System: Common
Prison Rate: High
Death Penalty: No
Corporal Punishment: No

Background

The Pitcairn Islands are situated in the South Pacific between New Zealand and Chile and even today remain remote from the rest of the world. In 1790, mutineers from HMAV *Bounty* and a group of Polynesian men and women occupied Pitcairn.

In 1898 the secretary of state directed that the 1893 Pacific Order in Council, which provided a system of government for British settlements in the Pacific, should apply to Pitcairn. The application of the Pacific Order in Council to Pitcairn was revoked by the 1952 Pitcairn Order in Council, which provided that the governing responsibilities of Pitcairn, along with some neighboring uninhabited islands, would fall to the governor of Fiji and that the governor would be endowed with lawmaking power for the "peace, order and good government" of the islands. A clause in the order included that the jurisdiction of the High Commissioner's Court and the law which it applied should continue to be in force until such time that the governor passed other provisions.

Judicature Ordinance 1961 replaced the jurisdiction of the High Commissioner with that of the Supreme Court of Fiji. Since Fiji achieved independence in 1970, the Pitcairn Order 1970 replaced the 1952 Pitcairn Order in Council and provided that Her Majesty appoint a governor and allow him similar power to enact laws for "the peace, order and good government of the Islands." The Judicature Ordinance of 1970 enacted by the sitting governor revoked the 1961 ordinance and gave a newly formed Supreme Court of Pitcairn jurisdiction equivalent to the jurisdiction of the High Court of Justice in England.

The governor of Pitcairn, Ducie, and Oeno Islands creates local law in the form of ordinances. The governor, also the British High Commissioner to New Zealand, acts within the power given to him by the Pitcairn Order 1970 (UK) and Orders in Council promulgated by the United Kingdom Executive. Thus, the statutory incorporation of English law into Pitcairn law has resulted in a mixed system combining domestic laws, local circumstances and customs with an adversarial system, English law.

There has been an island police officer present on Pitcairn for at least 70 years. Initially police officers were appointed by the island community; they were not trained professionals but local residents. Since 1950 the officer derived his authority from the high commissioner/governor. His role was to enforce all Pitcairn law, including English criminal law. Island police officers received guidelines of their responsibilities from the island magistrates, and at times, from the Suva administration. After 1970, the administration in New Zealand also offered occasional instruction to the officers. In fact, the island police officer had requested assistance from the Suva administration when investigating offenses such as rape and abortion in the 1950s. Crime and policing records after 1961 are not abundant in Pitcairn.

No professional English police were present on Pitcairn until 1996, when Constable Gail Cox, a British policewoman, visited Pitcairn and heard complaints of sexual assault. The resulting prosecution, which led to conviction of six male offenders, involved several inquiries conducted on the island by personnel from the Kent County Constabulary appointed by the governor of Pitcairn as Pitcairn police officers. Today, the duties of Pitcairn police officers are stipulated in Section 79 of the Justice Ordinance. The absence of an educated and effective English police force until 1996 has been invoked by the public defender in the above proceedings as indicating that Pitcairn islanders were not aware that English law could apply on the island and in any case that they could not have meaningful access to English law. Nevertheless, the Pitcairn Supreme Court rejected this argument in view of the evidence concerning the effectiveness of island police officers during the periods that the crimes had been committed.

Crime

Classification of Crimes

According to the 1952 Interpretation and General Clauses Ordinance, an "offense" is any crime, unlawful act, or contravention or other breach of, or failure to comply with, any provision of any law, for which a penalty is provided. There is no express legal classification of crimes in local Pitcairn law. To the extent that English law applies, such English law classification is transferred into local Pitcairn law.

The magistrates' court hears minor matters and preliminary hearings—including whether a *case is substantiated.* The Supreme Court hears serious offenses, including treason, piracy, murder, manslaughter, rape, or arson.

While the full range of offenses that might be regarded as serious has never been articulated on the island, there has been a long tradition of recognizing rape and other sexual offending, abortion, and murder among them. Sexual crimes have been most challenging for the island, especially in view of the small Pitcairn community. The landmark sexual crime that brought Pitcairn law to world attention was that of the *Seven named accused v. the Queen* when in 1999 two complaints of sexual assault were made to the UK police officer serving on Pitcairn. All offenses were alleged to have been committed at least 5 years before the investigation and some dating back 40 years. This case opened an international legal discourse about the defendants' rights in criminal proceedings, retrospective justice, and fundamental human rights protection; it revealed the importance of sovereignty, sovereign title, and self-determination and self-government. Six males were found guilty as a result of this famous trial.

The age of criminal responsibility is not expressly stipulated in domestic Pitcairn law. Children bear criminal responsibility and can be convicted of an offense. However, imprisonment of children is prohibited. If, at the time of the commission of the offense, the offender was under the age of 17 years, the courts can impose imprisonment only in respect of an offense that is triable by the Supreme Court. English law applies to the extent that Pitcairn law leaves gaps in this respect.

In the absence of a local ordinance or order on drug offenses, relevant English legislation applies, including inter alia the Misuse of Drugs Act 1971, the Misuse of Drugs Regulations 1985, and Drug Trafficking Act 1994. Drugs are classified as either A, B, or C depending on the degree of harm they are considered to cause to individuals or society. More severe penalties apply to *Class A*: among others, heroin, morphine, methadone, cocaine, opium, and hallucinogens, and any Class B drug prepared for injection. The maximum penalties are 7 years and/or unlimited fine for possession; life and/or unlimited fine for production or trafficking with a mandatory 7-year sentence for a third conviction for trafficking. *Class B* includes cannabis, cannabis resin, codeine, oral amphetamines, and sedatives (barbiturates). The maximum penalties are 5 years and/or unlimited fine for possession; and 14 years and/or unlimited fine for production or trafficking. *Class C* includes drugs that are considered the least harmful such as tranquilizers, some less potent stimulants, and mild opioid analgesics. The maximum penalties are 2 years and/or unlimited fine for possession; and 5 years and/or unlimited fine for trafficking.

Finding of Guilt

The Pitcairn judicature includes a Magistrates' Court, a Supreme Court, and the Court of Appeal. The magistrates' court hears minor cases; it has the same criminal jurisdiction as the Supreme Court except for the crimes of treason, piracy, murder, manslaughter, rape, or arson, which lie in the jurisdiction of the Supreme Court. The latter hears also appeals from the magistrates' court. Established in 2000, the Pitcairn Court of Appeal hears appeals from the Supreme Court and can sit in places other than the Pitcairn Islands—as determined by its president. Additionally, the Pitcairn (Appeals to Privy Council) Order 2000 grants the right of ultimate appeal to the United Kingdom Privy Council. Before these courts were established, the laws in Pitcairn offered no appeal for a Supreme Court ruling.

While trials before the Supreme Court are by a sole judge, the magistrates' court is presided over by the island magistrate, who is appointed by the governor from among the permanent residents of the islands at the time of his or her appointment for not less than five years. While the island magistrate is not required to be professionally qualified in law, the other magistrates of the court are to be qualified in law and to have practiced in any Commonwealth country for more than five years prior to their appointment. They should not necessarily be permanent residents of the islands. The Court of Appeal has a president and two or more judges from the Appeal Court and the chief of justice of the Supreme Court who is a member of the Court of Appeal *ex officio*.

The UK Human Rights Act 1998 gives effect in domestic law to the rights and freedoms guaranteed under the European Convention on Human Rights (ECHR). Nevertheless, the United Kingdom has not included Pitcairn Islands in the list of British Overseas Territories where the ECHR applies. In the *R v. Christian and other (No. 2)* judgment, the Pitcairn Supreme Court concluded that the accused were entitled to rely on the ECHR in these proceedings; the right to a hearing within a reasonable time was found to apply in Pitcairn as established in ECHR article 6 and further analyzed in the jurisprudence of the European Court of Human Rights.

Right to Trial by Jury

While the right to trial by jury is a central feature of common law tradition, it has not been introduced in domestic Pitcairn law. Judicature (Courts) Ordinance 2000 (Pitcairn Islands) and Justice Ordinance 2001 (Pitcairn Islands) are silent with respect to jury trials, but they do not explicitly exclude them. The Supreme Court of Pitcairn does not sit with a jury but may provide assessors to reside when it considers it "expedient and practicable" to do so. Assessors can be "not less than two nor more than four" and their role is advisory only.

Right to Appeal

Persons convicted by the magistrates' court have the right to appeal to the Supreme Court against conviction or sentence or both, on a question of fact as well as on a question of law. Any person convicted on a trial held by the Supreme Court may appeal to the Court of Appeal.

Legal Aid in Criminal Proceedings

The Legal Aid (Criminal Proceedings) Ordinance stipulates that any person committed for trial for an indictable offense shall be entitled to legal aid in the preparation and conduct of his or her defense at the trial. The magistrate or chief justice shall grant to such person a certificate for legal representation, if it appears that the person committed for trial has insufficient means to obtain such representation. The public defender has independent status and advisory function on behalf of defendants in relation to criminal proceedings. The same provisions apply to persons involved in extradition proceedings.

Police officers conduct investigations and in the name of Her Majesty the Queen, they conduct prosecutions provided that all prosecutions and applications made on behalf of the council under the provisions of any regulations made under the local government ordinance shall be conducted by a police officer in the name of the council.

Local Pitcairn law does not have a separate ordinance concerning criminal proceedings for juveniles. Nonetheless, special provisions regulate punishment of children. English law applies to the extent that local circumstances allow it.

Punishment

Types of Punishments

Monetary penalties include reparation and fines. Reparation is imposed unless the court is satisfied that such sentence would cause undue hardship for the offender or his or her dependants, or that it is inappropriate in view of any other special circumstances. It can be imposed on its own or cumulatively to any other sentence. A fine is imposed in addition to, or instead of, any other sentence. For those offenders who do not have the financial means to pay the fine, the court may consider not imposing the sentence.

Community-based sentences, such as supervision and community work, are imposed only if the court does not consider a fine the appropriate sentence or because the offender does not have the means to pay. For the imposition of imprisonment for any offense, the court must take into consideration the desirability of keeping offenders in the community as far as that is practicable and safe for the community. This is of particular concern in the Pitcairn context; the population of the island is so limited that imprisonment, for example, of male offenders could have an impact on the survival of the community.

Preventative detention is to be applied to (a) persons convicted of a qualifying sexual or violent offense, which is any sexual offense, or offense of violence against the person, punishable by seven or more years of imprisonment; (b) persons of 18 years of age or over at the time of committing the offense; and (c) persons who are likely to commit another qualifying sexual or violent offense if they are released at the date that their sentence expires.

Home detention can be imposed in case the offender has been sentenced to imprisonment less than two years. Nonassociation orders can be made by a court to offenders convicted of a crime punishable by imprisonment, if the nonassociation order is reasonably necessary to ensure that the offender does not commit further offenses punishable by imprisonment.

Punishment for Murder

Murder convictions carry a sentence of life imprisonment. The only exception depends on the circumstances of the offense and the offender and whether these would constitute the imprisonment for life being manifestly unjust; in that case, the court has to give written reasons for not doing so. Life imprisonment means 10 years' imprisonment, in case the court does not impose a minimum period of imprisonment of more than 10 years. For aggravated circumstances the court can impose imprisonment of a minimum 17 years.

While local Pitcairn law does not explicitly allow or prohibit the death penalty, English law does. Therefore, it is argued that the death penalty is prohibited in Pitcairn Islands through the incorporation of English law into Pitcairn laws as explained earlier.

Prison

There is only one prison on Pitcairn located in Adamstown. The six convicted males in the latest sexual offenses case mentioned above are serving their sentences in the Pitcairn prison, which is staffed by seven New Zealand prison officers. Since the population of Pitcairn is only 60 persons, this computes to a very high rate (one-tenth of the population!) compared to other countries.

Male and female prisoners are confined separately in any prison or in separate prisons. Female prisoners are supervised only by a female prison officer. Convicted prisoners often must do "useful work" but not for more than the whole of the morning on any weekday, and officials must arrange for prisoners to be able to work outside of their cells when possible and in association with one another. The medical officer may excuse a prisoner from work on medical grounds. Prisoners cannot work for other prisoners or for prison officers. Additionally, prisoners are not allowed to work for the private benefit of any person unless the authority of the governor specifically allows such an individualized occurrence. The governor approves the pay rates that prisoners receive in relation to the tasks they perform. Prisoners can work outside the prison but are at all times under supervision of a prison officer.

Education of prisoners is not mandatory, but prisoners are encouraged to benefit by the educational facilities at prison. Programs of daytime and evening educational classes may be arranged, and, subject to the directions of the superintendent, reasonable facilities may be provided for prisoners who wish to do so at their own expense to improve their education by correspondence courses or private study, or to practice handicrafts in their spare time. Special attention is given to the education of illiterate prisoners, and if deemed necessary, they are to be taught to read and write within the hours normally prearranged to work. Every prisoner is allowed to have library books and exchange them at the public library.

Except as explicitly provided in the Prisons Regulation found in Prisons Ordinance, prisoners are not permitted to communicate with any person outside the prison without the leave of the superintendent. Only family and friends can visit prisoners. Every letter or communication to and from a prisoner may be examined by the superintendent or a prison officer deputed by him or her, and the superintendent may, at his or her judgment, stop any letter or communication for the reason that its contents are disagreeable or could lead to a violation of prison security. Every visit to a prisoner shall take place within the sight and the hearing of a prison officer unless the superintendent otherwise directs. The superintendent may give instructions, generally or in relation to any visit or class of visit, concerning the days and times when prisoners may be visited.

While unconvicted prisoners are allowed to send and receive as many letters and receive as many visits as they wish within the superintendent's directions, convicted prisoners are entitled to send and receive a letter on admission into prison and thereafter once a week and to receive a visit every Sunday. The superintendent may allow a prisoner an extra letter or visit where necessary for the welfare of the prisoner or his or her family. The superintendent may allow a prisoner entitled to a visit to send and receive a letter instead. The 2003 Juridicature

Amendment Ordinance allows serving and enforcement in New Zealand of sentences imposed by Pitcairn courts sitting in New Zealand.

Danai Azaria

Further Reading

Angelo, A. H., and A. Townend. (2003). "Pitcairn: A Contemporary Comment." *New Zealand Journal of Public International Law* 1: 229–251.

Farran, S. (2007). "The Case of Pitcairn: A Small Island, Many Questions." *Journal of South Pacific Law* 11(2): 124–150.

Ntumy, Michael A. (1993). *South Pacific Islands Legal Systems.* Honolulu: University of Hawaii Press.

Power, H. (2007, August). "Pitcairn Island: Sexual Offending, Cultural Difference and Ignorance of the Law." *Criminal Law Review*, 609–629.

Polynesia

COOK ISLANDS

Legal System: Common
Prison Rate: Medium
Death Penalty: No
Corporal Punishment: Yes

FRENCH POLYNESIA

Legal System: Civil
Prison Rate: Medium
Death Penalty: No

NIUE

Legal System: Common
Death Penalty: No

SAMOA

Legal System: Civil/Customary
Murder: Low
Prison Rate: Medium
Death Penalty: No
Corporal Punishment: Maybe

TOKELAU

Legal System: Common
Death Penalty: No

TUVALU

Legal System: Common
Murder: Low
Death Penalty: No
Corporal Punishment: Yes

WALLIS AND FUTUNA

Legal System: Civil
Death Penalty: No

Background

Although originally introduced by the French writer Charles de Brosses in 1756 as a reference to all the islands in the Pacific Ocean, the term *Polynésie* (Polynesia) presently designates one of three subregions of Oceania that generally extends from Hawaii to the north, New Zealand to the southwest, and Easter Island to the southeast. Included within this Polynesian triangle are more than 1,000 islands covering a total of 24,135,000 square kilometers (9,318,576 square miles) of the Central and South Pacific Ocean. This section focuses on seven of the independent and freely associated states and territories in Polynesia: Tuvalu, Tokelau, the Cook Islands, Niue, Samoa, Wallis and Futuna, and French Polynesia.

Tuvalu is located north of New Zealand in the western boundary of Polynesia. It consists of nine islands with a total land area of 26 kilometers (10 square miles) and an estimated population of 12,373. East of Tuvalu is Tokelau, which consists of three islands and has the smallest total land area of 12 square kilometers (4.63 square miles). It has approximately 1,416 inhabitants. Wallis and Futuna lie southeast of Tuvalu and consist of two island archipelagoes with a total land area of 142 kilometers (54.83 square miles) and a population of 15,289. West of Tuvalu and south of Tokelau is Samoa, which consists of two main islands with a total land area of 2,831 square kilometers and a population of approximately 219,998 inhabitants. Nuie,

Armed villagers man a blockade on the outskirts of Valusu Village near the Western Samoa capital of Apia following the arrest of 21 villagers, including four chiefs, five women, and two children on charges of squatting in relation to a land dispute. (Ross Land/Getty Images)

which is a single island with an area of 260 square kilometers (100.39 square miles), lies south of Samoa and has the smallest population at about 1,398 inhabitants. The Cook Islands lie east of Samoa and Niue and consist of 15 islands with a total land area of 236 square kilometers (91.12 square miles). It has a population of approximately 11,870 inhabitants. Finally, French Polynesia forms the eastern border of Polynesia and includes five island archipelagoes with the largest total land area of 4,167 kilometers (1,608.89 square miles). It also has the largest population at approximately 287,032 inhabitants.

European contact with the Polynesian islands began as early as the 16th century with Spanish exploration in French Polynesia (which includes Tahiti) and continued throughout the 19th century, primarily through Dutch, British, and French expeditions. In the late 19th and early 20th centuries, various islands were granted British protectorate status—Rarotonga (the largest of the Cook Islands) in 1888, Tokelau in 1889, Tuvalu in 1892 (as part of the Gilbert and Ellice Islands administration), and Niue in 1900. New Zealand later assumed administrative control of the Cook Islands (1901), Niue (1901, as part of the Cook Islands), and Tokelau (1926). Meanwhile, Wallis was established as a French protectorate in 1887, followed by Futuna in 1888. Different islands in what is now collectively French Polynesia were claimed, colonized, or made protectorates of France in the mid- to late 19th century. Finally, from the mid-19th century until its colonization by Germany in 1900, Samoa engaged in political interactions with Britain and the United States. As a result of colonialism, most of Polynesia still retains either some form of political association with their former colonial administrative power or has adopted similar legal and political systems, albeit tailored to incorporate their own unique customary laws and traditions.

Government and Legal System

Tuvalu (formerly the Ellice Islands) gained independence from Great Britain in 1978 and is currently a member of the Commonwealth of Nations. It has a common law legal system and its sources of law include the Tuvalu Constitution, acts of the Tuvaluan Parliament, customary law, "applied laws" (certain imperial enactments), and English common law. Under the Constitution, the head of state is the British sovereign, Queen Elizabeth II, who is represented by the governor general of Tuvalu. As representative of the British sovereign, the governor general exercises executive authority along with the cabinet, which consists of the prime minister who is elected by the Tuvaluan Parliament and the other members of the cabinet who are appointed by the governor general upon the recommendation of the prime minister. Legislative authority is vested in the Parliament, or the *Fale I Fono,* which is a unicameral legislature with 15 members who are popularly elected to serve four-year terms. The judicial branch consists of local island courts, land courts, and magistrates' courts at the lower level; and a High Court, Court of Appeal, and Sovereign in Council (Privy Council [UK]) at the higher level.

With regard to criminal matters, island courts have jurisdiction over offenses for which the maximum penalty is a $100 fine, six months' imprisonment, or both. Appeals may go to the magistrates' courts, where there is a distinction between senior magistrates' courts and regular magistrates' courts. Senior magistrates' courts have jurisdiction over offenses for which the maximum penalty is 14 years' imprisonment, a fine, or both. However, senior magistrates' courts can only impose a maximum punishment of 5 years' imprisonment, a fine of $1,000, or both. Regular magistrates' courts have jurisdiction over offenses for which the maximum penalty is one year's imprisonment, a $200 fine, or both. Criminal cases may be further appealed to the High Court, which has unlimited original jurisdiction over criminal matters, and then to the Court of Appeal. The Sovereign in Council, for the most part, only hears cases involving constitutional issues. As of 2007, neither the Court of Appeal nor the Sovereign in Council had ever received a criminal appeal.

Tokelau (formerly the Union Islands) is a territory of New Zealand with a common law legal system. The head of state is the British monarch, Queen Elizabeth II, who is represented by the governor general of New Zealand. Executive authority also lies with the Council of *Faipule*, which consists of three elected elders and functions as a cabinet. The head of government is chosen from the council for a term of one year, followed by a rotation to the other members. The legislative branch consists of a unicameral legislature with 20 members called the General *Fono*. The judicial branch consists of a village council or *taupulega* on each island at the local level, with appeals to the New Zealand High Court and Court of Appeal. With regard to criminal matters, village councils have jurisdiction over offenses for which the maximum penalty is one year's imprisonment. In practice, nearly all matters are settled outside the formal judicial system.

The Cook Islands (formerly the Harvey Islands) became a self-governing state in "free association" with New Zealand in 1965. It has a common law legal system, and its sources of law are the Constitution of the Cook Islands, acts of the Legislative Assembly and later the Parliament of the Cook Islands, certain ordinances in effect before 1965, certain acts of the Parliament of New Zealand, as well as certain acts of the British Parliament in force in New Zealand in 1916. As a freely associated state, the Cook Islands are responsible for internal affairs while New Zealand, in consultation with the Cook Islands, is responsible for external affairs and defense. Under the Constitution, the executive branch consists of the British monarch, Queen Elizabeth II, who is head of state and is represented by the Queen's representative; the prime minister, who is the head of government and is appointed by the Queen's representative; and the Cabinet of Ministers, which includes the prime minister and other ministers who are appointed by the Queen's representative on the advice of the prime minister. The legislative branch consists of a unicameral Parliament with 25 members who are popularly elected to five-year terms. The House of *Arikis*, which is composed of chiefs appointed by the Queen's representative, functions in an advisory capacity to Parliament. It considers issues regarding the welfare and customs of the people, although it has no legislative authority. The judicial branch consists of the High Court (with a distinction between High Court presided by judges and High Court provided by justices of the peace), the Court of Appeal, and the Privy Council.

With regard to criminal offenses, the High Court presided by a single justice of the peace has jurisdiction over minor offenses and can impose a maximum penalty of two years' imprisonment, a $200 fine, or both; if presided by three justices, the maximum penalty that can be imposed is three years' imprisonment, a $300 fine, or both. If the High Court is presided by a judge, it has unlimited original jurisdiction and may hear appeals from decisions of the justices of the peace. The Court of Appeal decides constitutional issues and hears appeals from High Court decisions wherein the penalty is life imprisonment or imprisonment for a term exceeding six months or a fine of $200 or more, unless the sentence is fixed by law.

Niue (formerly Savage Island) became a self-governing state in free association with New Zealand in 1974. It has a common law legal system, and its sources of law are the Constitution of Niue, statutes, regulations, English common law, and custom. Under the Constitution, the head of state is Queen Elizabeth II, who is represented by the governor general of New Zealand. The executive branch also includes the premier, who is elected by the Legislative Assembly and is the head of government, and the Cabinet of Ministers, which consists of the premier and three other ministers chosen by the premier from among the members of the *Fono Ekepule* or Legislative Assembly. The legislative branch consists of the unicameral *Fono Ekepule*, which has 20 members who are popularly elected to serve three-year terms. The judicial branch consists of a High Court, which is divided into civil, criminal, and land divisions; the Court of Appeal, and the Privy Council. With regard to criminal matters, the High Court exercises unlimited original jurisdiction and the Court of Appeal hears appeals from High Court decisions.

Samoa (formerly Western Samoa) became an independent state in 1962 following the dissolution of the UN Trusteeship administered by New Zealand. It has a mixed system of common law and customary law, and sources of law include the Constitution, statute, English common law, and customary law. The chief of state is elected by the *Fono* or Legislative Assembly for a five-year term. With the approval of the *Fono*, the chief of state appoints the prime minister, who functions as the head of government and is included in the 12-member cabinet. Legislative authority rests with the unicameral *Fono*, which has 49 members who serve five-year terms. The judiciary consists of the local village *fonos*, the Land and Titles Court, the District Court, the Supreme Court, and the Court of Appeal. With regard to criminal matters, the village *fonos* have customary law jurisdiction and can impose punishments that range from fines to labor. District courts have jurisdiction over offenses where the maximum penalty does not exceed five years' imprisonment, and the Supreme Court has unlimited criminal jurisdiction and can hear appeals from district court decisions. Further appeals may go to the Court of Appeal.

Wallis and Futuna formally became an Overseas Territory of France in 1961. It has a civil law legal system, and its sources of law are the French Constitution, international treaties to which France is a signatory, legislation (executive and parliamentary legislation as well as the French Codes), "general principles of law," and administrative regulations. The head of state is the president of France, who is represented by the high administrator. The head of government is the president of the Territorial Assembly, and the Council of the Territory, which consists of three kings and three appointed members, functions as a cabinet. The legislative branch consists of the unicameral Territorial Assembly or *Assemblee Territoriale,* which has 20 members who are popularly elected to five-year terms. Wallis and Futuna also have a senator in the French Senate and a deputy in the French National Assembly. The judicial branch consists of Courts of First Instance, which deal with minor criminal matters; the Court of Assizes, which deals with more serious criminal offenses; and the Court of Appeal in Noumea, New Caledonia.

French Polynesia currently holds the political status of overseas lands of France. Sources of law are similar to those of other French territories such as Wallis and Futuna and New Caledonia. The head of state is the president of France, who is represented by a high commissioner. The head of government is the president of French Polynesia and the president of the Territorial Assembly, who are both elected to five-year terms by members of the Territorial Assembly. The legislative branch consists of the unicameral Territorial Assembly or *Assemblee Territoriale,* which has 57 members who are popularly elected for five-year terms. The judicial branch consists of the Court of Administrative Law, Courts of First Instance, and the Court of Appeal.

Police

None of the Polynesian states and territories covered in this section maintain a regular military force, primarily because most of them have formal agreements with their former colonial administrators that provide for external defense. France is responsible for the defense of Wallis and Futuna and French Polynesia, and New Zealand is responsible for the defense of Tokelau, Niue, and the Cook Islands (in consultation with the government of the Cook Islands and at its request). Regarding internal law enforcement, the Cook Islands has a National Police Department headed by a police commissioner and Niue has a Central Police Department headed by a chief of police. Tokelau has three local Tokelauan police officers stationed on each island—for a total of nine officers—who are responsible to local village authorities. Tuvalu has no regular military but has a national police force that had a total of 73 members in 2005. The Tuvaluan Constitution provides for a chief of police who is appointed by the head of state and whose office is within the Tuvalu Police Force. Finally, Samoa does not have a regular military force but maintains a national police force headed by a commissioner.

Crime

Due to limited resources and technology in Polynesia, detailed statistics about crime, law enforcement personnel, and correctional populations are generally unavailable or not updated on a regular basis. Compounding this issue is the reality that each state population is relatively small and divided among different islands, and each maintains a strong tradition of addressing criminal offenses through traditional means as opposed to resorting to the official government fora. As a result, the relatively few crimes that do occur are handled locally and are not always reported to national agencies. However, each of the states and territories has a national statistics office that coordinates with the Secretariat of the Pacific Community (SPC) to publish available statistical information in an online database called the Pacific Regional Information System (PRISM). Although the reporting system is not uniform with respect to the type of data collected and methodology used, it often provides the most updated statistical information available. Data on other aspects of the criminal justice systems of Polynesia may be obtained by government agencies and international organizations that collect information about world governments, such as the U.S. Department of State or the International Centre for Prison Studies, and from the national governments that administer the particular territories.

Crime Statistics

According to the Pacific Regional Information SysteM (PRISM), basic crime statistics are available for Tuvalu, Niue, Samoa, and French Polynesia. The most recent crime statistics from Tuvalu are from 2003, which recorded a total of 1,666 crimes against persons and 591 property crimes. The most recent statistics from Niue and Samoa were from 2002, during which 32 crimes against persons and 5 crimes against property were reported in Niue, and 41 crimes against persons and 23 crimes against property were reported in Samoa. Finally, the most recent statistics from French Polynesia came from 2006, which only reported 2,862 crimes against property. Tokelau has not reported any serious crimes other than property crimes such as petty theft, which are all handled locally and informally.

Classification of Crimes

The English common law, which influenced the criminal laws of all the former British territories in Polynesia, historically classified crimes as felonies or misdemeanors depending on the seriousness of the offense. This distinction was later removed in the United Kingdom under the Criminal Justice Act of 1967, although the terminology still remains in the Tuvalu Penal Code (Cap. 8), where a felony designates those offenses punishable by three years' imprisonment or more. In Niue, the distinction was expressly removed in the 1966 Niue Act, which was passed by the New Zealand Parliament before Niue gained self-governing status in 1974, but still remains the general criminal legislation for the island. The criminal laws of the Cook Islands (Crimes Act 1969), Samoa (Crimes Ordinance 1961), and Tokelau (Crimes, Procedure and Evidence Rules 2003) do not make distinctions between felonies and misdemeanors. Both French Polynesia and Wallis and Futuna adhere to the French Penal Code, which classifies offenses as contraventions (minor or petty offenses), *délits* (similar to misdemeanors), or crimes (serious offenses similar to felonies).

Finding of Guilt

Because the formal system of criminal laws and procedure of each state and territory either derive directly from, or are influenced by, the penal and procedural codes of former colonial administrators, the rights of the accused as articulated in their constitutions and/or codes closely resemble those of other Western nations. Foremost among these rights are the right to be informed promptly of charges and to be brought before a fair and impartial hearing or trial, the right to counsel and to have counsel appointed if the cost is prohibitive to a defendant, and to be presumed innocent until found guilty. (See, e.g., Constitution of Cook Islands, Part IVA—Fundamental Rights and Freedoms; Constitution of Tuvalu, Part II—Bill of Rights.)

Punishment

Punishment for criminal offenses varies among the different Polynesian states and territories depending on the gravity of the offense, as well as how or if it is handled locally and in accordance with custom and tradition. In Tokelau, most crimes are relatively minor offenses that do not require imprisonment, and punishments usually involve some form of public rebuke, labor, or a fine. There has been some controversy over certain traditional punishments such as banishment in Samoa or corporal punishment in Tuvalu, even though their occurrence is extremely rare. The French-affiliated territories follow the French Penal Code as the source of their criminal laws, including the types of punishments meted out for the various types of offenses. Overall, the penalties according to the state/territorial penal codes of the different jurisdictions share similarities and range from fines to community service to imprisonment, with the highest form of punishment being life imprisonment. There is no death penalty, although some places have only recently abolished capital punishment, such as the Cook Islands in 2007. In that case, however, although death was formally listed as a sentence for certain crimes such as treason—an import from old colonial/territorial laws—it was never actually practiced on the islands. Samoa also abolished capital punishment relatively recently in 2004.

In most jurisdictions, the punishment of life imprisonment is reserved only for the crime of culpable homicide, usually murder and manslaughter. (See Tuvalu—Penal Code, Cap. 8, §§ 192 and 193; Cook Islands—Crimes Act 1969, § 141(2); Niue Act 1966 [NZ], § 134; Samoa—Crimes Ordinance 1961, §§ 66 and 67.) A notable exception is Tokelau, where the penalty for murder is a minimum of 10 years' and a maximum of 20 years' imprisonment. (See Schedule 2, Crimes, Procedure, and Evidence Rules 2003.) In Tuvalu and Samoa, however, life imprisonment may also be a punishment for rape (Penal Code, Cap. 8, § 129; and Crimes Ordinance 1961, § 47(2), respectively). In other jurisdictions, such as the Cook Islands and Niue, the maximum penalty for rape is 14 years' imprisonment (Crimes Act 1969, § 141(2); Niue Act 1966 [NZ], § 162(2), respectively). The typical punishment for a serious property crime such as burglary is a term of imprisonment with a maximum that ranges from 5 to 10 years. (See Niue Act 1966 [NZ], § 204 [5 years]; Cook Islands—Crimes Act 1969, § 262 [10 years].)

Prison System

The International Centre for Prison Studies provides data on the penal systems of Tuvalu, the Cook Islands, Samoa, and French Polynesia. Tuvalu has a single prison facility, which in 2007 had a total population of 3 inmates. Prison administration is the responsibility of the Police, Immigration and Prisons Department under the Office of the Prime Minister. The Cook Islands also has a single facility that had a total population of 27 inmates in April 2005. Prison administration is handled by the Cook Islands Prison Service under the Ministry of Justice. Both Samoa and French Polynesia have three facilities, with a total 186 and 404 prisoners in September and January 2007, respectively. In Samoa, prison administration is handled by the Police and Prisons Department under the Ministry of Police, Prisons and Fire Services; and in French Polynesia the penal system is administered under the French Ministry of Justice. Tokelau does not have a prison as most of the crimes committed are not offenses that carry a term of imprisonment and are thus handled apart from the formal justice system. In Niue, people sentenced to a term of imprisonment are generally sent to New Zealand.

Estelle Hofschneider

Further Reading

Corrin, Jennifer, and Don Paterson. (2007). *Introduction to South Pacific Law.* New York: Routledge-Cavendish.

International Centre for Prison Studies: http://www.kcl.ac.uk/schools/law/research/icps.

Ntumy, M., ed. (1993). *South Pacific Islands Legal Systems.* Honolulu: University of Hawaii Press.

Pacific Islands Legal Information Institute (PacLII): http://www.paclii.org/.

Pacific Regional Information SysteM (PRISM): http://www.spc.int/PRISM/index.htm.

Tonga

Legal System: Common
Murder: Low
Corruption: High
Prison Rate: Medium
Death Penalty: Maybe
Corporal Punishment: Yes

Background

Tonga comprises 171 islands, of which 45 are inhabited, and is strategically located in the middle of the Pacific Ocean. Most people, more than 70,000, live on the main island, Tongatapu. In 2005 the United Nations estimated that Tonga had approximately 106,000 people; 40 percent of whom were aged under 15. Approximately 35,000 Tongans dwell in the capital, Nuku'alofa. About 2,500 Tongans emigrate every year. Most seek low-income jobs in New Zealand, Australia, and the United States. A significant number of young men, some with gang connections, have been deported back into Tonga, mainly for drug offenses.

The British explorer Captain Cook named Tonga the "Friendly Islands," but interisland fighting between the chiefs characterized centuries of history. In 1845, Tonga was created a Polynesian kingdom from disparate islands of the South Pacific archipelago. It became an hereditary constitutional monarchy in 1875 and then a British protectorate in 1900. Regaining its independence on June 4, 1970, Tonga remains an absolute monarchy, although there is increasing pressure for constitutional reform to curb the power of the wealthy aristocracy and monarchy.

Unlike much of Polynesia, Tonga has not adopted a Western form of governance. However, it has a written constitution and the king and Privy Council can make ordinances, but none have been made since independence. Some English statutory law remains in force in Tonga. The remaining body of written law consists of acts and regulations produced by the Legislative Assembly (see below) with the king's assent. Common law applies as far as local circumstances and legislation allow.

Structure and Role of Courts

The court structure of Tonga is based on the standard model of inferior court, superior court, and Court of Appeal. The Privy Council is the body appointed by the king to assist him, rather than a court. The Privy Council has jurisdiction to hear appeals from the Land Court in relation to hereditary estates and titles.

The Court of Appeal has all the powers of the Supreme Court and exclusive jurisdiction to determine criminal and civil appeals from the Supreme Court. Any person who has been convicted on trial in the Supreme Court may appeal to the Court of Appeal. It has jurisdiction to hear appeals from the Land Court except in matters relating to the determination of hereditary estates and titles, where appeals lie with the Privy Council. Judges of the Court of Appeal are empowered to give opinions on important or difficult matters when requested to do so by the king, the cabinet, or the Legislative Assembly.

The Supreme Court has all the powers of the magistrates' courts and appellate jurisdiction in relation to decisions of the magistrates' courts. The Supreme Court is empowered to try all indictable offenses and has criminal jurisdiction in relation to all offenses that carry a maximum penalty of a fine that is more than $500 pa'anga (US$252.25) or a period of imprisonment exceeding two years. Judges in Tonga determine that where there is a lack of definition in legislation, the English common law meaning is applied. Tonga's Supreme Court has been acknowledged as the top reformer in terms of case management. Despite 500 criminal prosecutions stemming from the 2006 November riots (see below), the World Bank cited Tonga's Supreme Court for best management, cutting the times to enforce contracts from 510 days to 350. A new chief justice, by introducing case management, oversaw the transferring of 90 percent of all cases—criminal, commercial, and land—from paper to computer. Cases are now monitored daily.

The magistrates' court handles matters not covered by the above courts and usually hears matters relating to theft, disputes, and other conflicts. A magistrates' court, constituted by the chief police magistrate, has jurisdiction throughout Tonga. Other magistrates may exercise jurisdiction within the district to which they are assigned. Every magistrate has the general powers and jurisdiction in civil cases to make orders for maintenance; issue subpoenas for witnesses; enforce payments; exercise powers set down by law; and make temporary orders where prompt action is required. All magistrates have jurisdiction with regard to hearing and determining criminal matters in which the prescribed punishment does not exceed a fine of $1,000 pa'anga (US$504.5) or a period of three years' imprisonment. In addition, the chief police magistrate has jurisdiction to hear cases in which the fine provided by law is no more than $2,000.

Political and Social Context of Criminal Justice System

The king has the power to dictate policy and purpose throughout Tonga. The Constitution provides for an independent judiciary whose ranks historically have been occupied by foreign nationals, but occasionally subject to royal influence. The prodemocracy reformers have achieved greatest impact by strengthening the role of the Tongan judiciary to act as a partial counterbalance to the king's power. The judiciary has attempted to protect individual rights granted in the Constitution of Tonga. As a result of cases involving freedom of the press, especially its role in the *Lali Media decisions,* the judiciary has provided some protection for Tongan prodemocracy citizens. It has also condemned censorship of political speech in Tonga.

In September 2006, King Taufa'ahau Tupou IV, who held power for nearly 40 years, died and was succeeded by his eldest son, King Siaosi Tupou V. The king holds the predominant place in Tongan politics and life and makes hereditary appointments to the token Parliament. The prime minister, deputy prime minister, and the minister of police are appointed for life. The king also appoints the cabinet. The nobility-dominated parliamentary system ensures that voters can only choose a minority of members of the Legislative Assembly. The king selects 12 of the 30 members of the Legislative Assembly, and 33 holders of noble titles select a further 9 members of Parliament, with only 9 members of Parliament being popularly elected. The 9 elected commoners, 7 of whom were elected in 2006, constitute a powerless minority in the Parliament. Universal suffrage applies to those of 21 years and above. The U.S. ambassador to Tonga has indicated that changes toward democracy "should happen at a pace appropriate for the society concerned."

Economic poverty is the major challenge for Tonga. The country remains dependent on external aid and remittances from exiled Tongan communities working abroad (mainly in New Zealand, Australia, and the United States) to offset its trade deficit. More nationals live outside the country than inside. Due to economic stagnation, Tonga requires extensive economic and public sector reform. In September 2005, a massive pay increase (60%–80% per worker) saw the Tongan government teetering on the edge of bankruptcy. Programs are in place to improve fiscal policies, develop a fairer taxation system, promote private sector growth, and create a streamlined public service. Environmentally, deforestation is a growing concern.

The previous king's government made problematic economic decisions that allegedly wasted millions of dollars. In the 1980s, Tongan passports were sold to Asian customers. Diplomatic sources indicated that the Kingdom of Tonga was nearing ruin after disastrous royal decisions, including investing A$35 million (approximately 40% of the government's revenue) in pyramid investment scam that was orchestrated by the king's court jester (the notorious Jesse Bogdonoff), who embezzled proceeds from the Tongan government. The court jester was tried for fraud, negligence, and conspiracy but, due to "retrospective amendments," the king avoided any such censure. The nation has a somewhat notorious reputation for "get-rich-quick" schemes. The Kingdom of Tonga was close to financial ruin, reportedly in debt to A$43 million.

For decades, sections of the population have been agitating for a more democratic constitution. Politically, the progress toward democracy has been slow and hazardous. Prodemocracy newspapers have been targeted by the government eager to silence dissent. In February 2003, the government declared the only independent Tongan-language newspaper, *Times of Tonga* (printed biweekly in Auckland with a circulation of more than 20,000 in Tonga), a prohibited import and made it a criminal offense to possess any copies of it. Despite years of harassment, the paper continued to report scandals of the royal family and government. Its editor successfully challenged the ban in the Tongan Supreme Court. However, the Privy Council issued another ban that exempted the newspaper from judicial review.

On March 10, 2003, a prodemocracy march advocating freedom of speech took place in the main street of Nuku'alofa. The march was reported as peaceful; the police helpful; and hundreds of people clapped the marchers. A second Order in Council placed a second ban on the newspaper, after a Supreme Court ruling that the earlier royal ban was unlawful. The paper reappeared on Tongan streets. In October 2003, an estimated 8,000 people marched through the capital of Nuku'alofa to the Legislative Assembly in protest at the king's plan to change the Constitution so that he can control newspapers and limit the rights of the courts to review his decisions. The amendment to the Constitution increased the state's control over the media and limited the rights of the courts to review royal decisions.

Some moves toward reform occurred in early 2005 when elected members of Parliament were appointed to the cabinet for the first time. The increasing desire to curb royal powers has already caused considerable civil instability and disobedience in Tonga with the first nationwide strike of public servants in 2005 and the rioting in the capital in November 2006 (see further below). After these prodemocracy riots, the government announced elections for April

2008, in which a majority of Parliament would be directly elected by a popular vote.

Role of Police

The Tonga Police Force is a national agency with jurisdiction throughout the kingdom. There are no separate local or municipal police agencies. Tongan law enforcement is focused on providing essential policing services. Tonga is a heavily policed country. According to the 1998 research questionnaire distributed to chief officers of police, it has 418 officers with a population ratio of approximately 1: 226. The same survey revealed a male-dominated force (82%).

The Tonga Police Force is commanded by a commissioner of police. The force is deployed in three territorial districts: Tongatapu, Haapai, and Vava'u island groups. Many remote small islands lack any police presence, so law and order is reliant upon the authority of the local chiefs. The regular police also issue fishermen's licenses, register bicycles, apprehend school truants, and enforce Tongan custom and tradition.

Tonga has been without a police commander since December 2006 when the police commander resigned shortly after the November 16 rioting. The Public Service Commission was unable to select a suitable local candidate from the seven applicants. The Tongan government requested that the New Zealand government provide an expatriate commander from within the New Zealand Police. In 2008, a New Zealand police officer has subsequently been appointed as the commissioner of police.

The Tongan police deputy commander, right, is joined by police superintendents from New Zealand, left, and Australia for a patrol of central Nuku'alofa, Tonga, on November 21, 2006. The Tongan government called in international troops to help its police force secure the capital following violent prodemocracy riots. (AP Photo/NZPA, Ross Setford)

Physical training for police recruits is estimated to comprise approximately 80 percent of the six-month initial training period conducted at the Police Training School in Tonga. Tongan police are relatively inexperienced and undertrained to maintain surveillance and intercept drug trafficking. Allegations of corruption and bribe taking in the police have been reported.

Section 7 of Tonga's Police Act states: "All members of the Force shall with the approval of the Prime Minister carry arms for the performance of their duties." Under what circumstances the prime minister has granted such approval is unknown. Batons are held in reserve and issued when required.

Tonga was one of seven founding members when the South Pacific Chiefs of Police Conference (SPCPC) began in 1970 in Fiji and determined the need for regional cooperation in law enforcement as a priority for its future endeavor. Tonga also belongs to the Pacific Islands Forum, an annual conference of the heads of states of 16 Pacific nations. The forum has been central to the development of a number of initiatives related to police work. Tonga is one of the Pacific regional members of INTERPOL, the global police organization that facilitates cooperation between police forces at the international level. Tonga sent police to the Solomon Islands to assist the implementation of the Townsville Peace Agreement in October 2000. Tonga has contributed and maintained a military presence as part of the Royal Assistance Mission to the Solomon Islands (RAMSI).

In February 2007, a seven-member team (three Australian, three New Zealanders, and one Tongan) conducted an assessment of the operation of the Tongan police. Tonga has signed a tripartite Memorandum of Agreement for a Tonga Police Force Development Programme, between Tonga, New Zealand, and Australia, and the program has been implemented. The objective is to improve operational standards of the Tongan police force. The program is funded by AusAID and NZAid and implemented by both the New Zealand Police and the Australian Federal Police.

The country's security agencies are the Tonga Defense Services (TDS) and the police force. The minister of defense controls the TDS force, which is directly responsible for external security. The police are under the control of the minister of police and prisons. The police are usually responsible for internal security, but under the state of emergency declared during the November 2006 rioting, the TDS shared domestic security duties with the police who were unable to control the large-scale rioting.

Crime

According to the United Nations Survey of Crime and Criminal Justice Systems, the total number of reported crimes in 1990 in Tonga was 1,434. Of these, 50.4 percent were theft offenses; 30.2 percent of the remaining reported crimes were assaults. According to INTERPOL data, in Tonga the rate for murder in 1999, the most recent year available, was 1.05 per 100,000 population; this represented a decrease of 49 percent on 1995 figures. For rape, the rate in 1999 was 2.11; this represented an increase of 78.8 percent on 1995 figures. Rates reported by INTERPOL for other crimes in 1999 were robbery 15.8, aggravated assault 108.5, burglary 541.65, and motor vehicle theft 14.8.

Gangs

A number of Pacific island cities or towns, including the Tongan capital, experience street gangs, the product of limited infrastructure, stagnant economy, unemployment, and dislocation from rural areas. Officials, such as a former police minister, have blamed Tongans who have been convicted of gang-related crimes in the United States and who have returned to Tonga and contributed to an upsurge in crime in Tonga in the last few years. Some reports have connected American gang membership with the return of some Tongan youth to Nuku'alofa for the November 2006 riots.

Money Laundering and Drug Trafficking

The extent of the transshipment of drugs through Tonga is unknown. Cannabis has been observed growing in Tonga, and the island state is known for the illicit commercial cultivation of marijuana. Also, a Tongan syndicate based in Hawaii has been connected to the trafficking of cocaine. Tonga has enacted money-laundering legislation that deals specifically with proceeds from narcotics-related crimes.

It is estimated that the bulk of migrant remittances to Tonga flows through illegal, unofficial, and informal channels. In 2005, remittances accounted for 50 percent of Tonga's Gross Domestic Product, with 75 percent of Tongan households receiving remittances from overseas.

Computer Crime

The Computer Act was enacted by the Tonga Legislative Assembly in September 2003. The act defined the following activities as crimes and offenders are subject to fines and/or imprisonment: obtaining illegal access to a computer; interfering with another's computer system; unlawfully intercepting computer data; and trafficking in illegal computer devices. Substantial procedural powers were granted to law enforcement authorities by the act.

Corruption

In July 2007, Parliament enacted legislation establishing a commissioner to investigate official corruption. Government tenders appear to unfairly benefit members of the royal family. A recent case of alleged fraud against a government minister was squashed by the prime minister. In 2008, the minister for tourism was accused of inappropriately using funds donated by the ambassador of China. The funds were deposited in the minister's personal account as part of his department's efforts to gain quicker access to the funds for government programs. The auditor general recommended that the minister be asked to resign "because he has broken the law." However, the prime minister rejected this recommendation on the grounds the minister's violation of the law was minor and did not constitute fraud, akin to driving with broken headlights or illegal parking. The prime minister refused to ask the tourism minister to resign but imposed a penalty of work without pay for three months.

Terrorism

Tonga, keen to pursue global moneymaking enterprises destined for the Middle East, was criticized by the United States for offering "flags of convenience" through an open shipping register. The CIA has claimed that al Qaeda has used as many as 62 Tongan-registered "flag-ships" to carry arms for terrorist purposes. In 2002, three foreign-owned Tongan "ships of shame" were caught ferrying terrorists, weapons, and explosives for al Qaeda, according to an Australian Institute of Criminology report. Tongan policy changed, and the 185 Tongan-registered ships were given 12 months' notice of termination. More conscious of the potential threat or consequences of inadvertently aiding possible terrorist groups, Tonga has eliminated its flag of convenience program, which was a major revenue generator for the impoverished country.

Riot and Sedition

As a result of the protest march in June 2006 about press freedoms, 32 protesters were charged, and most of the defendants were found guilty of obstructing police and were fined. On November 16, 2006, a peaceful protest in support of political reform descended into a riot that left the capital city badly damaged and burned, which destroyed about 80 percent of the capital's central business district. Looting and fires caused a huge amount of damage to businesses in the city. New Zealand and Tongan police arrested about 900 people for crimes connected to the "16/11" rioting and more than 500 were charged with offenses relating to the riot. The charges included murder, arson, sedition, and theft.

Five members of Parliament were charged with sedition related to public speeches they made at political rallies in November 2006. Another Tongan was sentenced to seven years in prison for his part in the riot. One man received an 11-year jail sentence for setting fire to a supermarket during the rioting.

In late November 2006, the Australian Federal Police deployed more than 60 members to Tonga in response to government calls for assistance. They investigated seven deaths and 87 separate crime scenes.

Murder

The first conviction for murder since 1981 occurred in October 2005 when a 26-year-old man was found guilty by a jury of seven for the murder of another male who had been repeatedly hit with an iron bar. In 1981 four men were sentenced to death and hung at the village of Vaini. Since 1981 there have been numerous jury trials in Tonga on the charge of murder, but no jury was prepared to pass a guilty verdict for murder, opting instead for the lesser charge of manslaughter.

Domestic Violence

Domestic violence against women is seldom reported, yet believed to be common. Women's groups claim that domestic violence is common, although it is seldom publicized. Domestic violence is prosecuted under laws against physical violence, but prosecutions are very rare. When abuse is reported to police, victims are often encouraged to return to their homes. In June 2005, Tonga's finance minister announced that the number of crimes being reported had increased significantly in recent years, especially domestic violence. Rape is punishable by up to 15 years' imprisonment. The law does not recognize spousal rape. There are no reliable statistics about the incidence of rape.

Illegal Firearms

Tonga has 500 licensed guns, mainly for the legitimate use of farmers. The penalty for anyone found in possession of an illegal firearm is a maximum of five years' imprisonment. There has been an increase in shooting incidents. An incident of an armed robbery at a gas station in March 2006 was believed to be the first, and two people were shot dead in January 2008 in the capital.

Finding of Guilt

The Constitution provides for the right of a fair trial, and an independent judiciary enforces this. The judiciary usually provides citizens with a fair and efficient legal process. Historically, the highest-ranking judges have been foreign nationals. Judges hold office "during good behaviour" and otherwise cannot be dismissed during their term of office. The Constitution prohibits arbitrary arrest and detention. However, human rights lawyers claimed that the arrests of the suspected November 16, 2006, rioters were illegal.

The law provides for the right to judicial determination of the legality of arrest. Under normal circumstances, police have the power to arrest detainees without a warrant, but detainees must be brought before a local magistrate within 24 hours. There are no statutory limits to the time that a suspect may be held prior to being charged. However, there is no evidence of preventative detention or other lengthy pretrial detention. In most cases, magistrates set bail. The law permits unlimited access by counsel, church and family members to detained persons.

A court may not summon anyone without providing a written indictment stating the charges. Trials are public, and defendants have the option to request a seven-member jury. Defendants are presumed innocent, may question witnesses against them, and have access to government-held evidence. Lawyers have free access to defendants. Public defenders are not provided, but local lawyers occasionally take pro bono cases. Defendants have the right of appeal. The king has the power to grant amnesty. Recently, the new rules of procedure for the Supreme Court provided for court referral to mediation in civil cases for the first time.

Partly as a response to the November 16, 2006, rioting, a youth diversionary pilot program was instigated in 2007. The scheme avoids long delays and cumbersome court procedures for young people involved in minor offenses, mostly theft or other property matters. The police prosecutor can refer young people aged 17 years and under who are not currently involved in serious offending for youth diversion. The young person must show remorse and admit his or her responsibility for harm caused. The youth must agree to complete community work. The alleged success of the program to date suggests that it will be further expanded for other offenders.

Punishment

Types of Punishment

The typical punishment for murder is imprisonment for life or any less period. The typical punishment for rape is imprisonment for any term not exceeding 15 years. However, in exceptional circumstances, the penalty can be life in prison. The typical punishment for theft, if the value of the stolen item does not exceed $500 pa'anga (US$252.25), is imprisonment for any period not exceeding 2 years. If the value of the thing stolen does exceed $500, punishment is imprisonment for any period not exceeding 7 years. In Tonga, the crimes of robbery and burglary are equal in meaning and punishment; the culprit for such crimes shall be liable for imprisonment for any period not exceeding 10 years. By comparison, a couple who obtained a $3000-pa'anga (about US$1,512) loan from the Westpac bank of Tonga by false pretenses and abetment received a suspended sentence and 80 hours of voluntary work.

The typical punishment for the most serious drug offense depends on the amount involved. For instance, possession of Indian hemp can result in a 7-years' sentence. In November 2003, the government enacted harsh penalties for drug offenders. A fine not exceeding $1 million pa'anga (about US$454,445) or 30 years' imprisonment or both can be imposed on any person convicted of importing or exporting illicit drugs.

Capital punishment is legal, but Tonga has not conducted an execution since 1982. Provisions exist for the head of state to commute the death sentence. Tongan legal legislation refers to the availability of whipping as a punishment either in relation to certain offenders or to certain offenses such as rape. Torture is prohibited by law. There were reports of gratuitous violence used during some routine arrests, detentions, and other encounters with the Tonga Defense Services and police after the rioting in Nuku'alofa in November 2006. A report of the Community Para-Legal Taskforce, an NGO, illustrated cases of physical abuse of some detainees while in custody. Both the police and the TDS conducted internal inquiries, but the findings were not made public.

Prison

As of June 2002, Tonga had six prisons holding some 113 prisoners. (i.e., 106 prisoners per 100,000 capita of population). Only 1.8 percent of prisoners were female. The total prison capacity of Tonga is 139 (81.3% of prison capacity was filled in 2002). The prison population has remained steady since 1992, around the 100 mark, although the rate dropped in 2006 to 89.

The main penal institution is at Hu'atolitoli, near Nuku'lofa. Prisoners are often required to undertake public works or work on government copra plantations. There are three classes of prisoners: debtors, prisoners awaiting trial or under remand, and prisoners sentenced to penal servitude or imprisonment. Those prisoners awaiting trial or under examination are allowed to receive visits from family and friends. All visiting is under the direction of the minister or head of department.

Prison conditions generally meet international standards, although they are basic and in line with local living standards. There are separate facilities for pretrial detainees and convicted prisoners, men and women, and adults and juveniles. The Tonga Red Cross in December 2006 visited three prisons to ascertain whether prisoners are appropriately looked after by the police. The society observed that the quality of water needed improvement and that prison sanitation was very poor and unhealthy. The Red Cross did not find any underage inmates and did not see any signs of abuse and torture.

The tiny island of Ata (30 acres) forms the smallest prison with about half a dozen residents. It was intended to be Tonga's only youth jail. By the end of 2002, about 50 convicted youth under 16 had spent their sentence on Ata. Inmates inhabit a two-room hut, and they receive home breaks once a month. The main communication is a basic radio telephone and a battery-powered radio.

David Baker

Further Reading

Australian Government AusAID: Tonga: http://www.ausaid.gov.au/country/country.cfm?CountryId=19

Care, Jennifer, Tess Newton, and Don Paterson. (1999). *Introduction to South Pacific Law.* London: Cavendish Publishing.

Maloney, John, and Jason Struble. (2007). "A New Day in Tonga: The Judiciary, the Reformers and the Future." *Journal of South Pacific Law* 11: 151–168.

Newton, Tess. (2000). "Policing in the South Pacific Region." Occasional Paper No. 1. Suva: School of Law, University of the South Pacific.

Pacific Islands Legal Information Institute: http://www.paclii.org.

Pacific Islands Report with Archives: http://www.pidp.ewc.hawaii.edu/pireport.

Tongan Government: http://www.pmo.gov.to.

General Bibliography

Books, Periodicals, and Articles

Aas, K. (2007). *Globalization and Crime*. Los Angeles, CA: Sage.

Adeyemi, A. (1990). "Crime and Development in Africa: Case Study of Nigeria." In *Essays on Crime and Development,* edited by U. Zvekic, pp. 135–193. Rome: United Nations Interregional Crime and Justice Institute.

ADT. (2006). *Anti-Social Behaviour across Europe:* http://www.jdi.ucl.ac.uk/downloads/publications/journal_articles/cc4416AD_ANTI_SOCIAL_Report_UK_fv.pdf

Aebi, M. F. (2010). "Methodological Issues in the Comparison of Police Recorded Crime Rates." In *International Handbook of Criminology,* edited by S. Shoham, P. Knepper, and M. Kett, pp. 209–226. London: Routledge.

Aebi, M. F., K. Aromaa, B. Aubusson de Cavarlay, G. Barclay, B. Gruszczynska, H. von Hofer, V. Hysi, J.-M. Jehle, M. Killias, P. Smit, and C. Tavares. (2006). *European Sourcebook of Crime and Criminal Justice Statistics—2006.* 3rd ed. Den Haag: Boom Juridische Uitgevers.

Aebi, M. F., and N. Delgrande. (2009). *Council of Europe Annual Penal Statistics SPACE I: Survey 2007.* Strasbourg: Council of Europe.

Aebi, M. F., and A. Linde. (2009). *Review of the Current Situation in Respect of the Collection of Survey Data on Victimization.* Lausanne: Université de Lausanne.

Alvazzi del Frate, A. (2004). "The International Crime Business Survey: Findings from Nine Central-Eastern European Cities." *European Journal on Criminal Policy and Research* 10(2–3): 137–161.

Archer, D., and R. Gartner. (1984). *Violence and Crime in Cross-National Perspective.* New Haven, CT: Yale University Press.

Aromaa, K., and M. Heiskanen, eds. (2008). *Crime and Criminal Justice Systems in Europe and North America 1995–2004. Publication 55.* Helsinki, Finland: European Institute for Crime Prevention and Control, Affiliated with the United Nations (HEUNI).

Barak, G., ed. (2000). *Crime and Crime Control: A Global View.* Westport, CT: Greenwood Press.

Bayley, D. H. (2006). *Changing the Guard: Developing Democratic Police Abroad.* New York: Oxford University Press.

Beirne, P., and D. Nelken. (1997). *Issues in Comparative Criminology.* Sudbury, MA: Dartmouth Publishing.

Bennett, R.R. (1997a). "Excessive Force: A Comparative Study of Police in the Caribbean." *Justice Quarterly* 14: 651–686.

Bennett, R.R. (1997b). "The Determinants of Job Satisfaction among Police Constables: A Comparative Study in Three Developing Nations." *Justice Quarterly* 14: 295–323.

Bennett, R.R. (2004). "Comparative Criminology and Criminal Justice Research: The State of Our Knowledge." *Justice Quarterly* 21: 1–21.

Botchkovar, E.V., C.R. Tittle, and O. Antonaccio. (2009). "General Strain Theory: Additional Evidence Using Cross-Cultural Data." *Criminology* 47(1): 131–165.

Caldwell. J., ed. (1994). *Networking and AIDS in Sub-Saharan Africa: Behavioral Research and the Social Context,* pp. 101–116. Canberra: Australian National Universities.

Care, Jennifer, Tess Newton, and Don Paterson. (1999). *Introduction to South Pacific Law.* London: Cavendish.

Chevigny, P. (1995). *Edge of the Knife: Police Violence in the Americas.* New York: Free Press.

Dalgleish, D. (2005). "Pre-Colonial Criminal Justice in West Africa: Eurocentric Thought versus Africentric Evidence." *African Journal of Criminology and Justice Studies* 1(1): 155–169.

Delgrande, N., and M.F. Aebi. (2009). "European Prisons: Stability or Change?" *Criminology in Europe: Newsletter of the European Society of Criminology* 8(3): 1, 17–19.

European Journal of Criminology. Various issues providing country profiles.

European Journal on Criminal Policy and Research, in particular those on crime trends in Western and Eastern European Countries (Vol. 10[2–3], 2004) and prosecution and diversion within criminal justice systems in Europe (Vol. 14[2–3], 2008).

Fairchild, Erika, and Harry Dammer. (2001). *Comparative Criminal Justice Systems.* 2nd ed. Belmont, CA: Wadsworth.

Fiala, R., and G. LaFree. (1988). "Cross-National Determinants of Child Homicide." *American Sociological Review* 53: 432–445.

Findlay, Mark. (2000). *Criminal Laws of the South Pacific.* Suva: University of the South Pacific.

Friedrichs, D. (2007). "Transnational Crime and Global Criminology: Definitional, Typological, and Contextual Conundrums." *Social Justice* 34(2): 4–18.

Howard, G.J., G. Newman, and W.A. Pridemore. (2000). "Theory, Method, and Data in Comparative Criminology" (excerpted from *Measurement and Analysis of Crime and Justice. Criminal Justice 2000*) 4: 139–211.

International Journal of Comparative and Applied Criminal Justice. Published and copyrighted by the School of Criminal Justice, Michigan State University. ISSN 0192–4036.

Johnson, H., N. Ollus, and S. Nevala. (2007). *Violence against Women: An International Perspective.* New York: Springer.

Joireman, Sandra F. (2004). "Colonization and the Rule of Law: Comparing the Effectiveness of Common Law and Civil Law Countries." *Constitutional Political Economy* 15: 315–338.

Junger-Tas, J., I. Haen Marshall, and D. Ribeaud. (2003). *Delinquency in an International Perspective: The International Self-Report Delinquency Study.* The Hague, The Netherlands: Kugler Publications.

Karstedt, S. (2001). "Comparing Cultures, Comparing Crime: Challenges, Prospects and Problems for a Global Criminology." *Crime, Law, and Social Change* 36(3): 285–308.

Karstedt, S., and G. LaFree. (2006). "Democracy, Crime, and Justice." *Annals of the American Academy of Political and Social Science* 605: 6–23.

Kury, H., ed. (2001). *International Comparison of Crime and Victimization: The ICVS.* Ontario, Canada: de Sitter Publications.

Kyle, D., and R. Koslowski. (2001). *Global Human Smuggling: Comparative Perspectives.* Baltimore, MD: Johns Hopkins University Press.

Larsen, N., and R. Smandych, eds. *Global Criminology and Criminal Justice: Current Issues and Perspectives.* Peterborough, Ontario: Broadview Press.

Lee, M. R., and T. Earnest. (2003). "Perceived Community Cohesion and Perceived Risk of Victimization: A Cross-National Study." *Justice Quarterly* 20: 131–157.

Lo, Stefan H. C., Ian Dobinson, and Wing Hong Chui. "Sentencing for Drug Offences in Hong Kong: An Overview." *Hong Kong Law Journal* 34 (2005): 13–46.

Mawby, R., ed. (1996). *Policing across the World,* pp. 3–12. London: Routledge.

Messner, S. F., and Richard R. Rosenfeld. (2007). *Crime and the American Dream.* 4th ed. Belmont, CA: Thomson Wadsworth.

Nalla, M. K. (2009) "Democratic Policing: A Comparison of Police Officers' Perceptions of Their Role and Functions in Transitional Societies." *Journal of Criminal Justice and Security* 11(4): 520–535.

Nalla, M. K., and J. Johnson. (2009). "Are Police and Security Personnel Warming up to Each Other? A Comparison of Officer's Attitudes in Developed, Emerging, and Transitional Economies." *Policing: An International Journal of Police Strategies and Management* 32(3): 508–525.

National Institute of Justice, Office of Justice Programs, U.S. Department of Justice: http://www.ncjrs.gov/criminal_justice2000/vol4_2000.html.

Neapolitan, J. L. (1997). *Cross-National Crime: A Research Review and Sourcebook.* Westport, CT: Greenwood Press.

Newburn, T., and R. Sparks. (2004). *Criminal Justice and Political Cultures: National and International Dimensions of Crime Control.* Devon, UK: Willan.

Newman, Graeme R. (1999). *Global Report on Crime and Justice.* New York: United Nations Office of Drug Control and Crime Prevention.

Newman, Graeme R. (2008). *Comparative Deviance: Perception and Law in Six Cultures.* Reprinted with new introduction. Piscataway, NJ: Transaction Press.

Owomero, B. (1987). "Crime Rates and Development in Africa: Empirical Analysis of Data from Nigeria, Kenya, and Tanzania." *Indian Journal of Criminology* 15: 107–120.

Pridemore, W.A. (2008). "A Methodological Addition to the Cross-National Empirical Literature on Social Structure and Homicide: A First Test of the Poverty-Homicide Thesis." *Criminology* 46: 133–154.

Rafter, N.H., and F. Heidensohn. (1995). *International Feminist Perspective in Criminology.* Buckingham, UK: Open University Press.

Reichel, P.L. (2004). *Comparative Criminal Justice Systems: A Topical Approach.* Upper Saddle River, NJ: Prentice Hall.

Reichel, Philip L. (2008). *Comparative Criminal Justice Systems.* Upper Saddle River, NJ: Prentice Hall.

Robert, P., ed. (2009a). *Comparing Crime Data in Europe: Official Crime Statistics and Survey Based Data.* Brussels: VUBPRESS Brussels University Press.

Robert, P., ed. (2009b). *Evaluating Safety and Crime Prevention Policies in Europe.* Brussels: VUBPRESS Brussels University Press.

Savage, J., R.R. Bennett, and M. Danner. (2008). "Economic Assistance and Crime: A Cross-National Investigation." *European Journal of Criminology* 5: 217–238.

Schwabach, Aaron. (2003. Rev. 2006). *Non-Western Philosophies of Law.* In *Encyclopedia of Life Support Systems (EOLSS),* edited by Aaron Schwabach and Arthur John Cockfield, topic 6.31.1. Developed under the Auspices of UNESCO. Oxford: Eolss: http://www.eolss.net.

Sheptycki, J., and A. Wardak, eds. (2005). *Transnational and Comparative Criminology*. London: Glasshouse.

Stamatel, Janet P. (2006). "Incorporating Socio-Historical Context and Temporal Variation into Quantitative Cross-National Criminology." *International Journal of Comparative and Applied Criminal Justice* 30(2): 177–208.

Stamatel, Janet P. (2009a). "Correlates of National-Level Homicide Variation in Post-Communist East-Central Europe." *Social Forces* 87(3), 1423–1448.

Stamatel, Janet P. (2009b). "Contributions of Cross-National Research at the Beginning of the 21st Century." In *Handbook on Criminology and Deviance,* edited by Marvin Krohn, Alan Lizotte, and Gina Penly-Hall, 3–18. New York: Springer Science + Business Media.

Stamatel, Janet P. (guest editor). (2009, December). "New Methodological Directions for International and Comparative Criminology." *International Journal of Comparative and Applied Criminal Justice* 33 (2): 167.

Sung, Hung-En. (2004a). "Democracy and Organized Crime: Evidence from Fifty-Nine Countries." *Security Journal* 17(4): 21–34.

Sung, Hung-En. (2004b). "State Failure, Economic Failure, and Predatory Organized Crime." *Journal of Research in Crime and Delinquency* 41(2): 111–129.

Sung, Hung-En. (2006a). "Democracy and Criminal Justice in Comparative Perspective: From Crime Control to Due Process." *The Annals of the American Academy of Political and Social Science* 605(1): 311–337.

Sung, Hung-En. (2006b). "Structural Determinants of Police Effectiveness in Market Democracies." *Police Quarterly* 9(1): 3–19.

Sung, Hung-En, and Jack Reed. (2006). "Migration and Crime in Europe." In *Crime and Immigration,* edited by Joshua Freilich Graeme R. Newman, 95–120. Hampshire, UK: Ashgate.

Terrill, Richard J. (2009). *World Criminal Justice System: A Survey.* 7th ed. Southington, CT: Anderson.

Uildriks, N. (2009). *Policing Insecurity: Police Reform, Security and Human Rights in Latin America.* Lanham, MD: Lexington Books.

United Nations Office on Drugs and Crime. (2005). *Crime and Development in Africa.* Vienna, Austria: United Nations: http://www.unodc.org/pdf/African_report.pdf.

United Nations Office on Drugs and Crime. (2008). *Crime and Its Impact on the Balkans and Affected Countries.* Vienna, Austria: United Nations: http://www.unodc.org/documents/data-and-analysis/Balkan_study.pdf.

United Nations Office on Drugs and Crime and the Latin America and the Caribbean Region of the World Bank. (2007). *Crime, Violence, and Development: Trends, Costs, and Policy Options in the Caribbean.* Vienna, Austria: United Nations: http://www.unodc.org/pdf/research/Cr_and_Vio_Car_E.pdf.

Van Dijk, Jan. (2008). *The World of Crime: Breaking the Silence of Security, Justice, and Development across the World.* Thousand Oaks, CA: Sage.

Van Dijk, J., J. Kesteren, and P. Smit. (2007). *Criminal Victimisation in International Perspective: Key Findings from the 2004–2005 ICVS and EU ICS.* WODC: http://www.nicis.nl/kenniscentrum/binaries/nicis/bulk/onderzoek/2008/2/3/icvs2004_05report.pdf.

Weitekamp, E. G. M., and H. Kerner. (1994). *Cross-National Longitudinal Research on Human Development and Criminal Behavior.* Dordrecht, Netherlands: Kluwer Academic.

Zauberman, R., ed. (2009a). *Self-Reported Crime and Deviance Studies in Europe.* Brussels: VUBPRESS Brussels University Press.

Zauberman, R., ed. (2009b). *Victimization and Insecurity in Europe.* Brussels: VUBPRESS Brussels University Press.

Zimring, Franklin E., and David T. Johnson. (2008). "Law, Society, and Capital Punishment in Asia." *Punishment and Society* 10(2): 103–115.

Web Sites

BBC News Country Profiles: http://news.bbc.co.uk/2/hi/country_profiles/default.stm. This site is very good for background information on history, geography, and politics. It's also good for links to internal national sites and news media sites.

Cecil Greek's Criminal Justice Resources on International Criminal Justice: http://www.criminology.fsu.edu/p/cjl-world.php. There is a good variety of sources here, from common to the unusual, such as, for example, South Africa's Crime Mysteries.

CIA World Factbook: https://www.cia.gov/library/publications/the-world-factbook/index.html. The information in this book tends to be regurgitated in many Web sites, but it contains useful background information and is updated annually. Sometimes there are crime data, but usually descriptive, without statistics.

Council of Europe Annual Penal Statistics: www.coe.int/prison. Detailed data on prisons in Europe since 1983 can be found here.

The Council of Europe, European Commission for the Efficiency of Justice. (2008): *Evaluation of European Judicial Systems:* http://www.coe.int/t/dghl/cooperation/cepej/evaluation/default_en.asp.

Country Report of the Justice Studies Center of the Americas: http://www.cejamericas.org. This research and advocacy group publishes online country-specific analysis of legal systems and their operations in Latin America.

The Economist: http://www.economist.com/countries/index.cfm. This Web site offers much economic, historical, and political information on many countries and often useful information in its city guides.

European Society of Criminology: http://www.esc-eurocrim.org. This site provides a lot of relevant information on crime and punishment in Europe, including the programs of the annual conferences.

European Sourcebook of Crime and Criminal Justice Statistics: www.europeansourcebook.org. This site provides databases on police, prosecution, conviction, and correctional statistics since 1990 as well as some data on victimization.

International Centre for Prison Studies: http://www.kcl.ac.uk/depsta/rel/icps/home.html. This is a good source for international prison statistics.

International Court of Justice: http://www.icj-cij.org/.

Library of Congress Area Studies: http://www.loc.gov/rr/.

Nationmaster: http://www.nationmaster.com/index.php. This interesting interactive site allows comparative statistics of countries on a wide range of topics, including criminal justice. However, the crime statistics tend to be outdated.

The New York Times Countries and Territories: http://topics.nytimes.com/topics/news/international/countriesandterritories/index.html. These pages contain both general background information and links to recent media stories.

United Nations Interregional Crime and Justice Research Institute (UNICRI): http://www.unicri.it/wwd/analysis/icvs/data.php. A wide variety of information, particularly data for many countries participating in the International Crime Victim Survey (ICVS), is available.

United Nations Office on Drugs and Crime: http://www.unodc.org/. This site contains a wealth of information on crime, with extensive databases of crime statistics from the UN Surveys of Crime and Criminal Justice Systems.

U.S. Library of Congress Country Studies: http://lcweb2.loc.gov/frd/cs/. These are much more detailed than the usual country profiles, such as the CIA Factbook.

U.S. National Institute of Justice International Center: http://www.ojp.usdoj.gov/nij/international/. This site offers a variety of reports, articles, and descriptions of transnational and international crime and justice.

Wikipedia: http://wikipedia.org/. There is much information on countries, including interesting descriptions of crime and criminal justice issues. One has to be careful of the sources, but often there are links that lead to useful and reasonable resources. This is particularly good for tracking down internal national news media Web sites (i.e., local newspapers and TV stations) that almost always have news on local crimes.

World Criminal Justice Library Network: http://andromeda.rutgers.edu/~wcjlen/WCJ/mainpages/statres.htm. This site contains excellent statistical data from 80 countries. Internal national publications are usually the source.

World Factbook of Criminal Justice Systems. U.S. NIJ. Bureau of Justice Statistics: http://bjs.ojp.usdoj.gov/index.cfm?ty=pbdetail&iid=1435.

About the Editors and Contributors

General Editor

Graeme R. Newman is a distinguished teaching professor at the School of Criminal Justice, University at Albany and the associate director of the Center for Problem-Oriented Policing. He has advised the United Nations on crime and justice issues over many years and in 1990 established the United Nations Crime and Justice Information Network.

Volume 3 Editor

Doris C. Chu is an associate professor in the Department of Criminology, Sociology, and Geography at Arkansas State University. She received her PhD in criminal justice from the State University of New York at Albany in 2003. Her research interests include religiosity and desistance, policing, and comparative criminal justice. Her recent articles have appeared in *Crime and Delinquency, International Journal of Offender Therapy and Comparative Criminology, Families in Society, International Criminal Justice Review*, *Policing: An International Journal of Police Strategies and Management*, and *Criminal Justice and Behavior.*

Volume 3 Contributors

Ahmad Ghazali bin Abu Hassan is an associate professor at the Department of Strategic Studies, Faculty of Defence Studies and Management, National Defence University of Malaysia. He teaches public international law and international humanitarian law.

Danai Azaria is a PhD candidate at University College London (UCL). She holds an LLM in public international law from UCL (2006) and a LLM in international studies from the National and Kapodistrian University of Athens, Greece (2005).

Yoko Baba received her PhD from the University of Oklahoma in 1987. Currently, she is a professor and chair of the sociology department at San José State University.

David Baker is the head of criminal justice at Monash University Gippsland, Australia. He is author of *Batons and Blockades: Policing Industrial Disputes in*

Australasia and has published in a variety of interdisciplinary journals. He is an associate investigator for the Australian Research Council's Centre of Excellence for Policing and Security.

Thierry Bouhours, PhD, is a research officer at the Centre of Excellence in Policing and Security, RegNet, Research School of Pacific and Asian Studies, Australian National University, Canberra, Australia.

Roderic Broadhurst is a professor, Australian Research Council, Centre for Excellence in Policing and Security, RegNet, Research School of Pacific and Asian Studies, Australian National University, Canberra, Australia.

Hoan N. Bui is an associate professor in the Department of Sociology, University of Tennessee, Knoxville. Her research has been published in major criminal justice journals, and she is the author of *In the Adopted Land: Abused Immigrant Women and the Criminal Justice System,* published in 2004 by Greenwood Press.

Tess Newton Cain, LLB, PhD, is a former lecturer in law at the University of the South Pacific (1997–2001).

Rolando V. del Carmen is Distinguished Professor of Criminal Justice (Law) and Regents Professor in the College of Criminal Justice, Sam Houston State University. He finished his BA and LLB degrees in the Philippines. He has an MCL from Southern Methodist University, an LLM from the University of California-Berkeley, and a JSD from the University of Illinois.

Charles K.M. Chang is a professor in the School of Police Policy, Central Police University, Taiwan. Professor Chang was the second president of the Asian Association of Police Studies (AAPS). His recent publications appeared in the *Journal of Asian Association of Police Studies, Journal of Policing (Taiwan), Third Sector Review (Taiwan), Journal of Central Police University (Taiwan),* and *Police Science Bio-Monthly.*

Sutham Cheurprakobkit is a professor in the Department of Sociology and Criminal Justice, Kennesaw State University. His research interests include community policing, comparative criminal justice, and computer crime.

Doris C. Chu is an associate professor in the Department of Criminology, Sociology, and Geography at Arkansas State University. Her recent publications appeared in *Criminal Justice and Behavior, International Journal of Offender Therapy and Comparative Criminology, International Criminal Justice Review,* and *Policing: An International Journal of Police Strategies and Management.*

Wing Hong Chui, PhD, is an associate professor in the Department of Social Work and Social Administration at the University of Hong Kong. His areas of interest include probation studies, youth justice, comparative criminal justice, and social work with offenders. He is the coeditor of five books, including *Understanding Criminal Justice in Hong Kong.*

Graham Farrell is a professor of criminology at Loughborough University. He has published widely in the fields of domestic and transnational criminology.

Narayanan Ganapathy is an assistant professor in the Department of Sociology, National University of Singapore.

Gilbert Geis is a professor emeritus, Department of Criminology, Law and Society, University of California, Irvine. He is former president of the American Society of Criminology and recipient of its Edwin H. Sutherland Award for outstanding research. His most recent books are *Criminal Justice and Moral Issues* (with Robert F. Meier) and *White-Collar and Corporate Crime.*

Heike Gramckow is senior legal counsel to the World Bank, Legal and Justice Sector Reform Group, Washington, D.C.

Hennessey Hayes is a senior lecturer in the School of Criminology and Criminal Justice at Griffith University. He is engaged in a program of research on restorative justice and reoffending.

Estelle Hofschneider has a master's degree in criminal justice from the State University of New York (SUNY) College at Buffalo. She is currently pursuing a JD at the University at Buffalo Law School (SUNY). Her research interests include criminal law, immigration law, and international human rights law.

Kristen Lee Hourigan is a graduate student at the State University of New York at Albany.

Syed Ejaz Hussain is Deputy Inspector General of Pakistan Police and currently a PhD candidate at the University of Pennsylvania.

Hee-Jong Joo is an associate professor in the College of Criminal Justice at Sam Houston State University.

Suman Kakar, PhD, is an associate professor in the School of Criminal Justice at Florida International University, Miami. Her research interests include child abuse, delinquency, juvenile delinquency, comparative criminal justice, law enforcement, and domestic violence.

Mohammed Bin Kashem is an associate professor of Sociology and dean (in-charge) of Curriculum Development and Evaluation Center at the National University, Gazipur, Bangladesh. He received his master's in criminal justice from the University of Baltimore, Maryland, in 1996.

Chenda Keo is a PhD student at the Research School of Pacific and Asian Studies, Australian National University, Canberra, Australia.

George Kikuchi received his PhD in Sociology from Purdue University in 2008. He currently works as a postdoctoral researcher at the National Research Institute of Police Science in Japan.

Helmut Kury is a professor of psychology, PhD in psychology, at the University of Freiburg. He has been a member of the research group at the Max Planck Institute for foreign and international penal law in Freiburg, Germany, and from 1980 to 1987, he was the founding director of the Research Institute of Lower Saxony in Germany.

Samson Chi-fai Kwan is an associate professor in the Department of Social Work, Macao Polytechnic Institute. His main research areas are social deviance, suicidology, and gender studies.

Chia-Wen Lee is an associate professor in the Department of Law, National Cheng-Kung University. She recently published *Punishment in the Neo-Liberal Order.* Her other publications appear in various law reviews published by universities, *EurAmerica,* and *Taiwan Law Review.*

Unisa Lerdtomornsakul is an assistant professor in the Department of Sociology and Anthropology, Chulalongkorn University, Thailand. Her main research areas include crime prevention and criminological theory.

Anna Margaryan is an associate professor of criminal law and criminology at Yerevan State University, Armenia. She has done research on the crime trends in Armenia, offense patterns, and juvenile criminality.

Andrew Marriott is a legal adviser to the Judicial System Monitoring Programme in Dili, Timor-Leste, and a doctoral candidate at Deakin University, Australia. His research draws on experience in Sierra Leone and Cambodia to examine the role of the legal profession in postconflict justice sector reform.

Muhammad Mustofa is a professor in the Department of Criminology at the University of Indonesia. His recent international publication appears in the *Journal of Labour and Development Management,* the University of Tasmania, Australia.

Graeme R. Newman is Distinguished Teaching Professor at the School of Criminal Justice, State University of New York at Albany. He has published widely on comparative criminal justice and punishment. His most recent book, with Pietro Marongiu, is *Beccaria, On Crimes and Punishment* (2009).

Claire Angelique Nolasco is a doctoral student in the College of Criminal Justice, Sam Houston State University. She obtained her bachelor's degree in political science and her JD from the University of the Philippines and her LLM in international economic and business law from Kyushu University, Japan. She is a practicing lawyer in the state of California and the Philippines and has served as chief legal officer for Senator Francis N. Pangilinan in the Philippine Senate.

Corina Oliver graduated cum laude from Arizona State University Barrett Honores College with a BA in journalism and mass communications. She currently directs a New Zealand marketing campaign for American Express International in the Auckland office.

Jennifer Lynn Owens is a PhD student at the School of Criminal Justice, State University of New York at Albany. Her research interests include capital punishment, comparative criminal justice, psychology and the law, sexual assault, and domestic violence.

Edisher Phutkaradze, JD, is a professor of law and has been director of the Chair for Penal Law and Criminology at the University in Tbilissi since 2001. In 2002, he became a member of the research group of the Institute for State and Law in Tbilissi. He also held positions in the courts of Georgia from 1992 to 1995, and was investigator for crime affairs from 1995 to 2002.

Tim Prenzler is a professor of criminology and criminal justice at Griffith University and is a member of the Australian Research Council Centre of Excellence in Policing and Security.

Prapon Sahapattana is an associate professor at the Police Management Department, Royal Thai Police Cadet Academy, Thailand. His research interests include GIS applications for criminal justice, crime mapping, police technology, and computer crime.

Paul Schupp is an associate professor in the Department of Criminal Justice at Niagara University. His primary scholarly interests are the sociology of punishment and the development of imprisonment patterns.

Erkan Sezgin holds a doctoral degree from Kent State University, Department of Political Science. He is a member of Turkish National Police.

Moris Shalikashvili holds a JD (LLM) from the University in Hamburg, Germany. He works in Tbilissi as an adviser to the public defender (Ombudsman) and at the Ivane Javachishvili State University in Tbilissi where he teaches criminology, juvenile law, and prison law.

Pamela Shultz is a graduate student at Arkansas State University. She received a Master's degree in Criminal Justice in 2009 and a Master's degree in Sociology in 2010. She is currently working towards a Specialist degree.

Julie Ahmad Siddique is a doctoral student at the City University of New York Graduate Center, John Jay College of Criminal Justice. Her research interests include comparative criminal justice, long-term trends in crime and victimization, sexual violence, and empirical testing of criminological theories.

Anil Singh Sona is a master's student in the Department of Sociology, National University of Singapore.

Janet P. Stamatel is an assistant professor at the School of Criminal Justice, State University of New York at Albany. Her main research area is cross-national criminology.

Elizabeth Stanley is a senior lecturer in criminology at Victoria University of Wellington, New Zealand. She has undertaken studies on rights and detention in New Zealand and the United Kingdom, and her work in South Africa, Chile, and Timor-Leste has focused on truth commissions and court processes.

Stephanie L. Stashenko is a graduate student at the State University of New York at Albany.

Jeremy Tasch is an assistant professor of Eurasian and global studies in the Department of Geography and Environmental Planning, Towson University.

Yik Koon Teh is a professor in criminology and sociology in the Department of Strategic Studies, Faculty of Defence Studies and Management, National Defence University of Malaysia. She obtained her PhD from the London School of Economics and Political Science and was a Fulbright Scholar at the University of California, Los Angeles, in 2002.

Sener Uludag holds a doctoral degree from Kent State University, Department of Political Science. He is a member of Turkish National Police Academy. He currently works as the director of Crime Prevention Research Center at Turkish National Police Academy.

Jayampathy Wickramaratne, PhD, is an attorney-at-law from Sri Lanka. In 2001, he was appointed president's counsel. He has extensive experience in Lao PDR, having been a consultant for the UNDP, UNODC, and Sida on legal reform, human rights, international law, and human trafficking.

James Windle is a PhD student at Loughborough University, Leicestershire, United Kingdom.

Minwoo Yun, PhD, is an assistant professor, Department of Social Science, Wheeling Jesuit University. He has published on terrorism, hostage taking, and Russian organized crime.

Lening Zhang, PhD, is a professor of sociology at Saint Francis University. Dr. Zhang has published more than 50 articles and co-edited a book on China's crime and criminal justice (2001).

Index

Boldface numbers refer to volume numbers. A key appears on all verso pages.

1: Africa and the Middle East **2:** The Americas **3:** Asia and Pacific **4:** Europe

1: Africa and the Middle East
2: The Americas
3: Asia and Pacific
4: Europe

1: Africa and the Middle East
2: The Americas
3: Asia and Pacific
4: Europe

1: Africa and the Middle East **2:** The Americas **3:** Asia and Pacific **4:** Europe

1: Africa and the Middle East
2: The Americas
3: Asia and Pacific
4: Europe

1: Africa and the Middle East
2: The Americas
3: Asia and Pacific
4: Europe

1: Africa and the Middle East
2: The Americas
3: Asia and Pacific
4: Europe

1: Africa and the Middle East
2: The Americas
3: Asia and Pacific
4: Europe

1: Africa and the Middle East
2: The Americas
3: Asia and Pacific
4: Europe

1: Africa and the Middle East
2: The Americas
3: Asia and Pacific
4: Europe

1: Africa and the Middle East
2: The Americas
3: Asia and Pacific
4: Europe

1: Africa and the Middle East
2: The Americas
3: Asia and Pacific
4: Europe

Crime and Punishment around the World

Crime and Punishment around the World

EUROPE

Volume 4

MARCELO F. AEBI AND VÉRONIQUE JAQUIER, VOLUME EDITORS
GRAEME R. NEWMAN, GENERAL EDITOR

ABC-CLIO

Santa Barbara, California • Denver, Colorado • Oxford, England

Copyright 2010 by Marcelo F. Aebi and Véronique Jaquier, Volume Editors

Graeme R. Newman, General Editor

All rights reserved. No part of this publication may be reproduced, stored in a retrieval system, or transmitted, in any form or by any means, electronic, mechanical, photocopying, recording, or otherwise, except for the inclusion of brief quotations in a review, without prior permission in writing from the publisher.

Library of Congress Cataloging-in-Publication Data

Crime and punishment around the world.
p. cm.
Includes bibliographical references and index.
ISBN 978-0-313-35133-4 (set : alk. paper) — ISBN 978-0-313-35134-1 (set ebook) — ISBN 978-0-313-35135-8 (vol. 1 : alk. paper) — ISBN 978-0-313-35136-5 (vol. 1 ebook) — ISBN 978-0-313-35137-2 (vol. 2 : alk. paper) — ISBN 978-0-313-35138-9 (vol. 2 ebook) — ISBN 978-0-313-35139-6 (vol. 3 : alk. paper) — ISBN 978-0-313-35140-2 (vol. 3 ebook) — ISBN 978-0-313-35141-9 (vol. 4 : alk. paper) — ISBN 978-0-313-35142-6 (vol. 4 ebook)
1. Crime. 2. Punishment. 3. Criminal justice, Administration of.
HV6025.C7115 2010
364—dc22 2010021159

ISBN (set): 978-0-313-35133-4
EISBN (set): 978-0-313-35134-1

14 13 12 11 10 1 2 3 4 5

This book is also available on the World Wide Web as an eBook.
Visit www.abc-clio.com for details.

ABC-CLIO, LLC
130 Cremona Drive, P.O. Box 1911
Santa Barbara, California 93116-1911

This book is printed on acid-free paper ∞

Manufactured in the United States of America

This volume set is dedicated to the memory of
Ali Sabeeh of Omara, Iraq, who, while preparing the entry on Iraq,
was kidnapped, tortured, and killed in October 2007

Editorial Advisory Board

Adam Bouloukos, Director of Outreach and Partnerships, UNOPS, Copenhagen, Denmark

Ronald V. Clarke, University Professor, Rutgers University

Adam Graycar, Professor, Australian National University

Martin Killias, Professor, University of Zurich

Jeremy Travis, President, John Jay College of Criminal Justice

Contents

Acknowledgments

The contribution made by the volume editors to this project has been inestimable. A project of this magnitude could not have been achieved without their unceasing efforts to find contributors for large and small countries alike, to manage their contributors' contributions, and to edit them into the style and format required by a publication of this type. They helped overcome a number of crises we met along the way. For this and for their always being on the receiving end of my constant e-mails, I express my sincere appreciation. I thank especially Janet Stamatel for producing the world and regional maps from my sometimes less than adequate databases.

Many authors have contributed to these volumes. Without them, of course, this project would not have been possible. The volume editors and I express our great admiration to our contributors and appreciation for their tolerance of our editorial demands, which oftentimes must have seemed unreasonable. We apologize if your chapter ended up a little shorter than you had wanted. We bear full responsibility for any misconceptions that may have occurred as a result of our at-times heavy editorial hand.

Finally, we thank the Editorial Advisory Board members for being there when we needed them.

—Graeme R. Newman
Albany, NY
December 31, 2009

General Introduction

We humans are fascinated by the diversity of cultures, climates, landscapes, and peoples. It is part of our deep human heritage that we have never been able to stay at home. Since the beginning of human time, our haplogroups have migrated far and wide, stumbling on new fauna and evolving with them, adapting to cold, hot, wet, and dry seasons and climates. Along the way, we have constructed societies and civilizations that have come and gone, none reaching perfection; each having tried its own solutions to the problem of order; each constructing rules, laws, customs, and ways of dealing with those who, for whatever reason, have broken with the sacred commandments of order. Somewhere along the way, no matter what the civilization or society, the idea of justice emerged, perhaps independently of the need for order and, indeed, every now and again in opposition to order. But whatever order's relationship to justice, one thing is certain: order is necessary for societies to survive. And embedded in this necessity is the inevitability that individuals will break laws, rules, and customs and will, as a matter of logic (and justice), be punished for it.

So law (so-called if it is written) and custom (embodying law and rules that may not be written but that are "practiced" and conveyed orally) is universal in all known societies. They are part of the "civilizing" process, which seeks to hold in check the tendency of humans to devour each other. It is true that great thinkers, philosophers, and even scientists have insisted—in the face of the overwhelming evidence of history that stands against them—that humans, if only given a chance, can or could work together for their common good without being coerced to do so. But we know of no society anywhere in which this utopian (if it is utopian) conception of human nature has produced a society without laws or customs and their concomitant punishments. And surely humans have had plenty of chances to construct such utopian societies. Yet each time they try, order takes over, because we know that individuals only grudgingly curb their own desires. They do not like the imposition of order, but they know that they cannot survive without it and its accoutrements. Or at least, we may say that life is much more comfortable if one gives into almost any kind of order. This observation probably applies even to the worst of tyrannical orders, for it is easier to remain in submission than it is to rise up and overthrow a very powerful authority. The 18th-century enlightenment thinkers upon whose ideas much of the world's criminal justice systems are based (whether civil or common) were clearly of the opinion that punishment was a necessary evil, a price paid for the

comfort of living in an ordered society. Its universality certainly attests to the truth of this assertion.

It should come as no surprise, therefore, that getting reliable information about such a touchy subject—essentially how a society, nation, or culture maintains order in the face of a populace that may secretly or even openly resent its imposition—is very difficult. Nations can be very secretive about their crime rates and their punishments, not to mention their procedures for finding guilt and their manner of interrogating suspects. Various organizations have set themselves up to monitor the most egregious violations of individuals in the name of order, such as Human Rights Watch and Amnesty International, but there is a far larger part of the maintenance of order and the processing of lawbreakers by nations and regional governments that also needs constant scrutiny. Violations of human rights in the name of order may easily be hidden inside the bureaucratic inertia and practices of even the most "enlightened" societies. To admit to having a very high rate of murder or incarceration—perhaps one of the highest—of its citizens is not something of which a nation can be especially proud. Such statistics say something about that nation, though what that something is, unfortunately, can be easily misinterpreted. For example, some countries may be criticized for having very high imprisonment rates, but their retort may be that this is because they have very high crime rates, to which it may be asked, but why do you have such high crime rates? The reply may be, "Because we have strict laws that are strictly enforced, which is for the good of our citizens, who are kept safer than those in other countries whose administration of criminal justice is too lax." Provided here is just a taste of the controversies and disagreements concerning the differing levels of crime and punishment in diverse countries, as well as the puzzling relationship or lack thereof between prison rates and crime rates. The riddle can be stated thus: more punishment should reduce crime, but more crime requires more punishment.

One would think that the costs in public relations to a nation would be far too high to allow for the publication of crime and punishment statistics. So it is an amazing achievement that the United Nations World Crime Surveys, whose mission is to collect the official statistics on crime and justice from member nations, have shown steady and significant increases in the number of countries submitting their statistics since they were first collected in the 1970s. From a handful of countries in the beginning, the number providing crime and punishment statistics had grown to about 50 as of 2005. That is the positive spin. In fact, this is only 50 out of 190 member UN nations, and there are signs of decreasing reporting by countries in recent years, according to Jan Van Dijk, author of *The World of Crime* and former UN expert on international crime and justice.

Although it is true that nations are reticent to make public their crime and punishment statistics for reasons of public image, there are many technical difficulties in making comparisons of officially collected crime and justice statistics across countries. Many of these difficulties are serious, and *the reader is warned to use considerable caution in making such comparisons across countries*. These technical difficulties include the following:

- Different legal definitions of offenses make it difficult to compare specific offenses across nations.
- Different reporting and recording practices of the police who generally have first official contact with a crime make comparing statistics from one country to another unreliable without knowledge of these practices.
- Different legal systems may affect the finding of guilt, recording and classification of offenses, and recording of arrests and convictions.
- Inconsistent classifications of crime records and frequent changes over time make it difficult to compare trends in crime or punishment.
- Different bureaucracies and government departments within each nation that collate and publish crime and punishment statistics may produce different statistics. For example, city- or state-level collection of crime rates or prison rates may differ from collection at the federal level, as in the United States.
- Inadequate infrastructure for collecting and processing crime and justice reports, including information technology, may hinder the amount or accuracy of criminal justice data.
- Lack of professionally trained crime analysts and statisticians may limit the reliability and depth of statistical data available.
- Local events or conditions may inflate crime and punishment statistics, such as genocidal events that may or may not be recorded as murders.
- Changing government policies about making crime and justice statistics public may affect trends and the amount and type of data made available. There have been instances where countries have revealed crime and justice statistics to the United Nations, but not to their own citizens. The reverse is also true. There was a time, for example, when the Soviet Union routinely collected crime statistics for its internal use but officially denied to the United Nations that there was any crime at all in the Soviet Union, because there could be no crime in a true communist society.
- In large populous countries, there may be vast differences within those countries. For example, the levels of crime and punishment vary enormously throughout the United States; some states still retain the death penalty, and many do not. There may also be huge differences in amounts and kinds of crime between urban and rural regions. There may even be different legal systems operating within the same country, such as, for example, Quebec in Canada or the several customary, Islamic, and civil law systems operating in Timor-Leste.

If one must make comparisons—and most people are unable to resist it—the best way to overcome these pitfalls is to make sure that one knows as much as possible about the historical and social context within which the statistics are collected. *Crime and Punishment around the World* provides just that context. This encyclopedia describes in detail the crime and punishment practices of each country and, in some instances, specific regions. The four volumes offer a glimpse of the ways in which all the nations around the world try to solve the basic problem

they all face: what to do with those who break the law? They have all enacted either customary or written criminal laws. They have all inherited their criminal laws from their ancestors near and far, not infrequently from other nations that either usurped them or overtook them through migration. They have all developed procedures for the finding of guilt of the accused, and all, of course, follow up the finding of guilt with legislated or customary punishments. These are all essentially the product of their legal systems.

World Legal Systems

For more than 1,000 years, the Roman Empire encompassed just about all the region around the Mediterranean and stretched as far north as Great Britain. Law was probably its major weapon against the peoples it subdued, bringing with it order and a stable means of commerce. Its concepts would form much of the basis of canon law and eventually much of the civil law of Europe. Furthermore, much of the Islamic and customary law of the countries surrounding the south and east of the Mediterranean was deeply affected by Roman law because those peoples were also subjects of the Roman Empire at various times for over 1,000 years. Those countries of Europe that retained more of the Roman law and its procedures would later come to be known as "civil law" countries. Those European countries that managed to put aside Roman law came to be known as "common law" countries. And those of North Africa and the Far East retained Islamic and customary law systems.

Civil law systems account for over 50 percent of the world's legal systems, although many such systems are mixed with other legal systems because of local and historical circumstance. In fact, as a result of constant reforms, it is likely that there are no purely civil law systems left in the world. Most countries have incorporated various aspects of the adversarial system. The main characteristics of civil law systems are the following:

1. Systematically written legal codes are the prime source of authority in legal decisions and procedures.
2. Their procedures are often (though not entirely) based on what is sometimes called the "inquisitorial system"—reaching back to the days of the Roman Catholic Inquisition—in which the process of finding of guilt is conducted by a judge or magistrate who both investigates and conducts the final trial. These trials are usually, though not always, conducted before a magistrate or panel of magistrates.

Probably the prime examples of European civil law systems are those of France and Germany and, to some extent, Italy, which has recently incorporated aspects of the adversarial system.

Common law systems account for another 20 percent of the world's legal systems. These are commonly referred to as "adversarial systems" because the finding of guilt is not conducted by the magistrate who decides and investigates the case as in civil law; rather, a prosecutor (or sometimes an investigating police officer) investigates the case and prepares the case for a trial by judge and jury

(although juries are not always required). The two significant features of common law systems are the following:

1. Cases are decided based on precedent, which views previous cases and decisions as a cumulative wisdom and authority.
2. Cases are a courtroom drama in which the prosecutor is pitted against the defense.

It should be noted, however, that in modern legal systems of common law, there are legal codes that systematize the law, and these may or may not be based on the codification of past legal practice. In the United States, for example, every state, in addition to the federal system, has its own written code. Cases are decided, however, based not only on how well the offender's acts match the written code but also on the cases that came before it—that is, precedent. One sees this tradition played out in the U.S. Supreme Court, which arduously scrutinizes past decisions to conclude whether a particular case was decided correctly or not, in accordance with the supreme law of the land, the U.S. Constitution. The popular view that contrasts these two legal traditions is that civil law is focused more on finding a probably guilty person guilty, whereas common law is focused more on defending a possibly innocent person from a guilty verdict. Both systems do, however, adhere to the presumption of innocence of the accused until proven guilty. The most typical examples of common law systems are those of the United Kingdom, the United States, and Australia.

Islamic legal systems account for about 10 percent of the world's legal systems, although there are probably no purely Islamic systems anywhere in the world. This is because of the early Roman influence on all countries surrounding the Mediterranean and because of the imperialism of the West during the 16th through 20th centuries. In its pure form, the Islamic system of law follows the exact law of God, as interpreted by experts (Mullahs), deriving from the Koran, the Bible, and other sacred texts. Islamic law is often called sharia—the path to follow. Perhaps the most contrasting feature of Islamic law is that it is more a way to live one's life than a set of prohibitions laid down by a state authority as in Roman law and its progenitors. Thus, not only does it include prohibitions, some of which are set out in the Ten Commandments, but it also includes exhortations to lead a good life (e.g., love thy neighbor). No such positive exhortations are found in other Western legal traditions, whose defining principle is prohibition. The procedural rules of Islamic law are those of human reasoning and consensus. One of the problems that faces legal theorists in Islamic law is that there are many offenses that are not specifically covered in any of the sacred texts. For example, sodomy is not mentioned in the Koran or Sunna (another sacred text), but adultery is. So the judge may reason that the two offenses are similar and the punishments prescribed for one may apply to the other. In practice, however, many cases are decided also on custom and precedent, given that in many Islamic countries, tribal customs concerning redress of wrongs (e.g., feuding and vengeance) have developed alongside Islamic and other kinds of law. The majority of countries with Islamic legal systems therefore also have customary law as a major component, especially in dealing with day-to-day infractions. Finally, most Islamic law

countries also have a considerable dose of civil law, especially in the field of commerce, though it has been necessary even there for such countries to develop ways to get around the Islamic prohibition of usury, defined rather broadly.

Customary law is the law that has arisen through oral tradition among tribes and cultures where law is not written down but rather communicated across generations by tribal elders. Village or regional chieftains are usually, though not always, the main repositories of such legal wisdom, and the finding of guilt usually occurs within an informal meeting of interested parties. In many countries of Africa and southern Asia, these kinds of local meetings occur and settlements are reached based on the hearing of all sides of the complaints. Depending on the culture, shamans or others thought to hold special powers may be brought in as expert witnesses and sometimes as judges. However, the most important attribute of customary law is its specificity to the local region or village. These traditions can be very deep and resistant to change or imposition from outside influences. Perhaps a prime example in the 21st century is that of the tribal villages in the mountains of Pakistan and parts of Afghanistan that have defied state authority for hundreds of years. Instead, these tribal areas have their own chiefs and their own informal ways of settling infractions and disputes.

Socialist legal systems are those that have arisen on top of civil law systems, for the most part. Certainly this was the case in the Soviet Union and continues to be the case in Cuba and other communist countries, although China is perhaps an exception. Yet even there, the customary legal system was usurped by Western powers in the 19th century and abolished by the revolution of 1949. However, the emergence in the 1980s of China as an industrial and trading nation required that it develop a legal system that would make commerce possible and more efficient. The result has been that its legal system is based essentially on civil law, with criminal law that codifies edicts of the State and procedures that are largely reflective of the inquisitorial system.

Finally, although there are probably no countries that are purely of one or the other legal system, there are quite a number of countries whose legal systems are mixtures of some or all of the preceding. Many African and some South Asian countries are mixtures of customary, civil, common, and Islamic law. Such countries would include, for example, India, Afghanistan, and maybe Egypt.

How Does Your Country Measure Up?

Although for the reasons recounted earlier, comparing the crime and punishment of countries to each other is a very difficult procedure, it is nevertheless important to get a rough idea of how one country compares to the rest of the world. It is probably one of the main reasons people refer to world encyclopedias of any kind, to get a sense of how one fits in the universe.

To provide a very rough glimpse of how a country's crime and punishment compare to the rest of the world, we have provided a snapshot of some major indicators of crime and punishment for each country at the start of each country essay. We have chosen these indicators because they are readily available and offer a reasonably approximate way of ranking countries along a continuum. Of

the crime indicators, murder is chosen as probably the most reliable for making comparisons because its definition is roughly similar across nations, and in most cases, the statistics have been adjusted to fit the UN standard definition of murder for countries reporting their murder rates. Nevertheless, many countries do not report their murder rates. Prison rates are also reasonably reliable for making comparisons, although they too involve great technical difficulties in measurement, considering that the counting of inmates may occur on different days of the year, and a simple accounting on a particular day does not give any indication of the flow of prisoners in and out of the prison over a given period of time. The snapshot indicators provided for each country or region when available are as follow:

- *Type of Legal System*
- *Murder*—murders per 100,000 people
- *Burglary*—those victimized by burglaries per thousand people
- *Corruption*—levels of perceived corruption
- *Human Trafficking*—how much the country is doing to control human trafficking
- *Prison*—number of prisoners per 100,000 population
- *Death Penalty*—whether the country has the death penalty
- *Corporal Punishment*—whether corporal punishment is available to the criminal justice system

Legal System

The types of legal system were compiled from the United Nations *Global Report on Crime and Justice,* supplemented by information from individual country Web sites and from the University of Ottawa Civil Law Section Web site on World Legal Systems at http://www.droitcivil.uottawa.ca/world-legal-systems/eng-tableau.php.

Murder

These are officially reported statistics on murder supplied by countries to the United Nations World Crime Surveys, supplemented where necessary by individual country information plus homicide statistics from the World Health Organization. Most of the statistics were taken from the revised listing supplied by Jan Van Dijk in his book *The World of Crime,* in which he reported the average murder rates for 1998–2002, supplemented by more recent United Nations surveys. Additional data from INTERPOL and individual country sources, where available, sometimes for a slightly different period of years, were also included. However, such small differences should not matter because we know that murder rates are fairly stable over time. The countries are ranked from highest to lowest murder rate (murders per 100,000 people) and then divided into quartiles, with the middle two quartiles classified as "Medium" and the two outer quartiles labeled "High" and "Low." The world distribution of murder rates can be seen in Map 1, Murder around the World.

Burglary

Obtaining reliable rates of property crime, the most common of which is usually referred to as theft, is especially difficult when relying on officially recorded statistics because definitions and enforcement practices vary enormously across nations. We have therefore included measures of victimization of individuals by burglary. These measures are derived from the International Crime Victim Surveys (ICVS), which are interviews or questionnaires asking samples of a population whether they have been victims of particular offenses over a particular number of years (usually the past year). In this case, the samples were households, and the survey was conducted in many countries, although *limited only to urban populations*. Therefore, they do not, of course, represent the country or region as a whole, though they do, perhaps in the case of burglary, represent most of the population of a given country that there are, generally, many more households in urban settings than in rural settings. These data are taken from Van Dijk's *World of Crime.* Countries were ranked according to their burglary rates (number of victimizations reported per 1,000 people) using quartiles, divided into High, Medium, and Low, with Medium defined by the two middle quartiles.

Corruption

The ways in which crime and punishment are eventually perceived by the public and administered by the State are affected by the level of corruption in a particular country. We have therefore included a measure of corruption, a kind of crime that is neither a violent crime nor, strictly speaking, a property crime. Rather, it is a crime against justice itself. There is also the advantage that data on perceived corruption in countries are much more available, thanks to the source of our data, Transparency International at http://www.transparency.org/policy_research/surveys_indices/cpi. This Corruption Perception Index (CPI) is based on the ranking of "180 countries by their perceived levels of corruption, as determined by expert assessments and opinion surveys" according to Transparency International. We have taken these rankings, added some additional countries in some cases where they were not included in the survey, and then divided them into Low, Medium, and High, using quartiles once again.

Human Trafficking

This measure is taken from the U.S. Department of State three-tier listing of countries it classifies as making a strong effort to control human trafficking, making some effort, or making very little effort. The classifications are taken from the U.S. Department of State *Trafficking in Persons Report 2008*, found at http://www.state.gov/g/tip/rls/tiprpt/2008/index.htm. The classification scheme is derived from the U.S. Trafficking Victims Protection Act of 2000 (TVPA), which defines the minimum standards for the elimination of trafficking. It should be noted, however, that our ratings of "High" "Medium," and "Low" in the rates of human trafficking are only very rough because they assume that countries that comply with the U.S. anti-trafficking standards of enforcement will therefore have low levels of human trafficking. This is not always true. The United States,

for example, is rated as low for human trafficking because it complies with the TVPA anti-trafficking act; however, we know that it is a major destination country for trafficked humans. The classifications are as follows:

- *Low Amount of Trafficking* (Tier 1): Countries that fully comply with the U.S. Department of State standards for anti-trafficking enforcement.
- *Medium Amount of Trafficking* (Tier 2): Countries that do not fully comply with the minimum standards but are making significant efforts to bring themselves into compliance.
- *Medium Amount of Trafficking* (Watch List): Countries on Tier 2 requiring special scrutiny because of a high or significantly increasing number of victims, failure to provide evidence of increasing efforts to combat trafficking in persons, or an assessment as Medium based on commitments to take action over the next year.
- *High Amount of Trafficking* (Tier 3): Countries that neither satisfy the minimum standards nor demonstrate a significant effort to come into compliance. Countries in this tier are subject to potential non-humanitarian and non-trade sanctions.

Prison

The prison rate assessments are derived from the International Center for Prison Studies, King's College, London, and found at http://www.kcl.ac.uk/schools/law/research/icps. The rates are of prisoners per 100,000 population, and countries are ranked from high to low and divided into High, Medium, and Low using the quartile method described previously. These were the most up-to-date and thorough statistics available as of 2008. The world distribution of prison rates is depicted in Map 2: Imprisonment around the World.

Death Penalty

About 65 percent of countries have abolished the death penalty either by legislation or in practice. A few have essentially abolished it while retaining it for especially heinous crimes, although it may not have been used for many years. These countries are classified as "maybe" in our assessment of whether the death penalty is available to countries. Thus, the classifications for whether countries have the death penalty as an available punishment are "Yes," "Maybe," and "No." The information has been taken from the Web site *Info Please* at http://www.infoplease.com/ipa/A0777460.html, which in turn has taken its statistics from Amnesty International. The world death penalty distribution may be seen in Map 3: Death Penalty around the World.

Corporal Punishment

The assessments as to whether countries have available to them the use of corporal punishment, either as a sentence for a crime or for use within the prison system for disciplinary purposes, is based on information provided by the Web site http://www.endcorporalpunishment.org/pages/frame.html, which assesses

mainly the legislative steps that countries have taken to prohibit the use of corporal punishment. The Web site covers the use of corporal punishment in homes and schools as well as in the criminal justice system. Its assessments of countries are based almost entirely on whether legislation has been passed prohibiting corporal punishment either as a sentence in criminal justice or as a means of discipline in prisons. The legal situation is often ambiguous because, as with the death penalty, many countries retain the possibility of corporal punishment's use either as a sentence or in prisons but rarely or never resort to it. Thus, there is a category of "maybe" for those countries. Perhaps surprisingly, less than 20 percent of the world's countries have prohibited by legislation the use of corporal punishment either as a sentence for a crime or for use in prison discipline. Like the death penalty, our classification of the availability of corporal punishment is "Yes," "No," or "Maybe." The world use of corporal punishment is presented in Map 4: Corporal Punishment around the World.

Regions of the Four Volumes

The four volumes are broken up into the following regions:

- Volume 1: Africa and the Middle East
- Volume 2: The Americas
- Volume 3: Asia and Pacific
- Volume 4: Europe

There are any number of ways to classify countries into regions of the world. We have mostly relied on a geographical classification based on the United Nations Statistics Division classification system (http://unstats.un.org/unsd/geoinfo/default.htm). But this method is far from satisfactory. Although geography (relatively speaking) remains the same, the borders of countries do not, mostly as a result of political conflict and other factors such as migration. Furthermore, the definition of what makes a country a country is also very difficult because there are many instances where "principalities" (e.g., San Marino) and "independent nations" (e.g., the Navajo Nation in the United States) exist inside larger nations or countries. The complex histories of colonialism and migration have resulted in particular countries containing a vast variety of peoples, cultures, and social arrangements, such that calling them a "country" or even "nation" gives a misleading impression of a cohesive national system governed by one set of laws. Bosnia and Herzogovina are perhaps a prime recent example of this difficulty.

Given the shifting boundaries and definitions of countries and the social, cultural, and political diversity contained in them, allocating such countries to broad regions of the world is obviously even less precise. The final allocation of countries that were hard to classify—Turkey, for example—was admittedly somewhat arbitrary. We finally placed Turkey, along with Georgia, in Asia, not Europe. And we located countries of the Middle East (itself a very difficult region to define in both geographical and political terms) along with Africa in Volume 1. A number of the countries classified in the Middle Eastern region could just

as easily be placed in Asia, and others are geographically located in North Africa. And the variety of countries found in the Asia and Pacific volume is also vast in terms of both geography and culture; New Zealand and Australia, for example, have much more in common with Europe, from a historical and cultural point of view, than they do with their near and distant neighbors in Asia (although this is probably changing). Thus, comparing regions on any number of crime and punishment factors is fraught with even greater difficulties than comparing individual countries. Some commonalities and patterns, however, do emerge when one peruses the world maps that are provided. It is likely, as editors to the respective volumes point out, that these patterns reflect the colonial past of these regions, although there are no doubt other explanations related to local culture, migration patterns, and political history.

About the Contributors

We have drawn on a variety of authors to contribute to these four volumes. In some cases, these authors are professionals who work for their governments, but in other cases (the majority), these authors are independent scholars. The objectivity of reports written by those who work for governments may perhaps be questioned, but on the other hand, government officials have much greater access to information and statistics than do outsiders. With a couple of important exceptions, all governments, by and large, have a monopoly on crime and punishment information. The exceptions are the international crime-victim surveys described earlier that are conducted mostly apart from governments, because they do not necessarily depend on officially recorded statistics by criminal justice officials. However, more government departments are conducting their own victimization surveys because some governments in the past have been embarrassed by the findings. Various nongovernmental watch groups, such as Amnesty International and Transparency International, also collect crime and punishment information and it is part of their mission to apply value judgments and criticism to governments and their administrators. As editors, we have tried in these chapters, as far as possible, to avoid either advocacy on behalf of the government's interest or criticism of governments, although in some cases the criminality and punitive practices of governments cannot be ignored.

—Graeme R. Newman
University at Albany

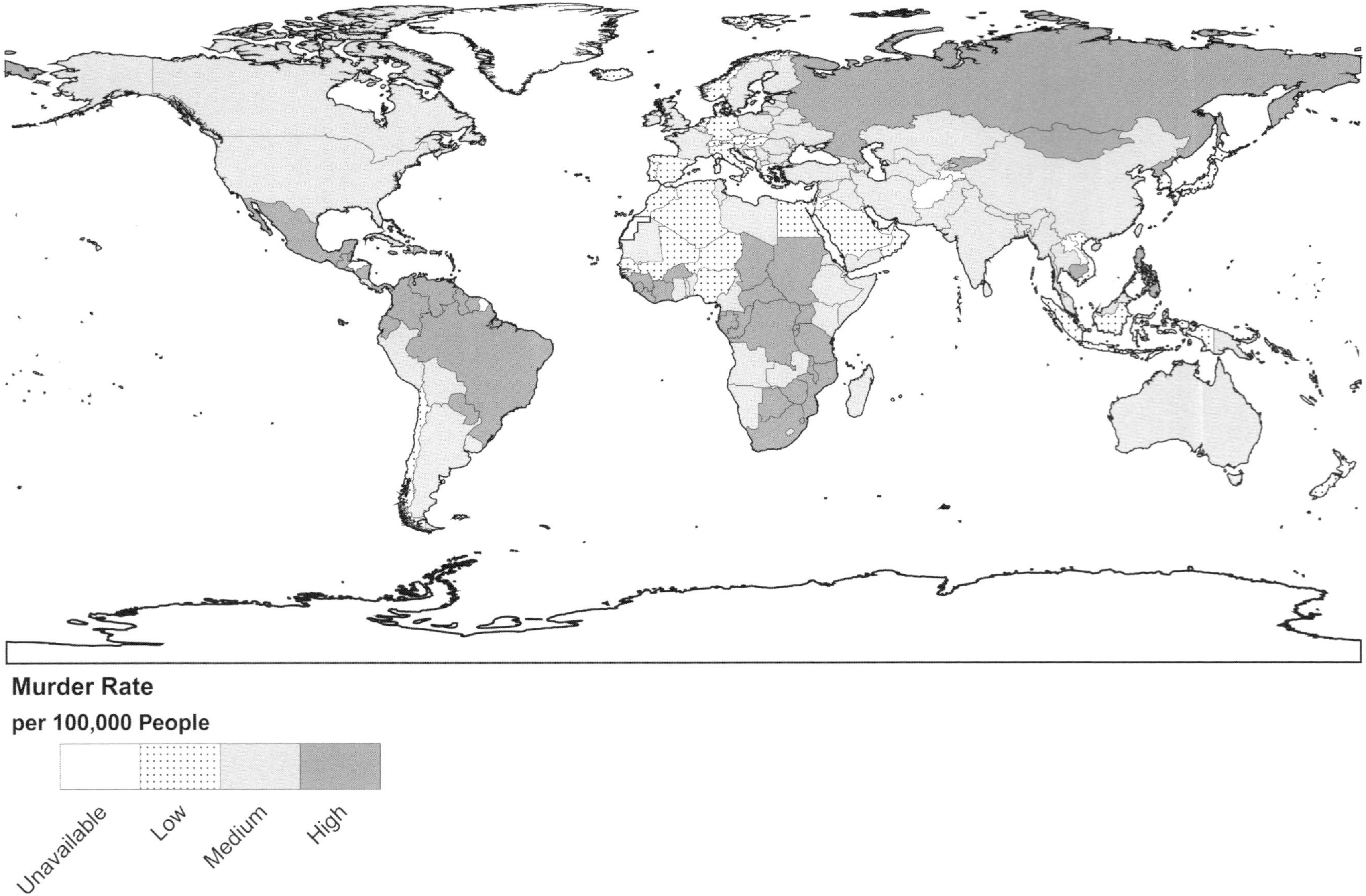

Murder around the World

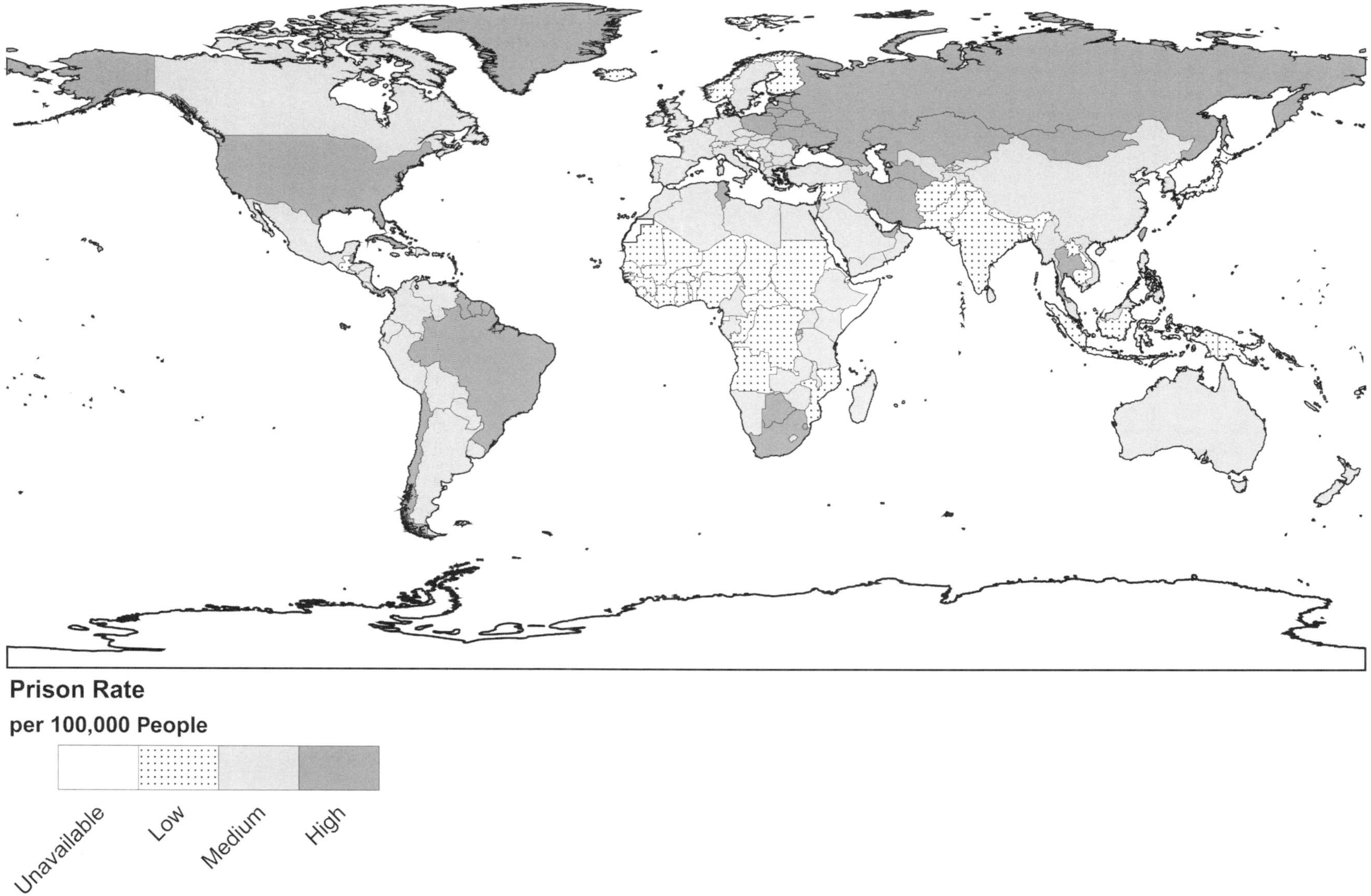

Imprisonment around the World

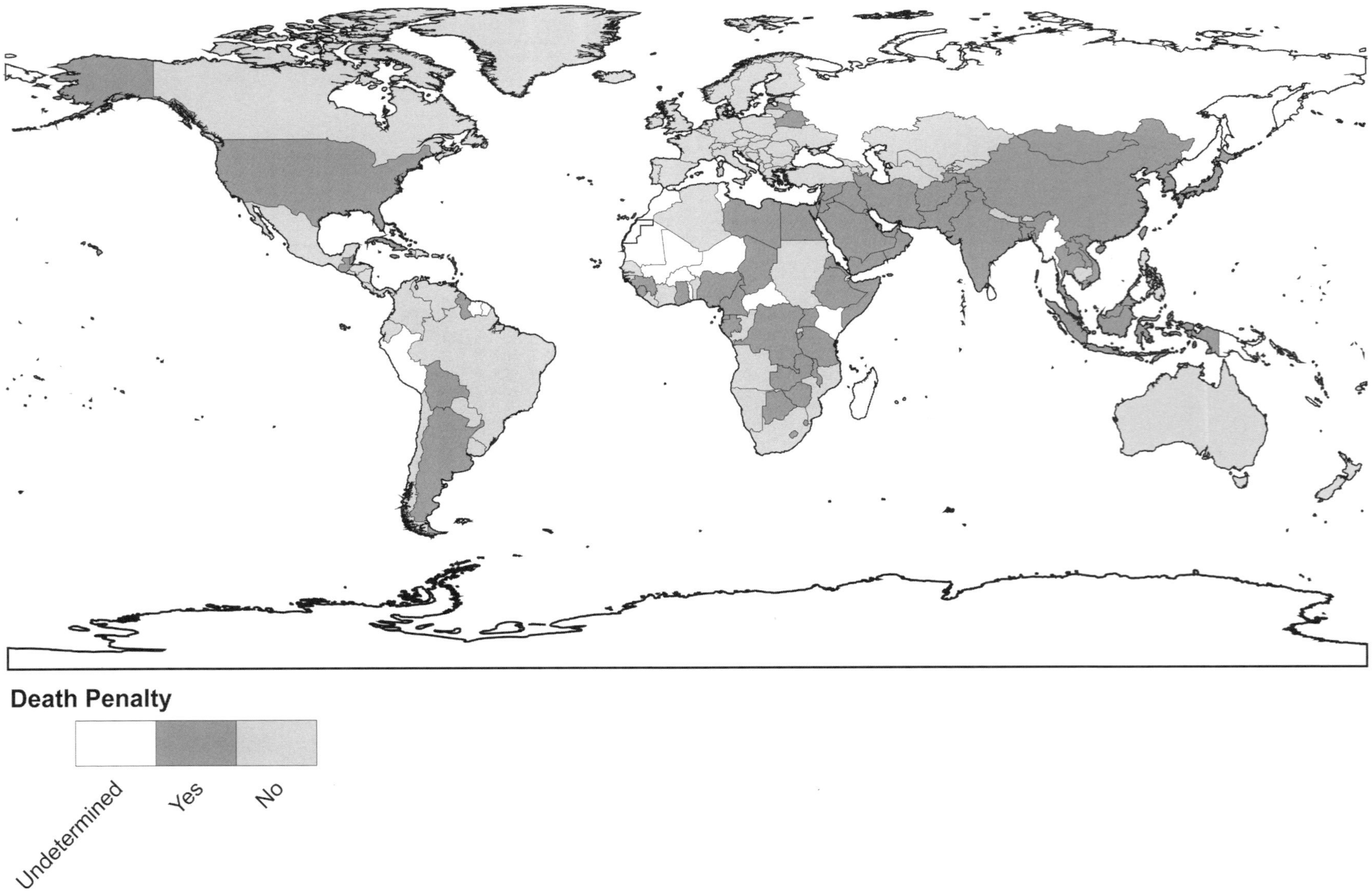

Death Penalty around the World

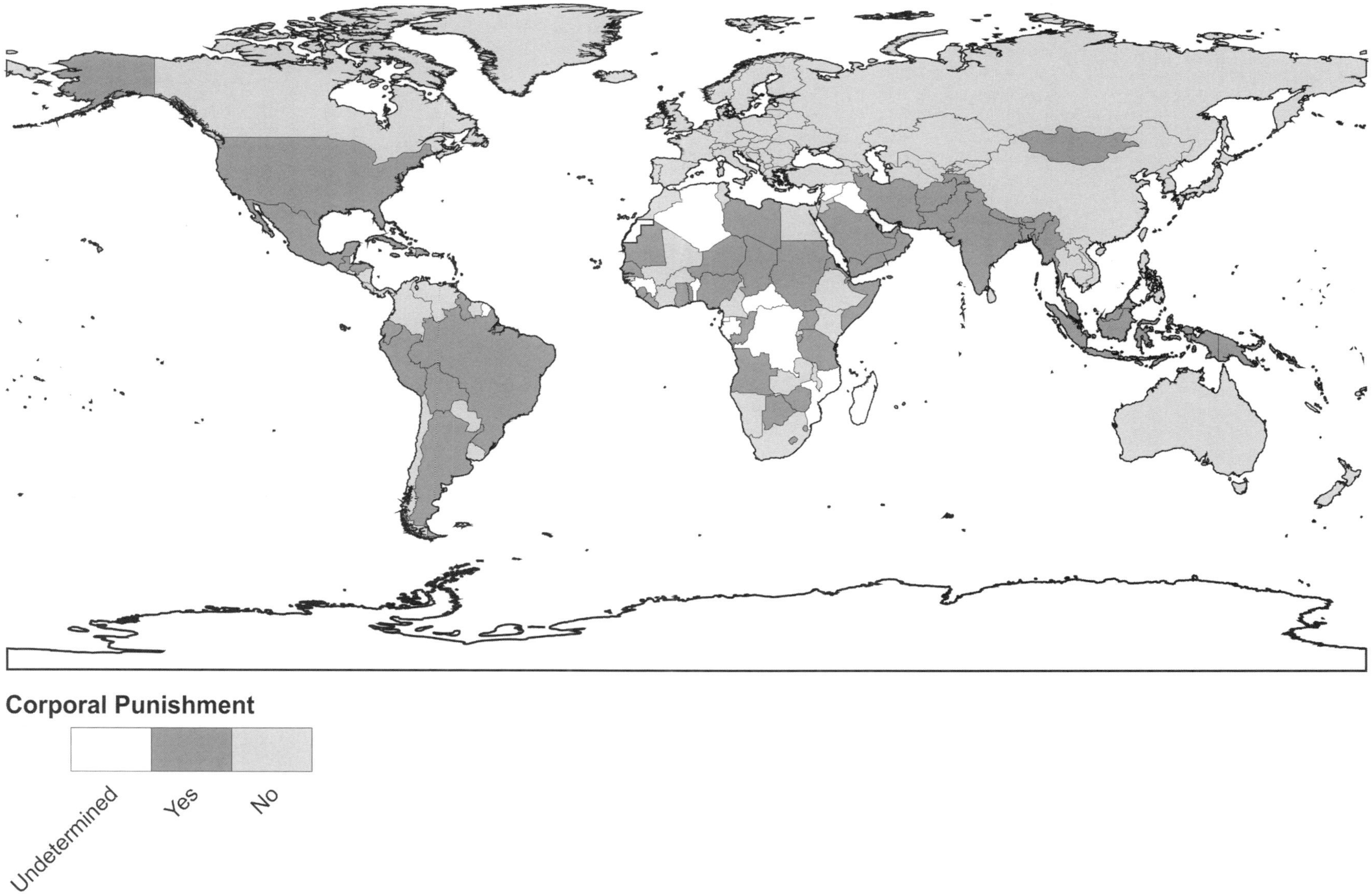

Corporal Punishment around the World

Introduction

Volume 4 of *Crime and Punishment around the World* includes entries on 56 European countries and legal entities. It contains all Member States of the Council of Europe, with the exceptions of Armenia, Georgia, and Azerbaijan—which, for technical reasons, were included in Volume 3: Asia and Pacific—and Iceland. It also includes essays on territories such as Gibraltar; the Åland, Faroe, Guernsey, Man, Svalbard and Jan Mayen Islands; as well as the Vatican; and four entries for the United Kingdom (England, Northern Ireland, Scotland, and Wales).

Going through these essays, the reader will probably be surprised by the huge diversity of the European criminal justice systems. A traditional distinction, whose origins can be traced back to Roman times, can be made between countries that apply the common law system (the United Kingdom and Ireland) and countries that apply the civil law system (the rest of Europe), which was inspired by Roman law. However, this apparent uniformity in continental Europe hides differences that in many cases are due to historical reasons. In this context, the collapse of the Soviet Union has played a major role on crime and justice in contemporary Europe. It had an influence on crime opportunities and crime rates, on the evolution of prison population rates, and on the criminal justice system in general because, since the 1990s, most Central and Eastern European countries have adopted new criminal codes.

In the following paragraphs, we will comment on the European situation according to the main snapshot indicators described by Graeme Newman in the General Introduction to *Crime and Punishment around the World.* We will also include a series of suggested readings on crime and justice in Europe and Web sites where data on these issues can be downloaded. Additional general works on world crime and punishment can be found in the General Bibliography.

Europe and the Death Penalty

One of the distinctive factors of Europe is that all countries have abolished corporal punishment and that all the Member States of the Council of Europe have abolished the death penalty or introduced a moratorium on its application. The Council of Europe is an international organization founded in 1949 by 10 countries and that, in 2010, has 47 member countries. Thus, it includes all European countries with the exception of Belarus. Its main mission is to protect human rights, pluralist democracy, and the rule of law.

The Council of Europe's Parliamentary Assembly has played a major role in the abolition of the death penalty, particularly through the adoption of Protocol No. 6 to the European Convention on Human Rights (ECHR), which entered into force on March 1, 1985, and provides for the abolition of the death penalty in peacetime. Article 1 of that protocol states that "The death penalty shall be abolished. No-one shall be condemned to such penalty or executed."

In 1985, the Council of Europe counted 21 Member States and, since then, it has been an obligation for all countries seeking membership of the council to comply with Protocol 6. As a consequence, with the exception of Belarus, there have been no executions in Europe since 1997.

Moreover, on July 1, 2003, Protocol No. 13 to the ECHR entered into force. This protocol abolishes the death penalty under all circumstances, which implies that such penalty shall be applied even for acts committed in time of war or imminent threat of war. Only Azerbaijan and Russia have not signed the protocol, while Armenia, Latvia, and Poland have signed it but not yet ratified it. However, with the exception of Russia, which introduced a moratorium on the death penalty, and Latvia, which abolished the death penalty for ordinary crimes but kept it for crimes committed in wartime, all the Council of Europe Member States have abolished the death penalty.

Homicide in Europe

In the 2000s, Europe had a median of less than 2 completed intentional homicides per 100,000 inhabitants. When attempts are included, the median is still lower than 4 homicides per 100,000 inhabitants, according to the 2006 *European Sourcebook of Crime and Criminal Justice Statistics.* This means that, in a comparative perspective, European homicide rates are quite low.

The information presented in the map on page xxxiv may be misleading because the rates have been calculated on the basis of both completed and attempted homicide, and the way in which the latter is registered varies widely across Europe. For example, in the Netherlands and Scotland, less than 20 percent of the total homicides are completed homicides, while in other countries they represent more than 80 percent of them. Thus, international comparisons of homicide rates should only be conducted using the rates for completed homicide, excluding attempts. When such comparisons are made, it can be seen that the rates in Central and Eastern Europe are slightly higher than in Western Europe.

Corruption in Europe

According to the 2009 Corruption Perceptions Index, 12 out of the 20 countries with the lowest levels of perceived corruption are Western European countries. This cluster includes the five Scandinavian countries, Switzerland, the Netherlands, Luxembourg, Germany, Ireland, Austria, and the United Kingdom. The only countries with a high level of perceived corruption are Russia (146 out of 180 countries) and Belarus (139). In the rest of the continent the rates are predominantly low, or medium.

European Prison Population Rates

In a comparative perspective, Europe is a continent with a low prison population rate. As shown in the map on page xxxv, the highest prison population rates can be found in Eastern Europe, in particular, in the former Soviet republics. However, a more detailed analysis of prison populations in Europe, based on the *Council of Europe Annual Penal Statistics* (SPACE), shows that between 2000 and 2007 the rates of these countries have been decreasing, while during the same period, prison population rates have slightly increased in Western Europe. The same analysis shows that the number of foreign detainees is very low in Central and Eastern European countries, while they are overrepresented in Western Europe, especially in countries exposed to important flows of illegal immigrants as well as in entry and transit countries for drug trafficking. The situation is aggravated by the fact that many foreigners cannot benefit from alternatives to pretrial and imprisonment because they are not legally established in the country where they are imprisoned.

Learn More

Both for authors who believe that criminology was born with the publication of *On Crimes and Punishments,* by Cesare Beccaria, in 1764, and for those who believe that the scientific era of criminology starts with the Italian Positivist School by the end of the 19th century, Europe, and in particular Italy, is the birthplace of criminology. Nowadays, the main forum for European criminologists is the European Society of Criminology (http://www.esc-eurocrim.org), and a lot of relevant information on crime and punishment in Europe, including the programs of the annual conferences, is available on its Web site.

Readers interested in obtaining data on crime in Europe can download the databases of the different editions of the *European Sourcebook of Crime and Criminal Justice Statistics* (www.europeansourcebook.org), which includes police, prosecution, conviction, and correctional statistics since 1990 as well as some data on victimization. Detailed data on prisons in Europe since 1983 can be found in the Council of Europe Annual Penal Statistics (www.coe.int/prison). Victimization data for many European countries are available through the databases of the International Crime Victim Survey (ICVS), which can be downloaded directly from the UNICRI Web site (http://www.unicri.it/wwd/analysis/icvs/data.php). Many European countries have also participated in the first and second wave of the International Self-Reported Delinquency Study (ISRD), but the databases are not available yet.

In recent years, a lot of publications have analyzed different aspects of crime and punishment in Europe. Of particular interest are the country reports included in different issues of the *European Journal of Criminology* as well as some special issues of the *European Journal on Criminal Policy and Research,* specifically the ones on crime trends in Western and Eastern European Countries (Vol. 10[2–3], 2004) and prosecution and diversion within criminal justice systems in Europe (Vol. 14[2–3], 2008). The European Commission for the Efficiency of Justice, which belongs to the Council of Europe, has conducted and published in 2008 an Evaluation of European Judicial Systems (http://www.coe.int/t/dghl/cooperation/cepej/evaluation/default_en.asp). Some other useful sources of information are listed below.

Aebi, M. F. (2010). "Methodological Issues in the Comparison of Police Recorded Crime Rates." In *International Handbook of Criminology,* edited by S. Shoham, P. Knepper, and M. Kett, pp. 209–226. London: Routledge.

Aebi, M. F., K. Aromaa, B. Aubusson de Cavarlay, G. Barclay, B. Gruszczynska, H. von Hofer, V. Hysi, J.-M. Jehle, M. Killias, P. Smit, and C. Tavares. (2006). *European Sourcebook of Crime and Criminal Justice Statistics—2006.* 3rd ed. Den Haag: Boom Juridische Uitgevers.

Aebi, M. F., and A. Linde. (2009). *Review of the Current Situation in Respect of the Collection of Survey Data on Victimization.* Lausanne: Université de Lausanne.

Aebi, M. F., and N. Delgrande. (2009). *Council of Europe Annual Penal Statistics SPACE I: Survey 2007.* Strasbourg: Council of Europe.

Delgrande, N., and M. F. Aebi. (2009). "European Prisons: Stability or Change?" *Criminology in Europe: Newsletter of the European Society of Criminology* 8(3), 1, 17–19.

Robert, P., ed. (2009a). *Comparing Crime Data in Europe: Official Crime Statistics and Survey Based Data.* Brussels: VUBPRESS Brussels University Press.

Robert, P., ed. (2009b). *Evaluating Safety and Crime Prevention Policies in Europe.* Brussels: VUBPRESS Brussels University Press.

Zauberman, R., ed. (2009a). *Self-Reported Crime and Deviance Studies in Europe.* Brussels: VUBPRESS Brussels University Press.

Zauberman, R., ed. (2009b). *Victimization and Insecurity in Europe.* Brussels: VUBPRESS Brussels University Press.

—Marcelo F. Aebi and Véronique Jaquier
University of Lausanne

Acknowledgements

The editors of this volume would like to thank Miriam Pina, currently at the University of Porto, who collaborated with us during the first steps of this project.

Country Key to Europe Maps

Åland Islands	AX	Latvia	LV
Albania	AL	Liechtenstein	LI
Andorra	AD	Lithuania	LT
Austria	AT	Luxembourg	LU
Belarus	BY	Macedonia, Former Yugoslav Republic of (FYRM)	MK
Belgium	BE	Malta	MT
Bosnia and Herzegovina	BA	Moldova	MD
Bulgaria	BG	Monaco	MC
Croatia	HR	Montenegro	ME
Cyprus	CY	Netherlands	NL
Czech Republic	CZ	Norway	NO
Denmark	DK	Poland	PL
Estonia	EE	Portugal	PT
Faroe Islands	FO	Romania	RO
Finland	FI	Russia	RU
France	FR	San Marino	SM
Germany	DE	Serbia	RS
Gibraltar	GI	Slovak Republic	SK
Greece	GR	Slovenia	SI
Guernsey	GG	Spain	ES
Hungary	HU	Svalbard and Jan Mayen Islands	SJ
Iceland	IS	Sweden	SE
Ireland	IE	Switzerland	CH
Man, Isle of	IM	Ukraine	UA
Italy	IT	United Kingdom	GB
Jersey	JE	Vatican City	VA

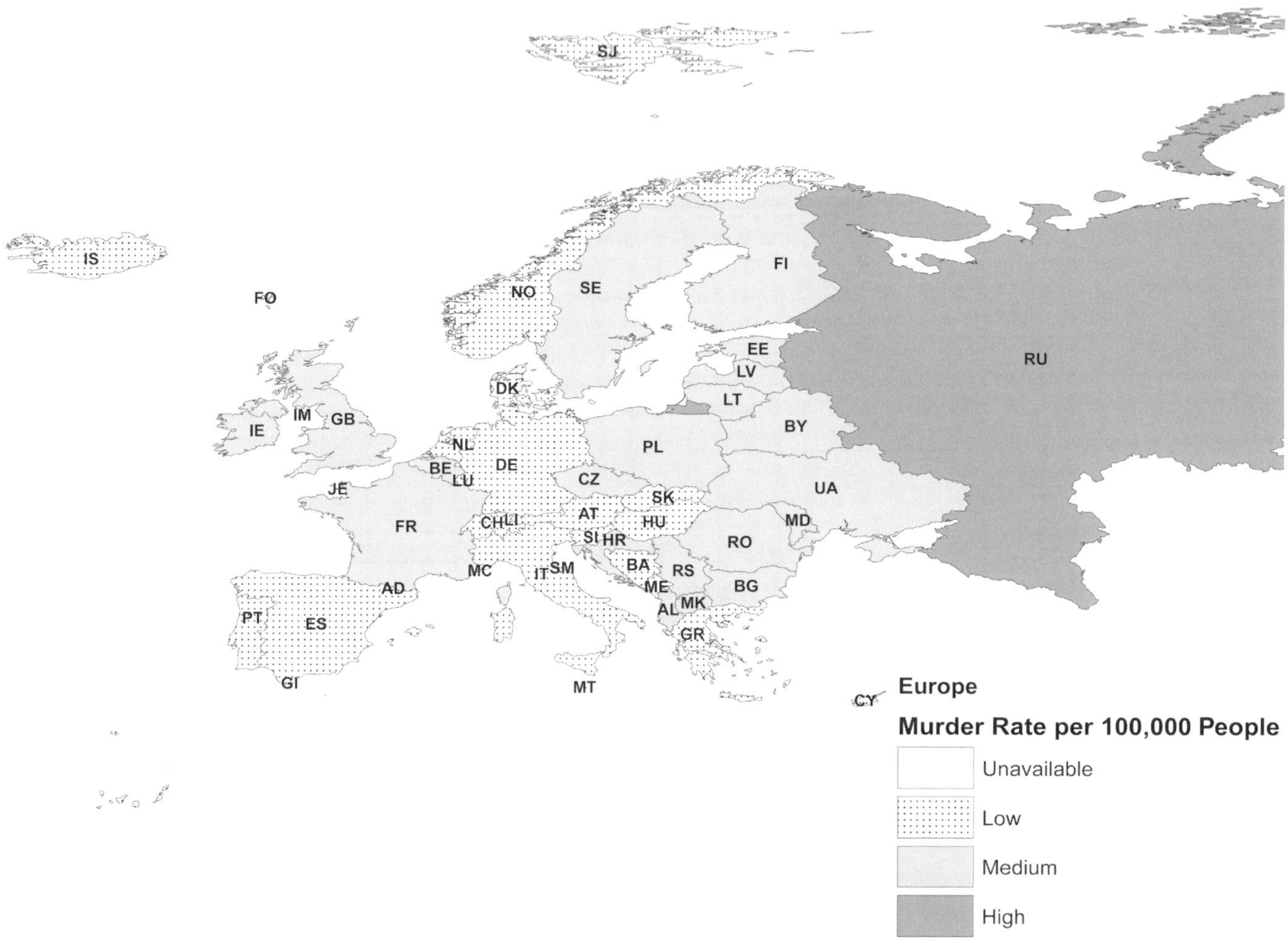

Murder in Europe

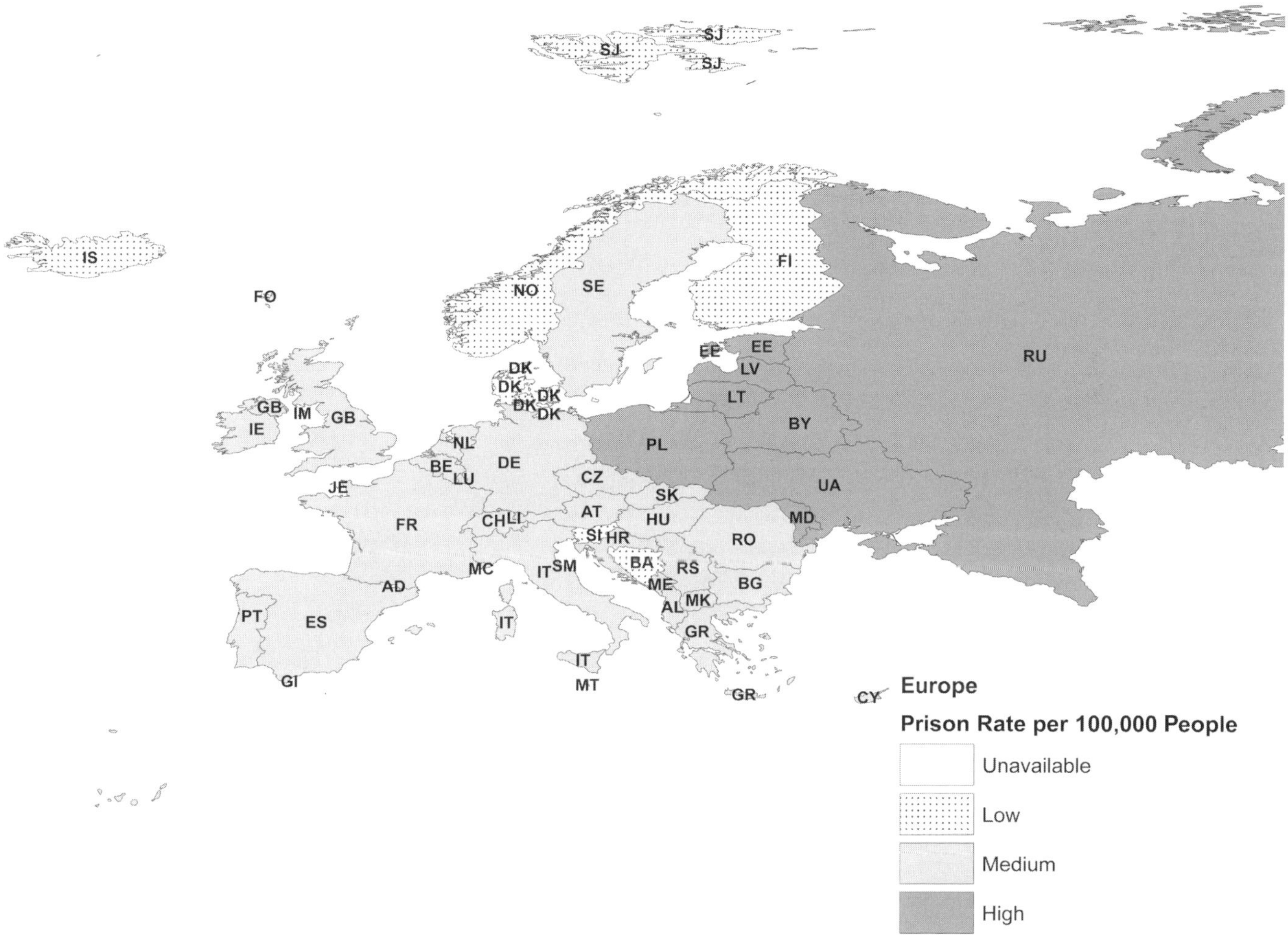

Imprisonment in Europe

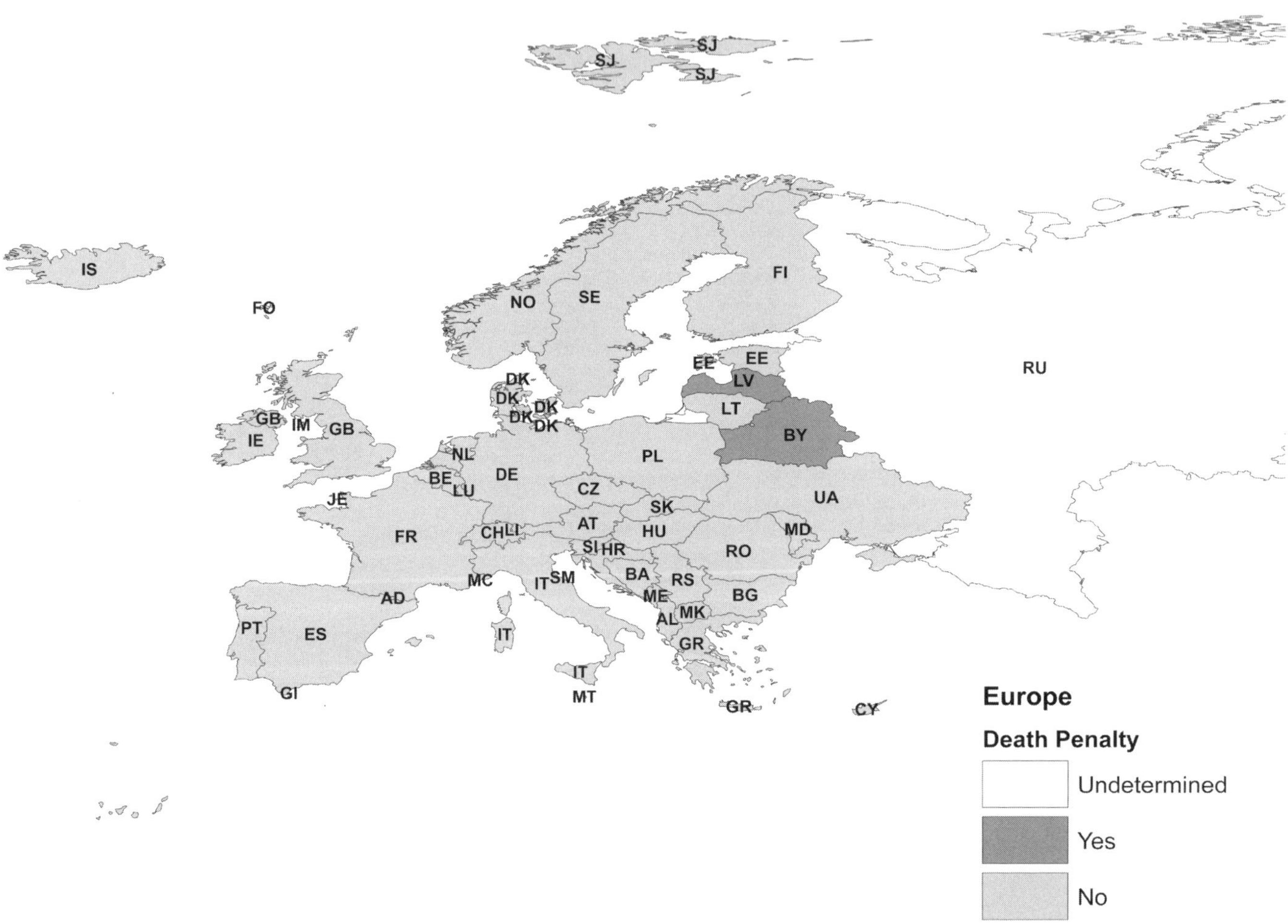

Death Penalty in Europe

Europe

Åland Islands

Legal System: Civil
Death Penalty: No
Corporal Punishment: No

Background

The Åland Islands became a self-governing part of Finland in 1922 after World War I. The islands have a home rule system, which means that they themselves pass legislation in a number of areas, whereas other fields are regulated by Finnish law. As a self-governing part of Finland, Åland has been authorized to consider certain types of international treaties by itself. Åland has, for instance, decided not to be a part of the European Union even if Finland joined it in 1994.

If you are born on the Åland Islands, you automatically have two citizenships, Finnish and the so-called homeland-right of the Åland Islands, *åländsk hembygdsrätt.* Without homeland-right, you are not able to buy land or residence on the islands. A person who has lived on the islands for five years can apply for citizenship, but it is quite difficult to receive. Young men with homeland-right are excused from joining the Finnish Army, which otherwise is mandatory for all men when reaching the age of 18.

Åland has its own police department, which is under the Ministry of Domestic Affairs, like all the other police districts in Finland. Its jurisdiction is the whole of Åland Islands, and it deals with keeping order, doing investigations, and other police work in connection with criminal cases. Because the landscape is so varied, the police force is split in three groups, one located in Mariehamn, one located in the archipelago, and one located in the countryside.

Crime

Classification of Crimes

Finnish law applies to crimes committed in Finland, to Finnish ships or aircrafts, to foreign ships on Finnish territorial waters, and foreign aircrafts in Finnish air territory. The Finnish Penal Code also applies to crimes committed against Finnish citizens by Finnish citizens in Finland or abroad whenever international commitments apply. People visiting the Åland Island are subject to the jurisdiction of the island, where the regulations differ from those of Finland. For instance, Åland has different punishments for traffic offenses. Most of the separate regulations for punishment are focused on crimes against the environment, road and sea traffic offenses as well as crimes against personal integrity.

A person may be found guilty of an offense only on the basis of an act that has been specifically criminalized in law at the time of its commission. The punishment and other sanction under criminal law must be based on law. Furthermore, the act has to be intentional to be punishable. Intent is based on the offender's idea whether or not the crime will be successful or at least most likely successful. If the consequence is the result of recklessness, the responsibility will be reduced considering the circumstances. An accident is not punishable. An attempt, however, is punishable but not as harsh as a completed offense and the sentence also depends on the type of crime and circumstances.

According to the Finnish Penal Code, the offender has to have reached the age of 15 at the time of the act to be criminally responsible. The offender is not criminally responsible, if he or she at the time of the act, due to mental illness, severe mental deficiency, a serious mental disturbance, or a serious disturbance of consciousness, is not able to understand the factual nature or unlawfulness of his or her act. Intoxication or other temporary mental disturbance induced by the offender is not taken into account in the assessment of criminal responsibility unless there are particularly weighty reasons for this. The court can waive the punishment due to the mental condition of the person accused of an offense, and the court shall then, unless this is obviously unnecessary, submit for clarification the question of the offender's needs.

Violent crimes between spouses have become more common. Crimes including alcohol and drugs as well as snuff are also more common. Snuff is illegal in Finland, but legal in Sweden and was legal to buy tax free on cruise ships going from Finland to Sweden when mooring in Mariehamn, but the Finnish government prohibited this two years ago. Smuggling snuff has been a big problem since. Nowadays one can possess snuff if it is bought outside Finland, but only for one's own use. Other drugs like cocaine, opium, khat (cathinone), cannabis, and psilocybe mushrooms (widely known as "magic mushrooms") are strictly forbidden to use, sell, grow, or transport.

Crime Statistics

Most crimes are committed by offenders between 21 and 39 years old. According to statistics from the Criminal Sanctions Agency covering early 2003 until the end of 2007, homicide and other crimes of violence were the most common committed by those convicted. Women are approximately 6.9 percent of all prisoners. Homicide and other violent crimes, represent 39 percent of all crimes. Theft, drunk driving, and drug offenses about 14 percent each. Burglary presented about 5 percent of all crimes. According to statistics from the Finnish Police Department, around 600 traffic offenses are reported every year on Åland Island. An average of 80 percent of all the cases are solved according to the Finnish Police Department. Statistics of all crimes committed on the Åland Islands show that most of the crimes are committed during the summer months, June, July, and August. Over 60 percent of about 600 criminal cases, in the district court on Åland during 2008, were related to alcohol. The rest were mostly drug-related offenses, drug offenses, and minor thefts to get money for drugs. The offender was intoxicated in almost every case concerning assault and battery, both when within the family or other cases.

Finding of Guilt

Finland has a number of different methods dealing with criminal offenses. The most common way is going to trial. Minor cases in the district court, where the highest sentence is a maximum of one year in prison, are resolved by one judge and three members of the community. If the vote is a draw the judge's opinion matters. Major offenses are handled by three judges. If the case is clear and both parties agree, the case can be settled by written consent. Another method to ease the burden on the courts is settlement or reconciliation between victim and offender. It is a voluntary process often used before going to court in minor criminal cases. It has been an effective way to make the court process faster and reduce costs. This process, however, has not been a part of the court system on Åland. In 2005 some members of the Åland Parliament proposed making dispute settlement a part of the system. The proposal was dismissed.

A person suspected of an offense has the right to take care of the defense on his or her own in criminal investigations and in a trial. On the request of the suspect, a defense counsel must be appointed. Depending on the offender's income, the state has a duty to provide the offender with legal assistance. To assist someone at a trial, one has to have a master's in law. The language of the trial is Finnish or

Swedish depending on the offender's mother tongue and if necessary the state has to provide an interpreter. Everyone also has the right to a speedy trial. The time between prosecution and trial must be within 2 weeks. If the charges are against a juvenile, the trial should preferably happen within 30 days.

A person suspected of an offense can be taken into custody by the police for no more than 72 hours. If no charges are brought before that, the police have to free the suspect. The public prosecutor must bring a charge always when there is a prima facia case against the suspect. But in case of a prosecution, the suspect can be held as long as the trial is not settled.

Juveniles are treated a little differently. Young offenders under the age of 18 can be sentenced to a juvenile sentence of a minimum of four months and maximum of one year. The punishment consists of supervised discussions, assignments, and programs that support and develop the social ability and capacity in society. Assistance at the workplace can also be a part of the punishment. Those juveniles who are sentenced to prison usually serve their time in special juvenile facilities.

Cases from Turku Court of Appeal and the Supreme Court that concern Åland are mostly offenses against the road traffic regulations, offenses against building regulations, or cases concerning homeland-right, though there are some exceptions. In one case from Turku Court of Appeal an offender had been driving a motorcycle that was not registered as it should be according to the law. The offender had been driving without a helmet with 1.18 percentage of alcohol in his blood. The highest amount allowed is 0.5. The Åland district court classed this as drunk driving and the other offenses as traffic misdemeanors and sentenced the man to a €1,050 (US$1,320) fine. The case was taken to the Turku Court of Appeal where it surprisingly was dismissed. After hearing a couple of witnesses and a statement from the offender, the court found that the offender had bought his motorcycle from a bicycle salesman, and that it had very low power and almost could be considered a bicycle. The court found further that the offender could not be held responsible since it was not obvious that the vehicle was a motorcycle that one has a duty to register. Furthermore, Finnish law allows people to ride bicycles while drunk as long as nobody else's life is at risk.

Punishment

Types of Punishment

The Åland Islands has for the most part the same kind of punishments as Finland. The general penalties are imprisonment, probation, community service, fines, and summary penal fees. The special penalties for public officials are dismissal and warning. The most common punishment in Finland is still fines. Almost all minor offenses are punished with day-fines. The system is progressive, meaning that the amount of one day-fine depends on the offender's daily income. One can be sentenced to pay a fine of 120 times the day-fine, based on the amount counted from the offender's income. Fines can also be converted to a prison sentence if necessary. Another type of fine is the summary penal fee, which is a fixed fine often given for minor offenses against road traffic or sea traffic regulations. A sentence of imprisonment may be passed either for a fixed period or for life. A sentence of imprisonment for a fixed period may be at least 14 days and at most 12 years or, when sentencing to a joint punishment, at most 15 years. For a killing to be considered as a murder and given a life sentence, the killing has to be very harsh, otherwise it is seen as manslaughter, for which the sentence is usually 8 to 12 years. Other prison sentences, for example, serious theft, burglary, or robbery can vary, depending if it is first time, or repeat offenders, from 2 to 4 or 6 years of prison. The Finnish Penal Code has a long chapter on drug offenses, which are considered as very serious offenses. For trying to produce or for producing, or for growing or dealing the sentences are up to 4 years of prison. If the crime is considered serious, the sentence can be as much as more than 10 years.

Prison

Finland has 41 prisons all over the country. The Åland Islands, though, has no prison. If an offender is sentenced to time in prison by the district court of Åland, he or she will spend time in the prison in Turku. Appeals go to the Turku Court of Appeal, mostly because the working language is Swedish, even though the district court on Åland Island comes under the administration of the Department of Justice in Helsinki. According to statistics from December 31, 2007, Finland held around 3,540 prisoners at that time, and 77 percent of them were doing their time in a closed facility, while 23 percent were placed in an open facility. People working in the prisons are almost as many; according to the same source there were around 2,818 officers and employees.

Anna Gustafson

Further Reading

Åland Parliament: http://www.government.ax.
Finnish Judicial System: http://www.oikeus.fi.
Finnish Penal Law and the Code of Judicial Procedure: http://www.finlex.fi.
Finnish Police Department: http://www.poliisi.fi.

Albania

Legal System: Civil
Murder: Medium
Burglary: Medium
Corruption: Medium
Human Trafficking: Medium
Prison Rate: Medium
Death Penalty: No
Corporal Punishment: No

Background

Albania, with Tirana as its capital, is situated in southeastern Europe, to the west of the Balkan Peninsula. Until 1912, Albania was under Ottoman rule. Albania proclaimed its independence on November 28, 1912, and fought against fascism in World War II. Up to 1992, it was under the dictatorship of the proletariat and was one of the most isolated countries in Eastern and Central Europe. With the fall of the Soviet system Albania took the path of pluralist democracy and a market economy. From 1990 to 1997, Albania went through several mass exoduses of Albanians chiefly toward Italy, Greece, and neighboring countries and several other countries of Europe. More than 1,200,000 Albanians live in Italy, Greece, and other countries of Europe, the United States, and Canada. In 2007, Albania's population was 3,601,000 inhabitants.

Legal System

Until the proclamation of independence, Ottoman laws were enforced in certain areas of Albania and the common law in others (not written, but later collected and codified). After the proclamation of independence, the first Albanian government, known by the name of *Vlora*, prepared several important laws concerning judicial organization, the establishment of a jury and the procedures for its selection.

During the period of the republic (1925–1928), there were also religious courts and juries. In the period of the monarchy (1928–1939), the judicial system was organized in the form of courts of peace, which deliberated on contraventions and small cases, first instance courts, courts of appeal, and the Supreme Court. The prosecution was under the authority of the chief prosecutor and under the management of the ministry of justice. Judges and prosecutors were selected by a commission and appointed by a royal decree.

During the fascist occupation of Albania (1939–1944), the existing judicial structures were left untouched. Meanwhile, partisan courts were established adjudicating crime and culpability in the context of the National Liberation War. Major reforms occurred in which regional courts, neighborhood courts, rural, and urban courts were reorganized in 1968 and 1973. The Constitution of 1976, known otherwise as the Constitution of the People's Socialist Republic of Albania, was introduced to overtly defend a state based on the dictatorship of the proletariat.

Having emerged from the totalitarian communist system in 1992, Albania today is a country with a new democracy. The Main Constitutional Provisions on Human Rights and Freedom were approved in 1993, and after 1995, all fundamental laws were approved such as the Criminal Code, the Civil Code, the Labor Code, the Family Code, the Criminal Procedure Code, and the Civil Procedure Code. The Constitution of the Republic of Albania approved on November 28, 1998, regulates the judiciary in Albania.

Courts

The judicial power in Albania is exercised by the first instance courts, courts of appeal, and the Supreme Court. Judicial district courts and the Court for Serious Crimes are first instance courts. Judicial district courts are organized and operate according to the judicial districts throughout the territory of Albania. The first instance courts handle preliminary investigations and juridical relations with foreign authorities. One judge adjudicates criminal offenses that are punishable by a fine or a prison term of no longer than 7 years, while a panel composed of three judges adjudicates the rest of the criminal offenses.

During the period of 2002–2007, there was an increase in the number of cases reviewed by the first instance courts. Criminal cases occupied 14–19 percent of the total of court-tried cases. The rest were civil, family, and trading cases. There was an increase of the volume of criminal cases from year to year, due to the rise in crime rates but also to changes in criminal procedures after 2001.

Courts of appeal and the Court of Appeal for Serious Crimes are second instance courts. Courts of appeal, composed of a panel of three judges, examine in second instance cases tried by the judicial district courts. Complaints against decisions of the first instance courts are also tried by these courts. During the period of 2005–2007, the number of appeals decreased from 2,608 in 2006 to 1,805 in 2007. The right to appeal rests with the prosecutor and the defendant. The defendants make the majority of complaints.

The Supreme Court has original jurisdiction in hearing by the General Prosecution Office on important cases involving members of the government, of Parliament, of the Supreme Court, deputy ministries, the general prosecutor, and his or her assistants (being judges or prosecutors), and it also has review jurisdiction. The Supreme Court is composed of a panel of five judges. During the period of 2005–2007, there was a decline in the number of appeals. The majority of appeals have been submitted by the defendants, though in 2007, the number of appeals registered was 54, with 31 of them exercised by the prosecutor.

In 2003, the Court for Serious Crimes and the Court of Appeal for Serious Crimes were established to examine high-risk crimes, defined in the law as crimes against humanity (murders, trafficking of human beings, trafficking of narcotics, trafficking of children, terrorism-related criminal offenses, etc.), and crimes committed by armed gangs and criminal organizations. These courts adjudicate also cases of such crimes committed by juveniles. Both courts are organized and function in one or more judicial districts. Currently, there is a Court of First Instance for Serious Crimes in Tirana, and a second one attached to the Court of Appeal in Tirana. The First Instance Court for Serious Crimes adjudicates by the means of a five-judge panel. During 2007, this court tried 124 cases and it had completed 62 of them.

In addition, there are currently 21 district courts. In 2007, there were 270 judges. There are also 6 courts of appeal and one Supreme Court. Military criminal courts continued to operate until 2007 when they were abolished. Criminal cases according to the military criminal code are currently tried by the criminal courts. The president of Albania, based on the proposal made by the High Council of Justice, appoints judges at first instance courts and courts of appeal, while the Assembly of Albania elects Supreme Court judges based on the proposal of the president.

There is a Constitutional Court, which is not part of the judiciary system but guarantees adherence to the Constitution and provides final interpretations of it. This court consists of nine members appointed by the president with the consent of Parliament. The right to put the Constitutional Court in motion rests with the president, the prime minister, no less than one-fifth of Parliament members, individuals, political parties, and other organizations. In 1999, the institution of the ombudsman was established as an independent constitutional institution protecting the rights, freedom, and legitimate interests of individuals from illegal and inappropriate actions or nonactions of the public administration.

Police

The Albanian police were founded in 1913. Initially part of the military, in 1999, the police became part of the public administration. The police are organized at a central and local level. The general directorate makes up the central level of the police, while regional police directorates, regional border and migration police directorates as well as their subordinate structures make up its local level. Regional police directorates, regional border and migration police directorates, police commissariats, border and migration police commissariats, police stations, and border and migration police stations are also part of the police.

In every region, there is a regional police directorate supporting and supervising police operational activities undertaken by the police commissariats and stations found within the region it manages. Every regional police directorate is composed of police commissariats carrying out operational tasks and duties in compliance with the functions of the police. Police stations are established and operate upon the order of the general director of state police and upon the proposal of the regional police director in certain geographical areas, within the territory of a commissariat. The number of police officers has declined from 12,394 in 2003 to 9,700 in 2007. Specialized departments deal with crime prevention and fight organized crime, financial crime, illegal trafficking, money laundering resulting from illegal activities, domestic violence, and juvenile crime. An Office of National Coordination was established at the Ministry of Interior to fight trafficking of human beings. The Training and Police Schooling Department, Support Services Department, and the Professional Standards' Department provide continuous development and training of police officers in the state police.

Crime

The current Criminal Code is based on the constitutional principles of the rule of law, equality before the law, justice in the assignment of culpability and punishment as well as humanism (article 1/c). The Criminal Code of 1995 lists criminal offenses against life (the person) after those against humanity, followed by criminal offenses against health, sexual crimes, criminal offenses against personal freedom, one's morality and dignity, and so forth.

Currently, there exists a Criminal Civil Code, a Criminal Military Code, and Criminal Procedure Code. After 2001, many new crimes have been legislated, such as illegal trafficking, corruption in the private and public sector, economic crime, and terrorism.

According to the Criminal Code of 1995, the age of criminal responsibility is 14 years old for crimes and 16 years old for criminal contraventions. The maximum juvenile age extends to 18 years old. In 2007, 198 minors were convicted of crimes and 13 for contraventions. The number of adult cases tried at courts in 2007 was 6,268 and the total number convicted was 5,678. In that same year 325 women were convicted of crimes and 130 convicted of contraventions.

Crimes of high social risks are murders, trafficking of human beings and of juveniles, crimes related to narcotics, money laundering, and so forth. Trafficking in human beings, women, and children has been a serious problem since the 1990s. The majority of victims come from the rural areas and from small and poor towns. In recent years, a decline in such crime has been observed. In 2007 there were 10 convictions for trafficking of women for prostitution and 2 for trafficking of minors, compared to 26 and 8, respectively, in 2003.

The most common crimes are offenses against property and economic crime, cultivation and trafficking of narcotics, and transporting of drugs such as heroin. Convictions in 2007 were as follows:

An Albanian police officer stands by new motorcycles, patrol cars, and four-wheel-drive vehicles, provided by the European Union to beef up the country's border security and aid its fight against gangs trafficking in humans, arms, and drugs, Tirana, February 27, 2006. (AP Photo/Hektor Pustina)

Trafficking of cars	17
Trafficking of firearms and ammunition	9
Money laundering	5
Trafficking of drugs	69

The Criminal Code has been amended several times regarding criminal offenses related to narcotics. The law punishes the sale, offer for sale, delivery or receipt in any form, distribution, trading, transport, sending, delivery and possession, except for personal use and in small doses, of narcotic and psychotropic substances as well as seeds of narcotic plants, in contravention to the law or in excess of its content. Trafficking of narcotics may receive harsh sentences with 10–15 years in prison and serious cases of from 10–20 years. Encouraging others to use narcotic or psychotropic substances or using or injecting others without their knowledge or consent is punishable by a prison sentence from 5 to 10 years.

Despite efforts made to fight criminal offenses motivated by vendetta and blood feuds, in some areas of the country murders are still committed out of vendetta and blood feud, although their number has been decreasing.

Finding of Guilt

Rights of the Accused

The criminal procedure system is mainly accusatorial, but there are also elements of the inquisitorial system. The Criminal Code of 1995, designed according to the principles of the European Convention of Human Rights, provides for the right to freedom and security of person, the right to be informed in a language one understands of the reasons for the arrest and any charge against the person, the right to stand trial within 48 hours of the arrest, the right to appeal a decision of the judge determining the security measure, the right to compensation in case of wrongful arrest or detention, the right to a fair and public trial, the right to a trial within a reasonable time, the right of juvenile defendants to legal assistance, presumption of innocence until proved guilty, the right to a review of the decision of the court, and the right not to be tried twice for the same offense.

Justice is administered by the courts through normal and special trials: direct and expedited trials. A direct trial can take place if a person is caught in the act of commission and the public prosecutor submits within 48 hours to the court a request for arrest and trial. An expedited trial can be requested by the defendant or his or her representative and is to be decided by the court. In practice, expedited trials are the more common.

The defendant has the right to defend himself or herself or through an attorney. If the person does not have the required means, he or she is provided free legal representation. The defendant is entitled to choose no more than two legal representatives. In the case of a defendant with no representation or left without an attorney, the proceeding body provides him or her with another attorney if he or she requests one. The courthouse or the prosecution cannot continue proceedings in absence of the attorney.

Legal and consultation services are also offered by several nonprofit organizations to the poor, children, victims of domestic violence and trafficking, victims of public administration violation of human rights. In December 2008, the Law on Legal Assistance was passed, enabling for the destitute free legal representation in criminal, civil, and administrative proceedings as well as juveniles in need of compulsory representation.

Investigation

Criminal investigations take place in two stages: preliminary investigations and court reviews. The prosecutor pursues criminal prosecution, conducts the investigation, checks on preliminary investigations, brings charges before the court, and takes measures for the execution of decisions in compliance with the rules determined in the Code of Criminal Procedure. Some cases may avoid the standard judicial procedure when the damaged accuser agrees to mediation or dispute resolution. These are mainly criminal contraventions and criminal offenses committed due to imprudence. Mediation is an out-of-court activity carried out by a third person.

If a person under investigation is suffering from an ailment, the investigation is interrupted and the person under investigation is sent for compulsory medical assessment. In the case of a mental illness requiring continuous treatment, the court has the right to declare the person irresponsible and exempt him or her from punishment, imposing instead medical measures.

The prosecution has the right to decide not to initiate prosecution or dismiss the criminal case under certain conditions, such as the person is deceased, not responsible, or has not reached the age of criminal responsibility, there is no indictment by the damaged party or when the latter withdraws the indictment, if the law does not determine the fact as a criminal offense or when it becomes clear that the fact does not exist, if the criminal offense has been terminated, if amnesty has been granted, and in all of the other cases prescribed by the law. The prosecutor can decide to dismiss charges or the case at any stage of the proceedings according to various conditions specified by law. In 2008, the prosecution decided not to initiate the prosecution of 446 persons, it terminated 4,325 criminal cases, and it suspended 4,647 cases due to the unknown identity of the perpetrator.

A person cannot be investigated while under a coercive measure such as prison or house arrest. Coercive measures are determined by a court order, after its evaluation in a court hearing. When the person to be arrested is mentally ill the court may order his or her temporary hospitalization in a psychiatric institution. During the preliminary investigations, the prosecutor asks the court to decide on the hospitalization of the defendant in a psychiatric institution and when delays present risks, it orders the temporary hospitalization until the court reaches a decision.

Duration of detention varies depending on whether the proceedings involve a contravention or a crime, according to the range of punishment provided for crimes. As a rule, detention cannot be longer than 3 months, when it is applied for a criminal contravention, 6 months for crimes punishable by a prison sentence of up to 10 years, and 12 months for crimes punishable by a minimum of 10 years of prison or life sentence.

Likewise, detention loses affect when particular time limits have expired without a decision: 2 months when it is proceeded for a criminal offense, 9 months when it is proceeded for crimes punishable by a prison sentence of up to 10 years, and 12 months when it is proceeded for crimes punishable by a prison sentence of no less than 10 years or life sentence. The total duration of detention is generally 2 years for crimes punishable by prison sentence of less than 10 years and 3 years for crimes punishable by a prison sentence of at least 10 years or life sentence. Court proceedings end in one of these ways: guilt, acquittal, termination, the case is returned to the prosecutor of the case to complete the investigation, or a decision on incompetence. In 2007, out of 6,896 cases heard, 5,221 cases ended with a decision of "found guilty," 1,280 cases were terminated, 233 were acquitted, and the remainder were undecided. Out of these cases, 4,368 involved crimes and the rest criminal offenses (2,528). In 2007, according to the civil and criminal codes 5,678 persons were punished, 211 of whom were juvenile and 455 female offenders. The majority of criminal cases (tried according to the criminal and civil code) ended with an acquittal decision.

Juveniles

In 2006, the president of Albania decreed the establishment of the juvenile divisions in some of the biggest courthouses in the country. Likewise, juvenile departments have also been established in some prosecution offices in the country. There is no special law in Albania regulating juvenile justice, but there exist certain provisions in the material law and the criminal procedure law as well as other laws regulating the treatment of detainees and prisoners.

The Code of Criminal Procedures contains several rules regarding the prosecution of juveniles. Juvenile offenders are tried by the relevant departments established in specific judicial district courts. Juvenile defendants are provided legal and psychological assistance at any stage of the proceedings. This assistance is provided in the presence of the parent or other persons whose presence is requested by the juvenile and approved by the proceeding authority. All acts and actions are taken in the presence of the attorney, but in the absence of other persons, when such a thing is in the interest of the juvenile or when delays might seriously impair proceedings.

The proceeding authority collects information on the personal, familial, and social life conditions of the defendant juvenile. The intention is to evaluate the responsibility and its extent, the importance of the fact, and to impose suitable criminal measures. The court must take into consideration the requirement concerning noninterruption of the educational programs.

A juvenile cannot be arrested when accused of a criminal offense; the prosecutor may order that he or she remain under surveillance inside his or her dwelling or in another place under surveillance. The parent or guardian must be notified. The Criminal Procedure Code does not draw any distinction between juvenile and adults regarding detention duration.

Court hearings are public. According to the Criminal Procedure Code, juveniles under 16 and those who are drunk, intoxicated, or mentally disabled shall not be allowed in the hearing. However, the trial or certain actions can be held behind closed doors, when it is judged necessary during the questioning of juvenile witnesses. It can be conducted by the chairperson who can be assisted by a family member or a specialist in the field of child education.

Punishment

Types of Punishment

Albanian criminal legislation has provided for principal and supplementary punishment. The main punishments for crimes are life sentence in prison, imprisonment, and fine. The death penalty was proclaimed unconstitutional in 1999. After the changes in the Criminal Code of 2001, the two main punishments for crimes such as smuggling, forgery, trafficking, or money laundering are a prison sentence and a fine.

Prison sentences are given for crimes and offenses. The minimum of a prison sentence is 5 days, and the maximum varies according to the offense, although for crimes it is 25 years, and for offenses, up to 2 years. A fine is given for crimes and offenses according to the seriousness of the crimes and offenses.

The prison sentence is applied in most of the cases by the Albanian courts for crimes, while fines are typical penalties for contraventions. In 2007, 1,847 out of 5,678 convicts were punished with a fine. Life prison sentences are given by the court for the commission of a serious crime. During 2007, this punishment was imposed in five cases.

The Criminal Code also allows for several supplementary punishments: revocation of the right to exercise public functions; confiscation of items used to commit the criminal offense and the products of the criminal offense; restriction to using vehicles; revocation of awards and titles of honor; revocation of the right to exercise a profession or trade, exercise management duties; prohibition to stay in one or several administrative units; expulsion from the territory and obligation to make public the court decision; and compulsory medical treatment.

The Criminal Code additionally provides for other alternatives to prison sentences, such as fragmentation of the prison sentence, suspension of the execution of a sentence, suspension of the execution of a prison sentence and performing compulsory public work, and release on parole. Currently the suspension of the execution of a prison sentence for a period of no more than five years is the most common measure applied by the courts. The rest of the measures have found little or no application due to the absence of adequate supervision. In March 2009, the Regulation on the Probation Services was approved and several changes were made in the Criminal Code and in the execution of criminal sentencing, allowing for wider application of the probation services.

Criminal offenses such as murders and armed robberies are punished by long prison sentences, even life in prison. Punishments for theft vary according to the risk level of the offense and the circumstances under which it was committed, recidivism, or collaboration.

Juveniles

Educational placement of a juvenile in an educational institution may be required, but there is currently no such institution for children. In 2009, a special penitentiary institution for juveniles sentenced to prison began to operate. Juvenile prison sentences do not exceed half of the term of punishment provided for by the relevant provision. The Criminal Code provides for the exclusion of juveniles from punishment and the reduction of sentences. Out of 211 juvenile offenders punished in 2007, only in 26 cases did the court punish with a fine.

The following punishments of offenders were handed down by the civil courts in 2007:

Fine	1,847
Imprisonment	
up to 2 years	2,980
2–5 years	430
5–10 years	246
10–25 years	170
Life imprisonment	5

Prison

Prisons and detention facilities are administered by the General Directorate of Prisons, which operates under the authority of the Ministry of Justice. Albanian prisons are classified according to the security level: high-security prisons, medium-security prisons, and low-security prisons. There are special institutions for sick and disabled people, one in the town of Kruja and another new institution in the town of Durres. There are also specific sections in prisons or hospitals outside for prisoners with special needs. Those offenders under investigation pending a final court decision are placed in detention institutions.

Perpetrators of organized crime and other convicts, who at the time of commission of the criminal offense or while serving their term, have been characterized by a behavior and attitude that makes their stay in other prison categories impossible serve their sentences in high-security prisons. Prisoners sentenced for criminal contraventions, criminal offenses committed out of negligence, or other criminal offenses punishable by a prison sentence of no more than five years are placed in low-security prisons. The law provides for the possibility of transferring to this type of prison prisoners convicted for criminal offenses different from those cited earlier, but when the following requirements are met: the prisoner must have less than two years of prison term left to serve and must have followed the internal prison regulations. The rest of the prisoners serve their prison sentence in medium-security prisons.

Juvenile offenders serve their prison sentences in special facilities separate from the adults; women and men serve their prison sentences in separate institutions. If placing juveniles and women in separate institutions is impossible, the law requires for them to be placed in separate sections of other institutions. Mothers with children under the age of three are allowed to keep their children with them. Today, there is only one female prisoner section in the low-security prison of Tirana and a female as well as a juvenile detention section in one of the detention facilities in Tirana. Life sentence prisoners serve their term in special institutions established for this specific purpose. They are mainly placed in the prison of Burrel, Peqin, and Tepelenë. A prisoner can be transferred from one prison to another for security reasons or to be closer to one's family.

Currently, penitentiary institutions in Albania are located in Burrel, Tepelenë, Tirana, Lushnjë, Rrogozhinë, Peqin, Lezhë, Korçë, Fushë-Krujë, and Kavajë. Several prisons also have detention sections. In some cities there are also detention institutions.

The Albanian prison system includes a prison hospital center and a training center for prison police based in Tirana. In recent years, Albanian prisons have faced overcrowding problems. In 2008, two new penitentiary institutions were established: one in Fushë-Krujë and another one in Korçë. The application of alternative sentences is expected to alleviate overcrowding in prisons.

The 2007 prison population was 2,735 representing a substantial increase over the 2003 number of 1,677. The proportion of inmates is roughly 90 percent male and 10 percent female. There were only 8 minors in prison in 2007.

A prisoner enjoys certain rights. The prisoner informs his or her family about the arrival at the institution or about his or her transfer. Family members are immediately notified in case of illness or death of the prisoner. The prisoner has the right to be informed on the death of a relative. Prisoners are entitled to four family visits a month. One of them is an extended visit (for married prisoners). Prisoners are allowed to meet and exchange correspondence with other persons. The right to preserve family contacts is recognized to all prisoners, even to those placed in high-security prisons.

Prisoners are allowed to read magazines, newspapers, books, and make use of any type of means of information (radio, television, etc.) available at the institution. Foreign prisoners are entitled to contact diplomatic or consular representatives of their country and have communication facilitated.

Prisoners may benefit from special furloughs in case of serious illness of a family member; in the case of birth of the child of a prisoner, or the birth of a child to the children of the prisoner, his or her brothers and sisters; or furlough as a reward for good behavior and when the prisoner does not present any social risk.

Prisoners have the right to use the common library and social areas, practice their religion, meet with representatives of their religious community, and so forth. According to the law, all prisoners are entitled to labor, according to their physical and psychological capabilities, guidelines and real possibilities of the prisoners, requirements and discipline regulations of the penitentiary institution.

Several categories of prisoners are not required to work during their prison term, such as prisoners who have met the requirements to benefit retirement, first and second group disabled people, pregnant women for the time period provided by the law, and those who do not have the necessary physical or health condition to complete the job offered. The stipend of a prisoner can be lower than the minimum wage determined upon the decision of the Council of Ministers. Until now, labor opportunities for prisoners have been very few and stipends have been extremely minimal ($1 per month). Starting from March 2009, a new Regulation of Prisons and Prisoner Labor has been approved that provides for special arrangements. Local organizations monitoring human rights employ various forms of control to guarantee the protection of prisoner and detainee rights.

Prisoners are entitled to address requests and complaints to the director of the institution, inspectors, the director general of prisons, the minister of justice, independent monitoring organizations and institutions, national or international, such as the ombudsman institution and the European Committee for the Prevention of Torture and Inhuman or Degrading Treatment or Punishment (CPT). The ombudsman plays a special role in monitoring penitentiary institutions. The ombudsman has the right to visit without prior authorization and at any time all penitentiary institutions where final court decisions are executed. The National Office for the Prevention of Torture and Cruel, Inhumane, or Degrading Treatment or Punishment, established in March 2008, supervises the fulfillment and the respect of the rights of persons deprived of their liberty.

The majority of prisoners have little or no education. The law requires that the administration create the necessary conditions for prisoners to complete their 9-year education and the necessary conditions, where possible, to attend high school or university. All persons under the age of 25 years old must undergo cultural and professional development programs. In fact, such programs find little application in the Albanian prisons due to the insufficient space and lack of the necessary funds. Human rights or religious organizations and associations, domestic and foreign, have undertaken several initiatives through which prisoners are offered various vocational courses.

Vasilika Hysi

Further Reading

Courts and Statistics: http://www.justice.gov.al.

Ministry of Interior: http://www.moi.gov.al.

Organization for Security and Co-operation in Europe: http://www.osce.org/albania/13143.html. It provides analysis of the criminal justice system and criminal appeal proceedings in Albania.

Andorra

Legal System: Customary/Civil
Murder: Medium
Prison Rate: Low
Death Penalty: No
Corporal Punishment: No

Background

The Principality of Andorra is located on the Mediterranean side of the eastern Pyrenees. It has an area of 468 square kilometers (approximately 17 square miles), and its territory is divided into seven parishes. On March 14, 1993, the first Constitution of Andorra was approved by referendum. According to its article 1, Andorra is proclaimed an independent democratic and social state based on the rule of law, with sovereignty vested in the people. Its political regime is a parliamentary co-principality.

As a result of its historical heritage, the head of state is dual, the co-princes being the bishop of Urgell and the president of France. According to the Constitution, the co-princes are the symbol and guarantee of the permanence and continuity of Andorra, as well as of its independence and its equality with regard to its traditional, balanced relations with neighboring states. The co-princes have limited and symbolic power, and their acts must be endorsed by the head of the government or by the Syndic General and in principle they do not have any political responsibility.

The Criminal Code in force in Andorra was issued under Law 9, 2005, which reforms the extinct Criminal Code of 1990. It was the consequence of a long process that originated in the need to harmonize criminal legislation with the Constitution of 1993 and with the principles of legality and subsidiarity of criminal law.

The Criminal Code begins with an enunciation of principles, among which are the following: penal guarantee, criminal guarantee, jurisdictional guarantee, prohibition of analogy, the principle of guilt, no double jeopardy, together with the judicial principle of the proportionality of sentences.

On the other hand, the existing Criminal Procedure Code of Andorra was issued in 1989 and amended on December 10, 1998, by virtue of the *Llei qualificada de modificació del Codi de procediment penal.* It was subsequently reformed in 2005 and 2008 under the *Llei 16 y qualificada de modificació del Codi de procediment penal.* These changes were consolidated by decree-in-session on December 17, 2008.

Police

For centuries there was no need to create a professional police force, as the people's militia was charged with maintaining order. In 1932, the *veguers*—delegates of the protecting countries—created the Service of Order, with a chief and six agents, to maintain order in the country when there was an increase in the floating population owing to works of the electricity company and the building of highways. The police followed the orders of the veguers and the mayors until the entry into force of the Constitution of 1933. With Law 8/2004, of May 27, known as the Police Corps Act, the police was recognized as an organic part of the public administration, reporting to the government through the Ministry of Justice. Nevertheless, in judicial matters, according to article 94 of the Constitution, the judges and the Public Prosecutor's Office direct the actions of the police.

The Police Corps is organized into the Directorate of Police and the following three broad areas:

1. The Area of Criminal Police has jurisdiction in judicial police matters: narcotics, crimes against persons, crimes against property, organized crime, technological crime, etc.
2. The Area of Public Security and Proximity guarantees the safety of citizens and immediate attention in all most evident aspects closest to citizens: deactivation of explosives, transport and control of explosives, interventions in the transfer of high-risk prisoners, maintaining order, protection of dignitaries, etc.
3. The Technical Area gives technical and operational support to the other two areas and to the Directorate: arms inspection, immigration, investigation into traffic accidents, etc.

Crime

Classification of Crimes

The Criminal Code defines criminal offenses as "purposeful or reckless actions or omissions punished by law," which can be classified into major crimes, minor crimes, and misdemeanors. This classification is made on the basis of the severity of the conduct. Such conducts are also classified as reckless, in which case they must be expressly established, and as purposeful, which the Court of Andorra defines as those in which the subject is "aware of infringing social values in relation to a material or at least a legal result."

The Criminal Code establishes an extensive number of crimes, including, in particular, the following:

- Crimes against human life—homicide, murder, induction to or cooperation with suicide, consent to homicide—and crimes against prenatal human life—nonconsensual abortion, consensual abortion.

- Crimes against freedom—illegal arrest, slavery, kidnapping, coercion, threats—and crimes against sexual freedom—sexual assault, sexual abuse, favoring prostitution, procuring, child pornography, exhibitionism, and distribution of pornography to minors.
- Crimes against honor—slander, insult, libel, and perjury.
- Crimes against property—larceny, theft, extortion, fraud, computer fraud, defrauding of communications systems and flows, misappropriation of funds, privileged appropriation, disloyal administration, receiving stolen property, punishable bankruptcy.
- Crimes against the socioeconomic order—crimes against intellectual property, crimes against rights patents and utility models, crimes against trademark rights, defrauding the *Caja Andorrana de Seguridad Social*, contraband, illegal financial activity, usury and tax fraud. In relation to the control of these forms of criminality, special laws have been passed such as the international criminal law to combat money laundering or proceeds of international crime in 2000.
- Crimes against security in legal traffic—counterfeiting, forgery of documents, suppression of documents, creation or alteration of computer data, use of false or adulterated computer data, usurping identity or infiltration.
- Crimes against public health that are classified in two groups: crimes against the health of consumers, and crimes relating to the illegal trafficking of toxic drugs. Under the Regulation of Toxic Drugs (art. 281 to 288), a toxic drug means any substance for consumption that produces an alteration in the state of consciousness and is damaging to the health of persons, if included in international agreements on this matter and is not considered legal by Andorran legislation, or, if not included, is in its nature and its effects similar to those included and its trafficking is unauthorized.

As a basic legal definition of drug-related crime, the conduct of one who "produces, makes, transports, imports, exports, sells or provides" toxic drugs is punished. In the case of cannabis or similar drugs, the sentence and fine will be less than those for conduct that involves drugs of greater toxicity. The above-mentioned types of conduct will carry a higher prison sentence and fine whenever certain circumstances concur, such as a large amount of drugs; providing minors or handicapped persons with drugs; provision of drugs at schools, recreation centers, welfare centers, or prisons, or to persons in treatment for detoxification or rehabilitation.

However, as addressed by Andorran criminal legislation, under article 284 of the Criminal Code, the consumption, introduction, or possession of toxic drugs for personal use is punished with a sentence of up to one year's imprisonment—less than the basic crime definition—and if the court so considers it, a fine of up to €1,200 (US$1,500). This situation is considered aggravated in cases where drugs are taken in public.

Juveniles

Regarding the age of criminal responsibility, the Criminal Code points out that for a minor who has not reached 18 years of age and has committed a criminal offense, a special law is applicable. Pursuant to the guidelines established by the Convention on the Rights of the Child of 1989, the *Llei qualificada de la jurisdicció de menors* was enacted on April 22, 1999. This provided for procedures and measures applicable to minors between the ages of 12 and 18 (in certain cases it can be applied to minors under 21) who commit offenses established by the Criminal Code. This implies that the offending minor between 12 and 18 years of age is subject to special procedures and measures, and therefore minors under 12 are understood to have no criminal responsibility.

Crime Statistics

In the report by Andorra's Public Prosecutor's Office reviewing the judicial year 2008–2009, some data should be highlighted. For example, some crimes, when compared with the year before, have given rise to the initiation of the following large number of judicial proceedings:

- Crimes against public health, 1,359 criminal proceedings having been initiated, and increased by 10.85 percent.
- Regarding crimes of theft, larceny, extortion, and receiving, a total of 1,192 cases have been tried, the majority involving larceny, with 1,162 cases. This represents an increase of 6.54 percent over the previous year.
- In the area of economic crimes, 94 cases were heard, up from 54.10 percent. Most of these were linked with counterfeiting.

More generally, crimes against human life and moral and physical integrity, as well as crimes against honor, privacy, and the inviolability of the home remained nearly unchanged. Compared to the year before, there has been a decrease in the following:

- Crimes against road safety, with 295 cases, a decrease of 31.87 percent.
- Crimes against sexual freedom, with 22 cases, have decreased by 47.62 percent.
- Crimes against collective security, with 21 proceedings, are down by 41.67 percent.

Finding of Guilt

Articles 9 and 10 of the Constitution of Andorra establish principles of guarantee for persons who are being investigated as suspects of a crime. These basic pillars have been developed by the law now in force: *Llei qualificada de modificació del codi de procediment penal.* This law is based on the Principle of Legality, according to which no one can be convicted of a crime unless in accordance with the provisions of the Criminal Code currently in force or with special laws and by virtue of a decision based on law and issued by a competent court.

These established guarantees also cover the statements to the police that anyone who is considered a suspect in a crime may be required to give. To this effect, suspects giving a statement to the police must be informed of the acts with which they are charged and the reasons for their possible detention, as well their rights. Those include the right not to testify against oneself and not to confess guilt, the right to a lawyer and to ask for him or her to be present after being detained for 24 hours to assist with the statement and to be present at any verification of identity that the suspect may be subject to as from that moment. If the suspect cannot afford a lawyer, one will be appointed by the court; this will be free of charge only for those persons who can prove their insolvency. Suspects must also be informed of their right to a free interpreter if they are foreigners who do not understand or speak the national language or one of the languages of the neighboring states. If it is decided that the suspect is to be detained, he or she shall be taken into custody for legal causes and not detained for more than 48 hours before being referred to a court authority.

The authority for administering justice in criminal matters pertains to the *Tribunal Superior de Justicia d'Andorra*, the *Tribunal de Corts*, the *presidente*, the *Tribunal de Batlles*, and the *batlles* or judges. The public prosecutor is responsible for the initiation of criminal proceedings and for the protection and implementation of the legal system.

Prosecution of a crime begins with the filing of an accusation or suit, is initiated *ex officio* by the public prosecutor. On this basis, criminal proceedings are opened, comprising the following three stages:

1. A preparatory stage, in which the judicial police inform the public prosecutor of the initiation of an investigation by means of *L'atestat.* This first stage may conclude with the withdrawal of the accusation, the refusal to admit a lawsuit, the temporary stay of proceedings, or the order of initiation of a preliminary investigation.
2. Stage of collecting evidence and specifying charges. This is about investigating the punishable action and its perpetrators, accomplices, or accessories and the establishment of responsibility for the offense. This stage concludes by giving 15 days to the public prosecutor, the civil claimant, the private complainant,

the counsel for the defense, and the counsel for any responsible third parties so that they may petition the court for examination of evidence, dismissal of the action, or any other appropriate ruling.

3. If the court orders the trial to commence, the trial stage begins. The parties have 15 days to submit briefs that should contain the facts deemed to be proved, statements of legal standing, the names of those purported to be responsible, the acquittal or sentence sought, any civil liabilities or claims, and the evidence requested.

Once the evidence has been examined, the final submissions of the prosecution and the defense are presented, and the ruling is pronounced.

Punishment

Types of Punishment

Taking into account the severity of the crime, the sentence will vary according to the legal definition of crime. The death penalty and any cruel, inhumane, or degrading punishment are prohibited by the Constitution.

In the case of major crimes, the prison sentence can be as high as 25 years, with the exception of the provisions for accumulation of sentences and of sentences envisaged for the crime of genocide and crimes against humanity. Also provided are fines; disqualification from the exercise of public rights, from holding office, from family and professional rights; and prohibition of entering into contract with public administrations. These crimes include homicide, with a 10- to 16-year prison sentence; murder, with a 14- to 25-year prison sentence; robbery—with violence or intimidation of persons—with a 2- to 6-year prison sentence. In the case of illegal drug trafficking involving large amounts or selling to minors, the prison sentence can range from 3 to 6 years.

For minor crimes, there are prison sentences of up to 2 years; weekend imprisonment; home detention; fines; community work; disqualification or suspension of the exercise of public rights, a public career, family or professional rights; revocation of driving license, of a license to carry arms, to hunt, or fish; and prohibition of entering into contract with the public administration. Among these crimes are larceny, that is, the taking of a movable object of another without the owner's consent but without violence or intimidation, which entails a prison sentence of up to 2 years; and the illegal trafficking of toxic drugs when the consumption, introduction, or possession of the toxic drug is for personal consumption, in which case the prison sentence can be up to 1 year.

For misdemeanors the following sentences are established: confinement on holidays of up to 8 weekends or an equivalent amount of time; home detention up to 1 month; partial daily confinement for up to 2 months; fines; community work; revocation of driving license, of a license to carry arms, to hunt, or fish; and prohibition of entering into contract with public administration, suspension from practicing one's profession, and public or private admonishment. Examples of misdemeanors are minor injuries caused by imprudence, which carry a fine of up to €3,000, and coercion or minor ill-treatment, which carries a sentence of confinement or a fine of up to €3,000.

Also established are security measures of confinement to a psychiatric institution, a detoxification, special education, or rehabilitation facility; outpatient treatment; following a special program; expulsion; prohibition of going to certain places or having contact with certain persons, of driving, of possessing or using arms, of drinking alcohol, of going out at certain hours; family custody; and disqualification from practicing one's profession or career.

Prison

In the Council of Europe Annual Penal Statistics, consulted on December 12, 2007, the most recent data for the Principality of Andorra in relation to the prison population corresponds to September 2006. At that time the total prison population (including pretrial detainees) numbered 30 people, for a prison population rate of 40.4 per 100,000 inhabitants. The percentage of female prisoners and foreign prisoners (including pretrial detainees in both cases) was 3.3 percent in the first case and an excessive 83.3 percent in the case of foreigners.

There is only one prison, the *Centre Penitenciari de la Comella* (built in 2004), which has capacity for 124 prisoners, and to which were transferred those prisoners formerly held in the *Casa de la Vall*. According to Bisbat D'Urgell (www.bisbaturgell.org) for November 2009, there was a total of 62 inmates in the *Centre Penitenciari de la Comella*.

Lina Mariola Díaz Cortés and Carlos Guillermo Castro Cuenca

Further Reading

Council of Europe Annual Penal Statistics: http://www.coe.int/t/e/legal_affairs/legal_co-operation/prisons_and_alternatives/Statistics_SPACE_I/List_Space_I.asp.

Jiménez Naudí, Jesús (2005). *Legislació penal del Principat d'Andorra* [Penal Legislation of the Principality of Andorra]. Andorra La Vell: Prensa Andorrana.

Memorias de la Fiscalía de Andorra (2008–2009): http://www.justicia.ad/web/php/memoria.php.

Police of Andorra: http://www.policia.ad/cat/organi.html.

Austria

Legal System: Civil
Murder: Low
Burglary: Medium
Corruption: Low
Human Trafficking: Low
Prison Rate: Medium
Death Penalty: No
Corporal Punishment: No

Background

The Republic of Austria—situated in Central Europe—is a relatively small country with a surface area of about 83,860 square kilometers (approximately 30,189 square miles). It shares borders with the EU member states Germany, the Czech Republic, Slovakia, Hungary, Slovenia, Italy, and with the non-EU countries Switzerland and Liechtenstein. Austria's total population is approximately 8,348,200, of whom about 10 percent are foreign citizens. The country's official language is German; Hungarian, Slovene, and Croatian are spoken by relatively small minorities. Austria's political system is that of a parliamentary representative democracy; it is a federal republic consisting of nine states (*Bundesländer*), Vienna, the capital, being one of them.

History of the Legal System

Austria has basically a civil law system. Criminal law currently in force dates back to legislation from the times of the monarchy, which ended in 1918. This applies in particular to the Code of Criminal Procedure, large portions of which have been in force since 1873. This procedural legislation was devised by the Liberal government of the time in contrast to the inquisitorial trial system and was subsequently modified and added to over the years.

After the Kaiser formally abdicated in 1918, Austria became a democratic republic. This was enshrined in the federal Constitution, which was presented two years later and which in principle is still in force today. In 1938 Austria became part of the *Deutsches Reich* and was subject to Hitler's regime until 1945, the end of World War II. During this time the Criminal Code remained in force in theory; in practice it was almost smothered by a very large number of new ordinances and administrative orders so that the legal situation became totally opaque.

Austria was relaunched as an independent state after the Nazi era, and both the Code of Criminal Procedure and the Criminal Code were repromulgated in 1945. The country was, however, divided into four zones of occupation where Allied forces were stationed. The State Treaty of 1955, which was followed by the evacuation of the occupation forces, made Austria a fully sovereign state again. The country declared itself permanently neutral and enshrined neutrality in its Constitution. The same year saw Austria's accession to the United Nations. The criminal laws, the Criminal Code, and the Code of Criminal Procedure were amended on an ongoing basis. A new Criminal Code, which is still in force today, entered into force in 1974; the Code of Criminal Procedure was merely repromulgated in 1975. Owing to Austria's accession to the European Union in 1995, a distinctive influence of European legislation on Austrian substantive law and increasingly also on procedural law has been in evidence.

Police

The police force is organized on a federal level in a sense that there are no autonomous entities. In the past Austria knew two different uniformed corps, the gendarmerie and the police. Now there is just one corps, called *Bundespolizei.* The political responsibility for police work in Austria belongs to the Home Office (Federal Ministry of the Interior). Subordinated to the Home Office, nine state directorates for public security are responsible for security administration in general. There are 14 federal police directorates and 9 state police headquarters, divided into 83 district police headquarters and 27 city police headquarters. Under these headquarters there are about 1,000 police stations in Austria competent for all matters of security, including fighting and preventing crime.

Traffic matters are dealt with by 9 state traffic departments, 35 highway patrol stations, and 15 traffic police stations. Criminal investigation is the focus of the Federal Criminal Investigation Service and nine state criminal investigation services. Also, there are a number of specialized units such as agencies for state protection and counterterrorism, SWAT units, alpine duties, narcotics units, or immigration authorities. All in all, the number of police in Austria in 2008 stood at more than 27,000 officers, thereof 10 percent female.

Crime

Classification of Crimes

Austrian law distinguishes between felonies (serious) and misdemeanors (less serious). According to article 17 of the Austrian Criminal Code, felonies are premeditated acts that carry a life sentence or a custodial sentence of more than three years. For example, genocide, homicide (any premeditated killing according to the Austrian Criminal Code), manslaughter (a premeditated killing that happens upon sudden heat of a kind that is generally considered understandable, such as despair), assisting suicide, causing bodily harm with fatal consequences, rape, sexual abuse of minors, kidnapping with extortion, robbery, aggravated theft, aggravated fraud (if the value of stolen and/or fraudulently obtained objects exceeds €50,000 [US$62,840]), membership in a terrorist organization, treason, violation of state secrets, civil disorder, arson, counterfeiting of money, or abuse of authority are classified as felonies on the basis of the long sentences they carry.

Misdemeanors are all other culpable acts (in particular, acts of negligence). These include all homicide by negligence, bodily injury caused by negligence as well as aggravated battery and such criminal offenses as deprivation of freedom, coercion, damage to property, theft, fraud, handling stolen goods, bigamy, perjury, and falsification of documents.

In many offenses against life and limb, against property, or in sexual offenses, the basic facts of the case may result in the offense being classified as a misdemeanor, which may be changed to a felony on the basis of additional aggravating circumstances. Battery, for instance, is a misdemeanor, whereas battery with serious lasting consequences (aggravated battery) is a felony.

Age of Criminal Responsibility

In Austria the age of criminal responsibility is 14. Juveniles between the ages of 14 and 17 are subject to the Juvenile Court Act. This act takes into account the special, development-related characteristics of juvenile delinquency by focusing on the transitional period between the ages of criminal minority of children and the full criminal majority of adults. From age 18 the criminal procedure regulations for adults apply in principle (but some provisions of the Juvenile Court Act also apply to so-called young adults aged 18 to 20).

At the moment, the political discussion in Austria concerning crime focuses on juvenile crime, mostly juvenile aggression, and burglary committed by foreign offenders. Apart from the fact that youth crime is primarily recorded as property crime (more than 50%)—mostly theft—in the last five years the number of juvenile suspects registered because of robbery reveals a sharp increase of more than 75 percent. Partly, this development is due to the popularity of mobile phones among juveniles resulting in a large number of juveniles committing robbery of these high-valued status symbols. The number of juvenile offenders registered because of (aggravated) assault increased from 2002 to 2007 by 42 percent. The scientific discussion mainly circulates around the question whether this increase represents a real growth in aggressive behavior of juveniles or is a result of a greater willingness to report these crimes to the police.

Another challenge is the rising number of (domestic) burglaries in recent years. On the one hand, the percentage of solved cases concerning burglary diminished from 14 percent in 2002 to 10 percent in 2007. On the other hand, the percentage of foreign offenders increased in this period by more than 60 percent. As a result, in 2007 nearly half of all offenders registered because of burglary were foreigners. One part of an explanation is the fall of the so-called iron curtain and the opening of borders in the course of the enlargement of the European Union.

Drug Offenses

In Austria, drug offenses are dealt with by a separate law, the Addictives Act. The latest amendment entered into force at the beginning of 2008 and was a reaction to the EU Council Framework Decision laying down minimum provisions on the constituent elements of criminal acts and penalties in the field of illicit drug trafficking.

The substances covered by the Austrian Drug Law are not comprehensively and explicitly listed in the act; instead of such a list there are references to international agreements, in particular to the UN Convention against Illicit Traffic in Narcotic Drugs and Psychotropic Substances, and to domestic statutory orders. In practice, marijuana, hashish, coca leaves, opium, and psilocybin mushrooms are relevant in criminal law contexts.

Anyone is liable to prosecution who purchases, possesses, produces, transports, imports, exports, offers to others, passes on to or procures for others psychotropic substances, or cultivates, for example, cannabis plants, with a view to producing a psychotropic substance. These acts are punishable in principle with detention of up to a year or with fines of up to 360 daily rates of fines. The threat of punishment increases as follow:

- To up to 3 years' imprisonment, e.g., if an adult enables a minor to use an illicit substance.
- To up to 5 years' imprisonment, depending on the amount of controlled substances involved; the greater the amount, the higher the threat of punishment.
- To up to 15 years' imprisonment, e.g., in the case of drug trafficking by a criminal organization.
- To up to 20 years' imprisonment or a life sentence for those who play a leading role in drug trafficking ("drug lords").

Lighter sentences are available to those who possess drugs exclusively for their own consumption or in cases of drug-related crime.

In fact, convictions in Austria in 2007 resulted in nearly 70 percent imprisonment and in 30 percent fines. In minor cases the majority of imprisonment cases were suspended, whereas in aggravated cases (e.g., drug trafficking of a great amount), the average imprisonment is 1 to 3 years going up to more than 5 years in exceptional cases. The rationale underlying the Addictives Act may be summed up as follows: priority is accorded to treatment over punishment. Ambulatory measures take precedence as far as possible and punishment is kept in reserve as a means of last resort.

Crime Statistics

The number of offenses recorded by the police is published roughly every month on the home page of the Home Office (http://www.bmi.gv.at). In a much more detailed way data are published annually in the so-called crime report (*Kriminalitätsbericht*). Information about persons who have been convicted can be found in the judicial conviction statistics (*Gerichtliche Kriminalstatistik*) published annually. The most important results concerning convictions and sentences are also published on the home page of Statistics Austria (http://www.statistik.at/web_en). Unfortunately, Austria doesn't carry out nationwide crime victimization surveys at regular intervals. Therefore, the explanatory power of statistics is limited.

In the last 15 years the number of offenses recorded by police increased from about 500,000 to 650,000 and dropped to 600,000 in the last 3 years. In 2007 the number of offenses equaled 594,240, thereof 22 percent felonies. Consequently, the crime rate climbed from 6,000 offenses per 100,000 persons of the population in the 1990s to nearly 8,000 in 2003 and 2004. After a decrease the latest crime rate for 2007 was 7,175. Finally, while Vienna holds only 20 percent of the population, 36 percent of all offenses are recorded in this urban area.

An overall view of the number of suspects and the number of convicted persons per 100,000 persons of the population reveals that the rate of suspects increased from 2002 to 2007 by 15 percent, while the rate of convicted offenders remained rather stable and increased by 3 percent only.

Presenting offenders and convictions in Austria doesn't show the whole picture. Since January 1, 2000, diversionary measures are applicable to juveniles and adults. Since 2003 more suspects are successfully diverted than finally convicted, thus showing the importance of diversion in Austria.

A look at the kind of offenses reveals that the great majority of recorded crime belongs to property crimes. In 2007 the proportion of this group of offenses amounted to 70 percent. Crimes against life and limbs are the second most categories, responsible for 15 percent of all offenses. Half of this group are traffic accidents causing injury or death. Of the total crimes registered, 4 percent were drug offenses, 3 percent crimes against freedom, and 1 percent sexual offenses; the remaining 7 percent covered a variety of offenses with a small number each.

Finally, in 2007 the police in Austria registered 121 cases of homicide, thereof 75 attempts, and 710 cases of rape, thereof 145 attempts. Furthermore, 8,660 offenses were registered as aggravated theft, thereof 629 attempts. The number of burglaries amounted to 104,860, thereof 18,144 attempts. Of the whole group of a little more than 24,000 drug offenses, 10 percent are felonies.

Finding of Guilt

Rights of the Accused

The minimum standards for rights of accused have been defined in article 6 of the European Convention on Human Rights, which has been elevated to constitutional rank in Austria. According to this article the accused is entitled to a fair and public hearing within a reasonable time by an independent and impartial tribunal established by law. The rights are further defined in Austria's Criminal Procedure Code, and are mostly also applied for suspects.

The accused is entitled to defend himself or herself and to the assistance of a defense lawyer at any stage of the proceedings. This right is strengthened by the provision that the accused must not be forced to incriminate himself or herself. If he or she pleads guilty, this is to be taken into account as an extenuating cause in fixing the sentence.

To enable him or her to defend himself or herself effectively, the accused has the right of obtaining information, of participation, and of a fair hearing. This is why the alleged offender has to be informed by the criminal police or the state prosecutor as early as possible of the proceedings opened against him or her, of the charges, and of his or her essential rights. In addition to this the accused has the right to be given access to his or her file. The right to ask questions—the accused is entitled at all hearings at which he or she may lawfully be present to put questions to the person under examination—and the right to demand a hearing of evidence enable the defendant to make sure that facts important to him or her are taken into account. People who are not sufficiently fluent in the language of the court are entitled to the assistance of a translator.

Until a legally valid verdict has been reached, the accused is presumed to be innocent, which means that the accused benefits from the presumption of innocence throughout the entire proceedings. Before

Psychological consultant Heidi Kastner, left, and defense lawyer Rudolf Mayer talk in court prior to the trial of Josef Fritzl in the provincial courthouse in St. Poelten, Austria, March 16, 2009. Fritzl is accused of imprisoning his daughter for nearly a quarter of a century and fathering her seven children. (AP Photo/Robert Jaeger)

a verdict is reached, the prosecution must not come down in favor of an appraisal of the evidence to the detriment of the accused or rashly present the accused as convicted, for instance, at a press conference. In the last resort the presumption of innocence will prevent the court from convicting the accused unless his or her guilt has been proved beyond reasonable doubt.

The accused is moreover entitled to the court case being terminated within a reasonable time frame, which applies in particular to accused persons in detention; the Austrian Code of Criminal Procedure does not, however, specify the criteria for what is reasonable in this context. Equally unknown to Austrian law are sanctions for unduly protracted proceedings, and it is also not a mitigating circumstance, which have to be taken into account; appeals to the European Court of Human Rights are, however, possible.

The accused is entitled at any stage of the trial to make use of one (or more) defense lawyer. Any person is eligible for the role of defense lawyer who has qualified as a lawyer, barring the case when a lawyer is himself or herself the object of legal investigations on account of the same crime.

The accused—already when he or she is a suspect—has to be informed of his or her rights in the criminal police proceedings. In case of arrest he or she has to be given the opportunity to contact a defense lawyer of his or her choice or the counsel who happens to be on duty at the lawyer emergency service. Until the alleged offender's commitment to prison (which may not be deferred for longer than 24 hours), the criminal police are entitled to monitor contacts between him or her and his or her counsel. Once he or she has been committed to prison, his or her exchanges with the defense lawyer are left unmonitored on principle, the exception being danger of collusion or danger of suppression of evidence or when there are especially serious reasons to fear that evidence might be tampered with in some way.

To guarantee an effective defense the alleged offender may be granted the right to have the assistance of his or her counsel at his or her very first interrogation (even though this can be ruled inadmissible if it may reasonably be concluded that the counsel's presence might be detrimental to the investigation). However, the Austrian Code of Criminal Procedure does not provide for an active part played by the defense lawyer during the first interrogation. It is only after the suspect has been questioned by the police that the defense lawyer is entitled to put supplementary questions to him or her.

In certain cases, such as a main trial before a court of lay assessors, a grand jury, or a single judge with an impending custodial sentence of more than three years, a defense lawyer is obligatory. If the accused opts against the involvement of a defense lawyer in a case of obligatory defense, he or she is assigned a court-appointed legal defender whose expenses have to be paid by the accused, though if unable to pay the costs of the counsel he or she is granted free legal assistance. Handicapped persons are also entitled to receive this legal assistance. In county court proceedings the accused may be represented by a *Machthaber,* a proxy acting on behalf of the accused; he or she is entitled to make depositions and perform other relevant acts.

Prosecution and Investigation

The first phase of the trial—the pretrial—is conducted by the public prosecutor, who also bears ultimate responsibility, in collaboration with the criminal police. The prosecution commences once the criminal police or the public prosecutor's office start a criminal investigation and/or use coercive measures against a person known or unknown, who is suspected of having committed a criminal act.

The Public Prosecutor's Office is entitled to carry out the investigation on its own; in practice, however, the taking of evidence is carried out by the criminal police, as they are entitled to carry out investigations independently. Certain types of evidence taking require the public prosecutor's prior directive. For the most invasive of coercive measures, such as arrests or house searches, the public prosecutor must seek the court's consent, with the exception of cases where there is danger in delay; here no directive is needed and the criminal police are entitled to use these coercive measures without formal authorization, but a subsequent permission is necessary.

The criminal police are obliged to keep the public prosecutor informed throughout to enable him or her to conduct and monitor the preliminary investigation. In the final report of the police the facts of the case are expected to be sufficiently clear for the public prosecutor to base a decision on them whether he or she is going to formally charge the suspect, recommend a diversionary process, or terminate the investigation.

Alternatives to Trial

Within the spectrum of lesser to medium crimes a criminal charge may be disposed of without a formal trial and without a traditional sentence, if the public prosecutor agrees to a diversionary procedure. Prosecution is temporarily deferred and the charge is ultimately dismissed if the conditions under which diversion was granted are successfully completed. In this way a criminal record is avoided. A diversionary procedure cannot be used if the maximum sentence that may be passed down exceeds 5 years of detention, and when the other preconditions are fulfilled. Diversionary procedures include the following:

- A probation period of up to 2 years. The temporary deferment of prosecution may be tied to the completion of certain tasks, such as, above all, the compensation of the victim and/or submission to a probation regime.

- The suspect may be charged with the payment of a sum of money to the treasury, if possible, under the auspices of compensation. This *Geldbuße* may not exceed a maximum of 180 daily rates of fine.
- Community service (at most 240 working hours) performed in the suspect's spare time within the framework of a social institution such as an old people's home or a hospital.
- Victim-offender mediation. For this it is necessary for the suspect to realize the extent of his or her culpability and to confront the consequences of his or her crime, and the victim must consent.
- A special provision—the first diversional provision in the Austrian Criminal Law—can be found in the Addictives Act, which requires the public prosecutor to defer prosecution for certain drug and drug-related offenses. The probation period must be combined with drug addiction treatment.

How Are the Majority of Criminal Cases "Solved"?

In 2007 the prosecution authorities in Austria had to deal with more than 300,000 known perpetrators. In 25 percent of the cases they brought in an accusation, in 13 percent they offered the suspect a diversionary measure, the great majority of them accepted by the perpetrators. Nearly 44 percent of all cases ended up by closing of the proceedings. The remaining share covers mainly waiver of prosecution concerning juveniles and the dropping of proceedings in the absence of the perpetrator.

Austrian courts registered in 2007 about 85,000 new cases requiring a decision of the trial court. In nearly 84,000 cases one judgment was rendered. Slightly more than 43,000 persons were found guilty and nearly 10,000 perpetrators accepted a diversionary measure offered by the judge.

Incarceration before or Awaiting Trial

The preconditions justifying arrest are a concrete suspicion and at least one of the following states of affairs that are taxatively listed by the law: for the suspect to be caught in the act; a high degree of probability that the suspect will abscond, suppress evidence, or attempt to enter into an agreement with witnesses or accomplices, commit another similar criminal act, or realize a threat (the chargeable criminal act must carry a threat of punishment of 6 or more months imprisonment). Arrest and pretrial custody are mandatory in cases of criminal acts that carry a minimum threat of punishment of 10 years (e.g., murder). Arrests are carried out by the police who are also entitled and obliged to act on their own initiative in cases of danger in delay. In all other cases a public prosecutor's arrest warrant authorized by the court is needed. The suspect has to be informed of his or her rights and imprisoned within 48 hours at the detention facility of the competent court, where he or she has to be questioned as soon as possible. The competent court has to reach a decision within 48 hours from the imposition of pretrial custody.

The imposition of pretrial custody has to be reviewed regularly, for a first time 14 days after the initial imposition; 1 month after the first prolongation; and then every 2 months. The Code of Criminal Procedure stipulates a maximum duration of pretrial custody (in cases where there is a danger of the suppression of evidence and/or collusion up to 2 months; in cases of misdemeanors up to 6 months; in cases of felonies up to 1 year; and in cases of aggravated felonies up to 2 years). After a verdict with a sentence to imprisonment, the pretrial custody term will be deducted from the term of imprisonment.

Criminal Court Judges

The number of professional and/or lay judges depends on the type of court. Three judges and eight jurors (district court as jury court) are required to deal with criminal acts that carry a threat of punishment of a life sentence or between a minimum of 5 to more than 10 years and for criminal acts explicitly specified in the Code of Criminal Procedure, such as treason.

Two judges and two lay assessors (district court as a court of lay assessors) are to be put in charge of criminal acts carrying a threat of punishment of more than 5 years' detention, for certain sex offenses and such crimes as voluntary euthanasia.

For prosecutions on account of sex offenses the law has provisions that ensure that a certain number of judges and of lay assessors belong to the same sex as the accused and the victim, respectively.

One single judge is required at regional court level to preside over trials that deal with criminal acts carrying a minimum threat of punishment of more than one year. All other criminal acts carrying a threat of punishment in the form of a fine or detention not exceeding one year also fall within the remit of a single judge but at district court level.

Appeal cases are heard by senates. At the higher district court the senates consist of 3 judges; at the Supreme Court, which is especially in charge of nullity appeals, there are 5 judge senates. To reach a decision in exemplary cases at the Supreme Court (if, for instance, there is no uniform jurisdiction), that number is increased to 11 judges.

Justices must have a master's law degree (in Austria called *Magister*) and must undergo a four-year training course at a court. To make sure prospective judges obtain a comprehensive overview of legal practice, they will be given the opportunity of first-hand experiences in different areas of judicature and at different levels within the court. After their appointment they are eligible for further training. According to the Juvenile Court Act, judges presiding over juvenile cases must have a certain amount of expertise in the areas of psychology and social work.

Juveniles

The Juvenile Court Act contains substantive and procedural regulations, including regulations on the enforcement of imprisonment. For all juveniles there is the possibility of nonintervention; the prosecutor and the judge may drop the case of a juvenile, if the offense is punishable by a fine or not more than five years of imprisonment and a diversion or a sentence is not necessary to prevent the juvenile from committing further crimes. Nonintervention is particularly recommended in cases of petty misdemeanors of nonproblem juveniles, for whom a special preventive effect results from the mere fact that the authorities have become involved with the attendant consequences in the social environment of the juvenile. If a nonintervention is not possible, then a diversion (see also above) has to be taken into account by the public prosecutor or by the judge. A broader application of the diversion than for adults is also possible. Fines and imprisonment may only be implemented as measures of last resort.

Punishment

Punishment aims above all at special or general prevention and at the protection of victims. According to law, the aspect of retribution has been eliminated almost completely.

Types of Punishment

Fines and Imprisonment

The law indicates in every case a range of sentences by stating minimum and maximum sentences (only in the case of minor misdemeanors no explicit minimum sentence is specified), which stake out the range within which courts must hand down a sentence that is proportionate to the criminality of the act and the culpability of the criminal. The two options that are available for sentencing according to Austria's Criminal Law are fines and prison sentences.

Imprisonment is either limited to a maximum of 20 years or it takes the form of a life sentence. The minimum term is one day. To prevent the potentially negative consequences of short prison sentences (up to 6 months), the Criminal Code allows under certain circumstances for the substitution of a fine for imprisonment.

A fine is fixed according to the daily rate of fine system; the number of daily rates depends on the seriousness of the crime and on the criminal's culpability, the amount of the specific daily rates on the criminal's income and his or her pecuniary circumstances. If the fine proves uncollectable, an alternative prison sentence is imposed, which is put into effect in the same manner as a normal prison sentence. Since 2008, the convict does, however, have the possibility of averting the alternative prison sentence by performing community service. Fines and prison sentences may be suspended under certain circumstances in connection with a probation period.

If a prison sentence is put into effect, the convict may be eligible for early release after serving at least one-half of his or her sentence in connection with a probation period. After 15 years of imprisonment even a convict sentenced to life imprisonment may be eligible for release. In addition to the sentence the Criminal Code and a number of auxiliary laws provide for so-called legal consequences, which enter into force automatically in the case of adults. Under certain conditions the sentence is followed by loss of office or of a business license.

Preventive Measures

Preventive measures do not focus on the culpability of the convict but on the danger that he or she poses to the public. The Criminal Code provides for the possibility of detention for three categories of convicts: the dangerously disturbed, addicts in need of drug detoxification, and dangerous recidivists. These preventative measures remain in effect as long as they are deemed necessary. Therefore, the judge does not order a temporal limit of the measure in the verdict. But there are regular reviews, whether the person can be released, and there is a maximum period of detention: 2 years for drug detoxification, and 10 years for dangerous recidivists.

Directives and Probation Services

If a sentence of imprisonment/fine or a preventive measure is suspended or the convict is released early after the setting of a probation period, the court will give the convict a directive. Among the directives explicitly mentioned in the law are an alcohol ban and the convict's consent to a psychotherapeutic and/or medical treatment.

Corporate Criminal Liability

Since 2005 corporations may also be prosecuted under penal law in Austria. A *Verbandsgeldbuße* may be imposed to which the daily rate of fine system is applicable. Here too a conditional suspension is possible together with the setting of a probation period and, if necessary, also the imposition of a directive.

Typical Punishments

Murder carries a prison sentence of 10 to 20 years or a life sentence. Manslaughter carries a sentence of 5 to 10 years' imprisonment. Whoever kills someone at his or her express and urgent request is to be punished with a prison sentence between 6 months and 5 years. The same applies to assisting suicide. For a mother who intentionally kills her child during or immediately after birth the Criminal Code specifies a sentence of up to 1 year in prison. In 2007 the typical punishment in practice for intentional homicide (not including attempts) was imprisonment of more than 5 years. Out of 81 convicted persons, 10 received a life sentence.

Rape carries imprisonment between 6 months and 10 years. If the rape results in grievous bodily harm or pregnancy, the sentence will range from 5 to 15 years' imprisonment. If the rape results in the victim's death, the threat of punishment is increased to imprisonment between 10 to 20 years or a life sentence. The typical punishment implemented for rape is imprisonment of more than 1 year. In 2007 30 percent of all convicts, mostly persons with no previous criminal record, were sentenced to a partly suspended prison sentence.

Serious theft (e.g., stolen value of more than €3,000, if the victim was helpless) receives a custodial sentence of up to 3 years. For theft committed on a professional basis or within the framework of a criminal organization, the threat of punishment is expanded to between 6 months and 5 years; if the value of the stolen object exceeds €50,000, the range of sentences is from 1 to 10 years in prison. The typical punishment is imprisonment, for convicts with no previous criminal record, mostly (partly) suspended. The length of imprisonment depends on the seriousness of the case but the average was 1 to 3 years in 2007. In exceptional cases we can find imprisonment with duration of more than 5 years, too.

Burglary receives from 6 months to 5 years, and if it is done on a professional basis, from 1 to 10 years. In 2007 in Austria 90 percent of all convictions accounted for imprisonment (partly) suspended for persons with no previous criminal record. The average prison length imposed by judges ranged from 6 months to 3 years.

Aggravated robbery receives between 5 and 15 years imprisonment. This increases to 10 to 20 years in prison or to a life sentence if the robbery resulted in a death. In 2007 in Austria mostly imprisonment of more than 5 years is registered in the statistics. Differentiating between perpetrators with and without a previous conviction reveals that nearly one-quarter of all persons with no previous criminal record were sentenced to partly suspended imprisonment, even for aggravated robbery.

Death Penalty

The death penalty, which held out longest in Military Law, was finally abolished in 1968. Its abolition is also enshrined in article 85 of Austria's Federal Constitution and in Additional Protocols of European Human Rights Convention Nos. 6 and 13 that have constitutional rank in Austria.

Prison

The number of inmates according to statistics published by the Ministry of Justice has increased dramatically since 2002. While the daily average of inmates in 2002 amounted to about 7,500, the number for 2007 was nearly 9,000. Nearly one-quarter of all arrests are pretrial detentions.

The total increase in the number of inmates is mainly due to an increase of foreign inmates. On January 1, 2008, the percentage of foreign inmates from more than 100 nations in Austrian prisons was 46 percent. Looking at pretrial detention only, the share of foreign inmates was 60 percent.

The total number of penal institutions in Austria adds up to 28. There are 9 prisons for convicted persons sentenced to imprisonment of more than 18 months. There are 16 prisons established at the seat of the provincial courts being competent for penal cases, and 3 institutions are specialized for the execution of preventive measures. The dimension of the institutions varies between 63 and 990 places.

The biggest prisons for inmates serving longer sentences are the penitentiaries in Stein, Graz-Karlau, and Garsten. Depending on the kind of offense, the personality of the convicted person, and the capacity, perpetrators are allocated to a single institution by decision of the Ministry of Justice.

Work in Prisons

The Prisons Act contains provisions that convicts and pretrial prisoners should have the opportunity to work. Useful and, in the case of juveniles, educationally meaningful tasks are supposed to be performed, such as helping in the kitchen or in renovation work in the institution or work in the institution's workshops (inter alia metalworking and woodwork shops, garages), which also accept orders from private businesses and clients. So-called day-release prisoners are entitled to accept jobs outside the institution. To the extent this is possible—this applies in particular to juveniles—convicts are to be given the opportunity to get vocational or further training that may improve their job prospects after their release. For this reason the time and conditions of work are supposed to be organized in a manner that corresponds to the situations of life outside the institution; juveniles are given longer breaks as a matter of principle. Convicts are entitled to pay (approx. €5 for light unskilled work and up to approx. €7 for skilled work and work as a foreman); after the deduction of their contribution toward costs and the unemployment insurance premium, this money is at the disposal of the convicts as inmates' allowance and as a set-aside for the time after their release. It is, however, not possible for organizational reasons (such as staff shortages) or owing to a lack of demand to provide work for all inmates. Depending on the institution, nonemployment rates may be as high as 40 percent.

For juvenile inmates school attendance is compulsory, which means that youth penitentiaries have to organize classes on a regular basis. The aim is to give inmates the possibility to obtain basic school leaving certificates or to attend vocational school as part of an apprenticeship. To avoid stigmatization school certificates contain no reference to where they were obtained. For adults, extra occupational courses are provided and they are entitled to enroll in distance learning or e-learning courses that they follow in their spare time.

Visiting Policies and Other Privileges in Prison

Convicts may become eligible for phone calls to their relatives even though there are no special circumstances, such as illness, to justify them. The law provides also for minimum entitlements regarding visits; these are expanded in the case of good conduct. Each penal institution has its fixed hours, when inmates are entitled to receive previously announced visits of at least half an hour's duration (for juveniles 1 hour) a week. Prisoners awaiting trial need court permission for visits. Visiting time is to be extended to 1 hour once every 6 weeks or in cases where visitors have a long way to travel to the prison. Important personal, economic, or legal reasons entitle convicts to receive visits outside the fixed times. These visits are moderately supervised and additional privileges such as the so-called table visits or 24-hour visits in so-called cuddle cells are possible.

Other types of privileges are the so-called interruptions of detention and the day-leaves; the convicts' conduct at the detention facility is one of the factors that is taken into account in granting these privileges. Under certain circumstances the prisoner may be granted (repeatedly) upon request an interruption of detention of up to 8 days or a day-leave of 12 hours (twice in 3 months at most).

Transfer of Prisoners

According to the Act on Extradition and Mutual Assistance a sentenced person can be transferred to his or her home country. According to the Council of European Convention on the Transfer of Sentenced Persons and to all bilateral treaties on mutual transfer, the sentenced person has to give his or her consent to the transfer. Without the consent of the person a transfer is allowed when the original sentence includes a deportation order.

Karin Bruckmüller and Christian Grafl

Further Reading

Bertel, Christian, and Klaus Schwaighofer. (2008). *Österreichisches Strafrecht. Besonderer Teil I (§§ 75 bis 168b StGB)* [Austrian Penal Law]. Vienna: Springer.

Bertel, Christian, and Andreas Venier. (2009). *Strafprozessrecht.* 3rd ed. Vienna: Manz.

Bruckmüller, Karin, Arno Pilgram, and Günther Stummvoll. (2010). "Juvenile Justice System in Austria." In *Juvenile Justice Systems in Europe: Current Situation, Reform, Developments and Good Practices,* edited by Frieder Dünkel, Joanna Grzywa, and Ineke Pruin, pp. 41–98. Mönchengladbach, Germany: Forum Verlag Godesberg.

Grafl, Christian. (2007). "Community Service in Austria: Main Results of a Feasibility Study." *Probation Journal* 54(3): 251–263.

Gratz, Wolfgang, Andreas Held, and Arno Pilgram. (2001). "Imprisonment in Austria." In *Imprisonment Today and Tomorrow: International Perspectives on Prisoners' Rights and Prison Conditions.* 2nd ed., edited by Dirk van Zyl and Frieder Dünkel, pp. 3–31. The Hague, the Netherlands: Kluwer Law International.

Kienapfel, Diethelm, and Frank Höpfel. (2007). *Grundriss des österreichischen Strafrechts: Allgemeiner Teil.* 12th ed. Vienna: Manz.

Belarus

Legal System: Civil
Murder: High
Burglary: Medium
Corruption: High
Human Trafficking: Medium
Prison Rate: High
Death Penalty: Yes
Corporal Punishment: No

Background

The Constitution of the Republic of Belarus of 1994, with amendments and additions adopted at the National Referendum of November 24, 1996, defines the Republic of Belarus as a unitary democratic social state. It is a presidential republic, with power residing strongly in the head of the state. Historically, the Belarusian legal system has developed within the continental legal tradition. However, the influence of the Soviet Union has deeply affected the structure and the contents of its legal sources. At present, Belarus is a country of written and codified law. A written constitution occupies the top of the pyramid of the Belarusian law. The first level beneath the Constitution is represented by codes and codified provisions that have prevalence over laws adopted by Parliament (the National Assembly).

After annexation of the actual East-Belarusian lands by the Russian Empire in the 16th century, the Russian Code of Penal Laws (1832) was introduced. Russian law made legal rules more organized and introduced in 1864 the Institute of Justice of Peace for treatment of minor offenses to relieve the overburdened judicial system. The Russian Code of Criminal and Correctional Punishments of 1903, with its classification of crimes and principles of penal responsibility, became then the prototype of the future criminal legislation in Belarus. The first decrees of the Soviet power established criminal responsibility for offenses against the new regime: counterrevolutionary activities, sabotage, corruption, profiteering, desertion, and so forth.

The adoption of the socialist Criminal Code marked a significant regression in the development of Belarusian legal tradition. This code allowed for applying its rules by analogy: if the code did not expressly provide for a certain offense, the courts could determine the punishment for it on the basis of rules that they deemed similar; in effect, the abandonment of *nulla poena sine lege* (no punishment without law) principle. The crimes were categorized into two groups: crimes against the Soviet regime and other crimes. For the first type of crimes, the code established a minimum threshold of punishment, and for the second type—only a maximum limit. Another peculiarity of the code was the rejection of a fundamental principle, that of individualized criminal responsibility. Restrictive measures could be applied not only to the culprit, but also to his or her immediate family who could be deported to remote regions of Siberia. The age threshold of criminal responsibility was lowered to 12 years. The number of criminally reprehensible actions was considerably enlarged during the 1930s: abortion, leaving the workplace without permission, absence at workplace without medical certificate, and so forth.

Most of the repressive trends in the criminal law development were reversed in 1958, with the adoption of the Model Criminal Law of the Soviet Union and Soviet Republics, proclaiming the adherence of the union to humanist principles, including *nulla poena sine lege.* In Belarus, this was followed by the adoption of the new Criminal Code in 1961. Despite the proclaimed decriminalization of a large number of offenses, some of them remained in the code, in violation of common principles of international human rights law: circulation without passport, vagrancy and mendicancy, private entrepreneurship and agency.

After the proclamation of independence of the Republic of Belarus in 1991, the Criminal Code of 1961 continued to be applied. It was subject to multiple modifications adapting Belarusian criminal law to the human rights and free market philosophy. In June 1999, the Chair of Criminal Law of Belarusian State University presented to Parliament a project of New Criminal Code of the Republic of Belarus, based on the new social and economic model. It was adopted by both chambers of Parliament, respectively, on June 2 and June 24, 1999, and promulgated by the president on July 9, 1999.

Crime

Types of Crimes

According to the Belarusian Criminal Code there are four requisite features of crime: social danger, unlawfulness, culpability, and punishability. The code classifies crimes according to the following four degrees of social danger.

- Crimes that do not represent considerable social danger. Offenses that traditionally fall within this group include inciting to suicide; illegal abortion; nonaccomplishment of parental duties; nonaccomplishment of the obligation of taking care of elderly parents; unauthorized disclosure of an adoption kept in secret; violation of the medical secrecy; defamation; coercion; threats of murder, of violence, or of destruction of property; slander; insult; and discrimination.
- Less serious crimes. This group traditionally includes murder in a fit of passion; assisted suicide; libel; public insult; torture; putting someone at risk of HIV contamination; violent coercion to donate organs or tissues for transplantation; consensual sexual intercourse or other sexual acts with a minor under 16 years of age; coercion to prostitution; inciting minors to regular consumption of alcohol, narcotic substances, to vagrancy or to mendicancy; theft; robbery; and car highjacking.
- Serious crimes traditionally include rape, intentional infliction of a severe bodily injury, intentional contamination by HIV, human trafficking, and kidnapping.
- Crimes of particular seriousness include murder, international terrorism, genocide, ecocide, preparing and leading an aggressive war.

Crimes recorded by the police and the number of offenders convicted in 2004, published by the Ministry of Internal Affairs, Information and Analytics Department, were as follows:

	Crimes	**Convictions**
Murder	1,010	1,058
Sexual crimes	1,102	660
(Rape)	386	357
Serious bodily injury	2,368	2,132
Theft and misappropriation	93,660	31,977
Robbery and plundering	10,692	6,891
Burglary	23,865	8,448
Car highjacking	1,260	1,798
Fraud	5,218	1,600
Counterfeit currency	2,844	2,118

Crimes of Particular Challenge

According to the Ministry of Internal Affairs, three types of crimes represent a real social scourge for Belarus: human trafficking, drug offenses, and economic crimes.

Human Trafficking

In Europe, Belarus is a recognized exporter of "live merchandise." During the 2000–2006 period, Belarusian investigation authorities revealed 3,162 human traffic offenses, 963 of which involved international trafficking. Since 2002, the investigation bodies, including the General Prosecutor's Office, have suppressed the trafficking activities of 48 organized groups and 10 criminal organizations. During the same reference period, 2,600 victims of human trafficking have been identified, 2,250 of which were forced into prostitution, and 350 were subject to forced labor.

Proliferation of human trafficking in the Belarusian territory is partially related to the low quality of the post-Soviet legislation. The low efficiency of anti-traffic measures provoked in the late 1990s an intensive legislative effort in this sphere. The reform started with the Ordinance of the Council of

Ministers of November 8, 2001, putting into effect the State Program on Complex Measures to Counter Proliferation of Human Traffic and Prostitution for the Period of 2002–2007. At the present day Belarus participates in all existing universal conventions in the sphere of human trafficking.

Human trafficking is punished exclusively by deprivation of liberty (imprisonment), which may eventually be supplemented with confiscation of property and revocation of rights to exercise certain activities or occupy certain positions. Today, the Criminal Code defines the following acts as human trafficking:

- Profiteering from or facilitating prostitution or coercion to prostitution.
- Involving minors into antisocial activities (prostitution, vagrancy, or mendicancy).
- Traffic of human beings.
- Kidnapping for exploitation purposes.
- Illegal assistance for employment abroad.
- Diffusion of pornographic materials.

In 2005, there were 650 recorded cases of human trafficking, while in 2006 there were 567, according to the Ministry of Internal Affairs. The Ordinance of the President No. 352 of August 8, 2005, On Preventing Negative Consequences of Human Traffic, established measures for the protection and rehabilitation of victims. Among these were nondisclosure of identity, exemption from being present during the court hearings, closed hearings, and surveillance of their domicile and property. The Ministry of Labor and Social Protection organizes centers of psychological aid and rehabilitation of victims. Trafficking victims not having reached the age of legal majority undergo rehabilitation programs in special pedagogical centers (total number of 101) and in social care centers (140), organized by the Ministry of Education.

Drug Offenses

According to official statistics, the number of drug addicts in Belarus remained stable in 2006 and 2007: around 127 persons per 100,000 inhabitants actually suffer addictions to narcotic or other psychotropic substances. There is an increasing accessibility to drugs principally due to Belarus's geographic situation on the crossroads of two principal traffic streams, one coming from Afghanistan, Central and Southeast Asia (heroin, hashish, marijuana) to Western and Northern Europe, and the other of synthetic drugs coming in the opposite direction. In recent years, Belarus seems to have ceased to be just a place of transit. A large part of the transiting "goods" actually remains in the internal market, where it easily finds consumers. The flooding of the market with new products (methadone and amphetamines) provoked a general fall of the drug prices, thus increasing their accessibility for younger consumers.

These trends are accompanied by a pronounced increase in the number of drug offenses. According to data of the Ministry of Internal Affairs, during the last five years, the number of drug offenses increased by 26.7 percent, and the number of convicted persons by 32.3 percent. In 2006, a total of 4,959 drug offenses were registered, 1,945 of which related to illegal sale. A total of 719 kilograms (1,584 pounds) of papaverous straw, 16,446 kilograms (36,246 pounds) of drugs ready for consumption, 9,014 kilograms (19,866 pounds) of psychotropic substances, and 7,846 kilograms (17,292 pounds) of precursors were confiscated.

The national strategy of struggling against drug offenses is established by the Law of May 22, 2002, on Narcotic Substances, Psychotropic Substances and Precursors. The law establishes the national classification of the above substances. The official list of narcotic substances, psychotropic substances, and precursors is established by the Ordinance of the Ministry of Public Health of May 28, 2003. Only the substances that are included in this regularly updated list may constitute the object of a criminal offense. The following types of offenses qualify as criminal by the Belarusian Criminal Code:

- Theft of narcotic substances, psychotropic substances, and precursors.
- Illegal circulation of narcotic substances, psychotropic substances, and precursors, including fabrication, processing, conservation, transportation, and conveyance thereof.

- Sowing or cultivation of prohibited plants containing narcotic substances.
- Violation of rules of treatment of narcotic or psychotropic substances.
- Inciting to consumption of narcotic substances, psychotropic substances, or derivatives thereof.
- Organization or keeping of dens for consumption of narcotic or other stupefying substances.

Economic Offenses

Economic offenses include corruption and abuse of power, coinage offenses, illegal circulation of precious metals and nonferrous metals, illegal production and sale of alcohol-containing products. In 2006, Belarus registered 8,000 new incoming cases as economic offenses. Among these, the share of serious and particularly serious offenses constituted 50.8 percent according to the Ministry of Internal Affairs. There were 980 cases of corruption, 82 of which were committed in the industrial sphere, 75 in the construction sector, and 70 in educational establishments. The construction sector seems particularly affected by the corruption problem. Cases of bribery are frequent to obtain a permission of construction and leasing lots for construction of houses or commercial premises.

In 2006, the authorities of primary investigation registered 2,118 cases of marketing counterfeit currency, 240 of which concerned national currency. In the first semester of 2007, the number of cases amounted to 922, 133 of which concerned national currency. In 2007, the authorities of preliminary investigation dismantled 19 criminal groups specialized in counterfeiting bank notes. Yet, the principal difficulty of these cases relates to the fact that a large majority of the group members are aged less than 16 years, and therefore may not be criminally liable.

Finding of Guilt

Rights of the Accused

The Code of Criminal Procedure of the Republic of Belarus specifies 28 rights to which the accused is entitled, of which the major ones are the following:

- To be immediately informed of the charges.
- To obtain written information on the rights of the accused.
- For family members to be informed of the place of his or her detention.
- In case of pretrial detention, to obtain a free legal consultation before the first interrogation.
- To testify and refuse to testify.
- To submit evidence.
- To use his or her native language and have an interpreter.
- To plead guilty or not guilty.
- To object against actions of the investigating authority and have the objections registered in the protocol of the proceedings.
- To contest before a court of law his or her arrest, preliminary detention, home arrest, or placement in a psychiatric establishment for examination.
- To have access to the files of the criminal case and make copies thereof, after the investigation is officially terminated.
- To get acquainted with the protocols of the court audience, submit objections in respect to correctness and exhaustiveness thereof, and complete the protocols.
- To take part in the court debate, if the accused chose to carry out his or her own defense.
- To submit objections against protests of the public prosecutor, prosecutors, and against complaints of other participants of criminal proceedings.
- To obtain full compensation of damage caused by illegal actions of the authority in charge of the criminal proceedings, and be entirely rehabilitated, if the accusation is not confirmed.

The accused is entitled to a defender. The defender must be a lawyer belonging to the National Bar Association and qualified to practice law. However, in-court representation by a lawyer is not mandatory. The accused may opt to be defended by a close relative or by a legal representative. The right to legal aid is guaranteed by the state. Free legal aid may be provided by local bar associations and is financed by the state budget.

A lawyer's participation is generally obligatory if solicited by the accused, or if the accused is a minor, physically or mentally impaired, illiterate or cannot speak the language. Total or partial exemption of legal fees is within the discretion of the president of the bar.

Prosecution and Investigation of Cases

Criminal investigation is carried out by prosecutors, as well as criminal investigators and officers of preliminary investigation. The prosecutors are in charge of investigation of the crimes of particular seriousness as described in an earlier section. Other offenses fall under the jurisdiction of criminal investigators and officers of preliminary investigation belonging to the Ministry of Internal Affairs.

Alternatives to Trial

In the present state of legislation, there are no alternative (nonjudiciary) methods of treating criminal cases. However, in cases called "of private accusation," the criminal proceedings are initiated by the victim and may be terminated by reconciliation. However, the parties may reconcile at any moment of the criminal proceedings, before the judge leaves the courtroom for final deliberation. Only in 1.8 percent of cases are criminal proceedings terminated before trial. According to official statistics (Ministry of Justice, first semester of 2007), the majority of cases end up with a verdict of "guilty" (96.6%).

Incarceration Awaiting Trial

Preliminary detention of suspects or the accused is permitted by article 126 of the Code of Criminal Procedure. This measure of procedural constraint is applied for the offenses punishable by imprisonment for a term exceeding two years or on the grounds of the particular seriousness of the suspected crime. Preliminary detention may be exceptionally applied in less serious cases, when the suspect or the accused has no permanent residence in the territory of Belarus. Preliminary detention must be sanctioned by the prosecutor general, regional prosecutors, municipal prosecutors, or prosecutors having an equivalent status.

Status of Criminal Judges

There are no judges specializing in criminal matters in common courts. Criminal cases, as well as civil and administrative ones, are handled by the same judges within the common courts. Regional courts, possessing a more complex structure, have civil and criminal collegiums allowing a specialized approach to criminal cases.

To access the judicial profession, a person must satisfy the following qualification requirements: be a citizen of the Republic of Belarus, be over 25 years of age, have an excellent knowledge of the national languages, have a university law degree, have no criminal record, have no less than three years of experience in legal practice, and have successfully passed the qualification exam. Judges of all courts are appointed by the president, according to the Constitution of the Republic of Belarus and the Code on the Judicial System and Status of Judges.

Juveniles

At present, there is no specialized system of juvenile justice. Cases involving minors fall under the jurisdiction of common courts. However, the Code of Criminal Procedure contains specific provisions for criminal proceedings instituted against minors (under 18 years of age). General rules of criminal procedure remain applicable, but they are adapted to the age and the special needs of the accused. Thus, juvenile participants (suspects, accused, victims, witnesses) are mandatorily accompanied by their legal representatives (parents or legal guardians) and a pedagogue (a psychologist). The participation of a lawyer is obligatory, if the accused has not reached the age of majority on the day of the trial.

Criminal cases against minors are entrusted to judges having special training and experience in the matter. If the charges are brought against several persons, one of which is minor, the case against the latter is detached into a separate procedure, provided that such separate investigation "will not hamper an exhaustive, thorough and objective study of the case" (art. 431 of the Code of Criminal Procedure).

Interrogation of minors may not last more than two hours without intermission and may not exceed four hours in total. During the trial, minors are removed from the courtroom whenever the proceedings may negatively affect him or her. When sentencing, the court must give first priority to sanctions that are not related to deprivation of liberty.

Punishment

Article 47 of the Belarusian Criminal Code gives a legal definition to punishment as applied to criminal matters: "Punishment is a coercive measure, provided for by criminal law and applied on the basis of a judicial decision to a person convicted for crime. It consists in limiting convicts' rights or depriving them thereof under conditions provided by law."

The peculiarity of the Belarusian law system is that coercive penalties are far from monopolizing the criminal law. In fact, some rules of administrative law also provide for sanctions that consist in limiting personal rights or depriving offenders of certain liberties, that is, administrative fines, administrative arrest, correctional services. These correctional measures are not defined as punishment under criminal law. They are subject to special regulations under the Code of Administrative Offenses of April 21, 2003.

System of Punishments

The Belarusian Criminal Code establishes a system of punishments, which is an exhaustive list of legally possible sanctions arranged in a definite order, according to the degree of their severity. The system of punishments outlined by article 48 of the Criminal Code is constructed upon the principle of increasing severity of sanction, as follows:

- Public works
- Fine
- Revocation of right to occupy certain positions or to exercise certain activities/occupations
- Correctional work period
- Restrictions in military service
- Arrest
- Limitation of liberty
- Assignment to a disciplinary military unit
- Deprivation of liberty
- Life sentence
- Capital punishment

The criminal sanctions are also categorized into three general types: principal punishments, complementary punishments, and mixed ones.

Principal punishments are assigned by the judge, where they are provided for by the Criminal Code, as basic sanctions and may not be assigned as penalties complementary to other punishments. The punishments situated on levels 4 to 11 in the system of punishments may only be applied as principal punishments. For every committed crime, the judge may assign only one principal punishment provided for by the relevant article of the Criminal Code.

Complementary punishments may not be applied as an independent sanction, but only as an adjunct to a principal punishment. Where the code provides for several possible complementary sanctions, the judge may assign one or multiple complementary punishments. The severity of the complementary punishment may not be greater or equal to that of the principal punishment.

Mixed punishments may be used as principal punishments or as complementary ones, depending upon the case. The punishments situated on levels 1 to 3 in the system of punishments outlined above are mixed punishments.

The general system of punishments is not applicable to juvenile offenders. The system of punishments for juveniles consists of the following sanctions:

- Public works
- Fine
- Revocation of right to occupy certain positions or to exercise certain activities/occupations
- Correctional work period
- Arrest
- Deprivation of liberty

The first three levels are considered mixed punishments, whereas the last three may only be applied as principal ones. Despite the fact that limitation of liberty may not be assigned to minor convicts, judicial practice allows it when minors have reached the full legal age on the date of pronouncement of the verdict.

Types of Punishment

Public works consists in compelling the convicts to carrying out community services or other works of public interest, free of charge and during their free time. In general, public works are applied in cases where convicts' modest income does not allow them to pay the fine and when there is no evidence of evasion from the punishment. The duration of public works varies from 60 to 240 hours (from 30 to 180 hours for minors).

Criminal fines are pecuniary sanctions considered as interchangeable with public works. A fine may be applied as a principal and as a complementary sanction. The articles of the Criminal Code do not establish the amount of the fine applicable for different offenses. The judge determines the concrete sum on a case-by-case basis, taking into consideration the nature and the seriousness of the offense, as well as the convicts' paying capacity. The concrete amount is calculated in "basic units," which are microeconomic indicators established and regularly revised by the National Bank, within the boundaries running from 30 to 1,000 basic units. The given maximum and minimum boundaries are doubled for lucrative crimes and crimes committed for mercenary ends.

The revocation of rights to occupy certain positions or to exercise certain activities/occupations is applied when the crime is directly connected with the convicts' activity or with their position. The punishment may be for a term of one to five years. A copy of the verdict is sent to the employer, which must suspend the convicted worker from his or her functions within three working days.

A correctional work period consists in putting the convicted persons under an obligation to pay 10 to 25 percent of their income to the state budget during the period running from six months to two years. Income retentions are carried out monthly by the employer. Correctional work periods are not applied to minors aged under 16, to women aged over 55, to men aged over 60, to pregnant women, to persons on parental leave, to handicapped persons having an established degree of invalidity, and to military personnel. In case of the convicted person's unemployment on the day of the verdict's pronouncement, the person is required to find an employment corresponding to his or her qualifications within a two-week period. If the employment search turns out be fruitless, the convict is directed to the Public Service of Employment to acquire a priority job placement.

Restrictions in military service, applicable to military personnel, are similar to correctional works. Restrictions in military service are assigned to officers and other military personnel undergoing their military service on contract basis. Restrictions consist in imposing income retentions running from 10 to 25 percent of monthly pay and in impossibility of career advancement during the restrictions period.

Criminal arrest consists in temporary detention, during which the convicts are kept in the conditions of strict isolation. The convicts serve their sentence in detention homes, located within the region of their primary domicile. Depending on the nature and the seriousness of the crime, the term of detention may vary from 1 to 6 months. Juvenile delinquents having reached 16 years of age may be assigned a term of arrest varying from 15 days to 3 months. During the detention period, the convicts are not entitled to visits, other than visits of their lawyers and legal advisors. They are not entitled to receive packages, except for those containing the objects of primary necessity and seasonal clothing. Junior inmates not having reached 18 years of age are entitled to a monthly 4-hour visit of their parents or legal guardians. The inmates enjoy the right of a 1-hour walk per day (1-and-a-half-hour walk for junior inmates).

Limitation of liberty consists in placing the detainees in an "open-campus" correctional establishment and imposing on them an obligation to work for a public or private enterprise designated by the correctional establishment. The punishment entails multiple limitations of personal freedoms: freedom of movement, freedom to choose one's domicile, freedom of labor, freedom to choose one's occupation, and so forth. Thus, the inmates may not leave the territory of the correctional establishment without special permission to do so. The inmates are placed under constant surveillance of the penitentiary establishment: their person, their room and personal effects may be subjected to a search at any moment without a prosecutor's warrant. The inmates live in special dormitories of the correctional establishment. However, upon permission of the director of the correctional establishment, the inmates may live with their families in rented apartments or in their personal domiciles, provided that they do not violate the conditions of their detention and their work for the assigned enterprise. For the term of detention, the inmates' passports are taken by the administration of the correctional establishment and temporarily replaced by inmates' identity cards. Limitation of liberty is usually assigned on the grounds that the convict's correction and resocialization is possible without his or her isolation from the society. It may only be applied as a principal punishment for the minimal term of six months and for the maximal term of five years.

Assignment to a disciplinary military unit is applied to military personnel on temporary service having committed a military crime or any other crime during their service. The term of detention is set between three months and two years.

Deprivation of liberty (imprisonment) consists in placing convicts in conditions of strict isolation from society and from their immediate entourage and keeping them in a correctional establishment of a determined regime during the term established in the verdict. Deprivation of liberty or imprisonment may only be assigned as a principal punishment. Deprivation of liberty is considered to be an exceptional measure and is applied only for crimes of a particular social danger, if the judge deems, considering all the circumstances of the case, that a milder sanction shall not be proportionate to the convict's measure of responsibility. Article 57 of the Criminal Code sets general guidelines for determining the term of imprisonment. The deprivation of liberty may be assigned for the minimum period of 6 months and for the maximum period of 12 years. However, for the crimes of particular seriousness, the maximum limit is extended to 15 years, or even 25 years of imprisonment if there was especially intentional human suffering inflicted by the offender. The term of imprisonment for nonintentional crimes may not exceed 7 years. Sentences of imprisonment are served in a variety of correctional establishments specifically designated to match the social danger of the convicted individuals and the eventual risk of flight.

A part of the imprisonment sentence may be served in prisons, but no longer than five years, by persons sentenced for crimes of particular seriousness and in case of multiple recidivism. Reinforced and special regime are not applied to women, who are placed into correctional establishments reserved for women. Minor convicts aged less than 18 years old on the day of the verdict serve imprisonment sentences in educational colonies.

Life imprisonment is applicable as an alternative to capital punishment for crimes connected with encroachment on human life in presence of aggravating circumstances. Life sentence may not be assigned to minors or to women and men having attained 65 years of age on the day of the verdict. Persons convicted to a life sentence serve their punishment in correctional colonies of special regime, in isolation from common inmates. They are usually kept in separate cells, with no more than two inmates per cell. The correctional colonies do not organize any continuing educational training for convicts sentenced to life. However, they are obliged to create all necessary facilities for self-education.

Revocation of a military title may be applied exclusively as a complementary punishment (art. 60 of the Criminal Code), but in very serious cases the court may order permanent revocation of the special or military title.

Confiscation consists in total or partial requisition by the state of the convicted person's property. It may be mandatory or alternative. The property subject to confiscation may not be substituted by a proportionate sum of money. When applying confiscation measures, the judge must take into consideration the convicted person's family situation, the level of income, and the number of eventual dependants.

Death Penalty

Capital punishment is still practiced in the Republic of Belarus. No moratorium on the application of capital punishment is envisaged in the near future. However, on March 11, 2004, the Constitutional Court rendered public its assessment of the compliance of the death-penalty provisions in the Criminal Code with the Constitution, following a request from the House of Representatives of the National Assembly. The court found a number of provisions of the Criminal Code to be inconsistent with the Constitution, thus providing for the possibility of either the abolition of the death penalty or the imposition of a moratorium on executions as a first step toward full abolition. The constitutional court's ruling provoked a legislative reform of the Criminal Code. The constitutional law adopted on June 23, 2006, supplemented the Criminal Code with a reference to the temporary character of the death penalty, which, until its abolition, may be assigned as "an exceptional measure which may only be applied for cases of premeditated murder with aggravating circumstances" (art. 59.1 of the Criminal Code). Thus, the actual wording of article 59.1 suggests that the evolution of the criminal legislation will ultimately lead to a total abolition of this type of punishment.

The Supreme Court has emphasized that capital punishment is to be applied in exceptional cases, when the crime was committed in aggravating circumstances, the seriousness of which characterizes the author of the crime as particularly dangerous for the society. If a life sentence is substituted for capital punishment, the judge must present clear and exhaustive reasons in the final verdict. The reason for the punishment is subject to thorough review by the superior jurisdictions, a procedure initiated by the prosecutor general.

In the present state of law, capital punishment may be applied for the following 14 types of crimes, directly provided for by the Criminal Code:

- Unleashing or leading an aggressive war
- Murder of an official representative of a foreign state or of an international organization with an aim to provoke international tensions or war)
- International terrorism
- Genocide
- Crimes against security of humanity
- Use of weapons of mass destruction
- Violation of laws and customs of war
- Aggravated murder
- Terrorism
- High treason associated with murder
- Conspiracy aiming at taking over state power, entailing accidental death, or associated with murder
- Act of terrorism
- Act of sabotage
- Murder of a police officer

Compared to the old legislation, the number of cases in which the law directly allows for application of capital punishment has considerably diminished (30 to 14). In addition, all of the aforementioned articles provide for life sentence as an alternative to capital punishment.

The law prohibits applying capital punishment to the following categories of convicts: (1) persons having committed a crime before having attained 18 years of age, (2) women, and (3) men having attained 65 years of age on the date of the verdict. If the convict has reached 60 years of age on the date of verdict enforcement, the court must substitute imprisonment.

Persons sentenced to a death penalty are entitled to file a clemency application. Appeals are initially considered by the Clemency Commission. If the application is granted, the death penalty is commuted to life imprisonment. In any case, death penalties may not be put into effect unless the clemency application is officially rejected. Since 1994, the cases of all individuals sentenced to death are automatically considered, regardless of whether the sentenced person has submitted an appeal for clemency. According to Organization for Security and Co-operation in Europe (OSCE) data, in the period from June 30, 2006, to June 30, 2007, the president did not grant clemency.

The method of execution of capital punishment in Belarus is death by shooting. The death penalty is executed in complete secrecy, in presence of the prosecutor, the penitentiary establishment director, and a doctor. Relatives are not informed in advance of the date of execution. The administration of the correctional institution where the execution is carried out is obliged to notify a close relative once the execution is realized. The body is not returned to the family, and the place of burial is not disclosed.

The number of death penalty sentences in Belarus is covered by state secret. The official statistics on the number of executions are therefore not available. According to United Nations data, five death sentences were executed in 2005. The number was brought down to three in 2006. According to the information provided by the Supreme Court, during the period from June 30, 2006, to June 30, 2007, one individual was executed. However, due to inaccessibility of the official data, the real number of executions may be considerably higher.

Typical Punishments

Murder

Murder is punishable by 6 to 15 years of imprisonment, 8 years to life imprisonment, or death penalty with aggravating circumstances. According to statistics of the Supreme Court for 2002, in 97 percent of nonaggravated murder cases and 99 percent of "aggravated" murder cases, the tribunals opted for imprisonment.

Rape

Rape entails limitation of liberty for maximum duration of 4 years or, alternatively, of imprisonment for the term of 3 to 7 years and in aggravating circumstances 5 to 13 years.

Serious Theft

Serious theft is punished by 2 to 7 years of imprisonment, with assorted confiscation or without such. Particularly large-scale theft, the economic value of which is beyond US$16,556 (1,000 basic units), and theft committed by an organized group are punished by 3 to 12 years of imprisonment, with assorted confiscation.

Drug Offenses

Manufacturing, processing, acquisition, storage, transportation, or remittance of narcotic or psychotropic substances with the aim of sale thereof, or sale of narcotic or psychotropic substances, is punishable by limitation of liberty for the maximum term of 5 years or, alternatively, by 2 to 5 years of imprisonment; if by an organized group, 10 to 15 years of imprisonment, with assorted confiscation. The most commonly applied punishment is imprisonment for the term of 1 to 2 years. In 2005, such sanction was assigned in 55.7 percent of cases.

Prison

The number of inmates kept in correctional colonies, educational colonies, and prisons on January 1, 2006, was 41,538, of which 19.6 percent was pretrial or remand prisoners, 7.5 percent were female, 2 percent juveniles, and 4 percent foreigners. The number of correctional institutions numbered 32, with an official capacity of 43,400.

Work in Prison

Socially useful work is considered to be the key to the prisoners' rehabilitation program. For this reason, inmates are required to work, while serving their sentence, for the enterprises officially operated by the Penitentiary Administration and equipped to accommodate prisoners. Prisoners work in workshops established in the confines of the penitentiary establishment, or in workshops situated outside of the penitentiary establishment. In general, all public and private enterprises may employ prisoners, provided that their factory premises are secured and isolated.

Male prisoners having reached 60 years of age, female prisoners having reached 55 years of age, and handicapped persons do not have an obligation to work. However, their employment is encouraged, as a measure of rehabilitation and reintegration in the society. Juvenile prisoners having reached 16 years of age are required to work on a regular basis, but no longer than 35 hours per week. Upon a written permission of parents, guardians, or educational establishment, juvenile prisoners not having reached 16 years of age may carry out easy tasks, which do not present any health risks and do not interfere with their studying process. The maximum length of the workweek may not exceed 23 hours for juvenile prisoners aged 14 to 16.

The time of work in prison is counted within the time of continuous service for the purposes of social security and retirement funding. Prisoners are entitled to an annual paid leave of 18 workdays for inmates of educational colonies, and of 12 workdays for inmates of correctional colonies. For prisoners serving their first sentence, paid leave may be granted outside of the correctional establishment.

Prisoners' labor is paid proportionately to their working time or to their output rate. In any case, the salary may not be lower than the level of the minimum monthly income established by law for the particular type of work. Monthly salaries are paid directly to prisoners' personal bank accounts. The correctional establishment deducts amounts for catering and clothing fees and costs of the communal services (gas, electricity, heating). However, the monthly deductions may not take more than 75 percent of a prisoner's salary. Prisoners subscribe to mandatory social insurance contracts and pay superannuation contributions to the Retirement Pensions Fund. According to article 101 of the Code of Execution of Punishments, prisoners' labor may be used free by the correctional establishment for cleaning, laundering, cooking, and other services.

Education in Prison

Considered as one of the principal means of the prisoners' correction, educational measures are mandatory. Correctional establishments, in cooperation with public organizations, nongovernment associations, and religious organizations, organize educational activities, aiming at providing prisoners with legal information; stimulating their interest in cultural, political, social life; involving them into team sport activities; and keeping them from losing touch with life outside prison. Educational activities in correctional colonies are supervised by section directors, and in educational colonies by special educators. A staff psychologist is present at every correctional establishment.

General secondary education is compulsory for all prisoners not having reached 30 years of age. Prisoners having reached 30 years of age and handicapped persons may attend the courses on a voluntary basis. Continuing education facilities are organized in cooperation with local executive authorities. Prisoners are offered a paid leave for the term of the examination period.

Article 108 of the Code of Execution of Punishment allows creation, within correctional establishments, of voluntary associations of prisoners, aiming at improvement of the quality of life in prison, organizing and diversifying leisure time, maintaining order and discipline, and carrying out other activities. Members of associations are not entitled to any privileges. However, participation in associations is taken into account when evaluating prisoners' degree of rehabilitation for the purposes of release on parole, reduction of the term of imprisonment, or substitution of imprisonment by a milder sanction.

Daria Solenik

Further Reading

General Prosecutor's Office: http://prokuratura.gov.by.

Krygier, Martin, and Adam Czarnota, eds. (1999). *The Rule of Law after Communism: Problems and Prospects in East-Central Europe.* Aldershot, UK: Ashgate.

Ministry of Internal Affairs: http://mvd.gov.by.

Ministry of Justice of the Republic of Belarus: http://www.minjust.by.

National Center of Legal Information: http://www.ncpi.gov.by.

Obokata, Tom. (2005). "Trafficking of Human Beings as a Crime against Humanity: Some Implications for the International Legal System." *International and Comparative Law Quarterly* 54(2): 445–457.

The Supreme Court of the Republic of Belarus: http://www.supcourt.by.

Szirmai, Zsolt, ed. (1994). *Law in Eastern Europe: A Series of Publications. Criminal Law.* Leyden: University of Leyden, the Documentation Office for East European Law; A. W. Sijthoff.

Belgium

Legal System: Civil
Murder: Medium
Burglary: Medium
Corruption: Low
Human Trafficking: Low
Prison Rate: Medium
Death Penalty: No
Corporal Punishment: No

Background

At the time of its independence in 1830, Belgium retained from its period of annexation to France (1792–1815) the repressive Napoleonic laws that were in vigor at that time, that is, the 1808 Code of Penal Procedure and the 1810 Penal Code that had basically not been changed during the reunion with the Netherlands (1815–1830). The adoption, in 1867, of the first Belgian Penal Code followed the spirit of the previously existing laws, although the severity of the punishments was somewhat moderated. With regard to penal procedure, the system proposed by the legislator in 1808 was retained, containing elements of both the accusatorial and inquisitorial systems. The preliminary phase of the penal process during which the repressive dossier is constituted is more of the inquisitorial type (secret, noncontradictory, and written), whereas the judgment phase is more of the accusatorial type (public, adversary, and oral).

Police

As of the law of December 7, 1998, a single integrated police service is organized and structured on two autonomous levels, the federal and the local level. The local police fulfill the basic police tasks at the level of the 196 police zones covering one or more municipalities. The federal police fulfills tasks on the whole territory, conducting specialized and supralocal tasks of administrative and judicial police, as well as tasks in support of the local police and of the police authorities. The Ministry of Interior and the Ministry of Justice are responsible for coordinating the general policy with respect to police and the management of the local and federal police forces.

The idea to reorganize the structure of the police followed a series of tragic events that have marked the history of Belgium during the 1980s and that have brought the shortcomings and dysfunctions of the administration of criminal justice, and of the police in particular, to the foreground of the political scene. This reform process, described very briefly here, did, however, not develop without friction and criticism.

At the time of the reform the local police comprised about 27,500 people and the federal police some 10,000 people, which brought the total number at close to 37,500, or about 3.7 policemen per 1,000 inhabitants. The overall numbers have hardly changed, but the reform is said to have resulted in a decrease of the proportion of policemen working at the local level from three-quarters to about two-thirds of the whole group. To these operational police officers, one has to add the civilian staff that resort under the administrative and logistical framework that are constantly on the rise (close to 7,500 in 2006). In a structural way, at the local level the police has gone from 586 municipal police brigades and 429 territorial gendarmerie brigades to 196 police zones. The federal police, on its side, has since its creation in 2001 undergone important structural reorganizations.

Crime

Classification of Crimes

Belgian penal law distinguishes between three categories of criminal acts in increasing order of seriousness: contraventions, misdemeanors, and felonies. The categories are defined in law not based on intrinsic characteristics of the behavior but based on the nature of the penalty applied to them. Contraventions attract police punishments, misdemeanors correctional punishments, and felonies criminal punishments. In principle, the police court presides over contraventions, the correctional court over misdemeanors, and the *cour d'assises* over felonies. However, acts that are normally classified as felonies can be subject to a process of "correctionalization" by applying mitigating circumstances and hence be judged by a correctional court. The possibilities for correctionalization have gradually been broadened over the last 30 years to such an extent that it is now possible for all felonies that do not attract a penalty of more than 20 years and for a certain number of felonies for which the legal penalty is more than 20 years. In the same manner mitigating circumstances can lead up to a misdemeanor being tried before the police court. This means that the division of criminal acts in three categories is constantly up for discussion through the continuous extension of the technique of correctionalization, and—to a lesser extent—of "contraventionalization." These processes make it virtually impossible to make a definitive list of criminal acts falling under the different categories.

Crime Statistics

Police crime statistics are only recently available in Belgium. The first were gathered for the year 1994. Since 2000, due to the police reform, a different system is used to produce the statistical data. Excluding traffic offenses, 1,002,829 cases were recorded by the police in 2007, of which 93.4 percent were completed acts and 6.6 percent attempts. The category that is represented the most in the police statistics is the one including all kinds of thefts, burglaries, and robberies: they comprise about 42 percent of registered crime in 2007. This proportion is slowly decreasing: it was 50 percent in 2000 and 52 percent in 1994. Next come the violent property crimes (vandalism, destruction, arson) amounting to 12 percent of registered crime in 2007, which represent a slight increase as compared to 2000 (10.5%). The group of offenses against physical integrity, consisting mainly of assaults but also of rapes and murders, represents about 9 percent of the criminality registered in 2007. This was 7 percent in 2000. Fraudulent crimes against property (fraud, breach of trust, receiving and concealing stolen goods, etc.) constitute about 5 percent of crimes registered in 2007, which was about 7 percent in 2000. Finally, drug-related criminality (possession, use, or trafficking) amount to a bit more than 4 percent of the crime registered in 2007, a proportion that has hardly changed since 2000. These five categories together represent 70 percent of the total amount of registered crime. Crimes (per 100,000 population, not including attempts) recorded by police in 2006 are as follows:

Homicide	2.1
Rape	27
Theft	3,533
Of which robbery	168
Bodily injury	674
Of which nonfamily	429
Of which in family	245
Drugs total	384
Of which traffic	112

A recent study of the National Institute for Criminalistics and Criminology, based on data of correctional and youth courts, shows that the portion of registered crime that can be attributed to minors is about 11 percent.

Finding of Guilt

Judicial Organization, Procedure, and Rights

The exercise of penal justice belongs in principle to the police courts for contraventions, to correctional courts and its court of appeal for misdemeanors, and to the *cour d'assises*—court with a jury—for felonies. This principle is modulated because of the application of a process of correctionalization or of contraventionalization due to the admission of mitigating circumstances.

Ronny Baudewyn, the lawyer for Marc Dutroux, speaks during a court session at the Palace of Justice in Arlon, Belgium, June 21, 2004. Prosecutors called for convicted pedophile Dutroux to spend the rest of his life behind bars for multiple counts of child rape and murder. Dutroux is seen at rear right. (AP Photo)

The burden of proof in penal matters rests exclusively with the prosecution authority. The public prosecutor plays an important role in the Belgian system: the police must inform him or her of every offense and he or she then decides which measures have to be taken by the police to gather the necessary elements related to the offense. The public prosecutor can also requisition an examining magistrate that will examine the case both for and against the offender.

The suspect or prosecuted person can rely on the presumption of innocence, on the right to a fair trial, and on the right to defend oneself according to the principles conferred by article 6 of the European Convention on Human Rights. The position of the parties is, however, very different depending on whether it is the preliminary phase of the penal process, which is of the inquisitorial type, or in the adversarial phase of the judgment. The Law on March 12, 1998 Concerning the Improvement of Penal Procedure at the Pre-trial Stage brought about important changes in the existing balance between the rights of the prosecution authorities, the victim, and the accused. At the stage of information gathering, the rights of the accused still remain almost nonexistent, except for the possibility to ask for a copy of one's interrogation. At the stage of the preliminary investigation, however, the position of the accused has been completely revisited. Thus from now on, the investigating judge has to formally charge the person against whom serious indications of guilt exist, which brings about a number of rights for the accused. The accused has the right to request access to the dossier or to ask for additional investigative acts to be undertaken. Whereas, at the time, the critics of the law saw it as only a tentative and partial reform, it has proven to be a stimulating factor in the next improvements of the penal procedure.

The role of the victim, especially since the Dutroux affair (a widely known case of a child murderer and sexual abuse that instigated a public outcry and the White March of 300,000 people in protest), has become more important. Since 1985, the state may compensate certain victims of intentional violent crimes. The provictim movement also resulted, in the 1990s, in a number of concrete actions in favor of victims and their need for recognition. In 1993, the Chamber of Representatives called for the creation of a national forum for a provictim policy and in 1996 the minister of justice established a victim aid service in every public prosecutor's office. The law of March 12, 1998, concerning the improvement of penal procedure aims to put victims on the same level as suspects in terms of rights and guarantees: their prerogatives are strengthened during the preliminary investigation and, to a lesser extent, at the stage of information gathering. Consideration of the victim was even accentuated further by the law of May 17, 2006, concerning the external status of persons convicted to deprivation of liberty and concerning the victim rights recognized in the framework of the modalities for executing a punishment.

Alternatives to Trial

In Belgium, the fact that an offense was committed, the identification of its author, and the collection of sufficient evidence against the offender do not in all cases lead to a criminal process. The public prosecutor indeed has the possibility to drop the case for various reasons. These can be linked to the nature of the facts themselves (limited social repercussions or very limited damage, for example), to the person of the offender (no prior record, disproportionate consequences, etc.), or to criminal policy considerations (priorities, investigative capacities). This possibility is used frequently: in 2007 it represented about 77 percent of the decisions to close a case at the level of the correctional court (excluding the decisions to dismiss a case because the offender could not be identified, because there was no crime, or because of insufficient evidence).

In 18 percent of these cases, a penal process takes place, and in another 5 percent an alternative way of handling the case is used, that is, a penal transaction (2.5%), penal mediation (1%), or praetorian probation (1.6%), according to prosecution authority sources. The *penal transaction* consists of the prosecutor inviting the offender to pay a certain sum, to give up certain objects that were seized or to return them. The fulfillment of the penal transaction leads to the extinction of the public action. *Penal mediation* encompasses a proposal to mediate between offender and victim in search of a negotiated solution, but also extinction of the public action as a result of performing community service, following a training, or following therapy. Finally, *praetorian probation* entails the postponement of the prosecutor's decision to prosecute following commitments made by the offender. Its use should remain exceptional (1.6% of the cases in 2007).

Incarceration before Trial

Detention before judgment is possible in the Belgian system. Its use is regulated by the law on detention on remand. The framework for pretrial detention is of the inquisitorial type even though the legislator of 1990 introduced a certain contradictory element during the required interrogation by the investigating judge.

In theory, pretrial detention has to remain exceptional: the law limits its use to cases where it is absolutely necessary for reasons of public safety and only if the fact would call for a detention of at least 1 year. In addition, if the maximum punishment would not surpass 15 years of imprisonment, there has to be a risk of reoffending, a risk for proof to disappear, or a risk of conspiracy with third parties. It is clear that these elements are susceptible to speculation.

In practice the use of pretrial detention may indeed be questioned due to its increasingly frequent use. Research conducted by the National Institute for Criminalistics and Criminology shows besides that for all arrest warrants issued in 2003, the proportion of arrest warrants that are not motivated by at least a violation of physical integrity is very variable depending on the judicial district. Whereas it is close to 30 percent in one of the 27 judicial districts, it reaches 75 percent in another, which indicates a strong divergence in judiciary practice.

Juveniles

The age of criminal majority is fixed at 18, which also corresponds to the age of civil majority. For acts committed before this age, the minor will fall under a specific jurisdiction, the youth court, which is one of the sections of the court of first instance. However, in certain cases the youth court can send the minor to adult court when it considers that a "safeguarding, protecting or educational measure" is not adequate and on the condition that the facts were committed by a minor more than 16 years of age.

Although they did not fundamentally touch upon the philosophy of this model, the recent laws of June 13 and 15, 2006, have, nevertheless, after decennia of critique, debates, and attempted reforms brought about important changes at the level of the range of measures available until then. The reference model remains protectionist even though both "restorative" and "punishment" approaches have been introduced.

Punishment

Types of Punishment

Belgian penal law basically allows distinguishing between the different existing punishments on the basis of two criteria: the relationship between the different punishments on the one hand, and their level of seriousness on the other hand. In function of the relationship between the punishments, Belgian penal law basically distinguishes between three categories: the principal punishments, the accessory punishments, and the subsidiary punishments. The *principal punishments,* which are the direct punishment for the offense, exist autonomously and can be imposed alone, without being accompanied by any of the other types. Following the law of July 10, 1996, that abolished the death penalty and modified the criminal sentences, the principal sentences are imprisonment, the work sentence, and the fine. The work sentence, considered to be more serious than a fine, was introduced in the penal code by the law of April 17, 2002. It has been foreseen as an alternative to imprisonment and can thus not be added to a term of imprisonment.

The effective application of these different sentences—or a part of them—can be made conditional on probation, in the form of a suspension or a postponement. In case of a suspension, the judge suspends the judgment during a fixed probationary period. In case of a postponement, he or she passes judgment and imposes a sentence but suspends its execution. Both suspension and postponement can be accompanied by probationary conditions. These can take different forms and can consist of either an interdiction (not being allowed to frequent certain places or people, a prohibition to perform certain activities, etc.) or an obligation (obligation to undergo medical or therapeutic follow-up, obligation to repair the harm caused, etc.). Before the introduction of the work sentence as an autonomous punishment in 2002, the performance of a community service was also a possible probationary condition.

The *accessory punishments* are punishments that necessarily owe their existence to the existence of a principal punishment to which they are being attached. The accessory punishments are notably the suspension of certain civil and political rights, the closing of an establishment, the dissolution of a driver's license, the publication or the distribution of judgments and arrests, the special confiscation, or the fine accompanying a prison sentence. Another accessory punishment is the order to remain at the disposal of the government—which was replaced recently by remaining at the disposal of the court for the application of sentences—with the aim to protect society against people who have committed certain serious acts that have touched upon the integrity of people and/or recidivist offenses. This complementary punishment takes place after the prison sentence and can last for a minimum of 5 years and a maximum of 15 years.

The *subsidiary punishments* are punishments that replace the ones pronounced if the latter are not being executed. Until recently only imprisonment could be used as a subsidiary punishment in case of nonpayment of fines. The duration of the subsidiary imprisonment is fixed in the sentence from the outset. Since the introduction of the work sentence, the fine may also constitute a subsidiary sentence to the work sentence, in the same manner as imprisonment. Finally, since 2003, in the case of traffic offenses, the dissolution of the right to drive can be applied in case a fine has not been paid.

In terms of their level of seriousness, one may distinguish—in decreasing order—three categories of sentences among the principal sentences: the criminal sentences, the correctional sentences, and the police sentences. Life imprisonment is at the top of the scale of punishments. Temporary criminal detention is of at least 5 years and can be pronounced for four different terms depending on the degree of seriousness: from 20 to 30 years, from 15 to 20 years, from 10 to 15 years, and from 5 to 10 years. In principle it is the *cour d'assises* that passes judgment over crimes. However, they can be the object of a process of correctionalization through the admission of mitigating circumstances for acts normally defined as crimes, in such a way that they can be tried before the correctional court. Correctional imprisonment can in that case be of 10 years, and exceptionally more due to the application of the rules on recidivism and on the convergence of offenses. The following three principal punishments can be *correctional punishments:* imprisonment of a minimum of 8 days and a maximum of 5 years, a work punishment of 46 to 300 hours, and a fine of a minimum €26 (US$33) (multiplied by a coefficient that is regularly adapted to the actual value of money). The same three punishments can be *police punishments* to respond to a contravention: imprisonment of 1 to 7 days, work punishment from 20 to 45 hours, and a fine of a maximum €25 (US$31).

When we consider all the cases in which judgment was passed by the different tribunals, and if we exclude the acquittals, about 95 percent of the cases lead to a sentence of punishment, close to 5 percent to a suspended sentence, and only 0.2 percent to an internment, according to figures of convictions (Ministry of Justice). Of all the punishments pronounced as a principal or accessory punishment, the fine is the most frequently used: of the 359,965 punishments pronounced in 2002, 179,897 were fines (in 164,514 distinct convictions), amounting to 50 percent. In 74 percent of cases the fine is imposed as a principal punishment. On the other hand, about 36 percent of the fines are postponed and this is more frequently done when the fine is imposed as a principal punishment (40%). The punishment that comes second in terms of being imposed the most is the dissolution of the right to drive, which represents 40 percent of the totality. For the same year, 2002, the deprivations of liberty represented 7.6 percent of all punishments. The work sentence, introduced quite recently, has known a rapid development: the mandates given to the justice assistants that are charged with their implementation increased from 556 in 2002—the first year in which the punishment was introduced—to 10,131 in 2008.

The predominance of the fines is, however, related to the high number of traffic offenses. If we leave out this category of offenses, and if we also do not consider the cases decided by the police courts, it is the deprivation of liberty that is by far the punishment being imposed the most: in 2002 deprivation of liberty was imposed by way of principal punishment in 77 percent of cases (23,510) whereas this was the case for fines in 19 percent of cases (5,854).

According to the Ministry of Justice figures available for the years 1995 to 2004, on average, 54 percent of the imprisonments imposed by correctional and police courts are accompanied by a postponement of either the whole punishment or a part of it. This proportion is almost identical for the imprisonments up to 6 months as for those between 6 months and 5 years. It is, on the other hand, only 1 percent for the punishments of 5 years and more. In terms of evolution (1995–2004), one can notice the downward trend of the prison sentences up until 6 months (34% less over 10 years), whereas the sentences from 6 months to less than 5 years have increased (13% more over 10 years). This increase is even more important for prison sentences of 5 years and more—of which 97 percent are sentences between 5 and 10 years—since they have increased 24 percent over this period. In regard to the prison sentences imposed for felonies by the *cour d'assises* one can see that 80 percent of the sentences imposed are longer than 10 years. Even though it is difficult to draw firm conclusions based on relatively weak numbers, we can nevertheless discern a general upward tendency in the number of long sentences imposed over this 10-year period (58 in 1995 and 93 in 2004).

Typical Punishments

While it is difficult to account for the different punishments for different crimes because of the use of accessory punishments and cumulated punishments, the proportions of those sentenced to prison for a selection of offenses is of interest. It is for homicide, and more particularly for completed homicide, that imprisonment is the most typical sentence. In this case it represents, in 2004, 78 percent of the 241 convictions. This compares to rape with 537 convictions and 36 percent sentenced to prison; 4,904 convictions for bodily injury with 28 percent sentenced to prison; robbery, 2,739 convictions and 43 percent sentenced to prison; theft with 8,446 convictions and 48 percent receiving prison; drug offenses, 4,317 and 31 percent receiving prison. The use of postponed detention, either totally or partially, was used the most in case of rape (or attempted rape) with 63 percent receiving suspended sentences. In the case of theft and violent theft, imprisonment is imposed in almost half of the cases.

Tribunals for the Application of Punishment

The recent law of May 17, 2006, established tribunals for the application of punishments, which now belong to a specific jurisdiction to decide on granting the different modalities to execute a prison sentence. These concern conditional release, but also limited detention (authorization for the inmate to leave the prison during 12 hours per day), electronic monitoring, provisional release with a view to leaving the territory (for convicted persons without a residence permit or who will be extradited or handed over as a result of a European arrest warrant), or still the replacement of the prison sentence with a work sentence. For the sentences of which the outstanding part is more than 3 years, the decision has to be made by the tribunal (one judge and two assessors). For the sentences of which the part that remains to be executed is below or equal to 3 years, the judge of application of punishment can decide alone. However, he or she will only be given these competencies starting from September 2012.

Since 1930, Belgium has had a specific regime for criminals who, because of mental problems, are not considered to be responsible for their acts. These do not receive a punishment but are imposed measures of internment that resemble much more safety measures and that aim at protecting society as well as at treating the ill. This regime has, however, been changed by the law of April 21, 2007, which has given the competence related to the execution of internment measures to the new tribunals for the application of punishments. These dispositions will, however, not enter into effect before January 1, 2012.

Prison

Prison Population

On March 1, 2008, the Belgian prison population amounted to 9,858 detainees or 93 detainees per 100,000 inhabitants. Compared to other European countries, this detention rate might seem moderate. However, when we consider the Belgian situation on its own and especially when we consider it from a long-term perspective, the inflation of the prison population is a striking phenomenon. An upward trend could already be observed in the 1980s but it was mainly from the 1990s on that the increase became important and continuous. The average population was close to 6,000 in 1991 but more than 10,000 in 2007, which is an increase of more than 60 percent in 16 years.

Over the long term of these last three decennia, the inflation of the prison population is not due to the incarceration of a higher number of people: the entries in detention are much higher in 1975 or 1980 than in 2007. Prison inflation is likely linked to the fact that the length of detention has in general increased considerably rather than to the actual sentencing of more individuals to prison. The average length of imprisonment, calculated on the whole prison population, has increased from 3.5 months in 1980 to 7.1 months in 2007.

There are two large categories of the population that also weigh the heaviest on the phenomenon of inflation of the prison population. The first of these are the convicted prisoners (51% of the population in March 2008), and the second the detainees whose conviction is not definite yet (34%, of whom 28% are detained before judgment and 6% have appealed against their judgment or are within the terms for doing so). The category of detainees that fall under the specific regime for persons having a mental illness represents 14 percent and is relatively more stable. Youth represent only a very small proportion of the Belgian prison population.

Between 1980 and 2007, the number of prisoners whose conviction was not final yet had multiplied by about 2.5. Before the 1990s the rise of this category of prisoners was linked to an increase in the duration of pretrial detention. However, since then two phenomena coincide: an increase in the number of arrest warrants and an increase in the duration of pretrial detention (1.6 months in 1980 and 3.2 months in 2005).

During the same period, the population with a final conviction has doubled. The observed inflation is mainly due to a rather phenomenal increase in the population of those sentenced to terms of more than 5 years of imprisonment. The number of prisoners convicted to long sentences was below 500 between 1975 and 1980. Afterward it increased to almost 3,000 in 2007, which means a multiplication by a factor of more than 6.5. The increase in the number of those purging a correctional sentence between 3 and 5 years is also considerable: the population has multiplied by 4. The category of those purging a correctional sentence between 1 and 3 years was relatively stable until the end of the 1990s and afterward shows a significant downward trend. The number of those serving a correctional sentence of less than 1 year of imprisonment is clearly decreasing. On the long term the above confirms the hypothesis of a bifurcation in the use of imprisonment, that is, a lower use of deprivation of liberty at the lower end of the penal sentences but longer prison sentences at the upper end.

Electronic monitoring was introduced in Belgium as an alternative way to undergo a prison sentence. It was first applied in 1998, as a pilot, and later became a legally recognized form of deprivation of liberty. It can, in principle, be applied to both the shortest and longest sentences. According to figures from the Prison Administration, the use of electronic monitoring has clearly not helped to stop the increase of those convicted to the longest sentences. It also cannot explain by itself the decrease in the group of those convicted to a sentence of less than 3 years in prison because of its relatively minor application. The introduction of electronic monitoring thus seems not to have had a real significant impact on the volume of the prison population.

The evolution of the convicted population can be explained by two types of factors: on the one hand, what happens at the level of imposing prison sentences, and on the other hand, what happens at the level of the practice of early release. The reconstruction of series (1975–2004 with a break within 1992 and 1994) clearly shows the important increase of the totality of the sentences of more than 5 years. The two series of those convicted to a long-term sentence and of those in prison convicted to a long-term sentence actually presents a high correlation ($R^2 = 0.76$). The rise of the population of detainees convicted to long sentences is thus certainly the reflection of an increased severity in the decisions by the courts and tribunals.

But a look at the data relating to early release will, however, show that this is not the only factor providing an explanation. Belgium has two main forms of early release. *Conditional release* exists since 1888 and may in principle be applied to all categories of convicted people. Whereas before it was a prerogative of the executive power (Ministry of Justice), it is now—since 1998—subject to a process of judiciarization. The decision to grant conditional release was first entrusted to commissions for the application of early release, and more recently, since 2007 (law of May 17, 2006), to the new courts for the application of sentences. *Provisional release* is a form of early release awarded by the minister of justice, and more precisely by his or her administration. Whereas before it was granted for special reasons, it has become—in the 1980s—a way to manage prison overcrowding and is applied in a systematic way to those convicted of a sentence of a maximum 3 years.

Available figures clearly show a considerable rise of the provisional releases over this period, that is, mainly benefiting those convicted to a sentence of less than 3 years, and on the other side, a significant downward trend of the conditional release since 1991. But a more useful indicator is the time span between the moment at which the prisoner is legally eligible for conditional release and the moment of the effective release. The results are striking: this time span evolves from an average of 5.2 months in 1990 to 14.4 months in 2007. The "waiting" time between the date at which the prisoner is eligible for conditional release and the conditional release in itself has thus been multiplied by 2.8 in 17 years. The transfer of the decision-making power relating to conditional release from the administration to the judiciary, which took place in the "after-Dutroux" context, has thus also been accompanied by a more restrictive use of releases. This observation helps to explain the previously established phenomenon of bifurcation.

Prison System

In 2007, there were 31 penitentiaries in Belgium for adult detainees, one (federal) center depending on the penitentiary administration for the placement of minors that cannot be placed in the institutions for the protection of minors, and three social defense institutions for mentally ill who have been placed on internment after having committed an offense. However, the current minister of justice announced a building plan in April 2008 to respond to a deficit that was evaluated at 1,500 cells.

The law of January 12, 2005, or the law Concerning the Principles of the Administration of the Penitentiary Institutions and Concerning the Legal Status of Detainees, saw a crucial improvement of the rights of detainees. For the first time, starting from the objective to limit the negative consequences of detention, the legislator defined the rights and duties of detainees, the basic principles of detention, and the organization of the prison system. Pushed by budgetary reality, the legislator has nevertheless left it up to the executive power to fix the dates of the entry into force of the different dispositions. In October 2008, this law is only very partially in application, the executive power having considered that a prior evaluation of the needs generated by the law, particularly in terms of personnel and infrastructure, was needed. It is quite evident that the overcrowding, but also—to a lesser extent—the resistance of the surveillance staff, is an important restraint for the concrete implementation of this law. Whereas the fundamental principles have effectively entered into force, important parts like the ones concerning the living conditions in prisons—material conditions or conditions related to living together—the detention plan, education and leisure activities, work, or the creation of consultative bodies are still not being applied. Thus, whereas the prisoner in principle has the right to participate in the available work in the prison, and in theory benefits of the widest possible access to education activities, these rights are in practice seriously limited because the prisons are not able to make these possibilities available. Currently, priority has been awarded to three issues: order and security, discipline of the inmates, and health care.

Charlotte Vanneste

Further Reading

Bosly, Henri, Georges Demanet, Jean-Michel Messine, and Michel Bernard, eds. (2007). *Cent ans de publication de droit pénal et de criminologie: Le centenaire de la Revue de Droit pénal et de Criminologie* [Hundred Years of Publications in Penal Law and Criminology: The Hundredth Anniversary of the *Revue de Droit pénal et de Criminologie*]. Brussels: La Charte.

Federal Police: http://www.polfed-fedpol.be.
Heirbaut, Dirk, Xavier Rousseaux, and Karel Velle, eds. (2004). *Histoire politique et sociale de la justice en Belgique de 1830 à nos jours* [Political and Social History of Justice in Belgium since 1830]. Brussels: La Charte.
Ministry of Justice: http://www.just.fgov.be.
National Institute for Criminalistics and Criminology: http://incc.fgov.be.
Snacken, Sonia. (2007). "Penal Policy and Practice in Belgium." In *Crime, Punishment and Politics in Comparative Perspective,* edited by Michael Tonry, pp. 127–215. Chicago: University of Chicago Press.
Van Outrive, Lode. (2005). *La nouvelle police belge: Désorganisation et improvisation* [The New Belgium Police: Disorganization and Improvisation]. Brussels: Bruylant.
Vanneste, Charlotte. (2001). *Les chiffres des prisons: Des logiques économiques à leur traduction pénale* [Prison Data: From the Logics of Economics to Their Penal Translation]. Paris: L'Harmattan.

Bosnia and Herzegovina

Legal System: Civil
Murder: Low
Corruption: Medium
Human Trafficking: Medium
Prison Rate: Low
Death Penalty: No
Corporal Punishment: No

Background

Bosnia and Herzegovina (BH) is a small country, situated in the Balkan Peninsula, with a population estimated at 3.85 million. It has a territory of 51,209 square kilometers (approximately 19,771 square miles). Per capita income in the country is US$3,815 (2006 est.), and the unemployment rate is among the highest in Europe, reaching 31.1 percent in 2007. As a result of the 1992–1995 war BH consists of two entities, the Federation of Bosnia and Herzegovina (FBH) and the Republic of Srpska, plus the Brčko District of Bosnia and Herzegovina (BDBH), each having an autonomous, separate administration and criminal justice system. Furthermore, FBH consists of 10 cantons, each with a high level of autonomy.

After the Ottoman conquest (1463–1878), Bosnia took on its unique character as a province with a large Slavic, Muslim population. Under Austrian rule, the Habsburg military code of law was introduced in 1878 and on January 1, 1930, the Criminal Code of the Kingdom of Yugoslavia came into effect. The Socialist Federative Republic of Yugoslavia (SFRY) introduced the Criminal Code in 1951, followed by the passage of the new SFRY Constitution in 1974, when the SFRY for the first time abandoned the centralized socialist criminal justice system and introduced nine separate criminal codes, one at the federal level (SFRY), six criminal codes at the level of socialist republics (Slovenia, Croatia, Bosnia and Herzegovina, Serbia, Montenegro, and Macedonia), and two province-level criminal codes (Kosovo and Vojvodina). After the dissolution of the SFRY in the early 1990s, Bosnia and Herzegovina, as a sovereign and independent state, introduced new criminal legislation based on the existing Criminal Code of the Socialistic Republic of Bosnia and Herzegovina and the Criminal Code of the Socialistic Federal Republic of Yugoslavia.

The Constitution of the FBH entailed that the FBH was itself only competent for a few crimes, such as terrorism, drug crime, organized crime, and the so-called intercantonal crime. All other crimes were in the competency of cantons (10 cantons in the FBH), so that each canton could introduce its own criminal code. Nevertheless, in 1998 the cantonal authorities realized that this was a major absurdity and transferred their legislative powers onto the FBH. Separate criminal codes were also introduced in 2002 by both the Republika Srpska and the Brčko District of BH, so that three criminal codes prevailed on the BH territory during this period. At the time, the Criminal Code of BH did not exist.

Eventually, on March 1, 2003, the High Representative of the International Community in BH imposed both the Criminal Code of BH and the Criminal Procedure Code of BH. This reform also initiated the establishment of the state-level prosecution office, state court, and some, although modest but important, police capacities at the level of the state of BH. BH became a full member of the Council of Europe in 2002, thereby committing it to harmonize its criminal legislation with the European Convention on Protection of Human Rights and other relevant documents. Today, BH is also seeking full membership in the EU.

There are courts of different jurisdictions in BH: (1) the Court of BH (the highest judicial instance) and (2) the Constitutional Court of BH. The Court of BH has a general department, criminal department, administrative department, and appeals department. It is the highest judiciary court in the state. In the FBH there are a Supreme Court, cantonal courts, and municipality courts. In the Republika Srpska there are a Supreme Court, district courts, and basic courts. Finally, Brčko District has an Appeals Court and a Basic Court. In October 2003, the Parliament of BH adopted the Law on the Prosecutor's Office of BH. In 2004 the Court of BH and the Prosecutor's Office of BH took jurisdiction over the prosecution of war crimes including the war crime cases from The Hague Tribunal.

Police

In BH, there are three levels of organization of police forces. At the level of the state of BH, there are several organizational units: the State Investigation and Protection Agency (SIPA) and the Border Police of BH. The Republika Srpska has a totally centralized system of police organization modeled after the socialist models from former Yugoslavia, while the police in the FBH is totally decentralized and divided into 10 ministries of interior with broad powers. The police forces of the Brčko District also constitute a separate police force.

In the FBH there are 9,574 police officers (1 per 242 citizens); in the Republika Srpska, 6,267 police officers (1 per 185 citizens); and in the Brčko District, there are 307 officers (1 per 350 citizens). This compares to the 2004 EU recommended standard of 1 police officer per 1,000 citizens in urban areas, and per 2,000 citizens in the rural areas.

While the conventional crime and traffic-related issues are in the competency of the local police forces in the Republika Srpska, that is to say, of the cantonal police forces in the FBH, for some more complex crimes, the competencies have been delegated to a small number of state-level police organizations.

SIPA is the first police agency at the state level. It is a governmental agency within the Ministry of Security of BH. This agency performs tasks within its jurisdiction on the territory of the whole of BH and has operational independence. SIPA deals with prevention, detection, and investigation of organized crime, terrorism, and illegal trade—war crimes and acts punishable according to international and humanitarian law, trafficking in human beings, as well as all other crimes within the jurisdiction of the Court of BH. SIPA has been a very successful agency, having begun with just 3 employees, whereas today it has more than 850 employees working in 11 organizational units at the headquarters of the agency and in 4 regional offices in Banja Luka, Mostar, Sarajevo, and Tuzla.

Finally, the Border Police of BH was established in 2004, with operational independence within the BH Ministry of Security. The Border Police was established for the purpose of performing police tasks linked to the BH border surveillance and border crossing control, implementation of the provisions of the Law on Movement and Stay of Aliens, and other matters regulated by the BH Criminal Code.

Crime

Classification of Crimes

Criminal legislation of BH is not applicable to children under 14 years old. Offenders who at the time of the commission of an offense were 14 or older, but still not 18, are considered juvenile offenders and they are considered criminally liable. Their criminal liability, however, is established in accordance with the procedure designed for juvenile offenders (see below). All perpetrators who at the time of the commission of an offense were 18 or older are considered adults.

Criminal legislation in BH does not differentiate between more and less serious offenses explicitly. Nevertheless, such distinction is implicitly introduced through several provisions. For example, there are many instances of crimes that merit prison and crimes for which prison cannot be imposed. At the state level, the number of "serious" criminal offenses listed by the criminal legislation is vast, including criminal offenses such as espionage, trafficking in human beings, or terrorism. Less serious offenses include unauthorized use of personal data and illegal manufacturing. On the local level of entities, murder, robbery, fraud, or arson would be considered serious criminal offenses whereas light bodily injury or serving alcohol to persons younger than 16 would be considered less serious offenses.

Challenging Crimes

Following the serious social, economic, and humanitarian problems caused by the four-year war in BH, and the political instability that followed, it may be said that criminality itself is overall the biggest challenge. Nevertheless, some forms of criminality are a special problem.

War crimes constitute one of the most frequently addressed topics in the postwar BH. The court procedures conducted before the International Criminal

Bosnian State Border Service officers display a load of marijuana, confiscated at the southeastern Bosnian border near the town of Trebinje, during a ceremony marking the first anniversary of the Bosnian State Border Service in Sarajevo, August 15, 2001. (AP Photo/Hidajet Delic)

Tribunal for the former Yugoslavia (ICTY) and the local courts against persons suspected for crimes of genocide, war crimes against civilian population and prisoners, involving mass expulsion and ethnic cleansing in some parts of the country, have been almost daily topics of the public life in BH. A special challenge for governmental response lies in some crimes involving concealment of war crimes or war crime perpetrators, support to perpetrators after commission of crimes, and harming or injuring of war crime victims or witnesses.

Corruption, economic, and organized crime are forms of crime primarily directed against the legally protected assets as particularly vulnerable targets for high-level perpetrators in a politically problematic transition process in BH. There has been an inadequate response by criminal prosecution authorities to perpetrators of such crimes. Harmful consequences of these crimes emerge in the struggling business, economic, and political development of BH, especially in regard to abuses in the privatization process, crimes involving money laundering, corruption, abuse of office, and so forth.

Terrorism and causing of public danger constitute crimes the commission of which in most cases requires firearms or explosives. Given that even 14 years after the end of war, BH still has major difficulties involving illegal holding of these materials (in the majority of cases, these involve arms left over from the war), a special challenge for the criminal justice authorities lies in the crimes related to terrorist activities and the crimes related to causing of public danger.

Human trafficking is a phenomenon strongly prevalent in southeastern and Eastern European countries, particularly those with major socioeconomic problems or political instability, such as BH. In addition to the fact that the citizens of BH are very frequently victim-clients of human trafficking, it often happens that the territory of this country is used as a transit route for trafficking of persons originating from East Europe and Asia too. The tasks faced by policy makers in BH pertain to reforms in regulating border and customs controls, and the issues related to visa system, citizen records and registries, and so forth.

Juvenile delinquency is a particularly distressing issue in BH because a large number of children have been left without one or both parents due to war consequences, and many families are in economic distress. These problems strongly influence the drastic increase in the rate of violent offenses among juveniles, abuse of narcotics, as well as the traditionally high rate of property offenses among this category of delinquents. The state has not yet developed the infrastructure required to respond to juvenile offenses both mild and serious.

Drug Offenses

The war as a factor in the etiology of crime in general has played a key role in the etiology of drug crime in BH and its emergence as international organized crime. The countries created through the dissolution of former Yugoslavia, and BH in particular, have been the most favorable ones as the primary destination on the Colombia-Europe drug trafficking route. The Albanian-Sanjak criminal organization has a major influence in the Balkans. This cartel has a strong association with the Albanian and Turkish mafia, and it is believed that some individuals from this criminal milieu have gained such influence in BH that they act as an extended arm of the Turkish mafia. Criminals originating from BH serve as contact points for Germany, Switzerland, and the Czech Republic.

And finally, it is estimated that BH is both a transit country and one in which drugs are stored waiting for further transport. Major quantities have been seized in the interior of the county, mainly on the territory of the Republika Srpska, or at the demarcation lines between the entities of the Republika Srpska and the FBH. The drugs most frequently enter BH from southern Serbia and from Montenegro and are bound for the three largest cities in BH, Sarajevo, Mostar, and Banja Luka, where they are stored until the continuation of transport into the countries of West Europe.

In mid-2003, the new state-level Criminal Code of BH in its article 195 provides the crime of unauthorized distribution of narcotic drugs to cover exclusively international illegal transactions involving drugs.

Possession of Narcotic Drugs

As a separate form of crime, the criminal code of FBH and the criminal code of BDBH provide the unauthorized possession of narcotic drugs. Previously, drug possession, without an intention to place it into distribution, was treated as a minor offense rather than as a crime. However, the fact is that there have been many difficulties involved in the efforts to prove the intention to distribute drugs in unauthorized possession. Furthermore, the quantity of drugs has always been questionable. As an example, there is no comparison between the harm that may come from one kilogram of heroin and one kilogram of marijuana. Thus, when unable to prove the intention to sell drugs, the court shall be able to qualify the offense as unauthorized drug possession.

Crime Statistics

According to the Ministry of Security of Bosnia and Herzegovina, *Information on Security Situation in Bosnia and Herzegovina,* 2007, crimes (not including attempts) registered by the police for 2006 for FBH, Republika Srpska, and BDBH combined were as follows:

Murder	74
Rape (all forms)	40
Car theft	2,439
Production and trafficking in drugs	486

Finding of Guilt

Criminal proceedings in BH are based on several important principles that stem primarily out of the Constitution of BH and the European Convention on the Protection of Human Rights and Fundamental Freedoms and its protocols. Some of the most important principles are the principle of legality, presumption of innocence, no crime without law, protection against double jeopardy, legally inadmissible evidence, and the accusatory principle.

Criminal proceedings in BH may only be initiated and conducted upon the request of the prosecutor. Upon receiving and analyzing a written or oral report that a crime is committed, the prosecutor shall order an investigation if grounds for suspicion that a criminal offense has been committed exist. In the course of the investigation, the prosecutor may undertake all investigative actions, including the questioning of the suspect and hearing of the injured party and witnesses, crime scene investigation and reconstruction of events, undertaking special measures to protect witnesses and information, and may order the necessary expert evaluation. However, if there are grounds for suspicion that a criminal offense has been committed that is punishable by more than five years of imprisonment, an authorized official (in most cases a police officer) shall immediately inform the prosecutor and shall under the prosecutor's direction take the steps necessary to apprehend the perpetrator, to detect and secure the clues to the criminal offense and objects which might serve as evidence, and to gather all information that might be of use for the criminal proceedings.

Once the prosecutor finds that there is enough evidence that the suspect has committed a criminal offense, he or she refers the indictment to the preliminary hearing judge who may confirm or discharge all or some of the counts in the indictment within 8 days from receipt of the indictment. Upon confirmation of some or all counts in the indictment, the accused and his or her defense attorney are presented with the indictment and a plea of guilty or not guilty on each count is required within 15 days. If the accused fails to enter a plea, the preliminary hearing judge shall record that the accused enters a plea of not guilty. If the accused enters a plea of guilty and thereby accepts the sentence proposed in the indictment, the preliminary hearing judge shall refer the case for a hearing at which it shall be determined whether the conditions for the acceptance of the plea exist. The court must ensure the following: (1) that the plea of guilty was entered voluntarily and that the accused was informed of the possible consequences; and (2) that there is enough evidence proving the guilt of the suspect or the accused. The date for the pronouncement of the sentence is scheduled within 3 days.

Plea bargaining may occur at any stage of the criminal proceedings. The prosecutor may propose an agreed sentence of less than the minimum prescribed by the law for the criminal offense(s) or a lesser penalty against the accused. Such agreement has to be prepared in writing and submitted to the preliminary hearing judge, who may sustain or reject the agreement. The court must ensure the following: (1) that the plea of guilty was entered voluntarily and that the accused was informed of the possible consequences; (2) that there is enough evidence proving the guilt of the suspect or the accused; and (3) that the suspect or the accused understands that by agreement on the admission of guilt he or she waives his or her right to trial and that he or she may not file an appeal against the pronounced criminal sanction. If the accused does not plead guilty or the court rejects the plea bargaining agreement, the case goes to trial, which is directed by a judge.

According to the Annual Report for 2007, the majority of indictments on the state level were confirmed by the court without the warrant for pronouncement of sentence (62.5%), while a smaller number was confirmed with the warrant for pronouncement of sentence (20.8%) and proposed plea bargaining agreement (16.7%). It is interesting to note, however, that the court only exceptionally rejects the plea bargaining agreement. When it comes to acceptance of the plea bargaining agreements, the situation is not significantly different on the level of FBH, Republika Srpska, and the Brčko District, where the plea bargaining agreements have been reached in 9.3 percent, 17.6 percent, and 23.7 percent of cases, respectively.

Rights of the Accused

The suspect or accused shall be entitled to have a defense attorney throughout the course of the criminal proceedings. If the accused does not hire a defense attorney, a defense attorney may be engaged for him or her by his or her legal representatives unless he or she does not explicitly oppose it. However, if the accused is mute or deaf or if he or she is suspected of a criminal offense for which a penalty of long-term imprisonment may be pronounced, a defense attorney at the first questioning is mandatory. Otherwise, a suspect or accused must have a defense attorney immediately after he or she has been put in to pretrial custody. After an indictment has been issued for a criminal offense for which a prison sentence of 10 years or more may be pronounced, the accused must have a defense attorney at the time of the delivery of the indictment.

Custody

Any person caught committing a criminal offense may be restricted in his or her movement by any other person. The person must be immediately turned over to the court, prosecutor, or to the nearest police authority. This general right to restrict someone's movement is different from taking an accused into custody. A person can be taken into pretrial custody if there is a grounded suspicion that he or she committed a criminal offense or if other circumstances exist that suggest a possibility of flight; or if there is a justified fear to believe that he or she will destroy, conceal, alter, or falsify evidence. Additionally, in exceptional circumstances, such as an offense for which 10 years or more severe punishment may be pronounced, a person can be taken into pretrial custody if the release would result in an actual threat to public order. Pretrial custody can only be ordered by a court's decision on a prosecutor's motion. The duration of the custody is determined by both the so-called functional and time limits defined in the legislation. Pretrial custody, after the indictment is confirmed, may be no longer than 1 month and can thereafter, should it be needed, be prolonged for another 2 months, and in the cases of criminal offenses calling for 10 years of imprisonment, for additional 3 months. This means that, under normal circumstances, pretrial custody cannot last longer than 6 months. However, in an extraordinarily complex case for which a long-term imprisonment is prescribed, custody may again be extended for no longer than 3 months. Such an extension may occur twice consecutively, following a motion of the prosecutor for each extension, so that pretrial custody can in fact last up to 12 months.

Juveniles

For criminal offenses punishable by up to three years of imprisonment or a fine, the prosecutor may decide not to file the indictment even though there is evidence that the minor committed the criminal offense if the prosecutor feels that it would be detrimental to conduct a criminal proceeding against the minor in view of the nature of the criminal offense and the circumstances under which it was committed, the minor's previous life, and his or her personal characteristics. The juvenile may be summoned via his or her parents, or decisions may be delivered in writing. In the trial, a judge can exclude the public and the presence of the representative of a social welfare center can be required. The minor must be separated from adults when in custody.

For criminal offenses for which a fine or a punishment of imprisonment for a term not exceeding three years is prescribed, educational recommendations may be imposed. The purpose of educational recommendations is to avoid initiation of criminal procedures against juveniles and to use the educational recommendations as a means of influencing them not to perpetrate criminal offenses in the future. For these recommendations to be applied, the juvenile has to admit that he or she has perpetrated the criminal offense and has to express willingness to make amends to the injured party. The catalog of recommendations includes personal apology; compensation; regular school attendance; working for a humanitarian organization or local community; accepting an appropriate job; being placed in another family or institution; treatment in an adequate health institution; attending instructive, educational, psychological, and other forms of counseling.

Taking the overall interests of both the juvenile (such as regular schooling or work) and the injured party, the competent prosecutor or judge for juveniles selects one educational recommendation in collaboration with the juvenile's parents or guardians and institutions of social care. The chosen educational recommendation may not last longer than one year. Upon becoming effective, one educational recommendation may be replaced with another, or it may be cancelled.

As far as the criminal sanctions are concerned, juveniles can be sentenced to educational measures or juvenile imprisonment. Educational measures include committal to a disciplinary center for juveniles; intensified supervision by parents, guardians, or foster home; and committal to an educational institution, educational-reformatory home, or some other training establishment. Which of these will be imposed depends on the age of the juvenile, the degree of his or her mental development, and other personal and social factors.

Whereas the educational recommendations and the educational measures can be imposed on all juvenile offenders, juvenile imprisonment can be imposed only on juveniles who at the time of the commission of the offense were 16 years or older and if they committed a criminal offense for which 5 years of imprisonment may be imposed. However, imprisonment may be imposed only if it would not be justifiable to apply an educational measure because of the grave consequences of the offense perpetrated and the high degree of criminal responsibility of the juvenile. The duration of juvenile imprisonment may not be shorter than 1 or longer than 10 years and is to be pronounced in full years or half-years.

Judges

The institution in charge of appointing all judges (including the court presidents, lay judges, and reserve judges) and prosecutors (including the chief prosecutors and deputy chief prosecutors and prosecutors) at all levels of judiciary in BH is the High Judicial and Prosecutorial Council (HJPC). The HJPC is additionally in charge of appointing international judges and prosecutors to the Court of BH and the Prosecutor's Office of BH, as well as to give proposals to relevant institutions for the appointment of judges in the entity constitutional courts and appointment of judicial associates. Based on the Annual Report for 2007, out of 885 available positions for judges in all courts in BH, 856 were occupied.

The basic requirements for appointment are citizenship, law school education, and the bar exam.

Other requirements are personal integrity, moral standing, professional ability and required training and qualifications, and work experience. The HJPC is also obliged to consider professional knowledge and performance, academic written works and activities within professional associations, communication abilities, and reputation, among other factors.

Punishment

Given the divisions in the legislative competency in BH, punishments are prescribed in the state-level or entity- or district-level laws. To avoid repetitive presentation of the systems of sanctions in all the criminal codes in force in BH, only the one contained in the criminal code of the FBH will be presented here.

Types of Punishment

The system of criminal sanctions in the FBH comprises penalties, warning (noncustodial) sentences, security measures, educational measures for juveniles, and educational recommendations for juveniles.

Penalties

Penalties include imprisonment and fine. Whereas imprisonment may only be imposed as principal punishment, a fine may be imposed both as a principal and as an accessory punishment. If both penalties are prescribed for a criminal offense, only one of them may be imposed as a principal punishment. For criminal offenses motivated by greed, a fine may be imposed as an accessory punishment even when that is not specifically prescribed by the law or in cases where the law prescribes that the perpetrator shall be punished by imprisonment or a fine, and the court decides to impose the punishment of imprisonment as the principal punishment. Prison is the core criminal sanction prescribed either as a sole sentence or as an alternative sanction with the fine. The prison sentence can be imposed for period ranging between 30 days and 20 years. For perpetrators of the aggravated forms of serious crimes, the prison sentence prescribed may even be in the duration from 20 to 45 years.

Short-term prison sentences (up to 6 months), as well as fines that are not paid in due time (see below), may be, with the consent of the accused, replaced with community service. The duration of the community service has to be proportional to the imposed imprisonment and can range, depending on the perpetrator's personal circumstances and employment, from a minimum of 10 to a maximum of 60 working days. The period in which the community service is to be performed shall be neither shorter than 1 month nor longer than 1 year.

Fine is pronounced in "daily amounts," and if this is not possible it may also be pronounced in a "fixed amount." If a perpetrator does not pay a fine in full or in part within the period determined in the judgment, the fine shall be substituted by imprisonment. One day of imprisonment is computed as about 50KM (US$38), but the period may not exceed one year.

Warning Sentences

In cases where imposing a penalty (imprisonment or a fine) is not needed, the judicial admonition and the suspended sentence (warning sanctions) can be imposed. In principle, a judicial admonition may be pronounced for criminal offenses for which an imprisonment for a term not exceeding one year or a fine is prescribed, also taking into account the perpetrator's attitude toward the injured party and compensation for the damage caused by the criminal offense.

For a suspended sentence the court determines a punishment, but at the same time orders that it shall not be executed if the convicted person does not perpetrate another offense over a period of time established by the court. In principle, a suspended sentence may be imposed only when a punishment of imprisonment for a term not exceeding two years is the case. The court may also order that the convicted person shall make a restitution and be placed under protective guardianship. The protective guardianship, which may not last less than six months nor exceed two years, encompasses treatment in an appropriate health institution, refraining from alcoholic drinks or opiates, attending psychiatric or other counseling centers, training for a certain profession, accepting employment and disposing with the salary or other income and property.

Security Measures

The purpose of security measures is to remove situations or conditions that might influence an offender to commit offenses in the future. The catalog of security measures that may be imposed on perpetrators of criminal offenses includes mandatory psychiatric treatment; mandatory medical treatment of addiction; ban on carrying out a certain occupation, activity, or duty; ban on driving a motor vehicle; forfeiture.

Typical Punishments

- Murder: a prison sentence of 5 to 20 years, extendable to 45 years for aggravating circumstances, reduced to 1–10 years for mitigating circumstances (manslaughter) and 6 months to 5 years for accidental murder, and for murder of child at birth in the maximum duration of 5 years.
- Rape: 1 to 10 years in prison.
- Theft: fine or up to 3 years' imprisonment. Burglary (a type of aggravated theft): Prison sentence in the duration of 6 months up to 5 years (FBH and BDBH, but in Republika Srpska 1 to 8 years in prison).
- Serious theft and robbery: 1 to 10 years in prison.
- Unauthorized production and distribution of narcotic drugs: 1 to 10 years in prison, if organized, 3 to 20 years.
- Allowing drug consumption to children, juveniles, or multiple persons: 1 to 10 years in prison.

Prison

As of July 31, 2007, the total prison population in BH was 2,668 persons. Of this number, 1,086 persons were placed in enclosed facilities, 1,210 in semi-open facilities, 146 persons in special institutional wards, 205 persons in district institutions, and 21 persons were placed in the preliminary investigation unit of the Court of BH.

In BH, there are 11 operating prison institutions with three separate departments. Of the total number of institutions, two are enclosed (Zenica and Foča), six are of semi-open type (Sarajevo, Banja Luka, East Sarajevo, Tuzla, Mostar, and Bihać), three institutions are district jails (Bijeljina, Trebinje, and Doboj), and three departments also function as separate units (Orašje, Busovača, and Ustikolina). Juveniles serve prison sentences and other institutional measures at separate wards of the prisons in Zenica, Foča, and Banja Luka, and the prison sentences for women are executed at wards of prison institutions in Tuzla and East Sarajevo.

The total capacity of the prisons in BH has been estimated at 2,700 persons, based on the standard of 4 square meters (42.9 square feet) of space per inmate. In BH a new prison is planned for 2011 to include 29 single and 156 double cells, with total capacity of up to 350 inmates, which should significantly lighten the burden of prisons in Zenica and Foča.

The largest prison in BH, the Penal and Correctional Institute of enclosed type, is located in the central town of Zenica, at one of the major intersections of roads connecting the northern and southern, or western and eastern, parts of the country. This prison is in the competency of the entity of the FBH, so that the majority of the inmates convicted at the courts of this entity are the ones serving sentences there.

The prison in Zenica includes several cellblocks for accommodation of inmates in various categories (adults, juveniles). Additionally, the prison contains the forensic cellblock, where security measures involving mandatory psychiatric medical treatment are executed. The prison includes a reception cellblock, labor unit, and custody unit. Convicts are accommodated in 38 single and 48 double cells, and the majority of them have been placed into group dormitories with a large number of beds, which is one of the major problems for this institution. The shortage of space and accommodation capacities are the biggest concerns for the prison in Zenica, resulting in inadequate facilities for problem inmates, guards, and for mentally incompetent inmates.

There are specific provisions on organization of labor for inmates, financial outputs of such labor, work hours, protection and security at work, and on the compensation for labor. The inmates should be assigned with the type of work in line with the needs of their treatment, mental and physical capacities, affiliations, personal properties, and their vocational training.

In relation to educational activities, special attention is paid to juvenile inmates as well as to junior adults who have not completed primary school. In such cases, institutes are mandated to organize training aimed at acquisition of primary education, as well as training for vocational education.

Inmates are entitled to maintain communication via mail (letters) and telephone without restrictions with their family members and with persons and representatives of organizations that can assist in their treatment. Close family members are allowed to visit inmates without any special consent from the administrator, whereas visits by other persons require the administrator's consent. Among other benefits that may be singled out are receipt of parcels with clothing, personal items, press, books, and money, but only from close family members. Special benefits that are subject to additional requirements pertain to free movement outside the site of the institution, city visits, leave of up to seven days and annual leave spent with family. Relocation of inmates from the institution located in one entity of BH into an institution located in the other entity is permitted only after half the time of the sentence has been served.

Almir Maljević, Elmedin Muratbegović, and Muhamed Budimlić

Further Reading

Court of Bosnia and Herzegovina: http://www.sudbih.gov.ba.

Functional Review of the BH Police Forces: Final Report. (2004). Sarajevo, Bosnia and Herzegovina: Ministry of Justice.

Petrović, Borislav, and Elmedin Muratbegović. (2008). "Criminology in Bosnia and Herzegovina: History, Recent Trends and Research." *Journal of Criminal Justice and Security* 10(2): 353–368.

Prosecutor's Office of Bosnia and Herzegovina: http://www.tuzilastvobih.gov.ba.

Sijerčić-Čolić, H., et al. (2005). *Komentari zakona o krivičnim postupcima u Bosni i Hercegovini* [Commentaries of the Criminal Procedure Codes in Bosnia and Herzegovina]. Sarajevo, Bosnia and Herzegovina: Vijeće Evrope/Evropska Komisija.

Vijeće Evrope/Evropska Komisija. (2005). *Komentari krivičnih/kaznenih zakona u Bosni i Hercegovini, Knjiga I. i II.* [Commentaries of the Criminal Codes in Bosnia and Herzegovina]. Sarajevo, Bosnia and Herzegovina: Vijeće Evrope/Evropska Komisija.

Bulgaria

Legal System: Civil
Murder: Medium
Burglary: Medium
Corruption: Medium
Human Trafficking: Medium
Prison Rate: Medium
Death Penalty: No
Corporal Punishment: No

Background

The modern Bulgarian legal system can be traced back to the end of the 1870s, where influences of continental traditions of the Russian, German, and French criminal justice systems are already visible. After the liberation of Bulgaria in 1878 the first step toward a comprehensive system was the bringing together of all authorities participating in judicial activities. This arrangement existed up to the adoption of the Tarnovo Constitution of Bulgaria, in force from April 1879 to December 1947. The text laid down the foundations for a modern constitutional state and the building of a legal system.

The structure of the judicial power has been formed by temporary rules at the end of 1878 with the institution of the Supreme Court in the city of Sofia. These rules prevailed until the adoption of the Courts Arrangement Act in 1880 and the Criminal Court Proceedings Act later in 1897. The Tarnovo Constitution established that the judicial power belonged to the judicial authorities, who acted on behalf of the Royal Prince; however, the judicial power was not subordinate to the prince. According to the provisions of the Constitution, the Royal Prince has the right to cancel punishments as well as the right to clemency. The right of amnesty belonged to the Royal Prince and the National Assembly. The notions of prosecution and investigation appeared, in a structured way, for the first time in the Courts Arrangement Act of 1880. Prosecutors worked both within the district court and the appellate court, as the structure somehow recreated the French model of the *ministère public*. At the same time, judicial investigators were officially declared "agents of the judicial police." They were subordinate to the prosecutor whose orders were mandatory. The prosecutors at the Supreme Court of Cassation and the ones at the appellate courts were appointed by and subordinate directly to the minister of justice.

After World War II, the organization of the Bulgarian judicial system gradually changed, in response to the Soviet legal system. It acquired characteristics such as, for example, an independent prosecution, a powerful investigation apparatus, a centralized administration, and the diminution of the rights of party litigants. The Constitution of the People's Republic of Bulgaria of 1947 upheld several principles such as the division of powers, the independence of judges, or the participation of jurors in the administration of justice. The prosecutor general was to be elected by the National Assembly and was to appoint and dismiss all other prosecutors. New laws on the structure of the courts entered into force, as well as the Law on the Prosecution.

The Modern Criminal Justice System

The building of the Bulgarian criminal justice system was further modified by the adoption of a new Constitution of the Republic of Bulgaria in 1991. The Constitution defines the judicial power as a system of authorities: the Supreme Judicial Council, the courts, the prosecution, and the investigation services, as well as the Supreme Judicial Council Inspectorate and the Bar. All these authorities are free, independent, and self-governing.

The Judicial Power Act of 2007 sets up in detail the structure and function of the different units, the status of the magistrates, their rights and duties, as well as the organization and activities of the Supreme Judicial Council (SJC) and its Inspectorate. The SJC is composed of 25 members; the chairman of the Supreme Court of Cassation, the chairman of the Supreme Administrative Court, and the prosecutor general are members by right. Other members of the SJC are elected among jurists of high professional and moral qualities who have a work experience of at least 15 years. Eleven members of the SJC are elected by the National Assembly and 11 by the judicial authorities for a term of five years. Justice is administered by the Supreme Court of Cassation, the Supreme Administrative Court, as well as the appellate, district, administrative, military, and regional courts. Special courts can be set up by means of an act, but extraordinary courts are not admitted.

In the period 2003–2007, three amendments related to the judicial power and connected with the reform of the judicial system have been made to the Constitution. The amendments referred to issues of immunity, irrevocability, mandate and responsibility of the magistrates, and the management of property. At the present stage, the recommendations of the European Commission and international acts do not require specific changes in the structure of the Bulgarian judicial system. The Constitution is fully harmonized with the democratic legal arrangement of the European states.

Some of the principal rights are set up in articles 30 to 35 of the Constitution. Everyone has the right to freedom and privacy. No one may be detained or subjected to inspection except on the conditions and in a manner established by law. In urgent cases explicitly stated by the law, the competent authorities may detain any citizen yet have to inform without delay the judicial authorities. Everyone has the right to a lawyer's defense from the moment of his or her detention or charging as defendant. Everyone has the right to meet in private the person defending him or her; the secret of their communication is guaranteed. Everyone accused of a criminal offense needs to be handed over to the competent judicial authorities within the term defined by the law. No one can be forced to plead guilty, nor be convicted on the sole basis of his or her confession. The defendant is deemed innocent until proven guilty by an effective sentence. Statutory limitation does not apply to war crimes and crimes against humanity. Fundamental constitutional rights of the citizens may be limited only by and with permission of the court.

The Bulgarian criminal law is intended to regulate the commission of negative acts that endanger or damage the society or the citizen. It is sanction-related, relies on strong pretrial proceedings, and ensures the protection of existing social relationships. Pretrial proceedings involve the process of investigation as well as the actions of the prosecutor upon the completion of the investigation. The investigation is performed by examining magistrates, investigators or investigating officers, while investigations in relation to materials received from the State Agency for National Security are conducted by a prosecutor, who may then assign the investigation of certain facts to an examining magistrate. The administration of justice in criminal cases is performed by courts only, as established by the Constitution. No extraordinary courts are admitted. Court proceedings are the key elements in the criminal process and are regulated by the Bulgarian Criminal Code of Procedure.

International Legislation

The Republic of Bulgaria has practically accepted and ratified all important international acts of the United Nations, the Council of Europe, and the European Union. Pursuant to article 5, paragraph 4, of the Constitution, the international agreements constitutionally ratified, published. and effective for the Republic of Bulgaria, are part of the domestic legislation. They have priority over the domestic legislation.

Criminal proceedings instituted by the authorities of another state or any effective sentence adjudicated by the court of another state and not recognized by this code is no impediment to the institution of criminal proceedings by the authorities of the Republic of Bulgaria for the same crime against the same person. However, if the sentence is not recognized in the way of the Criminal Code of Procedure, it is not subject to execution.

Police

The police in the Republic of Bulgaria are a state institution and part of the Ministry of Interior. The Minister of Interior is the sole central authority of the executive power that directs, coordinates, and controls the implementation of state policies for the protection of the rights and freedom of the citizens, the national security, and the public order.

The Criminal Police General Directorate is a national specialized operational search structure of the Ministry of Interior devoted to counteracting crime and to carrying out activities related to the detection and prevention of crime. The Pre-trial Proceedings General Directorate, another specialized structure, is in charge of the various activities surrounding crime prosecution. Crime investigations are conducted according to the Criminal Code of Procedure by the authorities of the respective units in the district directorates. The upholding of order and security in the Ministry of Defense and the Bulgarian Army is assigned to the Military Police Service.

Judicial Authorities

In all cases, judges, prosecutors, examining magistrates, administrative managers, and deputy administrative managers are appointed, promoted, transferred, and dismissed from duty by decision of the Supreme Judicial Council. The chairman of the Supreme Court of Cassation, the chairman of the Supreme Administrative Court, and the prosecutor general are appointed by the president on proposal of the Supreme Judicial Council for a term of seven years without the right to reelection. In 2007, there were 2,215 judges in Bulgaria, of which one-third works in the criminal field.

Judges, prosecutors, and investigators must have a Bulgarian citizenship, have completed higher legal education, have passed the required post-graduate training and have acquired a legal capacity, possess the required moral and professional knowledge of the rules for professional ethics, have never been sentenced to imprisonment for a premeditated crime, and do not suffer from any mental disorder.

Crime

Classification of Crimes

A crime is a socially dangerous act that has been committed by an offender and declared by the law as punishable. An act is not criminal if its criminal elements are of such minor importance that it is not socially dangerous or its social danger is obviously negligible. A socially dangerous act is one that threatens or harms the Constitution or other interests defended by the law.

Criminal offenses are defined in the Bulgarian Criminal Code. The concept of "serious crime" qualifies any criminal offense subject to a custodial sentence of 5 or more years. The concept of "particularly serious crime" refers to any criminal offense that constitutes an exceptionally high degree of social danger because of its consequences, aggravating circumstances of the act, or the perpetrator's character. The concept of "minor fact" qualifies any criminal offense that represents a low level of social danger because of insignificant harmful consequences.

A criminal act is intentional when the perpetrator has been aware of its socially dangerous character, foresaw its socially dangerous consequences, and yet he or she has accepted these consequences. A criminal act is negligent when the perpetrator has not foreseen the occurrence of socially dangerous consequences, however, he or she had been obliged and could have foreseen them, or when he or she had foreseen the occurrence of these consequences, however, he or she thought of preventing them. The negligent acts are punishable only in the cases stated by the law.

The Criminal Code applies to any adult who has committed a crime. Juveniles aged 14–17 are criminally liable only if they could understand the illicit character and the significance of their offense. If necessary, juvenile offenders, who cannot be charged for a criminal offense, can be placed in a correctional boarding school or in another suitable facility by a court decision.

A person is not criminally liable when he or she acted in a state of insanity because of mental underdevelopment or temporary/chronic mental disorder, as the person could not understand the quality or the meaning of the act perpetrated or could not manage his or her acts.

Crime Statistics

Statistics for the registered criminal and economic crime for 2008 are not yet available. The source is the Coordination and Information and Analysis Activities Directorate at the Ministry of Interior in agreement with other authorities. Criminal offenses (not including attempts) for the first six months of 2008 were as follows:

Crime against the personality	2,817
Homicide	247
Completed rape	113
Bodily injury	1,538
Trafficking in people	34
Property crimes	34,150
Robbery	1,323
Theft	28,479
Fraud	870
Drug-related crimes	1,312
Total	**70,883**

Drug Offenses

The strategic location of Bulgaria on the so-called Balkan drug route shapes the policy of the state in the field of countering illegal traffic of narcotic substances and precursors. The Balkan route is used mainly for illegal transportation of heroin. Drug trafficking is one of the most profitable spheres of organized crime, along with trafficking in human beings, smuggling, economic crime, and money laundering. At the same time, over the last 10 years, the country has evolved from a transit point into a final destination for various narcotic substances, in the sense that we are now witnessing how the inclusion of local criminal groups into international drug trafficking leads to the increase of drug distribution on the territory, as well as the increase of the number of people using drugs. State efforts are aimed at counteracting drug trafficking both on the territory of Bulgaria and in cooperation with international law enforcement authorities.

Corruption

The prosecution uses a working term for "corruption," which includes all forms of misuse of power aimed at acquiring personal or group benefiting. This includes a multitude of criminal offenses, for instance, articles 201–205—misappropriation in public office; article 219—careless management of public property; article 220—conclusion of unprofitable transaction by an official; article 225c—bribe when performing commercial activities; article 282—crime in public office by an official; articles 301–307a—bribe to an official.

Money Laundering

Who carries out a financial operation or a transaction with a property, or hides the origin, location, movement, or actual rights on a property about which he or she knows or suspects that it has been acquired through crime or another socially dangerous act is punished for money laundering by imprisonment of 1 to 6 years and a fine of 3,000 to 5,000 lev (US$1,925 to $3,209)—article 253 of the Criminal Code. The punishment shall be imprisonment of 1 to 8 years and a fine of 5,000 to 20,000 lev (US$3,209 to $12,838) if the act has been committed by two or more persons who have conspired in advance, or by a person acting on an errand or in fulfillment of a decision of an organized criminal group; two or more times; by an official within the scope of his or her office; by opening and maintaining an account in a financial institution under a fictitious name or under the name of a person who has not given consent for that. If the means or the property are of particularly large size and the case is particularly serious, the punishment is imprisonment of 5 to 15 years and a fine of 10,000 to 30,000 lev (US$6,419 to $19,258). The subject of the crime or the property into which it has been transformed is seized in favor of the state, and if it is missing or alienated, its equivalence is adjudged.

Finding of Guilt

Criminal Procedure

Within the framework of the judicial system, the Constitution shares out competences between the court, the prosecution, and the examining magistrates. The court administers justice, the prosecution charges the persons who have committed a crime and supports the indictment in criminal cases, and the examining magistrates, the officers of the Ministry of Interior and the Ministry of Defense investigate committed crimes.

Judges, court assessors, prosecutors, investigating authorities, lawyers, private plaintiffs, private prosecutors, civil claimants, and civil defendants and witnesses take part in the criminal proceedings. Only evidentiary material collected by the competent authorities and in conformity with the requirements of the Criminal Code of Procedure is admissible.

All criminal cases fall under the jurisdiction of regional courts, as courts of first instance, except some cases specially mentioned in the Criminal Code of Procedure that fall under the jurisdiction of the district courts. Court composition at the first level (i.e., number of judges and assessors) is decided upon the seriousness of the crime. Hearings at the appellate instance are conducted by three judges, similarly for cases heard at the Supreme Court of Cassation.

No one can be detained for more than 24 hours without authorization of the court. The prosecutor can order detention of the accused up to 72 hours. The defendant or the detained person has the right to be assisted by a defense counsel; however, in certain cases, his or her defense is mandatory.

The victim is granted the necessary procedural means for defense of his or her rights and lawful interests. The Legal Assistance Act provided for the building of a system and the setting up of a

National Bureau for Legal Assistance, which guarantees equal access to justice for all and effective assistance by lawyers.

The Functions of the Prosecutor

The prosecutor raises criminal charges and presents the indictment related to criminal offenses of general character. In the discharge of his or her duties, he or she does the following:

- Directs the investigation and exercises constant supervision for its lawful and timely conduct.
- May perform investigation or other investigative or procedural actions.
- Participates in court proceedings as accuser on behalf of the state.
- Takes measures for the elimination of law infringements.
- Exercises supervision for legality in the enforcement of coercive measures.

When the prosecutor withdraws from proceedings (i.e., in cases of complainant offenses), the victim may proceed with maintaining the accusation, acting as a private complainant. The Prosecutor-General of the Republic of Bulgaria provides methodological guidance for other prosecutors' actions and ensures respect of legal provisions.

Remand Measures

Remand measures are based upon the degree of social risk inherent to the criminal offense perpetrated and the evidence gathered against the accused party. His or her health condition, family status, occupation, age, and other personal characteristics shall be taken into consideration as well. Measures include, for example, signed promise for appearance, bail, house arrest, or remand in custody (i.e., pretrial detention). House arrest, as a remand measure in pretrial proceedings, is pronounced and supervised by the court of first instance at the prosecutor's request. The process is identical for pretrial detention; it is applied in cases that fulfill the following cumulative conditions: a reasonable assumption can be made that the accused party has committed a criminal offense subject to a custodial sentence or another more severe punishment, and a set of evidence indicates the person is at risk of absconding or reoffending. The measure of remand in custody may not exceed 1 year for serious intentional criminal offenses, 2 years for offenses subject to a custodial sentence of at least 15 years. In all other cases, remand in custody in the course of pretrial proceedings cannot exceed 2 months.

Juveniles

According to the Bulgarian Criminal Code of Procedure, one of the cases in which the participation of a defense counsel in criminal proceedings is mandatory is in cases where the accused party is a minor. The penal proceedings establish special rules for examination of cases of crimes committed by minors, taking into consideration the special features of the offense, the age of the perpetrators, and the particularities of their psychological development. In these cases, pretrial proceedings are conducted by specifically trained investigative bodies. Only the following remand measures can be applied to juveniles: supervision by the parents or guardian; supervision by the administration of the educational establishment where the minor has been placed; supervision by the inspector at the child pedagogical facility or by a member of the local Commission for Combating Anti-Social Acts of Minors and Underage Persons; remand in custody. The remand measure of custody is taken only in exceptional cases.

Where it is necessary, a pedagogue or a psychologist can take part in the interrogation of a juvenile offender; he or she may ask questions with the permission of the person in charge of the investigation. Court hearings in cases against juvenile offenders are conducted behind closed doors, unless the court finds it in the interest of the public to examine the case at an open court hearing.

To guarantee the minor perpetrator's rights and for the purpose of establishing an appropriate environment for the child, the parents or guardians are summoned to the hearings. They have the right to take part in the collection and verification of evidentiary materials and to make requests, remarks, and objections. In cases against underage persons, the participation of a prosecutor is mandatory.

A specialized state body, the Central Commission for Combating Juvenile Delinquency, and local commissions are being established at municipalities. The central commission develops, participates in the drafting, and proposes programs and activities to prevent and combat crime, such as outreach programs for juveniles to prevent and eliminate antisocial behavior; programs for their education and social integration; vocational training and employment programs; or outreach programs for parents whose children have committed misdemeanors or offenses. Only a limited number of punishments can be imposed on minors who have committed a criminal offense; all intend to reeducating and preparing juveniles for socially useful work. When the court decides to suspend a sentence, it should inform the local commission to make arrangements for educative care.

Punishment

Types of Punishment

Punishments can be of a criminal type, legal type, disciplinary type, or civil type. There is no death penalty in Bulgaria. Punishments are defined in the Criminal Code and include life imprisonment; imprisonment; probation; confiscation of available property; fine; revocation of the right to occupy a definite state or public position; revocation of the right to practice a definite profession or an activity; revocation of the right to received orders, honorary titles, and insignia of honor; revocation of military rank; and public reprobation.

Imprisonment

Life imprisonment without alternative, the most severe sentence, is a temporary and exceptional measure imposed only in cases of serious deliberate crimes threatening the basis of the republic and where no alternative lesser punishment is conceivable. Offenders sentenced to such punishment must be older than 20 at the time of offense, older than 18 during war time. Such punishment cannot be imposed on women pregnant at the commission of the offense or at the pronouncing of the sentence. Life imprisonment can be replaced by an imprisonment for a period of 30 years if the convict has served no less than 20 years.

Imprisonment can be from 3 months to 20 years. Exceptionally, it can be extended up to 30 years in replacement of life imprisonment for multiple crimes or for some particularly serious deliberate crimes in the cases specially determined in the Criminal Code. Imprisonment is the most common punishment imposed by courts. Custodial sentences not exceeding 3 years can be suspended for a period of 3 to 5 years. Stay of execution is applicable only if the offender has not been previously sentenced to imprisonment, and if the court finds it more appropriate for the objectives of the punishment and the rehabilitation of the offender. The stay of execution cannot exceed the term of the imposed punishment of imprisonment by more than 3 years. During that time, the convicted is obliged to study or work, unless mandatory medical treatment was decided.

Custodial sentences are served in prisons, correctional homes, or prisoners' boarding houses. Such sentences range from 3 months to 20 years (30 years in some cases defined in the Criminal Code). In these facilities, convicts are placed at a primary regime indicated in the sentence, which can be modified later depending on their behavior.

Imprisonment shall be accompanied by a suitable, respectively paid, and socially useful work, which shall aim at the rehabilitation of the convicted, as well as the creation and improvement of their professional qualifications. Work days are considered in reducing the term of the sentence, as two work days equal three days of imprisonment. Convicts who avoid socially useful work opportunities or intentionally commit an offense or a serious breach of the established order are considered as showing low probability of rehabilitation. Therefore, the court is allowed to ignore, partially or totally, work days accomplished during the two years following the offense in the count of time served. Decisions related to imprisonment and its administration are ruled by the Serving Sentences Act.

Probation Measures

Probation refers to a set of measures destined to control and have an influence on the convict. Probation measures can be imposed together or separately and include obligatory registration at the present address; obligatory periodical meetings with a probation employee; restrictions of free movement; attendance of courses for professional qualification or programs for public influence; community work; voluntary work. Probation measures are implemented in compliance with the law and their duration varies depending on the types of measure: between 6 months and 3 years for the first four measures, between 3 months and 2 years of community work, and between 100 and 320 hours per year for no more than 3 consecutive years of voluntary work. The first two measures shall be imposed to all individuals sentenced to probation. Community and voluntary work cannot be imposed on juvenile offenders under 16 years old. In case a probation measure is not respected and upon request of the Probation Council, the court can impose other probation measure(s), or pronounce a custodial sentence in partial or total replacement of the probation measure not carried out.

Monetary Sanctions

Confiscation is a compulsory and *ex gratia* requisition of a definite property of the convict, or parts of such properties, in favor of the state. Confiscation shall not be ruled if the convict does not possess available property that can be subject to this punishment. The belongings necessary for personal or family expenses, the objects necessary to the exercise of a profession, as well as any resources necessary to support of a family for a period of one year cannot be subject to confiscation. In case of confiscation, the state shall be liable up to the value of the confiscated property for recovery of the damages caused by the crime, and subsequently for the liabilities of the convicted that occurred before laying the indictment when the remaining available property is not enough for the recovery of the damages and for payment of the liabilities.

A fine is an enforcement of a monetary liability of the convicted for the criminal offense committed. When imposing this penalty the court has to comply with the property status of the sentenced, with his or her income and the family liabilities. The fine cannot be less than 100 lev (approx. US$64).

Revocations

The punishment of deprivation of the right to occupy a definite state or public position and deprivation of the right to practice a definite profession or activity is imposed in the cases stipulated by the law if the occupation of the respective position or the practicing of the respective profession or activity is incompatible with the nature of the committed crime and is adjudicated for a definite term of less than three years. However, where they are imposed together with imprisonment, the length of the punishment may not be more than the imprisonment by more than three years.

Public reprobation shall consist in a public reprobation of the convicted that shall be announced in a suitable way according to the instructions of the verdict. The punishment of deprivation of a right to received orders, honorary titles and distinction, and deprivation of military rank can be imposed only for conviction for serious crime.

Prison

The Execution of Punishments Directorate General is a specialized administrative structure whose activity is regulated by the Execution of Punishment and Take into Custody Law. It is connected with the execution of imprisonment, probation, and pretrial detention. Bulgaria counts 12 prisons, with 22 prison boarding houses of open, transitional, and closed type, and one correctional home for juvenile offenders. The latter accommodates juvenile convicts serving a custodial sentence. Prison boarding houses are not self-contained facilities but subunits of the respective prisons.

The prosecution exercises control over the observance of legality during the execution of punishments. The places of deprivation of liberty are set up and closed by order of the Minister of Justice. They need to comply with the security and health requirements and to have the necessary living, household, and other premises. The investigation detention facilities are places for deprivation of liberty of persons detained pursuant to the Criminal Code of Procedure. Women serve their term of imprisonment in separate prisons and correctional homes. Recidivists serve their sentence in separate prisons and prison boarding houses of closed type. Prisoners sentenced for the first time to imprisonment up to five years for premeditated crime and those sentenced for crime by negligence serve the punishment in prison boarding houses of open type. The prison boarding houses of transitional type accommodate convicts with good behavior, who have served at least six months of the imposed sentence in a prison or prison boarding house of closed type and the remainder of their punishment is not more than five years.

The prisoners are divided in groups, which are managed by inspectors in social activities and educational work. The medical assistance for the prisoners is rendered by medical facilities of the Ministry of Justice. The prisoners can receive medication from outside as prescribed by a doctor from the medical facility at the prison. Prisoners with psychiatric illnesses and serious chronic disorders enjoy special care. Where there is no condition in these facilities to perform the necessary treatment, the prisoners are sent to other hospitals. In emergency medical cases the prisoners have the same rights as the other citizens.

The newly arrived prisoners are placed in receiving units where they stay from 14 days to 1 month. The prisoners are allowed to inform their relatives of their arrival in the prison or the correctional home. The prisoners in the receiving units undergo sanitary and hygienic control, medical check-up, and psychological survey. The prisoners can enjoy all rights established by the law except the rights of which they have been deprived by the sentence, the rights taken away or restricted explicitly by the law or by another normative act, and the right the execution of which is incompatible with the execution of the punishment.

The inmates have the right to be given suitable jobs. For each job the prisoners receive a certain part, but not less than 30 percent of the remuneration for their labor. Inmates do not work in weekends, and students in education facilities can be exempted from work for a term of 30 days for preparation and taking of examinations and preparation of diploma works. Pregnant women and breast-feeding women are placed in suitably furnished premises conforming to the necessary hygienic requirements and are under systematic medical control.

The general education and professional technical schooling in the educational facilities is carried out without discontinuing work according to syllabuses and programs. The professional and technical training is carried out in qualification courses without discontinuing work as well as through brigade and individual training. The necessary conditions are created in the prisons and detention facilities for theoretical and practical mastering of the specialty or profession through ensuring training equipment, free manuals, school aids, textbooks and reference books, and so forth. Prisoners are given the opportunity to satisfy their religious need by participation in religious services and rituals, as well as by having access to religious literature.

Hristo Manchev and Tsveta Docheva

Further Reading

Ministry of Interior: http://www.mvr.bg.

Stankov, Boyan. (1996). *Criminal Justice Systems in Europe and North America: Bulgaria*. Helsinki: The European Institute for Crime Prevention and Control (HEUNI).

Supreme Judicial Council: http://www.vss.justice.bg.

Trendafilova, Ekaterina. (1995). "Criminal Procedure in Bulgaria." In *Legal Reform in Post-Communist Europe: The View from Within,* edited by Stanislas Frankowski and Paul B. Stephan, pp. 309–329. Boston, MA: Kluwer International.

Croatia

Legal System: Civil
Murder: Medium
Burglary: Low
Corruption: Medium
Human Trafficking: Low
Prison Rate: Medium
Death Penalty: No
Corporal Punishment: No

Background

The Republic of Croatia (Hrvatska) is located on the Adriatic Sea in Southeastern Europe. It has a total land area of 55,974 square kilometers (21,611 square miles) and shares a border with Bosnia and Herzegovina, Hungary, Montenegro, Serbia, and Slovenia. Prior to World War I, Croatia was part of the Austro-Hungarian Empire, therefore escaping Ottoman Turkish rule. By the end of World War I, it became part of the Kingdom of Serbs, Croats and Slovenes, which remained until 1929 when it became known as the Kingdom of Yugoslavia. After World War II, Yugoslavia became a federal Communist state under the rule of Josip Broz Tito. It remained part of Yugoslavia until the Balkan Wars in the 1990s. In 1991 Croatia declared its independence from Yugoslavia and became a separate state. It applied for European Union (EU) membership in 2003 and is still in the process of negotiating for accession into the EU. In April 2009, it became a member of NATO.

In 1990 Croatia adapted the Constitution of 1990, which was later amended in 1997 and 1999. It was altered once more when the Change of the Constitution of the Republic of Croatia was passed at the end of 2000. The final change to the Constitution took place in 2001 with the passing of the Change of the Constitution of the Republic of Croatia. The government is based on the tripartite principle, with the separation of power between the legislative, executive, and judicial branches and a checks and balances system, including an independent judiciary. The first democratic elections in Croatia since World War II were held in the spring of 1990. The president is the commander-in-chief of the armed forces and appoints a prime minister and cabinet members with the approval of Parliament. In 1992 and 1993 the Chamber of Deputies and Chamber of Counties, respectively, were created. In March 2001, the Chamber of Counties (upper house) was abolished and the Croatian Parliament (Sabor) became unicameral. The Chamber of Deputies (Representatives) remained, consisting of 153 members who are elected and serve 4-year terms. The Parliament, or Sabor, has 140 members, 10 members from each of the 14 geographic districts, who are also elected.

Police

The police in Croatia are under the command of the Ministry of Interior (*Ministarstvo Unutarnjih Poslova,* MUP). They have a criminal police directorate, border police unit, special police command, communication center, forensic center, and a police academy. The police are broken up over the 20 counties and divided into four police directorates, or police administrations. District One includes only the police directorate for Zagreb, the capital city of Croatia, and the largest of its cities. District Two includes four police directorates, District Three has six police directorates, and District Four has nine. Each of the counties is further broken down into police stations and includes various other police units based on the need of that county. The Split-Dalmatia County, which is located on the Adriatic coast in southeastern Croatia, for example, has various police stations, border police units that include a station in Trilj and one at the airport in Split, and a maritime unit.

Courts

The judiciary in the Republic of Croatia is independent and autonomous. The role of the court is to determine guilt and to impose sanctions and measures on criminal offenders for misdemeanors and petty offenses as specified by law; to review legality of acts of public administration; as well as to decide on cases involving personal relations, labor cases, commercial law, property, and other civil cases. There is also a Law on Juvenile Courts (*Narodne Novine*, no. 111/97), which contains provisions for juvenile offenders charged with criminal offenses. This special law creates provisions for courts that dictate the process in cases involving juveniles, as well as providing legal protection of minors throughout the criminal procedure and in the execution of sanctions.

The justice system is made up of misdemeanor courts, municipal courts, commercial courts, county courts, the High Commercial Court, the High Misdemeanor Court, the Administrative Court, and the Supreme Court of the Republic of Croatia. As of December 31, 2009, there were 215 courts in Croatia. Of these, 110 are misdemeanor courts, 67 are municipal courts, and 12 are commercial courts; at the appellate level there are 21 county courts, which also adjudicate certain court cases at the nonappellate level. There are a total of 8,754 employees of the court, including 1,886 judges, of which 66 percent or 1,251 are women. In 2009, a total of 2,475,293 cases were adjudicated before all the courts in Croatia. Of the total number of cases brought before the court in 2009, 1,667,955 cases were resolved by the courts, leaving nearly 800,000 cases pending.

Crime

Classifications of crime

A criminal offense cannot exist without being properly defined. In Croatia, criminal offenses and sanctions are prescribed by statute and are covered in the criminal code. The Criminal Code: The Official Gazette of the Republic of Croatia, passed in October 1997, went into effect in January 1998. This criminal code provides the basis and limitations of criminal law enforcement. It also outlines conduct that is considered criminal. Conduct that does not constitute a criminal offense will not be punishable by law. This criminal legislation is not applied to children who are under 14 years of age at the time the offense was committed. The code does, however, apply to juveniles who are 14 or over, unless they are otherwise protected by a special statute.

The first nine chapters of the code discuss basic provisions, what constitutes a criminal offense, culpability, types of punishment including noncustodial, and security measures. Chapters 10–26 describe various crimes and the sanctions for those crimes. According to Chapter 1, article 1:

> 1. Criminal offenses and criminal sanctions shall be prescribed only for acts threatening or violating personal liberties or human rights, as well as other rights and social values guaranteed and protected by the Constitution of the Republic of Croatia and international law in such a manner that their protection could not be realized without criminal law enforcement.
> 2. The prescribing of specific criminal offenses, as well as the types and the range of criminal sanctions against their perpetrators, shall be based upon the necessity for criminal law enforcement and its proportionality with the degree and nature of the danger against personal liberties, human rights and other social values.

Crimes are delineated between serious criminal offenses such as murder, and petty offenses, or misdemeanors. One of the major problems plaguing Croatia is its central location between the opium-producing Golden Crescent, particularly Afghanistan, and Western Europe. The Balkan Route, which runs through the former Yugoslavia, is a popular land route for transporting illegal contraband to Western Europe. This includes drug trafficking, human smuggling and trafficking, weapons trafficking, contraband cigarettes, stolen vehicles, and the trade in other illegal goods or services. This route is also used for synthetic drugs moving east from the Netherlands, and it has been increasingly used as an alternate route for Colombian cocaine trafficking, which is increasingly being trafficked through Western Africa and then up through the Balkan routes to Western Europe.

Human trafficking in Eastern Europe has also remained problematic. The revenue from human trafficking is estimated to be between $7 and $9.5 billion a year, according to the U.S. Department of Homeland Security. Some 200,000 women and children are trafficked through the Balkan region every year.

Hard economic times and exploitation of women and children have led to an increase in women coming from Moldova, the Ukraine, and Romania. Croatia, due to its central location between East and West, is used as a transit country for many criminal gangs operating networks throughout the Balkans. Also, with the recovery of tourism in Croatia, it is increasingly a destination country for human trafficking, according to *Jane's Sentinel Security Assessment* of 2009. Counterfeiting of passports is also a concern. Holders of a Croatian passport are not required to obtain visas for most European countries, which make it especially valuable, particularly for groups engaged in human trafficking or smuggling.

Crime Statistics

Criminal offenses are separated between serious criminal offenses and misdemeanors, as well as by adult and juvenile perpetrators. According to *Statistical Yearbook* 2009, there were 71,221 total criminal offenses reported in Croatia in 2008. There were another 277,631 adults accused of misdemeanor offenses in 2008, of which 46,944 were women. For juveniles, there were 3,419 criminal offenses reported in 2008, and 10,684 juveniles accused of misdemeanor offenses, of which 888 were females. Statistics from the Ministry of Interior Secretariat of the Ministry Department of Analytics are broken down by criminal offenses, based on the title of the criminal code. Title 10 includes criminal offenses against life and limb. In 2009 there were 2,171 crimes reported, of which 2,015 were resolved. In 2008 there were 51 murders, 119 attempted murders, 16 aggravated murders, and 18 attempted aggravated murders. In 2009 there were a total of 31 murders, 134 attempted murders, 18 aggravated murders, and 19 attempted aggravated murders. A majority of the criminal offenses against life and limb included bodily injury and aggravated bodily injury. In 2008 there were a total of 872 cases of bodily injury and 1,128 cases of aggravated bodily injury, while in 2009 there were a total of 810 cases of bodily injury and 1,059 cases of aggravated bodily injury.

In Title 13, criminal offenses against valuables protected by international law, the majority of offenses reported were for abuse of narcotic drugs. Of the 7,235 cases under Title 13 in 2009, 7,063 were cases involving illegal narcotics. In 2009, there were a total of 658 criminal offenses against sexual freedom and morality (Title 14) reported, of which 76 were rape, and 14 were attempted rape. In terms of property crimes, included in Title 17, there were a total of 37,788 offenses reported in 2009. A majority of these cases were theft, with 12,378 cases reported, and aggravated theft, which includes four subparagraphs for a total of 18,777 cases.

Finding of Guilt

The legal system in Croatia is based on the civil law system. In criminal cases in Croatia, investigations are led by investigative judges at the county courts, while trials are held at the municipal courts. The misdemeanor courts handle low-level offenses, which mostly lead to fines and up to two months incarceration. The municipal courts handle most criminal cases and general civil cases. The states attorney is responsible for initiating all criminal procedures.

Chapter 3, article 25 of the Criminal Code of the Republic of Croatia states that a criminal offense can be committed by an act or an omission to act. Chapter 3 continues to give exculpatory factors in crimes, such as self-defense, necessity, coercion or threat, lawful use of force, and similar instances. Chapter 4 discusses the culpability of the offender, including mental incapacity, diminished mental capacity, voluntary intoxication, intent, and negligence. The Criminal Procedure Act has 35 chapters, which protect a person during the trial phase. Chapter 1, article 1 states:

> This Act establishes the rules which guarantee that an innocent person shall not be convicted, and that a punishment or other criminal sanction shall be imposed on the person who commits a criminal offense, subject to the provisions of the criminal law and in lawful proceedings before the competent court.

Punishment

After the court finds an individual guilty of a criminal offense, Chapters 10 through 26 of the Criminal Code of the Republic of Croatia are used to mete out punishment for convicted perpetrators. Punishment prescribed for these offenses varies based on the seriousness of the crime, as well as taking into account mitigating and aggravating factors. According to article 50 of the Criminal Code, "the purpose of inflicting punishment is to express the community's condemnation of a committed criminal offense, to deter the perpetrator from committing criminal offenses in the future, to deter all others from committing criminal offenses," by carrying out sanctions to prevent such acts from occurring. The sanctions for committing crime in Croatia include: fines; imprisonment, including parole; noncustodial measures, such as admonition and suspended sentences, including guidelines for probation; security measures, which include mandatory psychiatric treatment, mandatory treatment of addiction, revoked driving privileges, forfeiture, and expulsion of aliens. There are also provisions for confiscating any monetary gains obtained by illicit means. For juvenile offenders the most common punishments include juvenile detention, suspended sentences, and educational measures.

Sentencing

The Criminal Code of the Republic of Croatia delineates a range of sentences for all criminal offenses. Croatia does not have the death penalty for any criminal acts. The sentence for murder is not less than 5 years. For aggravated murder, the minimum is 10 years. The sentence for manslaughter is between 1 and 10 years, while the sentences for infanticide and killing on request are both 1 to 8 years. Negligent homicide yields a sentence between 6 months and 5 years. The crime of bodily injury is punishable by the imposition of a fine or less than three years imprisonment. Aggravated bodily injury has three different sentences. If a person inflicts serious bodily injury or severely impairs a person's health, the perpetrator can be sentenced to between 6 months and 5 years; if the bodily injury is so severe that the life of the person is endangered, or causes permanent disfigurement or disability, the sentence is between 1 and 10 years; and if the person dies due to serious bodily injury, the sentence is between 3 and 15 years. The sentence for rape can range from 1 year to 15 years imprisonment depending on the situation surrounding the incident, the amount of injury received, and the age of the victim.

In looking at criminal offenses against property, the sentences vary a great deal based on circumstances surrounding the incident. Chapter 17, article 216 details the punishments for petty larceny, which include fines and between 6 months and 5 years imprisonment. Aggravated larceny, described as committing larceny by breaking in, entering by force, or in a dangerous manner, or by taking advantage of a natural disaster, or taking advantage of a helpless person, yields a sentence of between 6 months and 10 years. For those who commit aggravated larceny of items of great value, cultural heritage, or religious or other historical or technical significance, the sentence is 6 months to 5 years. If the aggravated larceny was committed by a perpetrator in possession of a weapon, or if the perpetrator is a member of an organized criminal group, the sentence is from 1 to 8 years. The sentence for robbery is between 1 and 10 years, unless the act was committed by a member of a group or criminal organization or in the circumstances of an armed robbery. In these cases the sentence is between 3 and 15 years.

The sentence for those individuals in possession of a controlled substance with intent to sell can range from 1 to 12 years. For those who manufacture or process with the intent to sell, or purchase with the intent to resell, the sentence is 3 to 15 years. Some major issues facing Croatia are from organized criminal groups; therefore, the sentences on controlled substances mentioned are elevated if they are committed by a perpetrator who is a member of a criminal organization. The sentences in those instances can range from 3 years to a life sentence. In cases of human trafficking, which also includes organ trafficking, the sentence is from 1 to 10 years. If the individuals trafficked are juveniles or minors, the sentence is from 3 to 15 years. If, however, the offender is a member of a criminal organization, the sentence ranges from 5 years to life imprisonment.

Prison

In 2008, there were over 70,000 criminal offenses reported. Of the 71,221 criminal offenses perpetrated by adults, only 4,384 were sentenced to prison. Another 16,922 received a suspended prison sentence. Of the 3,419 juvenile perpetrators charged with criminal offenses, only 9 were sentenced to juvenile detention. Of the 277,631 adults accused of misdemeanors, 185,494 were found guilty, and 7,836 received a sentence of imprisonment. Of the 10,684 juveniles accused of misdemeanors, 18 received a sentence of juvenile detention. These sentences of imprisonment are served in the Croatian penal system. Croatia's prison system is under the auspices of the Ministry of Justice and is controlled by the Directorate for the Prison System.

The penal system includes a central office, education center, penitentiaries, prisons, and reformatories. The central office includes the prison administration, human resources, service for treatment (which includes departments for special treatment programs and the department for juveniles), a security sector, and an analytical department. The education center includes a department for the development of work skills and another for the implementation of educational programs. There are 6 penitentiaries in Croatia, and 14 prisons, including a prison hospital in the capital city of Zagreb, as well as 2 reformatories. The penitentiaries house inmates who have been sentenced to criminal offenses and misdemeanors, people who have replaced their monetary fines with a sentence, a juvenile detention division, and pretrial detention. The prisons are used to execute sentences in misdemeanor cases and are also used for prison security, that is, maintaining internal order among prisoners. The prison also operates a Center of Training, which opened in October 1999, to provide continuous training for correctional officers. The training includes introductory course work, basic training, additional courses, and specialized training.

Vesna Markovic

Further Reading

Crostat. Republic of Croatia—Central Bureau of Statistics: http://www.dzs.hr/default_e.htm.

Government of the Republic Croatia: http://www.vlada.hr/en.

Jane's Sentinel Security Assessment. The Balkans, Security. Croatia, October 28, 2009.

Ministry of Interior for the Republic of Croatia (Ministarstvo Unutrasnjih Poslova Republike Hrvatske): http://www.mup.hr/default.aspx?id=1257.

Supreme Court of Croatia, Criminal Procedure Act: http://www.vsrh.hr/CustomPages/Static/HRV/Files/Legislation__Criminal-Procedure-Act.pdf.

Cyprus

Legal System: Common/Civil
Murder: Low
Corruption: Low
Human Trafficking: Medium
Prison Rate: Medium
Death Penalty: No
Corporal Punishment: No

Background

The history of Cyprus goes back to 9000 BC and the legal history of Cyprus is indeed extensive. While the origins of law in Cyprus are lost in the mist of time, historically speaking, the major phases in its development correspond to the powers that have ruled over the island since ancient times until its independence in 1960. Starting at approximately 1250 BC, legal authority was exercised by the kings in the various ancient Greek city-kingdoms in Cyprus, justice administration reflecting such neighboring legal orders as that of Egypt, Assyria, and Babylonia. During the Byzantine period

(330–1191), justice administration was the responsibility of local officials who applied Byzantine-Roman law and there was a right of appeal against their rulings to the higher authorities in Constantinople. Jurisdiction in family law matters, including mediation, was also exercised by the 12 Episcopal (Greek-Orthodox Church) courts. The crusader Richard the Lionhearted conquered Cyprus on his way to Jerusalem in 1291 and soon after transferred it to the knights and finally to the Loisignan kings (French origin). In 1373 the Genoans occupied Cyprus until the Venetians took control in 1489. The Frankish rule that lasted until 1489 introduced the feudal socioeconomic system that existed in Western Europe at the time and the applicable law took the form of the Assizes of Jerusalem and Cyprus. The Francophone law applicable to the landed gentry was the *Assises de la Haute Cour* and for the serfs the *Assises de la Basse Cour*. The latter was translated into the local Cypriot dialect in 1244. The Episcopal courts, however, continued to have jurisdiction in family law matters and their role grew in importance as far as justice administration for the local landless population is concerned when the Franks relinquished control of Cyprus to Venice in 1489. The Ottomans invaded and occupied the island from 1571–1878, and the Assizes were replaced by the Holy Muslim Law (sharia), exercised by the local *Kadi*, a Muslim judge, and the *Moufti*, a Muslim legal consultant. The Greek Orthodox Church Courts were allowed and continued to apply Byzantine family law.

Cyprus was leased by Turkey to Great Britain in 1878 in exchange for the protection of Turkey from the Russian czar. Britain proceeded to annex the island in 1914 and it became a Crown Colony in 1925. By 1882 the judicial system was revised, establishing assise courts, district courts, and a Supreme/High Court. In 1878, there was the Imperial Ottoman Penal Code, which the British, with some amendments, left as it was until 1928 when the Criminal Code of England (now in force in Cyprus) was introduced. The criminal justice system introduced by the British was an accusatorial one, similar to that at Common Law. Inter alia, the Criminal Code and the Criminal Procedure Law were codified in 1959. When Cyprus gained its independence in 1960, article 188 of its Constitution provided that all laws that applied previously would continue to do so until repealed or amended by law enacted by its Parliament. Thus, the Criminal Code of Cyprus embodies both the general principles and the main offenses of the Common Law of England. There are four criminal courts.

Legal System

Like the rest of the government administration, in terms of its legal framework and procedures, the contemporary criminal justice system of the Republic of Cyprus (criminal code, police structure and standard operating procedures, the prison, and the procedures followed by social workers in dealing with juveniles) reflects the significant influence of the British. It should be noted in this context that whereas criminal justice legislation and procedures in England have changed significantly since 1960 when Cyprus became independent, in the Republic of Cyprus a great deal has remained as it was inherited at the time. Also, with the exception of the judiciary, during the period from 1960 to the late 1990s recruitment and promotion into the police and prison services was largely determined by one's political party connections. Under pressure to harmonize legislation and practices in the aforementioned services in preparation for full membership of the European Union in 2004, entrance and promotion criteria for the police and the prison services became more objective. Nevertheless, the effectiveness and efficiency of the police and prison services have been adversely affected by the established practice by all political parties whereby selection and promotion into the public service generally should reflect their strength in national political elections. This practice was introduced in the late 1980s in an effort to avoid any one political party dominating the composition of the public service, as was the case with the right-wing until recently. Low morale and a certain degree of corruption in the police and prison services can arguably be said to be attributable to low salaries of the rank-and-file and the lack of meritocracy.

Police

The Cyprus police was first established as the Cyprus Military Police when the British took over control of Cyprus from the Ottomans in 1879. Its command structure, operating procedures, and training has been largely influenced by the British police model and its police culture reflects the political and social history of Cyprus. Today, it numbers 5,321 members, of whom 951 (17.8%) are specials, 3,312 (62.2%) police constables, 634 (11.9%) sergeants, 258 (4.8%) inspectors, 96 (1.8%) chief inspectors, 38 (0.7%) superintendents B, 13 (0.2%) superintendents A, 13 (0.2%) chief superintendents, 4 assistant chiefs of police, 1 deputy chief of police, and 1 chief of police. The command structure of the Cyprus police consists of the following:

- Under the chief: Executive Office, Strategic Planning Committee, Public Relations and Press Office, and Planning and Operations Planning.
- Under the deputy chief: staff officer.
- Assistant chief (Education): Police Academy, Recruitment Office.
- Assistant chief (Administration): Administration Department, Office for Inspections and Control, Finance Division, Research and Development Department, European Union and International Co-Operation Office.
- Assistant chief (Support): Traffic Department, Aliens and Immigration Service, Fire Brigade, Mechanized Rapid Response Unit, Central Information Service, Presidential Guard Unit, Port and Naval Police, Air Operations Unit, Equipment and Provisions Management Office, Airports Security Office.
- Assistant chief (Operations): Criminal Investigations Department (including Economic Crime Squad), Forensic Investigations Service, Operations Office, Drug Squad.

A similar structure underpins each district police officer in each of six police districts, namely, Nicosia, Limassol, Larnaca, Famagusta, Paphos, and Morphou. The police district of Kyrenia is not functioning due to the continuing occupation of the northern part of Cyprus by Turkey. Thus, the police command structure is organized at a national and district level. A total of 450 police personnel are assigned to traffic duties. The police has no organic relationship with the Cyprus National Guard other than collaboration in criminal investigations. As provided in the Constitution, the chief and the deputy chief of police are appointed by the president of the Republic of Cyprus and the assistant chiefs by the chief of police in consultation with the minister of justice and public order.

Crime

Classification of Crimes

The annual report of the Statistical Service entitled *Criminal Statistics* divides criminal offenses into "serious" and "minor" on the basis of offense seriousness, as used by the police. To illustrate, since 2003, a property offense is classified as "serious" if the value of property stolen or damaged is valued at €850 (US$1,052) or more. The following crimes categories are considered serious: against public order; against lawful authority; injurious to the public in general; sexual offenses; against the person; malicious injury to property; forgery, coining, counterfeiting, similar offenses, and criminal impersonation; and miscellaneous. The annual police serious crime index comprises homicide and attempted homicide, arson, robbery, drugs, criminal damage using explosives, burglaries, theft, and "other serious offenses." It should be noted that the age of criminal responsibility is 14 years. Of particular challenge to law enforcement in Cyprus are drug offenses, armed robberies, destroying property with explosives, economic crimes, illegal immigration from the Turkish-occupied northern part of Cyprus and, finally, serious traffic offenses that result in one of the worst annual road death tolls in the European Union. Interestingly, however, causing death by want of precaution or carelessness in a traffic accident is no longer classified under serious offenses against the person, as was the case in earlier years, but is treated as a minor offense for statistical purposes under the category of traffic offenses. Causing death by want of precaution or carelessness in all other instances excluding traffic accidents continues to be considered a serious offense against the person.

Cypriot Special Police officers investigate the house of Cypriot Dimitri Chrisanthou and his wife Monika of Slovakia, who were allegedly stabbed to death by a Chinese worker in Kathikas village near Paphos, Cyprus, February 23, 2007. (AP Photos/Andreas Lazarou)

Unless one can convince a criminal court otherwise, being in possession of or transporting prohibited narcotics is considered as doing so to supply it to a third person if (1) the quantity and the drug involved is as follows: cannabis (30 grams or more), reprocessed opium or its products (10 grams or more), processed cocaine or its products (10 grams or more), or any other prohibited substance (20 grams or more in solid form or 20 cubic centimeters or more in liquid form); and (2) if the number of plants is 3 or more in the case of cannabis, 20 or more plants of *papaver somniferum L* and, finally, 5 or more plants of the *erythroxylum coca* category.

Crime Statistics

In 2008, the following serious offenses were reported to and recorded by the police: murder (9), rape (30), burglaries (2,587), serious drug offenses (777). Crime rates have been increasing in Cyprus. More specifically, in a total population of 860,000 in the free areas of the republic, the number of adults (17 years of age and older) convicted of serious offenses per 100,000 of the population was as follows: 1976 (115), 1980 (120), 1990 (150), and 2005 (258). The most typical crime in rural areas is theft while in urban areas the most typical crimes are burglaries, malicious damage to property with explosives, drugs, and armed robberies.

Finding of Guilt

Article 12.4 of the Constitution of the Republic of Cyprus provides that every person is innocent until guilty. With the exception of some strict liability offenses, both *actus reus* as well as *mens rea* are required for a conviction. The rights of an accused to be found in the Criminal Procedure Law reflect provisions in the Constitution, international treaties, and the European Convention for the Protection of Human Rights. A person may only be arrested under the authority of a reasoned judicial warrant, with the exception of a flagrant offense punishable with detention or imprisonment. As far as detaining an arrested person and before charging him or her is concerned, it is provided in the Constitution that such a person must be brought before a judge within 24 hours the latest who will decide whether to release or to remand him or her in custody and on what conditions. An application for remand must be made by a police officer not below the rank of inspector. Within 3 days the judge must decide whether to release the person arrested from police custody or to remand him or her for up to 8 days. The remand periods cannot exceed 3 months from the date of arrest.

Following an application to a court, an accused of documented insufficient financial means is entitled to legal aid to have the services of a defense lawyer. Regarding plea bargaining, it does occur, albeit "unofficially," both between an accused and/or his or her defense lawyer and the police concerning the gravity of the charge as well as the judiciary regarding changing a not-guilty plea for a less severe sentence. In cases where the likely sentence upon conviction is a term of imprisonment of less than five years, an accused pleading guilty can apply for summary trial. There is no jury trial in Cyprus. Most cases are resolved by summary judgment and sentence. The police carry out investigations into alleged offenses and prepare a criminal file for the Legal Service of the Republic, headed by the attorney general who also acts as the director of public prosecutions. Cases are prosecuted by a public prosecutor in the Office of the Attorney General. Occasionally, nonserious offenses are prosecuted by the police themselves. Alternatives to going to trial exist only for juveniles such as an official police warning. In rare cases, the attorney general may decide not to prosecute a case, if it is deemed to be in the public interest. A court may decide that an accused is not to be released on bail but to be remanded in custody to await trial.

There are 32 criminal court judges, 38 percent of the total number of judges. The qualification for application to be appointed to the bench is six years' practice as a lawyer and all applicants are interviewed by the Supreme Court Bench. There is no separate juvenile court in Cyprus. A district court judge on a given day of the week simply sits as juvenile court.

Punishment

Types of Punishment

The punishments available for adults are absolute discharge, conditional discharge, binding over, fine, fine and binding over, probation order, suspended sentence of imprisonment, suspended sentence of imprisonment and fine, imprisonment, periodic imprisonment, imprisonment and fine, life sentence, and community service, all of which may be applied to juveniles who may also be committed to the care of a suitable person. Probation order and community service, fine and community service, suspended sentence of imprisonment and community service, and death sentence (only for high treason) are additional punishments.

The only sentence for murder is life imprisonment; the typical term of imprisonment in years for rape is 8, burglary 1.5, robbery 6, and trafficking in large quantities of heroin 12 years. The typical sentence for theft is 6 months' prison. The death penalty (by hanging) has been abolished and it was last used in 1961 for premeditated murder.

Prison

There is only one prison in Cyprus and it is in Nicosia, the capital city of Cyprus. On the basis of statistical data (unpublished) provided by the prison authorities, on July 31, 2009, the total number of persons held in prison was 718, comprising 563 (78.4%) prisoners serving their sentences and 155 persons on remand awaiting trial (21.6%). Of the 563 sentenced prisoners, 36 (6.4%) were women. The prison is increasingly seriously overcrowded.

All sentenced prisoners are required to work, except for medical reasons, as provided in the Prison (General) Regulations of 1997 and 1998. A large number of classes on a broad range of topics is available to prisoners who wish to take them. Unless the prison governor decides otherwise, prisoners held in the closed prison are entitled to eight visits a month and those in the open prison six. Prisoners and those on remand are entitled to and can apply for escorted or unescorted home leave and to be transported to hospital, on a home visit, or to visit a seriously ill close relative, or to attend the funeral of a close relative, or to get married, or to attend the wedding of a close relative, or to attend the birth or the baptism of their child, to attend court as accused or witnesses or, finally, to attend activities organized by the prison authorities. In those cases where a bilateral agreement exists for the exchange or transfer of prisoners, as in the case, for example, of other European member states or Australia, prisoners can be transferred to their home country to serve the remainder of their sentence. To illustrate, at the time of writing, a Greek-Cypriot serving a sentence in an Australian prison is the subject of a transfer procedure, while a national of Bulgaria convicted in Cyprus of trafficking in drugs and sentenced to 11 years in prison was transferred to Bulgaria 11 months after he was sentenced to serve the rest of his sentence there.

Andreas Kapardis

Further Reading

Artemis, P. (1989). "An Outline of Criminal Law and the Working of the Judicial System in Criminal Cases." *Cyprus Law Review* 26(2): 4016.

Kapardis, Andreas. (2001). *Society, Crime and Criminal Justice in Cyprus: The First Years of British Rule.* Athens: A. N. Sakkoulas.

Neocleous, Andreas, Eleni Christodoulidou, and Panayiotis Neocleous. (2000). *Introduction to Cyprus Law.* New York: Yorkhill Law.

Statistical Service, Ministry of Finance, Republic of Cyprus. (2006). *Criminal Statistics 2006* (series 1; report 33). Nicosia: Government Printing Office.

Czech Republic

Legal System: Civil
Murder: Medium
Burglary: High
Corruption: Low
Human Trafficking: Low
Prison Rate: Medium
Death Penalty: No
Corporal Punishment: No

Background

The Czech Republic is part of Central Europe and its neighbors include Germany, Poland, Slovakia, and Austria. The country's total area is 78,867 square kilometers (30,450 square miles). Until 1993, the Czech Republic and Slovakia formed a single country created after the break-up of the Austro-Hungarian Empire in 1918. On January 1, 1993, the two parts of the former federal republic parted ways to establish two independent national states—the Czech Republic and the Slovak Republic.

The Czech Republic is a parliamentary democracy. The country's current Constitution took effect on January 1, 1993. The president is the head of state, elected for five-year terms. The legislative branch is represented by a bicameral Parliament consisting of the Senate (81 senators elected for six-year terms) and the Chamber of Deputies (200 deputies elected for four-year terms). Executive power lies with the cabinet headed by the prime minister who is appointed by the president. The prime minister is usually chosen from the ranks of the political party that wins elections to the Chamber of Deputies. The Czech Republic is divided into 14 regions including the capital city of Prague, the only city to receive regional status. Each region has a governor and a Regional Assembly while towns are managed by mayors and local assemblies. It has been a NATO member since 1999 and an EU member since 2004.

The Czech Republic has a population of 10,220,911, including 5,253,606 women. Youth under 14 years of age represent 13.8 percent of the population, and people over 65 years of age 15.1 percent. Czechs' life expectancy is 76 years. The number of foreigners living in the Czech Republic has increased nearly 10 times since 1990, which is a natural consequence of the deep political and economic changes the country has seen since the collapse of socialism. Nevertheless, the Czech Republic still belongs to countries with a relatively low number of foreigners who currently represent only 2.9 percent of the Czech population. Ukrainians represent the largest group of foreign nationals in the Czech Republic (102,000), followed by citizens of the Slovak Republic (58,000) and Vietnam (41,000).

The Czech Republic is also a target country for some asylum seekers. Between 1998 and 2005, the number of asylum applicants fluctuated between 4,000 and 18,000 with a dropping trend since 2002; in 2006, the Czech Republic registered 3,016 asylum applications. In addition to legal aliens, the Czech Republic is also used as a transit or target country of illegal migration. However, the number of identified illegal foreign migrants has been declining since 2000 from approximately 53,000 persons in 2000 to less than 11,000 in 2006. The largest national group among illegal migrants are Ukrainians.

With the exception of the Roma (gypsy), there are no significant large ethnic minorities in the Czech Republic. The Roma live practically in all parts of the country. The exact number of their population is unknown but is estimated to be somewhere between 150,000 and 200,000 people. Generally speaking, this ethnic group shows lower levels of education and higher levels of unemployment. The Roma are also more vulnerable to social exclusion.

Legal System

The country's legal system is based on the continental legal tradition. After 1989, there have been numerous fundamental legislative changes aimed at removing legal deformities inherited from the previous socialist regime and implementing legal standards of the European Union. The Czech penal law is largely codified in a single law—the Criminal Act No. 140/1961 Coll., but it has seen many amendments, especially since 1990. The Chamber of Deputies approved a complete new version of the Criminal Act in 2009 and it came into force on January 1, 2010.

The current penal law does not divide crimes into several categories. Antisocial actions and behavior of lesser gravity are addressed in the Offences Act. The minimum age of criminal liability is 15 years with persons between 15 and 18 years of age defined as juveniles. The Czech penal law is based on the principle of personal criminal liability and does not recognize collective liability, liability for the guilt of another, and corporate criminal liability, but the latter has been the subject of extensive legal debate over the past few years. The key principle of criminal procedure is that a person may be prosecuted only on legal grounds as defined in the Bill of Rights and Freedoms (incorporated in the Czech Constitution), meaning that nobody may be prosecuted or incarcerated for reasons and in ways other than those defined by law. Criminal procedure is defined in Act No. 141/1961 Coll.—the Code of Criminal Procedure, which has also been subject to numerous amendments after 1991.

Justice System

The judicial system consists of a network of independent courts (the Supreme Court, the Supreme Administrative Court, two high courts, regional courts, and district courts); the system of public prosecutors shares a similar structure. Public prosecution is designed as a system of state offices whose purpose is to represent the state in the protection of public interest in cases defined by the law. Judges are appointed by the president of the republic while public prosecutors are nominated by the chief public prosecutor and appointed by the justice minister. The chief public prosecutor is appointed and dismissed by the cabinet at the suggestion of the justice minister.

Investigation is most usually conducted by the Criminal Police Service and the Police of the Czech Republic. Public prosecution is responsible for ensuring that the law is observed during pretrial procedures. Issues of constitutionality are the jurisdiction of the Constitutional Court that is not part of the regular court system. The basic principles of judiciary organization and practice are defined in Head IV of the Constitution of the Czech Republic and further addressed in other laws.

Police

A fundamental piece of police legislation is Act No. 283/1991 Coll., which regulates the organization and activity of the police of the Czech Republic. Police are under the jurisdiction of the Ministry of the Interior. The chief of police is appointed by the Minister of Interior with the approval of the Czech government.

Police are generally divided into the uniformed and nonuniformed police. Uniformed police are responsible above all for the public order and security, and they comprise the Police on the Beat, the Traffic Police, the Aliens and Border Police, the Railway Police, Air Service, and some special departments, as for example, the Department of the Protection of Constitutional Authorities. Nonuniformed police are responsible chiefly for the detection and investigation of crime and comprise above all the Criminal Police and Investigation Service. The scope of activity of some police departments and units covers the whole territory of the Czech Republic (e.g., Department for Detection of Organized Crime, Unit for the Detection of Corruption and Financial Crime, National Anti-Drug Headquarters, Air Service, Rapid Employment Unit, Institute of Criminalistics, Office for Documentation and Investigation of Communism Crimes); other police forces act within the regions and are managed by the regional police headquarters.

Local police in the CR may be established by the decision of the municipal council on the basis of the Act on the Local Police No. 553/1991 Coll. Local police is responsible for the public order, especially it assists in providing protection and safety of persons and property, to observe the rules of public peace and coexistence of citizens, traffic safety, and also to disclose the minor offenses and administrative misdemeanors. Local police is headed by the magistrate/mayor or by a selected member of the board of a municipal council. It collaborates closely with the police of the CR.

Local police is an armed service but the use of guns is allowed in case of urgent emergency only (life threat or the risk of escape of a dangerous offender). In addition to the police of the CR and local police, there are many private security agencies. They are defined as so-called licensed trade under the conditions regulated by the Act on Commercial Activity No. 455/1991 Coll.

Crime

Crime Statistics

Basic official data are to be found in the Report on Internal Security and Public Order in the Czech Republic." The report is based primarily on information in the Crime Statistics System of the Czech Police. Another source used in developing the annual reports is the Justice Ministry's statistics on persons prosecuted, charged, and sentenced on the territory of the Czech Republic during the given year.

The level of crime in the Czech Republic dramatically increased in the 1990s, culminating in 1999 with a total of 427,000 crimes investigated by the police, which was three times more than the level in the 1980s. After 1999, however, a decline in overall crime has been recorded and since 2001, the number of investigated crimes has stagnated at around 360,000 cases a year. At the peak of criminal activity in 1999, there were approximately 4,100 crimes per 100,000 inhabitants. In 2007, the figure dropped to approximately 3,500 crimes per 100,000 inhabitants.

Both the massive increase and later the decrease in investigated crimes were largely due to what the Czech police describes as "crime against property." Each year, one-quarter of all crimes occur in the capital city and only 20 percent of cases are solved—that is, the perpetrator is identified. Compared with other regions of the Czech Republic, the crime level in Prague is twice as high but the rate of solved cases is half as high. One interpretation of these findings may be that Prague is the most attractive place for crime (and criminals) in the entire country.

Property and Economic Crimes

Current police statistics on property crime include theft—the most common type of crime in the Czech Republic (in 2007, there were approximately 210,000 theft cases, or 58.5% of all crimes recorded that year), some types of fraud and embezzlement cases as well as other types of crime.

Economic crime constituted 11 percent of all cases recorded by the police in 2007. A dramatic increase in this type of criminality in 2005 was due to a major growth in credit fraud, the single most common type of economic crime in police statistics (32% of all cases described by the police as economic crime).

Personal Crimes

Violent crime constituted 5 percent of all cases recorded by the police in 2007. The most common types of violent crime are bodily harm and robbery. In the past decade, the lowest number of murders was recorded in 2005—186 cases (including cases of attempted murder and planned murder) and in 2007—196 cases. On the other hand, the highest number of murders was recorded in 1998—313 cases. The number of recorded robbery cases continued to grow until 2004 when it reached 6,107 cases; the first decrease (by approximately 600) was recorded in 2005 and another one in 2006 (by 900). In 2007, a total of 4,856 robbery cases were recorded (83 more than in the previous year).

Compared with 2006, the police recorded a significant increase in the number of rape cases in 2007 (from 530 to 637 cases). Crimes against morality constituted 0.5 percent of all cases recorded by the police in 2007. The number of cases reported under this category has remained more or less unchanged.

Miscellaneous Crime

This category (in order of frequency in 2007) includes the following types of criminal activity: driving a motor vehicle without license (18,098 cases recorded in 2007) and infringement of other people's rights (together the two types of criminal acts made up 38% of the "miscellaneous crime" category) as well as avoidance of alimony (20%), dangerous behavior under the influence of addictive substances and alcohol (20%), and road traffic accidents (20%).

The total number of persons affected by crime (victims) is reported only in police statistics. The number of victims has been slowly but steadily increasing and in 2004 and 2005 the minimum annual number already exceeded 50,000 people. In 2006 and 2007 it was again approximately 50,000. Men, specifically younger men, are victims of crime more often than women.

In 2007, approximately 139,000 crimes were solved, which represents 39 percent of all cases recorded that year.

Offenders' Profile

The number of known offenders stagnated between 2003 and 2007 at around 121,000–123,000 people with a long-term growth in the number of female offenders. Between 1993 and 2007, the annual number of female offenders increased from around 9,000 to approximately 16,500 persons, and their share of the total group of known offenders thus increased from 8 percent to 13 percent.

The number of adult offenders slightly increased while the number of offenders under the age of 18 dropped (with a significant drop in the under-15 category—i.e., persons without criminal liability). In 2007, a total of 9,000 child and juvenile offenders were identified (including nearly 3,000 individuals under 15 years of age). The number of foreign offenders has been relatively stable, and foreign nationals represent approximately 6 percent of all known offenders since 1993. In 2007, there were some 8,000 foreign offenders. Prague has the highest share of foreign offenders—around 15 percent of all known offenders in 2007.

The share of first-time offenders (i.e., persons who are entered in police files for the first time) on the total number of offenders still remains very high, around 50 percent a year. The share of recidivists (repeat offenders) on the total number of known offenders has started growing in recent years—there was a 46 percent increase in 2006, the highest figure in a decade. In 2007, it was approximately 44 percent.

Organized Crime

The phenomenon of organized crime first came to the attention of the general public soon after 1990. A key moment that prompted Czech authorities to take organized crime seriously was the World Inter-Ministerial Conference on international organized crime that took place in Naples, Italy, in 1994. Major legislative changes were made in relation to organized crime in the first half of the 1990s. First, punitive sanctions for crimes committed in organized groups were increased. In 1995, the Criminal Act was amended to include several new concepts such as participation in criminal conspiracy, effective repentance, immunity from prosecution for undercover agents, the possibility of sentencing an offender for a crime committed in favor of a criminal conspiracy and, above all, the definition of a criminal conspiracy.

The Code of Criminal Procedure was amended to improve protection of persons involved in criminal prosecution of organized crime such as witness protection, access to hitherto secret bank records, wiretapping, and so forth. The Czech Republic has signed but not yet ratified the UN Convention against Transnational Organized Crime. A key organizational change against organized crime was the creation of the Unit for Detection of Organized Crime of the Criminal Police on January 1, 1995, and the Police Service for Detection of Corruption and Serious Economic Crime on January 1, 1994. In 2000, specialized sections devoted to serious economic crime were created on the prosecution side as well, on the level of the chief public prosecutor and high public prosecutors.

The situation in the Czech Republic is further complicated by the fact that no cases of participation in criminal conspiracy (sec. 163a of the Criminal Act) were detected before 1998. After 1998, however, there were dozens of prosecuted and investigated persons. The number approached 100 a year in 2002–2004, exceeded 100 in 2005 and 2006 (it was as high as 181 in 2005), and once again fell to 78 in 2007. Unfortunately, the number of sentenced individuals was much lower. In 1999, only 1 person was sentenced for participation in criminal conspiracy, 2 persons in 2001, 5 in 2003, 10 in 2004, 9 in 2005, 21 in 2006, and 15 in 2007. Official documents of the Police Presidium indicate that approximately 75 organized groups with a total of 2,000 members were active on the territory of the Czech Republic in 2007.

By far the most common activities of organized crime are car theft, prostitution, and since 1994, drug production, smuggling, and distribution. Between 1993 and 1998, one of the most common types of criminal activities was theft of works of art. In 1996, 1997, 2002, and 2005, it was tax, credit, insurance, and foreign exchange fraud. Corruption occasionally comes to the fore, although its overall level greatly fluctuates. Between 1998 and 2004, one of the most common activities among organized crime groups was illegal migration. Since 2005, however, its extent has been falling and in 2006 it ranked 10th in the overall statistics. Several changes occurred in 2006. Money laundering and forgery of documents, bills, and coins is on the rise together with a major increase in computer crime. Since 2005, illegal production and smuggling of alcohol and cigarettes has gained in prominence as well.

Finding of Guilt

The law requires the police to investigate crime based on their own initiative to secure evidence necessary to detect facts important for the evaluation of a given case and suspect as soon as possible. The police detect and secure evidence regardless of whether it is in favor of or against the suspect. A suspect cannot be forced to testify or confess in any way. If identified facts indicate that a crime was committed and that it was committed by a specific person, the police immediately decide to start prosecution of the suspect as a person charged. A copy of the order to begin prosecution must be delivered to the person charged no later than on the day of first interrogation and to the public prosecutor and defense lawyer within 48 hours. Defendants may complain against the prosecution order to the public prosecutor. Supervision of the legality of crime investigation is exercised by the public prosecutor who also has the right to issue binding instructions to the investigating police units and cancel their illegal or groundless decisions or measures.

Each person charged must have a defense lawyer in cases where the maximum possible sentence is imprisonment for more than five years. Defense lawyers are also required in cases against juveniles; in cases where the court or the public prosecutor have doubts about the defendant's ability to defend himself or herself, especially due to physical or mental handicaps; and in other specified conditions.

Searches

In court procedures, a house search may be ordered by the presiding judge while in preliminary procedures it may be ordered at the request of a public prosecutor by a judge with territorial jurisdiction over the premises. A house search order must be in writing and must state the reasons and grounds for the search. Police officers may enter apartments and other residential premises and related land only in urgent cases where entry is necessary to protect the life or health of a person or to provide protection of other rights and freedoms or to avert serious threats to public safety and order. When entering such premises, the police officer must not perform any task or act other than those necessary to avert a threat or to arrest a person based on an arrest warrant or to arrest and deliver a person for execution of a prison sentence. In cases of prosecution of especially serious willful crimes, a judge may, at the request of a public prosecutor, order wiretapping and recording of telephone calls.

Arrest and Custody

A person charged may be taken into custody if his or her behavior or other pertinent circumstances give reason to believe that the person may attempt to flee, where the person's identity is not immediately established, if the person does not have a permanent residence, if there is risk of repeat offenses, if he or she is facing a severe sentence or could influence accomplices or witnesses. Custody is ordered by a court. Only persons subject to criminal prosecution may be committed to custody.

Arrest is executed by police officers who are also responsible for locating the person charged, if necessary. After arrest, the police officer who arrested the person charged based on an arrest warrant must immediately but no later than within 24 hours deliver the person to the court. If this does not take place, the arrested individual must be released. The judge receiving the arrested person must immediately interrogate him or her and decide whether the person should be taken into custody. The decision must be communicated to the person within 24 hours of his or her delivery to the court. If the judge decides for custody, at least one family member of the person charged as well as his or her employer must be informed of the fact without undue delay. However, the person may choose not to have his or her family and employer notified of his or her committal to custody. Juveniles do not have this option, though. Custody is executed in prisons managed by the Prison Service of the Czech Republic (for more details, see below).

If the total time of custody during preliminary procedures reaches 3 months, the public prosecutor has 5 days to decide whether to keep the person charged in custody or whether to release him or her. Once charges are brought against the person, the court has 30 days to decide whether to keep the person charged in custody or whether to release him or her.

The total time of custody during criminal procedure must not exceed 1 year in cases involving crimes that fall into jurisdiction of sole judges. The time limit is 2 years in cases heard by a senate and 3 years in cases of grave willful crimes. The longest possible time of custody is 4 years in cases that carry maximum possible sentence of 15–20 years in prison or a life sentence.

All bodies responsible for penal proceedings must continuously assess whether the reasons for custody still prevail or whether conditions have changed. The person charged may at any time request to be released and a court must decide about the request within 5 days. If a request is turned down, the person may repeat the request on the same grounds no sooner than after 14 days.

In some cases, custody may be replaced by guarantees, supervision, or promise. A court may also release a person charged from custody against a bail in an amount defined by the court. However, a person suspected of criminal activities may be arrested by police officers in urgent cases for up to 48 hours. Within this 48-period, the person must be either delivered to a court or released.

Summary Process

In simple criminal cases that carry maximum sentences of less than three years, a summary process is possible under certain circumstances. The police submit to the public prosecutor a brief report on their investigation and the prosecutor either recommends a sentence to the court or adjourns the case or transfers the case to the relevant body to try the case. Instead of recommending a sentence, the public prosecutor may decide to conditionally postpone such a recommendation if the suspect confesses, pays any damage caused, and agrees with the postponement of prosecution recommendation. The decision to suspend prosecution recommendation must set a probation period of six months to one year.

Criminal cases with summary preliminary procedure are heard by sole judges in a summary process. The sole judge may grant a court order without trial with a maximum sentence of one year in prison with conditional suspension of the sentence or a sentence of community service, a money penalty, forfeiture of property, deportation for five years, or five-year prohibition of stay. A sentence order has equivalent force to a conviction.

Juveniles

Procedure in cases of juvenile crime is addressed in a special law, that is, Act No. 218/2003 Coll., on juvenile liability for illegal actions and juvenile jurisdiction. Procedures on crimes committed by children under 15 years of age and juveniles (persons between 15 and 18 years of age) must be conducted with due regard to the age, health, mental and moral development of the offender to mitigate negative effects on his or her future growth. Personal data and privacy of these persons must be strictly protected.

The only sentences available for juvenile offenders are education correction, protective measures, and criminal measures. Education correction includes supervision of a probation officer, probation programs, educational obligations, educational restrictions, and reprehension with caution. Protective measures include reformative education, protective therapy, and confiscation of property.

Juveniles may receive only the following types of sentences if convicted of criminal activities: community service, fines, fines with probation period, confiscation of property, prohibition of activities, deportation, prison sentence with a trial probation period, or a trial probation with supervision and imprisonment without probation. A juvenile custody may be replaced by guarantees, supervision, promise, or remitting to custody of a trustworthy person. Bail is also possible. Children under 15 years of age do not have criminal liability. If a child under 15 years of age commits a crime, a court must decide on corrective measures, usually based on the results of a prior expert psychological examination. Judges, public prosecutors, police officers, and employees of the Probation and Mediation Service who deal with child and youth crime must go through special training on how to communicate with and handle youth.

Punishment

The fundamental purpose of punishment as defined in Section 23 of the Criminal Act is to protect society against crime and its perpetrators. The objective of punishment, therefore, is to prevent an offender from continuing with criminal activities and to assist in resocialization; a sentence must not debase human dignity.

When choosing the type and length of a sentence, a court must always consider the gravity of the crime from the point of view of society and likelihood of correction as well as the offender's social situation. Courts also consider mitigating and aggravating circumstances, listed in general terms in the Criminal Act (Sec. 33, 34).

Section 27 of the Criminal Act lists all the possible sentences, that is, imprisonment, community service, loss of honorary titles and distinctions, loss of military rank, prohibition of activity, confiscation of property, fines, confiscation of items, deportation, prohibition of stay. In addition, courts may use exceptional punishments under Section 29 of the Criminal Act.

The only types of sentence that a court may pass on a juvenile are imprisonment, community service, confiscation of item, deportation, and fines, if the juvenile already has his or her own income; prohibition of activity is possible only in cases where the sentence does not prevent the juvenile from learning a trade or acquiring education and the sentence cannot be longer than five years. Sentencing guidelines defined by law for judges are cut in half in juvenile cases but the maximum term of imprisonment cannot exceed five years and the minimum term must not be shorter than one year.

Protective measures represent a special type of legal sanction that may be issued both to persons with criminal liability and persons without criminal liability (either due to legal age or insanity). Personal measures are used by criminal courts and, in exceptional cases, by civil courts (in cases involving persons under 15 years of age) and may be issued alone or in conjunction with other types of punishment. The objective is not to restrict the offender but to provide treatment, education, or ensure the destruction of an item. Protective measures, therefore, include protective treatment, protective education, and confiscation of item; protective education may be imposed only on juvenile offenders.

Types of Punishment

Imprisonment

Basically, this form of punishment temporarily restricts the personal freedom of movement of offenders by incarceration in a prison facility and the related restrictions of other personal rights and freedoms. An exceptional punishment is understood to be imprisonment for 15–20 years and a life sentence. An exceptional punishment may be used only in cases specifically listed in a special section of the Criminal Act. Imprisonment for 15–20 years may be used only in cases where the threat posed by the crime to society is very high or where the chances of correcting the offender are very low. A life sentence may be used only for offenders who commit murder, treason, terrorist acts, or genocide.

A conditional stay of prison sentences is used when a court issues a guilty verdict and a prison sentence but waives the imprisonment under the condition that the offender behaves properly during the probation period and meets all conditions set by the court. Conditional stay of prison sentences is often provided in conjunction with supervision measures or certain other obligations and restrictions. If the court concludes that the offender on probation has proven his or her worth, the person is considered as never having been sentenced in the first place.

A court may also conditionally stay a prison sentence of more than three years provided that it imposes supervision for the offender. The purpose of supervision is to monitor the offender's behavior in greater detail during the trial period and provide the necessary assistance and psychological and social care. In addition, courts usually require offenders to pay, according to his or her financial possibilities, the damage or loss resulting from his or her criminal actions.

Fines

Fines from CZK2,000 up to CZK5,000,000 (US$97 to $242,724) are mainly used for crimes against property, the most common type of crime in the republic.

Diversion

In cases where the maximum prison sentence is less than five years, the court may approve a settlement with the consent of both the victim and the offender and stop criminal prosecution. The same can be done by a public prosecutor during preliminary procedures. In this out-of-court settlement, an offender admits to a crime for which he or she is being prosecuted, pays the damage or loss resulting from his or her criminal activity, and pays a certain amount to be used for publicly beneficial ends. However, this option is not widely used yet (in 2006 only 168 criminal cases were settled this way).

A new Criminal Act was adopted in 2009, and it introduces new alternative sanctions such as home confinement, including possible future use of electronic tagging devices. It also further increases community service options, with different regimes for performance and intensity of repression, and isolation such as weekend punishments or various forms of detention.

Prison

Prison sentences are served in facilities managed by the Czech Prison Service, which is part of the Justice Ministry. The justice minister appoints and dismisses the general director of the Prison Service. The general director is accountable to the justice minister for the operation of the Prison Service.

The basic organizational units of the Prison Service are the general directorate, remand prisons (for custody), and prisons (for execution of prison sentences). Prisons are managed by prison governors, appointed and dismissed by the general director of the Prison Service. The Prison Service also has a special, independent organization unit—the Education Institute—that provides professional training for prison employees.

The Prison Service is responsible for the execution of custody and prison sentences. It uses appropriate resocialization programs to help offenders improve their habits and quality of life after release. The Prison Service also carries out certain business activities necessary to allow inmates to work when serving their sentences (or during custody).

The Prison Service consists of prison guards, justice guards, and administration services. Prison guards and justice guards have the status of armed units. Prison guards guard, deliver, and escort persons in custody and persons serving prison sentences while justice guards provide order and security in court buildings and public prosecutor offices as well as on the premises of the Justice Ministry. The administration services is responsible for organizational, economic, and educational issues as well as professional assistance in prisons, including medical services.

When being admitted to prison, an offender must be clearly informed of his or her rights and obligations as defined by law and other regulations. Men and women are never placed in mixed-gender cells. Youth and adults are usually placed in different cells as well. The same applies to recidivists and first-time offenders and persons who committed premeditated crimes and persons who committed crimes from negligence. Persons suffering from mental disorders and behavior disorders as well as certain other groups of inmates who require special treatment are also housed separately from the general prison population. Inmates serving life sentences are a special group and are placed on separate premises in a few select prisons (with maximum level of security).

Naturally, the above general rules are in practice observed as the accommodation capacity of each prison allows. In a situation where the capacity of most prisons is exceeded and prisons are already full, it is hard to expect strict observance of such requirements. The system of "one cell—one inmate" cannot be fully applied because the interior layout of most prisons was designed with traditional group accommodation in mind. There are long-term problems with accommodation capacities, lack of leisure facilities as well as office space for prison employees.

Inmates may work either in the prison's own production facilities or at third-party employers. Work conditions for inmates are subject to the same rules and regulations as work conditions of other employees. Inmates are entitled to remuneration according the amount and quality of their work. Remuneration is lowered by alimony for dependent children, the cost of serving a prison sentence or custody as well as other liabilities of the inmate. The total deduction from an inmate's remuneration cannot exceed 86 percent of his or her net remuneration. A lack of jobs for inmates has been a long-term problem. Only around 50 percent of the current prison population is employed.

Inmates receive regular meals, get eight hours of sleep a day, at least an hour a day for outdoor exercise, and reasonable time for private matters. They may also get education of elementary and secondary vocational level and attend various other courses. Inmates may file complaints that prison governors are obliged to acknowledge without undue delay. The rights of inmates are guaranteed by the Act on Execution of Prison Sentences. The scope of inmate rights is in line with European Prison Rules and other international documents (UN Convention of Human Rights, among others).

Prisons are divided into four basic categories according to the level and type of security: prisons with supervision, prisons with surveillance, security prisons, and high security prisons. One prison facility may consist of areas with different levels of security.

The court chooses which type of prison an offender will be sent to and may decide to transfer an inmate from a prison of one category to a prison of another category, taking into account the progress in the person's correction.

There are 35 prisons in the Czech Republic (including remand prisons); four prisons have capacity over 1,000 inmates but most facilities have capacity between 300 and 600 inmates. The buildings of some prisons are in rather bad shape, especially in the case of historical sites.

Public prosecutors regularly inspect premises where custody and prison sentences are executed. The inspecting public prosecutor may issue orders requiring application of valid regulations directly at the prison. He or she may also order that a person held in prison or custody illegally be released immediately. Supervision by public prosecutors does not replace the Prison Service's obligation to conduct its own control and inspections. The Justice Ministry directly contributes to prison control and supervision through its General Inspector Department.

Approximately 10 percent of all inmates serving prison sentences in Czech prisons are foreigners. The population of remand prisons includes approximately 20 percent foreigners. The largest national group are Slovaks, followed by Ukrainians, Moldavians, Belarussians, Bulgarians, people from former Yugoslavia, as well as Vietnam, certain Arab countries, Poland, and Germany.

In the early 1990s, the Czech Republic signed the Treaty on Extradition (the treaty is valid in the Czech Republic since August 1, 1992). Extradition is also possible based on bilateral agreements on jurisdiction signed between the Czech Republic and a number of other countries. Each year, dozens of individuals are transferred to their home countries for the execution of sentences.

Parole

When an inmate serves half of his or her prison sentence and his or her behavior during incarceration and performance of obligations shows that the inmate has sufficiently corrected his or her ways, a court may conditionally release an offender if the court receives guarantees from a civic association. For these purposes, civic associations are to be understood as labor unions and other social organizations, work teams, and religious organizations but not political parties and movements.

Persons convicted of grave crimes listed in a special section of the act may be released on parole only after serving two-thirds of their sentence. Persons serving exceptional life sentences may be released on probation only after serving 20 years of the sentence. According to the Constitution, the president of the republic is the only person entitled to grant pardons (art. 69.g of the Constitution). The president may also grant across-the-board pardons (amnesty) but the decision requires a joint signature by the prime minister or another member of the cabinet appointed by the prime minister. This means that the cabinet shoulders a part of the responsibility for the president's decision.

Across-the-board pardons (amnesty) are a relatively common event in the Czech Republic. They are most often granted at the occasion of the election of a new head of state as well as important national holidays or other prominent events. For example, when the socialist regime was overthrown, the president granted a large-scale amnesty as of January 1, 1990, and nearly 24,000 inmates of the total prison population of 33,000 were released. This major amnesty caused certain problems as the society was not ready to receive such large numbers of former inmates to regular social life in a very short time.

Assistance to persons released from prison is the responsibility of social curators who are attached to district authorities and provide help to socially excluded citizens. The country also has special social curators for youth. When released from prison, each inmate is instructed to contact a social curator who will be able to help him or her adapt to everyday life again (accommodation, job, etc.). The main problem is that communication with social curators is not obligatory and many former inmates do not use this possibility despite the fact that they are clearly unable to deal with their new social situation. Prior to release, inmates are prepared for the change and social workers of the Prison Service are there to assist them. Furthermore, there are many nongovernmental and charitable organizations, religious organizations, foundations, and other groups that assist former inmates.

Probation

The Czech Republic has a Probation and Mediation Service whose responsibilities include the following:

- Gathering information about persons charged and about their family and social situation.
- Creating suitable conditions for decisions on conditional stay of criminal prosecution or approval of settlements.
- Supervision of charged persons' behavior in cases where custody was replaced by probation supervision, or where supervision is required by courts as part of the sentence.
- Monitoring and control of offenders' behavior during trial periods in cases of early conditional release from prison.

The Probation and Mediation Service plays an important role in providing and controlling alternative forms of punishment replacing incarceration. The most common type is community service (Sec. 45, Sec. 45a of the Criminal Act) and settlement (Sec. 309–314 of the Criminal Act).

Punishment in the form of community service is possible in cases with a maximum prison term of five years provided that no other type of punishment is deemed necessary to achieve the purpose of punishment. The court may impose community service in length from 50 to 400 hours and may include cleaning public premises, cleaning and maintenance of public buildings and roads or other small tasks for municipalities or state or publicly beneficial institutions, fire prevention, health protection, and many other charitable, religious, and athletic activities.

Martin Cejp, Zdeněk Karabec,
Alena Marešová, and Miroslav Scheinost

Further Reading

Aebi, Marcelo F., Kauko Aromaa, Bruno Aubusson de Cavarlay, Gordon Barclay, Beata Gruszczyñska, and Hanns von Hofer, et al. (2006). *European Sourcebook of Crime and Criminal Justice Statistics.* The Hague, the Netherlands: WODC.

Czech Ministry of Interior: http://www.mvcr.cz.

Czech Ministry of Justice: http://www.justice.cz.

Czech Statistical Office: http://www.czso.cz.

Institute of Criminology and Social Prevention, Prague: http://www.ok.cz/iksp/en/aboutus.html.

Karabec, Zdeněk, and Miroslav Scheinost. (2006). "Czech Correctional and Police System." In *World Encyclopedia of Police Forces and Correctional Systems,* edited by Georges Th. Kurian, pp. 335–341. Detroit, MI: Thomson Gale.

Denmark

Legal System: Civil
Murder: Medium
Burglary: Low
Corruption: Low
Human Trafficking: Low
Prison Rate: Low
Death Penalty: No
Corporal Punishment: No

Background

Denmark belongs to the Nordic countries that include Finland, Iceland, Norway, and Sweden. Greenland and the Faroe Islands are also Nordic but are not counted as independent countries. Since the Danish/Norwegian Vikings also conquered Iceland, Greenland, and the Faroe Islands in 800–1200, there have been strong connections and to some degree Danish dominance over those areas. Iceland became independent in 1944. Greenland and the Faroe Islands have a home rule system. Today Greenland and the Faroe Islands still have two members each in the Danish Parliament.

Denmark is a kingdom with 5.25 million inhabitants covering an area of 43,048 square kilometers (16,621 square miles). The biggest part is a peninsula, Jutland, on the "top" of Germany; there are also more than 400 islands around the peninsula, out of which 80 are inhabited. The biggest island is Zealand, where the capital, Copenhagen, with its 1.75 million inhabitants is located.

Denmark had its first Constitution in 1849. It was revised in 1915, when women gained the right to vote. There was a constitutional reform in 1953 after which Denmark had a Parliament with one chamber and a king or queen with mainly formal and ceremonial functions. Parliament has 175 members elected in Denmark plus the above-mentioned two members from, respectively, Greenland and Faroe Islands. Denmark has been a member of the United Nations since its foundation in 1945. In 1949, Denmark entered the North Atlantic Treaty Organization (NATO) and, in 1973, it became a member of the Common Market, now the European Union (EU).

It is not uncommon in Denmark for a government to rule on the basis of less than 50 percent of the votes in Parliament, so cooperation and consensus in policy making is a necessity. Before the 1990s crime policy was not only based on political consensus, it was also closely connected to scientific evidence. But in the last two decades crime policy has moved away from the experts into the hands of politicians and has become an issue in political election campaigns.

Crime

Reported crime has developed in different directions depending on the kind of crimes. The year 2000 had 500,000 reported breaches of the Criminal Code and 66,000 reported breaches of the so-called special codes, such as the Code against Drugs and the Code against Weapons. In 2007 the numbers were 445,000 and 69,000, respectively. The Traffic Code is a special code but not counted under reported crime as most of the reports are made by the police themselves. Crimes reported per 100,000 inhabitants over 15 years old for various Criminal Code offenses in 2007 were as follows:

Sexual crimes	59
Violence	437
Property crimes	9,366
Others	152
Total	**10,014**

The total number of responses to crime by the criminal justice system was 160,000 in 1997 and 176,567 in 2007, having reached a peak of 223,000 in 2005. By responses to crime is meant all kinds of reactions to reported crime. For instance, in 2007 the total includes 9,000 unconditional prison sentences and an equal amount of conditional prison sentences, whereas the amount of fines was 140,000, out of which 110,000 referred to breaches of the Traffic Code. The rest are mainly withdrawal or dropping of charges, not-guilty findings, and 550 sentences to mental treatment for mentally disturbed offenders. Out of 140,000 fines only about 15,000 are decided in a court, the rest are decided by the police and accepted by the offender.

In all years from 1997 to 2007 more than 50 percent of all criminal justice system responses concerned the Traffic Code. Criminal Code responses have declined from 35 percent to 25 percent in the same period. Furthermore, the proportion of criminal justice responses to women increased from 15 percent in 1997 to 21 percent in 2007. The share of juveniles receiving a response to crime has been stable between 11 and 13 percent for the last decade, whereas the proportion of persons over 40 years old has increased and the proportion of persons between 20 and 40 has slightly decreased. The overall clearance rate of all crime has been between 15 and 20 percent in the latest decades. This covers a most different picture from 98 percent of all reported murders being cleared up to not much more than 0 percent of thefts of bikes.

Police wait outside a bank in Copenhagen, Denmark, after three armed men robbed a bank van, September 4, 1997. (AP Photo/Bent Midstrup)

Finding of Guilt

Investigation of crime is carried out by the police who, in Denmark, are divided in 12 districts. Each district has its own director and the commissioner of police; the national head of the police works under the supervision of the minister of justice. Prosecution is carried out by the prosecutors, who are lawyers. The prosecutors are divided in a hierarchy with three levels: the director of public prosecution who is the prosecutor of the Supreme Court, the public prosecutor and the lawyers working with him or her who prosecute cases before one of the two High Courts and, finally, the district attorney who prosecutes cases in the 24 city courts. Exceptions to this main structure are more important jury cases carried out in city courts in first instance, where lawyers from the Office of the Director of Public Prosecution act as prosecutors. It is explicitly laid down in the Constitution that lay judges must be included in criminal court procedure. The Administration of Justice Act defines the scope and the competencies of the lay judges.

Suspects may be arrested by the police but must be let out after 24 hours. Pretrial detention is decided by the court and each decision cannot exceed a period of 4 weeks. The total duration of pretrial detention is limited to 1 year for adults and 8 months for suspects below the age of 18. These time limits may be prolonged by the court under special conditions. In serious cases, the court can decide that pretrial detention is to take place under solitary confinement. If the suspect is younger than 18, the reasons to place the person under solitary confinement must be extra strong, and only in cases concerning the security of the state, be prolonged for more than 4 weeks. For adults the maximum (if the court does not see special reasons) period of solitary confinement is 6 months, except for cases concerning the security of the state.

Punishment

Types of Punishment

The Criminal Code defines the legal limits of the sentencing for each crime. These limits form the starting point for each sentence but the court must also take into consideration past sentencing practice as well as the offenders' personal circumstances. There are two main ways of sentencing offenders, namely, fine, partly day-fine, and imprisonment. They are not seen as alternatives to each other. Fines are mainly used for breaches of the laws apart from the Criminal Code, such as the Traffic Code but they may also be used for minor breaches of the Criminal Code. Imprisonment is used for more serious breaches of the Criminal Code. It may happen very rarely that a person who does not pay a fine can be taken into prison to serve the sentence.

Comprehensively viewed prison sentences may be from 7 days to 16 years, and in some exceptional cases, up to 20 years. In some cases, for example, for murder and arson a sentence to lifetime imprisonment is a possibility. Furthermore, the Criminal Code opens the possibility of sentencing a person to secure imprisonment, which does not have a legal maximum. The duration of secure imprisonment is not fixed in the sentence but is on average about 7 years. Finally, the duration of the treatment of mentally ill people who are sentenced to treatment may also be indeterminate. The principal rule is that the duration of the treatment in hospital should be fixed but in practice the exceptions form the majority of the cases.

Juveniles

The legal age of criminal responsibility is 15 but may be lowered to 14, as this continues to be debated intensively in Parliament, as of autumn 2009. To put the age into a relevant perspective of today, it is worth mentioning that the age of (sexual) consent is 15 as well. However, a Dane achieves the right to vote, to marry, to withdraw/apply for membership of a church, to apply for a driver's license, and to decide on his or her own personal and financial circumstances at the age of 18. It is possible to buy cigarettes from the age of 18 and to buy beer in a store from the age of 16.

Denmark does not have a particular juvenile justice system, juvenile justice law, or youth prison. In principle juvenile offenders are treated within the same complex of codes and routines as anybody else. But in practice, offenders under the age of 18 benefit from a number of sentencing policies and practical options that are not available to adults. The extra options are, for instance, shorter sentences and diversion to the welfare authorities. Further, the Criminal Code states that persons who were not yet 18 years old when they committed their crime may in no case be convicted to more than eight years of imprisonment.

Extra efforts are made to divert the youngest offenders from prison and to keep them within the Child Welfare System. The fundamental consideration is that cases against the youngest citizens require rehabilitative rather than punitive responses. Therefore, alternatives to imprisonment, such as social measures and suspended sentences, are always available. To direct a person's conduct into a more appropriate direction, reactions toward juvenile crime are frequently of a noncustodial type.

From age 15 up to the age of 18 a criminal act may lead to a variety of noncustodial orders—supervised by the Child Welfare System. This age group may, however, be sentenced to prison and a prison sentence may be served either in a prison or in an alternative institution with different levels of security. The type of sentence depends on the circumstances of each given case, such as the type and nature of the committed offense, the criminal record, and the child welfare representative's assessment. Great efforts are made to divert juveniles away from prison. Persons under the age of 18 who receive a suspended sentence are under supervision by the Child Welfare System and not by the Probation Service.

Youth prison was introduced by the Criminal Code that came into force in 1933. The duration of youth prison sentences was not fixed in court, as it depended on when (within a period of one to three years) the prison administration found the person ready for release. In the 1960s youth prison was only rarely in use and was subsequently abolished in 1973 due to a massive critique that targeted in particular the unpredictable duration of such sentences.

Parallel to the rare use of youth prison during the second half of the 20th century, leading principles of offering help and support to deviant children and juveniles became more dominant. But within the last decade this principle has become increasingly challenged, as still more ways of providing help are edging closer and closer to the practical reality of punishment. A clear example of this tendency is the Youth Sanction, which does bear resemblance to the concept of youth imprisonment.

The Youth Sanction was implemented in the beginning of the 2000s to replace some prison sentences for 15- to 17-year-old offenders having "deserved" a prison sentence of 3–12 months. The sanction is said to be used when "appropriate" for the prevention of further offenses and the means is a structured and controlled social pedagogic treatment for 2 years divided into three phases. According to the rule in the Criminal Code, the maximum time to be spent in an institution is 1.5 years, with a maximum of 12 months in a secure residential institution (phase 1). After this follows a period in a more open institution (phase 2), and finally there is a period to be spent outside an institution but with support from the Child Welfare System. It is not explicitly stated in the law that the courts should determine the lengths of stay in each type of institution, but this is indirectly indicated in the law as the juvenile offender concerned is given the right to a judicial review of an administrative extension of a stay "beyond the period provided for in the judgment."

The level of criminality that will lead to the imposition of a Youth Sanction is the commission of a serious offense endangering persons, or some other serious offense, such as assault, robbery or rape, or a serious case of theft, embezzlement, or vandalism.

In addition to the requirements as to the seriousness and extent of the offense, it is assumed that the social profile of the young offender will show clear problems of social maladjustment and inappropriate or abnormal behavior, including criminal behavior of a particularly violent nature.

The Youth Sanction is meant for the more serious juvenile offenders but still the comparable sentence is expected to be up to one year, whereas the Youth Sanction has a fixed duration of two years. The introduction of the Youth Sanction has been criticized to be disproportionate and to create inequality in the sentencing system.

The number of sentences to deprivation of liberty (including imprisonment and Youth Sanction) has been increasing. Per 100,000 inhabitants over the age of 15 years, the number that had a sentence including deprivation of liberty in 1997 was 512. This number was 399 in 2007. Compared to this the numbers of juveniles in the age group 15–19 years old were 822 in 1997 and 1,014 in 2007.

The explanations of more juveniles being sentenced harder are several, as follow:

- There was a series of "fights" between police and juveniles about a house in Copenhagen having been occupied by juveniles for several years; the house is now emptied and overturned.
- There is a less tolerant policy against possession of small amounts of cannabis.
- There is a tendency of reporting more minor violence to the police.
- Responses to car theft have become tougher.

The length of unsuspended prison sentences varies within the framework as described above. The average length of the 8,800 unsuspended prison sentences in 2007 was 6.2 months; one had life imprisonment, and three were sentenced to secure imprisonment. About half of the sentences, namely 4,465, had a length of 60 days or less, whereas 76 sentences were at a length of more than 6 years of imprisonment.

The reconviction rate is increasing for all types of sentences. In 2008, there was a reconviction rate after having been in prison of 30 percent (closed and open prison together), after suspended sentence the rate was 17 percent, and after Community Service Orders the rate was 16 percent. The reconviction rate is highest for the youngest offenders: 15–19 years old at 26 percent, whereas 10 percent of the offenders at 50 years or older repeated crime.

Prison

With the exceptions of mentally ill offenders and the main part of the juvenile offenders, any detention connected to (suspicion of) criminality in Denmark takes place in institutions ruled and controlled by the Department of Corrections under the responsibility of the minister of justice. The two main categories of penal institutions are, first, the pretrial prisons, which are located nearby the court buildings in the cities and may house persons waiting for trial as well as convicted persons either serving a relatively short sentence (6 months or less) or waiting for a place in a prison; and second, the prisons, which solely house convicted persons serving a sentence. In the pretrial prisons there are about 1,700 places totally in the country, whereas there is a total of about 2,400 places in the prisons.

According to the main rule a prisoner is moved to either a closed or an open prison after he or she is sentenced. Most of the five closed prisons in Denmark are located in cities, whereas the open prisons are placed in the countryside. Closed prisons and pretrial prisons are of similar security degree. There are walls all the way round the prison and electronic surveillance on the top of the walls. The prison wards are separated from each other and each ward is locked.

Several of the eight open prisons were founded immediately after World War II as work camps for those who collaborated with the German occupying power. Open prisons are more campuslike. The inmates are not allowed to leave the prison area, but there are no perimeter walls and the prisoners can move (more or less) freely on the prison areas, for instance, they can go to work in the prison factory or walk to the prison school without being accompanied by a member of staff. From 9 or 10 P.M. until the following morning, the prisoners in open prisons are locked up in the wards or in the cells.

In open as well as closed facilities each ward is typically of 8–12 cells, and in case the prison houses women there will be wards where the sexes are separated and other wards where they are mixed. In the middle of the 1990s a number of open prisons established semi-open places. The Department of Corrections explained this decision with a lower utilization rate in the open prisons than in the closed facilities, which again was explained with the fact that the proportion of prisoners suited for open prisons was decreasing. In other words an upcoming proportional imbalance between the profile of the prisoners and the capacity of the prisons was foreseen. An inmate may only be placed in a semi-open block if he or she is "qualified" for closed prison but is not necessarily transferred to such a place.

All prisons run training programs and the like, such as cognitive skills programs. Further, all prisoners sentenced to three months or more must be offered treatment for drug or alcohol addiction if they ask for it. Including housing, guarding, occupation, and so on, a cell in an open prison costs about half as much as a cell in a closed prison. The daily price for a cell in an open prison is 1,158 Danish krone (DKK) (US$206) and the daily price of a cell in a closed prison is 1,973 DKK (US$351).

While the courts decide the length of the prison sentence, the type and location of prison is decided by the Department of Corrections. After having been sentenced in the court, the person is either moved to imprisonment via custody or released until he or she is called in to serve the sentence. The decision about where a sentence must be served must be made within the framework of Sections 20–30 of the Corrections Act, where guidelines for the choice of institution and the transfer of prisoners from one institution to another are laid down.

The main rule is that imprisonment is served in open prisons, unless the sentence is of five years or more. If—in spite of a sentence being of five years or more—it is considered unproblematic to let the person serve the sentence in open prison, this is also possible. Furthermore, a person may always be placed in closed prison instead of open for security reasons if the prisoner is seen as dangerous to himself or herself or others. More than 90 percent of all prison intakes are in open prisons.

When the choice between closed or open prison is made, it is the predominant principle that the prison of the relevant category closest to the prisoner's home is chosen. This principle can be deviated from for pedagogical, medical, prison capacity, or other reasons. The principle of choosing the prison closest to the prisoner's home is systematically broken in relation to young men below 23 years, who are collected in one closed and one open prison. The intention is to prevent young men from being badly influenced or exploited by older fellow prisoners.

The Danish prison system as a whole includes two different "alternatives" to imprisonment. First, there exist Community Service Orders, which were introduced in the 1980s. When the court is convinced that an unconditional prison sentence is deserved, it may change it into a Community Service Order if it is reasonable to believe it is not necessary to lock the person up. The court decides how many hours (between 30 and 240) the person has to do community service and the Probation Service finds a working place.

Second, there is the electronic foot-ring, which was introduced gradually from the beginning of the 2000s. Where the length of a sentence to unconditional imprisonment is three months or shorter, the convicted person may, shortly after being sentenced, receive a letter from the Department of Corrections informing him or her of the right to apply for a so-called home-serving. This implies that the person for the period of the sentence must wear an electronic foot-ring, making it possible for the Probation Service to monitor that he or she does not leave his or her home except for the periods of the day agreed upon, for instance, to frequent school or a job.

Everyday Life in Prison

The Program of Principles for the Department of Corrections, published in 1993, was the very first official definition of principles and functions for the sector. The program lays down that the main task is to execute penalties and that this task consists of two parallel components, namely, to exercise the control necessary for executing the penalty and to support and motivate the sentenced person to free himself or herself of criminality by developing socially and personally through work and education. This program can be seen as the beginning of strengthening the focus on education and social/cognitive training in the prisons. In the following years many prisons developed different concepts for supporting and motivating the prisoners.

Every prisoner under any kind of deprivation of liberty has the right and the obligation to take part in work, training/treatment, or school every day. Before the confirmation and implementation of the Corrections Act in 2000, the keyword was work, but now more possibilities of occupation are accepted—even recommended sometimes—and consequently paid for like work. Ordinary basic payment for prison work is 8 DKK (US$1.30) per hour. For extraordinary good or demanding work, the salary may go up to 12 DKK (US$2) per hour (2005). Full-time school, either in the prison school or in some cases in educational institutions outside the prison, or full-time participation in a structured treatment program is economically rewarded at the same level as ordinary prison work. Also individual activities, such as when a prisoner is elected as a spokesperson for the prisoners, are rewarded like work. Different activities for spare time may be organized by prisoners or by staff members. That might be sport, chess, handicraft, or sometimes drama or choir. Prisoners have the right to receive visits and may also be allowed to visit relatives in weekends or at special occasions.

On the condition that a mother or father is capable of taking care of her or his child, there is a possibility of having a child in the prison until the child reaches the age of three years. The presence of a baby may cause a placement of parent and child in an alternative institution, an infant home, or the like. This, however, is not in any case a legal right for the imprisoned mother/father but depends on the discretionary power of the prison authority. Some prisons have family wards where sometimes mother, father, and child are placed at the same time.

One very fundamental principle is that of normalization, which is laid down in the Corrections Act. The principle aims to create a prison life and prison conditions as close as possible to life and conditions in the Danish society. Normalization is consequently not a principle of "normalizing" the prisoners but of "normalizing" life in prison. The principle of normalization consists of at least two core elements, namely, the principles of self-management and supplying oneself with provisions. The idea is a kind of deinstitutionalization of the prisons, which means that even if the prisoners are locked up, they are neither sick nor unable to take care of their own needs during an ordinary day. In other words individual daily routines, as, for instance, cooking, washing, and so on, are to be carried through by every single person. Every prisoner takes care of his or her own cooking, cleaning, and personal hygiene. Except for clothes all necessities must be bought in the prison's store—including food, soap, toothpaste, and so on. A sum of 51 DKK per day (US$8.60) is paid to all prisoners—if they are working or not—to maintain these kinds of personal needs. In most prisons the prisoners form groups of buying food and cooking. In every prison block is a kitchen and one or two washing machines.

The Prison Situation

By the end of 2008 the prison capacity was about 4,000, divided into 1,400 places in open prisons, 1,000 places in closed prisons, and 1,700 in pretrial prison. One pretrial prison in Copenhagen has more than 500 places and many short prison sentences are served here. Apart from the Copenhagen custody, the majority of the prisons have up to 200 places. The average utilization rate in the prisons was 90 percent and 92 percent in the pretrial prisons in 2008. A few years ago the utilization rate was over 96 percent, which caused a major pressure on the prison system and resulted in the establishment of more prison places. Since then, a few places have been closed down as the pressure eased off in 2006–2007. The leveling off of the pressure on prison capacity was, among other things, due to the implementation of a police reform lowering the number of prosecutions and sentences.

The overall profile of the prisoners in this decade indicates that 20–25 percent are sentenced for violence, the same share is sentenced for drug crime, 2.5 percent are sentenced for rape, and 20–30 percent are sentenced for property crime, including robbery. The number of prisoners sentenced for all kinds of property crime has decreased during the last decade. The majority of all persons taken into prison in Denmark are Danish, namely 9,000 out of 11,000 persons received in the prisons in 2008. About 60 percent of all prisoners taken in report that they used illegal drugs within a period of 30 days up to admission. For almost 50 percent of the drug users, cannabis is their preferred drug, whereas 22 percent prefer alcohol.

There has been a noteworthy increase in the use of disciplinary measurements in the prisons during this decade from a total of 8,000 in 2000 to 15,300 in 2008. There has also been a noteworthy increase in refusals of release on parole from 21 percent in 2000 to 29 percent in 2008. The prisoner may have a refusal of release on parole tried in court. Out of a total of 48 such cases in 2008, two were changed by the court.

Sentenced Persons Outside Prison

Prisoners on parole as well as suspended sentenced persons, those with Community Service Orders, and persons carrying an electronic foot-ring are supervised by the Probation Service. In case they commit a new crime, it is more likely that they will go to prison for the whole or the rest of their time. In case they do not follow the instructions given by the Probation Service, such as attending drug or alcohol treatment, the Probation Service warns them and as the last resort if they do not succeed in following the guidelines, they may be taken into court to change the sentence into an unsuspended prison sentence. At the national level, the Probation Service opens a period of supervision in about 9,000 cases per year. The three main groups are, in order: Community Service Orders, parole, and suspended sentences.

Between 200 and 250 prisoners are not serving their sentence in prison but in an alternative institution. The two main reasons for placing a prisoner in another institution are drug addiction and young age, but also, for instance, mothers with babies or sex offenders may be placed in an alternative institution.

Anette Storgaard

Further Reading

Kyvsgaard, Britta. (2004). "Youth Justice in Denmark." In *Crime and Justice: A Review of Research,* edited by Michael Tonry and Anthony N. Doob, pp. 349–391. Chicago: University of Chicago Press.

Ministry of Justice: http://www.jm.dk.

Statistics Denmark: http://www.dst.dk.

Storgaard, Anette. (2004). "Juvenile Justice in Scandinavia." *Scandinavian Journal of Criminology and Crime Prevention* 5(2): 188–204.

Vestergaard, Jørn. (2003). Den særlige ungdomssanktion [The Special Youth Sanction]. *Tidsskrift for Kriminalret* 1: 1–24.

England. *See* United Kingdom/England

Estonia

Legal System: Civil/Common
Murder: Medium
Burglary: Medium
Corruption: Low
Human Trafficking: Medium
Prison Rate: High
Death Penalty: No
Corporal Punishment: No

Background

Estonia is a parliamentary state, situated in the northeastern part of Europe, at the Russian border and belongs to the most eastern EU states. Its territory is 45,000 square kilometers (17,374 square miles) and population 1.33 million (2008), of which about two-thirds are Estonians and about one-third consist mainly of various nationalities of the former Soviet Union, predominantly Russians. The capital, Tallinn, has 400,000 population.

In November 1917, after more than two centuries under the control of the Russian Empire, the Provisional Assembly of Estonia (*Maapäev*) declared itself to be the supreme power in Estonia. During the war between Germany and the Russian Army, on February 23, 1918, in Pärnu and on the next day in Tallinn, the *Maapäev*'s Committee of Elders issued the Estonian Declaration of Independence. As a consequence of the secret Molotov-Ribbentrop pact between Nazi Germany and the Soviet Union in August 1939, the Soviet Union occupied Estonia in June 1940 and annexed it as a Soviet republic (SSR) in August 1940. During World War II, German troops temporarily occupied Estonia but were defeated in autumn 1944 by the Soviet Army. About 70,000 people escaped to Western countries just before the new Soviet occupation.

During the following years, repression was widely used, including deportation of more than 20,000 people to Siberia on March 25, 1949. After the death of Josef Stalin in March 1953, hard repression ended. Social and economic conditions became better and, since the late 1950s until the early 1960s, several social problems (e.g., suicide and homicide rate, alcohol consumption) were at the lowest level of the whole Soviet period (1944–1991). Immigration from other republics of the Soviet Union intensified after the mid-1960s and was significant until the mid-1980s, causing a gradual increase of social problems, especially in Tallinn and in the cities of the northeastern part of Estonia (e.g., homicide rate among immigrants was about three times higher than among the native population).

In 1985, Mikhail Gorbachev came to power in Moscow. In the following years, he initiated several reforms, but always in the framework of the Soviet system. Censorship in mass media was substantially reduced and discussions on various problems in the society became possible. In the late 1980s, demands for more economic and political freedom from Moscow intensified in the Soviet republics. Estonia became relatively free in 1990, and the elected Supreme Soviet declared independence on August 20, 1991, during the military coup attempt in Moscow. In this way, the prewar independent state was formally reconstituted. The Estonian Constitution was adopted by a national referendum in June 1992 and the first completely free elections of Parliament (*Riigikogu*) took place in September 1992. The last Russian troops left Estonia in August 1994. In spring 2004, Estonia became a full member of NATO and the European Union.

Criminal Law

Inside the Soviet Union, criminal legislation was to a great extent similar in all Soviet republics. Their criminal codes were unified and included, inter alia, several articles on so-called political crimes (e.g., membership in an anti-Soviet organization, disparagement of the Soviet State) and illegal economic activities (e.g., private entrepreneurship, brokerage). Offenses against the state property received harder punishments than other similar offenses. Political articles in the Estonian SSR's Criminal Code (that entered into force in 1961) were abolished in 1990 and the whole code was revised in 1992. One of the key features of the new code was the abolition of the distinction between state and private ownership.

During the 1990s, several amendments to the Criminal Code were adopted. The goal was to adapt the criminal law to the rapid social and economic developments, including an increase in the recorded crime, and the intensifying international contacts between organized criminal groups in different countries (e.g., new Criminal Code articles were introduced to punish membership or development of a criminal organization in 1996, to harden the punishments for drug offenses in 1996–1998, and to introduce life imprisonment in 1996). Capital punishment was abolished in 1998. During the same year, the probation system was implemented on the basis of the Probation Supervision Act.

A completely new Penal Code replaced the old Criminal Code in September 2002. The new code implemented principles of continental Europe, particularly Germany's and France's criminal law. The Penal Code introduced several chapters on new types of crime (violation of competition rules, offenses against intellectual property, causing damage to environment, etc.). At the same time, use of illicit drugs or possession of a small amount of illicit drugs for personal use was decriminalized. Sentences for several offense types were increased and new types of supplementary punishment were enacted (fining to the extent of assets, compulsory dissolution of legal person, deprivation of certain rights, expulsion of foreign citizens).

Police

The police forces were formed on the basis of the former militia in 1992. The police is under the supervision of the Ministry of the Interior. The central agency is the Police Board, which manages, directs, and coordinates the activities of all police units under its administration. There are four territorial units (police prefectures) and two national units (the Central Criminal Police, the Personal Protection Service). Prefectures have specialized divisions to tackle crimes against the person, property crime, economic crime, drugs trafficking, traffic offenses, among others. The Central Criminal Police investigate most serious cases, including crimes committed by international organized criminal groups.

The highest-ranking police officer, the National Police Commissioner, is appointed to office for five years. The police prefectures are managed by prefects. At the end of 2007 there were a total 3,249 police officers. In 2007, the police initiated about 97 percent of criminal investigations, followed by prisons (1.5%), prosecutors' offices (0.7%), and Tax and Customs Board (0.4%). The role of other investigative bodies (Security Police Board, Border Guard Administration, Competition Board, and General Staff of the Defense Forces) was smaller.

Prosecutor's Office

Prosecutors conduct criminal proceedings in cooperation with the police and other investigative bodies; they guide the preliminary investigators in collecting evidence and decide whether to bring charges against the suspects. The prosecution system consists of four Circuit Prosecutor's Offices and their superior body, the Public Prosecutor's Office, headed by the chief public prosecutor. In 2007 there were in total 199 prosecutors.

Courts

The court system has three levels. The first level consists of four county and two administrative courts of first instance: Harju (in Tallinn), Viru (in the city of Jõhvi), Pärnu, and Tartu county courts with courthouses in each of the 15 counties, which hear civil, criminal, and misdemeanor matters, and administrative courts in Tallinn and Tartu. The second level includes Tallinn, Tartu, and Viru circuit courts, which review the decisions of county and administrative courts by way of appeal proceedings. The highest court is the Supreme Court in Tartu, which reviews decisions by way of cassation proceedings and is also the court of constitutional review. In 2008, there were 60 criminal judges in county courts and 16 in circuit courts, 6 justices belonged to the Criminal Chamber of the Supreme Court.

All judges must have an academic higher education in law, they are appointed to office for life, and they shall not hold any other elected or appointed office, except in the cases prescribed by law. Judges of first and second level are nominated by the president; justices of the Supreme Court are nominated by the Riigikogu. A judge can be removed from office only by a court judgment that has entered into force. Criminal charges may be brought against a judge during his or her term of office only on the proposal of the Supreme Court and with the consent of the president; in the case of justices of the Supreme Court it will be possible only on the proposal of the chancellor of justice and with the consent of the majority of the membership of the Riigikogu.

Crime

Classification of Crimes

In the Penal Code, offenses are divided into two categories: criminal offenses and misdemeanors. Typical criminal offenses are theft, robbery, fraud, assault, repeated drunken driving. Most common misdemeanors are traffic violations (except in the case of accidents resulting in death or serious injuries), violations of the Alcohol Act and Tobacco Act (e.g., drunkenness in public places, use of alcohol or tobacco by minors), breach of public order, and petty theft without aggravating circumstances. Sanctions for all criminal offenses and for some misdemeanors are prescribed in the Penal Code, but for the majority of misdemeanors in a large number of other acts (e.g., Traffic Act, Alcohol Act).

Criminal offenses are punishable by a pecuniary punishment or imprisonment, and in the case of corporations, by a pecuniary punishment or compulsory dissolution. Misdemeanors are punishable by a fine up to 300 daily rates (in 2008, one daily rate was 60 Estonian kroons [US$4.80]) or detention up to 30 days. The minimum age of liability for any offenses is 14 years of age.

There are two categories of criminal offenses according to the severity of punishment: the first-degree offense is punishable by imprisonment of more than 5 years and up to 20 years or life imprisonment; the second degree offense is punishable by imprisonment up to 5 years or a pecuniary punishment, which shall be calculated on the basis of the average daily income of the offender.

Crime Statistics

During almost the whole Soviet period crime statistics were substantially influenced by the political circumstances and consequently deliberate falsification, as unsolved crimes were often left unrecorded to get "better" clearance rates—although crime statistics were kept completely secret and data on crime were never published. For example, the clearance rate of thefts in Estonia was 98 percent in 1982, but dropped to the level of 51 percent in 1983, due to a drastic increase (2.3 times) in the number of recorded thefts, while the number of solved thefts increased only 21 percent. An obvious reason for such a change was that after the Soviet Communist Party leader Leonid Brezhnev's death in 1982, the former KGB Chief Yuri Andropov took over the leadership and started to demand reduction of corruption and more reliable information on the crime situation. Statistical manipulations were not so easily possible with the most serious crime like homicides. Since the late 1980s crime was no longer seen as a politically sensitive issue by the Soviet leadership and open discussions were allowed; crime statistics became more reliable and were made public.

The total recorded crimes in Estonia in 2007 was 50,375 compared with 40,972 in 1997. Essential changes in the society took place in the early 1990s. Political and economic liberalization, changes in legislation, reforms in the police, weak border control with increasing international communication, and other factors created favorable opportunities for illegal activities and produced an increase in the recorded crime. The police forces were in their early stage not able to control crime effectively. The number of recorded crimes remained relatively stable for some years in the mid-1990s, but increased again in 1997–2002. It is unclear how adequately the figures do reflect real trends, as crime victimization surveys in 1993–2004 do not show substantial changes in crime against private persons and against their households in the same time. The police became more efficient in tackling so-called victimless crimes (drug offenses, tax fraud, economic and occupational crimes, corruption, drunken driving, etc.) in the second half of the 1990s, and this may be one of the main reasons of increased crime figures. Simultaneously, public opinion polls showed significant increase in the people's respect toward the police.

In 2007, crimes against property (theft, robbery, fraud, etc.) comprised 55 percent of total registered crimes. Most common offenses were thefts (43% of all crimes), repeated drunk driving (10%), physical abuse (causing damage to the health of another person, beating, battery; 9%), frauds (5%), and aggravated breach of public order (use of violence in public places, resistance to a person protecting public order, threatening with a weapon; 4%). The recorded crimes, according to the Ministry of Justice, Police Board for 2007, were the following:

Murder (completed)	15
Manslaughter (completed)	78
Causing serious damage to health	145
Rape (including attempts)	122
Robbery	887
Theft	21,685
Fraud	2,481
Drug trafficking	1,048

Since the early 1990s, the crime rate has been the highest in Tallinn and the lowest in rural areas, especially in the islands of western Estonia. There have been no essential differences in the crime structure between towns and rural areas. The high crime rate in Tallinn has mainly been caused by the large number of thefts (particularly from shops and vehicles). In rural areas, thefts also dominate, usually followed by repeated drunk driving and use of violence or threat to use violence (physical abuse, aggravated breach of public order). The rate of robberies and drug offenses has been highest in Tallinn and other big cities.

Drug Offenses

Drug trafficking is among the crime types that have received particular attention during the last years. According to the Narcotic Drugs and Psychotropic Substances and Their Precursors Act, the handling of narcotic drugs and psychotropic substances is prohibited, regardless of the type of illicit substance. Also, cultivation of opium poppy or cannabis for the purpose of preparing narcotic substances is not allowed. Whether administrative or criminal liability is applied depends on the amount of illicit substance and the purpose of illegal activity, as follows:

- Illegal acquisition, possession, and use of a small amount of narcotic drugs and psychotropic substances for one's own consumption is punishable by a fine or detention up to 30 days (misdemeanors).
- Any act of illegal dealing with drugs not intended for personal use only, or handling of a large amount of drugs, is considered as a criminal offense (usually called "drug crimes") and is punishable by a pecuniary punishment or imprisonment.

A large quantity of narcotic drugs or psychotropic substances, plants, or mushrooms is an amount that is sufficient to cause intoxication of at least 10 persons. The same rule applies in case of mixtures. The most common drug crime, handling of large quantities without aggravating circumstances, is punishable by imprisonment from 1 to 10 years, but if such an offense is committed by an organized group, even up to 20 years or life imprisonment. The police have no discretion; all criminal offenses have to be investigated by the police or other investigative authorities and must be prosecuted by the prosecutor. The prosecutor's decision can either be a diversion from prosecution or an official charge.

Drug abusers commit a large proportion of property crimes (especially thefts from cars and shops, robberies, pickpocketing) and misdemeanors (e.g., petty thefts from shops). In 2007 the share of drug crimes from all criminal offenses was 3 percent, the majority of which were related to trafficking in large amounts, as the police have prioritized tackling of serious traffickers instead of arresting small-scale street dealers and simple users. In the same year 31 organized criminal groups were charged for large-scale drug trafficking, of which 5 groups had been active in international drug trafficking. In addition, a number of single drug couriers have been arrested. Drug offenses have been most frequent in big cities, but differences between urban and rural areas have decreased during the last decade.

The most common drugs in local markets in recent years have been amphetamine-type stimulants and Ecstasy, followed by cannabis. Stimulants have been smuggled from the other Eastern and Western European countries, and produced locally. Both in 2006 and 2007 three clandestine laboratories were discovered by the police. Precursors for producing synthetic drugs have been imported mainly from Russia. The majority of synthetic drugs produced in Estonia has been targeted at Nordic countries, but the importance of Russian markets has also increased in the last few years. Cannabis has been smuggled mainly from Spain to local markets and via Estonia to Nordic countries and Russia. Synthetic opiates (3-methylfentanyl, fentanyl) have become widespread and have almost completely replaced heroin in local markets, although heroin from Afghanistan is still smuggled via Russia and Estonia to Nordic countries. Cocaine use has increased due to direct contacts of Estonian traffickers with counterparts in the Central American countries, and it is also smuggled to the neighboring countries.

Finding of Guilt

Pretrial Criminal Proceedings

Pretrial criminal proceedings are led by the Prosecutor's Office, which also represents public prosecution in court. An arrested person has a right to notify a close person. The maximum length of custody permitted without a court order is 48 hours. He or she has also the right to choose and consult with counsel. If the defendant has not requested it but participation of a counsel in the criminal proceedings is mandatory (e.g., if defendant is a minor or has mental or physical disability), counsel must be appointed by the authorities. Also, in such circumstances the defendant may receive state legal aid regardless of his or her financial situation. If a convicted offender is unable to reimburse procedural expenses, part of the expenses may be covered by the state.

According to the Code of Criminal Procedure, the Prosecutor's Office may terminate criminal proceedings if the following conditions are fulfilled (as a general rule, only in the cases of second-degree offenses):

- Termination in event of lack of public interest in proceedings and in case of negligible guilt is possible if the defendant has compensated damages or promised to do it. The court may impose requirements such as compensations and/or performing community service.
- Termination of criminal proceedings due to lack of proportionality of punishment is possible if the punishment for the offense would be negligible compared to the punishment that has been or presumably will be imposed for another offense.
- Termination of criminal proceedings on the basis of conciliation is possible if there is no

public interest for prosecution and the defendant has reconciled with the victim, except in certain circumstances (e.g., violent crimes, crimes against the state, occupational crimes, offenses committed by an adult against a minor). In the case of a minor, the consent of his or her parent or a representative is also required.

If the offense is committed by a juvenile of less than 14 years, no proceedings are initiated and the materials are forwarded to the juvenile committee. Already initiated proceedings may be terminated and the materials forwarded to the juvenile committee also if the offense is committed by a minor of 14–18 years of age, if it appears that it is not necessary to impose a criminal penalty. Special nonpenal sanctions can be imposed on minors aged 7–18 years.

In 2007, termination of criminal proceedings was applied in 19 percent of cleared crimes (of which about 80% were terminated due to lack of public interest and 14% were sent to the juvenile committee).

Court Proceedings

Prosecutor (or, in most cases, defendant) may request to apply one of the following types of simplified proceedings instead of the general court procedure, if there are no legal obstacles (e.g., the proceeding concerns serious crime for which long imprisonment is stipulated).

- *Alternative ("short") proceedings* are carried out on the basis of the materials of the criminal file without summoning the witnesses or experts, and the principal punishment is reduced by one-third. If several persons are accused, there must be consensus to apply such proceedings.
- *Settlement proceedings* may be used at the request of the accused or the Prosecutor's Office, if all parties agree to apply such proceedings.
- *Summary proceedings* are possible if facts on the crime are explicit and the prosecutor considers application of a pecuniary punishment as the principal punishment, except if the suspect is a minor.
- *Expedited procedure* is possible if the facts on the crime are explicit and all necessary evidence have been collected. The prosecutor may request to apply such procedure within 48 hours after the suspect has been arrested.

Settlement proceedings counted 41 percent of all criminal court proceedings in 2007, followed by "short" proceedings (32%), general proceedings (15%), expedited proceedings (7%), and summary proceedings (5%). Pretrial detention is possible on the basis of a court ruling and it cannot last more than 6 months. In exceptional circumstances, if the case is particularly complex or due to international criminal proceedings, this term can be extended at the request of the chief public prosecutor. A preliminary investigation judge or court may impose bail instead of arrest, if requested by the offender. Bail cannot be used in the case of some serious offenses (e.g., murder, extortion, terrorism, membership in a criminal organization), and the amount of bail must be at least 500 days' wages.

Court sessions are usually public, but public access may be restricted to protect a state or business secret, in interests of family life or of a minor, or if publicity may endanger the security of a witness or other persons. Judgment is pronounced publicly, unless the interests of a minor, spouse, or victim require restrictions.

Punishment

Types of Punishment

A natural person can be punished for a criminal offense by a pecuniary punishment of 30 to 500 daily rates (average daily income), or by imprisonment from 30 days to 20 years or life imprisonment. Minors under 18 years of age can be sentenced by up to 10 years' imprisonment. In addition, various supplementary punishments can be imposed (e.g., occupational ban, deprivation of driving privileges, deprivation of right to hold weapons or ammunition). In the case of a legal person, a pecuniary punishment from 50,000 to 250,000,000 kroons and/or the compulsory dissolution can be imposed. Courts' decisions are publicly available at the Web site of the court judgments register.

Conditional sentencing or release from punishment is widely practiced. Probation (complete or partial suspension of the sentence) for a period of three to five years can be imposed instead of the imprisonment or the pecuniary punishment, and the imposed punishment will not be enforced if the convicted offender does not commit a new crime within the period of probation. This option can also require supervision of conduct, which may include certain requirements (e.g., remedy of damage caused by the offense, prohibition of consumption of alcohol or narcotics, prescription of treatment if the offender has previously consented to such treatment). The imprisonment can also be substituted by community service; in such a case one day of imprisonment corresponds to two hours of community service. Juvenile offenders may be released from punishment by the court and alternative sanctions may be used (admonition, subjection to supervision of conduct, placement in a youth home or in a school for pupils who need special treatment due to behavioral problems). A prisoner can be released on parole after serving the required minimum part of his or her imprisonment (depends on severity of the offense, but at least one-third of total sentence time). In certain conditions, earlier release on parole may be possible if the person agrees with electronic surveillance.

During the second half of the 1990s, the average numbers of offenders convicted for criminal offenses ranged from 8,000 to 9,000 a year. Since the year 2000 this number has been more than 10,000, particularly due to traffic offenses, as repeated drunken driving within 12 months was criminalized in 1999. In 2007, in total 11,889 persons were convicted, of which 3,565 persons for traffic offenses and 2,311 persons for thefts. The typical punishment for homicide, rape, theft, robbery, and serious drug offenses was imprisonment, but a considerable part of the convictions were conditional (except in the case of homicides), that is, not full prison term. Most frequently the prison terms for murder ranged from 10 to 12 years, for manslaughter from 6 to 8 years, for rape from 1 to 2 years (in the case of aggravating circumstances, 6 years), for robbery from 2 to 3 years, and for drug trafficking from 1 to 4 years (but in several cases up to 9 years). In the case of thefts (all criminal offenses, regardless of their seriousness), the majority of given prison terms was shorter than 1 year, and in rare cases more than 3 years.

Prison

During the Soviet period punishments were relatively hard and imprisonment was widely used (e.g., 61% of convicted persons in 1980 were sentenced to unconditional imprisonment). The number of convicted and imprisoned persons increased until the mid-1980s. In 1985, there were 8,600 prisoners (including 2,000 suspects under preliminary investigation), that is, 562 prisoners per 100,000 of population. The number of convicted and imprisoned persons decreased in 1987–1988, probably due to liberalization of sentencing practice, convicts from other regions of the Soviet Union were sent back to prisons in their native republics, and some prisoners were released by way of amnesties. From 1988 until 2006, the number of prisoners remained approximately the same, ranging from 4,200 to 4,800 persons. The number of prisoners declined substantially in 2007 due to increased use of parole and a decrease in the number of convictions. Also, electronic surveillance was introduced.

At the beginning of 2008, there were 3,456 prisoners: 2,540 convicted by a court and 916 persons in pretrial detention; that means in total 258 prisoners per 100,000 population. Taking into account the most serious crime only, 24 percent of total convicted persons were imprisoned for homicide, 17 percent for theft, 16 percent for robbery, 13 percent for drug crime, 7 percent for a traffic crime, 4 percent for rape, 4 percent for inflicting a serious bodily injury, and 15 percent for other types of offenses. According to imposed time of imprisonment, the distribution was 10 percent of convicted persons were imprisoned for less than 1 year,

49 percent for the term from 1 to 5 years, 28 percent for the term from 5 to 10 years, 12 percent for the term from 10 to 30 years, and 1 percent (35 persons) for life imprisonment. In most cases actual imprisonment time is expected to be shorter, due to likely conditional release on parole after the prisoner has served a certain part of the sentence imposed by the court. At the same time, about 8,500 sentenced persons were under probation, of those 70 percent had been released immediately after court proceedings, 15 percent had been released from prison on parole, 7 percent had served a short predetermined prison term, and 7 percent were under probation due to substitution of up to 2 years' imprisonment by community service.

There are six prisons that have places for 3,800 prisoners, including pretrial detainees. The two most modern prisons (Viru and Tartu) are cell-type, but other prisons were built in the Soviet period and are colony-type, that is, with common areas for a large number of prisoners. Viru Prison in the city of Jõhvi was opened in spring 2008. It has 1,075 places for convicted males, and for males and females in pretrial detention (both including male minors). There is also a special department for drug addicts. To ensure high-level security, all buildings are connected with special corridors. Inmates have possibilities for recreation and practicing religious activities. The prison offers jobs for 244 prison officers and 106 civilians. A new police detention house is also situated in the same area.

Prisons in Tartu and Tallinn have places for convicted male adults, and for persons in pretrial detention. In addition, Tartu Prison has a special unit for drug addicts, and at Tallinn Prison there is a hospital for prisoners from all prisons. Murru Prison is for convicted low-risk male adults, and Harku Prison for convicted female adults and minors (both are located in Harju County near Tallinn).

As a general rule, convicted inmates have an obligation to work or attend educational programs. Prisoners have the right to conjugal visits, that is, to meet a spouse or partner in a special room. All prisoners are entitled to correspondence, but only a message written on paper or a photograph is allowed (e.g., it is not allowed to receive money or magazines). The letters are opened by a prison officer in the presence of the prisoner to detect forbidden items, but the prison officer has no right to read the text of the letter. A convicted prisoner, who has served at least a year of his or her prison term, has a right for prison leave for up to 21 calendar days a year (except persons in pretrial detention and the persons convicted for life imprisonment). His or her arrival to and departure from the destination place must be registered at the local police station, and he or she must return to the prison in time and in a sober condition.

Andri Ahven

Further Reading

Leps, Ando. (1991). *Kuritegevus Eestis* [Crime in Estonia]. Tartu: Tartu Ülikool, Eesti Akadeemiline Õigusteaduse Selts.

Ministry of Justice of Estonia: http://www.just.ee. This site provides information on the criminal justice system and criminal policy; there is an English summary of publications.

Saar, Jüri, et al. (2003). *Kuritegevus Eestis 1991–2001* [Crime in Estonia 1991–2001]. Tallinn: Juura.

Saar, Jüri, et al. (2005). *Rahvusvaheline kuriteoohvrite uuring Eestis 2004.* [The Estonian Crime Victim Survey 2004]. Tallinn: Tartu Ülikooli Õigusinstituut, Justiitsministeerium, Siseministeerium.

Faroe Islands

Legal System: Civil
Prison Rate: Low
Death Penalty: No
Corporal Punishment: No

Background

The Faroe Islands, which are also part of the Danish Realm, are situated far from Denmark in the Atlantic. The 18 beautiful islands cover an area of 1,400 square kilometers (540 square miles) and hold

50,000 inhabitants. Approximately 17,000 of these live in the capital of Tórshavn. The Faroe Islands have had a home rule system since 1948, which means that they themselves pass legislation in a number of areas, whereas other areas are regulated by Danish law. Furthermore, the Faroe Islands are represented by two members of the *Folketing* (Danish Parliament) in Copenhagen.

The Faroe Islands has its own police district. The purpose of the police force is in general to maintain safety, security, peace, and order in society. The most important task, though, is to ensure the politicians abide by the Danish legislation. Furthermore, crime prevention, assistance, and law enforcement are important fields of work.

Crime

Classification of Crimes

The Faroe Islands have the same Penal Code and Administration of Justice Act as the rest of Denmark and the conditions are not different in principle. Some variations, though, have been made in a number of the amendments in the Danish Criminal Code that have not taken effect on the Faroe Islands.

According to the Danish Criminal Code only acts punishable under a statute or acts of entirely similar nature can be punished. Unless otherwise provided, legal consequences can always take effect, if provided by the law at the time of the criminal act. Danish criminal law is applicable on crimes committed within the territory of the Danish state, despite that of Greenland, which has its own criminal code. The law applies onboard any Danish vessel or aircraft within or outside the territory (if recognized by international law), abroad by a Danish citizen or any other person with domicile in Denmark if it is an offense against the state and punishable in the country committed.

According to the Danish Criminal Code, a person becomes criminally responsible when reaching the age of 15. Criminal offenses are defined either in the Criminal Code or in separate statutes. The general conditions for imposing criminal penalties can be found in the general part of the Criminal Code, which also apply to separately defined statutes. A criminal offense can consist of a violation of the code or be a violation of a separate statute. The substantive Danish criminal law is monistic, meaning that violations of the law have never been divided into categories like felonies or misdemeanors, but this does not mean that major offenses would be treated in the same manner as minor ones. The distinction exists, even though the violations are not categorized.

According to the Criminal Code the mere possession of drugs is criminalized. However, the law is not enforced regarding possession of very small amounts meant for the offenders' own consumption. Otherwise it is illegal to use, sell, manufacture, and to transfer narcotics. Danish drug policy has been quite liberal but has started to change during the past five years. New drug policies were drawn up in 2003, which were the first in decades. Denmark is heading more and more toward zero-tolerance drug policy. The policy covers all aspects of drug-related problems, like treatment, drug control, prevention, and harm reduction. What forms the basis of the new line in drug policy is the outspoken focus on zero-tolerance toward not only drug dealing and drug trafficking but also drug use. Minor drug offenses are usually punished by imprisonment from 2 to 6 years and for more serious drug offenses the sentence can be up to 16 years of imprisonment. Particularly serious drug crimes can nowadays receive as much as 24 years, which is much more than the maximum of 10 years that was the case 5 years ago.

Crime Statistics

Every year about 400,000 criminal offenses are reported to the police in Denmark. Some people also violate the sections of the traffic legislation and the road traffic regulations. Getting caught for speeding or drunk driving are the two most common offenses. Approximately 275,000 persons are charged with violation of the Road Traffic Act every year according to the Danish National Police. According to crime statistics and research made by the police in Denmark, a little under half of all crimes are never solved. Of all crimes, 60 percent are committed by men, 40 percent by women. Most of the crimes are committed in the home environment by 15- to 30-year-old offenders. Most crimes happen because of firearms and other violent hand weapons. Almost 50 percent of all crimes happen within the family, between parents and children. In approximately 40 percent of the crimes committed, the victim and the offender have some kind of a preexisting relationship. Only 10 percent of all crimes happen between strangers.

Finding of Guilt

In a situation of self-defense, the danger inherent in the attack, the person of the aggressor, and the social importance of the interests endangered by the attack are taken into consideration. A person cannot be punished for committing an act in saving a person or property from otherwise unavoidable danger. Neither are acts committed in self-defense punishable if it was necessary to resist or avert an unlawful attack, provided that such an act does not manifestly exceed what is normally considered reasonable. If the offender has a mental illness or is irresponsible due to a mental deficiency, he or she is not criminally responsible. Where the punishable nature of an act depends on or is influenced by an actual or intended consequence, the act shall also be deemed to have been committed where the consequence has taken effect or was intended to take effect.

The Administration of Justice Act sets out a wide range of detailed rules aimed to guarantee a fair trial for the accused and protecting the rights of the parties. The act also aims to strike a fair balance between the rights of the individual and the interests of society, including the necessary efficiency of the criminal justice system. Basic principles are, for example, the presumption of innocence until proven guilty, the burden of proof placed on the prosecution service, application of free assessment of evidence, the right of the defendant to remain silent, and equality of arms between prosecution and defense. Open justice covers both public access to attending legal proceedings and media access to courtroom coverage. Sometimes, however, it can be harmful for the parties or the investigation. In these situations, the court may decide to hear the case behind closed doors or impose restrictions on certain parts of the proceedings or the identity of the offender.

Faroe Islands has its own court situated in the capital. Its jurisdiction comprises all the islands. The court at Tórshavn has the same type of cases as do district courts in other regions of Denmark. Appeals go to the High Court of Eastern Denmark. Prosecutors on the Faroe Islands have the same authority as the regional public prosecutors, thus coming under the direct authority of the director of public prosecutions. In minor cases where the prosecution results in a fine, the case will be tried by a single judge. In more severe cases the judge sits with two lay judges, and they decide the question of guilt together and impose the sentence.

Punishment

Types of Punishment

Sanctions available to the court are imprisonment, fines, community service, and probation orders. A prison sentence can either be for a limited time from 7 days to 16 years or a life sentence. As of July 1, 2000, the Criminal Code was amended so that life prisoners can be released on parole when they have served a minimum of 12 years of their sentences. Within the first 12 years release can only take place through pardoning. The vast majority of pardons are granted before the actual imprisonment. Inmates sentenced to imprisonment for life can only be released by the pardon of royal resolution. In recent years Danish prisons have held between 10 and 13 inmates serving a life sentence.

Any person who kills another person will become guilty of homicide and liable to imprisonment for any term ranging from five years to life. Any person who negligently causes the death of some other person will become liable to simple detention or to a fine or, in case of aggravating circumstances, to imprisonment for any term not exceeding four years. The special part of the Criminal Code is very detailed and has many paragraphs concerning offenses against family relations, sex offenses, offenses of violence against a person, offenses against personal honor and certain individual rights, offenses against personal liberty, and others. The most common sanctions are imprisonment for a certain time limit.

Prison

The prison in Tórnshavn was built in 1976 and has capacity to accommodate 15 to 20 people. The prison in Copenhagen has a special unit where serious prisoners serve their sentences. The Prison Service (*Kriminalforsorgen*) is responsible for implementing new rules and regulations in prisons around Denmark. On the Faroe Islands rules and regulations are mostly within the director-general's responsibility. The Office of the Director-General of Prisons and Probation reports directly to the minister of justice concerning decisions on specific and general cases relating to enforcement of the punishments, as well as decisions concerning staffing matters.

The probation officers work with offenders released on parole, to which must be added the work with remand prisoners and the preparation of pretrial reports. Probation officers have a high degree of freedom to use their own judgment in their work with individual offenders as long as they respect the objectives of the Probation Service and the conditions imposed on the offender. They can even give advice and guidance, issue instructions and requirements, but also ultimately can report the offender to the department or the court if things are not working out. According to the Criminal Code, convicted offenders who have a special need for treatment might have an opportunity to serve their sentence at a hospital or another suitable institution, including different hostels belonging to the Prison and Probation Service. It may, for example, concern very young offenders or offenders who, because of health or abuse problems, have a special need for treatment. A great number of staff members work in crime prevention, especially with young serious offenders between 15 and 18.

Anna Gustafson

Further Reading

Danish Judicial System: http://www.justitsministeriet.dk.

Faroe Islands Government: http://www.faroeislands.org.uk and http://landsbank.fo. This site provides news concerning politics, government, culture, and statistical facts.

Statistics can be found at: http://www.hagstova.fo; http://www.nationmaster.com; and http://www.dst.dk.

Finland

Legal System: Civil
Murder: Medium
Burglary: Medium
Corruption: Low
Human Trafficking: Low
Prison Rate: Low
Death Penalty: No
Corporal Punishment: No

Background

Finland is situated in Northern Europe with a population of 5.3 million and is one of the Nordic countries (the others are Denmark, Iceland, Norway, and Sweden). Since the 1960s, the Nordic countries have been the leaders in developing the welfare state system, based on advanced social security, public health service, fair justice system with lenient punishments, equal income distribution, high GDP, democratically elected governance, and low corruption.

The Finnish judicial system is rooted in Western, Continental culture, and certain Scandinavian features have been prevalent in the Finnish legal system because Finland was part of Sweden for more than 700 years. Finland was under the Russian regime from 1809 to 1917, but retained its autonomous status and fundamental laws as the Grand Duchy under the Russian czar. After the independence declaration in 1917, Finland began to develop into one of the Western European democracies.

The Finnish Penal Code is one of the oldest in Europe. Published in 1889, it came into force in 1894. Along with the Penal Code, decrees concerning the implementation of the code and the enforcement of punishments were passed. Although the basic structure of the Penal Code has remained unchanged, the contents of the code have been greatly amended during the years. The total reform of the Criminal Code was based on the work of a committee that began its work in 1972. The task was finished in 1999.

Becoming a member of the European Union in 1995 has stabilized the financial situation of the country. Finland fulfilled the criteria for joining the European Monetary Union in 1999. In the future, the Finnish judicial system will be developed into a unified format along with Continental Europe.

Police

The Finnish police are subordinated to the Ministry of Interior. The Ministry of Interior comprises four departments: the Police Department, the Department for Rescue Services, the Migration Department, and the Border Guard Department. In 2006 Finnish police had 10,950 employees, of whom 8,206 were police officers, and the number of civilians was 2,744 persons. Police officers receive a professional training of 2.5 years, which comprises a field working period as junior officer. Civilians work mainly in administrative duties.

Police powers and the key principles of policing are laid down primarily in the Police Act, the Coercive Measures Act, and the Pre-Trial Investigation Act. Police powers have been formulated in accordance with constitutional and human rights and to ensure that the Finnish police are capable of effective cooperation in the fight against international crime. In addition to legislation, police operations are guided by police ethics and citizens' expectations.

According to the Police Act, the function of the police is to secure judicial and social order, to maintain public order and security, to prevent and investigate crimes, and to submit cases to prosecutors for decision. In practice, the Finnish police is divided into police districts that take care of the local tasks. Most severe and complicated cases are investigated by the National Bureau of Investigation (e.g., homicide, money laundering, organized crime, transnational crime) that operates throughout the country, as do also the National Traffic Police and the Security Police. The function of the National Traffic Police is to carry out traffic control and surveillance and improve traffic safety.

The task of the Security Police is to prevent schemes and crimes that may endanger the established governmental and social order or the internal and external security of the state, and to investigate such crimes. The Security Police must also maintain and develop general readiness to prevent actions that may endanger state security. Also the Finnish Border Guards and the Customs investigate independently crimes that are related to their field (illegal immigration, smuggling, human and drug trafficking). Criminal intelligence and analysis functions are carried out together by the police, the Customs, and the Border Guards when investigating cross-border crimes.

In Finland, the police authorities are mainly responsible for the pretrial investigation of crimes and, if crime is suspected, they deliver the pretrial investigation protocol to the prosecutor for public prosecution. If the legal conditions for prosecution exist, the prosecutor must prosecute for offenses that have come to his or her attention. However, there are offenses where prosecution is possible only on the request of the victim. These are mostly petty offenses that are of little public interest. The prosecutor can also waive the charges in case of lacking evidence and in a number of petty offenses.

The International Crime Victims Survey from 2005 shows that 90 percent of the Finnish respondents thought that the police do a good job in their living area in controlling crime. Reasons for the positive result could be the corruption-free reputation of the police. Police officers are recruited from the average population, and therefore, they represent the same values and have a similar background as the main population. The Finnish police operate on the basis of performance guidance procedures, and the main focus areas and targets are reevaluated annually in the performance plan.

Crime

Classification of Crimes

The Finnish Penal Code is divided into a general part and a special part. In the special part of the code, elements of the offenses are described, as well as the types of the punishments connected to the crimes, and the punishment scale. The criminal law of Finland classifies offenses into three levels of severity. The basic statutory offense is a crime in its most essential form. A criminal case is considered aggravated when it is particularly serious, harmful, and/or premeditated. When a crime is considered as petty, there are significant mitigating circumstances present. There is no lower limit for petty crimes; for example, petty theft can be stealing personal or company property of any value.

Petty crimes are classified as complainant offenses, which means that the victim is responsible for the decision whether to raise charges or not. More severe cases are taken to court despite the opinion of the victim. Previously, the basic form of an offense was a complainant offense (e.g., assault was a complainant offense according the former penal code but was changed into a public prosecution offense because it was considered to serve public wellbeing and justice).

The age of criminal responsibility is 15 years. Offenders younger than 15 years are responsible only for damages. If they commit a serious offense, they are handed over to the social services.

In 2003, according to the program of the Finnish government, a project was launched to map the present state and the development of internal security in Finland. In 2008, the program was updated. The new version emphasizes the following areas in crime control: social exclusion, injuries, relations between the population groups, violence, major accidents, vulnerability of the society, cross-border crime, information network criminality, terrorism, and violent radicalism.

Alcohol, Social Exclusion, and Male Homicide

The high prevalence of homicide in Finland has been concentrated on two groups: one group consists of men and is characterized by social exclusion, misuse of alcohol, unemployment, and low educational level. The other group is women who have been killed by their male partners. The number of manslaughters has risen among blue-collar workers in the past decades.

The drinking habits of Finnish men have traditionally been notoriously reckless. The increased availability of alcohol in the 1970s had its effect on consumption, which in turn reflected on homicide rates. Around 80 percent of perpetrators are inebriated during the time of the attack. It is also common that the victims are under the influence of alcohol. When violence against men by men is concerned, both the typical perpetrators as well as typical victims are 20- to 50-year-old males, who are often unemployed, but consider themselves as laborers or craftsmen. Alcohol-related homicide is often conducted with a knife or a blunt weapon and is often unplanned or unintentional.

Violence against Women

Each year, around 30 to 40 women are violently killed, which is more than twice as much as in other Nordic countries (men's homicides are three times more common). Of these women, 20 to 30 are killed by their current or former partners. According to the Finnish Violence against Women Surveys, approximately 8 percent of women face violence in the hands of a male partner in Finland every year. Violence in close relationships is common in all social, economic, and educational backgrounds.

Domestic violence has been traditionally regarded as a "private problem" but has gained more public attention during the past two decades. Rape in marriage was criminalized in 1994 and assault in a private place became an offense that is prosecuted under an official charge in 1995. Nongovernmental organizations and shelters have been established to protect victims of domestic violence and to provide legal assistance.

Violence at Work

According to victimization surveys, violence at work has increased in Finland during the last decades, while other forms of violence have remained on a rather stable level. It is common for both men and women, although women suffer more incidents. Violence at work rarely leads to severe injuries, and fatal workplace violence is uncommon. The national victimization survey from 2006 found that the amount of workplace violence is slightly decreasing. Although victimization surveys show that men and women experience violence equally often, the victimization situations differ. Men fall more often victims to violence on the streets by unknown offenders, at restaurants and in other public places, whereas women are assaulted at the workplace and in their close relations.

Drug Offenses

Probably because binge drinking is common in Finland, drugs have not become popular among the general public. The level of drug offenses in Finland is relatively low compared to other Western industrialized countries. The market consists mainly of cannabis and amphetamines, and smaller amounts of cocaine, heroin, Ecstasy, and prescription drugs. In the last few years *Subutex*®, which is used as a substitute treatment for heroin addiction, has become more common in the illegal trade. In 1991, certain immigrant groups brought a new type of mild narcotic, khat, into Finland. The use remains limited to their own ethnic group and it is not commonly available.

Efforts to control the drug market have increased in the past 10 years. Tapping phone calls of suspects has been possible from 1995. Since 2001 the police have been allowed to use unconventional methods for the investigation of drug offenses, such as fake purchases and undercover work, but such operations are still rarely used. The Finnish drug market is not highly organized. One of the reasons behind this is the corruption-free reputation of the Finnish police. Another cause is the small size of the Finnish drug market and the negative attitude against drugs among the general public.

There are several organizations that are dedicated to reducing the risks of drugs, such as needle exchange points and other outreach services. Voluntary access to government-funded rehabilitation programs is possible both in society and in prisons. In some cases, drug addiction is controlled with a substitute treatment, such as methadone or Subutex, but these are not widely accepted.

Crime Statistics

Homicide (Murder, Manslaughter, Killing)

In 2007, there were a total of 127 completed homicides (2.4 deaths/100,000 population). The rate has been quite steady for the past 20 years, although the trend is slightly downward. Most homicides are classified as manslaughters. Killings (homicide in mitigating circumstances) are rare, with only seven cases during the time period 1988–2007. The trend in murders is increasing. Numbers of manslaughter were high through the 1990s and the beginning of the new millennium, but have decreased significantly in the last few years. The trend in assaults resulting in death has been decreasing for the past 20 years. In 2007, 25 persons were killed in this kind of assault.

In Finland, for each homicide an extensive questionnaire is completed, and the data are recorded for research purposes. The homicide database comprises incidents beginning from the year 2002. The number of infanticides has been low during the last decades, on the average one incident per year. Reasons for this could be that babies are almost without exception delivered in general hospitals, contraceptives are widely used and, most important, abortion is allowed (the law of abortion was introduced in 1970).

Particular tragedies have a significant effect on murder rates. For example, the Jokela school shooting increased the number by 8, making 2007 the murder peak of 20 years. The homicide figures from 2008 are distorted by the Kauhajoki school shooting, in which 10 persons were murdered. The third massacre happened in 2002 in a shopping center. In a bomb explosion 7 persons were killed.

Rape and Sexual Violence

In 2007, a total of 2,326 sex offenses were recorded. Of these, one-third were rapes and nearly one-half were sexual abuse of children. The rest of the cases were cases such as coercion to a sexual act, sexual abuse, buying sexual services from a young person, and pandering. A total of 739 rape cases were reported to the police in 2007—over a hundred cases more than in the previous year or any given earlier year. In 2007, 80 percent of rapes were classified as basic rapes (no cases of aggravated rapes recorded in 2007), and 20 percent as coercion into sexual intercourse (attempts included). Cases of child sexual abuse have steadily increased over the past 10 years. The numbers for 2006 and 2007 have nearly doubled compared to the previous decades. The rate of other sex crimes has varied a lot during the last 10 years. The year 2006 stands out particularly: with more than 1,000 cases the number is two to three times as high as the average of the decade. In 2007 there were significantly less other reported sex crimes, but still a lot compared to the beginning of the new millennium.

Increase in sex crimes other than rape is likely to be explained by the new police unit specializing in tackling sexual abuse of children and teenage prostitution established in 2006. The statistical increase in rapes does not necessarily mean that the crime of rape is significantly more common than before. It tells more about an attitude change; in the past, rape victims were seen as guilty of provocation or false information.

Property Offenses

Nearly one-half of offenses against the Penal Code reported to the police are property offenses. Around one in five crimes (including traffic offenses) is a theft, or unauthorized use of a motor vehicle. The rate of property offenses rose steadily during the 1980s. Consumerism and urban development increased the potential targets and opportunities for stealing. However, the growth of property crimes stopped in the early 1990s, when Finland was struggling with severe financial depression. Since then the decrease in recorded property offenses has been replaced by an increase in drug offenses. Commonly, a large part of property crime is committed to finance a drug habit.

Only around 1.5 percent of theft offenses are defined as aggravated. The classification is based mainly on the value of the stolen items. A total of 251,000 property offenses were committed in 2007. Over half of them were thefts of different degrees. The number of robberies was just under 2,000, the number of burglaries 25,000 (6,500 domestic burglaries), and almost 15,000 unlawful uses of motor vehicles. The rest included offenses such as possession and hiding of stolen items.

Drug Offenses

In 2007 the total number of drug offenses published in crime statistics was 15,000 cases. A relatively small amount of all drug offenses recorded by the police are aggravated (during 1997–2006 on the average 5%). With 883 aggravated drug offenses, the year 2007 reached the peak of the decade. Basic drug offenses were committed over 4,000 times (nearly two-thirds of the drug offenses were drug use). The rate started to increase in the early 1990s and has remained high ever since. It is common for the same persons to have committed multiple offenses.

Urban and Rural Crimes

Homicides are slightly more common in the rural areas than in cities and large towns. On the other hand, assaults are less common in the periphery. There are at least two possible reasons; in the urban areas help arrives faster and the risk of dying of blood loss or other injury is smaller. In rural areas there are more weapons available in the households (e.g., shotguns). In urban areas there are more witnesses and more police officers and stations, so it is more likely that an assault will be reported. Also assaults by strangers are more often reported to the police and in rural areas the victim usually knows the offender and the crimes are perhaps settled in a more unofficial way. Property crime is more common in urban areas, simply because there are more opportunities. Shops and department stores are situated in larger towns and cities, and suburbs offer a chance for multiple burglaries.

Finding of Guilt

Rights of the Accused

Every person suspected of a crime has the right to a fair trial. The accused is seen as one party of the criminal process and must be treated as equal in relation to the complainant and the prosecutor. According to the presumption of innocence one must be considered innocent until proven guilty. The court must hold no presumptions about the outcome of the trial. The accused have the right to receive immediate and detailed information on what they are being charged for, in a language that they understand. They are entitled to a defense and there must be enough time and resources to prepare it. Also translation services must be provided in case where the accused does not understand or speak the language used in the court.

A person accused of a crime is not required to contribute to the finding of his or her guilt. The plaintiff and the witnesses are obligated to speak the truth during the hearing, but the accused is not. This is on the grounds that no person can be expected to act in a way that has a negative effect on his or her own situation.

Police escort former world champion ski jumper Matti Nykanen, head covered, to the court in Tampere, Finland, August 27, 2004. Nykanen and his wife, Mervi Tapola-Nykanen, were detained on suspicion of attempted homicide after a 59-year-old man was found severely stabbed at a summer cottage in Nokia, near Tampere. (AP Photo/Lehtikuva)

Assistance to the Accused

Right to assistance is one of the minimum rights of the accused in the human rights treaty. A qualified person can work either as an advocate or an assistant, depending on the needs and capabilities of the accused. The assistant is usually a lawyer, but he or she can also be another law practitioner or an adult civilian with an honest reputation, who has not declared bankruptcy or who has no other restrictions. When a person is suspected of a serious crime the advocate can be appointed by the court. His or her wages are paid by the government, but if the defendant is convicted of a crime, he or she will have to reimburse the amount. The accused also have the right to defend themselves should they wish.

Preliminary Investigation

The police must conduct a preliminary investigation on grounds of a reported crime or if there is some other reason to suspect that a crime has taken place. In case of a complainant crime, preliminary investigation will only be conducted if the complainant demands a punishment of the offender. The investigation process must be cancelled if the complainant requests so, except if public interest requires otherwise.

The purpose of a preliminary investigation is to find out whether there are grounds for a trial. It consists of finding out if a crime has been committed, in what circumstances, what kind of damage has been done, and what advantages gained. The possibilities of returning stolen goods and reimbursement of financial loss are also studied. A preliminary investigation is usually conducted by the police of the municipality where the suspected crime took place. If a crime is considered particularly serious (e.g., a complicated homicide case or organized crime), the investigation is carried out by the Federal Bureau of Investigation. A preliminary investigation consists of hearing the victim, the suspect, and the witnesses. All the issues both for and against the suspect must be taken into consideration. He or she must be informed about his or her status in the process. A suspect under 18 years of age must be interrogated in the presence of his or her assistant. If the preliminary investigation shows that a crime has not been committed or no one can be held responsible, the case is withdrawn. Otherwise the case will be forwarded to prosecution. There are two exceptions: canceling the reporting and restricting preliminary investigation.

Police have the right not to report the case if it is assessed as minor and would result in not more than a fine considering that the plaintiff does not have any demands. In around 10 percent of all crimes against the Penal Code, the reporting to the prosecutor is cancelled. Canceling reporting only applies to cases where the crime and the offender have been solved. In some cases the officer in charge of investigation proposes that the investigation be ended. The prosecutor gives out an order to restrict the investigation if he or she is not willing to press charges and public interest does not require so. This can be done even if the offender has been found out.

Prosecution

When the preliminary investigation is completed, the police deliver the record to the prosecutor. The main task of the prosecutor is to determine if there are grounds to press charges. He or she assesses whether there is sufficient evidence to support the case. Another primary task of the prosecutor is confirming punishment orders given by the police (e.g., penalty fines for traffic offenses).

If the offense is classified under public prosecution, charges will be pressed despite the opinion of the plaintiff. In some cases charges will not be pressed if the plaintiff wishes so and general benefit does not require it (e.g., petty assault). Charges must be pressed as soon as there is reliable evidence that suggest that the defendant is guilty and it must be based on probable causes. Charges can be dropped if the offense is in total considered as minor, the offender is young, or on the basis of consideration of equity. Plea bargaining is not practiced in Finland.

Mediation

Mediation is not an alternative to trial, because it does not solve the judicial side of the case, but it has been developed to function as a complementary means to trial. However, mediation can influence the outcome of the trial in a mitigating manner, or in some cases the charges can be completely dropped, or the punishment can be waived. An initiative regarding mediation can be done by either party of the case, police, prosecutor, or social service. If the suspect is a minor, his or her guardian or other legal representative has the right to suggest mediation. In case of a violent crime against the offender's partner, child, or other close person, only the police or the prosecutor can initiate mediation.

Mediation is voluntary and both parties must agree to it. Typical criminal cases where mediation is applicable are assaults, thefts, and malicious damage. The more aggravated the crime, the less suitable it is considered to be for mediation. In 2007, 6,825 crime cases were directed to mediation.

Incarceration before or Awaiting Trial

The police can hold a suspect in custody for a maximum of 4 days without pressing charges. If a person has been arrested for aggressive behavior or under the influence of alcohol or drugs, but he or she is not suspected of a crime, the person can be held in custody for no more than 12 hours. To hold a suspect for a longer time, the police must obtain an imprisonment order from the court. Remand imprisonment is not a punishment, but a coercive measure used during the preliminary investigation and trial. Its purpose is to secure the investigation and the trial and to discontinue possible criminal activity.

The remand prisoner must be placed in another prison or a different ward from prisoners serving a sentence. He or she should ideally be placed in a single cell. It is also possible that he or she will be kept in solitary confinement. A remand prisoner cannot be held for more than four weeks, unless there is a significant reason to do so. If the trial results in a prison sentence, the time spent on remand will be deducted from the total length.

Judges

In 2006, there were 691 professional judges or magistrates in Finland (officials authorized to hear civil, criminal, and other cases, including in appeal courts, and make dispositions in a court of law). Thirty-nine percent of the judges were female. Professional judges must have a master's degree in law; also training on the bench is required. In Finnish magistrate's courts there are also lay judges, who participate together with the judge in defining of the outcome of the case. In 2006 the number of lay judges was 3,671; of them 68 percent were women.

Juveniles

Juveniles are tried and punished under the same criminal justice system as adults. The age of criminal responsibility is 15 years, and 15- to 17-year-olds are tried as minors. They are sentenced to prison very rarely and never to a life sentence. Around one out of 10 prison sentences is unconditional. Minors represent only 0.1 percent of Finland's prison population, and 18- to 20-year-olds represent less than 2 percent.

Offenders who are over 15 but not yet 21 years old are considered young offenders. They receive custodial sentences less often than adults and are eligible for parole after one-third of the imprisonment has been served. The most common punishment for a young offender is a fine. It is more common that a young offender is sentenced as guilty but left without a punishment. Mediation is often used when dealing with juvenile offenders and it can be applied to under 15-year-olds as well. Under 15-year-olds cannot be tried in court but in serious cases they are put into the custody of social services. Offenders 15 to 17 years old can be treated both under the criminal justice and the child welfare systems.

In 1997, Finland introduced a special youth sentence for 15- to 17-year-old offenders. It was first limited to seven courts and became nationwide in 2005. It is considered a more serious punishment than probation. It consists of control meetings, exercises for developing social skills, support, guidance, and looking into employment opportunities. There are two meetings every week, which is considerably more than with an unconditional sentence, where the offender meets with a criminal justice officer only once a month. Youth sentence is typically used as a punishment for violent crime. The average length of a youth sentence has decreased from eight to four months. Around one in 10 is discontinued, most often due to a drug or alcohol problem of the offender. The youth sentence is still quite rarely used throughout Finland.

Punishment

Finland has pursued a conscious, systematic, long-term criminal policy. The decrease of the prison population is one of the outcomes of this policy. Several reasons can be found behind the decrease of the Finnish prison rates. Nordic penal policy has been described as a pragmatic, less politicized, and nonmoralistic approach, which has had a clear social policy orientation. There has been a strong political will among professionals and practitioners in Finland to decrease the prisoner rate. The comprehensive planning instruments of the welfare society have been utilized. The slogan "effective social policy is the best criminal policy" describes the intertwined structure of the areas: measures against social marginalization and inequality are also effective means against crime. At the same time there has been in the Nordic countries a strong debate emphasizing the ineffectiveness of an extensive use of the prison system.

In Finland, an extensive theoretical cost-benefit analysis was used aiming at the minimization of the costs and harmful effects of crime and of crime control, and the fair distribution of the costs among the offender, society, and the victim. Costs in this connection referred not only to the material costs, but also to the immaterial costs to all of the three parties. As a consequence, many laws have been enacted to decrease the prison population. The development of punishments has in practice been directed toward an increased use of fines.

Types of Punishment

The following financial punishments are described in the Finnish penal code:

- Day-fine. The idea of the day fine system is that the penalty is in relation to the offender's economic situation. One unit of fine represents approximately 1 out of 60 of the total monthly net income of the person.
- Conversion sentence. In case a fine cannot be collected, it can be transformed into a custodial sentence. One day in prison makes up for three day fines. A conversion punishment must last for at least 4 and no more than 60 days.
- Penalty fine. The penalty fine is a less serious financial punishment than a day fine. The sum is fixed and cannot be more than €200. The penalty fine varies and is always a set amount for a particular offense. An unpaid penalty fine cannot be converted into imprisonment. Police officers and other officials (carrying out a statutory function) have the right to issue penalty fines, while fines are imposed by the prosecutor or the court.

The following custodial punishments are described in the Finnish Penal Code:

- Conditional sentence. When a prison sentence is conditional the execution is postponed until the end of a probation period. The period lasts for at least one and no more than three years. At the end of the probation, the sentence is cancelled.
- Unconditional sentence. A custodial sentence consists of the loss or restriction of freedom. A prison sentence is either a temporary or a life sentence, although the latter is not to be taken literally in practice. An inmate serving a life sentence is eligible for parole after 12 years of incarceration. A single temporary sentence ranges from 14 days to 12 years, and the maximum length of a combined sentence is 15 years. Offenders who are classified by the health authorities as unaccountable are given psychiatric treatment in closed institutions, but this is not considered as a punishment.
- Probation. Most convicts are given the chance to spend the end of their sentence outside the prison. It is possible to apply for parole when two-thirds of the sentence are served. If the convict was younger than 21 years old at the time of the sentencing, he or she is eligible for parole after one-half of the custodial sentence.

- Trial freedom under surveillance. Since 2006, it has been possible, to facilitate social inclusion, to release a prisoner into the society no more than six months before probation, accompanied by an electronic surveillance device. The convict must commit to complete sobriety.
- Community service. Community service is a common punishment initiated in the 1990s, which can be applied instead of a no more than 8 months prison sentence. Depending on the length of the sentence the duration of the community service is 20–200 hours. When imprisonment is converted into community service, one day in prison equals to one hour of community service.
- Restraining order. Finland started using restraining orders in 1995 (extension involving family members in 1999). It is not a punishment, but a preventive measure to protect a potential victim. It states that the receiver is forbidden from approaching, contacting, following, or watching the claimant. The maximum length of a restraining order is one year, in cases involving family members, three months.

Typical Punishments

Typical punishments for crimes are as follows:

- Rape: at least 1 and no more than 6 years in prison, up to 8 years if aggravated.
- Murder: a life sentence, which is in practice at least 12 years in prison, less for killing with mitigating circumstances. In 2005 the average punishment for manslaughter was more than 9 years in prison. For an attempted manslaughter the punishment was around 3.5 years.
- Assault: a fine or custodial sentence of no more than 2 years; at least 1 and no more than 10 years in prison if aggravated. The average punishment for aggravated assault was just under 2 years in 2005.
- Theft/burglary and aggravated theft/burglary: varies from a fine to a 1-year-and-6-month custodial sentence. If the offense meets the conditions of an aggravated theft or burglary, the sentence goes up to 4 months to 4 years in prison.
- Serious drug offense: varies from 1 to 10 years in prison. In 2005 the average sentence was a little more than 3 years.

Prison

The imprisonment act was renewed on October 1, 2006. Five regional prisons were established. All prisoners begin their sentence in the regional prison of their residential location. A personal needs and risk assessment is made to measure the factors that have contributed to the development of the convict's criminality and the required level of security. The convicts must be placed in institutions near their homes to preserve relationships between inmates and their families. Other factors that are taken into account are age, gender, health, number of convictions, previous offenses, the convict's own preference, and possibilities to take part in productive activities while incarcerated. A convict can be placed directly into an open prison, if he or she is serving a conversion of a fine or less than one year's sentence and commits to sobriety.

There are in total 26 prisons in Finland, of which four are open. The largest prison is the Turku prison, which houses approximately 350 inmates. Inmates of all kinds are placed in the Turku prison, from juveniles and first timers to those serving life imprisonment, as well as people serving a fine conversion sentence.

In 2007, there were 3,551 prisoners on the average, out of which 7 percent were women and 9 percent foreign nationals. At the beginning of the 1950s Finland had about 200 prisoners per 100,000 inhabitants, while the figures in Denmark, Norway, and Sweden were around 50. By the beginning of the 1990s the prisoner rates in Finland had decreased to the Nordic level, which had during the years remained rather stable (about 60 prisoners per 100,000). The number of prisoners was lowest in 1999 (2,743 persons incarcerated on the average), and since 1999, it increased until 2005 (3,888 persons). The changes in the prisoner rates can partly be traced to changes in legislation. Most law reforms from the 1960s up to the beginning of the 1990s were launched to decrease the number of prisoners (more than 25 law reforms). However, from the middle of the 1990s, the punishments for assault, rape, and drug-related crimes increased.

In 2006 and 2007, the number of prisoners has been slightly lower than in the antecedent years. The reasons for the decline have been the decrease in theft convictions, while violence has not increased. At the same time the number of default prisoners has decreased. During the recent years, about 35 percent of the prison sentences up to eight months have been converted to community service. The number of community service sentences has been approximately 3,700 per year, and the share of successfully completed sentences has been about 80 percent. One-half of the crimes leading to community service were aggravated drunken driving cases.

Exchange and Extradition of Prisoners

Sentences given in other Nordic countries can be put into practice in Finland, if requested by the officials of the country. Similarly a Finnish custodial sentence can be transferred to another country. The transfer must be accepted by the officials of the sentencing country as well as the sentenced person. In 2007 Finland received 109 convicts from other Nordic countries and gave out 56. Extraditions to other countries are arranged by the International Department of the Ministry of Justice. The requirements for extradition are the acceptance of both legal parties, as well as the convict, and the nationality of the receiving country. Since 2001, it has been possible to extradite a sentenced person without his or her own agreement. It is possible in cases where the convict is avoiding going into prison or in cases of banishment.

Work and Education While Incarcerated

Approximately 40 percent of the prison population takes part in employment. About half of them work in maintenance and other activities related to the everyday running of the prison. Another half are employed in the production of goods sold in the prison shops and over the Internet. The prisons collaborate with local schools to provide teaching in both general knowledge and practical skills. It is not stated on the certificate that the degree was accomplished in prison. In 2007, a total of 1,737 inmates participated in education while incarcerated. One-third of them were heading for a vocational degree and almost as many for a high school diploma. Most of the teaching was arranged within the institution, but in some cases the inmates were granted the permission to take part in education outside the prison.

Keeping in Touch with the World Outside

An inmate can be awarded permission to make phone calls outside of the prison. The phone calls can be tapped in case there is a suspicion of misuse, but both the recipient and the caller must be informed about it. The inmates are allowed to exchange letters without any quantitative restrictions. They can be searched for illegal substances or read for security reasons. Friends and relatives are allowed to spend time with the prisoners during specified visiting hours. The prisons provide an apartment for family visits, for the prisoners to meet their loved ones in a more homelike environment. Family meetings are not monitored, therefore, the visitors must meet security requirements.

A prisoner can be granted a temporary leave after two-thirds of the sentence has been spent or if there are special circumstances. The reliability of the inmate is assessed and in some cases a chaperone (guard) is appointed for the duration of the leave. The maximum length of a leave is in total three days to two months.

Markku Heiskanen and Anna Vuorelainen

Further Reading

The European Institute for Crime Prevention and Control (HEUNI): www.heuni.fi.

Joutsen, Matti, Raimo Lahti, and Pasi Pölönen. (2001). *Crime and Justice Systems in Europe and North America: Finland.* Helsinki: The

European Institute for Crime Prevention and Control (HEUNI).

Lappi-Seppälä, Tapio. (2007). "Penal Policy in Scandinavia." In *Crime, Punishment and Politics in Comparative Perspective,* edited by Michael Tonry, pp. 217–295. Chicago: University of Chicago Press.

France

Legal System: Civil
Murder: Medium
Burglary: Low
Corruption: Low
Human Trafficking: Low
Prison Rate: Medium
Death Penalty: No
Corporal Punishment: No

Background

The main features of the French criminal justice system were established at the beginning of the 19th century through the Napoleonic codes. Three court levels (*cour d'assises, tribunal correctionnel,* and *tribunal de police*) correspond to three degrees of seriousness of offenses. For each level, there are specific rules about criminal investigation and proceedings. There have been many legal changes over the past two centuries concerning these rules but the dominant role of the public prosecutor remains. The police are made up mainly by the *Police nationale* and the *Gendarmerie nationale* but also of other public administrations for some specific offenses (customs, tax department, Department of Labor, for instance).

From the beginning of the 1980s, legal changes have become more and more frequent under the pressure of insecurity and political debates. Repeated modifications to the Code of Criminal Proceedings have resulted in a reinforcement of the influence of the police role in judicial decisions through the extension of police officers' powers (identity control, police data files, assistant police officers).

Crime

Classification of Crimes

According to the French Penal Code, criminal offenses fall into three categories depending on their seriousness. Felonies (*crimes* in French) are judged by *cours d'assises* (assises courts) where a popular jury sits. They are punishable by a prison term of 10 years to life. Misdemeanors (*délits*) are judged by *tribunaux correctionnels* (criminal courts) punishable by up to 10 years in prison or a fine of more than €1,500 (US$1,885). Petty offenses (*contraventions*) are judged by *tribunaux de police* (police courts) punishable by a fine.

Petty offenses are themselves divided into five classes from the first one (maximum fine of €38) to the fifth class punishable by a fine of €750 to €1,500 (US$942 to $1,885). These fifth class petty offenses and misdemeanors are prosecuted in the same way even if they are not judged by the same jurisdiction. They are recorded in the national criminal file. Other petty offenses from the first to the fourth class are also legally considered as criminal offenses but they are dealt with in a simplified way, often following administrative paper proceedings (set fines, penal orders). Some of them are breaches of the criminal code (battery, insults, slight deterioration) and may involve a victim, but most are traffic offenses and other kinds of breaches of specialized legislations (labor, health and environmental laws).

A general classification of offenses is as follows:

- Felonies (*crimes*): Homicide (*meurtre, assassinat, coups mortels*), rape, armed robbery.
- Misdemeanors (*délits*): Assault, threat, sexual assault, unintentional homicide, unintentional injury causing work disability over three months, theft (aggravated or simple), fraud, breach of trust, embezzlement, forgery, serious criminal damage, drunk driving, driving license–related offenses, drug consumption, possession, trafficking, firearms offenses, undeclared work, illegal immigration.
- Petty offenses fifth class (*contraventions de cinquième classe*): Minor assault, unintentional injury causing work disability less than

three months, minor criminal damage, trucking offenses, speed limit serious offenses.

Drug Offenses

In France, consuming any kind of prohibited drug (including cannabis) is a misdemeanor punishable by a prison term of one year or a fine. But, in principle, the priority is to require medical treatment of addicted persons. Drug trafficking is basically a misdemeanor punishable by longer prison sentences up to 10 years. Some kinds of organized international trafficking are legally considered as felonies and may receive longer sentences but, after complex judicial inquiries, very few cases end up in a judgment by a *cour d'assises*. France also adopted the European rules about the control and the repression of money laundering. They are enforced mainly for drug trafficking.

Crime Statistics

For a long time, police statistics, including cases reported to and recorded by the *Police Nationale* and *Gendarmerie Nationale* (the two main bodies acting as criminal police), have been the only statistical measurement of crime. Annual results are published each year by the Ministry of Interior including figures about offenses recorded (petty offenses and traffic offenses are excluded), clearance rates by offenses, offenders with a breakdown by gender, age (minor or adult), and citizenship (French citizen or foreigner), and also figures about the use of police custody. This situation has changed now since crime victim surveys are regularly conducted. In some cases, such as burglary, the two measures are similar, but in others there are considerable discrepancies.

The table below shows the number of offenses recorded by the police for the year 2007. In principle, from a legal point of view, there is no difference between attempts and completed offenses and police statistics include attempts. Homicide is the only offense type for which the number of completed offenses is collected. In this table assault leading to death is included with completed homicide.

Homicide	2,333
Of which completed	1,168
Bodily injury	228,675
Rape	10,946
Sexual assault	13,754
Robbery	116,978
Theft total	1,847,247
Of which motor vehicle theft	231,875
Of which burglary	336,240
Of which domestic burglary	174,707
Fraud	181,020
Drug offenses total	163,297
Of which trafficking	6,131
Offenses against immigration law	131,351
Total	**2,695,601**

As can be seen, the number of recorded offenses against property is far higher than the number of offenses against persons. Their long-term trends are also quite different. During the 1970s and 1980s, recorded thefts were growing quickly and recorded personal offenses were stable. From the mid-1980s, a regular significant increase in bodily injury and sexual assault appeared contrasting with fluctuations for property offenses followed by a clear decrease at least for burglary, motor vehicle theft, and other thefts in or from a car. Since 1995, this decrease is also shown by national crime victims' surveys, the situation being less clear for personal theft because the surveys do not allow an accurate breakdown of incidents among theft without violence, robbery and assault without theft, at least before 2005.

The rise in reported and recorded bodily injury shown by police statistics during the last 20 years may reflect changes in perception about violence and safety, in reporting and recording practices, and moreover from changes in legal categorization of bodily injury. Recorded homicides do not follow this trend. After a sharp increase between 1972 and 1984, they have been decreasing until 2007, with only some limited occasional upward movements. Since victimization surveys do not yield evidence for a significant variation in serious bodily injury, this may be due to changes in recording practices. For example, new tough official guidelines to police forces and prosecution services may have resulted in more recorded cases and more convictions for domestic violence.

Police statistics also show a growing number of offenses without individual victims: drug offenses, illegal entries of foreigners, public order offenses. For these offenses, levels and trends in recorded cases reflect variations in criminal law enforcement even if there are some independent sources also affecting changes. When counting offenses, the proportion of these cases resulting mainly from police control and investigation represents only about 10 percent of the total. But the number of *offenders* is proportionally quite higher, about one-third of the total. This is the consequence of a very low clearance rate for thefts, which still represent the main part of recorded crime (53% in 2007) but a limited proportion of offenders (20%). The shift in recorded crime from thefts to personal offenses and offenses detected by the police produces a significant increase in the number of offenders handled to the prosecution services.

Finding of Guilt

In 2007, about 470,000 cases were sent to the criminal courts by the public prosecutors for a normal judgment. Among these, only 2,450 were judged by *cours d'assises* (felonies) after a judicial inquiry conducted by the examining magistrate (a compulsory phase for felonies). Most of them were judged by *tribunaux correctionnels* (misdemeanors), sometimes also after the examining magistrate's involvement (optional) but usually directly after a short preliminary inquiry by the police. The global proportion of cases involving the examining magistrate for felonies and misdemeanors is decreasing (6% in 2007).

Direct summons are also the normal way for a judgment by *tribunaux de police* for petty offenses of the fifth class. But, for these petty offenses and for less serious misdemeanors (mainly traffic offenses), the public prosecutor can get a decision from a court without a hearing (penal orders mainly). Since 2004, they also have the opportunity to propose a court sentence or a kind of sanction to the offenders who admit their guilt. They also can avoid going to court by proposing to defendants any kind of "alternative" solution among the disposals that appeared in the Code of Criminal Procedure after 1970 and are still in expansion. And, last but not least, French public prosecutors have the legal possibility to drop cases not only for factual or technical reasons, but also in application of the expediency principle (see below). French prosecutors have in fact a key position in the French criminal justice system, not only regarding their role during the treatment of each case but also by selecting which cases will be prosecuted and along which paths in application of national or local guidelines.

Regular Court Proceedings

Before the trial by a *cour d'assises* of a person charged with felony, the examining magistrate conducts a judicial inquiry. During this period police officers are investigating under the supervision of this magistrate—a judge from the bench—and not under supervision of the public prosecutor. This feature seems to maintain the French procedure within an inquisitorial scheme but in practice judicial inquiry has become the procedural framework where accused persons have more rights. They have access to the written file as soon as they are accused or even before: the examining judge must involve any hypothetical offender whose name appears in the police report or in victim's complaint as *témoin assisté* (assisted witness). Assisted witnesses and accused persons will get the assistance of their personal advocate or can request for the automatic appointment of an advocate. Under personal resources conditions, they will receive financial help for their defense.

Accused persons have the right to ask for some specific police investigation, the hearing of witnesses, or to contest experts' reports. Their position could be comparable to the prosecutor's one: the examining magistrate can refuse these demands and the accused person or the prosecutor can appeal from such a refusal. The major difference is, of course, that the accused person is often in pretrial detention.

Cours d'assises verdicts are given by a popular jury (9 members) and three professional judges after long hearings. Since the jury was not involved during the judicial inquiry, all its findings must be summed up orally, the public prosecutor as well as the counsel for the defense calls in witnesses, experts, and even police officers who participate in the investigation. Victims joining the case on civil ground also play an important role. The court (jury and judges) decides whether the offender is guilty and sets the sentence. Since 2001, this decision (guilty and sentence) can be reviewed by an appeal assises court with a larger jury (12 members). As for other court decisions, the public prosecutor may appeal from a first judgment and the appeal court is not limited by the decision in the first instance. According to statistics related to the period 2001–2005, 23 percent of first *cours d'assises* decisions were reviewed. Among those who appeal after being found guilty in the first instance, 5 percent were discharged by the appeal court. But among those who were discharged after the first trial (representing 6% of the total number of appeals), 57 percent were found guilty following an appeal from the public prosecutor.

For misdemeanors proceedings can also take a long time if the case is transmitted to the examining magistrate before trial. Prosecutors will have to choose this path for complex and/or serious cases. The rights of accused persons are basically the same during the judicial inquiry but in general the trial will not be so long. The *tribunal correctionnel* includes three professional judges, at least when the maximum penalty is more than five years' imprisonment. Even in this case, hearings are normally shorter than for felonies and the court will get some evidence about the case directly from the written file.

At prosecutor's level, one reason to transfer a case of misdemeanor to the examining magistrate is to get the possibility of maintaining the offender in pretrial detention. This is possible when the maximum penalty incurred is three years' imprisonment.

Besides these long proceedings, accused persons can be prosecuted on the very fast summary trial track (*comparution immediate*). On this track a person may be tried within 2 days of his or her arrest by the police when the case has been handed over to the public prosecutor service. If the accused person asks for a delay or if some procedural supplement is required, the trial will be delayed for a maximum of 2 months and the court can issue a committal order. With this possible pretrial detention, such a summary trial for misdemeanors appears as an alternative to proceedings starting at the examining magistrate level, and actually during the last 20 years, the ministerial guidelines for prosecutors ask them to choose the fast track whenever possible.

Apart from these two solutions allowing pretrial detention, the normal way to prosecute misdemeanors and petty offenses of the fifth class is a direct summons following a preliminary investigation conducted by the police. Prosecutors still have an important role since the police forces investigate under their legal responsibility. Police power is more limited in this case but some procedural acts are allowed when offenders are arrested for flagrant violations (*flagrante delicto*). Such a possibility is widely used in practice and involves many road traffic offenses as well as less serious personal and property offenses for which the prosecutor will not ask for an unsuspended sentence.

From 2002, new simplified proceedings involving a judge and the extension of the existing simplified proceedings (penal order) are aimed at reaching court decisions (convictions) without full trials. In 2008, prosecutors have a wide range of solutions available. These include the following:

- Court decisions without hearings.
- Paper proceedings. For petty offenses, including the fifth class, the penal order (*ordonnance pénale*) was implemented in 1972. The prosecutor formulates a written recommendation to the judge, using a standard form. If the judge agrees and signs the order, it is sent to the accused. The offender can object to the decision and ask for a public hearing. Otherwise, the offender is viewed as consenting to the prosecutor's decision and the penal order will be enforced like an ordinary sentence.
- Admission of guilt. A specific kind of guilty plea was introduced in the French Code of Criminal Procedure in 2004 for misdemeanors punished by a principal penalty of a fine or a prison sentence not exceeding five years. The accused person will be heard by the prosecutor

who will suggest a penalty. The prosecutor's proposal is made in the presence of the offender's advocate. Offenders cannot wave this right to be assisted. Offenders who refuse prosecutors' proposals are prosecuted in a normal way. When the defendants accept the prosecutor's proposal, the final decision is made by the court. In 2007, the annual number of cases treated in this way (50,000) was slightly above the number of cases following the fast summary trial track (46,000).

Alternative Disposals

The French *Composition Pénale*

This procedure stipulates that the prosecutor may recommend an alternative to the normal penalty, such as fines, confiscation, immobilization of the vehicle for no more than 6 months, suspension of the driver's license for no more than 4 months, unpaid work for no more than 60 hours, and miscellaneous other measures involving prohibitions or obligations. This is sanction which, if accepted, would avoid prosecution. The offender must explicitly admit to guilt.

Other Alternative Disposals

Other alternative proceedings first appeared in 1970 to avoid prosecution of drug users. The measure was an order to undergo treatment, issued by the prosecutor only, but implemented in collaboration with the health services. If the person subjected to that order complies with the minimum medical requirements, the prosecutor does not institute prosecution for what is still, to this day (2008), a misdemeanor punishable by a one-year prison term. After some local experiences, the penal mediation for adults and reparation for juveniles were added in 1993. To get the offender to engage in a process also involving the victim, a person or an accredited nonprofit organization is designated by the prosecutor and the encounters involved normally take place outside the courthouse, in a *maison de justice.* These disposals rose constantly until 2004, but they now seem to follow an opposite trend. Since they have been frequently used for less serious violence (but repeated, in particular, within the family), the decrease can be seen as a consequence of more severe ministerial guidelines about this type of offense.

Dropping for Expediency

Simple drops "when justified by the particular circumstances surrounding the acts committed" (the expediency principle) have not yet disappeared even if they have been reduced. The most important decrease during the last 10 years appears for drops grounded on the low seriousness of the damage or of the trouble. Even for less serious cases, ministerial guidelines now enjoin prosecutors to choose a "penal response" among the other disposals. One of the key indicators of local prosecutors' efficiency is the global proportion of cases receiving a "penal response" among those that can be prosecuted. Simple drop is the only category of decision not counted as a "penal response." Moreover, to calculate a rate of "penal response," technical drops are not taken into account. Most of these are cases where the offender remains unknown (about 60% of all recorded cases in prosecution services).

Juveniles

The broad principles of criminal proceedings are applicable to juveniles but a specific law (the 1945 *Ordonnance*) calls for the intervention of specialized courts competent for judging offenders who were under age 18 when the offense was committed. The judge must prefer educational measures, and the maximum sentences incurred are shorter. Prosecutorial proceedings are also of a particular nature: the examining magistrate phase is compulsory, even if it is usually entrusted to the juvenile court judge. Delays may now be imposed on the judge for appearance in court and the prosecutor's role has been reinforced over the last decade. In the largest courts, prosecution sections specialized in dealing with cases involving juveniles work with the educational agencies in charge of conducting rapid socio-educational investigations for the juvenile court. These are compulsory whenever the prosecutor hands a juvenile over to the court and considers summoning the person shortly or issuing a committal order. The principle of a systematic penal response to the least serious kinds of delinquency was put into action sooner for juveniles, producing a considerable increase in the number of cases transmitted to a juvenile court judge. However, the most important change during this period has been the development of measures decided by the prosecutor alone. Court decisions without hearing are not available for juveniles.

Crime Trends

Between 1998 and 2007, the alternatives to proceedings and court decisions without hearings grew from 20 percent to 55 percent of all decisions. Simple drops decreased from 31 to 11 percent. The growing part of court decisions without hearing did not produce significant changes in the total proportion of cases transmitted to the courts (about 53%), but the proportion of normal judgments decreased from 49 to 34 percent. In absolute figures, whereas treated cases increased by 23 percent from 1.13 to 1.4 million, "normal" court proceedings were reduced by 15 percent from 552,000 to 470,000. But this trend did not produce a decrease in convictions counted in the national criminal record, which in 2007 remained at 685,335 for all offenses. These statistics reflect the stronger role of prosecution services since the new disposals give them a major role in the choice of the measures and sanctions.

Punishment

Types of Punishment

According to the Penal Code, different categories of crime receive different punishment. Basically, felonies are punished with criminal imprisonment (*réclusion criminelle*), ranging from a 15-year term to life sentence. Misdemeanors are defined according to the maximum penalty fixed by the law (imprisonment not exceeding 10 years or a fine of €1,500 [US$1,885] or more). Petty offenses are punished by a fine not exceeding €1,500. But the Penal Code and specific laws add a great variety of other penalties or allow the court to choose milder sentences. In case of reconviction for the same type of crime (recidivism), the maximum penalty is in general doubled. Since 2007, for some crimes minimum penalties have been introduced for recidivists (roughly one-third of the maximum), but courts are allowed to choose milder sentences according to the cases and the offenders' personal situation. When offenders are reconvicted after two previous convictions related to the same type of offense, courts are bound to the minimum penalty unless they show exceptionally high guarantees for their rehabilitation.

Apart from prison and fine, the available types of sanctions for misdemeanors are day-fine (fine converted into imprisonment if not paid), community service, citizenship course, and diverse penalties entailing forfeiture or restriction of rights. The last ones are linked to the committed crime (for instance, suspension of a driving license, confiscation, prohibition for a fixed term to exercise some professional or social activity, etc.) and the list may be extended when the law mentions some additional penalty for a specific offense. Courts can use one of them as a main sanction rather than prison or fine. This mechanism, known as substitute penalties, is also possible for petty offenses.

Prison and fine sentences may be suspended. Such sentences will not be enforced if the convicted persons do not commit within a period of five years any felony or misdemeanors leading to an unsuspended sentence entailing the revocation of the suspension. In addition to "ordinary" suspended prison sentences, probation appears in the French system as a condition for some suspended sentences. For these suspended prison sentences with supervision, the court can impose a wide variety of supervision measures and special obligations. For instance, convicted persons will have to exercise a professional activity or follow professional training, undergo medical treatment, make up for the damage caused by the offense, and so forth. Some obligations already appeared in the list of additional or substitute penalties. The difference is that they are linked to a suspended prison sentence that can be enforced when convicted persons do not comply with these obligations. Even community service can be imposed as a condition for suspended prison sentences. All suspended sentences but the last one can be combined with an unsuspended sentence (partially suspended sentences).

A prison guard walks inside the new Bourg-en-Bresse Prison, near Lyon, France, during a visit organized for the press, February 4, 2010. The prison can hold up to 690 inmates. (AP Photo/Laurent Cipriani)

Besides all these available type of sanctions, the court may exempt from penalty a convicted person where it appears that the damage caused has been made good and that the public disturbance generated by the offense has ceased.

With such a complexity of legal rules, it is not possible to give a precise quantitative picture about the actual sentencing practice. The usual way to describe it is to count "principal sanctions" only according to a legal order among sanctions. When a convicted person is sentenced to several sanctions, the most severe one only appears. Partially suspended sentences are counted with unsuspended sentences.

According to the Ministry of Justice annual report from the national criminal record, for adults and for the total of criminal offenses, fines are the most frequent sanctions (37.9% in 2006), reflecting the dominant part of traffic offenses. For other offenses fines are not so frequent. Long-term imprisonment is almost the only applicable sanction for felonies such as intentional homicide (96.5%) and rape (96.5%). But unsuspended imprisonment also comes first for drug trafficking (56.8%) and theft (40.5%). Suspended custodial sanctions with supervision (French form of probation) take a significant proportion for sexual assault (26%) and bodily injury (14.5%). They are also frequently used for drug-addicted convicted persons, including alcohol.

When minors are convicted they receive milder sanctions. For very young offenders (above 13 this is compulsory) or first-time offenders, the court favors educational measures that are the most frequent outcome of a criminal judgment for minors. For less serious cases, this decision is made by a single judge. Educational measures include supervision by social workers and full-time housing in youth centers. But the social concern for juvenile delinquency and the general climate about insecurity has led successive governments to add to the traditional educational centers some new measures, including more freedom restrictions. Known as "closed centers," their development did not reduce the frequency of unsuspended imprisonment among all sanctions and measures.

Prison

The total number of places in the 195 French prisons was 50,610 on January 1, 2008, as defined by administrative standards assessing their capacity. On the same day, the total prison population, excluding 2,927 persons under penitentiary legal responsibility but not staying in prison (electronic monitoring, for instance), was 61,076. These figures include all overseas territories (overseas departments and overseas communities). The average prison density per 100 places is 120.7, but this rate varies significantly among the different categories of facilities.

The *maisons centrales* hold convicted detainees for long-term sentences. The notion of long term is not very accurate. Legally, all convicted detainees sentenced for five years or over could be held in these facilities. But, as the number of these detainees has been increasing for decades, the corresponding 2,060 places are now managed according to security goals. The number of detainees is still lower (1,872) to avoid difficulties coming from overcrowding.

The other facilities for convicted detainees (*centres de détention*) represent the most important part for these detainees with 16,015 places. But, for the same security reasons, the penitentiary administration made the choice to limit the consequences of excess numbers of prisoners. On January 1, 2008, there were 15,446 staying in these *centres de détention*. The prison density is 96.5 per 100 places; that is a normal situation. But one cannot conclude that all convicted detainees (44,279 on January 1, 2008) are held in normal conditions since only 39 percent were staying in a *maison centrale* or a *centre de détention*.

The situation is not the same in the *maisons d'arrêt,* which were originally devoted to pretrial detention. Convicted detainees with short-term sentences (less than one year) are now also held there and even some detainees with long-term sentences. Pretrial detainees (16,797 detainees without final sentence on January 1, 2008) represent about 39 percent of the total number of detainees in the *maisons d'arrêt.* All these persons (42,860 on January 1, 2008) were put in for a capacity of 31,582—that is an average rate equal to 135.7 percent. But official reports point that in 62 prisons, the density was over 150 percent. The biggest French prisons fall in this category. Two of them are located in the Paris suburbs (Fleury-Merogis, 2,855 places, and Fresnes, 1,543 places). The third one is in Marseille (Les Baumettes, 1,288 places). On September 1, 2008, 7,922 detainees were staying in these three prisons for 5,686 places.

The consequences of this abnormal situation in the *maisons d'arrêt* have been pointed out for many years by the European Committee for the Prevention of Torture and Inhuman or Degrading Treatment or Punishment (Council of Europe) and by some NGOs. The French government response focuses on a program adopted in 2002 and planning new prisons for 2012 (13,200 places). Whereas some very old prisons will be necessarily closed before the end of this program, many commentators consider that France persists in a wrong choice, after the last two extension programs. In these overcrowded prisons, not only are housing conditions quite below ordinary standards, but most detainees cannot have access to work, education, or training. For instance, whereas legal rules provide that any (pretrial or convicted) detainee can work in prison, only 32 percent had this opportunity in 2008 for the *maisons d'arrêt* compared with 51 percent in other facilities.

Over the long term it appears that increases in prison population rate are not constant. From the mid-1970s to the beginning of the 1980s, the increase was indeed regular and prison population rose by 65 percent between January 1, 1976, and

January 1, 1988. After 1996, prison population began to decrease. From 1981 to 1996, the prison population (stock) has been growing but the annual number of entries was decreasing. The stock increase was the consequence of longer prison sentences. From 1996 to 2001, this lengthening was not strong enough to compensate the downward effect of a still decreasing entry flow. At the end of 2001, a sudden turn-up occurred and during the year 2002, the annual number of entries was 22 percent higher than in 2001. Between January 1, 2002, and January 1, 2007, the absolute number increased by 10,000. During the same time, only 1,000 new prison places were created.

Between January 1, 2001, and January 1, 2003, the number of convicted persons detained for sentences less than three years increased by 29 percent. During the same period, the number of convicted detainees with sentences of three years and above has been slightly decreasing. The number of pretrial detainees also moved upward between 2001 and 2003 (+31% on January 1), but after 2004, the trend was again downward whereas the total prison population was still significantly increasing. These changes are consistent with the growing use of fast summary trial and that changes occurred in the way sentences are enforced.

Two additional features of the French system need some explanation. The first one is the regular use of amnesties and collective pardons, at least until 2002, as a periodical solution to prevent the negative consequences of prison overcrowding. All the major decreases occurring in the total prison population over time are the direct consequence of amnesties following elections (1974, 1981, 1988). Though amnesties also occurred after the 1995 and 2002 elections (but not after the last one in 2007), their consequences on prison population were quite limited since only very short sentences (less than three months) were expunged and convicted persons probably would not have been in prison anyhow. The effects of collective pardons decided by the president of the republic every year (usually on July 14, a national holiday) were significant during the 1990s, most of the prisoners having their sentences reduced by some amount ranging from a few days to several months, in addition to the normal legal sentence reduction. During the last years, these collective decisions have been criticized because of their alleged effects, and the number of cases excluded from pardon became larger and larger. The main point is that they could undermine any attempt to achieve delinquents' rehabilitation by individual sentence adjustment decided by the judge in charge of sentence enforcement.

The second feature is the French sentencing system itself. The general rule is that sentences must fit the personal situation of convicted persons. The courts' decision must follow this principle but sentence enforcement also includes a wide range of disposals to achieve the same goal. All probation sentences (suspended prison sentences with supervision) are adapted to the personal situation of the convicted person, for instance. When convicted persons get an unsuspended sentence less than one year and were not detained before their judgment, they must be heard by the judge in charge of sentence enforcement who may propose an alternative solution (electronic monitoring) or a partial release, for instance.

Since 2005, prison overcrowding has reached such a high level that the official response to the critics about detainees' situation is to promote the development of prison sentences enforced without staying in prison. Electronic monitoring is the most frequent solution to keep the "detainees" out of prison and their number increased by 148 percent within two years (September 2006–September 2008). But the absolute number remains low: approximately 3,300 persons were on prison calendar without staying in prison on September 1, 2008; that is about 5 percent of all persons on the calendar. It is low in comparison to the 13,000 missing places in the 136 prisons showing a density rate above 100 percent.

Bruno Aubusson de Cavarlay

Further Reading

Aubusson de Cavarlay, Bruno. (2006). "The Prosecution Service Function within the French Criminal Justice System." In *Criminal Justice*

Systems: The Rise of Prosecutorial Power across Europe, edited by Jörg-Martin Jehle and Marianne Wade, pp. 185–206. Berlin: Springer.

Bastard, Benoît, and Christian Mouhanna. (2007). *Une justice dans l'urgence: Le traitement en temps réel des affaires pénales*. [A Justice System in Emergency: The Real Time Processing of Criminal Cases] Paris: PUF.

Kensey, Annie. (2007). *Prison et récidive* [Prison and Recidivism]. Paris: Armand Colin.

Mucchielli, Laurent, and Philippe Robert, eds. (2002). *Crime et sécurité: L'état des savoirs* [Crime and Security: Current State of Knowledge]. Paris: La Découverte.

Penal issues, the CESDIP Bulletin: http://www.cesdip.fr/spip.php?rubrique30.

Zauberman, Renée, ed. (2008). *Victimisation and Insecurity in Europe: A Review of Surveys and Their Use.* Brussels: VUB.

Germany

Legal System: Civil
Murder: Low
Burglary: Low
Corruption: Low
Human Trafficking: Low
Prison Rate: Medium
Death Penalty: No
Corporal Punishment: No

Background

The Federal Republic of Germany lies in the center of Europe and is a member of the European Union. Its nine neighbors are the Netherlands, Belgium, Luxembourg, France, Switzerland, Austria, the Czech Republic, Poland, and Denmark. Within an area of 357,020 square kilometers (137,838 square miles), the population is about 82 million, 10 percent of whom are non-German citizens; about 20 percent are or stem from immigrants, who arrived mostly in the 1960s or 1970s and then in a second wave in the 1990s of the last century.

The Federal Republic of Germany was established after World War II in 1949, originally only on the territory of West Germany (including West Berlin), but after the "reunification" in 1990, also including the territory of the former socialist German Democratic Republic (East Germany). According to the Constitution (the so-called Basic Law), the 16 federal *Länder* are not only provinces, but like states endowed with their own powers. The federal states have important jurisdiction, especially in the areas of education and cultural policy in their entirety as a manifestation of their "cultural sovereignty." They are also responsible for local government law, the police, and in general for the execution of federal legislation. The real strength of the federal states lies in their participation in the legislative process at the federal level through the second chamber of federal legislation, the Federal Council.

The federal constitutional bodies with primarily legislative functions are the Federal Parliament (*Bundestag*) and the Federal Council (*Bundesrat*). Executive responsibilities lie principally with the Federal Government (*Bundesregierung*), headed by the Federal Chancellor (*Bundeskanzler*). Judicial functions pertaining to the Constitution are performed by the Federal Constitutional Court (*Bundesverfassungsgericht*). The federation has its legislative powers in fields where it is necessary to have a uniform law for the whole country. The areas that fall into this category are, for example, foreign affairs, military, customs and taxes, traffic, civil and civil procedural law, and criminal and criminal procedural law.

German criminal procedure is fundamentally marked by the principle of legality and traditionally by the principle of mandatory prosecution, with the role of punishment reserved for the courts. The second main principle, the principle of material truth, means that the state is responsible for the investigation in finding the truth starting with the public prosecutor (PP) who has to search for evidence for prosecution as well as for exonerating evidence. At the court level he or she and the defense are not parties in the main proceedings, and the court itself has the full obligation *ex officio* to find the truth. This is usually called an inquisitorial system in contrast to the adversary character in common law countries.

Police

The police are assigned a supporting role in relation to the PP activities because the latter has no executing arm of its own. The police are organizationally answerable to the individual *Länder*'s ministries of the interior but made functionally subservient to the PP by law as far as the prosecution of offenses is concerned. The police can only take preliminary measures that cannot be delayed. Having carried these out, they are fundamentally required to inform the PP of their actions and to pass their records on to the latter so that the PP can decide how the investigations are to proceed. The police are also the executing organ during PP investigations. The law further assigns the PP auxiliary police officers (*Ermittlungspersonen*) with special powers and a closer relationship to the PP. In practice this difference is of little significance as almost all police officers are made *Ermittlungspersonen.* In relation to the prosecution of crimes, the police are viewed only as an organ serving the PP. In practice, however, German criminal procedure is a very different matter. Nowadays, the PP is by no means "ruler of the investigative stage" in most cases. In relation to less serious or mass crimes, this role has long been assumed by the police. They carry out investigations independently and only when these are finished is the file passed on to the PP, which is informed of the case in this way. Where the offense severity increases, so does the intensity of investigation. PP involvement is stronger here, at the same time, police independence wanes.

Crime

During the ancien régime, German criminal law was a mixture of common law principles (*jus commune*) and statutes of the many larger and often only tiny principalities and territories. Since the late 1700s and during the 1800s, most of the surviving principalities codified the criminal law in criminal codes. When the German Empire emerged in 1871, a new German Criminal Code (*Reichsstrafgesetzbuch*) was enacted, which largely resembled the criminal code of the Kingdom of Prussia of 1851. Despite all the dramatic shifts in German history since 1871, the Code of 1871 has remained in effect up to today.

The Criminal Code has undergone considerable revisions during its long history, for example, concerning the treatment of juveniles (14–17 years), the sanctions (the restrictive use of short prison terms and the introduction of day-fines), the scope of certain offenses (e.g., concerning sexual behavior), and so on. The major reforms of the Criminal Code have in particular changed the sanctions system to a great extent. The 1969 and 1975 reforms restricted short-term imprisonment, extended the scope of fines, moved to the day-fine system, and extended the suspended sentence and probation services. The 1990 reform of the Juvenile Justice Act extended diversion and community sanctions (mediation, social training courses, and community service orders), suspended sentences, and probation and reduced pretrial detention. The 1994 reform introduced mediation into the sentencing provisions. In several steps since 1997, the scope of the preventive measures, imposed besides or instead of punishment, especially preventive detention (after imprisonment), has been extended.

As far as the structure of offenses is concerned, a large number of offenses, previously considered criminal, were decriminalized in the 1970s and became offenses against order dealt with administratively. A large number of forms of behavior regarded as socially unacceptable fall into this category. There are two types of criminal offenses: misdemeanors (*Vergehen*) and crimes (*Verbrechen*). Crimes are punishable by a minimum of one year's imprisonment, misdemeanors by less.

During the last decades, modern forms of crimes have been introduced, such as money laundering, computer fraud, stalking or terrorist acts, and the penalties for violent and sexual crimes have been increased; especially rape and sexual assault have been redefined. Rape is defined as an aggravated form of a broader concept of sexual assault by means of force, threat, or using a helpless situation regardless of the gender and the marital status of the victim. Drug offenses include the whole range of production, trafficking, and selling, including the mere possession: Cases of mere consumption can be dismissed. Low forms of trafficking are seen as a misdemeanor. Aggravated circumstances lead to harsher penalties in three steps: not under one year, two years', and five years' imprisonment.

Crime Statistics

According to the German Police Crime Statistics of 2007, more than two-fifths of the detected cases are of theft. Serious offenses against the person such as homicide or offenses against sexual self-determination (sexual offenses) are relatively rare. For every 100,000 inhabitants, there are 4 homicides (including attempts), but almost 3,100 thefts, as can be seen in the following table:

Crimes	**Cases per 100,000 population**
Total crimes	7,635
Homicides	4
Sexual offenses	68
Bodily injury	665
Robbery, extortion resembling robbery, assault of a motor vehicle driver resembling robbery	64
Total theft	3,112
Theft under aggravating circumstances	1,515
Property offenses; forgery	1,375
Offenses under the Narcotics Act	302
Others	2,045

It should be noted that, in regard to total offenses, offenses against public order are excluded and traffic offenses, even if criminalized, are not counted in police statistics. From the beginning of the 1960s to the beginning of the 1990s, a tremendous increase of the crime rate took place: from about 3,000 to about 8,000 per 100,000 population. Since then figures have slightly decreased, due to the decrease of theft. But concerning violent offenses, there is the opposite trend: bodily injury has risen strongly over the last two decades, especially where young offenders are concerned.

Suspects

The suspect rates that are calculated only for German citizens show that 76 percent of all the suspects are men; women only account for almost one-quarter. As is to be expected, the vast majority of suspects are adults (21 and over). But the highest suspect rates are recorded for juveniles (14–17) and particularly young adults (18–20): of every 100,000 of the relevant age group, almost 12,000 of young male adults and more than 10,000 male juveniles, that is, roughly every 8 young adults and 1 in 10 juveniles, are on police records, which is the case for only 1 in 30 adults. However, it should be remembered that the crimes in which children and juveniles are mostly involved are generally less serious in nature, such as shoplifting, bicycle theft, or criminal damage, and that the vast majority of young suspects are only recorded once or during a short period of their lives.

Non-German suspects account for just 21 percent of all suspects; this is higher than their proportion of the population of approximately 9 percent. However, the different pattern of crime reporting in the population must be borne in mind here, as must the fact that the suspects include tourists, armed forces personnel and their families stationed in Germany, cross-border commuters, and persons staying illegally in Germany—none of whom are included in the population figures. Furthermore, the structure of this group is different from that of the German population (in terms of age, sex, and social structure).

Finding of Guilt

Prosecution

After the cases have been processed by the police, they have to be passed on to the PP even if no suspect has been found. The PP is also informed directly about certain cases, for example, because they are reported to it or it learns of them itself. As it is "in charge" of the investigation proceedings, the PP takes further steps to clear up the case and identify a suspect. The intention is to ascertain whether there is sufficient evidence against the accused for main proceedings to be opened, that is, a level of suspicion that makes a subsequent conviction likely.

If the investigations provide sufficient indications to assume that a criminal act has occurred and a suspect can be named, the PP will principally bring a charge against the accused at the relevant court. If it is a simple case that can be dealt with quickly, the PP can apply to the criminal judge or the *Schöffengericht* for "accelerated proceedings." In such cases, a formal charge will usually not be filed. In other simple cases, the PP can apply further for a penal order without previous trial. This simplified procedure, with no oral proceedings, makes it possible to deal with uncomplicated cases quickly. However, this approach cannot be applied to *Verbrechen* (offenses with a minimum punishment of a one-year prison sentence). Also, there are limits to the level of sanction that can be imposed in such proceedings: at most, this can be either a fine or a suspended custodial sentence of up to one year.

Penal orders and accelerated proceedings are not permitted in cases involving juveniles. Instead, the PP can apply for "simplified proceedings," as long as no period of custody in a young offender institution or measures to reform the offender or protect the public are likely. If no suspect is found, if the act is not criminal, or if there are other procedural impediments, for example, if the case falls under the statute of limitations, the PP will discontinue the proceedings.

The proceedings can also be terminated if the offender's guilt is of a minor nature and there is no public interest in prosecution. This termination can involve the imposition of certain conditions, such as financial redress for the injury caused by the act, the payment of a fine, the undertaking of community service, or, as of the year 2000, offender-victim

Defendant Sven K., center, faces photographers and TV crews in a courtroom in Munich, Germany, August 25, 2008. He is charged with armed theft during a money transport. (AP Photo/Matthias Schrader)

mediation. Furthermore, the PP can refrain from prosecution if the crimes involved are insignificant additional offenses compared with the main crime with which the accused is charged.

In the case of certain crimes (trespass, minor bodily injury, criminal damage, etc.), the PP can advise that a private prosecution be pursued if there is no public interest in prosecution; the injured party must then bring a charge himself or herself. This is not possible in cases involving juveniles. The approach taken by the PP in individual cases is recorded in the statistics of the courts and Public Prosecution Offices. In 2006 the PP at the regional courts and the local courts dealt with 4,876,989, and at the higher regional courts, with 3,267 investigative proceedings. Of a total of 5,770,785 persons, determination of their cases was as follows: public charge(s) 11.5 percent, application for a penal order 10.3 percent, conditional termination 4.4 percent, and other disposals 73.8 percent. The "other" ways of dealing with the case generally involve discontinuation because of insufficient evidence, unconditional disposals passing the proceedings on to another PP or—in the case of administrative offenses—to the administrative authority, or the recommendation that a private prosecution be brought.

Remand Custody

The PP can order coercive measures or apply for their imposition by a judge to secure the investigation. Such means can include the seizure of evidence, searches, measures for identification purposes and, the most intrusive, remand custody. Remand custody can only be ordered by a judge where the accused is strongly suspected of having committed the crime (i.e., it is very likely that he or she will be punished), where the detention is not disproportionate to the significance of the case and to the likely punishment, and there are grounds for remand custody, such as the accused's flight, the risk of flight, or the risk of evidence being tampered with. About 3 percent of all those judged in court were previously in remand custody; for females, the figure is only 1.1 percent. However, the detention rate fluctuates widely depending on the charge: it is particularly low in the case of traffic offenses, and particularly high in the case of homicides.

The suspect fleeing or the risk of flight is easily the main reason for imposing remand custody; there are far fewer cases where it is imposed because of a risk that evidence will be tampered with, that is, that evidence will be manipulated or witnesses influenced. There are even fewer cases where remand custody is imposed because of the seriousness of the crime or of the danger of recidivism in the case of sexual crimes or other serious crimes.

Courts

Once the charge has been filed by the PP, the court checks whether there are sufficient grounds to suspect the accused of the crime he or she is alleged to have committed and main proceedings can begin. Generally, the local court (*Amtsgericht*) is the court of first instance. If the crime is one where the punishment is not likely to be more than two years' imprisonment, the case is presided over by a single judge. If imprisonment of between two and four years is likely or an allegation of a *Verbrechen* (offenses with a minimum punishment of a one-year prison sentence) is to be heard, the case will normally come before a judge and two lay assistants (*Schöffengericht*). The regional court (*Landgericht*) is responsible for serious cases, and the Small Criminal Chamber at a regional court (*Strafkammer*) hears all cases in which imprisonment of more than four years or commitment to a psychiatric hospital or to preventive detention (postimprisonment) is to be expected. A court with three professional and two lay judges (*Schwurgericht*) hears particularly serious cases, above all, those resulting in a person's death. In exceptional cases, including crimes against the state, the Higher Regional Court (*Oberlandesgericht*) is responsible.

Appeals against judgments by the local court can be made to the Regional Court (Small Criminal Chamber), which will review the facts of the case. Instead of such an appeal (on the facts of the case), it is also possible to lodge an appeal with the Higher Regional Court on points of law regarding the ruling made in the first instance by the criminal judge or the *Schöffengericht*. Appeals on points of law can also be lodged against the appellate judgment by the Small Criminal Chamber at the Regional Court. If the court of first instance is the Grand Criminal Chambers at a Regional Court or the *Schwurgericht,* an appeal can be made on points of law to the Federal Court of Justice (in exceptional cases to the Higher Regional Court). If the court of first instance is the Higher Regional Court, appeal on points of law can only be made to the Federal Court of Justice. In all cases, an appeal on points of law can only be based on the argument that the judgment is based on a violation of the law.

There are special juvenile courts for cases against juveniles and young adult offenders. The distribution of responsibilities between the judge of a Juvenile Court (*Jugendrichter*), the Juvenile Court consisting of a judge and two lay assistants (*Jugendschöffengericht*), and the Juvenile Court Division (*Jugendkammer*) is governed by the Act on Juvenile Courts. If the only punishment is likely to be educative or disciplinary measures and the charge is filed with a criminal judge, the *Jugendrichter* is responsible. The *Jugendkammer* is primarily responsible in cases which (if they involved adults) would be heard by the *Schwurgericht.* However, the *Jugendkammer* also acts in cases involving the protection of young people, that is, crimes committed by adults who injure a child or a juvenile. Apart from that, cases against juveniles and young adult offenders are normally heard in the first instance by the *Jugendschöffengericht.*

In the juvenile court process, each person entitled to challenge a judgment has only one right of appeal: an appeal against judgments of a *Jugendrichter* or the *Jugendschöffengericht* regarding the facts of the case can be heard by the *Jugendkammer,* or an appeal on points of law can be made to the Higher Regional Court; an appeal on points of law can be made against judgments by the *Jugendkammer* to the Federal Court of Justice.

In 2006, the number of cases processed by local courts were as follows:

Criminal judge	518,554
Schöffengericht	41,298
Juvenile court judge	228,265
Jugendschöffengericht	61,628

The Criminal Division of Regional Courts processed 48,056 appeals, the Grand Criminal Division 11,978 cases, and the Juvenile Criminal Division 2,498 cases and 8,324 appeals. The Higher Regional Court processed 5,855 appeals and the Federal Court of Justice 3,326 appeals.

Rights of the Accused

The accused has the right to keep silence without negative consequences and to be supported by a defense lawyer; in serious cases or in cases of pretrial detention the court has to provide for a defense lawyer. The accused has to be informed about these rights from the very beginning of the investigative proceedings. Through his or her defense the accused is allowed to view the case files, and in main proceedings, he or she can interrogate witnesses and can ask the court to hear witnesses or order inquiries.

Victim Participation

The German Criminal Procedure Code has witnessed various changes in recent years to incorporate victim's interests. The most recent reform took place in 2004. The extent of victim participation legally provided for differs according to the seriousness of the offenses concerned.

First of all there is a group of offenses, the *Antragsdelikte* (application offenses) that will only be prosecuted if the victim requests this and that may well be dropped by the PP with a reference to private prosecution. The victim and close relatives may become joint plaintiffs in proceedings for particularly serious offenses. In these cases the victim has the possibility to suggest a prosecution at pretrial stage. As a joint plaintiff, the victim has participatory rights in the trial as well as a right to appeal and, in some cases, a right to a lawyer paid for by the state. Even if the victim decides not to participate as a joint plaintiff, this kind of victim has a positive right to be present during trial.

Furthermore the victim may file for joined proceedings in which he or she applies for civil damages and compensation to be judged in the course of criminal proceedings. These proceedings have been of little real importance in practice.

The victim also has a number of informational rights: he or she must be notified as to the date of main proceedings, of any decision not to bring the case to court, of the outcome of a trial, and of any measures involving the deprivation of liberty, that is, prison, committal, release, relaxation of or holiday from incarceration. If a case is dropped for evidential reasons, the victim can initiate proceedings to force a charge in more serious cases. The joint plaintiff victim can appeal against a court decision.

A victim has a general right to a lawyer and to be represented during criminal proceedings. Through his or her lawyer, he or she has a right to view case files and to be present at court and prosecutor interviews, provided this does not undermine the investigation. Criminal justice institutions are now obliged to inform the victim as soon as possible of his or her rights and the means of achieving them (e.g., to explain joined proceedings), as well as to indicate the potential for support through victim support organizations.

Punishment

The main punishments under general (i.e., adult) criminal law take the form of fines and prison sentences (with or without the sentence being suspended on probation). In certain cases, the law also permits additional penalties, such as a driving ban and/or a ban from holding public office. If the accused is sentenced to a prison sentence of up to two years, execution of the sentence can be suspended and the convicted person put on probation. In a period of probation to be determined by the court, the person sentenced should demonstrate that being sentenced was itself sufficient warning and that he or she will not commit any further crimes. At the same time, as the punishment is suspended, the negative effects of confinement are avoided, for example, that the individual is torn away from his or her previous life, work, and social contacts. In combination with suspending the sentence and imposing a period of probation, the court can impose conditions on the person sentenced (e.g., a fine) or issue instructions affecting his or her conduct, for example, he or she can be placed under the supervision of a probation officer for the period of probation. If the person sentenced reoffends during the probationary period, or if he or she fails to meet conditions or follow instructions, the suspension of the sentence can be revoked, meaning that he or she must now serve the prison sentence.

The longer the prison sentence, the more stringent are the preconditions for suspending the sentence and granting probation. Prison sentences of less than six months are suspended by the court and the individual put on probation if it is likely that he or she will not commit any further crimes without going to prison. Prison sentences of between six months and a year are suspended in the same way, unless it is necessary for the person to serve the sentence to preserve legal order. Prison sentences of between one and two years can be similarly suspended if, additionally, an overall assessment of the crime and the convict's character indicates special circumstances.

If the punishment cannot be suspended and the individual placed on probation, or if the suspension is revoked, for example, because the person has reoffended, the person must serve his or her sentence in a penal institution. After at least two-thirds of the term of imprisonment has been served, the remaining period is suspended and probation imposed—as long as the person agrees and this can legitimately be done in consideration of the interest of public safety. In exceptional cases, the remainder of the sentence can be suspended and probation imposed at an earlier stage, that is, once half of the term of imprisonment has been served. Similarly, the remainder of a sentence to life imprisonment can be suspended and probation imposed once 15 years have been served, if the particular gravity of the convicted offender's guilt does not necessitate his or her remaining in prison, and if the prognosis is favorable and the prisoner agrees.

In addition to the sanctions mentioned above, it is also possible for measures other than punishment to be imposed to reform the offender or protect the public (committal to a psychiatric hospital or institution for withdrawal treatment, preventive detention [postimprisonment], supervision of conduct, withdrawal of permission to drive, ban from the pursuit of certain occupations). Even if the person is acquitted due to lack of criminal responsibility, it may be possible for such measures to be imposed; for example, he or she can under certain conditions be committed to a psychiatric hospital or an institution for withdrawal treatment. These measures can be suspended on probation if there are special circumstances indicating that their objective can still be achieved.

In total 645,485 adults were sentenced under general criminal law in 2006. Of these, 19 percent were female (121,115). Easily the most frequent sentence imposed on adults is a fine, in 520,791 cases (or 81% of the total); in the other cases a prison sentence was imposed. Roughly two-thirds of the 124,694 prison sentences were suspended on probation, that is, 13 percent (87,112) of all sentences result in the person receiving a suspended sentence and being placed on probation, and 6 percent (37,582) are sent to prison without a suspension. With regard to the length of the prison sentences, most are under 12 months. One-third of the people are given short sentences of under 6 months and two-fifths are between 6 and 12 months; 16 percent are related to terms of between 1 and 2 years. The proportion of prison sentences that are suspended declines in line with the length of the term, but even for sentences of 1–2 years the proportion is above two-thirds. Seven percent of prison sentences are for terms of more than 2 years, and 1.4 percent of sentences are for more than 5 years, with 0.1 percent of prison sentences to life imprisonment.

Juveniles

In the case of juvenile offenders (14–17 years inclusive, children up to 13 years are not criminally responsible) and young adults (18–20 years inclusive) convicted under juvenile criminal law, the criminal justice system aims to educate the offender and provides for special sanctions: first, educative and disciplinary measures and, second, youth imprisonment with the possibility of suspension and probation. The imposition of additional legal consequences and measures to reform the offender and protect the public is only possible to a limited extent. A young adult offender is required to be processed under juvenile criminal law if he or she is like a juvenile in terms of his or her development or if the offense was a transgression of a juvenile nature.

The educative measures include the issuing of instructions and the requirement that the offender accept certain forms of educative assistance, that is, socio-educational support or in the form of residential accommodation with back-up support from social workers. These measures are not really intended to punish, but to promote the juvenile's upbringing in an educative dimension. For example, the instructions may refer to the place of residence, participation in a course of social training, work, or attempts to achieve offender-victim mediation.

In contrast, disciplinary measures are also intended as a sanctioning reaction. The juvenile is to be made aware of the injustice of his or her action, without this requiring youth imprisonment. Disciplinary measures include cautions, the imposition of conditions (reparations for the injury, apologies to the injured party, payment of a fine, work), and detention, which can range from a weekend to up to four weeks. Educative and disciplinary measures can be imposed simultaneously.

Youth imprisonment is the only real criminal punishment available under the Act on Juvenile Courts. There are differences compared with adult imprisonment rules. The length of the period is limited to between 6 months and 10 years. The judge imposes youth imprisonment when the criminal tendencies of the juvenile, which have become apparent as a result of his or her crime, indicate that educative or disciplinary measures will not suffice to reform the offender or when punishment is needed because of the seriousness of the offense. If it is not possible to ascertain with certainty during the main proceedings whether the criminal tendencies of the offender are such that youth imprisonment is actually needed, the judge will only pronounce the guilt of the juvenile. The decision as to whether a sentence to youth imprisonment should be imposed is suspended for a certain probationary period.

The proceedings can be dropped by the PP with the approval of the court and by the juvenile court itself (in 2006: 46,000 cases). Furthermore, the PP itself can decide to drop the case without referring to the court. These decisions can, where they are taken by the court or with the approval of the court, be linked to the imposition of certain conditions and instructions on the offender. In minor cases, it may be sufficient for other educative measures to be taken or introduced or for the offender to attempt to make good the injury suffered by the victim.

In 2006, 105,902 persons were convicted under juvenile criminal law. Nine-tenths of the juvenile and young adult offenders were male; one-tenth was female. In 84 percent of convictions educative and disciplinary measures were imposed, 10 percent of offenders were sentenced to youth imprisonment with the sentence suspended, and 6 percent were given a sentence to youth imprisonment without it being suspended.

Probation

The probation service's main task is to look after those offenders placed on probation. It also looks after persons whose conduct is subject to supervision. When the prison sentence is suspended, or the remainder of the sentence is suspended, the court can order that the offender be placed under the *supervision of a probation officer;* in the case of youth imprisonment this is obligatory. Other conditions (e.g., making good the injury caused, community service) or instructions (e.g., regarding place of residence, or regular reporting by the offender to the court or another agency) can also be imposed.

Supervision of conduct is one of the measures taken to reform the offender and protect the public. It is imposed when a sentence committing to an institution for withdrawal treatment or a psychiatric hospital is suspended or when continuing accommodation there is suspended, after a period of preventive detention (postimprisonment) has been served, or when the court expressly requires it for particular crimes. The most frequent case in practice is supervision of conduct following the full serving of a prison sentence of at least two years. The offender is then subject to the control and assistance of the supervisory agency and the probation officer. Supervision of conduct can also be linked to instructions. The office supervising the conduct monitors the behavior of the offender and compliance with any instructions.

The juvenile criminal justice system has a special feature. It is possible for the judge merely to declare the guilt of the juvenile in the main proceedings, but to leave open the decision as to whether to impose a prison sentence and to appoint a probation officer to supervise a period of probation. If, during that period, the bad behavior of the juvenile makes it clear that the offense was committed because of criminal tendencies, a prison sentence will be imposed. If this is not the case, the guilty verdict is extinguished after the probationary period has expired.

The probation officer assists and looks after the offender. With the approval of the court, he or she monitors compliance with the conditions and instructions. The period of probation either ends "successfully," with remission of the punishment or the end of supervision; or the court revokes the suspension of the sentence or of the remainder of the sentence under certain conditions—if the offender commits new crimes during the probationary period, seriously or continually violates conditions and instructions, or continually evades supervision by the probation officer.

The probation service keeps its own statistics. The number of probation orders recorded there is greater than the number of people subject to it. This is mainly because a single offender in court for several offenses in various trials can be placed on probation several times. Of a total of 174,207 probation orders in 2006, 21 percent of the probation orders in force on the fixed date result in accordance with juvenile criminal law, and 79 percent in accordance with adult criminal law. As the length of probation periods in accordance with juvenile criminal law is generally shorter than those in accordance with adult criminal law, the proportion of young probationers, who occupy the probation service personnel in the course of one year, is significantly higher.

Prison

Only a small proportion of those sentenced actually spend a period in prison: those sentenced to prison or to youth imprisonment without suspension, or those whose prison sentence was suspended but whose suspension was then revoked. In addition, there are those who are kept in preventive detention following a prison sentence. Finally, offenders sentenced to a fine end up in prison if they fail to pay their fine and have to serve a period of imprisonment instead.

However, the penal institutions also accommodate people not sentenced by the criminal courts: those in remand custody or those deprived of their freedom for other reasons. The latter include people in other judicially imposed forms of detention (e.g., under civil law—in very rare cases) and those in custody awaiting deportation (although the latter are not always housed in penal institutions).

Information about the prison system is to be found in the Federal Statistical Office's prison statistics. Part of the data refer to a fixed date, usually March 31 of the year. While interpreting these numbers it should be borne in mind that short-term prisoners are underrepresented in comparison to long-term prisoners; the likelihood of a prisoner serving a longer sentence being included in a count that is only carried out once a year is much higher than that of one sentenced to a short term of imprisonment.

On March 31, 2007, 75,756 people were imprisoned in 194 penal institutions, about three-fifths in single and two-fifths in shared cells, respectively. The total of 75,756 prisoners in 2007 equals a rate of 93 per 100,000 population. Of the people in prison, 79 percent are serving a prison sentence; approximately 17 percent are in remand custody. Prisoners detained for other reasons, for example, those in custody awaiting deportation, account for 3 percent of the prison population. The numbers of those in preventive detention (postimprisonment) are small (0.5%). Women account for a small proportion of the prison population: 95 percent of inmates are male.

According to the Code of Execution of Prison Sentence the prisoners have certain rights, especially regarding communication with the outside world. An important part of this is visits of family or friends within the prison. The legal minimum is one hour per month, but often this time span is extended. On the other hand the prisoner has the obligation to work or alternatively to undergo a job training. This is embedded in the context of the overall aim of imprisonment, namely, to improve the capacity of the prisoner to live his or her life after release without committing offenses.

Jörg-Martin Jehle

Further Reading

Elsner, Beatrix, and Julia Peters. (2006). "The Prosecution Service Function within the German Criminal Justice System." In *Coping with Overloaded Criminal Justice Systems,* edited by Jörg-Martin Jehle and Marianne Wade, pp. 207–236. Berlin: Springer.

Federal Statistical Office: http://www.destatis.de.

Jehle, Jörg-Martin. (2009). *Criminal Justice in Germany: Facts and Figures*. 5th ed. Mönchengladbach, Germany: Federal Ministry of Justice.

Kangaspunta, Kristiina, Matti Joutsen, Natalia Ollus, and Sami Nevala, eds. (1999). *Profiles of Criminal Justice Systems in Europe and Northern America, 1990–1994*. Helsinki: The European Institute for Crime Prevention and Control (HEUNI).

Weigend, Thomas. (2004). "The Prosecution Service in the German Administration of Criminal Justice." In *Tasks and Powers of the Prosecution Services in the EU Member States,* edited by Peter J. Tak, pp. 203–222. Nijmegen, the Netherlands: Wolf Legal.

Gibraltar

Legal System: Common
Prison Rate: Medium
Death Penalty: No

Background

Gibraltar is a largely self-governing territory of the United Kingdom, which assumes responsibility for Gibraltar's defense and international affairs.

Located on the southern tip of the Iberian Peninsula, it is surrounded by water on three sides. It sits strategically at the Strait of Gibraltar, the entrance to the Mediterranean Sea from the Atlantic Ocean, and shares a 1.2 kilometer (0.75 mile) land border with Spain to the north.

Gibraltar's territory is approximately 6.5 square kilometers (2.4 square miles). The *CIA World Factbook* estimates the population, all urban, at 28,034 for 2009. Two-thirds of the population is between the ages of 15 and 64. The remaining population is evenly divided between those under 15 and those over 64. Life expectancy is 80 years.

The 2001 Census counted the following national groups: Gibraltarian, Other British, Moroccan, Spanish, Other EU, and Other. English is the official language and is used in the schools. There is no significant migration into or out of Gibraltar, although tourism attracts a substantial number of foreign visitors.

Gibraltar was ceded to Britain by Spain in perpetuity under the terms of the Treaty of Utrecht in 1713. It continues to be a source of dispute between the two countries. In 2002, Gibraltarians voted overwhelmingly—17,900 (98.97%) votes to 187 (1.03%)—by referendum to reject any "shared sovereignty" arrangement with Spain. The British government has made further assurances that the will of the people of Gibraltar will be followed.

The legal system is British, and English common law applies. Laws enacted by the Gibraltar Parliament, such as the Criminal Offenses Act and the Criminal Procedure Act, provide reference to English sources. As part of the European Union (EU), Gibraltar is also required to implement all relevant EU directives.

Police

The Gibraltar police force was initially composed of citizens of Gibraltar commissioned to apprehend deserters from the British armed forces. For many years the British military saw to the maintenance of public safety and security. Policing became the domain of civilian authorities in 1830. On June 12, 1992, Queen Elizabeth II conferred the prefix "Royal" to the Gibraltar Police, thus renaming it the Royal Gibraltar Police (RGP).

The Gibraltar Services Police (GSP) is a civilian force employed by the Ministry of Defense, which guards and enforces law on military installations and adjacent to certain government buildings in Gibraltar. Regulation of the GSP is achieved by agreement between the Ministry of Defense and the Gibraltar Police Authority (GPA). All such agreements must be approved by the governor.

The Gibraltar Coordinating Centre for Criminal Intelligence and Drugs (GCID) was established in 1997 to cope with the increased drugs trafficking, money laundering, and other organized crime. It is composed of officers from the Royal Gibraltar Police, Gibraltar Services Police, and Gibraltar Customs and the United Kingdom's HM Customs and Excise.

The Gibraltar Police Authority (GPA) was established in the 2006 Constitution, and enabled by the Police Act, 2006. It is an independent body responsible for the efficiency and effectiveness of the RGP, for providing information on police issues to the community, for handling complaints against police officers, and for ensuring high standards of policing in Gibraltar.

The governor has ultimate responsibility for the integrity, probity, and independence of policing, and the policing aspects of national security, including internal security. He or she has the power to hold the GPA accountable for any matter under the Police Act, and for the professional standards of the force. The GPA is required to provide the governor, the Gibraltar government, and Parliament with annual plans and reports. The annual report includes statistics of "serious" and "minor" crimes and traffic offenses. Five-year comparisons of selected crimes are also reported. The commissioner of police is appointed by the governor with the advice of the Gibraltar Police Authority. By law, the commissioner is a member of the force and is responsible for command, supervision, direction, and control of the force, and for the proper expenditure of all public moneys appropriated to the force.

Crime

Classification of Crimes

The Criminal Offences Act provides 22 categories of crime in Gibraltar. However, as mentioned above, the annual reports of the GPA include statistics in three categories: serious crimes, minor crimes, and traffic offenses. Among the serious crimes are the following:

- Certain offenses against the person—murder, wounding, assault occasioning harm, child neglect.
- Burglary and attempted burglary.
- Robbery and attempted robbery.
- Sexual offenses—rape, indecent assault on a person under 16, unlawful sex with a female under 16.
- Theft—including motor vehicle theft, handling stolen goods, blackmail.
- Fraud and deception—including forgery, money laundering.
- Criminal damage.
- Firearms offenses—illegal possession, discharging.
- Drug offenses—cultivation of cannabis, possession, supplying, obstructing the Misuse of Drugs Act.
- Violence against police—escaping custody, assault, impersonation.

Certain other crimes, labeled by the authority as "miscellaneous offenses," but still categorized as "serious" include attempts to pervert the course of justice, breaking prison, conduct endangering ships, bomb hoaxes, harmful/obscene publications, interfering with a witness, false declaration, intimidating jurors/witnesses, oil spillage, taking photos within court precincts, contempt of court, assisting an offender, destroying electoral posters, and uttering counterfeit coins/notes.

Minor crimes include common assaults; theft from a motor vehicle; attempted theft; causing minor damage; certain antisocial behaviors such as disturbing the peace, loud noises, drunk and disorderly conduct; police-related offenses such as wasting police time; immigration offenses; tobacco smuggling; selling alcohol to a person under 16; licensing offenses; and a number of miscellaneous offenses.

Drugs are controlled under the Drugs (Misuse) Act and subsidiary legislation. Controlled drugs are classified A, B, and C within the act and regulations. Possession is distinguished from supplying or selling by the quantity of the drug. For most classes of drug, the quantity is at 2 grams (but some less), and cannabis at 20 grams. The age of criminal responsibility in Gibraltar is 8 years. Persons between the ages of 14 and 16 are categorized as "young persons." Charges brought against children and young persons are tried in the Magistrates' Court, acting as a juvenile court. Special rules under the Criminal Procedure Act apply to these proceedings.

Crime Statistics

As one might expect, the number of crimes committed in Gibraltar is low relative to the numbers of much larger jurisdictions. In the 2007–2008 report of the GPA, there were 103 reported serious crimes against the person, 83 of which were assaults that occasioned harm, 5 of grievous bodily harm, 1 threat to kill. There were 17 reported sexual offenses committed, of which 4 were rapes. Among property crimes, there were 194 burglaries and attempted burglaries, 15 reported cases of arson, and 33 cases reported of serious damage to property or motor vehicles. The GPA also reported 551 serious drug cases: 459 were for possession, 38 for possession with intent to supply, and 39 for obstructing the Drugs (Misuse) Act. There were a total of 1,209 serious crimes reported. The Government of Gibraltar Statistical Office also publishes in its *Abstract of Statistics* the number of criminal offenses committed in each year, with comparative statistics over several years.

Finding of Guilt

The Gibraltar Constitution provides the foundation for the rights of accused persons. Any person who is arrested or detained is to be informed as soon as reasonably practicable, in a language that he or she understands, of the reasons for his or her arrest or detention. Any person who is arrested or detained has the right to retain a legal practitioner of his or her own choice, and to hold private communication with that person. A minor is afforded a reasonable opportunity to communicate with his or her parent or guardian. Children and young persons are required to have representation. An accused who cannot afford to retain representation may have one provided for him or her at public expense. The accused has a right to a speedy trial.

Certain minor crimes are heard in Magistrates' Court in summary proceedings. Anyone who has reached the age of 14 and charged before the Magistrates' Court with a summary offense, or as an adult is liable to be sentenced to imprisonment for a term exceeding three months, may make a claim for a jury trial. Exceptions include assault or offenses related to prostitution or solicitation. The court has a duty to explain this right.

The Magistrates' Court is typically the court of first instance in many criminal proceedings. For many minor offenses, the court holds summary proceedings. Juvenile proceedings are heard before the Magistrates' Court in special juvenile session. The court is presided over by a stipendiary magistrate. Lay magistrates sit in his or her absence.

The Gibraltar Supreme Court has unlimited jurisdiction and is both a court of appeal and a court of first instance. As a court of appeal, it may hear appeals from the Magistrates' Court. Its criminal jurisdiction is similar to that of the English Crown Court.

The Gibraltar Court of Appeal hears cases on appeal from the Supreme Court. Appeals may be made from the Court of Appeal to the Queen in Council. Justices of the Court of Appeal are primarily drawn from the English Court of Appeal. It is not a resident court and sits three times per year.

Prosecution and investigation of criminal cases is performed by the attorney general (AG) and the police (under the terms of the Police Act). The AG may institute and undertake criminal proceedings before any court of law, except a court established by a disciplinary law; he or she may take over and continue any criminal proceeding that may have been instituted by any other person or authority; and discontinue at any stage before judgment is delivered any such criminal proceedings instituted or undertaken by himself or any other person or authority.

Incarceration before trial is permitted. There is provision for bail. Prosecution may verbally object to bail at the arraignment proceeding and has two hours within which to submit a written appeal. The accused continues to be held until the appeal is either successful or abandoned.

Punishment

Typical Punishments

Punishment in Gibraltar may take the form of imprisonment, imprisonment and fine, fine, probation, community service, or attendance center. A child may not be sentenced to prison and a young person may not be imprisoned for more than 2 years. Sentences are set by the Criminal Offences Act. The following represent the statutory set penalties for major crimes.

- Murder. A person who with malice aforethought causes the death of another person is guilty of murder and on conviction upon indictment is sentenced to imprisonment for life. The court may set a minimum period that should elapse before the governor orders his or her release on license under the Prison Act. The death penalty has been abolished.
- Rape. Rape is punishable with imprisonment for life.
- Theft/Burglary/Robbery. A person found guilty of theft is liable to imprisonment for 10 years. A person guilty of burglary is liable to imprisonment for 14 years. A person guilty of aggravated burglary is liable on conviction to imprisonment for life. A person guilty of robbery, or of an assault with intent to rob, is liable to imprisonment for life.
- Serious Drug Offenses. Production, supplying, offering to supply, possession with intent to supply Class A or B drugs, when convicted on indictment, can carry a life sentence and a

fine. Sentences for offenses related to Class C drugs vary between 2 and 5 years with fines if convicted on indictment, and 6 to 12 months if a summary conviction.

Alternatives to Imprisonment

Parole

The Gibraltar Parole Board may recommend to the governor the release of a prisoner after he or she has served at least one-third of the sentence, but a minimum of six months; the release of any person detained for consecutive sentences imposed by the Magistrates' Court; or, after consulting with the chief justice, anyone serving a life term. The governor may at any time release a person on license on compassionate grounds and may do so without the recommendation of the Parole Board if time is an essential factor.

Pardon

After consultation with the chief minister, the governor may also grant a pardon, either free or subject to conditions; may grant a respite from the execution of a punishment; may substitute a less severe form of punishment; or may remit the whole or any part of a punishment, penalty, or forfeiture.

Fines

Many offenses carry both a sentence of imprisonment and a fine, or a fine alone. Fines are set according to a standard scale established in the Criminal Offences Act.

Absolute and Conditional Discharge

Where a court convicts a person of an offense that is not fixed by law, and upon considering the circumstances, nature of the offense, and the character of the offender, and that probation is not appropriate, the court may make an order discharging him or her absolutely. The court may also order a conditional discharge if he or she commits no offense during a specified period of time not to exceed 12 months.

Probation

Like discharge, where the offense has no fixed term, the court may also issue on order of probation. Probation requires the offender to be under the supervision of a probation officer for a period of no less than 12 months, and no more than 3 years. If the probationer fails to comply with requirements of the order, the chief justice or justice may either impose a fine of 10 pounds (US$14.30), require him or her to attend an attendance center, or deal with him or her as if convicted of the offense. Violation of discharge and probation orders may result in their revocation. The court may deal with an offender who commits a violation as if he or she had just been convicted of the offenses.

Community Service

For persons 16 years or more, convicted of an offense punishable with imprisonment, the court may, if the convicted person consents, make a community service order requiring him or her to perform unpaid work. The court assigns an officer of the Social Services Agency to supervise the performance of the order.

Attendance Center

When dealing with persons between 12 and 20 years of age, the court may order the person to attend an attendance center for up to 36 hours. The activities and instruction given at the center are to be conducive to health of mind and body. If the offender fails to comply with the order or to follow the rules of the center, the court may revoke the order, and deal with him or her as if the order had not been made.

Prison

On September 24, 2008, the total prison population of Gibraltar was 43 (approximately 154 per 100,000 total population, based on Gibraltar's 2008 population of 28,010). Of those inmates, 53.5 percent were pretrial detainees/remand prisoners, and 25.6 percent were foreign prisoners. There were no female prisoners and none under the age of 18 years. Her Majesty's prison at Tarik Road is the only prison in Gibraltar. It is administered by the Gibraltar Prison Service within the Department of Social Services and has a total capacity of 69 inmates. All male prisoners over the age of 17 and under the age of 60 are required to work inside or outside the prison, subject to the approval of the governor, and prescribed by regulations or standing orders. An unconvicted prisoner is permitted, if he or she wishes, to work as if he or she were a convicted prisoner. Prisoners may be paid for their work at rates approved by the governor and may spend money on such articles and subject to conditions established by the governor. Prisoners are permitted a limited number of visitors at any one time and a limited number of visits per week. Regulation of prisons and rules regarding prisoners are available in the Prison Act and Prison Regulations.

Dennis C. Benamati

Further Reading

Archer, Edward G. (2006). *Gibraltar, Identity and Empire.* Abingdon, UK: Routledge.
Gibraltar Police Authority: http://www.gpa.gi.
Gibraltar Statistical Office: http://www.gibraltar.gov.gi.
Laws of Gibraltar: http://www.gibraltarlaws.gov.gi.
World Prison Brief, Kings College London: http://www.kcl.ac.uk/depsta/law/research/icps/worldbrief.

Greece

Legal System: Civil
Murder: Low
Burglary: Low
Corruption: Medium
Human Trafficking: Medium
Prison Rate: Medium
Death Penalty: No
Corporal Punishment: No

Background

Greece gained its independence under the London Protocol of 1830, by virtue of which France, Great Britain, and Russia recognized Greece as an independent state, after the Greek War of Independence against the Ottoman Empire in 1821. According to the latest official census (2001), the Greek population numbered 10,934,097 people. The official percentage of foreigners living in Greece is 6.9 percent but is probably higher due to the number of illegal immigrants. In the early 1990s most immigrants came to Greece from Albania and other Balkan countries, while recently most immigrants come from Asian and African countries. Greece became a full member of European Economic Community in 1981 and a full member of the European Monetary Union in 2002.

Criminal Law

Greece is a presidential parliamentary democracy. The Constitution establishes the system of representative democracy and the organic separation of powers. Following the tradition of other European continental legal systems, Greek criminal law is defined as a branch of civil law. The first criminal law of the modern Greek state, the "Criminal Statute," was promulgated in 1934, inspired by Ludwig von Maurer, a professor of law at the University of Munich, who came to Greece from Bavaria as a member of the three-member regency to Otto, the first king of the free modern Greek state. This work was based on a previous law named "Collection of Criminal Laws," which was composed by a nine-member committee in 1824 on the grounds of the French *Code d'instruction criminelle* of 1810. Ludwig von Maurer, who had received French legal education, prepared a criminal statute that prevailed in Greece for more than 100 years. After many amendments, the Greek Penal Code of 1950 still prevails, while recently two legislative committees

Police in riot gear await protestors in front of the parliament building in Athens, September 1, 2009. (Tissman/Dreamstime)

were entrusted by the Ministry of Justice with an amendment of the Penal Code and the Code of Criminal Procedure.

In Greece, the Courts of First Instance and the Office of Public Prosecutions are regarded as one entity. Greece is divided in 63 judicial districts. Each of them has a Court of First Instance/Office of Public Prosecutions and a Bar Association. Additionally, there are 299 justices of the peace, which belong to the aforementioned 63 judicial districts. Their main competence is to hear disputes of a civil nature. Second instance cases are tried in one of 13 courts of appeal. Finally, the jurisdiction of Supreme Court cases belongs to *Areios Pagos* (the Greek Supreme Court), which has a civil and a criminal division. Criminal offenses committed by officers and petty officers of the Greek Army as well as by civilians while serving their compulsory military service are tried by military courts.

Legal System

The Greek system of criminal procedure uses a mixed system, namely, inquisitorial in pretrial procedure and accusatorial in trial process. Prosecution and investigation on the one hand and trial on the other hand are fully separated. The prosecution is ordered by the public prosecutor of the Misdemeanour Court, who is responsible for the pretrial stage, and the judgment belongs to the judges of the court, who decide always after trial.

In many cases of serious crimes an intermediate stage (between the investigation and the trial) before the Judicial Council, which acts as an indicting chamber, is provided. The investigation is either ordinary or summary investigation. Investigating officials responsible for the pretrial procedures are the investigating judge in case of serious crimes, or the investigating magistrate and the police officers in case of misdemeanors. In both cases they are ordered by the public prosecutor.

The criminal process generally opens with a prosecution of a criminal offense by the public prosecutor of the Misdemeanour Court and comprises two basic stages: the investigation (pretrial proceedings) and the trial proceedings. In many cases of serious crimes an intermediate stage (between the investigation and the trial) before the Judicial Council, which acts as an indicting chamber, is provided. Prosecution of the offense does not require strong evidence that an offense has been committed. Even slim evidence suffices to open investigation proceedings. If the public prosecutor doubts that there is any evidence to open criminal proceedings, he or she orders a preliminary inquiry, aimed at collecting the evidence that would justify prosecution. The Public Prosecutor of Appeal Court can abstain from prosecution in some cases.

Pretrial proceedings have an inquisitorial character. They are written, not public, and nonadversarial. The trial before the Misdemeanour Court, in the Mixed Criminal Courts (three professional judges, four jurors) and in the Courts of Appeal, is public apart from cases of minors or of state security offenses, oral, and moderately adversarial. *Areios Pagos* sitting in camera as a three-member council of its criminal section decides on appeal after hearing the public prosecutor who submits a written recommendation. *Areios Pagos* or the Supreme Court may call the parties to appear to argue their case.

Police

The first Greek Policing Corps were organized soon after the Greek War of Independence during 1821–1827. They were the Greek Gendarmerie and the Municipal Police, which coexisted until 1906 when the former remained and the latter was dissolved. The City Police was established in 1920 in the then four large cities: Athens, Piraeus, Patra, and Corfu.

The Greek Police in its current form was established in 1984, when the Greek Gendarmerie and the City Police were merged. It is recognized as a security body responsible for all Greek territories except the ports and the sea, which are protected by the Port Police Corps. The hierarchical structure of the Greek police is determined by its organizational document, which aims at the following:

- Sustain public order and security and assist the country's defense in collaboration with the Armed Forces.
- Secure public peace, good order, and the citizens' undistracted social life, including general policing and roads traffic.
- Prevent and tackle crime and protect the state and democracy according to the Constitution, that is, offering protection both to the public and the state.

With respect to geography the police consists of 14 general police regions, which correspond to respective administrative regions, and they are further divided in 54 police directorates, which reflect the 52 municipalities of the country with an additional police directorate in Alexandroupolis (northeast) and separate ones for Athens and Piraeus, which form, however, a single municipality.

Crime

Criminal Responsibility

Criminal offenses are defined in the Greek Penal Code, which also defines the notion of criminal responsibility. A minor is considered to be anyone whose age is between 8 and 18 years old at the time of commission of an offense. Minors normally are criminally responsible. It follows that those offenders who are younger than 8 years may never be prosecuted and the state will take no action against them. Minors who have not completed their 13th year of age are not criminally responsible and those between the ages of 13 and 18 are called criminally responsible. Criminally responsible minors must be subjected to rehabilitative or therapeutic measures, unless the court believes that a confinement in a correctional institution is more appropriate.

Finally, there are also cases of adults, in which the Greek Penal Code provides impunity (grounds of excuse). Grounds of excuse amount to these circumstances that prevent the offender from assuming guilt either because, due to his or her mental health or maturity, he or she is not responsible for his or her actions or because unforeseen and unforeseeable events have rendered his or her state of mind not blameworthy. This happens in case of insanity at the moment of the act or omission or at the moment of the trial, intoxication, coercion, ignorance or mistake of law or mistake of fact, report of some criminal offenses to public authorities, remorse after the offense, and impunity based on personal grounds.

Crime Statistics

Crime statistics indicate that 139 completed intentional homicides were recorded in 2007 (0.03% of total recorded crimes). The number of homicides in Greece is generally low; the highest number for the period 1991–2007 was recorded in 1997 (203 homicides). In 2007, 185 rapes were recorded (0.04% of recorded crimes). The peak years were 1993 and 2004 with 204 and 191 rapes, respectively.

Thefts (vehicle theft is not included) are on the rise in recent years, but the highest number of incidents was recorded during the period 1995–1998. In 2007, they accounted for 13.9 percent (58,472) of all recorded crimes. In 2007, 2,823 robberies were recorded, which make up 0.67 percent of all recorded crimes, the highest numbers since the early 1990s.

Finally, police-recorded drug incidents in 2007 and 2006 were 9,271 and 9,600, respectively. Raw cannabis (5.902.861 grams) and heroin (236.504 grams) were the drugs mostly confiscated in 2007.

Criminal Organizations

The activities of criminal organizations in Greece include human trafficking, drug dealing, stolen car markets, illegal markets of cigarettes and cultural heritage pieces, fraud, forgery, intellectual property theft, robbery and theft, child pornography, and blackmailing.

One hundred thirty-nine cases with organized crime characteristics were investigated in 2005 according to the Ministry of Justice Report. In most cases the main crime, that is, the main activity of the organized crime group, referred to illegal immigration, human trafficking, and drug dealing. It should be noted that organized crime groups are increasingly international with cross-national border activities that tend to block their discovery. Domestic organized crime groups are rather easily broken up because they have loose bonds and hierarchy. By contrast, organized crime groups with origins from the Balkan, East European, and Southwest Asian countries are dynamic and constantly adapt to new conditions.

Human Trafficking

According to police records 162 individuals were arrested for human trafficking in 2008. Most arrestees were Greek, Romanians, Albanians, and Bulgarians. The 78 victims (men, women, and children) were mostly Romanians, Bulgarians, and Russians. Out of 40 recorded cases, 37 referred to sexual exploitation, 2 to labor exploitation, and 1 to trafficking of human body organs. In 14 cases organized criminal groups were involved.

The Greek Police Group against Human Trafficking and 14 anti-trafficking groups were established in 2001. In 2002 the penal framework was updated to encompass all modern forms of human trafficking and defined punishment appropriate to serious offense as well as the state's obligation to actively protect victims. Since 2007, victims of human trafficking are not deported and any prior deportation decision is annulled via special immigration policy clauses.

A number of barriers, however, prevent tackling human trafficking successfully. These include the dark but rather high figure of such crimes, a number of impracticalities in the relevant penal code, such as the definition of victim and the small number of convictions against "clients," as well as lack of well-developed victim support services, according to the National Commission for Human Rights.

Drug Offenses

Drug use is relatively low in Greece compared to other EU countries, although it has been increasing since the mid-1980s. Drug possession, use, production, and dealing are illegal. Drug-related offenses are addressed via penal and therapeutic measures that are implemented either alternatively or supplementary. Thus, a complicated penal framework coexists with a therapeutic one.

Drug dealing is dealt with more severely, since it is also covered by the 2001 Law on Organized Crime. A recent (2006) Law Code on Drugs offers a systematic codification of existing legislation, on the basis of which the public debate on the type, intensity, and characteristics of preventive drug policies is to be developed. Drug use is punished with 1 year's imprisonment. If the user is, however, deemed drug-dependent, he or she is offered the choice to opt for a drug rehabilitation program, in which case prosecution is postponed for a set period. The public prosecutor of misdemeanors in agreement with the public prosecutor of appeals court may further withhold prosecution indefinitely as long as the accused has successfully completed the drug rehabilitation program. Individuals prosecuted for import, export, possession, production, and selling of drugs are punished with imprisonment for at least 10 years and fines from €2,900 to €29,000 (US$3,644 to $36,447). These may increase due to additional incriminating evidence, such as drug dealing as profession or habit, involvement or employment of underage individuals during any of the above actions, firearm use during any of the above actions, or to escape the police.

Corruption

A central theme in the public debate of the last few years is corruption. High government officials, political parties, and multinational and domestic companies seem to be involved in such crimes, while citizens have become more sensitized to them than in the past. The most prominent corruption cases of recent years with roughly daily media coverage referred to business contracts in telecommunications between the public sector and a multinational company that paid large sums to political parties and the investment of public pension funds in the private sector with huge losses (pension funds bond scandal). Another high-profile case was the "judicial corruption network" of judges, lawyers, businessmen, and a former MP who were prosecuted on crimes such as abuse of authority, participation in money laundering, and attempted fraud.

The results of the National Survey on Corruption in Greece 2008 (commissioned by International Transparency-Hellas), showed that the estimated total corruption (in the public and private sectors) was between €681 and €815 million (US$855 to $1,024). Thirteen and a half percent of households reported corruption incidents, with respective 9.5 and 5.1 percent cases in the public and private sectors. According to the public, among the first in rank corruption cases in the public sector were in hospitals, city planning, and Inland Revenue Services, and in the private sector, in hospitals, doctors' surgeries and medical centers, banks, and lawyers.

Finding of Guilt

Rights of the Accused

The fundamental principles of the Greek Criminal Procedure define the procedural position of the defendant and allocate the rights of the accused. The main principles of criminal procedure include the principle of searching for truth, the principle of respect of human dignity, the principle of judicial hearing, the presumption of innocence, the principle of fair trial, the principle of justifying the decisions, the principle of a speedy trial or to be judged within a reasonable time and the principle of economy of trial, the principle of adversarial trial, the principle of equality of arms, the principle of judicial assistance, the principle of proportionality, the principle of due process of trial, and the principle of evidentiary law.

The Code of Criminal Procedure provides a well-developed system of defendant's rights at the pretrial as well as the trial stage. The defendant's rights in pretrial stage are as follows:

- The right to be informed by the investigating judge or other official of the charges against him or her in a language he or she understands, before being called to answer the charges.

- The right to be informed and receive copies of all evidence and to ask and take the adequate time (not less than 48 hours) to prepare his or her defense.
- The right to remain silent toward the charges or to submit a written defense statement.
- The right to appoint defense counsel (no more than two) from the beginning of the police investigation or to receive legal assistance if he or she is indigent and to communicate with counsel at any stage of the procedure.
- The right to be present at any stage of the criminal procedure, put questions to witnesses, and submit comments on the evidence collected.
- The right to present evidence defending himself or herself and to request the examination of witnesses, experts, and others.

The defendant's rights at the trial stage are as follows:

- The right to call witnesses of his or her choice and ask the public prosecutor to call witnesses he or she wishes (one in misdemeanor court and two in serious crimes trials).
- The right to examine witnesses and experts and to comment on all evidence.
- The right to defend himself or herself in person and/or through his or her counsel and to have the last word.
- The right to appeal against conviction and sentence by a first instance court.

It should also be added that, according to the Greek Constitution, everyone, namely the accused of an offense, may not be submitted to torture or other inhuman and degrading treatment abusing his or her dignity. Additionally, nobody shall be arrested without a warrant justifying his or her arrest and the Greek Constitution also protects a person's home asylum from any search that is not in accordance with the law.

Alternatives to Trial

Despite the fact that the Greek Constitution provides that the trial of cases belongs to criminal courts, the Greek legislature has already started to incorporate Recommendations R 68 (25) "for the creation of a simplified procedure regarding the light traffic offenses" and R (87) 20 "about the social reactions against juvenile criminality," as well as the Decision-Frame of the Council of European Community 15-3-2001 about the regime of victims in criminal procedures, which provided the adoption of the institution of reconciliation in criminal cases.

There are several provisions to relieve the criminal justice system from the burden of thousands of cases. The public prosecutor can abstain from prosecution, for example, and order educative or therapeutic measures for cases involving minors, or when a drug addict accused of drug use or supply or possession of drugs for personal use voluntary attends a therapeutic care organization. The vast majority of criminal cases are "resolved" with a court decision after trial. Despite the fact that there are provisions about the penal reconciliation, it is not applied in reality.

Special Matters

In Greece, pretrial incarceration is allowed but cannot last more than 6 months in misdemeanors and 12 months in serious offenses. In exceptional cases the maximum limits of pretrial incarceration can be exceeded by 3 and 6 months, respectively, if the Judicial Council in charge decides so. Greek judges are divided in judges of civil and criminal justice on the one hand and judges of administrative justice on the other hand. There is no specialization between the judges of criminal and civil justice. They can judge either a criminal or a civil case depending on the decision of their chief judge.

The appointment of a judge presupposes the success of the applicant in the annual national and official examinations that take place under the responsibility of the Ministry of Justice and the National School of Judges and after the successful one-year graduation from the school. The requirements for the application concentrate on the age (between 28 and 40 years old), the previous working experience as a lawyer, the fulfillment of military obligations for men applicants, and other factors.

There is a separate system for juveniles who are tried by juvenile courts. One-judge courts try petty offenses and appeals against decisions of petty offenses courts and impose therapeutic and educative measures of the Greek Penal Code in case of minors younger than 13 years old. Three-judge courts try juvenile offenses against which are threatened the penalty of confinement in special institution for young offenders. The Juvenile Courts of Appeals try the appeals against one-judge and three-judge courts. The appeal suspends the execution of the decision against the minor by the law in any case. Juvenile offenders enjoy most of the rights that adult offenders do, as far as these rights suit to the character of the juvenile trial. No trial precedent issues in case of juvenile offenses. No publicity is permitted during the procedure of the trial and the announcement of the judgment in minors' trials. The pretrial detention of juvenile offenders is an exception and it takes place under strict conditions. Confinement as a penalty for a minor must be the *ultimum refugium.* Juvenile offenders serve their penalty in separated prisons. In Greece, there are three juvenile detention centers all around the country.

Punishment

Type of Punishment

The Penal Code classifies criminal offenses into three categories according to the threatened penal sanctions: *serious crimes/felonies, misdemeanors,* and *petty offenses.* Petty offenses are punished with detention or fine. Misdemeanors are threatened with confinement or monetary punishment or confinement in special institutions for young offenders. Serious offenses/felonies are punished with confinement in a penitentiary for life or for a fixed term between 5 and 20 years. The death penalty provided against serious offenses/felonies was abrogated in 1994. The Greek Penal Code provides a dual system of sanctions: *penalties* and *measures of security and reform.*

Penalties

Penalty is a harm prescribed by the law and imposed by the penal judge according to a certain procedure against the culprit of an offense and because of it as an expression of a specific disapproval on behalf of the legal order. The Greek Penal Code provides principal and accessory penalties. Principal penalties are imposed without conditions while accessory penalties presuppose the enforcement of the principal penalty and are imposed additionally. Principal penalties include custodial penalties, pecuniary sanctions, and community service.

Custodial penalties are enlisted as follows: (1) confinement in a penitentiary for life or for a fixed term between 5 and 20 years and the so-called confinement of indefinite duration, where the court will determine only the minimum term of confinement. This rule is enforced against anyone, who having already been sentenced at least three times for serious crimes or misdemeanors committed with intent to custodial sentences, commits intentionally a new serious crime or misdemeanor; (2) imprisonment (the minimum term is 10 days and the maximum 5 years); (3) confinement in a psychiatric institution in case of defendants who have acted with diminished criminal responsibility due to psychological conditions when a mitigated penalty is imposed; (4) the confinement in a special institution for young offenders (from 5 to 20 years in case the law threatens against the offense committed a penalty of more than 10 years; in any other case confinement limits range from 6 months to 10 years); and (5) detention (from 1 day to 1 month).

Two pecuniary sanctions envisaged in the Penal Code are monetary penalties and fines. Usually, pecuniary sanctions are threatened as an alternative to a term of imprisonment. In case neither the custodial sentence nor the pecuniary sanction appears to be adequate punishment to prevent the defendant from offending again, the judge is empowered to impose both penalties. Monetary penalties range from €150 to €15,000 (US$188 to $18,852), unless other statutes contain heavier pecuniary penalties; fines range from €29 to €590 (US$36 to $740).

The ever-increasing prison population together with the lack of new penitentiaries to accommodate convicts has led the legislator to use the *conversion of custodial sentences into pecuniary sanctions* as a means to avert prison overcrowding. The Penal Code provides that a custodial sentence that does not exceed one year is automatically converted into a pecuniary penalty or fine.

Custodial sentences between one and two years are to be converted into a pecuniary sanction, unless the perpetrator is a recidivist. Custodial sentences exceeding two years can be converted if the convict has served half of the sentence and the remaining term is less than two years. Custodial sentences between two and five years can be converted into a pecuniary sanction, provided that the court considers such conversion sufficient to prevent the defendant from reoffending. Finally, custodial sentences between two and three years can be converted in *community service* upon request from the defendant or with his or her agreement.

There are four accessory penalties: (1) deprivation of political and civil rights, (2) incapacitation through revocation of the special permission for exercising a profession, (3) publication of the judgment of conviction, and (4) special confiscation of the offense's instrumentality or proceeds. The Penal Code perceives special confiscation as being both an accessory penalty and a security measure. According to the Greek Constitution, general confiscation is prohibited.

Measures of Security and Reform

As the punitive nature of punishment may not always be appropriate considering the personal circumstances of the offender, and since criminal law also aims at preventing reoffending through rehabilitation, the Penal Code prescribes a number of *measures of security and reform.* Such measures can substitute a penalty when the defendant cannot be punished as being of diminished responsibility or can supplement a sentence. The Penal Code distinguishes between measures:

- Applying to specific categories of offenders, namely, minors, abnormal persons, alcoholics and drug addicts, and foreigners:
    1. Protective/therapeutic and educational measures imposed to minors. All educative and therapeutic measures imposed by the court are subjected to amendment or revocation depending on the minor's future conduct or the development of his or her personality. Such measures are automatically revoked when the minor reaches age 21. These measures include, for example, reconciliation between the minor and the victim through expression of apologies and amicable settlement; compensation of the victim; community service; following social and psychological programs. Yet most common penalties in legal practice of juvenile courts entrust the minor's guardianship to probation officers and confinement in special establishments. Penal reconciliation is far beyond implementation due to practical difficulties (lack of probation officers' education).
    2. Protective measures against "abnormal" or habitual offenders.
    3. Protective measures against alcoholics and drug addicts.
    4. Deportation of foreigners.
- Applying only when the otherwise normal personality of the offender reveals a certain behavior that must be specifically addressed, namely, aversion to work (internment to work institutions), or when his or her residing in certain areas poses specific threats (prohibition of residing in certain areas).

Prison

Incarceration rates have increased in recent years. Specifically in 2001 there were 79 prisoners per 100,000 population, in 2004, the rate was 82 per 100,000 and in 2008, 109 per 100,000 residents. The total number of incarcerated was 12,300 in 2008, but during 2009, it has dropped.

On January 1, 2009, the total number of inmates in the Greek prisons was 11,736 and more recently, according to the Direction of Inspection of Prisons and Special Juvenile Detention Establishments, on September 19, 2009, it was 11,225. This slight reduction of prison population observed during 2009 is due to the recent legislation of the Ministry of Justice in an attempt to disburden the suffocating overcrowded Greek prisons. Over the total number of 11,225 prisoners, 5,182 were Greeks (1,448 pretrial detainees and 3,734 convicts) and 6,043 foreigners (2,183 pretrial detainees and 3,860 convicts).

There are 33 prisons in Greece. The biggest is Korydallos Prison in Athens, which is divided into six male wings and a separate wing for women who are pretrial detainees. There are 3 agricultural prisons, 3 special Juvenile Detention Establishments, 8 "closed" prisons, 3 therapeutic establishments, and 16 judicial prisons.

The possibility of work exists in all prisons with the availability of job vacancies. According to the Greek Penitentiary Code, the five-member Work Council of Prisoners (it consists of the judicial officer in charge as president, the prison warden, the senior social worker, the chief-guardian, and the agronomist or the manager of the technical office) in each prison decides for the organization of prisoners' employment. Prisoners are employed in accessory services contributing to the functional needs of the detention center, such as cleaning, working in the kitchen, laundry, food services, or in gardening. This employment can last a maximum of three months and can be renewed once. Prisoners can offer paid work outside prison, under specific conditions. In rural prisons, prisoners work in fields and crops and can take advantages of "beneficial calculation," namely, one day of work equals two or three days of imprisonment, which is equally reduced, so that the prisoner can be released from prison earlier.

The Institute of Continuous Education offers educational programs in nearly all prisons. The programs deliver language courses (Greek, English, and French), literature, information technology, physical and mental health, music, sign language, creative writing, and pottery, among others.

Christina Zarafonitou, Anastasia Chalkia, Maria Galanou, and Andromachi Tseloni

Further Reading

Anagnostopoulos, Elias, and Konstantinos D. Magliveras. (2000). *Criminal Law in Greece.* The Hague: Kluwer Law International.

Karras, Argyrios. (2007). *Criminal Procedural Law.* Athens: Sakkoulas.

Ministry of Citizen Protection, Greek Police: http://www.astynomia.gr.

Ministry of Justice, Transparency and Human Rights: http://www.ministryofjustice.gr.

Spyropoulos, Philippos C., and Theodore P. Fortsakis. (2009). *Constitutional Law in Greece.* Alphen aan den Rijn, the Netherlands: Kluwer Law International.

Guernsey

Legal System: Common/Customary
Prison Rate: Medium
Death Penalty: No
Corporal Punishment: No

Background

Guernsey is a small island located just south of the United Kingdom. The island is about 78 square kilometers (30 square miles) in total area with a population of about 65,726 people. Guernsey is a dependency of the British Crown. Wherever applicable, Guernsey follows all the laws of the United Kingdom, observing common law as well as its own practices. The judicial branch is that of the Royal Court, in which the judges are elected by an Electoral College voting system. All matters of justice in Guernsey are deliberated by the Royal Court. Although Guernsey relies heavily upon the United Kingdom, which also represents it in matters that deal with the United States and the United Nations, its criminal justice system has its own unique aspects. Guernsey has its own police force that is separate from that of the United Kingdom.

The Guernsey State Police Force is directed by the chief officer of police. In total, the Guernsey police have 177 officers, spread through seven different management levels, all with different titles. The titles, from top to bottom, are as follows: chief officer (1), chief superintendent (1), superintendent (1), chief inspectors (4), inspectors (15), sergeants (36), and constables (119). Each of these officers is assigned to different police units within the police force: the Criminal Investigation Department, Financial Intelligence Service, the Family Protection Unit, Force Intelligence Bureau, the Special Branch, Crime Management Unit, Crime Prevention, and the IT Department. The Guernsey Police Force also works very closely with the law officers of Guernsey. The law officers are the two persons who look over the Crown, the States of Guernsey, the States of Alderney, and the Chief Pleas of Sark. The law officers pledge to provide a comprehensive range of legal services for these areas, which includes provision of legal advice, drafting, crime, civil litigation, and constitutional and international work. Although there is a lot of international work done by the law officers, the State of Guernsey does not have its own military, so if it needs a military defense, it becomes the responsibility of the United Kingdom.

Crime

Classification of Crimes

Guernsey splits crimes into many categories, for which different police forces may be responsible. The Criminal Investigation Department (CID) deals with the serious offenses in Guernsey, including murder, robberies, and burglaries. A 2006 report states that the Criminal Investigation Department deals with a lot with high-profile crimes, which may not be necessarily violent, but are still considered to be quite serious. The CID usually takes on the investigation, but it must also work with other units of the police force to reach prosecution. For example, a serious offense that the Guernsey police deals with is fraud and money laundering, for which it must work closely with the Financial Intelligence Service Department. These cases also include situations like terrorism financing. These crimes are considered to be serious offenses and usually result in jail time for the offender. Although these serious crimes warrant a lot of attention, the Guernsey police department also deals with less serious misdemeanors, such as traffic violations, drug offenses, computer crimes, and others, which are usually dealt with by the Force Intelligence Bureau. The bureau operates under the detective inspector and is split into four different departments: Drugs Intelligence Unit, the Special Branch, Crime Management Unit, and Technical Support Unit. Drug offenses, Class A and B drugs, are a big problem in Guernsey, as well as internationally. According to the 2006 police report, two drugs of mention were marijuana and prescription drugs. From 2004 to 2005, there was a big increase in drug-related crimes, and after a 2006 survey by the Guernsey government, the police department developed a plan to crack down on drugs in the island. Another major issue that concerns Guernsey police is traffic violations, which account for a great deal of the police work and are also tied into drug usage. According to the 2006 survey, drinking/drug-impaired driving rose considerably since 2004.

Crime Statistics

Guernsey, although it does not experience much crime, did see an increase from 2004 to 2005. Of crimes that were reported to the police, Guernsey had 3,465, which was 386 more than the 2004 number of 3,079. There were 97 convictions handed down by the Royal Court, and of these, 27 were convictions of drug-related offenses. That means that close to one-third of all the convictions were related to drugs. The next highest convicted offense was of child pornography, of which there were 7 convictions of indecent photos of children. Finally, the third highest number was of money laundering. Close to half of all convictions were for nonviolent offenses.

Another problem in Guernsey is the number of children who are convicted of crimes. Of the 97 crimes recorded in 2004–2005, 21 were committed by children. These crimes were typically criminal damage or drug-related convictions. Thus, according to the 2006 police report, one of the main priorities of the police department's future policing plan is in drug- and alcohol-related crime where it plans "to increase the number of offenders dealt with for offenses involving Class A and B drugs" and, in particular, to increase the number of "stop/searches" conducted in respect to suspicion of drug offenses to 180 from 120 in 2005. The age of criminal responsibility is 12.

Finding of Guilt

As mentioned, Guernsey has a legal system patterned on that of the United Kingdom. It is not, however, identical. Guernsey has three different criminal parts to its criminal courts: magistrates' court, royal courts, and the Guernsey Court of Appeal. These courts have different types of legal jurisdiction. The magistrates' court has limited jurisdiction, the royal courts have unlimited jurisdiction, and finally the Court of Appeal oversees all appeals that need to be processed. The court services are overseen by the law officers, who are responsible for supervising all prosecutions that take place in Guernsey. They are given a great range of power to do what they think is necessary within the criminal law of Guernsey, which is why Guernsey can indict almost all of its cases, excluding usually only minor public offenses and traffic violations. After the collection of evidence by the Guernsey police, it then becomes the responsibility of the prosecutors to make the case. The prosecutors make requests for evidence, as well as witnesses, and statements by these witnesses. On the other side, the defense has advocates, who are lawyers who must be qualified in England and must have passed the local bar system. These advocates split the role of barrister and solicitor for the Guernsey courts, by sharing in advising their clients and preparing to present the case to the court. Unlike the advocates, the law officers usually do not provide advice or counsel to members of the public; they have to find their own.

Once a case is ready to be heard, it goes before the court, which includes a group of jurors who are elected officials and well-respected people of the community. They rely on precedents that have come prior to hearing the case because that is what the English law follows. These jurors are actually called jurats, which is from the Latin word *jurare* that means "an oath." On the opposing side are the law officers who will represent the state in the matters that are at hand. This court system is basically the same for juveniles, except it is carried out in a separate court where procedures are similar to the adult court, but not always resulting in the same punishment.

Punishment

In Guernsey the main type of punishment for serious crimes is prison, of which Guernsey has only one, called the Guernsey Prison. Of course, not all criminals are sent to prison, since fines and probation services are widely available. The Guernsey Prison plays a big part in punishing and rehabilitating its criminals. According to the Guernsey government Web site, its "objectives are to protect the public by holding those committed by the courts in a safe, decent, and healthy environment," as well as to "reduce crime by providing constructive regimes which address offending behavior, improve educational and work skills and promote law-abiding behavior in custody and after release." According to the yearly prison report, in 2005 there were 105 inmates in the prison compared to 93 in 2004.

The high level of drug crime in Guernsey also means that the prison system has the same problems. The prison takes extreme measures to prevent/limit the drug usage in the system. According to the prison Web site, "all prisoners are assessed [evaluated for drug usage/dependency] on reception." However, many of the incoming prisoners are already addicts, and unfortunately, there are limited detoxification facilities in the prison's health center for those who need it. There are drug awareness, drug actions, and drug education courses offered through the prison offices, which are designed not only for the good of the inmates but also to protect the workers and the quality of prison life in general. There is a strict policy against drugs either entering or leaving the prisons. According to the prison Web site, there are mandatory and voluntary drug tests, and drug-sniffing dogs are used constantly. Anyone caught attempting to smuggle drugs is handed over to the police. If an inmate is caught smuggling drugs, he or she will have his or her visitation rights stripped away.

The Guernsey Prison also works with many different agencies to better its system, including Drug Concern, Probation Service, College of Further Education, Children's Board, Samaritans, Alcoholics Anonymous (AA), Parole Review Committee, and the Education Department.

Timothy McCorry

Further Reading

Guernsey Island Government: http://www.gov.gg.
Island Life: http://www.islandlife.org/legal_gsy.

Hungary

Legal System: Civil
Murder: Low
Burglary: Low
Corruption: Medium
Human Trafficking: Low
Prison Rate: Medium
Death Penalty: No
Corporal Punishment: No

Background

Hungary is situated in Central Europe with a territory of approximately 93,000 square kilometers (36,000 square miles), and a population of about 10.1 million. Approximately two-thirds of the population lives in towns and cities, with 2 million residents in the capital of Budapest. The ethnic breakdown of present-day Hungary is as follows: 92 percent Hungarian, 5 percent Roma (gypsy), and 3 percent other ethnic minorities (e.g., German, Slovak, Romanian, Serb, Croat, Slovenian, etc.). In 2008, there were 174,000 foreign nationals (1.7% of the population) holding residence permits. Most of the population is Roman Catholic (nearly 70%), followed by a significant proportion of Protestant, Greek Catholic, Jewish, and other smaller denominations.

Following World War II, the country was brought into the Soviet sphere of interest between 1948 and 1989. During this period Hungary's legal system belonged to the so-called socialist legal system. The legal basis of the "socialist law" was the Constitution, approved in 1949, which was Hungary's first written constitution. This Constitution formed a governmental system based on the principle of unity of power rather than the principle of the division of powers. Parliament had a formal as against substantive role. Governance was realized mainly through decrees rather than through legislation. After collapse of the Soviet system, free parliamentary elections in the spring of 1990 ended 40 years of socialist rule. Hungary joined the Council of Europe on November 6, 1990, the North Atlantic Treaty Organization on March 12, 1999, and the European Union on May 1, 2004.

Legal System

A fundamental modification of the Constitution took place in 1989–1990 to comply with the requirements arising in connection with joining the Council of Europe and the ratification of the European Convention for the Protection of Human Rights and Fundamental Freedoms, as well as with certain historical traditions. For this reason, the change in the regime in 1989–1990 has been labeled a "constitutional revolution."

There was general agreement that even though the Hungarian socialist system before 1989 suffered from lack of legitimacy, the whole legal system could not be regarded as illegal. Thus, in present-day Hungary, there are a number of laws (acts) in effect that were drafted before 1989. Although amended to adjust to the requirements of the modified Constitution and the characteristics of the new state, the Penal Code of 1978 is still in force.

Upon the amendment of the Constitution in 1989–1990, the form of government of Hungary

Flanked by a prison guard, German defendant Dietmar Clodo, right, reads out his last statement to the judge, far left, before hearing his verdict in Metropolitan Court in Budapest, Hungary, December 29, 2001. Dubbed the "bomb manufacturer" by the media, Clodo and his accomplices were found guilty of explosive and shotgun abuse committed in criminal conspiracy as well as of faking private documents. (AP Photo/MTI/Tibor Rozsahegyi)

became republican. The president of the republic is elected by Parliament for five years. Parliament has one chamber with 386 members. Parliamentary elections are held every four years. The prime minister is elected upon the proposal of the president of the republic by the votes of the majority of Parliament. The basic administrative units of the country are the capital (Budapest) and 19 counties.

The legal system of Hungary now basically belongs to the civil law system again. Criminal justice is based on the mixed model of criminal procedure, the principle of legality, and mandatory prosecution. The Constitution contains the requirements of due process and limitations of criminal law contained in international conventions. The most important laws shaping the criminal justice system are the Penal Code of 1978, the Criminal Procedure Code of 1998, the Law on Prison Service of 1979, the Act on Victim Support and Victim Compensation of Crimes of 2005, and the Act on Mediation in Criminal Justice of 2006. In addition, separate laws apply to the courts, prosecutor service, the police, lawyers, and probation officers.

Courts

The Hungarian judicial system has four levels: local courts, county (metropolitan) courts, regional courts of appeal, and the Supreme Court. The local court is court of first instance, with competence in criminal cases of lower significance but higher frequency. There are 117 local courts in Hungary. The local court proceeds in chamber (one professional judge and two lay judges) if the statutory penalty for the offense is imprisonment for eight years or more, otherwise one professional judge conducts the procedure. The frequency of sole judge procedures at the first instance trial is approximately 60 percent.

The 20 county courts (19 county courts, 1 metropolitan court) have dual competence. First, they may handle appeals filed against the decisions of local courts operating in the county, and second, they may conduct proceedings in first instance in cases determined by law. As a court of first instance, the county court handles more serious cases such as offenses with statutory penalty of imprisonment up to 15 years or life imprisonment. These include acts of terrorism and participation in criminal organizations. The county court proceeds in chamber, most often consisting of one professional judge and two lay judges, and, in certain cases, two professional judges and three lay judges.

Local courts adjudicate 80,000 to 90,000 criminal cases yearly, while the county courts in the first instance handle about 900. The five regional courts of appeal (Gyprr, Debrecen, Budapest, Szeged, Pécs) are exclusively appellate courts. They adjudicate appeals filed against the decisions of local and county courts.

The Supreme Court hears cases of two types: first, appeals against the decisions of the regional courts of appeal in the form of ordinary or extraordinary remedies; and second, cases related to the uniform application of the law to ensure the harmonization of judicial practice. The president of the Supreme Court is appointed by Parliament for six years upon the proposal of the president of the republic. Professional judges are appointed by the president of the republic. The Constitution states that the judges are independent and shall be subjected to the laws, exclusively, and also states that they shall not be members of any party and shall not carry on political activities.

The Constitutional Court (11 members appointed by Parliament with majority voting) operates outside the general judicial organization for the purpose of reviewing the constitutionality of laws and statutes. In so doing, the court may declare a law as null and void, in part or in whole, effective immediately, or at a later date. Setting a later date provides the National Assembly with an opportunity to enact a new law to replace the unconstitutional one. The Constitutional Court has delivered numerous decisions in relation to criminal justice. As an example, the Constitutional Court abolished capital punishment in Hungary on October 31, 1990.

There are approximately 1,000 professional criminal court judges in Hungary. A professional judge must have obtained a university law degree (the university legal education lasts for five years), then worked as court clerk for three years and passed the bar examination. Following success with the bar exam, the aspirant shall work a year as court secretary before being appointed as judge. During this minimum four-year period, court clerks and secretaries are provided with continuous education at the Hungarian Judicial Academy.

Prosecution

The Prosecutor Service is a separate organization, independent from the government. In criminal procedure, the primary tasks of the Prosecutor Service are the supervision of the legality of investigation, and the representation of indictments arising from the public prosecutor. In certain cases, the Prosecutor Service may conduct investigations. Relative to criminal justice, the Prosecutor Service also supervises the legality of the execution of criminal sanctions and the operation of the correctional system.

The prosecutorial system is hierarchically structured, the head of which is the chief prosecutor who is appointed by Parliament for six years, upon the proposal of the president of the republic. The structure of the Prosecutor Service is composed of four levels: Chief Prosecutor's Office, Appellate Prosecutor's Offices at the seat of the regional courts of appeal, County Prosecutor's Offices in the 19 counties and the capital, and at the lowest level, the local prosecutors.

Police

The authority, tasks, organization, and rights of the police are stipulated in Act 34 of 1994 on the police. Broadly speaking, their tasks include the protection of public safety and public order, and protection of the state borders, supervision of frontier traffic, and maintenance of the order of the state border. The police operate independently from the professional army. As a unified police organization, separate organizational units perform the tasks related to the detection and investigation of crimes, trespass, traffic control, the maintenance of order of public domain, the supervision of persons, property protection and private investigator activities, and the protection and supervision of state borders.

The police organization is divided into National Police Headquarters, 19 county police headquarters and the Budapest Police Headquarters, local police headquarters, and border control branches. Special units within the National Police Headquarters perform the tasks of examining financial offenses, money laundering, and crime prevention and protection of victims.

The police are directed by the Minister of Justice and Law Enforcement (until 2006, the Minister of Internal Affairs). The national police commissioner is appointed and exempted from service by the prime minister upon the proposal of the minister. The police act without political influence in the performance of their duties. The total staff of the police, including the administrative personnel, is about 45,000, or 420 personnel per 100,000 inhabitants of Hungary.

Crime

Classification of Crimes

The Hungarian Penal Code (HPC) consists of two main parts: the General Part, and the Special Part. In accordance with the General Part, the age of criminal liability is 14 years at the time of committing the offense. Those between ages 14 and 18 are classified as juveniles and are subject to less severe penalties than adult offenders convicted of the same crime. Provisions regarding juveniles are contained in the HPC. There is no separate juvenile justice act in Hungary. In addition to considering the age of the offender, both the criminality of the act and criminal intent (or lack thereof) of the offender are considered.

The Hungarian Penal Code classifies crimes as either felonies or misdemeanors. A felony (art. 11 par. [2]) is an act of crime perpetrated intentionally, for which the statutory punishment is imprisonment for more than two years. All other crimes are misdemeanors. Thus, an intentional offense is a misdemeanor if the penalty is less than two years. A crime committed due to negligence, such as negligent homicide, is also a misdemeanor even though it carries a statutory punishment of five years' imprisonment.

Crimes, and the punishments ordered for them, are set out in individual chapters within the Special Part. The Penal Code is the only source of legally defined crimes, thus, drug-related crimes, economic crimes, and simple traffic offenses are all in one law.

Drug Offenses

Statutory drug offenses are found in the Title 4 (Crimes against Public Health) of Chapter 16 of the Penal Code. Most important characteristics of the law include statutory penalties for drug offenses that do not depend on the type or the harm of drug in question; the quantity of the drug influences the statutory penalty; and offenses committed by users and traffickers are punished differently. Coercive medical treatment as a criminal sanction for drug-addicted offenders does not exist.

In the HPC, all illegal drug-related activities are placed together under the heading "Drug Abuse." Within this, however, there are five different articles. Article 282 contains the so-called user or consumer-type offenses. The use of drugs per se is not a punishable criminal act, but the possession of drugs is. Article 282/A contains the statutory offense of illegal trafficking. The penalty range is 2–8 years of imprisonment. Article 282/B specifically addresses offenses for supplying drugs to a minor and for using a minor to supply them, which may be sentenced to up to 10 years. In the most severe cases, these offenses may also be punished with life imprisonment. Article 283 states that if an offender agrees to complete a treatment program of six months the sentence is suspended, and there will be no criminal record. If, however, the offender refuses treatment, or if he or she accepts, but later fails to comply, the appropriate criminal sentence will be imposed.

Crime Statistics

The official statistical system of recorded crimes and perpetrators was introduced in Hungary in 1964. The Integrated Criminal Statistics of the Police and the Public Prosecution contains, broken down by years, the number of recorded crimes and perpetrators, certain characteristics of crimes (e.g., place and time of perpetration), and certain data regarding the perpetrators (sex, age, etc.). Since 1993 the criminal statistics include the victims of recorded crimes. The system contains data in connection with criminal justice, namely, the number of prosecutorial decisions regarding indictment (e.g., postponement of indictment or filing charges) and of sentencing practice. The most important data are published in an information booklet by the Chief Prosecutor's Office and the Police, and since 2006 by the Ministry of Justice and Law Enforcement. There is no nationwide, regular crime survey in Hungary as yet.

In Hungary, the average number of recorded crimes between the middle of the 1960s and 1980 was approximately 120,000 yearly. In this period the annual average number of offenders was around 80,000. The number of juvenile offenders was typically about 7,000 per year. The number of recorded crimes increased gradually from 1980 to 1988. Subsequently, crime rates increased dramatically from just over 200,000 in 1989 to approximately 600,000 in 1998. The rate of crime detection, at the same time, decreased, and the structure of registered crimes altered.

The dramatic increase in criminality during the first decade following the change in the regime may be explained by the expanding possibilities in most fields of social life, and the inequalities that came with it, which increased the number of opportunities for crime and multiplied the risk factors of criminality. At the same time, however, external control on people weakened, and institutions for reacting to criminality outside the criminal justice system, such as community crime prevention, were not yet established. As the new system stabilized, the increase of recorded crimes subsided, and from 1998 to 2003 (with the exception of one year), the rate decreased. Since 2003, it has been steady.

In 2007 the number of recorded crimes was 426,914, and the number of recorded offenders 121,561. The number of juvenile crimes in the same year was 10,909. Almost two-thirds (64.7%) of the recorded crimes were crimes against property, 6.9 percent were violent crimes, and 5.4 percent traffic crimes. The typical criminal offense in Hungary is theft. In the past few years about 40 percent of the recorded crimes were theft, about 25 percent of which were burglary. One-third of thefts were less severe criminal offenses, that is, theft of money or goods with a value less than 200,000 HUF (US$900 or approx. €700).

Of recorded crimes, the proportion of drug-related crimes between 2003 and 2007 averaged 1.4 percent. In each year, among recorded drug abuse crimes, 90 percent were acts related to prohibited use, while less than 10 percent are attributed to supply and illicit trafficking. Among crimes classified as "violent," the least violent seem to dominate. One-third were attributed to "rowdyism." The level of robberies has not reached 10 percent, while the level of rape has not reached 1 percent in the past five years. Even though the proportion and number of rapes are low, extremely brutal forms of this offense occur each year. Armed bank robbery is considered a new and relatively frequent crime since the second part of the 1990s.

From the middle of the 1960s to 1980, the number of recorded murders never exceeded 237. In 1988 the number of murders was 206, and in 1989 it was 191. From 1990 to 1991, however, the number of murders increased by 50 percent (to 307), and the rate continued to increase from 1991 (307) to 1994 (313). Public opinion blamed the abolition of capital punishment by the Constitutional Court on October 31, 1990, for the increases.

In 1995, however, the increases stopped, and by the year 2000, a significant decrease occurred. By 2005, the number of murders decreased to a level even lower than that of the time of the change in the regime. There has been no research that attempts to explain this phenomenon. Some regional differences in crime rates are noticeable. Of the 19 counties and the capital, the rate of crime is by far the highest in Budapest, for example, 6,257 in 2007. The national average in the same year was 4,241.1, and the average of the counties was 3,828.8.

Finding of Guilt

The procedure for finding of guilt, and the rights and obligations of the participants in the procedure, are stipulated in Act 19 of 1998 on the Criminal Procedure Code (CPC), as amended. The content and structure of the CPC are fundamentally determined by provisions of the Constitution related to criminal justice, such as requirements for fair trial (e.g., Art. 57 of the Constitution). Criminal procedure is based on the principle of legality. This means that investigating authorities and the prosecutor shall commence procedure upon suspicion beyond reasonable doubt, and that they and the courts shall conduct procedure as stipulated by the law.

In Hungarian law criminal procedure consists of three phases: investigation, prosecution (filing of charges), and judicial. Investigation may be performed by the prosecutor, the police, and the customs and finance guards. The prosecutor supervises investigation or performs investigation himself or herself, but most are performed by the police (97%). Investigations are to be conducted in the shortest time possible, most often, within two months. In certain cases the period may be prolonged to one year, and in especially difficult cases, for two years. The prosecutor decides about indictment after the closure of investigation. Following the filing of charges, the court holds a trial to determine if evidentiary procedure shall be conducted for the establishment of criminal responsibility of the accused.

Rights of Accused and Legal Representation

According to the CPC, criminal procedure may be initiated against the person who is, beyond doubt, suspected to have committed a criminal offense. The accused is entitled to the following rights: right to court, and right to independent, impartial court in his or her case; right to remedies (two-level appeal in criminal cases); right to defense; presumption of innocence; prohibition of self-accusation; and right to the use of native language. The accused may perform his or her defense personally or through an authorized or appointed defender. In cases where defense is obligatory, and the accused does not have an authorized defender, the authority appoints one from a registry prepared by the bar.

Trial

According to the CPC, the determination of guilt, and the imposition of a penalty may take place only in trial. In Hungary there is no jury trial. Trial is conducted at local courts before a sole judge in cases for which the statutory penalty is up to eight years. In cases of more severe offenses, the local courts and the county courts proceed in judicial panel. In the local and county courts, the judicial panel is composed of two lay judges and a professional judge. Lay judges have the same rights as their professional counterparts in decision making and determining criminal responsibility. Lay judges may be persons between the ages of 30–70, who are elected from among the candidates by the local government or the county (metropolitan) general meeting.

The CPC provides the possibility for simplified forms of the procedure that ensure faster closure of the case. Arraignment occurs when the statutory penalty for the crime is not more than 8 years; the adjudication of the case is simple; all evidence is available; and the accused is caught in *flagrante delicto* or confessed to the crime. If all conditions are met, the prosecutor may bring the suspect to court within 15 days following the commission of the crime.

Proceedings against a defendant in absentia may be conducted in cases of criminal offenses punishable with imprisonment; when the accused or the defendant is staying at an unknown location or abroad with well-presumed intention of hiding from the authorities. The participation of prosecutor and defender in such cases is obligatory.

Waiver of the right to trial may be considered, to a certain extent, "limited plea bargaining." A prosecutor may terminate the investigation by offering a less strict sentence for a suspect who commits an offense in criminal organization, and the prosecutor received significant information from this person regarding the case or any other criminal cases.

Omission of trial occurs upon the proposal of the prosecutor when the offense has a penalty of imprisonment for less than three years; the facts of the case are simple and the defendant has confessed to the offense. This form is typical against perpetrators driving under the influence of alcohol, the most frequent penalty for which is pecuniary penalty or suspension of driving privileges.

Alternatives to Trial

In addition to the simplified court procedures described above, there are two methods by which material closure of criminal cases can take place outside the courtroom—mediation and postponement of indictment. Mediation may be applied if criminal procedure was initiated in cases of crimes against persons, property, or traffic crimes that demand a statutory penalty of imprisonment for less than five years. The consent of both the victim and the accused is necessary for the conduct of mediation. In the course of one criminal procedure mediation may be initiated only once. If the penalty is imprisonment three to five years, the criminal procedure cannot be terminated, but the least severe sentence may be applied.

Postponement of indictment may be applicable in two cases. In the first, if the offense carries a penalty of imprisonment for not more than three years and, weighing the significance of the offense and extraordinary mitigating circumstances, postponement may be presumed to have favorable effects on the future behavior of the accused. The other instance applies to certain cases of drug abuse in which the perpetrator undertakes to participate in drug dependency treatment, prevention, or counseling. These cases are accompanied by a period of probation and supervision by a probation officer. Criminal procedure is terminated if the period of postponement is passed successfully.

Incarceration before Trial

The law provides for limitations to remaining at large under certain conditions and procedures. *Detention* is applied in cases of suspicion beyond reasonable doubt of an offense punishable with imprisonment, especially when caught in *flagrante delicto,* provided that the pretrial detention of the accused may be presumed. Detention may be ordered by the court, the prosecutor service, or the police. Detention lasts for 72 hours, at most. Only judges may order pretrial detention. It is applicable only if the offense is punishable with imprisonment and the defendant escaped, or attempted to escape; if his or her presence cannot be ensured otherwise; if there is a presumption that if released, he or she would hamper the investigation; or if there is a presumption that he or she would commit the attempted offense. Strict rules apply to its length of time and supervision. Primarily, pretrial detention shall last for 1 month but may be extended under various conditions. The absolute upper limit of pretrial detention, with certain exceptions, is 3 years calculated from the date of the order. Pretrial detention is executed in a prison.

Juveniles

Juvenile criminal justice is not a separate system in Hungary. The judges and prosecutors of the juveniles operate within the criminal justice system. In the CPC, however, there are provisions different from the general rules regarding criminal procedure against juveniles. For example, the law stipulates that at first instance trials against juveniles, one lay judge of the court shall be a teacher. In procedures against juveniles, participation of a defender is obligatory. Among the different provisions, it may be highlighted that a juvenile may be placed into custody only if the severity of the crime justifies it. Postponement of indictment and mediation may also be applied more widely than in procedures against adults.

Punishment

Types of Punishment

The punishment system of the Hungarian Penal Code is a dual one. It contains both penalties and measures. The penalties are divided into principal penalties and secondary penalties. The principal penalties are community service, fine, and imprisonment, which may be for a definite period of time, or life imprisonment (since 1999, the court may exclude the possibility of parole in cases of life imprisonment). Secondary penalties include deprivation of basic rights, suspension of license to practice, suspension of driving privileges, ban, expulsion, fine as an ancillary punishment. Measures can be taken in the forms of admonition, release on parole, involuntary treatment in a mental institution, involuntary detoxification, confiscation, confiscation of property, and supervision by a probation officer, and, exclusively in cases of juveniles, corrective education.

Statistics show that approximately every second adult offender receives a fine. At the same time, however, it shall be mentioned that the punishment system of the HPC has two characteristics that have remained virtually the same since 1989–1990. First, it is extremely imprisonment-centered, and second, there is the shortage of noncustodial or alternative sanctions. This is why the penalty system was modified in June 2009 by Act 80. According to this new act, the principal penalties are imprisonment, community service, fine, suspension of license to practice, suspension of driving privileges, and ban. Secondary penalties are deprivation of basic rights and expulsion. The new rules on the penalty system entered into force May 1, 2010. Community service as a penalty is always an alternative punishment to imprisonment or fine. Fine is also primarily an alternative punishment to imprisonment. In a small number of statutory offenses, a fine can be found as individual penalty. Compensation has been available in the framework of criminal procedure since 2007. In this past year prosecutors postponed indictment in nearly 2,500 cases, to facilitate mediation, providing possibility for compensation.

Typical Punishments

Statutory penalties are set for each crime. For a "basic" case of murder, the statutory penalty is imprisonment from 5 to 15 years. The typical sentence in a basic case is 14–15 years. In "qualified" cases (e.g., "qualified" by the fact that the victim is under the age of 14), the statutory penalty shall be imprisonment from 10 to 15 years or life imprisonment. A sentence of life imprisonment is frequent. In a basic case of rape, the statutory penalty shall be imprisonment from 2 to 8 years. Imprisonment for 2 years is typical. Suspended imprisonment is frequent, especially if the victim is the spouse. For a qualified case of rape (e.g., many persons have sexual intercourse with the victim), the statutory penalty is imprisonment from 5 to 15 years, while the typical sentence is imprisonment for about 10 years.

Prison

Data regarding Hungarian prison population are available from statistics published by the National Headquarters of Prison Service (NHPC), supervised by the Minister of Justice and Law Enforcement; and the data of the King's College International Centre for Prison Studies. At the NHPC data regarding the daily population, annual average number of inmates, and the total number of inmates at the end of the relevant year are available. The service publishes the data in its yearbooks. The total number of inmates in Hungarian prisons on December 31, 2007, was 14,353, and the average number of inmates for the year was 14,897. The capacity of the prisons in 2007 was 11,252, and the occupancy level was 132 percent. Three-quarters of detainees are convicts, circa one-quarter are in pretrial detention. In the past years 97–98 percent of the inmates have typically been Hungarian nationals.

The prison population has significantly decreased compared to the period preceding the change in the regime. In the 1970s and 1980s, the annual average prison population was well above 20,000 and prison population rate per 100,000 inhabitants exceeded 200. As a consequence of modifications to the Penal Code in 1993, and the change in the sentencing practice, the prison population rate significantly decreased.

After 1995, the prison population and the prison population rate increased. In 1998 the number of detainees was 14,366 and the prison population rate 140. In 2002, it was 17,915 and 178, respectively. With the increase, the prison occupancy level rose from the 140 percent of 1998–1999 to 160 percent. From 2002 to 2006, both the number of detainees (14,821) and the prison population rate (147) fell.

Hungary has three levels of prisons. By increasing severity, they are jail, prison, and maximum security prison. There are 32 penitentiaries in total. Of these, 15 are national, 3 are regional, and 14 are county institutions. One of the national institutes and all three regional institutions serve for the placement of juvenile detainees. The largest institution of the country is the Central-Transdanubian National Penitentiary Institute, located in Dunaújváros-Pálhalma. It was established in August 2007 by the unification of two institutions. The institution is both a prison and maximum security prison with accommodations for 1,200 inmates. Along with farm buildings, there is a large area available for agricultural cultivation. An agricultural and trade limited liability company, operating next to the institution, provides employment for the inmates.

Nine industrial and three agricultural companies provide employment for inmates in Hungarian penitentiaries. Inmates have a right to remuneration for work they perform while incarcerated. However, just as in the private sphere, there are not enough jobs for everyone. In 2007 only about 4,000 detainees worked, which is approximately 30 percent of the annual average number of the detainees. Inmates may receive visitors, carry on education, practice religion, access the institution's library, communicate, receive food packets, and leave the institution for a short period of time to visit their relatives.

Miklós Lévay

Further Reading

Jakab, András. (2008). "The Republic of Hungary." In *Constitutions of the Countries of the World,* edited by Rudiger Wolfrum and Rainer Grote, pp. 1–46. New York: Oxford University.

Jakab, András, Péter Takàcs, and Allan F. Tatham. (2007). *The Transformation of the Hungarian Legal Order 1985–2005*. The Hague, the Netherlands: Kluwer Law International.

Kerezsi, Klára, and Miklós Lévay. (2008). "Criminology, Crime and Criminal Justice in Hungary." *European Journal of Criminology* 5(2): 239–260.

Lévay, Miklós. (2007). "'Social Exclusion': A Thriving Concept in Contemporary Criminology. Social Exclusion and Crime in Central and Eastern Europe." In *Penal Policy, Justice Reform, and Social Exclusion,* edited by Kauko Aromaa, pp. 7–26. Helsinki: The European Institute for Crime Prevention and Control (HEUNI).

Iceland

Legal System: Civil
Murder: Low
Burglary: Medium
Corruption: Low
Prison Rate: Low
Death Penalty: No
Corporal Punishment: No

Background

Settled by Norwegians and Celts in the ninth century B.C.E., Iceland is home to the world's oldest functioning legislative assembly, the *Althing,* established in 930. In the 12th century, the country came under Norwegian, and later Danish, rule, but regained home rule in 1874, and complete independence in 1944. Iceland is the most sparsely populated country in Europe. Roughly half of its 320,000 inhabitants live in and around the capital Reykjavik. The economy is heavily dependent on fishing, tourism, and energy production, and with its high literacy rate and life expectancy, strong social cohesion, and welfare-oriented profile, the country ranked first on the UN's Human Development index for 2007–2008. It is presently experiencing an economic downturn after the collapse of the banking sector in 2008. Many numbers in this article are therefore in flux, and there are calls for constitutional reforms.

Iceland is a neutral country with no military. It is a member of the UN, NATO, IMF, World Bank, Council of Europe, International Criminal Court, INTERPOL (and a 2001 cooperation agreement with Europol), Organization for Security and Cooperation in Europe (OSCE), Schengen, the European Free Trade Association (EFTA), and the European Economic Area (EEA). At the time of writing, an application for EU membership is pending. After centuries of ethnic homogeneity, the past few decades saw an increase in immigration, and in 2007, 6 percent of the population held foreign citizenship. A halting of the construction boom has again prompted many foreign workers to leave.

Legal System

Iceland is a constitutional republic with a parliamentary government. Its civil law system is modeled on the other Nordic systems, especially Denmark's. Sources of law are the Constitution of 1944 (Act No. 33, http://www.stjornarskra.is, amended seven times, e.g., to incorporate various provisions of human rights), statutes and regulations published in the Legal Gazette, custom, and tradition of culture (*eðli máls*), a Scandinavian concept akin to equity. Iceland takes a dualist approach to international law: ratified international treaties do not have direct effect until incorporated into domestic legislation. The European Convention on Human Rights was incorporated by Act No. 62/1994. Criminal law is governed by the General Penal Code (GPC), an official English translation of which is available on the Web site of the Ministry of Justice and Human Rights at http://www.domsmalaraduneyti.is/laws-and-regulations/english, as well as of Law on Criminal Procedure, No. 88/2008 (entered into force January 1, 2009).

Judiciary

Iceland's eight district courts (*héraðsdómur*) are of first instance in civil and criminal matters. District court judges are appointed for an indefinite term by the minister of justice. The Supreme Court (*Hæsti réttur*) is the only court of appeal. Its nine justices are nominated by the minister of justice and appointed for an indefinite term. All criminal judgments may be referred to the Supreme Court without restrictions. (District court decisions available, in Icelandic, at http://www.domstolar.is; Supreme Court decisions at http://www.haestirettur.is.)

In 1998, a Judicial Council was given oversight over matters pertaining to the district courts to safeguard their independence, and a committee was established to assess the qualifications of judicial appointees (Reg. No. 693/1999, judicial qualifications, and Reg. No. 436/2000, judges' part-time employment and ownership of companies: http://www.domsmalaraduneyti.is). In October 2009, it was proposed that the same rules apply to supreme and district court judges, and that while the appointing authority remain with the minister of justice, appointments of persons other than recommended by the committee be approved by the *Althing.* In his new year's address to the nation on January 1, 2010, the president of Iceland lamented the fact that judges are still politically appointed.

Police

The Ministry of Justice is responsible for the coast guard and police force (25 districts and police academy); and the Foreign Ministry for the police at the international airport in Keflavik. The entire police force is administered by the national police commissioner. A new law entered into effect on January 1, 2009, which restructures the respective spheres of prosecutors and police (Law on Criminal Procedure, No. 88/2008 replacing Law No. 19/1991). There are five main departments, each with subdivisions: (I) e.g., international cooperation and border control; (II) e.g., riot police, search and rescue; (III) e.g., alcohol and firearms; (IV) e.g., narcotics, crime prevention; (V) prosecutions, tax fraud, money laundering, and so forth. A new central police recording system was introduced in February 2005 to track crime data and the home page of the police includes comprehensive and up-to-date crime statistics, available in English at http://www.logreglan.is.

Crime

In Iceland, a person cannot be found guilty of a crime for acts committed while under 15 years of age. The criminal law is divided into two main categories: the General Penal Code (*hegningarlög*) and special laws (*sérrefsilög*) for violations of specific acts. The GPC applies to violations such as assaults, murder, sexual offenses, theft, destruction of property, and robbery. Drug offenses are covered by a special law on controlled substances No. 65/1974, and alcohol crimes by special law No. 75/1998.

Iceland maintains online statistics on offenses registered by the police in 1999–2008. The total numbers registered in 2008 were 39,734 in the capital region and 35,222 outside the capital region, approximately 75 percent being traffic offenses. (For further details, see http://www.statice.is and http://www.logreglan.is.) In 2008 no murder was reported, homicide cases in recent years having been between 0–3 annually. Due to the infrequency of certain serious offenses, the data may show apparent fluctuations where trends are in fact stable. The average number of offenses recorded by the police in some main categories for the period 2003–2007, according to the National Commission of Police, Crime Statistics 2008 (reported November 2009, http://www.logreglan.is) is as follows:

Unjust enrichment	7,722
Alcohol Act violations	1,648
Violations of privacy	737
Offenses against life and body	1,607
Vandalism	3,355
Drug offenses	1,763
Property theft	427
Forged documents	26
Traffic violations	53,668
Other	3,268

In 2003–2008, 75 percent of all drug offenses were for possession and use, but there was an increase in sale, distribution, and manufacturing. The number of violations is not indicative of the amount of narcotics seized, which can range from 1–2 grams to tens of kilos. Per capita, most deadly and serious assaults (82) occurred in the Westman Islands south of Iceland, and in the South-West peninsulas (62 and 61). In the capital region, there were 40 such violations per 10,000 inhabitants. There were also proportionately more sexual offenses outside the capital region. There were 257 thefts per 10,000 inhabitants in 2008, most in the capital region.

Particular Challenges

The crime rate in Iceland is relatively low; most violations are traffic-related, and only about 20 percent of recorded violations are GPC violations. Often, crime in Iceland has gone hand-in-hand with alcohol abuse, and most violent attacks still occur during weekend brawls. That said, the work environment of the police is rapidly changing. Crimes that were virtually unknown in Iceland, such as international money laundering, organized crime, drug trafficking, and online child pornography, now demand significant time and resources. Due to the financial crisis, the police department has been requested to cut its operating budget, and a recent report on its Web site lists its core tasks in order of priority with a view to identifying possible cutbacks. A new office of Special Prosecutor was established in 2009 to investigate possible criminal activities connected with the causes of the bank collapse.

Finding of Guilt

Assistance to the Accused

An arrested person has the right to contact an attorney immediately upon arrest. The police must grant the wish to appoint a defense attorney, and it may appoint one if not requested. The accused may act on his or her own behalf, and shall be provided with needed information if he or she is not legally trained. The accused may at any stage of a case hire an attorney, and the police and judges must inform the accused of such right.

Investigation and Prosecution

Criminal investigation is carried out by the police unless otherwise provided by law. Special investigative departments handle investigations of the most serious crimes. According to the new Law on Criminal

Procedure (88/2008), prosecuting authority is divided into three spheres. District attorneys prosecute in the first instance any major crimes such as homicides, sexual offenses, and assaults, and major fraud; the State Prosecutor's Office has an oversight role and decides whether to appeal district court criminal judgments; and police chiefs prosecute minor cases such as traffic violations and burglaries.

Pretrial Detention

Pretrial detention is only used if there is reasonable suspicion that the accused is guilty of an act punishable by prison. It is justified if the accused poses a threat to the investigation of the case or to public safety. Strict legal restrictions apply to detentions, and there are no limitations on their appeals. Pretrial detention must be ordered by a judge and shall not exceed four weeks, any extensions requiring a new court order. Trials are heard by a panel of judges who deliberate before closed doors and decide on the basis of majority vote.

Punishment

Under the Icelandic Constitution, the death penalty may never be stipulated by law. The two categories of punishment are imprisonment and fines. Imprisonment may be for life, or for a period not shorter than 30 days and not longer than 16 years. There is strong emphasis, as elsewhere in Scandinavia, on sentences being served outside prisons in the form of community service, release on probation, conditional arrangements, supervised work or study, and alcohol or substance abuse treatment. More than two-thirds of all sentences were served outside prison in the last decade.

Sentences are specified as either conditionally suspended (for less serious crimes) or unconditional imprisonment, for serious and premeditated offenses. Juveniles 15–18 years old who receive an unconditional prison sentence are referred to the Agency for Child Protection for internment in a treatment home.

An officially commissioned study of punishments in Iceland during 1951–2000 focused on murder, attempted murder, serious theft, and assault (excluding drug offenses—as these changed drastically in recent years—and sexual offenses, the lax punishments for which have been severely criticized, e.g., in a recent (2009) book by Þórdís Elva Þorvaldsdóttir). According to the study, punishment for murder is higher in Iceland than in neighboring countries, a typical sentence for murder being 14 years in prison, but then, homicides are rarer in Iceland than in other European countries (approximately one annually in 1955–2000). Punishment for assaults (nonsexual) varied greatly depending on the circumstances, as its sentencing framework is quite wide (up to 16 years). The maximum sentence for theft is 10 years and it is punished relatively strictly. Alcohol does not play as large a role in this category as in assaults. The report noted that tough sentences have not seemed to deter theft, as such offenses have increased with time. Other social factors are at play. Differences between judged sentences and time actually served were not great overall; the average time served for murder, for example, was 12 years.

According to another study, persons convicted of theft in Iceland tend to have grown up in broken families and be repeat offenders or habitual drug users, whereas prisoners found guilty of offenses such as fraud or sexual violence tend to be older, better educated, and from more stable family and work situations. A severe economic downturn could thus be expected to lead to an increase in theft and drug-related crime, and the police in March 2009 reported an increase in theft from the previous year.

Prison

There are five prisons operated by the Prison and Probation Administration (PPA), with a total of 85 staff. As of July 15, 2008, they were populated to 97.9 percent of their official capacity of 144 places. The oldest, *Hegningarhúsið,* built in 1874 is in Reykjavík city center. It is mainly a short-term and reception prison, with space for 14 prisoners and two solitary confinement cells. In Kópavogur, close to Reykjavík, is a women's prison with capacity for 12 prisoners. Litla-Hraun, on the south coast about 70 kilometers (42 miles) from Reykjavík, is Iceland's largest prison; 60–65 percent of all prisoners in Iceland serve their sentence there. The low-security prison Kvíabryggja on the west coast lies on 30 hectares of land to which the (maximum 14) prisoners have full access. Last and smallest is a prison within the Akureyri police station in the north, with room for 9 short-term prisoners.

All prisoners are obliged to work weekdays from 8 A.M. to 5 P.M., or pursue other approved activities while in prison. Consideration shall be given to their personal circumstances and wishes when it comes to work. They are also entitled to pursue studies or vocational training: each hour of study equaling one hour of work. Prisoners are remunerated for work or studies, or receive a per diem allowance for sick days or days on which work was unavailable. On September 1, 2008, the total prison population in Iceland was 140 (7.1% in pretrial detention/remand); representing 44 per 100,000 of the national population. As of July 15, 2008, female prisoners were 4.3 percent, juveniles (under 18) 2.1 percent, and foreigners 19.1 percent.

Visiting Policies, Leave, and Probation

Prisoners may receive visits (usually unsupervised) in prison at least once a week, or they can refuse to receive visits from persons other than those with whom they have official business. When a prisoner has served two-thirds of a sentence, the PPA may allow release on probation, and in special situations when one-half of a sentence has been served. It must be certain that the prisoner has a suitable place to stay, employment, and other necessary support.

The return to free society can be very challenging, so in addition to the service provided in the prisons, the PPA has for years sought to acclimatize prisoners gradually to society by allowing them to serve part of their sentences outside prison in treatment or rehabilitation.

Extradition

Icelandic citizens may not be extradited. Others may only be extradited if the offense involved, or a comparable offense, could be punishable by more than one year's imprisonment under Icelandic law unless otherwise agreed in an extradition treaty with other states. Extradition in connection with political offenses is not permitted, nor if there is a risk that the extradited person will be subjected to injustice or persecution on account of his or her race, nationality, belief, or political opinion in the requesting state. Iceland entered into an agreement with Eurojust in December 2005, for enhanced cooperation in combating serious international crime. An Icelandic citizen may be extradited to one of the Scandinavian countries if he or she has lived there for two years prior to committing a crime in such country and a stricter sentence than four years' imprisonment applies to the act under Icelandic law.

Edda Kristjansdottir

Further Reading

Gunnlaugsson, H., and J. F. Galliher. (2000). *Wayward Icelanders: Punishment, Boundary Maintenance, and the Creation of Crime.* Madison: University of Wisconsin Press.

Icelandic Government: http://www.government.is.

Ministry of Justice and Human Rights: http://www.domsmalaraduneyti.is.

Police Iceland: http://www.logreglan.is.

Scandinavian Research Council for Criminology: http://www.nsfk.org.

State Prison and Probation Administration: http://www.fangelsi.is.

Statistics Iceland: http://www.statice.is.

Ireland

Legal System: Common
Murder: Medium
Burglary: Medium
Corruption: Low
Human Trafficking: Medium
Prison Rate: Medium
Death Penalty: No
Corporal Punishment: No

Background

After a war of independence fought against Britain between 1919 and 1921, the island of Ireland was partitioned, with 26 of its 32 counties gaining a large measure of autonomy and becoming the Irish Free State. The remaining six counties, part of the historic province of Ulster, formed a region of the United Kingdom. In 1948, during a visit to Canada, the *Taoiseach* (prime minister) declared the Free State a republic and severed any remaining links to the crown. The decision to split the island led to a civil war and successive waves of agitation and terrorist activity that have continued, albeit at a greatly reduced level, up to the present. Organizations such as the Irish Republican Army (IRA) and the Irish National Liberation Army (INLA) strove to reunite what they saw as the national territory. There was a countermovement by groups wishing to maintain the union with Britain, most prominent among them the Ulster Volunteer Force (UVF) and the Ulster Defense Association (UDA). The British Army and the Royal Ulster Constabulary also contributed to the scale of the conflict. The violence associated with the national question, which was furious at times—there were 470 deaths in 1972—was nonetheless highly concentrated and rarely strayed south of the border.

Today, the island remains divided into two jurisdictions, the Republic of Ireland (Éire) and Northern Ireland. Since the declaration of a ceasefire in 1994, and the Good Friday Agreement that followed in 1998, the military fortifications that used to be in place along the country's internal border have been removed and the number of British soldiers stationed in Northern Ireland has been scaled down. Paramilitary prisoners who recognized the legitimacy of the peace process were released en masse and a new police force was established to replace the Royal Ulster Constabulary. Despite occasional atrocities perpetrated by militant splinter groups, the ceasefire has held firm.

The focus of this article is the Republic of Ireland, which has an area of 70,300 square kilometers (27,142 square miles) and, according to the census of 2006, a population of 4.2 million (the highest since 1861). Most of the population lives in, or near to, the major cities of Dublin (the capital), Cork, Galway, Limerick, and Waterford. The country includes a number of small inhabited offshore islands, which are home to around 9,000 hardy men, women, and children.

There is a bicameral parliamentary system with 166 members of Parliament directly elected by the people at least once every five years. The upper house comprises 60 senators who are elected by local political representatives, nominated by the *Taoiseach,* or voted in by graduates of Dublin University and the National University of Ireland.

The national languages are English and Irish (*Gaeilge*). A significant proportion of the population has a reasonable level of fluency in the latter, which is a compulsory subject in primary (age 4 to 12 years) and secondary (age 12 to 18 years) school and competency is required for entrance to the National University of Ireland and membership of the legal profession. Citizens are entitled to conduct legal proceedings in Irish and to use the language in any dealings with state agencies.

When the country achieved independence, it maintained the common law legal tradition and the criminal justice apparatus that it inherited from Britain. The legal process is adversarial and professional (there are no lay judges). Colonial legislative arrangements remained in place, courtrooms and penal institutions continued in use as before, and archaic forms of legal behavior were seamlessly transplanted onto the fledgling Free State. Some statutes introduced by the British Parliament in Westminster before independence are still in force, such as the Probation of Offenders Act 1907. Indeed, it is not just buildings and laws that have endured. So too have a number of administrative arrangements, such as the division of the legal profession.

The Royal Irish Constabulary that had policed Ireland prior to independence was disbanded in 1922, followed three years later by the Dublin Metropolitan Police, a dedicated force for the capital. The replacement organization was named *An Garda Siochána* (guardians of the peace) and, remarkably given the revolutionary context into which it emerged, it was unarmed virtually from its inception. The rationale for this decision was expressed by the first *Garda* commissioner, Michael Staines, as a desire for his men to "succeed not by force of arms, or numbers, but on their moral authority as servants of the people."

The criminal justice system exists within the context of a written Constitution, which was enacted by the people in 1937. This deals with the establishment and operation of the courts, the trial of offenses, and the fundamental rights of the person. There are other criminal justice–related provisions sprinkled throughout the text such as those giving the president the power to commute or remit punishment imposed by any court and prohibiting retrospective criminalization. Perhaps the most significant elements of the constitutional framework are that justice shall be administered in courts established by law; all judges shall be independent in the exercise of their judicial functions; no person shall be tried on any criminal charge save in due course of law; and no citizen shall be deprived of his or her personal liberty save in accordance with law.

The Minister for Justice, Equality and Law Reform has responsibility for setting the legislative and policy context according to which the criminal justice system functions. Traditionally this role has involved taking a close interest in operational matters. The minister is also the regular recipient of petitions from politicians on behalf of constituents who wish to have a penalty remitted (usually a fine reduced) or to see an increased police presence on the streets of their area. These factors allow the minister to stamp his or her personality on the portfolio with clearer definition than cabinet colleagues.

For about a decade beginning in the mid-1990s, the Republic of Ireland experienced a period of rapid economic growth. By the beginning of the 21st century, Ireland had been transformed from a failing economy that hemorrhaged many of its young people through emigration to a desirable destination for people seeking a better life. One statistic dramatically illustrates the scale of this change. It is the rise in the number of asylum applications from around half a dozen each month in 1993 to almost 1,000 each month by 2002.

Not unsurprisingly given the changed nature of the resident population, media reports of immigrant involvement in criminal activity began to appear in the late 1990s and prisons began to feel the presence of a more diverse clientele, with almost one-third of committals in 2007 being non-Irish nationals.

Crime

Broadly speaking, criminal cases are divided into two types, summary and indictable. Summary offenses are those of a minor nature and are tried in the district court by a judge sitting alone without a jury. They are usually prosecuted by *An Garda Síochána.* The maximum prison sentence that can be imposed for any one such offense is 12 months, and the maximum sentence available to the court for multiple offenders is 2 years. Motoring matters, public order offenses, criminal damage, and theft make up much of the daily business of the district court. Indictable offenses are more serious and can be heard by a judge and jury in the Circuit Court or the Central Criminal Court; the latter forum dealing exclusively with homicide and serious sexual violence. Any sentence can be imposed up to the statutory maximum, which for more serious offenses such as robbery and rape is life imprisonment. Murder carries a mandatory life sentence, and if the victim is an on-duty *Garda* or prison officer, the minimum term is 40 years.

The Offences against the State Act 1939 provided the legislative basis for a (juryless) Special Criminal Court. This was seen as an important weapon in the fight against subversion, to be deployed when the government was satisfied that the threat of juror intimidation was such that the ordinary courts were "inadequate to secure the effective administration of justice and the preservation of public peace and order." It was reinforced by internment, judicial execution and, in 1940, the establishment (for a brief period) of a Military Court. From its inception, the Special Criminal Court dealt with more than just subversion. While its jurisdiction was restricted to offenses that could not be dealt with by the ordinary courts, what was deemed to satisfy this standard was elastic. In the early years, most of the matters dealt with were economic, such as black market trading that exploited the rationing arrangements put in place during the Emergency (this is how World War II was described in Ireland).

In 1962, the Special Criminal Court was formally disestablished. It was brought back to life in 1972, in response to mounting violence in Northern Ireland, but in the absence of any evidence that the threat to jurors was such that special measures were required. It has been continuously in existence ever since. The resuscitated Special Criminal Court differs from its predecessor in that its members are drawn exclusively from the judiciary, with no military personnel involved. It is similar in the extent to which it has become a vehicle for dealing with persons (including drug dealers and members of criminal gangs) who have no relationship with unlawful organizations, thereby normalizing what were intended as exceptional measures.

Crime Statistics

The compilation and publication of crime statistics was taken over by the Central Statistics Office (CSO) in 2006. A major overhaul followed this transfer of function and in 2008 the figures were published for the first time according to a new scheme, based on the Australian model, and known as the Irish Crime Classification System (ICCS). The table below shows the main crime categories for 2007. It is important to note that, for the purposes of the ICCS, homicide is widely defined, including 78 murders, 6 cases of manslaughter, 1 infanticide, and 48 incidents of dangerous driving leading to death.

Homicide	133
Sexual offenses	1,368
Attempts/threats to murder, assault, etc.	17,550
Dangerous or negligent acts	21,014
Kidnapping and related offenses	108
Robbery, extortion, and hijacking	2,172
Burglary and related offenses	23,556
Theft and related offenses	75,239
Fraud, deception, and related offenses	5,848
Controlled drug offenses	18,588
Weapons and explosives offenses	3,593
Damage to property and to the environment	43,276
Public order and other social code offenses	60,703
Offenses against justice procedures, etc.	10,789

Turning our attention to the geographical distribution of crime, it is clear that for the majority of categories, the highest rates were to be found in the Dublin Metropolitan Region (DMR). Looking at the most prevalent crime types during 2006, the disadvantageous situation of Dublin residents is apparent. The rate of burglary per 1,000 population was 8.3 in the DMR and 3.0 in the predominantly rural, sparsely populated, Northern Region (the national average was 5.8). For theft, the DMR stood at 28.1 compared with 10.1 for the Northern Region and a national average of 17.6. For robbery, the DMR was top once again at 1.4 and the Northern Region was bottom once again at 0.1 (with a national average of 0.6). There was less variation to be found for the statistically infrequent offenses of homicide and sex crime.

Drug crime is a cause of concern, particularly in deprived parts of Dublin where opiate misuse is concentrated. Typically, heroin is administered intravenously with predictable consequences for the spread of diseases such as HIV and hepatitis, and a range of other adverse health effects such as ulcers and gangrene. The gaunt and pitted bodies of long-term heroin users are a regular sight in Dublin's city center. Methadone is widely prescribed as a heroin substitute and dispensed from community pharmacies as well as specialist clinics. The easy availability of methadone is associated with a decline in the kind of offending directly related to drug use. One measure of this is that robberies and aggravated burglaries involving syringes declined in frequency from 1,104 in 1996 to 115 in 2006. On the other hand, the financial attractiveness of the drug trade to criminal entrepreneurs has contributed to an upward trend in lethal violence as disputes about debts and distribution networks are increasingly resolved with guns. The schedule to the Misuse of Drugs Act 1977 sets out a long list of controlled drugs from acetorphine to trimeperidine. The most commonly used drugs, based on seizures by police and customs, are cannabis (resin and herbal), Ecstasy, cocaine, and heroin.

Law and Order Politics

Anxiety about crime reached a peak in June 1996 with the shooting death in the space of a fortnight of a crime journalist (Veronica Guerin) who wrote for the country's most-read newspaper, *The Sunday Independent,* and a *Garda* detective (Jerry McCabe) who was escorting a delivery of cash to a bank. The killing of the former was thought to have been arranged by a gangland figure about whom she was planning to write an exposé. The latter was shot by an IRA unit that was carrying out an unauthorized operation during a temporary break in the ceasefire that had been declared a couple of years earlier. These deaths raised the specter of gangland drug dealers acting with impunity and renegade paramilitaries continuing to pose a lethal threat to the state.

Parliament was recalled from its summer recess for a special debate in July 1996 and the government introduced a swathe of legislation to improve the efficacy of the criminal justice system. Most significant was the setting up of a Criminal Assets Bureau (CAB) to deny offenders the chance to benefit from the proceeds of their crimes. This was a hugely significant development as it meant that assets could be confiscated without a prior conviction or proof of criminal activity; the decision being made on the balance of probability. The onus is then placed on the citizens to establish the innocent provenance of their wealth. These powers have been used with considerable success against individuals believed to have amassed fortunes through the drug trade, extortion, or armed robbery. Often the accused is required to put his or her tax affairs in order by paying the revenue commissioners what the CAB estimates is owed on the basis of ill-gotten gains. There has been muted concern about the implications of this model of policing for civil liberties, especially the presumption of innocence and the burden of proof.

The apparatus of policing is skewed toward offenses such as theft, burglary, public disorder, and gun violence. There is little official recognition of the seriousness of white-collar offending. This is despite the fact that in its annual report for 2007 the revenue commissioners revealed that the cumulative yield from an ongoing investigation into money illegally invested in nonresident bank accounts, insurance policies, and offshore assets had reached €2.4 billion (US$3.02 billion), with just more than €132 million collected during the year in question.

Police

An Garda Síochána is a national body with a unified command structure. It is led by a commissioner who is appointed by the government. For policing purposes the country is divided into six regions. These in turn are divided into divisions, districts, and subdistricts. Each subdistrict usually has only one station, the strength of which can vary from 3 to 100 *Gardaí.* There are 703 *Garda* stations throughout the country and as at April 30, 2008, the personnel strength of *An Garda Síochána* was 13,874 with more than 1,000 recruits in training. Uniformed members of the force do not carry firearms. There are approximately 1,700 detectives who are armed and always work in plainclothes. They are available to support their uniformed colleagues should the need arise. There are a small number of specialist units that operate on a national basis dealing with matters such as drugs and immigration.

The Policing Plan 2008 set out six strategic goals for *An Garda Síochána.* These can be summarized as follows:

- Maintain national and international security.
- Significantly reduce the incidence of crime and criminal behavior.
- Significantly reduce the incidence of fatal and serious injuries and improve road safety.

- Significantly reduce the incidence of public disorder and antisocial behavior.
- Provide equal protection and appropriate service, while nurturing mutual respect and trust.
- Build a *Garda* service that reflects the needs and priorities of the people.

There has been a high level of concern about police indiscipline and the absence of an adequate framework to call errant officers to account. In combination with the lack of an adequate mechanism to handle complaints from members of the public (until the *Garda Síochána* Ombudsman Commission and the *Garda* Inspectorate were created by statute in 2005), this gave rise to a context where a culture of impunity could emerge. Nevertheless, opinion surveys show repeatedly that the police continue to be held in high regard by members of the public and the volume of applications to join the force greatly exceeds the number of available places.

Finding of Guilt

The Office of the Director of Public Prosecutions (DPP) decides whether to charge people with criminal offenses, and what the offenses should be; enforces the criminal law in the courts on behalf of the people; and directs and supervises prosecutions. Most of the cases dealt with by the DPP emanate from *An Garda Síochána.*

An Garda Síochána and the specialist investigating agencies conduct most of the summary prosecutions that take place in the district court in relation to minor offenses. For more serious matters directions are sought from the DPP about whether and how to proceed. There are general principles set out in *The Statement of General Guidelines for Prosecutors* published in 2001, which guide the initiation and conduct of prosecutions. The decision whether to prosecute is based on twin considerations: the strength of the evidence and the public interest.

In many cases the evidence will disclose a number of possible offenses. Determining the choice of charge is generally within the exclusive domain of the prosecutor. According to the guidelines, the charge should adequately reflect the seriousness of the criminal conduct for which there is evidence and provide the court with an appropriate basis for sentence. The charge or charges laid will ordinarily be the most serious disclosed by the evidence but there may also be circumstances that justify preferring a lesser charge than the evidence would support. The prosecutor should only prefer charges that are justified by the facts and must not "overcharge." In summary prosecutions the choice of charge will in most cases be made by a *Garda.* Some offenses can be tried either summarily or on indictment and the law provides for different sentences depending on the method of prosecution.

In 2007, the DPP gave directions on files relating to 10,500 suspects (for less serious crimes there is no need for *An Garda Síochána* to submit a file). In around one-third of these the direction given was not to prosecute, in another one-third the direction was to prosecute on indictment, and the remainder were deemed suitable for summary disposal. For prosecutions on indictment the conviction rate is typically over 90 percent, with the overwhelming majority of suspects entering guilty pleas. There is a strong incentive to do so as such a plea attracts a discount at the sentencing stage.

The DPP does not explain the decisions taken in individual cases. This is based on a concern not to condemn a person without a trial. However, in January 2008, the DPP initiated a dialogue about the propriety and practicality of giving reasons, signaling a willingness to consider reversing years of practice. A consultation process was initiated and a reform package may follow. In part this move to render decisions more transparent reflects a growing awareness of the importance of addressing the interests of victims of crime, who can be pivotal to the case for the prosecution but whose needs are often unrecognized or unmet. Organized support services for crime victims scarcely exist in the Republic of Ireland and compensation for criminal injuries, if not forthcoming from the offender, is available only on a trivial scale (and in selected cases) from the state.

In essence, the law permits any offense to be transferred to the Special Criminal Court if the DPP certifies that the ordinary courts are inadequate to deal with it. The DPP's discretion in this respect is virtually unlimited and there is no requirement to give reasons. The Special Criminal Court only deals with a handful of cases every year (it heard seven trials involving 10 accused persons in 2007), but each one raises serious questions about the integrity of the criminal justice system and the proper nature of the relationship between the state and the accused.

Suspects can be held for questioning by *An Garda Síochána* for maximum periods ranging from 24 hours to 7 days, depending on the nature of the charge. While being detained they are allowed reasonable access to a lawyer but lawyers are not entitled to be present when their client is being interrogated. When charged and produced in court the accused can be remanded in custody if the offense is serious and, in the terms of the Bail Act 1997, their detention is "reasonably considered necessary to prevent the commission of a serious offense by that person." Bail can also be denied if there is a risk that the accused will interfere with witnesses or not turn up for trial. If the offense is a serious one and the accused cannot afford to pay legal fees, then the court will grant a legal aid certificate, which meets the full cost of advice and representation. Some of the most able lawyers in the state provide their services to the defense and it would be fair to say that the opposing legal teams are usually of comparable caliber during a criminal trial on a matter of any consequence.

Judicial Authorities

Judges are not elected. Rather they are appointed by the government and thereafter almost impossible to remove from office. Although Irish judges are political appointees with a party pedigree that is usually obvious, there is a strong professional norm of autonomy and impartiality once they take office. The courts system comprises several layers.

The Supreme Court is made up of the chief justice and seven ordinary judges. The president of the High Court is *ex officio* an additional judge of the Supreme Court. This is the court of final appeal. In addition the president of Ireland may refer any bill (or any provision of a bill) to the Supreme Court for adjudication as to whether it is repugnant to the Constitution.

The Court of Criminal Appeal consists of a judge of the Supreme Court and two judges of the High Court. It hears appeals by persons convicted on indictment in the circuit, central, or special criminal courts.

The High Court (38 judges) exercising its criminal jurisdiction is known as the Central Criminal Court. Trials are conducted by a single judge sitting with a jury of 12 men and women. It deals with murder, rape, and allied offenses.

Two courts of limited jurisdiction are organized on a local basis. The first of these is the Circuit Court (38 judges), which deals with indictable offenses other than those that are reserved for the Central Criminal Court. The other is the district court (61 judges), which deals with minor crimes.

The Special Criminal Court tries cases where it is determined that the ordinary courts are inadequate to secure the effective administration of justice and the preservation of public peace and order. There is a panel of 11 judges appointed to the court who are drawn from the High, circuit, and district courts. It sits without a jury.

In 1995, the law was changed to allow solicitors of at least 10 years' standing to be considered for appointment to the Circuit Court (as well as barristers). The first solicitors were appointed to the Circuit Court in 1996. Circuit Court judges with at least 4 years' experience could also apply for appointment to the High Court, meaning that former solicitors could now be promoted to the High Court. In 2002 a further change was introduced to provide for direct appointments of both barristers and solicitors of not less than 12 years' standing to the superior courts. As a result, the same year, the first practicing solicitor was appointed directly to the High Court. Judges are appointed by the president on the nomination of the government. The government is assisted in this task by a Judicial Appointments Advisory Board, which is chaired by the chief justice.

Juveniles

The district court has jurisdiction to try a child or young person for any offense except homicide provided that, in the case of an indictable offense, the child's parent or the young person has been informed of his or her right to trial by jury and has consented to be dealt with summarily. In Dublin there is a dedicated Children Court, which sits on each working day of the week. In other cities, the courtrooms where ordinary sittings of the district court take place are used. In 2006 the age of criminal responsibility was raised from 7 to 12 years. There is an exception, however, for children aged 10 or 11 who can be charged with murder, manslaughter, rape, or aggravated sexual assault.

In December 2005, following a review of the youth justice system, the government agreed on a reform program. This included the establishment of the Irish Youth Justice Service (IYJS) to coordinate activities that had formerly straddled three government departments (Justice, Equality and Law Reform, Health and Children, Education and Science). The main responsibilities of the IYJS are to develop a unified youth justice policy and devise a strategy for its implementation; to manage and develop children detention facilities and a variety of community sanctions, restorative justice conferencing and diversion schemes; to coordinate service delivery at national and local level; and to produce and disseminate information about youth justice.

The approach to dealing with children who break the law is flexible. Unlike for adults, the desire to see detention used only as a "measure of last resort" is given statutory expression in the Children Act 2001. The same legislation allows for the expungement of most criminal convictions acquired when a person was aged less than 18 years as long as there are no further offenses for three years; for adults there is no facility for wiping the slate clean. Also for children there is a long-established scheme of cautioning and diversion that is operated by *An Garda Síochána,* and since 2006 the Probation Service has put in place a range of interventions and supports that have been designed specifically for young people. While there is some distance yet to travel, the response to youth offending is beginning to acquire distinctive characteristics.

Punishment

There is very little information available about sentencing and it is not possible to determine the average prison terms imposed for different categories of crime, let alone how penalties relate to offender characteristics. What we do know is that there is a great deal of variation. Looking at the district court, the likelihood of imprisonment following a conviction for public disorder or assault in 2007 ranged from 2 percent in one area to 26 percent in another. Turning to the more serious business dealt with by the Circuit Criminal Court, suspended sentences were twice as common outside Dublin (39.4% vs. 19.1%) and prison sentences of more than five years were half as common (6.6% vs. 15.3%). This may result from the balance of offenses coming before the courts, a difference in the characteristics of offenders, or a sterner judicial culture in the capital city.

There is perennial concern around consistency in sentencing and the almost unfettered discretion allowed to judges who, generally speaking, are free to impose whatever combination of sanctions or measures they believe best meets the demands of the individual case, subject only to the statutory maximum or the inherent limitation of the court's powers. They are unconstrained by guidelines. The Criminal Justice Act 1999 introduced presumptive minimum 10-year prison sentences for the possession of drugs worth €13,000 (US$16,338) or more. The clear intent of this legislation was to reduce judicial discretion. However, the court can decline to impose the 10-year minimum if it finds "exceptional and specific circumstances" that would make such a sentence unjust. This clause has been interpreted broadly and few eligible offenders have received the minimum sentence.

Penalties are used interchangeably rather than thought of hierarchically and related to offense seriousness. For example, when imposing a fine the number of days of imprisonment that must be served in default is stated. (It is not uncommon for fine defaulters to constitute up to one in

The interior of Kilmainham Jail in Dublin, Ireland. (Martin Novak/Dreamstime)

four of those committed to prison in a given year.) Similarly, community service is a direct alternative to prison and the judge must state the number of hours of community service to be carried out and how much prison time will be served if the order is not followed. Suspended prison sentences are popular, even for serious offenses. As judicial discretion is broad there is a great deal of variation in the selection of penalties thought to be appropriate even for similarly situated offenders.

But checks and balances are in place. Defense appeals against conviction and sentence have been possible for many years and the Criminal Justice Act 1993 allows the DPP to apply to the Court of Criminal Appeal to have a sentence reviewed on the grounds of undue leniency. Such applications were made infrequently at first (two or three times a year between 1994 and 1997) but have become more common recently, with 42 lodged in 2007. Most are successful.

Probation

The Probation Service in the Republic of Ireland continues to operate within the framework set out by the Probation of Offenders Act 1907. Although this legislation came into existence before independence was won from Britain, it remains in force. This serves as a reminder of the country's colonial heritage and the inertia that has characterized criminal justice policy making. The most significant change in the 20th century was the introduction of the Community Service Order under the Criminal Justice (Community Service) Act 1983, a piece of legislation imported almost in its entirety from England and Wales. Probation supervision consists primarily of individual casework.

Under the Probation Act there is scope for the district court to find an accused guilty but discharge them. This means that no penalty is imposed and the individual does not acquire a criminal record.

This option is regularly availed of because there is no facility for the expungement of adult convictions and courts are alive to the lasting ramifications of a criminal record, especially in terms of employment and travel opportunities.

In the absence of a modern legislative framework judges have tended to innovate, as evidenced by the popularity of what are known as orders for supervision during deferment of penalty. In such cases the judge postpones sentence until the offender has had an opportunity to demonstrate a willingness to respond to a specified intervention. This may involve the payment of compensation to the victim, participation on a drug or alcohol course, or engagement in mediation. The understanding is that if the offender complies, and the reports are favorable, a prison sentence will not be imposed.

Supervision during deferment of penalty is chosen more often by the courts than probation or community service. According to the annual report of the Probation Service, such orders were made on 3,402 occasions during 2007. This contrasts with a total of 2,756 Probation Orders and 1,519 Community Service Orders made the same year. (Imprisonment is more frequently resorted to than probation and community service combined; in 2007 there were 5,715 committals to prison under sentence.)

Another judicial innovation is the request to make a contribution to the court poor box. Although without any statutory basis, the poor box has been applied in a range of circumstances including public order offenses, minor theft and criminal damage, careless and dangerous driving, and possession of cannabis for personal use. The amounts are generally modest but in January 2003 a man convicted of possession of child pornography paid €40,000 (US$50,272) to a named charity in addition to receiving 240 hours community service (in lieu of a nine-month prison term).

Prison

From an overall daily average population of around 400 in the mid-1950s, by the 1970s, the daily average number of prisoners had begun to rise, exceeding 1,000 in 1975. Crime rates increased dramatically during this period, from, on average, less than 20,000 recorded indictable offenses each year in the 1960s to more than 100,000 in 1983. As the prison population grew, the penal system came under increasing strain. This situation was exacerbated by the outbreak of conflict in Northern Ireland in the 1970s, which contributed to an escalation in armed crime, an increased caseload for the Special Criminal Court, and the need to make special provision for politically motivated prisoners. By the mid-1990s, the crime rate was at an all-time high, the prisons were overcrowded, and the safety valve of temporary release (prisoners sent home without supervision before the end of their sentence) was bringing the system into disrepute. When the Department of Justice, Equality and Law Reform relinquished day-to-day responsibility for the management of prisons to the newly established Irish Prison Service in 1999, there were 15 prisons and a daily average population of nearly 3,000. By 2007 the stock of prisoners had grown to more than 3,300 (a rate of around 80 per 100,000 population). Portlaoise prison is the country's only high-security establishment. Its perimeter is patrolled by soldiers from the Irish Defense Forces.

Sentences tend to be short, with 60 percent of those received into prison in 2006 serving less than 6 months and only 4 percent serving 5 years or more (including life). All fixed-length prison sentences automatically attract 25 percent remission, which can be forfeit in the event of prisoner indiscipline. Life-sentence prisoners may apply to the Parole Board after 7 years. They are unlikely to be released before they have served at least 12 years and, when eventually returned to the community, always remain on license and subject to recall.

A delegation from the European Committee for the Prevention of Torture and Inhuman or Degrading Treatment or Punishment (CPT), a nonjudicial body established by the Council of Europe, visited the Republic of Ireland for the fourth time in October 2006. Its report depicted a prison system distorted by a climate of violence and fear. Beatings of prisoners were detailed, and the CPT expressed grave reservations about the effectiveness of *Garda* investigations into allegations of abuse by prison staff. In addition, there was a worrying level of interprisoner violence, with frequent stabbings and assaults, and increasing numbers of prisoners seeking protective custody—in reality 23-hour-a-day lock-up—out of fear for their safety. Limerick and Mountjoy prisons and St. Patrick's Institution for young offenders were deemed "unsafe" for both staff and inmates. The level of violence was attributed to the availability of drugs and the absence of meaningful activities.

The CPT found that conditions in prisons were variable, with some inmates enduring prolonged periods in small, dilapidated cells with another prisoner and a couple of stinking chamber pots for company. Hygiene problems were most acute in prisons like Cork and Limerick that also bear the brunt of routine overcrowding. Clearly, there is some way to go before the Irish Prison Service achieves its mission of providing "safe, secure and humane custody." An inspector of prisons was appointed in 2002 and the work of this office should help to hold the prison service to account by monitoring its activities closely and continuously.

Ian O'Donnell

Further Reading

The Central Statistics Office: http://www.cso.ie/statistics/crimeandjustice.htm.

Kilcommins, Shane, Ian O'Donnell, Eoin O'Sullivan, and Barry Vaughan. (2004). *Crime, Punishment and the Search for Order in Ireland.* Dublin: Institute of Public Administration.

O'Donnell, Ian. (2008). "Stagnation and Change in Irish Penal Policy." *The Howard Journal of Criminal Justice* 47: 121–133.

O'Donnell, Ian, Eric Baumer, and Nicola Hughes. (2008). "Recidivism in the Republic of Ireland." *Criminology and Criminal Justice* 8: 123–146.

Isle of Man

Legal System: Common/Customary
Prison Rate: Medium
Death Penalty: No
Corporal Punishment: Yes

Background

The Isle of Man is located in the Irish Sea just off the coast of the United Kingdom. The island is about 572 square kilometers (220 square miles) and has a population of 76,220. It is a dependency of the United Kingdom and therefore has a parliamentary democracy. Its legislative system is based on the laws of the UK but it also applies its own "Manx Statutes" that derive from the Isle of Man Constitution Act of 1961. The Constitution, like those of its fellow Channel Islands of Guernsey and Jersey, is unwritten. However, it has its own legislation that is issued by the Legislative Council and the House of Keys. The Legislative Council is composed of the president of Tynwald, the Lord Bishop of Sodor, and the attorney general (who does not vote), as well as eight other members named by the House of Keys. The House of Keys consists of 24 seats, which are elected by popular vote to serve five-year terms. Since the Isle of Man is a dependency of the United Kingdom, it does not have its own military, which is instead the responsibility of the United Kingdom. While the legal structure of the Isle of Man is similar to many other common law states, it nevertheless differs in many respects, and this is apparent in its police force.

In the Isle of Man, the police force is called a constabulary, a common European term. The constabulary in the Isle of Man is run by the chief constable and is composed of 379 officers, 29 of which are volunteers. The highest office is the chief constable, followed by the deputy chief constable, 2 superintendents, 4 chief inspectors, 14 inspectors, 39 sergeants, and 183 constables. In addition, there are the commandant (1), special constables (38), support staff (67), and finally, community volunteers (29). This staff deals with all crimes from the most important criminal offenses all the way down to the smallest traffic offenses. According to the 2007–2008 Annual Police Report, most crime statistics have dropped since previous years. The report also states that according to a recent survey, the morale of the squad and job satisfaction have increased substantially in recent years. The police report concludes that "people were feeling a much greater satisfaction toward the police force."

Crime

Classification of Crimes

In the most recent 2008 Crime Report, the Isle of Man reports the crimes according to 12 different categories. Surprisingly, murder and homicide are not included, even though according to the Isle of Man local newspaper Telegraph.co.uk, in February 2004, a man was convicted of a double murder and sentenced to 20 years in jail. Nor is money laundering included, which is also a crime problem in the Isle of Man and other off-coast dependencies that are widely acknowledged in the media. According to the U.S. Department of State, the Isle of Man is on its countries/jurisdictions money laundering list of primary concern. The categories reported instead are assault, domestic assault, burglary in a dwelling, burglary other than dwelling, criminal damage, deception, drug offenses, miscellaneous, acts against public order, robbery, sexual offenses, and theft. Each category receives equal recognition for protection, and each is monitored by the police force.

Crime Statistics

Overall crime rates have diminished over the last three years in the Isle of Man. In 2007–2008 there were 3,824 crimes recorded, which was a 9 percent decrease compared to the average over the last three years, according to the Isle of Man government Web site. In those three years, the greatest amount of crime was in criminal damage (damaging property). In 2007–2008, the number of criminal damages recorded was 1,228, a decrease of 23 percent over the previous year, with numbers lower than the previous year's in every month except March. The Isle of Man police force attributes this decline to the police crackdown on crime immediately after 2004, before which there had been considerable increases in crime. The next highest crime rate in the Isle of Man for the 2007–2008 year was theft. Theft fluctuated throughout the year in comparison with last year's numbers, with a 12 percent increase in the crime since the previous year.

The third most common crime in the Isle of Man in recent years is assault (not including domestic assault), which since 2004–2005 has been a growing problem. Over the last three years, it increased by 12 percent, though in 2008, there is a sign of decrease as a result of police crackdown, according to the police report. Finally, drug crimes in the three years prior to 2008 have been up a total of 52 percent. In 2003–2004, the amount of drug crimes reported was 113, which jumped to 276 in 2007–2008. The following year saw an increase of 10 percent in drug crimes.

Finding of Guilt

As noted above, the Isle of Man follows a legal system based on that of the United Kingdom. However, it has also developed what is called the Manx System that responds more closely to the island's social and political history and draws its authority from the Registry of Deeds. Thus, it does not follow the land laws of the United Kingdom. It still refers to the Parliament of the United Kingdom for certain matters that are based on common concerns, such as defense, nationality, and immigration. But in recent years, the changes in law in the United Kingdom have not been followed by the Isle of Man. The court systems in Isle of Man follow the Acts of Tynwald, which have the right to approve any act they want, and the Orders and Regulations made under those acts.

In Isle of Man there are many different courts that preside over cases. The lower courts are presided over by the high bailiff and the deputy high bailiff. The higher court is called the High Court and has jurisdiction over all criminal and civil cases. These courts have two trial judges that are called the two "Deemsters," a term that comes from Viking times. Next there is the Manx Appeal Court that is presided over by the Deemsters and the Judge of Appeal. They are the ones that see all appeals. If they consider the appeal and there is still room for doubt, there is one step higher to appeal, which is that of the Judicial Committee of the Privy Council in London, although that option is rarely pursued.

Punishment

Although the death penalty has been abolished, physical punishment has not been completely abandoned in the Isle of Man. Juveniles are allowed to be beaten with a cane or birch; however, the cane cannot exceed 4 feet in length or half an inch in diameter and the birch cannot weigh more than 9 ounces, have a length of 40 inches or more, or have a handle length of 15 inches or more. It is also not to have a circumference of more than 6 inches at the center or 3.5 inches at the butt of the handle. For any indictable offense, up to 6 strokes are permitted to a child and 12 strokes for any young adult.

Prisons have been considered fortresses from very early on in Isle of Man history. The first prison, Peel Castle, was used until 1780 as the only prison in Isle of Man. After that it switched to Castle Rushen, which became a prison instead of a castle. In the late 1700s and early 1800s, the government stopped using the court fines to help maintain the prison and so it started to deteriorate. By the 1880s it was deemed inadequate to house all its prisoners. In 1891, the government built a new prison and slowly started to expand it and integrate more and more prisoners into it. In 2005 the Isle of Man began a project to build a new prison, which was the island's biggest capital project, opening in July 2008 with 138 cells. The government transferred 90 inmates from the old prison to the new one to mark its opening. The prisoners are expected to participate in education and vocational training programs that include workshops for "painting and decorating, joinery, and plumbing skills," as well as classes in "basic literacy and numeracy, information technology, arts and crafts, music (practical guitar playing), P.S.H.E. (personal, social, and health education), and other academic subjects." According to the prison Web site, the prisons, although they are meant to be a punishment, also take great measures to reintegrate prisoners into society. This goal is also achieved through the probation system, which focuses on stopping alcohol or drug use, and family and community issues. The probation service works closely with the Isle of Man Prison Service, Drug and Alcohol Team, Parole, Parole Committee, and David Gray House (rehabilitation).

Timothy McCorry

Further Reading

Isle of Man Government: http://www.gov.im.
Isle of Man Police: http://www.gov.im/dha/police; http://www.gov.im/infocentre/faqs/police.xml.
World Corporal Punishment Research: http://www.corpun.com.

Italy

Legal System: Civil/Common
Murder: Low
Burglary: Low
Corruption: Medium
Human Trafficking: Low
Prison Rate: Medium
Death Penalty: No
Corporal Punishment: No

Background

Italy has a population of around 60.1 million people. The country is largely homogeneous linguistically and religiously but is culturally, economically, and politically diverse. Minority groups are relatively small, the largest being the German-speaking people of the Bolzano Province and the Slovenes around Trieste. Immigration has increased in recent years, but the Italian population is declining overall due to low birth rates. Although Roman Catholicism is the majority religion (85% of native-born citizens are nominally Catholic), the Constitution guarantees equal protection and freedom before the law for all religious faiths.

The Italian economy has changed dramatically since the end of World War II. From an agriculturally based economy, Italy has developed into an industrial state and ranks as the world's seventh-largest market economy. However, the Italian economy remains divided into a developed industrial north, dominated by private companies, and a less-developed, welfare-dependent, agricultural south, with 20 percent unemployment. Chronic problems of inadequate infrastructure, corruption, and organized crime act as disincentives to investment and job creation in the south. The country is also affected by a large underground economy, worth some 27 percent of Italy's GDP. This is not subject to taxation and thus remains a source of lost revenue to the local and central government.

Despite numerous recent institutional and legal reforms, the country's most pressing problem remains the inefficiency of the criminal justice system, as assessed by the 2006 Report of the European Commission for the Efficiency of Justice. The report shows that in regard to the annual budget spent on courts and prosecution without legal aid, Italy is second only to Germany but both civil and criminal decisions are rendered, on average, more slowly than by any other European country. The excessive duration of proceedings and the enormous judicial backlog are part of the problem. In the first semester of 2005, more than 3 million proceedings were pending before the criminal courts. In 2005, criminal proceedings averaged two years and five months for the first instance alone, and their duration reached an average of five years and six months for cases taken to appeal and to the Supreme Court of Cassation. Unsurprisingly, the European Court of Human Rights has repeatedly convicted Italy for violation of the European Convention's reasonable-time requirement.

Origins of the Italian Legal System

Although the origins of Italian law might be traced back to Roman and Middle Age law, the current system derives from the Enlightenment. Before its unification in 1861, Italy was divided in several kingdoms, duchies, and the so-called Papal States. The unification of the legal system was a serious challenge because each entity had its own codes of criminal law and procedure and its own judicial system. The Kingdom of Italy (1861–1946) developed as a progressive enlargement of the Kingdom of Piedmont-Sardinia, and its laws (mostly based upon the postrevolutionary French codifications) were initially extended to the newly acquired territories. From the early years of the Italian kingdom, the sources of criminal law and procedure have been codified. The first renowned Criminal Code, inspired by Justice Minister Giuseppe Zanardelli, was approved in 1889, the year that also marked the unification of all prior Supreme Courts in the *Corte di Cassazione,* based in the new state capital, Rome. In the following year a unified Code of Criminal Procedure came into force, to be replaced in 1913 by a new version that still subscribed to the French inquisitorial model embedded in the 1808 French *Code de l'instruction criminelle.*

During the Fascist period (1922–1943), new codes were enacted and although they both originally emphasized crime control to the detriment of civil liberties, they long survived the birth of the republic (June 2, 1946) and the Constitution (January 1, 1948). Since the 1960s, nonetheless, provisions of the substantive and procedural codes have been subject to the scrutiny of the Constitutional Court, the judicial body designed to ensure the alignment of statutory law with the provisions of the Constitution. A new code of criminal procedure came into force on October 24, 1989, a date that stands out as a turning point in the history of Italian law.

The 1989 code marked a departure from the inquisitorial French tradition and partly subscribed to adversarial assumptions. The new code opened the doors to cross-examination of witnesses by parties, private investigation by counsel and detectives, and alternative forms of proceedings (based upon negotiations on the evidence and the sentence between the counsel and prosecutor). More important, the phase of investigation was entirely restructured and the examining magistrate was replaced by a *judge of the preliminary investigation* with carefully defined tasks (issuing of warrants for searches, wiretaps, remanding of defendants in pretrial custody, etc.). A few remarkable features of the continental system, however, were maintained such as the professional judiciary supervised by the Superior Council of the Magistrates, with authority over both judges and prosecutors, the "right to lie" for defendants who give evidence, and the sentencing phase. Unique to Italy is the constitutional principle of mandatory prosecution (Art. 112 I-Constitution), according to which prosecutors are prevented from dropping charges out of their own discretion. However, the idea that discretion could be taken away by constitutional provision is unrealistic, as a prosecution office necessarily concentrates its effort in certain directions and not others, and must eventually make choices in the allocation of scarce resources.

The recent fall of corporate giants (such as Cirio and, more recently, Parmalat), as well as other scandals of mismanagement in public companies, has also led to the progressive surrender of another traditional principle of Italian law, according to which a corporation could not be subject to criminal prosecution. Pursuant to Decree No. 231/2001, corporations can now be brought before a criminal court for offenses committed on their behalf or to their advantage by directors, administrators, and other persons responsible for the governance of the corporation.

A crucial aspect in current Italian criminal policy is that although its crime rates often rank below the European average, public confidence in the criminal justice system is critically low. Low confidence originates from well-founded concerns over the inefficiencies of the criminal justice system (mainly due to inflated budgets and lengthy proceedings) and from the "uncertainty" of criminal penalties. Defendants seldom serve the prison time that the trial court imposed upon them as the law offers multiple ways to reduce jail time, get early release, and access probation—even in the case of serious offenses.

Police

The present organization of public security in Italy dates back to 1981. The National Authority for Public Security is the minister of the interior, responsible for public order and security and the coordination of police forces. Five separate national police forces provide law enforcement: *Polizia di Stato, Arma dei Carabinieri, Corpo Forestale dello Stato, Guardia di Finanza,* and the *Polizia Penitenziaria.*

The *Polizia di Stato* is Italy's national civilian police force. It performs common patrolling, investigative and law enforcement duties, and there are regional and provincial divisions of this force scattered throughout Italy. The *Arma dei Carabinieri* may be regarded as the Italian equivalent of the French *Gendarmerie,* a military corps with police duties. Unrivalled in popular affection and national pride, the *Carabinieri* perform the same duties as the state police, though some units have recently been dispatched in peacekeeping missions abroad, including Kosovo, Afghanistan, and Iraq. The *Guardia di Finanza* is a financial and customs police under the Ministry of the Economy. It is a military corps and its duties primarily involve investigating economic crimes, such as tax evasion, financial crimes, money laundering, smuggling, international drugs trafficking, credit-card fraud, anti-mafia operations, and counterfeiting. The *Guardia di Finanza* has a naval fleet for the overseeing of territorial waters and an air force. The *Polizia Penitenziaria* is a penitentiary body that operates the prison system and handles the transportation of inmates. And similar to park rangers in the United States, the *Corpo Forestale dello Stato* (National Forestry Police) controls Italian national parks and forests. Its duties include fighting poachers, safeguarding protected animal species, and preventing forest fires.

In addition, every Italian town and city operates its own municipal police force, primarily engaged with traffic patrolling, reporting of petty crimes, and combating antisocial behaviors. In recent years, a new program for a neighborhood police termed *Polizia di Quartiere* has been launched. The program consists of pairs of state police officers (or *carabinieri*) patrolling sensitive areas of major cities, on foot.

Crime

Classification of Crimes

The 1930 Criminal Code groups offenses into *delitti* (crimes) and *contravvenzioni* (misdemeanors). Offenses against persons, property, and the state are listed as crimes (e.g., murder, robbery, rape, drug offenses, theft, actual bodily harm), while misdemeanors include, among others, failure to comply with the order of a public authority (Art. 650 CC), failure to disclose one's identity when requested by a public officer, and a number of offenses aimed at protecting the general public and public safety.

The age of criminal responsibility is set at 18, pursuant to article 98 of the Criminal Code. For those who were under the age of 18 when they committed the offense, the law provides a mandatory one-third reduction in penalty. If the defendant is between the age of 14 and 18, however, the court must be satisfied that he or she was "mature" at the time of the offense. The state of maturity is to be determined by experts who are supposed to report on the criminological, psychological, and social aspects of the minor's personality and life. Crimes that are particularly challenging to Italy at present include mafia crimes, the crimes of immigrants, and the corruption in the public sector.

First, mafia-type organizations—which developed in the 20th century essentially as local and regional enterprises—are now multibillion Euro businesses established across the whole of Italy and even abroad. Besides the world-famous Sicilian Mafia, dating back to the 19th century, the list now includes the *Camorra* (based primarily in Campania and its capital, Naples), the *'Ndrangheta* (in Calabria), and the *Sacra Corona Unita* (in Puglia). Mafia-type organizations are characterized by their viciousness and their structural similarity, which is based on a network of secret associations of "men of honor" governed by a code of silence. One of the most significant features of these organizations has always been their aptitude for infiltrating public offices and exerting political influence. In the

A view of the courtroom during former Italian premier Silvio Berlusconi's trial in Milan, Italy, November 21, 2006. Berlusconi was charged with false accounting, embezzlement, and tax fraud. (AP Photo/Luca Bruno)

1990s, Italy adopted a number of measures (such as a tough prison regime for mafia detainees, the encouragement of defections through exceptionally early parole, and the requirement of a low standard of proof to allow the seizure of mafia assets).

Second, immigrant crime is currently a cause for serious public concern. While prisons are filled with foreign nationals (see below), figures for immigrant crime have continued to rise systematically in the last decade. Statistics from the Italian National Institute for Statistics (ISTAT) show that immigrants are especially active in thefts and burglaries in shops and apartments. In 2003, in the metropolitan areas of the central and northern regions (around Turin, Milan, Bologna, and Florence), more than 60 percent of all reported offenders were foreigners. Further, it appears that foreign criminals have learned their lessons from their Italian counterparts. As a result, expressions such as "Albanian mafia" and "Russian mafia" are used to describe ethnic criminal groups engaged in all sorts of criminal activities. To be accurate, however, these groups do not resemble the traditional structure of *Cosa Nostra* since they do not benefit from its political capital.

Third, while most if not all prime ministers and major politicians have been subject to criminal prosecution in the last decade—on different grounds and with remarkably different judicial outcomes—various theories have been put forward to explain the economic, political, and cultural causes of corruption in Italy. Some blame the Italians' poor sense of civic duty, while others suggest that corruption finds fertile soil in the typical Italian attitude of favoring friends and family in social and economic relations. Lack of transparency in the public administration, overly complex legal regulations, and inefficient bureaucracy also play a part.

Such challenges to the country's criminal policy should not, however, lead to underestimating some of the positive developments. The defeat of internal political terrorism, for example, was a major success in the early 1980s, while a number of prominent mafia leaders have been captured in the last 20 years (including godfathers Salvatore Riina, in 1993, and Bernardo Provenzano, in 2006). The last decade also marks a sharp decrease in kidnapping for ransom, once a profitable business—especially in the southern regions of Sardinia and Calabria.

Drug Crimes

The substantive and procedural aspects of drug crimes are governed by an entirely separate body of law (Decree 309/1990) and have been subject to swinging reforms amid heated public concern over the alleged primacy of mafia-type organizations and the role of illegal immigrants in drug trafficking. The personal use of all drugs was decriminalized following a national referendum held in 1993. Since then, only administrative sanctions (e.g., suspension of driving license or withdrawal of one's passport) may be imposed on drug users. Instead, the production, sale, or trafficking of drugs is regarded by the law as a very serious offense with a penalty of between 6 and 20 years of imprisonment (art. 73, Decree 309/1990). Conspiracy to commit drug trafficking is punishable by a prison sentence of no less than 20 years (art. 74, Decree 309/1990). Although personal consumption is not punishable per se, a 2003 statute has nonetheless made it harder for defendants to prove "personal use" when they are found in possession of a quantity of a drug exceeding the figures set in a dedicated ministerial chart. Illegal drugs include opium and its derivatives (morphine, heroin), cocaine and its derivatives, amphetamine, synthetic drugs, cannabis, and hashish.

Crime Statistics

According to the Annual Report of Judicial Statistics drafted by ISTAT, murders connected with organized crime (*Mafia, Camorra, 'Ndrangheta,* and *Sacra Corona Unita*) account for over one-sixth of the murders recorded in the entire country. As anticipated, there are major differences between the north and the south of the country. In the last 10 years, the southern regions account for 97.5 percent of the total mafia murders. In 2006, most murders occurred in Campania (140 out of 621, or 22.57% with less than 10% of Italy's population), while Calabria is the riskiest region, with almost 3 murders per 100,000 inhabitants. In stark contrast, however, figures for *domestic* murders are higher in the north.

Reported offenses for rape quadrupled in the last decade. The increase may be regarded as the direct result of a sharp increase in sexual offenses, although researchers argue that the figures must be placed in a broader context. First, several statutory reforms have introduced new sexual offenses in the Italian Criminal Code (1996, 1998, 2006). Second, the increase may signal the progressive erosion of the "dark figure," which used to keep most of women and minors from reporting sex offenders. Still to date, however, reports of sex offenders are more frequent proportionally in the north than in the south, possibly due to different social perception of sex offenses by region.

Statistics show a constant increase of robberies in the last decade, while theft remained stable. When broken into regional patterns, these data suggest that robberies are more frequent in the wealthy north, while record high figures have consistently been reported in Campania (the Region of Naples), followed by Lombardy (Milan) and Sicily (Palermo).

The ISTAT annual report combines serious drug-related offenses in one figure, which include both drug manufacturing and trafficking (art. 74 Decree 309/90) and conspiracy to commit drug-related offenses (art. 74 Decree 309/90). There are almost as many drug offenses as there are robberies. A snapshot of offenses recorded by police in 2004 is as follows:

Total murders	621
Mafia murders	138
Rape	3,734
Robbery	46,265
Serious drug offenses	30,053

Finding of Guilt

Rights of the Accused

Traditional constitutional guarantees include the principle of legality (no punishment without law), the presumption of innocence (art. 27), habeas corpus (art. 13), freedom from torture and inhuman and degrading treatment (art. 27), right to counsel (art. 24), and the right to appeal all judgments on matters of law before the Supreme Court of Cassation (art. 111 para. 6).

Human rights discourse in Italy has also focused—especially since the 1980s—on the need to align domestic law with the European Convention of Human Rights. The most noticeable reform was the 1999 "fair trial" amendment to the Constitution, inspired almost literally by article 6 of the European Convention. The amended version of article 111 now includes a blend of long-established domestic principles (i.e., the right to a public trial before an independent and impartial tribunal and the right to an interpreter) as well as new and improved guarantees. By way of illustration, the amendment specifies that every accused person has the right to be promptly informed of the accusations against him or her, to be given adequate time to prepare a defense, to summon witnesses on his or her own behalf, and to confront adverse witnesses before the court.

Following the 1999 constitutional amendment, Italian criminal proceedings are subject to principles of adversarial adjudication: an explicit clause prevents the use in evidence of any out-of-court statement made by those who have always avoided confrontation with the accused or counsel. Essentially, the amendment limits the use of prior inconsistent statements and prevents police officers from offering in evidence any statements that they collected from informants during the investigation (art. 195). Similarly, any statements made by co-defendants that refuse to take the stand at trial are inadmissible (art. 513).

The most striking deficiency of Italian criminal procedure remains the length of proceedings. The lack of an effective case management system has led over the years to an intolerable length of both civil and criminal proceedings—which can often last up to a decade (or even longer). The 1999 amendment, however, stops short of announcing a fundamental individual right to a speedy proceeding, which is nevertheless provided for by article 6 paragraph 1 of the European Convention.

With regard to the institutional arrangements of Italian criminal justice, one must be aware that criminal cases are heard by several different courts of justice. While minor offenses are tried before the lay justice of the peace, the majority of offenses are dealt with by the Tribunal of First Instance. Depending on the gravity of the offense, the tribunal sits either with a single judge or with a panel of three judges. In contrast, the Assize Court is given jurisdiction over extremely serious offenses (such as murder), and has a panel of eight judges (six lay, two professionals) who retire together and jointly deliberate on questions of both fact and law. Cases may also be dealt with by a single professional judge at a committal hearing if the defendant agrees to certain simplified proceedings. The Assize Court should not be compared to a jury, as no right to trial by jury is in fact ensured in the Constitution.

Legal aid is crucial in ensuring equal access to justice for all, as provided for by article 6 (paragraph 3, letter c) of the European Convention of Human Rights. Nevertheless, Italy does not operate a structured public defender system: instead, any lawyer may serve as a public defender when available or "on call." It comes as no surprise that public spending for legal aid is very limited. In 2004, the annual budget allocated to legal aid was €66 million (US$82 million), as against more than €3 billion (US$3.7 billion) in the UK. In the same year, the overall number of Italian legal aid cases for 10,000 inhabitants totaled 17, compared to 459 in the United Kingdom. To be eligible for legal aid defendants must prove an annual income below €9,723.84 (US$12,219), increased by around €1,000 (US$1,256) for each person of the household.

Prosecution

The authority to investigate a criminal case and to press charges against suspects rests with the public prosecutor's office, which is attached to the local *Tribunale* (the court of first instance). Prosecutors are *magistrati* (i.e., members of the judiciary) who have been recruited through the very same examination provided for judges (see below) and usually serve for life. In practice, however, investigations are often carried out by police officers and agents (usually referred to as the *polizia giudiziaria*). Appointed agents and officers from all national police corps may serve in criminal investigations under the direct supervision of the prosecution.

There are a few acts of investigation that may only be performed by the prosecutor in person. The most important is the interrogation of suspects and questioning of informants who are in custody. During interrogation, suspects must be assisted by counsel—whether their own or court-appointed—as the law does not permit waiver of the right to counsel. Further, the prosecutor has sole responsibility to issue certain types of search warrants and applications for a wiretap warrant to the judge of the preliminary investigation.

Alternatives to Trial

Drafters of the 1989 Code of Criminal Procedure were especially concerned with procedural economy since the success of an adversarial system of justice requires trial to be the exception rather than the rule. Along with the traditional accelerated proceedings for flagrant crimes and petty offenses, the new code entered the untested waters of plea bargaining–like procedures. Two procedures are available: the first based upon certain concessions to the defendant in exchange for the surrender of certain fundamental rights (*giudizio abbreviato*—summary trial), or the second, agreement with the prosecution on the sentence (*patteggiamento*—application for a penalty upon request).

A summary trial allows the findings of the preliminary investigation to be used in evidence, and may act as a waiver of the hearsay rules, and also triggers an automatic one-third reduction in penalty, should the defendant be found guilty.

Originally, the only offenses subject to *patteggiamento* were those that carried a maximum of a three-year term of imprisonment, in line with the idea that this mode of procedure was unsuited to the prosecution of serious offenses. This state of affairs, however, has significantly changed since 2003, when a statutory reform allowed defendants to file an application for a penalty upon request for offenses punishable by a term of up to seven and one-half years of imprisonment. In any case, negotiations are capped at a one-third reduction of penalty.

The efficacy of trial alternatives must be assessed against their actual use. The 2004 Annual Report for the Opening of the Judicial Year suggests that the prosecutors' offices initiated 561,000 criminal proceedings in 2003, 180,000 of which were eventually resolved either with a summary trial or an application of penalty upon request. These figures account for 32 percent of criminal litigation.

Pretrial Detention

While no right to bail is guaranteed to criminal defendants, any time served in prison before the passing of a final judgment is considered by the law as "preliminary detention." Preliminary detention may only be authorized when there is a probable cause that the defendant committed the crime and material danger that he or she may (1) escape, (2) corrupt the evidence, or (3) commit further crimes. Preliminary detention is permissible for offenses that carry more than a 3-year imprisonment and it must be authorized by a judge, upon the request of the prosecution. The detention order may be challenged within 10 days before the so-called Freedom Court (*Tribunale della libertà*).

Although the Constitution explicitly states that preliminary detention must be limited in length (Art. 13 para. 5), no further specification is provided therein and, as a result, defendants may in fact spend several years in prison awaiting the final judgment. Since 1989, however, the new code sets an accurate time frame for the overall duration of the preliminary detention as well as for the delay within the different phases of a proceeding. As a result, six months is the maximum duration allowed during the investigation stage, one year for the trial of first instance, and so forth. In total, for the most serious offenses preliminary detention may not exceed nine years.

Judicial Authorities

On December 31, 2007, Italy employed 6,377 professional court judges and around 3,200 justices of the peace engaged in both civil and criminal proceedings. Although no separate statistics are available to determine the exact number of professional judges involved in criminal cases, a reasonable figure should be around 2,000. To this figure one should add the lay citizens who are occasionally attached to the assize courts (440 units in 2007) and the nonprofessional judges in the juvenile courts and the supervisory penitentiary courts. As of December 31, 2007, there were 2,184 prosecutors.

All professional magistrates (judges and prosecutors) are chosen through a single public competitive examination. By tradition, all applicants must hold a law degree. Successful candidates are then trained by working for two years with established magistrates. Both the judges and the prosecutors have a lifetime tenure.

Juveniles

Italy operates an entirely separate system for the criminal prosecution of juveniles pursuant to the provisions of Decree No. 448/1988. Special offices of the prosecution and selected police officers and agents investigate juvenile crimes. Juvenile criminal courts sit in panels of four judges (two professionals and two lay persons, chosen from experts in psychiatry, psychology, criminology, and sociology). The lay expert serves in the court for a renewable three-year term.

Criminal proceedings against juveniles are designed to serve both as assessment of criminal liability and as a means of reeducating the offender. The law does not allow the trial of juveniles as if they were adults, no matter how serious the alleged offense is and how mentally "mature" the defendant appears to be. The Italian approach to juvenile justice is characterized by leniency, as pretrial detention is only applied under exceptional circumstances and an automatic one-third reduction in sentence applies. To minimize the stigma associated with the criminal charge, hearings against juveniles are usually held in camera and either a family member or expert provides the defendant with psychological assistance. Two alternatives to trial are available to the court in the case of juvenile crimes. First, the court may dismiss the case if the offense caused only minor damage or constituted an isolated instance of bad behavior. Second, even in cases of serious offenses (such as robberies and murder), the court may place the minor under a tailor-made program of pretrial probation. Under this program, the juvenile is returned to the community for a period in which he or she will have to abide to certain conditions set forth by the court under the supervision of the office for the administration of juvenile justice. General conditions may include enrolling in a study course or maintaining employment, abstaining from unlawful behavior, and so forth. If the probation period goes well, charges will be dropped and the criminal proceeding discontinued.

Punishment

Types of Punishment

The main penalties provided by Italian law for criminal offenders are imprisonment (including life in prison for adults) and/or fine. A number of ancillary sanctions may also be attached to a criminal conviction, such as deprivation of the right to vote; a ban on holding public office, exercising certain professions, or contracting with public authorities; and a suspension of parental rights. Corporal punishments and shame penalties are illegal, unless one considers the publication of the guilty sentence in the national and local press their contemporary equivalent. For minor offenses triable before the justice of the peace, the defendant's reparation to the victim may lead the court to dismiss the case, but this procedure is considered as a settlement of the matter between the alleged offender and the victim, rather than a criminal penalty.

In the absence of a prior criminal record, the court may place a sentence of two years or less on hold for a set period of time (two to five years). If, during that time, the convicted person commits no further offense, no punishment will be served. The law also disfavors short-term sentences on the assumption that incarceration undermines rehabilitation, especially in the case of first-time offenders. As a result, the court may apply substitute sanctions for short-term imprisonment (such as half-time custody and/or *libertà vigilata*, i.e., release under surveillance).

In addition to the aforementioned criminal penalties, a number of "security measures" are laid out by the criminal code with regard to offenders who are deemed socially dangerous. Only noncustodial safety measures—such as the release under surveillance—are served upon those who are found guilty of a criminal offense. Instead, custodial security measures—such as the prolonged confinement in mental hospitals for offenders—are applied in case of insanity acquittals.

Italian criminal law operates a "unitary" monophase sentencing model, according to which the court renders the verdict and sentence simultaneously. The model gives the court "guided" discretion within specified sentence ranges but also imposes upon the court an obligation to justify the sentence with reference to both the gravity of the offense and the character of the defendant. In the last two decades, severe mandatory minimums in the penal code have translated into a widespread court practice geared to the issuing of minimum sentence in most, if not all, cases. In this manner the courts essentially forego their discretionary authority and the entire purpose of sentencing is frustrated.

Further, the sentence imposed on the defendant at the end of the trial is subject to significant change during the term of that sentence. The Supervisory Penitentiary Court frequently grants good time credit (45 days every 6 months), half-time regimes, home detention, probation, and other benefits to those who qualify for them under the terms of the law (very strict limits on such benefits, however, are provided for mafia and terrorist offenses). In practice, a defendant who files for summary trial in the case of a "simple" murder may be sentenced to 14 years (considering the one-third reduction for summary trial) and then, subject to good conduct, apply for parole, early release, and/or other benefits as early as after 8–9 years of detention. In the case of murder of first degree, instead, application for summary trial would cut the sentence automatically down to 30 years, and the inmate will become eligible for half-time detention after 15 years and early release after 19 to 20 years.

Imprisonment

The Italian prison system is governed by Statute 354/1975, which is a body of law originally designed to guarantee requirements of article 27 of the Constitution, including freedom from inhumane and degrading treatment and the rehabilitation of offenders. Over the last several decades, the 1975 act has been amended by several major reforms to align prison policy with sometimes contradictory goals: at times, the additional protection of detainees' rights, and at other times, with public interest concerns for criminal emergencies like mafia and terrorism.

In an effort to reeducate offenders, prisons implement tailor-made treatment programs designed by professionals. Treatment includes work assignments, sport and recreational activities, contact with family, the encouragement of spirituality and religious beliefs, and a number of other benefits and privileges (good conduct time credit, release on special occasions, visits to family, and early parole). Italy also operates a maximum-security detention regime for dangerous inmates or detainees awaiting trial. This regime is usually referred to as "Article 41bis," the provision which governs the matter since the 1992 amendment to Statute 354/75. Article 41bis was introduced in 1986 as an emergency measure to deal with prison unrest and revolts in the age of domestic terrorism. On June 1992, after the killing of magistrate Giovanni Falcone by the Mafia, an amendment to Article 41bis allowed restrictive measures to be taken whenever there was "serious concern over the maintenance of order and security." The aim was to break the chain of command between Mafia bosses in prison and their subordinates in the outside world. In response to the killing of Falcone's colleague Paolo Borsellino, more than 400 Mafia inmates were transferred from Palermo to maximum-security prisons on both the mainland and the island prisons of Pianosa and Asinara, where the severity of the "41bis regime" was enhanced by geographical remoteness. Over the years, the "41bis regime" has gradually been relaxed in response to domestic court decisions and the European Committee for the Prevention of Torture and Inhuman or Degrading Treatment or Punishment recommendations, to ensure appropriate contacts and activities for prisoners subject to that regime. The prisons on the islands of Pianosa and Asinara were closed between 1997 and 1998.

Nonetheless, a discussion on contemporary prison policy would not be complete without a preliminary reference to the 2006 Pardon Act (*indulto*). Approved by a two-thirds parliamentary majority as required by the Constitution, the Pardon Act was specifically designed to reduce the inmate population in the light of the country's very limited prison capacity. Regrettably, Italy has been found in breach of the European Convention of Human Rights for the flagrantly insufficient amount of personal space given in 2002 to a detainee in the Rome-Rebibbia prison (the Sulejmanovic case). Under the terms of the 2006 Pardon Act, all inmates were eligible for pardon, with the sole exclusion of mafia and terrorist offenders. The immediate effects of the statute were remarkable: 61,264 inmates were detained on June 30, 2006, but by August 31, 2006, the figure had dropped to 38,847. A year later, on June 30, 2007, the inmate population had increased to 43,957, which may suggest that some former inmates had reoffended, but, on the other hand, national crime rates did not suffer any sudden increase. In July 2009, however, the prison population was back to pre-Pardon Act figures (63,574).

Some statistics may help clarify the current state of penitentiary affairs in Italy. For example, foreigners are disproportionately represented in Italian prisons; in 2007, 48 percent of the incoming inmate population was foreign. In contrast, women are underrepresented and only account for the 4.4 percent of the total inmate population. Additionally, the system is very reluctant to serve prison sentence on minors, as on June 30, 2007, only 393 minors were incarcerated in Italy (50.5% of whom were foreigners). With regard to adults, the most represented age group is 30–34 (at 17% of the total inmate population), and more than 50 percent of inmates are between 24 and 44 years old.

Prison

In 2007, there were 160 facilities for detainees awaiting trial and 37 penitentiaries for convicted inmates. To this figure one must add 8 facilities for custodial security measures, including 6 mental hospitals for offenders. All Italian prisons are administered directly by the state through the Department of Penitentiary Affairs, under the authority of the Ministry of Justice. Nonetheless, the regional and local governmental bodies have taken a keener interest in prison policy as of late. A 2005 regional statute for inmate rights in Lombardy, for instance, supplements national law and has paved the way for similar efforts in other regions.

The largest prisons in the country are located in Rome, Milan, and Naples. Milano-San Vittore and Roma Regina-Coeli are 18th-century panoptical prisons, and they host around 1,400 and 900 detainees awaiting trial, respectively. The detention center of Milano-Opera has more than 1,000 inmates and hosts a separate section for detainees in preliminary detention, a maximum-security compound as well as a separate section for female inmates. The prison operates a number of educational and work activities, including courses in creative writing, a tailoring workshop, and the Free Opera soccer team, which is enrolled in the local championship and is allowed to travel for away matches. The prison hospital has a section for infectious diseases. Additionally, a mosque is available for Muslim inmates. The newly built (2000) detention center of Milano-Bollate has a maximum capacity of 970 inmates and is among the largest and most innovative in Europe. Its prison cells are equipped with one, two, and four beds. All sections include kitchen facilities, common areas, and a gym. The inmates may work at the prison's call center, in the information technology department (the prison has a Web site: http://www.carcerebollate.it), in food services as well as at the carpentry workshop.

Convicted prisoners are under the obligation to work, while detainees awaiting trial may do so only upon request. On June 30, 2007, 28 percent of detainees reportedly had a job. Most inmates, however, were employed by the prison administration itself and served within the walls of the penitentiaries. In the first six months of 2007, there were 317 active professional courses, with a total figure of 3,667 inmate students. Courses include information technology (the most popular), cooking, gardening and farming, electricians, arts and culture, craftwork, textiles, construction, typography, and plumbing.

Visiting policies and privileges vary depending upon the prison. Broadly speaking, detainees are allowed six visits each month. Each visit has a maximum duration of 1 hour. For people in preliminary detention, visits must also be authorized by prosecution authorities. Visits take place in dedicated areas, under the visual surveillance of prison guards. Some prisons, such as Rome-Rebibbia, provide dedicated and closed rooms to allow for a more discreet setting for certain intimate meetings. In any case, wiretapping of conversation during visits requires a court warrant. Inmates are also allowed one 10-minute phone call per week. Restrictions do not apply to the visits and communication with counsel. Solitary confinement is allowed only in case of infectious diseases, as a disciplinary measure (for no longer than 15 days) and for detainees in pretrial detention, when the court finds it necessary for the investigation.

Italian law allows both the transfer of prisoners to foreign countries to serve the sentence imposed by an Italian court and the extradition of persons that must serve a custodial sentence imposed upon them by a foreign court. These procedures are governed in detail by the Code of Criminal Procedure (art. 697 746), unless otherwise specified by international agreements among the concerned countries. Generally, decisions on these matters are subject to both political and judicial scrutiny, by the minister of justice and the competent court of appeal, respectively. Under no circumstances will the transfer or extradition be allowed if there is reason to believe that the person may be subject to the death penalty, to cruel and degrading treatment, or discrimination on grounds of gender, race, religion, nationality, or political opinions.

It is worth noting that extradition within part of the European Union has recently been replaced by the simplified system of the European Arrest Warrant (EAW). Italy passed domestic legislation in 2005 to implement the EU directive concerning the EAW. In essence, the European Arrest Warrant means faster and simpler surrender procedures without political involvement. Member states can no longer refuse to surrender to another member state those citizens who have committed, or who are suspected of having committed, a serious crime in another EU country party to the EAW, on the ground that they are nationals.

Stefano Maffei and
Isabella Merzagora Betsos

Further Reading

Grande, Elisabetta. (2000). "Italian Criminal Justice: Borrowing and Resistance." *American Journal of Comparative Law* 48: 227–259.

Maffei, Stefano. (2004). "Negotiations 'on Evidence' and Negotiations 'on Sentence': Adversarial Experiments in Italian Criminal Procedure." *Journal of International Criminal Justice* 2(4): 1050–1069.

Maffei, Stefano, and Isabella Merzagora Betsos. (2007). "Crime and Criminal Policy in Italy: Tradition and Modernity in a Troubled Country." *European Journal of Criminology* 4(4): 461–482.

Perrodet, Antoinette. (2005). "The Italian System." In *European Criminal Procedures,* edited by Mireille Delmas-Marty and J. R. Spencer, pp. 348–414. Cambridge: Cambridge University Press.

Pizzi, William T., and Luca Marafioti. (1992). "The New Italian Code of Criminal Procedure: The Difficulties of Building an Adversarial Trial System on a Civil Law Foundation." *Yale Law Journal of International Law* 17: 1–40.

Note: The authors wish to thank Stephanie Watson for editing this essay and Mariel Covarrubias for research assistance in reviewing the 2006 Report of the European Commission for the Efficiency of Justice for findings relevant to Italy.

Jersey

Legal System: Common/Customary
Prison Rate: Medium

Background

Jersey is an island located just off the coast of the United Kingdom in the English Channel. The island is 116 square kilometers (44 square miles) and has a population of 91,533 and is the largest of the Channel Islands group, larger than its counterpart Guernsey Island of 78 square kilometers(30 square miles). Jersey is a dependency of the British Crown, and uses the UK laws, although it does have local statutes and its justice system is administered by its Royal Court. It does not have a written constitution and obeys both the statutes and the common law of England. The government is a parliamentary democracy, and Queen Elizabeth is the chief of state. Since it is a dependency, it relies on the United Kingdom for its foreign affairs; this includes any military action. The legislative branch of Jersey consists of the unicameral States of Jersey with 58 seats, but only 55 voters. The three nonvoters are the dean of jersey, the attorney general, and the solicitor general appointed by the monarch. Of the 55 voters, 43 are appointed to a three-year term, and 12 are appointed to a six-year term. The judicial branch, as mentioned above, follows the Royal Court, which has judges appointed by an Electoral College and the bailiff.

Police

The police force of Jersey Island consists of around 240 different officers. It consists of four different departments, the Community Safety Branch, the Drugs Squad, the Public Protection Unit, and the Joint Financial Crimes Unit. These different branches are what control all different aspects of crime in Jersey. Each department has its own officers whose duties depend on their respective unit.

According to the Jersey police Web site, the Community Safety Branch consists of many different groups of officers. These officers are community officers, licensing unit, crime reduction unit, road safety unit, the youth action team (YAT), the dog section, and also a charity group called "Prison! Me! No Way!" Each of these units has a different role in serving its community. The community officers try to build relationships with community members, all the way down to the dog unit. The Drugs Squad's mission is to control "all major drugs dealers involved in the supply of illegal drugs in Jersey, whether residing on the Island or in other jurisdictions." The Public Protection Unit deals with sexual and violent crimes, focusing especially on "dangerous offenders" defined as "people who physically abuse children in their care directly or indirectly—engage in the sexual abuse of children physically or mentally—Abuse intimate partners and adult family members—Commit serious sexual offense—Pose a threat to other members of the public through their tendency to use extreme violence." They are in charge of the most serious offenses that take place on the island. Finally, the Joint Financial Crimes Unit is the unit that focuses on financial crimes, especially operations that deal with drug money laundering as well as money laundering that supports terrorism.

Crime

While there are the usual property crimes and assaults in Jersey, probably the most significant type of crime occurring in Jersey (and other Channel Islands) is money laundering and tax evasion. In fact, these islands are widely considered to be the biggest source of off-shore wealth in the world. The UK government has threatened to impose new regulations and legislation on the Channel Islands, of which Jersey is a major player, to prevent and control money laundering and tax evasion. Jersey actually has about a 25 percent higher standard of living than its partner the United Kingdom, getting most of its money through money laundering. Due to taxes being so much lower in Jersey Island compared to the United Kingdom (no inheritance tax, no capital gains, and only 20% income tax), it is much cheaper to keep money in Jersey Island. Also it makes it very hard for the tax department in the United Kingdom to pick up on any "slip-ups" in tax write-offs that people may have taken. That is why many British people have off-shore bank accounts registered in Jersey Island. Nor is it just the British people, but more than 100,000 companies also have off-shore accounts registered in Jersey Island. It is good revenue for the island because having these bank accounts is not illegal, so they can charge for holding the money. So while the person who is money laundering can benefit from the possibility of avoiding taxation, Jersey Island makes money in a legal way.

Crime Statistics

The 2006 Crime Report for Jersey Island is the most complete, up-to-date report available. The crime report breaks down crime into five different categories: acquisitive crime, offenses against the person, offenses against property, illegal drug offenses, and financial crimes. Over the last three years on average, the most prevalent crimes were acquisitive crimes, followed by offenses against property, offenses against the person, then drugs, and financial crimes. In 2006, there were 5,030 crimes recorded in Jersey Island, a drop of some 5.6 percent from the previous three years. According to the crime report the number of "serious crimes" fell by 7 percent against the three-year average, and a total of 10 percent from the previous year. Also 18 percent of crimes were committed by children ages 14 to 17, which is a 7 percent decrease since 2004. Of all street violence, more than 100 assaults were reported, but no murders.

Finding of Guilt

The court system in Jersey Island consists of five different departments comprising Bailiffs Chambers, Law Officers, Viscount's Department, Judicial Greffe, and Probation and After-Care Service. Four of these divisions help in the court proceedings while the probation and after-care service deals with the offenders and the courts to make sure that the offender will not reoffend. The Bailiff's Chambers provides support to the bailiff. According to the Jersey Island government Web site, "the Bailiff is the one who is head of the judiciary, President of the States and civic head of Jersey." The law officers' duties are to protect the state by giving the Crown and states legal advice. Their role is essentially that of attorney general. The Viscount's Department is the administrative muscle of the departments, making sure that the convictions and decisions of the courts are carried out.

Six different courts make up the court system in Jersey Island. These courts are the Royal Court (High Court), the Court of Appeal, the Magistrate's Court, the Youth Court, and the Petty Debts Court. The High Court is the court that is presided over by the bailiff of Jersey. These courts hear different cases based on their respective jurisdictions. The Judicial Greffe is the department that looks over all these courts and can hear all general matters of the courts.

An important service of the Jersey Island legal system is the JLIB, or Jersey Law Information Board. The JLIB was developed in 1998, and has been a very important resource for legal information in Jersey. It can be used for legal issues, research, for businesses, or just for information that any person may seek. The JLIB Web page is one of its main assets, receiving more than 2 million page views per year. The site contains Jersey Law Reports, Royal Court Rules, directives of the Royal Court, and much other useful legal information.

Punishment

Jersey Island does not practice capital punishment. Its main punishment for serious crimes is imprisonment. The island has one prison, HM Prison La Moye. The prison can hold up to 184 inmates. Men, women, and juveniles are segregated into separate units. It also has a protective ward for vulnerable prisoners. The prison does have visitation hours but only two visitors over 16 years of age can visit at one time. If the person is under the age of 16, he or she must be accompanied by an adult.

Jersey practices an idea of ROTL, which is a Release on Temporary License. This is not a right of the prisoner, but it may be implemented as part of the sentence. It is a way to reintegrate the prisoner into society, providing funds for accommodation, helping with family relationships, or in obtaining employment. It is a way to help prisoners by allowing temporary release and slowly returning them to society instead of being suddenly faced with release.

Another way that Jersey Island helps its prisoners during their punishment period is through education. When prisoners first enter HM Prison La Moye, they must meet with someone from the Prison's Education Department. They are then encouraged to take tests and programs that best fit their appropriate level. The Prison Education Department offers six different programs. These are basic skills assessments/lessons, English for speakers of other languages, information communication technology (computers), open learning, and workshop training.

Timothy McCorry

Further Reading

Bailiff and Chief Justice of Jersey: http://www.jerseylaw.je.
Jersey Government: http://www.gov.je.
Jersey Police: http://www.jersey.police.uk.

Latvia

Legal System: Civil
Murder: Medium
Burglary: Low
Corruption: Medium
Human Trafficking: Medium
Prison Rate: High
Death Penalty: Maybe
Corporal Punishment: No

Background

The Republic of Latvia is a parliamentary, multiparty democracy with free and fair elections. The republic gained its independence from Soviet rule in 1991 and entered the European Union in 2004. The Interior Ministry operates under the basic principles of openness, the rule of law, proportionality, compatibility, reporting, and due regard to the constitutional rights of citizens. It oversees administrative rights (ensuring public order as well as democratic principles and human rights within relationships between the state and private individuals); criminal rights (focusing on reduction in crime rates; protection of victims; rectification of injustice; fair, speedy, and efficient judgment of individuals convicted of crime; and criminal resocialization); civil and commercial rights; international and European Union rights; and ensures an efficient and reliable court system. The Interior Ministry holds responsibility for upholding the law and oversees the national police, security police, special immigration police, and border guards, while municipal police are under local control. The Ministry of Defense supervises the Military Counterintelligence Service and the National Guard.

Police

Police are militarized civil servants tasked with the responsibility of the protection of life, health, rights and freedoms, property, and the interests of society and of the state from criminal and other illegal threats. There are a number of different types of police, including the state police, civil police, criminal police, and local government police. Police have the right to arrest, transport, and detain anyone they believe is acting or has acted unlawfully or is posing a danger to himself or herself or others. They also have the right to enter residential units by force without permission of the residents to arrest an occupant or if there is some danger. Police have the right to use physical force against others as well as weapons. No one has the right to interfere with the police while they are fulfilling their duties. As of

Riot police in Riga, Latvia, prepare for demonstrators at a commemoration of the Latvian Waffen SS unit, March 16, 2010. (Ints Vikmanis/Dreamstime)

2002, there were more than 10,000 police officers, just over 4.5 per 1,000 population.

Human Rights

The National Human Rights Office is independent from other public authorities and ensures essential human rights are upheld. However, some concerns remain, including police abuse, corruption and bribery within law enforcement ranks, poor conditions within detention facilities and prisons, prison overcrowding, judicial corruption, obstacles to due process, violence against women, child abuse, human trafficking, violence against ethnic minorities and homosexuals, and governmental discrimination against homosexuals. Another concern is the length of the investigatory process, as the average length of time a detainee spent awaiting trial under detention in investigatory jails was seven months.

Crime

Classification of Crimes

Criminal offenses are broken down into two categories, criminal violations and crimes. Punishment for criminal violations does not exceed 2 years' imprisonment. Crimes are classified as less serious, serious, and especially serious. Less serious crimes are punishable by 2 to 5 years' imprisonment. A serious crime is punishable with imprisonment from 5 to 10 years. Especially serious crimes are punishable from 10 years to life imprisonment.

Guilt is based on either intentional or negligent criminal offense. Anyone under 14 years of age cannot be held criminally liable for his or her actions. Individuals found to be in a state of mental incapacity at the time of the offense due to a mental disorder or disability also are not held liable for the offense. If it is determined by a court that the individual was incapable of fully understanding or controlling his or her actions the sentence may be reduced or reversed with compulsory medical measures.

Latvian Criminal Law prescribes the following crimes:

- Murder is the intentional illegal homicide of another person and is punishable by 5 to 15 years' imprisonment with or without subsequence police supervision. Aggravating circumstances can increase the maximum sentence for murder to life imprisonment with police supervision for up to 3 years and confiscation of property.
- The intentional serious bodily injury of another that is dangerous to life or causing disfigurement, loss of pregnancy, loss of vision, loss of hearing, or loss of any other bodily function is punishable by up to 10 years' imprisonment with police supervision for up to 3 years.
- Human trafficking carries a sentence of 3 to 8 years in prison, with or without confiscation of property.
- Rape, defined as sexual intercourse committed by means of violence, threats or taking advantage of the state of helplessness of a female victim, is punishable by up to 7 years' imprisonment and police supervision for up to 3 years. Subsequent rape convictions carry sentences up to 15 years' imprisonment. Rape of a minor female is punishable by life imprisonment.
- Theft is defined in the Criminal Code as concealed or overt stealing of movable property of another. This carries a maximum sentence of 4 years' imprisonment but is also punishable by custodial arrest, community service, or fine.
- Robbery is theft of movable property associated with violence or the threat of violence and is punishable by up to 10 years' imprisonment with confiscation of property and police supervision up to 3 years.
- Drugs: The unauthorized manufacturing, production, acquisition, storage, registration, dispensation, transportation, or conveyance of narcotic or psychotropic substances carries a wide array of sentences, including imprisonment up to 5 years, confiscation of property, custodial arrest, community service, and fine. Illegal substances include cocaine, synthetic drugs, opiates, and cannabis.

Crime Statistics

According to the Latvia 2007 Crime and Safety report issued by the Overseas Security Advisory

Council, in recent years crime rates in general have been on the rise in Latvia. Specifically, officials report increases in assault (intentional serious bodily injury), theft, residential break-ins, drug-related crime, and economic crime.

According to the Fifth Annual BSA and IDC Global Software Piracy Study, the total crimes reported for 2002 were 49,329. The Eighth United Nations Survey on Crime Trends and the Operations of Criminal Justice Systems reported that there were 1,718 robberies, down from 2,664 in 2000. The total number of adults prosecuted in 2002 was 15,508 and in 2000 the total females prosecuted was 2,014. The total number of adults convicted in 2002 was 12,615.

The Regional Security Office at the U.S. Embassy Riga, reported by the Overseas Security Advisory Council, reports the following for 2005:

- Juvenile crimes reported: 2,465 (1,427 were theft-related and 144 were more serious robberies)
- Murders: 106 with 75 more deaths resulting from intentional serious bodily injuries
- Rapes: 221
- Intentional serious bodily injury: 717

Finally, the World Development Indicators database reported that there were 629 drug offenses per 100,000 people in 2002.

Special Matters

Suicide is a significant societal problem in Latvia. According to the World Health Organization, the suicide rate in Latvia is one of the highest in the world (45 suicides per 100,000 citizens). Causes of this high suicide rate are thought to include high rates of alcoholism and unemployment.

With a high rate of alcoholism, driving under the influence is also of great concern in Latvia. Recidivism rates for DUI offenses are quite high as are rates of vehicular manslaughter taking place while the driver is under the influence of intoxicants. Latvia maintains its rank as having one of the highest per capita vehicle accident rates and vehicle death rates in Europe. According to the Regional Security Office at the U.S. Embassy Riga, reported by the Overseas Security Advisory Council, in a period of only one month (January 2005) there were 3,640 automobile accidents resulting in 431 injuries and 47 deaths. Reasons for this include the high rate of alcoholism, lack of adequate lighting of roads outside of city centers, and unsafe driving conditions during winter months.

Car theft is also a widespread problem in Latvia. Russian organized crime gangs are known to commit vehicle thefts and quickly transport the stolen property across the national border into the Russian Federation. For this reason, over 90 percent of stolen vehicles in Latvia are not recovered. It is also not uncommon for the offender to choose particularly expensive vehicles and contact the owner after the theft to negotiate a ransom for the return of the vehicle.

Finding of Guilt

Latvian law requires that all arrests be made openly and with official warrants. Detainees must be informed of the charges being placed against them and the Prosecutor's Office must either officially charge the individual or release him or her within 48 hours of arrest. Investigation is carried out by officials from state security and defense institutions, officials from those institutions designed for maintaining public order, and other specially authorized agents of the state. Detainees have the right to an attorney's presence at all times, but this right is often alienated by investigators who conduct interrogations without the detainee's legal representation present. Indigent detainees are provided legal counsel by the government. A bail system exists in Latvia, but other than in economic crimes, it is rarely used. Pretrial detention is allowed but is limited to 18 months, and this maximum stay is only allowable in cases of the most serious crimes.

According to the Overseas Security Advisory Council, reports by the Regional Security Office at the U.S. Embassy Riga indicated that in 2006 there were 76,480 criminal cases initiated in Latvia. Of these, 8,746 were sent to the Prosecutor's Office for prosecution and 20,599 were dismissed. Less than half of all crimes were resolved in 2006.

Judicial System

Latvia maintains an independent judiciary. The Latvian judicial system comprises district (city) courts, regional courts (which hear appeals from district courts), separate administrative courts, the Supreme Court (which is the highest appeals court), and the 7-member Constitutional Court responsible for hearing cases in which constitutional rights were violated. As of 2000, there were 315 judges in Latvia. Judges are appointed by the *Saeima* (Parliament) following the recommendation of the minister of justice. Those considered for appointment must be citizens of Latvia and deemed highly qualified and honest lawyers. District judges must have the following minimum qualifications: have obtained a law degree, be at least 25 years old, have at least two years of in-service time within the legal profession, and have successfully completed a qualification examination. Before appointment to the regional or Supreme Court, judges first serve at the lower level of court or as an attorney, prosecutor, or lecturer at the Department of Law at a higher educational institution. All requirements must also be met by judges appointed to the Constitutional Court. In 1998, the Disciplinary Board of Judges was established to ensure objective evaluation procedures and the Judicial Qualification Board was installed to grant qualification degrees after judicial training and enforce high standards for the appointment of judges.

Once appointed, judges have full security within their positions and can only be removed from office if convicted of committing a crime. The justice minister is responsible for overseeing court procedures including the discipline of judges. Courts and laws regarding civil, criminal, and administrative matters are regulated by the Constitution, the Act on Civil Procedures, the Act on Criminal Procedures, and the Act on Administrative Procedures.

Trials in Latvia are fair and public unless the protection of governmental secrets or minors is at issue. One trial judge hears the majority of cases, while in the most serious criminal and civil cases two lay assessors will join the professional judge on the bench in hearing the case at both the district and regional levels. In some cases, randomly selected citizens will make up a modified jury, having limited participation in the trial.

Defendants have the right to be present at their trial; read charges and view evidence against them; and call witnesses and offer evidence in their defense. There is a presumption of innocence until defendants are tried and proven guilty. However, it is the defendant's responsibility to collect and present evidence to substantiate his or her defense. If the defendant is unable to collect this evidence, a request can be made of the court after which the court will assume the responsibility. According to the European Commission Judicial Network, the evidence must be "integrally, fully and objectively" verified by the court and evaluated using logic, science, and experience. After the court has ruled, defendants have the right to appeal the decisions of their case.

Individuals committing offenses in Latvian territory but not under the jurisdiction of the Republic of Latvia are held liable for their offenses on an individual basis through agreements made between the states involved. Citizens of other states may be deported for criminal offenses.

Judges are held to high standards of conduct regarding fairness, integrity, impartiality, and diligence; however, corruption is a serious problem in Latvia as the judicial system is overburdened and understaffed. According to the European Commission, the Latvian court system is in need of reform as the process of hearing court cases takes an unreasonable amount of time. It is also its opinion that the enforcement of sentences is inefficient due to a lack of necessary enforcement instruments and a lack of authority over many public bodies that implement the court's decisions.

Punishment

Types of Punishment

According to the Criminal Law of the Republic of Latvia, the objective of punishment is not only to punish the offender of the criminal offense but also to dissuade the offender and others from committing such offenses in the future. The court system favors prison sentences over alternative forms of punishment, but a number of alternative punishments are at the court's disposal, including custodial arrest (the holding of a person in short-term compulsory imprisonment for up to one year), confiscation of property, community service (up to 280 hours), deportation, fine, limitation of rights (including the right to entrepreneurial activity, to specific employment, to the holding of certain positions, or the acquisition of permits), and police supervision (for up to three years). When sentences are determined, aggravating and mitigating circumstances are often considered. In 1999, Latvia ratified its Constitution, establishing a clemency board for decisions surrounding use of life imprisonment, which amounts to at least 20 years' incarceration.

Death by shooting was once allowed in cases of murder with especially aggravating circumstances. However, when joining the European Union, Latvia was required to abolish use of the death penalty, which it did in 1999. However, the country has still not ratified Protocol 13 of the European Convention of Human Rights that bans the death penalty for all crimes, including in times of war. Citizens of Latvia retain highly punitive attitudes toward criminal punishment.

According to the latest finding of Prison Watch Public Association, the average imprisonment sentence is 4.5 years for men and 3 years for women. In 1998, 5 percent of inmates were serving sentences that were longer than 10 years. However, in general, only 8 percent of all convicted individuals actually serve their full sentence.

Prison

In 1995, amendments were accepted to the Latvian Penal Code regarding the implementation of progressive punishment. Punishment is now based on the progressive English system of differentiating inmates into specified prison types. Adult prisons fall into three categories, closed, semiclosed, and open, while juveniles are held in educational facilities. The appointment of prisoners to each prison type as well as the transfer of prisoners between prison types is determined on the basis of such considerations as time served, behavior, crime type, previous convictions, attitude toward other inmates, and attitude toward prison staff. As of July 2008, of the 15 prisons in Latvia, 8 were closed prisons, 2 were semiclosed (including a women's prison), 2 were open facilities, 2 were investigatory jails, and 1 was a juvenile education institution. Untried detainees are kept separate from convicted inmates in separate sections within these institutions. The average prison holds between 470 and 970 inmates. The largest, the Central Prison, can hold more than 2,000 inmates. The women's prison is capable of holding 347.

In 2008, Latvia had 15 prisons operating at only 89 percent capacity. As of July 2009, there were 7,200 prisoners including pretrial detainees and remand prisoners. In recent years the prison population has been declining steadily. Convicted individuals are required to maintain employment throughout their sentence. However, in 2006, only 17.6 percent of prisoners were engaged in some form of prison employment. More than half of prisoners at this time were allowed only one hour out of their cells per day, as they were not involved in work or educational programs.

Inmates are expected to work an eight-hour workday, six days per week, with additional days off during holidays. Jobs include sewing, metal work, horticulture, and prison maintenance. Prisoner pay is unregulated by legislation but does not fall below minimum wage. Only three of the adult prisons include educational facilities in which prisoners can obtain general education or professional skills training.

Although oversight of the prisons passed from the Ministry of the Interior to the Ministry of Justice in 2000, the style of management within the prison system remains militaristic. Prisoners are rarely kept in individual cells and reports often indicate less than ideal conditions of both facilities and prisoner treatment. Some of the prisons are dilapidated and not properly maintained. One report indicated that prisoners were allowed only one shower per week. Poor facility conditions and prisoner treatment may be responsible for suicide being particularly problematic within the prison system.

Juveniles

Minors (those younger than 18 years of age at the time of the offense) are punishable for criminal offenses by deprivation of liberty, custodial arrest, community service, or fine. Imprisonment of minors cannot exceed 10 years, except in cases of especially serious crimes for which up to 15 years' imprisonment is allowable. Only one juvenile prison exists in Latvia, Cesu Correctional Institution for Juveniles, which is an educational facility. Cesu currently houses more than 100 inmates, ages 14 to 21. A grant from Norway Grants is currently being used to establish guidelines for prison-building standards as well as to begin a reform to this institute, renovating the dilapidated structures and erecting new buildings for pretrial detention as well as space for educational and rehabilitation activities. This institution will then serve as a pilot project for future improvements anticipated for the other Latvian prisons.

Kristen Lee Hourigan

Further Reading

European Judicial Network in Civil and Commercial Matters, "Taking of Evidence and Mode of Proof—Latvia": http://www.ec.europa.eu/civiljustice/evidence/evidence_lat_en.htm.

History of Latvian Prisons, Latvijas Republica: http://www.ievp.gov.lv.

Smart, Ursula. (2006). "A Visit to Latvian Prisons." *Justice of the Peace* 170(47): 810–813.

2008 Human Rights Report: Latvia. U.S. Department of State, Bureau of Democracy, Human Rights, and Labor: http://www.state.gov/g/drl/rls/hrrpt/2008/eur/119087.htm.

Liechtenstein

Legal System: Civil
Murder: Medium
Prison Rate: Low
Death Penalty: No
Corporal Punishment: No

Background

The Principality of Liechtenstein is one of a group of modern microstates with significant impact on the fabric of international criminal justice. More notable recently for its centrality in numerous international banking scandals than its thriving industrial sector and charming countryside, the tiny nation presents a rich amalgam of legal customs and practice worth considerable study. This is particularly so with regard to the inherently cosmopolitan obligations of the Liechtenstein economy. As Duursma (1996) states, "Due to the limited possibilities of internal trade . . . the economy is highly dependent on exports and the inflow of foreign capital. Consequently, the economy is more exposed to external influences than those of larger countries" (p. 148). Accordingly, this "exposure" has caused the Liechtensteiner government to reconsider its position regarding both internal legal regulations and its role as a member of the global criminal justice community. That Liechtenstein in all of its scant 160 square kilometers (61.7 square miles) and 35,200 inhabitants should be at the center of international affairs is nonetheless appropriate given its long history as a European crossroads.

Liechtenstein has a parliamentary form of government, but it is one situated inside a constitutional hereditary monarchy, according to which the power of the state is vested in both the prince and the people. The Constitution of Liechtenstein sets up a system of checks and balances between all sections of the government and the electorate. The Diet (Parliament) is composed of 25 directly elected representatives who serve four-year terms. Further, the government is led by a prime minister and 4 councilors who are appointed by the prince. This arrangement requires close cooperation between the various governing interests as well as the citizenry. On the matter of public participation, the people of Liechtenstein have the right of referendum, which appears to play a significant part in local politics.

The centrality of the Regnant is set down in article 7 of the Constitution of Liechtenstein, "The Prince Regnant is the head of state and shall exercise his sovereign authority in conformity with the provisions of the present Constitution and of the other laws." The only apparent limit to the governmental power of the monarchy was a single caveat that the prince could not appoint or dismiss the head of the government at will. According to a 2003 BBC news report, under threats the Liechtenstein royal family would otherwise "move to Austria," the people voted to make Prince Hans-Adam II an absolute monarch. While His Excellency already held the power to dissolve the national Parliament and to call elections, he also wanted the authority to remove any member of government at will.

The Judiciary

The Liechtenstein judicial system owes much to the Austrian system, on which it is largely based. If a presiding magistrate is acting as a so-called sole judge, that person is a professional magistrate appointed by the prince for life. Typically there are about eight sole judges, some of whom may be from Austria. This rather unusual arrangement stems from an 1884 treaty between the nations whereby Austria agreed to "lend" Liechtenstein judges. If the court consists of more than one judge, the majority will be laypersons. In no instance, however, are foreign judges allowed to comprise a majority on a court. Interestingly, every Liechtensteiner may be appointed for a four-year term as a judge.

In criminal proceedings of the first instance, there are four different courts empowered to hear cases. A sole judge is deemed competent to hear cases in which the maximum penalty could be six months' imprisonment or less. A Court of Aldermen Judges (*Schöffengerichtshof*) may hear indictable offenses; a Criminal Court (*Kriminalgerichtshof*) will hear the most serious allegations; and a Juvenile Court (*Jugendgerichtshof*) is reserved for matters dealing with people under the age of 18. It should be noted that cases of those persons accused of serious crimes (i.e., those heard by the *Kriminalgerichtshof*) will be conducted with a public jury as well as presiding judges. All court decisions and indeed all orders of the government may be appealed before the *Verwaltungsbeschwerdeinstanz,* an administrative tribunal. This body consists of a chairman (typically a trained jurist) and four appeal judges appointed by the prince on proposal of the Diet. The law also provides that each member shall have a substitute available and that the chairman be a Liechtensteiner.

This tribunal has executive authority in that its decisions take precedence over government orders. If a party to a civil, criminal, or administrative case claims that a given law or government order is unconstitutional, the matter is then referred to another body, the State Tribunal. This body consists of five judges each appointed by the Diet for five-year terms. The tribunal must include at least two professional jurists and its president is appointed by the prince. The president and at least two other members must be native Liechtensteiners.

The Council of Europe reports that the Liechtenstein government spent approximately 0.23 of its 2004 annual budget per inhabitant as percentage of per capita GDP for its courts. This level of expenditure puts Liechtenstein at the average for Europe. Spending per capita on legal aid is among the highest on the Continent.

For prosecution of criminal conduct beyond the immediate purview of the Liechtenstein state court system (i.e., matters such as genocide, crimes against humanity, and war crimes), the principality consults the International Criminal Court at The Hague. In 2001, Liechtenstein ratified the "Rome Statute" proffered by the United Nations Diplomatic Conference of Plenipotentiaries on the Establishment of an International Criminal Court.

On the matter of individual rights and fairness of criminal process, the Constitution and laws of Liechtenstein make extensive provisions. Individuals may not be subject to arbitrary arrest or detention. Within 24 hours of arrest, suspects must be brought before a magistrate (often at the behest of a prosecutor). The magistrate is obliged to either file charges or order the subject's release. An accused person has the right to legal counsel of his or her own choosing during pretrial detention. Moreover, counsel is provided indigent persons. This said, until very recent legal changes, suspects could gain access to a lawyer only after a magistrate had filed formal charges.

During pretrial detention, visits are not allowed except for some contact with family members. During investigative detention, visits may be monitored to prevent evidence tampering or other behavior that might interfere with administrative process. While awaiting trial, the accused may be released on bail or freed on his or her own recognizance, provided he or she is deemed neither a danger nor a flight risk.

At trial, defendants may challenge government witnesses and evidence as well as present witnesses or evidence on their own behalf. Defendants are presumed innocent and have access to government-held evidence relevant to their cases. A new provision, § 128a of the (amended) Code of Criminal Procedure (StPO), mandates that every apprehended person must be made aware, at the time of apprehension or immediately thereafter, of the offense of which he or she is suspected. Further, he or she must be apprised of the reason for his or her apprehension, his or her right to inform a relative or another person of trust and a defense lawyer, and of his or her right to remain silent. Additionally, the accused shall be made aware that any statement he or she makes may be used for his or her defense, but also as evidence against him or her.

The National Police

As with the judiciary, policing in the principality has a necessarily internationalist character. With a total personnel of approximately 130 persons (85 of whom are sworn), the National Police or *Landspolizei* have a broad range of tasks and obligations, including management of the nation's single correctional facility, the *Untersuchungsgefängnis.* Since 1960, the agency has been a member of INTERPOL and according to its Web site, "At the regional level, the trilateral police agreement with Switzerland and Austria guarantees cross-border cooperation in the field of crime fighting, mutual assistance in the case of major events as well as in conjunction with the search for suspects."

The *Landspolizei* are organized into three administrative divisions: Security and Traffic, the Executive Support, and Crime Investigation. Each of these reports to a bureau headed by a chief of staff and ultimately to a police commissioner. Each of the constituent divisions within the agency contains six specialized units tasked to deal with particular types of criminal activity or public service. The *Landspolizei* Web site indicates that the agency answers approximately 159 calls for service each day. The role of women in the *Landspolizei* has expanded in recent years. According to the agency, there are currently 5 female sworn officers, each of whom performs duties identical to those of male officers. The majority of the 48 support staff members (nonsworn civilian personnel) are female.

At a glance, the *Landspolizei* appear to be as thoroughly modern, well-equipped, and professionalized as any police agency in Europe. New police recruits attend a year-long training academy at the *Polizeischule Ostschweiz* in Kirchstrasse, Switzerland. The training curriculum consists of lessons covering 50 different topical areas. As of 2005, Liechtenstein and Switzerland have also agreed to share information regarding DNA and fingerprint identifiers relevant to criminal investigations. With regard to broader international criminal matters, the Office of Foreign Affairs for Liechtenstein notes that the principality is a signatory to the European Convention on Mutual Assistance in Criminal Matters as well as a member of INTERPOL. As will be discussed below, Liechtenstein's position in world banking and financial matters has strongly undercut the vitality of this participation.

With regard to the police use of deadly force, the United Nations Human Rights Committee reported, "The rate of use of firearms by national police in Liechtenstein was very low. The last case dated back to March 1996 when a police officer fired a warning shot to stop a robber." The committee further observed, "And in 1999 a weapon smuggler was shot by the Swiss border control forces after he shot a border control officer. There had been no more incidents of this kind in Liechtenstein during the last ten years."

Beyond observing professional proprieties, the *Landspolizei* appear to be engaged in an active program of what might be termed community-oriented policing. Current police campaigns include promotion of seatbelt use, encouraging respect and tolerance of diversity, home security, Internet safety, safety for elderly persons, drug abuse prevention, credit card fraud protection, violence prevention, and traffic safety.

The Correctional Institutions

Given the close connections with the Swiss and Austrian governments, it is not surprising that Liechtenstein has unique arrangements with regard to its correctional institutions. While the vast majority of prisoners are dealt with internally, starting in 1983 Liechtenstein has housed long-term prisoners (sentences longer than two years) in Austrian institutions. Since the enabling agreement went into force, Liechtenstein has referred only a few prisoners each year to Austria. According to a report entitled, *Ressortbericht: der liechtensteinischen Justiz aus dem Jahr,* in 2007, there were only three Liechtensteiner prisoners in Austrian facilities, representing a combined total of 870 days' imprisonment. There are, however, a couple of caveats to the bilateral agreement: the offense in question must also be punishable under Austrian law; the maximum period of detention cannot exceed that for which Austrian law would provide and; the prisoners may not be incarcerated for either tax crimes or political crimes.

As mentioned above, the *Landspolizei* are responsible for operation of the nation's single correctional facility, the *Untersuchungsgefängnis.* This facility is a part of the police facility and has capacity to house 22 prisoners. In addition to the director, there is a full-time staff of six and a varying number of part-time staff on an ad hoc basis.

Several sources indicate that Liechtenstein correctional facilities (inclusive of those prisoners sent to Austria) house as many as 90 prisoners. While this may be true in terms of the total number of individual persons serviced during a given year, it is likely more correct to state that there are approximately a dozen (or fewer) persons incarcerated at any one time. The Council of Europe Annual Penal Statistics report as of September 2006 notes there were 10 prisoners total in the *Untersuchungsgefängnis* (including pretrial detainees and remand prisoners). This report further states that 40 percent were pretrial detainees; 60 percent were foreigners; none were either female or juveniles. It is perhaps telling that in its most recent site-visit report, the European Committee for the Prevention of Torture and Inhuman or Degrading Treatment or Punishment states, "No-one was being held in the police cells located within the *Untersuchungsgefängnis* at the time of the visit."

While all correctional systems doubtless have room for improvement, it appears from a variety of impartial sources that the Liechtensteiner correctional facility is managed with an eye toward fair, humane, and publicly transparent operation. In its Committee against Torture report, the United Nations concluded favorably with regard to the preparation of officers assigned to the facility, "[The officers] are trained for three months in the area of the treatment of prisoners and other persons held in custody. This training includes studies of the relevant international law such as the European Convention on Human Rights, as well as the Penal Code and the Code of Criminal Procedure."

Upon examination of the Council of Europe report on conditions in the facility, it is clear that improvements might be made. On a number of frontiers including access to health care, conditions specific to female prisoners and juveniles, and use of observation cells, there is a need for additional attention. This being said, the report demonstrates that the problems found pale in comparison to those in many other nations; in fact, the relative treatment of Liechtenstein prisoners is arguably excellent as compared to many other correctional systems. According to the Council of Europe report, work opportunities for prisoners had improved over time. Some prisoners were able to secure employment assembling electric guitars. Prisoners are afforded work, recreational, educational, and other opportunities during their incarceration. However, sports activities were "underdeveloped." The report focused in particular on the absence of a promised, but unrealized table tennis table. In sum the report stated, "there was a pervasive air of boredom in the establishment, prisoners spending most of their time playing cards in the small common room, reading books and watching TV."

Crime

From the preceding mention of a national prison with no prisoners in residence, one may properly infer that Liechtenstein is blessed with an exceptionally low crime rate. Criminal statistics reveal that the occurrence of serious crime is so infrequent that to speak of Liechtenstein's crime in terms of "rates" is largely uninformative. During the seven years for which data were available, there was only one homicide and there were never more than five robberies per year. Also worthy of note is the fact drug crimes have declined during the last two years. Given the precipitous decline in drug crimes, one is given to wonder whether this change reflects a difference in reporting rather than occurrence, however, no information was available to provide clarification.

Moreover, the fact that overall crime has increased markedly during the last two years bears closer examination. Juvenile offending could provide one possible reason for this overall increase. In 2006 and 2007 there were approximately 200 youth crimes and an equal number of petty vandalism crimes each year. If one removes those two categories from the overall tallies, the apparent two-year upsurge vanishes. As with the drug crime anomaly, one wonders whether this also reflects a change in reporting strategies rather than actual occurrence.

While no explanation is readily available to account for the apparent drop in drug crimes, some light may be shed on the distribution of total offenses for 2006 and 2007. According to the *Landspolizei,* of the 134 and 132 drug-related arrests made during 2006 and 2007, respectively, approximately two-thirds were for simple possession or consumption offenses. There were three cases of smuggling in 2006 and two cases in 2007. There was only one so-called severe case (*schwere fälle*) in 2006.

Weapons cases follow a similar pattern with an average of 100 offenses each year. The incidence of frauds, thefts, assaults, arson, promotion of prostitution, and rape is equally stable year to year. In fact, just considering these two years (years for which the most complete statistics are available), most categories of crime show remarkably small variation.

Punishment

As a starting point for criminal prosecution, Liechtensteiner law is couched in the concept of *mens rea.* Section 5 of the Criminal Code speaks directly to the "willful," "knowing," or "intentional" commission of an act. Similarly, the perpetrators of inchoate or "attempted" offenses are criminally liable, "The penalties for willful acts shall not only apply to a completed offense, but also to an attempt and to any participation in an attempt." Likewise, criminal culpability extends not just to the immediate actor, but to all who assist in the crime, "Not only the immediate perpetrator shall be deemed to commit the punishable act, but also every person who directs another person to perform the act or who otherwise contributes to its performance."

For those persons convicted of crimes in Liechtenstein there exists a broad array of possible penalties. These sanctions range from small fines to life sentences in prison. Liechtenstein abolished the death penalty in the 1980s and according to Amnesty International, the last execution in Liechtenstein took place in 1785.

While Liechtenstein law does not permit plea bargains or negotiated sentences, the Criminal Code does permit "Diversion," which provides an array of alternative settlement mechanisms. According to the Liechtenstein Prosecutor's Office, "Well over 100 cases are solved like this annually. Typically applied to possession of small quantities of drugs, small thefts, domestic violence cases (mediation), but also in all kinds of other cases where suitable (not felonies)."

Liechtenstein also makes extensive use of probation for minor crimes and assignment to treatment facilities for many drug-related offenses. Likewise, Liechtensteiner Criminal Code provides for forfeiture, confiscation, and absorption of assets gained as the result of crime. The Liechtenstein Criminal Code is also structured to take into account mitigating and aggravating circumstances of the offense as well as the broader societal implications of a given course of formal sanction.

For typical ranges of sanctions for specific crimes, the Criminal Code prescribes the following: For murder, the range can be from 10 years' imprisonment to a term of life; for robbery, the possible sentences range from 1 to 10 years' imprisonment; for rape, the penalty is 1 to 15 years' imprisonment; promotion of prostitution carries a sentence as high as 2 years' incarceration; for violation of pornography laws, the violator can receive a sentence of up to 1 year's imprisonment; for the most serious drug offenses, the penalty can go as high as 20 years' imprisonment. As implied before, it is in some stead difficult to talk about "typical" penalties for many of the aforementioned offenses as they are rarely charged.

One category of offense, drug crime, is particularly interesting to discuss with regard to its enforcement in Liechtenstein. Predictably the possession, sale, transportation, manufacture, cultivation, and use of many substances is prohibited here as it is in many nations. All of the commonly thought of illicit substances—marijuana, opiates, hallucinogens, amphetamines, barbiturates—are strictly controlled by the government. For individuals convicted of use/possession, there are treatment programs. As stated above, for more serious offenses, long prison terms may result. Obviously, there are myriad variations on the severity and extent of sanction. What is perhaps most compelling about drug enforcement in the principality has very little to do with the end user, but a lot to do with the international community through which the drug trade is financed and operates.

Banking and secretive finance are arguably the cornerstone of the Liechtenstein economy, a fact that makes it very attractive to money launderers. As T. Patterson of *The Independent* newspaper of London reported on March 15, 2008, "Banks and 'discreet' financial services are the core of its economy. They account for 14.3 per cent of the workforce and contribute to 30 per cent of a gross domestic product of €2.7bn (£2bn)."

Following September 11, 2001, Liechtenstein was forced to acknowledge (at least tacitly) that banking practices inadvertently served to fund terrorist activities. As Komisar asserts in her article entitled "Dirty Money and Global Banking Secrecy," Liechtenstein belonged to a group of states that "offered state-of-the-art financial services for crooks." L. MacDonald of *The Guardian* summarized the principality's dealings on June 2, 2008, "Millions of dollars of South American drug money were allegedly laundered here; Saddam Hussein's government even registered a jet. In 2000 . . . the [OECD] named the country as the only money-laundering nation in Europe and put it on its blacklist."

Response from the global community was swift. Whether motivated by diplomatic pressure or economic necessity, the Liechtenstein government was obliged to reform its national banking practices and reassert its position as a responsible participant in global affairs. In October 2001, Liechtenstein established a Financial Intelligence Unit (FIU) as an early warning system for potential abuse of the country's banking practices.

In its fifth report to the UNCTC Liechtenstein cites, "a total revision of its Due Diligence Act." The necessity of a revision arose primarily from Liechtenstein's obligation to implement the second EU directive on money laundering. Among the measures taken were amendments to its Criminal Code, the Narcotics Act, and the Mutual Legal Assistance Act, all of which were directed toward implementation of the EU money laundering directive, and the requirements of the UN Convention against Transnational Organized Crime.

These changes in Liechtenstein national laws may represent a fundamental shift in at least one important area. Heretofore, the Liechtenstein government appeared extremely reluctant to address any matters of tax fraud. As such, one might cautiously conclude Liechtenstein has embarked upon a discernable change of course. All this said, recent reports indicate that, despite substantial changes in Liechtensteiner financial regulations, old habits die hard.

Matthew Pate

Further Reading

Beattie, David. (2004). *Liechtenstein: A Modern History.* London: I. B. Tauris Press.

Duursma, Jorri C. (1996). *Fragmentation and the International Relations of Micro-States.* Cambridge, UK: Cambridge University Press.

Raton, Pierre. (1970). *Liechtenstein: History and Institutions of the Principality.* Vaduz: Liechtenstein-Verlag.

Seger, Otto. (1984). *A Survey of Liechtenstein History.* Vaduz: Press and Information Office of the Principality of Liechtenstein.

Note: The author would like to provide a special thanks to Tina Enz, media specialist for the Liechtenstein National Police, whose help was invaluable in preparation of this article.

Lithuania

Legal System: Civil
Murder: High
Burglary: Medium
Corruption: Medium
Human Trafficking: Low
Prison Rate: High
Death Penalty: No
Corporal Punishment: No

Background

Lithuania is a small country situated on the coast of the Baltic Sea, covering 65,301 square kilometers (25,213 square miles). In 2008, 3.36 million inhabitants lived in Lithuania, comprising Lithuanians (83.5%), Poles (6.7%), Russians (6.3%), as well as other nationalities (3.5%). Vilnius is the capital of Lithuania (550,000 residents). The Grand Duchy of Lithuania was formed in the 12th century. It was a part of the Polish-Lithuanian Commonwealth Zecpospolita from 1569 to 1795. Following the destruction of the commonwealth by the Russian, Prussian, and Austro-Hungarian empires at the end of the 18th century, the territory of Lithuania remained a part of the Russian Empire until 1918, when the independent Republic of Lithuania was created. Independence lasted until 1940 when Lithuania was occupied by Soviet troops.

On March 11, 1990, Lithuania proclaimed its independence after the Soviet occupation, which lasted for almost 50 years, and since 2004 Lithuania has been a member of the European Union and NATO. In the referendum of October 25, 1992, Lithuanian citizens approved the Constitution. Lithuania is now a parliamentary republic, so Parliament (*Seimas*) is the most important national governmental institution. Foreign policy and state representation are among the principal functions of the directly elected president, although the president also has substantial power in the internal life of the state; for example, the president plays an important role in formation of the judicature.

History of the Legal System

Lithuania has a rich legal history with the first written laws (*Pamedes teisynas*) dating back to 1340, while the first three codifications of laws (Statutes of Lithuania) date from 1529, 1566, and 1588, respectively. However, after the occupation of the territory of Lithuania by the Russian Empire, the Russian legal system was introduced in Lithuania (in 1840) and the Russian Criminal Code of 1903 remained in force (although with many amendments and additions) in the Republic of Lithuania after the restoration of independence in 1918 up to the Soviet occupation in 1940. During the first decades of Soviet occupation the Criminal Code of the Russian Soviet Federal Socialist Republic was applied in Lithuania, while in 1961 the Penal Code and the Penal Procedure Code of the Lithuanian Soviet Socialist Republic were introduced. The codes literally repeated the corresponding codes of the Russian Soviet Federal Socialist Republic and can hardly be said to reflect the legal culture of Lithuania.

On May 1, 2003, the first national Criminal Code of the Republic of Lithuania came into force along with the Code of Criminal Procedure and the Code of Execution of Penalties. The structure and the system of criminal sanctions of the old Soviet code that applied with many changes up to 2003 did not conform to the needs of a free democratic country. Significant changes included the additions of new types of penalties and their application, limitations on the use of prison, the availability of reconciliation, and the separate treatment of minors, including alternatives to imprisonment.

The New Code of Criminal Procedure is also widely acknowledged to be more liberal in comparison to the one in force until 2003. However, although the Constitutional Court of the Republic of Lithuania has approved the adversarial principle to be one of the essential principles of criminal procedure, the Lithuanian Criminal Procedure Code remains inquisitorial. The code concedes a rather active role of judges both in pretrial investigations and trials.

Political and Social Context of the Criminal Justice System

In Soviet times, the extent of criminality was not revealed; criminals were depicted as "public enemies"; and a similar assessment of criminal conduct also prevails in the contemporary Lithuanian society, that is, intolerance. This intolerance combined with the fear of persecution in the previous Soviet society, in which confidence in other persons was undermined, have produced a distinct "us" and "them" psychology.

There are some indications that legislation is becoming more resistant to this "us" against "them" mindset. In 2007, among all the penalties imposed by Lithuanian courts, the penalty of fine came to 31 percent and, for the first time in Lithuanian history, it became the most frequent annually imposed penalty, ahead of imprisonment. Therefore, even though legal norms have changed and have had a visible effect, attitudes to criminal conduct and punishment ideas have changed slowly. The society tends to demand strict penalties and isolation of criminals and considers that the new Criminal Code is too mild. Up to early 2008, the new Criminal Code has been modified 14 times already, the Code of Criminal Procedure 15 times, and the Code of Execution of Penalties 5 times.

International legal events played an important role in changing the criminal justice policy and legal system of Lithuania. Lengthy international isolation, earlier absence of the rule of law, and the fall of the iron curtain evoked aspiration for international standards and unconditional belief in their power; especially prior to the membership of Lithuania in the European Council (1993) and the European Union (2004). International standards of human rights were immediately embraced, but in practice change came slowly. Moreover, it should be noted that as soon as Lithuania gained international recognition and joined the main international organizations, direct and constant encouragement to implement international requirements disappeared (as, for example, to reduce the number of prisoners, to improve their imprisonment conditions, etc.), with the possible exception of visits and reports by the European Committee for the Prevention of Torture and Inhuman or Degrading Treatment or Punishment (CPT).

Police

On January 1, 2009, in total there were 12,230 police positions compared to 15,100 on January 1, 1999. The number of police positions per 100,000 residents is approximately 364,322 taking into account vacant positions, based on Police Department records. There are two integrated units of the police in Lithuania: criminal and public. The Police Department is under the Ministry of Interior of the Republic of Lithuania. Besides this department, the Lithuanian police system comprises the following: territorial police units, police professional educational institutions, and specialized police units. There are 59 territorial police departments.

Approximately 30 percent of the police work as criminal police, approximately 60 percent in public police, and the remaining in other police units. In addition, there is one more small police unit comprising the military police subordinate to the Ministry of Defense and responsible for the prevention, disclosure, and investigation of crimes and other legal violations within the military territories and the army as well as for the supervision of military transport traffic safety.

Alongside the police officers, similar work is carried out by officers working in other related organizations. In 2007, there were 3,611 officers of state border guard, 232 officers of financial crime investigation service; in 2008, 2,690 officers in the prison system, 216 officers of special investigation service (investigating corruption cases) plus officers of some other specialized institutions (National Security Department, military police, Fire-Fighting and Rescue Department).

Disclosure of white collar and related crimes is mainly within the competency of two institutions not subordinate to the police, that is, Financial Crime Investigation Service under the Ministry of Interior and an independent Special Investigations Service. The Financial Crime Investigation Service is entitled to investigate and disclose criminal offenses that infringe upon the financial system. The Special Investigation Service is also entitled to investigate and disclose criminal offenses of corruption. Each of these services follows the law regulating activity of its service, which it is hoped ensures independence of these institutions. Both services conduct operative investigation and pretrial investigation in criminal cases.

Lithuanian residents have little trust in the police. In sociological polls regularly conducted since 1996, the proportion of those trusting the police ranged from 20 to 45 percent. However, the situation is changing for the better. During the last poll conducted in April 2009, 62 percent of participants stated that they trust the police, 30 percent did not trust them, and 8 percent did not have any opinion. This fact undoubtedly plays an important role when recording criminal offenses since during victimization surveys some of the residents state that they do not report offenses to the police because they have neither trust nor belief in their competence.

Crime

Classification of Crimes

The Penal Code of Lithuania distinguishes two types of criminal acts: crimes and criminal offenses. Crimes are classified into intentional and negligent crimes. Further, intentional crimes are classified into four categories, according to the severity of punishments foreseen in the Penal Code. Criminal acts that can be punished by a punishment not exceeding 3 years of deprivation of liberty are considered to be crimes of minor gravity (e.g., theft, fraud, destruction of property, bribery, etc.). Criminal acts that can be punished by a punishment exceeding 3 years but not exceeding 6 years of deprivation of liberty are considered to be crimes of middle gravity (e.g., assisted suicide, robbery, burglary, extortion of property, aggravated destruction of property, aggravated bribery, terror act, hostage taking, etc.). Criminal acts that can be punished by a punishment exceeding 6 years but not exceeding 10 years of deprivation of liberty are considered to be grave crimes (e.g., aggravated assault, trafficking in human beings, rape, aggravated robbery, aggravated extortion of property, aggravated fraud, smuggling, aggravated bribery, etc.). Criminal acts that can be punished by a punishment exceeding 10 years of deprivation of liberty or by a life sentence are considered to be crimes of extreme gravity (e.g., genocide, murder, aggravated espionage, rape of a preteen, trafficking in children, participation in criminal organization, aggravated terror act, aggravated hostage taking, aggravated trafficking in drugs, etc.).

Age of Criminal Liability

The Penal Code sets three age limits. First, there is a general rule that only persons who have reached the age of 16 can be responsible for criminal acts. However, part 2 of the code also lists 11 criminal acts that persons between 14 and 16 years of age can be sentenced for. These crimes are murder; aggravated bodily injury; rape; sexual coercion; theft; robbery; extortion of property; destruction or damage of property; plunder of a firearm, ammunition, or explosives; theft; extortion or other illegal acquisition of narcotic or psychotropic substances; destruction of vehicles, roads, or road equipment. The list has been created according to the dangerousness of the crime as well as its blatancy.

The Criminal Code has a separate section "Singularities of Minors' Criminal Liability." This section establishes the penalties applied only to minors (minors are eligible for a life sentence, and a provision stating that minors must receive milder penalties than adults); a separate system of educational treatment is applied only to minors; simplified criteria for release of minors from criminal liability and

A Lithuanian state border police officer shows smuggled cigarettes at a confiscated cigarettes storage area southwest of the national capital Vilnius, December 15, 2004. Shots are fired almost every night on the Nemunas River, as boats dodge the border patrol's searchlight. (AP Photo/Mindaugas Kulbis)

suspension of penalty for minors are provided for. Provisions of the section are applied with regard to all the persons who committed criminal offenses being under 18 years old. Despite this, the Criminal Code also specifies that provisions of the section may also be applied to person between 18 and 21 years old if the court decides that according to their social maturity, they are equal to minors.

Drug Crimes

Chapter 37 of the Criminal Code is dedicated to criminal offenses related to disposal of narcotic or psychotropic, toxic, or potent substances. Offenses provided for in this section differ in their hazardousness. The main criteria predetermining hazardousness of offenses comprise whether the offense was related to distribution of narcotic substances and what was the quantity of the substance present in the offense.

Production, processing, acquisition, storage, transport, or shipment of narcotic and psychotropic substances considered as crimes are classified according to small, large, and very large quantities approved by the order of the Minister of Health of the Republic of Lithuania in 2003.

According to data of the Drug Control Department for the year 2006, cannabis was the most prevalent drug, 7.6 percent of the Lithuanian population reported having used it at least once in their lifetimes. Men indicated three times more frequently than women having tried cannabis at least once in their lifetimes. Besides cannabis, the most prevalent drugs are amphetamine and Ecstasy. Their prevalence rates are very similar: 1.1 percent of the population used amphetamine at least once in their lifetimes, 1.0 percent—Ecstasy, 0.5 percent—hallucinogenic mushrooms, 0.4 percent—cocaine, 0.3 percent—heroin and LSD each.

Recorded criminal offenses related to narcotic or psychotropic substances within the period from 1990 to 2007 increased by more than 20 times (from 76 up to 1,724). These offenses have increased much more than any of the other types of criminal offenses. As soon as the totalitarian system collapsed, more opportunities occurred for the development of the drugs market.

Crime Statistics

The number of criminal offenses recorded by police for the period 1989 to 2008 increased from 31,238 to 78,060, having peaked in 2004 at 93,419. Two possible causes of this increase are: (1) failures and delays in creation of a democratic system of formal and informal social control after having passed from totalitarian to democratic system of the state, and (2) increased opportunities to commit criminal offenses (especially those related to property). Furthermore, factors affecting the recording of crimes by police are inhabitants' (mis)trust in the police (thus not reporting crimes to them) and also conduct of the police upon receipt of the information reported by a victim.

Out of the recorded criminal offenses, approximately 40 percent is cleared up in Lithuania. The number of persons accused of criminal offenses within the period 1989 to 2008 almost doubled (from 12,843 up to 23,235), although since 1993 no essential changes have taken place. The number of persons sentenced (i.e., those who received criminal penalties) has also doubled (from 7,546 up to 14,295). However, this number has been significantly decreasing since 2003, suggesting that more often various alternative sanctions have been applied.

The largest portion of criminal offenses comprises property-related criminal offenses. Out of all recorded criminal offenses, thefts come to approximately 50 percent. For example, in 2008 there were 38,422 thefts compared to 836 serious crimes of violence (homicide, sexual assault, bodily harm). However, it should be noted that the homicide rate per 100,000 residents ranges from 14 in 1994 through 11 in 2005 to 8 in 2007, possibly indicating a slight decrease.

Administrative Violations

The Code of Administrative Violations of Law is a single code remaining in force in Lithuania since Soviet times. This code comprises such offenses that in their essence are very similar to criminal offenses, although they are defined as administrative violations of law. Such violations exist in the field of property protection. For example, minor theft of a property belonging to another person is considered an administrative violation of law (up to 130 Litas [US$47.30]), as is intentional destruction or damage of property that did not cause large losses to an aggrieved person, and so forth. Approximately 15,000 administrative violations of law in the field of property protection are recorded in Lithuania every year and these are not included in the statistics of criminal offenses.

Urban and Rural Distribution of Crime

Property-related criminal offenses are the most prevalent in cities and towns. Approximately two-thirds of all residents live in Lithuanian cities and towns and approximately one-third of them in rural areas. Out of all criminal offenses recorded in Lithuania in 2008, 77 percent were registered in cities and towns and 23 percent in rural areas. Approximately 2,500 recoded criminal offenses per 100,000 city residents was almost double the rural rate of approximately 1,500 of recorded offenses per 100,000 rural residents. Relatively more robberies were registered in cities and towns than rural areas (88% and 12%). However, a disproportionately greater number of recorded homicides occurs in rural areas. This is probably because the most common case of homicide in Lithuania (almost two-thirds) is related to conflicts among individuals consuming alcohol. This problem is especially topical in Lithuanian villages where, due to the difficult economic situation, hopelessness, heavy physical work, and lack of leisure infrastructure, consumption of alcohol is a part of everyday life, not only at leisure but also at work.

Finding of Guilt

Prosecution

The prosecutor organizes pretrial investigation, starts pretrial investigation, assesses whether pretrial investigation was legally started by pretrial investigation officers, gives necessary instructions to pretrial investigations officials on how pretrial investigation should be conducted, and takes the most important decisions concerning suspension or termination of the investigation. At any time of pretrial investigation the prosecutor may decide to take over and to conduct the whole pretrial investigation. The prosecutor is also entitled to a wide range of powers to apply measures restricting the suspect's rights: bail, seizure of documents, obligation for the suspect to regularly register at a police station, to obtain a written commitment not to leave, to temporarily restrict the suspect's or (in exceptional cases) a third person's property rights.

Pretrial investigation officials include officers of police, military police, National Security Department, Special Investigation Service, Financial Crime Investigation Service, State Border Guards, Prison Department, Customs Department, Fire-Fighting and Rescue Department). They must abide by the prosecutor's instructions on all matters of pretrial investigation; despite this, they are entitled to carry out many procedural actions without coordination with the prosecutor. Pretrial investigation officials may carry out interrogations, confrontations, identification line-ups, and some other acts of investigation. Pretrial investigation officials may also apply separate measures of procedural constraint, such as temporary detention, delivery, examination of a person, among others. In exceptional, urgent cases, searches and seizures may be carried out on the decision of a pretrial investigation official.

Participation of a pretrial investigation judge is also important in pretrial process. First, the most severe preventive measures depend on the decision by the pretrial investigation judge, that is, detention on remand and house arrest. On the decision by the pretrial investigation judge, a suspect may also be temporarily removed from his or her current position or he or she may temporarily be denied the right to be engaged in some specific activity. Second, some specific acts of investigation restricting human rights may not be carried out without approval by the pretrial investigation judge, such as search and seizure, seizure of mail, control of the information transmitted by electronic means of communication, secret surveillance, actions not revealing the identity of pretrial investigation officials or sting operations, and seizure of documents kept in companies or institutions.

Trial

Jury trials are nonexistent in Lithuania. During the Soviet occupation, the system of sworn lay judges in session together with professional lawyers was tried, but discarded. Recently the introduction of a jury system has been raised more often, but the probability that it will be introduced is slight.

Criminal cases in regional and district courts of first instance are heard by one judge. A board of justices consisting of three judges hears cases in regional courts when cases are related to crimes for which a life sentence is provided or cases in which accused persons in the course of committing a criminal offense were the president, members of Parliament or the government, judges of the Constitutional Court, judges, or prosecutors. A board of justices may be formed in regional and district courts also for hearing of other cases. In the Court of Appeal all cases are heard by a board of justices consisting of three judges. In the Lithuanian Supreme Court criminal cases are heard by a board of justices consisting of three judges. Upon the decision by the chief justice of Lithuania or a chairman of criminal cases department of this court, such case may be handed over to be heard under the cassation procedure by an extended board of justices consisting of seven judges or by a plenary meeting of the Criminal Cases Department at the Supreme Court, when a judge responsible for hearing of the case establishes that in the course of investigation it may be necessary to formulate a new judicial interpretation of the legal norm applied or it may be necessary to deviate from the jurisprudence of the Supreme Court that has already been formed.

Right to Plead Guilty to Lesser Offense

The Code of Criminal Procedure establishes that in court of first instance an accused person is entitled to plead guilty, to give evidence and agree that other evidence is not investigated. In this case, a judge is obligated to familiarize the persons participating in the case with all the evidence and this way to finalize the investigation. However, such provision may not be applied when the accused person is accused of committing a medium and major crime or if a prosecutor or defender objects to such a shortened investigation.

At the same time pleading guilty and repentance may be the grounds to terminate the criminal process with regard to minors who are suspected or accused of having committed the criminal offense for the first time (except for the minors suspected or accused of committing a medium and major crime). In fact, criminal laws provide for the release from criminal liability of persons who plead guilty, if they assist relevant law enforcement officers to detect criminal offenses or a coup d'état being planned by an organized group. As a matter of fact, pleading guilty itself, if a person assists the law enforcement officers to solve a criminal offense committed by him or her is a palliative in every case; moreover, pleading guilty allows some release from criminal liability or mitigation of a person's liability.

Assistance Provided to the Accused

The Code of Criminal Procedure specifies that in some specific cases neither pretrial investigation nor trial investigation are possible if a defender is absent in the process. The defender's participation is essential and if an accused person does not have a defense counsel, one must be appointed by a pretrial investigation official, prosecutor, or the court. The decision to appoint the defense counsel is made by a lawyer appointed by the Lithuanian advocacy on behalf of the national guaranteed legal assistance service and paid from the funds of the state budget. The national guaranteed legal assistance in criminal cases in the major cities of Lithuania (Vilnius, Vilnius, Klaipėda, Šiauliai) is operated by public lawyers' offices dependent on the state.

Alternatives to Trial

The Code of Criminal Procedure (CCP) identifies certain formal alternatives for judicial proceedings: article 212 of CCP stipulates that pretrial investigation may be terminated if the perpetrator and the victim reconcile, also when the suspect helps to disclose criminal offenses committed by organized crime or criminal associations as well as in some other cases. These alternatives are only available, however, subject to a variety of conditions such as a very serious crime is involved or a previous case of reconciliation with the victim. A decision to dismiss the pretrial investigation if the accused and the victim are reconciled is taken by the prosecutor and in all cases such decision must be approved by the judge of pretrial investigation. If reconciliation takes place during the court hearing, a decision on the release from prosecution is made by the investigating judge and the board of justices.

Criminal cases are not very often dismissed for reasons of reconciliation, probably less than 4 percent of all pretrial investigations completed in 2008. This is because, although the laws of Lithuania specify the possibility of remission of persons from criminal liability after their reconciliation with the victim, there is no formal mechanism of mediation to bring it about.

Another basis of remission of criminal liability exists for juveniles. Article 93 of the Criminal Code specifies that a juvenile suspect or accused may be released from criminal liability even if a victim does not intend to reconcile with him or her—it is enough for a juvenile to apologize to the victim and to indemnify the property damage by means of his or her work and money. Moreover, other much simpler grounds for remission of criminal liability are applied. A juvenile may be released from criminal liability if he or she pleads guilty and expresses regret.

Finally, the criminal code leaves open the possibility for juveniles to receive remission on other grounds, particularly if it is assessed that the offender will not commit again. All decisions on remission, however, must be made by the prosecutor and must be approved by the pretrial investigation judge, or by the trial judge if the case has already gone to trial.

A person may be released from criminal liability on bail. Cases of persons who committed a criminal offense for the first time (except for serious and very serious ones) may be dismissed, when they plead guilty, show regret for committing criminal offenses, and indemnify damage caused. The court can request a bondsman to pledge a fixed amount as a condition for bail.

One more alternative for pretrial investigation is the procedure of penal order foreseen in article 418 of the CCP. By a penal order the Criminal Code assesses a fine that may be the only punishment foreseen for the corresponding criminal offense, or one of the several punishments foreseen for the act. This procedure may be applied to suspects who make up for the damage caused by a criminal offense or who reach an agreement with the victim regarding its indemnification. The content of the prosecutor's recommendation (as well as the size of a fine to be imposed) is negotiated with the suspect. If upon drawing up the penal order, the accused does not agree with it, he or she may demand to continue the judicial proceedings of the case. In 2008, 16 percent of all cases brought before the court were ended by a penal order.

Similar to drawing up a penal order is the hearing of cases in summary procedure. Even though the Code of Criminal Procedure specifies that the cases of serious and very serious crimes cannot be heard in summary procedure, exceptions are made in a large number of criminal offenses. In summary procedure, the pretrial investigation is not exercised; the case is at once heard in the court. This procedure is applied on the recommendation of the prosecutor and on agreement of the accused (though no requirement is set for the accused to plead guilty for having committed a criminal offense).

The Code of Criminal Procedure and the Criminal Code also allow discontinuance of the pretrial investigation by releasing from criminal liability persons who actively helped to disclose acts committed by an organized group or the criminal association. Article 39–1 of the CC specifies only the extreme restrictions of remission of criminal liability—persons who committed voluntary homicides, as well as persons who themselves were the organizers or leaders of the organized group or the criminal association cannot be released from criminal liability.

Pretrial Detention

Detention (also the two other most stringent pretrial detention measures—house arrest and obligation to live apart from the victim) may be imposed only by a decision of the judge of pretrial investigation, at the request of the prosecutor. Article 140 of the CCP stipulates that the prosecutor or the officer of pretrial investigation in particular cases is entitled to temporarily detain a person even though a suspicion for the commission of a criminal offense was not brought against him or her, but such custody may last no longer than for 48 hours.

The CCP allows for detention on remand if the judge of pretrial investigation finds that (1) a suspect will abscond from the pretrial investigation officers, prosecutors, or the court, (2) a suspect will obstruct the course of the proceedings, or (3) a suspect will commit new crimes.

Article 127 of the CCP also allows for a judge of pretrial investigation to impose custody lasting no longer than 3 months. Imposition of custody may be repeatedly extended by the judge of pretrial investigation for another 3 months, but cannot exceed the term of 6 months. Part 2 of the same article stipulates that due to the particular complexity of the case, the term of custody may be repeatedly extended by a decision of the district court judge up to 18 months (detention for juveniles in no cases may exceed the term of 12 months), but the term of each extension may be no longer than 3 months.

Judges

The Law on Courts of the Republic of Lithuania requires that separate departments of criminal and civil cases shall be formed at the Supreme Court of Lithuania (18 judges working in the department), the Court of Appeal of Lithuania (13 judges working in the department), district courts (in Lithuania, there are five district courts, in their departments of criminal cases with a total of 72 judges). In the regional courts, separate departments for different categories of cases are not formed; judges hear both criminal cases and cases of other categories.

In the Court of Appeal of Lithuania, in all district courts, in the major part of regional courts, judges specializing in juvenile civil and criminal cases are appointed. However, judges of regional courts hear both juvenile civil and criminal cases.

According to the Constitution of the Republic of Lithuania, the judges of the Supreme Court of Lithuania are appointed by the Seimas of the Republic of Lithuania on recommendation of the president; judges of the Court of Appeal of Lithuania are appointed by the president with the approval of the Seimas. Other judges are appointed by the president.

The Law on Courts of the Republic of Lithuania specifies that a judge must be a citizen of the Republic of Lithuania with a higher university education in law. Moreover, a person seeking judicial office as a regional court judge and thus starting his or her career as a judge should have at least five years' standing of judicial work. Requirements set for judges include impeccable reputation, reliability, and health. The Commission for Secrets Protection Co-ordination decides whether the person is reliable according to criteria laid down in the Law on State Secrets and Office Secrets. Persons possessing these qualifications take a qualifying examination, which is organized by the examination commission, formed by the Council of Justices, the self-governing institution of the courts. Doctors of social sciences in the field of law, as well as former judges (meeting certain formal requirements), may be appointed as regional court judges, without taking an examination.

Persons with no less than five years' standing as judges of regional courts may be appointed as judges of district courts. Judges of the Court of Appeal of Lithuania may be appointed if they have a four-year work record as judges of the district court. A judge of the Supreme Court of Lithuania may be appointed after having an eight-year work record as a judge of the district court or a five-year work record as a judge of the Court of Appeal.

Punishment

Types of Punishment

In 1991–2002, the major parts of the former punishments in the old Criminal Code were abolished. This included exile, deportation, public reprimand, and dismissal from office. In 1996 a moratorium on the death penalty was imposed, and in 1998 its abolition. Criminal offenses were punished most frequently by real deprivation of liberty. The absolute number of persons punished with the penalty of deprivation of liberty within this period increased by more than three times: from 2,787 (1990) to 8,677 (2002). Until 1994, the penalty of correctional works was quite frequently applied (21% in 1991, 10% in 1993, 7% in 1994), which later, even though foreseen by the law, was not applied because of the type of forced work and difficulties arising from its application under the conditions of a market economy (the convicted person had to work in his or her workplace and from his or her wages from 5 to 20 percent were deducted, therefore the aforementioned punishment was similar to a fine, not to a hard labor). The punishment of a fine only in the last years of the old Criminal Code constituted the more considerable part in the punishment practice (7% in 2001, 13.2% in 2002), and previously was imposed rarely due to a very high minimum limit of this punishment (100 minimum subsistence levels, i.e., Litas 12,500 [US$4,548]).

The situation changed with the adoption of the new Criminal Code, which became valid on May 1, 2003, where eight independent penalties were enforced, of which three (community service, restriction of liberty, apprehension) are completely new. The new Criminal Code of the Republic of Lithuania (article 42) foresees the following punishments:

- Deprivation of public rights (from 1 to 5 years)
- Deprivation of the right to perform a certain job or to engage in activities in certain areas (from 1 to 5 years)

- Community service (up to 480 hours)
- Fine (from 130 Litas [US$47] to 39,000 Litas [US$14,190])
- Restriction of liberty (otherwise, "house arrest," from 3 months to 2 years)
- Apprehension (from 5 to 90 days)
- Fixed-term imprisonment (3 months to 20 years)
- Life imprisonment (no parole, unless granted by the president or amnesty declared by the Seimas of Lithuania, though no person has benefited from this so far)

For the period 2003–2008 after the new Criminal Code was in place, the penalty of deprivation of liberty accounted for about 30–35 percent of all punishments while the penalty of restriction of liberty has become not an alternative but a replacement for adjournment of execution of imprisonment, which in the past years comprised about 15–20 percent. Fines in 2005–2008 increased to 31 percent. Arrest and restriction of liberty accounts for approximately 10 percent each in the structure of imposed penalties.

The Department of Prisons under the Ministry of Justice of the Republic of Lithuania calculates the terms of the penalty of deprivation of liberty of the convicts in the detention facilities by separate criminal offenses. The average time served (years/months) for a variety of offenses for persons released in 2007 was as follows:

Homicide	6/4
Rape	3/7
Robbery	2/1
Major theft	1/11
Drug related	2/1
Criminal association	4/3
Bribery	0/7

In general, the time served was roughly half to two-thirds the sentence actually imposed by the court.

Prison

According to statistics from the prison department from the Ministry of Justice, from the end of 2003, the average daily prison population has been approximately 8,000 prisoners, constituting 240 prisoners per 100,000 of the population. Distribution of prisoners by age and education has remained stable for many years. Prisoners are disproportionately young and poorly educated.

On September 1, 2000, control of the penal system was transferred to the Ministry of Justice from the Ministry of Interior, a major reform. In 2002–2003, the process of demilitarization of detention facilities was completed. It is notable that within the past years the government approved several programs, the implementation of which should improve considerably the infrastructure of detention facilities and incarceration conditions.

Detention facilities where convicted persons serve their terms of imprisonment at the present moment are not overcrowded, except for a hospital. Only remand prisons are considerably overcrowded. In mid-2002, the occupancy of detention facilities in Lithuania reached 114 percent, and at the beginning of 2009 the detention facilities were occupied 87 percent. There are a total of 15 detention facilities operating, including remand prisons and specialized medical establishments for prisoners. The three biggest detention facilities in Lithuania are Alytus Correctional House (1,512 official places and 1,201 persons serving their terms of imprisonment, January 1, 2009); Marijampolė Correctional House (1,115 places and 988 persons); and Pravieniškės Correctional House No. 2 (1,252 places and 1,171 persons). All of them are in the southwestern part from the geographical center of Lithuania.

According to the old system, persons sentenced to imprisonment are accommodated in big dormitories (approx. 20 in each, on the average), but during the day they can walk without restriction in the yard (in their local sector). In the Lukiškės prison only and in remand prisons and holding rooms (where a penalty of apprehension is served), several convicts are accommodated in one cell and may go for a walk in the closed yard for one or two hours a day.

Each convict serving his or her penalty of imprisonment must work, if it is offered to him or her by the administration of the detention facilities. The administration of the facilities must ensure that convicts would be involved in the work, taking into account their capacity for work and, as much as possible, their profession. In addition to the mentioned major detention facilities in Lithuania, another three state enterprises are operating, with branches in some other enterprises. Moreover, the prisoners may be involved in unpaid household work. The total number of the employed prisoners is one of the lowest in the European Union. This is predetermined by the shortage of well-organized work, the lack of motivation for the convicts, and low wages. Together with work, less than one-third of the prisoners are employed. The practice that is usually applied in West European countries of employing the prisoners outside the prison does not occur in Lithuania, even though the legal provisions allow for it.

In the detention facilities, the number of visits for the sentenced prisoners as well as contacts with the external world and other rights and duties depend on the group to which the prisoner is allocated (simple, light, and disciplinary). At the beginning of 2008, in all detention facilities the prisoners served their terms of imprisonment as follows: 85 percent in the simple group, 10 percent in the light group, and 5 percent in the disciplinary group. All start serving their terms in the simple group, and then depending on their behavior in the prison, they are allocated either to the light or disciplinary group.

Lithuania is a party to many international conventions in the field of criminal law, criminal procedure, and execution of penalties, including Convention on the Transfer of Sentenced Persons (ratified in 1996) and Additional Protocol to the Convention on the Transfer of Sentenced Persons (ratified in 2001). The transfer of sentenced persons is provided in bilateral treaties that Lithuania has concluded with Azerbaijan, Byelorussia, and the Russian Federation.

Algimantas Čepas and Gintautas Sakalauskas

Further Reading

The Centre for Crime Prevention in Lithuania: http://www.nplc.lt.

Morag, MacDonald. (2004). *Country Report for the CEENDPS Research in Lithuania: Research Project of the Central and Eastern European Network of Drug Services in Prison and HEUNI.* Birmingham: Centre for Research into Quality. The University of Central England in Birmingham.

Sakalauskas, Gintautas. (2000). "Crime: Patterns and Trends." In *Lithuanian Human Development Report* 1999, pp. 141–154. Vilnius: United Nations Development Programme.

Sakalauskas, Gintautas. (2005). "The Rights of the Persons with Restricted Freedom." In *Human Rights in Lithuania,* edited by Algimantas Čepas, pp. 304–331. Vilnius: United Nations Development Programme.

Statistics Lithuania: http://www.stat.gov.lt.

Švedas, Gintaras. (2000). *Criminal Justice Systems in Europe and North America: Lithuania.* Helsinki: The European Institute for Crime Prevention and Control (HEUNI).

Luxembourg

Legal System: Civil
Murder: Low
Corruption: Low
Human Trafficking: Low
Prison Rate: Medium
Death Penalty: No
Corporal Punishment: No

Background

Luxembourg has been considered a grand duchy since 1815 and is presently the only officially recognized grand duchy in existence. A grand duchy is a territory with a monarch as a head of state, specifically a grand duchess or grand duke. It has been an independent state under the Netherlands since 1835 as a result of the Treaty of London, although it was not until 1839 that it was granted political autonomy. Luxembourg was guaranteed perpetual neutrality and recognized as independent in 1867.

Luxembourg surrendered neutrality to become a charter member of NATO in 1949, following extensive occupation by Germany during both world wars. Today, Luxembourg is a constitutional monarchy whose current chief of state is Grand Duke Henri. It has a parliamentary system in which Prime Minister Jean-Claude Juncker is the current head of government. Executive power is performed by the grand duke and the cabinet including the prime minister.

With a land area of just 2,586 square kilometers (998 square miles), Luxembourg is located between France, Germany, and Belgium. As of 2009, The *CIA World Factbook* estimates a population of 491,775 people. Approximately two-thirds of the population are between the ages of 15 and 64 years old and the life expectancy is 79.33 years. The national language is Luxembourgish, which blends elements of German, French, and Frankish. German and French are recognized as administrative languages.

The judicial system of Luxembourg is an inquisitorial system that embodies influence from the French, German, and Belgian systems. The Superior Court of Justice rests at the top of the judicial system. Judges, at all levels of the court including justices of the peace, are appointed by the grand duke. It is a life appointment barring any misconduct. The Superior Court of Justice comprises the Court of Cassation, which reviews cases that are seeking to have the decision of the Court of Appeal overturned, the Court of Appeal, and a Department of Public Prosecution. There are 5 judges on the bench of the Court of Cassation and 27 judges on the bench of the Court of Appeal. Below the Superior Court of Justice are two district courts that hear more serious cases while there are 3 justices of the peace to deal with minor cases.

Police

The National Police of Luxembourg is structured with a general directorate that is in charge of overseeing the successful function of the National Police. There are five branches of the general directorate: Human Resources; Operations, which is in charge of managing larger events such as the National Emergency Center; Budget and Equipment; Information Technology; and Organization and Methodology, responsible for introducing new procedures with the goal of improving current procedures.

There are six subdivisions of the central units. The Criminal Investigation Unit is charged with preservation of the crime scene and collection and protection of evidence. This unit is further divided into specialized units such as organized crime and drug crime. Other units included Airport Control Unit, responsible for issues of immigration and border control; Central Unit of Traffic Police; Special Police Unit; Police School; the Mobile Supply and Guard Unit, which is responsible for securely transporting prisoners to various destinations.

Police are further broken down into regional units. There are 13 intervention centers that are responsible for preventing crimes and misdemeanors. As implied in the name they function on a regional level and for this reason often provide a vital link between the people and the larger branches of the police.

Luxembourg has a public unit that serves as an external overseer of police activities by investigating potential police misconduct as well as misdemeanors allegedly committed by police officers. This unit also provides audits and reports in hopes of improving police efficiency and supplies legal counsel when laws and regulations are introduced that will affect police personnel.

In 2007, there were 1,519 police officers according to Eurostat.

Crime

Classification of Crimes

Luxembourg has a civil law system. Crimes are labeled differently according to severity and also classified as crime, misdemeanor, and violation. Included crime categories are homicide, aggravated assault, robbery, rape and sexual assault, burglary, and some property crime, including theft, depending on the severity. Misdemeanors may include burglary and various property crimes and minor thefts; violations include traffic offenses and other minor offenses.

Luxembourg prohibits both the use and sale of drugs including, as of 2001, cannabis. Punishment

Armed undercover police officers rush toward a daycare center in Wasserbillig, Luxembourg, after two shots were heard, June 1, 2000. Police shot the hostage taker and freed 25 children and three teachers, ending the 30-hour standoff. (AP Photo/Yves Logghe)

for using cannabis is just a fine as long as there are no aggravating factors, while users of more illicit drugs can face a fine and/or a sentence of 8 days to 6 months in prison. Punishment for drug dealing is more concerned with the outcome of the drug deal than the amount of drugs dealt. Small- or large-scale drug deals carry the sentence of 1–5 years and/or a fine. If the drug sold causes severe damage to health the sentence increases to 5–10 years, and if the outcome is death for the user the sentence further increases to 15–20 years. Heroin is the drug responsible for the majority of drug offenses in Luxembourg.

Crime Statistics

According to Eurostat the total number of homicides reported to the police in 2007 was seven, representing a 1.09 percent increase in homicides from 2003. For 2003, the *European Sourcebook of Criminal Justice* reported the following crime statistics per 100,000 population:

Homicide (completed)	0.7
Assault	298
Rape	8
Robbery	95
Burglary	741
Domestic burglary	339
Theft (total)	3,150
Motor vehicle theft	115
Drug offenses	248
Drug trafficking	39

The *2006 Crime and Safety Report* recognized increasing nonviolent and violent crimes, although Luxembourg still remains reasonably safe. At that time there was also a visible increase in drug sales to youth. The most common nonviolent crime at the time was residential burglary.

In 2009, Luxembourg fought to be removed from a tax haven "grey list" maintained by the OECD. The country was originally placed on the list as a result of its bank secrecy laws. Luxembourg was one of three European Union countries to be added to this grey list. The prime minister was outraged to find his country on the list after a verbal agreement earlier in the year that Luxembourg would not be placed on the list. If Luxembourg does not allow more open information sharing regarding tax issues, it could face the consequences of legislative crackdowns from other countries, including the United States.

Finding of Guilt

Accused offenders are given the right to a fair trial. Defendants are presumed innocent and have the right to appeal the outcome of the trial. There are no jury trials. Defendants are allowed to confer with an attorney immediately. An attorney is provided by the government for indigent defendants. Prosecutors are appointed by the grand duke. There are two prosecutor's offices under the direction of the state prosecutor. There is also a General State Prosecutor's Office whose prosecutors are charged with overseeing the other prosecutors in the state. The criminal investigation may be carried out by either the police or an investigating judge depending on the nature and severity of the crime. There is no plea bargaining system in Luxembourg. It is, however, possible to exercise leniency toward persons who cooperate with the police.

Defendants may be detained in prison while awaiting trial, although they are kept separate from convicted offenders unless they consent to sharing accommodations with convicted offenders or overcrowding denies the existence of this consideration. There is also no guarantee against contact with convicted offenders while participating in various prison programs.

The age of responsibility in Luxembourg is 16 years old. In 2004 Luxembourg had committed to build a secure detention unit for minors. The construction was to commence in mid-2005; however, as of 2008, the unit had still not been completed. The demand for the secure unit for youths arose out of concern for contact between juvenile and adult prisoners while being incarcerated at Luxembourg Prison. While male and female youth offenders are separated, the lack of separate amenities for youths makes it hard to prevent interaction between youths and adults in the prison. Similarly, there is no segregation regarding placement of minors in trouble with the law and minors suffering from severe behavioral and social problems. Also as of 2007, juveniles accused of serious offenses were permitted to be tried as adults.

Punishment

There are eight recognized punishments in Luxembourg: prison (either life sentence or determined amount of time); fine; special confiscation; removal of degree, title, job, etc.; revocation of civil and political rights; closure of institution or enterprise; publication of sentencing decision; and exclusion from specific professional activities. Certain punishments may accompany imprisonment as opposed to being stand-alone punishments. Removal of degree is mandatory following a sentence to imprisonment and certain rights are revoked following a prison sentence of more than 10 years. The death penalty was abolished in Luxembourg in 1979 with the last execution occurring in 1949, according to Amnesty International.

Prison

According to Eurostat, in 2007 the prison population was 666 inmates. The *Centre Pénitentiaire de Luxembourg* (CPL) is the largest and possibly only true prison in the entire country of Luxembourg. It is located in Schrassig. As a result of being the main prison, it is responsible for housing not only convicted adult offenders, but also juvenile offenders and foreigners who are being administratively held until the time of their removal.

There is a smaller prison in the country, *Centre Pénitentiaire de Givenich*. This seems to be a prison with a more open set-up with the goal of putting the offenders to work in various trades. In fact, some offenders are permitted to leave the premises to perform jobs for minimum wage. This smaller prison is concerned with preparing individuals for release and reintegration into society.

Both prisons have work programs. The work at CPL is often related to upkeep and operation of the prison. In 2006, 106 prisoners worked 35 hours a week to build a new laundry room for the facility. Likewise, both prisons offer education courses for inmates. This is consistent with a recommendation of the Council of Europe, which regards education as a fundamental right and believes that education facilitates the return of the inmate to society. Participation in education or work is voluntary, not compulsory. Prisoners are allowed communication with the outside world except for an extreme situation where an investigating judge temporarily suspends communication privileges of pretrial detainees.

Raquel Moriarty

Further Reading

The Ministry of Justice: http://www.mj.public.lu.

Report by Mr. Alvaro Gil-Robles, Commissioner for Human Rights, on His Visit to the Grand Duchy of Luxembourg, 2–3 February 2004, Council of Europe, Commissioner for Human Rights: http://www.unhcr.org/refworld/docid/4159737b4.html.

2008 Human Rights Report of the Bureau of Democracy, Human Rights and Labor: http://www.state.gov/g/drl/rls/hrrpt/2008/eur/119090.htm.

Macedonia, Former Yugoslav Republic of

Legal System: Civil
Murder: Medium
Burglary: Medium
Corruption: Medium
Human Trafficking: Low
Prison Rate: Medium
Death Penalty: No
Corporal Punishment: No

Background

The Former Yugoslav Republic of Macedonia (FYRM) became an independent nation in 1991 when it successfully seceded from the former Yugoslavia in a referendum. It then ratified its new constitution. Since then, the country has evolved into a market-based, parliamentary democracy in which power rests largely with the prime minister's government while the president serves a largely ceremonial role. Its legal system is based upon civil law and the judicial review of legislation.

The UN officially recognized the new nation's sovereignty in 1993 as a conflict arose, in which Greece challenged the legitimacy of the country's name Macedonia. Greek authorities objected to what they have perceived to be the former Yugoslav republic's unwarranted appropriation of the Hellenic name and that the new nation to their north would develop territorial claims to Macedonian territories within Greece. After Greece's 1994 embargo of the new republic, the formal name Former Yugoslav Republic of Macedonia was agreed upon while diplomatic negotiations over the "name issue" continue.

Apart from the name issue, ethnic tensions have been particularly troublesome. The independence referendum was overwhelmingly ratified by voters, and it did secure independence without armed insurrection. However, ethnic Albanians, who today represent about 25 percent of the population, abstained from the voting because they felt threatened by the Slavic-speaking ethnic Macedonian majority.

Ethnic Macedonians today represent about 65 percent of the nation's population, and unlike ethnic Albanians, they are predominantly Eastern Orthodox Christians. Thus, ethnic Albanians did not democratically consent to the new nation's construction, and significant ethnic tensions have existed ever since.

In 2000, ethnic Albanians expressed grave concerns regarding the lack of minority protections and participation. During the first half of 2001, open hostilities ignited near the Kosovo border between the Albanian armed group National Liberation Army and the FYRM government. During the summer of 2001, the sides brokered a ceasefire and agreed to a peace accord within the Ohrid Framework. The framework facilitated a new governing coalition, led to the implementation of constitutional and legislative reforms to improve minority group civil rights, as well as new constitutional amendments. But by 2007, ethnic tensions had arisen, and rival Albanian parties deemed that the original agreement had broken down and protests reemerged.

The UN Committee on the Elimination of Racial Discrimination (CERD) recently found that the government was in breach of its obligations toward the minority Romani (gypsy) community, and expressed concerns for the treatment of both Albanian and Turkish children. As well, Amnesty International concluded that Romani females in particular continue to experience "double discrimination" as both minorities and as females. Ethnic tensions and discrimination have also been tied to the challenges posed by internally displaced persons and refugees resulting from various conflicts. During the 1999 Kosovo crisis, 360,000 refugees flooded into the country of just 2 million people, and about 1,800 predominantly Romani and Ashkalia remain under temporary "asylum for humanitarian protection." An estimated 1,000 persons remain internally displaced from the 2001 conflict.

Justice System

Since independence, the civil sector and the media have developed rather well compared with some other countries in the region. Adopted in 2004, Constitutional article 16 guarantees freedom of speech and access to information. But media outlets are highly partisan in their coverage of issues along ethnic and political lines. Reporters without Borders expressed concern that speech is prohibited that is deemed to invite national, religious, or ethnic hatred. As well, journalists and broadcasters are faced with suppressive libel suits, criminal prosecution resulting in onerous fines, and are frequently targets of physical harassment. Further, NGOs have warned that while civil institutions have developed rather well, the government appears to be setting up its own proxy organizations to crowd out legitimate independent governmental watchdogs.

To adjudicate legal disputes, the country has a three-tiered court system with trial courts, appellate courts, along with courts such as the new administrative court and the Supreme Court. Citizens can bring lawsuits through the appellate courts and the Supreme Court to try to stop various human rights violations or to receive compensation. The Constitutional Court handles matters that involve constitutional interpretation and certain human rights protections.

In 2007, the Law on Public Prosecution, the Law on the Council of Public Prosecutors, and changes in the Law on Courts were adopted to finish the legislative framework that was set out in the constitutional amendments of 2005. The changes to the Law on Courts provide for improved protection of citizens' rights to have their cases adjudicated in a timely manner. The judiciary also includes the Public Prosecutor's Office and the public attorney.

The Judicial Council is responsible for the election, discipline, and removal of judges. In 2007, the government authorized the new administrative court. This court is responsible for hearing cases against state institutions. Unfortunately, because of political battles over the membership of the Judicial Council, judges have not been appointed to the court, and by 2009 it had not yet processed any cases.

Outside the country, the International Criminal Tribunal for the former Yugoslavia (ICTY) has had jurisdiction in certain ongoing cases involving

Macedonian officials alleged to have had command involvement in serious violations of laws regulating the customs of war during the 2001 conflict. One high-profile case involves former Minister of Interior Ljube Boshkovski and Johan Tarchulovski for their alleged involvement in the deaths and inhuman treatment of ethnic Albanians. Although the U.S. State Department regards the government as generally complying with the ICTY, Amnesty International has expressed its concern over delays in the draft Law on Cooperation with the Tribunal and the country's recent amnesty legislation.

Police

The Macedonian police force is a centralized national force under the auspices of the Ministry of Interior. It consists of uniformed police, criminal (civilian) police, and the border police. The Eighth UN Survey on Crime Trends and Operations of Criminal Justice Systems (UNCTS) reported police manpower to be 9,789. Both the United States and EU have reportedly been actively involved in providing training and guidance in professionalizing and organizing the police forces, particularly with respect to policing corruption and organized crime. This responsibility officially rests with the Organized Crime Department, which is also under Ministry of Interior authority.

Part of the Ohrid Agreement was that the government would actively recruit ethnic Albanians into the police forces to better reflect their proportional representation in society. But they are still disproportionately represented. The U.S. State Department reports that in 2007, only 20.3 percent of police were minorities, short of the 25 percent government quota. While 25 percent of the population, Albanians are only 16 percent of the police force. Further, they are particularly underrepresented in the intelligence and counterintelligence agencies of the police and military.

Human rights groups have been particularly sensitive to matters of police misconduct and brutality, especially in light of ethnic tensions and past conflicts. For example, Amnesty International has expressed concern about police excessive use of force against people in the village of Brodec during Operation Mountain Storm aimed at recapturing members of armed opposition groups who had escaped from Dubrava Prison in Kosovo. As well, it has expressed concern about cases of past ill-treatment and torture by "Alpha" special police forces.

During the 2001 conflict the "Lions," a monoethnic paramilitary police unit, was set up by the Ministry of Interior following the National Liberation Army uprising. According to credible accounts reported by the ombudsperson, these too committed various human rights violations. The same was reportedly true for the "Tigers" commando military unit and the Security and Counter-espionage Service (DBK). Further, there still has been no progress made in resolving cases of enforced disappearances of ethnic Albanians during the 2001 conflict.

Based on testimony from former high-ranking officials, police informants, and victims, the Macedonian Helsinki Committee for Human Rights (MHC) has reported on the existence of a police infrastructure of torture and corruption. Although they did not operate secret prisons, both the Ministry of Interior and the DBK have owned roughly 40 secret apartments throughout the country. In them, they have tortured at least 15 individuals over the past 10 years. They have also used luxury apartments with cameras hidden within television sets to blackmail public figures, foreign diplomats, foreign intelligence services employees, among others.

The people's defender (ombudsperson) is responsible for reporting human rights violations and corrupt acts by various government agencies, including criminal justice, to the Ministry of Interior. The Professional Standards Unit (PSU) is responsible for investigating and preventing police misconduct. Unfortunately, NGOs cite corruption, the lack of transparency, and political pressure within the Ministry of Interior as having hindered crime-fighting efforts, especially against organized crime. The U.S. State Department believes that police impunity is still problematic, but that more aggressive internal investigations coupled with the ombudsperson's work have helped.

Crime

Various external agencies and internal NGOs have closely monitored corruption and organized crime in Macedonia. These problems remain serious and widespread, and this is particularly so with official corruption. In recent years, there have been high-profile arrests and investigations that the government has reported to the UN Office of Drugs and Crime (UNODC) regarding its efforts to abide by the UN Convention against Corruption. Unfortunately, some have accused officials of making partisan- and revenge-driven arrests in anticorruption cases, selectively prosecuting some while ignoring others.

Still, in 2007 the government launched its Macedonia without Corruption campaign. This included a media campaign and a special 199 telephone line for members of the public to report corruption. Due to efforts like these, organizations like America's Freedom House (FH) and the European Parliament report that the level of corruption is falling.

While attempting to deal with the serious corruption and organized crime problems, the government has been urged to seriously address crime involving trafficking in persons and prostitution. Illegal in FYRM, trafficking in persons usually involves people from the Balkans being trafficked to South Central and Western Europe. Less than a third of the potential victims eligible for government assistance in Macedonia actually avail themselves of it. In 2007, prosecutors brought 57 cases and put 184 suspects on trial. Prostitution is illegal, but laws are not always enforced. Some foreign women are deported, and some men are prosecuted for "mediating" in prostitution. Still, in 2008, Human Rights Watch (HRW) condemned the government's mass arrest of alleged sex workers in the capital city Skopje. The country is a major transit country for hashish and heroin, and to a lesser extent, cocaine, destined for Europe. As well, money laundering is believed to be problematic because the economy is so cash-dependent.

The prevalence of drug abuse appears to be relatively low. According to the World Drug Report 2008, the annual prevalence of abuse as a percentage of Macedonians aged 15–64 for opiates was 0.5 percent in 2005. For cocaine, it was even lower, 0.08 percent in 2007. Back in 1999, Ecstasy abuse was reported to be 0.1 percent of this population.

Intentional homicide rates in the country tend to be low. According to the UNODC International Homicide Statistics, estimates ranged from 2.4 to 5.2 intentional homicides per 100,000 people in 2004. The Eighth UN Survey of Crime Trends and Operations of Criminal Justice Systems (UNCTS) suggested that about 35 percent of the homicides result from firearms. The same survey data reported that there were 296 robberies and 27 rapes.

Rape, including spousal rape, is specifically prohibited. However, the crime requires a higher burden of proof than do other crimes. There must be evidence of both penetration and signs of physical resistance by the victim. Victims must overcome significant cultural stigma, and authorities seem reluctant to seriously investigate and prosecute these cases.

Domestic violence seems to be quite prevalent in FYRM. An NGO, the Association of Emancipation, Solidarity, and Equality of Women (ESE), provided research that estimates that as many as half of all women experience psychological abuse, and about a fifth experience physical abuse. AI estimates that Romani females suffer even more abuse, with an estimated 70 percent being abused. The Ministry of Interior statistics report that during the first six months of 2007, reports of abuse increased with 1,409 reports of psychological abuse, 130 reports of physical abuse, and 3 rapes.

The government operates six shelters while an NGO operates a hotline and a temporary crisis shelter in Skopje. Human rights investigators have generally viewed the government response as poor. Police officers are often unaware of provisions that authorize them to respond to domestic violence cases more assertively, although officer training programs are underway. Child abuse is problematic in some areas. The Ministry of Interior statistics recently included 96 cases of child sexual abuse. The Department of Juvenile Delinquency and the Ministry of Labor and Social Policy's (MLSP) Center for Social Work are responsible for child abuse cases.

Finding of Guilt

Macedonian law requires that police get arrest warrants from the investigating judge in each case, and police generally abide by this requirement. Prosecutors must arraign a detainee within 24 hours of arrest. Only an investigative judge, at the prosecutor's request, may order detention for longer than 24 hours. The judge may approve two additional 24-hour periods. Again, it is believed that authorities generally abide by these legal rules.

Defendants are legally entitled to be presumed innocent and have open court proceedings except for trials that involve minors, sexual offenses, or those in which the defendant's personal safety may be at risk. Defendants have the right to contact lawyers when they are arrested, questioned by police, and during any court proceedings. Although logistical challenges arise, authorities appear to generally abide by these rules.

Indigent clients are also legally entitled to defense attorneys. Defendants are entitled to question witnesses and present evidence. Although not always respected in practice, defendants have a right to access government-held evidence. They also have the right to appeal their convictions. Courts may try defendants in absentia as long as they repeat those trials if the convict returns for trial at a later date. Consistent with a civil law system, there are no juries. Two lay judges assist each judge in determining the verdicts. But the judges generally make the final decisions on sentences.

During pretrial detention, investigative judges have to grant permission for family members, physicians, diplomatic representatives, and representatives from the European Committee for the Prevention of Torture and Inhuman or Degrading Treatment or Punishment (CPT) or the International Committee of the Red Cross (ICRC) to access detainees. Judges typically grant access, but not always in a timely manner. The bail system is such that pretrial detainees may be held up to 30 days. There is then the possibility of up to 180 days of extensions if a council of three judges first orders a 60-day extension for further investigation, then a superior court orders an additional 90-day extension. This extension is only allowed in cases for which the crime under investigation is subject to a sentencing guideline of at least 5 years' imprisonment.

NGOs have expressed concern that judges are increasingly abusing their pretrial detention authority. They assert that judges are too often declining to grant bail or use alternative measures of guaranteeing that defendants show up to trial. These might include home confinement or having defendants relinquish their passports. Human rights groups are also concerned that there is undue pressure on judges in politically sensitive cases. The Constitution and the law provide for judicial independence. However, there is still significant political pressure, intimidation, and corrupting influences on the judiciary. For example, the government may manipulate the judicial budget, such as cutting funds available for the "goods and services" part of judicial operating budgets, which thus hinders the ability of the courts to operate efficiently.

FYRM has recognized the need to improve both judicial independence and efficiency. The problem stems partly from political disputes over the composition of the Judicial Council whose members must be elected by a two-thirds majority of Parliament. The council is supposed to be composed of 13 judges elected by their peers, the Ministry of Justice, and the president of the Supreme Court as *ex officio* members, all totaling 15 Judicial Council members. The delay in selecting members has resulted in delays in the appointment of judges needed to operate courts efficiently.

The Ministry of Justice reports that while many laws relating to the judicial system have been adopted lately, they still require implementation. Indeed, the U.S. State Department believes that the government continues to delay implementation of a number of 2006 judicial reform laws that were meant to enhance independence and efficiency. The government's unofficial reports show that during the first half of 2007, only about 30.6 percent of the 1.1 million cases were actually adjudicated. It is hoped that the 2006 Law on Mediation will reduce court workloads through the use of alternative dispute resolution. As well, the Academy of Judges and Prosecutors has been established to provide continuous training to promote professionalism and competence within the judiciary.

Some measures have been taken to improve the proper prosecution and adjudication of corruption and organized crime. In 2008, amendments were made to the Criminal Procedure Code and the law on monitoring of communications to allow special investigative measures in corruption cases, and law enforcement agencies seem more willing to coordinate their activities, resulting in more successful convictions. The Public Prosecutor's Office prosecutes those charged with organized crime and corruption. This can be done, for example, under article 357 of the Criminal Code. Further, the Law on Courts has been amended so that there will be only one specialized court department to deal with organized crime and corruption, instead of five. It is hoped this will improve efficiency in such cases.

Although arbitrary arrest and detention and police misconduct are prohibited by law, they still remain problematic. Police have been known to invite suspects to police stations for "informative talks" without informing suspects of their rights. Although it appears that such interviews do not result in suspects being arrested or held for any length of time, there are concerns that individuals are improperly questioned for political reasons.

The Macedonian Helsinki Committee for Human Rights (MHC) reports that there have been cases of torture and ill-treatment during arrest and detention, cases which the Ministry of Interior has failed to investigate according to provisions in its own internal procedures, domestic law, and international standards. Foreign governments and the EU continue to monitor the police and advise the Ministry of Interior on police reforms. Inside the country, the Professional Standards Unit (PSU) is responsible for conducting investigations into cases of police misconduct.

In 2007, the PSU reported that citizens filed 137 complaints of police misconduct, including 64 alleging excessive use of force. Citizens also filed 243 complaints of police misconduct with the ombudsperson. The PSU reportedly visited 20 police stations and made recommendations on preventative measures against misconduct in 2007. That same year, the PSU conducted investigation into 4 cases of police excessive use of force during the apprehension and detention of suspects.

According to the U.S. State Department, the PSU has been slow to complete investigations and bring charges. But it believes that there has been improvement in the MOI response to new cases as well as more frequent discipline. In 2007, the PSU recommended disciplinary action against police employees in 90 cases. The MOI reduced pay for 96 employees in 56 cases, suspended 39 employees in 10 cases, and reassigned 53 employees in 24 cases. The PSU also submitted criminal charges against 75 employees for 70 crimes. But it is not clear whether or not prosecutors actually prosecuted them.

Although torture and extrajudicial killings are clearly illegal, there is compelling evidence that in 2002 in the aftermath of the 9/11 terrorist attacks in New York, FYRM police ambushed and shot to death seven male Pakistani and Indian immigrants north of Skopje. Although police alleged that the men were plotting terrorist attacks and that security services had acted appropriately, Western diplomats expressed doubts. The Parliamentary Assembly of the Council of Europe reviewed the official FYRM account of the killings and concluded that it was "utterly untenable."

However, American officials appear to have been suitably impressed with the government's antiterrorism zeal and made the former Yugoslav republic a junior partner in its rendition program. In this program, American agents typically abduct persons whom they suspect of terrorist affiliation then deliver them to security service in governments who reliably torture them to produce the requisite "confessions."

In one notorious case, FYRM agents kidnapped Lebanese-German Khaled el-Masri on New Year's Eve 2003 during his holiday in Macedonia. They then delivered him to American CIA agents who allegedly took him to be tortured in Afghanistan. Convinced of his innocence and making little progress, they eventually released Masri on a deserted road near the Albanian border.

Punishment

FYRM law does not provide for the use of execution for any crime, and it prohibits the forced exile, either internally or externally, as a means of penal punishment. Imprisonment is available for criminal violations. For example, for a serious crime such as rape or forcible sexual assault the law imposes from 1 to 15 years' imprisonment.

The Ministry of Justice Directorate of Prison Administration operates eight facilities. According to the International Centre for Prison Studies, there were 2,200 prisoners for an imprisonment rate of 107 prisoners per 100,000 in 2008. The prison population has been rising since 2001, when there were 1,518 prisoners.

Within the overall population, the number of female prisoners is low, composing 2.7 percent of the total in 2007. That same year, juveniles and foreigners made up 0.8 percent and 4.1 percent, respectively. There is concern about the fact that juveniles and adults are being held together due to limited space. Pretrial/remand prisoners represented 8.9 percent of the total in 2007.

Prison officials usually allow groups such as the ICRC, the CPT, and the country's ombudsperson to visit the prisons and interview prisoners. As a result of their visits to prisons and detention facilities, the CPT expressed concern with the lack of progress that prison officials had made in addressing concerns that the CPT itself had previously raised. In particular, they condemned the practice of chaining prisoners to restrain them and the provision of too little prisoner supervision. The CPT described prison conditions as "inhuman and degrading."

According to the U.S. State Department, prison conditions barely met international standards in 2007. There have been serious problems with poor hygienic conditions, insufficient medical care, as well as inadequate funding and staffing in some facilities such as the Skopje detention center. Overcrowding appears to contribute to many of the problems within the prison system. The system's official capacity was reportedly 2,005 in 2007. Yet occupancy level was 102.2 percent. In that year, the Council of Europe Directorate of Legal Affairs reported that the Indrizovo and Skopje prisons, in particular, have been severely overcrowded.

Paul Schupp

Further Reading

Jelavich, Barbara. (1983). *History of the Balkans.* New York: Cambridge University Press.

Roma in Macedonia, (Gypsy) Rights Network. (2009): http://www.romarights.net.

WashLaw, Legal Research: http://www.washlaw.edu/forint/europe/macedoni.html.

Malta

Legal System: Civil/Common
Murder: Low
Burglary: Low
Corruption: Low
Human Trafficking: Medium
Prison Rate: Medium
Death Penalty: No
Corporal Punishment: No

Background

Malta is a small nation, or micro-state, in the center of the Mediterranean Sea. The country of Malta comprises a chain of five islands; most of the population resides on Malta, the largest of these islands, and some on Gozo, the second largest. Malta is the smallest state in the European Union (EU) with a population of 400,000 and a land area of 316 square kilometers (122 square miles). The economy is based on tourism, as well as financial and information technology services, some manufacturing, and a thriving film industry. Each year, more than a million tourists visit the islands.

History

From the 1800s until 1964, Malta was under British rule. In the administrative language of the British Empire, Malta fit into the category of Crown Colony, meaning the governor embodied the whole of civil and military authority. The Palace of the Grand Masters became the British governor's office and Castellania Palace served as the law courts under British rule until 1853. The first British governor, Sir Thomas Maitland, instituted a Constitution of the Criminal Court that abolished torture and established some rules of criminal procedure.

The Criminal Code

The first effort to write a criminal code occurred in 1826 during the administration of the second British governor, General Francis Rowden, who requested Ignazio Bonavita, senior judge of the Criminal Court of Malta, to prepare a report. Bonavita's criminal code relied on the Neapolitan Code and later revisions in the French code, both of which drew on Roman law. In 1842, the code was sent to Andrew Jameson, a Scottish lawyer. He sought to reconcile Bonavita's code with principles of English criminal law. The code was not brought into effect until 1854.

Over the years, numerous amendments have been made, although the framework of the original 1854 code remains. Legislation enacted in 2002 specified new procedural rights in favor of the accused and established several new offenses, including conspiracy. More recently introduced procedural rights relate to bail, habeas corpus, and redress against unlawful detention, consistent with requirements of the European Court of Human Rights. In addition, special laws define a variety of criminal offenses such as drug offenses or traffic offenses.

Police

The Malta police originated in 1814 when Maitland consolidated the Coast Artillery, the Provincial Corps, and the Police Corps into a single institution, the Police Corps. Several reorganizations took place in the first half of the 19th century. A significant reorganization of police followed the events of June 7, 1919. Known as the *Sette Guigno*, this is the day when a Maltese National Assembly formed to demand independence and British forces fired shots in the direction of a crowd, killing four Maltese. In the 1950s, in the years before independence, the organization of the police was further revised, which improved the standards of recruits, conditions of service, and collection of crime statistics. In 1956, the first female constables were appointed at the Malta police.

Currently, the Malta Police comprises about 1,600 officers of lower ranks (constables, sergeants, sergeant majors) and more than 100 senior officers (inspectors, superintendents, assistant commissioners, the deputy commissioner, and the commissioner). Police are deployed across regional districts, managing local police stations, or at general headquarters, carrying out administrative duties or working in specialized squads. Specialized squads include the cybercrime unit, homicide squad, drug squad, economic crimes squad, vice squad, antiterrorism unit, and immigration branch. The Police Academy has responsibility for training of the national police force. The academy, in conjunction with the Institute of Criminology of the University of Malta, provides a two-year, part-time intensive diploma course in policing for police inspectors.

Crime

Classification of Crimes

Maltese criminal law distinguishes between two categories of offenses: crime and contraventions. Although the Criminal Code does not delineate the specific offenses within each category, it is obvious that contraventions are offenses of a less serious nature than crimes. Other laws establish offenses (both crimes and contraventions) not found in the Criminal Code, such as drug trafficking, money laundering, and forgery of currency.

Terrorism, Immigration, and Money Laundering

Terrorism, illegal immigration, and money laundering present particular areas of concern. Concerns about terrorist violence had led to recent changes in legislation. Until the first half of 2005, activities related to terrorism were punishable under several Maltese laws. The absence of a counterterrorism act was not in conformity with EU standards. The Criminal Code was therefore amended in 2005, creating numerous terrorist offenses, such as hostage taking, hijacking of transport, and the manufacture of biological and chemical weapons.

The Malta Armed Forces Maritime Squadron assists would-be immigrants as they cling to tuna nets in the Mediterranean Sea not far from the coast of Malta, June 15, 2008. The 28 people were stranded when their boat allegedly capsized after colliding with the steel nets. (AP Photo/Rohan Dalli, Malta Armed Forces Maritime Squadron)

In recent years, there has been a sharp increase in the number of illegal immigrants arriving in Malta by boat, and this has raised concern within the government and general population. Given its geographic position, Malta finds itself at the crossroads of irregular migration. In 2006, the Malta police responded to 57 incidents involving some 1,780 persons who either had to be brought ashore or had landed illegally in Malta. About half of these so-called boat people were of Eritrean, Egyptian, Somali, or Moroccan nationality. Most sought to apply for asylum status and received assistance from the Ministry of Family and Social Solidarity. Malta accepts more than half of all asylum seekers, the highest acceptance rate in Europe, and questions have been raised in government and media circles about the extent to which this level of absorption can be sustained. Malta already has, by far, the greatest population density in the EU, with 1,250 persons per square kilometer.

Malta is keen to protect its expanding economy from international crime. The government has sought to establish and promote Malta as an international financial center. However, foreign investment increased fears that money obtained by drug trafficking, used to support terrorist financing, could be laundered through the banking system. To protect the integrity of the country's financial institutions, the government enacted the Professional Secrecy Act (1994) and Prevention of Money Laundering Act (1994). This was followed by creation of a national Financial Intelligence Analysis Unit in 2001. Malta has contributed to international efforts to suppress money laundering. International concerns led to creation of the multinational Financial Action Task Force in 1990, following the initiative taken at the G-7 summit in Paris the previous year. This organization urged criminalization of money laundering, confiscation of money laundering proceeds, and greater international cooperation in investigation and prosecution of money launderers.

Drugs and Alcohol

Malta has sought to contribute to international efforts to reduce drug-related crime. In 2006, the Drug Squad of the Malta Police seized various drugs, in amounts of 2 kilos or less, at the Luqa Airport. These included cocaine, cannabis, heroin, and Ecstasy tablets. New substances uncovered for the first time in Malta included benzylpiperazine (BZP) and khat. Overall, there were 361 convictions for possession and 96 for trafficking.

Drug use among young adults in Malta probably began during the 1970s. Pharmaceutical drugs, such as tranquilizers, made an appearance, as did cannabis smoking and inhalants among a limited group. Heroin has been in use since the 1980s. Caritas Malta opened a drug-rehabilitation center in 1985, and in 1994, the government established a national drug agency (*Sedqa*), which developed community-based programs, a prison-based facility, and extensive prevention programs. Much of the concern has focused on drug use among youth. Malta participated in European-wide school surveys of the use of alcohol and other drugs during the 1990s sponsored by the Council of Europe. Essentially, Maltese youth consume more alcohol, but less illicit drugs, than youth elsewhere in Europe. More than 90 percent of students in secondary schools in Malta report having consumed alcohol on more than one occasion. This places Malta in the top category of "drinking countries," alongside Denmark, the United Kingdom, and (the Republic of) Ireland. Maltese youth prefer wine and spirits rather than beer. A similar percentage of school-age youth in Malta report that they have *never* used an illicit drug during their lifetime. This is the lowest figure among students reporting illicit drug use across Europe. Lower use among Maltese youth, compared to European youth generally, is also true of tobacco. Nearly half of Maltese youth surveyed reported that they had *never* used tobacco; this is the lowest figure reported in school surveys across Europe.

Crime Statistics

Although the Malta police do not issue annual crime reports as such, statistics are easily accessible upon request. The limitations of police statistics as a valid indicator of crime are well known. That said, Malta has a relatively low crime rate as can be seen from the data collected in 2006 presented here.

Type of Crime	Number
Arson	2
Bodily harm	228
Property damage	356
Homicide	2
Prostitution	259
Sexual offenses	160
Theft	631
Violence against police	53
Total	**1,691**

In 2006, there were more than 16,000 reported crimes. Theft and damage to property account for most—about 80 percent—of these. Violent crime, particularly homicide, is rare. The Malta police does have a special squad for investigation of homicides, although there were years (e.g., 2006) when no homicide was reported. The single largest category of theft, about 28 percent, consists of theft from motor vehicles. Thefts from residences, bars, hotels, public beaches, and retail stores comprise about 22 percent of total recorded thefts, and holdups amount to less than 1 percent.

Criminologists in Malta have analyzed the geographic distribution of crime. St. Julian's, St. Paul's Bay, Sliema, and Valletta have been the areas of highest crime during the past decade. Marsaxlokk, Ta'Xbiex, Pembroke, and Gozo have been the areas of lowest crime. This pattern can be easily explained by the tourist and leisure economy. The hot spots are those areas with the greatest concentration of recreational and retail outlets and a high population density. The areas of lowest crime, Marsaxlokk, Ta'Xbiex, and Pembroke, are those with settled residential populations. The island of Gozo is a more tightly knit society than Malta—residents tend to leave doors unlocked, leave valuables in the open, and exhibit other behavior confident of secure surroundings. Although, it must also be said, that the criminal aspect in Gozo is covered by a veil of *omertà*.

Criminal victimization of tourists presents a special concern given its potential economic impact. Tourism is the strongest sector of the economy, with about half of the jobs in Malta connected directly or indirectly to tourism. Recent research carried out by Victim Support Malta shows that while Malta lives up to its reputation as a safe destination for tourists, the authorities could do more to assist those who are victimized. The research team interviewed persons departing from Malta's International Airport at Luqa during a 12-hour period and obtained 719 cases for analysis. Of these, 3 percent reported having experienced victimization while in the country; nearly all had been victims of theft at hotels. This figure is higher than the official tourist victimization rate derived from police statistics, which likely reflects the reality that reporting by tourists is low.

Some areas of Malta have been known for particular criminal activities. During the years when the British Navy maintained its Mediterranean Fleet in the Grand Harbour, *Strada Stretta* in Valletta, was notorious for prostitutes. This area contained many music halls catering to sailors and soldiers on shore leave. A number of young women from Poland, Russia, and elsewhere in Eastern Europe came to Malta to work in the music halls as artistes or barmaids The nighttime economy has now moved to St. Julian's and Sliema, and locations in adjacent areas of GŻira, Msida, Marsa, and Ta' Xbiex have become notorious for prostitutes. But some things have not changed: many of the allegations of prostitution continue to involve foreign women.

Finding of Guilt

The administration of justice presents a fusion of civil law and common law principles. There is an inquisitorial aspect of Maltese procedure nearly as strong as the Italian system, although the system also reflects nearly two centuries of British influence.

Criminal Responsibility

Onus probandi incumbit ei qui dicit non ei qui negat—the onus of proof is on the person who alleges, not who denies. Witnesses, evidential material, and forensic evidence in combination with circumstantial evidence are the necessary ingredients that may infuse the proof that laws have been breached. There are particular cases where the offenders can be exempted wholly or partially from the criminal responsibility; these take into account age, physical or physiological conditions, and insanity.

Children under 9 years are considered to be *doli incapax*. This means that according to the law, they are incapable of having a malicious intent, thus are exempted from criminal responsibility for any act or omission. Minors under 14 years of age are similarly exempted, unless there is a mischievous discretion. If the minor is between 14 and 18 years of age, the punishment applicable to the offense shall be decrease by one or two degrees.

Court Proceedings

The Criminal Court incorporates the inferior courts, which are convened by a magistrate, and the superior courts, which are convened by a judge. The majority of the criminal cases are tried by summary proceedings in the magistrates' courts. Few cases are tried by jury in the superior courts. The prosecution must prove its case beyond reasonable doubt, and in line with the principle *audi alteram parte,* the defendant has the right to bring forward any evidence to substantiate his or her defense.

The Maltese inferior courts are presided by 15 magistrates, 6 of whom are women. The superior courts are presided over by 19 judges including the chief justice, only 2 of whom are women. In the superior courts, 4 of the serving judges preside (separately) over the Criminal Court, hearing trials by jury and appeals from decisions of the inferior criminal courts. Appeals from decisions of the Criminal Court given in the first instance are decided by the Criminal Court of Appeal, which is presided by the chief justice and 2 other judges.

According to the Maltese Constitution, the president appoints the judges of the superior courts and the magistrates on the advice of the prime minister. To qualify as a judge of the superior courts, a person must have practiced as an advocate, or have served as a magistrate, for at least 12 years. To qualify a person must practice as an advocate in Malta for at least for 7 years. Both judges and magistrates shall vacate office by the age of 65 years. The Constitution provides that a judge may be removed from office by the president following a resolution supported by not less than two-thirds of the House of Representatives on the proven inability to perform functions of this office or on account of proven misbehavior.

Plea Bargaining

The concept of finding an agreement regarding punishment to be meted out in case of admission of guilt has been informally resorted to for many years in the Criminal Court. In 2002, plea bargaining was officially regulated with the introduction of Section 453A of the Criminal Code, which is called *Sentence at the request of the parties*.

If the accused pleads guilty, the accused and the attorney general may request the court to apply a sanction or measure agreed between them. Upon a plea of guilty by the accused the court can proceed to pass the sentence indicated to it by the parties. The court should declare in its judgment that the sentence is awarded on the request of the parties. However, the final decision is of the judge or magistrate, who has to consider the various circumstances that may have been involved in each individual case. Thus, the court may accept or reject the recommended sanction

Court Structure

The criminal courts are housed in the Courts of Justice building in Valletta, although the Juvenile Court is currently housed in Santa Venera. There is also a magistrates' court in Gozo. The magistrates' court (Court of Criminal Judicature and Court of Inquiry) has both civil and criminal jurisdiction. It is competent to try all offenses within its original jurisdiction that are punishable by up to 6 months imprisonment and acts as a court of inquiry in respect to indictable offenses dealt with by higher courts. It implies compiling evidence and deciding whether there are sufficient grounds for the defendant to be indicted. Conclusions of the court are transmitted to the attorney general. The attorney general may request that the case proceed summarily before the magistrates' court if the crime is punishable by imprisonment not exceeding 10 years. If the defendant has no objection to the case being dealt with summarily, the Court of Magistrates will become competent to try and judge the accused. The prosecutors in this court are police inspectors or police officers of a higher rank.

For offenses subject to a custodial sentence exceeding 10 years, or in case the defendant objects to being tried summarily, the case will be heard in the Criminal Court. This court is presided by a judge together with a jury of nine persons. The attorney general is the prosecutor before the Criminal Court. Appeals are tried by the Court of Criminal Appeal. Appeals from the decisions by the Court of Magistrates are heard by one of the judges sitting on the Criminal Court. Appeals from decisions of the Superior Court are heard by the Court of Criminal Appeal; this court is presided over by the chief justice and two other judges.

Finally, the Juvenile Court is presided over by a magistrate assisted by two persons. It is customary to hold sittings in a less formal environment than that of a courtroom, which is intended to make the juvenile offenders feel more at ease. The Juvenile Court hears charges against minors of less than 16 years of age

Use of Arrest and Pretrial Detention

The police may request a warrant of arrest from a magistrate. When the warrant of arrest cannot be obtained in such a short time, a police officer may arrest any person that is in the act, has committed, or is about to commit an unlawful act. When a person is arrested, the investigating officer may grant "police bail." Police bail is a break in the arrest where the person is released under particular conditions such as to return to the police station in a specific time and date and not to leave Malta. However, when a senior officer concludes that the arrested person is being investigated and it is necessary to detain the arrest person more than 6 hours, the duty magistrate is notified of the circumstances thereof. The magistrate may order the transfer of the arrested person in another place if it is deemed necessary. As prescribed by the Maltese Constitution, any person arrested for the purpose of being arraigned before a court and/or is suspected of having committed or was about to commit a criminal offense must be released within 48 hours of the arrest. The Police Act also prescribes that during these 48 hours, every 12 hours the custody officer has to verify with the investigating officer whether the continued detention is justified.

Thus the person under arrest must be brought before the court during the 48-hour period. On arraignment the court may release the person unconditionally or may impose conditions that ensure that this person appears for the trial and for any other court proceedings preliminary to the trial. If the person does not abide by these conditions, he or she is brought again before the court. One of the bail conditions that may be imposed is that the person is confined in his or her house and should inform the police every time that person needs to go out. It is commonly called "house arrest," although house arrest as such is not contemplated by Maltese law and the time during which these conditions are in force is not deducted from any term of imprisonment eventually given as is the case with preventive custody.

Together with the bail conditions the court may also issue a provisional order of supervision. If the person is granted bail he or she may be put under a provisional order of supervision. The accused will be under the supervision of a probation officer even during any criminal proceedings. A provisional order of supervision may be issued irrespective of the nature of the offense with which a person is charged, even if the penalty is more than 10 years of imprisonment such as drug trafficking or voluntary homicide.

Punishment

Types of Punishment

The Maltese criminal justice system provides for an extensive inventory of punishments for crimes, including imprisonment; solitary confinement; interdiction; pecuniary penalties; detention; suspended sentence; suspended sentence with a supervision order; probation order; community service order; combination order; absolute and conditional discharge; reprimand or admonition; interdiction and pecuniary penalties.

Imprisonment and Solitary Confinement

Persons sentenced to imprisonment shall be confined in the prison or in that part of the prison appointed for persons sentenced to that punishment. These persons are subject to the restrictions prescribed in the prison regulations, which are lawfully made. The duration of the punishment of imprisonment is specified for every individual case. The punishment of solitary confinement demands keeping the person in the course of an imprisonment sentence continuously closed in an appointed place within the prison. In such eventuality only persons assigned on duty are authorized to access that person. Solitary confinement shall not exceed 10 continuous days and can only be applied with an interval of 2 months between one term and another. This punishment can be inflicted in case of any infringement of the prison regulations, or for any other offense committed during the intervals. Before awarding the punishment of solitary confinement the court shall satisfy itself by medical evidence, which may include a medical examination, that the person convicted is fit to undergo this punishment. If the person is not fit to undergo such punishment the execution of this punishment shall be suspended until the person is considered medically fit to undertake such punishment.

Fines

The Maltese law distinguishes between a fine in case of a criminal offense, which is called *multa*, while for a contravention it is called *ammenda*. Fines serve as a sole punishment for misdemeanors or as part of a combination sentence in a more serious case. The fine shall be paid within a specific period of time. If a person is sentenced to pay a fine and is granted the benefit of time by order of the court and does not pay such fine, he or she is liable to be arrested and brought before the court. The court shall commit such person to undergo the detention or imprisonment prescribed in substitution for the fine or the still-unpaid balance as the case may be; maximum terms are prescribed according to the amounts of unpaid fine.

Suspended Sentence

When court awards a sentence of imprisonment of not more than two years for an offense, it may order that the imprisonment sentence shall not take effect immediately, and order a suspended sentence. The suspended sentence can be applied with some exceptions (the person is a recidivist, for example). The law provides that the court shall explain the suspended sentence in ordinary language so that the offender can understand better the imposed conditions.

Where the court awards a sentence of more than six months' imprisonment and suspended in accordance, the court may add a supervision order. In these circumstances the suspended sentence will be referred to as suspended sentence supervision order. The offender is placed under the supervision of a supervising officer for the period specified in the order, which does not exceed the operational period of the suspended sentence (from one to four years). The supervising officer is a probation officer appointed under the Probation Act and named in the supervision order. The supervision order requires the offender to comply, during the whole or any part of the period of supervision, with requirements as may be imposed by the court.

Probation Order

Instead of sentencing an offender the court may award a probation order. During this order the offender will be under the supervision of a probation officer for a period of not less than 1 year and not more than 3 years. This order can be made only if the offender is convicted of an offense that is not punishable only with a fine and it is not an offense that is punishable with imprisonment for not more than 7 years and, in particular circumstances, up to 10 years' imprisonment. The court is convinced that the supervision by a probation officer is in the interest of securing the rehabilitation of the offender while protecting the public and preventing the offender from committing further offenses; and it is considered appropriate when taking in consideration the circumstances of the case, including the nature of the offense and the character of the offender.

A probation order may require the offender to comply with a number of requirements during the whole or any part of the probation period. The court considers such requirements as necessary for securing the good conduct of the offender and preventing further repetition of the same or commission of other offenses. When the court considers the circumstances that surround an offender, these may include the home surroundings of the offender and the mental condition of the offender that may require treatment such as for drug addiction. A probation order may include a requirement that the offender shall undergo treatment during the probation period. During the treatment the offender can be a resident patient, a nonresident patient in a hospital or other appropriate agency or institution, or under the direction of a suitably qualified person as may be specified in the order or as indicated by the probation officer. Another important requirement that can be added to a probation order, community service order, combination order, or an order for conditional discharge or absolute discharge is that an offender may be required to compensate for the damages of the injured parties.

Community Service Order

The court may award a community service order to an offender aged 16 years and over. Such an offense must not be punishable only by a fine and cannot be an offense, which apart from any increase in punishment in view of the continuity or of previous convictions, is punishable with imprisonment exceeding 7 years but not exceeding 10 years, like in the probation order. In this case the court orders the offender to be placed on a community service order. This will require the offender to perform unpaid work for a number of hours as specified in the order. The number of hours ranges from 40 hours of work to 240 hours. These hours are to be performed in not less than 3 months and in not more than a year. However, the court may extend the period of 1 year by 6 months so that the order is carried out. The offender has to work the specified number of hours unless the order is revoked. These hours must not interfere with normal working hours or school attendance. The Probation Services reports that since 2003, when the community service order became effective, the total number of community service orders issued so far amount to 3,320 hours.

Prison

In the islands of Malta there is only one prison, the Corradino Correctional Facilities, built in the 1840s. Numerous additions have been undertaken since that time, such as facilities for secure confinement, a young offenders unit, and secure detention facilities for offenders with addiction or other psychiatric disorders.

Prison Population

The population of the prison on May 15, 2008, was 417 persons. This figure included 299 sentenced persons (283 men, 16 women) and 118 persons (113 men, 5 women) awaiting trial. Eight prisoners were serving a life sentence (5 Maltese, 3 foreign). Maltese prisoners numbered 258 or about 68 percent of the population; prisoners of foreign nationality numbered 132 or about 32 percent. Most of these came from North Africa and Eastern Europe.

Between 2004 and 2006, Malta had an average rate of 76 per 100,000, one of the lowest in Europe. Historically, imprisonment in Malta reached highest levels during World War II and in the 1990s. Imprisonment rose in the 1990s due to sentencing practices and changes in the population sent to prison.

Conditions of Confinement

Attending educational classes is not obligatory for adult inmates and there are no repercussions for those who choose not to participate in available educational opportunities. Young offenders and illiterate offenders are to be given special attention to their educational needs. In respect to work, both inmates serving a prison sentence and those awaiting trial are regulated by the Prison Regulations 1995. In no instance can the work provided be of an afflictive nature.

Inmates serving a prison sentence are allowed one contact visit a week, which lasts 45 minutes. If these inmates are working as part of the prison regime, then they are given an extra contact visit of 45 minutes per week. Inmates who are awaiting trial can also avail themselves of a daily 15-minute no-contact visit with only those persons that the police and the courts have issued a legal permit allowing the contact to take place. Additionally all inmates can benefit from a 2.5-hour unsupervised family extended visit with their loved ones, when certain criteria are met.

Paul Knepper and Trevor Calafato

Further Reading

Bell, A. (1995). *Changing Dimensions of Inmate Population in Malta.* Malta: Ministry for Home Affairs and Social Development.

Calafato, Trevor, and Paul Knepper. (2009). "Criminology and Criminal Justice in Malta." *European Journal of Criminology* 6(1): 89–108.

Grech, Jean-Paul. (2006). *Criminal Justice Systems in Europe and North America: Malta.* Helsinki: The European Institute for Crime Prevention and Control (HEUNI).

Moldova

Legal System: Civil
Murder: Medium
Corruption: Medium
Human Trafficking: High
Prison Rate: High
Death Penalty: No
Corporal Punishment: No

Background

In 1812, after Bessarabia was annexed by the Russian Empire, several attempts to apply Russian law were undertaken. The name of "Moldova" was changed, and the territory between Prut and Dniester was called "Bessarabia." In spite of the efforts of the local population to keep their own law, on April 29, 1818, the Act of Constitution of the Province of Bessarabia was approved. Since this date, the Russian judicial organization model has also applied in these territories. Three authorities were set up: district courts, regional criminal courts, and the Supreme Council.

The Russian Revolution of 1917 and the end of World War I in 1918 saw the return of the territory of Bessarabia to Romania. The modified Criminal Code of 1937 introduced the final distinction between the common law crimes and the offenses of a political nature. Impregnated with strong democratic ideas, Romanian law was used even as a source for certain European codifications of that time. But the period of progressive development was hampered by the beginning of World War II and by new annexation of the territory of Bessarabia in 1940, which became in short time the Moldavian Soviet Socialist Republic (MSSR).

The organization of the legal institutions in the MSSR was subjected to the same principles as in the majority of the republics of the Soviet Union (USSR). Primarily, the law applied to this territory was that of the Ukrainian Soviet Socialist Republic, taking up the generalized model of the USSR. Serious crimes were judged in accordance with the national USSR law, whereas sentences for less serious offenses were provided by the Criminal Code of the MSSR (CP MSSR). Even after the proclamation of independence, the CP MSSR of 1961, subject to important modifications and additions, was applied until 2003, when the new Criminal Code came into force. The legislative changes were very important compared to other former Soviet republics. For example, the Republic of Moldova (RM) was the first to abolish the death penalty.

The Constitution of the RM represents the primary source in the national legislation. The main constitutional standards constituting the base of the criminal procedure are access to justice, presumption of innocence, nonretroactivity, and the right to be informed of its rights and obligations. The Constitution of 1994, amended in 2001, specifies the conditions of arrest and the protection of the person during arrest.

Currently, the RM is carrying several legal reforms, in compliance with international European standards. At the present time the legal system is mixed, combining the principles of both the accusatorial and inquisitorial systems, thus moving away from the former Soviet system. However, distance from the Soviet tradition is still a long way off, taking into account the fact that the party in office since 2009 is the Communist Party.

Crime

Classification of Crimes

The Criminal Code of the Republic of Moldova (CP RM) defines crime as "a prejudicial act (action or failure to act), provided by the Criminal Law committed with guilt and subjected to criminal liability." In 2008, the Parliament adopted the new Code of Administrative Offences, which allows a more accurate specification of certain acts and the adjustment of the sanctions for a large category of offenses, which up to now were disproportionately too severe. The decision on whether an act constitutes a criminal or an administrative offense depends on the constituent elements and the seriousness of the prescribed sanction. The constituent elements of an offense must be identified by the court before they can be classified as a criminal act. Moreover, culpability is an essential component in the qualification of the crime. Cases without the intention to cause damages are, with some exceptions, omitted from the classifications of the crimes. According to the CP RM, offenses are classified into five categories: minor, less serious, serious, extremely serious, and exceptionally serious.

Acts that can be sentenced with a jail term not exceeding two years are considered minor offenses. Among these offenses are threatening to murder or inflict gross bodily or health harm, gross or medium bodily or health harm caused by negligence, the unlawful performance of an abortion, illegal imprisonment of a person, violation of labor protection regulations, violation of the right to freedom of assembly, the illegal practice of medicine, spreading diseases, illegal circulation of narcotics and psychotropic substances or precursors, illegal public use of narcotics, smuggling, illegal access to computerized information, and slandering a judge or a person performing criminal investigation.

Less serious offenses are acts prohibited by the criminal law, which can be sentenced by a jail term not exceeding five years; these are mostly the same acts as minor offenses, but perpetrated with aggravated circumstances or repeatedly. Offenses represented in this group include all acts categorized as "Crimes regarding sexual life" in Chapter 4 of the CP RM, for which sentences range from three to seven years. Other offenses include, for example, assault on the person, theft, robbery, damage through deception or abuse of trust, incest, child abuse, or luring of minors into illegal consumption of drugs. "Crimes against public health and social living," such as contaminating with AIDS, pimping, environmental crimes, fabrication of credit cards or checks, spreading of software viruses, hooliganism, or vandalism, are also included under this heading, similarly to an important part of "crimes against the State authority and against State security."

Serious crimes are criminal acts subject to a jail term from 5 to 15 years inclusively. More than half of offenses included in the category "Crimes against property" and most "crimes against peace or security of humanity and war crimes" are considered serious crimes. Other offenses included are, for example, kidnapping, burglary in aggravated circumstances, rape, counterfeiting, and terrorism. Some military crimes perpetrated during a war are also included. Extremely serious crimes subject to more than 15-year jail terms are deliberate murder, trafficking of human beings, rape, misappropriation of property on an especially large scale, child trafficking, and hostage taking.

Finally, exceptionally serious crimes are offenses for which the criminal law provides life detention, the most serious sentence available. These crimes include genocide; preparing, unleashing, or waging of a war; using forbidden means and methods in waging a war; deliberate murder; rape; child trafficking; terrorism; banditry; and attempt on the life of the president of the RM, of the president of Parliament, or the prime minister.

In spite of continual adjustment of the CP RM, inconsistencies remain. Several categories of minor offenses are subject to excessively severe punishments and the gap between European criminal legislation and that of the RM remains considerable. Thus, the experts of the Council of Europe recommended to the Moldavian authorities to set up a device for reform of the CP RM. The project aims at the modification of more than 200 articles as well as the drafting of 5 new ones.

Juveniles

The age of criminal responsibility is 16 years old. Juveniles between 14 and 16 years of age can be punished only for some offenses of certain gravity or perpetrated repeatedly, such as, for example, deliberate murder, murder of a newborn infant by the mother, deliberate gross bodily or health harm, deliberate medium bodily harm or health harm, kidnapping, rape, violent actions with a sexual character, perversion, theft, robbery, and burglary.

The age of full criminal responsibility is fixed at 18 years old. Juveniles under 18 cannot be sentenced to prison for more than 6 months; in case of plurality of crimes, the maximum sentence to be imposed is 15 years. Moreover, juveniles must be held in special penitentiary institutions for juvenile offenders. In particular, in cases of minor or less serious offenses, young adults (between 18 and 21 years old) may be treated as juvenile offenders and can be held in special penitentiary institutions for juveniles. On September 1, 2007, of 186 people detained in such institutions, 105 were more than 18 years old.

Organized Crime

The problem of organized crime is of undeniable importance. Today, criminal organizations operating on the territory of the RM, but also abroad, are numerous and hierarchically structured. The principal activities of these organizations are auto thefts, burglaries, blackmail, trafficking of human beings, smuggling, trafficking in human organs, corruption, and drug trafficking. Closely related to the quite unstable economic situation of the country, corruption is a major concern for the state.

Since the declaration of independence of the RM in 1991, and until 2006, the shadow economy has reached almost 70 percent of the economic activity of the country. The number of emigrations to Western Europe countries or large cities in Russia is estimated to exceed 500,000 people (i.e., more than 30% of the RM working population). People without an authorization of stay and with limited subsistence means are more easily recruited by criminal groups. Moldavian offenders perpetrate mainly car thefts with the goal to resell these in RM or in other adjoining countries. Since 2007 (accession of Romania, western RM's neighbor, to the European Union), when controls of the land borders improved, the criminals intensified the use of the sea and river ways (mainly through Ukraine). Today, while the western border is better protected, an alarming problem is the eastern border of the country. The Transdniestria separatist territory, located between RM and Ukraine, a 150-kilometer- (90-mile-) length area, is not controlled by the Moldavian authorities.

A great quantity of goods of smuggling passes through the territory of Transdniestria: cigarettes, alcohol, and other products. Moldavian authorities are mostly worried by the great proportions of the traffic of firearms, ammunition, and narcotic substances through this territory. Significant amounts of money are laundered annually in Transdniestria. Sanctions for these crimes in RM are considerable, but the offenders can hide from Moldavian justice in the territory of Transdniestria.

Trafficking in human beings, another aspect of organized criminality, consists in the recruiting of people in precarious financial situations for sexual exploitation or forced labor abroad. The RM is a source country of workers for the sex industry in countries that are in a state of military conflict or with a reduced policing capacity. Main destinations remain to date Turkey, the United Arab Emirates, Israel, and Afghanistan. Traffickers head also to countries with high economic levels and with a legal prohibition of prostitution, but where there exists opportunity of a criminal network.

In the CP RM, trafficking in human beings is subject to a jail term that ranges from 7 to 25 years. Given that half of trafficked victims are minors, the CP RM prescribes sentences between 10–25 years of imprisonment for this specific category of trafficking. In 2006, the RM ratified the Convention of the Council of Europe on the Fight against Trafficking in Human Beings. This allowed the creation of the Centre of Fight against Trafficking in Human Beings within the Ministry of Internal Affairs. According to the ministry, in 2008 there were 531 cases of trafficking recorded by the police, of which 215 were for human trafficking; 30 cases involved the trafficking of children, 159 pimping, and 112 illegal migration. In 2007, there were 51 offenders sentenced for human trafficking; 7 offenders had been involved in the trafficking of children, 130 in pimping, 27 in organized illegal migration, and 18 in organized begging and forced labor.

Corruption

In 1992, the Presidential Decrees, On the Measures of the Fight against Corruption within the State and Administrative Bodies, followed in 1996 by the Law on the Fight against Corruption and Protectionism, allowed the evaluation of the gravity of the situation regarding organized crime and corruption. The collaboration of the Moldavian authorities with the state and nongovernmental bodies of the member states of the European Union (EU), as well as the Council of Europe, allowed the draft of the projects of common work at the European level. In 2008 the new Law on the Prevention and Fight against Corruption came into force.

The Centre for Combating Economic Crimes and Corruption of the Republic of Moldova began its activity in 2002, and has since then become the central body for the eradication of the corruption in the RM. The number of the cases of corruption recorded by the police has been on the rise for a few years. In 2002 cases related to corruption recorded by the police represented 2.11 percent of the total number of cases; in 2007 the percentage was two times higher, 4.89 percent. Problems remain very important, because the cases of corruption are often not easily detectable, and the identification of the offenses of this type is sporadic. According to information of the General Prosecutor Office, between January and November 2008, 3,494 cases comprising the constitutive elements of the corruption offenses, or those of related offenses, were recorded. Approximately 20 percent of cases were perpetrated in the field of public administration, 16 percent within the bodies of criminal prosecution, 11 percent in the education area, nearly 9 percent in the field of justice, 9 percent within the Customs, and almost 30 percent in the private sector.

Drug Offenses

In June 2008, the total number of drug users recorded by Republican Narcological Dispensary was of 9,500 people, which represents approximately 230 people per 100,000 inhabitants. Most of these drug-addicted persons, 95 percent, were less than 30 years old. Even though drug use as such is punishable only administratively in the RM, the public consumption or the inducement of minors to consumption are criminal offenses. In 2006, the government approved a list of substances and identified new unit quantities for the qualification of drug offenses. Changes in the criminal legislation allowed a more accurate distinction between serious and minor drug offenses, in particular, introducing criminal responsibility for the cultivation of plants that contain drugs or psychotropic substances.

In 2006, 11 percent (2,087) of police-recorded drug offenses were classified as serious. Most arrested offenders were males (79.7%). Thereby, over the last 10 years, the proportion of female offenders has significantly decreased from 56.2 percent in 1997 to 20.3 percent in 2006, according to the *Moldova Annual Drug Report* of 2007. Over the period 2004–2007, the average number of offenders sentenced for drug crimes was 1,064.

The problem of drug trafficking is most important in the eastern part of the country, mostly explained by the impossibility of adequate border control between Transdniestria and the RM. Generally, narcotic substances imported to or transiting the RM are marijuana, heroin, and cocaine. Poppy and hemp precursors are frequently exported from the RM.

For several years, drug offenses were particularly frequent among prisoners in penal institutions. Such offenses were subject to up to 2 years of imprisonment, or under aggravated circumstances, up to 5 years. The fight against these practices is a priority of the Ministry of Justice and the Ministry of Internal Affairs. The total amount of drug seizures in penal institutions decreased from 14.533 kg in 2005 to 3.379 kg in 2006.

Crime Statistics

Crime data are recorded by the Ministry of Internal Affairs, the General Prosecutor Office, the Centre for Combating Economic Crimes and Corruption of the Republic of Moldova, the Customs Service, and the Information and Security Service. The highest rates of criminality are found in urban areas: 63.3 percent of all recorded offenses in 2007. Mostly affected are the capital of the country, Chisinau, and the "North capital," Balti, the third-largest city of the RM.

Almost 31 percent of recorded offenses in 2007 were classified as serious, of which 8 percent were extremely or exceptionally serious. Between 2004 and 2007, the total number of recorded offenses and more particularly the number of serious offenses continued to decrease. The general decrease exceeded 15 percent, and exceeded 60 percent for serious offenses. According to the Moldova Bureau of Statistics, the following offenses were recorded by police in 2007:

Murder	216
Deliberate serious injury	408
Rape	281
Theft	9,724
Robbery	868
Burglary	153
Fraud	860
Smuggling	493
Counterfeiting	87
Drug offenses	2,182
Against public health	194

Offenders in the RM are mostly nonworking (78.5%), young (59% are less than 30), and males (over 85%). Of offenders known to the police, 92.8 percent are first-time offenders. The proportion of juvenile offenders has been decreasing, from 14.6 percent of offenders in 2005 to 11.9 percent in 2007.

Finding of Guilt

Rights of the Accused

According to the Criminal Procedure Code (CPC RM), the accused has the right to defense, which must be ensured by the prosecution body or the court, and to be presumed innocent. Some other important rights are the following:

- To be told what he or she is accused of.
- Upon apprehension, to be informed of his or her rights, including the right to remain silent.
- Charges to be brought no later than 72 hours before a judge and to be tried within in a reasonable time.
- Upon indictment, to be assisted by a defense counsel and if he or she cannot pay a lawyer, to be assisted for free by an *ex officio* lawyer.
- To admit the accusation and to conclude a plea bargaining agreement.
- To accept an abbreviated procedure for the criminal prosecution.
- To have his or her close relatives informed of his or her place of arrest.
- To submit documents and other means of evidence for the purpose of investigation in the court hearing.
- To formulate objections to witnesses and prosecution procedures.
- To participate in the trial in the first instance and in appeal.
- To reconcile with the damaged party under the conditions provided by the law.
- To ask and get compensations for the damage caused as a consequence of illegal actions of the criminal prosecution body and the court.

Investigation and Prosecution

As a rule, prosecutors supervise and conduct the criminal prosecution actions. The criminal prosecution bodies are subdivisions organized within the Ministry of Internal Affairs, Information and Security Service, Customs Department, and Centre for Combating Economic Crimes and Corruption of the Republic of Moldova. All subdivisions are represented by criminal prosecution officers especially assigned by these institutions. Prosecution officers are generally law graduates. The powers of the prosecution officers are still very large, but are considerably limited compared to the Soviet period. They settle on the direction of the investigation, approve proceedings, check and evaluate the pieces of evidence. Moreover, they have authority to apply constraint measures. Prosecution officers from the Ministry of Internal Affairs are in charge of investigation and prosecution of approximately 90 percent of annually recorded criminal cases.

Alternatives to Trial

Mediation as an alternative to trial has been used by the Institute for Penal Reform (IRP) since 2005 though it was only officially recognized by Parliament in 2007. Mediation is suitable for cases qualified as minor or less serious and can be applied to both adult and juvenile offenders. From January 1, 2009, the mediator for criminal cases was paid by the state. The Council of Mediation is organized within the Ministry of Justice. Members of the Council of Mediation are designated for a term of four years. They have the prerogative to set up the Table of the Accredited Mediators, and to monitor the process of the practical implementation of the mediation. Between 2005 and October 2008, mediators from the IRP managed 282 criminal cases; in 70 percent of these cases an agreement was signed, and the criminal proceedings were stopped.

The use of the alternatives is in a phase of evaluation, therefore, the greatest part of criminal cases is terminated with sentences. In 2008, decisions reported were as follows: 69 percent—convictions, 2.17 percent—verdict not guilty, 28.2 percent—proceedings dropped, and 0.63 percent—constraint measures with medical supervision. The cases of mediation were not even considered in the official statistics.

Incarceration before or Awaiting Trial

Pretrial arrest is used for people who perpetrated offenses that can be sanctioned with a jail term of more than 2 years. In some cases, pretrial arrest can be ordered if the suspect may hide from the criminal investigation body or from the court, may impede the establishment of truth in the criminal proceedings, or may commit new crimes. Other circumstances for using the pretrial arrest are when the suspect does not have a permanent residence on the territory of the RM, the identity of the suspect is not known, or if the suspect violated the conditions of other preventive measures.

Holding a person under remand until sending the case to the court cannot exceed 30 days. In exceptional cases, depending on the complexity of the case, on the seriousness of the crime or risk of destroying evidence, the term for the pretrial arrest can be extended up to 6 months if the crime is punished by a maximum of 15 years of imprisonment, and to up to 12 months for a crime punishable by a maximum of 25 years of imprisonment or for life. For indicted minors the pretrial arrest can be ordered only in cases of serious, extremely serious, and exceptionally serious crimes, and cannot be extended for more than 4 months.

Pretrial detention facilities are under the control of the Department of Penitentiary Institutions of the Ministry of Justice. Nevertheless, there still exist more than 35 separate preventive custody facilities (isolators) under the Ministry of Internal Affairs. These establishments do not correspond to European criteria of the pretrial detention, and cases of torture have been recorded by the international bodies. As a result, the Moldova-European Union Action Plan makes provision for the construction of 8 new arrest houses on the territory of the RM.

Criminal Court Judges

Criminal judges in the RM are part of the general category of judges. All judges have a unique status, but different assignments and competencies. Qualifications for holding a judicial office are as follows: to be citizen of the RM with permanent residence in the territory, to have a university law degree, to have no criminal record, and to know the national language. Court judges can be nominated if they are more than 30 years of age, have no less than 5 years of legal practice, and have successfully passed the qualifying exam. Court of Appeal judges may be nominated if they have more than 6 years of judicial practice, and in the Supreme Court of Justice, more than 10 years' practice.

In 2007, there were 310 judges in the RM, 47 of whom were Supreme Court judges, at the Court of Appeal—60, and in courts—250 judges. The number of criminal actions that entered the courts in 2007 was about 12,800. The annual charge of criminal and civil actions to be solved by a judge was 66.6.

Juveniles

No specific juvenile justice exists in the RM. The criminal proceedings are applied in the same way to juveniles as to adults, though some mention is made in the CP RM and in the CPC RM with regard to the people up to 18 years of age. Juveniles under 14 years are not assimilated in the same category with juveniles between 16 to 18 years old. On the proceedings level separate consideration is done as much as possible in case of the mixed (juvenile and adult) commission of the offense. On the next judicial level, the participation of the defense counsel, teacher, or psychologist is mandatory. Only juveniles may be sent under supervision. Such decision implies the written obligation taken by one of the parents or guardian, as well as by the management of the special education institution.

Among all categories of punishment existing in the RM, four can be applied to juvenile offenders: fine, depriving the right to maintain certain positions or to exercise a certain activity, nonpaid work in the benefit of the community, and jail. The types of punishment practically applied to juveniles in the RM are mostly fines, nonpaid work between 60 and 240 hours for those who are 16 years and over, and, rarely, jail terms between 6 months and 15 years.

Punishment

Types of Punishment

Moldavian Criminal Law provides the definition of the punishment based on a combination of repression and prevention. Execution of the punishment must not cause physical suffering or affect the convict's dignity.

Punishments are main and complementary. Only jail terms and life imprisonment can be firmly classified as main punishments. Main punishments may include jail for a specific term or life imprisonment. Since many adjustments have been done on the CP RM, a new intermediate category has emerged. Intermediate punishments include fines, depriving of right to maintain certain positions, and nonpaid community service. Complementary punishments include withdrawal of military rank, special title, or honors. Offenders receiving the different kinds of punishments in 2007 under the new Criminal Code of 2003 were as follows: 23.2 percent imprisonment, fine 23.7 percent, nonpaid community work 24.1 percent, and conditional suspension of punishment 28.2 percent.

Nonpaid work for the benefit of the community is a new alternative to imprisonment. This is served outside the basic work or studies program. It can be ordered for a length between 60 and 240 hours, and calculated on the basis of 2 or 4 hours' daily work. If the convict fails to perform the nonpaid community service, this punishment will be replaced by jail, 2 hours of nonpaid work being equivalent to one day of jail.

The Probation Office under the Department of the Execution of the Sentences of the Ministry of Justice began its service in 2007. This office and 42 probation sections manage the noncustodial sentences. Probation mainly occurs following conditional suspension of the punishment. Conditional suspension of the punishment execution is applied to the offenders who deliberately perpetrated offenses and have been sentenced to jail terms up to 5 years or who committed offenses by negligence and were sentenced to jail for less than 7 years. The probation term is set by the court between 1 and 5 years. Adults make up a large part of clients to be supervised by the Probation Service (average ratio is 10 adults for 1 juvenile). The total number of people supervised by the Probation Office at the beginning of 2008 was 8,903.

Typical Punishments

All types of homicide (including euthanasia) are punished with different terms of jail. The maximum incurred for the act assessed as deliberate murder is life imprisonment. Minors who perpetrated homicide may also be sentenced to jail. Even so, juveniles less than 18 years of age cannot be sentenced to life imprisonment. They can get special jail terms and cannot serve the jail term in the prisons for adults.

Rape offenses are sentenced with jail terms from 3 to 5 years. In aggravated circumstances the sentence can be life imprisonment. Only for the category of offenses of compelling to sexual intercourse (i.e., homosexuality or committing other sexual actions by use of blackmail or taking advantage of the financial dependence, related to work, or any other kind of dependence of the victim) can noncustodial sentences be pronounced. Thus, these offenders may be sentenced to a fine in the amount from 300 to 500 Moldovan lei (MDL) (US$480 to $800) or to nonpaid community work from 140 to 240 hours. Serious theft (i.e., perpetrated by two or more persons, or causing substantial damages to the victim) is punished by a fine in the amount from MDL 300 to 1,000 (US$480 to $1,600), by nonpaid community work from 180 to 240 hours, or by a jail term up to 4 years.

Robbery is punished by a fine between MDL 200 and 500 (US$320 to $800), or by nonpaid work for the benefit of the community from 180 to 240 hours, or by a jail term up to 3 years. More serious types of robbery perpetrated in aggravated circumstances or on a large scale are punished only by jail terms. The maximum term of jail incurred is 15 years; jail terms can be complemented by fines. For burglary offenses only jail sentences are allowed. For less serious cases, the jail term ranges from 3 to 6 years, and for serious cases from 10 to 15 years.

For the most serious drug offenses the CP RM provides jail sentences up to 15 years (e.g., illegal circulation of narcotic and psychotropic substances or precursors on an especially large scale). Generally custodial sentences in drug offense cases do not exceed 5 years, but are accompanied by considerable fines.

Drug use is decriminalized in the RM. Nevertheless, a "security measure" may be imposed such as compulsory treatment in medical institutions. Those who have been sentenced to imprisonment are subject to compulsory treatment during the serving of the sentence, and after release may be subject to treatment in medical institutions with special treatment conditions. In 2006, 395 inmates sentenced with the compulsory measure for alcoholics and drug addicts were serving their terms in penal institutions. The total number of identified drug users incarcerated in penal institutions of the RM in 2006 was 935, representing 13.5 percent of the total number of prisoners.

Death penalty was abolished and removed from the Criminal Code in 1995. In the Constitution, death penalty is allowed in exceptional circumstances (e.g., in wartime). In 2006, amendments were unanimously voted by Parliament, and the definitive abolition of the death penalty is almost finalized. It is important to note that death penalty is allowed in Transdniestria; however, a moratorium on the execution of death penalties was pronounced in January 1999.

Prison

Punishment can be served in three types of institution: open, semiclosed, and closed. Open institutions hold inmates convicted for crimes committed by negligence; semiclosed institutions hold those sentenced for minor offenses; closed penitentiaries hold prisoners sentenced for extremely serious and heinous crimes, as well as recidivists. Special penitentiary institutions exist for juveniles less than 18 years of age and for female offenders.

Since January 1, 1996, the Department of the Penitentiary Institutions, which belonged to the Ministry of Interior, was placed under the authority of the Ministry of Justice. This change produced some structural adjustments within the department and also allowed a global reform of the penitentiary system.

The Department of Penitentiary Institutions manages 17 institutions, of which 5 are only for pretrial detention, 1 specially designed institution for juveniles, and 1 for female offenders. One of the largest prisons is a semiclosed institution at Cricova, located 11 kilometers (6.8 miles) from the capital. Another one is a closed institution at Soroca, situated in the northeastern part of the country. There is a big project of building one new pretrial detention facility, which will replace the highest existing one, located in the old town of Chisinau, and will be built outside the city.

The total number of prisoners on September 1, 2007, was 8,130. The occupancy rate was about 77.9 per 100 places. On January 1, 2008, the distribution of the prisoners by type of penitentiary institution was as follows: closed institutions held 3,675 prisoners, in semiclosed 2,507, and in open institutions 85 inmates. There were also 186 minors in special institutions. The decrease in the number of juveniles held in penitentiary institutions between 2002 and 2008 was about 25 percent.

In 2008, first-time sentenced prisoners were about 46.1 percent, sentenced twice 25.16 percent, sentenced three times 14.75 percent, and persistent offenders (four sentences and over) 14.08 percent. More than 67 percent of prisoners serving final sentences have very long lengths imposed (5 years and over); 1.32 percent are life prisoners.

The rate of imprisonment per 100,000 of population in 2007 was 187.8, though this rate has steadily decreased since 2001 by about 5 percent. According to the Council of Europe the majority of prisoners have been sentenced for various types of theft, followed by homicide (about one-third of prisoners), robbery, and rape and drug offenses.

Work in Prison

Sentenced prisoners may engage in nonpaid and paid work. The paid work depends on the regime under which the prisoner is placed. Prisoners can be engaged in paid work inside or outside the prison perimeter, in the prison or prison service enterprises, and also in businesses regardless of ownership. Detainees in pretrial detention facilities (isolators) and life prisoners may be involved in paid work only in cells or in workshops specially designed for this purpose. Work times and wages are in accordance with the laws on labor in effect. The minimum wage is guaranteed only if they fulfill the employment norms in the fixed time, established by law and contract. Wages are deposited in their personal bank accounts. Withholdings from the wages of a sentenced prisoner on the basis of the administrative acts may not exceed 75 percent of monthly earnings.

Education in Prison

Obligatory general secondary education for the sentenced prisoners is provided. Prisoners over the age of 50, disabled persons, and life prisoners may receive a general secondary education if they wish so. At the request of the prison administration and/or the local authorities, secondary vocational or higher education may be taken. Prisoners who work may obtain leave at the time of exams in accordance with the Labor Code.

Libraries exist in every prison and are designed for general use by all the categories of sentenced prisoners. Prisoners are encouraged to visit the library. The already existing libraries are mainly stocked by donations. The lack of books in Romanian and Russian languages remains important. Several district libraries organize once per week loan service directly to the penitentiary institutions.

Conditions for professional training and development of related programs are implemented in the manner agreed by the Ministry of Justice, in accordance with the Ministry of Education. Diplomas, certificates, or other acts confirming the acquirement of professional and vocational skills are recognized by the Ministry of Education and the Ministry of Economy and Trade. However, the educational work cannot be correctly performed in penal institutions because the conditions are not appropriate for individual work with the prisoner.

Visiting Policies

The prisoner has the right to short and long visits. In particular cases ordered by the director of the institution, long visits with sentenced prisoners' family members may take place outside the institution. Short-term visits from a spouse, relative, and in exceptional cases, with the permission of the prison administration, with another person chosen by the convict are for a period of 1 to 4 hours. Long-term visits are of 12 hours to 3 days.

The sentenced prisoner is entitled to not less than one short visit per month and no less than four long visits during the year. Long-term visits are not allowed for sentenced prisoners held in initial treatment, and for life prisoners. The number of visits with a lawyer, a person entitled to provide legal assistance, or a mediator is not limited. Prisoners with tuberculosis in an active form cannot receive long visits.

Transfers and Extraditions of Prisoners

Legal cooperation with other countries is carried out under bilateral or multilateral agreements. To unify and strengthen existing procedures for granting of international legal assistance in criminal matters, on December 1, 2006, the Law on International Legal Assistance in Criminal Matters was adopted.

In 2006, the total number of prisoners transferred to the RM was 97. In 2007, the number of prisoners transferred from other countries was 34, all of them being citizens of the RM; 19 detainees were transferred from the Russian Federation, 12 from Ukraine, and 3 from Austria. Six detainees were extradited to other countries, of which 4 went to the Russian Federation, one to Ukraine, and one to Poland. No prisoners have been transferred from other countries.

Natalia Delgrande

Further Reading

Blockmans, Steven, and Adam Lazowski. (2006). *The European Union and Its Neighbours: A Legal Appraisal of the EU's Policies of Stabilisation, Partnership and Integration.* Cambridge: Cambridge University Press.

The Drug Situation in the Republic of Moldova: Annual Report 2007: http://www.observator.mednet.md.

The Institute for Penal Reform: http://www.irp.md.

Lewis, Ann. (2007). *The EU and Moldova: On a Fault-Line of Europe*. London: Federal Trust for Education and Research.

The Ministry of Internal Affairs: http://www.mai.md.

The Ministry of Justice: http://www.justice.gov.md.

Popa, Vladimir, and Victor Zaharia. (2008). "Moldova." In *Probation in Europe,* edited by Anton van Kalmthout and Ioan Durnescu, pp. 639–675. Nijmegen, the Netherlands: Wolf Legal.

Note: The author is very grateful to Professor Igor Dolea (PhD Law), Director of the Institute for Penal Reform, Republic of Moldova, for his advice and assistance.

Monaco

Legal System: Civil
Murder: Medium
Prison Rate: Medium
Death Penalty: No
Corporal Punishment: No

Background

Monaco is a constitutional monarchy that has been under the rule of the Grimaldi family since its founding in 1287 with the exception of the period when it was under French rule from 1789 to 1814. While independent, a 1918 treaty solidified that many facets of Monaco such as politics and economy would be comparable to France and also offered limited protection from France.

Prince Albert II is the current Prince of Monaco. He gained the throne after the death of his father, Prince Rainier III. The justice system is under the power of the prince who was the absolute ruler until 1911 when Monaco's Constitution was declared. After the 1911 Constitution was proclaimed, the minister of state serves as a representative for the prince who oversees police and executive services. The minister of state is a French citizen who is appointed to a three-year term by the prince. In 1962 the Constitution was updated to include a National Council composed of 24 members elected to five-year terms who vote on laws.

Monaco is located on the coast of the Mediterranean Sea bordering southern France, close to Italy. It is a mere 2 square kilometers (0.77 square miles). After the Holy See, it is the smallest independent state in the world. According to the *CIA World Factbook* there are approximately 32,965 people living in Monaco. Life expectancy is 80.09 years. A majority of the population (47%) is French with an equal percent of the population (16%) being native to Monaco or Italian. The official language is French, but English, Italian, and Monegasque, a blend of Italian and French, are other languages common to the country.

Police

The Direction of Public Safety, a division within the Department of the Interior, is in charge of police tasks in Monaco. There are five policing divisions: criminal, urban, administrative, administrative and training, and maritime and airport police.

The criminal police division deals with criminal investigations that can include financial and economic investigations as well as research and intervention. The subdivision for criminal identity works on issues that are INTERPOL-related and there is also a resources division. The urban police division works on coordination between uniformed forces as well as special operations. The administrative division deals with civilian administrative

Police officers wait outside a police station in Monaco where alleged bank robber Toni Musulin had given himself up, November 16, 2009. Musulin vanished with $7.4 million in cash from a bank in Lyon, France. (AP Photo/Lionel Cironneau)

issues such as visas and residency. Administrative and training is concerned with issues pertaining to the functioning, training, and maintenance of police personnel. The maritime and airport police are most concerned with issues of border control and national security.

There are 519 police personnel in Monaco. The breakdown of the policing personnel is as follows:

- 370 uniformed personnel
- 93 civilian clothed personnel
- 50 administrative staff
- 6 high-ranking personnel including 1 director, 4 commissioners, and 1 senior inspector

The Prince's *Carabiniers* are entrusted with the protection of the Royal Family and the Palace. In addition it serves many public service functions, including order maintenance, law enforcement, humanitarian missions, and participation in various official ceremonies and parades. There are 112 men serving on the Prince's Carabiniers.

Crime

Classification of Crimes

Monegasque justice is heavily influenced by the Napoleonic code and the nation subscribes to a civil law system, following the system in France and its various departments and dependencies. Crimes are divided into the categories of felonies, misdemeanors, and violations. Monaco has taken an active role in the fight against money laundering. Multiple laws have been passed to prevent money laundering and financing terrorism. Monaco had developed a reputation for itself as a tax haven, but in March 2009 it adopted international standards for information sharing and bank openness. Prince Albert II has committed to cleaning up the reputation of Monaco when it comes to tax evaders.

Crime Statistics

Monaco has an overall crime rate for index offenses of 1,166.76 per 100,000 according to INTERPOL. In 2001 rates per 100,000 for major crimes were as follows:

Murder	3.33
Rape	0.0
Robbery	0.0
Aggravated assault	46.7
Burglary	180.0
Larceny	863.33
Motor vehicle theft	73.33

From 1996 to 2001 all crime rates including overall index offenses decreased with the exception of motor vehicle theft, which increased.

Finding of Guilt

Judicial independence is guaranteed by the Constitution; however, the judges are appointed by the prince and they deliver justice in his name. Arrest, prosecution, and bringing to trial generally follows that of the inquisitorial or civil system of France and other European nations. A suspect cannot be detained for more than 24 hours before appearing before a judge to hear the charges being levied against him or her and his or her rights. In most instances the detainees are released without bail unless they are deemed to be a flight risk or likely to interfere with the investigation.

Accused offenders are guaranteed a fair and public trial. Every defendant is entitled to legal counsel and if he or she is indigent, the state will provide counsel. The judiciary is made up entirely of French judges and is appointed by the prince. The defendant is presumed innocent and has the right to appeal a legal decision.

Punishment

Types of Punishment

The most severe punishment available is life imprisonment as the death penalty has been abolished. Other sentencing options include imprisonment for a particular amount of time, suspension of certain civil rights, and fines. Loss of civil rights is almost always accompanied by a term of imprisonment. The courts may also require compensation or restitution to the parties for whom the damage has been done. The Criminal Code has a clause that requires harsher punishment for repeat offending.

Corporal punishment of children is permitted at home and in alternative care systems; however, it is unlawful in schools and the penal system. It cannot be used as a sentence for a crime and is also not meant to be used for disciplinary measures in the prison; however, it is not expressly prohibited.

Prison

According to *Prison Brief for Monaco* provided by King's College London, the prison population rate for 2008 was 76 per 100,000. The government of Monaco noticed a more recent shift in the offenses for which prisoners were sentenced. White-collar crime and narcotic offenses have become increasingly responsible for the prison population.

There is one prison in Monaco that can hold up to 90 inmates. Women, men, and minors are housed separately within the prison. The prison is a less restrictive environment as the cells remain open for seven hours out of the day and inmates are free to visit other cells. The prisoners are allowed two daily showers and two daily walks. Each cell has a television, although it must be turned off at midnight. The philosophy of the prison is to try to maintain life as normal as possible so as not to impede an inmate's transition back to society. Although there is some opportunity to work, the jobs are limited and restricted to a small fee for onsite work such as laundry or housekeeping. There are classes and activities offered to the inmates. Once the prisoner receives his or her definite sentence, he or she is transferred to a prison in France to carry out the duration of the sentence if it is more than four months.

Raquel Moriarty

Further Reading

A Comparative Criminology Tour of the World: Monaco, by Robert Winslow: http://www.rohan.

sdsu.edu/faculty/rwinslow/europe/monaco.html.
Legislation: http://www.legimonaco.mc.

Montenegro

Legal System: Civil
Corruption: Medium
Human Trafficking: Medium
Prison Rate: Medium
Death Penalty: No
Corporal Punishment: No

Background

While Montenegro was recognized by Berlin as an independent principality in 1878, this tiny country has had a long and tumultuous road establishing itself apart from external rule. Following World War I, Montenegro was invaded and occupied by Austria. The Montenegrin king Nikola I was forced into exile. The Library of Congress Country Study on Yugoslavia (1980) notes "After World War I, political forces in Montenegro were deeply divided between the Greens, who supported an independent Montenegro, and the Whites, who advocated unification with Serbia" (http://memory.loc.gov/frd/cs/yutoc.html). During the interwar period the Whites prevailed and Montenegrins were classified as Serbs. It should be noted that Montenegro lost nearly one-quarter of its population during World War I.

By 1918, Montenegro was declared part of the Kingdom of Serbs, Croats and Slovenes and ruled by a Serbian king. A decade later, the name would be changed again to the Kingdom of Yugoslavia. The British Foreign and Commonwealth Office notes that the status of Montenegro would change again in 1945 when it became a republic, as did Croatia, Bosnia and Herzegovina, Slovenia, Serbia and Macedonia. The 1980s brought a union between Montenegro and Serbia, but that union was formally dissolved when Montenegro declared its independence on June 3, 2006.

According to the U.S. Department of State, present-day Montenegro is approximately 13,938 square kilometers (5,381 square miles). The total population is about 630,000, of which 43 percent identify as Montenegrin; Serbian (31%); Bosnian (8%); Albanian (5%); Muslim (5%); Croatian (1%); and Roma (gypsy) (0.5%). In terms of current governmental organization, Montenegro is a mixed parliamentary and presidential republic. A review of the 2009 elections by the Organization for Security and Cooperation in Europe and the Council of Europe noted that the elections met almost all the requirements for democratic elections. Despite this promising assessment of the political process, the U.S. Department of State Human Rights Report on Montenegro notes that police routinely abuse suspects, arbitrary arrests are common, and there is widespread corruption among law enforcement and the judiciary. This suggests that the road toward a fully democratic Montenegro may still be quite long.

Police

According to the Policing OnLine Information System (POLIS), the principal policing agency in Montenegro is the Police Directorate. The Police Directorate employs approximately 5,209 people, 2,473 of which are uniformed officers (94 of whom are female). POLIS notes that uniformed officers undergo two types of training. Basic training, for noncollege-educated staff, includes "12 months of theory, 3 months of 'in-field training', and 3 additional months back at the academy." Candidates entering police service with a college degree undergo training that is slightly shorter in duration at just 10 months. Specialized training is also available and varies both in subject matter and extent, depending on the nature of the training.

Given the prevalence of organized crime in the country, a special unit within the police was created in 2003 to combat organized crime. The Chr. Michelsen Institute (CMI) report, *Corruption in Montenegro 2007: Overview over Main Problems and Status of Reforms,* notes that considerable training and resources have been diverted to this special unit, but there is more work to be done.

Courts

The legal traditions of Montenegro can be traced back to the 13th and 14th centuries under the governance of Zeta rulers, Balsici and Crnojevici. In relatively modern times, a major turning point was the 1888 adoption of the General Property Law for the Principality of Montenegro, drafted by noted European legal expert Valtazar Bogisic.

The judicial system of Montenegro consists of a four-level court structure. The basic courts are the lowest level, serving as courts of the first instance for crimes with a maximum penalty of 10 years' imprisonment or less. Beyond criminal cases, basic courts also hear matters of civil, labor, and other disputes. The superior courts are the first appellate level for cases referred from basic court. Superior courts also act as courts of original jurisdiction for more serious crimes than are tried in basic court. The Montenegrin Court of Appeal decides appeals against the first instance rulings of the basic and superior courts (as well as appeals against the rulings of the commercial courts). The Court of Appeal also decides disputes relating to the conflict of jurisdiction between lower courts. The highest legal authority in Montenegro is the Supreme Court. This court, typically comprising three judges, reviews the decisions of all other courts and intervenes in disputes between departments/jurisdictions of the government.

Within the Prosecutor's Office, there exists a special unit tasked with combating organized crime. A special prosecutor heads this unit. This special prosecutor is assisted by a deputy prosecutor and three assistants who focus specifically on corruption.

Human Rights

Articles 28–38 of the Montenegrin Constitution provide many basic procedural safeguards for persons accused of crimes. Specifically, the accused are entitled to the following: a fair and public trial within a reasonable time frame, presumption of innocence, no double jeopardy, right to a defense, and compensation in the event of an illegal conviction.

Crime

Reliable criminal statistics are difficult to obtain for Montenegro, but the Overseas Security Advisory Council notes car theft and residential break-ins are among the most frequently occurring incidents. The U.S. State Department observes that violent crime tends to be quite rare. The prevalence of organized crime appears to be of greatest concern to both Montenegrin society and external international watchers. The Council of Europe's Group of States Against Corruption (GRECO) has reported that extortion, money laundering, illegal gambling, robbery, vehicle trafficking and prostitution are all linked to organized crime in Montenegro. Since 2003, however, Montenegro has made efforts to stamp out corruption, most notably with the development of special units within the police and Prosecutor's Office to investigate and combat organized crime. In 2007, the Montenegrin government established a working group devoted to organized crime and terrorism. This group is composed of representatives from the Police Directorate, Customs Administration, Tax Administration, and Agency for Anti-Money Laundering and Financing of Terrorism.

Punishment

While the Constitution of Montenegro stipulates that no degrading or inhumane punishments will be used, the U.S. State Department notes punishments tend to be quite severe relative to those available in the United States. Article 26 of the Montenegrin Constitution prohibits the use of the death penalty. Imprisonment is used as an alternative.

The 2008 World Prison Population List reports Montenegro has a total prison population of just 734 (including pretrial detainees) and the per 100,000 rate of imprisonment is 108. According to the U.S. Department of State Human Rights Report 2008, Montenegrin prisons are overcrowded and in generally poor condition, a situation that appears to be exacerbated by pretrial detainees.

A 2003 report of a prison hospital in Serbia and Montenegro appearing in *The Lancet* described the often brutal conditions awaiting most inmates, including overcrowding and inadequate insulation. Winters in Montenegro are frigid, often charting below-zero temperatures. This extreme cold often leads to frozen water systems in the facility, making cleaning during the winter months impossible. Summer brings relief from the cold, but also brings a host of other problems because there is little ventilation in the windowless cells. Predictably, the combination of overcrowding and minimal ventilation substantially increases the likelihood of contracting communicable diseases such as tuberculosis.

It should be noted that this report appeared in *The Lancet* in 2003 before Montenegro's independence. According to the U.S. Department of State Human Rights Report 2008, more recent indications suggest the situation inside some facilities does appear to have improved, particularly in some police detention facilities. Facilities in police stations in Podgorica, Budva, Bar, Herceg Novi, Niksic, Bijelo Polje, Berane, and Pljevlja have been renovated to include video surveillance and air conditioning. Additionally, funds have been made available to build a building at Bijelo Polje Prison.

Laurie Gould and Matthew Pate

Further Reading

Bieber, Florian. (2002). *Montenegro in Transition: Problems of Identity and Statehood.* Baden-Baden: Nomos Verlagsgesellschaft.

Boehm, Christopher. (1986). *Blood Revenge: The Enactment and Management of Conflict in Montenegro and Other Tribal Societies.* Philadelphia: University of Pennsylvania Press.

Flemming, Thomas. (1997). *Montenegro: The Divided Land.* Rockford, IL: Chronicles Press.

Morrison, Kenneth. (2009). *Montenegro: A Modern History.* London: I. B. Tauris Press.

Roberts, Elizabeth. (2007). *Realm of the Black Mountain: A History of Montenegro.* Ithaca, NY: Cornell University Press.

Stevenson, Francis Seymour. (2002). *A History of Montenegro.* Boston, MA: Adamant Media.

The Netherlands

Legal System: Civil
Murder: Low
Burglary: Medium
Corruption: Low
Human Trafficking: Low
Prison Rate: Medium
Death Penalty: No
Corporal Punishment: No

Background

The Netherlands is a Western European country and is one of the six founding members of the European Union. The capital of the Netherlands is Amsterdam, but it is not the seat of the government, which is The Hague. After having been a republic in the 17th and 18th century, the Netherlands became a constitutional monarchy after the Congress of Vienna in 1815. And it became a parliamentary democracy with the introduction of a new Constitution in 1848. The role of the monarch, at present Queen Beatrix, is mainly symbolic and ceremonial, although she does have some influence. Parliament consists of a lower house (*Tweede Kamer der Staten—Generaal*) with 150 members and an upper house (*Eerste Kamer der Staten—Generaal*) with 75 members. The lower house plays a more important role in controlling the government and legislation than the upper house. Traditionally, the Netherlands has many political parties and governments are always formed by a coalition, usually consisting of three parties.

The Netherlands is economically a prosperous country: according to the IMF, the GDP in 2007 was $640 billion, which puts the Netherlands on the 16th place in the ranking of all countries in the world, or on the 11th place if looking at GDP per capita. The population of the Netherlands is 16.4 million (January 1, 2008). This means that it is densely populated with 486 inhabitants per square kilometer (1,259 per square mile). The proportion of residents of nonethnic Dutch origin (according to either nationality or country of birth) has increased from 9.2 percent in 1972 to 19.6 percent in 2008. Of those nonethnic Dutch residents that have their country of origin outside Europe, the largest groups are people with a Moroccan, Turkish, or Surinam (Dutch Guyana, a former colony of the Netherlands) background. Each of these three groups consists of about 2 percent of the total population.

Until recently, the Netherlands could be seen as a tolerant and permissive society. Examples of this are same-sex marriages and the legalization of prostitution. Also euthanasia and abortion, although *not* legalized, are not prosecuted when certain well-defined conditions are met. Basically the same holds for the Dutch drug policy: while trafficking and using drugs is in general illegal, special legislation makes it possible to buy and use small quantities of less harmful drugs without being prosecuted. Another example could be the traditionally low sentences in the Netherlands, although this has changed dramatically since the mid-1980s.

However, this tolerant and permissive attitude seems to have changed considerably in the last few years. There are some possible causes for that and the most important could well be the increase of the nonethnic Dutch population as mentioned above, in combination with the attitude toward Islamic-oriented terrorism since 9/11 and the Madrid and London bombings. Also, two dramatic assassinations—that of the charismatic but controversial leader of one of the political parties, Pim Fortuyn in 2002, and the other of moviemaker Theo van Gogh in 2004—have had a considerable impact on Dutch society.

This attitude change in recent years coincided with more severe regulations and tighter control on individual citizens. The introduction of the obligation to carry an identification document for everyone above 14 years of age, the installation of closed circuit cameras in many public places, increasing the maximum statutory penalties for many crime types, the broadening of the possibilities the police have for stop and search, and extending the possibilities for the prosecution to start an investigation even before a crime has been committed (important for preventing terrorism) are examples of this. Also the policy for accepting asylum seekers has become more restricted, which was probably one of the reasons for the dramatic decrease of the number of people coming to the Netherlands to ask for asylum since 2000.

Criminal Justice System

The Dutch criminal justice system is characterized by large discretionary powers for the police, prosecutors, and judges and by the central role the Public Prosecution Service has. Originally based upon the Napoleonic system—both the French *Code Pénal* and the *Code d'instruction criminelle* were adopted in the beginning of the 19th century—this gradually changed during the 19th century. In 1881 a new Criminal Code was introduced and in 1926 the new Code of Criminal Procedure changed the system from a mainly inquisitorial one to a more accusatorial one. Both codes are still in use today but have been changed considerably over the years.

Police

The Netherlands is divided geographically into 25 police regions. In addition, there is a 26th separate police force dealing with issues at a national level, such as central criminal investigations and with international police cooperation. There is no hierarchical relation between this central police force and the 25 regional ones. The total number of employees—both police officers and civilians—in the police force is 51,000 (2006), which is about 312 per 100,000 inhabitants. The two main tasks of the police are maintaining public order and carrying out criminal investigations. While administratively the police organization as a whole falls under the responsibility of the minister of the interior, the operational management of the police reflects both the independence of each police region and the two different main tasks of the police: the mayors of the cities within each police region—with the mayor of the main city within the police region acting as formal head of the police—are responsible for maintaining public order and the prosecutor has the authority over the criminal investigations. The two tasks cannot be separated completely, however; therefore there is frequent consultation between the police, the mayors, and the Public Prosecution Service within each police region. The military police is a separate organization, supervised by the minister of defense. Apart from having the police task within the Dutch Army, the military police is also responsible for border control.

The police is not the only organization doing criminal investigations. There are four specialized agencies for offenses like tax offenses and social security fraud. Looking at offenders that are prosecuted, about 7 percent had their case investigated by one of these special agencies and not by the police.

By law the public prosecutor is in charge of the investigation in all criminal cases. But in the majority of cases the direct involvement of a prosecutor is negligible and the police will follow general guidelines from the Public Prosecution Service to investigate these cases. This could even mean not to investigate certain crimes at all if they have a low priority according to the Prosecution Service guidelines. Only in a few cases (the more serious or complicated ones) the prosecutor actually takes the lead in the investigation. For special investigative measures such as pretrial detention, telephone taps, searching of premises, and others, permission is needed from the prosecutor and/or a judge (the examining magistrate). The clear-up rate, defined as the percentage of recorded cases where at least one suspect has been found, is 10 percent for property crimes and 59 percent for violent crimes.

Formally, the police is not allowed to drop a case or to impose sanctions. In practice, however, there are some possibilities for the police to do this. Although it is technically under the responsibility of the prosecutor, for some not too serious offenses the police can impose a fine (this type of fine is called a *transactie*), and if some conditions are met the police can let a juvenile offender do a work or learning activity (together with compensation for damage done by his or her offense). Although a formal decision to drop a case, which is somewhere registered as such, does not exist, nevertheless, the police can decide just to stop investigative activities.

The Public Prosecution Service

The Public Prosecution Service is part of the judiciary. The highest authority within the service is the Board of Prosecutors General. The minister of justice has the final responsibility and political accountability for the Public Prosecution Service. The service is responsible for investigating criminal offenses, for prosecuting offenders, and for making sure that sentences are properly imposed. There are 675 prosecutors, which is about 4.1 per 100,000 inhabitants. Prosecutors are not elected but appointed by the Crown (in practice the minister of justice).

The Dutch Prosecution Service plays a very central role in dealing with criminal cases. It has the monopoly on prosecution—there is no such thing as "private" prosecution in the Netherlands—and because of the expediency principle it can also decide *not* to prosecute. Basically there are three options for the prosecution when a suspected offender is known: the prosecutor can drop the case, both for technical reasons (not enough evidence) or for policy reasons; the prosecutor can settle the case outside the court with a *transactie,* which is usually a fine or a community service; or the prosecutor can issue a writ of summons for a court hearing. Plea bargaining or guilty pleas are not known in the Netherlands.

In most cases a so-called police investigation to gather evidence suffices. There can be some involvement of the prosecutor, particularly when special investigatory measures are needed such as searching premises. In more serious cases the prosecutor can decide to start a "preliminary judicial investigation," which is carried out by an examining magistrate or a "criminal financial investigation" in preparation of a court verdict where (part of) the sentence could be that the offender has to pay back his or her illegally obtained financial gain.

During trial, the prosecutor presents the evidence gathered during the investigation. The judge will then examine the evidence and question the accused. If necessary he or she will also question witnesses and experts, however, since also written statements by witnesses or experts are accepted as evidence in court this will usually not happen, except in the most serious cases. The prosecutor (and the defense) may also ask additional questions but cross-examination is unknown.

A trial in the Netherlands is not purely adversarial, but has more a "truth finding" character. Being part of the judiciary and having as main task to "administer legal order," the prosecutor will theoretically also take the interests of the offender into account. So it is possible, and this does occasionally happen, that the prosecutor requests a nonguilty verdict.

Courts

There are 19 district courts, five courts of appeal, and a Supreme Court. There are no special juvenile courts, but within the normal courts there are judges handling juvenile cases only. Court sessions with juveniles are usually closed to the public.

Most cases are handled by a single judge. The maximum custodial sentence that can be given by this single judge is one year. More serious cases (and all appeals) will be done by a bench of three judges. There are no juries and—with a few exceptions—no lay judges. This way only professional judges decide on the verdict and the punishment. Judges are appointed by the Crown and the minister of justice. There are about 400 judges for criminal cases. Unlike prosecutors they are appointed for life, but usually retire at 70.

Sanctions

The three main sanctions in the Netherlands are prison sentences (about one-tenth of all sanctions), fines (about half of all sanctions), and community services (about one-third of all sanctions). Although formal sanctions can only be given by a court, fines and community services can also be part of a settlement outside the court. Legally these are seen as conditional disposals by the prosecutor. Combinations of sanctions are possible. For every type of crime there is a maximum sentence defined in the Criminal Code, but no minimum sentence. Capital punishment is not known in the Netherlands; the most severe sentence is life imprisonment. General amnesties do not occur, but pardoning in individual cases sometimes happens. For mentally ill offenders either a psychiatric hospital order or an entrustment order can be given. A psychiatric hospital order can be given when the mental illness of the offender is of such nature that the offender cannot be held responsible for the offense he or she committed. There were 118 of those measures in 2007. When the offender, despite his or her mental illness, *is* held responsible for committing the offense, then usually a penalty is imposed, but besides also an entrustment order, which is a compulsory treatment in a private or state institute after the punishment has been fulfilled. An entrustment order lasts for two years with the possibility of another one or two years. For serious and violent crimes the order can be extended indefinitely, but should be regularly evaluated. The number of entrustment orders in 2007 was 247.

Sanctions for juveniles are not different from those for adults, but less severe. The age of criminal responsibility is 12. Juveniles are those who, at the time the offense was committed, were at least 12 and not yet 18 years old. However, the judge can decide, depending on the severity of the offense or the personality of the offender, to apply adult criminal law for offenders aged 16 or 17. But he or she can also decide to apply juvenile law for those between 18 and 21. The maximum prison sentence for juveniles is one year (under age 16) or two years (age 16 or 17). The Netherlands had until very recently a system of automatic and unconditional early release, in general after about two-thirds of the sentence length. In 2008 this was replaced by a system of conditional release, but also after about two-thirds of the sentence length.

Crime

Classification of Crimes

All punishable acts (which is the literal translation of *strafbare feiten,* the Dutch term for offenses) can be divided into three broad categories based on the Dutch Criminal Code and procedural law. The first category consists of all those minor offenses (infractions or *overtredingen*) that are dealt with administratively, that is, without any involvement of the Public Prosecution Service or the courts, unless the offender decides to appeal. These are the majority of traffic offenses and the penalty is always a fine.

The second category consists of all other minor offenses (infractions) with the exception of those that are defined as infractions under the different laws for economic, environmental—where often the offender is not a person but a company—and drugs offenses. In this second category offenses like some more serious traffic offenses (excessive speeding, driving without insurance) or "being drunk and disorderly in a public place" or "travelling in public transport without a valid ticket" can be found. Almost always the penalty will be a fine, but other penalties such as the withdrawal of the driver's license or a (short) prison sentence are also possible.

The offenses in the third category are those that are defined in the Criminal Code as a crime (in Dutch *misdrijf*) and also the economic, environmental, and drugs infractions. Most Dutch crime statistics—also those presented in this article—refer to this third category only and Statistics Netherlands has defined a classification for all offenses in this category. Included in this category are the following:

- Violent crimes (homicide, rape, sexual assault, assault, threats, and robbery)
- Property crimes (theft and fraud)
- Public order crimes (vandalism, discrimination, arson)
- Serious traffic offenses (drunk driving, leaving scene of an accident)
- Economic and environmental crimes (shop open outside regular hours, pollution)
- Drug crimes and infractions (possession of large quantities, trafficking)
- Weapons crimes (illegal weapons possession)
- Crimes under military law

A common crime type that is missing in the classification is "burglary." In the Netherlands, as is the case in many other continental European countries, burglary is not recognized as a separate crime in the Criminal Code. Instead a distinction is made between "theft" and "aggravated theft." Most (but not all) burglaries will be considered aggravated theft; on the other hand many aggravated thefts (such as theft committed by more than one person) are not burglaries.

Since drugs possession and use—in small quantities and mainly for relatively harmless drugs—are not prosecuted, they will usually not be recorded by the police to begin with. This means that the statistics for drugs crimes reflect almost always drugs trafficking. The number of drugs crimes has increased considerably during the last years, reflecting the less-tolerant behavior by the authorities regarding drugs crimes.

Although violent crime is relatively low in the Netherlands compared to many other European countries (as both victim surveys and recorded crime statistics show), reduction of violent crimes (also domestic violence) is one of the priorities of the Dutch government. In particular violence on the street by nonethnic Dutch juveniles gets a lot of media attention. Other priorities are trafficking in human beings, organized crime, and terrorism. The nature of organized crime in the Netherlands is somewhat different from the common conception of so-called mafia-type organizations infiltrating in governments and companies. Criminal groups in the Netherlands can better be seen as networks with no real hierarchical structure. The main criminal activities of these networks are drugs trafficking, trafficking in human beings for sexual exploitation, smuggling of illegal immigrants, and so forth.

Crime Statistics

The Netherlands has a long tradition of victim surveys, the first was in 1973. According to these surveys the occurrence of crimes was stable between 1980 and 2000. After 2000 a decline in crime can be seen, mainly for property crime. The general level of crime as perceived by victims and also feelings of insecurity are the highest in the cities.

Police-recorded crime is a small part of all crimes experienced by victims. For a few crime types the recorded crimes for the year 2007 per 100,000 inhabitants, according to the Ministry of Justice/WODC and Statistics Netherlands, were as follows:

Homicide	0.9
Rape	7.7
Assault	370.2
Violent crimes total	682.2
Theft	3,918.6
Property crimes total	4,172.2
Drugs offenses	95.5

The number of homicides—less than 1 per 100,000—is low and has declined considerably during the last five years. This is remarkable because the general level of violent crime hardly decreased (according to victim surveys) or even increased (according to the statistics for police-recorded crime) during that period. As in all Western European countries the number of recorded theft offenses—and in general of property crimes—is high, but has decreased considerably since 2002.

The most common recorded theft offenses are theft from a car, bicycle theft, and theft from a private home. Looking at victim surveys, it is bicycle theft that is by far the most common theft offense, but most victims of bicycle theft do not bother to report the crime to the police. The decrease in property crimes since 2002 can be seen in all types of theft offenses. In particular the decrease in car theft is remarkable—the number of car thefts in 2007 is only about 40 percent of the level in 2002. Most probably this is due to better technical prevention.

The rise in recorded violent crime is hard to reconcile with the stability (or even decrease) found in the victim surveys. But when one looks at specific violent crime types it seems that there is indeed also a decrease in the more serious recorded violent crimes, such as homicide, rape, and robbery. The overall increase in recorded violent crime seems to be solely due to the less serious forms of violence like threats and less serious assaults. So it could well be that the police is now more inclined than it used to be to register less serious forms of violent crime.

Both recorded property and violent crime are typically city crimes. And the difference between larger cities and smaller communities is even more pronounced than the difference found in the victim surveys. Remarkably, however, for public order offenses—although there were indeed somewhat less recorded offenses in rural areas—there was no difference found between smaller and larger cities.

Finding of Guilt

Apart from a recent development that will be discussed later the only person deciding on the guilt of the accused, both in theory and in practice, is a professional judge (or a bench of three judges). Trial by jury is unknown in the Netherlands and neither is it possible for the accused to negotiate with the prosecutor on the crime type he or she will be accused of or the punishment he or she will get. Even an admittance of guilt by the accused could by itself not be enough for a guilty verdict by the judge. Also, an admittance of guilt does not influence the nature of the trial: there are no accelerated procedures. And they are not really needed: because there are no juries and written evidence is admitted at court, trials rarely last longer than a few hours. So in principle it is rather straightforward: the prosecutor—and no one else—decides if and for what crime the accused will be prosecuted, and the judge—and no one else—decides on the verdict and the punishment. However, this does not mean that only the court can make case-ending decisions: both police and prosecution can do this as well and can even impose conditions on the accused that could be seen as punishments, although in a legal sense they are not and in particular they are not seen as a legal declaration of guilt nor are they part of a criminal record.

In total there were about 330,000 case-ending decisions in the year 2007. One-fourth of those decisions did not lead to any punishment at all for various reasons. Some were dropped by the police or the prosecutor, possibly for lack of evidence. For others the prosecutor decided not to prosecute for reasons of public interest; perhaps because in his or her opinion the criminal act was not serious enough, or the offender had experienced already enough negative consequences of the act himself or herself. In about 11,000 cases the judge did not give a sanction; mostly because the verdict was "not guilty," but in some cases there was a guilty verdict but the judge apparently had reasons not to give a sanction at all.

Both the police—although under the responsibility of and following guidelines from the Public Prosecution Service—and the prosecution can end a case conditionally. Most conditional disposals are called *transacties* and they can take the form of a fine or a community service (*taakstraf*). Besides, the police can use a special kind of disposal for juveniles, mostly a work and/or learning activity. This is called a *HALT* measure. Conditional disposals are not really the result of any negotiating between police/prosecutor and the accused. It is an independent decision of the police or the prosecutor to give the accused the opportunity to avoid undergoing a court trial. The accused is free to accept this, but in doing so he or she does not formally admit guilt. If the accused does not accept the condition, or if he or she fails to meet the condition (e.g., by not paying the fine) the case will almost certainly go to court. The total number of all conditional disposals—which are essentially settlements outside court—is 132,000. This is 53 percent of all punishments.

The three main sanctions for the court are prison sentences, community services, and fines. Between 2000 and 2006 the number of community services imposed by the court increased from 20,000 to 40,000, whereas the number of prison sentences decreased in the last few years. Possibly this is due to a substitution effect: more community services are given where in previous years a prison sentence would have been seen as more appropriate. Another common sanction is the withdrawal of someone's driver's license.

Based on data (in some cases estimates) from Statistics Netherlands (Ministry of Justice/WODC) the following case-ending decisions and resulting punishments occurred:

- By police: 25,000 cases were dropped or dismissed and 58,000 cases given conditional disposal, resulting in 24,000 juvenile measures and 34,000 fines.
- By prosecution: 15,000 cases were dropped or dismissed, 30,000 disposed in the public interest and 74,000 on conditional disposal, resulting in 17,000 on community service, 45,000 fines, and 12,000 miscellaneous.
- By the courts: 1,000 guilty but no sanction, 10,000 not guilty, and 117,000 found guilty, resulting in prison for 26,000, community service for 40,000, 44,000 fines, 6,000 conditional sentences, and 1,000 other.

Starting in 2007 the system of *transacties* will be gradually replaced by a system using penal orders (*strafbeschikking*). Although in practice the differences are small—the accused will pay an amount of money or fulfill a community service as proposed by the prosecutor or the police—the legal differences are far-reaching. The most important difference between a *transactie* and a *strafbeschikking* is that a *strafbeschikking* is a formal declaration of guilt autonomously decided by the prosecutor with no court involvement at all. And the crime will be added to the criminal record of the accused. Also, if the accused does not agree with the proposed *strafbeschikking,* he or she has to make an appeal explicitly and within the time period where an appeal is possible. If he or she does nothing—by just not paying the fine—the case will *not* go to a penal court because after the appeal period, the case has become irrevocable. Instead, a civil lawsuit will follow for the amount of money due.

Rights of the Accused

Suspected offenders have certain rights, the most obvious being that there is no obligation to contribute to his or her own conviction (i.e., the right not to answer any questions). Other rights are the right to be heard, to have all relevant case files at his or her disposal, to be tried within a reasonable time frame, and the right to have an interpreter if necessary. And the accused has the right to have legal counsel. If there is some form of deprivation of liberty, the accused will get a lawyer appointed by the state and free of charge automatically. But the accused can always choose (and pay for) his or her own lawyer. A "no cure—no pay" system is not known in the Netherlands. Also, the accused can ask the examining magistrate to perform specific investigating activities, for example, hearing witnesses in favor of the accused.

An accused offender can be incarcerated before trial. This can be done through an arrest by the police, but this is only possible when the offender is caught red-handed and the deprivation of liberty can last 12 hours at most. If the offender is not caught red-handed or if further detention is needed after the 12-hour police arrest, the prosecutor has to decide on pretrial detention, but he or she can do this only for 6 days maximum. After 6 days the prosecutor has to make a request for extending the pretrial detention to the examining magistrate (for another 10 days) or to a full bench penal court (after that). Pretrial detention (apart from the 12-hour police arrest and the 6 days decided by the prosecutor) is only possible for more serious crimes. Bail, although the Code of Criminal Procedure gives some possibilities for a judge to suspend pretrial detention under certain guaranties provided by the accused—such as depositing an amount of money—is hardly ever used in the Netherlands.

Punishment

Types of Punishment

In the Netherlands there is a distinction between a penalty (*straf*) and a measure (*maatregel*). Penalties are seen as punishments and/or retribution and are also aimed at general prevention. Measures are more aimed at individual safety and security or at restoring the state of affairs before the crime was committed. Measures can also be imposed if the offender is not criminally responsible. The sanctions already mentioned—deprivation of liberty, community services, fines, and withdrawal of someone's driver's license—are all penalties. But various other sanctions are also possible. Among the other penalties are deprivation of the right to hold a public office or to practice certain professions. But also closure of a company can be, for specific crimes, a penalty.

Security guards practice camera surveillance at an experimental prison with minimum security in Lelystad, the Netherlands, January 16, 2006. Inmates wear electronic wristbands that register every movement and allow them to pass from room to room when authorized. (AP Photo/Cor de Kock)

Measures, except for the psychiatric hospital orders, are usually given in combination with a penalty. These measures can be entrustment orders, compulsory treatment for offenders with specific problems such as drug addicts, paying compensation for the benefit of the victim, and confiscation of illegally obtained profits.

For premeditated murder with no special circumstances the typical punishment would be about 15 years' imprisonment. But longer (until 30 years) or even life sentences are very well possible, in particular when there is more than one victim. For other crimes it is very hard to determine a typical punishment, but the average imposed prison sentence can be seen from the court statistics. For rape this is about 3 years, for qualified theft 1.5 years and for drugs offenses a little more than 1 year.

Prison

To count the number of prisoners at a certain moment seems a simple exercise, but it is not. In the Netherlands 18,680 persons were held in detention on September 30, 2007. However, only about 1 in 3 of these persons were actually convicted for a criminal offense with a prison sentence as penalty. There are many other reasons—such as pretrial detention—to deprive people of their liberty.

The first complication is that there are an estimated 4,400 persons who are convicted but for different reasons not (yet) imprisoned. Of those 4,400 there are about 3,500 with a (probably short) prison sentence who are waiting for a place in prison. The other 900 are mostly people not willing to pay a fine or another financial compensation and waiting for default detention.

Of the 18,680 total behind bars, there are 16,250 adults, 1,800 of whom are not convicted with a prison sentence—or their prison sentence was already executed—but are held in a special institution because they were sentenced with an entrustment order as a measure. Also 1,680 adults are not convicted at all but are held because of a civil law court decision. These are almost all illegal immigrants waiting for extradition. Of the 7,010 convicted adult offenders, 1,040 have not been punished with a prison sentence. However, they are detained because they did not pay their fine or did not fulfill their community service. Or in general did not meet the conditions imposed by the court verdict.

Of the 2,430 juveniles, there are 1,360 held under civil law who are mostly problem children, but they have not necessarily committed a crime. Of the remainder of 1,070 held under criminal law, 680 have been convicted and the remainder are in pretrial detention.

In total, 13,840 persons (12,770 adults and 1,070 juveniles) are in prison because of a criminal law offense. Almost half of them (6,150 persons: 5,760 adults and 390 juveniles) are not yet convicted but are in pretrial detention.

According to the Ministry of Justice/WODC and Statistics Netherlands, the number of prisoners increased considerably during the last three decades, from around 20 per 100,000 population in the 1970s to more than 100 in 2005, though with an apparent decrease after that year. Why the number of prisoners decreased since 2005 is not completely clear. The decrease in recorded crime in general and the increase in the number of community services are possible causes for this.

Prisons in the Netherlands are small, the largest prison has less than 400 cells. The standard prison regime consists of 26 hours' labor per week, visits, recreation, and sports. This standard regime applies to the majority of prisoners. Labor is compulsory, except for pretrial detainees who are not obliged to work. However, usually they do, because the only way to get money to spend in prison (to buy tobacco, extra food, telephone cards, renting televisions, etc.) is to work. Convicted prisoners have the right to receive visitors. These visits are supervised, but those serving a long prison sentence could be given the opportunity to receive nonsupervised visits. Pretrial detainees are dependent on a decision by the prosecutor or the examining judge to be allowed to receive visitors, but they can always have visits from their lawyer.

Since the Netherlands is part of the European Convention on the Transfer of Sentenced Persons, it is possible either for Dutch persons convicted abroad to be transferred to the Netherlands and for foreign persons convicted at a Dutch court to ask to serve their sentence in their home country. In 2007 there were 556 requests for transfer from abroad to the Netherlands, mainly from Germany, Spain, the United Kingdom, and France. There were 63 requests made for a transfer from the Netherlands to another country.

Paul R. Smit

Further Reading

Bijleveld, Catrien C. J. H., and Paul R. Smit. (2005). "Crime and Punishment in the Netherlands, 1980–1999." In *Crime and Punishment in Western Countries, 1980–1999,* edited by Michael Tonry and David P. Farrington, pp. 161–211. Chicago: University of Chicago Press.

Blom, Martine, and Paul R. Smit. (2006). "The Prosecution Service Function within the Dutch Criminal Justice System." In *Coping with Overloaded Criminal Justice Systems,* edited by Jörg-Martin Jehle and Marianne Wade, pp. 237–256. Berlin: Springer.

Tak, Peter J. (2003). *The Dutch Criminal Justice System, Organization and Operation.* The Hague, the Netherlands: Boom Juridische uitgevers.

Tonry, Michael, and Catrien C. J. H. Bijleveld, eds. (2007). *Crime and Justice in the Netherlands.* Chicago: University of Chicago Press.

Northern Ireland. *See* United Kingdom/Northern Ireland

Norway

Legal System: Civil
Murder: Low
Burglary: Low
Corruption: Low
Human Trafficking: Low
Prison Rate: Low
Death Penalty: No
Corporal Punishment: No

Background

Located on the Scandinavian Peninsula, with a population of approximately 4.8 million on 385,155 square kilometers (148,708 square miles) of land, the Kingdom of Norway is known for its rich Viking history, its fjords, and its snowcapped mountain ranges. The origin of its legal system and culture is similar to other Nordic countries such as Finland, Iceland, Denmark, and Sweden, which were united under a sole monarch from 1353–1412.

The Norwegian legal system is a civil system that has codified criminal and procedural laws that reflect centuries-old legal principles practiced by the *Althing*—a quasijudicial meeting of *yeomen* who gathered regularly to resolve disputes within their various communities. In the 10th century, formal institutions called the *Lagting* were developed to perform legislative, judicial, and executive functions and they consisted of elected officials, clergy, and representatives of the king.

King Magnus Lagabøte (Magnus the Law-Mender) played an important role in the development of the Norwegian legal system. In 1274, he revised the regional laws established by the *Lagting,* and compiled them as a single document of codified laws called the *Landslov*. Centuries later these laws were revised and codified again by King Christian V of Denmark.

The circumstances surrounding the establishment of the Norwegian Constitution are important in regard to the development of Norway's legal system. After the Napoleonic wars, Norway's union with Denmark was dissolved and a political union with Sweden was formed. Norway's king ceded his power to the king of Sweden who found it politically expedient to allow Norway to have its own constitution. As a result, the Norwegian Constituent Assembly at Eidsvoll successfully instituted the new Constitution on May 17, 1814; it is the oldest European constitution currently in force. Norway's Constitution established a constitutional monarchy and parliamentary democracy with the king serving as (a largely symbolic) chief of state and a prime minister as its executive head of the government. In 1905, the union with Sweden ended with Norway declaring its sovereignty. This signaled an important period in Norwegian history as the country experienced a social renaissance with unprecedented cultural development.

Police

Norway, like many other European countries, has a centralized national police force that is not linked to the military structure. The police employ approximately 12,000 citizens and are managed by the National Police Directorate (*Politidirektoratet*) under the Ministry of Justice and the Police. Structurally, the police are organized according to regional (local) and national scope of operations. There are 27 regional police districts throughout the country and several special agencies that provide assistance to police districts. Police officers are required to attend the Norwegian Police University College and complete three years of training and education. Some main areas of study include criminology, criminal law and criminal procedures, legal research methods, communication and conflict management, and forensic science.

The Constitution and the Criminal Procedure Act govern the police power of arrest. According to article 99 of the Norwegian Constitution, police can only take persons into custody in cases determined by law and only in a manner that is prescribed by law. Therefore, if there are any breaches of these rules, the officer concerned will be accountable to the person imprisoned. Additionally, article 102 states that police can only conduct searches of private homes within the context of criminal cases.

The Criminal Procedure Act provides a further breakdown of rules governing traffic stops, arrests, and searches. These may be carried out only when certain prerequisites and special conditions are present. Another noteworthy characteristic of the Norwegian police is that they do not carry guns and provide prosecuting services for minor crimes.

Courts

Norwegian courts have a three-tier structure consisting of lower courts, appellate courts, and a court of last resort. District courts are courts of first instance where questions of guilt in criminal cases are determined. Norway is currently divided into 66 judicial districts, with a lower court assigned to each district. The appellate court system, divided into six circuits throughout the country, hears cases where a judgment made by the district court is contested. Prosecutors and defendants can appeal their cases if they believe the sentence is unjust (too lenient or severe) or when there are problems with the determination of guilt. Finally, the highest court in Norway is the Supreme Court, which is located in Oslo. The chief justice chairs the Supreme Court and works alongside 18 judges, even though a panel of 5 judges decides most cases. Additionally, there is a committee of 3 judges that decides what cases will be heard in the Supreme Court.

Respecting criminal matters, court procedure generally involves the use of juries and also allows people without legal qualifications (lay judges) to sit with professional judges in the hearing of cases. Additionally, it is evident that judicial precedent (*stare decisis*) does not hold the same clout in the lower Norwegian courts as is the practice in common law countries, and generally the courts are not restricted by special rules regarding the admissibility of evidence. However, the rulings of the Supreme Court have a substantial effect on the lower courts and often deal with fundamental questions of law.

Prisons

Norway's correctional system embraces a philosophy of rehabilitation that is reinforced by initiatives instituted by the Ministry of Justice and the Norwegian Advisory Panel. An important goal of the correctional system is to equip offenders with tools that will allow them to become productive members of society upon their release.

Two types of prisons exist in Norway—high- or low-security facilities. High-security facilities, also known as closed prisons, have physical barriers such as barbed wire fences and are normally reserved for inmates who have been sentenced to more than two years' confinement. Inmates in high-security facilities can be considered for transfer to a lower-security facility, also known as open prisons, once they have served a portion of their prison sentence. In 2009, there were 47 prisons in operation.

Currently, there are more than 4,500 employees of the Correctional Service of Norway, with most working either in prison or probation. Employees must attend a two-year basic training program at the Prison Officer College where, for example, officers are trained in ethics, social work, human rights, criminology, psychology, and penal law.

Crime

Classification of Crimes

The General Civil Penal Code (hereinafter Penal Code) classifies crimes as either felonies (Part II) or misdemeanors (Part III) and only those who are 15 years of age or older, at the moment the crime was committed, are criminally liable for their actions. As a general rule, crimes that are punishable by more than three months' imprisonment are considered felonies. Felonies include violent and property offenses such as burglary, embezzlement, counterfeiting money, robbery, rape, and murder. Other felonies include narcotics offenses and discriminatory or hateful expression. Misdemeanors are crimes that are punishable by up to three months' imprisonment, although there are several exceptions. For example, pilfering carries a maximum penalty of six months' imprisonment.

Norway's drug laws are considered some of the strictest in Europe and are outlined in the Penal Code and the Act on Medicinal Products. Possession of small quantities and use of drugs, in violation of the act, is punishable by up to six months of imprisonment. Section 162 of the Penal Code prohibits the manufacture, storage, and trafficking of drugs and the penalties vary from fines to prison sentences up to 21 years. Judgments about the seriousness of the offense are based on the type and quantity of drugs as well as the nature of the crime. Norwegian law does not explicitly classify drugs in any systematic fashion (by harmfulness, for example) and, therefore, treats cannabis the same as cocaine, heroin, and LSD.

Crime Statistics

Statistics were drawn from two data sources: (1) Statistics Norway provided data on crimes reported to the police in 2008, and (2) the International Crime Victims Survey (ICVS, 2004/2005 sweep) furnished data on criminal victimizations for 2003. To facilitate meaningful comparisons between countries, the authors have computed standardized crime rates per 100,000 residents using population totals reported by Statistics Norway (as of January 1, 2008, there were 4,737,171 people living in Norway).

In 2008, there were a total of 386,251 offenses (8,153.62 per 100,000) reported to the police, of which 264,199 were felonies (5,577.14 per 100,000) and 122,052 were misdemeanors (2,576.47 per 100,000). In terms of total offenses reported to the police, the 2008 figures are at their lowest since 1996.

Focusing on select crimes, Statistics Norway reported 34 murders (0.71 per 100,000), 944 rapes (19.92 per 100,000), 1,229 robberies (25.94 per 100,000), 3,362 housebreaking and burglaries (70.97 per 100,000), and 6,942 automobile thefts (146.54 per 100,000) in 2008. In terms of crime trends, total murders have stabilized since peaking at 51 in 2003; rapes have increased almost threefold since 1993; robberies are at the highest levels since 1993; housebreaking/burglaries have decreased substantially since peaking in 2000; and automobile thefts are at their lowest levels since 1993.

As for drug offenses in violation of the Penal Code, there were 16,475 (347.78 per 100,000) offenses labeled as "crime of narcotics" and 1,072 (22.62 per 100,000) considered "serious crime of narcotics," while narcotic offenses in violation of the Act on Medicinal Goods totaled 19,191 (405.11 per 100,000). Among the offenses in violation of the act, 60 percent were for use of narcotics, 36.5 percent were reported as possession of narcotics, and 3.5 percent were listed as other. With respect to trends in reported drug offenses, all categories of narcotic offenses have increased since 1993. In particular, "crime of narcotics," "serious crime of narcotics," and "use of narcotics" has nearly tripled.

Additionally, there has been a sixfold increase in "possession of narcotics" offenses since 1995.

Since not all crimes are reported to and recorded by the authorities, it is particularly useful to examine victimization surveys to tap into the dark figure of crime. In terms of criminal victimizations, the ICVS program reported that 27 percent of participants were victimized in 2003 for a selection of common crimes: car theft, theft from a car, car vandalism, theft of a motorcycle, theft of a bicycle, burglary, attempted burglary, robbery, personal property theft, sexual incidents, and assault/threat. The prevalence of criminal victimization is higher as compared to the 1989 ICVS sweep (21.3%).

Finally, there are geographic variations in criminal offending in Norway that correspond to population density. Oslo, for example, has the highest reported felony rate (11,440 per 100,000) as compared to any other county with 2,000 inhabitants or more. Further analyses reveal that the mean felony rate for counties that have fewer than 75 percent of their population living in urban settlements is significantly lower (37.42 per 100,000) than as compared to counties with more than 75 percent of their population residing in urban settlements (59.16 per 100,000). As for variations in types of crimes by level of population density, there are no significant differences for violent and property crime rates. However, narcotic offending rates are higher for counties that have more than 75 percent of their population residing in urban settlements (918 per 100,000) than as compared to counties with less than 75 percent residing in urban settlements (660 per 100,000).

Finding of Guilt

Rights of the Accused

Due to the results of a referendum in 1996, Norway is not yet a member of the European Union. However, it is a founding member of the Council of Europe and therefore legally bound by the European Convention of Human Rights (ECHR). The ECHR has binding authority over all member states and grants European citizens the right to seek redress against human rights violations via the European Court of Human Rights located in Strasbourg, France. This is the general authority under which the fundamental rights and freedoms of Norwegians are enshrined. Therefore, the interpretation of Constitutional provisions and the actions of the state cannot contradict the ECHR.

However, the Constitution and the Criminal Procedure Act (CPA 1981) still speak directly to the rights of the accused and the finding of guilt in criminal proceedings in Norway. Article 96 of the Constitution deals with the presumption of innocence and the prohibition of torture. This provision makes three statements. First, convictions can only take place if there is proper adherence to the process of law. Second, the accused must not be punished until the completion of a court judgment. Third, the provision strictly prohibits the use of torture during interrogations.

The CPA 1981, last amended in 2006, gives a detailed description of the rights described above as well as the process of finding of guilt. It is stipulated in Section 90 that the accused must be informed of the nature of the charge and must be made aware of the fact that he or she has a right not to testify when attending court for the first time. Furthermore, according to Section 92, the person charged must be given the opportunity to refute the criminal allegations made against him or her.

Despite the provision that the person charged has the right to summon witnesses, he or she may be asked to leave the courtroom while a witness is being examined in special situations where it is likely that the testimony may be affected by the presence of the accused (Section 245). However, the accused must be subsequently informed of the proceedings that occurred in his or her absence.

Finally, Section 135 states that the person charged can be excluded from court proceedings if the content of the proceedings pose a national security risk. However, it is also stipulated that the accused must be made aware of the verdict, and there must be full disclosure of the defendant's right to an appeal. The reasons for the decision and the conclusion of the judgment must also be communicated to the accused (Section 39), and the court is bound by the decision after the verdict has been delivered (Section 42).

Right to Appeal

Regarding the right to an appeal, the accused can generally lodge appeals against court judgments based on questions of fact and law. However, appeals to the Supreme Court can only be based on errors of law and cannot proceed without the consent of the court's Appeal Committee. The Appeal Committee ultimately decides whether the substance of the appeal pertains to issues that have far-reaching consequences beyond the current case (Section 323).

Trial by Jury

It is noteworthy that the CPA 1981 does not grant the accused the right to a trial by jury. However, juries will be present to decide on questions of guilt in felony cases tried in the High Court that attract a sentence of more than six years.

Right to Choose an Attorney

Section 94 highlights the general rule that at every stage of a criminal case, and at every stage of the judicial process, the person charged has a right to defense counsel of his or her choosing. Exceptions and limitations to this rule arise in the district court with respect to minor offenses such as traffic violations, or in cases where the person charged is fully aware of his or her rights and makes a confession that is corroborated by evidence. Furthermore, if the accused does not choose defense counsel, the court will appoint a permanent defense counsel in proceedings where it is warranted (Section 103).

Prosecution

The prosecuting authority consists of three levels. The director of public prosecutions (DPP), public prosecutors, and the police prosecuting authority are all responsible for handling prosecutions. The DPP is ultimately responsible for directing the prosecution of all criminal cases but the majority of offenses, mostly minor crimes ranging from property crimes to falsification of documents, are handled by the police prosecuting authority. Prosecution of more serious offenses, such as murder, is handled by the DPP and public prosecutors.

Alternatives to Trial

There are many instances where a formal trial can be avoided and Norway relies heavily on this process. According to Section 248, the district court may decide on a matter summarily in the absence of an indictment or a hearing. This provision applies to cases that can be settled by arbitration, criminal acts that are not punishable by a sentence that exceeds 10 years, and traffic offenses in which the accused pleads guilty.

These matters can also be resolved when a judicial official or a police officer serves a penalty writ to the accused that will only require the payment of a fine, and after the fine is paid, there are no further judicial proceedings (Section 255).

Pretrial Incarceration

After a person has been arrested he or she will appear before a court of first instance with summary jurisdiction. At this stage it is decided whether or not the person should be remanded in custody. The CPA 1981 stipulates that pretrial incarceration must not exceed four weeks, and it insists that persons who are remanded in custody must be held for as short a time as possible (Sections 184 and 185). Additionally, persons cannot be held without charge unless it is legally justified and it is within a reasonable time period.

Juveniles

The juvenile justice system in Norway is still in the stages of development. Despite the fact that juvenile offenders charged with murder can be tried in ordinary courts, the overwhelming majority of cases are handled and determined by municipal juvenile welfare boards. The juvenile welfare boards comprise five members who are each elected by the municipal council to serve a four-year term. Standard procedure for a juvenile case is that the parents' right to custody is suspended, and the juvenile offender is placed in a youth center or a psychiatric institution pending further recommendations from the child welfare office. This office functions in an advisory role to the welfare board and is responsible for communicating all of the facts of the case prior to a quasijudicial hearing.

Some critics have contended, however, that juvenile justice in Norway is too harsh and does not provide opportunities for an appeal and bemoan the fact that juveniles seldom appear before the board with an attorney. Additionally, some have suggested that there needs to be more oversight in regard to how long juveniles must be "detained" in youth facilities before it is determined that treatment was successful.

Punishment

Types of Punishment

Norway abolished the death penalty in 1905. The harshest penalty currently allowed for the most serious of crimes, such as premeditated homicide, is 21 years of confinement. Other crimes that are eligible for the maximum prison sentence include rape and narcotic offenses deemed to be very serious. Criminal penalties, other than imprisonment, include payment of fines, community sentences, imprisonment, and suspended prison sentences.

According to Statistics Norway, in 2007, fines and unconditional prison sentences were the most prevalent forms of punishment for felony convictions. Suspended sentences (with or without a fine imposed) are the next most common disposition, followed by community sentences. Offenders who receive community sentences are expected to perform 30–340 hours of unpaid service that is beneficial to the community. In the event offenders do not fulfill their service commitments, they may be sent to prison to serve a subsidiary sentence.

Imprisonment

Norway's incarceration rate in 2009 is approximately 70 per 100,000 and has increased steadily since the 1980s. Prison capacity is about 3,600 and the total prison population, on any given day in 2009, was approximately 3,400 inmates. Recent data show that the vast majority of those sentenced to an unconditional prison term are there for driving under the influence of alcohol (22%), a drug offense (14%), larceny or motor vehicle theft (13%), or a crime of violence such as an assault or homicide (12%).

It is also interesting to note that the average amount of time spent in custody is about 70 days and that more than half of new entrances to prison are shorter than 60 days. Currently, female prisoners represent about 6 percent of the prison population, less than 1 percent of inmates are juveniles under the age of 18, and approximately 28 percent are foreign nationals.

Prison

As described by the Norwegian Correctional Services, each prison presents many opportunities for paid work, education, training, and rehabilitative programs to all inmates. Prisoners are required to either work or attend school. Treatment programs are offered individually or in groups and provide the knowledge, techniques, and motivation for changing lives by, for example, improving coping skills, confronting substance abuse, and managing anger or stress. Additionally, guards are expected to be actively involved in the rehabilitation process via a personal officer scheme. Under this system, correctional officers may personally supervise and motivate inmates by serving as role models and advisors through daily contact, personal conversations, and follow-up.

Prisons also offer inmates an assortment of physical, recreational, religious, and cultural activities. For example, Oslo Prison, a high-security facility, publicizes events that inmates have involved themselves with recently, including a televised preelection political debate that centered upon crime policy and a Christmas concert with the crown princess of Norway in attendance. Other privileges afforded to inmates include access to electronic devices, such as televisions and radios, and other forms of entertainment, such as magazines, in their prison cells.

Inmates also have a right to make phone calls (up to 20 minutes per week) and written correspondence (mail), and receive personal visitations from family and friends. Normally these activities are carefully monitored by correctional staff unless the correspondence or meeting is with an attorney. Prisoners are also granted the right to file complaints that are heard by the prison board first, then, if necessary, the prison governor, and finally, the regional director. Additionally, inmates have the right to be outdoors for a minimum of one hour a day.

Finally, it is interesting to note that inmate opinions matter to correctional authorities. Surveys have been administered to inmates to elicit feedback about their confinement experiences as well as to identify ways in which to improve correctional services.

Leave of Absence

The Execution of Sentences Act allows prisoners the opportunity for both day releases and short leaves of absences. Day release permits inmates to work, train, or otherwise participate in correctional programs off prison property. Short leaves of absences are permitted for up to 24 hours if justified while compassionate leave requests, to visit an ailing relative, for example, can be granted for longer periods of time.

Release

Inmates are normally released from confinement after serving two-thirds or at least 60 days of their sentence. If there is reason to believe that the prisoner will commit another crime while on probation, then consideration for early release can be revoked. Should an inmate breach the conditions of probation, he or she may be sent back to prison to serve the remainder of the sentence.

Transfer

Inmates who begin their confinement in high-security facilities are normally transferred to lower-security prisons a year before they are expected to be placed on probationary release to allow them to make a gradual transition from full custody to complete independence. However, the transfer may be denied if there is reason to believe the inmate will commit a criminal act, attempt an escape, or disrupt the peace of the institution. Transfers to more restrictive facilities are discouraged unless that it is determined to be absolutely necessary.

Prisoners may also request a transfer to execute their sentences at home after serving at least half of their original sentence. This type of transfer is permitted if the prisoner has a permanent residence and is employed or being trained. Transfers of this kind typically require additional conditions that must be met. For example, the inmate may be asked to continue pursuing a course of mental health treatment or participate in correctional programs.

Extradition

Norway has extradition agreements with many countries. In particular, Norway has firm extradition agreements with other Nordic countries. Norwegian nationals are able to serve their sentence in Norwegian correctional institutions if they have been convicted of a crime in Denmark, Finland, Iceland, or Sweden. The same applies to nationals of these countries who are convicted of a crime in Norway.

Norwegian nationals cannot be extradited. While Norway does cooperate with many foreign countries with extradition requests, Norwegian authorities reject petitions if the person is at risk of being tortured, sentenced to death, or other humanitarian concerns arise. For example, the Norwegian Supreme Court unanimously refused to extradite a drug trafficker, accused of smuggling 50 tons of hashish to the United States, because it argued that prison conditions in America were inhumane.

Tony R. Smith, Vaughn Crichlow, and Steven DeStefano

Further Reading

Bertnes, Pål A. *Legal Information in Norway and the Faculty of Law Library at the University of Oslo:* http://www.ub.uio.no/ujur/publikasjoner/skriftserie/13/index.html.

Bygrave, Lee. (1994). "Overview of Norway's Criminal Justice System." In *The World Factbook of Criminal Justice Systems*. Washington, DC: U.S. Department of Justice, Bureau of Justice Statistics.
Courts of Norway, Domstol Administrasjonen: http://www.domstol.no/upload/DA/Internett/da.no/Publikasjoner/Domstolene%20i%20Norge_ENG_OPPSL.pdf.
Criminal Procedure Act with Subsequent Amendments: http://www.ub.uio.no/ujur/ulovdata/lov-19810522-025-eng.pdf.
Norwegian Correctional Services: http://www.kriminalomsorgen.no.
Statistics Norway: http://www.ssb.no.

Poland

Legal System: Civil
Murder: Medium
Burglary: Low
Corruption: Medium
Human Trafficking: Low
Prison Rate: High
Death Penalty: No
Corporal Punishment: No

Background

Contemporary Poland is a country of 312,685 square kilometers (120,727 square miles) territory and population of 38,115,000 in 2007. Poland's history in the past 200 years has been quite turbulent. It was only in 1918 that Poland was able to regain independence, as a consequence of World War I, the collapse of all three partitioning powers, and the Versailles Treaty. One of the most serious tasks facing the so-called Second Republic (1918–1939) was to reestablish the national legal system. In the case of criminal law this happened relatively quickly, as the new Code of Criminal Procedure was adopted in 1928 and the new Criminal Code in 1932. The former was influenced by the French example, although Prussian and Austrian influences were noticeable. The latter, considered a very modern and original piece of legislation, remained within the framework of German legal concepts, and in particular of the so-called sociological school of criminal law.

These developments were interrupted again in 1939 by Nazi Germany's aggression, followed immediately by that of the Soviet Union, and yet another partition of the country between the two totalitarian regimes. The aftermath of World War II had profound consequences for the legal system, especially for criminal law and the criminal justice system, as both became mainly tools of oppression used to protect interests of the Communist Party and ruling elites. This changed somewhat after 1956. Liberalization of the system meant abandonment of outright terror as a method of government and rejection of most vivid excesses. Nevertheless, the political system remained authoritarian in its essence, and socialist criminal law was used in Poland until the end of the 1980s for the purpose of political repression. This could be seen not only in the wide use of the death penalty, but also in the large prison population and lack of effective alternatives to imprisonment. In the area of criminal procedure it meant lack of judicial independence, weak mechanisms to protect the rights of the accused, and crucial influence exerted by the police and public prosecutor. Despite an unquestionable "sovietization" of the criminal law and criminal justice system, this process in Poland was probably still less far-reaching than in some other neighboring countries. For instance, prewar criminal codes remained in force until the year 1969. This was unusual, as in other countries so-called capitalist criminal legislation was usually almost immediately replaced by a new, "progressive" one. Of course, communist authorities supplemented the old codes with various additional and special legislations. But the codes themselves remained in force, which for many years prevented direct introduction of various legal concepts of Soviet provenance. The prewar codes were replaced only in 1970. But even the new codes were not completely isolated from their prewar predecessors.

Carrying a banner that reads, "We want the reinstatement of the death penalty," taxi drivers demonstrate in the northwestern city of Szczecin, Poland, November 21, 1998. The taxi drivers, who are protesting a series of murders of their colleagues, demand reinstatement of capital punishment, which was abolished by Poland's new penal code in September 1998. (AP Photo/PAP, Jerzy Undro)

Political and Social Context of the Criminal Justice System

Since the fall of the communist regime in 1989, a process of political, social, and economic change, building democratic institutions, moving to an open society and market economy was started in Poland. This constituted, first of all, an attempt to cast off the Soviet inheritance, and to join, or as some prefer to say, to rejoin in every respect the Western world. Certainly this process culminated in Poland becoming in 1997 a NATO member, and in 2005, a member of the European Union.

All this applied equally to the specific areas of crime and criminal justice. As a result of the communist rule, Poland had no chance to undergo a specific "civilizing process" of penal policy that took place in Western Europe after World War II.

During the 1990s, Poland was confronted with completely new challenges, namely, serious quantitative and qualitative changes in the phenomenon of crime. Like other countries of the region, Poland experienced an almost constant substantial growth of crime. Crime changed also in qualitative terms, as organized and serious economic crime started to flourish amid economic transformation and privatization. Also street crime changed significantly. Violence, including its serious forms involving firearms—something unheard of before 1989—became much more common. Juvenile delinquency, traditionally dominated by petty property offenses, started to be more violent, and to grow in its volume. Also, drug problems, although not completely unknown earlier, established themselves in a pattern fairly similar to that of the Western world with all its consequences: from illegal drug trafficking and dealing to public health and public order problems. This took place amid radical economic reforms, which brought originally an economic slowdown, a drop of real income, huge unemployment, and "deindustrialization" in the areas of heavy industry, coal mining, and similar industries.

All this had significant influence on crime and the criminal justice system during the 1990s. Crime became a matter of serious concern for politicians, media, and the public, and Poland became a country characterized by a very high level of fear of crime. This influenced public perception of crime and punishment, meaning growing punitive attitudes, including widespread public support for the death penalty. During the first half of the 1990s reforms went on relatively undisturbed; at that time crime control policies were dominated by experts and were not subject to intensive political debate. However, at the end of the 1990s reform efforts started to encounter serious obstacles, as political parties began to indulge increasingly in "law and order politics" and "law and order rhetoric." Experts started to lose their influence and crime control policies became more populist.

One can speak about two contradictory tendencies in the area of crime control since 1989. On the one hand, there was a visible tendency for liberal criminal law reforms, resulting first of all from the need to overcome the communist past in this area and to catch up with the tendencies in the Western part of the continent. This tendency culminated in the adopting in 1997 of a completely new penal legislation package consisting of three codes: Criminal Code (further on CC), Code of Criminal Procedure (CCP), and Code of the Execution of Punishments (CEP), all entered into force on September 1, 1998. They represented a modern, liberal, and human rights–oriented approach to crime control. On the other hand, the growth of crime and public concern with it resulted in pressure to return to punitive policies. The last tendency brought about in recent years several amendments to the penal legislation and attempts to change it even more thoroughly in a more punitive way (although the most radical of them were so far unsuccessful).

Court System, Public Prosecution, and the Police

The court system in Poland consists of several types of courts dealing with various types of cases. Generally there are courts of three types, namely the general courts, special courts, and the Supreme Court, which has a distinct character. To the category of special courts belong military courts (having jurisdiction over offenses committed by the members of the military) and administrative courts.

Public prosecution in Poland is the task of the special public prosecution agency called *prokuratura*. It is a hierarchical four-tier system parallel to the court system: regional, district, appellate, and country *prokuratura* offices. The minister of justice is at the same time *prokurator generalny*, general public prosecutor, having broad powers of supervising and directing activities of all *prokurators* or public prosecutors in the country, including direct interference in any ongoing investigation or prosecution. The last has been strongly criticized in recent years, as it makes the system extremely prone to political interference in investigating cases. Because of this, legislation to separate *prokuratura* from the Office of the Minister of Justice is pending currently in Parliament.

Police in Poland are a national, centralized force organized as a hierarchical structure. Police units are organized according to the administrative structure of the country. This means there is the main police headquarters in Warsaw, 16 *woiwodship* police headquarters plus a separate police headquarters for Warsaw, and 321 county police headquarters (bigger cities have separate city police headquarters, and on their territory there are additionally several police precincts).

On December 31, 2007, there were 98,102 police officers in Poland, which means that there were 5,207 vacancies, as 103,309 police officers posts existed officially. The above numbers mean 257 police officers per 100,000 inhabitants.

Despite the centralized character of the Polish police force since the beginning of the 1990s, efforts continue to give it a more local character. So far these attempts have not been very successful. They are limited to separate forces, created in all major cities as well as in many towns, called municipal guards (they have no right to call themselves police). Municipal guards constitute primarily public order police. They enforce local laws, impose fines, and have the right to investigate and bring charges in cases of petty offenses. They have limited powers compared with the "regular" police. There are about 9,000 municipal guards in 500 Polish cities and towns.

Crime

Classification of Crimes

The Polish legal system differentiates between several categories of acts prohibited under the threat of punishment, depending on their gravity, or—under the existing legal terminology—degree of social harm resulting from them. Criminal offenses and contraventions—or petty offenses—are, in a legal sense, two absolutely separate categories, the latter constituting a separate category that is not considered to constitute "real" offenses. Both are regulated in separate codes.

Being convicted for a contravention does not result in a criminal record. Contraventions are not included in criminal records or in police statistics. Therefore, the overall statistical picture of crime in Poland is always a little bit misleading, as it does not include contraventions.

Drug offenses are dealt with separately in the Drug Abuse Counteraction Act of 2005. It is a comprehensive act dealing with practically all aspects of substance control, prevention of drug abuse, and fighting drug trafficking. This act has mainly administrative character and includes provisions on legal turnover with drugs for medical and scientific purposes, cultivation of some plants (like poppy or hemp), as well as education, prevention, and treatment of drug abuse. It contains also a separate chapter with penal provisions, that is, definitions of drug offenses connected to illicit drug trafficking and use.

The criminalization of the possession of small quantities of drugs for a person's own use has been widely discussed over the years in conjunction with the development of the black market of illicit drugs around 1989. In 1997, the Drug Abuse Counteraction Act made possession of drugs to constitute in principle a criminal offense. But it provided also that persons possessing illegal substances in small quantities for their own use should be generally exempted from punishment, and proceedings in such cases should be dismissed practically automatically. This solution lasted for only three years, as in 2000 the law has been amended again to the effect that the punishment exemption clause was deleted.

The Polish legal system provides for separate responsibility of juveniles. Children under 15 are not held criminally responsible and offenses committed by juveniles (persons between 15 and 18) are regulated by the Proceedings in Cases of Juveniles Act of 1982 based on the welfare model of juvenile justice and covering both substantive and procedural aspects of juvenile justice. Juveniles may be held criminally responsible only exceptionally in cases of the most serious offenses (e.g., homicide, rape, armed robbery), if the public prosecutor decides to use such possibility.

Crime Statistics

Crime trends and patterns in Poland, like in other postcommunist societies, changed in a significant way over the past 20 years. Before 1989, Poland was considered a "low crime country." Among the many factors contributing to the low official crime rate, two can be mentioned here. First was the differences in the structures of opportunity compared to developed market economies. Second was the "underregistration" of crime under communism, as the police and other state agencies indulged in various techniques aimed at limiting input to the criminal justice system. The real volume of crime was probably substantially higher than official statistics were showing.

Since 1989, Poland underwent a real explosion of the registered offenses rate. Alone in 1990, the first year of political, economic, and social transformation, the registered offenses rate grew by more than 60 percent (from 1,140 in 1989 to 2,314 per 100,000 inhabitants). After a stable period, it started to grow again during the second half of the 1990s, in an even more substantial way, with the crime rate reaching its peak in 2003 (3,840). Since that year crime trends seem to have reversed, and Poland entered a phase of crime drop (3,354 in 2006).

The crime rate in Poland is still rather low compared to other European countries. Paradoxically, and compared to other countries, Poland experiences a high level of fear of crime. Results of the International Crime Victims Survey conducted in Poland suggest that the proportion of unreported offenses is higher in Poland and in other countries of Central and Eastern Europe. Despite an increasing willingness of citizens to report victimizations, only about 30 percent of all offenses are reported to the police, while in many Western countries this proportion exceeds 50 percent.

Despite significant changes since the fall of the communist regime in the numbers of registered offenses and their patterns, the overall structure of registered offenses remained fairly stable, and was dominated by property offenses. In recent years, they constituted on average 62 percent of all registered offenses. Offenses against life and health represent 2.2 percent of all registered offenses. Adding robbery and rape to this group increase the proportion to 5.4 percent (2006).

Two changes are noticeable in recent years. First, the proportion of drug offenses has grown from insignificance to approximately 5.8 percent in 2006. Reasons for this increase include the criminalization of the possession of small quantities of drugs for personal use and a more proactive approach by the police. Second, the proportion of traffic offenses also increased up to 14.4 percent of all criminal offenses in 2006 (not counting minor traffic violations). Moreover, a single offense constitutes 12.9 percent of all offenses, namely drunk driving. In 2000, drunk driving was reclassified as a misdemeanor (earlier it constituted a contravention only), which resulted in an increase of crime statistics. As these do not register contraventions, the sudden inclusion of drunk driving significantly affected the overall structure of registered offenses.

Finding of Guilt

Polish criminal procedure belongs to civil law or a continental system often referred to in Anglo-American literature as an inquisitorial one. Preparatory proceedings may take two different forms, namely investigation and inquiry, the second one being more common. Investigation is conducted by the public prosecutor (*prokurator*), yet it can be partially or totally delegated to the police. The investigation often relies on the police, with the exception of some serious cases (e.g., white-collar crimes, organized crime). However, major decisions are always the responsibility of the prosecutor. The inquiry is a simplified form of preparatory proceedings that is used in the vast majority of cases (i.e., those decided by regional courts and others involving custodial sentences up to five years). Inquiries are always independently conducted by the police, whereas some decisions have to be formally approved by the prosecutor. Preparatory proceedings may end in various ways, namely discontinuation of the case or decision to prosecute. Polish criminal procedure is governed by the principle of mandatory prosecution, and the public prosecutor has very little discretionary powers not to prosecute. Such possibilities exist only, but in a very limited way, in cases of petty offenses.

There is no jury trial in Polish criminal procedure, but citizens may participate in the administration of justice as lay assessors. Cases are adjudicated either by a professional judge(s) or mixed panels of professional judges and lay assessors. Most cases are adjudicated by a single professional judge, except cases of felonies that are adjudicated by one professional judge and two lay assessors. The court's president may always set a panel of three professional judges when the case is difficult. Cases involving life imprisonment have to be adjudicated by two professional judges and three lay assessors. Professional judges and lay assessors are completely equal members of a judicial panel. Trials are in principle public.

The new CCP has recently introduced the possibility of "conviction without trial," a concept similar to the Anglo-American plea bargaining. Indeed, a motion for a sentence without trial can be included in the bill of indictment. There should be no doubt regarding the circumstances of the case, and the attitude of the defendant should suggest that the sentence will be enforced. Interestingly, relevant provisions do not explicitly refer to an accused pleading guilty and courts are not bound by such agreements. Such convictions without trial are possible only for misdemeanors carrying a custodial sentence not exceeding 10 years.

Parties are not in charge during the trial and the cross-examination of witnesses does not exist. The trial is led by the presiding judge who conducts most of the examinations using relevant information included in preparatory proceedings files. Despite the introduction, in the new CCP, of some elements borrowed from the adversarial trial (e.g., the order of interventions), the Polish criminal trial remains highly inquisitorial.

Polish criminal procedure does not know separate decisions on guilt and punishment and final decisions always include the verdict and, when guilty, the sentence. Appeals can be filed against every court decision on the verdict and/or the sentence by the public prosecutor and the accused. Courts of appeals rule on facts and laws. Depending on the circumstances, they may change decisions of courts of original jurisdiction on merits or reverse these judgments and send cases for retrial under the original jurisdiction.

Several rights of the accused have already been mentioned; most of them have a constitutional character (e.g., freedom and integrity, defense, legal assistance, prohibition of torture, compensation for unlawful deprivation of liberty). Provisions of the CCP also guarantee several rights to the accused (e.g., remaining silent, not testifying against himself or herself, and not telling the truth). The accused has the right to know charges against him or her from the beginning of the procedure and to be informed of all evidence collected against him or her. The accused has a constitutional right to defense and the right to be assisted by a counsel during both preparatory proceedings and trial, as well as during the execution of a possible sentence. The representation by a counsel is mandatory when the accused is a juvenile, physically handicapped (e.g., blind, deaf) or when his or her sanity is questionable. In such situations, the accused may always hire an attorney of his or her choice. If he or she doesn't, the court has the duty to appoint an attorney who will be paid by the state.

There is no general right to bail pending trial, and courts may use various "protective measures" (like pretrial detention, bail, or police supervision) to secure the presence of the accused during investigation or trial. But their application is not mandatory, and in a substantial proportion of cases no such measures are applied. The most serious protective measure constitutes pretrial detention and may be imposed by the court only, upon request of a public prosecutor. Pretrial detention is permissible, if the identity of the accused is unknown, he or she has no permanent residence, or there are good grounds to suspect that he or she may escape or try to influence witnesses or destroy or distort other evidence. It is possible to apply it if the accused is charged with an especially serious offense, but it is also prohibited to apply it in cases of offenses carrying punishment of no more than one year of imprisonment.

The uses and abuses of pretrial detention are subject to constant debate in Poland. It is a common complaint that courts are too ready to accept prosecutors' requests regarding preliminary detention, and prosecutors are too eager to have suspects in detention in the hope this may make them eventually confess. Consequently, about 25 percent of the Polish prison population consists in pretrial detainees. This is aggravated by the fact that Poland has serious problems with guaranties of speedy trial. In principle, first decision on preliminary detention may not exceed 3 months. But it may be prolonged by courts for up to 2 years, and under certain specified circumstances it is possible to prolong it even beyond that period (for a specified period of time), on the decision of an appropriate court of appeal. Such situations are by no means exceptional, and there are known cases of people spending in preliminary detention several years before investigation is finished, not to mention final judicial verdict. Generally, inefficiency and slowness (usually in very serious and complicated cases involving many accused, but sometimes also in very petty ones) constitute one of the gravest problems of the Polish criminal justice system. Both the long periods spent in preliminary detention and the enormously long time (in record cases up to 10 years) necessary to reach a final verdict constitute the most common ground for Poland being quite often convicted by the European Court of Human Rights. Despite various attempts to change this, both by legislative and organizational measures, the situation remains still rather unsatisfactory.

Punishment

Under current Polish law, there are four basic kinds of punishment, namely, deprivation of liberty or imprisonment, deprivation of liberty with conditional suspension of execution or suspended sentence, limitation of liberty, and fine. The death penalty was abolished in the 1998 CC. Yet, in practice, it was no longer used. After 1988, an informal moratorium was introduced; this lasted till 1995 when a formal moratorium was introduced by Parliament.

Deprivation of liberty or imprisonment may be imposed in principle for the duration from 1 month up to 15 years (lower and upper limits may be different by particular kinds of offenses, but cannot be lower than 1 month and higher than 15 years). Apart from this, in cases of some felonies (e.g., homicide), it is possible to impose either imprisonment for 25 years or life imprisonment. Imprisonment is imposed always in years and/or months.

Execution of imprisonment sentences of up to 2 years may be conditionally suspended. Such suspended sentence is always accompanied by a trial period from 2 up to 5 years. Suspension of sentence may be accompanied by supervision by a probation officer, although in most cases it is not mandatory. It means that in a certain proportion of suspended sentences there is only the trial period without supervision. Suspended sentence may be also accompanied by various kinds of obligations for the convicted person, as well as—in cases specified by the law—by supplementary fine.

Limitation of liberty constitutes an equivalent of community service known in many legal systems of the world. It may be imposed in cases of offenses carrying possibility of such a sanction, for a period from 1 month to up to 12 months. This sanction consists of the duty to perform unpaid work for the community (in a hospital, institution providing social services, or in a charitable organization). The work is to be performed for 20 to 40 hours per month (exact number is to be fixed in a sentence). The code provides also for another form of this sanction, namely, deduction of 10 to 25 percent of monthly wages for the state treasury or community purposes. This form, amounting in fact to a special type of fine, may be imposed only if a person is employed.

Finally, fines are imposed according to the day-fine system introduced by the new CC. It requires from the judge a two-step evaluation during the sentencing process. First, the number of (fine) days is to be established, within the limits of 10 (lowest) and 360 (highest). Then, the daily amount is to be established, again between 10 zlotys (US$5) and 2,000 zlotys (US$900). It is assumed that this system makes it easier to adjust the fine to the financial means of a convicted person. The day-fine system does not apply to supplementary fines accompanying suspended sentences, and—also possible in specified cases—accompanying immediate imprisonment. In such cases fines are always imposed as a concrete amount of money to be paid.

Apart from the above-mentioned kinds of punishments CC provides for various additional penal measures, like, for example, deprivation of public rights, prohibition to perform a profession or occupy certain positions, withdrawal of driving license, confiscation of property, obligation to repair the damage resulting from an offense, making the sentence public in a special way, and so forth. These measures may be imposed parallel to punishment or also as sole sanctions, depending on specific circumstances ascertained in the law. They may be imposed for a specific period of time, from 1 to 10 or from 1 to 15 years.

Under the communist regime imprisonment constituted no doubt *the* most common sanction. During the 1950s and 1960s, it amounted to more than 40 percent of all imposed sanctions. During the 1970s and 1980s, the proportion of prison sentences dropped somewhat, but still constituted well above 30 percent of all sanctions imposed by the courts. One of the consequences of this situation, that is, frequent use of imprisonment for relatively long periods of time, was an extremely high imprisonment rate (incomparable with any country of Western Europe at that time). This changed since 1989, as the proportion of imprisonment sentences started to drop. In recent years it amounts to about 10 percent of all sentences, or even less. This may be considered to constitute significant progress. However, it did not result in the expected drop of the imprisonment rate to the European average. Moreover, it contributed to the—often criticized—change in the role played by other kinds of punishment. The huge proportion of suspended sentences, which—as mentioned earlier—often mean simple suspended sentence with trial period only, but without any meaningful supervision by a probation officer (more often such sentences are accompanied by supplementary fines), was always considered to be somehow problematic. In recent years suspended sentences amount to about 60–65 percent of all sanctions. At the same time there are problems with broader application of such alternatives to imprisonment as fines and community service. Use of community service dropped significantly after 1989, mainly due to various problems with the organization of the execution of such sentences. Only in recent years have courts started to impose this sanction a little bit more often (in about 15% of all convictions), which marks a significant progress.

The proportion of fines during the early 1990s was growing steadily. Paradoxically, after introduction in 1998 of the day-fine system, intended to stimulate use of this sanction, just the opposite happened, as the proportion of fines dropped sharply after that date. Only in recent years has it started to grow again somewhat, but it is still lower than in 1997. It is usually assumed that there were two reasons for this. First, judges may have been somehow reluctant to accept the new system of imposing fines, finding it to be too complicated. Second, introduction of the new system coincided with a sharp increase of the unemployment rate, which meant that courts were facing higher numbers of accused with very low or no income and because of this presumably were unable to pay fines (in such circumstances CC prohibits imposing a fine, to avoid fine defaulters being sent to prison).

Nevertheless, broad use of suspended sentence is strongly criticized by some experts. It is claimed that simple suspended sentences have a very negative impact on the public perception of the criminal justice system in Poland. The public gets the impression that most of the offenders "get away" with the consequences of their acts, as suspended sentence is no "real" punishment. Of course, this is not completely correct, but it seems that Polish criminal law and its criminal justice system were unable so far to establish a firm pattern of using other alternatives to imprisonment such as fines and community service. In the judges' mentality imprisonment remains still *the* sanction, even if suspended. In case they face offenders who do not necessarily deserve to be sent to prison (and this is probably the majority of those accused of offenses, especially petty ones), they use predominantly the suspended sentence. It is such conservative attitudes that should be changed first of all, although changes in legal regulation of the sentencing process and development of a meaningful probation system may be of even greater significance.

In recent years many politicians, and media, but also some experts, complain about the alleged leniency of the Polish criminal justice system. It is generally true that since 1990 the enormous punitiveness of Polish criminal law has been reduced somewhat. Unfortunately, the absolutely necessary reductions in the severity of penal sanctions were accompanied by a significant growth of crime. In consequence some claim that the policy of liberalizing criminal law and the criminal justice system initiated after 1989 was completely unjustified, even irresponsible, and contributed significantly to the growth of crime. American-style crime control policies, mass imprisonment, the "three strikes and you are out" rule, and similar ideas are portrayed as examples of "good practice," which resulted in significant reduction of crime and are presented as a panacea also for Polish problems. Although such views are opposed by the majority of experts, in recent years there were several attempts to change sentencing rules and patterns, to increase significantly the severity of sanctions in the Criminal Code and to introduce even draconian punishments. So far none of these attempts was successful, but penal populism plays an increasing role in the area of crime control in Poland.

Such attempts to increase the level of repression are hardly justified as the Polish criminal justice system is still quite punitive, especially by the standards of Western Europe. Problems result mainly from the fact that a substantial proportion of petty offenders and perpetrators of medium-weight crimes are sent to serve prison sentences, instead of being treated with alternatives to imprisonment. This results in one of the highest imprisonment rates in Europe (372 per 100,000 inhabitants in the peak year 1973). There are several interesting features of the long-term trends in imprisonment in Poland. First, enormous dimensions of the prison population under the communist regime were accompanied by frequent, violent shifts of the curve. This was due to the fact that prisons suffered at that time under the consequences of permanent, severe overcrowding. This forced authorities to use quite often general amnesties as a means of dealing with this problem. However, the criminal justice system was usually able to fill in the consequences of every amnesty within 3–4 years, and soon new amnesty was necessary.

In the years 1989–1990 the prison population dropped significantly (to 106 in 1990), mainly due to yet another amnesty act adopted in the fall of 1989 (this was the last general amnesty in recent Polish history, adopted after the fall of communism). During the 1990s the imprisonment rate remained much lower than during the communist time, although it was still quite high by European standards. Despite some efforts it was not possible to reduce the prison population further, and at the end of the 1990s the reverse trend occurred. Mainly due to more restrictive policies on granting conditional release or parole (possible in principle after serving half of a sentence), initiated at the turn of the century, the average length of time served started to grow, and with it, the imprisonment rate. Since the beginning of the present decade, the imprisonment rate went up significantly, and now belongs to the highest not only in EU, but also in Central and Eastern Europe (220 in 2005). As a consequence prisons are facing again a serious overcrowding problem. According to data of the Polish prison administration on December 31, 2007, in all prisons there were 78,883 places but 87,462 inmates, which means that prisons functioned almost 11 percent over their maximum capacity (it is necessary to stress that during that year this indicator was much higher, and reached usually about 20%). Despite this every government for the past 10 years actually did very little to deal in a serious way with the problem of prison overcrowding by means of introducing necessary sentencing and other reforms.

In December 2007 there were altogether 187 penitentiary institutions in Poland. Of that number 85 were prisons where convicts were serving their sentences, 70 were detention centers accommodating persons in preliminary detention pending investigation and trial, and 32 were "external units," or institutions of special, usually open, character.

The communist prison system was notorious for its severity, stiff regime, and very poor conditions in every respect, aggravated by overcrowding. This resulted in various negative consequences, including widespread existence of gangs within prisons referred to in Polish literature as the "second life" phenomenon. It meant inmates with long prison experience, belonging to gangs dominating other inmates, and prison life in general, and being able to strike various "deals" with the guards. It resulted also in problems with prison violence, which escalated during the 1980s into several serious prison riots with loss of lives and serious damage to property. Because of this prison reform constituted a very important task after 1989. Necessary reforms were introduced very quickly immediately after the fall of the communist regime. As the amnesty of 1989 reduced significantly the prison population, it was possible to close some of the oldest prisons with the worst conditions and all local jails administered by the police. Subsequently broad prison reform has been introduced. Rules and regulations were relaxed significantly, and inmates obtained first of all much broader possibilities of contacts with the outside world. During the communist time there were very stiff limitations on the number of visits, letters, packages, and other forms of contacts per month, as well as purchases in prison canteens (depending on the type of regime). Most of them were lifted after 1990. Also—quite controversial among the public—the policy of generous granting of furloughs has been introduced (much restricted in recent years). Broad changes also occurred in prison administration. Some older officers and guards had to leave the service, and relations between inmates and guards became quite different with the stress on human rights and dignity of inmates. This changed prison conditions significantly, eased tensions, and reduced the phenomenon of "second life." Generally speaking prison reform of the early 1990s is considered to be one of the most successful reforms in postcommunist Poland, which changed deeply the realities of the prison system. These changes are reflected in the CEP of 1997, which stresses issues of prisoners' rights, prisoners' dignity, and imposes broader judicial control over penitentiaries.

Unfortunately, over the last 10 years the prison system has faced several new challenges. Due to growing numbers of convicts and detainees, overcrowding has become *the* problem again. Prisons are filled beyond their capacity, which means that security-related issues start to dominate over treatment and rehabilitation of offenders. There are growing numbers of inmates considered to be dangerous. There are some serious violent offenders, but foremost among them are members of organized crime groups serving usually long sentences. This particular group of convicts seems to have changed in a very significant way the functioning of Polish prisons. Polish penitentiaries face also the growing problem of drug use and abuse, as it is practically impossible to control effectively the smuggling of illicit drugs if inmates are to maintain contacts with the outside world.

Krzysztof Krajewski

Further Reading

Frankowski, Stanislaw, and Andrzej Wasek. (1993). "Evolution of the Polish Criminal Justice System after World War Two: An Overview." *European Journal of Crime, Criminal Law and Criminal Justice* 1(2): 143–166.

Krajewski, Krzysztof. (2004). "Crime and Criminal Justice in Poland." *European Journal of Criminology* 1(3): 377–407.

Krajewski, Krzysztof. (2004). "Polish Drug Policies: Between 'Hard' and 'Soft' Prohibition." *Journal of Drug Issues* 34(3): 587–622.

Krajewski, Krzysztof. (2006). "The Juvenile Justice System in Poland." In *Juvenile Law Violators, Human Rights, and the Development of New Juvenile Justice Systems,* edited by Eric L. Jensen and Jorgen Jepsen, pp. 155–186. Portland, OR: Hart.

Portugal

Legal System: Civil
Murder: Low
Burglary: Low
Corruption: Low
Human Trafficking: Medium
Prison Rate: Medium
Death Penalty: No
Corporal Punishment: No

Background

For more than 30 years Portugal has been a democratic republic based on the rule of law with a clear separation between legislative, executive, and judicial powers. It has been a member of the European Union (EU) since 1986. After the military dictatorship of Salazar ended in 1974, free and multiparty elections forged a new Constitution in 1976, replacing the preceding one of 1933. Under this new constitutional framework, a new Criminal Code (CC) emerged in 1982.

A new Criminal Procedure Code (CPC) was also introduced in 1988. It represented a transition to a model of accusatorial legal system with certain judicial investigative powers. In spite of three profound amendments in 1995, 1998, and 2007, the modular structure of the CPC has been retained: the public organism charging the defendant is separated from the one trialing the case, thus ensuring impartiality and independence in the process of assessing criminal responsibility. The Public Prosecution Service, the *Ministério Público* (MP), conducts pretrial investigations, representing the state, and is regulated in accordance with the Constitution and the CPC. However, the Portuguese system is not a pure accusatorial model such as in common law. Judges are expected not only to base their decisions on the proofs furnished by the parties, but also themselves to gather other evidence as relevant.

Crime

Classification of Crimes

Apart from criminal offenses expressly described in the CC and other criminal legislation, there are also violations that are regulated by "administrative penal law," which punishes offenses through monetary coercive measures and accessory penalties regulated by various administrative agencies.

Criminal procedure law identifies "public," "semipublic," or "private" offenses. "Public crimes" are the ones in which major "legal interests" are violated, such as life or legal state goods, insofar as punishment is deemed necessary, even against the victim's will. "Semipublic crimes" are those that demand a concrete act from the offended person showing he or she wants criminal action against the offender. Only after pressing charges can the MP carry out investigations. "Private offenses" are those in which the MP's legitimacy to continue penal action depends on the previous criteria, to which is added the need to present a private accusation in the end of the investigative phase. In these crimes, victims must constitute themselves as *assistentes.* The status of assistant to the public prosecutor entails the right to intervene during the two pretrial phases by offering evidence or petitioning other investigative measures or to appeal from a decision even if MP does not. Victims in this particular role have to be represented by lawyers. One should underline that in all types of crime, investigative powers are exercised by public prosecutors (and police) and not by private citizens.

Note that there is no real burden of proof in Portuguese criminal procedure law. The MP supports its version of the facts written in the accusation and the defendant, suspect, or "person of interest" points out contrary elements. However, in a state of judicial doubt, magistrates have to decide according to the principle of the presumption of innocence, if prosecution cannot convince judges of the fact that the defendant has committed the offense.

The CC is divided into two parts: a general and a special one. The first contains not only the "general doctrine of the crime" (i.e., the elements that constitute the violation of the criminal law: its description, the illicit behavior, and guilt), but also legal consequences—penalties and "security measures."

Specific types of criminal offenses are described in the Special Part of the CC and in other statutes (from such diverse areas as the national economy's protection, public health, environment, driving, enterprises, and stock exchange markets). The CC defines five main types of crimes:

- Crimes against persons involving life protection (e.g., murder) and, in defined conditions, intra-uterine life. In 2007, after a disputed referendum, the law was changed to permit women to interrupt pregnancy by their option, in an appropriate medical facility, during the first 10 weeks. Assaults, domestic violence, and crimes against personal freedom (e.g., threat, coercion, kidnapping, slavery, human trafficking) are examples of other crimes against persons. Crimes against honor (e.g., defamation, offenses to a deceased person's honor), against privacy (e.g., house trespassing, mail and telecommunications' violation, secrecy violation), and other personal legal interests (e.g., illegal recording and photography) complete the catalog of crimes against persons.
- Patrimony wrongdoings include crimes against property (e.g., theft, robbery, damage, embezzlement) and crimes against patrimony in general. The latter are connected to frauds (false pretenses).
- Crimes against peace, cultural identity, and personal integrity. Offenses violating international humanitarian law are not subjected to any statute of limitations (e.g., genocide, crimes against humanity—slavery, deportation—and war crimes).

- Crimes against life in society that include offenses against family (e.g., bigamy, parental kidnapping), religious beliefs, and violation of respect of the dead (e.g., corpse profanation), forgeries, fake coin, arson, crimes against nature (e.g., pollution), crimes against the security in using means of transportation, reckless driving, and driving under alcohol or other drugs' influence.
- Crimes against the state. These include offenses against national sovereignty, such as treason, violation of state's secret, espionage, unlawful exercise of diplomatic office. Also within the range of crimes against the state, there are those against rule of law's enforcement and electoral crimes. Closely connected to these are offenses committed during the exercise of public office or activities, such as corruption, abuse of authority, and mail and telecommunication secrecy violation.

"Intentional crimes" have graduations in terms of offense seriousness concerning the personal and individual blame for the concrete action (or omission) performed. Guilt cannot be ascribed if the criminal lacks responsibility (in terms of age and mental condition) or if the offender had acted under mistaken knowledge.

Negligent crimes are those in which the defendant has violated an "objective duty," that is, all citizens are expected to perform their behaviors in such a manner that they do not constitute special dangers to others. Negligence can only be affirmed in situations in which the offender acts contrary to how others could reasonably be expected to behave.

The criminal justice system and law administration in general are considered one of the less developed areas in Portuguese democracy. Law cases are generally longer than what would be a "reasonable time" (as the Portuguese Constitution proclaims, repeating the European Convention on Human Rights), not only due to material conditions of scarcity, insufficient number of judges and prosecutors (in the present years there has been an increase in public recruitment), but also owing to a burdensome judicial tradition, many times favored by complex legislation. Most recently, controversy has arisen on the considerable increase of judicial costs.

Particular challenges placed to Portuguese criminal law include money laundering, corruption, drug offenses, and gun control. Although being a country with strict regulations on the use of guns, recent years have shown they are more widespread than originally thought, moving the legislator toward enacting a new law with more severe penalties.

Age of Criminal Responsibility and Juveniles in the Justice System

Portugal enacted the Child Protection Law in 1911, which provided a different legal framework in dealing with juvenile offenders. The age of criminal responsibility was set at 16 years and the first juvenile courts were created together with the correctional institutions for juveniles. The essence of the legislation was that a juvenile delinquent under 16 should not be treated as an adult offender in need of punishment but as a child who needs to be protected and educated by the state. This system of "paternal" justice was subsequently reformed in 1962 and 1978, accentuating the main features of the protection model. This model emphasized individualized sentencing (systematic consideration of the minor's living conditions and personality), reliance on child care experts and youth workers and informality of handling. All the measures were indistinctly applied both to children simply in need of protection and to deviant or delinquent youngsters. Their duration was indeterminate. As the intervention was intended to protect instead of punish the minor, the rights and guarantees before the law were not provided.

The most recent juvenile justice reform was introduced in 1999 with the *Lei Tutelar Educativa* (LTE, Law nr. 66/99, September 14), which dealt with juvenile delinquents between the ages of 12 and 16. The provisions of the LTE regime can be enforced until the age of 18 for deeds committed before the age of 16 and that can be executed until 21. Minors under the age of 12 who have committed an offense punishable by criminal law cannot be held responsible before LTE. Those cases evaluated as endangered minors are referred to administrative agencies and social welfare authorities.

This new legislation, which came into force in 2001, reinforced the role of the public prosecutor. Under certain conditions the prosecutor can dismiss the case or he or she can refer the case to the juvenile judge if he or she assesses the need of a judicial measure. The cases referred to the judge can be handled in an informal session, which happens in most cases, or in a formal one. The aims of the 1999 reform were to ensure the basic principles of due process (legality, legal assistance, proportionality, determinate sanctions) and to react to the "leniency" of the protection model. Nevertheless the primacy of educational aims over punishment was maintained.

The educative measures are ranged by gravity from admonition to detention order in appropriate facilities for minors. The detention order of less than three months and up to two years (three years in exceptional cases) provides for three types of regimes (open, semi-open, and closed), the most common being the semi-open regime.

The situation of young adults (from the age of 16 to less than 21) falls within the penal jurisdiction. In 1982 an intermediate regime was created regulating the sanctioning of young adults. Guided by a concern to put minors over the age of 16 under the sway of criminal law but wishing to spare them the hardships of prison, the statutory order provides for reduced prison sentences and gives the judge the possibility of replacing prison sentences of less than two years with the placement in a detention center. This regime has not truly been applied since the detention centers were never built. That means that young people under civil majority age (18 years) continue to serve their prison sentences in common prisons, without any true distinction between their conditions and those for adults.

Drug Offenses

Trafficking and criminal organizations connected with illicit substances trade are considered one of the most serious offenses in Portugal, especially because of the country's geographical location, as a gateway to Europe of drugs coming from, among other locations, South America. If trafficking occurs in jails (a major concern in Portugal) or if it is carried out by medical doctors or other professionals, punishments are much more severe. In contrast "trafficker-consumers," that is, persons who traffic drugs mainly to have money to buy them for their own consumption, have less harsh penalties. Since 2001, Portugal decriminalized, through the law (not through guidelines), drug use and possession of all drugs (defined as the average individual quantity for 10 days' usage for one person) for personal use, including cocaine and heroin (Law nr. 30/2000, of November 29). The behavior remains illegal but it is completely removed from criminal realm. The violations of those prohibitions are subjected to the application of administrative sanctions. However, drug trafficking is still a criminal offense.

Decriminalization occurred in a moment when Portugal presented one of the highest rates of heroin consumption in Europe. Contrary to what might have been expectable, its effects do not support an increased drug usage. In fact, a general decrease in the consumption of heroin and cocaine was observed, alongside with an increase in the consumption of cannabis and methamphetamines. In terms of the justice system, after the law, the level of drug trafficking (convictions) has declined. The sanitary conditions, using deaths related to AIDS and those related to drugs as indicators, have considerably improved. For an in-depth analysis of the Portuguese drug decriminalization, see Agra 2009.

Crime Statistics

The type of crimes most frequently recorded by the police in 2007 were theft (161,150, or 1,590 crimes per 100,000 population), of this theft from vehicle (39,781), theft of vehicle (23,986), and burglary (22,343) are the most common. In addition, road crimes such as driving without legal permission (21,313) and driving under the influence of alcohol (20,612) were also very frequent.

According to the Portuguese Directorate-General for Justice Policy–Ministry of Justice, the following number of crimes were reported by police in 2007:

	Murder	Aggravated Assault	Rape	Robbery	Drug Dealing
Crimes Reported	133	665	305	13,008	3,281
Rate per 100,000 Inhabitants	1.31	6.57	3.01	128.45	32.40

Finding of Guilt

The MP conducts crime investigations once having received any victim complaint or report from police agencies. This first investigation phase aims to gather evidence to determine whether a crime has occurred or not and who have been its perpetrators. The Public Prosecution Office is in charge with the support of police agencies. Judicial Police is responsible for the investigation of the most serious crimes such as murder, robbery, assault, sexual offenses, corruption, money laundering, drugs trafficking. Other illicit behaviors are investigated, always under the MP's supervision, by other police agencies, namely, Public Security Police, National Republican Guard (a military organization similar to Italian *Carabinieri* or French *Gendarmerie*) and the Borders Service. The MP generally delegates investigative authority to the police.

When the investigation requires a particular fundamental rights' restriction (e.g., wiretapping, certain searches and seizures), permission of a judge is obligatory. The public prosecutor analyzes proof and decides whether or not there is sufficient evidence to support a public accusation. This sufficiency is defined as a strong suspicion that the person has committed the crime, but not yet a proof "beyond any reasonable doubt." When evidence could not be gathered, the MP drops charges. If the sanction is mild (imprisonment up to six months or fine up to 120 days), a judge may determine a sentence but, if there are no preventive concerns, the actual penalty may not be carried out.

"Provisional suspension" applies to offenses punishable with imprisonment up to five years or with a sanction other than prison, provided the judge, MP, and victim agree. In this case, the defendant has to fulfill one or more requirements (e.g., paying compensation or apologizing to the victim, living in a certain place, not having certain jobs, not being in certain places or accompanying certain persons). In most cases, these demands can be imposed for up to two years. If the defendant complies with all conditions, the case is closed and cannot be reopened.

Most recently, through law in compliance with an EU's Council Framework Decision, a system of mediation in criminal matters has been introduced. Mediation is limited to "private" and "semipublic" crimes that protect people or patrimony and punished with up to five years' imprisonment. If there is an agreement with the victim on the way the defendant will repair the consequences of his or her actions, and if the MP does not have any formal objections to it, the agreement is equivalent to dropping charges.

After ending the investigation, a new phase may be opened that is directed by a judge. Its function is to ascertain whether the investigation's final decision was correctly based. At least one accusatory debate between the MP, the defendant, and eventually the victim is held, in which all of them expound their case, drawing the judge's attention to whether there is sufficient evidence to subject the defendant to a public trial. Apart from this debate, new investigations may be carried out when instructed by the judge or required by any of the "parties" involved. This phase ends by means of a decision to send the case to trial or not. If not sent to trial and if no appeals are presented or if they are denied, the case is closed.

After this pretrial procedure, a trial phase is opened by another judge's decision to accept accusation. The defendant may present a written statement on the facts opposed to him or her and may offer other evidence. A trial date is scheduled and if the defendant is not yet represented by a lawyer, the court nominates one. When the defendant does not appear in court, a judgment in absence can be held.

Depending on the seriousness of the offense (generally, if the crime is punishable by imprisonment from five years up), the case is judged by a single judge or by three judges. Jury trials are rare in the

Portuguese legal system. It is only reserved for very serious offenses (normally punishable with imprisonment of more than eight years) and upon specific request of the MP, the defendant, or the victim. Its intervention having been requested, a jury court is formed by four citizens randomly selected within electoral registers and three career judges. The jurors intervene in determining guilt and penalty.

Judges conduct the hearing or hearings, interrogating the defendant, witnesses, experts and allowing or refusing other means of proof presented by the defense, the MP, or the victim. In the Portuguese system judges do not have a passive role as they have in common law tradition countries.

After closing the hearings the court issues a decision of guilt or innocence. Except in special procedures (e.g., "summary procedure" applied to arrest in the course of the illicit behavior), sentences are issued on another date after the trial. At the sentencing hearing, the court determines, based on the specific statute, whether imprisonment or a fine ("main penalties") are to be imposed or if a "substitution penalty" should be established. Most of the cases end by trial or dropping of charges. As mentioned before, consensual ways of dealing with crime are not ignored of the Portuguese CPC, but they are not yet so widely used.

There is a specific system of appeals. Apart from special cases in which a "jurisdiction privilege" is prescribed to the highest state office holders (e.g., president of the republic, government member, Parliament member, judges of the highest courts), all criminal procedures start in a "first jurisdiction" court. Only by means of appeal are higher courts called upon to judge them. Roughly, if the appeal is based on factual issues, the appeals court is a "second jurisdiction" one. In case the appeal is solely restricted to law interpretation issues, the appeal is judged by the highest judicial court in Portugal, the Supreme Court of Justice.

Rights of the Accused

Accordingly to the CPC, the defendant's rights include the following:

- Being present in all procedure acts.
- Being informed of the facts before making any statement to any authorities.
- Not answering any questions.
- Being assisted by a lawyer during all procedure acts and hearings.
- Offering proofs and demanding any procedure actions.
- Being informed of his or her rights.
- Appealing unfavorable decisions.

Incarceration before or awaiting trial is allowed under strict conditions. Pretrial arrest (possible even without a formal accusation being issued) can be determined if other measures are inappropriate, provided there are grave suspicions that the suspect has committed an intentional crime punishable with more than five years' imprisonment, if there are strong suspicions of terrorism, organized criminality or risk of escape, danger to the public, or destruction of evidence.

Courts

Except for very particular cases (already mentioned), all criminal matters are judged by the lowest courts within the jurisdictional order. Those courts are competent to trial offenses committed within their territorial jurisdiction. Depending on the number of cases usually processed by a particular jurisdiction, those first-degree courts may be of "generic competence" (judging all areas of the law) or "specialized competence" (trialing certain phases within the criminal procedure law). There are also "specific competence courts," which are organized according to penalties' severity and that only exist in jurisdictions with higher case volume (major Portuguese cities such as Lisbon and Porto and the surrounding metropolitan areas). The most serious offenses are tried by courts composed of three judges who assess proofs and dictate sentences. The less serious crimes are judged by lower criminal courts and many of those are special procedures characterized by a "speed trial."

A second degree of jurisdiction, hierarchically superior only in terms of appeal, is constituted by one or more higher courts in each jurisdiction. Normally they judge appeals from lower courts, not only in terms of ascertaining facts, but also the law's interpretation. Finally, at the top there is a Supreme Court. It judges appeals coming from the high courts and, in certain cases, from first jurisdiction courts. Generally, the Supreme Court only deals with matters of the law's interpretation.

In Portugal, one can find two different magistrates' bodies: judges and the MP's magistrates. The first ones are independent from legislative and executive powers and cannot be transferred, expelled, or sanctioned except after a specific process ruled by an agency constituted by other elected judges and members appointed by the president of the republic and Parliament. This Superior Council of Magistrates, presided by the president of the Supreme Court, applies disciplinary action over judges and evaluates them for career progression purposes. The MP's magistrates, whose competencies are, in the field of criminal law, to conduct investigations (helped by police agencies) and to represent the state's interest in pursuing and sanctioning offenders, are a body whose head is the republic's attorney general, nominated by the president of the republic and the government.

In 2008, there was a profound change in selection of judges to the profession. Candidates are now required to have a master's degree or a PhD. The selection procedure involves written exams on several areas of the law, oral exams, and psychological tests. Those having at least five years of experience in a law-related job can also apply by performing a written exam on Civil or Penal Law and an interview to defend their qualifications and experience. Succeeding this phase and after choosing between a judge career or a MP's magistrate career, they undergo training to prepare themselves for the practical aspects of the profession, followed by some months working in a court under the supervision of a judge or a MP's magistrate.

Punishment

Types of Punishment

There are two major sanctions: penalties and "security measures" (the latter sanctions are applied to defendants that technically cannot commit "crimes" due to their severe psychological condition or their age under 16, therefore lacking "guilt" as a necessary element of "crime").

Portugal completely abolished the death penalty in 1870. The main penalties are prison and fines. Prison has a length varying from 1 month to 25 years' maximum, even in case of several perpetrated crimes. There is no imprisonment for life in Portugal. Fines are defined in days according to a daily rate from €5 to €500 (US$6 to $628). Fines can be transformed into prison in lieu of payment.

There is a wide range of "substitution penalties" applied instead of imprisonment or monetary sanctions. Some of them are suspended sentence (in certain aspects of its regime a similar institute to probation), community work, house arrest with electronic surveillance, and professional activities interdiction.

The most common punishment is fine, representing 73 percent of the measures. Around 6 percent of all the convictions result in effective prison. Based on 2006 data on court sentencing from the Bureau of Justice Statistics (DGPJ), the typical punishment for those convicted of violent offenses such as murder or rape is incarceration, 86 percent and 75 percent of the convictions, respectively. The remaining cases were given suspended prison. Of those convicted of robbery, 39 percent were sentenced to incarceration and 57.4 percent to suspended prison. In the case of serious theft, from the 2,284 convictions, 32.8 percent were sentenced to prison and 50.6 percent to suspended prison. In drug trafficking offenses, 70.7 percent of the cases tried were sentenced to prison and 28.7 percent to suspended prison.

Parole is generally granted, preceded by a favorable appreciation from a panel composed by a judge, prison's administration and other officers, at the middle of imprisonment's length, provided the inmate has served at least six months in jail. Whenever the criteria are not fulfilled, parole may be also granted when two-thirds or five-sixths of imprisonment length are accomplished. In the latter case, parole is mandatory if the convict was punished with prison of more than six years, even when there is no favorable judgment in terms of general and special prevention. In any case, parole demands the inmate's consent and it cannot last for more than the remaining imprisonment time, up to a five years' maximum.

Judicial decisions concerning crimes against honor may be published in newspapers whenever required by the victim. In 2007, the CPC's amendment has introduced the possibility of the MP communicating to the victim of sexual crimes the date (and never the place) in which the offender is released on parole or after having served his or her time in jail. CC's 2007 amendment has introduced a wider liability in what concerns corporate crime.

Prison

The prison facilities are classified as regional prisons (for preventive custody and prison sentences up to 6 months); central prisons (for sentences greater than 6 months), and special prisons, for prisoners with special needs (women, young adults, and inmates with special health needs). The law states that the penitentiary staff should elaborate for sentenced inmates a reintegration plan to attend their needs and to prepare the release of the offenders.

In spite of legal reforms, there are several problems that have persisted over the years and have been aggravated by the increase of custody use during the 1980s. This fact, partially due to the expansion of offenses related to drugs, had a major impact on the penitentiary system, particularly in overcrowding. In the late 1980s and during the 1990s, an important effort was made to improve living conditions inside prisons. Beyond the improvement of sanitary conditions of the facilities, a focused attention was given to health care, education, professional training, and working conditions. The implementation of programs oriented to special needs is very recent (e.g., programs for sexual offenders and driving offenders). The creation of the National Probation Service in 1983 made it possible for probation officers to work on a full-time basis, including inside prisons.

Types of Prisons

At present, Portugal has a total of 49 prisons, classified as central prisons (17 facilities), regional prisons (28 facilities), and special prisons (4 facilities). Two of them are exclusively for women, 8 are mixed, and the remaining 39 for men. There is one high-security prison and the others can have maximum security annexes. All of them are regulated by the Directorate-General for Prison Services.

Prison Population and Overcrowding

According to the last Prison Services (DGSP) official statistics from the end of 2008, Portuguese inmate population is constituted by 10,807 inmates (101.7 per 100,000 inhabitants), of those 10,160 (94%) being male. The most represented age group in inmate population (52.7%) is between 25 and 39 years, 30.7 percent are aged between 40 and 59 years, 12.6 percent between 19 and 24 years, 3.3 percent are more than 60 years old and, finally, 0.7 percent between 16 and 18. Most, 79.7 percent, have Portuguese nationality with the remaining 20.3 percent being foreign nationals.

Regarding penal situation, 19.5 percent (2,108 inmates) are in preventive custody, 78.1 percent (8,443 inmates) have been convicted, and 2.4 percent (256 inmates) serve a custodial "security measure." For the convicted inmates, 99.3 percent (8,387) of them are serving a determined sentence and 0.7 percent (56 inmates) an undetermined sentence. In terms of the length of the sentence, 5.4 percent are convicted to a sentence up to six months, 17.2 percent to sentences between six months and three years, 53.9 percent to sentences between three and nine years, and 23.5 percent to sentences more than nine years. In 2007, roughly 1,189 inmates were serving time for murder, 377 for aggravated assault, 194 for rape, 1,284 for robbery, and 2,459 for drug dealing.

The total capacity of the penitentiary system is 12,294 inmates according to the last statistical data from December 31, 2008. The prison of Lisbon (Central prison) has the greatest capacity (887 inmates) with the total number of inmates being 929. The prison of Porto (also a Central prison) possesses the biggest discrepancy between its capacity (686 inmates) and the number of current inmates (823 inmates), showing the highest overcrowding rate in the Portuguese prison system (corresponding to 120%).

Labor

Prison work is not mandatory; the inmates can serve their sentence without undertaking any labor activity. Statistics from December 31, 2008, indicate that 45.7 percent of the inmates are engaged in work in the prisons. Regarding academic education and professional training, the proportion of inmates attending such activities is, respectively, 14.7 percent and 8.9 percent. The labor is assured in the prison industries and in some prisons there is also agriculture-based labor. Many of the industries inside prison are functioning through contracts with outside businesses. To promote the social reintegration of inmates, there are two kinds of open regime, inside and outside the prison, and the temporary licenses. In the first, open regime inside prison allows circulation inside the perimeter of the prison under mitigated surveillance. According to the DGSP, about 2,000 inmates are in this regime. The other kind of open regime allows work or education experience outside the prison. However, the inmates can only have this possibility after a substantial portion of the prison sentence has been served.

Temporary licenses may serve different purposes: there are special licenses up to 12 hours for exceptional personal reasons such as to visit dying relatives, attend funerals, to receive medical treatment, and to attend court, tribunal, or inquiry proceedings. These visits are made under custody and are authorized by the prison's warden. The other licenses are focused in promoting the social reintegration of inmates, namely through the restoration of family and community ties. After having served a quarter of the sentence, inmates may be allowed temporary licenses up to 16 days per year. The management of family and friend visits is regulated by each prison administration. Some prisons allow "intimate partner visits" provided certain criteria are fulfilled. Inmates also have rights to correspondence, to telephone calls, and telegrams.

Extradition

The Portuguese Constitution prohibits extradition for political offenses or to countries where the crime is punishable with death penalty. Whenever the specific crime is punishable with imprisonment for life, extradition can only be authorized by a court order provided there is reciprocal agreement between nations.

Portuguese citizens can only be extradited in cases of terrorism or highly organized criminality, if there are reciprocity conditions stated in an international convention. There are also special rules regarding extradition within the EU.

André Lamas Leite, Josefina Castro, Carla Cardoso, Miriam Pina, and Cândido da Agra

Further Reading

Agra, Cândido da (2009). "Requiem pour la guerre à la drogue: L'expérimentation portugaise de décriminalisation" [Requiem for the Fight against Drugs: The Portuguese Experiment of Decriminalization] *Déviance et Société* 33(1): 27–49.

Agra, Cândido da, and Josefina Castro. (2007). "La justice pénale des mineurs au Portugal: Risque, responsabilité et réseau" [Juvenile Justice in Portugal: Risk, Responsibility and Network]. In *La justice pénale des mineurs en Europe: Entre modèle 'Welfare' et inflexions néolibérales,* edited by Francis Bailleau and Yves Cartuyvels, pp. 229–246. Paris: L'Harmattan.

Figueiredo Dias, Jorge de. (2007). *Direito Penal. Parte Geral.* [Criminal Law: General Part] Vol. I. 2nd ed. Coimbra: Coimbra Editora.

Jurisprudence of Portuguese Superior Courts: http://www.dgsi.pt.

Ministério da Justiça. Relatório Final da Comissão de Estudo e Debate da Reforma do Sistema Prisional [Ministry of Justice: Final report of the Commission Relative to the Study and Debate of the Reform of the Correctional System]: http://www.dgpj.mj.pt.

Portuguese Ministry of Justice and Other State Departments: http://www.mj.gov.pt.

Portuguese Official Journal—Diário da República (for legislation): http://www.dre.pt.

Prison Services Directorate-General: http://www.dgsp.mj.pt.

Silva, Germano Marques da. (2008). *Curso de Processo Penal* [Course of Criminal Proceedings]. Lisbon: Verbo.
Statistical Data: http://www.dgpj.mj.pt.

Romania

Legal System: Civil
Murder: Medium
Burglary: Low
Corruption: Medium
Human Trafficking: Medium
Prison Rate: Medium
Death Penalty: No
Corporal Punishment: No

Background

The origins of the contemporary Romanian legal system can be traced to the mid-19th century, when the independent principalities of Moldavia and Wallachia were united to form the first incarnation of the present-day Romanian state. Soon after declaring statehood, Romanian authorities laid the groundwork for a modern legal system by adopting the first Romanian codes of criminal law and criminal procedure in 1864. These early codes borrowed heavily from the French model, with only minor adaptations to fit the Romanian context. However, Romanian criminal law and procedure was not fully unified until the adoption of the 1936 Criminal Code and Code of Criminal Procedure. Until that time, the territories of Transylvania and Bucovina, which were incorporated into the Romanian state at the end of World War I, operated according to separate legal regulations.

With the advent of communist rule in the post–World War II period, Romanian law was modified several times according to a quick succession of communist-era constitutions in 1948, 1952, and 1965. These constitutions had many superficial commonalities with the constitutions of Western liberal democracies. However, a tremendous gap existed between the rights and procedures stipulated by Romanian law and the actual practices of the communist authorities. During the communist period, Romanian courts and prosecutorial offices were politicized and co-opted as instruments of the Communist Party, political dissidents were intimidated and imprisoned, and Romanian police and security forces curtailed the basic liberties of association and expression in one of the most repressive regimes in all of Eastern Europe.

Immediately following the revolutionary overthrow of communist dictator Nicolae Ceauşescu in December 1989, a number of important pieces of legislation were passed to bring Romania's criminal justice system in line with international standards. Two of the most important changes to the Romanian Criminal Code were Law No. 104/1992, which updated existing methods of criminal punishment, and Law No. 140/1996, introducing new offenses and aggravated penalties. A number of notable new laws were also passed to combat specific types of criminal activity, including laws on money laundering (21/1998), official corruption (78/2000), drug trafficking (143/2000), and human trafficking (678/2001). In addition, several reform packages in the early and mid-1990s brought important changes to the Code of Criminal Procedure, which provided more guarantees for the accused, increased the competency of the courts vis-à-vis state prosecutors, and refined regulations related to the collection of evidence.

To be sure, many of the most important legal and institutional changes in the postcommunist period have come (often begrudgingly) at the behest of the European Union, which Romania joined as a full Member State in January 2007. Yet, as the EU's influence over the transition process has waned, many problems remain. Notwithstanding the previously mentioned reforms, the 1969 communist-era Criminal Code and Code of Criminal Procedure are still in force in Romania, as lawmakers have yet to pass a comprehensive legislative reform bill. Thus, while new criminal and procedural codes have been in development for several years, the justice system currently operates according to a confusing patchwork of revised and amended codes. Moreover, the justice system continues to be dogged by corruption scandals and poor conditions in courts and prisons, which are chronically underfunded and poorly managed. Further, nearly 20 years after the revolution, very little has been done to prosecute or even censure the perpetrators of communist-era crimes, or to compensate the victims of communist oppression.

Courts

The court system in Romania follows a unitary four-tier structure, according to Law No. 92/1992 and Law No. 304/2004 on the organization of the judiciary. This structure includes several local courts and at least one regional court in each of Romania's 41 counties, as well as 15 courts of appeal in major municipalities around the country and a Supreme Court in Bucharest. In addition, Romania has a separate system of military courts (five regional courts and one appellate court), as well as a Constitutional Court, which reviews the constitutionality of laws passed by the Romanian Parliament and supervises national elections and referendums.

Local courts (*judecătorii*), of which there are currently 178, act as the first instance for most criminal and civil matters. Cases are decided by a single judge, who may specialize in a particular type of law in high-volume courts. However, many local courts have only a handful of judges who must handle all types of cases. Currently, approximately 2,155 judges (about half of all judges) work in local courts throughout Romania.

Regional courts or tribunals (*tribunale*), presently 46 in number, handle intermediate appeals of local court decisions. They also act as courts of first instance for administrative and commercial law cases, as well as more serious civil and criminal cases, including homicide, rape, robbery, and fraud. Tribunal judges are organized into specialized sections (civil, criminal, commercial, administrative, minors, and family). Cases are tried before a single judge when acting as a court of first instance, while appeals are heard by panels of two or three judges. At present, there are approximately 1,430 judges working at tribunals in Romania.

Courts of appeal (*curţi de apel*), which currently number 15, handle intermediate appeals for cases begun in tribunals, as well as final appeals for local court cases. They also act as the first instance for very serious cases, including offenses against state security and offenses committed by judges and prosecutors in the lower courts. As in the tribunals, judges are organized into specialized sections and usually sit in panels of three. According to the most recent figures, there are approximately 755 appeals court judges in Romania.

The High Court of Cassation and Justice (*Înalta Curtea de Casaţie şi Justiţie a României*), located in Bucharest, acts as Romania's supreme court. As the court of last instance, it hears appeals from the appellate courts and military courts. It also acts as the court of first instance under unusual circumstances, such as cases in which high public officials are charged with serious crimes. The High Court of Cassation and Justice is divided into specialized sections, where judges sit in panels of nine.

As in many modern justice systems, criminal investigations and trials in Romania exhibit characteristics of both the inquisitorial and accusatorial models. Reflecting the inquisitorial nature of the system, investigations and court proceedings are still regulated by the communist-era Code of Criminal Procedure, which assigns prosecutors and judges (both enjoying the same official status as magistrates) an active role in securing evidence with the ultimate goal of ascertaining the "truth" in criminal cases.

Police

Despite some initial reform measures immediately following the revolution of 1989, the most important steps toward restructuring and modernizing Romania's law enforcement sector came in 2002 with the passage of two major reform laws—Law No. 218/2002 on the organization and functioning of the police, and Law No. 360/2002 on the status of the police. In accordance with the new laws, Romania's National Police became the first fully demilitarized professional police force in Eastern Europe. The reform legislation also laid out new codes dictating the rights and responsibilities of police personnel and establishing new career guidelines and disciplinary sanctions in an attempt to professionalize the police corps.

At present, Romania is policed by three major law enforcement bodies—the National Police, the Border Police, and the Romanian Gendarmerie—all organized under the authority of the Ministry of Administration and Interior. The National Police (*Poliţia Română*), the largest of the three, is primarily responsible for law enforcement activities in Romania. The National Police is headed by a General Inspectorate of Romanian Police, who is aided by a number of administrative directorates in Bucharest. However, most of the day-to-day work of the National Police is carried out by officers working in territorial units in each of Romania's 41 counties. Each territorial unit is headed by a county inspectorate, who commands the county's general officer corps, as well as an emergency rapid reaction unit. The National Police organization also includes several specialized central command units, including the Organized Crime and Narcotics Directorate, the Public Order Directorate, and the Traffic Police Directorate. According to the most recent statistics available, the total police personnel in Romania in 2004 was 45,777, or approximately 209 per 100,000 inhabitants.

The second major police body, the Romanian Border Police (*Poliţia de Frontieră Română*), is charged with monitoring borders and regulating the movement of people and goods across approximately 3,100 kilometers (1,926 miles) of national boundary lines. In 2005, the Border Police launched an initiative to ramp up border security, increasing the number of guards, officers, and staff by some 1,400

Members of the Romanian SWAT team prepare for a public demonstration. (Pepine/Dreamstime)

positions. Corruption and bribe-taking among border guards is also reported to be a significant problem, given the high rate of cross-border smuggling of drugs and other goods.

The Romanian Gendarmerie (*Jandarmerie Română*), the third major law enforcement body in Romania, is a national paramilitary police force responsible for maintaining public order and security among the country's civilian population. Though distinct from the National Police in terms of its specialized military training and status, the Romanian Gendarmerie is subordinate to the Ministry of Administration and Interior and acts as an exclusively domestic security force, specifically created to handle disturbances and security operations within the national borders of Romania. Among its major duties, the Gendarmerie is charged with maintaining and restoring order during public events and demonstrations, including crowd and riot control. It is also responsible for securing important public buildings and institutions and is actively involved in the country's counterterrorism efforts. The Gendarmerie is headed by the General Inspectorate of the Romanian Gendarmerie, appointed by the Minister of Administration and Interior, who manages 41 territorial inspectorates, 8 Gendarmerie Mobile Groups, and a national Special Intervention Brigade.

In addition to the three main law enforcement bodies, national police forces in Romania are assisted by Local Police (*Poliţia Comunitară*) in towns and municipalities throughout the country. Created in 2004 according to Law No. 371/2004, each community police force is subordinated to the mayor of its respective locality. The main duties of the Local Police are to enforce local ordinances and assist the National Police and the Gendarmerie in maintaining and restoring the public order.

Romania has also witnessed an explosion of private security firms in the years immediately following the communist collapse. As of 2005, approximately 1,000 private security firms were registered in Romania, employing more than 37,000 private security personnel—an average of 1 private security guard for every 1.2 National Police officers. While the private security industry is relatively well regulated by Law No. 333/2003, which requires all companies to obtain an operating license from the National Police and mandates police-issued background checks for all private security firm employees, some concerns remain. In particular, employees of private security firms are authorized to carry lethal firearms in Romania, despite widespread concerns about inadequate training and several high-profile cases of private security firms using excessive force against members of the public. Moreover, as elsewhere in the region, allegations have surfaced linking certain private security firms with organized crime groups in Romania.

Crime

Classification of Crimes

The Romanian Criminal Code does not distinguish between felonies and misdemeanors or indictable versus nonindictable offenses. Rather, the code refers to all violations as "offenses" (*infracţiune*), categorizing them according to the general type of crime. Among the major categories of crime included in this classification system are crimes against state security (espionage, treason, political assassination), crimes against the individual (homicide, rape, assault), crimes against property (theft, robbery, vandalism), forgery (of money, documents, etc.), and crimes against peace and mankind (incitement to violence, genocide, torture).

The age of criminal responsibility in Romania varies depending on the circumstances of the crime. Offenders under the age of 14 are not subject to criminal liability under any conditions. However, between the ages of 14 and 16, offenders are held criminally responsible only if it can be proven that the offense was committed intentionally, while offenders 16 and older are subject to criminal liability in all cases. Regardless of the circumstances, persons under 18 are treated as juvenile offenders, entailing certain rights detailed later in this article.

While the use of illegal narcotics is not explicitly prohibited in Romania, the possession, cultivation, production, transportation, and sale of such substances is expressly forbidden. In recent years, Romanian authorities have amended the country's outdated drug laws with several pieces of new legislation that specify more severe sanctions for offenders involved in drug trafficking, as opposed to those charged with possession of drugs for personal consumption. The new legislation also distinguishes between different categories of illegal substances.

Crime Statistics

As in much of the postcommunist region, violent crime in Romania increased significantly in the 1990s, following the collapse of communism and the tumultuous transition period thereafter. However, as the situation has normalized over the last decade, crime rates have by and large subsided to pretransition levels or below. For example, Romania saw a significant increase in the homicide rate in the early 1990s, from 3.87 homicides per 100,000 inhabitants during the late 1980s to 4.70 in the first half of the 1990s. More recent statistics show a dramatic decline, however, averaging a rate of 2.20 homicides per 100,000 during the five-year period from 2003 to 2007—well below pretransition levels. Similarly, the 1990s witnessed a sharp rise in the number of reported rapes in Romania, jumping from 947 in 1990 to a high of 1,687 in 1997—an increase of nearly 80 percent. However, rape rates also declined to near pretransition levels during the last decade, hovering around 1,000 per year from 2003 onward.

Unfortunately, as traditional crime rates have subsided, Romania has seen a recent increase in both drug trafficking and human trafficking activities. Romania is mainly involved in the illegal drug trade as a transit country along the "Northern Balkan Route," linking heroin and opium suppliers in Afghanistan and Pakistan with consumers in Central and Western Europe. In recent years, it has also emerged as a developing route for synthetic drugs from Western and Northern Europe to destinations in the east, as well as a transit hub for South American cocaine destined for Western Europe. Though Romania is not a major source country for illegal narcotics, a small amount of domestic amphetamine production has been reported in recent years.

In terms of domestic drug consumption, marijuana and heroin are the primary drugs of choice in Romania, while synthetic drugs such as Ecstasy are on the rise among certain segments of the youth population. Huffing of glue, paint thinner, and other common solvents is also a serious problem among the country's substantial street population. However, Romania remains primarily a transit country rather than a destination for drug traffickers, with more than 80 percent of the illegal drugs entering Romania continuing on to destinations in Western Europe, according to police estimates.

In response to the recent increase in drug-related crime, the Romanian government established a National Anti-Drug Agency in 2002, following Government Decision No. 1489/2002. Among its responsibilities, the agency is charged with monitoring and assessing illegal drug use in Romania, developing a National Anti-Drug Strategy, and coordinating the antidrug trafficking activities of Romanian law enforcement bodies. According to the most recent statistics available, Romanian authorities reported 1,449 drug possession offenses and 1,223 drug trafficking offenses in 2006.

Romania has also witnessed a startling rise in human trafficking activity in recent years, as a major country of origin for victims of trafficking to Western Europe. In 2005, when the problem appears to have reached its peak, Romanian authorities estimate that 2,551 men, women, and children in Romania fell victim to trafficking, primarily for the purposes of forced labor and commercial sexual exploitation. While the numbers have steadily declined in subsequent years, with 2,285 reported victims in 2006 and 1,780 confirmed trafficking cases in 2007, official statistics only scratch the surface of what is clearly a very serious problem.

According to government statistics, of the 1,780 reported trafficking victims in 2007, 54 percent were female (compared to 74% in 2006). More than half of those women were aged 14 to 25, and well over half were trafficked for the purpose of sexual exploitation. Of the male trafficking victims, the vast majority (85%) were used for forced labor, while a small minority were used in forced street begging operations. The primary destinations for trafficking victims were Italy and Spain, where approximately half of all Romanian trafficking victims were sent in both 2006 and 2007. Illustrating the magnitude of the problem, official statistics from the Italian government reveal that Romanians accounted for one-third (34%) of all reported trafficking victims in Italy between 2003 and 2006.

In 2001, the Romanian government passed Law No. 678/2001 to allow for the prosecution of suspects believed to be involved in the trafficking of persons. That law was later amended by Government Decision No. 1584/2005, establishing the National Agency against Trafficking in Persons, which is charged with monitoring and preventing human trafficking offenses in Romania.

Finding of Guilt

According to the Romanian Constitution, individuals accused of a criminal offense are guaranteed the right to a "fair and speedy hearing." Upon arrest or detention, any person held in police custody must be promptly informed of the grounds of the arrest, as well as the charges against that person, which must be presented in the presence of a lawyer chosen by the suspect or appointed by the court. The accused is also guaranteed the right to remain silent at all phases of the investigation and trial, according the Romanian Code of Criminal Procedure. However, this right does not apply to the provision of personal data used to identify the suspect.

The presumption of innocence is guaranteed by article 23 of the Constitution, which places the burden of proof on the prosecution in criminal cases. During the investigatory phase of a case, prosecutors and police are forbidden from procuring evidence through the use of violence, threats, constraints, promises, or encouragement.

Criminal investigations are run by the local prosecutors' office, which works in permanent cooperation with the police. In general, police carry out much of the investigatory work, while the prosecutor in charge coordinates and supervises the activities of the police, ensuring that the investigation is conducted according to the law. If necessary, the prosecutor can step in at any point to help out or take over an ongoing investigation.

If a prosecutor decides to detain or arrest a suspect, article 23 of the Constitution stipulates that police custody cannot exceed 24 hours without an arrest warrant. Until recently, arrest warrants could be issued directly by prosecutors, who hold the official title of magistrates in Romania. However, a recent amendment requires that all arrest warrants must henceforth be issued by a court of justice, in line with the European Convention on Human Rights, to which Romania is a signatory. Once an arrest warrant is issued, police can hold a suspect up to 30 days. This period can be extended as necessary, but it must be reconfirmed by the court every 30 days. After being arrested, detainees are typically held in lockups (jails) until they are charged or released. If formal charges are issued at the conclusion of the prosecutor's investigation, the suspect is transferred to a prison, where defendants awaiting trial are held in separate facilities from convicts.

Article 24 of the Romanian Constitution guarantees the right of defense and the right to legal counsel for the accused during all phases of a criminal investigation and trial. Moreover, the Code of Criminal Procedure lays out specific circumstances under which legal counsel is compulsory, including when the accused is a minor, a student, an inmate in a correctional or pretrial detention facility, or when the penalty associated with the charges may exceed five years' imprisonment. If the judge or prosecutor in a case decides that the defendant cannot secure his or her own defense, the accused is entitled to a court-appointed attorney.

In cases where legal assistance is provided by a court-appointed attorney, the court instructs the local bar association to appoint a lawyer to assist the defendant, who is paid from the budget of the Ministry of Justice. Though all licensed attorneys are required by law to provided legal counsel in the case of a court-issued appointment, in practice, legal aid cases are typically assigned to apprentice lawyers, as the financial compensation is rather small and does not account for the number of hearings or length of the trial in a given case.

Romania does not currently have a separate juvenile justice system for underage offenders, though a specialized court system for minors has been under discussion since 2006. For the time being, most juvenile cases are tried in regular courtrooms before judges who may or may not specialize in juvenile or family law. Trials involving underage offenders are required by law to be held in closed-door private hearings, and in most cases, the parents or guardians of the accused are called to participate on behalf of the child.

Punishment

Types of Punishment

Though the death penalty was abolished in Romania in 1990, the country's criminal justice system is quite strict in terms of the severity of punishments dealt to convicted criminal offenders. According to statistics maintained by the Council of Europe, detainees in Romanian penitentiaries serve some of the harshest prison sentences in all of Europe—both in terms of the length of initial sentences and the average number of days spent behind bars. Moreover, while the number of detainees in Romanian prisons has been decreasing steadily since 2002, Romania maintains a comparatively high prison population rate of 166.8 prisoners per 100,000 inhabitants—well above the European average of 142.1 per 100,000.

In part, these statistics reflect a long-standing pattern in the Romanian justice system of applying strict sanctions for relatively minor crimes. Illustrating the point, in 2005, more than 35 percent of all prison inmates in Romania were serving sentences for nonviolent theft offenses. That number was nearly 50 percent as recently as 2001, when Romanian prisons held more than 18,500 convicted "thieves"—second only to Ukraine in terms of the total number of prisoners held for nonviolent theft. Prison sentences have actually became more punitive during the 1990s and early 2000s, as authorities attempted to deter rising crime rates.

Though statistics regarding the average length of prison sentences are not readily available, the Romanian Criminal Code provides some guidance as to the standard sentences for various types of contraventions. According to the law, intentional homicide is punishable by 10 to 15 years' imprisonment, and aggravated intentional homicide (including premeditated homicide, multiple homicide, and homicide against a magistrate, policeman, or armed service person) garners 15 to 25 years' imprisonment. Forcible rape is punishable with imprisonment of 3 to 10 years, or 10 to 20 years if the victim is under 14 years old. Robbery is punishable by 3 to 18 years' imprisonment, while offenders convicted of nonviolent theft are subject to 1 to 12 years' imprisonment.

There is no specified punishment for drug use. However, unlawful possession, cultivation, or production of illegal substances for personal use is punishable by 6 months to 2 years' incarceration for drugs in the "risk" category, and 2 to 5 years' imprisonment for drugs classified as "high risk." Drug trafficking offenses carry more severe penalties: 3 to 15 years' imprisonment for "risk" drugs, and 10 to 20 years' imprisonment for "high risk" substances.

Prison

At the present time, there are 44 penal institutions in Romania, including 32 prisons, 1 women's penitentiary (Târgşor), 2 juvenile detention centers (Craiova and Tichileşti), 3 juvenile reeducation facilities (Buziaş, Gaeşti, and Târgu Ocna), and 6 prison hospitals (Bucureşti-Jilava, Bucureşti-Rahova, Colibaşi, Dej, Poarta Albă, and Târgu Ocna). The largest of these facilities is the Poarta Albă Prison near the Black Sea port city of Constanţa, with a capacity of approximately 2,360 inmates. However, Romania has several large prisons housing between 1,000 and 2,000 inmates each.

For much of the 1990s and early 2000s, international observers criticized the conditions in Romania's overcrowded, understaffed prisons, denouncing them as inhumane at worst and unfit for a modern European nation at best. In 2002, when the Romanian prison population reached its peak, the country had a detention rate of nearly 230 prisoners per 100,000 inhabitants—one of the highest in all of Europe. Prisons were filled well over capacity, while a shortage of prison staff meant that detainees were afforded few opportunities to venture outside their overcrowded cells.

In recent years, Romania has witnessed a sea change in prison conditions around the country, as the total prison population has been drastically reduced—dropping by more 30 percent from 2002 to 2006. As a result, as of September 1, 2006, Romania's penitentiaries were running below capacity with an official prison population of 35,910 inmates, including pretrial detainees and juvenile offenders.

Inmates in good physical condition may take advantage of opportunities to work in many of Romania's prisons. For example, nearly all of the country's penitentiaries have farms on which inmates can find employment. However, prisoners are paid at the minimum national wage and are only allowed to keep a portion of their earnings, with the rest going to the penitentiary.

Not surprisingly, despite recent improvements in prison conditions, many challenges remain. Cultural and educational programs remain limited and job training programs are frequently out of date with current labor market conditions. Medical staff are overloaded and in many cases do not have access to the necessary equipment or facilities to provide comprehensive treatment. Basic living conditions in many of the country's prisons are poor and in some cases unsanitary. Moreover, numerous incidents of prisoner abuse have been reported by prison watchdog organizations—including at least one death resulting from violence suffered at the hands of prison staff.

Despite the relatively harsh sentencing guidelines stipulated by Romanian law, detainees serving prison sentences are often eligible for parole, which is used to regulate prison overcrowding and provide an incentive for good behavior among inmates. According to estimates published in 2004, approximately 70 percent of those released from Romanian prisons each year are discharged on parole.

Daniel J. Beers

Further Reading

Association for the Defense of Human Rights in Romania—The Helsinki Committee. (2005). *The Penitentiary System in Romania: 1995–2004.* Bucharest: APADOR-CH.

Küpper, Herbert. (2003). "Romania's Legal System: Transition Halfway on Its Road to Modernity." In *Consolidating Legal Reform in Central and Eastern Europe: An Anthology,* edited by Anders Fogelklou and Fredrik Sterzel, pp. 103–144. Uppsala, Sweden: Rättsfonden.

Romanian National Agency against Trafficking in Persons: http://anitp.mai.gov.ro.

Russia

Legal System: Civil
Murder Rate: High
Burglary: Low
Corruption: High
Human Trafficking: Medium
Prison Rate: High
Death Penalty: Maybe
Corporal Punishment: No

Background

The Russian Federation came into existence in 1991 when the Union of Soviet Socialist Republics (USSR), of which the Russian Soviet Federative Socialist Republic (RSFSR) was the largest constituent part, was formally dissolved. The collapse of the Soviet Union brought to an end more than 70 years of authoritarian rule, during which dictate and decree had prevailed over the rule of law. On December 12, 1993, Russia adopted a new Constitution, according to which justice is based on the equality of all citizens. However, the rights enshrined in Russia's Constitution and other legislative documents are not always translated into practice, particularly with regard to the various component parts of its criminal justice system.

Geography and Demography

There are around 142 million people living in Russia—the world's largest country—which spans 11 time zones across two continents, Europe and Asia, and has borders with 14 countries. Its largest cities are Moscow—the capital—which has a population of around 10.5 million people, and St. Petersburg, which has a population of around 4.5 million. A key issue for the state in recent years has been steeply declining birth rates, coupled with higher death rates, partly caused by a catastrophic fall in

Russian militia officers and a secret service collaborator in civilian clothing detain political protesters in downtown Moscow on October 2, 2006. (Kojoku/Dreamstime)

the life expectancy of men in particular, leading to an overall reduction in population figures. This trend has slowed somewhat in recent years.

The Structure of the State

In Russia executive power lies with the president, who is directly elected by the population for a period of four years for a maximum of two terms (to be increased to six years from the next presidential elections due in 2012). The current president is Dmitriy Medvedev, who was elected in May 2008 for the first time with 70 percent of the popular vote. The government is headed by the prime minister, currently Vladimir Putin, who was appointed in May 2008, having previously served two terms as president.

The legislature comprises the upper and lower houses of the Federal Assembly. The upper house—the Federation Council—is made up of delegates from all of Russia's 83 federal subjects, which (as of December 2009) include 2 federal cities (Moscow and St. Petersburg), 46 provinces (*oblast*), 21 republics (*respublika*), 9 territories (*krai*), 4 autonomous districts (*okrug*), and 1 autonomous province, and each benefits from the same representation at federal level. The lower house—the State *Duma* (Parliament)—has 450 seats that are allocated in proportion to the percentage of votes obtained by each party. The political scene in Russia is dominated by the United Russia Party, which won 64 percent of the popular vote (compared to 11% for the Communist Party) in the last election. Questions have been raised about the fairness of elections given the party/government's influence over, for example, the media.

The judiciary in Russia consists of the Constitutional Court (which interprets the Constitution and tests the constitutionality of laws and normative acts of the president and Council of Ministers, as well as the constitutions and laws of the federal subjects), the Supreme Court, and the Supreme Court of Arbitration (which deals with commercial disputes).

All higher court judges are appointed for life by the Federation Council on the recommendation of the president. Most other judges are appointed by the president after they have passed a qualifying exam and been through a formal or informal vetting procedure. The minimum requirement for new judges is five years of relevant government work (for example, as a court secretary, police officer, judicial assistant, investigator, or assistant procurator). Justices of the peace, who preside over small claims courts, are appointed for five-year terms. According to the Ministry of Justice as of 2007 there were 30,539 professional judges (23,172 judges and 7,367 justices of the peace) working in around 9,800 courts as well as an additional number of specialized courts of first instance, military and other courts.

Although independent in theory, in practice judges presiding over certain cases may find themselves under pressure from the authorities at various levels to return a particular verdict (so-called telephone justice). Bribery and other forms of corruption have also been the focus of media reports and complaints. Against this background, it is interesting to note that Russian citizens are increasingly turning to the European Court of Human Rights when they feel their cases have not been heard fairly in domestic courts.

Recent History

Following the collapse of the Soviet Union, the Russian Federation underwent a period of extreme economic crisis during the early to mid-1990s. This was caused inter alia by the collapse of the state sector, the implementation of rapid privatization, and trade and price liberalization, which led both directly and indirectly to high levels of unemployment, huge delays in the payment of wages/salaries—particularly, but not exclusively among state employees—and a concomitant increase in poverty rates. This proved catastrophic for the country's social services, which struggled to cope but were eventually reconfigured to provide a social safety net of sorts.

Crime rates also increased steeply during the early to mid-1990s as organized crime and corruption took hold in what was described as a state verging on lawlessness. In particular violent crime, including murders, increased significantly and the Ministry of Internal Affairs was seen to be somewhat powerless in terms of dealing with the onslaught of criminal behavior. In effect the Ministry of Internal Affairs went through its own period of crisis, one that continues, in spite of several years of attempts to reform various aspects of its work.

The Ministry of Internal Affairs (MVD) is headed by the minister of interior, currently Rashid Nurgaliyev (since 2004). Traditionally the minister is an experienced functionary who has come up through the ranks of the MVD or a related organization. Only one exception to this rule has occurred in recent years: prior to Nurgaliyev being appointed MVD chief, it was headed by Boris Gryzlov (the current speaker in the lower house, the State *Duma,* and deputy head of the United Russia Party), an "outsider" from industry appointed by President Putin to reform the MVD, with mixed results. The heads of regional police departments are also appointed—and dismissed—by the president.

The minister of interior is assisted in his or her work by a first deputy minister, a state secretary/deputy minister, and five other deputy ministers. The ministry is located in Moscow and houses the main directorates (offices) of its various support and operational departments. Support departments include the Administrative Department, Human Resources, the Legal Department, Finance, and Logistics. The main operational directorates located here include the Department of Public Security, the Criminal Investigations Department, the Federal Migration Service, and other independent services.

The Department for the Protection of Public Security includes the main office for the maintenance of public order (the uniformed officers who patrol communities on foot and by car), the main office of the State Inspection of Road Traffic Safety (the Traffic Police), and the Interdepartmental Guard Service (a semi-independent police service that provides security services to individuals, households, schools, businesses, etc., on a commercial basis).

The Criminal Investigations Department includes the Main Office for Criminal Investigations, the Main Office for Combating Economic and Tax Crimes, and previously (until 2008) the Main Office for Combating Organized Crime, which has undergone a change of name and remit and is now the Department for Counteracting Extremism. (Although it was announced at the time that organized crime was no longer a problem in Russia and combating extremism was seen to be a much more pressing issue, this is not necessarily borne out by official statistics—see below.)

The Federal Migration Service includes the Passport and Visa Office, which regulates the system of internal passports, which all Russian citizens have, and of residence permits. Independent services regulated from Moscow include the Internal Troops (a military/paramilitary branch of the Russian police used to support the regular forces in dealing with large-scale incidences of public disorder, such as riots); the Special Designation Police Units (*Otryad Militsii Osobogo Naznacheniya*, OMON), the Office of Internal Affairs, and the National Central Bureau for INTERPOL.

These offices also exist at other levels (regional/district/local) throughout the Russian Federation. Various sources put the number of personnel employed by the ministry at around 2 million, which includes just under 1 million police personnel. However, it is unlikely that the police are operating at full strength: conditions in the force mean that turnover remains high and some areas encounter particular difficulties in recruiting and maintaining staff.

The Russian Police—The Militia

Owing to their historical development (organizations created in the wake of the Russian Revolution on the basis of worker and other militia groups), in Russia the police are still known formally as the Militia (*Militsiya*). Their work is regulated by the 1991 Law on the Militia, which defined the role of the police as protecting the state and individuals from crime and guaranteeing the safety of every Russian citizen. It also established the militia's guiding values as legitimacy, humanism, social justice, political neutrality, impartiality, and respect for, and observance of, human rights. Most significantly from the perspective of establishing democratic values, the law states that militia personnel must themselves uphold the law, and thus provides the legal framework for the development of democratic policing in Russia. However, laws can be rendered meaningless if they are not effectively monitored and enforced, which is a systemic problem in Russia.

Research conducted on the process of reform suggests that while there has been a lot of change to militia structures and procedures, the legacy of the Soviet system and its czarist predecessor continues to influence both what the militia do and how they do it. Consequently, the militia still lack legitimacy in the eyes of the public, as witnessed by the fact that opinion polls routinely suggest that they are the agency least trusted by them. This is partly the result of well-documented police corruption, both smaller-scale, including routine abuse of power by the notoriously corrupt traffic police, and larger-scale corruption by so-called werewolves in epaulettes.

Added to this, during 2009 some well-publicized cases of criminal behavior, including several murders of civilians by serving (both off and on duty) police officers, have brought the need for reform back to the fore. Indeed calls were made in late 2009 to eliminate the police force as a whole and start again. While this is clearly impossible, it seems likely that the training and education system will now be subject to systematic review. In the meantime new initiatives introduced in 2009 to try to tackle elements of police corruption include making officers wear name badges (for ease of identification) and fitting cameras to police vehicles to record interactions between officers and members of the public.

The Legal System

The Russian legal system is based on civil law and the judicial review of legislative acts. Under Soviet rule, the legal system relied on an inquisitorial approach, but this changed with the introduction of the 2001 Criminal Procedure Code, which aimed to provide for more adversarial principles at every stage of the criminal process. Research suggests that Russia now has a mixed legal system that encompasses principles of both adversarial and inquisitorial systems, not necessarily to good effect.

The main codes that regulate deviant and criminal behavior in Russia are the Code of Administrative Offences (nonindictable) and the Criminal Code of the Russian Federation (indictable offenses). The Code of Administrative Offences (2001) deals with violations of the law rather than criminal acts, for example, traffic violations and environmental breaches and provides for such penalties as warnings and administrative fines, among others. The Criminal Code was adopted in 1996 and came into force in 1997. It replaced the Soviet Criminal Code of 1960 and as such introduced various amendments relating to criminal offenses not previously covered, for example, economic and property crime.

Crime

Classification of Crimes

The Criminal Code distinguishes four different categories of crime: less serious crimes, crimes of medium severity, serious, and very serious crimes, which attract the following range of possible punishments/sentences:

- Less serious crimes are those committed unintentionally or through carelessness and for which the maximum sentence is 2 years of imprisonment.
- Crimes of medium severity are those for which the maximum sentence is 5 years of imprisonment, and also those committed through careless acts for which the punishment exceeds 2 years.
- Serious crimes are intentional acts where the maximum penalty does not exceed 10 years of deprivation of liberty.
- Very serious crimes are those for which the maximum penalty either exceeds 10 years of imprisonment or takes the form of a more severe punishment.

Crime Issues

Key crime issues worthy of note are violent crime, trafficking, corruption, terrorism, and drugs, although these are not necessarily reflected in crime or trial statistics. During the 1990s violent crime, including murder, increased significantly in Russia. Much of the increase was the result of contract shootings among/between organized crime fraternities, but also of more legitimate entrepreneurs and businessmen, bankers, and of opponents of the government/regime, including politicians, human rights' activists, and journalists. Murder rates are still very high.

Given its size and geography, it is not surprising that Russia is believed to be a major player in human trafficking—as both a source and destination, but also as a transit country—and that organized crime is likely to be heavily involved in this area. In this regard both organized crime and corruption have been endemic in Russia for many years, with the fight against both being the focus of successive government policies. The change of focus of the main department responsible for organized crime (mentioned above) suggests that the battle against the former is over, although the struggle with the latter goes on: in fact President Medvedev has made rooting out corruption the focus of his presidency.

Russia also faces terrorism problems—mainly linked to the separatist movement fighting for independence for the Chechen Republic. Events such as the apartment bombings in 1999, the Moscow Theatre siege in 2002, and the Beslan School siege in 2004 resulted in more than 750 deaths and many more casualties. More recently in November 2009 a passenger train traveling between Moscow and St. Petersburg was partially derailed as a result of an explosion on the line—for which Chechen separatists subsequently claimed responsibility.

Drugs have become more of a problem in recent years. For several decades Russia has served as a transit country for drugs moving from their place of production in Afghanistan to Europe, as a consequence of which Russia has developed its own drug "habit." Most drug offenses involve the acquisition, storage, and sale of narcotics or psychotropic substances. As in many countries, however, it is alcohol, rather than drugs, that is often a mitigating factor in criminal behavior: according to crime data for 2008 from the Ministry of Internal Affairs, 16 percent of detected offenses were committed by people under the influence of alcohol, compared with only 1 percent under the influence of drugs.

Crime Statistics

As with all official sources of crime data, Russian criminal statistics must be viewed with caution as they are unlikely to provide a full picture of crime for all the usual reasons, but also because of the way police bonuses are largely based on performance indicators. This makes it an attractive option for the police not to register crimes they know they are unlikely to be able to solve. Moreover, recent media reports have suggested that they may also invent fake crimes to solve to meet targets, further obscuring the picture of crime obtained from statistics.

The data available from the Ministry of Internal Affairs does not distinguish between actual crimes and attempts, so the figures given below include both. According to MVD data during 2008 the police recorded a total of 3,209,862 criminal offenses, of which 851,392 (27%) were deemed "serious" or "very serious." One-half of all registered crimes were property-related, including 1,326,342 thefts, 243,957 robberies, and 35,366 aggravated robberies. Domestic burglary accounted for around 5 percent of all crimes recorded by the police, which was a reduction of 18 percent on the previous year. Violent crimes included 20,056 murders and attempted murders, 45,436 cases of grievous bodily harm, and 6,208 rapes and attempted rapes. Drug-related crime accounted for around 232,600 crimes, only 0.6 percent higher than in 2007. Vehicle-related crime included 24,326 traffic infringements and 50,313 cases of illegally driving cars without the aim of stealing them. It is interesting to note that only 642 acts of a "terrorist nature" were recorded, along with 460 of an "extremist character."

These figures only offer a snapshot of recorded crime statistics in Russia: perhaps more revealing (of recording practices if nothing else) are the trends revealed by overall crime figures, which increased by 5 percent between 2003–2004 (from around 2.8 to 2.9 million), 23 percent in 2004–2005 (to 3.6 million), and 8 percent in 2005–2006 (to 3.8 million), but decreased by 7 percent in 2006–2007 (to 3.6 million) and fell by a further 10 percent (to 3.2 million) in 2007–2008. In addition to changes to recording practices, these fluctuations are also likely to reflect in part changes to legislation in terms of how certain crimes are defined and punished, as Russia seeks to "humanize" the law (see below) via measures of decriminalization.

Offender Statistics

In terms of the socio-demographic and economic characteristics of detected offenders, according to MVD figures for 2008, 16 percent of offenders were female and 9 percent under the age of 18. A further 61 percent had no regular income, including 5 percent who were registered unemployed and 30 percent who had previous convictions; 16 percent committed offenses in groups, but only 1 percent of offenders were identified as committing their offenses as part of organized criminal groups.

Finding of Guilt

Upon being detained for questioning about an offense, in Russia a suspect can be held for up to 5 days without being charged. According to the new Criminal Procedure Code (2001), they are entitled to legal counsel within 24 hours of being detained. Where deemed necessary, a suspect can be held on remand in pretrial detention, but since the introduction of the Criminal Procedure Code, this can only be done upon application to a judge. This and other changes introduced as a result of the code reduced the number of suspects held in pretrial detention, which was a positive development given routine overcrowding in such facilities (see below).

Investigating Crime

When a crime is reported or discovered and recorded by the police, a case may be formally opened and be subject to an inquiry (*doznanie*) by a detective. Previously the police could open a criminal case on their own initiative, but they now require the agreement of the Prosecutor's Office. Since 1990 all suspects have had the right to legal counsel, but only since 2002 has it been mandatory for the police/courts to inform suspects of this right, and research suggests this is still not always enacted according to the law. In a criminal case any individual without sufficient financial resources can request legal aid (which is partly means tested, but also automatically available to certain categories of citizens, such as war veterans), which covers legal advice and representation in court in both criminal and other cases. According to the Ministry of Justice, in 2007 more than 57,000 cases were granted legal aid, although it is likely that many more would have been provided with a court-appointed advocate for the trial phase.

Trials

During the Soviet era trials were often held in front of a judicial panel of one judge and two lay assessors rather than a jury. However, jury trials began to be reintroduced to Russia at the end of 1993, and at the defendant's request a jury of 12 people may now consider certain types of cases—usually for more serious offenses (e.g., murder and rape) tried at regional court level. According to the Ministry of Justice in 2007, 18,450 people served as jurors in trials across Russia, but this represented only around 1 percent of all criminal cases. Data from the Legal Department of the Supreme Court show that during the first nine months of 2009 only 421 jury trials took place, involving 748 accused persons, resulting in 168 acquittals (i.e., a 22% acquittal rate). It is possible that the number of jury trials will decline in the future as proposals have been put forward to remove this right for certain serious offenses, including terrorism and treason.

For serious cases the right to trial by jury exists alongside the old system of judicial panel of one judge and two lay assessors or a bar of three professional judges. Minor cases are most likely to be heard before a justice of the peace.

Plea Bargaining

Russian legal codes allow for simplified proceedings to take place for certain offenses—if the defendant does not contest the charge against him or her. Termed "special trial procedures" and first introduced in 2002 for "less serious crimes" and crimes of "medium severity," they allow a person accused of such offenses to plead guilty in exchange for some leniency in sentencing (the upper third of the sentencing range is excluded). These special procedures were extended to cover serious crimes in 2005, and in 2009 such "plea bargaining" was extended to all offenses—even serious crimes that may result in life sentences. It is estimated that special trial procedures now account for around 45 percent of all cases (which nonetheless still go to trial).

Mediation

Mediation as a form of alternative dispute resolution is also provided for by the Russian legal system: private or court-annexed mediation is possible in civil and commercial cases, family law cases (e.g., divorce), and in criminal cases. Public authorities can also organize mediation in criminal cases, and prosecutors can be involved in the organization of mediation in family law cases and criminal cases. Reconciliation and mediation are recommended for all less serious crimes and crimes of medium severity and therefore it is almost standard practice for justices of the peace to attempt to resolve cases in this way.

Court Cases and Outcomes

According to data for the first nine months of 2009 from the Supreme Court Legal Department, theft accounts for around 24 percent of all criminal trial proceedings, drugs for 9 percent, robbery and aggravated robbery for 8 percent, grievous bodily harm for 5 percent, and homicide, rape, extortion, bribe-taking/giving and arms-related offenses for less than 1 percent each. First-degree murder represents just over 1 percent of all criminal trials.

According to data published in the Russian media, of those cases that went to trial in 2007 45 percent resulted in a suspended sentence, 33 percent in imprisonment, 13 percent in a fine, and 4 percent in corrective labor without imprisonment (i.e., community service). Data from the Legal Department of the Supreme Court show that for the first nine months of 2009 fewer than 1 percent of those accused at (nonjury) trial were acquitted, while around 30 percent had the cases against them stopped, and 32 percent were imprisoned, including 55 people for life.

Juveniles

The age of criminal responsibility in Russia is 16, but for many serious crimes such as murder, rape, grievous bodily harm, and robbery, it is 14 and children of this age are held criminally responsible for their offenses. As there is no separate court system for juveniles, they are processed through the regular criminal justice system, although trials involving minors are usually held in camera and are handled by experienced judges, increasingly with the help of social workers. Those found guilty of a crime and sentenced to deprivation of liberty may be sent to a juvenile penal colony (or corrective educational facilities), of which there are 64 in Russia, including 3 for girls. They may remain there till the age of 18 and sometimes until the age of 20.

Punishment

Types of Punishment

The Criminal Code of the Russian Federation provides for a range of punishments commonly found in other countries. There are three types of penalties: basic, additional, and those that can serve as either/both:

- Basic penalties include compulsory work, corrective labor, restrictions in military service or service in a disciplinary military unit (for serving military personnel), restricted liberty, arrest, deprivation of liberty for a specific period, deprivation of liberty for life, and capital punishment (but see below).
- Additional penalties include confiscation of property, and deprivation of special military ranks or honor titles, class ranks, or government decorations.
- Penalties that can be either "basic" or "additional" include fines and deprivation of the right to hold a specified office or to engage in specific activities.

Capital Punishment

Although Russia has had a moratorium on the death penalty since 1996, when it joined the Council of Europe, this provision remains on the statutes. The moratorium was originally in place until such a time as all of the country's federal subjects had introduced the possibility of trial by jury: as the final subject—the Chechen Republic—introduced jury trials in January 2010, which fulfils the abovementioned condition, this raised the possibility of a return to the use of the death penalty. However, as the Constitutional Court ruled in November 2009 that Russia's international obligations take precedence over domestic legislation, even after the moratorium expires the death penalty will not be an option.

Typical Punishments

For most types of crime the punishment depends on both the nature of the offense and of the victim, as a result of which there is not necessarily a "typical punishment," but rather a range that varies accordingly. Some examples of offenses and punishments are given below:

- Murder is defined as the intentional taking of another person's life and is punishable by deprivation of liberty for a period of between 6 and 15 years. In special circumstances, including the murder of two or more people, of someone acting in the course of his or her official duty (e.g., a police officer), a pregnant woman, or when committed with particular cruelty or maliciousness, murder is punishable by longer periods of incarceration—between 8 and 20 years, or for life, or can (in theory) attract the death penalty.
- Rape is defined as sexual relations with the use/threat of violence against the victim or

other persons or taking advantage of a victim's helpless condition. It is punishable by deprivation of liberty of between 3 and 6 years, 4 and 10 years, or 8 and 15 years, depending upon the nature of the offense, offender, and victim of the crime.

- Robbery is defined as the open theft of other people's property and is punishable by corrective labor for between 1 and 2 years; by arrest for 4–6 months; or by deprivation of liberty for a term of up to 4 years. More serious cases (e.g., large-scale robberies, committed by groups of organized criminals, or by repeat offenders) are punishable by deprivation of liberty of between 6 and 12 years, with or without confiscation of property.
- The illegal acquisition or storage of narcotic drugs and psychotropic substances on a large scale is punishable by up to 3 years of deprivation of liberty in cases without the purpose of sale and by 3–7 years for cases with the purpose of sale.

Prison

Previously under the control of the Ministry of Internal Affairs, in 1998 the Federal Service for the Implementation of Punishment was transferred to the Ministry of Justice. According to the Ministry of Justice, on October 1, 2009, there were 877,595 persons in all types of penal institutions in Russia, including pretrial detainees and those on remand. Russia therefore has one of the biggest prison populations in the world, both in absolute terms (second only to the United States) and per 100,000 of the population (620). However, it should be noted that numbers have fallen in recent years: according to the International Centre for Prison Studies (ICPS), 2009, they fell from a high of more than a million in the late 1990s to the present-day figures, as a result of which they now suggest an occupancy level of around 91.6 percent, based on an official capacity of the prison system of 955,421.

While occupancy levels are a quantitative indicator, they do not allow for any qualitative evaluation of space in penal institutions. Reports from Russia speak overwhelmingly of serious overcrowding in prison institutions, and particularly in pretrial detention centers (SIZOs), where prisoners may be allocated one square meter of space or less and may find themselves sitting and/or sleeping in shifts owing to a shortage of beds. High infection rates for contagious diseases such as tuberculosis and HIV have also been reported, partly owing to the sheer numbers of people living in extremely close proximity to each other.

Of the total number stated above, around 15.6 percent were pretrial or remand prisoners, including 4.7 percent who were untried, 5.2 percent who had been convicted but were awaiting sentencing, and 5.6 percent who had been sentenced but were awaiting confirmation of their sentences. According to the ICPS's World Prison Brief, 2009, around 8 percent of the total prison population were females, 1.8 percent were juveniles (under the age of 18), and 2.8 percent were foreign nationals. There are more than 1,000 penal establishments in Russia, including around 225 pretrial detention centers (SIZOs), 755 correctional "colonies" (including 45 for women and 62 for juveniles), and 7 prisons.

Pretrial detention centers (SIZOs) hold people on remand who are awaiting trial and investigation. Reports suggest the worst conditions exist in such establishments, mainly because of overcrowding. Upon sentencing, inmates can be sent to one of several types of penal institution, depending on the nature of the offense for which they have been found guilty, the length of their sentence, and the ruling of the court.

Prisons are penitentiary-type institutions reserved for those who have been found guilty of committing serious or very serious crimes and sentenced to at least five years. Other inmates of prisons include those who have been transferred for persistently breaching the rules and regulations of other penal establishments, who can be sentenced to prison for a maximum of three years. Prisons house inmates serving time at various security levels: minimum, medium, and maximum. A relatively low percentage of the country's penal population are held in prisons. One of the country's oldest and largest prisons is located in the historic city of Vladimir, around 100 miles from Moscow. It opened in 1783 and currently houses more than 1,000 "dangerous" criminals.

Correctional colonies can be either open or closed facilities. Correctional colony settlements are similar to open prison establishments, where there are few guards and uniforms do not have to be worn by inmates, who live in dormitories or in rented accommodation within the boundaries of the open settlement. Inmates' relatives are permitted to live with them within settlements. Such open institutions only house low-risk inmates, including first-time offenders convicted of certain types of crime and sentenced to no more than five years. In contrast correctional colonies are closed institutions guarded by armed officers and where inmates have to wear uniforms. There are three different categories of closed correctional institutions: general, strict, and special regime: (1) the general regime is a minimum security regime for most male and female prisoners not sentenced to higher regimes; (2) the strict regime involves medium to maximum security; and (3) the special regime is a maximum security regime for inmates convicted of the repeated commission of serious crimes and sentenced to life imprisonment. There are separate general regime colonies for women with children under the age of 3 and also separate colonies for inmates who previously worked in the area of law enforcement and criminal justice (for their own protection it is assumed).

Work in Prison

According to Laura Piacentini (2004), the aim of the Soviet penal system was to both correct and punish deviant behavior (considered to be "anti-Soviet") through enforced hard labor, which had the added benefit of simultaneously contributing to the Soviet economy. After the collapse of the Soviet Union certain practices continued in terms of prison labor; however, this was perhaps more a function of financial necessity on the part of the woefully underfunded penal institutions than of punishment, rehabilitation, or national economic needs. Many different approaches have been recorded across Russia's penal institutions, where prison labor remains a necessity in many areas, but opportunities tend to be dictated by available natural resources, competition, and supply and demand.

Policies on Visitors and Privileges

In the Russian penal system convicted prisoners are entitled to six family visits per year—more if governors allow them as a reward, for good behavior, for example. Each visit—for close relatives only—can last up to 72 hours, during which time visitors live in specially provided subsidized accommodation with the prisoner. The aim of such visits is to allow for family links to be preserved—which is seen to have short- as well as long-term benefits in terms of rehabilitation and reintegration at the end of a prisoner's sentence. However, owing to the geography of Russia's penal system, which means that prisoners can be sent to institutions far from their homes and families, as well as financial issues associated with traveling long distances, taking time off work and other schedules, and paying for the special accommodation, making the most of these permitted visits may be problematic for many prisoners and their families. Prisoners are also entitled to receive letters and parcels—but this is restricted to a certain number each year.

Annette Robertson

Further Reading

Piacentini, Laura. (2004). *Surviving Russian Prisons: Punishment, Politics, and Economy in Transition.* Devon, UK: Willan.

Pridemore, William A., ed. (2005). *Ruling Russia: Law, Crime and Justice in a Changing Society.* New York: Rowman and Littlefield.

Roudik, Peter. (2008). "Policing the Russian Federation." In *Comparative Policing: The Struggle for Democratization,* edited by Mika Haberfield, pp. 139–167. London: Sage.

Russian Ministry of the Interior: http://www.mvdrf.ru.

Solomon, Peter H., and Todd S. Foglesong. (2000). *Courts and Transition in Russia: The Challenge of Judicial Reform.* Boulder, CO: Westview.

Note: The author would like to thank Professor Peter H. Solomon, Jr., Professor of Political Science, Law and Criminology at the University of Toronto, Canada, for his very helpful comments on the first draft of this essay.

San Marino

Legal System: Civil
Corruption: Medium
Death Penalty: No
Corporal Punishment: No

Background

The Republic of San Marino is a landlocked country in central Italy of roughly 61 square kilometers (24 square miles) and claims to be the world's oldest republic. The *CIA World Factbook* estimates the population at 30,324 as of July 2009, with 94 percent urbanization. Roughly, two-thirds of the population is between the ages of 15 and 64. There is a migration rate of 10.32 per 1,000 people and tourism adds about 3 million visitors a year.

San Marino is a parliamentary democracy. The republican form of government and the protection of civil and political rights are constant features in the history of San Marino. Though it does not have an official written constitution, there is legislation and statues, dating from the initial formation on October 8, 1600, that serve a similar purpose. The 1974 Declaration of Human Rights Law No. 59 clarified the Citizens' Rights and of the Fundamental Principles of the San Marinese Legal Order and formalized certain constitutional matters. Article 5 of the Declaration of Rights declares human rights as inviolable and articles 6–11 enumerate the most important of these rights.

The San Marino legal system is a mixture of the old and new. The country has preserved the traditional system of *jus commune* in noncriminal matters and civil procedure. *Jus commune* is commonly thought of as a combination of Canon law and Roman law and remained in force in Italy and Europe before the development of the Napoleonic code. Private law, which is noncriminal law, is based on a combination of *leges statutae,* customary law, and the Justinian Code. Private law in San Marino is not codified. However, there are a number of legislative instruments that explicate the law in San Marino, the most significant being the Statutes of 1600, known as *Statutae Leges Republicae Sancti Marini.* The Statutes of 1600 is written in Latin and contained in six books, the third of which is known as the *maleficiorum.* The *maleficiorum* includes 74 articles and covers the criminal law of San Marino. Criminal matters of law are dealt with under a penal code adopted in 1974 and a Code of Penal Procedure that dates from 1878. This code was amended in the late 20th century.

Police

Law enforcement in San Marino is divided among the centralized Civil Police, the Corps of Gendarmerie, and the *Guardie di Rocca* or Guardians of the Rock. The Civil Police are a nonmilitary police force that works with the Gendarmerie when necessary. They deal with civil, commercial, and tax/revenue matters along with traffic control issues. The Gendarmerie was instituted in 1824 and addresses problems concerning public safety, criminal investigation, and drug enforcement activity. The Gendarmerie is primarily responsible for the reduction of crime, the safety of citizens, the respect of the laws, and emergency relief. The Guardians of the Rock protect important state institutional buildings, control and police customs, escort valuable goods and securities, verify any administrative infringements, and help with border control. There is no regular military force, only a voluntary military force known as *Corpi Militari Voluntar.* The voluntary military performs ceremonial duties and limited police support functions. The San Marino police forces are trained by the Italian police and have a mutual agreement for cooperation and aid when needed. Italy's armed forces are responsible for defense during hostile or aggressive conflicts. San Marino defense is the responsibility of Italy.

The Financial Intelligence Unit (FIU) under Law 92 of June 17, 2008, works under the Central Bank of San Marino. The responsibilities tasked include preventing and fighting money laundering and terrorism. The FIU cooperates with the other San Marino police forces and international agencies.

Crime

Classification of Crimes

The San Marino Criminal Code, enacted on January 1, 1975, includes all criminal offenses; however, the only clear classification is based on the punishment rather than the crime. A misdemeanor is any crime that does not require imprisonment. Although not officially categorized, the major criminal offenses include the following:

- Murder, manslaughter, reckless homicide.
- Intentional and unintentional personal injuries, instigating and/or assisting with suicide, personal violence, fraud in marriage.
- Enslaving, trafficking and trade in slaves, abduction, violation of sexual freedom.
- Housebreaking.
- Disclosure of correspondence, defamation, slander, libel, public defamation of religion, violation of religious freedom, interference with religious rites.
- Attack on the free exercise of the right to vote, violation of secret ballot, violation of political rights.

The minimum age of criminal responsibility in San Marino is 12 years of age. Minors over the age of 12 but under 18 who have had their mental capacity ascertained may receive a penalty reduced by one or two degrees. The mental capacity of a minor is established through a bio-physical examination.

Human rights are protected under San Marino law and all behaviors that constitute violations of these rights are subject to punishment by criminal regulations. Under the San Marino Criminal Code criminal offenses include murder, manslaughter, reckless homicide, intentional and unintentional personal injuries, instigating and assisting the commission of suicide, enslaving, trafficking and trade in slaves, abduction, violation of sexual freedom, private violence, housebreaking, slander, libel, public defamation of religion, arbitrary arrest and failure to release from jail, and arbitrary treatment of detainees.

Crime Statistics

According to European Committee on Crime Problems, in 2002 the most serious crimes in San Marino were fraud (36 cases), counterfeiting (11 cases), possession of drugs (12 cases), smuggling (1 case), extortion (3 cases), and bankruptcy (1 case). The committee also reported that San Marino has not experienced drugs or arms trafficking, kidnapping, robbery, or bag snatching for 2003.

On October 18, 2007, the media reported that 60 cases of violence against women occurred in the first eight months of the year, according to the U.S. Department of State, Bureau of Democracy, Human Rights, and Labor. According to the Central Bank Services, the headquarters of the Financial Intelligence Unit, for 2006 there were 55 reports received of money laundering, the increase attributed to heightened awareness of money laundering. The Financial Intelligence Unit investigated 1 money laundering, 1 robbery, 9 thefts, and 2 drug-related crimes for the first half of 2009. The Gendarmerie between January 1, 2008 and July 31, 2009, arrested 11 people for theft, 2 for robbery, and none for narcotic-related offenses.

According to the International Labour Standards Department for 2004, there were no problems with human trafficking and in 2006, no cases of child labor. San Marino's Minors' Service, formed in 1977, is responsible for formal child protective systems; it reports that cases of abuse and neglect are rare, and most of its funds are directed toward disabled minors.

Money Laundering and Tax Evasion

The biggest challenge to the San Marino government is money laundering, mainly due to the open borders with Italy and the lax banking regulations, banking secrecy, and a developed financial system that is very attractive to the business sector.

Offshore crackdown of institutes that conduct tax dodging initially began with the international fight against organized crime. The crackdown especially affected the local market when the largest bank in San Marino, *Cassa di Risparmio Della Repubblica di San Marino* (CRSM), lost its top five executives when they were arrested for money laundering by Italian prosecutors. CRSM's consumer finance group Delta was placed under bankruptcy proceedings by the Italians, which placed more tension on the banking system of San Marino consisting of 12 banks and 55 financial groups. San Marino responded by creating the Financial Intelligence Unit in 2008; this specialized unit is devoted to the challenges raised by money laundering.

San Marino's policy of offering tax clients anonymity and secrecy is approaching its end. With pressures mounting from the European Union and Italian government, the San Marino government has taken steps to alleviate money laundering problems, including the ratification of the 1990 Council of Europe Convention on Laundering, Search, Seizure and Confiscation of Proceeds from Crime, and the adoption of corresponding domestic legislation in the area of criminal procedural law. In 2002 the country signed a treaty with the Organization for Economic Cooperation and Development (OECD) in an effort to provide greater transparency in banking and taxation. This treaty removed San Marino from the OECD's blacklist of tax havens and placed the country on the grey list. The grey list consists of countries who have pledged to comply with the rules on sharing tax information but have not yet taken action. Recently, the OECD has established the Global Forum on Transparency and Exchange of Information for Tax Purposes. The global forum accomplishes its mission through in-depth monitoring and peer review, and San Marino is listed as a participating member country.

Finding of Guilt

The Declaration of Citizens' Rights and of the Fundamental Principles of the San Marinese Legal Order effective on July 8, 1974, under Law No. 59 provides the rights of all citizens including accused persons. The declaration prohibits arbitrary arrest and detention. Communication to relatives is compulsory for any police stop or arrest and if the accused is a minor, this is immediate. Any arrested or detained person is entitled to defend himself or herself during the entire proceedings. An accused is afforded an advocate of his or her choice, allowed private communications with the advocate, and is accompanied by the advocate during all interrogations. The judicial system provides an advocate free of charge for an accused that requires legal assistance. Innocence is presumed until convicted. Trials are public and with the exception of the Council of Twelve, all courts function with a single judge making decisions.

If the offense involves violence, including domestic violence, the victim is afforded confidentiality and privacy including protection for the victim's children. The guardianship judge assigns a minor representative to all juvenile cases involving maltreatment from the parent, guardian, relative, or parties with significant relationship to the family to protect the minor's rights. The declaration guarantees a fair, speedy, and cost-effective trial including an independent judiciary. The accused is allowed to conduct his or her own investigation through access to all government-held evidence and question witnesses. Trials are public and presided by a single judge with no jury trial.

Regulations require police officers to record the stop and/or arrest. All interested parties, including the advocate, can freely access this report. The investigation and prosecution are assigned to the prosecutor, while the judge supervises the entire investigation to guarantee certainty of the law and protection for the defense.

Prosecution and Investigation

San Marino's legal system is basically inquisitorial in nature and judicial authority is responsible for inquiring about criminal activities by way of an investigation to uncover the truth. Any person whose rights have been violated can go to the criminal court to prosecute the offender. Judicial authority is obligated to provide an investigation into criminal activity in the absence of a complaint in instances where a *notitia criminis* is received. A *notitia criminis* is a notice conveyed to a judicial authority that a crime has allegedly transpired. The law commissioner is responsible for criminal investigations and has a duty to begin a diligent search upon receipt of a *notitia criminis*. The accused may be interrogated as soon as possible and retains the right to have an advocate of his or her choosing or a public defender present during the questioning.

After all evidence is collected the investigating judge determines if there is an adequate amount of evidence for an arraignment. If there is not sufficient evidence then the case is dismissed after a second opinion from the *procuratore del fisco*. With sufficient evidence the investigating judge shall issue a summons describing the nature and cause of the charge. At this time the defendant will be informed of his or her right to counsel. The defendant then has 30 days from notification of the summons to appear in court. The summons issued by the investigating judge terminates the inquiry stage. The defendant is then given a full hearing, which is public and oral. The judgment shall be delivered by a law commissioner different from the one responsible for the initial inquiry.

Deprivations of Liberty

Deprivations of liberty prior to conviction include preventative detention in prison or a treatment facility, house arrest, the obligation to stay on the territory of the republic or part of it, and the prohibition to expatriate. The deprivation of personal liberty prior to a final judgment is regarded as an extraordinary measure in San Marino. This measure may be adopted only under special circumstances. A judge will order a deprivation of liberty only if it is determined that the defendant may harm the community or there is a risk of withholding evidence of the defendant's escape. The judge bases the decision by evaluating the regulatory measures that least affect the accused and his or her family, provided it proves to be effective. Preventative detention can also be ordered in cases where an individual is accused of a crime punishable by first-degree or second-degree imprisonment.

Courts

There are at least four levels of courts within San Marino. At the bottom of the hierarchy are the conciliatory judges. The conciliatory judges handle only civil cases that do not exceed €12,000 (US$15,000). Noncriminal cases can go to the conciliatory judge or a law commissioner depending on the amount of money in controversy. Appeals from the conciliatory judges go to a law commissioner and can further advance to a civil appeals judge. The Council of Twelve sits at the top of the legal institution and may choose between the two lower court opinions. The final court of review is the College of Guarantors, appointed from the members of the Great and General Council, each serving four-year terms. The College of Guarantors was institutionalized in 2002 under Law No. 36, replacing the original Council of Twelve, which was composed of 12 judges. The college is composed of 6 judges and decides on constitutional rules and procedures, considers conflicts of competency, determines if a referendum is admissible by law, and intervenes with the Regents as needed.

In criminal matters, a case can be decided either by a law commissioner or by a criminal appeals judge. The criminal appeals judge handles all cases where a prison sentence of more than three years is possible. An appeal from a law commissioner to a criminal appeals judge is possible; however, there is no appeal available for a sentence imposed by a criminal appeals judge. The Great and General Council deal with constitutional matters. There is a separate judicial hierarchy that deals with administrative matters. There is a juvenile court in San Marino, known as the *tribunal dei minori*.

Judges

Up until 2004, the judicial system required judges to be noncitizens for the lower courts to assure impartiality due to the size of the population. Reform legislation in 2004 reversed that decision; however, most judges are generally Italian citizens and serve under contract through the government. Justices of the peace are the only judgeships that have ever been solely open to San Marino citizens since the justice system formed. All judges are appointed by two-thirds majority ruling from the Great and General Council. Judges of appeal and the judge of administrative appeal are typically chosen from among magistrates, tenured professors of law, or attorneys with at least 15 years' experience in the practice of law. Law commissioners and administrators who have served for at least 10 years may also be appointed. Conciliating judges, who can be San Marino citizens, are selected from the attorneys having experience of at least 5 years, or from clerks having served for at least 2 years.

Punishment

Types of Punishment

Punishment in San Marino takes the following forms, according to the Criminal Code, from most severe to least:

- Imprisonment not to exceed 35 years, ranging from 1st degree (3 months–6 months) to 8th degree (25 years) punishments.
- Disqualification from public offices, political rights, or a profession/trade not to exceed 5 years.
- House arrest is permitted depending on special circumstances, including family or work needs and required for women who are pregnant, breastfeeding, or responsible for the care of children under 3 years old, physically or mentally handicapped persons, or semi-invalid or invalid persons more than 65 years of age.
- Fines between €103.81 (US$130) to a maximum of €1,549.37 (US$1,947).
- Fine by day depending on the judge's discretion.
- Reprimand in a public hearing.

Probation is under the discretion of the judge for a two- or three-year imprisonment sentence. The criminal is placed in either house arrest or under the supervision of Social Services. Drug or alcohol addicts are permitted to serve a portion of their sentence in rehabilitative probation under the supervision of Social Services or in a public institute for treatment and assistance.

Penalties are to be humane and rehabilitative, considered only through the discretion of the court. A pardon or mercy application can be submitted to the Great and General Council. A pardon completely or partially terminates the remaining portion of the punishment or transfers the punishment to another form. Mercy allows the convict to receive a reprieve from his or her punishment. Typically, juveniles are assigned probation or to the care of the Minors' Service rather than minor detentions.

Sentences are provided by the Criminal Code, which prohibits life imprisonment and restricts the maximum sentence of imprisonment to 35 years. The following are the penalties set by the Criminal Code for major crimes.

The typical punishment for murder is 20–25 years' imprisonment, a seventh- or eighth-degree punishment. Other penalties can change the imprisonment based on aggravating and mitigating circumstances. Rape, including spousal rape, is punished by 2 to 6 years' imprisonment, second- or third-degree punishments. If the circumstance is aggravating, the punishment is increased to 4 to 10 years. Theft is typically punished based on the weight of the stolen goods; under 25 pounds, 1–3 months' imprisonment; between 25–250 pounds, 3 months–1 year; and more than 250 pounds, 1–3 years.

According to Law No. 139, enacted in 1997, drug offenses are entitled to a second-degree imprisonment, especially if the accused produces narcotics or is in possession of drugs. If the accused has large quantities of the drugs, has the sole intention of profit, or a youth is involved, the punishment increases by one to three degrees. The death penalty was abolished in 1848 for ordinary crimes and completely in 1865. The last recorded execution in San Marino was in 1468.

Prison

The secretary of state for justice is responsible for the only prison, San Marino Prison, which has an official capacity of 12 and includes one visiting room. The San Marino Prison meets all international standards, including separate cells for males, females, and juveniles. An agreement with Italy allows San Marino prisoners to serve their sentences in Italy, where most of the criminals serve.

According to the *ICPS World Prison Brief* as of January 2007, the San Marino Prison had one prisoner, including pretrial detainees, and no female, juvenile, foreign, or political prisoners and an 8.3 percent official occupancy level. By agreement with the Italian government, institutions in Italy are used to hold most persons imprisoned by San Marino. An imposed prison sentence can be served in the prison of San Marino, though the Criminal Code provides for the execution of a prison sentence of more than six months in a foreign prison on the basis of international conventions.

A convicted person serving a term of imprisonment for a maximum of two or three years who also suffers from drug or alcohol addiction may request to undergo a rehabilitation program. The person would then be placed on probation and under the supervision of social services to start an agreed-upon treatment program. A judge may also authorize the leave of a convicted person from the place of detention during the day for an amount of time necessary to perform a working activity essential for his or her personal and family maintenance.

The Criminal Code prohibits forced labor. Inmates are allowed regular exercise and visits. All measures involving inmates, including restraints, are only allowed through written permission from the council. San Marino has bilateral extradition treaties with the United States, Italy, France, Belgium, the Netherlands, and the United Kingdom. Any other countries requesting extraditions are granted solely on necessary political authority. In general, San Marino citizens are prohibited from extradition except with countries connected by the bilateral extradition treaties. According to the *Third Compliance Report for MONEYVAL* between January 1, 2009, and August 15, 2009, two extraditions were granted for the Italian government for money laundering and human trafficking.

Nazmia E. Alqadi and Jessica Gentile

Further Reading

Astuti, Guido. (1987). "San Marino." In *International Encyclopedia of Comparative Law.* Vol. 1, edited by Viktor Knapp, pp. S13-S15. Dordrecht, the Netherlands: Martinus Nijhoff.

Duursma, Jorri. (1996). *Fragmentation and the International Relations of Micro-States: Self-Determination and Statehood.* Cambridge: Cambridge University Press.

Giannini, Torquato C., and Menetto Bonelli. (1900). *Raccolta delle leggi e descreti della Republica di San Marino* [Collection of Laws and Decrees of the Republic of San Marino]. San Marino: Città Di Castello S. Lapi Tipografo.

San Marino official Web site: http://www.sanmarinosite.com.

Scotland. *See* United Kingdom/Scotland

Serbia

Legal System: Civil
Murder: Medium
Burglary: Medium
Corruption: Medium
Human Trafficking: Medium
Prison Rate: Medium
Death Penalty: No
Corporal Punishment: No

Background

Serbian current criminal legislation is compatible with democratization and in compliance with international standards. Important legislative changes have occurred over the years, especially in the 1990s. Several political crimes were decriminalized in 1990; the death penalty was abolished in 1993, as well as the prohibition of public speech. In addition, important legal changes were initiated after the collapse of Milosevic's regime in 2000, and particularly with the adoption of a new Criminal Code and other laws related to prosecution in 2005.

In 2005, the Serbian criminal legislation was reformed in compliance with European criminal laws and traditions, but also to gather criminal law provisions scattered in different acts. The new modern

Criminal Code of the Republic of Serbia entered into force on January 1, 2006. As for procedural provisions, the Serbian Criminal Code of Procedure of 2001 has been amended several times over the years until a new Criminal Code of Procedure was adopted in 2005. However, the so-called *new* Code has never been applied, and the latest amendments to the Criminal Code of Procedure adopted on August 31, 2009, nullified it definitely.

Recent reforms of criminal legislation are certainly placing Serbia more in line with contemporary civilized democratic countries. Nevertheless, one should note that, throughout history, the Serbian criminal legislation almost always used criminal and other relevant codes of Western European countries as a model (Austrian, German, French, and Swiss codes, in particular). Due to that, it is disputable whether we can speak of just the current criminal justice system as a democratic and modern one, or we may assume that it was rather "contemporary and modern" throughout its development.

The Serbian legal system shares the characteristics of the European (Continental) model. It is based exclusively on written laws (the core texts are the Criminal Code and the Criminal Procedure Code). Criminal court decisions (i.e., the outcome of a particular case) are not considered a source of law.

The criminal procedural system is mixed; a combination of accusatorial and inquisitorial principles regulate the position of the main participants in the criminal justice process. The main accusatorial characteristic of the proceedings is the complete seclusion of the procedural functions and subjects, which is the guarantee of fair trial. Inquisitorial elements are mostly present at the investigation stage (e.g., limited publicity, investigation that can be undertaken before the official start of criminal proceeding). A major inquisitorial characteristic of the Serbian proceedings relates to the obligation for the court to establish all facts necessary to the rendering of a truthfully and completely lawful decision. Thus, relevant facts can be investigated by court *ex officio,* that is apart from the initiative of the party litigants.

The number of criminal offenses included in the Criminal Code is constantly increasing and the Serbian criminal justice system is still rather repressive. A constant strengthening of criminal protection in the normative field can be an obstacle for an efficient and effective work of the judiciary, which is facing a lack of both human and technical resources. However, during recent years some changes toward implementing elements of restorative justice into the criminal justice system are also visible, suggesting that recent reforms are taking a progressive direction.

Police

The Serbian police are a service organized within the Ministry of Interior and independent from the military or other relevant institutions. The Police Directorate, a division of the Ministry of Interior, is responsible for the organization of police work. The Police Directorate is organized at a state level and comprises several departments, for example, a Department of Criminal Investigation, a Security Department, a Border Police Department, a Department of Information Technology, a Special Anti-Terrorist Division, and the Gendarmerie. Police units are organized on a territorial basis, for either one or more municipalities, and/or on the city level. There is a strong hierarchy between police units and officers from different levels. According to the Law on the Police (2005), the Serbian police forces are to protect the life, rights, and freedom of citizens; to prevent, discover, and investigate criminal offenses; and to apprehend offenders. The police are bound to protect public order and provide assistance whenever needed.

In 2007, the Serbian police took over the protection of the state border from the military, which resulted in a demilitarization of the Serbian borders after 94 years of military control. The police now control some 2,100 kilometers (1,304 miles) of borders that separate Serbia from Bosnia and Herzegovina, Croatia, Romania, Hungary, Bulgaria, and Macedonia. Unfortunately, no data on the number of officers working in the different police structures are available.

Crime

Classification of Crimes

According to the Serbian legislation, illicit acts can be divided into three groups: criminal offenses, economic violations, and misdemeanors. The term "criminal offense" is defined in the 2005 Criminal Code as comprising the following elements: the prescription of a certain behavior by the law as a criminal offense, an act that is against the law, and the dimension of guilt. The first two elements are objective and formal components of the law, while the last one is subjective. In comparison to previous legislations, the definition of a criminal offense in the 2005 Criminal Code does not include the notion of social danger of a certain behavior anymore. Most criminal offenses are defined in the Criminal Code, although they might be foreseen in some other laws regulating certain specific fields.

The Serbian criminal legislation is characterized by the constant increase of the number of behaviors that are considered criminal offenses by either the Criminal Code or other laws. In the current Criminal Code, there are more than 1,000 different criminal offenses proscribed either in their basic or qualified forms. Nevertheless, in the Serbian criminal jurisdiction, there is no formal or terminology distinction between serious and less serious crimes. In practice, a crime is considered more or less serious depending on the prescribed sentence, which then determines the court jurisdiction or a form of prosecution. Beside some exceptions, municipal prosecution offices and courts will be authorized to prosecute criminal offenses punishable with a fine or a custodial sentence of less than 10 years. Other cases are settled by courts of higher jurisdiction. On the other hand, most criminal offenses are prosecuted *ex officio* by the public prosecutor. However, there are some explicitly determined criminal offenses for which the prosecution can be undertaken by a private prosecutor (i.e., the injured party or another authorized person). Finally, for some also explicitly determined criminal offenses, the injured party's consent to prosecution is a condition to the undertaking of a prosecution by a public prosecutor.

Age of Criminal Responsibility

The age of criminal responsibility set forth in the Serbian criminal justice system is 14, whereas juveniles from 14 to 18 years old are considered minors. Minors are divided into two groups: juniors and seniors. The latter distinction relates to the types of sanctions that can be imposed. Namely, educative measures are the only sanctions that can be pronounced against junior juvenile offenders, while senior juvenile offenders can be sentenced to both educative measures and juvenile imprisonment.

Crime Statistics

According to the latest available data of the Serbian Statistical Office, in 2005, 112 persons (103 adults and 9 minors) were convicted for murder, 61 (57 adults and 4 minors) for rape, 683 (561 adults and 122 minors) for robbery, and 1,850 (1,790 adults and 60 minors) for unauthorized production, possession, and sale of narcotics.

While urban areas tend to have higher crime rates, the most typical offenses in both rural and urban areas are property offenses—mainly thefts. Burglaries and robberies are more common in urban areas, as well as economic crime and crime against public order and legal transactions. Finally, arsons are the typical rural crimes.

Trafficking in Persons

At the end of the 20th century, trafficking in persons became a growing problem in southeastern Europe, equally affecting countries of origin, transit, and destination. During the past two decades, trafficking in human beings, primarily in women and children, developed in two main directions. At the beginning of the 1990s, due to political factors, there was an opening of Eastern and Central European borders that translated into waves of trafficked victims entering the West. At the same time, human trafficking benefited from restrictive immigration policies of Western countries that prevented legal immigration. Consequently, trafficking markets changed and moved from Asia to Central, Eastern, and southeastern Europe. On the other hand, the Balkans, once predominantly a transit zone, increasingly became a destination for numerous victims of trafficking.

The geographical position of Serbia, as a part of the Balkans, makes it an important route for various forms of illegal trafficking, including human trafficking. Main trafficking routes go from East to West, positioning Serbia as mostly a transit country and a country of temporary destination. However, with a worsening of the economic situation, Serbia became a country of origin for either transnational or internal trafficking as well. The first survey on the prevalence, structure, and characteristics of trafficking in human beings, conducted in 2003 by the Victimology Society of Serbia, identified 1,134 victims of trafficking (940 women, 100 men, and 94 children) on the territory of Serbia during 2002 and the first six months of 2003. Consequently, social visibility and social response to human trafficking in Serbia has improved over recent years.

Trafficking in human beings was included in the Criminal Code as a separate criminal offense in 2003. According to data of the Serbian Statistics Office, in 2003, there were 10 criminal reports of human trafficking, yet no indictment nor conviction. Comparatively, in 2006, 50 criminal reports were filed; there were 18 indictments and 13 convictions. Data on victims of human trafficking are not available in the Statistics Office but can be gathered from other sources. The Ministry of Interior identified 35 victims of human trafficking in 2004, 26 in 2005, 56 in 2006, 96 in 2007, and 55 in 2008. Most of these victims were females, although in 2007 two-thirds of the victims were males. The Agency for Coordination of Protection of Victims of Human Trafficking identified 38 victims of human trafficking in 2004, 53 in 2005, 62 in 2006, 60 in 2007, and 55 in 2008. Over 90 percent of the victims identified by the latter institution were adult women or girls. However, it is estimated that the number of victims is 10 times higher than the number of officially recognized victims.

Drug Offenses

The Serbian Criminal Code foresees two drug-related criminal offenses: the unauthorized production, possession, or trafficking in narcotics and the enabling of drug use (inducing and aiding consumption of narcotics). Possession of narcotics for personal use is not prosecuted to avoid punishing actual drug addiction.

Finding of Guilt

The right to defense is the basic right of the defendant that generates all of the other rights. The right to defense includes, for example, the right to be heard in the presence of the chosen defense counsel, the right not to be interfered/impeded in communication with a defense counsel, the right to be informed of criminal charges at the first interrogation, and the right to refuse to answer questions, including those related to identification.

The right to fair trial is a complex concept encompassing several principles and rights envisaged by the Constitution, the Criminal Procedure Code, and other acts. It includes, among others, the principle of publicity, the presumption of innocence, the principle not to be tried twice for the same crime, the principle no crime without law, the principle of due process, the right to appeal, and the right to compensation in case of wrongful conviction. The right to a trial by jury, as known in common law systems, does not exist as such in the Serbian criminal legislation. However, the principle is that, in criminal proceedings, the courts of law adjudicate a council. Thus, councils in first instance courts are composed of two judges and three lay judges to decide on sanctions exceeding 15 years of imprisonment, and one judge and two lay judges in less serious cases.

A single judge adjudicates in the first instance court when special provisions on summary proceedings are applicable. This is the case for criminal offenses punishable by a fine or custodial sentence not exceeding three years and, exceptionally, upon request of an authorized prosecutor and with the defendant's explicit consent. Consequently, the judge may issue a penal order event without holding a trial. The defendant can object to the order, thus forcing the judge to schedule a trial.

A Serbian police officer stands guard in front of the Special Court in Belgrade, October 2, 2007, during reading of the verdicts to three suspects in Japan's biggest ever jewelry heist after they were convicted in their native Serbia and sentenced to up to seven years in prison. (AP Photo/Srdjan Ilic)

The defendant has the right to defend himself or herself or to be assisted by a defense counsel member of the Bar Association of Serbia. During the interrogation, the defendant has the right to be assisted by a defense counsel; the defendant shall be informed of this right. If the defendant does not retain a defense counsel by himself or herself, the court shall appoint a defense counsel. The defendant must be offered adequate time and facilities to prepare the defense.

Criminal offenses subject to official prosecution are prosecuted by the public prosecutor and cases subject to a private claim are prosecuted by a private prosecutor. If the public prosecutor determines that there is no ground for prosecution, the injured party may act as a subsidiary prosecutor according to the provisions of the Criminal Procedure Code.

The public prosecutor is bound to institute the prosecution when there is a reasonable suspicion that a certain person has committed a criminal offense subject to official prosecution. The public prosecutor shall be competent to do the following:

- Conduct a preinvestigation procedure.
- Request that an investigation be carried out and direct a pretrial procedure.
- Prefer an indictment before the court having jurisdiction.

- File an appeal against a decision of the court of first instance or contest final decisions by an extraordinary legal remedy.
- Perform any other functions defined by the code.

Investigation

Requests for investigations are sent to the investigating judge who shall examine the request and render a ruling whenever agreeing with the request. The ruling shall be delivered to the state prosecutor, the defendant, and the defense counsel. If clarification is needed or if a preliminary hearing seems appropriate, the investigating judge may summon the state prosecutor and the suspect before the court. Preliminary hearings are conducted orally. The state prosecutor can use this opportunity to alter or complete his or her request; he or she may also suggest the request be conducted upon an indictment without investigation.

Party litigants may appeal against the ruling of the investigating judge. In such cases, the judge shall refer to the council without further delay. The appeal does not stay the execution of the ruling. If the investigating judge does not agree with the state prosecutor's request for investigation, he or she shall, upon questioning of the suspect, request the council to make a disposition. The council shall dismiss the request for investigation if there are circumstances that temporarily prevent the prosecution and shall reject the request for investigation if there is no sufficient evidence. The defendant, the state prosecutor, and the injured party may appeal against the ruling of the council, which does not stay its execution.

Most criminal cases in Serbian jurisdiction are closed after trial. According to the latest available official statistics, in 2005, 43.4 percent of criminal reports filed against an adult were prosecuted, while the largest part resulted in a court trial. The same year, offenders were pronounced guilty in 77.1 percent of the cases brought to court.

Alternatives to Trial

In 2002, the Criminal Code of Procedure introduced the principle of opportunity in the criminal prosecution of adult offenders. The public prosecutor may decide to delay prosecution in certain cases. Such possibility exists only for criminal offenses subject to a fine or a custodial sentence not exceeding three years, and just exceptionally for the criminal offenses for which a custodial sentence of more than three and less than five years could be imposed. The defendant must, however, agree to fulfill one of the following conditions set by the law:

- To remove harmful consequences resulting from the criminal offense.
- To pay a financial compensation to a humanitarian organization, fund, or a public institution.
- To carry out community or humanitarian work.
- To fulfill the obligations of paying alimony.
- To treat an alcohol or drug addiction problem.
- To undertake a psychosocial therapy.
- To fulfill the duty set forth by the irrevocable judgment.
- To get a driver's license, go for additional driving lessons, or to finish other appropriate course.

Imposing conditions such as a donation to a humanitarian organization or a public institution, or ordering community work, are dependent on the consent of the victim. The time frame for carrying out imposed conditions cannot exceed six months. If the defendant fulfils the commitment within the set time period, the public prosecutor will drop criminal charges. The possibility of lifting criminal charges is foreseen even in the case when the defendant, truly remorseful, has prevented the damage from occurring or has already fully compensated for the damage, and the public prosecutor has in accordance with the circumstances evaluated that setting a criminal sanction would not be just. However, one should note that the principle of opportunity is very rarely applied in practice, as public prosecutors are not interested in the application of these regulations. They consider these too complicated and, above all, are afraid that not pressing charges might be considered corruption.

The juvenile justice system also provides alternatives to criminal procedure: the principle of opportunity in prosecuting juvenile offenders, and educative (diversion) orders. In case of criminal offenses subject to a fine or a custodial sentence not exceeding 5 years, the prosecutor can decide not to press charges if considering it not suitable. To assess the situation, the prosecutor can ask the juvenile's parents or guardians, other persons or institutions, particularly social welfare services, to provide the necessary information. If the juvenile's personal conditions need to be examined, he or she may be placed in an institution for children and youths or in another educative institution for a maximum of 30 days.

Educative (diversion) orders are also an alternative to criminal procedure. Educative orders are foreseen as special measures. The juvenile public prosecutor or the juvenile judge may impose one or more educative orders to a juvenile who committed a crime subject to a fine or a custodial sentence not exceeding five years. Whether this measure will ever be applied depends, among other things, on whether the juvenile admitted to a criminal offense and on the person's regard toward the criminal offense and the injured party. The basic purpose of these orders is not to bring criminal charges against a juvenile or its suspension, but they aim at improving the development of the juvenile and strengthening his or her personal responsibility. The legislator has foreseen the following diversion orders: settlement with the injured party (i.e., financial compensation of damage), apologies, mandatory attendance of classes, voluntary humanitarian or community work (e.g., welfare, local or environmental), mandatory alcohol or drug treatment program, or individual/group counseling. Diversion orders can last up to six months; during that time, orders can be replaced by another measure or suspended.

Pretrial Detention

In the Serbian criminal justice system, incarceration before or awaiting trial is possible. Pretrial detention is regulated by the Criminal Code of Procedure and can be used only as a last resort. Therefore, pretrial detention is used in two different types of situation: first, when the criminal offense is really serious, second, to guarantee undisturbed criminal proceedings.

The investigating judge can pronounce pretrial detention for a period no longer than one month after the arrest. The prolongation of the incarceration is dependent upon a formal decision of the council and limited to a period of two months. Finally, the Supreme Court Council can extend the incarceration for three additional months for cases subject to a custodial sentence of at least five years.

Judiciary

The latest official data from the Statistics Office of the Republic, in 2005, reports that there were 138 municipal courts, 30 district courts, and one Supreme Court in Serbia. There were 2,698 judges, including both criminal and civil suit judges, and 7,374 judge assessors. Besides, there were 17 economic courts where worked 268 judges and 780 judge assessors. However, there are no precise data on the number of criminal court judges. In practice, judges often change affiliation; so that civil judges become criminal judges and inversely.

According to the Law on Judges (2002), any Serbian citizen can become a judge as long as he or she fulfills the following criteria: meets the conditions to work within a state agency, has obtained a law degree, has passed the judiciary exam, and is capable to accomplish the duties of judge. In addition, a certain work experience is necessary as well: after the judicial exam, the candidate will need 2 years of experience in legal affairs to be appointed at a municipal court; 4 years to be appointed at an economic court; 6 years to be appointed at a district court; 8 years at the Court of Appeal, Higher Economic Court, or the Administrative Court; and 12 years to be appointed at the Supreme Court of Serbia.

At the prosecution stage, in 2005, there were 109 municipal public prosecutor's offices, 30 district offices, and 1 republic office. Altogether, 767 public prosecutors and deputies were working during that year.

Juveniles

The juvenile justice system in Serbia is regulated by a separate code, the Law on Juvenile Offenders and the Criminal Protection of Juveniles, which entered into force in 2006. Although juvenile offenders have always been treated differently from adults, with the adoption of that law, juvenile justice was for the first time regulated as a completely separate system. The legal text contains provisions on both the position of juvenile offenders in the criminal procedure and the position of juveniles injured by a set of explicitly defined criminal offenses.

The law on juveniles envisages diversion orders and criminal sanctions for juveniles, including educational measures and juvenile prison. In cases involving juvenile offenders, the criminal procedure at first instance is run by either a juvenile court judge or a council, but proceedings are always conducted in a district court. When the hearing is run by a council, it is composed of one juvenile court judge and two lay judges of different sexes. The jurisdiction of the Supreme Court is set as second instance; the proceedings are conducted by a council consisting of three professional judges.

A criminal procedure against a juvenile may only be initiated by a juvenile prosecutor. It cannot be initiated upon the sole request of an injured party, although in some cases the consent of the injured party is required. All persons involved in juvenile criminal justice are specifically trained. Police officers, lawyers, prosecutors, investigating judges, and court judges have attended training on children's rights, juvenile delinquency, and issues related to the protection of juveniles.

As mentioned previously, a section of the Law on Juvenile Offenders and the Criminal Protection of Juveniles is devoted to the protection of juvenile victims. Legal provisions are applicable for a list of criminal offenses explicitly defined in the law (including rape and other forms of sexual offenses, domestic violence, human trafficking, trafficking for the purpose of adoption, murder, kidnapping, child abuse and neglect, incest, burglary, arson, and enabling the use of narcotics). In these cases, victimized juveniles must have a legal representative from the very beginning of the procedure (i.e., the first time a suspect is questioned).

The law additionally envisages special rules to be applied for the questioning of a juvenile offender to avoid any negative impact on the juvenile's personality and development. These rules and guidelines include the following: questionings of juvenile offenders are conducted in presence of an expert; juvenile offenders cannot be questioned more than twice; questionings are recorded and can later be used in courts; and questionings conducted outside the courtroom (e.g., parents' house, institution) are authorized.

Punishment

Types of Punishment

Criminal sanctions foreseen in the Criminal Code include punishments, warning measures (i.e., suspended sentence and judicial admonition), and security measures. Educational measures and juvenile custodial sentences are envisaged in the Law on Juvenile Offenders and the Criminal Protection of Juveniles.

According to available data of the Serbian Statistics Office (for the period 2002–2006), the most typical form of punishment is imprisonment, and short-term sentences (i.e., less than six months) are the most frequent custodial sentences. However, the sentences are suspended most of the time (51.9% of all pronounced sentences in 2006).

Custodial sentences range from 30 days to 20 years. A convict can be released on parole at the halfway point of the sentence if one can reasonably expect that he or she will behave well and especially that he or she will not reoffend.

According to conviction data, in 2005, the following punishments can be considered typical. The typical punishment for murder was imprisonment, mostly for a period of 5 to 10 years. Rape offenders were usually sentenced to 1 or 2 years of imprisonment. Typical punishments for the perpetration of aggravated theft or robbery were custodial sentences, ranging from 6 to 12 months for aggravated theft and from 1 to 2 years for robbery. The perpetration of drug offenses was most of the time accompanied by a prison sentence ranging from 6 to 12 months.

Suspension can be pronounced for any custodial sentence not exceeding two years. Suspended sentences are pronounced by the court and the sentence is not carried out unless the convict commits a new criminal offense over the period of probation decided by the court. The probation period ranges from one to five years.

Prison

Data provided by the Ministry of Justice indicate that 9,068 persons (i.e., 8,768 males and 300 females) were detained in Serbian penal institutions at the end of August 2008. Among the male adults, 6,199 convicted offenders were serving a sentence, 2,148 were held in pretrial detention, 183 were held in misdemeanor proceedings, and the remainder are unclassified. Similarly, the female detainees were mostly convicted offenders, 211 were females serving a sentence, and 89 were held in pretrial detention. In addition, 219 juveniles were held in a juvenile correctional facility, and 19 were held in pretrial detention.

Prisons in Serbia consist of 9 penal-correctional facilities, among which there is 1 facility for female offenders and 1 correctional facility for juvenile offenders. Beside these, the Republic of Serbia also counts a special prison hospital and 17 district prisons. The largest Serbian prison is the penal-correctional facility of Požarevac-Zabela, an institution for male adult offenders that can accommodate up to 2,400 convicts.

Rights of convicted offenders are numerous. For example, convicted offenders have, as a rule, the right to work. Unfortunately, work and occupation opportunities for convicted offenders in Serbian prisons have decreased drastically in recent years, resulting in an increase of the problems associated with the issue of spare time in prison. A convict who behaves particularly well, or makes particular effort at work, should be awarded special privileges, inside or outside the institution by the governor of the penal institution. Convicts also have the right to primary and secondary education, and penal institutions may also organize additional forms of education.

Convicted offenders have the right to be visited by their spouse, children, parents, or any other relative. Obviously, they have the right to see a defense attorney or legal counsel; such visits may be supervised only visually, discussions are private. Any foreign citizen detained in a Serbian correctional facility has, under conditions of reciprocity, the right to be visited by a diplomatic-consular representative of his or her own country. The governor of the penal institution may allow a convict to be visited by other persons as well.

Sanja Copic, Biljana Simeunovic-Patic, and Sladjana Jovanovic

Further Reading

Grubac, Momcilo. (2006). *Krivicno procesno pravo* [Criminal Procedure Law]. Beograd: Pravni fakultet Univerziteta Union i Sluzbeni glasnik.

Ignjatovic, Djordje, ed. (2007). *Stanje kriminaliteta u Srbiji i pravna sredstva reagovanja, Deo I, II i III* [Crime in Serbia and Legal Means of Reaction, Parts I–III]. Beograd: Pravni fakultet Univerziteta u Beogradu.

Mrvic-Petrovic, Natasa. (2006). *Krivicno pravo* [Criminal Law]. Beograd: Pravni fakultet Univerziteta Union i Sluzbeni glasnik.

Nikolic-Ristanovic, Vesna, Sanja Copic, Sanja Milivojevic, Biljana Simeunovic-Patic, and Biljana Mihic. (2004). *Trafficking in People in Serbia*. Belgrade: Organization for Security and Co-operation in Europe.

Sokovic, Snezana. (2008). *Izvrsenje krivicnih sankcija* [Execution of Penal Sanctions]. Kragujevac: Pravni fakultet Univerziteta u Kragujevcu and JP Sluzbeni glasnik.

Shetland

Legal System: Civil/Common
Prison Rate: Medium
Death Penalty: No

Background

Shetland is an archipelago in Scotland that is 80 kilometers (50 miles) north of the Orkney Islands. It divides the Atlantic Ocean on its west shore and the North Sea on its east shore. Shetland's territory stretches 1,247 square kilometers (551 square miles) over more than 100 islands. Archaeological sites such as at Jarlshof, Mousa, and Clickhimin are rich in prehistoric and Scandinavian relics. The dialect and names of places reflect a strong Norse influence.

The 2007 mid-year estimates from General Register Office for Scotland estimated the population at 21,950–11,037 males and 10,913 females. The most populous five-year age group is 40- to 44-year-olds at 1,726. Shetland has suffered from volatile population levels in the last several decades, a fact that is attributed to changes in oil-related employment off the North Sea.

The population plummeted for several decades before plateauing under 17,000 in the mid-1960s. Demand for oil workers caused a 31 percent spike in population from 1971 to 1981. Oil construction halted in the early 1980s, causing a migration and overall waning population. The population stabilized during the mid-1980s to the early 1990s. Mainland is the most populous of the 16 inhabited islands and had a population of 17,575 according to the 2001 Census.

Shetland is one of Scotland's 32 unitary authorities, which are also referred to as local councils. Located in Mainland, the burg of Lerwick is a hub for oil extraction activities and serves as Shetland's capital. Administrative functions for the Shetland Local Council are executed from Lerwick. It has a population of 6,830. The Shetland Council area is divided into seven wards that are represented by 22 elected members. Each ward has 3 elected members, except for Ward 7, Lerwick South, which has 4 elected members. The chief executive of Shetland is Morgan Goodlad.

The major sources of employment in Shetland include oil, agriculture, fishing, and knitwear. Efforts to extract oil from the North Sea rely on pipelines that cross the Brent and Ninian fields and extend to the largest terminal of its type in the continent, which is at Sullom Voe. Much of the farming involves crofting and is aided by large herds of sheep. Fair Isle and Unst have traditionally been involved with handknitting. Mechanization of these services to produce garment items is more common today, however. Fish-processing factories are also a major source of employment.

Legal System

Shetland uses the Scottish legal system, which has major differences from English common law in terms of the law, judiciary, and courts. All prosecution in Scotland is directed by the lord advocate, who is responsible for prosecutions in the High Court, sheriff courts, and district courts. He or she acts without influence from the police, who do not have authority in the decision to prosecute. The lord advocate serves through the Crown Office in Edinburgh.

There are six full-time sheriff principals in Scotland and they each head one of Scotland's six sheriffdoms. These sheriffdoms are divided into sheriff court districts. Legally qualified resident sheriff or sheriffs are a part of each sheriff court district and serve as judges. Shetland is part of the sheriffdom known as Grampian, Highland, and Islands.

Police

The secretary of state is responsible for police power and law enforcement in Scotland. This position is accountable to Parliament. The terms of the Police Act 1967 created Her Majesty's Inspectors of Constabulary (HMIC), a statutory agency with the paramount goal of improving efficiency and cooperation among Scotland's various police organizations. Under the auspices of the secretary of state, HMIC visits police forces and assesses their progress. HMIC publish its findings on an annual basis in a report directed to the secretary of state.

In 1857, the General Police Act mandated each county and burgh to establish a police force, or to join with an adjacent county for policing. In 1883 the County of Zetland created its own County Force, as did the Burgh of Lerwiock in 1892. These two forces coalesced in 1892 to form the Zetland Constabulary, extending the 1857 act to the county. County Forces of Caithness, Orkney, and Zetland were blended into the first Northern Constabulary, founded in 1940 and headquartered in Wick, Caithness. The present Northern Constabulary force traces its beginnings to the restructuring of local government that merged Northern (Caithness-Orkney-Shetland) Constabulary, Ross and Sutherland Constabulary, and Inverness Constabulary on May 16, 1975.

Today, Scotland comprises eight police forces. In all but two of these forces, their jurisdiction is the same as government regional boundaries in the main. Lothian and Borders Police and Northern Constabulary are the two exceptions. Northern Constabulary polices Shetland in addition to Highland Region, Western Isles, and Orkney. The small town nature of Northern Constabulary drives a responsive, localized strategy to policing that keeps the force attuned to the needs of its communities. It serves a population of 300,000 scattered across the region's 10,000 square miles. As of September 30, 2009, there were 17,217 police officers (full-time equivalent) in Scotland. This dwarfs the 400 support staff and slightly more than 700 police officers that combine to make up about Northern Constabulary's 1,100 law enforcement employees. The Northern Force made up 5.5 percent of the police officers in Scotland and had a rate of 25.0 police officers per 10,000 population. The challenge of policing the small towns in the 10,000 square miles that span Northern Highlands from the Outer Hebrides in the west, Glencoe and Newtonmore in the south, and the northern range of the Orkney and Shetland islands, requires a policy grounded in the needs of the various communities. Northern Constabulary's headquarters are located in Inverness, an urban hub with a population of 76,000. Lerwick is Northern Constabulary's designated urban center for Shetland.

The force review program created three geographic divisions, North, Central, and East, in an effort to emphasize an overall structure without hindering local police control. The communities of Caithness, Sutherland and East Ross, Shetland, and Orkney constitute the North Division. Each division is headed by a superintendent and composed of eight area commands. A chief inspector and inspector teams are responsible for policing the area commands, which are supported by local police units to provide continuous policing coverage. An area commander is assigned to each of the eight area commands. The Shetland Area Command of the Northern Constabulary is headed by the Northern Joint Police Board, which is spearheaded by Highland Council. The Shetland Islands Council demanded £2,034,671 (US$2,296,498) in 2007–2008 toward the budget.

Crime

The Scottish government relies on a framework of 350 codes in classifying crimes and offenses. Crimes are matched with a specific classification code using seven major groupings. These groupings include the following:

- Nonsexual crimes of violence—homicide, serious assault, attempted murder.
- Crimes of indecency—rape and indecent assault.
- Crimes involving dishonesty—theft, housebreaking, fraud.
- Fire-raising, vandalism, etc.—malicious mischief, vandalism, reckless conduct with firearms.
- Other crimes—crimes against public justice, handling an offensive weapon, drugs, other.
- Miscellaneous offenses—common assault, breach on the peace, drunkenness, other.
- Motor vehicle offenses—dangerous and careless driving, driving drunk, speeding, etc.

Crime Statistics

For 2008–2009 police in the Shetland Islands Council Area recorded a total of 887 crimes across all categories except miscellaneous and motor vehicle offenses, which were unavailable for this year. The 2007 data include all categories and indicate 2,022 crimes were reported to police. Crimes of dishonesty made up separate statistics for crimes and included 4 serious assault, 20 offensive weapon, 15 domestic housebreaking, and 321 vandalism. The rate per 100,000 population was recorded for those crimes at 2 for serious assault, 9 for offensive weapons, 7 for domestic housebreaking, 146 for vandalism, and 404 for all crimes. The index of rate per

100,000 population was recorded at 16 for serious assault, 52 for offensive weapons, 20 for domestic housebreaking, 75 for vandalism, and 55 for all crimes. The Shetland Islands Council recorded among the least crimes and lowest rate of crimes of all the councils for 2008–2009.

The Northern Police Force Area includes the Shetland Islands and had 561 crimes reported per 10,000 population in 2008–2009. The 76 percent crime clear-up rate experienced by the Shetland Islands in 2008–2009 was higher than every other local authority in Scotland. Police recorded seven crimes of domestic housebreaking per population of 10,000 for the Shetland Islands in 2008–2009. Eilean Siar had five and was the only local council with a lower rate than the Shetland Islands. Shetland was the home area of 12 (10 males and 2 females) out of the 6,681 adult offenders and 3 (all males) out of 1,080 young offenders. Twenty-two individuals with the home address of the Shetland Islands were remanded in 2008–2009.

Punishment

The punishment regime in Shetland is the same as that for all of Scotland. (See the United Kingdom/Scotland.) A brief summary of punishment features that apply to Shetland is as follows.

Custodial Sentences

There were 16,700 convictions that led to a custodial sentence in 2007–2008, about the same as the previous year and the second highest year for this sentence in the 10 years prior. Crimes of violence and crimes of indecency were the two categories that most likely resulted in a custodial sentence. Males constituted 85 percent of convictions, yet represented 92 percent of the custodial sentences for 2007–2008 in Scotland. In 2007–2008, 244 days marked the average custodial sentence. The average custodial sentence in the decade prior ranged from 7½ to 8½ months, and 2007–2008 represented a 7 percent increase in average custodial sentence from the previous year.

In March 2008, the Scottish government approved the Northern Community Justice Authority's Area Plan for 2008–2011. The Shetland Islands Council's Criminal Justice Social Work Service Local Plan for 2008–2009 revolves around priorities of improving public safety and reducing recidivism. The Management of Offenders Act 2005 created Community Justice Authorities (CJAs) in a cooperative effort to aid offender management across criminal justice systems. Eight CJAs were established and the Northern CJA represented the Shetland Islands as well as other areas.

Alternatives to Imprisonment

Courts in Scotland are afforded wide discretion in their choice of sentence. These may include the following:

- Absolute discharge. The accused is not convicted and is discharged from the court without any offense recorded.
- Admonition. The accused is convicted but dismissed and may receive a verbal warning.
- Compensation order. Introduced in Part IV of the Criminal Justice Act 1980, compensation orders mandate a compensation for loss, damage, or personal injury caused by the convicted offender. The average compensation order imposed by courts either as main or secondary penalty was £331 (US$476) in 2007–2008, representing a decrease of 4 percent from the 2006–2007 average of £344.
- Community service orders and probation orders. Community sentences were imposed as the result of 16,700 convictions, with probation (9,000) and community service (5,600) making up the bulk of this number. Other formats used by the courts included restriction of liberty orders (1,151 sentences), drug treatment and testing orders (817 sentences), and supervised attendance orders of first instance (129 sentences).

Fines

The most common punishment for individuals convicted of a criminal offense in Scotland for the years 1998–1999 through 2008–2009 was financial penalty. Financial penalty was the outcome of 83,100 (or 62%) convictions in 2007–2008. Excluding companies, the average fine leveled was £220 (US$316). Of the 16,700 custodial sentences for 2007–2008, 76 percent were for six months or less. Motor vehicle offenses (92%), "other" miscellaneous offenses (77%), drunkenness (70%), drugs offenses (60%), and breach of the peace (56%) were the most likely convictions to result in a fine.

Prison

For the year reported as 2008–2009 the Shetland rate of imprisonment was 85 per 100,000, markedly lower than the rate of 109 per 100,000 for the Northern Community Justice Authority. In 2008 there were 15 penal establishments in Scotland. The penal establishment in Inverness, a city that is part of Northern Constabulary's jurisdiction, had an average daily prison population of 148 men and 3 women in 2008–2009, for a total of 151. The maximum number of prisoners for any day in 2008–2009 was 173 men and 14 women and a total of 180 in 2008–2009.

Prisoners liberated after serving sentence included 8 within six months, 8 between six months and less than one year, 11 between one year and less than four years, and 1 from four years of more. Additionally, one individual was recalled from supervision/license. The 51 prisoners who came from the Shetland Islands and were liberated into the community make up a tiny fraction of Scotland's total of 21,994 for this category.

Nathaniel Kip Arnold

Further Reading

Prison Statistics Scotland, 2007–2008 (Statistical Bulletin—Crime and Justice Series). Published August 29, 2008: http://www.scotland.gov.uk/Resource/Doc/235546/0064616.pdf.

Shetland in Statistics 2008. Published by Shetland Islands Council: http://www.shetland.gov.uk/documents/sins2008.pdf.

Shetland Islands Criminal Justice Social Work Service Local Plan for 2008–2009. Published by Shetland Islands Council: http://www.shetland.gov.uk/performance/documents/CriminalJusticeServicePlan1.pdf.

Slovak Republic

Legal System: Civil
Murder: Low-Medium
Burglary: High
Corruption: Medium
Human Trafficking: Medium
Prison Rate: Medium
Death Penalty: No
Corporal Punishment: No

Background

The Slovak Republic became an independent state in 1993, following the dissolution of the Czech and Slovak Federal Republic, a successor of the former Czechoslovak Republic created after the breakdown of the Austria-Hungary kingdom in 1918. On May 1, 2004, the Slovak Republic became a member of the European Union. It is likewise a member state of the Council of Europe and many other international organizations, such as North Atlantic Treaty Organization, United Nations, Organization for Economic Co-operation and Development, or World Trade Organization.

Legal System

The Slovak legal system is a civil law system. Its main characteristics are the following: (1) principal areas of law and procedure are codified (Civil and Criminal Codes, Codes of Criminal, Civil and Administrative Procedure, etc.); (2) the system of legal sources is hierarchical, forming a pyramidal structure of legal force within the legal system with the Constitution of the Slovak Republic (hereafter the "Constitution") being on the top; and finally (3) only written law (legislation) is, at least in theory, recognized as source of law.

The Constitution adopted by the Slovak National Council on September 1, 1992, defines the Slovak Republic as a sovereign, democratic state governed by the rule of law. The political system of the Slovak Republic is a parliamentary democracy where the legislative power is vested with the National Council of the Slovak Republic, the executive power with the government (as the highest body of the executive power) and the head of state (president of the Slovak Republic), and the judicial power with the courts of general jurisdiction and the Constitutional Court.

Courts

The system of general courts comprises (1) the Supreme Court of the Slovak Republic (hereafter the "Supreme Court") with its seat in Bratislava, (2) 8 regional courts, and (3) 54 district courts. In general, district courts conduct proceedings at first instance in all civil, criminal, commercial, and administrative cases. Regional courts hear these cases as appellate courts. The Supreme Court has the function of an appellate review court. Being the supreme judicial body, it never acts as a first instance court. The Specialized Court with its seat in Pezinok likewise falls within the general courts system and deals with organized crime and corruption cases. Judges of the general courts are appointed by the president of the Slovak Republic for an indefinite period of time on the basis of a proposal of the Judiciary Council of the Slovak Republic. Every citizen of the Slovak Republic who is eligible for election to the National Council of the Slovak Republic, has attained the age of 30 years, and who has a university education in law may be appointed as a judge. The Constitutional Court is composed of 13 judges who are appointed by the president of the Slovak Republic for a 12-year term on a proposal of the National Council of the Slovak Republic. A judge of the Constitutional Court must be a citizen of the Slovak Republic, eligible to be elected to the National Council of the Slovak Republic, not younger than 40 years, and a law-school graduate with 15 years of experience in the legal profession.

Criminal Law

The Criminal Code and the Code of Criminal Procedure are the primary legal sources of the criminal law in the Slovak Republic. Until 2005, the Slovak Criminal Code and the Code of Criminal Procedure were based on the Acts No. 140/1961 Coll. and No. 141/1961 Coll., which had been adopted during the communist period and amended several times since then. Notwithstanding the numerous amendments, however, a completely new recodification of the Slovak criminal law had to be initiated in 2000 to adequately reflect the process of transformation and democratization of the Slovak society after 1989 (need for the removal of the residue of the criminal system of the communist regime, impact of the EU accession, etc.). In 2005, this new recodification resulted in the adoption of new criminal codes—the Criminal Code (Act No. 300/2005 Coll.) (hereafter the "CC") and the Code of Criminal Procedure (Act No. 301/2005 Coll.) (hereafter the "CCP"). Both codes came into effect on January 1, 2006. The basic principles on which these codes are based include, inter alia, no crime without law, no punishment without law; proportionality, publicity, and legality of the criminal proceedings; protection against double jeopardy; presumption of innocence; or accusatorial nature of the criminal proceedings. In this respect, it should be noted that the Slovak law distinguishes between criminal offenses and wrongful acts (the so-called administrative delicts). The administrative delicts are considered less dangerous for the society than the criminal offenses and are governed by the Minor Offences Act No. 372/1990 Coll. or by other, more specific acts, rather than the criminal codes. The administrative delicts fall within the competence of the administrative authorities and wrongdoers are liable to fines. Decisions taken by administrative authorities are reviewable by the courts.

Police

The main law enforcement body in the Slovak Republic is the National Police. The National Police is subordinated to the Ministry of Interior of the Slovak Republic with several special police units reporting to other authorities, such as the Local Police (reporting to local governments), the Railway Police (reporting to the Ministry of Transport, Posts and Telecommunications of the Slovak Republic), the Military Police (reporting to the Ministry of

Defense of the Slovak Republic), the Customs Authority (reporting to the Ministry of Finance of the Slovak Republic), or Corps of Prison and Court Guard (reporting to the Ministry of Justice of the Slovak Republic). The organization of the Slovak National Police follows the administrative division of the country into eight regions and 79 districts. According to the relevant law, the National Police is an armed security corps with duties in the field of internal order, security, and fight against crime, including organized and international crime. It also has other tasks in coherence with international affairs. The activities of the National Police are controlled by the National Council of the Slovak Republic and the Slovak government.

Crime

Classification of Crimes

A criminal offense is an unlawful act that meets the elements set out in the CC. The CC defines two forms of criminal offense—minor offense and crime. A minor offense involves either a criminal offense committed by negligence or an intentional criminal act liable to a sentence of deprivation of liberty for a term not exceeding five years. A minor offense is not regarded as a criminal offense provided it was committed by a minor under the age of 18 and its seriousness (gravity) of the act was small. A crime is an intentional criminal act that is liable to a sentence of deprivation of liberty for period exceeding five years. In this context, it should be noted that the CC specifically defines a so-called aggravated crime, which is an intentional criminal act liable to a sentence of deprivation of liberty for a period of no less than eight years.

Pursuant to the relevant provisions of the CC, nobody can be held criminally responsible for an act committed before reaching the age of 14. In the case of a crime of sexual abuse a person must be at least 15 years old to be held responsible for the crime. Moreover, a person under 15 years of age cannot be held responsible for his or her actions if his or her intellectual or moral state of mind would not allow him or her to recognize the illegality of a criminal act.

Regarding drug offenses, pursuant to the relevant provisions of the CC, criminal sanctions can be imposed for the possession of a narcotic drug, psychotropic substance, poison, or precursor for own consumption. Here, the CC defines two offenses: possession for own consumption (defined as no more than three times one single dose), which has a maximum 3-year sentence; and possession of a larger amount for own consumption (defined as no more than 10 times one single dose), which has a maximum 5-year sentence. Two other penalties can also be given to those charged with possession for personal use: monitored home imprisonment for up to 1 year, or community service of 40 to 300 hours. Unauthorized possession of a greater amount of drug, that is, more than 10 times the usual single dose, will not be considered as possession of such substance for own consumption but as an offense of unlawfully manufacturing, importing, exporting, transporting or causing to be transported, purchasing, selling, exchanging, procuring, or possessing a narcotic drug, a psychotropic substance, poison, or precursor, or brokering such activity (i.e., drug trafficking). In such cases, an offender can be held liable to sanction of 4 to 10 years of imprisonment. The penalty increases if the offender is a repeat offender or if other aggravating circumstances are present (see below).

The Act No. 139/1998 Coll. on Narcotic Drugs, Psychotropic Matters and Substances defines the types of drugs for which it is criminal either to sell or use. The objective of this law is to strictly define conditions for cultivation, producing, control, stockpiling, distribution, application for scientific purposes and research, export and import, and transit of controlled substances. The cultivation of poppy seeds is allowed under legally defined conditions, and cultivation of cocaine and cannabis is prohibited with the exception of their cultivation for industrial purposes. The Act No. 219/2003 Coll. on the Chemical Substances Misused for Illicit Production of Narcotic Drugs and Psychotropic Substances sets out the requirements governing the production, market introduction, and use of chemical substances that may be diverted for illicit production of narcotic drugs and psychotropic substances, including their import, export, transit, and transportation with a view to prevent their misuse for illicit production of narcotic drugs, psychotropic substances, and preparations containing such substances.

Crime Statistics

According to the statistical data of the Office of the General Prosecutor of the Slovak Republic, the most numerous criminal offenses committed in 2008 were of a violent nature, such as illegal infliction of bodily harm, illegal intrusion into private homes, and assault (threatening). In comparison with preceding years, there has been a growth in the number of persons prosecuted for maltreatment of a close and entrusted person, murder of a newborn baby, sexual abuse, kidnapping, and gross coercion. Since the accession of the Slovak Republic to the European Union in 2004, there has also been a moderate growth of drug criminality. In 2008, there were 43 persons convicted of murder, 59 persons convicted of rape, 489 persons convicted of robbery, and 979 persons convicted of drug offenses. According to the statistics collected by the Statistical Office of the Slovak Republic, a great majority of criminal offenses of 2008 were recorded in the capital city region.

Finding of Guilt

Pursuant to the Slovak Constitution, only courts can decide about the guilt and punishment for criminal offenses in the criminal proceedings. Pursuant to the relevant provisions of the CCP, there are two stages of criminal proceedings: pretrial and trial. The pretrial stage includes criminal investigation by police and prosecutor. The police work on their own initiative so that all important facts of the case are clarified as soon as possible, including the identification of the perpetrator (accused) and consequences of the criminal act. Transparency and legality of individual investigative operations and the overall investigative procedure is controlled by the prosecutor. Upon completion of the investigation, unless agreed otherwise, the police authority submits the outcomes of investigation to a district prosecutor who has to decide whether there is sufficient evidence to bring an accused to court charging him or her with a specific crime (the indictment). In certain cases, the prosecutor may decide to end the prosecution by approving the out-of-court settlement (only with respect to less serious crimes and subject to strict conditions). Alternatively, the prosecutor may ask the court to approve the so-called agreement on guilt and penalty. The purpose of this agreement is to speed up the criminal proceeding provided that the accused individual recognizes his or her guilt and consents to the proposed penalty (in some other jurisdictions, commonly referred to as a "plea bargain"). Following a court decision approving any such agreement on guilt and penalty, this agreement has the nature of an enforceable judgment.

The trial stage begins with the court reviewing the indictment submitted by the prosecutor and, in principle, scheduling a hearing. In general, the courts hold their hearings in public. The public may only be excluded subject to special circumstances listed in the CCP (e.g., need to preserve the confidentiality of the facts, etc.). The judgment must always be pronounced publicly. In the judgment, an individual can either be acquitted or found guilty. Alternatively, the courts may decide to discontinue the prosecution, transfer the case to a different authority, or to cease the prosecution by approving an out-of-court settlement.

Pretrial Detention

A person suspected of a criminal offense may be detained subject to conditions provided by law. These are listed in the CCP. Pursuant to the relevant provisions of the CCP, a police officer may detain a person suspected of having committed a crime (even before any charges have been brought) provided there are reasonable grounds to believe that the person would (1) escape or go into hiding to avoid persecution or punishment, (2) try to influence witnesses, or (3) continue his or her criminal activities. The police officer who detained a person or to whom a person caught while committing a crime was handed over shall notify the prosecutor of the detention and draw up a report containing the detailed description of all circumstances, information on the place and time of detention, grounds for detention, and so forth. A detained person must be informed of the grounds for detention immediately. The detained person shall have the right choose a legal representative and consult him or her from the very moment of detention. After interrogation, within 48 hours at the latest, the detainee must be either released or brought before a court. The pretrial judge has then 48 hours (72 hours in the case of especially serious criminal offenses carrying a penalty of more than 10 years' imprisonment) to hear the detainee and decide on his or her release or remand. The court can also decide on alternatives to pretrial detention. Alternatives are monetary bail, guarantee, written promise by the accused, or probation. Whenever the judge decides about an alternative to pretrial detention, he or she can, in addition, impose one or more duties and/or restrictions on the person concerned. These may include a duty to maintain regular contacts with certain authorities or ban to travel abroad, visit certain places, leave the place of residence, drive a car, contact certain people, carry a gun, among others.

Juveniles

There are some specific procedural rules that apply to juveniles in the criminal proceedings. Besides the aforementioned rules on criminal responsibility (i.e., a juvenile may be held criminally liable at the age of 14 unless he or she has been held criminally liable for sexual abuse), the CCP sets out that in the criminal proceedings against a juvenile, parents or other individuals who have the legal responsibility for the child are entitled to lodge an appeal against the decision that involves the juvenile, to attend the trial at the court, to present a speech in the course of the proceedings in the court, among others. A juvenile may only be taken into custody when the purpose for deprivation of liberty cannot be reached in another (i.e., noncustodial) way. However, there are no specific (additional) alternatives to custody for juveniles, and there also no specific grounds that have to be met to take a juvenile offender into custody. Thus, rules applicable to the criminal proceedings in general likewise apply to the proceedings involving juveniles.

Rights of the Accused

In general, the Slovak Constitution as well as the relevant provisions of the CCP set out, inter alia, that only law shall lay down which conduct is a criminal offense and which punishment; only courts shall decide about the guilt and punishment for criminal offenses; and the jurisdiction of courts shall be laid down by the law. Everyone has the right to have his or her case tried publicly without undue delay, to be present at the proceedings, and to comment on any evidence given in the course of such proceedings. Everyone shall be presumed innocent until proved guilty by a final judgment of the court. Everyone charged with a criminal offense shall be entitled to have time and facilities for the preparation of his or her defense and to defend himself or herself in person or through legal assistance. Everyone shall have the right to legal advice from the commencement of proceedings before courts, other public authorities, or bodies of public administration, under the conditions laid down by the law. Everyone charged with a criminal offense shall have the right to refuse to give testimony. No one may be prosecuted for the same criminal offense again. A law adopted after the commission of the criminal offense shall be used if it is more beneficial to the offender.

Pursuant to the CCP, an accused has the right to free legal aid once his or her case enters the trial stage (i.e., once an indictment in which the prosecutor charges the accused with a specific crime is submitted to the court) and he or she proves an inability (complete or partial) to pay the costs of legal representation. In such event, the state will cover the costs (in full or partially). However, this applies only to cases where legal representation is compulsory under the CCP (e.g., in the proceedings against juveniles, fugitives, or individuals with no legal capacity, etc.). In all other cases, the state will not bear the costs of legal representation of the accused.

Punishment

Types of Punishment

Once found guilty of an offense, an individual may be subjected to the following types of punishment: imprisonment, home arrest, community service, fine, property forfeiture, forfeiture of a thing, ban on engaging in professional activity, residence ban, loss of military rank, loss of honorary titles and, finally, expulsion. Along with these punishments, the court may decide to impose other restrictions and obligations, as appropriate (obligation to undergo a drug treatment, etc.). Imprisonment is regarded as the most severe form of punishment and is considered only if all other types of punishments enforced outside prison are considered insufficient for the purpose of punishment. Imprisonment may have either the form of imprisonment for a fixed term not exceeding 25 years or the form of life imprisonment. Provided the term of imprisonment does not exceed 2 years, its execution may be suspended for a probationary period (from 1 to 5 years) during which the sentenced person must lead a law-abiding life and fulfill the conditions that the court may decide to prescribe (i.e., obligation to participate in re-education program, etc.).

The sanction of imprisonment between 15 and 20 years will be imposed on an offender convicted of murder. The offense of a predetermined murder is punishable by 20 to 25 years of imprisonment. An intentional murder of a newborn baby by the mother in distress is liable to 4 to 8 years of imprisonment. A person who was found guilty of rape will be sentenced to 5 to 10 years in prison. The punishment for theft or robbery increases with the amount of damage caused by the offense. For the most aggravated offense, the punishment is imprisonment of up to 12 years, a fine between €130 and €130,000 (US$163 and $163,384), and confiscation. The punishment for fraud is the same, but the court may also impose a ban on engaging in professional activity for up to 10 years. Serious drug offenses may incur 10 to 15 years of imprisonment for a repeat offender; 15 to 20 years if it causes grievous bodily harm or death, or if committed against a person under the age of 15 or on a large scale; 20 to 25 years or life imprisonment if grievous bodily harm occurs to several persons or the death of several persons thereby or when he or she commits it as a member of a dangerous group.

Prison

According to the data collected by the International Centre for Prison Studies (ICPS) and the Ministry of Justice of the Slovak Republic, the total prison population in the Slovak Republic was 8,166 on December 31, 2008. The prison population rate per 100,000 of national population in the Slovak Republic was thus 151 (based on Eurostat's estimated number of national population, which was 5.41 million at the end of 2008). The ICPS's data furthermore state that on September 1, 2007, the number of female prisoners was 4.6 percent and juveniles 0.6 percent of total prison population in the Slovak Republic. There are 18 prisons in the Slovak Republic. According to the ICPS, on December 31, 2007, the total prisons' official capacity was 10,588 and about 75.4 percent of such capacity was used. The biggest and oldest Slovak prison is situated in Leopoldov. The Leopoldov prison is a high-security prison situated some hundred miles north-east of the capital city Bratislava. It is built on a site that had been used as a military fortress since the 17th century. It is made up of two establishments: a pretrial section with a capacity of 341 places and a section for sentenced prisoners with 1,053 places.

Pursuant to the Act No. 475/2005 Coll. on Execution of Punishment of Imprisonment, which sets out basic rights and obligations of the prisoners, the accommodation space in a cell or room should be at least 37.6 square feet (3.5 square meters) for a sentenced man and 43 square feet (4 square meters) for a sentenced woman or adolescent. Prisoners are provided with regular meals three times a day and consideration is given to the state of their health, age, type of work they carry out and, if possible, also to their cultural traditions and religious customs. Prisoners are entitled to 8 hours of an uninterrupted sleep a day. Prisoners are provided with the prison clothes suitable for the actual weather conditions and sufficient to protect their health. They are entitled to free medical care and treatment. Prisoners are entitled to receive and send correspondence at their own expense without any restrictions unless stated otherwise. The prison service officer is entitled to check and read the correspondence but is banned from doing so with respect to the correspondence between a prisoner and his or her legal representative, state authorities, international institutions, and others. Prisoners have the right to call their relatives or other close persons twice a month for the duration of 15 minutes and are entitled to a monthly visit of at least 2 hours. Prisoners who have the required aptitude are enabled to undertake studies in the primary or secondary school as well as attend various courses to master their skills. Prisoners are required to work subject to their health, working skills, and other conditions. In this respect, the provisions of the Labour Code governing working hours and rest periods, overtime work, occupational safety and health, and employers' accountability for damages caused by occupational accidents and diseases are applicable to the prisoners at work. Prisoners are entitled to a wage depending on the kind of work carried out, the time worked, or the labor consumption standard. Deductions from such wages are made to cover the costs of imprisonment and pay child maintenance or debts (if applicable). In 2008, the rate of employment in the Slovak prisons was 76.58 percent. Prisoners are entitled to file various complaints with the authorities to ensure a proper exercise of their human rights.

Jana Gajdošová

Further Reading

Bahtiyar, Z., P.S. Lambertina, W.A.M. van der Linden, and M. Roze. (2009). "Slovakia." In *Pre-Trial Detention in the European Union,* edited by A.M. van Kalmthout, M.M. Knapen, and C. Morgenstern, pp. 817–839. Nijmegen, the Netherlands: Wolf Legal.

Ministry of Justice of the Slovak Republic: http://www.justice.sk.

Office of the General Prosecutor of the Slovak Republic: http://www.genpro.gov.sk.

Statistical Office of the Slovak Republic: http://portal.statistics.sk.

Trnkócyová, Vladimíra. (2005). "Criminal Investigation in the Slovak Republic." In *Judicial Reform: The Prosecution Office and Investigation Authorities in the Context of EU Membership,* edited by Maria Yordanova and Dimitar Markov, pp. 124–129. Sofia, Bulgaria: The Center for the Study of Democracy.

Slovenia

Legal System: Civil
Murder: Low
Burglary: Medium
Corruption: Low
Human Trafficking: Low
Prison Rate: Low
Death Penalty: No
Corporal Punishment: No

Background

Slovenia underwent the path from being a constituent part of the Federal Socialist Republic of Yugoslavia, a semi-authoritarian one-party state, to becoming an independent country (1991) governed by the rule of law and a member of the European Community (2004). Dramatic changes during the transitional period and the proximity of armed conflicts in the Balkans resulted in uncertainty in many fields of social and economic life as well as in crime control policies, strategies, and operations.

The first Slovenian Penal Code was incorporated in September 1941 under the auspices of the Slovenian Liberation Committee. It included some provisions on criminal offenses, criminal sanctions, and criminal procedure but did not have its own criminal legislation until 1977 when the Federal Penal Code and Slovenian Penal Code were introduced. In 1989 an amendment to the Yugoslavian Constitution (1974) was passed that abolished the death penalty in Slovenia in spite of the fact that the Federal Penal Code still sustained it. In fact, from the beginning, the Federal Penal Code was in discord with the values and legal system of the

Three Slovenian police officers hide in a wooden bus shelter, while aiming a laser radar device at speeding drivers on the road to Kocevje, Slovenia, March 1, 2005. (AP Photo/Denis Sarkic)

Republic of Slovenia. With establishment of the Slovenian Constitution, the right of secession from Yugoslavia was established and, in 1994, the Penal Code of Slovenia was adopted and came into force on January 1, 1995. Recently a new Penal Code was adopted and came into force in November 2008.

The first Code of Criminal Procedure, adopted in 1953, was similar to that of the Soviet Union. In particular, the public prosecutors had a very broad and relatively unchecked jurisdiction. The amendment of 1967 imported the Western-based adversarial process: the rights of the victim were broadened and criminal prosecution was led by the principle of legality, and conditions for detention became more restrictive. Four years after Slovenian independence (in 1994), a new Code of Criminal Procedure was adopted and came into force in 1995. Since then 11 amendments were adopted. The new Code of Criminal Procedure is still under discussion in the academic and legal community.

Police

Through the Police Act that came into force July 18, 1998, the police service became a body within the Ministry of Interior of the Republic of Slovenia but was given more autonomy than it had in the past. The police perform their tasks at three levels: state, regional, and local. Organizationally, it is composed of General Police Directorate, Police Directorates, and Police Stations. The national police headquarters are in Ljubljana. The police service is headed by the director general of the police, who also conducts the work of the General Police Directorate.

The Criminal Police is a specialized division for fighting crime. It is headed by the Criminal Police Directorate, which coordinates, monitors, analyzes, and evaluates situations in the area of criminal offenses. In cooperation with judicial and other state bodies (such as Ministry of Defense) as well as foreign competent authorities, it ensures effective and lawful implementation of activities against various forms of crime. The Criminal Police are composed of several divisions including Organized Crime Division, General Crime Division, Economic Crime Division and Special Task Division, International Police Cooperation Division, and Criminal Analysis Division. The criminal police cooperate with uniformed police officers in uncovering criminal offenses and perpetrators.

The Uniformed Police Division is responsible for the areas of public order and the safeguarding of lives, personal safety and the property of people. It is composed of the Public Order Section, the General Safety Section, the Traffic Police Division, and the Border Police Division. The Public Order Section analyzes and evaluates security situations and the success and effectiveness of police work in the areas of public order and peace, safeguarding of lives, personal safety, and the property of people. The General Safety Section analyzes and evaluates the security situation, successfulness and effectiveness of police work in the field of public order and safeguarding lives, personal safety, property of people and personal security, and detective activities. The Traffic Police Division comprises road traffic safety and the regulation of traffic. The Border Police Division performs tasks in the field of state border security, illegal migrations and foreigners, and Section for the Security of People.

Crime

Classification of Crimes

Criminal offenses are classified in chapters within the Penal Code (2008) in accordance with generally recognized social values. Categorization regarding the age of offender (juvenile or adult) is used for some offenses, but it is useful only for cleared criminal offenses. Children (under age 14) are not subject to criminal liability. Those aged 14 to 17 come under the juvenile justice provisions, and a less strict approach is given to adolescents from 18 to 21 years old.

In 2008, adjustments to the Penal Code introduced additional changes in divisions of the criminal offenses indictable by official duty and criminal offenses indictable by civil lawsuit of victims. More forms of less serious criminal offenses (chiefly against property) are indictable by civil law than before. The lowest limit of the harm is set at €200 (US$251) for offenses against property. For extremely severe criminal offenses, life sentence has been introduced.

Crime Statistics Trends

The main sources of official (police) statistical data are articles (shortened and interpreted version of the official report to the Slovenian Parliament), which appear yearly beginning in 1959 in the *Slovenian Journal of Criminalistics and Criminology.*

With the exception of a brief decline toward the middle of the 1990s, general crime has increased steadily from a low of 37,173 in 1997 to a high of 90,354 in 2006, leveling off to 88,192 in 2007. The fluctuations are a consequence of changes in criminal activity, changes of perceptions and reactions to crime, and changes of activities of political and law enforcement agencies. The greatest increase occurs in the category of criminal offenses against property. Economic crime also increased from 2,222 crimes in 1990 to 8,471 in 2006, leveling off to 7,962 in 2007. Organized crime, when first recorded in 1995, revealed 735 crimes, peaking at 1,116 in 1999, dropping to 225 in 2004, peaking again at 499 in 2006, dropping again to 293 in 2007. These fluctuations probably reflect changes of definitions of "organization" of the criminal activity.

General crime includes offenses against private property and against life and limb. Economic crime includes offenses against the social ownership of the means of production and public property. Newer categories of economic and organized crime are not always explicitly and clearly defined, so data should be interpreted carefully. The reported crimes for 2007, according to particular crime categories defined by the Penal Code (1995), is as follows (compiled from the police Web site and various journal articles):

Life and limb	2,776
Human rights	4,656
Sexual integrity	216
Property	63,158
Public order	1,366
Safety of traffic	342
Other	13,783

For the period 1990 to 2007, offenses against property increased from 30,787 to 63,158; offenses against human rights and liberties increased from 586 to 4,656; offenses against legal transactions increased from 820 to 2,111; and offenses against life and limb increased from 1,718 to 2,776. Looking more closely at offenses against life and limb, murders have decreased from 37 in 1990 to 24 in 2007 but serious grievous bodily harms have increased from 389 to 2,803 for the same period.

The Slovenian Penal Code treats sexual integrity (women, children, and other vulnerable groups) as an important social value. The number of offenses against sexual integrity grew until 2002, and then decreased. However, the decrease in number does not give a complete picture, because the "dark figure" of crime is probably the greatest with respect to this type of crime. There were 62 rapes in 1990, increasing to 85 in 2007, and 100 offenses of sexual violence, assault, and abuse, increasing to 279 in 2007.

In 2001 there were 1,140 offenses of unlawful manufacture and trade of narcotic drugs, increasing to 1,429 in 2007, and there were 397 offenses enabling opportunities for consumption of narcotic drugs, decreasing to 183 in 2007. More than half of criminal offenses (50.7%) occurred in the Ljubljana area (which has approximately one-quarter of the population of the country). Such results are generally confirmed by victimization studies conducted in Ljubljana.

In regard to offenders, there were 27,559 suspects apprehended in 1990, of which 22.1 percent were juveniles. This compares to 17,478 suspects in 2007, of which 8.6 percent were juveniles. The clearance rate for all cases in 1990 was 61.7 percent, compared to 38.2 percent in 2007. Data from the *Statistical Yearbook of Republic of Slovenia* (2008) show that the number of convicted persons more than doubled in the period from 1995 to 2007, after the introduction of the Penal Code (1995): from 3,462 convicted adults to 8,685 convicted adults.

Finding of Guilt

The Slovenian Code of Criminal Procedure is composed of three main parts. The first includes general provisions, the second consists of typical ordinary criminal procedure, and the third contains special procedures. Human rights and fundamental freedoms of the accused are described in the Slovenian Constitution and more precisely in the general principles of the Code of Criminal Procedure. The right to a fair trial is prescribed in articles 6 and 13 of the European Convention on Human Rights. Articles 2–4 of Protocol 7 are not emphasized in the Code of Criminal Procedure but evident from other provisions.

Rights of the Accused

Only an independent, impartial, and lawful court can judge a criminal case. In those settings, defendants whose rights, freedoms, and legal interests are the substance of legal procedure have the opportunity to confront evidence and produce evidence in their own behalf. In addition, Slovenian criminal defendants are entitled to the following rights:

- To be acquainted with circumstances, facts, and evidence that incriminate them.
- To know their rights and use them in their language.
- To remain silent and are not obligated to plead guilty.
- To have adequate time and facilities to prepare defense as provided by law.
- To conduct their own defense or to be defended by a defense counsel.
- To know that no one may be deprived of their freedom except in such cases and pursuant to such procedures as are provided by law.
- To an independent, impartial court constituted by law.

- To be physically present at their trial.
- To exclude illegally obtained evidence.
- To appeal against conviction.

Article 23 of the Slovenian Constitution requires that a main hearing must take place "within a reasonable time."

The accused may spend a long period of time in detention in both the pretrial and trial phase. Bail and other mechanisms that may replace the use of detention are possible. Even with a confession by the accused during the process of pretrial investigation, the investigating magistrate and the state prosecutor must still collect evidence. During the trial (a main hearing) the state prosecutor (or private prosecutor) has the primary responsibility to produce the evidence. The court has a discretionary power by virtue of which the judge may, in honor and good conscience, take any measures (e.g., examination of the witnesses) that can be useful to enable the truth to be discovered.

Both the offender and the prosecutor have the right to produce evidence, and the judge has the right to produce evidence as well (the latter is the exception from the usual adversary procedure). The accused have the right to counsel and to have legal aid. In the police proceedings (before the criminal procedure), the suspect cannot be interrogated without the presence of a defense counsel.

Prosecution and Investigation

Criminal procedure is started on the demand of the prosecutor or on the proposal of the victim. This can be either a state prosecutor or private prosecutor. If the state prosecutor realizes that there is no reason to start or continue the criminal procedure, the victim can step in as the prosecutor under provisions by law. In contrast to the former inquisitorial procedure, all three basic functions of criminal procedure are divided: prosecution, defense, and trial.

Alternatives to Trial

After the reception of criminal complaint, the state prosecutor must drop the complaint if the act is not a criminal act, if the prosecution for the act is under limitation or under amnesty or pardon or there are other circumstances that exclude prosecution, or there is no probable cause that the accused committed a crime. Successful alternatives to trials can result in avoiding one or more phases of criminal procedure. Mediation between the victim and accused is possible in the presence of an independent mediator appointed by a state prosecutor. According to substantive law the sentence can or has to be dropped if the prosecutor estimates that the sanction is unnecessary.

The case can also be dropped if the criminal act is punishable by fine or imprisonment of up to one year and the accused, with remorse, prevents harm or fully compensates the damage.

Incarceration before and during Trial

The Slovenian Code of Criminal Procedure distinguishes between police custody, pretrial detention, and detention during the trial. Detailed provisions allow the suspect to be held by the police for up to 48 hours. The police can authorize this detention by issuing a warrant. It must fully identify the suspect and provide details of the offense, statutory basis and the facts upon which both these and the need for urgency are based. Immediately after these grounds no longer exist, the suspect must be released or be brought without a delay before an investigating magistrate. However, pretrial detention may be deemed necessary for identification, for the checking of an alibi, for the collecting of information and items of evidence for the criminal offense in question, if there is good reason to fear that the person might destroy traces of the crime, and if reasons provided by law for detention during the trial exist as well (e.g., of defendant).

Police can arrest the suspect with a warrant. Without the warrant they can make an arrest under conditions provided by law. The suspects have to be read their rights when they are to be placed in detention or brought to an investigating magistrate. The suspects must be advised immediately of the reasons for their loss of freedom. They have the right to know that they may remain silent and that they are entitled to the legal assistance of a lawyer of their own choice. Upon request of the suspect, the competent body (the police) is bound to inform the suspect's family of the arrest. If suspects cannot afford to hire a defense counsel, one shall be appointed to represent them before any questioning.

The police must have probable cause that the suspect committed a crime, and there are reasons for detention before arresting the suspect and bringing him or her to an investigating magistrate. The police detention is only for a short time period. It is not meant to elicit a confession of the crime by the suspect or to gather evidence but to take him or her to the court that issued the warrant.

The accused detained under the ruling of the investigating magistrate may be remanded in custody for a maximum of one month from the day they were arrested. After that, they may be kept in custody only under a ruling ordering the extension of remand in custody. Remand in custody may be extended under a ruling of the judicial panel by two months at the longest, and the Supreme Court may extend it for another three months as well.

Judges

For appointment, a judge must fulfill the following general criteria:

- To be a citizen of Republic of Slovenia and actively speak the Slovenian language.
- To have business capacity and is in a general healthy condition.
- To be more than 30 years old.
- To have acquired the title of a lawyer in Slovenia or an equivalent abroad recognized by the law.
- To have passed special state juridical exams.

Juveniles

The Slovenian Code of Criminal Procedure defines a special procedure for juvenile offenders. Differences between juvenile criminal procedure and ordinary criminal procedure are numerous. First, only district courts handle criminal offenses by juveniles in a procedure that is a part of the code using the juvenile criminal law as a part of substantive criminal law. State prosecutors are the only authorized prosecutors in juvenile procedures. If state prosecutors do not want to begin with the criminal procedure and the victim disagrees, the victim may demand from the court (judicial panel) a commencement of prosecution against the juvenile in question. The juvenile cannot be judged by the court in his or her absence. The social welfare agency collects data on the social behavior of the offender, and a criminological evaluation may also be conducted. During the criminal procedure, the defendant is entitled to formal defense counsel, if he or she committed a crime punishable by imprisonment for more than three years.

Juveniles may be detained up to three months in a facility where separation from adult convicts is possible. The alternative to detention is removal from their social environment. After the main hearing or after the judicial panel session, they may be sentenced by educational measure, imprisonment, or fine.

Punishment

Prisoners

The Slovenian Prison Administration has faced an increase in the prison population in the last 10 years and overcrowding has recently occurred for the first time in the history of Slovenian prisons. However, the imprisonment rate is still quite low with a rate of 66 per 100,000. The current prison population of 1,339 exceeds the design capacity of 1,094 by nearly 22 percent in 2007, according to the National Prison Administration. The majority of persons deprived of liberty are classified as sentenced prisoners (70%), followed by detainees (25%), persons imprisoned for a misdemeanor (3%), and juveniles in the correctional home (2%). Less than 4 percent of inmates are female, about 40 percent of inmates have not finished elementary school, and 44 percent of prisoners were sentenced for offenses against property.

Prison

The Prison Administration of the Republic of Slovenia is administratively housed within the Ministry of Justice, which has been responsible for the prison system since 1968. The current Prison Administration was established in 1995 by joining eight authorities into a single, central entity. Certain tasks previously carried out by the Ministry of Justice were also taken over by the Prison Administration.

The main mission of Prison Administration is the implementation of various penal sanctions and pretrial detention. The Prison Administration also works for the benefit of the community as an alternative to prison and educational measures implemented within a correctional institution. It makes every effort to ensure that the prisons are safe for society, inmates, and employees; and provides the possibility of resocialization. This means that the treatment of inmates must be organized in such manner as to provide them with training for their return to life in society, and to particularly dissuade them from future criminal offenses.

The Prison Administration has a prison staff of more than 800 people. Three basic services exist within prisons in Slovenia: prison officers, treatment staff, and labor instructors. Approximately half of the staff is prison officers. The organizational structure is nearly the same in all prisons. The Treatment Department employs pedagogues, psychologists, social workers, medical staff, leisure activities staff, educators, and other professionals carrying out treatment programs. The Penal Sanction Enforcement Act states that prisons must prepare prisoners for normal life after prison using programs of individual, group, and community treatment. These programs are established on a case-by-case basis and include a written agreement between prisoners and the prison.

Prison sentences are executed in 6 prisons, at 13 locations, 2 of which are open departments. The largest prison is at Dob, where male prisoners serve prison sentences from 1.5 to 30 years. The central institution for women prisoners is at Ig. In Celje there is an institution for juveniles and young adults, and a juvenile correctional institution is located at Radeče. In the regional prisons of Koper, Maribor, and Ljubljana, sentenced persons serve their prison terms of up to 1.5 years. Every institution has an open, half-open, and a closed unit that are distinguished according to their security level and the restriction of freedom of movement. Detention departments are organized within particular institutions at 9 locations. Slovenia prisons are smaller than those in other European countries. Out of the 13 prisons, only 3 have the capacity of more than 100 inmates (233 at the most). Most prisons are located in old buildings built before and after World War II, and the buildings only partially meet the current demands for penal institutions. The central prison for men at Dob was built in 1963. A program for developing the capacities of the prisons was adopted in 2003. During the last 10 years, more than 40 percent of all present-day accommodation facilities for prisoners have been built or refurbished. The most important completed project is the new prison in Koper, which meets regulatory standards. A new open department at Slovenska Vas at Dob is among the most modern in Europe.

There are nine jails or regional prisons that also house pretrial detainees. Out of the nine pretrial detention facilities, five are for men, one for women, and three are mixed facilities. The average daily number of pretrial detainees in 2004 was 280, equivalent to 14 detainees per 100,000 inhabitants. The country's total pretrial detention capacity had been exceeded by 9 percent. About 80 percent of pretrial facilities had been renovated or newly built over the previous 10 years (National Prison Administration, 2005; CCPR, 2005). The most significant characteristic of the Slovenian pretrial detention is that there is no classification of prisoners (CCPR, 2005).

Slovenian courts may hand down a maximum prison sentence of 30 years; general minimum prison sentences are 15 days. There is no death penalty, but life sentence for the most extreme cases was introduced in November 2008.

Life in Prison

Prisoners in Slovenia serve their prison sentence in different prisons according to different criteria:

- Sex—as a rule there are separate prisons for men and women; in some cases they are only separated within a prison.

- Duration of the sentence—prisons for serving long and short prison sentences.
- Age of the convict—prisons for adult prisoners and prisons for juveniles and young adults.
- Degree of security—closed, semi-open, and open institutions or departments.

Those convicted of serious criminal offenses are separated from detainees, persons sentenced to prison in misdemeanors procedures, and juvenile prisoners. There are no separate institutions for repeat or first-time offenders. In all Slovenian prisons there is a vertical classification into closed, semi-open, and open units. The regime in individual units differs according to the degree of restriction of freedom of prisoners. Prisoners are not classified by category of criminal offense, but there are drug-free units where differentiated treatment of drug addicts in the sense of separated residence is carried out.

If a prisoner is given a prison sentence of up to 3 years, the court can order the sentence to be served in an open institution. If the imposed prison sentence is up to 5 years, the court can order the sentence to be served in a semi-open institution. The court can decide to replace a prison sentence of less than 3 months with performing community work for humanitarian organizations or for the local community (community service order). The offender is ordered to perform unpaid work from 80 to 240 hours in 6 months.

Transfer between individual prisons is within the jurisdiction of the director general of the Prison Administration. Most transfers are the result of requests by prisoners or their relatives, but they also can happen *ex-officio* (for security reasons, overcrowding, etc.).

The director general may allow prisoners sentenced for a criminal act committed out of negligence to a prison term of up to six months. If they are orderly and have regular employment or attend school and are serving a prison sentence for the first time, they may be allowed to continue working while serving the sentence and to reside at home, except on nonwork days, as a rule at the weekend, when they must reside in prison.

The prison in which the convicted person begins the sentence shall, with written consent, notify the responsible center for social work in the area of the prisoner's residence at the start of the sentence. The centers for social work, together with other services in the field and in cooperation with the prison, must prepare a program of necessary measures at least three months prior to the prisoner's release. This process starts at the beginning of the sentence. They set up the social network in the local community and plan the resolution of problems of the prisoner's family (child protection, material situation, interpersonal relationships, etc.).

Various programs are conducted in prisons in the area of education, work, leisure activities, health care, special programs concentrating on providing help to inmates addicted to drugs or alcohol, programs of social learning, preparations for release, and special programs connected with inmates' specific needs, but there are no programs for pretrial detainees.

Each individual treatment program includes decisions on allocation of the prisoner in question to a particular unit and cell, methods of managing the prisoner, the prisoner's health, and the prisoner's work. Integral parts of the individual treatment program are the social programs and the postpenal plans. They are prepared by the social workers and pedagogues employed in prisons, in cooperation with the prisoner and the external service providers.

Group treatment programs are carried out in small therapeutic groups. They are heterogeneous and open. Groups include prisoners who differ with regard to age, previous sentences, and the type of offense they had committed, recidivism, personality structure, and social status. They may involve elements of reality therapy, transaction analysis, family therapy, painting therapy, and other therapies.

Prisoners have an opportunity to acquire education while in prison, especially for the completion of obligatory primary education and to train for a profession. Prisoners are motivated to participate in educational processes from their first day in prison. Prisoners are allowed to attend lectures and participate in other educational activities outside of the prison without accompaniment if they meet the conditions for award of out-of-prison privileges. Prisoners who complete their schooling are issued a certificate that must not indicate that it was acquired in prison. A prisoner who attends schooling may be granted the right to a part-time job.

Prisons organize sports and recreational activities, cultural-educational activities, concerts, special volunteer work projects, and so on. Prisoners can regularly borrow books from prison libraries as well as from local and traveling libraries. Prisons publish their own newsletters, and daily and weekly newspapers are available to prisoners.

Medical Care

Prisoners are guaranteed the right to health care. Every prison provides basic health and dental care and has separate rooms for those who suffer from long-term illness. A pregnant woman prisoner or woman who has given birth during imprisonment is guaranteed suitable medical care and conditions to care for the child. The child may stay with the mother until it is one year old, and on special grounds, the child can stay until two years of age. Prisoners must be provided confidential testing for HIV and hepatitis infections, and receive special health consultations. They are also provided with disability insurance.

The treatment of alcohol and drug addiction is carried out in all prisons according to the national program based on expert positions, similar to medical and psychosocial programs of treatment provided by the centers for the treatment of alcohol and drug addicts outside the prison. These programs are carried out in drug-free units. Counseling is provided for all prisoners with psychological problems and especially to those who have committed certain criminal offenses (sex crimes, violent crimes, etc.).

Work

Employment of prisoners may be within the prison's commercial units, on tasks required in the prison, or on contractual work outside the prison. Prisoners who are fully employed during the serving of their sentence are entitled to all of the rights deriving from employment (salary, annual leave). Apart from the regular working hours (eight hours per day), the prisoner may be employed for no more than two hours in maintaining cleanliness and order in the prison. The basis for payment of salary is 25 percent of the basic salary of civil servants. The commercial units of the prisons sell their projects to the market, having long-term contracts with various external partners for whom they manufacture products or parts. They provide work in metal, carpentry, timber, plastic and wood-turning factories, agricultural work, electrical engineering, and a variety of other occupations.

Spiritual/Religious Services

Inmates are entitled to spiritual/religious services of the main religions in Central and Eastern Europe. A priest is employed by the Slovenian Prison Administration and provides prisoners with spiritual services as well as counseling.

Release Procedures

Slovenia does not have an organized parole administration. Aftercare must be provided by prisons (preparation for the release) and by centers for social work, which are organized as local community public services in the field of social assistance and whose operation is supervised by the Ministry of Labor, family, and social affairs.

Prisoners may be released conditionally after serving half of their sentence. In exceptional cases, a prisoner may be conditionally released after serving one-third of their sentence. A prisoner sentenced to more than 15 years may be conditionally released after serving three-quarters of the sentence. Older young offenders in juvenile prisons may be conditionally released after serving one-third of their sentences, though not until they have served at least six months. The court may order the juvenile to be supervised by a center for social work during the conditional release period.

The release decision for each individual case is made by the Commission for Conditional Releases at the Ministry of Justice on the request of the prisoner or their family members, or on the proposal of the governor. The commission meets every three months in each institution. A formal complaint against the decision of the commission is not allowed, but an administrative appeal is possible.

The prison governor is authorized to release prisoners up to one month before the completion of their sentence if they have served at least three-quarters of the period of the imposed imprisonment. The terms are appropriate behavior, striving at work, and active participation in the prison-sponsored programs.

If the conditionally released prisoner commits at least one criminal offense for which a prison sentence of more than one year may be imposed, or if he or she is convicted for the same type of criminal offense for which he or she had been convicted and imprisoned, the court may revoke the conditional release.

Gorazd Meško, Miran Mitar, and Sonja Kotnik

Further Reading

Meško, Gorazd, Bojan Dobovšek, and Milan Pagon. (2004). *Policing in Central and Eastern Europe: Dilemmas of Contemporary Criminal Justice.* Maribor, Slovenia: Faculty of Criminal Justice, University of Maribor.

Ministry of Interior, Police of the Republic of Slovenia: http://www.policija.si.

Mitar, Miran, and Gorazd Meško. (2008). "Reported Crime. Indications from Crime Victims Surveys and Fear of Crime Studies: An Attempt to Make a Clearer Picture of the Extent and Nature of Crime in Slovenia." In *Forecasting Crime and Control of Crime in Central and Eastern European Countries: Proceedings of the International Conference, Bratislava, November 14–16, 2007,* edited by Daniela Košecka, pp. 45–64. Bratislava, Slovak Republic: School of Law.

The Pipeline Project: http://www.pipeline-project.org.

The Statistical Yearbook of Republic of Slovenia: http://www.stat.si/eng/pub_letopis_prva.asp.

Šugman, Katja, Matjaž Jager, Nina Peršak, and Katja Filipčič. (2004). *Criminal Justice Systems in Europe and North America: Slovenia.* Helsinki: The European Institute for Crime Prevention and Control (HEUNI).

Note: The authors wish to thank Colby Eisenhart and Chris Eskridge of the University of Nebraska for their assistance in preparing this essay.

Spain

Legal System: Civil
Murder: Medium
Burglary: Low
Corruption: Low
Human Trafficking: Low
Prison Rate: Medium
Death Penalty: No
Corporal Punishment: No

Background

Spain is a constitutional kingdom situated in Western Europe on the Iberian Peninsula. It extends over 504,782 square kilometers (194,896 square miles). The Spanish Constitution is the highest legal authority, to which all others must accommodate. The most recent constitution dates from 1978, although the history of constitutional Spain goes as far back as 1812. The legal system is Continental, written laws and codes being the most important sources of rights and justice. The monarchy follows an hereditary model, and Juan Carlos I has been the king and head of the state since 1975. In that year, Spain experienced a very important political and social change that brought democracy to its citizens.

The political administration of Spain is made up of the Central Government and 17 autonomous regions (*Comunidades Autónomas*), plus 2 autonomous cities (Ceuta and Melilla, on the north African coast). There are three branches of the government: the executive, legislative, and judicial. The executive branch is organized around the *Consejo de Ministros* (Council of Ministers). The legislative branch is organized around the *Cortes Generales* (General Courts), and consists of two chambers, the *Congreso de Diputados* (Deputies Congress) and the *Senado* (Senate). Judges are governed by the *Consejo General del Poder Judicial* (General Council of the Judicial Power). Political parties play a key role in the designation of the members of these institutions, including the General Council of the Judicial Power.

Political life is strongly influenced by the two large national parties—the *Partido Socialista Obrero Español* (Spanish Socialist Party, ruling at the moment in the national government) and the *Partido Popular* (Popular Party)—and by a number of so-called nationalist parties.

The population of Spain has recently reached 46 million. Immigration has played a very important role in this achievement, especially in the last decade. According to different sources, there were between 4.5 and 5 million foreign residents in Spain in 2008. There are many reasons for this immigrant phenomenon. For many Europeans, Spain's weather and the relatively affordable prices make it a nice place for retirement. The Spanish language is an advantage for Latin Americans considering emigration, not to mention the traditional bonds with Spain. Finally, Spain's proximity to North Africa has led to a sizable number of immigrants entering illegally by sea. Moroccans and Ecuadorians represent around 10 percent each of the foreign population. Other sizeable communities include Romanians, Peruvians, Colombians, British, and Germans.

Crime

Classification of Crimes

From the early 1980s to the mid-1990s, an important item on the Spanish agenda had been to provide a new code to replace the 1973 *Texto Refundido* (Unified Text), associated with the Franco regime. The current Spanish Criminal Code dates from 1995. Although the 1995 code was entitled the *Código Penal de la Democracia* (Democracy's Code), there is strong debate regarding its necessity and its character. In general, it was probably necessary to have a new criminal code even though the important reforms of 1983 and 1989 had cleared most of the technical and material inconsistencies of the former legal body. At the same time, however, it is difficult to see anything new in the 1995 code since its structure can easily be traced to the original 1848 code.

The Criminal Code is the main Spanish body of criminal law, with the exception of a few *Leyes Penales Especiales* (Special Criminal Laws). These latter laws are criminal dispositions to be found outside the Criminal Code. They include the Military Criminal Code, the *Ley Penal del Menor* (Juveniles Criminal Law), and a few other laws that include crimes and criminal punishments. The Criminal Code is organized in three books. The first includes the so-called General Part and the second and third, the so-called Special Part. Crimes are classified in three categories: *delitos graves, menos graves,* and *faltas* (serious offenses, less serious offenses, and misdemeanors). This classification, however, is much more procedural in nature than it is substantive.

Liberal criminal law has developed strongly in Spain over the last few decades. As a result, a system respectful of suspected and convicted criminals has grown. In the last few years, nevertheless, this system seems to be in a deep crisis, and some commentators suggest that Spain no longer has a liberal criminal law and that, at the same time, it does not seem to be coming back in the future.

Three principles apply to Spain's Criminal Law: the principles of legality, culpability, and proportionality. To be considered a crime, the principle of legality dictates that a behavior should be defined as "criminal" in a written Organic Law. The same applies to penalties—there can be no punishment without crime. And without culpability, there is no criminal responsibility. This principle has many important consequences, including the exclusion of objective responsibility, as in other branches of the law.

The Spanish Criminal Law is in a process of expansion, and the principle of proportionality has probably been abandoned. As is the case in many European countries, a process of increasing punitivity at the level of the state can be observed in Spain. Scholars have studied these developments and tied them to changes in late-modern societies. For example, in recent years, there has been an increasing inclusion in the Criminal Code of so-called risk crimes, that is, behavior causing risk but not actual damage. This is part of the process of expansion of criminal law and includes cases in which there is no effect upon any person or object, but the probability that damage can take place.

Police inspect the scene of a car bomb explosion near a trade fair center on Madrid's outskirts, February 9, 2009. The armed Basque group ETA is believed to have planted the bomb, which blew a three-foot hole in the ground, destroyed some 30 cars, and blew out windows at nearby offices, though no one was hurt. (AP Photo/Arturo Rodriguez)

The Spanish Criminal Code includes, among the offenses against individuals (homicide, murder, bodily harm), sexual offenses including forcible rape, offenses against honor, offenses against personal security, property offenses, including many examples of reckless offenses, offenses against the state security, offenses against the administration of justice, drug offenses, terrorism, and so forth.

Drug offenses, as in many other countries, play an important role in explaining the large inmate populations in prisons. According to the Spanish Criminal Code, the acts of growing, processing, trafficking, promoting, and facilitating the consumption of illegal drugs are punishable. In certain cases, a higher penalty can be imposed. Such is the case for members of permanent or temporary organizations involved in trafficking of drugs. Personal consumption of drugs is not punishable according to the Criminal Law.

Crimes of terrorism are also important for the Spanish Criminal Law, due to the traditional problems faced by Spain. The legal regulation is complex and includes cases of the individual terrorist.

Penalties include prison sentences lasting up to 40 years (though this penalty can be imposed in very exceptional cases), fine, suspension of public office, revocation of driving license, and suspension of other rights. The Criminal Code provides maximum and minimum limits on penalties, and a catalog of circumstances that may mitigate or exacerbate the exact amount of penalty to be imposed. Capital punishment was abolished by the Spanish Constitution in 1978, although before that date executions were very rare.

The age of criminal responsibility in Spain is 8 years. Cases involving individuals between 14 and 18 can be adjudicated in the juvenile courts according to the Juvenile Criminal Law. Delinquents between 18 and 21 years old can as well be judged according to this law (Criminal Code, article 19).

Since 1995, the Criminal Code has experienced no less than 20 reforms, some of them very extensive. This is especially the case of changes made in 2003. An example will be helpful here. The 1995 Spanish Criminal Code increased the punishment in cases of recidivism. By comparison, the 1983 reform did not include recidivism as a special qualification. Punishment in the case of recidivism was increased again in the 2003 reform.

Crime Statistics

There seems to be some agreement that crime trends have not increased in Spain in any significant way in the last several years. However, it must first be stated that there is an important problem regarding the sources of data on crime in Spain. Social sciences, and especially criminology, are not well developed in Spain. The causes usually mentioned in the literature have to do with traditional anti-empirical bias and the imperialism of certain disciplines as is the case of criminal law. At the same time, since corruption is rampant in the field of human sciences and the university, criminology as a positivist science has not had a chance to develop. As a result, there is little sound scientific research on the extent and evolution of crime in Spain. The best approach, in any case, is to collect as many sources of information regarding the evolution of crime, and then compare them.

In general, the state of Spanish criminal statistics is quite confusing. For many years, statistics were not published in any systematic way. Some scientific journals tried to fill this gap by gathering data through informal means. The best examples are the *Revista de Derecho Penal y Criminología* (*Review of Criminal Law and Criminology*), a well-known journal edited by the Criminal Law and Criminology Department of the *Universidad Nacional de Educación a Distancia* (National University of Distance Education) in Madrid. One may find data in its section on statistics since the early 1990s. In the last few years, the Spanish *Ministerio del Interior* (Ministry of Interior) has tried to improve Spanish statistics. Regular information is now available in a few sources, including its Web page. It is hoped that in a few years the process of official data collection will improve.

Regarding the validity and reliability of official statistics, some Spanish criminologists express little confidence. Some seem to suggest that statistics are occasionally made up. In fact, official data from the police are compiled and reported by a small working group that in a certain way is dependent upon the Ministry of Interior. At any rate, without viable alternatives, it seems that there is not much of a choice but to rely on official data.

Criminologists in Spain have generally relied on two sources of official data to measure crime: crimes known to the police—just mentioned—and *Diligencias previas incoadas por presuntos delitos* (Previous measures taken for suspected offenses). These previous measures refer to the actuation of the *Fiscalías* (Prosecutors) when a would-be crime comes to their knowledge, to prosecute it or not (actually it is a judge—the *Juez Instructor* (Examining Magistrate)—who decides whether to prosecute or not, and this for historical and political reasons). Crimes known to the police fall under the competence of the Spanish Ministry of Interior, and previous measures under that of the *Fiscalía General del Estado* (General Prosecution Services of the State). It is probably true that both sources of information regarding the extent of crime have their own strengths and weaknesses. Criminologists have demonstrated the problems that account for the differences between previous measures and crimes known to the police (mainly, that some crimes are counted more than once in the case of previous measures). As can be seen in the following table, the two different measures reveal quite different trend patterns in crime. Previous measures displays a clear bulge in incidence in the late 1990s, but by 2005 falls back to the level of the early 1990s. In contrast, offenses known to police have remained stable, and misdemeanors known to police have gradually increased over the same period. Whether these statistics represent actual changes in crime as against changes in workload of judges or recording practices by police remains unknown.

Offenses and Misdemeanors Known to the Police and Previous Measures Taken by the Prosecution Services, 1991–2005 (per 100,000 pop.)

YEAR	OFFENSES KNOWN TO THE POLICE	MISDEMEANORS KNOWN TO THE POLICE	PROSECUTION SERVICES
1991	2,547	1,388	6,525
1992	2,386	1,398	6,988
1993	2,359	1,524	7,478
1994	2,241	1,641	7,675
1995	2,245	1,717	7,978
1996	2,346	1,927	8,764
1997	2,325	2,017	8,866
1998	2,424	2,150	10,129
1999	2,392	2,191	10,110
2000	2,280	2,140	9,817
2001	2,470	2,337	9,622
2002	2,480	2,480	9,791
2003	2,237	2,442	5,938
2004	2,168	2,427	6,331
2005	2,110	2,503	6,746

Source: Fernández Villazala, T. 2008. *La medición del delito en la seguridad pública.* Madrid: Dykinson; *Fiscalía General del Estado* (Prosecution Services of the State).

Finding of Guilt

According to the Spanish Procedure Law, the investigation of crimes in the criminal process is carried out by a judge (*Juez de instrucción,* examining magistrate), though critical voices suggest that this role should be played by a prosecutor. Actually, there is an important debate on the issue in Spain. Some authors insist on the technical benefits of an investigation by a prosecutor, while others fear the influence of politicians since prosecutors are not independent and must follow the direction of their chiefs—needless to say, usually with strong political bonds.

Suspects are protected by procedural guarantees and rights. Any accused has the right to be defended by a public attorney. Arrested individuals have the right to remain silent, to be informed in a clear and understandable way of charges against them, to provide and ask for evidence, to a speedy trial, to legal assistance including public assistance when they do not have means, that relatives or acquaintances are informed of the detention, and so forth. Judicial warrants are required for entrance to search and seize evidence.

There are multiple police agencies in Spain. The *Guardia Civil* (Civil Guard) and *Policía Nacional* (National Police) are national forces and represent the largest of all agencies. There are other police corps in some autonomous regions such as the *Mossos d'Esquadra* in Catalonia and *Ertzaintza* in the Basque Country. There are also local police in many cities. Brief legal information about two forms of detention will be provided here: *detención* (arrest) and *prisión preventiva* (pretrial detention), both regulated by the Spanish Law of Criminal Procedure (*Ley de Enjuiciamiento Criminal*, LECrim).

It is the duty of the police to arrest suspects of crimes of certain severity, as well as cases where the suspect is unlikely to appear in court when required (art. 494 LECrim). In these cases, the police are to bring the suspect to the judge within 72 hours of arrest. There exists the possibility of extending this time by 48 hours in the case of terrorism (LECrim, article 520bis). Pretrial detention (*prisión provisional*) can only apply to crimes with punishments of 2 or more years imprisonment, except in the case of suspects with records that have not been cancelled or cannot be cancelled; only when there is "enough reason" (*motivos bastantes*) to believe the suspect is responsible for the crime; and only when pretrial detention is a means to avoid escape; the concealment, destruction, or alteration of evidence; or the commission of further crimes against the victim. In general, pretrial detention will only take place when there are no other measures to meet the same ends (LECrim, Art. 503 y 520). In practice, judges have no obligation to make use of pretrial detention. They tend not to apply this measure because they understand suspects often are unlikely to commit any other crime, hide evidence, and will appear in court when required to do so.

Punishment

We have seen that, according to the Criminal Code (art. 33), there are many different types of punishment. At the same time, imprisonment is the best-known form, and the one citizens have in their minds when they think about punishing criminals. With the exception of Catalonia, the prison system depends on the central government. Prison conditions are in general acceptable in Spain in comparison with other countries, although there is a problem of overpopulation. The government has announced new prisons. Whether this will reduce overpopulation remains to be seen.

There are two important ways for a convicted criminal to avoid imprisonment. In cases of first-time offenders, with prison sentences not exceeding two years, the penalty can be suspended. Another requirement is payment of civil responsibilities (Criminal Code, art. 80 ff.). The idea is that a prison term shorter than two years might have a negative impact on the individual, for example, cutting his or her social bonds or losing his or her job. This impact is not compatible with the potential general deterrent effect of the punishment. It is a clear example of a punishment philosophy that places retribution at the center of the system, but gives a role to deterrence too. In practice, judges apply this rule in an automatic way. In similar cases, when suspension of a prison sentence cannot be applied, a substitution may be in order. Fines or community service are potential substitutes for imprisonment here (Criminal Code, art. 808 ff.). Finally, another important institution for tempering the effects of imprisonment is *libertad condicional* (conditional release). It is possible for prisoners to be released after a certain portion of the sentence has been served, usually three-fourths (Criminal Code, art. 90 ff.). Work in prisons is very common for inmates, although since the 1995 Code, it does not translate automatically in a reduction of time in prison in the traditional form of one day for every two of work (known as *redención de penas por el trabajo*, "redemption of sanctions through work").

Empirical evidence suggests that levels of punitivity have steadily increased, at least in many Western countries, in the last few years, possibly as a result of citizens being worried, fearful, and insecure of a loss of quality in their lives. Indeed, the 1995 Spanish Criminal Code was more punitive than the previous, which paradoxically dated from 1973, still in the Franco era. Since 1995, most of the reforms of the Criminal Code followed a punitive trend. Whatever the reason, the mean number of persons incarcerated in Spanish prisons has increased from 36.5 in 1991 to 68.9 as of July 2008, according to the director general of penitentiary institutions.

In regard to the death penalty, forbidden in Spain since the 1978 Constitution, surveys conducted by the *Centro de Investigaciones Sociológicas* have shown that consistently over 70 percent of respondents are against it. This would lend credence to the claim that increases in punishments as measured by incarceration are not the result of a general punitivity of citizens but to either political or legislative changes in criminal law and its administration.

Alfonso Serrano Maíllo

Further Reading

Aebi, Marcelo F., and Marc Balcells. (2008). "The Prosecution Service Function within the Spanish Criminal Justice System." *European Journal on Criminal Policy and Research* 14(2–3): 311–331.

Aebi, Marcelo F., and Gonzalo Jar-Couselo. (2006). "Spain." In *World Police Encyclopedia,* edited by Dillip K. Das, pp. 773–780. New York: Routledge

Barberet, Rosemary. (2005). "Spain." *European Journal of Criminology* 2(3): 341–368.

Mendoza Buergo, Blanca. (2001). *El Derecho penal en la sociedad del riesgo* [Criminal Law in the Risk Society]. Madrid: Civitas.

Serrano Gómez, Algonso. (2006). "Prólogo" [Prologue]. In *Derecho penal. Parte especial,* edited by Alfonso Serrano Gómez and Alfonso Serrano Maíllo, 11th ed. Madrid: Dykinson.

Serrano Maíllo, Alfonso. (2006). "Punitivität und Gesetzgebung: Die Situation in Spanien" [Punitivity and Legislation: The Situation in Spain]. In *Kriminalität und Kriminalprävention in Ländern des Umbruchs,* edited by Helmut Kury and Elmar Karimov, pp. 721–745. Bochum, Germany: Brockmeyer.

Stangeland, Per. (1995). "La delincuencia en España: Un análisis crítico de las estadísticas judiciales y policiales" [Delinquency in Spain: A Critical Analysis of Crime and Criminal Justice Statistics]. *Revista de Derecho Penal y Criminología* 5: 803–839.

Svalbard and Jan Mayen Islands

Legal System: Civil/Common
Murder: Low
Corruption: Low
Human Trafficking: Low
Prison Rate: Low
Death Penalty: No
Corporal Punishment: No

Background

Both Svalbard (*Spitzbergen*) and Jan Mayen Islands are nowadays two *distinct* dependencies of the Kingdom of Norway, but there are different theories about their discovery. The Danish-Norwegian Kingdom claimed its sovereignty during the 16th, 17th, and 18th centuries, finding resistance from both the English and the Dutch. A conference between the three states was arranged in Oslo in 1910, but nothing came out of it. At a closed meeting in November 1918, the Standing Committee of Foreign Affairs announced that Norway should acquire sovereignty over Svalbard. The Norwegian Svalbard Act was enacted in 1925. Section 2 of the act set out that even though Svalbard has some legislative power, Norwegian civil law, criminal law, and the Norwegian regulations concerning legal procedure applied to Svalbard. Until 1994, Jan Mayen and Svalbard were governed by the governor of Svalbard, an officer known as the *sysselmannen.* From August 1994 the administration of Jan Mayen was taken over by a county governor of Nordland, an office called *fylkesmann.* Svalbard was home to 2,321 inhabitants in 2007, whereas the only inhabitants on Jan Mayen are personnel working for the Norwegian military or the Norwegian Meteorological Institute. They all work on the LORAN-C base, which is a radio navigation center.

The *sysselmann* on Svalbard has both administrative and police authority. He or she may even function as a judge. Svalbard has no ordinary local democracy, but different governmental bodies are, however, represented; for instance, the Svalbard Council in Longyearbyen, whose representatives are elected by the Norwegian population. Svalbard is demilitarized and has no army of its own. Svalbard has, on the other hand, Norway's biggest coast guard ships that serve the seas in the north and operate closely with the police force, that handles the entire archipelago to the territorial limits of 12 nautical miles outside of Svalbard.

Crime

Classification of Crimes

Norwegian criminal law is applicable on crimes committed in the realm, on any Norwegian vessel or aircraft, by any member of its crew or by any person traveling on it or abroad by a Norwegian citizen or any other person with domicile in Norway, if it is a felony or misdemeanor against the state and punishable in the country committed. Criminal law defines most of the offenses that are against the law. It also defines a number of other regulations, which are not necessarily a crime but which still lead to a penalty. Norwegian legislators are trying to reflect society's morals through the Penal Code and the code is therefore changing with the society. At the moment a criminal act is defined as an act carried out against the current Norwegian law and which is followed by a penalty. Offenses can include a number of different acts, with various motives for the offender. A person has to have reached the age of 15 to be held criminally responsible.

The Norwegian Penal Code groups criminal offenses into felonies, *forbrytelser,* and misdemeanors, *forseelser.* Felonies are, with some exceptions, offenses with a maximum penalty of three months' imprisonment or more. The majority of felonies are defined and listed in the Penal Code, where one can find, for example, perjury, arson, racial discrimination, rape, slander and libel, larceny, embezzlement, damaging information and communication systems, murder, blackmail and robbery, fraud, breach of trust, and so forth. Misdemeanors are generally minor offenses carrying a maximum penalty of three months' imprisonment. Examples of these types of offenses can also be found in the Penal Code. All breaches of the Road Traffic Act are defined as misdemeanors irrespective of whether or not they carry a maximum penalty of more than three months' imprisonment.

The Penal Code and the Medicine Goods Act cover drug offenses. It is illegal to use, sell, manufacture, store (as opposed to possess), and to transport narcotics. Drug offenses are usually punished by a fine or by imprisonment up to 2 years. For a serious drug offense the offender can be given a sentence up to 10 years. The degree of seriousness depends on the type of drug involved. If the quantity is seen as very significant, imprisonment can be imposed for as long as 3 to 15 years. Under "particularly aggravating circumstances," the punishment can be as much as 21 years. Illegal drugs are listed in the Narcotic Regulations by the Ministry of Social Affairs and cover approximately 250 substances. Even some kind of salts and derivatives are categorized as narcotics.

Crime Statistics

According to *Statistisk sentralbyrå,* Oslo, during 2005 the total number of crimes reported to the police in Norway was 394,301. Svalbard only had 88 crimes reported during 2005. Of all crimes reported, 62 percent were classified as crimes and 38 percent as misdemeanors. The breakdown was as follows: 40 percent of the crimes were property offenses, 17 percent traffic offenses, 15 percent vandalism and environment-related offenses, and only a few were crimes of violence and other sexual crimes. The prosecution authority, the district court, or the Lower Court of Appeal punished as few as 31 of the offenders, of which 2 were female offenders, 23 were sentenced with a fine, 2 with a probation sentence; 6 offenders were sent to prison.

According to Statistics Norway, most of the crimes in Norway are committed by male offenders, surprisingly enough, by offenders who are between 30 and 60 years old. The majority of prison inmates, on the other hand, around 65 percent, are men aged 25–44. Around 100–150 criminal cases are charged in Svalbard every year. Although most of them are minor cases of theft or vandalism, occasional incidents of serious violence or work-related accidents occur quite often. Special attention has lately been devoted to environmental crime. As the situation is now, about every 5 to 10 cases of environmental crime are investigated and punished with a fine.

Finding of Guilt

According to the General Civil Penal Code, no person can be criminally responsible before reaching the age of 15. No person may either be punished for committing an act in self-defense or for saving a person or property from otherwise unavoidable danger. No one who acts unintentionally is liable under Norwegian criminal law, unless it is expressly or unambiguously provided that also negligent acts are punishable. If the offender is intoxicated by alcohol or any other means, the court will not take this into consideration when judging the willfulness of the act. Also a misdemeanor consisting of failure to act is punishable under the law. A person acting in a state of ignorance, concerning the circumstances in the case, is always liable for the consequences. If the offender has a mental disturbance, like psychosis or another mental illness, he or she is not criminally responsible.

The rights of the accused are described in the Criminal Procedure Act. The most basic right is to have one's case tried in front of a judge. The offender has also the right to attend the court proceedings, if there are not any special circumstances. Further, the suspect has the right to know what charges are being brought against him or her and has to be given a chance to refute the grounds of which the charges are being based. As a general rule, the suspect is always entitled to legal assistance during all stages of the process. During the main hearing the court shall provide free assistance to the suspect, if the case is complicated. Finally, the suspect has the right to bring appeals against court verdicts, both on questions concerning facts and questions of law. The time limit for an appeal is two weeks from the judgment. There are, however, several limitations on the exercise of this right. For example, appeals to the Supreme Court, which is the highest judicial body, can only take place if the appeal is permitted by the court's Appeals Selection Committee.

A criminal case in the district court is being solved with one professional judge and two lay judges. In particularly complex cases or if for some other reason it is necessary, the court can decide to sit with two professional judges and three lay judges. All lay judges shall be experts in their fields.

Criminal investigation is instituted and carried out by the police. Examination and investigation of suspects under the age of 18 can be carried out, but the guardian shall be informed and given opportunity to participate. If the case is trivial, the police shall inform the child welfare services.

Punishment

Types of Punishment

The general punishments, according to the Norwegian Penal Code, are imprisonment, preventive detention, detention, community service, and fines. In special cases loss of civil rights can be imposed in addition to or instead of other penalties. A sentence of imprisonment is always a limited time, from 14 days to 15 years, and in special cases 20 or 21 years. A prisoner can be released on probation in accordance with the provision of a special act. An offender can be sentenced to detention from 14 days up to 20 years. Detention can be converted to imprisonment, where 2 days of detention are equivalent to 1 day of prison. Under certain conditions community service can be given as a sentence by the court instead of imprisonment. First, a more severe sentence than 1 year of imprisonment would not have been given. Second, the purpose of the sentence cannot contradict a noncustodial sanction, and finally, the offender has to be resident in Norway. Community service can be given for a maximum 420 hours and cannot exceed 120 days. When a fine is imposed, consideration must be given not only to the nature of the offense but also especially to the financial position of the offender and to what he or she could presumably afford to pay under the circumstances.

Prison

Norway is divided into six prison districts. Inmates in Norwegian prisons are usually in a bad situation already before imprisonment. According to a survey done by Statistics Norway, inmates reported that they had difficult and complex living conditions outside prison. Many of them were unemployed and had no permanent accommodation. The education level among inmates is poor. Most of them have only lower secondary school; as a consequence these people are not attractive on the labor market, since they have little to offer, compared with an average Norwegian citizen. Norwegian prisons held around 3,250 prisoners in 2006, and the number keeps increasing. There have been two prisons, one on Svalbard and one on Jan Mayen Island, but they are just tourist attractions nowadays.

Anna Gustafson

Further Reading

Domstoladministrasjonen, the National Court Administration: http://www.domstol.no.

Intro, a Web site on the Norwegian society: http://www.introengelsk.cappelen.no.
Ministry of Justice and the Norwegian Police: http://www.regjeringen.no/en/dep.

Sweden

Legal System: Civil
Murder: Medium
Burglary: Medium
Corruption: Low
Human Trafficking: Low
Prison Rate: Medium
Death Penalty: No
Corporal Punishment: No

Background

Sweden is a small country with about 9.2 million inhabitants located on the outskirts of Northern Europe. Sweden has until recently been regarded as the welfare state *par excellence,* exhibiting high employment rates and social expenditure but weak family ties, lower poverty rates, and lower income inequality. The political wing of the labor movement, the Social Democratic Party, has long dominated Swedish politics. The Social Democrats have governed since the 1930s, with the exception of the periods 1976–1982, 1991–1994, and from 2006, when center-right blocs were elected into office.

Modern Swedish criminal law is based on written rules and is rooted in a European civil law tradition. Some written local codification already existed prior to 1350; major "modern" codifications originate from 1736, 1865, and 1965, when the present Penal Code came into force. The rules of the European Convention on Human Rights (ECHR) have constituted part of the Swedish law since 1995.

Police

The police service is one of the largest public employers in Sweden. However, in a European perspective, the number of police per inhabitants is low. In 2007, there were a total of 18,000 sworn police officers. The first policewoman was employed in 1957. Today, 22 percent of all sworn police officers and 14 percent of the commanding police officers are women. The police have been state-financed since 1965. Municipal police, city guards, border police, gendarmerie, fiscal, or court police do not exist in Sweden. The police budget amounts presently to about €1.7 billion (US$2.14 billion).

Each of the 21 counties in Sweden constitutes a police district. In each district, there is a police authority responsible for the policing of the district. A police authority is led by a Police Board made up of the county police commissioner and a number of politically appointed members. Each police authority decides how its work is to be organized. The National Audit Office has repeatedly criticized the complicated structures of the Swedish police.

The style of policing is civilian; there is no barracked police force, and the existing military police has no civilian functions. The powers of the police are regulated by written laws. There is no empirical evidence of systematic police brutality or police corruption. According to a Danish investigation regarding the years 1996–2006, the annual average of civilians killed or wounded by Swedish police officers using a firearm has been one and five persons, respectively. It is difficult to get into the National Police Academies: only about 5 to 10 percent of applicants can be offered a place. Efforts are being made to increase the proportion of women and ethnic minority officers. The Police Training Program comprises two years of full-time studies and six months of field training at a police authority.

Crime

Classification of Crimes

The Swedish system makes no formal distinction between serious and minor offenses (e.g., felonies and misdemeanors). Both are classified as "crime." However, the Penal Code usually divides offenses of major importance into three categories: minor, normal, and serious infractions of the law. Since the year 2000 all findings of guilt are registered in a central register and held for a period of 5 to 10 years. Prior to 2000, only more serious infractions were registered. It is possible to grade offenses according to their (abstract) sanctioning scale, because certain coercive procedural measures only apply in the case of more serious infractions; the pretrial detention of a suspect in principle presupposes an offense that is punishable by imprisonment, for example.

The exact number of punishable offenses in Sweden is not known. A study conducted in the early 1990s counted more than 400 laws—in addition to the Penal Code—that contained punishment clauses. The Penal Code itself specifies some 150 different criminal offenses. Thus, it is clear that the authorities have to set priorities. Violence against women, juvenile offending, serious economic criminality, and other forms of crime deemed to present a threat to the nation's economic and political infrastructure are currently prioritized. A national strategy to meet the threat of terrorism has been formulated.

In practice, property offenses, major traffic offenses, drug offenses and violence are the most frequent offenses for which people are punished. At least every fourth adjudicated offense is directly connected to narcotics. As of 2006, 55 percent of the daily prison population was considered by the prison authorities to have a history of drug use. Swedish drug policy is based on the principle of total prohibition. All nonmedical handling of drugs is a punishable offense. The unrelenting view on drugs, which is shared by both politicians and the public, may be seen as partly being a consequence of the strong temperance tradition in Swedish history, dating back to the mid-1800s. The drug policy has been one of the core reasons for the recent shift in Swedish criminal justice policy toward

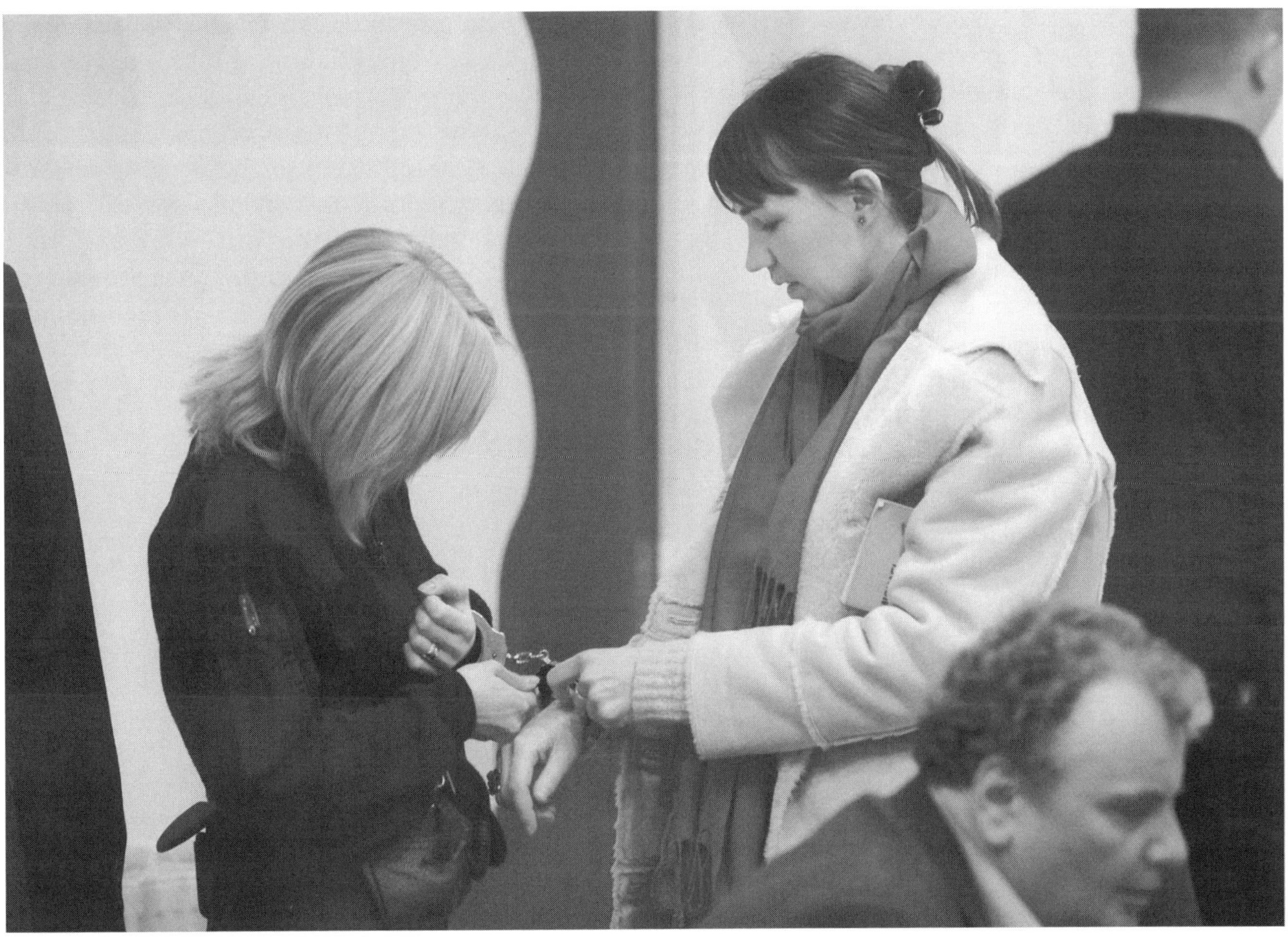

Christine Schuerrer, right, is handcuffed at the end of a hearing in the Svea Court of Appeal in Vasteras, Sweden, January 19, 2009. Schuerrer, a German citizen, has been sentenced to life in prison for killing two toddlers in Arboga, Sweden, in March 2008. (AP Photo/Jessica Gow)

a more punitive approach. Regrettably, Sweden scores high when it comes to drug-related deaths.

Crime Statistics

Sweden has a well-developed system of criminal justice statistics. Yearly data on homicide can be traced back as far as to the 1750s. Today, homicide rates lie at about the same level (at about 1 per 100,000 population) as in the 1870s, the 1830s, and the 1750s. Court statistics have been published annually since the 1830s, following the French model. National data on police-recorded offenses are available since the early 1950s. Nationwide victim surveys have been conducted on a regular basis since the late 1970s, and regular nationwide self-report studies among pupils started in 1995. Sweden has also participated in the International Crime Victims Surveys (ICVS) since 1992. The most recent sweep (2004–2005) showed that crime peaked around 2000 and is now at a level similar to that of the early 1990s. In the European Union (EU) context the level of crime in Sweden is medium high. Public exposure to drugs-related problems is relatively rare. The prevalence of hate crimes is just above the EU average.

Sweden is known for its comprehensive way of counting offenses in police statistics, which makes it appear to be a high-crime country. Comparisons with victim surveys do not corroborate this picture. Therefore, no detailed information is provided here about offenses reported to the police, which conforms to Jan van Dijk's recent criticism against the use of police statistics in an international comparative frame of reference.

However, it is meaningful to describe the *structure* of police-recorded criminality. Thus, in 2007, 65 percent of all recorded crimes comprised crimes against property (including fraud, criminal damage, etc.), 16 percent comprised crimes against the person (violent offenses and sex offenses), 6 percent comprised drug crimes or serious traffic offenses. The high proportion of property offenses is partly related to the fact that almost all Swedish households have a home insurance that covers incidents of crime. To receive compensation, the insurance companies require that the crime is first reported to the police.

Since living conditions in modern Sweden are much the same in the cities and in rural areas, the crime profiles are not very different between geographical regions. According to recent victim surveys, crime is less than twice as frequent in densely populated areas in comparison to less densely populated areas.

The ICVS project as well as the Eurobarometer surveys not only monitor events of criminal victimization but also other related matters such as levels of fear, crime-preventive measures, and attitudes toward and experiences of the police. Asked whether they felt they were at risk of being burgled during the following year, respondents from Sweden ranked low or average in an international perspective. Feelings of insecurity were consistently low among Swedish respondents, when asked how safe they felt outside in their own neighborhood after dark. In response to the question of whether they had installed various kinds of anti-break-in devices (such as burglar alarms, special locks, or bars on windows and doors), Swedish respondents scored in the middle. According to the Spring 2008 Eurobarometer, Swedish respondents ranked, somewhat surprisingly, the health care system and crime as the two most important issues facing Sweden at the moment (while the average EU citizen was most concerned about rising prices and unemployment).

Finding of Guilt

According to article 6(2) ECHR, a person suspected of a crime is legally considered innocent until proven otherwise. The burden of proof lies with the state (prosecution and courts). However, a suspected person can—under circumstances qualified by law—be placed in pretrial detention. Other coercive measures are also lawful. Inter alia, the following measures are applicable according to Swedish law:

- Capture, arrest, and detention
- Travel bans and a duty to report to the police
- Sequestration
- Seizure
- Searches of premises and body searches
- Public camera surveillance

- Secret camera surveillance, wiretapping, etc.
- Concealed microphones, bugging, etc.
- Blood tests, breath tests, saliva tests for DNA analysis

Sweden has often been criticized for its practice of imposing unnecessary isolation and other restrictions on pretrial detainees. In its report of 2008, the UN Committee against Torture (CAT) expressed concern regarding information that still between 40 and 50 percent of remand prisoners are subjected to restrictions and that remand prisoners are currently unable to effectively challenge and appeal decisions to impose or to maintain specific restrictions. The committee also complained of the lack of official statistics on the use of such restrictions.

The actual time spent in pretrial detention amounts on average to 45 days and is regularly deducted from the final prison sentence. According to article 5(5) ECHR, everyone who has been the victim of arrest or detention in contravention of the provisions of article 5 ECHR shall have an enforceable right to compensation. In 2007, about 1,200 persons were compensated for unlawful arrest or detention. Usually, the state pays between €50–70 per day as compensation. According to official statistics for 2006, about 30,000 persons (gross number) had been taken into custody by the police, and 11,500 persons (gross number) had been placed in pretrial detention by the courts. Despite the presumed innocence of crime suspects, there is a growing trend in the Swedish media to name them, sooner or later, and to publish their pictures.

Crime Investigation

As a rule, crimes are investigated by the police. In more serious cases, a prosecutor can lead the investigation. There are about 850 prosecutors in Sweden assisted by 400 staff. Fifty-two percent of prosecutors are women (2007). A prosecutor in Sweden is not elected but is rather a civil servant. Becoming a trainee public prosecutor requires a law degree and formal court practice as a law clerk. The Prosecution Authority's budget amounts presently to about €90 million.

Once a criminal investigation has been finalized, the prosecutor decides whether the case should be brought before the court or settled in another way. However, police have in minor cases the legal power to decide not to open a case for investigation or to close an investigation without the consent of the prosecutor. The right of the crime victim to prosecute a case as an individual remains only in rare cases.

If the prosecutor considers a person guilty of an offense, there are three possibilities to proceed, depending on the circumstances of the case: the prosecutor can (1) issue a waiver of prosecution, (2) fine the guilty suspect, or (3) go to court. Waivers and fines require the suspect to consent to being guilty. If the person does not consent, the case goes to court.

Plea bargaining is not known in Sweden. In 2002, mediation (restorative justice) was introduced into the Swedish system. However, it does not replace a criminal sanction, and it is only used in connection with juveniles and only for nonserious offenses. In 2007, a total of 416,000 persons (gross number) were found guilty of a criminal offense (minor traffic offense included). The distribution was as follows (rounded numbers):

- Summary fines (by police; Swedish customs): 292,000
- Waivers of prosecution (by prosecutor): 21,000
- Day-fines (by prosecutor): 41,000
- Sentences (by court): 62,000

Court sentences are relatively rare. This is because the crime picture is dominated by less serious mass criminality ("volume crime"), which for practical and economic reasons should not burden the courts. The first rules regarding summary fines were introduced in the late 1940s and their area of application has been consistently broadened since that time. The police were given the right to issue summary fines in the late 1960s. Today the majority of people found guilty of a criminal offense in Sweden are found guilty outside the courts. Due process had to make way for economic considerations.

From a European perspective, Sweden ranks high among countries punishing people found guilty of a criminal offense. A study of a Swedish birth cohort showed that as much as 37 percent of the males and 10 percent of the females were registered for at least one nontrivial criminal offense up to age 37. Most frequent were registrations for theft, major traffic offense, drug crime, criminal assault, inflicting damage, public order disturbances, fraud, and violence against a public servant.

Courts

There are 53 judicial districts in Sweden, each one with a district court and six courts of appeal. The Supreme Court is located in Stockholm. The courts hear both criminal and civil cases. In 2008, there were a total of 527 permanent judges, 137 trainee judges, and 660 law clerks. The corresponding numbers at appeal courts were 197 judges and 280 trainee judges. Unfortunately, their distribution according to gender is not easily available. At the levels of the district and appeal courts, Sweden uses a mix of permanent and lay judges. In district courts, the criminal court consists of three lay judges and one permanent judge. In appeal courts, the criminal court consists of three permanent and two lay judges. The lay judges are elected by the local government on a political party basis and serve a term of four years. Permanent judges must have a law degree and are appointed by the government. In principle, a permanent judge cannot be dismissed other than in specific cases set out in the Instrument of Government. Lay judges have the same functions as permanent judges, although they cannot chair a court session. The courts decide according to a one-person-one-vote rule.

The basic provisions on proceedings in criminal (and civil) cases are to be found in the Swedish Code of Judicial Procedure. This means that the court rules on cases after a main hearing attended by both parties who orally state their claims and other circumstances relating to the case. During the main hearing any witnesses and experts are heard and other evidence is presented. There are no particular rules on the assessment of evidence. Hearsay testimony is principally admissible and so is evidence gathered unlawfully.

Seventy-five percent of criminal cases are generally settled within 6 months at the district courts and within another 10 months at the courts of appeal. Cases where the defendant is detained or is young have priority and are settled in a shorter period of time. Bail is not known in Sweden. On average, a district court case costs €1,300 as compared with €3,450 in courts of appeal.

The typical court session lasts for 1.5 hours. In 5 percent of cases the court session exceeds 6 hours. In about 12 percent of cases, the defendant is on pretrial remand. Thirteen percent of cases are usually dismissed by the courts. Another 12 percent of cases are appealed to the Court of Appeal. The appeal sessions last about 2.3 hours on average. The defendant appeals more often than the public prosecutor. The verdict is changed in roughly one-third of the cases. The odds are higher for the public prosecutor to get the verdict changed than they are for the defendant. Only very few cases (about 2%) are finally decided by the Supreme Court. The Supreme Court reviews only legal and procedural questions, never the facts of the case.

In cases of a simple nature, the court normally delivers its judgment immediately. If the defendant is detained, the court must pronounce its judgment no later than one week after the completion of the hearing. Special rules apply to young offenders; for instance, such cases are to be dealt with promptly.

Defense Counsel and Legal Aid

Private defense counsels are always admissible. The police are not legally obligated to inform the suspect of the right to have a lawyer present. According to a recent study in Gothenburg, a lawyer was present in 7 percent of police interrogations. However, anyone suspected of a serious crime or taken into custody is always entitled to a public defense counsel. In the case of minor offenses, it is up to the court to determine whether or not the suspect needs a defense counsel. Suspects who are sentenced for a crime are obliged to cover the state's costs for their defense counsel, although the sum may not exceed the equivalent costs for legal aid (explained below). Those who are acquitted do not have to pay the costs of their defense counsel.

Legal Aid

In Sweden legal aid constitutes a form of statutory social protection legislation that aims to help an individual who cannot obtain legal support in any other way. The right to legal aid is governed by the Legal Aid Act. In practice, legal aid is financial support provided by the state to those who are unable to pay for a legal representative. Legal aid covers part of the costs for the legal representative and also costs relating to evidence and other expenditure. Being granted legal aid does not automatically mean that the state pays all the costs for the legal representative. The basic idea is that one should contribute to the cost to the extent one can afford. One can receive legal aid for the whole or part of the cost of a legal representative for up to 100 hours. In special cases the court can extend legal aid.

Crime Victims

As a rule, victims of serious crimes are entitled to free counsel and support services in connection with the preliminary investigation and trial. If it is suspected that a child is the victim of an offense by one of its guardians, the child may receive more extensive support from a special representative for children. Special support to witnesses has also been introduced at most district courts and at all courts of appeal to make proceedings easier for injured parties and witnesses.

Juveniles

The age of criminal responsibility has long been 15 years in Sweden. According to the Penal Code, persons under 15 who have committed an offense cannot be sentenced to any criminal sanction. If the underage offender is in need of corrective measures as a result of the crime, it is the responsibility of the local social welfare board to take appropriate action, for example, by ordering that he or she be placed in a family home or a home with special supervision.

Full criminal responsibility is not reached until the age of 21. Offenders between 15 and 21 are subject to special provisions with regard to choice of sanctions and measures. Only under very exceptional circumstances can a person under 18 years be sentenced to imprisonment. Restrictions are also applicable to sentence young adults (18–20 years) to imprisonment. Furthermore, persons under 21 may never be sentenced to life imprisonment. In 2007, four persons aged 15–20 years and 721 persons aged 18–20 years were sentenced to imprisonment.

A new custodial sanction called youth custody was introduced in 1999. The Youth Custody Act reintroduced the juvenile prison sentence that had been abolished in the early 1980s. The purpose of this new sanction is to keep the youngest offenders (15–17 years old) out of prison. The sentence is served in special youth homes under the responsibility of the National Board of Institutional Care. The sanction is time-limited (maximum 4 years; no conditional release) and is applied by the court in accordance with the seriousness of the crime. Youth custody is part of a larger reform that aims to make the response to youth crime more consistent and firm. In 2007, 89 young, mostly male persons were sentenced to youth custody by the courts. The average daily number of inmates in such institutions was 60. The average length of the sentence added up to 8 to 9 months.

Offenders aged between 15 and 17 (at the time of the offense) can also be subject to sanctions under the Care of Young Persons (Special Provisions) Act. Thus, Sweden applies a dual system regarding those offenders.

Which sanction or measure is applied in the individual case depends to a large extent on whether the prosecutor decides to start criminal proceedings or not. If this step is not taken, it is the responsibility of the local social welfare board to see that appropriate measures are taken. The prosecutor can decide against initiating criminal proceedings if the offender was under 18 at the time of the offense and measures are taken according to the Care of Young

Persons Act, if he or she receives other help and support, or if the offense was committed in haste or ignorance. If the prosecutor decides on legal proceedings, the court can, as mentioned above, place the offender in care in accordance with the Care of Young Persons Act under certain circumstances, but criminal sanctions may also be applied. If criminal sanctions are chosen, the penalty applied is—in accordance with the law—milder than normally stipulated.

Sweden does not operate a separate juvenile court system. In 2007, the majority of cases involving juveniles 15–17 years of age ended with a fine (37%), a waiver of prosecution (36%), or measures in accordance with the Care of Young Persons (Special Provisions) Act (26%). Correspondingly, cases involving young persons 18–20 years of age ended usually with a fine (53%), a waiver of prosecution (12%), a suspended sentence (12%), or probation (11%).

Punishment

Types of Punishment

The most common penalties are *fines*—monetary fines or "day-fines" determined on the basis of the defendant's daily income. A prison sentence for nonpayment of fines (between 14 days and 3 months) is only awarded if the debtor evades his or her obligations to pay *with intent to deceive*. The imprisonment of fine defaulters has become practically obsolete after the mid-1980s.

For more serious crimes or in the case of reoffending, the penalty prescribed may be imprisonment. The shortest prison sentence is 14 days, the longest 10 years (in exceptional cases 18 years) or life imprisonment.

Instead of prison, the court may also prescribe a *conditional sentence* (i.e., a court warning) if the person convicted has no previous record, or *probation,* for example, if the individual has an abuse problem and needs supervision. The court can also commit a person to *special care*. Individuals who are mentally ill can receive forensic psychiatric care, while young offenders may be sentenced to institutional youth care or to community service for young offenders.

Both conditional sentences and probation can be combined with fines or an order to perform unpaid work—community service. Probation can also be combined with different orders for special care, such as treatment for alcohol or drug addiction. This rich variety of sanctions and combinations of sanctions is the result of the treatment ideology that characterized Swedish criminal policy throughout most of the 20th century.

Aside from the penalties listed above, and in accordance with appropriate statutory provisions, the crime may also incur forfeiture of property, corporate fines, a trading ban, deportation (of a foreign citizen), the rescinding of a driver's license, and liability for the payment of damages. Such damages may, for example, be compensation for destroyed clothing, medical costs, pain and suffering, or personal violation. The issue of damages can be considered in conjunction with the criminal trial. In certain cases, the prosecutor is under an obligation to represent the victim. The amount of the damages is determined by the court.

A person who has been awarded damages receives a written offer from the enforcement services to assist with collection of the debt. If the perpetrator is not able to pay, or if a perpetrator has not been found, and there is no insurance that can cover all the damages, the crime victim may receive compensation from the state in the form of criminal injury compensation. This compensation is intended primarily for personal injury and violation. The Crime Victim Compensation and Support Authority reviews cases involving criminal injuries compensation. It also administers the Fund for the Victims of Crime. This is funded by means of special payments charged to convicted perpetrators (€50 each). The resources of the fund are distributed to different types of projects and activities directed at victims of crime under the auspices both of nonprofit organizations and public agencies. Money from the fund also goes to research on crime victims. In the budget for 2008, roughly €12 million were allocated for criminal injury compensation.

Typical Punishments

Murder

Until the 1980s, the typical sentence in a normal murder case was residential psychiatric care. By the early 2000s, the typical sentence had changed to life imprisonment. The actual time served by those serving a life sentence has varied greatly during the last 50 years or so. It decreased from 10–15 years in the 1950s to about 8 years in the 1980s. Today conditional release is granted after about 17 years.

Rape

In nonaggravated rape cases the average sentence length of imprisonment amounts to 27 months, in aggravated cases to 59 months. Offenders are only rarely sentenced to forensic psychiatric care.

Serious Theft and Robbery

The typical punishment for serious theft (including burglary)—in contrast to violent offenses—has decreased over the decades. Today, only about one-half of all serious theft cases result in a prison sentence. The average sentence length is about 11 months. The typical punishment for robbery is imprisonment. Simple robbery renders usually 16 months of imprisonment, while aggravated robbery renders 48 months.

Serious Drug Offense

The typical punishment for a serious drug offense is 57 months of imprisonment. Drug offenses have been the principal force behind the increasing prison population in Sweden. Drug offenses are also one reason for the increasing numbers of women in Swedish prisons. It should be noted that all prisoners who have served at least 1 month in prison are, in principle, entitled to early release after having served two-thirds of their sentence.

Prison

There are presently 55 correctional institutions. Swedish prisons remain small, usually with less than 100 inmates. The largest prison—Kumla—holds 231 places. Single cells of 64.5 square feet (6 square miles) are the rule. Open prisons, where security is minimal, account for about a quarter of all prison places. Closed institutions have a high degree of security to prevent inmates from escaping. Some of them house special high-security units. Inmates are placed in accordance with risk assessments. In 2007, 10 escapes were recorded from closed prisons and 64 from open prisons. Swedish prisons are not guarded by armed guards, and escape from prison is not a criminal offense, but can lead to a prolongation of the sentence.

On June 1, 2008, the number of prison inmates stood at approximately 5,050 sentenced offenders (55 per 100,000 of population) and 1,870 pretrial detainees (20 per 100,000 of population). However, up to 10 percent of prison inmates are usually absent due to periods of leave, work outside the prison during the day, treatment programs, and so forth. Between 1997 and 2004, the number of inmates rose by 40 percent. Overcrowding occurred for a short period. Presently, Sweden is said to have the most ambitious prison-building program in Europe.

Organization and Employees

The Prison and Probation Service is organized into a headquarters, six regional offices, and a Transport Service. Each region has remand prisons, prisons, and probation units. In terms of administration, the National Prison and Probation Service is also the supreme authority for the National Parole Board and the 30 probation committees. In the Prison and Probation Service there are some 50 different professions including prison officers, inspectors, transport staff, nurses, kitchen staff, cleaning staff, and office workers. The majority are prison officers, whose work also entails planning leave or organizing treatment of the inmates, in cooperation with other authorities. Almost 9,000 staff are employed in the prisons and remand prisons; 45 percent are women. The staff/prisoner ratio is high. Prison and Probation Service staff undergo paid basic training of between 20 and 28 weeks' duration.

The Inmates

Ninety-three percent of all inmates are men, of whom 46 percent have previously been in prison. Foreign citizens account for 28 percent of the prison population. Eight percent of inmates are 55 years of age or older; 6 percent are under the age of 20. The median age is 35 years. Research on the backgrounds of prison inmates reveals that as a group the inmates may still be described as marginalized and/or socially excluded.

Prisoners are obliged to engage in some form of activity, which may include usual work, training, or treatment. The Prison and Probation Service has treatment programs for drug abusers, sex offenders, and men using violence against their partners. The programs are often imported from the English-speaking world, especially Canada. Presently, the Prison and Probation Service lists 14 different programs in use (such as cognitive skills, enhanced thinking skills, aggression replacement training, 12-step program, and programs for reducing individual substance abuse). According to official data, between 2005 and 2007, the annual number of prison inmates who have completed such programs has doubled from about 1,000 to 2,000 inmates.

Other top priority areas are security and keeping the prison free from drugs. Drug testing is mandatory. On average, each inmate is tested every third week, but samples are taken much more often in treatment wings for drug abusers. Over the course of a year, the Prison and Probation Service conducts approximately 100,000 drug tests. Twenty-one sniffing dogs are employed. Since April 1, 2008, the Prison and Probation Service can use additional, but less intrusive, methods for drug testing such as taking saliva, sweat, and hair samples. On September 1, 2008, the Prison and Probation Service introduced also a smoke-free working environment. It is not allowed to smoke within the confines of the prison/remand center.

Prisoners' Rights

Prisoners have the conditional right to send and receive mail from persons outside of the prison. Prisoners are also allowed the use of a telephone unless the telephone call is believed to jeopardize prison security or counteract the prisoner's adjustment in society. All prisoners have, as a rule, opportunities to follow events in the outside world through newspapers, magazines and other publications, radio, and television. According to a law from 2008, the possession of publications may be prevented if they may be viewed as having a negative effect on any treatment that the inmate is undergoing or if they represent a threat to order or security at the institution in question.

Conjugal visits have been allowed for many decades. The rights of the inmates' children have become a focal concern in recent years to adhere to the UN Convention on the Rights of the Child (CRC). In 2007, the Prison and Probation Service granted 36,000 applications for visits and 16,000 applications for the use of a telephone. A total of just more than 35,000 instances of prison leave were granted, with leave conditions being breached in 770 cases.

Inmates in Swedish prisons have the right, guaranteed by law, to meet and discuss grievances and other issues of mutual interest and to present their views to the warden of the prison. Prisoners who are Swedish citizens have the right to participate in parliamentary elections. The complaints procedures are laid down in the Prison Treatment Act and the Prison Treatment Ordinance. Decisions in individual cases decided by the Prison and Probation Service can be sent on appeal to the administrative court. Like every other citizen, prisoners also have the option to complain to the parliamentary ombudsman. The number of complaints has increased in recent years, but almost all cases are dismissed without any action being taken.

According to the law, there are only two formal disciplinary measures applicable: a written warning and the postponement of early release. In 2006, about 2,500 warnings were filed and early release was postponed in about 1,800 cases (for eight days on average).

Release

There are several possibilities available for gradual release from prison. These include extended day release, electronic monitoring (see below), and halfway houses with special support and supervision. Nevertheless, Swedish data on reconviction have consistently shown that institutional treatment does not produce lower reconviction rates than noninstitutional treatment—controlling for other factors. For prisoners serving more than two months and up to two years of imprisonment, the probability of a reconviction for a nontrivial offense is presently about 70–75 percent within a three-year follow-up period.

Exchange of Prisoners

Prison sentences awarded in Sweden can be transferred in accordance with the Nordic law on the implementation of sentences, the Convention on the Transfer of Sentenced Persons, and the additional protocol to this convention. In 2007, 153 prison sentences were transferred to other Nordic countries. Another 37 were transferred to other European countries and Morocco, following an application from the sentenced person. An additional 43 convicted persons were transferred against their will, largely to Poland and Lithuania.

Suicide

The number of suicides in remand prisons amounts to 5 to 6 suicides per year and in common prisons, 1 or 2. Between 20 and 30 attempted suicides are recorded annually. The latest case known that a prisoner was killed by another prisoner occurred in the mid-1990s.

Noninstitutional Treatment

Noninstitutional treatment is provided at 35 noninstitutional treatment agencies with a staff of about 1,000 executing officers (the majority of them being women). There are also about 6,000 lay supervisors. Together, they monitor an average of 13,500 clients every day. The agencies' task is to monitor clients sentenced to sanctions other than prison (probation with or without contract care/community service and conditional sentences to community service), and also to monitor offenders who have been released on parole. The period of probation is three years and monitoring by noninstitutional treatment agencies is normally carried out for one year. In the case of release on parole, the probation period is equivalent to the remainder of the prison sentence, but not less than one year. Those who are placed under supervision are assigned a probation officer who offers support and helps to facilitate the convicted person's adaptation to society.

Contract care is primarily intended for drug or alcohol abusers, if they committed the crime in relation to their substance abuse. Instead of prison, the court sentences the individual to probation with treatment at a treatment center. Community service is another alternative to prison and is a supplement to conditional sentences or probation. Community service means that the convicted person carries out unpaid work during his or her spare time. The court decides on the number of hours, between a minimum of 40 hours and a maximum of 240 hours, that the convicted person is to work.

A further alternative to prison is electronic monitoring. A person sentenced up to 6 months in prison (and early release up to, as a rule, 18 months) can apply to serve his or her sentence at home fitted with an electronic ankle bracelet. The transmitter on the bracelet is connected to a computer, which checks that the client follows an established timetable. If the client does not follow the timetable, the responsible noninstitutional treatment agency is alerted. The convicted person is monitored 24 hours a day. The freedom of movement of clients is strictly regulated and noninstitutional treatment agencies regularly check that the clients are drug- and alcohol-free. However, Swedish legislation has been very clear that electronic monitoring may not take the form of house arrest. One of the groups that often serve its prison sentences via electronic monitoring comprises those convicted of drunk driving. This punishment is then combined with treatment.

Costs

According to official calculations, the average cost per client per day adds up to €20 in noninstitutional treatment, €160 in an open prison, €230 in a closed prison, and €240 in a remand prison. The Prison and Probation Service's budget amounts to approximately €650 million per year.

Hanns von Hofer

Further Reading

Crime Victim Compensation and Support Authority: http://www.brottsoffermyndigheten.se.

Ministry of Justice. (2007). *The Swedish Judicial System: A Brief Presentation.* Stockholm: Ministry of Justice.

Pratt, John. (2008). "Scandinavian Exceptionalism in an Era of Penal Excess: The Nature and Roots of Scandinavian Exceptionalism." *British Journal of Criminology* 48: 119–137.

Swedish Prison and Probation Service publishes different documents, such as the *Basic Facts of the Swedish Prison and Probation Service* or *The Swedish System of Sanctions:* http://www.kriminalvarden.se.

Note: Changes of the law after December 31, 2008, are not incorporated in this essay. The exchange rate has been set to 10 SEK = €1 (US$1.26).

Switzerland

Legal System: Civil
Murder: Low
Burglary: Medium
Corruption: Low
Human Trafficking: Low
Prison Rate: Medium
Death Penalty: No
Corporal Punishment: No

Background

Switzerland is a small European country of 7.5 million people sharing a mountainous land of 41,288 square kilometers (15,941 square miles), of which 25.5 percent are nonproductive. In 2008, 21.7 percent of the Swiss resident population were foreign nationals, a relatively high proportion compared to other European countries, a situation explained by the strict rules that apply to the obtaining of Swiss citizenship. Foreign nationals come principally from the 27 European Union (EU) countries (62.1%); the most represented nationalities are Italians (17.5%), Germans (14.1%), and Portuguese nationals (11.8%). Besides, almost 25 percent of foreign nationals come from European countries outside the EU, mostly from former Yugoslavian republics, less than 4 percent come from the African continent, and less than 6 percent from Asia.

The political organization of the country is characterized by its federalism—a direct democracy highly decentralized—as it is divided into 26 autonomous cantons and half-cantons, each with its own constitution. Switzerland has four national languages: German, French, Italian, and Romansh. Most cantons have one official language, with German being predominant in the eastern cantons (63.7%), French in the west (20.4%), and Italian (6.4%) in the canton of Ticino, in the south; Romansh is spoken by less than 1 percent of the population. As a result of the large degree of political autonomy of the cantons, the Swiss criminal justice system is probably the most highly fragmented system in Europe, which makes it, to some extent, a comparative lawyer's dream.

The structure of police forces in Switzerland reflects the organization of the country in three levels: federal, cantonal, and municipal. Thus, Switzerland has no national police force, but a Federal Police, 26 cantonal police forces, and more than 100 municipal police forces. Cantonal and municipal police forces are responsible for law and order, while the Federal Police (with only 870 employees) is responsible for national security as well as for the most serious cases of organized and economic criminality, such as international drug trafficking, trafficking of human beings, or money laundering. On December 31, 2007, cantonal police forces had 12,147 sworn officers, and municipal forces 4,311. Thus, there were 219 police sworn officers per 100,000 inhabitants, which represents a low rate compared to other European countries.

Likewise, prison administration and noncustodial sanctions are run by the cantons. On September 3, 2008, Switzerland counted 124 penal institutions;

most of these are small local institutions for pretrial detention or people serving short sentences. The majority of these institutions have less than 100 places and only two prisons offer a capacity of more than 300 prisoners.

History of the Legal System

Swiss criminal laws and sentencing practices have been influenced by different legal traditions, including French and German legislations. The first approximation of a criminal code in Switzerland was written in 1799, mostly inspired by the French Code of 1791. After 1830, many cantons passed their own criminal code, even though some did maintain the use of the *Code pénal helvétique* for some time. French-speaking cantons generally followed the French tradition, whereas German-speaking cantons were more inspired by the German criminal legislation.

The idea to codify criminal law at the national level emerged in 1898 with the introduction of a new article in the Constitution that instituted the competence of legislation in the field of criminal law to the Confederation. As a result, the Confederation had the competence to pass legislation regarding substantive law; yet courts organization, criminal procedures, and criminal justice administration were left to the cantons. However, as will be seen in the next paragraphs, all this is about to change.

The Swiss Criminal Code and Other Criminal Laws

Offenses definitions are contained in the Swiss Criminal Code (CP), which recently underwent a major revision. The new code is depicted as "modern," mainly because it accords a special attention to the rehabilitative dimension of the sentence and favors—some—alternative sanctions (e.g., community work orders). Indeed, the new code no longer considers prison sentences as central to the system of sanctions, but as a last choice in an era emphasizing alternative sanctions. Sentencing practices are modified: fines are calculated with the new concept of day-fines up to 360 days. The amount of day-fines is computed according to the economic situation of the person sentenced, with the maximum amount being 3,000 Swiss francs (CHF) per day (approximately US$2,636). Community work orders up to 720 hours were introduced in replacement of short custodial sentences (i.e., less than 6 months) or sentences up to 180 day-fines. Indeed, short custodial sentences are basically suppressed unless particular cases properly motivated. Finally, suspended sentences are applicable to fines, community work orders, and custodial sentences between 1 and 3 years. In addition to its CP, Switzerland counts a Military Criminal Code—dealing with military-related offenses as well as common offenses perpetrated by a person on duty.

The three major federal laws contributing to criminal convictions are the Road Traffic Act, the Federal Act on Narcotics and Psychotropic Substances, and the Federal Act on Foreign Nationals regulating offenses related to immigration and residence of aliens and asylum seekers. In addition, many administrative laws, at both the cantonal and federal levels, contain dispositions related to criminal offenses. Cantonal criminal laws usually regulate police contraventions, contraventions to the administrative or procedural cantonal prescriptions, and contraventions to fiscal legislations.

The Future Swiss Code of Criminal Procedure

Switzerland currently has a typical continental system, one criminal code at the federal level and 26 autonomous procedural systems, one in each canton. Whereas offenders can easily circulate across cantons, judicial authority stops at the borders. In March 2000, Switzerland extended the federal competence to legislation to include the criminal procedure and, after a long legislative process, usual in Switzerland, a unified Swiss Code of Criminal Procedure (CPP) should become effective at the earliest in January 2011. One can note, among other interesting changes, the extension of the principle of opportunity, which allows the law enforcement authorities to waive prosecution under certain circumstances. The rights of the accused will be reinforced as well, with the admission of the "attorney of the first hour" and the right to call a defender at any stage of the proceedings. On the Public Prosecution Service (PPS) side, the monitoring of bank accounts will constitute a new compulsory measure.

Crime

Classification of Crimes

Based on the seriousness of the sanction associated with an offense, the CP defines three categories of offenses: felonies (i.e., *crimes* in French, *Verbrechen* in German, and *crimini* in Italian), misdemeanors (i.e., *délits, Vergehen, delitti*), and contraventions (i.e., *contraventions, Übertretungen, contravvenzioni*). The first category encompasses offenses liable to imprisonment of more than three years, whereas the sanction for the misdemeanors is up to three years of imprisonment or a fine. Contraventions are only liable to a fine, while petty offenses can be dealt with by administrative proceedings with the police institutions, as long as the fine does not exceed CHF 300 (approximately US$264).

Crime Trends According to Police Crime Statistics

The Swiss police crime statistics system was initiated in 1982. Until recently, statistics were managed by police authorities of each of the 26 cantons on behalf of the Swiss Federal Office of Police, who was in charge of compiling the data; therefore, these statistics have always been limited as they consist of a statistical aggregation of data based on police crime reports. This statistic was based on a selection of offenses (36) from the CP; not all offenses were considered and many offenses were aggregated, because the distinction between them was not consistent across police authorities. Furthermore, there was no standardization of data collection procedures or written guidelines on how to record and count offenses. For example, it was shown that some departments were counting offenses when they were reported to the police (input) while others were counting them at the end of the police intervention (output). Because of several shortcomings, the crime statistics system underwent a major revision that started at the end of the 1990s. The main goal of the revision was to achieve a centralized database recording all criminal offenses through the use of standardized evaluation principles and data captures rules. The new statistical system was gradually implemented in each canton and the first national-level crime data, covering the year 2009, were published in March 2010. Besides the crime statistics related to offenses defined in the CP, data on police-recorded offenses under the Federal Act on Narcotics and Psychotropic Substances are collected, as well as data on traffic offenses recorded by the police. These have been incorporated into the new national statistic with the addition of police-recorded offenses under the Federal Act on Foreign Nationals.

Because of the aggregate nature of police-recorded crime data, as well as its shortcomings, looking at overall trends is not of any interest. Trends for specific offenses are more informative. For example, the rate of vehicle theft, mostly theft of scooters and motorbikes, has fallen over time. Improved security devices are largely responsible for the drop of car thefts, whereas the introduction of compulsory helmet legislation has played a role in the drop of scooters and motorbikes thefts. Other forms of theft show less consistent trends over time, with a significant rise in 2004. This inconsistency may be a methodological artifact related to changes in recording practices of minor theft (i.e., theft of value of less than CHF 300). Burglary rate almost doubled between 1985 and 1997, and then decreased up to 1999. The fact that burglary, motor vehicle theft, and personal crime differ in trends is not surprising as these differ in situational characteristics as well.

The trends for police-recorded violent offenses are different. The intentional homicide rate is stable over time, whereas assault rates have been going up since the mid-1990s and two important increases arose in 2004 and 2006, respectively. Assault rates according to surveys have also increased around 1995, and later after 1999. The existence of large open drug scenes was among the main factors for the increase of street crime in Swiss major cities between 1989 and 1995. In urban areas with high concentration of activities related to drugs or prostitution, offenders are more likely to find potential victims; hence, these areas were more attractive to offenders than more wealthy neighborhoods. In 1994, the adoption of a new drug policy that included harm reduction (through exchange of needles as well as methadone and heroin prescription) led to the closing of open drug scenes and to a drastic reduction of street crime as well as deaths by overdose. The number of rapes recorded by the police decreased between the 1980s up to the mid-1990s (from 6.6 per 100,000 inhabitants in 1982 to 3.9 in 1994); however, it has been increasing since then (up to 8.5 per 100,000 inhabitants in 2007). Over time, the pattern is similar for other sexual offenses.

Drug Offenses and Drug-Related Problems

The rates of drug-related offenses are increasing. Obviously police-recorded data on drug offenses reflect underlying changes in drug use and trafficking only to a limited degree. Since the beginning of the 1990s, the number of offenses related to drug consumption has been going up: from 189 offenses per 100,000 inhabitants in 1990 to 484.3 in 2007. In addition, the trends for trafficking offenses are also going up.

According to the most recent data published by the Swiss Institute for the Prevention of Alcoholism and Other Drug Problems (ISPA), more than one out of three men, and one out of five women, had ever used an illegal drug. Between 1992 and 2002, drug use remained stable in Switzerland, with the exception of the use of cannabis, which increased. Indeed, as in many countries, cannabis is today the most widely used illegal drug in Switzerland; according to ISPA data, about one-fifth of the Swiss population aged 15 to 74 has ever used cannabis. In 2006, 34 percent of the male students aged 15, and 27 percent of the female students of the same age group, had ever used cannabis.

Heroin Prescription Program and Offending Behavior

In 1994, the federal government introduced a new drug policy based on a four-pillar strategy (prevention, treatment, harm reduction, and enforcement). As mentioned before, harm reduction included heroin prescription programs. A few weeks later, open drug scenes in Zurich and other cities were closed. Between 1995 and 1996, more than 800 drug addicts started programs based on heroin prescription, whereas, simultaneously, methadone substitution was extended to approximately 15,000 drug addicts. These programs had several consequences, including a major decrease of deaths by overdose (from 419 in 1992 to 152 in 2007) and, from a criminal policy point of view, a drastic drop in criminal involvement among beneficiaries of the heroin prescription program and, to a lesser extent, among those enrolled in the methadone substitution program, as well as an immediate reduction in the concentration of drug addicts in urban centers. All this led to a reduction of crime. In 1999, a referendum against heroin prescription programs was rejected by the population. In 2008, almost 70 percent of the voters approved the new law on drugs that consolidates the four-pillar strategy. The law entered into force in January 2010. Heroin prescription is currently a recognized form of treatment followed by 1,300 persons, while 17,500 others participate in methadone substitution programs.

Juvenile Delinquency According to Official and Self-reported Data

According to a compilation of data by the Federal Statistical Office, 12,920 youths were suspected by the police of having committed an offense in 2007, 27 percent of them for a violent offense. These juveniles account for approximately 3 percent of the age group 13–17 in the population. During the same year, juvenile judges issued more than 14,000 court orders involving minors; over 90 percent of orders involved criminal sanctions and about 15 percent involved educational measures. Less than 12 percent of court orders involved female juveniles; over 75 percent of youths were aged 15 or older. At the same time, 4,825 juveniles attended a consultation at a victim's crisis center, approximately half of the consultations concerned violent offenses. Suspected offenders were known to the victim in 80 percent of the cases; in half of the cases, there was even a family relationship between the victim and the suspected offender.

Switzerland participated in the first and the second International Self-Reported Delinquency Survey (ISRD-1 and ISRD-2), conducting national surveys on juvenile delinquency in 1992 and 2006. The Swiss ISRD-2 was administered to a national random sample of more than 3,600 juveniles attending the seventh, eighth, and ninth grade (i.e., juveniles aged 13 to 16). Lifetime and 12-month prevalence rates were computed for a range of problematic behaviors and offenses, including questions on alcohol and drug consumption, property offenses (e.g., shoplifting, burglary, robbery/extortion), drug-related offenses (i.e., selling drugs), and personal offenses (e.g., assault, group fight).

The most common offense committed is theft, as over 23 percent of youths have ever perpetrated a theft. The study reveals that 9.1 percent of juveniles have stolen from a shop in the last 12 months, whereas 7.8 percent have been involved in vandalism, and 3.7 in bicycle/motorbike theft. More serious property offenses concerns 0.9 percent of juveniles who have completed a burglary in the past year. Juveniles have also been involved in violent offenses: 8.4 percent have engaged in a group fight, whereas around 2 percent of them have assaulted someone (1.2%), snatched a purse (1.1%), or robbed someone (0.9%). Altogether, 15.5 percent of youths have been involved in a group fight. Only 2.8 percent of the sample have been dealing drugs in the past year. During the last month, 39 percent of students have drunk wine or beer—a percentage that is not unusual in a wine-producer country—and 16 percent strong spirits. In fact, almost all students who consumed strong spirits during that period have also been drinking wine or beer. Lifetime hard drug use (i.e., Ecstasy/speed, LSD, heroin, and cocaine) concern only 2 percent of the sample. Victimization is relatively common, with almost a quarter of juveniles having had something stolen from them in the last 12 months, and 12.4 percent reporting they have been victims of bullying. Robbery and assault were experienced by 2.3 percent and 2.4 percent of the students, respectively.

Victimization Surveys in Switzerland

National Crime Victimization Surveys

The first national crime victimization survey conducted in Switzerland was administered in two waves in 1984 (French-speaking cantons) and in 1987 (German- and Italian-speaking cantons). It was one of the first major crime surveys to use computer-assisted telephone interviews (CATI). Similar national surveys were conducted in 1996, 1998, 2000, and 2005, usually as a part of the International Crime Victims Survey (ICVS) and using the ICVS core questionnaire with a few additional questions. A recent comprehensive analysis of all sweeps of the Swiss crime victim surveys yielded interesting findings, especially with respect to putting crime trends into a wider perspective. Overall, survey trends and trends for police-recorded offenses are congruent, yet the magnitude of crime is different according to both indicators. Burglary, a crime that became transnational after the fall of the Berlin Wall in 1989, doubled from the late 1980s to 1997, decreased in 1999, and remained stable in 2004. Motorcycle theft decreased for the reasons explained before. Violent offenses like robbery/mugging and assault increased until the mid-1990s, decreased at that time—reflecting the changes in drug policy that have already been explained—and increased since then. The latter trend appears to be due to an increase of youth violence, reflected also in the data from self-reported delinquency surveys. Reporting to the police has been decreasing for most offenses, including violent ones.

Swiss Component of the International Violence against Women Survey

In 2003, Switzerland took part in the International Violence against Women Survey (IVAWS), an international project coordinated by the European Institute for Crime Prevention and Control. Between April and August, 1,975 women aged 18 or older took part in the survey and answered questions about their lifetime experiences of partner and non-partner victimization as well as their feelings of personal safety. This study was the first national-level report on violence against women.

According to these victimization data, 4 out of 10 women report having ever experienced threats, physical, and/or sexual violence since the age of 16. Prevalence rates for the last 12 months ranged from 0.5 percent for completed and attempted rape to

1.9 percent for physical violence and threats. As for victim-offender relationship, the Swiss study reveals that 32 percent of women have been assaulted by a nonpartner, namely, a friend or an acquaintance (18.9%), a stranger (14.4%), or a relative (4.3%), whereas 10.5 percent of victims were assaulted by a partner. Intimate partner violence consists mostly of assaults by ex-partners; most common types of assault include slapping and hitting, then pushing and grabbing one's spouse.

Other analyses reveal that most cases are not reported to the police: only 23 percent of women victimized in the preceding five years reported the incident to the police. Female victims are more likely to contact the police when physically assaulted than when sexually assaulted. Official complaints were filed in less than 15 percent of the cases; women are more likely to file a complaint against a stranger (complaint was filed in 29% of the cases) or an acquaintance (18%) than against a partner (7%). However, when victimized, women were very likely to disclose the abuse to someone. Violence incidents are principally disclosed to different family members (60%) or friends (25%); this is also the case for intimate partner violence. Victim's crisis centers or shelters were contacted by approximately 20 percent of the victims. Multivariate analyses revealed that the strongest predictors of partner violence were the partner's characteristics, among which are a violent and aggressive behavior outside the family and excessive drinking.

Finding of Guilt

Criminal Proceedings under the Future Swiss Code of Criminal Procedure

The Swiss Code of Criminal Procedure (CPP) follows an inquiry model that gives extended powers to the Public Prosecution Services (PPS), a system that also exists in Germany, Italy, and the United States. Cases are carried out by the same person throughout the criminal procedure that comprises two phases: police investigation and case instruction. A criminal procedure can be decided by the police, the PPS, or the competent penal authorities for the sanctioning of contraventions. Usually, the police investigate an affair and inform the PPS about the findings; the PPS then decides whether to conduct an investigation. The police do have some autonomy during the preliminary investigations, but always act under the surveillance of the PPS. The PPS can also order the police to start an investigation. Petty offenses (i.e., contraventions) are prosecuted by specific administrative authorities designated by each canton.

Whenever a formal instruction is opened by the PPS, it must be conducted against and in defense of the accused (i.e., exonerating facts and circumstances that incriminate the defendant). The instruction follows the inquisitorial model of procedure, which means it is secret—without the participation of the public—written, and noncontradictory. During this process, the rights of the defendant include the right to read his or her case file, the right to be assisted by an attorney, the right to take part in criminal proceedings, and obviously the right to oppose any PPS decision.

The PPS is granted different judicial powers during the distinct phases of the criminal procedure. During the instruction phase, the PPS can resort to all legal means of investigation to establish the truth. The PPS can summon the parties, a witness, or an expert, and can go to the crime scene or request an official report. In addition, the PPS can also pronounce different measures of constraint, such as police search, DNA analyses, or monetary impoundment. However, the PPS is not allowed to send the defendant in pretrial detention; to avoid the concentration of powers in the hand of a single entity, a special court—the Court of Coercive Measures—has been instituted, whose powers include sending a defended in pretrial detention.

Police are allowed to keep a suspect under arrest for 24 hours, but they must inform the PPS within this period. The PPS then has 48 hours to ask the court to order pretrial detention. The court has 48 hours to rule; without a decision within the deadline, the suspect must be released. The instruction ends with the PPS dropping the charges, with the PPS wording a penal order, or with the case being transferred to court accompanied by an act of indictment. Once the case is transferred to court, the PPS becomes one of the parties. He or she then represents the state as he or she is prosecuting the case and calling the sentence. At this stage, the PPS is only acting against the defendant.

Party Litigants and Rights

Any party litigant has several rights, among which are the right to be heard, the right to read his or her case file, and the right to be assisted by an attorney. Swiss criminal law recognizes the defendant and the victim as parties in the criminal procedure. The PPS is considered a party litigant only during the trial. In addition, each canton is allowed to give the right to some authorities to act as a party litigant; this could include social welfare services, child protection services, or even authorities protecting the environment.

The rights of the accused—among which the right to be heard, the right to read his or her case file, and the right to be legally assisted—exist right from the beginning of the criminal procedure. Indeed, a person is considered the accused as soon as he or she is suspected of having committed an offense. The suspicion can arise from an official complaint, a denunciation, or be the result of an official procedure. The injured party becomes a party litigant as soon as he or she expresses the desire to enter the criminal procedure, then becoming a plaintiff. Only the plaintiff can intervene in the criminal procedure and join a civil claim to the criminal proceedings. The status of *victim* refers to the definition encompassed in the Swiss Victim Aid Act. In Switzerland, this act has existed since 1995, but was recently entirely revised; the updated legislation entered into force in January 2009.

The injured party is defined a direct victim whenever there is a criminal offense as defined by the CP. Abuses against the physical, sexual, or psychological integrity must reach a certain level of seriousness and be in direct causal relation with the offense committed. The aid includes advice provided by staff of victim crisis centers, protection, and the preservation of victim's rights during criminal proceedings. The act also regulates claims for reparation and compensation. The victim can contact a victim crisis center whether he or she reports the incident to the police or not. The advice is free of charge and anonymous. Beside other rights, the victim may be accompanied by a person during the criminal proceedings, the right not to be confronted with the offender, the right to be informed about the state of the proceedings, the right to be heard by a person of the same gender, and the right to have a trial in camera.

The help given by the centers covers three dimensions. First they include socio-psychological advice, including listening to the victim, giving information on how to file a complaint, or the organization of a criminal proceeding. The centers can also address the victim to health care specialists or psychologists whenever the trauma of the attack requires it; the psychological assistance is financed by the centers up to 10 sessions. The staff can also provide the victim with other immediate financial help, such as emergency accommodation, medical or transportation costs that arose directly from the offense. Legal advice is also part of the center's tasks, although victims are likely to be addressed to an attorney for serious cases. Here also, the Swiss Victim Aid Act allows the centers to offer a free legal consultation with a registered attorney, up to six hours total. The last part of this legislation contains dispositions related to compensation claims. The victim is indeed allowed to claim, first, for a compensation of the costs consecutive to the offense and, second, for reparations of the prejudice. Financial help is subsidiary, which means it will be paid by the state only if neither the accused nor insurance bear the costs.

Courts and Judicial Authorities

Judicial organization is one of the tasks devoted to the cantons; therefore, the courts are organized in a different way from one canton to another and often named differently. However, the CPP enumerates four entities intervening in criminal proceedings. The PPS refer a case to a court of first instance. There are two distinct appeal jurisdictions depending on the object of the appeal, that can be generally described as follows. The *autorité de recours* (*Beschwerdeinstanz* in German, and *Giurisdizione di reclamo* in Italian) gives a ruling on any appeal against decisions and procedural acts of the police, the PPS, or the authorities dealing with contraventions (art. 20 and 393 CPP). The *juridiction d'appel* (*Berufungsgericht*, *Tribunale d'appello*) reviews first instance closing decisions that are contested in matters of law or of fact (art. 21 and 398 CPP). Finally, a court of coercive measures, the *tribunal des mesures de contrainte* (*Zwangsmassnahmengericht*, *Giudice dei provvedimenti coercitivi*) regulates cases of pretrial detention or involving measures such as hospitalization of the accused person, DNA sampling in major investigations, or peace bond; attacks on fundamental rights of the accused are usually also ruled by the court of coercive measures (art. 18 CPP). As the judicial organization will remain, the competence of the cantons, names, and internal organization are likely to differ across cantons.

The structure of judicial authorities differs not only across cantons but also within the different legal domains (e.g., criminal, civil, or administrative). In Swiss criminal proceedings, judicial authorities can consist of one single person (single judge for criminal matters) or multiple individuals (collegiate body). Most often the judge who sits alone in a court of first instance is competent to try contraventions, and minor felonies and misdemeanors, whereas a collegiate body tries more serious cases. Appeals are almost always tried by a collegiate body.

In Switzerland judges are not always jurists (i.e., law graduates). For example, many cantons possess a justice of the peace in which works a peace commissioner, a magistrate who has the jurisdiction to judge small claims actions, and which is also an arbitration court to which parties bring their cases for conciliation purposes before being referred to the higher court with appropriate jurisdiction. However, the actual complexity of law, as well as the facilitated access to law studies, has increased the presence of lawyers with judicial authorities. Judges do not always work full-time, especially in the courts of higher instances and especially when they are not jurists.

The number of female judges has increased over time, yet only 27 percent of criminal judges are women. Federal law requires that, for criminal proceedings concerning sexual offenses, the victim can request to be heard by a person of the same gender. Similarly, during the trial, at least one of the judges has to be of the same gender as the victim.

Pretrial Detention

The CPP distinguishes between pretrial detention (i.e., up to the end of the instruction phase) and preventive detention (i.e., during the trial). The first aims at safeguarding the goals of the investigation process; the latter is used to ensure the availability of the accused and the execution of possible custodial sanctions. Pretrial detention is ordered by the PPS for reasons that include, among others, flight, collusion, or repeat offending.

A survey conducted by the Federal Statistical Office in 2006 revealed that, on the reference day, 29 percent of all detainees were in pretrial detention. Among these suspects, 21 percent were Swiss citizens, 22 percent were foreign nationals with a residency permit, 16 percent were asylum seekers or persons admitted upon provisional authorization, and 45 percent were foreign nationals without residence permit (persons living near the border, illegal migrants, tourists). Whereas the proportion of Swiss citizen in pretrial detention has remained stable since 2001, the proportion of foreign nationals with a residency permit has decreased more than 12 points since 2004. During the same period, the proportion of illegal migrants has increased more than 11 points.

Criminal Justice for Juveniles

In Switzerland, the minimum age of criminal responsibility is 10 years. If the competent authority learns that an offense has been committed by a child aged less than 10, the legal representatives of the child are informed. When it appears that the child needs particular attention, the guardianship authority or child welfare services, as designated in cantonal legislation, are informed.

The offenses that can be committed by a juvenile consist solely of the offenses defined in the CP; there are no special offenses like status offenses as in some states of the United States. Since January 2007, articles related to juvenile law have been taken out of the CP and formulated into a special federal law setting up the sanctions applicable to any offender aged 10 to 17. The law is considered perpetrator-oriented as the person of the child or the adolescent is in the forefront. The appropriate decision is made based on the personality of the juvenile rather than on the seriousness of the offense; in this sense, Switzerland follows the general rehabilitative principles of juvenile justice. Therefore, the law distinguishes between corrective methods, special (therapeutic) treatment, and punishment. As of January 2007, the following penalties may be imposed on juvenile offenders: a reprimand, a personal work order, fines up to CHF 2,000 (approximately US$ 1,757) for offenders between 15 and 18 years old, a custodial sentence of up to 1 year for offenders between 15 and 18 years old, or up to 4 years for juveniles, from the age of 16 on, who have committed a serious felony. Finally, a major difference with the regular criminal law is that the juvenile law offers the possibility to convict the offender but to suspend the decision on the sanction for a given time. It applies, for example, when the judge is not sure whether a measure or a punishment would be adequate.

Official Data on Court Orders Involving Minors

Since 1999, the Federal Statistical Office annually computes a database on juvenile justice. Data include all sentences imposed on minors from 10 years old to less than 18 years old. All offenses are considered, that is, offenses defined by the CP, the Federal Act on Narcotics and Psychotropic Substances, the Road Traffic Act, or the Federal Act on Foreign Nationals. Most sentences consist of disciplinary penalties: 12,328 disciplinary penalties were imposed in 2006. There is an important gap between rates of boys' and girls' delinquency. For example, in 2007, out of 14,404 sentenced cases, only 2,831 concerned a girl, that is, 19.7 percent. Over the past 9 years, on average, 18.9 percent of sentences cases dealt with girl delinquency.

Punishment

Types of Punishment

Sanctions (i.e., punishments and measures) are defined in the CP. The first ones intend to punish the accused, whereas the latter are designated to heal the defendant or protect the society. The Swiss system counts three distinct types of punishment—fines, community service, and custodial sentence—and five different types of measures—treatment for psychological disorders, treatment for addictions, measures for young adults, out-care treatment, and internment. In addition, a sanction may be suspended, as long as the custodial sentence is longer than 6 months, whereas partial suspension is possible for fines or community services. Contraventions may be sentenced with up to a CHF 10,000 (approximately US$8,786) fine or a community service order of up to 360 hours. Imprisonment is considered only if the accused cannot pay the fine. Sanctions for serious offenses and crimes differ according to the length of the sentence. The rule is to avoid short custodial sentences; therefore, the judge should always try to "convert" the sanction into a fine or a community service order.

There are no sentencing guidelines in Switzerland, but there are some general rules in the CP referring to aggravating/mitigating factors and a few broad principles. In practice, judges are nevertheless required to provide the criteria that determine their sentence and choice of sanction. Although the Supreme Court does not review sentences as such, it has to guarantee the conformity of the sentences imposed by lower courts.

Conviction Data

Convictions data encompass criminal convictions registered in the police record of each individual; contraventions are not registered in police records, unless they were sanctioned by a short prison sentence. The number of convictions has continuously increased over time, with the exception of a drop in the middle of the 1990s due to changes in recording practices (i.e., the definition of minor theft was enlarged, resulting in more thefts being sanctioned by fines and therefore not registered in conviction data). The constant increase in the number of convictions is partially explained by the inclusion of new offenses and by demographic growth. According to analysts from the Federal Statistical Office, the slight drop in 2005 parallels a drop in drug offenses and traffic offenses. This drop, as we have mentioned before, is related to the modification of the federal drug policy. The trend did not maintain in 2006.

Over time, the average length of unsuspended custodial sentence has increased or decreased depending on the offense. Sentences for homicide fluctuate within a 10 to 15 percent range (3,574.4 days in 2006), whereas sentences for rape increased by 26 percent since 1984, with an average sentence of 1,073 days in 2006. On the opposite, the average length decreased for theft and robbery (40.7 and 705.2 days respectively, in 2006). Length patterns for drug-related offenses show a certain stability over time, although sentences have become less severe after 1994. In 2006, drug trafficking punishment was imposed an average of 394.9 days of imprisonment, 962.5 for aggravated drug trafficking.

Correction Data

In 2007, the Federal Statistical Office carried out a survey on 115 prison facilities and institutions. On the reference day, 5,715 places were occupied for a total capacity of 6,654 places, that is, an occupation rate of 86 percent. Compared with a previous study conducted in 2005, it is a 7 point decrease consecutive to a diminution of the number of both pretrial detainees and detainees serving a sentence. Among the 5,715 detainees, 63 percent were serving a sentence, 29 percent were in pretrial detention, and 7 percent were detained for administrative purpose (i.e., waiting for an expulsion/extradition). These percentages have been stable over time since 2001.

According to the Council of Europe Penal Statistics (SPACE), the Swiss prison population rate increased from 4,000 detainees in 1983 to 6,390 in 2000. An important decrease was registered in 2001 and continued in 2002 when there were 4,987 detainees. However, the prison population raised again in 2003 and 2004 (6,021 detainees) before decreasing slightly in 2005 and remaining more or less stable since then. While the increase in 2003–2004 seems to be due to a harsher criminal policy, the overall evolution of the prison population is related to the implementation of alternatives to imprisonment in the 21st century. Currently, community work orders and electronic monitoring are more frequently imposed as alternatives to custodial sanctions. In 1984, 70 percent of detainees were serving their sentence in a prison facility, whereas they were only 54 percent in 2004. According to the Federal Statistical Office, in 2007, detainees were mostly males (94%), foreigners (70%), and serving an unsuspected custodial sentence (52%). Mean age for detainees was 34 years old. According to our interpretation, the high percentage of foreign prisoners seems due to the transnational character of some offenses (mainly drug trafficking and burglary) as well as to the fact that alternatives to imprisonment are seldom used for nonresidents.

The median length of stay in prison has increased over time: from four weeks in 1984 to six weeks in 2004. Therefore, even though the number of persons sent to prison has decreased, the mean number of detainees in prison facilities and institutions increased up to 5,715 in 2007.

In 2006, 4,087 community work orders were served, in majority by Swiss male citizens aged 35 on average. Orders required on average 90 hours of community work. Electronic monitoring was introduced in the CP in 1999. In 2006, 506 custodial sentences were, in part or totally, carried out under electronic monitoring. The profile of the offenders was similar to the one of offenders serving community work orders: 95 percent were males, 63 percent were Swiss citizens aged 35 on average.

Véronique Jaquier and Marcelo F. Aebi

Further Reading

Eisner, Manuel, and Martin Killias. (2004). "Switzerland." *European Journal of Criminology* 1(2): 257–293.

Haymoz, Sandrine, Marcelo F. Aebi, Martin Killias, and Philippe Lamon. (2009). "Comparisons of Crime Data Based on General Population Surveys with Criminal Statistics in Switzerland." In *Comparing Crime Data in Europe: Official Crime Statistics and Survey Based Data,* edited by Philippe Robert, pp. 127–140. Brussels: VUBPRESS Brussels University Press.

Killias, Martin, Marcelo F. Aebi, Sonia Lucia, Leslie Herrmann, and Carine Dilitz. (2010). "Self-Reported Juvenile Delinquency in Switzerland in 2006: Overview and Explanations." In *Juvenile Delinquency in Europe and Beyond: Results of the Second International Self-Report Delinquency Study,* edited by Josine Junger-Tas, pp. 79–95. New York: Springer.

Killias, Martin, Mathieu Simonin, and Jacqueline De Puy. (2005). *Violence Experienced by Women in Switzerland over Their Lifespan.* Bern: Staempfli.

Ribeaud, Denis, Martin Killias, and Marcelo F. Aebi. (2004). "Long-Term Effects of Heroin Prescription on Patients' Offending Behavior." In *Crime Policy in Europe: Good Practices and Promising Examples,* edited by Council of Europe, pp. 27–36, Strasbourg: Council of Europe Publishing.

Ukraine

Legal System: Civil
Murder: Medium
Burglary: Medium
Corruption: Medium
Human Trafficking: Medium
Prison Rate: High
Death Penalty: No
Corporal Punishment: No

Background

Ukraine became an independent state in 1991, following the dissolution of the Soviet Union and, as a republic, is composed of 24 *oblasts* (provinces), one autonomous republic (Crimea), and two cities with special status: Kyiv, its capital, and Sevastopol. The country is home to 46.4 million people, 77.8 percent of whom are ethnic Ukrainians, with sizable minorities of Russians, Belarusians, and Romanians. The Ukrainian language is the only official language in Ukraine, while Russian is also widely spoken. The dominant religion in the country is Eastern Orthodox Christianity.

The Constitution of Ukraine was adopted in June 1996 and defines the state institutions and deals with human right of citizens. As a republic, Ukraine has a mixed semiparliamentary, semipresidential system with separate legislative, executive, and judicial branches. The president is elected by popular vote for a five-year term and is the formal head of state. Ukraine's legislative branch includes the 450-seat unicameral Parliament, the *Verkhovna Rada*. Parliament is primarily responsible for the formation of the executive branch and the Cabinet of Ministers, which is headed by the prime minister.

Legal System

Ukraine's judicial system is made up of courts of general jurisdiction and the Constitutional Court of Ukraine. The Ukrainian Law on Judicial System of 2002 establishes the principle of the division of the legislative, executive, and judiciary powers. Judicial authorities shall exercise their power exclusively on this basis, according to the Constitution and laws of Ukraine. Judicial power shall be exercised by the administration of justice in the form of civil, commercial, administrative, criminal, as well as constitutional, legal proceedings. Legal proceedings shall be undertaken by the Constitutional Court and courts of general jurisdiction.

Laws, acts of Parliament and the cabinet, presidential decrees, and acts of the Crimean Parliament may be abrogated by the Constitutional Court, if they should be found to violate the Constitution. Other normative acts are subject to judicial review. The Supreme Court is the main authority in the system of courts of general jurisdiction.

Courts

In administering justice, courts shall ensure the protection of human and civil rights and freedoms, rights and interests of legal entities, as well as public and state interests that are guaranteed by the Constitution and Ukrainian laws. Ukraine's judicial system is made up of courts of general jurisdiction and the Constitutional Court. The system of courts of general jurisdiction is made up from local courts; courts of appeal and the Court of Appeal; highest specialized courts; and the Supreme Court. Powers of specialized courts cover commercial, military, and administrative cases. Those jurisdictions comprise separate court subsystems. In courts of general jurisdiction judges specialize in hearing criminal, civil, and juvenile cases.

The court system of Ukraine counts 783 courts, including 15 military courts, 39 commercial courts, and 35 administrative courts. More than 6,600 judges work under the administration of the court system. Professional judges are appointed by the president for a period of five years; other judges are elected without a time limit by the *Verkhovna Rada*. Justice in Ukraine shall be administered exclusively by courts whose functions cannot be delegated. Nor may other bodies or officials appropriate these functions. Consideration of cases in courts shall be open, except for cases envisaged by procedural law.

Law Enforcement

The system of law-enforcement bodies of Ukraine is complex and consists of numerous agencies of general and specialized jurisdiction. There are two principal law enforcement agencies, which share responsibility for internal security: the Ministry of Internal Affairs, which controls the various police forces, and the Security Service of Ukraine, which guaranties the state security of Ukraine.

The militia is a single system subordinate to the Ministry of Internal Affairs and incorporated into its structure. The major militia's tasks are defined in the 1991 Law on Militia and include the following:

- Providing personal security for citizens
- Protecting their rights and freedoms
- Preventing crime
- Maintaining public order
- Revealing and detecting crime
- Arresting offenders
- Maintaining safety on the roads
- Protecting public and private property
- Executing administrative penalties

The protection of state sovereignty, the constitutional system, the state's territorial integrity, maintaining the interests of society and the state in and out of Ukraine are among the main tasks of the Security Service. The Security Service of Ukraine is intended to carry out intelligence activities in compliance with the law, as well as uncovering criminal activities whose investigation is within its competence. Objectives also include the prevention, detection, interruption, and investigation of crimes against the peace and security of mankind, terrorism, corruption, and organized criminal activities in the sphere of management and economy.

Prosecuting Authorities

The public prosecution of Ukraine is a centralized system under the supervision of the general prosecutor and representing the state in the process of prosecution. The general prosecutor is nominated by the president and approved by the *Verkhovna Rada.* The General Prosecutor's Office supports the accusation in court and represents the interests of the citizen and the state. The general prosecutor may enter the case at any stage of the proceedings, if it appears necessary for the preservation of constitutional rights. Prosecutor's requests are mandatory. Unfortunately, a complete reformation of the public prosecution system in accordance with principles and standards of the Council of Europe has not yet been accomplished.

Crime

Classification of Crimes

The new Criminal Code of Ukraine was enacted in 2001. It marked significant humanization of the criminal legislation. The system of punishment and rules of its imposition were significantly modified to prioritize noncustodial sentences. New types of offenses were introduced in the code in compliance with international standards (e.g., human trafficking, money laundering). In addition, some types of offenses (e.g., administrative offenses) are treated under special proceedings.

The Criminal Code applies to all persons 16 years or older. Criminal liability of juvenile ages 14–16 depends on the type of offenses (e.g., murder, intended grievous bodily injury, rape, theft, or seizure of railroad rolling stock, hooliganism). Depending on the situation, juveniles are subject to punishment or special measures, such as educational measures. Criminal offenses committed by juveniles are treated by the criminal justice system within general proceedings. The Criminal Procedural Code includes special rules regarding criminal proceedings involving juveniles.

Crime Statistics

Crime statistics are recorded by official agencies, namely, the Ministry of Internal Affairs, the Prosecutors' Office, and the Supreme Court of Ukraine. It should be remembered that official statistics do not accurately reveal the actual crime rate, especially economic, organized, and white-collar crime. The main reason for this phenomenon is a high level of latent crime that is not known to the investigation authorities.

The crime rate increased after the independence of Ukraine up to 1995 then stabilized. In 2003, the crime rate increased by 20 percent, yet this is partially due to a change in the procedure of crime recording. In 2007 the crime rate for the first time revealed a 1 percent reduction in comparison with 1991. However, it should be taken into account that simultaneously the country's population declined by about 10 percent.

Statistics show that, in 2007, law enforcement agencies uncovered 420 organized crime groups. Of the crimes committed by organized groups 64 percent belong to common delinquency (e.g., thefts, robberies) and 36 percent are economic crimes. Corruption remains a major, widespread problem in Ukraine that has a very negative impact on detection of organized crime.

Economic crime constitutes another great challenge for Ukraine. Various illicit activities sustain the shadow economy, which has been estimated to constitute approximately 30 percent or 40 percent of the economy. Looking back at the Soviet period, such crime was never a law enforcement priority, as the official doctrine denied private commercial relations. When this changed in 1991, a time of wild business and semicriminal activities began. No strict rules of commerce existed and people lacked traditions of civilized market economies. The situation, however, changed over time: new legislation was enforced and state agencies started to control financial interactions. Nevertheless, a significant proportion of the profit economy remains hidden behind semilegal schemes. Entrepreneurs are avoiding taxation, hiding part of their income, abusing labor and social security legislation. Targeting such illicit activities and other grey business transactions has become a state agencies' priority. In 2007, 42,755 offenses related to economic crime were recorded, which represents 10.6 percent of total offenses.

Property offenses are also common in Ukraine, especially thefts and robberies. Property offenses traditionally make up the largest proportion of nonviolent offenses. Between 1991 and 1995, thefts made up over 50 percent of registered crime. According to crime statistics, this increase was followed by a drastic drop: in 2007, the proportion of thefts accounted for 28.4 percent of all offenses. This phenomenon does not reflect a real change in the extent of property crime, but a change in legislation as the lower limit for a theft to be considered a criminal offense was raised to 772.7 Hryvnia (approximately US$97). The largest increase in the number of robberies registered by the police was observed in 1993. Proactive law enforcement policies aimed at reducing the number of robberies have been carried out recently and robberies have decreased. It represents approximately 1.5 percent of registered crime. Property offenses trends are closely connected to the financial situation of the country. The economic crisis and inflation in the 1990s resulted in high unemployment, lack of social payments, and slowing down of industry. People committed offenses to survive.

Drug offenses also make up a significant proportion of crime in Ukraine and the number of drug offenses has increased over the years. Between 1991 and 2007, the rate of drug offenses was multiplied by a factor 6. Drug abuse was recently recognized as a public health issue: in 2007, 173,323 drug addicts have been recorded, that is, an increase of over 40 percent in less than five years. Moreover, official statistics underestimate the extent of drug addiction as many addicts are not officially registered. Public organizations estimate that approximately 2 million people have addiction problems. As drug addicts are often involved in delinquency (i.e., both criminal and noncriminal offenses), the Ukrainian criminal procedure includes measures of compulsory treatment of drug addiction that can be pronounced in association with a custodial sentence.

Finally, human trafficking constitutes a serious problem whose importance has been increasing since the beginning of the 1990s. In 1998, human trafficking was introduced in the Criminal Code as an individual article that was later amended in 2001 and 2006 in compliance with international standards. The proportion of recorded offenses increased four times between 2001 and 2007 (89 and 359 cases, respectively). The International Organization for Migration estimates that about 100,000 Ukrainians have been victims of human trafficking over the period 2001–2008.

Finding of Guilt

The Criminal Procedural Code of Ukraine is intended for the determination of criminal proceedings. It applies to the inquest, pretrial investigation, and judicial consideration of the case. The Ukrainian criminal justice system is based on both the inquisitorial and adversarial justice principles.

Police custody cannot exceed 72 hours. After that time, the prosecutor has to file a petition to court to prolong detention. Other measures of restraint can be chosen; these include, for example, house arrest, bail (i.e., personal or by organization/institution), pledge, or pretrial detention up to 2 months. House arrest is the most common measure of restraint, whereas pledge is a relatively new measure that has not been widely used to date.

Pretrial investigation ends with the drafting of an indictment, a resolution on closing the case, or a resolution on transferring the case to court. The accused is then informed of the closure of the investigation and presented with all investigation material. Petitions for additional pretrial investigation measures can be presented at this time.

The indictment should be approved by the prosecutor before the case is brought to court. Justice in criminal cases is executed on the principles of equality of the citizens before law and court. Consideration of cases in courts is open, except when it runs counter to the interests of protection of state secret or other protected information. Criminal cases are considered in the court of primary jurisdiction by a sole judge as long as the possible punishment does not exceed a 10-year custodial sentence; other cases are considered by the court collectively.

The Criminal Procedural Code contains the list of participants of criminal procedure and determines their rights and duties, namely, the suspect or defendant, the defense lawyer, the victim or civil plaintiff, the prosecutor, the investigator, the judge, the witnesses, and the legal experts.

The prosecutor is a central figure in criminal proceedings as he or she supervises all decisions taken during criminal proceedings and has to approve each bill of indictment. After that he or she files the case to court and supports public accusation in all criminal cases. Investigative authorities (i.e., the police and the Security Service of Ukraine) have powers to drop proceedings only in a limited number of situations (e.g., unknown offender, lack of evidence, absence of criminal action). Such decisions are supervised by the prosecutor and other decisions implying the dropping of a case can only be taken by the court.

The prosecution and the defense enjoy equal rights to present evidence, participate in the investigation, speak during proceedings, and appeal of court. The accused has to take part in the trial. He or she can defend himself or herself or be assisted by a legal representative. If he or she cannot financially afford to hire a counsel, the latter will be paid by the state.

Ukrainian Supreme Court judges Anatoliy Yarema, left, and Viktor Kryvenko vote during a court hearing of an appeal by former prime minister Viktor Yanukovych, in Kiev, Ukraine, January 17, 2005. Yanukovych, the losing candidate, had appealed to the court over alleged fraud in the recent presidential election. (AP Photo/Sergei Chuzavkov)

The judgment of the court shall be legal and grounded. The court shall evaluate evidence according to the extent to which it is grounded on comprehensive, full, and objective consideration of all circumstances of the case and guided by law. The judgment of the court may be accusatory or justificatory. A justificatory judgment is made if the event of the crime has not been found out, when there is no clear evidence of the culprit's actions, as well as when participation of the culprit in commitment of crime has not been proved. In all other cases the accusatory judgment shall be made. The copy of the judgment must be served to the convict or to the justified person in a three-day term after its passing.

Court decisions can be appealed by the convict and his or her counsel, the plaintiff, or the victim and their representatives. Courts of appeal can decide the following:

- To retain the ruling
- To cancel the ruling and order a new investigation or judicial consideration
- To cancel the ruling and close the case
- To modify the ruling

Juvenile justice in Ukraine does not make up a separate jurisdiction and cases involving juvenile offenders are tried in courts of primary jurisdiction. The Criminal Procedural Code provides several extra guarantees to protect accused juveniles (e.g., mandatory legal counsel, authorization to be assisted by a third person such as a parent or a psychiatrist during interviews, investigation guidelines). Juvenile justice is handled as a rule by specialized judges. Finally, the Ukrainian criminal justice system does not recognize alternatives to trial such as mediation procedures. However, this might be included in the next revision of the criminal procedure.

Punishment

Types of Punishment

Types of punishment are listed in the Criminal Code. Punishment is defined as a coercive measure imposed in a judgment of court on behalf of the state upon a person found guilty of a criminal offense. Punishment aims not only at sanctioning but also at preventing recidivism and rehabilitating the offender.

The Criminal Code of Ukraine defines general principles of imposition of punishment. The punishment imposed on an offender should be adequate and sufficient to reform the offender and prevent new offenses. The Criminal Code describes the following types of punishment: fines; downgrading of military rank, title, or qualification class; depriving of the right to take certain positions or to perform certain activities; community service; correctional works; service restriction for military personnel; forfeiture of property; arrest; restraint of liberty; retention in a disciplinary battalion for military personnel; imprisonment for a definite period; and life imprisonment.

The existing types of punishment have been significantly modified in the reform of the Criminal Code in 2001. The main objective of the reform was to develop alternative sanctions such as community service and correctional works. The death penalty was abolished in 1999 after Ukraine faced strong political pressures when applying to join the Council of Europe. The death penalty was recognized unconstitutional and immoral, and commuted to life-term imprisonment.

The code provides clear instructions on application of punishments. For instance, community service may not be imposed upon persons who have been certified to have a first- or a second-degree disability, pregnant women, persons of retirement age, or military personnel in active duty. Correctional work labor may not be imposed upon pregnant women, women on maternity leave, disabled persons, persons under 16 years of age, persons of retirement age, military servants, law enforcement officers, notaries, judges, prosecutors, defense attorneys, civil servants, or local government officials. Life imprisonment may not be imposed on persons who committed offenses under 18 years of age and to persons more than 65 years of age, and women who were pregnant at the time of offense or at the time of sentencing.

The amount of a monetary fine is determined by a court based on the severity of the offense committed and the income status of the guilty person, but within the limits of 30 to 1,000 tax-free minimum individual income. The judge can impose a larger amount of a fine if it is prescribed by articles of the special part of the Criminal Code of Ukraine. A fine may be imposed as an additional penalty only if it is specifically sanctioned by an article in the special part of the Criminal Code of Ukraine.

When imposing a punishment, a court may find aggravating circumstances such as recidivism, an offense committed in a group, an offense committed against a minor or a helpless person, as well as the violent character of an offense. Inversely, when imposing a punishment, a court may find mitigating circumstances such as voluntary compensation, offenses committed in excess of necessary defense or as a consequence of adverse personal, familial, or other circumstances. The code also recognizes the possibility to impose a milder punishment than that prescribed by law based upon the personality of offender and the nature of the offense.

According to the Criminal Procedural Code, the type and the measure (including the term) of punishment is defined exclusively by the court. If the sanction implies a deprivation of liberty, the type of the correctional establishment is defined by the agencies of the State Department of Ukraine for the Execution of Sentences—the central official body of executive power with special status.

Conviction statistics over the period 2002–2007 show interesting trends. Custodial sentences are the most common sanctions, making up 24–26 percent of all sanctions, whereas community service does not exceed 2.5 percent. The latter being a relatively new type of punishment, this is not surprising. Indeed, custodial sentences were far more numerous in the 1990s as they represented approximately 35 percent of all convictions.

Finally, as defined in the Criminal Code, probation can be pronounced up to a period of 3 years and be associated with specific conditions such as the obligation to reside in the country or to undergo a medical treatment. Such court decisions are based on the personality of the culprit, the seriousness of the offense, and the circumstances of the crime. Probation in Ukraine differs from probation rules in other countries as it is a type of discharge from punishment that does imply criminal liability. Putting a culprit on probation does not prevent him or her from conviction. The strategic goal of reforming the system of enforcement of sentences in Ukraine is the establishment of the Probation Service in accordance with the European standards on the basis of the Criminal Executive Inspection.

Prison

The Criminal Executive Code of Ukraine of 2004 regulates the procedure and conditions of the execution of custodial sentences. It serves the interests of the individuals and the state in creating conditions that ensure correction, favor resocialization, and prevent recidivism. Sentences are administered in dignity and torture and humiliations are prohibited.

The institutions where sentences can be carried out are arrest facilities, criminal facilities, special facilities, and educational facilities (i.e., educational colonies). Criminal facilities are divided into open criminal facilities (i.e., correctional centers) and closed criminal facilities (i.e., correctional colonies). Different types of correctional colonies exist according to their level of security, namely, colonies of minimum, medium, and maximum security.

The execution of sentences is controlled by the State Department for the Execution of Sentences and its management bodies, as well as the Criminal Executive Inspection. The State Executive Service executes punishments in the form of penalty and confiscation of property in cases and procedure stipulated by the code and laws of Ukraine. The Criminal Executive Inspection executes punishments in the form of deprivation of right to hold certain positions or carry out certain activities, social work, and correctional work. Arrest houses execute punishments in the form of arrest. Correctional centers execute punishments in the form of limitation of freedom in relation to the persons condemned for crimes of small and middle gravity. Correctional colonies execute punishment in the form of imprisonment for a certain term or lifelong imprisonment. Isolation wards perform the functions of correctional colonies of minimum safety level with general conditions of holding and of correctional colonies of middle safety level in relation to the condemned that do economic service. Educational colonies execute punishment in the form of imprisonment for a certain term in relation to the condemned minors.

The system of correctional institutions in Ukraine comprises 186 bodies of execution of punishment and 704 departments of criminal executive inspection and educational establishments. In 2006, this system housed 160,725 convicts, of which 32,600 persons were placed in centers of pretrial detention, 125,600 persons (of which 7,600 females) in correctional institutions, 2,200 juveniles in educational colonies, and 285 persons in medical centers for convicts. It should be noted that the number of convicts has significantly decreased over the last years. In 2007, 0.32 percent of the Ukrainian population was incarcerated.

Correction policies aim at resocializing and rehabilitating the convicted person. To achieve this, the execution of the sanction should include socially useful work, educational work, general education, and vocational training. The convicted offender shall enjoy all rights of a human being and a citizen except limitations inscribed by the laws of Ukraine and this code and set by sentence of court.

The regime in correctional and educational colonies is set by law and other legal procedures on sentence execution, which ensures isolation of convicts, permanent supervision; fulfillment of their duties; exercise of their rights and legal interests; safety of convicts and staff; separate keeping of different categories of convicts; different conditions of keeping of convicts based on the type of colony; change of terms of holding of convicts.

To stop illegal actions and prevent both direct and indirect harm, physical strength, special devices, straitjackets, and weapons can be used under the following conditions: the convicts physically resist, do not perform legal requirements, show disorderly conduct, participate in mass disturbances, capture hostages, or commit other violent actions, as well as in case of escape.

Convicts have the right to acquire food and basic items for the money earned in colonies. Condemned men older than 60 years old, women more than 55 years old, the disabled, pregnant women who have children in child care establishments at correctional colonies, minors, and the condemned who stay in medical preventive establishments of places of imprisonment have the above right also for the money obtained by orders, at the expense of pensions and other incomes. Convicts have the right to receive in book-posts, packages, parcels, as well as without limitation to acquire literature through a bookselling network, writing facilities, subscribe to newspapers and magazines for money that they have on their personal accounts.

Convicts have the right to short meetings—up to four hours long, and long meetings—up to three days and nights. Short meetings may be with relatives or other persons in presence of a representative of the colony. Long meetings may be given with the right of joint living and only with close relatives (married couple, parents, children, foster parents, adopted children, own brothers and sisters, grandfather, grandmother, grandchildren). Long meetings may also be provided for the spouse who lived together as one family but was not married provided that they have common minor children. Services for use of rooms for short and long meetings are paid for by the convicts, their relatives, or other persons from their own funds.

Convicts work in places and on works that are determined by the administration of the colonies. Convicts must be engaged in socially useful labor, taking into account available production capacities, sex, age, ability to work, health condition, and specialty. As a rule the condemned shall be engaged in labor on enterprises, in workshops of colonies, as well as on state or private enterprises, if the required conditions of protection and isolation are provided. For the persons who serve sentence in the form of imprisonment, the working week must not exceed the norm of working time that is set by regular labor legislation. Time of beginning and end of work (shift) shall be determined by the administration of the colony. The condemned shall be freed from work on weekends, holidays, and days off, which are determined by labor legislation.

According to the law, colonies must provide for moral, legal, labor, aesthetic, physical, and sanitary hygienic education of the condemned, as well as other types of education that help to establish with the condemned such viewpoints that correspond to legal norms and requirements of socially useful activity. Freedom to profess any religion or express beliefs related to attitude toward religion shall be limited only in the part that is necessary for ensuring isolation and public security. The limitations are established by this code.

Offenders sentenced to lifelong imprisonment serve sentence in correctional colonies of maximum safety level. They must be placed in camera-type rooms, as a rule, for two persons and wear clothes of set style. Confinement in a solitary cell might be envisaged to protect the convict from violence by other offenders, prevention of the commission of crime by the convict, or for any other medical reason.

The Criminal Executive Code of Ukraine determines the procedure of discharge from serving sentence and aid to the persons who are freed from serving sentence, control and supervision. Grounds for discharge from serving sentence are completing the term of sentence given by the court, the law of Ukraine on amnesty, pardon act, cancellation of court decision and closing of criminal case, end of prescription term for execution of sentence, grant of parole from serving sentence, disease, or other grounds stipulated by law. Persons who have served the sentence shall bear responsibilities and enjoy rights that are established for Ukrainian citizens with limitations envisaged for the persons who have previous convictions. Such limitations shall be stipulated only by law.

Not later than three months prior to the termination of the sentence, the administration, through territorial departments of domestic affairs and employment centers of population, must take measures to ensure labor and everyday settlement of the convict in a chosen place of residence.

In conclusion, it must be noted that the transfer of the system of the execution of sentences to the Ministry of Justice has not yet been achieved. The State Department for the Execution of Sentences has continued and even extended its practice of adopting departmental procedures that violate the rights of convicted prisoners. At the present time there is no real effective mechanism for safeguarding the rights of prisoners to turn to the court to protect their violated rights and legitimate interests. The major unsolved problem now is the prisoners suffering from an active form of tuberculosis. The penitentiary system remains closed to society.

Olena Shostko and Olena Ovcharenko

Further Reading

Dremin, Viktor. (2004). "Organized Crime and Corruption in Ukraine as a System Phenomenon." In *Organized Crime, Trafficking, Drugs: Selected Papers Presented at the Annual Conference of the European Society of Criminology, Helsinki 2003,* edited by Sami Nevala and Kauko Aromaa, pp. 49–59. Helsinki: The European Institute for Crime Prevention and Control (HEUNI).

Foglesong, Todd S., and Peter H. Solomon. (2001). *Crime, Criminal Justice and Criminology in Post-Soviet Ukraine.* Washington, DC: National Institute of Justice.

Shostko, Olena. (2004). "Organized Crime in Ukraine: Contemporary Situation and Methods of Counteraction." In *Organized Crime, Trafficking, Drugs: Selected Papers Presented at the Annual Conference of the European Society of Criminology, Helsinki 2003,* edited by Sami Nevala and Kauko Aromaa, pp. 216–225. Helsinki: The European Institute for Crime Prevention and Control (HEUNI).

United Kingdom/England

Legal System: Common
Murder: Medium
Burglary: Medium
Corruption: Low
Human Trafficking: Low
Prison Rate: Medium
Death Penalty: No
Corporal Punishment: No

Background

England's population (2006 estimate) is 50,762,900, of which approximately 92 percent are white, while 8 percent are of immigrant or ethnic origin including Asian, African, or Chinese. England is a representative democracy. There is a two-house system: the House of Commons and the House of Lords. The three main political parties in England are Labour, Conservative, and Liberal Democrats, and are represented in both houses. The House of Commons consists of publicly elected Members of Parliament (MPs). The political party with the largest number of members in the House of Commons forms the government. At the heart of the government is the cabinet, consisting of the most senior ministers who each advise the prime minister on their specialist areas of responsibility. The House of Commons debates new laws and key political issues. It is also solely responsible for decisions on financial bills. The House of Lords consists mostly of those appointed by the queen on the advice of the prime minister. It is the highest court in England (Supreme Court of Appeal) and revises legislation. Decisions made in one house generally have to be approved by the other: the two-chamber system acts as a check for both houses. The House of Commons is generally considered to be the more powerful of the two.

History of the Criminal Justice System

The English criminal justice system has existed for centuries and is the forerunner of many other such systems around the world. Some key dates in its development include the following:

- 1215: The *Magna Carta*, a document that limited the king's powers by law, was signed.
- 1723: The Black Act, which created 50 new capital offenses, was passed.
- Late 1700s to early 1800s: Capital punishment was in decline and the modern prison was established: Reformers such as John Howard and Elizabeth Fry were key figures in England during this time.
- 1829: The Metropolitan Police Act established professional policing.
- 1837–1901 (Victorian period): A consensus evolved on sanctions to address criminal behavior. Workhouses and prisons were designed to have conditions harsher than those experienced by the lowest worker outside. An ethos of control was enforced over prisoners.
- 1863: Broadmoor Criminal Lunatic Asylum opened. It was one of the first institutions for the treatment of those who had committed crimes while mentally ill.
- 1895: Gladstone Committee on Prisons recommended a more rehabilitative system.
- 1908: Borstal schools—prisons for youths—were introduced. This signified the beginning of separating juvenile justice from the adult system.
- 1960s: This period saw the strengthening of drug laws, the decriminalization of homosexuality, and the abolition of the death penalty.
- Present day: There has been an increase in the prison population, an increase in the fear of crime, and politicians have put crime at the heart of their election manifestos.

Legal System

England works on a common law system, using the adversarial principle. A judge and jury, or bench of magistrates, listen to evidence presented by both parties: prosecution and defense. Safeguards are provided within the system to prevent an abuse of power by either the state or its agents. To this end there is a separation of powers, with executive, legislative, and judiciary branches all having independent decision-making powers. There are restrictions on the way evidence can be gathered and how long suspects can be held for questioning. The inclusion of strict procedures aims to increase fairness and reliability within the criminal justice system in England.

Previously all responsibilities fell under the Home Office, but a new Ministry of Justice was launched on May 9, 2007. The aim of this new department was to create coherency across all aspects of the criminal justice system. The Ministry of Justice employs 77,000 people, with funding available for a further 21,000 members of staff. The ministry incorporates a variety of organizations from across the criminal justice system. It brings them together under one umbrella to improve the way that offenders, victims, and staff are dealt with. The core components of the Ministry of Justice are as follows:

- The National Offender Management Service: administration of correctional services
- Youth Justice Board
- Inspectorates of Prison and Probation and the Prison and Probation Ombudsmen
- Criminal, civil, family, and administrative law, including sponsorship of the Sentencing Guidelines Council
- The Office for Criminal Justice Reform
- Her Majesty's Courts Service
- The Tribunals Service
- Legal Aid and Legal Services Commission
- Judicial Appointments Commission, the Judicial Office, and Judicial Communications Office
- The Privy Council
- Constitutional affairs: electoral reform and democratic engagement
- Ministry of Justice corporate center

The Attorney General's Office has existed in some form since 1315. Since 1461 there has been both an attorney general and a solicitor general, although they did not assume their current form until 1885. They are now jointly known as the Law Officers of the Crown; the solicitor general deputizes for the attorney general. They are guardians of the public interest to which end they can, for example, appeal against unduly lenient sentences, or bring proceedings under the Contempt of Court Act 1981. They are also chief legal advisers to the government, and they are criminal justice ministers. Questions of law arising on government bills and with issues of legal policy are referred to the law officers. The law officers are responsible for all Crown litigation and have overall responsibility for the work of the Treasury Solicitors Department, Crown Prosecution Service, Serious Fraud Office, Revenues and Customs Prosecution Office, and Her Majesty's Crown Prosecution Service Inspectorate.

Police

As of 2007, the Police Service employed 232,948 full-time equivalent staff, of which the majority are police officers. In addition to the staff employed by the Police Service, there are 14,021 Special Constables. These have all the powers of regular police officers but are volunteers who give up a minimum of four hours of their time each week.

Police Community Support Officers do not have the same powers as police officers. They provide support to the police and act as a high-visibility foot patrol. They focus predominantly on lower-level crime, disorder, and antisocial behavior. They have standard enforcement powers to allow them to carry out their duties, for example, serving fixed penalty notices and seizing illegal drugs.

The extent of police powers is laid out in the Police and Criminal Evidence Act (PACE) 1984. This piece of legislation sets out to strike the right balance between public rights and the powers of the police. PACE codes of practice are periodically reviewed and updated to ensure this balance is maintained. They include rules on stopping and searching persons, premises, and vehicles; detention, treatment, and questioning of suspects; keeping accurate and reliable criminal records; recording of interviews with suspects; powers of arrest.

As of 2008, there are 43 police forces across England and Wales. The Police Service is entirely separate from the military. The Metropolitan Police is England's largest police force, covering an area of 620 square miles with a population of 7.2 million. This compares to England's smallest force, the City of London Police, who have responsibility for London's Square Mile, comprising just 8,600 residents, alongside some 350,000 commuters.

There is a three-way system of responsibility to allow the police to run smoothly without any political interference. This also avoids giving any one organization absolute power over the Police Service. The Home Office funds just over half of police costs, and so has the lead responsibility. Chief police officers take responsibility for regional police forces, and police authorities ensure that local forces work effectively. In addition to this three-way system, regional forces are monitored by Her Majesty's Inspectorate of Constabulary. This is an independent body, separate from the Home Office and from the police, which examines and improves the Police Service. Since 2004, specific complaints have been referred to the Independent Police Complaints Commission (IPCC). The IPCC can investigate or manage complaints and helps the police to improve on the basis of their findings. Decisions on cases are free from government involvement.

The Serious Organized Crime Agency (SOCA) was established in 2006. SOCA has law enforcement powers, harm reduction responsibilities, and is an intelligence-led agency. Current areas of focus for SOCA include trafficking of people and drugs, fraud, and other organized crimes. SOCA brings together expertise from areas as diverse as immigration, e-crime, and finance. Like the Police Service, SOCA is independent of government involvement, is funded by the Home Office, and complaints can be investigated by the IPCC. Unlike the Police Service, SOCA is exempt from the Freedom of Information requirement due to the sensitive nature of much of its information and sources.

Crime

Classification of Crimes

There are three categories of offenses in England: summary, triable either way, and indictment only. Summary offenses include the less serious crimes.

This group includes road traffic offenses, common assault, being drunk and disorderly, and criminal damage where the value of the property destroyed or damaged is less than £5,000 (US$7,191). These offenses are tried in a magistrates' court.

Offenses that are classed as triable either way are those that may be dealt with at either the magistrates' court or the Crown Court. Proceedings for these offenses begin at the magistrates' court where it is decided whether the case needs to be referred up to the Crown Court, or whether it can be dealt with by the magistrates. Offenses in this category include theft, criminal damage (where costs are estimated above £5,000), deception, and handling stolen property.

The term "indictable offense" refers to all cases tried by the Crown Court, therefore "indictable only" is a term used to distinguish those offenses that can only be tried by the Crown Court. These are the most serious offenses as recognized under English law and include rape, murder, robbery, and serious firearms offenses.

The age of criminal responsibility in England is 10. From the age of 10 to 13, defendants are classified as children, and from the age of 14 to 17 they are classed as young people, though in practice both groups are often referred to as juveniles. Children and young people will normally appear in the youth court, except where the youth court declines jurisdiction or where the crime is of a serious nature.

Police wearing body armor search a young man for drugs in Brixton, South London, July 10, 2002. The British government has announced its intention to downgrade marijuana from a Class B drug to a Class C drug, making possession and use a less serious offense. (AP Photo/Steve Holland)

Terrorism

Following coordinated terrorist attacks in London on July 7, 2005, terrorism has been increasingly debated in the public forum. In a speech on January 17, 2008, the Home Secretary reported the Security Service's estimate that in 2007, the United Kingdom had 2,000 operating terrorists, up from 1,600 on the previous year. In the wake of the Home Secretary's speech there has been extensive discussion of possibilities for expanding the powers of police and security services in relation to terrorist offenses, suspects, and sentencing.

Antisocial Behavior

Antisocial behavior includes activities such as vandalism, antisocial drinking, the misuse of fireworks, rowdy behavior, and nuisance neighbors. In a one-day count carried out by the Anti Social Behavior Unit (ASBU) on September 10, 2003, the number of complaints about antisocial behavior across England and Wales was recorded as 66,000. It is considered a cause of an increasing fear of crime in England. Since the Anti Social Behavior Act 2003 was introduced, failure to comply with an official request to abstain from the undesirable behavior automatically upgrades many of these behaviors to a criminal offense. Antisocial drinking of alcohol is considered a problem in many towns and city centers in England, particularly over the weekend evenings.

Drug Offenses

The Misuse of Drugs Act is the main piece of legislation relating to drugs. It sets out drug-related offenses, and categorizes drugs as one of Class A, B, or C. Class A drugs are considered the most harmful, and so attract more severe sentences upon conviction. Trafficking is dealt with much more harshly than possession, with life imprisonment and an unlimited fine possible for individuals dealing Class A drugs (heroin, cocaine, etc.).

In addition to trafficking, other offenses recognized under the Misuse of Drugs Act include the following:

- Possession
- Possession with intent to supply
- Supplying/offering to supply (even where no payment for the drugs has been received)
- Allowing premises to be used for the production or supply of controlled drugs

The police have special powers in relation to controlled drugs. They may stop, detain, and search people on "reasonable suspicion" that they are in possession of a controlled drug.

Drugs can be reclassified as new evidence emerges about the harm they cause and to reflect changes in the cultures and attitudes in England. In 2004, cannabis was reclassified from a Class B to a Class C drug, a controversial move said to cause confusion as to the harm and legal status of the drug. Cannabis is the most widely used recreational illegal drug in England, and several cabinet ministers have admitted to occasional use in their youth.

Crime Statistics

The most recently available crime statistics (2007–2008) for a selection of offenses that were reported to and recorded by the police are as follows:

Homicide	784
Rape (of female)	11,648
Rape (of male)	1,006
Domestic burglary	280,704
Trafficking in drugs	28,130

In addition, the British Crime Survey, which collects information from interviews of household members, reported 729,000 domestic burglaries. The British Crime Survey has also found for several years that there is a lower risk of being a victim of household crime (including vandalism, vehicle-related theft, and burglary) in rural areas than urban areas. There is also a lower risk of experiencing violence against the person in rural areas. However, variation in most crime types tends to be masked when examining broad regions, as most crimes in England tend to be geographically concentrated in smaller areas.

Finding of Guilt

The criminal justice system works on the assumption that an individual is innocent until proven guilty. While a person is awaiting trial, he or she may be either remanded on bail or remanded in custody. The Bail Act 1967 advises that unless there are strong reasons why this should not be allowed, an individual will be remanded on conditional bail. The severity of the alleged offense may result in bail being refused, for example, the crimes of murder, rape, or manslaughter. Bail may also be refused where the individual has prior convictions; it is likely that he or she will commit further offenses before trial; the accused is likely to interfere with witnesses; or there is reason to believe the individual may disappear before the trial.

If a person is remanded in custody, he or she is treated differently from those who have been sentenced, to reflect the presumption of innocence. These persons retain their entitlement to vote, can wear their own clothes, and can take reasonable activity to maintain their business interests. They also retain benefit entitlements where applicable, and do not have to work or attend education classes. Free legal advice and representation is available for everybody under investigation or facing criminal charges. During questioning at a police station, detainees are entitled to consult either a solicitor of their choice or the duty solicitor. The role of the attending solicitor is to protect the legal rights of his or her client.

For certain proceedings at a magistrates' court or the Crown Court, the cost of a solicitor preparing a case and initial representation may be offered. Full legal representation for defense in criminal cases at all court levels is available. These services are provided nationally by the Criminal Defense Service (CDS). This provision of legal aid helps the courts and the police to operate fairly. Although legal aid can be offered to all defendants, a court order can be issued to recover legal aid costs if it is found the defendant could have paid for his or her own representation.

The Crown Prosecution Service (CPS) was created by the Prosecution of Offences Act 1985. It is responsible for determining the charge and for prosecuting criminal cases investigated by the police. It is an independent body but works closely with other organizations within the criminal justice system.

Crown prosecutors are responsible for making the decision on whether to prosecute. The decision is broadly based on whether there is enough evidence for a reasonable chance of conviction, and whether the prosecution would be "in the public interest." The term "public interest" can be controversial, particularly where it does not coincide with that of the victim.

England has a hierarchical system of courts. The Supreme Court of Judicature of England and Wales consists of the Court of Appeal, High Court of Justice, and the Crown Court. Subordinate courts include the magistrates' courts, family proceedings courts, youth courts, and county courts. There are 650 Crown, county, and magistrates' courts throughout England and Wales, all of which have been run by Her Majesty's Courts Service since 2005.

A criminal trial is required to be fair by both English common law and more recently the European Convention on Human Rights. Fairness does not require trial by jury. Any defects that occur during a trial can be rectified by a later appearance before the Court of Appeal: what matters is the fairness of the proceedings as a whole.

The most commonly used court is the magistrates' court, which sees around 95 percent of all criminal cases through to completion. Almost all cases are initially heard at a magistrates' court, but may then be passed to the Crown Court for sufficiently serious offenses, for triable-either-way offenses, where the accused requests trial by jury, or where the magistrate believes a Crown Court trial is more appropriate.

The magistrates' court usually consists of three magistrates who are laypersons, that is, they are not lawyers or professional judges and are unpaid for their services. The three magistrates are collectively known as the bench. Magistrates are also known as justices of the peace. These are voluntary posts but all lay magistrates undergo mandatory training and have access to legal advice. There are around 30,000 magistrates in England and Wales, each of whom usually attends 35–45 half-day sittings each year. In addition to lay magistrates, there are around 130 district judges (formerly known as stipendiary magistrates) in England and Wales. These sit alone and must have at least seven years' experience as either a solicitor or barrister and have two years' experience as a deputy district judge. District judges deal with particularly sensitive or complex cases such as extradition hearings.

The magistrates' court tries and sentences summary offenses, as well as some triable-either-way offenses. The bench has the power to order sentences of up to six months, or fines of up to £5,000. In triable-either-way offenses, where the magistrates believe that the offense requires a more serious penalty than they can enjoin, the case may be referred to a Crown Court for sentencing.

The Crown Court is a national institution based across 77 centers throughout England and Wales. It deals with all indictment offenses, which includes indictment-only offenses as well as those triable-either-way offenses that have been referred upward by a magistrates' court. In addition, the Crown Court may handle summary offenses where these can be dealt with at the same time as more serious allegations and appeals against sentencing or conviction decisions by the magistrates' court.

Trials at a Crown Court are heard by a judge and a 12-person jury. Jurors are randomly selected from the electoral roll. Once summoned, jurors are legally obliged to serve on the jury unless they are ineligible for or disqualified from jury duty. Ineligibility is relatively rare, but may occur where the person summoned is on bail, has been sentenced, or suffers from certain categories of mental illness.

The Crown Court has four options open to it should the defendant be found guilty. These are discharge, fines, community sentences, or imprisonment. Although the Crown Court has less restrictions on the sentence it can impose than a magistrates' court, judges are still given sentencing guidelines that are designed to ensure consistency. There are maximum penalties designated to offenses, alongside minimum penalties for certain serious offenses.

The Judicial Appointments Commission was launched on April 3, 2006. It has taken responsibility for choosing candidates for judicial appointments away from the Lord Chancellor for the first time in more than 900 years. This shift of responsibility aims to make the appointment process clearer and more accountable. The Lord Chancellor still has final veto over the appointment, but must provide reasons if rejecting the recommendation for appointment. To ensure judicial independence, once appointed, a judge has "security of position" and cannot be forced to leave his or her post. Therefore, appointing the right candidate is crucial.

The 218 county courts throughout England and Wales deal with civil matters such as debt repayments, divorce, and personal injury claims. Unlike the magistrates' court and the Crown Court, hearings are not accessible to the public and instead are heard privately in front of a judge. The Court of Appeal is the highest court within the Supreme Court of Judicature. Although in some cases a further appeal to the House of Lords is possible, in practice, for the majority of cases the Court of Appeal is the final opportunity for appeal. The prime minister recommends judges for appointment to the Court of Appeal, and they are appointed by the monarch (Queen Elizabeth II at the time of writing). All are senior judges with extensive judicial experience. The Bench normally consists of two High Court judges and a Lady or Lord Justice.

An appeal against conviction should take no longer than eight months, and that against a sentence no longer than five months, providing the case is straightforward. Should the conviction be quashed, and "the interests of justice so require," the court can order a retrial. In recent years this has occurred in around a third of all quashed convictions.

When an offender pleads guilty to a charge, a reduction in sentence is normally applied. The reduction is on a sliding scale depending on how soon the guilty plea was submitted. The maximum sentence reduction is one-third, where the offender pleads guilty at the first available opportunity. A reduction in sentence is considered appropriate as it allows justice to be administered more quickly and reduces costs. A guilty plea is not considered a mitigating factor. Reductions in sentence will be withheld where the court determines there should be a whole life minimum term.

The youth court is used for nearly all offenses committed by persons aged from 10 years to 18 years. A very small number are tried in the Crown Court. This occurs where a "grave crime" has been committed. A grave crime normally consists of an offense that would carry a sentence of 14 years or more for a convicted adult. Three magistrates make up the bench in a youth court. These are specially trained "lay" magistrates and must include representation from both sexes. The youth court has three key principles that it abides by: ensuring welfare of the child or young person, the prevention of offending, and proportionality of the sentence to the offense.

Unlike an adult court, members of the public are not permitted access to a youth court. There are restrictions on reporting that prevent the name of the child or young person being revealed either directly or indirectly. These restrictions can be lifted in some circumstances, for instance, where the juvenile is a persistent offender. However, in practice the restrictions on reporting are rarely removed.

Punishment

Types of Punishment

There are four sentencing levels available. From greatest to least punishment, these are imprisonment, community sentence, fine, or discharge.

Guidelines issued by the Sentencing Guidelines Council must be adhered to in all but exceptional circumstances. Sentences must address four key areas: protection of the public, fair and appropriate punishment of the offender, encouraging the offender to make amends for the crime, and reducing crime by stopping reoffending. All offenses have a maximum penalty applicable under law. Some offenses also have a mandatory minimum sentence associated with them. As of 2008 these are the following:

- There must be a life sentence for murder.
- There is an automatic life sentence for a second serious sexual or violent offense (there is a list of qualifying offenses, all of which have a maximum penalty of life). For offenses committed after April 4, 2005, this penalty has been replaced with new public protection sentences.
- A minimum 7-year prison sentence for third-time trafficking in Class A drugs (this provision applies to importation, production, supplying, and possession with intent to supply Class A drugs. The maximum penalty for these offenses is life imprisonment).
- A minimum 3-year prison sentence for third-time domestic burglary. The maximum penalty for burglary is 14 years' imprisonment.
- A minimum 5-year prison sentence for possession or distribution of prohibited weapons or ammunition. The maximum penalty is 10 years' imprisonment.

Custodial sentences are reserved for the most serious offenses. They can be imposed where the court assesses the offender as posing a risk of a sexual or violent nature to public safety. A custodial sentence can also be used where the offender refuses to comply with a community order, or if the offense is so serious that neither a fine nor a community sentence is an adequate response to the offense. The prison an offender is allocated to depends on a risk assessment. Different prisons have different levels of security. Since 2005, offenders serving determinate sentences of more than 12 months have served the second half of their sentence on a conditional license in the community.

Community sentences combine punishment with making amends and changing offenders' behavior. The community order has different elements that are tailored to the offender and the offense. Some of these are enforced using new technologies. For example, a curfew may be enforced using electronic tagging. The elements available to make up a community order may include compulsory (unpaid) work; curfew; exclusion from certain areas; residence requirement; mental health, drug, or alcohol treatment.

Fines are the sentence most commonly imposed by the courts. The Crown Court may impose an unlimited fine, taking into account the seriousness of the offense and the offender's ability to pay. The magistrates' court has limits on the fines it may issue according to the level of the offense, up to a maximum of £5,000. Less serious offenses such as speeding, graffiti, and public disorder are often dealt with by a fixed penalty notice. These fines can be contested, but otherwise do not require attendance at court. The fine must be paid within a fixed period, and there is no criminal record associated with the fixed penalty notice.

A discharge can be chosen by the court where punishment is not considered appropriate. The court must take into account the nature and circumstances of the crime and the character of the offender. An absolute discharge is given where the offense is very minor, and/or the court considers that the experience has been enough of a deterrent for the offender. In this case no further action is taken. A conditional discharge is similar, except that further action on the original offense is taken if another offense is committed within a period decided by the court, up to a maximum of three years. A discharge will still show up on an offender's criminal record.

Alternative arrangements exist in England for offenders who are mentally ill. Under the 1983 Mental Health Act, an accused person can be remanded to a secure hospital for either treatment or for a report on his or her mental disorder. Where appropriate, once an individual has been convicted of a crime, the court can make an order for the individual to be detained in a secure hospital for treatment and care. The discharge and movements of the patient can then be restricted, and any movement may require the approval of the Home Secretary. There are three high secure hospitals in England: Rampton, Broadmoor, and Ashworth. In addition there are a number of medium and low secure units around the country, as well as six Secure Forensic Services for Young People. The last execution in England took place in 1964, but it was not until 1998 that the death penalty was formally abolished for all crimes. There are provisions under English law to allow the reinstatement of the death penalty in times of war, or where war is imminent.

A young person in England either committing a first minor offense or behaving antisocially will usually be kept out of the youth court. Instead, the police and relevant local authority will use a variety of orders and agreements to keep them out of the youth justice system. These enable help and support to be given to try to divert these young people away from criminal activity. The level of intervention used depends on both the young person and the offense.

The least serious step that may be taken is the issuing of a reprimand. This is a formal verbal warning issued when a young person admits his or her guilt to a minor offense. Sometimes the person may also be referred to the local Youth Offending Team (YOT) to take part in a voluntary program designed to address the young person's offending behavior.

A final warning is similar to a reprimand in that it is a formal verbal warning issued to a young person. It is given when there is an admittance of guilt to a first or second minor offense. It differs from a reprimand in that the young person also undergoes a mandatory assessment to determine a program of activities to address the offending behavior.

Antisocial behavior may be addressed by an acceptable behavior contract (ABC), an antisocial behavior order, or an individual support order (ISO). An acceptable behavior contract is targeted at those young people who are behaving in a low level antisocial manner. The local authority and YOT draw up a contract with the young person and his/her parents or care-givers to stop the troublesome behavior. A breach of this contract can lead to the imposition of an antisocial behavior order (ASBO). This prohibits the young person from going to certain places, taking part in certain activities, or meeting up with specified people. If the young person does not comply with the ASBO, he or she can face prosecution.

An individual support order (ISO) can be attached to an ASBO. This imposes conditions on the young person designed to address the antisocial behavior. An ISO typically requires the young person to attend up to two sessions a week supervised by his or her local Youth Offending Team (YOT). Failure to comply with an ISO may be punished by a financial order.

There are 10 community sentences that can be applied to young people. Community sentences can be subject to additional orders: a curfew order, a parenting order, and/or a drug treatment and testing order. A curfew order requires a young person to be in a specified place for 2 to 12 hours of the day. It lasts for up to 3 months for those under 16, or 6 months for young people aged 16 or over. A parenting order places requirements on the parent of the young offender, for example, to attend guidance or counseling sessions, to meet regularly with their child's teacher, or to ensure the child is at home at specified times. These conditions can last for up to 12 months. Although the parent does not get a criminal record, failure to comply with the order can result in prosecution. Drug treatment and testing orders are supervised by the Probation Service. With the young person's agreement, regular drug testing and treatment is provided in the community for a period of between 6 months and 3 years.

National Offender Management Service

The National Offender Management Service (NOMS), set up in 2004, was incorporated into the newly formed Ministry of Justice in 2007. NOMS collaborates with a variety of offender management services across public, private, community, and voluntary arenas to bridge the divide between custody and community.

Within the National Offender Management Service in England there are nine regional offender managers (ROMs). These managers coordinate delivery of prison and probation services. Each ROM is responsible for developing a regional plan for reducing reoffending, commissioning services for their region, and coordinating regional and local partnerships. The seven areas of focus that NOMS targets to reduce reoffending are accommodation; education, training, and employment; health; drugs and alcohol; finance, benefit, and debt; children and families; and attitudes, thinking, and behavior.

Prison

There are four security categories of prisons for adult male prisoners in England. These categories are fluid: a prisoner often moves into an open prison close to his release date to acclimatize to life on the outside. Prisoners can also be moved into a higher-security prison should they attempt to escape, or they are assessed as posing more of a risk. The four levels of security range from Category A for the most serious offenders who would pose a threat to public, police, or national security should they escape, through to Category D for prisoners who are trusted not to attempt to escape and may be allowed day release or to work in the community.

Women and young offenders are not subject to security classification unless they are assessed as Category A offenders. They are instead kept in either an open or a closed prison. Remand prisoners are usually treated as Category B offenders; unconvicted women and young offenders are kept in closed conditions.

England and Wales currently imprison 148 people per 100,000 of the population. The prison population on February 15, 2008, stood at 81,918, with the total operational capacity available (including 400 places in police cells) on the same date of 82,020. This compares to a prison population in 1998 of 65,727.

Prison overcrowding poses a continuous challenge to Her Majesty's Prison Service. At the end of October 2007, 85 out of the 141 prisons in England and Wales were overcrowded according to the Bromley Briefing Paper, a publication issued twice annually by the Prison Reform Trust. Wandsworth Prison in London is the largest in England, with a capacity of 1,416 inmates. It is also one of the largest prisons in Western Europe. Wandsworth Prison was built in 1851, though a modernization program upgraded the accommodation to include in-cell sanitation and privacy screens for cells housing more than one prisoner. More recently, a rolling program has provided electricity installation in individual cells.

Wandsworth Prison runs a variety of workshops and day classes. The prison houses two gymnasiums and a sports hall, and also runs two accredited offending behavior programs: enhanced thinking skills and a sex offender treatment program. A dedicated chaplaincy team caters for a variety of faiths, and meals provided by the prison take into account most dietary and religious requirements.

All prisoners in England have access to an educational and training service. This assesses need and teaches basic and key skills where appropriate. Some prisons have further education facilities, which may include provision for academic as well as vocational qualifications. Gymnasium access is provided to all prisoners in England to encourage fitness.

Workshops in prisons vary across establishments. They range from craft workshops, where charities sell the finished products, to car maintenance, contract cleaning, and masonry. Although only token wages are earned, skills learned in these workshops may help a prisoner work toward a qualification or potentially gain employment on release.

Convicted prisoners are permitted a minimum of a one-hour visit every two weeks. Only three people may visit at any one time, although children under the age of 10 are allowed in addition to this maximum. Unconvicted (remand) prisoners are entitled to at least one and a half hours of visits each week. Visiting times vary depending on the individual prison. Most visits take place in a relaxed open setting, which allows the prisoner and visitor to have some physical contact. However, this is not possible for some prisoners who are separated from the visitor by a screen. Conjugal visits are not permitted for any prisoners. In most prisons, visitors can give prisoners items such as CDs and books. The nature of permitted items varies depending on the individual prison.

Prisoners can sometimes earn additional visiting time through the Incentives and Earned Privileges Scheme. This is a system run throughout the Prison Service that places the inmate on one of three levels: basic, standard, or enhanced. Prisoners move up and down through these levels depending on their behavior. Privileges earned as the levels increase can include access to more of their own money to spend in the prison shop or on telephone calls, more hours out of their cell, the opportunity to wear their own clothes and cook their own food, and the chance to pay for a television in their own cell.

The Parole Board is responsible for risk assessing prisoners to decide whether they can be safely released into the community. It is an independent body that was set up in 1968 and works closely with other organizations within the criminal justice system. The Parole Board has responsibility for determining the release of prisoners on both indeterminate and determinate sentences.

Parole Board decisions are made by a panel consisting of a selection of members from different backgrounds, including independent members, psychologists, criminologists, probationers, and judicial members. Oral hearings normally have three members on the panel while paper hearings can consist of one, two, or three members. Oral hearings are generally used for prisoners on indeterminate sentences and normally take place in prison. Paper hearings are used for most prisoners on determinate sentences, and decisions are based on a dossier containing a variety of reports, risk assessments, and occasionally victim statements.

Probation

The National Probation Service (NPS) is part of the National Offender Management Service. It has responsibility for supervising offenders in the community. The duties of NPS include the following:

- Providing presentence reports and bail information reports to magistrates and judges.
- Finding and supervising unpaid work by offenders.
- Creating reports of risk and dangerousness assessments to allow decisions to be made about early release of prisoners.

Probation can take two forms: criminal supervision, the supervision of an offender for a fixed period of time, or pre- and postrelease supervision, where the offender is supervised before or after release from custody. The latter is statutory for all young offenders and adults sentenced to 12 months or over. All offenders in custody, or up to 12 months after release, can opt to be voluntarily supervised.

The caseload of the NPS on any given day is more than 200,000. Of these, approximately 90 percent are male, and 10 percent female; 70 percent are supervised on a community sentence, and 30 percent are imprisoned with supervision in the community as part of the license.

Extradition

England has extradition agreements with more than 100 countries worldwide. Each case for extradition is heard before a judge. Extradition will be carried out only in cases where the judge decides there are no bars to this. Bars to extradition include the person's age, or where the person may face punishment or a prejudiced trial on the grounds of his or her political opinions, sexual orientation, gender, nationality or race, or where extradition would otherwise contravene the 1998 Human Rights Act.

Louise Grove and Graham Farrell

Further Reading

Criminal Justice System: http://www.cjsonline.gov.uk.

Home Office: http://www.homeoffice.gov.uk.

Kershaw, Chris, Sian Nicholas, and Alison Walker, eds. (2008). *Crime in England and Wales 2007/08: Findings from the British Crime Survey and Police Recorded Crime.* London: Home Office, Ministry of Justice.

Sanders, Andrew, and Richard Young. (2006). *Criminal Justice.* 3rd ed. Oxford, UK: Oxford University Press.
Youth Justice Board: http://www.yjb.gov.uk.

United Kingdom/Northern Ireland

Legal System: Common
Murder: Low
Corruption: Low
Human Trafficking: Low
Prison Rate: Medium
Death Penalty: No
Corporal Punishment: No

Background

At the time of the last UK census (2001), Northern Ireland had a population of 1,685,000. This comprises nearly one-third of the total population on the island of Ireland and approximately 3 percent of the population of the United Kingdom. In ethnic terms 99.15 percent of the population of Northern Ireland is white and due to historically low levels of immigration, there is a relatively small minority-ethnic population. Research conducted by the Office of the First and Deputy First Minister (OFMDFM) in 2002 estimated that there are 16,000 people from minority-ethnic community backgrounds in Northern Ireland. The largest group is Chinese, followed by those from the Indian subcontinent, and lastly those from a number of North African countries. In recent years, improved economic conditions have witnessed a net influx of economic migrants, mainly from Portugal and the recently accessioned countries of the European Union (EU), such as Poland, Latvia, Lithuania, and Estonia. Northern Ireland is a constituent region of the United Kingdom along with England, Wales, and Scotland. Between 1921 and 1972 it had its own Parliament in Belfast, which was deferred in 1973 until Direct Rule was introduced from Westminster in 1998. Following the peace negotiations (1994–1997) and the signing of the Belfast Agreement in 1998, a new Northern Ireland Assembly was established that reintroduced devolved government to Northern Ireland based on power-sharing principles. As of 2009, the majority of governmental functions (health, education, environment, etc.) have been devolved to the assembly; however, the British government still maintains overall control of policing and criminal justice matters. These are due to be devolved to the Northern Ireland Assembly in 2010.

Legal System

As a common law jurisdiction the legal system in Northern Ireland is similar to that in England and Wales—but not Scotland—although there are some important differences in law and criminal procedure. It is an adversarial system with the prosecution and defense presenting evidence to magistrates in the lower courts or judges in the higher courts. Statute law in Northern Ireland derives from a number of sources: the UK Parliament at Westminster, the current Northern Ireland Assembly, the Northern Ireland Parliament between 1921 and 1972, and legislation passed by the Irish Parliament in Dublin before the Act of Union in 1800. Many of the statutes governing criminal procedure and police powers are derived from those found in England and Wales also. There is an independent public prosecution service while the age of criminal responsibility is 10. In the financial year 2009–2010 the annual budget to administer the criminal justice system in Northern Ireland stood at £1.3 billion (US$148.12 billion). One of the most significant differences between Northern Ireland and the rest of the United Kingdom in terms of the sentencing framework concerns the existence of a statutory system for restorative and reparative youth conferencing in relation to juvenile offenders—laid down by the Justice (Northern Ireland) Act 2002. However, it is important to recognize that considered historically, many aspects of policing, criminal justice, and legal powers were modified in Northern Ireland to deal with the political conflict. For more than 70 years between 1922 and 1998, Northern Ireland was governed almost continuously under state-of-emergency legislation such as the Civil Authorities (Special Powers)

Act (Northern Ireland) [1922] and the Northern Ireland (Emergency Provisions) Act [1973].

Political Conflict in Northern Ireland

Following the War of Independence with Britain in 1920, Ireland was partitioned. The southern 26 counties seceded from British rule to become the Irish Free State, with a Catholic majority, while 6 of the northeasterly counties were annexed to form the new state of Northern Ireland, which continued under British rule. This compromise situation was to sow the seeds of future instability, however. While the population of Northern Ireland was predominantly Protestant and unionist, it contained a significant Catholic minority, many of whom were Irish nationalists. Tensions between the unionist and nationalist communities were exacerbated during a phase of nationalist civil rights mobilization in the mid-1960s over what was perceived as discrimination by the Unionist government and the repressive character of the local police, the predominantly Protestant Royal Ulster Constabulary (RUC) and the exclusively Protestant police auxiliary, the Ulster Special Constabulary (USC). Toward the end of the 1960s these tensions spilled over into violent ethnosectarian conflict and political unrest. This unrest culminated in a campaign of political violence led by the Irish Republican Army (IRA), which sought to bring about a British withdrawal from Northern Ireland by violent means and that sparked a counterreaction from the RUC and British Army. In addition, loyalist paramilitary organizations—those who wanted to maintain the link with Britain by recourse to violent tactics—embarked on an indiscriminate campaign of targeting and murdering Catholic civilians. The conflict reached its most violent nadir between 1969 and 1994—a period that is colloquially referred to as "The Troubles." The conflict had an undoubted impact on the nature of criminal justice and policing and led to a number of practices that were condemned by national and international human and civil rights organizations. These included the use of torture in obtaining confession evidence, claims of a shoot-to-kill policy against republican suspects, collusion with prostate loyalist paramilitary organizations, the use of indefinite detention without trial, as well as modifications to the legal and criminal justice system, which among other things abolished jury trials for those charged with terrorist-related offenses (the so-called *Diplock* Courts). Between 1969 and the signing of the Belfast Agreement in 1998, just under 3,300 people had lost their lives due to the conflict while 41,837 were seriously injured. Based on population size, the corresponding scale of violence in Britain would have yielded more than 100,000 deaths and 1,406,000 serious injuries, while figures for the United States would have been 500,000 and 6,673,000, respectively.

The Peace Process: Criminal Justice and Policing Reform

The Belfast Agreement, signed in 1998 as part of the developing peace process, resulted in a number of proposals for the restructuring of the criminal justice system, the reform of public policing structures, the release of paramilitary prisoners, and a review of the operation of antiterrorism legislation in Northern Ireland. The Independent Commission on Policing (ICP) was established to investigate police reform; the Criminal Justice Review (CJR) to consider criminal justice reform; while a senior British judge, Lord Lloyd, was charged with reviewing the operation of antiterror legislation. The ICP reported in September 1999 and made 175 recommendations for the reform of the RUC, including the renaming of the force to the Police Service of Northern Ireland (PSNI), as well as introducing a raft of new mechanisms to enhance the governance and accountability of the police, including the introduction of a fully independent police complaints machinery. The ICP proposals were given legislative effect in the Police (Northern Ireland) Act 2000 and 2003 as well as two Implementation Plans drawn up by the Northern Ireland Office (2000 and 2001). In addition, an international Oversight Commission was established to monitor the progress of police reform across a number of benchmark indicators and completed its work in 2007. The Criminal Justice Review reported in March 2000 and put forward

294 recommendations for reform across the system as a whole. These included the development of innovative youth justice strategies; improved support for victims and witnesses; and major changes to the public prosecution service, judicial appointments, prisons, and sentencing frameworks. The proposals were given legislative effect in the Justice (Northern Ireland) Act 2002 and 2004. The legislative basis for counterterrorist operations in Northern Ireland was rationalized and brought within the remit of the UK-wide Terrorism Act (2000) on the advice of the senior judge Lord Lloyd.

Terrorism

The signing of the Belfast Agreement and the declaration of an end to armed conflict by the majority of paramilitary organizations in Northern Ireland has resulted in a considerable easing of the security situation and a reduction in the threat from terrorist attack. However, more recently, "dissident republicans"—those who oppose the leadership of Sinn Féin and mainstream republicanism—have become much more active. Such groups are numerically small and splintered into various factions such as Continuity IRA and Real IRA. The latter group was responsible for one of the biggest single atrocities of the entire conflict, the Omagh bombing of 1998, in which 29 people died and a further 220 were left seriously injured or maimed. More recently, in March 2009, the Real IRA also claimed responsibility for the killing of two British soldiers from the 38 Engineer Regiment at a military base in Antrim, while a few days later, Continuity IRA were involved in the shooting death of a PSNI officer in Craigavon. Constable Stephen Carroll was the first police officer to be killed in Northern Ireland since 1998. The threat from dissident republican groups has resulted in security measures being stepped up in Northern Ireland for the first time in over a decade.

Police

Policing in Northern Ireland, as is the situation elsewhere in the United Kingdom, is separate and distinct from the military. In addition, there is no gendarmerie or its equivalent as is found in some continental European jurisdictions. The new Police Service of Northern Ireland (PSNI) is the "national" police force. As of late 2009, there were just over 9,000 officers in the PSNI, composed of 7,542 in the regular force and 1,539 in the full and part-time Reserve. The full-time Reserve force is due to be phased out by the end of 2010. There are currently plans to supplement regular officers with several hundred Police Community Support Officers (PCSOs) who will deal mainly with low-level crime and antisocial behavior. Policing is coordinated from PSNI Headquarters in Belfast and organized into a number of District Command Units (DCUs), which provide the bulk of operational policing at the local level. PSNI Headquarters in Belfast provides specialist technical and logistical support in relation to forensics, crime analysis, counterterrorism, and organized crime as well as having overall responsibility for the direction and management of force policy and ensuring compliance with directives emanating from the Home Office in London. Currently, the emphasis for the PSNI, as with all UK police forces, is on the development of Neighborhood Policing and various "partnership" initiatives.

Unlike the rest of the United Kingdom, all police officers in Northern Ireland carry guns (sidearms), although their discharge necessitates an automatic investigation by the Office of the Police Ombudsman for Northern Ireland (OPONI). In the most recent period for which data are available (2007–2008), firearms were discharged by PSNI officers on four occasions; however, there were no fatalities. Between 2001 and 2009 there has been one fatality in Northern Ireland due to the police use of lethal force following what appeared to be a covert operation. The PSNI have had access to CS Spray (from 2003) and to the Taser electroshock weapon (from 2007). The police ombudsman automatically investigates all instances where the Taser is deployed. Since April 2009 there is no longer a requirement on the part of the PSNI to forward incidents involving the use of CS Spray to the ombudsman.

One of the most deep-seated historical problems with policing in Northern Ireland has been the persistently low proportion of Catholic/nationalist recruits. To meet the targets proposed by the ICP, the PSNI was given a specific exemption from EU fair employment directives to embark on a program of positive discrimination to increase the number of Catholic officers. Catholic recruitment to the PSNI currently stands at just over 26 percent (October 2009) compared to less than 8 percent for the old RUC pre-2001, and the force seems on track to meet its 30 percent target for Catholic recruitment by 2011. Currently, the percentage of female officers in the PSNI stands at just over 20 percent, and the force has recently announced the establishment of a Gay and Lesbian Police Officers Association—a development that would have been unthinkable just a few years ago.

The statutory powers of the police are laid down in the Police and Criminal Evidence (Northern Ireland) Order [1989], which is virtually identical to legislation adopted elsewhere in the United Kingdom. Likewise, the police accountability and governance structures are modeled on the Tripartite arrangements that are found in England and Wales and that establishes a three-way system of checks and balances between government, the police, and local communities. However, in Northern Ireland there have been some significant enhancements introduced as a result of the ICP reforms, which mean that the PSNI is subject to arguably more robust mechanisms for the democratic oversight of policing than exist in any other region of the UK. For example, a Policing Board comprising elected political representatives and independent members performs a similar role to Police Authorities in England and Wales but has considerably more powers to initiate inquiries into police actions. The Policing Board performs a number of statutory functions such as securing an effective and efficient police service, appointing and dismissing senior officers, developing long- and short-term policing plans in conjunction with the chief constable, monitoring the performance of the police in relation to these policing plans, and monitoring the police's compliance with the provisions of the Human Rights Act. The Policing Board is also under a statutory obligation to convene public meetings during which community members may question senior police managers about the performance of the PSNI. At the local level, there are 26 District Policing Partnerships (DPPs) in each local council area, again composed of elected representatives and independent members, and which monitor the performance of the local police. The investigation of complaints against PSNI officers is the responsibility of the Office of the Police Ombudsman for Northern Ireland (OPONI), which unlike the situation in England and Wales and Scotland, is modeled on a system of fully independent investigation and oversight of all complaints. Other oversight and accountability mechanisms such as Her Majesty's Inspectorate of Constabulary (HMIC) also operate in Northern Ireland, while the PSNI are also subject to periodic inspection by the Northern Ireland Criminal Justice Inspectorate and the National Audit Office.

The Serious Organised Crime Agency (SOCA), which was established in England and Wales to deal with serious organized crime, has a restricted jurisdiction in Northern Ireland but works closely with the Northern Ireland Organized Crime Taskforce. In April 2008 the Northern Ireland Assets Recovery Agency (ARA) merged with SOCA, which now undertakes civil recovery and tax investigations in Northern Ireland. In 2007 the UK security service, MI5, has established a regional headquarters in Belfast. Currently around 90 PSNI officers are seconded to MI5 to deal with the threat from local terrorism.

One other notable feature of policing in Northern Ireland concerns the establishment of a Historical Enquiries Team (HET) as a unit of the PSNI to investigate a number of unsolved "cold cases"—specifically 3,369 murders—committed during the conflict. The HET has a team of 100 investigators and support staff and a budget of £30 million (US$43 million). It is divided into separate Review and Investigation teams, and the aim is to bring some closure to the relatives of those who died. Sophisticated data-mining software is used to piece together shreds of evidence from events stretching back over 30 or 40 years.

Crime

Making direct comparisons between the levels of crime in different jurisdictions is difficult because of differing counting rules, definitions of crime, and the contrasting ways criminal justice systems operate and measure crime. However, the official crime data suggest that Northern Ireland has lower levels of police-recorded crime than other regions of the UK, at about half that of England and Wales.

Recently recorded crime levels have increased from 62,222 offenses in 1997 to 110,094 in 2008–2009. This has meant that the crime rate has increased from around 37 crimes per 1,000 of the population in 1997 to 62 per 1,000 population in 2008–2009. These changes appear to have largely been caused by new counting rules that came into effect in 1998, which record crimes that were not previously part of the official figures, and together with the introduction of a new data collection system, have had a significant impact on recorded crime levels. Despite these changes, however, Northern Ireland still has a lower level of recorded crime than England and Wales. Victimization surveys also confirm the view that Northern Ireland has a relatively low level of recorded crime. The International Crime Victimization Survey that surveyed victims of crime in a number of different countries in Europe and North America showed that Northern Ireland had the lowest victimization rate of any of the participating countries. Only 15 percent of those questioned in Northern Ireland (for the 2000 survey) had been a victim, compared with an international average of 21 percent. Earlier surveys confirm these findings and the 1995 International Crime Victims Survey showed Northern Ireland to have the lowest incidence rate of criminal victimization (at 27 crimes per 100 population) of the 11 industrialized countries surveyed. Indeed, the rate of victimization in Northern Ireland was considerably lower than in the United States, Canada, or England and Wales.

A comparison of the Northern Ireland Crime Survey 2007–2008 (NIO Research Bulletin 1/2009) with the British Crime Survey (BCS 2007/08) also shows that the risk of becoming a victim of crime is lower in Northern Ireland (13.8%) than in England and Wales (22.1%). While England and Wales had higher rates than Northern Ireland for burglary (2.4% vs. 1.2%), the two jurisdictions had similar rates of violent crime (3.3% vs. 2.2%).

However, these recent statistics mask other aspects of victimization that are not directly reflected in official crime statistics or addressed in the International Victims Survey; namely, the social and human costs associated with 30 years of violent conflict and that continue to exert a deep impact. There are also continuing problems of sectarian crime that blight communities across Northern Ireland. Many miles of euphemistically named "peace lines"—32-foot (10-meter) high walls—intersect Protestant and Catholic working-class areas of Belfast and in spite of the peace process of recent years, levels of sectarian and intercommunal violence still continue. Of course, violence such as this tends to be concentrated in specific geographical areas, but it remains an important corrective to the general view of Northern Ireland as a "low crime" society.

Juveniles

Northern Ireland has adopted a radically different form of youth justice to the rest of Europe. This new system of justice was introduced following recommendations of the Criminal Justice Review, and it embraces a restorative model of justice. Unlike most criminal justice systems, it places a very strong emphasis on victims and offenders coming together in a meeting to deal with the crime and its aftermath. This system of "youth conferencing" was established under Justice (Northern Ireland) Act 2002 and began operation as a pilot project in December 2003 dealing with juveniles (10–16-year-olds). It was extended to the whole of Northern Ireland, including 10–17 year olds, in 2005.

There are two distinctive types of conference available: diversionary conferences and court-ordered conferences. In either case, a conference co-coordinator is responsible for submitting a plan to the prosecutor or court on how the young person should be dealt with for his or her offense. A decision to hold a diversionary conference is taken by the Public Prosecution Service. Unlike many restorative schemes elsewhere, diversionary conferences are not intended for first-time minor offenders. Instead, the program is aimed at young offenders who would normally be considered for prosecution through the courts. Providing a conference plan is agreed and successfully completed, the young person will avoid a court appearance and a subsequent criminal conviction. Two preconditions must be in place before a diversionary conference can proceed. First, the young person must admit to the offense, and second, he or she must consent to the process. If both these conditions are not in place, the offense will be disposed of in the normal way through prosecution in the youth court.

Court-ordered youth conferences, on the other hand, are referred through the courts and take place with a view to a youth conference co-coordinator providing a recommendation to the court on how the young person should be dealt with for his or her offense. Again, the admission or establishment of guilt and consent of the young person are prerequisites for such a conference to take place. A distinctive feature of the Northern Ireland system is that a court *must* refer a young person to a youth conference. This is subject to certain restrictions: when a magistrate refers a case, he or she must take into account the type of offense committed. Only offenses with a penalty of life imprisonment, offenses that are triable, in the case of an adult, on indictment only (very serious offenses), and scheduled offenses that fall under the Terrorism Act are not automatically eligible for youth conferencing. In effect, the vast majority of young offenders have to be referred for the youth conferencing process. The mandatory nature of court-ordered referrals highlights the intended centrality of youth conferencing to the youth justice system.

Restorative youth conferencing has changed the landscape of the youth justice system in Northern Ireland, and although it has only been in operation for a few years, early indications appear to be positive. The youth conferencing scheme has been subject to a major evaluation in which the proceedings of 185 conferences were observed and personal interviews were completed with 171 young people and 125 victims who participated in conferences (O'Mahony and Campbell 2006). The research findings were generally very positive concerning the impact of the scheme on victims and offenders, and found it to operate with relative success. Importantly, the research showed that youth conferencing considerably increased levels of participation for both offenders and victims in the process of seeking a just response to offending. The scheme engaged a high proportion of victims in the process: over two-thirds of conferences (69%) had a victim of some sort in attendance, which is high compared with other restorative-based programs. Of these 40 percent were personal victims and 60 percent were victim representatives (such as in cases where there was damage to public property or there was no directly identifiable victim). Indeed, nearly half of personal victims attended as a result of assault, while the majority (69%) of victim representatives attended for thefts (typically shoplifting) or criminal damage.

Nearly all of the plans (91%) following conferences were agreed by participants, and importantly, victims were on the whole happy with the content of the plans. Interestingly, many of the plans centered on elements that were designed to help the young person and victim, such as reparation to the victim, or attendance at programs to help the young person. Recent research suggests that conferencing schemes have a positive impact on recidivism rates. These encouraging findings, which compare reconviction rates for young offenders given different disposals, including custodial and community orders, show those given restorative conferences had a one-year reconviction rate of 38 percent, while those given custodial sentences and community disposals had reconviction rates of 73 percent and 47 percent, respectively.

Courts

Historically, Northern Ireland has a special procedure for dealing with terrorist (scheduled) offenses and such cases were tried in Diplock courts, where a judge sat without a jury. Diplock courts were abolished in Northern Ireland in July 2007, although in rare instances terrorist offenses may still be tried by a judge sitting without a jury. Nonterrorist indictable offenses are heard in the Crown Court and involve a trial by judge and jury. But the vast majority of all criminal offenses are tried summarily in a magistrates' court and do not involve a jury trial. Over half of the offenses dealt with in the magistrates' court relate to road traffic incidents. In 2006, 29,749 defendants were dealt with through the magistrates' courts, of which 84 percent were found guilty, whereas only 1,625 defendants were proceeded against in the Crown Court.

The sentencing power of the magistrates' court is restricted to 12–18 months' imprisonment. However, the Crown Court can impose lengthy and life sentences. Any appeals that are made have to go to the Court of Appeal. The Court of Appeal's ruling may be further challenged in the House of Lords, with leave from the Court of Appeal or the House of Lords. The Public Prosecution Service (formerly the Department of the Director of Public Prosecutions) is generally responsible for preparing the indictment or charges that the accused will face in Northern Ireland.

A third level of the court system is the youth court, which is a special magistrates' court. It is constituted to deal with proceedings against juveniles between the ages of 10 and 17. The youth court operates along broadly similar lines to the adult court, but with some differences. It consists of a bench of three members, of whom the chairman is a resident magistrate, who sits with two lay magistrates, including at least one woman. Proceedings are less formal than the adult magistrates' court and are held in private. Only persons connected with the case and court officials are usually present. The youth court can deal with any offense other than murder if it thinks that such a course is expedient and if the prosecution and the juvenile's parents or the juvenile consents.

Punishment

Types of Punishment

Imprisonment is the most severe penalty available to the courts. The length of a term of imprisonment is determined either by statute or a judge or magistrate in a common law case. It can vary from a few days to life, which is mandatory for a person convicted of murder. In Northern Ireland, the maximum length of sentence that can be given by a magistrate is 12 months for an indictable offense or 18 months if the person is convicted of more than one indictable offense. Following the enactment of the Life Sentences (NI) Order 2001, a court passing a life sentence must state the period that should be served to satisfy the requirements of retribution and deterrence. This is referred to as the "tariff." Following the expiry of the tariff, a life sentence prisoner may require the secretary of state to refer his or her case to the Life Sentence Review Commissioners for consideration for release. In exceptional circumstances a "whole life" tariff may be imposed where the court is of the view that due to the seriousness of the offense, the offender should not be considered for release on license.

Imprisonment is a sentence mostly confined to persons aged 21 and over, but there is provision for detention of persons under 21 in a prison where the circumstances warrant it. Such detention is included in the statistics of imprisonment and can be for a stipulated sentence of more than four years or at the secretary of state's pleasure—analogous to a life sentence for persons under 18 when their crime was committed. Prison sentences are rarely served in full. Remission is the cancellation of part of a term of imprisonment and may be granted at up to 50 percent of the sentence depending upon the circumstances.

Detention in the young offenders' center is instead of imprisonment for offenders of not less than 16 years but under 21 years who have been convicted of an offense that is punishable with imprisonment in the case of a person of at least 21 years of age. The maximum term is four years.

Other types of sanctions include:

- *Custody Probation Order.* This is an order unique to Northern Ireland, reflecting the different regime that applies in respect of remission and the general absence of release on license. They are only available where a period in custody of more than 12 months would otherwise be justified. The custodial sentence, which can be of any length, is followed by a period of supervision by a probation officer for a period between 12 months and 3 years. Such an order cannot be made unless the offender consents.

- *Juvenile Justice Centre Order.* This order was introduced in 1999 under the Criminal Justice (Children's Northern Ireland Order 1998) to replace the training school order. It is available for children under the age of 17 and is for a period of six months unless the court specifies a longer period not exceeding two years. The period of detention is for one-half of the period of the order, with the remainder comprising a period of close supervision in the community.
- *Community Sentences.* The Community Service Order is a community sentence that requires the offender to do unpaid work in the community. It can be given to someone aged 16 or over convicted of an imprisonable offense if the offender consents and may be between 40 and 240 hours' duration. The Probation Order is a community sentence in which the offender is placed under the supervision of a probation officer for a period of between 6 months to 3 years. It puts the offender under supervision, during which probation personnel act as a source of guidance to avoid reoffending. The order may have extra requirements, for example, treatment for alcohol, or anger management. Offender consent is required. The Combination Order comprises a Probation Order and a Community Service Order and is intended for offenders who the courts believe should make some reparation to the community and who need probation supervision to reduce the risk of reoffending in the future. The order requires the offender to be under the supervision of a probation officer for a period between 12 months to 3 years and to perform unpaid work in the community for between 40 and 100 hours. Attendance Orders are used in the case of a juvenile aged under 17 and require the offender to attend a designated place and undertake a structured program of activities. The order should not be less than 12 hours and no more than 24 hours. The times at which the offender attends the center should avoid interference, so far as practicable, with school hours or working hours.
- *Youth Conference Order.* This is available to juvenile offenders (10–17 years). It aims to balance the needs of the victim and the young offender by agreeing to plans of action that satisfy the victim and create opportunities for the young person to make amends and stop committing crime.
- *Suspended Sentence.* The suspended sentence operates as a deterrent measure. Where a court sentencing an offender for an offense that is not a "serious offense" (i.e., an offense which a person aged 21 or over could, on indictment, be sentenced to prison for a term of five years or more) passes a sentence of imprisonment or makes an order for detention in a young offenders' center for a term not exceeding two years, the court may suspend the sentence for between one and three years. Alternatively, where a court sentencing an offender for a "serious offense" passes a prison sentence for a term of not more than seven years, the court may suspend the sentence for between one and five years.
- *Fines.* This is a financial punishment, the maximum level of which is generally set by statute. In the Crown Court the amount is unlimited. It is not a part of the principle of this sentence to fine a wealthy person according to his or her means; rather, the court must inquire into the financial circumstances of the offender, for the purposes of increasing or reducing the amount of the fine. The fine is the most common disposal given in Northern Ireland, and of 26,363 persons sentenced in 2006, 66 percent were fined.
- *Conditional Discharge.* This order imposes a condition upon the offender that he or she commits no further offense for a specified period up to three years. If the condition is

broken, the person may be dealt with for the earlier and the current offense.

- *Absolute Discharge.* This may be imposed where following conviction, punishment is considered inappropriate. The offender while found guilty is not further liable for the offense.
- *Deferred Sentence.* After conviction, a person may have his or her sentence deferred for a period of up to six months. Sentence is passed after changes (if any) in the circumstances of the case have been assessed. For example, the offender may have made some form of reparation.

Prison

Northern Ireland's prison system has altered dramatically in recent years, primarily because of the developing peace process and the recommendations of the Criminal Justice Review published in March 2000. The prison population has decreased from a peak of approximately 3,000 in 1979 to currently around 1,500 prisoners. At the height of the conflict, paramilitary prisoners convicted of terrorist offenses made up nearly two-thirds of the entire prison population. However, as a key component of the peace process, paramilitary prisoners were released from prison and by July 2000, some 450 prisoners were released on license back into the community.

There are three prison establishments: Maghaberry, Magilligan, and Hydebank Wood. Maghaberry is a high-security prison, housing long-term and remand prisoners and those charged or convicted of the most serious offenses. Magilligan is a medium-security prison, housing lower-security prisoners, and Hydebank Wood is medium security, accommodating young male offenders (aged between 17 and 21 years) and female prisoners. As of October 2009, there were approximately 1,500 prisoners held across the Northern Ireland prison system, of which 500 were being held on remand. There were 26 female prisoners, and 82 young offenders aged between 17 and 21 at the time of conviction. The rate of imprisonment in Northern Ireland is 84 per 100,000 population, lower than the rate for England and Wales (148) and Scotland (139). There are several anomalies in the Northern Irish prison system compared to other UK regions. For example, remand prisoners comprise a higher proportion of the prison population—34 percent compared to 15 percent in England and Wales. Also, fine defaulters amount to 59 percent of *all* prison receptions in Northern Ireland, a figure that is considerably higher than England (2.2%). This situation has recently been addressed by the Northern Ireland Courts Service.

Recently, the Northern Ireland Prison Service has been heavily criticized for its general failure to provide a duty of care to inmates in a report commissioned by the Northern Ireland Human Rights Commission following a spate of suicides in prison establishments. There are also issues concerning a lack of effective and transparent oversight, and while this is provided by the Prison Ombudsman—an independent agency that has responsibility for investigating a prisoner's complaints—its powers are largely limited to examining individual cases rather than having any overt role in shaping prison policy.

Graham Ellison and David O'Mahony

Further Reading

Ellison, Graham. (2007). "A Blueprint for Democratic Policing Anywhere in the World? Police Reform, Political Transition and Conflict Resolution in Northern Ireland." *Police Quarterly* 10(3): 243–269.

Northern Ireland Criminal Justice Inspectorate: http://www.cjini.org.

Northern Ireland Office, Criminal Justice Directorate: http://www.cjsni.gov.uk.

O'Mahony, David, and Catriona Campbell. (2006). "Mainstreaming Restorative Justice for Young Offenders through Youth Conferencing: The Experience of Northern Ireland." In *International Handbook of Juvenile Justice,* edited by Josine Junger-Tas and Scott H. Decker, pp. 93–116. New York: Springer.

United Kingdom/Scotland

Legal System: Common/Civil
Murder: Medium
Prison Rate: Medium
Death Penalty: No

Background

Scotland is a country that forms part of the United Kingdom (alongside England, Wales, and Northern Ireland). It lies to the north of England, making up around one-third of the island of Great Britain. With a population of some 5 million people, the majority are concentrated in the two main cities of Edinburgh and Glasgow. The population is over 98 percent Caucasian, with a small ethnic minority chiefly of Pakistani heritage. Scotland has also recently experienced a notable influx of people from Poland and the Baltic states, whether for shorter or longer periods of work or to settle permanently.

Although Scotland has been part of the United Kingdom for the past 300 years, it has retained its own identity and culture and a separate legal system, reflecting its very different historical and constitutional evolution. During the later Middle Ages, there was development of a form of parliament (the Assembly of the Three Estates), a supreme civil court (the Court of Session), and a further institution (the College of Justice) with powers to enact laws for the administration of justice. During this period, Scots common law came under the influence of Roman and continental law and contributed to the development of Scots law as a "mixed system." The Acts of Union of 1707, while creating the United Kingdom of Great Britain and a shared legislature at Westminster, preserved the independence and integrity of Scots law. This endures today and is evident in Scotland's distinctive court systems, legal professions, and procedures and remedies. Distinctive features of Scottish criminal law include the requirement of corroboration, the jury system, and the third verdict of "not proven." The criminal procedure is accusatorial in form, placing the onus on the prosecutor to provide sufficient relevant evidence against the accused. There is no criminal or penal code.

Scotland's relative autonomy has been bolstered in the last 10 years following the devolution of significant legislative and executive powers and the (re)creation of a Scottish Parliament in the capital city of Edinburgh in 1999. However, evidence from opinion polling and voting patterns suggests that Scotland does not want full independence from the United Kingdom, although there is a settled majority in Scotland in favor of greater autonomy and the transfer of some additional powers to the Scottish Parliament and government.

The Scottish Parliament has jurisdiction over a number of key policy areas, including education, health, and crime and justice (though not drugs laws, laws relating to firearms, border controls, and other issues considered to touch the security of the United Kingdom as a whole). Since 1999, there has been a marked escalation in the volume of legislation passed, particularly for criminal justice. Young offenders, persistent offenders, and those considered as presenting higher risk were among the chief targets of new legislation.

Crime

Crime Statistics

The two main sources of information on levels of crime in Scotland are from police-recorded data and information gathered from victimization surveys, the latter of which also gathers a wide range of information about the public's attitudes to crime and punishment. Police-recorded data show that recorded crime has decreased almost continuously since the early 1990s, with the latest figures putting recorded crime at its lowest level for 30 years. The Scottish Crime and Justice Survey provides a more holistic picture of crime in Scotland, in that it includes crimes that are not reported to the police. Of crimes reported in the survey, 34 percent were incidents of vandalism (to an individual's property or vehicle), 26 percent were minor assaults, 17 percent were thefts from the home (but not including housebreaking), 9 percent were theft from the person (excluding robbery, which involves violence), 7 percent were motor vehicle thefts, 2 percent were housebreaking (burglary), 2 percent were robbery, and 2 percent were serious assault. Sexual offending was not covered in the most recent publication.

The survey showed that the group most likely to be victimized were people aged between 16 and 24, particularly males, and that the most deprived areas of Scotland also experienced higher levels of crime. Although the rate of murder is low by global standards at just over 2 per 100,000, it is slightly higher than that in England and Wales. Many observers attribute this to the existence in some areas of a "knife culture"—an embedded practice of carrying knives and blades. Nearly half of all homicides in Scotland are committed with knives and blades, with firearms causing only 2 percent of the overall number. The majority of murders were carried out by someone known to the victim, and the typical victims are males between the ages of 16–30. As one would expect, there is substantial variation between levels of crime between rural and urban Scotland, with the vast majority of crime committed in cities, particularly in the cities of Glasgow and Edinburgh.

Drugs, Alcohol, and Crime

Crime in Scotland is widely considered to be closely linked to the twin public health concerns of drug and alcohol abuse. The former has long been within the ambit of criminal justice institutions, with drug policies having formed a central plank of crime control strategies since the 1980s. Latterly, however, Scotland has begun to acknowledge, and take some tentative steps toward addressing, the connection between alcohol, public disorder, and crime.

Scotland has long had a problem with drugs, particularly with heroin, which ravaged many economically deprived communities during the 1980s and 1990s. Heroin continues to be a problem and is the drug associated with most other drug offending, particularly for female offenders. In recent years there has also been a sharp rise in the numbers taking cocaine due to a reduction in its street value, and other recreation drugs such as Ecstasy becoming less fashionable. Despite occasional media scare stories, synthetic drugs such as "crystal meth" have yet to take hold in Scotland.

Research on the prison population shows that nearly all female prisoners (98%) test positive for drugs on admission to prison, the vast majority for heroin, and nearly two-thirds of prisoners reported that they were under the influence of drugs at the time of the offense. While awareness of drug issues in Scotland remains high, recognition of the relationship between alcohol and offending has increased over recent years as well. Scotland's relationship with alcohol is complex in that it is very much linked to the country's culture. Not only is an alcoholic drink one of the country's most iconic (and lucrative) exports—the connoisseur's tipple of malt whisky—but for many Scots, getting very drunk is traditionally closely associated with having a good time.

The connection between alcohol and offending (particularly violent offending) is strong, most particularly for young offenders (aged 16–20). Recent research shows that for this younger age group, the consumption of alcohol played a more important role in their offending than did drugs, with 81 percent saying they consumed alcohol prior to their offense, and 79 percent blaming alcohol for the offense for which they were serving their sentence.

There have been recent moves to address the issue of problematic drinking, with much stricter enforcement of the prohibition on the sale of alcohol to anyone under the age of 18. At the time of writing the Scottish government is seeking to introduce a "minimum pricing" policy, which would price drink per unit of alcohol it contained. This is very controversial, however, and it remains to be seen whether or not it becomes law.

Police

Police in Scotland are organized into eight police forces. These vary considerably in size: the largest, Strathclyde Police, employs half of all police officers in Scotland, and the smallest has fewer officers than one of Strathclyde's divisions. Each force is afforded a considerable degree of operational independence in determining how to police its

A protester is removed by British police officers during the "carnival for full enjoyment" demonstration in Edinburgh, Scotland, ahead of the forthcoming G8 summit, July 4, 2005. (AP Photo/Matt Dunham)

territory. Strathclyde Police, for example, has developed innovative initiatives to tackle gang culture and violence reduction, working together with other agencies such as social work and education departments.

There are more than 16,000 officers throughout all the forces, with this number projected to increase by another 1,000 by 2011. Only 22 percent of the police are female, and only 1 of the 8 chief constables (the most senior officer of a police force) is a woman. Increasing demands for efficiency have led to a significant rise in the numbers of civilians also employed in the service, who carry out functions such as clerical work and technical analysis. There are now more than 7,000 civilians in Scottish police forces. Police forces are divided in terms of general operations and specialist operations. General operations are routine tasks undertaken by uniformed patrol officers in the divisions (where "division" refers to a territorial fraction of a police force area). Specialist operations concern tasks that require specific training and experience, such as the Criminal Investigations Department (CID), traffic, child protection units, and wildlife crime. In 2001, the Scottish Crime and Drug Enforcement Agency (SCDEA) was established. SCDEA focuses on tackling serious and organized crime in Scotland. SCDEA also works together with the Serious and Organised Crime Agency (SOCA), which is UK-wide.

Recent research shows that 63 percent of the public think that the police do a "good job" in their local area (although those who have been victims of crime are less likely to say that the police in their area do a good job—51%). Adults living in the most deprived areas of Scotland were also less positive about the performance of their local police force compared with the rest of Scotland (56%), and those living in accessible small towns were also less positive than the average (49%).

Finding of Guilt

There are two types of criminal procedure: "solemn" and "summary." Solemn procedure is trial on indictment before a judge of the High Court of Justiciary or a sheriff in the Sheriff Court, sitting with a jury of 15 people. This form of procedure is reserved for more serious crimes. Certain crimes such as murder, rape, and incest fall within the exclusive jurisdiction of the High Court and can only be tried on indictment there. Armed robbery and the most serious sexual offense would also be prosecuted in the High Court. More generally, crimes such as serious assault and drug trafficking would be dealt with under solemn procedure in either the High Court or Sheriff Court.

Summary procedure is trial on complaint before a sheriff in the Sheriff Court, or before a bench of one or more "lay" justices in the district court and is used for less serious crimes. ("Lay" justices are volunteers drawn from local communities. They receive training and are advised in court by a professional clerk. They need have no legal background themselves and are unpaid.) The types of offenses that are prosecuted under summary procedure include breach of the peace (a crime of disorder), shoplifting, theft, and fraud, but also assault and some offenses involving weapons. Most road traffic contraventions and minor drug offenses are dealt with by way of summary procedure.

System of Public Prosecution

Scotland has a system of public prosecution by independent lawyers, managed by the Crown Office and Procurator Fiscal Service (COPFS). This organization is headed by the Lord Advocate and the Solicitor General, Scotland's law officers. These are political appointments and change at the time of a general election for the Scottish Parliament. The permanent local public prosecutor is the procurator fiscal.

The discretionary powers of the public prosecutor are considerable and include the decision to take no action, to offer an alternative to prosecution, or to otherwise divert the case. If prosecution is thought to be in the public interest, the decision by the prosecutor as to forum, or court, and hence mode of trial (solemn or summary) is an important one given the different sentencing powers exercised by each court. The accused has no right to elect for trial by jury. The public prosecutor conducts all cases in court and has the right to discontinue proceedings or accept a plea to a reduced charge at any stage.

The Judiciary

The High Court of Justiciary is Scotland's supreme criminal court. There are 34 judges, known as senators of the College of Justice, of whom at present 4 are female. All judges are legally qualified and are drawn from the ranks of experienced advocates or solicitor-advocates (solicitors with extended rights of audience) with at least five years' experience. In a criminal trial the judge sits alone with a jury. In the Sheriff Court, the judicial position of sheriff is held by 140 experienced solicitors and advocates, of whom 26 are female. The sheriff sits with a jury when hearing solemn cases and alone in summary cases.

The neutrality and impartiality of the individual judge is integral to the judicial role. It is also considered essential for the doctrine of the separation of powers and the rule of law that the collective judicial body is independent of the other branches of government and not placed under any undue influence, control, or pressure from the other branches. This principle was recently invoked by the judiciary in its opposition to proposed sentencing reforms aimed at "structuring" judicial discretion by the introduction of sentencing guidelines. While declaring its commitment to the principle of judicial independence, the government asserted its right to legislate in sentencing policy, one of which aims was the reduction of the prison population.

Investigation

The procurator fiscal is responsible for the investigation and prosecution of all crime in Scotland. In practice, most preliminary investigation are carried out by the police or other specialist reporting agency. The police have discretion in some minor cases to take no action, give informal warnings, or issue fixed penalty notices. In the most serious types of cases, the procurator fiscal is likely to become involved at an early stage of the investigation and may direct the police in their inquiries.

In all cases the procurator fiscal must consider first whether there is sufficient evidence of a crime committed by the accused, and if so, what action is appropriate in the public interest. In less serious cases, no action may be taken or an alternative to prosecution offered, as follows:

- A written or personal warning may be issued.
- A "fixed penalty conditional offer" (fine) at a level between £50–£300 (US$72–$430) may be given.
- There may be a compensation offer in cases where an individual has suffered monetary or personal loss, or alarm and distress. The maximum level of compensation is £3,000 (US$4,314). Compensation offers and fixed penalties are not criminal convictions but are recorded and can be disclosed to a court for up to two years.
- Diversion from prosecution may be offered in suitable cases and may involve referral to psychiatric, psychological, or social work agencies.
- Road traffic fixed penalties are routinely offered in less serious cases.
- Reparation and mediation schemes may be available in some areas.

The majority of cases reported to the procurator fiscal do not result in court proceedings. In 2008–2009, a total of 284,859 cases were reported and 58 percent were marked for no action or dealt with by way of alternatives to prosecution.

Rights of the Accused

A person in custody has the right to have a solicitor (lawyer) informed without delay and to have a private consultation with that solicitor. A duty solicitor under the Legal Aid scheme will be made available. Thereafter, eligibility for legal aid for the cost of representation by a solicitor or advocate at trial is determined first according to whether it is believed to be "in the interests of justice" for the accused to be so represented. This is usually granted in any of the following circumstances: where an accused person is remanded in custody before trial, is likely to go to prison if convicted, or to lose a job, if he or she has a mental or physical disability that prevents him or her from following proceedings, where English is not his or her first language, or in an appeal against a decision. The grant of legal aid is also subject to a financial assessment as to whether the expenses of the case would cause "undue hardship" to the accused person or his or her dependants without assistance.

All crimes in Scotland are eligible for bail, consistent with the presumption of innocence in Scots law. The decision to grant bail is within the judge's discretion and release on bail may be subject to conditions such as not to commit further offenses or interfere with witnesses in the case. In the period 2001–2008 the remand population (i.e., accused persons refused bail before trial) increased by 78 percent, contributing significantly to the problem of overcrowding in Scotland's prisons. Notwithstanding governmental will to reduce the overall size of the prison population, higher prison sentences for breaches of bail were introduced in 2007, along with measures to limit the granting of bail to persons accused of serious, violent, or sexual offenses or of drug dealing with similar previous convictions.

Under summary procedure, an accused person can be remanded for no more than 40 days after the first calling of the case in court. Under solemn procedure in the Sheriff Court, the trial must start within 110 days of the person's full committal in court and within 140 days in the High Court. These are among the strictest time limits in the world.

Trial and Sentence

Almost all cases that are prosecuted in court proceed by way of summary complaint. In 2008–2009, these accounted for 95 percent of all court disposals. Of summary cases, less than 5 percent resulted in a trial, and in solemn procedure only 18 percent of cases in the same period proceeded to trial. The Scottish criminal justice system allows an informal system of plea negotiation between prosecutor and defense lawyer (but with no judicial participation) in the expectation that lesser charges will attract a reduced sentence. In addition, there is now statutory inducement in the form of a sentencing discount for an early plea. Alongside recent reform of summary justice aimed at increasing the efficiency of the courts, this appears to signal an open acknowledgment of the benefits to the system of early pleas. However, there may be concern at the lack of due process safeguards that arise.

Juveniles: The Children's Hearings System

The age of criminal responsibility in Scotland is currently 8, one of the lowest in Europe, although it is planned to raise it to 12. In practice, very few children under the age of 16 are prosecuted in court and only on the instructions of the Lord Advocate. Instead, children who offend are dealt with in the Children's Hearings System.

The Children's Hearings System is Scotland's distinctive way of dealing with young people under the age of 16 who offend. Introduced in 1971, it represented a radical departure from a court-based system to one in which an informal tribunal consisting of three trained volunteers from the local community considers the child's needs with the participation of the child and their carers. The court is used only to determine grounds of referral where disputed. The guiding philosophy is that those children who commit offenses and those who require care and protection are often the same child and should therefore be dealt with in the same system.

The Reporter to the Children's Hearing, to whom all cases are reported, has wide discretion and most cases are dealt with other than by referral to a hearing, often by way of informal measures of supervision. The most common outcome of a Children's Hearing is the making of a supervision requirement, usually involving the child remaining at home but taking part in some type of program or intervention, or being subject to restrictions on his or her movements. The child may also be placed with foster carers, in a residential unit, or rarely, in secure accommodation.

In recent years, the UK's ratification of the United Nation Convention on the Human Rights of the Child and the incorporation of the European Convention of Human Rights have brought new challenges for the Children's Hearings System, requiring more consideration of due process rights and for any intervention in the life of the child or family to be proportionate. Moreover, recent political imperatives such as antisocial behavior legislation and the requirement in some cases for a Children's Hearing to consider society's need for protection sit uneasily with the still-central principle that the welfare of the child is of paramount interest.

It is perhaps remarkable that this essentially caring, welfare-oriented rather than punitive response to offending in young people still retains considerable cultural force and political commitment during a period in which other features of contemporary crime and punishment in Scotland appear to have succumbed to a measure of what has been called the "penal temptation."

Punishment

Types of Punishment

Broadly, four types of punishment are used in Scotland: imprisonment, community sentences, financial penalties, and cautions or admonitions. The last execution in Scotland was carried out on August 15, 1963. The death penalty was first suspended for the whole of the UK in 1965 and finally officially abolished in 1998.

The Scottish judiciary has wide sentencing discretion, with no formal sentencing guidelines in place. The only mandatory sentences are life imprisonment for murder and a minimum of seven years' imprisonment for a third offense of Class A drug trafficking. When life sentences are imposed, the judge specifies the minimum amount of time offenders will spend in prison (the punishment part of the sentence), after which they are entitled to apply to the Parole Board for release. In 1999, mandatory life sentence prisoners spent just more than 11 years on average in custody.

Financial penalties are the most common sentence imposed overall—in 2007–2008 they accounted for 62 percent of all punishments. There are two types of financial penalties: the fine paid to the state and compensation orders, where the money goes to the victim. The average amounts ordered to be paid in 2007–2008 were £220 (US$316) and £331 (US$476), respectively.

Imprisonment is the most usual sentence for murder, (attempted) rape, and most violent offenses. In addition, almost half of those convicted of housebreaking receive a custodial sentence. In total, imprisonment was imposed in 13 percent of all convictions in 2007–2008.

Community sentences were imposed in a similar number of cases, also accounting for 13 percent of all sentences imposed in 2007–2008. The most common types of community sentence are community service and probation; other community disposals available to the courts are drug treatment and testing orders, supervised attendance orders, and restriction of liberty orders.

Admonitions (judicial reproofs stated in open court) are noted on the offenders' criminal record in case of their returning to court for a further offense, when they will be taken into account. Orders to find caution require the offender to pay a sum of money to the court as a safeguard of good behavior for up to a year. At the end of the specified period, the person can apply to be refunded the money if he or she has not offended again. Together, these orders made up 13 percent of the sentences imposed in 2007–2008.

Community Sentences

Unlike in England and Wales, community sentences in Scotland are carried out by criminal justice social work services, delivered by local authorities. This has been the case since the Scottish Probation Service was disbanded in 1969, following recommendations made in the Kilbrandon Report in 1964. Historically, the placement of offender services under the social work umbrella has meant that offenders have been seen as in need of help and rehabilitation, although more recently the meaning of community sentences has undergone a transformation, with the underlying rationale shifting toward one of protecting the public. In 2005 provision was made to organize the local authorities delivering criminal justice social work services into eight Community Justice Authorities (CJAs), to facilitate the delivery of offender services and coordination with the Scottish Prison Service (SPS).

There is a wide array of noncustodial sentences in Scotland, most of which can carry conditions that resemble other community sentences, and there have been suggestions that the situation should be simplified. A bill currently before Parliament proposes the creation of the "Community Payback Order" as the single community sentence, to which sentencers would be able to attach the conditions they considered most appropriate. This order would have an increased emphasis on reparative actions to be undertaken by the offender. Also, because of low levels of public confidence in community penalties, the aim would be to make Community Payback Orders more visible and better understood by the public. Currently available community disposals are briefly discussed below, in order of prevalence.

The most frequently used community sentence, the Probation Order, can only be imposed with the consent of the offender and is intended to tackle offending behavior. These orders can last from six months to three years, and their content can range from very minimal contact between the practitioner and probationers who are deemed to be at low risk of reoffending to quite intensive programs of group work and one-to-one contact for medium- or high-risk offenders. Conditions that can be attached to probation include unpaid work, curfews (which can be enforced through electronic monitoring), and statutory drug and alcohol treatment. Community Service Orders require the offender to carry out between 80 and 300 hours of unpaid work in the community within 12 months. They are only meant to be imposed as an alternative to custody and require the consent of the offender.

Supervised Attendance Orders are imposed when an offender ordered by the court to pay a fine defaults on this payment. They are meant to provide an alternative to (brief periods of) imprisonment in these cases. Since 2003 they can also be imposed as an alternative to a fine, although this happens in only a small number of cases. Offenders who are given a Supervised Attendance Order are required to take part in constructive activity for between 10 and 100 hours.

Restriction of Liberty Orders were introduced in 2002 and can be imposed for up to a year, but only with the consent of the offender. Offenders are ordered to either stay within their homes for up to 12 hours per day or to stay away from a certain area for up to 24 hours per day. They are required to wear an electronic tag, which allows monitoring of their movements.

The Drug Treatment and Testing Order (DTTO) is another relatively new disposal, rolled out across Scotland between 1999 and 2006. It is reserved for offenders who commit crimes to fund their drug habit. As the name suggests, it requires such offenders to undergo treatment for their drug problem and submit to frequent random drug tests. Uniquely, DTTOs are reviewed by the judge who imposed the order, allowing progress to be encouraged and lapses to be criticized. DTTOs can last from six months to three years.

Prison

In 2007, Scotland imprisoned 139 people per 100,000 of the population, a rate slightly lower than in neighboring England and Wales. According to the most recent prison statistics compiled by the Scottish government, on June 30, 2007, 7,154 people were incarcerated, 334 of whom were female. The number of prisoners has increased by 22 percent over the previous nine years. This rise in imprisonment is predominantly fuelled by the increasing imprisonment of women (up by 87%) and the use of remand (up by 60%), alongside a huge increase in the reincarceration of those who have been released on license (up by 790%).

Generally, the most disadvantaged are imprisoned to a far greater extent than others. Inspections have found that 90 percent of female prisoners are addicted to drugs or alcohol and 75 percent have histories of abuse and/or health problems, and that in male prisons, too, many prisoners have problems with addiction and/or their physical and mental health. However, only 4.5 percent of adult prisoners were found to have severe and enduring mental health problems. When prisoners require psychiatric treatment, they can be transferred to secure mental health facilities. Those with drug addictions, mainly heroin, can be prescribed methadone within the prison.

In 2007–2008, half of all prison sentences imposed were for periods of up to three months, while 76 percent of all sentences were for six months or less. In Scotland, a distinction is made between short-term prisoners, those serving less than four years, and long-term prisoners, who are imprisoned for four years or over. While the latter made up 42 percent of prisoners in 2007–2008, only 3 percent of those with a charge proved against them in Scottish courts in the same period were given a long-term prison sentence.

Prison Conditions

There are 16 penal establishments in Scotland, including 2 open prisons (Castle Huntley and Noranside). Two of the prisons are operated by private companies, including the most recent addition to the prison estate, Addiewell, which was opened on December 12, 2008. Male young offenders aged 16–20 are detained in a Young Offenders Institute (YOI Polmont) and part of 1 other prison (Perth). There is also a dedicated prison for female prisoners and young offenders (Cornton Vale), with some of the more remote other prisons having small units for females. To ease overcrowding at Cornton Vale, one hall in Her Majesty's Prison (HMP) Greenock is now also used to house short-term female prisoners.

Experiences of imprisonment can vary widely in Scotland, due to variable pressures on the system and to contrasts in entitlements and provisions between prisoner categories. The system is overburdened; in February 2008, 11 of Scotland's prisons were holding more prisoners than their design allowed for. This has a negative impact on the availability of work, education, and rehabilitation for many prisoners. In the worst situations, prisoners spend most of their time, as much as 22 hours per day, locked up. On the other hand, there are positive developments and examples of good practice. Many prisons are being refurbished and most run accredited programs that address offending behavior, such as the Violence Prevention Programme and Constructs: Positive Steps to Stop Offending. Vocational training opportunities are varied in many prisons and focus on such employment areas as engineering, construction, horticulture, cleaning, forestry, and catering. Prisoners are also entitled to at least 1 hour's exercise a day. Importantly, relationships between staff and prisoners are rated as at least satisfactory by almost all prisoners.

The largest prison in Scotland is HMP Barlinnie, first opened in 1882. It is located in Glasgow and houses 20 percent of all Scottish prisoners. It holds remand and short-term prisoners, while also temporarily accommodating those serving more than 4 years until they can be transferred to the long-term prisoner system. Barlinnie is one of the most overcrowded prisons in the Scottish estate: its average population was 1,462 during 2007–2008, 45 percent more than the 1,018 it is designed to hold. Consequently, its prisoners only spend 20 minutes per day on average on meaningful activity (employability training, education, exercise) compared to a national average of 50 minutes per day. During the last inspection in 2006, on average only 127 prisoners were working outside of their hall each day and 27 were attending education. Vocational training programs include industrial cleaning, hairdressing, bricklaying, and joinery. Other courses available are in English, information technology (computing), modern studies, art, creative writing, and communication.

Entitlement to visits varies between prisons, but convicted prisoners are allowed a minimum of one half-hour visit per week. This allowance can be saved up in most prisons to one two-hour visit every four weeks. Up to three adults can visit at a time, with no restriction on the number of children visiting. Visits ordinarily take place in visiting rooms, with no physical barrier between the prisoners and their families. Where there are particular security concerns, prisoners and visitors may be separated by a glass barrier. Prisoners book the visits themselves and it is their responsibility to inform visitors of the date and time. There is no provision for conjugal visits.

As extradition is dealt with by the Home Office for the UK as a whole, the arrangements in Scotland are the same as those in England and Wales.

Throughcare and Release

While practice in preparing prisoners for their release into the community varies somewhat between establishments, the following is an attempt to describe usual practice. All prisoners who are serving more than seven days have their needs assessed when they first come into the prison to facilitate referral to specialist services within the prison. For short-term prisoners, this information feeds into a Community Integration Plan, which is updated prior to their release. Short-term prisoners are routinely released at the halfway point of their sentence (with the exception of sex offenders serving more than six months). Since 2006 short-term prisoners serving more than three months can be released up to four and a half months before the halfway point of their sentence on Home Detention Curfew (HDC). The curfew requires them to stay at their home address or hostel from 7:00 p.m. to 7:00 a.m., with their movements monitored by means of an electronic tag. If the curfew is breached, the prisoner is recalled to prison until the halfway point of his or her sentence. Released short-term prisoners are not subject to statutory supervision.

For long-term prisoners, a multidisciplinary Action Planning Case Conference takes place at most six months after the start of their sentence and at least yearly thereafter. They can apply to the Parole Board once they have served half their sentence to be released on license. If they are rejected for this, they are automatically released on license after two-thirds of their sentence. Any prisoner released on license is subject to statutory throughcare: he or she has to maintain contact with criminal justice social workers and may have to attend group programs and take other steps to reduce the risk of future offending. Released prisoners can be returned to prison if they breach a condition of their license or commit another imprisonable offense before their original sentence has expired.

Fiona Jamieson, Katrina Morrison, Marguerite Schinkel, and Richard Sparks

Further Reading

CJScotland: http://www.cjscotland.org.uk/. This a regularly updated, independent Web resource on crime and criminal justice in Scotland, providing both news and commentary.

Scottish Centre for Crime and Justice Research: http://www.sccjr.ac.uk.
Scottish Government's Research on Crime and Justice: http://www.scotland.gov.uk/Topics/Research/by-topic/crime-and-justice

United Kingdom/Wales

Legal System: Common
Murder: Medium (England and Wales)
Burglary: Medium (England and Wales)
Corruption: Low (England and Wales)
Human Trafficking: Low (England and Wales)
Prison Rate: Low
Death Penalty: No
Corporal Punishment: No

Background

Wales is a country with a population of 3 million, situated as a large peninsula in the west of Great Britain. It is about 270 kilometers (162 miles) long and about 100 kilometers (60 miles) wide, bordering England to the east and surrounded by sea on the other three sides, with more than 1,200 kilometers (720 miles) of coastline. Much of the country is rural, with agriculture and tourism the main industries. The main population and industrial areas are in the south of the country and consist of the areas around the three cities of Cardiff, Swansea, and Newport. Here, during the last 50 years the traditional extractive industries of coal and iron ore have been almost entirely replaced with service industries and tourism. Parts of the north and center of Wales are quite mountainous with low population density, where access to local communities is poor with few motorways or railways.

Wales has a long unique cultural tradition, including four universities and its own language and literature. The resurgence of Welsh pride since 1950 has led to a rediscovery of old traditions. This is particularly the case with the Welsh language, which is one of a family of similar languages spoken in Scotland, through Ireland, Wales, and Cornwall to northern France. Although the populations of Wales all speak English, Welsh is now spoken by around 20 percent of the population and around 40 percent of those aged under 20. The Wales Language Act of 1993 had the function of promoting the use of the Welsh language and giving effect to the principle that in the conduct of public business and the administration of justice in Wales the English and Welsh languages should be treated on a basis of equality.

There is a long tradition of population movement both ways between Wales and England so that many Welsh people are educated outside Wales, work or live outside Wales, and vice versa. The 20th- and 21st-century immigration from other parts of the world into England has also affected Wales, but to a lesser extent so that today 4 percent of the Welsh resident population is of minority ethnic origin compared to 8 percent in England.

Wales was entirely part of England and Wales from 1534 to 1997. However, there was a movement toward more autonomy for Wales during the latter half of the 20th century, spurred on by the large number of countries of similar size throughout the world that had themselves become independent following the end of the various European empires. Cardiff was named the capital of Wales in 1955; the political party Plaid Cymru, aiming for independence for Wales, achieved growing support: a special government office (the Welsh Office) was created in 1964 with gradually increasing powers, and a television channel in Welsh was established (S4C). A referendum for a move toward Welsh independence was rejected in 1976 but passed in 1997, leading to the creation in 1999 of a Welsh Assembly with limited legislative powers, which were enhanced in 2007.

Criminal Law

Before 1534, Wales had its own body of criminal and civil law *Cyfraith Hywel*, set up during the rule of King Hywel between 904 and 949, a time when the country was peaceful and conducive to the working out of a code of law. This was a remarkably detailed set of laws, laying down the obligations of the king and his officers and covering every likely social situation. Penalties were often quite light by the standards of the time. Homicide was punished by payment of recompense to the victim's family. Certain serious thefts could be punished by death but most other offenses were punished by a fine. In court the accused gave evidence under oath, as long as he or she could find a number of men to swear that he or she could be trusted. A judge decided on guilt and sentence. The law also set down the rights and obligations of women and husbands, the law of contracts, and the law of inheritance.

The law was continually revised and updated until Wales was absorbed into the wider jurisdiction of England and Wales. By the 12th century, the English had moved away from a code of law, especially one as liberal as Hywel's. The Statute of Wales (1284) introduced the English Common Law System into the courts and Hywel's criminal law lapsed. However, much civil law, especially laws of inheritance, remained untouched until the 16th century. The Act of Uniformity in 1534 replaced the Welsh Penal Code by the Anglo-Saxon Law of England, and from then until 1997 there was one jurisdiction run from London. During much of this time the Welsh population remained poor in comparison with the ruling English who were the main landowners. Much crime involved typical rural crime in such a country: stealing animals or robbing rich travelers; those who robbed the English often achieved some fame and were written about as folk heroes. One such hero, Twn Sion Catti, was an outlaw, a robber, and a highwayman of the 16th century whose exploits compare with the English Robin Hood.

The current Welsh legal system follows that of England. Petty offenses, especially traffic violations, are dealt with by fixed penalties, imposed by the police or other authorities. Police also give warnings or cautions after admission of guilt, often as agents of the prosecutor (the Crown Prosecution Service or CPS). Of the cases that are prosecuted in court, the minor offenses are dealt with by the magistrates' courts in the common law tradition in which suspects are tried and sentenced (mainly) by nonlegal members of the public who have volunteered for this (unpaid) role.

More serious offenses come before the Crown Court. Appeals from the Crown Court go to the Court of Appeal and eventually to the highest court in the jurisdiction. At present the highest court is composed of Law Lords, sitting as a committee of the Upper House of the London Parliament, the House of Lords. In 2009, this almost-medieval English concept will be renamed the Supreme Court and its links with Parliament severed. All appeal courts are situated in London, the capital of England, reflecting the current single jurisdiction of England and Wales.

Courts are conducted on an adversarial basis, where the prosecution has to prove the case against the accused according to a set of firm rules on admissibility of evidence. All evidence can be challenged in court, through cross-examination, which leads to lengthy trials in many cases. There is no career judiciary. In many magistrates' courts, guilt and sentence are given by lay magistrates representative of their local communities. At the Crown Court guilt is determined by a lay jury of 12 members from the local community; admissibility of evidence and sentence is determined by the judge, a trained lawyer of many years' standing.

Welsh criminal law, in common with any other country following a common law tradition, develops through the use of precedent, particularly by referring to decisions and opinions of judges that have been made in similar cases. For example in 1991, Welsh Law was changed by a decision of the Court of Appeal that reversed a long-held legal rule that a man could not be legally found guilty of raping his wife. This was entirely because of the judges' reactions to cultural changes in society that relegated such a legal rule to the category of actions that could no longer be tolerated in a society where the position of women had changed out of all recognition.

Welsh criminal law also develops by changing the context in which it operates. Although it is too early to say if or when the Welsh Assembly will have substantive legislative powers over Welsh criminal law, it already exercises many powers influencing the crime situation; for example, it sets drugs policies, defines crime reduction initiatives, and intervenes to deal with young offending through such instruments as the Substance Misuse Action Fund, the Safer Communities Fund, and the All Wales Youth Offending Strategy.

Welsh law also develops through the setting up of new institutions. Occasionally, despite the appeal process having been exhausted, a criminal case is still thought to involve a miscarriage of justice. This can lead to a media campaign or result from the discovery of new evidence or an improvement in detection technology, such as the coming of DNA analysis. Such a case can be referred to the Criminal Cases Review Commission, often many years after the case has first been concluded. The Criminal Cases Review Commission is an independent body that has the resources to review such a case. If the new material is thought to be significant, then this commission will send it back to the Court of Appeal in London. If this court finds the new circumstances compelling, then it can quash the original verdict or order a new trial.

Welsh criminal law also develops through legislative change. And in recent years Wales has achieved a degree of legal autonomy from London. This is likely to grow in the next generation. Acts of 1998 and 2006 set out limited areas of devolved responsibility for the Welsh Assembly to draft laws. On July 9, 2008, the assembly passed the first new Welsh law since Cyfraith Hywel in the 10th century. Where powers have not been devolved, they can now be requested from London, if public interest is sufficiently large. A consultation is underway, with a recommendation from the current Welsh ruling political coalition, that criminal justice be devolved.

Police

Policing is not a devolved service in Wales but follows law and guidelines set down by London. However, everything the police in Wales do impacts on all the services already devolved to the Welsh Assembly government. A Police Liaison Team works closely with the Welsh Assembly to ensure the police play a full part in all assembly activities, including taking part in the Local Service Boards that are Wales's new model for engaging the whole of the Wales public service by integrating services and responding more effectively to citizens' needs.

Police in Wales are a completely civilian group, divided into four forces: South Wales, Gwent, covering mainly urban areas, and North Wales and Dyfed-Powys, covering mainly rural areas. Low-level crimes are dealt with by these four forces with special arrangements for cooperation with other forces if needed. More serious crime involving more than one force or international agents is dealt with by national organizations such as the Serious Organised Crime Agency (SOCA) in London. In 2008, there were 7,500 police in Wales, a ratio of 253 per 100,000 population. Of these, 1,800 were female. In addition, there were 870 special (voluntary) constables and 700 community support officers who assisted the police on the streets and 3,800 civilians who assisted with administrative tasks.

Police in Wales are overseen by Her Majesty's Inspectorate of Constabulary (HMIC) in London. The police service has seen a major cultural change since 1990 and has become part of a wider police family, including not only the police service with full powers to arrest offenders but also community support officers who have a more on-the-street presence, although they have limited police powers, and neighborhood wardens who have more limited, discretionary powers. Since 1994, all police activity has to be conducted in Welsh if a victim, witness, or defendant wishes it to be done that way. Police are also very active in crime prevention and reduction, keeping in close touch with other agencies and community groups and issuing a large amount of guidance to individuals and businesses.

Crime

Classification of Crimes

Crimes in Wales are classified into the following three broad groups:

- *Indictable:* The most serious offenses, only triable at the higher courts. The main indictable offenses are homicide, robbery, and rape.

- *Either-way:* Less serious offenses, which can be tried at either the higher court or the magistrates' courts. This includes all forms of theft, burglary (theft from a building), criminal damage, less serious offenses of violence, fraud offenses, trafficking offenses, offenses involving firearms and knives, less serious sex offenses, drug offenses, and some motoring offenses.
- *Summary:* Least serious offenses. This includes nearly all traffic offenses that can be dealt with outside the court process or through a court trial, administrative offenses such as not possessing licenses, offenses against various acts such as environmental offenses, trading offenses, and prostitution offenses.

The age of criminal responsibility is 10 years, extremely low by international standards, although there are special court arrangements for children up to the age of 18, and penalties for younger people are lower than those for adults.

There is particular concern about violent crime, especially those committed in a public place, using weapons such as guns or knives, or by young people. Wales has generally managed to avoid the high rates of many English cities, and gun and knife crime is quite low. However, the urban areas around the ports in the south of Wales have a much longer tradition of violence and upsurges in violent crime occur from time to time. Violent crimes against women or against young children also attract considerable attention in Wales, as do drug offenses that drive much of property crime. Although security is high, Wales has also avoided any significant terrorist incidents or conspiracies. As much of Wales is composed of rural areas, crime in general is lower than in England.

Police-recorded crime in Wales follows the counting rules laid down by London, which include attempts. According to the Home Office, total police-recorded crimes in Wales for the 2007–2008 period were 243,623, a decrease of 6 percent from the previous year (compared with a decrease of 9 percent for England and Wales). Rates per 1,000 population for the same period for major offense categories were as follows:

All offenses	82
Violence	17
Burglary	9
Vehicle offenses	12
Theft	16
Criminal damage	20

These figures have been falling for about 10 years, reflecting intensive crime prevention activity by law enforcement authorities and the population alike. Theft and criminal damage are typical crimes in the extensive rural areas of Wales; urban areas are characterized by more examples of robbery and street violence; domestic violence and hate crime are found in all areas and are offenses of particular interest to the police. All cultivation, sale, and use of unprescribed drugs is illegal, and drugs are divided into three bands, according to their seriousness, with penalties ranging from fines, fines with periods in prison, and for the most serious, up to life in prison.

About 15 percent of all households in Wales experienced a crime in 2007, and 5 percent of households experienced a crime against the person. Both these figures are slightly less than the English situation, reflecting the fact that Wales is basically a rural nation. In particular vehicle crime in Wales affected 5.0 percent of the population compared to 6.4 percent in England, with the rural parts of central and north Wales having rates of just under 3 percent.

Levels of worry about burglary and car crime are similar to England with about 10 percent having a high concern. However, other concerns were higher in Wales: 18 percent of households were worried about antisocial behavior, 32 percent about drug dealing, and 28 percent worried about young people drinking in public and rowdy behavior. In total 48 percent of people thought the police were doing a good job and this rose to 56 percent in rural areas. The Welsh police forces are recruited locally, and 62 percent of people thought the police in Wales understood local concerns well. All these perceptions had remained stable over the last few years.

Investigation of Crimes

Offenses in Wales are investigated by the police. However, the Crown Prosecution Service is organized within the same four regions as the police and works closely with them, with most large police stations having a resident prosecutor to give advice on criminal investigations. At present the CPS does not carry out any investigations itself, although it is conducting some experiments in interviewing rape victims. However, the police will consult closely with the CPS from the earlier stages of the investigation. The case file will then be sent to the local CPS, who will decide on what action to be taken. In most cases the CPS will decide to charge the suspect and take the case to court, but the CPS can also ask the police to conduct more investigation before a decision is taken.

An important characteristic of criminal justice in Wales is that resources to deal with known offenses are limited. Thus, in 2006–2007, of the quarter of a million offenses known to have been committed, around a third of these offenses were brought to justice. However, not all of these were due to findings of guilt at a court. Authorities in Wales follow English procedures regarding case ending that enable cases to be finalized without a full court trial. These alternative procedures all involve the accused admitting his or her guilt. The procedures comprise final warnings issued by the police to juveniles or cautions issued to adults on admission of guilt; penalty notices ("on the spot fines") issued by police for disorderly behavior, including shoplifting, mainly used for juveniles, on admission of guilt; formal warnings for cannabis possession, issued by the police; other offenses taken into account by the court, without extra penalty, when the offender is found guilty of another crime. For many of these alternative procedures, legal representation is not easily available or is discouraged in the interests of speedy conclusion of the case. Of the 252,473 recorded offenses in 2006–2007, 80,546 of these were brought to justice. Of these, 41,248 resulted in convictions, and the remainder were dealt with by police and court actions such as penalty notices and warnings.

For those cases where police feel that further action is necessary, they pass the case file to the prosecution service (CPS). The CPS in Wales then decides what further action is necessary and in 2006 took the following actions:

- In 28 percent of cases a charge was brought and the case proceeded against in court.
- In 4.8 percent of cases they were sent back to the police for further investigation.
- In 2.5 percent of cases they were sent back to the police to finalize the case through a caution or other means.
- In 36.9 percent of cases the CPS decided no further action was to be taken on grounds that evidence was not strong enough to give a good chance of conviction.
- In 3.2 percent of cases the CPS decided no further action was to be taken in the public interest.
- In 24 percent of cases action was postponed until further information was available.

The accused has the right to a full trial in all cases where a charge is brought. However, there is often some pressure by the courts to go along with alternative procedures, such as pleading guilty to a less serious offense for a lower penalty, rather than pleading not guilty as charged. An accused also has the right to legal representation, first at the police station and then when represented at court.

For cases that do go to trial at court, most of these are dealt with in front of a panel of 3 lay magistrates, chosen to be aware of local concerns. For the more serious offenses, or if the accused insists, trial is before a jury of 12 lay people, chosen by lot from the local electoral registers. The jury decides on the facts, and the judge will decide on what evidence is allowed to be put before them and on sentence, if the accused is found guilty. Legal defense is provided by the public, if the accused is unable to pay for such defense himself or herself. A Legal Service Commission decides on the accused's eligibility for legal assistance; 55,000 defendants were so assisted in Wales in 2007.

Most cases are decided before a magistrates' court in a summary trial. In 2006–2007, 208,816 persons were found guilty of less serious offenses at magistrates' courts in Wales, and 2,906 were found guilty of the more serious offenses at the Crown Court. Court authorities encourage guilty pleas by judges giving a "discount" of one-third on sentence for a guilty plea, as long as it is made in good time.

Thus, at the magistrates' courts most cases involve a plea of guilty and at the Crown Court about one-half of cases involve a guilty plea. At the Crown Court, depending on the seriousness of the case and of the strength of the evidence, there is scope for informal hearings between the judge and the prosecution and defense lawyers; these hearings aim to reduce length and cost of the trial and can discuss any possibility connected with a guilty plea for a lesser offense, including an informal statement from the judge as to the type of sentence that he or she would give in certain cases.

For serious cases, the accused is held in custody before trial. However, there is a presumption that bail will be granted before trial unless the police object, for example, on the grounds that the suspect will leave the country or intimidate witnesses.

At most magistrates' courts, all judges are nonlawyers, chosen from volunteers from the local Welsh community, although a growing number of magistrates' courts are now presided over by a qualified (district) judge. The numbers of Crown Court judges in Wales are as follows: 36 circuit judges, 69 recorders (less senior judges), and 68 district judges or their deputies. There is no career judiciary but Crown Court judges are chosen from qualified lawyers who have had considerable experience of court work in Wales. There are no appeal court judges in Wales as the Appeal Court sits in London. Most judges sit on civil as well as criminal cases.

All agencies of law enforcement have the ability to look for alternative case resolutions, especially for young people or for less serious offenses. There are separate courts for young people that, especially for first offenders, refer cases to social authorities for alternative dispute resolution, for example, an offender can offer an apology or some restitution to the victim or to the community at large.

Punishment

Punishments follow the general laws of England and Wales. There is no corporal punishment, capital punishment, or banishment to another country. The legal age of responsibility is 10 years old, although juveniles up to 18 are treated differently from adults, with special courts, offender programs, and custodial establishments.

For traffic offenses, fixed penalty fines are laid down in law, including a penalty points system that can add up to suspension of the offender's driving license. The fixed penalty system has recently been extended to a number of public order offenses including theft from shops.

Most offenses dealt with at the magistrates' courts result in fines, although magistrates can award probation, electronic monitoring, and imprisonment. The higher Crown Court is much more likely to award probation or imprisonment. Electronic monitoring can involve restriction to one's home for much of the day. The proportions awarded imprisonment and the lengths of imprisonment have increased considerably in the last 15 years.

In addition to these punishments, compensation to the victim can be awarded, assets can be confiscated in some circumstances, or offenders can be forced to attend offender programs, either in the community or in prison. Compensation can be awarded to victims of violent crime, even if the offender is not caught. Offender programs can involve such areas as drug therapy, anger management, cognitive behavioral work, alcohol therapy, better driving, or sex offender treatment. Also, many offenders, especially young offenders, are encouraged to make reparation to their victims.

The very few mandatory sentences in Welsh courts are the following:

- A life sentence for murder.
- An automatic life sentence for a second serious sexual or violent offense called a public protection sentence.
- A minimum 7-year prison sentence for third-time trafficking in Class A drugs (this provision applies to importation, production, supplying, and possession with intent to supply Class A drugs. The maximum penalty for these offenses is life imprisonment).

- A minimum 3-year prison sentence for third-time domestic burglary. The maximum penalty is 14 years' imprisonment.
- A minimum 5-year prison sentence for possession or distribution of prohibited weapons or ammunition. The maximum penalty is 10 years' imprisonment.

Apart from these judges have full flexibility in their sentences up to the maximum set by law. A judge can give a very low penalty or even none at all, even though the defendant has been found guilty. However, guidelines are set and published for typical offenses and a judge has to justify deviation from these.

Life imprisonment tends to mean at least 15 years, and this has grown considerably over the last 10 years as penality has increased. A recent change in the law has resulted in indefinite custodial sentences being given to very serious offenders, who will not be released if they are judged to be of serious risk to the public. The indefinite nature of this law is presently being challenged in the courts as being against human rights legislation.

Prison

Wales has only four prisons: Swansea, Cardiff, Usk (for young offenders), and the Parc, a private prison within the public prison system. There is not an exact match between those sentenced to imprisonment in Wales and these four prisons. Many of those sentenced in Wales in fact end up in English prisons. On the other hand, some prisoners sentenced in English courts can be sent to Welsh prisons, depending on the available prison spaces, at a time of acute overcrowding within the English and Welsh system. In July 2008, there were 2,635 prisoners in Welsh prisons, which were running at nearly full capacity.

The largest prison in Wales, the Parc, is situated to the north of the industrial area in south Wales, near Bridgend. It is a Category B local prison housing approximately 1,126 male adults (convicted only), young offenders (convicted and remand), and young people (convicted and remand). The prison opened in November 1997 and is the only private prison in Wales. It is managed by Group 4 Securicor on behalf of the Prison Service. The prison employs 580 members of staff, many of whom are recruited from the local area.

The Parc offers a progressive and challenging regime in a modern environment. A range of activities aim to equip offenders with the key skills necessary to reduce the risk of reoffending after release. Education is provided for all subjects and for all qualifications up to and including university courses. The gymnasium is in use up to 10 hours every day. There are nine workshops employing 40 people. Health care is provided through an inpatient ward with 24 beds, as well as routine visits from local hospitals, dentists, opticians, and psychiatrists.

The prison does not tolerate the presence and use of illicit drugs and has effective security measures to restrict smuggling of drugs. Drug services include routine drug testing, both mandatory and voluntary, clinical provision for maintenance management programs, detoxification, and management of stimulant withdrawal and naltraxone prescriptions prerelease is provided. A range of one-to-one interventions (harm reduction, overdose awareness, drug use and offending, relapse prevention, relationships, and drug use and safer injecting) is provided to individuals. Counseling and group work is provided for those assessed as needing these types of intervention. There is also a cognitive behavioral group work program designed to address drug dependence and related offending.

Interventions are designed specifically to address and promote change with regard to the particular cognitive deficits and criminogenic attitudes that are common within the majority of offenders serving a custodial sentence. Services comprise a mixture of programs accredited nationally and innovative pilot schemes exclusively developed within the Parc. The Parc is also committed to the effective resettlement of offenders back into the community, offering offending behavior courses, prerelease training programs, and workshops to prisoners nearing their date of release.

All Welsh prisons offer similar arrangements for their prisoners, in so far as resources are available. However, there is no prison at all in North Wales and those sentenced in the north have to be sent to prisons across the border in England. Also, all women sentenced to imprisonment in Wales have to go to English prisons as there are no women's prisons within Wales. For the families of such people, there is considerable extra traveling to see their relatives in prison in England. Full religious behavior is possible within prisons, for all faiths.

Prison visiting is possible from family and friends of the prisoner, on at least a monthly basis. Visitor centers are usually available where visits can take place in comfort and a certain amount of privacy. Most Welsh prisons are quite close to urban areas and can be accessed easily by public or special transport. Other privileges allowed include short-term release as a preparation before final release; also, in many cases, prisoners are released early and made to stay in their homes on home detention curfew orders.

The British Prison Service has prisoner transfer agreements with 96 countries and territories. Statistics are not available for Wales alone but in 2006, 109 prisoners were transferred from prisons in England and Wales to prisons in other countries to continue serving their sentences of imprisonment, and 43 prisoners were transferred from prisons abroad to prisons in England and Wales to serve the remainder of their prison sentences here. On average about 3 percent of these will have been from/to Welsh prisons.

Community Sentences

There are also many community sentences awarded in Wales. In 2006, there were 2,259 community penalties awarded in magistrates' courts in Wales. These combine punishment with making amends to the victim or to society and in trying to change the offender's behavior, while encouraging the offender to deal with any problems that might be making him or her commit crime—like drugs. Technological advances, such as electronic tagging and voice recognition, provide ways to restrict liberty and reduce crime without requiring a prison sentence. The previous diversity of community order for adults has now been replaced by a single generic community order with a range of possible requirements.

Courts are able to choose different elements to make up a bespoke community order that is relevant to that particular offender and the crime(s) committed. The range of requirements that are available with a generic community sentence or community order are compulsory (unpaid) work; participation in any specified activities; programs aimed at changing offending behavior; prohibition from certain activities; curfew; exclusion from certain areas; residence requirement; mental health treatment (with consent of the offender); drug treatment and testing (with consent of the offender); alcohol treatment (with consent of the offender); supervision; and attendance orders. These penalties are served under the supervision of the Welsh Probation Service.

Offenders under 18 are dealt with by various Welsh Youth Offending Teams, which exist in all areas. These teams are multiagency partnerships with staff drawn from children's services, the schools service, the police, probation service, and health services, from Careers Wales, the Crime Reduction Initiative, and local street drugs projects. Their principal aim is to prevent offending by children and young people by working with young people aged 10–17 who have offended, giving support and guidance to their parents and carers, and by offering restorative justice, general advice, and support to victims of crimes committed by young people.

Modern technologies are also used to supervise offenders. Electronic monitoring of adult offenders provides value for money and a cost-effective alternative to custody for low-risk offenders. Research has shown that three months of an electronically monitored curfew are nearly five times cheaper than three months in custody. Thus, each month, a small number of prisoners, judged safe to be released up to three months early are allowed to complete their sentence in their own homes on electronic curfew arrangements. Electronic monitoring is also used extensively by the Probation Service in Wales, for example, if the offender has been given a curfew order or a community rehabilitation order with electronic monitoring requirements by the Crown Court.

Chris Lewis

Further Reading

Annual Criminal Statistics, the Ministry of Justice: http://www.justice.gov.uk/publications/criminal annual.htm.

Crime Statistics in Wales, the Home Office: http:// www.homeoffice.gov.uk/rds.

Jenkins, Dafydd, ed. (1986). *Law of Hywel Dda: Law Texts of Medieval Wales.* Ceredigion, Wales: Gomer.

Public Order, Justice and Rights, the Welsh Assembly: http://wales.gov.uk/publications/accessinfo/drnewhomepage/publicorderdrs2/?lang=en.

Sandars, Andrew, and Richard Young. (2006). *Criminal Justice.* Oxford, UK: Oxford University Press.

Vatican City and the Holy See

Legal System: Civil
Death Penalty: No

Background

The Vatican is a sovereign and independent city-state. It is an enclave located on Vatican Hill, west of the Tiber River, within the city of Rome, Italy. The name "Vatican" derives from the ancient Latin *Mons Vaticanus,* where allegedly the Roman emperor Caligula built his private circus, in which a number of the early Christians were martyred and which was later completed by Nero. The Christian Church attained the status of a sovereign political entity with the emergence of the Papal States in mid-eighth century, ruling a considerable part of the Italian peninsula for more than a thousand years, although during this period the regions over which the Church had secular control have varied notably in extent.

In the 18th century, at the height of their power, the Papal States embraced modern Latium, Umbria, Marche, and other areas in continental Italy and around Avignon in France. As a result of the process of Italian unification, from 1860 to 1870, most of the Papal States, that in 1859 still encompassed a territory of about 44,030 square kilometers (17,000 square miles) across central Italy, were absorbed into the newly created Kingdom of Italy. The temporal power of the Pope was subsequently abrogated and much Church property confiscated. The problem of the Pope's status and his relation to the Italian state between 1870 and 1929 is historically known as the "Roman Question," which began in 1870 with the annexation of Rome to Italy and was not resolved until February 11, 1929, when the Italian government and the Holy See signed in the Lateran Palace in Rome an agreement of mutual recognition between Italy and the Holy See known as the "Lateran Pacts." The Lateran Treaty was incorporated into the Italian Republican Constitution in 1947.

The State of the Vatican City was therefore founded with the signing of the Lateran Pacts between the Holy See and the Kingdom of Italy. They provided the Holy See with a temporal jurisdiction and independence, full property rights, and exclusive sovereignty on the Vatican, also definitely establishing its territorial extent, by assigning 108.7 acres of Rome to the Holy See. Hence, the world's smallest sovereign nation, both by size and population, was created.

Territory

The State of Vatican City has a total border of 3.2 kilometers (2.0 miles) almost totally surrounded by medieval and Renaissance walls (*mura leonine*) and includes St. Peter's Square, whose border is just outside the oval formed by Bernini's impressive colonnade. There are five entrances to Vatican City, each of them patrolled by the Pontifical Swiss Guards and by the Gendarmes Corps of Vatican City State. The villas and the palace of Castel Gandolfo, which is the summer residence of the Pope, the complex of patriarchal basilicas, and some other belongings of the Holy See that are located outside Vatican territory, enjoy extraterritorial rights. Castel Gandolfo and the basilicas are patrolled internally by police agents of the Vatican City State and not by Italian police. St. Peter's Square is ordinarily policed jointly.

Population and Languages

The total population of Vatican City is 779, of whom 527 have Vatican citizenship, while the rest have permission to reside there, either temporarily or permanently, without the benefit of citizenship. The Vatican citizenry essentially consists of clergy, generally working in the service of the Holy See, a few officials of the state, and the Swiss Guard. Only a part of Vatican City's 527 citizens live within the Vatican's walls. In fact, about half of them (287) serve (mostly as diplomatic personnel) in Vatican embassies around the world. The total resident population of Vatican City consists of 492 persons. Most of the more than 3,000 Vatican lay workers are Italian citizens residing outside the Vatican territory. Each year some 18 million tourists and pilgrims visit Vatican City.

Although Latin is the official language of Vatican City, Italian is the everyday language most used in the state. Laws and regulations are also published in Italian in the *Supplemento per le leggi e disposizioni dello Stato della Città del Vaticano,* attached to the official state bulletin *Acta Apostolicae Sedis.* Many languages are used within the state. The Pontifical Swiss Guard use German, French, or Italian, which are three of the four official languages of Switzerland. The Holy See's newspaper, *L'Osservatore Romano,* is published in Italian, English, French, German, Polish, Portuguese, and Spanish. The Holy See uses Latin for its official documents, which are published in the *Acta Apostolicae Sedis.*

Institutional and Political Contexts

The Vatican City State and the Holy See are two distinct entities. The Holy See, or *Apostolica Sedes,* is the seat of the Pope, as Bishop of Rome, the Roman Curia, and the various bodies that assist the pontiff in carrying out his pastoral mission. The term therefore defines the supreme authority and the central government of the Roman Catholic Church. The Holy See is a religious entity that does not occupy a temporal location. The Vatican City State is the territorial unit where the Holy See is located, providing it with the territorial sovereignty necessary to exist alongside other states. According to the Lateran Treaty, the Holy See has "full ownership, exclusive and absolute power and sovereign jurisdiction" over the Vatican City State. The state of Vatican City and the Holy See are recognized sovereign subjects of international law. Unlike the Holy See, the state of Vatican City is not a diplomatic entity and therefore does not receive or send diplomatic representatives. Foreign ambassadors are accredited not to the Vatican City State, but to the Holy See. Although the Vatican City State is a distinct legal jurisdiction, its intrinsic connection with the Holy See renders it difficult to separate the temporal functions of the state from the functions and government of the Catholic Church. The institutional system of the Vatican City State is not based on separation of the legislative, executive, and judicial powers of the governmental body.

The Holy See is ruled by the Pope through the Roman Curia and the Papal Civil Service. The Roman Curia consists of the secretariat of state, 6 congregations, 3 tribunals, 12 pontifical councils, and a system of administrative offices and structures. The congregations and councils consist of cardinals, archbishops, bishops, and laypeople selected from the worldwide Catholic Church, and each is chaired by a cardinal prefect or president who is assisted on the practical level by officials responsible for administrative tasks and by a body of consulters chosen for their specific skills and knowledge.

The Vatican City is the sovereign territory of the Holy See (*Sancta Sedes*) and the location of the Pope's residence, referred to as the Apostolic Palace. It is an absolute elective monarchy that is ruled by the Bishop of Rome, the Pope, who is elected for a life term in conclave by cardinals under the age of 80. As head of state and head of government, the Pope has *ex officio* full legislative, executive, and judicial power over Vatican City. His official title is Sovereign of the State of the Vatican City. The highest state functionaries are all clergymen of the Catholic Church.

Legislative power, except for those cases that the Pope intends to reserve to himself or to others, is exercised by a commission composed of a cardinal president and other cardinals, all appointed by the Pope for a five-year term. The commission can seek the advice of the "Consulta," a group of experts on legislative matters appointed by the Pope. The cardinal president of the commission is also president of the governorate of the state of Vatican City.

Executive authority is delegated to the governorate of Vatican City. The governorate consists of the president, a general secretary, and a deputy general secretary, each appointed by the Pope for five-year terms. Important actions of the governorate must be confirmed by the Pontifical Commission and by the Pope through the State Secretariat. The governorate oversees the central governmental functions through several departments and offices. The directors and officials of these offices are appointed by the Pope for five-year terms. These organs concentrate on material questions concerning the state's territory, including local security, records, transportation, and finances.

The Prefecture for Economic Affairs of the Holy See, one of the offices of the Roman Curia, is in charge of the Vatican City State budget, coordinates the finances of the Holy See departments, manages the fiscal affairs of the Roman Curia, and supervises the administration of the patrimony of the Holy See.

Military and Police

The Vatican's security and police corps is the *Corpo della Gendarmeria dello Stato della Città del Vaticano* (Corps of Gendarmes of the Vatican City State), or Gendarmerie, of about 100 officers, which is in charge for all regular police duties, such as public order, law enforcement, crowd, traffic and border control, security, crime prevention and investigations, enforcement of financial and commercial regulations in Vatican City. The Corps of Gendarmes is a part of the Security and Civil Defense Services Department (which also includes the Vatican Fire Brigade), an organ of the governorate of Vatican City State. The chief of the Vatican gendarmerie is appointed personally by the Pope, as is the chief of the Swiss Guard.

The Corps of the Pontifical Swiss Guard, or Swiss Guard, is a small military force of the Holy See, consisting of some 110 members, responsible for the safety of the Pope, the security of the Apostolic Palace, and Vatican City's border patrol. The Swiss Guard carry modern efficient arms like SIG P225 semiautomatic pistols and SIG SG 550 assault rifles, the same weapons that are used in the Swiss Army. The guard also engages in yearly rifle competition, enhanced training in unarmed combat, and defensive bodyguard tactics similar to those used in the protection of many heads of state. Notwithstanding such strong protective measures, allegedly the Pope entrusts himself almost entirely to Divine Providence.

Security in the State of Vatican City is also taken care of by the Italian Inspectorate of Public Security to the Vatican. This special section of the Italian State Police, of about 150 selected officers, is in charge of the protection of the Pope during his traveling in the Italian territory. It is also in charge of policing in St. Peter's Square, which, according to the Lateran Pacts, is subject to supervision by the Italian police authorities.

Legal System

The Vatican legal system can be defined as a civil law (Romano-Germanic law or Continental law as opposed to common law) system, based on Canon Law. Under the current Law of the Sources of Laws, the principal sources of Vatican City law are as follows:

- The *Codex Iuris Canonici* (Code of Canon Law), which has to be regarded as the first source of Vatican law and the first principle of its juridical interpretation. In this sense the Vatican legal system can be defined as based on the Code of Canon Law and revisions to it.
- The Fundamental Law of Vatican City State, along with the other constitutional laws.
- The laws promulgated either directly by the Pope or through the Pontifical Commission or other delegated legislative organs; these include the Vatican Code of Civil Procedure (May 1, 1946), administrative acts and regulations, apostolic constitutions, and conventions and agreements with other states.

The use of Italian and local laws as well is allowed, providing that they do not conflict with Canon Law, the rules of the Lateran Treaty (and its revisions), or Divine Law. These include the following:

- The Italian Civil Code
- The Italian 1899 Penal Code
- The Italian 1913 Code of Penal Procedure
- Other laws relating to public works, transportation, telecommunications, health and sanitation

Under the current Law of the Sources, all Italian laws have to be examined (and, if necessary, modified) by Vatican authorities before they are adopted as part of the city state's own legislation. The Vatican's new statute also states that the Holy See will scrutinize international treaties before deciding whether to sanction "the explicit admission of conformity of the Holy See"—a measure that has been implicit in the past. Great care is taken to ensure that Italian law is not applied in instances where it might conflict with pontifical or Canon Law. The Pope, as noted, enjoys full legislative, executive, and judicial power and, consequently, he can use any means in keeping with or opposed to positive law to resolve individual cases. The legislative regulations are published in a special supplement of the *Acta Apostolicae Sedis.*

Finding of Guilt

Judicial power is exercised by the juridical organs established by the Pope, which exercise their authority in his name. The Vatican City's court system is similar to the Italian judicial system. Specific procedures and responsibilities are established by the codes currently in force in Vatican City. Four judicial organs are responsible for civil and criminal matters:

- A Judge (*Giudice Unico*)
- A Tribunal (*Tribunale*)
- A Court of Appeal (*Corte d'Appello*)
- A Supreme Court (*Corte di Cassazione*)

Judges and prosecutors, as noted, are directly appointed by the Pope, at his complete discretion. As a rule, they are, however, distinguished jurists in both Canon and Civil Law. The Giudice Unico mostly handles minor crimes and violations, which are punished with administrative sanctions. The judge, directly appointed by the Pope, must be a citizen of the Vatican City State, and must also serve as a judge on the other courts. The tribunal consisting of a president and of three judges, all designated by the Pope, has jurisdiction over both civil and penal matters. Each year one of the three judges is appointed by the president as investigating judge (*giudice istruttore*) for a one-year term. The tribunal is also competent to handle appeals from any decisions of the Giudice Unico.

The president and the three other judges of the Court of Appeal are appointed for a five-year term by the Pope. The Giudice Unico and the judges of the tribunal are laypersons, while the Court of Appeal is composed partly of lay judges and partly of judges who are members of the clergy. The president of the Supreme Court is the cardinal prefect of the *Apostolic Signatura*, the highest canon law court in the Catholic Church. The two other judges of the court are also cardinals and members of the Apostolic Signatura. The Corte di Cassazione is responsible for hearing appeals from the Court of Appeal and has jurisdiction over penal matters against high-rank ecclesiastics, unless the Pope decides to handle the case personally. Many of the judges from the canon law courts serve a dual function as judges on the Vatican courts. With respect to criminal procedure, the Vatican City's judicial system is based upon a variant of the inquisitorial system, being a kind of "bench" trial made up of a single judge or a judicial panel, which includes the inquisitorial figure of the investigating judge and does not provide for a jury of peers.

The Vatican City State has full penal jurisdiction on its territory and therefore can sentence offenders to prison. However, in practice, such jurisdiction is not exercised for crimes punished with imprisonment. Offenders sentenced to prison in the Vatican would have to serve time in Italy, at the Vatican's expense, since in fact the Vatican has no prison facilities. Important criminal cases are mostly tried in Italy, also because, according to the Lateran Pacts, anyone who commits a crime on Vatican territory can be handed over to Italian police and prosecuted in an Italian court. That is why in 1981 Italians carried out the investigation and trial of Mehmet Ali Ağca, who shot and seriously wounded Pope John Paul II in St. Peter's Square.

Rights of the accused may be generally summarized as follows:

- The accused has the right to be tried by a single judge or by a judicial panel.
- Under the 1913 Code of Penal Procedure, currently in force in Vatican City, a public defender assistance is provided.
- The chief prosecutor is the Vatican's "Promoter of Justice," corresponding to the Italian attorney general, and conducts the prosecution, while the investigation is conducted by the investigating judge.
- Under the 1913 Code of Penal Procedure, currently in force in Vatican City, no "plea bargain," nor negotiated settlement, is allowed.
- Most criminal cases are "resolved" without resorting to a prison sentence. The most common sanctions are fines or deprivation of financial privileges normally granted to Vatican residents.
- Incarceration before trial is in theory allowed. In practice it is not carried out, since, as noted, the Vatican has no prison system, although it does maintain a small jail facility, located just to the south of St. Peter's Basilica, off St. Martha's Square, which is rarely used.

Crime

Classification of Crimes

The age of full penal responsibility is 21 years. Under the Penal Code currently in force in Vatican City, the so-called 1899 Zanichelli Code, there is a basic distinction between serious and less serious offenses. All criminal offenses are divided into two broad categories: *delitti,* which are serious offenses and *contravvenzioni,* which are less serious offenses. The distinction between *delitti* and *contravvenzioni* is based on the seriousness of the crime and on the severity of punishment. The crime categories are described in the second and third books of the Penal Code, entitled *Libro secondo: Dei delitti in ispecie* (in particular) and *Libro terzo: Delle contravvenzioni in ispecie* (in particular), respectively. Although they are both punishable by imprisonment and/or fine, the sentences for *delitti* are more severe than those for the *contravvenzioni.* The Penal Code generally classifies each criminal offense under the following specific headings:

- Crimes against the safety of the state, for example, espionage, armed bands, terrorism.
- Crimes against religious, and individual freedom, for example, offenses against religious feelings, profanation of a tomb, reduction to slavery, abduction, kidnapping, threat/intimidation, unlawful entering, offenses against secrecy (such as confidentiality of correspondence).
- Crimes against public authority, for example, corruption, bribery, embezzlement of public property by an officer, resisting and/or insulting a public officer on duty, breaking of seals, destroying crime evidence.
- Crimes against judicial authority, for example, simulation of offense, slander, perjury, prevarication, subornation, aiding and abetting, prison escape, duels.
- Crimes against the public order/breach of the peace, for instance, criminal association/incitement.
- Crimes against public faithfulness, for example, forgery and counterfeiting.
- Crimes against public safety, for instance, arson, bombing, provoking a railway or air disaster, adulteration/poisoning of food, water, and drugs.
- Crimes against public and family morality, for example, rape, indecent assault, abduction, adultery, bigamy.
- Crimes against the person, for example, murder, assault/bodily harm, abortion, child abandonment/abuse, defamation.
- Crimes against property, for example, theft, robbery, extortion, ransom kidnapping, fraud, embezzlement, receiving stolen property, penal damages.

- Offenses concerning public order, for example, mendicity, disturbing the peace.
- Offenses concerning public safety, for example, infringement of laws/regulations on weapons and explosives.
- Offenses concerning public morality, for example, gambling, drunkenness and disorderedly conduct, indecent exposure, maltreatment of animals.
- Offenses concerning the public protection of property, for example, unjustified possession of money/goods/burglary tools.

Drug Offenses

In Vatican City there is a lack of legislation regarding the possession and sale of illegal drugs, that is, there is no specific legal provision against this offense. This became apparent in 2008 after a Vatican employee was caught with 87 grams of cocaine. As a result of that case, Nicola Picardi, promoter of justice in the tribunal of Vatican City State, said that, since the Vatican employee could only be sentenced to the maximum of six months' imprisonment, the sentence was "completely inadequate to the seriousness of the crime and not in line with the legislation of other states," according to VaticanNews.com.

Crime Statistics

No crimes of murder, rape, serious property offenses, and serious drug offenses have been reported in Vatican City in recent years, though there have been occasional murders celebrated in the media, in particular the May 4, 1998, murders of Swiss Guard Commander Alois Estermann, his wife, and a young guard, all shot by Swiss Guard Vice-Corporal Cedric Tornay. The killings of the Estermanns were, ostensibly, the first to take place in the state since its creation. The case was eventually pronounced by the Vatican's investigation as a murder suicide, though many rumors and controversies surround the episode to this day.

According to the Vatican, almost all crimes consist of petty theft, especially pickpockets, whose perpetrators are rarely caught, with about 90 percent of complaints not leading to a prosecution. Other crimes include embezzlement, fraud, and insulting the police and civil servants. The number of cases involving Vatican residents is insignificant. Although most of Vatican City crime seems to be of trivial nature, the city state has more criminal cases per capita (per unit of inhabitants) than any other state of the world. According to the Vatican's promoter of justice (the equivalent to the Italian attorney general), Chief Prosecutor Nicola Picardi, the Vatican's justice department in 2008 had to contend with 549 civil and 486 criminal cases. In a population of 492 residents, this amounts approximately to one criminal case per person—20 times the corresponding rate in Italy, notwithstanding the fact that the Vatican City State has about one Swiss Guard or police officer for each citizen. These figures are, of course, deceptive: such a high crime rate in fact derives from what has been called "a handful of black sheep" among the some 18 million pilgrims and tourists who visit Vatican City every year.

Punishment

Types of Punishment

There is no "typical" or commonly used punishment for murder, rape, and serious theft/burglary/robbery, since, as noted, there is no recorded evidence of the occurrence of these crimes in Vatican's territory. As far as serious drug crimes are concerned, as noted, there is a lack of legislation in the Vatican regarding the possession and sale of illegal drugs; there is no specific legal provision against this crime. The death penalty, originally provided only for attempted assassination of the Pope, has been definitely removed for all crimes in Vatican City State with the 2001 Fundamental Law. No execution was carried out since the creation of the state in 1929.

Prison

The Vatican has no prison facilities. Persons sentenced to prison in the Vatican have to serve their sentence in Italy, at the Vatican City State's expense.

Pietro Marongiu and Graeme R. Newman

Further Reading

Vatican, the Holy See: http://www.vatican.va.

Vatican Publishing House (*Libreria Editrice Vaticana*) publishes the *Acta Apostolicae Sedis* (AAS), together with its supplements, on a periodic basis. AAS constitutes the official bulletin for the Holy See. The Vatican Publishing House also publishes Vatican City's newspaper *The Roman Observer.* The daily edition is in Italian. A weekly, English-language compendium edition is also published.

Wales. *See* United Kingdom/Wales

General Bibliography

Books, Periodicals, and Articles

Aas, K. (2007). *Globalization and Crime*. Los Angeles, CA: Sage.

Adeyemi, A. (1990). "Crime and Development in Africa: Case Study of Nigeria." In *Essays on Crime and Development,* edited by U. Zvekic, pp. 135–193. Rome: United Nations Interregional Crime and Justice Institute.

ADT. (2006). *Anti-Social Behaviour across Europe:* http://www.jdi.ucl.ac.uk/downloads/publications/journal_articles/cc4416AD_ANTI_SOCIAL_Report_UK_fv.pdf

Aebi, M. F. (2010). "Methodological Issues in the Comparison of Police Recorded Crime Rates." In *International Handbook of Criminology,* edited by S. Shoham, P. Knepper, and M. Kett, pp. 209–226. London: Routledge.

Aebi, M. F., K. Aromaa, B. Aubusson de Cavarlay, G. Barclay, B. Gruszczynska, H. von Hofer, V. Hysi, J.-M. Jehle, M. Killias, P. Smit, and C. Tavares. (2006). *European Sourcebook of Crime and Criminal Justice Statistics—2006.* 3rd ed. Den Haag: Boom Juridische Uitgevers.

Aebi, M. F., and N. Delgrande. (2009). *Council of Europe Annual Penal Statistics SPACE I: Survey 2007.* Strasbourg: Council of Europe.

Aebi, M. F., and A. Linde. (2009). *Review of the Current Situation in Respect of the Collection of Survey Data on Victimization.* Lausanne: Université de Lausanne.

Alvazzi del Frate, A. (2004). "The International Crime Business Survey: Findings from Nine Central-Eastern European Cities." *European Journal on Criminal Policy and Research* 10(2–3): 137–161.

Archer, D., and R. Gartner. (1984). *Violence and Crime in Cross-National Perspective.* New Haven, CT: Yale University Press.

Aromaa, K., and M. Heiskanen, eds. (2008). *Crime and Criminal Justice Systems in Europe and North America 1995–2004. Publication 55.* Helsinki, Finland: European Institute for Crime Prevention and Control, Affiliated with the United Nations (HEUNI).

Barak, G., ed. (2000). *Crime and Crime Control: A Global View.* Westport, CT: Greenwood Press.

Bayley, D. H. (2006). *Changing the Guard: Developing Democratic Police Abroad.* New York: Oxford University Press.

Beirne, P., and D. Nelken. (1997). *Issues in Comparative Criminology.* Sudbury, MA: Dartmouth.

Bennett, R. R. (1997a). "Excessive Force: A Comparative Study of Police in the Caribbean." *Justice Quarterly* 14: 651–686.

Bennett, R. R. (1997b). "The Determinants of Job Satisfaction among Police Constables: A Comparative Study in Three Developing Nations." *Justice Quarterly* 14: 295–323.

Bennett, R. R. (2004). "Comparative Criminology and Criminal Justice Research: The State of Our Knowledge." *Justice Quarterly* 21: 1–21.

Botchkovar, E. V., C. R. Tittle, and O. Antonaccio. (2009). "General Strain Theory: Additional Evidence Using Cross-Cultural Data." *Criminology* 47(1): 131–165.

Caldwell. J., ed. (1994). *Networking and AIDS in Sub-Saharan Africa: Behavioral Research and the Social Context,* pp. 101–116. Canberra: Australian National Universities.

Care, Jennifer, Tess Newton, and Don Paterson. (1999). *Introduction to South Pacific Law.* London: Cavendish.

Chevigny, P. (1995). *Edge of the Knife: Police Violence in the Americas.* New York: Free Press.

Dalgleish, D. (2005). "Pre-Colonial Criminal Justice in West Africa: Eurocentric Thought versus Africentric Evidence." *African Journal of Criminology and Justice Studies* 1(1): 155–169.

Delgrande, N., and M. F. Aebi. (2009). "European Prisons: Stability or Change?" *Criminology in Europe: Newsletter of the European Society of Criminology* 8(3): 1, 17–19.

European Journal of Criminology. Various issues providing country profiles.

European Journal on Criminal Policy and Research, in particular those on crime trends in Western and Eastern European Countries (Vol. 10[2–3], 2004) and prosecution and diversion within criminal justice systems in Europe (Vol. 14[2–3], 2008).

Fairchild, Erika, and Harry Dammer. (2001). *Comparative Criminal Justice Systems.* 2nd ed. Belmont, CA: Wadsworth.

Fiala, R., and G. LaFree. (1988). "Cross-National Determinants of Child Homicide." *American Sociological Review* 53: 432–445.

Findlay, Mark. (2000). *Criminal Laws of the South Pacific.* Suva: University of the South Pacific.

Friedrichs, D. (2007). "Transnational Crime and Global Criminology: Definitional, Typological, and Contextual Conundrums." *Social Justice* 34(2): 4–18.

Howard, G. J., G. Newman, and W. A. Pridemore. (2000). "Theory, Method, and Data in Comparative Criminology" (excerpted from *Measurement and Analysis of Crime and Justice. Criminal Justice 2000*) 4: 139–211.

International Journal of Comparative and Applied Criminal Justice. Published and copyrighted by the School of Criminal Justice, Michigan State University. ISSN 0192–4036.

Johnson, H., N. Ollus, and S. Nevala. (2007). *Violence against Women: An International Perspective.* New York: Springer.

Joireman, Sandra F. (2004). "Colonization and the Rule of Law: Comparing the Effectiveness of Common Law and Civil Law Countries." *Constitutional Political Economy* 15: 315–338.

Junger-Tas, J., I. Haen Marshall, and D. Ribeaud. (2003). *Delinquency in an International Perspective: The International Self-Report Delinquency Study.* The Hague, The Netherlands: Kugler Publications.

Karstedt, S. (2001). "Comparing Cultures, Comparing Crime: Challenges, Prospects and Problems for a Global Criminology." *Crime, Law, and Social Change* 36(3): 285–308.

Karstedt, S., and G. LaFree. (2006). "Democracy, Crime, and Justice." *Annals of the American Academy of Political and Social Science* 605: 6–23.

Kury, H., ed. (2001). *International Comparison of Crime and Victimization: The ICVS.* Ontario, Canada: de Sitter Publications.

Kyle, D., and R. Koslowski. (2001). *Global Human Smuggling: Comparative Perspectives.* Baltimore, MD: Johns Hopkins University Press.

Larsen, N., and R. Smandych, eds. *Global Criminology and Criminal Justice: Current Issues and Perspectives.* Peterborough, Ontario: Broadview Press.

Lee, M. R., and T. Earnest. (2003). "Perceived Community Cohesion and Perceived Risk of Victimization: A Cross-National Study." *Justice Quarterly* 20: 131–157.

Lo, Stefan H.C., Ian Dobinson, and Wing Hong Chui. "Sentencing for Drug Offences in Hong Kong: An Overview." *Hong Kong Law Journal* 34 (2005): 13–46.

Mawby, R., ed. (1996). *Policing across the World,* pp. 3–12. London: Routledge.

Messner, S. F., and Richard R. Rosenfeld. (2007). *Crime and the American Dream.* 4th ed. Belmont, CA: Thomson Wadsworth.

Nalla, M. K. (2009) "Democratic Policing: A Comparison of Police Officers' Perceptions of Their Role and Functions in Transitional Societies." *Journal of Criminal Justice and Security* 11(4): 520–535.

Nalla, M. K., and J. Johnson. (2009). "Are Police and Security Personnel Warming up to Each Other? A Comparison of Officer's Attitudes in Developed, Emerging, and Transitional Economies." *Policing: An International Journal of Police Strategies and Management* 32(3): 508–525.

National Institute of Justice, Office of Justice Programs, U.S. Department of Justice: http://www.ncjrs.gov/criminal_justice2000/vol4_2000.html.

Neapolitan, J. L. (1997). *Cross-National Crime: A Research Review and Sourcebook.* Westport, CT: Greenwood Press.

Newburn, T., and R. Sparks. (2004). *Criminal Justice and Political Cultures: National and International Dimensions of Crime Control.* Devon, UK: Willan.

Newman, Graeme R. (1999). *Global Report on Crime and Justice.* New York: United Nations Office of Drug Control and Crime Prevention.

Newman, Graeme R. (2008). *Comparative Deviance: Perception and Law in Six Cultures.* Reprinted with new introduction. Piscataway, NJ: Transaction Press.

Owomero, B. (1987). "Crime Rates and Development in Africa: Empirical Analysis of Data from Nigeria, Kenya, and Tanzania." *Indian Journal of Criminology* 15: 107–120.

Pridemore, W.A. (2008). "A Methodological Addition to the Cross-National Empirical Literature on Social Structure and Homicide: A First Test of the Poverty-Homicide Thesis." *Criminology* 46: 133–154.

Rafter, N.H., and F. Heidensohn. (1995). *International Feminist Perspective in Criminology.* Buckingham, UK: Open University Press.

Reichel, P.L. (2004). *Comparative Criminal Justice Systems: A Topical Approach.* Upper Saddle River, NJ: Prentice Hall.

Reichel, Philip L. (2008). *Comparative Criminal Justice Systems.* Upper Saddle River, NJ: Prentice Hall.

Robert, P., ed. (2009a). *Comparing Crime Data in Europe: Official Crime Statistics and Survey Based Data.* Brussels: VUBPRESS Brussels University Press.

Robert, P., ed. (2009b). *Evaluating Safety and Crime Prevention Policies in Europe.* Brussels: VUBPRESS Brussels University Press.

Savage, J., R.R. Bennett, and M. Danner. (2008). "Economic Assistance and Crime: A Cross-National Investigation." *European Journal of Criminology* 5: 217–238.

Schwabach, Aaron. (2003. Rev. 2006). *Non-Western Philosophies of Law.* In *Encyclopedia of Life Support Systems (EOLSS),* edited by Aaron Schwabach and Arthur John Cockfield, topic 6.31.1. Developed under the Auspices of UNESCO. Oxford: Eolss: http://www.eolss.net.

Sheptycki, J., and A. Wardak, eds. (2005). *Transnational and Comparative Criminology*. London: Glasshouse.

Stamatel, Janet P. (2006). "Incorporating Socio-Historical Context and Temporal Variation into Quantitative Cross-National Criminology." *International Journal of Comparative and Applied Criminal Justice* 30(2): 177–208.

Stamatel, Janet P. (2009a). "Correlates of National-Level Homicide Variation in Post-Communist East-Central Europe." *Social Forces* 87(3), 1423–1448.

Stamatel, Janet P. (2009b). "Contributions of Cross-National Research at the Beginning of the 21st Century." In *Handbook on Criminology and Deviance,* edited by Marvin Krohn, Alan Lizotte, and Gina Penly-Hall, 3–18. New York: Springer Science + Business Media.

Stamatel, Janet P. (guest editor). (2009, December). "New Methodological Directions for International and Comparative Criminology." *International Journal of Comparative and Applied Criminal Justice* 33 (2): 167.

Sung, Hung-En. (2004a). "Democracy and Organized Crime: Evidence from Fifty-Nine Countries." *Security Journal* 17(4): 21–34.

Sung, Hung-En. (2004b). "State Failure, Economic Failure, and Predatory Organized Crime." *Journal of Research in Crime and Delinquency* 41(2): 111–129.

Sung, Hung-En. (2006a). "Democracy and Criminal Justice in Comparative Perspective: From Crime Control to Due Process." *The Annals of the American Academy of Political and Social Science* 605(1): 311–337.

Sung, Hung-En. (2006b). "Structural Determinants of Police Effectiveness in Market Democracies." *Police Quarterly* 9(1): 3–19.

Sung, Hung-En, and Jack Reed. (2006). "Migration and Crime in Europe." In *Crime and Immigration,* edited by Joshua Freilich Graeme R. Newman, 95–120. Hampshire, UK: Ashgate.

Terrill, Richard J. (2009). *World Criminal Justice System: A Survey.* 7th ed. Southington, CT: Anderson.

Uildriks, N. (2009). *Policing Insecurity: Police Reform, Security and Human Rights in Latin America.* Lanham, MD: Lexington Books.

United Nations Office on Drugs and Crime. (2005). *Crime and Development in Africa.* Vienna, Austria: United Nations: http://www.unodc.org/pdf/African_report.pdf.

United Nations Office on Drugs and Crime. (2008). *Crime and Its Impact on the Balkans and Affected Countries.* Vienna, Austria: United Nations: http://www.unodc.org/documents/data-and-analysis/Balkan_study.pdf.

United Nations Office on Drugs and Crime and the Latin America and the Caribbean Region of the World Bank. (2007). *Crime, Violence, and Development: Trends, Costs, and Policy Options in the Caribbean.* Vienna, Austria: United Nations: http://www.unodc.org/pdf/research/Cr_and_Vio_Car_E.pdf.

Van Dijk, Jan. (2008). *The World of Crime: Breaking the Silence of Security, Justice, and Development across the World.* Thousand Oaks, CA: Sage.

Van Dijk, J., J. Kesteren, and P. Smit. (2007). *Criminal Victimisation in International Perspective: Key Findings from the 2004–2005 ICVS and EU ICS.* WODC: http://www.nicis.nl/kenniscentrum/binaries/nicis/bulk/onderzoek/2008/2/3/icvs2004_05report.pdf.

Weitekamp, E. G. M., and H. Kerner. (1994). *Cross-National Longitudinal Research on Human Development and Criminal Behavior.* Dordrecht, Netherlands: Kluwer Academic.

Zauberman, R., ed. (2009a). *Self-Reported Crime and Deviance Studies in Europe.* Brussels: VUBPRESS Brussels University Press.

Zauberman, R., ed. (2009b). *Victimization and Insecurity in Europe.* Brussels: VUBPRESS Brussels University Press.

Zimring, Franklin E., and David T. Johnson. (2008). "Law, Society, and Capital Punishment in Asia." *Punishment and Society* 10(2): 103–115.

Web Sites

BBC News Country Profiles: http://news.bbc.co.uk/2/hi/country_profiles/default.stm. This site is very good for background information on history, geography, and politics. It's also good for links to internal national sites and news media sites.

Cecil Greek's Criminal Justice Resources on International Criminal Justice: http://www.criminology.fsu.edu/p/cjl-world.php. There is a good variety of sources here, from common to the unusual, such as, for example, South Africa's Crime Mysteries.

CIA World Factbook: https://www.cia.gov/library/publications/the-world-factbook/index.html. The information in this book tends to be regurgitated in many Web sites, but it contains useful background information and is updated annually. Sometimes there are crime data, but usually descriptive, without statistics.

Council of Europe Annual Penal Statistics: www.coe.int/prison. Detailed data on prisons in Europe since 1983 can be found here.

The Council of Europe, European Commission for the Efficiency of Justice. (2008): *Evaluation of European Judicial Systems:* http://www.coe.int/t/dghl/cooperation/cepej/evaluation/default_en.asp.

Country Report of the Justice Studies Center of the Americas: http://www.cejamericas.org. This research and advocacy group publishes online country-specific analysis of legal systems and their operations in Latin America.

The Economist: http://www.economist.com/countries/index.cfm. This Web site offers much economic, historical, and political information on many countries and often useful information in its city guides.

European Society of Criminology: http://www.esc-eurocrim.org. This site provides a lot of relevant information on crime and punishment in Europe, including the programs of the annual conferences.

European Sourcebook of Crime and Criminal Justice Statistics: www.european-sourcebook.org. This site provides databases on police, prosecution, conviction, and correctional statistics since 1990 as well as some data on victimization.

International Centre for Prison Studies: http://www.kcl.ac.uk/depsta/rel/icps/home.html. This is a good source for international prison statistics.

International Court of Justice: http://www.icj-cij.org/.

Library of Congress Area Studies: http://www.loc.gov/rr/.

Nationmaster: http://www.nationmaster.com/index.php. This interesting interactive site allows comparative statistics of countries on a wide range of topics, including criminal justice. However, the crime statistics tend to be outdated.

The New York Times Countries and Territories: http://topics.nytimes.com/topics/news/international/countriesandterritories/index.html. These pages contain both general background information and links to recent media stories.

United Nations Interregional Crime and Justice Research Institute (UNICRI): http://www.unicri.it/wwd/analysis/icvs/data.php. A wide variety of information, particularly data for many countries participating in the International Crime Victim Survey (ICVS), is available.

United Nations Office on Drugs and Crime: http://www.unodc.org/. This site contains a wealth of information on crime, with extensive databases of crime statistics from the UN Surveys of Crime and Criminal Justice Systems.

U.S. Library of Congress Country Studies: http://lcweb2.loc.gov/frd/cs/. These are much more detailed than the usual country profiles, such as the CIA Factbook.

U.S. National Institute of Justice International Center: http://www.ojp.usdoj.gov/nij/international/. This site offers a variety of reports, articles, and descriptions of transnational and international crime and justice.

Wikipedia: http://wikipedia.org/. There is much information on countries, including interesting descriptions of crime and criminal justice issues. One has to be careful of the sources, but often there are links that lead to useful and reasonable resources. This is particularly good for tracking down internal national news media Web sites (i.e., local newspapers and TV stations) that almost always have news on local crimes.

World Criminal Justice Library Network: http://andromeda.rutgers.edu/~wcjlen/WCJ/mainpages/statres.htm. This site contains excellent statistical data from 80 countries. Internal national publications are usually the source.

World Factbook of Criminal Justice Systems. U.S. NIJ. Bureau of Justice Statistics: http://bjs.ojp.usdoj.gov/index.cfm?ty=pbdetail&iid=1435.

About the Editors and Contributors

General Editor

Graeme R. Newman is a distinguished teaching professor at the School of Criminal Justice, University at Albany, and the associate director of the Center for Problem-Oriented Policing. He has advised the United Nations on crime and justice issues over many years and in 1990 established the United Nations Crime and Justice Information Network.

Volume 4 Editors

Marcelo F. Aebi, PhD, is a professor of criminology at the University of Lausanne, Switzerland. He is also a scientific expert for the Council of Europe, the European Union, and the United Nations Office on Drugs and Crime, as well as a part-time professor at the Autonomous University of Barcelona, Spain. His main fields of expertise include comparative criminology and victimology, drugs and crime, and juvenile delinquency.

Véronique Jaquier, PhD, is a lecturer and senior researcher at the University of Lausanne, School of Criminal Sciences. She has trained in social psychology and criminology both in Switzerland and the United States. Her fields of expertise include violence against women—especially methodological problems arising in the measurement of victimization and comparative research—as well as issues surrounding the policing and sentencing of domestic violence.

Volume 4 Contributors

Cândido da Agra holds a PhD in psychology from the Catholic University of Louvain-la-Neuve, Belgium, and is a full professor and director of the School of Criminology, Faculty of Law, University of Porto.

Andri Ahven is an adviser to the criminal policy department at the Estonian Ministry of Justice. His research is related to crime victimization surveys and interpretation of crime statistics.

Nazmia E. Alqadi is a graduate student at the School of Criminal Justice, State University of New York at Albany.

Nathaniel Kip Arnold is a graduate student at the School of Criminal Justice, State University of New York at Albany and is a librarian at Schenectady County Community College of New York State.

Bruno Aubusson de Cavarlay, research director at the Centre national de la recherche scientifique (CNRS, National Center for Scientific Research), works at the Center for Sociological Research on Law and Penal Institutions (CESDIP) on criminal statistics and the functioning of the criminal justice system. He is a member of the Experts Group of the *European Sourcebook of Crime and Criminal Justice Statistics* project.

Daniel J. Beers is a visiting lecturer in the Department of Political Science and International Relations at Knox College. During the 2007–2008 academic year, he conducted dissertation field research in Romania and the Czech Republic with the support of a Fulbright-Hays Doctoral Dissertation Research Abroad Fellowship.

Dennis C. Benamati is library director, Jamestown Community College, Jamestown, New York.

Karin Bruckmüller is a university assistant at the Institute of Criminal Law and Criminology at the University of Vienna, and a research associate for the Austrian Criminal Bar Association and the Victim Support Organization "Weisser Ring."

Muhamed Budimlić is an assistant professor of criminology, Faculty of Criminal Justice, Criminology and Security Studies, University of Sarajevo.

Trevor Calafato is an assistant lecturer, Institute of Criminology, University of Malta. His research interests include crime prevention, community-based sanctions, security and terrorism.

Carla Cardoso holds a master's degree in biology and a PhD in biomedical sciences from the University of Porto. She is an invited professor at the Faculty of Law, University of Porto. Her main research interests are experimental criminology, security, and statistics.

Josefina Castro holds a degree in psychology and a master's in criminology from the University of Porto. She is an assistant professor at the Faculty of Law, University of Porto. Her main research interests are juvenile delinquency and social control.

Carlos Guillermo Castro Cuenca holds a doctorate in criminal law from the University of Salamanca and is a lecturer at the Universidad del Rosario in Colombia.

Martin Cejp is a researcher at the Institute of Criminology and Social Prevention, Prague.

Algimantas Čepas is a researcher at the Law Institute of Lithuania.

Anastasia Chalkia, a sociologist, is currently studying for a PhD on punitive attitudes at Panteion University in Athens, Greece. Prior to this, she gained an MA in criminology at the same university.

Sanja Copic, LLM, is a researcher at the Institute for Criminological and Sociological Research in Belgrade, as well as a researcher and president of the Executive Board of the Victimology Society of Serbia. Her research interests cover the following topics: trafficking in human beings, domestic violence, juvenile delinquency, crime victims' position in the criminal justice system, and restorative justice.

Vaughn Crichlow earned an MA in Criminal Justice from Rowan University, LLB from the University of London, and a BA in English at the University of the West-Indies, Trinidad.

Natalia Delgrande is a researcher at the School of Criminal Sciences of the University of Lausanne in Switzerland. She is a scientific expert for the Council for Penological Co-operation (PC-CP) of the Council of Europe and voluntary project-adviser for the Probation Office in Chisinau, Republic of Moldova.

Steven DeStefano is a law and justice studies student at Rowan University.

Lina Mariola Díaz Cortés holds a doctorate in criminal Law from the University of Salamanca, Spain, and is a lecturer in special criminal law in the Security Sciences Degree Programme-CISE-of the University of Salamanca.

Tsveta Docheva works as chief expert in the section International Relations and Projects at the Administration of the Prosecutor General in Bulgaria.

Graham Ellison is a senior lecturer in the School of Law, Queen's University Belfast.

Graham Farrell, PhD, is a professor of criminology at the Midlands Centre for Criminology and Criminal Justice at Loughborough University. He has previously worked at the universities of Cincinnati, Oxford, and Manchester, Rutgers University, the Police Foundation (Washington, D.C.), and the United Nations.

Jana Gajdošová has a Master of Law from Comenius University, Faculty of Law, in Bratislava (Slovakia), and a PhD in law from the University of East Anglia, Norwich Law School (United Kingdom). She has published several articles on the European human rights law and currently works as a legal advisor to the Agent of the Slovak Republic before the European Court of Human Rights.

Maria Galanou, MA in criminal law-criminal procedure, MA in criminology, is a PhD student at the Law School of Athens University.

Jessica Gentile is a graduate student at the School of Criminal Justice, State University of New York at Albany.

Laurie Gould is an assistant professor at the University of Texas at Arlington in the criminology and criminal justice department. She has previously published on a variety of topics including the use of strategic planning by state correctional agencies and the availability of jail visitation information.

Christian Grafl is an associate professor of criminology and criminalistics at the Institute of Criminal Law and Criminology at the University of Vienna. He is head of the Department of Criminology and deputy head of the Institute of Criminal Law and Criminology.

Louise Grove is a PhD student funded by the Economic and Social Research Council (ESRC) at the Midlands Centre for Criminology and Criminal Justice at Loughborough University.

Anna Gustafson has a Bachelor of Law from Abo Akademi University in Finland and is working toward a master's degree in law. She is currently working at the District Court of Parainen.

Markku Heiskanen, PhD, is a senior researcher at the European Institute for Crime Prevention and Control, affiliated with the United Nations (HEUNI). His research activity has focused on victimization surveys, violence against women, national and international crime statistics, social surveys, drinking habit surveys, survey methodology, and statistical analysis.

Kristen Lee Hourigan is a graduate student at the State University of New York at Albany.

Vasilika Hysi is an associate professor of criminology and penology and crime policy, Law Faculty, Tirana University, Albania.

Fiona Jamieson is a research student at the University of Edinburgh and an affiliated researcher of the Scottish Centre for Crime and Justice Research.

Jörg-Martin Jehle is director of the Institute for Criminal Law and Justice, head of the Department for Criminology, University of Göttingen, and member of the Experts Group of the *European Sourcebook of Crime and Criminal Justice Statistics* project.

Sladjana Jovanovic, PhD, is an assistant professor at the Law School of Union University in Belgrade. She has been publishing and doing research in the following areas: gender equality, domestic violence, trafficking in human beings, violence in the workplace.

Andreas Kapardis is a professor at the University of Cyprus, Department of Law.

Zdeněk Karabec is a researcher at the Institute of Criminology and Social Prevention, Prague.

Paul Knepper is a senior lecturer, Department of Sociological Studies, University of Sheffield, and a visiting professor, Institute of Criminology, University of Malta. His research involves the historical origins of contemporary crime problems, conceptual foundations of crime prevention, and the racialization of crime. His recent book is *The Invention of International Crimes* (Basingstoke: Palgrave Macmillan, 2010).

Sonja Kotnik, LLM, is a senior lecturer in criminal law on the Faculty of Criminal Justice and Security, University of Maribor, Slovenia. Her research field is mainly criminal procedure law, criminal substantive law, and partly private security sector. Currently, her interest is summary criminal proceeding and its impact on crime in Slovenia.

Krzysztof Krajewski is head of the Chair of Criminology at Jagiellonian University in Krakow, Poland. He is a fellow of the Alexander von Humboldt Foundation and spent several longer research periods at the Max Planck Institute for International and Foreign Penal Law in Freiburg, Germany. He has served as president of the European Society of Criminology and president of the Polish Criminological Association.

Edda Kristjansdottir is a member of the Faculty of Public International Law at the University of Amsterdam, the Netherlands.

André Lamas Leite holds a degree in law from the University of Porto and a master's in law–criminal sciences from the University of Coimbra. He is an assistant professor at the Faculty of Law, University of Porto. His main research interests include penalties' system and criminal procedure law.

Miklós Lévay is a judge of the Constitutional Court of Hungary, a professor of criminology at the Eötvös Loránd University, and general secretary of the Hungarian Society for Criminology. He also teaches criminal law at the University of Miskolc and is a member of the Scientific Committee of the International Society for Criminology.

Chris Lewis is a senior research fellow and a visiting professor at the Institute of Criminal Justice Studies at the University of Portsmouth. He was born in Wales, studied in England, and became first chief statistician at the British Home Office and later assistant director of research from 1976 to 2003. He continues to work and write on criminal statistics and justice policies throughout the world, especially Europe, Africa, and Japan.

Stefano Maffei (DPhil, Oxford) is a lecturer in criminal procedure at the University of Parma, Italy, and was a visiting professor at the University of the Pacific McGeorge School of Law in fall 2008 and summer 2009 (Salzburg Programme).

Almir Maljević is a senior lecturer of criminal law, Faculty of Criminal Justice, Criminology and Security Studies, University of Sarajevo.

Hristo Manchev is deputy prosecutor general at the Supreme Cassation Public Prosecutor's Office in Bulgaria.

Alena Marešová is a researcher at the Institute of Criminology and Social Prevention, Prague.

Vesna Markovic is the director of collection for the Institute for the Study of Violent Groups at Sam Houston State University. She earned her PhD in criminal justice from Sam Houston, and her research interest focus is on terrorism, transnational crime, and comparative criminal justice systems.

Pietro Marongiu is an associate professor of criminology, School of Medicine, University of Cagliari, Italy.

Timothy McCorry is a graduate of the State University of New York at Albany, having majored in criminal justice and informatics. He is currently working for the New York State Office of Cyber Security and Critical Infrastructure Coordination (CSCIC).

Isabella Merzagora Betsos is professor of criminology at the State University of Milan, Italy.

Gorazd Meško, PhD, is a professor of criminology and dean on the Faculty of Criminal Justice and Security, University of Maribor, Slovenia. His research interests include criminology theory, modes of social control in contemporary society, fear of crime, crime in countries in transition, and violence.

Miran Mitar, PhD, is an assistant professor of methodology on the Faculty of Criminal Justice and Security, University of Maribor, Slovenia. His research interests are in the field of evidence-based crime prevention and security policies in the framework of modern systems theory.

Raquel Moriarty is a graduate student in the School of Criminal Justice, State University of New York at Albany.

Katrina Morrison is a research student at the University of Edinburgh and an affiliated researcher of the Scottish Centre for Crime and Justice Research.

Elmedin Muratbegović is an assistant professor of criminal justice, Faculty of Criminal Justice, Criminology and Security Studies, University of Sarajevo.

Ian O'Donnell is a professor of criminology at University College Dublin. His recent books include *Prison Violence: The Dynamics of Conflict, Fear and Power* (Willan, 2003) and *Child Pornography: Crime, Computers and Society* (Willan, 2007).

David O'Mahony is a reader in Durham Law School, Durham University, and codirector of the Centre for Criminal Law and Criminal Justice.

Olena Ovcharenko is an assistant professor at Yaroslav Mudry National Law Academy of Ukraine.

Matthew Pate is a doctoral candidate in the School of Criminal Justice at the State University of New York at Albany. His academic interests include cross-national studies of criminal justice, policing, and media depictions of criminal justice. He has previously published on topics as varied as the Alger Hiss affair, search and seizure litigation as well as Neighborhood Watch program evaluation.

Miriam Pina holds a degree in psychology from the University of Porto and a master's in criminology and security from the University of Lausanne. She is an assistant professor at the Faculty of Law, University of Porto. Her main research interests are clinical criminology and victimology.

Annette Robertson, PhD, is a senior lecturer in criminology in the Department of Law, School of Law and Social Sciences, Glasgow Caledonian University, Scotland.

Gintautas Sakalauskas is a researcher at the Law Institute of Lithuania.

Miroslav Scheinost is a researcher at the Institute of Criminology and Social Prevention, Prague.

Marguerite Schinkel is a research student at the University of Edinburgh and an affiliated researcher of the Scottish Centre for Crime and Justice Research.

Paul Schupp is an assistant professor in the Department of Criminal Justice at Niagara University. His primary scholarly interests are the sociology of punishment and the development of imprisonment patterns.

Alfonso Serrano Maíllo is a professor at Universidad Nacional de Educación a Distancia, Madrid.

Olena Shostko is an associate professor at the Yaroslav Mudry National Law Academy of Ukraine. She has also been head of the Laboratory of International Cooperation of the Institute for the Study of Crime Problems, Ukrainian Academy of Legal Sciences. She is the national correspondent of Ukraine for the *European Sourcebook of Crime and Criminal Justice Statistics* project.

Biljana Simeunovic-Patic, PhD, is a researcher at the Institute of Criminological and Sociological Research in Belgrade. Her main research interests include crimes of violence, theoretical criminology, juvenile delinquency, and trafficking in human beings.

Paul R. Smit is a researcher at the Ministry of Justice in the Netherlands. His main research topic is international comparisons of crime statistics, and he is a member of the *European Sourcebook of Crime and Criminal Justice Statistics* project group.

Tony R. Smith is an assistant professor in the Department of Law and Justice Studies at Rowan University, Glassboro, New Jersey.

Daria Solenik is a legal advisor, Eastern Europe and French-Speaking Countries, Swiss Institute of Comparative Law, Lausanne, Switzerland; a scientific expert, Directorate General of Human Rights and Legal Affairs, Council of Europe, Strasbourg, France; a lecturer in law, University of Nancy, France, and European Humanities University in Vilnius, Lithuania.

Richard Sparks is a professor of criminology in the School of Law, University of Edinburgh, and a codirector of the Scottish Centre for Crime and Justice Research (http://www.sccjr.ac.uk). He is author or editor of a number of books including (with Ian Loader) *Public Criminology?* (Routledge, 2010).

Anette Storgaard, PhD, is an assistant professor in criminology and criminal law at the University of Aarhus, School of Law, Denmark.

Andromachi Tseloni, PhD, is a professor in criminology at Nottingham Trend University, UK.

Charlotte Vanneste, PhD, is director of the Department of Criminology of the National Institute for Criminalistics and Criminology in Brussels. She is also a national correspondent for the *European Sourcebook of Crime and Criminal Justice Statistics* project.

Hanns von Hofer is a professor of criminology at the Department of Criminology, Stockholm University, Sweden.

Anna Vuorelainen, BA, worked in 2008 as a research assistant at the European Institute for Crime Prevention and Control (HEUNI).

Christina Zarafonitou, PhD, is a professor in criminology and director of the postgraduate program "The Contemporary Criminality and Its Confrontation" at Panteion University in Athens, Greece.

Categorical Index

AFRICA

THE AMERICAS

ASIA

EUROPE

MIDDLE EAST AND NORTH AFRICA

THE PACIFIC

Index

Boldface numbers refer to volume numbers. A key appears on all verso pages.

1: Africa and the Middle East **2:** The Americas **3:** Asia and Pacific **4:** Europe

1: Africa and the Middle East
2: The Americas
3: Asia and Pacific
4: Europe

1: Africa and the Middle East
2: The Americas
3: Asia and Pacific
4: Europe

1: Africa and the Middle East
2: The Americas
3: Asia and Pacific
4: Europe

1: Africa and the Middle East
2: The Americas
3: Asia and Pacific
4: Europe

1: Africa and the Middle East
2: The Americas
3: Asia and Pacific
4: Europe

1: Africa and the Middle East
2: The Americas
3: Asia and Pacific
4: Europe

1: Africa and the Middle East
2: The Americas
3: Asia and Pacific
4: Europe

1: Africa and the Middle East
2: The Americas
3: Asia and Pacific
4: Europe

1: Africa and the Middle East
2: The Americas
3: Asia and Pacific
4: Europe

1: Africa and the Middle East
2: The Americas
3: Asia and Pacific
4: Europe